OXFORD

ESSENTIAL
WORLD
ATLAS

The editors are grateful to the following for acting as specialist geography consultants on "The World in Focus" front section:

Professor D. Brunsden, Kings College, University of London, UK
Dr C. Clarke, Oxford University, UK
Dr I. S. Evans, Durham University, UK
Professor P. Haggett, University of Bristol, UK
Professor K. McLachlan, University of London, UK
Professor M. Monmonier, Syracuse University, New York, USA
Professor M-L. Hsu, University of Minnesota, Minnesota, USA
Professor M. J. Tooley, University of St Andrews, UK
Dr T. Unwin, Royal Holloway, University of London, UK

THE WORLD IN FOCUS
Cartography by Philip's

Picture Acknowledgements:
Robin Scagell/Galaxy Picture Library page 3
Thinkstock/iStockphoto page 7 (bottom left & bottom right), /Digital Vision
    page 7 (center)

WORLD CITIES
Cartography by Philip's

Page 10, Dublin: The town plan of Dublin is based on Ordnance Survey Ireland by permission of the Government Permit Number 8798. © Ordnance Survey Ireland and Government of Ireland.

OS Ordnance Survey®   **Page 11, Edinburgh, and page 15, London:**
                **This product includes mapping data licensed from Ordnance Survey® with
the permission of the Controller of Her Majesty's Stationery Office. © Crown copyright 2012.
All rights reserved. Licence number 100011710.**

**All satellite images in this section courtesy of Fugro NPA Ltd, Edenbridge, Kent, UK
(www.fugro-npa.com).**

Philip's, a division of Octopus Publishing Group Limited
(www.octopusbooks.co.uk)
Endeavour House, 189 Shaftesbury Avenue, London WC2H 8JY
An Hachette UK Company (www.hachette.co.uk)

Published in North America by
Oxford University Press USA
198 Madison Avenue,
New York, NY 10016

www.oup.com/us

OXFORD   Oxford is a registered trademark
UNIVERSITY PRESS   of Oxford University Press

Library of Congress Cataloging-in-Publication Data available

ISBN 978–0–19–997155–8

Printing (last digit):
9 8 7 6 5 4 3 2 1

Printed in Singapore

OXFORD

ESSENTIAL WORLD ATLAS

SEVENTH EDITION

Contents

World Statistics

Countries   vi
Physical Dimensions   vii
User Guide   viii

The World in Focus

Planet Earth   2–3
Restless Earth   4–5
Landforms   6–7
Oceans   8–9
Climate   10–11
Water and Vegetation   12–13
Environment   14–15
Population   16–17
The Human Family   18–19
Wealth   20–21
Quality of Life   22–23
Energy   24–25
Production   26–27
Trade   28–29
Travel and Tourism   30–31

World Cities

Amsterdam   2
Athens   2
Atlanta   3
Baghdad   3
Bangkok   3
Barcelona   4
Beijing   4
Berlin   5
Boston   6
Brussels   6
Budapest   7
Buenos Aires   7
Cairo   7
Cape Town   8
Copenhagen   8
Chicago   9
Dubai   9
Delhi   10
Dublin   10
Edinburgh   11
Guangzhou (Canton)   11
Helsinki   11
Hong Kong   12
Istanbul   12
Jakarta   12
Jerusalem   13
Johannesburg   13
Karachi   13
Kolkata (Calcutta)   14
Lagos   14
Las Vegas   14
Lima   14
London   15
Lisbon   16
Los Angeles   16
Madrid   17
Manila   17
Melbourne   18
Mexico City   18
Milan   18
Miami   19
Moscow   19
Montréal   20
Mumbai (Bombay)   20
Munich   21
New Orleans   21
New York   22
Orlando   23
Osaka   23
Oslo   23
Paris   24
Prague   25
Rio de Janeiro   25
Rome   26
San Francisco   26
St Petersburg   27
Santiago   27
São Paulo   27
Seoul   27
Shanghai   28
Singapore   28
Stockholm   29
Sydney   29
Tokyo   30
Tehran   31
Toronto   31
Venice   32
Vienna   32
Warsaw   33
Washington   33
Index to City Maps   34–39
World Cities Satellite Images   40–48

World Maps

Map Symbols   1

The World: Political
1:95 000 000   2–3

Arctic Ocean
1:35 000 000   4

Antarctica
1:35 000 000   5

Europe

Europe: Physical
1:20 000 000   6

Europe: Political
1:20 000 000   7

Scandinavia 1:6 000 000
Iceland 1:6 000 000
Færoe Islands 1:6 000 000
                                   8–9

Ireland 1:2 000 000
                                   10

Scotland 1:2 000 000
                                   11

England and Wales
1:2 000 000
                                   12–13

British Isles 1:5 000 000
                                   14

Netherlands, Belgium and
Luxembourg 1:2 500 000
                                   15

Central Europe 1:5 000 000
                                   16–17

Eastern Europe and Turkey
1:10 000 000
                                   18–19

France   1:5 000 000
                                   20

Spain and Portugal
1:5 000 000
                                   21

Italy and the Balkan States
1:5 000 000
                                   22–23

Asia

Asia: Physical 1:47 000 000   24

Asia: Political 1:47 000 000   25

Russia and Northern Asia
1:20 000 000
                                   26–27

Japan 1:5 000 000
                                   28–29

China and the Far East
1:15 000 000
Hong Kong, Macau and Shenzhen
1:1 000 000
                                   30–31

Northern China and Korea
1:6 000 000
                                   32–33

Southern China
1:6 000 000
                                   34–35

Indonesia and the Philippines
1:12 500 000
Java and Madura 1:7 500 000
Bali 1:2 000 000
                                   36–37

Mainland Southeast Asia
1:6 000 000
Ko Phuket 1:1 000 000
Ko Samui 1:1 000 000
Pinang 1:1 000 000
Singapore 1:1 000 000
                                   38–39

South Asia 1:10 000 000
                                   40–41

Northern India, Pakistan
and Nepal
1:6 000 000
Jammu and Kashmir 1:6 000 000
                                   42–43

Southern India and Sri Lanka
1:6 000 000
Andaman and Nicobar Islands
1:6 000 000

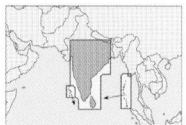

44–45

The Middle East
1:7 000 000

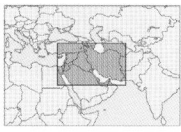

46–47

The Near East 1:2 500 000

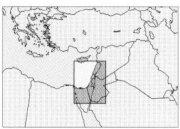

48

**Arabia and the Horn
of Africa** 1:15 000 000

49

Africa

Africa: Physical
1:42 000 000   50

Africa: Political
1:42 000 000   51

Northern Africa
1:15 000 000
Azores 1:15 000 000
Cape Verde Islands 1:10 000 000

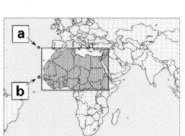

52–53

Central and Southern Africa
1:15 000 000
Comoros 1:8 000 000
Seychelles 1:2 500 000
Réunion 1:2 500 000
Mauritius 1:2 500 000
Madagascar 1:15 000 000

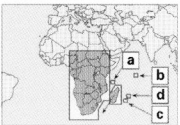

54–55

Southern Africa
1:8 000 000

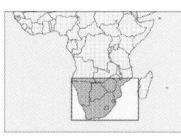

56–57

Australia and Oceania

**Australia and Oceania:
Physical and Political**
1:50 000 000   58

New Zealand 1:6 000 000
Fiji 1:6 000 000
Samoan Islands 1:6 000 000
Tonga 1:6 000 000
Tahiti and Moorea 1:1 000 000

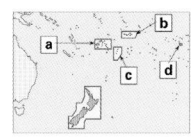

59

Western Australia
1:8 000 000

60–61

Eastern Australia
1:8 000 000
Torres Strait 1:8 000 000
Whitsunday Islands 1:2 500 000
Tasmania 1:8 000 000

62–63

Pacific Ocean
1:54 000 000   64–65

North America

North America: Physical
1:35 000 000   66

North America: Political
1:35 000 000   67

Canada 1:15 000 000

68–69

Western Canada 1:7 000 000

70–71

Eastern Canada 1:7 000 000

72–73

United States 1:15 000 000
Hawai'i 1:15 000 000
Alaska 1:15 000 000

74–75

United States – West
1:6 700 000

76–77

**Central and Southern
California and Western
Washington**
1:2 500 000

78–79

**United States – Midwest and
Northeast**
1:6 700 000

80–81

Northeastern United States
1:2 500 000

82–83

United States – South
1:6 700 000

84–85

Mexico 1:8 000 000

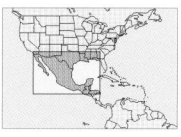

86–87

**Central America and the
West Indies** 1:8 000 000
Jamaica 1:3 000 000
Guadeloupe 1:2 000 000
Martinique 1:2 000 000
Puerto Rico 1:3 000 000
Virgin Islands 1:2 000 000
St Lucia 1:1 000 000
Barbados 1:1 000 000

88–89

South America

South America: Physical
1:35 000 000   90

South America: Political
1:35 000 000   91

South America – North
1:16 000 000
Trinidad and Tobago 1:2 500 000

92–93

Central South America
1:8 000 000

94–95

South America – South
1:16 000 000

96

Index to World Maps

97–176

World Statistics: Countries

This alphabetical list includes the principal countries and territories of the world. If a territory is not completely independent, the country it is associated with is named. The area figures give the total area of land, inland water, and ice. The population figures are 2011 estimates where available. The annual income is the Gross Domestic Product per capita in US dollars. The figures are the latest available, usually 2011 estimates.

Country/Territory	Area km² *Thousands*	Area miles² *Thousands*	Population *Thousands*	Capital	Annual Income US $
Afghanistan	652	252	29,835	Kabul	1,000
Albania	28.7	11.1	2,995	Tirana	7,800
Algeria	2,382	920	34,995	Algiers	7,200
American Samoa (US)	0.20	0.08	67	Pago Pago	8,000
Andorra	0.47	0.18	85	Andorra La Vella	37,200
Angola	1,247	481	13,339	Luanda	5,900
Anguilla (UK)	0.10	0.04	15	The Valley	12,200
Antigua & Barbuda	0.44	0.17	88	St John's	22,100
Argentina	2,780	1,074	41,770	Buenos Aires	17,400
Armenia	29.8	11.5	2,968	Yerevan	5,400
Aruba (Netherlands)	0.19	0.07	106	Oranjestad	21,800
Australia	7,741	2,989	21,767	Canberra	40,800
Austria	83.9	32.4	8,217	Vienna	41,700
Azerbaijan	86.6	33.4	8,372	Baku	10,200
Azores (Portugal)	2.2	0.86	236	Ponta Delgada	15,000
Bahamas	13.9	5.4	313	Nassau	30,900
Bahrain	0.69	0.27	1,215	Manama	27,300
Bangladesh	144	55.6	158,571	Dhaka	1,700
Barbados	0.43	0.17	287	Bridgetown	23,600
Belarus	208	80.2	9,578	Minsk	14,900
Belgium	30.5	11.8	10,431	Brussels	37,600
Belize	23.0	8.9	321	Belmopan	8,300
Benin	113	43.5	9,325	Porto-Novo	1,500
Bermuda (UK)	0.05	0.02	70	Hamilton	69,900
Bhutan	47.0	18.1	708	Thimphu	6,000
Bolivia	1,099	424	10,119	La Paz/Sucre	4,800
Bosnia-Herzegovina	51.2	19.8	4,622	Sarajevo	8,200
Botswana	582	225	2,065	Gaborone	16,300
Brazil	8,514	3,287	203,430	Brasília	11,600
Brunei	5.8	2.2	395	Bandar Seri Begawan	49,400
Bulgaria	111	42.8	7,149	Sofia	13,500
Burkina Faso	274	106	16,751	Ouagadougou	1,500
Burma (Myanmar)	677	261	53,414	Rangoon/Naypyidaw	1,300
Burundi	27.8	10.7	10,216	Bujumbura	400
Cambodia	181	69.9	14,702	Phnom Penh	2,300
Cameroon	475	184	19,711	Yaoundé	2,300
Canada	9,971	3,850	34,031	Ottawa	40,300
Canary Is. (Spain)	7.2	2.8	2,117	Las Palmas/Santa Cruz	19,900
Cape Verde Is.	4.0	1.6	516	Praia	4,000
Cayman Is. (UK)	0.26	0.10	51	George Town	43,800
Central African Republic	623	241	4,950	Bangui	800
Chad	1,284	496	10,759	Ndjaména	1,900
Chile	757	292	16,889	Santiago	16,100
China	9,597	3,705	1,336,718	Beijing	8,400
Colombia	1,139	440	44,726	Bogotá	10,100
Comoros	2.2	0.86	795	Moroni	1,200
Congo	342	132	4,244	Brazzaville	4,600
Congo (Dem. Rep. of the)	2,345	905	71,713	Kinshasa	300
Cook Is. (NZ)	0.24	0.09	11	Avarua	9,100
Costa Rica	51.1	19.7	4,577	San José	11,500
Croatia	56.5	21.8	4,484	Zagreb	18,300
Cuba	111	42.8	11,087	Havana	9,900
Curaçao (Netherlands)	0.44	0.17	142	Willemstad	15,000
Cyprus	9.3	3.6	1,120	Nicosia	29,100
Czech Republic	78.9	30.5	10,190	Prague	25,900
Denmark	43.1	16.6	5,530	Copenhagen	40,200
Djibouti	23.2	9.0	757	Djibouti	2,600
Dominica	0.75	0.29	73	Roseau	13,600
Dominican Republic	48.5	18.7	9,957	Santo Domingo	9,300
East Timor	14.9	5.7	1,178	Dili	3,100
Ecuador	284	109	15,007	Quito	8,300
Egypt	1,001	387	82,080	Cairo	6,500
El Salvador	21.0	8.1	6,072	San Salvador	7,600
Equatorial Guinea	28.1	10.8	668	Malabo	19,300
Eritrea	118	45.4	5,939	Asmara	700
Estonia	45.1	17.4	1,283	Tallinn	20,200
Ethiopia	1,104	426	90,874	Addis Ababa	1,100
Falkland Is. (UK)	12.2	4.7	3	Stanley	35,400
Faroe Is. (Denmark)	1.4	0.54	49	Tórshavn	30,500
Fiji	18.3	7.1	883	Suva	4,600
Finland	338	131	5,259	Helsinki	38,300
France	552	213	65,312	Paris	35,000
French Guiana (France)	90.0	34.7	229	Cayenne	8,300
French Polynesia (France)	4.0	1.5	295	Papeete	18,000
Gabon	268	103	1,577	Libreville	16,000
Gambia, The	11.3	4.4	1,798	Banjul	2,100
Gaza Strip (OPT)*	0.36	0.14	1,657	–	2,900
Georgia	69.7	26.9	4,586	Tbilisi	5,400
Germany	357	138	81,472	Berlin	37,900
Ghana	239	92.1	24,791	Accra	3,100
Gibraltar (UK)	0.006	0.002	29	Gibraltar Town	43,000
Greece	132	50.9	10,760	Athens	27,600
Greenland (Denmark)	2,176	840	58	Nuuk	37,400
Grenada	0.34	0.13	108	St George's	13,300
Guadeloupe (France)	1.7	0.66	452	Basse-Terre	7,900
Guam (US)	0.55	0.21	183	Agana	15,000
Guatemala	109	42.0	13,824	Guatemala City	5,000
Guinea	246	94.9	10,601	Conakry	1,100
Guinea-Bissau	36.1	13.9	1,597	Bissau	1,100
Guyana	215	83.0	775	Georgetown	7,500
Haiti	27.8	10.7	9,720	Port-au-Prince	1,200
Honduras	112	43.3	8,144	Tegucigalpa	4,300
Hungary	93.0	35.9	9,976	Budapest	19,600
Iceland	103	39.8	311	Reykjavik	38,000
India	3,287	1,269	1,189,173	New Delhi	3,700
Indonesia	1,905	735	245,613	Jakarta	4,700
Iran	1,648	636	77,891	Tehran	12,200
Iraq	438	169	30,400	Baghdad	3,900
Ireland	70.3	27.1	4,671	Dublin	39,500
Israel	20.6	8.0	7,473	Jerusalem	31,000
Italy	301	116	61,017	Rome	30,100
Ivory Coast (Côte d'Ivoire)	322	125	21,504	Yamoussoukro	1,600
Jamaica	11.0	4.2	2,868	Kingston	9,000
Japan	378	146	126,476	Tokyo	34,300
Jordan	89.3	34.5	6,508	Amman	5,900
Kazakhstan	2,725	1,052	15,522	Astana	13,000
Kenya	580	224	41,071	Nairobi	1,700
Kiribati	0.73	0.28	101	Tarawa	6,200
Korea, North	121	46.5	24,457	Pyŏngyang	1,800
Korea, South	99.3	38.3	48,755	Seoul	31,700
Kosovo	10.9	4.2	1,826	Pristina	6,500
Kuwait	17.8	6.9	2,596	Kuwait City	40,700
Kyrgyzstan	200	77.2	5,587	Bishkek	2,400
Laos	237	91.4	6,477	Vientiane	2,700

*OPT = Occupied Palestinian Territory

Country/Territory	Area km² *Thousands*	Area miles² *Thousands*	Population *Thousands*	Capital	Annual Income US $
Latvia	64.6	24.9	2,205	Riga	15,400
Lebanon	10.4	4.0	4,143	Beirut	15,600
Lesotho	30.4	11.7	1,925	Maseru	1,400
Liberia	111	43.0	3,787	Monrovia	400
Libya	1,760	679	6,598	Tripoli	14,100
Liechtenstein	0.16	0.06	35	Vaduz	141,100
Lithuania	65.2	25.2	3,536	Vilnius	18,700
Luxembourg	2.6	1.0	503	Luxembourg	84,700
Macedonia (FYROM)	25.7	9.9	2,077	Skopje	10,400
Madagascar	587	227	21,926	Antananarivo	900
Madeira (Portugal)	0.78	0.30	267	Funchal	22,700
Malawi	118	45.7	15,879	Lilongwe	900
Malaysia	330	127	28,729	Kuala Lumpur/Putrajaya	15,600
Maldives	0.30	0.12	395	Malé	8,400
Mali	1,240	479	14,160	Bamako	1,300
Malta	0.32	0.12	408	Valletta	25,700
Marshall Is.	0.18	0.07	67	Majuro	2,500
Martinique (France)	1.1	0.43	397	Fort-de-France	14,400
Mauritania	1,026	396	3,282	Nouakchott	2,200
Mauritius	2.0	0.79	1,304	Port Louis	15,000
Mayotte (France)	0.37	0.14	231	Mamoudzou	4,900
Mexico	1,958	756	113,714	Mexico City	15,100
Micronesia, Fed. States of	0.70	0.27	107	Palikir	2,200
Moldova	33.9	13.1	4,314	Kishinev	3,400
Monaco	0.001	0.0004	31	Monaco	63,400
Mongolia	1,567	605	3,133	Ulan Bator	4,500
Montenegro	14.0	5.4	662	Podgorica	11,200
Montserrat (UK)	0.10	0.39	5	Brades	3,400
Morocco	447	172	31,968	Rabat	5,100
Mozambique	802	309	22,949	Maputo	1,100
Namibia	824	318	2,148	Windhoek	7,300
Nauru	0.02	0.008	9	Yaren	5,000
Nepal	147	56.8	29,392	Katmandu	1,300
Netherlands	41.5	16.0	16,847	Amsterdam/The Hague	42,300
Netherlands Antilles (Neths)	0.8	0.31	229	Willemstad	1,600
New Caledonia (France)	18.6	7.2	256	Nouméa	15,000
New Zealand	271	104	4,290	Wellington	27,900
Nicaragua	130	50.2	5,666	Managua	3,200
Niger	1,267	489	16,469	Niamey	800
Nigeria	924	357	155,216	Abuja	2,600
Northern Mariana Is. (US)	0.46	0.18	46	Saipan	12,500
Norway	324	125	4,692	Oslo	53,300
Oman	310	119	3,028	Muscat	26,200
Pakistan	796	307	187,343	Islamabad	2,800
Palau	0.46	0.18	21	Melekeok	8,100
Panama	75.5	29.2	3,460	Panamá	13,600
Papua New Guinea	463	179	6,188	Port Moresby	2,500
Paraguay	407	157	6,459	Asunción	5,500
Peru	1,285	496	29,249	Lima	10,000
Philippines	300	116	101,834	Manila	4,100
Poland	323	125	38,442	Warsaw	20,100
Portugal	88.8	34.3	10,760	Lisbon	23,200
Puerto Rico (US)	8.9	3.4	3,989	San Juan	16,300
Qatar	11.0	4.2	848	Doha	102,700
Réunion (France)	2.5	0.97	839	St-Denis	6,200
Romania	238	92.0	21,905	Bucharest	12,300
Russia	17,075	6,593	138,740	Moscow	16,700
Rwanda	26.3	10.2	11,370	Kigali	1,300
St Kitts & Nevis	0.26	0.10	50	Basseterre	16,400
St Lucia	0.54	0.21	162	Castries	12,900
St Vincent & Grenadines	0.39	0.15	104	Kingstown	11,700
Samoa	2.8	1.1	193	Apia	6,000
San Marino	0.06	0.02	32	San Marino	36,200
São Tomé & Príncipe	0.96	0.37	180	São Tomé	2,000
Saudi Arabia	2,150	830	26,132	Riyadh	24,000
Senegal	197	76.0	12,644	Dakar	1,900
Serbia	77.5	29.9	7,311	Belgrade	10,700
Seychelles	0.46	0.18	89	Victoria	24,700
Sierra Leone	71.7	27.7	5,364	Freetown	800
Singapore	0.68	0.26	4,741	Singapore City	59,900
Slovak Republic	49.0	18.9	5,477	Bratislava	23,400
Slovenia	20.3	7.8	2,003	Ljubljana	29,100
Solomon Is.	28.9	11.2	572	Honiara	3,300
Somalia	638	246	9,926	Mogadishu	600
South Africa	1,221	471	49,004	Cape Town/Pretoria	11,000
Spain	498	192	46,755	Madrid	30,600
Sri Lanka	65.6	25.3	21,284	Colombo	5,600
Sudan	1,886	728	35,680	Khartoum	3,000
Sudan, South	620	239	8,260	Juba	1,500
Suriname	163	63.0	492	Paramaribo	9,500
Swaziland	17.4	6.7	1,370	Mbabane	5,200
Sweden	450	174	9,089	Stockholm	40,600
Switzerland	41.3	15.9	7,640	Bern	43,400
Syria	185	71.5	22,518	Damascus	5,100
Taiwan	36.0	13.9	23,072	Taipei	37,900
Tajikistan	143	55.3	7,627	Dushanbe	2,000
Tanzania	945	365	42,747	Dodoma	1,500
Thailand	513	198	66,720	Bangkok	9,700
Togo	56.8	21.9	6,772	Lomé	900
Tonga	0.65	0.25	106	Nuku'alofa	7,500
Trinidad & Tobago	5.1	2.0	1,228	Port of Spain	20,300
Tunisia	164	63.2	10,629	Tunis	9,500
Turkey	775	299	78,786	Ankara	14,600
Turkmenistan	488	188	4,998	Ashkhabad	7,500
Turks & Caicos Is. (UK)	0.43	0.17	45	Cockburn Town	11,500
Tuvalu	0.03	0.01	11	Fongafale	3,400
Uganda	241	93.1	34,612	Kampala	1,300
Ukraine	604	233	45,135	Kiev	7,200
United Arab Emirates	83.6	32.3	5,149	Abu Dhabi	48,500
United Kingdom	242	93.4	62,698	London	35,900
United States of America	9,629	3,718	313,232	Washington, DC	48,100
Uruguay	175	67.6	3,309	Montevideo	15,400
Uzbekistan	447	173	28,129	Tashkent	3,300
Vanuatu	12.2	4.7	225	Port-Vila	4,900
Venezuela	912	352	27,636	Caracas	12,400
Vietnam	332	128	90,549	Hanoi	3,300
Virgin Is. (UK)	0.15	0.06	25	Road Town	38,500
Virgin Is. (US)	0.35	0.13	110	Charlotte Amalie	14,500
Wallis & Futuna Is. (France)	0.20	0.08	15	Mata-Utu	3,800
West Bank (OPT)*	5.9	2.3	2,569	–	2,900
Western Sahara	266	103	507	El Aaiún	2,500
Yemen	528	204	24,133	Sana'	2,500
Zambia	753	291	13,881	Lusaka	1,600
Zimbabwe	391	151	12,084	Harare	500

World Statistics: Physical Dimensions

Each topic list is divided into continents and within a continent the items are listed in order of size. The bottom part of many of the lists is selective in order to give examples from as many different countries as possible. The order of the continents is the same as in the atlas, beginning with Europe and ending with South America. The figures are rounded as appropriate.

World, Continents, Oceans

	km²	miles²	%
The World	509,450,000	196,672,000	–
Land	149,450,000	57,688,000	29.3
Water	360,000,000	138,984,000	70.7
Asia	44,500,000	17,177,000	29.8
Africa	30,302,000	11,697,000	20.3
North America	24,241,000	9,357,000	16.2
South America	17,793,000	6,868,000	11.9
Antarctica	14,100,000	5,443,000	9.4
Europe	9,957,000	3,843,000	6.7
Australia & Oceania	8,557,000	3,303,000	5.7
Pacific Ocean	155,557,000	60,061,000	46.4
Atlantic Ocean	76,762,000	29,638,000	22.9
Indian Ocean	68,556,000	26,470,000	20.4
Southern Ocean	20,327,000	7,848,000	6.1
Arctic Ocean	14,056,000	5,427,000	4.2

Ocean Depths

Atlantic Ocean

	m	ft
Puerto Rico (Milwaukee) Deep	8,605	28,232
Cayman Trench	7,680	25,197
Gulf of Mexico	5,203	17,070
Mediterranean Sea	5,121	16,801
Black Sea	2,211	7,254
North Sea	660	2,165

Indian Ocean

	m	ft
Java Trench	7,450	24,442
Red Sea	2,635	8,454

Pacific Ocean

	m	ft
Mariana Trench	11,022	36,161
Tonga Trench	10,882	35,702
Japan Trench	10,554	34,626
Kuril Trench	10,542	34,587

Arctic Ocean

	m	ft
Molloy Deep	5,608	18,399

Southern Ocean

	m	ft
South Sandwich Trench	7,235	23,737

Mountains

Europe

		m	ft
Elbrus	Russia	5,642	18,510
Dykh-Tau	Russia	5,205	17,076
Shkhara	Russia/Georgia	5,201	17,064
Koshtan-Tau	Russia	5,152	16,903
Kazbek	Russia/Georgia	5,047	16,558
Pushkin	Russia/Georgia	5,033	16,512
Katyn-Tau	Russia/Georgia	4,979	16,335
Shota Rustaveli	Russia/Georgia	4,860	15,945
Mont Blanc	France/Italy	4,808	15,774
Monte Rosa	Italy/Switzerland	4,634	15,203
Dom	Switzerland	4,545	14,911
Liskamm	Switzerland	4,527	14,852
Weisshorn	Switzerland	4,505	14,780
Taschorn	Switzerland	4,490	14,730
Matterhorn/Cervino	Italy/Switzerland	4,478	14,691
Grossglockner	Austria	3,797	12,457
Mulhacén	Spain	3,478	11,411
Zugspitze	Germany	2,962	9,718
Olympus	Greece	2,917	9,570
Galdhøpiggen	Norway	2,469	8,100
Ben Nevis	UK	1,344	4,409

Asia

		m	ft
Everest	China/Nepal	8,850	29,035
K2 (Godwin Austen)	China/Kashmir	8,611	28,251
Kanchenjunga	India/Nepal	8,598	28,208
Lhotse	China/Nepal	8,516	27,939
Makalu	China/Nepal	8,481	27,824
Cho Oyu	China/Nepal	8,201	26,906
Dhaulagiri	Nepal	8,167	26,795
Manaslu	Nepal	8,156	26,758
Nanga Parbat	Kashmir	8,126	26,660
Annapurna	Nepal	8,078	26,502
Gasherbrum	China/Kashmir	8,068	26,469
Broad Peak	China/Kashmir	8,051	26,414
Xixabangma	China	8,012	26,286
Kangbachen	Nepal	7,858	25,781
Trivor	Pakistan	7,720	25,328
Pik Imeni Ismail Samani	Tajikistan	7,495	24,590
Demavend	Iran	5,604	18,386
Ararat	Turkey	5,165	16,945
Gunong Kinabalu	Malaysia (Borneo)	4,101	13,455
Fuji-San	Japan	3,776	12,388

Africa

		m	ft
Kilimanjaro	Tanzania	5,895	19,340
Mt Kenya	Kenya	5,199	17,057
Ruwenzori (Margherita)	Ug./Congo (D.R.)	5,109	16,762
Meru	Tanzania	4,565	14,977
Ras Dashen	Ethiopia	4,553	14,937
Karisimbi	Rwanda/Congo (D.R.)	4,507	14,787
Mt Elgon	Kenya/Uganda	4,321	14,176
Batu	Ethiopia	4,307	14,130
Toubkal	Morocco	4,165	13,665
Mt Cameroun	Cameroon	4,070	13,353

Oceania

		m	ft
Puncak Jaya	Indonesia	4,884	16,024
Puncak Trikora	Indonesia	4,730	15,518
Puncak Mandala	Indonesia	4,702	15,427
Mt Wilhelm	Papua New Guinea	4,508	14,790
Mauna Kea	USA (Hawai'i)	4,205	13,796
Mauna Loa	USA (Hawai'i)	4,169	13,678
Aoraki Mt Cook	New Zealand	3,753	12,313
Mt Kosciuszko	Australia	2,228	7,310

North America

		m	ft
Mt McKinley (Denali)	USA (Alaska)	6,194	20,321
Mt Logan	Canada	5,959	19,551
Pico de Orizaba	Mexico	5,610	18,405
Mt St Elias	USA/Canada	5,489	18,008
Popocatépetl	Mexico	5,452	17,887
Mt Foraker	USA (Alaska)	5,304	17,401
Iztaccíhuatl	Mexico	5,286	17,342
Mt Lucania	Canada	5,226	17,146
Mt Steele	Canada	5,073	16,644
Mt Bona	USA (Alaska)	5,005	16,420
Mt Whitney	USA	4,418	14,495
Tajumulco	Guatemala	4,220	13,845
Chirripó Grande	Costa Rica	3,837	12,589
Pico Duarte	Dominican Rep.	3,175	10,417

South America

		m	ft
Aconcagua	Argentina	6,962	22,841
Bonete	Argentina	6,872	22,546
Ojos del Salado	Argentina/Chile	6,863	22,516
Pissis	Argentina	6,779	22,241
Mercedario	Argentina/Chile	6,770	22,211
Huascarán	Peru	6,768	22,204
Llullaillaco	Argentina/Chile	6,723	22,057
Nevado de Cachi	Argentina	6,720	22,047
Yerupaja	Peru	6,632	21,758
Sajama	Bolivia	6,520	21,391
Chimborazo	Ecuador	6,267	20,561
Pico Cristóbal Colón	Colombia	5,800	19,029
Pico Bolivar	Venezuela	5,007	16,427

Antarctica

		m	ft
Vinson Massif		4,897	16,066
Mt Kirkpatrick		4,528	14,855

Rivers

Europe

		km	miles
Volga	Caspian Sea	3,700	2,300
Danube	Black Sea	2,850	1,770
Ural	Caspian Sea	2,535	1,575
Dnieper	Black Sea	2,285	1,420
Kama	Volga	2,030	1,260
Don	Black Sea	1,990	1,240
Petchora	Arctic Ocean	1,790	1,110
Oka	Volga	1,480	920
Dniester	Black Sea	1,400	870
Vyatka	Kama	1,370	850
Rhine	North Sea	1,320	820
N. Dvina	Arctic Ocean	1,290	800
Elbe	North Sea	1,145	710

Asia

		km	miles
Yangtse	Pacific Ocean	6,380	3,960
Yenisey–Angara	Arctic Ocean	5,550	3,445
Huang He	Pacific Ocean	5,464	3,395
Ob–Irtysh	Arctic Ocean	5,410	3,360
Mekong	Pacific Ocean	4,500	2,795
Amur	Pacific Ocean	4,442	2,760
Lena	Arctic Ocean	4,402	2,735
Irtysh	Ob	4,250	2,640
Yenisey	Arctic Ocean	4,090	2,540
Ob	Arctic Ocean	3,680	2,285
Indus	Indian Ocean	3,100	1,925
Brahmaputra	Indian Ocean	2,900	1,800
Syrdarya	Aralkum Desert	2,860	1,775
Salween	Indian Ocean	2,800	1,740
Euphrates	Indian Ocean	2,700	1,675
Amudarya	Aralkum Desert	2,540	1,575

Africa

		km	miles
Nile	Mediterranean	6,695	4,160
Congo	Atlantic Ocean	4,670	2,900
Niger	Atlantic Ocean	4,180	2,595
Zambezi	Indian Ocean	3,540	2,200
Oubangi/Uele	Congo (D.R.)	2,250	1,400
Kasai	Congo (D.R.)	1,950	1,210
Shaballe	Indian Ocean	1,930	1,200
Orange	Atlantic Ocean	1,860	1,155
Cubango	Okavango Delta	1,800	1,120
Limpopo	Indian Ocean	1,770	1,100
Senegal	Atlantic Ocean	1,640	1,020

Australia

		km	miles
Murray–Darling	Southern Ocean	3,750	2,330
Darling	Murray	3,070	1,905
Murray	Southern Ocean	2,575	1,600
Murrumbidgee	Murray	1,690	1,050

North America

		km	miles
Mississippi–Missouri	Gulf of Mexico	5,971	3,710
Mackenzie	Arctic Ocean	4,240	2,630
Missouri	Mississippi	4,088	2,540
Mississippi	Gulf of Mexico	3,782	2,350
Yukon	Pacific Ocean	3,185	1,980
Rio Grande	Gulf of Mexico	3,030	1,880
Arkansas	Mississippi	2,340	1,450

		km	miles
Colorado	Pacific Ocean	2,330	1,445
Red	Mississippi	2,040	1,270
Columbia	Pacific Ocean	1,950	1,210
Saskatchewan	Lake Winnipeg	1,940	1,205

South America

		km	miles
Amazon	Atlantic Ocean	6,450	4,010
Paraná–Plate	Atlantic Ocean	4,500	2,800
Purus	Amazon	3,350	2,080
Madeira	Amazon	3,200	1,990
São Francisco	Atlantic Ocean	2,900	1,800
Paraná	Plate	2,800	1,740
Tocantins	Atlantic Ocean	2,750	1,710
Orinoco	Atlantic Ocean	2,740	1,700
Paraguay	Paraná	2,550	1,580
Pilcomayo	Paraná	2,500	1,550
Araguaia	Tocantins	2,250	1,400

Lakes

Europe

		km²	miles²
Lake Ladoga	Russia	17,700	6,800
Lake Onega	Russia	9,700	3,700
Saimaa system	Finland	8,000	3,100
Vänern	Sweden	5,500	2,100

Asia

		km²	miles²
Caspian Sea	Asia	371,000	143,000
Lake Baikal	Russia	30,500	11,780
Tonlé Sap	Cambodia	20,000	7,700
Lake Balqash	Kazakhstan	18,500	7,100
Aral Sea	Kazakhstan/Uzbekistan	17,160	6,625

Africa

		km²	miles²
Lake Victoria	East Africa	68,000	26,300
Lake Tanganyika	Central Africa	33,000	13,000
Lake Malawi/Nyasa	East Africa	29,600	11,430
Lake Chad	Central Africa	25,000	9,700
Lake Bangweulu	Zambia	9,840	3,800
Lake Turkana	Ethiopia/Kenya	8,500	3,290

Australia

		km²	miles²
Lake Eyre	Australia	8,900	3,400
Lake Torrens	Australia	5,800	2,200
Lake Gairdner	Australia	4,800	1,900

North America

		km²	miles²
Lake Superior	Canada/USA	82,350	31,800
Lake Huron	Canada/USA	59,600	23,010
Lake Michigan	USA	58,000	22,400
Great Bear Lake	Canada	31,800	12,280
Great Slave Lake	Canada	28,500	11,000
Lake Erie	Canada/USA	25,700	9,900
Lake Winnipeg	Canada	24,400	9,400
Lake Ontario	Canada/USA	19,500	7,500
Lake Nicaragua	Nicaragua	8,200	3,200

South America

		km²	miles²
Lake Titicaca	Bolivia/Peru	8,300	3,200
Lake Poopo	Bolivia	2,800	1,100

Islands

Europe

		km²	miles²
Great Britain	UK	229,880	88,700
Iceland	Atlantic Ocean	103,000	39,800
Ireland	Ireland/UK	84,400	32,600
Novaya Zemlya (N.)	Russia	48,200	18,600
Sicily	Italy	25,500	9,800
Corsica	France	8,700	3,400

Asia

		km²	miles²
Borneo	Southeast Asia	744,360	287,400
Sumatra	Indonesia	473,600	182,860
Honshu	Japan	230,500	88,980
Celebes	Indonesia	189,000	73,000
Java	Indonesia	126,700	48,900
Luzon	Philippines	104,700	40,400
Hokkaido	Japan	78,400	30,300

Africa

		km²	miles²
Madagascar	Indian Ocean	587,040	226,660
Socotra	Indian Ocean	3,600	1,400
Réunion	Indian Ocean	2,500	965

Oceania

		km²	miles²
New Guinea	Indonesia/Papua NG	821,030	317,000
New Zealand (S.)	Pacific Ocean	150,500	58,100
New Zealand (N.)	Pacific Ocean	114,700	44,300
Tasmania	Australia	67,800	26,200
Hawai'i	Pacific Ocean	10,450	4,000

North America

		km²	miles²
Greenland	Atlantic Ocean	2,175,600	839,800
Baffin Is.	Canada	508,000	196,100
Victoria Is.	Canada	212,200	81,900
Ellesmere Is.	Canada	212,000	81,800
Cuba	Caribbean Sea	110,860	42,800
Hispaniola	Dominican Rep./Haiti	76,200	29,400
Jamaica	Caribbean Sea	11,400	4,400
Puerto Rico	Atlantic Ocean	8,900	3,400

South America

		km²	miles²
Tierra del Fuego	Argentina/Chile	47,000	18,100
Falkland Is. (E.)	Atlantic Ocean	6,800	2,600

User Guide

The reference maps which form the main body of this atlas have been prepared in accordance with the highest standards of international cartography to provide an accurate and detailed representation of the Earth. The scales and projections used have been carefully chosen to give balanced coverage of the world, while emphasizing the most densely populated and economically significant regions. A hallmark of Philip's mapping is the use of hill shading and relief coloring to create a graphic impression of landforms: this makes the maps exceptionally easy to read. However, knowledge of the key features employed in the construction and presentation of the maps will enable the reader to derive the fullest benefit from the atlas.

Map sequence

The atlas covers the Earth continent by continent: first Europe; then its land neighbor Asia (mapped north before south, in a clockwise sequence), then Africa, Australia and Oceania, North America, and South America. This is the classic arrangement adopted by most cartographers since the 16th century. For each continent, there are maps at a variety of scales. First, physical relief and political maps of the whole continent; then a series of larger-scale maps of the regions within the continent, each followed, where required, by still larger-scale maps of the most important or densely populated areas. The governing principle is that by turning the pages of the atlas, the reader moves steadily from north to south through each continent, with each map overlapping its neighbors.

Map presentation

With very few exceptions (for example, for the Arctic and Antarctica), the maps are drawn with north at the top, regardless of whether they are presented upright or sideways on the page. In the borders will be found the map title; a locator diagram showing the area covered; continuation arrows showing the page numbers for maps of adjacent areas; the scale; the projection used; the degrees of latitude and longitude; and the letters and figures used in the index for locating place names and geographical features. Physical relief maps also have a height reference panel identifying the colors used for each layer of contouring.

Map symbols

Each map contains a vast amount of detail which can only be conveyed clearly and accurately by the use of symbols. Points and circles of varying sizes locate and identify the relative importance of towns and cities; different styles of type are employed for administrative, geographical, and regional place names. A variety of pictorial symbols denote features such as glaciers and marshes, as well as man-made structures including roads, railroads, airports, and canals.

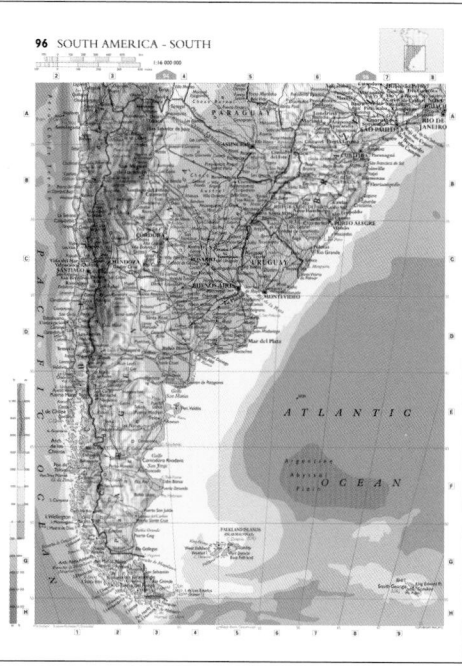

International borders are shown by red lines. Where neighboring countries are in dispute, for example in the Middle East, the maps show the *de facto* boundary between nations, regardless of the legal or historical situation. The symbols are explained on the first page of the World Maps section of the atlas.

Map scales

The scale of each map is given in the numerical form known as the "representative fraction." The first figure is always one, signifying one unit of distance on the map; the second figure, usually in millions, is the number by which the map unit must be multiplied to give the equivalent distance on the Earth's surface. Calculations can easily be made in centimeters and kilometers, by dividing the Earth units figure by 100 000 (i.e. deleting the last five 0s). Thus 1:1 000 000 means 1 cm = 10 km. The calculation for inches and miles is more laborious, but 1 000 000 divided by 63 360 (the number of inches in a mile) shows that the ratio 1:1 000 000 means approximately 1 inch = 16 miles. The table below provides distance equivalents for scales down to 1:50 000 000.

LARGE SCALE		
1:1 000 000	1 cm = 10 km	1 inch = 16 miles
1:2 500 000	1 cm = 25 km	1 inch = 39.5 miles
1:5 000 000	1 cm = 50 km	1 inch = 79 miles
1:6 000 000	1 cm = 60 km	1 inch = 95 miles
1:8 000 000	1 cm = 80 km	1 inch = 126 miles
1:10 000 000	1 cm = 100 km	1 inch = 158 miles
1:15 000 000	1 cm = 150 km	1 inch = 237 miles
1:20 000 000	1 cm = 200 km	1 inch = 316 miles
1:50 000 000	1 cm = 500 km	1 inch = 790 miles
SMALL SCALE		

Measuring distances

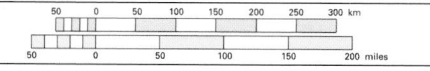

Although each map is accompanied by a scale bar, distances cannot always be measured with confidence because of the distortions involved in portraying the curved surface of the Earth on a flat page. As a general rule, the larger the map scale (i.e. the lower the number of Earth units in the representative fraction), the more accurate and reliable will be the distance measured. On small-scale maps such as those of the world and of entire continents, measurement may only be accurate along the "standard parallels," or central axes, and should not be attempted without considering the map projection.

Latitude and longitude

Accurate positioning of individual points on the Earth's surface is made possible by reference to the geometrical system of latitude and longitude. Latitude *parallels* are drawn west–east around the Earth and numbered by degrees north and south of the Equator, which is designated 0° of latitude. Longitude *meridians* are drawn north–south and numbered by degrees east and west of the *prime meridian*, 0° of longitude, which passes through Greenwich in England. By referring to these coordinates and their subdivisions of minutes ($1/60$th of a degree) and seconds ($1/60$th of a minute), any place on Earth can be located to within a few hundred meters. Latitude and longitude are indicated by blue lines on the maps; they are straight or curved according to the projection employed. Reference to these lines is the easiest way of determining the relative positions of places on different maps, and for plotting compass directions.

Name forms

For ease of reference, both English and local name forms appear in the atlas. Oceans, seas, and countries are shown in English throughout the atlas; country names may be abbreviated to their commonly accepted form (for example, Germany, not The Federal Republic of Germany). Conventional English forms are also used for place names on the smaller-scale maps of the continents. However, local name forms are used on all large-scale and regional maps, with the English form given in brackets only for important cities – the large-scale map of Russia and Central Asia thus shows Moskva (Moscow). For countries which do not use a Roman script, place names have been transcribed according to the systems adopted by the British and US Geographic Names Authorities. For China, the Pin Yin system has been used, with some more widely known forms appearing in brackets, as with Beijing (Peking). Both English and local names appear in the index, the English form being cross-referenced to the local form.

THE
WORLD
IN FOCUS

PLANET EARTH	2	WATER AND VEGETATION	12	QUALITY OF LIFE	22
RESTLESS EARTH	4	ENVIRONMENT	14	ENERGY	24
LANDFORMS	6	POPULATION	16	PRODUCTION	26
OCEANS	8	THE HUMAN FAMILY	18	TRADE	28
CLIMATE	10	WEALTH	20	TRAVEL AND TOURISM	30

Planet Earth

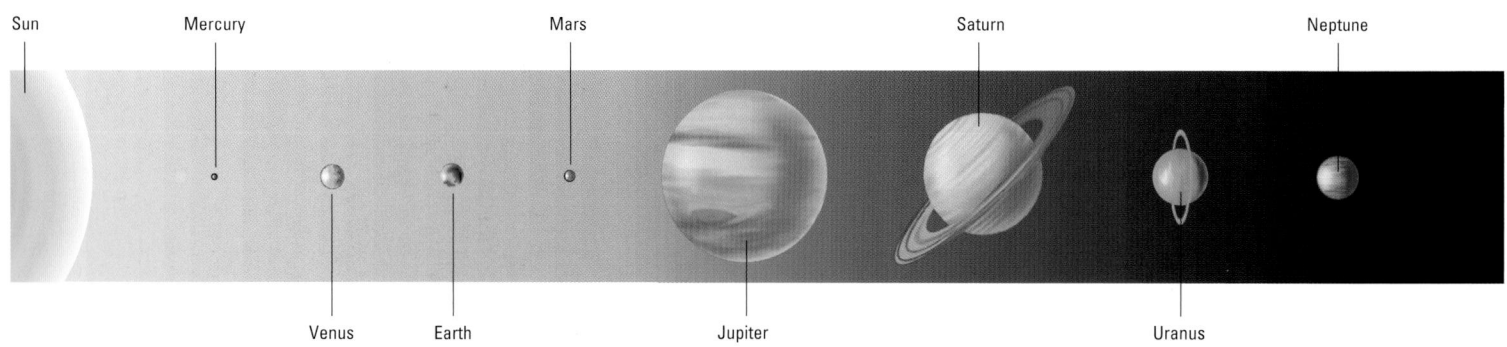

Sun   Mercury   Mars   Saturn   Neptune
Venus   Earth   Jupiter   Uranus

THE SOLAR SYSTEM

A minute part of one of the billions of galaxies (collections of stars) that populate the Universe, the Solar System lies about 26,000 light-years from the center of our own Galaxy, the "Milky Way." Thought to be about 5 billion years old, it consists of a central Sun with eight planets and their moons revolving around it, attracted by its gravitational pull. The planets orbit the Sun in the same direction – counterclockwise when viewed from above the Sun's north pole – and almost in the same plane. Their orbital distances, however, vary enormously.

The Sun's diameter is 109 times that of the Earth, and the temperature at its core – caused by continuous thermonuclear fusions of hydrogen into helium – is estimated to be 27 million degrees Fahrenheit. It is the Solar System's only source of light and heat.

PROFILE OF THE PLANETS

	Mean distance from Sun (million miles)	Mass (Earth = 1)	Period of orbit (Earth days/years)	Period of rotation (Earth days)	Equatorial diameter (miles)	Number of known satellites*
Mercury	36.0	0.06	87.97 days	58.65	3,032	0
Venus	67.2	0.82	224.7 days	243.02	7,521	0
Earth	93.0	1.00	365.3 days	1.00	7,926	1
Mars	141.6	0.11	687.0 days	1.029	4,220	2
Jupiter	483.7	317.8	11.86 years	0.411	88,848	67
Saturn	886.6	95.2	29.45 years	0.428	74,900	62
Uranus	1,784	14.5	84.02 years	0.720	31,764	27
Neptune	2,795	17.2	164.8 years	0.673	30,776	13

* Number of known satellites at mid-2012

All planetary orbits are elliptical in form, but only Mercury follows a path that deviates noticeably from a circular one. In 2006, Pluto was demoted from its former status as a planet and is now regarded as a member of the Kuiper Belt of icy bodies at the fringes of the Solar System.

THE SEASONS

Seasons occur because the Earth's axis is tilted at an angle of approximately 23½°. When the northern hemisphere is tilted to a maximum extent toward the Sun, on June 21, the Sun is overhead at the Tropic of Cancer (latitude 23½° North). This is midsummer, or the summer solstice, in the northern hemisphere.

On September 22 or 23, the Sun is overhead at the Equator, and day and night are of equal length throughout the world. This is the autumnal equinox in the northern hemisphere. On December 21 or 22, the Sun is overhead at the Tropic of Capricorn (23½° South), the winter solstice in the northern hemisphere. The overhead Sun then tracks north until, on March 21, it is overhead at the Equator. This is the spring (vernal) equinox in the northern hemisphere.

In the southern hemisphere, the seasons are the reverse of those in the north.

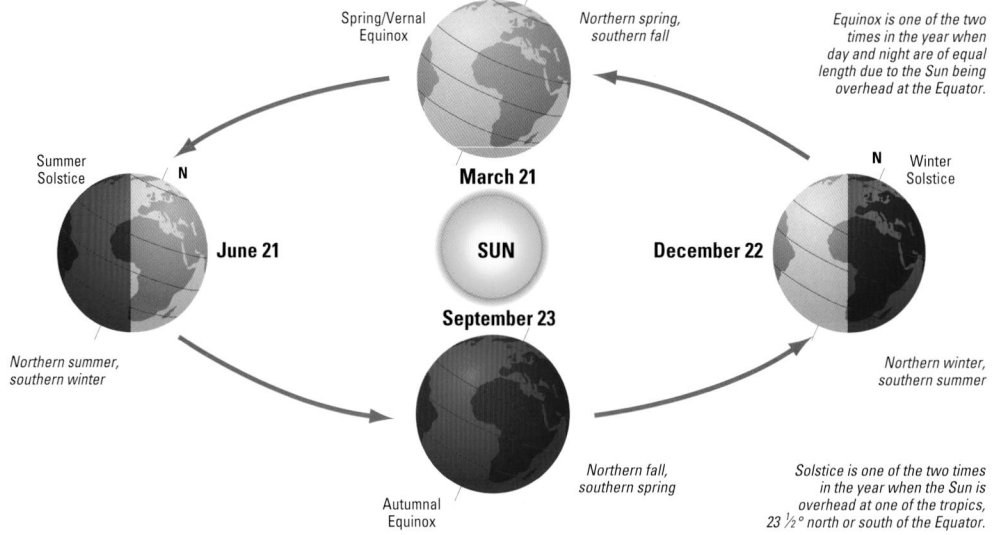

Spring/Vernal Equinox | Northern spring, southern fall
Equinox is one of the two times in the year when day and night are of equal length due to the Sun being overhead at the Equator.
Summer Solstice | N
March 21
June 21 | SUN | December 22
September 23
N | Winter Solstice
Northern summer, southern winter
Northern winter, southern summer
Northern fall, southern spring
Autumnal Equinox
Solstice is one of the two times in the year when the Sun is overhead at one of the tropics, 23 ½° north or south of the Equator.

DAY AND NIGHT

The Sun appears to rise in the east, reach its highest point at noon, and then set in the west, to be followed by night. In reality, it is not the Sun that is moving but the Earth rotating from west to east. The moment when the Sun's upper limb first appears above the horizon is termed sunrise; the moment when the Sun's upper limb disappears below the horizon is sunset.

At the summer solstice in the northern hemisphere (June 21), the Arctic has total daylight and the Antarctic total darkness. The opposite occurs at the winter solstice (December 21 or 22). At the Equator, the length of day and night are almost equal all year.

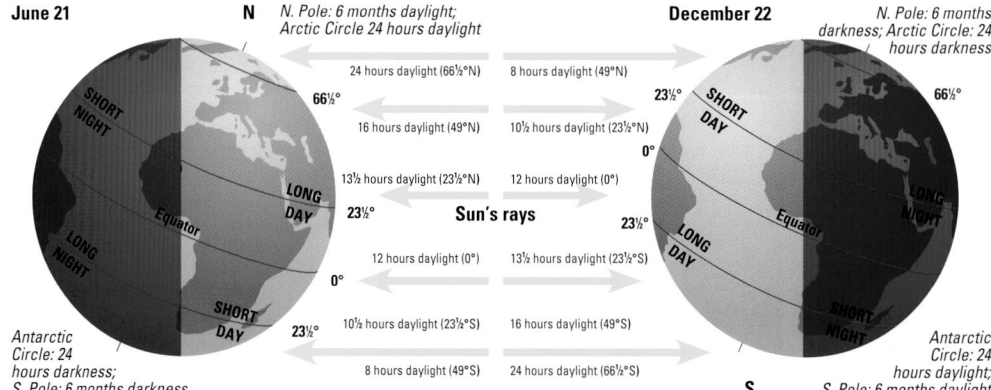

June 21 | N | N. Pole: 6 months daylight; Arctic Circle 24 hours daylight | December 22 | N. Pole: 6 months darkness; Arctic Circle: 24 hours darkness
24 hours daylight (66½°N) | 8 hours daylight (49°N)
66½° | 23½° | 66½°
16 hours daylight (49°N) | 10½ hours daylight (23½°N)
0°
13½ hours daylight (23½°N) | 12 hours daylight (0°)
23½° | Sun's rays | 23½°
12 hours daylight (0°) | 13½ hours daylight (23½°S)
0°
10½ hours daylight (23½°S) | 16 hours daylight (49°S)
23½°
8 hours daylight (49°S) | 24 hours daylight (66½°S)
Antarctic Circle: 24 hours darkness; S. Pole: 6 months darkness | S | Antarctic Circle: 24 hours daylight; S. Pole: 6 months daylight

2

TIME

Year: The time taken by the Earth to revolve around the Sun, or 365.24 days.

Leap Year: A calendar year of 366 days, February 29 being the additional day. It offsets the difference between the calendar and the solar year.

Month: The 12 calendar months of the year are approximately equal in length to a lunar month.

Week: An artificial period of 7 days, not based on astronomical time.

Day: The time taken by the Earth to complete one rotation on its axis.

Hour: 24 hours make one day. The day is divided into hours a.m. (ante meridiem or before noon) and p.m. (post meridiem or after noon), although most timetables now use the 24-hour system, from midnight to midnight.

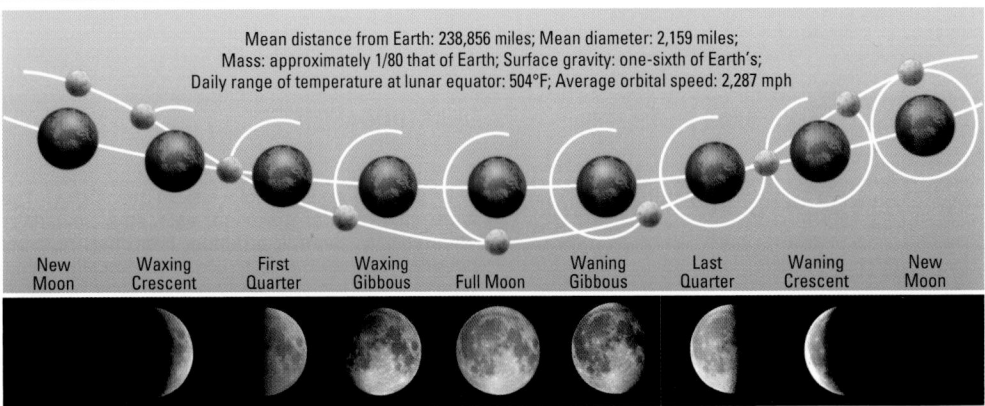

THE MOON

The Moon rotates more slowly than the Earth, taking just over 27 days to make one complete rotation on its axis. This corresponds to the Moon's orbital period around the Earth, and therefore the Moon always

PHASES OF THE MOON

Mean distance from Earth: 238,856 miles; Mean diameter: 2,159 miles;
Mass: approximately 1/80 that of Earth; Surface gravity: one-sixth of Earth's;
Daily range of temperature at lunar equator: 504°F; Average orbital speed: 2,287 mph

| New Moon | Waxing Crescent | First Quarter | Waxing Gibbous | Full Moon | Waning Gibbous | Last Quarter | Waning Crescent | New Moon |

presents the same hemisphere toward us; some 41% of the Moon's far side is never visible from the Earth. The interval between one New Moon and the next is 29½ days – this is called a lunation, or lunar month.

The Moon shines only by reflected sunlight, and emits no light of its own. During each lunation the Moon displays a complete cycle of phases, caused by the changing angle of illumination from the Sun.

ECLIPSES

When the Moon passes between the Sun and the Earth, the Sun becomes partially eclipsed (1). A partial eclipse becomes a total eclipse if the Moon proceeds to cover the Sun completely (2) and the dark central part of the lunar shadow touches the Earth. The broad geographical zone covered by the Moon's outer shadow (P) has only a very small central area (often less than 62 miles never last for more than 7½ minutes at maximum, but is usually much briefer than this. Lunar eclipses take place when the Moon moves through the shadow of the Earth, and can be partial or total. Any single location on Earth can experience a maximum of four solar and three lunar eclipses in any single year, while a total solar eclipse occurs an average of once every 360 years for any given location.

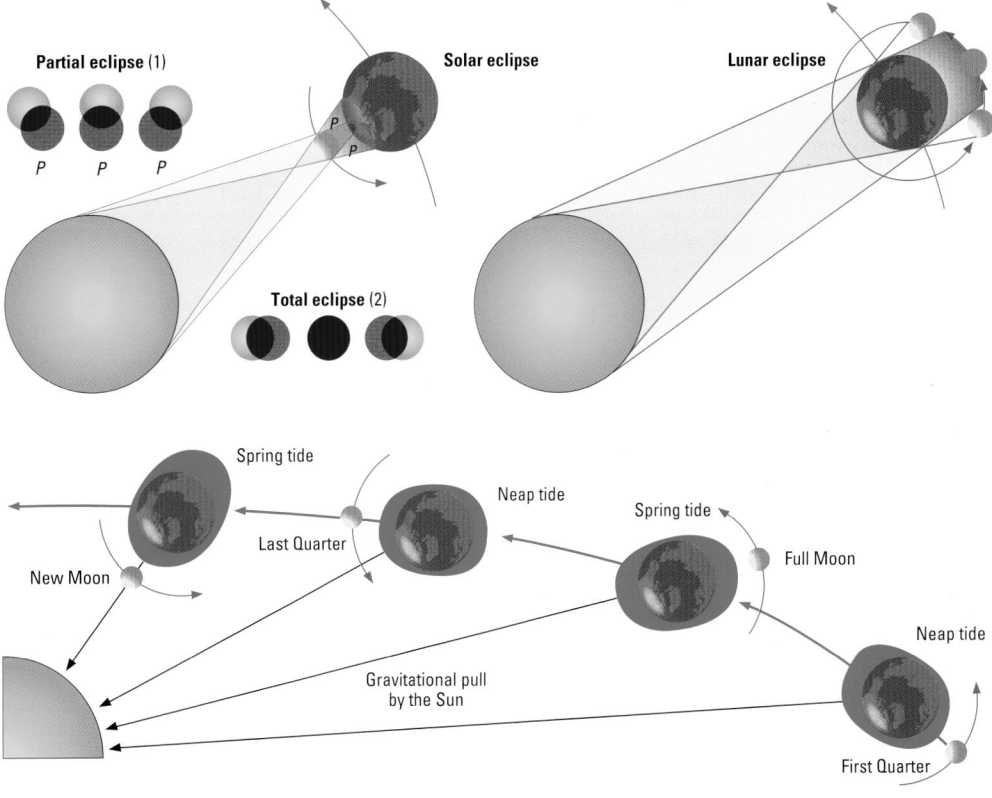

TIDES

The daily rise and fall of the ocean's tides are the result of the gravitational pull of the Moon and that of the Sun, though the effect of the latter is not as strong as that of the Moon. This effect is greatest on the hemisphere facing the Moon and causes a tidal "bulge."

Spring tides occur when the Sun, Earth, and Moon are aligned; high tides are at their highest, and low tides fall to their lowest. When the Moon and Sun are furthest out of line (near the Moon's First and Last Quarters), neap tides occur, producing the smallest range between high and low tides.

Restless Earth

THE EARTH'S STRUCTURE

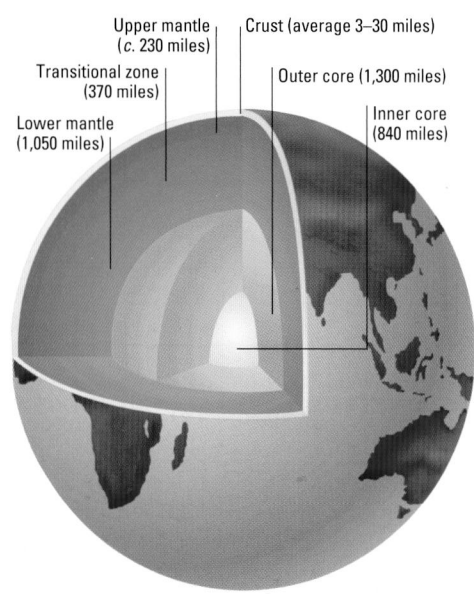

Upper mantle (c. 230 miles)
Crust (average 3–30 miles)
Transitional zone (370 miles)
Outer core (1,300 miles)
Lower mantle (1,050 miles)
Inner core (840 miles)

CONTINENTAL DRIFT

About 200 million years ago the original Pangaea land mass began to split into two continental groups, which further separated over time to produce the present-day configuration.

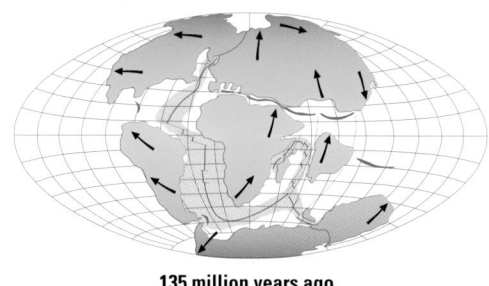

135 million years ago

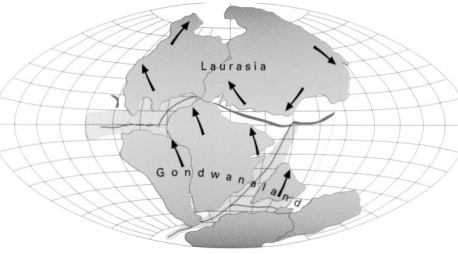

Laurasia

Gondwanaland

180 million years ago

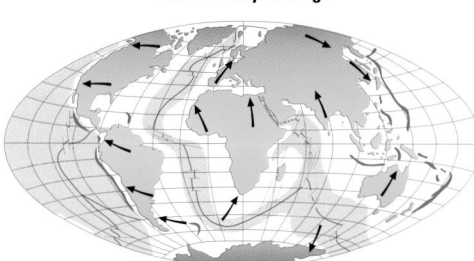

Present day

———— Trench
———— Rift
New ocean floor
Zones of slippage

NOTABLE EARTHQUAKES SINCE 1900

Year	Location	Richter Scale	Deaths
1906	San Francisco, USA	8.3	3,000
1906	Valparaiso, Chile	8.6	22,000
1908	Messina, Italy	7.5	83,000
1915	Avezzano, Italy	7.5	30,000
1920	Gansu (Kansu), China	8.6	180,000
1923	Yokohama, Japan	8.3	143,000
1927	Nan Shan, China	8.3	200,000
1932	Gansu (Kansu), China	7.6	70,000
1933	Sanriku, Japan	8.9	2,990
1934	Bihar, India/Nepal	8.4	10,700
1935	Quetta, India (now Pakistan)	7.5	60,000
1939	Chillan, Chile	8.3	28,000
1939	Erzincan, Turkey	7.9	30,000
1960	S. W. Chile	9.5	2,200
1960	Agadir, Morocco	5.8	12,000
1962	Khorasan, Iran	7.1	12,230
1964	Anchorage, USA	9.2	125
1970	N. Peru	7.8	70,000
1972	Managua, Nicaragua	6.2	5,000
1976	Guatemala	7.5	22,500
1976	Tangshan, China	8.2	255,000
1978	Tabas, Iran	7.7	25,000
1980	El Asnam, Algeria	7.3	20,000
1985	Mexico City, Mexico	8.1	4,200
1988	N.W. Armenia	6.8	55,000
1990	N. Iran	7.7	36,000
1993	Maharashtra, India	6.4	30,000
1994	Los Angeles, USA	6.6	51
1995	Kobe, Japan	7.2	5,000
1998	Rostaq, Afghanistan	7.0	5,000
1999	Izmit, Turkey	7.4	15,000
1999	Taipei, Taiwan	7.6	1,700
2001	Gujarat, India	7.7	14,000
2003	Bam, Iran	6.6	30,000
2004	Sumatra, Indonesia	9.0	250,000
2005	N. Pakistan	7.6	74,000
2006	Java, Indonesia	6.4	6,200
2007	S. Peru	8.0	600
2008	Sichuan, China	7.9	70,000
2010	Haiti	7.0	230,000
2011	Christchurch, New Zealand	6.3	182
2011	N. Japan	9.0	28,000

EARTHQUAKES

Earthquake magnitude is usually rated according to either the Richter or the Modified Mercalli scale, both devised by seismologists in the 1930s. The Richter scale measures absolute earthquake power with mathematical precision: each step upward represents a tenfold increase in shockwave amplitude. Theoretically, there is no upper limit, but most of the largest earthquakes measured have been rated at between 8.8 and 8.9. The 12–point Mercalli scale, based on observed effects, is often more meaningful, ranging from I (earthquakes noticed only by seismographs) to XII (total destruction); intermediate points include V (people awakened at night; unstable objects overturned), VII (collapse of ordinary buildings; chimneys and monuments fall), and IX (conspicuous cracks in ground; serious damage to reservoirs).

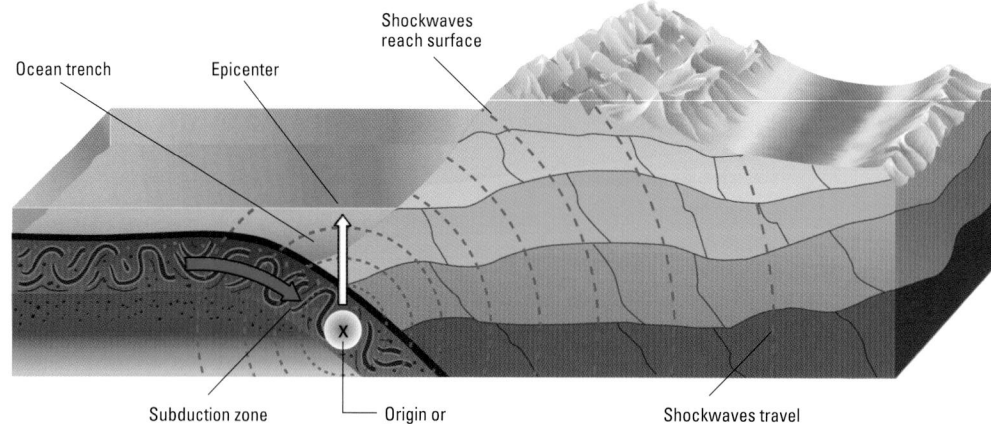

Ocean trench
Epicenter
Shockwaves reach surface
Subduction zone
Origin or focus
Shockwaves travel away from focus

DISTRIBUTION OF EARTHQUAKES

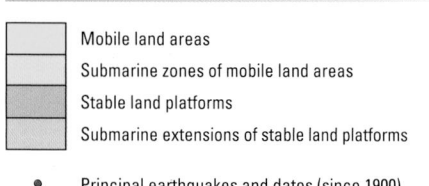

Mobile land areas
Submarine zones of mobile land areas
Stable land platforms
Submarine extensions of stable land platforms

• 1995 Principal earthquakes and dates (since 1900)

Earthquakes are a series of rapid vibrations originating from the slipping or faulting of parts of the Earth's crust when stresses within build up to breaking point. They usually happen at depths varying from 5 miles to 20 miles. Severe earthquakes cause extensive damage when they take place in populated areas, destroying structures and severing communications. Most initial loss of life occurs due to secondary causes such as falling masonry, fires, and flooding.

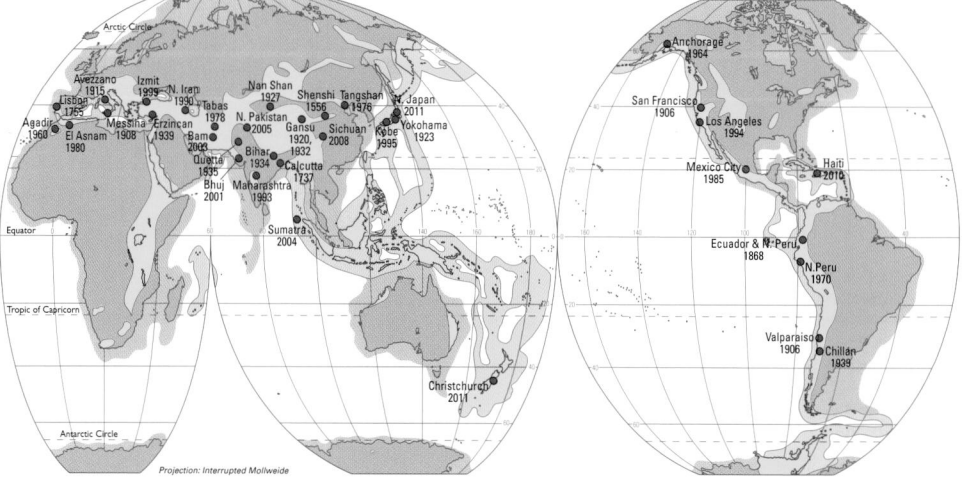

Projection: Interrupted Mollweide

4

PLATE TECTONICS

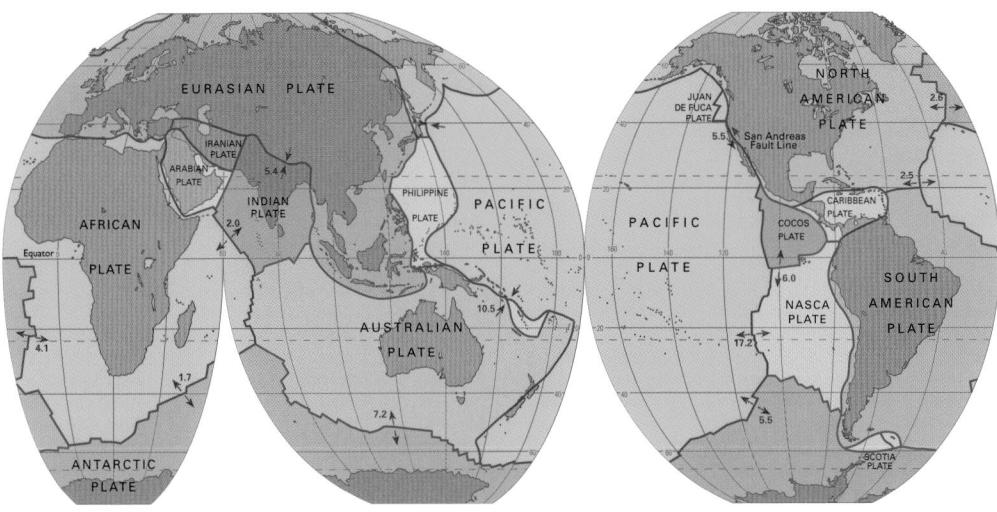

— Plate boundaries

↙ Direction of plate movements and rate of movement (cm/year)

The drifting of the continents is a feature that is unique to planet Earth. The complementary, almost jigsaw-puzzle fit of the coastlines on each side of the Atlantic Ocean inspired Alfred Wegener's theory of continental drift in 1915. The theory suggested that the ancient supercontinent, which Wegener named Pangaea, incorporated all of the Earth's land masses and gradually split up to form today's continents.

The original debate about continental drift was a prelude to a more radical idea: plate tectonics. The basic theory is that the Earth's crust is made up of a series of rigid plates which float on a soft layer of the mantle and are moved about by continental convection currents within the Earth's interior. These plates diverge and converge along margins marked by seismic activity. Plates diverge from mid-ocean ridges where molten lava pushes upward and forces the plates apart at rates of up to 1.6 inches [40 mm] a year.

The three diagrams, left, give some examples of plate boundaries from around the world. Diagram (a) shows sea-floor spreading at the Mid-Atlantic Ridge as the American and African plates slowly diverge. The same thing is happening in (b) where sea-floor spreading at the Mid-Indian Ocean Ridge is forcing the Indian plate to collide into the Eurasian plate. In (c) oceanic crust (sima) is being subducted beneath lighter continental crust (sial).

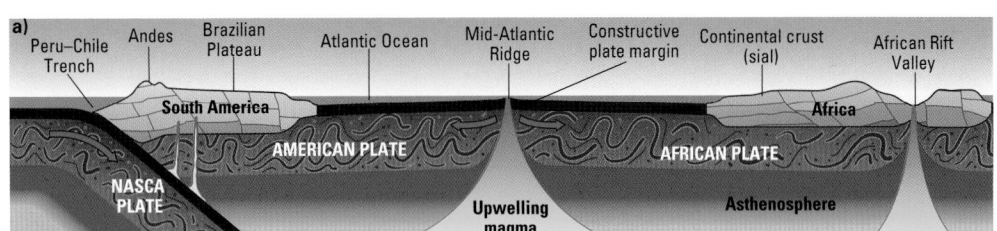

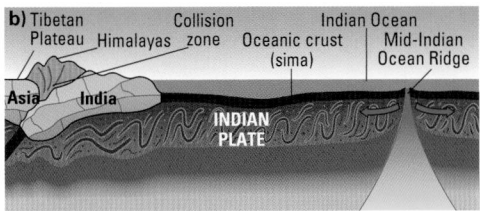

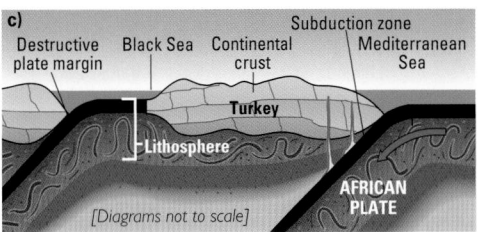

VOLCANOES

Volcanoes occur when hot liquefied rock beneath the Earth's crust is pushed up by pressure to the surface as molten lava. Some volcanoes erupt in an explosive way, throwing out rocks and ash, whilst others are effusive and lava flows out of the vent. There are volcanoes which are both, such as Mount Fuji. An accumulation of lava and cinders creates cones of variable size and shape. As a result of many eruptions over centuries, Mount Etna in Sicily has a circumference of more than 75 miles [120 km].

Climatologists believe that volcanic ash, if ejected high into the atmosphere, can influence temperature and weather for several years afterwards. The 1991 eruption of Mount Pinatubo in the Philippines ejected more than 20 million tonnes of dust and ash 20 miles [32 km] into the atmosphere and is believed to have accelerated ozone depletion over a large part of the globe.

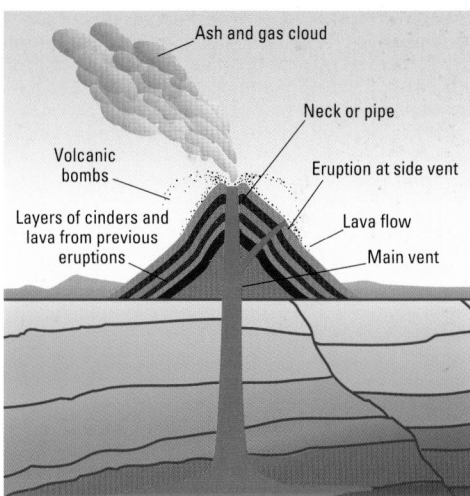

DISTRIBUTION OF VOLCANOES

Volcanoes today may be the subject of considerable scientific study but they remain both dramatic and unpredictable: in 1991 Mount Pinatubo, 62 miles [100 km] north of the Philippines capital Manila, suddenly burst into life after lying dormant for more than six centuries. Most of the world's active volcanoes occur in a belt around the Pacific Ocean, on the edge of the Pacific plate, called the "ring of fire." Indonesia has the greatest concentration with 90 volcanoes, 12 of which are active. The most famous, Krakatoa, erupted in 1883 with such force that the resulting tidal wave killed 36,000 people, and tremors were felt as far away as Australia.

▬▬ "Ring of Fire"

∘ Submarine volcanoes

▲ Land volcanoes active since 1700

— Boundaries of tectonic plates

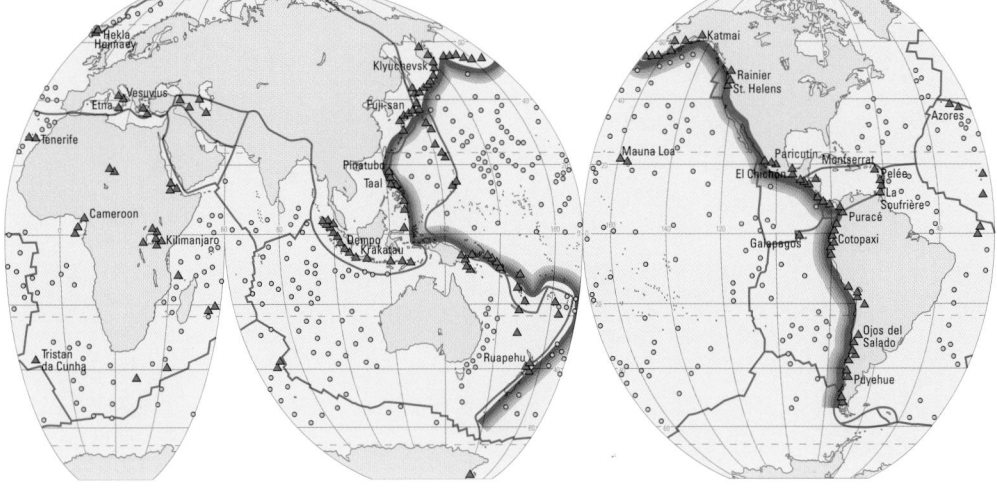

5

Landforms

THE ROCK CYCLE

James Hutton first proposed the rock cycle in the late 1700s after he observed the slow but steady effects of erosion.

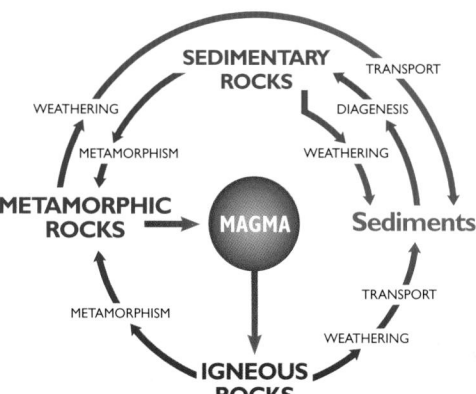

Above and below the surface of the oceans, the features of the Earth's crust are constantly changing. The phenomenal forces generated by convection currents in the molten core of our planet carry the vast segments or "plates" of the crust across the globe in an endless cycle of creation and destruction. A continent may travel little more than 1 inch [25 mm] per year, yet in the vast span of geological time this process throws up giant mountain ranges and creates new land.

Destruction of the landscape, however, begins as soon as it is formed. Wind, water, ice, and sea, the main agents of erosion, mount a constant assault that even the most resistant rocks cannot withstand. Mountain peaks may dwindle by as little as a few fractions of an inch each year, but if they are not uplifted by further movements of the crust they will eventually be reduced to rubble and transported away.

Water is the most powerful agent of erosion – it has been estimated that 100 billion tonnes of sediment are washed into the oceans every year.

Three Asian rivers account for 20% of this total: the Huang He, in China, and the Brahmaputra and the Ganges in Bangladesh.

Rivers and glaciers, like the sea itself, generate much of their effect through abrasion – pounding the land with the debris they carry with them. But as well as destroying they also create new landforms, many of them spectacular: vast deltas like those of the Mississippi and the Nile, or the deep fjords cut by glaciers in British Columbia, Norway, and New Zealand.

Geologists once considered that landscapes evolved from "young," newly uplifted mountainous areas, through a "mature," hilly stage, to an "old age" stage when the land was reduced to an almost flat plain, or peneplain. This theory, called the "cycle of erosion," fell into disuse when it became evident that so many factors, including the effects of plate tectonics and climatic change, constantly interrupt the cycle, which takes no account of the highly complex interactions that shape the surface of our planet.

MOUNTAIN BUILDING

Mountains are formed when pressures on the Earth's crust caused by continental drift become so intense that the surface buckles or cracks. This happens where oceanic crust is subducted by continental crust or, more dramatically, where two tectonic plates collide: the Rockies, Andes, Alps, Urals, and Himalayas resulted from such impacts. These are all known as fold mountains because they were formed by the compression of the rocks, forcing the surface to bend and fold like a crumpled rug. The Himalayas were formed from the folded former sediments of the Tethys Sea, which was trapped in the collision zone between the Indian and Eurasian plates.

The other main mountain-building process occurs when the crust fractures to create faults, allowing rock to be forced upward in large blocks; or when the pressure of magma within the crust forces the surface to bulge into a dome, or erupts to form a volcano. Large mountain ranges may reveal a combination of these features; the Alps, for example, have been compressed so violently that the folds are fragmented by numerous faults and intrusions of molten igneous rock.

Over millions of years, even the greatest mountain ranges can be reduced by the agents of erosion (most notably rivers) to a low rugged landscape known as a peneplain.

Types of faults: Faults occur where the crust is being stretched or compressed so violently that the rock strata break in a horizontal or vertical movement. They are classified by the direction in which the blocks of rock have moved. A normal fault results when a vertical movement causes the surface to break apart; compression causes a reverse fault. Horizontal movement causes shearing, known as a strike-slip fault. When the rock breaks in two places, the central block may be pushed up in a horst fault, or sink (creating a rift valley) in a graben fault.

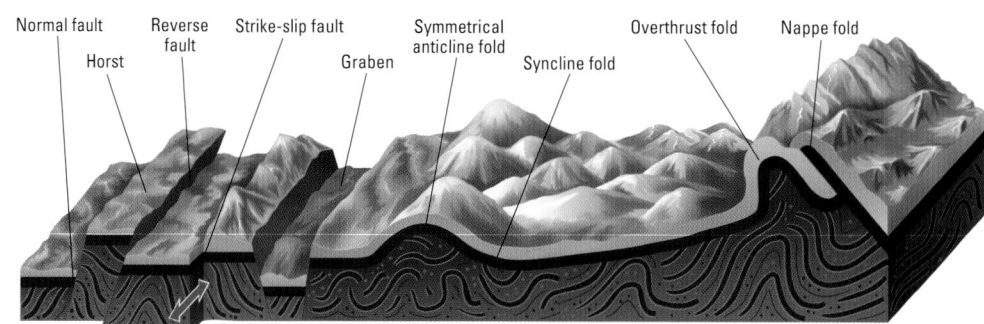

Types of fold: Folds occur when rock strata are squeezed and compressed. They are common, therefore, at destructive plate margins and where plates have collided, forcing the rocks to buckle into mountain ranges. Geographers give different names to the degrees of fold that result from continuing pressure on the rock. A simple fold may be symmetric, with even slopes on either side, but as the pressure builds up, one slope becomes steeper and the fold becomes asymmetric. Later, the ridge or "anticline" at the top of the fold may slide over the lower ground or "syncline" to form a recumbent fold. Eventually, the rock strata may break under the pressure to form an overthrust and finally a nappe fold.

CONTINENTAL GLACIATION

Ice sheets were at their greatest extent about 200,000 years ago. The maximum advance of the last Ice Age was about 18,000 years ago, when ice covered virtually all of Canada and reached as far south as the Bristol Channel in Britain.

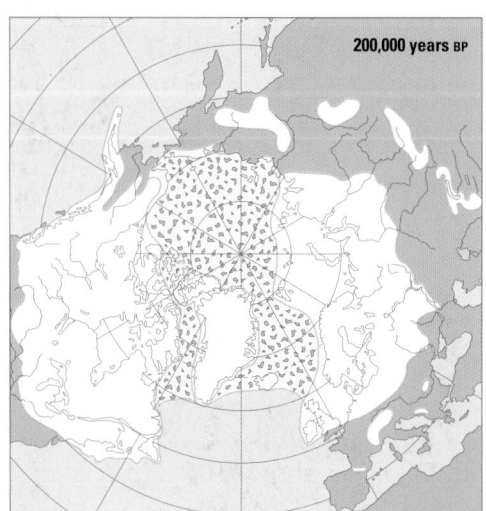

200,000 years BP

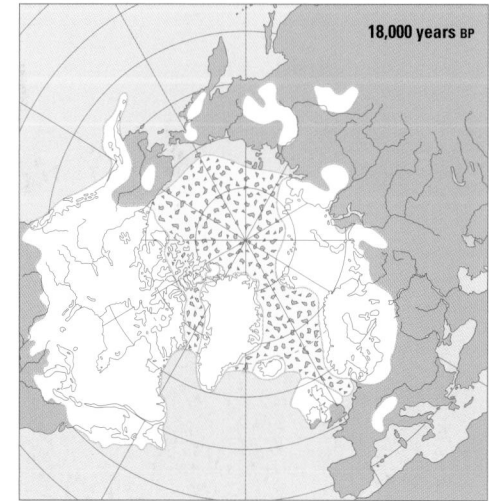

18,000 years BP

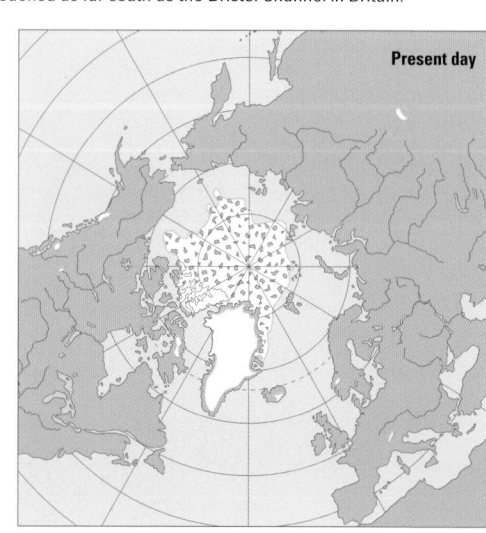

Present day

NATURAL LANDFORMS

A stylized diagram to show some of the major natural landforms found in the mid-latitudes.

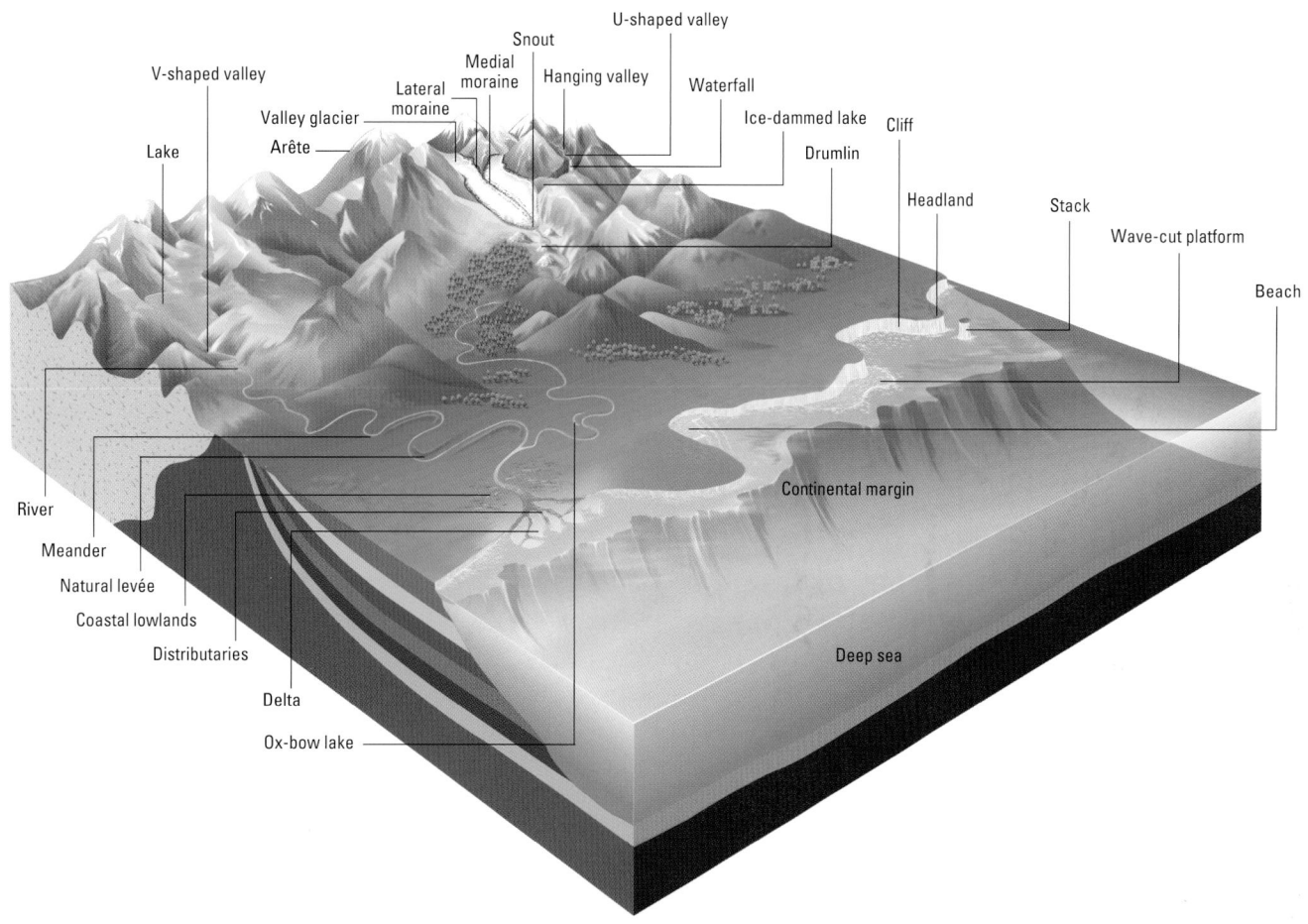

DESERT LANDSCAPES

The popular image that deserts are all huge expanses of sand is wrong. Despite harsh conditions, deserts contain some of the most varied and interesting landscapes in the world. They are also one of the most extensive environments – the hot and cold deserts together cover almost 40% of the Earth's surface.

The three types of hot desert are known by their Arabic names: sand desert, called *erg*, covers only about one-fifth of the world's desert; the rest is divided between *hammada* (areas of bare rock) and *reg* (broad plains covered by loose gravel or pebbles).

In areas of *erg*, such as the Namib Desert, the shape of the dunes reflects the character of local winds. Where winds are constant in direction, crescent-shaped *barchan* dunes form. In areas of bare rock, wind-blown sand is a major agent of erosion. The erosion is mainly confined to within 6.5 ft [2 m] of the surface, producing characteristic mushroom-shaped rocks.

Erg

Hammada

Reg

SURFACE PROCESSES

Catastrophic changes to natural landforms are periodically caused by such phenomena as avalanches, landslides and volcanic eruptions, but most of the processes that shape the Earth's surface operate extremely slowly in human terms. One estimate, based on a study in the United States, suggested that 3 ft [1 m] of land was removed from the entire surface of the country, on average, every 29,500 years. However, the time-scale varies from 1,300 years to 154,200 years depending on the terrain and climate.

In hot, dry climates, mechanical weathering, a result of rapid temperature changes, causes the outer layers of rock to peel away, while in cold mountainous regions, boulders are prised apart when water freezes in cracks in rocks. Chemical weathering, at its greatest in warm, humid regions, is responsible for hollowing out lime-stone caves and decomposing granites.

The erosion of soil and rock is greatest on sloping land and the steeper the slope, the greater the tendency for mass wasting – the movement of soil and rock downhill under the influence of gravity. The mechanisms of mass wasting (ranging from very slow to very rapid) vary with the type of material, but the presence of water as a lubricant is usually an important factor.

Running water is the world's leading agent of erosion and transportation. The energy of a river depends on several factors, including its velocity and volume, and its erosive power is at its peak when it is in full flood. Sea waves also exert tremendous erosive power during storms when they hurl pebbles against the shore, undercutting cliffs and hollowing out caves.

Glacier ice forms in mountain hollows and spills out to form valley glaciers, which transport rocks shattered by frost action. As glaciers move, rocks embedded into the ice erode steep-sided, U-shaped valleys. Evidence of glaciation in mountain regions includes cirques, knife-edged ridges, or arêtes, and pyramidal peaks.

Oceans

THE GREAT OCEANS

Relative sizes of the world's oceans

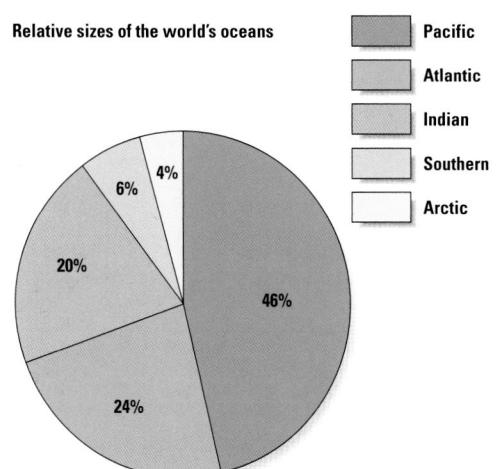

- Pacific
- Atlantic
- Indian
- Southern
- Arctic

From ancient times to about the 15th century, the legendary "Seven Seas" comprised the Red Sea, Mediterranean Sea, Persian Gulf, Black Sea, Adriatic Sea, Caspian Sea, and Indian Sea.

The Earth is a watery planet: more than 70% of its surface – over 140,000,000 sq miles [360,000,000 sq km] – is covered by the oceans and seas. The mighty Pacific alone accounts for nearly 36% of the total, and more than 46% of the sea area. Gravity holds in around 320 million cubic miles [1,400 million cubic km] of water, of which over 97% is saline.

The vast underwater world starts in the shallows of the seaside and plunges to depths of more than 36,000 ft [11,000 m]. The continental shelf, part of the land mass, drops gently to around 650 ft [200 m]; here the seabed falls away suddenly at an angle of 3° to 6° – the continental slope. The third stage, called the continental rise, is more gradual with gradients varying from 1 in 100 to 1 in 700. At an average depth of 16,500 ft [5,000 m] there begins the aptly-named abyssal plain – massive submarine depths where sunlight fails to penetrate and few creatures can survive.

From these plains rise volcanoes which, taken from base to top, rival and even surpass the tallest continental mountains in height. Mauna Kea, on Hawai'i, reaches a total of 33,400 ft [10,203 m], some 4,500 ft [1,355 m] higher than Mount Everest, though scarcely 40% is visible above sea level.

In addition, there are underwater mountain chains up to 600 miles [1,000 km] across, whose peaks sometimes appear above sea level as islands, such as Iceland and Tristan da Cunha.

OCEAN DEPTHS

Average and maximum depths of the world's great oceans, in meters

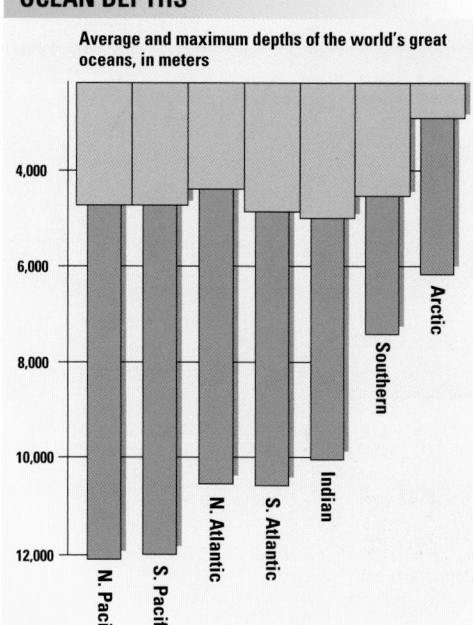

OCEAN CURRENTS

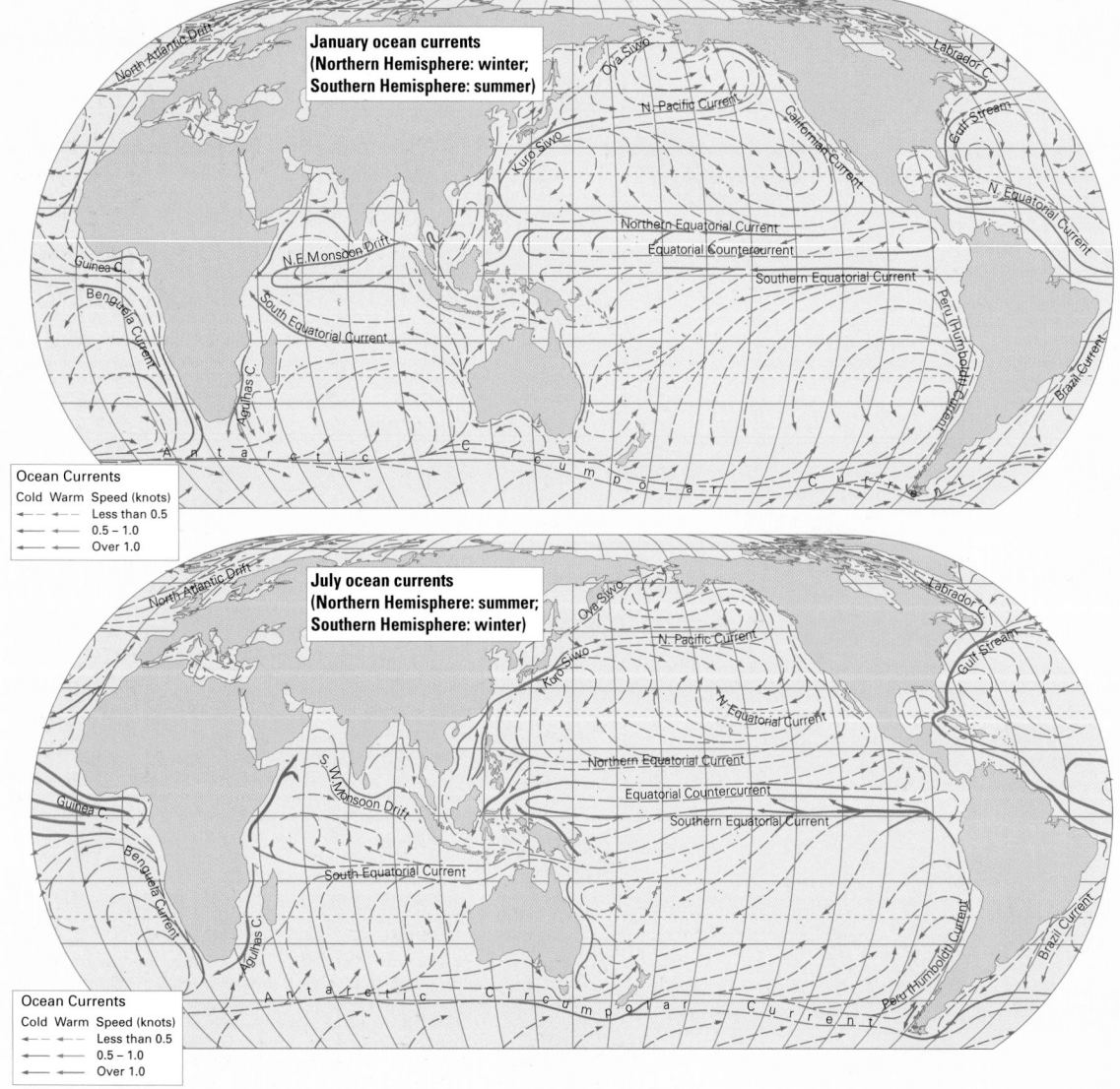

January ocean currents (Northern Hemisphere: winter; Southern Hemisphere: summer)

Ocean Currents
Cold Warm Speed (knots)
Less than 0.5
0.5 – 1.0
Over 1.0

July ocean currents (Northern Hemisphere: summer; Southern Hemisphere: winter)

Ocean Currents
Cold Warm Speed (knots)
Less than 0.5
0.5 – 1.0
Over 1.0

Moving immense quantities of energy as well as billions of tonnes of water every hour, the ocean currents are a vital part of the great heat engine that drives the Earth's climate. They themselves are produced by a twofold mechanism. At the surface, winds push huge masses of water before them; in the deep ocean, below an abrupt temperature gradient that separates the churning surface waters from the still depths, density variations cause slow vertical movements.

The pattern of circulation of the great surface currents is determined by the displacement known as the Coriolis effect. As the Earth turns beneath a moving object – whether it is a tennis ball or a vast mass of water – it appears to be deflected to one side. The deflection is most obvious near the Equator, where the Earth's surface is spinning eastward at 1,050 mph [1,700 km/h]; currents moving poleward are curved clockwise in the northern hemisphere and counterclockwise in the southern.

The result is a system of spinning circles known as "gyres." The Coriolis effect piles up water on the left of each gyre, creating a narrow, fast-moving stream that is matched by a slower, broader returning current on the right. North and south of the Equator, the fastest currents are located in the west and in the east respectively. In each case, warm water moves from the Equator and cold water returns to it. Cold currents often bring an upwelling of nutrients with them, supporting the world's most economically important fisheries.

Depending on the prevailing winds, some currents on or near the Equator may reverse their direction in the course of the year – a seasonal variation on which Asian monsoon rains depend, and whose occasional failure can bring disaster to millions of people.

WORLD FISHING AREAS

Main commercial fishing areas (numbered FAO regions)

Catch by top marine fishing areas, million tonnes (2009)

		% world catch by area
1.	North Pacific	23.6%
2.	Central Pacific	11.6%
3.	South Pacific	12.3%
4.	Indian	11.2%
5.	North Atlantic	11.0%
6.	Central Atlantic	3.5%
7.	South Atlantic	2.5%

Principal fishing areas

Leading fishing nations

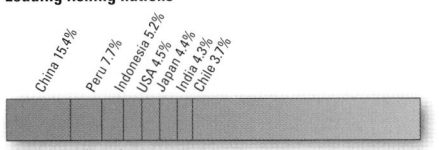

China 15.4% | Peru 7.7% | Indonesia 5.2% | USA 4.5% | Japan 4.4% | India 4.3% | Chile 3.7%

World total (2009): 96.1 million tonnes
(Marine catch 90% : Inland catch 10%)

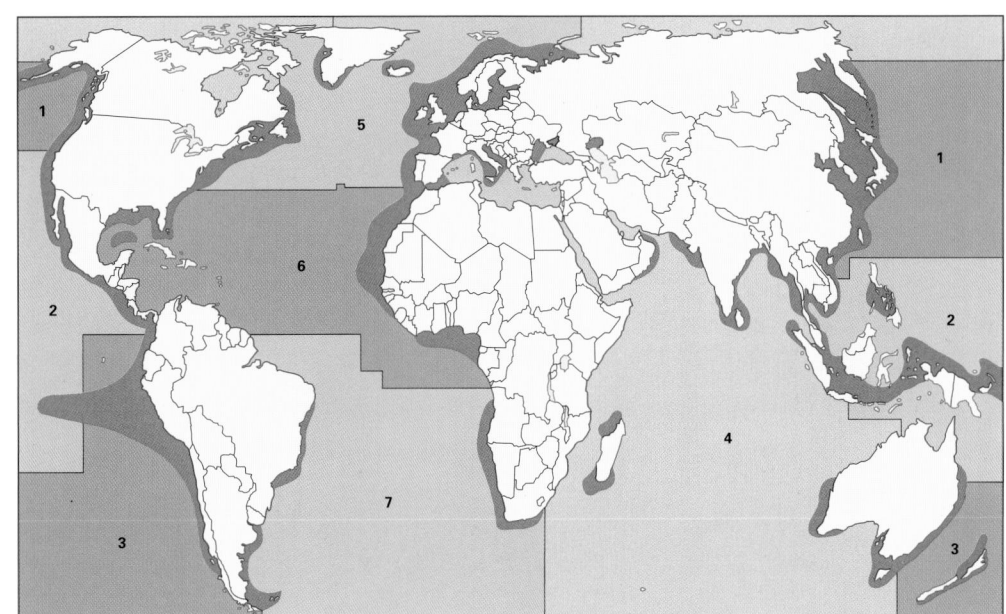

MARINE POLLUTION

Sources of marine oil pollution

- Tanker operations
- Municipal wastes
- Tanker accidents
- Bilge and fuel oils
- Natural seeps
- Industrial waste
- Urban runoff
- Coastal oil refining
- Offshore oil rigs
- River runoffs
- Other

OIL SPILLS

Major oil spills from tankers and combined carriers

Year	Vessel	Location	Spill (barrels)*	Cause
1979	Atlantic Empress	West Indies	1,890,000	collision
1983	Castillo De Bellver	South Africa	1,760,000	fire
1978	Amoco Cadiz	France	1,628,000	grounding
1991	Haven	Italy	1,029,000	explosion
1988	Odyssey	Canada	1,000,000	fire
1967	Torrey Canyon	UK	909,000	grounding
1972	Sea Star	Gulf of Oman	902,250	collision
1977	Hawaiian Patriot	Hawaiian Is.	742,500	fire
1979	Independenta	Turkey	696,350	collision
1993	Braer	UK	625,000	grounding
1996	Sea Empress	UK	515,000	grounding
2002	Prestige	Spain	463,250	storm

Other sources of major oil spills

1983	Nowruz oilfield	Persian Gulf	4,250,000†	war
1979	Ixtoc 1 oilwell	Gulf of Mexico	4,200,000	blowout
2010	Deepwater Horizon	Gulf of Mexico	3.6 - 4,610,000	blowout

* 1 barrel = 0.136 tonnes/159 lit./35 Imperial gal./42 US gal. † estimated

RIVER POLLUTION

Sources of river pollution, USA

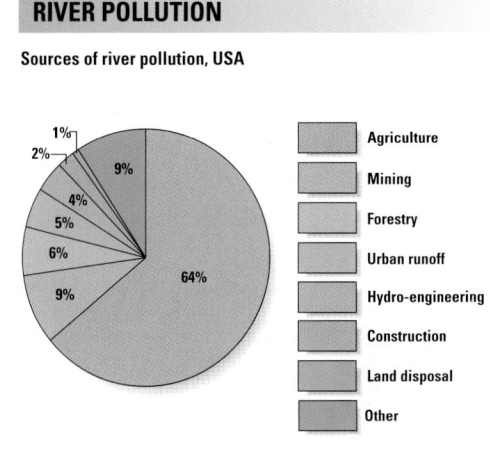

- Agriculture
- Mining
- Forestry
- Urban runoff
- Hydro-engineering
- Construction
- Land disposal
- Other

EL NIÑO

El Niño, "The Little Boy" in Spanish, was originally the name given by local fishermen to the warm current that can appear off the Pacific coast of South America. In a normal year, southeasterly trade winds drive surface waters westward off the coast of South America, drawing cold, nutrient-rich water up from below. In an El Niño year, warm water from the west Pacific suppresses upwelling in the east, depriving the region of nutrients and driving the fish away. The water is warmed by as much as 13°F, disturbing the tropical atmosphere circulation. During an intense El Niño, the southeast trade winds change direction and become equatorial westerlies, resulting in climatic extremes in many regions of the world, such as drought in parts of Australia and India, and heavy rainfall in southeastern USA.

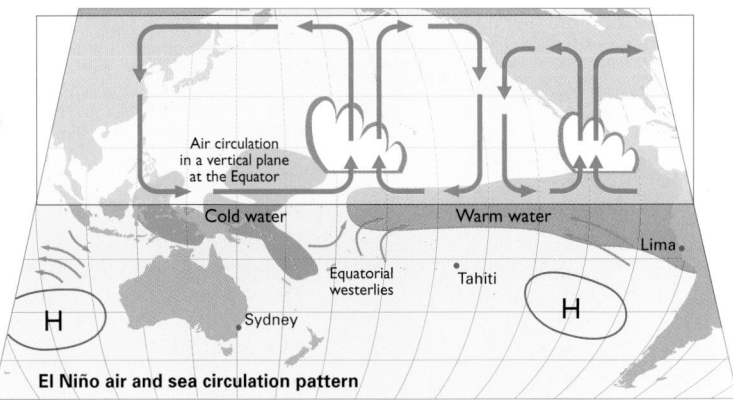

El Niño air and sea circulation pattern

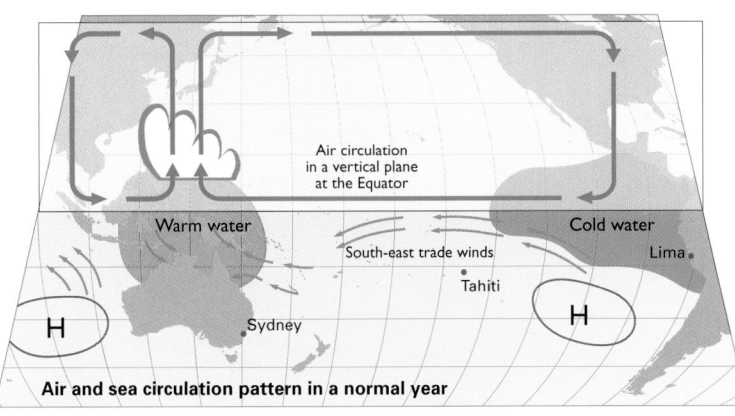

Air and sea circulation pattern in a normal year

El Niño events occur about every 4 to 7 years and typically last for around 12 to 18 months. El Niño usually results in reduced rainfall across northern and eastern Australia. This can lead to widespread and severe drought, as well as increased temperatures and bushfire risk. However, each El Niño event is unique in terms of its strength as well as its impact. It is measured by the Southern Oscillation Index (SOI) and the changes in ocean temperatures.

La Niña, or "The Little Girl," is associated with cooler waters in the central and eastern Pacific. A La Niña year can result in cooler land temperatures across the tropics and subtropics, and more storms in the North Atlantic.

Climate

CLIMATE REGIONS

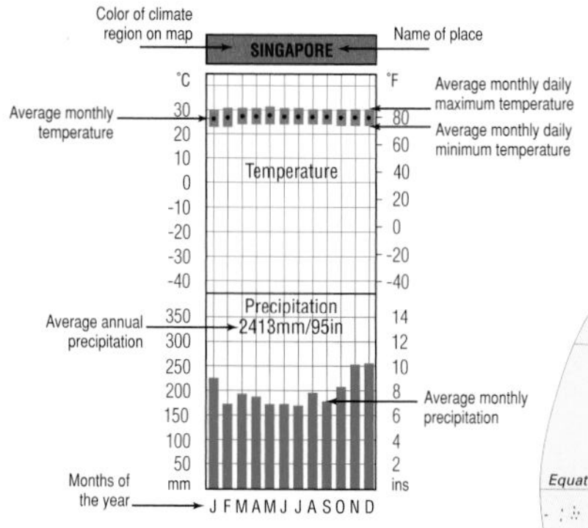

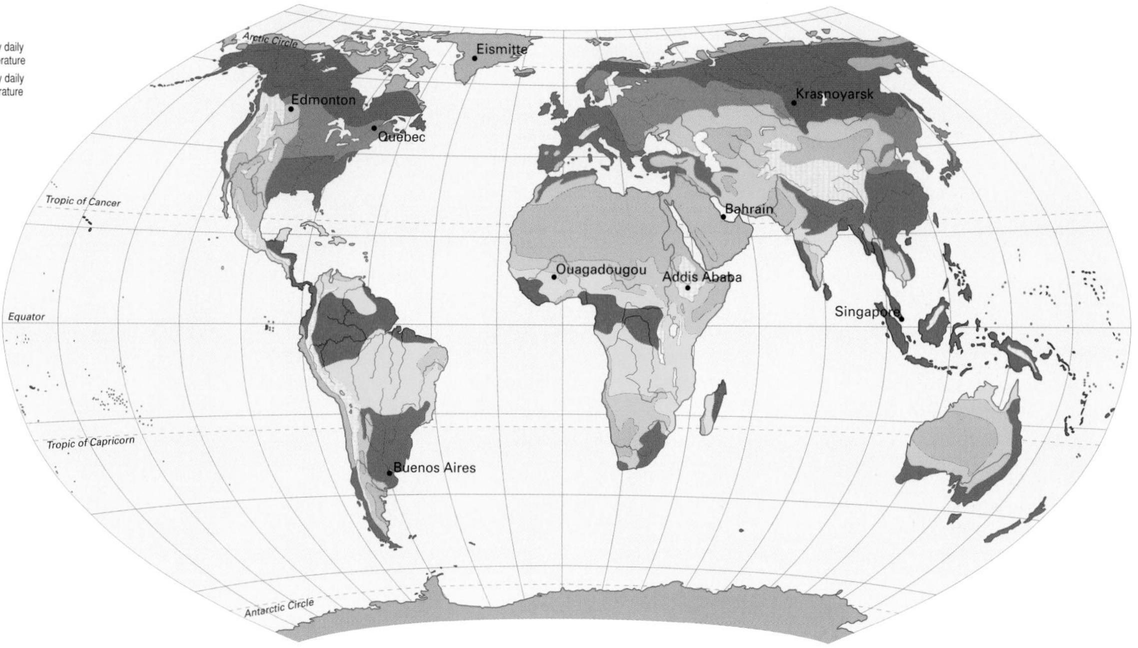

Color of climate region on map
SINGAPORE ← Name of place

°C / °F
Average monthly temperature — 30 20 10 0 -10 -20 -30 -40 — Average monthly daily maximum temperature / Average monthly daily minimum temperature

Temperature

80 60 40 20 0 -20 -40

Average annual precipitation — 350 300 250 200 150 100 50 mm

Precipitation 2413mm/95in

14 12 10 8 6 4 2 ins — Average monthly precipitation

Months of the year → J F M A M J J A S O N D

(World map with locations: Arctic Circle, Eismitte, Edmonton, Québec, Krasnoyarsk, Tropic of Cancer, Bahrain, Ouagadougou, Addis Ababa, Singapore, Equator, Tropic of Capricorn, Buenos Aires, Antarctic Circle)

Tropical climate (hot with rain all year)

Desert climate (hot and very dry)

Savanna climate (hot with dry season)

Steppe climate (warm and dry)

Mild climate (warm and wet)

Continental climate (wet with cold winter)

Subarctic climate (very cold winter)

Polar climate (very cold and dry)

Mountainous climate (altitude affects climate)

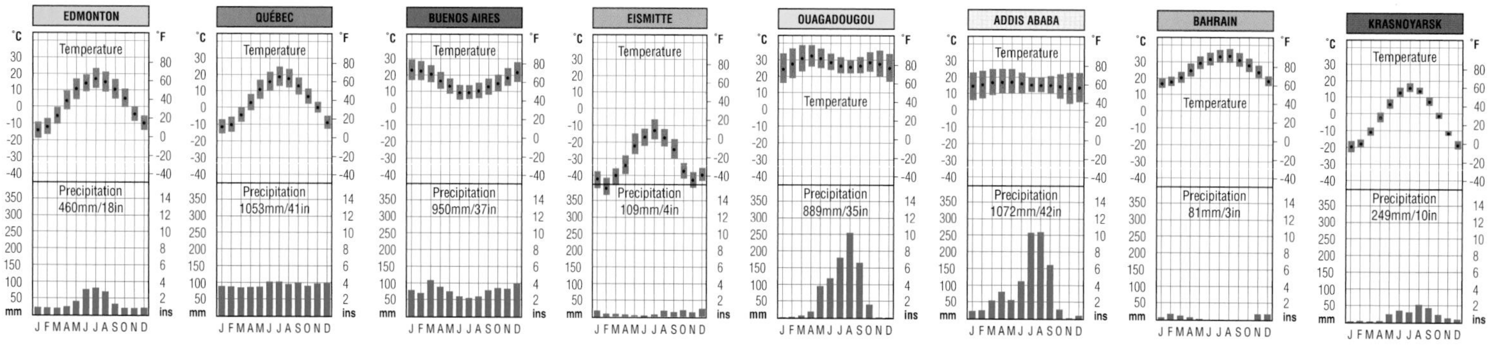

EDMONTON
Temperature
Precipitation 460mm/18in
J F M A M J J A S O N D

QUÉBEC
Temperature
Precipitation 1053mm/41in
J F M A M J J A S O N D

BUENOS AIRES
Temperature
Precipitation 950mm/37in
J F M A M J J A S O N D

EISMITTE
Temperature
Precipitation 109mm/4in
J F M A M J J A S O N D

OUAGADOUGOU
Temperature
Precipitation 889mm/35in
J F M A M J J A S O N D

ADDIS ABABA
Temperature
Precipitation 1072mm/42in
J F M A M J J A S O N D

BAHRAIN
Temperature
Precipitation 81mm/3in
J F M A M J J A S O N D

KRASNOYARSK
Temperature
Precipitation 249mm/10in
J F M A M J J A S O N D

THE MONSOON

Monthly rainfall
mm		mm
400		50
200		25
100		0

→ Wind direction

ITCZ (intertropical convergence zone)

In early March, which normally marks the end of the subcontinent's cool season and the start of the hot season, winds blow outward from the mainland. But as the overhead sun and the ITCZ move northward, the land is intensely heated, and a low-pressure system develops. The southeast trade winds, which are drawn across the Equator, change direction and are sucked into the interior, bringing heavy rain. By November, the overhead sun and the ITCZ have again moved southward and the wind directions are again reversed. Cool winds blow from the Asian interior to the sea, losing any moisture on the Himalayas before descending to the coast.

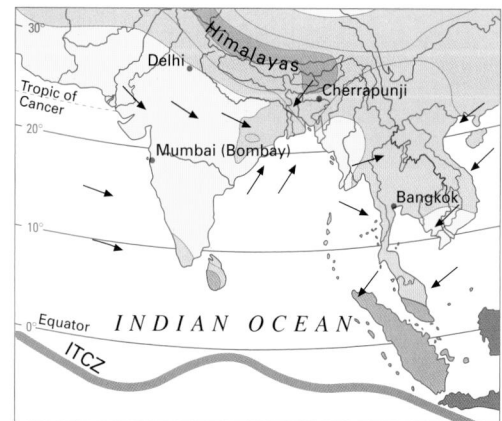

March – Start of the hot, dry season, the ITCZ is over the southern Indian Ocean.

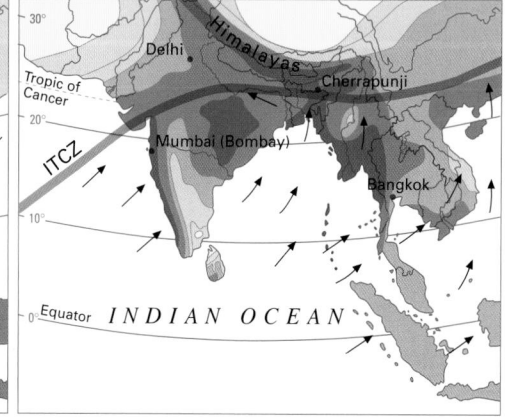

July – The rainy season, the ITCZ has migrated northward; winds blow onshore.

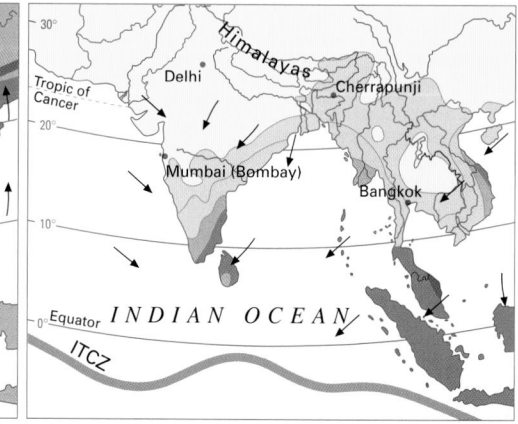

November – The ITCZ has returned south, the offshore winds are cool and dry.

CLIMATE

Climate is weather in the long term: the seasonal pattern of hot and cold, wet and dry, averaged over time (usually 30 years). At the simplest level, it is caused by the uneven heating of the Earth. Surplus heat at the Equator passes toward the poles, leveling out the energy differential. Its passage is marked by a ceaseless churning of the atmosphere and the oceans, further agitated by the Earth's diurnal spin and the motion it imparts to moving air and water. The heat's means of transport – by winds and ocean currents, by the continual evaporation and recondensation of water molecules – is the weather itself. There are four basic types of climate, each of which can be further subdivided: tropical, desert (dry), temperate, and polar.

COMPOSITION OF DRY AIR

Nitrogen	78.09%	Sulfur dioxide	trace
Oxygen	20.95%	Nitrogen oxide	trace
Argon	0.93%	Methane	trace
Water vapor	0.2–4.0%	Dust	trace
Carbon dioxide	0.03%	Helium	trace
Ozone	0.00006%	Neon	trace

CLIMATE RECORDS

Temperature
Highest recorded shade temperature: Al Aziziyah, Libya, 135.9°F [57.7°C], September 13, 1922.

Highest mean annual temperature: Dallol, Ethiopia, 94°F [34.4°C], 1960–66.

Longest heatwave: Marble Bar, W. Australia, 162 days over 100°F [38°C], October 23, 1923 to April 7, 1924.

Lowest recorded temperature (outside poles): Verkhoyansk, Siberia, –93.6°F [–68°C], February 7, 1982.

Lowest mean annual temperature: Polus Nedostupnosti, Pole of Cold, Antarctica, –72°F [–57.8°C].

Precipitation
Driest place: Quillagua, Chile, mean annual rainfall 0.02 inches [0.5 mm], 1964–2001.

Wettest place (average): Mt Wai-ale-ale, Hawai'i, USA, mean annual rainfall 459.8 inches [11,680 mm].

Wettest place (12 months): Cherrapunji, Meghalaya, N. E. India, 1,042 inches [26,461 mm], August 1860 to July 1861. Cherrapunji also holds the record for the most rainfall in one month: 115 inches [2,930 mm], July 1861.

Wettest place (24 hours): Fac Fac, Réunion, Indian Ocean, 71.9 inches [1,825 mm], March 15–16, 1952.

Heaviest hailstones: Gopalganj, Bangladesh, up to 2.25 lb [1.02 kg], April 14, 1986 (killed 92 people).

Heaviest snowfall (continuous): Bessans, Savoie, France, 68 inches [1,730 mm] in 19 hours, April 5–6, 1969.

Heaviest snowfall (season/year): Mt Baker, Washington, USA, 1,140 inches [28,956 mm], June 1998 to June 1999.

Pressure and winds
Highest barometric pressure: Agata, Siberia (at 862 ft [262 m] altitude), 1,083.8 mb, December 31, 1968.

Lowest barometric pressure: Typhoon Tip, Guam, Pacific Ocean, 870 mb, October 12, 1979.

Highest recorded wind speed: Bridge Creek, Oklahoma, USA, 318 mph [512 km/h], May 3, 1999. Measured by Doppler radar monitoring a tornado.

Windiest place: Port Martin, Antarctica, where winds of more than 40 mph [64 km/h] occur for not less than 100 days a year.

Conversions
°C = (°F − 32) × 5/9; °F = (°C × 9/5) + 32; 0°C = 32°F
1 in = 25.4 mm; 1 mm = 0.0394 in; 100 mm = 3.94 in

TEMPERATURE

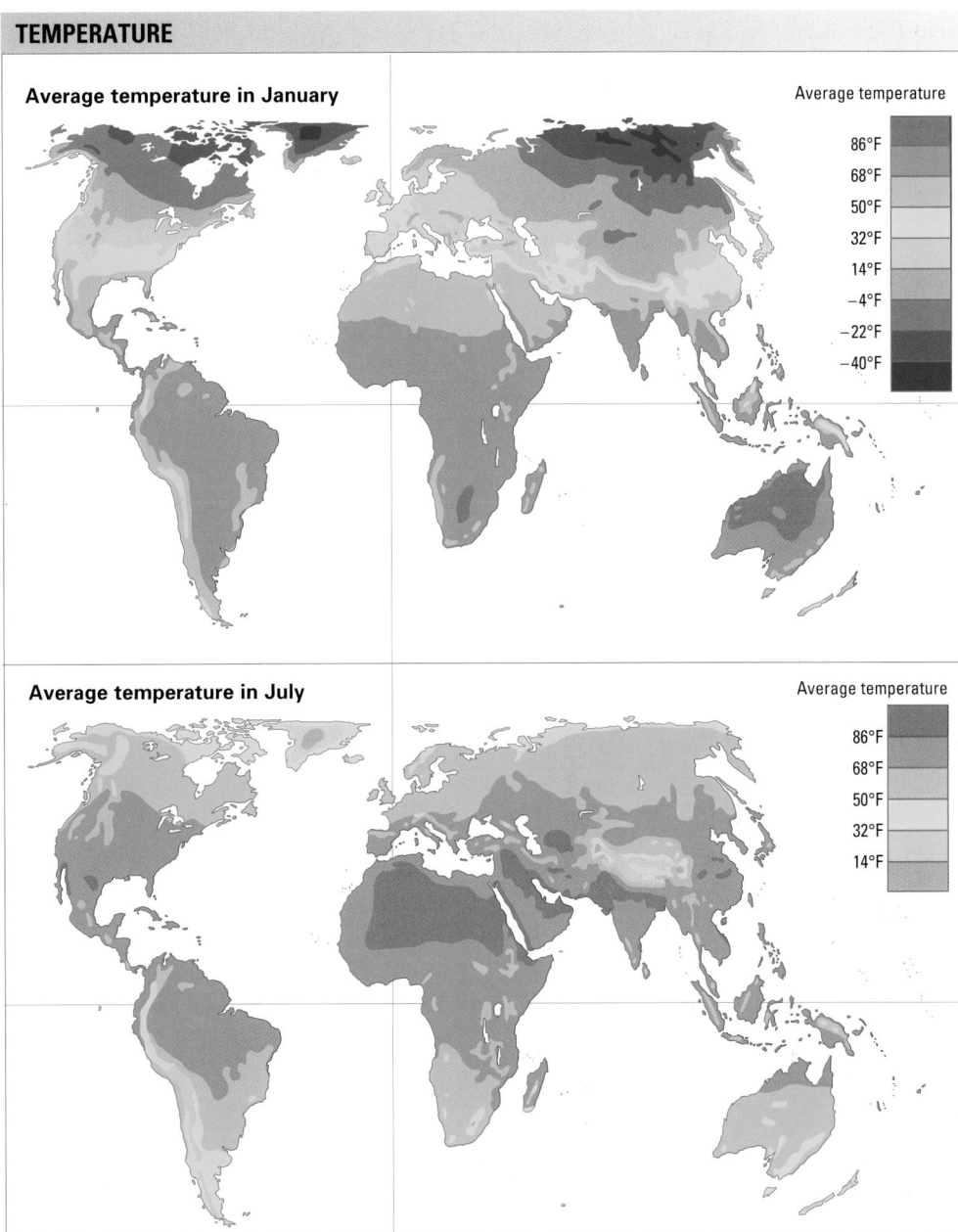

Average temperature in January

Average temperature

- 86°F
- 68°F
- 50°F
- 32°F
- 14°F
- −4°F
- −22°F
- −40°F

Average temperature in July

Average temperature

- 86°F
- 68°F
- 50°F
- 32°F
- 14°F

PRECIPITATION (RAINFALL AND SNOW)

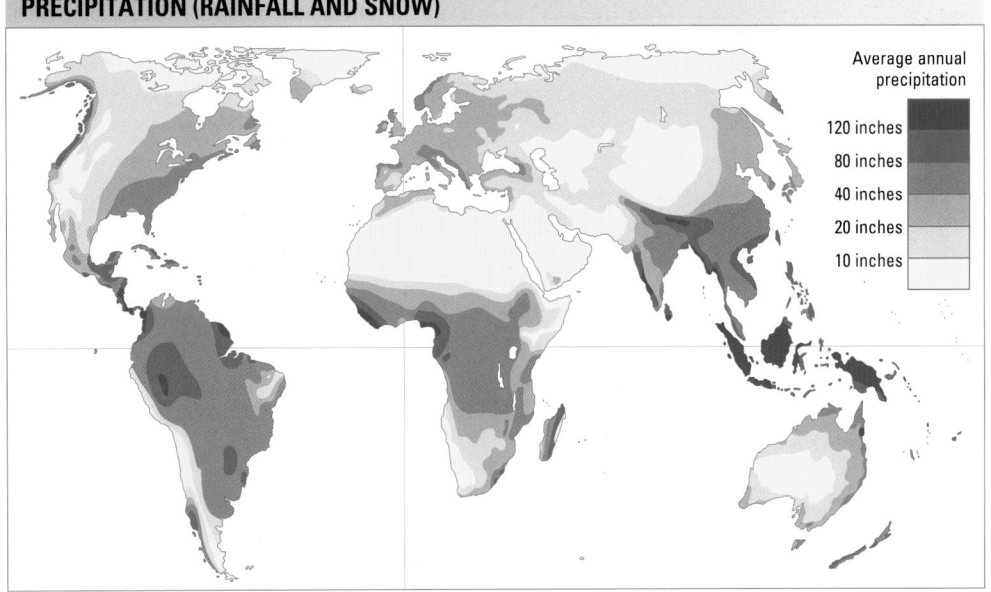

Average annual precipitation

- 120 inches
- 80 inches
- 40 inches
- 20 inches
- 10 inches

Water and Vegetation

THE HYDROLOGICAL CYCLE

The world's water balance is regulated by the constant recycling of water between the oceans, atmosphere and land. The movement of water between these three reservoirs is known as the hydrological cycle. The oceans play a vital role in the hydrological cycle: 74% of the total precipitation falls over the oceans and 84% of the total evaporation comes from the oceans.

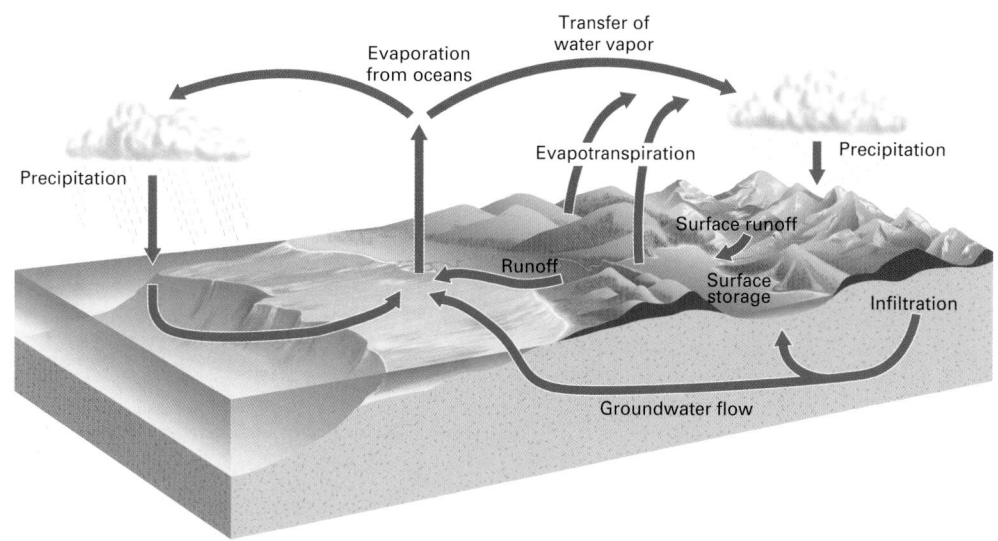

WATER DISTRIBUTION

The distribution of planetary water, by percentage. Oceans and ice caps together account for more than 99% of the total; the breakdown of the remainder is estimated.

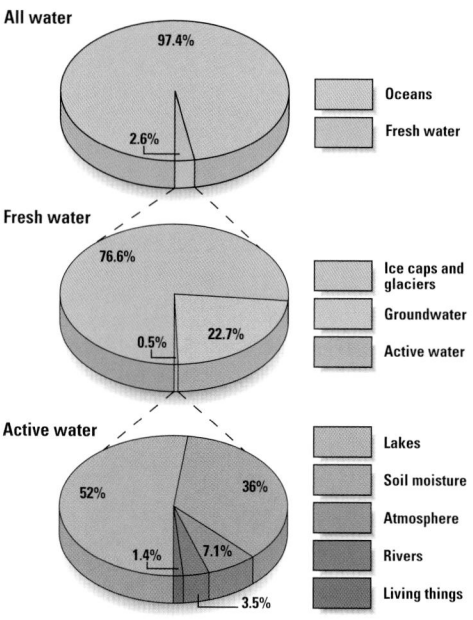

All water
- Oceans
- Fresh water

Fresh water
- Ice caps and glaciers
- Groundwater
- Active water

Active water
- Lakes
- Soil moisture
- Atmosphere
- Rivers
- Living things

WATER UTILIZATION

The percentage breakdown of water usage by sector, selected countries (2009)

Domestic | Industrial | Agriculture

Algeria
Australia
Egypt
France
Ghana
India
Mexico
Poland
Russia
Saudi Arabia
UK
USA

0   20   40   60   80   100

WATER USAGE

Almost all the world's water is 3,000 million years old, and all of it cycles endlessly through the hydrosphere, though at different rates. Water vapor circulates over days or even hours, deep ocean water circulates over millennia, and ice-cap water remains solid for millions of years.

Fresh water is essential to all terrestrial life. Humans cannot survive more than a few days without it, and even the hardiest desert plants and animals could not exist without some water. Agriculture requires huge quantities of fresh water: without large-scale irrigation most of the world's people would starve. In the USA, agriculture uses 40% and industry 46% of all water withdrawals.

According to the latest figures, the average North American uses 1.5 million liters of water per year. This is more than six times the average African, who uses just 186,000 liters of water each year. Europeans and Australians use 694,000 liters per year.

WATER SUPPLY

Percentage of total population with access to safe drinking water (2008)

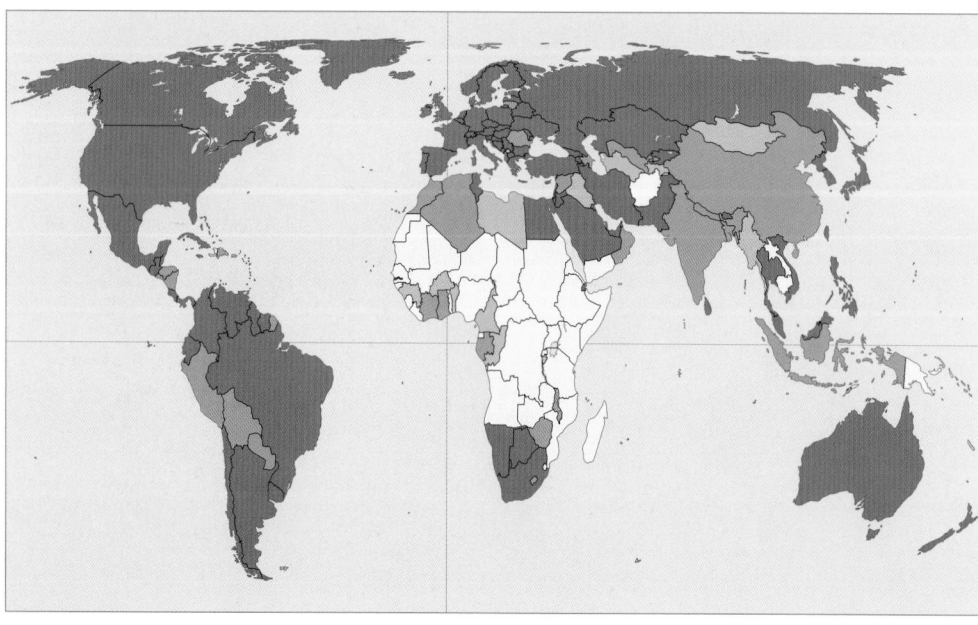

- Over 90% with safe water
- 80 – 90% with safe water
- 70 – 80% with safe water
- Less than 70% with safe water
- No data available

Least well-provided countries

Niger	48%	Madagascar	41%
Fiji	47%	Papua New Guinea	41%
Mozambique	47%	Ethiopia	38%
Congo (Dem. Rep.)	46%	Somalia	30%
Equatorial Guinea	43%	Western Sahara	26%

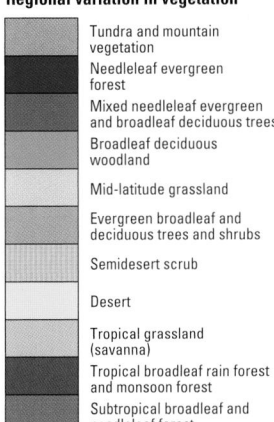

NATURAL VEGETATION

Regional variation in vegetation

- Tundra and mountain vegetation
- Needleleaf evergreen forest
- Mixed needleleaf evergreen and broadleaf deciduous trees
- Broadleaf deciduous woodland
- Mid-latitude grassland
- Evergreen broadleaf and deciduous trees and shrubs
- Semidesert scrub
- Desert
- Tropical grassland (savanna)
- Tropical broadleaf rain forest and monsoon forest
- Subtropical broadleaf and needleleaf forest

The map shows the natural "climax vegetation" of regions, as dictated by climate and topography. In most cases, however, agricultural activity has drastically altered the vegetation pattern. Western Europe, for example, lost most of its broadleaf forest many centuries ago, while irrigation has turned some natural semidesert into productive land.

LAND USE BY CONTINENT (2010)

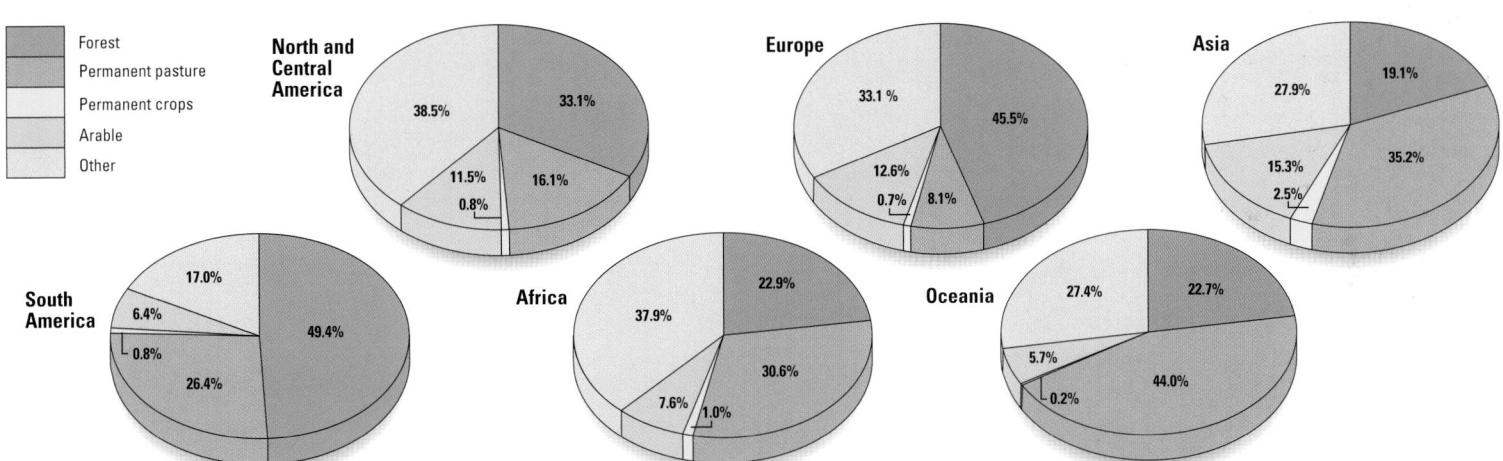

Legend:
- Forest
- Permanent pasture
- Permanent crops
- Arable
- Other

North and Central America: 33.1%, 16.1%, 0.8%, 11.5%, 38.5%

Europe: 45.5%, 8.1%, 0.7%, 12.6%, 33.1%

Asia: 19.1%, 35.2%, 2.5%, 15.3%, 27.9%

South America: 49.4%, 26.4%, 0.8%, 6.4%, 17.0%

Africa: 22.9%, 30.6%, 1.0%, 7.6%, 37.9%

Oceania: 22.7%, 44.0%, 0.2%, 5.7%, 27.4%

FORESTRY: PRODUCTION

	Forest and woodland (million hectares)	Annual production (2010; million cubic meters)	
		Fuelwood	Industrial roundwood*
World	*4,038.7*	*1,868.0*	*1,616.3*
Europe	1,004.2	149.5	504.2
S. America	867.9	197.9	196.2
Africa	677.9	616.7	74.2
N. & C. America	705.4	128.4	520.2
Asia	590.8	765.0	268.0
Oceania	192.5	10.5	53.5

Paper and Board

Top producers (2010)**		Top exporters (2010)**	
China	96.5	Germany	13,254
USA	75.7	Finland	11,851
Japan	27.3	USA	11,707
Germany	23.2	Canada	10,910
Canada	12.7	Sweden	10,579
Finland	11.7		
World	399.8		

* roundwood is timber as it is felled
** in million tonnes

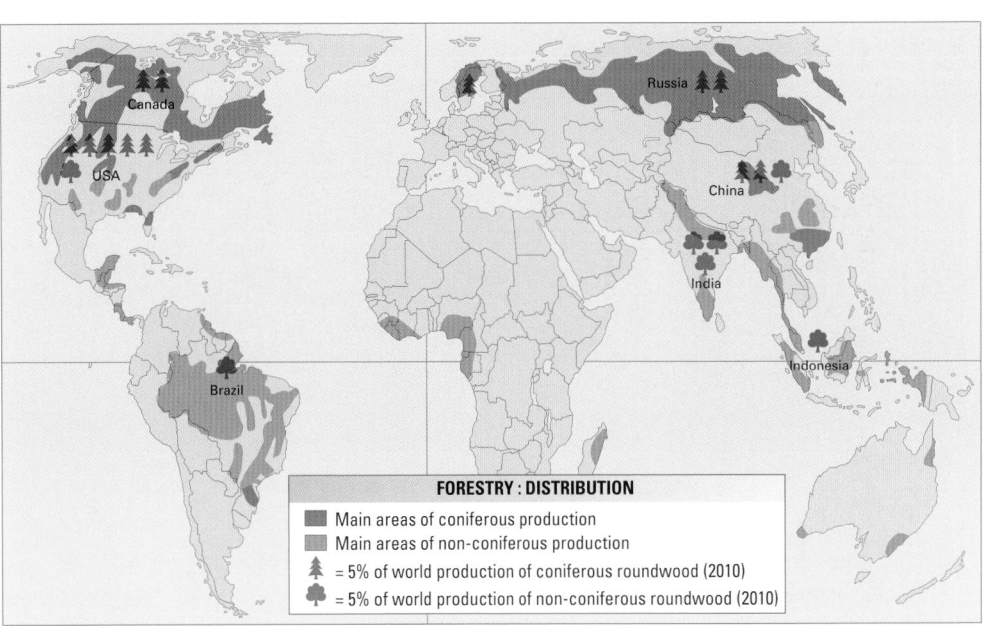

FORESTRY : DISTRIBUTION

- Main areas of coniferous production
- Main areas of non-coniferous production
- 🌲 = 5% of world production of coniferous roundwood (2010)
- 🌳 = 5% of world production of non-coniferous roundwood (2010)

Environment

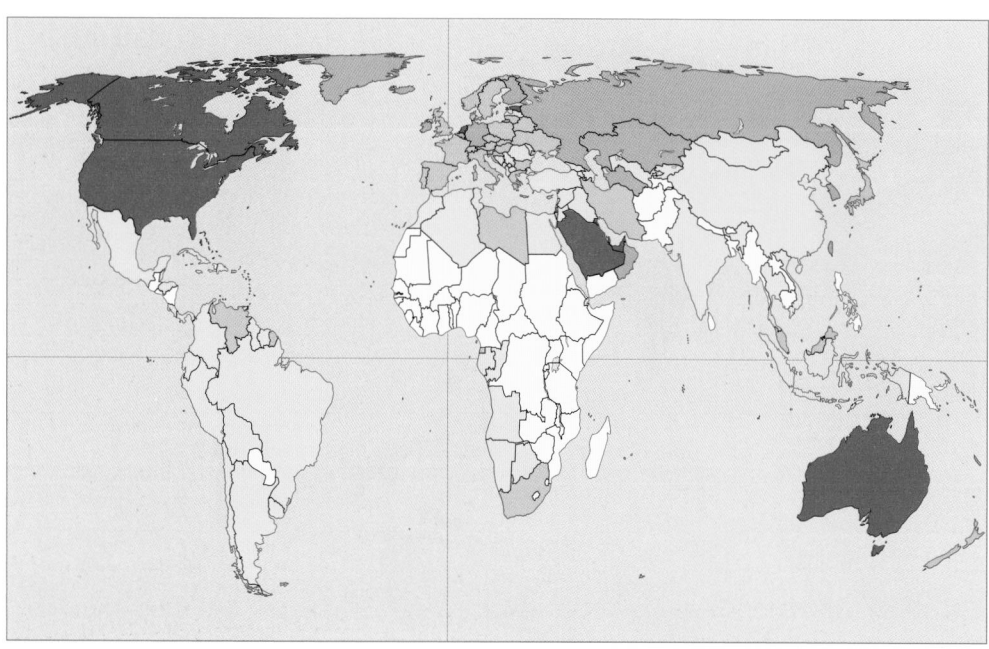

GLOBAL WARMING

Carbon dioxide emissions in tonnes per capita (2009)

- Over 15
- 10 – 15
- 5 – 10
- 1 – 5
- Under 1
- No data available

CARBON DIOXIDE EMISSIONS

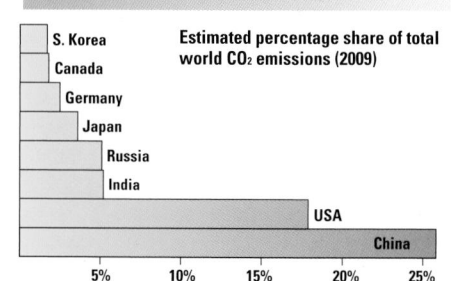

Estimated percentage share of total world CO_2 emissions (2009)

- S. Korea
- Canada
- Germany
- Japan
- Russia
- India
- USA
- China

5%　10%　15%　20%　25%

PREDICTED CHANGE IN PRECIPITATION

The difference between actual annual average precipitation, 1960–1990, and the predicted annual average precipitation, 2070–2100. It should be noted that these predicted annual mean changes mask quite significant seasonal detail.

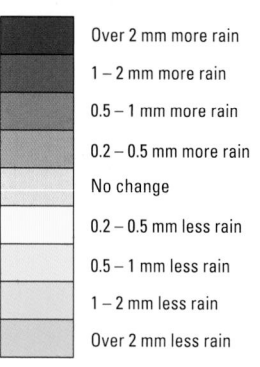

- Over 2 mm more rain
- 1 – 2 mm more rain
- 0.5 – 1 mm more rain
- 0.2 – 0.5 mm more rain
- No change
- 0.2 – 0.5 mm less rain
- 0.5 – 1 mm less rain
- 1 – 2 mm less rain
- Over 2 mm less rain

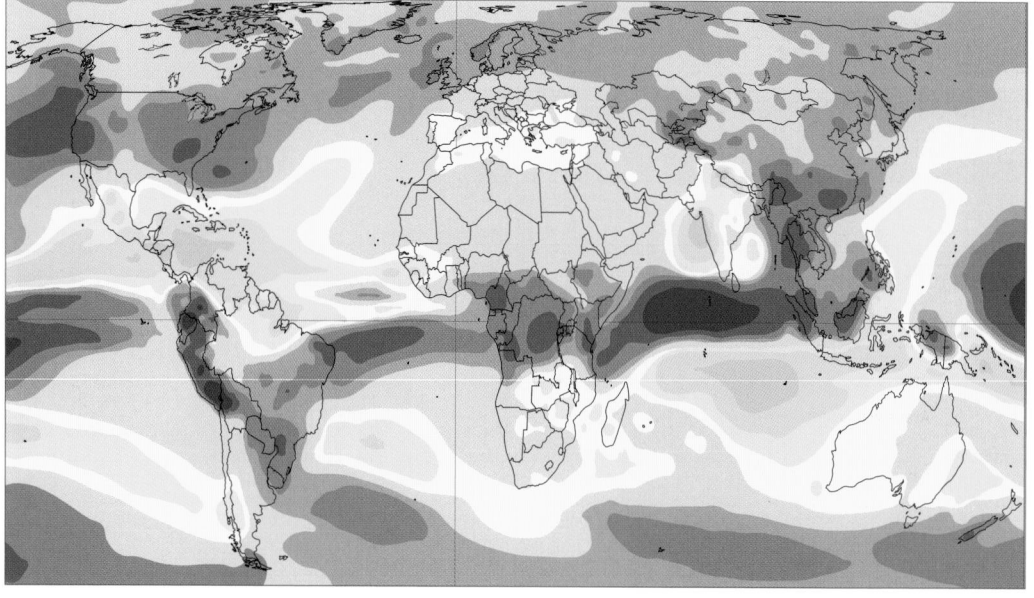

PREDICTED CHANGE IN TEMPERATURE

The difference between actual annual average surface air temperature, 1960–1990, and the predicted annual average surface air temperature, 2070–2100. This map shows the predicted increase, assuming a "medium growth" of global economy and assuming that no measures are taken to combat the emission of greenhouse gases.

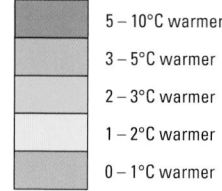

- 5 – 10°C warmer
- 3 – 5°C warmer
- 2 – 3°C warmer
- 1 – 2°C warmer
- 0 – 1°C warmer

Source: The Hadley Centre of Climate Prediction and Research, The Met. Office

GLOBAL WARMING PROJECTIONS

Projected Change in Global Warming

⋀ Rise in average temperatures assuming present trends in CO_2 emissions continue

⋀ Assuming some cuts are made in emissions

⋀ Assuming drastic cuts are made in emissions

Climate models are used to provide the best scientifically-based estimates of the future global climate. A typical method is to run the models for some decades ahead and then to compare the predicted average with a past 30-year period. A range of climate models are used, run with different scenarios that express the breadth of possibilities of, for example, industrial development and the degree of atmospheric pollution "clean-up" by industrial nations.

The diagram on the right shows global observed and predicted surface mean temperature change from 1950 to 2070 with three prediction scenarios. The first (red) assumes rapid economic growth and continued population increases. The second (blue) assumes some attempts are made to cut greenhouse gas emissions, while the green line involves the greater use of cleaner technologies, with global population peaking mid-century then declining.

C°
+3.0
+2.5
+2.0
+1.5
+1.0
+0.5
0
−0.5

1950 1970 1990 2010 2030 2050 2070

GREENHOUSE EFFECT

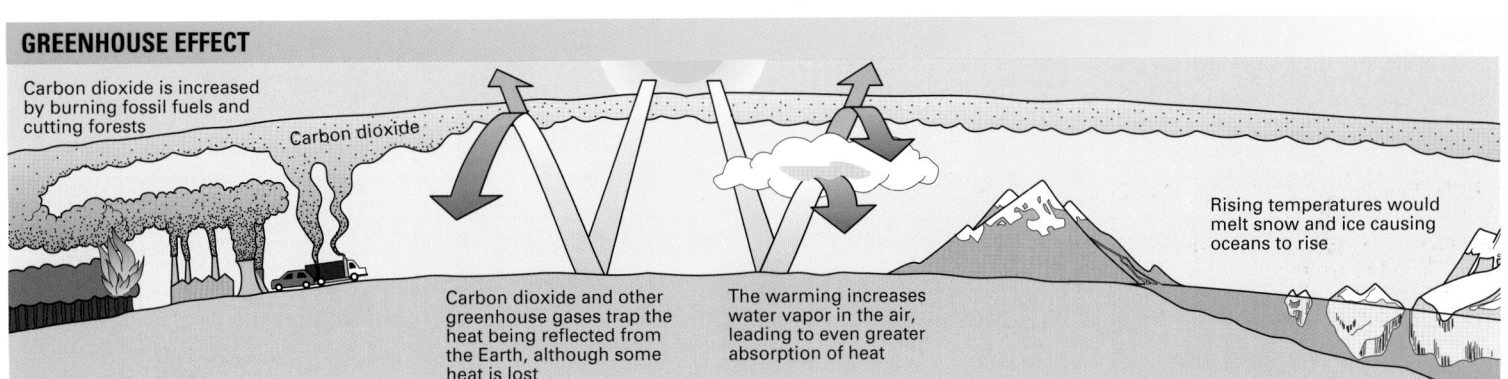

Carbon dioxide is increased by burning fossil fuels and cutting forests

Carbon dioxide

Rising temperatures would melt snow and ice causing oceans to rise

Carbon dioxide and other greenhouse gases trap the heat being reflected from the Earth, although some heat is lost

The warming increases water vapor in the air, leading to even greater absorption of heat

DESERTIFICATION AND DEFORESTATION

- Existing deserts
- Areas with a high risk of desertification
- Areas with a moderate risk of desertification
- Former areas of rain forest
- Existing rain forest

FOREST CLEARANCE

Thousands of hectares of forest cleared annually, tropical countries surveyed 1980–85, 1990–95, 2000–2005 and 2005–10. Loss as a percentage of remaining stocks is shown in figures on each column. Gain is indicated as a minus figure.

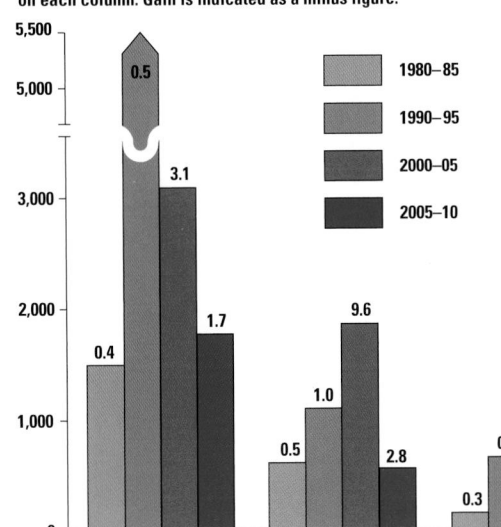

- 1980–85
- 1990–95
- 2000–05
- 2005–10

5,500
5,000
3,000
2,000
1,000
0

Brazil 0.4, 0.5, 3.1, 1.7
Indonesia 0.5, 1.0, 9.6, 2.8
India 0.3, 0.0, 0.7, −0.9
Burma 0.3, 1.4, 4.7, 3.7
Thailand 2.4, 2.6, 2.0, −0.3
Vietnam 0.7, 1.4, −12.2, −4.4
Philippines 1.0, 3.5, 4.2, −3.0
Costa Rica 4.0, 3.0, −0.6, −3.7

DEFORESTATION

The Earth's remaining forests are under attack from three directions: expanding agriculture, logging, and growing consumption of fuelwood, often in combination. Sometimes deforestation is the direct result of government policy, as in the efforts made to resettle the urban poor in some parts of Brazil; just as often, it comes about despite state attempts at conservation.

Loggers, licensed or unlicensed, blaze a trail into virgin forest, often destroying twice as many trees as they harvest. Landless farmers follow, burning away most of what remains to plant their crops, completing the destruction. However, some countries such as Vietnam, Philippines and Costa Rica have successfully implemented reafforestation programs.

Population

COPYRIGHT PHILIP'S

DEMOGRAPHIC PROFILES

Developed nations such as the UK have populations evenly spread across the age groups and, usually, a growing proportion of elderly people. The great majority of the people in developing nations, however, are in the younger age groups, about to enter their most fertile years. In time, these population profiles should resemble the world profile (even Nigeria has made recent progress by reducing its birth rate), but the transition will come about only after a few more generations of rapid population growth.

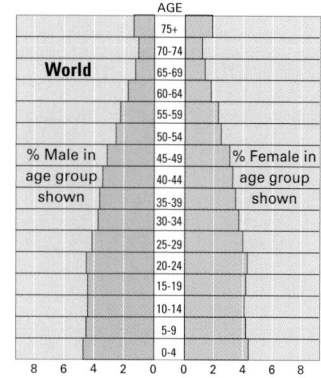

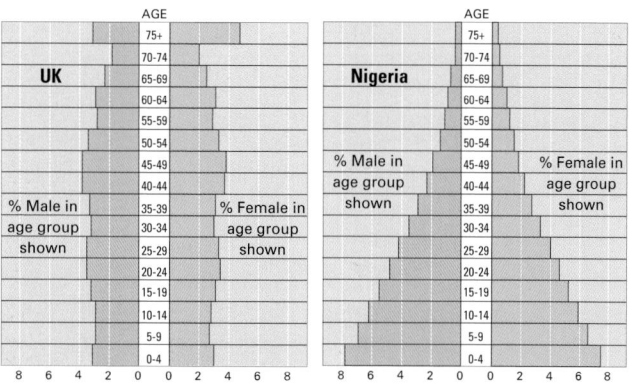

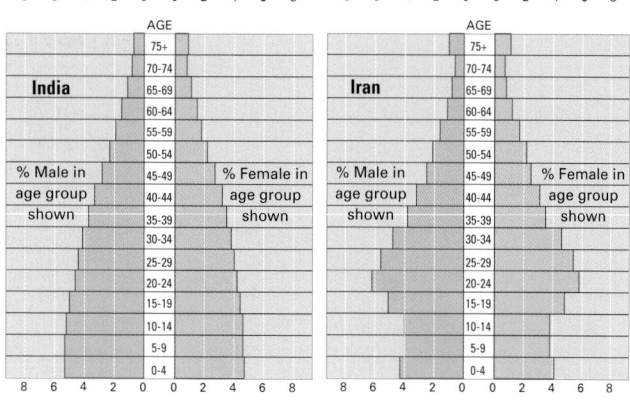

MOST POPULOUS NATIONS

Totals in millions (2011 estimates)

1. China	1,337	9. Russia	139	17. Turkey	79
2. India	1,189	10. Japan	126	18. Iran	78
3. USA	313	11. Mexico	113	19. Congo (Dem. Rep.)	72
4. Indonesia	246	12. Philippines	101	20. Thailand	67
5. Brazil	203	13. Vietnam	91	21. France	65
6. Pakistan	187	14. Ethiopia	91	22. UK	63
7. Bangladesh	159	15. Egypt	82	23. Italy	61
8. Nigeria	155	16. Germany	81	24. Burma (Myanmar)	53

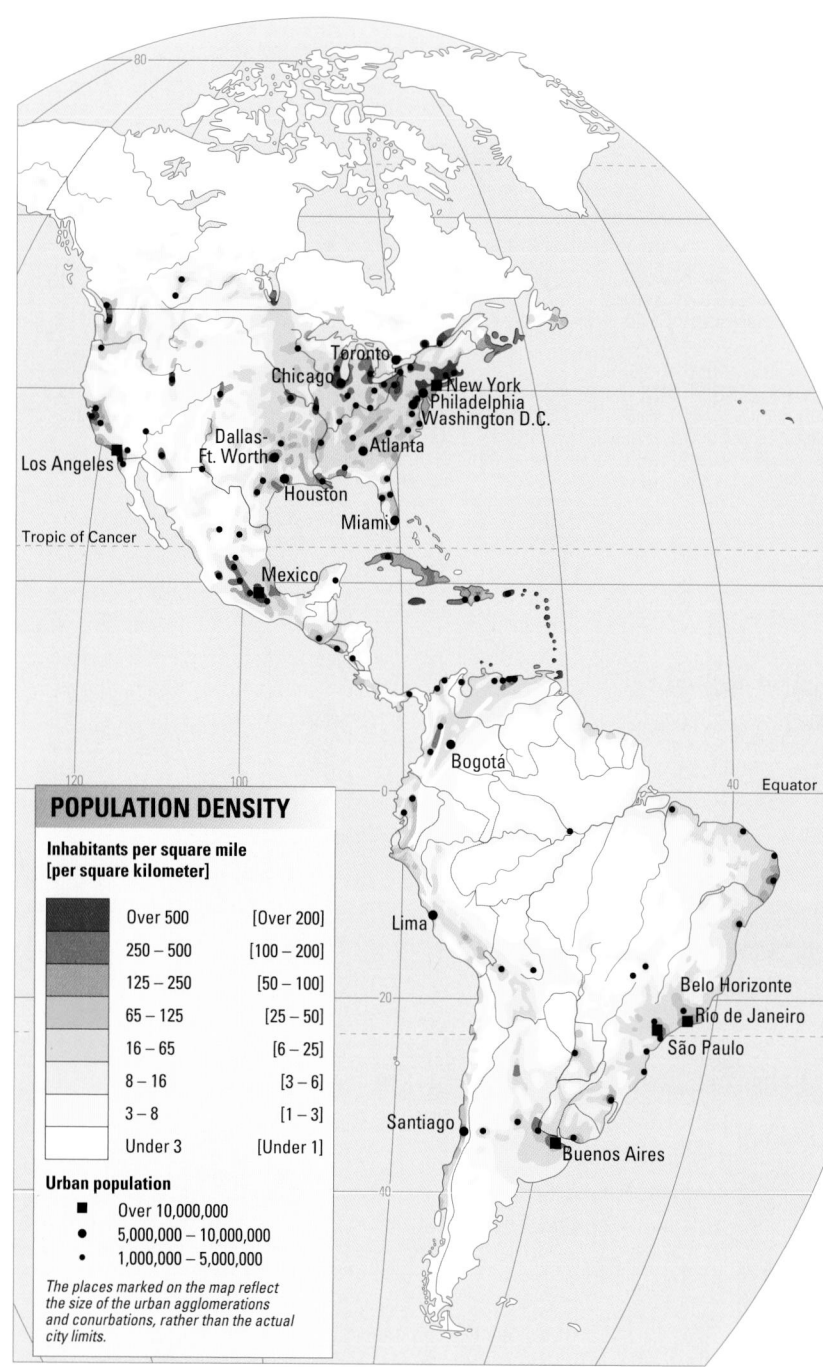

POPULATION DENSITY

Inhabitants per square mile
[per square kilometer]

Over 500	[Over 200]
250 – 500	[100 – 200]
125 – 250	[50 – 100]
65 – 125	[25 – 50]
16 – 65	[6 – 25]
8 – 16	[3 – 6]
3 – 8	[1 – 3]
Under 3	[Under 1]

Urban population

- ■ Over 10,000,000
- ● 5,000,000 – 10,000,000
- • 1,000,000 – 5,000,000

The places marked on the map reflect the size of the urban agglomerations and conurbations, rather than the actual city limits.

Projection: Interrupted Mollweide's Homolographic

CONTINENTAL COMPARISONS

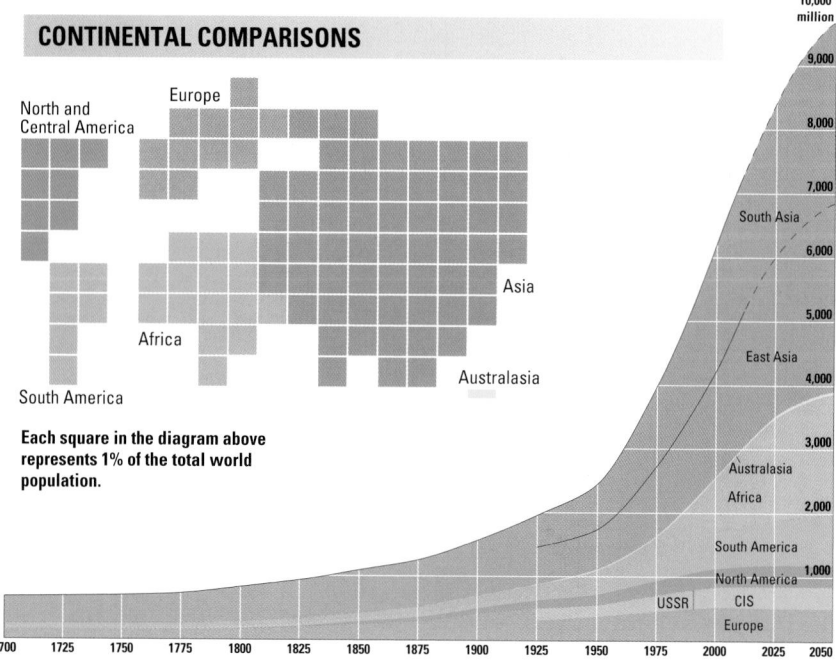

Each square in the diagram above represents 1% of the total world population.

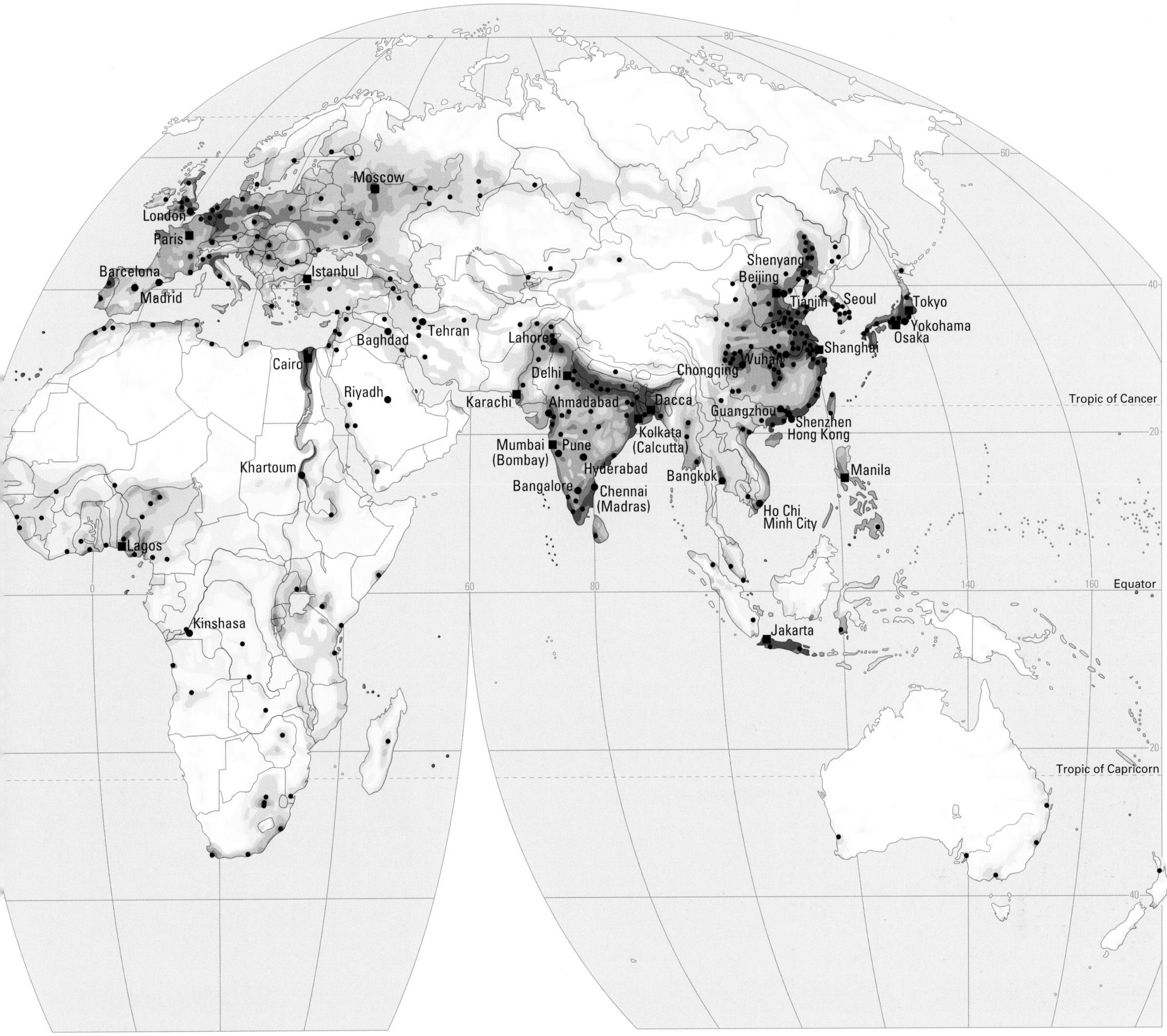

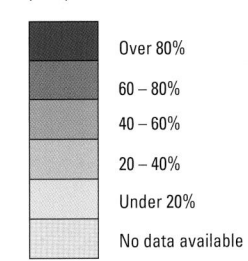

London
Paris
Barcelona
Madrid
Moscow
Istanbul
Cairo
Baghdad
Tehran
Riyadh
Lahore
Delhi
Khartoum
Karachi
Ahmadabad
Mumbai (Bombay)
Pune
Hyderabad
Bangalore
Chennai (Madras)
Kolkata (Calcutta)
Dacca
Bangkok
Shenyang
Beijing
Tianjin
Seoul
Tokyo
Yokohama
Osaka
Wuhan
Shanghai
Chongqing
Guangzhou
Shenzhen
Hong Kong
Manila
Ho Chi Minh City
Jakarta
Lagos
Kinshasa

Tropic of Cancer
Equator
Tropic of Capricorn

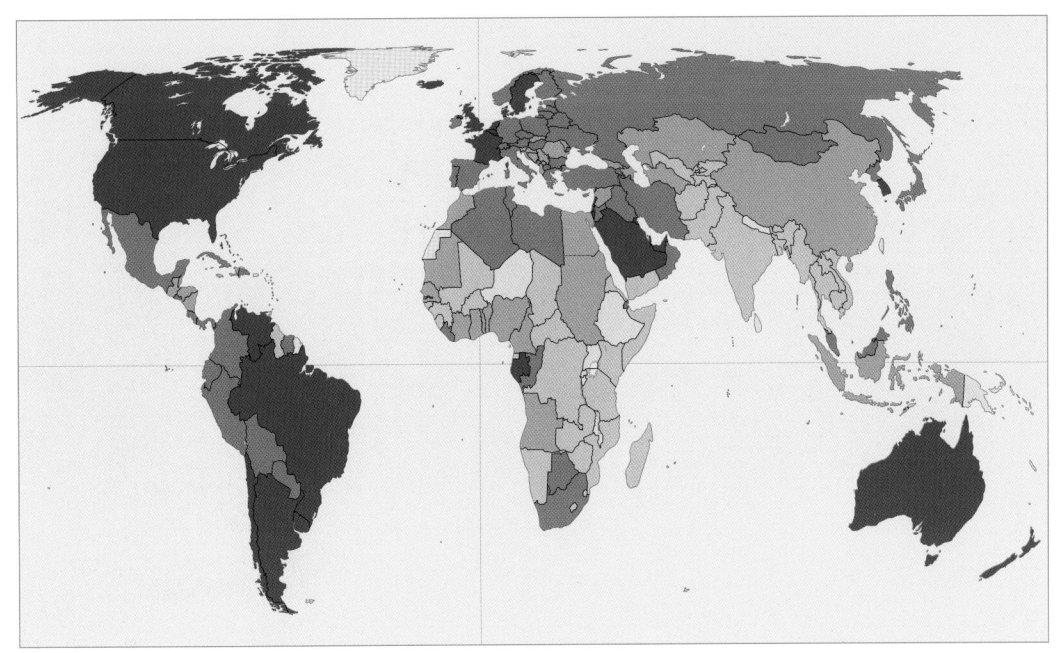

URBAN POPULATION

Percentage of total population living in towns and cities (2010)

- Over 80%
- 60 – 80%
- 40 – 60%
- 20 – 40%
- Under 20%
- No data available

Most urbanized		Least urbanized	
Singapore	100%	Burundi	11%
Kuwait	98%	Papua New Guinea	13%
Belgium	97%	Uganda	13%
Qatar	96%	Trinidad & Tobago	14%
Malta	95%	Sri Lanka	15%

17

The Human Family

PREDOMINANT LANGUAGES

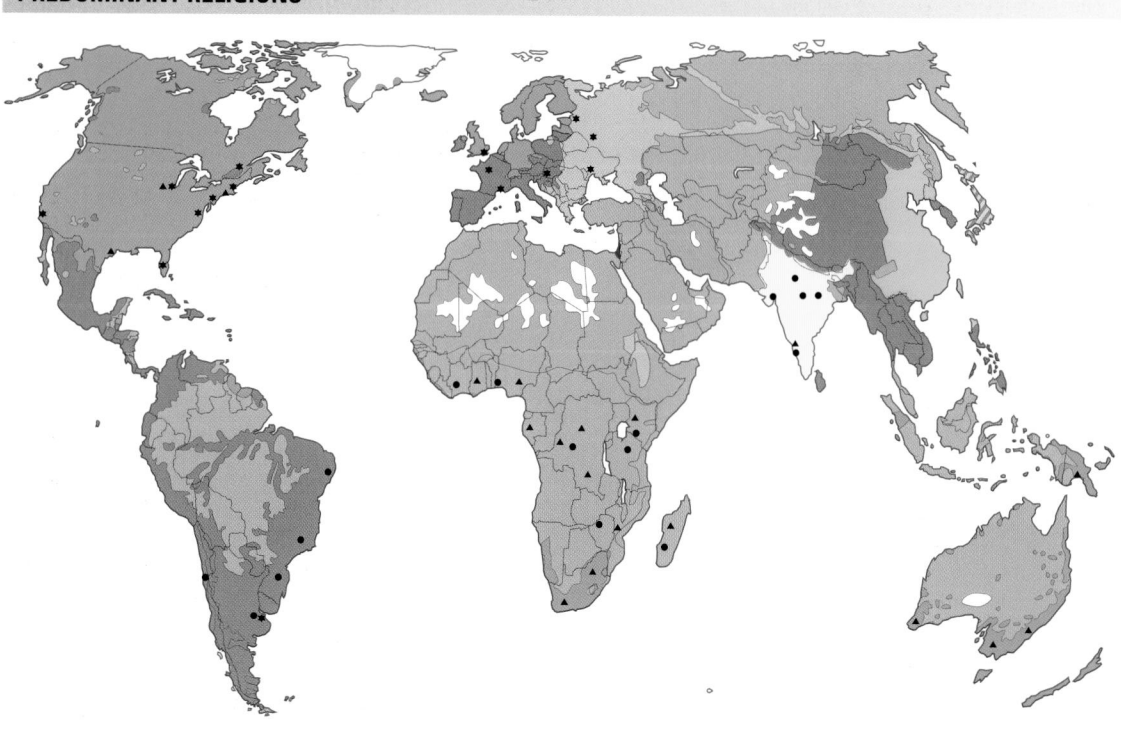

LANGUAGES OF THE WORLD

Language can be classified by ancestry and structure. For example, the Romance and Germanic groups are both derived from an Indo-European language believed to have been spoken 5,000 years ago.

First-language speakers, in millions (2009)
Mandarin Chinese 845, Spanish 329, English 328, Arabic 221, Hindi 182, Bengali 181, Portuguese 178, Russian 144, Japanese 122, German 90, Javanese 85, Wu Chinese 77, Telugu 70, Vietnamese 69, Marathi 68, French 68, Korean 66, Tamil 66, Punjabi 63, Italian 62.

Distribution of Living Languages

The figures refer to the number of languages currently in use in the regions shown

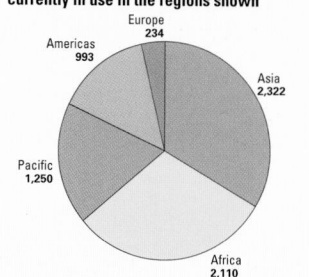

Europe 234
Americas 993
Asia 2,322
Pacific 1,250
Africa 2,110

INDO-EUROPEAN FAMILY

1	Balto-Slavic group (incl. Russian, Ukrainian)
2	Germanic group (incl. English, German)
3	Celtic group
4	Greek
5	Albanian
6	Iranian group
7	Armenian
8	Romance group (incl. Spanish, Portuguese, French, Italian)
9	Indo-Aryan group (incl. Hindi, Bengali, Urdu, Punjabi, Marathi)
10	CAUCASIAN FAMILY

AFRO-ASIATIC FAMILY

11	Semitic group (incl. Arabic)
12	Kushitic group
13	Berber group
14	KHOISAN FAMILY
15	NIGER-CONGO FAMILY
16	NILO-SAHARAN FAMILY
17	URALIC FAMILY

ALTAIC FAMILY

18	Turkic group (incl. Turkish)
19	Mongolian group
20	Tungus-Manchu group
21	Japanese and Korean

SINO-TIBETAN FAMILY

22	Sinitic (Chinese) languages (incl. Mandarin, Wu, Yue)
23	Tibetic-Burmic languages
24	TAI FAMILY

AUSTRO-ASIATIC FAMILY

25	Mon-Khmer group
26	Munda group
27	Vietnamese
28	DRAVIDIAN FAMILY (incl. Telugu, Tamil)
29	AUSTRONESIAN FAMILY (incl. Malay-Indonesian, Javanese)
30	OTHER LANGUAGES

PREDOMINANT RELIGIONS

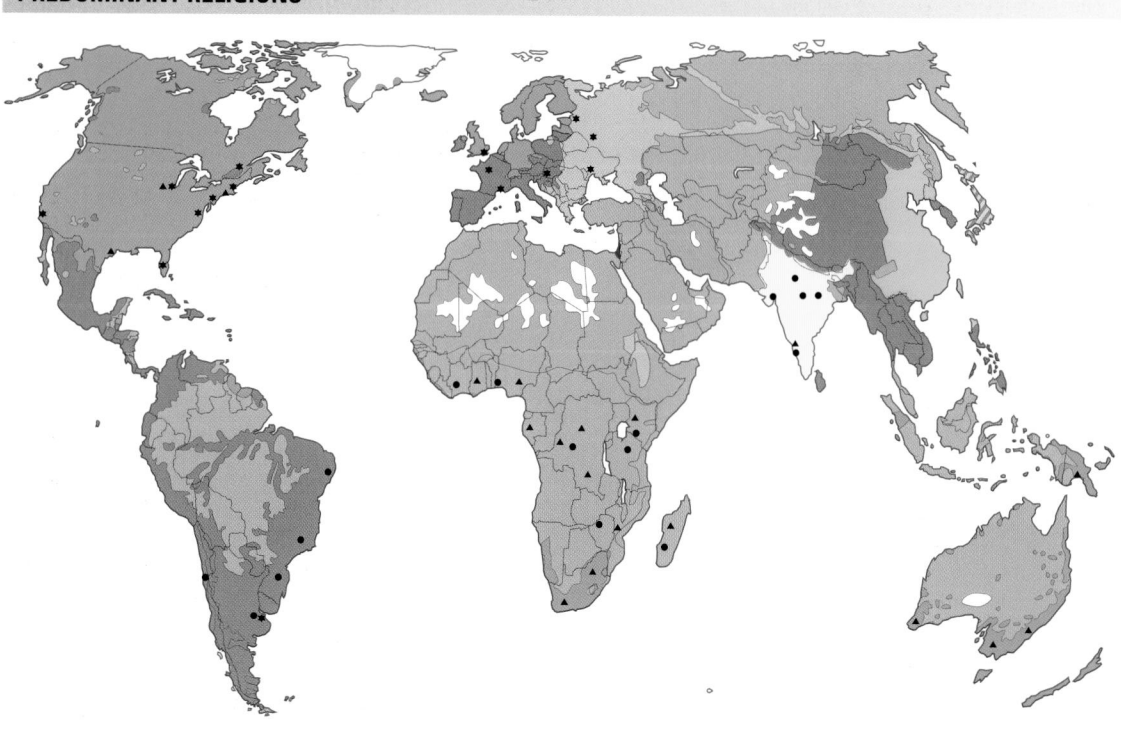

RELIGIOUS ADHERENTS

Religious adherents in millions (2009)

Christianity	2,264	Buddhism	484
Roman Catholic	*1,143*	Chinese folk	455
Protestant	*413*	Ethnic religions	259
Orthodox	*273*	New religions	64
Anglican	*85*	Sikhism	24
Islam	1,523	Spiritism	14
Sunni	*1,279*	Judaism	15
Shi'ite	*213*	Taoism	9
Hinduism	935	Baha'i	7
Non-religious/		Confucianism	6
Agnostic/Atheist	779	Jainism	6

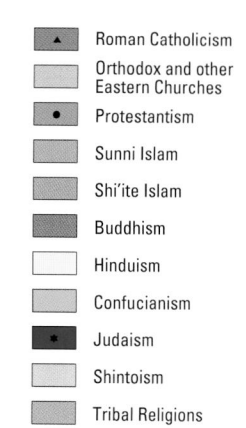

- ▲ Roman Catholicism
- Orthodox and other Eastern Churches
- • Protestantism
- Sunni Islam
- Shi'ite Islam
- Buddhism
- Hinduism
- Confucianism
- ✳ Judaism
- Shintoism
- Tribal Religions

UNITED NATIONS

Created in 1945 to promote peace and cooperation, and based in New York, the United Nations is the world's largest international organization, with 193 members and an annual budget of US $5.2 billion (2012). Each member of the General Assembly has one vote, while the five permanent members of the 15-nation Security Council – China, France, Russia, the UK, and the USA – each hold a veto. The Secretariat is the UN's principal administrative arm. The 54 members of the Economic and Social Council are responsible for economic, social, cultural, educational, health, and related matters. The UN has 16 specialized agencies – based in Canada, France, Switzerland, and Italy, as well as the USA – which help members in fields such as education (UNESCO), agriculture (FAO), medicine (WHO), and finance (IFC). By the end of 1994, all the original 11 trust territories of the Trusteeship Council had become independent.

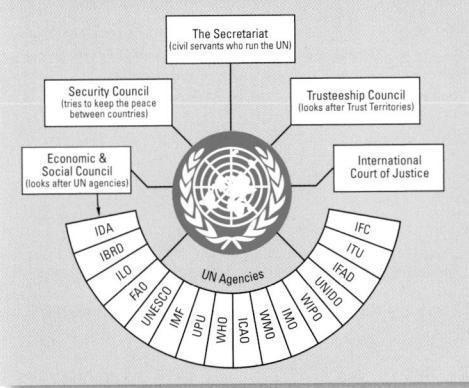

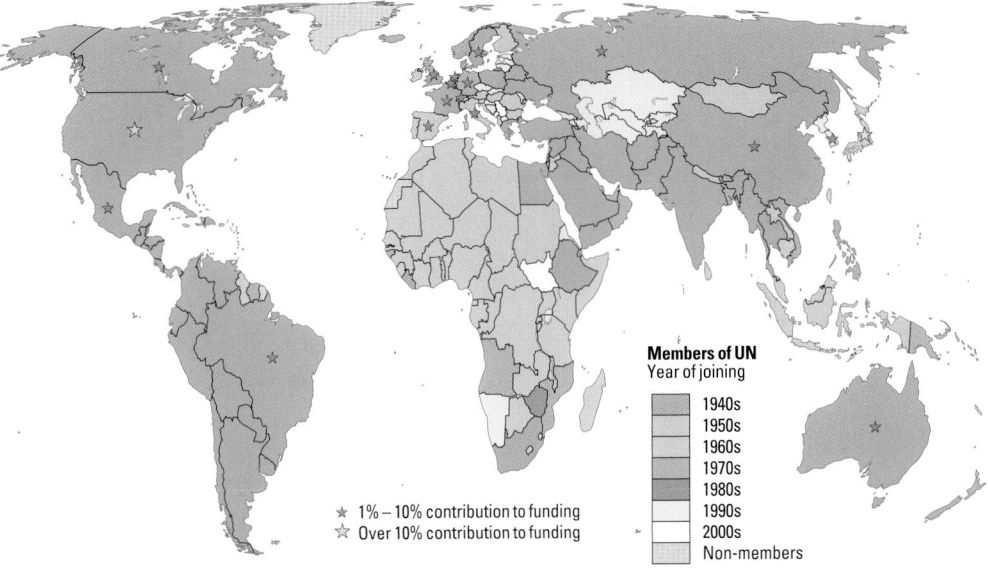

Members of UN
Year of joining

- 1940s
- 1950s
- 1960s
- 1970s
- 1980s
- 1990s
- 2000s
- Non-members

★ 1% – 10% contribution to funding
☆ Over 10% contribution to funding

MEMBERSHIP OF THE UN   From the original 51, membership of the UN has now grown to 193. Recent additions include East Timor, Switzerland, Montenegro, and South Sudan. There are only two independent states which are not members of the UN – Taiwan and the Vatican City. All the successor states of the former USSR had joined by the end of 1992. The official languages of the UN are Chinese, English, French, Russian, Spanish, and Arabic.

FUNDING   The UN budget for 2012 was US $5.2 billion. Contributions are assessed by the members' ability to pay, with the maximum 22% of the total (USA's share), and the minimum 0.001%. The 27-member EU pays 40% of the budget.

PEACEKEEPING   The UN has been involved in 67 peacekeeping operations worldwide since 1948.

INTERNATIONAL ORGANIZATIONS

ACP   African-Caribbean-Pacific (formed in 1963). Members have economic ties with the EU.
APEC   Asia-Pacific Economic Cooperation (formed in 1989). It aims to enhance economic growth and prosperity for the region and to strengthen the Asia-Pacific community. APEC is the only intergovernmental grouping in the world operating on the basis of non-binding commitments, open dialogue, and equal respect for the views of all participants. There are 21 member economies.
ARAB LEAGUE   (formed in 1945). The League's aim is to promote economic, social, political, and military cooperation. There are 22 member nations.
ASEAN   Association of Southeast Asian Nations (formed in 1967). Cambodia joined in 1999.
AU   The African Union replaced the Organization of African Unity (formed in 1963) in 2002. Its 53 members represent over 94% of Africa's population. Arabic, English, French, and Portuguese are recognized as working languages.
COLOMBO PLAN   (formed in 1951). Its 25 members aim to promote economic and social development in Asia and the Pacific.
COMMONWEALTH   The Commonwealth of Nations evolved from the British Empire. Pakistan was suspended in 1999, but reinstated in 2004. Zimbabwe was suspended in 2002 and, in response to its continued suspension, Zimbabwe left the Commonwealth in 2003. Fiji was suspended in 2006 following a military coup. Rwanda joined the Commonwealth in 2009, as the 54th member state, becoming only the second country which was not formerly a British colony to be admitted to the group.
EU   European Union (evolved from the European Community in 1993). Cyprus, the Czech Republic, Estonia, Hungary, Latvia, Lithuania, Malta, Poland, the Slovak Republic, and Slovenia joined the EU in May 2004; Bulgaria and Romania joined in 2007. The other 15 members of the EU are Austria, Belgium, Denmark, Finland, France, Germany, Greece, Ireland, Italy, Luxembourg, Netherlands, Portugal, Spain, Sweden, and the UK. Together, the 27 members aim to integrate economies, coordinate social developments, and bring about political union.
LAIA   Latin American Integration Association (1980). Its aim is to promote freer regional trade.
NATO   North Atlantic Treaty Organization (formed in 1949). It continues despite the winding-up of the Warsaw Pact in 1991. Bulgaria, Estonia, Latvia, Lithuania, Romania, the Slovak Republic, and Slovenia became members in 2004, Albania and Croatia in 2009.

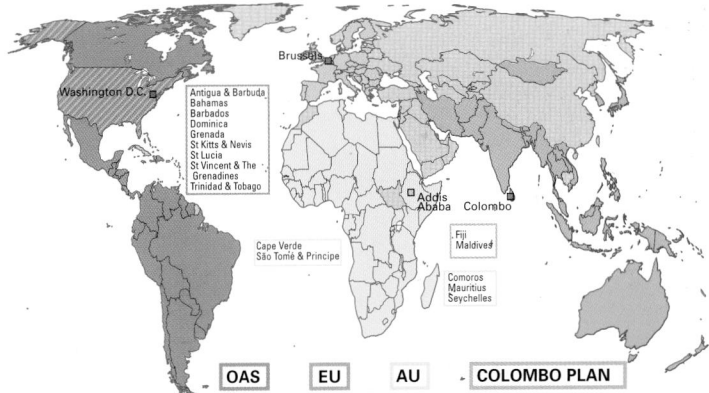

OAS | EU | AU | COLOMBO PLAN

OAS   Organization of American States (formed in 1948). It aims to promote social and economic cooperation between countries in developed North America and developing Latin America.
OECD   Organization for Economic Cooperation and Development (formed in 1961). It comprises 30 major free-market economies. Poland, Hungary, and South Korea joined in 1996, and the Slovak Republic in 2000. The "G8" is its "inner group" of leading industrial nations, comprising Canada, France, Germany, Italy, Japan, Russia, the UK, and the USA.
OPEC   Organization of Petroleum Exporting Countries (formed in 1960). It controls about three-quarters of the world's oil supply. Gabon formally withdrew from OPEC in August 1996.

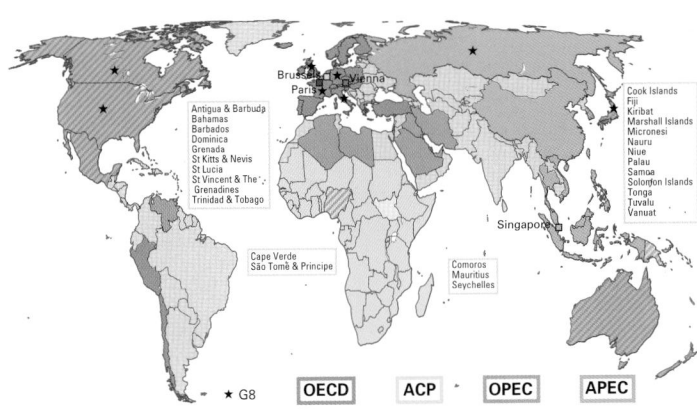

★ G8   OECD | ACP | OPEC | APEC

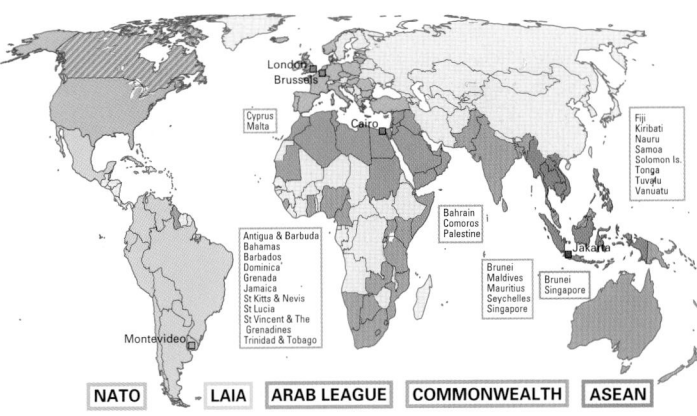

NATO | LAIA | ARAB LEAGUE | COMMONWEALTH | ASEAN

Wealth

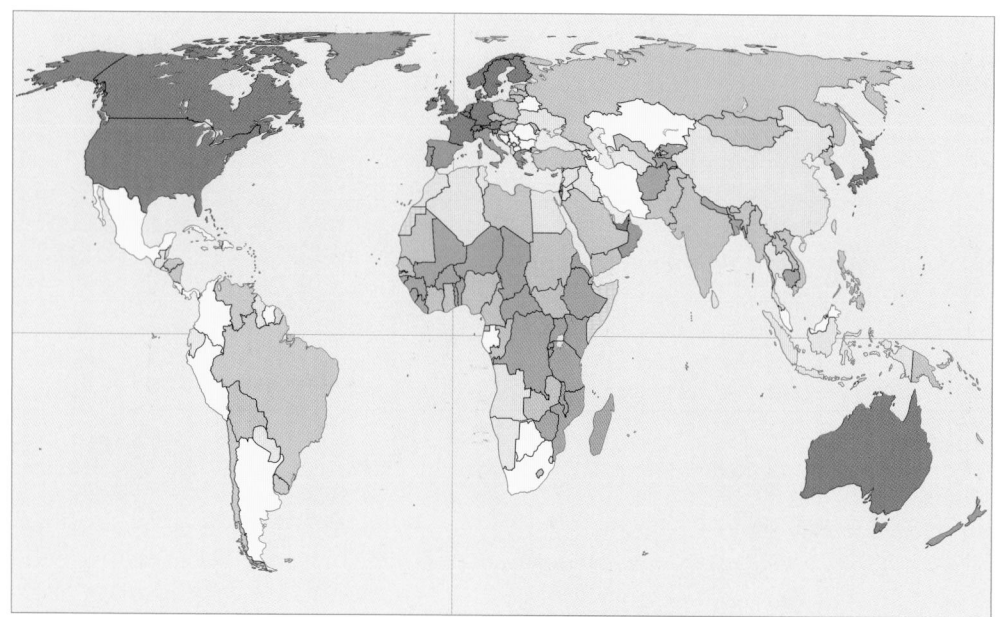

LEVELS OF INCOME

Gross National Income per capita: the value of total production divided by the population (2010)

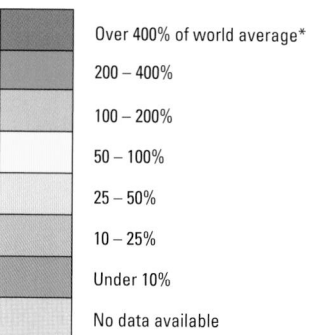

- Over 400% of world average*
- 200 – 400%
- 100 – 200%
- 50 – 100%
- 25 – 50%
- 10 – 25%
- Under 10%
- No data available

*World average = US$ 9,135

WEALTH CREATION

The Gross National Income (GNI) of the world's largest economies, US $ million (2010)

1.	USA	14,645,600	21. Belgium	499,500
2.	China	5,720,800	22. Poland	474,900
3.	Japan	5,334,400	23. Sweden	470,000
4.	Germany	3,522,000	24. Saudi Arabia	439,000
5.	France	2,749,800	25. Norway	411,800
6.	UK	2,387,100	26. Austria	394,600
7.	Italy	2,125,800	27. Argentina	348,400
8.	Brazil	1,830,400	28. Venezuela	334,100
9.	India	1,553,900	29. Iran	330,600
10.	Canada	1,475,900	30. Denmark	327,400
11.	Spain	1,462,900	31. Greece	305,000
12.	Russia	1,403,800	32. South Africa	304,600
13.	Taiwan	1,016,400	33. Thailand	286,600
14.	Mexico	1,008,000	34. Finland	256,000
15.	South Korea	972,300	35. Colombia	255,300
16.	Australia	957,500	36. Portugal	232,900
17.	Netherlands	814,800	37. Hong Kong (China)	231,700
18.	Turkey	719,900	38. Malaysia	220,400
19.	Indonesia	599,200	39. Israel	207,200
20.	Switzerland	559,700	40. North Korea	205,000

THE WEALTH GAP

The world's richest and poorest countries, by Gross National Income (GNI) per capita in US $ (2010)

Richest countries		Poorest countries	
1. Monaco	183,150	1. Burundi	170
2. Liechtenstein	137,070	2. Congo (Dem. Rep.)	180
3. Norway	84,290	3. Liberia	200
4. Luxembourg	77,160	4. Malawi	330
5. Switzerland	71,530	5. Eritrea	340
6. Denmark	59,050	6. Sierra Leone	340
7. San Marino	50,670	7. Niger	370
8. Sweden	50,110	8. Ethiopia	390
9. Netherlands	49,050	9. Guinea	400
10. Finland	47,720	10. Afghanistan	410
11. USA	47,390	11. Madagascar	430
12. Austria	47,060	12. Mozambique	440
13. Belgium	45,910	13. Nepal	440
14. Australia	43,590	14. Togo	440
15. Canada	43,270	15. Gambia, The	450
16. Germany	43,110	16. Zimbabwe	460
17. France	42,390	17. Central African Rep.	470
18. United Arab Emirates	41,930	18. Uganda	500
19. Japan	41,850	19. Rwanda	520
20. Andorra	41,130	20. Tanzania	530

CONTINENTAL SHARES

Shares of population and of wealth (GNI) by continent (2010)

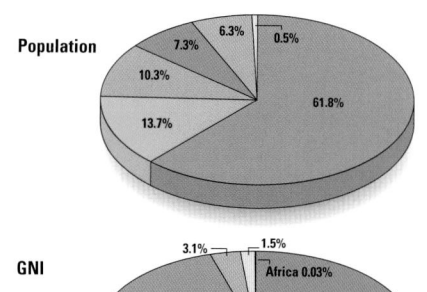

Population

GNI

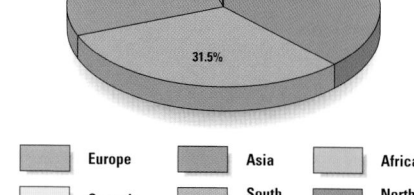

- Europe
- Asia
- Africa
- Oceania
- South America
- North America

INFLATION

Average annual rate of inflation (2011)

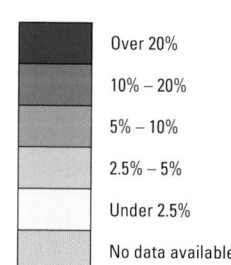

- Over 20%
- 10% – 20%
- 5% – 10%
- 2.5% – 5%
- Under 2.5%
- No data available

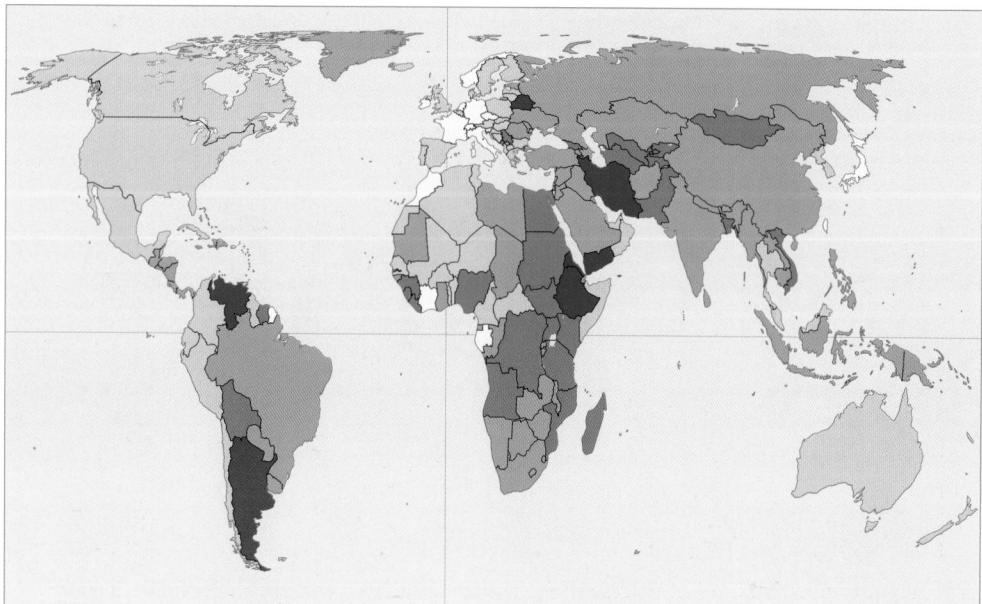

Highest average inflation		Lowest average inflation	
Belarus	41%	Bahrain	0.3%
Venezuela	29%	Switzerland	0.4%
Ethiopia	29%	Japan	0.4%

INTERNATIONAL AID

Official Development Assistance (ODA) provided and received, per capita (2010)

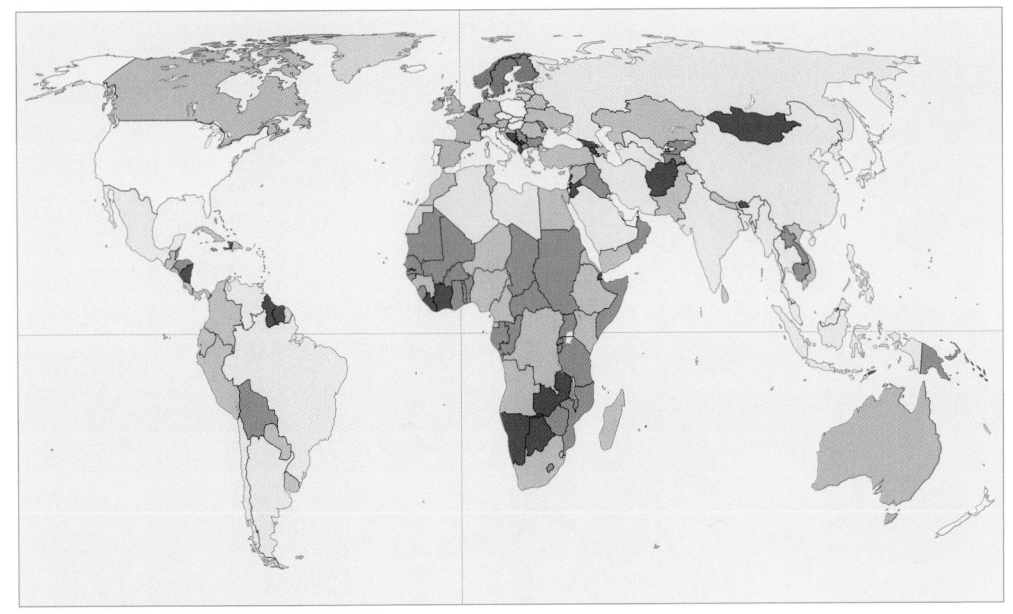

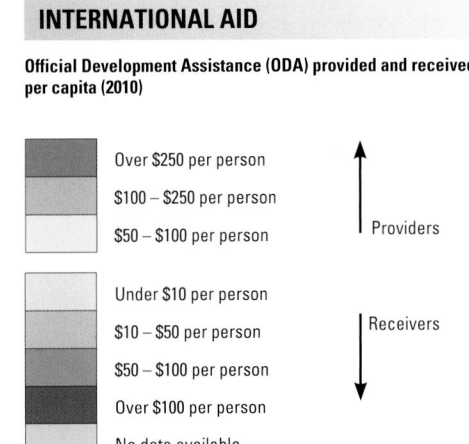

Over $250 per person

$100 – $250 per person

$50 – $100 per person

↑ Providers

Under $10 per person

$10 – $50 per person

$50 – $100 per person

Over $100 per person

No data available

↓ Receivers

DEBT AND AID

International debtors and the aid they receive

Although aid grants make a vital contribution to many of the world's poorer countries, they are usually dwarfed by the burden of debt that the developing economies are expected to repay. It is estimated that the total debt burden of developing countries is US$4,000 billion.

Debt, US$ per capita (2009)

Aid, US$ per capita (2009)

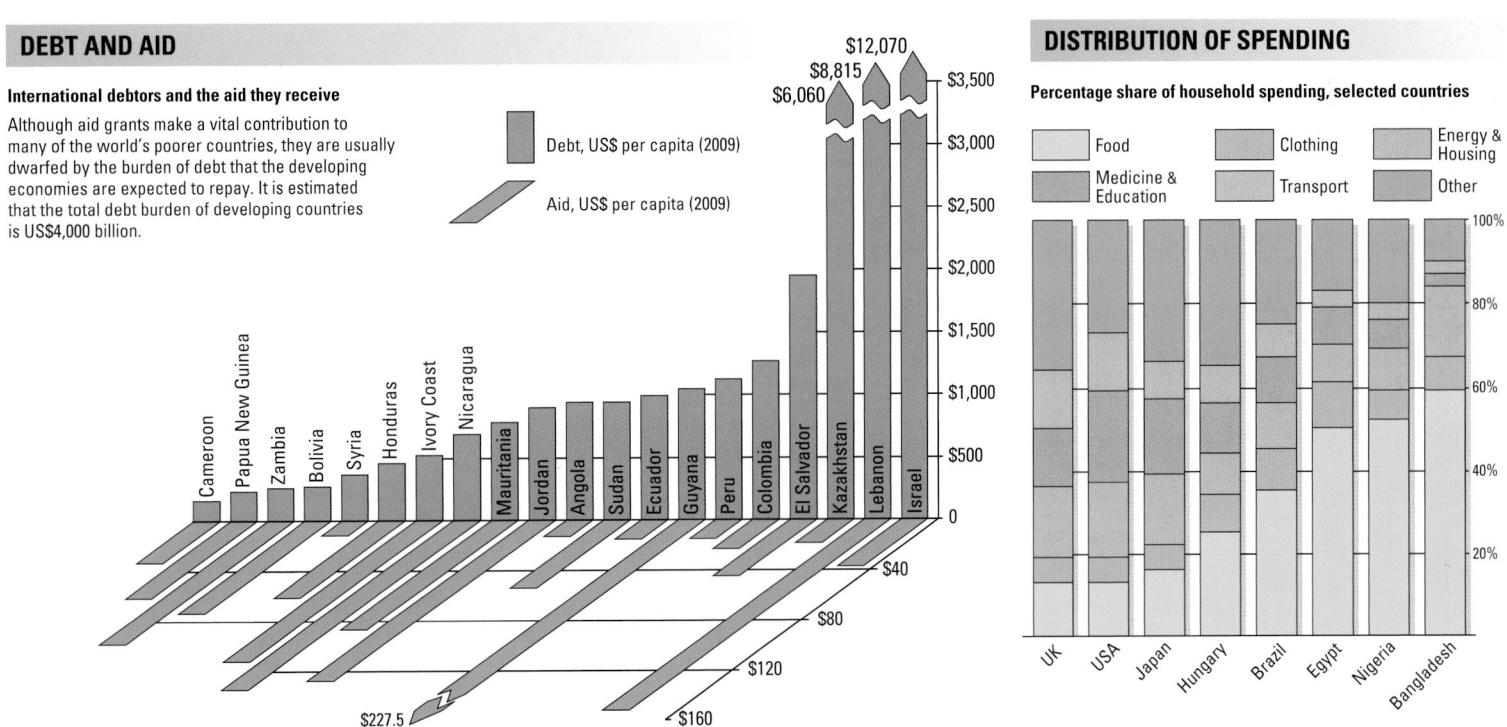

$12,070
$8,815
$6,060

DISTRIBUTION OF SPENDING

Percentage share of household spending, selected countries

Food

Clothing

Energy & Housing

Medicine & Education

Transport

Other

UK USA Japan Hungary Brazil Egypt Nigeria Bangladesh

WEALTH INDICATORS

Number of passenger vehicles, Internet users and mobile phones for each 1,000 people, selected countries (2010)

Passenger vehicles   Internet users   Mobile phones

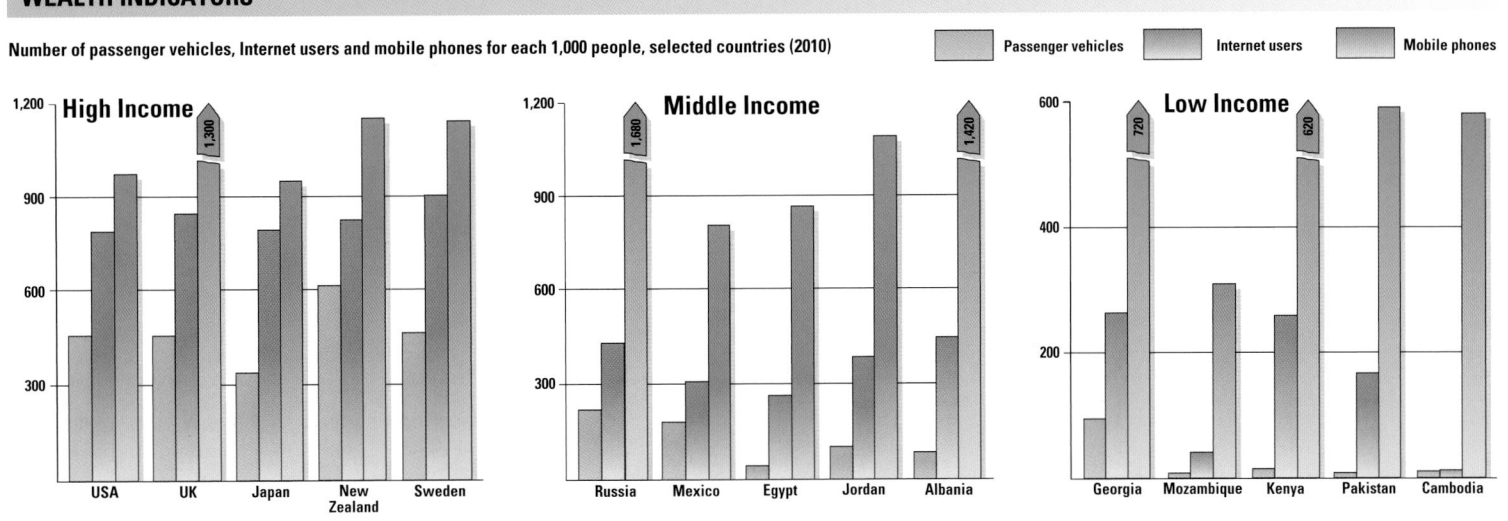

High Income

USA UK Japan New Zealand Sweden

Middle Income

Russia Mexico Egypt Jordan Albania

Low Income

Georgia Mozambique Kenya Pakistan Cambodia

21

Quality of Life

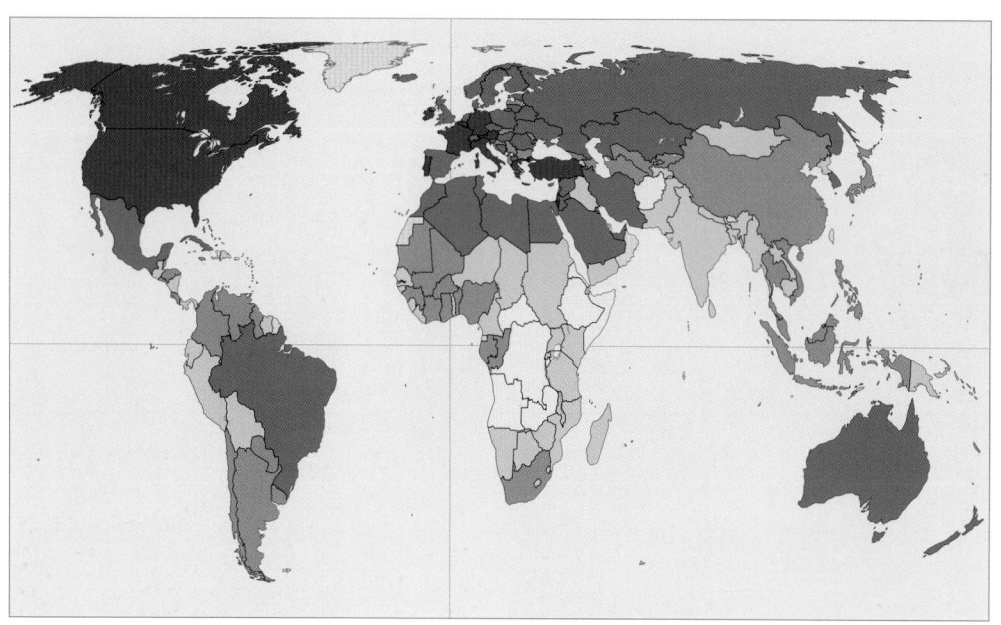

DAILY FOOD CONSUMPTION

Average daily food intake in calories per person (2007)*

- Over 3,500 calories per person
- 3,000 – 3,500 calories per person
- 2,500 – 3,000 calories per person
- 2,000 – 2,500 calories per person
- Under 2,000 calories per person
- No data available

A man needs, on average, 2,500 calories per day; a woman needs 2,000.

HOSPITAL CAPACITY

Hospital beds available for each 1,000 people (2009)

Highest capacity		Lowest capacity	
Japan	13.8	Cambodia	0.1
North Korea	12.3	Ethiopia	0.2
South Korea	12.2	Madagascar	0.3
Belarus	11.2	Niger	0.3
Russia	9.7	Guinea	0.3
Ukraine	8.7	Senegal	0.3
Germany	8.2	Uganda	0.4
Azerbaijan	7.7	Bangladesh	0.4
Austria	7.7	Mauritania	0.4
Barbados	7.6	Afghanistan	0.4
Kazakhstan	7.6	Ivory Coast	0.4
Czech Republic	7.2	Somalia	0.4
France	7.1	Sierra Leone	0.4
Hungary	7.0	Chad	0.4
Lithuania	6.8	Philippines	0.5

Although the ratio of people to hospital beds gives a good approximation of a country's health provision, it is not an absolute indicator. Raw numbers may mask inefficiency and other weaknesses: the high availability of beds in Belarus, for example, has not prevented infant mortality rates over three times as high as in the United States and the United Kingdom.

LIFE EXPECTANCY

Years of life expectancy at birth, selected countries (2012)

The chart shows combined data for both sexes. On average, women live longer than men worldwide, even in developing countries with high maternal mortality rates. Overall, life expectancy is steadily rising, though the difference between rich and poor nations remains dramatic.

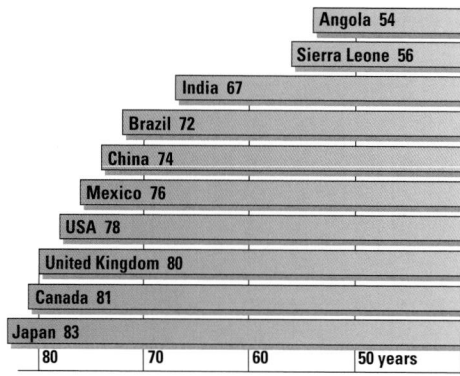

- Angola 54
- Sierra Leone 56
- India 67
- Brazil 72
- China 74
- Mexico 76
- USA 78
- United Kingdom 80
- Canada 81
- Japan 83

80 70 60 50 years

CAUSES OF DEATH

Causes of death for selected countries by percentage

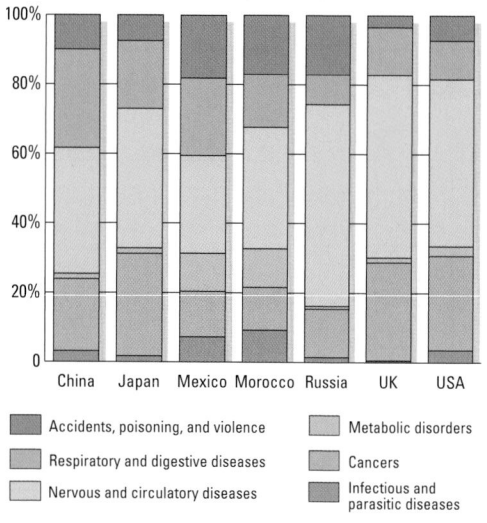

China Japan Mexico Morocco Russia UK USA

- Accidents, poisoning, and violence
- Respiratory and digestive diseases
- Nervous and circulatory diseases
- Metabolic disorders
- Cancers
- Infectious and parasitic diseases

INFANT MORTALITY

Number of babies who died under the age of one, per 1,000 live births (2011)

- Over 100 deaths per 1,000 births
- 50 – 100 deaths per 1,000 births
- 20 – 50 deaths per 1,000 births
- 10 – 20 deaths per 1,000 births
- Under 10 deaths per 1,000 births
- No data available

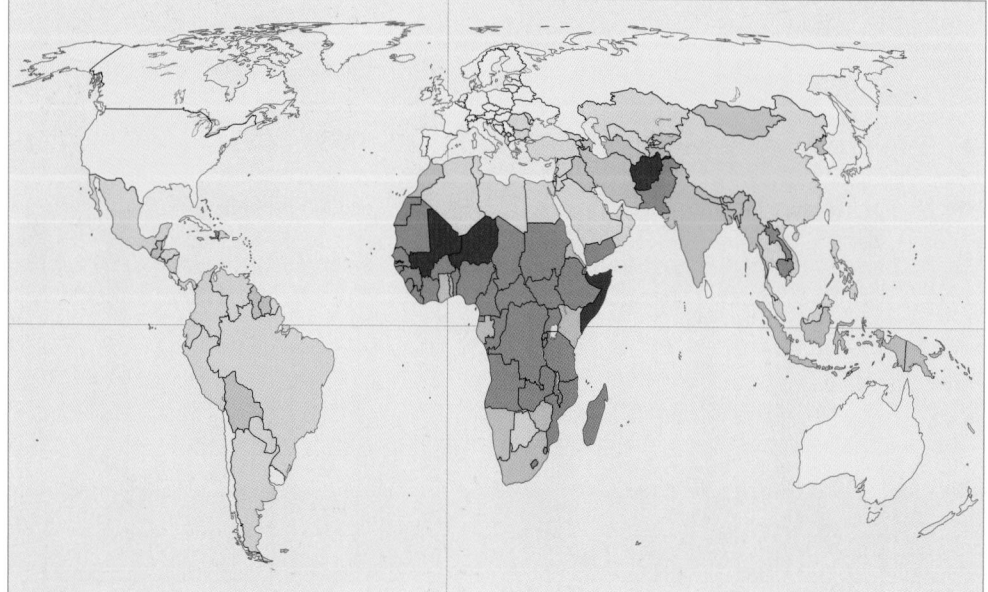

Highest infant mortality		Lowest infant mortality	
Afghanistan	122 deaths	Japan	2 deaths
Niger	110 deaths	Singapore	3 deaths
Mali	109 deaths	Sweden	3 deaths

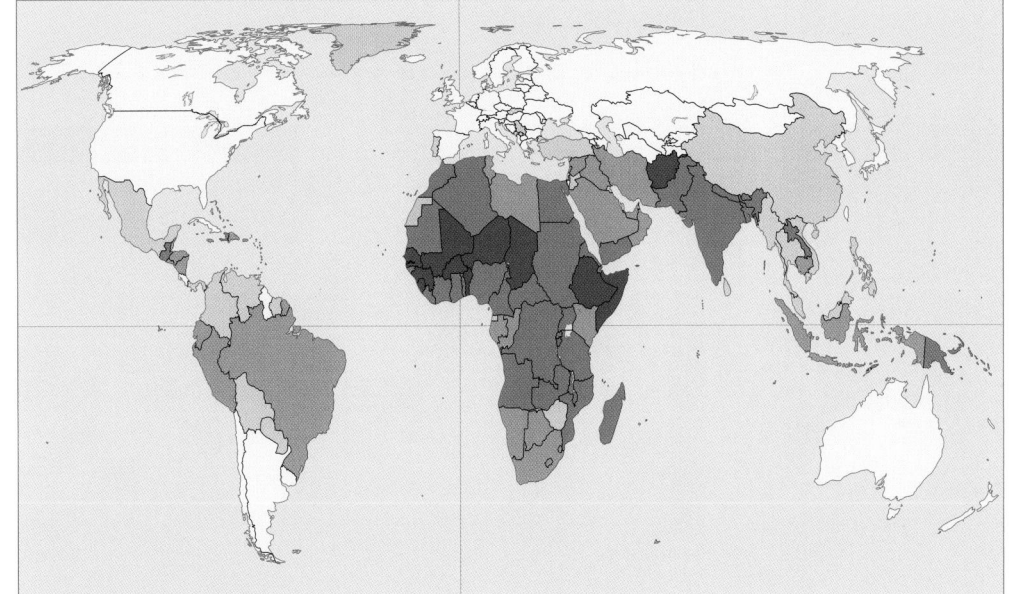

ILLITERACY

Percentage of the total adult population unable to read or write (2010)

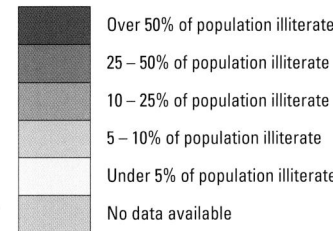

Over 50% of population illiterate

25 – 50% of population illiterate

10 – 25% of population illiterate

5 – 10% of population illiterate

Under 5% of population illiterate

No data available

Countries with the highest and lowest illiteracy rates as percentage of population

Highest		Lowest	
Mali	74%	Australia	0%
Burkina Faso	71%	Denmark	0%
Niger	71%	Finland	0%
Ethiopia	70%	Liechtenstein	0%
Chad	66%	Luxembourg	0%

FERTILITY AND EDUCATION

Fertility rates compared with female education, selected countries (2010)

Percentage of females aged 12–17 in secondary education

Fertility rate: average number of children borne per woman

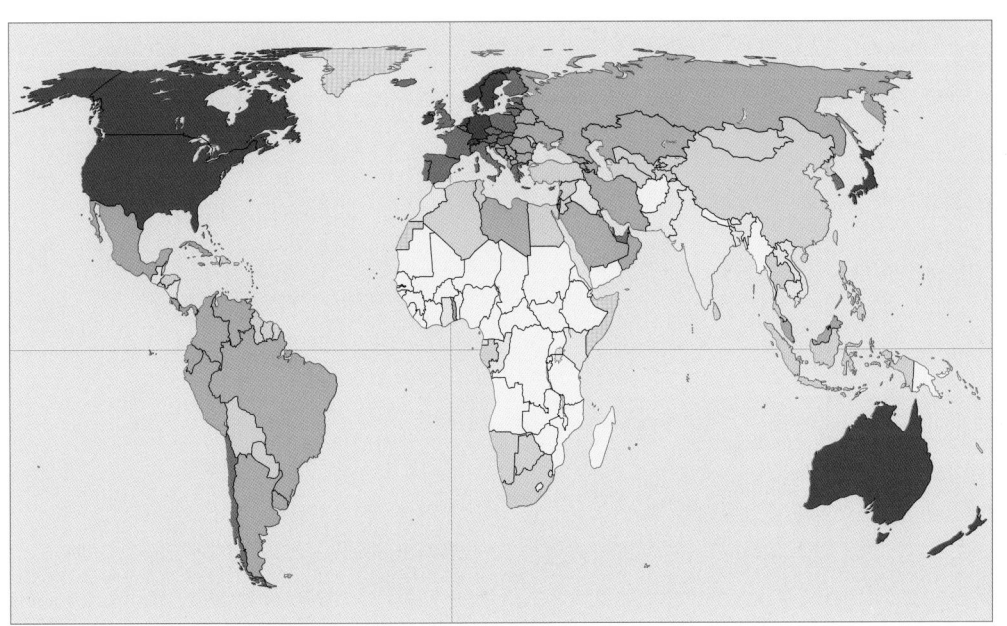

LIVING STANDARDS

At first sight, most international contrasts in living standards are swamped by differences in wealth. The rich not only have more money, they have more of everything, including years of life. Those with only a little money are obliged to spend most of it on food and clothing, the basic maintenance costs of their existence; air travel and tourism are unlikely to feature on their expenditure lists. However, poverty and wealth are both relative: slum dwellers living on social security payments in an affluent industrial country have far more resources at their disposal than an average African peasant, but feel their own poverty nonetheless. A middle-class Indian lawyer cannot command the earnings of a counterpart living in New York, London or Rome; nevertheless, he rightly sees himself as prosperous.

The rich not only live longer, on average, than the poor, they also die from different causes. Infectious and parasitic diseases, all but eliminated in the developed world, remain a scourge in the developing nations. On the other hand, more than two-thirds of the populations of OECD nations eventually succumb to cancer or circulatory disease.

HUMAN DEVELOPMENT INDEX

The Human Development Index (HDI), calculated by the UN Development Program (UNDP), gives a value to countries using indicators of life expectancy, education and standards of living (2011). Higher values show more developed countries.

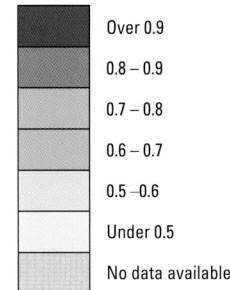

Over 0.9

0.8 – 0.9

0.7 – 0.8

0.6 – 0.7

0.5 – 0.6

Under 0.5

No data available

Highest values		Lowest values	
Norway	0.943	Congo (Dem. Rep.)	0.286
Australia	0.929	Niger	0.295
Netherlands	0.910	Burundi	0.316
USA	0.910	Mozambique	0.322
Canada	0.908	Chad	0.328

Energy

ENERGY PRODUCTION

Each square represents 1% of world primary energy production, by region (2009)

North America Western Europe Eastern Europe & Russia

Middle East

Africa Asia

South America

Oceania

ENERGY CONSUMPTION

Each square represents 1% of world primary energy production, by region (2009)

North America Western Europe Eastern Europe & Russia

Middle East

Africa Asia

South America

Oceania

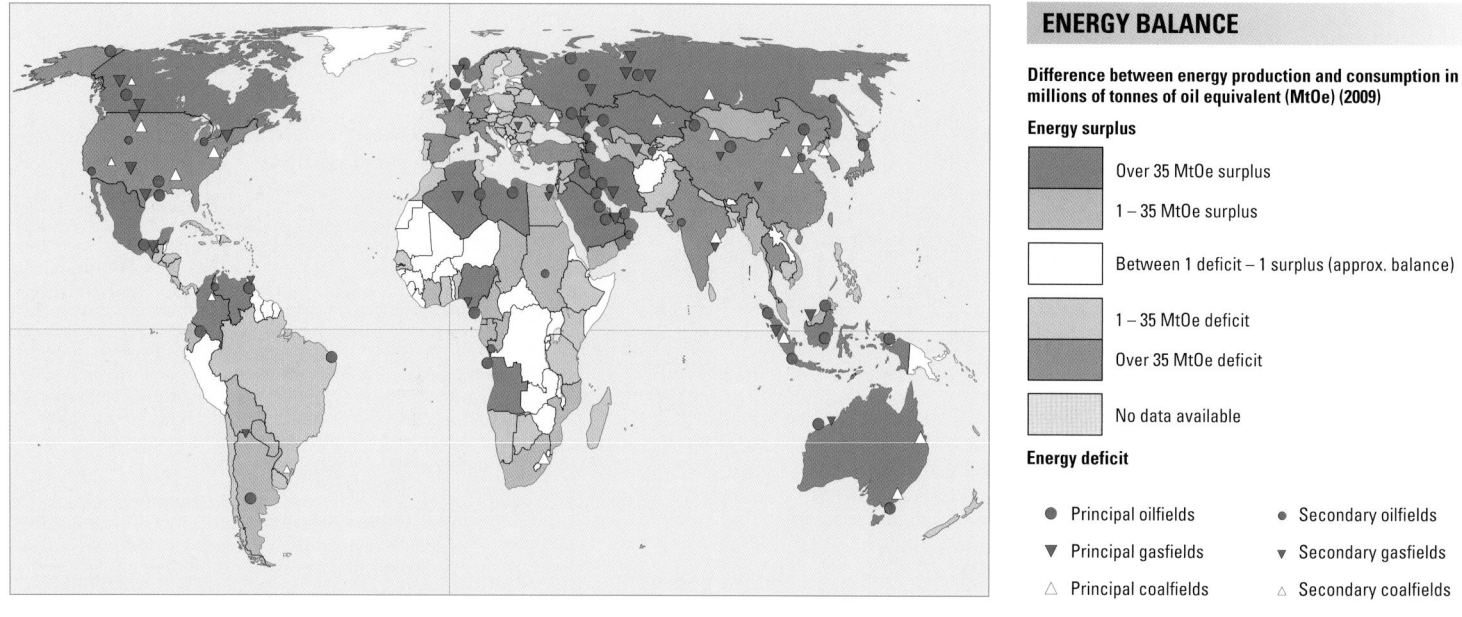

ENERGY BALANCE

Difference between energy production and consumption in millions of tonnes of oil equivalent (MtOe) (2009)

Energy surplus

- Over 35 MtOe surplus
- 1 – 35 MtOe surplus
- Between 1 deficit – 1 surplus (approx. balance)
- 1 – 35 MtOe deficit
- Over 35 MtOe deficit
- No data available

Energy deficit

- ● Principal oilfields   ● Secondary oilfields
- ▼ Principal gasfields   ▼ Secondary gasfields
- △ Principal coalfields   △ Secondary coalfields

WORLD ENERGY CONSUMPTION

Energy consumed by world regions, measured in million tonnes of oil equivalent (2010)
Total world consumption was 11,843 MtOe. Only energy from oil, natural gas, coal, nuclear, and hydroelectric sources are included. Excluded are biomass fuels such as wood, peat and animal waste, and wind, solar, and geothermal energy which, though important locally in some countries, are not always reliably documented statistically.

Oil   Gas   Coal   Nuclear   Hydro

World energy consumption, by source (2010)

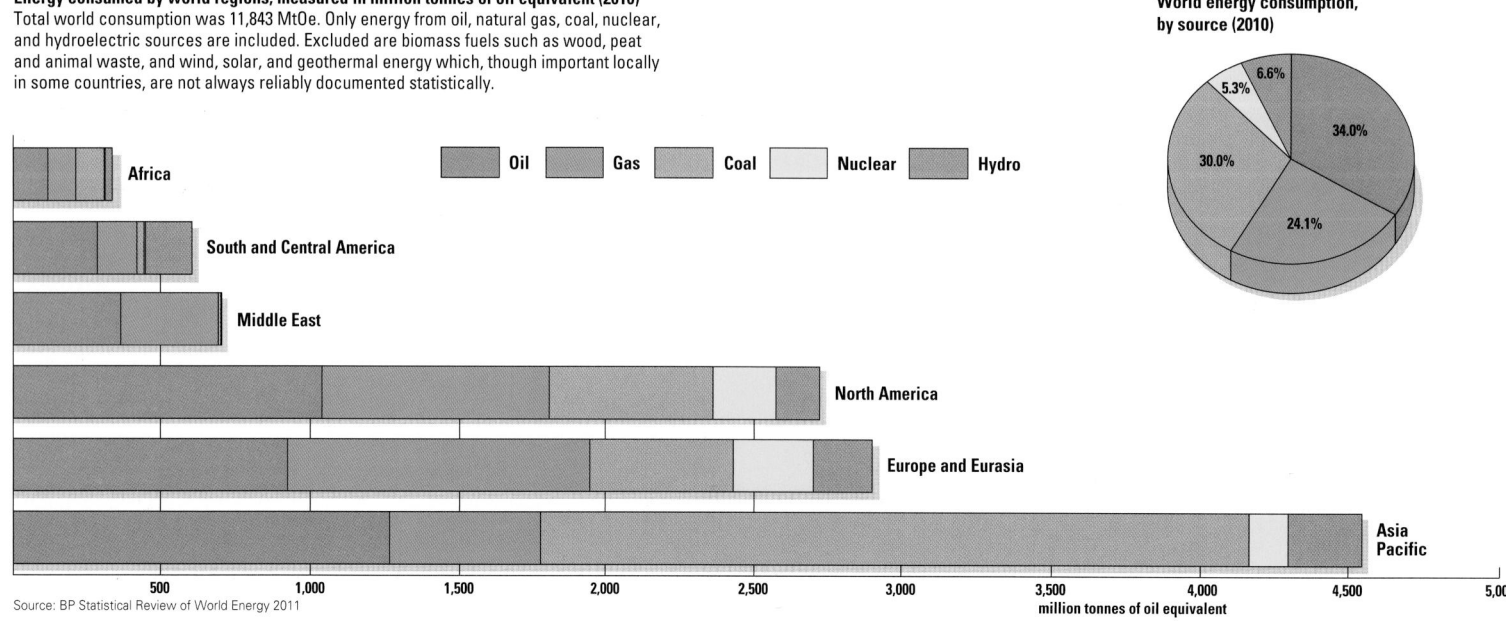

- 6.6%
- 5.3%
- 34.0%
- 30.0%
- 24.1%

Africa

South and Central America

Middle East

North America

Europe and Eurasia

Asia Pacific

500   1,000   1,500   2,000   2,500   3,000   3,500   4,000   4,500   5,000

million tonnes of oil equivalent

Source: BP Statistical Review of World Energy 2011

ENERGY

Energy is used to keep us warm or cool, fuel our industries and our transport systems, and even feed us; high-intensity agriculture, with its use of fertilizers, pesticides and machinery, is heavily energy-dependent. Although we live in a high-energy society, there are vast discrepancies between rich and poor; for example, a North American consumes six times as much energy as a Chinese person. But even developing nations have more power at their disposal than was imaginable a century ago.

The distribution of energy supplies, most importantly fossil fuels (coal, oil, and natural gas), is very uneven. In addition, the diagrams and map opposite show that the largest producers of energy are not necessarily the largest consumers. The movement of energy supplies around the world is therefore an important component of international trade.

As the finite reserves of fossil fuels are depleted, renewable energy sources, such as solar, hydro-thermal, wind, tidal, and biomass, will become increasingly important around the world.

NUCLEAR POWER

Major producers by percentage of world total and by percentage of domestic electricity generation (2010)

Country	% of world total production	Country	% of nuclear as proportion of domestic electricity
1. USA	30.7%	1. France	74.7%
2. France	15.5%	2. Slovakia	53.1%
3. Japan	10.6%	3. Belgium	49.2%
4. Russia	6.2%	4. Ukraine	47.4%
5. South Korea	5.3%	5. Hungary	42.1%
6. Germany	5.1%	6. Sweden	37.7%
7. Canada	3.2%	7. Switzerland	37.3%
8. Ukraine	3.2%	8. Bulgaria	33.1%
9. China	2.7%	9. Czech Republic	32.6%
10. UK	2.2%	10. South Korea	29.7%

Although the 1980s were a bad time for the nuclear power industry (fears of long-term environmental damage were heavily reinforced by the 1986 disaster at Chernobyl), the industry picked up in the early 1990s. Despite this, growth has recently been curtailed whilst countries review their energy mix, in light of the March 2011 Japanese earthquake and tsunami which seriously damaged the Fukushima nuclear power station.

HYDROELECTRICITY

Major producers by percentage of world total and by percentage of domestic electricity generation (2010)

Country	% of world total production	Country	% of hydroelectric as proportion of domestic electricity
1. China	21.0%	1. Norway	94.8%
2. Brazil	11.6%	2. Brazil	81.7%
3. Canada	10.7%	3. Colombia	70.7%
4. USA	7.6%	4. Venezuela	65.8%
5. Russia	4.9%	5. Canada	58.1%
6. Norway	3.4%	6. New Zealand	56.4%
7. India	3.2%	7. Peru	56.0%
8. Japan	2.5%	8. Switzerland	50.6%
9. Venezuela	2.2%	9. Austria	48.9%
10. Sweden	2.0%	10. Ecuador	44.3%

Countries heavily reliant on hydroelectricity are usually small and non-industrial: a high proportion of hydroelectric power more often reflects a modest energy budget than vast hydroelectric resources. The USA, for instance, produces only 6% of its power requirements from hydroelectricity; yet that 6% amounts to almost half the hydropower generated by most of Africa.

ELECTRICITY PRODUCTION

Percentage of electricity generated by source (2010)

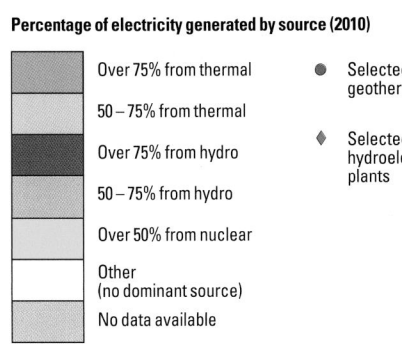

- Over 75% from thermal
- 50 – 75% from thermal
- Over 75% from hydro
- 50 – 75% from hydro
- Over 50% from nuclear
- Other (no dominant source)
- No data available
- ● Selected geothermal plants
- ◆ Selected hydroelectric plants

Conversion Rates

1 barrel = 0.136 tonnes or 159 liters or 35 Imperial gallons or 42 US gallons

1 tonne = 7.33 barrels or 1,185 liters or 256 Imperial gallons or 261 US gallons

1 tonne oil = 1.5 tonnes hard coal or 3.0 tonnes lignite or 12,000 kWh

1 Imperial gallon = 1.201 US gallons or 4.546 liters or 277.4 cubic inches

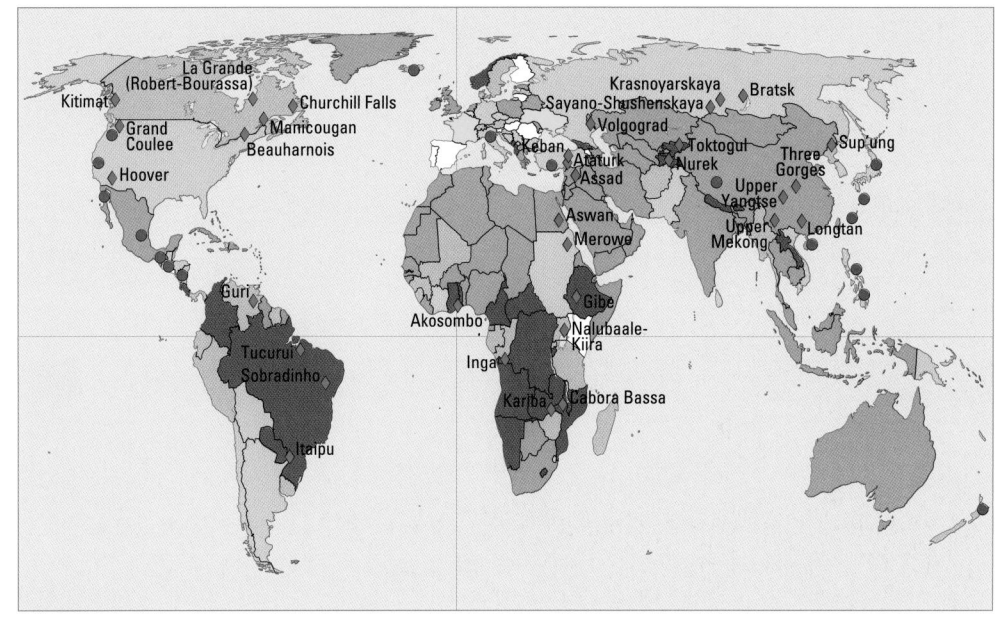

Measurements
For historical reasons, oil is traded in "barrels." The weight and volume equivalents (shown right) are all based on average-density "Arabian light" crude oil.

The energy equivalents given for a tonne of oil are also somewhat imprecise: oil and coal of different qualities will have varying energy contents, a fact usually reflected in their price on world markets.

ENERGY RESERVES

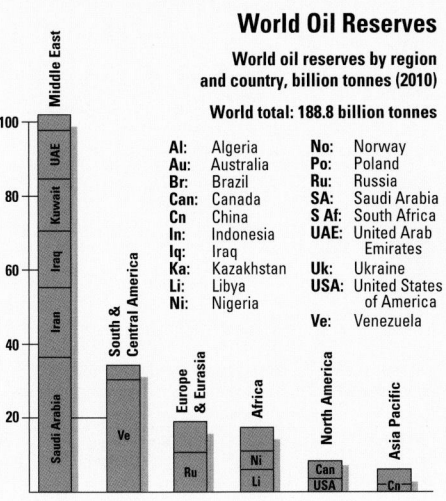

World Oil Reserves

World oil reserves by region and country, billion tonnes (2010)

World total: 188.8 billion tonnes

Al:	Algeria
Au:	Australia
Br:	Brazil
Can:	Canada
Cn:	China
In:	Indonesia
Iq:	Iraq
Ka:	Kazakhstan
Li:	Libya
Ni:	Nigeria
No:	Norway
Po:	Poland
Ru:	Russia
SA:	Saudi Arabia
S Af:	South Africa
UAE:	United Arab Emirates
Uk:	Ukraine
USA:	United States of America
Ve:	Venezuela

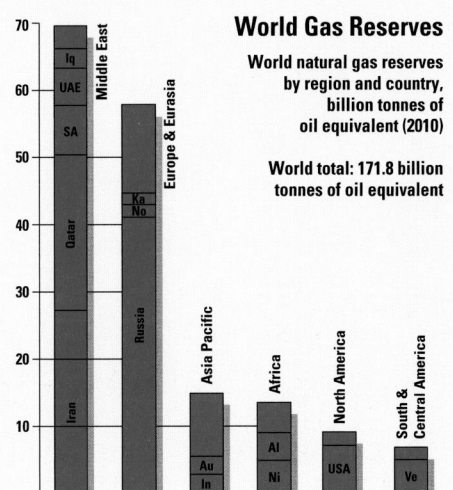

World Gas Reserves

World natural gas reserves by region and country, billion tonnes of oil equivalent (2010)

World total: 171.8 billion tonnes of oil equivalent

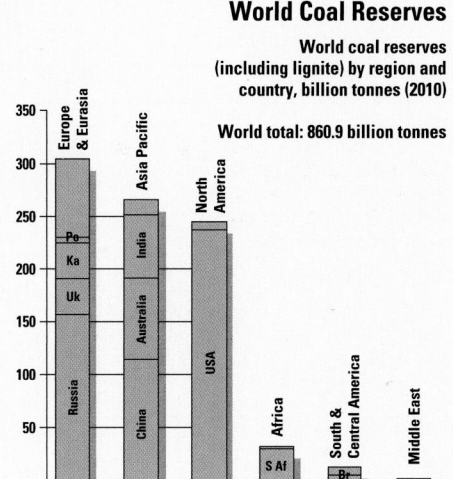

World Coal Reserves

World coal reserves (including lignite) by region and country, billion tonnes (2010)

World total: 860.9 billion tonnes

Production

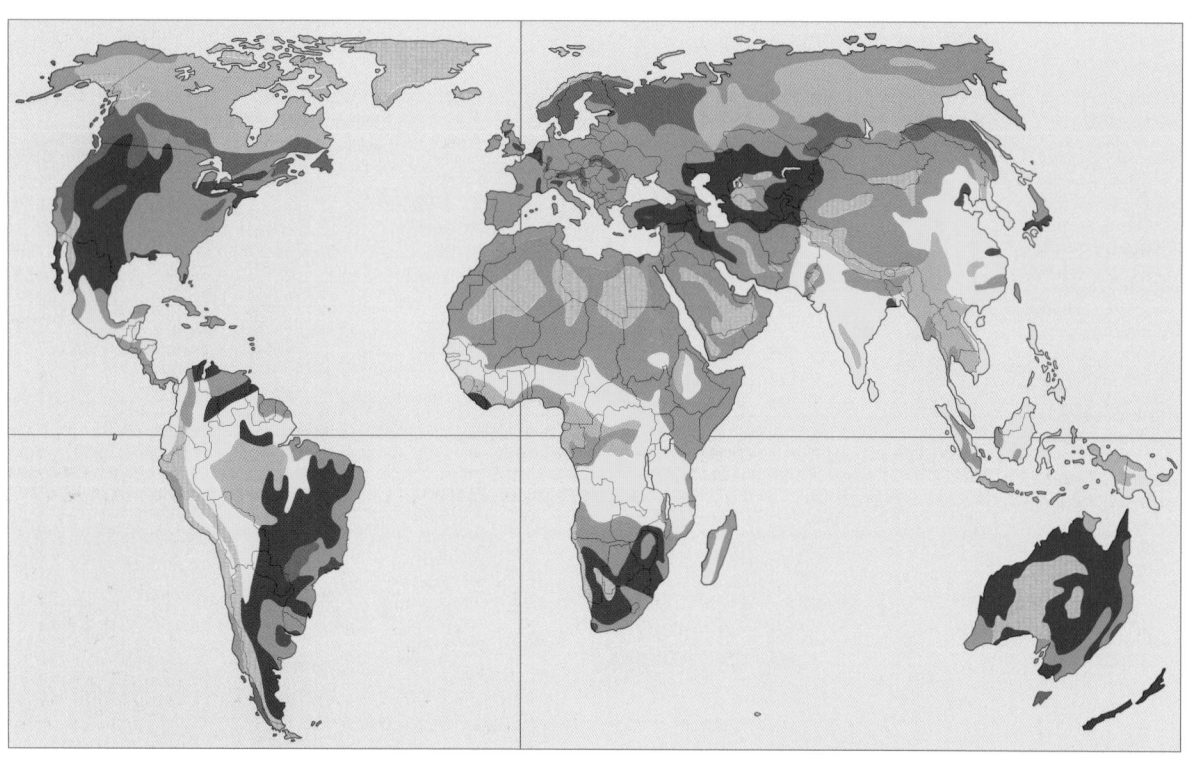

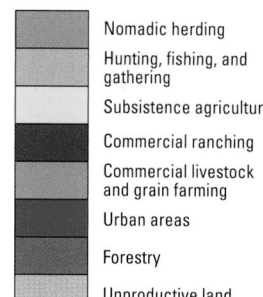
STAPLE CROPS

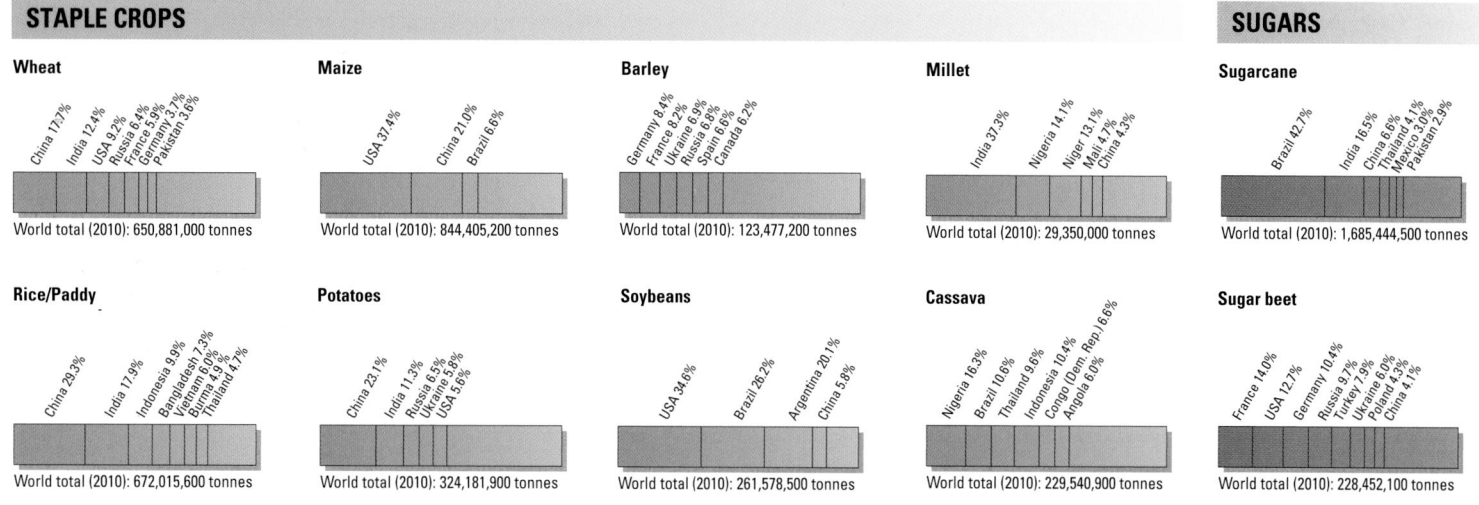

Wheat

China 17.7% | India 12.4% | USA 9.2% | Russia 6.4% | France 5.9% | Germany 3.7% | Pakistan 3.6%

World total (2010): 650,881,000 tonnes

Maize

USA 37.4% | China 21.0% | Brazil 6.6%

World total (2010): 844,405,200 tonnes

Barley

Germany 8.4% | France 8.2% | Ukraine 6.9% | Russia 6.8% | Spain 6.6% | Canada 6.2%

World total (2010): 123,477,200 tonnes

Millet

India 37.3% | Nigeria 14.1% | Niger 13.1% | Mali 4.7% | China 4.3%

World total (2010): 29,350,000 tonnes

Rice/Paddy

China 29.3% | India 17.9% | Indonesia 9.9% | Bangladesh 7.3% | Vietnam 6.0% | Burma 4.9% | Thailand 4.7%

World total (2010): 672,015,600 tonnes

Potatoes

China 23.1% | India 11.3% | Russia 6.5% | Ukraine 5.6% | USA 5.6%

World total (2010): 324,181,900 tonnes

Soybeans

USA 34.6% | Brazil 26.2% | Argentina 20.1% | China 5.6%

World total (2010): 261,578,500 tonnes

Cassava

Nigeria 16.3% | Brazil 10.6% | Thailand 9.6% | Indonesia 10.4% | Congo (Dem. Rep.) 6.6% | Angola 6.0%

World total (2010): 229,540,900 tonnes

SUGARS

Sugarcane

Brazil 42.7% | India 18.5% | China 6.6% | Thailand 4.1% | Mexico 3.0% | Pakistan 2.9%

World total (2010): 1,685,444,500 tonnes

Sugar beet

France 14.0% | USA 12.7% | Germany 10.4% | Russia 9.7% | Turkey 7.9% | Ukraine 6.0% | Poland 4.3% | China 4.1%

World total (2010): 228,452,100 tonnes

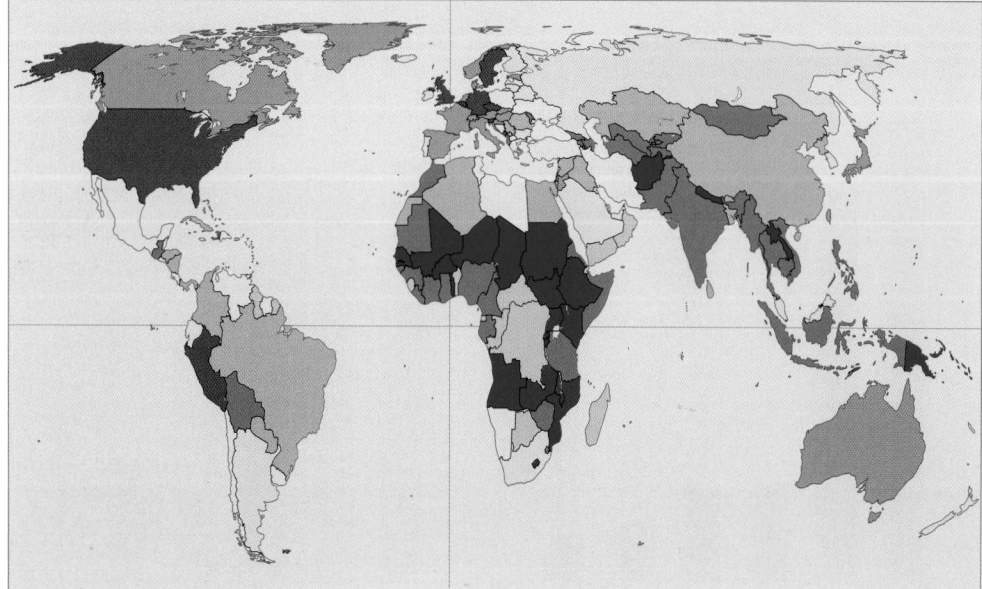

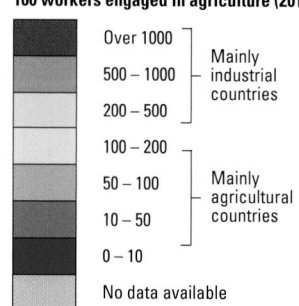

MINERAL PRODUCTION

Aluminum
China 39.7%, Russia 9.7%, Canada 7.9%, Australia 4.7%, USA 4.2%, Brazil 3.6%, India 3.6%
World total (2010): 40,800,000 tonnes

Bauxite
Australia 29.9%, China 17.1%, Brazil 10.7%, India 10.3%, Guinea 9.0%, Jamaica 6.8%, Russia 3.1%, Venezuela 2.7%
World total (2010): 205,000,000 tonnes

Chromium
South Africa 35.5%, India 19.5%, Kazakhstan 17.3%
World total (2010): 19,300,000 tonnes

Copper
Chile 33.9%, Peru 8.0%, USA 7.4%, China 6.3%, Indonesia 5.4%, Russia 4.6%
World total (2010): 15,900,000 tonnes

Diamonds
Congo (Dem. Rep.) 29.9%, Australia 23.4%, Russia 19.5%, S. Africa 11.7%, Botswana 10.4%
World total (2010): 169,000,000 carats

Gold
China 13.5%, Australia 10.2%, USA 9.0%, Russia 7.5%, S. Africa 7.4%, Peru 6.4%
World total (2010): 2,560,000 kg (metal content)

Iron Ore
China 41.3%, Australia 16.7%, Brazil 14.3%, India 8.9%, Russia 3.9%, Ukraine 3.0%, S. Africa 2.9%
World total (2010): 2,590,000,000 tonnes

Lead
China 44.7%, Australia 15.1%, USA 8.9%, Peru 6.3%, Mexico 5.8%
World total (2010): 4,140,000 tonnes

Manganese
Australia 22.3%, South Africa 20.9%, China 18.7%, Gabon 10.2%, India 7.2%, Brazil 5.6%
World total (2010): 13,900,000 tonnes

Mercury
China 71.1%, Kyrgyzstan 11.1%
World total (2010): 2,220,000 tonnes (metal content)

Nickel
Russia 16.9%, Indonesia 14.6%, Philippines 10.9%, Australia 10.7%, Canada 9.9%, New Caledonia 8.2%, China 5.0%, Colombia 4.5%
World total (2010): 1,590,000 tonnes

Silver
Mexico 19.1%, Peru 15.9%, Australia 8.1%, Chile 5.5%, China 5.5%, USA 5.5%, Bolivia 5.5%
World total (2010): 23,100 tonnes (metal content)

Tin
China 45.3%, Indonesia 21.1%, Peru 12.8%, Bolivia 7.6%, Brazil 4.2%, USA 2.6%
World total (2010): 265,000 tonnes

Uranium
Kazakhstan 33.2%, Canada 18.2%, Australia 11.0%, Namibia 8.4%, Niger 7.8%, Russia 6.6%
World total (2010): 53,700 tonnes

Zinc
China 30.8%, Australia 12.3%, Peru 12.3%, USA 6.2%, India 5.6%, Canada 5.4%, Mexico 4.3%
World total (2010): 12,000,000 tonnes

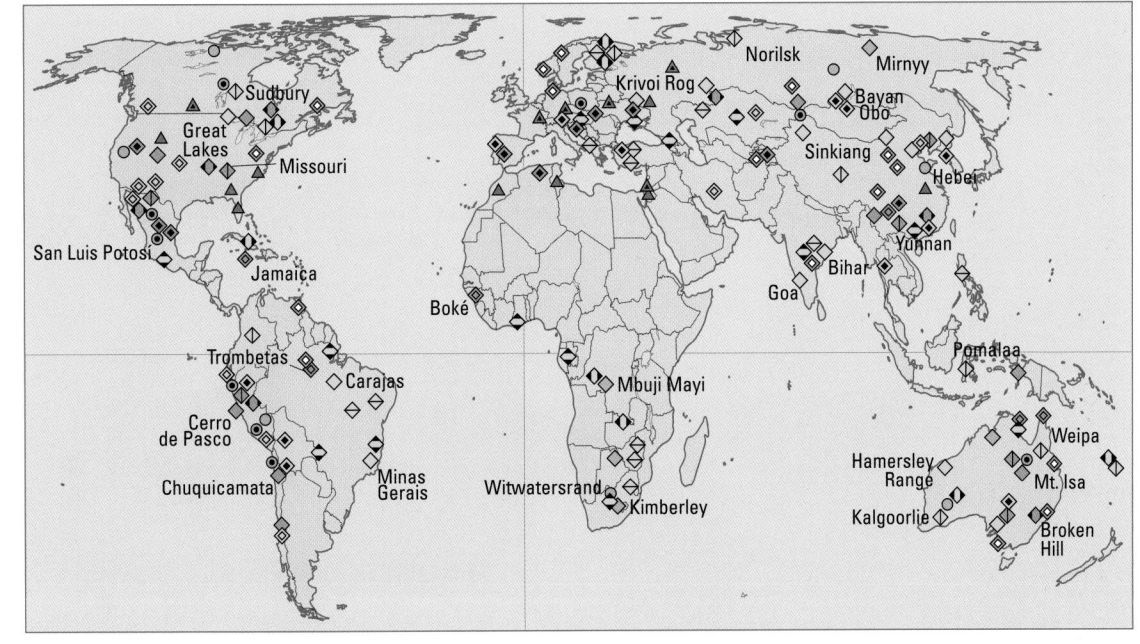

MINERAL DISTRIBUTION

The map shows the richest sources of the most important minerals

Precious metals
◇ Diamonds
○ Gold
◉ Silver

Iron and ferro-alloys
◇ Chromium
◈ Cobalt
◇ Iron ore
◇ Manganese
◈ Molybdenum
◈ Nickel ore
◈ Tungsten

Non-ferrous metals
◈ Bauxite
(◈ Aluminum)
◇ Copper
◈ Lead
◈ Mercury
◇ Zinc

Fertilizers
▲ Phosphates
▲ Potash

The map does not show undersea deposits, most of which are currently inaccessible.

INDUSTRIAL PRODUCTION

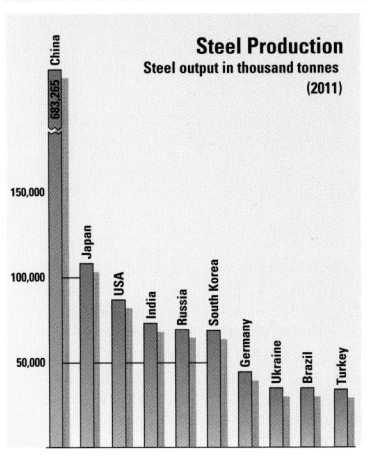

Steel Production
Steel output in thousand tonnes (2011)
China 683,265, Japan, USA, India, Russia, South Korea, Germany, Ukraine, Brazil, Turkey

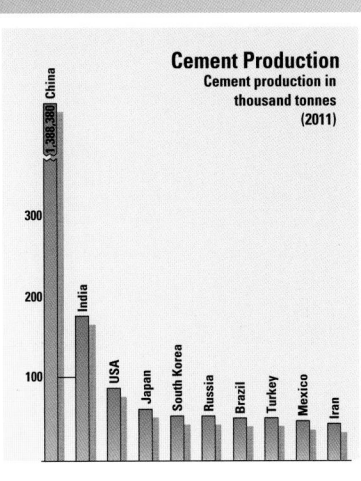

Cement Production
Cement production in thousand tonnes (2011)
China 2,068,360, India, USA, Japan, South Korea, Russia, Brazil, Turkey, Mexico, Iran

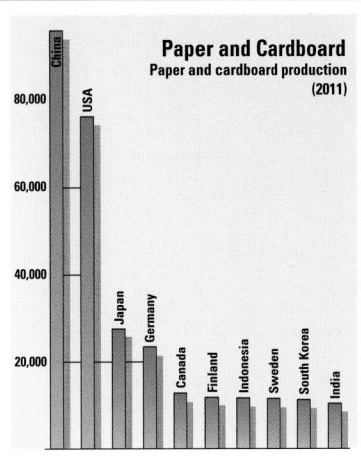

Paper and Cardboard
Paper and cardboard production (2011)
China, USA, Japan, Germany, Canada, Finland, Indonesia, Sweden, South Korea, India

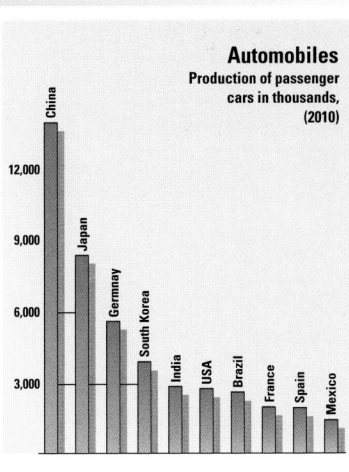

Automobiles
Production of passenger cars in thousands, (2010)
China, Japan, Germany, South Korea, India, USA, Brazil, France, Spain, Mexico

27

Trade

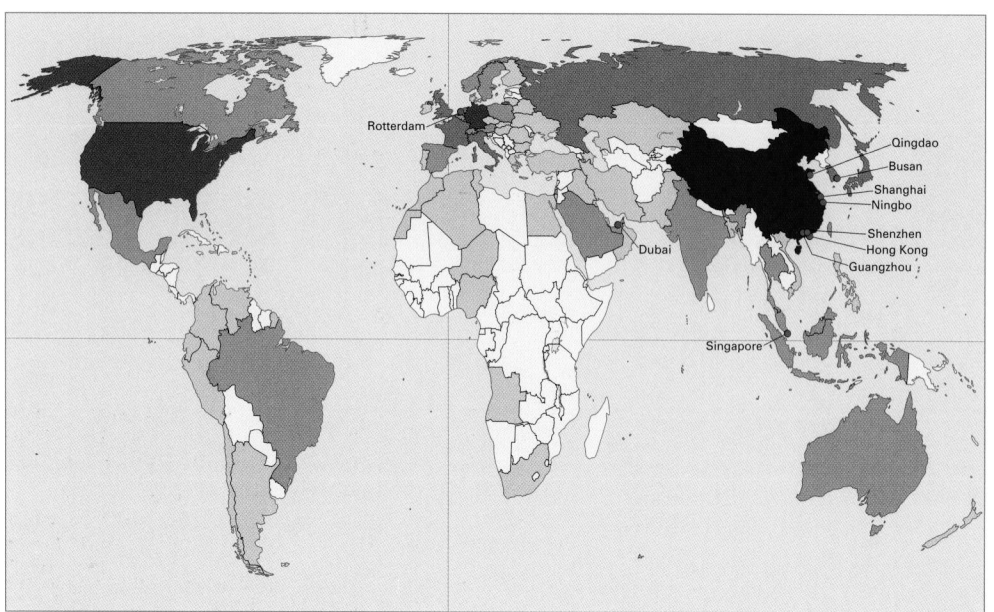

Percentage share of total world exports by value (2011)

- Over 10% of world trade
- 5 – 10% of world trade
- 2.5 – 5% of world trade
- 1.0 – 2.5% of world trade
- 0.1 – 1.0% of world trade
- Under 0.1% of world trade
- No data available
- ● Top ten container ports

Countries with the largest share of world trade

1. China	10.5%	6. Netherlands	3.2%
2. Germany	8.5%	7. South Korea	3.1%
3. USA	8.3%	8. Italy	2.8%
4. Japan	4.4%	9. UK	2.7%
5. France	3.2%	10. Russia	2.7%

THE MAIN TRADING NATIONS

The imports and exports of the top ten trading nations as a percentage of world trade (2010). Each country's trade in manufactured goods is shown in dark blue

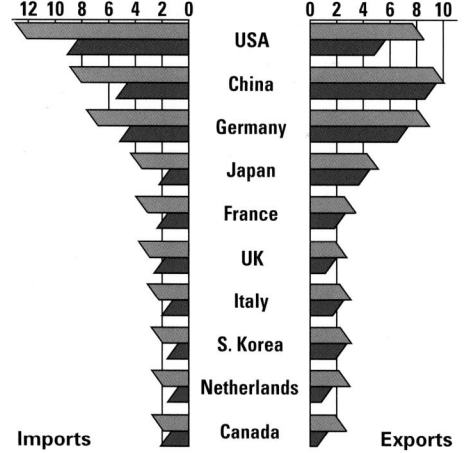

Imports / Exports

MAJOR EXPORTS

Leading manufactured items and their exporters

Motor Vehicles
World total (2010): US$ 3,502,062 million

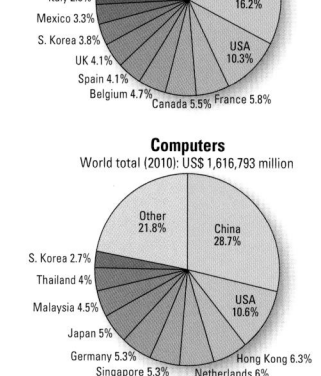

Computers
World total (2010): US$ 1,616,793 million

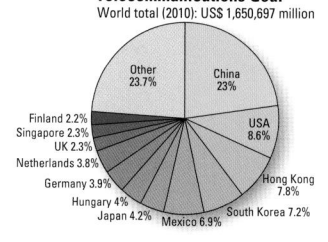

Telecommunications Gear
World total (2010): US$ 1,650,697 million

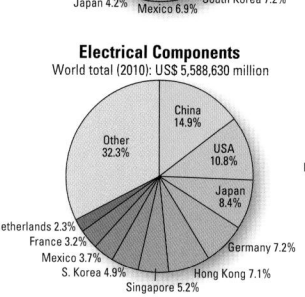

Electrical Components
World total (2010): US$ 5,588,630 million

Petrol Products
World total (2010): US$ 2,100,016 million

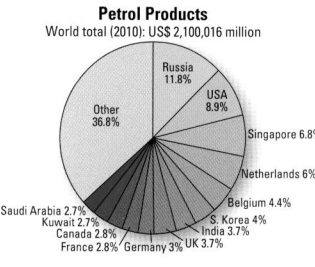

Pharmaceuticals
World total (2010): US$ 1,436,679 million

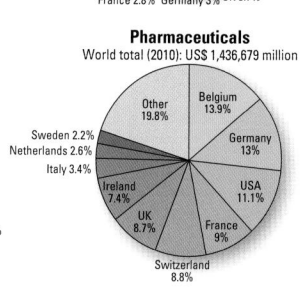

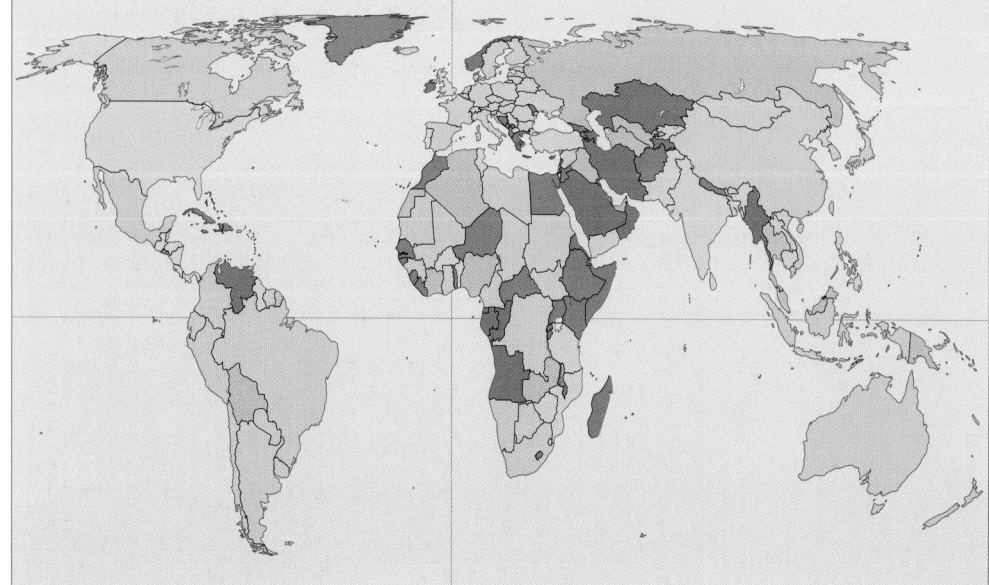

BALANCE OF TRADE

Value of exports in proportion to the value of imports (2011)

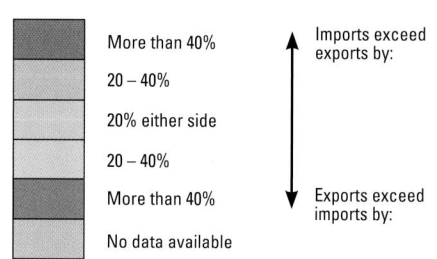

- More than 40% — Imports exceed exports by:
- 20 – 40%
- 20% either side
- 20 – 40%
- More than 40% — Exports exceed imports by:
- No data available

The total world trade balance should amount to zero, since exports must equal imports on a global scale. In practice, at least $100 billion in exports go unrecorded, leaving the world with an apparent deficit and many countries in a better position than public accounting reveals. However, a favorable trade balance is not necessarily a sign of prosperity: many poorer countries must maintain a high surplus in order to service debts, and do so by restricting imports below the levels needed to sustain successful economies.

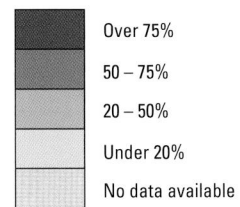

TRADE IN PRIMARY EXPORTS

Primary exports as a percentage of total export value (2009)

- Over 75%
- 50 – 75%
- 20 – 50%
- Under 20%
- No data available

Primary exports are raw materials or partly processed products that form the basis for manufacturing. They are the necessary requirements of industries and include agricultural products, minerals, fuels and timber, as well as many semi-manufactured goods such as cotton, which has been spun but not woven, wood pulp or flour. Many developed countries have few natural resources and rely on imports for the majority of their primary products. The countries of Southeast Asia export hardwoods to the rest of the world, while some South American countries are heavily dependent on coffee exports.

MERCHANT FLEETS

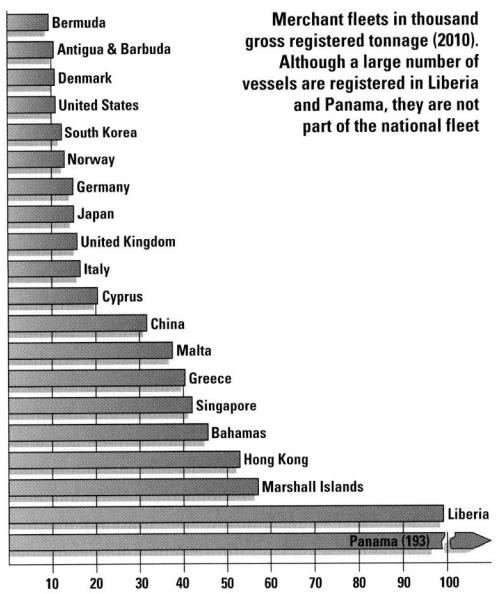

Merchant fleets in thousand gross registered tonnage (2010). Although a large number of vessels are registered in Liberia and Panama, they are not part of the national fleet

Bermuda
Antigua & Barbuda
Denmark
United States
South Korea
Norway
Germany
Japan
United Kingdom
Italy
Cyprus
China
Malta
Greece
Singapore
Bahamas
Hong Kong
Marshall Islands
Liberia
Panama (193)

TOP TEN PORTS

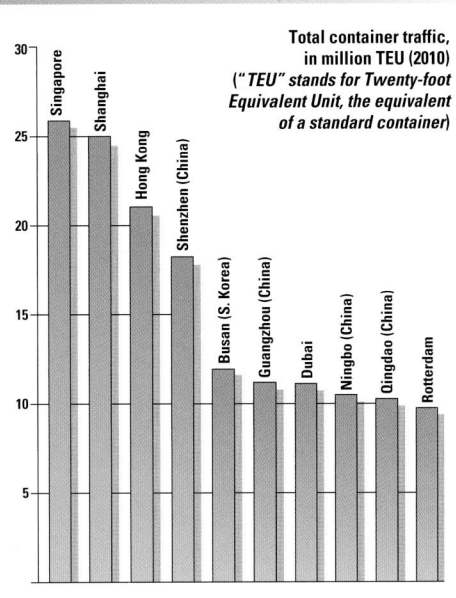

Total container traffic, in million TEU (2010) ("TEU" stands for Twenty-foot Equivalent Unit, the equivalent of a standard container)

Singapore
Shanghai
Hong Kong
Shenzhen (China)
Busan (S. Korea)
Guangzhou (China)
Dubai
Ningbo (China)
Qingdao (China)
Rotterdam

TYPES OF VESSELS

World fleet by type of vessel (2010)

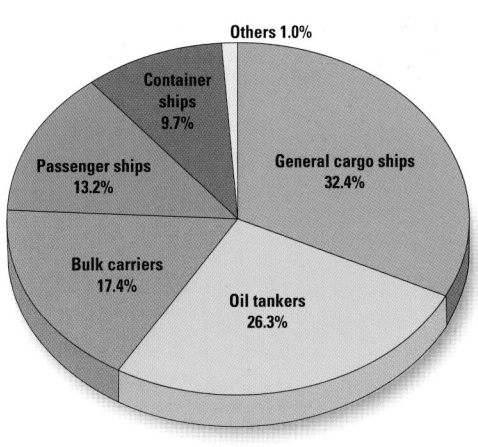

- Others 1.0%
- Container ships 9.7%
- Passenger ships 13.2%
- Bulk carriers 17.4%
- Oil tankers 26.3%
- General cargo ships 32.4%

EXPORTS PER CAPITA

Value of exports in US $, divided by total population (2011)

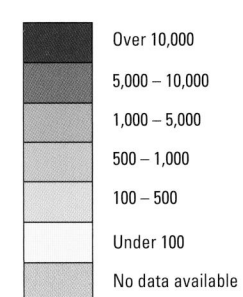

- Over 10,000
- 5,000 – 10,000
- 1,000 – 5,000
- 500 – 1,000
- 100 – 500
- Under 100
- No data available

Countries with highest exports per capita

Qatar	$122,993
Singapore	$91,146
Liechtenstein	$80,316
San Marino	$77,223
Norway	$55,373
UAE	$51,528

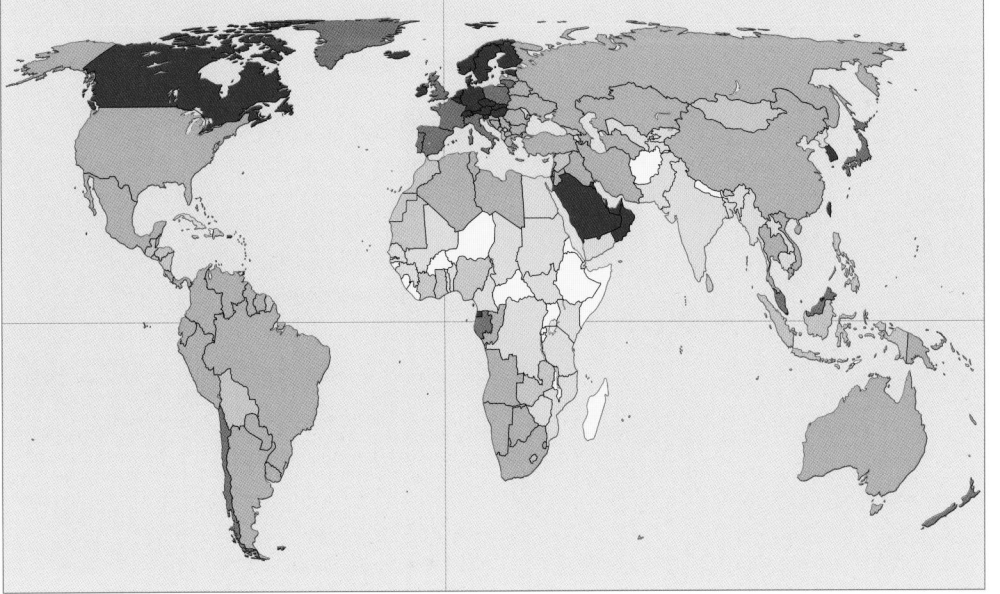

29

Travel and Tourism

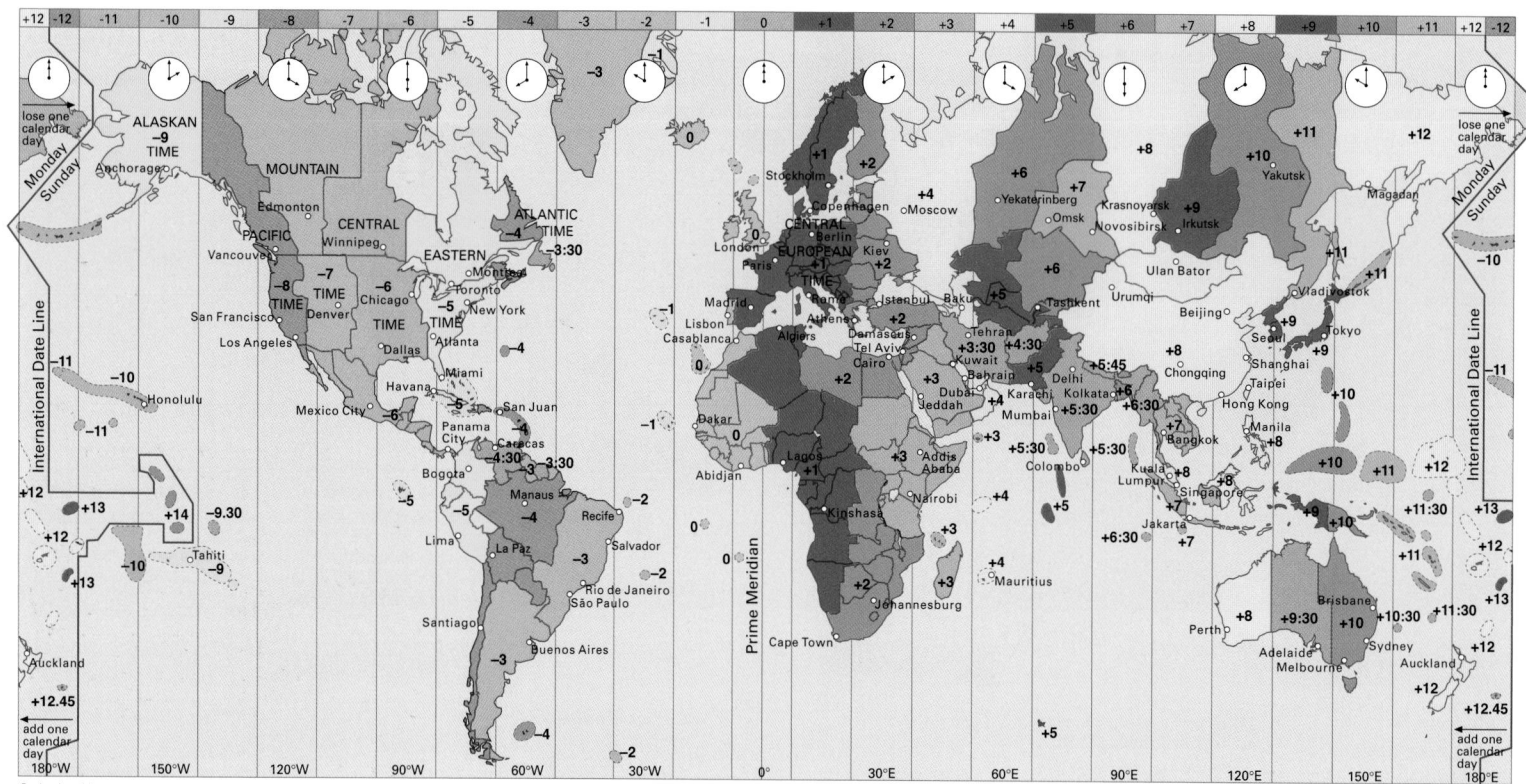

Projection: Mercator

TIME ZONES

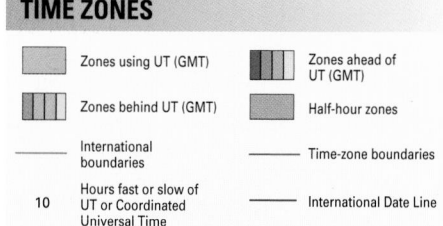

Zones using UT (GMT)	Zones ahead of UT (GMT)
Zones behind UT (GMT)	Half-hour zones
International boundaries	Time-zone boundaries
10 Hours fast or slow of UT or Coordinated Universal Time	International Date Line

Certain time zones are affected by the incidence of daylight saving time in countries where it is adopted.

Actual solar time, when it is noon at Greenwich, is shown along the top of the map.

The world is divided into 24 time zones, each centered on meridians at 15° intervals, which is the longitudinal distance the sun travels every hour. The meridian running through Greenwich, London, passes through the middle of the first zone.

RAIL AND ROAD: THE LEADING NATIONS

	Total rail network ('000 km), 2010	Passenger km per head per year, 2010		Total road network ('000 km), 2009	Vehicle km per head per year, 2009	Number of vehicles per km of roads, 2009
1.	USA....................228.5	Switzerland 2,258	USA................ 6,486.2	Peru 38,553	Kuwait 271
2.	Russia 85.3	Japan 1,910	China 3,799.4	USA.....................34,560	Hong Kong..........241
3.	China 65.5	Slovakia 1,420	India............... 3,428.0	Tunisia................25,225	Macau.................238
4.	India...................63.3	Denmark 1,322	Brazil 1,841.5	Pakistan.............25,199	UAE.....................220
5.	Canada 58.3	France 1,320	Canada 1,419.3	Ecuador.............23,570	Singapore 218
6.	Germany 33.7	Austria 1,227	Japan 1,201.3	Chile...................22,671	Taiwan 170
7.	France 33.6	Ukraine................1,097	France 1,030.2	South Korea 21,763	South Korea 157
8.	UK 31.5	Russia.................1,075	Russia 953.0	Singapore 21,563	ABC Islands 154
9.	Brazil 29.8	Belgium 972	Australia 815.5	Morocco.............18,455	Israel 128
10.	Mexico 26.7	Germany 961	Sweden 697.8	Croatia...............17,723	Malta 123
11.	Argentina 25.0	Netherlands 922	Spain 680.3	Finland...............17,639	Thailand 121
12.	South Africa 22.1	UK 887	Germany 644.8	Canada 17,498	Bahrain 114
13.	Ukraine 21.7	Kazakhstan 879	Italy 490.0	Denmark 16,903	Jordan 112
14.	Japan 20.0	Belarus 779	Turkey 427.2	Thailand 16,823	Puerto Rico 110
15.	Poland 19.7	Italy 735	Indonesia 404.3	Isreal 16,721	Dom. Rep. 105

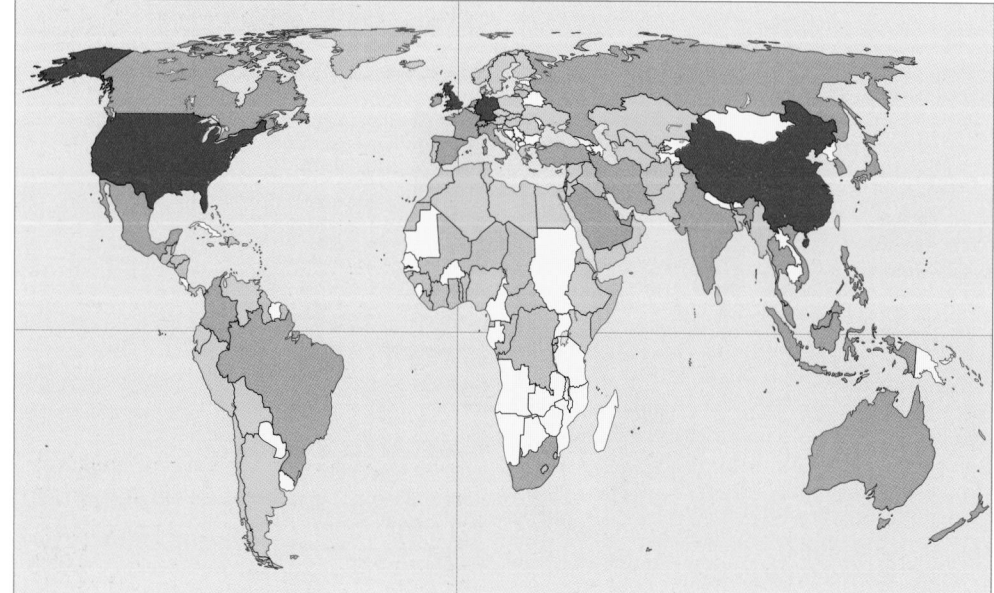

AIR TRAVEL

Number of air passengers carried (2009)

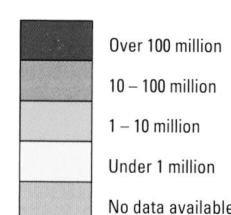

	Over 100 million
	10 – 100 million
	1 – 10 million
	Under 1 million
	No data available

World's busiest airports (2011) – total passengers

1. Atlanta Hartsfield Internat'l.
2. Beijing Capital International
3. London Heathrow
4. Chicago O'Hare International
5. Tokyo Haneda
6. Los Angeles International
7. Paris Charles de Gaulle
8. Dallas Fort Worth Internat'l.
9. Frankfurt International
10. Hong Kong International

World's busiest airports (2011) – international passengers

1. London Heathrow
2. Paris Charles de Gaulle
3. Hong Kong International
4. Dubai International
5. Amsterdam
6. Frankfurt International
7. Singapore Changi
8. Bangkok Suvarnabhumi
9. Incheon International
10. Madrid Barajas

TOURIST CENTRES

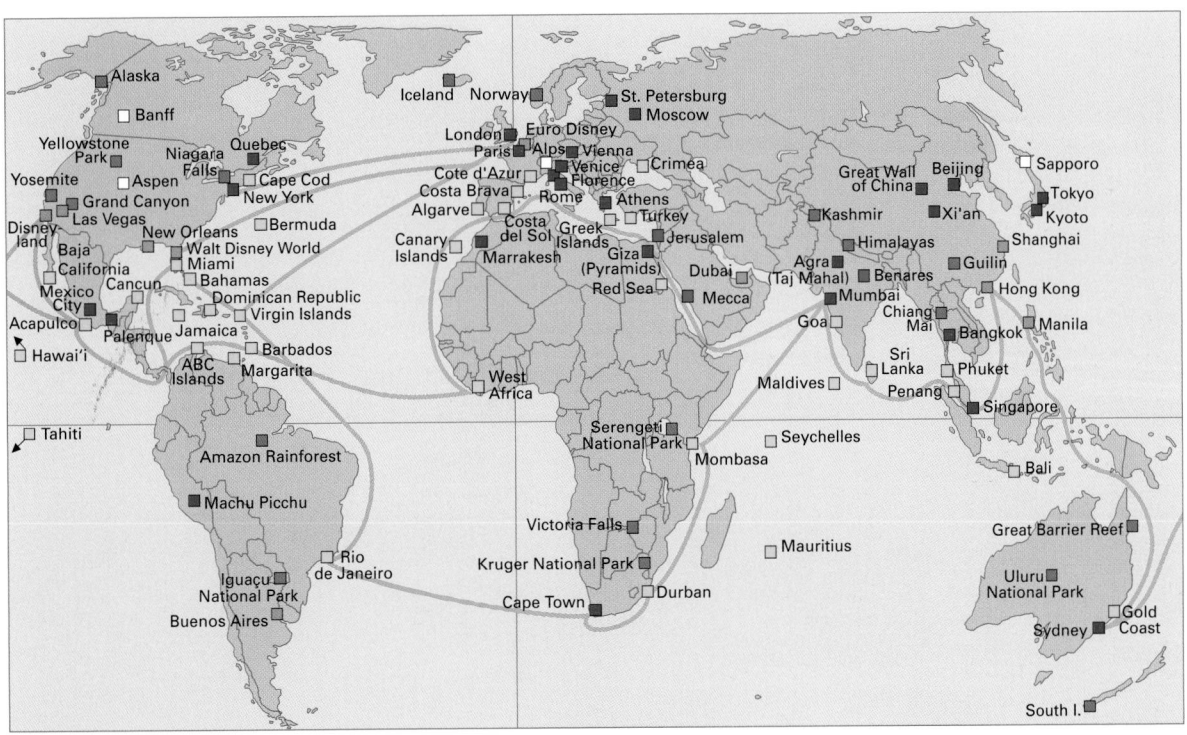

- ■ Cultural and historical centers
- ☐ Coastal resorts
- ☐ Ski resorts
- ■ Centers of entertainment
- ■ Places of pilgrimage
- ■ Places of great natural beauty
- ～ Popular holiday cruise routes

VISITORS TO THE USA

Overseas arrivals to the USA, in thousands (2011)

1.	Canada	21,028
2.	Mexico	13,414
3.	UK	3,835
4.	Japan	3,249
5.	Germany	1,823
6.	Brazil	1,508
7.	France	1,504
8.	South Korea	1,145
9.	China	1,089
10.	Australia	1,037

TOURIST SPENDING

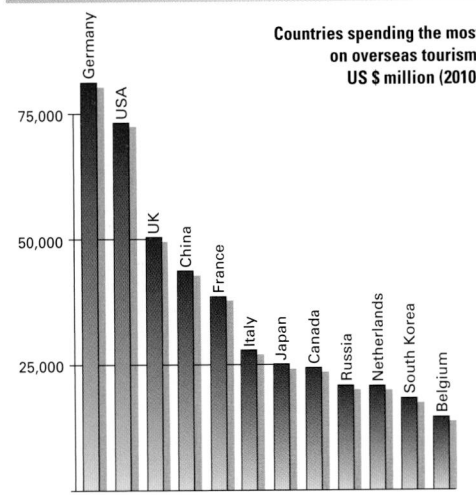

Countries spending the most on overseas tourism, US $ million (2010)

THE MAIN DESTINATIONS

		Arrivals from abroad millions (2010)	% of world total (2010)
1.	France	76.8	9.0%
2.	USA	59.7	6.4%
3.	China	55.7	5.9%
4.	Spain	52.7	5.6%
5.	Italy	43.6	4.6%
6.	UK	28.1	3.0%
7.	Turkey	27.0	2.9%
8.	Germany	26.9	2.6%
9.	Malaysia	24.6	2.6%
10.	Mexico	22.4	2.4%

The 940 million international arrivals in 2010 represented an additional 62 million over the 2009 level – making a new record year for the industry. Growth was common to all regions, but was particularly strong in Asia and the Pacific, and in the Middle East.

TOURIST EARNINGS

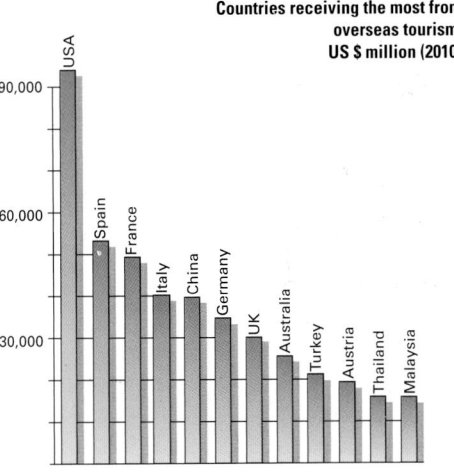

Countries receiving the most from overseas tourism, US $ million (2010)

IMPORTANCE OF TOURISM

Tourism receipts as a percentage of Gross National Income (2010)

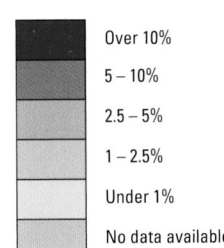

- Over 10%
- 5 – 10%
- 2.5 – 5%
- 1 – 2.5%
- Under 1%
- No data available

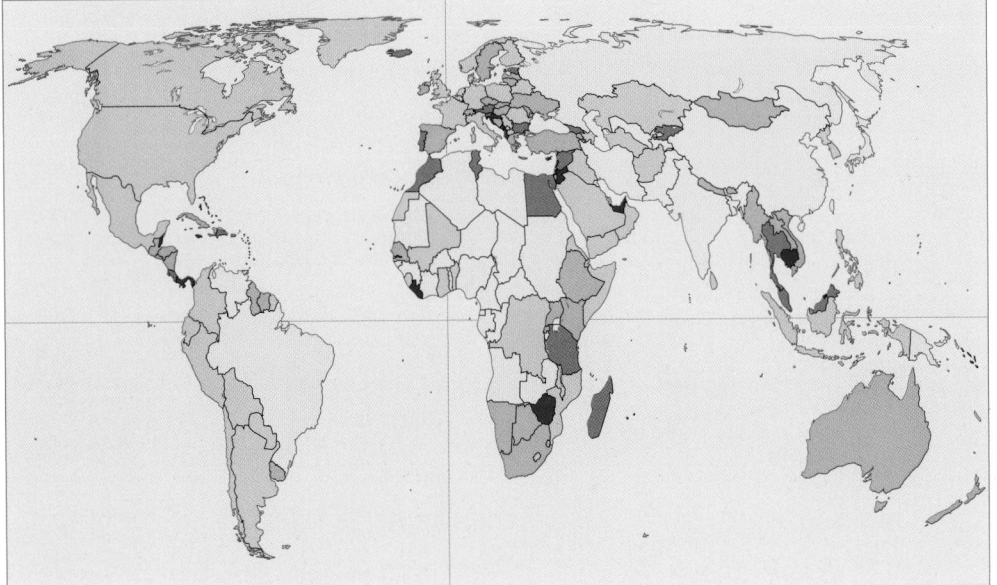

Countries with the highest tourism receipts as % of GNI (2010)

1. Bermuda (UK)	90.8		6. Virgin Is. (UK)	32.6
2. Palau	53.9		7. Barbados	30.4
3. Maldives	39.3		8. St Lucia	28.8
4. Cayman Is. (UK)	38.8		9. Liechtenstein	27.2
5. Seychelles	35.7		10. Antigua & Barbuda	25.8

31

HONG KONG, CHINA

© RapidEye AG/Fugro NPA

WORLD CITIES

Amsterdam	2	Helsinki	11	Montréal	20	Tokyo	30
Athens	2	Hong Kong	12	Mumbai	20	Tehran	31
Atlanta	3	Istanbul	12	Munich	21	Toronto	31
Baghdad	3	Jakarta	12	New Orleans	21	Venice	32
Bangkok	3	Jerusalem	13	New York	22	Vienna	32
Barcelona	4	Johannesburg	13	Orlando	23	Warsaw	33
Beijing	4	Karachi	13	Osaka	23	Washington	33
Berlin	5	Kolkata	14	Oslo	23		
Boston	6	Lagos	14	Paris	24	Index	34–39
Brussels	6	Las Vegas	14	Prague	25		
Budapest	7	Lima	14	Rio de Janeiro	25	WORLD CITIES	
Buenos Aires	7	London	15	Rome	26	SATELLITE IMAGES	
Cairo	7	Lisbon	16	San Francisco	26	Beijing	40
Cape Town	8	Los Angeles	16	St Petersburg	27	Cape Town	41
Copenhagen	8	Madrid	17	Santiago	27	Las Vegas	42
Chicago	9	Manila	17	São Paulo	27	London	43
Dubai	9	Melbourne	18	Seoul	27	Mexico City	44
Delhi	10	Mexico City	18	Shanghai	28	Mumbai	45
Dublin	10	Milan	18	Singapore	28	New York	46
Edinburgh	11	Miami	19	Stockholm	29	Rio de Janeiro	47
Guangzhou	11	Moscow	19	Sydney	29	Sydney	48

CITY MAPS

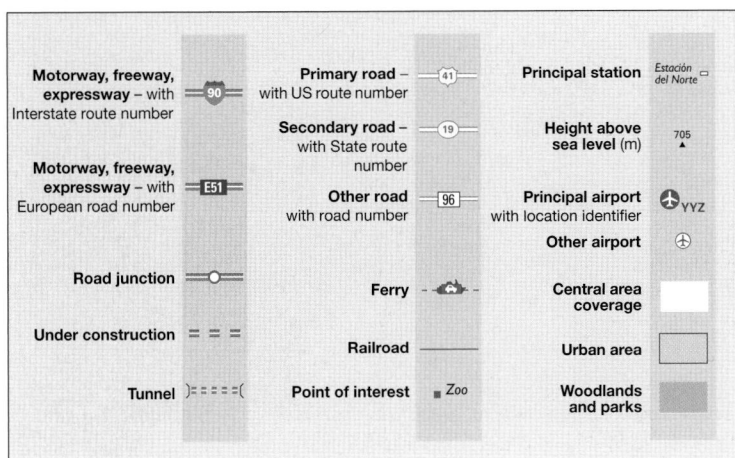

Motorway, freeway, expressway – with Interstate route number

Motorway, freeway, expressway – with European road number

Road junction

Under construction

Tunnel

Primary road – with US route number

Secondary road – with State route number

Other road – with road number

Ferry

Railroad

Point of interest

Principal station

Height above sea level (m)

Principal airport with location identifier

Other airport

Central area coverage

Urban area

Woodlands and parks

CENTRAL AREA MAPS

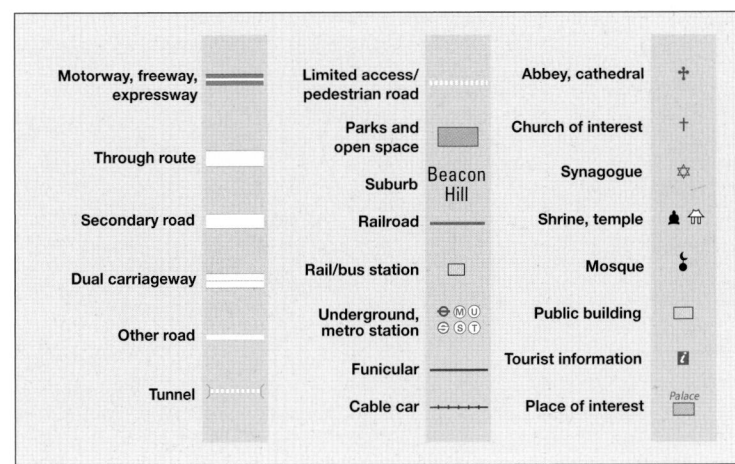

Motorway, freeway, expressway

Through route

Secondary road

Dual carriageway

Other road

Tunnel

Limited access/ pedestrian road

Parks and open space

Suburb

Railroad

Rail/bus station

Underground, metro station

Funicular

Cable car

Abbey, cathedral

Church of interest

Synagogue

Shrine, temple

Mosque

Public building

Tourist information

Place of interest

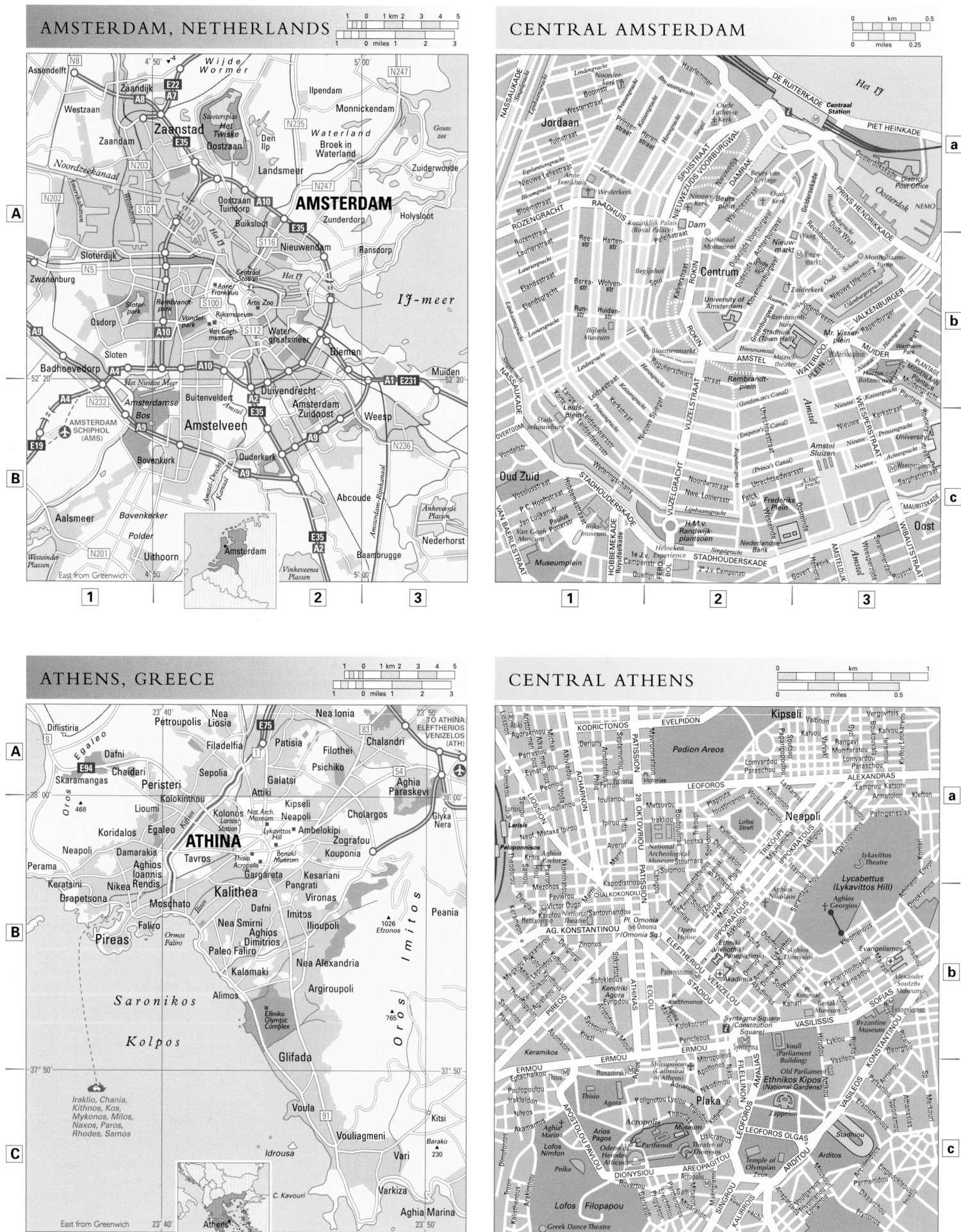

ATLANTA, GEORGIA

Interstate route numbers · U.S. route numbers · State route numbers

BAGHDAD, IRAQ

International Zone (Green Zone)

BANGKOK, THAILAND

CENTRAL BANGKOK

Skytrain · Shrine · Temple

COPYRIGHT PHILIP'S

BARCELONA, SPAIN

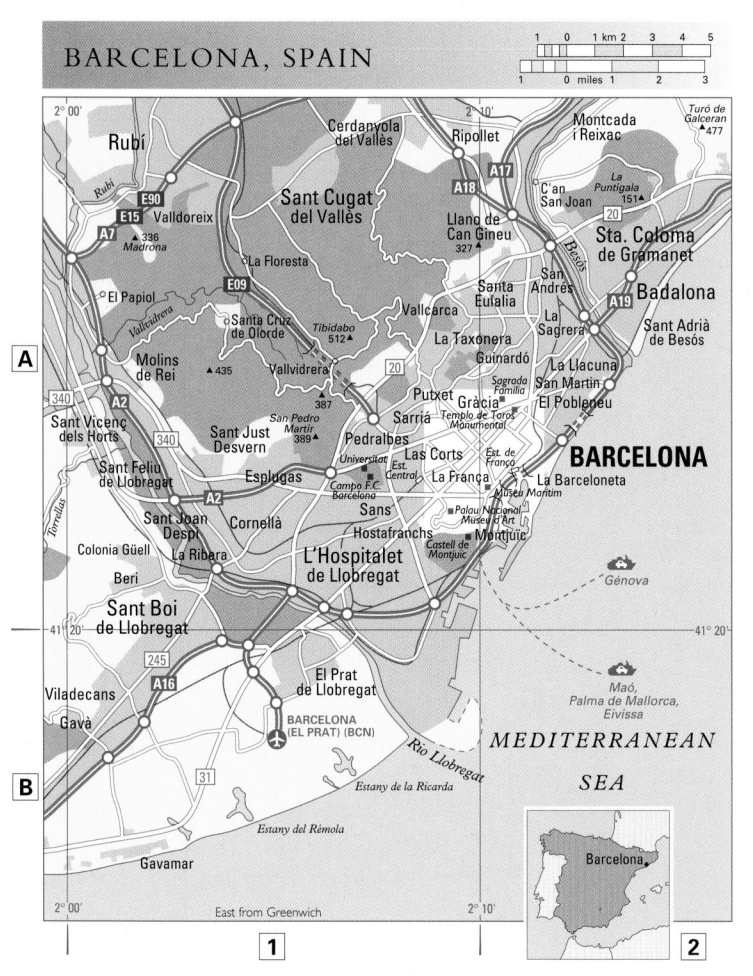

CENTRAL BARCELONA

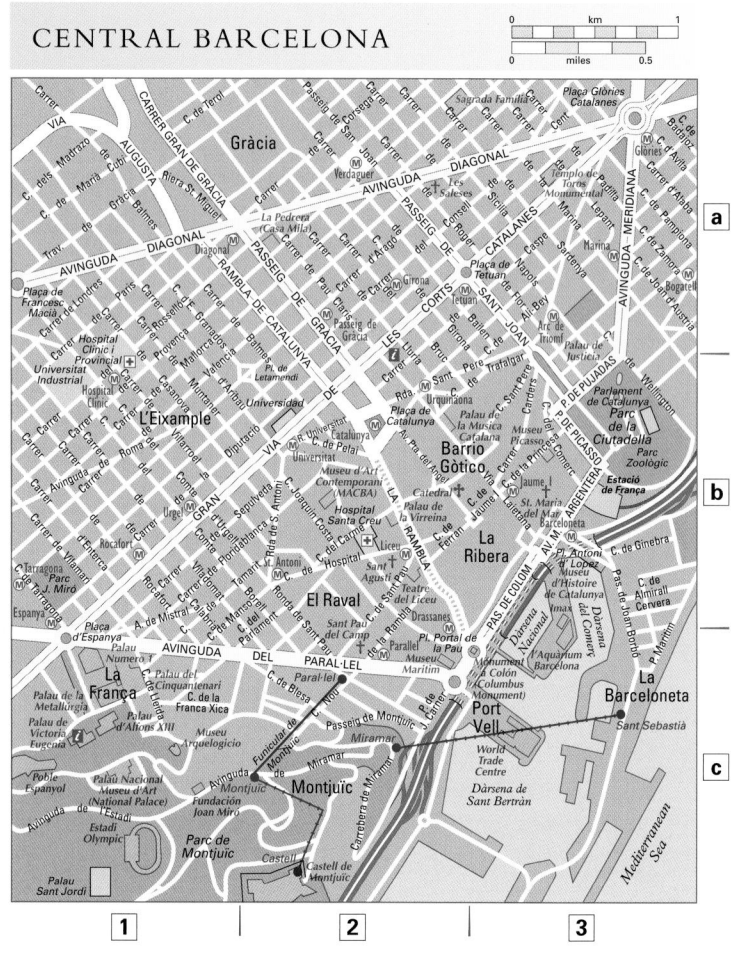

BEIJING, CHINA

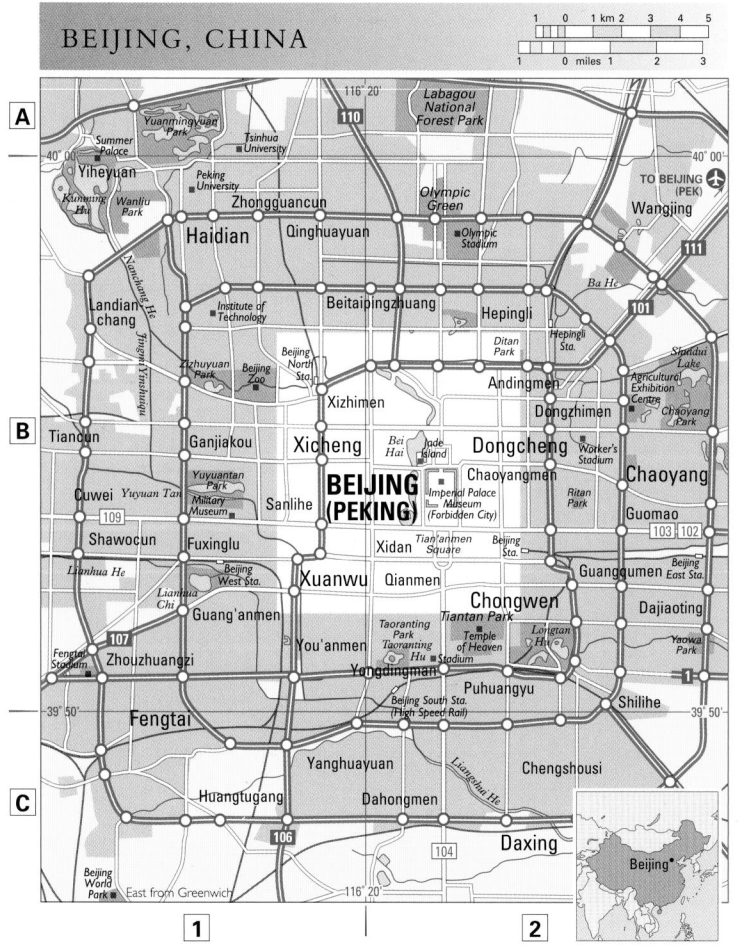

CENTRAL BEIJING

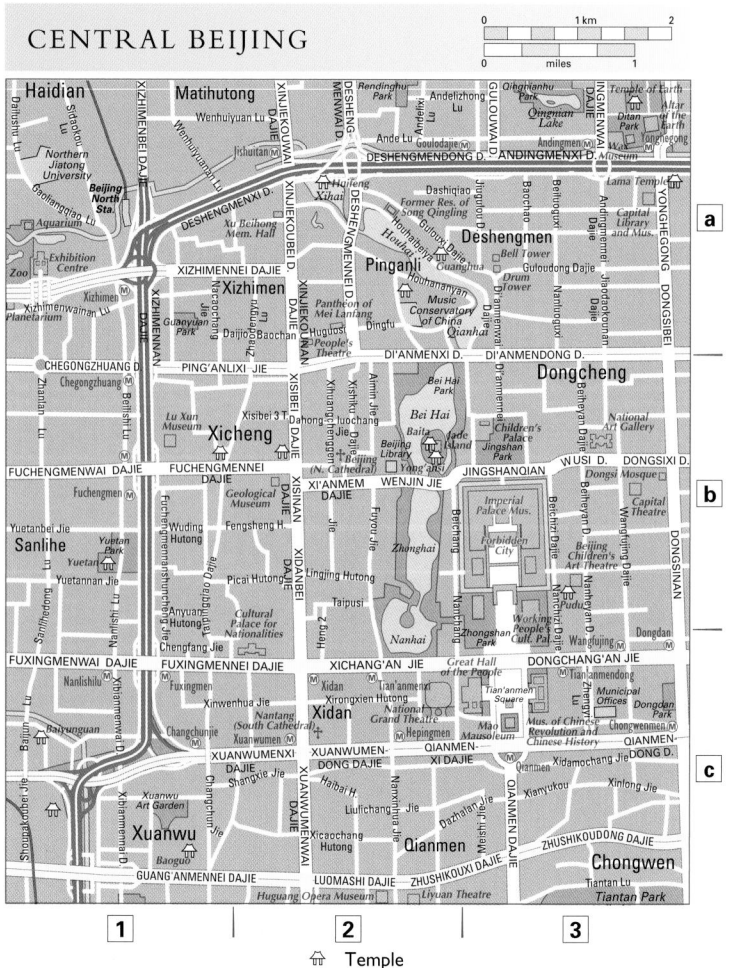

⛩ Temple

BERLIN, GERMANY

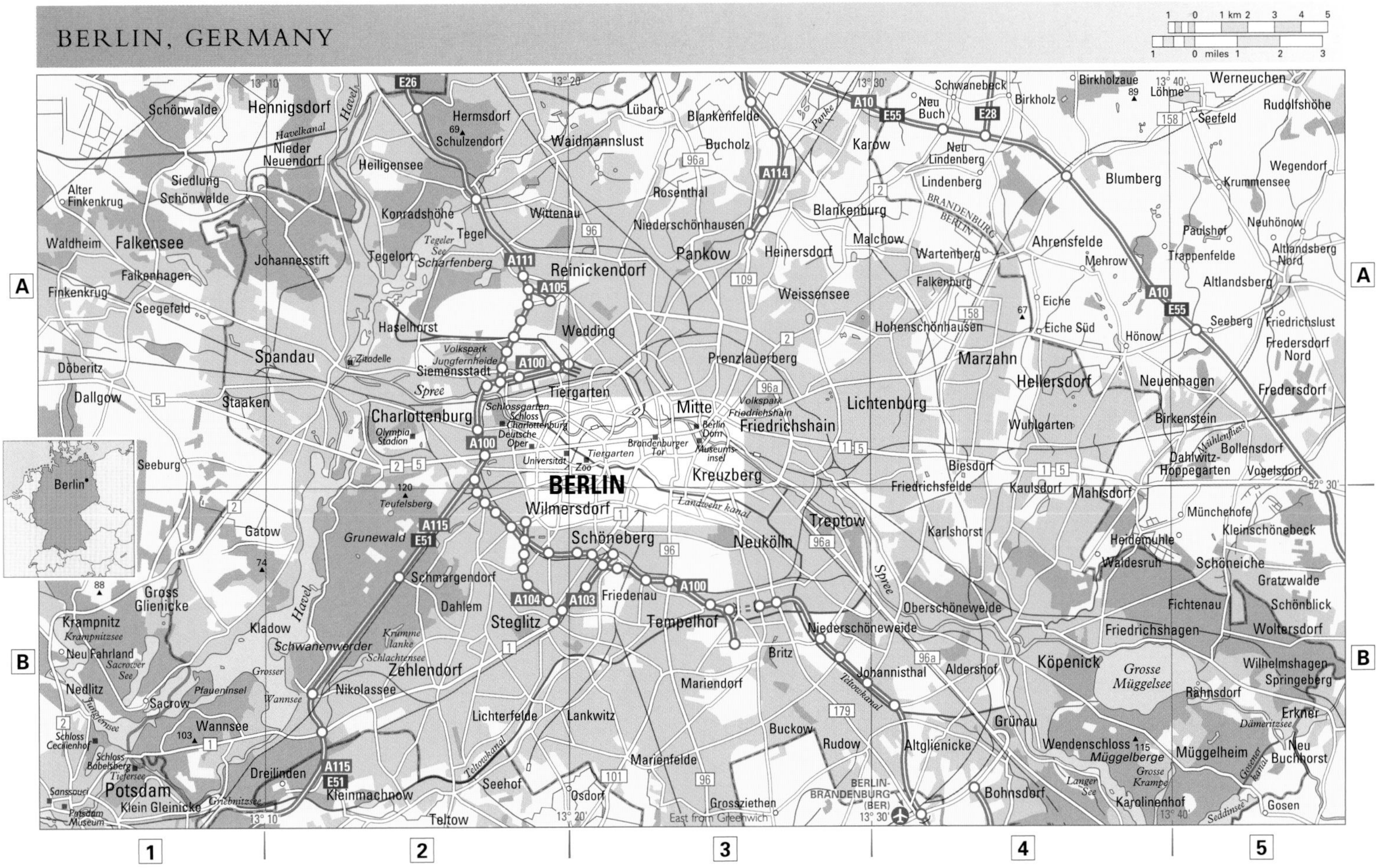

CENTRAL BERLIN

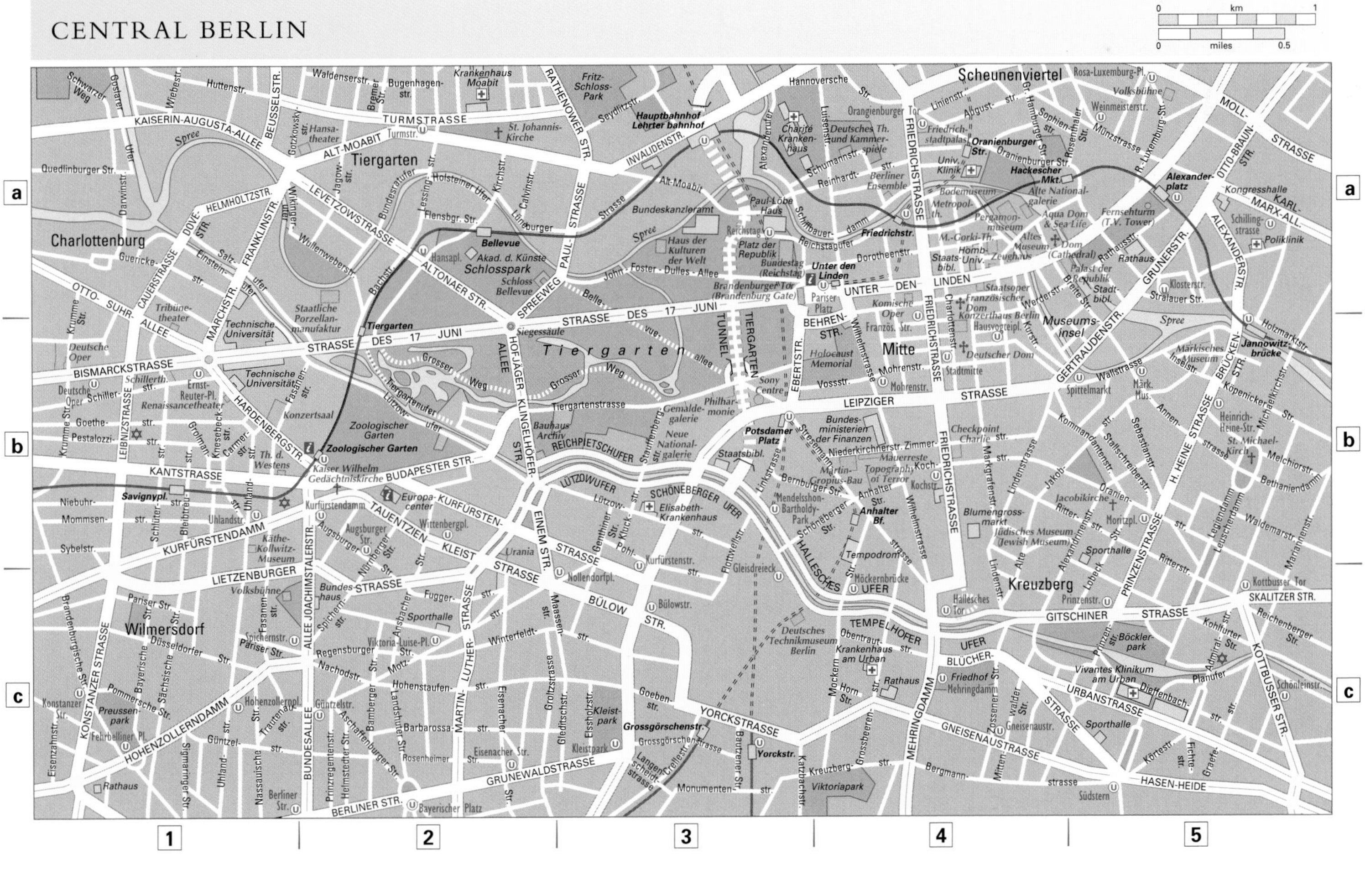

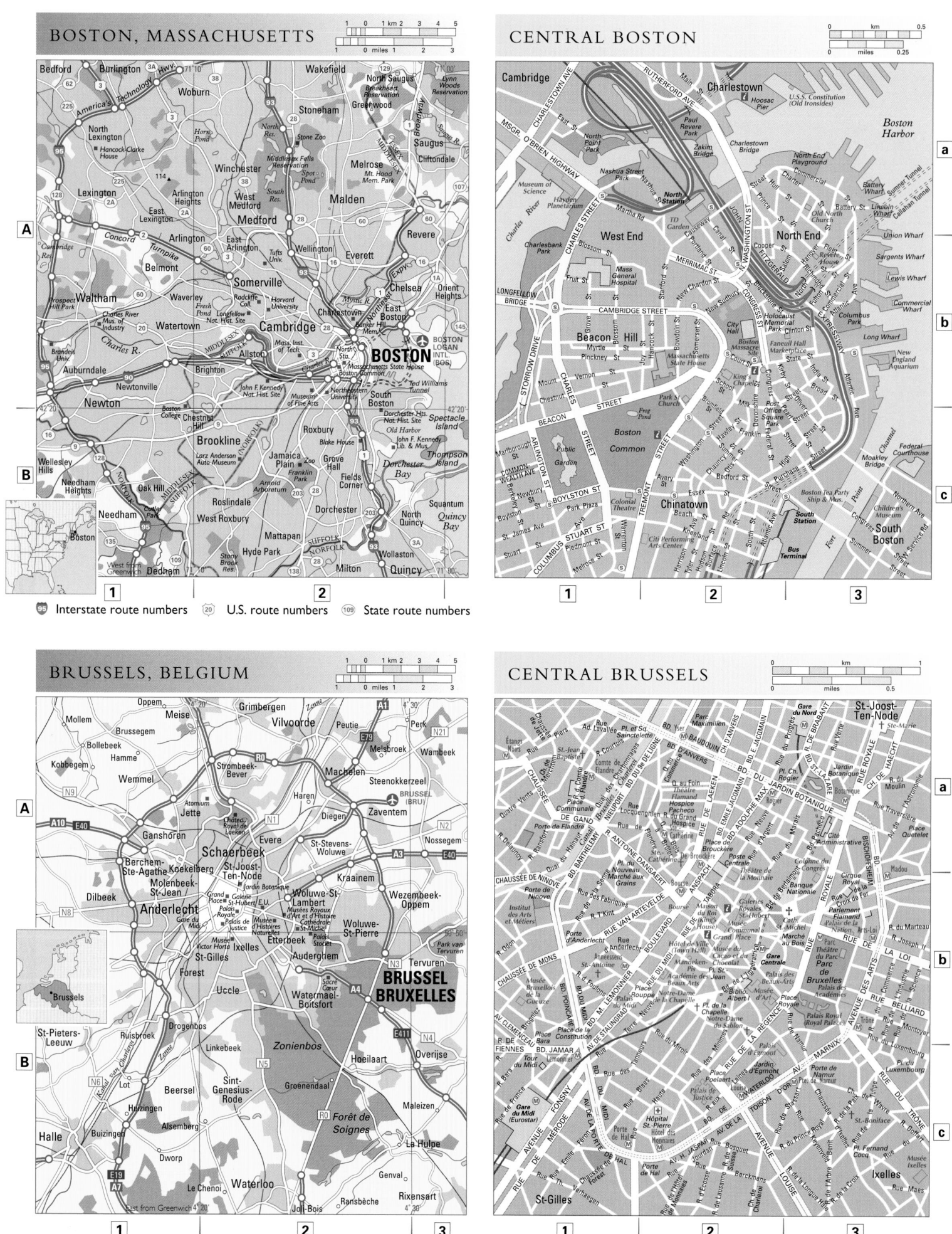

BOSTON, MASSACHUSETTS

Bedford · Burlington · Woburn · Wakefield · Stoneham · Greenwood · Melrose · Saugus · Cliftondale · Revere · North Lexington · Winchester · West Medford · Malden · Orient Heights · Lexington · East Lexington · Arlington Heights · Medford · Everett · East Boston · Chelsea · Arlington · Belmont · Somerville · Wellington · Waltham · Waverley · Watertown · Cambridge · Charlestown · East Boston · BOSTON · Auburndale · Allston · Brighton · South Boston · Newton · Newtonville · Chestnut Hill · Roxbury · Spectacle Island · Brookline · Jamaica Plain · Grove Hall · Fields Corner · Dorchester Bay · Wellesley Hills · Needham Heights · Roslindale · Dorchester · North Quincy · Quincy Bay · Needham · West Roxbury · Mattapan · Squantum · West from Greenwich · Dedham · Hyde Park · Wollaston · Milton · Quincy

Interstate route numbers · U.S. route numbers · State route numbers

CENTRAL BOSTON

Cambridge · Charlestown · U.S.S. Constitution (Old Ironsides) · Boston Harbor · North End · West End · Beacon Hill · Boston Common · Chinatown · South Station · Bus Terminal · South Boston

BRUSSELS, BELGIUM

Oppem · Meise · Grimbergen · Vilvoorde · Peutie · Perk · Mollem · Brussegem · Bollebeek · Hamme · Wemmel · Strombeek-Bever · Machelen · Steenokkerzeel · Kobbegem · Haren · Diegem · Wambeek · Atomium · Jette · BRUSSEL (BRU) · Zaventem · Ganshoren · Evere · St-Stevens-Woluwe · Nossegem · Schaerbeek · Berchem-Ste-Agathe · Koekelberg · St-Joost-Ten-Node · Kraainem · Molenbeek-St-Jean · Woluwe-St-Lambert · Wezembeek-Oppem · Dilbeek · Anderlecht · Woluwe-St-Pierre · Etterbeek · Ixelles · Auderghem · St-Gilles · Tervuren · Park van Tervuren · Forest · Uccle · BRUSSEL BRUXELLES · Watermael-Boitsfort · St-Pieters-Leeuw · Drogenbos · Zonienbos · Overijse · Ruisbroek · Linkebeek · Hoeilaart · Halle · Buizingen · Lot · Beersel · Sint-Genesius-Rode · Groenendaal · Forêt de Soignes · La Hulpe · Dworp · Alsemberg · Genval · Rixensart · Waterloo · Jol-Bois · Ransbèche · East from Greenwich

CENTRAL BRUSSELS

St-Joost-Ten-Node · Gare du Nord · Parc de Bruxelles · Ixelles · St-Gilles · Gare du Midi (Eurostar)

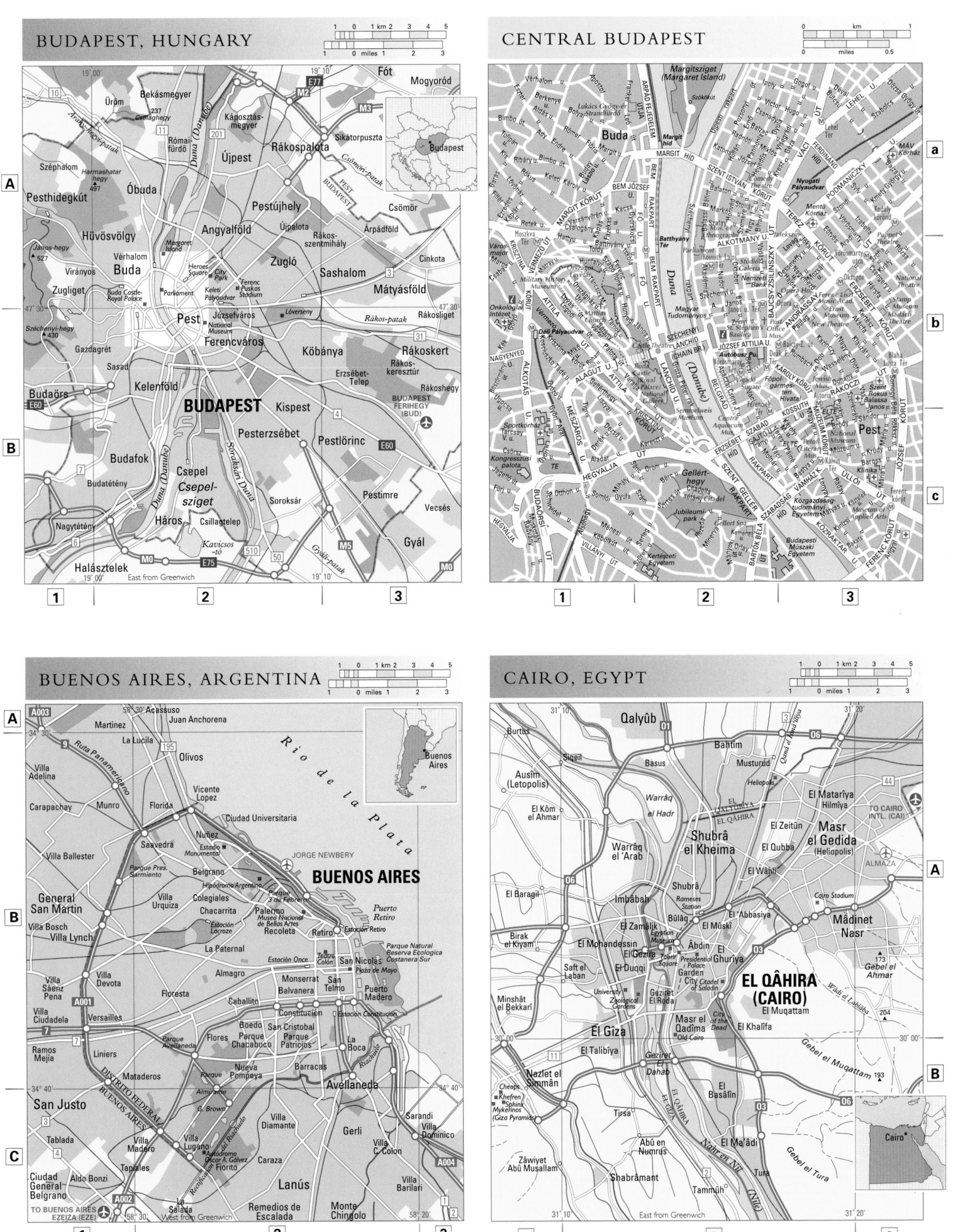

BUDAPEST, HUNGARY

CENTRAL BUDAPEST

BUENOS AIRES, ARGENTINA

CAIRO, EGYPT

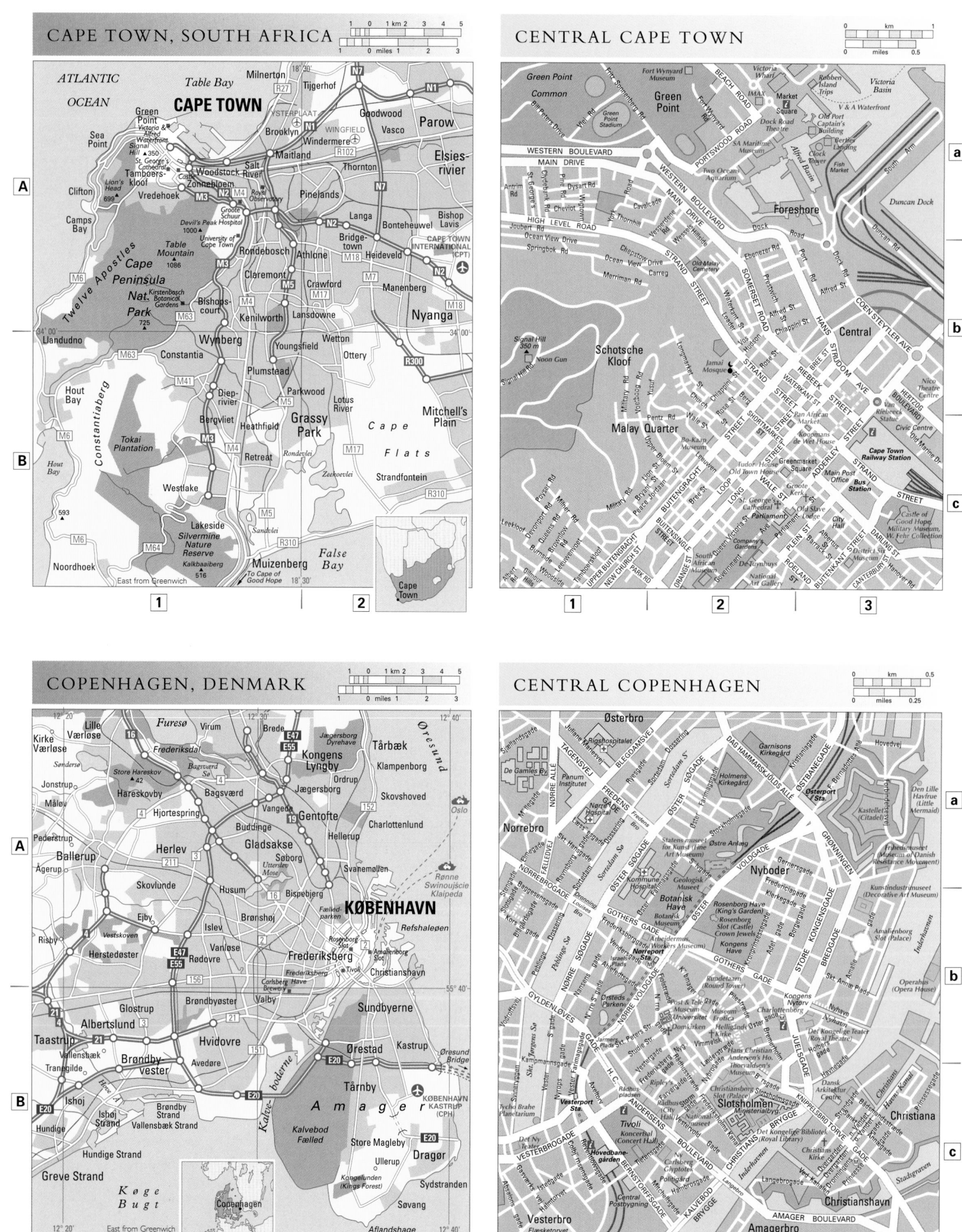

CENTRAL CHICAGO

km 0   0.5

miles 0   0.25

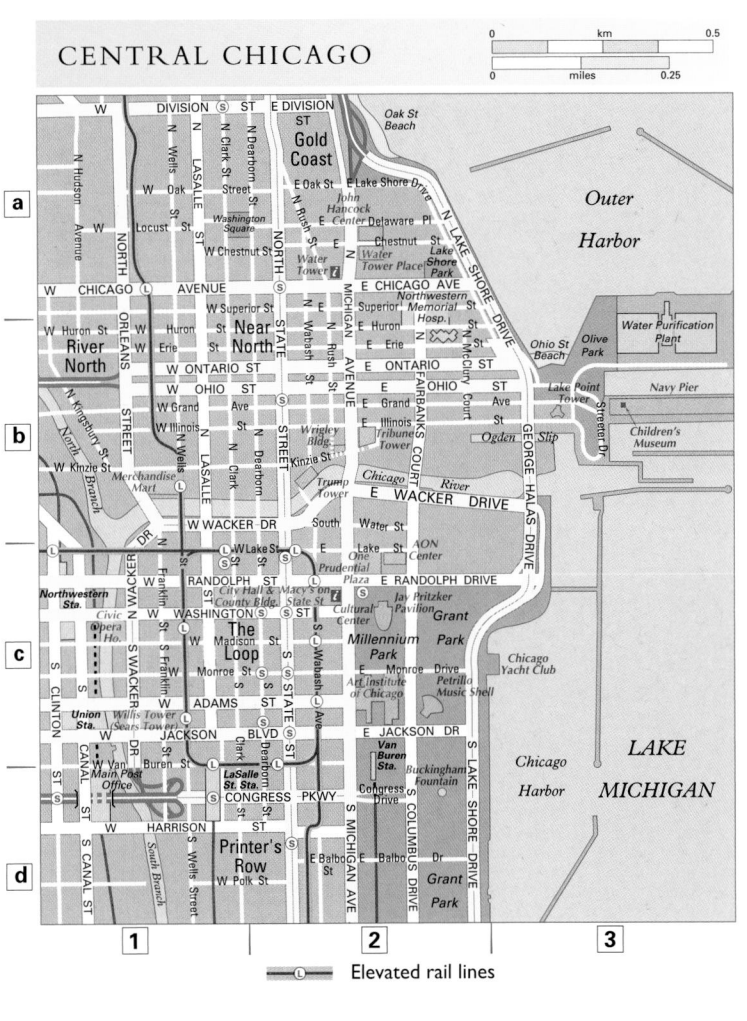

—Ⓛ— Elevated rail lines

DUBAI, U.A.E.

1   0   1 km 2   3   4   5

1   0   miles 1   2   3

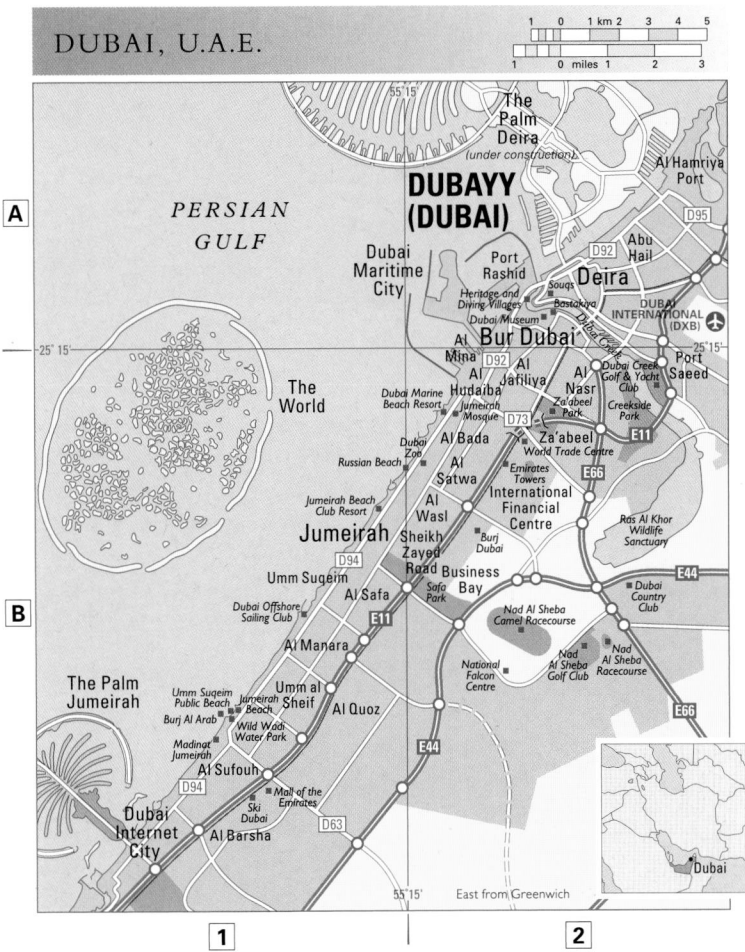

East from Greenwich

CHICAGO, ILLINOIS

1   0   1 km 2   3   4   5

1   0   miles 1   2   3

West from Greenwich

🛡 Interstate route numbers   ⬭ U.S. route numbers   ⬭ State route numbers

COPYRIGHT PHILIP'S

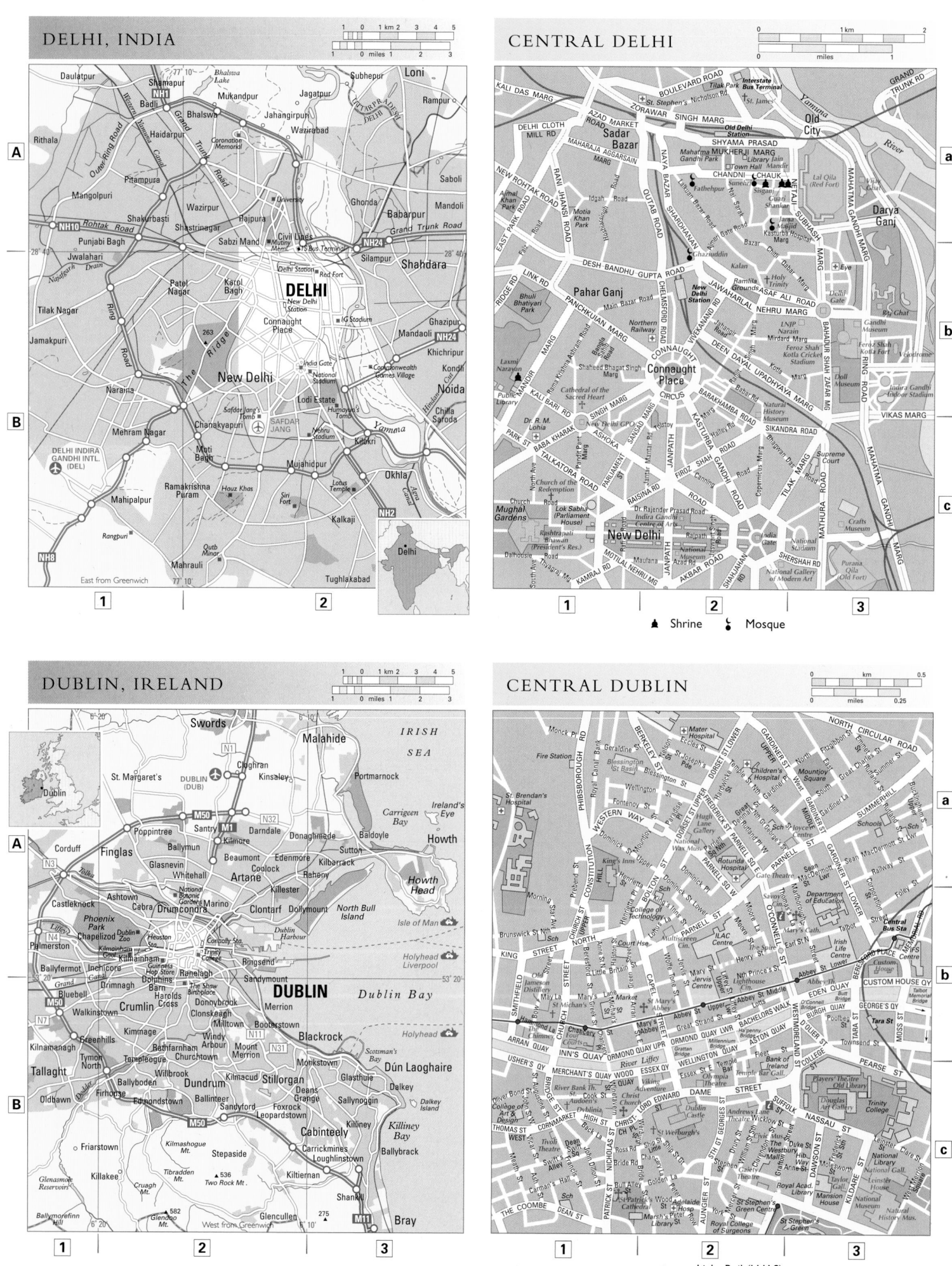

DELHI, INDIA

CENTRAL DELHI

▲ Shrine   ♦ Mosque

DUBLIN, IRELAND

CENTRAL DUBLIN

Light Rail (LUAS)

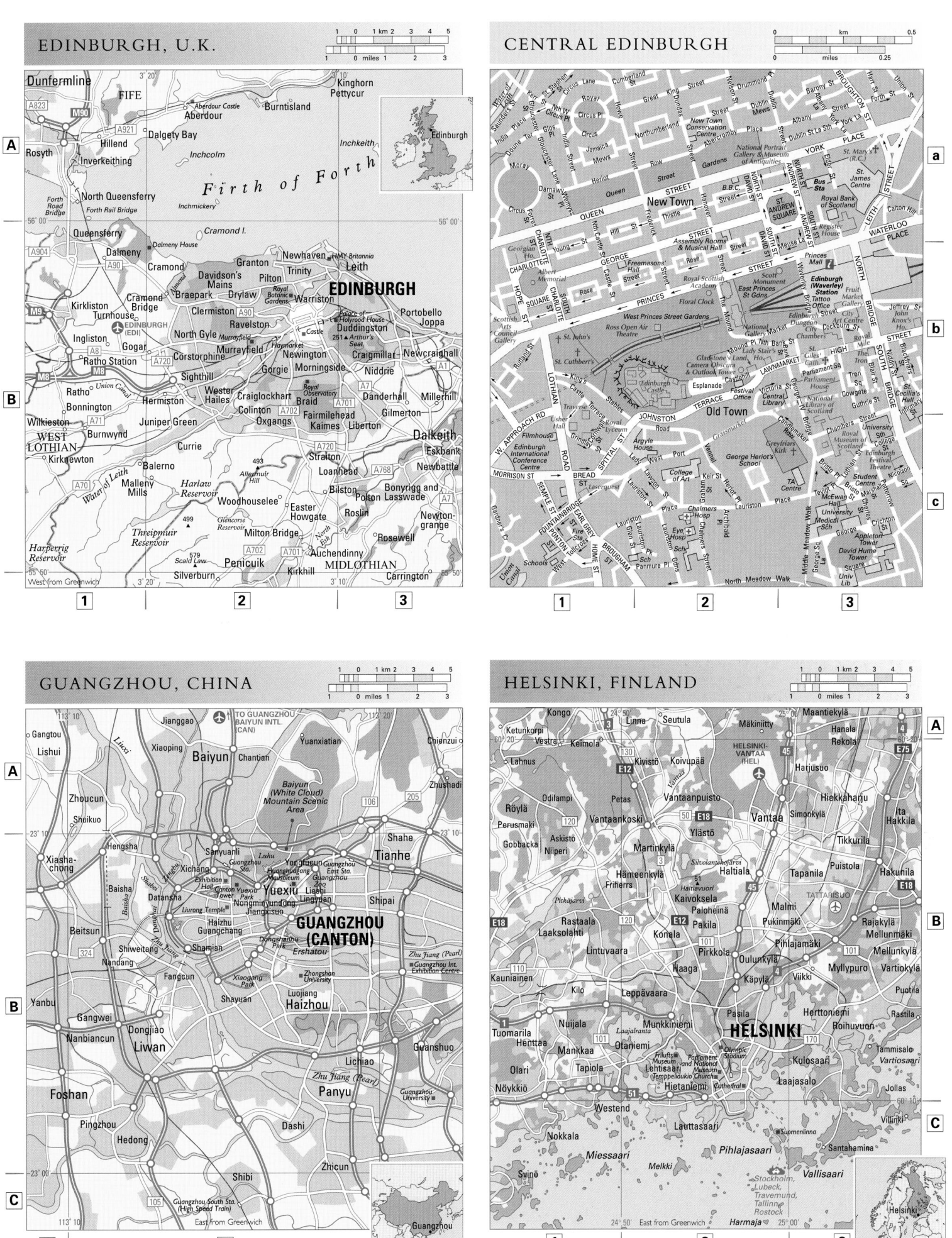

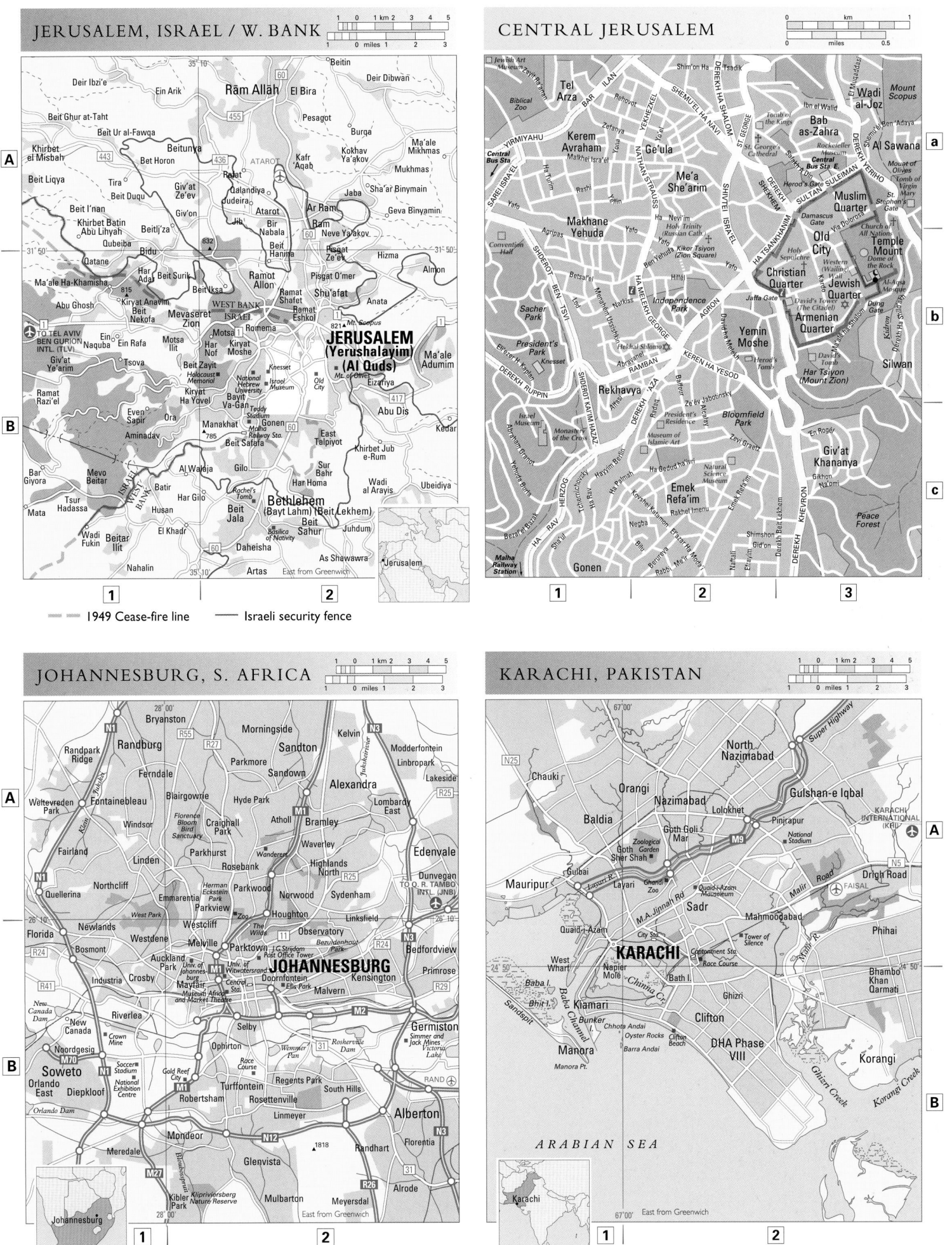

JERUSALEM, ISRAEL / W. BANK

1 0 1 km 2 3 4 5
1 0 miles 1 2 3

Deir Ibzi'e   Beitin
Deir Dibwan
Ein Arik   Rām Allāh   El Bira   60
455   Pesagot   Burqa
Beit Ghur at-Taht   Bet Ur al-Fawqa   Ma'ale Mikhmas
443   Beitunya   436   Kokhav Ya'akov   Mukhmas
Khirbet el Misbah   Bet Horon   ATAROT   Rafat   Kafr Aqab
Beit Liqya   Giv'at Ze'ev   Qalandiya Judeira   Jaba   Sha'ar Binymain
Tira   Beit Duqu   Atarot   Ar Ram   Geva Binyamin
Beit I'nan   Giv'on   Jib   Bir Nabala   60   Neve Ya'akov.
Khirbet Batin   Beitlj'za   Ram   Beit Hanina
Abu Lihyah   Qubeiba   832   Bidu   Pisgat Ze'ev   Hizma   Almon
Qatane   31° 50'   Har Adar   Beit Surik   Ramot Allon   Pisgat O'mer   Anata   31° 50'
Ma'ale Ha-Khamisha   815   Beit Iksa   Ramat Shafet   Shu'afat
Abu Ghosh   Kiryat Anavim   Beit Nekofa   WEST BANK   Ramat Eshkol   Mt. Scopus   1
TO TEL AVIV   Mevaseret Zion   ISRAEL   Romema   JERUSALEM
BEN GURION   Ein Naquba   Motsa   Har Nof   (Yerushalayim)   Ma'ale
INTL. (TLV)   Ein Rafa   Motsa Ilit   Kiryat Moshe   (Al Quds)   Adumim
Giv'at Ye'arim   Tsova   Beit Zayit   Holocaust Memorial   Knesset   Old   Mt. of Olives   Eizariya
Ramat Razi'el   National Hebrew University   Israel Museum   City
Even Sapir   Kiryat   Ha Yovel   417
Ora   Bayit Va-Gan   785   Teddy Stadium   East   Kedar
Aminadav   Manakhat   Gonen   Talpiyot
Bar Giyora   Mevo Beitar   Beit Safafa   Sur Bahr   Abu Dis
Mata   Tsur Hadassa   Al Walaja   Gilo   Har Homa   Khirbet Jub e-Rum
Batir   Rachel's Tomb   Wadi al Arayis   Ubeidiya
Wadi Fukin   Beitar Ilit   Husan   Har Gilo   Bethlehem   Beit Sahur   Juhdum
El Khadr   Beit Jala   (Bayt Lahm) (Beit Lekhem)
Nahalin   Daheisha   Basilica of Nativity   As Shawawra
60   Artas   East from Greenwich

1   2

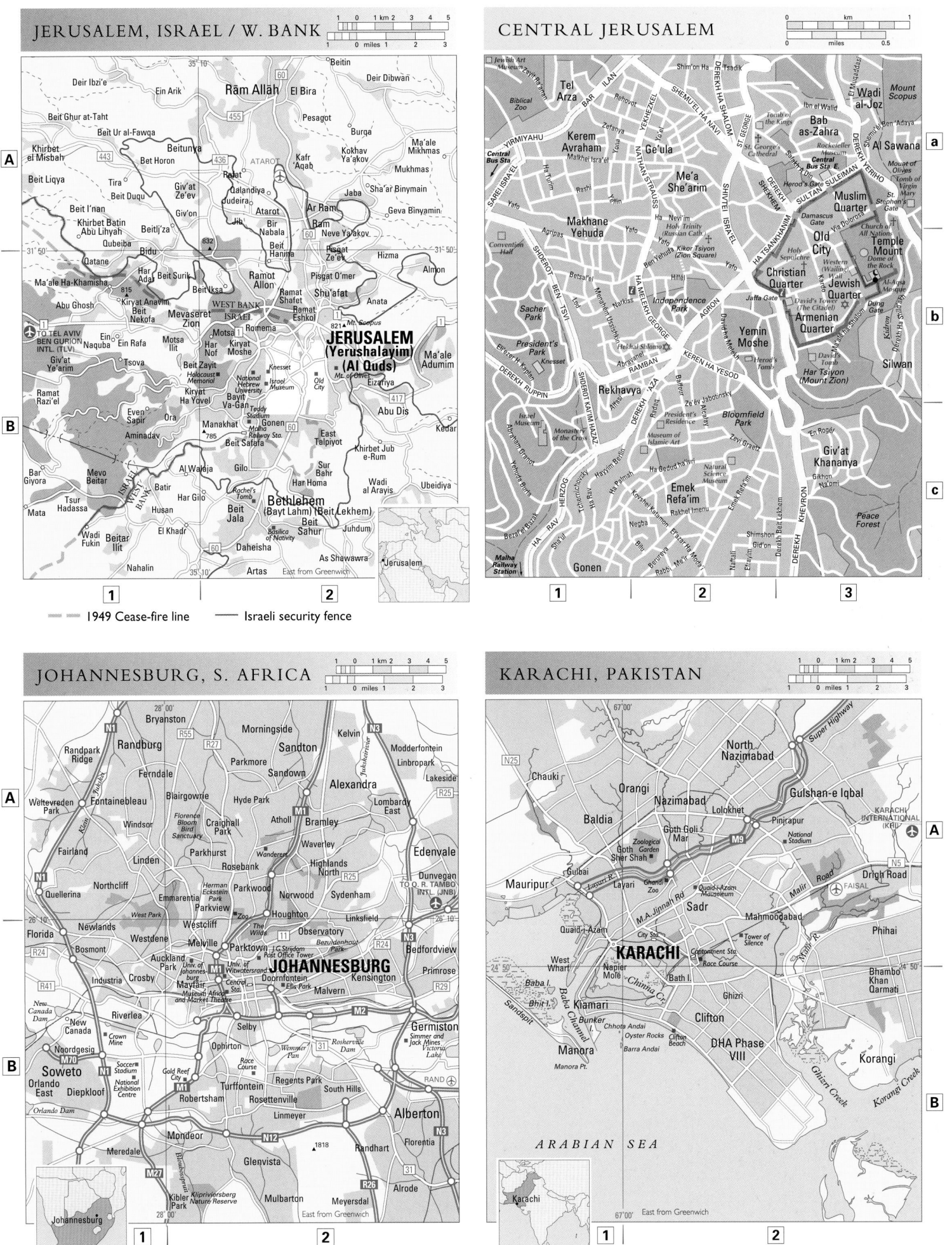

--- 1949 Cease-fire line   — Israeli security fence

CENTRAL JERUSALEM

0 km 1
0 miles 0.5

Jewish Art Museum   Shim'on Ha Tsadik   Ibn el Walid   Mount Scopus
Tel Arza   BAR ILAN   Rehovot   ST. GEORGE   Tomb of the Kings   Wadi al-Joz   a
Biblical Zoo   Zefanya   Rockefeller Museum   Bab as-Zahra   Al Sawana
YIRMIYAHU   Kerem Avraham   Malkhei Isra'el   Central Bus Sta. E.   Mount of Olives   St. Stephen's Gate
Central Bus Sta   Ge'ula   Herod's Gate   Tomb of Virgin Mary
Makhane Yehuda   Me'a She'arim   SULTAN SULEIMAN   Muslim Quarter   Church of All Nations
Convention Hall   Holy Trinity (Russian Cath.)   Damascus Gate   Old   Temple   b
Sacher Park   Independence Park   Holy Sepulchre   City   Mount
President's Park   Kikar Tsiyon (Zion Square)   Christian Quarter   Dome of the Rock
Israel Museum   Knesset   Jaffa Gate   Jewish Quarter   Al-Aqsa Mosque
Monastery of the Cross   Museum of Islamic Art   Yemin Moshe   Armenian Quarter   Silwan
Rekhavya   David's Tomb   Dung Gate
President's Residence   Bloomfield Park   Har Tsiyon (Mount Zion)   En Rogel   c
Natural Science Museum   Giv'at Khananya
Emek Refa'im   Peace Forest
Malha Railway Station   Gonen

1   2   3

JOHANNESBURG, S. AFRICA

1 0 1 km 2 3 4 5
1 0 miles 1 2 3

N1   Bryanston   28° 00'   R55   R27   Kelvin   N3
Randpark Ridge   Randburg   Morningside   Modderfontein
Weltevreden Park   Fontainebleau   Ferndale   Sandton   Linbropark   A
Fairland   Windsor   Blairgowrie   Parkmore   Sandown   Lakeside
Blairgowrie   Hyde Park   Atholl   Bramley   Alexandra   R25
N1   Linden   Florence Bloom Bird Sanctuary   Craighall Park   Waverley   Lombardy East
Quellerina   Northcliff   Parkhurst   Rosebank   Highlands North   Edenvale
Newlands   Emmarentia   Parkwood   Norwood   R25   Dunvegan
Florida   Westdene   West Park   Parkview   Houghton   Sydenham   TO O. R. TAMBO   26° 10'
R24   Bosmont   Melville   Zoo   The Wilds   Observatory   Linksfield   INTL. (JNB)   N3
Auckland Park   Parktown   11   Bezuidenhout Park   R24
Crosby   Univ. of Johannesburg   J.G.Strijdom Post Office Tower   Bedfordview
Industria   Mayfair   Univ. of Witwatersrand   JOHANNESBURG   Primrose
New Canada Dam   Crown Mine   Central Sta.   Doornfontein   Kensington   R29
New Canada   Riverlea   Museum Africa and Market Theatre   Ellis Park   Malvern   M2
Noordgesig   Selby   M2   Germiston
M70   Ophirton   Simmer and Jack Mines   R
Soweto   M1   Soccer City Stadium   Wemmer Pan   Rosherville Dam   Victoria Lake
Orlando East   Gold Reef City   National Exhibition Centre   Turffontein   Regents Park   South Hills   RAND
Diepkloof   Robertsham   Rosettenville
Orlando Dam   Linmeyer   Alberton
Mondeor   N12   1818   Randhart   N3
M27   Meredale   Florentia   31
Kibler Park   Klipriviersberg Nature Reserve   Glenvista   Mulbarton   Meyersdal   R26   Alrode
28° 00'   East from Greenwich

1   2

KARACHI, PAKISTAN

1 0 1 km 2 3 4 5
1 0 miles 1 2 3

67° 00'   Super Highway
Chauki   North Nazimabad
N25   Orangi   Gulshan-e Iqbal   KARACHI INTERNATIONAL (KHI)
Baldia   Nazimabad   Lolokhet   Pinjrapur
Goth Goli Mar   M9   National Stadium   A
Mauripur   Gubai   Zoological Garden Goth Sher Shah   Ghandi Zoo   Quaid-i-Azam Mausoleum   Malir Road   Drigh Road   N5
Lasbari R.   Layari   Quaid-i-Azam   M.A. Jinnah Rd   Sadr   Mahmoodabad   FAISAL
West Wharf   City Sta.   Tower of Silence   Phihai
Napier Mole   KARACHI   Cantonment Sta.   Ghizri   Malir R.
24° 50'   Baba I.   Bath I.   Race Course   Bhambo Khan Qarmati   24° 50'
Baba I.   Bhit I.   Kiamari   Clifton
Sandspit   Bunker   Chhota Andai   Clifton Beach   DHA Phase VIII   Korangi
Manora   Oyster Rocks   Korangi Creek
Manora Pt.   Barra Andai   Ghizri Creek
ARABIAN SEA

1   2

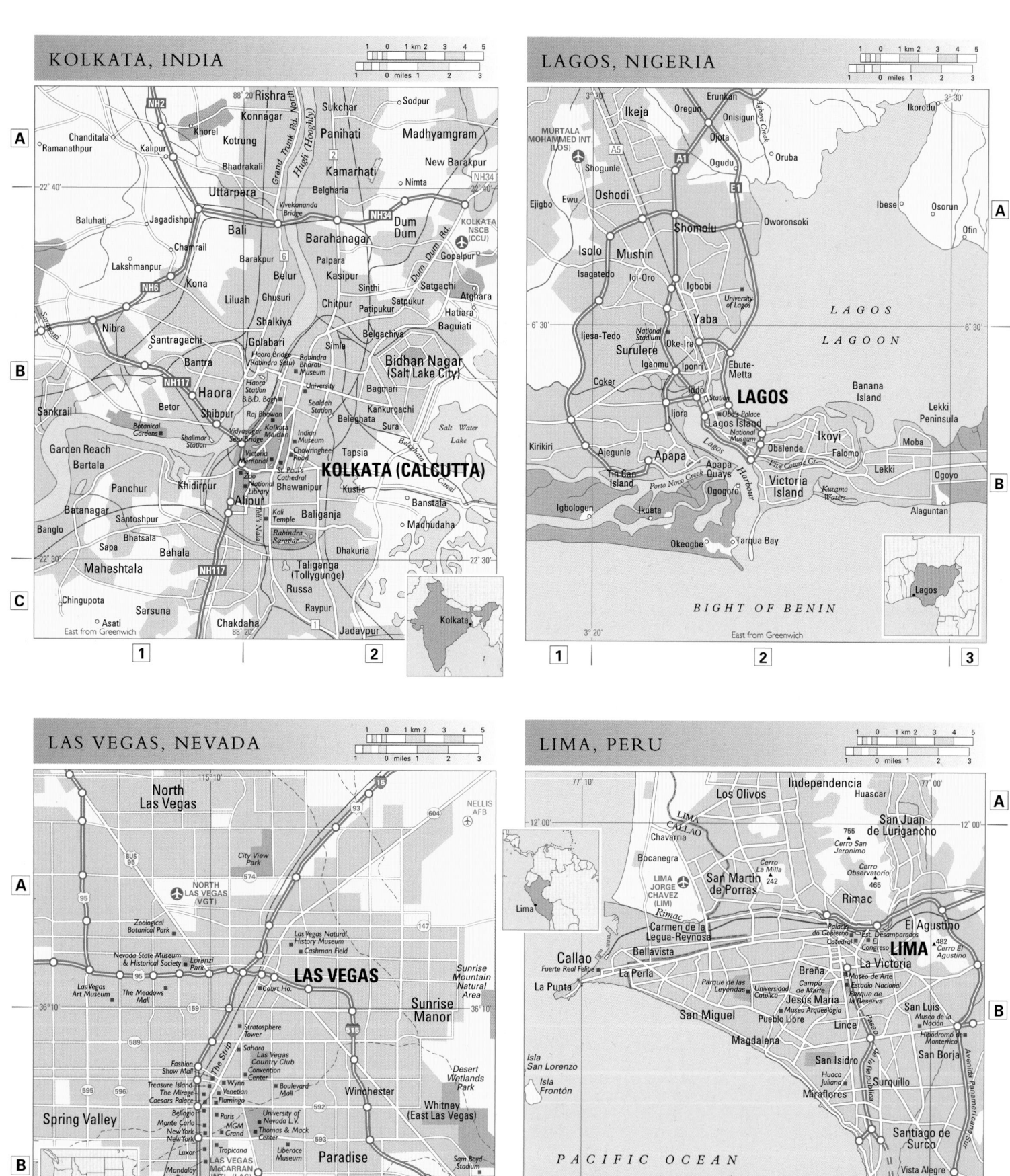

Interstate route numbers   U.S. route numbers   State route numbers

COPYRIGHT PHILIP'S

LONDON, U.K.

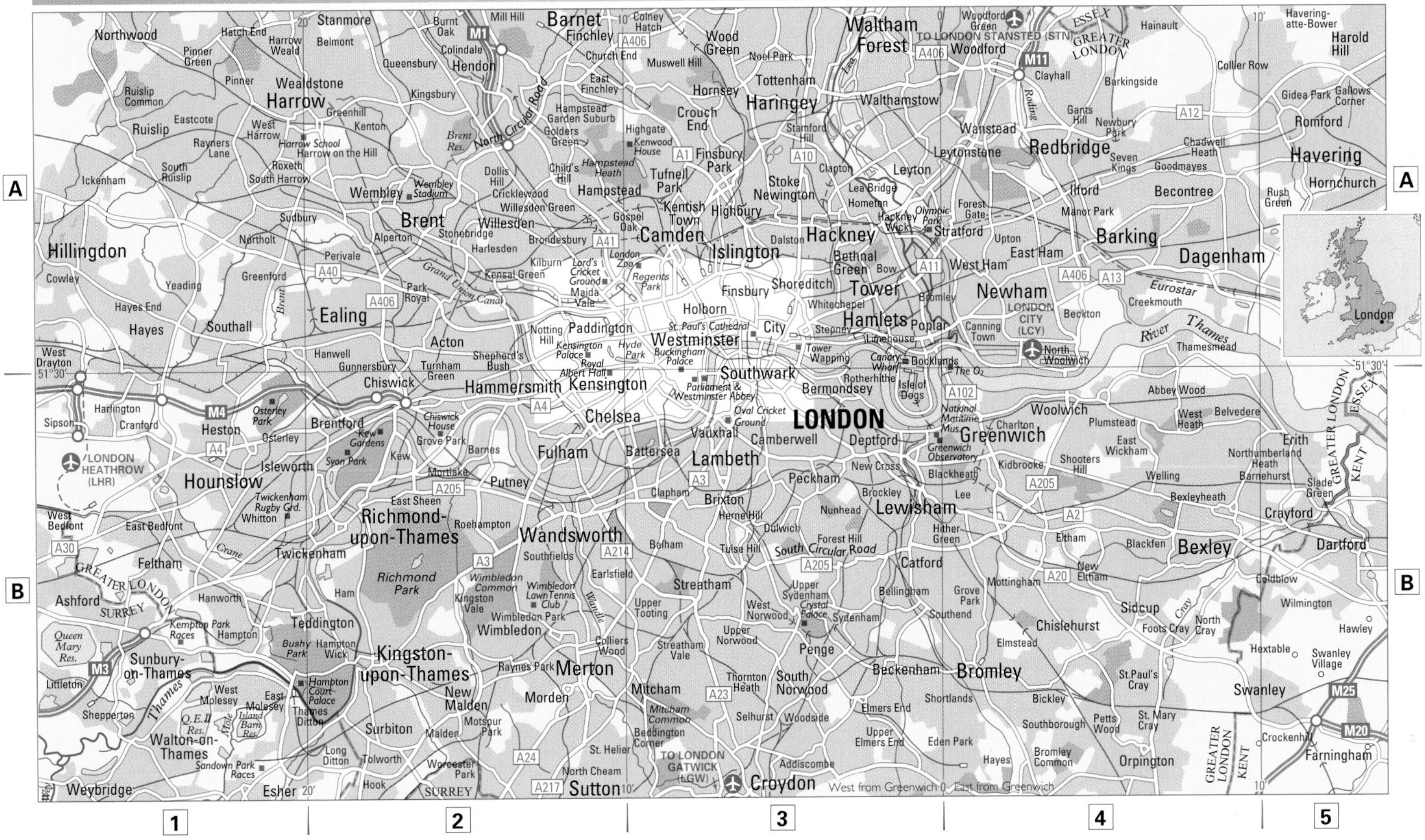

CENTRAL LONDON

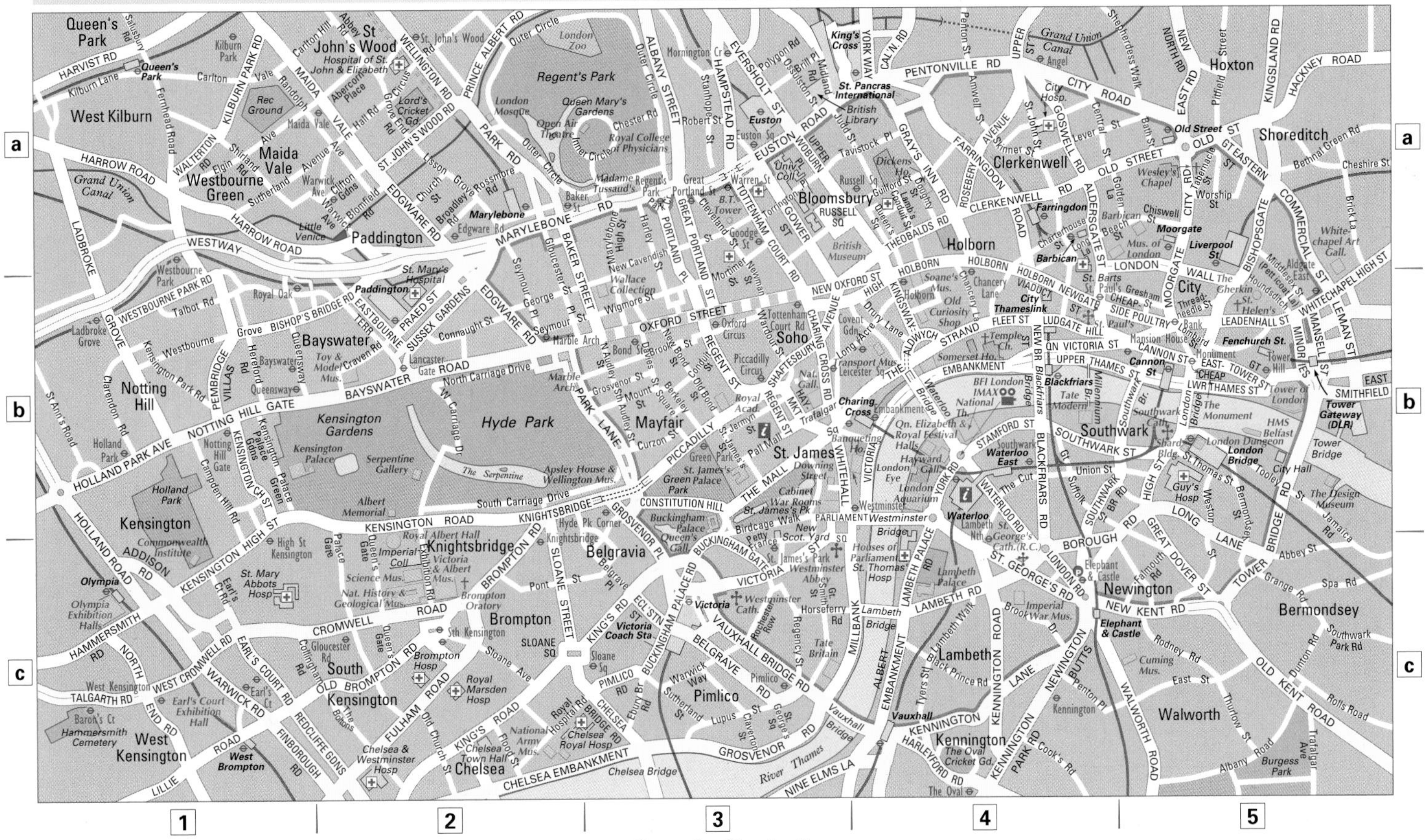

Congestion Charging Zone

COPYRIGHT PHILIP'S

LISBON, PORTUGAL

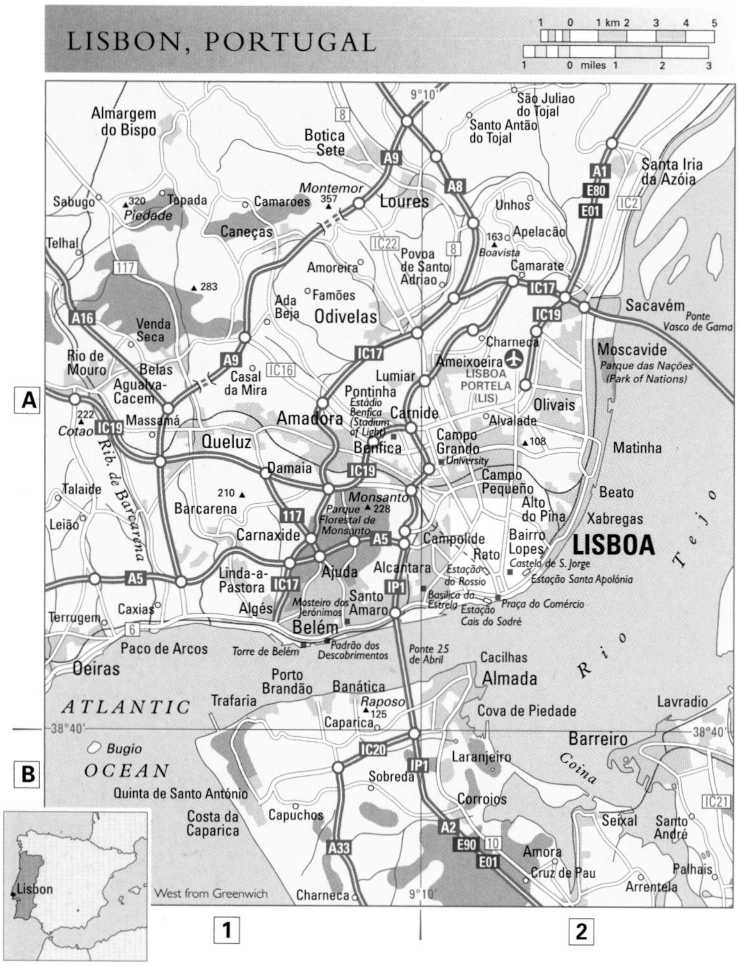

Almargem do Bispo, Botica Sete, São Julião do Tojal, Santo Antão do Tojal, Santa Iria da Azóia, Sabugo, Piedade, Topada, Camarões, Montemor, Loures, Unhos, Apelação, Telhal, Caneças, Póvoa de Santo Adrião, Camarate, Amoreira, Boavista, Famões, Ada Beja, Odivelas, Sacavém, Ponte Vasco da Gama, Rio de Mouro, Venda Seca, Casal da Mira, Lumiar, Charneca, Moscavide, Parque das Nações (Park of Nations), Belas, Aguava-Cacem, Massamá, Pontinha, Ameixoeira, LISBOA PORTELA (LIS), Olivais, Cotão, Queluz, Amadora, Catnide, Estádio Benfica (Stadium of Light), Campo Grande University, Alvalade, Matinha, Damaia, Barcarena, Monsanto Parque Florestal de Monsanto, Campo Pequeno, Beato, Alto do Pina, Xabregas, Carnaxide, Campolide, Rato, Bairro Lopes, **LISBOA**, Leião, Talaide, Linda-a-Pastora, Ajuda, Alcântara, Castelo de S. Jorge, Estação do Rossio, Estação Santa Apolónia, Terrugem, Caxias, Algés, Santo Amaro, Mosteiro dos Jerónimos, Basílica da Estrela, Praça do Comércio, Oeiras, Paço de Arcos, Porto Brandão, Belém, Torre de Belém, Padrão dos Descobrimentos, Ponte 25 de Abril, Cacilhas, **ATLANTIC OCEAN**, Trafaria, Banática, Raposo, Almada, Lavradio, Bugio, Caparica, Cova de Piedade, Barreiro, Quinta de Santo António, Sobreda, Laranjeiro, Coina, Costa da Caparica, Capuchos, Corroios, Seixal, Santo André, Palhais, Amora, Cruz de Pau, Arrentela, Charneca, West from Greenwich

Lisbon (inset)

CENTRAL LISBON

Penitenciária, Palácio de Justiça, S. Sebastião, Praça Duque de Saldanha, Instituto Superior Técnico, Parque Eduardo VII, Estefânia, Maternidade, Hospital de Estefânia, Penha França, Amoreiros, Praça Marquês de Pombal, Rato, Anjos, Hospital de Santa Marta, Hospital dos Capuchos, Academia das Ciências, Jardim Botânico, Bairro Lopes, Palácio da Assembleia Nacional, Graça, Bairro Alto, Museu do Arqueologia, Baixa, Estação do Rossio, Castelo de São Jorge (St. George's Castle), Alfama, Igreja Sta. Engrácia, Estação Santa Apolónia, Elevador de Santa Justa, Teatro Nac. de São Carlos, Sé Catedral, Praça do Comércio, Biblioteca Nacional, Chiado, Estação Cais do Sodré, Estação Fluvial, **Rio Tejo (Tagus)**

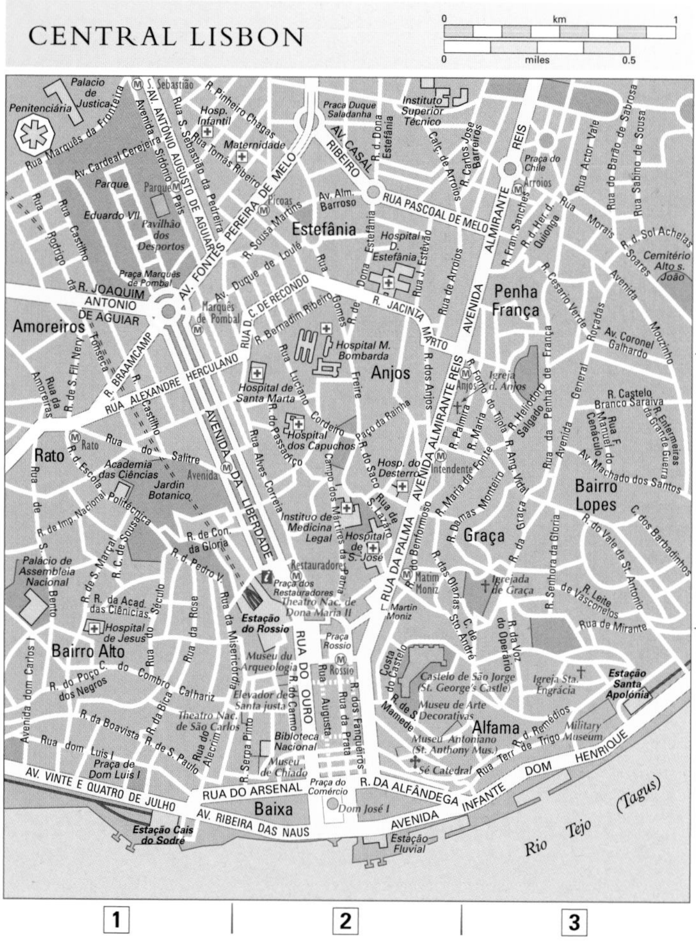

LOS ANGELES, CALIFORNIA

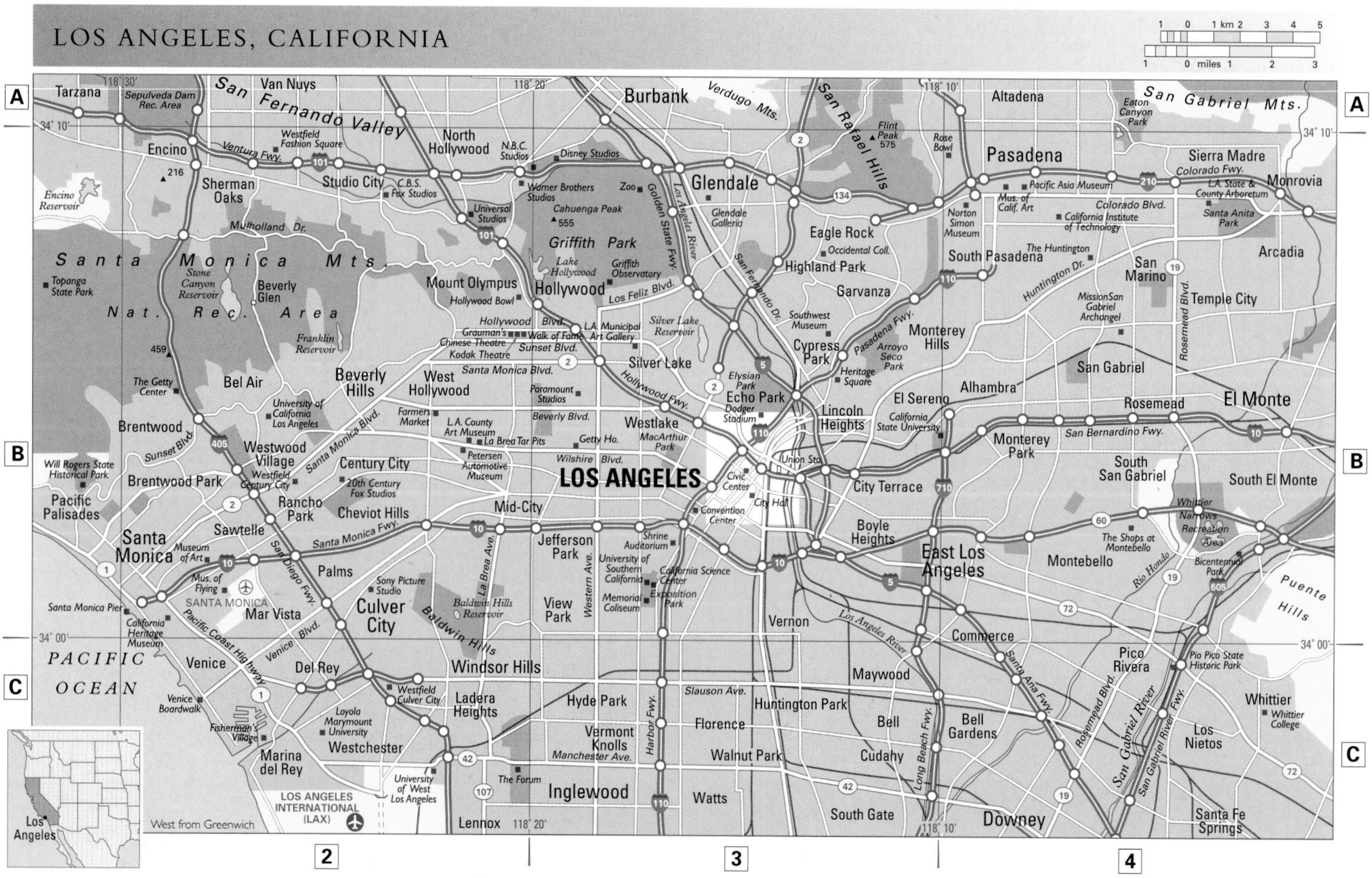

Tarzana, Sepulveda Dam Rec. Area, Van Nuys, Burbank, Verdugo Mts., Altadena, San Gabriel Mts., Eaton Canyon Park, Encino, San Fernando Valley, North Hollywood, N.B.C. Studios, Disney Studios, Glendale, Pasadena, Sierra Madre, Monrovia, Sherman Oaks, Studio City, C.B.S., Fox Studios, Warner Brothers Studios, Zoo, Golden State Fwy, Rose Bowl, L.A. State & County Arboretum, Encino Reservoir, Universal Studios, Cahuenga Peak, Griffith Park, Eagle Rock, Occidental Coll., South Pasadena, The Huntington, San Marino, Arcadia, Santa Monica Mts., Topanga State Park, Stone Canyon Reservoir, Beverly Glen, Mount Olympus, Lake Hollywood, Griffith Observatory, Hollywood, Highland Park, Garvanza, California Institute of Technology, Santa Anita Park, Nat. Rec. Area, Franklin Reservoir, Hollywood Bowl, Grauman's Chinese Theatre, Walk of Fame, Sunset Blvd., L.A. Municipal Art Gallery, Silver Lake Reservoir, Los Feliz Blvd., Southwest Museum, Monterey Hills, Mission San Gabriel Archangel, Temple City, The Getty Center, Bel Air, Beverly Hills, West Hollywood, Santa Monica Blvd., Silver Lake, Elysian Park Dodger Stadium, Cypress Park, Heritage Park, El Sereno, Alhambra, San Gabriel, Rosemead, El Monte, University of California Los Angeles, Westwood Village, Century City, Paramount Studios, Beverly Blvd., Getty Ho., Westlake MacArthur Park, Echo Park, Lincoln Heights, California State University, Monterey Park, South San Gabriel, South El Monte, Brentwood, Farmers Market, L.A. County Art Museum, La Brea Tar Pits, Petersen Automotive Museum, Wilshire Blvd., **LOS ANGELES**, Civic Center, City Hall, City Terrace, Boyle Heights, Will Rogers State Historical Park, Brentwood Park, Westwood, 20th Century Fox Studios, Rancho Park, Cheviot Hills, Mid-City, Convention Center, East Los Angeles, Montebello, The Shops at Montebello, Pacific Palisades, Santa Monica, Museum of Art, Mus. of Flying, Sawtelle, Palms, Sony Picture Studio, Baldwin Hills Reservoir, Jefferson Park, University of Southern California, Shrine Auditorium, California Science Center, Memorial Coliseum, Vernon, Commerce, Pico Rivera, Pio Pico State Historic Park, Puente Hills, California Heritage Museum, Santa Monica Pier, Mar Vista, Culver City, View Park, Whittier, **PACIFIC OCEAN**, Venice, Venice Boardwalk, Del Rey, Windsor Hills, Maywood, Whittier Narrows Recreation Area, Bicentennial Park, Whittier College, Fisherman's Village, Ladera Heights, Hyde Park, Huntington Park, Bell, Bell Gardens, Los Nietos, Marina del Rey, Loyola Marymount University, Westfield Culver City, Vermont Knolls, Manchester Ave., Florence, Cudahy, Walnut Park, Westchester, University of West Los Angeles, LOS ANGELES INTERNATIONAL (LAX), The Forum, Inglewood, Lennox, Watts, South Gate, Downey, Santa Fe Springs, West from Greenwich

Los Angeles (inset)

85 Interstate route numbers 166 State route numbers

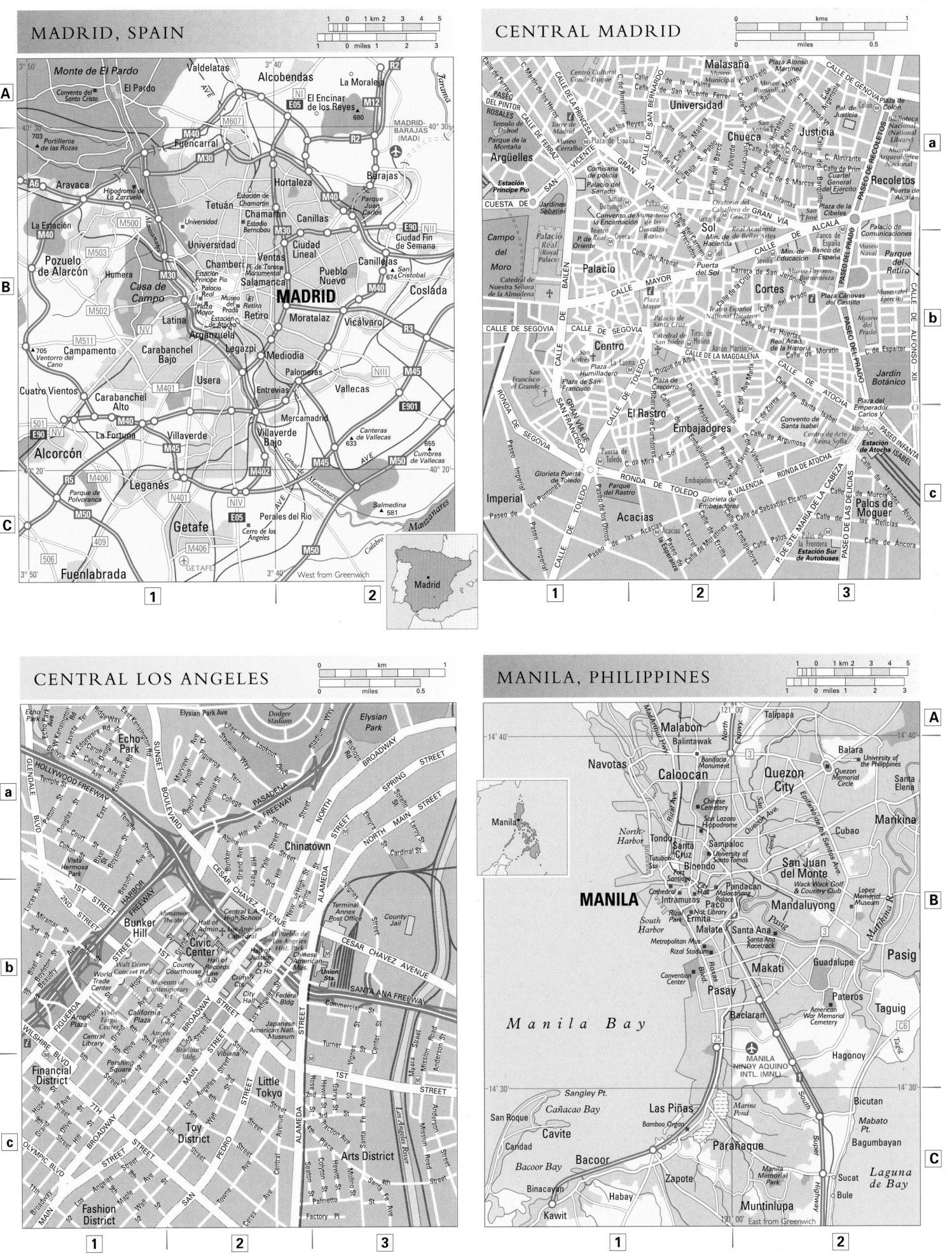

MADRID, SPAIN

CENTRAL MADRID

CENTRAL LOS ANGELES

MANILA, PHILIPPINES

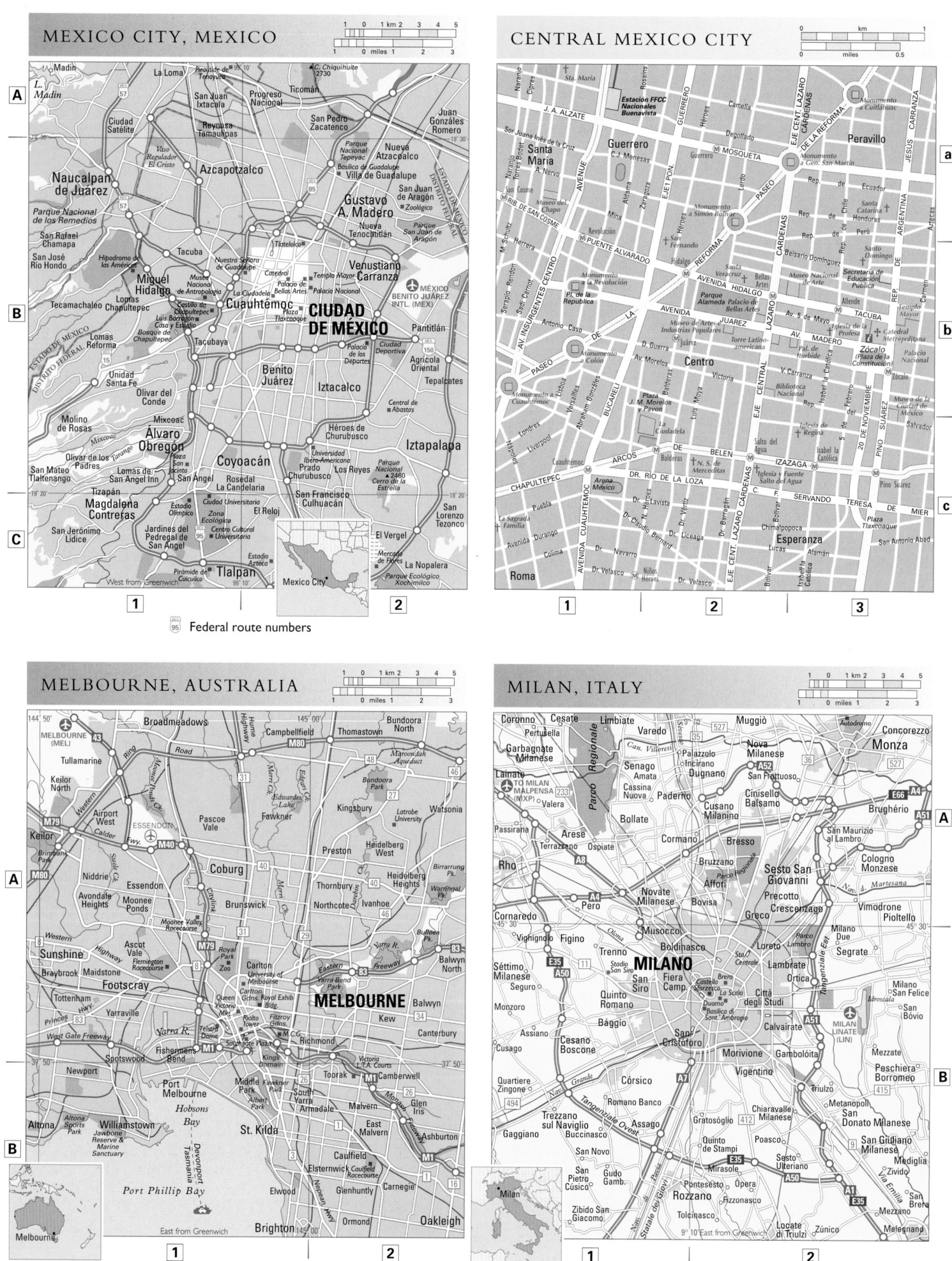

MEXICO CITY, MEXICO

1 0 1 km 2 3 4 5
0 miles 1 2 3

CENTRAL MEXICO CITY

km 1
0 miles 0.5

Federal route numbers

MELBOURNE, AUSTRALIA

1 0 1 km 2 3 4 5
1 0 miles 1 2 3

MILAN, ITALY

1 0 1 km 2 3 4 5
1 0 miles 1 2 3

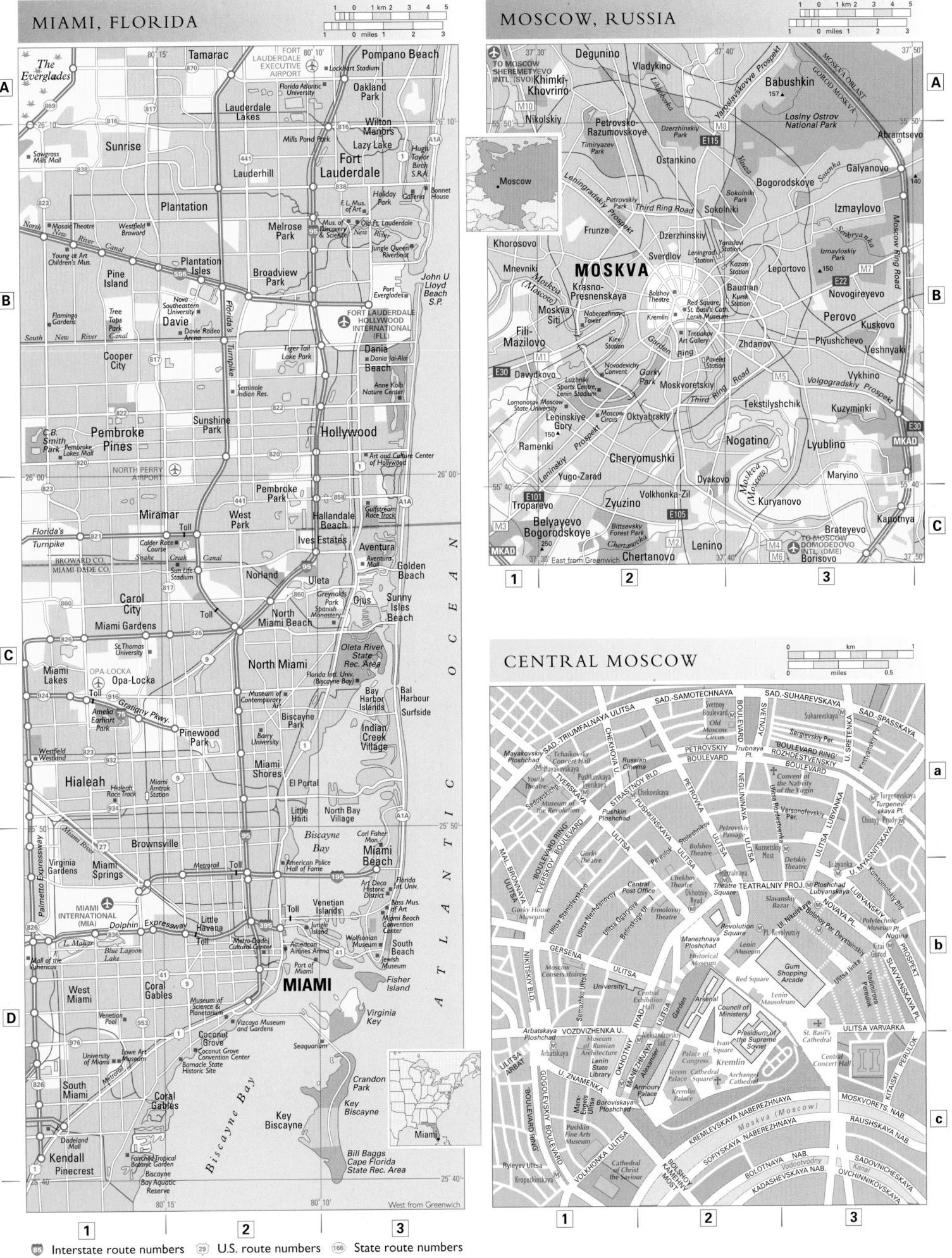

MIAMI, FLORIDA

The Everglades
Tamarac
Pompano Beach
FORT LAUDERDALE EXECUTIVE AIRPORT
Lockhart Stadium
Oakland Park
Florida Atlantic University
Lauderdale Lakes
Wilton Manors
Lazy Lake
Mills Pond Park
Fort Lauderdale
Sunrise
Lauderhill
Melrose Park
Holiday Park
Galleria
Mus. of Discovery & Science
Old Ft. Lauderdale
Hugh Taylor Birch S.R.A.
Bonnet House
Plantation
Plantation Isles
Mosaic Theatre
North New River Canal
Westfield Broward
Young at Art Children's Mus.
F.L. Mus. of Art
Broadview Park
Jungle Queen Riverboat
Port Everglades
Pine Island
Nova Southeastern University
Davie
Tree Tops Park
Flamingo Gardens
South New River Canal
Davie Rodeo Arena
John U Lloyd Beach S.P.
Cooper City
Tiger Tail Lake Park
Seminole Indian Res.
Anne Kolb Nature Center
FORT LAUDERDALE HOLLYWOOD INTERNATIONAL (FLL)
Dania Beach
Dania Jai-Alai
C.B. Smith Park
Pembroke Pines
Sunshine Park
Hollywood
Art and Culture Center of Hollywood
Pembroke Lakes Mall
NORTH PERRY AIRPORT
Pembroke Park
West Park
Hallandale Beach
Gulfstream Race Track
Miramar
Florida's Turnpike
Calder Race Course
Ives Estates
Aventura
Aventura Mall
Golden Beach
BROWARD CO. MIAMI-DADE CO.
Snake Creek Canal
Sun Life Stadium
NoRand
Uleta
Ojus
Sunny Isles Beach
Carol City
Greynolds Park Spanish Monastery
Miami Gardens
North Miami Beach
St. Thomas University
Oleta River State Rec. Area
OPA-LOCKA
Opa-Locka
North Miami
Florida Intl. Univ. (Biscayne Bay)
Museum of Contemporary Art
Bay Harbor Islands
Bal Harbour
Surfside
Miami Lakes
Gratigny Pkwy.
Biscayne Park
Indian Creek Village
Amelia Earhart Park
Pinewood Park
Barry University
Miami Shores
Westfield Westland
Hialeah
Hialeah Race Track
Miami Amtrak Station
El Portal
Little Haiti
North Bay Village
Brownsville
Biscayne Bay
Carl Fisher Mon.
Miami Springs
Virginia Gardens
Miami River
Metrorail
American Police Hall of Fame
Miami Beach
MIAMI INTERNATIONAL (MIA)
Dolphin Expressway
Little Havana
Metro-Dade Cultural Center
American Airlines Arena
Art Deco Historic District
Bass Mus. of Art
Miami Beach Convention Center
Florida Intl. Univ.
Jungle Island
Wolfsonian Museum
South Beach
Jewish Museum
Mall of the Americas
L. Mabar
Blue Lagoon Lake
MIAMI
Port of Miami
Fisher Island
West Miami
Venetian Islands
Venetian Pool
Coral Gables
Museum of Science & Planetarium
Vizcaya Museum and Gardens
Virginia Key
University of Miami
Lowe Art Museum
Coconut Grove
Coconut Grove Convention Center
Barnacle State Historic Site
Seaquarium
Crandon Park
South Miami
Coral Gables
Fairchild Tropical Botanic Garden
Biscayne Bay Aquatic Reserve
Key Biscayne
Key Biscayne
Bill Baggs Cape Florida State Rec. Area
Dadeland Mall
Kendall
Pinecrest
Miami
West from Greenwich

ATLANTIC OCEAN

Interstate route numbers   U.S. route numbers   State route numbers

MOSCOW, RUSSIA

TO MOSCOW SHEREMETYEVO INTL. (SVO)
Degunino
Vladykino
Khimki-Khovrino
Babushkin
GOROD MOSKVA
MOSKVA OBLAST
Nikolskiy
Petrovsko-Razumovskoye
Dzerzhinskiy Park
Losiny Ostrov National Park
Abramtsevo
Timiryazev Park
Ostankino
Bogorodskoye
Galyanovo
Khorosovo
Leningradsky Prospekt
Petrovsky Park
Sokolniki Park
Sokolniki
Izmaylovo
Frunze
Dzerzhinskiy
Yaroslav Station
Serebryanka
Izmayloskiy Park
Mnevniki
Sverdlov
Leningrad Station
Kazan Station
Leportovo
MOSKVA
Krasno-Presnenskaya
Bolshoy Theatre
Red Square, St. Basil's Cath. Lenin Museum
Bauman Kursk Station
Novogireyevo
Fili-Mazilovo
Moskva Siti
Kremlin
Garden Ring
Zhdanov
Perovo
Kuskovo
Kiev Station
Tretiakov Art Gallery
Pavelet Station
Plyushchevo
Veshnyaki
Davydkovo
Novodevichy Convent
Gorky Park
Moskvoretskiy
Third Ring Road
Vykhino
Volgogradskiy Prospekt
Luzhniki Sports Centre, Lenin Stadium
Moscow Circus
Kuzminki
Lomonosov Moscow State University
Leninskiye Gory
Oktyabrskiy
Tekstilyshchik
Ramenki
Nogatino
Lyublino
Yugo-Zarad
Cheryomushki
Dyakovo
Maryino
Troparevo
Zyuzino
Volkhonka-Zil
Kuryanovo
Kapotnya
Belyayevo Bogorodskoye
Bittsevsky Forest Park
Chertanovo
Brateyevo
Lenino
Borisovo
Chertanovo
TO MOSCOW DOMODEDOVO INTL. (DME)
East from Greenwich

CENTRAL MOSCOW

SAD.-SAMOTECHNAYA
SAD.-SUHAREVSKAYA
SAD.-SPASSKAYA
Svetnoy Boulevard
Suharevskaya
Mayakovskiy Ploshchad
Tchaikovsky Concert Hall
Old Moscow Circus
PETROVSKY
Sergievskiy Per.
Mayakovskaya
SVETNOY BOULEVARD
Trubnaya Pl.
U. SRETENKA
Youth Theatre
Pushkinskaya Tverskaya
Russian Cinema
'BOULEVARD RING' ROZHDESTVENSKY
Convent of the Nativity of the Virgin
Sadovnichiy
Museum of the Revolution
STRASTNOY BLD.
Chekovskaya
PETROVKA
NEGLINNAYA
U. Rozhdestvenki
Varsonofyevsky Per.
U. LUBYANKA
Turgenevskaya
Turgenev-skaya Pl.
Chisty Prudy
BOULEVARD RING
TVERSKOY BOULEVARD
PUSHKINSKAYA ULITSA
Gorky Theatre
Stoleshnikov
Petrovsky Passage
Kuznetsky Most
Detskiy Mir
ULITSA LUBYANKA
MAL BRONNAYA ULITSA
Perelok
Bolshoy Theatre
Tralnaya
Teatralniy Proj.
U. MYASNITSKAYA
NIKITSKY BLD.
Ulitsa Nezhdanoy
ULITSA Bolshaya
Chekhov Theatre
Okhotny Ryad
Theatre TEATRALNIY PROJ.
Ploshchad Lubyanskaya
Komsomolsky Bld.
GERSENA
Moscow Conservatoire
University
Central Post Office
Ermolovoy Theatre
Slavanskiy Bazar
NOVAYA PL.
Polytechnic Museum Pl.
Ulitsa Ostyanoy
Belinskogo
Revolution Square
Manezhnaya Ploshchad
U. Nikolskaya
Bolshoy Per. Devyatinsky
Nogina
Gorky House Museum
Ploshchad Revolyutsiy
Lenin Museum
Gum Shopping Arcade
Kitai Gorod
Arbatskaya Ploshchad
VOZDVIZHENKA U.
Central Exhibition Hall
Historical Museum
PROSPEKT
Museum of Russian Architecture
OKHOTNY RYAD
 MANEZNAYA
Red Square
Lenin Mausoleum
SLAVYANSKAYA PL.
Arbatskaya
Aleksandrovsky Garden
Arsenal
Council of Ministers
ULITSA VARVARKA
ULITSA ARBAT
U. ZNAMENKA
Ivan the Great
Ivan Square
Presidium of the Supreme Soviet
St. Basil's Cathedral
Lenin State Library
Palace of Congress
Cathedral Square
Archangel Cathedral
Central Concert Hall
Teren Palace
KITAISKI PEROULOK
GOGOLEVSKY BOULEVARD
Marx-Engels Ploshchad
Palace of Facets
Kremlin
MOSKVORETS. NAB.
BOULEVARD RING
Borovitskaya Ploshchad
Borovitskaya Palace
Kremlin Palace
Vladimirov Pereulok
Pushkin Fine Arts Museum
Moskva (Moscow)
KREMLEVSKAYA NABEREZHNAYA
RAUSHSKAYA NAB.
Ryleyev Ulitsa
VOLKHONKA ULITSA
SOFIYSKAYA NABEREZHNAYA
SADOVNICHESKAYA
Kropotkinsky
Cathedral of Christ the Saviour
NAB.
BOLSHOY KAMENIY MOST
Vodootvodny
BOLOTNAYA NAB.
Kanal
OVCHINNIKOVSKAYA
KADASHEVSKAYA NAB.

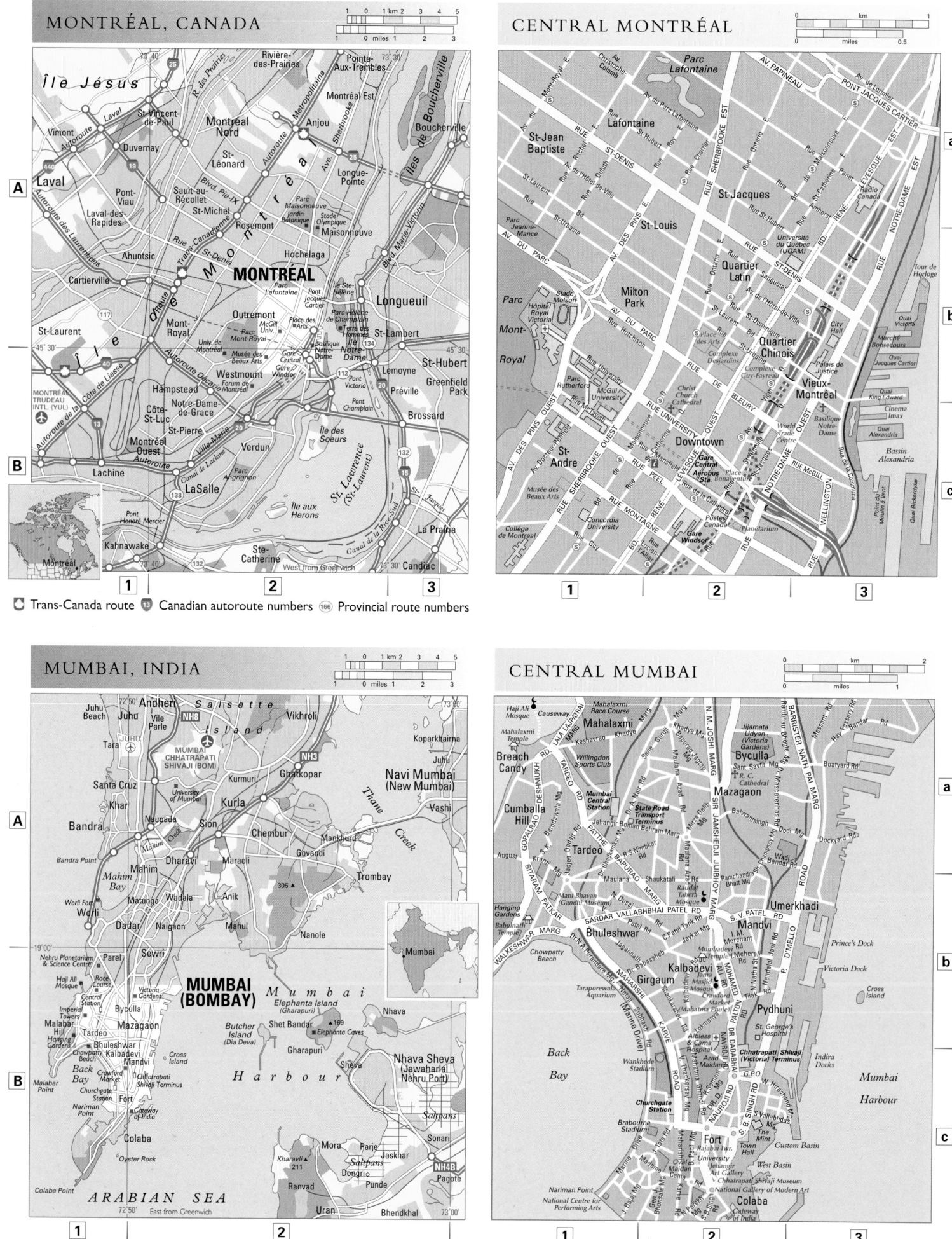

MONTRÉAL, CANADA

Île Jésus
Laval
Vimont
St-Vincent-de-Paul
Duvernay
Pont-Viau
Laval-des-Rapides
Ahuntsic
Cartierville
St-Laurent
A
MONTRÉAL TRUDEAU INTL. (YUL)
Côte-St-Luc
Hampstead
Notre-Dame-de-Grace
Westmount
Montréal Ouest
St-Pierre
B
Lachine
LaSalle
Kahnawake
Montréal
Rivière-des-Prairies
Pointe-Aux-Trembles
Montréal Est
Anjou
Longue-Pointe
Boucherville
Montréal Nord
St-Léonard
Sault-au-Récollet
St-Michel
Rosemont
Hochelaga
Maisonneuve
Parc Maisonneuve
Jardin Botanique
Stade Olympique
Outremont
Mont-Royal
McGill Univ.
Parc Mont-Royal
Univ. de Montréal
Place des Arts
Terre des Hommes
Parc Hélène-de-Champlain
Longueuil
St-Lambert
St-Hubert
Greenfield Park
Préville
Lemoyne
Brossard
Verdun
Île des Soeurs
Île aux Herons
Île Ste-Hélène
Basilique Notre-Dame
Gare Windsor
Musée des Beaux Arts
Forum de Montréal
Pont Victoria
Pont Champlain
St-Laurent (St-Laurent)
La Prairie
Ste-Catherine
Candiac
West from Greenwich

🍁 Trans-Canada route   13 Canadian autoroute numbers   166 Provincial route numbers

CENTRAL MONTRÉAL

Parc Lafontaine
St-Jean Baptiste
Lafontaine
St-Jacques
St-Louis
Quartier Latin
Milton Park
Parc Jeanne-Mance
Parc Mont-Royal
Stade Molson
Hôpital Royal Victoria
Université du Québec (UQAM)
Quartier Chinois
City Hall
Vieux-Montréal
St-Andre
Downtown
Gare Central Aerobus Sta.
Place des Arts
Complexe Desjardins
World Trade Centre
Christ Church Cathedral
McGill University
Place Bonaventure
Basilique Notre-Dame
Palais de Justice
Marché Bonsecours
Musée des Beaux Arts
Concordia University
Collège de Montréal
Gare Windsor
Postes Canada
Planétarium
Cinema Imax
Bassin Alexandria
Tour de Horloge
a
b
c

MUMBAI, INDIA

Andheri
Juhu Beach
Juhu
Vile Parle
Tara
Santa Cruz
Khar
Bandra
Bandra Point
Salsette Island
Vikhroli
Koparkhairna
MUMBAI CHHATRAPATI SHIVAJI (BOM)
Kurmuri
Ghatkopar
Juhu
Navi Mumbai (New Mumbai)
Vashi
University of Mumbai
Kurla
Naupada
Sion
Chembur
Mankhurd
Govandi
Mahim
Dharavi
Maraoli
Trombay
Mahim Bay
Matunga
Wadala
Anik
305
Worli Fort
Worli
Dadar
Naigaon
Mahul
Nanole
Parel
Sewri
Nehru Planetarium & Science Centre
MUMBAI (BOMBAY)
Haji Ali Mosque
Race Course
Victoria Gardens
Byculla
Mazagaon
Central Station
Imperial Towers
Malabar Hill
Hanging Gardens
Tardeo
Bhuleshwar
Chowpatty Beach
Kalbadevi
Mandvi
Back Bay
Crawford Market
Chhatrapati Shivaji Terminus
Malabar Point
Churchgate Station
Fort
Nariman Point
Gateway of India
Colaba
Oyster Rock
Co.laba Point
ARABIAN SEA
East from Greenwich
Mumbai
Elephanta Island (Gharapuri)
Butcher Island (Dia Deva)
Shet Bandar
Elephanta Caves
Gharapuri
Nhava
Sheva
Nhava Sheva (Jawaharlal Nehru Port)
Harbour
Cross Island
Mora
Parje
Jaskhar
Saltpans
Sonari
Kharavli 211
Dongrio
Ranvad
Punde
NH4B
Pagote
Uran
Bhendkhal

CENTRAL MUMBAI

Haji Ali Mosque
Causeway
Mahalaxmi Race Course
Mahalaxmi
Mahalaxmi Temple
Breach Candy
Willingdon Sports Club
Jijamata Udyan (Victoria Gardens)
Byculla
Mazagaon
Cumballa Hill
Mumbai Central Station
State Road Transport Terminus
R. C. Cathedral
Tardeo
Hanging Gardens
Mani Bhavan (Gandhi Museum)
Rashid Tahera Mosque
Umerkhadi
Mandvi
Prince's Dock
Babulnath Temple
Bhuleshwar
Chowpatty Beach
Girgaum
Kalbadevi
Crawford Market
Pydhuni
Victoria Dock
Taraporewala Aquarium
Jama Masjid
St. George's Hospital
Cross Island
Back Bay
Wankhede Stadium
Albless & Cama Hospital
Azad Maidan
Chhatrapati Shivaji (Victoria Terminus)
G.P.O.
Indira Docks
Mumbai Harbour
Churchgate Station
Brabourne Stadium
Rajabai Twr.
University
Fort
Town Hall
The Mint
Custom Basin
West Basin
Jehangir Art Gallery
Chhatrapati Shivaji Museum
National Gallery of Modern Art
Nariman Point
National Centre for Performing Arts
Colaba
Gateway of India
a
b
c

MUNICH, GERMANY

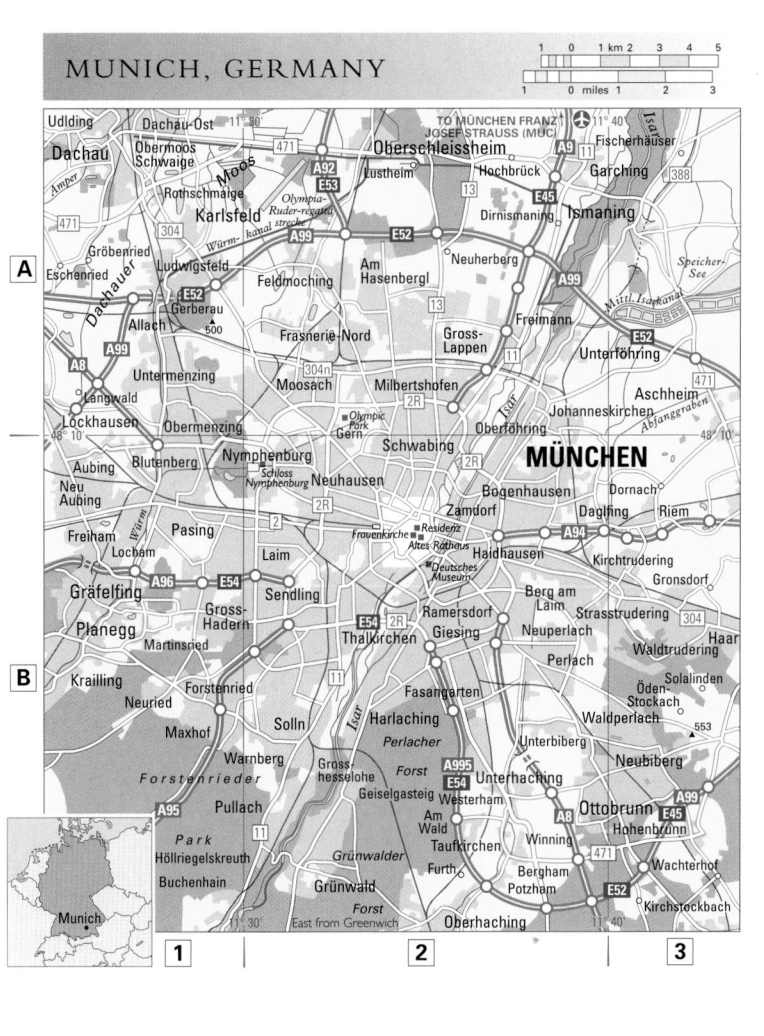

CENTRAL MUNICH

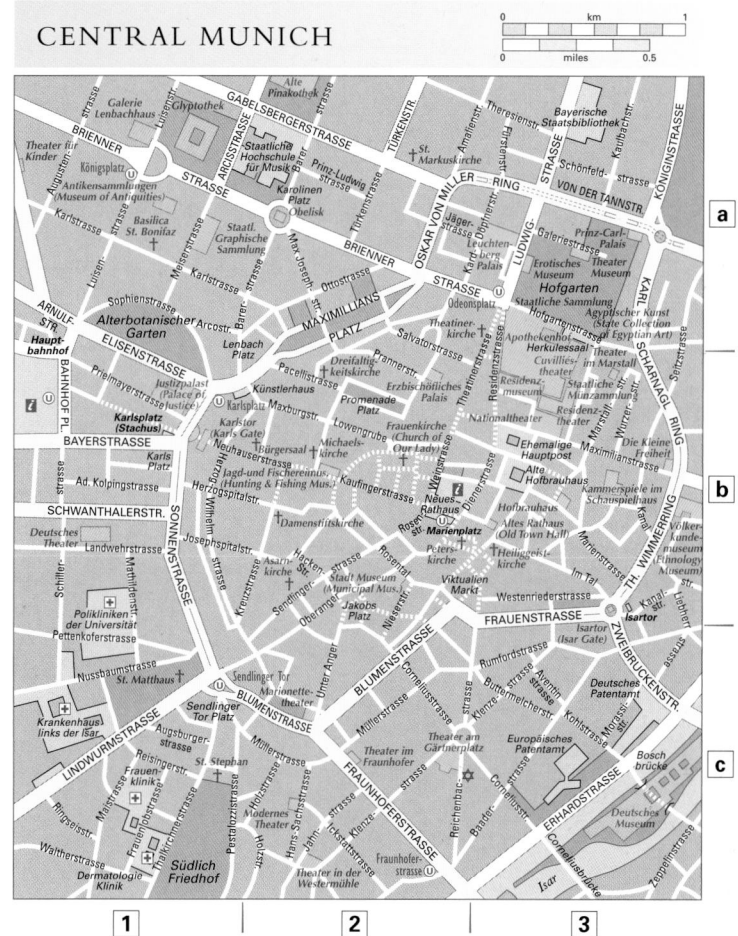

NEW ORLEANS, LOUISIANA

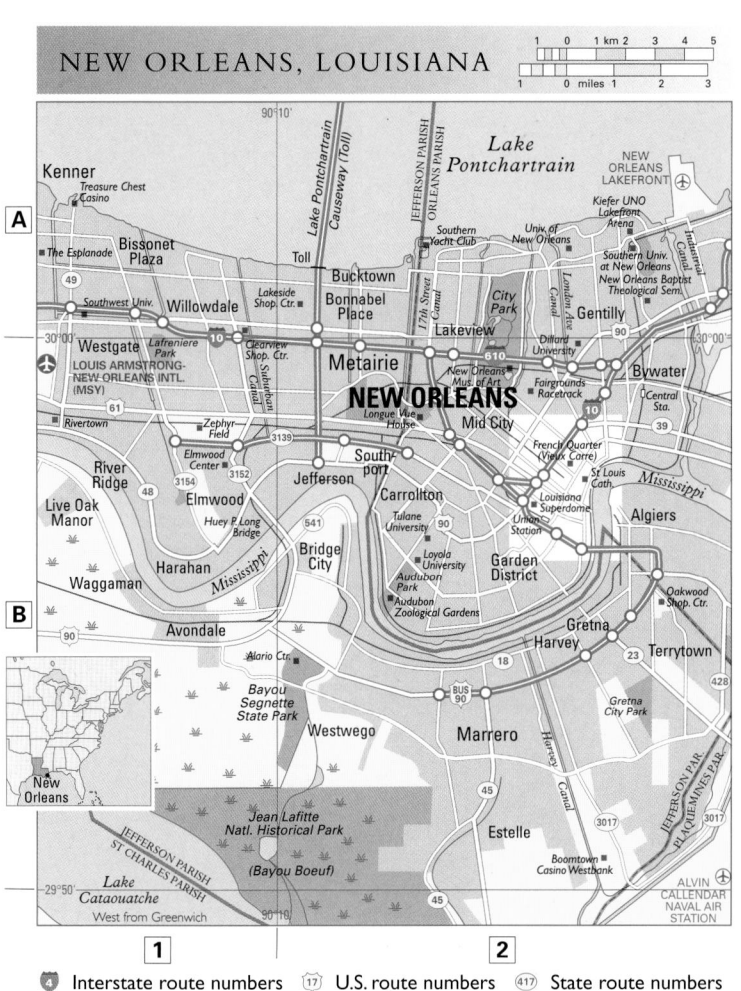

CENTRAL NEW ORLEANS

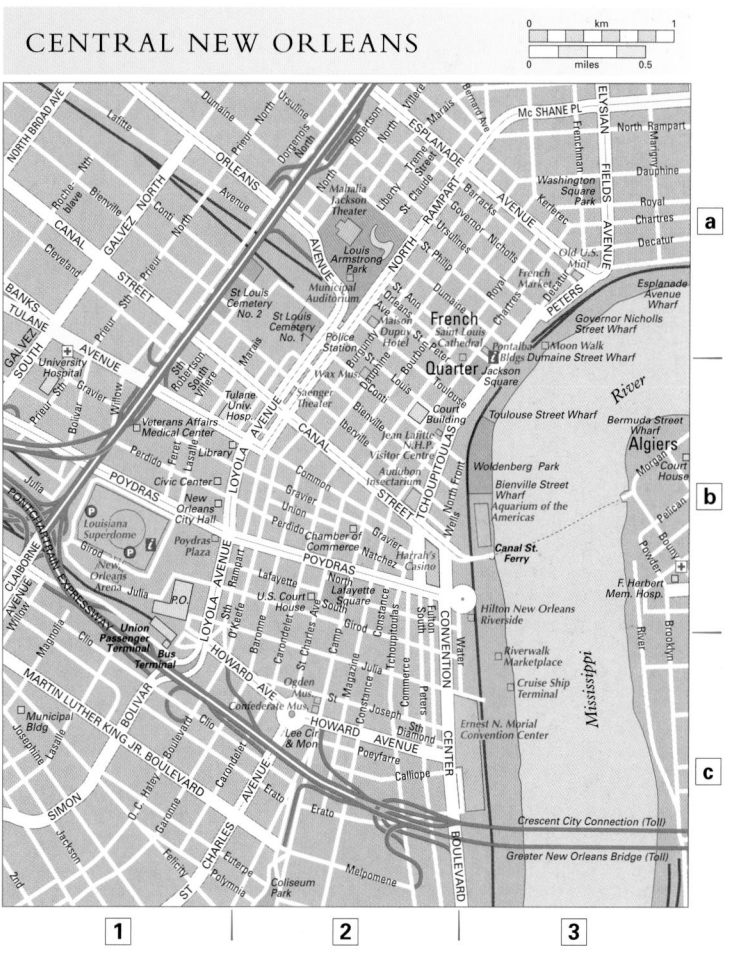

Interstate route numbers   U.S. route numbers   State route numbers

NEW YORK, NEW YORK

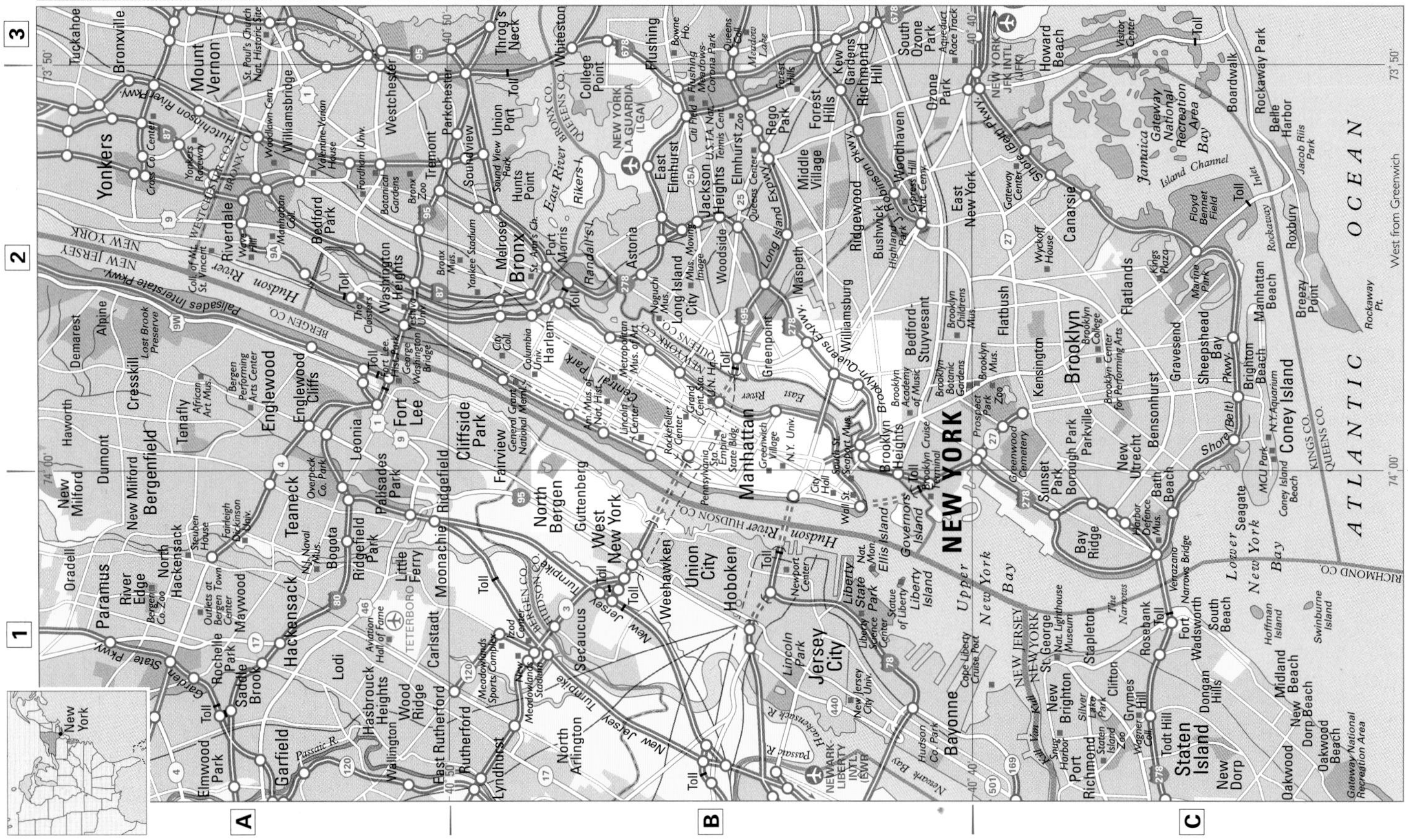

CENTRAL NEW YORK

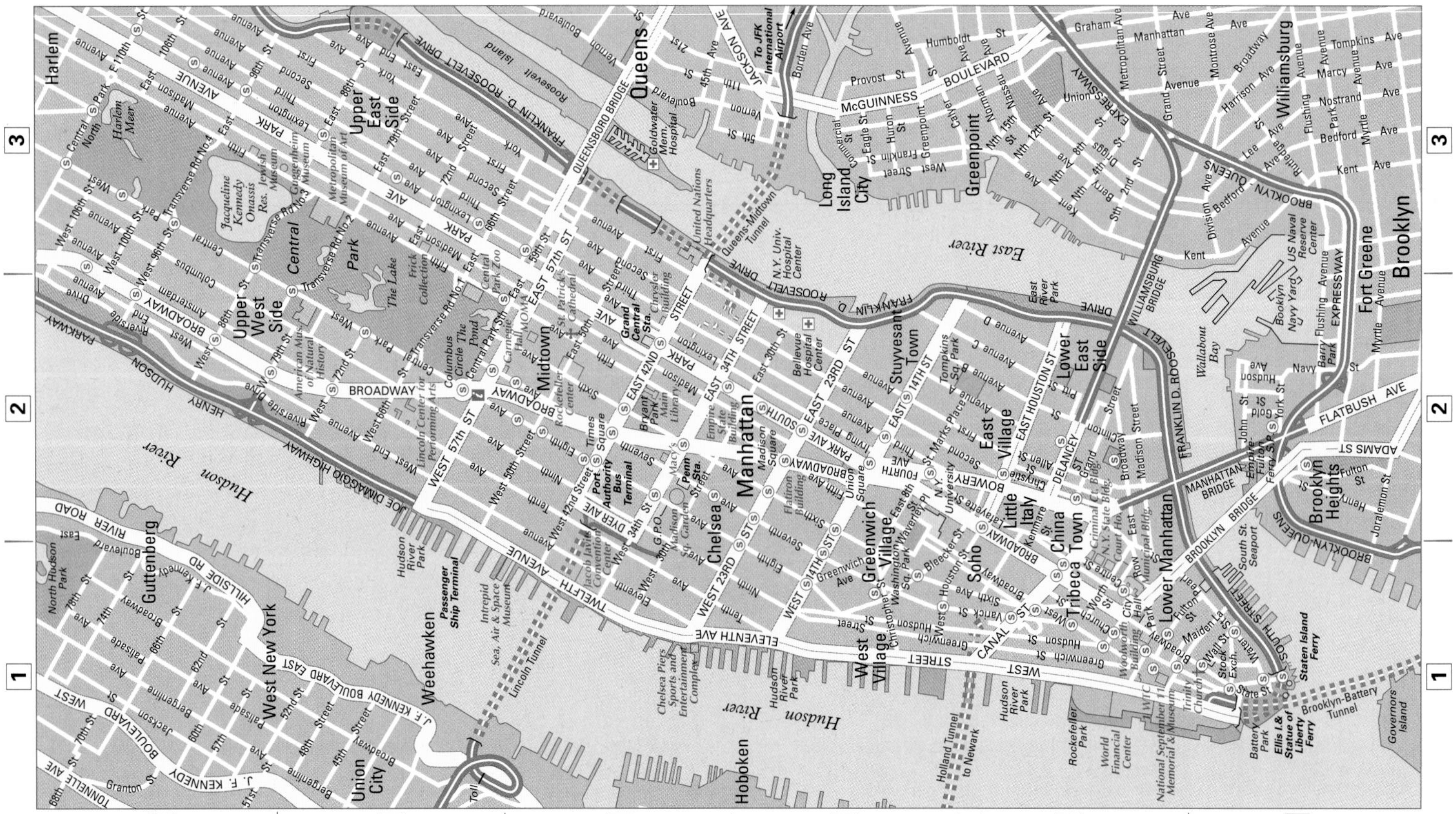

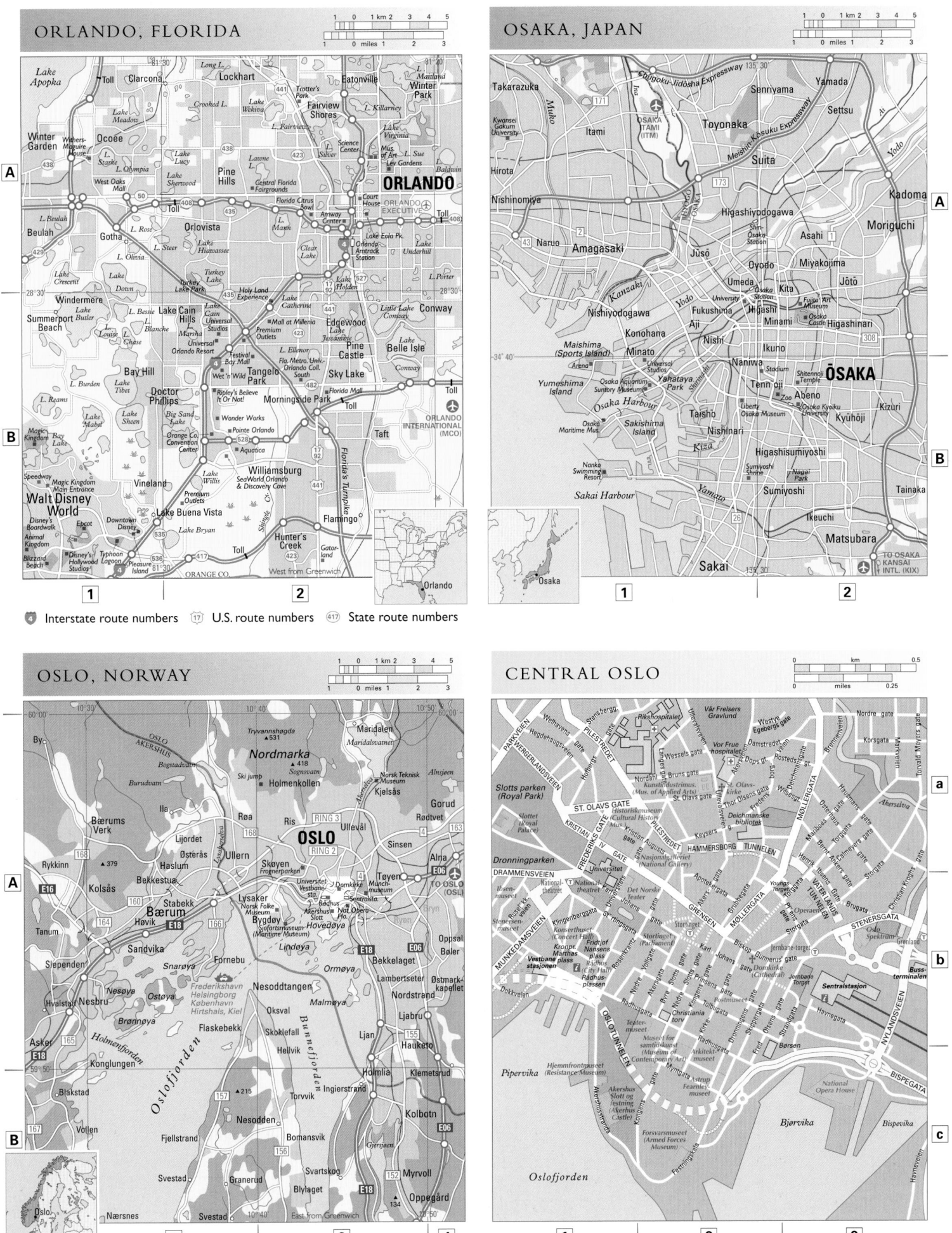

ORLANDO, FLORIDA

Lake Apopka, Toll, Clarcona, Long L., Lockhart, Eatonville, L. Maitland, Winter Park, Ocoee, Lake Meadow, Crooked L., Trotter's Park, Fairview Shores, L. Killarney, Winter Garden, Withers-Maguire House, Lake Wekiva, L. Fairview, Science Center, L. Virginia, Mus. of Art, Leu Gardens, L. Sue, Baldwin, West Oaks Mall, Lake Lucy, Pine Hills, Central Florida Fairgrounds, Florida Citrus Bowl, Amway Center, ORLANDO EXECUTIVE, Toll, Beulah, L. Beulah, Gotha, L. Rose, L. Steer, Lake Hiawassee, Lake Mann, Clear Lake, Orlando Amtrak Station, Lake Eola Pk., Lake Underhill, L. Porter, Windermere, Lake Crescent, L. Olivia, Lake Down, Turkey Lake Park, Holy Land Experience, Lake Catherine, Conway, Summerport Beach, L. Bessie, L. Blanche, Lake Cain Hills, Marsha, Lake Cain, Universal Studios, Mall at Millenia, Edgewood, Lake Jessamine, Little Lake Conway, Bay Hill, L. Burden, Lake Tibet, Universal Orlando Resort, Festival Bay Mall, Premium Outlets, L. Ellenor, Fla. Metro. Univ. Orlando Coll. South, Pine Castle, Belle Isle, Wet 'n' Wild, Doctor Phillips, L. Reams, Lake Sheen, Big Sand Lake, Tangelo Park, Ripley's Believe It Or Not!, Morningside Park, Sky Lake, Florida Mall, Conway, Toll, Magic Kingdom, Bay Lake, Wonder Works, Orange Co. Convention Center, Pointe Orlando, Aquatica, Taft, ORLANDO INTERNATIONAL (MCO), Speedway, Magic Kingdom Main Entrance, Vineland, Williamsburg, SeaWorld Orlando & Discovery Cove, Premium Outlets, Lake Willis, Walt Disney World, Disney's Boardwalk, Epcot, Downtown Disney, Lake Buena Vista, Lake Bryan, Flamingo, Animal Kingdom, Blizzard Beach, Disney's Hollywood Studios, Typhoon Lagoon, Pleasure Island, Hunter's Creek, Gatorland, ORANGE CO., West from Greenwich, Orlando

🛡4 Interstate route numbers   ⑰ U.S. route numbers   ④¹⁷ State route numbers

OSAKA, JAPAN

Takarazuka, Chugoku-Jidōsha Expressway, Yamada, Senriyama, Settsu, Itami, OSAKA ITAMI (ITM), Toyonaka, Kwansei Gakuin University, Meishin-Kosoku Expressway, Hirota, Suita, Yodo, Kadoma, Nishinomiya, Higashiyodogawa, Moriguchi, Naruo, Amagasaki, Jusō, Asahi, Miyakojima, Jōtō, Oyodo, Umeda, Kita, Fujita Art Museum, Nishiyodogawa, University, Kanzaki, Fukushima, Higashi, Ōsaka Castle, Higashinari, Konohana, Aji, Nishi, Minami, Ikuno, Kizuri, Maishima (Sports Island), Arena, Universal Studios, Suntory Museum, Yahataya Park, Tennōji, ŌSAKA, Kyūhōji, Yumeshima Island, Osaka Aquarium, Shitennōji Temple, Osaka Harbour, Liberty Osaka Museum, Zoo, Osaka Kyoiku University, Abeno, Taishō, Osaka Maritime Mus., Sakishima Island, Nishinari, Sumiyoshi Shrine, Nagai Park, Tainaka, Sakai Harbour, Nanko Swimming Pool, Kiza, Yamato, Higashisumiyoshi, Sumiyoshi, Ikeuchi, Matsubara, Sakai, TO OSAKA KANSAI INTL. (KIX), Osaka

OSLO, NORWAY

By, Maridalen, Maridalsvatnet, Tryvannshøgda ▲531, Nordmarka ▲418, Sognsvatn, Norsk Teknisk Museum, Alnsjøen, Bogstadvatn, Ski jump, Holmenkollen, Kjelsås, Gorud, Bærums Verk, Ila, Røa, Ris, RING 3, Ullevål, Rødtvet, Rykkinn ▲379, Østerås, OSLO, Sinsen, Lijordet, Haslum, Ullern, Skøyen, RING 2, Alna, E06, Kolsås, Bekkestua, Universitet Vestbane Stn., Frognerparken, Toyen, Munch-museet, TO OSLO (OSL), Stabekk, Lysaker, Norsk Folke Museum, Bygdøy, Bygdøy, Byørtsmuseum (Maritime Museum), Rådhus, Akershus Slott, Ny Opera Ho., Sentralstn., Bryn, Tanum, Hovedøya, Bærum, Hovik, Lindøya, Oppsal, Bøler, Sandvika, Fornebu, Ormøya, Bekkelaget, Slependen, Snarøya, Nesoddtangen, Malmøya, Lambertseter, Østmarkkapellet, Nesøya, Frederikshavn, Helsingborg, København, Hirtshals, Kiel, Nordstrand, Hvalstad, Nesbru, Ostøya, Oksval, Ljabru, Brønnøya, Flaskebekk, Skokelefall, Ljan, Hauketo, Asker, E18, Holmenfjorden, Hellvik, Holmlia, Klemetsrud, Konglungen, Bunnefjorden, Holmlia, Blåstad, ▲215, Torvik, Ingierstrand, Vollen, Oslofjorden, Nesodden, Kolbotn, E06, Fjellstrand, Bomansvik, Svartskog, Myrvoll, Svestad, Granerud, Gjersjøen, ▲134, Oppegård, Næsnes, Blylaget, East from Greenwich, Oslo

CENTRAL OSLO

Wergelandsveien, Welhavens gate, Storebergg., Vår Frelsers Gravlund, Westye Egebergs gate, Nordre gate, Korsgata, Markveien, Torvald Meyers gate, Parkveien, Hegdehaugsveien, Pilestredet, Rikshospitalet, Vor Frue hospitalet, Damstredet, Bremsengen, Wessels gate, Dops gt., Rostedsgt., Akerselva, Slotts parken (Royal Park), ST. OLAVS GATE, Nordahl Brun Kunstindustrimus. (Mus. of Applied Arts), St. Olavs kirke, St. Olavs gt., Thor Olsens gate, Deichmanske bibliotek, Møllergata, Hausmanns gate, Kristian IV Gate, Frederiks Gate, Historisk museum (Cultural History), Kristian Augusts, Keysers, Hammersborg, Tunnelen, Dronningparken, Universitet, Nasjonalgalleriet (National Gallery), Vaterlands Tunnelen, Stenersgata, DRAMMENSVEIEN, Nasjonal-theatret, Nationaltheatret, Det Norske Teater, Apotergata, Møllergata, Youngs Torget, Operaen, Oslo Spektrum, Grenland, Ibsen-museet, Johans, GRENSEN, Karl Johans, Stortinget (Parliament), Bisp, Jernbane-torget, Stenersgata, MUNKEDAMSVEIEN, Klingenberggata, Konserthuset (Concert Hall), Fridtjof Nansens plass, Rådhus (City Hall), Bispetorget, Jernbane Torget, Sentralstasjon, Buss-terminalen, Vestbane plass stasjonen, Kronpr. Marthas, Rådhus-plassen, NYLANDSVEIEN, Teater-museet, Christiania torv, Doktveien, Rådhusgata, Myntgata, Tollbugata, Museet for samtidskunst (Museum of Contemporary Art), Arkitekt-museet, Børsen, Havnegata, Pipervika, Hjemmefrontmuseet (Resistance Museum), Akershus Slott og festning (Akershus Castle), Fearnley museet, National Opera House, BISPEGATA, Forsvarsmuseet (Armed Forces Museum), Festningsalm., Oslofjorden, Bjørvika, Bispevika

COPYRIGHT PHILIP'S

PARIS, FRANCE

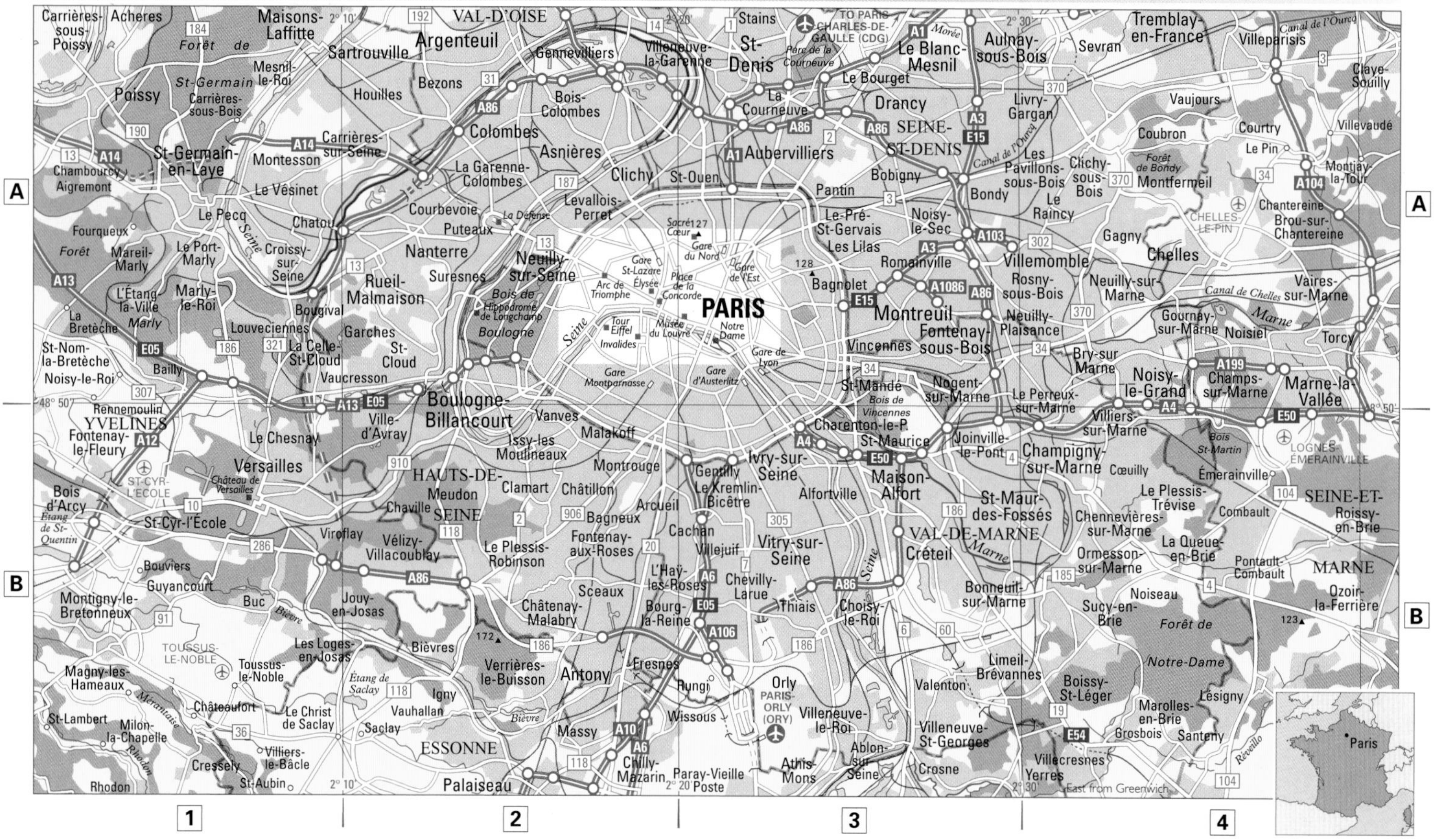

1 0 1 km 2 3 4 5
1 0 miles 1 2 3

CENTRAL PARIS

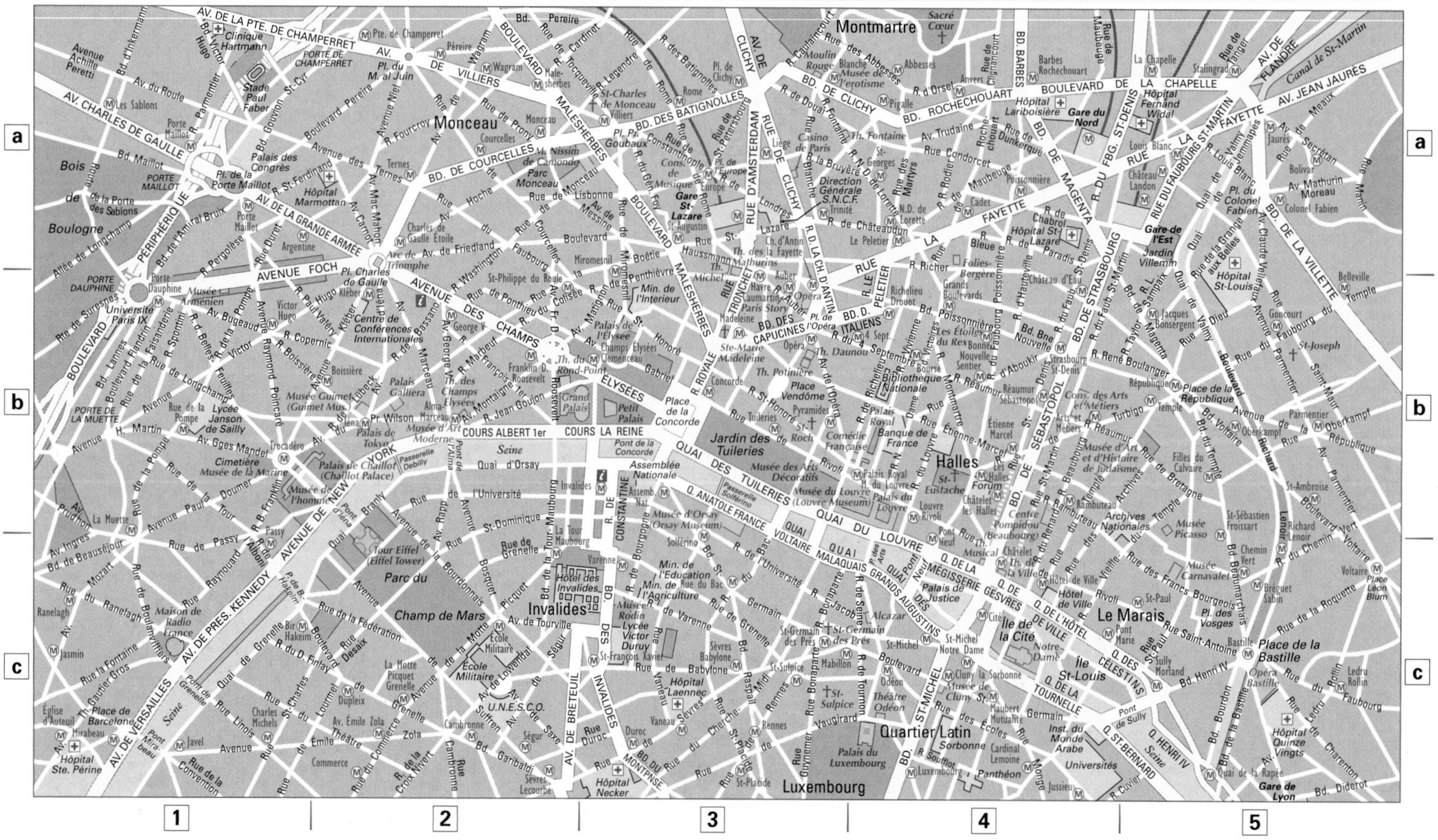

0 km 1
0 miles 0.5

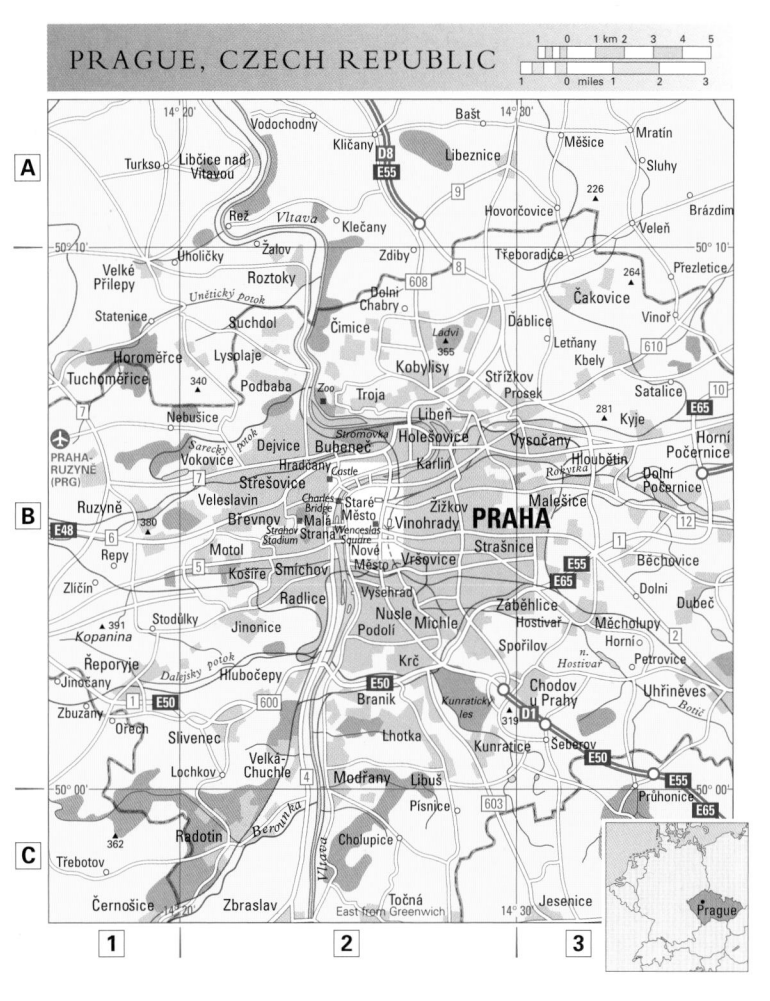

PRAGUE, CZECH REPUBLIC

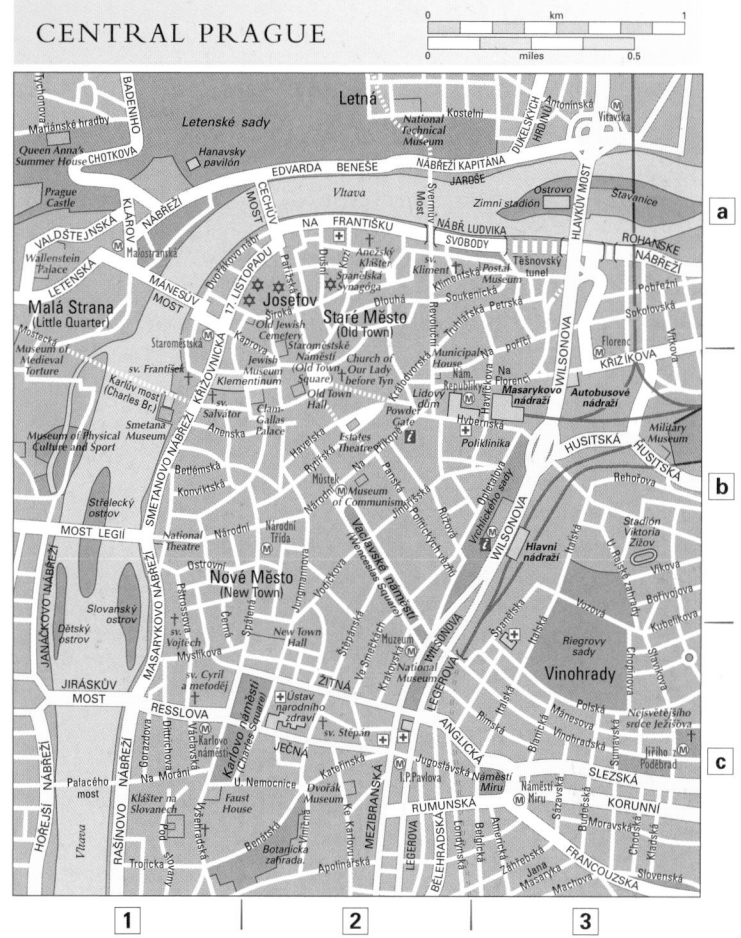

CENTRAL PRAGUE

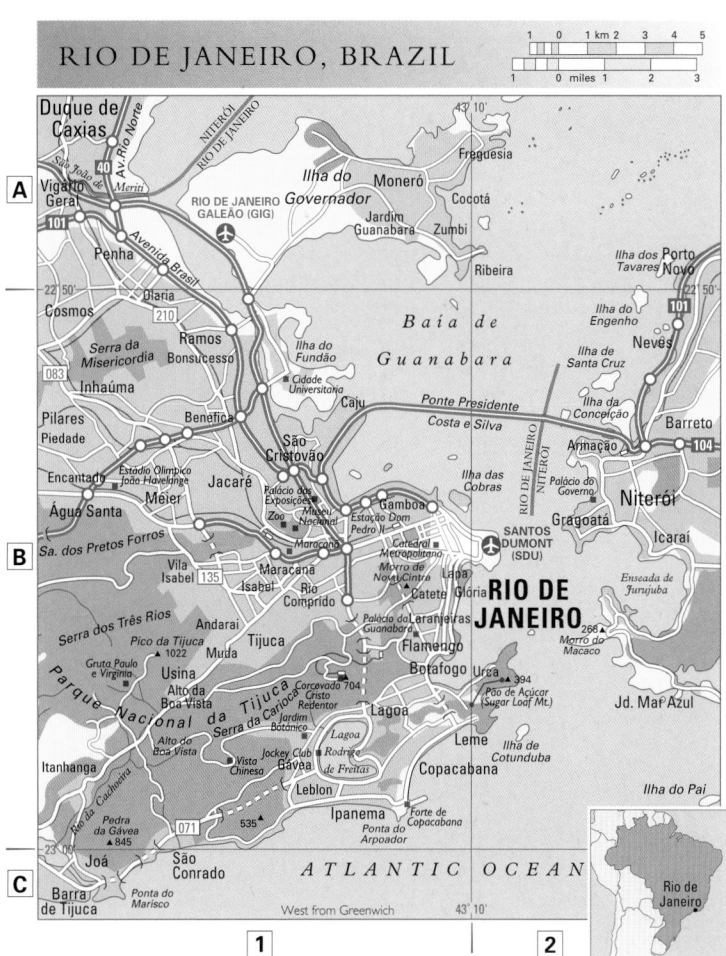

RIO DE JANEIRO, BRAZIL

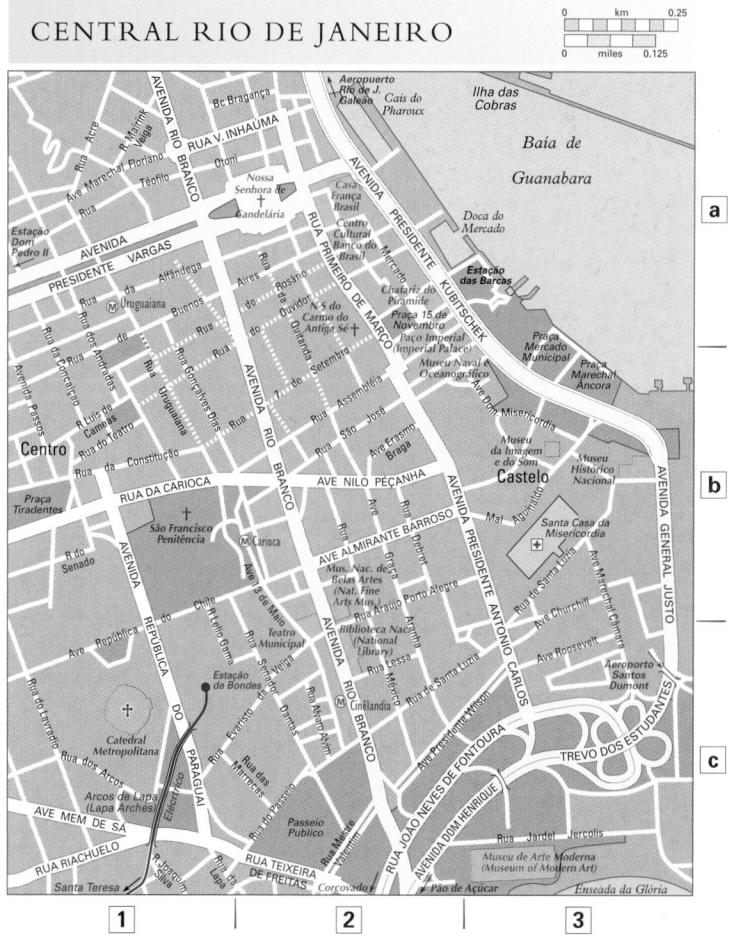

CENTRAL RIO DE JANEIRO

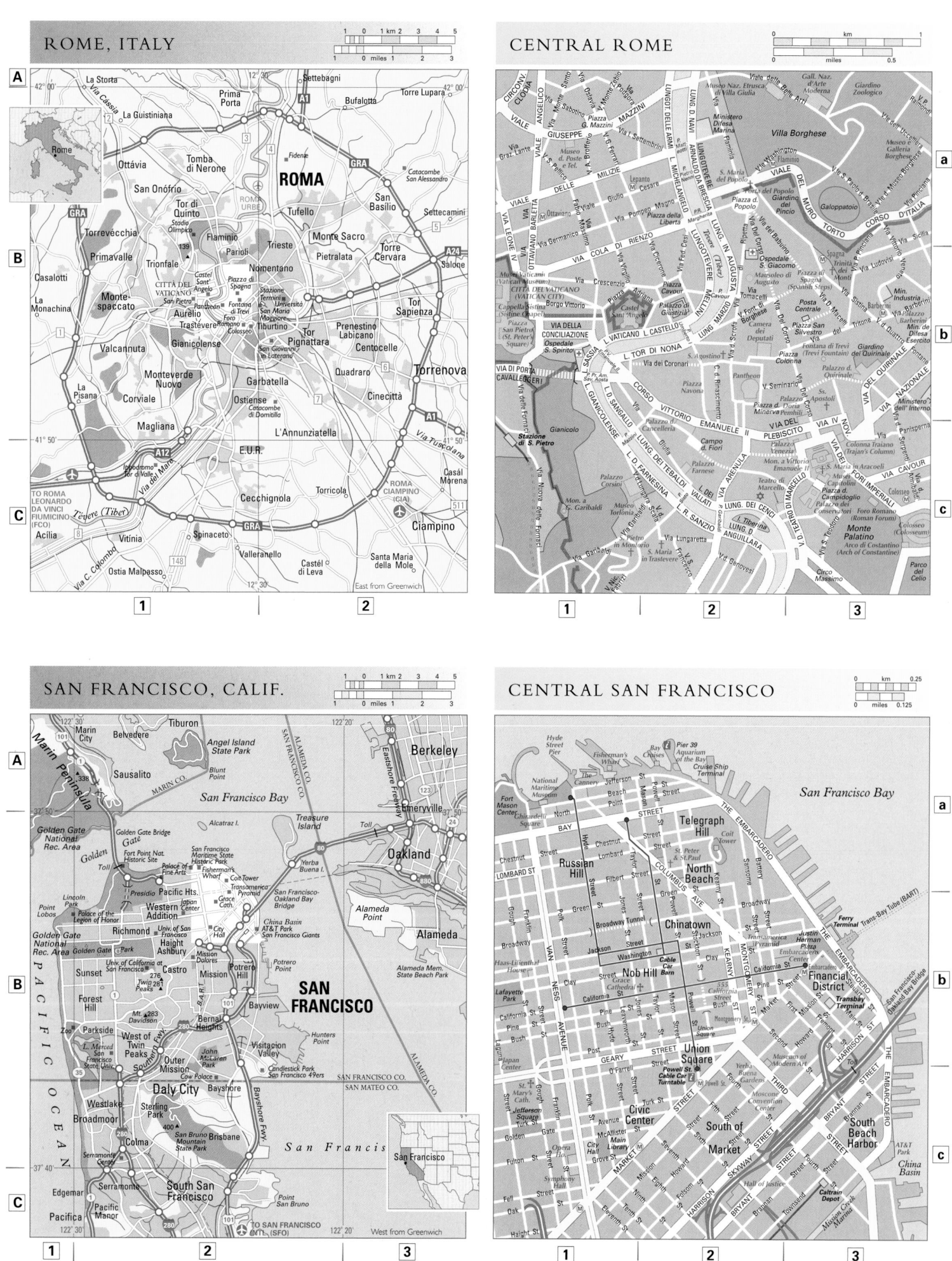

ROME, ITALY

CENTRAL ROME

SAN FRANCISCO, CALIF.

CENTRAL SAN FRANCISCO

Interstate route numbers   U.S. route numbers   State route numbers

Cable Car route

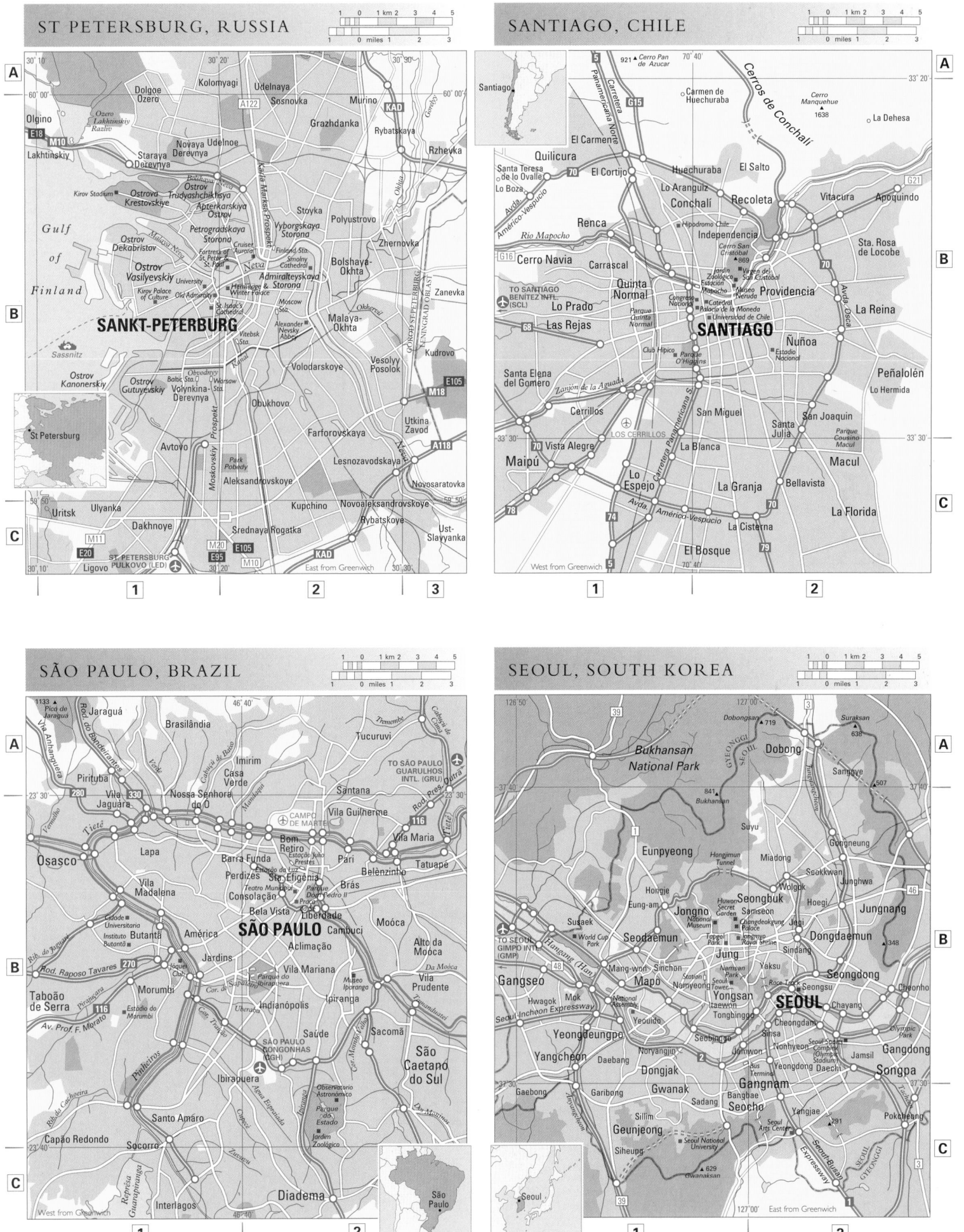

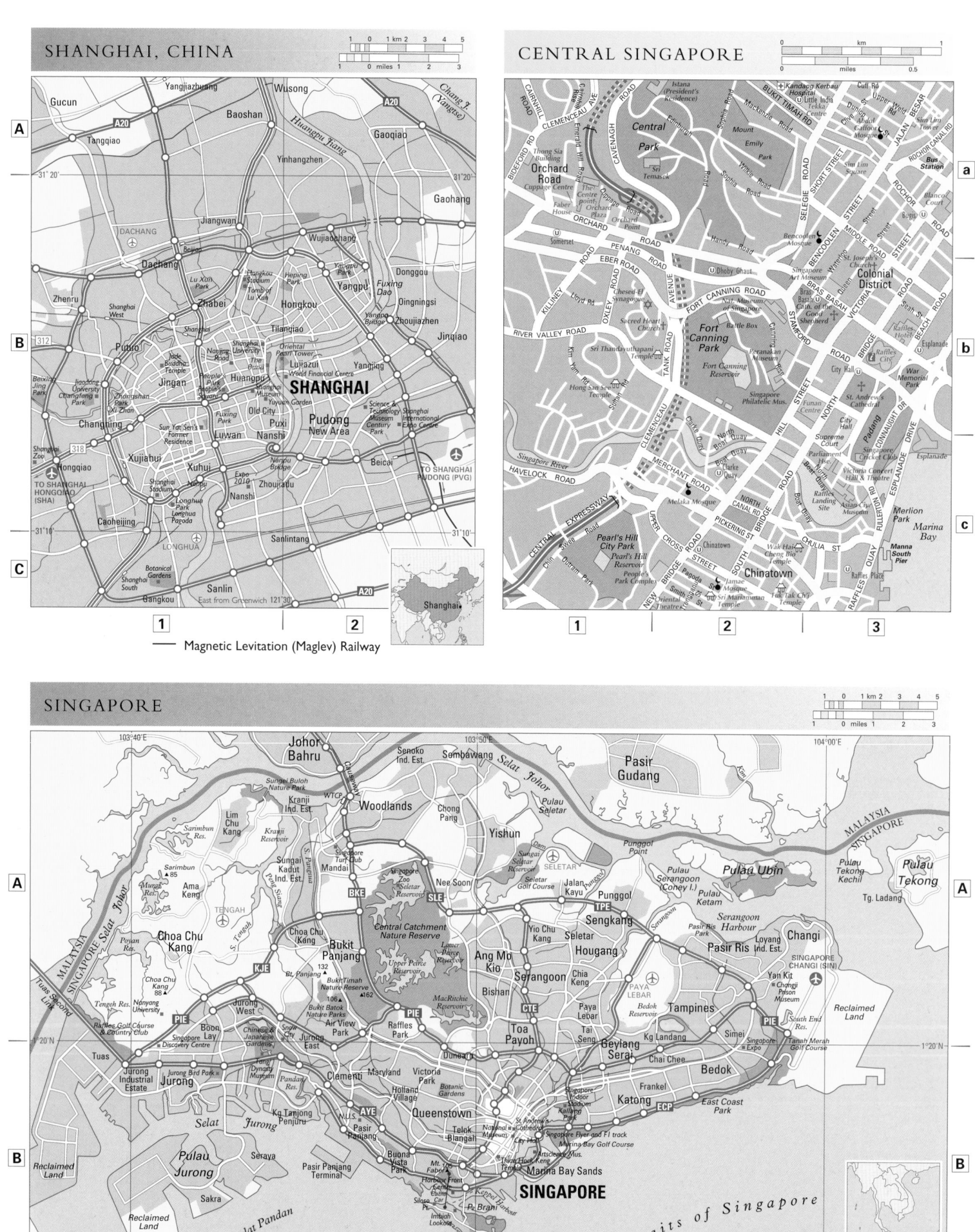

SHANGHAI, CHINA

Magnetic Levitation (Maglev) Railway

CENTRAL SINGAPORE

SINGAPORE

TOKYO, JAPAN

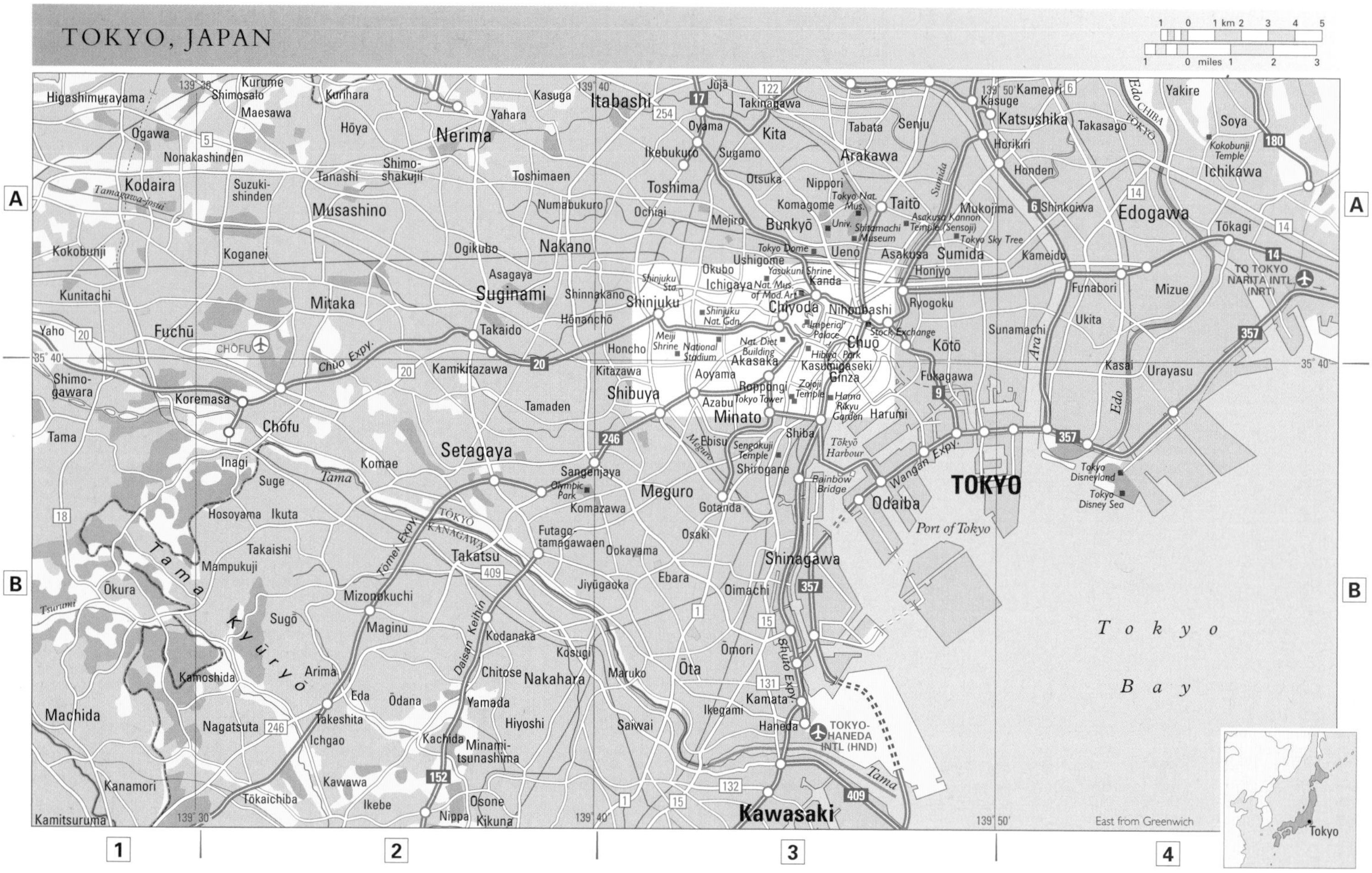

1 0 1 km 2 3 4 5
0 miles 1 2 3

Higashimurayama · Kurume · Shimosato · Shimosalo · Kunihara · Kasuga · 139°40 · Jūjō · Takinagawa · 122 · 50 Kameari · 6 · Yakire
Ogawa · Kurumi · Maesawa · Hōya · Yahara · 254 · Ōyama · Kita · Tabata · Senju · Kasuge · Katsushika · Takasago · Soya
Kodaira · Suzuki-shinden · Tanashi · Shimo-shakujii · Nerima · Ikebukuro · Sugamo · Arakawa · Horikiri · Honden · Shinkoiwa · Ichikawa · 180
Nonakashinden · 5 · Musashino · Numabukuro · Toshimaen · Toshima · Otsuka · Nippori · Komagome · Tokyo Nat. Mus. · Mukojima · Kameido · Tōkagi · Kokobunji Temple
Kokobunji · Koganei · Ochiai · Mejiro · Bunkyō · Univ. · Asakusa Kannon Temple (Sensoji) · Tokyo Sky Tree · Edogawa · 14
Kunitachi · Mitaka · Ogikubo · Nakano · Asagaya · Shinnakano · Shinjuku Sta. · Okubo · Yasukuni Shrine · Ushigome · Ueno · Asakusa · Sumida · Honjyo · 14
Yaho · Fuchū · Takaido · Honancho · Shinjuku · Ichigaya · Nat. Mus. of Mod. Art · Kanda · Nihonbashi · Ryogoku · Funabori · Mizue · TO TOKYO NARITA INTL (NRT)
CHOFU · Kamikitazawa · Kitazawa · Shinjuku Nat. Gdn. · Chiyoda · Imperial Palace · Stock Exchange · Kōtō · Sunamachi · Ukita · 357
Shimogawara · 20 · 20 · Aoyama · Nat. Diet Building · National Stadium · Akasaka · Kasumigaseki · Ginza · Chūō · Fukagawa · Kasai · Urayasu · 35° 40
Koremasa · Chōfu · Setagaya · Tamaden · Shibuya · Roppongi · Zoo Temple · Tokyo Tower · Hama Rikyu Garden · Harumi · 9
Tama · Inagi · Suge · Komae · Sangenjaya · Meguro · Minato · Azabu · Ebisu · Sengoku-ji Temple · Shiba · Tōkyō Harbour · TOKYO · Tokyo Disneyland
Hosoyama · Ikuta · Komazawa · Sangen-jaya · Gotanda · Shirogane · Rainbow Bridge · Odaiba · Port of Tokyo · Tokyo Disney Sea
Takaishi · Mampukuji · Maginu · Futago-tamagawaen · Ookayama · Osaki · Shinagawa
Okura · Arima · Mizonokuchi · Kodanaka · Kōsugi · Jiyūgaoka · Ebara · Oimachi · 357
Kamoshida · Sugō · Eda · Ōdana · Yamada · Nakahara · Maruko · Ōta · Ōmori · 15
Machida · Nagatsuta · Takeshita · Chitose · Hiyoshi · Saiwai · Kamata · 131 · Ikegami · Haneda · TOKYO-HANEDA INTL (HND)
Kanamori · Ichgao · 246 · Kachida · Minami-tsunashima · Kawawa · 152 · 132 · 409
Kamitsuruma · 139°30 · Tōkaichiba · Ikebe · Nippa · Osone · Kikuna · 139°40 · **Kawasaki** · 139°50 · East from Greenwich

Tama River · Tama Kyūryō · Tokyo Kanagawa Expwy · Tomei Expwy · Daisan Keihin · Tama · Edo River · Tokyo Bay · Tōkyō · Bay

Tokyo (inset map)

CENTRAL TOKYO

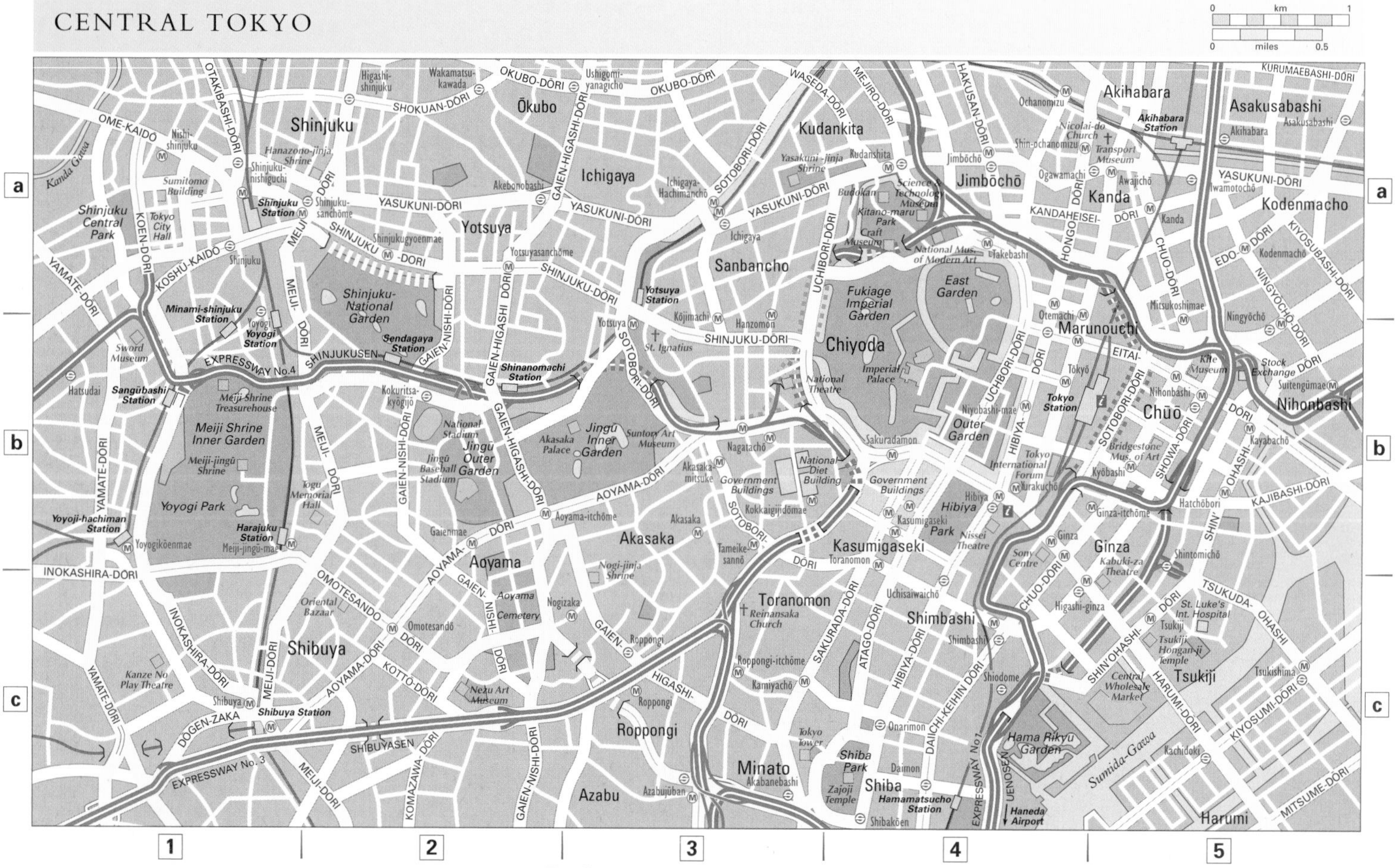

0 km 1
0 miles 0.5

OME-KAIDO · OTAKIBASHI-DORI · Higashi-shinjuku · Wakamatsu-kawada · SHOKUAN-DORI · Ushigomi-yanagicho · OKUBO-DORI · WASEDA-DORI · MEJIRO-DORI · HAKUSAN-DORI · KURUMAEBASHI-DORI
Nishi-shinjuku · **Shinjuku** · Hanazono-jinja Shrine · **Ōkubo** · OKUBO-DORI · Ochanomizu · Nicolai-do Church · **Akihabara** · **Asakusabashi**
Sumitomo Building · Shinjuku-nishiguchi · Ichigaya · YASUKUNI-DORI · Yasukuni-jinja Shrine · Kudankita · Science · Akihabara Station · Asakusabashi
Shinjuku Central Park · Tokyo City Hall · **Shinjuku Station** · Shinjuku-sanchōme · Yotsuya · Ichigaya-Hachimancho · Kudanshita · Buddhist · Technology Museum · Jimbōchō · KANDAHEISEI · Iwamotocho · YASUKUNI-DORI
Shinjuku · Shinjuku-gyoenmae · SHINJUKU-DORI · Sanbancho · Kitano-maru Park · Nat. Mus. of Modern Art · Takebashi · Kanda · YASUKUNI-DORI · Kodenmacho
Shinjuku City Hall · **Minami-shinjuku Station** · **Yoyogi Station** · Yotsuya Station · Kōjimachi · Hanzomon · Awanichō · KYOBASHI-DORI
Sword Museum · Shinjuku-National Garden · SOTOBORI-DORI · **Fukiage Imperial Garden** · **East Garden** · Ōtemachi · Mitsukoshimae · Ningyōchō
KOSHU-KAIDO · Sendagaya Station · Shinanomachi Station · St. Ignatius · **Chiyoda** · Imperial Palace · Tōkyō · KKE Museum · Stock Exchange · Sutengūmae
Meiji Shrine Treasurehouse · National Stadium · National Theatre · Outer Garden · **Tokyo Station** · **Marunouchi** · Nihonbashi
Sangubashi Station · Meiji Shrine · Kokuritsa-kyōgijō · Jingū Outer Garden · Akasaka Palace · Suntory Art Museum · Nagatachō · **Chūō** · **Nihonbashi**
Meiji Shrine Inner Garden · Jingū Baseball Stadium · **Jingū Inner Garden** · National Diet Building · Government Buildings · Kasumigaseki Park · Hibiya · Bridgestone Mus. of Art · Kayabachō
Yoyoji-hachiman Station · Togu Memorial Hall · Gaienmae · Akatsutsumi-mitsuke · Government Buildings · Hibiya · Tokyo International Forum · Kyūbashi
Yoyogi Park · Harajuku Station · Meiji-jingū-mae · AOYAMA-DORI · Aoyama-itchōme · Akasaka · Tameike-sannō · Hibiya Park · Sony Centre · **Ginza** · Ginza-itchōme
INOKASHIRA-DORI · Oriental Bazaar · Omotesandō · Nogizaka · Nogi-jinja Shrine · Toranomon · Kasumigaseki · Nissei Theatre · Kabuki-za Theatre · Shintomichō
Kanze No Play Theatre · OMOTESANDŌ · Aoyama Cemetery · **Toranomon** · Reinansaka Church · Uchisaiwaicho · St. Luke's Int. Hospital · **Tsukiji**
Nezu Art Museum · **Aoyama** · **Akasaka** · **Shimbashi** · Shimbashi · Tsukiji Honganji Temple
YAMATE-DORI · **Shibuya** · KOTTO-DORI · Roppongi-itchōme · Shiodome · Central Wholesale Market
DOGEN-ZAKA · **Shibuya Station** · Roppongi · HIGASHI-DORI · **Roppongi** · Onarimon · Hama Rikyū Garden
SHIBUYASEN · KOMAZAWA-DORI · MEIJI-DORI · Tokyo Tower · Shiba Park · Daimon · HARUMI-DORI
EXPRESSWAY No. 3 · GAIEN-NISHI-DORI · **Minato** · Akabanebashi · Hamamatsucho Station · **Harumi**
Azabu · Azabujūban · Zōjōji Temple · **Shiba** · Shibakōen · Haneda Airport · EXPRESSWAY No. 1 · MITSUME-DORI

⊖ Toei Subway   Ⓜ Tokyo Metro

TEHRAN, IRAN

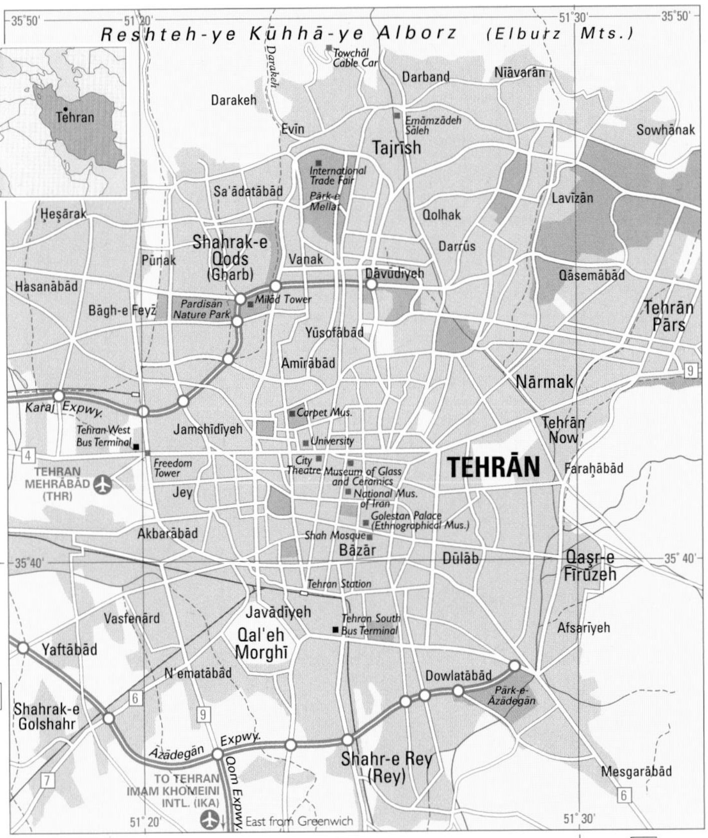

Reshteh-ye Kūhhā-ye Alborz (Elburz Mts.)

Towchal Cable Car
Darband
Niāvarān
Darakeh
Sowhānak
Evīn
Emāmzādeh Sāleh
Tajrīsh
International Trade Fair
Park-e Mellat
Sa'ādatābād
Qolhak
Lavīzān
Vanak
Dāvūdīyeh
Qāsemābād
Shahrak-e Qods (Gharb)
Pardisan Nature Park
Mīlād Tower
Hasanābād
Pūnak
Yūsofābād
Tehrān Pārs
Bāgh-e Feyż
Amīrābād
Nārmak
Karaj Expwy.
Corpet Mus.
Tehran-West Bus Terminal
Jamshīdīyeh
University
Tehrān Now
Freedom Tower
City Theatre
Museum of Glass and Ceramics
National Mus. of Iran
Golestan Palace (Ethnographical Mus.)
Farahābād
TEHRAN MEHRĀBĀD (THR)
Jey
Akbarābād
Shah Mosque
Bāzār
Dūlāb
Qasr-e Fīrūzeh
Tehran Station
Vasfenārd
Javādīyeh
Qal'eh Morghī
Afsarīyeh
Yaftābād
Tehran South Bus Terminal
N'ematābād
Dowlatābād
Park-e Āzādegān
Shahrak-e Golshahr
Āzādegān Expwy.
Shahr-e Rey (Rey)
Mesarābād
TO TEHRAN IMAM KHOMEINI INTL. (IKA)
East from Greenwich

CENTRAL TORONTO

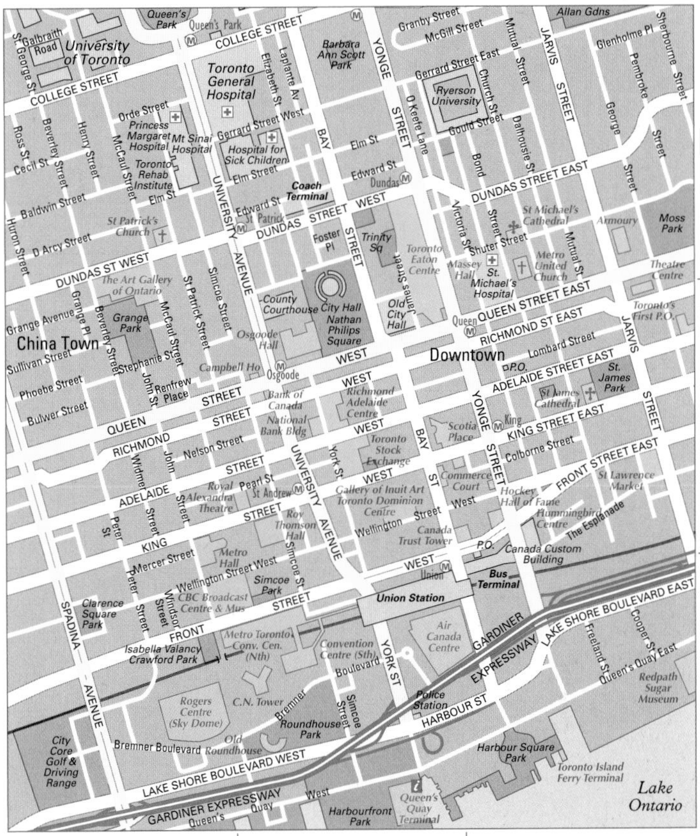

University of Toronto
Queen's Park
College Street
Granby Street
McGill Street
Yonge Street
Jarvis Street
Allan Gdns
Gerrard Street East
Glenholme Pl
Sherbourne Street
Toronto General Hospital
Ryerson University
Barbara Ann Scott Park
College Street
Orde Street
Princess Margaret Hospital
Mt Sinai Hospital
Hospital for Sick Children
Elm St
Edward St
Dundas
Coach Terminal
St Michael's Cathedral
Moss Park
Armour
Dundas Street West
St Patrick's Church
D'Arcy Street
Toronto Eaton Centre
Metro United Church
Theatre Centre
Dundas Street East
The Art Gallery of Ontario
China Town
County Courthouse
City Hall
Nathan Philips Square
Old City Hall
Queen Street East
Toronto's First P.O.
Downtown
Grange Park
Campbell Ho.
Osgoode Hall
Queen Street West
Richmond St East
Adelaide Street East
St James Park
Phoebe Street
Bank of Nova Scotia
Richmond Adelaide Centre
Scotia Place
King Street East
Colborne Street
Bulwer Street
National Bank Bldg
Toronto Stock Exchange
Royal Alexandra Theatre
St Andrew
Gallery of Inuit Art
Toronto Dominion Centre
Commerce Court
St Lawrence Market
Mercer Street
Roy Thomson Hall
Canada Trust Tower
Hockey Hall of Fame
Hummingbird Centre
The Esplanade
Clarence Square Park
Wellington Street West
Front Street East
CBC Broadcast Centre & Mus.
Union Station
Canada Custom Building
Bus Terminal
Isabella Valancy Crawford Park
Metro Toronto Conv. Cen. (Nth)
Convention Centre (Sth)
Air Canada Centre
Gardiner Expressway
Lake Shore Boulevard East
Redpath Sugar Museum
Rogers Centre (Sky Dome)
C.N. Tower
Police Station
Harbour St
Queen's Quay East
City Core Golf & Driving Range
Bremner Boulevard
Roundhouses
Roundhouse
Harbour Square Park
Toronto Island Ferry Terminal
Lake Ontario
Lake Shore Boulevard West
Gardiner Expressway
Quay
Harbourfront Park
Queen's Quay Terminal

TORONTO, CANADA

Boyd Conservation Area
Vaughan
Thornhill
The Promenade
East Don
Markham
Toronto Zoo
Brown
Rouge
Fairport
Rouge Hill
Concord
Newtonbrook
West Rouge
Pine Grove
Edgeley
Fisherville
Willowdale
Agincourt
Malvern
Highland Creek
Port Union
Woodbridge
York University
G. Ross Lord Park
East Don Parkland
Fairview Mall
Morningside Park
Black Creek Pioneer Village
Northmount
Macdonald-Cartier Frwy
Scarborough Town Centre
Woburn
West Hill
Humber Summit
North York
Lansing
York Mills
Wexford
Bendale
Eastpoint Park
Beaumonde Heights
Downsview Park
Armour Heights
Creek Hague Park
Scarborough
Thistletown
Northwood Park
Don Mills
Cliffside
Claireville Reservoir
Downsview
Lawrence Heights
Yorkdale Shopping Centre
Wilket Creek Park
Sunnybrook Health Science Centre
Ontario Science Centre
Humberwood Park
Kipling Heights
Humberlea
Forest Hill
Leaside
Thorncliffe
Danforth
Malton
Woodbine Centre
Rexdale
Weston
Cedarvale Park
Bluffers Park
Woodbine Race Track
Dentonia Park
Scarborough Bluffs
York
Casa Loma
East York
Birch Cliff
TORONTO LESTER B. PEARSON INTL. (YYZ)
Humber Valley Village
Mount Dennis
Royal Ontario Museum
Riverdale Park
Kew Gardens
Hanlon
Lambton Mills
Swansea
University of Toronto
Old City Hall
Parliament Buildings
Ashbridge's Bay Park
Etobicoke
High Park
C.N. Tower & Rogers Centre
Union Sta.
TORONTO
Islington
Kingsway
Old Fort York
Gardiner Expy.
Burnhamthorpe
Markland Wood
Humber Bay
Parkdale
Exhibition Place
TORONTO CITY (ISLAND)
Tommy Thompson Park
Summerville
Humber Bay Park
Ontario Place
Island Park
Toronto Harbour
Mimico
Toronto Islands
Cooksville
New Toronto
Samuel Smith Park
Gibraltar Point
LAKE ONTARIO
Mississauga
Long Branch
West from Greenwich
Toronto

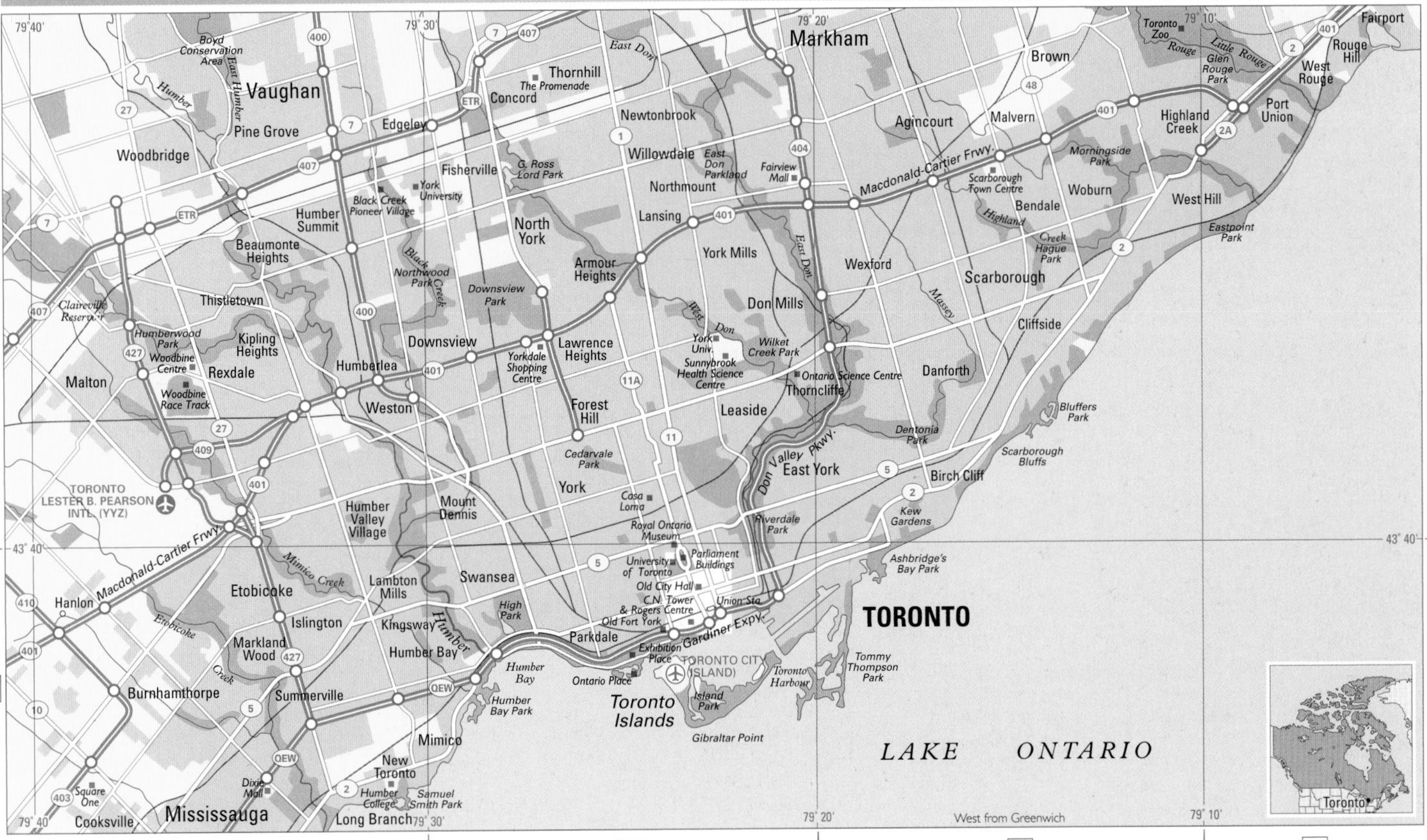

Provincial route numbers

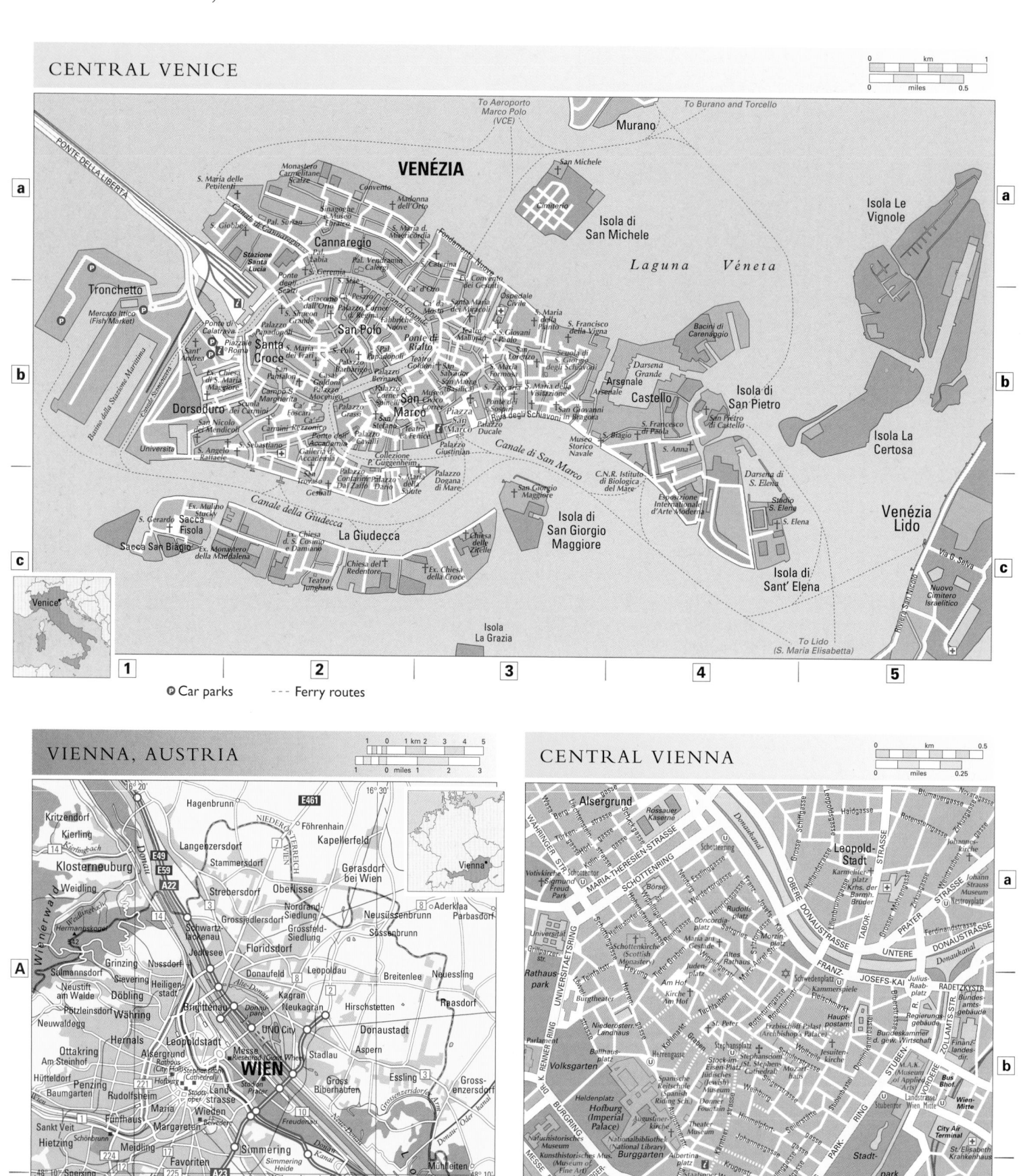

CENTRAL VENICE

To Aeroporto Marco Polo (VCE)

To Burano and Torcello

Murano

VENÉZIA

San Michele

Cimitero

Isola di San Michele

Isola Le Vignole

Laguna Véneta

PONTE DELLA LIBERTA

S. Maria delle Penitenti

Monastero Carmelitani Scalze

Convento

Madonna dell'Orto

Sinagoghe e Museo Ebraico

S. Marziale

Cannaregio

S. Giobbe

Canale di Cannaregio

Pal. Surian

Stazione Santa Lucia

Labia

S. Geremia

Pal. Vendramin Calergi

S. Caterina

Convento dei Gesuiti

Ospedale Civile

S. Maria dei Miracoli

S. Maria della Pietà

Tronchetto

Mercato Ittico (Fish Market)

Ponte degli Scalzi

Giacomo dall'Orto

S. Simeon Grande

Palazzo Corner Regina

Ca' d'Oro

Santa Maria dei Frari

Fabbriche Nuove

S. Maria d. Misericordia

Fondamente Nuove

S. Francisco della Vigna

Bacini di Carenaggio

Ponte di Calatrava

Palazzo Papadopoli

S. Pietro

Canal Grande

S. Lorenzo

SS. Giovanni e Paolo

Scuola di S. Giorgio degli Schiavoni

Darsena Grande

Isola di San Pietro

Sant' Andrea

Piazzale Roma

Santa Croce

San Polo

S. Maria dei Frari

S. Polo

Pal. Papadopoli

Rialto

Ponte di Rialto

Fabbriche Vecchie

Teatro Goldoni

S. Salvador

S. Zaccaria

Arsenale

Arsenale

Castello

P

Dorsoduro

Ex. Chiesa di S. Maria Maggiore

Pantalon

Campo S. Margherita

Palazzo Mocenigo

Palazzi Corner Spinelli

Museo Correr

San Marco Basilica

Ponte dei Sospiri

S. Giovanni in Bragora

S. Francesco di Paola

S. Biagio

Scuola dei Carmini

Ca' Foscari

San Marco

S. Stefano

Piazza S. Marco

Riva degli Schiavoni

S. Anna

Università

Carmini

Rezzonico

S. Sebastiano

S. Angelo Raffaele

Galleria d. Accademia

Teatro La Fenice

Palazzo Grassi

Palazzo Cavalli

Palazzo Ducale

Museo Storico Navale

C.N.R. Istituto di Biologia del Mare

Darsena di S. Elena

San Nicolo dei Mendicoli

Collezione P. Guggenheim

Palazzo Contarini Dal Zaffo

Palazzo Dario

S. Maria della Salute

Palazzo Dogana di Mare

Maria della Salute

S. Giorgio Maggiore

Esposizione Internazionale d'Arte Moderna

Stadio S. Elena

Venézia Lido

Via G. Selva

Canale della Giudecca

Ex. Mulino Stucky

S. Gerardo

Sacca Fisola

Sacca San Biagio

Ex. Monastero della Maddalena

Ex. Chiesa d. S. Cosimo e Damiani

Chiesa d. S. Zitelle

Isola di San Giorgio Maggiore

Isola di Sant' Elena

S. Elena

Nuovo Cimitero Israelitico

Teatro Junghans

Chiesa del Redentore

Chiesa della Croce

La Giudecca

Isola La Grazia

To Lido (S. Maria Elisabetta)

Venice

⊙ **Car parks** --- **Ferry routes**

a b c — 1 2 3 4 5

VIENNA, AUSTRIA

1 0 1 km 2 3 4 5 / 1 0 miles 1 2 3

Vienna

Kritzendorf

Kierling

Klostermühlbach

Hagenbrunn

E461

NIEDERÖSTERREICH

Föhrenhain

Kapellerfeld

Langenzersdorf

Stammersdorf

Gerasdorf bei Wien

Klosterneuburg

Weidling

S. Weidling

Wienerwald

E49 E59 A22

Streberdorf

ObeNisse

Nordrand-Siedlung

Grossjedlersdorf

Aderklaa

Parbasdorf

Hermannskogel

Schwartz-lackenau

14

Jedlesee

Grossfeld-Siedlung

Floridsdorf

Neusüssenbrunn

Süssenbrunn

Grinzing

Nussdorf

Donaufeld

Kagran

Leopoldau

Breitenlee

Neuessling

Sievering

Heiligen-stadt

Neukagran

Hirschstetten

Reasdorf

A Sulmannsdorf

Neustift am Walde

Pötzleinsdorf

Döbling

Brigittenau

UNO City

Donaustadt

Aspern

Neuwaldegg

Währing

Leopoldstadt

Messe

Stadlau

Ottakring

Am Steinhof

Hernals

Rathaus (City Hall)

WIEN

Essling

Gross-enzersdorf

Hüttldorf

Penzing

Baumgarten

Rudolfsheim

Hofburg

Fünfhaus

Maria

Wieden

Gross Biberhaufen

Sankt Veit

Schönbrunn

Meidling

Margareten

Freudenau

Hietzing

Mariahilf

Favoriten

224

Simmering

Simmering Heide

Mühlleiten

Lainz

Spersing

Atzgersdorf

Hetzendorf

Erlaa

225

A23

Kaiserebersdorf

Albern

48° 10'

Mauer

Rodaun

Liesing

Inzersdorf

Oberlaa

Kledering

Schwechat

B Perchtoldsdorf

E60 A21

Vösendorf

A2 E59

Siebenhirten

Rothneusiedl

Unterlaa

Rannersdorf

Neukettenhof

WIEN SCHWECHAT (VIE)

Mödling

Leopoldsdorf

Zwölfaxing

Himberg

16° 20' 16° 30'

East from Greenwich

1 2 3

CENTRAL VIENNA

km 0.5 / miles 0.25

Alsergrund

Rossauer Kaserne

Leopold-Stadt

WÄHRINGER STR.

Votivkirche

Sigmund Freud Park

Schottenring

Börse

MARIA-THERESIEN-STRASSE

SCHOTTENRING

TABOR

PRATER STRASSE

Johann Strauss Museum

Universität

Rathaus-park

Schottenkirche (Scottish Monastery)

Concordia platz

Rudolfs platz

Maria am Gestade

Altes Rathaus

Juden platz

Morzin Platz

a Burgtheater

Parlament

Am Hof

Kirche Am Hof

St. Peter

Erzbischöf. Palast (Archbishop's Palace)

Haupt Postamt

Bundeskammer d. gew. Wirtschaft

Finanz-landes-dir.

Volksgarten

Niederösterr. Landhaus

Graben

Stephansplatz

St. Stephen Cathedral

Jesuiten Kirche

R. Regierungs-gebäude

RADETZKYSTR.

ZOLLAMTS-STR.

b Heldenplatz

Hofburg (Imperial Palace)

Spanische Reitschule (Spanish Riding Sch.)

Donner Fountain

Himmelpfort

Stephansdom

Stock-im-Eisen Platz

Jüdisches Museum (Jewish Museum)

Mozartplatz

Stubentor

Wien Mitte

M.A.K. (Museum of Applied Arts)

Bus Bhof.

Nationalbibliothek (National Library)

Augustiner Kirche

Theater Museum

Albertina platz

Johannesgasse

STUBEN RING

City Air Terminal

St. Elisabeth Krankenhaus

Naturhistorisches Museum

Burggarten

Kunsthistorisches Mus. (Museum of Fine Art)

Staatsoper (Nat. Opera House)

OPERNRING

KÄRNTNER RING

SCHUBERTRING

Stadt-park

c Museums-quartier

Schiller platz

Ak. der Bildenden Künste (Acad. of Fine Arts)

Hotel Bristol

Akademie-theater

Technische Universität

Musikverein

LOTHRINGERSTR.

Schwarzenbergplatz

Konzerthaus

Lehár-Theater an der Wien

Ressel park

Hist. Mus. der Stadt

Karlskirche

Karlsplatz

Palais Schwarzenberg (Schwarzenberg Palace)

LINKE WIENZEILE

RECHTE WIENZEILE

OPERNGASSE

WIEDNER HAUPTSTRASSE

Technische Universität

Veterinär-medizin. Universität

Jaurès-gasse

COPYRIGHT PHILIP'S

1 2 3

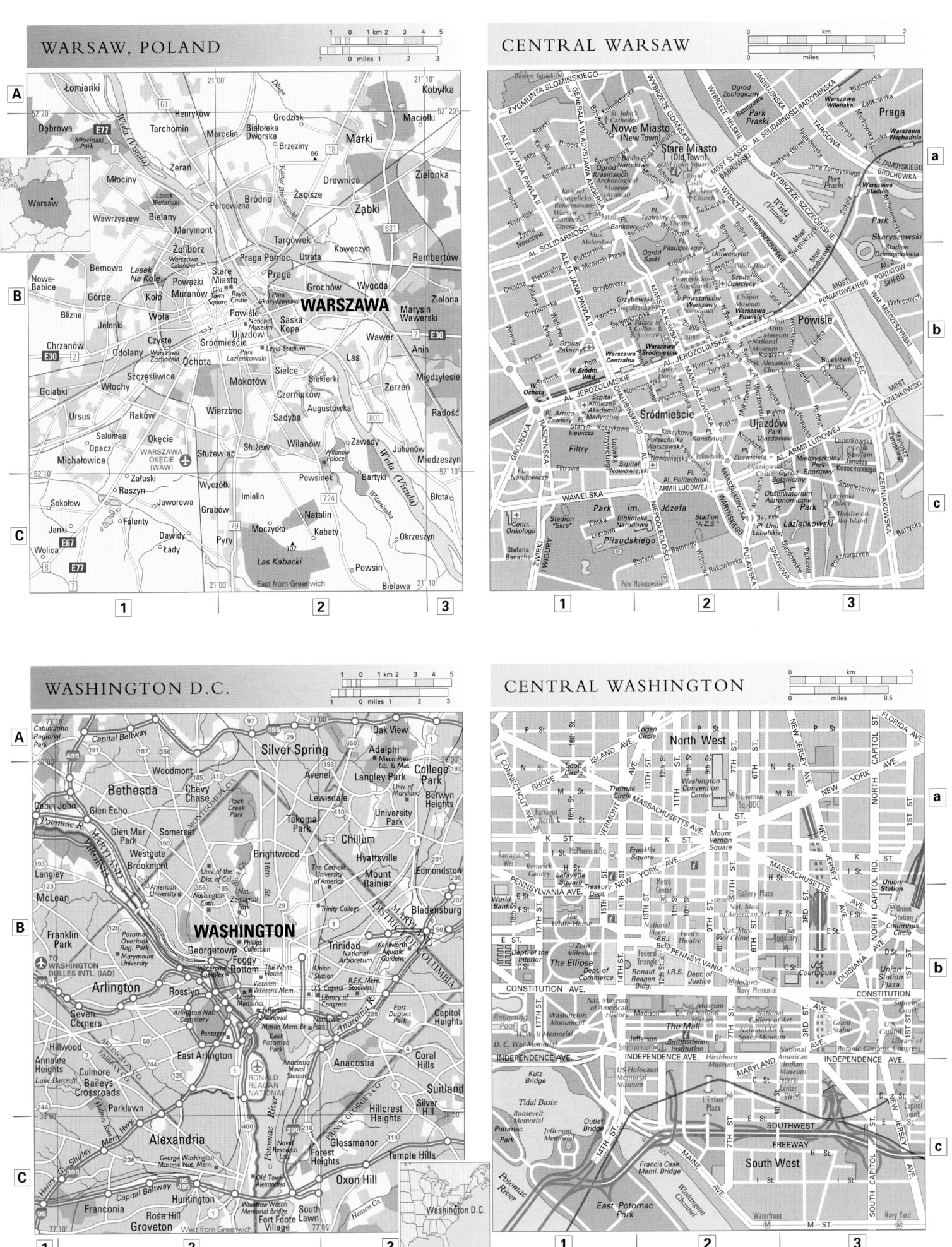

WARSAW, POLAND

A Łomianki Kobyłka
Henryków Grodzisk Maciołki
Dąbrowa Tarchomin Marcelin Białołeka Dworska Brzeziny Marki
Żerań Drewnica Zielonka
Młociny Pelcowizna Ząbki
Wawrzyszew Bielany Żacisze
Żoliborz Targówek Kawęczyn
B Bemowo Praga Północ Utrata Rembertów
Górce Koło Stare Miasto Praga Wygoda
Blizne Jelonki Wola Powiśle Grochów Zielona
Chrzanów Czyste Ujazdów Saska Kępa Marysin Wawerski
Odolany Śródmieście Wawer Anin
Szczęśliwice Włochy Ochota Sielce Las Międzylesie
Golabki Raków Mokotów Czerniaków Zerzeń Radość
Ursus Salomea Okęcie Sadyba Augustówka Zawady Julianów
Michałowice Służewiec Służew Wilanów Miedzeszyn
C Sokołów Załuski Raszyn Jaworowa Grabów Imielin Powsinek Bartyki Błota
Janki Falenty Dawidy Moczydło Natolin Okrzeszyn
Wolica Łady Pyry Kabaty Powsin
Las Kabacki Bielawa

1 2 3

CENTRAL WARSAW

(as a city-center map with street names)

a Praga Warszawa Wileńska Warszawa Wschodnia
Nowe Miasto (New Town) Stare Miasto (Old Town)
b Powiśle Śródmieście Ujazdów
c Lazienkowski

1 2 3

WASHINGTON D.C.

A Cabin John Regional Park Capital Beltway Oak View
Silver Spring Adelphi Nixon Pres. Lib. & Mus.
Woodmont Avenel Langley Park College Park
Bethesda Chevy Chase Lewisdale Berwyn Heights
Cabin John Glen Echo Rock Creek Park Takoma Park University Park
Glen Mar Park Somerset Chillum
Langley Westgate Brookmont Brightwood Hyattsville Mount Rainier Edmondston
McLean Univ. of the Dist. of Col. Washington Cath. Trinity College
B Franklin Park WASHINGTON Kenworth Aquatic Gardens Capitol Park
Baileys Georgetown Foggy Bottom The White House Trinidad
Arlington Rosslyn Union Station Fort Dupont Park Capitol Heights
Seven Corners Pentagon Anacostia Coral Hills
Hillwood East Arlington Anacostia Suitland
Annalee Heights Culmore Ronald Reagan National Hillcrest Heights Silver Hill
Baileys Crossroads Parklawn Glassmanor Temple Hills
C Alexandria Forest Heights
Franconia Huntington Fort Foote Village Oxon Hill
Rose Hill Groveton South Lawn

● 85 Interstate route numbers ㉙ U.S. route numbers ⑯⑥ State route numbers

1 2 3

CENTRAL WASHINGTON

a North West Logan Circle Washington Convention Center Mount Vernon Square
Thomas Circle McPherson Sq. Franklin Square Union Station
b Farragut Lafayette Square The White House Metro Center Gallery Place Judiciary Sq.
The Ellipse Federal Triangle F.B.I. Bldg.
c Washington Monument The Mall National Gallery of Art U.S. Capitol
Tidal Basin Jefferson Memorial Smithsonian Hirshhorn Museum
SOUTH WEST FREEWAY South West Navy Yard

1 2 3

INDEX TO CITY MAPS

The index contains the names of all the principal places and features shown on the City Maps. Each name is followed by an additional entry in italics giving the name of the City Map within which it is located.

The number in bold type which follows each name refers to the number of the City Map page where that feature or place will be found.

The letter and figure which are immediately after the page number give the grid square on the map within which the feature or place is situated.

The letter represents the latitude and the figure the longitude. The full geographic reference is provided in the border of the City Maps.

The location given is the centre of the city, suburb or feature and is not necessarily the name. Rivers, canals and roads are indexed to their name. Rivers carry the symbol ➔ after their name.

An explanation of the alphabetical order rules and a list of the abbreviations used are to be found at the beginning of the World Map Index.

A

Aaläm *Baghdad* 3 B2
Aalsmeer *Amsterdam* 2 B1
Abbey Wood *London* 15 B4
Abcoude *Amsterdam* 2 B2
Âbdin *Cairo* 7 A2
Abeno *Osaka* 23 B2
Aberdeen *Hong Kong* 12 B2
Aberdour *Edinburgh* 11 A2
Aberdour Castle *Edinburgh* 11 A3
Abfanggraben ➔ *Munich* 21 A3
Ablon-sur-Seine *Paris* 24 B3
Abramtsevo *Moscow* 19 B3
Abu Dis *Jerusalem* 13 B2
Abū en Numrus *Cairo* 7 B2
Abu Ghosh *Jerusalem* 13 B1
Abu Hail *Dubai* 9 A2
Acassuso *Buenos Aires* 7 A2
Achères *Paris* 24 A1
Acília *Rome* 26 C1
Aclimação *São Paulo* 27 B2
Acropolis *Athens* 2 B2
Acton *London* 15 A2
Açúcar, Pão de
 Rio de Janeiro 25 B2
Ada Beja *Lisbon* 16 A1
Adams Park *Atlanta* 3 B2
Addiscombe *London* 15 B3
Adelphi *Washington* 33 A3
Aderklaa *Vienna* 32 A3
Adler Planetarium *Chicago* 9 B3
Admiralteyskaya Storona
 St. Petersburg 27 B2
Àffori *Milan* 18 A2
Aflandshage *Copenhagen* 8 B3
Afsariyeh *Tehran* 31 B2
Agboyi Cr. ➔ *Lagos* 14 A2
Agerup *Copenhagen* 8 A1
Agesta *Stockholm* 29 B2
Aghia Marina *Athens* 2 C3
Aghia Paraskevi *Athens* 2 A2
Aghios Dimitrios *Athens* 2 B2
Aghios Ioannis Rendis
 Athens 2 B2
Agincourt *Toronto* 31 A3
Agra Canal *Delhi* 10 B2
Agricola Oriental
 Mexico City 18 B2
Água Espraiada ➔
 São Paulo 27 B2
Agualva-Cacem *Lisbon* 16 A1
Ahrensfelde *Berlin* 5 A4
Ahuntsic *Montreal* 20 A1
Ai ➔ *Osaka* 23 A2
Aigremont *Paris* 24 A1
Air View Park *Singapore* 28 A2
Airport West *Melbourne* 18 A1
Ajegunle *Lagos* 14 B2
Aji *Osaka* 23 A1
Ajuda *Lisbon* 16 A1
Akalla *Stockholm* 29 A1
Akasaka *Tokyo* 30 A3
Akbarābād *Tehran* 31 A2
Akershus Slott *Oslo* 23 A3
Al 'Azamīyah *Baghdad* 3 A2
Al Bada *Dubai* 9 B2
Al Barsha *Dubai* 9 B1
Al Hamriya Port *Dubai* 9 A2
Al Hudaiba *Dubai* 9 B2
Al Jafiliya *Dubai* 9 B2
Al Manara *Dubai* 9 B1
Al Mina *Dubai* 9 B2
Al Nasr *Dubai* 9 B2
Al Quds = Jerusalem
 Jerusalem 13 B2
Al Quoz *Dubai* 9 B1
Al Safa *Dubai* 9 B1
Al Satwa *Dubai* 9 B2
Al Sufouh *Dubai* 9 B1
Al Walaja *Jerusalem* 13 B1
Al Wasl *Dubai* 9 B2
Alaguntan *Lagos* 14 B2
Alameda *San Francisco* 26 B3
Alameda Memorial State
 Beach Park *San Francisco* 26 B3
Albern *Vienna* 32 B2
Albert Park *Melbourne* 18 B1
Alberton *Johannesburg* 13 B2
Albertslund *Copenhagen* 8 B2
Alcantara *Lisbon* 16 A1
Alcatraz I. *San Francisco* 26 B2
Alcobendas *Madrid* 17 A2
Alcorcón *Madrid* 17 B1
Aldershof *Berlin* 5 B4
Aldo Bonzi *Buenos Aires* 7 C1
Aleksandrovskoye
 St. Petersburg 27 B2
Alexander Nevsky Abbey
 St. Petersburg 27 B2
Alexandra *Johannesburg* 13 A2
Alexandra *Singapore* 28 B2
Alexandria *Washington* 33 C2
Alfortville *Paris* 24 B3
Algés *Lisbon* 16 A1
Algiers *New Orleans* 21 B2
Alhambra *Los Angeles* 16 B4
Alibey ➔ *Istanbul* 12 B1
Alibey Baraji *Istanbul* 12 B1
Alibeyköy *Istanbul* 12 B1
Alimos *Athens* 2 B2
Alipur *Kolkata* 14 B1
Allach *Munich* 21 A1
Allambie Heights *Sydney* 29 A2
Allermuir Hill *Edinburgh* 11 B2
Allston *Boston* 6 A2
Almada *Lisbon* 16 A2
Almagro *Buenos Aires* 7 B2
Almargem do Bispo *Lisbon* 16 A1

Almirante G. Brown,
 Parque *Buenos Aires* 7 C2
Almon *Jerusalem* 13 B2
Almond ➔ *Edinburgh* 11 B2
Alna *Oslo* 23 A4
Alnsjøen *Oslo* 23 A4
Alperton *London* 15 A2
Alpine *New York* 22 A2
Alrode *Johannesburg* 13 B2
Alsemberg *Brussels* 6 B2
Alsergrund *Vienna* 32 A2
Alsip *Chicago* 9 C2
Ålsten *Stockholm* 29 B1
Ålta *Stockholm* 29 B1
Altadena *Los Angeles* 16 A4
Alte-Donau ➔ *Vienna* 32 A2
Alter Finkenkrug *Berlin* 5 A1
Altes Rathaus *Munich* 21 B2
Altglienicke *Berlin* 5 B4
Altlandsberg *Berlin* 5 A5
Altlandsberg Nord *Berlin* 5 A5
Altmannsdorf *Vienna* 32 B1
Alto da Boa Vista
 Rio de Janeiro 25 B1
Alto da Mooca *São Paulo* 27 B2
Alto do Pina *Lisbon* 16 A2
Altona *Melbourne* 18 B1
Alvalade *Lisbon* 16 A2
Alvik *Stockholm* 29 B1
Alvin Callendar Naval Air
 Station *New Orleans* 21 B2
Älvsjö *Stockholm* 29 B2
Älvvik *Stockholm* 29 A3
Am Hasenbergl *Munich* 21 A2
Am Steinhof *Vienna* 32 A1
Am Wald *Munich* 21 B2
Ama Keng *Singapore* 28 A2
Amadora *Lisbon* 16 A1
Amagasaki *Osaka* 23 A1
Amager *Copenhagen* 8 B3
Amâl Qâdisiya *Baghdad* 3 B2
Amalienborg Slot *Copenhagen* 8 A3
Amata *Milan* 18 A1
Ambelokipi *Athens* 2 B2
Ameixoeira *Lisbon* 16 A2
Amelia Earhart Park *Miami* 19 C1
América *São Paulo* 27 B1
American Univ. *Washington* 33 B2
Amin *Baghdad* 3 B2
Aminadav *Jerusalem* 13 B1
Amirābād *Tehran* 31 A2
Amora *Lisbon* 16 A2
Amoreira *Lisbon* 16 A1
Amper ➔ *Munich* 21 A1
Amstel-Drecht-Kanaal
 Amsterdam 2 B2
Amstelveen *Amsterdam* 2 B2
Amsterdam *Amsterdam* 2 A2
Amsterdam ✈ (AMS)
 Amsterdam 2 B1
Amsterdam-Rijnkanaal
 Amsterdam 2 B3
Amsterdam Zuidoost
 Amsterdam 2 B2
Amsterdamse Bos
 Amsterdam 2 B1
Anacostia *Washington* 33 B3
Anacostia ➔ *Washington* 33 B3
Anadoluhisarı *Istanbul* 12 B2
Anadolukavağı *Istanbul* 12 A2
Anata *Jerusalem* 13 B2
Ancol *Jakarta* 12 A1
'Andalus *Baghdad* 3 B1
Andarai *Rio de Janeiro* 25 B1
Anderlecht *Brussels* 6 A1
Anderson Park *Atlanta* 3 B2
Andingmen *Beijing* 4 B2
Ang Mo Kio *Singapore* 28 A2
Ängby *Stockholm* 29 A1
Angel I. *San Francisco* 26 A2
Angel Island State Park △
 San Francisco 26 A2
Angke, Kali ➔ *Jakarta* 12 A1
Angyalföld *Budapest* 7 A2
Anik *Mumbai* 20 A2
Anin *Warsaw* 33 B2
Anjou *Montreal* 20 A2
Annalee Heights
 Washington 33 B1
Antony *Paris* 24 B2
Aoyama *Tokyo* 30 A3
Ap Lei Chau *Hong Kong* 12 B1
Apapa *Lagos* 14 B2
Apapa Quays *Lagos* 14 B2
Apelação *Lisbon* 16 A2
Apopka, L. *Orlando* 23 A1
Apoquindo *Santiago* 27 B2
Apterkarskiy Ostrov
 St. Petersburg 27 B2
Ar Kazimiyah *Baghdad* 3 B1
Ar Ram *Jerusalem* 13 B2
Ara ➔ *Tokyo* 30 A4
Arakawa *Tokyo* 30 A3
Arany-hegyi-patak ➔
 Budapest 7 A2
Aravaca *Madrid* 17 B1
Arbataash *Baghdad* 3 A1
Arc de Triomphe *Paris* 24 A2
Arcadia *Los Angeles* 16 B4
Arcueil *Paris* 24 B2
Arese *Milan* 18 A1
Arganzuela *Madrid* 17 B1
Argenteuil *Paris* 24 A2
Argiroupoli *Athens* 2 B2
Arima *Tokyo* 30 A3
Arlanda, Stockholm ✈
 (ARN) *Stockholm* 29 A2
Arlington *Boston* 6 A1
Arlington *Washington* 33 B2
Arlington Heights *Boston* 6 A1

Arlington Nat. Cemetery
 Washington 33 B2
Bagsværd Sø *Copenhagen* 8 A2
Armação *Rio de Janeiro* 25 B2
Armadale *Melbourne* 18 B2
Armour Heights *Toronto* 31 A2
Arncliffe *Sydney* 29 B1
Arnold Arboretum *Boston* 6 B2
Árpádföld *Budapest* 7 A3
Arrentela *Lisbon* 16 B2
Arroyo Seco Park
 Los Angeles 16 B3
Årsta *Stockholm* 29 B2
Artane *Dublin* 10 A2
Artas *Jerusalem* 13 B2
Arthur's Seat *Edinburgh* 11 B3
Arts, Place des *Montreal* 20 A2
As Shawawra *Jerusalem* 13 B2
Asagaya *Tokyo* 30 A2
Asahi *Osaka* 23 A2
Asakusa *Tokyo* 30 A3
Asati *Kolkata* 14 C1
Aschheim *Munich* 21 A3
Ascot Vale *Melbourne* 18 A1
Ashbridge's Bay Park
 Toronto 31 B3
Ashburn *Chicago* 9 C2
Ashburton *Melbourne* 18 B2
Ashfield *Sydney* 29 B1
Ashford *London* 15 B1
Ashtown *Dublin* 10 A2
Asisto *Helsinki* 11 B1
Askrikefjärden *Stockholm* 29 A3
Asnières *Paris* 24 A2
Aspern *Vienna* 32 A3
Assago *Milan* 18 B1
Assendelft *Amsterdam* 2 A1
Assiano *Milan* 18 B1
Astoria *New York* 22 B2
Astrolabe Park *Sydney* 29 B2
Atarot *Jerusalem* 13 A2
Atarot ✈ (JRS) *Jerusalem* 13 A2
Atghara *Kolkata* 14 B2
Athens = Athína *Athens* 2 B2
Athína *Athens* 2 B2
Athína ✈ (ATH) *Athens* 2 A3
Athinai = Athína *Athens* 2 B2
Athis-Mons *Paris* 24 B3
Athlone *Cape Town* 8 A2
Atholl *Johannesburg* 13 A2
Atifiya *Baghdad* 3 B2
Atişalen *Istanbul* 12 B1
Atlanta *Atlanta* 3 B2
Atlanta Hartsfield-Jackson
 Int. ✈ (ATL) *Atlanta* 3 C2
Atlanta History Center
 Atlanta 3 B2
Atlanta Zoo *Atlanta* 3 B2
Atomium *Brussels* 6 A2
Attiki *Athens* 2 B2
Atzgersdorf *Vienna* 32 B1
Aubervilliers *Paris* 24 A3
Aubing *Munich* 21 B1
Auburndale *Boston* 6 A1
Auchendinny *Edinburgh* 11 B2
Auckland Park
 Johannesburg 13 B2
Auderghem *Brussels* 6 B2
Audubon Park *New Orleans* 21 B2
Augustówka *Warsaw* 33 B2
Aulnay-sous-Bois *Paris* 24 A3
Aurelio *Rome* 26 B1
Ausím *Cairo* 7 A1
Austerlitz, Gare d' *Paris* 24 A3
Austin *Chicago* 9 B2
Avedøre *Copenhagen* 8 B2
Avellaneda *Buenos Aires* 7 C2
Avenel *Washington* 33 B3
Aventura *Miami* 19 C3
Avondale *Chicago* 9 B2
Avondale *New Orleans* 21 B1
Avondale Heights
 Melbourne 18 A1
Avtovo *St. Petersburg* 27 B1
Ayazağa *Istanbul* 12 B1
Ayer Chawan, Pulau
 Singapore 28 B2
Ayer Merbau, Pulau
 Singapore 28 B2
Azabu *Tokyo* 30 B3
Azcapotzalco *Mexico City* 18 B1
Azteca, Estadia *Mexico City* 18 C2
Azucar, Cerro Pan de
 Santiago 27 B2

B

Baambrugge *Amsterdam* 2 B2
Baba Channel *Karachi* 13 B1
Baba I. *Karachi* 13 B1
Babarpur *Delhi* 10 A2
Babushkin *Moscow* 19 A3
Back B. *Mumbai* 20 B1
Baclaran *Manila* 17 C1
Bacoor B. *Manila* 17 C1
Badalona *Barcelona* 4 A2
Badhoevedorp *Amsterdam* 2 A1
Badli *Delhi* 10 A1
Bærum *Oslo* 23 A2
Bağcılar *Istanbul* 12 B1
Bağgio *Milan* 18 B1
Bāgh-e-Feyz *Tehran* 31 A1
Baghdād *Baghdad* 3 B2
Baghdād al Muthana ✈
 (BGW) *Baghdad* 3 B2
Baghdad Int. ✈ (SDA)
 Baghdad 3 B1
Bagmari *Kolkata* 14 B2
Bagneux *Paris* 24 B2
Bagnolet *Paris* 24 A3

Bagsværd *Copenhagen* 8 A2
Baguiati *Kolkata* 14 B2
Bagumbayan *Manila* 17 C2
Baha'i Temple *Chicago* 9 A2
Bahçeköy *Istanbul* 12 A1
Bahçelievler *Istanbul* 12 B1
Bahtîm *Cairo* 7 A2
Baile Átha Cliath = Dublin
 Dublin 10 A2
Baileys Crossroads
 Washington 33 B2
Bailly *Paris* 24 A1
Bairro Lopes *Lisbon* 16 A2
Baisha *Guangzhou* 11 B2
Baiyun *Guangzhou* 11 A2
Baiyun Mountain Scenic
 Area *Guangzhou* 11 A2
Bakırköy *Istanbul* 12 C1
Bal Harbor *Miami* 19 C3
Balara *Manila* 17 B2
Baldia *Karachi* 13 A1
Baldoyle *Dublin* 10 A3
Baldwin, L. *Orlando* 23 A3
Baldwin Hills *Los Angeles* 16 B2
Baldwin Hills Res.
 Los Angeles 16 B2
Balgowlah *Sydney* 29 A2
Balgowlah Heights *Sydney* 29 A2
Balham *London* 15 B3
Bali *Kolkata* 14 B1
Baliganja *Kolkata* 14 B2
Balingsnäs *Stockholm* 29 B3
Balingsta *Stockholm* 29 A2
Balintawak *Manila* 17 B1
Ballerup *Copenhagen* 8 A2
Ballinteer *Dublin* 10 B2
Ballyboden *Dublin* 10 B1
Ballybrack *Dublin* 10 B3
Ballyfermot *Dublin* 10 A1
Ballymorefinn Hill *Dublin* 10 B1
Ballymun *Dublin* 10 A2
Balmain *Sydney* 29 B2
Baluhati *Kolkata* 14 B1
Balvanera *Buenos Aires* 7 B2
Balwyn *Melbourne* 18 A2
Balwyn North *Melbourne* 18 A2
Banana Island *Lagos* 14 B2
Banática *Lisbon* 16 A1
Bandra *Mumbai* 20 A1
Bandra Pt. *Mumbai* 20 A1
Bang Kapi *Bangkok* 3 B2
Bang Na *Bangkok* 3 B2
Bangbae *Seoul* 27 C1
Bangkhen *Bangkok* 3 A2
Bangkok *Bangkok* 3 B2
Bangkok Don Muang
 Int. ✈ (BKK) *Bangkok* 3 A2
Bangkok Noi *Bangkok* 3 B1
Bangkok Yai *Bangkok* 3 B1
Banglo *Kolkata* 14 B1
Bangrak *Bangkok* 3 B2
Bangsu *Bangkok* 3 B2
Banks, C. *Sydney* 29 C2
Banksmeadow *Sydney* 29 B2
Banstala *Kolkata* 14 B2
Bantra *Kolkata* 14 B1
Baoshan *Shanghai* 28 A1
Bar Giyora *Jerusalem* 13 B1
Barahanagar *Kolkata* 14 B2
Barajas *Madrid* 17 B2
Barajas, Madrid ✈ (MAD)
 Madrid 17 B2
Barakpur *Kolkata* 14 B2
Barcarena *Lisbon* 16 A1
Barcarena, Rib. de ➔
 Lisbon 16 A1
Barcelona *Barcelona* 4 A2
Barcelona ✈ (BCN) *Barcelona* 4 B1
Barcroft, L. *Washington* 33 B2
Barking *London* 15 A4
Barkingside *London* 15 A4
Barnes *London* 15 B2
Barnet *London* 15 A2
Barra Andai *Karachi* 13 B2
Barra Funda *São Paulo* 27 B2
Barracas *Buenos Aires* 7 B2
Barrackpur = Barakpur
 Kolkata 14 A2
Barranco *Lima* 34 B2
Barreiro *Lisbon* 16 B2
Barreto *Rio de Janeiro* 25 B2
Bartala *Kolkata* 14 B2
Barton Park *Sydney* 29 B1
Bartyki *Warsaw* 33 C2
Basus *Cairo* 7 A2
Batanagar *Kolkata* 14 B1
Bath Beach *New York* 22 C1
Bath I. *Karachi* 13 B2
Batir *Jerusalem* 13 B1
Batok, Bukit *Singapore* 28 A2
Battersea *London* 15 B3
Bauman *Moscow* 19 B3
Baumgarten *Vienna* 32 A1
Bay, L. *Orlando* 23 A2
Bay Harbor Islands *Miami* 19 C3
Bay Hill *Orlando* 23 A2
Bay Ridge *New York* 22 C1
Bayit Va-Gan *Jerusalem* 13 B2
Bayonne *New York* 22 B1
Bayou Boeuf *New Orleans* 21 A1
Bayou Segnette State
 Park △ *New Orleans* 21 B1
Bayrampaşa *Istanbul* 12 B1
Bayshore *San Francisco* 26 B2
Bayt Lahm *Jerusalem* 13 B2
Bayview *San Francisco* 26 B2
Bāzār *Tehran* 31 A2
Beacon Hill *Hong Kong* 12 A2
Beato *Lisbon* 16 A2
Beaumont *Dublin* 10 A2

Beaumonte Heights *Toronto* 31 A1
Bebek *Istanbul* 12 B2
Běchovice *Prague* 25 B3
Beckenham *London* 15 B3
Beckton *London* 15 A4
Becontree *London* 15 A4
Beddington Corner *London* 15 B3
Bedford *Boston* 6 A1
Bedford Park *Chicago* 9 C2
Bedford Park *New York* 22 A2
Bedford Stuyvesant
 New York 22 B2
Bedford View *Johannesburg* 13 B2
Bedok *Singapore* 28 B3
Bedok, Res. *Singapore* 28 A3
Beersel *Brussels* 6 B1
Behala *Kolkata* 14 B1
Bei Hai *Beijing* 4 B2
Beicai *Shanghai* 28 B2
Beijing *Beijing* 4 B1
Beit Duqu *Jerusalem* 13 A1
Beit Ghur at-Taht *Jerusalem* 13 A1
Beit Ghur el-Fawqa
 Jerusalem 13 A1
Beit Hanina *Jerusalem* 13 B2
Beit Ij'za *Jerusalem* 13 A1
Beit Iksa *Jerusalem* 13 B2
Beit I'nan *Jerusalem* 13 A1
Beit Jala *Jerusalem* 13 B2
Beit Lekhem = Bayt Lahm
 Jerusalem 13 B2
Beit Liqya *Jerusalem* 13 A1
Beit Nekofa *Jerusalem* 13 B1
Beit Safafa *Jerusalem* 13 B2
Beit Surik *Jerusalem* 13 B1
Beit Ur al-Fawqa *Jerusalem* 13 A1
Beit Zayit *Jerusalem* 13 B1
Beitaipingzhuan *Beijing* 4 B1
Beitar Ilit *Jerusalem* 13 B1
Beitin *Jerusalem* 13 A2
Beitsun *Guangzhou* 11 B2
Beitunya *Jerusalem* 13 A2
Beixing Jing Park *Shanghai* 28 B1
Bèkásmegyer *Budapest* 7 A2
Bekkelaget *Oslo* 23 A4
Bekkestua *Oslo* 23 A2
Bel Air *Los Angeles* 16 B2
Bela Vista *São Paulo* 27 B2
Bélanger *Montreal* 20 A1
Belas *Lisbon* 16 A1
Beleghata *Kolkata* 14 B2
Belém *Lisbon* 16 A1
Belém, Torre de *Lisbon* 16 A1
Belènzinho *São Paulo* 27 B2
Belgachiya *Kolkata* 14 B2
Belgharia *Kolkata* 14 B2
Belgrano *Buenos Aires* 7 B2
Bell *Los Angeles* 16 C3
Bell Gardens *Los Angeles* 16 C4
Bellavista *Lima* 34 B2
Bellavista *Santiago* 27 C2
Belle Harbor *New York* 22 C2
Bellingham *London* 15 B3
Belmont *Boston* 6 A1
Belmont *London* 15 A2
Belmont *London* 15 B4
Belmont Cragin *Chicago* 9 B2
Belmont Harbor *Chicago* 9 B3
Belmore *Sydney* 29 B1
Belur *Kolkata* 14 B1
Belvedere *London* 15 B4
Belvedere *San Francisco* 26 A2
Belvedere Park *Atlanta* 3 B3
Belyayevo Bogorodskoye
 Moscow 19 B3
Bemowo *Warsaw* 33 B1
Benaki Museum *Athens* 2 B2
Bendale *Toronto* 31 A3
Benefica *Rio de Janeiro* 25 B1
Benfica *Lisbon* 16 A1
Benitez Int. ✈ (SCL)
 Santiago 27 B1
Benito Juárez, Int. ✈
 (MEX) *Mexico City* 18 B2
Bensonhurst *New York* 22 C2
Berchem-Ste-Agathe
 Brussels 6 A1
Berg am Laim *Munich* 21 B2
Bergenfield *New York* 22 A2
Bergham *Munich* 21 B3
Bergvliet *Cape Town* 8 B1
Beri *Barcelona* 4 A1
Berkeley *San Francisco* 26 A3
Berlin *Berlin* 5 A3
Berlin Brandenburg ✈
 (BER) *Berlin* 5 B4
Berlin Dom *Berlin* 5 A3
Bermondsey *London* 15 B3
Bernabeu, Estadio *Madrid* 17 B1
Bernal Heights
 San Francisco 26 B2
Berwyn *Chicago* 9 B2
Berwyn Heights *Washington* 33 B3
Beşiktaş *Istanbul* 12 B2
Besòs ➔ *Barcelona* 4 A2
Bessie, L. *Orlando* 23 B1
Bet Horon *Jerusalem* 13 A1
Bethesda *Washington* 33 B2
Bethlehem = Bayt Lahm
 Jerusalem 13 B2
Bethnal Green *London* 15 A3
Betor *Kolkata* 14 B1
Beulah *Orlando* 23 A1
Beulah, L. *Orlando* 23 A1
Beverley Hills *Sydney* 29 B1
Beverley Park *Sydney* 29 B1
Beverly *Chicago* 9 C2
Beverly Arts Center *Chicago* 9 C2
Beverly Glen *Los Angeles* 16 B2
Beverly Hills *Los Angeles* 16 B2

Beverly Hills -Morgan
 Park Historic District
 Chicago 9 C2
Beverly Hills *Sydney* 29 B1
Bexley *Sydney* 29 B1
Bexley *London* 15 B4
Bexleyheath *London* 15 B4
Beykoz *Istanbul* 12 B2
Beylerbeyi *Istanbul* 12 B2
Beyoğlu *Istanbul* 12 B1
Bezons *Paris* 24 A2
Bezuidenhout Park
 Johannesburg 13 B2
Bhadrakali *Kolkata* 14 A2
Bhalswa *Delhi* 10 A2
Bhambo Khan Qarmati
 Karachi 13 B2
Bhatsala *Kolkata* 14 B1
Bhawanipur *Kolkata* 14 B2
Bhendkhal *Mumbai* 20 A2
Bhit I. *Jerusalem* 13 B1
Bhuleshwar *Mumbai* 20 B1
Białoleka Dworska *Warsaw* 33 B2
Bicentennial Park
 Los Angeles 16 B4
Bicentennial Park *Sydney* 29 B1
Bickley *London* 15 B4
Bicutan *Manila* 17 C2
Bidhan Nagar *Kolkata* 14 B2
Bidu *Jerusalem* 13 B1
Bielany *Warsaw* 33 B1
Bielawa *Warsaw* 33 C2
Biesdorf *Berlin* 5 A4
Bièvre ➔ *Paris* 24 B1
Bièvres *Paris* 24 B2
Big Sand L. *Orlando* 23 B2
Bill Baggs Cape Florida
 State Recr. Area △
 Miami 19 D3
Bilston *Edinburgh* 11 B2
Binacayan *Manila* 17 C1
Binondo *Manila* 17 B1
Bintaro Jaya *Jakarta* 12 B1
Bir Nabala *Jerusalem* 13 B1
Birak el Kiyam *Cairo* 7 A1
Birch Cliff *Toronto* 31 A3
Birkenstein *Berlin* 5 A5
Birkholz *Berlin* 5 A4
Birkholzaue *Berlin* 5 A4
Birrarrung Park *Melbourne* 18 A2
Biscayne Bay Aquatic
 Reserve *Miami* 19 C2
Biscayne Park *Miami* 19 C2
Bishop Lavis *Cape Town* 8 A2
Bishopscourt *Cape Town* 8 A1
Bispebjerg *Copenhagen* 8 A3
Bissonet Plaza *New Orleans* 21 A1
Bittsevsky Forest Park
 Moscow 19 C2
Björknas *Stockholm* 29 B3
Black Cr. ➔ *Toronto* 31 A2
Black Creek Pioneer
 Village *Toronto* 31 A1
Blackfen *London* 15 B4
Blackheath *London* 15 B4
Blackrock *Dublin* 10 B2
Bladensburg *Washington* 33 B3
Blair Village *Atlanta* 3 C2
Blairgowrie *Johannesburg* 13 A2
Blake House *Boston* 6 B2
Blakehurst *Sydney* 29 B1
Blakstad *Oslo* 23 B1
Blanche, L. *Orlando* 23 B1
Blankenburg *Berlin* 5 A3
Blankenfelde *Berlin* 5 A3
Blizne *Warsaw* 33 B1
Blota *Warsaw* 33 C1
Blue Island *Chicago* 9 D2
Blue Lagoon L. *Miami* 19 D1
Blue Mosque =
 Sultanahme Camil
 Istanbul 12 B1
Bluebell *Dublin* 10 B1
Bluff Hd. *Hong Kong* 12 B2
Bluffers Park *Toronto* 31 A3
Blumberg *Berlin* 5 A4
Blunt Pt. *San Francisco* 26 A2
Blutenberg *Munich* 21 B1
Blylaget *Oslo* 23 B3
Boa Vista, Alto do
 Rio de Janeiro 25 B1
Boardwalk *New York* 22 C3
Boavista *Lisbon* 16 A2
Bobigny *Paris* 24 A3
Bocanegra *Lima* 34 B2
Boedo *Buenos Aires* 7 B2
Bogenhausen *Munich* 21 B2
Bogorodskoye *Moscow* 19 B3
Bogota *New York* 22 A1
Bogstadvatnet *Oslo* 23 A2
Bohnsdorf *Berlin* 5 B4
Bois-Colombes *Paris* 24 A2
Bois-d'Arcy *Paris* 24 B1
Boissy-St-Léger *Paris* 24 B4
Boldinasco *Milan* 18 B1
Bøler *Oslo* 23 A4
Bollate *Milan* 18 A1
Bollebeek *Brussels* 6 A1
Bollensdorf *Berlin* 5 A5
Bollmora *Stockholm* 29 B3
Bolshaya Okhta
 St. Petersburg 27 B2
Bolton *Milan* 18 A2
Bom Retiro *São Paulo* 27 B2
Bombay = Mumbai
 Mumbai 20 B2
Bondi *Sydney* 29 B2
Bondi Beach *Sydney* 29 B2
Bondy *Paris* 24 A3
Bondy, Forêt de ➔ *Paris* 24 A4
Bonifacio Monument
 Manila 17 B1
Bonnabel Place *New Orleans* 21 A2

Bonneuil-sur-Marne *Paris* 24 B4
Bonnington *Edinburgh* 11 B1
Bonnyrigg and Lasswade
 Edinburgh 11 B3
Bonsucesso *Rio de Janeiro* 25 B1
Bonteheuwel *Cape Town* 8 A2
Boo *Stockholm* 29 A3
Booterstown *Dublin* 10 B2
Borisovo *Moscow* 19 C3
Borle *Mumbai* 20 A2
Boronia Park *Sydney* 29 A1
Bosmont *Johannesburg* 13 B1
Bosön *Stockholm* 29 A3
Bosporus = İstanbul
 Boğazı *Istanbul* 12 B2
Bostancı *Istanbul* 12 C2
Boston *Boston* 6 A2
Boston Common *Boston* 6 A2
Boston Logan Int. ✈ (BOS)
 Boston 6 A2
Botafogo *Rio de Janeiro* 25 B1
Botany *Sydney* 29 B2
Botany B. *Sydney* 29 B2
Botany Bay △ *Sydney* 29 B2
Botič ➔ *Prague* 25 B3
Botica Sete *Lisbon* 16 A1
Boucherville *Montreal* 20 A3
Boucherville, Îs. de
 Montreal 20 A3
Bougival *Paris* 24 A1
Boulder Pt. *Hong Kong* 12 B1
Boulogne, Bois de *Paris* 24 A2
Boulogne-Billancourt *Paris* 24 A2
Bourg-la-Reine *Paris* 24 B2
Bouviers *Paris* 24 B1
Bovenkerk *Amsterdam* 2 B2
Bovenkerker Polder
 Amsterdam 2 B2
Bovisa *Milan* 18 A2
Bow *London* 15 A3
Boyacıköy *Istanbul* 12 B2
Boyd Conservation Area
 Toronto 31 A1
Boyle Heights *Los Angeles* 16 B3
Braepark *Edinburgh* 11 B2
Braid *Edinburgh* 11 B2
Bramley *Johannesburg* 13 A2
Brandeis Univ. *Boston* 6 A1
Brandenburger Tor *Berlin* 5 A3
Brani, Pulau *Singapore* 28 B3
Branik *Prague* 25 B2
Brännkyrka *Stockholm* 29 B2
Brás *São Paulo* 27 B2
Brasilândia *São Paulo* 27 A1
Brateyevo *Moscow* 19 C3
Braybrook *Melbourne* 18 A1
Brázdim *Prague* 25 A3
Breakheart Reservation
 Boston 6 A2
Brede *Copenhagen* 8 A2
Breezy Point *New York* 22 C2
Breitenlee *Vienna* 32 A3
Breña *Lima* 34 B2
Brent □ *London* 15 A2
Brent Res. *London* 15 A2
Brentford *London* 15 B2
Brentwood *Los Angeles* 16 B2
Brentwood Park *Los Angeles* 16 B2
Brera *Milan* 18 B2
Bresso *Milan* 18 A2
Brevik *Stockholm* 29 A3
Břevnov *Prague* 25 B2
Brickyard, The *Chicago* 9 B2
Bridge City *New Orleans* 21 B2
Bridgeport *Chicago* 9 B3
Bridgeview *Chicago* 9 C2
Brighton *Cape Town* 8 A2
Brighton *Melbourne* 18 B1
Brighton Beach *New York* 22 C2
Brighton Park *Chicago* 9 C2
Brighton-Le-Sands *Sydney* 29 B1
Brightwood *Washington* 33 B2
Brigittenau *Vienna* 32 A2
Brimbank Park *Melbourne* 18 A1
Brisbane *San Francisco* 26 B2
Britz *Berlin* 5 B3
Brixton *London* 15 B3
Broadmeadows *Melbourne* 18 A1
Broadmoor *San Francisco* 26 B2
Broadview *Chicago* 9 B1
Broadview Park *Miami* 19 B2
Brockley *London* 15 B3
Bródno *Warsaw* 33 B2
Bródnowski, Kanal *Warsaw* 33 B2
Broek *Amsterdam* 2 B2
Bromley □ *London* 15 B4
Bromley Common *London* 15 B4
Bromma *Stockholm* 29 A1
Bromma ✈ (BMA)
 Stockholm 29 A1
Brøndby Strand *Copenhagen* 8 B2
Brøndbyøster *Copenhagen* 8 B2
Brøndbyvester *Copenhagen* 8 B2
Brondesbury *London* 15 A2
Brønnøya *Oslo* 23 B2
Brønshøj *Copenhagen* 8 A2
Bronxville *New York* 22 A2
Brookfield Zoo *Chicago* 9 B1
Brookhaven *Atlanta* 3 A2
Brookline *Boston* 6 B2
Brooklyn *Cape Town* 8 A1
Brooklyn = Kolkata *Kolkata* 14 B2
Brooklyn *New York* 22 C2
Brooklyn Heights *New York* 22 B2
Brookmont *Washington* 33 B2
Brossard *Montreal* 20 B4
Brou-sur-Chantereine *Paris* 24 A4
Brown *Toronto* 31 A2
Brownsville *Miami* 19 D1
Brughério *Milan* 18 A2
Brunswick *Melbourne* 18 A1

Brussegem *Brussels* 6 A1
Brussel *Brussels* 6 A2
Brussel ✈ (BRU) *Brussels* 6 A2
Brussels = Brussel *Brussels* 6 A2
Bruxelles = Brussel *Brussels* 6 A2
Bruzzano *Milan* 18 A2
Bry-sur-Marne *Paris* 24 A4
Bryan, L. *Orlando* 23 B2
Bryanston *Johannesburg* 13 A1
Bryn *Oslo* 23 A4
Brzeziny *Warsaw* 33 B2
Bubeneč *Prague* 25 B2
Buc *Paris* 24 B1
Buchenhain *Munich* 21 B1
Buchholz *Berlin* 5 A3
Buckhead *Atlanta* 3 A2
Buckingham Palace *London* 15 A3
Buckow *Berlin* 5 B3
Bucktown *New Orleans* 21 A2
Buda *Budapest* 7 A2
Buda Castle =
 Budaváripalota *Budapest* 7 A2
Budafok *Budapest* 7 B2
Budaörs *Budapest* 7 B1
Budapest *Budapest* 7 B2
Budapest ✈ (BUD) *Budapest* 7 B3
Budatétény *Budapest* 7 B2
Budaváripalota *Budapest* 7 A2
Buddinge *Copenhagen* 8 A3
Buenos Aires *Buenos Aires* 7 B2
Buenos Aires Ezeiza ✈
 (EZE) *Buenos Aires* 7 C1
Bufalotta *Rome* 26 B2
Bugio *Lisbon* 16 B1
Buiksloot *Amsterdam* 2 A2
Buitenveldert *Amsterdam* 2 B2
Buizingen *Brussels* 6 B1
Bukhansan *Seoul* 27 B1
Bukit Panjang *Singapore* 28 A2
Bukit Panjang Nature
 Reserve *Singapore* 28 A2
Bukit Timah Nature
 Reserve *Singapore* 28 A2
Bukum, Pulau *Singapore* 28 B2
Bûlâq *Cairo* 7 A2
Bule *Manila* 17 C2
Bullen Park *Melbourne* 18 A2
Bund, The *Shanghai* 28 B1
Bundoora North *Melbourne* 18 A2
Bundoora Park *Melbourne* 18 A2
Bunker Hill Memorial
 Boston 6 A2
Bunker I. *Karachi* 13 B1
Bunkyō *Tokyo* 30 A3
Bunnefjorden *Oslo* 23 A3
Buona Vista Park *Singapore* 28 B2
Bur Dubai *Dubai* 9 B2
Burbank *Chicago* 9 C2
Burbank *Los Angeles* 16 B3
Burden, L. *Orlando* 23 B1
Burj Al Arab *Dubai* 9 B1
Burj Dubai *Dubai* 9 B2
Burlington *Boston* 6 A1
Burnham Park *Chicago* 9 C3
Burnham Park Harbor
 Chicago 9 B3
Burnhamthorpe *Toronto* 31 B1
Burnt Oak *London* 15 A2
Burntisland *Edinburgh* 11 A2
Burnwynd *Edinburgh* 11 B1
Burqa *Jerusalem* 13 A2
Burtus *Cairo* 7 A1
Burudvatn *Oslo* 23 A2
Burwood *Sydney* 29 B1
Bushwick *New York* 22 B2
Bushy Park *London* 15 B1
Business Bay *Dubai* 9 B2
Butantã *São Paulo* 27 B1
Butcher I. *Mumbai* 20 A2
Butler, L. *Orlando* 23 B1
Büyükdere *Istanbul* 12 B2
Byculla *Mumbai* 20 B2
Bygdøy *Oslo* 23 A3
Bywater *New Orleans* 21 B2

C

C.B.S. Fox Studios
 Los Angeles 16 B2
C.N. Tower *Toronto* 31 B2
Caballito *Buenos Aires* 7 B2
Cabin John *Washington* 33 B1
Cabin John Regional
 Park △ *Washington* 33 A1
Cabinteely *Dublin* 10 B3
Cabra *Dublin* 10 A2
Cabuçú de Baixo ➔
 São Paulo 27 A1
Cabuçú de Cima ➔
 São Paulo 27 A2
Cachan *Paris* 24 B2
Cachoeira, Rib. da ➔
 São Paulo 27 B2
Cacilhas *Lisbon* 16 A2
Cahuenga Park *Los Angeles* 16 B3
Cain, L. *Orlando* 23 B2
Cairo = El Qâhira *Cairo* 7 A2
Cairo Int. ✈ (CAI) *Cairo* 7 A3
Caju *Rio de Janeiro* 25 B1
Čakovice *Prague* 25 B3
Calcutta = Kolkata *Kolkata* 14 B2
California Inst. of Tech.
 Los Angeles 16 B4
California Los Angeles,
 Univ. of *Los Angeles* 16 B2
California State Univ.
 Los Angeles 16 B4
Callao *Lima* 34 B2
Caloocan *Manila* 17 B1
Calumet, L. *Chicago* 9 C3

Calumet City Chicago 9 D3
Calumet Park Chicago 9 C3
Calumet Sag Channel → Chicago 9 C2
Calvairate Milan 18 B2
Camarate Lisbon 16 A2
Camaroes Lisbon 16 A1
Camberwell London 15 B3
Camberwell Melbourne 18 B2
Cambridge Boston 6 A2
Cambuci São Paulo 27 B2
Camden □ London 15 A3
Çamlıca Istanbul 12 B2
Camp Springs Washington 33 C3
Campamento Madrid 17 B1
Campbellfield Melbourne 18 A1
Camperdown Sydney 29 B2
Campo, Casa de Madrid 17 B1
Campo F.C. Barcelona Barcelona 4 A1
Campo Grande Lisbon 16 A2
Campo Pequeño Lisbon 16 A2
Campolide Lisbon 16 A2
Camps Bay Cape Town 8 A1
C'an San Joan Barcelona 4 A2
Cañacao B. Manila 17 C1
Canarsie New York 22 C2
Canary Wharf London 15 A3
Candiac Montreal 20 B3
Caneças Lisbon 16 A1
Canillas Madrid 17 B2
Canillejas Madrid 17 B2
Canning Town London 15 A4
Canteras de Vallecas Madrid 17 B2
Canterbury Melbourne 18 A2
Canterbury Sydney 29 B1
Canton = Guangzhou Guangzhou 11 B2
Canton Tower Guangzhou 11 B2
Caoheijing Shanghai 28 B1
Capão Redondo São Paulo 27 B1
Caparica Lisbon 16 A2
Caparica, Costa da Lisbon 16 B1
Cape Flats Cape Town 8 B2
Cape Town Cape Town 8 A1
Cape Town Int. ✕ (CPT) Cape Town 8 A2
Capitol Heights Washington 33 B3
Captain Cook Bridge Sydney 29 C1
Captain Cook Landing Place Park Sydney 29 C2
Capuchos Lisbon 16 B1
Carabanchel Alto Madrid 17 B1
Carabanchel Bajo Madrid 17 B1
Carapachay Buenos Aires 7 B1
Caraza Buenos Aires 7 C2
Caridad Manila 17 C1
Carioca, Sa. da Rio de Janeiro 25 B1
Carlstadt New York 22 A1
Carlton Melbourne 18 A1
Carlton Gardens Melbourne 18 A1
Carmen de Huechuraba Santiago 27 B1
Carmen de la Legua -Reynosa Lima 14 B2
Carnaxide Lisbon 16 A1
Carnegie Melbourne 18 B2
Carnide Lisbon 16 A1
Carol City Miami 19 C1
Carrollton New Orleans 21 B2
Carrascal Santiago 27 B1
Carrickmines Dublin 10 B3
Carrières-sous-Bois Paris 24 A1
Carrières-sous-Poissy Paris 24 A1
Carrières-sur-Seine Paris 24 A2
Carrigeen B. Dublin 10 A3
Cartierville Montreal 20 A1
Casa Loma Toronto 31 A2
Casa Verde São Paulo 27 A1
Casal da Mira Lisbon 16 A1
Casal Morena Rome 26 C2
Casalotti Rome 26 B1
Cascade Heights Atlanta 3 B2
Castèl di Leva Rome 26 C2
Castèl Sant'Angelo Rome 26 B1
Castleknock Dublin 10 A1
Castleton Corners New York 22 C1
Cataouatche, L. New Orleans 21 B1
Catete Rio de Janeiro 25 B1
Catford London 15 B3
Catherine, L. Orlando 23 B2
Caulfield Melbourne 18 B2
Cavite Manila 17 C1
Caxias Lisbon 16 A1
Cebecci Istanbul 12 B1
Cecchignola Rome 26 C2
Cecilienhof, Schloss Berlin 5 B1
Cedar Grove Atlanta 3 C3
Cedarvale Park Toronto 31 A2
Cempaka Putih Jakarta 12 B2
Çengelköy Istanbul 12 B2
Cengkareng Jakarta 12 A1
Centennial Olympic Park Atlanta 3 B2
Centennial Park Sydney 29 B2
Center Hill Atlanta 3 B2
Centocelle Rome 26 B2
Central, Gare Montreal 20 B2
Central Park New York 22 B2
Century City Los Angeles 16 B2
Cerdanyola del Vallès Barcelona 4 A1
Cerillos Santiago 27 B1
Cerro de la Estrella △ Mexico City 18 B2
Cerro de los Angeles Madrid 17 C1
Cerro Navia Santiago 27 B1
Cesano Boscone Milan 18 B1
Cesate Milan 18 A1
Cha Kwo Ling Hong Kong 12 B2
Chacarita Buenos Aires 7 B2
Chadwell Heath London 15 A4
Chai Chee Singapore 28 B3
Chai Wan Hong Kong 12 B2
Chai Wan Kok Hong Kong 12 A1
Chaidari Athens 2 A1
Chakdaha Kolkata 14 C1
Chalandri Athens 2 A2
Chamartin Madrid 17 B1
Chamberi Madrid 17 B1
Chambourcy Paris 24 A1
Champigny-sur-Marne Paris 24 B4
Champlain, Pont Montreal 20 B2
Champs-sur-Marne Paris 24 A4
Chamrail Kolkata 14 B1
Chanakyapuri Delhi 10 B2
Chanditala Kolkata 14 A1
Changfeng Park Shanghai 28 B1
Changhai = Shanghai Shanghai 28 B2
Changi Singapore 28 A3
Changi, Singapore ✕ (SIN) Singapore 28 A3
Changning Shanghai 28 B1
Chantereine Paris 24 A4
Chantian Guangzhou 11 A2
Chaoyang Beijing 4 B2
Chaoyangmen Beijing 4 B2
Chapelizod Dublin 10 A1
Chapultepec, Bosque de Mexico City 18 B1
Chapultepec, Castillo de Mexico City 18 B1
Charenton-le-Pont Paris 24 B3
Charleroi, Kanal de → Brussels 6 B1
Charles Bridge = Karlův most Prague 25 B2
Charles Gates Dawes House Chicago 9 A2
Charlestown Boston 6 A2
Charlottenburg Berlin 5 A2
Charlottenburg, Schloss Berlin 5 A2
Charlottenlund Copenhagen 8 A3
Charlton London 15 B4
Charneca Lisbon 16 A2
Charneca Lisbon 16 B1
Chase, L. Orlando 23 B1
Châteaufort Paris 24 B1
Châtenay-Malabry Paris 24 B2
Chatham Chicago 9 C3
Châtillon Paris 24 B2
Chatou Paris 24 A1
Chatpur Kolkata 14 B2
Chatswood Sydney 29 A2
Chatuchak Bangkok 3 B2
Chatuchak Park Bangkok 3 B2
Chauki Karachi 13 A1
Chavarria Lima 14 B2
Chaville Paris 24 B2
Chayang Seoul 27 B2
Chelles Paris 24 A4
Chelles, Canal de Paris 24 A4
Chells-le-Pin ✕ Paris 24 A4
Chelsea Boston 6 A2
Chelsea London 15 B2
Chembur Mumbai 20 A2
Chengshousi Beijing 4 C2
Chennevières-sur-Marne Paris 24 B4
Cheongdam Seoul 27 B2
Cheonho Seoul 27 B2
Cheops Cairo 7 B1
Chertanovka → Moscow 19 C2
Chertanovo Moscow 19 C2
Cheryomushki Moscow 19 B2
Chestnut Hill Boston 6 B1
Cheung Sha Wan Hong Kong 12 A1
Cheverly Washington 33 B3
Chevilly-Larue Paris 24 B3
Cheviot Hills Los Angeles 16 B2
Chevy Chase Washington 33 B2
Chhatrapati Shivaji, Mumbai ✕ (BOM) Mumbai 20 A2
Chhatrapati Shivaji Terminus Mumbai 20 B2
Chia Keng Singapore 28 A3
Chiaravalle Milanese Milan 18 B2
Chicago Chicago 9 B3
Chicago, Univ. of Chicago 9 C3
Chicago Harbor Chicago 9 B3
Chicago Lawn Chicago 9 C2
Chicago Ridge Chicago 9 C2
Chicago River, North Branch → Chicago 9 B2
Chicago Sanitary and Ship Canal Chicago 9 C2
Chicago State Univ. Chicago 9 C3
Chienzui Guangzhou 11 A3
Chik Sha Hong Kong 12 B2
Child's Hill London 15 A2
Chile, Univ. de Santiago 27 B2
Chilla Saroda Delhi 10 B2
Chillum Washington 33 B3
Chilly-Mazarin Paris 24 B2
Chingupota Kolkata 14 C1
Chinna Cr. → Karachi 13 B2
Chiquihuite, Cerro Mexico City 18 A2
Chislehurst London 15 B4
Chiswick London 15 B2
Chiswick House London 15 B2
Chitose Tokyo 30 B2
Chitralada Palace Bangkok 3 B2
Chiyoda Tokyo 30 A3
Choa Chu Kang Singapore 28 A2
Chodov u Prahy Prague 25 B3
Chōfu Tokyo 30 B2
Choisy-le-Roi Paris 24 B3
Cholargos Athens 2 B2
Cholupice Prague 25 C2
Chom Thong Bangkok 3 B1
Chong Pang Singapore 28 A2
Chongwen Beijing 4 B2
Chorrillos Lima 14 C2
Chowpatty Beach Mumbai 20 B1
Christianshavn Copenhagen 8 A3
Chrzanów Warsaw 33 B1
Chuen Lung Hong Kong 12 A1
Chuk Kok Hong Kong 12 A2
Chulalongkorn Univ. Bangkok 3 B2
Chuō Tokyo 30 A3
Church End London 15 A2
Church of our Lady = Frauenkirche Munich 21 B2
Churchtown Dublin 10 B2
Ciampino Rome 26 C2
Ciampino ✕ (CIA) Rome 26 C2
Cicero Chicago 9 B2
Cilandak Jakarta 12 B1
Cilincing Jakarta 12 A2
Ciliwung → Jakarta 12 B2
Čimice Prague 25 B2
Cinecittà Rome 26 B2
Cinisello Bálsamo Milan 18 A2
Cinkota Budapest 7 A3
Cipete Jakarta 12 B1
Città degli Studi Milan 18 B2
Città del Vaticano = Vatican City ■ Rome 26 B1
City, The London 15 A3
City Hall = Rådhus Oslo 23 A3
City Hall = Stadshuset Stockholm 29 B2
City of the Dead Cairo 7 A2
City Park New Orleans 21 B2
City Terrace Los Angeles 16 B3
Ciudad de México Mexico City 18 B2
Ciudad Deportiva Mexico City 18 B2
Ciudad Fin de Semana Madrid 17 B2
Ciudad General Belgrano Buenos Aires 7 C1
Ciudad Lineál Madrid 17 B2
Ciudad Satélite Mexico City 18 A1
Ciudad Universitaria Buenos Aires 7 B2
Ciudad Universitaria Mexico City 18 C1
Claireville Res. Toronto 31 A1
Clamart Paris 24 B2
Clapham London 15 B3
Clapton London 15 A3
Claremont Cape Town 8 A1
Clayhall London 15 A4
Clear, L. Orlando 23 A2
Clermiston Edinburgh 11 B2
Clichy Paris 24 A2
Clichy-sous-Bois Paris 24 A4
Cliffside Toronto 31 A3
Cliffside Park New York 22 B2
Clifton Cape Town 8 A1
Clifton Karachi 13 B2
Clifton New York 22 A1
Clifton Beach Karachi 13 B2
Cliftondale Boston 6 A2
Cloghran Dublin 10 A2
Clonskeagh Dublin 10 B2
Clontarf Dublin 10 A2
Clontarf Sydney 29 A2
Clovelly Sydney 29 B2
CNN Center Atlanta 3 B2
Cobras, I. das Rio de Janeiro 25 B2
Coburg Melbourne 18 A1
Coconut Grove Miami 19 D2
Cocotá Rio de Janeiro 25 A1
Cœuilly Paris 24 B4
Coina Lisbon 16 B2
Coker Lagos 14 B2
Colaba Mumbai 20 B1
Colaba Pt. Mumbai 20 B1
Colegiales Buenos Aires 7 B2
Colindale London 15 A2
Colinton Edinburgh 11 B2
College Park Atlanta 3 C2
College Park Washington 33 B3
College Point New York 22 B2
Collégien Paris 24 A4
Collier Row London 15 A4
Colliers Wood London 15 B2
Colma San Francisco 26 B2
Colney Hatch London 15 A3
Cologno Monzese Milan 18 A2
Colombes Paris 24 A2
Colonia Güell Barcelona 4 A1
Colosseo Rome 26 B1
Colosseum = Colosseo Rome 26 B1
Combault Paris 24 B4
Comércio, Praça do Lisbon 16 A2
Commerce Los Angeles 16 B4
Conceição, I. da Rio de Janeiro 25 B2
Conchali Santiago 27 B2
Concord Sydney 29 B1
Concord Toronto 31 A2
Concorde, Place de la Paris 24 A2
Concorezzo Milan 18 A2
Condet Jakarta 12 A2
Coney I. = Serangoon, Pulau Singapore 28 A3
Coney Island New York 22 C2
Congonhas São Paulo ✕ (CGH) São Paulo 27 B2
Conley → Atlanta 3 C3
Connaught Place Delhi 10 B2
Consolação São Paulo 27 B2
Constantia Cape Town 8 B1
Constitución Buenos Aires 7 B2
Constitution Atlanta 3 B2
Conway Orlando 23 B2
Conway, L. Orlando 23 B2
Coogee Sydney 29 B2
Cooksville Toronto 31 B1
Coolock Dublin 10 A2
Cooper City Miami 19 B1
Copacabana Rio de Janeiro 25 B1
Copenhagen = København Copenhagen 8 A2
Coral Gables Miami 19 D1
Coral Hills Washington 33 B3
Corcovado, Cristo Redentor Rio de Janeiro 25 B1
Corduff Dublin 10 A1
Cormano Milan 18 A2
Cornaredo Milan 18 A1
Córsico Milan 18 B1
Corstorphine Edinburgh 11 B2
Corviale Rome 26 B1
Coslada Madrid 17 B2
Cossigny Paris 24 B4
Cotao Lisbon 16 A1
Côte-St-Luc Montreal 20 B2
Cotunduba, I. de Rio de Janeiro 25 B2
Coubron Paris 24 A4
Courbevoie Paris 24 A2
Courtry Paris 24 A4
Cowley London 15 A1
Coyoacán Mexico City 18 B2
Craighall Park Johannesburg 13 A2
Craiglockhart Edinburgh 11 B2
Craigmillar Edinburgh 11 B3
Cramond Edinburgh 11 B2
Cramond Bridge Edinburgh 11 B1
Cramond I. Edinburgh 11 B2
Crandon Park Miami 19 D3
Cranford London 15 B1
Crawford Cape Town 8 A2
Crayford London 15 B5
Creekmouth London 15 A4
Crescent, L. Orlando 23 A1
Crescenzago Milan 18 A2
Cressely Paris 24 B1
Cresskill New York 22 A2
Crestwood Chicago 9 D2
Créteil Paris 24 B3
Cricklewood London 15 A2
Cristo Redentor, Corcovado Rio de Janeiro 25 B1
Crockenhill London 15 B4
Croissy-Beaubourg Paris 24 B4
Croissy-sur-Seine Paris 24 A1
Crosby Johannesburg 13 B1
Crosne Paris 24 B3
Cross I. Mumbai 20 B2
Crouch End London 15 A3
Crown Mine Johannesburg 13 B1
Crows Nest Sydney 29 A2
Croydon London 15 B3
Croydon Park Sydney 29 B1
Crugh Mt. Dublin 10 B2
Crumlin Dublin 10 B2
Cruz de Pau Lisbon 16 B2
Crystal Palace London 15 B3
Csepel Budapest 7 B2
Csepelsziget Budapest 7 B2
Csillaghegy Budapest 7 A2
Csillagtelep Budapest 7 B2
Csömör Budapest 7 A3
Csömöri-patak → Budapest 7 A3
Cuatro Vientos Madrid 17 B1
Cuauhtémoc Mexico City 18 B2
Cubao Manila 17 B2
Çubuklu Istanbul 12 B2
Cudahy Los Angeles 16 C3
Cuicuilco, Pirámide de Mexico City 18 C1
Culmore Washington 33 B2
Culver City Los Angeles 16 B2
Cupecê → São Paulo 27 B1
Currie Edinburgh 11 B2
Cusago Milan 18 B1
Cusano Milanino Milan 18 A2
Cutler Park Boston 6 B1
Çuvuşabaşı → Istanbul 12 B1
Cuwei Beijing 4 B1
Cypress Hills New York 22 B2
Cypress Park Los Angeles 16 B3
Czerniaków Warsaw 33 B2
Czyste Warsaw 33 B1

D

D.H.A. Phase VIII Karachi 13 B2
Da Moóca → São Paulo 27 B2
Ďablice Prague 25 B2
Dąbrowa Warsaw 33 B1
Dachang Shanghai 28 B1
Dachang ✕ Shanghai 28 B1
Dachau Munich 21 A1
Dachau-Ost Munich 21 A1
Dachauer Moos Munich 21 A1
Dadar Mumbai 20 A1
Daebang Seoul 27 B1
Daechi Seoul 27 B2
Dafni Athens 2 B2
Dagenham London 15 A4
Daglfing Munich 21 B2
Dahab, Gezîret el Cairo 7 B2
Daheisha Jerusalem 13 B2
Dahlem Berlin 5 B2
Dahlwitz-Hoppegarten Berlin 5 A5
Dahongmen Beijing 4 C2
Daiba = Odaiba Tokyo 30 B3
Dajiaoting Beijing 4 B2
Dakhnoye St. Petersburg 27 C1
Dalejsky potok → Prague 25 B2
Dalgety Bay Edinburgh 11 A1
Dalkeith Edinburgh 11 B3
Dalkey Dublin 10 B3
Dalkey I. Dublin 10 B3
Dallgow Berlin 5 A1
Dalmeny Edinburgh 11 B1
Dalston London 15 A3
Daly City San Francisco 26 B2
Damaia Lisbon 16 A1
Damarakia Athens 2 B1
Dämeritzsee Berlin 5 B5
Dan Ryan Woods Chicago 9 C2
Danderhall Edinburgh 11 B3
Danderyd Stockholm 29 A2
Danforth Toronto 31 A3
Dania Beach Miami 19 B3
Darakeh Tehran 31 A2
Darband Tehran 31 A2
Darling Point Sydney 29 B2
Darndale Dublin 10 A2
Darrūs Tehran 31 A2
Dartford London 15 B5
Dashi Guangzhou 11 B2
Datansha Guangzhou 11 B2
Datun Beijing 4 B2
Daulatpur Delhi 10 A1
Davidson, Mt. San Francisco 26 B2
Davidson's Mains Edinburgh 11 B2
Davie Miami 19 B2
Dāvūdiyeh Tehran 31 A2
Davydkovo Moscow 19 B1
Dawidy Warsaw 33 C1
Daxing Beijing 4 C2
Decatur Atlanta 3 B3
Dedham Boston 6 B1
Degunino Moscow 19 A2
Deir Dibwan Jerusalem 13 A2
Deir Ibzi'e Jerusalem 13 A1
Deira Dubai 9 A2
Dejvice Prague 25 B2
Dekabristov, Ostrov St. Petersburg 27 B1
Del Rey Los Angeles 16 C2
Delhi Delhi 10 B2
Delhi Indira Gandhi Int. ✕ (DEL) Delhi 10 B1
Demarest New York 22 A2
Den Ilp Amsterdam 2 A2
Denistone Heights Sydney 29 A1
Dentonia Park Toronto 31 A3
DePaul Univ. Chicago 9 B3
Deptford London 15 B3
Desert Wetlands Park Las Vegas 14 B2
Deutsche Oper Berlin 5 A2
Deutsches Museum Munich 21 B2
Devil's Peak Cape Town 8 A1
Dhakuria Kolkata 14 B2
Dharavi Mumbai 20 A2
Dia Deva = Butcher I. Mumbai 20 B2
Diadema São Paulo 27 C2
Diegem Brussels 6 A2
Diemen Amsterdam 2 A2
Diepkloof Johannesburg 13 B1
Dieprivier Cape Town 8 B1
Dilbeek Brussels 6 A1
Dilli = Delhi Delhi 10 B2
Dirnismaning Munich 21 A2
Disney-M.G.M. Studios Orlando 23 B1
Disney Studios Los Angeles 16 B3
Dixmoor Chicago 9 D2
Djakarta = Jakarta Jakarta 12 A2
Djursholm Stockholm 29 A2
Döberitz Berlin 5 A1
Döbling Vienna 32 A2
Dobong Seoul 27 B2
Dobongsan Seoul 27 A2
Docklands London 15 A3
Doctor Phillips Orlando 23 B2
Dodder → Dublin 10 B1
Dodger Stadium Los Angeles 16 B3
Dogs, Isle of London 15 B3
Dolgoe Ozero St. Petersburg 27 A1
Dollis Hill London 15 A2
Dollymount Dublin 10 A2
Dolní Prague 25 B3
Dolní Chabry Prague 25 B2
Dolní Počernice Prague 25 B3
Dolphins Barn Dublin 10 B2
Dolton Chicago 9 D3
Dom Pedro II, Parque São Paulo 27 B2
Don Mills Toronto 31 A2
Don Muang Int. ✕ (BKK) Bangkok 3 A2
Donaghmede Dublin 10 A3
Donau-Oder Kanal Vienna 32 A3
Donaufeld Vienna 32 A2
Donaupark Vienna 32 A2
Donaustadt Vienna 32 A2
Dongan Hills New York 22 C1
Dongcheng Beijing 4 B2
Dongdaemung Seoul 27 B2
Donggou Shanghai 28 B2
Dongjak Seoul 27 B1
Dongjiao Guangzhou 11 B2
Dongri Mumbai 20 B2
Dongshanhu Park Guangzhou 11 B2
Dongzhimen Beijing 4 B2
Donnybrook Dublin 10 B2
Doornfontein Johannesburg 13 B2
Dorchester Boston 6 B2
Dorchester B. Boston 6 B2
Dorchester Heights Nat. Historical Site ⌂ Boston 6 B2
Dornach Munich 21 B3
Dorval Int., Montréal ✕ (YUL) Montreal 20 B1
Dos Moninos → São Paulo 27 B2
Douglas Park Chicago 9 B2
Dover Heights Sydney 29 B2
Dowlatābād Tehran 31 B2
Down, L. Orlando 23 A1
Downey Los Angeles 16 C4
Downsview Toronto 31 A2
Downsview Park Toronto 31 A2
Dragør Copenhagen 8 B3
Drancy Paris 24 A3
Drapetsona Athens 2 B1
Dreilinden Berlin 5 B2
Drewnica Warsaw 33 B2
Drigh Road Karachi 13 A2
Drimnagh Dublin 10 B2
Drogenbos Brussels 6 B1
Drottningholm Stockholm 29 B1
Druid Hills Atlanta 3 B2
Drumcondra Dublin 10 A2
Drummoyne Sydney 29 B1
Drylaw Edinburgh 11 B2
Dubai = Dubayy Dubai 9 A2
Dubai Creek Dubai 9 A2
Dubai Int. ✕ (DXB) Dubai 9 A2
Dubai Int. Financial Centre Dubai 9 B2
Dubai Internet City Dubai 9 B1
Dubai Maritime City Dubai 9 A2
Dubayy Dubai 9 A2
Dubeč Prague 25 B3
Dublin Dublin 10 A2
Dublin ✕ (DUB) Dublin 10 A2
Dublin B. Dublin 10 B3
Dublin Harbour Dublin 10 A2
Duddingston Edinburgh 11 B3
Dugnano Milan 18 A2
Duivendrecht Amsterdam 2 B2
Dūlāb Tehran 31 B2
Dulwich London 15 B3
Dum Dum Kolkata 14 B2
Dumont New York 22 A2
Dún Laoghaire Dublin 10 B3
Dundrum Dublin 10 B2
Dunearn Singapore 28 B2
Dunleary = Dún Laoghaire Dublin 10 B3
Dunning Chicago 9 B2
Dunvegan Johannesburg 13 A2
Duomo Milan 18 B2
Duque de Caxias Rio de Janeiro 25 A1
Duren Sawit Jakarta 12 B2
Dusit Bangkok 3 B2
Dworp Brussels 6 B1
Dyakovo Moscow 19 B2
Dyker Beach Park New York 22 C1
Dzerzhinskiy Moscow 19 B2
Dzerzhinskiy Park Moscow 19 B2

E

E.U.R. = Esposizione Universale di Roma Rome 26 C1
Eagle Rock Los Angeles 16 B3
Ealing □ London 15 A2
Earlsfield London 15 B2
Earlwood Sydney 29 B1
East Arlington Boston 6 A2
East Arlington Washington 33 B2
East Bedfont London 15 B1
East Boston Boston 6 A2
East Don → Toronto 31 A2
East Don Parkland Toronto 31 A2
East Elmhurst New York 22 B2
East Finchley London 15 A2
East Flatbush New York 22 C2
East Ham London 15 A4
East Humber → Toronto 31 A1
East Lamma Channel Hong Kong 12 B1
East Las Vegas = Whitney Las Vegas 14 B2
East Lexington Boston 6 A1
East Los Angeles Los Angeles 16 B3
East Molesey London 15 B1
East New York New York 22 B2
East Pines Washington 33 B3
East Point Atlanta 3 B2
East Potomac Park Washington 33 B2
East River → New York 22 B2
East Rutherford New York 22 A1
East Sheen London 15 B2
East Talpiyot Jerusalem 13 B2
East Wickham London 15 B4
East York Toronto 31 A2
Eastcote London 15 A1
Easter Howgate Edinburgh 11 B2
Eastpoint Park Toronto 31 A4
Eastwood Sydney 29 A1
Eaton Canyon Park Los Angeles 16 A4
Ebara Tokyo 30 B3
Ebisu Tokyo 30 B3
Ebute-Metta Lagos 14 B2
Eda Tokyo 30 B2
Edendale Johannesburg 13 A2
Edenmore Dublin 10 A2
Edgars Cr. → Melbourne 18 A1
Edgeley Toronto 31 A1
Edgemar San Francisco 26 C2
Edgewater New York 22 B2
Edgewood Orlando 23 B2
Edinburgh Edinburgh 11 B2
Edinburgh ✕ (EDI) Edinburgh 11 B1
Edinburgh Castle Edinburgh 11 B2
Edison Park Chicago 9 A2
Edmondston Washington 33 B3
Edmondstown Dublin 10 B2
Edo → Tokyo 30 B4
Edogawa Tokyo 30 A4
Edsberg Stockholm 29 A1
Edwards L. Melbourne 18 A1
Efxonos Athens 2 B2
Egaleo Athens 2 B1
Egaleo, Oros Athens 2 B1
Eiche Berlin 5 A4
Eiche Süd Berlin 5 A4
Eiffel, Tour Paris 24 A2
Ein Arik Jerusalem 13 A1
Ein Naquba Jerusalem 13 B1
Ein Rafa Jerusalem 13 B1
Eizariya Jerusalem 13 B2
Ejby Copenhagen 8 A2
Ejigbo Lagos 14 A1
Ekeberg Oslo 23 A3
Ekenäs Stockholm 29 B3
El 'Abbasiya Cairo 7 A2
El Agustino Lima 14 B2
El Agustino, Cerro Lima 14 B3
El Baragil Cairo 7 A1
El Basâtîn Cairo 7 B2
El Bira Jerusalem 13 A2
El Bosque Santiago 27 C2
El Carmen Santiago 27 B1
El Cortijo Santiago 27 B1
El Cristo, Vaso Regulador Mexico City 18 B1
El Duqqi Cairo 7 A2
El Encinar de los Reyes Madrid 17 A2
El Gezira Cairo 7 A2
El Ghurîya Cairo 7 A2
El Gîza Cairo 7 A2
El Khadr Jerusalem 13 B1
El Khalîfa Cairo 7 A2
El Kôm el Ahmar Cairo 7 A2
El Ma'âdi Cairo 7 B2
El Matarîya Cairo 7 A2
El Mohandessin Cairo 7 A2
El Monte Los Angeles 16 B4
El Muqattam Cairo 7 A2
El Mûski Cairo 7 A2
El Pardo Madrid 17 A1
El Pobleneu Barcelona 4 A2
El Portal Miami 19 C2
El Prat Barcelona ✕ (BCN) Barcelona 4 B1
El Prat de Llobregat Barcelona 4 B1
El Qâhira Cairo 7 A2
El Qubba Cairo 7 A2
El Reloj Mexico City 18 C2
El Retiro Madrid 17 B1
El Salto Santiago 27 B2
El Sereno Los Angeles 16 B3
El Talibîya Cairo 7 B2
El Vergel Mexico City 18 C2
El Wâhli Cairo 7 A2
El Zamâlik Cairo 7 A2
El Zeitûn Cairo 7 A2
Eleftherios Venizelos ✕ (ATH) Athens 2 A3
Elephanta Caves Mumbai 20 B2
Elephanta I. Mumbai 20 B2
Ellboda Stockholm 29 A3
Ellenor, L. Orlando 23 B2
Elliniko Olympic Complex Athens 2 B2
Ellis I. New York 22 B1
Elmers End London 15 B3
Elmhurst New York 22 B2
Elmstead London 15 B4
Elmwood New Orleans 21 B1
Elmwood Park Chicago 9 B2
Elmwood Park New York 22 A1
Elsiesrivier Cape Town 8 A2
Elsternwick Melbourne 18 B2
Eltham London 15 B4
Elwood Melbourne 18 B1
Élysée Paris 24 A2
Elysian Park Los Angeles 16 B3
Emāmzādeh Sāleh Tehran 31 A2
Émerainville Paris 24 B4
Emeryville San Francisco 26 A3
Eminönü Istanbul 12 B1
Emirates, Mall of the Dubai 9 B1
Emirgan Istanbul 12 B2
Emmarentia Johannesburg 13 A2
Empire State Building New York 22 B2
Encantado Rio de Janeiro 25 B1
Encino Los Angeles 16 B2
Encino Res. Los Angeles 16 B1
Enebyberg Stockholm 29 A1
Enfield Sydney 29 B1
Engenho, I. do Rio de Janeiro 25 B2
Englewood Chicago 9 C3
Englewood New York 22 A2
Englewood Cliffs New York 22 A2
Enmore Sydney 29 B2
Enskede Stockholm 29 B2
Enterprise Las Vegas 14 B1
Entrevias Madrid 17 B1
Epcot Orlando 23 B1
Epping Sydney 29 A1
Erenköy Istanbul 12 C2
Erith London 15 B5
Erlaa Vienna 32 B1
Ermington Sydney 29 A1
Ermita Manila 17 B1
Ershatou Guangzhou 11 B2
Erskineville Sydney 29 B2
Erunkan Lagos 14 A2
Erzsébet-Telep Budapest 7 B3
Eschenried Munich 21 A1
Esenler Istanbul 12 B1
Esher London 15 B1
Eskbank Edinburgh 11 B3
Esplanade Shanghai 28 C3
Esplugas Barcelona 4 A1
Esposizione Universale di Roma Rome 26 C1
Essendon Melbourne 18 A1
Essendon ✕ (MEB) Melbourne 18 A1
Essingen Stockholm 29 B1
Essling Vienna 32 A3
Est, Gare de l' Paris 24 A3
Estado, Parque do São Paulo 27 B2
Estelle New Orleans 21 B2
Estrela, Basilica da Lisbon 16 A2
Etobicoke Toronto 31 B1
Etobicoke Cr. → Toronto 31 B1
Etterbeek Brussels 6 B2
Eung-am Seoul 27 B1
Eunpyeong Seoul 27 B1
Evanston Chicago 9 A2
Even Sapir Jerusalem 13 B1
Evere Brussels 6 A2
Everett Boston 6 A2
Evergreen Park Chicago 9 C2
Evīn Tehran 31 A2
Ewu Lagos 14 A1
Exhibition Place Toronto 31 B2
Expo 2010 Shanghai 28 B1
Exposições, Palácio das Rio de Janeiro 25 B1
Eyüp Istanbul 12 B1
Ezeiza ✕ (EZE) Buenos Aires 7 C1

F

Faber, Mt. Singapore 28 B2
Fælledparken Copenhagen 8 A3
Fågelön Stockholm 29 B1
Fagersjö Stockholm 29 B2
Fairland Johannesburg 13 A1
Fairmilehead Edinburgh 11 B2
Fairport Toronto 31 A4
Fairview New York 22 B2
Fairview, L. Orlando 23 A2
Falenty Warsaw 33 C1
Faliro Athens 2 B1
Faliro, Ormos Athens 2 B2
Falkenburg Berlin 5 A4
Falkenhagen Berlin 5 A1
Falkensee Berlin 5 A1
Falomo Lagos 14 B2
False Bay Cape Town 8 B2
Famões Lisbon 16 A1
Fangcun Guangzhou 11 B2
Farahābād Tehran 31 A2
Farforovskaya St. Petersburg 27 B2
Farningham London 15 B5
Farsta Stockholm 29 B2
Fasanerie-Nord Munich 21 A2
Fasangarten Munich 21 B2
Fatih Istanbul 12 B1
Favoriten Vienna 32 B2
Fawkner Melbourne 18 A1
Fawkner Park Melbourne 18 B1
Feldkirchen Munich 21 B3
Feldmoching Munich 21 A2
Feltham London 15 B1
Fener Istanbul 12 B1
Fenerbahçe Istanbul 12 C2
Fengtai Beijing 4 C1
Fengtai Stadium Beijing 4 B1
Ferencváros Budapest 7 B2
Ferihegy, Budapest ✕ (BUD) Budapest 7 B3
Ferndale Johannesburg 13 A2
Fichtenau Berlin 5 B5
Field Museum of Natural History Chicago 9 B3
Fields Corner Boston 6 B2
Fiera Camp Milan 18 B1
Figino Milan 18 B1
Fijir Baghdad 3 A2
Filadelfia Athens 2 A2
Fili-Mazilovo Moscow 19 B1
Filothei Athens 2 A2
Finchley London 15 A2
Fine Arts, Museum of Boston 6 A2
Finglas Dublin 10 A2
Finsbury London 15 A3
Finsbury Park London 15 A3
Fiorito Buenos Aires 7 C2
Firhouse Dublin 10 B2
Fischerhäuser Munich 21 A3
Fisher I. Miami 19 D3
Fishermans Bend Melbourne 18 A1
Fisherman's Village Los Angeles 16 C2
Fisherville Toronto 31 A2
Fisksätra Stockholm 29 B3
Fitzroy Gardens Melbourne 18 A1
Five Cowrie Cr. → Lagos 14 B2
Five Dock Sydney 29 B1
Fjellstrand Oslo 23 B2
Flamengo Rio de Janeiro 25 B1
Flamingo Orlando 23 B2
Flaminio Rome 26 B1
Flaskebekk Oslo 23 A2
Flatbush New York 22 C2
Flaten Stockholm 29 B2
Flatlands New York 22 C2
Flemington Racecourse Melbourne 18 A1
Flint Pk. Los Angeles 16 B3
Florence Los Angeles 16 C3
Florence Bloom Bird Sanctuary ⌂ Johannesburg 13 A2
Florentia Johannesburg 13 B2
Flores Buenos Aires 7 B2
Flores, Mercado de Mexico City 18 C2
Floresta Buenos Aires 7 B2
Florida Buenos Aires 7 B2
Florida Johannesburg 13 B1
Floridsdorf Vienna 32 A2
Flushing New York 22 B3
Flushing Meadows Corona Park New York 22 B2
Flysta Stockholm 29 A1
Fo Tan Hong Kong 12 A2
Foggy Bottom Washington 33 B2
Föhrenhain Vienna 32 A2
Fontainebleau Johannesburg 13 A1
Fontenay-aux-Roses Paris 24 B2
Fontenay-le-Fleury Paris 24 B1
Fontenay-sous-Bois Paris 24 A3
Foots Cray London 15 B4
Footscray Melbourne 18 A1
Forbidden City = Imperial Palace Museum Beijing 4 B2
Forest Brussels 6 B1
Forest Gate London 15 A4
Forest Heights Washington 33 C2
Forest Hill London 15 B3
Forest Hill Toronto 31 A2
Forest Hills New York 22 B2
Forest Park Chicago 9 B2
Forest Park New York 22 B2
Forest View Chicago 9 C2
Fornebu Oslo 23 A2
Foro Romano Rome 26 B1
Forstenried Munich 21 B1
Forstenrieder Park Munich 21 B1
Fort Mumbai 20 B1
Fort Dupont Park Washington 33 B3
Fort Foote Village Washington 33 C2
Fort Lauderdale Miami 19 B3
Fort Lauderdale Executive ✕ (FXE) Miami 19 A2
Fort Lauderdale-Hollywood Int. ✕ (FLL) Miami 19 B3
Fort Lee New York 22 A2
Forth, Firth of Edinburgh 11 A3
Forth Rail Bridge Edinburgh 11 A1
Forth Road Bridge Edinburgh 11 A1
Foshan Guangzhou 11 B1
Fót Budapest 7 A3
Fourqueux Paris 24 A1
Fox Studios Sydney 29 B2
Foxrock Dublin 10 B2
Franconia Washington 33 C2
Frank Lloyd Wright Home Chicago 9 B2
Frankel Singapore 28 B3
Franklin Park Boston 6 B2
Franklin Park Washington 33 B2
Franklin Res. Los Angeles 16 B2
Franz Josef Strauss ✕ (MUC) Munich 21 A2
Frauenkirche Munich 21 B2
Frederiksberg Copenhagen 8 A3
Frederiksdal Copenhagen 8 A2
Fredersdorf Berlin 5 A5
Freguesia Rio de Janeiro 25 A1
Freidrichshain, Volkspark Berlin 5 A3
Freiham Munich 21 B1
Freimann Munich 21 A2
French Quarter New Orleans 21 B2
Fresh Pond Boston 6 A2
Fresnes Paris 24 B2
Freudenau Vienna 32 A2
Friarstown Dublin 10 B1
Friedenau Berlin 5 B3
Friedrichsfelde Berlin 5 B4
Friedrichshagen Berlin 5 B4
Friedrichshain Berlin 5 A3
Friedrichslust Berlin 5 A5
Friherrs Helsinki 11 B1
Frilufts Museum Helsinki 11 B2
Frontón, I. Lima 14 B1
Frunze Moscow 19 B2
Fuchū Tokyo 30 A1
Fuencarral Madrid 17 B1
Fuenlabrada Madrid 17 C1
Fukagawa Tokyo 30 B3
Fukushima Osaka 23 A1
Fulham London 15 B2
Funabori Tokyo 30 A4
Fundão, I. do Rio de Janeiro 25 B1
Fünfhaus Vienna 32 A2
Furesø Copenhagen 8 A2
Fürth Munich 21 B2
Futago-tamagawaen Tokyo 30 B2
Fuxing Dao Shanghai 28 B2
Fuxing Park Shanghai 28 B1
Fuxinglu Beijing 4 B1

G

G. Ross Lord Park Toronto 31 A2
Gaebong Seoul 27 C1
Gage Park Chicago 9 C2
Gagny Paris 24 A4
Galata Istanbul 12 B1
Galata Tower Istanbul 12 B1
Galatsi Athens 2 A2
Galeão, Int. de ✕ (GIG) Rio de Janeiro 25 A1
Galyanovo Moscow 19 B3
Gambir Jakarta 12 A1
Gamboa Rio de Janeiro 25 B1
Gamboloita Milan 18 B2
Gamlebyen Oslo 23 A3
Gangdong Seoul 27 B2
Gangnam Seoul 27 B1
Gangseo Seoul 27 B1
Gangtou Guangzhou 11 A1
Gangwei Guangzhou 11 B2
Ganjiakou Beijing 4 B1
Ganshoren Brussels 6 A1
Gants Hill London 15 A4
Gaohang Shanghai 28 B2
Gaoqiao Shanghai 28 A2
Garbagnate Milanese Milan 18 A1
Garbatella Rome 26 B2
Garches Paris 24 A2
Garching Munich 21 A3
Garden City Cairo 7 A2
Garden District New Orleans 21 B2
Garden Reach Kolkata 14 B1
Garder Oslo 23 B2
Garfield New York 22 A1
Garfield Park Chicago 9 B2
Gargareta Athens 2 B2
Garibong Seoul 27 B1
Garvanza Los Angeles 16 B3
Gåshaga Stockholm 29 A3
Gateway ⌂ New York 22 C2
Gateway of India Mumbai 20 B2
Gatow Berlin 5 B1
Gavà Barcelona 4 B1
Gavamar Barcelona 4 B1
Gávea Rio de Janeiro 25 B1
Gávea, Pedra da Rio de Janeiro 25 B1
Gazdagrét Budapest 7 B1
Gaziosmanpaşa Istanbul 12 B1
Gebel el Ahmar Cairo 7 A3
Gebel el Muqattam Cairo 7 A2
Gebel el Tura Cairo 7 B2
Geiselgasteig Munich 21 B2
General San Martin Buenos Aires 7 B1
Gennevilliers Paris 24 A2
Gentilly New Orleans 21 A2
Gentilly Paris 24 B3
Gentofte Copenhagen 8 A3
Genval Brussels 6 B2
George I. Hong Kong 12 B1
Georges River Bridge Sydney 29 C1
Georgetown Washington 33 B2
Georgia Dome Atlanta 3 B2
Gerasdorf bei Wien Vienna 32 A2
Gerberau Munich 21 A1
Gerli Buenos Aires 7 C2
Germiston Johannesburg 13 B2
Gern Munich 21 B2
Getafe Madrid 17 C1
Getty Center, The Los Angeles 16 B2
Geumjeong Seoul 27 C1
Geva Binyamin Jerusalem 13 A2
Geylang Serai Singapore 28 B3
Gharapuri = Elephanta I. Mumbai 20 B2
Gharapuri Mumbai 20 B2
Gharb = Shahrak-e Qods Tehran 31 A2
Ghatkopar Mumbai 20 A2
Ghazipur Delhi 10 B2
Ghizri Karachi 13 B2
Ghizri Cr. → Karachi 13 B2
Ghonda Delhi 10 A2
Ghusuri Kolkata 14 B2
Gianicolense Rome 26 B1
Giant Wheel = Riesenrad Vienna 32 A2
Gibraltar Pt. Toronto 31 B2
Gidea Park London 15 A5
Giesing Munich 21 B2
Gilmerton Edinburgh 11 B3
Gilo Jerusalem 13 B2
Gimmersta Stockholm 29 B3
Ginza Tokyo 30 B3
Giv'at Ram Jerusalem 13 B2
Giv'at Ye'arim Jerusalem 13 B1
Giv'at Ze'ev Jerusalem 13 A2
Giv'on Jerusalem 13 A1
Giza = El Gîza Cairo 7 A2
Giza Pyramids Cairo 7 B1
Gjersjøen Oslo 23 B3
Gladesville Sydney 29 B1
Gladsakse Copenhagen 8 A2
Glasnevin Dublin 10 A2
Glassmanor Washington 33 C3
Glasthule Dublin 10 B3
Glen Iris Melbourne 18 B2
Glen Mar Park Washington 33 B2
Glen Rouge Park Toronto 31 A4
Glenasmole Reservoirs Dublin 10 B1
Glencoe Chicago 9 A2
Glencorse Res. Edinburgh 11 B2
Glencullen Dublin 10 B2
Glendale Los Angeles 16 B3
Glendoo Mt. Dublin 10 B2
Glenhuntly Melbourne 18 B2
Glenview Chicago 9 A2
Glenview Countryside Chicago 9 A2
Glenvista Johannesburg 13 B2
Glifada Athens 2 B2
Glostrup Copenhagen 8 B2
Gogar Edinburgh 11 B2
Göktürk Istanbul 12 A1
Golabari Kolkata 14 B2
Golabki Warsaw 33 B1
Gold Coast Chicago 9 B3
Golden Beach Miami 19 C3
Golden Gate San Francisco 26 B2
Golden Gate ⌂ San Francisco 26 A2
Golden Gate Bridge San Francisco 26 B2

Golden Gate Park San Francisco 26 B2
Golden Horn = Haliç Istanbul 12 B1
Golders Green London 15 A2
Golestan Palace Tehran 31 A2
Golf Chicago 9 A2
Gonen Jerusalem 13 B2
Gongneung Seoul 27 B2
Goodmayes London 15 A4
Goodwood Cape Town 8 A2
Gopalpur Kolkata 14 B2
Górce Warsaw 33 B1
Gore Hill Sydney 29 A2
Gorelyy → St. Petersburg 27 A3
Gorgie Edinburgh 11 B2
Gorky Park Moscow 19 B2
Gosen Berlin 5 B5
Gosener kanal Berlin 5 B5
Gospel Oak London 15 A3
Gotanda Tokyo 30 B3
Goth Goli Mar Karachi 13 A2
Goth Sher Shah Karachi 13 A1
Gotha Orlando 23 A1
Gournay-sur-Marne Paris 24 A4
Governador, I. do Rio de Janeiro 25 A1
Governors I. New York 22 B1
Grabów Warsaw 33 C1
Gràcia Barcelona 4 A2
Gräfelfing Munich 21 B1
Gragoatá Rio de Janeiro 25 B2
Grand Bazaar = Kapali Carsi Istanbul 12 B1
Grand Central Station New York 22 B2
Grand Palace Bangkok 3 B1
Grand Place Brussels 6 A2
Grande Place Brussels 6 A2
Grankulla = Kauniainen Helsinki 11 B1
Grant Park Chicago 9 B3
Granton Edinburgh 11 B2
Grassy Park Cape Town 8 B2
Gratosóglio Milan 18 B2
Gratzwalde Berlin 5 B5
Gravesend New York 22 C2
Grazhdanka St. Petersburg 27 B2
Great Western Forum Los Angeles 16 C2
Greco Milan 18 A2
Green I. Hong Kong 12 B1
Green Point Cape Town 8 A1
Green Point Stadium Cape Town 8 A1
Greenfield Park Montreal 20 B3
Greenford London 15 A1
Greenhill London 15 A2
Greenhills Dublin 10 B1
Greenwich □ London 15 B3
Greenwich Observatory London 15 B3
Greenwich Village New York 22 B2
Greenwood Boston 6 A2
Grefsen Oslo 23 A3
Gresham Park Atlanta 3 B2
Gretna New Orleans 21 B2
Gretna City Park New Orleans 21 B2
Greve Strand Copenhagen 8 B1
Greynolds Park Miami 19 C3
Griebnitzsee Berlin 5 B1
Griffith Park Los Angeles 16 B3
Grimbergen Brussels 6 A2
Grinzing Vienna 32 A2
Gröbenried Munich 21 A1
Grochów Warsaw 33 B2
Grodzisk Warsaw 33 B2
Groenendaal Brussels 6 B2
Grogol Petamburin Jakarta 12 A1
Gronsdorf Munich 21 B3
Grorud Oslo 23 A4
Gross-Glienicke Berlin 5 B1
Gross-Hadern Munich 21 B1
Gross-Lappen Munich 21 A2
Grosse Krampe Berlin 5 B5
Grosse Müggelsee Berlin 5 B4
Grosse Point Lighthouse Chicago 9 A2
Grossenzersdorf Vienna 32 A3
Grossenzersdorfer Arm → Vienna 32 A3
Grosser Biberhaufen Vienna 32 A2
Grosser Wannsee Berlin 5 B2
Grossfeld-Siedlung Vienna 32 A2
Grosshesselohe Munich 21 B2
Grossjedlersdorf Vienna 32 A2
Grossziethen Berlin 5 B3
Ground Zero = National September 11 Memorial and Museum New York 22 B1
Grove Hall Boston 6 B2
Grove Park Atlanta 3 B2
Grove Park London 15 B4
Grove Park London 15 B2
Groveton Washington 33 C2
Grünau Berlin 5 B4
Grunewald Berlin 5 B2
Grünwald Munich 21 B2
Grünwalder Forst Munich 21 B2
Grymes Hill New York 22 C1
Guadalupe Manila 17 B2
Guadalupe, Basilica de Mexico City 18 B2
Guanabara, B. de Rio de Janeiro 25 B1
Guanabara, Jardim Rio de Janeiro 25 A1
Guanabara, Palácio da Rio de Janeiro 25 B1
Guang'anmen Beijing 4 B1
Guangqumen Beijing 4 B2
Guangzhou Guangzhou 11 B2
Guanshuo Guangzhou 11 B3
Gucun Shanghai 28 A1
Gudö Stockholm 29 B3
Güell, Parque de Barcelona 4 A2
Guinardó Barcelona 4 A2
Gulbai Karachi 13 A1
Gulshan-e Iqbal Jerusalem 13 A2
Güngören Istanbul 12 B1
Gunnersbury London 15 B2
Guomao Beijing 4 B2
Gustavo A. Madero Mexico City 18 B2
Guttenberg New York 22 B1
Gutuyevskiy, Ostrov St. Petersburg 27 B1
Guyancourt Paris 24 B1
Gwanak Seoul 27 C1
Gwanaksan Seoul 27 C1
Gyál Budapest 7 B3
Gyáli-patak → Budapest 7 B2

H

Haaga Helsinki 11 B2
Haar Munich 21 B3
Habay Manila 17 C1
Hackbridge London 15 B3
Hackensack New York 22 A1
Hackensack → New York 22 B1
Hackney □ London 15 A3
Hackney Wick London 15 A3
Hadr, Warrâq el Cairo 7 A2
Haga Stockholm 29 A2
Hagenbrunn Vienna 32 A2
Hägersten Stockholm 29 B1
Häggvik Stockholm 29 A1
Hagonoy Manila 17 B2
Hague Park Toronto 31 A3
Haidari = Chaidari Athens 2 A1
Haidarpur Delhi 10 A1
Haidhausen Munich 21 B2
Haidian Beijing 4 B1
Haight-Ashbury San Francisco 26 B2
Hainault London 15 A4
Haizhou Guangzhou 11 B2
Haizhu Guangchang Guangzhou 11 B2
Hakunila Helsinki 11 B3
Halandri = Chalandri Athens 2 A2
Halásztelek Budapest 7 B1
Haliç Istanbul 12 B1
Halim Perdana Kusuma Int. ✕ (HLP) Jakarta 12 B2
Hallandale Beach Miami 19 C3
Halle Brussels 6 B1
Haltiala Helsinki 11 B2
Haltiavuori Helsinki 11 B2
Ham London 15 B2
Hämeenkylä Helsinki 11 B1
Hammarby Stockholm 29 B2
Hamme Brussels 6 A1
Hammersmith London 15 B2
Hampstead London 15 A2
Hampstead Montreal 20 B2
Hampstead Garden Suburb London 15 A2
Hampstead Heath London 15 A2
Hampton London 15 B1
Hampton Court Palace London 15 B1
Hampton Wick London 15 B2
Hamrā' Baghdad 3 B1
Hanala Helsinki 11 A3
Haneda Tokyo 30 B3
Haneda, Tōkyō ✕ (HND) Tokyo 30 B3
Hang Hau Hong Kong 12 B2
Hanging Gardens Mumbai 20 B1
Hanlon Toronto 31 B1
Hanwell London 15 A1
Hanworth London 15 B1
Haora Kolkata 14 B1
Hapeville Atlanta 3 C2
Happy Valley Hong Kong 12 B2
Har Adar Jerusalem 13 B1
Har Gilo Jerusalem 13 B2
Har Homa Jerusalem 13 B2
Har Nof Jerusalem 13 B2
Harahan New Orleans 21 B1
Harbour Front Centre Singapore 28 B2
Haren Brussels 6 A2
Hareskovby Copenhagen 8 A2
Haringey □ London 15 A3
Harjusuo Helsinki 11 B3
Harlaching Munich 21 B2
Harlaw Res. Edinburgh 11 B2
Harlem New York 22 B2
Harlesden London 15 A2
Harlington London 15 B1
Harmaja Helsinki 11 C2
Harmashatar hegy Budapest 7 A2
Harolds Cross Dublin 10 B2
Háros Budapest 7 B2
Harperrig Res. Edinburgh 11 B1
Harrow □ London 15 A1
Harrow on the Hill London 15 A1
Harrow School London 15 A1
Harrow Weald London 15 A1
Hartsfield-Jackson Atlanta Int. ✕ (ATL) Atlanta 3 C2
Harumi Tokyo 30 B3
Harvard Univ. Boston 6 A2
Harvey Chicago 9 D3
Harvey New Orleans 21 B2
Harwood Heights Chicago 9 B2
Ḥasanābād Tehran 31 A1
Hasbrouck Heights New York 22 A1
Haselhorst Berlin 5 A2
Hasköy Istanbul 12 B1
Hasle Oslo 23 B2
Haslum Oslo 23 A2
Hästhagen Stockholm 29 B2
Hatch End London 15 A1
Hatiara Kolkata 14 B2
Hauketo Oslo 23 A3
Hauz Khas Delhi 10 B2
Havel → Berlin 5 A2
Havelkanal Berlin 5 A2
Havering □ London 15 A5
Havering-atte-Bower London 15 A5
Haworth New York 22 A2
Hawthorne Racecourse Chicago 9 C2
Hayes London 15 B4
Hayes London 15 A1
Hayes End London 15 A1
Hayford Chicago 9 C2
Heathfield Cape Town 8 B1
Heathrow, London ✕ (LHR) London 15 B1
Hebe Haven Hong Kong 12 A2
Hedong Guangzhou 11 B2
Heidelberg Heights Melbourne 18 A2
Heidelberg West Melbourne 18 A2
Heidemühle Berlin 5 B5
Heideveld Cape Town 8 A2
Heiligensee Berlin 5 A2
Heiligenstadt Vienna 32 A2
Heinersdorf Berlin 5 A3
Hélène de Champlain, Parc △ Montreal 20 A2
Helenelund Stockholm 29 A1
Heliopolis = Masr el Gedida Cairo 7 A2
Hellersdorf Berlin 5 A4
Hellerup Copenhagen 8 A3
Helsingfors = Helsinki Helsinki 11 B2
Helsinki Helsinki 11 B2
Helsinki-Vantaa ✕ (HEL) Helsinki 11 B2
Hen and Chicken B. Sydney 29 B1
Henderson Las Vegas 14 B2
Hendon London 15 A2
Hengsha Guangzhou 11 B2
Hennigsdorf Berlin 5 A2
Henryków Warsaw 33 B1
Henson Cr. → Washington 33 C3
Henttaa Helsinki 11 B1
Heping Park Shanghai 28 B2
Hepingli Beijing 4 B2
Herlev Copenhagen 8 A2
Herman Eckstein Park Johannesburg 13 A2
Hermannskogel Vienna 32 A1
Hermiston Edinburgh 11 B2
Hermitage and Winter Palace St. Petersburg 27 B2
Hermsdorf Berlin 5 A2
Hernals Vienna 32 A2
Herne Hill London 15 B3
Héroes de Churubusco Mexico City 18 B2
Herons, Î. aux Montreal 20 B2
Herstedøster Copenhagen 8 A2
Herttoniemi Helsinki 11 B3
Ḥeşārak Tehran 31 A1
Heston London 15 B1
Hetzendorf Vienna 32 B1
Hextable London 15 B5
Hialeah Miami 19 C1
Hialeah Race Track Miami 19 C1
Hiawassa, L. Orlando 23 A2
Hickory Hills Chicago 9 C2
Hiekkaharju Helsinki 11 B3
Hietaniemi Helsinki 11 B2
Hietzing Vienna 32 A1
Higashi Osaka 23 A2
Higashimurayama Tokyo 30 A1
Higashinari Osaka 23 A2
Higashisumiyoshi Osaka 23 B2
Higashiyodogawa Osaka 23 A1
High Park Toronto 31 B2
Highbury London 15 A3
Highgate London 15 A3
Highland Cr. → Toronto 31 A3
Highland Creek Toronto 31 A3
Highland Park Los Angeles 16 B3
Highlands North Johannesburg 13 A2
Hillcrest Heights Washington 33 C3
Hillend Edinburgh 11 A1
Hillingdon □ London 15 A1
Hillwood Washington 33 B2
Hilmīya Cairo 7 A2
Hin Keng Hong Kong 12 A2
Hirota Osaka 23 A1
Hirschstetten Vienna 32 A2
Hither Green London 15 B3
Hiyoshi Tokyo 30 B2
Hizma Jerusalem 13 B2
Hjortekær Copenhagen 8 A3
Hjortespring Copenhagen 8 A2
Hlubočepy Prague 25 B2
Ho Chung Hong Kong 12 A2
Hoboken New York 22 B1
Hobsons B. Melbourne 18 B1
Hochbrück Munich 21 A2
Hochelaga Montreal 20 A2
Hoegi Seoul 27 B2
Hoeilaart Brussels 6 B2
Hofburg Vienna 32 A2
Hoffman I. New York 22 C1
Hohenbrunn Munich 21 B3
Hohenschönhausen Berlin 5 A4
Holargos = Cholargos Athens 2 B2
Holborn London 15 A3
Holden, L. Orlando 23 B2
Holešovice Prague 25 B2
Holiday Park Miami 19 B3
Holland Village Singapore 28 B2
Höllriegelskreuth Munich 21 B1
Hollywood Los Angeles 16 B3
Hollywood Miami 19 B3
Hollywood Bowl Los Angeles 16 B2
Holmenkollen Oslo 23 A3
Holmgård Stockholm 29 B1
Holmlia Oslo 23 B3
Holocaust Memorial Jerusalem 13 B2
Holyrood House, Palace of Edinburgh 11 B3
Holysloot Amsterdam 2 A3
Homerton London 15 A3
Hometown Chicago 9 C2
Hōnanchō Tokyo 30 A2
Honcho Tokyo 30 A3
Honden Tokyo 30 A4
Hondo, Rio → Los Angeles 16 B4
Hong Kong Hong Kong 12 B1
Hong Kong, Univ. of Hong Kong 12 B1
Hong Kong I. Hong Kong 12 B2
Hongje Seoul 27 B1
Hongjimun Tunnel Seoul 27 B1
Hongkou Shanghai 28 B1
Hongqiao Shanghai 28 B1
Honjyo Tokyo 30 A3
Honoré Mercier, Pont Montreal 20 B1
Hönow Berlin 5 A4
Hook London 15 B2
Horikiri Tokyo 30 A4
Horn Pond Boston 6 A1
Hornchurch London 15 A5
Horní Prague 25 B3
Horní Počernice Prague 25 B3
Hornsey London 15 A3
Horoměřice Prague 25 B1
Hortaleza Madrid 17 B2
Hosoyama Tokyo 30 B2
Hostafrancs Barcelona 4 A1
Hostivař Prague 25 B3
Houbětin Prague 25 B3
Hougang Singapore 28 A3
Houghton Johannesburg 13 B2
Houilles Paris 24 A2
Hounslow □ London 15 B1
Hout Bay Cape Town 8 B1
Hove Å → Copenhagen 8 B2
Hovedøya Oslo 23 B3
Høvik Oslo 23 A2
Hovorčovice Prague 25 A3
Howard Beach New York 22 C2
Howrah = Haora Kolkata 14 B1
Howth Dublin 10 A3
Howth Hd. Dublin 10 A3
Hōya Tokyo 30 A2
Hradčany Prague 25 B2
Huanghuagang Mausoleum Guangzhou 11 B2
Huangpu Shanghai 28 B2
Huangpu Jiang → Shanghai 28 B1
Huangtugang Beijing 4 C1
Huascar Lima 14 A2
Huay Khwang Bangkok 3 B2
Huddinge Stockholm 29 B2
Huechuraba Santiago 27 B1
Hugh Taylor Birch State Recr. Area △ Miami 19 B3
Huizingen Brussels 6 B1
Humayun's Tomb Delhi 10 B2
Humber → Toronto 31 A1
Humber B. Toronto 31 B2
Humber Bay Toronto 31 B2
Humber Bay Park Toronto 31 B2
Humber College Toronto 31 A1
Humber Summit Toronto 31 A1
Humber Valley Village Toronto 31 A1
Humberlea Toronto 31 A1
Humberwood Park Toronto 31 A1
Humboldt Park Chicago 9 B2
Humera Madrid 17 B1
Hunaydī Baghdad 3 B2
Hundige Copenhagen 8 B1
Hundige Strand Copenhagen 8 B2
Hung Hom Hong Kong 12 B2
Hunters Hill Sydney 29 B1
Hunters Pt. San Francisco 26 B2
Huntington Washington 33 C2
Huntington Park Los Angeles 16 C3
Hurīya Baghdad 3 A1
Hurstville Sydney 29 B1
Husan Jerusalem 13 B1
Husby Stockholm 29 A1
Husum Copenhagen 8 A2
Hütteldorf Vienna 32 A1
Hüvösvölgy Budapest 7 A2
Huwon Secret Garden Seoul 27 B1
Hvalstad Oslo 23 A1
Hvalstrand Oslo 23 A2
Hvidovre Copenhagen 8 B2
Hwagok Seoul 27 B1
Hyattsville Washington 33 B3
Hyde Park Boston 6 B2
Hyde Park Chicago 9 C3
Hyde Park Johannesburg 13 A2
Hyde Park London 15 A2
Hyde Park Los Angeles 16 C3

I

Ibese Lagos 14 A2
Ibirapuera São Paulo 27 B1
Ibirapuera, Parque do São Paulo 27 B2
Icarai Rio de Janeiro 25 B2
Içerenköy Istanbul 12 C2
Ichgao Tokyo 30 B2
Ichigaya Tokyo 30 A3
Ichikawa Tokyo 30 A4
Ickenham London 15 A1
Iddo Lagos 14 B2
Idi-Oro Lagos 14 A2
Iganmu Lagos 14 B2
Igbobi Lagos 14 A2
Igbologun Lagos 14 B1
Igny Paris 24 B2
IJ, Het → Amsterdam 2 A2
IJ-meer Amsterdam 2 A3
Ijesa-Tedo Lagos 14 B1
Ijora Lagos 14 B2
Ikebe Tokyo 30 B2
Ikebukuro Tokyo 30 A3
Ikegami Tokyo 30 B3
Ikeja Lagos 14 A2
Ikeuchi Osaka 23 B2
Ikorodu Lagos 14 A2
Ikoyi Lagos 14 B2
Ikuata Lagos 14 B2
Ikuno Osaka 23 A2
Ikuta Tokyo 30 B2
Ila Oslo 23 A2
Ilford London 15 A4
Ilioupoli Athens 2 B2
Illinois at Chicago, Univ. of Chicago 9 B3
Illinois Institute of Technology Chicago 9 B3
Ilpendam Amsterdam 2 A2
Ilsos → Athens 2 B2
Imbābah Cairo 7 A2
Imbiah Lookout Singapore 28 B2
Imielin Warsaw 33 C2
Imirim São Paulo 27 A2
Imitos Athens 2 B2
Imitos, Oros Athens 2 B2
Imperial Palace Museum Beijing 4 B2
Inagi Tokyo 30 B2
Inchcolm Edinburgh 11 A2
Inchicore Dublin 10 A1
Inchkeith Edinburgh 11 A3
Inchmickery Edinburgh 11 A2
Incirano Milan 18 A1
Independencia Lima 14 A2
Independencia Santiago 27 B2
India Gate Delhi 10 B2
Indian Creek Village Miami 19 C3
Indianópolis São Paulo 27 B2
Indira Gandhi Int. ✕ (DEL) Delhi 10 B1
Industria Johannesburg 13 B1
Industrial Canal New Orleans 21 A2
Ingierstrand Oslo 23 B3
Inglewood Los Angeles 16 C3
Ingliston Edinburgh 11 B1
Inhaúma Rio de Janeiro 25 B1
Inner Port Shelter Hong Kong 12 A2
Interlagos São Paulo 27 C1
Intramuros Manila 17 B1
Invalides Paris 24 A2
Inverkeithing Edinburgh 11 A1
Inzersdorf Vienna 32 B2
Ipanema Rio de Janeiro 25 B1
Ipiranga São Paulo 27 B2
Ipiranga → São Paulo 27 B2
Iponri Lagos 14 B2
Ireland's Eye Dublin 10 A3
Irving Park Chicago 9 B2
Isabel Rio de Janeiro 25 B1
Isagatedo Lagos 14 A1
Isar → Munich 21 A3
Ishbīliya Baghdad 3 A2
Ishøj Strand Copenhagen 8 B2
Islands Park Toronto 31 B2
Islev Copenhagen 8 A2
Isleworth London 15 B2
Islington Toronto 31 B1
Islington □ London 15 A3
Ismā'ilīya, Qanâ el Cairo 7 A2
Ismaning Munich 21 A3
Ismayloskiy Park Moscow 19 B3
Isolo Lagos 14 A1
Issy-les-Moulineaux Paris 24 B2
İstanbul Istanbul 12 C1
İstanbul Boğazı Istanbul 12 B2
İstinye Istanbul 12 B2
Itä Hakkila Helsinki 11 B3
Itaewon Seoul 27 B1
Itami Osaka 23 A1
Itanhanga Rio de Janeiro 25 B1
Ivanhoe Melbourne 18 A2
Ives Estates Miami 19 C3
Ivry-sur-Seine Paris 24 B3
Ixelles Brussels 6 B2
Izmaylovo Moscow 19 B3
Iztacalco Mexico City 18 B2
Iztapalapa Mexico City 18 B2

J

Jaba Jerusalem 13 A2
Jabotabek = Jakarta Jakarta 12 A2
Jacaré Rio de Janeiro 25 B1
Jackson Heights New York 22 B2
Jackson Park Chicago 9 C3
Jacques-Cartier Montreal 20 A3
Jacques-Cartier, Pont Montreal 20 A2
Jadavpur Kolkata 14 C2
Jade Buddha Temple Shanghai 28 B1
Jægersborg Copenhagen 8 A3
Jægersborg Dyrehave Copenhagen 8 A3
Jagadishpur Kolkata 14 B1
Jagatpur Delhi 10 A2
Jaguaré, Rib. do → São Paulo 27 B1
Jahangirpur Delhi 10 A2
Jakarta Jakarta 12 A2
Jakarta, Teluk Jakarta 12 A1
Jakarta Halim Perdana Kusuma Int. ✕ (HLP) Jakarta 12 B2
Jalan Kayu Singapore 28 A3
Jamaica B. New York 22 C3
Jamaica Plain Boston 6 B2
Jamakpuri Delhi 10 B1
Jamshīdīyeh Tehran 31 A2
Jamsil Seoul 27 B2
Jamwon Seoul 27 B2
Janki Warsaw 33 C1
Jaraguá São Paulo 27 A1
Jaraguá, Pico de São Paulo 27 A1
Jardim Paulista São Paulo 27 B1
Järvatältet Stockholm 29 A1
Jaskhar Mumbai 20 B2
Jatinegara Jakarta 12 B2
Javādīyeh Tehran 31 B2
Jawaharlal Nehru Port = Nhava Sheva Mumbai 20 B2
Jaworowa Warsaw 33 C1
Jean Lafitte Nat. Historical Park △ New Orleans 21 B1
Jedlesee Vienna 32 A2
Jefferson New Orleans 21 B2
Jefferson Memorial Washington 33 B2
Jefferson Park Chicago 9 B2
Jefferson Park Los Angeles 16 B3
Jegi Seoul 27 B2
Jelambar Jakarta 12 A1
Jelonki Warsaw 33 B1
Jerónimos, Mosteiro dos Lisbon 16 A1
Jersey City New York 22 B1
Jerusalem Jerusalem 13 B2
Jessamine, L. Orlando 23 B2
Jésus, Î. Montreal 20 A1
Jesús María Lima 14 B2
Jette Brussels 6 A1
Jey Tehran 31 B2
Jianggao Guangzhou 11 A2
Jiangwan Shanghai 28 B1
Jib Jerusalem 13 A2
Jihād Baghdad 3 B1
Jingan Shanghai 28 B1
Jinočany Prague 25 B1
Jinonice Prague 25 B2
Jinqiao Shanghai 28 B2
Jiulong = Kowloon Hong Kong 12 B1
Jiyūgaoka Tokyo 30 B3
Jiżā'ir Baghdad 3 B2
Jizira Baghdad 3 B2
Joglo Jakarta 12 B1
Johannesburg Johannesburg 13 B2
Johannesburg, Univ. of Johannesburg 13 B2
Johanneskirchen Munich 21 A2
Johannesstift Berlin 5 A2
Johannisthal Berlin 5 B4
John F. Kennedy Nat. Historic Site △ Boston 6 A2
John McLaren Park San Francisco 26 B2
John U. Lloyd Beach △ Miami 19 B3
Joinville-le-Pont Paris 24 B3
Joli-Bois Brussels 6 B2
Jollas Helsinki 11 B3
Jongmyo Royal Shrine Seoul 27 B1
Jongno Seoul 27 B1
Jonstrup Copenhagen 8 A2
Joppa Edinburgh 11 B3
Jorge Chavez, Int. ✕ (LIM) Lima 14 B2
Jorge Newbery ✕ (AEP) Buenos Aires 7 B2
Józefa Piłsudskiego Park Warsaw 33 B1
Jōtō Osaka 23 A2
Jouy-en-Josas Paris 24 B2
Juan Anchorena Buenos Aires 7 A2
Juan González Romero Mexico City 18 A2
Juárez Int. ✕ (MEX) Mexico City 18 B2
Judeira Jerusalem 13 A2
Juhdum Jerusalem 13 B2
Juhu Mumbai 20 A2
Jūjā Tokyo 30 A3
Jukskeirivier → Johannesburg 13 A2
Julianów Warsaw 33 B2
Jumeirah Dubai 9 B1
Jung Seoul 27 B1
Jungfernheide, Volkspark Berlin 5 A2
Jungfernsee Berlin 5 B1
Junghwa Seoul 27 B2
Jungnang Seoul 27 B2
Jungnangcheon → Seoul 27 B1
Juniper Green Edinburgh 11 B2
Junk B. Hong Kong 12 B2
Jurong Singapore 28 B2
Jurong, Selat Singapore 28 B2
Jurong Industrial Estate Singapore 28 B1
Jurujuba, Enseada de Rio de Janeiro 25 B2
Jūsō Osaka 23 A1
Justice Chicago 9 C2
Jwalahari Delhi 10 B1

K

Kaapstad = Cape Town Cape Town 8 A1
Kabaty Warsaw 33 C2
Kadıköy Istanbul 12 C2
Kadoma Osaka 23 A2
Kafr 'Aqab Jerusalem 13 A2
Kāğithane Istanbul 12 B1
Kāğithane → Istanbul 12 B1
Kagran Vienna 32 A2
Kahnawake Montreal 20 B1
Kaimes Edinburgh 11 B2
Kaiserebersdorf Vienna 32 B2
Kaivoksela Helsinki 11 B2
Kalamaki Athens 2 B2
Kalbadevi Mumbai 20 B1
Kalipur Kolkata 14 A1
Kalithea Athens 2 B2
Kalkaji Delhi 10 B2
Kalookan = Caloocan Manila 17 B1
Kalvebod Fælled Copenhagen 8 B3
Kalveboderne Copenhagen 8 B3
Kamarhati Kolkata 14 A2
Kamata Tokyo 30 B3
Kameari Tokyo 30 A4
Kameido Tokyo 30 A4
Kami-Itabashi Tokyo 30 A3
Kamikitazawa Tokyo 30 B2
Kamitsuruma Tokyo 30 B1
Kamoshida Tokyo 30 B2
Kampong Landang Singapore 28 A3
Kampong Tanjong Penjuru Singapore 28 B2
Kampung Bali Jakarta 12 B1
Kanamori Tokyo 30 B1
Kanda Tokyo 30 A3
Kandilli Istanbul 12 B2
Kankurgachi Kolkata 14 B2
Kanlıca Istanbul 12 B2
Kanonerskiy, Ostrov St. Petersburg 27 B1
Kansai Int. ✕ (KIX) Osaka 23 B2
Kanzaki → Osaka 23 A1
Kapali Carsi Istanbul 12 B1
Kapellerfeld Vienna 32 A2
Káposztásmegyer Budapest 7 A2
Kapotnya Moscow 19 C3
Käppala Stockholm 29 A3
Kapuk Jakarta 12 A1
Käpylä Helsinki 11 B2
Karachi Karachi 13 A2
Karachi Int. ✕ (KHI) Karachi 13 A2
Karkh Baghdad 3 A2
Karlin Prague 25 B2
Karlsfeld Munich 21 A1
Karlshorst Berlin 5 B4
Karlův most Prague 25 B2
Karol Bagh Delhi 10 B2
Karolinenhof Berlin 5 B4
Karow Berlin 5 A3
Karrādah Baghdad 3 B2
Kärsön Stockholm 29 B1
Kasai Tokyo 30 B4
Kasipur Kolkata 14 B2
Kastrup Copenhagen 8 B3
Kastrup, København ✕ (CPH) Copenhagen 8 B3
Kasuga Tokyo 30 A2
Kasuge Tokyo 30 A3
Kasumigaseki Tokyo 30 B3
Katong Singapore 28 B3
Katsushika Tokyo 30 A4
Kau Pai Chau Hong Kong 12 B2
Kau Yi Chau Hong Kong 12 B1
Kaulsdorf Berlin 5 B4
Kauniainen Helsinki 11 B1
Kawasaki Tokyo 30 B3
Kawawa Tokyo 30 B2
Kawęczyn Warsaw 33 B2
Kayu Putih Jakarta 12 B2
Kbely Prague 25 B3
Kebayoran Baru Jakarta 12 B1
Kebayoran Lama Jakarta 12 B1
Kebon Jeruk Jakarta 12 B1
Kedar Jerusalem 13 B2
Kedoya Jakarta 12 B1
Keilor Melbourne 18 A1
Keilor North Melbourne 18 A1
Keimola Helsinki 11 A1
Kelapa Gading Jakarta 12 A2
Kelenföld Budapest 7 B2
Kelvin Johannesburg 13 A2
Kemang Jakarta 12 B1
Kemayoran Jakarta 12 B2
Kemerburgaz Istanbul 12 B1
Kempton Park Races London 15 B1
Kendall Miami 19 D1
Kenilworth Cape Town 8 A1
Kenilworth Chicago 9 A2
Kennedy Town Hong Kong 12 B1
Kenner New Orleans 21 A1
Kensal Green London 15 A2
Kensington Johannesburg 13 B2
Kensington London 15 B2
Kensington New York 22 C2
Kensington Sydney 29 B2
Kensington Palace London 15 A2
Kentish Town London 15 A3
Kenton London 15 A2
Kenwood House London 15 A3
Kepa Warsaw 33 B2
Keppel Harbour Singapore 28 B2
Kesariani Athens 2 B2
Kew London 15 B2
Kew Melbourne 18 A2
Kew Gardens London 15 B2
Kew Gardens Toronto 31 A3
Key Biscayne Miami 19 D3
Khalīj Baghdad 3 B2
Khansā' Baghdad 3 A2
Kharavli Mumbai 20 B2
Khefren Cairo 7 B1
Khichripur Delhi 10 B2
Khidirpur Kolkata 14 B1
Khimki-Khovrino Moscow 19 A2
Khirbet Batin Abu Lihyah Jerusalem 13 A1
Khirbet el-Misbah Jerusalem 13 A1
Khirbet Jub e-Rum Jerusalem 13 B2
Khlong San Bangkok 3 B2
Khlong Toey Bangkok 3 B2
Khorel Kolkata 14 A1
Khorosovo Moscow 19 B1
Kiamari Karachi 13 B1
Kierling Vienna 32 A1
Kierlingbach → Vienna 32 A1
Kifisos → Athens 2 B2
Kikuna Tokyo 30 B2
Kilbarrack Dublin 10 A3
Kilburn London 15 A2
Killakee Dublin 10 B2
Killester Dublin 10 A2
Killiney Dublin 10 B3
Killiney B. Dublin 10 B3
Kilmacud Dublin 10 B2
Kilmainham Dublin 10 A2
Kilmainham Gaol Dublin 10 A2
Kilmashogue Mt. Dublin 10 B2
Kilmore Dublin 10 A2
Kilnamanagh Dublin 10 B1
Kilo Helsinki 11 B1
Kilokri Delhi 10 B2
Kiltiernan Dublin 10 B2
Kimmage Dublin 10 B2
Kindi Baghdad 3 B2
Kinghorn Edinburgh 11 A2
Kings Domain Melbourne 18 A1
Kings Forest = Kongelunden Copenhagen 8 B3
Kingsbury London 15 A2
Kingsbury Melbourne 18 A2
Kingsford Sydney 29 B2
Kingsford Smith, Sydney ✕ (SYD) Sydney 29 B2
Kingston-upon-Thames □ London 15 B2
Kingston Vale London 15 B2
Kingsway Toronto 31 B1
Kinsaley Dublin 10 A2
Kipling Heights Toronto 31 A1
Kipseli Athens 2 B2
Kirchstockbach Munich 21 B3
Kirchtrudering Munich 21 B3
Kirikiri Lagos 14 B1
Kirke Værløse Copenhagen 8 A1
Kirkhill Edinburgh 11 B2
Kirkliston Edinburgh 11 B1
Kirknewton Edinburgh 11 B1
Kirov Palace of Culture St. Petersburg 27 B1
Kiryat Anavim Jerusalem 13 B1
Kiryat Ha Yovel Jerusalem 13 B1
Kısıklı Istanbul 12 B2
Kispest Budapest 7 B2
Kista Stockholm 29 A1
Kita Osaka 23 A2
Kita Tokyo 30 A3
Kitazawa Tokyo 30 B3
Kiu Tsiu Hong Kong 12 A2
Kivistö Helsinki 11 B2
Kiza → Osaka 23 B1
Kızıltoprak Istanbul 12 C2
Kizuri Osaka 23 B2
Kjelsås Oslo 23 A3
Kladow Berlin 5 B1
Klampenborg Copenhagen 8 A3
Klečany Prague 25 A2
Kledering Vienna 32 B2
Klein Jukskei → Johannesburg 13 A1
Kleinmachnow Berlin 5 B2
Kleinschönebeck Berlin 5 B5
Klemetsrud Oslo 23 A4
Klender Jakarta 12 A2
Kličany Prague 25 A2
Klipriviersberg Nature Reserve Johannesburg 13 B2
Klosterneuburg Vienna 32 A1
Köbánya Budapest 7 B2
Kobbegem Brussels 6 A1
København Copenhagen 8 A2
København ✕ (CPH) Copenhagen 8 B3
Kobylisy Prague 25 B2
Kobyłka Warsaw 33 A3
Kodaira Tokyo 30 A1
Kodanaka Tokyo 30 B2
Koekelberg Brussels 6 A1
Koganei Tokyo 30 A2
Kogarah Sydney 29 B1
Koivupää Helsinki 11 B2
Koja Jakarta 12 A2
Koja Utara Jakarta 12 A2
Kokhav Ya'akov Jerusalem 13 A2
Kokobunji Tokyo 30 A1
Kokobunji-Temple Tokyo 30 A4
Kolarängen Stockholm 29 B3
Kolbotn Oslo 23 B3
Kolkata Kolkata 14 B2
Kolkata Maidan Kolkata 14 B1
Kolkata Netaji Subhash Chandra Bose Int. ✕ (CCU) Kolkata 14 B2
Kolo Warsaw 33 B1
Kolokinthou Athens 2 B2
Kolomyagi St. Petersburg 27 A1
Kolonos Athens 2 B2
Kolsås Oslo 23 A2
Komae Tokyo 30 B2
Komagome Tokyo 30 A3
Komazawa Tokyo 30 B3
Kona Kolkata 14 B1
Konala Helsinki 11 B2
Kondli Delhi 10 B2
Kongelunden Copenhagen 8 B3
Kongens Lyngby Copenhagen 8 A3
Kongo Helsinki 11 A1
Konnagar Kolkata 14 A2
Konohana Osaka 23 A1
Konradshöhe Berlin 5 A2
Kopanina Prague 25 B1
Koparkhairna Mumbai 20 A2
Köpenick Berlin 5 B4
Korangi Karachi 13 B2
Koremasa Tokyo 30 B1
Koridalos Athens 2 B1
Kosino Moscow 19 B4
Kosugi Tokyo 30 B2
Kota Jakarta 12 A1
Kōtō Tokyo 30 A3
Kotrung Kolkata 14 A2
Kouponia Athens 2 B2
Kowloon Hong Kong 12 B1
Kowloon Peak Hong Kong 12 A2
Kowloon Res. Hong Kong 12 A1
Kowloon Tong Hong Kong 12 A2
Kraainem Brussels 6 A2
Krailling Munich 21 B1
Krampnitz Berlin 5 B1
Krampnitzsee Berlin 5 B1
Kranji Industrial Estate Singapore 28 A2
Kranji Res. Singapore 28 A2
Krasno-Presnenskaya Moscow 19 B2
Krč Prague 25 B2
Kremlin Moscow 19 B2
Krestovskiye, Ostrov St. Petersburg 27 B1
Kreuzberg Berlin 5 A3
Kritzendorf Vienna 32 A1
Krumme Lanke Berlin 5 B2
Krummensee Berlin 5 A5
Krung Thep = Bangkok Bangkok 3 B2
Krusboda Stockholm 29 B3
Kuangchou = Guangzhou Guangzhou 11 B2
Küçükköy Istanbul 12 B1
Küçüksu Istanbul 12 B2
Kudrovo St. Petersburg 27 B3
Kulosaari Helsinki 11 B3
Kumla Stockholm 29 B3
Kungens kurva Stockholm 29 B1
Kungliga Slottet Stockholm 29 B2
Kungshatt Stockholm 29 B1
Kungsholmen Stockholm 29 A2
Kuningan Jakarta 12 B1
Kunitachi Tokyo 30 A1
Kunming Hu Beijing 4 B1
Kunratice Prague 25 B2
Kupchino St. Petersburg 27 B2
Kuramo Waters Lagos 14 B2
Kurbağalı → Istanbul 12 C2
Kurihara Tokyo 30 A2
Kurla Mumbai 20 A2
Kurmuri Mumbai 20 A2
Kurume Tokyo 30 A2
Kuryanovo Moscow 19 C3
Kuskovo Moscow 19 B3
Kustia Kolkata 14 B2
Kuzguncuk Istanbul 12 B2
Kuzyminki Moscow 19 B3
Kwai Chung Hong Kong 12 A1
Kwangchow = Guangzhou Guangzhou 11 B2
Kwun Tong Hong Kong 12 B2
Kyje Prague 25 B3
Kyūhōji Osaka 23 B2

L

L.A. County Art Museum Los Angeles 16 B2
La Barceloneta Barcelona 4 A2
La Blanca Santiago 27 C2
La Boca Buenos Aires 7 B2
La Bretèche Paris 24 A1
La Campiña Lima 14 C2
La Celle-St-Cloud Paris 24 A1
La Cisterna Santiago 27 C2
La Courneuve Paris 24 A3
La Dehesa Santiago 27 B2
La Encantada Lima 14 C2
La Estación Madrid 17 B1
La Floresta Barcelona 4 A1
La Florida Santiago 27 C2
La Fortuna Madrid 17 B1
La Franca Barcelona 4 A1
La Garenne-Colombes Paris 24 A2
La Giustiniana Rome 26 B1
La Granja Santiago 27 C2
La Guardia, New York ✕ (LGA) New York 22 B2
La Hulpe Brussels 6 B2
La Llacuna Barcelona 4 A2
La Loma Mexico City 18 A1
La Lucila Buenos Aires 7 B2
La Maladrerie Paris 24 B1
La Milla, Cerro Lima 14 B2
La Monachina Rome 26 B1
La Moraleja Madrid 17 A2
La Nopalera Mexico City 18 C2
La Paternal Buenos Aires 7 B2
La Perla Lima 14 B2
La Perouse Sydney 29 B2
La Pisana Rome 26 B1
La Prairie Montreal 20 B3
La Punta Lima 14 B1
La Puntigala Barcelona 4 A2
La Queue-en-Brie Paris 24 B4
La Reina Santiago 27 B2
La Ribera Barcelona 4 A1
La Sagrera Barcelona 4 A2
La Salada Buenos Aires 7 C2
La Scala Milan 18 B2
La Storta Rome 26 A1
La Taxonera Barcelona 4 A2
La Victoria Lima 14 B2
La Vista Atlanta 3 B2
Laajalahti Helsinki 11 B1
Laajasalo Helsinki 11 B3
Laaksolahti Helsinki 11 B1
Labagou Nat. Forest Park Beijing 4 A2
Lablāba, W. el → Cairo 7 A2
Lachine Montreal 20 B1
Lachine, Canal de Montreal 20 B2
Lad Phrao Bangkok 3 B2
Ladera Heights Los Angeles 16 C2
Ládví Prague 25 B2
Lady Warsaw 33 C1
Lafontaine, Parc Montreal 20 A2
Lagoa Rio de Janeiro 25 B1
Lagos Lagos 14 B2
Lagos Harbour Lagos 14 B2
Lagos-Ikeja ✕ (LOS) Lagos 14 A1
Lagos Island Lagos 14 B2
Lagos Lagoon Lagos 14 B2
Laguna de B. Manila 17 C2
Laim Munich 21 B2
Lainate Milan 18 A1
Lainz Vienna 32 B1
Lake Buena Vista Orlando 23 B1
Lake Cain Hills Orlando 23 B2
Lakemba Sydney 29 B1
Lakeside Cape Town 8 B1
Lakeside Johannesburg 13 A2
Lakeview Chicago 9 B3
Lakeview New Orleans 21 A2
Lakewood Park Atlanta 3 B2
Lakhtinskiy St. Petersburg 27 B1
Lakhtinskiy Razliv, Oz. St. Petersburg 27 B1
Lakshmanpur Kolkata 14 B1
Laksi Bangkok 3 A2
Lal Qila Delhi 10 B2
Lam Tin Hong Kong 12 B2
Lambert Oslo 23 A3
Lambeth □ London 15 B3
Lambrate Milan 18 B2
Lambro, Parco Milan 18 B2
Lambton Mills Toronto 31 B1
Lamma I. Hong Kong 12 B1
Landianchang Beijing 4 B1
Landsmeer Amsterdam 2 A2
Landstrasse Vienna 32 A2
Landwehr kanal Berlin 5 B3
Lane Cove Sydney 29 A1
Lane Cove Nat. Park △ Sydney 29 A1
Langa Cape Town 8 A2
Langenzersdorf Vienna 32 A2
Langer See Berlin 5 B4
Langley Washington 33 B1
Langley Park Washington 33 B3
Langwald Munich 21 B1
Lankwitz Berlin 5 B3
L'Annunziatella Rome 26 C2
Lansdowne Cape Town 8 A2
Lansing Toronto 31 A2
Lanus Buenos Aires 7 C2
Lapa Rio de Janeiro 25 B1
Laranjeiras Rio de Janeiro 25 B1
Las Warsaw 33 B2
Las Corts Barcelona 4 A1
Las Kabacki Warsaw 33 C2
Las Pinas Manila 17 C1
Las Rejas Santiago 27 B1
Las Vegas Las Vegas 14 A2
Las Vegas McCarran Int. ✕ (LAS) Las Vegas 14 B2
LaSalle Montreal 20 B2
LaSalle Street Station Chicago 9 B3
Lasek Bielański Warsaw 33 B1
Lasek Na Kole Warsaw 33 B1
Latina Madrid 17 B1
Lauderdale Lakes Miami 19 B1
Lauderhill Miami 19 B2
Lauttasaari Helsinki 11 C2
Laval-des-Rapides Montreal 20 A1
Lavīzān Tehran 31 A2
Lavradio Lisbon 16 A2
Lawndale Chicago 9 B2
Lawne L. Orlando 23 A2
Lawrence Heights Toronto 31 A2
Layari Karachi 13 A2
Layari → Karachi 13 A1
Lazienkowski Park Warsaw 33 B2
Lazy Lake Miami 19 B3
Le Blanc-Mesnil Paris 24 A3
Le Bourget Paris 24 A3
Le Chenoi Brussels 6 B2
Le Chesnay Paris 24 B1
Le Christ de Saclay Paris 24 B2
Le Kremlin-Bicêtre Paris 24 B3
Le Mesnil-le-Roi Paris 24 A1
Le Pecq Paris 24 A1
Le Perreux Paris 24 A3
Le Pin Paris 24 A4

Le Plessis-Robinson *Paris* 24 B2
Le Plessis-Trévise *Paris* 24 B4
Le Port-Marly *Paris* 24 A1
Le Pré-St-Gervais *Paris* 24 A3
Le Raincy *Paris* 24 A4
Le Vésinet *Paris* 24 A1
Lea Bridge *London* 15 A3
Leaside *Toronto* 31 A2
Leblon *Rio de Janeiro* 25 B1
Lee *London* 15 B4
Leganés *Madrid* 17 B1
Legazpi *Madrid* 17 B1
Lehtisaari *Helsinki* 11 B2
Lei Yue Mun *Hong Kong* 12 B2
Leião *Lisbon* 16 A1
Leichhardt *Sydney* 29 B1
Leith *Edinburgh* 11 B3
Lekki *Lagos* 14 B2
Lekki Peninsula *Lagos* 14 B2
Lemoyne *Montreal* 20 B3
Lenino *Moscow* 19 C2
Lenino *Moscow* 19 B2
Leninskiye Gory *Moscow* 19 B2
Lennox *Los Angeles* 16 C2
Leopardstown *Dublin* 10 B2
Leopoldau *Vienna* 32 A2
Leopoldo-Perret *Paris* 24 B2
Leopoldstadt *Vienna* 32 A2
Leportovo *Moscow* 19 B2
Leppävaara *Helsinki* 11 B1
Les Lilas *Paris* 24 A3
Les Loges-en-Josas *Paris* 24 B1
Les Pavillons-sous-Bois
  Paris 24 A4
Lésigny *Paris* 24 B4
Lesnozavodskaya
  St. Petersburg 27 B2
Lester B. Pearson Int.,
  Toronto ✈ (YYZ) *Toronto* 31 A1
L'Étang-la-Ville *Paris* 24 A1
Letňany *Prague* 25 B2
Letopolis = Ausim *Cairo* 7 A1
Levallois-Perret *Paris* 24 A2
Levent *Istanbul* 12 B2
Lewisdale *Washington* 33 B3
Lewisham □ *London* 15 B3
Leyton *London* 15 A3
Leytonstone *London* 15 A4
L'Haÿ-les-Roses *Paris* 24 B3
L'Hospitalet de Llobregat
  Barcelona 4 A1
Lhotka *Prague* 25 B2
Liangshui He → *Beijing* 4 C2
Lianhua Chi *Beijing* 4 B1
Lianhua He → *Beijing* 4 B1
Libčice nad Vltavou *Prague* 25 A2
Liběn *Prague* 25 B2
Liberdade *São Paulo* 27 B2
Liberton *Edinburgh* 11 B3
Liberty I. *New York* 22 C1
Liberty Ōsaka Museum
  Osaka 23 B2
Liberty State Park △
  New York 22 B1
Libeznice *Prague* 25 A2
Libuš *Prague* 25 B2
Lichiao *Guangzhou* 11 B2
Lichtenberg *Berlin* 5 A4
Lichterfelde *Berlin* 5 B2
Lidingö *Stockholm* 29 A2
Lieshi Lingyuan *Guangzhou* 11 B2
Liesing → *Vienna* 32 B1
Liesing *Vienna* 32 B2
Ligovo *St. Petersburg* 27 C1
Lijordet *Oslo* 23 A2
Likhoborka → *Moscow* 19 A2
Lilla Värtan *Stockholm* 29 A3
Lille Værløse *Copenhagen* 8 A2
Liluah *Kolkata* 14 B1
Lim Chu Kang *Singapore* 28 A2
Lima *Lima* 14 ...
Lima Jorge Chavez, Int. ✈
  (LIM) *Lima* 14 C2
Limbiate *Milan* 18 A1
Limehouse *London* 15 A3
Limeil-Brévannes *Paris* 24 B3
Linate, Milano ✈ (LIN)
  Milan 18 B2
Linbropark *Johannesburg* 13 A2
Lincoln Center for
  Performing Arts
  New York 22 B2
Lincoln Heights *Los Angeles* 16 B3
Lincoln Memorial
  Washington 33 B2
Lincoln Park *Chicago* 9 B3
Lincoln Park *New York* 22 B1
Lincoln Park *San Francisco* 26 B1
Lincoln Park Zoo *Chicago* 9 B3
Lincolnwood *Chicago* 9 A2
Linda-a-Pastora *Lisbon* 16 A1
Linden *Johannesburg* 13 A2
Lindenberg *Berlin* 5 A4
Lindoya *Oslo* 23 A3
Liniers *Buenos Aires* 7 B1
Linkebeek *Brussels* 6 B2
Linksfield *Johannesburg* 13 A2
Linmeyer *Johannesburg* 13 B2
Linna *Helsinki* 11 A2
Lintuvaara *Helsinki* 11 B1
Lion Rock Country
  Park △ *Hong Kong* 12 A2
Lion's Head *Cape Town* 8 A1
Lionch *Athens* 2 B2
Lisboa *Lisbon* 16 A2
Lisboa ✈ (LIS) *Lisbon* 16 A2
Lisboa = Lisboa *Lisbon* 16 A1
Lishui *Guangzhou* 11 A1
Little B. *Sydney* 29 B2
Little Calumet → *Chicago* 9 C2
Little Ferry *New York* 22 A1
Little Haiti *Miami* 19 D1
Little Havana *Miami* 19 D1
Little India *Shanghai* 28 a2
Little Lake Conway *Orlando* 23 B2
Little Rouge → *Toronto* 31 A4
Liuhang *Shanghai* 28 B1
Liurong Temple *Guangzhou* 11 B2
Live Oak Manor
  New Orleans 21 B1
Livry-Gargan *Paris* 24 A4
Liwan *Guangzhou* 11 B2
Ljan *Oslo* 23 A3
Llano de Can Gineu
  Barcelona 4 A1
Lo Aranguiz *Santiago* 27 B2
Lo Boza *Santiago* 27 B1
Lo Chau *Hong Kong* 12 B2
Lo Chau Pak Mai
  Hong Kong 12 B1
Lo Espejo *Santiago* 27 C2
Lo Hermida *Santiago* 27 B2
Lo So Shing *Hong Kong* 12 B1
Lo Wai *Hong Kong* 12 A2
Loanhead *Edinburgh* 11 B3
Locham *Munich* 21 B1

Lochkov *Prague* 25 B2
Lockhausen *Munich* 21 A1
Lodi *New York* 22 A1
Lodi Estate *Delhi* 10 B2
Logan Intn., Boston ✈
  (BOS) *Boston* 6 A2
Logan Square *Chicago* 9 B2
Lognes-Émerainville ✈
  (XLG) *Paris* 24 A4
Löhme *Berlin* 5 A5
Lokelet *Karachi* 13 A2
Lomas Chapultepec
  Mexico City 18 B1
Lomas de San Angel Inn
  Mexico City 18 B1
Lombardy East *Johannesburg* 13 A2
Łomianki *Warsaw* 33 B1
Lomus Reforma *Mexico City* 18 B1
London *London* 15 B3
London Avenue Canal
  New Orleans 21 B2
London City ✈ (LCY)
  London 15 B4
London Heathrow ✈
  (LHR), *London* 15 B1
London Zoo *London* 15 A3
Long B. *Sydney* 29 B2
Long Branch *Toronto* 31 B1
Long Ditton *London* 15 B2
Long Island City *New York* 22 B2
Longchamp, Hippodrome
  de *Paris* 24 A2
Longhua Pagoda *Shanghai* 28 B1
Longhua Park *Shanghai* 28 B1
Longtan Hu → *Beijing* 4 B2
Longue-Pointe *Montreal* 20 A2
Longueuil *Montreal* 20 A3
Loni *Delhi* 10 A2
Lord's Cricket Ground
  London 15 A2
Loreto *Milan* 18 A2
Los Angeles *Los Angeles* 16 B3
Los Angeles Int. ✈ (LAX)
  Los Angeles 16 C2
Los Cerrillos ✈ (ULC)
  Santiago 27 B1
Los Nietos *Los Angeles* 16 C4
Los Olivos *Lima* 14 A2
Los Remedios △ *Mexico City* 18 B1
Los Reyes *Mexico City* 18 B2
Losiny Ostrov △ *Moscow* 19 A3
Lot *Brussels* 6 B1
Lotus River *Cape Town* 8 B2
Lotus Temple *Delhi* 10 B2
Loughlinstown *Dublin* 10 B3
Louis Armstrong New
  Orleans Int. ✈ (MSY)
  New Orleans 21 B1
Louise, L. *Orlando* 23 B2
Louisiana Superdome
  New Orleans 21 B2
Loures *Lisbon* 16 A1
Louveciennes *Paris* 24 A1
Louvre, Musée du *Paris* 24 A3
Lower B. *New York* 22 C1
Lower New York B.
  New York 22 C1
Lower B. = *New York* 22 C1
Lower Peirce Res. *Singapore* 28 A2
Lower Shing Mun Res.
  Hong Kong 12 A1
Loyola Univ. *Chicago* 9 A2
Lu Xun, Tomb of *Shanghai* 28 B1
Lu Xun Park *Shanghai* 28 B1
Lübars *Berlin* 5 A3
Lucy, L. *Orlando* 23 A2
Ludwigsfeld *Munich* 21 A1
Luhu *Guangzhou* 11 B2
Lumiar *Lisbon* 16 A1
Lundtofte *Copenhagen* 8 A3
Lung Mei *Hong Kong* 12 A2
Luojiang *Guangzhou* 11 B2
Lustheim *Munich* 21 A2
Luwan *Shanghai* 28 B1
Luzhniki Sports Centre
  Moscow 19 B2
Lyndhurst *New York* 22 B1
Lynn Woods Res. *Boston* 6 A2
Lyon, Gare de *Paris* 24 A3
Lyons *Chicago* 9 C2
Lysaker *Oslo* 23 A2
Lysakerselva → *Oslo* 23 A2
Lysolaje *Prague* 25 B2
Lyublino *Moscow* 19 B3

M

Ma Nam Wat *Hong Kong* 12 A2
Ma On Shan Country
  Park △ *Hong Kong* 12 A2
Ma'ale Adumim *Jerusalem* 13 B2
Ma'ale Ha Khamisha
  Jerusalem 13 B1
Ma'ale Mikhmas *Jerusalem* 13 A2
Maantiekylä *Helsinki* 11 A3
Maarifa *Baghdad* 3 B2
Mabato Pt. *Manila* 17 C2
Mabel, L. *Orlando* 23 B1
Macaco, Morro do
  Rio de Janeiro 25 B2
McCarran Int., Las
  Vegas ✈ (LAS) *Las Vegas* 14 B2
McCook *Chicago* 9 C2
McGill Univ. *Montreal* 20 A2
Machelen *Brussels* 6 A2
Machida *Tokyo* 30 B1
Maciolki *Warsaw* 33 B1
McKinley Park *Chicago* 9 C2
McLean *Washington* 33 B1
Macopocho → *Santiago* 27 B1
MacRitchie Res. *Singapore* 28 A2
Macul *Santiago* 27 C2
Madhudaha *Kolkata* 14 B2
Madhyamgram *Kolkata* 14 A2
Madin *Mexico City* 18 A1
Madin, L. *Mexico City* 18 A1
Madinah Al Mansūr
  Baghdad 3 B2
Mâdinet Nasr *Cairo* 7 A2
Madrid *Madrid* 17 B1
Madrid Barajas ✈ (MAD)
  Madrid 17 B2
Madrona *Barcelona* 4 A1
Maesawa *Tokyo* 30 A3
Magdalena *Lima* 14 B2
Magdalena Contreras
  Mexico City 18 C1
Magellangrund *Stockholm* 29 B2
Maghreb *Baghdad* 3 A2
Maginu *Tokyo* 30 B2
Magliana *Rome* 26 B1
Magny-les-Hameaux *Paris* 24 B1
Mahar, L. *Miami* 19 C1
Maheshtala *Kolkata* 14 B2
Mahim *Mumbai* 20 A1
Mahim B. *Mumbai* 20 A1
Mahipalpur *Delhi* 10 B1
Mahlsdorf *Berlin* 5 A4
Mahmoodabad *Karachi* 13 A2
Mahrauli *Delhi* 10 B1
Mahul *Mumbai* 20 A2
Maida Vale *London* 15 A2

Maidstone *Melbourne* 18 A1
Maipú *Santiago* 27 C1
Maisonneuve, Parc
  Montreal 20 A2
Maisons-Alfort *Paris* 24 B3
Maisons-Laffitte *Paris* 24 A1
Maissoneuve *Montreal* 20 A2
Maitland *Cape Town* 8 A1
Makasar *Jakarta* 12 A2
Makati *Manila* 17 B2
Makarong → *Manila* 17 B2
Makarong *Sydney* 29 B2
Meguro *Tokyo* 30 B3
Meguro → *Tokyo* 30 B3
Mehrābād ✈ (THR) *Tehran* 31 A1
Mehram Nagar *Delhi* 10 B1
Mehrow *Berlin* 5 A4
Meidling *Vienna* 32 A2
Méier *Rio de Janeiro* 25 B1
Meiji Shrine *Tokyo* 30 A3
Meise *Brussels* 6 A1
Mejiro *Tokyo* 30 A3
Melbourne *Melbourne* 18 A1
Melbourne ✈ (MEL)
  Melbourne 18 A1
Melkki *Helsinki* 11 C2
Mellunkylä *Helsinki* 11 B3
Mellunmäki *Helsinki* 11 B3
Melrose *Boston* 6 A2
Melrose *New York* 22 B2
Melrose Park *Chicago* 9 B1
Melrose Park *Miami* 19 B3
Melsbroek *Brussels* 6 A2
Melville *Johannesburg* 13 B2
Menteng *Jakarta* 12 B2
Mérantaise → *Paris* 24 B1
Mercamadrid *Madrid* 17 B2
Merced, L. *San Francisco* 26 B2
Meredale *Johannesburg* 13 B1
Mérida △ *São Paulo* 27 B2
Merlimau, Pulau *Singapore* 28 B2
Merri Cr. → *Melbourne* 18 A1
Merrion *Dublin* 10 B2
Merrionette Park *Chicago* 9 C2
Merton □ *London* 15 B2
Merton □ *London* 15 B2
Mesgarābād *Tehran* 31 B3
Messe *Vienna* 32 A2
Metairie *New Orleans* 21 B2
Metanópoli *Milan* 18 B2
Metro Toronto Zoo *Toronto* 31 A3
Metropolitan Museum of
  Art *New York* 22 B2
Meudon *Paris* 24 B2
Mevaseret Zion *Jerusalem* 13 B1
Mevo Beitar *Jerusalem* 13 B1
México, Ciudad de
  Mexico City 18 B1
Mexico City Int. ✈ (MEX)
  Mexico City 18 B2
Meyersdal *Johannesburg* 13 B2
Mezzate *Milan* 18 B2
Miadong *Seoul* 27 B2
Miami *Miami* 19 D2
Miami → *Miami* 19 D1
Miami Beach *Miami* 19 D3
Miami Gardens *Miami* 19 C2
Miami Int. ✈ (MIA) *Miami* 19 D1
Miami Lakes *Miami* 19 C1
Miami Shores *Miami* 19 C2
Miami Springs *Miami* 19 D1
Miasto *Warsaw* 33 B2
Michałowice *Warsaw* 33 B1
Michle *Prague* 25 B2
Mid-City *Los Angeles* 16 B2
Mid City *New Orleans* 21 B2
Middle Hd. *Sydney* 29 A2
Middle Park *Melbourne* 18 A1
Middle Village *New York* 22 B2
Middlesex Fells
  Reservation *Boston* 6 A2
Midland Beach *New York* 22 C1
Midlothian *Chicago* 9 C2
Midwood *New York* 22 C2
Miedzeszyn *Warsaw* 33 B3
Miedzylesie *Warsaw* 33 B3
Miessaari *Helsinki* 11 C1
Miguel Hidalgo *Mexico City* 18 B1
Milan = Milano *Milan* 18 B1
Milanese, Parco
  Regionale △ *Milan* 18 A1
Milano *Milan* 18 B1
Milano Due *Milan* 18 B2
Milano Linate ✈ (LIN)
  Milan 18 B2
Milano Malpense ✈
  (MXP) *Milan* 18 A1
Milano San Felice *Milan* 18 B2
Milbertshofen *Munich* 21 A2
Mill Hill *London* 15 A2
Millennium Dome *London* 15 A4
Miller Meadow *Chicago* 9 B1
Millerhill *Edinburgh* 11 B3
Milltown *Dublin* 10 B2
Milnerton *Cape Town* 8 A1
Milon-la-Chapelle *Paris* 24 B1
Milton *Boston* 6 B2
Milton Bridge *Edinburgh* 11 B2
Mimico *Toronto* 31 B1
Mimico Creek → *Toronto* 31 B1
Minami *Osaka* 23 B1
Minamitsunashima *Tokyo* 30 B2
Minato *Osaka* 23 B1
Minato *Tokyo* 30 B3
Minshât el Bekkarī *Cairo* 7 A1
Miraflores *Lima* 14 B2
Miramar *Miami* 19 C1
Misericordia, Sa. da
  Rio de Janeiro 25 B1
Mission *San Francisco* 26 B2
Mississauga *Toronto* 31 B1
Mitaka *Tokyo* 30 A2
Mitcham *London* 15 B3
Mitcham Common *London* 15 B3
Mitchell Museum of the
  American Indian *Chicago* 9 A2
Mitchell's Plain *Cape Town* 8 B2
Mitte *Berlin* 5 A3
Mittel Isarkanal → *Munich* 21 A3
Mixcoac *Mexico City* 18 B1
Miyakojima *Osaka* 23 A2
Mizonokuchi *Tokyo* 30 B2
Mizue *Tokyo* 30 A4
Młociński, Park *Warsaw* 33 B1
Młociny *Warsaw* 33 B1
Mnevniki *Moscow* 19 B1
Moba *Lagos* 14 A2
Moczydło *Warsaw* 33 A1
Modderfontein *Johannesburg* 13 A2
Modřany *Prague* 25 B2
Mogyoród *Budapest* 7 A3
Moinho Velho, Cor. →
  São Paulo 27 B2
Mok *Seoul* 27 B1
Mokotów *Warsaw* 33 B2
Molenbeek-St-Jean *Brussels* 6 A1
Molino de Rosas
  Mexico City 18 B1
Mollem *Brussels* 6 A1
Mollins de Rey *Barcelona* 4 A1
Mondeor *Johannesburg* 13 B2
Moneda, Palacio de la
  Santiago 27 B2
Monerò *Rio de Janeiro* 25 A1
Mong Kok *Hong Kong* 12 B2

Monkstown *Dublin* 10 B3
Monnickendam *Amsterdam* 2 A3
Monrovia *Los Angeles* 16 B4
Monsanto *Lisbon* 16 A1
Monsanto, Parque
  Florestal de *Lisbon* 16 A1
Mont-Royal *Montreal* 20 A2
Mont-Royal, Parc *Montreal* 20 A2
Montcada i Reixac *Barcelona* 4 A2
Monte Chingolo *Buenos Aires* 7 C2
Montebello *Los Angeles* 16 B3
Montemor *Lisbon* 16 A1
Monterey Hills *Los Angeles* 16 B3
Monterey Park *Los Angeles* 16 B4
Montespaccato *Rome* 26 B1
Montesson *Paris* 24 A1
Monteverde Nuovo *Rome* 26 B1
Montfermeil *Paris* 24 A4
Montigny-le-Bretonneux
  Paris 24 B1
Montjay-la-Tour *Paris* 24 A4
Montjuïc *Barcelona* 4 A2
Montparnasse, Gare *Paris* 24 A2
Montréal *Montreal* 20 A2
Montréal, Î. de *Montreal* 20 A2
Montréal Est *Montreal* 20 A3
Montréal Nord *Montreal* 20 A2
Montréal Ouest *Montreal* 20 B2
Montréal Trudeau Int. ✈
  (YUL) *Montreal* 20 B1
Montreuil *Paris* 24 A3
Montrouge *Paris* 24 B2
Montserrat *Buenos Aires* 7 B2
Monza *Milan* 18 A2
Monzoro *Milan* 18 B1
Moóca *São Paulo* 27 B2
Moonachie *New York* 22 B1
Moonee Ponds *Melbourne* 18 A1
Moonee Valley
  Racecourse *Melbourne* 18 A1
Moosach *Munich* 21 A2
Mora *Mumbai* 20 B2
Moratalaz *Madrid* 17 B2
Mörby *Stockholm* 29 A2
Morden *London* 15 B2
Morée → *Paris* 24 A3
Morgan Park *Chicago* 9 C3
Moriguchi *Osaka* 23 A2
Morivione *Milan* 18 B2
Morningside *Edinburgh* 11 B2
Morningside *Johannesburg* 13 A2
Morningside Park *Orlando* 23 B2
Morningside Park *Toronto* 31 A3
Morro Solar, Cerro *Lima* 14 C2
Mortlake *London* 15 B2
Mortlake *Sydney* 29 B1
Morton Grove *Chicago* 9 A2
Morumbi *São Paulo* 27 B1
Moscavide *Lisbon* 16 A2
Moschato *Athens* 2 B1
Moscow = Moskva *Moscow* 19 B2
Moskva *Moscow* 19 B2
Moskvoretskiy *Moscow* 19 B2
Mosman *Sydney* 29 B2
Moti Bagh *Delhi* 10 B2
Motol *Prague* 25 B1
Motsa *Jerusalem* 13 B1
Motsa Ilit *Jerusalem* 13 B1
Motspur Park *London* 15 B2
Mottingham *London* 15 B4
Mount Dennis *Toronto* 31 A1
Mount Greenwood *Chicago* 9 C2
Mount Hood Memorial
  Park △ *Boston* 6 A2
Mount Merrion *Dublin* 10 B2
Mount Olympus *Los Angeles* 16 B2
Mount Rainier *Washington* 33 B3
Mount Vernon *New York* 22 A3
Müggelberge *Berlin* 5 B4
Müggelheim *Berlin* 5 B5
Muggiò *Milan* 18 A2
Mühleiten *Vienna* 32 A3
Mühlenfliess → *Berlin* 5 A5
Muiden *Amsterdam* 2 A3
Muizenberg *Cape Town* 8 B1
Mujahidpur *Delhi* 10 B2
Mukandpur *Delhi* 10 A2
Mukhmas *Jerusalem* 13 A2
Muko → *Osaka* 23 A1
Mukojima *Tokyo* 30 A3
Mulbarton *Johannesburg* 13 B2
Mullach Íde = Malahide
  Dublin 10 A3
Mumbai *Mumbai* 20 B2
Mumbai Chhatrapati
  Shivaji Int. ✈ (BOM)
  Mumbai 20 A2
Mumbai Harbour *Mumbai* 20 B2
Munch-museum *Oslo* 23 A3
Münchehofe *Berlin* 5 B5
München *Munich* 21 B2
München Franz Josef
  Strauss Int. ✈ (MUC)
  Munich 21 A2
Munich = München
  Munich 21 B2
Munkkiniemi *Helsinki* 11 B2
Munro *Buenos Aires* 7 B1
Muntinlupa *Manila* 17 C2
Murai Res. *Singapore* 28 A2
Muranów *Warsaw* 33 B2
Murino *St. Petersburg* 27 B2
Murrayfield *Edinburgh* 11 B3
Murtala Mohammed
  Int. ✈ (LOS) *Lagos* 14 A2
Musashino *Tokyo* 30 A2
Museumsinsel *Berlin* 5 A3
Mushin *Lagos* 14 A2
Musocco *Milan* 18 B1
Mustansiriya *Baghdad* 3 A2
Musturud *Cairo* 7 A2
Muswell Hill *London* 15 A3
Mutanabi *Baghdad* 3 B2
Muthana *Baghdad* 3 B2
Myllypuro *Helsinki* 11 B3
Mystic → *Boston* 6 A2

N

N.S.C.B. Int. ✈ (CCU)
  Kolkata 14 B2
Naberezhnaya Tower
  Moscow 19 B2
Nacka *Stockholm* 29 B3
Nærnes *Oslo* 23 B1
Nagatsuta *Tokyo* 30 B2
Nagytétény *Budapest* 7 B2
Nahakara *Tokyo* 30 B2
Nakano *Tokyo* 30 A3
Namsan Park *Seoul* 27 B1
Namyeong *Seoul* 27 B1
Nanbiancun *Guangzhou* 11 B1
Nanchang He → *Beijing* 4 B1
Nandang *Guangzhou* 11 B2
Nangal Dewat *Delhi* 10 B1
Naniwa *Osaka* 23 B1
Nanole *Mumbai* 20 A2
Nanpu Bridge *Shanghai* 28 B1

Nanshi *Shanghai* 28 B1
Nanterre *Paris* 24 A2
Napier Mole *Karachi* 13 B1
Naraina *Delhi* 10 B2
Nariman T. *Mumbai* 20 C2
Naruo *Osaka* 23 A1
Närmak *Tehran* 31 A2
Näsby *Stockholm* 29 A2
Näsbypark *Stockholm* 29 A2
National Arboretum
  Washington 33 B3
National Maritime
  Museum *London* 15 B3
National September 11
  Memorial and Museum
  New York 22 B1
National University
  (N.U.S.) *Singapore* 28 B2
National Zoological Park
  Washington 33 B2
Nationals Park *Washington* 33 B2
Nativity, Basilica of
  Jerusalem 13 B2
Natolin *Warsaw* 33 C2
Naucalpan de Juárez
  Mexico City 18 B1
Naupada *Mumbai* 20 A2
Navi Mumbai *Mumbai* 20 A2
Naviglio di Pavia *Milan* 18 B1
Naviglio Grande *Milan* 18 B1
Navotas *Manila* 17 B1
Navy Pier *Chicago* 9 B3
Nazal Hikmat Beg *Baghdad* 3 A2
Nazimabad *Karachi* 13 B1
Nazlet el Simmân *Cairo* 7 B1
Nea Alexandria *Athens* 2 B2
Nea Ionia *Athens* 2 A2
Nea Liosia *Athens* 2 A2
Nea Smirni *Athens* 2 B2
Neapoli *Athens* 2 B2
Near North *Chicago* 9 B3
Nebušice *Prague* 25 B1
Nederhorst *Amsterdam* 2 A3
Nedlitz *Berlin* 5 A1
Nee Soon *Singapore* 28 A2
Needham *Boston* 6 B1
Needham Heights *Boston* 6 A1
Nellis Air Force Base ✈
  (LSV) *Las Vegas* 14 A2
N'emátābād *Tehran* 31 B2
Nerima *Tokyo* 30 A3
Nesodden *Oslo* 23 B3
Nesoddtangen *Oslo* 23 B3
Nesoya *Oslo* 23 A2
Netaji Subhash Chandra
  Bose Int. ✈ (CCU) *Kolkata* 14 B2
Neu Aubing *Munich* 21 B1
Neu Buch *Berlin* 5 A4
Neu Buchhorst *Berlin* 5 B5
Neu Fahrland *Berlin* 5 A1
Neu Lindenberg *Berlin* 5 A4
Neubiberg *Munich* 21 B2
Neuenhagen *Berlin* 5 A4
Neuessling *Vienna* 32 A3
Neuhausen *Munich* 21 B2
Neuherberg *Munich* 21 A2
Neuhönow *Berlin* 5 A5
Neukölln *Berlin* 5 B3
Neukuchen *Vienna* 32 A3
Neukettenhof *Vienna* 32 B2
Neukölln *Berlin* 5 B3
Neuperlach *Munich* 21 B2
Neuried *Munich* 21 B1
Neusiedl am Walde *Vienna* 32 A1
Neusüssenbrunn *Vienna* 32 A3
Neuwaldegg *Vienna* 32 A1
Neve Ya'akov *Jerusalem* 13 A2
Neves *Rio de Janeiro* 25 B2
New Baghdâd *Baghdad* 3 B2
New Barakpur *Kolkata* 14 A2
New Brighton *New York* 22 C1
New Canada *Johannesburg* 13 B1
New Canada Dam
  Johannesburg 13 B1
New Cross *London* 15 B3
New Delhi *Delhi* 10 B2
New Dorp *New York* 22 C1
New Dorp Beach *New York* 22 C1
New Malden *London* 15 B2
New Milford *New York* 22 A1
New Mumbai = Navi
  Mumbai *Mumbai* 20 A2
New Orleans *New Orleans* 21 B2
New Orleans Int. ✈ (MSY)
  New Orleans 21 B1
New River → *Miami* 19 B3
New Territories *Hong Kong* 12 A1
New Toronto *Toronto* 31 B1
New Utrecht *New York* 22 C2
New York *New York* 22 B2
New York La Guardia ✈
  (LGA) *New York* 22 B2
Newark B. *New York* 22 B1
Newbattle *Edinburgh* 11 B3
Newbury Park *London* 15 A4
Newcraighall *Edinburgh* 11 B3
Newham □ *London* 15 A4
Newhaven *Edinburgh* 11 B2
Newington *Edinburgh* 11 B3
Newlands *Johannesburg* 13 B1
Newport *Melbourne* 18 A1
Newton *Boston* 6 B1
Newtonbrook *Toronto* 31 A2
Newtongrange *Edinburgh* 11 B3
Newtonville *Boston* 6 A1
Newtown *Sydney* 29 B2
Ngau Chi Wan *Hong Kong* 12 A2
Ngau Tau Kok *Hong Kong* 12 B2
Ngong Shuen Chau
  Hong Kong 12 A1
Ngua Kok Wan *Hong Kong* 12 A1
Nhava Sheva *Mumbai* 20 B2
Niävärän *Tehran* 31 A2
Nibra *Kolkata* 14 B1
Nidâl *Baghdad* 3 A2
Niddrie *Edinburgh* 11 B3
Niddrie *Melbourne* 18 A1
Nieder Neuendorf *Berlin* 5 A2
Niederschönhausen *Berlin* 5 A3
Niederschönweide *Berlin* 5 B3
Niemeyer *Rio de Janeiro* 25 B1
Nieuwendam *Amsterdam* 2 A2
Nihonbashi *Tokyo* 30 A3
Niipperi *Helsinki* 11 B1
Nikéa *Athens* 2 B1
Nikolassee *Berlin* 5 B2
Nikolskiy *Moscow* 19 B1
Niles *Chicago* 9 A2
Nimta *Kolkata* 14 A2
Ninoy Aquino Int. ✈
  (MNL) *Manila* 17 B1
Nippa *Tokyo* 30 B2
Nippori *Tokyo* 30 A3
Nishi *Osaka* 23 B1
Nishinari *Osaka* 23 B1
Nishinomiya *Osaka* 23 A1
Nishiyodogawa *Osaka* 23 A1
Niterói *Rio de Janeiro* 25 B2
Nockeby *Stockholm* 29 B1

Noel Park *London* 15 A3
Nogatino *Moscow* 19 B3
Nogent-sur-Marne *Paris* 24 A3
Noida *Delhi* 10 B2
Noiseau *Paris* 24 B4
Noisiel *Paris* 24 A4
Noisy-le-Grand *Paris* 24 A4
Noisy-le-Roi *Paris* 24 A1
Noisy-le-Sec *Paris* 24 A3
Nokkala *Helsinki* 11 C1
Nomentano *Rome* 26 B2
Nonakashinden *Tokyo* 30 A2
Nongminyundong
  Jiangxisuo *Guangzhou* 11 B2
Nonhyeon *Seoul* 27 B2
Nonthaburi *Bangkok* 3 A1
Noordgezig *Johannesburg* 13 B1
Noordzeekanaal *Amsterdam* 2 A1
Nord, Gare du *Paris* 24 A3
Nordmarka *Oslo* 23 A2
Nordrand-Siedlung *Vienna* 32 A2
Nordstrand *Oslo* 23 A3
Norland *Oslo* 23 A2
Norridge *Chicago* 9 B2
Norrmalm *Stockholm* 29 B2
North Arlington *New York* 22 B1
North Atlanta *Atlanta* 3 A3
North Bay Village *Miami* 19 C3
North Bergen *New York* 22 B1
North Bull I. *Dublin* 10 A3
North Cheam *London* 15 B2
North Cray *London* 15 B4
North Decatur *Atlanta* 3 B3
North Druid Hills *Atlanta* 3 B3
North Esk → *Edinburgh* 11 B2
North Gyle *Edinburgh* 11 B2
North Hackensack
  New York 22 A1
North Harbor *Manila* 17 B1
North Hd. *Sydney* 29 A2
North Hollywood
  Los Angeles 16 B2
North Las Vegas *Las Vegas* 14 A1
North Las Vegas ✈ (VGT)
  Las Vegas 14 A1
North Lexington *Boston* 6 A1
North Miami *Miami* 19 C2
North Miami Beach *Miami* 19 C2
North Nazimabad *Karachi* 13 A2
North Perry ✈ (HWO)
  Miami 19 B2
North Pt. *Hong Kong* 12 B2
North Quincy *Boston* 6 B2
North Queensferry
  Edinburgh 11 A2
North Riverside *Chicago* 9 B2
North Saugus *Boston* 6 A2
North Shore Channel →
  Chicago 9 B2
North Sydney *Sydney* 29 B2
North Woolwich *London* 15 A4
North York *Toronto* 31 A2
Northbridge *Sydney* 29 A2
Northbridge Park *Sydney* 29 A2
Northbrook *Chicago* 9 A2
Northcliff *Johannesburg* 13 A1
Northcote *Melbourne* 18 A2
Northeastern Univ. *Boston* 6 A2
Northfield *Chicago* 9 A2
Northmount *Toronto* 31 A2
Northolt *London* 15 A2
Northumberland Heath
  London 15 B5
Northwestern Station
  Chicago 9 B3
Northwestern Univ. *Chicago* 9 A2
Northwood *London* 15 A1
Northwood Park *Toronto* 31 A1
Norwood Park *Chicago* 9 B2
Noryangjin *Seoul* 27 B1
Nossa Senhora do Ó
  São Paulo 27 B1
Nossegem *Brussels* 6 A2
Notre-Dame *Paris* 24 A3
Notre-Dame, Basilique
  Montreal 20 A2
Notre-Dame, Bois *Paris* 24 B4
Notre-Dame-de-Grâce
  Montreal 20 B2
Notting Hill *London* 15 A2
Nova Milanese *Milan* 18 A2
Novate Milanese *Milan* 18 A1
Novaya Derevnya
  St. Petersburg 27 A1
Nové Mĕsto *Prague* 25 B2
Novoaleksandrovskoye
  St. Petersburg 27 B2
Novodevichy Convent
  Moscow 19 B2
Novogireyevo *Moscow* 19 B3
Novosaratovka
  St. Petersburg 27 B2
Nowe-Babice *Warsaw* 33 B1
Nöykkiö *Helsinki* 11 B1
Nueva Atzacoalco
  Mexico City 18 B2
Nueva Pompeya *Buenos Aires* 7 C2
Nueva Tenochtitlán
  Mexico City 18 B2
Nuijala *Helsinki* 11 B1
Numabukuro *Tokyo* 30 A3
Nuñez *Buenos Aires* 7 B2
Nunhead *London* 15 B3
Ñuñoa *Santiago* 27 C2
Nusle *Prague* 25 B2
Nussdorf *Vienna* 32 A2
Nyanga *Cape Town* 8 A2
Nymphenburg *Munich* 21 B1
Nymphenburg, Schloss
  Munich 21 B2

O

O.R. Tambo Int. ✈ (JNB)
  Johannesburg 13 A2
Oak Forest *Chicago* 9 D2
Oak Grove *Atlanta* 3 A3
Oak Hill *Boston* 6 B1
Oak Lawn *Chicago* 9 C2
Oak Park *Chicago* 9 B2
Oak View *Washington* 33 B3
Oakdale *Atlanta* 3 A2
Oakland *San Francisco* 26 B2
Oaklawn *Washington* 33 C3
Oakleigh *Melbourne* 18 B2
Oakwood Beach *New York* 22 C1
Oatley *Sydney* 29 B1
Obalende *Lagos* 14 B2
Oba's Palace *Lagos* 14 B2
Oberföhring *Munich* 21 B2
Oberhaching *Munich* 21 B2
Oberlaa *Vienna* 32 B2
Oberlisse *Vienna* 32 A3
Obermenzing *Munich* 21 B1
Obermoos Schwaige
  Munich 21 A1
Oberschleissheim *Munich* 21 A2

Oberschöneweide *Berlin* 5 B4
Observatory *Johannesburg* 13 B2
Óbuda *Budapest* 7 A2
Obukhovo *St. Petersburg* 27 B2
Obvodnyy Kanal
  St. Petersburg 27 B2
Ocean Park *Hong Kong* 12 B2
Ochota *Warsaw* 33 B1
Ocoee *Orlando* 23 A1
Odaiba *Tokyo* 30 B3
Ōdana *Tokyo* 30 B2
Öden-Stockach *Munich* 21 A3
Odilampfi *Helsinki* 11 B1
Odivelas *Lisbon* 16 A1
Odolany *Warsaw* 33 B1
Oeiras *Lisbon* 16 A1
Ofin *Lagos* 14 A2
Ogawa *Tokyo* 30 A1
Ogden Park *Chicago* 9 C2
Ogogoro *Lagos* 14 B2
Ogoyo *Lagos* 14 B2
Ogudu *Lagos* 14 A2
Oimachi *Tokyo* 30 B3
Ojota *Lagos* 14 A2
Ojus *Miami* 19 C2
Oke-Ira *Lagos* 14 A2
Okęcie *Warsaw* 33 B1
Okęcie, Warszawa ✈
  (WAW) *Warsaw* 33 B1
Okeogbe *Lagos* 14 B2
Okhla *Delhi* 10 B2
Okhta → *St. Petersburg* 27 B2
Okkervil → *St. Petersburg* 27 B2
Okrzeszyn *Warsaw* 33 C2
Oksval *Oslo* 23 A2
Oktyabrskiy *Moscow* 19 B1
Ōkubo *Tokyo* 30 A3
Ōkura *Tokyo* 30 B2
Olari *Helsinki* 11 B1
Olaria *Rio de Janeiro* 25 B1
Old Admiralty *St. Petersburg* 27 B1
Old City *Jerusalem* 13 B2
Old City *Shanghai* 28 B1
Old Fort York *Toronto* 31 B2
Old Harbor *Boston* 6 A2
Old Town = Stare Miasto
  Warsaw 33 B2
Old Town *Chicago* 9 B3
Old Town Hall = Altes
  Rathaus *Munich* 21 B2
Oldbawn *Dublin* 10 B1
Oleta River State Rec.
  Area *Miami* 19 C3
Olgino *St. Petersburg* 27 B1
Olímpico, Estadio
  Mexico City 18 C1
Olivais *Lisbon* 16 A2
Olivar de los Padres
  Mexico City 18 B1
Olivar del Conde
  Mexico City 18 B1
Olives, Mt. of *Jerusalem* 13 B2
Olivia, L. *Orlando* 23 A1
Olivos *Buenos Aires* 7 B2
Olona → *Milan* 18 B1
Olympia, L. *Orlando* 23 A1
Olympic Green *Beijing* 4 B2
Olympic Park *London* 15 A3
Olympic Stadium =
  Turner Field *Atlanta* 3 B2
Olympic Stadium *Beijing* 4 B2
Olympic Stadium *Helsinki* 11 B2
Olympique, Stade *Montreal* 20 A2
Ōmori *Tokyo* 30 B3
One World Trade Center
  New York 22 B1
Onisigun *Lagos* 14 A2
Ontario Science Centre
  Toronto 31 A2
Ōokayama *Tokyo* 30 B3
Oostzaan Tuindorp
  Amsterdam 2 A2
Opa-Locka *Miami* 19 C1
Opa-Locka ✈ (OPF) *Miami* 19 C1
Opacz *Warsaw* 33 B1
Ophirton *Johannesburg* 13 B2
Oppegård *Oslo* 23 B3
Oppem *Brussels* 6 A1
Oppsal *Oslo* 23 A3
Ora *Jerusalem* 13 B1
Oradell Res. *New York* 22 A1
Orangi *Karachi* 13 A1
Ordrup *Copenhagen* 8 A3
Ōrechi *Prague* 25 B1
Oregun *Lagos* 14 A2
Orestad *Copenhagen* 8 A3
Orient Heights *Boston* 6 A3
Oriental Pearl Tower
  Shanghai 28 B2
Orland Park *Chicago* 9 D2
Orlando *Orlando* 23 B2
Orlando Dam *Johannesburg* 13 B1
Orlando East *Johannesburg* 13 B1
Orlando Executive ✈
  (ORL) *Orlando* 23 B2
Orlando Int. ✈ (MCO)
  Orlando 23 B2
Orlovista *Orlando* 23 B1
Orly Paris 24 B3
Orly, Paris ✈ (ORY) *Paris* 24 B3
Ormesson-sur-Marne *Paris* 24 B4
Ormond *Melbourne* 18 B2
Ormøya *Oslo* 23 A3
Orpington *London* 15 B4
Ortaköy *Istanbul* 12 B2
Ortica *Milan* 18 B2
Oruba *Lagos* 14 A2
Osaka *Osaka* 23 B2
Ōsaka Castle *Osaka* 23 A2
Ōsaka Harbour *Osaka* 23 B1
Ōsaka Itami Int. ✈ (ITM)
  Osaka 23 A2
Ōsaka Kansai Int. ✈ (KIX)
  Osaka 23 ...
Ōsaki *Tokyo* 30 B3
Osasco *São Paulo* 27 B1
Osdorp *Amsterdam* 2 A1
Oshodi *Lagos* 14 A2
Oslo *Oslo* 23 A3
Oslo ✈ (OSL) *Oslo* 23 A4
Ōsone *Tokyo* 30 B2
Osorun *Lagos* 14 A2
Ospiate *Milan* 18 A1
Ostankino *Moscow* 19 B2
Osterley *London* 15 B1
Osterley Park *London* 15 B1
Östermalm *Stockholm* 29 B2
Österskär *Stockholm* 29 A3
Ostia Malpasso *Rome* 26 C1
Ostiense *Rome* 26 B1
Østmarkkapellet *Oslo* 23 A4
Øståya *Oslo* 23 A2
Ōta *Tokyo* 30 B3
Otaniemi *Helsinki* 11 B1
Otsuka *Tokyo* 30 A3
Ottakring *Vienna* 32 A1
Ottávia *Rome* 26 B1
Ottery *Cape Town* 8 B2

Ottobrunn Munich 21 B3
Ouderkerk Amsterdam 2 B2
Oulunkylä Helsinki 11 B2
Ourcq, Canal de l' Paris 24 A3
Outer Mission San Francisco 26 B2
Outremont Montreal 20 A2
Overijse Brussels 6 B3
Oworonsoki Lagos 14 A2
Oxgangs Edinburgh 11 B2
Oxon Hill Washington 33 C3
Oyodo Osaka 23 A1
Oyster Rock Mumbai 20 B1
Oyster Rocks Karachi 13 B2
Ozoir-la-Ferrière Paris 24 B4
Ozone Park New York 22 B2

P

Pacific Heights San Francisco 26 B2
Pacific Manor San Francisco 26 C2
Pacific Palisades Los Angeles 16 B1
Pacifica San Francisco 26 C2
Paco Manila 17 B1
Paco de Arcos Lisbon 16 A1
Paddington London 15 A2
Paddington Sydney 29 B2
Paderno Milan 18 A1
Pagewood Sydney 29 B2
Pagote Mumbai 20 B2
Pai, I. do Rio de Janeiro 25 B2
Pak Kok Hong Kong 12 B1
Pak Kong Hong Kong 12 A2
Pakila Helsinki 11 B2
Palacio Real Madrid 17 B1
Palaiseau Paris 24 B2
Palazzolo Milan 18 A1
Paleo Faliro Athens 2 B2
Palermo Buenos Aires 7 B2
Palhais Lisbon 16 B2
Palisades Park New York 22 A1
Palm Deira, The Dubai 9 A2
Palm Jumeirah, The Dubai 9 B1
Palmerston Dublin 10 A1
Palms Los Angeles 16 B2
Paloheinä Helsinki 11 B2
Palomeras Madrid 17 B2
Palos Heights Chicago 9 D2
Palos Hills Chicago 9 C2
Palos Park Chicago 9 C1
Palpara Kolkata 14 B2
Panchur Kolkata 14 B1
Pandacan Manila 17 B2
Pandan, Selat Singapore 28 B2
Pandan Res. Singapore 28 B2
Pangrati Athens 2 B2
Pangsua, Sungei → Singapore 28 A2
Panihati Kolkata 14 A2
Panjang, Bukit Singapore 28 A2
Panke → Berlin 5 A3
Pankow Berlin 5 A3
Pantheon Rome 26 B1
Panthersville Atlanta 3 B3
Pantin Paris 24 A3
Pantitlán Mexico City 18 B2
Panyu Guangzhou 11 B2
Papiol Barcelona 4 A1
Paradise Las Vegas 14 B2
Paramount Studios Los Angeles 16 B3
Paramus New York 22 A1
Paranaque Manila 17 B1
Paray-Vieille-Poste Paris 24 B3
Pardisān Nature Park Tehran 31 A2
Parel Mumbai 20 B1
Pari São Paulo 27 B2
Parioli Rome 26 B1
Paris Paris 24 A3
Paris Orly ✈ (ORY) Paris 24 B3
Parje Mumbai 20 B2
Pārk-e Āzādegān Tehran 31 B2
Pārk-e Mellat Tehran 31 A2
Park Ridge Chicago 9 A1
Park Royal London 15 A2
Parkchester New York 22 B2
Parkdale Toronto 31 B2
Parkhurst Johannesburg 13 A2
Parklawn Washington 33 B2
Parkmore Johannesburg 13 A2
Parkside San Francisco 26 B2
Parktown Johannesburg 13 B2
Parkview Johannesburg 13 A2
Parkville New York 22 C2
Parkwood Cape Town 8 B1
Parkwood Johannesburg 13 A2
Parow Cape Town 8 A2
Parque Chacabuco Buenos Aires 7 B2
Parque Patricios Buenos Aires 7 B2
Parramatta → Sydney 29 A1
Paşabahçe Istanbul 12 B2
Pasadena Los Angeles 16 B4
Pasar Minggu Jakarta 12 B1
Pasay Manila 17 B1
Pascoe Vale Melbourne 18 A1
Pasig Manila 17 B2
Pasig → Manila 17 B2
Pasila Helsinki 11 B2
Pasing Munich 21 B1
Pasir Panjang Singapore 28 B2
Pasir Ris Singapore 28 A3
Passaic New York 22 A1
Passaic → New York 22 B1
Passirana Milan 18 A1
Patel Nagar Delhi 10 B1
Pateros Manila 17 B2
Pathumwan Bangkok 3 B2
Patipukur Kolkata 14 B2
Patisia Athens 2 A2
Paulo E. Virginia, Gruta Rio de Janeiro 25 B1
Paulshof Berlin 5 A5
Paya Lebar Singapore 28 A3
Peakhurst Sydney 29 B1
Peania Athens 2 B3
Pearson Int. Toronto ✈ (YYZ) Toronto 31 A1
Peckham London 15 B3
Pederstrup Copenhagen 8 A2
Pedralbes Barcelona 4 A1
Pedregal de San Angel, Jardines del Mexico City 18 C1
Peip'ing = Beijing Beijing 4 B1
Peking = Beijing Beijing 4 B1
Pelcowizna Warsaw 33 B2
Pembroke Park Miami 19 C2
Pembroke Pines Miami 19 B1
Peñalolén Santiago 27 B2
Peng Siang → Singapore 28 A2
Penge London 15 B3
Penha Rio de Janeiro 25 A1
Penicuik Edinburgh 11 B2
Penjaringan Jakarta 12 A1
Pentagon Washington 33 B2
Penzing Vienna 32 A1
People's Park Shanghai 28 B1
People's Square Shanghai 28 B1
Perales del Rio Madrid 17 C2
Perchtoldsdorf Vienna 32 B1
Perdizes São Paulo 27 B2
Peristeri Athens 2 A2
Perivale London 15 A2
Perk Brussels 6 A2
Perlach Munich 21 B2
Perlacher Forst Munich 21 B2
Pero Milan 18 A1
Peropok, Bukit Singapore 28 B2
Perovo Moscow 19 B3
Pertusella Milan 18 A1
Pesagot Jerusalem 13 A2
Pesanggrahag, Kali → Jakarta 12 B1
Peschiera Borromeo Milan 18 B2
Pesek, Pulau Singapore 28 B2
Pest Budapest 7 B2
Pesterzsébet Budapest 7 B2
Pesthidegkút Budapest 7 A1
Pestimre Budapest 7 B3
Pestlőrinc Budapest 7 B3
Pestújhely Budapest 7 A2
Petas Helsinki 11 B2
Petrogradskaya Storona St. Petersburg 27 B2
Petroupoli Athens 2 A2
Petrovice Prague 25 B3
Petrovskiy Park Moscow 19 B2
Petrovsko-Razumovskoye Moscow 19 B2
Pettycur Edinburgh 11 A2
Peutie Brussels 6 A2
Pfaueninsel Berlin 5 B1
Phaya Thai Bangkok 3 B2
Phihai Karachi 13 A2
Phillip B. Sydney 29 B2
Phoenix Chicago 9 D3
Phoenix Park Dublin 10 A2
Phra Khanong Bangkok 3 B2
Phra Nakhon Bangkok 3 B2
Phra Pradaeng Bangkok 3 C2
Phranakhon Bangkok 3 B1
Pico Rivera Los Angeles 16 C4
Piedade Lisbon 16 A1
Piedade Rio de Janeiro 25 B1
Piedade, Cova da Lisbon 16 A2
Piedmont Park Atlanta 3 B2
Pierre Elliott Trudeau ✈ (YUL) Montreal 20 B1
Pietralata Rome 26 B2
Pihlajamäki Helsinki 11 B2
Pihlajasaari Helsinki 11 C2
Pilares Rio de Janeiro 25 B1
Pilton Edinburgh 11 B2
Pine Castle Orlando 23 B2
Pine Grove Toronto 31 A1
Pine Hills Orlando 23 A2
Pine Island Miami 19 B1
Pinecrest Miami 19 D1
Pinewood Park Miami 19 C2
Pingzhou Guangzhou 11 B2
Pinheiros → São Paulo 27 B1
Pinjrapur Karachi 13 A2
Pinner London 15 A1
Pinner Green London 15 A1
Pioltello Milan 18 A2
Piræus = Pireas Athens 2 B1
Piraiévs = Pireas Athens 2 B1
Pirajuçara → São Paulo 27 B1
Pireas Athens 2 B1
Pirinçi Istanbul 12 B1
Pirituba São Paulo 27 A1
Pirkkola Helsinki 11 B2
Pisgat O'mer Jerusalem 13 B2
Pisgat Ze'ev Jerusalem 13 B2
Písnice Prague 25 C2
Pitampura Delhi 10 A1
Pitkäjärvi Helsinki 11 B1
Planegg Munich 21 B1
Plantation Miami 19 B2
Plantation Isles Miami 19 B2
Plaza Mayor Madrid 17 B1
Pleasure Island Orlando 23 B1
Plumstead Cape Town 8 B1
Plumstead London 15 B4
Plyushchevo Moscow 19 B3
Po Toi Hong Kong 12 B2
Po Toi O Hong Kong 12 B2
Poasco Milan 18 B2
Podbaba Prague 25 B2
Podoli Prague 25 B2
Pointe-Aux-Trembles Montreal 20 A2
Poissy Paris 24 A1
Pok Fu Lam Hong Kong 12 B1
Pokcheong Seoul 27 C2
Polton Edinburgh 11 B3
Polvoranca, Parque de Madrid 17 C1
Polyustrovo St. Petersburg 27 B2
Pompano Beach Miami 19 A3
Pomprap Bangkok 3 B2
Pondok Gede Jakarta 12 A2
Pondok Indah Jakarta 12 B1
Pont-Viau Montreal 20 A1
Pontault-Combault Paris 24 B4
Pontinha Lisbon 16 A1
Poplar London 15 A3
Poppintree Dublin 10 A2
Port Botany Sydney 29 B2
Port Mearnóg = Portmarnock Dublin 10 A3
Port Melbourne Melbourne 18 B1
Port Rashid Dubai 9 A2
Port Richmond New York 22 C1
Port Saeed Dubai 9 B2
Port Shelter Hong Kong 12 A2
Port Union Toronto 31 A4
Portage Park Chicago 9 B2
Portela, Lisboa ✈ (LIS) Lisbon 16 A2
Porter, L. Orlando 23 A3
Portmarnock Dublin 10 A3
Porto Brandão Lisbon 16 A1
Pôrto Novo Rio de Janeiro 25 A2
Porto Novo Cr. → Lagos 14 B2
Portobello Edinburgh 11 B3
Portrero San Francisco 26 B3
Posen Chicago 9 D2
Potomac Overlook Reg. Park ⌂ Washington 33 B2
Potrero Pt. San Francisco 26 B2
Potsdam Berlin 5 B1
Potzham Munich 21 B2
Pötzleinsdorf Vienna 32 A1
Póvoa de Santo Adriao Lisbon 16 A2
Powązki Warsaw 33 B1
Powiśle Warsaw 33 B2
Powsin Warsaw 33 C2
Powsinek Warsaw 33 C2
Poyan Res. Singapore 28 A2
Pozuelo de Alarcón Madrid 17 B1
Prado, Museo del Madrid 17 B1
Prado Churubusco Mexico City 18 B2
Praga Warsaw 33 B2
Prague = Praha Prague 25 B2
Praha Prague 25 B2
Praha ✈ (PRG) Prague 25 B1
Praires, R. des → Montreal 20 A2
Prater Vienna 32 A2
Precotto Milan 18 A2
Prenestino Labicano Rome 26 B2
Prenzlauerberg Berlin 5 A3
Preston Melbourne 18 A1
Pretos Forros, Sa. dos Rio de Janeiro 25 B1
Préville Montreal 20 B3
Přezletice Prague 25 B3
Prima Porta Rome 26 B1
Primavalle Rome 26 B1
Primrose Johannesburg 13 B2
Progreso Nacional Mexico City 18 A2
Prosek Prague 25 B3
Prospect Hill Park Boston 6 A1
Providencia Santiago 27 B2
Průhonice Prague 25 C3
Psichiko Athens 2 A2
Pudong New Area Shanghai 28 B2
Pueblo Libre Lima 14 B2
Pueblo Nuevo = El Pobleneu Barcelona 4 A2
Pueblo Nuevo Madrid 17 B2
Puerto Madero Buenos Aires 7 B2
Puhuangyu Beijing 4 B2
Puistola Helsinki 11 B3
Pukinmäki Helsinki 11 B2
Pulkovo Int. ✈ (LED) St. Petersburg 27 C1
Pullach Munich 21 B1
Pullman Historic District Chicago 9 C3
Pulo Gadung Jakarta 12 B2
Pūnak Tehran 31 A2
Punchbowl Sydney 29 B1
Punde Mumbai 20 B2
Punggol Singapore 28 A3
Punggol, Sungei → Singapore 28 A3
Punggol Pt. Singapore 28 A3
Punjabi Bagh Delhi 10 A1
Puotila Helsinki 11 B3
Puteaux Paris 24 A2
Putney London 15 B2
Putuo Shanghai 28 B1
Putxet Barcelona 4 A1
Puxi Shanghai 28 B1
Pyramids Cairo 7 B1
Pyry Warsaw 33 C1

Q

Qalandiya Jerusalem 13 A2
Qal'eh Morghī Tehran 31 B2
Qāsemābād Tehran 31 A3
Qasr-e Firūzeh Tehran 31 B3
Qatane Jerusalem 13 B1
Qianmen Beijing 4 B2
Qinghuayuan Beijing 4 B1
Qingningsi Shanghai 28 B2
Qolhak Tehran 31 A2
Quadraro Rome 26 B2
Quaid-i-Azam Karachi 13 A1
Quartiere Zingone Milan 18 B1
Qubeiba Jerusalem 13 A1
Quds Baghdad 3 A2
Queen Mary Res. London 15 B1
Queen Victoria Market Melbourne 18 A1
Queensbury London 15 A2
Queenscliffe Sydney 29 A2
Queensferry Edinburgh 11 B1
Queenstown Singapore 28 B2
Quellerina Johannesburg 13 A1
Queluz Lisbon 16 A1
Quezon City Manila 17 B2
Quilicura Santiago 27 B1
Quincy Boston 6 B2
Quincy B. Boston 6 B3
Quinta Normal Santiago 27 B1
Quinto de Stampi Milan 18 B2
Quinto Romano Milan 18 B1
Quirinale Rome 26 B1
Qutb Minar Delhi 10 B2

R

R.F.K. Memorial Stadium Washington 33 B3
Raasdorf Vienna 32 A3
Radcliffe College Boston 6 A2
Rådhus Oslo 23 A3
Radlice Prague 25 B2
Radość Warsaw 33 B3
Radotin Prague 25 C2
Rafat Jerusalem 13 A2
Raffles Park Singapore 28 B2
Raheny Dublin 10 A3
Rahnsdorf Berlin 5 B5
Rajakylä Helsinki 11 B3
Rajpura Delhi 10 A2
Rákos-patak → Budapest 7 B3
Rákoshegy Budapest 7 B3
Rákoskeresztúr Budapest 7 B3
Rákoskert Budapest 7 B3
Rákosliget Budapest 7 B3
Rákospalota Budapest 7 A2
Rákosszentmihály Budapest 7 A2
Raków Warsaw 33 B1
Ram Jerusalem 13 A2
Rām Allāh Jerusalem 13 A2
Ramadān Baghdad 3 B2
Ramakrishna Puram Delhi 10 B1
Rāmallāh = Rām Allāh Jerusalem 13 A2
Ramanathpur Kolkata 14 A1
Ramat Allon Jerusalem 13 B2
Ramat Eshkol Jerusalem 13 B2
Ramat Razi'el Jerusalem 13 B1
Ramat Shafet Jerusalem 13 B2
Rambler Channel Hong Kong 12 A1
Ramenki Moscow 19 B1
Ramersdorf Munich 21 B2
Rameses Station Cairo 7 A2
Ramos Rio de Janeiro 25 B1
Ramos Mejía Buenos Aires 7 B1
Ramot Jerusalem 13 B2
Rampur Delhi 10 A2
Ramsgate Sydney 29 B1
Rancho Park Los Angeles 16 B2
Rand ✈ (QRA) Johannesburg 13 B2
Randalls I. New York 22 B2
Randburg Johannesburg 13 A1
Randhart Johannesburg 13 B2
Randpark Ridge Johannesburg 13 A1
Randwick Sydney 29 B2
Ranelagh Dublin 10 A2
Rangpuri Delhi 10 B1
Rannersdorf Vienna 32 B2
Ransbèche Brussels 6 B2
Ransdorp Amsterdam 2 A2
Ranvad Mumbai 20 B2
Raposo Lisbon 16 A1
Rastaala Helsinki 11 B1
Rastila Helsinki 11 B3
Raszyn Warsaw 33 C1
Rathfarnham Dublin 10 B2
Ratho Edinburgh 11 B1
Ratho Station Edinburgh 11 B1
Rato Lisbon 16 A2
Ravelston Edinburgh 11 B2
Rawamangun Jakarta 12 B2
Rayners Lane London 15 A1
Raynes Park London 15 B2
Raypur Kolkata 14 C2
Real Felipe, Fuerte Lima 14 B2
Reams, L. Orlando 23 B1
Reclining Buddha = Wat Pho Bangkok 3 B1
Recoleta Buenos Aires 7 B2
Recoleta Santiago 27 B2
Red Fort = Lal Qila Delhi 10 B2
Red Square Moscow 19 B2
Redbridge ☐ London 15 A4
Redfern Sydney 29 B2
Refshaleøen Copenhagen 8 A3
Regents Park Johannesburg 13 B2
Regent's Park London 15 A3
Rego Park New York 22 B2
Reinickendorf Berlin 5 A3
Rekola Helsinki 11 B3
Rembertów Warsaw 33 B2
Rembrandtpark Amsterdam 2 A2
Remedios de Escalada Buenos Aires 7 C2
Rémola, Estany del Barcelona 4 B1
Renca Santiago 27 B1
Rennemoulin Paris 24 A1
Řeporyje Prague 25 B1
Repulse Bay Hong Kong 12 B2
Repy Prague 25 B1
Residenz Munich 21 B2
Retiro Buenos Aires 7 B2
Retiro Madrid 17 B1
Retiro, Puerto Buenos Aires 7 B2
Retreat Cape Town 8 B1
Reutov Moscow 19 B4
Réveillon → Paris 24 B4
Revere Boston 6 A2
Rexdale Toronto 31 A1
Reynosa Tamaulipas Mexico City 18 A1
Rho Milan 18 A1
Rhodes Sydney 29 A1
Rhodon Paris 24 B1
Rhodon → Paris 24 B1
Rialto Towers Melbourne 18 A1
Ribeira Rio de Janeiro 25 A1
Ricarda, Estany de la Barcelona 4 B1
Richmond Melbourne 18 A2
Richmond San Francisco 26 B2
Richmond Hill New York 22 B2
Richmond Park London 15 B2
Richmond-upon-Thames ☐ London 15 B2
Ridge, The Delhi 10 B2
Ridgefield New York 22 B1
Ridgefield Park New York 22 A1
Ridgewood New York 22 B2
Riem Munich 21 B3
Riesenrad Vienna 32 A2
Rijksmuseum Amsterdam 2 A2
Rikers I. New York 22 B2
Rimac Lima 14 B2
Ringsend Dublin 10 A2
Rinkeby Stockholm 29 A1
Rio Comprido Rio de Janeiro 25 B1
Rio de Janeiro Rio de Janeiro 25 B1
Rio de Janeiro Galeão ✈ (GIG) Rio de Janeiro 25 A1
Rio de Mouro Lisbon 16 A1
Ripollet Barcelona 4 A1
Ris Oslo 23 A3
Risby Copenhagen 8 A1
Rishra Kolkata 14 A2
Rithala Delhi 10 A1
Rive Sud, Canal de la Montreal 20 B2
River Edge New York 22 A1
River Forest Chicago 9 B2
River Grove Chicago 9 B1
River Ridge New Orleans 21 B1
Riverdale Chicago 9 D3
Riverdale New York 22 A2
Riverdale Washington 33 B3
Riverdale Park Toronto 31 A2
Riverlea Johannesburg 13 B1
Riverside Chicago 9 C2
Riverwood Sydney 29 B1
Rivière-des-Praires Montreal 20 A2
Rixensart Brussels 6 B3
Riyad Baghdad 3 B2
Rizal Park Manila 17 B1
Rizal Stadium Manila 17 B1
Røa Oslo 23 A2
Robbins Chicago 9 D2
Robertsham Johannesburg 13 B2
Rochelle Park New York 22 A1
Rock Cr. → Washington 33 B2
Rock Creek Park Washington 33 B2
Rockaway Beach New York 22 C3
Rockaway Pt. New York 22 C2
Rockdale Sydney 29 B1
Rockefeller Center New York 22 B2
Roda, Gezîret el Cairo 7 A2
Roda I. = Roda, Gezîret el Cairo 7 A2
Rodaon Vienna 32 B1
Rødovre Copenhagen 8 A2
Rodrigo de Freitas, L. Rio de Janeiro 25 B1
Roehampton London 15 B2
Rogers Park Chicago 9 A3
Roihuvuori Helsinki 11 B3
Roissy-en-Brie Paris 24 B4
Rokytka → Prague 25 B3
Roma Rome 26 B1
Roma Urbe ✈ Rome 26 B2
Római-Fürdö Budapest 7 A2
Romainville Paris 24 A3
Roman Forum = Foro Romano Rome 26 B1
Romano Banco Milan 18 B1
Rome = Roma Rome 26 B1
Romema Jerusalem 13 B2
Romford London 15 A5
Ronald Reagan Nat. Washington ✈ (DCA) Washington 33 B2
Rondebosch Cape Town 8 A1
Roppongi Tokyo 30 B3
Rose, L. Orlando 23 A1
Rose Bowl Los Angeles 16 B4
Rose Hill Washington 33 C2
Rosebank Johannesburg 13 A2
Rosebank New York 22 C1
Rosebery Sydney 29 B2
Rosedal La Candelaria Mexico City 18 B2
Roseland Chicago 9 C3
Rosemead Los Angeles 16 B4
Rosemont Chicago 9 B1
Rosemont Montreal 20 A2
Rosenborg Slot Copenhagen 8 A3
Rosenthal Berlin 5 A3
Rosettenville Johannesburg 13 B2
Rosewell Edinburgh 11 B3
Rosherville Dam Johannesburg 13 B2
Rösjön Stockholm 29 A2
Roslags-Näsby Stockholm 29 A2
Roslin Edinburgh 11 B3
Roslindale Boston 6 B2
Rosny-sous-Bois Paris 24 A4
Rosslyn Washington 33 B2
Rosyth Edinburgh 11 A1
Rotherhithe London 15 B3
Rothneusiedl Vienna 32 B2
Rothschmaige Munich 21 A1
Rouge Hill Toronto 31 A4
Round I. Hong Kong 12 B2
Roxbury Boston 6 B2
Roxeth London 15 A1
Royal Botanic Gardens Edinburgh 11 B2
Royal Exhibition Building Melbourne 18 A1
Royal Observatory Edinburgh 11 B2
Royal Palace = Kungliga Slottet Stockholm 29 B2
Royal Palace = Palacio Real Madrid 17 B1
Royal Park Melbourne 18 A1
Röylä Helsinki 11 B1
Rozas, Portilleros de las Madrid 17 B1
Roztoky Prague 25 B2
Rozzano Milan 18 B1
Rubí → Barcelona 4 A1
Rudolfsheim Vienna 32 A2
Rudolfshöhe Berlin 5 A5
Rudow Berlin 5 B3
Rueil-Malmaison Paris 24 A2
Ruisbroek Brussels 6 B1
Ruislip London 15 A1
Rumelihisarı Istanbul 12 B2
Rungis Paris 24 B3
Rusāfa Baghdad 3 A2
Rush Green London 15 A5
Russa Kolkata 14 C2
Rutherford New York 22 B1
Ruzyně Prague 25 B1
Ruzyne, Praha ✈ (PRG) Prague 25 B1
Rybatskaya St. Petersburg 27 B2
Rydboholm Stockholm 29 A3
Ryde Sydney 29 A1
Ryogoku Tokyo 30 A3
Rzhevka St. Petersburg 27 B3

S

Sa'ādatābād Tehran 31 A2
Saadūn Baghdad 3 B2
Saavedra Buenos Aires 7 B2
Saboli Delhi 10 A2
Sabugo Lisbon 16 A1
Sabzi Mand Delhi 10 A2
Sacavém Lisbon 16 A2
Saclay Paris 24 B2
Saclay, Étang de Paris 24 B1
Sacomã São Paulo 27 B2
Sacré Cœur Paris 24 A3
Sacrow Berlin 5 B1
Sacrower See Berlin 5 B1
Sadang Seoul 27 C1
Saddle → New York 22 A1
Saddle Brook New York 22 A1
Sadr Karachi 13 A2
Sadr City Baghdad 3 A2
Sadyba Warsaw 33 B2
Safdar Jang's Tomb Delhi 10 B2
Saft el Laban Cairo 7 A2
Sagene Oslo 23 A3
Sagrada Família, Templo de Barcelona 4 A2
Sahar, Mumbai ✈ (BOM) Mumbai 20 A2
Sai Kung Hong Kong 12 A2
Sai Wan Ho Hong Kong 12 B2
Sai Ying Pun Hong Kong 12 B1
St-Aubin Paris 24 B1
St-Cloud Paris 24 A2
St-Cyr-l'École Paris 24 B1
St-Cyr-l'École ✈ Paris 24 B1
St-Denis Paris 24 A3
St-Germain, Forêt de Paris 24 A1
St-Germain-en-Laye Paris 24 A1
St-Gilles Brussels 6 B2
St. Helier London 15 B2
St-Hubert Montreal 20 B3
St-Hubert, Galeries Royales Brussels 6 A2
St. Isaac's Cathedral St. Petersburg 27 B1
St-Jacques → Montreal 20 B3
St-Joost-Ten-Node Brussels 6 A2
St. Kilda Melbourne 18 B1
St-Lambert Montreal 20 A3
St-Lambert Paris 24 B1
St-Laurent Montreal 20 A1
St-Léonard Montreal 20 A2
St-Mandé Paris 24 A3
St. Margaret's Dublin 10 A2
St-Martin, Bois Paris 24 B4
St. Mary Cray London 15 B4
St-Maur-des-Fossés Paris 24 B3
St-Maurice Paris 24 B3
St-Michel Montreal 20 A2
St-Ouen Paris 24 A3
St. Paul's Cray London 15 B4
St. Peters Sydney 29 B2
St. Peter's Square = San Pietro, Piazza Rome 26 B1
St. Petersburg = Sankt-Peterburg St. Petersburg 27 B1
St. Petersburg Pulkovo Int. ✈ (LED) St. Petersburg 27 C1
St-Pierre Montreal 20 B2
St-Pieters Leew Brussels 6 B1
St-Quentin, Étang de Paris 24 B1
St. Stephen's Cathedral = Stephansdom Vienna 32 A2
St-Stevens-Woluwe Brussels 6 A2
St-Vincent-de-Paul Montreal 20 A2
St. Xavier Univ. Chicago 9 C2
Ste-Catherine Montreal 20 B2
Ste-Hélène, Î. Montreal 20 A2
Saiwai Tokyo 30 B3
Sakai Osaka 23 B1
Sakai Harbour Osaka 23 B1
Sakra, Pulau Singapore 28 B2
Salam Baghdad 3 A2
Salamanca Madrid 17 B1
Sallynoggin Dublin 10 B3
Salmannsdorf Vienna 32 A1
Salmedina Madrid 17 C2
Salomea Warsaw 33 B1
Salsette I. Mumbai 20 A2
Salt Lake City = Bidhan Nagar Kolkata 14 B2
Salt River Cape Town 8 A1
Salt Water L. Kolkata 14 B2
Saltsjö-Duvnäs Stockholm 29 B3
Samatya Istanbul 12 C1
Sampaloc Manila 17 B1
Samphan Thawong Bangkok 3 B2
Samseon Seoul 27 B2
Samuel Smith Park Toronto 31 B1
Samut Prakan Bangkok 3 B2
San Andrés Barcelona 4 A2
San Angel Mexico City 18 B1
San Basilio Rome 26 B2
San Borja Lima 14 B3
San Bóvio Milan 18 B2
San Bruno, Pt. San Francisco 26 C2
San Bruno Mountain State Park ⌂ San Francisco 26 B2
San Cristóbal Buenos Aires 7 B2
San Cristobal Madrid 17 B2
San Cristóbal, Cerro Santiago 27 B2
San Cristóbal, Virgen del Santiago 27 B2
San Cristoforo Milan 18 B1
San Donato Milanese Milan 18 B2
San Francisco San Francisco 26 B2
San Francisco B. San Francisco 26 B3
San Francisco Culhuacán Mexico City 18 C2
San Fruttuoso Milan 18 A2
San Gabriel Los Angeles 16 B4
San Gabriel → Los Angeles 16 C4
San Giuliano Milanese Milan 18 B2
San Isidro Lima 14 B2
San Jerónimo Lidice Mexico City 18 C1
San Joaquín Santiago 27 B2
San José Río Hondo Mexico City 18 B1
San Juan → Manila 17 B2
San Juan de Aragón Mexico City 18 B2
San Juan de Aragón, Parque Mexico City 18 B2
San Juan de Lurigancho Lima 14 A2
San Juan del Monte Manila 17 B2
San Juan Ixtacala Mexico City 18 A1
San Just Desvern Barcelona 4 A1
San Justo Buenos Aires 7 C1
San Lorenzo Tezonco Mexico City 18 C2
San Luis Lima 14 B2
San Marino Los Angeles 16 B4
San Martín Barcelona 4 A2
San Martín de Porras Lima 14 B2
San Mateo Tlaltenango Mexico City 18 B1
San Miguel Lima 14 B2
San Miguel Santiago 27 B2
San Nicolás Buenos Aires 7 B2
San Onófrio Rome 26 B1
San Pedro Mártir Barcelona 4 A1
San Pedro Zacatenco Mexico City 18 A2
San Pietro, Piazza Rome 26 B1
San Po Kong Hong Kong 12 A2
San Rafael Chamapa Mexico City 18 B1
San Rafael Hills Los Angeles 16 A3
San Roque Manila 17 B2
San Siro Milan 18 B1
San Souci Sydney 29 B1
San Telmo Buenos Aires 7 B2
San Vicenç dels Horts Barcelona 4 A1
Sandown Johannesburg 13 A2
Sandown Park Races London 15 B1
Sandton Johannesburg 13 A2
Sandvika Oslo 23 A2
Sandyford Dublin 10 B2
Sandymount Dublin 10 B2
Sangenjaya Tokyo 30 B2
Sanggye Seoul 27 B2
Sangley Pt. Manila 17 C1
Sankrail Kolkata 14 B1
Sankt-Peterburg St. Petersburg 27 B1
Sankt Veit Vienna 32 A1
Sanlihe Beijing 4 B1
Sanlin Shanghai 28 C1
Sanlintang Shanghai 28 C1
Sans Barcelona 4 A1
Sanssouci Berlin 5 B1
Sant Ambrogio, Basilica di Milan 18 B2
Sant Boi de Llobregat Barcelona 4 A1
Sant Cugat Barcelona 4 A1
Sant Feliu de Llobregat Barcelona 4 A1
Sant Joan Despi Barcelona 4 A1
Santa Ana Manila 17 B2
Santa Anita Park Los Angeles 16 B4
Santa Coloma de Gramenet Barcelona 4 A2
Santa Cruz Manila 17 B1
Santa Cruz Mumbai 20 A1
Santa Cruz, I. de Rio de Janeiro 25 B2
Santa Cruz de Olorde Barcelona 4 A1
Santa Efigénia São Paulo 27 B2
Santa Elena Manila 17 B2
Santa Elena del Gomero Santiago 27 B1
Santa Eulalia Barcelona 4 A2
Santa Fe Springs Los Angeles 16 C4
Santa Iria da Azóia Lisbon 16 A2
Santa Julia Santiago 27 C2
Santa Monica Los Angeles 16 B2
Santa Monica Mts. Los Angeles 16 B2
Santa Rosa de Locobe Santiago 27 B2
Santa Teresa de la Ovalle Santiago 27 B1
Santahamina Helsinki 11 C3
Santana São Paulo 27 A2
Santeny Paris 24 B4
Santiago Santiago 27 B2
Santiago Benítez ✈ (SCL) Santiago 27 B1
Santiago de Surco Lima 14 B2
Santo Amaro Lisbon 16 A1
Santo Amaro São Paulo 27 B1
Santo André Lisbon 16 B2
Santo Antão do Tojal Lisbon 16 A2
Santo Antônio, Qta. de Lisbon 16 B1
Santo Tomas, Univ. of Manila 17 B1
Santos Dumont ✈ (SDU) Rio de Janeiro 25 B2
Santoshpur Kolkata 14 B1
Santragachi Kolkata 14 B1
Santry Dublin 10 A2
Sanyuanli Guangzhou 11 B2
São Caetano do Sul São Paulo 27 B2
São Conrado Rio de Janeiro 25 B1
São Cristóvão Rio de Janeiro 25 B1
São Jorge, Castelo de Lisbon 16 A2
São Juliao do Tojal Lisbon 16 A2
São Paulo São Paulo 27 B2
São Paulo Congonhas ✈ (CGH) São Paulo 27 B2
Sapa Kolkata 14 B1
Sapateiro, Cor. do → São Paulo 27 B1
Sarandi Buenos Aires 7 C2
Saraswati → Kolkata 14 A1
Sarecky potok → Prague 25 B2
Sarimbun Singapore 28 A2
Sarimbun Res. Singapore 28 A2
Sarıyer Istanbul 12 A2
Sarriá Barcelona 4 A1
Sarsuna Kolkata 14 C1
Sartrouville Paris 24 A2
Sasad Budapest 7 B2
Sashalom Budapest 7 A3
Saska Warsaw 33 B2
Satalice Prague 25 B3
Satgachi Kolkata 14 B2
Satpukur Kolkata 14 B2
Sätra Stockholm 29 B1
Saúde São Paulo 27 B2
Saugus Boston 6 A2
Saugus → Boston 6 A2
Sault-au-Récollet Montreal 20 A2
Sausalito San Francisco 26 A2
Sawah Besar Jakarta 12 A1
Sawtelle Los Angeles 16 B2
Scald Law Edinburgh 11 B2
Scarborough Toronto 31 A3
Scarborough Bluffs Toronto 31 A3
Sceaux Paris 24 B2
Schaerbeek Brussels 6 A2
Scharfenberg Berlin 5 A2
Schiller Woods Chicago 9 B1
Schiphol, Amsterdam ✈ (AMS) Amsterdam 2 B1
Schlachtensee Berlin 5 B2
Schlossgarten Berlin 5 A2
Schmargendorf Berlin 5 B2
Schönblick Berlin 5 B5
Schönbrunn Vienna 32 A1
Schöneberg Berlin 5 B3
Schönefeld Berlin 5 B4
Schöneiche Berlin 5 B5
Schönwalde Berlin 5 A1
Schulzendorf Berlin 5 A2
Schwabing Munich 21 B2
Schwanebeck Berlin 5 A4
Schwanenwerder Berlin 5 B2
Schwarzlackenau Vienna 32 A2
Schwechat Vienna 32 B2
Schwechat, Wien ✈ (VIE) Vienna 32 B3
Science and Industry, Museum of Chicago 9 C3
Scopus, Mt. Jerusalem 13 B2
Scottdale Atlanta 3 B3
Scutari = Üsküdar Istanbul 12 B2
Sea Point Cape Town 8 A1
Seacliff San Francisco 26 B2
Seaforth Sydney 29 A2
Seagate New York 22 C1
SeaWorld Orlando 23 B2
Šeberov Prague 25 B3
Secaucus New York 22 B1
Seddinsee Berlin 5 B5
Seeberg Berlin 5 A5
Seeburg Berlin 5 A1
Seefeld Berlin 5 A5
Seegefeld Berlin 5 A1
Seehof Berlin 5 B2
Segeltorp Stockholm 29 B1
Segrate Milan 18 B2
Seguro Milan 18 B1
Seixal Lisbon 16 B2
Selby Johannesburg 13 B2
Seletar Singapore 28 A3
Seletar, Pulau Singapore 28 A3
Seletar Hills Singapore 28 A3
Seletar Res. Singapore 28 A2
Selhurst London 15 B3
Sembawang Singapore 28 A2
Senago Milan 18 A1
Sendling Munich 21 B2
Senju Tokyo 30 A3
Senkang Singapore 28 A3
Senriyama Osaka 23 A2
Sentosa Singapore 28 B2
Seobinggo Seoul 27 B1
Seocho Seoul 27 C1
Seodaemun Seoul 27 B1
Seokkwan Seoul 27 B2
Seongbuk Seoul 27 B2
Seongdong Seoul 27 B2
Seongsu Seoul 27 B2
Seoul Seoul 27 B2
Seoul Nat. Univ. Seoul 27 C1
Seoul Tower Seoul 27 B1
Sepolia Athens 2 A2
Sepulveda Dam Rec. Area ⌂ Los Angeles 16 A2
Serangoon Singapore 28 A3
Serangoon, Pulau Singapore 28 A3
Serangoon, Sungei → Singapore 28 A3
Serangoon Harbour Singapore 28 A3
Seraya, Pulau Singapore 28 B2
Serebryanka → Moscow 19 B3
Serramonte San Francisco 26 C2
Sesto San Giovanni Milan 18 A2
Sesto Ulteriano Milan 18 B2
Setagaya Tokyo 30 B2
Seter Oslo 23 A3
Setia Budi Jakarta 12 B1
Settebagni Rome 26 A2
Settecamini Rome 26 B2
Séttimo Milanese Milan 18 B1
Settsu Osaka 23 A2
Seutula Helsinki 11 A2
Seven Corners Washington 33 B2
Seven Kings London 15 A4
Seventeenth Street Canal New Orleans 21 A2
Séveso → Milan 18 A1
Sevran Paris 24 A4
Sewri Mumbai 20 B2
Sforzesso, Castello Milan 18 B2
Sha Kok Mei Hong Kong 12 A2
Sha Tin Hong Kong 12 A2
Sha'ar Binyamin Jerusalem 13 A2
Shabrâmant Cairo 7 B2
Shah Mosque Tehran 31 A2
Shahdara Delhi 10 A2
Shahe Guangzhou 11 B2
Shahr-e Rey Tehran 31 B2
Shahrak-e Golshahr Tehran 31 B1
Shahrak-e Qods Tehran 31 A2
Shaikh Aomar Baghdad 3 A2
Shakurbasti Delhi 10 A1
Shalkiya Kolkata 14 B2
Sham Shui Po Hong Kong 12 B1
Shamapur Delhi 10 A1
Shamian Guangzhou 11 B2
Shan Mei Hong Kong 12 A2
Shanghai Shanghai 28 B2
Shanghai Hongqiao Int. ✈ (SHA) Shanghai 28 B1
Shanghai Pudong Int. ✈ (PVG) Shanghai 28 B2
Shankill Dublin 10 B3
Sharp I. Hong Kong 12 A2
Shastrinagar Delhi 10 A2
Shau Kei Wan Hong Kong 12 B2
Shawocun Beijing 4 B1
Shayuan Guangzhou 11 B2
Sheen, L. Orlando 23 B1
Sheepshead Bay New York 22 C2
Sheikh Zayed Road Dubai 9 B2
Shek O Hong Kong 12 B2
Shelter I. Hong Kong 12 B2
Shepherds Bush London 15 A2
Shepperton London 15 B1
Sheremetyevo ✈ (SVO) Moscow 19 A1
Sherman Oaks Los Angeles 16 B2
Sherman Park Chicago 9 C2
Sherwood, L. Orlando 23 A2
Shet Bandar Mumbai 20 B2
Sheung Fa Shan Hong Kong 12 A1
Sheung Lau Wan Hong Kong 12 B2
Sheung Wan Hong Kong 12 B1
Sheva Mumbai 20 B2
Sheva Nhava Mumbai 20 B2
Shiba Tokyo 30 B3
Shibpur Kolkata 14 B1
Shibuya Tokyo 30 B3
Shilihe Beijing 4 B2
Shimogawara Tokyo 30 B1
Shimosalo Tokyo 30 A2
Shimoshakujii Tokyo 30 A2
Shinagawa Tokyo 30 B3
Shing Mun Res. Hong Kong 12 A1
Shinjuku Tokyo 30 A3
Shinjuku Nat. Garden Tokyo 30 A3
Shinkoiwa Tokyo 30 A4
Shinnakano Tokyo 30 A3
Shipai Guangzhou 11 B3
Shirinashi → Osaka 23 B1
Shirogane Tokyo 30 B3
Shitennoji Temple Osaka 23 B2
Shiweitang Guangzhou 11 B2
Shogunle Lagos 14 A2
Shomolu Lagos 14 A2
Shooters Hill London 15 B4
Shoreditch London 15 A3
Shortlands London 15 B4
Shu'afat Jerusalem 13 B2
Shubrâ Cairo 7 A2
Shubrâ el Kheima Cairo 7 A2
Shuikou Guangzhou 11 A2
Sidcup London 15 B4
Siebenhirten Vienna 32 B1
Siedlung Berlin 5 A1
Siekierki Warsaw 33 B2
Sielce Warsaw 33 B2
Siemensstadt Berlin 5 A2
Sierra Madre Los Angeles 16 B4
Sievering Vienna 32 A2
Sighthill Edinburgh 11 B2
Signal Hill Cape Town 8 A1
Siheung Seoul 27 C1
Sikátorpuszta Budapest 7 A3
Silampur Delhi 10 B2
Sillim Seoul 27 C1
Silver, L. Orlando 23 A2
Silver Hill Washington 33 B3
Silver Lake Los Angeles 16 B3
Silver Spring Washington 33 A2
Silvermine Nature Reserve Cape Town 8 B1
Silvolantekojärvi Helsinki 11 B2
Simei Singapore 28 A3
Simla Kolkata 14 B2
Simmering Vienna 32 A2
Simmering Heide Vienna 32 A2
Simonkylä Helsinki 11 B3
Sinchon Seoul 27 B1
Sindang Seoul 27 B2
Singapore ■ Singapore 28 B3
Singapore Changi ✈ (SIN) Singapore 28 A3
Sinki, Selat Singapore 28 B2
Sinsa Seoul 27 B2
Sint-Genesius-Rode Brussels 6 B2
Sion Mumbai 20 A2
Sipson London 15 B1
Siqeil Cairo 7 A1
Şişli Istanbul 12 B1
Skansen Stockholm 29 B2
Skärholmen Stockholm 29 B1
Skarpäng Stockholm 29 A2
Skarpnäck Stockholm 29 B2
Skaryszewski, Park Warsaw 33 B2
Skogskyrkogården Stockholm 29 B2
Skokie Chicago 9 A2
Skokie → Chicago 9 A2
Skokie Heritage Museum Chicago 9 A2
Skoklefall Oslo 23 A3
Sköndal Stockholm 29 B2
Skovlunde Copenhagen 8 A2
Skovshoved Copenhagen 8 A3
Skuru Stockholm 29 B3
Sky Lake Orlando 23 B2
Slade Green London 15 B5
Slependen Oslo 23 A2
Slipi Jakarta 12 B1
Slivenec Prague 25 B2
Sloten Amsterdam 2 A1
Sloterdijk Amsterdam 2 A1
Sloterpark Amsterdam 2 A1
Sluhy Prague 25 A3
Służew Warsaw 33 B2
Służewiec Warsaw 33 B2
Smíchov Prague 25 B2
Smith Forest Preserve Chicago 9 B2
Smolny St. Petersburg 27 B2
Smolny Cathedral St. Petersburg 27 B2
Snake Creek Canal Miami 19 C2
Snarøya Oslo 23 A2
Snättringe Stockholm 29 B1
Søborg Copenhagen 8 A2
Sobreda Lisbon 16 B1
Söderby Stockholm 29 A3
Södermalm Stockholm 29 B2
Sodpur Kolkata 14 A2
Soeurs, Î. des Montreal 20 B2
Sognsvatn Oslo 23 A3
Soignes, Forêt de Brussels 6 B2
Sok Kwu Wan Hong Kong 12 B1
Sokolniki Moscow 19 B3
Sokolniki Park Moscow 19 B3
Sokołów Warsaw 33 C1
Solalinden Munich 21 B3
Sollentuna Stockholm 29 A1
Solln Munich 21 B2
Solna Stockholm 29 A1
Somerset Washington 33 B2
Somerville Boston 6 A2

Sonari Mumbai 20 B2
Søndersø Copenhagen 8 A2
Songpa Seoul 27 B2
Sony Picture Studio
Los Angeles 16 B2
Sord = Swords Dublin 10 A2
Soroksár Budapest 7 B2
Soroksari Duna → Budapest 7 B2
Sosenka → Moscow 19 B3
Sosnovka St. Petersburg 27 B2
Sŏul = Seoul Seoul 27 B2
Soundview New York 22 B2
South Beach Miami 19 D3
South Beach New York 22 C1
South Bend Park Atlanta 3 B2
South Boston Boston 6 A2
South Decatur Atlanta 3 B3
South Deering Chicago 9 C3
South El Monte Los Angeles 16 B4
South Gate Los Angeles 16 C3
South Harbor Manila 17 B1
South Harrow London 15 A1
South Hd. Sydney 29 B2
South Hills Johannesburg 13 B2
South Holland Chicago 9 D3
South Lawn Washington 33 C2
South Miami Miami 19 D1
South Norwood London 15 B3
South of Market
San Francisco 26 B2
South Ozone Park
New York 22 B3
South Pasadena Los Angeles 16 B4
South Res. Boston 6 A2
South Ruislip London 15 A1
South San Francisco
San Francisco 26 C2
South San Gabriel
Los Angeles 16 B4
South Shore Chicago 9 C3
Southall London 15 A1
Southborough London 15 B4
Southend London 15 B3
Southern California, Univ.
of Los Angeles 16 B3
Southfields London 15 B2
Southport New Orleans 21 B2
Southwark □ London 15 B3
Southwest Museum
Los Angeles 16 B3
Søvang Copenhagen 8 B3
Soweto Johannesburg 13 B1
Sowhānak Tehran 31 A3
Soya Tokyo 30 A4
Spandau Berlin 5 A1
Spånga Stockholm 29 A1
Spectacle I. Boston 6 A3
Speicher-See Munich 21 A3
Speising Vienna 32 B1
Sphinx Cairo 7 B1
Spinaceto Rome 26 C1
Spit Junction Sydney 29 A2
Spořilov Prague 25 B3
Spot Pond Boston 6 A2
Spotswood Melbourne 18 B1
Spring Valley Las Vegas 14 B1
Springeberg Berlin 5 B5
Springfield Washington 33 C1
Squantum Boston 6 B2
Srednaya Rogatka
St. Petersburg 27 C2
Śródmieście Warsaw 33 B2
Staaken Berlin 5 A1
Stabekk Oslo 23 A2
Stadlau Vienna 32 A2
Stadshuset Stockholm 29 B2
Stains Paris 24 A3
Stamford Hill London 15 A3
Stammersdorf Vienna 32 A2
Stanley Hong Kong 12 B2
Stanley Pen. Hong Kong 12 B2
Stanmore London 15 A2
Stapleton New York 22 C1
Staraya Derevnya
St. Petersburg 27 B1
Staré Město Prague 25 B2
Stare Miasto Warsaw 33 B2
Starke, L. Orlando 23 A1
Staten Island Zoo New York 22 C1
Staten Islands Ferry
Terminal New York 22 C1
Statenice Prague 25 B1
Stedelijk Museum
Amsterdam 2 A2
Steele Creek Melbourne 18 A1
Steenokkerzeel Brussels 6 A2
Steer, L. Orlando 23 A2
Steglitz Berlin 5 B2
Stepaside Dublin 10 B2
Stephansdom Vienna 32 A2
Stepney London 15 A3
Sterling Park San Francisco 26 B2
Stickline udde Stockholm 29 A2
Stickney Chicago 9 C2
Stillorgan Dublin 10 B2
Stockholm Stockholm 29 B2
Stockholm Arlanda ✈
(ARN) Stockholm 29 A1
Stocksund Stockholm 29 A2
Stoclet, Palais Brussels 6 B2
Stodůlky Prague 25 B1
Stoke Newington London 15 A3
Stone Canyon Res.
Los Angeles 16 B2
Stone Zoo Boston 6 A2
Stonebridge London 15 A2
Stoneham Boston 6 A2
Stony Brook Res. Boston 6 B2
Stony Creek → Chicago 9 C2
Stora Värtan Stockholm 29 A2
Store Hareskov Copenhagen 8 A2
Store Magleby Copenhagen 8 B3
Storholmen Stockholm 29 A2
Stoyka St. Petersburg 27 B2
Straiton Edinburgh 11 B3
Strandfontein Cape Town 8 B2
Strašnice Prague 25 B2
Strassтrudering Munich 21 B3
Stratford London 15 A4
Strathfield Sydney 29 B1
Streatham London 15 B3
Streatham Vale London 15 B3
Strebersdorf Vienna 32 A2
Střešovice Prague 25 B2
Strip, The Las Vegas 14 B2
Střížkov Prague 25 B2
Strombeek-Bever Brussels 6 A2
Stromovka Prague 25 B2
Studio City Los Angeles 16 B2
Stureby Stockholm 29 B2
Stuvsta Stockholm 29 B2
Subhepur Delhi 10 A2
Suburban Canal
New Orleans 21 B1
Sucat Manila 17 C2
Suchdol Prague 25 B2
Sucy-en-Brie Paris 24 B4
Sue, L. Orlando 23 A2
Sugamo Tokyo 30 A3
Sugar Loaf Mt. = Açúcar,
Pão de Rio de Janeiro 25 B2
Suge Tokyo 30 B2
Suginami Tokyo 30 A2
Sugō Tokyo 30 B2
Sui Sai Wan Hong Kong 12 B1
Suita Osaka 23 A2
Suitland Washington 33 B3
Sukchar Kolkata 14 A2
Sultanahme Camil Istanbul 12 B1
Sumida Tokyo 30 A3
Sumida → Tokyo 30 A3
Sumiyoshi Osaka 23 B2
Sumiyoshi Shrine Osaka 23 B1
Summerville Toronto 31 B1
Summit Chicago 9 C2
Sunamachi Tokyo 30 A4
Sunbury-on-Thames
London 15 B1
Sundbyberg Stockholm 29 A1
Sundbyerne Copenhagen 8 B3
Sung Kong Hong Kong 12 B2
Sungei Kadut Industrial
Estate Singapore 28 A2
Sungei Selatar Res.
Singapore 28 A3
Sunny Isles Beach Miami 19 C3
Sunrise Miami 19 B2
Sunrise Manor Las Vegas 14 A2
Sunrise Mountain Natural
Area Las Vegas 14 A2
Sunset Park Las Vegas 14 B2
Sunset Park New York 22 C2
Sunshine Park Miami 19 B2
Sunter Jakarta 12 A2
Sunter, Kali → Jakarta 12 B2
Suomenlinna Helsinki 11 C2
Sur Bahr Jerusalem 13 B2
Sura Kolkata 14 B2
Suraksan Seoul 27 A2
Surbiton London 15 B2
Suresnes Paris 24 A2
Surfside Miami 19 C3
Surquillo Lima 14 B2
Surrey Hills Sydney 29 B2
Surulere Lagos 14 B2
Susaek Seoul 27 B1
Süssenbrunn Vienna 32 A2
Sutton Dublin 10 A3
Sutton London 15 B2
Suyu Seoul 27 B2
Suzukishinden Tokyo 30 A2
Svanemøllen Copenhagen 8 A3
Sveaborg = Suomenlinna
Helsinki 11 C2
Sverdlov Moscow 19 B2
Svestad Oslo 23 B2
Svinö Helsinki 11 C1
Swanley London 15 B4
Swansea Toronto 31 B2
Swinburne I. New York 22 C1
Swords Dublin 10 A2
Sydenham Johannesburg 13 A2
Sydney Sydney 29 B2
Sydney, Univ. of Sydney 29 B2
Sydney Harbour △ Sydney 29 B2
Sydney Harbour Bridge
Sydney 29 B2
Sydney Kingsford Smith ✈
(SYD) Sydney 29 B2
Sydstranden Copenhagen 8 B3
Sylvania Sydney 29 C1
Syon Park London 15 B2
Szczęśliwice Warsaw 33 B1
Széchnenyi-hegy Budapest 7 B1
Széphalom Budapest 7 A1

T

Taastrup Copenhagen 8 B1
Tabata Tokyo 30 A3
Tablada Buenos Aires 7 C1
Table B. Cape Town 8 A1
Table Mountain △
Cape Town 8 A1
Table Mt. Cape Town 8 A1
Taboão da Serra São Paulo 27 B1
Täby Stockholm 29 A2
Tacuba Mexico City 18 B1
Tacubaya Mexico City 18 B1
Tafelbaai = Table B.
Cape Town 8 A1
Taft Orlando 23 B2
Tagig → Manila 17 B2
Taguig Manila 17 B2
Tahrir Square Cairo 7 A2
Tai Lo Shan Hong Kong 12 A2
Tai Po Tsai Hong Kong 12 A2
Tai Seng Singapore 28 A3
Tai Shui Hang Hong Kong 12 A2
Tai Tam B. Hong Kong 12 B2
Tai Tam Tuk Res.
Hong Kong 12 B2
Tai Wai Hong Kong 12 A2
Tai Wan Tau Hong Kong 12 B2
Tai Wo Hau Hong Kong 12 A1
Tainaka Osaka 23 B2
Taishō Osaka 23 B1
Tajrish Tehran 31 A2
Takaido Tokyo 30 A2
Takaishi Tokyo 30 B3
Takarazuka Osaka 23 A1
Takasago Tokyo 30 A4
Takatsu Tokyo 30 B2
Takeshita Tokyo 30 B2
Takinegawa Tokyo 30 A3
Takoma Park Washington 33 B2
Taksim Istanbul 12 B1
Talaide Lisbon 16 A1
Taliganga Kolkata 14 B2
Talipapa Manila 17 A2
Tallaght Dublin 10 B1
Tallkrogen Stockholm 29 B2
Tama Tokyo 30 B1
Tama → Tokyo 30 B2
Tama Kyūryō Tokyo 30 B2
Tamaden Tokyo 30 B2
Tamagawa-josui → Tokyo 30 A1
Taman Sari Jakarta 12 A1
Tamanduateí → São Paulo 27 B2
Tamarac Miami 19 A1
Tamboerskloof Cape Town 8 A1
Tambora Jakarta 12 A1
Tammisalo Helsinki 11 B3
Tammūh Cairo 7 B2
Tampines Singapore 28 A3
Tanah Abang Jakarta 12 B1
Tanah Kusir Jakarta 12 B1
Tangelo Park Orlando 23 B2
Tanjung Duren Jakarta 12 B1
Tanjung Priok Jakarta 12 A2
Tanum Oslo 23 A1
Tapada Lisbon 16 A1
Tapanila Helsinki 11 B3
Tapiales Buenos Aires 7 C1
Tapiola Helsinki 11 B1
Tapsia Kolkata 14 B2
Tara Mumbai 20 A1
Tarabya Istanbul 12 B2
Tårbæk Copenhagen 8 A3
Tarchomin Warsaw 33 B1
Tardeo Mumbai 20 B1
Targówek Warsaw 33 B2
Tårnby Copenhagen 8 B3
Tarqua Bay Lagos 14 B2
Tathong Channel
Hong Kong 12 B2
Tathong Pt. Hong Kong 12 B2
Tatuapé São Paulo 27 B2
Taufkirchen Munich 21 B2
Tavares, I. dos Rio de Janeiro 25 A2
Tavros Athens 2 B2
Teaneck New York 22 A1
Tebet Jakarta 12 B2
Tecamachalco Mexico City 18 B1
Ted Williams Tunnel Boston 6 A2
Teddington London 15 B1
Tegel Berlin 5 A2
Tegeler See Berlin 5 A2
Tegelort Berlin 5 A2
Teheran = Tehrān Tehran 31 A2
Tehrān Tehran 31 A2
Tehrān Mehrābād ✈
(THR) Tehran 31 A1
Tehrān Pārs Tehran 31 A3
Tei Tong Tsui Hong Kong 12 B2
Tejo, Rio → Lisbon 16 A2
Tekstilyshchik Moscow 19 B3
Telhal Lisbon 16 A1
Telok Blangah Singapore 28 B2
Teltow Berlin 5 B2
Teltow kanal Berlin 5 B3
Tempelhof Berlin 5 B3
Temple City Los Angeles 16 B4
Temple Hills Washington 33 C3
Temple of Heaven Beijing 4 B2
Templeogue Dublin 10 B2
Temppeliaukio Church
Helsinki 11 B2
Tenafly New York 22 A2
Tenayuca, Piramide de
Mexico City 18 A1
Tengah → Singapore 28 A2
Tennoji Osaka 23 B2
Tepalcates Mexico City 18 B2
Tepeyac △ Mexico City 18 B2
Terrazzano Milan 18 A1
Terre des Hommes Montreal 20 A2
Terrugem Lisbon 16 A1
Terrytown New Orleans 21 B2
Tervuren Brussels 6 B3
Tervuren, Park van Brussels 6 B3
Tetuán Madrid 17 B1
Teufelsberg Berlin 5 B2
Thalkirchen Munich 21 B2
Thames Ditton London 15 B1
Thamesmead London 15 A4
Thana Cr. → Mumbai 20 A2
Thiais Paris 24 B3
Thisio Athens 2 B2
Thistletown Toronto 31 A1
Thomastown Melbourne 18 A2
Thompson I. Boston 6 B3
Thon Buri Bangkok 3 B1
Thornbury Melbourne 18 A2
Thorncliffe Toronto 31 A2
Thornhill Toronto 31 A2
Thornton Cape Town 8 A2
Thornton Heath London 15 B3
Threipmuir Res. Edinburgh 11 B2
Throg's Neck New York 22 B3
Tiancun Beijing 4 B1
Tianhe Guangzhou 11 B3
Tibet, L. Orlando 23 B1
Tibidabo Barcelona 4 A1
Tibradden Mt. Dublin 10 B2
Tiburon San Francisco 26 A2
Tiburtino Rome 26 B2
Ticomán Mexico City 18 A2
Tiefersee Berlin 5 B1
Tiergarten Berlin 5 A3
Tijgerhof Cape Town 8 A2
Tijuca Rio de Janeiro 25 B1
Tijuca, Pico da Rio de Janeiro 25 B1
Tijuca △ Rio de Janeiro 25 B1
Tikkurila Helsinki 11 B3
Tilak Nagar Delhi 10 B1
Tilanqiao Shanghai 28 B1
Timah, Bukit Singapore 28 A2
Timiryazev Park Moscow 19 B2
Tin Can I. Lagos 14 B2
Ting Kau Hong Kong 12 A1
Tira Jerusalem 13 A1
Tirsa Cairo 7 B2
Tishrīyaa Baghdad 3 B2
Tiu Keng Leng Hong Kong 12 B2
Tizapán Mexico City 18 C1
Tlalnepantla → Mexico City 18 A1
Tlalpan Mexico City 18 C2
To Kwai Wan Hong Kong 12 B2
Toa Payoh Singapore 28 A3
Točná Prague 25 C2
Toco Hills Atlanta 3 B2
Todt Hill New York 22 C1
Tōkagi Tokyo 30 A4
Tokai Plantation Cape Town 8 B1
Tōkaichiba Tokyo 30 B2
Tōkyō Tokyo 30 B3
Tōkyō B. = Tōkyō-Wan
Tokyo 30 B4
Tōkyō Disneyland Tokyo 30 B4
Tōkyō Haneda ✈ (HND)
Tokyo 30 B3
Tōkyō Harbour Tokyo 30 B3
Tōkyō Sky Tree Tokyo 30 A3
Tōkyō-Wan Tokyo 30 B4
Tolka → Dublin 10 A1
Tollygunge = Taliganga
Kolkata 14 B2
Tolworth London 15 B2
Tomba di Nerone Rome 26 B1
Tommy Thompson Park
Toronto 31 B3
Tondo Manila 17 B1
Tongbinggo Seoul 27 B1
Tongqiao Shanghai 28 A1
Toorak Melbourne 18 B2
Topanga State Park ⌓
Los Angeles 16 B1
Topkapı Istanbul 12 B1
Topkapı Palaca Istanbul 12 B1
Tor di Quinto Rome 26 B1
Tor Pignattara Rome 26 B2
Tor Sapienza Rome 26 B2
Torcy Paris 24 A4
Toronto Toronto 31 B2
Toronto, Univ. of Toronto 31 B2
Toronto City Centre ✈
(YTZ) Toronto 31 B2
Toronto Harbour Toronto 31 B2
Toronto I. Toronto 31 B2
Toronto Lester B. Pearson
Int. ✈ (YYZ) Toronto 31 A1
Torre Lupara Rome 26 B2
Torre Nova Rome 26 B2
Torrellas → Barcelona 4 A1
Torrevecchia Rome 26 B1
Toshima Tokyo 30 A3
Toshimaen Tokyo 30 A2
Tottenham London 15 A3
Tottenham Melbourne 18 A1
Toussus-le-Noble Paris 24 B1
Toussus-le-Noble ✈ (TNF)
Paris 24 B1
Towchāl Cable Car Tehran 31 A2
Tower Hamlets □ London 15 A3
Tower of London London 15 A3
Towra Pt. Sydney 29 C2
Tøyen Oslo 23 A3
Toyonaka Osaka 23 A1
Trafaria Lisbon 16 A1
Traição, Cor. → São Paulo 27 B2
Tranegilde Copenhagen 8 B2
Trångsund Stockholm 29 B2
Trappenfelde Berlin 5 A4
Trastévere Rome 26 B1
Treasure I. San Francisco 26 B2
Třeboradice Prague 25 B3
Třebotov Prague 25 C1
Tree Tops Park Miami 19 B1
Tremblay-en-France Paris 24 A4
Tremembe → São Paulo 27 A2
Tremont New York 22 A2
Trenno Milan 18 B1
Treptow Berlin 5 B3
Três Rios, Sa. dos
Rio de Janeiro 25 B1
Trevi, Fontana di Rome 26 B1
Trezzano sul Naviglio Milan 18 B1
Trieste Rome 26 B2
Trinidad Washington 33 B3
Trinity Edinburgh 11 B2
Trinity College Dublin 10 A2
Trionfale Rome 26 B1
Triulzo Milan 18 B2
Troja Prague 25 B2
Trollbäcken Stockholm 29 B3
Trombay Mumbai 20 A2
Troparevo Moscow 19 C1
Trudeau, Montréal ✈
(YUL) Montreal 20 B1
Trudyashchikhsya,
Ostrov St. Petersburg 27 B1
Tryvasshøgda Oslo 23 A3
Tseng Lan Shue Hong Kong 12 A2
Tseung Kwan Hong Kong 12 B2
Tsim Sha Tsui Hong Kong 12 B2
Tsing Yi Hong Kong 12 A1
Tsova Jerusalem 13 B1
Tsuen Wan Hong Kong 12 A1
Tsur Hadassa Jerusalem 13 B1
Tsurumi → Tokyo 30 B3
Tsz Wan Shan Hong Kong 12 A2
Tuas Singapore 28 B1
Tuchoměřice Prague 25 B1
Tuckahoe New York 22 A3
Tucuruvi São Paulo 27 A2
Tufello Rome 26 B2
Tufnell Park London 15 A3
Tufts Univ. Boston 6 A2
Tughlakabad Delhi 10 B2
Tullamarine Melbourne 18 A1
Tulse Hill London 15 B3
Tung Lung Chau Hong Kong 12 B2
Tung O Hong Kong 12 B1
Tunis Baghdad 3 A2
Tuomarila Helsinki 11 B1
Tureberg Stockholm 29 A1
Turffontein Johannesburg 13 B2
Turkey L. Orlando 23 A2
Turkey Lake Park Orlando 23 A2
Turner Field Atlanta 3 B2
Turnham Green London 15 B2
Turnhouse Edinburgh 11 B1
Tuscolana, Via Rome 26 B2
Twelve Apostles Cape Town 8 A1
Twentieth Century Fox
Studios Los Angeles 16 B2
Twickenham London 15 B1
Twickenham Rugby
Ground London 15 B1
Twin Peaks San Francisco 26 B2
Two Rock Mt. Dublin 10 B2
Tymon North Dublin 10 B1

U

U.S. Capitol Washington 33 B2
U.S. Cellular Field Chicago 9 C3
Ubeidiya Jerusalem 13 B2
Uberaba → São Paulo 27 B2
Ubin, Pulau Singapore 28 A3
Uccle Brussels 6 B2
Udelnaya St. Petersburg 27 A2
Udelnoe St. Petersburg 27 B1
Udlding Munich 21 A1
Ueno Tokyo 30 A3
Úholičky Prague 25 B1
Uhříněves Prague 25 B3
Uithoorn Amsterdam 2 B1
Ujazdów Warsaw 33 B2
Újpalota Budapest 7 A3
Újpest Budapest 7 A2
Ukita Tokyo 30 A4
Uleta Miami 19 C2
Ullerup Copenhagen 8 B3
Ullevål Oslo 23 A3
Ulriksdal Stockholm 29 A1
Ulyanka St. Petersburg 27 B1
Um Al Khanazir I. Baghdad 3 B2
Umeda Osaka 23 A1
Umm al Sheif Dubai 9 B1
Umm Suqeim Dubai 9 B1
Ümraniye Istanbul 12 B2
Underground Atlanta
Atlanta 3 B2
Underhill, L. Orlando 23 A3
Uněticky potok → Prague 25 B2
Unhos Lisbon 16 A2
Unidad Santa Fe
Mexico City 18 B1
Union City New York 22 B1
Union Port New York 22 B2
Union Square Hong Kong 12 B2
Union Station Toronto 31 B2
United Center Chicago 9 B2
United Nations
Headquarters New York 22 B2
Universal Studios
Los Angeles 16 B2
Universal Studios Orlando 23 B2
Universidad Madrid 17 B1
University Park Washington 33 B3
Unterbiberg Munich 21 B2
Unterföhring Munich 21 A3
Unterhaching Munich 21 B2
Unterlaa Vienna 32 B2
Untermenzing Munich 21 A1
Upper B. New York 22 C1
Upper Elmers End London 15 B3
Upper New York B. =
Upper B. New York 22 C1
Upper Norwood London 15 B3
Upper Peirce Res. Singapore 28 A2
Upper Sydenham London 15 B3
Upper Tooting London 15 B3
Upton London 15 A4
Uptown Chicago 9 B2
Uran Mumbai 20 B2
Urayasu Tokyo 30 B4
Urbe ✈ Rome 26 B2
Urca Rio de Janeiro 25 B2
Uritsk St. Petersburg 27 C1
Üröm Budapest 7 A2
Ursus Warsaw 33 B1
Ursvik Stockholm 29 A1
Usera Madrid 17 B1
Ushigome Tokyo 30 A3
Usina Rio de Janeiro 25 B1
Üsküdar Istanbul 12 B2
Ust-Slavyanka
St. Petersburg 27 C3
Uteke Stockholm 29 A3
Utrata Warsaw 33 B2
Uttarpara Kolkata 14 B1
Utterslev Mose Copenhagen 8 A2

V

Vaclavské náměstí Prague 25 B2
Vadaul Mumbai 20 A2
Vaires-sur-Marne Paris 24 A4
Valby Copenhagen 8 B2
Valcannuta Rome 26 B1
Valdelatas Madrid 17 A1
Valenton Paris 24 B3
Valera Milan 18 A1
Vallcarca Barcelona 4 A1
Valldoreix Barcelona 4 A1
Vallecas Madrid 17 B2
Vallecas, Cumbres de
Madrid 17 B2
Vallensbæk Copenhagen 8 B2
Vallensbæk Strand
Copenhagen 8 B2
Vallentunasjön Stockholm 29 A2
Valleranello Rome 26 C1
Vallisaari Helsinki 11 C3
Vallvidrera Barcelona 4 A1
Valvidrera → Barcelona 4 A1
Van Gogh Museum
Amsterdam 2 A2
Vanak Tehran 31 A2
Vanda = Vantaa Helsinki 11 B2
Vangede Copenhagen 8 A3
Vaniköy Istanbul 12 B2
Vanløse Copenhagen 8 A2
Vantaa Helsinki 11 B2
Vantaankoski Helsinki 11 B2
Vantaanpuisto Helsinki 11 B2
Vanves Paris 24 B2
Varedo Milan 18 A1
Varkiza Athens 2 C2
Vartiokylä Helsinki 11 B3
Vartiosaari Helsinki 11 B3
Vasamuseet Stockholm 29 B2
Vasco Cape Town 8 A2
Vasfenārd Tehran 31 B2
Vashi Mumbai 20 A2
Vasilyevskiy, Ostrov
St. Petersburg 27 B1
Vatican City ■ Rome 26 B1
Vaucluse Sydney 29 B2
Vaucluse House Sydney 29 B2
Vaucresson Paris 24 A1
Vaughan Toronto 31 A1
Vauhallan Paris 24 B2
Vaujours Paris 24 A4
Vauxhall London 15 B3
Vecsés Budapest 7 B3
Veleň Prague 25 A3
Veleslavin Prague 25 B2
Vélizy-Villacoublay Paris 24 B2
Velka-Chuchle Prague 25 B2
Velké Přilepy Prague 25 B1
Venda Seca Lisbon 16 A1
Venetian Islands Miami 19 D3
Venice Los Angeles 16 C2
Ventas Madrid 17 B1
Ventorro del Cano Madrid 17 B1
Venustiano Carranza
Mexico City 18 B2
Verde → São Paulo 27 A1
Verdi Athens 2 A2
Verdugo Mts. Los Angeles 16 A2
Verdun Montreal 20 B2
Vérhalom Budapest 7 A2
Vermelho → São Paulo 27 B1
Vermont Knolls Los Angeles 16 C3
Vernon Los Angeles 16 B3
Verrières-le-Buisson Paris 24 B2
Versailles Buenos Aires 7 B1
Versailles Paris 24 B1
Veshnyaki Moscow 19 B3
Vesolyy Posolok
St. Petersburg 27 B2
Vestra Helsinki 11 B1
Vestskoven Copenhagen 8 A2
Vicálvaro Madrid 17 B2
Vicente Lopez Buenos Aires 7 B2
Victoria Hong Kong 12 B2
Victoria, Pont Montreal 20 B2
Victoria and Alfred
Waterfront Cape Town 8 A1
Victoria Gardens Mumbai 20 B2
Victoria Harbour Hong Kong 12 B1
Victoria Island Lagos 14 B2
Victoria L. Johannesburg 13 B2
Victoria Lawn Tennis
Courts Melbourne 18 B2
Victoria Park Singapore 28 B2
Victoria Peak Hong Kong 12 B1
Victoria Terminus =
Chhatrapati Shivaji
Terminus Mumbai 20 B2
Vienna = Wien Vienna 32 A2
Vietnam Veterans
Memorial Washington 33 B2
Vietnam War Museum
Chicago 9 B3
Vieux Carré = French
Quarter New Orleans 21 B2
View Park Los Angeles 16 B3
Vigário Geral Rio de Janeiro 25 A1
Vigentino Milan 18 B2
Viggbyholm Stockholm 29 A2
Vighignolo Milan 18 B1
Viikki Helsinki 11 B3
Vikhroli Mumbai 20 A2
Vila Guilherme São Paulo 27 B2
Vila Isabel Rio de Janeiro 25 B1
Vila Jaguára São Paulo 27 B1
Vila Madalena São Paulo 27 B1
Vila Maria São Paulo 27 B2
Vila Mariana São Paulo 27 B2
Vila Prudente São Paulo 27 B2
Viladecans Barcelona 4 A1
Vile Parle Mumbai 20 A2
Villa Adelina Buenos Aires 7 B1
Villa Ballester Buenos Aires 7 B1
Villa Barilari Buenos Aires 7 C2
Villa Bosch Buenos Aires 7 B1
Villa C. Colon Buenos Aires 7 C2
Villa Ciudadela Buenos Aires 7 B1
Villa de Guadalupe
Mexico City 18 B2
Villa Devoto Buenos Aires 7 B1
Villa Diamante Buenos Aires 7 C2
Villa Dominico Buenos Aires 7 C3
Villa Lugano Buenos Aires 7 C2
Villa Lynch Buenos Aires 7 B1
Villa Madero Buenos Aires 7 C1
Villa Sáenz Pena
Buenos Aires 7 B1
Villa Urquiza Buenos Aires 7 B2
Villaverde Madrid 17 B1
Villaverde Bajo Madrid 17 B1
Ville-d'Avray Paris 24 B2
Villecresnes Paris 24 B4
Villejuif Paris 24 B3
Villemomble Paris 24 A4
Villeneuve-la-Garenne
Paris 24 A2
Villeneuve-le-Roi Paris 24 B3
Villeneuve-St-Georges Paris 24 B3
Villeparisis Paris 24 A4
Villevaudé Paris 24 A4
Villiers-le-Bâcle Paris 24 B1
Villiers-sur-Marne Paris 24 B4
Villinki Helsinki 11 C3
Villoresi, Canale Milan 18 A1
Vilvoorde Brussels 6 A2
Vimodrone Milan 18 A2
Vimont Montreal 20 A1
Vincennes Paris 24 A3
Vincennes, Bois de Paris 24 B3
Vineland Orlando 23 B1
Vinings Atlanta 3 A2
Vinohrady Prague 25 B2
Vinoř Prague 25 B3
Violet Hill Hong Kong 12 B2
Virányos Budapest 7 A1
Virginia, L. Orlando 23 A2
Virginia Gardens Miami 19 D1
Virginia Key Miami 19 D3
Viroflay Paris 24 B2
Vironas Athens 2 B2
Virum Copenhagen 8 A2
Visitacion Valley
San Francisco 26 B2
Vista Alegre Lima 14 B3
Vista Alegre Santiago 27 C1
Vista Grove Atlanta 3 A3
Vitacura Santiago 27 B2
Vitinia Rome 26 C1
Vitry-sur-Seine Paris 24 B3
Vladykino Moscow 19 A2
Vokovice Prague 25 B2
Volgelsdorf Berlin 5 B5
Volkhonka-Zil Moscow 19 C2
Vollen Oslo 23 B1
Volodarskoye St. Petersburg 27 B2
Volynkina-Derevnya
St. Petersburg 27 B1
Vondelpark Amsterdam 2 A2
Vösendorf Vienna 32 B2
Voula Athens 2 C2
Vouliagmeni Athens 2 C2
Vredehoek Cape Town 8 A1
Vršovice Prague 25 B2
Vyborgskaya Storona
St. Petersburg 27 B2
Vykhino Moscow 19 B3
Vyšehrad Prague 25 B2

W

Wachterhof Munich 21 B3
Wadala Mumbai 20 A2
Wadi al-Arayis Jerusalem 13 B2
Wadi Fukin Jerusalem 13 B1
Waduk Pluit Jakarta 12 A1
Waggaman New Orleans 21 B1
Wah Fu Hong Kong 12 B1
Wahda Baghdad 3 B2
Währing Vienna 32 A2
Waidmannslust Berlin 5 A3
Wakefield Boston 6 A2
Waldesruh Berlin 5 B4
Waldperlach Munich 21 B3
Waldtrudering Munich 21 B3
Walkinstown Dublin 10 B1
Wall Street New York 22 B1
Walt Disney World Orlando 23 B1
Waltham Boston 6 A1
Waltham Forest □ London 15 A3
Walthamstow London 15 A3
Walton-on-Thames London 15 B1
Wambeek Brussels 6 A3
Wan Chai Hong Kong 12 B2
Wandle → London 15 B2
Wandsworth □ London 15 B2
Wangjing Beijing 4 B2
Wannsee Berlin 5 B1
Wansdorf Berlin 5 A1
Wanstead London 15 A4
Wapping London 15 A3
Wards I. New York 22 B2
Warnberg Munich 21 B2
Warner Brothers Studios
Los Angeles 16 B2
Warrâq el 'Arab Cairo 7 A2
Warringal Park Melbourne 18 A2
Warriston Edinburgh 11 B2
Warsaw = Warszawa
Warsaw 33 B2
Warszawa Warsaw 33 B2
Warszawa ✈ (WAW)
Warsaw 33 B1
Wartenberg Berlin 5 A4
Washington Washington 33 B2
Washington Heights
New York 22 A2
Washington Park Chicago 9 C3
Washington Ronald
Reagan Nat. ✈ (DCA)
Washington 33 B2
Wat Pho Bangkok 3 B1
Water of Leith → Edinburgh 11 B1
Watergraafsmeer Amsterdam 2 A2
Waterland Amsterdam 2 A2
Waterloo Brussels 6 B2
Watermeal-Boitsfort Brussels 6 B2
Watertown Boston 6 A1
Watsonia Melbourne 18 A2
Watts Los Angeles 16 C3
Waverley Boston 6 A1
Waverley Johannesburg 13 A2
Waverley Sydney 29 B2
Wawer Warsaw 33 B2
Wawrzyszew Warsaw 33 B1
Wazirabad Delhi 10 A2
Wazīrīya Baghdad 3 A2
Wazirpur Delhi 10 A2
Wealdstone London 15 A1
Wedding Berlin 5 A3
Weehawken New York 22 B1
Weesp Amsterdam 2 B3
Weidling Vienna 32 A1
Weidlingbach Vienna 32 A1
Weissensee Berlin 5 A3
Wellesley Hills Boston 6 B1
Welling London 15 B4
Wellington Boston 6 A2
Weltevreden Park
Johannesburg 13 A1
Wembley London 15 A2
Wemmel Brussels 6 A1
Wemmer Pan Johannesburg 13 B2
Wenceslas Square =
Vaclavské náměstí
Prague 25 B2
Wendenschloss Berlin 5 B4
Wennington London 15 A5
Werneuchen Berlin 5 A5
West Don → Toronto 31 A2
West Drayton London 15 A1
West Ham London 15 A4
West Harrow London 15 A1
West Heath London 15 B4
West Hill Toronto 31 A3
West Hollywood Los Angeles 16 B2
West Lamma Channel
Hong Kong 12 B1
West Los Angeles, Univ. of
Los Angeles 16 C2
West Medford Boston 6 A2
West Miami Miami 19 D1
West Molesey London 15 B1
West New York New York 22 B1
West of Twin Peaks
San Francisco 26 B2
West Park Johannesburg 13 A1
West Park Miami 19 C2
West Rouge Toronto 31 A4
West Roxbury Boston 6 B2
West Town Chicago 9 B2
West Wharf Karachi 13 B1
Westchester Los Angeles 16 C2
Westchester New York 22 A2
Westcliff Johannesburg 13 B2
Westdene Johannesburg 13 B1
Westend Helsinki 11 C1
Wester Hailes Edinburgh 11 B2
Westerham Munich 21 B2
Western Addition
San Francisco 26 B2
Westgate New Orleans 21 A1
Westgate Washington 33 B2
Westlake Cape Town 8 B1
Westlake Los Angeles 16 B3
Westlake San Francisco 26 B2
Westminster London 15 A3
Westmount Montreal 20 B2
Weston Toronto 31 A1
Westwego New Orleans 21 B2
Westwood Village
Los Angeles 16 B2
Westzaan Amsterdam 2 A1
Wetton Cape Town 8 B2
Wexford Toronto 31 A3
Weybridge London 15 B1
Wezembeek-Oppem Brussels 6 A2
White Cloud Hill = Baiyun
Mountain Scenic Area
Guangzhou 11 B2
White House, The
Washington 33 B2
Whitechapel London 15 A3
Whitehall Dublin 10 A2
Whitney Las Vegas 14 B2
Whittier Los Angeles 16 C4
Whittier Narrows
Recreation Area ⌓
Los Angeles 16 B4
Whitton London 15 B1
Wieden Vienna 32 A2
Wien Vienna 32 A2
Wien-Schwechat ✈ (VIE)
Vienna 32 B3
Wienerberg Vienna 32 B2
Wierzbno Warsaw 33 B2
Wijde Wormer Amsterdam 2 A2
Wilanów Warsaw 33 B2
Wilanówka → Warsaw 33 C2
Wilds, The Johannesburg 13 B2
Wilhelmshagen Berlin 5 B5
Wilket Creek Park Toronto 31 A2
Wilkieston Edinburgh 11 B1
Will Rogers State
Historical Park ⌓
Los Angeles 16 B1
Willbrook Dublin 10 B2
Willesden London 15 A2
Willesden Green London 15 A2
Williamsbridge New York 22 A2
Williamsburg New York 22 B2
Williamsburg Orlando 23 B2
Williamstown Melbourne 18 B1
Willis, L. Orlando 23 B2
Willoughby Sydney 29 A2
Willowdale New Orleans 21 A1
Willowdale Toronto 31 A2
Wilmersdorf Berlin 5 B2
Wilmette Chicago 9 A2
Wilmington London 15 B5
Wilton Manors Miami 19 B3
Wimbledon London 15 B2
Wimbledon Common
London 15 B2
Wimbledon Park London 15 B2
Wimbledon Tennis
Ground London 15 B2
Winchester Boston 6 A2
Winchester Las Vegas 14 B2
Windermere Cape Town 8 A2
Windermere Orlando 23 B1
Windsor Johannesburg 13 A1
Windsor, Gare Montreal 20 B2
Windsor Hills Los Angeles 16 C2
Windy Arbour Dublin 10 B2
Winnetka Chicago 9 A2
Winning Munich 21 B2
Wissous Paris 24 B2
Wittenau Berlin 5 A2
Witwatersrand, Univ. of
Johannesburg 13 B2
Włochy Warsaw 33 B1
Wo Mei Hong Kong 12 A2
Wo Yi Hop Hong Kong 12 A1
Woburn Boston 6 A2
Woburn Toronto 31 A3
Woła Warsaw 33 B1
Wolgok Seoul 27 B2
Wolica Warsaw 33 C1
Wollaston Boston 6 B2
Woltersdorf Berlin 5 B5
Woluwe-St-Lambert Brussels 6 A2
Woluwe-St-Pierre Brussels 6 A2
Wong Chuk Hang
Hong Kong 12 B2
Wong Chuk Wan
Hong Kong 12 A2
Wong Chuk Yeung
Hong Kong 12 A2
Wood Green London 15 A3
Wood Ridge New York 22 A1
Woodbine Race Track
Toronto 31 A1
Woodbridge Toronto 31 A1
Woodford London 15 A4
Woodford Bridge London 15 A4
Woodford Green London 15 A4
Woodhaven New York 22 B2
Woodhouselee Edinburgh 11 B2
Woodlands Singapore 28 A2
Woodmont Washington 33 B2
Woodside London 15 B3
Woodside New York 22 B2
Woodstock Cape Town 8 A1
Woollahra Sydney 29 B2
Woolooware B. Sydney 29 C1
Woolwich London 15 B4
Worker's Stadium Beijing 4 B2
World Financial Centre
Shanghai 28 B2
World Trade Center, Site
of former = 11 Memorial
September 11 Memorial
and Museum New York 22 B1
Worli Mumbai 20 A1
Worth Chicago 9 C2
Wren's Nest Atlanta 3 B2
Wrigley Field Chicago 9 B3
Wuhlgarten Berlin 5 A4
Wujiaochang Shanghai 28 B2
Würm → Munich 21 B1
Würm-kanal Munich 21 A1
Wusong Shanghai 28 A1
Wyczólki Warsaw 33 C1
Wygoda Warsaw 33 B2
Wynberg Cape Town 8 B1

X

Xabregas Lisbon 16 A2
Xiaogang Park Guangzhou 11 B2
Xiaoping Guangzhou 11 A2
Xiashachong Guangzhou 11 B1
Xichang Guangzhou 11 B2
Xicheng Beijing 4 B1
Xidan Beijing 4 B2
Xizhimen Beijing 4 B1
Xochimilco, Parque
Ecológico Mexico City 18 C2
Xuanwu Beijing 4 B1
Xuhui Shanghai 28 B1
Xujiahui Shanghai 28 B1

Y

Yaba Lagos 14 A2
Yaftābād Tehran 31 B1
Yahara Tokyo 30 A2
Yaho Tokyo 30 A1
Yakire Tokyo 30 A4
Yaksu Seoul 27 B2
Yamada Osaka 23 A2
Yamada Tokyo 30 B2
Yamato → Osaka 23 B1
Yan Kit Singapore 28 A3
Yanbu Guangzhou 11 B1
Yangcheon Seoul 27 B1
Yanghuayuan Beijing 4 C1
Yangjae Seoul 27 C2
Yangjiazhuang Shanghai 28 A1
Yangjing Shanghai 28 B2
Yangpu Shanghai 28 B2
Yangpu Park Shanghai 28 B2
Yannawa Bangkok 3 B2
Yarmūk Baghdad 3 B1
Yarra Bend Park Melbourne 18 A2
Yarraville Melbourne 18 A1
Yauza → Moscow 19 B4
Yeading London 15 A1
Yedikule Istanbul 12 C1
Yenikapı Istanbul 12 B1
Yeniköy Istanbul 12 B2
Yeongdeungpo Seoul 27 B1
Yeongdong Seoul 27 B2
Yeouido Seoul 27 B1
Yerba Buena I.
San Francisco 26 B2
Yerres Paris 24 B4
Yerushalayim =
Jerusalem Jerusalem 13 B2
Yiheyuan Beijing 4 B1
Yıldız Park Istanbul 12 B2
Yinhangzhen Shanghai 28 A2
Yishun Singapore 28 A3
Ylästö Helsinki 11 B2
Yodo → Osaka 23 A2
Yongdingman Beijing 4 B2
Yongfucun Guangzhou 11 B2
Yongsan Seoul 27 B1
Yonkers New York 22 A2
York Toronto 31 A2
York Mills Toronto 31 A2
York Univ. Toronto 31 A2
You'anmen Beijing 4 B1
Youngsfield Cape Town 8 B2
Yuanmingyuan Park Beijing 4 A1
Yuanxiatian Guangzhou 11 A2
Yuexiu Guangzhou 11 B2
Yuexiu Park Guangzhou 11 B2
Yugo-Zarad Moscow 19 B2
Yung Shue Wan Hong Kong 12 B1
Yūsofābād Tehran 31 A2

Z

Za'abeel Dubai 9 B2
Zaandam Amsterdam 2 A1
Zaandijk Amsterdam 2 A1
Zaanstad Amsterdam 2 A1
Zāběhlice Prague 25 B2
Zabki Warsaw 33 B2
Zacisze Warsaw 33 B2
Zahrā Baghdad 3 A1
Žalov Prague 25 A2
Załuski Warsaw 33 C1
Zamdorf Munich 21 B2
Zanevka St. Petersburg 27 B3
Zapote Manila 17 C1
Zaventem Brussels 6 A2
Zawady Warsaw 33 B2
Zāwiyet Abū Musallam
Cairo 7 B1
Zawrā' Park Baghdad 3 B2
Zbraslav Prague 25 C2
Zbuzany Prague 25 B1
Zdiby Prague 25 B2
Zeekoevlei Cape Town 8 B2
Zehlendorf Berlin 5 B2
Zenne → Brussels 6 A2
Zephyr Field New Orleans 21 B1
Żerań Warsaw 33 B1
Zerzeń Warsaw 33 B2
Zeytinburnu Istanbul 12 C1
Zhabei Shanghai 28 B1
Zhdanov Moscow 19 B3
Zhenru Shanghai 28 B1
Zhernovka St. Petersburg 27 B2
Zhicun Guangzhou 11 B2
Zhongguancun Beijing 4 B1
Zhongshan Park Shanghai 28 B1
Zhoucun Guangzhou 11 A2
Zhoujiadu Shanghai 28 B1
Zhoujiazhen Shanghai 28 A2
Zhouzhuangzi Beijing 4 B1
Zhulebino Moscow 19 B4
Zhushadi Guangzhou 11 A3
Zielona Warsaw 33 B3
Zielonka Warsaw 33 B2
Zizhuyuan Park Beijing 4 B1
Žižkov Prague 25 B2
Zličín Prague 25 B1
Zografou Athens 2 B2
Żoliborz Warsaw 33 B1
Zonnebloem Cape Town 8 A1
Zugliget Budapest 7 B1
Zugló Budapest 7 A2
Zuiderwoude Amsterdam 2 A3
Zumbi Rio de Janeiro 25 A1
Zunderdorp Amsterdam 2 A2
Zuvvu → São Paulo 27 C1
Zwanenburg Amsterdam 2 A1
Zwölfaxing Vienna 32 B2

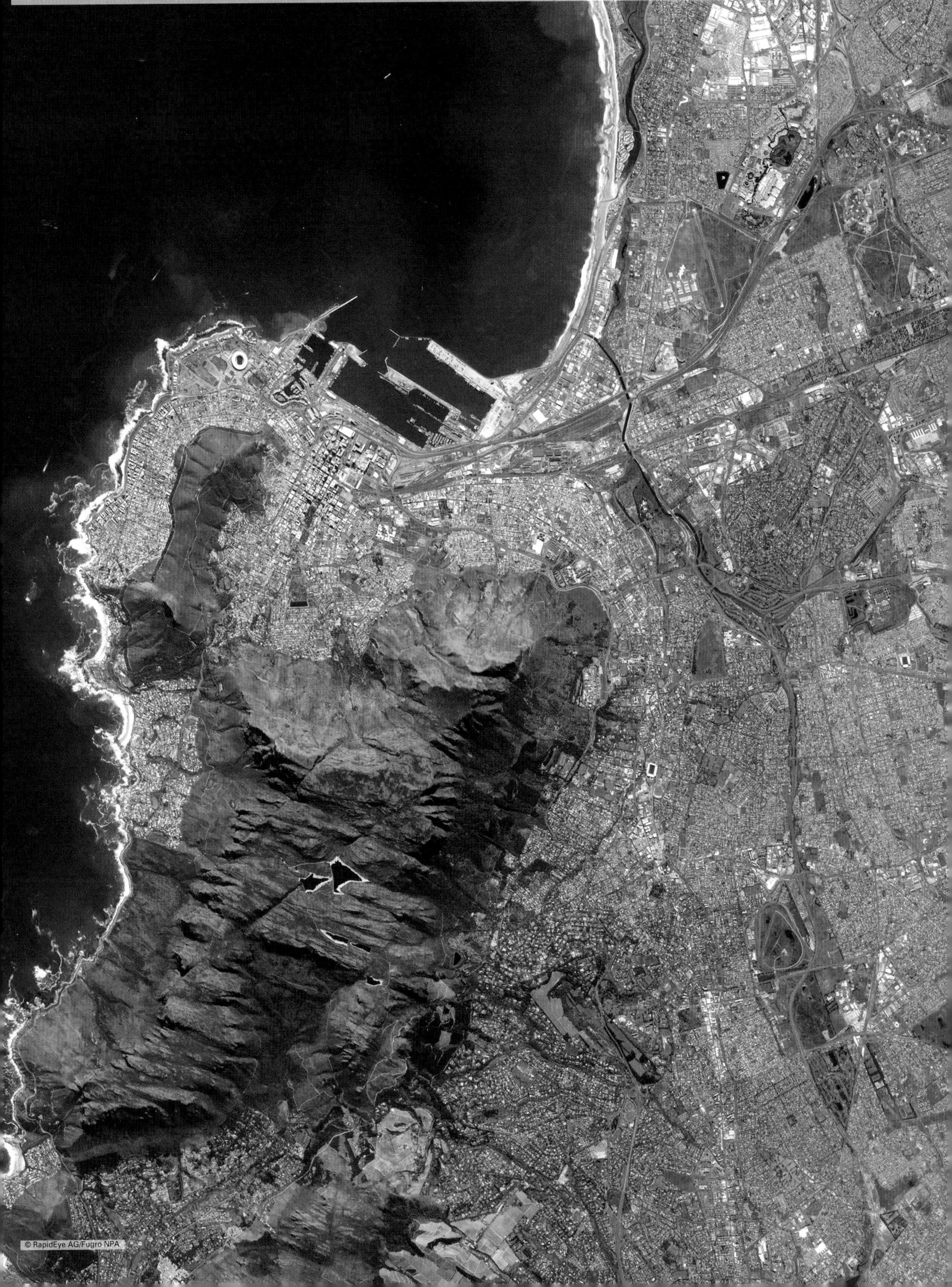
© RapidEye AG/Fugro NPA

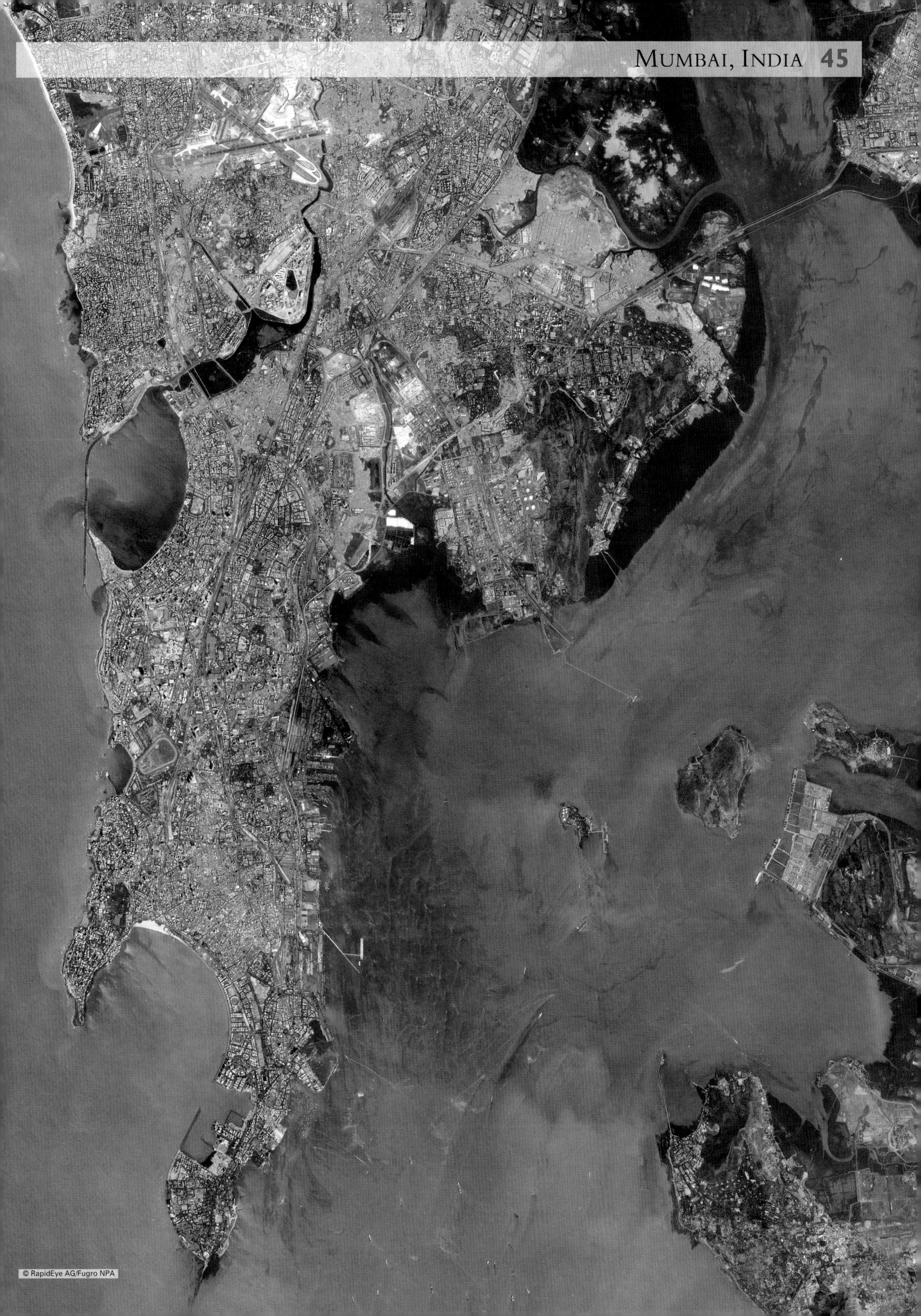

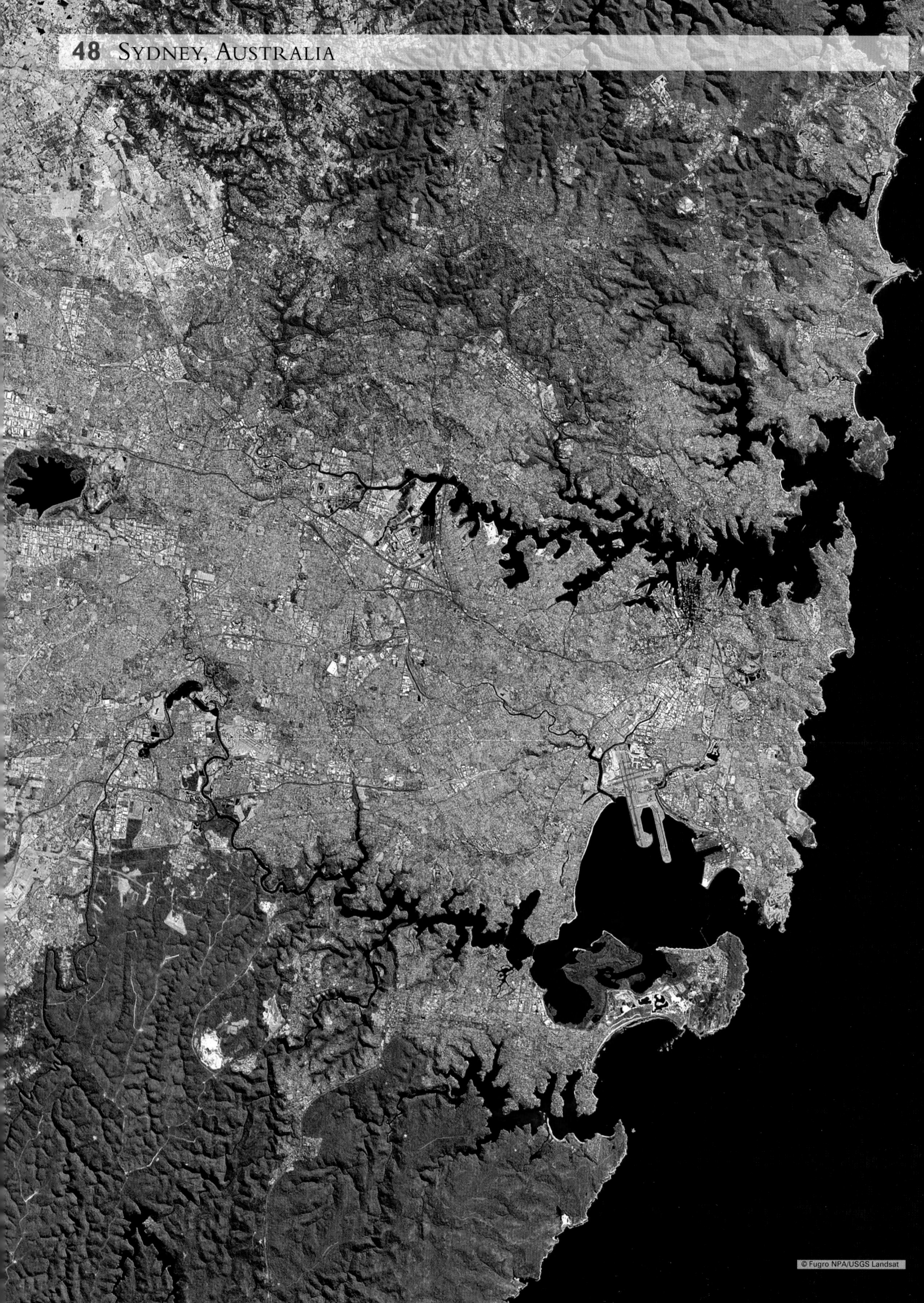

WORLD
MAPS

SETTLEMENTS

■ **PARIS**   ◉ **Rotterdam**   ◉ **Livorno**   ◉ **Brugge**   ◎ Exeter   ◦ *Torremolinos*   ◦ *Oberammergau*   ◦ *Thira*

Settlement symbols and type styles vary according to the scale of each map and indicate the importance
of towns on the map rather than specific population figures

● *Vaduz*   Capital cities have red infills   ∴   Ruins or archaeological sites

⬠   Urban agglomerations   Wells in desert

ADMINISTRATION

—————   International boundaries   ⋯⋯⋯   Internal boundaries   PERU   Country names

- - - - -   International boundaries
(undefined or disputed)   ⬡   National parks   KENT   Administrative
area names

International boundaries show the *de facto* situation where there are rival claims to territory

COMMUNICATIONS

═════   Motorways, freeways
and expressways   ———   Principal railways   LHR ✈   Principal airports

—————   Principal roads   - - - -   Railways
under construction   ⊕   Other airports

—————   Other roads   ———   Other railways   ⋯⋯⋯   Principal canals

+--+   Road tunnels   +--+   Railway tunnels   )(Passes

PHYSICAL FEATURES

〜〜   Perennial streams   ⬭   Intermittent lakes   ▲ 8850   Elevations in metres

- - - -   Intermittent streams   Swamps and marshes   ▼ 8500   Sea depths in metres

◯   Perennial lakes   Permanent ice
and glaciers   *1134*   Height of lake surface
above sea level in metres

Sand deserts

ELEVATION AND DEPTH TINTS

Height of land above sea level   Land below sea level   Depth of sea

in metres   6000 4000 3000 2000 1500 1000 400 200   0

                                                        6000 12 000 15 000 18 000 24 000   in feet

in feet   18 000 12 000 9000 6000 4500 3000 1200 600

                                                        0   200 2000 4000 5000 6000 8000   in metres

Some of the maps have different contours to highlight and clarify the principal relief features

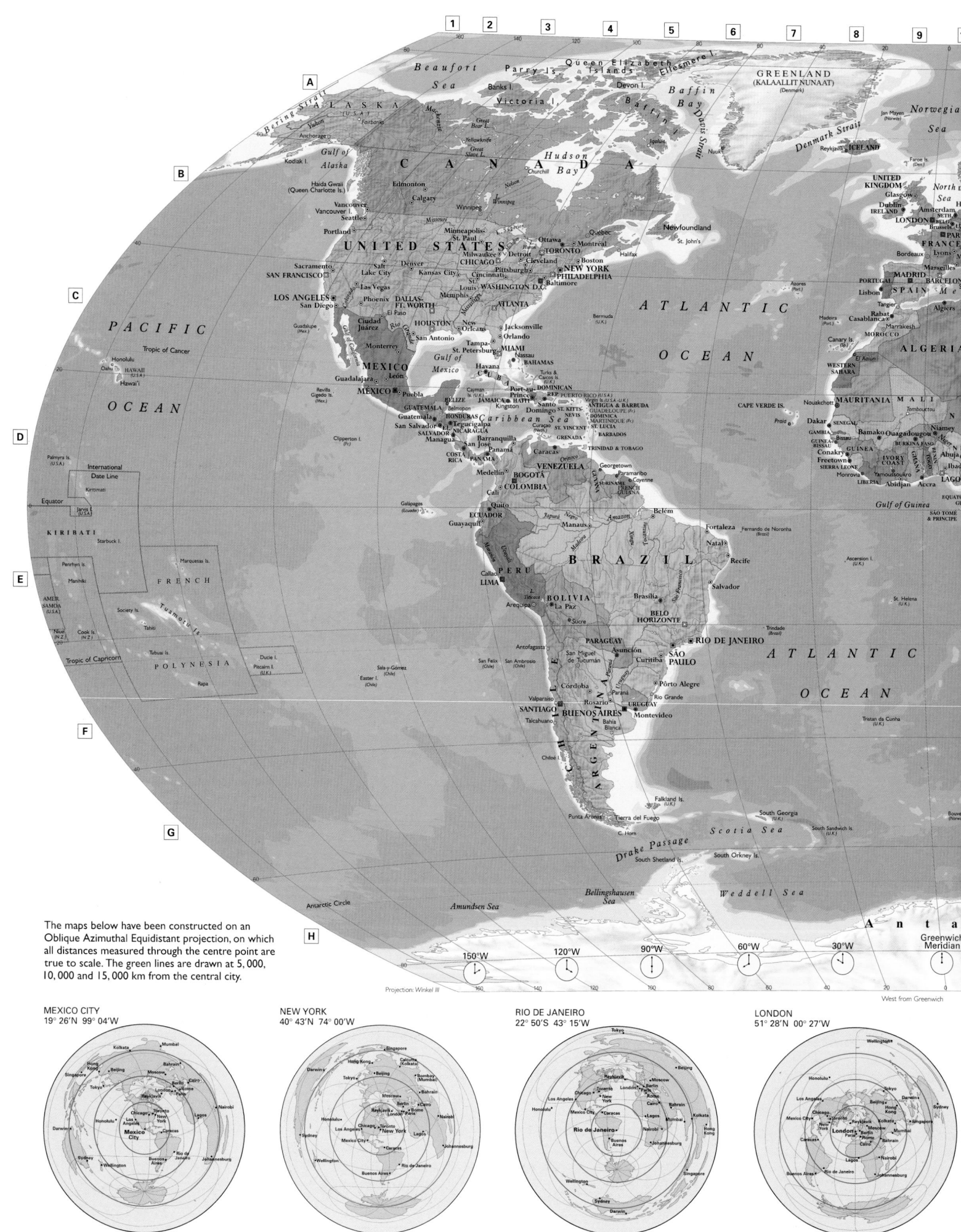

The maps below have been constructed on an Oblique Azimuthal Equidistant projection, on which all distances measured through the centre point are true to scale. The green lines are drawn at 5,000, 10,000 and 15,000 km from the central city.

Projection: Winkel III

West from Greenwich

MEXICO CITY
19° 26′N 99° 04′W

NEW YORK
40° 43′N 74° 00′W

RIO DE JANEIRO
22° 50′S 43° 15′W

LONDON
51° 28′N 00° 27′W

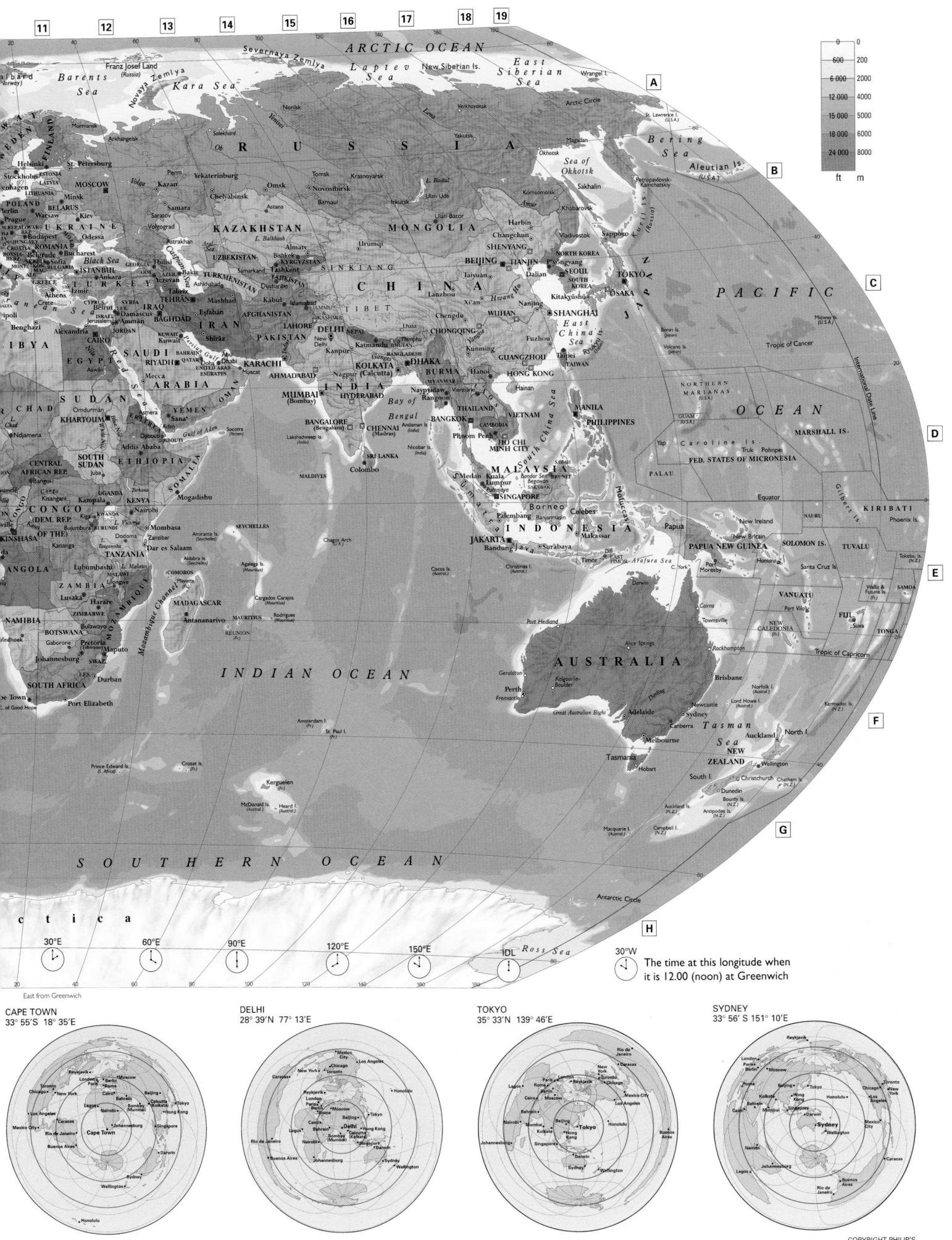

CAPE TOWN
33° 55'S 18° 35'E

DELHI
28° 39'N 77° 13'E

TOKYO
35° 33'N 139° 46'E

SYDNEY
33° 56' S 151° 10'E

The time at this longitude when it is 12.00 (noon) at Greenwich

East from Greenwich

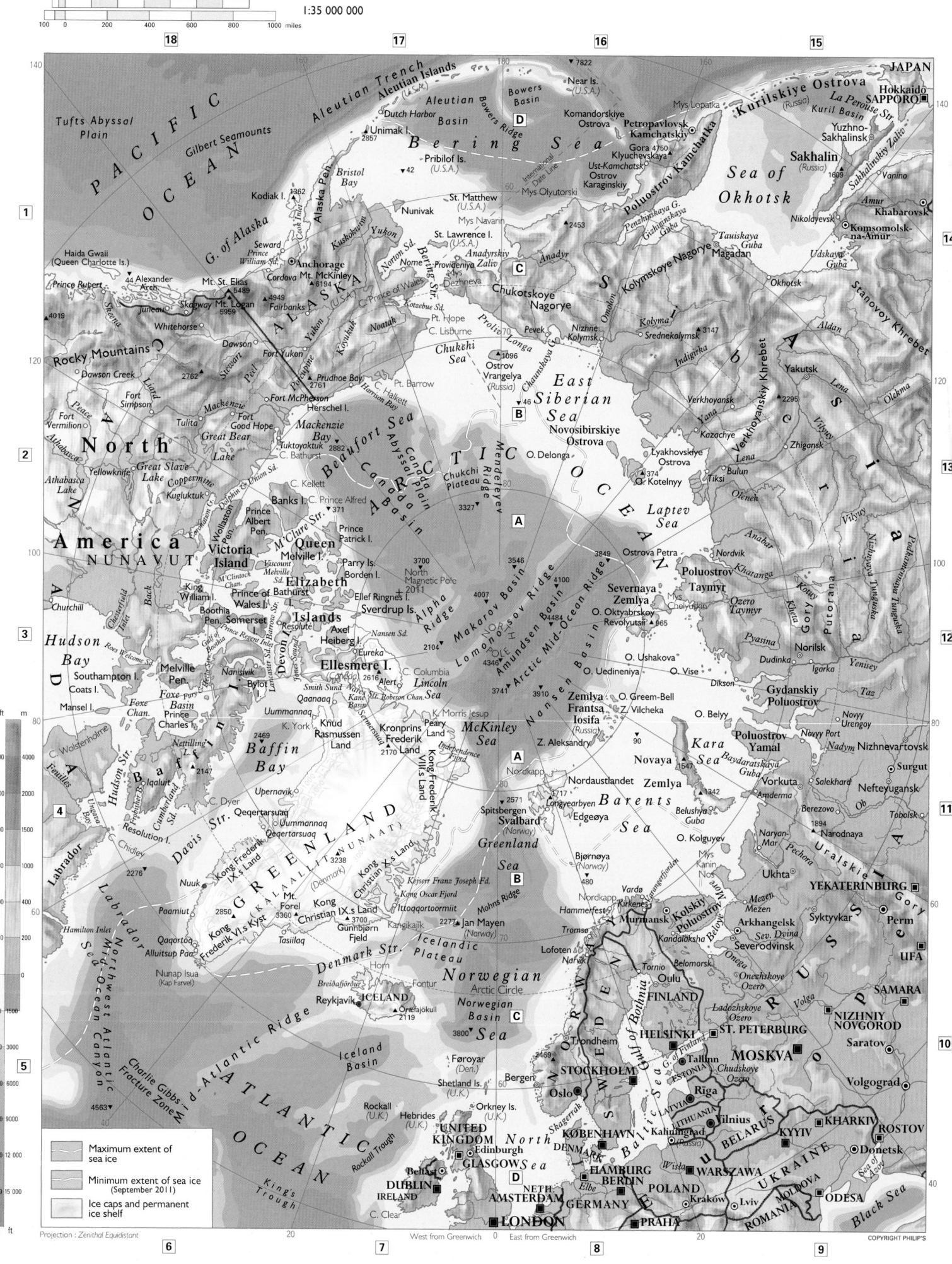

100 0 200 400 600 800 1000 1200 1400 km
1:35 000 000
100 0 200 400 600 800 1000 miles

Maximum extent of sea ice

Minimum extent of sea ice (September 2011)

Ice caps and permanent ice shelf

Projection : Zenithal Equidistant

West from Greenwich   East from Greenwich

COPYRIGHT PHILIP'S

1:35 000 000

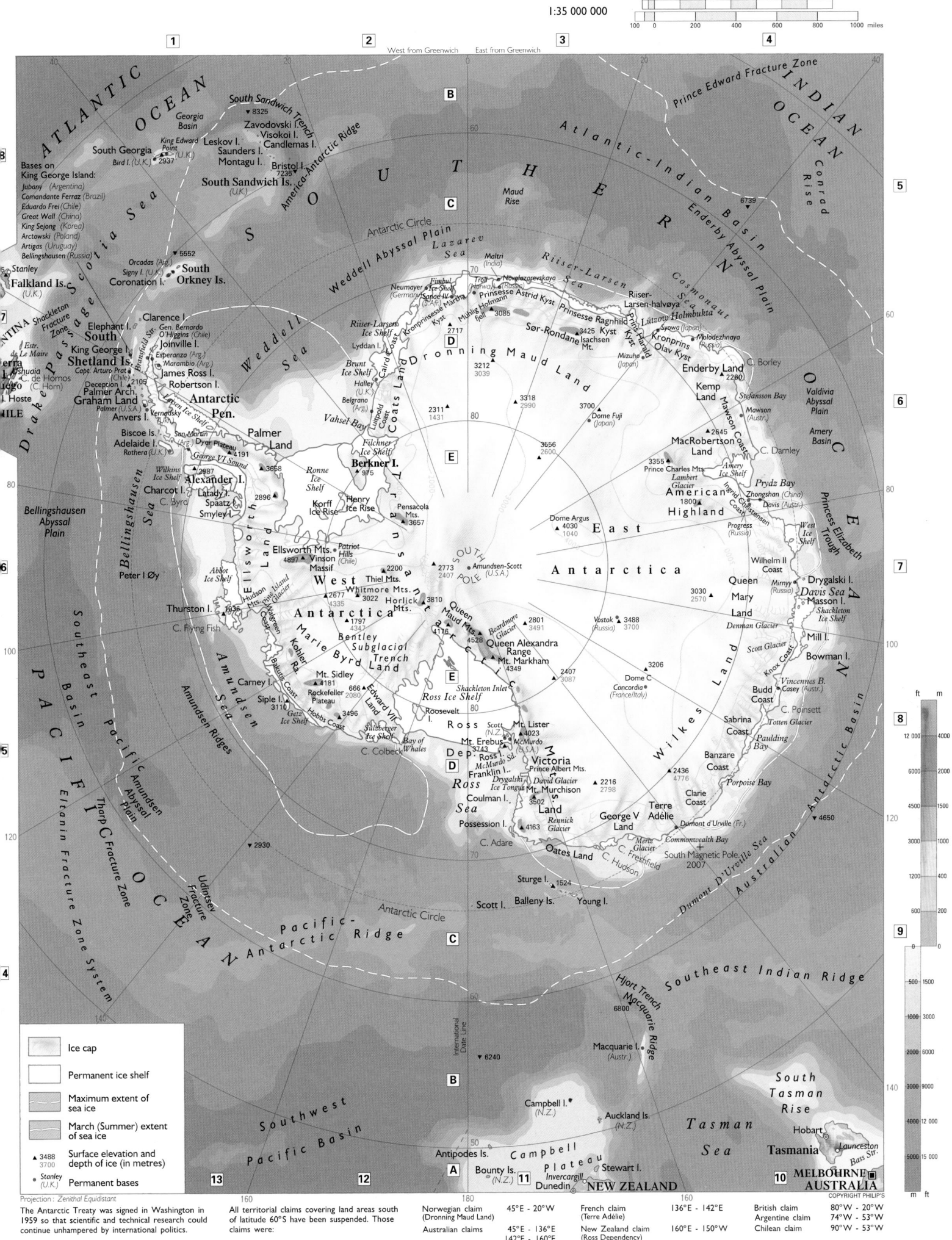

Legend:

- Ice cap
- Permanent ice shelf
- Maximum extent of sea ice
- March (Summer) extent of sea ice
- ▲ 3488 / 3700 Surface elevation and depth of ice (in metres)
- • Stanley (U.K.) Permanent bases

Projection : Zenithal Equidistant

The Antarctic Treaty was signed in Washington in 1959 so that scientific and technical research could continue unhampered by international politics.

All territorial claims covering land areas south of latitude 60°S have been suspended. Those claims were:

Norwegian claim (Dronning Maud Land)	45°E - 20°W
Australian claims	45°E - 136°E / 142°E - 160°E
French claim (Terre Adélie)	136°E - 142°E
New Zealand claim (Ross Dependency)	160°E - 150°W
British claim	80°W - 20°W
Argentine claim	74°W - 53°W
Chilean claim	90°W - 53°W

COPYRIGHT PHILIP'S

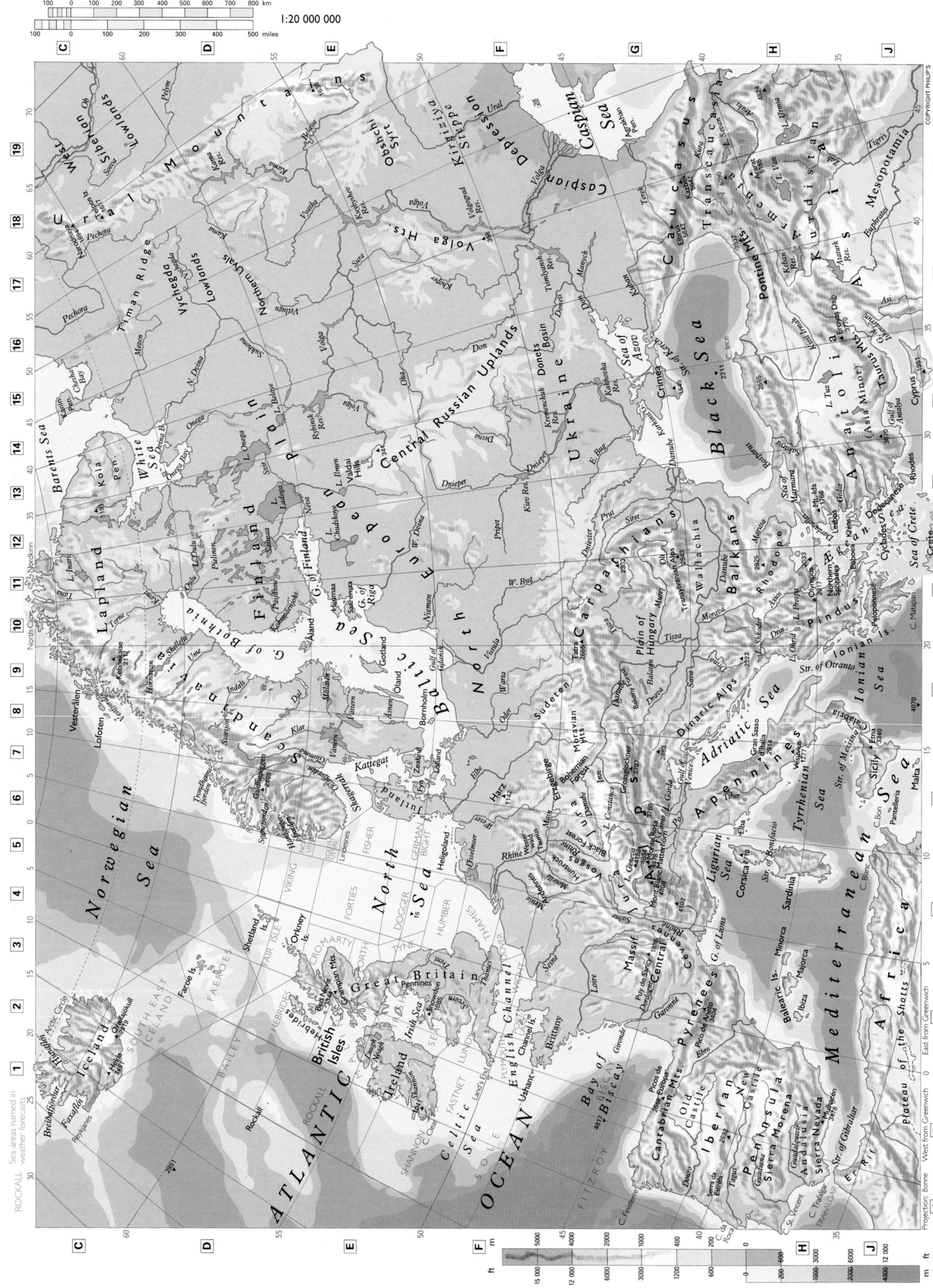

1:20 000 000

1:20 000 000

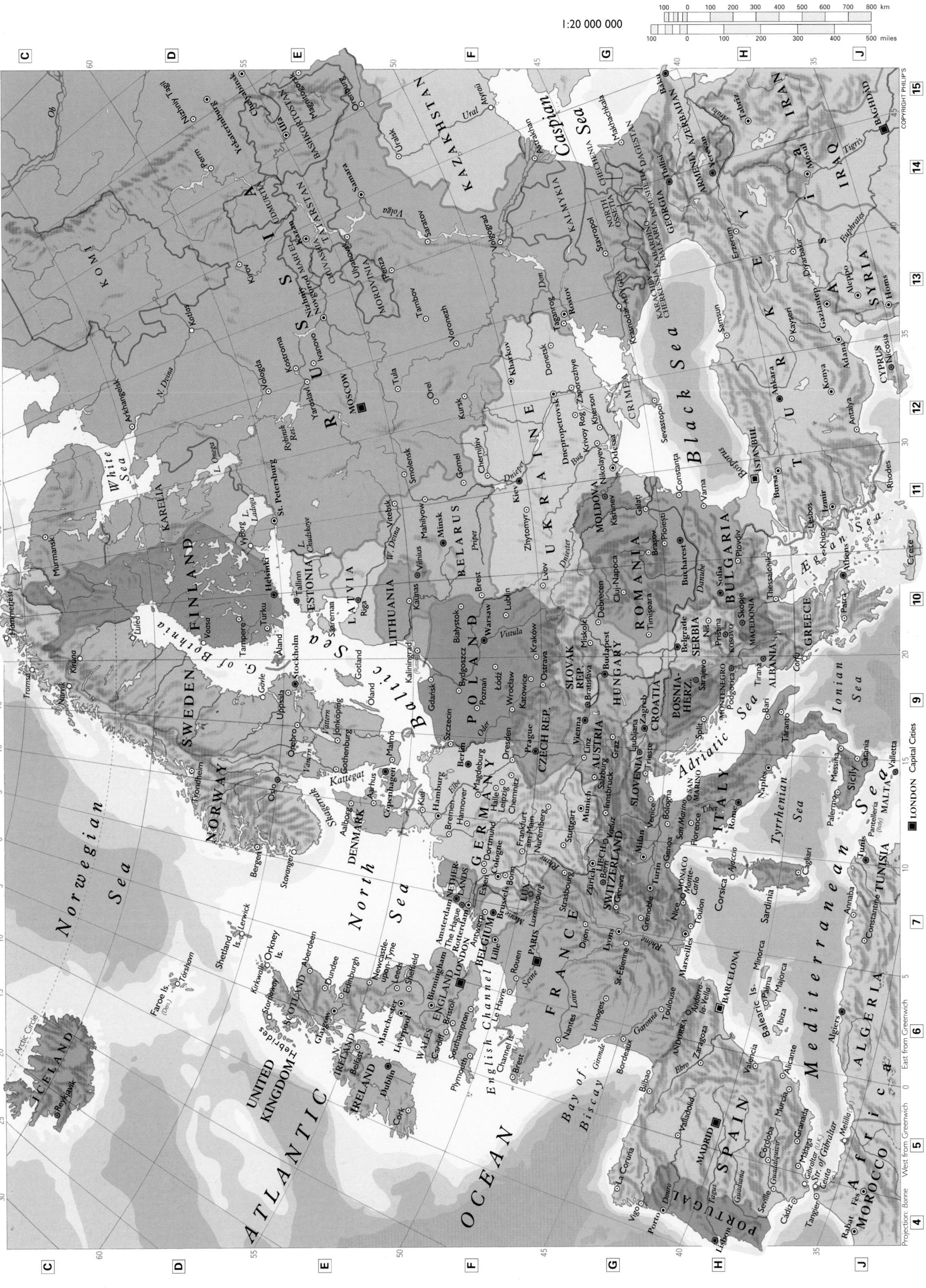

100 0 100 200 300 400 500 600 700 800 km
100 0 100 200 300 400 500 miles

COPYRIGHT PHILIPS

ATLANTIC OCEAN

Norwegian Sea

North Sea

White Sea

Baltic Sea

Black Sea

Caspian Sea

Mediterranean Sea

Adriatic Sea

Tyrrhenian Sea

Ionian Sea

Aegean Sea

English Channel

Gulf of Bothnia

Bay of Biscay

ICELAND — Reykjavik

UNITED KINGDOM — SCOTLAND, ENGLAND, WALES, IRELAND

NORWAY — Oslo, Bergen, Trondheim

SWEDEN — Stockholm, Gothenburg

FINLAND — Helsinki

DENMARK — Copenhagen

GERMANY — Berlin, Hamburg, Munich, Cologne, Frankfurt am Main

FRANCE — PARIS, Lyons, Marseilles, Bordeaux, Toulouse

SPAIN — MADRID, BARCELONA, Valencia, Seville

PORTUGAL — Lisbon, Porto

ITALY — Rome, Milan, Naples, Turin, Florence, Genoa, Venice

POLAND — Warsaw, Kraków, Łódź, Poznań, Wrocław, Gdańsk

RUSSIA — MOSCOW, St. Petersburg

UKRAINE — Kiev, Kharkov, Donetsk, Odessa

BELARUS — Minsk

LITHUANIA — Kaunas, Vilnius

LATVIA — Riga

ESTONIA — Tallinn

MOLDOVA — Kishinev

ROMANIA — Bucharest

BULGARIA — Sofia, Plovdiv, Varna

GREECE — Athens, Thessaloníka

TURKEY — Ankara, Istanbul, Izmir

CYPRUS — Nicosia

SYRIA — Aleppo, Homs

IRAQ — BAGHDAD, Mosul

IRAN

GEORGIA — Tbilisi

ARMENIA — Yerevan

AZERBAIJAN — Baku

KAZAKHSTAN

MOROCCO — Rabat, Tangier

ALGERIA — Algiers, Constantine, Annaba

TUNISIA — Tunis

MALTA — Valletta

Africa

CZECH REP. — Prague

SLOVAK REP. — Bratislava

AUSTRIA — Vienna, Linz, Salzburg, Innsbruck, Graz

HUNGARY — Budapest, Debrecen, Miskolc

SWITZERLAND — Zürich, Geneva, Basle, Berne

SLOVENIA — Ljubljana

CROATIA — Zagreb, Split

BOSNIA-HERZ. — Sarajevo

SERBIA — Belgrade, Niš

MONTENEGRO — Podgorica

MACEDONIA — Skopje

ALBANIA — Tirana

KOMI, KARELIA, MORDOVIA, BASHKORTOSTAN, TATARSTAN, UDMURTIA, MARI EL, CHUVASHIA

CRIMEA

KALMYKIA, DAGESTAN, CHECHNYA, NORTH OSSETIA, INGUSHETIA, KABARDINO-BALKARIA, KARACHAI-CHERKESSIA, ADYGEA

BELGIUM — Brussels, Antwerp

NETHERLANDS — Amsterdam, The Hague, Rotterdam

LUXEMBOURG

Arctic Circle

East from Greenwich / West from Greenwich

Projection: Bonne

■ LONDON Capital Cities

ICELAND
on same scale

FÆROE ISLANDS
on same scale

1:6 000 000

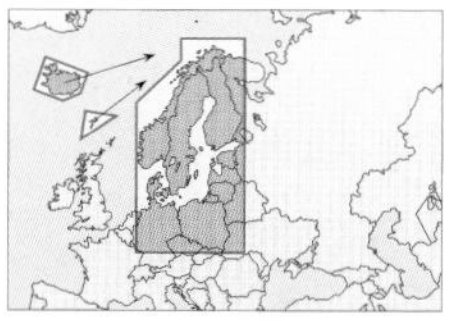

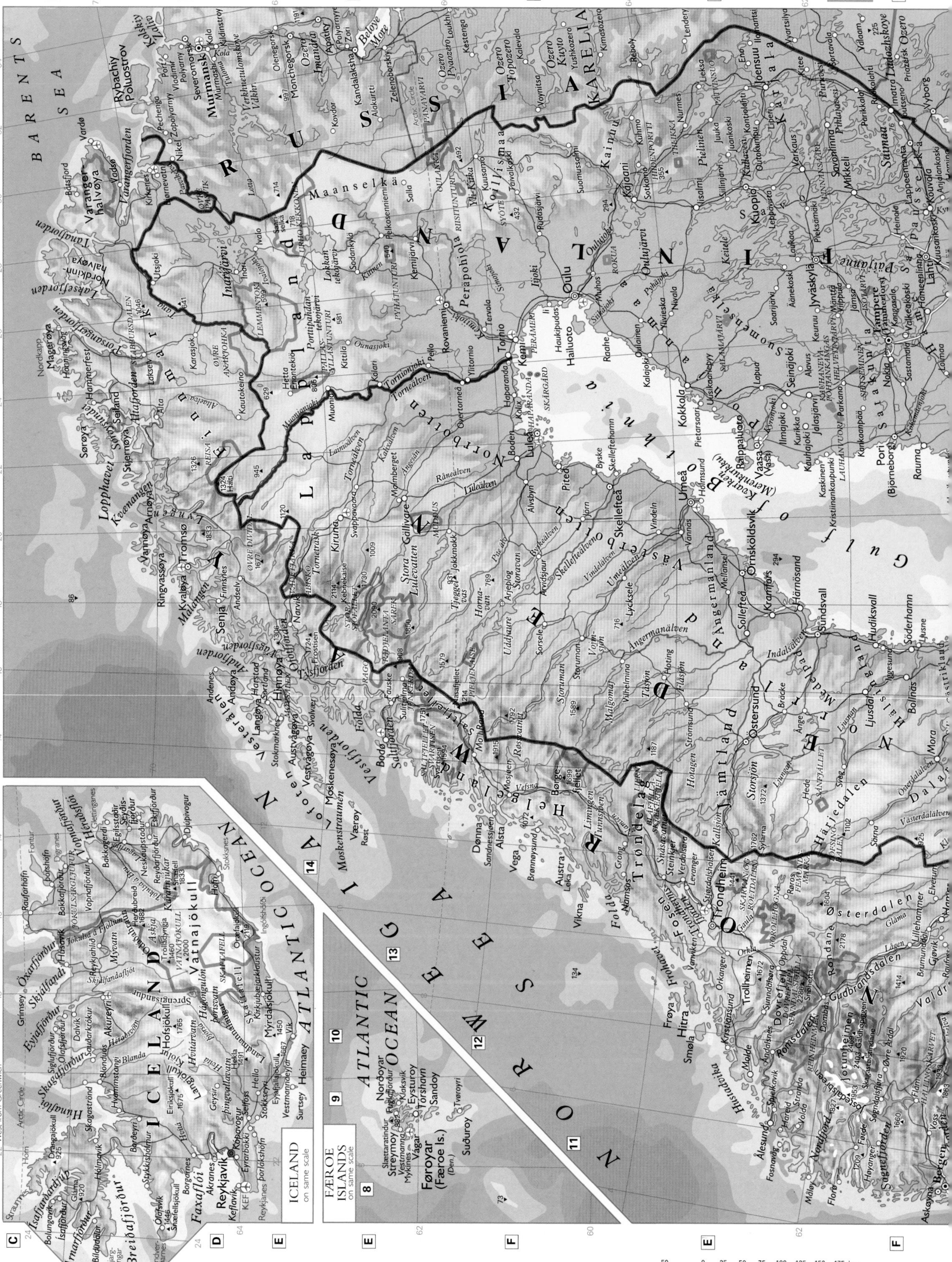

| 50 | 0 | 25 | 50 | 75 | 100 | 125 | 150 | 175 km |
| 50 | 0 | 25 | 50 | 75 | 100 | 125 miles |

1:2 000 000

10   0   10   20   30   40   50   60   70   80 km
10   0   10   20   30   40   50 miles

Projection: Lambert's Conformal Conic

West from Greenwich

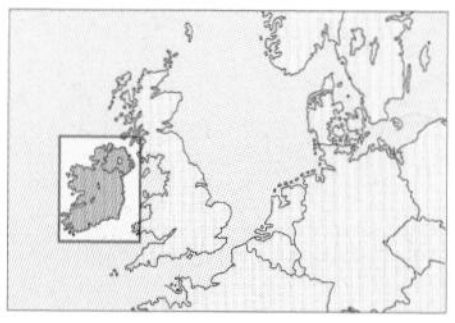

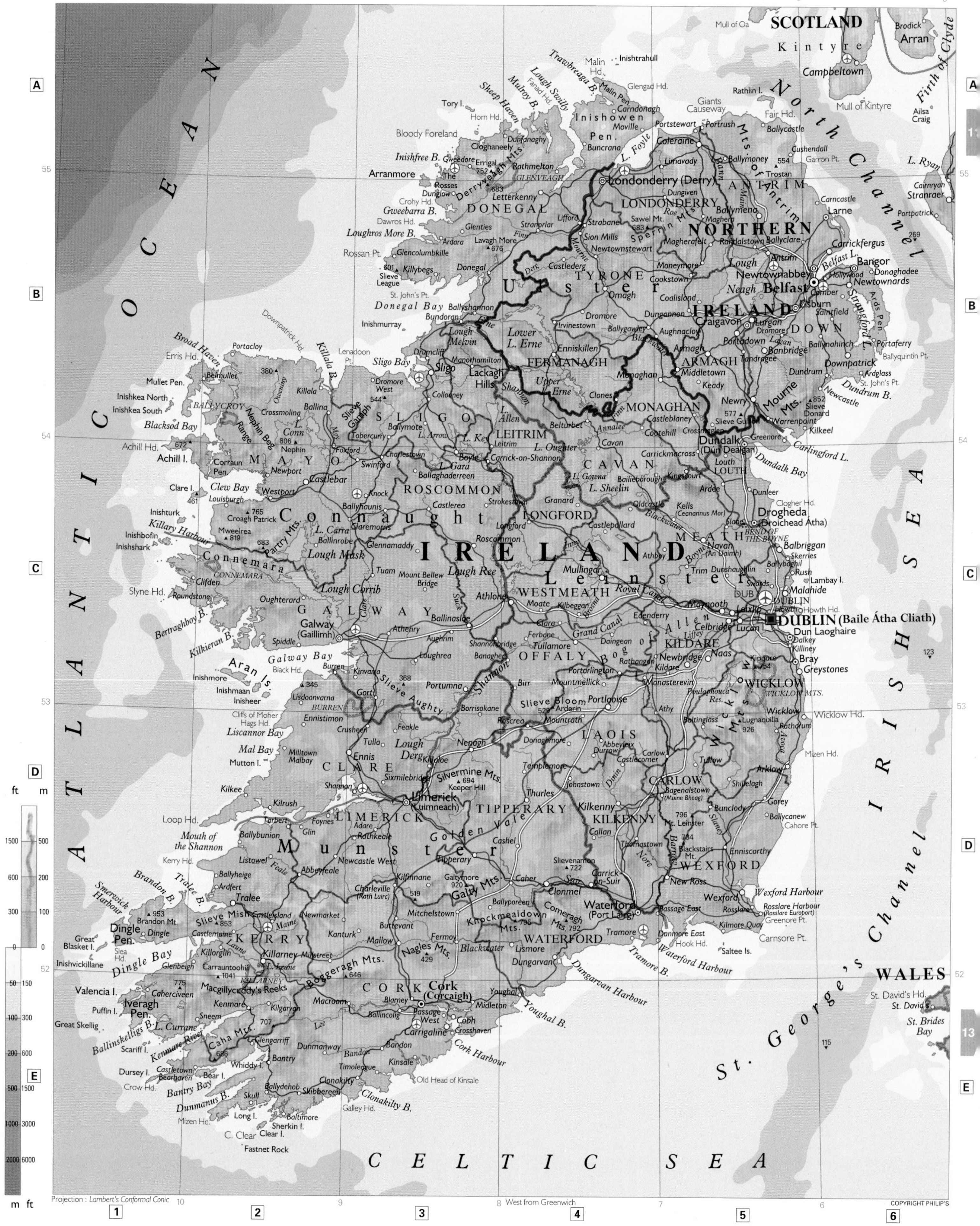

COPYRIGHT PHILIP'S

ATLANTIC OCEAN

CELTIC SEA

IRISH SEA

NORTH CHANNEL

St. George's Channel

SCOTLAND

WALES

IRELAND

NORTHERN IRELAND

Ulster — Connaught — Leinster — Munster

DUBLIN (Baile Átha Cliath)

Belfast

Londonderry (Derry)

Cork (Corcaigh)

Limerick (Luimneach)

Waterford (Port Láirge)

Galway (Gaillimh)

Counties: DONEGAL, TYRONE, FERMANAGH, ANTRIM, DOWN, ARMAGH, MONAGHAN, CAVAN, LEITRIM, SLIGO, MAYO, ROSCOMMON, LONGFORD, WESTMEATH, MEATH, LOUTH, GALWAY, OFFALY, KILDARE, DUBLIN, WICKLOW, CLARE, TIPPERARY, LAOIS, CARLOW, KILKENNY, WEXFORD, LIMERICK, KERRY, CORK, WATERFORD

ft   m
1500 500
600   200
300   100
0   0
50   150
100   300
200   600
500   1500
1000 3000
2000 6000
m   ft

1:2 000 000

Key to Scottish unitary
authorities on map
1 CITY OF ABERDEEN   8 EAST RENFREWSHIRE
2 DUNDEE CITY   9 NORTH LANARKSHIRE
3 WEST DUNBARTONSHIRE   10 FALKIRK
4 EAST DUNBARTONSHIRE   11 CLACKMANNANSHIRE
5 CITY OF GLASGOW   12 WEST LOTHIAN
6 INVERCLYDE   13 CITY OF EDINBURGH
7 RENFREWSHIRE   14 MIDLOTHIAN

ORKNEY IS.
on same scale

ORKNEY

SHETLAND IS.
on same scale

SHETLAND

Projection : Lambert's Conformal Conic

West from Greenwich

COPYRIGHT PHILIP'S

1:2 000 000

10 0 10 20 30 40 50 60 70 80 km
10 0 10 20 30 40 50 miles

Key to English unitary authorities on map

25 HARTLEPOOL
26 DARLINGTON
27 STOCKTON-ON-TEES
28 MIDDLESBROUGH
29 REDCAR AND CLEVELAND
30 BLACKPOOL
31 BLACKBURN WITH DARWEN
32 HALTON
33 WARRINGTON
34 KINGSTON UPON HULL
35 NORTH EAST LINCOLNSHIRE
36 STOKE-ON-TRENT
37 TELFORD AND WREKIN
38 DERBY CITY
39 CITY OF NOTTINGHAM
40 LEICESTER CITY
41 RUTLAND
42 PETERBOROUGH
43 MILTON KEYNES
44 LUTON
45 NORTH SOMERSET
46 CITY OF BRISTOL
47 BATH AND NORTH EAST SOMERSET
48 SWINDON
49 READING
50 WOKINGHAM
51 WINDSOR AND MAIDENHEAD
52 SLOUGH
53 BRACKNELL FOREST
54 THURROCK
55 SOUTHEND-ON-SEA
56 MEDWAY
57 PLYMOUTH
58 TORBAY
59 POOLE
60 BOURNEMOUTH
61 SOUTHAMPTON
62 PORTSMOUTH
63 BRIGHTON AND HOVE
64 BEDFORD
65 CENTRAL BEDFORDSHIRE

Key to Welsh unitary authorities on map

15 SWANSEA
16 NEATH PORT TALBOT
17 BRIDGEND
18 RHONDDA CYNON TAFF
19 MERTHYR TYDFIL
20 CAERPHILLY
21 BLAENAU GWENT
22 TORFAEN
23 CARDIFF
24 NEWPORT

NORTH SEA

IRISH SEA

North Channel

SCOTLAND

NORTHERN IRELAND

ISLE OF MAN

Edinburgh Glasgow Newcastle-upon-Tyne Sunderland Middlesbrough Hartlepool Kingston upon Hull Leeds Bradford Sheffield Manchester Liverpool Nottingham Derby Stoke-on-Trent Lincoln

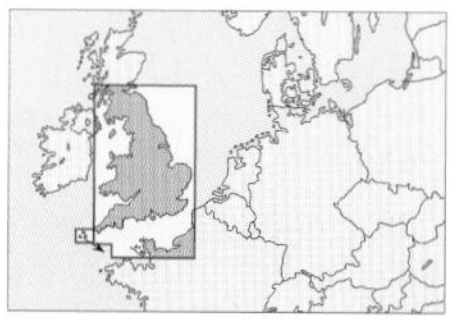

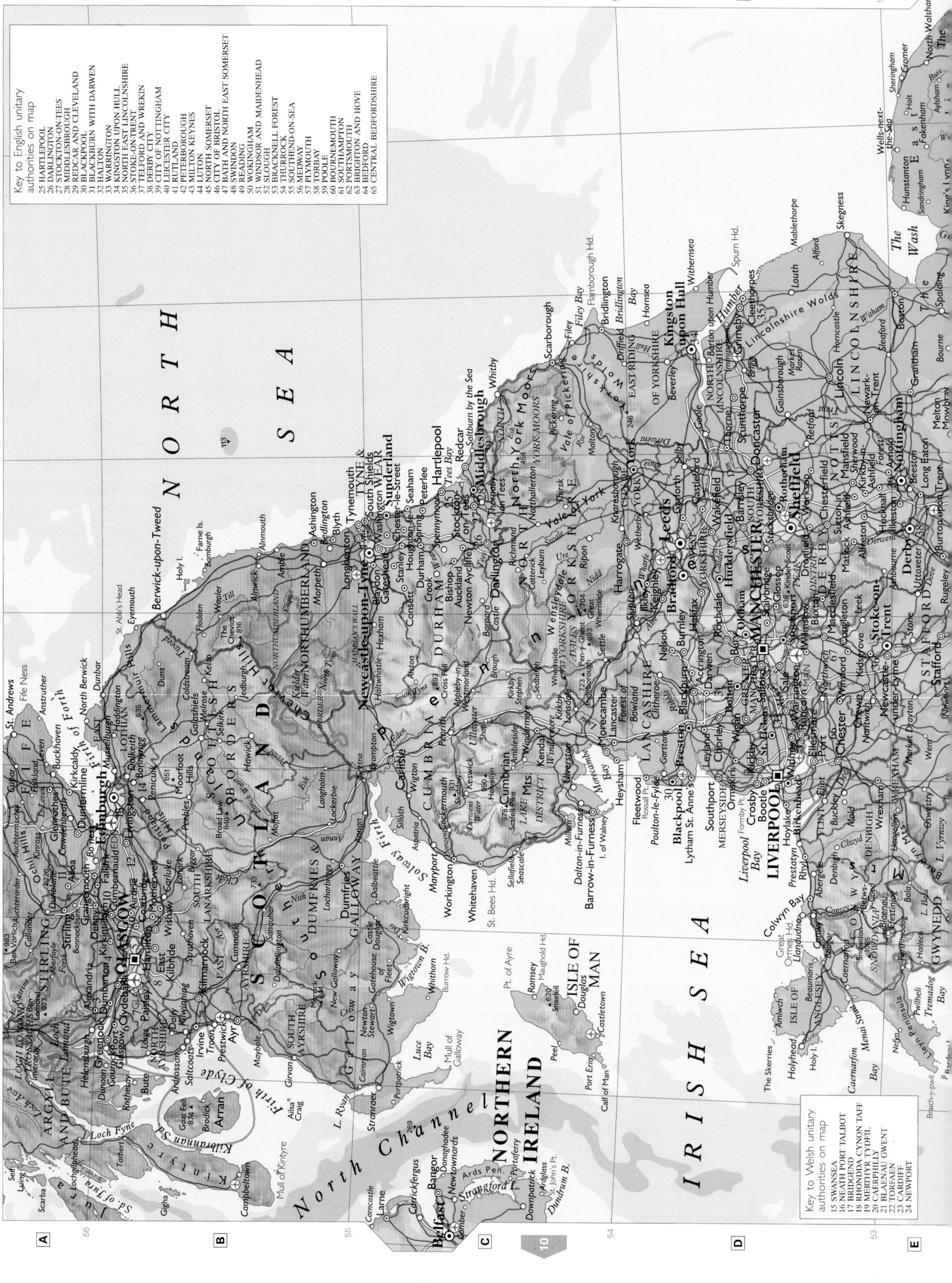

50   0   25   50   75   100   125   150   175 km

50   0   25   50   75   100   125 miles

1:5 000 000

Projection: Conical with two standard parallels

East from Greenwich   COPYRIGHT PHILIP'S

West from Greenwich

1:2 500 000

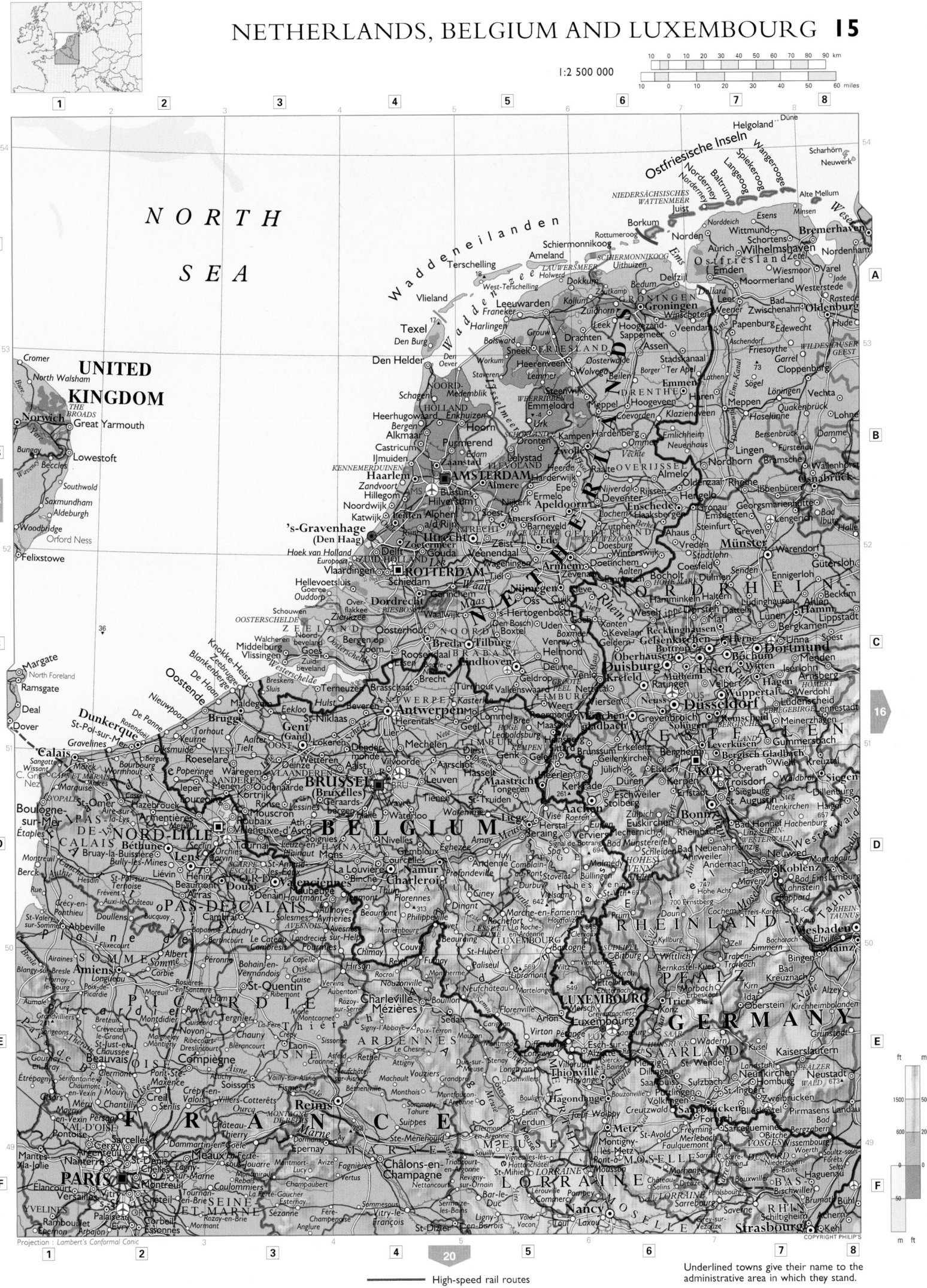

COPYRIGHT PHILIP'S

—— High-speed rail routes

Underlined towns give their name to the
administrative area in which they stand.

1:5 000 000

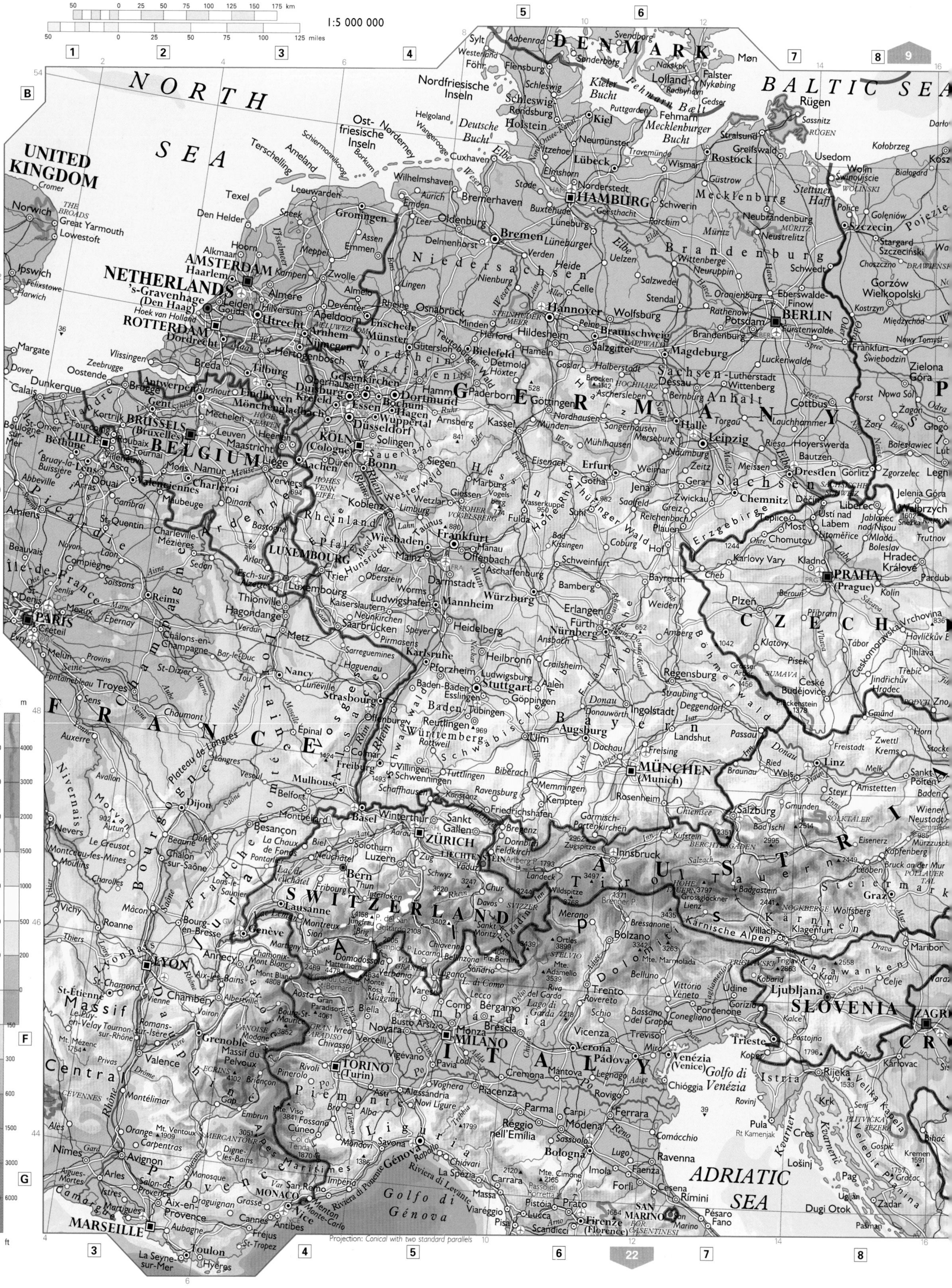

NORTH SEA
BALTIC SEA
ADRIATIC SEA
UNITED KINGDOM
NETHERLANDS
BELGIUM
LUXEMBOURG
FRANCE
GERMANY
DENMARK
CZECH
SWITZERLAND
AUSTRIA
ITALY
SLOVENIA
AMSTERDAM
BRUSSELS (Bruxelles)
PARIS
BERLIN
HAMBURG
MÜNCHEN (Munich)
PRAHA (Prague)
ZÜRICH
MILANO
TORINO (Turin)
LYON
MARSEILLE
Golfo di Génova
Golfo di Venézia
Projection: Conical with two standard parallels

Zatoka
Gdańska

LITHUANIA

BELARUS

MINSK

POLAND

**WARSZAWA
(Warsaw)**

Wrocław

Kraków

UKRAINE

**KYYIV
(Kiev)**

**Lviv
(Lvov)**

SLOVAK REP.

Bratislava

BUDAPEST

HUNGARY

MOLDOVA

**Chişinău
(Kishinev)**

ROMANIA

**BUCUREŞTI
(Bucharest)**

**BOSNIA-
HERZEGOVINA**

**BEOGRAD
(Belgrade)**

SERBIA

BULGARIA

East from Greenwich

COPYRIGHT PHILIP'S

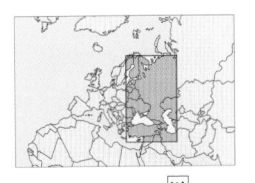

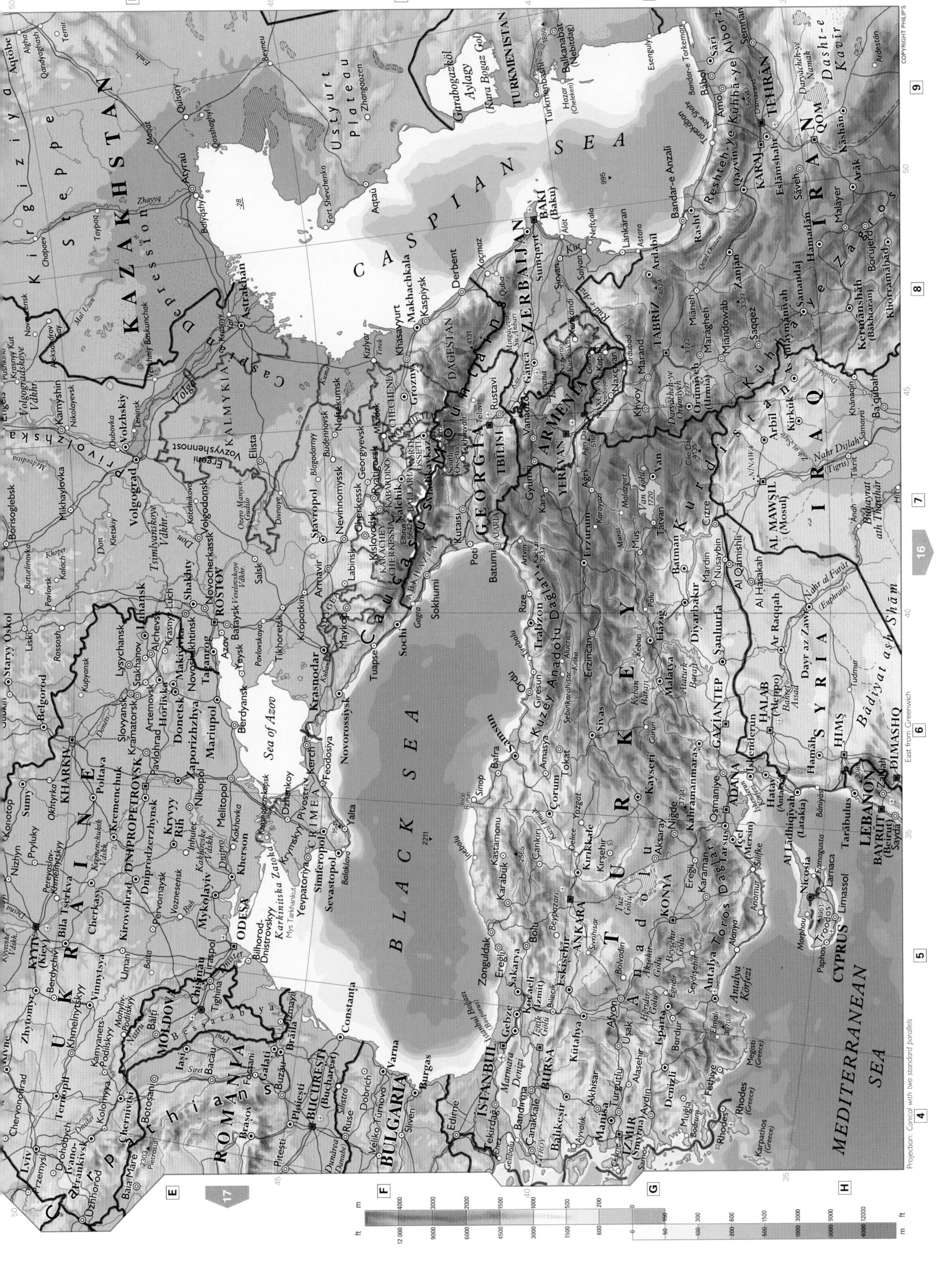

50 0 25 50 75 100 125 150 175 km

50 0 25 50 75 100 125 miles

1:5 000 000

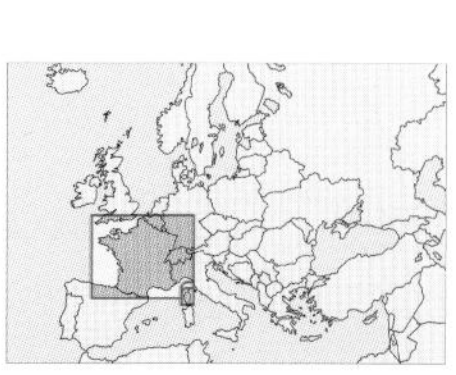

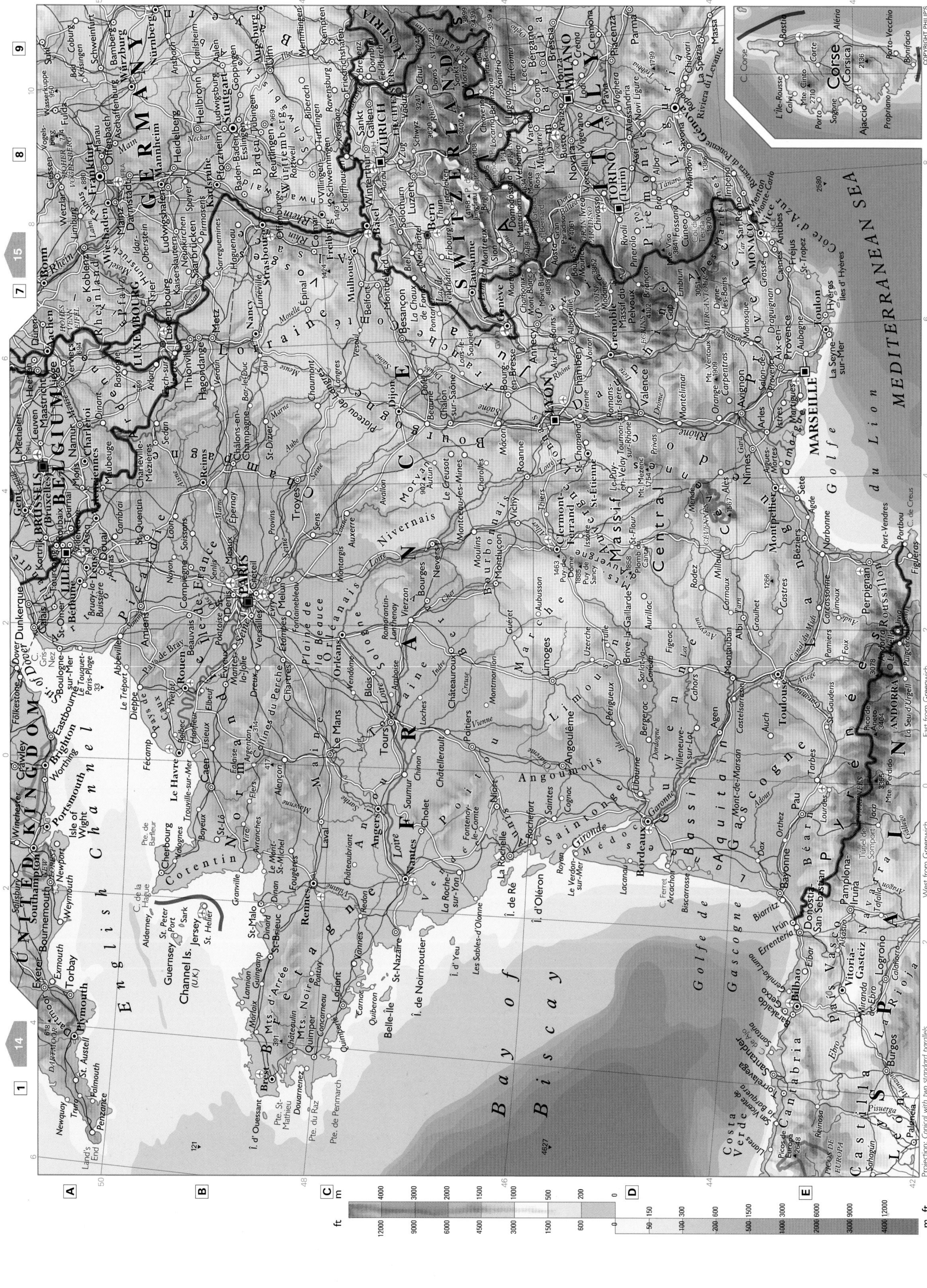
UNITED KINGDOM
FRANCE
BELGIUM
LUXEMBOURG
GERMANY
SWITZERLAND
ITALY
SPAIN
ANDORRA
MONACO
AUSTRIA
PARIS
LYON
MARSEILLE
BRUSSELS
MILANO
TORINO (Turin)
ZÜRICH
Bern
English Channel
Bay of Biscay
Golfe de Gascogne
Golfe du Lion
MEDITERRANEAN SEA
Massif Central
Corse (Corsica)
Bordeaux
Toulouse
Nantes
Rennes
Brest
Strasbourg
Lille
Nice
Montpellier
Projection: Conical with two standard parallels
East from Greenwich
West from Greenwich
COPYRIGHT PHILIP'S
m ft

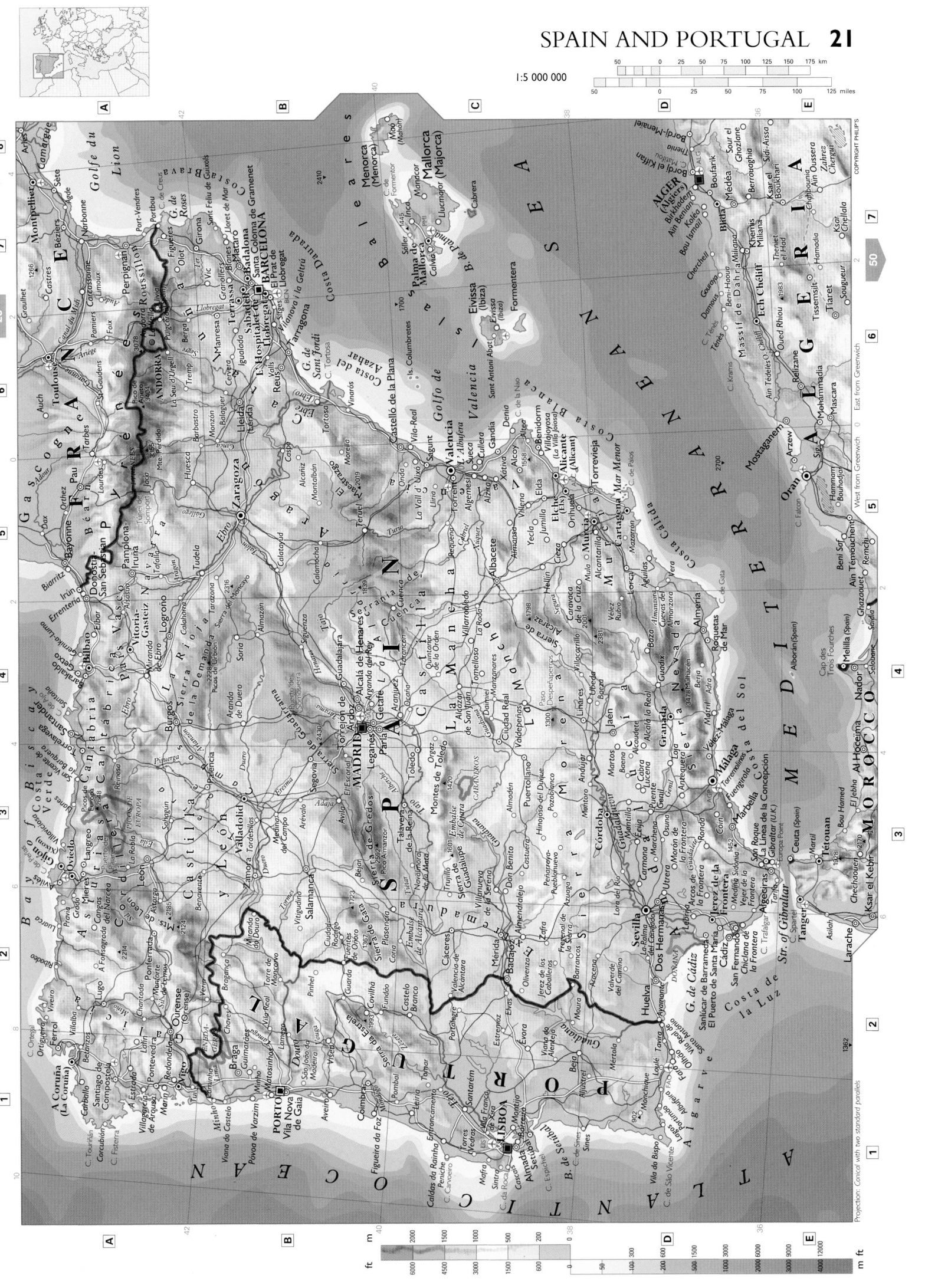

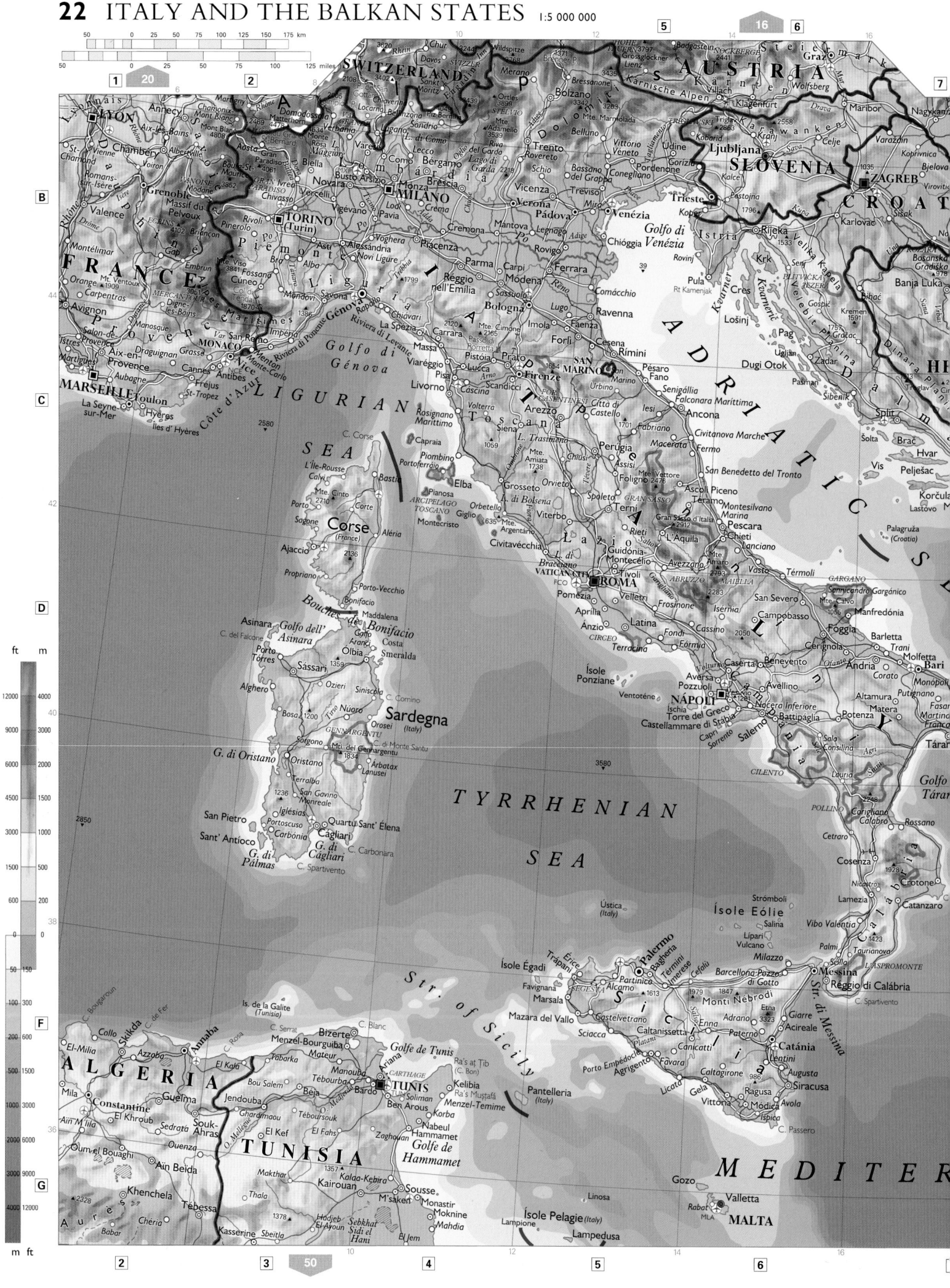

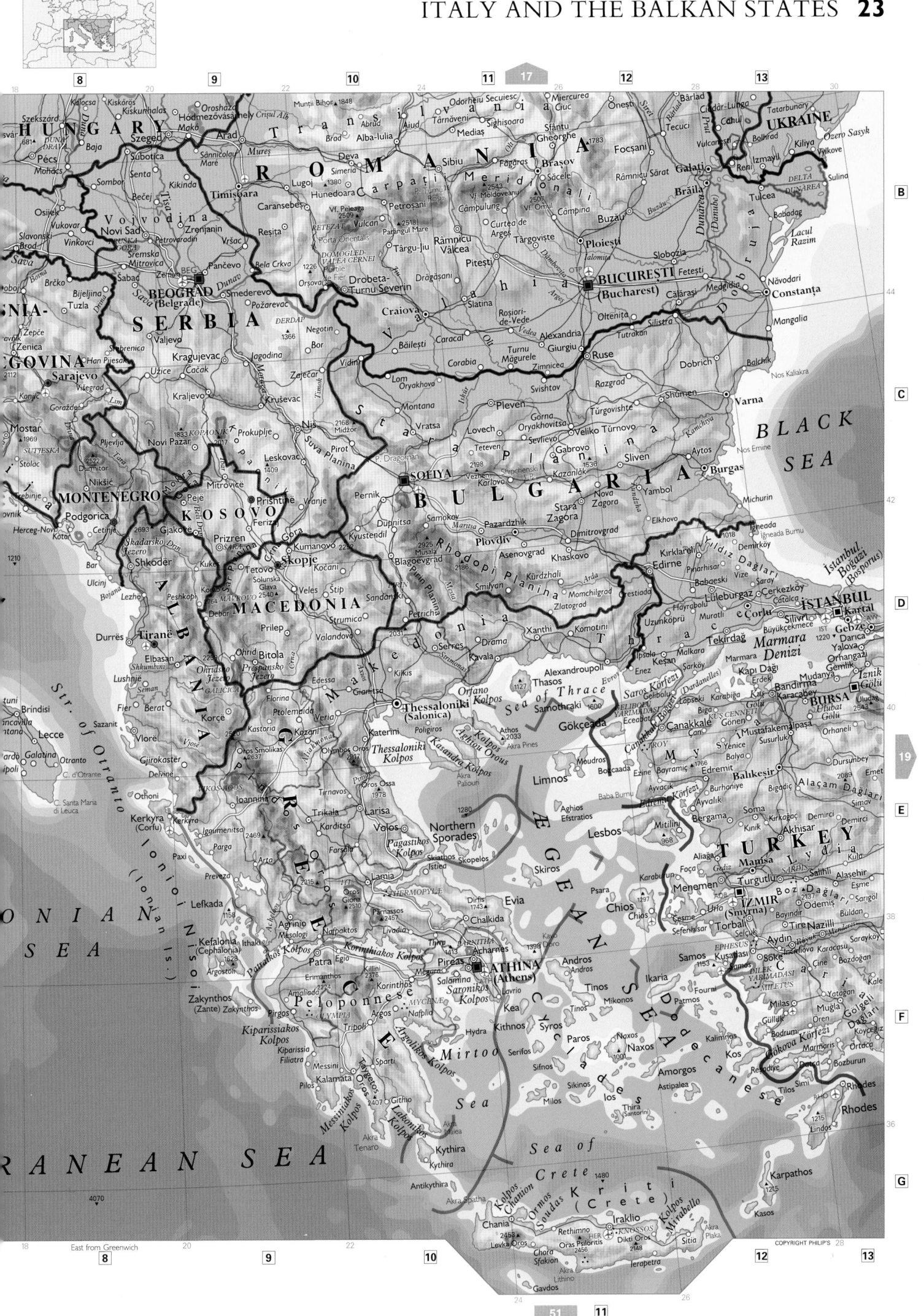

100 0   200 400 600 800 1000 1200 1400 km

1:47 000 000

100 0   200   400   600   800   1000 miles

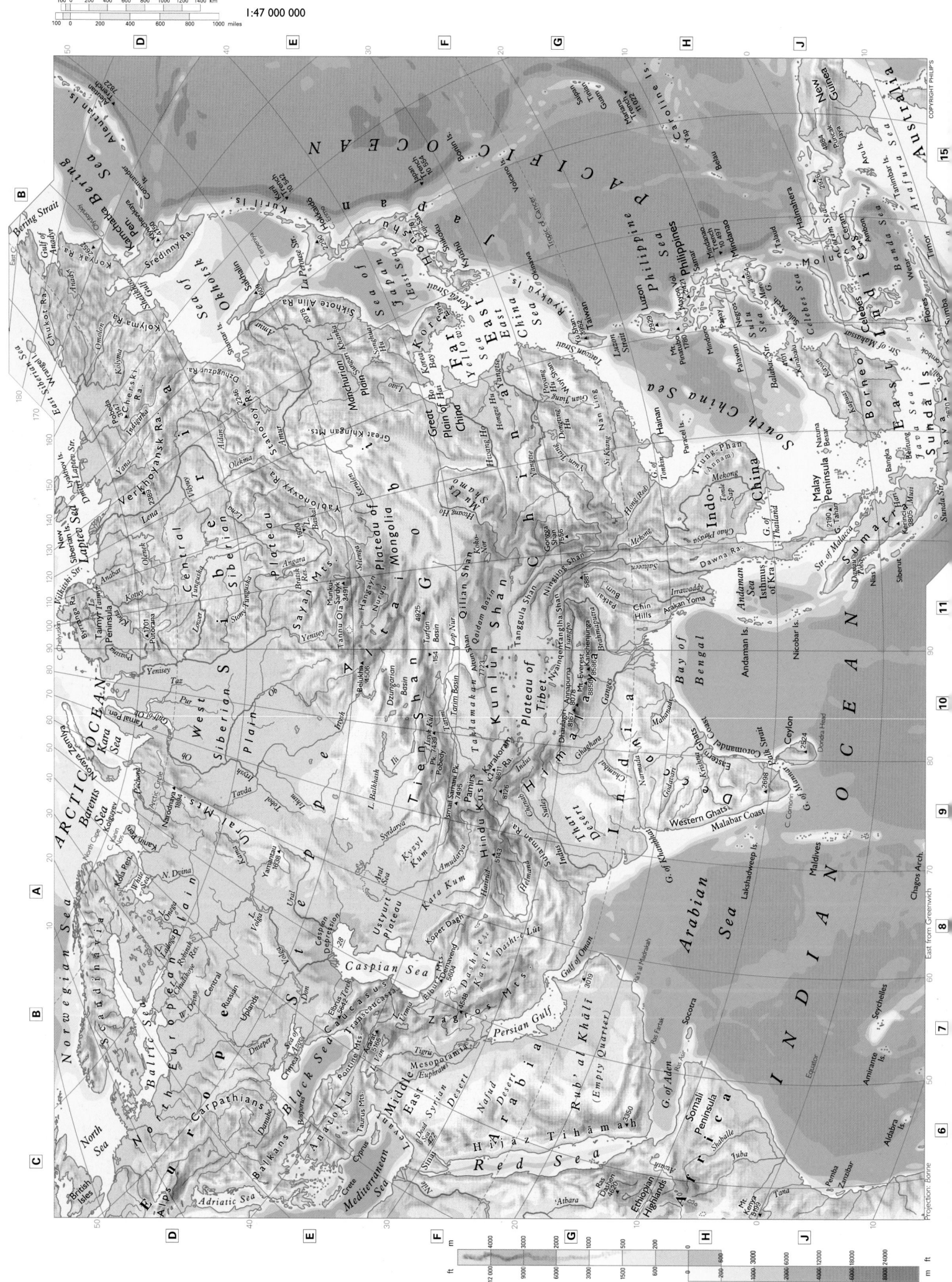

Projection: Bonne

m   ft
4000 12 000
3000 9000
2000 6000
1500 4500
1000 3000
500   1500
200   600
0
200   600
1000 3000
2000 6000
3000 9000
4000 12 000
6000 18 000
8000 24 000
m   ft
ft   m

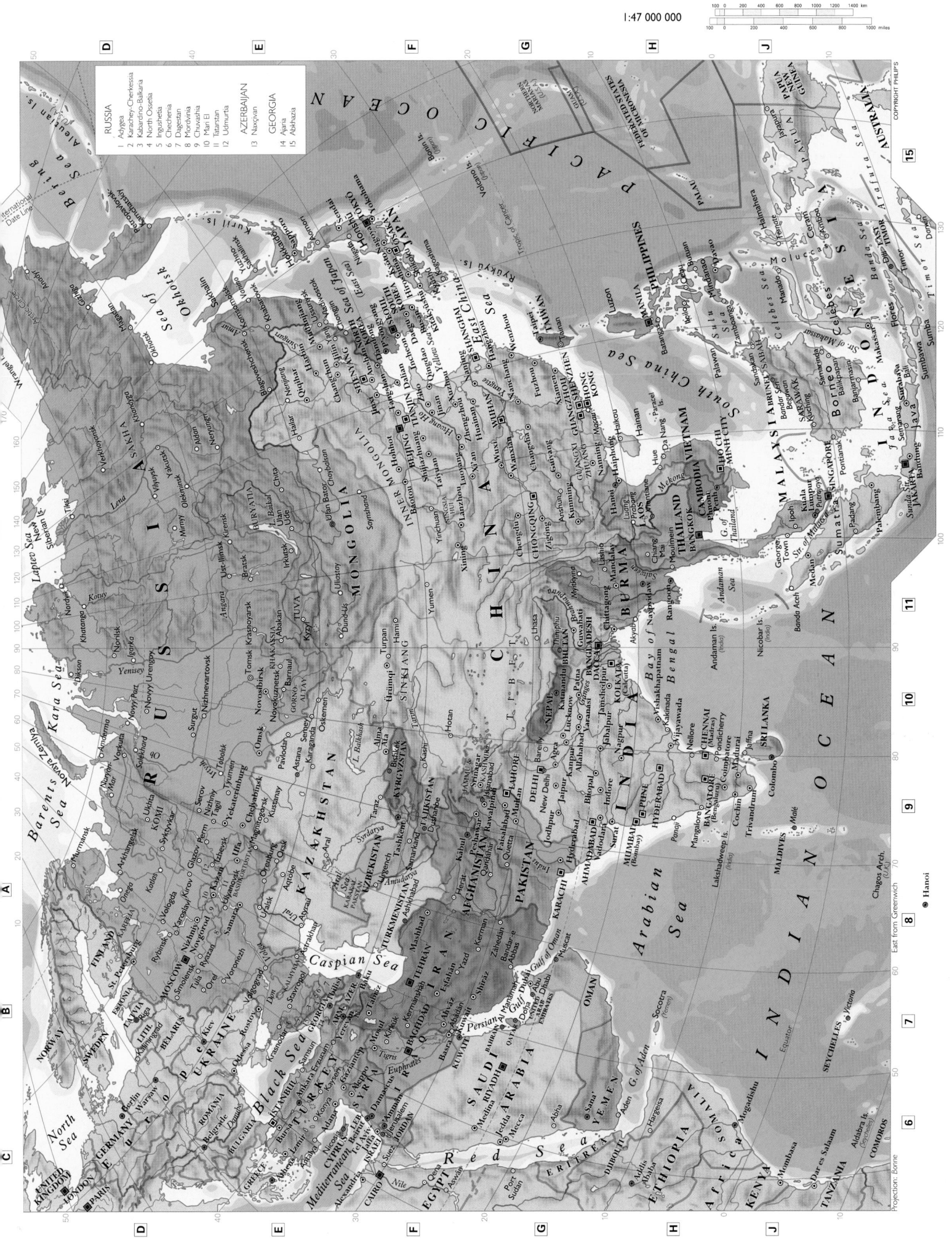

1:47 000 000

RUSSIA
1 Adygea
2 Karachey-Cherkessia
3 Kabardino-Balkaria
4 North Ossetia
5 Ingushetia
6 Chechenia
7 Dagestan
8 Mordvinia
9 Chuvashia
10 Mari El
11 Tatarstan
12 Udmurtia

AZERBAIJAN
13 Naxçivan

GEORGIA
14 Ajaria
15 Abkhazia

ARCTIC OCEAN

Severnaya Zemlya
Mys Arkticheskiy
Ostrov Shmidta
Ostrov Komsomolets
Ostrov Oktyabrskoy Revolyutsii
Ostrov Bolshevik
Ostrov Pioner
Ostrov Malyy Taymyr

Poluostrov Taymyr
Gory Byrranga
Nordvik
Khatanga
Kheta
Volochanka
Novorybnoye
Khatanga

Ostrov Bolshoy Begichev
Ostrova Petra
Prolив Vilkitskogo
Mys Chelyuskin

Laptev Sea
Tiksi
Ust Olenek
Bulun
Tit-Ary
Kyusyur
Zhilinda

Novosibirskiye Ostrova
Ostrov Kotelnyy
Lyakhovskiye Ostrova
Ostrov Bolshoy Lyakhovskiy
Ostrov Malyy Lyakhovskiy
Novaya Sibir
Ostrov Faddeyevskiy
Ostrov Belkovskiy
Ostrov Stolbovoy
Prolив Dmitriya Lapteva

Ostrova Delonga
Ostrov Bennetta
Ostrov Genriyetty
Ostrov Zhannetty
Ostrov Zhokhova

East Siberian Sea
Ostrov Vrangelya
Prolив Longa
Mys Shmidta
Chaunskaya Guba
Pevek
Nizhne Kolymsk

Chukchi Sea
Mys Dezhneva (East C.)
Uelen
Chukotskoye Nagorye
Vankarem
Egvekinot
Anadyrskiy Zaliv
Anadyr
Ust-Chaun

Bering Strait
St. Lawrence I. (U.S.A.)
International Date Line

Providenya
Beringovsky

Koryakskoye Nagorye
Bering Sea

Kolymskoye Nagorye
Srednekolymsk
Zyryanka
Kolyma
Chokurdakh
Indigirka
Omolon
Markovo
Penzhino
Gizhiga
Paren
Evensk

Sredinnyy Khrebet
Poluostrov Kamchatka
Petropavlovsk-Kamchatskiy
Klyuchi
Ust-Kamchatsk

Verkhoyansk
Khrebet Cherskogo
Verkhoyanskiy Khrebet
Batagay
Ust-Nera
Oymyakon
Gora Chen
Ust-Maya
Yagodnoye
Susuman
Magadan
Ola

Sea of Okhotsk
Okhotsk
Ayan
Khrebet Dzhugdzur

Zhigansk
Sangar
Batamay
Yakutsk
Pokrovsk
Namtsy
Vilyuysk
Verkhnevilyuysk
Nyurba
Suntar
Mirnyy
Chernyshevskiy
Vilyuyskoye Vdkhr.
Lensk
Olekminsk
Tommot
Aldan
Neryungri
Nagornyy

Udachnyy
Arctic Circle
Aykhal

Olenek

Shantarskiye Ostrova
Nikolayevsk-na-Amure
Okha
Sakhalin
Aleksandrovsk-Sakhalinskiy
Poronaysk
Yuzhno-Sakhalinsk
Kholmsk
Tatarskiy Proliv

Kurilskiye Ostrova

Komsomolsk-na-Amure
Khabarovsk
Sikhote Alin

Vanavara
Podkamennaya Tunguska
Tura
Nizhnyaya Tunguska
Yessey
Gory Putorana
Talnakh
Norilsk

Yeniseysk
Lesosibirsk
Krasnoyarsk
Kansk
Ilanskiy
Zelenogorsk
Minusinsk
Sayan
Abakan
Kyzyl

Bratsk
Taishet
Ust-Ilimsk
Nizhneudinsk
Tulun
Zima
Cheremkhovo
Usolye Sibirskoye
Angarsk
Irkutsk
Ulan Ude

Yablonovyy Khrebet
Chita
Nerchinsk
Sretensk
Shilka
Borzya

Stanovoy Khrebet
Tynda
Skovorodino
Mogocha
Zeya
Svobodnyy
Belogorsk
Blagoveshchensk
Amur
Birobidzhan

Severobaykalsk
Bodaybo
Chara
Ust-Kut
Magistralnyy
Kirensk
Lena

Baykal
Slyudyanka
Kyakhta
Gusinoozersk
Darhan

MONGOLIA
Ulaanbaatar
Hangayn Nuruu
Aerhtai Shan (Altay)
Bayankhongor
Arvayheer
Uliastay
Tsetserleg
Moron
Erdenet
Baruun-Urt
Choybalsan
Ondorhaan
Tamsagbulag
Choyr
Mandalgovi
Buyant-Uhaa
Dalandzadgad

Gobi

CHINA
Hulun Nur
Manzhouli
Hailar
Zalantun
Baicheng
Taonan
QIQIHAR
DAQING
HARBIN
JIAMUSI
Hegang
JIXI
MUDANJIANG
JILIN
CHANGCHUN
Siping
Dongbei (Manchuria)
Dalian
SHENYANG
ANSHAN
FUSHUN
BENXI
JINXI
CHIFENG
ZHANGJIAKOU
BEIJING
BAOTOU
HOHHOT
TANGSHAN
Chengde
Xilinhot
Linxi
Erenhot

Vladivostok
Nakhodka
Ussuriysk
Partizansk

NORTH KOREA
PYONGYANG
NAMPO
Hamhung
Wonsan
Chongjin

SOUTH KOREA
SEOUL
INCHEON
DAEJEON
DAEGU
BUSAN
GWANGJU

JAPAN
SAPPORO
Hokkaido
Hakodate
Aomori
Akita
Niigata
Honshu
TOKYO
KYOTO
OSAKA
KOBE

Sea of Japan (East Sea)

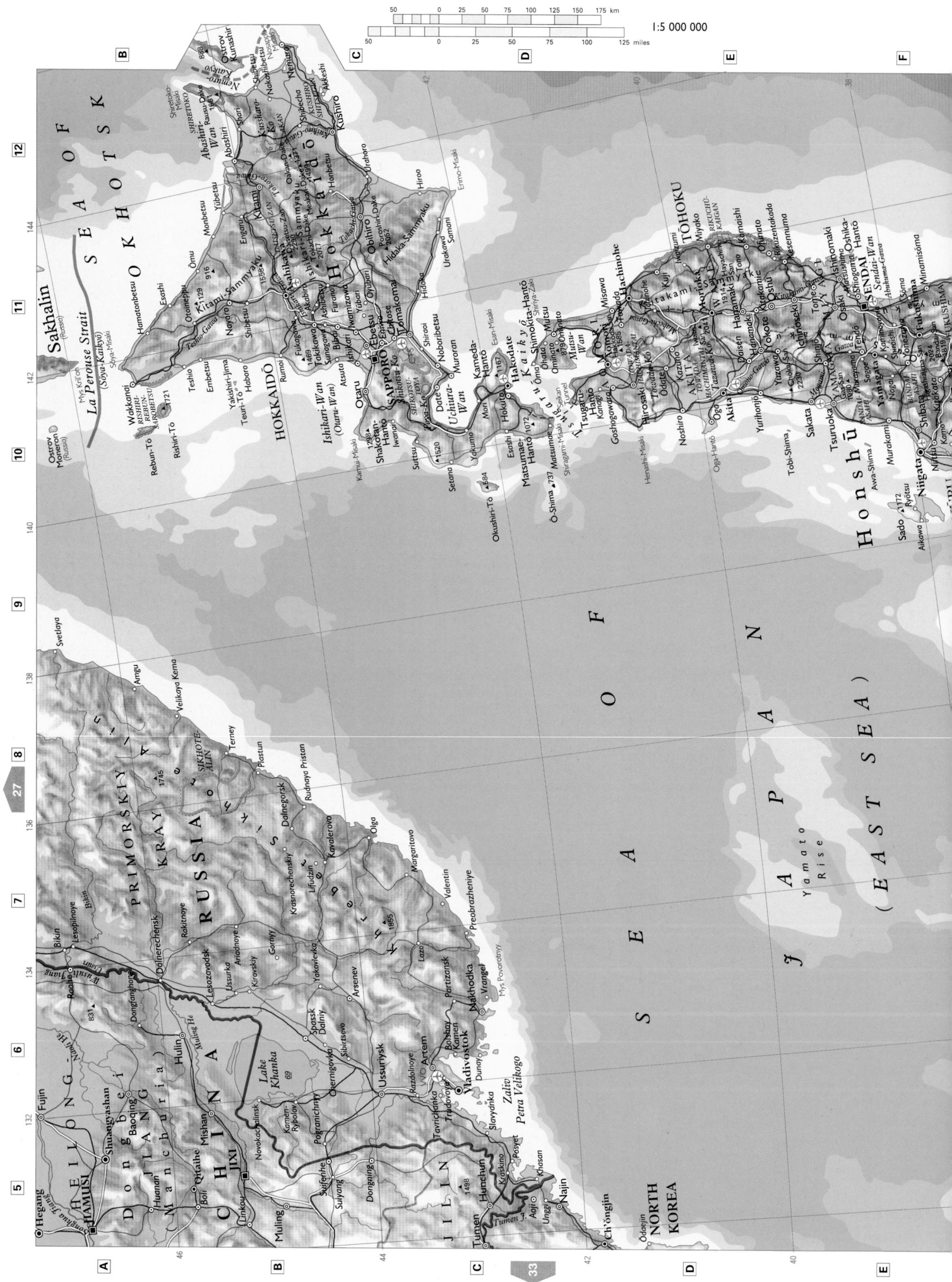

1:5 000 000

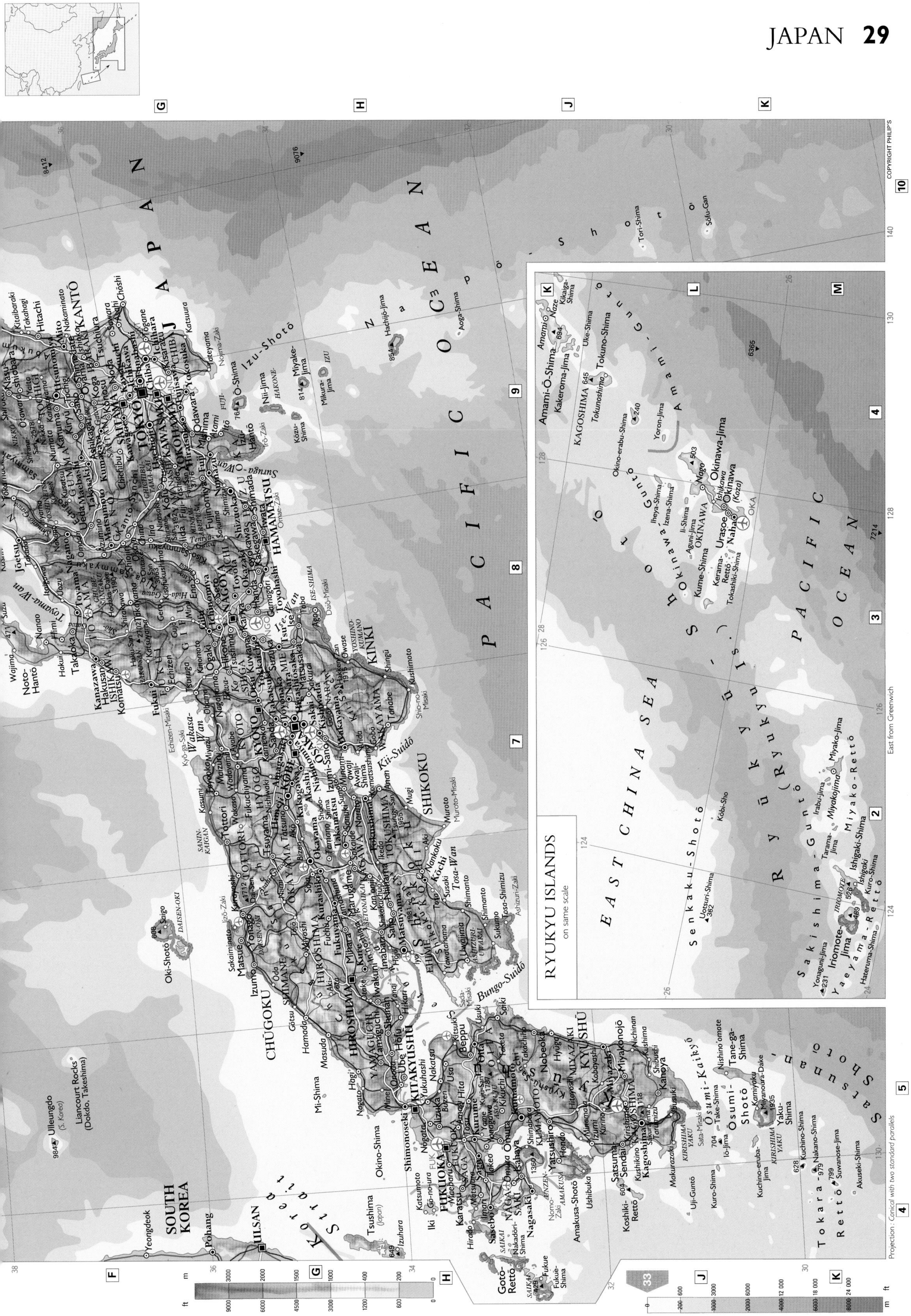

1:15 000 000

Projection: Bonne

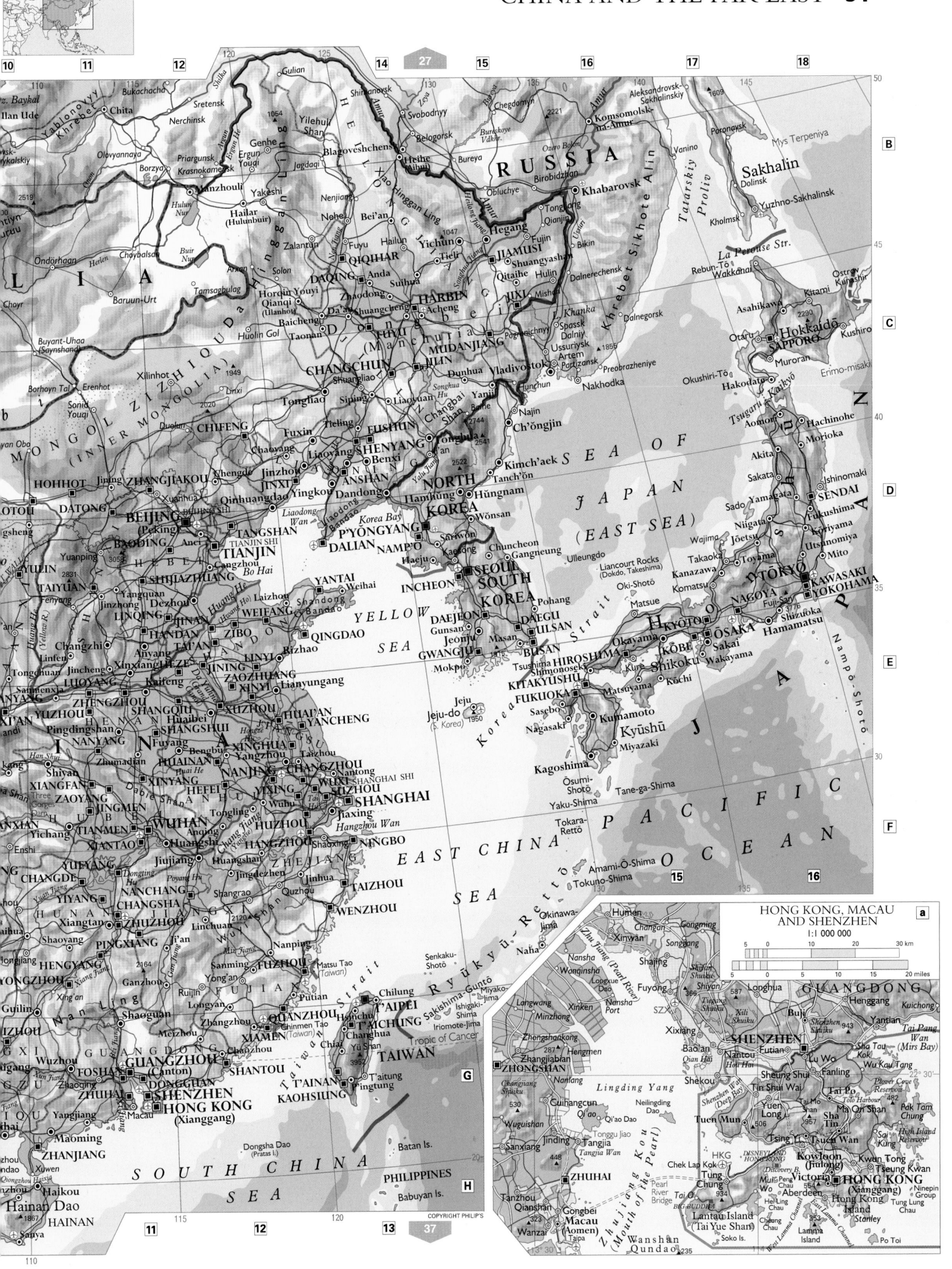

B

C

D

E

F

G

H

RUSSIA

Sakhalin

Hokkaidō
SAPPORO

SEA OF
JAPAN
(EAST SEA)

NORTH
KOREA

SOUTH
KOREA
SEOUL

YELLOW
SEA

BEIJING
(Peking)

SHANGHAI

J A P A N

TŌKYŌ

PACIFIC
OCEAN

EAST CHINA
SEA

TAIWAN

HONG KONG
(Xianggang)

SOUTH CHINA
SEA

PHILIPPINES

Tropic of Cancer

COPYRIGHT PHILIP'S

HONG KONG, MACAU AND SHENZHEN

1:1 000 000

GUANGDONG

SHENZHEN

HONG KONG
(Xianggang)

ZHUHAI

Macau
(Aomen)

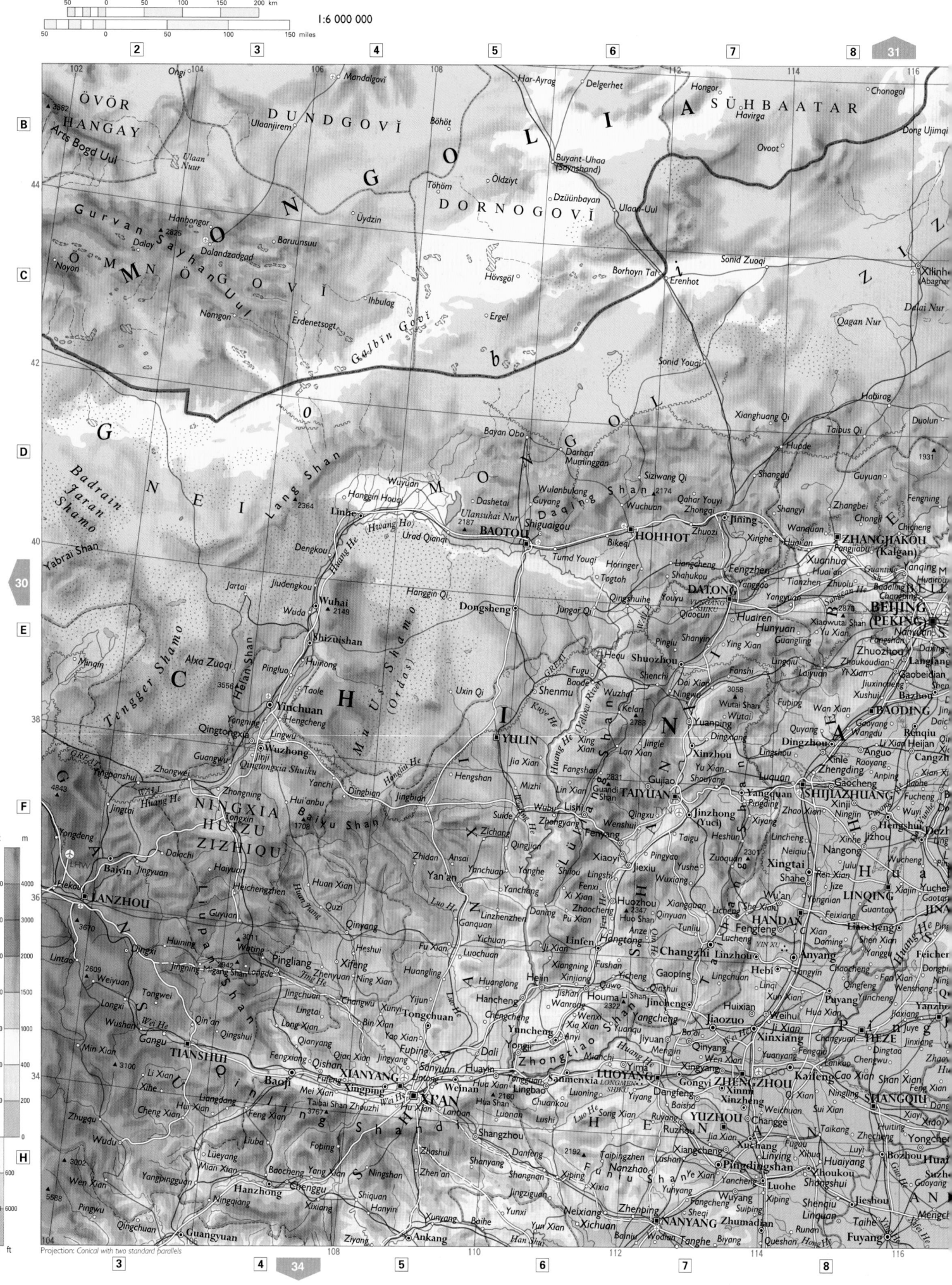

1:6 000 000

Projection: Conical with two standard parallels

1:6 000 000

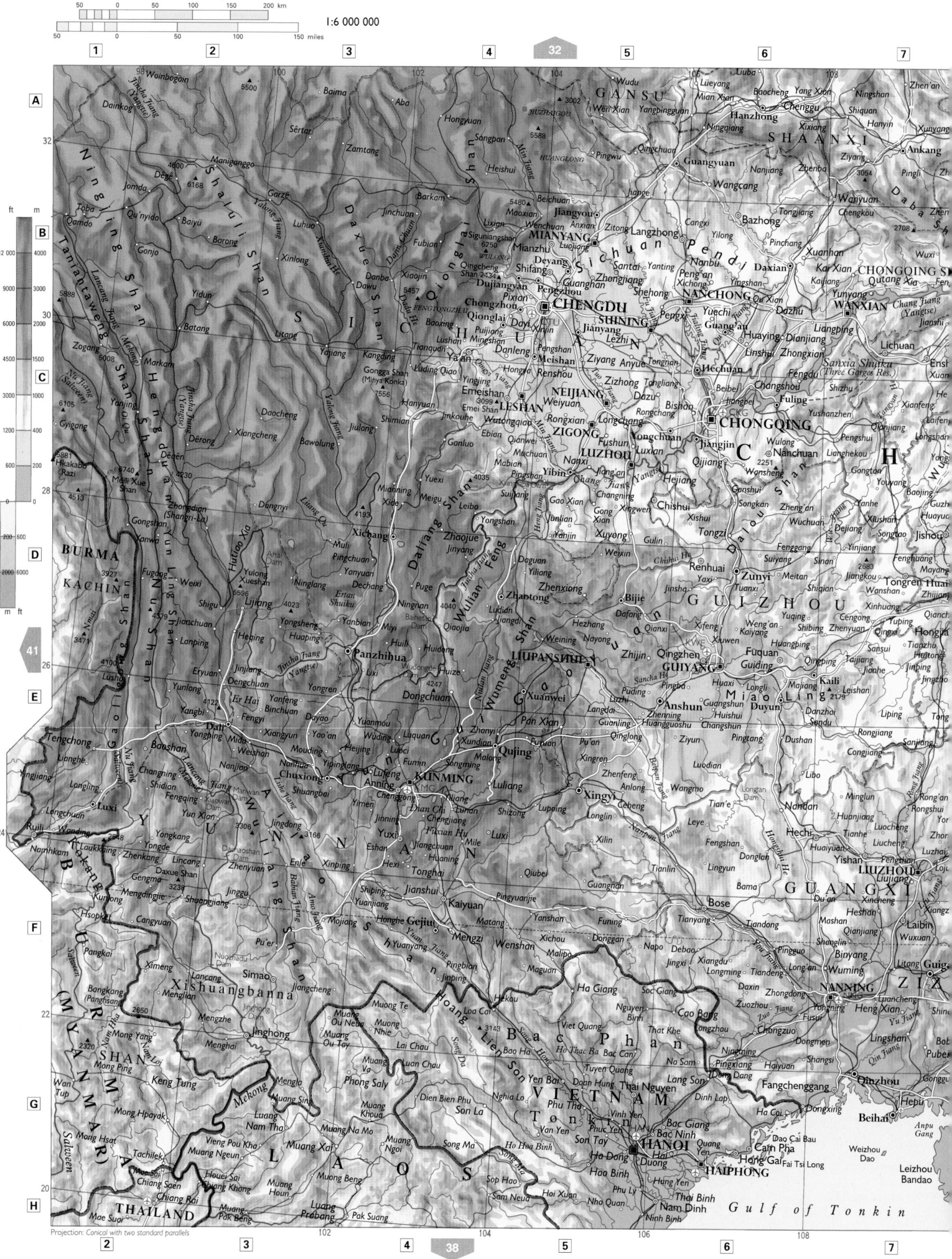

Projection: Conical with two standard parallels

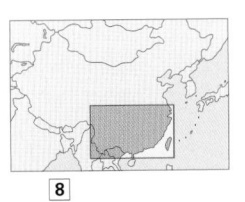

1:12 500 000

Projection: Mercator

East from Greenwich

JAVA AND MADURA
1:7 500 000

50 0 50 100 150 200 250 300 km
50 0 50 100 150 200 miles

BALI
1:2 000 000

10 0 10 20 30 km
10 0 10 20 miles

Oceans and Seas

CELEBES SEA

PACIFIC OCEAN

MOLUCCA SEA

CERAM SEA

BANDA SEA

FLORES SEA

SAVU SEA (Sawu Sea)

ARAFURA SEA

INDIAN OCEAN

BALI SEA

Major places — Philippines (Luzon / Mindanao)

Claveria, Babuyan Chan., C. Engaño, Bacarra, Laoag, Aparri, Tuguegarao, Vigan, Batac 2360, Tudo, Bangued, Bontoc, Ilagan, Palanan Pt., San Fernando, Pulag 2928, Santiago, Palanan, Lingayen, Bolinao, Baguio, Bayombong, Casiguran, Dagupan, Tarlac, Cabanatuan, C. San Ildefonso, Mt. Pinatubo 1759, San Fernando, Polillo Is., Olongapo, Malolos, QUEZON CITY, Lamon Bay, MANILA, Cavite, Santa Cruz, Daet, Virac, Bataan, Manila B., Lubang I., Lucena, Calauag, Naga, Tabaco, Marinduque, Legazpi, Sorsogon, Calapan, Mayon Volcano 2462, Burias, Masbate, Lipa, Batangas, C. Calavite 5245, Mamburao, Mindoro, Halcon 2586, Sablayan, San Jose, Romblon, Tablas, Sibuyan Sea, Laoang, Catarman, Catbalogan, Taft, General MacArthur, Busuanga, Culion, Cuyo Is., San Jose de Buenavista, Iloilo, Bacolod, Dumaguete, Tagbilaran, Cebu, Bohol, Mandaue, Maasin, Tacloban, Baybay, Guiuan, Ormoc, Leyte, Dinagat 10 497, Siargao, Tandag, Lianga, Butuan, Cagayan de Oro, Iligan, Malaybalay, Gateel, Baganga, Cateel, Ozamiz, Pagadian, Mindanao, Tagum, DAVAO, Mati, Zamboanga, Cotabato, Datu Piang, Digos, Isabela, Basilan, Lebak, Koronadal, Malita, C. Agustin, General Santos, Kiamba, Kiambaan, Sarangani B., Tinaca Pt., Sarangani Is., Jolo, Parang, Siasi, Tapul Group, Tawi-tawi, Sibutu Passage

SULU SEA, SULU ARCHIPELAGO

Java / Madura

JAKARTA, Tangerang, Bekasi, Karawang, Merak, Banten, Anyer, Pandeglang, Serang, Rangkasbitung, BANTEN, Bogor, Purwakarta, Subang, Indramayu, Cianjur, Sukabumi, Sumedang, Majalengka, Cirebon, Brebes, Tegal, Pemalang, Pekalongan, Jepara, Rembang, Tuban, Madura, Sumenep, Sampang, Bangkalan, Pamekasan, BANDUNG, Garut, Tasikmalaya, Ciamis, Kuningan, Purwokerto, Purbalingga, Wonosobo, Salatiga, Kudus, Demak, Semarang, Pati, Blora, Bojonegoro, Ngawi, Mojokerto, Gresik, SURABAYA, Sidoarjo, Pasuruan, Genteng, Cilacap, Purworejo, Yogyakarta, Surakarta, Madiun, Kediri, Ponorogo, Trenggalek, Tulungagung, Blitar, Malang, Lumajang, Jember, Probolinggo, Situbondo, Bondowoso, Banyuwangi, JAWA TIMUR, JAWA TENGAH, JAWA BARAT, Borobudur, Prambanan, Merapi 2911, Lawu, Arjuna, Semeru, Bromo, Tengger, Bali

KEPULAUAN KARIMUNJAWA, Bawean, Sangkapura

Bali

Singaraja, Kubutambahan, Tejakula, Gunung Raung, Banyuwangi, Gerokgak, Gilimanuk, Pulau Menjangan, Lovina, Seririt, Kintamani, Tianyar, Kubu, BALI BARAT, Ketapang, Gunung Batur, Songan, Culik, Amed, Melaya, Merebuk 1385, Busungbiu, Bedugul, Penelokan, Gunung Agung 3142, Tirtagangga, Negara, Yehbuah, Batukaru 2276, Baturiti, Rendang, Karangasem (Amlapura), Mendoyo, Belimbing, Tegallalang, Saren, Bangli, Klungkung (Semarapura), Candi Dasa, Monggis, Gianyar, Kusamba, Ubud, Sukawati, BALI, Tabanan, Blahkiuh, Sibang, Bangli, Badung, Denpasar, Legian, Kuta, Sanur, Kusamba, Jimbaran, Uluwatu, Bukit Badung, Nusa Dua, Nusa Lembongan, Nusa Penida, Tanjung Abah, LOMBOK, Senggigi, Montongbuwoh, Ampenan, Mataram, Lembuak, Gerung, Lembar, Blongas, Teluk Terang

Sulawesi (Celebes) and eastern islands

Manado, Bunaken, Kema, Tondano, Bitung, Amurang, Kotamobagu, GORONTALO, Gorontalo, UTARA, Tanjung Flesko, Toli-toli, Buol, Paleleh, Sumalata, Kwandang, Tilamuta, Moutong, Teluk Tomini, SULAWESI TENGAH, Palu, Parigi, Poso, Donggala, Toboli, Luwuk, Banggai, KEPULAUAN BANGGAI, Kolonodale, Danau Poso, Danau Towuti, Malili, Kendari, SULAWESI TENGGARA, Kolaka, Pomalaa, Mondeodo, Parepare, Pinrang, Rantepao, Makale, Palopo, Watampone, Teluk Bone, Sengkang, Pangkajene, Sinjai, Bulukumba, Bantaeng, MAKASSAR, Selayar, Muna, Raha, Buton, Baubau, Wangiwangi, KEPULAUAN TUKANGBESI, KEPULAUAN BONERATE, Kalaotoa

Maluku / Irian Jaya (Papua)

Halmahera, HALMAHERA UTARA, Morotai, Tobelo, Galela, Akelamo, Ternate, Tidore, Weda, Teluk Weda, Makian, Kayoa, KEPULAUAN SULA, Sanana, Mangole, Taliabu, Obi, Bacan, Mandioli, Gani, Bisa, KEPULAUAN BACAN, Buru, Namlea, Ambon, MALUKU, Seram (Ceram), Wahai, Amahai, Masohi, Geser, Bula, Waru, Tehoru, KEPULAUAN BANDA, Banda, Bandanaira, Tanjung Libobo, Misool, Sorong, Sele, JAZIRAH DOBERAI, Teminabuan, Fakfak, Kaimana, IRIAN JAYA BARAT, Kokas, Babo, Bintuni, Wendesi, Manokwari, Numfor, Biak, Supiori, KEPULAUAN PADAIDO, Serui, Nabire, PEGUNUNGAN MAOKE, PAPUA, Pegunungan Sudirman, Puncak Jaya 4884, Enarotali, Wamena, Timika, Tembagapura, Agats, Amamapare, Tanahmerah, Merauke, Muting, Okaba, Bade, Mindiptana, Pulau Dolak, Pulau Kimaam, Pulau Komoran, PAPUA NEW GUINEA, Jayapura, Genyem, Sarmi

Nusa Tenggara / Timor

Flores, Maumere, Ende, Ruteng, Bajawa, Reo, NUSA TENGGARA TIMUR, Sumba, Waingapu, Waikabubak, Melolo, Kupang, SAVU SEA, Sawu, Baing, Raijua, Rote, Lembata, Alor, Kalabahi, Pantar, Larantuka, Adonara, Solor, Wetar, Kisar, Moa, Leti, Romang, Damar, Teun, Nila, Serua, Gunungapi 5888, Wuliaru, Larat, KEPULAUAN TANIMBAR, Saumlaki, Yamdena, Selaru, Trangan, KEPULAUAN ARU, Dobo, Kai Besar, Kai Kecil, KEPULAUAN KAI, Tual, East Timor, Dili, Baucau, Viqueque, Atapupu, Kefamenanu

EQUATOR

COPYRIGHT PHILIP'S

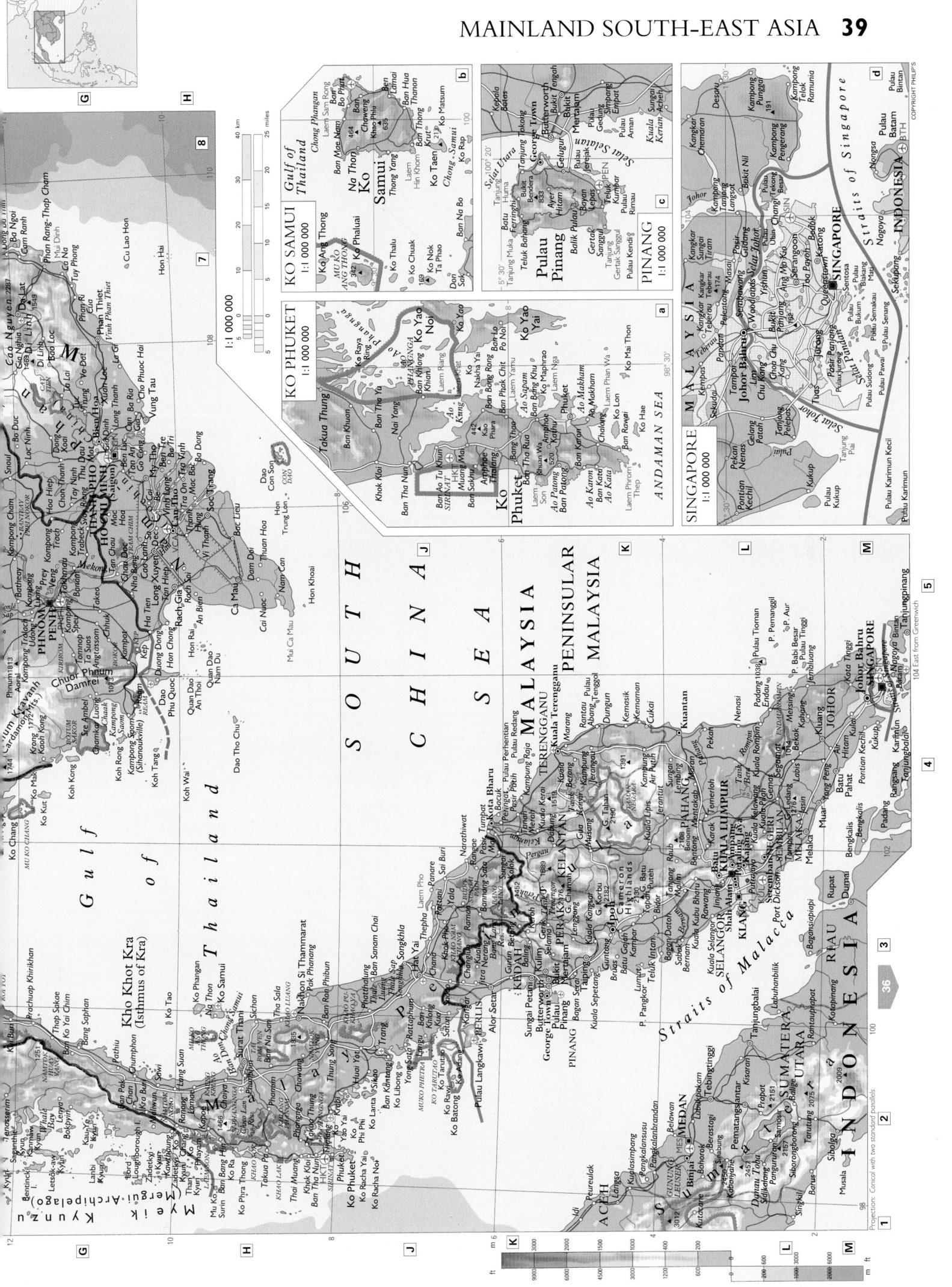

G H

8

40 km
30
20
25 miles
20
10
15
10
5
1:1 000 000
0
5
5

7

KO SAMUI
1:1 000 000

Gulf of Thailand

Ko Pha Ngan
Laem Sam Rong
Ban Mae Nam
Ban Bo Phut
Chong Phangan
Ben Lamai
Ban Hua Thanon
Chaweng
635
464
Na Thon
Ko Samui
Thong Yang
HKT
Hin Khom
Ko Taen
Ko Matsum
213
Ko Rap
Chong Samui

b

PINANG
1:1 000 000

Selat Utara
Kepala Batas
Butterworth
Bukit Tengah
George Town
454
Tanjung Tokong
Pulau Bunting
Bukit Mertajam
Gelugur
Teluk Bahang
Selat Selatan
Tanjung Muka
Batu Feringghi
342
Ayer Hitam
Bendera
833
Balik Pulau
Pulau Jerejak
Bayan Lepas
PEN
Teluk Kumbar
Gertak Sanggul
169
Pulau Kendi
Pulau Betong

c

d

Desaru
Kampong Punggai
Kampong Telok Ramunia
191
Pulau Bintan
Nongsa
Pulau Batam
INDONESIA
BTH
COPYRIGHT PHILIP'S

Straits of Singapore

KO PHUKET
1:1 000 000

Ao Phangnga
Ko Raya Ring
Ko Yao Yai
Ko Yao Noi
Phangnga
Nakha Yai
Takua Thung
Ban Thao Yu
Ban Khilong Khian
Ko Lon
Ban Bang Rong
Ban Phak Chit
Khok Kloi
Nai Yang
Ban Khuan
Ao Sapam
Ko Maphrao
Laem Yamu
442
Kao Phara
520
Ban Pak
Ban Tha Rua
Amphoe Thalang
Ao Makham
Ao Kung
Ban Pa Khlok
Muang Mai
Ko Mai Thon
HKT
SIREN'AT
Ban Ao Tu Khun
Laem Riang
Amphoe Kathu
Laem Phan Wa
Ban Karon
Ban Sakhu
Ao Chalong
Ko Hae
Ko Phuket
Laem Ka
Ao Patong
Ao Makham
Ban Patong
Ao Karon
Ao Kata
Laem Phromthep
Ban Kata
Ban Rawai

a

ANDAMAN SEA

SINGAPORE
1:1 000 000

MALAYSIA
Kulai
Ulu Tiram
Pasir Gudang
Kota Tinggi
Johor Bahru
Woodlands
Changi
SINGAPORE
Sentosa
INDONESIA
Straits of Singapore

L

M

6

SOUTH
CHINA
SEA

J

K

MALAYSIA

PENINSULAR
MALAYSIA

5

104 East from Greenwich

4

3

36

2

1

m 6

Projection: Conical with two standard parallels

G H J K L M

12 10 8 6 4 2

G H J K M

ft m
9000 3000
6000 2000
4500 1500
3000 1000
1800 600
1200 400
600   200
200   0
0   200
600   3000
3000 6000
m   ft

110 108 106 104 102 100 98

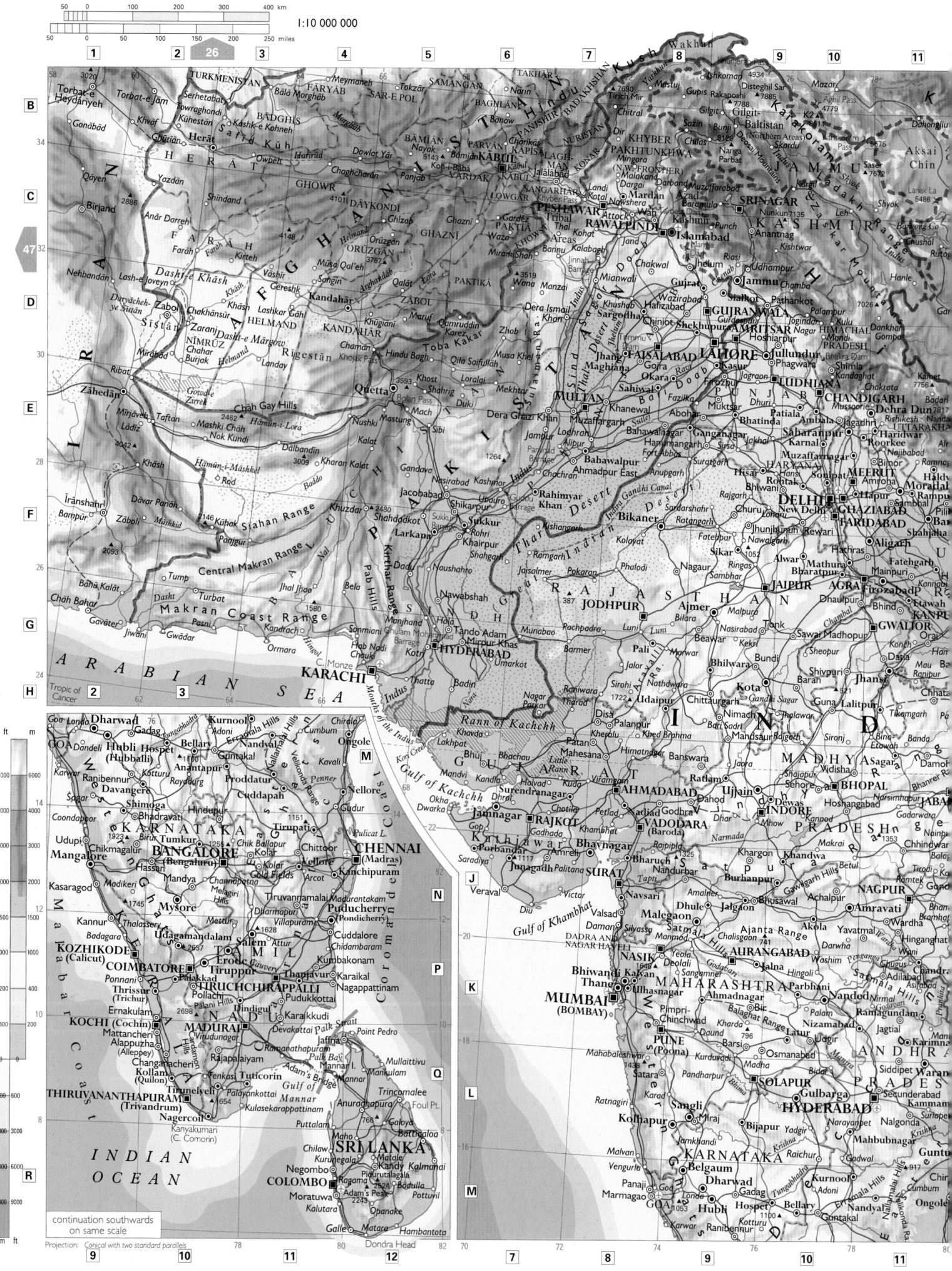

1:10 000 000

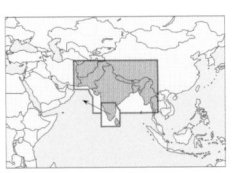

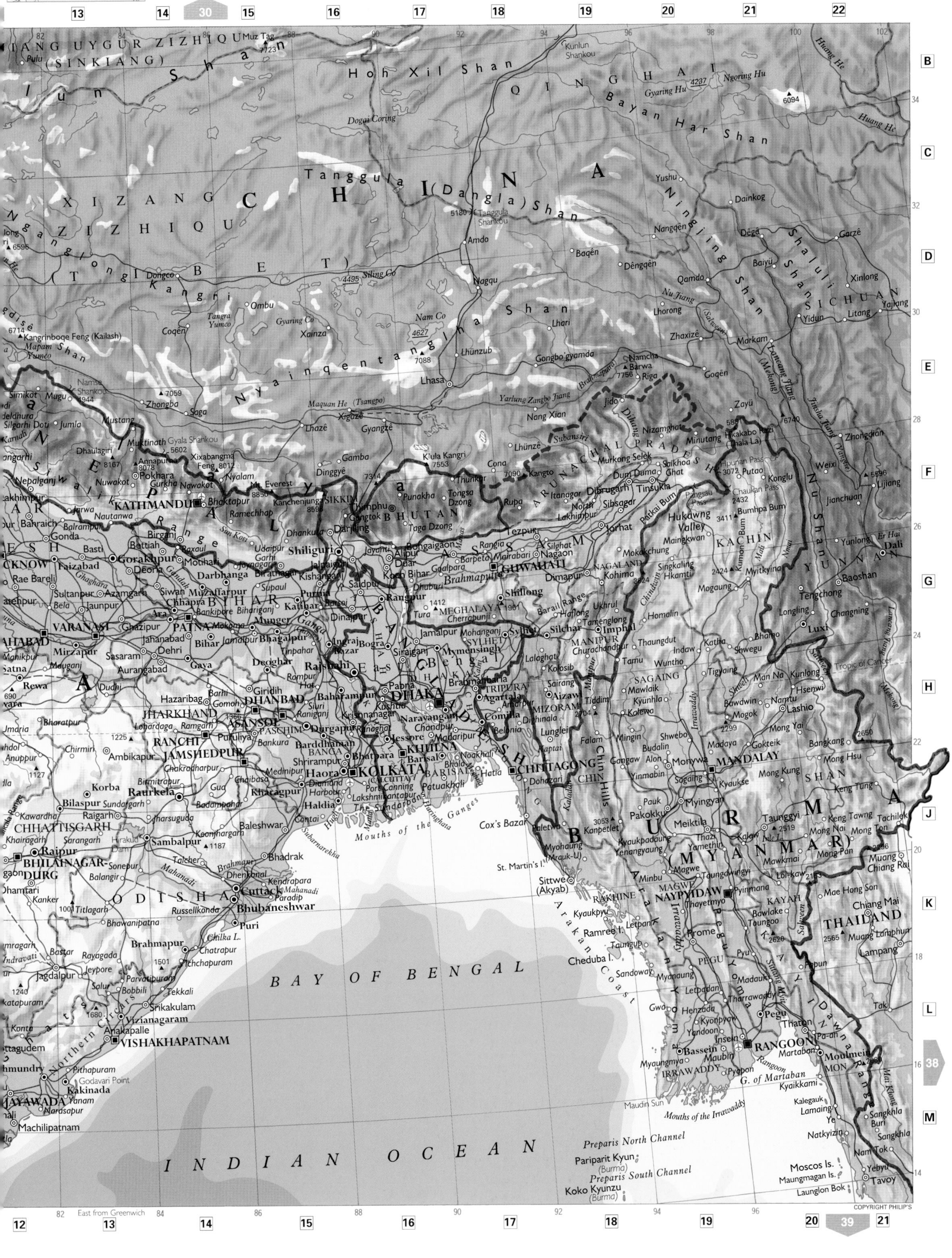

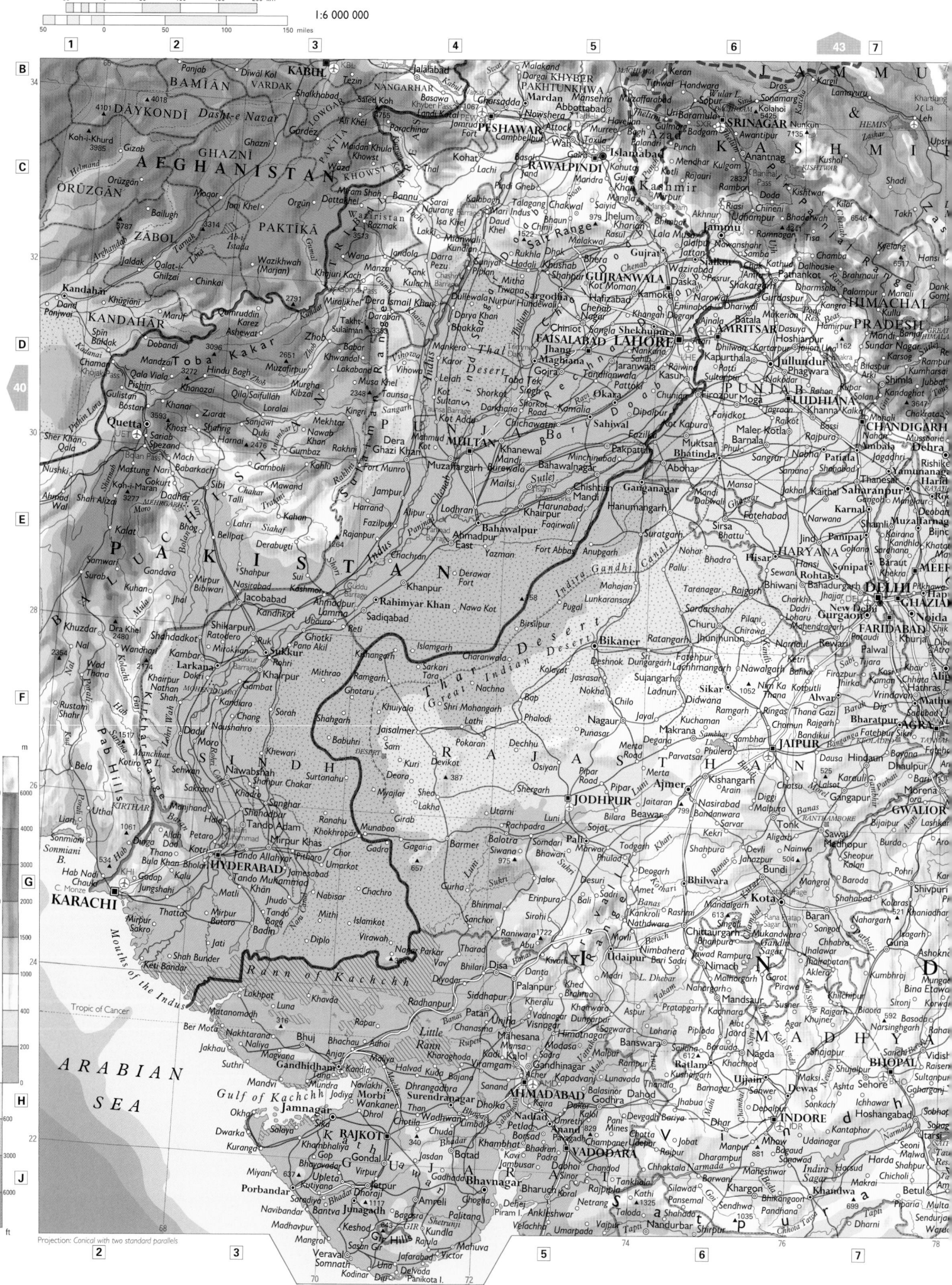

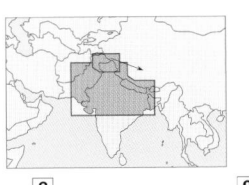

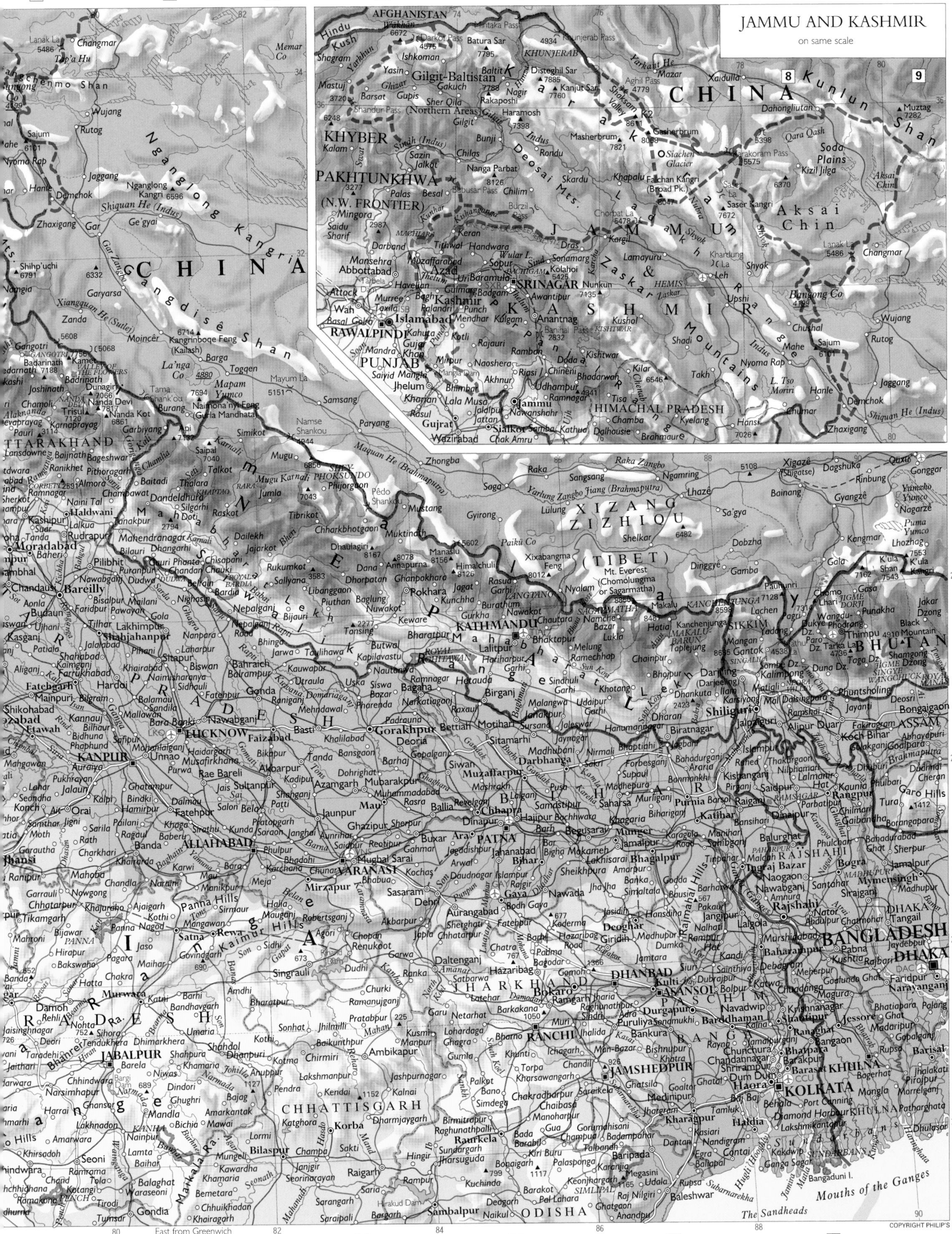

JAMMU AND KASHMIR
on same scale

AFGHANISTAN

CHINA

Hindu Kush

Gilgit-Baltistan (Northern Areas)

KHYBER PAKHTUNKHWA (N.W. FRONTIER)

Nanga Parbat

K2

Karakoram Range

Siachen Glacier

Aksai Chin

Soda Plains

Deosai Mts.

JAMMU & KASHMIR

Zaskar Range

Ladakh

SRINAGAR

Kashmir

Leh

Islamabad

RAWALPINDI

PUNJAB

Jammu

HIMACHAL PRADESH

CHINA

Ngangong Kangri

Tangdise Shan

Nanda Devi

UTTARAKHAND

Gangotri

N E P A L

Mahabharat Lekh

Dhaulagiri

Annapurna

Mt. Everest (Chomolungma or Sagarmatha)

Manaslu

KATHMANDU

Pokhara

XIZANG ZIZHIQU (TIBET)

Yarlung Zangbo Jiang (Brahmaputra)

Kangchenjunga

SIKKIM

BHUTAN

Thimphu

Makalu

MORADABAD

Bareilly

LUCKNOW

KANPUR

U T T A R   P R A D E S H

ALLAHABAD

VARANASI

Gorakhpur

PATNA

B I H A R

Darbhanga

Muzaffarpur

ASSAM

Koch Bihar

Siliguri

Darjeeling

Rangpur

Mymensingh

DHAKA

BANGLADESH

JABALPUR

M A D H Y A   P R A D E S H

CHHATTISGARH

JHARKHAND

DHANBAD

ASANSOL

RANCHI

JAMSHEDPUR

Durgapur

BARDDHAMAN

KOLKATA

Haora

KHULNA

ODISHA

Raurkela

SUNDARBANS

Mouths of the Ganges

The Sandheads

East from Greenwich

COPYRIGHT PHILIP'S

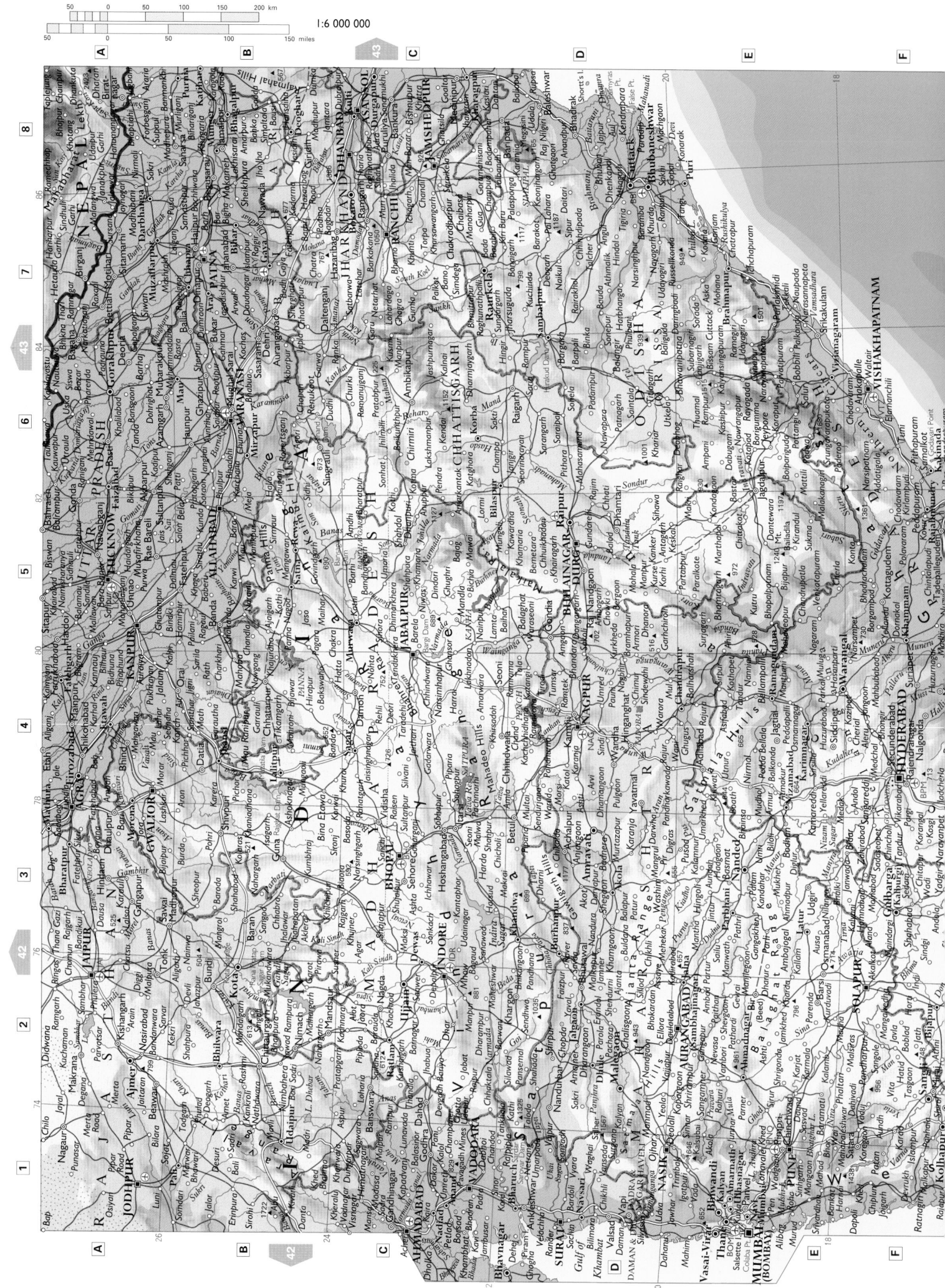

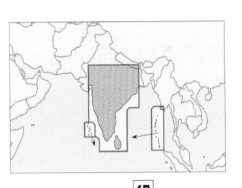

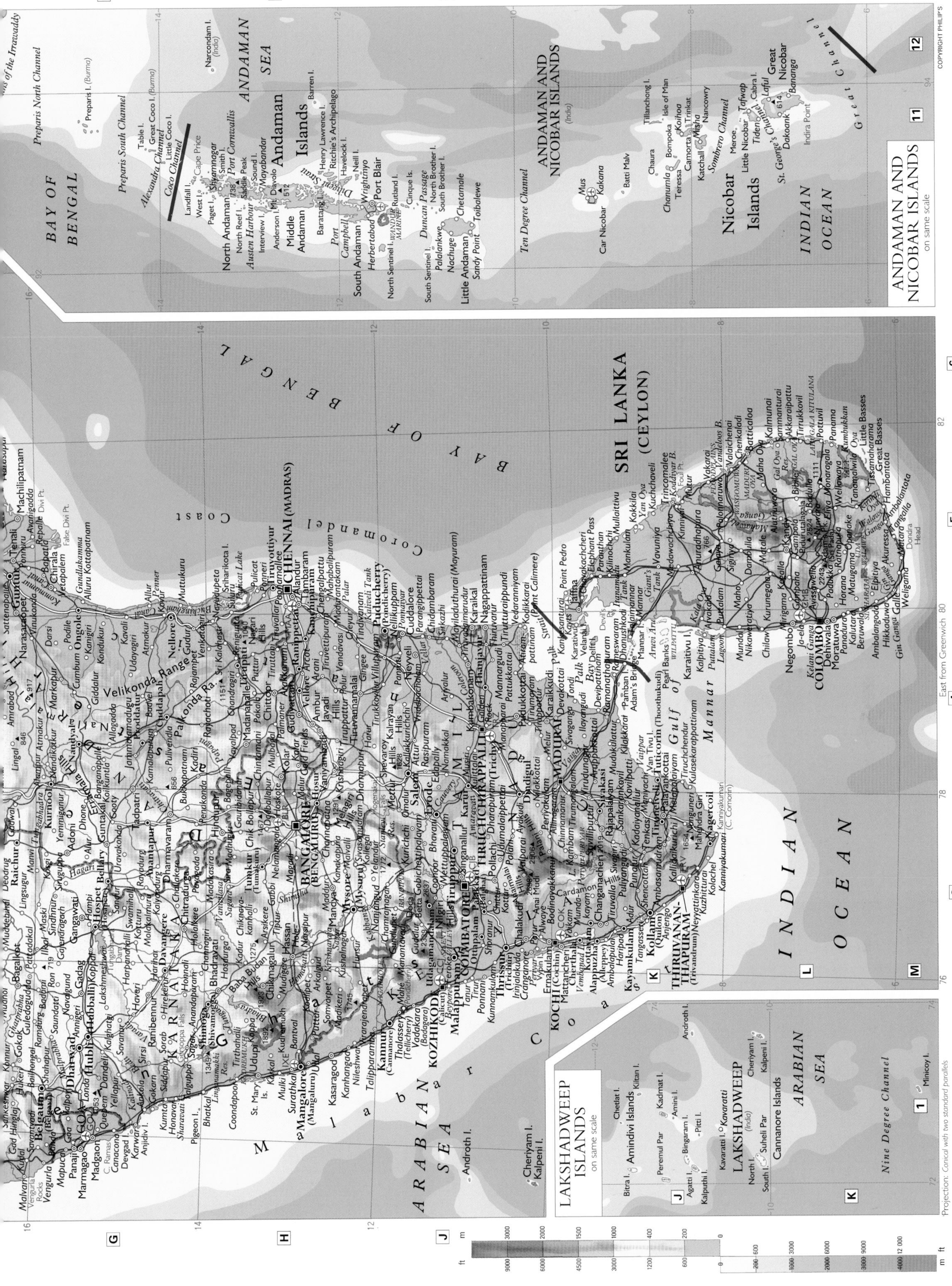

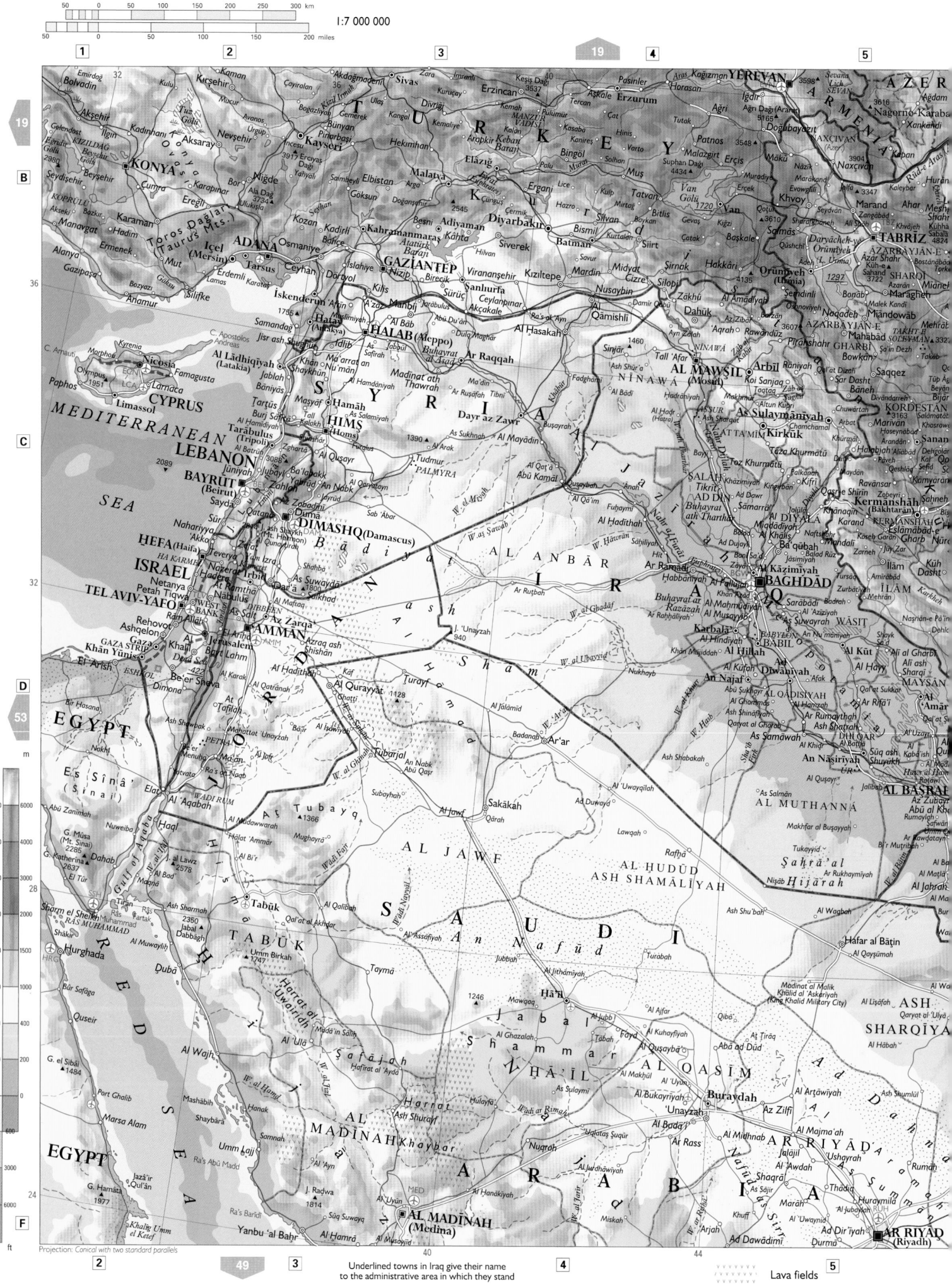

Lava fields

Projection: Conical with two standard parallels

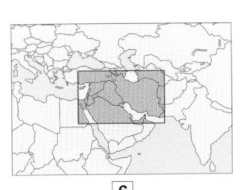

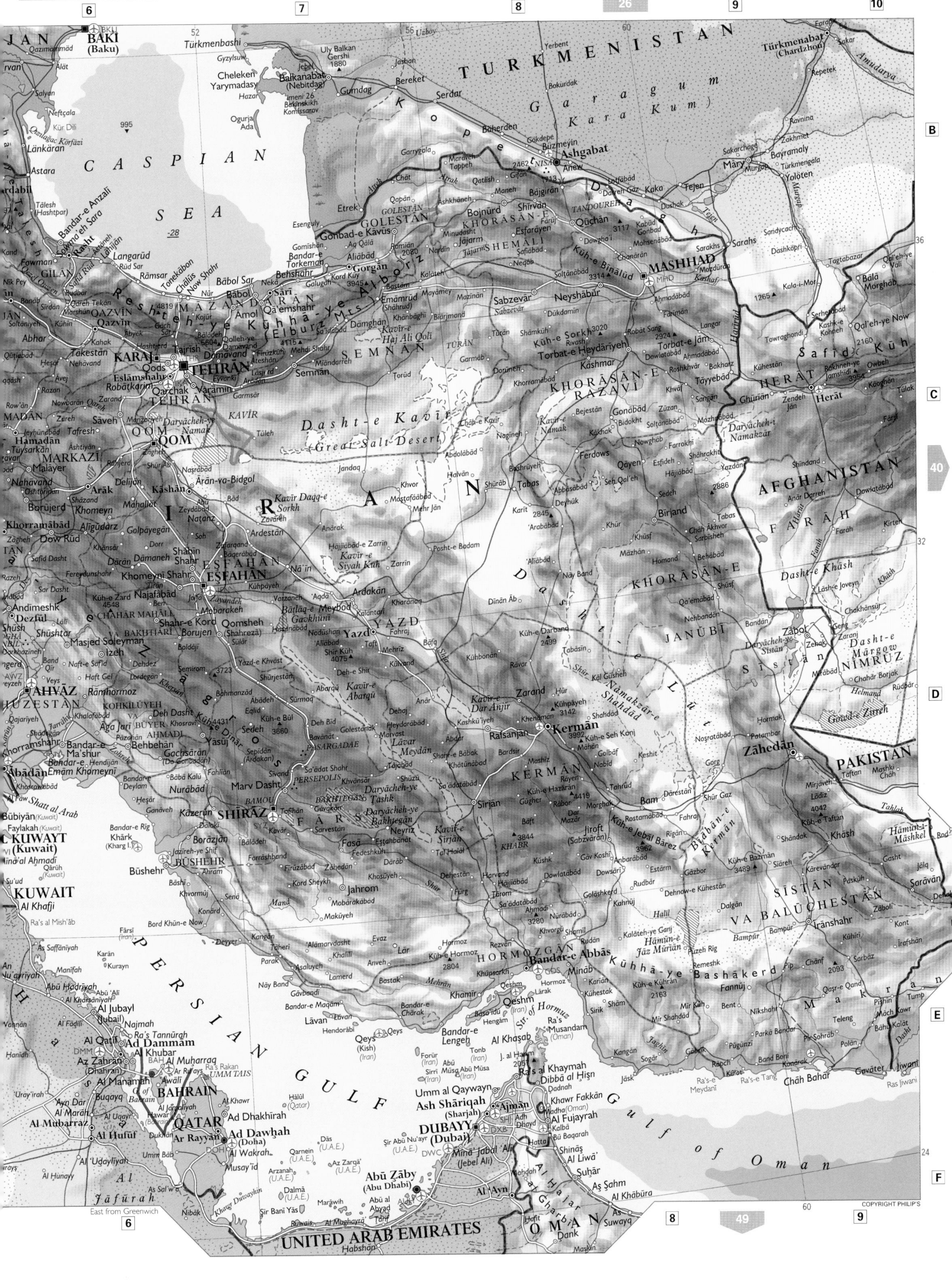

1:2 500 000

10 0 10 20 30 40 50 60 70 80 100 km
10 0 10 20 30 40 50 60 miles

1   **2**   **3**   **4**   46   **5**   **6**

Paphos
Episkopi
PFO
Kivides
Zyyi
CYPRUS
Limassol
Akrotiri
Episkopi
Bay
Akrotiri
Bay
C. Gata

▽2775

M E D I T E R R A N E A N

2089▽

S E A

Al Ḥamidiyah
Ḥimṣ (Homs)
Tall Kalakh
Ḥalbā
Shinshār
Furqlus
HIMṢ
Al Minā'
ASH SHAMĀL
Al Hirmil
Al Quṣayr
Ṭarābulus (Tripoli)
Zgharta
Qurnat as Sawdā' 3088▲
Al Buṭayj
Al Qaryatayn
Al Batrūn
Bsharri
2464▲ Al Labwah
Jubayl
Qarṭaba
An Nabk
Bi'r Ghadir
Ibrāhīm
AL BIQĀ 2616▲
Jūniyah
BAYRŪT
(Beirut) BEY
Biḳfayyā
2628▲ Sannīn
Ba'labakk
Yabrūd
SYRIA
Ash Shuwayfāt
Alayh
Zaḥlah
Ḥawsh Mūssā
Al Quṭayfah
Dumayr
Khān Abū Shāmat
Ad Dāmūr
JABAL LUBNĀN
Az Zabadānī
LEBANON
1942 J. al Bārūk
DIMASHQ
Qaṭanā
Al Hājānah
Ṣaydā (Sidon)
Jazzīn
J. ash Shaykh (Mt. Hermon) 2814▲
Dārayyā
DIMASHQ (Damascus)
Jaramānah
An Nabaṭiyah at Taḥtā
Marj 'Uyūn
Al Kiswah
Burāq
AL JANŪB
Ṣūr (Tyre)
Al Qunayṭirah
As Sanamayn
Qiryat Shemona
Golan Hts.
1197▲
DARʿĀ
AS SUWAYDĀ
Ma'alot-Tarshiha
Hagalil (Galilee)
Zefat
Yeḥi'am
Kinneret
Ar Rafid
Izra'
Shahbā
Nahariyya
1208▲
Karmi'el
Sea of Galilee
Fiq
Shaykh Miskīn
1900
'Akko (Acre)
Qiryat Ata
Teverya (Tiberias)
Saham al Jowlān
Qarā
Mifraz Hefa
-210
HAZAFON
As Suwaydā
Salah
Hefa (Haifa)
Qiryat Ata
Nazerat (Nazareth)
Afula
Ṭafas
IRBID
Malaḥ
Har HaKarmel 546▲
KARMEL
JABAL AD DURŪZ
Umm el Fahm
CAESAREA *TEL MEGIDDO*
Pardes
Jenin
Bet She'an
Irbid
Al Ramtha
Sālkhad
Hadera
Hanna-Karkur
SHOMRON
'Ajlūn
Buṣrā ash Shām
ISRAEL
Netanya
Tulkarm
Tubas
SAMARIA
'AJLŪN
Umm al Qiṭṭayn
HAMERKAZ
Nābulus
Ra'ananna
AJLŪN
Jarash
Al Mafraq
Herzliyya
Kefar Sava
JARASH
Az Zarqā
Benē Beraq
Petaḥ Tiqwa
SHILO
AL MAFRAQ
TEL AVIV-YAFO
Ramat Gan
N. az Zarqā
Bat Yam
Lod
WEST BANK
As Salṭ
AL BALQĀ
Az Zarqā
Holon
Ramla
Tila' al Alī
Ar Ruṣayfah
Azraq ash Shīshān
Rishon le Ziyyon
Rām Allah
AMMAN
Yavne
El Arīḥa (Jericho)
Wādī as Sīr
Al Quwaysimah
Reḥovot
Na'ūr
AZ ZARQĀ
Ashdod
Jerusalem
(Yerushalayim) (Al Quds)
Ma'daba
AMM
Qiryat Malakhi
Bayt Laḥm (Bethlehem)
Ma'dabā
Ashqelon
Qiryat Gat
MA'DABA
'AMMAN
Beit Lāhiyā
Al Khalīl (Hebron)
W. al Ḥaydān
GAZA STRIP
Jabālya
Gaza
Sederot
Dhibān
UMM AR RASAS
Deir al Balaḥ
Nuṣeirat
Rahat
Az Zāhiriya
En Gedi
Al Ḥadīthah
Khān Yūnis
ESHKOL
Besor
'En Boqeq
Al Qaṭrānah
Rafaḥ
Be'er Sheva (Beersheba)
Arad
Al Karak
W. al Mawjib
Al Mazār
El Daheir
AL KARAK
Bûr Saʿîd (Port Said)
Bûr Fu'ad
BŪR SAʿĪD
Khalîg el Tîna
Sabkhet el Bardawîl
El 'Arîsh
1305▲
Bor Mashash
Sedom
Dimona
Rās Burûn
Bir el 'Abd
Bîr el Garārât
Bîr Lahfan
Dimona
HADAROM
W. al Ḥasā
Romani
Bîr Qaṭia
Bîr Kaseiba
-333
JORDAN
El Qantara
Bir el Duweidar
W. al Ḥasā
Wāḥid
Bîr el Jafir
Qezi'ot
Sedē Boqer
At Ṭafīlah
W. Bā'ir
Bîr Madkûr
SHAMÂL SÎNÎ
At Ṭafīlah
Dana
Ismâ'ilîya
Talâta
892▲
Abu Aweigila
-121
AT TAFĪLAH
ISMÂ'ILÎYA
Khamsa
El Murrat
Muweilih
Mizpe Ramon
Nijil
Shawmari
El Buheirat el Murra el Kubra (Great Bitter L.)
Bîr el Mâlḥi
El Quseima
1072
1735
Hanegev (Negev Desert)
Rujm Tal'at al Jamāah
Bîr Hasana
Gineifa
Bîr Beiḍa
El 'Agrûd
N. Puran
PETRA
Wādī Mūsā
MA'ĀN
E G Y P T
Mamarr Mitlā
Bîr el Thamâda
W. el Brûk
El Agrûd
N. Hiyyon
Ma'ān
Al Jafr
Qa'el Jafr
E S S Î N Â' (Sinai)
Bîr Gebeil Ḥisn
N. Ḥavaṭ
El Kuntilla
Yotvata
Bi'r al Mārī
El Suweis (Suez)
Bûr Taufîq
Adabiya
Uyûn Mûsa
948▲ G. el Kabrît
Nakhl
W. el Ruag
Ra's an Naqb
Mahattat ash Shidīyah
Ain Sudr
'En 'Avrona
Bi'r al Qaṭṭār
Rās Sudr
W. el Aqaba
W. al Jirāfi
Bi'r Abu Muḥammad
Bi'r Buṭayḥāt
SAUDI ARABIA
Ghubbet el Bûs
1272▲
1592▲
Rum 1754▲
Baṭn al Ghūl
Gebel el Tih
Bîr Abu Shaqa
Rās Maṭarma
Elat
QI
WADI RUM
At Tubayq
EL SUWEIS
Bîr Wuseit
J A N Û B S Î N Î
W. Abu Ga'da
W. Abu el Gurn
Bîr el Biorât
Khalîg el 'Aqaba
Al 'Aqabah
Al Mudawwarah
1165▲
W. el Heisi
Bîr el Ḥeisi
Gulf of Aqaba
Ḥaql

⊐⊐⊐ 1974 Cease Fire Lines

ft   m
9000   3000
6000   2000
4500   1500
3000   1000
1200   400
600   200
0   0
100   300
200   600
500   1500
1000   3000
2000   6000
m   ft

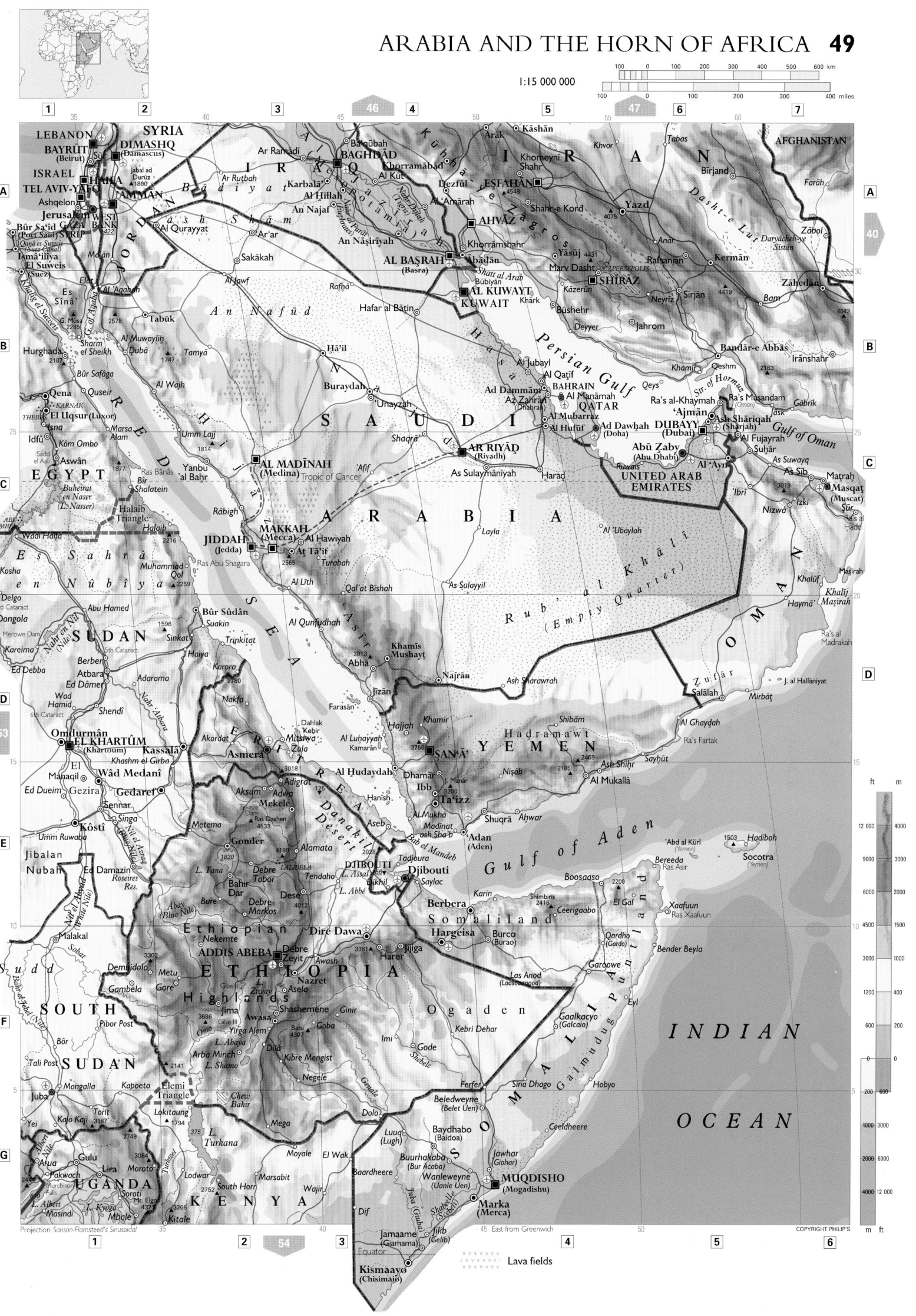

1:15 000 000

1:42 000 000

Projection: Azimuthal Equidistant

COPYRIGHT PHILIP'S

ATLANTIC OCEAN

Europe

British Isles

B. of Biscay

Azores

Iberian Peninsula

Pyrénées

Mont Blanc 4808

Alps

Apennines

Dinaric Alps

Adriatic Sea

Carpathians

Black Sea

Caucasus

Elbrus 5633

Aral Sea

Caspian Sea

Madeira

Str. of Gibraltar

6578

Corsica

Sardinia

Balearic Is.

Sicily

Malta

Crete

Cyprus

5121

Asia

Bon

Mediterranean Sea

Levant

Mesopotamia

Tigris

Euphrates

Syrian Desert

Dead Sea

Canary Is.
Tenerife 3718

C. Juby

Middle Atlas 4165
High Atlas
Toubkal

Maghreb

High Plateaux
Saharan Atlas

Chott Melrhir
Chott Djerid

G. of Gabès
Djerba

Oued Saoura

Moulouya

G. of Sidra

Tripolitania

Cyrenaica

Nile Delta
Suez
Canal
Mt.
Sinai 2285

Egypt

Persian Gulf

C. Bojador

C. Timiris

Ras Nouâdhibou

Adrar 485

El Djouf

S

Erg Iguidi

Erg Chech

Great Western Erg

Great Eastern Erg

Tasili Plateau

Hoggar 2918

a

598
Adrar
des Iforas

Aïr 2022

Ténéré

h

Bilma

Tibesti 3415

a

Al Kufrah

Libyan Desert

El Khârga

Nile

Eastern Desert

L. Nasser

1893

r

Nubian Desert

Nubia

Ras Banâs

Red Sea

Dahlak Is.

Ras Dashen 4533

-125

3350

Cape Verde Is.
2829

C. Vert

Senegal

Senegambia

Gambia

Bijagos Is.

Fouta Djallon

Niger

Bani

White Volta

Black Volta

L. Faguibine

El Mreyye

L. Débo

S

a

h

e

l

Hadejia

L. Chad

Bahr el Ghazal

Chari

Wadai

Dârfûr 3088

1310

Kordofan

White Nile

Blue Nile

Atbara

Sobat

Ethiopian Highlands

4307

L. Tana

Barîm

Bab el Mandeb

G. of Aden

Ras Asir

Ras Hafun

Somali Peninsula

Ogaden

Shabelle

Juba

L. Abbe

-156

1752

Kainji Res.
1780

G

u

i

n

e

a

Niger

Benue

Adamawa Highlands

Mt. Cameroon 4070

Bioko 3008

Bight of Benin

Bight of Bonny

Niger Delta

Oshun

Bahr Aouk

1330

Dar Banda

Bomu

Uele

Bahr el Arab

Sudd

Jur

Bahr el Ghazâl

Bahr el Jebel

Sherbro I.

Grain Coast

Ivory Coast

Gold Coast

Slave Coast

L. de Kossou

L. Volta

C. Palmas

C. Three Points

Gulf of Guinea

São Tomé

C. Lopez

I. de Principe

Annobón

Ogooué

Equator

Congo

L. Mai-Ndombe

Kasai

Sankuru

Lomami

Congo

Congo

Basin

Chutes
Boyoma

L. Albert
Ruwenzori
5109

L. Edward

L. Kivu

L. Kyoga
4321

Mt. Elgon

L. Turkana

Lach Dera

1134

L. Victoria

Mt. Kenya
5199

Kilimanjaro 5895
Meru 4564

Pemba I.

Zanzibar I.

Pangani

Seychelle

INDIAN

OCEAN

Aldabra Is.

Comoros

Mayotte

C. Delgado

C. d'Ambre

Ascension I.

Palmeirinhas Pt.

Cuanza

Cuango

Kwango

Katanga

L. Mweru

L. Tanganyika

Mitumba Mts.

Luvua

Luapula

L. Rukwa

Rungwe 2961

Great Ruaha

L. Bangweulu

L. Malawi
(L. Nyasa)

Ruvuma

Lúrio

2361

Mangoky 2643

Madagascar

Mauritius 3070

Réunion

2658

C. Ste. Marie

St. Helena

2619

Bié Plateau

Cunene

Kafue

Luangwa

L. Cabora Bassa

Shire

L. Kariba

Zambezi

Cuanza

Cuando

Chobe

Cubango

Victoria Falls

2593

Mozambique Channel

C. Fria

Etosha Pan

Okavango Delta

Makgadikgadi Salt Pans

Limpopo

ATLANTIC

OCEAN

Tristan da Cunha

Tropic of Capricorn

Namib Desert

Skeleton Coast

Walvis Bay

2483

Nossob

Kalahari

Vaal

Orange

High Veld

Thabana Ntlenyana 3482

Maputo Bay

Drakensberg

St. Helena Bay

Great Nwveveldberge

Compass Mt. 2502

Karoo

Swartberge

Orange

Algoa B.

C. of Good Hope

C. Agulhas

West from Greenwich

East from Greenwich

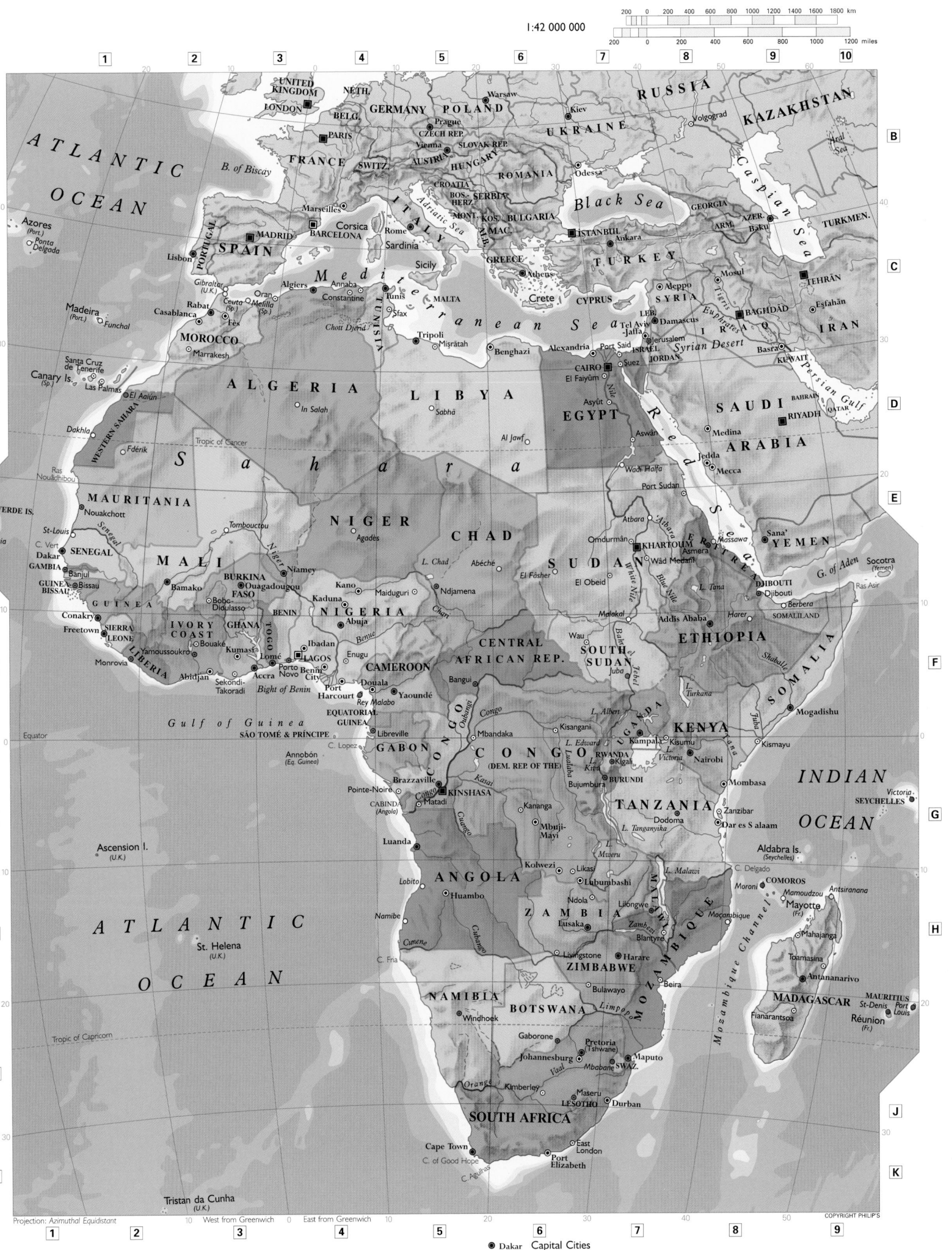

1:42 000 000

Political : AFRICA

ATLANTIC OCEAN

Azores (Port.)
Ponta Delgada

Madeira (Port.)
Funchal

Canary Is. (Sp.)
Santa Cruz de Tenerife
Las Palmas

VERDE IS.

St-Louis
C. Vert
Dakar
SENEGAL
GAMBIA
Banjul
GUINEA-BISSAU
Bissau
Conakry
Freetown
SIERRA LEONE
Monrovia
LIBERIA

UNITED KINGDOM
LONDON
NETH.
BELG.
PARIS
FRANCE
B. of Biscay
Marseilles
PORTUGAL
Lisbon
MADRID
SPAIN
BARCELONA
Corsica
Gibraltar (U.K.)
Oran
Algiers
Ceuta (Sp.)
Melilla (Sp.)
Rabat
Casablanca
Fès
MOROCCO
Marrakesh
Ras Nouâdhibou
El Aaiún
WESTERN SAHARA
Dakhla
Fdérik

GERMANY POLAND
Warsaw
Prague
CZECH REP.
Vienna
SLOVAK REP.
SWITZ. AUSTRIA HUNGARY
ROMANIA
CROATIA
BOS.-HERZ.
SERBIA
MONT. KOS.
ITALY
Rome
Sardinia
Sicily
MALTA
Tunis
TUNISIA
Annaba
Constantine
Sfax
Tripoli
Mişrātah
Benghazi

RUSSIA
Kiev
UKRAINE
Volgograd
Odessa
Black Sea
GEORGIA
ISTANBUL
Ankara
TURKEY
GREECE
Athens
Crete
CYPRUS
LEB.
Aleppo
SYRIA
Damascus
Tel Aviv-Jaffa
ISRAEL
Jerusalem
JORDAN

KAZAKHSTAN
Aral Sea
ARM. AZER.
Baku
TURKMEN.
Caspian Sea
Mosul
Tigris
BAGHDĀD
Eşfahān
IRAQ
Euphrates
Basra
KUWAIT
Persian Gulf
BAHRAIN
QATAR
RIYADH
SAUDI ARABIA
Medina
Mecca
Jedda

TEHRĀN
IRAN

Mediterranean Sea

ALGERIA
LIBYA
EGYPT
In Salah
Sabhā
Al Jawf
Alexandria
Port Said
CAIRO
Suez
El Faiyûm
Asyût
Aswân
Wadi Halfa
Port Sudan
Nile

Sahara

Tropic of Cancer

MAURITANIA
Nouakchott
Tombouctou
NIGER
Agadès
L. Chad
CHAD
Abéché
Ndjamena
El Fâsher
El Obeid
Omdurmán
KHARTOUM
Wād Medani
Atbara
Red Sea
ERITREA
Asmara
Massawa
YEMEN
Sana'
G. of Aden
Socotra (Yemen)
Ras Asir

MALI
Senegal
Niger
Bamako
BURKINA
FASO
Ouagadougou
Bobo-Dioulasso
Niamey
Kano
Kaduna
NIGERIA
Abuja
Maiduguri
BENIN
TOGO
GHANA
Kumasi
Bouaké
IVORY COAST
Yamoussoukro
Abidjan
Sekondi-Takoradi
Accra
Lomé
Porto Novo
Benin City
Ibadan
LAGOS
Enugu
Port Harcourt
Bight of Benin
Gulf of Guinea
CAMEROON
Douala
Yaoundé
Rey Malabo
EQUATORIAL GUINEA
SÃO TOMÉ & PRÍNCIPE
Annobón (Eq. Guinea)
C. Lopez
Libreville
GABON
Chari
Benue
Bangui
CENTRAL AFRICAN REP.
Wau
SUDAN
SOUTH SUDAN
Juba
Malakal
White Nile
Blue Nile
L. Tana
Bahr el Jebel
DJIBOUTI
Djibouti
Berbera
SOMALILAND
Addis Ababa
Harer
ETHIOPIA
Shabelle
SOMALIA
L. Turkana

Equator

Oubangui
Congo
Kisangani
L. Albert
L. Edward
UGANDA
Kampala
L. Victoria
Kisumu
Nairobi
KENYA
Juba
Mogadishu
INDIAN OCEAN
Kismayu
Mombasa

CONGO
Brazzaville
Pointe-Noire
CABINDA (Angola)
KINSHASA
Matadi
Congo
CONGO (DEM. REP. OF THE)
Mbandaka
Kananga
Mbuji-Mayi
Kasai
RWANDA
Kigali
BURUNDI
Bujumbura
L. Kivu
L. Tanganyika
TANZANIA
Dodoma
Zanzibar
Dar es Salaam
SEYCHELLES
Victoria

ATLANTIC OCEAN

Ascension I. (U.K.)

St. Helena (U.K.)

Luanda
ANGOLA
Lobito
Huambo
Namibe
C. Fria
Cunene
Cuango
Kasai
Kwanza
Cuanza
Kolwezi
Likasi
Lubumbashi
Ndola
ZAMBIA
Lusaka
L. Mweru
L. Malawi
MALAWI
Lilongwe
Blantyre
Moçambique
COMOROS
Moroni
Mamoudzou
Mayotte (Fr.)
Antsiranana
C. Delgado
Aldabra Is. (Seychelles)

Zambezi
Livingstone
Harare
ZIMBABWE
Bulawayo
Beira
MOZAMBIQUE
Mozambique Channel
Mahajanga
Toamasina
Antananarivo
MADAGASCAR
MAURITIUS
St-Denis
Port Louis
Réunion (Fr.)
Fianarantsoa

NAMIBIA
Windhoek
BOTSWANA
Gaborone
Limpopo
Orange
Vaal
Kimberley
Johannesburg
Pretoria (Tshwane)
Maputo
SWAZ.
Mbabane
Maseru
LESOTHO
Durban
East London
SOUTH AFRICA
Port Elizabeth
Cape Town
C. of Good Hope
C. Agulhas

Tropic of Capricorn

Tristan da Cunha (U.K.)

Projection: Azimuthal Equidistant
West from Greenwich
East from Greenwich

COPYRIGHT PHILIP'S

● Dakar Capital Cities

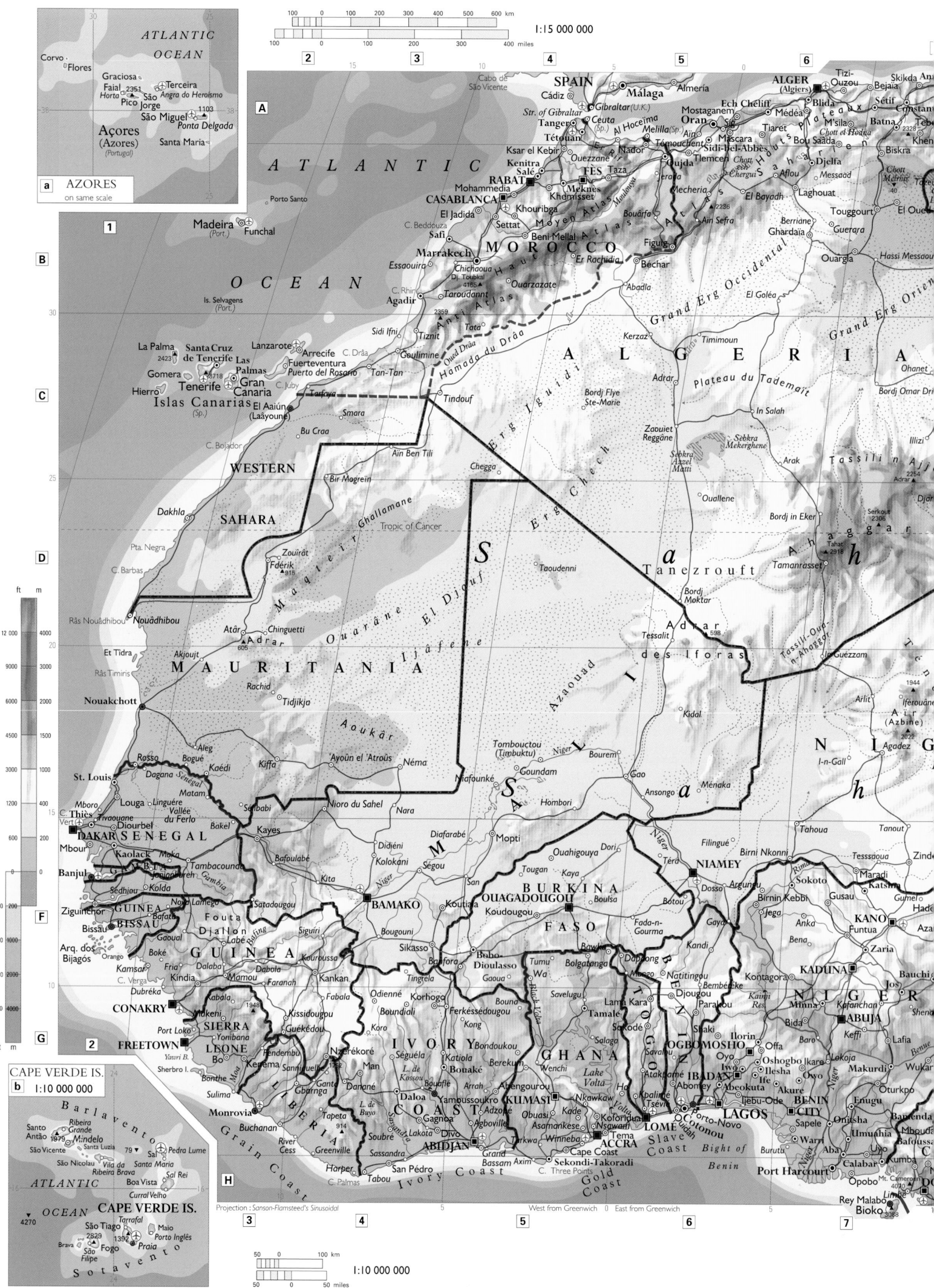

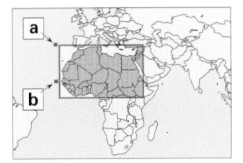

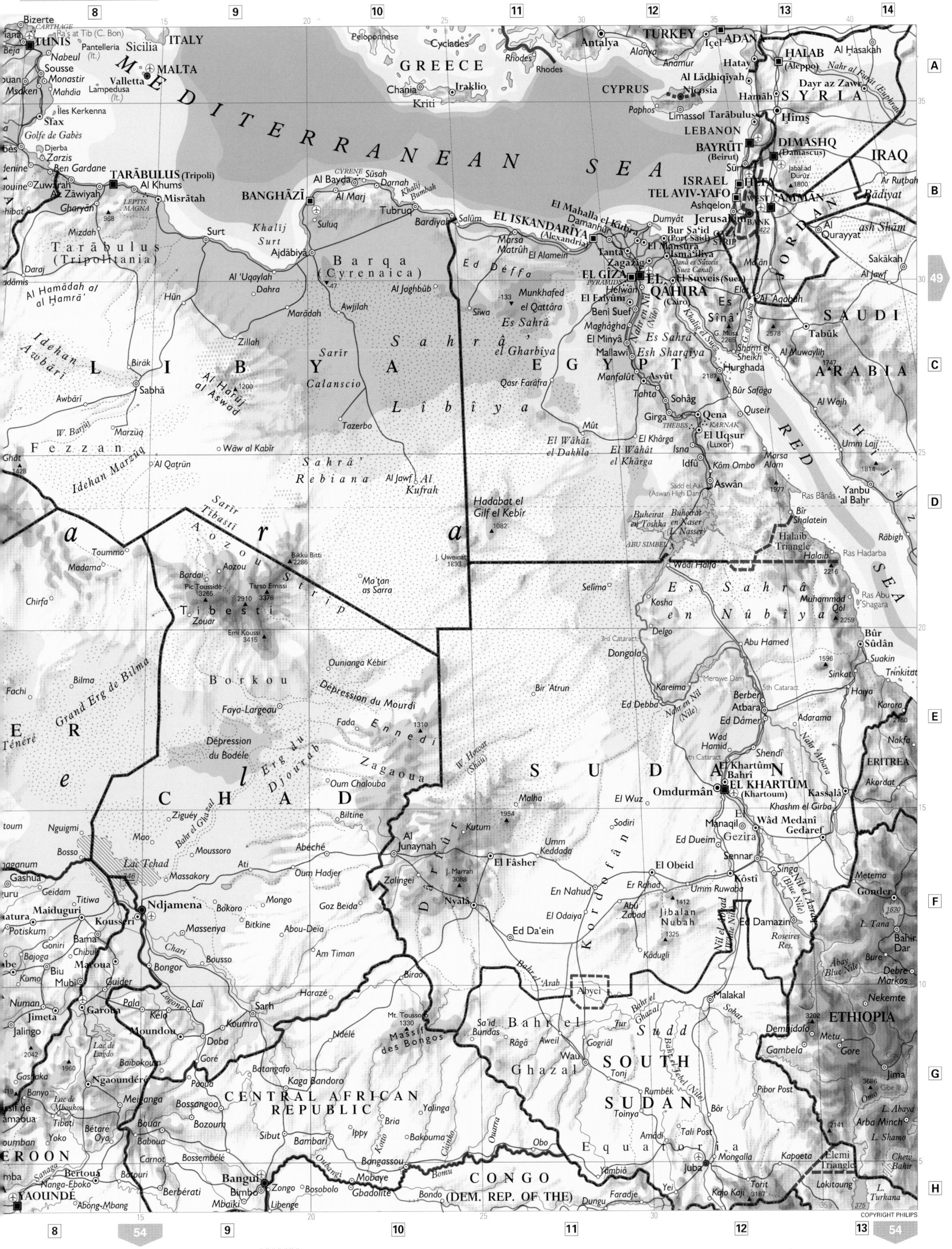

Lava fields

1:15 000 000

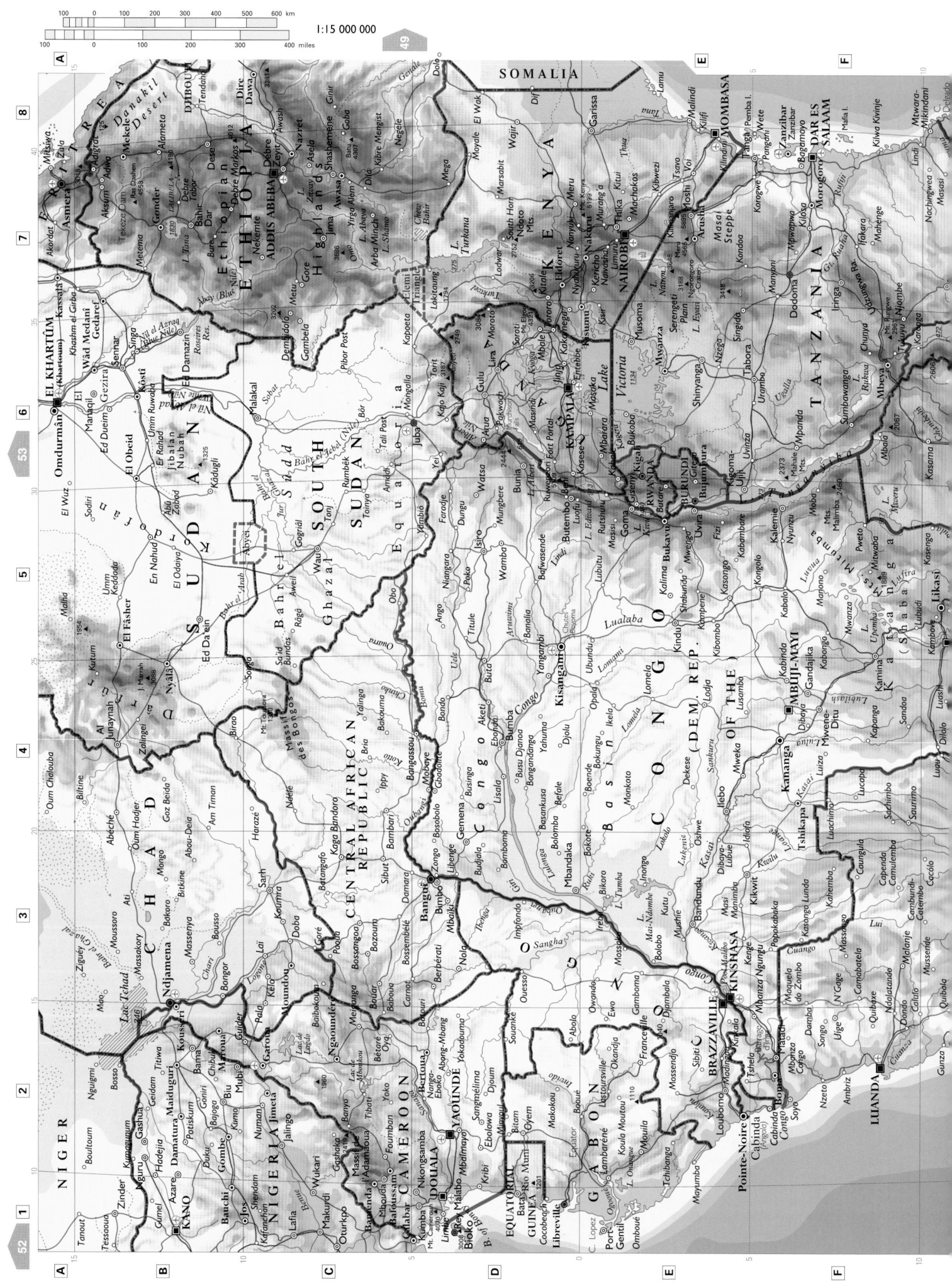

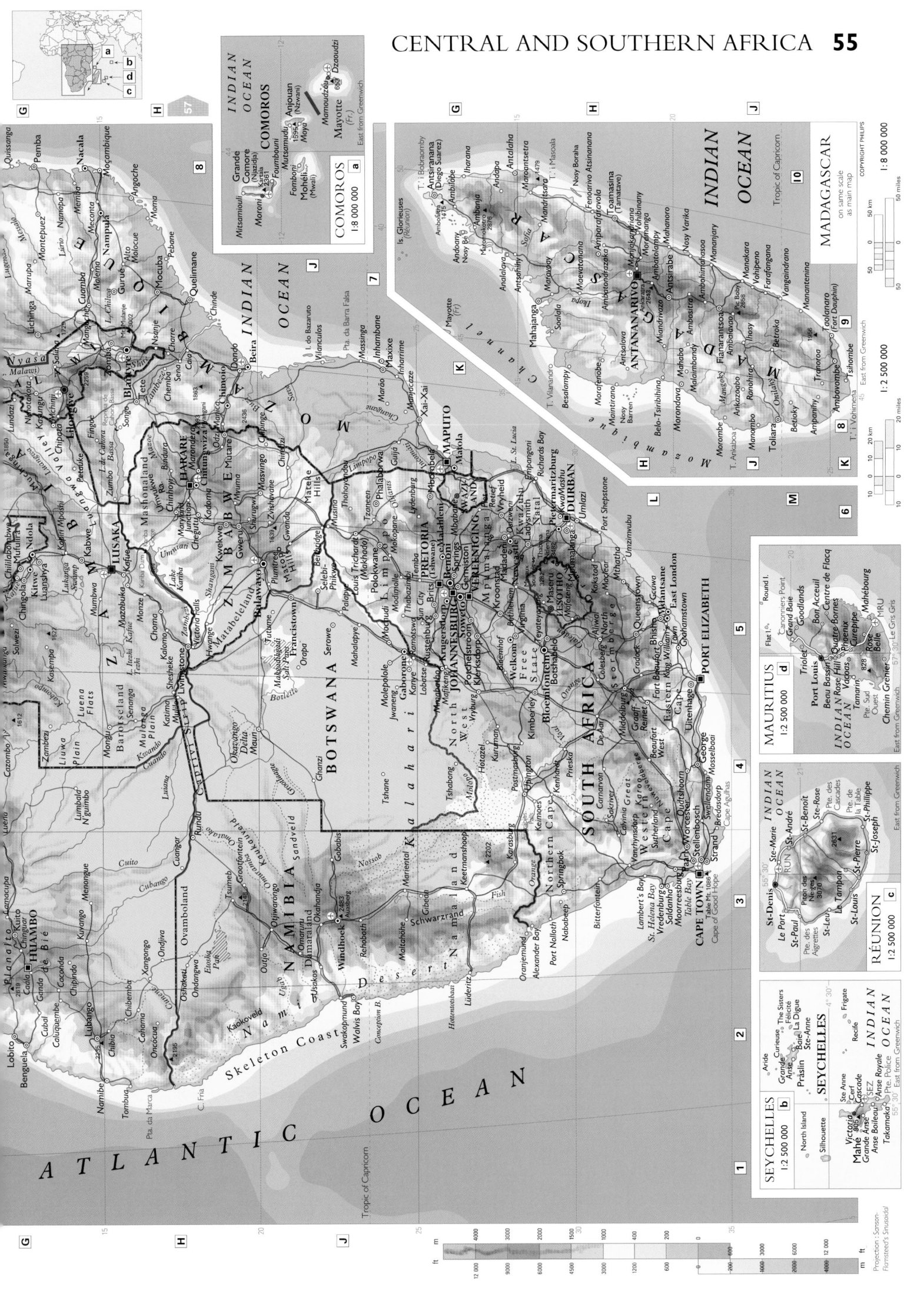

1:8 000 000

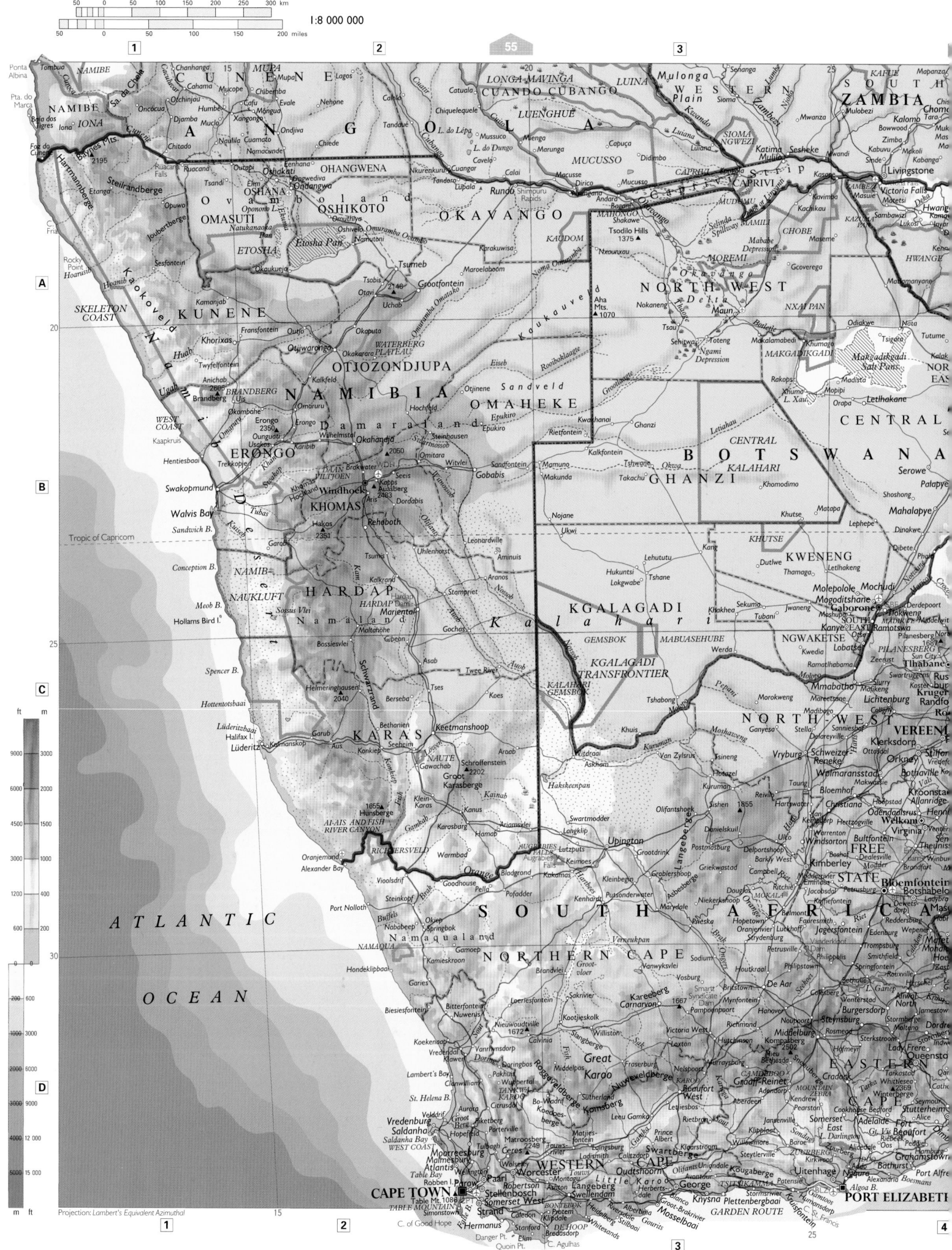

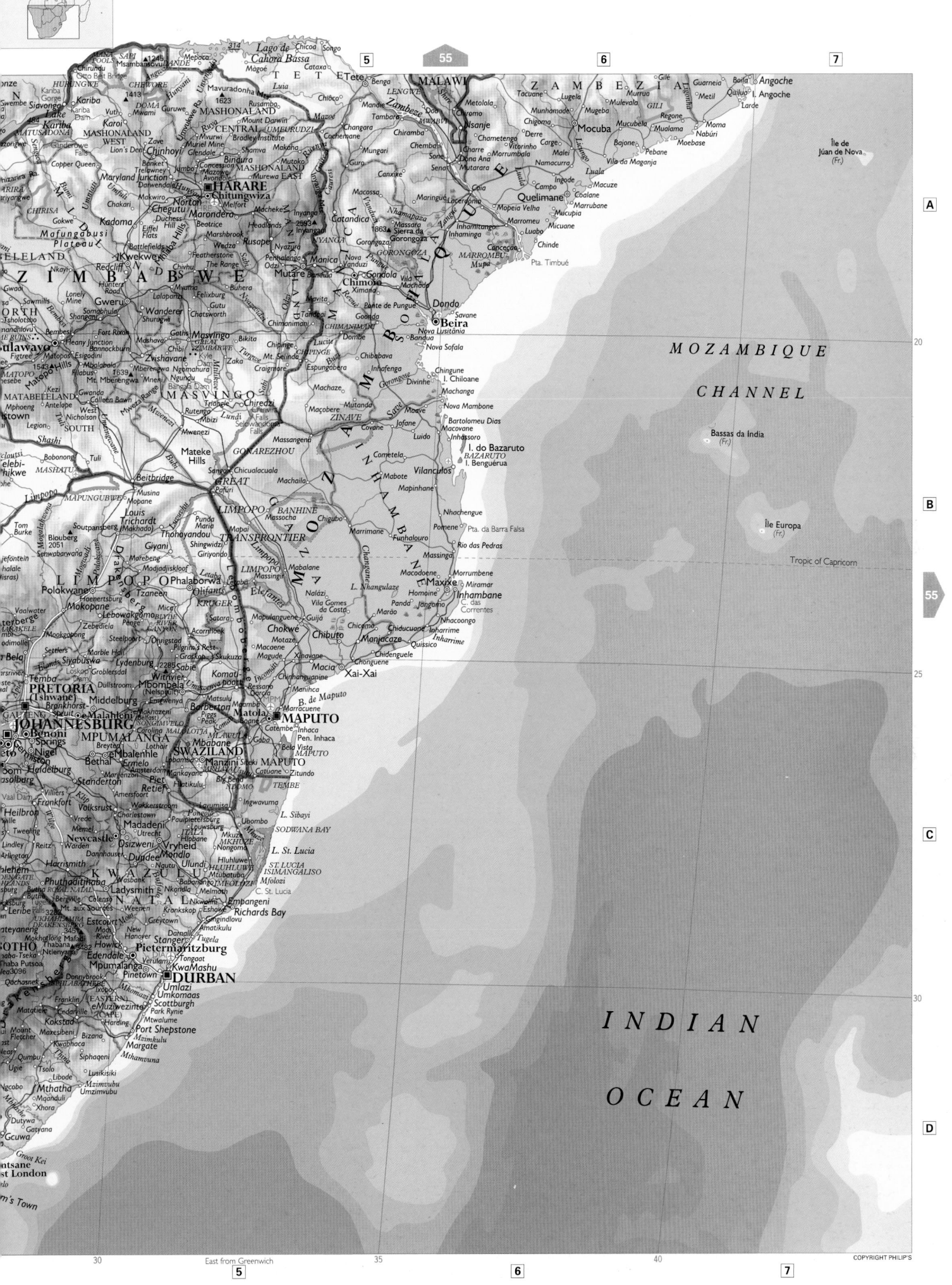

MOZAMBIQUE CHANNEL

Île de Júan de Nova (Fr.)

Bassas da India (Fr.)

Île Europa (Fr.)

Tropic of Capricorn

INDIAN

OCEAN

COPYRIGHT PHILIP'S

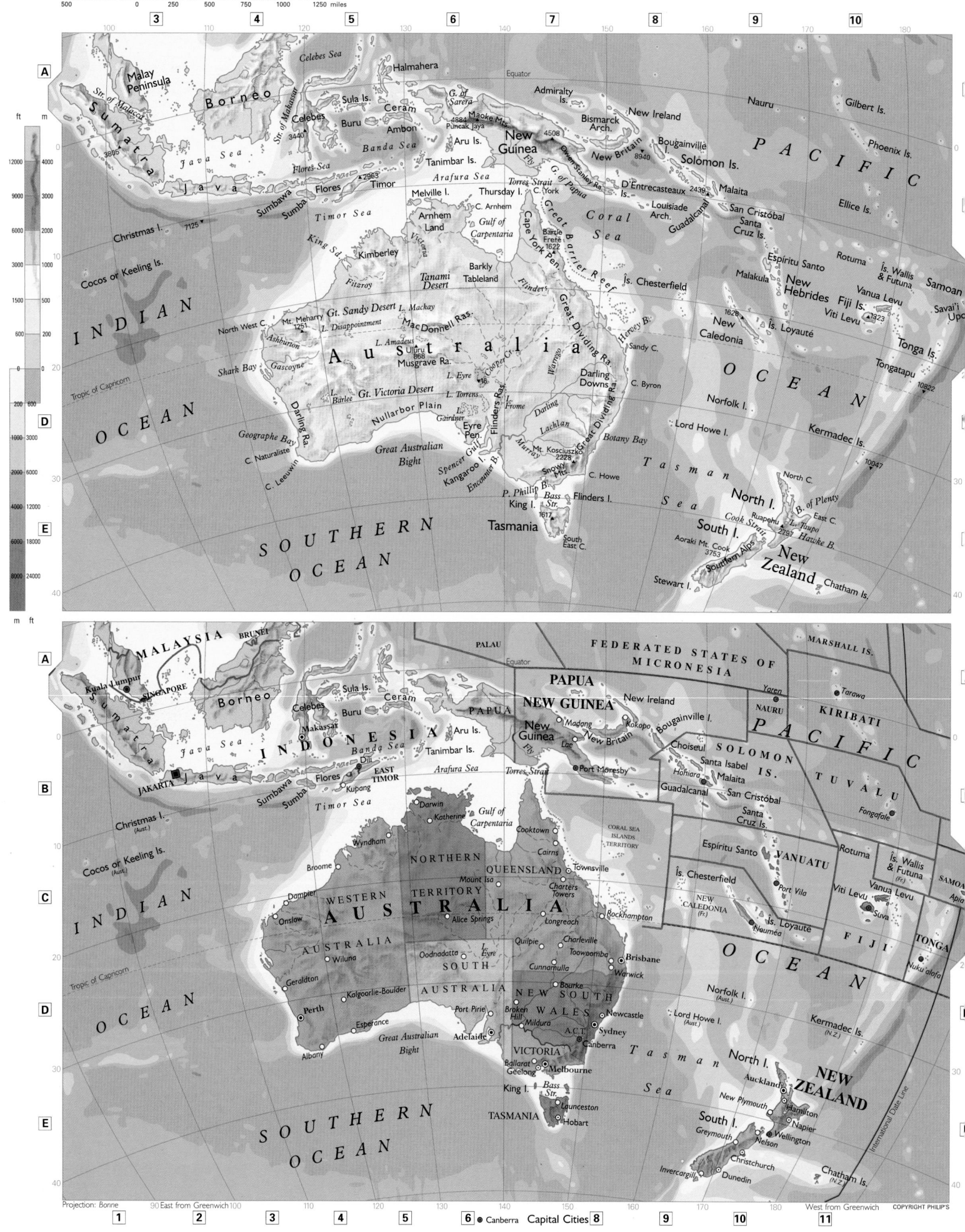

1:6 000 000

50 0 50 100 150 200 km
50 0 50 100 150 miles

64

FIJI a
on same scale

PACIFIC OCEAN

Great Sea Reef
Kia Udu Pt. Ringgold Is.
Yaqaga Labasa Rabi
Yasawa Group Yadua Bua Savusavu Qamea
Naviti Nabouwalu Taveuni Naitaba
Nacula Buca BOUMA
Viwa Naval △1031 Samosamo Vanua Balavu
Waya Tavua Tomanivi △1323 Iawaki Levuka Wayaka Vacata Namenalala Koro Vatu Vara Mago Cicia Tuvuca
Lautoka Mba KOROYANITU Korovou Nairai Vanua Levu Ovalau Nasori Gau Nayau
Nadi Keiyasi Viti Levu Yanuca Batiki Sawaleke Lakeba Passage Tubou Lakeba
Sigatoka Korolevu Beqa Oneata Moce
Vatulele Ono Moala Southern Lau Group Namuka-i-Lau Yagasa Cluster
Kadavu Totoya Kabara Fulaga Levu
Tavuki Vunisea Matuku Ogea Driki Ogea Levu

Vanua Levu Natewa Bay
KORO SEA

PACIFIC OCEAN

SAMOA
Falelima Asau Safune Pu'apu'a
Savai'i △1858 Salelologa Manono Falefa
Taga Satupa'itea Apia Amaile
Falelatai 'Upolu Siumu
OLE PUPU PUE Safata Bay

AMERICAN SAMOA (U.S.A.)
AMERICAN SAMOA Ofu Olosega
Tutuila Pago Pago Ta'u
Leone Vaitogi Aunu'u Manu'a Is. AMERICAN SAMOA
International Date Line

West from Greenwich

SAMOAN ISLANDS b
on same scale

TONGA c
on same scale

PACIFIC OCEAN

Fonualei Toku
Vava'u Neiafu
Late Vava'u Group
Home Reef
Disney Reef
Ofolanga Ha'ano
Tofua Kao Foa Ha'apai
Lifuka Group
Kotu Group Uiha
Fonuafo'ou Nomuka Oto Tolu Group
Nomuka Group Mango Tonumea
Hunga Ha'apai

TONGA
Nuku'alofa Tongatapu
Tongatapu Group Eua

West from Greenwich

PACIFIC OCEAN

TASMAN SEA

North Island

C. Reinga North C.
C. Maria van Diemen Rangaunu B. Doubtless B.
Houhora Heads Kaitaia Mangonui Mangaroa Harb.
Ahipara B. Okaihau Waitangi B. of Islands
Tauroa Pt. Rawene C. Brett
Hokianga Harbour Kaikohe Opua
Waipoua Forest Kawakawa Hikurangi
Dargaville Whangarei
Whangarei Harb. Bream Hd. Bream B.
Waipu Little Barrier I.
Warkworth Great Barrier I.
Kaipara Harbour C. Rodney
Helensville C. Colville Cuvier I.
Hauraki Gulf Coromandel Whitianga
Takapuna Whangamata
AUCKLAND Mayor I.
Manukau Papakura Thames Whangamata Tauranga Harb.
Waiuku Pukekohe Waihi Mount Maunganui
Waikato Mercer Paeroa Te Aroha Tauranga Whakaari (White I.) Runaway
Huntly Morrinsville Te Puke Bay of Plenty East C.
Hamilton Cambridge Whakatane Opotiki Raukumara Ra. Hikurangi △1753
Raglan Te Awamutu Rotorua Kawerau Waipiro
Kawhia Harbour Tirau L. Tarawera Te Kaha Motu Tolaga Bay
Putaruru Rotorua Waikaremoana UREWERA Ormond
Otorohanga Tokoroa Murupara Gisborne
Te Kuiti Kinleith Poverty Bay
Waitomo Caves Mokai Wairakei Nuhaka Waikokopu
North Taranaki Bight Mokau Taupo Wairoa Mahia Pen.
New Plymouth WHANGANUI Turangi Tarawera Mahia Pen.
Inglewood Whangamomona Kaimanawa Mts. Bay View
Waitara Ongarue Taumarunui Ruapehu △2797 Hawke Bay
Mt. Taranaki or Mt. Egmont △2518 TONGARIRO Napier
Stratford Ohakune Waiouru Hastings
Opunake EGMONT Raetihi C. Kidnappers
Kapuni Eltham Waipawa
Hawera Waverley Taihape Waipukurau
South Taranaki Bight Mangaweka Waipawa
Patea Wanganui Hunterville Dannevirke
Marton Halcombe Woodville
Bulls Feilding Pahiatua
Palmerston North Pahiatua
Foxton Shannon Eketahuna
Levin C. Turnagain
Paraparaumu Otaki Masterton
Kapiti I. Carterton
Upper Hutt Martinborough
Petone Featherston Wairarapa
Lower Hutt Greytown
Wellington
Cook Strait

PACIFIC OCEAN

South Island

C. Farewell
Golden B. D'Urville I.
Collingwood ABEL TASMAN Tasman B.
Takaka Tasman Pelorus
KAHURANGI Motueka Picton
Karamea Tasman Mts. Havelock Blenheim
Karamea Bight Nelson Richmond Seddon
Seddonville Wakefield Ward
Granity NELSON LAKES Clarence
Westport Lyell Murchison L. Rotoiti Kaikoura
Inangahua Reefton Tapuae-o-Uenuku △2885
PAPAROA Spenser Mts. △2337
Punakaiki Blackball Hanmer Springs
Runanga Grey Waiau
Greymouth Stillwater Culverden
Kumara L. Brunner Amberley
Hokitika Jacksons ARTHUR'S PASS Oxford Pegasus Bay
Ross Arthur's Pass Waikari Rangiora New Brighton
Whitcliffs Springfield Kaiapoi Christchurch
Abut Hd. Methven Darfield Riccarton Lyttelton
WESTLAND Aoraki/Mt. Cook △3753 Staveley Lincoln Banks Pen.
Jackson B. Haast MT. COOK Rakaia Southbridge Akaroa
Okuru Tekapo Canterbury Plains Little River
MOUNT ASPIRING L. Pukaki Ashburton Ashburton Bight
Mt. Aspiring △3033 Ohau Fairlie Rangitata
Earnslaw △2819 Wanaka Temuka Canterbury Bight
Milford Sd. △M416 Timaru
Sutherland Falls Arrowtown St. Andrews
Bligh Sound Wanaka Waimate
George Sound Queenstown Cromwell Oamaru
Secretary I. Te Anau Wakatipu Clyde Maheno
Doubtful Sd. L. Te Anau Alexandra Hampden
FIORDLAND Kingston Roxburgh Palmerston
Resolution I. Manapouri Waikouaiti
Breaksea Sd. Mossburn Lawrence Port Chalmers
Dusky Sd. Lumsden Kelso Otago Harbour
Chalky Inlet Clifden Edievale Clinton Dunedin
Preservation Inlet Tuatapere Nightcaps Gore Milton
Te Waewae B. Orepuki Winton Mataura Balclutha
Riverton Wyndham Kaitangata Nugget Pt.
Invercargill Edendale Owaka
South Invercargill Tahakopa
Bluff Ruapuke I.
Solander I. Foveaux Str.
Halfmoon Bay
Stewart I. (Rakiura) RAKIURA
Port Pegasus South West C.

Southern Alps (Tiritiri o te Moana)
Westland Bight

Projection: Conical with two standard parallels
East from Greenwich

TAHITI & MOOREA
1:1 000 000

Pte. Aroa
Papetoai Paopao B. de Matavai Pte. Vénus
Mt. Tohiea △1207 Arue Mahina
Moorea (France) Afareaitu Papeete Pirae Papenoo
Haapiti Pte. Nuupere Faaa Tiarei
Punaauia Mt. Aorai △2060 Mt. Orohena △2241 Hitiaa
Paea Mt. Tetufera △1799 Lac Vaihiria Faaone Afaahiti
PACIFIC OCEAN Maraa Papara Taravao Isthme de Taravao
Atimaono Mataiea Afaahiti Pte. Tatatua
Vairao Pueu Tautira
Mt. Rooniu △1332
Teahupoo
Presqu'île de Taiarapu
West from Greenwich

COPYRIGHT PHILIP'S

10 0 10 km
10 0 10 miles
1:1 000 000

ft m
9000 3000
6000 2000
3000 1000
1200 400
600 200
0 0
200 600
2000 6000
4000 12 000
6000 18 000
m ft

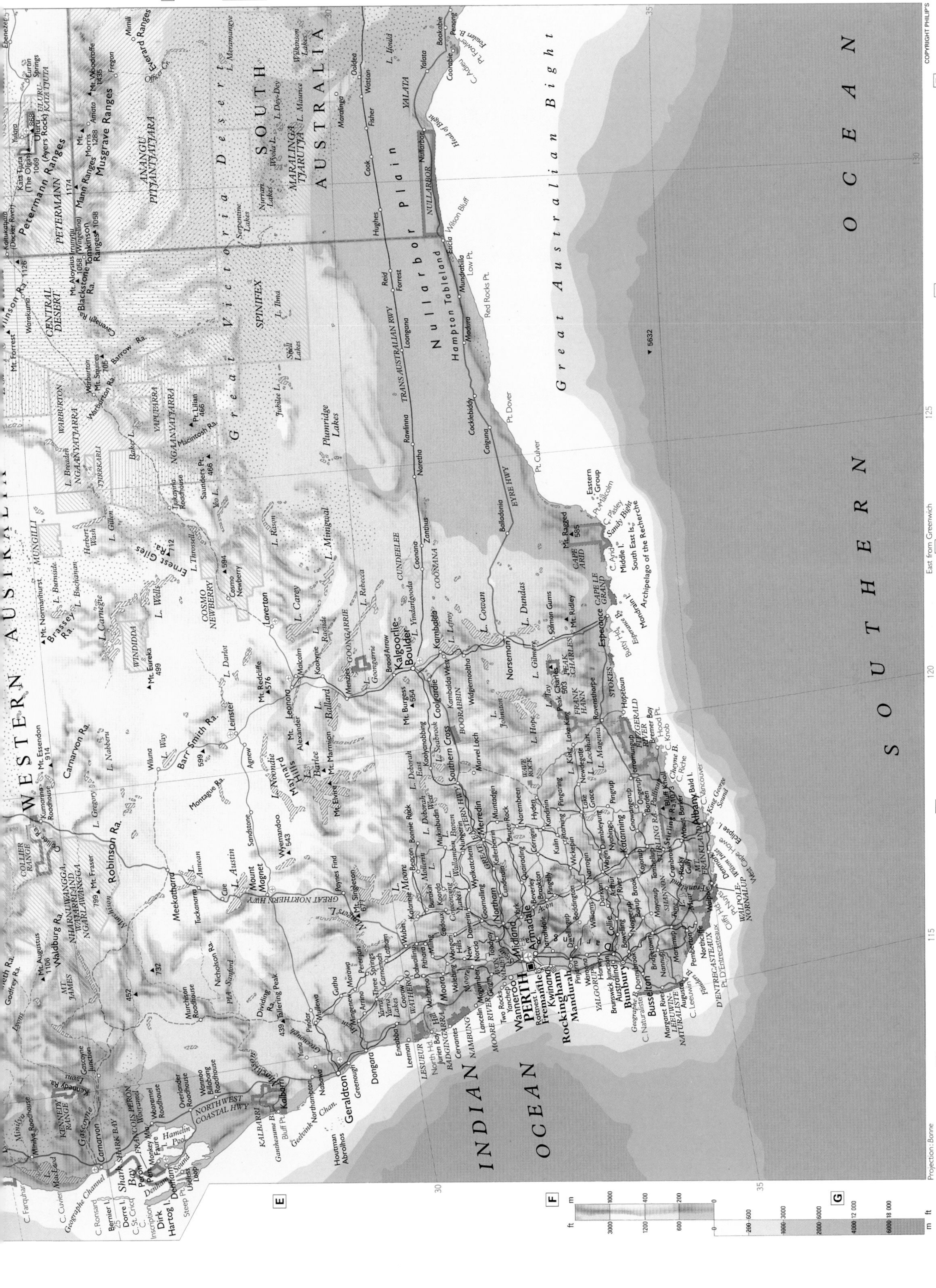

E · 63 · F · G · 5 · 4 · 3 · 2 · 1

COPYRIGHT PHILIP'S

Projection: Bonne

East from Greenwich

Aboriginal lands

1. NGALIWURRU / NUNGALI
2. WINIMYN
3. WAMBARDI
4. LIIALALITUMA
5. RODNA
6. NTJIRLA
7. ROULPMAULPMA
8. URUNA

Map labels

WESTERN AUSTRALIA

SOUTH AUSTRALIA

INDIAN OCEAN

SOUTHERN OCEAN

Great Australian Bight

Nullarbor Plain

Hampton Tableland

Great Victoria Desert

SPINIFEX

CENTRAL DESERT

WARBURTON

COLLIER RANGE

KENNEDY RANGE

Carnarvon Ra.

Robinson Ra.

Barr Smith Ra.

Musgrave Ranges

Mann Ranges

Petermann Ranges

ANANGU PITJANTJATJARA

MARALINGA TJARUTJA

YALATA

NGAANYATJARRA

YAPURARRA

MUNGILLI

WINDIDDA

COSMO NEWBERRY

NHARNUWANGGA WAJARRI NGARLAWANGGA

MT JAMES

PERTH
Fremantle
Rockingham
Mandurah
Midland
Armadale

Geraldton
Dongara
Kalbarri
Carnarvon
Shark Bay

Kalgoorlie-Boulder
Coolgardie
Norseman
Esperance
Albany

Kats Tjuta (The Olgas) 1069
Uluru (Ayers Rock) 863
ULURU · KATA TJUTA

Mt Woodroffe 1435

Mt Aloysius 1125
Mt Squires 705
Mt Fraser 799

Mt Redcliffe 576
Mt Leonora
Wiluna
Leinster
Laverton

TRANS-AUSTRALIAN RWY
GREAT NORTHERN HWY
NORTHWEST COASTAL HWY
EYRE HWY
Nullarbor

Mt Ragged 585
CAPE ARID
CAPE LE GRAND
Archipelago of the Recherche

▼5632

Elevation scale

ft / m

18 000 / 6000
12 000 / 4000
6000 / 2000
3000 / 1200
1000 / 400
600 / 200
0

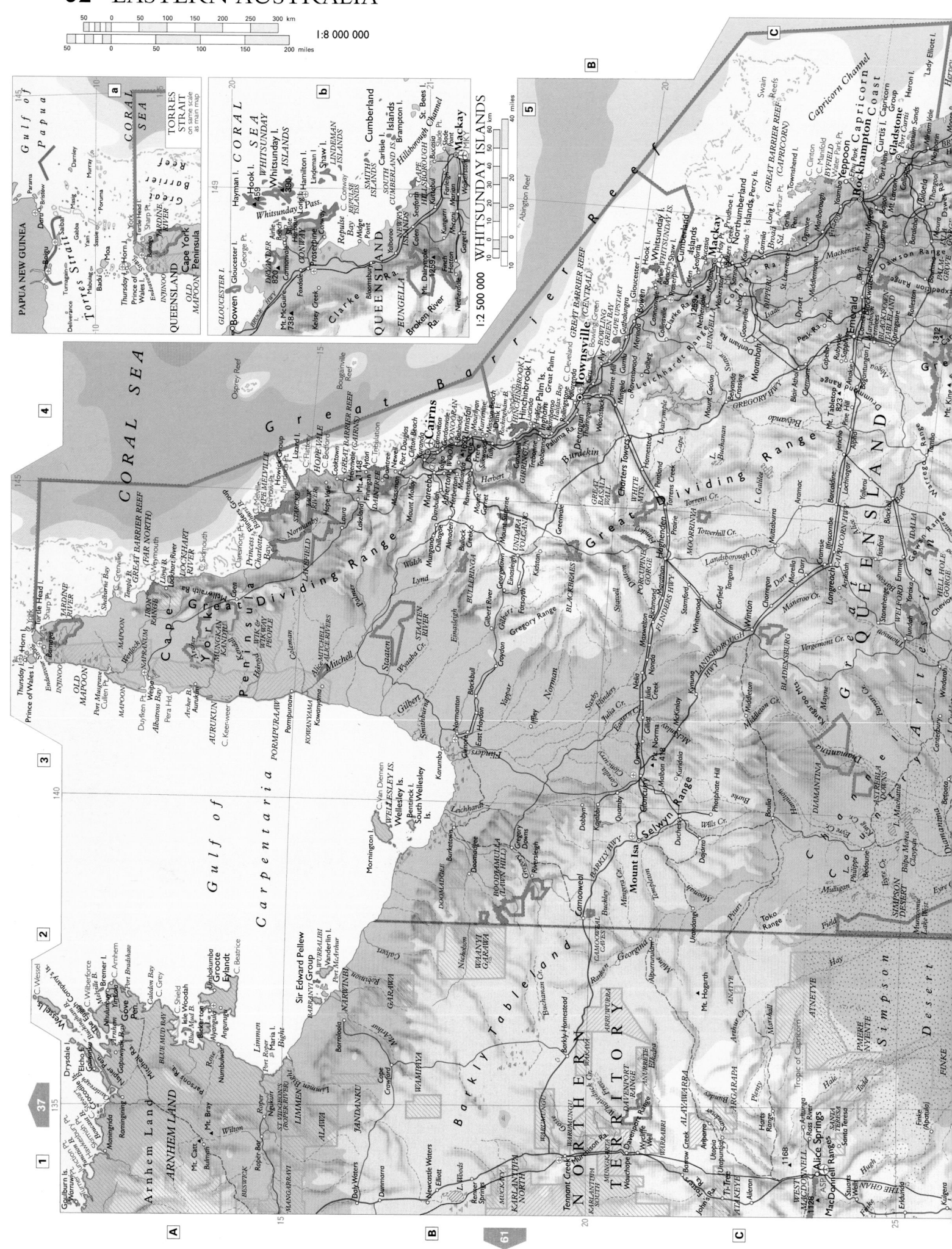

1:8 000 000

TORRES STRAIT
on same scale
as main map

WHITSUNDAY ISLANDS

1:2 500 000

TASMAN

SEA

SOUTH AUSTRALIA

NEW SOUTH WALES

BRISBANE
Gold Coast
Sunshine Coast
Coral Coast
Toowoomba
Warwick

Coffs Harbour
Port Macquarie
Taree
Newcastle
SYDNEY
Wollongong
Canberra
Nowra
Shellharbour
Kiama

Broken Hill

Dubbo
Orange
Bathurst
Parkes
Wagga Wagga
Griffith

ADELAIDE
Port Augusta
Whyalla
Port Pirie
Port Lincoln

MELBOURNE
Geelong
Ballarat
Warrnambool
Mount Gambier

Bass Strait

King Island
(Tasmania)

Flinders Island
Furneaux
Group
Cape Barren I.

Aboriginal lands

East from Greenwich

on same scale

TASMANIA

Launceston

Hobart

Bass Strait
King Island
Furneaux
Group
Flinders Island
Cape Barren I.

Projection: Bonne

RUSSIA

Yekaterinburg
Tomsk
Moskva
Novosibirsk
Irkutsk
Chita
Oz. Baykal
Ob
Lena
Volga

Okhotsk
Sea of Okhotsk

Poluostrov Kamchatka
Shirshov Ridge
Bering Basin
Komandorskiye Ostrova (Russia)
Petropavlovsk-Kamchatskiy
Near Is. (U.S.A.)
Andreanof (U.S.A.)
Aleutian Is.
Bert Sea

KAZAKHSTAN
Astana (Aqmola)
Semey
Almaty
Toshkent
Aral Sea
Balqash Köl
Altay
KYRGYZSTAN
Ürümqi
Ulaanbaatar
MONGOLIA
Blagoveshchensk
Amur
Khabarovsk
Sakhalin
La Perouse Str.
Kuril'skiye Ostrova
Kuril-Kamchatka Trench
7822
Aleutia
Aleutian Trench

Sapporo
Changchun
Shenyang
Vladivostok
Hakodate
Sea of Japan
NORTH KOREA
Harbin
7,542
Northwest
Emperor Trough
Emperor Seamount Chain
Chinook Trough

Beijing
Tianjin
Taiyuan
Huang He
Dalian
Qingdao
SOUTH KOREA
Seoul
Nagoya
Kyoto
Sendai
Tōkyō
Yokohama
Osaka
JAPAN
Shikoku
Kyūshū
Fuji-San 3776
Shatsky Rise
Pacific
Basin
Midway Is. (U.S.A.)
Howland

CHINA
Kabul
Srinagar
AFGHANISTAN
PAKISTAN
Lahore
Delhi
Kanpur
Kunlun Shan
XIZANG
Himalaya
Lanzhou
Xi'an
Nanjing
Chongqing
Wuhan
Hangzhou
Changsha
Chang
Lhasa
Everest 8850
NEPAL
Brahmaputra
Ganga
Shanghai
East China Sea
10,554
Japan Trench
Okinawa
Ryūkyū-retto (Japan)
Ogasawara Gunto (Japan)
Minami-Tori-Shima (Japan)
Lisianski I. (U.S.A.)

Kolkata (Calcutta)
Dhaka
BANGLADESH
Mandalay
BURMA
Kunming
Fuzhou
Guangzhou
Hong Kong
Macau
Taipei
TAIWAN
Iwo-Jima (Japan)
Kazan-Retto (Japan)
Wake I. (U.S.A.)
Mid-Pacific Mou

INDIA
Hyderabad
Chennai (Madras)
Hanoi
Hainan
LAOS
Irrawaddy
Salween
Mekong
Luzon
C. Engano
Paracel Is.
Philippine Sea
West Mariana Basin
NORTHERN MARIANAS (U.S.A.)
Tinian
Saipan
East Mariana Basin
MARSHALL IS.
Enewetak Atoll
Bikini Atoll
Kwajalein
P
A

Rangoon
Bay of Bengal
THAILAND
Bangkok
Mindoro
Manila
PHILIPPINES
Samar
Palawan
Philippine Basin
GUAM (U.S.A.)
Challenger 11,022 Deep
Mariana Trench
10,497
Yap
Caroline Is.
Micronesia
Majuro
Jaluit I.
Central Pacific

SRI LANKA
Colombo
Nicobar Is. (India)
Andaman Is. (India)
CAMBODIA
Phnom Penh
Thanh Pho Ho Chi Minh
South China Sea
G. of Thailand
Sulu Sea
Mindanao
Davao
Mindanao Trench
Melekeok
FED. STATES OF MICRONESIA
PALAU
Chuuk
Pohnpei
Palikir
Butaritari
Howland I. (U.S.A.)
Baker I. (U.S.)

MALAYSIA
Celebes Sea
4101
SABAH
BRUNEI
SARAWAK
Kuala Lumpur
Singapore
PEN. MALAYSIA
Sumatera
Palembang
Borneo
Sulawesi
Halmahera
Buru
Seram
West Caroline Basin
Eauripik Rise
Yap
East Caroline Basin
Solomon Rise
Melanesian Basin
Tarawa
Yaren
Banaba
Gilbert Is.
Nauru
Phoenix Is.
Abariringa
Enderbury
O

Sunda Ridge
Jakarta
Jawa
Surabaya
Bali
INDONESIA
Makassar
Java Sea
Flores Sea
Banda Sea
7440
Flores
Sumbawa
Sumba
Dili
EAST TIMOR
Timor
Puncak Jaya 4884
PAPUA
New Guinea
Admiralty Is.
Bismarck Arch.
New Ireland
PAPUA NEW GUINEA
Kokopo
New Britain
Bougainville
Lae
8940
SOLOMON IS.
Honiara
Guadalcanal
Santa Cruz I.
9165
Melanesia
Fongafale
TUVALU
Tokelau (N.Z.)
Kiribati

INDIAN
Cocos Is. (Austral.)
Christmas I. (Austral.)
Selat Sunda
Java Trench
North Australian Basin
C. Arnhem
Darwin
Gulf of Carpentaria
Torres Strait
C. York
Port Moresby
Louisiade Arch.
Coral Sea Basin
Rotuma
Îs. Wallis & Futuna (Fr.)
SAMOA
Apia

Wharton Basin
Exmouth Plateau
North West C.
Broome
Cairns
Townsville
Coral Sea
Great Barrier Reef
Îs. Chesterfield
VANUATU
Espíritu Santo
Port Vila
NEW CALEDONIA (Fr.)
Nouméa
Vanua Levu
West Fiji Basin
Viti Levu
Suva
FIJI
7570
Nuku'alofa
TONG

OCEAN
Ninetyeast Ridge
Geraldton
Mount Isa
Alice Springs
AUSTRALIA
L. Eyre
Rockhampton
Brisbane
Middleton Basin
Lord Howe I. (Austral.)
Norfolk I. (Austral.)
South Fiji Basin
Kermadec Is. (N.Z.)
Kermadec Trench 10,047

Broken Ridge
Perth Basin
Perth
Naturaliste Plateau
Great Australian Bight
Albany
Murray
Darling
Adelaide
Sydney
Canberra
Mt. Kosciuszko 2228
Lord Howe Rise
New Caledonia Trough
Norfolk Ridge
Tasman Sea
NEW ZEALAND
Auckland
Cook Strait
Wellington

Nouvelle Amsterdam (Fr.)
I. St. Paul (Fr.)
Melbourne
Bass Str.
Tasmania
Hobart
East Tasman Plateau
Aoraki Mt. Cook 3753
Tasman Basin
Christchurch
Chatham Rise
Chatham Is. (N.Z.)

Is. Crozet (Fr.)
Mid-Indian Ridge
SOUTHERN OCEAN
South Tasman Rise
South Tasman Basin
Dunedin
Invercargill
Bounty Trough
Bounty Is. (N.Z.)

Kerguelen (Fr.)
Antipodes Is. (N.Z.)
Campbell (N.Z.)
Auckland Is. (N.Z.)
Campbell Plateau
Macquarie I. (Austral.)
Campbell I. (Austral.)

Heard I. (Austral.)

ft m
12 000 4000
9000 3000
6000 2000
3000 1000
1500 500
600 200
0 0
200 600
1000 3000
2000 6000
4000 12 000
6000 18 000
8000 24 000
m ft

Projection: Mollweide's Homolographic   East from Greenwich

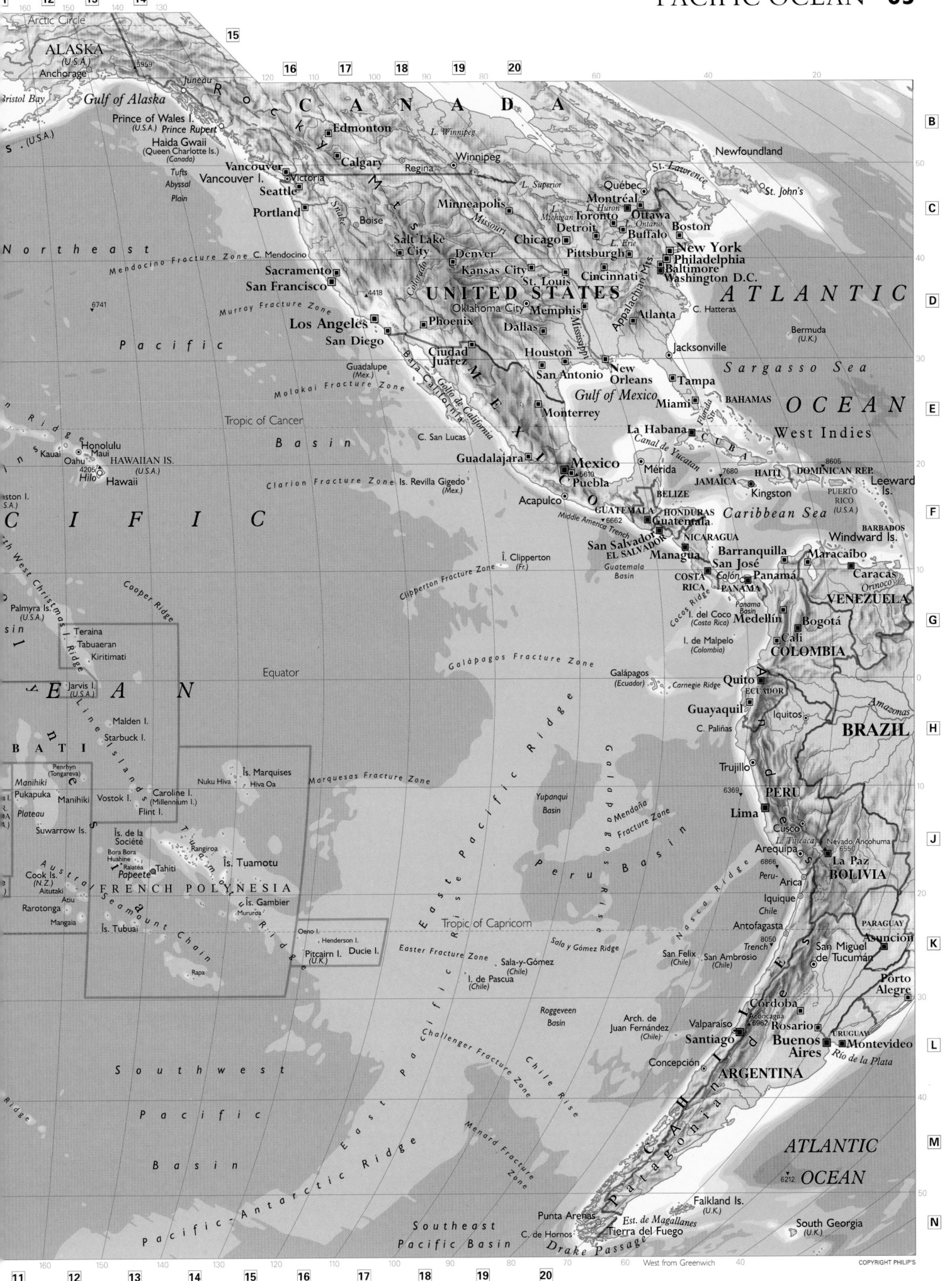

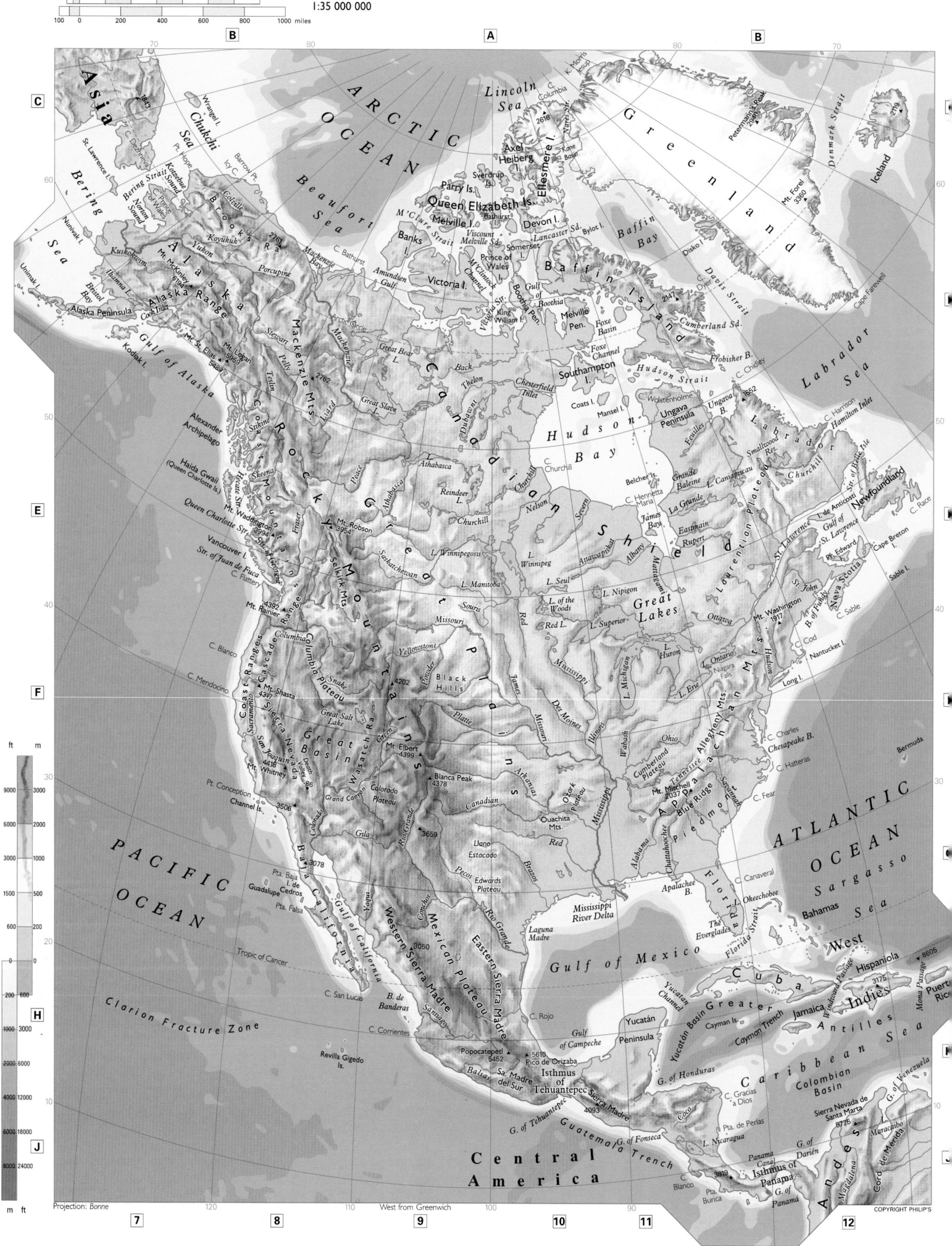

1:35 000 000

| 100 | 0 | 200 | 400 | 600 | 800 | 1000 | 1200 | 1400 km |
| 100 | 0 | 200 | 400 | 600 | 800 | 1000 miles |

B **A** **B**

C

RUSSIA

Asia

St. Lawrence I.

Bering Strait

ARCTIC OCEAN

International Date Line

Beaufort Sea

Queen Elizabeth Is.

Ellesmere I.

Victoria I.

GREENLAND

(Denmark)

Denmark Strait

ICELAND

Reykjavik

Baffin Bay

Nuuk

D

Bering Sea

ALASKA
(U.S.A.)

Yukon

Porcupine

Anchorage

Fairbanks

Kodiak I.

Gulf of Alaska

Whitehorse

Juneau

YUKON TERRITORY

NORTHWEST

Arctic Circle

Mackenzie

Great Bear L.

Back

NUNAVUT

Baffin Island

Davis Strait

Hudson Strait

Iqaluit

D

BRITISH COLUMBIA

Skeena

Fraser

Liard

TERRITORIES

Great Slave L.

Yellowknife

Dubawnt

CANADA

Hudson Bay

Eastmain

NEWFOUNDLAND &

St John's

LABRADOR

E

Victoria

Vancouver

Calgary

Edmonton

ALBERTA

Peace

Athabasca

Athabasca

SASKATCHEWAN

Saskatchewan

Regina

MANITOBA

Churchill

Nelson

L. Winnipeg

Winnipeg

ONTARIO

QUÉBEC

St. Lawrence

PRINCE EDWARD I.

Charlottetown

St-Pierre et Miquelon (Fr.)

Québec

Fredericton

NEW BRUNSWICK

MAINE

Augusta

NOVA SCOTIA

Halifax

E

Olympia

Seattle

WASHINGTON

Portland

Salem

Columbia

OREGON

Missouri

MONTANA

Helena

IDAHO

Boise

Snake

WYOMING

NORTH DAKOTA

Bismarck

SOUTH DAKOTA

MINNESOTA

Minneapolis-St. Paul

WISCONSIN

Madison

Milwaukee

L. Superior

L. Michigan

L. Huron

MICHIGAN

Lansing

Detroit

Ottawa

Montréal

TORONTO

L. Ontario

Buffalo

Erie

Cleveland

NEW YORK

Toledo

Pittsburgh

PA.

Concord

Boston

MASS.

Providence

Hartford

NEW YORK

Baltimore

PHILADELPHIA

N.J.

F

Sacramento

SAN FRANCISCO

San Jose

CALIFORNIA

Carson City

NEVADA

Salt Lake City

UTAH

Denver

COLORADO

NEBRASKA

Lincoln

IOWA

CHICAGO

ILLINOIS

INDIANA

Indianapolis

OHIO

Columbus

Cincinnati

WASHINGTON D.C.

W.V.

VIRGINIA

Richmond

MD.

Bermuda (U.K.)

F

UNITED STATES

Kansas City

Topeka

KANSAS

MISSOURI

St. Louis

Springfield

KENTUCKY

Nashville

TENNESSEE

NORTH CAROLINA

Raleigh

Charlotte

Columbia

SOUTH CAROLINA

G

LOS ANGELES

San Diego

Tijuana

Las Vegas

ARIZONA

Phoenix

Tucson

Mexicali

Santa Fe

Albuquerque

NEW MEXICO

Colorado

El Paso

Ciudad Juárez

OKLAHOMA

Oklahoma City

ARKANSAS

Little Rock

Memphis

Birmingham

MISSISSIPPI

Jackson

ALABAMA

Montgomery

GEORGIA

ATLANTA

Charleston

ATLANTIC OCEAN

G

PACIFIC OCEAN

Guadalupe (Mex.)

Hermosillo

Rio Grande

DALLAS-FT. WORTH

TEXAS

Austin

San Antonio

HOUSTON

Baton Rouge

LOUISIANA

New Orleans

Tallahassee

Jacksonville

FLORIDA

Orlando

Tampa-St. Petersburg

MIAMI

Nassau

BAHAMAS

Turks & Caicos Is. (U.K.)

Florida Str.

H

Tropic of Cancer

MEXICO

Culiacán

Torreón

Monterrey

San Luis Potosí

Mérida

Gulf of Mexico

Havana

CUBA

Cayman Is. (U.K.)

JAMAICA

Kingston

HAITI

Port-au-Prince

DOMINICAN REP.

Santo Domingo

PUERTO RICO (U.S.A.)

San Juan

Caribbean Sea

H

Revilla Gigedo Is. (Mex.)

León

Guadalajara

Querétaro

MÉXICO

Toluca

Puebla

Acapulco

BELIZE

Belmopan

GUATEMALA

Guatemala

San Salvador

EL SALVADOR

HONDURAS

Tegucigalpa

NICARAGUA

Managua

L. Nicaragua

Barranquilla

Maracaibo

VENEZUELA

J

COSTA RICA

San José

Panamá

PANAMA

COLOMBIA

Medellín

South America

J

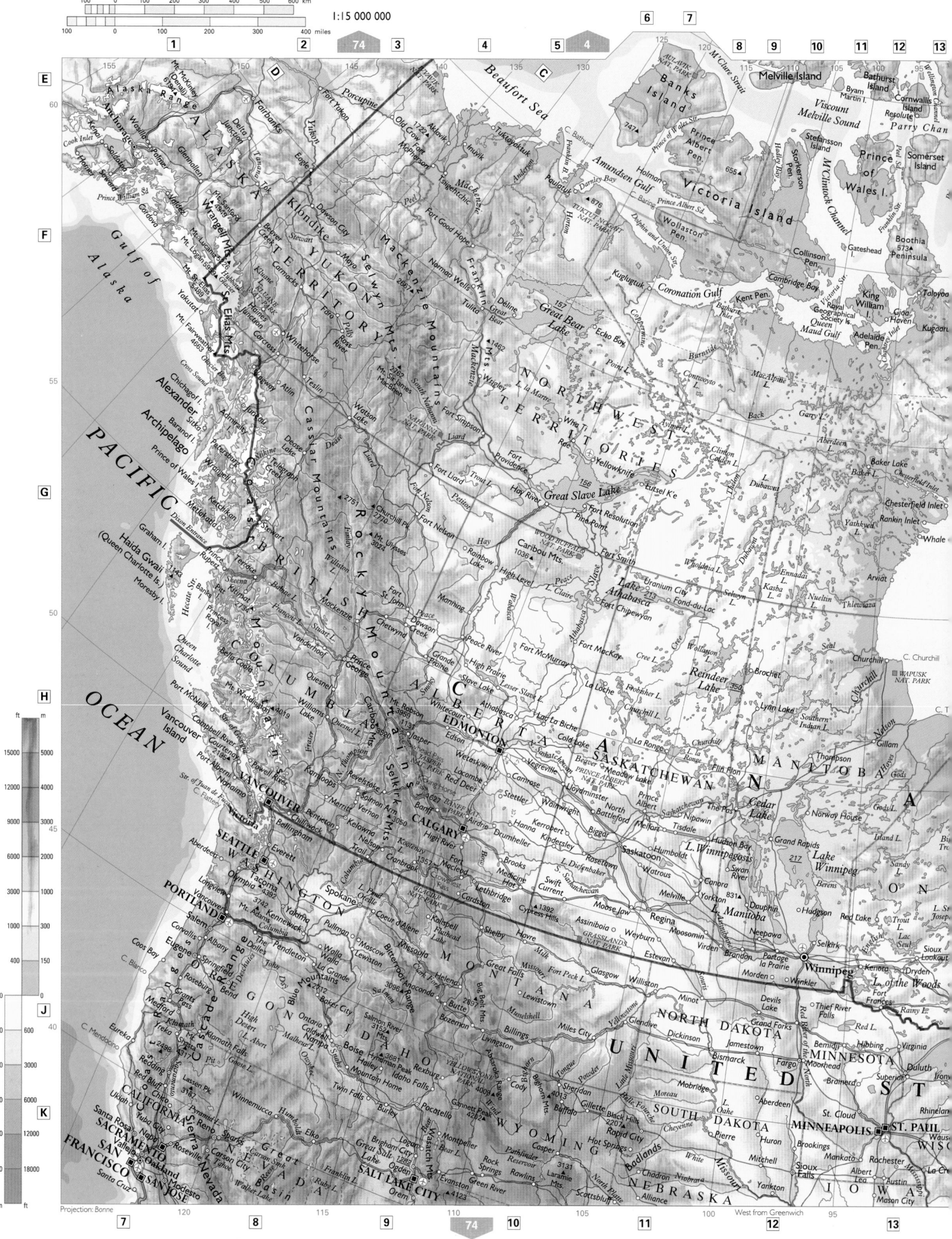

1:15 000 000

Projection: Bonne

West from Greenwich

NORTHERN CANADA
continuation northwards on same
scale as main map

ARCTIC OCEAN

GREENLAND
(KALAALLIT NUNAAT)

Kronprins
Frederik
Land

North Magnetic Pole
2011

1626

Queen Elizabeth Islands

N.W.T.

NUNAVUT

Parry Islands

Melville Island

Viscount Melville Sound

Parry Channel

Prince of Wales I.

Somerset Island

Devon Island

Lancaster Sound

Baffin Bay

Baffin Bay

GREENLAND (Denmark)

Nunavik

Lancaster Sound

Davis Strait

Baffin Island

NUNAVUT

Foxe Basin

Southampton I.

Hudson Strait

Foxe Channel

Péninsule d'Ungava

Ungava Bay

Labrador Sea

ATLANTIC

James Bay

Hudson Bay

QUEBEC

Labrador

NEWFOUNDLAND & LABRADOR

Newfoundland

ATLANTIC OCEAN

Gulf of St. Lawrence

PRINCE EDWARD I.

NEW BRUNSWICK

NOVA SCOTIA

MAINE

St. Lawrence (St-Laurent)

Québec

MONTREAL

OTTAWA

VERMONT

NEW HAMPSHIRE

MASS.

BOSTON

TORONTO

ROCHESTER

BUFFALO

NEW YORK

Lake Huron

L. Ontario

L. Michigan

DETROIT

CLEVELAND

Lake Erie

PENNSYLVANIA

CONN. R.I.

PROVIDENCE

HARTFORD

New Haven

Labrador Sea

COPYRIGHT PHILIP'S

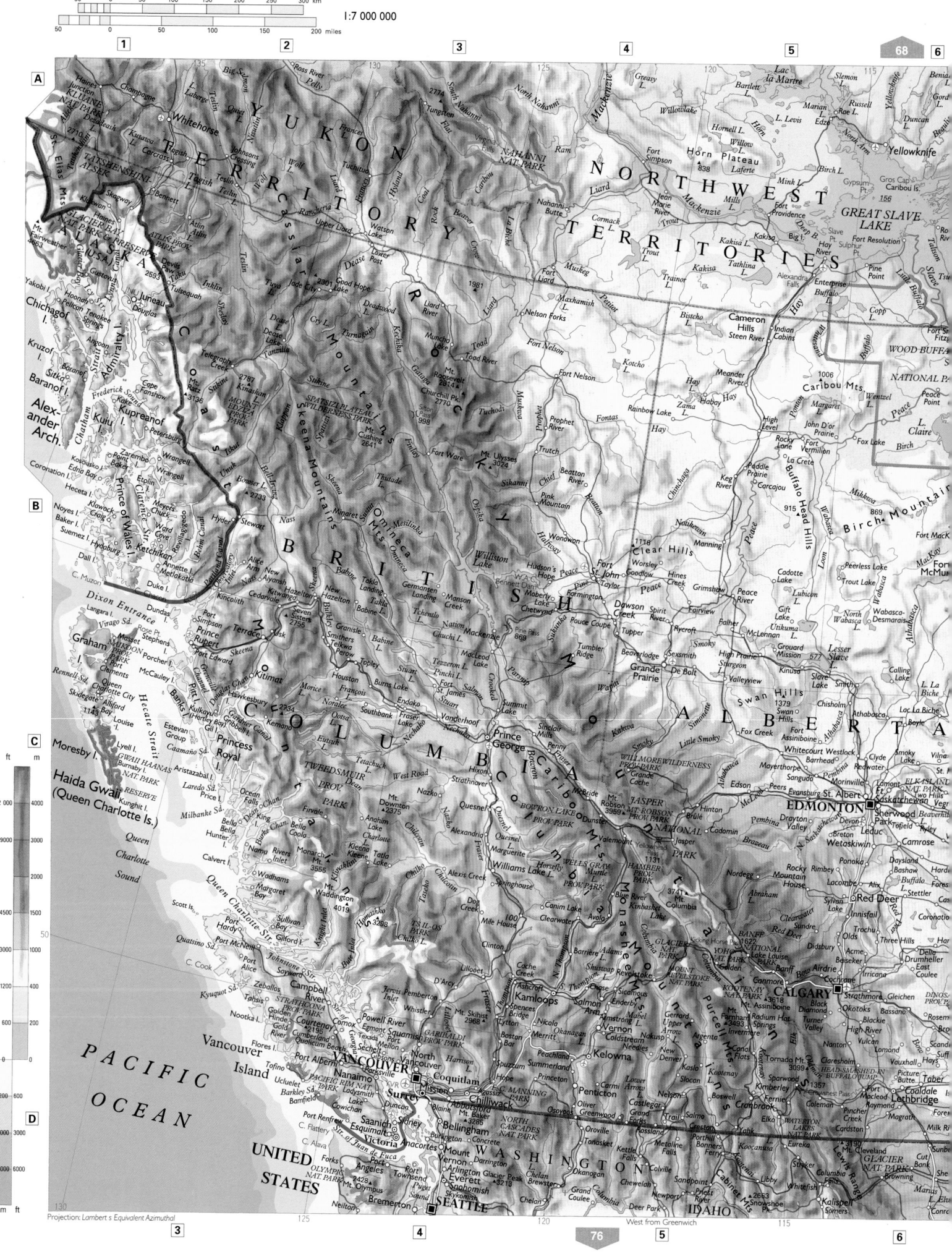

1:7 000 000

Projection: Lambert's Equivalent Azimuthal

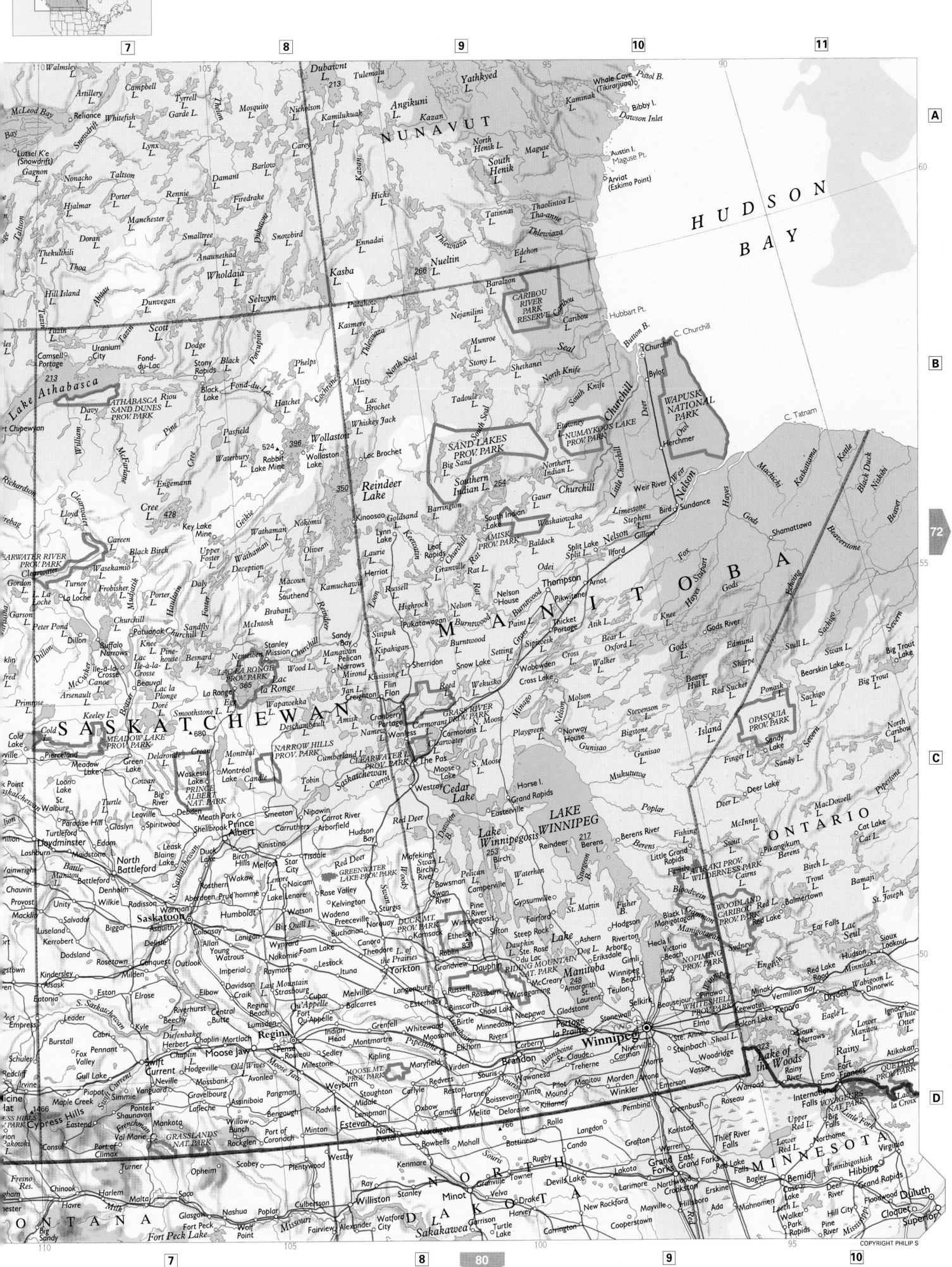

COPYRIGHT PHILIP'S

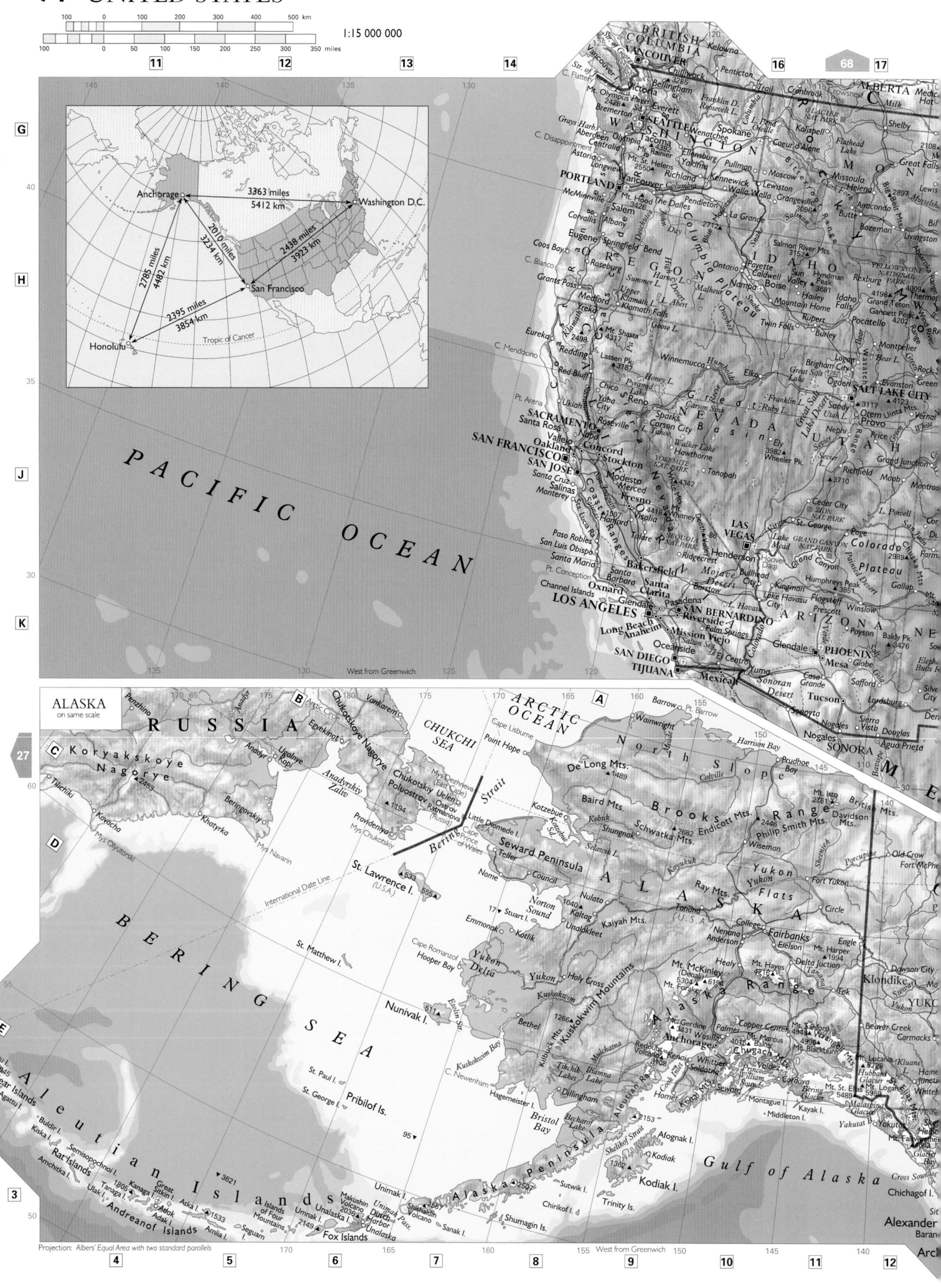

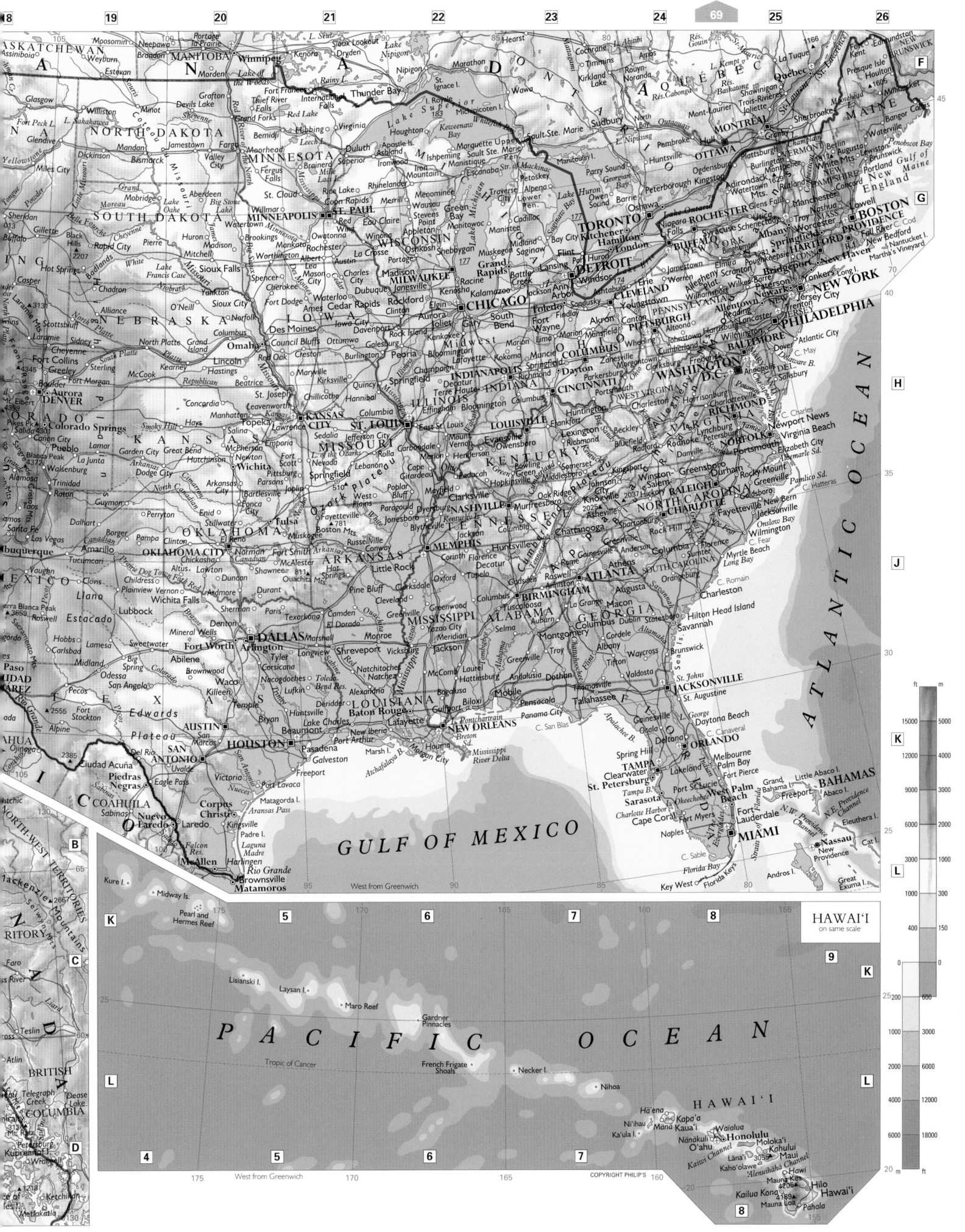

HAWAI'I
on same scale

COPYRIGHT PHILIP'S

1:6 700 000

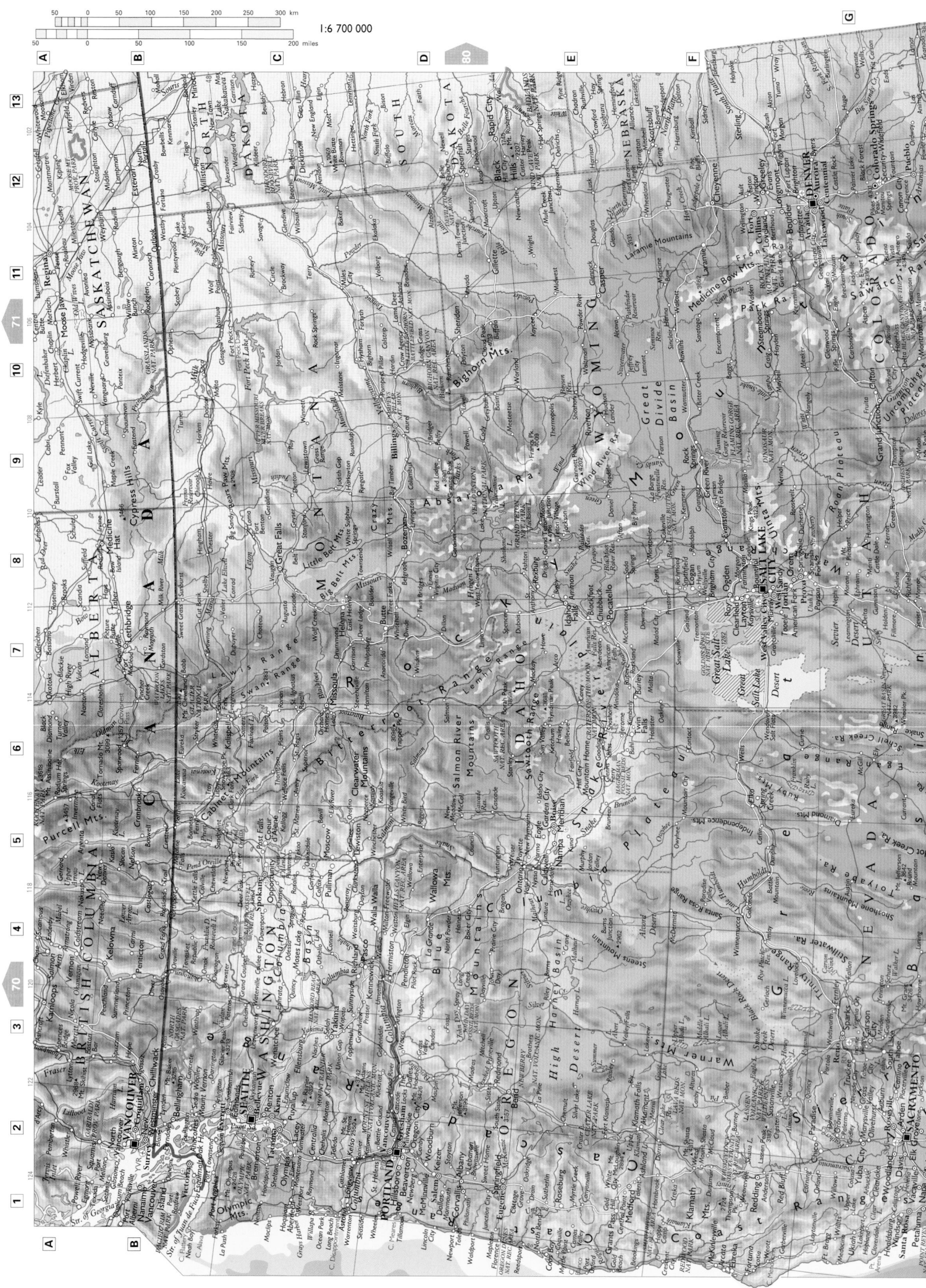

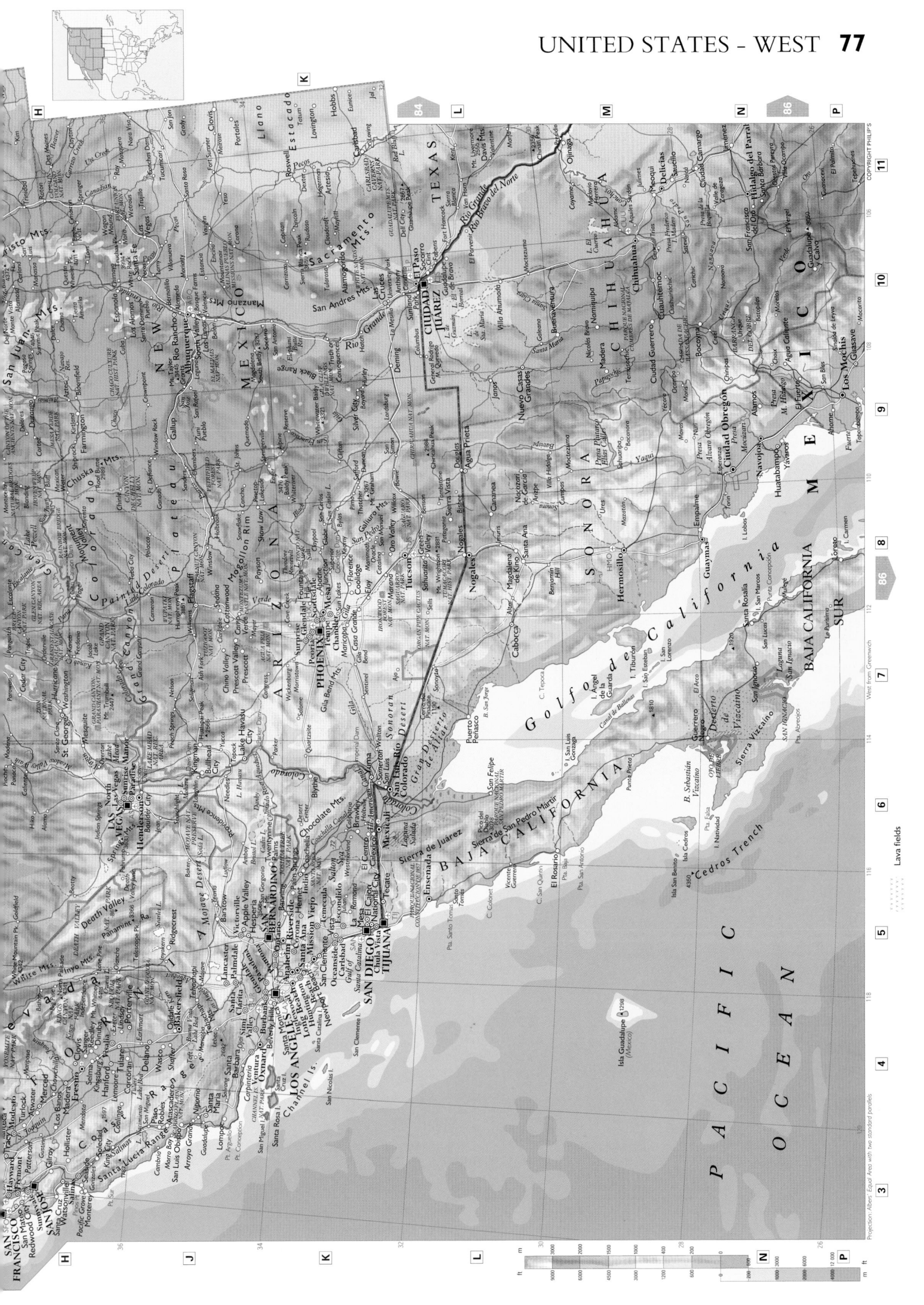

WESTERN WASHINGTON
REGION on same scale

1:2 500 000

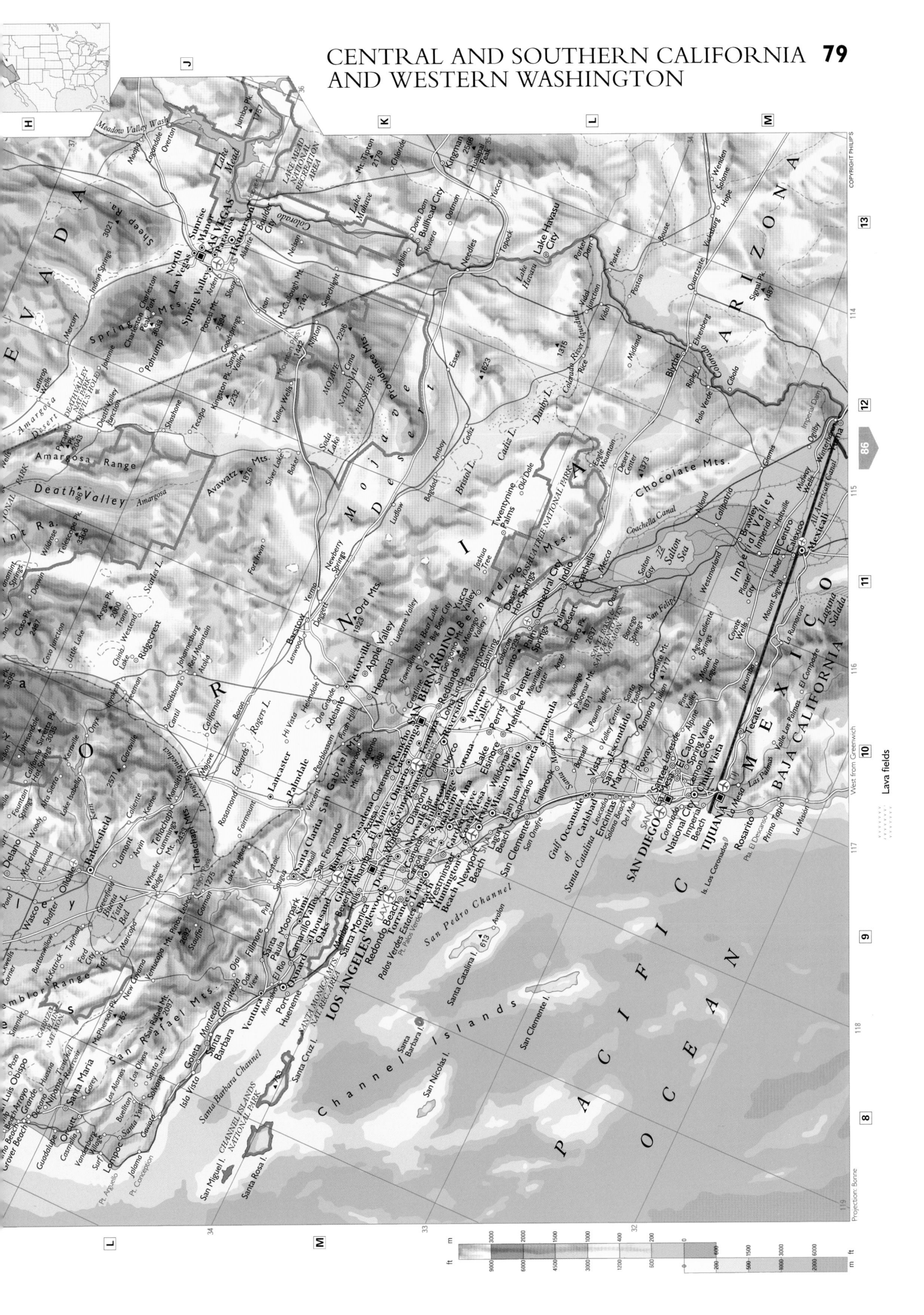

COPYRIGHT PHILIP'S

Lava fields

West from Greenwich

Projection: Bonne

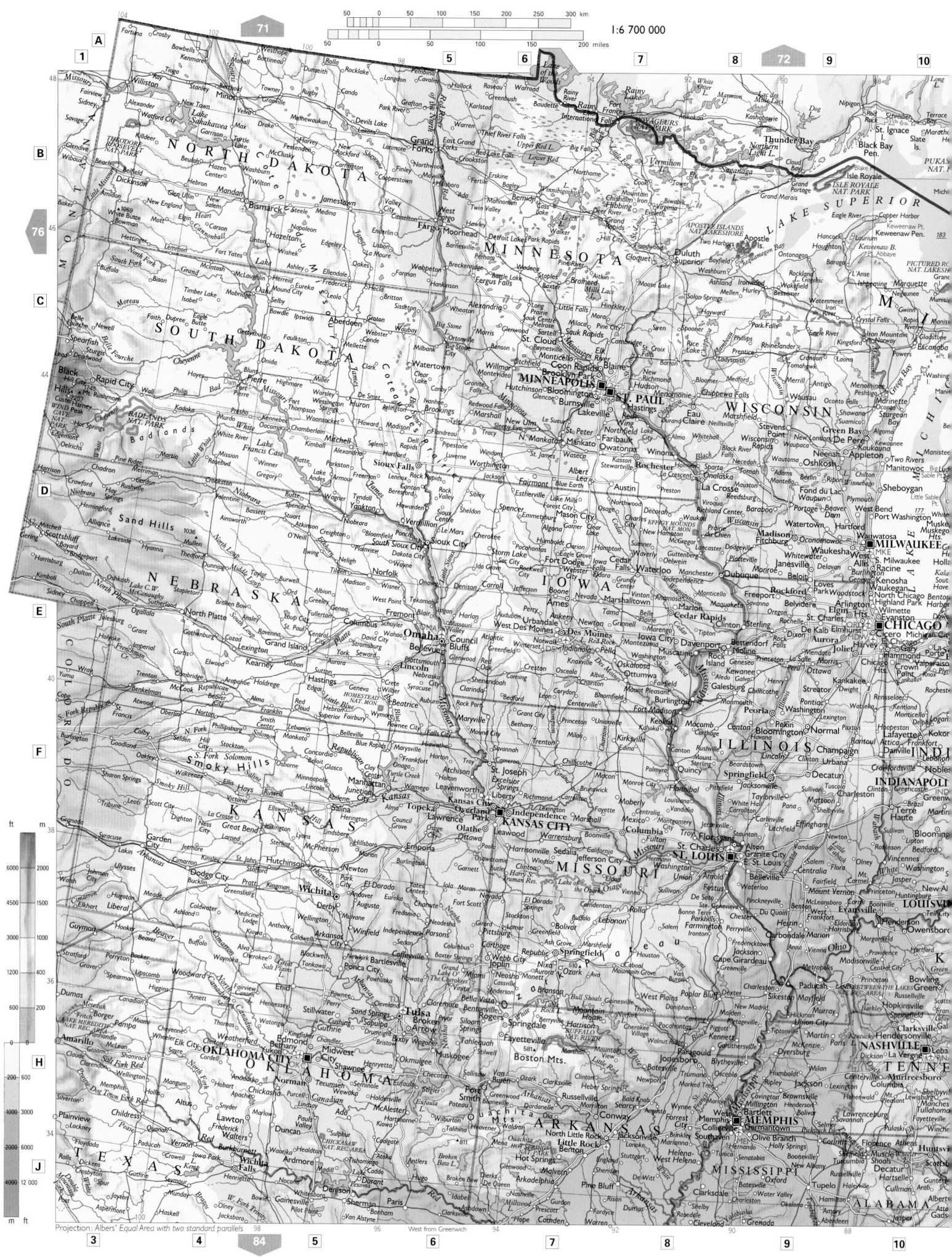

1:2 500 000

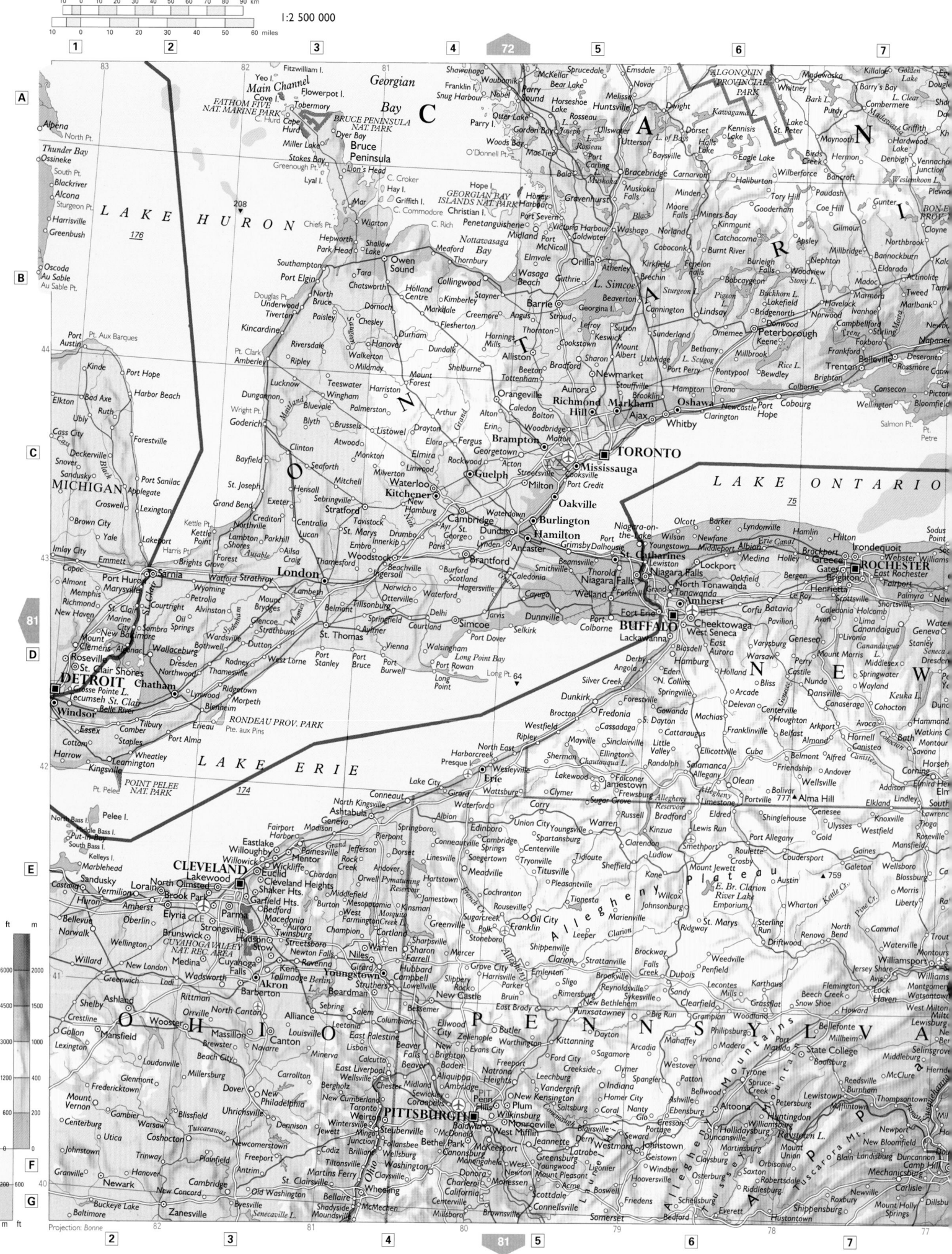

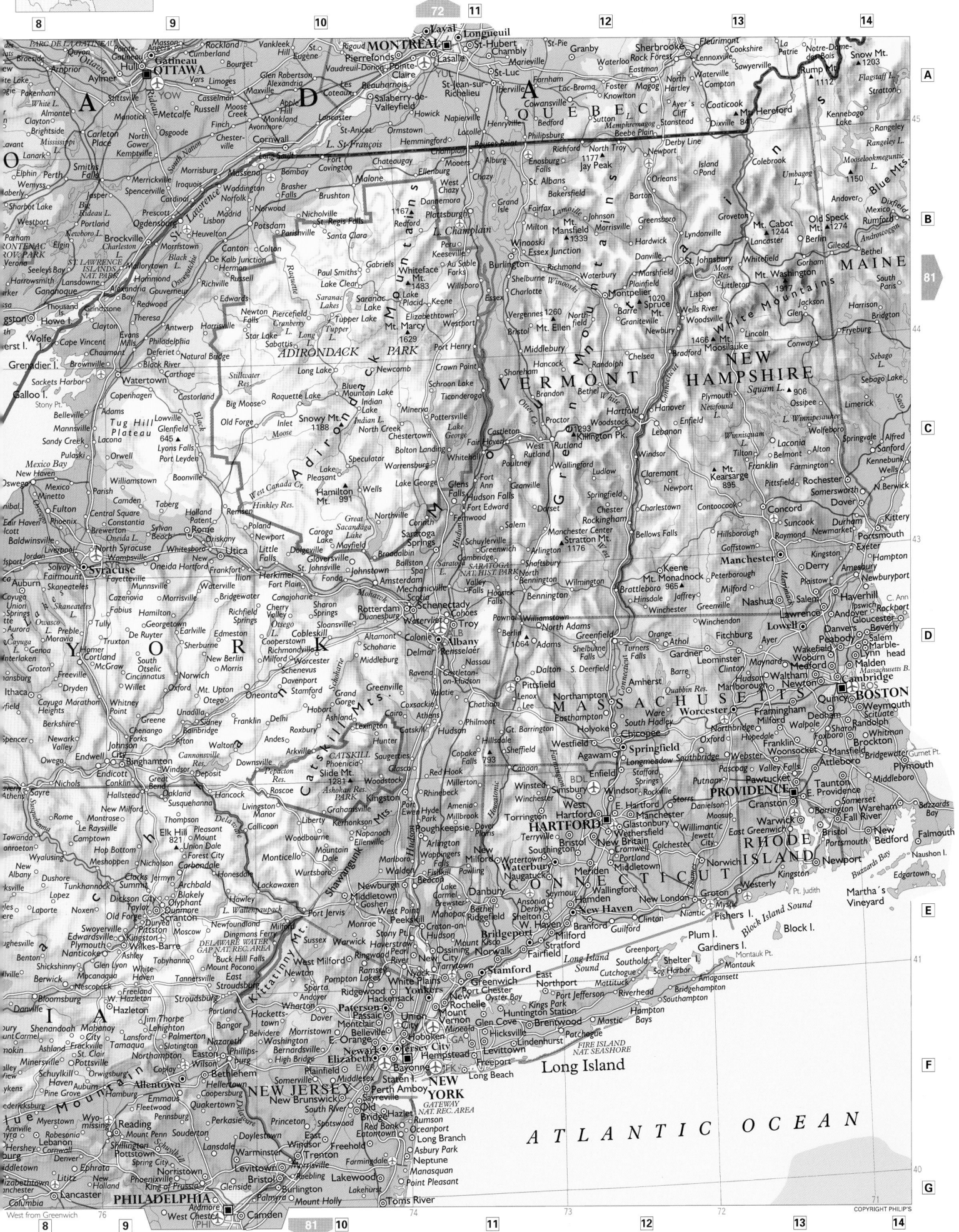

Projection: Bi-polar oblique Conical Orthomorphic

State names in Central Mexico

1 DISTRITO FEDERAL	3 GUANAJUATO	5 MÉXICO	7 QUERÉTARO
2 AGUASCALIENTES	4 HIDALGO	6 MORELOS	8 TLAXCALA

A

B

C

88

D

E

88

Wichita
Falls
Denison
Paris
Camden
Greenville
Tuscaloosa
Opelika
McRae
Sherman
ARKANSAS
Texarkana
El Dorado
Meridian
Montgomery
Americus
Columbus
Cordele
Possum
Kingdom
Denton
Greenville
MISSISSIPPI
ALABAMA
Phenix City
Albany
Tifton
Waycross
Fort Worth
DALLAS
Longview
Marshall
Monroe
Vicksburg
Jackson
Selma
Troy
Dothan
GEORGIA
Valdosta
Cleburne
Tyler
Corsicana
Shreveport
Tallulah
Natchez
Laurel
Hattiesburg
Brewton
Chattahoochee
Tallahassee
Waco
Hillsboro
Palestine
Lufkin
Nacogdoches
Alexandria
McComb
Bogalusa
Mobile
Pensacola
FLORIDA
Lake
City
Temple
Bryan
Huntsville
Lake
Livingston
Baton
Rouge
Hammond
Biloxi
Gulfport
Panama City
Apalachee
Bay
AUSTIN
HOUSTON
College Station
LOUISIANA
NEW
ORLEANS
Breton Sd.
C. San Blas
Suwannee
SAN
ANTONIO
Port
Arthur
Beaumont
Lake Charles
Lafayette
Atchafalaya
Bay
Terrebonne Bay
Mississippi
River Delta
Clearwater
Victoria
Galveston
32
35
Corpus Christi
PADRE ISLAND
NAT. SEASHORE
Laguna Madre
GULF
OF
82
Laredo
Kingsville
Alice
Nuevo Laredo
Zapata
McAllen
Harlingen
Brownsville
Reynosa
Rio Bravo
Matamoros
Valle Hermoso
Santa Teresa
Laguna Madre
MEXICO
25
Linares
San Fernando
M
3750
Ciudad
Victoria
Santander Jiménez
La Pesca
Soto la Marina
Sigsbee Deep
Tropic of Cancer
Banco
Campeche
75
CUBA
La Esperanza
Guane
La Fé
C. Cornentes
C. San Antonio
Canal de Yucatán
Aldama
I. Desterrada
Ciudad Mante
Ciudad Madero
Altamira
Ebano
Tampico
I. Pérez
(Mexico)
Pta.
Yalkubul
Río Lagartos
El Cuyo
C. Catoche
Isla
Mujeres
Cancún
González
Pánuco
47
Dzilam
de Bravo
Tizimin
Puerto Morelos
Tempoal
de Sánchez
L. de Tamiahua
Naranjos
Tantoyuca
C. Rojo
Progreso
Motul
Temax
Espita
Playa del Carmen
Isla
Cozumel
Cozumel
Tamazunchale
Chicontepec
Tuxpan
Mérida
Moxcanú
Izamal
Valla-
dolid
Zimapán
Poza Rica
Papantla
Nautla
Ticul
Peto
Tekax
Felipe
B. de la Ascensión
SIAN KA'AN
B. del Espíritu Santo
Huauchinango
Tulancingo
Teziutlán
Misantla
Tenabo
Bolonchén
Hopelchén
Carrillo
Puerto
Costa Maya
Yucatan
Basin
Pachuca
Xalapa
Golfo
de
Campeche
Campeche
QUINTANA
ROO
Banco
Chinchorro
EXICO
Veracruz
Boca del Río
Alvarado
Champotón
Chetumal
B. de
Chetumal
PUEBLA
Orizaba
Córdoba
Ciudad del
Carmen
L. de
Términos
Escárcega
Corozal
Ambergris Cay
Belize
Guernavaca
Tehuacán
San Andrés
Tuxtla
Paraíso
Frontera
CAMPECHE
Orange Walk
Belize
City
Turneffe Is.
Coatzacoalcos
TABASCO
Villahermosa
Belmopan
BELIZE
Barrier
Is. de
la Bahía
Guanaja
Oaxaca
Istmo
de
Tehuantepec
Cárdenas
Macuspana
Palenque
Teapa
CALAKMUL
Uaxactún
San Ignacio
Benque
Viejo
Dangriga
Roatán
Puerto
Castilla
Iriona
Tuxtla
Gutiérrez
San Cristóbal
de las Casas
Ocosingo
Flores
TIKAL
Monkey River
Golfo de Honduras
Puerto
Cortés
La
Ceiba
Trujillo
OAXACA
CHIAPAS
Comitán
de Domínguez
San Luis
San Antonio
Livingston
Barrios
Chokoma
San Pedro Sula
El Progreso
Tela
Olanchito
Acapulco
GUATEMALA
Huehuetenango
Cobán
HONDURAS
Juticalpa
Catacamas
TEGUCIGALPA
Puerto
Escondido
Golfo de
Tehuantepec
Tapachula
GUATEMALA

COPYRIGHT PHILIP'S

1:8 000

JAMAICA
1:3 000 000

GUADELOUPE AND MARTINIQUE
1:2 000 000

5

PUERTO RICO
d
1:3 000 000

ATLANTIC OCEAN
PUERTO RICO
(U.S.A.)
Pta. Agujereada
Isabela
Aguadilla
Barceloneta
Arecibo
Manati
Vega
Baja
Bayamón
SAN JUAN
Rio Grande
Carolina
Fajardo
Dewey
San Sebastian
Utuado
Sierra de
Luquillo
Puerca
Culebra
Mayagüez
Adjuntas
Cordillera Central
Cerro
de Punta
Caguas
Naguabo
Vieques
San German
Uroyan
Yauco
Cayey
Humacao
Esperanza
Yabucoa
Ponce
Coamo
Guayama
Pta. Aguila
Guanica
I. Caja de Muertos

VIRGIN ISLANDS
e
1:2 000 000

Rufiing Pt.
The Settlement
Anegada
East Pt.
Virgin Islands
(U.K.)
Great
Camanoe
Jost Van
Dyke I.
Guana I.
Virgin Gorda
Haos
Tortola
Beef
Virgin Is.
(U.S.A.)
Lollik I.
Cruz
Bay
Road Town
Spanish Town
Charlotte
Amalie
VIRGIN IS.
Peter I.
St.
Thomas I.
St. John I.

ST. LUCIA
f
1:1 000 000

Cap Point
Pte. Hardy
Gros Islet
Esperance Bay
Castries
Marquis
Girard
Anse la Raye
Canaries
Dennery
Millet
Soufrière
Soufrière
Bay
750
Petit Piton
Trou Gras Pt.
Micoud
Gros Piton Pt.
796
Gros Piton
Vierge Pt.
Choiseul
UVF
ST. LUCIA
Laborie
Vieux Fort
C. Moule à Chique

ATLANTIC
OCEAN
Crab Hill
North Point
Fustic
Spring Hall
Portland
245
Boscobelle
Belleplaine
Speightstown
BARBADOS
Westmoreland
Bathsheba
Hillcrest
Alleynes Bay
840
Martin's Bay
Holetown
Mt. Hillaby
Massiah
Street
Black Rock
Jackson
Bridgefield
Six Cross Roads
Ellerton
The Crane
Bridgetown
Ivy
Edey
St. Martins
Carlisle Bay
BGI
Worthing
Oistins
Bay
Chancery Lane
South Point

BARBADOS
g
1:1 000 000

6

7

A

ATLANTIC
OCEAN

MAS

Hur's Town
New Bight
Cat I.
San Salvador I.
Conception I.
Tropic of Cancer
Rum Cay
Long I.
Clarence
Town
Samana Cay
Crooked I.
Albert
Town
Plana Cays
Snug
Corner
Mayaguana I.
Acklins I.
Mira por vos Cay
Cay Verde
Hogsty Reef
Little Inagua I.
Turks & Caicos Is.
(U.K.)
Santa
PLS
Caicos Is.
Cockburn Town
la
Lucrecia
INAGUA
Lake Rose
Turks Island
Turks Is.
Moa
Matthew
Town
yari
Baracoa
Great
Inagua I.
Mouchoir
Bank
Silver
Bank

Navidad
Bank

Puerto Rico Trench

B

Guantanamo
Paso de los Vientos
(Windward Passage)
Cap-
Haïtien
Monte
Cristi
LA ISABELA
Santiago de
los Caballeros
Bayamón
SAN JUAN
Anegada
Virgin Is.
Sombrero (U.K.)
Jean Rabel
Port-de-
Paix
Fort Liberté
Puerto
Plata
San Francisco de Macorís
La Vega
Milwaukee
Deep
8605
Arecibo
Carolina
St. Thomas
Virgin Gorda
Road Town
Anguilla (U.K.)
Cap-à-
Foux
G. de la
Gonâve
Gonaïves
Hinche
Central
Cord.
Nagua
Samana
Sánchez
Sabana de la Mar
San Juan
Fajardo
Tortola
Charlotte Amalie
St.-Martin
St.-Barthélemy (Fr.)
HAITI
3175
Hato Mayor
Culebra
Virgin Is.
(U.S.A.)
St. Maarten (Neth.)
Saba (Neth.)
Barbuda
Jérémie
PORT-
AU-PRINCE
DOMINICAN
REP.
San Pedro
de Macorís
Higüey
Aguadilla
Ponce
Caguas
Vieques
St. Croix
St. Eustatius (Neth.)
Mt. Liamuiga
ANTIGUA
& BARBUDA
Dame
I. de la Gonâve
San Juan
1338
La Romana
Mayagüez
Guayama
Frederiksted
Christiansted
Basseterre
ST. KITTS
& NEVIS
St. John's
Antigua
Massif de la Hotte
Petit
Goâve
Jacmel
2680
SANTO
DOMINGO
B. de
Yuma
PUERTO
RICO
(U.S.A.)
Nevis (U.K.)
Redonda
SKB
ANU
Les Cayes
Aquin
Barahona
San Cristóbal
Isla
Saona
Montserrat
(U.K.)
Soufrière
914
Guadeloupe
Passage
Pointe-à-Pitre
Pointe-à-Gravois
I. à Vache
Pedernales
Isla
Mona
(U.S.A.)
Ste-Rose
1467
GUADELOUPE
(Fr.)
Le Moule
La Désirade
C. Carcasse
Hispaniola
I. Beata
C. Beata
5500
Muertas Trough
Basse-Terre
I. des Saintes
Marie-Galante (Fr.)
Grand-Bourg
Portsmouth
1447
DOMINICA
Antilles
Morne
Diablotin
DOM
Roseau
Dominica Passage

C

4530
Beata Ridge
Venezuelan
I. de Aves
(Venezuela)
TROIS PITONS
MORNE
Martinique Passage
Mt. Pelée
1397
Ste-Marie
Le Robert

BEAN
SEA
Basin
Fort-de-
France
FDF
Rivière-Pilote
MARTINIQUE
(Fr.)

ombian
5420
Aves Ridge
St. Lucia Channel
Castries
UVF
ST. LUCIA
Soufrière
850

asin
St. Vincent Passage
Soufrière
1234
St. Vincent
Speightstown
BGI

ABC
Lesser
Islands
Antilles
Kingstown
SVD
Bridgetown
BARBADOS
Oranjestad
Aruba
(Neth.)
Curaçao
Bonaire
Bequia I.
Tobago
ST. VINCENT
& THE
GRENADINES

D

AUA
Willemstad
CUR
ARC. LOS
ROQUES
(Ven.)
I. Orchila
(Ven.)
I. Blanquilla (Ven.)
Is. Los Hermanos
(Ven.)
Is. Los Testigos
(Ven.)
Canouan
The Grenadines
Carriacou
Basin
Tobago
GUAJIRA
Pta. Gallinas
MACURIA
C. San Román
Is. Las Aves
(Ven.)
Is. Los Roques
(Ven.)
St. George's
GND
GRENADA
Scarborough
Pen. de la
Guajira
Pta.
Espada
Pen. de
Paraguaná
Punto Fijo
NUEVA
ESPARTA
I. de Margarita
Galera
Pt.
Port of
Spain
TAB
COLOMBIA
Santa
Marta
Ríohacha
Uribia
Maicao
Golfo de
Venezuela
Punta
Cardón
Puerto Cumarebo
La Asunción
920
Porlamar
Pen. de Paria
POS
Trinidad
RRAN-
UILLA
TAYRONA
SA. NEVADA DE
STA. MARTA
5775
San
Rafael
Coro
La Vela
MÉDANOS DE CORO
CUEVA DE LA
QUEBRADA
DEL TORO
Tucacas
Puerto
Cabello
Carúpano
Caribe
Güiria
San
Fernando
TRINIDAD
& TOBAGO
Baranoa
Ciénaga
Sierra Nevada de
Santa Marta
FALCÓN
HENRI
PITTIER
Maiquetía
La Guaira
Cumaná
G. de Paria
Río Claro
SOLEDAD
ATICO
Sabanalarga
CESAR
Fundación
Villa del
Rosario
Machiques
Lago de
Maracaibo
La Concepción
Cabimas
LARA
YARACUY
Mene Grande
SA. DE SAN LUIS
Altagracia
Mene de Mauroa
Baragua
CARABOBO
MIRANDA
CARACAS
VARGAS
Higuerote
Puerto
La Cruz
Barcelona
SUCRE
Caripito
Maturín
MONAGAS
MARACAIBO
MAR
Santa Rita
Ciudad
Ojeda
CERRO
TOTUMO
BARQUISIMETO
VALENCIA
Villa
de Cura
San Juan
de los Morros
Aragua de
Barcelona
Anaco
Caicara
El Tigre
AMACURO
Magangué
El Banco
ZULIA
PERIJÁ
Trujillo
TRUJILLO
Carora
Araure
Acarigua
COJEDES
El Sombrero
Valle de
la Pascua
Santa María
de Ipire
ANZOÁTEGUI
Soledad
DELTA
Tucupita
Plato
CIÉNAGAS DE
CATATUMBO
Betijoque
PORTUGUESA
GUÁRICO
Ciudad Guayana
MÉRIDA
MÉRIDA
Guanare
Portuguesa
Calabozo
El Baúl
Sierra Imataca
BOLIVAR
Ocaña
Santa
SIERRA DE
SANTANDER
Encontrados
CORD. DE LA COSTA
SA. DE LA
CULATA
Pico Bolívar
Ciudad
Bolivia
BARINAS
BARINAS
Ciudad de Nutrias
El GUACHE
San Fernando
de Apure
Embalse de Guri
Ciudad
Bolívar
El Pao
El Callao
Guasipati
Tumeremo
TÁCHIRA
Cúcuta
Simití
BOLÍVAR
West from Greenwich
Bruzual
Achaguas
APURE
Apure
Mapire
Caicara
Orinoco

E

92
COPYRIGHT PHILIP'S

4000 3000 2000 1500 1000 600 400 200
12 000 9000 6000 4500 3000 1200 600
600 1200 6000 12 000 18 000 24 000 ft
0 200 2000 4000 6000 8000 m

5
6
7

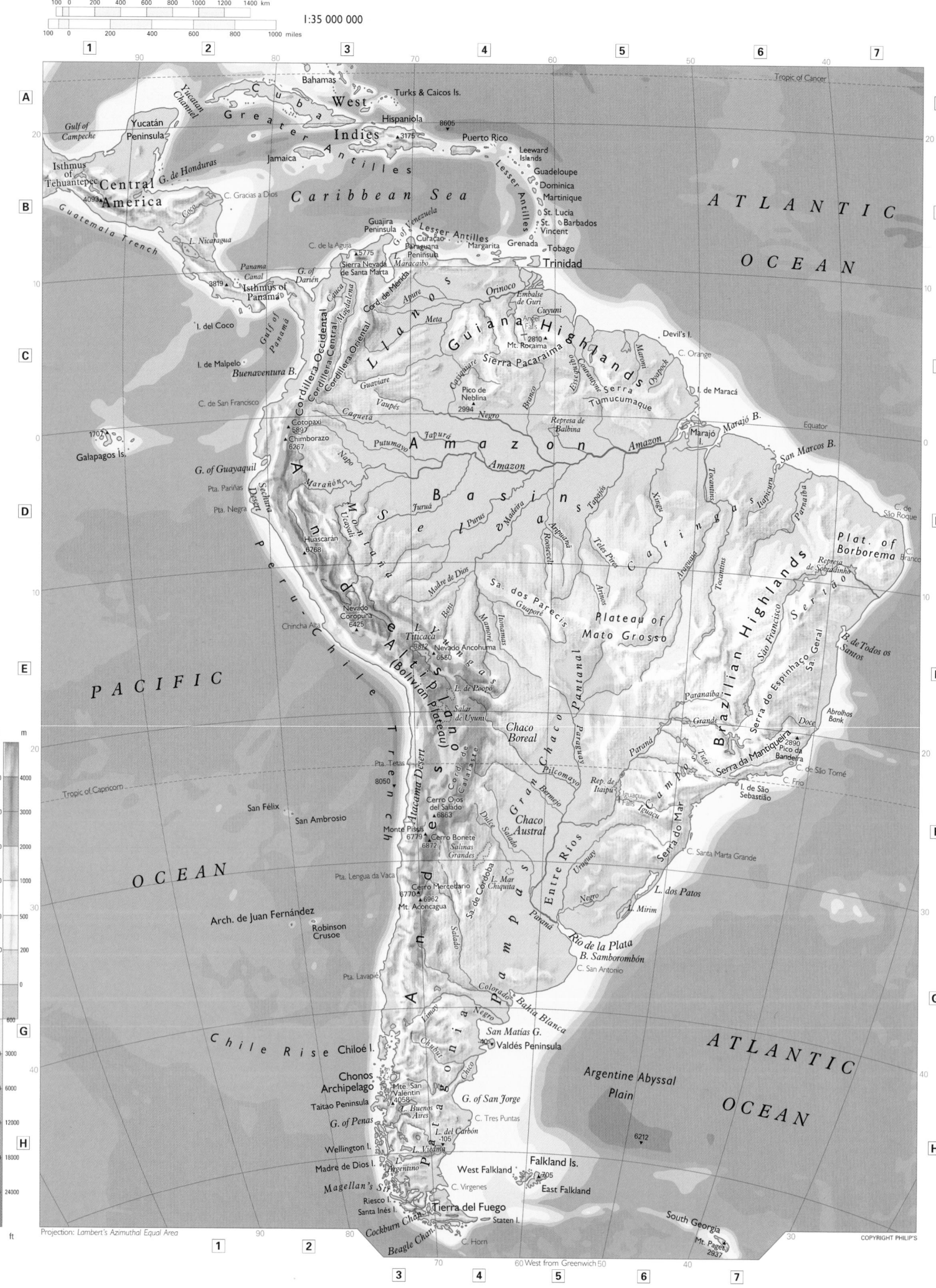

100 0   200   400   600   800   1000   1200   1400 km

1:35 000 000

100 0   200   400   600   800   1000 miles

Projection: Lambert's Azimuthal Equal Area

COPYRIGHT PHILIP'S

Tropic of Cancer

Bahamas

Cuba

West

Greater

Turks & Caicos Is.

Indies

Yucatán Channel

Gulf of
Campeche

Yucatán
Peninsula

Hispaniola

8605

3175

Puerto Rico

Antilles

Isthmus
of
Tehuantepec

Central

G. de Honduras

Leeward
Islands

Guadeloupe

Dominica

Martinique

4093

America

C. Gracias a Dios

Lesser

St. Lucia

St.
Vincent

Barbados

Guatemala Trench

Coco

Caribbean   Sea

Grenada

Tobago

Guajira
Peninsula

G. of Venezuela

Lesser Antilles

L. Nicaragua

C. de la Aguja

Curaçao
Paraguaná
Peninsula

Margarita

Trinidad

Panama
Canal

Sierra Nevada
de Santa Marta

5775

Maracaibo

Orinoco

Embalse
de Guri

Devil's I.

3819

Isthmus of
Panama

G. of
Darién

Cauca

Cord. de Mérida

Apure

Meta

Llanos

Angel
Falls

Cuyuni

Mt. Roraima

2810

Guiana

Highlands

Maroni

C. Orange

I. del Coco

Cordillera Occidental

Cordillera Central

Magdalena

Cordillera Oriental

Sierra Pacaraima

Branco

Essequibo

Serra

Oyapock

Courantyne

I. de Maracá

I. de Malpelo

Buenaventura B.

Guaviare

Pico de
Neblina
2994

Tumucumaque

C. de San Francisco

Caquetá

Vaupés

Negro

Represa de
Balbina

Marajó
I.

Marajó B.

Equator

Cotopaxi
5897

Chimborazo
6267

Napo

Putumayo

Japurá

Amazon

Amazon

San Marcos B.

1707

Galapagos Is.

G. of Guayaquil

Marañón

Montaña

Ucayali

Juruá

Purus

Amazon

Madeira

Roosevelt

Basin

Aripuanã

Tapajós

Xingu

Tocantins

Araguaia

Iriri

Parnaíba

C. de
São Roque

C. Branco

Pta. Pariñas

Pta. Negra

Sechura
Desert

Huascarán
6768

Madre de Dios

Beni

Sa. dos Parecis

Guaporé

Teles Pires

Arinos

Caatinga

Plat. of
Borborema

Represa
de Sobradinho

Chincha Alta

Nevado
Coropuna
6425

L. Titicaca
5812

Nevado Ancohuma
6560

Altiplano

Mamoré

Iténez

Plateau of
Mato Grosso

São Francisco

Serra do Espinhaço

Serra Geral

B. de Todos os
Santos

PACIFIC

Peru – Chile

(Bolivian Plateau)

L. de Poopó

Salar
de Uyuni

Chaco
Boreal

Paraguay

Paranaíba

Brazilian Highlands

Abrolhos
Bank

2890

Pta. Tetas
8050

Atacama Desert

Cord. de
Calalaste

Chaco

Grande

Serra da Mantiqueira

Pico da
Bandeira

Tropic of Capricorn

San Félix

San Ambrosio

Cerro Ojos
del Salado
6863

Gran

Chaco

Paraguay

Rep. de
Itaipú

Iguaçu
Falls

C. de São Tomé

Iguaçu

C. Frio

Monte Pissis
6779

Cerro Bonete
6872

Salinas
Grandes

Chaco
Austral

Dulce

Bermejo

Pilcomayo

Entre Ríos

Paraná

Uruguay

Serra do Mar

C. Santa Marta Grande

OCEAN

Pta. Lengua da Vaca

Cerro Mercedario
6770

6962

Mt. Aconcagua

Sa. de Córdoba

L. Mar
Chiquita

Salado

Paraná

Negro

I. de São
Sebastião

Arch. de Juan Fernández

Robinson
Crusoe

Salado

Pampas

L. dos Patos

L. Mirim

Pta. Lavapié

Colorado

Rio de la Plata

B. Samborombón

C. San Antonio

Andes

Bahía Blanca

ATLANTIC

Limay

Negro

San Matías G.

Chile Rise

Chiloé I.

Chubut

Valdés Peninsula

Argentine Abyssal
Plain

OCEAN

Chonos
Archipelago

Chico

Patagonia

San Jorge

Taitao Peninsula

Mte. San
Valentín
4058

L. Buenos
Aires

G. of San Jorge

C. Tres Puntas

G. of Penas

L. del Carbón
-105

6212

Wellington I.

L. Viedma

Madre de Dios I.

L.
Argentino

West Falkland

Falkland Is.

705

Magellan's Str.

C. Virgenes

East Falkland

Riesco I.

Santa Inés I.

Tierra del Fuego

Staten I.

South Georgia

Cockburn Chan.

Mt. Paget
2937

Beagle Chan.

C. Horn

ft   m
20

12000 4000

9000 3000

6000 2000

3000 1000

600 500

200

0   0

200 600

1000 3000

2000 6000

4000 12000

6000 18000

8000 24000

m   ft

1:35 000 000

100 0   200   400   600   800   1000   1200   1400 km
100 0   200   400   600   800   1000 miles

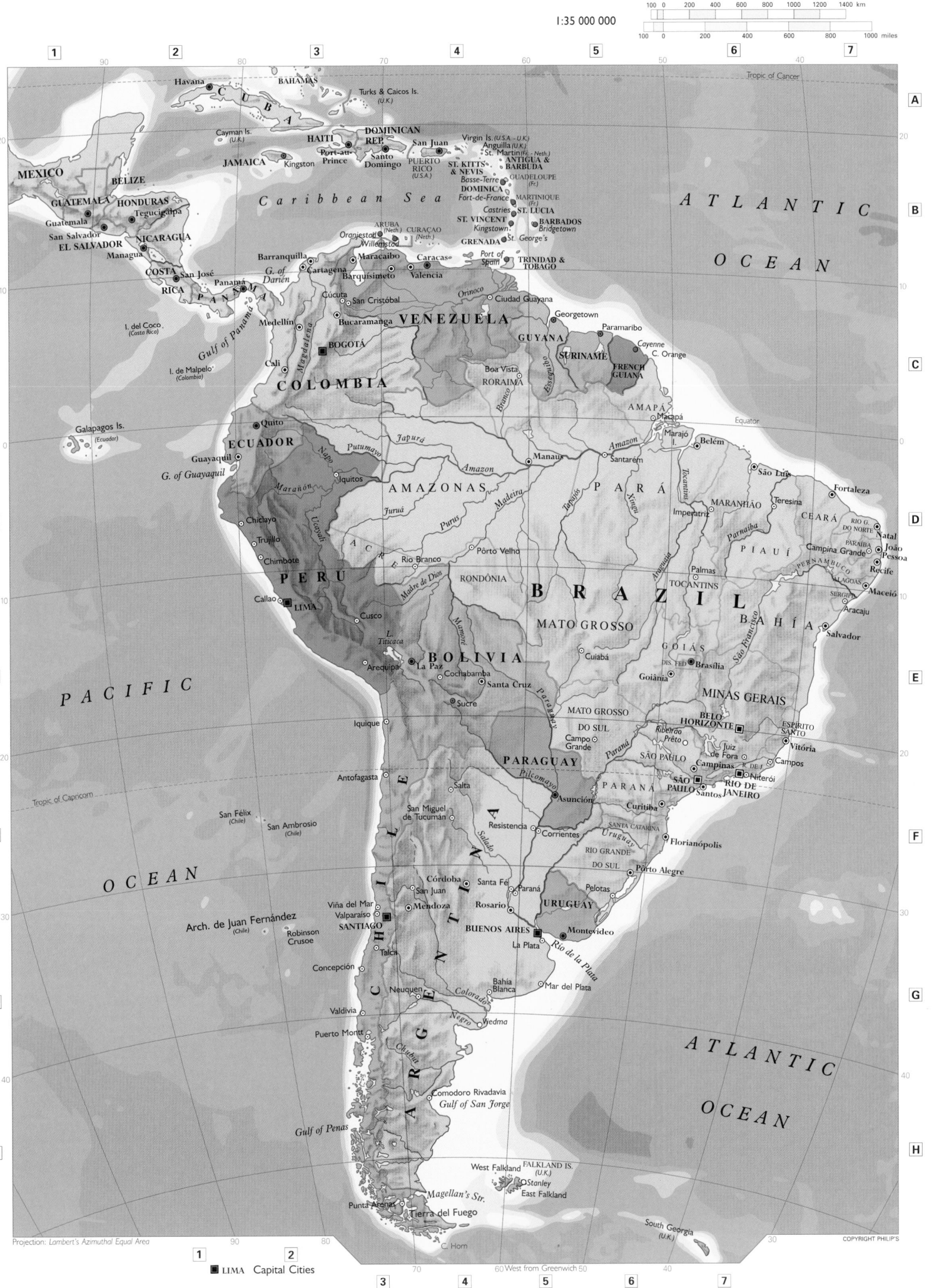

1   90   **2**   80   **3**   70   **4**   60   **5**   50   **6**   40   **7**

Tropic of Cancer

Havana   BAHAMAS
CUBA   Turks & Caicos Is.
(U.K.)

Cayman Is.   HAITI   Virgin Is. (U.S.A.-U.K.)
(U.K.)   DOMINICAN   Anguilla (U.K.)
JAMAICA   Kingston   REP.   San Juan   St. Martin (Fr. - Neth.)
MEXICO   Port-au-   Santo   PUERTO   ANTIGUA &
Prince   Domingo   RICO   ST. KITTS   BARBUDA
BELIZE   (U.S.A.)   & NEVIS   GUADELOUPE
Basse-Terre   (Fr.)
GUATEMALA   DOMINICA   MARTINIQUE
Guatemala   HONDURAS   Caribbean   Sea   Fort-de-France   (Fr.)
San Salvador   Tegucigalpa   Castries   ST. LUCIA
EL SALVADOR   ST. VINCENT   BARBADOS
Managua   NICARAGUA   ARUBA   CURAÇAO   Kingstown   Bridgetown
COSTA   San José   (Neth.)   (Neth.)   GRENADA   St. George's
RICA   Panamá   Oranjestad   Port of
PANAMA   Willemstad   Spain   TRINIDAD &
Barranquilla   Maracaibo   Caracas   TOBAGO
I. del Coco   G. of   Cartagena   Valencia
(Costa Rica)   Darién   Barquisimeto
Cúcuta   San Cristóbal   Orinoco   Ciudad Guayana
Medellín   Bucaramanga   VENEZUELA   Georgetown
I. de Malpelo   BOGOTÁ   GUYANA   Paramaribo
(Colombia)   Cali   SURINAME   Cayenne
COLOMBIA   Boa Vista   C. Orange
FRENCH
RORAIMA   GUIANA
Galapagos Is.   Quito   AMAPÁ   Macapá   Equator
(Ecuador)   ECUADOR   Japurá   Marajó   Belém
Guayaquil   Putumayo   I.
Napo   Amazon   Santarém   São Luís
G. of Guayaquil   Iquitos   Amazon   Fortaleza
Marañón   AMAZONAS   Manaus   PARÁ   MARANHÃO   Teresina   CEARÁ
Chiclayo   Juruá   Madeira   Tapajós   Xingu   Tocantins   RIO G.   Natal
Trujillo   Purus   Imperatriz   DO NORTE   João
Chimbote   ACRE   PIAUÍ   PARAÍBA   Pessoa
PERU   Rio Branco   Pôrto Velho   RONDÔNIA   Campina Grande   Recife
Callao   Madre de Dios   Palmas   PERNAMBUCO
LIMA   B R A Z I L   TOCANTINS   ALAGOAS   Maceió
Cusco   MATO GROSSO   BAHÍA   SERGIPE   Aracaju
L.   Mamoré   GOIÁS   São Francisco   Salvador
Titicaca   BOLIVIA   Cuiabá   DIS. FED.   Brasília
Arequipa   La Paz   Cochabamba   Goiânia   MINAS GERAIS
Santa Cruz   ESPÍRITO
MATO GROSSO   BELO   SANTO
Iquique   Sucre   DO SUL   Campo   Ribeirão   HORIZONTE   Vitória
Grande   Prêto   Juiz   Campos
de Fora   R. DE J.
Antofagasta   PARAGUAY   Paraná   SÃO PAULO   Campinas
Pilcomayo   SÃO   RIO DE
Salta   Asunción   PARANÁ   PAULO   JANEIRO
San Miguel   Santos   Niterói
San Félix   de Tucumán   Curitiba   SANTA CATARINA
(Chile)   San Ambrosio   Resistencia   Corrientes   Florianópolis
(Chile)   Uruguay   RIO GRANDE
Córdoba   DO SUL   Pôrto Alegre
San Juan   Santa Fé   Pelotas
Arch. de Juan Fernández   Viña del Mar   Paraná
(Chile)   Valparaíso   Mendoza   Rosario   URUGUAY
Robinson   SANTIAGO   BUENOS AIRES   Montevideo
Crusoe   Talca   La Plata   Río de la Plata
Concepción   Bahía   Mar del Plata
Neuquen   Blanca
Colorado
Valdivia   Negro   Viedma
Puerto Montt

Comodoro Rivadavia
Gulf of San Jorge

Gulf of Penas

ATLANTIC

OCEAN

West Falkland   FALKLAND IS.
(U.K.)
Magellan's Str.   Stanley
East Falkland
Punta Arenas   Tierra del Fuego
C. Horn   South Georgia
(U.K.)

PACIFIC

OCEAN

ATLANTIC

OCEAN

Tropic of Capricorn

A R G E N T I N A

C H I L E

Saladó

Salado

Chubut

Esequibo

Branco

Magdalena

Tocantins

Araguaia

Paraguay

Paraná

Parnaíba

Ucayali

Projection: Lambert's Azimuthal Equal Area

1   90   **2**   80

■ LIMA   Capital Cities

COPYRIGHT PHILIP'S

3   70   **4**   60   **5**   50   **6**   40   **7**

60 West from Greenwich 50

A   B   C   D   E   F   G   H

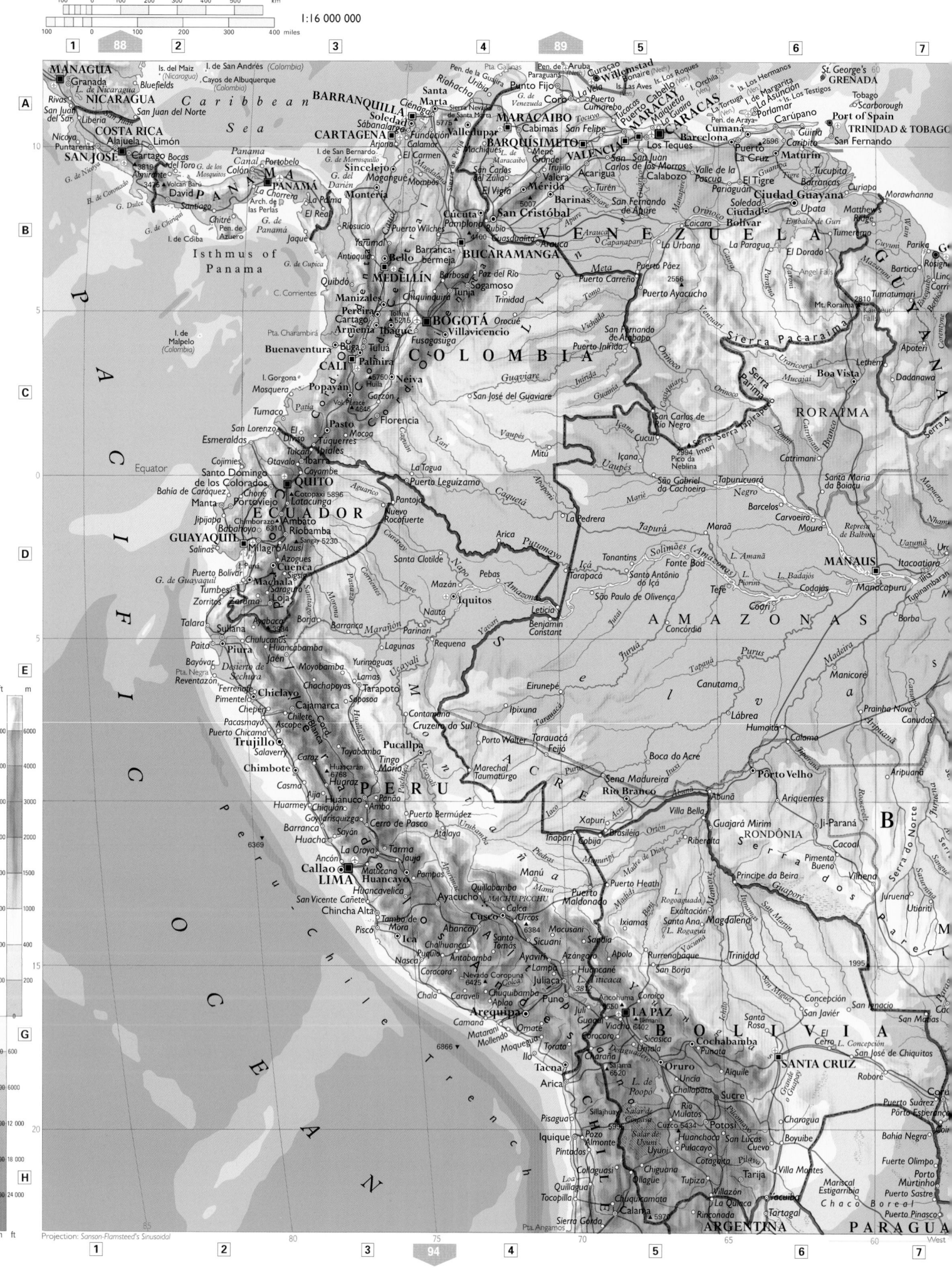

1:16 000 000

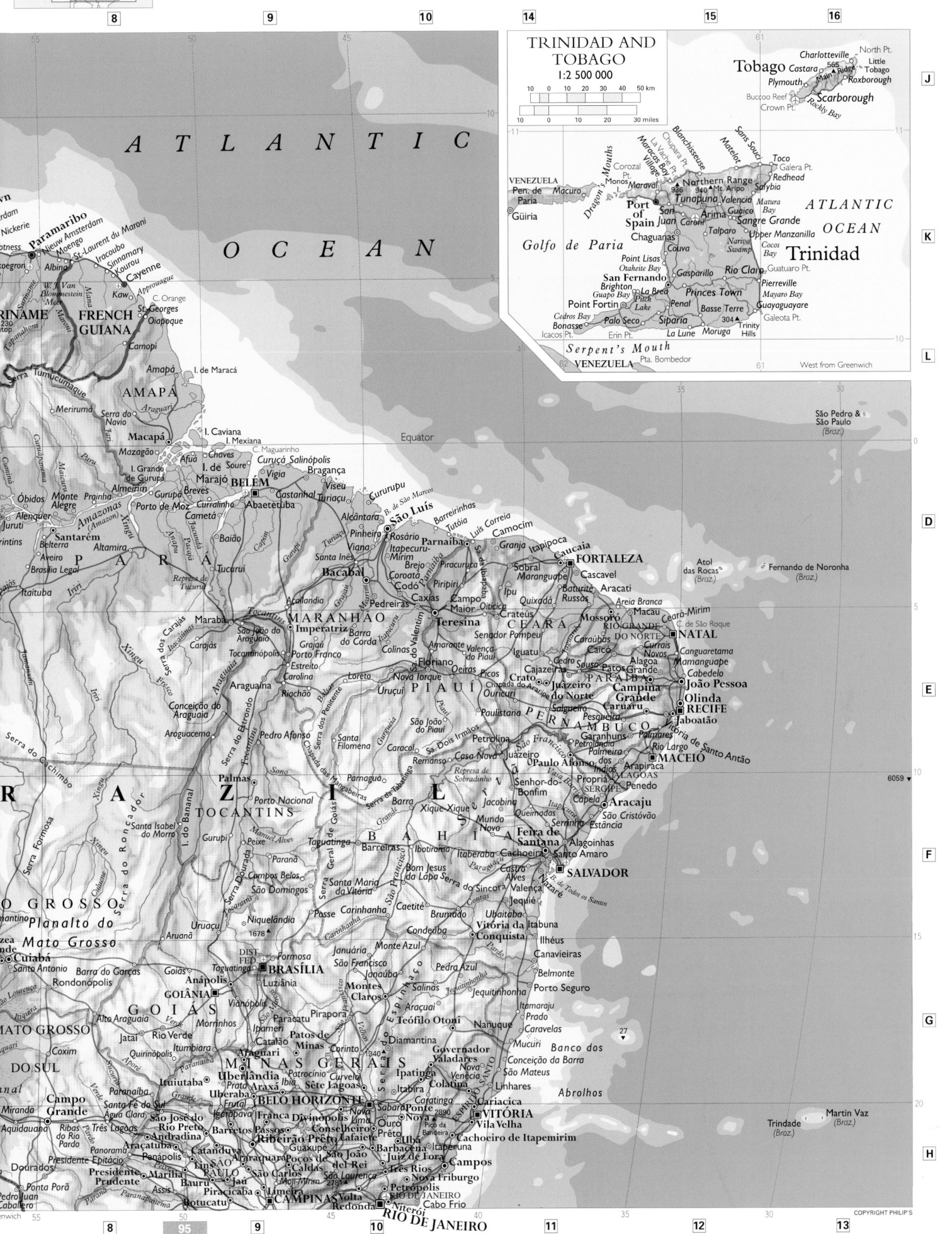

TRINIDAD AND TOBAGO
1:2 500 000

10 0 10 20 30 40 50 km
10 0   10   20   30 miles

ATLANTIC OCEAN

A T L A N T I C

O C E A N

Tobago Castara
Plymouth
Buccoo Reef
Crown Pt.

Charlotteville North Pt.
565 Ridge Little
Main Tobago
Rockly Bay Roxborough
Scarborough

J

VENEZUELA
Pen. de
Paria
Güiria

Dragon's Mouths
Monos
Maracas Village
La Vache Pt.
Maraval
Corozal Pt.

Blanchisseuses
Chupara Pt.
Matelot
Northern Range
940 Mt. Aripo
Tunapuna Valencia
Port of Spain San Juan
Chaguanas Caroni
Arima Guaico
Talparo

Sans Souci
Toco
936 Galera Pt.
Redhead
Salybia

ATLANTIC
OCEAN

Trinidad

Golfo de Paria

Point Lisas
Otaheite Bay
San Fernando Gasparillo
Brighton La Brea
Guapo Bay Penal
Point Fortin Siparia
Cedros Bay Palo Seco
Bonasse La Lune
Icacos Pt. Erin Pt.

Rio Claro
Princes Town
Basse Terre
Moruga
304 Trinity
Hills

Matura
Bay
Sangre Grande
Upper Manzanilla
Nariva
Swamp

Pierreville
Mayaro Bay
Guayaguayare
Galeota Pt.

Cocos
Bay
Guataro Pt.

Pitch
Lake

K

L

Serpent's Mouth
Pta. Bombedor
VENEZUELA

West from Greenwich

L

São Pedro &
São Pedro &
São Paulo
(Braz.)

Paramaribo
Nickerie
Nieuw Amsterdam
Moengo St-Laurent du Maroni
Iracoubo
Albina Sinnamary
Kourou
W.J. Van
Blommestein
Meer
Kaw Approuague
St-Georges
C. Orange
Oiapoque

**FRENCH
GUIANA**

SURINAME
koegroni
Camopi

AMAPÁ
Merirumã
Serra do
Navio
Macapá
Mazagão
I. Caviana
I. Mexiana
C. Maguarinho

Amapá
Araguari
I. de Maracá

BRAZIL

I. Grande
de Gurupá
Almeirim
Porto de Moz
Prainha
Monte
Alegre
Juruti
Óbidos
Alenquer

Afuá
I. de Soure
Breves
Curralinho
Cametá
Abaetetuba
Gurupá-de-Moz
Marajó
BELEM
Castanhal
Vigia
Bragança
Viseu
Turiaçu

Salinópolis
Curuçá

Equator

Fernando de Noronha
(Braz.)

Atol
das Rocas
(Braz.)

D

Santarém
Belterra
Aveiro
Altamira
Brasília Legal
Itaituba
Iriri

PARÁ
Tucuruí
Represa de
Tucuruí

Baião
Repartimento

Alcântara
Pinheiro
São Luís
Rosário
Pindaré-Mirim
Santa Inês
Viana
Bacabal
Acailândia
Pedreiras
Codó
Coroatá
Caxias
Piripiri
Campo
Maior
Teresina

Barreirinhas
Tutóia
B. de São Marcos
Parnaíba
Itapecuru-
Mirim
Brejo
Cururupu

Luís Correia
Camocim
Granja
Itapipoca
Sobral
Piracuruca
Marangupe
Ipu
Quixadá
Oiticica

CEARÁ
Baturité
Russas
FORTALEZA
Caucaia
Cascavel
Aracati

MARANHÃO
Maraba
São João do
Araguaia
Carajás
Serra dos Carajás
Tocantinópolis
Porto Franco
Estreito
Carolina
Riachão
Loreto

Imperatriz
Grajaú
Barra
do Corda
Colinas
Floriano
Oeiras
Picos
Uruçuí
Nova Iorque

PIAUÍ

Amarante
Valença
do Piauí
Cajazeiras

Crateús
Iguatu
Crato
Juazeiro
do Norte

Areia Branca
Macau
Mossoró
**RIO GRANDE
DO NORTE**
Caraúbas
Caicó
Patos
NATAL
Canguaretama
Mamanguape
Currais
Novos
Alagoa
Grande
Cabedelo
João Pessoa
C. de São Roque
Ceará-Mirim

E

São João
do Piauí
Caracol
Remanso
Casa Nova
Juàzeiro
Petrolina

Ouricuri
Paulistana
Sta. Dois Irmãos

Salgueiro
Pesqueira
Garanhuns
Arcoverde
Palmeira
dos Índios
Arapiraca
Propriá
Penedo
PERNAMBUCO
Campina
Grande
Caruaru
RECIFE
Olinda
Jaboatão
Palmares
Vitória de Santo Antão
Rio Largo
MACEIÓ
ALAGOAS

6059

Palmas
Porto Nacional
TOCANTINS
Gurupi
Peixe
Formosa
Taguatinga
Barreiras

Parnaguá
Barra
Xique-Xique
Ibotirama
Bom Jesus
da Lapa
Serra do Sincorá

Casa Nova
Senhor-do-
Bonfim
Jacobina
Mundo
Novo
Queimadas
Serrinha
Feira de
Santana
Itaberaba
Cachoeira
Castro
Alves
Valença

São Francisco
Capela
SERGIPE
São Cristóvão
Aracaju
Estância

F

BAHIA
Santa Maria
da Vitória
Caetité
Brumado
Condeúba
Vitória da
Conquista
Ubaitaba
Ilhéus
Canavieiras

Santo Amaro
SALVADOR
Nazaré
Jequié
B. de Todos os Santos

Mato Grosso
Planalto do
Mato Grosso
Cuiabá
Santo Antônio
Rondonópolis
Coxim

Niquelândia
Aruanã
1678
Uruaçu
São Domingos
Posse
Carinhanha
Januária
São Francisco
BRASÍLIA
DIST.
FED.
Taguatinga
Luziânia

Monte Azul
Salinas
Montes
Claros
Araçuaí
Pedra Azul
Jequitinhonha

Belmonte
Porto Seguro
Itamaraju
Prado
Caravelas

Banco dos
Abrolhos
27

G

GOIÁS
Anápolis
GOIÂNIA
Vianópolis
Alto Araguaia
Jataí
Quirinópolis
Campo
Grande
Aquidauana
Miranda
**MATO GROSSO
DO SUL**
Coxim

Morrinhos
Paracatu
Ipameri
Catalão
Itumbiara
Rio Verde

Piranga
Piracanjuba
Patos de
Minas
Patrocínio
Araxá
Ibiá
Sete Lagoas

Corinto
Diamantina
1340
Curvelo
Itabira

Teófilo Otoni
Governador
Valadares
Nova
Venécia
Colatina
Linhares

Conceição
da Barra
São Mateus

Nanuque
Mucuri

Trinidade
(Braz.)

Martin Vaz
(Braz.)

G

MINAS GERAIS
Uberlândia
Uberaba
Frutal
Prata
São José do
Rio Preto
Barretos
Andradina
Araçatuba
Penápolis
Marília
Bauru
Jaú

Araguari
Franca Divinópolis
Ribeirão Prêto
Passos
Pocos de
Caldas
São Carlos
Araraquara
Limeira
Piracicaba
CAMPINAS
Botucatu

Ituiutaba
Paranaíba
Santa Fé do Sul
Água Clara
Três Lagoas
Presidente
Prudente
Presidente
Epitácio
Panorama
Assis

Belo Horizonte
Sabará
Ponte
Nova
Ouro
Prêto
Barbacena
Conselheiro
Lafaiete
Pico da
2890 Bandeira
São João
del Rei
Mogi-Mirim

Caratinga
Ipatinga

Cachoeiro de Itapemirim

Cariacica
VITÓRIA
Vila Velha
**ESPÍRITO
SANTO**

Juiz de Fora
Três Rios
São Laurenço
Petrópolis
Volta
Redonda
Nova Friburgo
RIO DE JANEIRO
Cabo Frio
Niterói

Campos

H

8   95   9   10   11   12   13

RIO DE JANEIRO

COPYRIGHT PHILIP'S

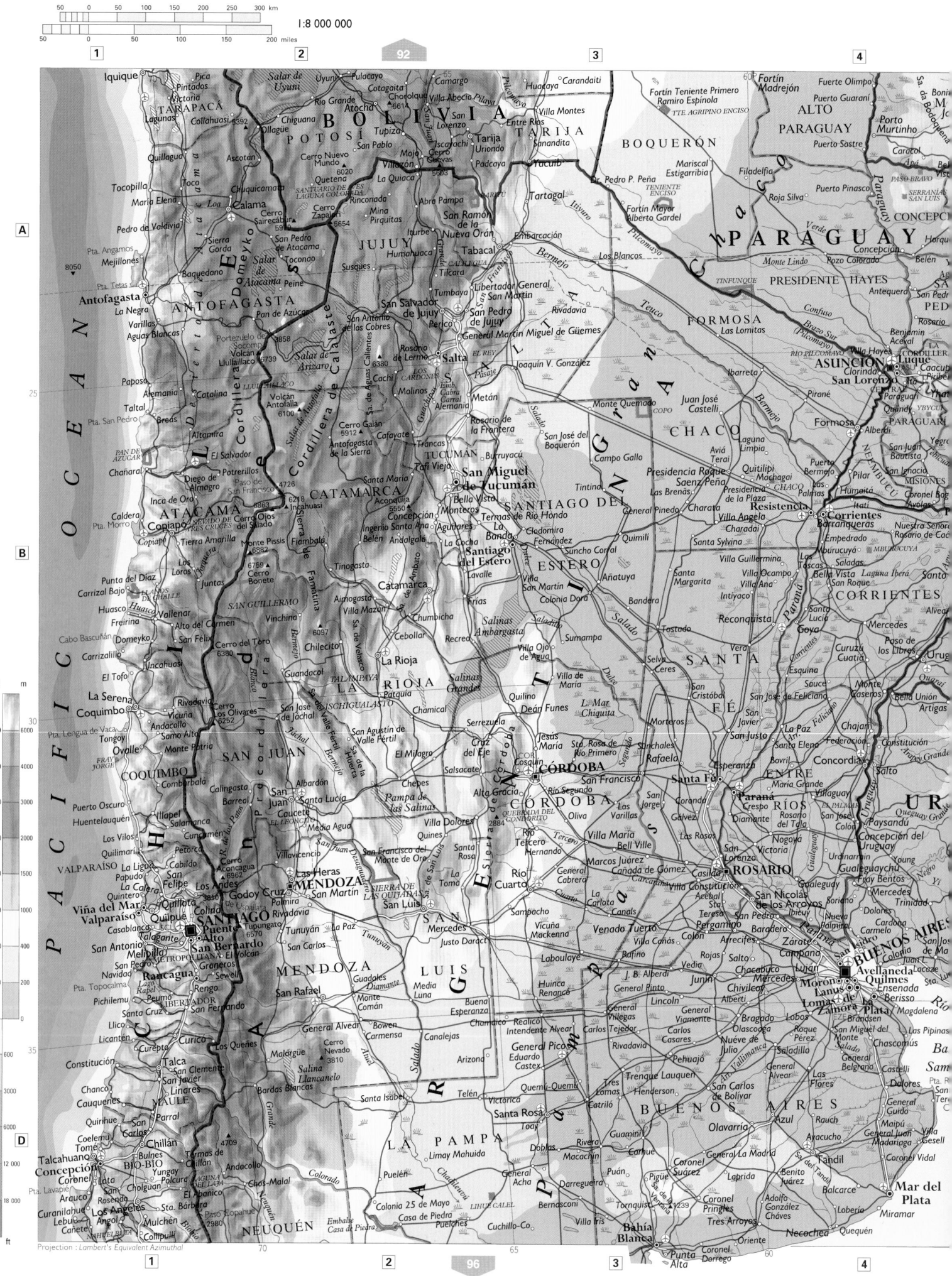

1:8 000 000

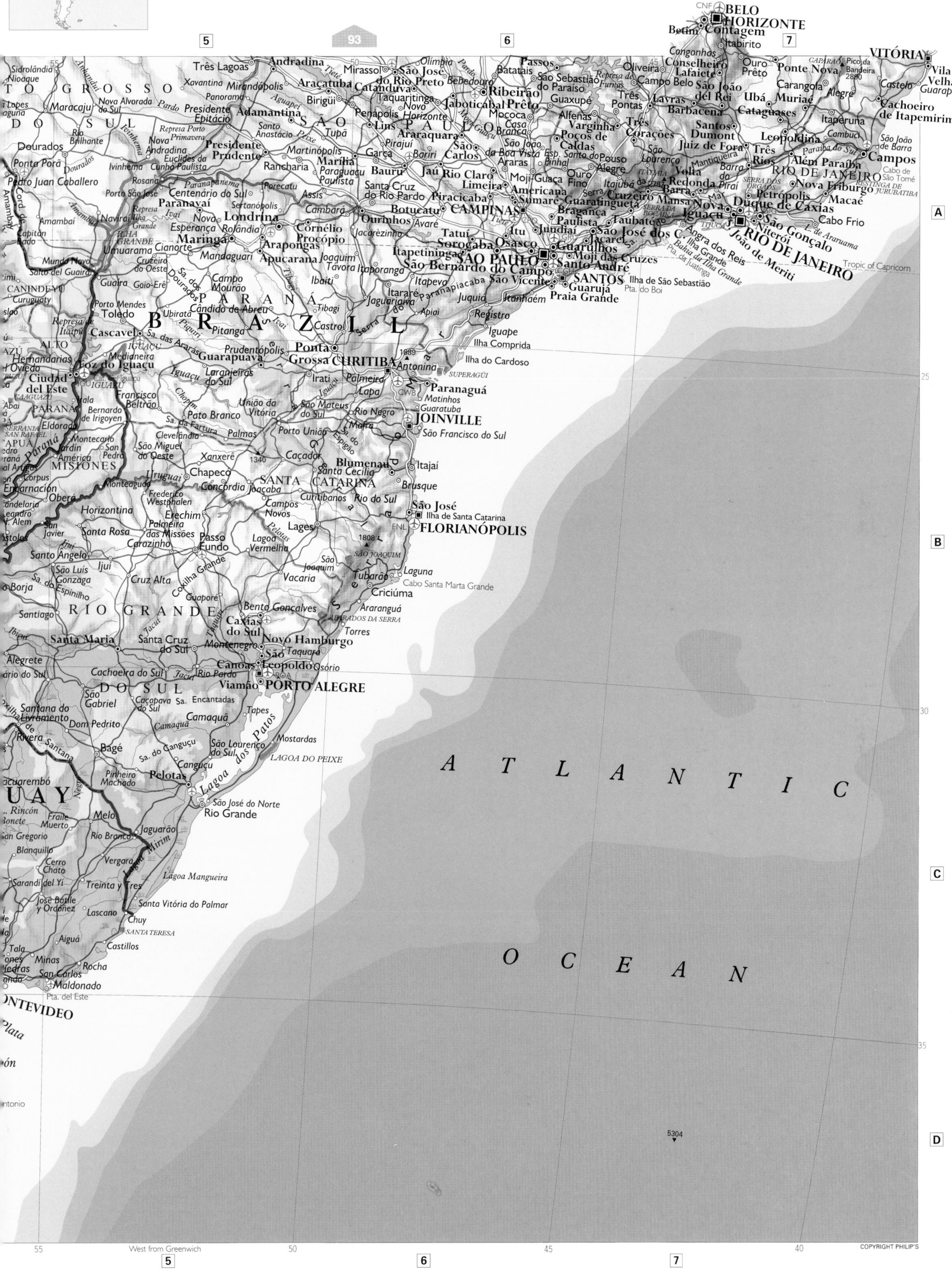

5   6   7

A
B
C
D

CNF BELO
HORIZONTE
Betim Contagem
Itabirito
VITÓRIA
Vila
Velha
Guarapari

TO GROSSO
DO SUL

Sidrolândia
Nioaque
Lopes
aguna
Maracaju
Nova Alvorada
do Sul
Dourados
Ponta Porã
Pedro Juan Caballero
Amambaí
Amambay
Nova
Andradina
Euclides da
Cunha Paulista
Presidente
Epitácio
Presidente
Prudente
Três Lagoas
Andradina
Mirandópolis
Panorama
Aracatuba
Birigüi
Araçatuba
Catanduva
Mirasso
do Rio Preto
São José
do Rio Preto
Olímpia
Passos
Batatais
São Sebastião
do Paraíso
Ribeirão Prêto
Guaxupé
Taquaritinga
Jaboticabal
Mococa
Casa
Branca
Alfenas
São João
da Boa Vista
Poços de
Caldas
Oliveira
Conselheiro
Lafaiete
Congonhas
Campo Belo
São João
del Rei
Barbacena
Três
Pontas
Varginha
Santo do
Pinhal
Lavras
Ubá
Muriaé
Cataguases
Leopoldina
Itaperuna

São João
de Barra
Campos
Cambuci

Martinópolis
Rancharia
Marília
Garça
Bauru
Jaú
Rio Claro
Limeira
Americana
Sumaré
Campinas
Atu
Jundiaí
Moji Guaçu
Mogi
Espirito
Santo do
Pouso
Alegre
São
Lourenço
Três
Corações
Juiz de Fora
Volta
Redonda
Barra
do
Piraí
Paraíba do Sul
Três
Rios
Além Paraíba
Petrópolis
Nova Friburgo
Macaé

Esp. Santo do
Botucatu
Avaré
Tatuí
Sorocaba
Itapetininga
Osasco
SÃO PAULO
São Bernardo do Campo
Santo André
São José dos C.
Moji das Cruzes
Guarulhos
Taubaté
Jacareí
Guaratinguetá
Cruzeiro
Mansa
Nova
Iguaçu
Duque de Caxias
São Gonçalo
Niterói
RIO DE JANEIRO
Cabo Frio

Paranaíba
Cornélio
Londrina
Procópio
Rolândia
Maringá
Apucarana
Arapongas
Mandaguari
Joaquim
Távora
Itaporanga
Ibaiti
Itararé
Itapeva
São Vicente
Juquiá
Santos
Guarujá
Praia Grande
Itanhaém
Angra dos Reis
João de Rio de Janeiro
Ilha Grande
Baía de Ilha Grande

BRAZIL

PARANÁ

Cândido de Abreu
Pitanga
Prudentópolis
Guarapuava
Ponta
Grossa
CURITIBA
Antonina
Paranaguá
Matinhos
Guaratuba
Ilha do Cardoso
Ilha Comprida
Iguape
Registro

Castro
Tibagi
Apiaí

Cascavel
Foz do Iguaçu
Ciudad
del Este
Francisco
Beltrão
Pato Branco
Palmas
São Mateus
do Sul
União da
Vitória
Porto União
Palmeira
Lapa
Irati
Rio Negro
Mafra
São Francisco do Sul
JOINVILLE
Itajaí

Xanxerê
Caçador
Santa Cecília
Blumenau
Brusque

Chapecó
Concórdia
Joaçaba
Curitibanos
Rio do Sul
São José
Ilha de Santa Catarina
FLORIANÓPOLIS

SANTA
CATARINA

Campos
Novos
Lages

Erechim
Passo
Fundo
Vacaria
Laguna

Santa Rosa
Carazinho
Bento Gonçalves
Criciúma
Araranguá

RIO GRANDE
Cruz Alta
Caxias
do Sul
Novo Hamburgo
Torres

DO SUL
Santa Maria
Santa Cruz
do Sul
Cachoeira do Sul
Montenegro
Canoas
São
Leopoldo
Osório
Taquara
Viamão
PORTO ALEGRE

Santana do
Livramento
Bagé
Pelotas
Rio Grande
São José do Norte

MONTEVIDEO

UAY

Melo
Rio Branco
Jaguarão
Santa Vitória do Palmar
Chuy

ATLANTIC

OCEAN

5304

1:16 000 000

100 0 100 200 300 400 500 km
100 0 100 200 300 400 miles

ATLANTIC

OCEAN

Argentine
Abyssal
Plain

BOLIVIA

PARAGUAY

Asunción

URUGUAY

MONTEVIDEO

BUENOS AIRES
La Plata

Mar del Plata

Bahía Blanca

Neuquén

CÓRDOBA

ROSARIO

Santa Fe
Paraná

MENDOZA
Godoy Cruz

SANTIAGO
Valparaíso
Viña del Mar

Concepción
Talcahuano

Temuco

Valdivia

Puerto Montt

Comodoro Rivadavia

Río Gallegos

SÃO PAULO
RIO DE JANEIRO
CAMPINAS
CURITIBA
JOINVILLE
FLORIANÓPOLIS
PORTO ALEGRE
Pelotas
Rio Grande

BRAZIL
ARGENTINA
CHILE

Tropic of Capricorn

PACIFIC OCEAN

Peru – Chile Trench

Golfo
San Matías

Golfo
San Jorge

Pen. Valdés

FALKLAND ISLANDS
(ISLAS MALVINAS) (U.K.)
West Falkland
East Falkland
Stanley

South Georgia
(U.K.)
Grytviken
King Edward Pt.
Mt. Paget 2934

Isla Grande de
Tierra del Fuego

Estrecho de Magallanes
(Magellan's Str.)

C. de Hornos (C. Horn)

Projection: Sanson-Flamsteed's Sinusoidal

West from Greenwich

COPYRIGHT PHILIP'S

ft m
12 000 4000
9000 3000
6000 2000
4500 1500
3000 1000
1200 400
600 200
0 0
200 600
2000 6000
4000 12 000
6000 18 000
8000 24 000
m ft

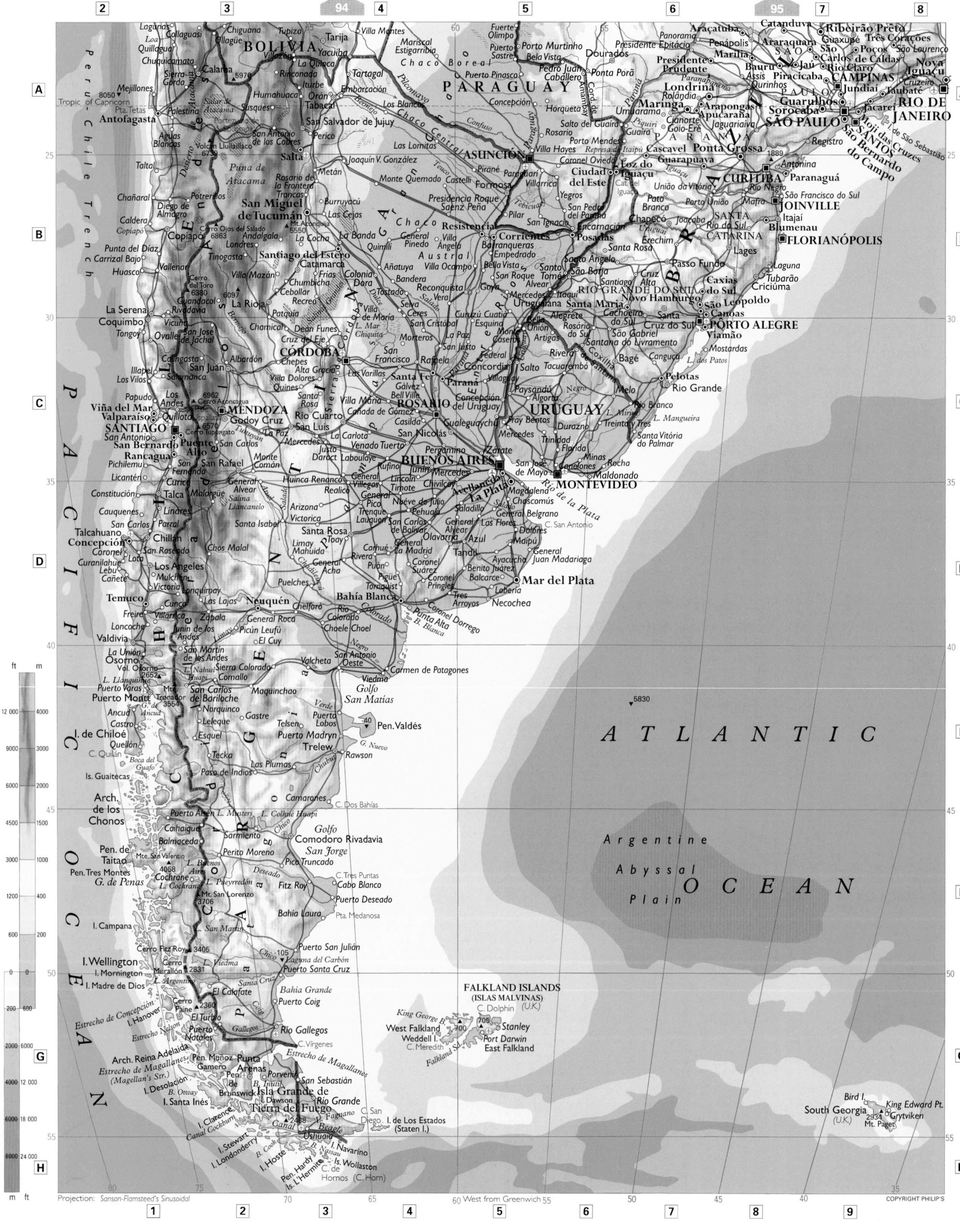

INDEX TO WORLD MAPS

The index contains the names of all the principal places and features shown on the World Maps. Each name is followed by an additional entry in italics giving the country or region within which it is located. The alphabetical order of names composed of two or more words is governed primarily by the first word, then by the second, and then by the country or region name that follows. This is an example of the rule:

Mīr Kūh *Iran*	26°22N 58°55E	**47** E8
Mīr Shahdād *Iran*	26°15N 58°29E	**47** E8
Mira *Italy*	45°26N 12°8E	**22** B5
Mira por vos Cay *Bahamas*	22°9N 74°30W	**89** B5

Physical features composed of a proper name (Erie) and a description (Lake) are positioned alphabetically by the proper name. The description is positioned after the proper name and is usually abbreviated:

Erie, L. *N. Amer.*	42°15N 81°0W	**82** D4

Where a description forms part of a settlement or administrative name, however, it is always written in full and put in its true alphabetical position:

Mount Morris *U.S.A.*	42°44N 77°52W	**82** D7

Names beginning with M' and Mc are indexed as if they were spelled Mac. Names beginning St. are alphabetized under Saint, but Sankt, Sint, Sant', Santa and San are all spelt in full and are alphabetized accordingly. If the same place name occurs two or more times in the index and all are in the same country, each is followed by the name of the administrative subdivision in which it is located.

The geographical co-ordinates which follow each name in the index give the latitude and longitude of each place. The first co-ordinate indicates latitude – the distance north or south of the Equator. The second co-ordinate indicates longitude – the distance east or west of the Greenwich Meridian. Both latitude and longitude are measured in degrees and minutes (there are 60 minutes in a degree).

The latitude is followed by N(orth) or S(outh) and the longitude by E(ast) or W(est).

The number in bold type which follows the geographical co-ordinates refers to the number of the map page where that feature or place will be found. This is usually the largest scale at which the place or feature appears.

The letter and figure that are immediately after the page number give the grid square on the map page, within which the feature is situated. The letter represents the latitude and the figure the longitude. A lower-case letter immediately after the page number refers to an inset map on that page.

In some cases the feature itself may fall within the specified square, while the name is outside. This is usually the case only with features that are larger than a grid square.

Rivers are indexed to their mouths or confluences, and carry the symbol ➔ after their names. The following symbols are also used in the index: ■ country, ☑ overseas territory or dependency, ☐ first-order administrative area, △ national park, ◠ other park (provincial park, nature reserve or game reserve), ✘ (LHR) principal airport (and location identifier), ✿ Australian aboriginal land.

Abbreviations used in the index

A.C.T. – Australian Capital Territory
A.R. – Autonomous Region
Afghan. – Afghanistan
Afr. – Africa
Ala. – Alabama
Alta. – Alberta
Amer. – America(n)
Ant. – Antilles
Arch. – Archipelago
Ariz. – Arizona
Ark. – Arkansas
Atl. Oc. – Atlantic Ocean
B. – Baie, Bahía, Bay, Bucht, Bugt
B.C. – British Columbia
Bangla. – Bangladesh
Barr. – Barrage
Bos.-H. – Bosnia-Herzegovina
C. – Cabo, Cap, Cape, Coast
C.A.R. – Central African Republic
C. Prov. – Cape Province
Calif. – California
Cat. – Catarata
Cent. – Central
Chan. – Channel
Colo. – Colorado
Conn. – Connecticut
Cord. – Cordillera
Cr. – Creek
Czech. – Czech Republic
D.C. – District of Columbia
Del. – Delaware
Dem. – Democratic
Dep. – Dependency
Des. – Desert
Dét. – Détroit
Dist. – District
Dj. – Djebel
Dom. Rep. – Dominican Republic

E. – East
El Salv. – El Salvador
Eq. Guin. – Equatorial Guinea
Est. – Estrecho
Falk. Is. – Falkland Is.
Fd. – Fjord
Fla. – Florida
Fr. – French
G. – Golfe, Golfo, Gulf, Guba, Gebel
Ga. – Georgia
Gt. – Great, Greater
Guinea-Biss. – Guinea-Bissau
H.K. – Hong Kong
H.P. – Himachal Pradesh
Hants. – Hampshire
Harb. – Harbor, Harbour
Hd. – Head
Hts. – Heights
I.(s). – Île, Ilha, Insel, Isla, Island, Isle
Ill. – Illinois
Ind. – Indiana
Ind. Oc. – Indian Ocean
Ivory C. – Ivory Coast
J. – Jabal, Jebel
Jaz. – Jazīrah
Junc. – Junction
K. – Kap, Kapp
Kans. – Kansas
Kep. – Kepulauan
Ky. – Kentucky
L. – Lac, Lacul, Lago, Lagoa, Lake, Limni, Loch, Lough
La. – Louisiana
Ld. – Land
Liech. – Liechtenstein
Lux. – Luxembourg
Mad. P. – Madhya Pradesh
Madag. – Madagascar
Man. – Manitoba
Mass. – Massachusetts

Md. – Maryland
Me. – Maine
Medit. S. – Mediterranean Sea
Mich. – Michigan
Minn. – Minnesota
Miss. – Mississippi
Mo. – Missouri
Mont. – Montana
Mozam. – Mozambique
Mt.(s) – Mont, Montaña, Mountain
Mte. – Monte
Mti. – Monti
N. – Nord, Norte, North, Northern, Nouveau, Nahal, Nahr
N.B. – New Brunswick
N.C. – North Carolina
N. Cal. – New Caledonia
N. Dak. – North Dakota
N.H. – New Hampshire
N.I. – North Island
N.J. – New Jersey
N. Mex. – New Mexico
N.S. – Nova Scotia
N.S.W. – New South Wales
N.W.T. – North West Territory
N.Y. – New York
N.Z. – New Zealand
Nac. – Nacional
Nat. – National
Nebr. – Nebraska
Neths. – Netherlands
Nev. – Nevada
Nfld & L. – Newfoundland and Labrador
Nic. – Nicaragua
O. – Oued, Ouadi
Occ. – Occidentale
Okla. – Oklahoma
Ont. – Ontario
Or. – Orientale

Oreg. – Oregon
Os. – Ostrov
Oz. – Ozero
P. – Pass, Passo, Pasul, Pulau
P.E.I. – Prince Edward Island
Pa. – Pennsylvania
Pac. Oc. – Pacific Ocean
Papua N.G. – Papua New Guinea
Pass. – Passage
Peg. – Pegunungan
Pen. – Peninsula, Péninsule
Phil. – Philippines
Pk. – Peak
Plat. – Plateau
Prov. – Province, Provincial
Pt. – Point
Pta. – Ponta, Punta
Pte. – Pointe
Qué. – Québec
Queens. – Queensland
R. – Rio, River
R.I. – Rhode Island
Ra. – Range
Raj. – Rajasthan
Recr. – Recreational, Récréatif
Reg. – Region
Rep. – Republic
Res. – Reserve, Reservoir
Rhld-Pfz. – Rheinland-Pfalz
S. – South, Southern, Sur
Si. Arabia – Saudi Arabia
S.C. – South Carolina
S. Dak. – South Dakota
S.I. – South Island
S. Leone – Sierra Leone
Sa. – Serra, Sierra
Sask. – Saskatchewan
Scot. – Scotland
Sd. – Sound
Sev. – Severnaya
Sib. – Siberia

Sprs. – Springs
St. – Saint
Sta. – Santa
Ste. – Sainte
Sto. – Santo
Str. – Strait, Stretto
Switz. – Switzerland
Tas. – Tasmania
Tenn. – Tennessee
Terr. – Territory, Territoire
Tex. – Texas
Tg. – Tanjung
Trin. & Tob. – Trinidad & Tobago
U.A.E. – United Arab Emirates
U.K. – United Kingdom
U.S.A. – United States of America
Ut. P. – Uttar Pradesh
Va. – Virginia
Vdkhr. – Vodokhranilishche
Vdskh. – Vodoskhovyshche
Vf. – Vîrful
Vic. – Victoria
Vol. – Volcano
Vt. – Vermont
W. – Wadi, West
W. Va. – West Virginia
Wall. & F. Is. – Wallis and Futuna Is.
Wash. – Washington
Wis. – Wisconsin
Wlkp. – Wielkopolski
Wyo. – Wyoming
Yorks. – Yorkshire

A

A Coruña Spain 43°20N 8°25W 21 A1
A Estrada Spain 42°43N 8°27W 21 A1
A Fonsagrada Spain 43°8N 7°4W 21 A2
A Shau Vietnam 16°6N 107°22E 38 D6
Aabenraa Denmark 55°3N 9°25E 9 J13
Aachen Germany 50°45N 6°6E 16 C4
Aalborg Denmark 57°2N 9°54E 9 H13
Aalen Germany 48°51N 10°6E 16 D6
Aalst Belgium 50°56N 4°2E 15 D4
Aalten Neths. 51°56N 6°35E 15 C6
Aalter Belgium 51°5N 3°28E 15 C3
Äänekoski Finland 62°36N 25°44E 8 E21
Aarau Switz. 47°23N 8°4E 20 C8
Aare → Switz. 47°33N 8°14E 20 C8
Aarhus Denmark 56°8N 10°11E 9 H14
Aarschot Belgium 50°59N 4°49E 15 D4
Aba China 32°59N 101°42E 34 A3
Aba Nigeria 5°10N 7°19E 52 G7
Abaco I. Bahamas 26°25N 77°10W 88 A4
Ābādān Iran 30°22N 48°20E 47 D6
Ābādeh Iran 31°8N 52°40E 47 D7
Abadla Algeria 31°2N 2°45W 52 B5
Abaetetuba Brazil 1°40S 48°50W 93 D9
Abagnar Qi = Xilinhot China 43°52N 116°2E 32 C9
Abah, Tanjung Indonesia 8°46S 115°38E 37 K18
Abai Paraguay 25°58S 55°54W 95 B4
Abakan Russia 53°40N 91°10E 27 D10
Abancay Peru 13°35S 72°55W 92 F4
Abang, Gunung Indonesia 8°16S 115°25E 37 J18
Abariringa Kiribati 2°50S 171°40W 64 H10
Abarqū Iran 31°10N 53°20E 47 D7
Abashiri Japan 44°0N 144°15E 28 B12
Abashiri-Wan Japan 44°0N 144°30E 28 C12
Ābay = Nîl el Azraq → Sudan 15°38N 32°31E 53 E12
Abay Kazakhstan 49°38N 72°53E 26 E8
Abaya, L. Ethiopia 6°30N 37°50E 49 F2
Abaza Russia 52°39N 90°6E 26 D10
'Abbāsābād Iran 33°34N 58°23E 47 C8
Abbay = Nîl el Azraq → Sudan 15°38N 32°31E 53 E12
Abbaye, Pt. U.S.A. 46°58N 88°8W 80 B9
Abbé, L. Ethiopia 11°8N 41°47E 49 E3
Abbeville France 50°6N 1°49E 20 A4
Abbeville Ala., U.S.A. 31°34N 85°15W 85 F12
Abbeville La., U.S.A. 29°58N 92°8W 84 G8
Abbeville S.C., U.S.A. 34°11N 82°23W 85 D13
Abbeyfeale Ireland 52°23N 9°18W 10 D2
Abbeyleix Ireland 52°54N 7°22W 10 D4
Abbot Ice Shelf Antarctica 73°0S 92°0W 5 D16
Abbotsford Canada 49°5N 122°20W 70 D4
Abbottabad Pakistan 34°10N 73°15E 42 B5
ABC Islands W. Indies 12°15N 69°0W 89 D6
Abd al Kūrī Yemen 12°5N 52°20E 49 E5
Ābdar Iran 30°16N 55°19E 47 D7
'Abdolābād Iran 34°12N 56°30E 47 C8
Abdulpur Bangla. 24°15N 88°59E 43 G13
Abéché Chad 13°50N 20°35E 53 F10
Abel Tasman △ N.Z. 40°59S 173°3E 59 D4
Abengourou Ivory C. 6°42N 3°27W 52 G5
Åbenrå = Aabenraa Denmark 55°3N 9°25E 9 J13
Abeokuta Nigeria 7°3N 3°19E 52 G6
Aberaeron U.K. 52°15N 4°15W 13 E3
Aberayron = Aberaeron U.K. 52°15N 4°15W 13 E3
Aberchirder U.K. 57°34N 2°37W 11 D6
Abercorn Australia 25°12S 151°5E 63 D5
Aberdare U.K. 51°43N 3°27W 13 F4
Aberdaugleddau = Milford Haven U.K. 51°42N 5°7W 13 F2
Aberdeen Australia 32°9S 150°56E 63 E5
Aberdeen Canada 52°20N 106°8W 71 C7
Aberdeen S. Africa 32°28S 24°2E 56 D3
Aberdeen U.K. 57°9N 2°5W 11 D6
Aberdeen Idaho, U.S.A. 42°57N 112°50W 76 E7
Aberdeen Md., U.S.A. 39°31N 76°10W 81 F15
Aberdeen Miss., U.S.A. 33°49N 88°33W 85 E10
Aberdeen S. Dak., U.S.A. 45°28N 98°29W 80 C4
Aberdeen Wash., U.S.A. 46°59N 123°50W 78 D3
Aberdeen, City of □ U.K. 57°10N 2°10W 11 D6
Aberdeen L. Canada 64°30N 99°0W 68 E12
Aberdeenshire □ U.K. 57°17N 2°36W 11 D6
Aberdovey = Aberdyfi U.K. 52°33N 4°3W 13 E3
Aberdyfi U.K. 52°33N 4°3W 13 E3
Aberfeldy U.K. 56°37N 3°51W 11 E5
Aberfoyle U.K. 56°11N 4°23W 11 E4
Abergavenny U.K. 51°49N 3°1W 13 F4
Abergele U.K. 53°17N 3°35W 12 D4
Abergwaun = Fishguard U.K. 52°0N 4°58W 13 E3
Aberhonddu = Brecon U.K. 51°57N 3°23W 13 F4
Abermaw = Barmouth U.K. 52°44N 4°4W 12 E3
Abernathy U.S.A. 33°50N 101°51W 84 E4
Aberpennar = Mountain Ash U.K. 51°40N 3°23W 13 F4
Abert, L. U.S.A. 42°38N 120°14W 76 E3
Abertawe = Swansea U.K. 51°37N 3°57W 13 F4
Aberteifi = Cardigan U.K. 52°5N 4°40W 13 E3
Aberystwyth U.K. 52°25N 4°5W 13 E3
Abhā Si. Arabia 18°0N 42°34E 49 D3
Abhar Iran 36°9N 49°13E 47 B6
Abhayapuri India 26°24N 90°38E 43 F14
Abidjan Ivory C. 5°26N 3°58W 52 G5
Abilene Kans., U.S.A. 38°55N 97°13W 80 F5
Abilene Tex., U.S.A. 32°28N 99°43W 84 E5
Abingdon U.K. 51°40N 1°17W 13 F6
Abingdon U.S.A. 36°43N 81°59W 81 G13
Abington Reef Australia 18°0S 149°35E 62 B4
Abitau → Canada 59°53N 109°3W 71 B7
Abitibi → Canada 51°3N 80°55W 72 B3
Abitibi, L. Canada 48°40N 79°40W 72 C4
Abkhaz Republic = Abkhazia □ Georgia 43°12N 41°5E 19 F7
Abkhazia □ Georgia 43°12N 41°5E 19 F7
Abminga Australia 26°8S 134°51E 63 D1
Åbo = Turku Finland 60°30N 22°19E 9 F20
Abohar India 30°10N 74°10E 42 D6
Abomey Benin 7°10N 2°5E 52 G6
Abong-Mbang Cameroon 4°0N 13°8E 54 D2
Abou-Deïa Chad 11°20N 19°20E 53 F9
Aboyne U.K. 57°4N 2°47W 11 D6
Abra Pampa Argentina 22°43S 65°42W 94 A2
Abraham L. Canada 52°15N 116°35W 70 C5
Abreojos, Pta. Mexico 26°50N 113°40W 86 B2
Abrolhos, Banco dos Brazil 18°0S 38°0W 90 E7
Abrud Romania 46°19N 23°5E 17 E12
Absaroka Range U.S.A. 44°45N 109°50W 76 D9
Abu India 24°41N 72°50E 42 G5
Abū al Abyad U.A.E. 24°11N 53°50E 47 E7
Abū al Khaşīb Iraq 30°25N 48°0E 46 D5
Abū 'Alī Si. Arabia 27°20N 49°27E 47 E6
Abū 'Alī → Lebanon 34°25N 35°50E 48 A4
Abu Dhabi = Abū Ẓāby U.A.E. 24°28N 54°22E 47 E7
Abū Du'ān Syria 36°25N 38°15E 46 B3
Abu el Gaīn, W. → Egypt 29°35N 33°30E 48 F2
Abu Ga'da, W. → Egypt 29°15N 32°53E 48 F1
Abū Ḩadrīyah Si. Arabia 27°20N 48°58E 47 E6
Abu Hamed Sudan 19°32N 33°13E 53 E12
Abū Kamāl Syria 34°30N 41°0E 46 C4
Abū Madd, Ra's Si. Arabia 24°50N 37°7E 46 E3
Abū Mūsā U.A.E. 25°52N 55°3E 47 E7
Abū Qaşr Si. Arabia 30°21N 38°34E 46 D3
Abu Shagara, Ras Sudan 21°4N 37°19E 53 D13
Abu Simbel Egypt 22°18N 31°40E 53 D12
Abū Şukhayr Iraq 31°54N 44°30E 46 D5
Abû Zabad Sudan 12°25N 29°10E 53 F11
Abū Ẓāby U.A.E. 24°28N 54°22E 47 E7
Abū Zeydābād Iran 33°54N 51°45E 47 C6
Abuja Nigeria 9°5N 7°32E 52 G7
Abukuma-Gawa → Japan 38°6N 140°52E 28 E10
Abukuma-Sammyaku Japan 37°30N 140°45E 28 F10
Abunã Brazil 9°40S 65°20W 92 E5
Abunã → Brazil 9°41S 65°20W 92 E5
Abut Hd. N.Z. 43°7S 170°15E 59 E3
Abyei ☒ Sudan 9°30N 28°30E 53 G11
Ābyek Iran 36°4N 50°33E 47 B6
Acadia △ U.S.A. 44°20N 68°13W 81 C19
Açailândia Brazil 4°57S 47°0W 93 D9
Acajutla El Salv. 13°36N 89°50W 88 D2
Acámbaro Mexico 20°2N 100°44W 86 D4
Acaponeta Mexico 22°30N 105°22W 86 C3
Acapulco Mexico 16°51N 99°55W 87 D5
Acaraí, Serra Brazil 1°50N 57°50W 92 C7
Acarigua Venezuela 9°33N 69°12W 92 B5
Acatlán Mexico 18°12N 98°3W 87 D5
Acayucán Mexico 17°57N 94°55W 87 D6
Accomac U.S.A. 37°43N 75°40W 81 G16
Accra Ghana 5°35N 0°6W 52 G5
Accrington U.K. 53°45N 2°22W 12 D5
Acebal Argentina 33°20S 60°50W 94 C3
Aceh □ Indonesia 4°15N 97°30E 36 D1
Achalpur India 21°22N 77°32E 44 D3
Acharnes Greece 38°5N 23°44E 23 E10
Acheloos → Greece 38°19N 21°7E 23 E9
Acheng China 45°30N 126°58E 33 B14
Acher India 23°10N 72°32E 42 H5
Achill Hd. Ireland 53°58N 10°15W 10 C1
Achill I. Ireland 53°58N 10°1W 10 C1
Achinsk Russia 56°20N 90°20E 27 D10
Acireale Italy 37°37N 15°10E 22 F6
Ackerman U.S.A. 33°19N 89°11W 85 E10
Acklins I. Bahamas 22°30N 74°0W 89 B5
Acme Canada 51°33N 113°30W 70 C6
Acme U.S.A. 40°8N 79°26W 82 F5
Aconcagua, Cerro Argentina 32°39S 70°0W 94 C2
Aconquija, Mt. Argentina 27°0S 66°0W 94 B2
Açores, Is. dos Atl. Oc. 38°0N 27°0W 52 a
Acornhoek S. Africa 24°37S 31°2E 57 B5
Acraman, L. Australia 32°2S 135°23E 63 E2
Acre = 'Akko Israel 32°55N 35°4E 48 C4
Acre □ Brazil 9°1S 71°0W 92 E4
Acre → Brazil 8°45S 67°22W 92 E5
Actinolite Canada 44°32N 77°19W 82 B7
Acton Canada 43°38N 80°3W 82 C4
Ad Dammām Si. Arabia 26°20N 50°5E 47 E6
Ad Dāmūr Lebanon 33°43N 35°27E 48 B4
Ad Dawādimī Si. Arabia 24°35N 44°15E 46 E5
Ad Dawḩah Qatar 25°15N 51°35E 47 E6
Ad Dawr Iraq 34°27N 43°47E 46 C4
Ad Dhakhīrah Qatar 25°44N 51°33E 47 E6
Ad Dir'īyah Si. Arabia 24°44N 46°35E 46 E5
Ad Dīwānīyah Iraq 32°0N 45°0E 46 D5
Ad Dujayl Iraq 33°51N 44°14E 46 C5
Ad Duwayd Si. Arabia 30°15N 42°17E 46 D4
Ada Minn., U.S.A. 47°18N 96°31W 80 B5
Ada Okla., U.S.A. 34°46N 96°41W 84 D6
Adabiya Egypt 29°53N 32°28E 48 F1
Adair, C. Canada 71°30N 71°34W 69 C17
Adaja → Spain 41°32N 4°52W 21 B3
Adak U.S.A. 51°45N 176°45W 74 E4
Adak I. U.S.A. 51°45N 176°45W 74 E4
Adamaoua, Massif de l' Cameroon 7°20N 12°20E 53 G8
Adamawa Highlands = Adamaoua, Massif de l' Cameroon 7°20N 12°20E 53 G8
Adamello, Mte. Italy 46°9N 10°30E 20 C9
Adaminaby Australia 36°0S 148°45E 63 F4
Adams Mass., U.S.A. 42°38N 73°7W 83 D11
Adams N.Y., U.S.A. 43°49N 76°1W 83 C8
Adams Wis., U.S.A. 43°57N 89°49W 80 D9
Adams, Mt. U.S.A. 46°12N 121°30W 78 D5
Adam's Bridge Sri Lanka 9°15N 79°40E 45 K4
Adams L. Canada 51°10N 119°40W 70 C5
Adam's Peak Sri Lanka 6°48N 80°30E 45 L5
'Adan Yemen 12°45N 45°0E 49 E4
Adana Turkey 37°0N 35°16E 46 B2
Adang, Ko Thailand 6°33N 99°18E 39 J2
Adapazarı = Sakarya Turkey 40°48N 30°25E 19 F5
Adarama Sudan 17°10N 34°52E 53 E12
Adare Ireland 52°34N 8°47W 10 D3
Adare, C. Antarctica 71°0S 171°0E 5 D11
Adaut Indonesia 8°8S 131°7E 37 F8
Adavale Australia 25°52S 144°32E 63 D3
Adda → Italy 45°8N 9°53E 20 D8
Addatigala India 17°31N 82°3E 44 F6
Addis Ababa = Addis Abeba Ethiopia 9°2N 38°42E 49 F2
Addis Abeba Ethiopia 9°2N 38°42E 49 F2
Addison U.S.A. 42°1N 77°14W 82 D7
Addo S. Africa 33°32S 25°45E 56 D4
Addo △ S. Africa 33°30S 25°50E 56 D4
Ādeh Iran 37°42N 45°11E 46 B5
Adel U.S.A. 31°8N 83°25W 85 F13
Adelaide Australia 34°52S 138°30E 63 E2
Adelaide S. Africa 32°42S 26°20E 56 D4
Adelaide I. Antarctica 67°15S 68°30W 5 C17
Adelaide Pen. Canada 68°15N 97°30W 68 D12
Adelaide River Australia 13°15S 131°7E 60 B5
Adelaide Village Bahamas 25°0N 77°31W 88 A4
Adelanto U.S.A. 34°35N 117°22W 79 L9
Adele I. Australia 15°32S 123°9E 60 C3
Adélie, Terre Antarctica 68°0S 140°0E 5 C10
Adelie Land = Adélie, Terre Antarctica 68°0S 140°0E 5 C10
Aden = 'Adan Yemen 12°45N 45°0E 49 E4
Aden, G. of Ind. Oc. 12°30N 47°30E 49 E4
Adendorp S. Africa 32°15S 24°30E 56 D3
Adh Dhayd U.A.E. 25°17N 55°53E 47 E7
Adhoi India 23°26N 70°32E 42 H4
Adi Indonesia 4°15S 133°30E 37 E8
Adieu, C. Australia 32°0S 132°10E 61 F5
Adieu Pt. Australia 15°14S 124°35E 60 C3
Adige → Italy 45°9N 12°20E 22 B5
Adigrat Ethiopia 14°20N 39°26E 49 E2
Adilabad India 19°33N 78°20E 44 E4
Adirondack ⌂ U.S.A. 44°0N 74°20W 83 C10
Adirondack Mts. U.S.A. 44°0N 74°0W 83 C10
Adis Abeba = Addis Abeba Ethiopia 9°2N 38°42E 49 F2
Adjuntas Puerto Rico 18°10N 66°43W 89 d
Adlavik Is. Canada 55°0N 58°40W 73 B8
Admiralty G. Australia 14°20S 125°55E 60 B4
Admiralty Gulf ✪ Australia 14°16S 125°52E 60 B4
Admiralty I. U.S.A. 57°30N 134°30W 70 B2
Admiralty Inlet Canada 72°30N 86°0W 69 C14
Admiralty Is. Papua N. G. 2°0S 147°0E 58 B7
Adolfo González Chaves Argentina 38°2S 60°5W 94 D3
Adolfo Ruiz Cortines, Presa Mexico 27°15N 109°6W 86 B3
Adonara Indonesia 8°15S 123°5E 37 F6
Adoni India 15°33N 77°18E 45 G3
Adour → France 43°32N 1°32W 20 E3
Adra India 23°30N 86°42E 43 H12
Adra Spain 36°43N 3°3W 21 D4
Adrano Italy 37°40N 14°50E 22 F6
Adrar Algeria 27°51N 0°11E 52 C6
Adrar Mauritania 20°30N 7°30W 52 D3
Adrar des Iforas Africa 19°40N 1°40E 52 E6
Adrian Mich., U.S.A. 41°54N 84°2W 81 E11
Adrian Tex., U.S.A. 35°16N 102°40W 84 D3
Adriatic Sea Medit. S. 43°0N 16°0E 22 C6
Adua Indonesia 1°45S 129°50E 37 E7
Adur India 9°8N 76°40E 45 K3
Adwa Ethiopia 14°15N 38°52E 49 E2
Adygea □ Russia 45°0N 40°0E 19 F7
Adzhar Republic = Ajaria □ Georgia 41°30N 42°0E 19 F7
Adzopé Ivory C. 6°7N 3°49W 52 G5
Ægean Sea Medit. S. 38°30N 25°0E 23 E11
Aerhtai Shan Mongolia 46°40N 92°45E 30 B7
Afaahiti Tahiti 17°45S 149°17W 59 d
'Afak Iraq 32°4N 45°15E 46 C5
Afareaitu Moorea 17°33S 149°47W 59 d
Afghanistan ■ Asia 33°0N 65°0E 40 C4
Aflou Algeria 34°7N 2°3E 52 B6
Afognak I. U.S.A. 58°15N 152°30W 74 D9
Africa 10°0N 20°0E 50 E6
'Afrīn Syria 36°32N 36°50E 46 B3
Afton N.Y., U.S.A. 42°14N 75°32W 83 D9
Afton Wyo., U.S.A. 42°44N 110°56W 76 E8
Afuá Brazil 0°15S 50°20W 93 D8
'Afula Israel 32°37N 35°17E 48 C4
Afyon Turkey 38°45N 30°33E 19 G5
Afyonkarahisar = Afyon Turkey 38°45N 30°33E 19 G5
Āgā Jarī Iran 30°42N 49°50E 47 D6
Agadès = Agadez Niger 16°58N 7°59E 52 E7
Agadez Niger 16°58N 7°59E 52 E7
Agadir Morocco 30°28N 9°55W 52 B4
Agalega Is. Mauritius 11°0S 57°0E 3 E12
Agar India 23°40N 76°2E 42 H7
Agar → India 21°0N 82°57E 44 D6
Agartala India 23°50N 91°23E 41 H17
Agassiz Canada 49°14N 121°46W 70 D4
Agassiz Icecap Canada 80°15N 76°0W 69 A16
Agats Indonesia 5°33S 138°0E 37 F9
Agatti I. India 10°50N 72°12E 45 J1
Agattu I. U.S.A. 52°25N 173°35E 74 E2
Agawam U.S.A. 42°5N 72°37W 83 D12
Agboville Ivory C. 5°55N 4°15W 52 G5
Ağdam Azerbaijan 40°0N 46°58E 46 B5
Agde France 43°19N 3°28E 20 E5
Agen France 44°12N 0°38E 20 D4
Āgh Kand Iran 37°15N 48°4E 47 B6
Aghios Efstratios Greece 39°34N 24°58E 23 E11
Aghiou Orous, Kolpos Greece 40°6N 24°0E 23 D11
Aginskoye Russia 51°6N 114°32E 27 D12
Agnew Australia 28°1S 120°31E 61 E3
Agori India 24°33N 82°57E 43 G10
Agra India 27°17N 77°58E 42 F7
Ağri Turkey 39°44N 43°3E 19 G7
Agri → Italy 40°13N 16°44E 22 D7
Ağrı Dağı Turkey 39°50N 44°15E 46 B5
Ağri Karakose = Ağri Turkey 39°44N 43°3E 19 G7
Agrigento Italy 37°19N 13°34E 22 F5
Agrinio Greece 38°37N 21°27E 23 E9
Agua Caliente Mexico 32°29N 116°59W 79 N10
Agua Caliente Springs U.S.A. 32°56N 116°19W 79 N10
Água Clara Brazil 20°25S 52°45W 93 H8
Agua Fria ⌂ U.S.A. 34°14N 112°0W 77 J8
Agua Hechicera Mexico 32°28N 116°15W 79 N10
Agua Prieta Mexico 31°18N 109°34W 86 A3
Aguadilla Puerto Rico 18°26N 67°10W 89 d
Aguadulce Panama 8°15N 80°32W 88 E3
Aguanga U.S.A. 33°27N 116°51W 79 M10
Aguanish Canada 50°14N 62°2W 73 B7
Aguanish → Canada 50°13N 62°5W 73 B7
Aguapey → Argentina 29°7S 56°36W 94 B4
Aguaray Guazú → Paraguay 24°47S 57°19W 94 A4
Aguarico → Ecuador 0°59S 75°11W 92 D3
Aguaro-Guariquito △ Venezuela 8°20N 66°35W 89 E6
Aguas Blancas Chile 24°15S 69°55W 94 A2
Aguas Calientes, Sierra de Argentina 25°26S 66°40W 94 B2
Aguascalientes Mexico 21°53N 102°18W 86 C4
Aguascalientes □ Mexico 22°0N 102°20W 86 C4
Aguila, Punta Puerto Rico 17°57N 67°13W 89 d
Aguilares Argentina 27°26S 65°35W 94 B2
Águilas Spain 37°23N 1°35W 21 D5
Aguja, C. de la Colombia 11°18N 74°12W 90 B3
Agujereada, Pta. Puerto Rico 18°30N 67°8W 89 d
Agulhas, C. S. Africa 34°52S 20°0E 56 D3
Agung, Gunung Indonesia 8°20S 115°28E 37 J18
Aguni-Jima Japan 26°30N 127°10E 29 L3
Agusan → Phil. 9°0N 125°30E 37 C7
Aha Mts. Botswana 19°45S 21°0E 56 A3
Ahaggar Algeria 23°0N 6°30E 52 D7
Ahai Dam China 27°21N 100°30E 34 D3
Ahar Iran 38°35N 47°0E 46 B5
Ahipara B. N.Z. 35°5S 173°5E 59 A4
Ahiri India 19°30N 80°0E 44 E5
Ahmad Wal Pakistan 29°18N 65°58E 42 E1
Ahmadabad India 23°0N 72°40E 42 H5
Aḩmadābād Khorāsān, Iran 35°3N 60°50E 47 C9
Aḩmadābād Khorāsān, Iran 35°49N 59°42E 47 C8
Aḩmadī Iran 27°56N 56°42E 47 E8
Ahmadnagar India 19°7N 74°46E 44 E2
Ahmadpur India 18°40N 76°57E 44 E3
Ahmadpur East Pakistan 29°12N 71°10E 42 E4
Ahmadpur Lamma Pakistan 28°19N 70°3E 42 E4
Ahmedabad = Ahmadabad India 23°0N 72°40E 42 H5
Ahmednagar = Ahmadnagar India 19°7N 74°46E 44 E2
Ahome Mexico 25°55N 109°11W 86 B3
Ahoskie U.S.A. 36°17N 76°59W 85 C16
Ahram Iran 28°52N 51°16E 47 D6
Ahuachapán El Salv. 13°54N 89°52W 88 D2
Ahvāz Iran 31°20N 48°40E 47 D6
Ahvenanmaa = Åland Finland 60°15N 20°0E 9 F19
Aḩwar Yemen 13°30N 46°40E 49 E4
Ai → India 26°26N 90°44E 43 F14
Ai-Ais Namibia 27°54S 17°59E 56 C2
Ai-Ais and Fish River Canyon △ Namibia 24°45S 17°15E 56 B2
Aichi □ Japan 35°0N 137°15E 29 G8
Aigrettes, Pte. des Réunion 21°3S 55°13E 55 c
Aiguá Uruguay 34°13S 54°46W 95 C5
Aigues-Mortes France 43°35N 4°12E 20 E6
Aihui = Heihe China 50°10N 127°30E 31 A14
Aija Peru 9°50S 77°45W 92 E3
Aikawa Japan 38°2N 138°15E 28 E9
Aiken U.S.A. 33°34N 81°43W 85 E14
Ailao Shan China 24°0N 101°20E 34 F3
Aileron Australia 22°39S 133°20E 62 C1
Aillik Canada 55°11N 59°18W 73 A8
Ailsa Craig Canada 43°8N 81°33W 82 C3
Ailsa Craig U.K. 55°15N 5°6W 11 F3
Aim Russia 59°0N 133°55E 27 D14
Aimogasta Argentina 28°33S 66°50W 94 B2
Aïn Ben Tili Mauritania 25°59N 9°27W 52 C4
Aïn Sefra Algeria 32°47N 0°37W 52 B5
Ain Sudr Egypt 29°50N 33°6E 48 F2
Aïn Témouchent Algeria 35°16N 1°8W 52 A5
Ainaži Latvia 57°50N 24°24E 9 H21
Ainsworth U.S.A. 42°33N 99°52W 80 D4
Aiquile Bolivia 18°10S 65°10W 92 G5
Aïr Niger 18°30N 8°0E 52 E7
Air Force I. Canada 67°58N 74°5W 69 D17
Air Hitam Malaysia 1°55N 103°11E 39 M4
Airdrie Canada 51°18N 114°2W 70 C6
Airdrie U.K. 55°52N 3°57W 11 F5
Aire → U.K. 53°43N 0°55W 12 D7
Airlie Beach Australia 20°16S 148°43E 62 b
Aisne → France 49°26N 2°50E 20 B5
Ait India 25°54N 79°14E 43 G8
Aitkin U.S.A. 46°32N 93°42W 80 B7
Aitutaki Cook Is. 18°52S 159°45W 65 J12
Aiud Romania 46°19N 23°44E 17 E12
Aix-en-Provence France 43°32N 5°27E 20 E6
Aix-la-Chapelle = Aachen Germany 50°45N 6°6E 16 C4
Aix-les-Bains France 45°41N 5°53E 20 D6
Aizawl India 23°40N 92°44E 41 H18
Aizkraukle Latvia 56°36N 25°11E 9 H21
Aizpute Latvia 56°43N 21°40E 9 H19
Aizuwakamatsu Japan 37°30N 139°56E 28 F9
Ajaccio France 41°55N 8°40E 20 F8
Ajaigarh India 24°52N 80°16E 43 G9
Ajalpan Mexico 18°22N 97°15W 87 D5
Ajanta India 20°30N 75°48E 44 D2
Ajanta Ra. India 20°28N 75°50E 44 D2
Ajari Rep. = Ajaria □ Georgia 41°30N 42°0E 19 F7
Ajaria □ Georgia 41°30N 42°0E 19 F7
Ajax Canada 43°50N 79°1W 82 C5
Ajdābiyā Libya 30°54N 20°4E 53 B10
Ajka Hungary 47°4N 17°31E 17 E9
'Ajlūn Jordan 32°18N 35°47E 48 C4
'Ajlūn □ Jordan 32°18N 35°47E 48 C4
'Ajmān U.A.E. 25°25N 55°30E 47 E7
Ajmer India 26°28N 74°37E 42 F6
Ajnala India 31°50N 74°48E 42 D6
Ajo U.S.A. 32°22N 112°52W 77 K7
Ajo, C. de Spain 43°31N 3°35W 21 A4
Akabira Japan 43°33N 142°5E 28 C11
Akalkot India 17°32N 76°13E 44 F3
Akan △ Japan 43°20N 144°20E 28 C12
Akaroa N.Z. 43°49S 172°59E 59 E4
Akashi Japan 34°45N 134°58E 29 G7
Akbarpur Bihar, India 24°39N 83°58E 43 G10
Akbarpur Ut. P., India 26°25N 82°32E 43 F10
Akçakale Turkey 36°41N 38°56E 46 B3
Akelamo Indonesia 1°35N 129°40E 37 D7
Akeru → India 17°25N 80°5E 44 F5
Aketi Dem. Rep. of the Congo 2°38N 23°47E 54 D4
Akhisar Turkey 38°56N 27°48E 23 E12
Akhnur India 32°52N 74°45E 43 C6
Akhtyrka = Okhtyrka Ukraine 50°25N 35°0E 19 D5
Aki Japan 33°30N 133°54E 29 H6
Akimiski I. Canada 52°50N 81°30W 72 B3
Akiōta Japan 34°36N 132°19E 29 G6
Akita Japan 39°45N 140°7E 28 E10
Akita □ Japan 39°40N 140°30E 28 E10
Akjoujt Mauritania 19°45N 14°15W 52 E3
Akkaraipattu Sri Lanka 7°13N 81°51E 45 L5
Akkeshi Japan 43°2N 144°51E 28 C12
'Akko Israel 32°55N 35°4E 48 C4
Aklavik Canada 68°12N 135°0W 68 D4
Aklera India 24°26N 76°32E 42 G7
Akō Japan 34°45N 134°24E 29 G7
Akola Maharashtra, India 20°42N 77°2E 44 D3
Akola Maharashtra, India 19°32N 74°3E 44 E2
Akordat Eritrea 15°30N 37°40E 49 D2
Akot India 21°10N 77°10E 44 D3
Akpatok I. Canada 60°25N 68°8W 69 E18
Åkrahamn Norway 59°15N 5°10E 9 G11
Akranes Iceland 64°19N 22°5W 8 D2
Akron Colo., U.S.A. 40°10N 103°13W 76 F12
Akron Ohio, U.S.A. 41°5N 81°31W 82 E3
Aksai Chin China 35°15N 79°55E 43 B8
Aksaray Turkey 38°25N 34°2E 46 B2
Aksay = Aqsay Kazakhstan 51°11N 53°0E 19 D9
Akşehir Turkey 38°18N 31°30E 46 B1
Akşehir Gölü Turkey 38°30N 31°25E 19 G5
Aksu China 41°5N 80°10E 30 C5
Aksum Ethiopia 14°5N 38°40E 49 E2
Aktsyabrski Belarus 52°38N 28°53E 17 B15
Aktyubinsk = Aqtöbe Kazakhstan 50°17N 57°10E 19 D10
Akure Nigeria 7°15N 5°5E 52 G7
Akuressa Sri Lanka 6°5N 80°29E 45 L5
Akureyri Iceland 65°40N 18°6W 8 D4
Akuseki-Shima Japan 29°27N 129°37E 29 K4
Akyab = Sittwe Burma 20°18N 92°45E 41 J18
Al 'Adan = 'Adan Yemen 12°45N 45°0E 49 E4
Al Aḩsā = Hasa Si. Arabia 25°50N 49°0E 47 E6
Al Ajfar Si. Arabia 27°26N 43°0E 46 E4
Al Amādīyah Iraq 37°5N 43°30E 46 B4
Al 'Amārah Iraq 31°55N 47°15E 46 D5
Al Anbār □ Iraq 33°25N 42°0E 46 C4
Al 'Aqabah Jordan 29°31N 35°0E 48 F4
Al 'Aqabah □ Jordan 29°30N 35°0E 48 F4
Al Arak Syria 34°38N 38°35E 46 C3
Al 'Aramah Si. Arabia 25°30N 46°0E 46 E5
Al Arţāwīyah Si. Arabia 26°31N 45°20E 46 E5
Al 'Āşimah = 'Ammān □ Jordan 31°40N 36°30E 48 D5
Al 'Assāfīyah Si. Arabia 28°17N 38°59E 46 D3
Al 'Awdah Si. Arabia 25°32N 45°41E 46 E5
Al 'Ayn Si. Arabia 25°4N 38°6E 46 E3
Al 'Ayn U.A.E. 24°15N 55°45E 47 E7
Al 'Azīzīyah Iraq 32°54N 45°4E 46 C5
Al Bāb Syria 36°23N 37°29E 46 B3
Al Bad' Si. Arabia 28°28N 35°1E 46 D2
Al Bada'i' Si. Arabia 26°2N 43°33E 46 E4
Al Bādī Iraq 35°56N 41°32E 46 C4
Al Baḩrah Kuwait 29°40N 47°52E 46 D5
Al Baḩral Mayyit = Dead Sea Asia 31°30N 35°30E 48 D4
Al Balqā' □ Jordan 32°5N 35°45E 48 C4
Al Bārūk, J. Lebanon 33°39N 35°40E 48 B4
Al Başrah Iraq 30°30N 47°50E 46 D5
Al Baţḩā Iraq 31°6N 45°53E 46 D5
Al Batrūn Lebanon 34°15N 35°40E 48 A4
Al Bayḍā Libya 32°50N 21°44E 53 B10
Al Biqā Lebanon 34°10N 36°10E 48 A5
Al Bi'r Si. Arabia 28°51N 36°16E 46 D3
Al Bukayrīyah Si. Arabia 26°9N 43°40E 46 E4
Al Burayj Syria 34°15N 36°46E 48 A5
Al Faḍilī Si. Arabia 26°58N 49°10E 47 E6
Al Fallūjah Iraq 33°20N 43°55E 46 C4
Al Fāw Iraq 30°0N 48°30E 47 D6
Al Fujayrah U.A.E. 25°7N 56°18E 47 E8
Al Ghadaf, W. → Jordan 31°26N 36°43E 48 D5
Al Ghammās Iraq 31°45N 44°37E 46 D5
Al Ghazālah Si. Arabia 26°48N 41°19E 46 E4
Al Ḩadīthah Iraq 34°0N 41°13E 46 C4
Al Ḩadīthah Si. Arabia 31°28N 37°8E 48 D6
Al Ḩaḍr Iraq 35°35N 42°44E 46 C4
Al Ḩājānah Syria 33°20N 36°33E 48 B5
Al Ḩajar al Gharbī Oman 24°10N 56°15E 47 E8
Al Ḩāmad Si. Arabia 31°30N 39°30E 46 D3
Al Ḩamdānīyah Syria 35°25N 36°50E 46 C3
Al Ḩamīdīyah Syria 34°42N 35°57E 48 A4

Al Ḥammār Iraq 30°57N 46°51E 46 D5
Al Ḥamrā' Si. Arabia 24°2N 38°55E 46 E3
Al Ḥamzah Iraq 31°43N 44°58E 46 D5
Al Ḥanākīyah Si. Arabia 24°51N 40°31E 46 E4
Al Harūj al Aswad Libya 27°0N 17°10E 53 C9
Al Ḥasakah Syria 36°35N 40°45E 46 B4
Al Ḥayy Iraq 32°5N 46°5E 46 C5
Al Ḥijarah Asia 30°0N 44°0E 46 D4
Al Ḥillah Iraq 32°30N 44°25E 46 C5
Al Hindīyah Iraq 32°30N 44°10E 46 C5
Al Hirmil Lebanon 34°26N 36°24E 48 A5
Al Hoceïma Morocco 35°8N 3°58W 52 A5
Al Ḥudaydah Yemen 14°50N 43°0E 49 E3
Al Ḥudūd ash Shamālīyah □
  Si. Arabia 29°10N 42°30E 46 D4
Al Hufūf Si. Arabia 25°25N 49°45E 47 E6
Al Ḥumaydah Si. Arabia 29°14N 34°56E 46 D2
Al Ḥunayy Si. Arabia 25°58N 48°45E 47 E6
Al Ïsāwīyah Si. Arabia 30°43N 37°59E 46 D3
Al Jafr Jordan 30°18N 36°14E 48 E5
Al Jāfūrah Si. Arabia 25°0N 50°15E 47 E7
Al Jaghbūb Libya 29°42N 24°38E 53 C10
Al Jahrah Kuwait 29°25N 47°40E 46 D5
Al Jalāmīd Si. Arabia 31°20N 40°6E 46 D3
Al Jamalīyah Qatar 25°37N 51°5E 47 E6
Al Janūb □ Lebanon 33°20N 35°20E 48 B4
Al Jawf Libya 24°10N 23°24E 53 D10
Al Jawf Si. Arabia 29°55N 39°40E 46 D3
Al Jawf □ Si. Arabia 29°30N 39°30E 46 D3
Al Jazair = Algeria ■ Africa 28°30N 2°0E 52 C6
Al Jazirah Iraq 33°30N 44°0E 46 C5
Al Jithāmīyah Si. Arabia 27°41N 41°43E 46 E4
Al Jubayl Si. Arabia 27°0N 49°50E 47 E6
Al Jubaylah Si. Arabia 24°55N 46°25E 46 E5
Al Jubb Si. Arabia 27°11N 42°17E 46 E4
Al Junaynah Sudan 13°27N 22°45E 53 F10
Al Kabā'ish Iraq 30°58N 47°0E 46 D5
Al Karak Jordan 31°11N 35°42E 48 D4
Al Karak □ Jordan 31°0N 36°0E 48 E5
Al Kāzimīyah Iraq 33°22N 44°18E 46 C5
Al Khābūrah Oman 23°57N 57°5E 47 F8
Al Khafji Si. Arabia 28°24N 48°29E 47 E6
Al Khalīl West Bank 31°32N 35°6E 48 D4
Al Khāliṣ Iraq 33°49N 44°32E 46 C5
Al Kharsānīyah Si. Arabia 27°13N 49°18E 47 E6
Al Khaṣab Oman 26°14N 56°15E 47 E8
Al Khawr Qatar 25°41N 51°30E 47 E6
Al Khiḍr Iraq 31°12N 45°33E 46 D5
Al Khiyām Lebanon 33°20N 35°36E 48 B4
Al Khubar Si. Arabia 26°17N 50°12E 47 E6
Al Khums Libya 32°40N 14°17E 53 B8
Al Kiswah Syria 33°23N 36°14E 48 B5
Al Kūfah Iraq 32°2N 44°24E 46 C5
Al Kufrah Libya 24°17N 23°15E 53 D10
Al Kuhayfiyah Si. Arabia 27°12N 43°3E 46 E4
Al Kūt Iraq 32°30N 46°0E 46 C5
Al Kuwayt Kuwait 29°30N 48°0E 46 D5
Al Labwah Lebanon 34°11N 36°20E 48 A5
Al Lādhiqīyah Syria 35°30N 35°45E 46 C2
Al Līth Si. Arabia 20°9N 40°15E 49 C3
Al Liwā' Oman 24°31N 56°36E 47 E8
Al Luḥayyah Yemen 15°45N 42°40E 49 D3
Al Madīnah Iraq 30°57N 47°16E 46 D5
Al Madīnah Si. Arabia 24°35N 39°52E 46 E3
Al Mafraq Jordan 32°17N 36°14E 48 C5
Al Mafraq □ Jordan 32°17N 36°15E 48 C5
Al Maghreb = Morocco ■
  N. Afr. 32°0N 5°50W 52 B4
Al Maḥmūdīyah Iraq 33°3N 44°21E 46 C5
Al Majma'ah Si. Arabia 25°57N 45°22E 46 E5
Al Makhruq, W. →
  Jordan 31°28N 37°0E 48 D6
Al Makhūl Si. Arabia 26°37N 42°39E 46 E4
Al Manāmah Bahrain 26°10N 50°30E 47 E6
Al Maqwa' Kuwait 29°10N 47°59E 46 D5
Al Marāḥ Si. Arabia 25°35N 49°35E 47 E6
Al Marj Libya 32°25N 20°30E 53 B10
Al Maṭlā Kuwait 29°24N 47°40E 46 D5
Al Mawṣil Iraq 36°15N 43°5E 46 B4
Al Mayādin Syria 35°1N 40°27E 46 C4
Al Mazār Jordan 31°4N 35°41E 48 D4
Al Midhnab Si. Arabia 25°50N 44°18E 46 E5
Al Minā' Lebanon 34°24N 35°49E 48 A4
Al Miqdādīyah Iraq 34°0N 45°0E 46 C5
Al Mubarraz Si. Arabia 25°30N 49°40E 47 E6
Al Mudawwarah Jordan 29°19N 36°0E 48 F5
Al Mughayrā' U.A.E. 24°5N 53°32E 47 E7
Al Muḥarraq Bahrain 26°15N 50°40E 47 E6
Al Mukallā Yemen 14°33N 49°2E 49 E4
Al Mukhā Yemen 13°18N 43°15E 49 E3
Al Musayjīd Si. Arabia 24°5N 39°5E 46 E3
Al Musayyib Iraq 32°49N 44°20E 46 C5
Al Muthanná □ Iraq 30°30N 45°15E 46 D5
Al Muwaylih Si. Arabia 27°40N 35°30E 46 E2
Al Qādisīyah □ Iraq 32°0N 45°0E 46 D5
Al Qā'im Iraq 34°21N 41°7E 46 C4
Al Qalībah Si. Arabia 28°24N 37°42E 46 D3
Al Qāmishlī Syria 37°2N 41°14E 46 B4
Al Qaryatayn Syria 34°12N 37°13E 48 A6
Al Qaṭ'ā Syria 34°40N 40°48E 46 C4
Al Qaṭīf Si. Arabia 26°35N 50°0E 47 E6
Al Qaṭrānah Jordan 31°12N 36°6E 48 D5
Al Qaṭrūn Libya 24°56N 15°3E 53 D9
Al Qayṣūmah Si. Arabia 28°20N 46°7E 46 D5
Al Qunayṭirah Syria 33°5N 35°45E 48 B4
Al Qunfudhah Si. Arabia 19°3N 41°4E 49 D3
Al Qurayyāt Si. Arabia 31°20N 37°20E 46 D3
Al Qurnah Iraq 31°1N 47°25E 46 D5
Al Quṣayr Iraq 30°39N 45°50E 46 D5
Al Quṣayr Syria 34°31N 36°34E 48 A5
Al Qutayfah Syria 33°44N 36°36E 48 B5
Al Quwaysimah Jordan 31°55N 35°57E 48 D4
Al 'Ubaylah Si. Arabia 21°59N 50°57E 49 D5
Al 'Udaylīyah Si. Arabia 25°8N 49°18E 47 E6
Al 'Ulā Si. Arabia 26°35N 38°0E 46 E3
Al 'Uqayr Si. Arabia 25°40N 50°15E 47 E6
Al 'Uwaynid Si. Arabia 24°50N 46°0E 46 E5
Al 'Uwayqīlah Si. Arabia 30°30N 42°10E 46 D4

Al 'Uyūn Ḥijāz, Si. Arabia 24°33N 39°35E 46 E3
Al 'Uyūn Najd, Si. Arabia 26°30N 43°50E 46 E4
Al 'Uzayr Iraq 31°19N 47°25E 46 D5
Al Wajh Si. Arabia 26°10N 36°30E 46 E3
Al Wakrah Qatar 25°10N 51°40E 47 E6
Al Waqbah Si. Arabia 28°48N 45°33E 46 D5
Al Wari'ah Si. Arabia 27°51N 47°25E 46 D5
Al Yaman = Yemen ■ Asia 15°0N 44°0E 49 E3
Ala Dağ Turkey 37°44N 35°9E 46 B2
Ala Tau Asia 45°30N 80°40E 30 B5
Ala Tau Shankou = Dzungarian
  Gate Asia 45°10N 82°0E 30 B5
Alabama □ U.S.A. 33°0N 87°0W 85 E11
Alabama → U.S.A. 31°8N 87°57W 85 F11
Alabaster U.S.A. 33°15N 86°49W 85 E11
Alaçam Dağları Turkey 39°18N 28°49E 23 E13
Alacant = Alicante Spain 38°23N 0°30W 21 C5
Alachua U.S.A. 29°47N 82°30W 85 G13
Alagoa Grande Brazil 7°3S 35°35W 93 E11
Alagoas □ Brazil 9°0S 36°0W 93 E11
Alagoinhas Brazil 12°7S 38°20W 93 F11
Alahaeiaetnu = Altaelva →
  Norway 69°54N 23°17E 8 B20
Alajuela Costa Rica 10°2N 84°8W 88 D3
Alaknanda → India 30°8N 78°36E 43 D8
Alakurtti Russia 66°58N 30°25E 8 C24
Alamarvdasht Iran 27°37N 52°59E 47 E7
Alameda U.S.A. 35°11N 106°37W 77 J10
Alamo U.S.A. 37°22N 115°10W 79 H11
Alamogordo U.S.A. 32°54N 105°57W 77 K11
Alamos Mexico 27°1N 108°56W 86 B3
Alamosa U.S.A. 37°28N 105°52W 77 H11
Alampur India 15°55N 78°6E 45 G4
Åland Finland 60°15N 20°0E 9 F19
Aland India 17°36N 76°35E 44 F3
Ålands hav Europe 60°0N 19°30E 9 G18
Alandur India 13°0N 80°15E 45 H5
Alania = North Ossetia □
  Russia 43°30N 44°30E 19 F7
Alanya Turkey 36°38N 32°0E 46 B1
Alapayevsk Russia 57°52N 61°42E 26 D7
Alappuzha India 9°30N 76°28E 45 K3
Alaşehir Turkey 38°23N 28°30E 23 E13
Alaska □ U.S.A. 64°0N 154°0W 74 C9
Alaska, G. of Pac. Oc. 58°0N 145°0W 68 F3
Alaska Peninsula U.S.A. 56°0N 159°0W 74 D8
Alaska Range U.S.A. 62°50N 151°0W 68 E1
Ālāt Azerbaijan 39°58N 49°25E 47 B6
Alatau Shan = Ala Tau
  Asia 45°30N 80°40E 30 B5
Alatyr Russia 54°55N 46°35E 18 D8
Alausi Ecuador 2°0S 78°50W 92 D3
Alava, C. U.S.A. 48°10N 124°44W 78 B2
Alavo = Alavus Finland 62°35N 23°36E 8 E20
Alavus Finland 62°35N 23°36E 8 E20
Alawa ◇ Australia 15°42S 134°39E 62 B1
Alawoona Australia 34°45S 140°30E 63 E3
Alayawarra ◇ Australia 22°0S 134°30E 62 C1
Alba Italy 44°42N 8°2E 20 D8
Alba-Iulia Romania 46°8N 23°39E 17 E12
Albacete Spain 39°0N 1°50W 21 C5
Albacutya, L. Australia 35°45S 141°58E 63 F3
Albanel, L. Canada 50°55N 73°12W 72 B5
Albania ■ Europe 41°0N 20°0E 23 D9
Albany Australia 35°1S 117°58E 61 G2
Albany Ga., U.S.A. 31°35N 84°10W 85 F12
Albany N.Y., U.S.A. 42°39N 73°45W 83 D11
Albany Oreg., U.S.A. 44°38N 123°6W 76 D2
Albany Tex., U.S.A. 32°44N 99°18W 84 E5
Albany → Canada 52°17N 81°31W 72 B3
Albardón Argentina 31°20S 68°30W 94 C2
Albatross B. Australia 12°45S 141°30E 62 A3
Albemarle U.S.A. 35°21N 80°12W 85 D14
Albemarle Sd. U.S.A. 36°5N 76°0W 85 C16
Alberche → Spain 39°58N 4°46W 21 C3
Alberdi Paraguay 26°14S 58°20W 94 B4
Alberga → Australia 27°6S 135°33E 63 D2
Albert, L. Africa 1°30N 31°0E 54 D6
Albert, L. Australia 35°30S 139°10E 63 F2
Albert Edward Ra.
  Australia 18°17S 127°57E 60 C4
Albert Lea U.S.A. 43°39N 93°22W 80 D7
Albert Nile → Uganda 3°36N 32°2E 54 D6
Albert Town Bahamas 22°37N 74°33W 89 B5
Alberta □ Canada 54°40N 115°0W 70 C6
Alberti Argentina 35°1S 60°16W 94 D3
Albertinia S. Africa 34°11S 21°34E 56 D3
Alberton Canada 46°50N 64°0W 73 C7
Albertville France 45°40N 6°22E 20 D7
Albertville U.S.A. 34°16N 86°13W 85 D11
Albi France 43°56N 2°9E 20 E5
Albia U.S.A. 41°2N 92°48W 80 E7
Albina Suriname 5°37N 54°15W 93 B8
Albina, Ponta Angola 15°52S 11°44E 56 A1
Albion Mich., U.S.A. 42°15N 84°45W 81 D11
Albion Nebr., U.S.A. 41°42N 98°0W 80 E4
Albion Pa., U.S.A. 41°53N 80°22W 82 E4
Alborán Medit. S. 35°57N 3°0W 21 E4
Ålborg = Aalborg Denmark 57°2N 9°54E 9 H13
Alborz, Reshteh-ye Kūhhā-ye
  Iran 36°0N 52°0E 47 C7
Albufeira Portugal 37°5N 8°15W 21 D1
Albuquerque U.S.A. 35°5N 106°39W 77 J10
Albuquerque, Cayos de
  Caribbean 12°10N 81°50W 88 D3
Alburg U.S.A. 44°59N 73°18W 83 B11
Albury Australia 36°3S 146°56E 63 F4
Alcalá de Henares Spain 40°28N 3°22W 21 B4
Alcalá la Real Spain 37°27N 3°57W 21 D4
Álcamo Italy 37°59N 12°55E 22 F5
Alcañiz Spain 41°2N 0°8W 21 B5
Alcântara Brazil 2°20S 44°30W 93 D10
Alcántara, Embalse de
  Spain 39°44N 6°50W 21 C2
Alcantarilla Spain 37°59N 1°12W 21 D5
Alcaraz, Sierra de Spain 38°40N 2°20W 21 C4
Alcaudete Spain 37°35N 4°5W 21 D3
Alcázar de San Juan
  Spain 39°24N 3°12W 21 C4

Alchevsk Ukraine 48°30N 38°45E 19 E6
Alcira = Alzira Spain 39°9N 0°30W 21 C5
Alcova U.S.A. 42°34N 106°43W 76 E10
Alcoy Spain 38°43N 0°30W 21 C5
Aldabra Is. Seychelles 9°22S 46°28E 51 G8
Aldama Mexico 22°55N 98°4W 87 C5
Aldan Russia 58°40N 125°30E 27 D13
Aldan → Russia 63°28N 129°35E 27 C13
Aldeburgh U.K. 52°10N 1°37E 13 E9
Alder Pk. U.S.A. 35°53N 121°22W 78 K5
Alderney U.K. 49°42N 2°11W 13 H5
Aldershot U.K. 51°15N 0°44W 13 F7
Aledo U.S.A. 41°12N 90°45W 80 E8
Aleg Mauritania 17°3N 13°55W 52 E3
Alegre Brazil 20°50S 41°30W 95 A7
Alegrete Brazil 29°40S 56°0W 95 B4
Aleksandriya = Oleksandriya
  Ukraine 50°37N 26°19E 17 C14
Aleksandrov Gay Russia 50°9N 48°34E 19 D8
Aleksandrovsk-Sakhalinskiy
  Russia 50°50N 142°20E 31 A17
Aleksandry, Zemlya
  Russia 80°25N 48°0E 26 A5
Além Paraíba Brazil 21°52S 42°41W 95 A7
Alemania Argentina 25°40S 65°30W 94 B2
Alemania Chile 25°10S 69°55W 94 B2
Alençon France 48°27N 0°4E 20 B4
Alenquer Brazil 1°56S 54°46W 93 D8
'Alenuihāhā Channel
  U.S.A. 20°30N 156°0W 75 L8
Aleppo = Ḥalab Syria 36°10N 37°15E 46 B3
Aléria France 42°5N 9°26E 20 E9
Alert Canada 83°2N 60°0W 69 A17
Aleru India 17°39N 79°3E 44 F4
Alès France 44°9N 4°5E 20 D6
Alessándria Italy 44°54N 8°37E 20 D8
Ålesund Norway 62°28N 6°12E 8 E12
Aleutian Basin Pac. Oc. 57°0N 177°0E 64 B9
Aleutian Is. Pac. Oc. 52°0N 175°0W 64 D17
Aleutian Range U.S.A. 60°0N 154°0W 74 D9
Aleutian Trench Pac. Oc. 48°0N 180°0E 64 C10
Alexander U.S.A. 47°51N 103°39W 80 B2
Alexander, Mt. Australia 28°58S 120°16E 61 E3
Alexander Arch. U.S.A. 56°0N 136°0W 68 F4
Alexander Bay S. Africa 28°40S 16°30E 56 C2
Alexander City U.S.A. 32°56N 85°58W 85 E12
Alexander I. Antarctica 69°0S 70°0W 5 C17
Alexandra Australia 37°8S 145°40E 63 F4
Alexandra N.Z. 45°14S 169°25E 59 F2
Alexandra Channel
  Burma 14°7N 93°13E 45 G11
Alexandra Falls Canada 60°29N 116°18W 70 A5
Alexandria = El Iskandarīya
  Egypt 31°13N 29°58E 53 B11
Alexandria B.C., Canada 52°35N 122°27W 70 C4
Alexandria Ont., Canada 45°19N 74°38W 83 A10
Alexandria Romania 43°57N 25°24E 17 G13
Alexandria S. Africa 33°38S 26°28E 56 D4
Alexandria U.K. 55°59N 4°35W 11 F4
Alexandria La., U.S.A. 31°18N 92°27W 84 F8
Alexandria Minn., U.S.A. 45°53N 95°22W 80 C6
Alexandria S. Dak.,
  U.S.A. 43°39N 97°47W 80 D5
Alexandria Bay U.S.A. 44°20N 75°55W 83 B9
Alexandrina, L. Australia 35°25S 139°10E 63 F2
Alexandroupoli Greece 40°50N 25°54E 23 D11
Alexis → Canada 52°33N 56°8W 73 B8
Alexis Creek Canada 52°10N 123°20W 70 C4
Aleysk Russia 52°40N 83°0E 26 D9
Alfenas Brazil 21°20S 46°10W 95 A6
Alford Aberds., U.K. 57°14N 2°41W 11 D6
Alford Lincs., U.K. 53°15N 0°10E 12 D8
Alfred Maine, U.S.A. 43°29N 70°43W 83 C14
Alfred N.Y., U.S.A. 42°16N 77°48W 82 D7
Alfreton U.K. 53°6N 1°24W 12 D6
Ålgård Norway 58°46N 5°53E 9 G11
Algarve Portugal 36°58N 8°20W 21 D1
Algeciras Spain 36°9N 5°28W 21 D3
Algemesí Spain 39°11N 0°27W 21 C5
Alger Algeria 36°42N 3°8E 52 A6
Algeria ■ Africa 28°30N 2°0E 52 C6
Alghero Italy 40°33N 8°19E 22 D3
Algiers = Alger Algeria 36°42N 3°8E 52 A6
Algoa B. S. Africa 33°50S 25°45E 56 D4
Algoma U.S.A. 44°36N 87°26W 80 C10
Algona U.S.A. 43°4N 94°14W 80 D6
Algonac U.S.A. 42°37N 82°32W 82 D2
Algonquin △ Canada 45°50N 78°30W 72 C4
Algorta Uruguay 32°25S 57°23W 96 C5
Alhucemas = Al Hoceïma
  Morocco 35°8N 3°58W 52 A5
'Alī al Gharbī Iraq 32°30N 46°45E 46 C5
'Alī ash Sharqī Iraq 32°7N 46°44E 46 C5
Āli Bayramlı = Şirvan
  Azerbaijan 39°59N 48°52E 47 B6
'Alī Khēl Afghan. 33°57N 69°43E 42 C3
Alī Shāh Iran 38°9N 45°50E 44 B5
'Aliābād Golestān, Iran 36°40N 54°33E 47 B7
'Aliābād Khorāsān, Iran 35°4N 59°16E 47 C8
'Aliābād Kordestān, Iran 35°4N 46°58E 46 C5
'Aliābād Yazd, Iran 31°41N 53°49E 47 D7
Aliağa Turkey 38°47N 26°59E 23 E12
Aliakmonas → Greece 40°30N 22°36E 23 D10
Alibag India 18°38N 72°56E 44 E1
Alicante Spain 38°23N 0°30W 21 C5
Alice S. Africa 32°48S 26°55E 56 D4
Alice U.S.A. 27°45N 98°5W 84 H5
Alice → Queens., Australia 24°2S 144°50E 62 C3
Alice → Queens.,
  Australia 15°35S 142°20E 62 B3
Alice Arm Canada 55°29N 129°31W 70 B3
Alice Springs Australia 23°40S 133°50E 62 C1
Alicedale S. Africa 33°15S 26°4E 56 D4
Aliceville U.S.A. 33°8N 88°9W 85 E10
Aliganj India 27°30N 79°10E 43 F8
Aligarh Raj., India 25°55N 76°15E 42 G7
Aligarh Ut. P., India 27°55N 78°10E 42 F8
Alīgūdarz Iran 33°25N 49°45E 47 C6

Alingsås Sweden 57°56N 12°31E 9 H15
Alipur Pakistan 29°25N 70°55E 42 E4
Alipur Duar India 26°30N 89°35E 41 F16
Aliquippa U.S.A. 40°37N 80°15W 82 F4
Alishan Taiwan 23°31N 120°48E 35 F13
Alitus = Alytus Lithuania 54°24N 24°3E 9 J21
Aliwal North S. Africa 30°45S 26°45E 56 D4
Alix Canada 52°24N 113°11W 70 C6
Aljustrel Portugal 37°55N 8°10W 21 D1
Alkmaar Neths. 52°37N 4°45E 15 B4
All American Canal
  U.S.A. 32°45N 115°15W 79 N11
Allagadda India 15°8N 78°30E 45 G4
Allagash → U.S.A. 47°5N 69°3W 81 B19
Allah Dad Pakistan 25°38N 67°34E 42 G2
Allahabad India 25°25N 81°58E 43 G9
Allan Canada 51°53N 106°4W 71 C7
Allanridge S. Africa 27°45S 26°40E 56 C4
Allegany U.S.A. 42°6N 78°30W 82 D6
Allegheny → U.S.A. 40°27N 80°1W 82 F5
Allegheny Mts. U.S.A. 38°15N 80°10W 81 F13
Allegheny Plateau
  U.S.A. 41°30N 78°30W 81 E14
Allegheny Res. U.S.A. 41°50N 79°0W 82 E6
Allen, Bog of Ireland 53°15N 7°0W 10 C5
Allen, L. Ireland 54°8N 8°4W 10 B3
Allendale U.S.A. 33°1N 81°18W 85 E14
Allende Mexico 28°20N 100°51W 86 B4
Allentown U.S.A. 40°37N 75°29W 83 F9
Alleppey = Alappuzha
  India 9°30N 76°28E 45 K3
Aller → Germany 52°56N 9°12E 16 B5
Alleynes B. Barbados 13°13N 59°39W 89 g
Alliance Nebr., U.S.A. 42°6N 102°52W 80 D2
Alliance Ohio, U.S.A. 40°55N 81°6W 82 F3
Allier → France 46°57N 3°4E 20 C5
Alliford Bay Canada 53°12N 131°58W 70 C2
Alligator Pond Jamaica 17°52N 77°34W 88 a
Allinagaram India 10°2N 77°30E 45 J3
Alliston Canada 44°9N 79°52W 82 B5
Alloa U.K. 56°7N 3°47W 11 E5
Allora Australia 28°2S 152°0E 63 D5
Alluitsup Paa Greenland 60°30N 45°35W 4 C5
Allur India 14°40N 80°4E 45 G5
Alluru Kottapatnam India 15°24N 80°7E 45 G5
Alma Canada 48°35N 71°40W 73 C5
Alma Ga., U.S.A. 31°33N 82°28W 85 F13
Alma Kans., U.S.A. 39°1N 96°17W 80 F5
Alma Mich., U.S.A. 43°23N 84°39W 81 D11
Alma Nebr., U.S.A. 40°6N 99°22W 80 E4
Alma Wis., U.S.A. 44°20N 91°55W 80 C8
Alma Ata = Almaty
  Kazakhstan 43°15N 76°57E 30 C4
Alma Hill U.S.A. 42°2N 78°0W 82 D7
Almada Australia 17°22S 144°40E 62 B3
Almadén Spain 38°49N 4°52W 21 C3
Almalyk = Olmaliq
  Uzbekistan 40°50N 69°35E 26 E7
Almanor, L. U.S.A. 40°14N 121°9W 76 F3
Almansa Spain 38°51N 1°5W 21 C5
Almanzor, Pico Spain 40°15N 5°18W 21 B3
Almanzora → Spain 37°14N 1°46W 21 D5
Almaty Kazakhstan 43°15N 76°57E 30 C4
Almazán Spain 41°30N 2°30W 21 B4
Almeirim Brazil 1°30S 52°34W 93 D8
Almelo Neths. 52°22N 6°42E 15 B6
Almendralejo Spain 38°41N 6°26W 21 C2
Almere Neths. 52°20N 5°15E 15 B5
Almería Spain 36°52N 2°27W 21 D4
Almirante Panama 9°10N 82°30W 88 E3
Almond U.S.A. 42°19N 77°44W 82 D7
Almonte Canada 45°14N 76°12W 83 A8
Almora India 29°38N 79°40E 43 E8
Alness U.K. 57°41N 4°16W 11 D4
Alnmouth U.K. 55°24N 1°37W 12 B6
Alnwick U.K. 55°24N 1°42W 12 B6
Alon Burma 22°12N 95°5E 41 H19
Alor Indonesia 8°15S 124°30E 37 F6
Alor Setar Malaysia 6°7N 100°22E 39 J3
Alot India 23°56N 75°40E 42 H6
Aloysius, Mt. Australia 26°0S 128°38E 61 E4
Alpaugh U.S.A. 35°53N 119°29W 78 K7
Alpena U.S.A. 45°4N 83°27W 82 A1
Alpha Australia 23°39S 146°37E 62 C4
Alpha Ridge Arctic 84°0N 118°0W 4 A2
Alphen aan den Rijn Neths. 52°7N 4°40E 15 B4
Alpine Ariz., U.S.A. 33°51N 109°9W 77 K9
Alpine Calif., U.S.A. 32°50N 116°46W 79 N10
Alpine Tex., U.S.A. 30°22N 103°40W 84 F3
Alps Europe 46°30N 9°30E 16 E5
Alpurrurulam Australia 20°59S 137°50E 62 C2
Alsace □ France 48°15N 7°25E 20 B7
Alsask Canada 51°21N 109°59W 71 C7
Alsasua Spain 42°54N 2°10W 21 A4
Alsek → U.S.A. 59°10N 138°12W 70 B1
Alsta Norway 65°58N 12°40E 8 D15
Alston U.K. 54°49N 2°25E 12 C5
Alta Norway 69°57N 23°10E 8 B20
Alta Gracia Argentina 31°40S 64°30W 94 C3
Alta Sierra U.S.A. 35°42N 118°33W 79 K8
Altaelva → Norway 69°54N 23°17E 8 B20
Altafjorden Norway 70°5N 23°5E 8 A20
Altai = Aerhtai Shan
  Mongolia 46°40N 92°45E 30 B7
Altai = Gorno-Altay □
  Russia 51°0N 86°0E 26 D9
Altamaha → U.S.A. 31°20N 81°20W 85 F14
Altamira Brazil 3°12S 52°10W 93 D8
Altamira Chile 25°47S 69°51W 94 B2
Altamira Mexico 22°24N 97°55W 87 C5
Altamont U.S.A. 42°42N 74°3W 83 D10
Altamura Italy 40°49N 16°33E 22 D7
Altar Mexico 30°43N 111°44W 86 A2
Altar, Gran Desierto de
  Mexico 31°50N 114°10W 86 B2
Altata Mexico 24°40N 107°55W 86 C3

Altavista U.S.A. 37°6N 79°17W 81 G14
Altay China 47°48N 88°10E 30 B6
Altay Mongolia 46°22N 96°15E 30 B7
Altea Spain 38°38N 0°2W 21 C5
Altiplano Bolivia 17°0S 68°0W 92 G5
Alto Araguaia Brazil 17°15S 53°20W 93 G8
Alto Cuchumatanes =
  Cuchumatanes, Sierra de los
  Guatemala 15°35N 91°25W 88 C1
Alto del Carmen Chile 28°46S 70°30W 94 B1
Alto Molocue Mozam. 15°50S 37°35E 55 H7
Alto Paraguay □
  Paraguay 21°0S 58°30W 94 A4
Alto Paraná □ Paraguay 25°30S 54°50W 95 B5
Alton Canada 43°54N 80°5W 82 C4
Alton U.K. 51°9N 0°59W 13 F7
Alton Ill., U.S.A. 38°53N 90°11W 80 F8
Alton N.H., U.S.A. 43°27N 71°13W 83 C13
Altona Canada 49°6N 97°33W 71 D9
Altoona U.S.A. 40°31N 78°24W 82 F6
Altun Kupri Iraq 35°45N 44°9E 46 C5
Altun Shan China 38°30N 88°0E 30 D6
Alturas U.S.A. 41°29N 120°32W 76 F3
Altus U.S.A. 34°38N 99°20W 84 D5
Alucra Turkey 40°22N 38°47E 19 F6
Alūksne Latvia 57°24N 27°3E 9 H22
Alunite U.S.A. 35°59N 114°55W 79 K12
Alur India 15°24N 77°15E 45 E3
Alusi Indonesia 7°35S 131°40E 37 F8
Alutgama Sri Lanka 6°26N 79°59E 45 L4
Alutnuwara Sri Lanka 7°19N 80°59E 45 L5
Aluva = Alwaye India 10°8N 76°24E 45 J3
Alva U.S.A. 36°48N 98°40W 84 C5
Alvarado Mexico 18°46N 95°46W 87 D5
Alvarado U.S.A. 32°24N 97°13W 84 E6
Alvaro Obregón, Presa
  Mexico 27°52N 109°52W 86 B3
Alvear Argentina 29°5S 56°30W 94 B4
Alvesta Sweden 56°54N 14°35E 9 H16
Alvinston Canada 42°49N 81°52W 82 D3
Älvkarleby Sweden 60°34N 17°26E 9 F17
Alvord Desert U.S.A. 42°30N 118°25W 76 E4
Älvsbyn Sweden 65°40N 21°0E 8 D19
Alwar India 27°38N 76°34E 42 F7
Alwaye India 10°8N 76°24E 45 J3
Alxa Zuoqi China 38°50N 105°40E 32 E3
Alyangula Australia 13°55S 136°30E 62 A2
Alyata = Ālāt Azerbaijan 39°58N 49°25E 47 B6
Alyth U.K. 56°38N 3°13W 11 E5
Alytus Lithuania 54°24N 24°3E 9 J21
Alzada U.S.A. 45°2N 104°25W 76 D11
Alzamay Russia 55°33N 98°39E 27 D10
Alzira Spain 39°9N 0°30W 21 C5
Am Timan Chad 11°0N 20°10E 53 F10
Amadeus, L. Australia 24°54S 131°0E 61 D5
Amâdi South Sudan 5°29N 30°25E 53 G12
Amadjuak L. Canada 65°0N 71°8W 69 E17
Amagansett U.S.A. 40°59N 72°9W 83 F12
Amagi Japan 33°25N 130°39E 29 H5
Amahai Indonesia 3°20S 128°55E 37 E7
Amaile Samoa 13°59S 171°22W 59 b
Amakusa = Hondo
  Japan 32°27N 130°12E 29 H5
Amakusa-Shotō Japan 32°15N 130°10E 29 H5
Åmål Sweden 59°3N 12°42E 9 G15
Amaliada Greece 37°47N 21°22E 23 F9
Amalner India 21°5N 75°5E 44 D2
Amamapare Indonesia 4°53S 136°38E 37 E9
Amambaí Brazil 23°5S 55°13W 95 A4
Amambaí → Brazil 23°22S 53°56W 95 A5
Amambay, Cordillera de
  S. Amer. 23°0S 55°45W 95 A4
Amami Japan 28°22N 129°27E 29 K4
Amami-Guntō Japan 27°16N 129°21E 29 L4
Amami-Ō-Shima Japan 28°16N 129°21E 29 L4
Aman, Pulau Malaysia 5°16N 100°24E 39 c
Amaná, L. Brazil 2°35S 64°40W 92 D6
Amanat → India 24°7N 84°4E 43 G11
Amanda Park U.S.A. 47°28N 123°55W 78 C3
Amankeldi Kazakhstan 50°10N 65°10E 26 D7
Amapá Brazil 2°5N 50°50W 93 C8
Amapá □ Brazil 1°40N 52°0W 93 C8
Amarante Brazil 6°14S 42°50W 93 E10
Amaranth Canada 50°36N 98°43W 71 C9
Amargosa → U.S.A. 36°14N 116°51W 79 J10
Amargosa Desert
  U.S.A. 36°40N 116°30W 79 J10
Amargosa Range
  U.S.A. 36°20N 116°45W 79 J10
Amarillo U.S.A. 35°13N 101°50W 84 D4
Amarkantak India 22°40N 81°45E 43 H9
Amarnath India 19°12N 73°22E 44 E1
Amaro, Mte. Italy 42°5N 14°5E 22 C6
Amarpur India 25°5N 87°0E 43 G12
Amarwara India 22°18N 79°10E 43 H8
Amasya Turkey 40°40N 35°50E 19 F6
Amata Australia 26°9S 131°9E 61 E5
Amatikulu S. Africa 29°3S 31°33E 57 C5
Amatitlán Guatemala 14°29N 90°38W 88 D1
Amay Belgium 50°33N 5°19E 15 D5
Amazon = Amazonas →
  S. Amer. 0°5S 50°0W 93 D8
Amazonas □ Brazil 5°0S 65°0W 92 E6
Amazonas → S. Amer. 0°5S 50°0W 93 D8
Ambad India 19°38N 75°50E 44 E2
Ambagarh Chowki India 20°47N 80°43E 44 D5
Ambah India 26°43N 78°13E 42 F8
Ambahta India 29°53N 77°15E 42 E7
Ambala India 30°23N 76°56E 42 D7
Ambalangoda Sri Lanka 6°15N 80°5E 45 L5
Ambalantota Sri Lanka 6°7N 81°1E 45 L5
Ambalapulai India 9°25N 76°25E 45 K3
Ambalavao Madag. 21°50S 46°56E 55 J9
Ambanja Madag. 13°40S 48°27E 55 G9
Ambarchik Russia 69°40N 162°20E 27 C17
Ambasamudram India 8°43N 77°25E 45 K3

Ambato *Ecuador* 1°5S 78°42W **92** D3
Ambato, Sierra de *Argentina* 28°25S 66°10W **94** B2
Ambatolampy *Madag.* 19°20S 47°35E **55** H9
Ambatondrazaka *Madag.* 17°55S 48°28E **55** H9
Amberg *Germany* 49°26N 11°52E **16** D6
Ambergris Cay *Belize* 18°0N 87°55W **87** D7
Amberley *Canada* 44°2N 81°42W **82** B3
Amberley *N.Z.* 43°9S 172°44E **59** E4
Ambikapur *India* 23°15N 83°15E **43** H10
Ambilobé *Madag.* 13°10S 49°3E **55** G9
Amble *U.K.* 55°20N 1°36W **12** B6
Ambleside *U.K.* 54°26N 2°58W **12** C5
Ambo *Peru* 10°5S 76°10W **92** F3
Ambohitra *Madag.* 12°30S 49°10E **55** G9
Amboise *France* 47°24N 1°2E **20** C4
Ambon *Indonesia* 3°43S 128°12E **37** E7
Ambositra *Madag.* 20°31S 47°25E **55** J9
Ambovombe *Madag.* 25°11S 46°5E **55** K9
Amboy *U.S.A.* 34°33N 115°45W **79** L11
Amboyna Cay *S. China Sea* 7°50N 112°50E **36** C4
Ambridge *U.S.A.* 40°36N 80°14W **82** F4
Ambriz *Angola* 7°48S 13°8E **54** F2
Ambur *India* 12°48N 78°43E **45** H4
Amchitka I. *U.S.A.* 51°32N 179°0E **74** E3
Amderma *Russia* 69°45N 61°30E **26** C7
Amdhi *India* 23°51N 81°27E **43** H9
Amdo *China* 32°20N 91°40E **30** E7
Ameca *Mexico* 20°33N 104°2W **86** C4
Ameca → *Mexico* 20°41N 105°18W **86** C3
Amecameca de Juárez *Mexico* 19°8N 98°46W **87** D5
Amed *Indonesia* 8°19S 115°39E **37** J18
Ameland *Neths.* 53°27N 5°45E **15** A5
Amenia *U.S.A.* 41°51N 73°33W **83** E11
America-Antarctica Ridge *S. Ocean* 59°0S 16°0W **5** B2
American Falls *U.S.A.* 42°47N 112°51W **76** E7
American Falls Res. *U.S.A.* 42°47N 112°52W **76** E7
American Fork *U.S.A.* 40°23N 111°48W **76** F8
American Highland *Antarctica* 73°0S 75°0E **5** D6
American Samoa ☐ *Pac. Oc.* 14°20S 170°0W **59** b
American Samoa △ *Amer. Samoa* 14°15S 170°28W **59** b
Americana *Brazil* 22°45S 47°20W **95** A6
Americus *U.S.A.* 32°4N 84°14W **85** E12
Amersfoort *Neths.* 52°9N 5°23E **15** B5
Amersfoort *S. Africa* 26°59S 29°53E **57** C4
Amery Basin *S. Ocean* 68°15S 74°30E **5** C6
Amery Ice Shelf *Antarctica* 69°30S 72°0E **5** C6
Ames *U.S.A.* 42°2N 93°37W **80** D7
Amesbury *U.S.A.* 42°51N 70°56W **83** D14
Amet *India* 25°18N 73°56E **42** G5
Amga *Russia* 60°50N 132°0E **27** C14
Amga → *Russia* 62°38N 134°32E **27** C14
Amgaon *India* 21°22N 80°22E **44** D5
Amgu *Russia* 45°45N 137°15E **28** B8
Amgun → *Russia* 52°56N 139°38E **27** D14
Amherst *Canada* 45°48N 64°8W **73** C7
Amherst *Mass., U.S.A.* 42°23N 72°31W **83** D12
Amherst *N.Y., U.S.A.* 42°59N 78°48W **82** D6
Amherst *Ohio, U.S.A.* 41°24N 82°14W **82** E2
Amherst I. *Canada* 44°8N 76°43W **83** B8
Amherstburg *Canada* 42°6N 83°6W **72** D3
Amiata, Mte. *Italy* 42°53N 11°37E **22** C4
Amidon *U.S.A.* 46°29N 103°19W **80** B2
Amiens *France* 49°54N 2°16E **20** B5
Amindivi Is. *India* 11°23N 72°23E **45** J1
Amini I. *India* 11°6N 72°45E **45** J1
Aminuis *Namibia* 23°43S 19°21E **56** B2
Amīrābād *Iran* 33°20N 46°16E **46** C5
Amirante Is. *Seychelles* 6°0S 53°0E **24** J7
Amisk ⌂ *Canada* 56°43N 98°0W **71** B9
Amisk L. *Canada* 54°35N 102°15W **71** C8
Amistad, Presa de la *Mexico* 29°26N 101°3W **86** B4
Amistad ⌂ *U.S.A.* 29°32N 101°12W **84** G4
Amite *U.S.A.* 30°44N 90°30W **85** F9
Amla *India* 21°56N 78°7E **42** J8
Amlapura *Indonesia* 8°27S 115°37E **37** J18
Amlia I. *U.S.A.* 52°4N 173°30W **74** E5
Amlwch *U.K.* 53°24N 4°20W **12** D3
'Ammān *Jordan* 31°57N 35°52E **48** D4
'Ammān ☐ *Jordan* 31°40N 36°30E **48** D5
'Ammān ✈ (AMM) *Jordan* 31°45N 36°2E **48** D5
Ammanford *U.K.* 51°48N 3°59W **13** F4
Ammassalik = Tasiilaq *Greenland* 65°40N 37°20W **4** C6
Ammochostos = Famagusta *Cyprus* 35°8N 33°55E **46** C2
Ammon *U.S.A.* 43°28N 111°58W **76** E8
Amnat Charoen *Thailand* 15°51N 104°38E **38** E5
Amnura *Bangla.* 24°37N 88°25E **43** G13
Amo Jiang → *China* 23°0N 101°50E **34** F3
Āmol *Iran* 36°23N 52°20E **47** B7
Amorgos *Greece* 36°50N 25°57E **23** F11
Amory *U.S.A.* 33°59N 88°29W **85** E10
Amos *Canada* 48°35N 78°5W **72** C4
Åmot *Norway* 59°57N 9°54E **9** G13
Amoy = Xiamen *China* 24°25N 118°4E **35** E12
Ampang *Malaysia* 3°8N 101°45E **39** L3
Ampani *India* 19°35N 82°38E **44** E6
Ampanihy *Madag.* 24°40S 44°45E **55** J8
Ampenan *Indonesia* 8°34S 116°4E **37** K18
Amper → *Germany* 48°29N 11°55E **16** D6
Amphoe Kathu *Thailand* 7°55N 98°21E **39** a
Amphoe Thalang *Thailand* 8°1N 98°20E **39** a
Amqui *Canada* 48°28N 67°27W **73** C6
Amrabad *India* 16°23N 78°50E **45** F4
Amravati *India* 20°55N 77°45E **44** D3
Amreli *India* 21°35N 71°17E **42** J4
Amritsar *India* 31°35N 74°57E **42** D6
Amroha *India* 28°53N 78°30E **43** E8
Amsterdam *U.S.A.* 42°56N 74°11W **83** D10
Amsterdam I. = Nouvelle Amsterdam, Î. *Ind. Oc.* 38°30S 77°30E **3** F13
Amstetten *Austria* 48°7N 14°51E **16** D8
Amudarya → *Uzbekistan* 43°58N 59°34E **26** E6
Amund Ringnes I. *Canada* 78°20N 96°25W **69** B12
Amundsen Abyssal Plain *S. Ocean* 65°0S 125°0W **5** C14
Amundsen Basin *Arctic* 87°30N 80°0E **4** A
Amundsen Gulf *Canada* 71°0N 124°0W **68** C7
Amundsen Ridges *S. Ocean* 69°15S 123°0W **5** C14
Amundsen-Scott *Antarctica* 90°0S 166°0E **5** E
Amundsen Sea *Antarctica* 72°0S 115°0W **5** D15
Amuntai *Indonesia* 2°28S 115°25E **36** E5
Amur → *Russia* 52°56N 141°10E **27** D15
Amurang *Indonesia* 1°5N 124°40E **37** D6
Amursk *Russia* 50°14N 136°54E **27** D14
Amyderya = Amudarya → *Uzbekistan* 43°58N 59°34E **26** E6
An Bien *Vietnam* 9°45N 105°0E **39** H5
An Hoa *Vietnam* 15°40N 108°5E **38** E7
An Khe *Vietnam* 13°57N 108°51E **38** F7
An Nabatīyah at Tahta *Lebanon* 33°23N 35°27E **48** B4
An Nabk *Syria* 34°2N 36°44E **48** A5
An Nafūd *Si. Arabia* 28°15N 41°0E **46** D4
An Najaf *Iraq* 32°3N 44°15E **46** C5
An Nāṣirīyah *Iraq* 31°0N 46°15E **46** D5
An Nhon = Binh Dinh *Vietnam* 13°55N 109°7E **38** F7
An Nu'ayrīyah *Si. Arabia* 27°30N 48°30E **47** E6
An Nu'mānīyah *Iraq* 32°32N 45°25E **46** C5
An Ros = Rush *Ireland* 53°31N 6°6W **10** C5
An Thoi, Quan Dao *Vietnam* 9°58N 104°0E **39** H5
Anabar → *Russia* 73°8N 113°36E **27** B12
Anaconda *U.S.A.* 46°8N 112°57W **76** C7
Anacortes *U.S.A.* 48°30N 122°37W **78** B4
Anadarko *U.S.A.* 35°4N 98°15W **84** D5
Anadolu *Turkey* 39°0N 30°0E **19** G5
Anadyr *Russia* 64°35N 177°20E **27** C18
Anadyr → *Russia* 64°55N 176°5E **27** C18
Anadyrskiy Zaliv *Russia* 64°0N 180°0E **27** C19
'Ānah *Iraq* 34°25N 42°0E **46** C4
Anaheim *U.S.A.* 33°50N 117°55W **79** M9
Anahim Lake *Canada* 52°28N 125°18W **70** C3
Anai Mudi *India* 10°12N 77°4E **45** J3
Anaimalai Hills *India* 10°20N 76°40E **45** J3
Anakapalle *India* 17°42N 83°6E **44** F6
Anakie *Australia* 23°32S 147°45E **62** C4
Analalava *Madag.* 14°35S 48°0E **55** G9
Anambar → *Pakistan* 30°15N 68°50E **42** D3
Anambas, Kepulauan *Indonesia* 3°20N 106°30E **36** D3
Anambas Is. = Anambas, Kepulauan *Indonesia* 3°20N 106°30E **36** D3
Anamosa *U.S.A.* 42°7N 91°17W **80** D8
Anamur *Turkey* 36°8N 32°58E **46** B2
Anan *Japan* 33°54N 134°40E **29** H7
Anand *India* 22°32N 72°59E **42** H5
Anandapuram *India* 14°5N 75°12E **45** G2
Anandpur *India* 21°16N 86°13E **44** D8
Anangu Pitjantjatjara ✪ *Australia* 27°0S 132°0E **61** E5
Anantapur *India* 14°39N 77°42E **45** G3
Anantnag *India* 33°45N 75°10E **43** C6
Ananyiv *Ukraine* 47°44N 29°58E **17** E15
Anápolis *Brazil* 16°15S 48°50W **93** G9
Anapu → *Brazil* 1°53S 50°53W **93** D8
Anār *Iran* 30°55N 55°13E **47** D7
Anārak *Iran* 33°25N 53°40E **47** C7
Anas → *India* 23°26N 74°0E **42** H5
Anatolia = Anadolu *Turkey* 39°0N 30°0E **19** G5
Añatuya *Argentina* 28°20S 62°50W **94** B3
Anatye ✪ *Australia* 22°29S 137°3E **62** C2
Anaunethad L. *Canada* 60°55N 104°25W **71** A8
Anbyŏn *N. Korea* 39°1N 127°35E **33** E14
Ancaster *Canada* 43°13N 79°59W **82** C5
Anchor Bay *U.S.A.* 38°48N 123°34W **78** G3
Anchorage *U.S.A.* 61°13N 149°54W **68** E2
Anchuthengu *India* 8°40N 76°46E **45** K3
Anci *China* 39°20N 116°40E **32** E9
Ancohuma, Nevado *Bolivia* 16°0S 68°50W **92** G5
Ancón *Peru* 11°50S 77°10W **92** F3
Ancona *Italy* 43°38N 13°30E **22** C5
Ancud *Chile* 42°0S 73°50W **96** E2
Ancud, G. de *Chile* 42°0S 73°0W **96** E2
Anda *China* 46°24N 125°19E **31** B14
Andacollo *Argentina* 37°10S 70°42W **94** D1
Andacollo *Chile* 30°14S 71°6W **94** C1
Andalgalá *Argentina* 27°40S 66°30W **94** B2
Åndalsnes *Norway* 62°35N 7°43E **8** E12
Andalucía ☐ *Spain* 37°35N 5°0W **21** D3
Andalusia = Andalucía ☐ *Spain* 37°35N 5°0W **21** D3
Andalusia *U.S.A.* 31°18N 86°29W **85** F11
Andaman & Nicobar Is. ☐ *India* 10°0N 93°0E **45** K11
Andaman Is. *Ind. Oc.* 12°30N 92°45E **45** H11
Andaman Sea *Ind. Oc.* 13°0N 96°0E **36** B1
Andamooka *Australia* 30°27S 137°9E **63** E2
Andapa *Madag.* 14°39S 49°39E **55** G9
Andara *Namibia* 18°2S 21°9E **56** A3
Andenes *Norway* 69°19N 16°18E **8** B17
Andenne *Belgium* 50°28N 5°5E **15** D5
Anderson *Alaska, U.S.A.* 64°25N 149°15W **74** C10
Anderson *Calif., U.S.A.* 40°27N 122°18W **76** F2
Anderson *Ind., U.S.A.* 40°10N 85°41W **81** E11
Anderson *Mo., U.S.A.* 36°39N 94°27W **80** G6
Anderson *S.C., U.S.A.* 34°31N 82°39W **85** D13
Anderson → *Canada* 69°42N 129°0W **68** D6
Anderson I. *India* 12°46N 92°43E **45** H11
Andes *U.S.A.* 42°12N 74°47W **83** D10
Andes, Cord. de los *S. Amer.* 20°0S 68°0W **92** H5
Andfjorden *Norway* 69°10N 16°20E **8** B17
Andhra, L. *India* 18°54N 73°32E **44** E1
Andhra Pradesh ☐ *India* 18°0N 79°0E **44** F4
Andijon *Uzbekistan* 41°10N 72°15E **30** C3
Andikíthira = Antikythira *Greece* 35°52N 23°15E **23** G10
Andīmeshk *Iran* 32°27N 48°21E **47** C6
Andizhan = Andijon *Uzbekistan* 41°10N 72°15E **30** C3
Andoany *Madag.* 13°25S 48°16E **55** G9
Andol *India* 17°51N 78°4E **44** F4
Andola *India* 16°57N 76°50E **44** F3
Andong *S. Korea* 36°40N 128°43E **33** F15
Andorra ■ *Europe* 42°30N 1°30E **20** E4
Andorra La Vella *Andorra* 42°31N 1°32E **20** E4
Andover *U.K.* 51°12N 1°29W **13** F6
Andover *Kans., U.S.A.* 37°43N 97°7W **80** G5
Andover *Maine, U.S.A.* 44°38N 70°45W **83** B14
Andover *Mass., U.S.A.* 42°40N 71°8W **83** D13
Andover *N.J., U.S.A.* 40°59N 74°45W **83** F10
Andover *N.Y., U.S.A.* 42°10N 77°48W **82** D7
Andover *Ohio, U.S.A.* 41°36N 80°34W **82** E4
Andøya *Norway* 69°10N 15°50E **8** B16
Andradina *Brazil* 20°54S 51°23W **93** H8
Andreanof Is. *U.S.A.* 51°30N 176°0W **74** E4
Andrews *S.C., U.S.A.* 33°27N 79°34W **85** E15
Andrews *Tex., U.S.A.* 32°19N 102°33W **84** E3
Ándria *Italy* 41°13N 16°17E **22** D7
Andros *Greece* 37°50N 24°57E **23** F11
Andros I. *Bahamas* 24°30N 78°0W **88** B4
Andros Town *Bahamas* 24°43N 77°47W **88** B4
Androscoggin → *U.S.A.* 43°58N 69°52W **83** C14
Androth I. *India* 10°50N 73°41E **45** J1
Andselv *Norway* 69°4N 18°34E **8** B18
Andújar *Spain* 38°3N 4°5W **21** C3
Andulo *Angola* 11°25S 16°45E **54** G3
Anegada *Br. Virgin Is.* 18°45N 64°20W **89** e
Anegada Passage *W. Indies* 18°15N 63°45W **89** C7
Aneto, Pico de *Spain* 42°37N 0°40E **21** A6
Anfu *China* 27°21N 114°40E **35** D10
Ang Thong *Thailand* 14°35N 100°31E **38** E3
Ang Thong, Ko *Thailand* 9°37N 99°41E **39** b
Ang Thong, Mu Ko △ *Thailand* 9°40N 99°43E **39** b
Angamos, Punta *Chile* 23°1S 70°32W **94** A1
Angara → *Russia* 58°5N 94°20E **27** D10
Angarsk *Russia* 52°30N 104°0E **30** A9
Angas Hills *Australia* 23°0S 127°50E **60** D4
Angaston *Australia* 34°30S 139°8E **63** E2
Ånge *Sweden* 62°31N 15°35E **8** E16
Ángel, Salto = Angel Falls *Venezuela* 5°57N 62°30W **92** B6
Ángel de la Guarda, I. *Mexico* 29°20N 113°25W **86** B2
Angel Falls *Venezuela* 5°57N 62°30W **92** B6
Angeles *Phil.* 15°9N 120°33E **37** A6
Ängelholm *Sweden* 56°15N 12°50E **9** H15
Angels Camp *U.S.A.* 38°4N 120°32W **78** G6
Ångermanälven → *Sweden* 64°0N 17°20E **8** E17
Ångermanland *Sweden* 63°36N 17°45E **8** E17
Angers *Canada* 45°31N 75°29W **83** A9
Angers *France* 47°30N 0°35W **20** C3
Ängesån → *Sweden* 66°16N 22°47E **8** C20
Angikuni L. *Canada* 62°12N 99°59W **71** A9
Angkor *Cambodia* 13°22N 103°50E **38** F4
Angledool *Australia* 29°5S 147°55E **63** D4
Anglesey *U.K.* 53°17N 4°20W **12** D3
Anglesey, Isle of ☐ *U.K.* 53°16N 4°18W **12** D3
Angleton *U.S.A.* 29°10N 95°26W **84** G7
Angmagssalik = Tasiilaq *Greenland* 65°40N 37°20W **4** C6
Ango *Dem. Rep. of the Congo* 4°10N 26°5E **54** D5
Angoche *Mozam.* 16°8S 39°55E **55** H7
Angol *Chile* 37°56S 72°45W **94** D1
Angola *Ind., U.S.A.* 41°38N 85°0W **81** E11
Angola *N.Y., U.S.A.* 42°38N 79°2W **82** D5
Angola ■ *Africa* 12°0S 18°0E **55** G3
Angoulême *France* 45°39N 0°10E **20** D4
Angoumois *France* 45°50N 0°25E **20** D3
Angra do Heroismo *Azores* 38°39N 27°13W **52** a
Angra dos Reis *Brazil* 23°0S 44°10W **95** A7
Angtassom *Cambodia* 11°1N 104°41E **39** G5
Anguang *China* 45°15N 123°45E **33** B12
Anguilla ☑ *W. Indies* 18°14N 63°5W **89** C7
Angul *India* 20°51N 85°6E **44** D7
Anguo *China* 38°28N 115°15E **32** E8
Angurugu *Australia* 14°0S 136°25E **62** A2
Angus *Canada* 44°19N 79°53W **82** B5
Angus ☐ *U.K.* 56°46N 2°56W **11** E6
Angwa → *Zimbabwe* 16°0S 30°23E **57** A5
Anhanduí → *Brazil* 21°46S 52°9W **95** A5
Anholt *Denmark* 56°42N 11°33E **9** H14
Anhua *China* 28°23N 111°12E **35** C8
Anhui ☐ *China* 32°0N 117°0E **35** B11
Anhwei = Anhui ☐ *China* 32°0N 117°0E **35** B11
Anichab *Namibia* 21°0S 14°46E **56** B1
Animas → *U.S.A.* 36°43N 108°13W **77** H9
Anin *Burma* 15°36N 97°50E **38** E1
Anjalankoski *Finland* 60°45N 26°51E **8** F22
Anjangaon *India* 21°10N 77°20E **44** D3
Anjar = Hawsh Mūssá *Lebanon* 33°45N 35°55E **48** B4
Anjar *India* 23°6N 70°10E **42** H4
Anjengo = Anchuthengu *India* 8°40N 76°46E **45** K3
Anji *China* 30°46N 119°40E **35** B12
Anjidiv I. *India* 14°40N 74°10E **45** G2
Anjou *France* 47°20N 0°15W **20** C3
Anjouan *Comoros Is.* 12°15S 44°20E **55** a
Anju *N. Korea* 39°36N 125°40E **33** E13
Ankaboa, Tanjona *Madag.* 21°58S 43°20E **55** J8
Ankang *China* 32°40N 109°1E **32** H5
Ankara *Turkey* 39°57N 32°54E **19** G5
Ankaratra *Madag.* 19°25S 47°12E **55** H9
Ankazoabo *Madag.* 22°18S 44°31E **55** J8
Ankeny *U.S.A.* 41°44N 93°36W **80** E7
Ankleshwar *India* 21°38N 73°3E **44** D1
Ankola *India* 14°40N 74°18E **45** G2
Anlong *China* 25°2N 105°27E **34** E5
Anlong Veng *Cambodia* 14°14N 104°5E **38** E5
Anlu *China* 31°15N 113°45E **35** B9
Anmyeondo *S. Korea* 36°25N 126°25E **33** F14
Ann, C. *U.S.A.* 42°38N 70°35W **83** D14
Ann Arbor *U.S.A.* 42°17N 83°45W **81** D12
Anna *U.S.A.* 37°28N 89°15W **80** G9
Annaba *Algeria* 36°50N 7°46E **52** A7
Annalee → *Ireland* 54°2N 7°24W **10** B4
Annam = Trung-Phan *Vietnam* 17°0N 109°0E **38** D6
Annamitique, Chaîne *Asia* 17°0N 106°40E **38** D6
Annan *U.K.* 54°59N 3°16W **11** G5
Annan → *U.K.* 54°58N 3°16W **11** G5
Annapolis *U.S.A.* 38°59N 76°30W **81** F15
Annapolis Royal *Canada* 44°44N 65°32W **73** D6
Annapurna *Nepal* 28°34N 83°50E **43** E10
Annean, L. *Australia* 26°54S 118°14E **61** E2
Annecy *France* 45°55N 6°8E **20** D7
Annette I. *U.S.A.* 55°9N 131°28W **70** B2
Annigeri *India* 15°26N 75°26E **45** G2
Anning *China* 24°55N 102°26E **34** E4
Anniston *U.S.A.* 33°39N 85°50W **85** E12
Annobón *Atl. Oc.* 1°25S 5°36E **51** G4
Annotto B. *Jamaica* 18°17N 76°45W **88** a
Annville *U.S.A.* 40°20N 76°31W **83** F8
Anping *Hebei, China* 38°15N 115°30E **32** E8
Anping *Liaoning, China* 41°5N 123°30E **33** D12
Anpu Gang *China* 21°25N 109°50E **34** G7
Anqing *China* 30°30N 117°3E **35** B11
Anqiu *China* 36°25N 119°10E **33** F10
Anren *China* 26°43N 113°18E **35** D9
Ansai *China* 36°50N 109°20E **32** F5
Ansan *S. Korea* 37°21N 126°52E **33** F14
Ansbach *Germany* 49°28N 10°34E **16** D6
Anse Boileau *Seychelles* 4°43S 55°29E **55** b
Anse la Raye *St. Lucia* 13°55N 61°3W **89** f
Anse Royale *Seychelles* 4°44S 55°31E **55** b
Anshan *China* 41°5N 122°58E **33** D12
Anshun *China* 26°18N 105°57E **34** D5
Ansley *U.S.A.* 41°18N 99°23W **80** E4
Anson *U.S.A.* 32°45N 99°54W **84** E5
Anson B. *Australia* 13°20S 130°6E **60** B5
Ansongo *Mali* 15°25N 0°35E **52** E6
Ansonia *U.S.A.* 41°21N 73°5W **83** E11
Anstruther *U.K.* 56°14N 2°41W **11** E6
Ansudu *Indonesia* 2°11S 139°22E **37** E9
Antabamba *Peru* 14°40S 73°0W **92** F4
Antagarh *India* 20°6N 81°9E **44** D5
Antakya = Hatay *Turkey* 36°14N 36°10E **46** B3
Antalaha *Madag.* 14°57S 50°20E **55** G10
Antalya *Turkey* 36°52N 30°45E **19** G5
Antalya Körfezi *Turkey* 36°15N 31°30E **19** G5
Antananarivo *Madag.* 18°55S 47°31E **55** H9
Antarctic Pen. *Antarctica* 67°0S 60°0W **5** C18
Antarctica 90°0S 0°0 **5** E3
Antep = Gaziantep *Turkey* 37°6N 37°23E **46** B3
Antequera *Paraguay* 24°8S 57°7W **94** A4
Antequera *Spain* 37°5N 4°33W **21** D3
Antero, Mt. *U.S.A.* 38°41N 106°15W **76** G10
Anthony *Kans., U.S.A.* 37°9N 98°2W **80** G4
Anthony *N. Mex., U.S.A.* 32°0N 106°36W **77** K10
Anti Atlas *Morocco* 30°0N 8°30W **52** C4
Anti-Lebanon = Sharqi, Al Jabal ash *Lebanon* 33°40N 36°10E **48** B5
Antibes *France* 43°34N 7°6E **20** E7
Anticosti, Î. d' *Canada* 49°30N 63°0W **73** C7
Antigo *U.S.A.* 45°9N 89°9W **80** C9
Antigonish *Canada* 45°38N 61°58W **73** C7
Antigua *Guatemala* 14°34N 90°41W **88** D1
Antigua *W. Indies* 17°0N 61°50W **89** C7
Antigua & Barbuda ■ *W. Indies* 17°20N 61°48W **89** C7
Antikythira *Greece* 35°52N 23°15E **23** G10
Antilla *Cuba* 20°40N 75°50W **88** B4
Antilles = West Indies *Cent. Amer.* 15°0N 65°0W **89** D7
Antioch *U.S.A.* 38°1N 121°48W **78** G5
Antioquia *Colombia* 6°40N 75°55W **92** B3
Antipodes Is. *Pac. Oc.* 49°45S 178°40E **64** M9
Antlers *U.S.A.* 34°14N 95°37W **84** D7
Antofagasta *Chile* 23°50S 70°30W **94** A1
Antofagasta ☐ *Chile* 24°0S 69°0W **94** A2
Antofagasta de la Sierra *Argentina* 26°5S 67°20W **94** B2
Antofalla *Argentina* 25°30S 68°5W **94** B2
Antofalla, Salar de *Argentina* 25°40S 67°45W **94** B2
Anton *U.S.A.* 33°49N 102°10W **84** E3
Antonina *Brazil* 25°26S 48°42W **95** B6
Antrim *U.K.* 54°43N 6°14W **10** B5
Antrim *U.S.A.* 40°7N 81°21W **82** F3
Antrim ☐ *U.K.* 54°56N 6°25W **10** B5
Antrim, Mts. of *U.K.* 55°3N 6°14W **10** A5
Antrim Plateau *Australia* 18°8S 128°20E **60** C4
Antsalova *Madag.* 18°40S 44°37E **55** H8
Antsirabe *Madag.* 19°55S 47°2E **55** H9
Antsiranana *Madag.* 12°25S 49°20E **55** G9
Antsohihy *Madag.* 14°50S 47°59E **55** G9
Antu *China* 42°30N 128°20E **33** C15
Antwerp = Antwerpen *Belgium* 51°13N 4°25E **15** C4
Antwerp *U.S.A.* 44°12N 75°37W **83** B9
Antwerpen *Belgium* 51°13N 4°25E **15** C4
Antwerpen ☐ *Belgium* 51°15N 4°40E **15** C4
Anupgarh *India* 29°10N 73°10E **42** E5
Anuppur *India* 23°6N 81°41E **43** H9
Anuradhapura *Sri Lanka* 8°22N 80°28E **45** K5
Anurrete ✪ *Australia* 20°50S 135°38E **62** C2
Anveh *Iran* 27°23N 54°11E **47** E7
Anvers = Antwerpen *Belgium* 51°13N 4°25E **15** C4
Anvers I. *Antarctica* 64°30S 63°40W **5** C17
Anwen *China* 29°4N 120°26E **35** C13
Anxi *Fujian, China* 25°2N 118°12E **35** E12
Anxi *Gansu, China* 40°30N 95°43E **30** C8
Anxian *China* 31°40N 104°25E **34** B5
Anxiang *China* 29°27N 112°11E **35** C9
Anxious B. *Australia* 33°24S 134°45E **63** E1
Anyang *China* 36°5N 114°21E **32** F8
Anyang *S. Korea* 37°23N 126°55E **33** F14
Anyer *Indonesia* 6°4S 105°53E **37** G11
Anyi *Jiangxi, China* 28°49N 115°25E **35** C10
Anyi *Shanxi, China* 35°2N 111°2E **32** G6
Anyuan *China* 25°9N 115°21E **35** E10
Anyue *China* 30°9N 105°50E **34** B5
Anza *U.S.A.* 33°35N 116°39W **79** M10
Anze *China* 36°10N 112°12E **32** F7
Anzhero-Sudzhensk *Russia* 56°10N 86°0E **26** D9
Ánzio *Italy* 41°27N 12°37E **22** D5
Ao Makham *Thailand* 7°50N 98°24E **39** a
Ao Phangnga △ *Thailand* 8°10N 98°32E **39** a
Aoga-Shima *Japan* 32°28N 139°46E **29** H9
Aohan Qi *China* 43°18N 119°43E **33** C10
Aoji *N. Korea* 42°31N 130°23E **33** C16
Aomen = Macau *China* 22°12N 113°33E **35** F9
Aomori *Japan* 40°45N 140°45E **28** D10
Aomori ☐ *Japan* 40°45N 140°40E **28** D10
tAonach, An = Nenagh *Ireland* 52°52N 8°11W **10** D3
Aonla *India* 28°16N 79°11E **43** E8
Aorai, Mt. *Tahiti* 17°34S 149°30W **59** d
Aoraki Mount Cook *N.Z.* 43°36S 170°9E **59** E3
Aoral, Phnum *Cambodia* 12°0N 104°15E **39** G5
Aosta *Italy* 45°45N 7°20E **20** D7
Aotearoa = New Zealand ■ *Oceania* 40°0S 176°0E **59** D6
Aoukâr *Mauritania* 17°40N 10°0W **52** E4
Aozou, Couloir d' *Chad* 22°0N 19°0E **53** D9
Apá → *S. Amer.* 22°6S 58°2W **94** A4
Apache *U.S.A.* 34°54N 98°22W **84** D5
Apache Junction *U.S.A.* 33°25N 111°33W **77** K8
Apalachee B. *U.S.A.* 30°0N 84°0W **85** G13
Apalachicola *U.S.A.* 29°43N 84°59W **85** G12
Apalachicola → *U.S.A.* 29°43N 84°58W **85** G12
Apaporis → *Colombia* 1°23S 69°25W **92** D5
Aparados da Serra △ *Brazil* 29°10S 50°8W **95** B5
Aparri *Phil.* 18°22N 121°38E **37** A6
Apatity *Russia* 67°34N 33°22E **8** C25
Apatula = Finke *Australia* 25°34S 134°35E **62** D1
Apatzingán *Mexico* 19°5N 102°21W **86** D4
Apeldoorn *Neths.* 52°13N 5°57E **15** B5
Apennines = Appennini *Italy* 44°30N 10°0E **22** B4
Api *Nepal* 30°0N 80°57E **30** F5
Apia *Samoa* 13°50S 171°50W **59** b
Apiacás, Serra dos *Brazil* 9°50S 57°0W **92** E7
Apies → *S. Africa* 25°15S 28°8E **57** C4
Apizaco *Mexico* 19°25N 98°8W **87** D5
Aplao *Peru* 16°0S 72°40W **92** G4
Apo, Mt. *Phil.* 6°53N 125°14E **37** C7
Apollonia = Sūsah *Libya* 32°52N 21°59E **53** B10
Apolo *Bolivia* 14°30S 68°30W **92** F5
Apopa *El Salv.* 13°48N 89°10W **88** D2
Aporé → *Brazil* 19°27S 50°57W **93** G8
Apostle Is. *U.S.A.* 47°0N 90°40W **80** B8
Apostle Islands ⌂ *U.S.A.* 46°55N 91°0W **80** B8
Apóstoles *Argentina* 28°0S 56°0W **95** B4
Apostolos Andreas, C. *Cyprus* 35°42N 34°35E **46** C2
Apoteri *Guyana* 4°2N 58°32W **92** C7
Appalachian Mts. *U.S.A.* 38°0N 80°0W **81** G14
Appennini *Italy* 44°30N 10°0E **22** B4
Apple Hill *Canada* 45°13N 74°46W **83** A10
Apple Valley *U.S.A.* 34°32N 117°14W **79** L9
Appleby-in-Westmorland *U.K.* 54°35N 2°29W **12** C5
Appledore *U.K.* 51°3N 4°13W **13** F3
Appleton *U.S.A.* 44°16N 88°25W **80** C9
Approuague → *Fr. Guiana* 4°30N 51°57W **93** C8
Aprília *Italy* 41°36N 12°39E **22** D5
Apsley *Canada* 44°45N 78°6W **82** B6
Apucarana *Brazil* 23°55S 51°33W **95** A5
Apure → *Venezuela* 7°37N 66°25W **92** B5
Apurímac → *Peru* 12°17S 73°56W **92** F4
Āq Qālā *Iran* 37°10N 54°30E **47** B7
Aqaba = Al 'Aqabah *Jordan* 29°31N 35°0E **48** F4
Aqaba, G. of *Red Sea* 29°0N 34°40E **46** D2
'Aqabah, Khalīj al = Aqaba, G. of *Red Sea* 29°0N 34°40E **46** D2
'Aqdā *Iran* 32°26N 53°37E **47** C7
'Aqrah *Iraq* 36°46N 43°45E **46** B4
Aqsay *Kazakhstan* 51°11N 53°0E **19** D9
Aqtaū *Kazakhstan* 43°39N 51°12E **19** F9
Aqtöbe *Kazakhstan* 50°17N 57°10E **19** D10
Aqtoghay *Kazakhstan* 46°57N 79°40E **26** E8
Aqua = Sokhumi *Georgia* 43°0N 41°0E **19** F7
Aquidauana *Brazil* 20°30S 55°50W **93** H7
Aquila *Mexico* 18°36N 103°30W **86** D4
Aquiles Serdán *Mexico* 28°36N 105°53W **86** B3
Aquin *Haiti* 18°16N 73°24W **89** C5
Aquitain, Bassin *France* 44°0N 0°30W **20** D3
Ar Horqin Qi *China* 43°45N 120°0E **33** C11
Ar Rafīd *Syria* 32°57N 35°52E **48** C4
Ar Raḥḥālīyah *Iraq* 32°44N 43°23E **46** C4
Ar Ramādī *Iraq* 33°25N 43°20E **46** C4
Ar Ramthā *Jordan* 32°34N 36°0E **48** C5
Ar Raqqah *Syria* 35°59N 39°8E **46** C3
Ar Rashidiya = Er Rachidia *Morocco* 31°58N 4°20W **52** B5
Ar Rass *Si. Arabia* 25°50N 43°40E **46** E4
Ar Rayyan *Qatar* 25°17N 51°25E **47** E6
Ar Rifā'ī *Iraq* 31°50N 46°10E **46** D5
Ar Riyāḍ *Si. Arabia* 24°41N 46°42E **46** E5
Ar Ru'ays *Qatar* 26°8N 51°12E **47** E6
Ar Rukhaymīyah *Iraq* 29°22N 45°38E **46** D5
Ar Rumaythah *Iraq* 31°31N 45°12E **46** D5

Ar Ruṣāfah *Syria* 35°45N 38°49E **46 C3**
Ar Ruṭbah *Iraq* 33°0N 40°15E **46 C4**
Ara *India* 25°35N 84°32E **43 G11**
Arab *U.S.A.* 34°19N 86°30W **85 D11**
'Arab, Bahr el →
  South Sudan 9°0N 29°30E **53 G11**
Arab, Shatt al → *Asia* 29°57N 48°34E **47 D6**
'Arabābād *Iran* 33°2N 57°41E **47 C8**
Arabia *Asia* 25°0N 45°0E **24 F6**
Arabian Desert = Es Sahrâ' Esh
  Sharqîya *Egypt* 27°30N 32°30E **53 C12**
Arabian Gulf = Persian Gulf
  Asia 27°0N 50°0E **47 E6**
Arabian Sea *Ind. Oc.* 16°0N 65°0E **24 G8**
Aracaju *Brazil* 10°55S 37°4W **93 F11**
Aracati *Brazil* 4°30S 37°44W **93 D11**
Araçatuba *Brazil* 21°10S 50°30W **95 A5**
Aracena *Spain* 37°53N 6°38W **21 D2**
Araçuaí *Brazil* 16°52S 42°4W **93 G10**
'Arad *Israel* 31°15N 35°12E **48 D4**
Arad *Romania* 46°10N 21°20E **17 E11**
Arādān *Iran* 35°21N 52°30E **47 C7**
Arafura Sea *E. Indies* 9°0S 135°0E **58 B6**
Aragón □ *Spain* 41°25N 0°40W **21 B5**
Aragón → *Spain* 42°13N 1°44W **21 A5**
Araguacema *Brazil* 8°50S 49°20W **93 E9**
Araguaia → *Brazil* 5°21S 48°41W **93 E9**
Araguaína *Brazil* 7°12S 48°12W **93 E9**
Araguari *Brazil* 18°38S 48°11W **93 G9**
Araguari → *Brazil* 1°15N 49°55W **93 C9**
Arain *India* 26°27N 75°2E **42 F6**
Arak *Algeria* 25°20N 3°45E **52 C6**
Arāk *Iran* 34°0N 49°40E **47 C6**
Arakan = Rakhine □
  Burma 19°0N 94°15E **41 K18**
Arakan Coast *Burma* 19°0N 94°0E **41 K19**
Arakan Yoma *Burma* 20°0N 94°40E **41 K19**
Arakkonam *India* 13°7N 79°43E **45 H4**
Araks = Aras, Rūd-e →
  Asia 40°5N 48°29E **46 B5**
Aral *Kazakhstan* 46°41N 61°45E **26 E7**
Aral Sea *Asia* 45°0N 58°20E **26 E7**
Aral Tengizi = Aral Sea
  Asia 45°0N 58°20E **26 E7**
Aralsk = Aral *Kazakhstan* 46°41N 61°45E **26 E7**
Aralskoye More = Aral Sea
  Asia 45°0N 58°20E **26 E7**
Aramac *Australia* 22°58S 145°14E **62 C4**
Aran → *India* 19°55N 78°12E **44 E4**
Aran I. = Arranmore
  Ireland 55°0N 8°30W **10 A3**
Aran Is. *Ireland* 53°6N 9°38W **10 C2**
Aranda de Duero *Spain* 41°39N 3°42W **21 B4**
Arandān *Iran* 35°23N 46°55E **46 C5**
Arani *India* 12°43N 79°19E **45 H4**
Aranjuez *Spain* 40°1N 3°40W **21 B4**
Aranos *Namibia* 24°9S 19°7E **56 B2**
Aransas Pass *U.S.A.* 27°55N 97°9W **84 H6**
Aranyaprathet *Thailand* 13°41N 102°30E **38 F4**
Arapahoe *U.S.A.* 40°18N 99°54W **80 E4**
Arapey Grande →
  Uruguay 30°55S 57°49W **94 C4**
Arapgir *Turkey* 39°5N 38°30E **46 B3**
Arapiraca *Brazil* 9°45S 36°39W **93 E11**
Arapongas *Brazil* 23°29S 51°28W **95 A5**
Ar'ar *Si. Arabia* 30°59N 41°2E **46 D4**
Araranguá *Brazil* 29°0S 49°30W **95 B6**
Araraquara *Brazil* 21°50S 48°0W **93 H9**
Araras, Serra das *Brazil* 25°0S 53°10W **95 B5**
Ararat, Mt. = Ağrı Dağı
  Turkey 39°50N 44°15E **46 B5**
Araria *India* 26°9N 87°33E **43 F12**
Araripe, Chapada do
  Brazil 7°20S 40°0W **93 E11**
Araruama, L. de *Brazil* 22°53S 42°12W **95 A7**
Aras, Rūd-e → *Asia* 40°5N 48°29E **46 B5**
Arauca *Colombia* 7°0N 70°40W **92 B4**
Arauca → *Venezuela* 7°24N 66°35W **92 B5**
Arauco *Chile* 37°16S 73°25W **94 D1**
Aravalli Range *India* 25°0N 73°30E **42 G5**
Araxá *Brazil* 19°35S 46°55W **93 G9**
Araya, Pen. de *Venezuela* 10°40N 64°0W **92 A6**
Arba Minch *Ethiopia* 6°0N 37°30E **49 F2**
Arbat *Iraq* 35°25N 45°35E **46 C5**
Árbatax *Italy* 39°56N 9°42E **22 E3**
Arbīl *Iraq* 36°15N 44°5E **46 B5**
Arborfield *Canada* 53°6N 103°39W **71 C8**
Arborg *Canada* 50°54N 97°13W **71 C9**
Arbroath *U.K.* 56°34N 2°35W **11 E6**
Arbuckle *U.S.A.* 39°1N 122°3W **78 F4**
Arcachon *France* 44°40N 1°10W **20 D3**
Arcade *U.S.A.* 42°32N 78°25W **82 D6**
Arcadia *Fla., U.S.A.* 27°13N 81°52W **85 H14**
Arcadia *La., U.S.A.* 32°33N 92°55W **84 E8**
Arcadia *Pa., U.S.A.* 40°47N 78°51W **82 F6**
Arcata *U.S.A.* 40°52N 124°5W **76 F1**
Archangel = Arkhangelsk
  Russia 64°38N 40°36E **18 B7**
Archer → *Australia* 13°28S 141°41E **62 A3**
Archer B. *Australia* 13°20S 141°30E **62 A3**
Archer Bend = Mungkan
  Kandju △ *Australia* 13°35S 142°52E **62 A3**
Arches △ *U.S.A.* 38°45N 109°25W **76 G9**
Archipel-de-Mingan △
  Canada 50°13N 63°10W **73 B7**
Archipiélago Los Roques △
  Venezuela 11°50N 66°44W **89 D6**
Arckaringa Cr. →
  Australia 28°10S 135°22E **63 D2**
Arco *U.S.A.* 43°38N 113°18W **76 E7**
Arcos de la Frontera
  Spain 36°45N 5°49W **21 D3**
Arcot *India* 12°53N 79°20E **45 H4**
Arctic Bay *Canada* 73°1N 85°7W **69 C14**
Arctic Mid-Ocean Ridge
  Arctic 87°0N 90°0E **4 A**
Arctic Ocean *Arctic* 78°0N 160°0W **4 B18**

Arctic Red River = Tsiigehtchic
  Canada 67°15N 134°0W **68 D5**
Arctowski *Antarctica* 62°30S 58°0W **5 C18**
Arda → *Bulgaria* 41°40N 26°30E **23 D12**
Ardabīl *Iran* 38°15N 48°18E **47 B6**
Ardabīl □ *Iran* 38°15N 48°20E **47 B6**
Ardakān = Sepīdān *Iran* 30°20N 52°5E **47 D7**
Ardakān *Iran* 32°19N 53°59E **47 C7**
Ardara *Ireland* 54°46N 8°25W **10 B3**
Ardee *Ireland* 53°52N 6°33W **10 C5**
Arden *Canada* 44°43N 76°56W **82 B8**
Arden *Calif., U.S.A.* 38°36N 121°33W **78 G5**
Arden *Nev., U.S.A.* 36°1N 115°14W **79 J11**
Ardenne *Belgium* 49°50N 5°5E **15 E5**
Ardennes = Ardenne
  Belgium 49°50N 5°5E **15 E5**
Arderin *Ireland* 53°2N 7°39W **10 C4**
Ardestān *Iran* 33°20N 52°25E **47 C7**
Ardfert *Ireland* 52°20N 9°47W **10 D2**
Ardglass *U.K.* 54°16N 5°36W **10 B6**
Ardivachar Pt. *U.K.* 57°23N 7°26W **11 D1**
Ardlethan *Australia* 34°22S 146°53E **63 E4**
Ardmore *Okla., U.S.A.* 34°10N 97°8W **84 D6**
Ardmore *Pa., U.S.A.* 40°2N 75°17W **83 F9**
Ardnamurchan, Pt. of
  U.K. 56°43N 6°14W **11 E2**
Ardnave Pt. *U.K.* 55°53N 6°20W **11 F2**
Ardrossan *Australia* 34°26S 137°53E **63 E2**
Ardrossan *U.K.* 55°39N 4°49W **11 F4**
Ards Pen. *U.K.* 54°33N 5°34W **10 B6**
Arecibo *Puerto Rico* 18°29N 66°43W **89 d**
Areia Branca *Brazil* 5°0S 37°0W **93 E11**
Arena, Pt. *U.S.A.* 38°57N 123°44W **78 G3**
Arenal *Honduras* 15°21N 86°50W **88 C2**
Arendal *Norway* 58°28N 8°46E **9 G13**
Arequipa *Peru* 16°20S 71°30W **92 G4**
Arévalo *Spain* 41°3N 4°43W **21 B3**
Arezzo *Italy* 43°25N 11°53E **22 C4**
Arga *Turkey* 38°21N 37°59E **46 B3**
Arganda del Rey *Spain* 40°19N 3°26W **21 B4**
Argarapa ☉ *Australia* 22°20S 134°58E **62 C1**
Argenta *Canada* 50°11N 116°56W **70 C5**
Argentan *France* 48°45N 0°1W **20 B3**
Argentário, Mte. *Italy* 42°24N 11°9E **22 C4**
Argentia *Canada* 47°18N 53°58W **73 C9**
Argentina ■ *S. Amer.* 35°0S 66°0W **96 D3**
Argentine Basin *Atl. Oc.* 45°0S 45°0W **96 F6**
Argentino, L. *Argentina* 50°10S 73°0W **96 G2**
Argeș → *Romania* 44°5N 26°38E **17 F14**
Arghandab → *Afghan.* 31°30N 64°15E **42 D1**
Argolikos Kolpos *Greece* 37°20N 22°52E **23 F10**
Argos *Greece* 37°40N 22°43E **23 F10**
Argostoli *Greece* 38°11N 20°29E **23 E9**
Arguello, Pt. *U.S.A.* 34°35N 120°39W **79 L6**
Argun → *Russia* 53°20N 121°28E **31 A13**
Argungu *Nigeria* 12°40N 4°31E **52 F6**
Argus Pk. *U.S.A.* 35°52N 117°26W **79 K9**
Argyle, L. *Australia* 16°20S 128°40E **60 C4**
Argyll & Bute □ *U.K.* 56°13N 5°28W **11 E3**
Århus = Aarhus *Denmark* 56°8N 10°11E **9 H14**
Ariadnoye *Russia* 45°8N 134°25E **28 B7**
Ariamsvlei *Namibia* 28°9S 19°51E **56 C2**
Ariana *Tunisia* 36°52N 10°12E **53 A8**
Arica *Chile* 18°32S 70°20W **92 G4**
Arica *Colombia* 2°0S 71°50W **92 D4**
Arid, C. *Australia* 34°1S 123°10E **61 F3**
Arida *Japan* 34°5N 135°8E **29 G7**
Aride *Seychelles* 4°13S 55°40E **55 b**
Ariège → *France* 43°30N 1°25E **20 E4**
Arima *Trin. & Tob.* 10°38N 61°17W **93 K15**
Arinos → *Brazil* 10°25S 58°20W **92 F7**
Ario de Rosales *Mexico* 19°12N 101°43W **86 D4**
Aripo, Mt. *Trin. & Tob.* 10°45N 61°15W **93 K15**
Aripuanã *Brazil* 9°25S 60°30W **92 E6**
Aripuanã → *Brazil* 5°7S 60°25W **92 E6**
Ariquemes *Brazil* 9°55S 63°6W **92 E6**
Arisaig *U.K.* 56°55N 5°51W **11 E3**
Aristazabal I. *Canada* 52°40N 129°10W **70 C3**
Ariyalur *India* 11°8N 79°8E **45 J4**
Arizaro, Salar de
  Argentina 24°40S 67°50W **94 A2**
Arizona *Argentina* 35°45S 65°25W **94 D2**
Arizona □ *U.S.A.* 34°0N 112°0W **77 J8**
Arizpe *Mexico* 30°20N 110°10W **86 A2**
'Arjah *Si. Arabia* 24°43N 44°17E **46 E5**
Arjeplog *Sweden* 66°3N 17°54E **8 C17**
Arjepluovve = Arjeplog
  Sweden 66°3N 17°54E **8 C17**
Arjona *Colombia* 10°14N 75°22W **92 A3**
Arjuna *Indonesia* 7°49S 112°34E **37 G15**
Arka *Russia* 60°15N 142°0E **27 C15**
Arkadelphia *U.S.A.* 34°7N 93°4W **84 D8**
Arkaig, L. *U.K.* 56°59N 5°10W **11 E3**
Arkalgud *India* 12°46N 76°3E **45 H3**
Arkalyk = Arqalyk
  Kazakhstan 50°13N 66°50E **26 D7**
Arkansas □ *U.S.A.* 35°0N 92°30W **84 D8**
Arkansas → *U.S.A.* 33°47N 91°4W **84 E9**
Arkansas City *U.S.A.* 37°4N 97°2W **80 G5**
Arkaroola *Australia* 30°20S 139°22E **63 E2**
Arkhangelsk *Russia* 64°38N 40°36E **18 B7**
Arki *India* 31°9N 76°58E **42 D7**
Arklow *Ireland* 52°48N 6°10W **10 D5**
Arkport *U.S.A.* 42°24N 77°42W **82 D7**
Arkticheskiy, Mys *Russia* 81°10N 95°0E **27 A10**
Arkville *U.S.A.* 42°9N 74°37W **83 D10**
Arlanzón → *Spain* 42°3N 4°17W **21 A3**
Arlbergpass *Austria* 47°9N 10°12E **16 E6**
Arlbergtunnel *Austria* 47°9N 10°12E **16 E6**
Arles *France* 43°41N 4°40E **20 E6**
Arlington *S. Africa* 28°1S 27°53E **57 D4**
Arlington *N.Y., U.S.A.* 41°42N 73°54W **83 E11**
Arlington *Oreg., U.S.A.* 45°43N 120°12W **76 D3**
Arlington *S. Dak., U.S.A.* 44°22N 97°8W **80 C5**
Arlington *Tex., U.S.A.* 32°44N 97°6W **84 E6**
Arlington *Vt., U.S.A.* 43°5N 73°9W **83 C11**
Arlington *Wash., U.S.A.* 48°12N 122°8W **78 B4**
Arlington Heights
  U.S.A. 42°5N 87°59W **80 D10**

Arlit *Niger* 19°0N 7°38E **52 E7**
Arlon *Belgium* 49°42N 5°49E **15 E5**
Arlparra *Australia* 22°11S 134°30E **62 C1**
Arltunga *Australia* 23°26S 134°41E **62 C1**
Armadale *Australia* 32°9S 116°0E **61 F2**
Armagh *U.K.* 54°21N 6°39W **10 B5**
Armagh □ *U.K.* 54°18N 6°37W **10 B5**
Armando Bermudez △
  Dom. Rep. 19°3N 71°0W **89 C5**
Armavir *Russia* 45°2N 41°7E **19 E7**
Armenia *Colombia* 4°35N 75°45W **92 C3**
Armenia ■ *Asia* 40°20N 45°0E **19 F7**
Armidale *Australia* 30°30S 151°40E **63 E5**
Armori *India* 20°28N 79°59E **44 D4**
Armour *U.S.A.* 43°19N 98°21W **80 D4**
Armstrong *B.C., Canada* 50°25N 119°10W **70 C5**
Armstrong *Ont., Canada* 50°18N 89°4W **72 B2**
Armur *India* 18°48N 78°16E **44 E4**
Arnarfjörður *Iceland* 65°48N 23°40W **8 D2**
Arnaud → *Canada* 59°59N 69°46W **69 F18**
Arnauti, C. *Cyprus* 35°6N 32°17E **46 C2**
Arnett *U.S.A.* 36°8N 99°46W **84 C5**
Arnhem *Neths.* 51°58N 5°55E **15 C5**
Arnhem, C. *Australia* 12°20S 137°30E **62 A2**
Arnhem B. *Australia* 12°20S 136°10E **62 A2**
Arnhem Land *Australia* 13°10S 134°30E **62 A1**
Arnhem Land ☉
  Australia 12°50S 134°50E **62 A1**
Arno → *Italy* 43°41N 10°17E **22 C4**
Arno Bay *Australia* 33°54S 136°34E **63 E2**
Arnold *U.K.* 53°1N 1°7W **12 D6**
Arnold *Calif., U.S.A.* 38°15N 120°21W **78 G6**
Arnold *Mo., U.S.A.* 38°26N 90°23W **80 F8**
Arnot *Canada* 55°56N 96°41W **71 B9**
Arnøya *Norway* 70°9N 20°40E **8 A19**
Arnprior *Canada* 45°26N 76°21E **83 A8**
Arnsberg *Germany* 51°24N 8°5E **16 C5**
Aroa, Pte. *Moorea* 17°28S 149°46W **59 d**
Aroab *Namibia* 26°41S 19°39E **56 C2**
Aron *India* 25°57N 77°56E **42 G6**
Aros → *Mexico* 29°9N 107°57W **86 B3**
Arqalyk *Kazakhstan* 50°13N 66°50E **26 D7**
Arrah = Ara *India* 25°35N 84°32E **43 G11**
Arrah *Ivory C.* 6°40N 3°58W **52 G5**
Arran *U.K.* 55°34N 5°12W **11 F3**
Arranmore *Ireland* 55°0N 8°30W **10 A3**
Arras *France* 50°17N 2°46E **20 A5**
Arrecife *Canary Is.* 28°57N 13°37W **52 C3**
Arrecifes *Argentina* 34°6S 60°9W **94 C3**
Arrée, Mts. d' *France* 48°26N 3°55W **20 B2**
Arriaga *Mexico* 16°14N 93°54W **87 D6**
Arrilalah *Australia* 23°43S 143°54E **62 C3**
Arrino *Australia* 29°30S 115°40E **61 E2**
Arrow, L. *Ireland* 54°3N 8°19W **10 B3**
Arrowtown *N.Z.* 44°57S 168°50E **59 F2**
Arroyo Grande *U.S.A.* 35°7N 120°35W **79 K6**
Ars *Iran* 37°9N 47°46E **46 B5**
Arsenault L. *Canada* 55°6N 108°32W **71 B7**
Arsenev *Russia* 44°10N 133°15E **28 B6**
Arsikere *India* 13°15N 76°15E **45 H3**
Arta *Greece* 39°8N 21°2E **23 E9**
Arteaga *Mexico* 18°28N 102°25W **86 D4**
Artem *Russia* 43°22N 132°13E **28 C6**
Artemovsk *Russia* 54°45N 93°35E **27 D10**
Artemovsk *Ukraine* 48°35N 38°0E **19 E6**
Artesia = Mosomane
  Botswana 24°2S 26°19E **56 B4**
Artesia *U.S.A.* 32°51N 104°24W **77 K11**
Arthur *Canada* 43°50N 80°32W **82 C4**
Arthur → *Australia* 41°2S 144°40E **63 G3**
Arthur Cr. → *Australia* 22°30S 136°25E **62 C2**
Arthur Pt. *Australia* 22°7S 150°3E **62 C5**
Arthur River *Australia* 33°20S 117°2E **61 F2**
Arthur's Pass *N.Z.* 42°54S 171°35E **59 E3**
Arthur's Pass △ *N.Z.* 42°53S 171°42E **59 E3**
Arthur's Town *Bahamas* 24°38N 75°42W **89 B4**
Artigas *Antarctica* 62°30S 58°0W **5 C18**
Artigas *Uruguay* 30°20S 56°30W **94 C4**
Artillery L. *Canada* 63°9N 107°52W **71 A7**
Artois *France* 50°20N 2°30E **20 A5**
Arts Bogd Uul *Mongolia* 44°40N 102°20E **32 B2**
Artsyz *Ukraine* 46°4N 29°26E **17 E15**
Artux *China* 39°40N 76°10E **32 B2**
Artvin *Turkey* 41°14N 41°44E **19 F7**
Aru, Kepulauan *Indonesia* 6°0S 134°30E **37 F8**
Aru Is. = Aru, Kepulauan
  Indonesia 6°0S 134°30E **37 F8**
Arua *Uganda* 3°1N 30°58E **54 D6**
Aruanã *Brazil* 14°54S 51°10W **93 F8**
Aruba ☑ *W. Indies* 12°30N 70°0W **89 D6**
Arué *Tahiti* 17°31S 149°30W **59 d**
Arun → *Nepal* 26°55N 87°10E **43 F12**
Arun → *U.K.* 50°49N 0°33W **13 G7**
Arunachal Pradesh □
  India 28°0N 95°0E **41 F19**
Aruppukkottai *India* 9°31N 78°8E **45 K4**
Arusha *Tanzania* 3°20S 36°40E **54 E7**
Aruvi → *Sri Lanka* 8°48N 79°53E **45 K4**
Aruwimi →
  Dem. Rep. of the Congo 1°13N 23°36E **54 D4**
Arvada *Colo., U.S.A.* 39°48N 105°5W **76 G11**
Arvada *Wyo., U.S.A.* 44°39N 106°8W **76 D10**
Arvayheer *Mongolia* 46°15N 102°48E **32 B5**
Arvi *India* 20°59N 78°16E **44 D4**
Arviat *Canada* 61°6N 93°59W **71 A10**
Arvidsjaur *Sweden* 65°35N 19°10E **8 D18**
Arvika *Sweden* 59°40N 12°36E **9 G15**
Arvin *U.S.A.* 35°12N 118°50W **79 K8**
Arwal *India* 25°15N 84°41E **43 G11**
Arxan *China* 47°11N 119°57E **31 B12**
Arys *Kazakhstan* 42°26N 68°48E **26 E7**
Arzamas *Russia* 55°27N 43°55E **18 C7**
Arzanah *U.A.E.* 24°47N 52°34E **47 E7**
Aş Şafā *Syria* 33°10N 37°0E **48 B6**
As Saffānīyah *Si. Arabia* 28°5N 48°50E **47 E6**
As Safirah *Syria* 36°5N 37°21E **46 B3**
Aş Şahm *Oman* 24°10N 56°53E **47 E8**

As Sājir *Si. Arabia* 25°11N 44°36E **46 E5**
As Salamīyah *Syria* 35°1N 37°2E **46 C3**
As Salmān *Iraq* 30°30N 44°32E **46 D5**
As Salṭ *Jordan* 32°2N 35°43E **48 C4**
As Sal'w'a *Qatar* 24°23N 50°50E **47 E6**
As Samāwah *Iraq* 31°15N 45°15E **46 D5**
As Sanamayn *Syria* 33°3N 36°10E **48 B5**
As Sukhnah *Syria* 34°52N 38°52E **46 C3**
As Sulaymānīyah *Iraq* 35°35N 45°29E **46 C5**
As Sulaymī *Si. Arabia* 26°17N 41°21E **46 E4**
As Sulayyil *Si. Arabia* 20°27N 45°34E **49 C4**
As Summān *Si. Arabia* 25°0N 47°0E **46 E5**
As Suwaydā' *Syria* 32°40N 36°30E **48 C5**
As Suwaydā' □ *Syria* 32°45N 36°45E **48 C5**
As Suwayq *Oman* 23°51N 57°26E **47 F8**
Aş Şuwayrah *Iraq* 32°55N 45°0E **46 C5**
Asab *Namibia* 25°30S 18°0E **56 C2**
Asad, Buḥayrat al *Syria* 36°0N 38°15E **46 C3**
Asahi *Japan* 35°43N 140°39E **29 E10**
Asahi-Gawa → *Japan* 34°36N 133°58E **29 G6**
Asahigawa = Asahikawa
  Japan 43°46N 142°22E **28 C11**
Asahikawa *Japan* 43°46N 142°22E **28 C11**
Asaluyeh *Iran* 27°29N 52°37E **47 E7**
Asamankese *Ghana* 5°50N 0°40W **52 G5**
Asan → *India* 26°37N 78°24E **43 F8**
Asansol *India* 23°40N 87°1E **43 H12**
Asau *Samoa* 13°27S 172°33W **59 b**
Asbesberge *S. Africa* 29°0S 23°0E **56 D3**
Asbestos *Canada* 45°47N 71°58W **73 C5**
Asbury Park *U.S.A.* 40°13N 74°1W **83 F10**
Ascensión *Mexico* 31°6N 107°59W **86 A3**
Ascensión, B. de la
  Mexico 19°40N 87°30W **87 D7**
Ascension I. *Atl. Oc.* 7°57S 14°23W **51 G2**
Aschaffenburg *Germany* 49°58N 9°6E **16 D5**
Aschersleben *Germany* 51°45N 11°29E **16 C6**
Áscoli Piceno *Italy* 42°51N 13°34E **22 C5**
Ascope *Peru* 7°46S 79°8W **92 E3**
Ascotán *Chile* 21°45S 68°17W **94 A2**
Aseb *Eritrea* 13°0N 42°40E **49 E3**
Asela *Ethiopia* 8°0N 39°0E **47 F2**
Asenovgrad *Bulgaria* 42°1N 24°51E **23 C11**
Aşgabat = Ashgabat
  Turkmenistan 37°58N 58°24E **47 B8**
Ash Fork *U.S.A.* 35°13N 112°29W **77 J7**
Ash Grove *U.S.A.* 37°19N 93°35W **80 G7**
Ash Shabakah *Iraq* 30°49N 43°39E **46 D4**
Ash Shamāl □ *Lebanon* 34°25N 36°0E **48 A5**
Ash Shāmīyah *Iraq* 31°55N 44°35E **46 D5**
Ash Shāriqah *U.A.E.* 25°23N 55°26E **47 E7**
Ash Sharmah *Si. Arabia* 28°1N 35°16E **46 D2**
Ash Sharqāt *Iraq* 35°27N 43°16E **46 C4**
Ash Shaṭrah *Iraq* 31°30N 46°10E **46 D5**
Ash Shawbak *Jordan* 30°32N 35°34E **46 D2**
Ash Shiḥr *Yemen* 14°45N 49°36E **49 E4**
Ash Shināfiyah *Iraq* 31°35N 44°39E **46 D5**
Ash Shu'bah *Si. Arabia* 28°54N 44°44E **46 D5**
Ash Shumlūl *Si. Arabia* 26°31N 47°20E **46 E5**
Ash Shūr'a *Iraq* 35°58N 43°13E **46 C4**
Ash Shurayf *Si. Arabia* 25°43N 39°14E **46 E3**
Ash Shuwayfāt *Lebanon* 33°45N 35°30E **48 B4**
Asha *Russia* 55°0N 57°16E **18 D10**
Ashbourne *U.S.A.* 53°2N 1°43W **12 D6**
Ashburn *U.S.A.* 31°43N 83°39W **85 F13**
Ashburton *N.Z.* 43°53S 171°48E **59 E3**
Ashburton → *Australia* 21°40S 114°56E **60 D1**
Ashcroft *Canada* 50°40N 121°20W **70 C4**
Ashdod *Israel* 31°49N 34°35E **48 D3**
Ashdown *U.S.A.* 33°40N 94°8W **84 E7**
Asheboro *U.S.A.* 35°43N 79°49W **85 D15**
Ashern *Canada* 51°11N 98°21W **71 C9**
Asherton *U.S.A.* 28°27N 99°46W **84 G5**
Asheville *U.S.A.* 35°36N 82°33W **85 D13**
Ashewat *Pakistan* 31°22N 68°32E **42 D3**
Asheweig → *Canada* 54°17N 87°12W **72 B2**
Ashford *Australia* 29°15S 151°3E **63 D5**
Ashford *U.K.* 51°8N 0°53E **13 F8**
Ashgabat *Turkmenistan* 37°58N 58°24E **47 B8**
Ashibetsu *Japan* 43°31N 142°11E **28 C11**
Ashikaga *Japan* 36°28N 139°29E **29 F9**
Ashington *U.K.* 55°11N 1°33W **12 B6**
Ashizuri-Uwakai △
  Japan 32°56N 132°32E **29 H6**
Ashizuri-Zaki *Japan* 32°44N 133°0E **29 H6**
Ashkarkot *Afghan.* 33°3N 67°58E **42 C2**
Ashkhabad = Ashgabat
  Turkmenistan 37°58N 58°24E **47 B8**
Äshkhāneh *Iran* 37°26N 56°55E **47 B8**
Ashland *Kans., U.S.A.* 37°11N 99°46W **80 G4**
Ashland *Ky., U.S.A.* 38°28N 82°38W **81 F12**
Ashland *Maine, U.S.A.* 46°38N 68°24W **81 B19**
Ashland *Mont., U.S.A.* 45°36N 106°16W **76 D10**
Ashland *Ohio, U.S.A.* 40°52N 82°19W **82 F2**
Ashland *Oreg., U.S.A.* 42°12N 122°43W **76 E2**
Ashland *Pa., U.S.A.* 40°45N 76°22W **83 F8**
Ashland *Va., U.S.A.* 37°46N 77°29W **81 G15**
Ashland *Wis., U.S.A.* 46°35N 90°53W **80 B8**
Ashley *N. Dak., U.S.A.* 46°2N 99°22W **80 B4**
Ashley *Pa., U.S.A.* 41°12N 75°55W **83 E9**
Ashmore Reef *Australia* 12°15S 123°0E **60 B3**
Ashmyany *Belarus* 54°26N 25°52E **17 A13**
Ashokan Res. *U.S.A.* 41°56N 74°13E **83 E10**
Ashoknagar *India* 24°34N 77°43E **44 D3**
Ashqelon *Israel* 31°42N 34°35E **48 D3**
Ashta *India* 23°1N 76°43E **42 H7**
Ashtabula *U.S.A.* 41°52N 80°47W **82 E4**
Ashti *Maharashtra, India* 21°21N 78°11E **44 D4**
Ashti *Maharashtra, India* 18°50N 75°15E **44 E2**
Ashton *S. Africa* 33°50S 20°5E **56 D3**
Ashton *U.S.A.* 44°4N 111°27W **76 D8**
Ashuanipi, L. *Canada* 52°45N 66°15W **73 B6**
Ashur = Assur *Iraq* 35°27N 43°15E **46 C4**
Ashville *U.S.A.* 40°34N 78°33W **82 F6**

Asia 45°0N 75°0E **24 E9**
Asia, Kepulauan *Indonesia* 1°0N 131°13E **37 D8**
Asifabad *India* 19°20N 79°24E **44 E4**
Asinara *Italy* 41°4N 8°16E **22 D3**
Asinara, G. dell' *Italy* 41°0N 8°30E **22 D3**
Asino *Russia* 57°0N 86°0E **26 D9**
Asipovichy *Belarus* 53°19N 28°33E **17 B15**
'Asīr *Si. Arabia* 18°40N 42°30E **49 D3**
Asir, Ras *Somalia* 11°55N 51°10E **49 E5**
Aska *India* 19°2N 84°42E **44 E7**
Askham *S. Africa* 26°59S 20°47E **56 C3**
Askim *Norway* 59°35N 11°10E **9 G14**
Askja *Iceland* 65°3N 16°48W **8 D5**
Askøyna *Norway* 60°29N 5°10E **8 F11**
Asmara = Asmera
  Eritrea 15°19N 38°55E **49 D2**
Asmera *Eritrea* 15°19N 38°55E **49 D2**
Åsnen *Sweden* 56°37N 14°45E **9 H16**
Aso Kujū △ *Japan* 32°53N 131°6E **29 H5**
Aspatria *U.K.* 54°47N 3°19W **12 C4**
Aspen *U.S.A.* 39°11N 106°49W **76 G10**
Aspermont *U.S.A.* 33°8N 100°14W **84 E4**
Aspiring, Mt. *N.Z.* 44°23S 168°46E **59 F2**
Aspur *India* 23°58N 74°7E **42 H6**
Asquith *Canada* 52°8N 107°13W **71 C7**
Assab = Aseb *Eritrea* 13°0N 42°40E **49 E3**
Assal, L. *Djibouti* 11°40N 42°26E **49 E3**
Assam □ *India* 26°0N 93°0E **41 G18**
Assateague Island △
  U.S.A. 38°15N 75°10W **81 F16**
Assaye *India* 20°15N 75°53E **44 D2**
Asse *Belgium* 50°24N 4°10E **15 D4**
Assen *Neths.* 53°0N 6°35E **15 A6**
Assiniboia *Canada* 49°40N 105°59W **71 D7**
Assiniboine → *Canada* 49°53N 97°8W **71 D9**
Assiniboine, Mt. *Canada* 50°52N 115°39W **70 C5**
Assis *Brazil* 22°40S 50°20W **95 A5**
Assisi *Italy* 43°4N 12°37E **22 C5**
Assur *Iraq* 35°27N 43°15E **46 C4**
Assynt, L. *U.K.* 58°10N 5°3W **11 C3**
Astana *Kazakhstan* 51°10N 71°30E **30 A3**
Åstäneh *Iran* 37°17N 49°59E **47 B6**
Astara *Azerbaijan* 38°30N 48°50E **47 B6**
Astaraboad = Gorgān *Iran* 36°55N 54°30E **47 B7**
Asti *Italy* 44°54N 8°12E **20 D8**
Astipalea *Greece* 36°32N 26°22E **23 F12**
Astorga *Spain* 42°29N 6°8W **21 A2**
Astoria *U.S.A.* 46°11N 123°50W **78 D3**
Astrakhan *Russia* 46°25N 48°5E **19 E8**
Astrebla Downs
  Australia 24°12S 140°34E **62 C3**
Asturias □ *Spain* 43°15N 6°0W **21 A3**
Asunción *Paraguay* 25°10S 57°30W **94 B4**
Asunción Nochixtlán
  Mexico 17°28N 97°14W **87 D5**
Aswân *Egypt* 24°4N 32°57E **53 D12**
Aswan High Dam = Sadd el Aali
  Egypt 23°54N 32°54E **53 D12**
Asyût *Egypt* 27°11N 31°4E **53 C12**
At Ṭafilah *Jordan* 30°45N 35°30E **48 E4**
At Ṭafilah □ *Jordan* 30°45N 35°30E **48 E4**
Aṭ Ṭā'if *Si. Arabia* 21°5N 40°27E **49 C3**
At Ta'mīm □ *Iraq* 35°30N 44°20E **46 C5**
Aṭ Ṭiraq *Si. Arabia* 27°19N 44°33E **46 E5**
Aṭ Ṭubayq *Si. Arabia* 29°30N 37°0E **46 D3**
Aṭ Ṭunayb *Jordan* 31°48N 35°57E **48 D4**
Atacama □ *Chile* 27°30S 70°0W **94 B2**
Atacama, Desierto de
  Chile 24°0S 69°20W **94 A2**
Atacama, Salar de *Chile* 23°30S 68°20W **94 A2**
Atakeye ☉ *Australia* 22°30S 133°45E **60 D5**
Atakpamé *Togo* 7°31N 1°13E **52 G6**
Atalaya *Peru* 10°45S 73°50W **92 F4**
Atami *Japan* 35°5N 139°4E **29 G9**
Atamyrat *Turkmenistan* 37°50N 65°12E **28 F7**
Atapupu *Indonesia* 9°0S 124°51E **37 F6**
Atâr *Mauritania* 20°30N 13°5W **52 D3**
Atari *Pakistan* 30°56N 74°2E **42 D6**
Atascadero *U.S.A.* 35°29N 120°40W **78 K6**
Atasū *Kazakhstan* 48°30N 71°0E **26 E8**
Atatürk Baraji *Turkey* 37°28N 38°30E **19 G6**
Atauro *E. Timor* 8°10S 125°30E **37 F7**
Atbara *Sudan* 17°42N 33°59E **53 E12**
'Atbara, Nahr → *Sudan* 17°40N 33°56E **53 E12**
Atbasar *Kazakhstan* 51°48N 68°20E **26 D7**
Atchafalaya B. *U.S.A.* 29°25N 91°25W **84 G9**
Atchison *U.S.A.* 39°34N 95°7W **80 F6**
Äteshän *Iran* 35°35N 52°37E **47 C7**
Ath *Belgium* 50°38N 3°47E **15 D3**
Athabasca *Canada* 54°45N 113°20W **70 C6**
Athabasca → *Canada* 58°40N 110°50W **71 B6**
Athabasca, L. *Canada* 59°15N 109°15W **71 B7**
Athabasca Sand Dunes △
  Canada 59°4N 108°43W **71 B7**
Athagarh *India* 20°30N 85°33E **44 D7**
Athboy *Ireland* 53°36N 6°56W **10 C5**
Athenry *Ireland* 53°18N 8°44W **10 C3**
Athens *Ala., U.S.A.* 34°48N 86°58W **85 D11**
Athens *Ga., U.S.A.* 33°57N 83°23W **85 E13**
Athens *N.Y., U.S.A.* 42°16N 73°49W **83 D11**
Athens *Ohio, U.S.A.* 39°20N 82°6W **81 F12**
Athens *Pa., U.S.A.* 41°57N 76°31W **83 E8**
Athens *Tenn., U.S.A.* 35°27N 84°36W **85 D12**
Athens *Tex., U.S.A.* 32°12N 95°51W **84 E7**
Atherley *Canada* 44°37N 79°20E **82 B5**
Atherton *Australia* 17°17S 145°30E **62 B4**
Athlone *Ireland* 53°25N 7°56W **10 C4**
Athmalik *India* 20°43N 84°32E **44 D7**
Athni *India* 16°44N 75°6E **44 F2**
Athol *U.S.A.* 42°36N 72°14W **83 D12**
Atholl, Forest of *U.K.* 56°51N 3°50W **11 E5**
Atholville *Canada* 47°59N 66°43W **73 C6**
Athos *Greece* 40°9N 24°22E **23 D11**
Athy *Ireland* 53°0N 7°0W **10 C5**
Ati *Chad* 13°13N 18°20E **53 F9**
Atik L. *Canada* 52°40N 64°32W **72 B4**
Atikaki ☉ *Canada* 51°30N 95°31W **71 C9**
Atikameg → *Canada* 52°30N 82°46W **72 B3**
Atikokan *Canada* 48°45N 91°37W **72 C1**

Atikonak L. *Canada*   52°40N 64°32W **73** B7
Atimaono *Tahiti*   17°46S 149°28W **59** d
Atirampattinam *India*   10°28N 79°20E **45** J4
Atiu *Cook Is.*   20°0S 158°10W **65** J12
Atka *Russia*   60°50N 151°48E **27** C16
Atka I. *U.S.A.*   52°7N 174°30W **74** E5
Atkinson *U.S.A.*   42°32N 98°59W **80** D4
Atlanta *U.S.A.*   33°7N 94°10W **84** E7
Atlantic *U.S.A.*   41°24N 95°1W **80** E6
Atlantic City *U.S.A.*   39°21N 74°27W **81** F16
Atlantic-Indian Basin
  Antarctica   60°0S 30°0E **5** B4
Atlantic Ocean   0°0 20°0W **2** D8
Atlantis *S. Africa*   33°34S 18°29E **56** D2
Atlas Mts. = Haut Atlas
  Morocco   32°30N 5°0W **52** B4
Atlin *Canada*   59°31N 133°41W **70** B2
Atlin, L. *Canada*   59°26N 133°45W **70** B2
Atlin △ *Canada*   59°10N 134°30W **70** B2
Atmakur *Andhra Pradesh,*
  India   18°45N 78°39E **44** E4
Atmakur *Andhra Pradesh,*
  India   14°37N 79°40E **45** G4
Atmakur *Andhra Pradesh,*
  India   15°53N 78°35E **45** G4
Atmore *U.S.A.*   31°2N 87°29W **85** F11
Atoka *U.S.A.*   34°23N 96°8W **84** D6
Atolia *U.S.A.*   35°19N 117°37W **79** K9
Atqasuk *U.S.A.*   70°28N 157°24W **74** A8
Atrai → *Bangla.*   24°7N 89°22E **43** G13
Atrak = Atrek →
  Turkmenistan   37°35N 53°58E **47** B8
Atrauli *India*   28°2N 78°20E **42** E8
Atrek → *Turkmenistan*   37°35N 53°58E **47** B8
Atsuta *Japan*   43°24N 141°26E **28** C10
Attalla *U.S.A.*   34°1N 86°6W **85** D11
Attapeu *Laos*   14°48N 106°50E **38** E6
Attawapiskat *Canada*   52°56N 82°24W **72** B3
Attawapiskat → *Canada*   52°57N 82°18W **72** B3
Attawapiskat L. *Canada*   52°18N 87°54W **72** B2
Attica *Ind., U.S.A.*   40°18N 87°15W **80** E10
Attica *Ohio, U.S.A.*   41°4N 82°53W **82** E2
Attikamagen L. *Canada*   55°0N 66°30W **73** B6
Attleboro *U.S.A.*   41°57N 71°17W **83** E13
Attock *Pakistan*   33°52N 72°20E **42** C5
Attopu = Attapeu *Laos*   14°48N 106°50E **38** E6
Attu I. *U.S.A.*   52°55N 172°55E **74** E2
Attur *India*   11°35N 78°30E **45** J4
Atuel → *Argentina*   36°17S 66°50W **94** D2
Åtvidaberg *Sweden*   58°12N 16°0E **9** G17
Atwater *U.S.A.*   37°21N 120°37W **78** H6
Atwood *Canada*   43°40N 81°1W **82** C3
Atwood *U.S.A.*   39°48N 101°3W **80** F3
Atyraū *Kazakhstan*   47°5N 52°0E **19** E9
Au Sable *U.S.A.*   44°25N 83°20W **82** B1
Au Sable → *U.S.A.*   44°25N 83°20W **82** B1
Au Sable Forks *U.S.A.*   44°27N 73°41W **83** B11
Au Sable Pt. *U.S.A.*   44°20N 83°20W **82** B1
Auas *Honduras*   15°29N 84°20W **88** C3
Auasberg *Namibia*   22°37S 17°13E **56** B2
Aubagne *France*   43°17N 5°37E **20** E6
Aube → *France*   48°34N 3°43E **20** B5
Auberry *U.S.A.*   37°7N 119°29W **78** H7
Auburn *Ala., U.S.A.*   32°36N 85°29W **85** E12
Auburn *Calif., U.S.A.*   38°54N 121°4W **78** G5
Auburn *Ind., U.S.A.*   41°22N 85°4W **81** E11
Auburn *Maine, U.S.A.*   44°6N 70°14W **81** C18
Auburn *N.Y., U.S.A.*   42°56N 76°34W **83** D8
Auburn *Nebr., U.S.A.*   40°23N 95°51W **80** E7
Auburn *Pa., U.S.A.*   40°36N 76°6W **83** F8
Auburn *Wash., U.S.A.*   47°18N 122°14W **78** C4
Auburn Ra. *Australia*   25°15S 150°30E **63** D5
Auburndale *U.S.A.*   28°4N 81°48W **85** G14
Aubusson *France*   45°57N 2°11E **20** D5
Auch *France*   43°39N 0°36E **20** E4
Auchterarder *U.K.*   56°18N 3°41W **11** E5
Auchtermuchty *U.K.*   56°18N 3°13W **11** E5
Auckland *N.Z.*   36°52S 174°46E **59** B5
Auckland Is. *Pac. Oc.*   50°40S 166°5E **64** N8
Aude → *France*   43°13N 3°14E **20** E5
Auden *Canada*   50°14N 87°53W **72** B2
Audubon *U.S.A.*   41°43N 94°56W **80** E6
Augathella *Australia*   25°48S 146°35E **63** D4
Aughnacloy *U.K.*   54°25N 6°59W **10** B5
Aughrim *Ireland*   53°18N 8°19W **10** C3
Augrabies Falls *S. Africa*   28°35S 20°20E **56** D3
Augrabies Falls △
  S. Africa   28°40S 20°22E **56** C3
Augsburg *Germany*   48°25N 10°52E **16** D6
Augusta *Australia*   34°19S 115°9E **61** F2
Augusta *Italy*   37°13N 15°13E **22** F6
Augusta *Ark., U.S.A.*   35°17N 91°22W **84** D9
Augusta *Ga., U.S.A.*   33°28N 81°58W **85** E14
Augusta *Kans., U.S.A.*   37°41N 96°59W **80** G5
Augusta *Maine, U.S.A.*   44°19N 69°47W **81** C19
Augusta *Mont., U.S.A.*   47°30N 112°24W **76** C7
Augustów *Poland*   53°51N 23°0E **17** B12
Augustus, Mt. *Australia*   24°20S 116°50E **61** D2
Augustus I. *Australia*   15°20S 124°30E **60** C3
Aujuittuq = Grise Fiord
  Canada   76°25N 82°57W **69** B15
Aukštaitija △ *Lithuania*   55°15N 26°0E **9** J22
Aukum *U.S.A.*   38°34N 120°43W **78** G6
Aul *India*   20°41N 86°39E **44** D8
Aulavik △ *Canada*   73°42N 119°55W **68** C8
Auld, L. *Australia*   22°25S 123°50E **60** D3
Ault *U.S.A.*   40°35N 104°44W **76** F11
Aundah *India*   19°32N 77°3E **44** E3
Aundh *India*   17°33N 74°23E **44** F2
Aunis *France*   46°5N 0°50W **20** C3
Aunu'u *Amer. Samoa*   14°20S 170°31W **59** b
Auponhia *Indonesia*   1°58S 125°27E **37** E7
Aur, Pulau *Malaysia*   2°35N 104°10E **39** L5
Auraiya *India*   26°28N 79°33E **43** F8
Aurangabad *Bihar, India*   24°45N 84°18E **43** G11
Aurangabad *Maharashtra,*
  India   19°50N 75°23E **44** E2
Aurich *Germany*   53°28N 7°28E **16** B4
Aurillac *France*   44°55N 2°26E **20** D5

Aurora *Canada*   44°0N 79°28W **82** C5
Aurora *S. Africa*   32°40S 18°29E **56** D2
Aurora *Colo., U.S.A.*   39°43N 104°49W **76** G11
Aurora *Ill., U.S.A.*   41°45N 88°19W **80** E9
Aurora *Mo., U.S.A.*   36°58N 93°43W **80** G7
Aurora *N.Y., U.S.A.*   42°45N 76°42W **83** D8
Aurora *Nebr., U.S.A.*   40°52N 98°0W **80** E5
Aurora *Ohio, U.S.A.*   41°21N 81°20W **82** E3
Aurukun *Australia*   13°20S 141°45E **62** A3
Aurukun ♦ *Australia*   13°36S 141°48E **62** A3
Aus *Namibia*   26°35S 16°12E **56** C2
Ausa *India*   18°15N 76°30E **44** E3
Ausable → *Canada*   43°19N 81°46W **82** C3
Auschwitz = Oświęcim
  Poland   50°2N 19°11E **17** C10
Auski Roadhouse
  Australia   22°22S 118°41E **60** D2
Austen Harbour *India*   12°55N 92°45E **45** H11
Austin *Minn., U.S.A.*   43°40N 92°58W **80** D7
Austin *Nev., U.S.A.*   39°30N 117°4W **76** G5
Austin *Pa., U.S.A.*   41°38N 78°6W **82** E6
Austin *Tex., U.S.A.*   30°17N 97°45W **84** F6
Austin, L. *Australia*   27°40S 118°0E **61** E2
Austin I. *Canada*   61°10N 94°0W **71** A10
Austra *Norway*   65°8N 11°55E **8** D14
Austral Is. = Tubuaï, Îs.
  French Polynesia   25°0S 150°0W **65** K13
Austral Seamount Chain
  Pac. Oc.   24°0S 150°0W **65** K13
Australia ■ *Oceania*   23°0S 135°0E **58** D6
Australian-Antarctic Basin
  S. Ocean   60°0S 120°0E **5** C9
Australian Capital Territory □
  Australia   35°30S 149°0E **63** F4
Australind *Australia*   33°17S 115°42E **61** F2
Austria ■ *Europe*   47°0N 14°0E **16** E8
Austvågøya *Norway*   68°20N 14°40E **8** B16
Autlán de Navarro
  Mexico   19°46N 104°22W **86** D4
Autun *France*   46°58N 4°17E **20** C6
Auvergne □ *France*   45°20N 3°15E **20** D5
Auvergne, Mts. d' *France*   45°20N 2°55E **20** D5
Auxerre *France*   47°48N 3°32E **20** C5
Auyuittuq △ *Canada*   67°30N 66°0W **69** D18
Av-Dovurak *Russia*   51°17N 91°35E **27** D10
Ava *U.S.A.*   36°57N 92°40W **80** G7
Avallon *France*   47°30N 3°53E **20** C5
Avalon *U.S.A.*   33°21N 118°20W **79** M8
Avalon Pen. *Canada*   47°30N 53°20W **73** C9
Avanigadda *India*   16°0N 80°56E **45** G5
Avanos *Turkey*   38°43N 34°51E **46** B2
Avaré *Brazil*   23°4S 48°58W **95** A6
Avawatz Mts. *U.S.A.*   35°40N 116°30W **79** K10
Aveiro *Brazil*   3°10S 55°5W **93** D7
Aveiro *Portugal*   40°37N 8°38W **21** B1
Åvej *Iran*   35°40N 49°15E **47** C6
Avellino *Italy*   40°54N 14°47E **22** D6
Avenal *U.S.A.*   36°0N 120°8W **78** K6
Aversa *Italy*   40°58N 14°12E **22** D6
Avery *U.S.A.*   47°15N 115°49W **76** C6
Aves, I. de *W. Indies*   15°45N 63°55W **89** C7
Aves, Is. las *Venezuela*   12°0N 67°30W **89** D6
Avesta *Sweden*   60°9N 16°10E **9** F17
Aveyron → *France*   44°5N 1°16E **20** D4
Avezzano *Italy*   42°2N 13°25E **22** C5
Aviá Terai *Argentina*   26°45S 60°50W **94** B3
Aviemore *U.K.*   57°12N 3°50W **11** D5
Avignon *France*   43°57N 4°50E **20** E6
Ávila *Spain*   40°39N 4°43W **21** B3
Avila Beach *U.S.A.*   35°11N 120°44W **79** K6
Avilés *Spain*   43°35N 5°57W **21** A3
Avis *U.S.A.*   41°11N 77°19W **82** E7
Avissawella *Sri Lanka*   6°56N 80°11E **45** L5
Avoca *U.S.A.*   42°25N 77°25W **82** D7
Avoca → *Australia*   35°40S 143°43E **63** F3
Avoca → *Ireland*   52°48N 6°10W **10** D5
Avola *Canada*   51°45N 119°19W **70** C5
Avola *Italy*   36°56N 15°7E **22** F6
Avon *U.S.A.*   42°55N 77°45W **82** D7
Avon → *Australia*   31°40S 116°7E **61** F2
Avon → *Bristol, U.K.*   51°29N 2°41W **13** F5
Avon → *Dorset, U.K.*   50°44N 1°46W **13** G6
Avon → *Warks., U.K.*   52°0N 2°8W **13** E5
Avon Park *U.S.A.*   27°36N 81°31W **85** H14
Avonlea *Canada*   50°0N 105°0W **71** D8
Avonmore *Canada*   45°10N 74°58W **83** A10
Avonmouth *U.K.*   51°30N 2°42W **13** F5
Avranches *France*   48°40N 1°20W **20** B3
Awa-Shima *Japan*   38°27N 139°14E **28** E9
A'waj → *Syria*   33°23N 36°20E **48** B5
Awaji-Shima *Japan*   34°30N 134°50E **29** G7
'Awālī *Bahrain*   26°0N 50°30E **47** E6
Awantipur *India*   33°55N 75°3E **43** C6
Awarja → *India*   17°5N 76°15E **44** F3
Awasa *Ethiopia*   7°2N 38°28E **49** F2
Awash *Ethiopia*   9°1N 40°10E **49** F3
Awatere → *N.Z.*   41°37S 174°10E **59** D5
Awbārī *Libya*   26°46N 12°57E **53** C8
Awbārī, Idehan *Libya*   27°10N 11°30E **53** C8
Awe, L. *U.K.*   56°17N 5°16E **11** E3
Awjilah *Libya*   29°8N 21°7E **53** C10
Axe → *U.K.*   50°42N 3°4W **13** G5
Axel Heiberg I. *Canada*   80°0N 90°0W **69** B14
Axim *Ghana*   4°51N 2°15W **52** H5
Axios → *Greece*   40°57N 22°35E **23** D10
Axminster *U.K.*   50°46N 3°0W **13** G4
Ayabaca *Peru*   4°40S 79°53W **92** D3
Ayabe *Japan*   35°20N 135°20E **29** G7
Ayacucho *Argentina*   37°5S 58°20W **94** D4
Ayacucho *Peru*   13°0S 74°0W **92** F4
Ayaguz = Ayaköz
  Kazakhstan   48°10N 80°10E **30** B5
Ayakkum Hu *China*   37°30N 89°20E **30** D6
Ayakudi *India*   10°28N 77°56E **45** J3
Ayamonte *Spain*   37°12N 7°24W **21** D2
Ayan *Russia*   56°30N 138°16E **27** D14
Ayaviri *Peru*   14°50S 70°35W **92** F4
Aydın *Turkey*   37°51N 27°51E **23** F12

Aydingkol Hu *China*   42°40N 89°15E **30** C6
Ayer *U.S.A.*   42°34N 71°35W **83** D13
Ayer Hitam *Malaysia*   5°24N 100°16E **39** c
Ayer's Cliff *Canada*   45°10N 72°3W **83** A12
Ayers Rock = Uluru
  Australia   25°23S 131°5E **61** E5
Ayeyarwady = Irrawaddy →
  Burma   15°50N 95°6E **41** M19
Aykhal *Russia*   66°0N 111°30E **27** C12
Aykino *Russia*   62°15N 49°56E **18** B8
Aylesbury *U.K.*   51°49N 0°49W **13** F7
Aylmer *Canada*   42°46N 80°59W **82** D4
Aylmer, L. *Canada*   64°5N 108°30W **68** E10
'Ayn, Wādī al *Oman*   22°15N 55°28E **47** F7
Ayn Dār *Si. Arabia*   25°55N 49°10E **47** E7
Ayn Zālah *Iraq*   36°45N 42°35E **46** B4
Ayolas *Paraguay*   27°10S 56°59W **94** B4
Ayon, Ostrov *Russia*   69°50N 169°0E **27** C17
Ayr *Australia*   19°35S 147°25E **62** B4
Ayr *Canada*   43°17N 80°27W **82** C4
Ayr *U.K.*   55°28N 4°38W **11** F4
Ayr → *U.K.*   55°28N 4°38W **11** F4
Ayre, Pt. of *I. of Man*   54°25N 4°21W **12** C3
Ayton *Australia*   15°56S 145°22E **62** B4
Aytos *Bulgaria*   42°42N 27°16E **23** C12
Ayu, Kepulauan *Indonesia*   0°35N 131°5E **37** D8
Ayutla *Guatemala*   14°40N 92°10W **88** D1
Ayutla de los Libres
  Mexico   16°54N 99°13W **87** D5
Ayutthaya = Phra Nakhon Si
  Ayutthaya *Thailand*   14°25N 100°30E **38** E3
Ayvacık *Turkey*   39°36N 26°24E **23** E12
Ayvalık *Turkey*   39°20N 26°46E **23** E12
Az Zabadānī *Syria*   33°43N 36°5E **48** B5
Aẕ Ẕāhirīyah *West Bank*   31°25N 34°58E **48** D3
Aẕ Ẕahrān *Si. Arabia*   26°10N 50°7E **47** E6
Az Zarqā *Jordan*   32°5N 36°4E **48** C5
Az Zarqā *U.A.E.*   24°53N 53°4E **47** E7
Az Zarqā □ *Jordan*   32°5N 36°4E **48** C5
Az Zāwiyah *Libya*   32°52N 12°56E **53** B8
Az Zibār *Iraq*   36°52N 44°4E **46** B5
Az Zilfī *Si. Arabia*   26°12N 44°52E **46** E5
Az Zubayr *Iraq*   30°26N 47°40E **46** D5
Azad Kashmir □ *Pakistan*   33°50N 73°50E **43** C5
Azamgarh *India*   26°5N 83°13E **43** F10
Azangaro *Peru*   14°55S 70°13W **92** F4
Āzār Shahr *Iran*   37°45N 45°59E **46** B5
Azarān *Iran*   37°25N 47°16E **46** B5
Azärbayjan = Azerbaijan ■
  Asia   40°20N 48°0E **19** F8
Āzarbāyjān-e Gharbī □
  Iran   37°0N 44°30E **46** B5
Āzarbāyjān-e Sharqī □
  Iran   37°20N 47°0E **46** B5
Azare *Nigeria*   11°55N 10°10E **52** F8
A'zāz *Syria*   36°36N 37°4E **46** B3
Azbine = Aïr *Niger*   18°30N 8°0E **52** E7
Azerbaijan ■ *Asia*   40°20N 48°0E **19** F8
Azogues *Ecuador*   2°35S 78°0W **92** D3
Azores = Açores, Is. dos
  Atl. Oc.   38°0N 27°0W **52** a
Azov *Russia*   47°3N 39°25E **19** E6
Azov, Sea of *Europe*   46°0N 36°30E **19** E6
Azovskoye More = Azov, Sea of
  Europe   46°0N 36°30E **19** E6
Azraq ash Shīshān *Jordan*   31°50N 36°49E **48** D5
Aztec *U.S.A.*   36°49N 107°59W **77** H10
Azua de Compostela
  Dom. Rep.   18°25N 70°44W **89** C5
Azuaga *Spain*   38°16N 5°39W **21** C3
Azuero, Pen. de *Panama*   7°30N 80°30W **88** E3
Azul *Argentina*   36°42S 59°43W **94** D4
Azumino *Japan*   36°20N 137°50E **29** F8
Azusa *U.S.A.*   34°8N 117°52W **79** L9
Azzel Matti, Sebkra
  Algeria   26°10N 0°43E **52** C6

B

Ba Be △ *Vietnam*   22°25N 105°37E **38** A5
Ba Don *Vietnam*   17°45N 106°26E **38** D6
Ba Dong *Vietnam*   9°40N 106°33E **39** H6
Ba Ngoi *Vietnam*   11°54N 109°10E **39** G7
Ba Ria *Vietnam*   10°30N 107°10E **39** G6
Ba Tri *Vietnam*   10°2N 106°36E **39** G6
Ba Vì △ *Vietnam*   21°1N 105°22E **38** B5
Ba Xian = Bazhou *China*   39°8N 116°22E **32** E9
Baa *Indonesia*   10°50S 123°0E **60** B3
Baalbek = Ba'labakk
  Lebanon   34°0N 36°10E **48** B5
Baardheere *Somalia*   2°20N 42°27E **49** G3
Baarle-Nassau *Belgium*   51°27N 4°56E **15** C4
Bab el Mandeb *Red Sea*   12°35N 43°25E **49** E3
Bābā, Koh-i- *Afghan.*   34°30N 67°0E **40** B5
Baba Budan Hills *India*   13°30N 75°44E **45** H2
Baba Burnu *Turkey*   39°29N 26°2E **23** E12
Bābā Kalū *Iran*   30°7N 51°0E **47** D6
Babadag *Romania*   44°53N 28°44E **17** F15
Babaeski *Turkey*   41°26N 27°6E **23** D12
Babahoyo *Ecuador*   1°40S 79°30W **92** D3
Babai = Sarju → *India*   27°21N 81°23E **43** F9
Babai → *Nepal*   28°10N 82°21E **43** E10
Babar *Indonesia*   8°0S 129°30E **37** F7
Babar *Pakistan*   31°7N 69°32E **42** D3
Babarkach *Pakistan*   29°45N 68°0E **42** E3
Babb *U.S.A.*   48°51N 113°27W **76** B7
Baberu *India*   25°33N 80°43E **43** G9
Babi Besar, Pulau
  Malaysia   2°25N 103°59E **39** L4
Babian Jiang → *China*   22°55N 101°47E **34** F3
Bābil □ *Iraq*   32°30N 44°30E **46** C5
Babinda *Australia*   17°20S 145°56E **62** B4
Babine *Canada*   55°22N 126°37W **70** B3
Babine → *Canada*   55°45N 127°44W **70** B3
Babine L. *Canada*   54°48N 126°0W **70** C3
Babo *Indonesia*   2°30S 133°30E **37** E8
Babol *Iran*   36°40N 52°50E **47** B7
Bābol Sar *Iran*   36°45N 52°45E **47** B7
Baboua *C.A.R.*   5°49N 14°58E **54** C2
Babruysk *Belarus*   53°10N 29°15E **17** B15
Babuhri *India*   26°49N 69°43E **42** F3
Babusar Pass *Pakistan*   35°12N 73°59E **43** B5
Babuyan Chan. *Phil.*   18°40N 121°30E **37** A6
Babylon *Iraq*   32°34N 44°22E **46** C5
Bac Can *Vietnam*   22°8N 105°49E **34** F5
Bac Giang *Vietnam*   21°16N 106°11E **34** G6
Bac Lieu *Vietnam*   9°17N 105°43E **39** H5
Bac Ninh *Vietnam*   21°13N 106°4E **34** G6
Bac Phan *Vietnam*   22°0N 105°0E **34** G5
Bacabal *Brazil*   4°15S 44°45W **93** D10
Bacalar *Mexico*   18°43N 88°27W **87** D7
Bacan, Kepulauan
  Indonesia   0°35S 127°30E **37** E7
Bacarra *Phil.*   18°15N 120°37E **37** A6
Bacău *Romania*   46°35N 26°55E **17** E14
Bacerac *Mexico*   30°18N 108°50W **86** A3
Bach Long Vi, Dao
  Vietnam   20°10N 107°40E **38** B6
Bach Ma △ *Vietnam*   16°11N 107°49E **38** D6
Bachhwara *India*   25°35N 85°54E **43** G11
Back → *Canada*   65°10N 104°0W **68** D11
Bacolod *Phil.*   10°40N 122°57E **37** B6
Bacuk *Malaysia*   6°4N 102°25E **39** J4
Bácum *Mexico*   27°33N 110°5W **86** B2
Bād *Iran*   33°41N 52°1E **47** C7
Bad → *U.S.A.*   44°21N 100°22W **80** C3
Bad Axe *U.S.A.*   43°48N 83°0W **82** C2
Bad Ischl *Austria*   47°44N 13°38E **16** E7
Bad Kissingen *Germany*   50°11N 10°4E **16** C6
Bada Barabil *India*   22°7N 85°24E **43** H11
Badagara = Vadakara
  India   11°35N 75°40E **45** J2
Badain Jaran Shamo
  China   40°23N 102°0E **30** C9
Badajós, L. *Brazil*   3°15S 62°50W **92** D6
Badajoz *Spain*   38°50N 6°59W **21** C2
Badakhshān □ *Afghan.*   36°30N 71°0E **40** A7
Badaling *China*   40°20N 116°0E **32** D9
Badalzai *Afghan.*   29°50N 65°35E **42** E1
Badami *India*   15°55N 75°41E **45** G2
Badampahar *India*   22°10N 86°10E **44** D8
Badanah *Si. Arabia*   30°58N 41°30E **46** D4
Badarinath *India*   30°45N 79°30E **43** D8
Badas, Kepulauan
  Indonesia   0°45N 107°5E **36** D3
Baddo → *Pakistan*   28°0N 64°20E **40** F4
Bade *Indonesia*   7°10S 139°35E **37** F9
Baden *Austria*   48°1N 16°13E **16** D9
Baden *U.S.A.*   40°38N 80°14W **82** F4
Baden-Baden *Germany*   48°44N 8°13E **16** D5
Baden-Württemberg □
  Germany   48°20N 8°40E **16** D5
Badgam *India*   34°1N 74°45E **43** B6
Badgastein *Austria*   47°7N 13°9E **16** E7
Badger *Canada*   49°0N 56°4W **73** C8
Badger *U.S.A.*   36°38N 119°1W **78** J7
Bādghīs □ *Afghan.*   35°0N 63°0E **40** B3
Badgingarra △ *Australia*   30°23S 115°22E **61** F2
Badin *Pakistan*   24°38N 68°54E **42** G3
Badlands *U.S.A.*   43°55N 102°30W **80** D2
Badlands △ *U.S.A.*   43°38N 102°56W **80** D2
Badnera *India*   20°48N 77°44E **44** D3
Badrah *Iraq*   33°6N 45°58E **46** C5
Badrain Jaran Shamo
  China   40°40N 103°20E **32** D2
Badrinath *India*   30°44N 79°29E **43** D8
Badu *Australia*   10°7S 142°11E **62** a
Badulla *Sri Lanka*   7°1N 81°7E **45** L5
Badung, Bukit *Indonesia*   8°49S 115°10E **37** K18
Badung, Selat *Indonesia*   8°40S 115°22E **37** K18
Badvel *India*   14°45N 79°3E **45** G4
Baena *Spain*   37°37N 4°20W **21** D3
Baengnyeongdo
  S. Korea   37°57N 124°40E **33** F13
Baeza *Spain*   37°57N 3°25W **21** D4
Bafatá *Guinea-Biss.*   12°8N 14°40W **52** F3
Baffin B. *N. Amer.*   72°0N 64°0W **66** B13
Baffin I. *Canada*   68°0N 75°0W **69** D17
Bafing → *Mali*   13°49N 10°50W **52** F3
Bafliyūn *Syria*   36°37N 36°59E **46** B3
Bafoulabé *Mali*   13°50N 10°55W **52** F3
Bafoussam *Cameroon*   5°28N 10°25E **54** C7
Bāfq *Iran*   31°40N 55°25E **47** D7
Bafra *Turkey*   41°34N 35°54E **19** F6
Bāft *Iran*   29°15N 56°38E **47** D8
Bafwasende
  Dem. Rep. of the Congo   1°3N 27°5E **54** D5
Bagaha *India*   27°6N 84°5E **44** A7
Bagalkot *India*   16°10N 75°40E **45** F2
Bagamoyo *Tanzania*   6°28S 38°55E **54** F7
Bagan Datoh *Malaysia*   3°59N 100°47E **39** L3
Bagan Serai *Malaysia*   5°1N 100°32E **39** K3
Baganga *Phil.*   7°34N 126°33E **37** C7
Bagani *Namibia*   18°7S 21°41E **56** A3
Bagansiapiapi *Indonesia*   2°12N 100°50E **36** D2
Bagasra *India*   21°30N 71°0E **42** J4
Bagaud *India*   22°19N 75°53E **42** H6
Bagdad *U.S.A.*   34°35N 115°53W **79** L11
Bagdarin *Russia*   54°26N 113°36E **27** D12
Bagé *Brazil*   31°20S 54°15W **95** C5
Bagenalstown *Ireland*   52°42N 6°58W **10** D5
Bagepalli *India*   13°47N 77°47E **45** H3
Bageshwar *India*   29°51N 79°46E **43** E8
Bagevadi *India*   16°35N 75°58E **44** F2
Baggs *U.S.A.*   41°2N 107°39W **76** F10
Bagh *Pakistan*   33°59N 73°45E **43** C5
Baghain → *India*   25°32N 81°1E **43** G9
Bagheria *Italy*   38°5N 13°30E **22** E5
Baghlān *Afghan.*   32°12N 68°46E **40** A6
Baghlān □ *Afghan.*   36°0N 68°30E **40** B6
Bagley *U.S.A.*   47°32N 95°24W **80** B6
Baglung *Nepal*   28°16N 83°36E **43** E10
Bago = Pegu *Burma*   17°20N 96°29E **41** L20
Bagodar *India*   24°5N 85°52E **43** G11
Bagrationovsk *Russia*   54°23N 20°39E **9** J19

Bābol *Iran*   36°40N 52°50E **47** B7
Baguio *Phil.*   16°26N 120°34E **37** A6
Bahadurganj *India*   26°16N 87°49E **43** F12
Bahadurgarh *India*   28°40N 76°57E **42** E7
Bahama, Canal Viejo de
  W. Indies   22°10N 77°30W **88** B4
Bahamas ■ *N. Amer.*   24°0N 75°0W **89** B5
Bahār *Iran*   34°54N 48°26E **47** C6
Baharampur *India*   24°2N 88°27E **43** G13
Baharu Pandan = Pandan
  Malaysia   1°32N 103°46E **39** d
Bahawalnagar *Pakistan*   30°0N 73°15E **42** E5
Bahawalpur *Pakistan*   29°24N 71°40E **42** E4
Bäherden *Turkmenistan*   38°25N 57°26E **47** B8
Baheri *India*   28°45N 79°34E **43** E8
Bahgul → *India*   27°45N 79°36E **43** F8
Bahía = Salvador *Brazil*   13°0S 38°30W **93** F11
Bahía □ *Brazil*   12°0S 42°0W **93** F10
Bahía, Is. de la *Honduras*   16°45N 86°15W **88** C2
Bahía Blanca *Argentina*   38°35S 62°13W **94** D3
Bahía de Caráquez
  Ecuador   0°40S 80°27W **92** D2
Bahía de Los Angeles
  Mexico   28°56N 113°34W **86** B2
Bahía Kino *Mexico*   28°47N 111°58W **86** B2
Bahía Laura *Argentina*   48°10S 66°30W **96** F3
Bahía Negra *Paraguay*   20°5S 58°5W **92** H7
Bahir Dar *Ethiopia*   11°37N 37°10E **49** E2
Bahmanzād *Iran*   31°15N 51°47E **47** D6
Bahraich *India*   27°38N 81°37E **43** F9
Bahrain ■ *Asia*   26°0N 50°35E **47** E6
Bahror *India*   27°51N 76°20E **42** F7
Bāhū Kalāt *Iran*   25°43N 61°25E **47** E9
Bai Bung, Mui = Ca Mau, Mui
  Vietnam   8°38N 104°44E **39** H5
Bai Thuong *Vietnam*   19°54N 105°23E **38** C5
Baia Mare *Romania*   47°40N 23°35E **17** E12
Baião *Brazil*   2°40S 49°40W **93** D9
Baïbokoum *Chad*   7°46N 15°43E **53** G9
Baicheng *China*   45°38N 122°42E **33** B12
Baidoa = Baydhabo
  Somalia   3°8N 43°30E **49** G3
Baie-Comeau *Canada*   49°12N 68°10W **73** C6
Baie-St-Paul *Canada*   47°28N 70°32W **73** C5
Baie Ste-Anne *Seychelles*   4°18S 55°45E **55** b
Baie-Trinité *Canada*   49°25N 67°20W **73** C6
Baie Verte *Canada*   49°55N 56°12W **73** C8
Baihar *India*   22°6N 80°33E **43** H9
Baihe *Hubei, China*   32°50N 110°5E **34** A6
Baihe *Jilin, China*   42°27N 128°9E **33** C15
Baiheitan Dam *China*   27°11N 102°54E **34** D4
Ba'ījī *Iraq*   35°0N 43°30E **46** C4
Baijnath *India*   29°55N 79°37E **43** E8
Baikal, L. = Baykal, Oz.
  Russia   53°0N 108°0E **27** D11
Baikonur = Bayqonyr
  Kazakhstan   45°40N 63°20E **26** E7
Baikunthpur *India*   23°15N 82°33E **43** H10
Bailadila, Mt. *India*   18°43N 81°15E **44** E5
Baile Átha Fhirdhia = Ardee
  Ireland   53°52N 6°33W **10** C5
Baile Átha Í = Athy *Ireland* 53°0N 7°0W **10** C5
Baile Átha Luain = Athlone
  Ireland   53°25N 7°56W **10** C4
Baile Átha Troim = Trim
  Ireland   53°33N 6°48W **10** C5
Baile Brigín = Balbriggan
  Ireland   53°37N 6°11W **10** C5
Baile Sear = Baleshare
  U.K.   57°31N 7°22W **11** D1
Băileşti *Romania*   44°1N 23°20E **17** F12
Bailhongal *India*   15°55N 74°53E **45** G2
Bailieborough *Ireland*   53°56N 6°59W **10** C5
Baima *China*   33°0N 100°26E **34** A3
Bainbridge *Ga., U.S.A.*   30°55N 84°35W **85** F12
Bainbridge *N.Y., U.S.A.*   42°18N 75°29W **83** D9
Bainbridge Island
  U.S.A.   47°38N 122°32W **78** C4
Baine *China*   42°0N 128°0E **31** C14
Baing *Indonesia*   10°14S 120°34E **37** F6
Bainiu *China*   32°50N 112°15E **32** H7
Baird Mts. *U.S.A.*   67°0N 160°0W **74** B8
Bairiki = Tarawa *Kiribati*   1°30N 173°0E **64** G9
Bairin Youqi *China*   43°30N 118°35E **33** C10
Bairin Zuoqi *China*   43°58N 119°15E **33** C10
Bairnsdale *Australia*   37°48S 147°36E **63** F4
Baisha *China*   34°20N 112°32E **32** G7
Baisha Li *China*   19°12N 109°20E **38** C7
Baishan = Hunjiang
  China   41°54N 126°26E **33** D14
Baishan *China*   42°43N 127°14E **33** C14
Baitadi *Nepal*   29°35N 80°25E **43** E9
Baitarani → *India*   20°45N 86°48E **44** D8
Baiyin *China*   36°45N 104°14E **32** F3
Baiyü *China*   31°16N 98°50E **34** B2
Baiyu Shan *China*   37°15N 107°30E **32** F4
Baj Baj *India*   22°30N 88°5E **43** H13
Baja *Hungary*   46°12N 18°59E **17** E10
Baja, Pta. *Mexico*   29°58N 115°49W **86** B1
Baja California *Mexico*   31°10N 115°12W **86** A1
Baja California □ *Mexico*   30°0N 115°0W **86** B2
Baja California Sur □
  Mexico   25°50N 111°50W **86** B2
Bajag *India*   22°40N 81°21E **43** H9
Bajana *India*   23°7N 71°49E **42** H4
Bajatrejo *Indonesia*   8°29S 114°19E **37** J17
Bajawa *Indonesia*   8°47S 120°59E **37** F6
Bajera *Indonesia*   8°31S 115°2E **37** J18
Bājgīrān *Iran*   37°36N 58°24E **47** B8
Bajimba, Mt. *Australia*   29°17S 152°6E **63** D5
Bajo Boquete *Panama*   8°46N 82°27E **94** E3
Bajo Nuevo *Caribbean*   15°40N 78°50W **88** C4
Bajool *Australia*   23°40S 150°35E **62** C5
Bakel *Senegal*   14°56N 12°20W **52** F3
Baker *Calif., U.S.A.*   35°16N 116°4W **79** K10
Baker *Mont., U.S.A.*   46°22N 104°17W **76** C11
Baker, L. *Canada*   64°0N 96°0W **68** E12
Baker, Mt. *U.S.A.*   48°50N 121°49W **76** B3

INDEX TO WORLD MAPS
Barotseland 103

Baker City U.S.A. 44°47N 117°50W 76 D5
Baker I. Pac. Oc. 0°10N 176°35W 64 G10
Baker I. U.S.A. 55°20N 133°40W 70 B2
Baker L. Australia 26°54S 126°5E 61 E4
Baker Lake Canada 64°20N 96°3W 68 E12
Bakers Creek Australia 21°13S 149°7E 62 C4
Bakers Dozen Is. Canada 56°45N 78°45W 72 A4
Bakersfield Calif., U.S.A. 35°23N 119°1W 79 K8
Bakersfield Vt., U.S.A. 44°45N 72°48W 83 B12
Bākharden = Bäherden Turkmenistan 38°25N 57°26E 47 B8
Bākhtarān = Kermānshāh Iran 34°23N 47°0E 46 C5
Bākhtarān = Kermānshāh □ Iran 34°0N 46°30E 46 C5
Bakhtegān, Daryācheh-ye Iran 29°40N 53°50E 47 D7
Bakhtegān △ Iran 29°51N 53°40E 47 D7
Bakı Azerbaijan 40°29N 49°56E 47 A6
Bakkafjörður Iceland 66°2N 14°48W 8 C6
Bakkagerði Iceland 65°31N 13°49W 8 D7
Bakony Hungary 47°10N 17°30E 17 E9
Bakony Forest = Bakony Hungary 47°10N 17°30E 17 E9
Bakouma C.A.R. 5°40N 22°56E 54 C4
Bakswaho India 24°15N 79°18E 43 G8
Baku = Bakı Azerbaijan 40°29N 49°56E 47 A6
Bakutis Coast Antarctica 74°0S 120°0W 5 D15
Baky = Bakı Azerbaijan 40°29N 49°56E 47 A6
Bala Canada 45°1N 79°37W 82 A5
Bala U.K. 52°54N 3°36W 12 E4
Bala, L. U.K. 52°53N 3°37W 12 E4
Balabac I. Phil. 8°0N 117°0E 36 C5
Balabac Str. E. Indies 7°53N 117°5E 36 C5
Balabagh Afghan. 34°25N 70°12E 42 B4
Ba'labakk Lebanon 34°0N 36°10E 48 B5
Balabalangan, Kepulauan Indonesia 2°20S 117°30E 36 E5
Balad Iraq 34°0N 44°9E 46 C5
Balad Rūz Iraq 33°42N 45°5E 46 C5
Bālādeh Fārs, Iran 29°17N 51°56E 47 D6
Bālādeh Māzandaran, Iran 36°12N 51°48E 47 B6
Balaghat India 21°49N 80°12E 44 D5
Balaghat Ra. India 18°50N 76°30E 44 E3
Balaguer Spain 41°50N 0°50E 21 B6
Balaklava Ukraine 44°30N 33°30E 19 F5
Balakovo Russia 52°4N 47°55E 18 D8
Balamau India 27°10N 80°21E 43 F9
Balancán Mexico 17°48N 91°32W 87 D6
Balangir India 20°43N 83°35E 44 D6
Balapur India 20°40N 76°45E 44 D3
Balashov Russia 51°30N 43°10E 19 D7
Balasinor India 22°57N 73°23E 42 H5
Balasore = Baleshwar India 21°35N 87°3E 44 D8
Balaton Hungary 46°50N 17°40E 17 E9
Balbina, Represa de Brazil 2°0S 59°30W 92 D7
Balboa Panama 8°57N 79°34W 88 E4
Balbriggan Ireland 53°37N 6°11W 10 C5
Balcarce Argentina 38°0S 58°10W 94 D4
Balcarres Canada 50°50N 103°35W 71 C8
Balchik Bulgaria 43°28N 28°11E 23 C13
Balclutha N.Z. 46°15S 169°45E 59 G2
Balcones Escarpment U.S.A. 29°30N 99°15W 84 G5
Bald I. Australia 34°57S 118°27E 61 F2
Bald Knob U.S.A. 35°19N 91°34W 84 D9
Baldock L. Canada 56°33N 97°57W 71 B9
Baldwin Mich., U.S.A. 43°54N 85°51W 81 D11
Baldwin Pa., U.S.A. 40°21N 79°58W 82 F5
Baldwinsville U.S.A. 43°10N 76°20W 83 C8
Baldy Peak U.S.A. 33°54N 109°34W 77 K9
Baleares, Is. Spain 39°30N 3°0E 21 C7
Balearic Is. = Baleares, Is. Spain 39°30N 3°0E 21 C7
Baleine → Canada 58°15N 67°40W 73 A6
Baleine, Petite R. de la → Canada 56°0N 76°45W 72 A4
Baler Phil. 15°46N 121°34E 37 A6
Baleshare U.K. 57°31N 7°22W 11 D1
Baleshwar India 21°35N 87°3E 44 D8
Baley Russia 51°36N 116°37E 27 D12
Balfate Honduras 15°48N 86°25W 88 C2
Balgo Australia 20°9S 127°58E 60 D4
Balharshah India 19°50N 79°23E 44 E4
Bali India 25°11N 73°17E 42 G5
Bali Indonesia 8°20S 115°0E 37 J18
Bali □ Indonesia 8°20S 115°0E 37 J17
Bali, Selat Indonesia 8°18S 114°25E 37 J17
Bali Barat △ Indonesia 8°12S 114°35E 37 J17
Bali Sea Indonesia 8°0S 115°0E 37 J17
Baliapal India 21°40N 87°17E 43 J12
Baliguda India 20°12N 83°55E 44 D6
Balik Pulau Malaysia 5°21N 100°14E 39 c
Balıkeşir Turkey 39°39N 27°53E 23 E12
Balikpapan Indonesia 1°10S 116°55E 36 E5
Balimbing Phil. 5°5N 119°58E 37 C5
Baling Malaysia 5°41N 100°55E 39 K3
Balkan Mts. = Stara Planina Bulgaria 43°15N 23°0E 23 C10
Balkanabat Turkmenistan 39°30N 54°22E 47 B7
Balkhash = Balqash Kazakhstan 46°50N 74°50E 26 E8
Balkhash, Ozero = Balqash Köli Kazakhstan 46°0N 74°50E 30 B3
Balkonda India 18°52N 78°21E 44 E4
Ballachulish U.K. 56°41N 5°8W 11 E3
Balladonia Australia 32°27S 123°51E 61 F3
Ballaghaderreen Ireland 53°55N 8°34W 10 C3
Ballarat Australia 37°33S 143°50E 63 F3
Ballard, L. Australia 29°20S 120°40E 61 E3
Ballater U.K. 57°3N 3°3W 11 D5
Ballenas, Canal de Mexico 29°10N 113°29W 86 B2
Balleny Is. Antarctica 66°30S 163°0E 5 C11
Ballia India 25°46N 84°12E 43 G11
Ballina Australia 28°50S 153°31E 63 D5
Ballina Ireland 54°7N 9°9W 10 B2
Ballinasloe Ireland 53°20N 8°13W 10 C3
Ballincollig Ireland 51°53N 8°33W 10 E3
Ballinger U.S.A. 31°45N 99°57W 84 F5
Ballinrobe Ireland 53°38N 9°13W 10 C2
Ballinskelligs B. Ireland 51°48N 10°13W 10 E1
Ballston Spa U.S.A. 43°0N 73°51W 83 D11
Ballyboghil Ireland 53°32N 6°16W 10 C5
Ballybunion Ireland 52°31N 9°40W 10 D2
Ballycanew Ireland 52°37N 6°19W 10 D5
Ballycastle U.K. 55°12N 6°15W 10 A5
Ballyclare U.K. 54°46N 6°0W 10 B5
Ballycroy △ Ireland 54°5N 9°50W 10 B2
Ballydehob Ireland 51°34N 9°28W 10 E2
Ballygawley U.K. 54°27N 7°2W 10 B4
Ballyhaunis Ireland 53°46N 8°46W 10 C3
Ballyheige Ireland 52°23N 9°49W 10 D2
Ballymena U.K. 54°52N 6°17W 10 B5
Ballymoney U.K. 55°5N 6°31W 10 A5
Ballymote Ireland 54°5N 8°31W 10 B3
Ballynahinch U.K. 54°24N 5°54W 10 B6
Ballyporeen Ireland 52°16N 8°6W 10 D3
Ballyquintin Pt. U.K. 54°20N 5°30W 10 B6
Ballyshannon Ireland 54°30N 8°11W 10 B3
Balmaceda Chile 46°0S 71°50W 96 F2
Balmertown Canada 51°4N 93°41W 71 C10
Balmoral Australia 37°15S 141°48E 63 F3
Balmorhea U.S.A. 30°59N 103°45W 84 F3
Balochistan = Baluchistan □ Pakistan 27°30N 65°0E 40 F4
Balod India 20°44N 81°13E 44 D5
Balonne → Australia 28°47S 147°56E 63 D4
Balotra India 25°50N 72°14E 42 G5
Balqash Kazakhstan 46°50N 74°50E 26 E8
Balqash Köli Kazakhstan 46°0N 74°50E 30 B3
Balrampur India 27°30N 82°20E 43 F10
Balranald Australia 34°38S 143°33E 63 E3
Balsas → Brazil 7°15S 44°35W 93 E9
Balsas → Mexico 17°55N 102°10W 86 D4
Balsas del Norte Mexico 18°0N 99°46W 87 D5
Balta Ukraine 47°56N 29°45E 17 D15
Bălţi Moldova 47°48N 27°58E 17 E14
Baltic Sea Europe 57°0N 19°0E 9 H18
Baltimore Ireland 51°29N 9°22W 10 E2
Baltimore Md., U.S.A. 39°17N 76°36W 81 F15
Baltimore Ohio, U.S.A. 39°51N 82°36W 82 G2
Baltinglass Ireland 52°56N 6°43W 10 D5
Baltit Pakistan 36°15N 74°40E 43 A6
Baltiysk Russia 54°41N 19°58E 9 J18
Baluchistan □ Pakistan 27°30N 65°0E 40 F4
Balurghat India 25°15N 88°44E 43 G13
Balvi Latvia 57°8N 27°15E 9 H22
Balya Turkey 39°44N 27°35E 23 E12
Balykchy Kyrgyzstan 42°26N 76°12E 30 C4
Balyqshy Kazakhstan 47°4N 51°52E 19 E9
Bam Iran 29°7N 58°14E 47 D8
Bama China 24°8N 107°12E 34 E6
Bama Nigeria 11°33N 13°41E 53 F8
Bamaga Australia 10°50S 142°25E 62 A3
Bamaji L. Canada 51°9N 91°25W 72 B1
Bamako Mali 12°34N 7°55W 52 F4
Bambari C.A.R. 5°40N 20°35E 54 C4
Bambaroo Australia 18°50S 146°10E 62 B4
Bamberg Germany 49°54N 10°54E 16 D6
Bamberg U.S.A. 33°18N 81°2W 85 E14
Bamburgh U.K. 55°37N 1°43W 12 B6
Bamenda Cameroon 5°57N 10°11E 54 C2
Bamfield Canada 48°45N 125°10W 70 D3
Bāmīān □ Afghan. 35°0N 67°0E 40 B5
Bamiancheng China 43°15N 124°2E 33 C13
Bamou △ Iran 29°45N 52°35E 47 D7
Bampūr Iran 27°15N 60°21E 47 E9
Bampūr → Iran 27°24N 59°0E 47 E8
Ban Ao Tu Khun Thailand 8°9N 98°20E 39 a
Ban Ban Laos 19°31N 103°30E 38 C4
Ban Bang Hin Thailand 9°32N 98°35E 39 H2
Ban Bang Khu Thailand 7°57N 98°23E 39 a
Ban Bang Rong Thailand 8°3N 98°25E 39 a
Ban Bo Phut Thailand 9°33N 100°2E 39 b
Ban Chaweng Thailand 9°32N 100°3E 39 b
Ban Chiang Thailand 17°30N 103°10E 38 D4
Ban Chiang Klang Thailand 19°25N 100°55E 38 C3
Ban Choho Thailand 15°2N 102°9E 38 E4
Ban Dan Lan Hoi Thailand 17°0N 99°35E 38 D2
Ban Don = Surat Thani Thailand 9°6N 99°20E 39 H2
Ban Don Vietnam 12°53N 107°48E 38 F6
Ban Don, Ao → Thailand 9°20N 99°25E 39 H2
Ban Dong Thailand 19°30N 100°59E 38 C3
Ban Hong Thailand 18°18N 98°50E 38 C2
Ban Hua Thanon Thailand 9°26N 100°1E 39 b
Ban Kantang Thailand 7°25N 99°31E 39 J2
Ban Karon Thailand 7°51N 98°18E 39 a
Ban Kata Thailand 7°50N 98°18E 39 a
Ban Keun Laos 18°22N 102°35E 38 C4
Ban Khai Thailand 12°46N 101°18E 38 F3
Ban Kheun Laos 20°13N 101°7E 38 B3
Ban Khlong Khian Thailand 8°10N 98°26E 39 a
Ban Khlong Kua Thailand 6°57N 100°8E 39 J3
Ban Khuan Thailand 8°20N 98°25E 39 a
Ban Ko Yai Chim Thailand 11°17N 99°26E 39 G2
Ban Laem Thailand 13°13N 99°59E 38 F2
Ban Lamai Thailand 9°28N 100°3E 39 b
Ban Lao Ngam Laos 15°28N 106°10E 38 E6
Ban Le Kathe Thailand 15°49N 98°53E 38 E2
Ban Lo Po Noi Thailand 8°1N 98°34E 39 a
Ban Mae Chedi Thailand 19°11N 99°31E 38 C2
Ban Mae Nam Thailand 9°34N 100°0E 39 b
Ban Mae Sariang Thailand 18°10N 97°56E 38 C1
Ban Mê Thuôt = Buon Ma Thuot Vietnam 12°40N 108°3E 38 F7
Ban Mi Thailand 15°3N 100°32E 38 E3
Ban Muang Mo Laos 19°4N 103°58E 38 C4
Ban Na Bo Thailand 9°19N 99°41E 39 b
Ban Na San Thailand 8°53N 99°52E 39 H2
Ban Na Tong Laos 20°56N 101°47E 38 B3
Ban Nam Bac Laos 20°38N 102°20E 38 B4
Ban Nammi Laos 17°7N 105°40E 38 D5
Ban Nong Bok Laos 17°5N 104°48E 38 D5
Ban Nong Pling Thailand 15°40N 100°10E 38 E3
Ban Pak Chan Thailand 10°32N 98°51E 39 G2
Ban Patong Thailand 7°54N 98°18E 39 a
Ban Phai Thailand 16°4N 102°44E 38 D4
Ban Phak Chit Thailand 8°0N 98°24E 39 a
Ban Pong Thailand 13°50N 99°55E 38 F2
Ban Rawai Thailand 7°47N 98°20E 39 a
Ban Ron Phibun Thailand 8°9N 99°51E 39 H2
Ban Sakhu Thailand 8°4N 98°18E 39 a
Ban Sanam Chai Thailand 7°33N 100°25E 39 J3
Ban Tak Thailand 17°2N 99°4E 38 D2
Ban Tako Thailand 14°5N 102°40E 38 E4
Ban Tha Nun Thailand 8°12N 98°18E 39 a
Ban Tha Rua Thailand 7°59N 98°22E 39 a
Ban Tha Yu Thailand 8°17N 98°22E 39 a
Ban Thong Krut Thailand 9°25N 99°57E 39 b
Ban Xien Kok Laos 20°54N 100°39E 38 B3
Ban Yen Nhan Vietnam 20°57N 106°2E 38 B6
Banaba Kiribati 0°45S 169°50E 64 H8
Banagher Ireland 53°11N 7°59W 10 C3
Banalia Dem. Rep. of the Congo 1°32N 25°5E 54 D5
Banam Cambodia 11°20N 105°17E 39 G5
Bananal, I. do Brazil 11°30S 50°30W 93 F8
Bananga India 6°57N 93°54E 45 L11
Banaras = Varanasi India 25°22N 83°0E 43 G10
Banas → Gujarat, India 23°45N 71°25E 42 H4
Banas → Mad. P., India 24°15N 81°30E 43 G9
Bânâs, Ras Egypt 23°57N 35°59E 53 D13
Banbridge U.K. 54°22N 6°16W 10 B5
Banbury U.K. 52°4N 1°20W 13 E6
Banchory U.K. 57°3N 2°29W 11 D6
Bancroft Canada 45°3N 77°51W 82 A7
Band Bonī Iran 25°30N 59°33E 47 E8
Band Qīr Iran 31°39N 48°53E 47 D6
Banda Mad. P., India 24°3N 78°57E 43 G8
Banda Maharashtra, India 15°49N 73°52E 45 G1
Banda Ut. P., India 25°30N 80°26E 43 G9
Banda, Kepulauan Indonesia 4°37S 129°50E 37 E7
Banda Aceh Indonesia 5°35N 95°20E 36 C1
Banda Banda, Mt. Australia 31°10S 152°28E 63 E5
Banda Elat Indonesia 5°40S 133°5E 37 F8
Banda Is. = Banda, Kepulauan Indonesia 4°37S 129°50E 37 E7
Banda Sea Indonesia 6°0S 130°0E 37 F8
Bandai-Asahi △ Japan 37°38N 140°5E 28 F10
Bandai-San Japan 37°36N 140°4E 28 F10
Bandān Iran 31°23N 60°44E 47 D9
Bandanaira Indonesia 4°32S 129°54E 37 E7
Bandanwara India 26°9N 74°38E 42 F6
Bandar = Machilipatnam India 16°12N 81°8E 45 F5
Bandar-e Abbās Iran 27°15N 56°15E 47 E8
Bandar-e Anzalī Iran 37°30N 49°30E 47 B6
Bandar-e Bushehr = Būshehr Iran 28°55N 50°55E 47 D6
Bandar-e Chārak Iran 26°45N 54°20E 47 E7
Bandar-e Deylam Iran 30°5N 50°10E 47 D6
Bandar-e Emām Khomeynī Iran 30°30N 49°5E 47 D6
Bandar-e Lengeh Iran 26°35N 54°58E 47 E7
Bandar-e Maqām Iran 26°56N 53°29E 47 E7
Bandar-e Ma'shur Iran 30°35N 49°10E 47 D6
Bandar-e Rīg Iran 29°29N 50°38E 47 D6
Bandar-e Torkeman Iran 37°0N 54°10E 47 B7
Bandar Labuan Malaysia 5°20N 115°14E 36 C5
Bandar Lampung Indonesia 5°20S 105°10E 36 F3
Bandar Maharani = Muar Malaysia 2°3N 102°34E 39 L4
Bandar Penggaram = Batu Pahat Malaysia 1°50N 102°56E 39 M4
Bandar Seri Begawan Brunei 4°52N 115°0E 36 D5
Bandar Sri Aman Malaysia 1°15N 111°32E 36 D4
Bandeira, Pico da Brazil 20°26S 41°47W 95 A7
Bandera Argentina 28°55S 62°20W 94 B3
Banderas, B. de Mexico 20°40N 105°25W 86 C3
Bandhavgarh India 23°40N 81°2E 43 H9
Bandhavgarh △ India 23°45N 81°10E 44 C5
Bandi → India 26°12N 75°47E 42 F6
Bandia → India 19°2N 80°28E 44 E5
Bandikui India 27°3N 76°34E 42 F7
Bandipur △ India 11°45N 76°30E 45 J3
Bandırma Turkey 40°20N 28°0E 23 D13
Bandjarmasin = Banjarmasin Indonesia 3°20S 114°35E 36 E4
Bandon Ireland 51°44N 8°44W 10 E3
Bandon → Ireland 51°43N 8°37W 10 E3
Bandundu Dem. Rep. of the Congo 3°15S 17°22E 54 E3
Bandung Indonesia 6°54S 107°36E 37 G12
Bāneh Iran 35°59N 45°53E 46 C5
Banes Cuba 21°0N 75°42W 89 B4
Banff Canada 51°10N 115°34W 70 C5
Banff U.K. 57°40N 2°33W 11 D6
Banff △ Canada 51°30N 116°15W 70 C5
Bang Fai → Laos 16°57N 104°45E 38 D5
Bang Hieng → Laos 16°10N 105°10E 38 D5
Bang Krathum Thailand 16°34N 100°18E 38 D3
Bang Lamung Thailand 13°3N 100°56E 38 F3
Bang Lang △ Thailand 5°58N 101°19E 39 K3
Bang Lang Res. Thailand 6°6N 101°17E 39 J3
Bang Mun Nak Thailand 16°2N 100°23E 38 D3
Bang Pa In Thailand 14°14N 100°35E 38 E3
Bang Rakam Thailand 16°45N 100°7E 38 D3
Bang Saphan Thailand 11°14N 99°28E 39 G2
Bang Thao Thailand 7°59N 98°18E 39 a
Bangaduni I. India 21°34N 88°52E 43 J13
Bangalore India 12°59N 77°40E 45 H3
Banganapalle India 15°19N 78°14E 45 G4
Banganga → India 27°6N 77°25E 42 F6
Bangaon India 23°0N 88°47E 43 H13
Bangassou C.A.R. 4°55N 23°7E 54 D4
Banggai Indonesia 1°34S 123°30E 37 E6
Banggai, Kepulauan Indonesia 1°40S 123°30E 37 E6
Banggai Arch. = Banggai, Kepulauan Indonesia 1°40S 123°30E 37 E6
Banggi, Pulau Malaysia 7°17N 117°12E 36 C5
Banghāzī Libya 32°11N 20°3E 53 B10
Bangka Sulawesi, Indonesia 1°50N 125°5E 37 D7
Bangka Sumatera, Indonesia 2°0S 105°50E 36 E3
Bangka, Selat Indonesia 2°30S 105°30E 36 E3
Bangka-Belitung □ Indonesia 2°30S 107°0E 36 E3
Bangkalan Indonesia 7°2S 112°46E 37 G15
Bangkang Burma 22°4N 99°1E 34 F2
Bangkinang Indonesia 0°18N 101°5E 36 D2
Bangko Indonesia 2°5S 102°9E 36 E2
Bangkok, Bight of Thailand 12°55N 100°30E 38 F3
Bangla = Paschimbanga □ India 23°0N 88°0E 43 H13
Bangladesh ■ Asia 24°0N 90°0E 41 H17
Bangli Indonesia 8°27S 115°21E 37 J18
Bangong Co China 33°45N 78°43E 43 C8
Bangor Down, U.K. 54°40N 5°40W 10 B6
Bangor Gwynedd, U.K. 53°14N 4°8W 12 D3
Bangor Maine, U.S.A. 44°48N 68°46W 81 C19
Bangor Pa., U.S.A. 40°52N 75°13W 83 F9
Bangued Phil. 17°40N 120°37E 37 A6
Bangui C.A.R. 4°23N 18°35E 54 D3
Bangweulu, L. Zambia 11°0S 30°0E 54 G6
Banhine △ Mozam. 22°49S 32°55E 57 B5
Baní Dom. Rep. 18°16N 70°22W 89 C5
Banī Sa'd Iraq 33°34N 44°32E 46 C5
Banihal Pass India 33°30N 75°12E 43 C6
Bāniyās Syria 35°10N 36°0E 46 C3
Banja Luka Bos.-H. 44°49N 17°11E 22 B7
Banjar India 31°38N 77°21E 42 D7
Banjar → India 22°36N 80°22E 43 H9
Banjarmasin Indonesia 3°20S 114°35E 36 E4
Banjul Gambia 13°28N 16°40W 52 F2
Banka India 24°53N 86°55E 43 G12
Bankipore India 25°35N 85°10E 41 G14
Bankot India 17°58N 73°2E 44 F1
Banks I. = Moa Australia 10°11S 142°16E 62 a
Banks I. B.C., Canada 53°20N 130°0W 70 C3
Banks I. N.W.T., Canada 73°15N 121°30W 68 C7
Banks Pen. N.Z. 43°45S 173°15E 59 E4
Banks Str. Australia 40°40S 148°10E 63 G4
Bankura India 23°11N 87°18E 43 H12
Banmankhi India 25°53N 87°11E 43 G12
Bann → Armagh, U.K. 54°30N 6°31W 10 B5
Bann → L'derry., U.K. 55°8N 6°41W 10 A5
Bannang Sata Thailand 6°16N 101°16E 39 J3
Banning U.S.A. 33°56N 116°53W 79 M10
Bannockburn Canada 44°39N 77°33W 82 B7
Bannockburn U.K. 56°5N 3°55W 11 E5
Bannu Pakistan 33°0N 70°18E 40 C7
Bano India 22°40N 84°55E 43 H11
Bansagar Dam India 24°11N 81°17E 44 B5
Bansgaon India 26°33N 83°21E 43 F10
Banská Bystrica Slovak Rep. 48°46N 19°14E 17 D10
Banswara India 23°32N 74°24E 42 H6
Bantaeng Indonesia 5°32S 119°56E 37 F5
Banteay Prei Nokor Cambodia 11°56N 105°40E 39 G5
Banten □ Indonesia 6°30S 106°0E 37 G11
Bantry Ireland 51°41N 9°27W 10 E2
Bantry B. Ireland 51°37N 9°44W 10 E2
Bantva India 21°29N 70°12E 42 J4
Bantval India 12°55N 75°0E 45 H2
Banyak, Kepulauan Indonesia 2°10N 97°10E 36 D1
Banyo Cameroon 6°52N 11°45E 54 C2
Banyuwangi Indonesia 8°13S 114°21E 37 J17
Banzare Coast Antarctica 68°0S 125°0E 5 C9
Bao Ha Vietnam 22°11N 104°21E 34 F5
Bao Lac Vietnam 22°57N 105°40E 38 A5
Bao Loc Vietnam 11°32N 107°48E 39 G6
Bao'an China 22°34N 113°52E 31 a
Baocheng China 33°12N 106°56E 34 A6
Baode China 39°1N 111°5E 32 E6
Baodi China 39°38N 117°20E 33 E9
Baoding China 38°50N 115°28E 32 E8
Baoji China 34°20N 107°5E 32 G4
Baojing China 28°45N 109°41E 34 C7
Baokang China 31°54N 111°12E 35 B8
Baoshan China 25°10N 99°5E 34 E2
Baotou China 40°32N 110°2E 32 D6
Baoxing China 30°24N 102°50E 34 B4
Baoying China 33°17N 119°20E 33 H10
Baoyou = Ledong China 18°41N 109°5E 38 C7
Bap India 27°23N 72°18E 42 F5
Bapatla India 15°55N 80°30E 45 G5
Bāqerābād Iran 33°2N 51°58E 47 C6
Ba'qūbah Iraq 33°45N 44°50E 46 C5
Baquedano Chile 23°20S 69°52W 94 A2
Bar Montenegro 42°8N 19°6E 23 C8
Bar Ukraine 49°4N 27°40E 17 D14
Bar Bigha India 25°21N 85°47E 43 G11
Bar Harbor U.S.A. 44°23N 68°13W 81 C19
Bar-le-Duc France 48°47N 5°10E 20 B6
Bara India 25°16N 81°43E 43 G9
Bara Banki India 26°55N 81°12E 43 F9
Barabai Indonesia 2°32S 115°34E 36 E5
Baraboo U.S.A. 43°28N 89°45W 80 D9
Baracoa Cuba 20°20N 74°30W 89 B5
Baradā → Syria 33°33N 36°34E 48 B5
Baradero Argentina 33°52S 59°29W 94 C4
Baraga U.S.A. 46°47N 88°30W 80 B9
Barah → India 27°42N 77°5E 42 F6
Barahona Dom. Rep. 18°13N 71°7W 89 C5
Barail Range India 25°15N 93°20E 41 G18
Barakaldo Spain 43°18N 2°59W 21 A4
Barakar → India 24°7N 86°14E 43 G12
Barakot India 21°33N 84°59E 43 J11
Baralaba Australia 24°13S 149°50E 62 C4
Baralzon L. Canada 60°0N 98°3W 71 B9
Baramati India 18°11N 74°33E 44 E2
Baramba India 20°25N 85°23E 44 D7
Baramula India 34°15N 74°20E 43 B6
Baran India 25°9N 76°40E 42 G7
Baran → Pakistan 25°13N 68°17E 42 G3
Baranavichy Belarus 53°10N 26°0E 17 B14
Baranof U.S.A. 57°5N 134°50W 70 B2
Baranof I. U.S.A. 57°0N 135°0W 68 F4
Barapasi Indonesia 2°15S 137°5E 37 E9
Barasat India 22°46N 88°31E 43 H13
Barat Daya, Kepulauan Indonesia 7°30S 128°0E 37 F7
Baratang I. India 12°13N 92°45E 45 H11
Barataria B. U.S.A. 29°20N 89°55W 85 G10
Barauda India 23°33N 75°15E 42 H6
Baraut India 29°13N 77°7E 42 E7
Barbacena Brazil 21°15S 43°56W 95 A7
Barbados ■ W. Indies 13°10N 59°30W 89 g
Barbas, C. W. Sahara 22°20N 16°42W 52 D2
Barbastro Spain 42°2N 0°5E 21 A6
Barbeau Pk. Canada 81°54N 75°1W 69 A16
Barberton S. Africa 25°42S 31°2E 57 C5
Barberton U.S.A. 41°1N 81°39W 82 E3
Barbosa Colombia 5°57N 73°37W 92 B4
Barbourville U.S.A. 36°52N 83°53W 81 G12
Barbuda W. Indies 17°30N 61°40W 89 C7
Barcaldine Australia 23°43S 145°6E 62 C4
Barcellona Pozzo di Gotto Italy 38°9N 15°13E 22 E6
Barcelona Venezuela 10°10N 64°40W 92 A6
Barceloneta Puerto Rico 18°27N 66°32W 89 d
Barcelos Brazil 1°0S 63°0W 92 D6
Barcoo → Australia 25°30S 142°50E 62 D3
Bardaï Chad 21°25N 17°0E 53 D9
Bardas Blancas Argentina 35°49S 69°45W 94 D2
Bardawīl, Sabkhet el Egypt 31°10N 33°15E 48 D2
Barddhaman India 23°14N 87°39E 43 H12
Bardejov Slovak Rep. 49°18N 21°15E 17 D11
Bardera = Baardheere Somalia 2°20N 42°27E 49 G3
Bardīyah Libya 31°45N 25°5E 53 B10
Bardoli India 21°12N 73°5E 44 D1
Bardsey I. U.K. 52°45N 4°47W 12 E3
Bardstown U.S.A. 37°49N 85°28W 81 G11
Bareilly India 28°22N 79°27E 43 E8
Barela India 23°6N 80°3E 43 H9
Barents Sea Arctic 73°0N 39°0E 4 B9
Barfleur, Pte. de France 49°42N 1°16W 20 B3
Bargara Australia 24°50S 152°25E 62 C5
Bargarh India 21°20N 83°37E 44 D6
Bargi Dam India 22°59N 80°0E 44 C5
Barguzin Russia 53°37N 109°37E 27 D11
Barh India 25°29N 85°46E 43 G11
Barhaj India 26°18N 83°44E 43 F10
Barharwa India 24°52N 87°47E 43 G12
Barhi India 24°15N 85°25E 43 G11
Bari India 26°39N 77°39E 42 F7
Bari Italy 41°8N 16°51E 22 D7
Bari Doab Pakistan 30°20N 73°0E 42 D5
Bari Sadri India 24°28N 74°30E 42 G6
Barīdī, Ra's Si. Arabia 24°17N 37°31E 46 E3
Barīm Yemen 12°39N 43°25E 50 E8
Barinas Venezuela 8°36N 70°15W 92 B4
Baring, C. Canada 70°0N 117°30W 68 D8
Baripada India 21°57N 86°45E 44 D8
Barisal Bangla. 22°45N 90°20E 41 H17
Barisal □ Bangla. 22°45N 90°20E 41 H17
Barisan, Pegunungan Indonesia 3°30S 102°15E 36 E2
Barito → Indonesia 4°0S 114°50E 36 E4
Baritú △ Argentina 23°43S 64°40W 94 A3
Barjūj, Wadi → Libya 25°26N 12°12E 53 C8
Bark L. Canada 45°27N 77°51W 82 A7
Barkakana India 23°37N 85°29E 43 H11
Barkam China 31°51N 102°28E 34 B4
Barker U.S.A. 43°20N 78°33W 82 C6
Barkley, L. U.S.A. 37°1N 88°14W 85 C10
Barkley Sound Canada 48°50N 125°10W 70 D3
Barkly East S. Africa 30°58S 27°33E 56 D4
Barkly Homestead Australia 19°52S 135°50E 62 B2
Barkly Tableland Australia 17°50S 136°40E 62 B2
Barkly West S. Africa 28°5S 24°31E 56 C3
Barkol Kazak Zizhixian China 43°37N 93°2E 30 C7
Bârlad Romania 46°15N 27°38E 17 E14
Bârlad → Romania 45°38N 27°32E 17 F14
Barlee, L. Australia 29°15S 119°30E 61 E2
Barlee, Mt. Australia 24°38S 128°13E 61 D4
Barletta Italy 41°19N 16°17E 22 D7
Barlovento C. Verde Is. 17°0N 25°0W 52 b
Barlow L. Canada 62°0N 103°0W 71 A8
Barmedman Australia 34°9S 147°21E 63 E4
Barmer India 25°45N 71°20E 42 G4
Barmera Australia 34°15S 140°28E 63 E3
Barmouth U.K. 52°44N 4°4W 12 E3
Barna → India 25°21N 83°3E 43 G10
Barnagar India 23°7N 75°19E 42 H6
Barnala India 30°23N 75°33E 42 D6
Barnard Castle U.K. 54°33N 1°55W 12 C6
Barnaul Russia 53°20N 83°40E 26 D9
Barnesville Ga., U.S.A. 33°3N 84°9W 85 E12
Barnesville Minn., U.S.A. 46°43N 96°28W 80 B5
Barnet □ U.K. 51°38N 0°9W 13 F7
Barneveld Neths. 52°7N 5°36E 15 B5
Barnhart U.S.A. 31°8N 101°10W 84 F4
Barnsley U.K. 53°34N 1°27W 12 D6
Barnstable U.S.A. 41°42N 70°18W 81 E18
Barnstaple U.K. 51°5N 4°4W 13 F3
Barnstaple Bay = Bideford Bay U.K. 51°5N 4°20W 13 F3
Barnwell U.S.A. 33°15N 81°23W 85 E14
Baro Nigeria 8°35N 6°18E 52 G7
Baroda = Vadodara India 22°20N 73°10E 42 H5
Baroda India 25°29N 76°35E 42 G7
Baroe S. Africa 33°13S 24°33E 56 D3
Baron Ra. Australia 23°30S 127°45E 60 D4
Barong China 31°3N 99°20E 34 B2
Barotseland Zambia 15°0S 24°0E 55 H4

Barpali India 21°11N 83°35E 44 D6
Barpeta India 26°20N 91°10E 41 F17
Barqa Libya 27°0N 23°0E 53 C10
Barques, Pt. Aux U.S.A. 44°4N 82°58W 82 B2
Barquísimeto Venezuela 10°4N 69°19W 92 A5
Barr Smith Range Australia 27°4S 120°20E 61 E3
Barra Brazil 11°5S 43°10W 93 F10
Barra U.K. 57°0N 7°29W 11 E1
Barra, Sd. of U.K. 57°4N 7°25W 11 D1
Barra de Navidad Mexico 19°12N 104°41W 86 D4
Barra do Corda Brazil 5°30S 45°10W 93 E9
Barra do Garças Brazil 15°54S 52°16W 93 G8
Barra do Piraí Brazil 22°30S 43°50W 95 A7
Barra Falsa, Pta. da Mozam. 22°58S 35°37E 57 B6
Barra Hd. U.K. 56°47N 7°40W 11 E1
Barra Mansa Brazil 22°35S 44°12W 95 A7
Barraba Australia 30°21S 150°35E 63 E5
Barranca Lima, Peru 10°45S 77°50W 92 F3
Barranca Loreto, Peru 4°50S 76°50W 92 D3
Barranca del Cobre ⌂ Mexico 27°18N 107°40W 86 B3
Barrancabermeja Colombia 7°0N 73°50W 92 B4
Barrancas Venezuela 8°55N 62°5W 92 B6
Barrancos Portugal 38°10N 6°58W 21 C2
Barranqueras Argentina 27°30S 59°0W 94 B4
Barranquilla Colombia 11°0N 74°50W 92 A4
Barraute Canada 48°26N 77°38W 72 C4
Barre Mass., U.S.A. 42°25N 72°6W 83 D12
Barre Vt., U.S.A. 44°12N 72°30W 83 B12
Barreal Argentina 31°33S 69°28W 94 C2
Barreiras Brazil 12°8S 45°0W 93 F10
Barreirinhas Brazil 2°30S 42°50W 93 D10
Barren, Nosy Madag. 18°25S 43°40E 55 H8
Barren I. India 12°16N 93°51E 45 H11
Barretos Brazil 20°30S 48°35W 93 H9
Barrhead Canada 54°10N 114°24W 70 C6
Barrie Canada 44°24N 79°40W 82 B5
Barrier Ra. Australia 31°0S 141°30E 63 E3
Barrière Canada 51°12N 120°7W 70 C4
Barrington U.S.A. 41°44N 71°18W 83 E13
Barrington L. Canada 56°55N 100°15W 71 B8
Barrington Tops Australia 32°6S 151°28E 63 E5
Barringun Australia 29°1S 145°41E 63 D4
Barron U.S.A. 45°24N 91°51W 80 C8
Barrow U.S.A. 71°18N 156°47W 74 A8
Barrow → Ireland 52°25N 6°58W 10 D5
Barrow, Pt. U.S.A. 71°23N 156°29W 74 A8
Barrow Creek Australia 21°30S 133°55E 62 C1
Barrow I. Australia 20°45S 115°20E 60 D2
Barrow-in-Furness U.K. 54°7N 3°14W 12 C4
Barrow Pt. Australia 14°20S 144°40E 62 A3
Barrow Ra. Australia 26°0S 127°40E 61 E4
Barrow Str. Canada 74°20N 95°0W 4 B3
Barry U.K. 51°24N 3°16W 13 F4
Barry's Bay Canada 45°29N 77°41W 82 A7
Barsat Pakistan 36°10N 72°45E 43 A5
Barsi India 18°10N 75°50E 44 E2
Barsoi India 25°48N 87°57E 41 G15
Barstow U.S.A. 34°54N 117°1W 79 L9
Bartica Guyana 6°25N 58°40W 92 B7
Bartle Frere Australia 17°27S 145°50E 62 B4
Bartlesville U.S.A. 36°45N 95°59W 84 C7
Bartlett Calif., U.S.A. 36°29N 118°2W 78 J8
Bartlett Tenn., U.S.A. 35°12N 89°52W 85 D10
Bartlett, L. Canada 63°5N 118°20W 70 A5
Barton U.S.A. 44°45N 72°11W 83 B12
Barton upon Humber U.K. 53°41N 0°25W 12 D7
Bartow U.S.A. 27°54N 81°50W 85 H14
Barú, Volcan Panama 8°55N 82°35W 88 E3
Barung, Nusa Indonesia 8°30S 113°30E 37 H15
Baruun Urt Mongolia 46°46N 113°15E 31 B11
Baruunsuu Mongolia 43°43N 105°35E 32 C3
Barwani India 22°2N 74°57E 42 H6
Barysaw Belarus 54°17N 28°28E 17 A15
Barzān Iraq 36°55N 44°3E 46 B5
Bāsa'idū Iran 26°35N 55°20E 47 E7
Basal Pakistan 33°33N 72°13E 42 C5
Basankusa Dem. Rep. of the Congo 1°5N 19°50E 54 D3
Basarabeasca Moldova 46°21N 28°58E 17 E15
Basarabia = Bessarabiya Moldova 47°0N 28°10E 17 E15
Basawa Afghan. 34°15N 70°50E 42 B4
Bascuñán, C. Chile 28°52S 71°35W 94 B1
Basel Switz. 47°35N 7°35E 20 C7
Bashākerd, Kūhhā-ye Iran 26°42N 58°35E 47 E8
Bashaw Canada 52°35N 112°58W 70 C6
Bāshī Iran 28°41N 51°4E 47 D6
Bashkir Republic = Bashkortostan □ Russia 54°0N 57°0E 18 D10
Bashkortostan □ Russia 54°0N 57°0E 18 D10
Basilan I. Phil. 6°35N 122°0E 37 C6
Basilan Str. Phil. 6°50N 122°0E 37 C6
Basildon U.K. 51°34N 0°28E 13 F8
Basim = Washim India 20°3N 77°0E 44 D3
Basin U.S.A. 44°23N 108°2W 76 D9
Basingstoke U.K. 51°15N 1°5W 13 F6
Baskatong, Rés. Canada 46°46N 75°50W 72 C4
Basle = Basel Switz. 47°35N 7°35E 20 C7
Basmat India 19°15N 77°12E 44 E3
Basoda India 23°52N 77°54E 42 H7
Basque Provinces = País Vasco □ Spain 42°50N 2°45W 21 A4
Basra = Al Başrah Iraq 30°30N 47°50E 46 D5
Bass Str. Australia 39°15S 146°30E 63 F4
Bassano Canada 50°48N 112°20W 70 C6
Bassano del Grappa Italy 45°46N 11°44E 22 B4
Bassas da India Ind. Oc. 22°0S 39°0E 57 B6
Basse-Pointe Martinique 14°52N 61°8W 88 c
Basse-Terre Guadeloupe 16°0N 61°44W 88 b
Basse Terre Trin. & Tob. 10°7N 61°19W 93 K15
Bassein Burma 16°45N 94°30E 41 L19
Basses, Pte. des Guadeloupe 15°52N 61°17W 88 b
Basseterre St. Kitts & Nevis 17°17N 62°43W 89 C7
Bassett U.S.A. 42°35N 99°32W 80 D4
Bassi India 30°44N 76°21E 42 D7
Bastak Iran 27°15N 54°25E 47 E7
Baştām Iran 36°29N 55°4E 47 B7
Bastar India 19°15N 81°40E 44 E5
Basti India 26°52N 82°55E 43 F10
Bastia France 42°40N 9°30E 20 E8
Bastogne Belgium 50°1N 5°43E 15 D5
Bastrop La., U.S.A. 32°47N 91°55W 84 E9
Bastrop Tex., U.S.A. 30°7N 97°19W 84 F6
Basuo = Dongfang China 18°50N 108°33E 38 C7
Bat Yam Israel 32°2N 34°44E 48 C3
Bata Eq. Guin. 1°57N 9°50E 54 D1
Bataan □ Phil. 14°40N 120°25E 37 B6
Batabanó Cuba 22°41N 82°18W 88 B3
Batabanó, G. de Cuba 22°30N 82°30W 88 B3
Batac Phil. 18°3N 120°34E 37 A6
Batagai Russia 67°38N 134°38E 27 C14
Batala India 31°48N 75°12E 42 D6
Batamay Russia 63°30N 129°15E 27 C13
Batang China 30°1N 99°0E 34 B2
Batang Indonesia 6°55S 109°45E 37 G13
Batangafo C.A.R. 7°25N 18°20E 54 C3
Batangas Phil. 13°35N 121°10E 37 B6
Batanta Indonesia 0°55S 130°40E 37 E8
Batatais Brazil 20°54S 47°37W 95 A6
Batavia U.S.A. 43°0N 78°11W 82 D6
Batchelor Australia 13°4S 131°1E 60 B5
Batdambang Cambodia 13°7N 103°12E 38 F4
Batemans B. Australia 35°40S 150°12E 63 F5
Batemans Bay Australia 35°44S 150°11E 63 F5
Batesburg-Leesville U.S.A. 33°54N 81°33W 85 E14
Batesville Ark., U.S.A. 35°46N 91°39W 84 D9
Batesville Miss., U.S.A. 34°19N 89°57W 85 D10
Batesville Tex., U.S.A. 28°58N 99°37W 84 G5
Bath Canada 44°11N 76°47W 83 B8
Bath U.K. 51°23N 2°22W 13 F5
Bath Maine, U.S.A. 43°55N 69°49W 81 D19
Bath N.Y., U.S.A. 42°20N 77°19W 82 D7
Bath & North East Somerset □ U.K. 51°21N 2°27W 13 F5
Batheay Cambodia 11°59N 104°57E 39 G5
Bathsheba Barbados 13°13N 59°32W 89 g
Bathurst Australia 33°25S 149°31E 63 E4
Bathurst Canada 47°37N 65°43W 73 C6
Bathurst S. Africa 33°30S 26°50E 56 D4
Bathurst, C. Canada 70°34N 128°0W 68 C6
Bathurst B. Australia 14°16S 144°25E 62 A3
Bathurst Harb. Australia 43°15S 146°10E 63 G4
Bathurst I. Australia 11°30S 130°10E 60 B5
Bathurst I. Canada 76°0N 100°30W 69 B11
Bathurst Inlet Canada 66°50N 108°1W 68 D10
Batiki Fiji 17°48S 179°10E 59 a
Batlow Australia 35°31S 148°9E 63 F4
Batman Turkey 37°55N 41°5E 46 B4
Baṭn al Ghūl Jordan 29°36N 35°56E 48 F4
Batna Algeria 35°34N 6°15E 52 A7
Baton Rouge U.S.A. 30°27N 91°11W 84 F9
Batong, Ko Thailand 6°32N 99°12E 39 J2
Batopilas Mexico 27°1N 107°44W 86 B3
Batouri Cameroon 4°30N 14°25E 54 D2
Båtsfjord Norway 70°38N 29°39E 8 A23
Battambang = Batdambang Cambodia 13°7N 103°12E 38 F4
Batti Malv India 8°50N 92°51E 45 K11
Batticaloa Sri Lanka 7°43N 81°45E 45 L5
Battipáglia Italy 40°37N 14°58E 22 D6
Battle U.K. 50°55N 0°30E 13 G8
Battle → Canada 52°43N 108°15W 71 C7
Battle Creek U.S.A. 42°19N 85°11W 81 D11
Battle Ground U.S.A. 45°47N 122°32W 78 E4
Battle Harbour Canada 52°16N 55°35W 73 B8
Battle Lake U.S.A. 46°17N 95°43W 80 B6
Battle Mountain U.S.A. 40°38N 116°56W 76 F5
Battleford Canada 52°45N 108°15W 71 C7
Batu Ethiopia 6°55N 39°45E 49 F2
Batu Malaysia 3°15N 101°40E 39 L3
Batu, Kepulauan Indonesia 0°30S 98°25E 36 E1
Batu Ferringhi Malaysia 5°28N 100°15E 39 c
Batu Gajah Malaysia 4°28N 101°3E 39 K3
Batu Is. = Batu, Kepulauan Indonesia 0°30S 98°25E 36 E1
Batu Pahat Malaysia 1°50N 102°56E 39 M4
Batu Puteh, Gunung Malaysia 4°15N 101°31E 39 K3
Batuata Indonesia 6°12S 122°42E 37 F6
Batugondang, Tanjung Indonesia 8°6S 114°29E 37 J17
Batukaru, Gunung Indonesia 8°20S 115°5E 37 J18
Batumi Georgia 41°39N 41°44E 19 F7
Batur, Gunung Indonesia 8°14S 115°23E 37 J18
Batura Sar Pakistan 36°30N 74°31E 43 A6
Baturaja Indonesia 4°11S 104°15E 36 E2
Baturité Brazil 4°28S 38°45W 93 D11
Baturiti Indonesia 8°19S 115°11E 37 J18
Bau Malaysia 1°25N 110°9E 36 D4
Baubau Indonesia 5°25S 122°38E 37 F6
Baucau E. Timor 8°27S 126°27E 37 F7
Bauchi Nigeria 10°22N 9°48E 52 F7
Bauda India 20°50N 84°25E 44 D7
Baudette U.S.A. 48°43N 94°36W 80 A6
Bauer, C. Australia 32°44S 134°4E 63 E1
Bauhinia Australia 24°35S 149°18E 62 C4
Baukau = Baucau E. Timor 8°27S 126°27E 37 F7
Bauld, C. Canada 51°38N 55°26W 69 G20
Bauru Brazil 22°10S 49°0W 95 A6
Bausi India 24°48N 87°1E 43 G12
Bauska Latvia 56°24N 24°15E 9 H21
Bautzen Germany 51°10N 14°26E 16 C8
Bavānāt Iran 30°28N 53°27E 47 D7
Bavaria = Bayern □ Germany 48°50N 12°0E 16 D6
Bavispe → Mexico 29°15N 109°11W 86 B3
Bawdwin Burma 23°5N 97°20E 41 H20
Bawean Indonesia 5°46S 112°35E 36 F4
Bawku Ghana 11°3N 0°19W 52 F5
Bawlakhe Burma 19°11N 97°21E 41 K20
Bawolung China 28°50N 101°16E 34 C3
Baxley U.S.A. 31°47N 82°21W 85 F13
Baxter U.S.A. 46°21N 94°17W 80 B6
Baxter Springs U.S.A. 37°2N 94°44W 80 G6
Baxter State ⌂ U.S.A. 46°5N 68°57W 81 B19
Bay City Mich., U.S.A. 43°36N 83°54W 81 D12
Bay City Tex., U.S.A. 28°59N 95°58W 84 G7
Bay Minette U.S.A. 30°53N 87°46W 85 F11
Bay Roberts Canada 47°36N 53°16W 73 C9
Bay St. Louis U.S.A. 30°19N 89°20W 85 F10
Bay Springs U.S.A. 31°59N 89°17W 85 F10
Bay View N.Z. 39°25S 176°50E 59 C6
Bayamo Cuba 20°20N 76°40W 88 B4
Bayamón Puerto Rico 18°24N 66°9W 89 d
Bayan Har Shan China 34°0N 98°0E 30 E8
Bayan Hot = Alxa Zuoqi China 38°50N 105°40E 32 E3
Bayan Lepas Malaysia 5°17N 100°16E 39 c
Bayan Obo China 41°52N 109°59E 32 D5
Bayan-Ovoo = Erdenetsogt Mongolia 42°55N 106°5E 32 C4
Bayana India 26°55N 77°18E 42 F7
Bayanaūyl Kazakhstan 50°45N 75°45E 26 D8
Bayanhongor Mongolia 46°8N 102°43E 30 B9
Bayard N. Mex., U.S.A. 32°46N 108°8W 77 K9
Bayard Nebr., U.S.A. 41°45N 103°20W 80 E2
Baybay Phil. 10°40N 124°55E 37 B6
Baydaratskaya Guba Russia 69°0N 67°30E 26 C7
Baydhabo Somalia 3°8N 43°30E 49 G3
Bayern □ Germany 48°50N 12°0E 16 D6
Bayeux France 49°17N 0°42W 20 B3
Bayfield Canada 43°34N 81°42W 82 C3
Bayfield U.S.A. 46°49N 90°49W 80 B8
Bayındır Turkey 38°13N 27°39E 23 E12
Baykal, Oz. Russia 53°0N 108°0E 27 D11
Baykan Turkey 38°7N 41°44E 46 B4
Baymak Russia 52°36N 58°19E 18 D10
Baynes Mts. Namibia 17°15S 13°0E 56 A1
Bayombong Phil. 16°30N 121°10E 37 A6
Bayonne France 43°30N 1°28W 20 E3
Bayovar Peru 5°50S 81°0W 92 E2
Bayqonyr Kazakhstan 45°40N 63°20E 26 E7
Bayram-Ali = Baýramaly Turkmenistan 37°37N 62°10E 47 B9
Baýramaly Turkmenistan 37°37N 62°10E 47 B9
Bayramiç Turkey 39°48N 26°36E 23 E12
Bayreuth Germany 49°56N 11°35E 16 D6
Bayrūt Lebanon 33°53N 35°31E 48 B4
Bays, L. of Canada 45°15N 79°4W 82 A5
Baysville Canada 45°9N 79°7W 82 A5
Baytown U.S.A. 29°43N 94°59W 84 G7
Baza Spain 37°30N 2°47W 21 D4
Bazaruto, I. do Mozam. 21°40S 35°28E 57 B6
Bazaruto △ Mozam. 21°42S 35°26E 57 B6
Bazhong China 31°52N 106°46E 34 B6
Bazhou China 39°8N 116°22E 32 E9
Bazmān, Kūh-e Iran 28°4N 60°1E 47 D9
Bé, Nosy Madag. 13°25S 48°15E 55 G9
Beach U.S.A. 46°58N 104°0W 80 B2
Beach City U.S.A. 40°39N 81°35W 82 F3
Beachport Australia 37°29S 140°0E 63 F3
Beachville Canada 43°5N 80°49W 82 C4
Beachy Hd. U.K. 50°44N 0°15E 13 G8
Beacon Australia 30°26S 117°52E 61 F2
Beacon U.S.A. 41°30N 73°58W 83 E11
Beaconsfield Australia 41°11S 146°48E 63 G4
Beagle, Canal S. Amer. 55°0S 68°30W 96 H3
Beagle Bay Australia 16°58S 122°40E 60 C3
Beagle Bay ✿ Australia 16°53S 122°40E 60 C3
Beagle G. Australia 12°15S 130°25E 60 B5
Béal an Átha = Ballina Ireland 54°7N 9°9W 10 B2
Béal Átha na Sluaighe = Ballinasloe Ireland 53°20N 8°13W 10 C3
Beals Cr. → U.S.A. 32°10N 100°51W 84 E4
Beamsville Canada 43°12N 79°28W 82 C5
Bear → Calif., U.S.A. 38°56N 121°36W 78 G5
Bear → Utah, U.S.A. 41°30N 112°8W 74 G17
Bear I. Ireland 51°38N 9°50W 10 E2
Bear L. Canada 55°8N 96°0W 71 B9
Bear L. U.S.A. 41°59N 111°21W 76 F8
Bear Lake Canada 45°27N 79°35W 82 A5
Beardmore Canada 49°36N 87°57W 72 C2
Beardmore Glacier Antarctica 84°30S 170°0E 5 E11
Beardstown U.S.A. 40°1N 90°26W 80 E8
Bearma → India 24°20N 79°51E 43 G8
Béarn France 43°20N 0°30W 20 E3
Bearpaw Mts. U.S.A. 48°12N 109°30W 76 B9
Bearskin Lake Canada 53°58N 91°2W 72 B1
Beas → India 31°10N 74°59E 42 D6
Beata, C. Dom. Rep. 17°40N 71°30W 89 C5
Beata, I. Dom. Rep. 17°34N 71°31W 89 C5
Beatrice U.S.A. 40°16N 96°45W 80 E5
Beatrice, C. Australia 14°20S 136°55E 62 A2
Beatton → Canada 56°15N 120°45W 70 B4
Beatton River Canada 57°26N 121°20W 70 B4
Beatty U.S.A. 36°54N 116°46W 78 J10
Beau Bassin Mauritius 20°13S 57°27E 55 d
Beauce, Plaine de la France 48°10N 1°45E 20 B4
Beauceville Canada 46°13N 70°46W 73 C5
Beaudesert Australia 27°59S 153°0E 63 D5
Beaufort Malaysia 5°30N 115°40E 36 C5
Beaufort N.C., U.S.A. 34°43N 76°40W 85 D16
Beaufort S.C., U.S.A. 32°26N 80°40W 85 E14
Beaufort Sea Arctic 72°0N 140°0W 66 B5
Beaufort West S. Africa 32°18S 22°36E 56 D3
Beauharnois Canada 45°20N 73°52W 83 A11
Beaulieu → Canada 62°3N 113°11W 70 A6
Beauly U.K. 57°30N 4°28W 11 D4
Beauly → U.K. 57°29N 4°27W 11 D4
Beaumaris U.K. 53°16N 4°6W 12 D3
Beaumont Belgium 50°15N 4°14E 15 D4
Beaumont Calif., U.S.A. 33°57N 116°59W 79 M9
Beaumont Tex., U.S.A. 30°5N 94°6W 84 F7
Beaune France 47°2N 4°50E 20 C6
Beaupré Canada 47°3N 70°54W 73 C5
Beauraing Belgium 50°7N 4°57E 15 D4
Beausejour Canada 50°5N 96°35W 71 C9
Beauvais France 49°25N 2°8E 20 B5
Beauval Canada 55°9N 107°37W 71 B7
Beaver Okla., U.S.A. 36°49N 100°31W 84 C4
Beaver Pa., U.S.A. 40°42N 80°19W 82 F4
Beaver Utah, U.S.A. 38°17N 112°38W 76 G7
Beaver → B.C., Canada 59°52N 124°20W 70 B4
Beaver → Ont., Canada 55°55N 87°48W 72 A2
Beaver → Sask., Canada 55°26N 107°45W 71 B7
Beaver → U.S.A. 36°35N 99°30W 84 C5
Beaver City U.S.A. 40°8N 99°50W 80 E4
Beaver Creek Canada 63°0N 141°0W 68 E3
Beaver Dam U.S.A. 43°28N 88°50W 80 D9
Beaver Falls U.S.A. 40°46N 80°20W 82 F4
Beaver Hill L. Canada 54°5N 94°50W 71 C10
Beaver I. U.S.A. 45°40N 85°33W 81 C11
Beavercreek U.S.A. 39°43N 84°11W 81 F11
Beaverhill L. Canada 53°27N 112°32W 70 C6
Beaverlodge Canada 55°11N 119°29W 70 B5
Beaverstone → Canada 54°59N 89°25W 72 B2
Beaverton Canada 44°26N 79°9W 82 B5
Beaverton U.S.A. 45°29N 122°48W 78 E4
Beawar India 26°3N 74°18E 42 F6
Bebedouro Brazil 21°0S 48°25W 95 A6
Bebera, Tanjung Indonesia 8°44S 115°51E 37 K18
Becán Mexico 18°34N 89°31W 87 D7
Bécancour Canada 46°20N 72°26W 81 B17
Beccles U.K. 52°27N 1°35E 13 E9
Bečej Serbia 45°36N 20°3E 23 B9
Béchar Algeria 31°38N 2°18W 52 B5
Becharof L. U.S.A. 57°56N 156°23W 74 D8
Becharre = Bsharri Lebanon 34°15N 36°0E 48 A5
Beckley U.S.A. 37°47N 81°11W 81 G13
Beddouza, C. Morocco 32°33N 9°9W 52 B4
Bedford Canada 45°7N 72°59W 83 A12
Bedford S. Africa 32°40S 26°10E 56 D4
Bedford U.K. 52°8N 0°28W 13 E7
Bedford Ind., U.S.A. 38°52N 86°29W 80 F10
Bedford Iowa, U.S.A. 40°40N 94°44W 80 E6
Bedford Ohio, U.S.A. 41°23N 81°32W 82 E3
Bedford Pa., U.S.A. 40°1N 78°30W 82 F6
Bedford Va., U.S.A. 37°20N 79°31W 81 G14
Bedford □ U.K. 52°4N 0°28W 13 E7
Bedford, C. Australia 15°14S 145°21E 62 B4
Bedourie Australia 24°30S 139°30E 62 C2
Bedti → India 14°50N 74°44E 45 G2
Bedugul Indonesia 8°17S 115°10E 37 J18
Bedum Neths. 53°18N 6°36E 15 A6
Beebe Plain Canada 45°1N 72°9W 83 A12
Beech Creek U.S.A. 41°5N 77°36W 82 E7
Beechy Canada 50°53N 107°24W 71 C7
Beed = Bir India 19°4N 75°46E 44 E2
Beef I. Br. Virgin Is. 18°26N 64°30W 89 e
Beenleigh Australia 27°43S 153°10E 63 D5
Be'er Menuḥa Israel 30°19N 35°8E 46 D2
Be'er Sheva Israel 31°15N 34°48E 48 D3
Beersheba = Be'er Sheva Israel 31°15N 34°48E 48 D3
Beestekraal S. Africa 25°23S 27°38E 57 C4
Beeston U.K. 52°56N 1°14W 12 E6
Beeton Canada 44°5N 79°47W 82 B5
Beeville U.S.A. 28°24N 97°45W 84 G6
Befale Dem. Rep. of the Congo 0°25N 20°45E 54 D4
Bega Australia 36°41S 149°51E 63 F4
Begusarai India 25°24N 86°9E 43 G12
Behābād Iran 32°24N 59°47E 47 C8
Behbehān Iran 30°30N 50°15E 47 D6
Behm Canal U.S.A. 55°10N 131°0W 70 B2
Behshahr Iran 36°45N 53°35E 47 B7
Bei Jiang → China 23°2N 112°58E 35 F9
Bei Shan China 41°30N 96°0E 30 C8
Bei'an China 48°10N 126°20E 31 B14
Beibei China 29°47N 106°22E 34 C6
Beichuan China 31°55N 104°39E 34 B5
Beihai China 21°28N 109°6E 34 G7
Beijing China 39°55N 116°20E 32 E9
Beijing □ China 39°55N 116°20E 32 E9
Beilen Neths. 52°52N 6°27E 15 B6
Beiliu China 22°41N 110°21E 35 F8
Beilpajah Australia 32°54S 143°52E 63 E3
Beinn na Faoghla = Benbecula U.K. 57°26N 7°21W 11 D1
Beipan Jiang → China 24°55N 106°5E 34 E6
Beipiao China 41°52N 120°32E 33 D11
Beira Mozam. 19°50S 34°52E 55 H6
Beirut = Bayrūt Lebanon 33°53N 35°31E 48 B4
Beiseker Canada 51°23N 113°32W 70 C6
Beit Lāhīyā Gaza Strip 31°33N 34°30E 48 D3
Beitaolaizhao China 44°58N 125°58E 33 B13
Beitbridge Zimbabwe 22°12S 30°0E 55 J6
Beizhen = Binzhou China 37°20N 118°2E 33 F10
Beizhen China 41°38N 121°54E 33 D11
Beizhengzhen China 44°31N 123°30E 33 B12
Beja Portugal 38°2N 7°53W 21 C2
Béja Tunisia 36°43N 9°12E 53 A7
Bejaïa Algeria 36°42N 5°2E 52 A7
Béjar Spain 40°23N 5°46W 21 B3
Bejestān Iran 34°30N 58°5E 47 C8
Bekaa Valley = Al Biqā Lebanon 34°10N 36°10E 48 A5
Bekasi Indonesia 6°14S 106°59E 37 G12
Békéscsaba Hungary 46°40N 21°5E 17 E11
Bekok Malaysia 2°20N 103°7E 39 L4
Bela India 25°50N 82°0E 43 G10
Bela Pakistan 26°12N 66°20E 42 F2
Bela Bela S. Africa 24°51S 28°19E 57 B4
Bela Crkva Serbia 44°55N 21°27E 23 B9
Bela Vista Brazil 22°12S 56°20W 94 A4
Bela Vista Mozam. 26°10S 32°44E 57 C5
Belan → India 24°2N 81°45E 43 G9
Belarus ■ Europe 53°30N 27°0E 17 B14
Belau = Palau ■ Palau 7°30N 134°30E 58 A6
Belawan Indonesia 3°33N 98°32E 36 D1
Belaya → Russia 54°40N 56°0E 18 C9
Belaya Tserkov = Bila Tserkva Ukraine 49°45N 30°10E 17 D16
Belaya Zemlya, Ostrova Russia 81°36N 62°18E 26 A7
Belcher Is. Canada 56°15N 78°45W 72 A3
Belden U.S.A. 40°2N 121°17W 78 E5
Belebey Russia 54°7N 54°7E 18 D9
Beledweyne Somalia 4°30N 45°5E 49 G4
Belém Brazil 1°20S 48°30W 93 D9
Belén Argentina 27°40S 67°5W 94 B2
Belén Paraguay 23°30S 57°6W 94 A4
Belen U.S.A. 34°40N 106°46W 77 J10
Belet Uen = Beledweyne Somalia 4°30N 45°5E 49 G4
Belev Russia 53°50N 36°5E 18 D6
Belfair U.S.A. 47°27N 122°50W 78 C4
Belfast = eMakhazeni S. Africa 25°42S 30°2E 57 C5
Belfast U.K. 54°37N 5°56W 10 B6
Belfast Maine, U.S.A. 44°26N 69°1W 81 C19
Belfast N.Y., U.S.A. 42°21N 78°7W 82 D6
Belfast L. U.K. 54°40N 5°50W 10 B6
Belfield U.S.A. 46°53N 103°12W 80 B2
Belfort France 47°38N 6°50E 20 C7
Belfry U.S.A. 45°9N 109°1W 76 D9
Belgaum India 15°55N 74°35E 45 G2
Belgavi = Belgaum India 15°55N 74°35E 45 G2
Belgium ■ Europe 50°30N 5°0E 15 D4
Belgorod Russia 50°35N 36°35E 19 D6
Belgorod-Dnestrovskiy = Bilhorod-Dnistrovskyy Ukraine 46°11N 30°23E 19 E5
Belgrade = Beograd Serbia 44°50N 20°37E 23 B9
Belgrade U.S.A. 45°47N 111°11W 76 D8
Belgrano Antarctica 77°52S 34°37W 5 D1
Belhaven U.S.A. 35°33N 76°37W 85 D16
Beli Drim → Europe 42°6N 20°25E 23 C9
Belimbing Indonesia 8°24S 115°2E 37 J18
Belinyu Indonesia 1°35S 105°50E 36 E3
Beliton Is. = Belitung Indonesia 3°10S 107°50E 36 E3
Belitung Indonesia 3°10S 107°50E 36 E3
Belize ■ Cent. Amer. 17°0N 88°30W 87 D7
Belize Barrier Reef Belize 17°9N 88°3W 87 D7
Belize City Belize 17°25N 88°10W 87 D7
Belkovskiy, Ostrov Russia 75°32N 135°44E 27 B14
Bell → Canada 49°48N 77°38W 72 C4
Bell I. Canada 50°46N 55°35W 73 B8
Bell-Irving → Canada 56°12N 129°5W 70 B3
Bell Peninsula Canada 63°50N 82°0W 69 E15
Bell Ville Argentina 32°40S 62°40W 94 C3
Bella Bella Canada 52°10N 128°10W 70 C3
Bella Coola Canada 52°25N 126°40W 70 C3
Bella Unión Uruguay 30°15S 57°40W 94 C4
Bella Vista Corrientes, Argentina 28°33S 59°0W 94 B4
Bella Vista Tucuman, Argentina 27°10S 65°25W 94 B2
Bella Vista U.S.A. 36°28N 94°16W 80 G6
Bellaire U.S.A. 40°1N 80°45W 82 F4
Bellary India 15°10N 76°56E 45 G3
Bellata Australia 29°53S 149°46E 63 D4
Belle Fourche U.S.A. 44°40N 103°51W 80 C2
Belle Fourche → U.S.A. 44°26N 102°18W 80 C2
Belle Glade U.S.A. 26°41N 80°40W 85 H14
Belle-Île France 47°20N 3°10W 20 C2
Belle Isle Canada 51°57N 55°25W 73 B8
Belle Isle, Str. of Canada 51°30N 56°30W 73 B8
Belle Plaine U.S.A. 41°54N 92°17W 80 E7
Belle River Canada 42°18N 82°43W 82 D2
Bellefontaine U.S.A. 40°22N 83°46W 81 E12
Bellefonte U.S.A. 40°55N 77°47W 82 F7
Belleoram Canada 47°31N 55°25W 73 C8
Belleplaine Barbados 13°15N 59°34W 89 g
Belleville Canada 44°10N 77°23W 82 B7
Belleville Ill., U.S.A. 38°31N 89°59W 80 F9
Belleville Kans., U.S.A. 39°50N 97°38W 80 F5
Belleville N.J., U.S.A. 40°47N 74°9W 83 F10
Belleville N.Y., U.S.A. 43°46N 76°10W 83 C8
Bellevue Idaho, U.S.A. 43°28N 114°16W 76 E6
Bellevue Nebr., U.S.A. 41°9N 95°54W 80 E6
Bellevue Ohio, U.S.A. 41°17N 82°51W 82 E2
Bellevue Wash., U.S.A. 47°37N 122°12W 78 C4
Bellin = Kangirsuk Canada 60°0N 70°0W 69 F18
Bellingen Australia 30°25S 152°50E 63 E5
Bellingham U.S.A. 48°46N 122°29W 78 B4
Bellingshausen Abyssal Plain S. Ocean 64°0S 90°0W 5 C16
Bellingshausen Sea Antarctica 66°0S 80°0W 5 C17
Bellinzona Switz. 46°11N 9°1E 20 C8
Bello Colombia 6°20N 75°33W 92 B3
Bellows Falls U.S.A. 43°8N 72°27W 83 C12
Bellpat Pakistan 29°0N 68°5E 42 E3
Belluno Italy 46°9N 12°13E 22 A5
Bellwood U.S.A. 40°36N 78°20W 82 F6
Belmont Canada 42°53N 81°5W 82 D3
Belmont S. Africa 29°28S 24°22E 56 C3
Belmont U.S.A. 42°14N 78°2W 82 D6
Belmonte Brazil 16°0S 39°0W 93 G11
Belmopan Belize 17°18N 88°30W 87 D7
Belmullet Ireland 54°14N 9°58W 10 B2
Belo Horizonte Brazil 19°55S 43°56W 93 G10
Belo-Tsiribihina Madag. 19°40S 44°30E 55 H8
Belogorsk Russia 51°0N 128°20E 27 D13
Beloit Kans., U.S.A. 39°28N 98°6W 80 F4
Beloit Wis., U.S.A. 42°31N 89°2W 80 D9
Belokorovichi Ukraine 51°7N 28°2E 17 C15
Belomorsk Russia 64°35N 34°54E 18 B5
Belonia India 23°15N 91°30E 41 H17
Beloretsk Russia 53°58N 58°24E 18 D10
Belorussia = Belarus ■ Europe 53°30N 27°0E 17 B14
Belovo Russia 54°30N 86°0E 26 D9

Beloyarskiy Russia 63°42N 66°40E **26 C7**
Beloye, Ozero Russia 60°10N 37°35E **18 B6**
Beloye More Russia 66°30N 38°0E **18 A6**
Belozersk Russia 60°1N 37°45E **18 B6**
Belpre U.S.A. 39°17N 81°34W **81 F13**
Belrain India 28°23N 80°55E **43 E9**
Belt U.S.A. 47°23N 110°55W **76 C8**
Beltana Australia 30°48S 138°25E **63 E2**
Belterra Brazil 2°45S 55°0W **93 D8**
Belton Brazil 31°3N 97°28W **84 F6**
Belton L. U.S.A. 31°6N 97°28W **84 F6**
Beltsy = Bălți Moldova 47°48N 27°58E **17 E14**
Belturbet Ireland 54°6N 7°26W **10 B4**
Belukha Russia 49°50N 86°50E **30 E9**
Beluran Malaysia 5°48N 117°35E **36 C5**
Belushya Guba Russia 71°32N 52°19E **26 B6**
Belvidere Ill., U.S.A. 42°15N 88°50W **80 D9**
Belvidere N.J., U.S.A. 40°50N 75°5W **83 F9**
Belyando → Australia 21°38S 146°50E **62 C4**
Belyando Crossing
  Australia 21°32S 146°51E **62 C4**
Belyuen Australia 12°34S 130°42E **60 B5**
Belyy, Ostrov Russia 73°30N 71°0E **26 B8**
Belyy Yar Russia 58°26N 84°39E **26 D9**
Belzoni U.S.A. 33°11N 90°29W **85 E9**
Bembéréke Benin 10°11N 2°43E **52 F6**
Bemetara India 21°42N 81°32E **43 J9**
Bemidji U.S.A. 47°28N 94°53W **80 B6**
Ben Iran 32°32N 50°45E **47 C6**
Ben Cruachan U.K. 56°26N 5°8W **11 E3**
Ben Dearg U.K. 57°47N 4°56W **11 D4**
Ben En △ Vietnam 19°37N 105°30E **38 C5**
Ben Gardane Tunisia 33°11N 11°11E **53 B8**
Ben Hope U.K. 58°25N 4°36W **11 C4**
Ben Lawers U.K. 56°32N 4°14W **11 E4**
Ben Lomond N.S.W.,
  Australia 30°1S 151°43E **63 E5**
Ben Lomond Tas.,
  Australia 41°38S 147°42E **63 G4**
Ben Lomond U.K. 56°11N 4°38W **11 E4**
Ben Lomond △ Australia 41°33S 147°39E **63 G4**
Ben Luc Vietnam 10°39N 106°29E **39 G6**
Ben Macdhui U.K. 57°4N 3°40W **11 D5**
Ben Mhor U.K. 57°15N 7°18W **11 D1**
Ben More Argyll & Bute,
  U.K. 56°26N 6°1W **11 E2**
Ben More Stirling, U.K. 56°23N 4°32W **11 E4**
Ben More Assynt U.K. 58°8N 4°52W **11 C4**
Ben Nevis U.K. 56°48N 5°1W **11 E3**
Ben Quang Vietnam 17°3N 106°55E **38 D6**
Ben Tre Vietnam 10°14N 106°23E **39 G6**
Ben Vorlich U.K. 56°21N 4°14W **11 E4**
Ben Wyvis U.K. 57°40N 4°35W **11 D4**
Bena Nigeria 11°20N 5°50E **52 F7**
Benalla Australia 36°30S 146°0E **63 F4**
Benares = Varanasi India 25°22N 83°0E **43 G10**
Benavente Spain 42°2N 5°43W **21 A3**
Benavides U.S.A. 27°36N 98°25W **84 H5**
Benbecula U.K. 57°26N 7°21W **11 D1**
Benbonyathe Hill
  Australia 30°25S 139°11E **63 E2**
Bend U.S.A. 44°4N 121°19W **76 D3**
Bender Beyla Somalia 9°30N 50°48E **49 F5**
Bendery = Tighina
  Moldova 46°50N 29°30E **17 E15**
Bendigo Australia 36°40S 144°15E **63 F3**
Bene Beraq Israel 32°6N 34°51E **48 C3**
Benevento Italy 41°8N 14°45E **22 D6**
Beng Mealea Cambodia 13°28N 104°14E **38 F5**
Bengal, Bay of Ind. Oc. 15°0N 90°0E **41 M17**
Bengaluru = Bangalore
  India 12°59N 77°40E **45 H3**
Bengbu China 32°58N 117°20E **33 H9**
Benghazi = Banghāzī
  Libya 32°11N 20°3E **53 B10**
Bengkalis Indonesia 1°30N 102°10E **39 M4**
Bengkulu Indonesia 3°50S 102°12E **36 E2**
Bengkulu □ Indonesia 3°48S 102°16E **36 E2**
Bengough Canada 49°25N 105°10W **71 D7**
Benguela Angola 12°37S 13°25E **55 G2**
Benguérua, I. Mozam. 21°58S 35°28E **57 B6**
Beni Dem. Rep. of the Congo 0°30N 29°27E **54 D5**
Beni → Bolivia 10°23S 65°24W **92 F5**
Beni Mellal Morocco 32°21N 6°21W **52 B4**
Beni Suef Egypt 29°5N 31°6E **53 C12**
Beniah L. Canada 63°23N 112°17W **70 A6**
Benidorm Spain 38°33N 0°9W **21 C5**
Benin ■ Africa 10°0N 2°0E **52 G6**
Benin, Bight of W. Afr. 5°0N 3°0E **52 H6**
Benin City Nigeria 6°20N 5°31E **52 G7**
Benito Juárez Argentina 37°40S 59°43W **94 D4**
Benjamin Aceval
  Paraguay 24°58S 57°34W **94 A4**
Benjamin Constant Brazil 4°40S 70°15W **92 D4**
Benjamín Hill Mexico 30°9N 111°7W **86 A2**
Benkelman U.S.A. 40°3N 101°32W **80 E3**
Bennett Canada 59°51N 135°0W **70 B2**
Bennett, L. Australia 22°50S 131°2E **60 D5**
Bennetta, Ostrov
  Russia 76°21N 148°56E **27 B15**
Bennettsville U.S.A. 34°37N 79°41W **85 D15**
Bennington N.H., U.S.A. 43°N 71°55W **83 D12**
Bennington Vt., U.S.A. 42°53N 73°12W **83 D11**
Benom Malaysia 3°50N 102°6E **39 L4**
Benoni S. Africa 26°11S 28°18E **57 C4**
Benque Viejo del Carmen
  Belize 17°5N 89°8W **87 D7**
Benson Ariz., U.S.A. 31°58N 110°18W **77 L8**
Benson Minn., U.S.A. 45°19N 95°36W **80 C6**
Bent Iran 26°20N 59°31E **47 E8**
Benteng Indonesia 6°10S 120°30E **37 F6**
Bentinck I. Australia 17°3S 139°35E **62 B2**
Bentinck I. Burma 11°45N 98°3E **39 G2**
Bentley Subglacial Trench
  Antarctica 80°0S 115°0W **5 E15**
Bento Gonçalves Brazil 29°10S 51°31W **95 B5**
Benton Ark., U.S.A. 34°34N 92°35W **84 D8**
Benton Calif., U.S.A. 37°48N 118°32W **78 H8**
Benton Ill., U.S.A. 38°0N 88°55W **80 F9**

Benton Pa., U.S.A. 41°12N 76°23W **83 E8**
Benton Harbor U.S.A. 42°6N 86°27W **80 D10**
Bentong Malaysia 3°31N 101°55E **39 L3**
Bentonville U.S.A. 36°22N 94°13W **84 C7**
Benue → Nigeria 7°48N 6°46E **52 G7**
Benxi China 41°20N 123°48E **33 D12**
Beo Indonesia 4°25N 126°50E **37 D7**
Beograd Serbia 44°50N 20°37E **23 B9**
Beolgyo S. Korea 34°51N 127°21E **33 G14**
Beppu Japan 33°15N 131°30E **29 H5**
Beqa Fiji 18°23S 178°8E **59 a**
Beqaa Valley = Al Biqâ
  Lebanon 34°10N 36°10E **48 A5**
Ber Mota India 23°27N 68°34E **42 H3**
Bera, Tasik Malaysia 3°5N 102°38E **39 L4**
Berach → India 25°15N 75°2E **42 G6**
Berastagi Indonesia 3°11N 98°31E **39 L2**
Berat Albania 40°43N 19°59E **23 D8**
Berau = Tanjungredeb
  Indonesia 2°9N 117°29E **36 D5**
Berau, Teluk Indonesia 2°30S 132°30E **37 E8**
Berber Sudan 18°0N 34°0E **53 E12**
Berbera Somalia 10°30N 45°2E **49 E4**
Berbérati C.A.R. 4°15N 15°40E **54 D3**
Berbice → Guyana 6°20N 57°32W **92 B7**
Berdichev = Berdychiv
  Ukraine 49°57N 28°30E **17 D15**
Berdsk Russia 54°47N 83°2E **26 D9**
Berdyansk Ukraine 46°45N 36°50E **19 E6**
Berdychiv Ukraine 49°57N 28°30E **17 D15**
Berea U.S.A. 37°34N 84°17W **81 G11**
Berebere Indonesia 2°25N 128°45E **37 D7**
Bereeda Somalia 11°45N 51°0E **49 E5**
Berehove Ukraine 48°15N 22°35E **17 D12**
Bereket Turkmenistan 39°16N 55°32E **47 B7**
Berekum Ghana 7°29N 2°34W **52 G5**
Berens → Canada 52°25N 97°2W **71 C9**
Berens I. Canada 52°18N 97°18W **71 C9**
Berens River Canada 52°25N 97°0W **71 C9**
Beresford U.S.A. 43°5N 96°47W **80 D5**
Berestechko Ukraine 50°22N 25°5E **17 C13**
Bereza = Byaroza
  Belarus 52°31N 24°51E **17 B13**
Berezhany Ukraine 49°26N 24°58E **17 D13**
Berezina = Byarezina →
  Belarus 52°33N 30°14E **17 B16**
Bereznik Russia 62°51N 42°40E **18 B7**
Berezniki Russia 59°24N 56°46E **18 C10**
Berezovo Russia 64°0N 65°0E **26 C7**
Berga Spain 42°6N 1°48E **21 A6**
Bergama Turkey 39°8N 27°11E **23 E12**
Bérgamo Italy 45°41N 9°43E **20 D8**
Bergaon India 20°41N 80°27E **44 D5**
Bergen Neths. 52°40N 4°43E **15 B4**
Bergen Norway 60°20N 5°20E **8 F11**
Bergen U.S.A. 43°5N 77°57W **82 C7**
Bergen op Zoom Neths. 51°28N 4°18E **15 C4**
Bergerac France 44°51N 0°30E **20 D4**
Bergholz U.S.A. 40°31N 80°53W **82 F4**
Bergville S. Africa 28°52S 29°18E **57 C4**
Berhala, Selat Indonesia 1°0S 104°15E **36 E2**
Berhampore = Baharampur
  India 24°2N 88°27E **43 G13**
Berhampur = Brahmapur
  India 19°15N 84°54E **44 E7**
Bering Glacier U.S.A. 60°20N 143°30W **74 C11**
Bering Sea Pac. Oc. 58°0N 171°0W **66 D2**
Bering Strait Pac. Oc. 65°30N 169°0W **74 B6**
Beringovskiy Russia 63°3N 179°19E **27 C18**
Berisso Argentina 34°56S 57°50W **94 C4**
Berja Spain 36°50N 2°56W **21 D4**
Berkner I. Antarctica 79°30S 50°0W **5 D18**
Berkshire U.S.A. 42°19N 76°11W **83 D8**
Berkshire Downs U.K. 51°33N 1°29W **13 F6**
Berlin Md., U.S.A. 38°20N 75°13W **81 F16**
Berlin N.H., U.S.A. 44°28N 71°11W **83 B13**
Berlin N.Y., U.S.A. 42°42N 73°23W **83 D11**
Berlin Wis., U.S.A. 43°58N 88°57W **80 D9**
Berlin L. U.S.A. 41°3N 81°0W **82 E4**
Bermejo → Formosa,
  Argentina 26°51S 58°23W **94 B4**
Bermejo → San Juan,
  Argentina 32°30S 67°30W **94 C2**
Bermejo, Paso = Uspallata, P. de
  Argentina 32°37S 69°22W **94 C2**
Bermen, L. Canada 53°35N 68°55W **73 B6**
Bermuda ☑ Atl. Oc. 32°18N 64°45W **67 F13**
Bern Switz. 46°57N 7°28E **20 C7**
Bernalillo U.S.A. 35°18N 106°33W **77 J10**
Bernardo de Irigoyen
  Argentina 26°15S 53°40W **95 B5**
Bernardsville U.S.A. 40°43N 74°34W **83 F10**
Bernburg Germany 51°47N 11°44E **16 C6**
Berne = Bern Switz. 46°57N 7°28E **20 C7**
Berneray U.K. 57°43N 7°11W **11 D1**
Bernier I. Australia 24°50S 113°12E **61 D1**
Bernina, Piz Switz. 46°20N 9°54E **20 C8**
Beroun Czech Rep. 49°57N 14°5E **16 D8**
Berri Australia 34°14S 140°35E **63 E3**
Berriane Algeria 32°50N 3°46E **52 B6**
Berry Australia 34°46S 150°43E **63 E5**
Berry France 46°50N 2°0E **20 C5**
Berry Is. Bahamas 25°40N 77°50W **88 A4**
Berryessa, L. U.S.A. 38°31N 122°6W **78 G4**
Berryville U.S.A. 36°22N 93°34W **84 C8**
Bershad Ukraine 48°22N 29°31E **17 D15**
Berthold U.S.A. 48°19N 101°44W **80 A3**
Berthoud U.S.A. 40°19N 105°5W **76 F11**
Bertoua Cameroon 4°30N 13°45E **54 D2**
Bertraghboy B. Ireland 53°22N 9°54W **10 C2**
Beruwala Sri Lanka 6°30N 80°0E **45 L4**
Berwick U.S.A. 41°3N 76°14W **83 E8**
Berwick-upon-Tweed U.K. 55°46N 2°0W **12 B6**
Berwyn Mts. U.K. 52°54N 3°26W **12 E4**
Besal Pakistan 35°4N 73°56E **43 B5**
Besalampy Madag. 16°43S 44°29E **55 H8**
Besançon France 47°15N 6°2E **20 C7**

Besar Indonesia 2°40S 116°0E **36 E5**
Besnard L. Canada 55°25N 106°0W **71 B7**
Besni Turkey 37°41N 37°52E **46 B3**
Besor, N. → Egypt 31°28N 34°22E **48 D3**
Bessarabiya Moldova 47°0N 28°10E **17 E15**
Bessarabka = Basarabeasca
  Moldova 46°21N 28°58E **17 E15**
Bessemer Ala., U.S.A. 33°24N 86°58W **85 E11**
Bessemer Mich., U.S.A. 46°29N 90°3W **80 B8**
Bessemer Pa., U.S.A. 40°59N 80°30W **82 F4**
Beswick Australia 14°34S 132°53E **60 B5**
Beswick ⊙ Australia 14°31S 132°51E **60 B5**
Bet She'an Israel 32°30N 35°30E **48 C4**
Bet Shemesh Israel 31°44N 35°0E **48 D4**
Betanzos Spain 43°15N 8°12W **21 A1**
Bétaré Oya Cameroon 5°40N 14°5E **54 C2**
Bethal S. Africa 26°27S 29°28E **57 C4**
Bethanien Namibia 26°31S 17°8E **56 C2**
Bethany Canada 44°11N 78°34W **82 B6**
Bethany Mo., U.S.A. 40°16N 94°2W **80 E6**
Bethany Okla., U.S.A. 35°31N 97°38W **84 D6**
Bethel Alaska, U.S.A. 60°48N 161°45W **74 C7**
Bethel Conn., U.S.A. 41°22N 73°25W **83 E11**
Bethel Maine, U.S.A. 44°25N 70°47W **83 B14**
Bethel Vt., U.S.A. 43°50N 72°38W **83 C12**
Bethel Park U.S.A. 40°19N 80°2W **82 F4**
Bethlehem S. Africa 28°14S 28°18E **57 C4**
Bethlehem = Bayt Lahm
  West Bank 31°43N 35°12E **48 D4**
Bethlehem U.S.A. 40°37N 75°23W **83 F9**
Bethulie S. Africa 30°30S 25°59E **56 D4**
Béthune France 50°30N 2°38E **20 A5**
Betioky Madag. 23°48S 44°20E **55 J8**
Betong Malaysia 1°24N 111°31E **36 D4**
Betong Thailand 5°45N 101°5E **39 K3**
Betoota Australia 25°45S 140°42E **62 D3**
Betpaqdala Kazakhstan 45°45N 70°30E **30 B3**
Betroka Madag. 23°16S 46°0E **55 J9**
Betsiamites Canada 48°56N 68°40W **73 C6**
Betsiamites → Canada 48°56N 68°38W **73 C6**
Bettendorf U.S.A. 41°32N 90°30W **80 E8**
Bettiah India 26°48N 84°33E **43 F11**
Betul India 21°58N 77°59E **44 D3**
Betws-y-Coed U.K. 53°5N 3°48W **12 D4**
Beulah Mich., U.S.A. 44°38N 86°6W **80 C10**
Beulah N. Dak., U.S.A. 47°16N 101°47W **80 B3**
Beveren Belgium 51°12N 4°16E **15 C4**
Beverley Australia 32°9S 116°56E **61 F2**
Beverley U.K. 53°51N 0°26W **12 D7**
Beverly U.S.A. 42°33N 70°53W **83 D14**
Beverly Hills U.S.A. 28°55N 82°28W **85 G13**
Bewas → India 23°59N 79°21E **43 H8**
Bewdley Canada 44°5N 78°19W **82 B6**
Bexhill U.K. 50°51N 0°29E **13 G8**
Beyānlū Iran 36°0N 47°51E **46 C5**
Beyneu Kazakhstan 45°18N 55°9E **19 E10**
Beypazarı Turkey 40°10N 31°56E **19 F5**
Beypore India 11°10N 75°47E **45 J2**
Beyşehir Gölü Turkey 37°41N 31°33E **46 B1**
Béziers France 43°20N 3°12E **20 E5**
Bezwada = Vijayawada
  India 16°31N 80°39E **44 F5**
Bhabua India 25°3N 83°37E **43 G10**
Bhachau India 23°20N 70°16E **42 H4**
Bhadar → Gujarat, India 22°17N 72°20E **42 H5**
Bhadar → Gujarat, India 21°27N 69°47E **42 J3**
Bhadarwah India 32°58N 75°46E **43 C6**
Bhadgaon = Bhaktapur
  Nepal 27°38N 85°24E **43 F11**
Bhadohi India 25°25N 82°34E **43 G10**
Bhadra India 29°8N 75°14E **42 E6**
Bhadra → India 14°0N 75°20E **45 H2**
Bhadrachalam India 17°40N 80°53E **44 F5**
Bhadrak India 21°10N 86°30E **44 D8**
Bhadran India 22°19N 72°6E **42 H5**
Bhadravati India 13°49N 75°40E **45 H2**
Bhag Pakistan 29°2N 67°49E **42 E2**
Bhagalpur India 25°10N 87°0E **43 G12**
Bhagirathi → Paschimbanga,
  India 23°25N 88°23E **43 H13**
Bhagirathi → Uttarakhand,
  India 30°8N 78°35E **43 D8**
Bhainsa India 19°10N 77°58E **44 E3**
Bhakkar Pakistan 31°40N 71°5E **42 D4**
Bhakra Dam India 31°30N 76°45E **42 D7**
Bhaktapur Nepal 27°38N 85°24E **43 F11**
Bhalki India 18°2N 77°13E **44 E3**
Bhamo Burma 24°15N 97°15E **41 G20**
Bhamragarh India 19°30N 80°40E **44 E5**
Bhandara India 21°5N 79°42E **44 D4**
Bhanpura India 24°31N 75°44E **42 G6**
Bhanrer Ra. India 23°40N 79°45E **43 H8**
Bhaptiahi India 26°16N 86°44E **43 F12**
Bharat = India ■ Asia 20°0N 78°0E **40 K11**
Bharatpur Chhattisgarh,
  India 23°44N 81°46E **43 H9**
Bharatpur Raj., India 27°15N 77°30E **42 F7**
Bharatpur Nepal 27°34N 84°10E **43 F11**
Bharno India 23°14N 84°53E **43 H11**
Bharuch India 21°47N 73°0E **44 D1**
Bhatghar L. India 18°10N 73°48E **44 E1**
Bhatinda India 30°15N 74°57E **42 D6**
Bhatkal India 13°58N 74°35E **45 H2**
Bhatpara India 22°50N 88°25E **43 H13**
Bhattu India 29°36N 75°19E **42 E6**
Bhaun Pakistan 32°55N 72°40E **42 C5**
Bhaunagar = Bhavnagar
  India 21°45N 72°10E **44 D1**
Bhavani India 11°27N 77°43E **45 J3**
Bhavnagar India 21°45N 72°10E **44 D1**
Bhawanipatna India 19°55N 83°10E **44 E5**
Bhayavadar India 21°51N 70°15E **42 J4**
Bhearnaraigh = Berneray
  U.K. 56°55N 7°32W **11 E1**
Bhera Pakistan 32°29N 72°57E **42 C5**

Bheri → Nepal 28°47N 81°18E **43 E9**
Bhikangaon India 21°52N 75°57E **42 J6**
Bhilai = Bhilainagar-Durg
  India 21°13N 81°26E **44 D5**
Bhilainagar-Durg India 21°13N 81°26E **44 D5**
Bhilsa = Vidisha India 23°28N 77°53E **42 H7**
Bhilwara India 25°25N 74°38E **42 G6**
Bhima → India 16°25N 77°17E **44 F3**
Bhimavaram India 16°30N 81°30E **45 F5**
Bhimbar Pakistan 32°59N 74°3E **43 C6**
Bhind India 26°30N 78°46E **43 F8**
Bhinga India 27°43N 81°56E **43 F9**
Bhinmal India 25°0N 72°15E **42 G5**
Bhisho S. Africa 32°50S 27°23E **56 D4**
Bhiwandi India 19°20N 73°0E **44 E1**
Bhiwani India 28°50N 76°9E **42 E7**
Bhogava → India 22°26N 72°20E **42 H5**
Bhojpur Nepal 27°10N 87°3E **43 F12**
Bhokardan India 20°16N 75°46E **44 D2**
Bhola Bangla. 22°45N 90°35E **41 H17**
Bholari Pakistan 25°19N 68°13E **42 G3**
Bhongir India 17°30N 78°56E **44 F4**
Bhopal India 23°20N 77°30E **42 H7**
Bhopalpatnam India 18°52N 80°23E **44 E5**
Bhor India 18°12N 73°53E **44 E1**
Bhuban India 20°53N 85°50E **44 D7**
Bhubaneshwar India 20°15N 85°50E **44 D7**
Bhuj India 23°15N 69°49E **42 H3**
Bhumiphol Res. Thailand 17°20N 98°40E **38 D2**
Bhusawal India 21°3N 75°46E **44 D2**
Bhutan ■ Asia 27°25N 90°30E **41 F17**
Biafra, B. of = Bonny, Bight of
  Africa 3°30N 9°20E **54 D1**
Biak Indonesia 1°10S 136°6E **37 E9**
Biała Podlaska Poland 52°4N 23°6E **17 B12**
Białogard Poland 54°2N 15°58E **16 A8**
Białystok Poland 53°10N 23°10E **17 B12**
Biaora India 23°56N 76°56E **42 H7**
Bīārjmand Iran 36°6N 55°53E **47 B7**
Biaro Indonesia 2°5N 125°26E **37 D7**
Biarritz France 43°29N 1°33W **20 E3**
Bibai Japan 43°19N 141°52E **28 C10**
Bibby I. Canada 61°55N 93°0W **71 A10**
Biberach Germany 48°5N 9°47E **16 D5**
Bibile Sri Lanka 7°10N 81°25E **45 L5**
Bicester U.K. 51°54N 1°9W **13 F6**
Bicheno Australia 41°52S 148°18E **63 G4**
Bichia India 22°27N 80°42E **43 H9**
Bickerton I. Australia 13°45S 136°10E **62 A2**
Bid = Bir India 19°4N 75°46E **44 E2**
Bida Nigeria 9°3N 5°58E **52 G7**
Bidar India 17°55N 77°35E **44 F3**
Biddeford U.S.A. 43°30N 70°28W **81 D18**
Bideford U.K. 51°1N 4°13W **13 F3**
Bideford Bay U.K. 51°5N 4°20W **13 F3**
Bidhuna India 26°49N 79°31E **43 F8**
Bidor Malaysia 4°6N 101°15E **39 K3**
Bidyadanga Australia 18°45S 121°43E **60 C3**
Bié, Planalto de Angola 12°0S 16°0E **55 G3**
Bieber U.S.A. 41°7N 121°8W **76 F3**
Biel Switz. 47°8N 7°14E **20 C7**
Bielefeld Germany 52°1N 8°33E **16 B5**
Biella Italy 45°34N 8°3E **20 D8**
Bielsk Podlaski Poland 52°47N 23°12E **17 B12**
Bielsko-Biała Poland 49°50N 19°2E **17 D10**
Bien Hoa Vietnam 10°57N 106°49E **39 G6**
Bienne = Biel Switz. 47°8N 7°14E **20 C7**
Bienville, L. Canada 55°5N 72°40W **72 A5**
Biesbosch △ Neths. 51°45N 4°48E **15 C4**
Biesiesfontein S. Africa 30°57S 17°58E **56 D2**
Big → Canada 54°50N 58°55W **73 B8**
Big B. Canada 55°43N 60°35W **73 A7**
Big Bear City U.S.A. 34°16N 116°51W **79 L10**
Big Bear Lake U.S.A. 34°15N 116°56W **79 L10**
Big Belt Mts. U.S.A. 46°30N 111°25W **76 C8**
Big Bend Swaziland 26°50S 31°58E **57 D5**
Big Bend △ U.S.A. 29°20N 103°5W **84 G3**
Big Black → U.S.A. 32°3N 91°4W **85 F9**
Big Blue → U.S.A. 39°35N 96°34W **80 F5**
Big Buddha
  Hong Kong, China 22°15N 113°54E **31 a**
Big Creek U.S.A. 37°11N 119°14W **78 H7**
Big Cypress ∆ U.S.A. 26°0N 81°10W **85 H14**
Big Desert Australia 35°45S 141°10E **63 F3**
Big Falls U.S.A. 48°12N 93°48W **80 A7**
Big Fork → U.S.A. 48°31N 93°43W **80 A7**
Big I. Canada 61°7N 116°45W **70 A5**
Big Lake U.S.A. 31°12N 101°28W **84 F4**
Big Moose U.S.A. 43°49N 74°58W **83 C10**
Big Muddy Cr. →
  U.S.A. 48°8N 104°36W **76 B11**
Big Pine U.S.A. 37°10N 118°17W **78 H8**
Big Piney U.S.A. 42°32N 110°7W **76 E8**
Big Quill L. Canada 51°55N 104°30W **71 C8**
Big Rapids U.S.A. 43°42N 85°29W **81 D11**
Big Rideau L. Canada 44°40N 76°15W **83 B8**
Big River Canada 53°50N 107°0W **71 C7**
Big Run U.S.A. 40°57N 78°55W **82 F6**
Big Sable Pt. U.S.A. 44°3N 86°1W **80 C10**
Big Salmon → Canada 61°52N 134°55W **70 A2**
Big Sand L. Canada 57°45N 99°45W **71 B9**
Big Sandy U.S.A. 48°11N 110°7W **76 B8**
Big Sandy → U.S.A. 38°25N 82°36W **81 F12**
Big Sandy Cr. = Sandy Cr. →
  U.S.A. 41°51N 109°47W **76 F9**
Big Sandy Cr. → U.S.A. 38°7N 102°29W **76 G12**
Big Sioux → U.S.A. 42°29N 96°27W **80 D5**
Big South Fork △
  U.S.A. 36°27N 84°47W **85 C12**
Big Spring U.S.A. 32°15N 101°28W **84 E4**
Big Stone City U.S.A. 45°18N 96°28W **80 C6**
Big Stone Gap U.S.A. 36°52N 82°47W **81 G12**
Big Stone L. U.S.A. 45°18N 96°27W **80 C6**
Big Sur U.S.A. 36°15N 121°48W **78 J5**
Big Timber U.S.A. 45°50N 109°57W **76 D9**
Big Trout L. Canada 53°40N 90°0W **72 B2**

Big Trout Lake Canada 53°45N 90°0W **72 B2**
Biğa Turkey 40°13N 27°14E **23 D12**
Bigadiç Turkey 39°22N 28°7E **23 E13**
Biggar Canada 52°4N 108°0W **71 C7**
Biggar U.K. 55°38N 3°32W **11 F5**
Bigge I. Australia 14°35S 125°10E **60 B4**
Biggenden Australia 25°31S 152°4E **63 D5**
Biggleswade U.K. 52°5N 0°14W **13 E7**
Biggs U.S.A. 39°25N 121°43W **78 F5**
Bighorn U.S.A. 46°10N 107°27W **76 C10**
Bighorn → U.S.A. 46°10N 107°28W **76 C10**
Bighorn Canyon △
  U.S.A. 45°10N 108°0W **76 D10**
Bighorn L. U.S.A. 44°55N 108°15W **76 D9**
Bighorn Mts. U.S.A. 44°25N 107°0W **76 D10**
Bigstone L. Canada 53°42N 95°44W **71 C9**
Bihać Bos.-H. 44°49N 15°57E **16 F8**
Bihar India 25°5N 85°40E **43 G11**
Bihar □ India 25°0N 86°0E **43 G12**
Bihariganj India 25°44N 86°59E **43 G12**
Bihor, Munții Romania 46°29N 22°47E **17 E12**
Bijagós, Arquipélago dos
  Guinea-Biss. 11°15N 16°10W **52 F2**
Bijaipur India 26°2N 77°20E **42 F7**
Bijapur Chhattisgarh, India 18°50N 80°50E **44 E5**
Bijapur Karnataka, India 16°50N 75°55E **44 F2**
Bījār Iran 35°52N 47°35E **46 C5**
Bijauri Nepal 28°6N 82°20E **43 E10**
Bijawar India 24°38N 79°30E **43 G8**
Bijeljina Bos.-H. 44°46N 19°14E **23 B8**
Bijie China 27°20N 105°16E **34 D5**
Bijnor India 29°27N 78°11E **42 E8**
Bikaner India 28°2N 73°18E **42 E5**
Bikapur India 26°30N 82°7E **43 F10**
Bikeqi China 40°43N 111°20E **32 D6**
Bikfayyā Lebanon 33°55N 35°41E **48 B4**
Bikin Russia 46°50N 134°20E **28 A7**
Bikin → Russia 46°51N 134°2E **28 A7**
Bikini Atoll Marshall Is. 12°0N 167°30E **64 F8**
Bikita Zimbabwe 20°6S 31°41E **57 B5**
Bīkkū Bīttī Libya 22°0N 19°12E **53 D9**
Bila Tserkva Ukraine 49°45N 30°10E **17 D16**
Bilara India 26°14N 73°53E **42 F5**
Bilaspur Chhattisgarh,
  India 22°2N 82°15E **43 H10**
Bilaspur Punjab, India 31°19N 76°50E **42 D7**
Bilauk Taungdan Thailand 13°0N 99°0E **38 F2**
Bilauri Nepal 28°41N 80°21E **43 E9**
Bilbao Spain 43°16N 2°56W **21 A4**
Bilbo = Bilbao Spain 43°16N 2°56W **21 A4**
Bildudalur Iceland 65°41N 23°36W **8 D2**
Bílé Karpaty Europe 49°5N 18°0E **17 D9**
Bilecik Turkey 40°5N 30°5E **19 F5**
Bilgram India 27°11N 80°2E **43 F9**
Bilhaur India 26°51N 80°5E **43 F9**
Bilhorod-Dnistrovskyy
  Ukraine 46°11N 30°23E **19 E5**
Bilibino Russia 68°3N 166°20E **27 C17**
Bilimora India 20°45N 72°57E **44 D1**
Billiluna Australia 19°37S 127°41E **60 C4**
Billings U.S.A. 45°47N 108°30W **76 D9**
Billiton Is. = Belitung
  Indonesia 3°10S 107°50E **36 E3**
Bilma Niger 18°50N 13°30E **53 E8**
Bilma, Grand Erg de Niger 18°30N 14°0E **53 E8**
Biloela Australia 24°24S 150°31E **62 C5**
Biloli India 18°46N 77°44E **44 E3**
Biloxi U.S.A. 30°24N 88°53W **85 F10**
Bilpa Morea Claypan
  Australia 25°0S 140°0E **62 D3**
Biltine Chad 14°40N 20°50E **53 F10**
Bim Son Vietnam 20°4N 105°51E **38 B5**
Bima Indonesia 8°22S 118°49E **37 F5**
Bimbo C.A.R. 4°15N 18°33E **54 D3**
Bimini Is. Bahamas 25°42N 79°25W **88 A4**
Bin Xian Heilongjiang,
  China 45°42N 127°32E **33 B14**
Bin Xian Shaanxi, China 35°2N 108°4E **32 G5**
Bina-Etawah India 24°13N 78°14E **42 G8**
Binalong Australia 34°40S 148°39E **63 E4**
Bīnālūd, Kūh-e Iran 36°30N 58°30E **47 B8**
Binatang = Bintangau
  Malaysia 2°10N 111°40E **36 D4**
Binche Belgium 50°26N 4°10E **15 D4**
Binchuan China 25°42N 100°38E **34 E3**
Bindki India 26°2N 80°36E **43 F9**
Bindura Zimbabwe 17°18S 31°18E **55 H6**
Bingara Australia 29°52S 150°36E **63 D5**
Bingaram I. India 10°56N 72°17E **45 J1**
Bingham U.S.A. 45°3N 69°53W **81 C19**
Binghamton U.S.A. 42°6N 75°55W **83 D9**
Bingöl Turkey 38°53N 40°29E **46 B4**
Binh Dinh Vietnam 13°55N 109°7E **38 F7**
Binh Son Vietnam 15°20N 108°40E **38 E7**
Binhai China 34°2N 119°49E **33 G10**
Binjai Indonesia 3°20N 98°30E **36 D1**
Binka India 21°2N 83°48E **44 D6**
Binnaway Australia 31°28S 149°24E **63 E4**
Binongko Indonesia 5°57S 124°2E **37 F6**
Binscarth Canada 50°37N 101°17W **71 C8**
Bintan Indonesia 1°0N 104°0E **36 D2**
Bintangau Malaysia 2°10N 111°40E **36 D4**
Bintulu Malaysia 3°10N 113°0E **36 D4**
Bintuni Indonesia 2°7S 133°32E **37 E8**
Binyang China 23°12N 108°47E **34 F7**
Binzert = Bizerte Tunisia 37°15N 9°50E **53 A7**
Binzhou China 37°20N 118°2E **33 F10**
Bío Bío □ Chile 37°35N 72°0W **94 D1**
Biobío → Chile 36°49S 73°10W **94 D1**
Bioko Eq. Guin. 3°30N 8°40E **54 D1**
Bir India 19°4N 75°46E **44 E2**
Bîr Abu Muḥammad
  Egypt 29°44N 34°14E **48 F3**
Bi'r al Butayyihāt Jordan 29°47N 35°20E **48 F4**
Bi'r al Mārī Jordan 30°4N 35°33E **48 E4**
Bi'r Atrun Sudan 18°15N 26°40E **53 E11**
Bîr Beïda Egypt 30°25N 34°29E **48 E3**
Bîr el 'Abd Egypt 31°2N 33°0E **48 D2**

Bîr el Biarât Egypt 29°30N 34°43E 48 F3
Bîr el Duweidar Egypt 30°56N 32°32E 48 E1
Bîr el Garârât Egypt 31°3N 33°34E 48 D2
Bîr el Heisi Egypt 29°22N 34°36E 48 F3
Bîr el Jafir Egypt 30°50N 32°41E 48 E1
Bîr el Mâlḥi Egypt 30°38N 33°19E 48 E2
Bîr el Thamâda Egypt 30°12N 33°27E 48 E2
Bîr Gebeil Ḥiṣn Egypt 30°2N 33°18E 48 E2
Bi'r Ghadīr Syria 34°6N 37°3E 48 A6
Bîr Ḥasana Egypt 30°29N 33°46E 48 E2
Bîr Kaseiba Egypt 31°0N 33°17E 48 E2
Bîr Lahfân Egypt 31°0N 33°51E 48 E2
Bîr Madkûr Egypt 30°44N 32°33E 48 E1
Bîr Mogreïn Mauritania 25°10N 11°25W 52 C3
Bi'r Muṭribah Kuwait 29°54N 47°17E 46 D5
Bîr Qaṭia Egypt 30°58N 32°45E 48 E1
Bîr Shalatein Egypt 23°5N 35°25E 53 D13
Birāk Libya 27°31N 14°20E 53 C8
Biratnagar Nepal 26°27N 87°17E 43 F12
Birch → Canada 58°28N 112°17W 70 B6
Birch Hills Canada 52°59N 105°25W 71 C7
Birch I. Canada 52°26N 99°54W 71 C9
Birch L. N.W.T., Canada 62°4N 116°33W 70 A5
Birch L. Ont., Canada 51°23N 92°18W 72 B1
Birch Mts. Canada 57°30N 113°10W 70 B6
Birch River Canada 52°24N 101°6W 71 C8
Birchip Australia 35°56S 142°55E 63 F3
Bird Canada 56°30N 94°13W 71 B10
Bird I. = Aves, I. de W. Indies 15°45N 63°55W 89 C7
Bird I. S. Georgia 54°0S 38°3W 96 G9
Birds Creek Canada 45°6N 77°52W 82 A7
Birdsville Australia 25°51S 139°20E 62 D2
Birdum Cr. → Australia 15°14S 133°0E 60 C5
Birecik Turkey 37°2N 38°0E 46 B3
Bireim Israel 30°50N 34°28E 48 E3
Bireuen Indonesia 5°14N 96°39E 36 C1
Birganj Nepal 27°1N 84°52E 43 F11
Birigüi Brazil 21°18S 50°16W 95 A5
Bīrjand Iran 32°53N 59°13E 47 C8
Birkenhead U.K. 53°23N 3°2W 12 D4
Bîrlad = Bârlad Romania 46°15N 27°38E 17 E14
Birmingham U.K. 52°29N 1°52W 13 E6
Birmingham U.S.A. 33°31N 86°48W 85 E11
Birmingham Int. ✕ (BHX) U.K. 52°26N 1°45W 13 E6
Birmitrapur India 22°24N 84°46E 44 C7
Birni Nkonni Niger 13°55N 5°15E 52 F7
Birnin Kebbi Nigeria 12°32N 4°12E 52 F6
Birobidzhan Russia 48°50N 132°50E 31 B15
Birr Ireland 53°6N 7°54W 10 C4
Birrie → Australia 29°43S 146°37E 63 D4
Birsilpur India 28°11N 72°15E 42 E5
Birsk Russia 55°25N 55°30E 18 C10
Birtle Canada 50°30N 101°5W 71 C8
Birur India 13°30N 75°55E 40 N9
Biržai Lithuania 56°11N 24°45E 9 H21
Bisa Indonesia 1°15S 127°28E 37 E7
Bisalpur India 28°14N 79°48E 43 E8
Bisbee U.S.A. 31°27N 109°55W 77 L9
Biscarrosse France 44°22N 1°20W 20 D3
Biscay, B. of Atl. Oc. 45°0N 2°0W 20 D1
Biscayne B. U.S.A. 25°40N 80°12W 85 J14
Biscoe Is. Antarctica 66°0S 67°0W 5 C17
Biscotasing Canada 47°18N 82°9W 72 C3
Bishan China 29°33N 106°12E 34 C6
Bishkek Kyrgyzstan 42°54N 74°46E 30 C3
Bishnupur India 23°8N 87°20E 43 H12
Bisho = Bhisho S. Africa 32°50S 27°23E 56 D4
Bishop Calif., U.S.A. 37°22N 118°24W 78 H8
Bishop Tex., U.S.A. 27°35N 97°48W 84 H6
Bishop Auckland U.K. 54°39N 1°40W 12 C6
Bishop's Falls Canada 49°2N 55°30W 73 C8
Bishop's Stortford U.K. 51°52N 0°10E 13 F8
Biskra Algeria 34°50N 5°44E 52 B7
Bismarck U.S.A. 46°48N 100°47W 80 B3
Bismarck Arch. Papua N. G. 2°30S 150°0E 58 B7
Bison U.S.A. 45°31N 102°28W 80 C2
Bīsotūn Iran 34°23N 47°26E 46 C5
Bissagos = Bijagós, Arquipélago dos Guinea-Biss. 11°15N 16°10W 52 F2
Bissam Cuttack India 19°31N 83°31E 44 E6
Bissau Guinea-Biss. 11°45N 15°45W 52 F2
Bistcho L. Canada 59°45N 118°50W 70 B5
Bistriṭa Romania 47°9N 24°35E 17 E13
Bistriṭa → Romania 46°30N 26°57E 17 E14
Biswan India 27°29N 81°2E 43 F9
Bitam Gabon 2°5N 11°25E 54 D2
Bitkine Chad 11°59N 18°13E 53 F9
Bitlis Turkey 38°20N 42°3E 46 B4
Bitola Macedonia 41°1N 21°20E 23 D9
Bitolj = Bitola Macedonia 41°1N 21°20E 23 D9
Bitra I. India 11°33N 72°9E 45 J1
Bitter Creek U.S.A. 41°33N 108°33W 76 F9
Bitterfontein S. Africa 31°1S 18°32E 56 D2
Bitterroot → U.S.A. 46°52N 114°7W 76 C6
Bitterroot Range U.S.A. 46°0N 114°20W 76 D6
Bitterwater U.S.A. 36°23N 121°0W 78 J6
Biu Nigeria 10°40N 12°3E 53 F8
Biwa-Ko Japan 35°15N 136°10E 29 G8
Biwabik U.S.A. 47°32N 92°21W 80 B7
Bixby U.S.A. 35°57N 95°53W 84 D7
Biyang China 32°38N 113°21E 32 H7
Biysk Russia 52°40N 85°0E 26 D9
Bizana S. Africa 30°50S 29°52E 57 D4
Bizen Japan 34°43N 134°8E 29 G7
Bizerte Tunisia 37°15N 9°50E 53 A7
Bjargtangar Iceland 65°30N 24°30W 8 D1
Bjelovar Croatia 45°56N 16°49E 22 B7
Björneborg = Pori Finland 61°29N 21°48E 8 F19
Bjørnevatn Norway 69°40N 30°0E 8 B24
Bjørnøya Arctic 74°30N 19°0E 4 B8
Black = Da → Vietnam 21°15N 105°20E 34 G5
Black → Canada 44°42N 79°19W 82 B5
Black → Ariz., U.S.A. 33°44N 110°13W 77 K8
Black → Ark., U.S.A. 35°38N 91°20W 84 D9
Black → La., U.S.A. 31°16N 91°50W 84 F9
Black → Mich., U.S.A. 42°59N 82°27W 82 D2
Black → N.Y., U.S.A. 43°59N 76°4W 83 C8
Black → Wis., U.S.A. 43°57N 91°22W 80 D8
Black Bay Pen. Canada 48°38N 88°21W 72 C2
Black Birch L. Canada 56°53N 107°45W 71 B7
Black Canyon of the Gunnison ⌂ U.S.A. 38°40N 107°35W 76 G10
Black Diamond Canada 50°45N 114°14W 70 C6
Black Duck → Canada 56°51N 89°2W 72 A2
Black Forest = Schwarzwald Germany 48°30N 8°20E 16 D5
Black Forest U.S.A. 39°0N 104°43W 76 G11
Black Hd. Ireland 53°9N 9°16W 10 C2
Black Hills U.S.A. 44°0N 103°45W 80 D2
Black I. Canada 51°12N 96°30W 71 C9
Black L. Canada 59°12N 105°15W 71 B7
Black L. Mich., U.S.A. 45°28N 84°16W 81 C11
Black L. N.Y., U.S.A. 44°31N 75°36W 83 B9
Black Lake Canada 59°11N 105°20W 71 B7
Black Mesa U.S.A. 36°58N 102°58W 84 C3
Black Mt. = Mynydd Du U.K. 51°52N 3°50W 13 F4
Black Mts. U.K. 51°55N 3°7W 13 F4
Black Range U.S.A. 33°15N 107°50W 77 K10
Black River Jamaica 18°0N 77°50W 88 a
Black River U.S.A. 44°0N 75°47W 83 C9
Black River Falls U.S.A. 44°18N 90°51W 80 C8
Black Rock Barbados 13°7N 59°37W 89 g
Black Rock Desert U.S.A. 41°10N 118°50W 76 F4
Black Sea Eurasia 43°30N 35°0E 19 F6
Black Tickle Canada 53°28N 55°45W 73 B8
Black Volta → Africa 8°41N 1°33W 52 G5
Black Warrior → U.S.A. 32°32N 87°51W 85 E11
Blackall Australia 24°25S 145°45E 62 C4
Blackball N.Z. 42°22S 171°26E 59 E3
Blackbraes △ Australia 19°10S 144°10E 62 B3
Blackbull Australia 17°55S 141°45E 62 B3
Blackburn U.K. 53°45N 2°29W 12 D5
Blackburn, Mt. U.S.A. 61°44N 143°26W 74 C11
Blackburn with Darwen □ U.K. 53°45N 2°29W 12 D5
Blackdown Tableland △ Australia 23°52S 149°8E 62 C4
Blackfoot U.S.A. 43°11N 112°21W 76 E7
Blackfoot → U.S.A. 46°52N 113°53W 76 C7
Blackfoot Res. U.S.A. 42°55N 111°39W 76 E8
Blackpool U.K. 53°49N 3°3W 12 D4
Blackpool □ U.K. 53°49N 3°3W 12 D4
Blackriver U.S.A. 44°46N 83°17W 82 B1
Blacks Harbour Canada 45°3N 66°49W 73 C6
Blacksburg U.S.A. 37°14N 80°25W 81 G13
Blacksod B. Ireland 54°6N 10°0W 10 B1
Blackstairs Mt. Ireland 52°33N 6°48W 10 D5
Blackstone U.S.A. 37°5N 78°0W 81 G14
Blackstone Ra. Australia 26°0S 128°30E 61 E4
Blackwater = West Road → Canada 53°18N 122°53W 70 C4
Blackwater Australia 23°35S 148°53E 62 C4
Blackwater → Meath, Ireland 53°39N 6°41W 10 C4
Blackwater → Waterford, Ireland 52°4N 7°52W 10 D4
Blackwater → U.K. 54°31N 6°35W 10 B5
Blackwell U.S.A. 36°48N 97°17W 84 C6
Blackwells Corner U.S.A. 35°37N 119°47W 79 K7
Bladensburg △ Australia 22°30S 142°59E 62 C3
Blaenau Ffestiniog U.K. 53°0N 3°56W 12 E4
Blaenau Gwent □ U.K. 51°48N 3°12W 13 F4
Blagodarnoye = Blagodarnyy Russia 45°7N 43°37E 19 E7
Blagodarnyy Russia 45°7N 43°37E 19 E7
Blagoevgrad Bulgaria 42°2N 23°5E 23 C10
Blagoveshchensk Russia 50°20N 127°30E 31 A14
Blahkiuh Indonesia 8°31S 115°12E 37 J18
Blain U.S.A. 40°20N 77°31W 82 F7
Blaine Minn., U.S.A. 45°10N 93°13W 80 C7
Blaine Wash., U.S.A. 48°59N 122°45W 78 B4
Blaine Lake Canada 52°51N 106°52W 71 C7
Blair U.S.A. 41°33N 96°8W 80 E5
Blair Athol Australia 22°42S 147°31E 62 C4
Blair Atholl U.K. 56°46N 3°50W 11 E5
Blairgowrie U.K. 56°35N 3°21W 11 E5
Blairsden U.S.A. 39°47N 120°37W 78 F6
Blairsville U.S.A. 40°26N 79°16W 82 F5
Blakang Mati, Pulau Singapore 1°15N 103°50E 39 d
Blake Pt. U.S.A. 48°11N 88°25W 80 A9
Blakely Ga., U.S.A. 31°23N 84°56W 85 F12
Blakely Pa., U.S.A. 41°28N 75°37W 83 E9
Blambangan, Semenanjung Indonesia 8°42S 114°29E 37 K17
Blanc, Mont Europe 45°48N 6°50E 20 D7
Blanca, B. Argentina 39°10S 61°30W 96 D4
Blanca, Cord. Peru 9°10S 77°35W 92 E3
Blanca Peak U.S.A. 37°35N 105°29W 77 H11
Blanche, C. Australia 33°1S 134°9E 63 E1
Blanche, L. S. Austral., Australia 29°15S 139°40E 63 D2
Blanche, L. W. Austral., Australia 22°25S 123°17E 60 D3
Blanchisseuse Trin. & Tob. 10°48N 61°18W 93 K15
Blanco S. Africa 33°55S 22°23E 56 D3
Blanco U.S.A. 30°6N 98°25W 84 F5
Blanco → Argentina 30°20S 68°42W 94 C2
Blanco, C. Costa Rica 9°34N 85°8W 88 E2
Blanco, C. U.S.A. 42°51N 124°34W 76 E1
Blanda → Iceland 65°37N 20°9W 8 D3
Blandford Forum U.K. 50°51N 2°9W 13 G5
Blanding U.S.A. 37°37N 109°29W 77 H9
Blanes Spain 41°40N 2°48E 21 B7
Blankenberge Belgium 51°20N 3°9E 15 C3
Blanquilla, I. Venezuela 11°51N 64°37W 89 D7
Blanquillo Uruguay 32°53S 55°37W 95 C4
Blantyre Malawi 15°45S 35°0E 55 H7
Blarney Ireland 51°56N 8°33W 10 E3
Blasdell U.S.A. 42°48N 78°50W 82 D6
Blåvands Huk Denmark 55°33N 8°4E 9 J13
Blaydon U.K. 54°58N 1°42W 12 C6
Blayney Australia 33°32S 149°14E 63 E4
Blaze, Pt. Australia 12°56S 130°11E 60 B5
Blekinge Sweden 56°25N 15°20E 9 H16
Blenheim Canada 42°20N 82°0W 82 D3
Blenheim N.Z. 41°38S 173°57E 59 D4
Bletchley U.K. 51°59N 0°44W 13 F7
Blida Algeria 36°30N 2°49E 52 A6
Bligh Sound N.Z. 44°47S 167°32E 59 F1
Bligh Water Fiji 17°0S 178°0E 59 a
Blind River Canada 46°10N 82°58W 72 C3
Bliss Idaho, U.S.A. 42°56N 114°57W 76 E6
Bliss N.Y., U.S.A. 42°34N 78°15W 82 D6
Blissfield U.S.A. 40°24N 81°58W 82 F3
Blitar Indonesia 8°5S 112°11E 37 H15
Block I. U.S.A. 41°11N 71°35W 83 E13
Block Island Sd. U.S.A. 41°15N 71°40W 83 E13
Bloemfontein S. Africa 29°6S 26°7E 56 C4
Bloemhof S. Africa 27°38S 25°32E 56 C4
Blois France 47°35N 1°20E 20 C4
Blönduós Iceland 65°40N 20°12W 8 D3
Blongas Indonesia 8°53S 116°2E 37 K19
Bloodvein → Canada 51°47N 96°43W 71 C9
Bloody Foreland Ireland 55°10N 8°17W 10 A3
Bloomer U.S.A. 45°6N 91°29W 80 C8
Bloomfield Canada 43°59N 77°14W 82 C7
Bloomfield Iowa, U.S.A. 40°45N 92°25W 80 E7
Bloomfield N. Mex., U.S.A. 36°43N 107°59W 77 H10
Bloomfield Nebr., U.S.A. 42°36N 97°39W 80 D5
Bloomington Ill., U.S.A. 40°28N 89°0W 80 E9
Bloomington Ind., U.S.A. 39°10N 86°32W 80 F10
Bloomington Minn., U.S.A. 44°50N 93°17W 80 C7
Bloomsburg U.S.A. 41°0N 76°27W 83 F8
Bloomsbury Australia 20°48S 148°38E 62 b
Blora Indonesia 6°57S 111°25E 37 G14
Blossburg U.S.A. 41°41N 77°4W 82 E7
Blouberg S. Africa 23°8S 28°59E 57 B4
Blountstown U.S.A. 30°27N 85°3W 85 F12
Blue Earth U.S.A. 43°38N 94°6W 80 D6
Blue Hole △ Belize 17°24N 87°30W 88 C2
Blue Mesa Res. U.S.A. 38°28N 107°20W 76 G10
Blue Mountain Lake U.S.A. 43°51N 74°27W 83 C10
Blue Mountain Pk. Jamaica 18°3N 76°36W 88 a
Blue Mt. U.S.A. 40°30N 76°30W 83 F8
Blue Mts. Jamaica 18°3N 76°36W 88 a
Blue Mts. Maine, U.S.A. 44°50N 70°35W 83 B14
Blue Mts. Oreg., U.S.A. 45°0N 118°20W 76 D4
Blue Mud B. Australia 13°30S 136°0E 62 A2
Blue Mud Bay ☼ Australia 13°25S 136°2E 62 A2
Blue Nile = Nîl el Azraq → Sudan 15°38N 32°31E 53 E12
Blue Rapids U.S.A. 39°41N 96°39W 80 F5
Blue Ridge U.S.A. 36°40N 80°50W 81 G13
Blue River Canada 52°6N 119°18W 70 C5
Bluefield U.S.A. 37°15N 81°17W 81 G13
Bluefields Nic. 12°20N 83°50W 88 D3
Bluevale Canada 43°51N 81°15W 82 C3
Bluff Australia 23°35S 149°4E 62 C4
Bluff N.Z. 46°37S 168°20E 59 G2
Bluff U.S.A. 37°17N 109°33W 77 H9
Bluff Knoll Australia 34°24S 118°15E 61 F2
Bluff Pt. Australia 27°50S 114°5E 61 E1
Bluffton Ind., U.S.A. 40°44N 85°11W 81 E11
Bluffton S.C., U.S.A. 32°14N 80°52W 85 E14
Blumenau Brazil 27°0S 49°0W 95 B6
Blunt U.S.A. 44°31N 99°59W 80 C4
Bly U.S.A. 42°24N 121°3W 76 E3
Blyde River Canyon ⌂ S. Africa 24°37S 31°2E 57 B5
Blyth Canada 43°44N 81°26W 82 C3
Blyth U.K. 55°8N 1°31W 12 B6
Blythe U.S.A. 33°37N 114°36W 79 M12
Blytheville U.S.A. 35°56N 89°55W 85 D10
Bo S. Leone 7°55N 11°50W 52 G3
Bo Duc Vietnam 11°58N 106°50E 39 G6
Bo Hai China 39°0N 119°0E 33 E10
Bo Hai Haixia Asia 38°25N 121°10E 33 E11
Bo Xian = Bozhou China 33°55N 115°41E 32 H8
Boa Vista Brazil 2°48N 60°30W 92 C6
Boa Vista C. Verde Is. 16°0N 22°49W 52 b
Boaco Nic. 12°29N 85°35W 88 D2
Bo'ai China 35°10N 113°3E 32 G7
Boalsburg U.S.A. 40°47N 77°49W 82 F7
Boane Mozam. 26°6S 32°19E 57 C5
Boao China 19°8N 110°34E 38 C8
Boardman U.S.A. 41°2N 80°40W 82 E4
Boath India 19°20N 78°20E 44 E4
Bobadah Australia 32°19S 146°41E 63 E4
Bobai China 22°17N 109°59E 34 F7
Bobbili India 18°35N 83°30E 44 E6
Bobcaygeon Canada 44°33N 78°33W 82 B6
Boblad India 17°13N 75°26E 44 F2
Bobo-Dioulasso Burkina Faso 11°8N 4°13W 52 F5
Bobonong Botswana 21°58S 28°20E 57 B4
Bóbr → Poland 52°4N 15°4E 16 B8
Bobraomby, Tanjon' i Madag. 12°40S 49°10E 55 G9
Bobruysk = Babruysk Belarus 53°10N 29°15E 17 B15
Boby, Pic Madag. 22°12S 46°55E 55 J9
Boca del Río Mexico 19°5N 96°4W 87 D5
Boca do Acre Brazil 8°50S 67°27W 92 E5
Boca Raton U.S.A. 26°21N 80°5W 85 H14
Bocas del Dragón = Dragon's Mouths Trin. & Tob. 11°0N 61°50W 93 K15
Bocas del Toro Panama 9°15N 82°20W 88 E3
Bochnia Poland 49°58N 20°27E 17 D11
Bochum = Senwabarana S. Africa 23°17S 29°7E 57 B4
Bochum Germany 51°28N 7°13E 16 C4
Bocoyna Mexico 27°52N 107°35W 86 B3
Bodaybo Russia 57°50N 114°0E 27 D12
Boddam U.K. 59°56N 1°17W 11 B7
Boddington Australia 32°50S 116°30E 61 F2
Bodega Bay U.S.A. 38°20N 123°3W 78 G3
Boden Sweden 65°50N 21°42E 8 D19
Bodensee Europe 47°35N 9°25E 20 C8
Bodh Gaya India 24°41N 84°59E 43 G11
Bodhan India 18°40N 77°44E 44 E3
Bodinayakkanur India 10°2N 77°10E 45 J3
Bodmin U.K. 50°28N 4°43W 13 G3
Bodmin Moor U.K. 50°33N 4°36W 13 G3
Bodø Norway 67°17N 14°24E 8 C16
Bodrog → Hungary 48°11N 21°22E 17 D11
Bodrum Turkey 37°3N 27°30E 23 F12
Boende Dem. Rep. of the Congo 0°24S 21°12E 54 E4
Boerne U.S.A. 29°47N 98°44W 84 G5
Boesmans → S. Africa 33°42S 26°39E 56 D4
Bogalusa U.S.A. 30°47N 89°52W 85 F10
Bogan → Australia 30°20S 146°55E 63 D4
Bogan Gate Australia 33°7S 147°49E 63 E4
Bogantungan Australia 23°41S 147°17E 62 C4
Bogata U.S.A. 33°28N 95°13W 84 E7
Bogda Shan China 43°35N 89°40E 30 C6
Boggabilla Australia 28°36S 150°24E 63 D5
Boggabri Australia 30°45S 150°5E 63 E5
Boggeragh Mts. Ireland 52°2N 8°55W 10 D3
Boglan = Solhan Turkey 38°57N 41°3E 46 B4
Bognor Regis U.K. 50°47N 0°40W 13 G7
Bogo Phil. 11°3N 124°0E 37 B6
Bogong, Mt. Australia 36°47S 147°17E 63 F4
Bogor Indonesia 6°36S 106°48E 37 G12
Bogotá Colombia 4°34N 74°0W 92 C4
Bogotol Russia 56°15N 89°50E 26 D9
Bogra Bangla. 24°51N 89°22E 41 G16
Boguchany Russia 58°40N 97°30E 27 D10
Bogué Mauritania 16°45N 14°10W 52 E3
Bohemian Forest = Böhmerwald Germany 49°8N 13°14E 16 D7
Böhmerwald Germany 49°8N 13°14E 16 D7
Bohol □ Phil. 9°50N 124°10E 37 C6
Bohol Sea Phil. 9°0N 124°0E 37 C6
Bohorok Indonesia 3°30N 98°12E 39 L2
Böhöt Mongolia 45°13N 108°16E 32 B5
Bohuslän Sweden 58°25N 12°0E 9 G15
Boi, Pta. do Brazil 23°55S 45°15W 95 A6
Boiaçu Brazil 0°27S 61°46W 92 D6
Boigu Australia 9°16S 142°13E 62 a
Boileau, C. Australia 17°40S 122°7E 60 C3
Boipariguda India 18°46N 82°26E 44 E6
Boise U.S.A. 43°37N 116°13W 76 E5
Boise City U.S.A. 36°44N 102°31W 84 C3
Boissevain Canada 49°15N 100°5W 71 D8
Bojador, C. W. Sahara 26°0N 14°30W 52 C3
Bojana → Albania 41°52N 19°22E 23 D8
Bojnūrd Iran 37°30N 57°20E 47 B8
Bojonegoro Indonesia 7°11S 111°54E 37 G14
Bokaro India 23°46N 85°55E 43 H11
Boké Guinea 10°56N 14°17W 52 F3
Bokhara → Australia 29°55S 146°42E 63 D4
Boknafjorden Norway 59°14N 5°40E 9 G11
Bokor △ Cambodia 10°50N 104°1E 39 G5
Bokoro Chad 12°25N 17°14E 53 F9
Bokpyin Burma 11°18N 98°42E 39 G2
Bokungu Dem. Rep. of the Congo 0°35S 22°50E 54 E4
Bolan → Pakistan 28°38N 67°42E 42 E2
Bolan Pass Pakistan 29°50N 67°20E 40 E5
Bolaños → Mexico 21°12N 104°5W 86 C4
Bolbec France 49°30N 0°30E 20 B4
Boldājī Iran 31°56N 51°3E 47 D6
Bole China 44°55N 81°37E 30 C5
Bolekhiv Ukraine 49°0N 23°57E 17 D12
Bolesławiec Poland 51°17N 15°37E 16 C8
Bolgatanga Ghana 10°44N 0°53W 52 F5
Bolgrad = Bolhrad Ukraine 45°40N 28°32E 17 F15
Bolhrad Ukraine 45°40N 28°32E 17 F15
Bolinao Phil. 16°23N 119°54E 37 A5
Bolivar Mo., U.S.A. 37°37N 93°25W 80 G7
Bolivar N.Y., U.S.A. 42°4N 78°10W 82 D6
Bolivar Tenn., U.S.A. 35°12N 89°0W 85 D10
Bolívar, Pico Venezuela 8°32N 71°2W 89 E5
Bolivia ■ S. Amer. 17°6S 64°0W 92 G6
Bolivian Plateau = Altiplano Bolivia 17°0S 68°0W 92 G5
Bollnäs Sweden 61°21N 16°24E 8 F17
Bollon Australia 28°2S 147°29E 63 D4
Bolmen Sweden 56°55N 13°40E 9 H15
Bolobo Dem. Rep. of the Congo 2°6S 16°20E 54 E3
Bologna Italy 44°29N 11°20E 22 B4
Bologoye Russia 57°55N 34°5E 18 C5
Bolomba Dem. Rep. of the Congo 0°35N 19°0E 54 D3
Bolonchén Mexico 20°1N 89°45W 87 D7
Boloven, Cao Nguyen Laos 15°10N 106°30E 38 E6
Bolpur India 23°40N 87°45E 43 H12
Bolsena, L. di Italy 42°36N 11°56E 22 C4
Bolshevik, Ostrov Russia 78°30N 102°0E 27 B11
Bolshoy Anyuy → Russia 68°30N 160°49E 27 C17
Bolshoy Begichev, Ostrov Russia 74°20N 112°30E 27 B12
Bolshoy Kamen Russia 43°7N 132°19E 28 C6
Bolshoy Kavkas = Caucasus Mountains Eurasia 42°50N 44°0E 19 F7
Bolshoy Lyakhovskiy, Ostrov Russia 73°35N 142°0E 27 B15
Bolshoy Tyuters, Ostrov Russia 59°51N 27°13E 9 G22
Bolsward Neths. 53°3N 5°32E 15 A5
Bolt Head U.K. 50°12N 3°48W 13 G4
Bolton Canada 43°54N 79°45W 82 C5
Bolton U.K. 53°35N 2°26W 12 D5
Bolton Landing U.S.A. 43°32N 73°35W 83 C11
Bolu Turkey 40°45N 31°35E 19 F5
Bolungavík Iceland 66°9N 23°15W 8 C2
Boluo China 23°3N 114°21E 35 F10
Bolvadin Turkey 38°45N 31°4E 46 B1
Bolzano Italy 46°31N 11°22E 22 A4
Bom Jesus da Lapa Brazil 13°15S 43°25W 93 F10
Boma Dem. Rep. of the Congo 5°50S 13°4E 54 F2
Bombala Australia 36°56S 149°15E 63 F4
Bombay U.S.A. 44°56N 74°34W 83 B10
Bombedor, Pta. Venezuela 9°53N 61°37W 93 L15
Bomberai, Semenanjung Indonesia 3°0S 133°0E 37 E8
Bomboma Dem. Rep. of the Congo 2°25N 18°55E 54 D3
Bomi China 29°50N 95°45E 30 F8
Bømlo Norway 59°37N 5°13E 9 G11
Bompoka India 8°15N 93°13E 45 K11
Bomu → C.A.R. 4°40N 22°30E 54 D4
Bon, C. = Ra's aṭ Tib Tunisia 37°1N 11°2E 22 F4
Bon Acceuil Mauritius 20°10S 57°39E 55 d
Bon Echo ⌂ Canada 44°55N 77°16W 82 B7
Bon Sar Pa Vietnam 12°24N 107°35E 38 F6
Bonāb Iran 36°35N 48°41E 47 B6
Bonaigarh India 21°50N 84°57E 43 J11
Bonaire W. Indies 12°10N 68°15W 89 D6
Bonampak Mexico 16°44N 91°5W 87 D6
Bonang Australia 37°11S 148°41E 63 F4
Bonanza Nic. 13°54N 84°35W 88 D3
Bonaparte Arch. Australia 14°0S 124°30E 60 B3
Bonar Bridge U.K. 57°54N 4°20W 11 D4
Bonasse Trin. & Tob. 10°5N 61°54W 93 K15
Bonaventure Canada 48°5N 65°32W 73 C6
Bonavista Canada 48°40N 53°5W 73 C9
Bonavista, C. Canada 48°42N 53°5W 73 C9
Bonavista B. Canada 48°45N 53°25W 73 C9
Bondo Dem. Rep. of the Congo 3°55N 23°53E 54 D4
Bondokodi Indonesia 9°33S 119°0E 60 A2
Bondoukou Ivory C. 8°2N 2°47W 52 G5
Bondowoso Indonesia 7°55S 113°49E 37 G15
Bone, Teluk Indonesia 4°10S 120°50E 37 E6
Bonerate Indonesia 7°25S 121°5E 37 F6
Bonerate, Kepulauan Indonesia 6°30S 121°10E 37 F6
Bo'ness U.K. 56°1N 3°37W 11 E5
Bonete, Cerro Argentina 27°55S 68°40W 94 B2
Bong Son = Hoai Nhon Vietnam 14°28N 109°1E 38 E7
Bongaigaon India 26°28N 90°34E 30 F7
Bongandanga Dem. Rep. of the Congo 1°24N 21°3E 54 D4
Bongor Chad 10°35N 15°20E 53 F9
Bongos, Massif des C.A.R. 8°40N 22°25E 54 C4
Bonham U.S.A. 33°35N 96°11W 84 E6
Bonifacio France 41°24N 9°10E 20 F8
Bonifacio, Bouches de Medit. S. 41°12N 9°15E 22 D3
Bonin Is. = Ogasawara Gunto Pac. Oc. 27°0N 142°0E 64 E6
Bonn Germany 50°46N 7°6E 16 C4
Bonne Terre U.S.A. 37°55N 90°33W 80 G8
Bonners Ferry U.S.A. 48°42N 116°19W 76 B5
Bonney, L. Australia 37°50S 140°20E 63 F3
Bonnie Rock Australia 30°29S 118°22E 61 F2
Bonny, Bight of Africa 3°30N 9°20E 54 D1
Bonnyrigg U.K. 55°53N 3°6W 11 F5
Bonnyville Canada 54°20N 110°45W 71 C6
Bonoi Indonesia 1°45S 137°41E 37 E9
Bonsall U.S.A. 33°16N 117°14W 79 M9
Bontang Indonesia 0°10N 117°30E 36 D5
Bontebok △ S. Africa 34°5S 20°28E 56 D3
Bonthe S. Leone 7°30N 12°33W 52 G3
Bontoc Phil. 17°7N 120°58E 37 A6
Bonython Ra. Australia 23°40S 128°45E 60 D4
Boodjamulla △ Australia 18°15S 138°6E 62 B2
Bookabie Australia 31°50S 132°41E 61 F5
Booker U.S.A. 36°27N 100°32W 84 C4
Booligal Australia 33°58S 144°53E 63 E3
Böön Tsagaan Nuur Mongolia 45°35N 99°9E 30 B8
Boonah Australia 27°58S 152°41E 63 D5
Boone Iowa, U.S.A. 42°4N 93°53W 80 D7
Boone N.C., U.S.A. 36°13N 81°41W 85 C14
Booneville Ark., U.S.A. 35°8N 93°55W 84 D8
Booneville Miss., U.S.A. 34°39N 88°34W 85 D10
Boonville Calif., U.S.A. 39°1N 123°22W 78 F3
Boonville Ind., U.S.A. 38°3N 87°16W 80 F10
Boonville Mo., U.S.A. 38°58N 92°44W 80 F7
Boonville N.Y., U.S.A. 43°29N 75°20W 83 C9
Boorabbin △ Australia 31°30S 120°10E 61 F3
Boorindal Australia 30°22S 146°11E 63 E4
Boorowa Australia 34°28S 148°44E 63 E4
Boosaaso Somalia 11°12N 49°18E 49 E4
Boothia, Gulf of Canada 71°0N 90°0W 68 C14
Boothia Pen. Canada 71°0N 94°0W 68 C13
Bootle U.K. 53°28N 3°1W 12 D4
Booué Gabon 0°5S 11°55E 54 E2
Boquilla, Presa de la Mexico 27°31N 105°30W 86 B3
Boquillas del Carmen Mexico 29°11N 102°58W 86 B4
Bor Serbia 44°5N 22°7E 23 B10
Bôr South Sudan 6°10N 31°40E 53 G12
Bor Mashash Israel 31°7N 34°50E 48 D3
Bora Bora French Polynesia 16°30S 151°45W 65 J12
Borah Peak U.S.A. 44°8N 113°47W 76 D7
Boraha, Nosy Madag. 16°50S 49°55E 55 H9
Borås Sweden 57°43N 12°56E 9 H15
Borāzjān Iran 29°22N 51°10E 47 D6
Borba Brazil 4°12S 59°34W 92 D7
Borborema, Planalto da Brazil 7°0S 37°0W 90 D7
Bord Khūn-e Now Iran 28°3N 51°28E 47 D6
Borda, C. Australia 35°45S 136°34E 63 F2
Bordeaux France 44°50N 0°36W 20 D3
Borden Australia 34°3S 118°12E 61 F2
Borden-Carleton Canada 46°18N 63°47W 73 C7
Borden I. Canada 78°30N 111°30W 69 B9
Borden Pen. Canada 73°0N 83°0W 69 C15

Border Ranges △ Australia 28°24S 152°56E **63 D5**
Borders = Scottish Borders □ U.K. 55°35N 2°50W **11 F6**
Bordertown Australia 36°19S 140°45E **63 F3**
Borðeyri Iceland 65°12N 21°6W **8 D3**
Bordj Flye Ste-Marie Algeria 27°19N 2°32W **52 C5**
Bordj in Eker Algeria 24°9N 5°3E **52 D7**
Bordj Mokhtar Algeria 21°20N 0°56E **52 D6**
Bordj Omar Driss Algeria 28°10N 6°40E **52 C7**
Borehamwood U.K. 51°40N 0°15W **13 F7**
Borgampad India 17°39N 80°52E **44 F5**
Borgarnes Iceland 64°32N 21°55W **8 D3**
Børgefjellet Norway 65°20N 13°45E **8 D15**
Borger Neths. 52°54N 6°44E **15 B6**
Borger U.S.A. 35°39N 101°24W **84 D4**
Borgholm Sweden 56°52N 16°39E **9 H17**
Borhoyn Tal Mongolia 43°50N 111°58E **32 C6**
Borigumma India 19°3N 82°33E **44 H7**
Borikhane Laos 18°33N 103°43E **38 C4**
Borisoglebsk Russia 51°27N 42°5E **19 D7**
Borisov = Barysaw Belarus 54°17N 28°28E **17 A15**
Borja Peru 4°20S 77°40W **92 D3**
Borkou Chad 18°15N 18°50E **53 E9**
Borkum Germany 53°34N 6°40E **16 B4**
Borlänge Sweden 60°29N 15°26E **9 F16**
Borley, C. Antarctica 66°15S 52°30E **5 C5**
Borneo E. Indies 1°0N 115°0E **36 D5**
Bornholm Denmark 55°10N 15°0E **9 J16**
Borobudur △ Indonesia 7°36S 110°12E **37 G14**
Borogontsy Russia 62°42N 131°8E **27 C14**
Borohoro Shan China 44°6N 83°10E **30 C5**
Boron U.S.A. 35°0N 117°39W **79 L9**
Borongan Phil. 11°37N 125°26E **37 B7**
Borovichi Russia 58°25N 33°55E **18 C5**
Borrego Springs U.S.A. 33°15N 116°23W **79 M10**
Borrisokane Ireland 53°0N 8°7W **10 D3**
Borroloola Australia 16°4S 136°17E **62 B2**
Borşa Romania 47°41N 24°50E **17 E13**
Borsad India 22°25N 72°54E **42 H5**
Bortala = Bole China 44°55N 81°37E **30 C5**
Borth U.K. 52°29N 4°2W **13 E3**
Borūjerd Iran 33°55N 48°50E **47 C6**
Boryeong S. Korea 36°21N 126°36E **33 F14**
Boryslav Ukraine 49°18N 23°28E **17 D12**
Borzya Russia 50°24N 116°31E **31 A12**
Bosa Italy 40°18N 8°30E **22 D3**
Bosanska Gradiška Bos.-H. 45°10N 17°15E **22 B7**
Boscastle U.K. 50°41N 4°42W **13 G3**
Boscobelle Barbados 13°17N 59°35W **89 g**
Bose China 23°53N 106°35E **34 F6**
Boseong S. Korea 34°46N 127°5E **33 G14**
Boshan China 36°28N 117°49E **33 F9**
Boshof S. Africa 28°31S 25°13E **56 C4**
Boshrūyeh Iran 33°50N 57°30E **47 C8**
Bosna → Bos.-H. 45°4N 18°29E **23 B8**
Bosna i Hercegovina = Bosnia-Herzegovina ■ Europe 44°0N 18°0E **22 B7**
Bosnia-Herzegovina ■ Europe 44°0N 18°0E **22 B7**
Bosnik Indonesia 1°5S 136°10E **37 E9**
Bosobolo Dem. Rep. of the Congo 4°15N 19°50E **54 D3**
Bosque Farms U.S.A. 35°51N 106°42W **77 J10**
Bosra = Buşra ash Shām Syria 32°30N 36°25E **48 C5**
Bossangoa C.A.R. 6°35N 17°30E **54 C3**
Bossier City U.S.A. 32°31N 93°44W **84 E8**
Bossiesvlei Namibia 25°1S 16°44E **56 C2**
Bosso Niger 13°43N 13°19E **53 F8**
Bostan Pakistan 30°26N 67°2E **42 D2**
Bostānābād Iran 37°50N 46°50E **46 B5**
Bosten Hu China 41°55N 87°40E **30 C6**
Boston U.K. 52°59N 0°2W **12 E7**
Boston Bar Canada 49°52N 121°30W **70 D4**
Boston Mts. U.S.A. 35°42N 93°15W **84 D8**
Boswell Canada 49°28N 116°45W **70 D5**
Boswell U.S.A. 40°10N 79°2W **82 F5**
Botad India 22°15N 71°40E **42 H4**
Botene Laos 17°35N 101°12E **38 D3**
Bothaville S. Africa 27°23S 26°34E **56 C4**
Bothnia, G. of Europe 62°0N 20°0E **8 F19**
Bothwell Australia 42°20S 147°1E **63 G4**
Bothwell Canada 42°38N 81°52W **82 D3**
Botletle → Botswana 20°10S 23°15E **56 B3**
Botoşani Romania 47°42N 26°41E **17 E14**
Botou Burkina Faso 12°42N 1°59E **52 F6**
Botou China 38°4N 116°34E **32 E9**
Botshabelo S. Africa 29°14S 26°44E **56 D4**
Botswana ■ Africa 22°0S 24°0E **56 B3**
Bottineau U.S.A. 48°50N 100°27W **80 A3**
Botucatu Brazil 22°55S 48°30W **95 A6**
Botum Sakor △ Cambodia 11°5N 103°15E **39 G4**
Botwood Canada 49°6N 55°23W **73 C8**
Bou Saâda Algeria 35°11N 4°9E **52 A6**
Bouaflé Ivory C. 7°1N 5°47W **52 G4**
Bouaké Ivory C. 7°40N 5°2W **52 G4**
Bouar C.A.R. 6°0N 15°40E **54 C3**
Bouârfa Morocco 32°32N 1°58W **52 B5**
Boucaut B. Australia 12°0S 134°25E **62 A1**
Bouctouche Canada 46°30N 64°45W **73 C7**
Bougainville, C. Australia 13°57S 126°4E **60 B4**
Bougainville I. Papua N. G. 6°0S 155°0E **58 B8**
Bougainville Reef Australia 15°30S 147°5E **62 B4**
Bougie = Bejaïa Algeria 36°42N 5°2E **52 A7**
Bougouni Mali 11°30N 7°20W **52 G4**
Bouillon Belgium 49°44N 5°3E **15 E5**
Boulder Colo., U.S.A. 40°1N 105°17W **76 F11**
Boulder Mont., U.S.A. 46°14N 112°7W **76 C7**
Boulder City U.S.A. 35°58N 114°49W **79 K12**
Boulder Creek U.S.A. 37°7N 122°7W **78 H4**
Boulder Dam = Hoover Dam U.S.A. 36°1N 114°44W **79 K12**
Boulia Australia 22°52S 139°51E **62 C2**

Boulogne-sur-Mer France 50°42N 1°36E **20 A4**
Boulsa Burkina Faso 12°39N 0°34W **52 F5**
Boultoum Niger 14°45N 10°25E **53 F8**
Bouma △ Fiji 16°50S 179°52E **59 a**
Boun Neua Laos 21°38N 101°54E **38 B3**
Boun Tai Laos 21°23N 101°58E **38 B3**
Bouna Ivory C. 9°10N 3°0W **52 G5**
Boundary Peak U.S.A. 37°51N 118°21W **78 H8**
Boundiali Ivory C. 9°30N 6°20W **52 G4**
Bountiful U.S.A. 40°53N 111°52W **76 F8**
Bounty Is. Pac. Oc. 48°0S 178°30E **64 M9**
Bounty Trough Pac. Oc. 46°0S 178°0E **64 M9**
Bourbonnais France 46°28N 3°0E **20 C5**
Bourdel L. Canada 56°43N 74°10W **72 A5**
Bourem Mali 17°0N 0°24W **52 E5**
Bourg-en-Bresse France 46°13N 5°12E **20 C6**
Bourg-St-Maurice France 45°35N 6°46E **20 D7**
Bourgas = Burgas Bulgaria 42°33N 27°29E **23 C12**
Bourges France 47°9N 2°25E **20 C5**
Bourget Canada 45°26N 75°9W **83 A9**
Bourgogne France 47°0N 4°50E **20 C6**
Bourke Australia 30°8S 145°55E **63 E4**
Bourne U.K. 52°47N 0°22W **12 E7**
Bournemouth U.K. 50°43N 1°52W **13 G6**
Bournemouth □ U.K. 50°43N 1°52W **13 G6**
Bouse U.S.A. 33°56N 114°0W **79 M13**
Bousso Chad 10°34N 16°52E **53 F9**
Bouvet I. = Bouvetøya Antarctica 54°26S 3°24E **2 G10**
Bouvetøya Antarctica 54°26S 3°24E **2 G10**
Bovill U.S.A. 46°51N 116°24W **76 C5**
Bovril Argentina 31°21S 59°26W **94 C4**
Bow → Canada 49°57N 111°41W **70 C6**
Bow Island Canada 49°50N 111°23W **76 B8**
Bowbells U.S.A. 48°48N 102°15W **80 A2**
Bowdle U.S.A. 45°27N 99°39W **80 C4**
Bowelling Australia 33°25S 116°30E **61 F2**
Bowen Argentina 35°0S 67°31W **94 D2**
Bowen Australia 20°0S 148°16E **62 J6**
Bowen Mts. Australia 37°0S 147°50E **63 F4**
Bowers Basin Pac. Oc. 53°45N 176°0E **4 D16**
Bowers Ridge Pac. Oc. 54°0N 180°0E **4 D17**
Bowie Ariz., U.S.A. 32°19N 109°29W **77 K9**
Bowie Tex., U.S.A. 33°34N 97°51W **84 E6**
Bowkān Iran 36°31N 46°12E **46 B5**
Bowland, Forest of U.K. 54°0N 2°30W **12 D5**
Bowling Green Ky., U.S.A. 36°59N 86°27W **80 G10**
Bowling Green Ohio, U.S.A. 41°23N 83°39W **81 E12**
Bowling Green, C. Australia 19°19S 147°25E **62 B4**
Bowling Green Bay △ Australia 19°26S 146°57E **62 B4**
Bowman U.S.A. 46°11N 103°24W **80 B2**
Bowman I. Antarctica 65°0S 104°0E **5 C8**
Bowmanville = Clarington Canada 43°55N 78°41W **82 C6**
Bowmore U.K. 55°45N 6°17W **11 F2**
Bowral Australia 34°26S 150°27E **63 E5**
Bowraville Australia 30°37S 152°52E **63 E5**
Bowron → Canada 54°3N 121°50W **70 C4**
Bowron Lake △ Canada 53°10N 121°5W **70 C4**
Bowser L. Canada 56°30N 129°30W **70 B3**
Bowsman Canada 52°14N 101°12W **71 C8**
Bowwood Australia 34°10S 143°50E **63 E3**
Boxmeer Neths. 51°38N 5°56E **15 C5**
Boxtel Neths. 51°36N 5°20E **15 C5**
Boyang China 29°0N 116°38E **35 C11**
Boyce U.S.A. 31°23N 92°40W **84 F8**
Boyd L. Canada 52°46N 76°42W **72 B4**
Boyle Canada 54°35N 112°49W **70 C6**
Boyle Ireland 53°59N 8°18W **10 C3**
Boyne → Ireland 53°43N 6°15W **10 C5**
Boyne, Bend of the Ireland 53°41N 6°27W **10 C5**
Boyne City U.S.A. 45°13N 85°1W **81 C11**
Boynton Beach U.S.A. 26°32N 80°4W **85 H14**
Boyoma, Chutes Dem. Rep. of the Congo 0°35N 25°23E **50 F6**
Boysen Res. U.S.A. 43°25N 108°11W **76 E9**
Boyuibe Bolivia 20°25S 63°17W **92 G6**
Boyup Brook Australia 33°50S 116°23E **61 F2**
Boz Dağları Turkey 38°20N 28°0E **23 E13**
Bozburun Turkey 36°43N 28°4E **23 F13**
Bozcaada Turkey 39°49N 26°3E **23 E12**
Bozdoğan Turkey 37°40N 28°17E **23 F13**
Bozeman U.S.A. 45°41N 111°2W **76 D8**
Bozhou China 33°55N 115°41E **32 H8**
Bozoum C.A.R. 6°25N 16°35E **54 C3**
Bozyazı Turkey 36°6N 33°0E **46 B2**
Bra Italy 44°42N 7°51E **20 D7**
Brabant □ Belgium 50°46N 4°30E **15 D4**
Brabant L. Canada 55°58N 103°43W **71 B8**
Brač Croatia 43°20N 16°40E **22 C7**
Bracadale, L. U.K. 57°20N 6°30W **11 D2**
Bracciano, L. di Italy 42°7N 12°14E **22 C5**
Bracebridge Canada 45°2N 79°19W **82 A5**
Bräcke Sweden 62°45N 15°26E **8 E16**
Brackettville U.S.A. 29°19N 100°25W **84 G4**
Bracknell U.K. 51°25N 0°43W **13 F7**
Bracknell Forest □ U.K. 51°25N 0°44W **13 F7**
Brad Romania 46°10N 22°50E **17 E12**
Bradenton U.S.A. 27°30N 82°34W **85 H13**
Bradford Canada 44°7N 79°34W **82 B5**
Bradford U.K. 53°47N 1°45W **12 D6**
Bradford Pa., U.S.A. 41°58N 78°38W **82 E6**
Bradford Vt., U.S.A. 43°59N 72°9W **83 C12**
Bradley Ark., U.S.A. 33°6N 93°39W **84 E8**
Bradley Calif., U.S.A. 35°52N 120°48W **78 K6**
Brady U.S.A. 31°9N 99°20W **84 F5**
Braeside Canada 45°28N 76°24W **83 A8**
Braga Portugal 41°35N 8°25W **21 B1**
Bragado Argentina 35°2S 60°27W **94 D3**
Bragança Brazil 1°0S 47°2W **93 D9**
Bragança Portugal 41°48N 6°50W **21 B2**
Bragança Paulista Brazil 22°55S 46°32W **95 A6**
Brahestad = Raahe Finland 64°40N 24°28E **8 D21**

Brahmanbaria Bangla. 23°58N 91°15E **41 H17**
Brahmani → India 20°39N 86°46E **44 D8**
Brahmapur India 19°15N 84°54E **44 E7**
Brahmaputra → Asia 23°40N 90°35E **43 H13**
Braich-y-pwll U.K. 52°47N 4°46W **12 E3**
Braidwood Australia 35°27S 149°49E **63 F4**
Brăila Romania 45°19N 27°59E **17 F14**
Brainerd U.S.A. 46°22N 94°12W **80 B6**
Braintree U.K. 51°53N 0°34E **13 F8**
Braintree U.S.A. 42°13N 71°0W **83 D14**
Brak → S. Africa 29°35S 22°55E **56 C3**
Brakwater Namibia 22°28S 17°3E **56 B2**
Bramhapuri India 20°36N 79°52E **44 D4**
Brampton Canada 43°45N 79°45W **82 C5**
Brampton U.K. 54°57N 2°44W **12 C5**
Brampton I. Australia 20°49S 149°16E **62 b**
Branco → Brazil 1°20S 61°50W **92 D6**
Branco, C. Brazil 7°9S 34°47W **90 D7**
Brandberg Namibia 21°10S 14°33E **56 B1**
Brandenburg = Neubrandenburg Germany 53°33N 13°15E **16 B7**
Brandenburg Germany 52°25N 12°33E **16 B7**
Brandenburg □ Germany 52°50N 13°0E **16 B6**
Brandfort S. Africa 28°40S 26°30E **56 D4**
Brandon Canada 49°50N 99°57W **71 D9**
Brandon B. U.S.A. 43°48N 73°6W **83 C11**
Brandon B. Ireland 52°17N 10°8W **10 D1**
Brandon Mt. Ireland 52°15N 10°15W **10 D1**
Brandsen Argentina 35°10S 58°15W **94 D4**
Brandvlei S. Africa 30°25S 20°30E **56 D3**
Branford U.S.A. 41°17N 72°49W **83 E12**
Braniewo Poland 54°25N 19°50E **17 A10**
Bransfield Str. Antarctica 63°0S 59°0W **5 C18**
Branson U.S.A. 36°39N 93°13W **80 G7**
Brantford Canada 43°10N 80°15W **82 C4**
Bras d'Or L. Canada 45°50N 60°50W **73 C7**
Brasher Falls U.S.A. 44°49N 74°47W **83 B10**
Brasil = Brazil ■ S. Amer. 12°0S 50°0W **93 F9**
Brasil, Planalto Brazil 18°0S 46°30W **90 E6**
Brasiléia Brazil 11°0S 68°45W **92 F5**
Brasília Brazil 15°47S 47°55W **93 G9**
Brasília Legal Brazil 3°49S 55°36W **93 D7**
Braslaw Belarus 55°38N 27°0E **9 J22**
Braşov Romania 45°38N 25°35E **17 F13**
Brasschaat Belgium 51°19N 4°27E **15 C4**
Brassey, Banjaran Malaysia 5°0N 117°15E **36 D5**
Brassey Ra. Australia 25°8S 122°15E **61 E3**
Brasstown Bald U.S.A. 34°53N 83°49W **85 D13**
Brastad Sweden 58°23N 11°30E **9 G14**
Bratislava Slovak Rep. 48°10N 17°7E **17 D9**
Bratsk Russia 56°10N 101°30E **27 D11**
Bratskoye Vdkhr. Russia 56°0N 101°40E **27 D11**
Brattleboro U.S.A. 42°51N 72°34W **83 D12**
Braunau Austria 48°15N 13°3E **16 D7**
Braunschweig Germany 52°15N 10°31E **16 B6**
Braunton U.K. 51°7N 4°10W **13 F3**
Brava C. Verde Is. 15°0N 24°40W **52 b**
Bravo del Norte, Rio = Grande, Rio → N. Amer. 25°58N 97°9W **84 J6**
Brawley U.S.A. 32°59N 115°31W **79 N11**
Bray, Mt. Australia 14°0S 134°30E **62 A1**
Bray, Pays de France 49°46N 1°26E **20 B4**
Brazeau → Canada 52°55N 115°14W **70 C5**
Brazil U.S.A. 39°32N 87°8W **80 F10**
Brazil ■ S. Amer. 12°0S 50°0W **93 F9**
Brazilian Highlands = Brasil, Planalto Brazil 18°0S 46°30W **90 E6**
Brazo Sur → S. Amer. 25°21S 57°42W **94 B4**
Brazos → U.S.A. 28°53N 95°23W **84 G7**
Brazzaville Congo 4°9S 15°12E **54 E3**
Brčko Bos.-H. 44°54N 18°46E **23 B8**
Bré = Bray Ireland 53°13N 6°7W **10 C5**
Breaden, L. Australia 25°51S 125°28E **61 E4**
Breaksea Sd. N.Z. 45°35S 166°35E **59 F1**
Bream B. N.Z. 35°56S 174°28E **59 A5**
Bream Hd. N.Z. 35°51S 174°36E **59 A5**
Breas Chile 25°29S 70°24W **94 B1**
Brebes Indonesia 6°52S 109°3E **37 G13**
Brechin Canada 44°32N 79°10W **82 B5**
Brechin U.K. 56°44N 2°39W **11 E6**
Brecht Belgium 51°21N 4°38E **15 C4**
Breckenridge Colo., U.S.A. 39°29N 106°3W **76 G10**
Breckenridge Minn., U.S.A. 46°16N 96°35W **80 B5**
Breckenridge Tex., U.S.A. 32°45N 98°54W **84 E5**
Breckland U.K. 52°30N 0°40E **13 E8**
Brecon U.K. 51°57N 3°23W **13 F4**
Brecon Beacons U.K. 51°53N 3°26W **13 F4**
Brecon Beacons △ U.K. 51°50N 3°30W **13 F4**
Breda Neths. 51°35N 4°45E **15 C4**
Bredasdorp S. Africa 34°33S 20°2E **56 D3**
Bree Belgium 51°8N 5°35E **15 C5**
Bregenz Austria 47°30N 9°45E **16 E5**
Breiðafjörður Iceland 65°15N 23°15W **8 D2**
Brejo Brazil 3°41S 42°47W **93 D10**
Bremen Germany 53°4N 8°47E **16 B5**
Bremer Bay Australia 34°21S 119°16E **61 F2**
Bremer I. Australia 12°5S 136°45E **62 A2**
Bremerhaven Germany 53°33N 8°36E **16 B5**
Bremerton U.S.A. 47°34N 122°37W **78 C4**
Brenham U.S.A. 30°10N 96°24W **84 F6**
Brennerpass Austria 47°2N 11°30E **16 E6**
Brent Canada 46°2N 78°30W **82 A6**
Brentwood U.K. 51°37N 0°19E **13 F8**
Brentwood Calif., U.S.A. 37°56N 121°42W **78 H5**
Brentwood N.Y., U.S.A. 40°47N 73°15W **83 F11**
Bréscia Italy 45°33N 10°15E **20 D9**
Breskens Neths. 51°23N 3°33E **15 C3**
Breslau = Wrocław Poland 51°5N 17°5E **17 C9**
Bressanone Italy 46°43N 11°39E **22 A4**
Bressay U.K. 60°9N 1°6W **11 A7**
Brest Belarus 52°10N 23°40E **17 B12**
Brest France 48°24N 4°31W **20 B1**
Brest □ Belarus 52°30N 26°10E **17 B13**

Brest-Litovsk = Brest Belarus 52°10N 23°40E **17 B12**
Bretagne □ France 48°10N 3°0W **20 B2**
Breton Canada 53°7N 114°28W **70 C6**
Breton Sd. U.S.A. 29°35N 89°15W **85 G10**
Brett, C. N.Z. 35°10S 174°20E **59 A5**
Brevard U.S.A. 35°14N 82°44W **85 D13**
Breves Brazil 1°40S 50°29W **93 D8**
Brewarrina Australia 30°0S 146°51E **63 E4**
Brewer U.S.A. 44°48N 68°46W **81 C19**
Brewer, Mt. U.S.A. 36°44N 118°28W **78 J8**
Brewster N.Y., U.S.A. 41°24N 73°36W **83 E11**
Brewster Ohio, U.S.A. 40°43N 81°36W **82 F3**
Brewster Wash., U.S.A. 48°6N 119°47W **76 B4**
Brewster, Kap = Kangikajik Greenland 70°7N 22°0W **4 B6**
Brewton U.S.A. 31°7N 87°4W **85 F11**
Breyten S. Africa 26°16S 30°0E **57 C5**
Bria C.A.R. 6°30N 21°58E **54 C4**
Briançon France 44°54N 6°39E **20 D7**
Bribie I. Australia 27°0S 153°10E **63 D5**
Bribri Costa Rica 9°38N 82°50W **88 E3**
Bridgefield Barbados 13°9N 59°36W **89 g**
Bridgehampton U.S.A. 40°56N 72°19W **83 F12**
Bridgend U.K. 51°30N 3°34W **13 F4**
Bridgend □ U.K. 51°36N 3°36W **13 F4**
Bridgenorth Canada 44°23N 78°23W **82 B6**
Bridgeport Calif., U.S.A. 38°15N 119°14W **78 G7**
Bridgeport Conn., U.S.A. 41°11N 73°12W **83 E11**
Bridgeport N.Y., U.S.A. 43°9N 75°58W **83 C9**
Bridgeport Nebr., U.S.A. 41°40N 103°6W **80 E2**
Bridgeport Tex., U.S.A. 33°13N 97°45W **84 E6**
Bridger U.S.A. 45°18N 108°55W **76 D9**
Bridgeton U.S.A. 39°26N 75°14W **81 F16**
Bridgetown Australia 33°58S 116°7E **61 F2**
Bridgetown Barbados 13°6N 59°37W **89 g**
Bridgetown Canada 44°55N 65°18W **73 D6**
Bridgewater Australia 42°44S 147°14E **63 G4**
Bridgewater Canada 44°25N 64°31W **73 D7**
Bridgewater Mass., U.S.A. 41°59N 70°58W **83 E14**
Bridgewater N.Y., U.S.A. 42°53N 75°15W **83 D9**
Bridgewater, C. Australia 38°23S 141°23E **63 F3**
Bridgnorth U.K. 52°32N 2°25W **13 E5**
Bridgton U.S.A. 44°3N 70°42W **83 B14**
Bridgwater U.K. 51°8N 2°59W **13 F5**
Bridgwater B. U.K. 51°15N 3°15W **13 F4**
Bridlington U.K. 54°5N 0°12W **12 C7**
Bridlington B. U.K. 54°4N 0°10W **12 C7**
Bridport Australia 40°59S 147°23E **63 G4**
Bridport U.K. 50°44N 2°45W **13 G5**
Brig Switz. 46°18N 7°59E **20 C7**
Brigg U.K. 53°34N 0°28E **12 D7**
Brigham City U.S.A. 41°31N 112°1W **76 F7**
Bright Australia 36°42S 146°56E **63 F4**
Brighton Canada 44°2N 77°44W **82 B7**
Brighton Trin. & Tob. 10°15N 61°39W **93 K15**
Brighton U.K. 50°49N 0°7W **13 G7**
Brighton Colo., U.S.A. 43°8N 77°34W **82 C7**
Brightside Canada 45°7N 76°29W **83 A8**
Brilliant Canada 40°15N 80°39W **82 F4**
Brindisi Italy 40°39N 17°55E **23 D7**
Brinkley U.S.A. 34°53N 91°12W **84 D9**
Brinnon U.S.A. 47°41N 122°54W **78 C4**
Brion, Î. Canada 47°46N 61°26W **73 C7**
Brisay → Canada 54°26N 70°31W **73 B5**
Brisbane Australia 27°25S 153°2E **63 D5**
Brisbane → Australia 27°24S 153°9E **63 D5**
Bristol U.K. 51°26N 2°35W **13 F5**
Bristol Conn., U.S.A. 41°40N 72°57W **83 E12**
Bristol Pa., U.S.A. 40°6N 74°51W **83 F10**
Bristol R.I., U.S.A. 41°40N 71°16W **83 E13**
Bristol Tenn., U.S.A. 36°36N 82°11W **85 C13**
Bristol Vt., U.S.A. 44°8N 73°4W **83 B11**
Bristol, City of □ U.K. 51°27N 2°36W **13 F5**
Bristol B. U.S.A. 58°0N 160°0W **74 D8**
Bristol Channel U.K. 51°18N 4°30W **13 F3**
Bristol I. Antarctica 58°45S 28°0W **5 B1**
Bristol L. U.S.A. 34°28N 115°41W **79 L11**
Bristow U.S.A. 35°50N 96°23W **84 D6**
Britain = Great Britain Europe 54°0N 2°15W **6 E5**
British Columbia □ Canada 55°0N 125°15W **70 C3**
British Indian Ocean Terr. = Chagos Arch. ☑ Ind. Oc. 6°0S 72°0E **25 J9**
British Isles Europe 54°0N 4°0W **14 D5**
British Mts. N. Amer. 68°50N 140°0W **74 B12**
British Virgin Is. ☑ W. Indies 18°30N 64°30W **89 e**
Brits S. Africa 25°37S 27°48E **57 C4**
Britstown S. Africa 30°37S 23°30E **56 D3**
Britt Canada 45°46N 80°34W **72 C3**
Brittany = Bretagne □ France 48°10N 3°0W **20 B2**
Britton U.S.A. 45°48N 97°45W **80 C5**
Brive-la-Gaillarde France 45°10N 1°32E **20 D4**
Brixen = Bressanone Italy 46°43N 11°39E **22 A4**
Brixham U.K. 50°23N 3°31W **13 G4**
Brno Czech Rep. 49°10N 16°35E **17 D9**
Broach = Bharuch India 21°47N 73°0E **44 D1**
Broad → U.S.A. 34°1N 81°4W **85 D14**
Broad Arrow Australia 30°23S 121°15E **61 F3**
Broad B. U.K. 58°14N 6°18W **11 C2**
Broad Haven Ireland 54°20N 9°55W **10 B2**
Broad Law U.K. 55°30N 3°21W **11 F5**
Broad Pk. = Faichan Kangri India 35°48N 76°34E **43 B7**
Broad Sd. Australia 22°0S 149°45E **62 C4**
Broadalbin U.S.A. 43°4N 74°12W **83 C10**
Broadback → Canada 51°21N 78°52W **72 B4**
Broadhurst Ra. Australia 22°30S 122°30E **60 D3**
Broads, The U.K. 52°45N 1°30E **12 E9**
Broadus U.S.A. 45°27N 105°25W **76 D11**
Brochet Canada 57°53N 101°40W **71 B8**
Brochet, L. Canada 58°36N 101°35W **71 B8**
Brock I. Canada 77°52N 114°19W **69 B9**

Brocken Germany 51°47N 10°37E **16 C6**
Brockport U.S.A. 43°13N 77°56W **82 C7**
Brockton U.S.A. 42°5N 71°1W **83 D13**
Brockville Canada 44°35N 75°41W **83 B9**
Brockway Mont., U.S.A. 47°18N 105°45W **76 C11**
Brockway Pa., U.S.A. 41°15N 78°47W **82 E6**
Brodeur Pen. Canada 72°30N 88°10W **69 C14**
Brodick U.K. 55°35N 5°9W **11 F3**
Brodnica Poland 53°15N 19°25E **17 B10**
Brody Ukraine 50°5N 25°10E **17 C13**
Brogan U.S.A. 44°15N 117°31W **76 D5**
Broken Arrow U.S.A. 36°3N 95°48W **84 C7**
Broken Bow Nebr., U.S.A. 41°24N 99°38W **80 E4**
Broken Bow Okla., U.S.A. 34°2N 94°44W **84 D7**
Broken Bow Lake U.S.A. 34°9N 94°40W **84 D7**
Broken Hill Australia 31°58S 141°29E **63 E3**
Broken Ridge Ind. Oc. 30°0S 94°0E **64 L1**
Broken River Ra. Australia 21°0S 148°22E **62 b**
Bromo Tengger Semeru △ Indonesia 7°56S 112°57E **37 H15**
Bromsgrove U.K. 52°21N 2°2W **13 E5**
Brønderslev Denmark 57°16N 9°57E **9 H13**
Bronkhorstspruit S. Africa 25°46S 28°45E **57 C4**
Brønnøysund Norway 65°28N 12°14E **8 D15**
Brook Park U.S.A. 41°23N 81°48W **82 E4**
Brookhaven U.S.A. 31°35N 90°26W **85 F9**
Brookings Oreg., U.S.A. 42°3N 124°17W **76 E1**
Brookings S. Dak., U.S.A. 44°19N 96°48W **80 C5**
Brooklin Canada 43°55N 78°55W **82 C6**
Brooklyn Park U.S.A. 45°6N 93°23W **80 C7**
Brooks Canada 50°35N 111°55W **70 C6**
Brooks Range U.S.A. 68°0N 152°0W **74 B9**
Brooksville U.S.A. 28°33N 82°23W **85 G13**
Brookton Australia 32°22S 117°0E **61 F2**
Brookville U.S.A. 41°10N 79°5W **82 E5**
Broom, L. U.K. 57°55N 5°15W **11 D3**
Broome Australia 18°0S 122°15E **60 C3**
Brora U.K. 58°0N 3°52W **11 C5**
Brora → U.K. 58°0N 3°51W **11 C5**
Brosna → Ireland 53°14N 7°58W **10 C4**
Brothers U.S.A. 43°49N 120°36W **76 E3**
Brough U.K. 54°32N 2°18W **12 C5**
Brough Hd. U.K. 59°8N 3°20W **11 B5**
Broughton Island = Qikiqtarjuaq Canada 67°33N 63°0W **69 D19**
Brown, L. Australia 31°5S 118°15E **61 F2**
Brown, Pt. Australia 32°32S 133°50E **63 E1**
Brown City U.S.A. 43°13N 82°59W **82 C2**
Brown Willy U.K. 50°35N 4°37W **13 G3**
Brownfield U.S.A. 33°11N 102°17W **84 E3**
Browning U.S.A. 48°34N 113°1W **76 B7**
Brownsville Oreg., U.S.A. 44°24N 122°59W **76 D2**
Brownsville Pa., U.S.A. 40°1N 79°53W **82 F5**
Brownsville Tenn., U.S.A. 35°36N 89°16W **85 D10**
Brownsville Tex., U.S.A. 25°54N 97°30W **84 J6**
Brownville U.S.A. 44°0N 75°59W **83 C9**
Brownwood U.S.A. 31°43N 98°59W **84 F5**
Browse I. Australia 14°7S 123°33E **60 B3**
Bruas Malaysia 4°30N 100°47E **39 K3**
Bruay-la-Buissière France 50°29N 2°33E **20 A5**
Bruce, Mt. Australia 22°37S 118°8E **60 D2**
Bruce Pen. Canada 45°0N 81°30W **82 B3**
Bruce Peninsula △ Canada 45°14N 81°36W **82 A3**
Bruce Rock Australia 31°52S 118°8E **61 F2**
Bruck an der Leitha Austria 48°1N 16°47E **17 D9**
Bruck an der Mur Austria 47°24N 15°16E **16 E8**
Brue → U.K. 51°13N 2°59W **13 F5**
Bruges = Brugge Belgium 51°13N 3°13E **15 C3**
Brugge Belgium 51°13N 3°13E **15 C3**
Bruin U.S.A. 41°3N 79°43W **82 E5**
Brûk, W. el → Egypt 30°15N 33°50E **48 E2**
Brûlé Canada 53°15N 117°58W **70 C5**
Brûlé, L. Canada 53°35N 64°4W **73 B7**
Brumado Brazil 14°14S 41°40W **93 F10**
Brumunddal Norway 60°53N 10°56E **8 F14**
Bruneau U.S.A. 42°53N 115°48W **76 E6**
Bruneau → U.S.A. 42°56N 115°57W **76 E6**
Brunei = Bandar Seri Begawan Brunei 4°52N 115°0E **36 D5**
Brunei ■ Asia 4°50N 115°0E **36 D5**
Brunner, L. N.Z. 42°37S 171°27E **59 E3**
Brunssum Neths. 50°57N 5°59E **15 D5**
Brunswick = Braunschweig Germany 52°15N 10°31E **16 B6**
Brunswick Ga., U.S.A. 31°10N 81°30W **85 F14**
Brunswick Maine, U.S.A. 43°55N 69°58W **81 D19**
Brunswick Md., U.S.A. 39°19N 77°38W **81 F15**
Brunswick Mo., U.S.A. 39°26N 93°8W **80 F7**
Brunswick Ohio, U.S.A. 41°14N 81°51W **82 E3**
Brunswick, Pen. de Chile 53°30S 71°30W **96 G2**
Brunswick B. Australia 15°15S 124°50E **60 C3**
Brunswick Junction Australia 33°15S 115°50E **61 F2**
Brunt Ice Shelf Antarctica 75°30S 25°0W **5 D2**
Brus Laguna Honduras 15°47N 84°35W **88 C3**
Brush U.S.A. 40°15N 103°37W **76 F12**
Brushton U.S.A. 44°50N 74°31W **83 B10**
Brusque Brazil 27°5S 49°0W **95 B6**
Brussels = Bruxelles Belgium 50°51N 4°21E **15 D4**
Brussels Canada 43°44N 81°15W **82 C3**
Bruthen Australia 37°42S 147°50E **63 F4**
Bryan Ohio, U.S.A. 41°28N 84°33W **81 E11**
Bryan Tex., U.S.A. 30°40N 96°22W **84 F6**
Bryan, Mt. Australia 33°30S 139°5E **63 E2**
Bryansk Russia 53°13N 34°25E **18 D4**
Bryce Canyon △ U.S.A. 37°30N 112°10W **77 H7**
Bryne Norway 58°44N 5°38E **9 G11**
Bryson City U.S.A. 35°26N 83°27W **85 D13**
Bsharri Lebanon 34°15N 36°0E **48 A5**
Bū Baqarah U.A.E. 25°35N 56°25E **47 E8**
Bu Craa W. Sahara 26°45N 12°50W **52 C3**

Bū Ḥaṣā U.A.E. 23°30N 53°20E **47 F7**
Bua Fiji 16°48S 178°37E **59 a**
Bua Yai Thailand 15°33N 102°26E **38 E4**
Buan S. Korea 35°44N 126°44E **33 G14**
Buapinang Indonesia 4°40S 121°30E **37 E6**
Bubi → Zimbabwe 22°20S 31°7E **57 B5**
Buca Fiji 16°38S 179°52E **59 a**
Bucaramanga Colombia 7°0N 73°0W **92 B4**
Bucasia Australia 21°2S 149°10E **62 b**
Buccaneer Arch.
  Australia 16°7S 123°20E **60 C3**
Buccoo Reef Trin. & Tob. 11°10N 60°51W **93 J16**
Buchach Ukraine 49°5N 25°25E **17 D13**
Buchan U.K. 57°32N 2°21W **11 D6**
Buchan Ness U.K. 57°29N 1°46W **11 D7**
Buchanan Canada 51°40N 102°45W **71 C8**
Buchanan Liberia 5°57N 10°2W **52 G3**
Buchanan, L. Queens.,
  Australia 21°35S 145°52E **62 C4**
Buchanan, L. W. Austral.,
  Australia 25°33S 123°2E **61 E3**
Buchanan, L. U.S.A. 30°45N 98°25W **84 F5**
Buchanan Cr. →
  Australia 19°13S 136°33E **62 B2**
Buchans Canada 48°50N 56°52W **73 C8**
Bucharest = București
  Romania 44°27N 26°10E **17 F14**
Bucheon S. Korea 37°28N 126°45E **33 F14**
Buchon, Pt. U.S.A. 35°15N 120°54W **78 K6**
Buck Hill Falls U.S.A. 41°11N 75°16W **83 E9**
Buckeye Lake U.S.A. 39°55N 82°29W **82 G2**
Buckhannon U.S.A. 39°0N 80°8W **81 F13**
Buckhaven U.K. 56°11N 3°3W **11 E5**
Buckhorn L. Canada 44°29N 78°23W **82 B6**
Buckie U.K. 57°41N 2°58W **11 D6**
Buckingham Canada 45°37N 75°24W **72 C4**
Buckingham U.K. 51°59N 0°57W **13 F7**
Buckingham B.
  Australia 12°10S 135°40E **62 A2**
Buckingham Canal India 14°0N 80°5E **45 H5**
Buckinghamshire □ U.K. 51°53N 0°55W **13 F7**
Buckle Hd. Australia 14°26S 127°52E **60 B4**
Buckleboo Australia 32°54S 136°12E **63 E2**
Buckley U.K. 53°10N 3°5W **12 D4**
Buckley → Australia 20°10S 138°49E **62 C2**
Bucklin U.S.A. 37°33N 99°38W **80 G4**
Bucks L. U.S.A. 39°54N 121°12W **78 F5**
București Romania 44°27N 26°10E **17 F14**
Bucyrus U.S.A. 40°48N 82°59W **81 E12**
Budalin Burma 22°20N 95°10E **41 H19**
Budaun India 28°5N 79°10E **43 E8**
Budd Coast Antarctica 68°0S 112°0E **5 C8**
Bude U.K. 50°49N 4°34W **13 G3**
Budennovsk Russia 44°50N 44°10E **19 F7**
Budge Budge = Baj Baj
  India 22°30N 88°5E **43 H13**
Budgewoi Australia 33°13S 151°34E **63 E5**
Budjala
  Dem. Rep. of the Congo 2°50N 19°40E **54 D3**
Budo-Sungai Padi △
  Thailand 6°19N 101°42E **39 J3**
Buellton U.S.A. 34°37N 120°12W **79 L6**
Buena Esperanza
  Argentina 34°45S 65°15W **94 C2**
Buena Park U.S.A. 33°52N 117°59W **79 M9**
Buena Vista Colo.,
  U.S.A. 38°51N 106°8W **76 G10**
Buena Vista Va., U.S.A. 37°44N 79°21W **81 G14**
Buena Vista Lake Bed
  U.S.A. 35°12N 119°18W **79 K7**
Buenaventura Colombia 3°53N 77°4W **92 C3**
Buenaventura Mexico 29°51N 107°29W **86 B3**
Buenos Aires Costa Rica 9°10N 83°20W **88 E3**
Buenos Aires △ Argentina 36°30S 60°0W **94 D4**
Buenos Aires, L. = General
  Carrera, L. S. Amer. 46°35S 72°0W **96 F2**
Buffalo Mo., U.S.A. 37°39N 93°6W **80 G7**
Buffalo N.Y., U.S.A. 42°53N 78°53W **82 D6**
Buffalo Okla., U.S.A. 36°50N 99°38W **84 C5**
Buffalo S. Dak., U.S.A. 45°35N 103°33W **80 C2**
Buffalo Wyo., U.S.A. 44°21N 106°42W **76 D10**
Buffalo → Canada 60°5N 115°5W **70 A5**
Buffalo → S. Africa 28°43S 30°37E **57 C5**
Buffalo △ U.S.A. 36°14N 92°36W **84 C8**
Buffalo Head Hills
  Canada 57°25N 115°55W **70 B5**
Buffalo L. Alta., Canada 52°27N 112°54W **70 C6**
Buffalo L. N.W.T.,
  Canada 60°12N 115°25W **70 A5**
Buffalo Narrows Canada 55°51N 108°29W **71 B7**
Buffels → S. Africa 29°36S 17°3E **56 C2**
Buford U.S.A. 34°7N 83°59W **85 D12**
Bug = Buh → Ukraine 46°59N 31°58E **19 E5**
Bug → Poland 52°31N 21°5E **17 B11**
Buga Colombia 4°0N 76°15W **92 C3**
Bugel, Tanjung Indonesia 6°26S 111°3E **37 G14**
Bugsuk I. Phil. 8°12N 117°18E **36 C5**
Bugulma Russia 54°33N 52°48E **18 D9**
Buguruslan Russia 53°39N 52°26E **18 D9**
Buh → Ukraine 46°59N 31°58E **19 E5**
Buhera Zimbabwe 19°18S 31°29E **57 A5**
Buhl U.S.A. 42°36N 114°46W **76 E6**
Builth Wells U.K. 52°9N 3°25W **13 E4**
Buir Nur Mongolia 47°50N 117°42E **31 B12**
Buji China 22°37N 114°5E **31 a**
Bujumbura Burundi 3°16S 29°18E **54 E5**
Bukachacha Russia 52°55N 116°50E **27 D12**
Bukavu
  Dem. Rep. of the Congo 2°20S 28°52E **54 E5**
Bukhara = Buxoro
  Uzbekistan 39°48N 64°25E **26 F7**
Bukhoro = Buxoro
  Uzbekistan 39°48N 64°25E **26 F7**
Bukhtarma Res. = Zaysan Köli
  Kazakhstan 48°0N 83°0E **26 E9**
Bukit Bendera Malaysia 5°25N 100°15E **39 c**
Bukit Mertajam Malaysia 5°22N 100°28E **39 c**
Bukit Nil Malaysia 1°22N 104°12E **39 d**

Bukit Tengah Malaysia 5°22N 100°25E **39 c**
Bukittinggi Indonesia 0°20S 100°20E **36 E2**
Bukkapatnam India 14°14N 77°46E **45 G3**
Bukoba Tanzania 1°20S 31°49E **54 E6**
Bül, Kuh-e Iran 30°48N 52°45E **47 D7**
Bula Indonesia 3°6S 130°30E **37 E8**
Bulahdelah Australia 32°23S 152°13E **63 E5**
Bulan Phil. 12°40N 123°52E **37 B6**
Bulawayo Zimbabwe 20°7S 28°32E **55 J5**
Buldan Turkey 38°2N 28°50E **23 E13**
Buldana India 20°30N 76°18E **44 D3**
Buldir I. U.S.A. 52°21N 175°56E **74 E3**
Bulgan Mongolia 48°45N 103°34E **30 B9**
Bulgar Russia 54°57N 49°4E **18 D8**
Bulgaria ■ Europe 42°35N 25°30E **23 C11**
Buli, Teluk Indonesia 0°48N 128°25E **37 D7**
Buliluyan, C. Phil. 8°20N 117°15E **36 C5**
Bull Shoals L. U.S.A. 36°22N 92°35W **84 C8**
Bulleringa △ Australia 17°39S 143°56E **62 B3**
Bullhead City U.S.A. 35°8N 114°32W **79 K12**
Büllingen Belgium 50°25N 6°16E **15 D6**
Bullock Creek Australia 17°43S 144°31E **62 B3**
Bulloo → Australia 28°43S 142°30E **63 D3**
Bulloo L. Australia 28°43S 142°25E **63 D3**
Bulls N.Z. 40°10S 175°24E **59 D5**
Bulman Australia 13°39S 134°20E **62 A1**
Bulnes Chile 36°42S 72°19W **94 D1**
Bulsar = Valsad India 20°40N 72°58E **44 D1**
Bultfontein S. Africa 28°18S 26°10E **56 D4**
Bulukumba Indonesia 5°33S 120°11E **37 F6**
Bulun Russia 70°37N 127°30E **27 B13**
Bumba
  Dem. Rep. of the Congo 2°13N 22°30E **54 D4**
Bumbah, Khalīj Libya 32°20N 23°15E **53 B10**
Bumhpa Bum Burma 26°51N 97°14E **41 F20**
Bunaken Indonesia 1°37N 124°46E **37 D6**
Bunbury Australia 33°20S 115°35E **61 F2**
Bunclody Ireland 52°39N 6°40W **10 D5**
Buncrana Ireland 55°8N 7°27W **10 A4**
Bundaberg Australia 24°54S 152°22E **63 C5**
Bundey → Australia 21°46S 135°37E **62 C2**
Bundi India 25°30N 75°35E **42 G6**
Bundjalung △ Australia 29°16S 153°21E **63 D5**
Bundoran Ireland 54°28N 8°18W **10 B3**
Bung Kan Thailand 18°23N 103°37E **38 C4**
Bungay U.K. 52°27N 1°28E **13 E9**
Bungil Cr. → Australia 27°5S 149°5E **63 D4**
Bungle Bungle = Purnululu △
  Australia 17°20S 128°20E **60 C4**
Bungo-Suidō Japan 33°0N 132°15E **29 H6**
Bungotakada Japan 33°35N 131°25E **29 H5**
Bunia
  Dem. Rep. of the Congo 1°35N 30°20E **54 D6**
Bunji Pakistan 35°45N 74°40E **43 B6**
Bunkie U.S.A. 30°57N 92°11W **84 F8**
Bunnell U.S.A. 29°28N 81°16W **85 G14**
Buntok Indonesia 1°40S 114°58E **36 E4**
Bunya Mts. △ Australia 26°51S 151°34E **63 D5**
Bunyu Indonesia 3°35N 117°50E **36 D5**
Buon Brieng Vietnam 13°9N 108°12E **38 F7**
Buon Ho Vietnam 12°57N 108°18E **38 F7**
Buon Ma Thuot Vietnam 12°40N 108°3E **38 F7**
Buong Long Cambodia 13°44N 106°59E **38 F6**
Buorkhaya, Mys
  Russia 71°50N 132°40E **27 B14**
Buqayq Si. Arabia 26°0N 49°45E **47 E6**
Bur Acaba = Buurhakaba
  Somalia 3°12N 44°20E **49 G3**
Bûr Safâga Egypt 26°43N 33°57E **46 E2**
Bûr Sa'îd Egypt 31°16N 32°18E **53 B12**
Bûr Sûdân Sudan 19°32N 37°9E **53 E13**
Burakin Australia 30°31S 117°10E **61 F2**
Burang China 30°15N 81°10E **30 E5**
Burao = Burco Somalia 9°32N 45°32E **49 F4**
Burāq Syria 33°11N 36°29E **48 B5**
Burathum Nepal 28°4N 84°50E **43 E11**
Buraydah Si. Arabia 26°20N 43°59E **46 E4**
Burco Somalia 9°32N 45°32E **49 F4**
Burda India 25°50N 77°35E **42 G7**
Burdekin → Australia 19°38S 147°25E **62 B4**
Burdur Turkey 37°45N 30°17E **19 G5**
Burdwan = Barddhaman
  India 23°14N 87°39E **43 H12**
Bure Ethiopia 10°40N 37°4E **46 E2**
Bure → U.K. 52°38N 1°43E **12 E9**
Bureskoye Vdkhr.
  Russia 50°16N 130°20E **27 D14**
Bureya → Russia 49°27N 129°30E **27 E13**
Burford Canada 43°7N 80°27W **82 C4**
Burgas Bulgaria 42°33N 27°29E **23 C12**
Burgeo Canada 47°37N 57°38W **73 C8**
Burgersdorp S. Africa 31°0S 26°20E **56 D4**
Burgess, Mt. Australia 30°50S 121°5E **61 F3**
Burghead U.K. 57°43N 3°30W **11 D5**
Burgos Spain 42°21N 3°41W **21 A4**
Burgsvik Sweden 57°3N 18°19E **9 H18**
Burgundy = Bourgogne □
  France 47°0N 4°50E **20 C6**
Burhaniye Turkey 39°30N 26°58E **23 E12**
Burhanpur India 21°18N 76°14E **44 J3**
Burhi Gandak → India 25°20N 86°37E **43 G12**
Burhner → India 22°43N 80°31E **43 H9**
Burias I. Phil. 12°55N 123°5E **37 B6**
Burica, Pta. Costa Rica 8°3N 82°51W **88 E3**
Burien U.S.A. 47°28N 122°20W **78 C4**
Burin Canada 47°1N 55°14W **73 C8**
Buriram Thailand 15°0N 103°0E **38 E4**
Burkburnett U.S.A. 34°6N 98°34W **84 D5**
Burke → Australia 23°12S 139°33E **62 C2**
Burke Chan. Canada 52°10N 127°30W **70 C3**
Burketown Australia 17°45S 139°33E **62 B2**
Burkina Faso ■ Africa 12°0N 1°0W **52 F5**
Burk's Falls Canada 45°37N 79°24W **72 C4**
Burleigh Falls Canada 44°33N 78°12W **82 B6**
Burley U.S.A. 42°32N 113°48W **76 E7**
Burlingame U.S.A. 37°35N 122°21W **78 H4**
Burlington Canada 43°18N 79°45W **82 C5**

Burlington Colo.,
  U.S.A. 39°18N 102°16W **76 G12**
Burlington Iowa, U.S.A. 40°49N 91°14W **80 E8**
Burlington Kans., U.S.A. 38°12N 95°45W **80 F6**
Burlington N.C., U.S.A. 36°6N 79°26W **85 C15**
Burlington N.J., U.S.A. 40°4N 74°51W **83 F10**
Burlington Vt., U.S.A. 44°29N 73°12W **83 B11**
Burlington Wash.,
  U.S.A. 48°28N 122°20W **78 B4**
Burlington Wis., U.S.A. 42°41N 88°17W **80 D9**
Burma ■ Asia 21°0N 96°30E **41 J20**
Burnaby I. Canada 52°25N 131°19W **70 C2**
Burnet U.S.A. 30°45N 98°14W **84 F5**
Burnham U.S.A. 40°53N 77°34W **82 F7**
Burnham-on-Sea U.K. 51°14N 3°0W **13 F5**
Burnie Australia 41°4S 145°56E **63 G4**
Burnley U.K. 53°47N 2°14W **12 D5**
Burns U.S.A. 43°35N 119°3W **76 E4**
Burns Junction U.S.A. 42°47N 117°51W **76 E5**
Burns Lake Canada 54°14N 125°45W **70 C3**
Burnside → Canada 66°51N 108°4W **68 D9**
Burnside, L. Australia 25°22S 123°0E **61 E3**
Burnsville U.S.A. 44°47N 93°17W **80 C7**
Burnt River Canada 44°41N 78°42W **82 B6**
Burntwood → Canada 56°8N 96°34W **71 B9**
Burntwood L. Canada 55°22N 100°26W **71 B8**
Burqān Kuwait 29°0N 47°57E **46 D5**
Burqin China 47°43N 87°0E **30 B6**
Burra Australia 33°40S 138°55E **63 E2**
Burray U.K. 58°51N 2°54W **11 C6**
Burren △ Ireland 53°9N 9°5W **10 C2**
Burren Junction Australia 30°7S 148°58E **63 E4**
Burrinjuck, L. Australia 35°0S 148°36E **63 F4**
Burro, Serranías del
  Mexico 28°56N 102°5W **86 B4**
Burrow Hd. U.K. 54°41N 4°24W **11 G4**
Burruyacú Argentina 26°30S 64°40W **94 B3**
Burry Port U.K. 51°41N 4°15W **13 F3**
Bursa Turkey 40°15N 29°5E **23 D13**
Burstall Canada 50°39N 109°54W **71 C7**
Burton Ohio, U.S.A. 41°28N 81°8W **82 E3**
Burton S.C., U.S.A. 32°26N 80°43W **85 E14**
Burton, L. Canada 54°45N 78°20W **72 B4**
Burton upon Trent U.K. 52°48N 1°38W **12 E6**
Buru Indonesia 3°30S 126°30E **37 E7**
Burûn, Râs Egypt 31°14N 33°7E **48 D2**
Burundi ■ Africa 3°15S 30°0E **54 E6**
Burutu Nigeria 5°20N 5°29E **52 G7**
Burwash Canada 46°13N 80°51W **82 A5**
Burwell U.S.A. 41°47N 99°8W **80 E4**
Burwick U.K. 58°45N 2°58W **11 C5**
Bury U.K. 53°35N 2°17W **12 D5**
Bury St. Edmunds U.K. 52°15N 0°43E **13 E8**
Buryatia □ Russia 53°0N 110°0E **27 D12**
Busan S. Korea 35°5N 129°0E **33 G15**
Busaso = Boosaaso
  Somalia 11°12N 49°18E **49 E4**
Buşayrah Syria 35°9N 40°26E **46 C4**
Büshehr Iran 28°55N 50°55E **47 D6**
Büshehr □ Iran 28°20N 51°45E **47 D6**
Bushire = Büshehr Iran 28°55N 50°55E **47 D6**
Busira →
  Dem. Rep. of the Congo 3°16N 20°59E **54 D4**
Buşra ash Shām Syria 32°30N 36°25E **48 C5**
Busselton Australia 33°42S 115°15E **61 F2**
Bussum Neths. 52°16N 5°10E **15 B5**
Busto Arsízio Italy 45°37N 8°51E **20 D8**
Busu Djanoa
  Dem. Rep. of the Congo 1°43N 21°23E **54 D4**
Busuanga I. Phil. 12°10N 120°0E **37 B6**
Busungbiu Indonesia 8°16S 114°58E **37 J17**
Buta Dem. Rep. of the Congo 2°50N 24°53E **54 D4**
Butare Rwanda 2°31S 29°52E **54 E5**
Butaritari Kiribati 3°30N 174°0E **64 G9**
Bute U.K. 55°48N 5°2W **11 F3**
Bute Inlet Canada 50°40N 124°53W **70 C4**
Butembo
  Dem. Rep. of the Congo 0°9N 29°18E **54 D5**
Butha-Buthe Lesotho 28°47S 28°14E **57 C4**
Butler Mo., U.S.A. 38°16N 94°20W **80 F6**
Butler Pa., U.S.A. 40°52N 79°54W **82 F5**
Buton Indonesia 5°0S 122°45E **37 E6**
Butte Mont., U.S.A. 46°0N 112°32W **76 C7**
Butte Nebr., U.S.A. 42°58N 98°51W **80 D4**
Butte Creek → U.S.A. 39°12N 121°56W **78 F5**
Butterworth = Gcuwa
  S. Africa 32°20S 28°11E **57 E4**
Butterworth Malaysia 5°24N 100°23E **39 c**
Buttevant Ireland 52°14N 8°40W **10 D3**
Buttfield, Mt. Australia 24°45S 128°9E **61 D4**
Button B. Canada 58°45N 94°23W **71 B10**
Buttonwillow U.S.A. 35°24N 119°28W **79 K7**
Butty Hd. Australia 33°54S 121°39E **61 F3**
Butuan Phil. 8°57N 125°33E **37 C7**
Butung = Buton Indonesia 5°0S 122°45E **37 E6**
Buturlinovka Russia 50°50N 40°35E **19 D7**
Butwal Nepal 27°38N 83°31E **43 F10**
Buxa Duar India 26°45N 89°35E **43 F13**
Buxar India 25°34N 83°58E **43 G10**
Buxoro Uzbekistan 39°48N 64°25E **26 F7**
Buxtehude Germany 53°28N 9°39E **16 B5**
Buxton U.K. 53°16N 1°54W **12 D6**
Buy Russia 58°28N 41°28E **18 C7**
Buyant-Uhaa Mongolia 44°55N 110°11E **32 B6**
Buyo, L. de Ivory C. 6°16N 7°10W **52 G4**
Büyük Menderes →
  Turkey 37°28N 27°11E **23 F12**
Büyükçekmece Turkey 41°2N 28°35E **23 D13**
Buyun Shan China 40°4N 122°43E **33 D12**
Buzău Romania 45°10N 26°50E **17 F14**
Buzău → Romania 45°26N 27°44E **17 F14**
Buzen Japan 33°35N 131°5E **29 H5**
Buzi → Mozam. 19°50S 34°43E **55 H6**
Buzuluk Russia 52°48N 52°12E **18 D9**
Būzmeyn Turkmenistan 38°3N 58°12E **47 B8**
Buzzards Bay U.S.A. 41°45N 70°37W **83 E14**

Byam Martin I. Canada 75°15N 104°15W **69 B11**
Byarezina → Belarus 52°33N 30°14E **17 B16**
Byaroza Belarus 52°31N 24°51E **17 B13**
Byblos = Jubayl Lebanon 34°5N 35°39E **48 A4**
Bydgoszcz Poland 53°10N 18°0E **17 B9**
Byelorussia = Belarus ■
  Europe 53°30N 27°0E **17 B14**
Byers U.S.A. 39°43N 104°14W **76 G11**
Byesville U.S.A. 39°58N 81°32W **82 G3**
Byfield △ Australia 22°52S 150°45E **62 C5**
Bykhaw Belarus 53°31N 30°14E **17 B16**
Bykhov = Bykhaw
  Belarus 53°31N 30°14E **17 B16**
Bylas U.S.A. 33°8N 110°7W **77 K8**
Bylot Canada 58°25N 94°8W **71 B10**
Bylot I. Canada 73°13N 78°34W **69 C16**
Byram U.S.A. 32°11N 90°15W **85 E9**
Byrd, C. Antarctica 69°38S 76°7W **5 C17**
Byrock Australia 30°40S 146°27E **63 E4**
Byron, C. Australia 28°43S 153°37E **63 D5**
Byron Bay Australia 28°43S 153°37E **63 D5**
Byrranga, Gory Russia 75°0N 100°0E **27 B11**
Byrranga Mts. = Byrranga, Gory
  Russia 75°0N 100°0E **27 B11**
Byske Sweden 64°57N 21°11E **8 D19**
Byskeälven → Sweden 64°57N 21°13E **8 D19**
Bytom Poland 50°25N 18°54E **17 C10**
Bytów Poland 54°10N 17°30E **17 A9**

C

C.W. McConaughy, L.
  U.S.A. 41°14N 101°40W **80 E3**
Ca → Vietnam 18°45N 105°45E **38 C5**
Ca Mau Vietnam 9°7N 105°8E **39 H5**
Ca Mau, Mui Vietnam 8°38N 104°44E **39 H5**
Ca Na Vietnam 11°20N 108°54E **39 G7**
Caacupé Paraguay 25°23S 57°5W **94 B4**
Caaguazú □ Paraguay 26°5S 55°31W **95 B4**
Caála Angola 12°46S 15°30E **55 G3**
Caamaño Sd. Canada 52°55N 129°25W **70 C3**
Caazapá Paraguay 26°8S 56°19W **94 B4**
Caazapá □ Paraguay 26°10S 56°0W **95 B4**
Cabanatuan Phil. 15°30N 120°58E **37 A6**
Cabano Canada 47°40N 68°56W **73 C6**
Cabazon U.S.A. 33°55N 116°47W **79 M10**
Cabedelo Brazil 7°0S 34°50W **93 E12**
Cabhán, An = Cavan
  Ireland 54°0N 7°22W **10 B4**
Cabildo Chile 32°30S 71°5W **94 C1**
Cabimas Venezuela 10°23N 71°25W **92 A4**
Cabinda Angola 5°33S 12°11E **54 F2**
Cabinda □ Angola 5°0S 12°30E **54 F2**
Cabinet Mts. U.S.A. 48°10N 115°50W **76 B6**
Cabo Blanco Argentina 47°15S 65°47W **96 F3**
Cabo Frio Brazil 22°51S 42°3W **95 A7**
Cabo Pantoja Peru 1°0S 75°10W **92 D3**
Cabo San Lucas Mexico 22°53N 109°54W **86 C3**
Cabo Verde = Cape Verde Is. ■
  Atl. Oc. 16°0N 24°0W **52 b**
Cabonga, Réservoir
  Canada 47°20N 76°40W **72 C4**
Cabool U.S.A. 37°7N 92°6W **80 G7**
Caboolture Australia 27°5S 152°58E **63 D5**
Cabora Bassa Dam = Cahora
  Bassa, Lago de Mozam. 15°20S 32°50E **55 H6**
Caborca Mexico 30°37N 112°6W **86 A2**
Cabot, Mt. U.S.A. 44°30N 71°25W **83 B13**
Cabot Hd. Canada 45°14N 81°17W **82 A3**
Cabot Str. Canada 47°15N 59°40W **73 C8**
Cabra Spain 37°30N 4°28W **21 D3**
Cabra I. India 7°18N 93°50E **45 L11**
Cabrera Spain 39°8N 2°57E **21 C7**
Cabri Canada 50°35N 108°25W **71 C7**
Cabriel → Spain 39°14N 1°3W **21 C5**
Caçador Brazil 26°47S 51°0W **95 B5**
Čačak Serbia 43°54N 20°20E **23 C9**
Caçapava do Sul Brazil 30°30S 53°30W **95 C5**
Cáceres Brazil 16°5S 57°40W **92 G7**
Cáceres Spain 39°26N 6°23W **21 C2**
Cache Bay Canada 46°22N 80°0W **72 C4**
Cache Cr. → U.S.A. 38°42N 121°42W **78 G5**
Cache Creek Canada 50°48N 121°19W **70 C4**
Cachi Argentina 25°5S 66°10W **94 B2**
Cachimbo, Serra do Brazil 9°30S 55°30W **93 E7**
Cachinal de la Sierra
  Chile 24°58S 69°32W **94 A2**
Cachoeira Brazil 12°30S 39°0W **93 F11**
Cachoeira do Sul Brazil 30°3S 52°53W **95 C5**
Cachoeiro de Itapemirim
  Brazil 20°51S 41°7W **95 A7**
Cacoal Brazil 11°32S 61°18W **92 F6**
Cacólo Angola 10°9S 19°21E **54 G3**
Caconda Angola 13°48S 15°8E **55 G3**
Caddo U.S.A. 34°7N 96°16W **84 D6**
Cader Idris U.K. 52°42N 3°53W **13 E4**
Cadereyta de Jiménez
  Mexico 25°36N 100°0W **86 B5**
Cadibarrawirracanna, L.
  Australia 28°52S 135°27E **63 D2**
Cadillac U.S.A. 44°15N 85°24W **81 C11**
Cádiz Phil. 10°57N 123°15E **37 B6**
Cádiz Spain 36°30N 6°20W **21 D2**
Cadiz Calif., U.S.A. 34°30N 115°29W **79 L11**
Cadiz Ohio, U.S.A. 40°22N 81°0W **82 F4**
Cádiz, G. de Spain 36°40N 7°0W **21 D2**
Cadiz L. U.S.A. 34°18N 115°24W **79 L11**
Cadney Park Australia 27°55S 134°3E **63 D1**
Cadomin Canada 53°2N 117°20W **70 C5**
Cadotte Lake Canada 56°26N 116°23W **70 B5**
Cadoux Australia 30°46S 117°7E **61 F2**
Caen France 49°10N 0°22W **20 B3**
Caernarfon U.K. 53°8N 4°16W **12 D3**
Caernarfon B. U.K. 53°4N 4°40W **12 D3**
Caernarvon = Caernarfon

Caernarvon = Caernarfon
  U.K. 53°8N 4°16W **12 D3**
Caerphilly U.K. 51°35N 3°13W **13 F4**
Caerphilly □ U.K. 51°37N 3°12W **13 F4**
Caesarea Israel 32°30N 34°53E **48 C3**
Caetité Brazil 13°50S 42°32W **93 F11**
Cafayate Argentina 26°2S 66°0W **94 B2**
Cafu Angola 16°30S 15°8E **56 A2**
Cagayan de Oro Phil. 8°30N 124°40E **37 C6**
Cágliari Italy 39°13N 9°7E **22 E3**
Cágliari, G. di Italy 39°8N 9°11E **22 E3**
Caguán → Colombia 0°8S 74°18W **92 D4**
Caguas Puerto Rico 18°14N 66°2W **89 d**
Caha Mts. Ireland 51°45N 9°40W **10 E2**
Cahama Angola 16°17S 14°19E **56 A1**
Cahir Ireland 52°22N 7°56W **10 D4**
Cahirciveen Ireland 51°56N 10°14W **10 E1**
Cahora Bassa, Lago de
  Mozam. 15°20S 32°50E **55 H6**
Cahore Pt. Ireland 52°33N 6°12W **10 D5**
Cahors France 44°27N 1°27E **20 D4**
Cahul Moldova 45°50N 28°15E **17 F15**
Cai Bau, Dao Vietnam 21°10N 107°27E **34 G6**
Cai Be Vietnam 10°20N 106°2E **39 G6**
Cai Nuoc Vietnam 8°56N 105°1E **39 H5**
Caia Mozam. 17°51S 35°24E **55 H7**
Caianda Angola 11°2S 23°31E **54 G4**
Caibarién Cuba 22°30N 79°30W **88 B4**
Caicara Venezuela 7°38N 66°10W **92 B5**
Caicó Brazil 6°20S 37°0W **93 E11**
Caicos Is. Turks & Caicos 21°40N 71°40W **89 B5**
Caicos Passage W. Indies 22°45N 72°45W **89 B5**
Caidian China 30°35N 114°2E **35 B10**
Caiguna Australia 32°16S 125°29E **61 F4**
Caird Coast Antarctica 75°0S 25°0W **5 D1**
Cairn Gorm U.K. 57°7N 3°39W **11 D5**
Cairngorm Mts. U.K. 57°6N 3°42W **11 D5**
Cairngorms △ U.K. 57°10N 3°50W **11 D5**
Cairnryan U.K. 54°59N 5°1W **11 G3**
Cairns Australia 16°57S 145°45E **62 B4**
Cairns L. Canada 51°42N 94°30W **71 C10**
Cairo Ga., U.S.A. 30°52N 84°13W **85 F12**
Cairo Ill., U.S.A. 37°0N 89°11W **80 G9**
Cairo N.Y., U.S.A. 42°18N 74°0W **83 D11**
Caiseal = Cashel Ireland 52°32N 7°53W **10 D4**
Caisleán an Bharraigh = Castlebar
  Ireland 53°52N 9°18W **10 C2**
Caithness U.K. 58°25N 3°35W **11 C5**
Caithness, Ord of U.K. 58°8N 3°36W **11 C5**
Caja de Muertos, I.
  Puerto Rico 17°54N 66°32W **89 d**
Cajamarca Peru 7°5S 78°28W **92 E3**
Cajazeiras Brazil 6°52S 38°30W **93 E11**
Calabar Nigeria 4°57N 8°20E **52 H7**
Calabogie Canada 45°18N 76°43W **83 A8**
Calabozo Venezuela 9°0N 67°28W **92 B5**
Calábria □ Italy 39°0N 16°30E **22 E7**
Calahorra Spain 42°18N 1°59W **21 A5**
Calais France 50°57N 1°56E **20 A4**
Calais U.S.A. 45°11N 67°17W **81 C20**
Calakmul △ Mexico 18°14N 89°48W **87 D7**
Calalaste, Cord. de
  Argentina 25°0S 67°0W **94 B2**
Calama Brazil 8°0S 62°50W **92 E6**
Calama Chile 22°30S 68°55W **94 A2**
Calamar Colombia 10°15N 74°55W **92 A4**
Calamian Group Phil. 11°50N 119°55E **37 B5**
Calamocha Spain 40°50N 1°17W **21 B5**
Calang Indonesia 4°37N 95°37E **36 D1**
Calanscio, Sarīr Libya 27°30N 22°30E **53 C10**
Calapan Phil. 13°25N 121°7E **37 B6**
Călărași Romania 44°12N 27°20E **17 F14**
Calatayud Spain 41°20N 1°40W **21 B5**
Calauag Phil. 13°55N 122°15E **37 B6**
Calavite, C. Phil. 13°26N 120°20E **37 B6**
Calbayog Phil. 12°4N 124°38E **37 B6**
Calca Peru 13°22S 72°0W **92 F4**
Calcasieu L. U.S.A. 29°55N 93°18W **84 G8**
Calcium U.S.A. 44°1N 75°50W **83 B9**
Calcutta U.S.A. 40°40N 80°34W **82 F4**
Caldas da Rainha Portugal 39°24N 9°8W **21 C1**
Calder → U.K. 53°44N 1°22W **12 D6**
Caldera Chile 27°5S 70°55W **94 B1**
Caldwell Idaho, U.S.A. 43°40N 116°41W **76 E5**
Caldwell Kans., U.S.A. 37°2N 97°37W **80 G5**
Caldwell Tex., U.S.A. 30°32N 96°42W **84 F6**
Caledon S. Africa 34°14S 19°26E **56 E2**
Caledon → S. Africa 30°31S 26°5E **56 D4**
Caledon B. Australia 12°45S 137°0E **62 A2**
Caledonia Canada 43°7N 79°58W **82 C5**
Caledonia U.S.A. 42°58N 77°51W **82 D7**
Calemba Angola 16°0S 15°44E **56 A2**
Calen Australia 20°56S 148°48E **62 b**
Caletones Chile 34°6S 70°27W **94 C1**
Calexico U.S.A. 32°40N 115°30W **79 N11**
Calf of Man I. of Man 54°3N 4°48W **12 C3**
Calgary Canada 51°0N 114°10W **70 C6**
Calhoun U.S.A. 34°30N 84°57W **85 D12**
Cali Colombia 3°25N 76°35W **92 C3**
Calicut = Kozhikode
  India 11°15N 75°43E **45 J2**
Caliente U.S.A. 37°37N 114°31W **77 H6**
California Mo., U.S.A. 38°38N 92°34W **80 F7**
California Pa., U.S.A. 40°4N 79°54W **82 F5**
California □ U.S.A. 37°30N 119°30W **78 H7**
California, Baja, T.N. = Baja
  California □ Mexico 30°0N 115°0W **86 B2**
California, Baja, T.S. = Baja
  California Sur □
  Mexico 25°50N 111°50W **86 B2**
California, G. de Mexico 27°0N 111°0W **86 B2**
California City U.S.A. 35°10N 117°55W **79 K9**
California Hot Springs
  U.S.A. 35°51N 118°41W **79 K8**
Calilegua △ Argentina 23°36S 64°50W **94 B3**
Calingasta Argentina 31°15S 69°30W **94 C2**
Calipatria U.S.A. 33°8N 115°31W **79 M11**
Calistoga U.S.A. 38°35N 122°35W **78 G4**

Calitzdorp *S. Africa* 33°33S 21°42E **56** D3
Callabonna, L. *Australia* 29°40S 140°5E **63** D3
Callan *Ireland* 52°32N 7°24W **10** D4
Callander *U.K.* 56°15N 4°13W **11** E4
Callicoon *U.S.A.* 41°46N 75°3W **83** E9
Calling Lake *Canada* 55°15N 113°12W **70** B6
Calliope *Australia* 24°0S 151°16E **62** C5
Calne *U.K.* 51°26N 2°0W **13** F6
Calola *Angola* 16°25S 17°48E **56** A2
Caloundra *Australia* 26°45S 153°10E **63** D5
Calpella *U.S.A.* 39°14N 123°12W **78** F3
Calpine *U.S.A.* 39°40N 120°27W **78** F6
Calstock *Canada* 49°47N 84°9W **72** C3
Caltagirone *Italy* 37°14N 14°31E **22** F6
Caltanissetta *Italy* 37°29N 14°4E **22** F6
Calulo *Angola* 10°1S 14°56E **54** G2
Calvert → *Australia* 16°17S 137°44E **62** B2
Calvert I. *Canada* 51°30N 128°0W **70** C3
Calvert Ra. *Australia* 24°0S 122°30E **60** D3
Calvi *France* 42°34N 8°45E **20** E8
Calvià *Spain* 39°34N 2°31E **21** C7
Calvillo *Mexico* 21°51N 102°43W **86** C4
Calvinia *S. Africa* 31°28S 19°45E **56** D2
Calwa *U.S.A.* 36°42N 119°46W **78** J7
Cam → *U.K.* 52°21N 0°16E **13** E8
Cam Lam = Ba Ngoi *Vietnam* 11°54N 109°10E **39** G7
Cam Pha *Vietnam* 21°7N 107°18E **34** G6
Cam Ranh *Vietnam* 11°54N 109°12E **39** G7
Cam Xuyen *Vietnam* 18°15N 106°0E **38** C6
Camabatela *Angola* 8°20S 15°26E **54** F3
Camacupa *Angola* 11°58S 17°22E **55** G3
Camagüey *Cuba* 21°20N 77°55W **88** B4
Camaná *Peru* 16°30S 72°50W **92** G4
Camanche Res. *U.S.A.* 38°14N 121°1W **78** G6
Camaquã *Brazil* 30°51S 51°49W **95** C5
Camaquã → *Brazil* 31°17S 51°47W **95** C5
Camargo *Mexico* 26°19N 98°50W **87** B5
Camarillo *U.S.A.* 34°13N 119°2W **79** L7
Camarón, C. *Honduras* 16°0N 85°5W **88** C2
Camarones *Argentina* 44°50S 65°40W **96** E3
Camas *U.S.A.* 45°35N 122°24W **78** E4
Camas Valley *U.S.A.* 43°2N 123°40W **76** E2
Camballin *Australia* 17°59S 124°12E **60** C3
Cambará *Brazil* 23°2S 50°5W **95** A5
Cambay = Khambhat *India* 22°23N 72°33E **42** H5
Cambay, G. of = Khambhat, G. of *India* 20°45N 72°30E **40** J8
Cambodia ■ *Asia* 12°15N 105°0E **38** F5
Camborne *U.K.* 50°12N 5°19W **13** G2
Cambrai *France* 50°11N 3°14E **20** A5
Cambria *U.S.A.* 35°34N 121°5W **78** K5
Cambrian Mts. *U.K.* 52°3N 3°57W **13** E4
Cambridge *Canada* 43°23N 80°15W **82** C4
Cambridge *Jamaica* 18°18N 77°54W **88** a
Cambridge *N.Z.* 37°54S 175°29E **59** B5
Cambridge *U.K.* 52°12N 0°8E **13** E8
Cambridge *Minn., U.S.A.* 45°34N 93°13W **80** C7
Cambridge *N.Y., U.S.A.* 43°2N 73°22W **83** C11
Cambridge *Nebr., U.S.A.* 40°17N 100°10W **80** E3
Cambridge *Ohio, U.S.A.* 40°2N 81°35W **82** F3
Cambridge Bay *Canada* 69°10N 105°0W **68** D11
Cambridge G. *Australia* 14°55S 128°15E **60** B4
Cambridge Springs *U.S.A.* 41°48N 80°4W **82** E4
Cambridgeshire □ *U.K.* 52°25N 0°7W **13** E7
Cambuci *Brazil* 21°35S 41°55W **95** A7
Cambundi-Catembo *Angola* 10°10S 17°35E **54** G3
Camdeboo △ *S. Africa* 32°28S 24°25E **56** D3
Camden *Australia* 34°1S 150°43E **63** B5
Camden *Ala., U.S.A.* 31°59N 87°17W **85** F11
Camden *Ark., U.S.A.* 33°35N 92°50W **84** E8
Camden *Maine, U.S.A.* 44°13N 69°4W **81** C19
Camden *N.J., U.S.A.* 39°55N 75°7W **83** G9
Camden *N.Y., U.S.A.* 43°20N 75°45W **83** C9
Camden *S.C., U.S.A.* 34°16N 80°36W **85** D14
Camden Sd. *Australia* 15°27S 124°25E **60** C3
Camdenton *U.S.A.* 38°1N 92°45W **80** F7
Camelford *U.K.* 50°37N 4°42W **13** G3
Cameron *Ariz., U.S.A.* 35°53N 111°25W **77** J8
Cameron *La., U.S.A.* 29°48N 93°20W **84** G8
Cameron *Mo., U.S.A.* 39°44N 94°14W **80** F6
Cameron *Tex., U.S.A.* 30°51N 96°59W **84** F6
Cameron Highlands *Malaysia* 4°27N 101°22E **39** K3
Cameron Hills *Canada* 59°48N 118°0W **70** B5
Cameroon ■ *Africa* 6°0N 12°30E **53** G7
Cameroun, Mt. *Cameroon* 4°13N 9°10E **54** D1
Cametá *Brazil* 2°12S 49°30W **93** D9
Camilla *U.S.A.* 31°14N 84°12W **85** F12
Caminha *Portugal* 41°50N 8°50W **21** B1
Camino *U.S.A.* 38°44N 120°41W **78** G6
Cammal *U.S.A.* 41°24N 77°28W **82** E7
Camocim *Brazil* 2°55S 40°50W **93** D10
Camooweal *Australia* 19°56S 138°7E **62** B2
Camooweal Caves △ *Australia* 20°1S 138°11E **62** C2
Camopi *Fr. Guiana* 3°12N 52°17W **93** C8
Camorta *India* 8°8N 93°30E **45** K11
Camp Hill *U.S.A.* 40°14N 76°55W **82** F8
Camp Nelson *U.S.A.* 36°8N 118°39W **79** J8
Camp Pendleton *U.S.A.* 33°13N 117°24W **79** M9
Camp Verde *U.S.A.* 34°34N 111°51W **77** J8
Camp Wood *U.S.A.* 29°40N 100°1W **84** G4
Campana *Argentina* 34°10S 58°55W **94** C4
Campana, I. *Chile* 48°20S 75°20W **96** F1
Campánia □ *Italy* 41°0N 14°30E **22** D6
Campbell *S. Africa* 28°48S 23°44E **56** C3
Campbell *Calif., U.S.A.* 37°17N 121°57W **78** H5
Campbell *Ohio, U.S.A.* 41°5N 80°37W **82** E4
Campbell I. *Pac. Oc.* 52°30S 169°0E **64** N8
Campbell L. *Canada* 63°14N 106°55W **71** A7
Campbell Plateau *S. Ocean* 50°0S 170°0E **5** A11
Campbell River *Canada* 50°5N 125°20W **70** C3
Campbellford *Canada* 44°18N 77°48W **82** B7
Campbellpur *Pakistan* 33°46N 72°26E **42** C5
Campbellsville *U.S.A.* 37°21N 85°20W **81** G11
Campbellton *Canada* 47°57N 66°43W **73** C6
Campbelltown *Australia* 34°4S 150°49E **63** E5
Campbeltown *U.K.* 55°26N 5°36W **11** F3
Campeche *Mexico* 19°51N 90°32W **87** D6
Campeche □ *Mexico* 19°0N 90°30W **87** D6
Campeche, Golfo de *Mexico* 19°30N 93°0W **87** D6
Camperdown *Australia* 38°14S 143°9E **63** F3
Camperville *Canada* 51°59N 100°9W **71** C8
Câmpina *Romania* 45°10N 25°45E **17** F13
Campina Grande *Brazil* 7°20S 35°47W **93** E11
Campinas *Brazil* 22°50S 47°0W **95** A6
Campo Grande *Brazil* 20°25S 54°40W **93** H8
Campo Maior *Brazil* 4°50S 42°12W **93** D10
Campo Mourão *Brazil* 24°3S 52°22W **95** A5
Campobasso *Italy* 41°34N 14°39E **22** D6
Campos *Brazil* 21°50S 41°20W **95** A7
Campos Belos *Brazil* 13°10S 47°3W **93** F9
Campos Novos *Brazil* 27°21S 51°50W **95** B5
Camptonville *U.S.A.* 39°27N 121°3W **78** F5
Camptown *U.S.A.* 41°44N 76°14W **83** E8
Câmpulung *Romania* 45°17N 25°3E **17** F13
Camrose *Canada* 53°0N 112°50W **70** C6
Camsell Portage *Canada* 59°37N 109°15W **71** B7
Çan *Turkey* 40°2N 27°3E **23** D12
Can Gio *Vietnam* 10°25N 106°58E **39** G6
Can Tho *Vietnam* 10°2N 105°46E **39** G5
Canaan *U.S.A.* 42°2N 73°20W **83** D11
Canacona *India* 15°1N 74°4E **45** G2
Canada ■ *N. Amer.* 60°0N 100°0W **68** G11
Canada Abyssal Plain *Arctic* 80°0N 140°0W **4** B18
Canada Basin *Arctic* 75°0N 145°0W **4** B18
Cañada de Gómez *Argentina* 32°40S 61°30W **94** C3
Canadian *U.S.A.* 35°55N 100°23W **84** D4
Canadian → *U.S.A.* 35°28N 95°3W **84** D7
Canadian Shield *Canada* 53°0N 75°0W **66** D12
Canajoharie *U.S.A.* 42°54N 74°35W **83** D10
Çanakkale *Turkey* 40°8N 26°24E **23** D12
Çanakkale Boğazı *Turkey* 40°17N 26°32E **23** D12
Canal Flats *Canada* 50°10N 115°48W **70** C5
Canalejas *Argentina* 35°15S 66°34W **94** D2
Canals *Argentina* 33°35S 62°53W **94** C3
Canandaigua *U.S.A.* 42°54N 77°17W **82** D7
Canandaigua L. *U.S.A.* 42°47N 77°19W **82** D7
Cananea *Mexico* 31°0N 110°18W **86** A2
Canarias, Is. *Atl. Oc.* 28°30N 16°0W **52** C2
Canaries *St. Lucia* 13°55N 61°4W **89** f
Canarreos, Arch. de los *Cuba* 21°35N 81°40W **88** B3
Canary Is. = Canarias, Is. *Atl. Oc.* 28°30N 16°0W **52** C2
Canaseraga *U.S.A.* 42°27N 77°45W **82** D7
Canatlán *Mexico* 24°31N 104°47W **86** C4
Canaveral, C. *U.S.A.* 28°27N 80°32W **85** G14
Canaveral ⌂ *U.S.A.* 28°28N 80°34W **85** G14
Canavieiras *Brazil* 15°39S 39°0W **93** G11
Canberra *Australia* 35°15S 149°8E **63** F4
Canby *Calif., U.S.A.* 41°27N 120°52W **76** F3
Canby *Minn., U.S.A.* 44°43N 96°16W **80** C5
Canby *Oreg., U.S.A.* 45°16N 122°42W **78** E4
Cancún *Mexico* 21°8N 86°44W **87** C7
Candelaria *Argentina* 27°29S 55°44W **95** B4
Candelo *Australia* 36°47S 149°43E **63** F4
Candi Dasa *Indonesia* 8°30S 115°34E **37** J18
Candia = Iraklio *Greece* 35°20N 25°12E **23** G11
Candle L. *Canada* 53°50N 105°18W **71** C7
Candlemas I. *Antarctica* 57°3S 26°40W **5** B1
Cando *U.S.A.* 48°32N 99°12W **80** A4
Canea = Chania *Greece* 35°30N 24°4E **23** G11
Canelones *Uruguay* 34°32S 56°17W **95** C4
Cañete *Chile* 37°50S 73°30W **94** D1
Cangas del Narcea *Spain* 43°10N 6°32W **21** A2
Cangnan *China* 27°30N 120°23E **35** D13
Cangshan *China* 34°50N 118°2E **33** G10
Canguaretama *Brazil* 6°20S 35°5W **93** E11
Canguçu *Brazil* 31°22S 52°43W **95** C5
Canguçu, Serra do *Brazil* 31°20S 52°40W **95** C5
Cangxi *China* 31°47N 105°59E **34** B5
Cangyuan *China* 23°12N 99°14E **34** F2
Cangzhou *China* 38°19N 116°52E **32** E9
Caniapiscau → *Canada* 56°40N 69°30W **73** A6
Caniapiscau, L. *Canada* 54°10N 69°55W **73** B6
Canicattì *Italy* 37°21N 13°51E **22** F5
Canim Lake *Canada* 51°47N 120°54W **70** C4
Canindeyu □ *Paraguay* 24°10S 55°0W **95** A5
Canisteo *U.S.A.* 42°16N 77°36W **82** D7
Canisteo → *U.S.A.* 42°7N 77°8W **82** D7
Cañitas de Felipe Pescador *Mexico* 23°36N 102°43W **86** C4
Çankırı *Turkey* 40°40N 33°37E **19** F5
Canmore *Canada* 51°7N 115°18W **70** C5
Cann River *Australia* 37°35S 149°7E **63** F4
Canna *U.K.* 57°3N 6°33W **11** D2
Cannanore = Kannur *India* 11°53N 75°27E **45** J2
Cannanore Is. *India* 10°30N 72°30E **45** J1
Cannes *France* 43°32N 7°1E **20** E7
Canning Town = Port Canning *India* 22°23N 88°40E **43** H13
Cannington *Canada* 44°20N 79°2W **82** B5
Cannock *U.K.* 52°41N 2°1W **13** E5
Cannonball → *U.S.A.* 46°26N 100°35W **80** B3
Cannondale Mt. *Australia* 25°13S 148°57E **62** D4
Cannonsville Res. *U.S.A.* 42°4N 75°22W **83** D9
Cannonvale *Australia* 20°17S 148°43E **62** b
Canoas *Brazil* 29°56S 51°11W **95** B5
Canoe L. *Canada* 55°10N 108°15W **71** B7
Cañon City *U.S.A.* 38°27N 105°14W **76** G11
Cañón del Río Blanco △ *Mexico* 18°43N 97°15W **87** D5
Canonniers Pt. *Mauritius* 20°2S 57°32E **55** d
Canora *Canada* 51°40N 102°30W **71** C8
Canowindra *Australia* 33°35S 148°38E **63** E4
Canso *Canada* 45°20N 61°0W **73** C7
Cantabria □ *Spain* 43°10N 4°0W **21** A4
Cantabrian Mts. = Cantábrica, Cordillera *Spain* 43°0N 5°10W **21** A3
Cantábrica, Cordillera *Spain* 43°0N 5°10W **21** A3
Cantal, Plomb du *France* 45°3N 2°45E **20** D5
Canterbury *Australia* 25°23S 141°53E **62** D3
Canterbury *U.K.* 51°16N 1°6E **13** F9
Canterbury Bight *N.Z.* 44°16S 171°55E **59** F3
Canterbury Plains *N.Z.* 43°55S 171°22E **59** E3
Cantil *U.S.A.* 35°18N 117°58W **79** K9
Canton *Ga., U.S.A.* 34°14N 84°29W **85** D12
Canton *Ill., U.S.A.* 40°33N 90°2W **80** E8
Canton *Miss., U.S.A.* 32°37N 90°2W **85** E9
Canton *Mo., U.S.A.* 40°8N 91°32W **80** E8
Canton *N.Y., U.S.A.* 44°36N 75°10W **83** B9
Canton *Ohio, U.S.A.* 40°48N 81°23W **82** F3
Canton *Pa., U.S.A.* 41°39N 76°51W **82** E8
Canton *S. Dak., U.S.A.* 43°18N 96°35W **80** D5
Canton L. *U.S.A.* 36°6N 98°35W **84** C5
Canudos *Brazil* 7°13S 58°5W **92** E7
Canumã → *Brazil* 3°55S 59°10W **92** D7
Canutama *Brazil* 6°30S 64°20W **92** E6
Canutillo *U.S.A.* 31°55N 106°36W **84** F1
Canvey *U.K.* 51°31N 0°37E **13** F8
Canyon *U.S.A.* 34°59N 101°55W **84** D4
Canyon De Chelly ⌂ *U.S.A.* 36°10N 109°20W **77** H9
Canyonlands △ *U.S.A.* 38°15N 110°0W **77** G9
Canyons of the Ancients ⌂ *U.S.A.* 37°30N 108°55W **77** H9
Canyonville *U.S.A.* 42°56N 123°17W **76** E2
Cao Bang *Vietnam* 22°40N 106°15E **34** F6
Cao He → *China* 40°10N 124°32E **33** D13
Cao Lanh *Vietnam* 10°27N 105°38E **39** G5
Cao Xian *China* 34°50N 115°35E **32** G8
Cap-aux-Meules *Canada* 47°23N 61°52W **73** C7
Cap-Chat *Canada* 49°6N 66°40W **73** C6
Cap-de-la-Madeleine *Canada* 46°22N 72°31W **72** C5
Cap-Haïtien *Haiti* 19°40N 72°20W **89** C5
Cap Pt. *St. Lucia* 14°7N 60°57W **89** f
Capac *U.S.A.* 43°1N 82°56W **82** C2
Capanaparo → *Venezuela* 7°1N 67°7W **92** B5
Cape → *Australia* 20°59S 146°51E **62** C4
Cape Arid △ *Australia* 33°58S 123°13E **61** F3
Cape Barren I. *Australia* 40°25S 148°15E **63** G4
Cape Breton Highlands △ *Canada* 46°50N 60°40W **73** C7
Cape Breton I. *Canada* 46°0N 60°30W **73** C7
Cape Charles *U.S.A.* 37°16N 76°1W **81** G15
Cape Coast *Ghana* 5°5N 1°15W **52** G5
Cape Cod ⌂ *U.S.A.* 41°56N 70°6W **81** E18
Cape Coral *U.S.A.* 26°33N 81°57W **85** H14
Cape Crawford *Australia* 16°41S 135°43E **62** B2
Cape Dorset = Kinngait *Canada* 64°14N 76°32W **69** E16
Cape Fear → *U.S.A.* 33°53N 78°1W **85** E15
Cape Girardeau *U.S.A.* 37°19N 89°32W **80** G9
Cape Hatteras ⌂ *U.S.A.* 35°30N 75°28W **85** D17
Cape Hillsborough △ *Australia* 20°54S 149°2E **62** b
Cape Le Grand △ *Australia* 33°54S 122°26E **61** F3
Cape Lookout ⌂ *U.S.A.* 35°45N 76°25W **85** D16
Cape May *U.S.A.* 38°56N 74°56W **81** F16
Cape May Point *U.S.A.* 38°56N 74°58W **81** F16
Cape Melville △ *Australia* 14°26S 144°28E **62** A3
Cape Range △ *Australia* 22°3S 114°0E **60** D1
Cape St. George *Canada* 48°28N 59°14W **73** C8
Cape Tormentine *Canada* 46°8N 63°47W **73** C7
Cape Upstart △ *Australia* 19°45S 147°48E **62** B4
Cape Verde Is. ■ *Atl. Oc.* 16°0N 24°0W **52** b
Cape Vincent *U.S.A.* 44°8N 76°20W **83** B8
Cape York Peninsula *Australia* 12°0S 142°30E **62** A3
Capela *Brazil* 10°30S 37°0W **93** F11
Capella *Australia* 23°2S 148°1E **62** C4
Capesterre-Belle-Eau *Guadeloupe* 16°4N 61°36W **88** b
Capesterre-de-Marie-Galante *Guadeloupe* 15°53N 61°14W **88** b
Capim → *Brazil* 1°40S 47°47W **93** D9
Capitan *U.S.A.* 33°35N 105°35W **77** K11
Capitán Arturo Prat *Antarctica* 63°0S 61°0W **5** C17
Capitol Reef △ *U.S.A.* 38°15N 111°10W **77** G8
Capitola *U.S.A.* 36°59N 121°57W **78** J5
Capraia *Italy* 43°2N 9°50E **20** E8
Capri *Italy* 40°33N 14°14E **22** D6
Capricorn Coast *Australia* 23°16S 150°49E **62** C5
Capricorn Group *Australia* 23°30S 151°55E **62** C5
Capricorn Ra. *Australia* 23°20S 116°50E **60** D2
Caprivi □ *Namibia* 18°0S 23°30E **56** A3
Caprivi ⌂ *Namibia* 17°55S 22°37E **56** A3
Caprivi Strip *Namibia* 18°0S 23°0E **56** A3
Captains Flat *Australia* 35°35S 149°27E **63** F4
Capulin Volcano ⌂ *U.S.A.* 36°47N 103°58W **84** C3
Caquetá → *Colombia* 1°15S 69°15W **92** D5
Car Nicobar *India* 9°10N 92°47E **45** K11
Caracal *Romania* 44°8N 24°22E **17** F13
Caracas *Venezuela* 10°30N 66°55W **92** A5
Caracol *Belize* 16°45N 89°6W **88** C2
Caracol *Mato Grosso do Sul, Brazil* 22°18S 57°1W **94** A4
Caracol *Piauí, Brazil* 9°15S 43°22W **93** E10
Carajas *Brazil* 6°5S 50°23W **93** E8
Carajás, Serra dos *Brazil* 6°0S 51°30W **93** E8
Carangola *Brazil* 20°44S 42°5W **95** A7
Caransebeş *Romania* 45°28N 22°18E **17** F12
Caraquet *Canada* 47°48N 64°57W **73** C6
Caratasca, L. de *Honduras* 15°20N 83°40W **88** C3
Caratinga *Brazil* 19°50S 42°10W **93** G10
Caraúbas *Brazil* 5°43S 37°33W **93** E11
Caravaca de la Cruz *Spain* 38°8N 1°52W **21** C5
Caravelas *Brazil* 17°45S 39°15W **93** G11
Caraveli *Peru* 15°45S 73°25W **92** G4
Caravelle, Presqu'île de la *Martinique* 14°46N 60°48W **88** c
Caraz *Peru* 9°3S 77°47W **92** E3
Carazinho *Brazil* 28°16S 52°46W **95** B5
Carballo *Spain* 43°13N 8°41W **21** A1
Carberry *Canada* 49°50N 99°25W **71** D9
Carbó *Mexico* 29°42N 110°58W **86** B2
Carbón, L. del *Argentina* 49°35S 68°21W **90** G3
Carbonara, C. *Italy* 39°6N 9°31E **22** E3
Carbondale *Colo., U.S.A.* 39°24N 107°13W **76** G10
Carbondale *Ill., U.S.A.* 37°44N 89°13W **80** G9
Carbondale *Pa., U.S.A.* 41°35N 75°30W **83** E9
Carbonear *Canada* 47°42N 53°13W **73** C9
Carbónia *Italy* 39°10N 8°30E **22** E3
Carcajou *Canada* 57°47N 117°6W **70** B5
Carcarana → *Argentina* 32°27S 60°48W **94** C3
Carcasse, C. *Haiti* 18°30N 74°28W **89** C5
Carcassonne *France* 43°13N 2°20E **20** E5
Carcross *Canada* 60°13N 134°45W **70** A2
Cardamon Hills *India* 9°30N 77°15E **45** K3
Cardamon Mts. = Kravanh, Chuor Phnum *Cambodia* 12°0N 103°32E **39** G4
Cárdenas *Cuba* 23°0N 81°30W **88** B3
Cárdenas *San Luis Potosí, Mexico* 22°0N 99°38W **87** C5
Cárdenas *Tabasco, Mexico* 17°59N 93°22W **87** D6
Cardiff *U.K.* 51°29N 3°10W **13** F4
Cardiff □ *U.K.* 51°31N 3°12W **13** F4
Cardiff-by-the-Sea *U.S.A.* 33°1N 117°17W **79** M9
Cardigan *U.K.* 52°5N 4°40W **13** E3
Cardigan B. *U.K.* 52°30N 4°30W **13** E3
Cardinal *Canada* 44°47N 75°23W **83** B9
Cardona *Uruguay* 33°53S 57°18W **94** C4
Cardoso, Ilha do *Brazil* 25°8S 47°58W **95** B5
Cardston *Canada* 49°15N 113°20W **70** D6
Cardwell *Australia* 18°14S 146°2E **62** B4
Careen L. *Canada* 57°0N 108°11W **71** B7
Carei *Romania* 47°40N 22°29E **17** E12
Carey *U.S.A.* 43°19N 113°57W **76** E7
Carey, L. *Australia* 29°0S 122°15E **61** E3
Carey L. *Canada* 62°12N 102°55W **71** A8
Carhué *Argentina* 37°10S 62°50W **94** D3
Caria *Turkey* 37°20N 28°10E **23** F13
Cariacica *Brazil* 20°16S 40°25W **93** H10
Caribbean Sea *W. Indies* 15°0N 75°0W **89** D5
Caribou Mts. *Canada* 53°0N 121°0W **70** C4
Caribou *U.S.A.* 46°52N 68°1W **81** B19
Caribou → *Man., Canada* 59°20N 94°44W **71** B10
Caribou → *N.W.T., Canada* 61°27N 125°45W **70** A3
Caribou I. *Canada* 47°22N 85°49W **72** C2
Caribou Is. *Canada* 61°55N 113°15W **70** A6
Caribou L. *Man., Canada* 59°21N 96°10W **71** B9
Caribou L. *Ont., Canada* 50°25N 89°5W **72** B2
Caribou Mts. *Canada* 59°12N 115°40W **70** B5
Caribou River ⌂ *Canada* 59°35N 96°35W **71** B9
Carichic *Mexico* 27°56N 107°3W **86** B3
Carinda *Australia* 30°28S 147°41E **63** E4
Carinhanha *Brazil* 14°15S 44°46W **93** F10
Carinhanha → *Brazil* 14°20S 43°47W **93** F10
Carinthia = Kärnten □ *Austria* 46°52N 13°30E **16** E8
Caripito *Venezuela* 10°8N 63°6W **92** A6
Carleton, Mt. *Canada* 47°23N 66°53W **73** C6
Carleton Place *Canada* 45°8N 76°9W **83** A8
Carletonville *S. Africa* 26°23S 27°22E **56** C4
Carlin *U.S.A.* 40°43N 116°7W **76** F5
Carlingford L. *U.K.* 54°3N 6°9W **10** B5
Carlinville *U.S.A.* 39°17N 89°53W **80** F9
Carlisle *U.K.* 54°54N 2°56W **12** C5
Carlisle *U.S.A.* 40°12N 77°12W **82** F7
Carlisle B. *Barbados* 13°5N 59°37W **89** g
Carlisle I. *Australia* 20°49S 149°18E **62** b
Carlos Casares *Argentina* 35°32S 61°20W **94** D3
Carlos Tejedor *Argentina* 35°25S 62°25W **94** D3
Carlow *Ireland* 52°50N 6°56W **10** D5
Carlow □ *Ireland* 52°43N 6°50W **10** D5
Carlsbad *Calif., U.S.A.* 33°10N 117°21W **79** M9
Carlsbad *N. Mex., U.S.A.* 32°25N 104°14W **77** K11
Carlsbad Caverns △ *U.S.A.* 32°10N 104°35W **77** K11
Carluke *U.K.* 55°45N 3°50W **11** F5
Carlyle *Canada* 49°40N 102°20W **71** D8
Carmacks *Canada* 62°5N 136°16W **68** E4
Carman *Canada* 49°30N 98°0W **71** D9
Carmarthen *U.K.* 51°52N 4°19W **13** F3
Carmarthen B. *U.K.* 51°40N 4°30W **13** F3
Carmarthenshire □ *U.K.* 51°55N 4°13W **13** F3
Carmaux *France* 44°3N 2°10E **20** D5
Carmel *U.S.A.* 41°26N 73°41W **83** E11
Carmel, Mt. = Hā Karmel, Har *Israel* 32°44N 35°3E **48** C4
Carmel-by-the-Sea *U.S.A.* 36°33N 121°55W **78** J5
Carmel Valley *U.S.A.* 36°29N 121°43W **78** J5
Carmelo *Uruguay* 34°0S 58°20W **94** C4
Carmen *Paraguay* 27°13S 56°12W **95** B4
Carmen, I. *Mexico* 25°57N 111°12W **86** B2
Carmen de Patagones *Argentina* 40°50S 63°0W **96** E4
Carmensa *Argentina* 35°15S 67°40W **94** D2
Carmi *Canada* 49°36N 119°8W **70** D5
Carmi *U.S.A.* 38°5N 88°10W **80** F9
Carmila *Australia* 21°55S 149°24E **62** C4
Carmona *Costa Rica* 10°0N 85°15W **88** E2
Carmona *Spain* 37°28N 5°42W **21** D3
Carn Ban *U.K.* 57°7N 4°15W **11** D4
Carn Eige *U.K.* 57°17N 5°8W **11** D3
Carnamah *Australia* 29°41S 115°53E **61** E2
Carnarvon *Australia* 24°51S 113°42E **61** D1
Carnarvon *Canada* 45°3N 78°41W **82** A6
Carnarvon *S. Africa* 30°56S 22°8E **56** D3
Carnarvon △ *Australia* 24°54S 148°2E **62** C4
Carnarvon Ra. *Queens., Australia* 25°15S 148°30E **62** D4
Carnarvon Ra. *W. Austral., Australia* 25°20S 120°45E **61** E3
Carnatic *India* 9°40N 77°50E **45** K3
Carnation *U.S.A.* 47°39N 121°55W **78** C5
Carncastle *U.K.* 54°54N 5°53W **10** B6
Carndonagh *Ireland* 55°16N 7°15W **10** A4
Carnduff *Canada* 49°10N 101°50W **71** D8
Carnegie *U.S.A.* 40°24N 80°5W **82** F4
Carnegie, L. *Australia* 26°5S 122°30E **61** E3
Carnegie Ridge *Pac. Oc.* 1°0S 87°0W **65** H19
Carney I. *Antarctica* 74°0S 121°0W **5** D14
Carnic Alps = Karnische Alpen *Europe* 46°36N 13°0E **16** E7
Carniche Alpi = Karnische Alpen *Europe* 46°36N 13°0E **16** E7
Carnot *C.A.R.* 4°59N 15°56E **54** D3
Carnot, C. *Australia* 34°57S 135°38E **63** E2
Carnot B. *Australia* 17°20S 122°15E **60** C3
Carnoustie *U.K.* 56°30N 2°42W **11** E6
Carnsore Pt. *Ireland* 52°10N 6°22W **10** D5
Caro *U.S.A.* 43°29N 83°24W **81** D12
Caroga Lake *U.S.A.* 43°8N 74°28W **83** C10
Carolina *Brazil* 7°10S 47°30W **93** E9
Carolina *Puerto Rico* 18°23N 65°58W **89** d
Carolina *S. Africa* 26°5S 30°6E **57** C5
Caroline I. *Kiribati* 9°58S 150°13W **65** H12
Caroline Is. *Micronesia* 8°0N 150°0E **64** G6
Caroni *Trin. & Tob.* 10°34N 61°23W **93** K15
Caroní → *Venezuela* 8°21N 62°43W **92** B6
Caronie = Nébrodi, Monti *Italy* 37°54N 14°35E **22** F6
Caroona *Australia* 31°24S 150°26E **63** E5
Carpathians *Europe* 49°30N 21°0E **17** D11
Carpaţii Meridionali *Romania* 45°30N 25°0E **17** F13
Carpentaria, G. of *Australia* 14°0S 139°0E **62** A2
Carpentras *France* 44°3N 5°2E **20** D6
Carpi *Italy* 44°47N 10°53E **22** B4
Carpinteria *U.S.A.* 34°24N 119°31W **79** L7
Carr Boyd Ra. *Australia* 16°15S 128°35E **60** C4
Carra, L. *Ireland* 53°41N 9°14W **10** C2
Carrabelle *U.S.A.* 29°51N 84°40W **85** G12
Carraig Mhachaire Rois = Carrickmacross *Ireland* 53°59N 6°43W **10** C5
Carraig na Siúire = Carrick-on-Suir *Ireland* 52°21N 7°24W **10** D4
Carranya ✪ *Australia* 19°13S 127°46E **60** C4
Carrara *Italy* 44°5N 10°6E **20** D9
Carrauntoohill *Ireland* 52°0N 9°45W **10** D2
Carrick-on-Shannon *Ireland* 53°57N 8°7W **10** C3
Carrick-on-Suir *Ireland* 52°21N 7°24W **10** D4
Carrickfergus *U.K.* 54°43N 5°49W **10** B6
Carrickmacross *Ireland* 53°59N 6°43W **10** C5
Carrieton *Australia* 32°25S 138°31E **63** E2
Carrigaline *Ireland* 51°48N 8°23W **10** E3
Carrillo *Mexico* 26°54N 103°55W **86** B4
Carrington *U.S.A.* 47°27N 99°8W **80** B4
Carrizal Bajo *Chile* 28°5S 71°20W **94** B1
Carrizalillo *Chile* 29°5S 71°30W **94** B1
Carrizo Cr. → *U.S.A.* 36°55N 103°55W **77** H12
Carrizo Plain ⌂ *U.S.A.* 35°11N 119°47W **78** K7
Carrizo Springs *U.S.A.* 28°31N 99°52W **84** G5
Carrizozo *U.S.A.* 33°38N 105°53W **77** K11
Carroll *U.S.A.* 42°4N 94°52W **80** D6
Carrollton *Ga., U.S.A.* 33°35N 85°5W **85** E12
Carrollton *Ill., U.S.A.* 39°18N 90°24W **80** F8
Carrollton *Ky., U.S.A.* 38°41N 85°11W **81** F11
Carrollton *Mo., U.S.A.* 39°22N 93°30W **80** F7
Carrollton *Ohio, U.S.A.* 40°34N 81°5W **82** F3
Carron → *U.K.* 57°53N 4°22W **11** D4
Carron, L. *U.K.* 57°22N 5°35W **11** D3
Carrot → *Canada* 53°50N 101°17W **71** C8
Carrot River *Canada* 53°17N 103°35W **71** C8
Carruthers *Canada* 52°52N 109°16W **71** C7
Carson *Calif., U.S.A.* 33°49N 118°16W **79** M8
Carson *N. Dak., U.S.A.* 46°25N 101°34W **80** B3
Carson → *U.S.A.* 39°45N 118°40W **78** F8
Carson City *U.S.A.* 39°10N 119°46W **78** F7
Carson Sink *U.S.A.* 39°50N 118°25W **76** G4
Cartagena *Colombia* 10°25N 75°33W **92** A3
Cartagena *Spain* 37°38N 0°59W **21** D5
Cartago *Colombia* 4°45N 75°55W **92** C3
Cartago *Costa Rica* 9°50N 83°55W **88** E3
Cartersville *U.S.A.* 34°10N 84°48W **85** D12
Carterton *N.Z.* 41°2S 175°31E **59** D5
Carthage *Tunisia* 36°52N 10°20E **22** F4
Carthage *Ill., U.S.A.* 40°25N 91°8W **80** E8
Carthage *Mo., U.S.A.* 37°11N 94°19W **80** G6
Carthage *N.Y., U.S.A.* 43°59N 75°37W **83** C9
Carthage *Tex., U.S.A.* 32°9N 94°20W **84** E7
Cartier I. *Australia* 12°31S 123°29E **60** B3
Cartwright *Canada* 53°41N 56°58W **73** B8
Caruaru *Brazil* 8°15S 35°55W **93** E11
Carúpano *Venezuela* 10°39N 63°15W **92** A6
Caruthersville *U.S.A.* 36°11N 89°39W **80** G9
Carvoeiro *Brazil* 1°30S 61°59W **92** D6
Carvoeiro, C. *Portugal* 39°21N 9°24W **21** C1
Cary *U.S.A.* 35°47N 78°46W **85** D15
Cas-gwent = Chepstow *U.K.* 51°38N 2°41W **13** F5
Casa de Piedra *Argentina* 38°5S 67°28W **94** D2
Casa de Piedra, Embalse *Argentina* 38°5S 67°32W **94** D2
Casa Grande *U.S.A.* 32°53N 111°45W **77** K8
Casa Nova *Brazil* 9°25S 41°5W **93** E10
Casablanca *Chile* 33°20S 71°25W **94** C1
Casablanca *Morocco* 33°36N 7°36W **52** B4
Cascada de Basaseachic △ *Mexico* 28°9N 108°15W **86** B3
Cascade *Seychelles* 4°39S 55°29E **55** b
Cascade *Idaho, U.S.A.* 44°31N 116°2W **76** D5
Cascade *Mont., U.S.A.* 47°16N 111°42W **76** C8
Cascade Locks *U.S.A.* 45°40N 121°54W **78** E5
Cascade Ra. *U.S.A.* 47°0N 121°30W **78** D5
Cascade Res. *U.S.A.* 44°32N 116°3W **76** D5
Cascades, Pte. des *Réunion* 21°9S 55°51E **55** c
Cascais *Portugal* 38°41N 9°25W **21** C1
Cascavel *Brazil* 24°57S 53°28W **95** A5

Cáscina *Italy* 43°41N 10°33E **22** C4
Casco B. *U.S.A.* 43°45N 70°0W **81** D19
Caserta *Italy* 41°4N 14°20E **22** D6
Casey *Antarctica* 66°0S 76°0E **5** C8
Caseyr, Raas = Asir, Ras
　Somalia 11°55N 51°10E **49** E5
Cashel *Ireland* 52°30N 7°53W **10** D4
Casiguran *Phil.* 16°22N 122°7E **37** A6
Casilda *Argentina* 33°10S 61°10W **94** C3
Casino *Australia* 28°52S 153°3E **63** D5
Casiquiare → *Venezuela* 2°1N 67°7W **92** C5
Casma *Peru* 9°30S 78°20W **92** E3
Casmalia *U.S.A.* 34°50N 120°32W **79** L6
Casnewydd = Newport
　U.K. 51°35N 3°0W **13** F5
Caspe *Spain* 41°14N 0°1W **21** B5
Casper *U.S.A.* 42°51N 106°19W **76** E10
Caspian Depression *Eurasia* 47°0N 48°0E **19** E8
Caspian Sea *Eurasia* 43°0N 50°0E **19** F9
Cass City *U.S.A.* 43°36N 83°10W **82** C1
Cass Lake *U.S.A.* 47°23N 94°37W **80** B6
Cassadaga *U.S.A.* 42°20N 79°19W **82** D5
Casselman *Canada* 45°19N 75°5W **83** A9
Casselton *U.S.A.* 46°54N 97°13W **80** B5
Cassiar Mts. *Canada* 59°30N 130°30W **70** B2
Cassino *Italy* 41°30N 13°49E **22** D5
Cassville *U.S.A.* 36°41N 93°52W **80** G7
Castaic *U.S.A.* 34°30N 118°38W **79** L8
Castalia *U.S.A.* 41°24N 82°49W **82** E2
Castanhal *Brazil* 1°18S 47°55W **93** D9
Castara *Trin. & Tob.* 11°17N 60°42W **93** J16
Castell-Nedd = Neath
　U.K. 51°39N 3°48W **13** F4
Castellammare di Stábia
　Italy 40°42N 14°29E **22** D6
Castelli *Argentina* 36°7S 57°47W **94** D4
Castelló de la Plana *Spain* 39°58N 0°3W **21** C5
Castelo *Brazil* 20°33S 41°14W **95** A7
Castelo Branco *Portugal* 39°50N 7°31W **21** C2
Castelsarrasin *France* 44°2N 1°7E **20** E4
Castelvetrano *Italy* 37°41N 12°47E **22** F5
Casterton *Australia* 37°30S 141°30E **63** F3
Castile *U.S.A.* 42°38N 78°3W **82** D6
Castilla-La Mancha □
　Spain 39°30N 3°30W **21** C4
Castilla y Leon □ *Spain* 42°0N 5°0W **21** B3
Castillos *Uruguay* 34°12S 53°52W **95** C5
Castle Dale *U.S.A.* 39°13N 111°1W **76** G8
Castle Douglas *U.K.* 54°56N 3°56W **11** G5
Castle Rock *Colo.*,
　U.S.A. 39°22N 104°51W **76** G11
Castle Rock *Wash.*,
　U.S.A. 46°17N 122°54W **78** D4
Castlebar *Ireland* 53°52N 9°18W **10** C2
Castlebay *U.K.* 56°57N 7°31W **11** E1
Castleblayney *Ireland* 54°7N 6°44W **10** B5
Castlederg *U.K.* 54°42N 7°36W **10** B4
Castleford *U.K.* 53°43N 1°21W **12** D6
Castlegar *Canada* 49°20N 117°40W **70** D5
Castleisland *Ireland* 52°14N 9°28W **10** D2
Castlemaine *Australia* 37°2S 144°12E **63** F3
Castlemaine *Ireland* 52°10N 9°42W **10** D2
Castlepollard *Ireland* 53°41N 7°19W **10** C4
Castlerea *Ireland* 53°46N 8°29W **10** C3
Castlereagh → *Australia* 30°12S 147°32E **63** E4
Castlereagh B. *Australia* 12°10S 135°10E **62** A2
Castleton *U.S.A.* 43°37N 73°11W **83** C11
Castleton-on-Hudson
　U.S.A. 42°31N 73°45W **83** D11
Castletown *I. of Man* 54°5N 4°38W **12** C3
Castletown Bearhaven
　Ireland 51°39N 9°55W **10** E2
Castor *Canada* 52°15N 111°50W **70** C6
Castor → *Canada* 53°24N 78°58W **72** B4
Castorland *U.S.A.* 43°53N 75°31W **83** C9
Castres *France* 43°37N 2°13E **20** E5
Castricum *Neths.* 52°33N 4°40E **15** B4
Castries *St. Lucia* 14°2N 60°58W **89** f
Castro *Brazil* 24°45S 50°0W **95** A6
Castro *Chile* 42°30S 73°50W **96** E2
Castro Alves *Brazil* 12°46S 39°33W **93** F11
Castro Valley *U.S.A.* 37°41N 122°5W **78** H4
Castroville *U.S.A.* 36°46N 121°45W **78** J5
Castuera *Spain* 38°43N 5°37W **21** C3
Cat Ba, Dao *Vietnam* 20°50N 107°0E **38** B6
Cat Ba △ *Vietnam* 20°47N 107°3E **38** B6
Cat I. *Bahamas* 24°30N 75°30W **89** B4
Cat L. *Canada* 51°40N 91°50W **72** B1
Cat Lake *Canada* 51°40N 91°50W **72** B1
Cat Tien △ *Vietnam* 11°25N 107°17E **39** G6
Catacamas *Honduras* 14°54N 85°56W **88** D2
Cataguases *Brazil* 21°23S 42°39W **95** A7
Catalão *Brazil* 18°10S 47°57W **93** G9
Çatalca *Turkey* 41°8N 28°27E **23** D13
Catalina *Canada* 48°31N 53°4W **73** C9
Catalina *Chile* 25°13S 69°43W **94** B2
Catalina *U.S.A.* 32°30N 110°50W **77** K8
Catalonia = Cataluña □
　Spain 41°40N 1°15E **21** B6
Cataluña □ *Spain* 41°40N 1°15E **21** B6
Catamarca *Argentina* 28°30S 65°50W **94** B2
Catamarca □ *Argentina* 27°0S 65°50W **94** B2
Catanduanes □ *Phil.* 13°50N 124°20E **37** B6
Catanduva *Brazil* 21°5S 48°58W **95** A6
Catánia *Italy* 37°30N 15°6E **22** F6
Catanzaro *Italy* 38°54N 16°35E **22** E7
Cataraman *Phil.* 12°28N 124°35E **37** B6
Catatumbo-Bari △
　Colombia 9°3N 73°12W **89** E5
Catchacoma *Canada* 44°44N 78°19W **82** B6
Cateel *Phil.* 7°47N 126°24E **37** C7
Catembe *Mozam.* 26°0S 32°33E **57** C5
Caterham *U.K.* 51°15N 0°4W **13** F7
Cathair na Mart = Westport
　Ireland 53°48N 9°31W **10** C2
Cathcart *S. Africa* 32°18S 27°10E **56** D4
Cathedral City *U.S.A.* 33°47N 116°28W **79** M10
Cathlamet *U.S.A.* 46°12N 123°23W **78** D3

Catlettsburg *U.S.A.* 38°25N 82°36W **81** F12
Catoche, C. *Mexico* 21°35N 87°5W **87** C7
Catriló *Argentina* 36°26S 63°24W **94** D3
Catrimani *Brazil* 0°27N 61°41W **92** C6
Catrimani → *Brazil* 0°28N 61°44W **92** C6
Catskill *U.S.A.* 42°14N 73°52W **83** D11
Catskill △ *U.S.A.* 42°8N 74°39W **83** D10
Catskill Mts. *U.S.A.* 42°10N 74°25W **83** D10
Catt, Mt. *Australia* 13°49S 134°23E **62** A1
Cattaraugus *U.S.A.* 42°20N 78°52W **82** D6
Catterick *U.K.* 54°23N 1°37W **12** C6
Catuala *Angola* 16°25S 19°2E **56** A2
Catuane *Mozam.* 26°48S 32°18E **57** C5
Caubvick, Mt. = Iberville, Mt. d'
　Canada 58°50N 63°50W **69** F19
Cauca → *Colombia* 8°54N 74°28W **92** B3
Caucaia *Brazil* 3°40S 38°35W **93** D11
Caucasus Mountains
　Eurasia 42°50N 44°0E **19** F7
Caucete *Argentina* 31°38S 68°20W **94** C2
Caungula *Angola* 8°26S 18°38E **54** F3
Cauquenes *Chile* 36°0S 72°22W **94** D1
Caura → *Venezuela* 7°38N 64°53W **92** B6
Cauvery → *India* 11°9N 78°52E **45** J4
Caux, Pays de *France* 49°38N 0°35E **20** B4
Cavalier *U.S.A.* 48°48N 97°37W **80** A5
Cavan *Ireland* 54°0N 7°22W **10** B4
Cavan □ *Ireland* 54°1N 7°16W **10** C4
Cave Creek *U.S.A.* 33°50N 111°57W **77** K8
Cavenagh Ra. *Australia* 26°12S 127°55E **61** E4
Cavendish *Australia* 37°31S 142°2E **63** F3
Caviana, I. *Brazil* 0°10N 50°10W **93** C8
Cawndilla L. *Australia* 32°30S 142°15E **63** E3
Cawnpore = Kanpur
　India 26°28N 80°20E **43** F9
Caxias *Brazil* 4°55S 43°20W **93** D10
Caxias do Sul *Brazil* 29°10S 51°10W **95** B5
Cay Sal Bank *Bahamas* 23°45N 80°0W **88** B4
Cayambe *Ecuador* 0°3N 78°8W **92** C3
Cayenne *Fr. Guiana* 5°5N 52°18W **93** B8
Cayey *Puerto Rico* 18°7N 66°10W **89** d
Cayman Brac *Cayman Is.* 19°43N 79°49W **88** C4
Cayman Is. ☑ *W. Indies* 19°40N 80°30W **88** C3
Cayman Trench *Caribbean* 17°0N 83°0W **66** H11
Cayuga *Canada* 42°59N 79°50W **82** D5
Cayuga *U.S.A.* 42°54N 76°44W **83** D8
Cayuga Heights *U.S.A.* 42°27N 76°29W **83** D8
Cayuga L. *U.S.A.* 42°41N 76°41W **83** D8
Cazenovia *U.S.A.* 42°56N 75°51W **83** D9
Cazombo *Angola* 11°54S 22°56E **55** G4
Ceanannus Mor = Kells
　Ireland 53°44N 6°53W **10** C5
Ceará = Fortaleza *Brazil* 3°45S 38°35W **93** D11
Ceará □ *Brazil* 5°0S 40°0W **93** E11
Ceará-Mirim *Brazil* 5°38S 35°25W **93** E11
Ceatharlach = Carlow
　Ireland 52°50N 6°56W **10** D5
Cébaco, I. de *Panama* 7°33N 81°9W **88** E3
Cebollar *Argentina* 29°10S 66°35W **94** B2
Cebu *Phil.* 10°18N 123°54E **37** B6
Cecil Plains *Australia* 27°30S 151°11E **63** D5
Cedar → *U.S.A.* 41°17N 91°21W **80** E8
Cedar City *U.S.A.* 37°41N 113°4W **77** H7
Cedar Creek Res. *U.S.A.* 32°11N 96°4W **84** E6
Cedar Falls *Iowa, U.S.A.* 42°32N 92°27W **80** D7
Cedar Falls *Wash.*,
　U.S.A. 47°25N 121°45W **78** C5
Cedar Key *U.S.A.* 29°8N 83°2W **85** G13
Cedar L. *Canada* 53°10N 100°0W **71** C9
Cedar Park *U.S.A.* 30°30N 97°49W **84** F6
Cedar Rapids *U.S.A.* 41°59N 91°40W **80** E8
Cedartown *U.S.A.* 34°1N 85°15W **85** D12
Cedarvale *Canada* 55°1N 128°22W **70** B3
Cedarville *S. Africa* 30°23S 29°3E **57** D4
Cedral *Mexico* 23°50N 100°45W **86** C4
Cedro *Brazil* 6°34S 39°3W **93** E11
Cedros, I. *Mexico* 28°12N 115°15W **86** B1
Cedros B. *Trin. & Tob.* 10°16N 61°54W **93** K15
Ceduna *Australia* 32°7S 133°46E **63** E1
Ceel Gaal *Somalia* 10°58N 50°20E **49** E5
Ceel Waaq *Kenya* 2°49N 40°56E **54** D8
Ceeldheere *Somalia* 3°50N 47°8E **49** G4
Ceerigaabo *Somalia* 10°35N 47°20E **49** E4
Cefalù *Italy* 38°2N 14°1E **22** E6
Cegléd *Hungary* 47°11N 19°47E **17** E10
Ceheng *China* 24°58N 105°48E **34** E5
Cekik *Indonesia* 8°12S 114°27E **37** J17
Celaque △ *Honduras* 14°30N 88°43W **88** D2
Celaya *Mexico* 20°31N 100°37W **86** C4
Celbridge *Ireland* 53°20N 6°32W **10** C5
Celebes = Sulawesi
　Indonesia 2°0S 120°0E **37** E6
Celebes Sea *Indonesia* 3°0N 123°0E **37** D6
Celina *U.S.A.* 40°33N 84°35W **81** E11
Celje *Slovenia* 46°16N 15°18E **16** E8
Celle *Germany* 52°37N 10°4E **16** B6
Celtic Sea *Atl. Oc.* 50°9N 9°34W **14** F2
Cenderawasih, Teluk
　Indonesia 3°0S 135°20E **37** E9
Cengong *China* 27°13N 108°44E **34** D7
Centennial *U.S.A.* 39°34N 104°52W **76** G11
Center *N. Dak., U.S.A.* 47°7N 101°18W **80** B3
Center *Tex., U.S.A.* 31°48N 94°11W **84** F7
Centerburg *U.S.A.* 40°18N 82°42W **82** F2
Centerville *Calif., U.S.A.* 36°44N 119°30W **78** J7
Centerville *Iowa, U.S.A.* 40°44N 92°52W **80** E7
Centerville *Pa., U.S.A.* 40°3N 79°59W **82** F5
Centerville *Tenn., U.S.A.* 35°47N 87°28W **85** D11
Centerville *Tex., U.S.A.* 31°16N 95°59W **84** F7
Central = Tsentralnyy □
　Russia 52°0N 40°0E **26** D4
Central □ *Botswana* 22°0S 26°30E **56** B4
Central, Cordillera *Colombia* 5°0N 75°0W **92** C4
Central, Cordillera
　Costa Rica 10°10N 84°5W **88** D3
Central, Cordillera
　Dom. Rep. 19°15N 71°0W **89** C5
Central, Cordillera
　Puerto Rico 18°8N 66°35W **89** d

Central African Rep. ■
　Africa 7°0N 20°0E **53** G9
Central America *America* 12°0N 85°0W **66** H11
Central Australia ◎
　Australia 22°30S 128°30E **60** D4
Central Bedfordshire □
　U.K. 52°5N 0°20W **13** E7
Central Butte *Canada* 50°48N 106°31W **71** C7
Central City *Colo.*,
　U.S.A. 39°48N 105°31W **76** G11
Central City *Ky., U.S.A.* 37°18N 87°7W **80** G10
Central City *Nebr., U.S.A.* 41°7N 98°0W **80** E4
Central Desert ◎
　Australia 19°56S 130°46E **60** C5
Central Japan Int. ✈ (NGO)
　Japan 34°53N 136°45E **29** G8
Central Kalahari ◎
　Botswana 22°36S 23°58E **56** B3
Central Makran Range
　Pakistan 26°30N 64°15E **40** F4
Central Pacific Basin
　Pac. Oc. 8°0N 175°0W **64** G10
Central Patricia *Canada* 51°30N 90°9W **72** B1
Central Point *U.S.A.* 42°23N 122°55W **76** E2
Central Russian Uplands
　Europe 54°0N 36°0E **6** E13
Central Siberian Plateau
　Russia 65°0N 105°0E **24** B12
Central Square *U.S.A.* 43°17N 76°9W **83** C8
Centralia *Canada* 43°17N 81°28W **82** C3
Centralia *Ill., U.S.A.* 38°32N 89°8W **80** F9
Centralia *Mo., U.S.A.* 39°13N 92°8W **80** F7
Centralia *Wash., U.S.A.* 46°43N 122°58W **78** D4
Centre de Flacq *Mauritius* 20°12S 57°43E **55** d
Centreville *N.Y., U.S.A.* 42°28N 78°14W **82** D6
Centreville *Pa., U.S.A.* 41°44N 79°45W **82** E5
Cenxi *China* 22°57N 110°57E **35** F8
Cephalonia = Kefalonia
　Greece 38°15N 20°30E **23** E9
Cepu *Indonesia* 7°9S 111°35E **37** G14
Ceram = Seram *Indonesia* 3°10S 129°0E **37** E7
Ceram Sea = Seram Sea
　Indonesia 2°30S 128°30E **37** E7
Ceredigion □ *U.K.* 52°16N 4°15W **13** E3
Ceres *Argentina* 29°55S 61°55W **94** B3
Ceres *S. Africa* 33°21S 19°18E **56** D2
Ceres *U.S.A.* 37°35N 120°57W **78** H6
Cerf *Seychelles* 4°38S 55°40E **55** b
Cerignola *Italy* 41°17N 15°53E **22** D6
Cerigo = Kythira *Greece* 36°8N 23°0E **23** F10
Çerkezköy *Turkey* 41°17N 28°0E **23** D12
Cerralvo, I. *Mexico* 24°15N 109°55W **86** C3
Cerritos *Mexico* 22°25N 100°16W **86** C4
Cerro Chato *Uruguay* 33°6S 55°8W **95** C4
Cerro Cofre de Perote △
　Mexico 19°29N 97°8W **87** D5
Cerro Corá △ *Paraguay* 22°35S 56°2W **95** A4
Cerro de Pasco *Peru* 10°45S 76°10W **92** F3
Cerro el Copey △
　Venezuela 10°59N 63°53W **89** D7
Cerro Hoya △ *Panama* 7°7N 80°45W **88** E3
Cerro Saroche △
　Venezuela 10°8N 69°38W **89** D6
Cerventes *Australia* 30°31S 115°3E **61** F2
Cervera *Spain* 41°40N 1°16E **21** B6
Cesena *Italy* 44°8N 12°15E **22** B5
Cēsis *Latvia* 57°18N 25°15E **9** H21
Česká Rep. = Czech Rep. ■
　Europe 50°0N 15°0E **16** D8
České Budějovice
　Czech Rep. 48°55N 14°25E **16** D8
Českomoravská Vrchovina
　Czech Rep. 49°30N 15°40E **16** D8
Çeşme *Turkey* 38°20N 26°23E **23** E12
Cessnock *Australia* 32°50S 151°21E **63** E5
Cetinje *Montenegro* 42°23N 18°59E **23** C8
Cetraro *Italy* 39°31N 15°55E **22** E6
Ceuta *N. Afr.* 35°52N 5°18W **21** E3
Cévennes *France* 44°10N 3°50E **20** D5
Ceyhan *Turkey* 37°4N 35°47E **46** B2
Ceylanpınar *Turkey* 36°50N 40°2E **46** B4
Ceylon = Sri Lanka ■ *Asia* 7°30N 80°50E **45** L5
Cha-am *Thailand* 12°48N 99°58E **38** F2
Chacabuco *Argentina* 34°40S 60°27W **94** C3
Chachapoyas *Peru* 6°15S 77°50W **92** E3
Chachoengsao *Thailand* 13°42N 101°5E **38** F3
Chachran *Pakistan* 28°55N 70°30E **42** E4
Chachro *Pakistan* 25°5N 70°15E **42** G4
Chaco □ *Argentina* 26°30S 61°0W **94** B3
Chaco □ *Paraguay* 26°0S 60°0W **94** B3
Chaco → *U.S.A.* 36°46N 108°39W **77** H9
Chaco Austral *S. Amer.* 27°0S 61°30W **96** B4
Chaco Boreal *S. Amer.* 22°0S 60°0W **92** H6
Chaco Central *S. Amer.* 24°0S 61°0W **96** A4
Chaco Culture △ *U.S.A.* 36°3N 107°58W **77** H10
Chacon, C. *U.S.A.* 54°42N 132°0W **70** C2
Chad ■ *Africa* 15°0N 17°15E **53** F8
Chad, L. = Tchad, L. *Chad* 13°30N 14°30E **53** F8
Chadileuvú → *Argentina* 37°46S 66°0W **94** D2
Chadron *U.S.A.* 42°50N 103°0W **80** D2
Chadyr-Lunga = Ciadâr-Lunga
　Moldova 46°3N 28°51E **17** E15
Chae Hom *Thailand* 18°43N 99°35E **38** C2
Chae Son △ *Thailand* 18°42N 99°20E **38** C2
Chaem → *Thailand* 18°11N 98°38E **38** C2
Chaeryŏng *N. Korea* 38°24N 125°36E **33** E13
Chagai Hills = Chāh Gay Hills
　Afghan. 29°30N 64°0E **40** E3
Chagda *Russia* 58°45N 130°38E **27** D14
Chaghcharān *Afghan.* 34°31N 65°15E **40** B4
Chagos Arch. ☑ *Ind. Oc.* 6°0S 72°0E **25** J9
Chagres △ *Panama* 9°33N 79°37W **88** E4
Chaguanas *Trin. & Tob.* 10°30N 61°26W **93** K15
Chang, Ko *Thailand* 12°0N 102°23E **39** G4
Chang, Ko *Thailand* 9°50N 98°27E **39** H2
Ch'ang Chiang = Chang Jiang →
　China 31°48N 121°10E **35** B13
Chang Jiang → *China* 31°48N 121°10E **35** B13
Chāh Ākhvor *Iran* 32°41N 59°40E **47** C8
Chāh Bahar *Iran* 25°20N 60°40E **47** E9
Chāh-e Kavīr *Iran* 34°29N 56°52E **47** C8
Chāh Gay Hills *Afghan.* 29°30N 64°0E **40** E3
Chahar Borjak *Afghan.* 30°17N 62°3E **40** D3

Chahār Mahāll va Bakhtīārī □
　Iran 32°0N 49°0E **47** C6
Chai Badan *Thailand* 15°12N 101°8E **38** E3
Chaibasa *India* 22°42N 85°49E **43** H11
Chainat *Thailand* 15°11N 100°8E **38** E3
Chainpur *Nepal* 27°17N 87°19E **43** F12
Chaiya *Thailand* 9°23N 99°14E **39** H2
Chaiyaphum *Thailand* 15°48N 102°2E **38** E4
Chaj Doab *Pakistan* 32°15N 73°0E **42** C5
Chajari *Argentina* 30°42S 58°0W **94** C4
Chak Amru *Pakistan* 32°22N 75°11E **42** C6
Chakar → *Pakistan* 29°29N 68°2E **42** E3
Chakari *Zimbabwe* 18°5S 29°51E **57** A4
Chakhānsūr *Afghan.* 31°10N 62°0E **40** D3
Chakonipau, L. *Canada* 56°18N 68°30W **73** A6
Chakradharpur *India* 22°45N 85°40E **43** H11
Chakrata *India* 30°42N 77°51E **42** D7
Chakwal *Pakistan* 32°56N 72°53E **42** C5
Chala *Peru* 15°48S 74°20W **92** G4
Chalakudi *India* 10°18N 76°20E **45** J3
Chalchihuites *Mexico* 23°29N 103°53W **86** C4
Chaleur B. *Canada* 47°55N 65°30W **73** C6
Chalfant *U.S.A.* 37°32N 118°21W **78** H8
Chalhuanca *Peru* 14°15S 73°15W **92** F4
Chaling *China* 26°58N 113°30E **35** D9
Chalisgaon *India* 20°30N 75°10E **44** D2
Chalk River *Canada* 46°1N 77°27W **72** C4
Chalkida *Greece* 38°27N 23°42E **23** E10
Chalky Inlet *N.Z.* 46°3S 166°31E **59** G1
Challakere *India* 14°19N 76°39E **45** G3
Challapata *Bolivia* 18°53S 66°50W **92** G5
Challenger Deep *Pac. Oc.* 11°30N 142°0E **64** F6
Challenger Fracture Zone
　Pac. Oc. 35°0S 105°0W **65** L17
Challis *U.S.A.* 44°30N 114°14W **76** D6
Chalmette *U.S.A.* 29°56N 89°57W **85** G10
Chaloem Rattanakosin △
　Thailand 14°40N 99°17E **38** E2
Chalon-sur-Saône *France* 46°48N 4°50E **20** C6
Chalong *Thailand* 7°50N 98°22E **39** a
Châlons-en-Champagne
　France 48°58N 4°20E **20** B6
Chálten, Cerro = Fitz Roy, Cerro
　Argentina 49°17S 73°5W **96** F2
Chālūs *Iran* 36°38N 51°26E **47** B6
Cham, Cu Lao *Vietnam* 15°57N 108°30E **38** E7
Chama → *U.S.A.* 36°54N 106°35W **77** H10
Chamaicó *Argentina* 35°3S 64°58W **94** D3
Chaman *Pakistan* 30°58N 66°25E **40** D5
Chamba *India* 32°35N 76°10E **42** C7
Chamba *Tanzania* 11°37S 37°0E **55** E4
Chambal → *India* 26°29N 79°15E **43** F8
Chamberlain →
　Australia 15°30S 127°54E **60** C4
Chamberlain *U.S.A.* 43°49N 99°20W **80** D4
Chamberlain L. *Canada* 46°14N 69°19W **81** B19
Chambers *U.S.A.* 35°11N 109°26W **77** J9
Chambersburg *U.S.A.* 39°56N 77°40W **81** F15
Chambéry *France* 45°34N 5°55E **20** D6
Chambeshi → *Zambia* 11°53S 29°48E **54** G6
Chambly *Canada* 45°27N 73°17W **83** A11
Chambord *Canada* 48°25N 72°6W **73** C5
Chamchamal *Iraq* 35°32N 44°50E **46** C5
Chamela *Mexico* 19°32N 105°5W **86** D3
Chamical *Argentina* 30°22S 66°27W **94** C2
Chamkar Luong
　Cambodia 11°0N 103°45E **39** G4
Chamoli *India* 30°24N 79°21E **43** D8
Chamonix-Mont Blanc
　France 45°55N 6°51E **20** D7
Chamouchuane =
　Ashuapmushuan →
　Canada 48°37N 72°20W **72** C5
Champa *India* 22°2N 82°43E **43** H10
Champagne *Canada* 60°49N 136°30W **70** A1
Champagne *France* 48°40N 4°20E **20** B6
Champaign *U.S.A.* 40°7N 88°15W **80** E9
Champaner *India* 22°29N 73°32E **42** H5
Champassak *Laos* 14°53N 105°52E **38** E5
Champawat *India* 29°20N 80°6E **43** E9
Champdoré, L. *Canada* 55°55N 65°49W **73** A6
Champion *U.S.A.* 41°19N 80°51W **82** E4
Champlain *U.S.A.* 44°59N 73°27W **83** B11
Champlain, L. *U.S.A.* 44°40N 73°20W **83** B11
Champotón *Mexico* 19°21N 90°43W **87** D6
Champua *India* 22°5N 85°40E **43** H11
Chamrajnagar *India* 11°52N 76°52E **45** J3
Chana *Thailand* 6°55N 100°44E **39** J3
Chañaral *Chile* 26°23S 70°40W **94** B1
Chanārān *Iran* 36°39N 59°6E **47** B8
Chanasma *India* 23°44N 72°5E **42** H5
Chancery Lane *Barbados* 13°3N 59°30W **89** g
Chanco *Chile* 35°44S 72°32W **94** D1
Chand *India* 21°57N 79°7E **43** J8
Chandan Chauki *India* 28°33N 80°47E **43** E9
Chandannagar *India* 22°52N 88°24E **43** H13
Chandausi *India* 28°27N 78°49E **43** E8
Chandeleur Is. *U.S.A.* 29°55N 88°57W **85** G10
Chandeleur Sd. *U.S.A.* 29°55N 89°0W **85** G10
Chandigarh *India* 30°43N 76°47E **42** D7
Chandil *India* 22°58N 86°3E **43** H12
Chandler *Australia* 27°0S 133°19E **63** D1
Chandler *Canada* 48°18N 64°46W **73** C7
Chandler *Ariz., U.S.A.* 33°18N 111°50W **77** K8
Chandler *Okla., U.S.A.* 35°42N 96°53W **84** D6
Chandod *India* 21°59N 73°28E **42** J5
Chandpur *Bangla.* 23°8N 90°45E **41** H17
Chandpur *India* 13°35N 79°19E **45** H4
Chandrapur *India* 19°57N 79°25E **44** E4
Chandrupatla *India* 18°33N 80°42E **44** E5
Chandui *India* 21°23N 71°17E **42** J4
Chanf *Iran* 26°38N 60°29E **47** E9
Chang *Pakistan* 26°59N 68°30E **42** F3
Chang, Ko *Thailand* 12°0N 102°23E **39** G4

Changan *China* 22°48N 113°48E **31** a
Changanacheri *India* 9°25N 76°31E **45** K3
Changanassery = Changanacheri
　India 9°25N 76°31E **45** K3
Changane → *Mozam.* 24°30S 33°30E **57** B5
Changbai *China* 41°25N 128°5E **33** C15
Changbai Shan *China* 42°20N 129°0E **33** C15
Changchiak'ou = Zhangjiakou
　China 40°48N 114°55E **32** D8
Ch'angchou = Changzhou
　China 31°47N 119°58E **35** B12
Changchun *China* 43°57N 125°17E **33** C13
Changchunling *China* 45°18N 125°27E **33** B13
Changde *China* 29°4N 111°35E **35** C8
Changdo-ri *N. Korea* 38°30N 127°40E **33** E14
Changfeng *China* 32°28N 117°10E **35** A11
Changge *China* 34°13N 113°46E **32** G7
Changhua *China* 30°12N 119°12E **35** B12
Changhua *Taiwan* 24°2N 120°30E **35** E13
Changhũngni *N. Korea* 40°24N 128°19E **33** D15
Changji *China* 44°1N 87°19E **30** C6
Changjiang *China* 19°20N 108°55E **38** C7
Changjiang Shuiku
　China 22°29N 113°27E **31** a
Changjin *N. Korea* 40°23N 127°15E **33** D14
Changjin-ho *N. Korea* 40°30N 127°15E **33** D14
Changle *China* 25°59N 119°27E **35** E12
Changli *China* 39°40N 119°13E **33** E10
Changling *China* 44°20N 123°58E **33** B12
Changlun *Malaysia* 6°25N 100°26E **39** J3
Changning *Hunan, China* 26°28N 112°22E **35** D9
Changning *Sichuan,*
　China 28°40N 104°56E **34** C5
Changning *Yunnan, China* 24°45N 99°30E **34** E2
Changping *China* 40°14N 116°12E **32** D9
Changsha *China* 28°12N 113°0E **35** C9
Changshan *China* 28°55N 118°27E **35** C12
Changshan Qundao
　China 39°11N 122°32E **33** E12
Changshou *China* 29°50N 107°4E **34** C6
Changshu *China* 31°38N 120°43E **35** B13
Changshun *China* 26°3N 106°25E **34** D6
Changtai *China* 24°35N 117°42E **35** E11
Changting *China* 25°50N 116°22E **35** E11
Changtu *China* 42°46N 124°0E **33** C12
Changuinola *Panama* 9°26N 82°31W **88** E3
Changwu *Guangxi Zhuangzu,*
　China 23°25N 111°17E **35** F8
Changwu *Shaanxi, China* 35°10N 107°45E **32** G4
Changxing *China* 31°0N 119°55E **35** B12
Changyang *China* 30°30N 111°10E **35** B8
Changyi *China* 36°40N 119°30E **33** F10
Changyŏn *N. Korea* 38°15N 125°6E **33** E13
Changyuan *China* 35°15N 114°42E **32** G8
Changzhi *China* 36°10N 113°6E **32** F7
Changzhou *China* 31°47N 119°58E **35** B12
Chanhanga *Angola* 16°0S 14°8E **56** A1
Chania *Greece* 35°30N 24°4E **23** G11
Chanion, Kolpos *Greece* 35°33N 23°55E **23** G10
Channagiri *India* 14°2N 75°56E **45** G2
Channapatna *India* 12°40N 77°15E **45** H3
Channel Is. *U.K.* 49°19N 2°24W **13** H5
Channel Is. *U.S.A.* 33°40N 119°15W **79** M7
Channel Islands △
　U.S.A. 34°0N 119°24W **79** L7
Channel-Port aux Basques
　Canada 47°30N 59°9W **73** C8
Channel Tunnel *Europe* 51°0N 1°30E **13** F9
Channing *U.S.A.* 35°41N 102°20W **84** D3
Chantada *Spain* 42°36N 7°46W **21** A2
Chanthaburi *Thailand* 12°38N 102°12E **38** F4
Chantrey Inlet *Canada* 67°48N 96°20W **68** D12
Chanumla *India* 8°19N 93°5E **45** K11
Chanute *U.S.A.* 37°41N 95°27W **80** G6
Chao Hu *China* 31°30N 117°30E **35** B11
Chao Phraya →
　Thailand 13°40N 100°31E **38** F3
Chao Phraya Lowlands
　Thailand 15°30N 100°0E **38** E3
Chaocheng *China* 36°4N 115°37E **32** F8
Chaohu *China* 31°38N 117°50E **35** B11
Chaoyang *Guangdong,*
　China 23°17N 116°30E **35** F11
Chaoyang *Liaoning,*
　China 41°35N 120°22E **33** D11
Chaozhou *China* 23°42N 116°32E **35** F11
Chapaev *Kazakhstan* 50°25N 51°10E **19** D9
Chapais *Canada* 49°47N 74°51W **72** C5
Chapala, L. de *Mexico* 20°15N 103°0W **86** C4
Chapayev = Chapaev
　Kazakhstan 50°25N 51°10E **19** D9
Chapayevsk *Russia* 53°0N 49°40E **18** D8
Chapecó *Brazil* 27°14S 52°41W **95** B5
Chapel Hill *U.S.A.* 35°55N 79°4W **85** D15
Chapleau *Canada* 47°50N 83°24W **72** C3
Chaplin *Canada* 50°28N 106°40W **71** C7
Chaplin L. *Canada* 50°22N 106°36W **71** C7
Chappell *U.S.A.* 41°6N 102°28W **80** E2
Chapra = Chhapra *India* 25°48N 84°44E **43** G11
Chara *Russia* 56°54N 118°20E **27** D12
Charadai *Argentina* 27°35S 59°55W **94** B4
Charagua *Bolivia* 19°45S 63°10W **92** G6
Charambirá, Punta
　Colombia 4°16N 77°32W **92** C3
Charaña *Bolivia* 17°30S 69°25W **92** G5
Charanwala *India* 27°51N 72°10E **42** F5
Charata *Argentina* 27°13S 61°14W **94** B3
Charcas *Mexico* 23°8N 101°7W **86** C4
Charcot I. *Antarctica* 70°0S 70°0W **5** C17
Chard *U.K.* 50°52N 2°58E **13** G5
Chardon *U.S.A.* 41°35N 81°12W **82** E3
Chardzhou = Türkmenabat
　Turkmenistan 39°6N 63°34E **47** B9
Charente → *France* 45°57N 1°5W **20** D3
Chari → *Chad* 12°58N 14°31E **53** F8
Chārīkār *Afghan.* 35°0N 69°10E **40** B6
Chariton → *U.S.A.* 41°1N 93°19W **80** E7
Chariton *U.S.A.* 39°19N 92°58W **80** E7
Chärjew = Türkmenabat
　Turkmenistan 39°6N 63°34E **47** B9

Charkhari India 25°24N 79°45E **43 G8**
Charkhi Dadri India 28°37N 76°17E **42 E7**
Charleroi Belgium 50°24N 4°27E **15 D4**
Charleroi U.S.A. 40°9N 79°57W **82 F5**
Charles, C. U.S.A. 37°7N 75°58W **81 G16**
Charles, Peak Australia 32°52S 121°11E **61 F3**
Charles City U.S.A. 43°4N 92°41W **80 D7**
Charles I. Canada 62°39N 74°15W **69 E17**
Charles L. Canada 59°50N 110°33W **71 B6**
Charles Town U.S.A. 39°17N 77°52W **81 F15**
Charlesbourg Canada 46°51N 71°16W **81 B18**
Charleston Ill., U.S.A. 39°30N 88°10W **80 F9**
Charleston Miss., U.S.A. 34°1N 90°4W **85 D9**
Charleston Mo., U.S.A. 36°55N 89°21W **80 G9**
Charleston S.C., U.S.A. 32°46N 79°56W **85 E15**
Charleston W. Va., U.S.A. 38°21N 81°38W **81 F13**
Charleston L. Canada 44°32N 76°0W **83 B9**
Charleston Peak U.S.A. 36°16N 115°42W **79 J11**
Charlestown Ireland 53°58N 8°48W **10 C3**
Charlestown S. Africa 27°26S 29°53E **57 C4**
Charlestown Ind., U.S.A. 38°27N 85°40W **81 F11**
Charlestown N.H., U.S.A. 43°14N 72°25W **83 C12**
Charlestown of Aberlour U.K. 57°28N 3°14W **11 D5**
Charleville Australia 26°24S 146°15E **63 D4**
Charleville Ireland 52°21N 8°40W **10 D3**
Charleville-Mézières France 49°44N 4°40E **20 B6**
Charlevoix U.S.A. 45°19N 85°16W **81 C11**
Charlotte Mich., U.S.A. 42°34N 84°50W **81 D11**
Charlotte N.C., U.S.A. 35°13N 80°50W **85 D14**
Charlotte Vt., U.S.A. 44°19N 73°16W **83 B11**
Charlotte Amalie U.S. Virgin Is. 18°21N 64°56W **89 e**
Charlotte Harbor U.S.A. 26°57N 82°4W **85 H13**
Charlotte L. Canada 52°12N 125°19W **70 C3**
Charlottesville U.S.A. 38°2N 78°30W **81 F14**
Charlottetown Nfld. & L., Canada 52°46N 56°7W **73 B8**
Charlottetown P.E.I., Canada 46°14N 63°8W **73 C7**
Charlotteville Trin. & Tob. 11°20N 60°33W **93 J16**
Charlton Australia 36°16S 143°24E **63 F3**
Charlton I. Canada 52°0N 79°20W **72 B4**
Charny France 46°43N 71°15W **73 C5**
Charolles France 46°27N 4°16E **20 C6**
Charre Mozam. 17°13S 35°10E **55 H7**
Charsadda Pakistan 34°7N 71°45E **42 B4**
Charters Towers Australia 20°5S 146°13E **62 C4**
Chartres France 48°29N 1°30E **20 B4**
Chascomús Argentina 35°30S 58°0W **94 D4**
Chase Canada 50°50N 119°41W **70 C5**
Chashma Barrage Pakistan 32°27N 71°20E **42 C4**
Chāt Iran 37°59N 55°16E **47 B7**
Châteaubriant France 47°43N 1°23W **20 C3**
Chateaugay U.S.A. 44°56N 74°5W **83 B10**
Châteauguay, L. Canada 56°26N 70°3W **73 A5**
Châteaulin France 48°11N 4°8W **20 B1**
Châteauroux France 46°50N 1°40E **20 C4**
Châteaux, Pte. des Guadeloupe 16°15N 61°10W **88 b**
Châtellerault France 46°50N 0°30E **20 C4**
Chatham = Miramichi Canada 47°2N 65°28W **73 C6**
Chatham Canada 42°24N 82°11W **82 D2**
Chatham U.K. 51°22N 0°32E **13 F8**
Chatham U.S.A. 42°21N 73°36W **83 D11**
Chatham Is. Pac. Oc. 44°0S 176°40W **64 M10**
Chatham Rise Pac. Oc. 43°0S 180°0E **64 M10**
Chatmohar Bangla. 24°15N 89°15E **43 G13**
Chatra India 24°12N 84°56E **43 G11**
Chatrapur India 19°22N 85°2E **44 E7**
Chats, L. des Canada 45°30N 76°20W **83 A8**
Chatsu India 26°36N 75°57E **42 F6**
Chatsworth Canada 44°27N 80°54W **82 B4**
Chāttagâm = Chittagong Bangla. 22°19N 91°48E **41 H17**
Chattahoochee U.S.A. 30°42N 84°51W **85 F12**
Chattahoochee → U.S.A. 30°54N 84°57W **85 F12**
Chattanooga U.S.A. 35°3N 85°19W **85 D12**
Chatteris U.K. 52°28N 0°2E **13 E8**
Chatturat Thailand 15°40N 101°51E **38 E3**
Chau Doc Vietnam 10°42N 105°7E **39 G5**
Chaukan Pass Burma 27°8N 97°10E **41 F20**
Chaumont France 48°7N 5°8E **20 B6**
Chaumont U.S.A. 44°4N 76°8W **83 B8**
Chaunskaya G. Russia 69°0N 169°0E **27 C17**
Chaura India 8°27N 93°2E **45 K11**
Chautara Nepal 27°46N 85°42E **43 F11**
Chautauqua L. U.S.A. 42°10N 79°24W **82 D5**
Chauvin Canada 52°45N 110°10W **71 C6**
Chavakachcheri Sri Lanka 9°39N 80°9E **45 K5**
Chaves Brazil 0°15S 49°55W **93 D9**
Chaves Portugal 41°45N 7°32W **21 B2**
Chawang Thailand 8°25N 99°30E **39 H2**
Chaykovskiy Russia 56°47N 54°9E **18 C9**
Chazy U.S.A. 44°53N 73°26W **83 B11**
Cheb Czech Rep. 50°9N 12°28E **16 C7**
Cheboksary Russia 56°8N 47°12E **18 C8**
Cheboygan U.S.A. 45°39N 84°29W **81 C11**
Chech, Erg Africa 25°0N 2°15W **52 D5**
Chechenia □ Russia 43°30N 45°29E **19 F8**
Checheno-Ingush Republic = Chechenia □ Russia 43°30N 45°29E **19 F8**
Chechnya = Chechenia □ Russia 43°30N 45°29E **19 F8**
Checotah U.S.A. 35°28N 95°31W **84 D7**
Chedabucto B. Canada 45°25N 61°8W **73 C7**
Cheduba I. Burma 18°45N 93°40E **41 K18**
Cheektowaga U.S.A. 42°54N 78°45W **82 D6**
Cheepie Australia 26°33S 145°1E **63 D4**
Chegdomyn Russia 51°7N 133°1E **27 D14**

Chegga Mauritania 25°27N 5°40W **52 C4**
Chegutu Zimbabwe 18°10S 30°14E **55 H6**
Chehalis U.S.A. 46°40N 122°58W **78 D4**
Chehalis → U.S.A. 46°57N 123°50W **78 D3**
Cheju = Jeju S. Korea 33°31N 126°32E **33 H14**
Cheju-do = Jeju-do S. Korea 33°29N 126°34E **33 H14**
Chek Lap Kok China 22°18N 113°56E **31 a**
Chek Lap Kok ✈ (HKG) China 22°19N 113°57E **31 a**
Chekiang = Zhejiang □ China 29°0N 120°0E **35 C13**
Chela, Sa. da Angola 16°20S 13°20E **56 A1**
Chelan U.S.A. 47°51N 120°1W **76 C3**
Chelan, L. U.S.A. 48°11N 120°30W **76 B3**
Cheleken = Hazar Turkmenistan 39°34N 53°16E **19 G9**
Cheleken Yarymadasy Turkmenistan 39°30N 53°15E **47 B7**
Chelforó Argentina 39°0S 66°33W **96 D3**
Chelkar = Shalqar Kazakhstan 47°48N 59°39E **26 E6**
Chelm Poland 51°8N 23°30E **17 C12**
Chelmno Poland 53°20N 18°30E **17 B10**
Chelmsford U.K. 51°44N 0°29E **13 F8**
Chelsea Australia 38°5S 145°8E **63 F4**
Chelsea U.S.A. 43°59N 72°27W **83 C12**
Cheltenham U.K. 51°54N 2°4W **13 F5**
Chelyabinsk Russia 55°10N 61°24E **26 D7**
Chelyuskin, C. = Chelyuskin, Mys Russia 77°30N 103°0E **27 B11**
Chelyuskin, Mys Russia 77°30N 103°0E **27 B11**
Chemainus Canada 48°55N 123°42W **78 B3**
Chemba Mozam. 17°9S 34°53E **55 H6**
Chemin Grenier Mauritius 20°29S 57°28E **55 d**
Chemnitz Germany 50°51N 12°54E **16 C7**
Chemult U.S.A. 43°14N 121°47W **76 E3**
Chen, Gora Russia 65°16N 141°50E **27 C15**
Chenab → Pakistan 30°23N 71°2E **42 D4**
Chenab Nagar Pakistan 31°45N 72°55E **42 D5**
Chenango Forks U.S.A. 42°15N 75°51W **83 D9**
Chenchiang = Zhenjiang China 32°11N 119°26E **35 A12**
Cheney U.S.A. 47°30N 117°35W **76 C5**
Cheng Xian China 33°43N 105°42E **32 H3**
Chengbu China 26°18N 110°16E **35 D8**
Chengcheng China 35°8N 109°56E **32 G5**
Chengchou = Zhengzhou China 34°45N 113°34E **32 G7**
Chengde China 40°59N 117°58E **33 D9**
Chengdong Hu China 32°15N 116°20E **35 A11**
Chengdu China 30°38N 104°2E **34 B5**
Chenggong China 24°52N 102°56E **34 E4**
Chenggu China 33°10N 107°21E **34 A6**
Chenghai China 23°30N 116°42E **35 F11**
Chengjiang China 24°39N 103°0E **34 E4**
Chengkou China 31°54N 108°31E **34 B6**
Chengmai China 19°50N 109°58E **38 C7**
Chengshan Jiao China 37°25N 122°44E **33 F12**
Ch'engtu = Chengdu China 30°38N 104°2E **34 B5**
Chengwu China 34°58N 115°50E **32 G8**
Chengxi Hu China 32°15N 116°10E **35 A11**
Chengyang China 36°18N 120°21E **33 F11**
Chenjiagang China 34°23N 119°47E **33 G10**
Chenkaladi Sri Lanka 7°47N 81°35E **45 L5**
Chennai India 13°8N 80°19E **45 H5**
Chenxi China 28°2N 110°12E **35 C8**
Chenzhou China 25°47N 113°1E **35 E9**
Cheò, Eilean a' = Skye U.K. 57°15N 6°10W **11 D2**
Cheo Reo Vietnam 13°20N 108°25E **38 F7**
Cheom Ksan Cambodia 14°13N 104°56E **38 E5**
Cheonan S. Korea 36°48N 127°9E **33 F14**
Cheongdo S. Korea 35°38N 128°42E **33 G15**
Cheongju S. Korea 36°39N 127°27E **33 F14**
Cheorwon S. Korea 38°15N 127°10E **33 E14**
Chepén Peru 7°15S 79°23W **92 E3**
Chepes Argentina 31°20S 66°35W **94 C2**
Chepo Panama 9°10N 79°6W **88 E4**
Chepstow U.K. 51°38N 2°41W **13 F5**
Chequamegon B. U.S.A. 46°39N 90°51W **80 B8**
Cher → France 47°21N 0°29E **20 C4**
Cheraw U.S.A. 34°42N 79°53W **85 D15**
Cherbourg France 49°39N 1°40W **20 B3**
Cherdyn Russia 60°24N 56°29E **18 B10**
Cheremkhovo Russia 53°8N 103°1E **30 A9**
Cherepovets Russia 59°5N 37°55E **18 C6**
Chergui, Chott ech Algeria 34°21N 0°25E **52 B6**
Cherial India 17°55N 78°59W **44 F4**
Cherikov = Cherykaw Belarus 53°32N 31°20E **17 B16**
Cheriyam I. India 10°9N 73°40E **45 J1**
Cherkasy Ukraine 49°27N 32°4E **19 E5**
Cherkessk Russia 44°15N 42°5E **19 F7**
Cherla India 18°5N 80°49E **44 E5**
Cherlak Russia 54°15N 74°55E **26 D8**
Chernaya Russia 70°30N 89°10E **27 B9**
Chernigov = Chernihiv Ukraine 51°28N 31°20E **18 D5**
Chernigovka Russia 44°19N 132°34E **28 B6**
Chernihiv Ukraine 51°28N 31°20E **18 D5**
Chernivtsi Ukraine 48°15N 25°52E **17 D13**
Chernobyl = Chornobyl Ukraine 51°20N 30°15E **17 C16**
Chernogorsk Russia 53°49N 91°18E **27 D10**
Chernovtsy = Chernivtsi Ukraine 48°15N 25°52E **17 D13**
Chernyakhovsk Russia 54°36N 21°48E **9 J19**
Chernysheyskiy Russia 63°0N 112°30E **27 C12**
Cherokee Iowa, U.S.A. 42°45N 95°33W **80 D6**
Cherokee Okla., U.S.A. 36°45N 98°21W **84 C5**
Cherokee Village U.S.A. 36°18N 91°31W **84 C9**
Cherokees, Grand Lake O' The U.S.A. 36°28N 94°55W **84 C7**
Cherrapunji India 25°17N 91°47E **41 G17**
Cherry Valley U.S.A. 42°48N 74°45W **83 D10**
Cherskiy Russia 68°45N 161°18E **27 C17**

Cherskogo Khrebet Russia 65°0N 143°0E **27 C15**
Cherthala India 9°42N 76°22E **45 K3**
Cherven Belarus 53°45N 28°28E **17 B15**
Chervonohrad Ukraine 50°25N 24°10E **17 C13**
Cherwell → U.K. 51°44N 1°14W **13 F6**
Cherykaw Belarus 53°32N 31°20E **17 B16**
Chesapeake U.S.A. 36°49N 76°16W **81 G15**
Chesapeake B. U.S.A. 38°0N 76°10W **81 F14**
Cheshire East □ U.K. 53°15N 2°15W **12 D5**
Cheshire West and Chester □ U.K. 53°15N 2°40W **12 D5**
Cheshskaya Guba Russia 67°20N 47°0E **18 A8**
Cheshunt U.K. 51°43N 0°1W **13 F7**
Chesil Beach U.K. 50°37N 2°33W **13 G5**
Chesley Canada 44°17N 81°5W **82 B3**
Chester U.K. 53°12N 2°53W **12 D5**
Chester Calif., U.S.A. 40°19N 121°14W **76 F3**
Chester Ill., U.S.A. 37°55N 89°49W **80 G9**
Chester Mont., U.S.A. 48°31N 110°58W **76 B8**
Chester Pa., U.S.A. 39°51N 75°22W **81 F16**
Chester S.C., U.S.A. 34°43N 81°12W **85 D14**
Chester Vt., U.S.A. 43°16N 72°36W **83 C12**
Chester W. Va., U.S.A. 40°37N 80°34W **82 F4**
Chester-le-Street U.K. 54°51N 1°34W **12 C6**
Chesterfield U.K. 53°15N 1°25W **12 D6**
Chesterfield, Îs. N. Cal. 19°52S 158°15E **58 C8**
Chesterfield Inlet Canada 63°30N 90°45W **68 E13**
Chesterton Ra. Australia 25°30S 147°27E **63 D4**
Chesterton Range △ Australia 26°16S 147°22E **63 D4**
Chestertown U.S.A. 43°40N 73°48W **83 C11**
Chesterville Canada 45°6N 75°14W **83 A9**
Chesuncook L. U.S.A. 46°0N 69°21W **81 C19**
Chetamale India 10°43N 92°33E **45 J11**
Chéticamp Canada 46°37N 60°59W **73 C7**
Chetlat I. India 11°42N 72°42E **45 J1**
Chetumal Mexico 18°30N 88°20W **87 D7**
Chetumal, B. de Cent. Amer. 18°40N 88°10W **87 D7**
Chetwynd Canada 55°45N 121°36W **70 B4**
Cheung Chau China 22°13N 114°1E **31 a**
Cheviot, The U.K. 55°29N 2°9W **12 B5**
Cheviot Hills U.K. 55°20N 2°30W **12 B5**
Cheviot Ra. Australia 25°20S 143°45E **62 D3**
Chew Bahir Ethiopia 4°40N 36°50E **49 G2**
Chewelah U.S.A. 48°17N 117°43W **76 B5**
Cheyenne Okla., U.S.A. 35°37N 99°40W **84 D5**
Cheyenne Wyo., U.S.A. 41°8N 104°49W **76 F11**
Cheyenne → U.S.A. 44°41N 101°18W **80 C3**
Cheyenne Wells U.S.A. 38°49N 102°21W **76 G12**
Cheyne B. Australia 34°35S 118°50E **61 F2**
Cheyur India 12°21N 80°0E **45 H5**
Chhabra India 24°40N 76°54E **42 G7**
Chhaktala India 22°6N 74°11E **42 H6**
Chhapra India 25°48N 84°44E **43 G11**
Chhata India 27°42N 77°30E **42 F7**
Chhatarpur Jharkhand, India 24°23N 84°11E **43 G11**
Chhatarpur Mad. P., India 24°55N 79°35E **43 G8**
Chhati India 20°47N 81°40E **44 D5**
Chhattisgarh □ India 22°0N 82°0E **43 J10**
Chhep Cambodia 13°45N 105°24E **38 F5**
Chhindwara Mad. P., India 23°3N 79°29E **43 H8**
Chhindwara Mad. P., India 22°2N 78°59E **43 H8**
Chhinhdipada India 21°6N 84°52E **44 D7**
Chhlong Cambodia 12°15N 105°58E **39 F5**
Chhota Tawa → India 22°14N 76°36E **42 H7**
Chhoti Kali Sindh → India 24°2N 75°31E **42 G6**
Chhuikhadan India 21°32N 80°59E **43 J9**
Chhuk Cambodia 10°46N 104°28E **39 G5**
Chi → Thailand 15°11N 104°43E **38 E5**
Chi Thanh Vietnam 13°17N 109°16E **38 F7**
Chiai Taiwan 23°29N 120°25E **35 F13**
Chiali Taiwan 23°9N 120°10E **35 F13**
Chiang Dao Thailand 19°22N 98°58E **38 C2**
Chiang Dao, Doi Thailand 19°23N 98°54E **38 C2**
Chiang Kham Thailand 19°32N 100°18E **38 C3**
Chiang Khan Thailand 17°52N 101°36E **38 D3**
Chiang Khong Thailand 20°17N 100°24E **34 G3**
Chiang Mai Thailand 18°47N 98°59E **38 C2**
Chiang Rai Thailand 19°52N 99°50E **34 H2**
Chiang Saen Thailand 20°16N 100°5E **34 G3**
Chiapa de Corzo Mexico 16°42N 92°58E **87 D6**
Chiapas □ Mexico 16°30N 92°30W **87 D6**
Chiapas, Sa. Madre de Mexico 15°40N 93°0W **87 D6**
Chiautla de Tapia Mexico 18°18N 98°36W **87 D5**
Chiávari Italy 44°19N 9°19E **20 D8**
Chiavenna Italy 46°19N 9°24E **20 D8**
Chiba Japan 35°30N 140°7E **29 G10**
Chiba □ Japan 35°30N 140°20E **29 G10**
Chibabava Mozam. 20°17S 33°35E **57 B5**
Chibemba Cunene, Angola 15°48S 14°8E **55 H2**
Chibemba Huila, Angola 16°20S 15°20E **56 A2**
Chibi Zimbabwe 20°18S 30°25E **57 B5**
Chibia Angola 15°10S 13°42E **55 H2**
Chibougamau Canada 49°56N 74°24W **72 C5**
Chibougamau, L. Canada 49°50N 74°20W **72 C5**
Chibuk Nigeria 10°52N 12°50E **53 F8**
Chibuto Mozam. 24°40S 33°33E **57 B5**
Chic-Chocs, Mts. Canada 48°55N 66°0W **73 C6**
Chicacole = Srikakulam India 18°14N 83°58E **44 E6**
Chicago Heights U.S.A. 41°30N 87°38W **80 E10**
Chichagof I. U.S.A. 57°30N 135°30W **68 C6**
Chichaoua Morocco 31°32N 8°44W **52 B4**
Chichawatni Pakistan 30°23N 72°42E **42 D5**
Chichén-Itzá Mexico 20°38N 88°35W **87 C7**
Chicheng China 40°55N 115°55E **32 D8**
Chichester U.K. 50°50N 0°47W **13 G7**
Chichester Ra. Australia 22°12S 119°15E **60 D2**
Chichibu Japan 35°59N 139°10E **29 F9**
Chichibu-Tama-Kai △ Japan 35°52N 138°42E **29 G9**

Ch'ich'ihaerh = Qiqihar China 47°26N 124°0E **31 B13**
Chicholi India 22°1N 77°40E **42 H8**
Chickasaw △ U.S.A. 34°26N 97°0W **84 D6**
Chickasha U.S.A. 35°3N 97°58W **84 D6**
Chiclana de la Frontera Spain 36°26N 6°9W **21 D2**
Chiclayo Peru 6°42S 79°50W **92 E3**
Chico U.S.A. 39°44N 121°50W **78 F5**
Chico → Chubut, Argentina 44°0S 67°0W **96 E3**
Chico → Santa Cruz, Argentina 50°0S 68°30W **96 G3**
Chicoa Mozam. 15°36S 32°20E **57 A5**
Chicomo Mozam. 24°31S 34°6E **57 B5**
Chicomostoc Mexico 22°28N 102°46W **86 C4**
Chicontepec Mexico 20°58N 98°10W **87 C5**
Chicopee U.S.A. 42°9N 72°37W **83 D12**
Chicoutimi Canada 48°28N 71°5W **73 C5**
Chicualacuala Mozam. 22°6S 31°42E **57 C5**
Chidambaram India 11°20N 79°45E **45 J4**
Chidenguele Mozam. 24°55S 34°11E **57 B5**
Chidley, C. Canada 60°23N 64°26W **69 E19**
Chiducuane Mozam. 24°35S 34°25E **57 B5**
Chiede Angola 17°15S 16°22E **56 A2**
Chiefs Pt. Canada 44°41N 81°18W **82 B3**
Chiem Hoa Vietnam 22°12N 105°17E **38 A5**
Chiemsee Germany 47°53N 12°28E **16 E7**
Chiengmai = Chiang Mai Thailand 18°47N 98°59E **38 C2**
Chiese → Italy 45°8N 10°25E **20 D9**
Chieti Italy 42°21N 14°10E **22 C6**
Chifeng China 42°18N 118°58E **33 C10**
Chignecto B. Canada 45°30N 64°40W **73 C7**
Chiguana Bolivia 21°0S 67°58W **94 A2**
Chigwell U.K. 51°37N 0°6E **13 F8**
Chihli, G. of = Bo Hai China 39°0N 119°0E **33 E10**
Chihuahua Mexico 28°38N 106°5W **86 B3**
Chihuahua □ Mexico 28°30N 106°0W **86 B3**
Chiili = Shīeli Kazakhstan 44°20N 66°15E **26 E7**
Chik Ballapur India 13°25N 77°45E **45 H3**
Chikalda India 21°24N 77°19E **44 D3**
Chikmagalur India 13°15N 75°45E **45 H2**
Chikodi India 16°26N 74°38E **45 G2**
Chilapa Mexico 17°36N 99°10W **87 D5**
Chilas Pakistan 35°25N 74°5E **43 B6**
Chilaw Sri Lanka 7°30N 79°50E **45 L4**
Chilcotin → Canada 51°44N 122°23W **70 C4**
Childers Australia 25°15S 152°17E **63 D5**
Childress U.S.A. 34°25N 100°13W **84 D4**
Chile ■ S. Amer. 35°0S 72°0W **96 D2**
Chile Rise Pac. Oc. 38°0S 92°0W **65 L18**
Chilecito Argentina 29°10S 67°30W **94 B2**
Chilete Peru 7°10S 78°50W **92 E3**
Chililabombwe Zambia 12°18S 27°43E **55 G5**
Chilim Pakistan 35°5N 75°5E **43 B6**
Chilin = Jilin China 43°44N 126°30E **33 C14**
Chilka L. India 19°40N 85°25E **44 E7**
Chilko → Canada 52°0N 123°40W **70 C4**
Chilko L. Canada 51°20N 124°10W **70 C4**
Chillagoe Australia 17°7S 144°33E **62 B3**
Chillán Chile 36°40S 72°10W **94 D1**
Chillicothe Ill., U.S.A. 40°55N 89°29W **80 E9**
Chillicothe Mo., U.S.A. 39°48N 93°33W **80 F7**
Chillicothe Ohio, U.S.A. 39°20N 82°59W **81 F12**
Chilliwack Canada 49°10N 121°54W **70 D4**
Chilo India 27°25N 73°32E **42 F5**
Chiloane, I. Mozam. 20°40S 34°55E **57 B5**
Chiloé, I. de Chile 42°30S 73°50W **96 E2**
Chilpancingo Mexico 17°33N 99°30W **87 D5**
Chiltern Hills U.K. 51°40N 0°53W **13 F7**
Chilton U.S.A. 44°2N 88°10W **80 C9**
Chilung Taiwan 25°3N 121°45E **35 E13**
Chilwa, L. Malawi 15°15S 35°40E **55 H7**
Chimaltitán Mexico 21°35N 103°50W **86 C4**
Chimán Panama 8°45N 78°40W **88 E4**
Chimanimani Zimbabwe 19°48S 32°52E **57 A5**
Chimanimani △ Zimbabwe 19°48S 33°0E **57 A5**
Chimay Belgium 50°3N 4°20E **15 D4**
Chimayo U.S.A. 36°0N 105°56W **77 J11**
Chimborazo Ecuador 1°29S 78°55W **92 D3**
Chimbote Peru 9°0S 78°35W **92 E3**
Chimboy Uzbekistan 42°57N 59°47E **26 E6**
Chimkent = Shymkent Kazakhstan 42°18N 69°36E **26 E7**
Chimoio Mozam. 19°4S 33°30E **55 H6**
Chimur India 20°30N 79°23E **44 D4**
Chin □ Burma 22°0N 93°0E **41 J18**
Chin Hills Burma 22°30N 93°30E **41 H18**
Chin Ling Shan = Qinling Shandi China 33°50N 108°10E **32 H5**
China Mexico 25°42N 99°14W **87 B5**
China ■ Asia 30°0N 110°0E **31 E11**
China, Great Plain of Asia 35°0N 115°0E **24 E13**
China Lake U.S.A. 35°44N 117°37W **79 K9**
Chinan = Jinan China 36°38N 117°1E **32 F9**
Chinandega Nic. 12°35N 87°12W **88 D2**
Chinati Peak U.S.A. 29°57N 104°29W **84 G2**
Chincha Alta Peru 13°25S 76°7W **92 F3**
Chinchaga → Canada 58°53N 118°20W **70 B5**
Chinchilla Australia 26°45S 150°38E **63 D5**
Chincholi India 17°28N 77°26E **44 F3**
Chinchorro, Banco Mexico 18°35N 87°20W **87 D7**
Chinchou = Jinzhou China 41°5N 121°3E **33 D11**
Chincoteague U.S.A. 37°56N 75°23W **81 G16**
Chinde Mozam. 18°35S 36°30E **55 H7**
Chindwin → Burma 21°26N 95°15E **41 J19**
Chineni India 33°2N 75°15E **43 C6**
Chingola Zambia 12°31S 27°53E **55 G5**
Ch'ingtao = Qingdao China 36°5N 120°20E **33 F11**
Chinguetti Mauritania 20°25N 12°24W **52 D3**
Chingune Mozam. 20°33S 34°58E **57 B5**

Chinhanguanine Mozam. 25°21S 32°30E **57 C5**
Chinhoyi Zimbabwe 17°20S 30°8E **55 H6**
Chiniot Pakistan 31°45N 73°0E **42 D5**
Chínipas Mexico 27°23N 108°32W **86 B3**
Chinji Pakistan 32°42N 72°22E **42 C5**
Chinju = Jinju S. Korea 35°12N 128°2E **33 G15**
Chinko → C.A.R. 4°50N 23°53E **54 D4**
Chinle U.S.A. 36°9N 109°33W **77 H9**
Chinmen Taiwan 24°26N 118°19E **35 E13**
Chinmen Tao Taiwan 24°26N 118°22E **35 E12**
Chinnamanur India 9°50N 77°24E **45 K3**
Chinnampo = Namp'o N. Korea 38°52N 125°10E **33 E13**
Chino Japan 35°59N 138°9E **29 G9**
Chino U.S.A. 34°1N 117°41W **79 L9**
Chino Valley U.S.A. 34°45N 112°27W **77 J7**
Chinon France 47°10N 0°15E **20 C4**
Chinook U.S.A. 48°35N 109°14W **76 B9**
Chinook Trough Pac. Oc. 44°0N 175°0W **64 C10**
Chinsura = Chunchura India 22°53N 88°27E **43 H13**
Chintalapudi India 17°4N 80°59E **44 F5**
Chintamani India 13°26N 78°3E **45 H4**
Chióggia Italy 45°13N 12°17E **22 B5**
Chios Greece 38°27N 26°9E **23 E12**
Chipata Zambia 13°38S 32°28E **55 G6**
Chipindo Angola 13°49S 15°48E **55 G3**
Chipinge Zimbabwe 20°13S 32°28E **55 J6**
Chipley U.S.A. 30°47N 85°32W **85 F12**
Chiplun India 17°31N 73°34E **44 F1**
Chipman Canada 46°6N 65°53W **73 C6**
Chippenham U.K. 51°27N 2°6W **13 F5**
Chippewa → U.S.A. 44°25N 92°5W **80 C7**
Chippewa Falls U.S.A. 44°56N 91°24W **80 C8**
Chipping Norton U.K. 51°56N 1°32W **13 F6**
Chiputneticook Lakes N. Amer. 45°35N 67°35W **81 C20**
Chiquián Peru 10°10S 77°0W **92 F3**
Chiquibul △ Belize 16°49N 88°52W **88 C2**
Chiquimula Guatemala 14°51N 89°37W **88 D2**
Chiquinquira Colombia 5°37N 73°50W **92 B4**
Chirala India 15°50N 80°26E **45 G5**
Chirawa India 28°14N 75°42E **42 E6**
Chirchiq Uzbekistan 41°29N 69°35E **26 E7**
Chiredzi Zimbabwe 21°0S 31°38E **57 B5**
Chiricahua △ U.S.A. 32°0N 109°20W **77 K9**
Chiricahua Peak U.S.A. 31°51N 109°18W **77 L9**
Chirikof I. U.S.A. 55°50N 155°40W **74 D8**
Chiriquí, G. de Panama 8°0N 82°10W **88 E3**
Chiriquí, L. de Panama 9°10N 82°0W **88 E3**
Chirmiri India 23°15N 82°20E **43 H10**
Chirripó Grande, Cerro Costa Rica 9°29N 83°29W **88 E3**
Chirundu Zimbabwe 16°3S 28°50E **57 A4**
Chisapani Nepal 28°37N 81°16E **43 E9**
Chisasibi Canada 53°50N 79°0W **72 B4**
Ch'ishan Taiwan 22°44N 120°31E **35 F13**
Chisholm U.S.A. 54°55N 114°10W **70 C6**
Chisholm U.S.A. 47°29N 92°53W **80 B7**
Chishtian Mandi Pakistan 29°50N 72°55E **42 E5**
Chishui China 28°30N 105°42E **34 C5**
Chishui He → China 28°49N 105°50E **34 C5**
Chisimaio = Kismaayo Somalia 0°22S 42°32E **49 H3**
Chişinău Moldova 47°2N 28°50E **17 E15**
Chisos Mts. U.S.A. 29°5N 103°15W **84 G3**
Chistopol Russia 55°25N 50°38E **18 C9**
Chita Russia 52°0N 113°35E **31 A11**
Chitapur India 17°10N 77°5E **44 F3**
Chitose Japan 42°49N 141°39E **28 C10**
Chitradurga India 14°14N 76°24E **45 H3**
Chitrakot India 19°10N 81°40E **44 E5**
Chitral Pakistan 35°50N 71°56E **40 B7**
Chitravati → India 14°45N 78°15E **45 G4**
Chitré Panama 7°59N 80°27W **88 E3**
Chittagong Bangla. 22°19N 91°48E **41 H17**
Chittagong □ Bangla. 24°5N 91°0E **41 G17**
Chittaurgarh India 24°52N 74°38E **42 G6**
Chittoor India 13°15N 79°5E **45 H4**
Chittur India 10°40N 76°45E **45 J3**
Chitungwiza Zimbabwe 18°0S 31°6E **55 H6**
Chiusi Italy 43°1N 11°57E **22 C4**
Chivasso Italy 45°11N 7°53E **20 D7**
Chivilcoy Argentina 34°55S 60°0W **94 C4**
Chixi China 22°0N 112°58E **35 G9**
Chkalov = Orenburg Russia 51°45N 55°6E **18 D10**
Chloride U.S.A. 35°25N 114°12W **79 K12**
Cho-do N. Korea 38°30N 124°40E **33 E13**
Cho Phuoc Hai Vietnam 10°26N 107°18E **39 G6**
Chobe △ Botswana 18°25S 24°25E **56 A4**
Chocolate Mts. U.S.A. 33°15N 115°15W **79 M11**
Choctawhatchee → U.S.A. 30°25N 86°8W **85 F11**
Chodavaram Andhra Pradesh, India 17°50N 82°57E **44 F6**
Chodavaram Andhra Pradesh, India 17°27N 81°46E **44 F5**
Choele Choel Argentina 39°11S 65°40W **96 D3**
Choghá Zanbil Iran 32°1N 48°32E **47 C6**
Choiseul St. Lucia 13°47N 61°3W **89 f**
Choiseul Solomon Is. 7°0S 156°40E **58 B8**
Choix Mexico 26°43N 108°17W **86 B3**
Chojnice Poland 53°42N 17°32E **17 B9**
Chok Chai Thailand 14°44N 102°10E **38 E4**
Chōkai-San Japan 39°6N 140°3E **28 E10**
Choke Canyon Res. U.S.A. 28°30N 98°20W **84 G5**
Chokurdakh Russia 70°38N 147°55E **27 B15**
Chokwé Mozam. 24°32S 32°59E **57 C5**
Cholame U.S.A. 35°44N 120°18W **78 K6**
Cholet France 47°4N 0°52W **20 C3**
Cholguan Chile 37°10S 72°3W **94 D1**
Choloma Honduras 15°37N 87°57W **88 C2**
Choluteca Honduras 13°20N 87°14W **88 D2**
Choluteca → Honduras 13°0N 87°20W **88 D2**
Chom Bung Thailand 13°37N 99°36E **38 F2**
Chom Thong Thailand 18°25N 98°41E **38 C2**
Choma Zambia 16°48S 26°59E **55 H5**

Chomolungma = Everest, Mt.
  Nepal 28°5N 86°58E **43** E12
Chomun India 27°15N 75°40E **42** F6
Chomutov Czech Rep. 50°28N 13°23E **16** C7
Chon Buri Thailand 13°21N 101°1E **38** F3
Chon Thanh Vietnam 11°24N 106°36E **39** G6
Chone Ecuador 0°40S 80°0W **92** D3
Chong Kai Cambodia 13°57N 103°35E **38** F4
Chong Mek Thailand 15°10N 105°27E **38** E5
Chong Phangan Thailand 9°39N 100°0E **39** b
Chong Samui Thailand 9°21N 99°50E **39** b
Chongde China 30°32N 120°26E **35** B13
Ch'ŏngjin N. Korea 41°47N 129°50E **33** D15
Chŏngju N. Korea 39°40N 125°5E **33** E13
Chongli China 40°58N 115°15E **32** D8
Chongming China 31°38N 121°23E **35** B13
Chongming Dao China 31°40N 121°30E **35** B13
Chongqing Chongqing,
  China 29°35N 106°25E **34** C6
Chongqing Sichuan,
  China 30°38N 103°40E **34** B4
Chongqing Shi □ China 30°0N 108°0E **34** C6
Chongren China 27°46N 116°3E **35** D11
Chonguene Mozam. 25°3S 33°49E **57** C5
Chongyi China 25°45N 114°29E **35** E10
Chongzuo China 22°23N 107°20E **34** F6
Chonogol Mongolia 45°54N 115°22E **32** B8
Chonos, Arch. de los Chile 45°0S 75°0W **96** F2
Chop Ukraine 48°26N 22°12E **17** D12
Chopda India 21°20N 75°15E **44** D2
Chopim → Brazil 25°35S 53°5W **95** B5
Chor Pakistan 25°31N 69°46E **42** G3
Chora Sfakion Greece 35°15N 24°9E **23** G11
Chorbat La India 34°42N 76°37E **43** B7
Chorley U.K. 53°39N 2°38W **12** D5
Chornobyl Ukraine 51°20N 30°15E **17** C16
Chorolque, Cerro Bolivia 20°59S 66°5W **94** A2
Chorregon Australia 22°40S 143°32E **62** C3
Chorro el Indio △
  Venezuela 7°43N 72°9W **89** E5
Chortkiv Ukraine 49°2N 25°46E **17** D13
Chorzów Poland 50°18N 18°57E **17** C10
Chos-Malal Argentina 37°20S 70°15W **94** D1
Ch'osan N. Korea 40°50N 125°47E **33** D14
Choszczno Poland 53°7N 15°25E **16** B8
Choteau U.S.A. 47°49N 112°11W **76** C7
Chotila India 22°23N 71°15E **42** H4
Chotta Udepur India 22°19N 74°1E **42** H6
Chowchilla U.S.A. 37°7N 120°16W **78** H6
Choybalsan Mongolia 48°4N 114°30E **31** B11
Choyr Mongolia 46°24N 108°30E **31** B10
Christchurch N.Z. 43°33S 172°47E **59** E4
Christchurch U.K. 50°44N 1°47W **13** G6
Christian I. Canada 44°50N 80°12W **82** B4
Christian Sd. U.S.A. 55°56N 134°40W **75** D13
Christiana S. Africa 27°52S 25°8E **56** C4
Christiansted
  U.S. Virgin Is. 17°45N 64°42W **89** C7
Christie B. Canada 62°32N 111°10W **71** A6
Christina → Canada 56°40N 111°3W **71** B6
Christmas Cr. →
  Australia 18°29S 125°23E **60** C4
Christmas I. = Kiritimati
  Kiribati 1°58N 157°27W **65** G12
Christmas I. Ind. Oc. 10°30S 105°40E **64** J2
Christopher, L. Australia 24°49S 127°42E **61** D4
Chū = Shū Kazakhstan 43°36N 73°42E **26** E8
Chu → Vietnam 19°53N 105°45E **38** C5
Chu Lai Vietnam 15°28N 108°45E **38** E7
Chu Mom Ray △
  Vietnam 14°29N 107°38E **38** E6
Chu Se Vietnam 13°40N 108°8E **38** F7
Chuadanga Bangla. 23°38N 88°51E **43** H13
Chuak, Ko Thailand 9°28N 99°41E **39** b
Ch'uanchou = Quanzhou
  China 24°55N 118°34E **35** E12
Chuankou China 34°20N 110°59E **32** G6
Chubbuck U.S.A. 42°55N 112°28W **76** E7
Chūbu □ Japan 36°45N 137°30E **29** F8
Chūbu-Sangaku △
  Japan 36°30N 137°40E **29** F8
Chubut → Argentina 43°20S 65°5W **96** E3
Chuchi L. Canada 55°12N 124°30W **70** B4
Chuda India 22°29N 71°41E **42** H4
Chudskoye, Ozero Russia 58°13N 27°30E **9** G22
Chugach Mts. U.S.A. 60°45N 147°0W **74** C10
Chūgoku □ Japan 35°0N 133°0E **29** G6
Chūgoku-Sanchi Japan 35°0N 133°0E **29** G6
Chugwater U.S.A. 41°46N 104°50W **76** F11
Chukchi Plateau Arctic 78°0N 165°0W **4** B17
Chukchi Sea Russia 68°0N 175°0W **27** C19
Chukotskiy Mys Russia 64°14N 173°8W **74** C5
Chukotskiy Poluostrov
  Russia 66°0N 174°0W **74** B5
Chukotskoye Nagorye
  Russia 68°0N 175°0E **27** C18
Chula Vista U.S.A. 32°38N 117°5W **79** N9
Chulband → India 20°40N 79°54E **44** D4
Chulucanas Peru 5°8S 80°10W **92** E2
Chulym → Russia 57°43N 83°51E **26** D9
Chum Phae Thailand 16°40N 102°6E **38** D4
Chum Saeng Thailand 15°55N 100°15E **38** E3
Chumar India 32°40N 78°35E **43** C8
Chumbicha Argentina 29°0S 66°10W **94** B2
Chumikan Russia 54°40N 135°10E **27** D14
Chumphon Thailand 10°35N 99°14E **39** G2
Chuna → Russia 57°47N 94°37E **27** D10
Chun'an China 29°35N 119°3E **35** C12
Chuncheon S. Korea 37°58N 127°44E **33** F14
Chunchura India 22°53N 88°27E **43** H13
Chunggang-ŭp
  N. Korea 41°48N 126°48E **33** D14
Chunghwa N. Korea 38°52N 125°47E **33** E13
Chungju S. Korea 36°58N 127°58E **33** F14
Chungking = Chongqing
  China 29°35N 106°25E **34** C6
Chungli Taiwan 24°57N 121°13E **35** E13
Chungt'iaoshan = Zhongtiao Shan
  China 35°0N 111°10E **32** G6

Chungyang Shanmo
  Taiwan 23°10N 121°0E **35** F13
Chunian Pakistan 30°57N 74°0E **42** D6
Chunya Tanzania 8°30S 33°27E **54** F6
Chunyang China 43°38N 129°23E **33** C15
Chupara Pt. Trin. & Tob. 10°49N 61°22W **93** K15
Chuquibamba Peru 15°47S 72°44W **92** G4
Chuquicamata Chile 22°15S 69°0W **94** A2
Chur Switz. 46°52N 9°32E **20** C8
Churachandpur India 24°20N 93°40E **41** G18
Church Stretton U.K. 52°32N 2°48W **13** E5
Churchill Canada 58°47N 94°11W **71** B10
Churchill → Man.,
  Canada 58°47N 94°12W **71** B10
Churchill, C. Canada 58°46N 93°12W **71** B10
Churchill Falls Canada 53°36N 64°19W **73** B7
Churchill L. Canada 55°55N 108°20W **71** B7
Churchill Pk. Canada 58°10N 125°10W **70** B3
Churki India 23°50N 83°12E **43** H10
Churu India 28°20N 74°50E **42** E6
Churún Merú = Angel Falls
  Venezuela 5°57N 62°30W **92** B6
Chushal India 33°40N 78°40E **43** C8
Chuska Mts. U.S.A. 36°15N 108°50W **77** H9
Chusovoy Russia 58°22N 57°50E **18** C10
Chute-aux-Outardes
  Canada 49°7N 68°24W **73** C6
Chuuk = Truk Micronesia 7°25N 151°46E **64** G7
Chuvash Republic = Chuvashia □
  Russia 55°30N 47°0E **18** C8
Chuvashia □ Russia 55°30N 47°0E **18** C8
Chuwārtah Iraq 35°43N 45°34E **46** C5
Chuxiong China 25°2N 101°28E **34** E3
Chuy Uruguay 33°41S 53°27W **95** C5
Chuzhou China 32°19N 118°20E **35** A12
Ci Xian China 36°20N 114°25E **32** F8
Ciadâr-Lunga Moldova 46°3N 28°51E **17** E15
Ciamis Indonesia 7°20S 108°21E **37** G13
Cianjur Indonesia 6°49S 107°8E **37** G12
Cianorte Brazil 23°37S 52°37W **95** A5
Cibola U.S.A. 33°17N 114°42W **79** M12
Cicia Fiji 17°45S 179°18W **59** a
Ciéagas del Cataumbo △
  Venezuela 9°25N 71°54W **89** E5
Ciechanów Poland 52°52N 20°38E **17** B11
Ciego de Ávila Cuba 21°50N 78°50W **88** B4
Ciénaga Colombia 11°1N 74°15W **92** A4
Cienfuegos Cuba 22°10N 80°30W **88** B3
Cieszyn Poland 49°45N 18°35E **17** D10
Cieza Spain 38°17N 1°23W **21** C5
Cihuatlán Mexico 19°14N 104°35W **86** D4
Cijara, Embalse de Spain 39°18N 4°52W **21** C3
Cijulang Indonesia 7°42S 108°27E **37** G13
Cilacap Indonesia 7°43S 109°0E **37** G13
Cili China 29°30N 111°8E **35** C8
Cill Airne = Killarney
  Ireland 52°4N 9°30W **10** D2
Cill Chainnigh = Kilkenny
  Ireland 52°39N 7°15W **10** D4
Cill Dara = Kildare Ireland 53°9N 6°55W **10** C5
Cill Droichid = Celbridge
  Ireland 53°20N 6°32W **10** C5
Cill Mhantáin = Wicklow
  Ireland 52°59N 6°3W **10** D5
Cilo Dağı Turkey 37°28N 43°55E **19** G7
Cima U.S.A. 35°14N 115°30W **79** K11
Cimarron Kans., U.S.A. 37°48N 100°21W **80** G3
Cimarron N. Mex.,
  U.S.A. 36°31N 104°55W **77** H11
Cimarron → U.S.A. 36°10N 96°16W **84** C6
Cimişlia Moldova 46°34N 28°44E **17** E15
Cimone, Mte. Italy 44°12N 10°42E **22** B4
Cinca → Spain 41°26N 0°21E **21** B6
Cîncar Bos.-H. 43°55N 17°5E **22** C7
Cincinnati U.S.A. 39°9N 84°27W **81** F11
Cincinnatus U.S.A. 42°33N 75°54W **83** D9
Çine Turkey 37°37N 28°2E **23** F13
Ciney Belgium 50°18N 5°5E **15** D5
Cinque I. India 11°16N 92°42E **45** J11
Cinto, Mte. France 42°24N 8°54E **20** E8
Circle Alaska, U.S.A. 65°50N 144°4W **74** B11
Circle Mont., U.S.A. 47°25N 105°35W **76** C11
Circleville U.S.A. 39°36N 82°57W **81** F12
Cirebon Indonesia 6°45S 108°32E **37** G13
Cirencester U.K. 51°43N 1°57W **13** F6
Cisco U.S.A. 32°23N 98°59W **84** E5
Citlaltépetl = Orizaba, Pico de
  Mexico 18°58N 97°15W **87** D5
Citrus Heights U.S.A. 38°42N 121°17W **78** G5
Citrusdal S. Africa 32°35S 19°0E **56** D2
Città di Castello Italy 43°27N 12°14E **22** C5
Ciudad Acuña Mexico 29°18N 100°55W **86** B4
Ciudad Altamirano
  Mexico 18°20N 100°40W **86** D4
Ciudad Anáhuac Mexico 27°14N 100°7W **86** B4
Ciudad Bolívar Venezuela 8°5N 63°36W **92** B6
Ciudad Camargo
  Mexico 27°40N 105°10W **86** B3
Ciudad Cortés Costa Rica 8°55N 84°0W **88** E3
Ciudad del Carmen
  Mexico 18°38N 91°50W **87** D6
Ciudad del Este Paraguay 25°30S 54°50W **95** B5
Ciudad Delicias = Delicias
  Mexico 28°13N 105°28W **86** B3
Ciudad Frontera Mexico 26°56N 101°27W **86** B4
Ciudad Guayana Venezuela 8°0N 62°30W **92** B6
Ciudad Guerrero
  Mexico 28°33N 107°28W **86** B3
Ciudad Guzmán Mexico 19°41N 103°29W **86** D4
Ciudad Juárez Mexico 31°44N 106°29W **86** A3
Ciudad Lerdo Mexico 25°32N 103°32W **86** B4
Ciudad Madero Mexico 22°19N 97°50W **87** C5
Ciudad Mante Mexico 22°44N 98°59W **87** C5
Ciudad Obregón Mexico 27°29N 109°56W **86** B3
Ciudad Real Spain 38°59N 3°55W **21** C4
Ciudad Rodrigo Spain 40°35N 6°32W **21** B2
Ciudad Valles Mexico 21°59N 99°1W **87** C5

Ciudad Victoria Mexico 23°44N 99°8W **87** C5
Civitanova Marche Italy 43°18N 13°44E **22** C5
Civitavécchia Italy 42°6N 11°48E **22** C4
Cixi China 30°17N 121°9E **35** B13
Cizre Turkey 37°19N 42°10E **46** B4
Clackmannanshire □
  U.K. 56°10N 3°43W **11** E5
Clacton-on-Sea U.K. 51°47N 1°11E **13** F9
Claire, L. Canada 58°35N 112°5W **70** B6
Clairton U.S.A. 40°18N 79°53W **82** F5
Clallam Bay U.S.A. 48°15N 124°16W **78** B2
Clanton U.S.A. 32°51N 86°38W **85** E11
Clanwilliam S. Africa 32°11S 18°52E **56** D2
Clara Ireland 53°21N 7°37W **10** C4
Claraville U.S.A. 35°24N 118°20W **79** K8
Clare Australia 33°50S 138°37E **63** E2
Clare □ Ireland 52°45N 9°0W **10** D3
Clare → Ireland 53°20N 9°2W **10** C2
Clare I. Ireland 53°47N 10°0W **10** C1
Claremont Calif., U.S.A. 34°6N 117°43W **79** L9
Claremont N.H., U.S.A. 43°23N 72°20W **83** C12
Claremont Pt. Australia 14°1S 143°41E **62** A3
Claremore U.S.A. 36°19N 95°36W **84** C7
Claremorris Ireland 53°45N 9°0W **10** C3
Clarence → Australia 29°25S 153°22E **63** D5
Clarence → N.Z. 42°10S 173°56E **59** E4
Clarence, I. Chile 54°0S 72°0W **96** G2
Clarence I. Antarctica 61°10S 54°0W **5** C18
Clarence Str. Australia 12°0S 131°0E **60** B5
Clarence Town Bahamas 23°6N 74°59W **89** B5
Clarendon Pa., U.S.A. 41°47N 79°6W **82** E5
Clarendon Tex., U.S.A. 34°56N 100°53W **84** D4
Clarenville Canada 48°10N 54°1W **73** C9
Claresholm Canada 50°2N 113°33W **70** D6
Clarie Coast Antarctica 68°0S 135°0E **5** C9
Clarinda U.S.A. 40°44N 95°2W **80** E6
Clarington Canada 43°55N 78°41W **82** C6
Clarion Iowa, U.S.A. 42°44N 93°44W **80** D7
Clarion Pa., U.S.A. 41°13N 79°23W **82** E5
Clarion → U.S.A. 41°7N 79°41W **82** E5
Clarion Fracture Zone
  Pac. Oc. 20°0N 120°0W **66** H7
Clark U.S.A. 44°53N 97°44W **80** C5
Clark, Pt. Canada 44°4N 81°45W **82** B3
Clark Fork U.S.A. 48°9N 116°11W **76** B5
Clark Fork → U.S.A. 48°9N 116°15W **76** B5
Clarkdale U.S.A. 34°46N 112°3W **77** J7
Clarke City Canada 50°12N 66°38W **73** B6
Clarke I. Australia 40°32S 148°10E **63** G4
Clarke Ra. Australia 20°40S 148°30E **62** b
Clarks Fork Yellowstone →
  U.S.A. 45°32N 108°50W **76** D9
Clark's Harbour Canada 43°25N 65°38W **73** D6
Clarks Hill L. = J. Strom Thurmond
  L. U.S.A. 33°40N 82°12W **85** E13
Clarksburg U.S.A. 39°17N 80°30W **81** F13
Clarksdale U.S.A. 34°12N 90°35W **85** D9
Clarkston U.S.A. 46°25N 117°3W **76** C5
Clarksville Ark., U.S.A. 35°28N 93°28W **84** D8
Clarksville Tenn., U.S.A. 36°32N 87°21W **85** C11
Clarksville Tex., U.S.A. 33°37N 95°3W **84** E7
Claude U.S.A. 35°7N 101°22W **84** D4
Claveria Phil. 18°37N 121°4E **37** A6
Clay U.S.A. 38°17N 121°10W **78** G5
Clay Center U.S.A. 39°23N 97°8W **80** F5
Claypool U.S.A. 33°25N 110°51W **77** K8
Claysburg U.S.A. 40°17N 78°27W **82** F6
Claysville U.S.A. 40°7N 80°25W **82** F4
Clayton Canada 45°11N 76°19W **83** A8
Clayton N. Mex., U.S.A. 36°27N 103°11W **77** H12
Clayton N.Y., U.S.A. 44°14N 76°5W **83** B8
Clear, C. Ireland 51°25N 9°32W **10** E2
Clear, L. Canada 45°26N 77°12W **82** A7
Clear Hills Canada 56°40N 119°30W **70** B5
Clear I. Ireland 51°26N 9°30W **10** E2
Clear L. U.S.A. 39°2N 122°47W **78** F4
Clear Lake Iowa, U.S.A. 43°8N 93°23W **80** D7
Clear Lake S. Dak., U.S.A. 44°45N 96°41W **80** C6
Clear Lake Res. U.S.A. 41°56N 121°5W **76** F3
Clearfield Pa., U.S.A. 41°2N 78°27W **82** E6
Clearfield Utah, U.S.A. 41°7N 112°2W **76** F7
Clearlake U.S.A. 38°57N 122°38W **78** G4
Clearwater Canada 51°38N 120°2W **70** C4
Clearwater U.S.A. 27°59N 82°48W **85** H13
Clearwater → Alta.,
  Canada 52°22N 114°57W **70** C6
Clearwater → Alta.,
  Canada 56°44N 111°23W **71** B6
Clearwater L. Canada 53°34N 99°49W **71** C9
Clearwater Lake △
  Canada 54°0N 101°0W **71** C8
Clearwater Mts. U.S.A. 46°5N 115°20W **76** C6
Clearwater River △
  Canada 56°55N 109°10W **71** B7
Cleburne U.S.A. 32°21N 97°23W **84** E6
Clee Hills U.K. 52°26N 2°35W **13** E5
Cleethorpes U.K. 53°33N 0°3W **12** D7
Cleeve Cloud U.K. 51°56N 2°0W **13** F6
Clemson U.S.A. 34°41N 82°50W **85** D13
Clerke Reef Australia 17°22S 119°20E **60** C2
Clermont Australia 22°49S 147°39E **62** C4
Clermont U.S.A. 28°33N 81°46W **85** G14
Clermont-Ferrand France 45°46N 3°4E **20** D5
Clervaux Lux. 50°4N 6°2E **15** D6
Clevedon U.K. 51°26N 2°52E **13** F5
Cleveland Miss., U.S.A. 33°45N 90°43W **85** E9
Cleveland Ohio, U.S.A. 41°29N 81°41W **82** E3
Cleveland Okla., U.S.A. 36°19N 96°28W **84** C6
Cleveland Tenn., U.S.A. 35°10N 84°53W **85** D12
Cleveland Tex., U.S.A. 30°21N 95°5W **84** F7
Cleveland, C. Australia 19°11S 147°1E **62** B4
Cleveland, Mt. U.S.A. 48°56N 113°51W **76** B7
Cleveland Heights U.S.A. 41°31N 81°33W **82** E3
Clevelândia Brazil 26°24S 52°23W **95** B5
Clew B. Ireland 53°50N 9°49W **10** C2
Clewiston U.S.A. 26°45N 80°56W **85** H14

Clifden Ireland 53°29N 10°1W **10** C1
Clifden N.Z. 46°1S 167°42E **59** G1
Cliffdell U.S.A. 46°56N 121°5W **78** D5
Cliffy Hd. Australia 35°1S 116°29E **61** G2
Clifton Australia 27°59S 151°53E **63** D5
Clifton Ariz., U.S.A. 33°3N 109°18W **77** K9
Clifton Colo., U.S.A. 39°7N 108°25W **76** G9
Clifton Tex., U.S.A. 31°47N 97°35W **84** K9
Clifton Beach Australia 16°46S 145°39E **62** B4
Clinch → U.S.A. 35°53N 84°29W **85** D12
Clingmans Dome
  U.S.A. 35°34N 83°30W **85** D13
Clint U.S.A. 31°35N 106°14W **84** F1
Clinton B.C., Canada 51°6N 121°35W **70** C4
Clinton Ont., Canada 43°37N 81°32W **82** C3
Clinton N.Z. 46°12S 169°23E **59** G2
Clinton Ark., U.S.A. 35°36N 92°28W **84** D8
Clinton Conn., U.S.A. 41°17N 72°32W **83** E12
Clinton Ill., U.S.A. 40°9N 88°57W **80** E9
Clinton Ind., U.S.A. 39°40N 87°24W **80** F10
Clinton Iowa, U.S.A. 41°51N 90°12W **80** E8
Clinton Mass., U.S.A. 42°25N 71°41W **83** D13
Clinton Miss., U.S.A. 32°20N 90°20W **85** E9
Clinton Mo., U.S.A. 38°22N 93°46W **80** F7
Clinton N.C., U.S.A. 35°0N 78°22W **85** D15
Clinton Okla., U.S.A. 35°31N 98°58W **84** D5
Clinton S.C., U.S.A. 34°29N 81°53W **85** D14
Clinton Tenn., U.S.A. 36°6N 84°8W **85** C12
Clinton Wash., U.S.A. 47°59N 122°21W **78** C4
Clinton, C. Australia 22°30S 150°45E **62** C5
Clinton Colden L.
  Canada 63°58N 107°27W **68** E10
Clipperton, Î. Pac. Oc. 10°18N 109°13W **65** F17
Clipperton Fracture Zone
  Pac. Oc. 19°0N 122°0W **65** G16
Clisham U.K. 57°58N 6°49W **11** D2
Clitheroe U.K. 53°53N 2°22W **12** D5
Clo-oose Canada 48°39N 124°49W **78** B2
Cloates, Pt. Australia 22°43S 113°40E **60** D1
Clocolan S. Africa 28°55S 27°34E **57** C4
Clodomira Argentina 27°35S 64°14W **94** B3
Cloghaneely Ireland 55°8N 8°5W **10** A3
Clogher Hd. Ireland 53°48N 6°14W **10** C5
Clonakilty Ireland 51°37N 8°53W **10** E3
Clonakilty B. Ireland 51°35N 8°51W **10** E3
Cloncurry Australia 20°40S 140°28E **62** C3
Cloncurry U.S.A. 35°25N 6°48W **10** C5
Cloncurry → Australia 18°37S 140°40E **62** B3
Clondalkin Ireland 53°19N 6°25W **10** C5
Clones Ireland 54°11N 7°15W **10** B4
Clonmel Ireland 52°21N 7°42W **10** D4
Cloppenburg Germany 52°50N 8°3E **16** B5
Cloquet U.S.A. 46°43N 92°28W **80** B7
Clorinda Argentina 25°16S 57°45W **94** B4
Cloud Peak U.S.A. 44°23N 107°11W **76** D10
Cloudcroft U.S.A. 32°58N 105°45W **77** K11
Cloverdale U.S.A. 38°48N 123°1W **78** G4
Clovis Calif., U.S.A. 36°49N 119°42W **78** J7
Clovis N. Mex., U.S.A. 34°24N 103°12W **77** J12
Cloyne Canada 44°49N 77°11W **82** B7
Cluain Meala = Clonmel
  Ireland 52°21N 7°42W **10** D4
Cluj-Napoca Romania 46°47N 23°38E **17** E12
Clunes Australia 37°20S 143°45E **63** F3
Clutha → N.Z. 46°20S 169°49E **59** G2
Clwyd → U.K. 53°19N 3°31W **12** D4
Clyde Canada 54°9N 113°39W **70** C6
Clyde N.Z. 45°12S 169°20E **59** F2
Clyde U.S.A. 43°5N 76°52W **82** C8
Clyde → U.K. 55°55N 4°30W **11** F4
Clyde, Firth of U.K. 55°22N 5°1W **11** F3
Clyde River Canada 70°30N 68°30W **69** C18
Clydebank U.K. 55°54N 4°23W **11** F4
Clymer N.Y., U.S.A. 42°1N 79°37W **82** D5
Clymer Pa., U.S.A. 40°40N 79°1W **82** D5
Coachella U.S.A. 33°41N 116°10W **79** M10
Coachella Canal
  U.S.A. 32°43N 114°57W **79** N12
Coahoma U.S.A. 32°18N 101°18W **84** E4
Coahuayana → Mexico 18°41N 103°45W **86** D4
Coahuila □ Mexico 27°0N 102°0W **86** B4
Coal → Canada 59°39N 126°57W **70** B3
Coalcomán Mexico 18°47N 103°9W **86** D4
Coaldale Canada 49°45N 112°35W **70** D6
Coalgate U.S.A. 34°32N 96°13W **84** D6
Coalinga U.S.A. 36°9N 120°21W **78** J6
Coalisland U.K. 54°33N 6°42W **10** B5
Coalville U.K. 52°44N 1°23W **12** E6
Coalville U.S.A. 40°55N 111°24W **76** F8
Coamo Puerto Rico 18°5N 66°22W **89** d
Coari Brazil 4°8S 63°7W **92** D6
Coast Mts. Canada 55°0N 129°20W **70** C3
Coast Ranges U.S.A. 39°0N 123°0W **78** G4
Coatbridge U.K. 55°52N 4°6W **11** F4
Coatepec Mexico 19°27N 96°58W **87** D5
Coatepeque Guatemala 14°46N 91°55W **88** D1
Coatesville U.S.A. 39°59N 75°50W **81** F16
Coaticook Canada 45°10N 71°46W **83** A13
Coats I. Canada 62°30N 83°0W **69** E15
Coats Land Antarctica 77°0S 25°0W **5** D1
Coatzacoalcos Mexico 18°7N 94°25W **87** D6
Cobá Mexico 20°31N 87°45W **87** C7
Cobalt Canada 47°25N 79°42W **72** C4
Cobán Guatemala 15°30N 90°21W **88** C1
Cobar Australia 31°27S 145°48E **63** E4
Cobh Ireland 51°51N 8°17W **10** E3
Cóbh, An = Cobh Ireland 51°51N 8°17W **10** E3
Cobija Bolivia 11°0S 68°50W **92** F5
Cobleskill U.S.A. 42°41N 74°29W **83** D10
Coboconk Canada 44°39N 78°48W **82** B6
Cobourg Canada 43°58N 78°10W **82** C6
Cobourg Pen. Australia 11°20S 132°15E **60** B5
Cobram Australia 35°54S 145°40E **63** F4
Coburg Germany 50°15N 10°58E **16** C6
Coburg I. Canada 75°57N 79°26W **69** B16
Cocanada = Kakinada
  India 16°57N 82°11E **44** F6
Cochabamba Bolivia 17°26S 66°10W **92** G5
Cochin = Kochi India 9°58N 76°20E **45** K3
Cochin China = Nam-Phan
  Vietnam 10°30N 106°0E **39** G6

Cochran U.S.A. 32°23N 83°21W **85** E13
Cochrane Alta., Canada 51°11N 114°30W **70** C6
Cochrane Ont., Canada 49°0N 81°0W **72** C3
Cochrane Chile 47°15S 72°33W **96** F2
Cochrane → Canada 59°0N 103°40W **71** B8
Cochrane, L. Chile 47°10S 72°0W **96** F2
Cochranton U.S.A. 41°31N 80°3W **82** E4
Cockburn Australia 32°5S 141°0E **63** E3
Cockburn, Canal Chile 54°30S 72°0W **96** G2
Cockburn I. Canada 45°55S 83°22W **72** C3
Cockburn Ra. Australia 15°46S 128°0E **60** C4
Cockermouth U.K. 54°40N 3°22W **12** C4
Cockpit Country, The
  Jamaica 18°15N 77°45W **88** a
Coco → Cent. Amer. 15°0N 83°8W **88** D3
Coco, I. del Pac. Oc. 5°25N 87°55W **65** G19
Coco Channel Asia 13°45N 93°10E **45** H11
Cocoa U.S.A. 28°21N 80°44W **85** G14
Cocobeach Gabon 0°59N 9°34E **54** D1
Cocos B. Trin. & Tob. 10°24N 61°2W **93** K15
Cocos I. = Coco, I. del
  Pac. Oc. 5°25N 87°55W **65** G19
Cocos Is. Ind. Oc. 12°10S 96°55E **64** J1
Cocos Ridge Pac. Oc. 4°0N 88°0W **65** G19
Cod, C. U.S.A. 42°5N 70°10W **81** D18
Codajás Brazil 3°55S 62°0W **92** D6
Codó Brazil 4°30S 43°55W **93** D10
Cody U.S.A. 44°32N 109°3W **76** D9
Coe Hill Canada 44°52N 77°50W **82** B7
Coelemu Chile 36°30S 72°48W **94** D1
Coen Australia 13°52S 143°12E **62** A3
Coeur d'Alene U.S.A. 47°41N 116°46W **76** C5
Coeur d'Alene L. U.S.A. 47°32N 116°49W **76** C5
Coevorden Neths. 52°40N 6°44E **15** B6
Coffeyville U.S.A. 37°2N 95°37W **80** G6
Coffin B. Australia 34°38S 135°28E **63** E2
Coffin Bay Australia 34°37S 135°29E **63** E2
Coffin Bay → Australia 34°34S 135°19E **63** E2
Coffin Bay Peninsula
  Australia 34°32S 135°15E **63** E2
Coffs Harbour Australia 30°16S 153°5E **63** E5
Cognac France 45°41N 0°20W **20** D3
Cohocton U.S.A. 42°30N 77°30W **82** D7
Cohocton → U.S.A. 42°9N 77°6W **82** D7
Cohoes U.S.A. 42°46N 73°42W **83** D11
Cohuna Australia 35°45S 144°15E **63** F3
Coiba, I. de Panama 7°30N 81°40W **88** E3
Coig → Argentina 51°0S 69°10W **96** G3
Coigeach, Rubha U.K. 58°6N 5°26W **11** C3
Coihaique Chile 45°30S 71°45W **96** F2
Coimbatore India 11°2N 76°59E **45** J3
Coimbra Brazil 19°55S 57°48W **92** G7
Coimbra Portugal 40°15N 8°27W **21** B1
Coín Spain 36°40N 4°48W **21** D3
Coipasa, Salar de Bolivia 19°26S 68°9W **92** G5
Cojimíes Ecuador 0°20N 80°0W **92** C3
Cojutepequé El Salv. 13°41N 88°54W **88** D2
Cokeville U.S.A. 42°5N 110°57W **76** E8
Colac Australia 38°21S 143°35E **63** F3
Colachel = Kolachel India 8°10N 77°15E **45** K3
Colatina Brazil 19°32S 40°37W **93** G10
Colbeck, C. Antarctica 77°6S 157°48W **5** D13
Colborne Canada 44°0N 77°53W **82** C7
Colby U.S.A. 39°24N 101°3W **80** F3
Colca → Peru 15°55S 72°43W **92** G4
Colchester U.K. 51°54N 0°55E **13** F8
Colchester U.S.A. 41°35N 72°20W **83** E12
Cold L. Canada 54°33N 110°5W **71** C7
Cold Lake Canada 54°27N 110°10W **71** C6
Coldstream Canada 50°13N 119°11W **70** C5
Coldstream U.K. 55°39N 2°15W **11** F6
Coldwater Canada 44°42N 79°40W **82** B5
Coldwater Kans., U.S.A. 37°16N 99°20W **80** G4
Coldwater Mich., U.S.A. 41°57N 85°0W **81** E11
Colebrook U.S.A. 44°54N 71°30W **83** B13
Coleman Canada 49°40N 114°30W **70** D6
Coleman U.S.A. 31°50N 99°26W **84** F5
Coleman → Australia 15°6S 141°38E **62** B3
Colenso S. Africa 28°44S 29°50E **57** D4
Coleraine Australia 37°36S 141°40E **63** F3
Coleraine U.K. 55°8N 6°41W **10** A5
Coleridge, L. N.Z. 43°17S 171°30E **59** E3
Coleroon → India 11°25N 79°50E **45** J4
Colesberg S. Africa 30°45S 25°5E **56** E4
Coleville U.S.A. 38°34N 119°30W **78** G7
Colfax Calif., U.S.A. 39°6N 120°57W **78** F6
Colfax La., U.S.A. 31°31N 92°42W **84** F8
Colfax Wash., U.S.A. 46°53N 117°22W **76** C5
Colhué Huapi, L.
  Argentina 45°30S 69°0W **96** F3
Coligny S. Africa 26°17S 26°15E **57** C4
Colima Mexico 19°14N 103°43W **86** D4
Colima □ Mexico 19°10N 104°0W **86** D4
Colima, Nevado de
  Mexico 19°33N 103°38W **86** D4
Colina Chile 33°13S 70°45W **94** C1
Colinas Brazil 6°0S 44°10W **93** E10
Coll U.K. 56°39N 6°34W **11** E2
Collahuasi Chile 21°5S 68°45W **94** A2
Collarenebri Australia 29°33S 148°34E **63** D4
College Alaska, U.S.A. 64°52N 147°49W **74** B10
College Station U.S.A. 30°37N 96°21W **84** F6
Collie Australia 33°22S 116°8E **61** F2
Collier B. Australia 16°10S 124°15E **60** C3
Collier Ra. Australia 24°45S 119°10E **61** D2
Collier Range △ Australia 24°39S 119°7E **61** D2
Collierville U.S.A. 35°3N 89°40W **85** D10
Collina, Passo di Italy 44°2N 10°56E **22** B4
Collingwood Canada 44°29N 80°13W **82** B4
Collingwood N.Z. 40°41S 172°40E **59** D4
Collins Canada 50°17N 89°27W **72** B2
Collins Bay Canada 44°14N 76°36W **83** B8
Collinson Pen. Canada 69°58N 101°24W **68** D11
Collinsville Australia 20°30S 147°56E **62** C4
Collipulli Chile 37°55S 72°30W **94** D1
Collooney Ireland 54°11N 8°29W **10** B3
Colmar France 48°5N 7°20E **20** B7
Colo → Australia 33°25S 150°52E **63** E5

Cologne = Köln *Germany* 50°56N 6°57E **16** C4
Coloma *U.S.A.* 38°48N 120°53W **78** G6
Colomb-Béchar = Béchar
 Algeria 31°38N 2°18W **52** B5
Colombia ■ *S. Amer.* 3°45N 73°0W **92** C4
Colombian Basin *Caribbean* 14°0N 76°0W **88** D4
Colombo *Sri Lanka* 6°56N 79°58E **45** L4
Colón *B. Aires, Argentina* 33°53S 61°7W **94** C3
Colón *Entre Ríos,*
 Argentina 32°12S 58°10W **94** C4
Colón *Cuba* 22°42N 80°54W **88** B3
Colón *Panama* 9°20N 79°54W **88** E4
Colón, Arch. de *Ecuador* 0°0 91°0W **90** D1
Colonia del Sacramento
 Uruguay 34°25S 57°50W **94** C4
Colonia Dora *Argentina* 28°34S 62°59W **94** B3
Colonial Beach *U.S.A.* 38°15N 76°58W **81** F15
Colonie *U.S.A.* 42°43N 73°50W **83** D11
Colonsay *Canada* 51°59N 105°52W **71** C7
Colonsay *U.K.* 56°5N 6°12W **11** E2
Colorado □ *U.S.A.* 39°30N 105°30W **76** G11
Colorado → *Argentina* 39°50S 62°8W **96** D4
Colorado → *N. Amer.* 31°45N 114°40W **77** L6
Colorado → *U.S.A.* 28°36N 95°59W **84** G7
Colorado City *U.S.A.* 32°24N 100°52W **84** E4
Colorado Plateau *U.S.A.* 37°0N 111°0W **77** H8
Colorado River Aqueduct
 U.S.A. 33°50N 117°23W **79** L12
Colorado Springs
 U.S.A. 38°50N 104°49W **76** G11
Colotlán *Mexico* 22°6N 103°16W **86** C4
Colstrip *U.S.A.* 45°53N 106°38W **76** D10
Colton *U.S.A.* 44°33N 74°56W **83** B10
Columbia *Ky., U.S.A.* 37°6N 85°18W **81** G11
Columbia *La., U.S.A.* 32°6N 92°5W **84** E8
Columbia *Miss., U.S.A.* 31°15N 89°50W **85** F10
Columbia *Mo., U.S.A.* 38°57N 92°20W **80** F7
Columbia *Pa., U.S.A.* 40°2N 76°30W **83** F8
Columbia *S.C., U.S.A.* 34°0N 81°2W **85** D14
Columbia *Tenn., U.S.A.* 35°37N 87°2W **85** D11
Columbia → *N. Amer.* 46°15N 124°5W **78** D2
Columbia, C. *Canada* 83°6N 69°57W **69** A18
Columbia, District of □
 U.S.A. 38°55N 77°0W **81** F15
Columbia, Mt. *Canada* 52°8N 117°20W **70** C5
Columbia Basin *U.S.A.* 46°45N 119°5W **76** C4
Columbia Falls *U.S.A.* 48°23N 114°11W **76** B6
Columbia Mts. *Canada* 52°0N 119°0W **70** C5
Columbia Plateau *U.S.A.* 44°0N 117°30W **76** E5
Columbiana *U.S.A.* 40°53N 80°42W **82** F4
Columbretes, Is. *Spain* 39°50N 0°50E **21** C6
Columbus *Ga., U.S.A.* 32°28N 84°59W **85** E12
Columbus *Ind., U.S.A.* 39°13N 85°55W **81** F11
Columbus *Kans., U.S.A.* 37°10N 94°50W **80** G6
Columbus *Miss., U.S.A.* 33°30N 88°25W **85** E10
Columbus *Mont., U.S.A.* 45°38N 109°15W **76** D9
Columbus *N. Mex.,*
 U.S.A. 31°50N 107°38W **77** L10
Columbus *Nebr., U.S.A.* 41°26N 97°22W **80** E5
Columbus *Ohio, U.S.A.* 39°58N 83°0W **81** F12
Columbus *Tex., U.S.A.* 29°42N 96°33W **84** G6
Colusa *U.S.A.* 39°13N 122°1W **78** F4
Colville *U.S.A.* 48°33N 117°54W **76** B5
Colville → *U.S.A.* 70°25N 150°30W **74** A9
Colville, C. *N.Z.* 36°29S 175°21E **59** B5
Colwood *Canada* 48°26N 123°29W **78** B3
Colwyn Bay *U.K.* 53°18N 3°44W **12** D4
Comácchio *Italy* 44°42N 12°11E **22** B5
Comalcalco *Mexico* 18°16N 93°13W **87** D6
Comallo *Argentina* 41°0S 70°5W **96** E2
Comanche *U.S.A.* 31°54N 98°36W **84** F5
Comandante Ferraz
 Antarctica 62°30S 58°0W **5** C18
Comayagua *Honduras* 14°25N 87°37W **88** D2
Combahee → *U.S.A.* 32°31N 80°31W **85** E14
Combarbalá *Chile* 31°11S 71°2W **94** C1
Combe Martin *U.K.* 51°12N 4°3W **13** F3
Comber *Canada* 42°14N 82°33W **82** D2
Comber *U.K.* 54°33N 5°45W **10** B6
Combermere *Canada* 45°22N 77°37W **82** A7
Comblain-au-Pont
 Belgium 50°29N 5°35E **15** D5
Comeragh Mts. *Ireland* 52°18N 7°34W **10** D4
Comet *Australia* 23°36S 148°38E **62** C4
Comilla *Bangla.* 23°28N 91°10E **41** H17
Comino, C. *Italy* 40°32N 9°49E **22** D3
Comitán de Domínguez
 Mexico 16°15N 92°8W **87** D6
Commerce *Ga., U.S.A.* 34°12N 83°28W **85** D13
Commerce *Tex., U.S.A.* 33°15N 95°54W **84** E7
Committee B. *Canada* 68°30N 86°30W **69** D14
Commodore, C. *Canada* 44°47N 80°54W **82** B4
Commonwealth B.
 Antarctica 67°0S 144°0E **5** C10
Commoron Cr. →
 Australia 28°22S 150°8E **63** D5
Communism Pk. = imeni Ismail
 Samani, Pik Tajikistan 39°0N 72°2E **26** F8
Como *Italy* 45°47N 9°5E **20** D8
Como, Lago di *Italy* 46°0N 9°11E **20** D8
Comodoro Rivadavia
 Argentina 45°50S 67°40W **96** F3
Comorin, C. = Kannyakumari
 India 8°3N 77°40E **45** K3
Comoros ■ *Ind. Oc.* 12°10S 44°15E **55** a
Comox *Canada* 49°42N 124°55W **70** D4
Compiègne *France* 49°24N 2°50E **20** B5
Compostela *Mexico* 21°14N 104°55W **86** C4
Compton *Canada* 45°14N 71°49W **83** A13
Compton *U.S.A.* 33°53N 118°13W **79** M8
Comrat *Moldova* 46°18N 28°40E **17** E15
Con Cuong *Vietnam* 19°2N 104°54E **38** C5
Con Son, Dao *Vietnam* 8°41N 106°37E **39** H6
Conakry *Guinea* 9°29N 13°49W **52** G3
Conceição da Barra
 Brazil 18°35S 39°45W **93** G11

Conceição do Araguaia
 Brazil 8°0S 49°2W **93** E9
Concepción *Argentina* 27°20S 65°35W **94** B2
Concepción *Bolivia* 16°15S 62°8W **92** G6
Concepción *Chile* 36°50S 73°0W **94** D1
Concepción *Paraguay* 23°22S 57°26W **94** A4
Concepción □ *Chile* 37°0S 72°30W **94** D1
Concepción, Est. de *Chile* 50°30S 74°55W **96** G2
Concepción, L. *Bolivia* 17°20S 61°20W **92** G6
Concepción, Pta.
 Mexico 26°53N 111°50W **86** B2
Concepción del Oro
 Mexico 24°38N 101°25W **86** C4
Concepción del Uruguay
 Argentina 32°35S 58°20W **94** C4
Conception, Pt. *U.S.A.* 34°27N 120°28W **79** L6
Conception B. *Canada* 47°45N 53°0W **73** C9
Conception B. *Namibia* 23°55S 14°22E **56** B1
Conchas Dam *U.S.A.* 35°22N 104°11W **77** J11
Concho *U.S.A.* 34°28N 109°36W **77** J9
Concho → *U.S.A.* 31°34N 99°43W **84** F5
Conchos → *Chihuahua,*
 Mexico 29°35N 104°25W **86** B4
Conchos → *Tamaulipas,*
 Mexico 24°55N 97°38W **87** B5
Concord *Calif., U.S.A.* 37°59N 122°2W **78** H4
Concord *N.C., U.S.A.* 35°25N 80°35W **85** D14
Concord *N.H., U.S.A.* 43°12N 71°32W **83** C13
Concordia *Antarctica* 75°6S 123°23E **5** D9
Concordia *Argentina* 31°20S 58°2W **94** C4
Concórdia *Amazonas,*
 Brazil 4°36S 66°36W **92** D5
Concórdia *Sta. Catarina,*
 Brazil 27°14S 52°1W **95** B5
Concordia *Mexico* 23°17N 106°4W **86** C3
Concordia *U.S.A.* 39°34N 97°40W **80** F5
Concrete *U.S.A.* 48°32N 121°45W **76** B3
Condamine *Australia* 26°56S 150°9E **63** D5
Conde *U.S.A.* 45°9N 98°6W **80** C4
Condeúba *Brazil* 14°52S 42°0W **93** F10
Condobolin *Australia* 33°4S 147°6E **63** E4
Condon *U.S.A.* 45°14N 120°11W **76** D3
Conegliano *Italy* 45°53N 12°18E **22** B5
Conejos *Mexico* 26°14N 103°53W **86** B4
Conemaugh → *U.S.A.* 40°28N 79°19W **82** F5
Confuso → *Paraguay* 25°9S 57°34W **94** B4
Conghua *China* 23°36N 113°31E **35** F9
Congjiang *China* 25°43N 108°52E **34** E7
Congleton *U.K.* 53°10N 2°13W **12** D5
Congo (Brazzaville) = Congo ■
 Africa 1°0S 16°0E **54** E3
Congo (Kinshasa) = Congo, Dem.
 Rep. of the ■ *Africa* 3°0S 23°0E **54** E4
Congo ■ *Africa* 1°0S 16°0E **54** E3
Congo → *Africa* 6°4S 12°24E **54** F2
Congo, Dem. Rep. of the ■
 Africa 3°0S 23°0E **54** E4
Congo Basin *Africa* 0°10S 24°30E **54** E4
Congonhas *Brazil* 20°30S 43°52W **95** A7
Congress *U.S.A.* 34°9N 112°51W **77** J7
Coniston *Canada* 46°29N 80°51W **72** C3
Conjeeveram = Kanchipuram
 India 12°52N 79°45E **45** H4
Conklin *Canada* 55°38N 111°5W **71** B6
Conklin *U.S.A.* 42°2N 75°49W **83** D9
Conn, L. *Ireland* 54°3N 9°15W **10** B2
Connacht □ *Ireland* 53°43N 9°12W **10** C2
Conneaut *U.S.A.* 41°57N 80°34W **82** E4
Conneautville *U.S.A.* 41°45N 80°22W **82** E4
Connecticut □ *U.S.A.* 41°30N 72°45W **83** E12
Connecticut → *U.S.A.* 41°16N 72°20W **83** E12
Connell *U.S.A.* 46°40N 118°52W **76** C4
Connellsville *U.S.A.* 40°1N 79°35W **82** F5
Connemara □ *Ireland* 53°29N 9°45W **10** C2
Connemara △ *Ireland* 53°32N 9°52W **10** C2
Connersville *U.S.A.* 39°39N 85°8W **81** F11
Connors Ra. *Australia* 21°40S 149°10E **62** C4
Conquest *Canada* 51°32N 107°14W **71** C7
Conrad *U.S.A.* 48°10N 111°57W **76** B8
Conran, C. *Australia* 37°49S 148°44E **63** F4
Conroe *U.S.A.* 30°19N 95°27W **84** F7
Consecon *Canada* 44°0N 77°31W **82** C7
Conselheiro Lafaiete
 Brazil 20°40S 43°48W **95** A7
Consett *U.K.* 54°51N 1°50W **12** C6
Consort *Canada* 52°1N 110°46W **71** C6
Constance = Konstanz
 Germany 47°40N 9°10E **16** E5
Constance, L. = Bodensee
 Europe 47°35N 9°25E **20** C8
Constanța *Romania* 44°14N 28°38E **17** F15
Constantine *Algeria* 36°25N 6°42E **52** A7
Constitución *Chile* 35°20S 72°30W **94** D1
Constitución *Uruguay* 31°0S 57°50W **94** C4
Constitución de 1857 △
 Mexico 32°4N 115°55W **86** A1
Consul *Canada* 49°20N 109°30W **71** D7
Contact *U.S.A.* 41°46N 114°45W **76** F6
Contai *India* 21°54N 87°46E **43** J12
Contamana *Peru* 7°19S 74°55W **92** E4
Contas → *Brazil* 14°17S 39°1W **93** F11
Contoocook *U.S.A.* 43°13N 71°45W **83** C13
Contra Costa *Mozam.* 25°9S 33°30E **57** C5
Contwoyto L. *Canada* 65°42N 110°50W **68** D8
Conway = Conwy *U.K.* 53°17N 3°50W **12** D4
Conway = Conwy →
 U.K. 53°17N 3°50W **12** D4
Conway *Ark., U.S.A.* 35°5N 92°26W **84** D8
Conway *N.H., U.S.A.* 43°59N 71°7W **83** C13
Conway *S.C., U.S.A.* 33°51N 79°3W **85** E15
Conway, C. *Australia* 20°34S 148°46E **62** b
Conway, L. *Australia* 28°17S 135°35E **63** D2
Conwy *U.K.* 53°17N 3°50W **12** D4
Conwy □ *U.K.* 53°10N 3°44W **12** D4
Conwy → *U.K.* 53°17N 3°50W **12** D4

Coober Pedy *Australia* 29°1S 134°43E **63** D1
Cooch Behar = Koch Bihar
 India 26°22N 89°29E **41** F16
Cooinda *Australia* 13°15S 130°5E **60** B5
Cook *Australia* 30°37S 130°25E **61** F5
Cook *U.S.A.* 47°51N 92°41W **80** B7
Cook, B. *Chile* 55°10S 70°0W **96** H3
Cook, C. *Canada* 50°8N 127°55W **70** C3
Cook, Mt. = Aoraki Mount Cook
 N.Z. 43°36S 170°9E **59** E3
Cook Inlet *U.S.A.* 60°0N 152°0W **68** F1
Cook Is. ☑ *Pac. Oc.* 17°0S 160°0W **65** J12
Cook Strait *N.Z.* 41°15S 174°29E **59** D5
Cookeville *U.S.A.* 36°10N 85°30W **85** C12
Cookhouse *S. Africa* 32°44S 25°47E **56** D4
Cooks Harbour *Canada* 51°36N 55°52W **73** B8
Cookshire *Canada* 45°25N 71°38W **83** A13
Cookstown *Canada* 44°11N 79°42W **82** B5
Cookstown *U.K.* 54°38N 6°45W **10** B5
Cooktown *Australia* 15°30S 145°16E **62** B4
Coolabah *Australia* 31°1S 146°43E **63** E4
Cooladdi *Australia* 26°37S 145°23E **63** D4
Coolah *Australia* 31°48S 149°41E **63** E4
Coolamon *Australia* 34°46S 147°8E **63** E4
Coolgardie *Australia* 30°55S 121°8E **61** F3
Coolidge *U.S.A.* 32°59N 111°31W **77** K8
Coolidge Dam *U.S.A.* 33°10N 110°32W **77** K8
Cooma *Australia* 36°12S 149°8E **63** F4
Coon Rapids *U.S.A.* 45°9N 93°19W **80** C7
Coonabarabran
 Australia 31°14S 149°18E **63** E4
Coonamble *Australia* 30°56S 148°27E **63** E4
Coonana *Australia* 31°0S 123°0E **61** F3
Coonana ☉ *Australia* 30°51S 122°53E **61** F3
Coondapoor *India* 13°42N 74°40E **45** H2
Cooninnie, L. *Australia* 26°4S 139°59E **63** D2
Coonoor *India* 11°21N 76°45E **45** J3
Cooper *U.S.A.* 33°23N 95°42W **84** E7
Cooper Cr. → *Australia* 28°29S 137°46E **63** D2
Cooper Ridge *Pac. Oc.* 10°0N 150°30W **65** G12
Cooperstown *N. Dak.,*
 U.S.A. 47°27N 98°8W **80** B4
Cooperstown *N.Y.,*
 U.S.A. 42°42N 74°56W **83** D10
Coorabie *Australia* 31°54S 132°18E **61** F5
Coorong, The *Australia* 35°50S 139°20E **63** F2
Coorow *Australia* 29°53S 116°2E **61** E2
Cooroy *Australia* 26°22S 152°54E **63** D5
Coos Bay *U.S.A.* 43°22N 124°13W **76** E1
Coosa → *U.S.A.* 32°30N 86°16W **85** E11
Cootamundra *Australia* 34°36S 148°1E **63** E4
Cootehill *Ireland* 54°4N 7°5W **10** B4
Copahue Paso *Argentina* 37°49S 71°8W **94** D1
Copainalá *Mexico* 17°4N 93°18W **87** D6
Copake *U.S.A.* 42°7N 73°31W **83** D11
Copán *Honduras* 14°50N 89°9W **88** D2
Cope *U.S.A.* 39°40N 102°51W **76** G12
Copenhagen *U.S.A.* 43°54N 75°41W **83** C9
Copiapó *Chile* 27°30S 70°20W **94** B1
Copiapó → *Chile* 27°19S 70°56W **94** B1
Coplay *U.S.A.* 40°44N 75°29W **83** F9
Copo △ *Argentina* 25°53S 61°41W **94** B3
Copp L. *Canada* 60°14N 114°40W **70** A6
Coppename → *Suriname* 5°48N 55°55W **93** B7
Copper Canyon = Barranca del
 Cobre △ *Mexico* 27°18N 107°40W **86** B3
Copper Center *U.S.A.* 61°58N 145°18W **74** C10
Copper Harbor *U.S.A.* 47°28N 87°53W **80** B10
Copperas Cove *U.S.A.* 31°8N 97°54W **84** F6
Coppermine = Kugluktuk
 Canada 67°50N 115°5W **68** D8
Coppermine → *Canada* 67°49N 116°4W **68** D8
Copperopolis *U.S.A.* 37°58N 120°38W **78** H6
Coquet → *U.K.* 55°20N 1°32W **12** B6
Coquille *U.S.A.* 43°11N 124°11W **76** E1
Coquimbo *Chile* 30°0S 71°20W **94** C1
Coquimbo □ *Chile* 31°0S 71°0W **94** C1
Coquitlam *Canada* 49°17N 122°45W **70** D4
Corabia *Romania* 43°48N 24°30E **17** G13
Coracora *Peru* 15°5S 73°45W **92** G4
Coraki *Australia* 28°59S 153°17E **63** D5
Coral *U.S.A.* 40°29N 79°10W **82** F5
Coral Bay *Australia* 23°8S 113°46E **60** D1
Coral Harbour *Canada* 64°8N 83°10W **69** E15
Coral Sea *Pac. Oc.* 15°0S 150°0E **58** C8
Coral Sea Basin *Pac. Oc.* 14°0S 152°0E **64** J7
Coral Sea Islands Terr. □
 Australia 20°0S 155°0E **58** C8
Coral Springs *U.S.A.* 26°16N 80°16W **85** H14
Coraopolis *U.S.A.* 40°31N 80°10W **82** F4
Corato *Italy* 41°9N 16°25E **22** D7
Corbett △ *India* 29°20N 79°0E **43** E8
Corbin *U.S.A.* 36°57N 84°6W **81** G11
Corby *U.K.* 52°30N 0°41W **13** E7
Corcaigh = Cork *Ireland* 51°54N 8°29W **10** E3
Corcoran *U.S.A.* 36°6N 119°33W **78** J7
Corcovado △ *Costa Rica* 8°33N 83°35W **88** E3
Corcubión *Spain* 42°56N 9°12W **21** A1
Cordele *U.S.A.* 31°58N 83°47W **85** F13
Cordell *U.S.A.* 35°17N 98°59W **84** D5
Córdoba *Argentina* 31°20S 64°10W **94** C3
Córdoba *Mexico* 18°53N 96°56W **87** D5
Córdoba *Spain* 37°50N 4°50W **21** D3
Córdoba □ *Argentina* 31°22S 64°15W **94** C3
Córdoba, Sierra de
 Argentina 31°10S 64°25W **94** C3
Cordova *U.S.A.* 60°33N 145°45W **68** E2
Corella *Australia* 19°34S 140°47E **62** B3
Corentyne → *S. Amer.* 5°50N 57°8W **92** B7
Corfield *Australia* 21°40S 143°21E **62** C3
Corfu = Kerkyra *Greece* 39°38N 19°50E **23** E8
Corfu ☑ *Greece* 39°27N 78°24W **82** D6
Coria *Spain* 39°58N 6°33W **21** C2
Corigliano Cálabro *Italy* 39°36N 16°31E **22** E7
Coringa Is. *Australia* 16°58S 149°58E **62** B4
Corinth = Korinthos
 Greece 37°56N 22°55E **23** F10
Corinth *Miss., U.S.A.* 34°56N 88°31W **85** D10
Corinth *N.Y., U.S.A.* 43°15N 73°49W **83** C11

Corinth, G. of = Korinthiakos
 Kolpos *Greece* 38°16N 22°30E **23** E10
Corinto *Brazil* 18°20S 44°30W **93** G10
Corinto *Nic.* 12°30N 87°10W **88** D2
Cork *Ireland* 51°54N 8°29W **10** E3
Cork □ *Ireland* 51°57N 8°40W **10** E3
Cork Harbour *Ireland* 51°47N 8°16W **10** E3
Çorlu *Turkey* 41°11N 27°49E **23** D12
Cormack L. *Canada* 60°56N 121°37W **70** A4
Cormorant *Canada* 54°14N 100°35W **71** C8
Cormorant L. *Canada* 54°15N 100°50W **71** C8
Corn Is. = Maíz, Is. del
 Nic. 12°15N 83°4W **88** D3
Cornélio Procópio *Brazil* 23°7S 50°40W **95** A5
Corner Brook *Canada* 48°57N 57°58W **73** C8
Corneşti *Moldova* 47°21N 28°1E **17** E15
Corning *Ark., U.S.A.* 36°25N 90°35W **85** C9
Corning *Calif., U.S.A.* 39°56N 122°11W **76** G2
Corning *Iowa, U.S.A.* 40°59N 94°44W **80** E6
Corning *N.Y., U.S.A.* 42°9N 77°3W **82** D7
Cornwall *Canada* 45°2N 74°44W **83** A10
Cornwall *U.S.A.* 40°17N 76°25W **83** F8
Cornwall □ *U.K.* 50°26N 4°40W **13** G3
Cornwall I. *Canada* 77°37N 94°38W **69** B13
Cornwallis I. *Canada* 75°8N 95°0W **69** B13
Corny Pt. *Australia* 34°55S 137°0E **63** E2
Coro *Venezuela* 11°25N 69°41W **92** A5
Coroatá *Brazil* 4°8S 44°0W **93** D10
Corocoro *Bolivia* 17°15S 68°28W **92** G5
Coroico *Bolivia* 16°0S 67°50W **92** G5
Coromandel *N.Z.* 36°45S 175°31E **59** B5
Coromandel Coast *India* 12°30N 81°0E **45** H5
Corona *Calif., U.S.A.* 33°53N 117°34W **79** M9
Corona *N. Mex., U.S.A.* 34°15N 105°36W **77** J11
Coronado *U.S.A.* 32°41N 117°10W **79** N9
Coronado, B. de *Costa Rica* 9°0N 83°40W **88** E3
Coronados, Is. Los
 Mexico 32°26N 117°19W **79** N9
Coronation *Canada* 52°5N 111°27W **70** C6
Coronation Gulf *Canada* 68°25N 110°0W **68** D10
Coronation I. *Antarctica* 60°45S 46°0W **5** C18
Coronation Is. *Australia* 14°57S 124°55E **60** B3
Coronda *Argentina* 31°58S 60°56W **94** C3
Coronel *Chile* 37°0S 73°10W **94** D1
Coronel Bogado
 Paraguay 27°11S 56°18W **94** B4
Coronel Dorrego
 Argentina 38°40S 61°10W **94** D3
Coronel Oviedo *Paraguay* 25°24S 56°30W **94** B4
Coronel Pringles
 Argentina 38°0S 61°30W **94** D3
Coronel Suárez *Argentina* 37°30S 61°52W **94** D3
Coronel Vidal *Argentina* 37°28S 57°45W **94** D4
Coropuna, Nevado *Peru* 15°30S 72°41W **92** G4
Corowa *Australia* 35°58S 146°21E **63** F4
Corozal *Belize* 18°23N 88°23W **87** D7
Corozal Pt. *Trin. & Tob.* 10°45N 61°37W **93** K15
Corpus *Argentina* 27°10S 55°30W **95** B4
Corpus Christi *U.S.A.* 27°47N 97°24W **84** H6
Corpus Christi, L. *U.S.A.* 28°2N 97°52W **84** G6
Corrabiedo, C. das *Mozam.* 24°6S 35°34E **57** B6
Corrib, L. *Ireland* 53°27N 9°16W **10** C2
Corrientes *Argentina* 27°30S 58°45W **94** B4
Corrientes □ *Argentina* 28°0S 57°0W **94** B4
Corrientes → *Argentina* 30°42S 59°38W **94** C4
Corrientes → *Peru* 3°43S 74°35W **92** D4
Corrientes, C. *Colombia* 5°30N 77°34W **92** B3
Corrientes, C. *Cuba* 21°43N 84°30W **88** B3
Corrientes, C. *Mexico* 20°25N 105°42W **86** C3
Corrigan *U.S.A.* 31°0N 94°52W **84** F7
Corrigin *Australia* 32°20S 117°53E **61** F2
Corriverton *Guyana* 5°55N 57°20W **92** B7
Corry *U.S.A.* 41°55N 79°39W **82** E5
Corse *France* 42°0N 9°0E **20** F8
Corse, C. *France* 43°1N 9°25E **20** E8
Corsica = Corse □ *France* 42°0N 9°0E **20** F8
Corsicana *U.S.A.* 32°6N 96°28W **84** E6
Corte *France* 42°19N 9°11E **20** E8
Cortés, Mar de = California, G. de
 Mexico 27°0N 111°0W **86** B2
Cortez *U.S.A.* 37°21N 108°35W **77** H9
Cortland *N.Y., U.S.A.* 42°36N 76°11W **83** D8
Cortland *Ohio, U.S.A.* 41°20N 80°44W **82** E4
Çorum *Turkey* 40°30N 34°57E **19** F5
Corumbá *Brazil* 19°0S 57°30W **92** G7
Corunna = A Coruña
 Spain 43°20N 8°25W **21** A1
Corvallis *U.S.A.* 44°34N 123°16W **76** D2
Corvette, L. de la *Canada* 53°25N 74°3W **72** B5
Corvo *Azores* 39°43N 31°8W **52** a
Cosalá *Mexico* 24°23N 106°41W **86** C3
Cosamaloapan de Carpio
 Mexico 18°22N 95°48W **87** D5
Cosenza *Italy* 39°18N 16°15E **22** E7
Coshocton *U.S.A.* 40°16N 81°51W **82** F3
Cosmo Newberry
 Australia 28°0S 122°54E **61** E3
Cosmo Newberry ☉
 Australia 27°59S 122°53E **61** E3
Cosmonaut Sea *S. Ocean* 66°30S 40°0E **5** C5
Coso Junction *U.S.A.* 36°3N 117°57W **79** J9
Coso Pk. *U.S.A.* 36°13N 117°44W **79** J9
Cosquín *Argentina* 31°15S 64°30W **94** C3
Costa Blanca *Spain* 38°25N 0°10W **21** C5
Costa Brava *Spain* 41°30N 3°0E **21** B7
Costa Cálida *Spain* 37°30N 1°30W **21** D5
Costa Daurada *Spain* 41°12N 1°15E **21** B6
Costa de la Luz *Spain* 36°15N 5°58W **21** D2
Costa del Azahar *Spain* 39°39N 0°13W **21** B6
Costa del Sol *Spain* 36°30N 4°30W **21** D3
Costa Maya *Mexico* 18°44N 87°42W **87** D7
Costa Mesa *U.S.A.* 33°38N 117°55W **79** M9
Costa Rica ■ *Cent. Amer.* 10°0N 84°0W **88** E3
Costa Smeralda *Italy* 41°5N 9°35E **22** D3
Costa Verde *Spain* 43°24N 4°14W **21** A3

Cosumnes → *U.S.A.* 38°16N 121°26W **78** G5
Cotabato *Phil.* 7°14N 124°15E **37** C6
Cotagaita *Bolivia* 20°45S 65°40W **94** A2
Côte d'Azur *France* 43°25N 7°10E **20** E7
Côte-d'Ivoire = Ivory Coast ■
 Africa 7°30N 5°0W **52** G4
Coteau des Prairies
 U.S.A. 45°20N 97°50W **80** C5
Coteau du Missouri
 U.S.A. 47°0N 100°0W **80** B4
Cotentin *France* 49°15N 1°30W **20** B3
Cotonou *Benin* 6°20N 2°25E **52** G6
Cotopaxi *Ecuador* 0°40S 78°30W **92** D3
Cotswold Hills *U.K.* 51°42N 2°10W **13** F5
Cottage Grove *U.S.A.* 43°48N 123°3W **76** E2
Cottam *Canada* 42°8N 82°45W **82** D2
Cottbus *Germany* 51°45N 14°20E **16** C8
Cottonwood *U.S.A.* 34°45N 112°1W **77** J7
Cotulla *U.S.A.* 28°26N 99°14W **84** G5
Couedic, C. du *Australia* 36°5S 136°40E **63** F2
Coulee City *U.S.A.* 47°37N 119°17W **76** C4
Coulee Dam Nat. Recr. Area =
 Lake Roosevelt △
 U.S.A. 48°5N 118°14W **76** B4
Coulman I. *Antarctica* 73°35S 170°0E **5** D11
Coulonge → *Canada* 45°52N 76°46W **72** C4
Coulterville *U.S.A.* 37°43N 120°12W **78** H6
Council *Alaska, U.S.A.* 64°53N 163°41W **74** C7
Council *Idaho, U.S.A.* 44°44N 116°26W **76** D5
Council Bluffs *U.S.A.* 41°16N 95°52W **80** E6
Council Grove *U.S.A.* 38°40N 96°29W **80** F5
Coupeville *U.S.A.* 48°13N 122°41W **78** B4
Courantyne = Corentyne →
 S. Amer. 5°50N 57°8W **92** B7
Courcelles *Belgium* 50°28N 4°22E **15** D4
Courtenay *Canada* 49°45N 125°0W **70** D4
Courtland *Canada* 42°51N 80°38W **82** D4
Courtland *U.S.A.* 38°20N 121°34W **78** G5
Courtrai = Kortrijk
 Belgium 50°50N 3°17E **15** D3
Courtright *Canada* 42°49N 82°28W **82** D2
Coushatta *U.S.A.* 32°1N 93°21W **84** E8
Coutts Crossing
 Australia 29°49S 152°55E **63** D5
Couva *Trin. & Tob.* 10°25N 61°27W **93** K15
Couvin *Belgium* 50°3N 4°29E **15** D4
Cove I. *Canada* 45°17N 81°44W **82** A3
Coventry *U.K.* 52°25N 1°28W **13** E6
Covilhã *Portugal* 40°17N 7°31W **21** B2
Covington *Ga., U.S.A.* 33°36N 83°51W **85** E13
Covington *Ky., U.S.A.* 39°5N 84°30W **81** F11
Covington *Tenn., U.S.A.* 35°34N 89°39W **85** D10
Covington *Va., U.S.A.* 37°47N 79°59W **81** G14
Cowal, L. *Australia* 33°40S 147°25E **63** E4
Cowan, L. *Australia* 31°45S 121°45E **61** F3
Cowan L. *Canada* 54°0N 107°15W **71** C7
Cowangie *Australia* 35°12S 141°26E **63** F3
Cowansville *Canada* 45°14N 72°46W **83** A12
Coward Springs
 Australia 29°24S 136°49E **63** D2
Cowcowing Lakes
 Australia 30°55S 117°20E **61** F2
Cowdenbeath *U.K.* 56°7N 3°21W **11** E5
Cowell *Australia* 33°39S 136°56E **63** E2
Cowes *U.K.* 50°45N 1°18W **13** G6
Cowichan L. *Canada* 48°53N 124°17W **78** B2
Cowlitz → *U.S.A.* 46°6N 122°55W **78** D4
Cowra *Australia* 33°49S 148°42E **63** E4
Coxilha Grande *Brazil* 28°18S 51°30W **95** B5
Coxim *Brazil* 18°30S 54°55W **93** G8
Cox's Bazar *Bangla.* 21°26N 91°59E **41** J17
Coyote Wells *U.S.A.* 32°44N 115°58W **79** N11
Coyuca de Benitez *Mexico* 17°2N 100°4W **87** D4
Coyuca de Catalán
 Mexico 18°20N 100°39W **86** D4
Cozad *U.S.A.* 40°52N 99°59W **80** E4
Cozumel *Mexico* 20°31N 86°55W **87** C7
Cozumel, Isla *Mexico* 20°30N 86°40W **87** C7
Crab Hill *Barbados* 13°19N 59°38W **89** g
Cracow = Kraków
 Poland 50°4N 19°57E **17** C10
Cracow *Australia* 25°17S 150°17E **63** D5
Cradle Mt.-Lake St. Clair △
 Australia 41°49S 147°56E **63** G4
Cradock *Australia* 32°6S 138°31E **63** E2
Cradock *S. Africa* 32°8S 25°36E **56** D4
Craig *U.S.A.* 40°31N 107°33W **76** F10
Craigavon *U.K.* 54°27N 6°23W **10** B5
Craik *Canada* 51°3N 105°49W **71** C7
Crailsheim *Germany* 49°8N 10°5E **16** D6
Craiova *Romania* 44°21N 23°48E **17** F12
Cramsie *Australia* 23°20S 144°15E **62** C3
Cranberry L. *U.S.A.* 44°11N 74°50W **83** B10
Cranberry Portage
 Canada 54°35N 101°23W **71** C8
Cranbrook *Australia* 34°18S 117°33E **61** F2
Cranbrook *Canada* 49°30N 115°46W **70** D5
Crandon *U.S.A.* 45°34N 88°54W **80** C9
Crane *Oreg., U.S.A.* 43°25N 118°35W **76** E4
Crane *Tex., U.S.A.* 31°24N 102°21W **84** F3
Crane, The *Barbados* 13°6N 59°27W **89** g
Cranganore *India* 10°13N 76°13E **45** J3
Cranston *U.S.A.* 41°47N 71°26W **83** E13
Crater L. *U.S.A.* 42°56N 122°6W **76** E2
Crater Lake △ *U.S.A.* 42°55N 122°10W **76** E2
Craters of the Moon △
 U.S.A. 43°25N 113°30W **76** E7
Crateús *Brazil* 5°10S 40°39W **93** E10
Crato *Brazil* 7°10S 39°25W **93** E11
Craven, L. *Canada* 54°20N 76°56W **72** B4
Crawford *U.S.A.* 42°41N 103°25W **80** D2
Crawfordsville *U.S.A.* 40°2N 86°54W **80** E10
Crawley *U.K.* 51°7N 0°11W **13** F7
Crazy Mts. *U.S.A.* 46°12N 110°20W **76** C8
Crean L. *Canada* 54°5N 106°9W **71** C7
Crediton *Canada* 43°17N 81°33W **82** C3
Crediton *U.K.* 50°47N 3°40W **13** G4
Cree → *Canada* 58°57N 105°47W **71** B7

Cree → U.K. 54°55N 4°25W 11 G4
Cree L. Canada 57°30N 106°30W 71 B7
Creede U.S.A. 37°51N 106°56W 77 H10
Creekside U.S.A. 40°40N 79°11W 82 F5
Creel Mexico 27°45N 107°38W 86 B3
Creemore Canada 44°19N 80°6W 82 B4
Creighton Canada 54°45N 101°54W 71 C8
Creighton U.S.A. 42°28N 97°54W 80 D5
Crema Italy 45°22N 9°41E 20 D8
Cremona Italy 45°7N 10°2E 20 D9
Cres Croatia 44°58N 14°25E 16 F8
Crescent City U.S.A. 41°45N 124°12W 76 F1
Crespo Argentina 32°2S 60°19W 94 C3
Cresson U.S.A. 40°28N 78°36W 82 F6
Crestline Calif., U.S.A. 34°14N 117°18W 79 L9
Crestline Ohio, U.S.A. 40°47N 82°44W 82 F2
Creston Canada 49°10N 116°31W 70 D5
Creston Calif., U.S.A. 35°32N 120°33W 78 K6
Creston Iowa, U.S.A. 41°4N 94°22W 80 E6
Crestview Calif., U.S.A. 37°46N 118°58W 78 H8
Crestview Fla., U.S.A. 30°46N 86°34W 85 F11
Crete = Kriti Greece 35°15N 25°0E 23 G11
Crete U.S.A. 40°38N 96°58W 80 E5
Creus, C. de Spain 42°20N 3°19E 21 A7
Creuse → France 47°0N 0°34E 20 C4
Crewe U.K. 53°6N 2°26W 12 D5
Crewkerne U.K. 50°53N 2°48W 13 G5
Crianlarich U.K. 56°24N 4°37W 11 E4
Criciúma Brazil 28°40S 49°23W 95 B6
Crieff U.K. 56°22N 3°50W 11 E5
Crimea □ Ukraine 45°30N 33°10E 19 E5
Crimean Pen. = Krymskyy
  Pivostriv Ukraine 45°0N 34°0E 19 F5
Crişul Alb → Romania 46°42N 21°17E 17 E11
Crişul Negru →
  Romania 46°42N 21°16E 17 E11
Crna → Macedonia 41°33N 21°59E 23 D9
Crna Gora = Montenegro ■
  Europe 42°40N 19°20E 23 C8
Crna Gora Macedonia 42°10N 21°30E 23 C9
Crna Reka = Crna →
  Macedonia 41°33N 21°59E 23 D9
Croagh Patrick Ireland 53°46N 9°40W 10 C2
Croatia ■ Europe 45°20N 16°0E 16 F9
Crocker, Banjaran
  Malaysia 5°40N 116°30E 36 C5
Crockett U.S.A. 31°19N 95°27W 84 F7
Crocodile = Umgwenya →
  Mozam. 25°14S 32°18E 57 C5
Crocodile → S. Africa 24°12S 26°53E 56 B4
Crocodile Is. Australia 12°3S 134°58E 62 A1
Crohy Hd. Ireland 54°55N 8°26W 10 B3
Croix, L. la Canada 48°20N 92°15W 72 C1
Croker, C. Australia 10°58S 132°35E 60 B5
Croker, C. Canada 44°58N 80°59W 82 B4
Croker I. Australia 11°12S 132°32E 60 B5
Croker Islands Seas ◊
  Australia 11°20S 132°30E 60 B5
Cromarty U.K. 57°40N 4°2W 11 D4
Cromer U.K. 52°56N 1°17E 12 E9
Cromwell N.Z. 45°3S 169°14E 59 F2
Cromwell U.S.A. 41°36N 72°39W 83 E12
Crook U.K. 54°43N 1°45W 12 C6
Crooked → Canada 54°50N 122°54W 70 C4
Crooked → U.S.A. 44°32N 121°16W 76 D3
Crooked I. Bahamas 22°50N 74°10W 89 B5
Crooked Island Passage
  Bahamas 22°55N 74°35W 89 B5
Crookston Minn., U.S.A. 47°47N 96°37W 80 B5
Crookston Nebr., U.S.A. 42°56N 100°45W 80 D3
Crookwell Australia 34°28S 149°24E 63 E4
Crosby U.K. 53°30N 3°3W 12 D4
Crosby N. Dak., U.S.A. 48°55N 103°18W 80 A2
Crosby Pa., U.S.A. 41°45N 78°23W 82 E6
Crosbyton U.S.A. 33°40N 101°14W 84 E4
Cross City U.S.A. 29°38N 83°7W 85 G13
Cross Fell U.K. 54°43N 2°28W 12 C5
Cross L. Canada 54°45N 97°30W 71 C9
Cross Lake Canada 54°37N 97°47W 71 C9
Cross Sound U.S.A. 58°0N 135°0W 68 F4
Crossett U.S.A. 33°8N 91°58W 84 E9
Crosshaven Ireland 51°47N 8°17W 10 E3
Crossmaglen U.K. 54°5N 6°36W 10 B5
Crossmolina Ireland 54°6N 9°20W 10 B2
Crossville U.S.A. 35°57N 85°2W 85 D12
Croswell U.S.A. 43°16N 82°37W 82 C2
Croton-on-Hudson
  U.S.A. 41°12N 73°55W 83 E11
Crotone Italy 39°5N 17°8E 22 E7
Crow → Canada 59°41N 124°20W 70 B4
Crow Agency U.S.A. 45°36N 107°28W 76 D10
Crow Hd. Ireland 51°35N 10°9W 10 E1
Crowell U.S.A. 33°59N 99°43W 84 E5
Crowley U.S.A. 30°13N 92°22W 84 F8
Crowley, L. U.S.A. 37°35N 118°42W 78 H8
Crown Point Ind., U.S.A. 41°25N 87°22W 80 E10
Crown Point N.Y.,
  U.S.A. 43°57N 73°26W 83 C11
Crownpoint U.S.A. 35°41N 108°9W 77 J9
Crows Landing U.S.A. 37°23N 121°6W 78 H5
Crows Nest Australia 27°16S 152°4E 63 D5
Crowsnest Pass Canada 49°40N 114°40W 70 D6
Croydon Australia 18°13S 142°14E 62 B3
Croydon □ U.K. 51°22N 0°5W 13 F7
Crozet, Îs. Ind. Oc. 46°27S 52°0E 3 G12
Crusheen Ireland 52°57N 8°53W 10 D3
Cruz, C. Cuba 19°50N 77°50W 88 C4
Cruz Alta Brazil 28°45S 53°40W 95 B5
Cruz Bay U.S. Virgin Is. 18°20N 64°48W 89 e
Cruz del Eje Argentina 30°45S 64°50W 94 C3
Cruzeiro Brazil 22°33S 45°0W 95 A7
Cruzeiro do Oeste Brazil 23°46S 53°4W 95 A5
Cruzeiro do Sul Brazil 7°35S 72°35W 92 E4
Cry L. Canada 58°45N 129°0W 70 B3
Crystal Bay U.S.A. 39°15N 120°0W 78 F7
Crystal Brook Australia 33°21S 138°12E 63 E2
Crystal City U.S.A. 28°41N 99°50W 84 G5
Crystal Falls U.S.A. 46°5N 88°20W 80 B9

Crystal River U.S.A. 28°54N 82°35W 85 G13
Crystal Springs U.S.A. 31°59N 90°21W 85 F9
Csongrád Hungary 46°43N 20°12E 17 E11
Cu Lao Hon Vietnam 10°54N 108°18E 39 G7
Cua Rao Vietnam 19°16N 104°27E 38 C5
Cuamato Angola 17°2S 15°7E 56 A2
Cuamba Mozam. 14°45S 36°22E 55 G7
Cuando → Angola 17°30S 23°15E 55 H4
Cuando Cubango □
  Angola 16°25S 20°0E 56 A3
Cuangar Angola 17°36S 18°39E 56 A2
Cuango = Kwango →
  Dem. Rep. of the Congo 3°14S 17°22E 54 E3
Cuanza → Angola 9°21S 13°9E 54 F2
Cuarto → Argentina 33°25S 63°2W 94 C3
Cuatrociénegas Mexico 26°59N 102°5W 86 B4
Cuauhtémoc Mexico 28°25N 106°52W 86 B3
Cuba N. Mex., U.S.A. 36°1N 107°4W 77 H10
Cuba N.Y., U.S.A. 42°13N 78°17W 82 D6
Cuba ■ W. Indies 22°0N 79°0W 88 B4
Cubango → Africa 18°50S 22°25E 56 B3
Cuc Phuong △ Vietnam 20°17N 105°38E 38 B5
Cuchumatanes, Sierra de los
  Guatemala 15°35N 91°25W 88 C1
Cuckfield U.K. 51°1N 0°8W 13 F7
Cucuí Brazil 1°12N 66°50W 92 C5
Cucurpé Mexico 30°20N 110°43W 86 A2
Cúcuta Colombia 7°54N 72°31W 92 B4
Cuddalore India 11°46N 79°45E 45 J4
Cuddapan, L. Australia 25°45S 141°26E 62 D3
Cue Australia 27°25S 117°54E 61 E2
Cuenca Ecuador 2°50S 79°9W 92 D3
Cuenca Spain 40°5N 2°10W 21 B4
Cuenca, Serranía de Spain 39°55N 1°50W 21 C5
Cuernavaca Mexico 18°55N 99°15W 87 D5
Cuero U.S.A. 29°6N 97°17W 84 G6
Cueva de la Quebrada del Toro △
  Venezuela 10°46N 69°3W 89 D6
Cuevas del Almanzora
  Spain 37°18N 1°58W 21 D5
Cuevo Bolivia 20°15S 63°30W 92 H6
Cuiabá Brazil 15°30S 56°0W 93 G7
Cuiabá → Brazil 17°5S 56°36W 93 G7
Cuihangcun China 22°27N 113°32E 31 a
Cuijk Neths. 51°44N 5°50E 15 C5
Cuilco Guatemala 15°24N 91°58W 88 C1
Cuillin Hills U.K. 57°13N 6°15W 11 D2
Cuillin Sd. U.K. 57°4N 6°20W 11 D2
Cuilo = Kwilu →
  Dem. Rep. of the Congo 3°22S 17°22E 54 E3
Cuito → Angola 18°1S 20°48E 56 A3
Cuitzeo, L. de Mexico 19°55N 101°5W 86 D4
Cukai Malaysia 4°13N 103°25E 39 K4
Culbertson U.S.A. 48°9N 104°31W 76 B11
Culcairn Australia 35°41S 147°3E 63 F4
Culebra Puerto Rico 18°19N 65°18W 89 d
Culgoa → Australia 29°56S 146°20E 63 D4
Culgoa Flood Plain △
  Australia 28°58S 147°5E 63 D4
Culiacán Mexico 24°50N 107°23W 86 C3
Culiacán → Mexico 24°30N 107°42W 86 C3
Culik Indonesia 8°21S 115°37E 37 J18
Culion Phil. 11°54N 119°58E 37 B6
Cullarin Ra. Australia 34°30S 149°30E 63 E4
Cullen U.K. 57°42N 2°49W 11 D6
Cullen Pt. Australia 11°57S 141°54E 62 A3
Cullera Spain 39°9N 0°17W 21 C5
Cullman U.S.A. 34°11N 86°51W 85 D11
Cullompton U.K. 50°51N 3°24W 13 G4
Culpeper U.S.A. 38°30N 78°0W 81 F14
Culuene → Brazil 12°56S 52°51W 93 F8
Culver, Pt. Australia 32°54S 124°43E 61 F3
Culverden N.Z. 42°47S 172°49E 59 E4
Cumaná Venezuela 10°30N 64°5W 92 A6
Cumberland B.C., Canada 49°40N 125°0W 70 D4
Cumberland Ont., Canada 45°29N 75°24W 83 A9
Cumberland U.S.A. 39°39N 78°46W 81 F14
Cumberland → U.S.A. 37°9N 88°25W 80 G9
Cumberland, L. U.S.A. 36°52N 85°9W 81 G11
Cumberland Gap △
  U.S.A. 36°36N 83°40W 81 G12
Cumberland I. U.S.A. 30°50N 81°25W 85 F14
Cumberland Is. Australia 20°35S 149°10E 62 b
Cumberland Island △
  U.S.A. 30°12N 81°24W 85 F14
Cumberland L. Canada 54°3N 102°18W 71 C8
Cumberland Pen. Canada 67°0N 64°0W 69 D19
Cumberland Plateau
  U.S.A. 36°0N 85°0W 85 D12
Cumberland Sd. Canada 65°30N 66°0W 69 D18
Cumbernauld U.K. 55°57N 3°58W 11 F5
Cumborah Australia 29°40S 147°45E 63 D4
Cumbres de Majalca △
  Mexico 28°48N 106°30W 86 B3
Cumbres de Monterrey △
  Mexico 25°26N 100°25W 86 B4
Cumbria □ U.K. 54°42N 2°52W 12 C5
Cumbrian Mts. U.K. 54°30N 3°0W 12 C5
Cuminá → Brazil 1°30S 56°0W 93 D7
Cummings Mt. U.S.A. 35°2N 118°34W 79 K8
Cummins Australia 34°16S 135°43E 63 E2
Cumnock Australia 32°59S 148°46E 63 E4
Cumnock U.K. 55°28N 4°17W 11 F4
Cumpas Mexico 30°2N 109°48W 86 B3
Cunco Chile 38°55S 72°2W 96 D2
Cumcumén Chile 31°53S 70°38W 94 C1
Cundeelee ◊ Australia 30°43S 123°25E 61 F3
Cunderdin Australia 31°37S 117°12E 61 F2
Cunene → Angola 17°20S 11°50E 56 A1
Cúneo Italy 44°23N 7°32E 20 D7
Cung Son Vietnam 13°2N 108°58E 38 F7
Çüngüş Turkey 38°13N 39°17E 46 B3
Cunnamulla Australia 28°2S 145°38E 63 D4
Cupar Canada 50°57N 104°10W 71 C8
Cupar U.K. 56°19N 3°1W 11 E5
Cupertino U.S.A. 37°19N 122°2W 78 H4
Cupica, G. de Colombia 6°25N 77°30W 92 B3

Curaçao W. Indies 12°10N 69°0W 89 D6
Curanilahue Chile 37°29S 73°28W 94 D1
Curaray → Peru 2°20S 74°5W 92 D4
Curepipe Mauritius 20°19S 57°31E 55 d
Curiapo Venezuela 8°33N 61°5W 92 B6
Curicó Chile 34°55S 71°20W 94 C1
Curitiba Brazil 25°0S 49°10W 95 B6
Curitibanos Brazil 27°18S 50°36W 95 B5
Currabubula Australia 31°16S 150°44E 63 E5
Currais Novos Brazil 6°13S 36°30W 93 E11
Curral Velho C. Verde Is. 16°8N 22°48W 52 b
Curralinho Brazil 1°45S 49°46W 93 D9
Currane, L. Ireland 51°49N 10°4W 10 E1
Currant U.S.A. 38°44N 115°28W 76 G6
Currarinya △ Australia 28°55S 144°27E 63 D3
Current → U.S.A. 36°15N 90°55W 84 C9
Currie Australia 39°56S 143°53E 63 F3
Currie U.S.A. 40°16N 114°45W 76 F6
Curtea de Argeş
  Romania 45°12N 24°42E 17 F13
Curtin Springs Australia 25°20S 131°45E 61 E5
Curtis U.S.A. 40°38N 100°31W 80 E3
Curtis Group Australia 39°30S 146°37E 63 F4
Curtis I. Australia 23°35S 151°10E 62 C5
Curuápanema → Brazil 2°25S 55°2W 93 D7
Curuçá Brazil 0°43S 47°50W 93 D9
Curuguaty Paraguay 24°31S 55°42W 95 A4
Çürüksu Çayı = Büyük
  Menderes → Turkey 37°28N 27°11E 23 F12
Curup Indonesia 3°26S 102°13E 36 E2
Cururupu Brazil 1°50S 44°50W 93 D10
Curuzú Cuatiá Argentina 29°50S 58°5W 94 B4
Curvelo Brazil 18°45S 44°27W 93 G10
Cusco Peru 13°32S 72°0W 92 F4
Cushendall U.K. 55°5N 6°4W 10 A5
Cushing U.S.A. 35°59N 96°46W 84 D6
Cushing, Mt. Canada 57°35N 126°57W 70 B3
Cusihuiriáchic Mexico 28°14N 106°50W 86 B3
Custer U.S.A. 43°46N 103°36W 80 D2
Cut Bank U.S.A. 48°38N 112°20W 76 B7
Cutchogue U.S.A. 41°1N 72°30W 83 E12
Cuthbert U.S.A. 31°46N 84°48W 85 F12
Cutler U.S.A. 36°31N 119°17W 78 J7
Cuttaburra → Australia 29°43S 144°22E 63 D3
Cuttack India 20°25N 85°57E 44 D7
Cuvier, C. Australia 23°14S 113°22E 61 D1
Cuvier I. N.Z. 36°27S 175°50E 59 B5
Cuxhaven Germany 53°51N 8°41E 16 B5
Cuyahoga Falls U.S.A. 41°8N 81°29W 82 E3
Cuyahoga Valley △
  U.S.A. 41°24N 81°33W 82 E3
Cuyo Phil. 10°51N 121°2E 37 B6
Cuyuni → Guyana 6°23N 58°41W 92 B7
Cuzco = Cusco Peru 13°32S 72°0W 92 F4
Cuzco Bolivia 20°0S 66°50W 92 H5
Cwmbran U.K. 51°39N 3°2W 13 F4
Cyclades Greece 37°0N 24°30E 23 F11
Cygnet Australia 43°8S 147°1E 63 G4
Cynthiana U.S.A. 38°23N 84°18W 81 F11
Cypress Hills Canada 49°40N 109°30W 71 D7
Cypress Hills △ Canada 49°40N 109°30W 71 D7
Cyprus ■ Asia 35°0N 33°0E 46 C2
Cyrenaica = Barqa Libya 27°0N 23°0E 53 C10
Cyrene Libya 32°53N 21°52E 53 B10
Czar Canada 52°27N 110°50W 71 C6
Czech Rep. ■ Europe 50°0N 15°0E 16 D8
Częstochowa Poland 50°49N 19°7E 17 C10

D

Da → Vietnam 21°15N 105°20E 34 G5
Da Hinggan Ling China 48°0N 121°0E 31 B13
Da Lat Vietnam 11°56N 108°25E 39 G7
Da Nang Vietnam 16°4N 108°13E 38 D7
Da Qaidam China 37°50N 95°15E 30 D8
Da Yunhe → Hopei,
  China 39°10N 117°10E 33 E9
Da Yunhe → Jiangsu,
  China 34°25N 120°5E 33 G11
Da'an China 45°30N 124°7E 33 B13
Daan Viljoen △ Namibia 22°2S 16°45E 56 B2
Daba Shan China 32°0N 109°0E 34 B7
Dabbagh, Jabal Si. Arabia 27°52N 35°45E 46 E2
Dabhoi India 22°10N 73°20E 42 H5
Dabie Shan China 31°20N 115°20E 35 C10
Dabola Guinea 10°50N 11°5W 52 F3
Dabu China 24°22N 116°41E 35 E11
Dabung Malaysia 5°23N 102°1E 39 K4
Dacca = Dhaka Bangla. 23°43N 90°26E 43 H14
Dachang China 31°40N 121°24E 35 A12
Dachaoshan Dam China 24°1N 100°22E 34 E3
Dachigam △ India 34°10N 75°0E 42 B6
Dacre Canada 45°22N 76°57W 82 A8
Dadanawa Guyana 2°50N 59°30W 92 C7
Dade City U.S.A. 28°22N 82°11W 85 G13
Dadhar Pakistan 29°28N 67°39E 42 E2
Dadnah U.A.E. 25°32N 56°22E 47 E8
Dadra & Nagar Haveli □
  India 20°5N 73°0E 44 D1
Dadri = Charkhi Dadri
  India 28°37N 76°17E 42 E7
Dadu Pakistan 26°45N 67°45E 42 F2
Dadu He → China 29°31N 103°46E 34 C4
Daegu S. Korea 35°50N 128°37E 33 G15
Daegwanryeong S. Korea 37°40N 128°42E 33 E15
Daejeon S. Korea 36°20N 127°28E 33 F14
Daejeong S. Korea 33°13N 126°19E 33 H14
Daet Phil. 14°2N 122°55E 37 B6
Dafang China 27°9N 105°39E 34 D5
Dafeng China 33°3N 120°45E 35 H11
Dagana Senegal 16°30N 15°35W 52 E2
Dagestan □ Russia 42°30N 47°0E 19 F8
Daggett U.S.A. 34°52N 116°52W 79 L10
Daghestan Republic = Dagestan □
  Russia 42°30N 47°0E 19 F8
Dağlıq Qarabağ = Nagorno-
  Karabakh □ Azerbaijan 39°55N 46°45E 46 B5

Dagö = Hiiumaa Estonia 58°50N 22°45E 9 G20
Dagu China 38°59N 117°40E 33 E9
Daguan China 27°43N 103°56E 34 D4
Dagupan Phil. 16°3N 120°20E 37 A6
Daguragu Australia 17°33S 130°30E 60 C5
Daguragu ◊ Australia 17°24S 130°48E 60 C5
Dahab Egypt 28°31N 34°31E 46 D2
Dahanu India 19°58N 72°44E 44 E1
Dahivadi India 17°43N 74°33E 44 F2
Dahlak Kebir Eritrea 15°50N 40°10E 49 D3
Dahlonega U.S.A. 34°32N 83°59W 85 D13
Dahod India 22°50N 74°15E 42 H6
Dahong Shan China 31°25N 113°0E 35 B9
Dahongliutan China 35°45N 79°20E 43 B8
Dahra Libya 29°30N 17°50E 53 C9
Dahūk Iraq 36°50N 43°1E 46 B3
Dai Hao Vietnam 18°1N 106°25E 38 C6
Dai-Sen Japan 35°22N 133°32E 29 G6
Dai Shan China 30°25N 122°10E 35 B14
Dai Xian China 39°4N 112°58E 32 E7
Daicheng China 38°42N 116°38E 32 E9
Daikondi = Dāykondī □
  Afghan. 34°0N 66°0E 40 C5
Dailekh Nepal 28°50N 81°44E 43 E9
Daingean Ireland 53°18N 7°17W 10 C4
Daingean, An = Dingle
  Ireland 52°9N 10°17W 10 D1
Dainkog China 32°30N 97°58E 34 A1
Daintree Australia 16°20S 145°20E 62 B4
Daintree △ Australia 16°8S 145°2E 62 B4
Daiō-Misaki Japan 34°15N 136°45E 29 G8
Daisen Japan 39°27N 140°29E 28 E10
Daisen-Oki △ Japan 35°23N 133°34E 29 G6
Daisetsu-Zan Japan 43°30N 142°57E 28 C11
Daisetsu-Zan △ Japan 43°30N 142°55E 28 C11
Daitari India 21°10N 85°46E 44 D7
Daiyun Shan China 25°50N 118°15E 35 E12
Dajarra Australia 21°42S 139°30E 62 C2
Dajiawa China 37°9N 119°0E 33 F10
Dajin Chuan → China 31°16N 101°59E 34 B3
Dak Dam Cambodia 12°20N 107°21E 38 F6
Dak Nhe Vietnam 15°28N 107°48E 38 E6
Dak Pek Vietnam 15°4N 107°44E 38 E6
Dak Song Vietnam 12°19N 107°35E 39 F6
Dak Sui Vietnam 14°55N 107°43E 38 E6
Dakar Senegal 14°34N 17°29W 52 F2
Dakhla W. Sahara 23°50N 15°53W 52 D2
Dakhla, El Wâhât el
  Egypt 25°30N 28°50E 53 C11
Dakoank India 7°2N 93°43E 45 L11
Dakor India 22°45N 73°11E 42 H5
Dakota City U.S.A. 42°25N 96°25W 80 D5
Dakovica = Gjakovë
  Kosovo 42°22N 20°26E 23 C9
Dakovo China 32°40N 92°10E 30 E7
Dalachi China 36°48N 105°0E 32 F3
Dalai Nur China 43°20N 116°45E 32 C9
Dālakī Iran 29°26N 51°17E 47 D6
Dälälven → Sweden 60°12N 16°43E 9 F17
Dalaman Turkey 36°41N 28°43E 23 F13
Dalandzadgad Mongolia 43°27N 104°30E 32 C3
Dalap-Uliga-Darrit = Majuro
  Marshall Is. 7°9N 171°12E 64 G9
Dalarna Sweden 61°0N 14°0E 8 F16
Dalay Mongolia 43°28N 103°30E 32 C2
Dālbandīn Pakistan 29°0N 64°23E 40 E4
Dalbeattie U.K. 54°56N 3°50W 11 G5
Dalbeg Australia 20°16S 147°18E 62 C4
Dalby Australia 27°10S 151°17E 63 D5
Dale City U.S.A. 38°38N 77°19W 81 F15
Dale Hollow L. U.S.A. 36°32N 85°27W 85 C12
Dalgān Iran 27°31N 59°19E 47 E8
Dalhart U.S.A. 36°4N 102°31W 84 C3
Dalhousie Canada 48°5N 66°26W 73 C6
Dalhousie India 32°38N 75°58E 42 C6
Dali Shaanxi, China 34°48N 109°58E 32 G5
Dali Yunnan, China 25°40N 100°10E 34 E3
Dalian China 38°50N 121°40E 33 E11
Daliang Shan China 28°0N 102°45E 34 D4
Daling He → China 40°55N 121°40E 33 D11
Dāliyat el Karmel Israel 32°43N 35°2E 48 C4
Dallas Oreg., U.S.A. 44°55N 123°19W 76 D2
Dallas Tex., U.S.A. 32°47N 96°48W 84 E6
Dalles, The U.S.A. 45°36N 121°10W 76 D3
Dalmā U.A.E. 24°30N 52°20E 47 E7
Dalmacija Croatia 43°20N 17°0E 22 C7
Dalmas, L. Canada 53°30N 71°50W 73 B5
Dalmatia = Dalmacija
  Croatia 43°20N 17°0E 22 C7
Dalmau India 26°4N 81°2E 43 F9
Dalmellington U.K. 55°19N 4°23W 11 F4
Dalnegorsk Russia 44°32N 135°33E 28 B7
Dalnerechensk Russia 45°50N 133°40E 28 A7
Dalnevostochnyy □
  Russia 67°0N 140°0E 27 C14
Daloa Ivory C. 7°0N 6°30W 52 G4
Dalou Shan China 28°15N 107°0E 34 C6
Dalry U.K. 55°42N 4°43W 11 F4
Dalrymple, L. Australia 20°40S 147°0E 62 C4
Dalrymple, Mt. Australia 21°1S 148°39E 62 b
Dalsland Sweden 58°50N 12°15E 9 G15
Daltenganj India 24°0N 84°4E 43 H11
Dalton Ga., U.S.A. 34°46N 84°58W 85 D12
Dalton Mass., U.S.A. 42°28N 73°11E 83 D11
Dalton Nebr., U.S.A. 41°25N 102°58W 80 E2
Dalton-in-Furness U.K. 54°10N 3°11W 12 C4
Dalvík Iceland 65°58N 18°32W 8 D4
Dalwallinu Australia 30°17S 116°40E 61 F2
Daly → Australia 13°35S 130°19E 60 B5
Daly L. Canada 56°32N 105°39W 71 B7
Daly River Australia 13°46S 130°42E 60 B5
Daly River-Port Keats ◊
  Australia 13°15S 129°36E 60 B4
Daly Waters Australia 16°15S 133°24E 62 B1

Dāmaneh Iran 33°1N 50°29E 47 C6
Damanganga → India 20°25N 72°56E 44 D1
Damanhûr Egypt 31°0N 30°30E 53 B12
Damant L. Canada 61°45N 105°5W 71 A7
Damar Indonesia 7°7S 128°40E 37 F7
Damara C.A.R. 4°58N 18°42E 54 D3
Damaraland Namibia 20°0S 15°0E 56 B2
Damascus = Dimashq
  Syria 33°30N 36°18E 48 B5
Damaturu Nigeria 11°45N 11°55E 54 B2
Damāvand Iran 35°47N 52°0E 47 C7
Damāvand, Qolleh-ye
  Iran 35°56N 52°10E 47 C7
Damba Angola 6°44S 15°20E 54 F3
Dâmboviţa → Romania 44°12N 26°26E 17 F14
Dambulla Sri Lanka 7°51N 80°39E 45 L5
Dame Marie Haiti 18°34N 74°26W 89 C5
Dāmghān Iran 36°10N 54°17E 47 B7
Damiel Spain 39°4N 3°37W 21 C4
Damietta = Dumyât
  Egypt 31°24N 31°48E 53 B12
Daming China 36°15N 115°6E 32 F8
Damir Qâbû Syria 36°58N 41°51E 46 B4
Dammam = Ad Dammām
  Si. Arabia 26°20N 50°5E 47 E6
Damodar → India 23°17N 87°35E 43 H12
Damoh India 23°50N 79°28E 43 H8
Dampier Australia 20°41S 116°42E 60 D2
Dampier, Selat Indonesia 0°40S 131°0E 37 E8
Dampier Arch. Australia 20°38S 116°32E 60 D2
Damrei, Chuor Phnum
  Cambodia 11°30N 103°0E 39 G4
Damyang S. Korea 35°19N 126°59E 33 G14
Dana Indonesia 11°0S 121°15E 37 F6
Dana Jordan 30°41N 35°37E 48 E4
Dana Nepal 28°32N 83°37E 43 E10
Dana, L. Canada 50°53N 77°20W 72 B4
Dana, Mt. U.S.A. 37°54N 119°12W 78 H7
Danakil Desert Ethiopia 12°45N 41°0E 49 E3
Danané Ivory C. 7°16N 8°9W 52 G4
Danba China 30°54N 101°48E 34 B3
Danbury U.S.A. 41°24N 73°28W 83 E11
Danby L. U.S.A. 34°13N 115°5W 79 L11
Dand Afghan. 31°28N 65°32E 42 D1
Dandeldhura Nepal 29°20N 80°35E 43 E9
Dandeli India 15°5N 74°30E 45 G2
Dandenong Australia 38°0S 145°15E 63 F4
Dandong China 40°10N 124°20E 33 D13
Danfeng China 33°45N 110°25E 32 H6
Dangan Liedao China 22°2N 114°8E 35 F10
Danger Is. = Pukapuka
  Cook Is. 10°53S 165°49W 65 J11
Danger Pt. S. Africa 34°40S 19°17E 56 E2
Dangla Shan = Tanggula Shan
  China 32°40N 92°10E 30 E7
Dangrek, Mts. = Dangrek, Phnom
  Thailand 14°20N 104°0E 38 E5
Dangrek, Phnom
  Thailand 14°20N 104°0E 38 E5
Dangriga Belize 17°0N 88°13W 87 D7
Dangshan China 34°27N 116°22E 32 G9
Dangtu China 31°32N 118°25E 35 B12
Dangyang China 30°52N 111°44E 35 B8
Daniel U.S.A. 42°52N 110°4W 76 E8
Daniel's Harbour Canada 50°13N 57°35W 73 B8
Danielskuil S. Africa 28°11S 23°33E 56 C3
Danielson U.S.A. 41°48N 71°53W 83 E13
Danilov Russia 58°16N 40°13E 18 C7
Daning China 36°28N 110°45E 32 F6
Danjiangkou China 32°31N 111°30E 34 A8
Danjiangkou Shuiku
  China 32°37N 111°30E 35 A8
Dank Oman 23°33N 56°16E 47 F8
Dankhar Gompa India 32°10N 78°10E 42 C8
Danleng China 30°1N 103°31E 34 B4
Danli Honduras 14°4N 86°35W 88 D2
Danmark = Denmark ■
  Europe 55°45N 10°0E 9 J14
Dannemora U.S.A. 44°43N 73°44W 83 B11
Dannevirke N.Z. 40°12S 176°8E 59 D6
Dannhauser S. Africa 28°0S 30°3E 57 C5
Dansville U.S.A. 42°34N 77°42W 82 D7
Danta India 24°11N 72°46E 42 G5
Dantan India 21°57N 87°20E 43 J12
Dante = Xaafuun Somalia 10°25N 51°16E 49 E5
Dantewara India 18°54N 81°21E 44 E5
Danube = Dunărea →
  Europe 45°20N 29°40E 17 F15
Danvers U.S.A. 42°34N 70°56W 83 D14
Danville Ill., U.S.A. 40°8N 87°37W 80 E10
Danville Ky., U.S.A. 37°39N 84°46W 81 G11
Danville Pa., U.S.A. 40°58N 76°37W 83 F8
Danville Va., U.S.A. 36°36N 79°23W 81 G14
Danville Vt., U.S.A. 44°25N 72°9W 83 B12
Danyang China 32°0N 119°31E 35 B12
Danzhai China 26°11N 107°48E 34 D6
Danzhou China 19°31N 109°33E 38 C7
Danzig = Gdańsk Poland 54°22N 18°40E 17 A10
Dao Xian China 25°36N 111°31E 35 E8
Daocheng China 29°0N 100°10E 34 C3
Dapaong Togo 10°55N 0°16E 52 F6
Dapoli India 17°46N 73°11E 44 F1
Daqing China 46°35N 125°0E 31 B13
Daqing Shan China 40°40N 111°0E 32 D6
Daqu Shan China 30°25N 122°20E 35 B14
Dar Banda Africa 8°0N 23°0E 50 F6
Dar el Beida = Casablanca
  Morocco 33°36N 7°36W 52 B4
Dar es Salaam Tanzania 6°50S 39°12E 54 F7
Dar Mazār Iran 29°14N 57°20E 47 D8
Dar'ā Syria 32°36N 36°7E 48 C5
Dar'ā □ Syria 32°55N 36°10E 48 C5
Dārāb Iran 28°50N 54°30E 47 D7
Daraban Pakistan 31°44N 70°20E 42 D4
Daraj Libya 30°10N 10°28E 53 B8
Dārān Iran 33°17N 50°38E 47 C6
Dārayyā Syria 33°28N 36°15E 48 B5
Darband Pakistan 34°20N 72°50E 42 B5

Darband, Kūh-e *Iran*	31°34N 57°8E	47 D8
Darbhanga *India*	26°15N 85°55E	43 F11
D'Arcy *Canada*	50°33N 122°29W	70 C4
Dardanelle *Ark., U.S.A.*	35°13N 93°9W	84 D8
Dardanelle *Calif., U.S.A.*	38°20N 119°50W	78 G7
Dardanelles = Çanakkale Boğazı *Turkey*	40°17N 26°32E	23 D12
Dārestān *Iran*	29°9N 58°42E	47 D8
Dārfūr *Sudan*	13°40N 24°0E	53 F10
Dargai *Pakistan*	34°25N 71°55E	42 B4
Dargaville *N.Z.*	35°57S 173°52E	59 A4
Darhan *Mongolia*	49°37N 106°21E	30 B10
Darhan Muminggan *China*	41°40N 110°28E	32 D6
Darıca *Turkey*	40°45N 29°23E	23 D13
Darién, G. del *Colombia*	9°0N 77°0W	92 B3
Darién △ *Panama*	7°36N 77°57W	88 E4
Dariganga = Ovoot *Mongolia*	45°21N 113°45E	32 B7
Daringbadi *India*	19°54N 84°8E	44 E7
Darjeeling = Darjiling *India*	27°3N 88°18E	43 F13
Darjiling *India*	27°3N 88°18E	43 F13
Darkan *Australia*	33°20S 116°43E	61 F2
Darkhana *Pakistan*	30°39N 72°11E	42 D5
Darkhazineh *Iran*	31°54N 48°39E	47 D6
Darkot Pass *Pakistan*	36°45N 73°26E	43 A5
Darling → *Australia*	34°4S 141°54E	63 E3
Darling Downs *Australia*	27°30S 150°30E	63 D5
Darling Ra. *Australia*	32°30S 116°20E	61 F2
Darlington *U.K.*	54°32N 1°33W	12 C6
Darlington *U.S.A.*	34°18N 79°52W	85 D15
Darlington □ *U.K.*	54°32N 1°33W	12 C6
Darlington, L. *S. Africa*	33°10S 25°9E	56 D4
Darlot, L. *Australia*	27°48S 121°35E	61 E3
Darłowo *Poland*	54°25N 16°25E	16 A9
Darmstadt *Germany*	49°51N 8°39E	16 D5
Darnah *Libya*	32°45N 22°45E	53 B10
Darnall *S. Africa*	29°23S 31°18E	57 C5
Darnley *Australia*	9°35S 143°46E	62 a
Darnley, C. *Antarctica*	68°0S 69°0E	5 C6
Darnley B. *Canada*	69°30N 123°30W	68 D7
Darr → *Australia*	23°39S 143°50E	62 C3
Darra Pezu *Pakistan*	32°19N 70°44E	42 C4
Darrequeira *Argentina*	37°42S 63°10W	94 D3
Darrington *U.S.A.*	48°15N 121°36W	76 B3
Darsi *India*	15°46N 79°44E	45 G4
Dart → *U.K.*	50°24N 3°39W	13 G4
Dartmoor *U.K.*	50°38N 3°57W	13 G4
Dartmoor △ *U.K.*	50°37N 3°59W	13 G4
Dartmouth *Canada*	44°40N 63°30W	73 D7
Dartmouth *U.K.*	50°21N 3°36W	13 G4
Dartmouth, L. *Australia*	26°4S 145°18E	63 D4
Darvel, Teluk = Lahad Datu, Telok *Malaysia*	4°50N 118°20E	37 D5
Darwen *U.K.*	53°42N 2°29W	12 D5
Darwendale *Zimbabwe*	17°41S 30°33E	57 A5
Darwha *India*	20°15N 77°45E	44 D3
Darwin *Australia*	12°25S 130°51E	60 B5
Darwin *U.S.A.*	36°15N 117°35W	79 J9
Darya Khan *Pakistan*	31°48N 71°6E	42 D4
Daryapur *India*	20°55N 77°20E	44 D3
Daryoi Amu = Amudarya → *Uzbekistan*	43°58N 59°34E	26 E6
Dās *U.A.E.*	25°20N 53°30E	47 E7
Dashen, Ras *Ethiopia*	13°8N 38°26E	49 E2
Dashetai *China*	41°0N 109°5E	32 D5
Dashiqiao *China*	40°38N 122°30E	33 D12
Dashköpri *Turkmenistan*	36°16N 62°8E	47 B9
Dasht → *Pakistan*	25°10N 61°40E	40 G2
Daska *Pakistan*	32°20N 74°20E	42 C6
Daşoguz *Turkmenistan*	41°49N 59°58E	26 E6
Dasuya *India*	31°49N 75°38E	42 D6
Datça *Turkey*	36°46N 27°40E	23 F12
Date *Japan*	42°28N 140°52E	28 C10
Datia *India*	25°39N 78°27E	43 G8
Datian *China*	25°40N 117°50E	35 E11
Datong *Anhui, China*	30°48N 117°44E	35 B11
Datong *Qinghai, China*	36°20N 102°50E	30 D9
Datong *Shanxi, China*	40°6N 113°18E	32 D7
Dattakhel *Pakistan*	32°54N 69°46E	42 C3
Dattapur = Dhamangaon *India*	20°48N 78°9E	44 D4
Datu, Tanjung *Indonesia*	2°5N 109°39E	36 D3
Datu Piang *Phil.*	7°2N 124°30E	37 C6
Datuk, Tanjong = Datu, Tanjung *Indonesia*	2°5N 109°39E	36 D3
Daud Khel *Pakistan*	32°53N 71°34E	42 C4
Daudnagar *India*	25°2N 84°24E	43 G11
Daugava → *Latvia*	57°4N 24°3E	9 H21
Daugavpils *Latvia*	55°53N 26°32E	9 J22
Daulatabad *India*	19°57N 75°15E	44 E2
Daulpur *India*	26°45N 77°59E	42 F7
Daund *India*	18°26N 74°40E	44 E2
Daung Kyun *Burma*	12°13N 98°4E	39 F1
Dauphin *Canada*	51°9N 100°5W	71 C8
Dauphin *U.S.A.*	40°22N 76°56W	82 F8
Dauphin L. *Canada*	51°20N 99°45W	71 C9
Dauphiné *France*	45°15N 5°25E	20 D6
Dausa *India*	26°52N 76°20E	42 F7
Davanagere *India*	14°25N 75°55E	45 G2
Davao *Phil.*	7°0N 125°40E	37 C7
Davao G. *Phil.*	6°30N 125°48E	37 C7
Dāvar Panāh = Sarāvān *Iran*	27°25N 62°15E	47 E9
Davenport *Calif., U.S.A.*	37°1N 122°12W	78 H4
Davenport *Iowa, U.S.A.*	41°32N 90°35W	80 E8
Davenport *Wash., U.S.A.*	47°39N 118°9W	76 C4
Davenport Ra. *Australia*	20°28S 134°0E	62 C1
Davenport Range △ *Australia*	20°36S 134°22E	62 C1
Daventry *U.K.*	52°16N 1°10W	13 E6
David *Panama*	8°30N 82°30W	88 E3
David City *U.S.A.*	41°15N 97°8W	80 E5
David Glacier *Antarctica*	75°20S 162°0E	5 D11
David Gorodok = Davyd Haradok *Belarus*	52°4N 27°8E	17 B14
Davidson *Canada*	51°16N 105°59W	71 C7
Davidson Mts. *U.S.A.*	68°41N 142°22W	74 B11
Davis *Antarctica*	68°34S 77°55E	5 C6
Davis *U.S.A.*	38°33N 121°44W	78 G5
Davis Dam *U.S.A.*	35°12N 114°34W	79 K12
Davis Inlet *Canada*	55°50N 60°59W	73 A7
Davis Mts. *U.S.A.*	30°50N 103°55W	84 F3
Davis Sea *Antarctica*	66°0S 92°0E	5 C7
Davis Str. *N. Amer.*	65°0N 58°0W	69 D19
Davos *Switz.*	46°48N 9°49E	20 C8
Davy L. *Canada*	58°53N 108°18W	71 B7
Davyd Haradok *Belarus*	52°4N 27°8E	17 B14
Dawei = Tavoy *Burma*	14°2N 98°12E	38 E2
Dawes Ra. *Australia*	24°40S 150°40E	62 C5
Dawlish *U.K.*	50°35N 3°28W	13 G4
Dawna Ra. *Burma*	16°30N 98°30E	38 D2
Dawros Hd. *Ireland*	54°50N 8°33W	10 B3
Dawson *U.S.A.*	31°46N 84°27W	85 F12
Dawson, I. *Chile*	53°50S 70°50W	96 G2
Dawson B. *Canada*	52°53N 100°49W	71 C8
Dawson City *Canada*	64°10N 139°30W	68 E4
Dawson Creek *Canada*	55°45N 120°15W	70 B4
Dawson Inlet *Canada*	61°50N 93°25W	71 A10
Dawson Ra. *Australia*	24°30S 149°48E	62 C4
Dawu *Hubei, China*	31°34N 114°7E	35 B9
Dawu *Sichuan, China*	30°55N 101°10E	34 B3
Dax *France*	43°44N 1°3W	20 E3
Daxian *China*	31°15N 107°23E	34 B6
Daxin *China*	22°50N 107°11E	34 F6
Daxindian *China*	37°30N 120°50E	33 F11
Daxinggou *China*	43°25N 129°40E	33 C15
Daxue Shan *Sichuan, China*	30°30N 101°30E	34 B3
Daxue Shan *Yunnan, China*	23°42N 99°48E	34 F2
Dayao *China*	25°43N 101°20E	34 E3
Daye *China*	30°6N 114°58E	35 B10
Dayi *China*	30°41N 103°29E	34 B4
Dāykondī □ *Afghan.*	34°0N 66°0E	40 C5
Daylesford *Australia*	37°21S 144°9E	63 F3
Dayong *China*	29°11N 110°30E	35 C8
Dayr az Zawr *Syria*	35°20N 40°5E	46 C4
Daysland *Canada*	52°50N 112°20W	70 C6
Dayton *Nev., U.S.A.*	39°14N 119°36W	78 F7
Dayton *Ohio, U.S.A.*	39°45N 84°12W	81 F11
Dayton *Pa., U.S.A.*	40°53N 79°15W	82 F5
Dayton *Tenn., U.S.A.*	35°30N 85°1W	85 D12
Dayton *Wash., U.S.A.*	46°19N 117°59W	76 C5
Dayton *Wyo., U.S.A.*	44°53N 107°16W	76 D10
Daytona Beach *U.S.A.*	29°13N 81°1W	85 G14
Dayu *China*	25°24N 114°22E	35 E10
Dayville *U.S.A.*	44°28N 119°32W	76 D4
Dazhu *China*	30°41N 107°15E	34 B6
Dazu *China*	29°40N 105°42E	34 C5
De Aar *S. Africa*	30°39S 24°0E	56 D3
De Funiak Springs *U.S.A.*	30°43N 86°7W	85 F11
De Grey → *Australia*	20°12S 119°13E	60 D2
De Haan *Belgium*	51°16N 3°2E	15 C3
De Hoop *S. Africa*	34°30S 20°28E	56 D3
De Kalb Junction *U.S.A.*	44°30N 75°16W	83 B9
De Land *U.S.A.*	29°2N 81°18W	85 G14
De Leon *U.S.A.*	32°7N 98°32W	84 E5
De Long Mts. *U.S.A.*	68°10N 163°30W	74 B7
De Panne *Belgium*	51°6N 2°34E	15 C2
De Pere *U.S.A.*	44°27N 88°4W	80 C9
De Queen *U.S.A.*	34°2N 94°21W	84 D7
De Quincy *U.S.A.*	30°27N 93°26W	84 F8
De Ruyters *U.S.A.*	42°45N 75°53W	83 D9
De Smet *U.S.A.*	44°23N 97°33W	80 C5
De Soto *U.S.A.*	38°8N 90°34W	80 F8
De Tour Village *U.S.A.*	46°0N 83°56W	81 B12
De Witt *U.S.A.*	34°18N 91°20W	84 D9
Dead Sea *Asia*	31°30N 35°30E	48 D4
Deadwood *U.S.A.*	44°23N 103°44W	80 C2
Deadwood L. *Canada*	59°10N 128°30W	70 B3
Deal *U.K.*	51°13N 1°25E	13 F9
Deal I. *Australia*	39°30S 147°20E	63 F4
Dealesville *S. Africa*	28°41S 25°44E	56 D4
De'an *China*	29°21N 115°46E	35 C10
Dean → *Canada*	52°49N 126°58W	70 C3
Dean, Forest of *U.K.*	51°45N 2°33W	13 F5
Dean Chan. *Canada*	52°30N 127°15W	70 C3
Deán Funes *Argentina*	30°20S 64°20W	94 C3
Dease → *Canada*	59°56N 128°32W	70 B3
Dease L. *Canada*	58°40N 130°5W	70 B2
Dease Lake *Canada*	58°25N 130°6W	70 B2
Death Valley *U.S.A.*	36°15N 116°50W	79 J10
Death Valley △ *U.S.A.*	36°29N 117°6W	79 J9
Death Valley Junction *U.S.A.*	36°20N 116°25W	79 J10
Deatnu = Tana → *Norway*	70°30N 28°14E	8 A23
Debagram *India*	23°41N 88°18E	43 H13
Debao *China*	23°21N 106°46E	34 F6
Debar *Macedonia*	41°31N 20°30E	23 D9
Debden *Canada*	53°30N 106°50W	71 C7
Dębica *Poland*	50°2N 21°25E	17 C11
DeBolt *Canada*	55°12N 118°1W	70 B5
Deborah East, L. *Australia*	30°45S 119°30E	61 F2
Deborah West, L. *Australia*	30°45S 119°5E	61 F2
Debre Markos *Ethiopia*	10°20N 37°40E	49 E2
Debre Tabor *Ethiopia*	11°50N 38°26E	49 E2
Debre Zeyit *Ethiopia*	8°50N 39°0E	49 F2
Debrecen *Hungary*	47°33N 21°42E	17 E11
Decatur *Ala., U.S.A.*	34°36N 86°59W	85 D11
Decatur *Ill., U.S.A.*	39°51N 88°57W	80 F9
Decatur *Ind., U.S.A.*	40°50N 84°56W	81 E11
Decatur *Tex., U.S.A.*	33°14N 97°35W	84 E6
Deccan *India*	18°0N 79°0E	44 F4
Deception Bay *Australia*	27°10S 153°5E	63 D5
Deception I. *Antarctica*	63°0S 60°15W	5 C17
Deception L. *Canada*	56°33N 104°13W	71 B8
Dechang *China*	27°25N 102°11E	34 D4
Dechhu *India*	26°46N 72°20E	42 F5
Děčín *Czech Rep.*	50°47N 14°12E	16 C8
Deckerville *U.S.A.*	43°32N 82°44W	82 C2
Decorah *U.S.A.*	43°18N 91°48W	80 D8
Dedéagach = Alexandroupoli *Greece*	40°50N 25°54E	23 D11
Dee → *Aberds., U.K.*	57°9N 2°5W	11 D6
Dee → *Dumf. & Gall., U.K.*	54°51N 4°3W	11 G4
Dee → *Wales, U.K.*	53°22N 3°17W	12 D4
Deep B. *Canada*	61°15N 116°35W	70 A5
Deep Bay = Shenzhen Wan *China*	22°27N 113°55E	31 a
Deepwater *Australia*	29°25S 151°51E	63 D5
Deer → *Canada*	58°23N 94°13W	71 B10
Deer L. *Canada*	52°40N 94°20W	71 C10
Deer Lake *Nfld. & L., Canada*	49°11N 57°27W	73 C8
Deer Lake *Ont., Canada*	52°36N 94°20W	71 C10
Deer Lodge *U.S.A.*	46°24N 112°44W	76 C7
Deer Park *U.S.A.*	47°57N 117°28W	76 C5
Deer River *U.S.A.*	47°20N 93°48W	80 B7
Deeragun *Australia*	19°16S 146°33E	62 B4
Defiance *U.S.A.*	41°17N 84°22W	81 E11
Degana *India*	26°50N 74°20E	42 F6
Dêgê *China*	31°44N 98°39E	34 B2
Dégelis *Canada*	47°30N 68°35W	73 C6
Deggendorf *Germany*	48°50N 12°57E	16 D7
Degh → *Pakistan*	31°3N 73°21E	42 D5
Deh Bīd *Iran*	30°39N 53°11E	47 D7
Deh Dasht *Iran*	30°47N 50°33E	47 D6
Deh-e Shīr *Iran*	31°29N 53°45E	47 D7
Dehaj *Iran*	30°42N 54°53E	47 D7
Dehak *Iran*	27°11N 62°37E	47 E9
Dehdez *Iran*	31°43N 50°17E	47 D6
Dehej *India*	21°44N 72°40E	42 J5
Dehestān *Iran*	28°30N 55°35E	47 D7
Dehgolān *Iran*	35°17N 47°25E	46 C5
Dehibat *Tunisia*	32°0N 10°47E	53 B8
Dehiwala *Sri Lanka*	6°50N 79°51E	45 L4
Dehlorān *Iran*	32°41N 47°16E	46 C5
Dehnow-e Kühestān *Iran*	27°58N 58°32E	47 E8
Dehra Dun *India*	30°20N 78°4E	42 D8
Dehri *India*	24°50N 84°15E	43 G11
Dehua *China*	25°26N 118°1E	35 E12
Dehui *China*	44°30N 125°40E	33 B13
Deinze *Belgium*	50°59N 3°32E	15 D3
Deir al Balah *Gaza Strip*	31°25N 34°21E	48 D3
Dej *Romania*	47°10N 23°52E	17 E12
Dejiang *China*	28°18N 108°7E	34 C7
Deka → *Zimbabwe*	18°4S 26°42E	56 A4
DeKalb *U.S.A.*	41°56N 88°46W	80 E9
Dekese *Dem. Rep. of the Congo*	3°24S 21°24E	54 E4
Del Mar *U.S.A.*	32°58N 117°16W	79 N9
Del Norte *U.S.A.*	37°41N 106°21W	77 H10
Del Rio *U.S.A.*	29°22N 100°54W	84 G4
Delambre I. *Australia*	20°26S 117°5E	60 D2
Delano *U.S.A.*	35°46N 119°15W	79 K7
Delano Peak *U.S.A.*	38°22N 112°22W	76 G7
Delareyville *S. Africa*	26°41S 25°26E	56 C4
Delaronde L. *Canada*	54°3N 107°3W	71 C7
Delavan *U.S.A.*	42°38N 88°39W	80 D9
Delaware *U.S.A.*	40°18N 83°4W	81 E12
Delaware □ *U.S.A.*	39°0N 75°20W	81 F16
Delaware → *U.S.A.*	39°15N 75°20W	83 G9
Delaware B. *U.S.A.*	39°0N 75°10W	81 F16
Delaware Water Gap △ *U.S.A.*	41°10N 74°55W	83 E10
Delay → *Canada*	56°56N 71°28W	73 A5
Delegate *Australia*	37°4S 148°56E	63 F4
Delevan *U.S.A.*	42°29N 78°29W	82 D6
Delft *Neths.*	52°1N 4°22E	15 B4
Delft I. *Sri Lanka*	9°30N 79°40E	45 K4
Delfzijl *Neths.*	53°20N 6°55E	15 A6
Delgado, C. *Mozam.*	10°45S 40°40E	54 G8
Delgerhet *Mongolia*	45°50N 110°30E	32 B6
Delgo *Sudan*	20°6N 30°40E	53 D12
Delhi *Canada*	42°51N 80°30W	82 D4
Delhi *India*	28°38N 77°17E	42 E7
Delhi *La., U.S.A.*	32°28N 91°30W	84 E9
Delhi *N.Y., U.S.A.*	42°17N 74°55W	83 D10
Delia *Canada*	51°38N 112°23W	70 C6
Delice *Turkey*	39°54N 34°2E	19 G5
Delicias *Mexico*	28°13N 105°28W	86 B3
Delījān *Iran*	33°59N 50°40E	47 C6
Delisle *Canada*	51°55N 107°8W	71 C7
Deliverance I. *Australia*	9°31S 141°34E	62 a
Dell City *U.S.A.*	31°56N 105°12W	84 F2
Dell Rapids *U.S.A.*	43°50N 96°43W	80 D5
Delmar *U.S.A.*	42°37N 73°47W	83 D11
Delmenhorst *Germany*	53°3N 8°37E	16 B5
Delonga, Ostrova *Russia*	76°40N 149°20E	27 B15
Deloraine *Australia*	41°30S 146°40E	63 G4
Deloraine *Canada*	49°15N 100°29W	71 D8
Delphi *U.S.A.*	40°36N 86°41W	80 E10
Delphos *U.S.A.*	40°51N 84°21W	81 E11
Delportshoop *S. Africa*	28°22S 24°20E	56 C3
Delray Beach *U.S.A.*	26°28N 80°4W	85 H14
Delta *Colo., U.S.A.*	38°44N 108°4W	76 G9
Delta *Utah, U.S.A.*	39°21N 112°35W	76 G7
Delta Dunărea △ *Romania*	45°15N 29°25E	17 F15
Delta Junction *U.S.A.*	64°2N 145°44W	68 E2
Deltona *U.S.A.*	28°54N 81°16W	85 G14
Delungra *Australia*	29°39S 150°51E	63 D5
Delvada *India*	20°46N 71°2E	42 J4
Delvinë *Albania*	39°59N 20°6E	23 E9
Demak *Indonesia*	6°53S 110°38E	37 G14
Demanda, Sierra de la *Spain*	42°15N 3°0W	21 A4
Demavend = Damāvand, Qolleh-ye *Iran*	35°56N 52°10E	47 C7
Dembidolo *Ethiopia*	8°34N 34°50E	49 F1
Demchok *India*	32°42N 79°29E	43 C8
Demer → *Belgium*	50°57N 4°42E	15 D4
Deming *N. Mex., U.S.A.*	32°16N 107°46W	77 K10
Deming *Wash., U.S.A.*	48°50N 122°13W	78 B4
Demini → *Brazil*	0°46S 62°56W	92 D6
Demirci *Turkey*	39°2N 28°38E	23 E13
Demirköy *Turkey*	41°49N 27°45E	23 D12
Demopolis *U.S.A.*	32°31N 87°50W	85 E11
Dempo *Indonesia*	4°2S 103°15E	36 E2
Den Bosch = 's-Hertogenbosch *Neths.*	51°42N 5°17E	15 C5
Den Burg *Neths.*	53°3N 4°47E	15 A4
Den Chai *Thailand*	17°59N 100°4E	38 D3
Den Haag = 's-Gravenhage *Neths.*	52°7N 4°17E	15 B4
Den Helder *Neths.*	52°57N 4°45E	15 B4
Den Oever *Neths.*	52°56N 5°2E	15 B5
Denair *U.S.A.*	37°32N 120°48W	78 H6
Denali = McKinley, Mt. *U.S.A.*	63°4N 151°0W	68 E1
Denau = Denov *Uzbekistan*	38°16N 67°54E	26 F7
Denbigh *Canada*	45°8N 77°15W	82 A7
Denbigh *U.K.*	53°12N 3°25W	12 D4
Denbighshire □ *U.K.*	53°8N 3°22W	12 D4
Dendang *Indonesia*	3°7S 107°56E	36 E3
Dendermonde *Belgium*	51°2N 4°5E	15 C4
Dengchuan *China*	25°59N 100°3E	34 E3
Dengfeng *China*	34°25N 113°2E	32 G7
Dengkou *China*	40°18N 106°55E	32 D4
Dengzhou *China*	32°34N 112°4E	32 H7
Denham *Australia*	25°56S 113°31E	61 E1
Denham, Mt. *Jamaica*	18°13N 77°32W	88 a
Denham Ra. *Australia*	21°55S 147°46E	62 C4
Denham Sd. *Australia*	25°45S 113°15E	61 E1
Denholm *Canada*	52°39N 108°1W	71 C7
Denia *Spain*	38°49N 0°8E	21 C6
Denial B. *Australia*	32°14S 133°32E	63 E1
Deniliquin *Australia*	35°30S 144°58E	63 F3
Denimoo = Fort Resolution *Canada*	61°10N 113°40W	70 A6
Denison *Iowa, U.S.A.*	42°1N 95°21W	80 D6
Denison *Tex., U.S.A.*	33°45N 96°33W	84 E6
Denison Plains *Australia*	18°35S 128°0E	60 C4
Deniyaya *Sri Lanka*	6°21N 80°33E	45 L5
Denizli *Turkey*	37°42N 29°2E	19 G4
Denman Glacier *Antarctica*	66°45S 100°0E	5 C8
Denmark *Australia*	34°59S 117°25E	61 F2
Denmark ■ *Europe*	55°45N 10°0E	9 J14
Denmark Str. *Atl. Oc.*	66°0N 30°0W	66 C17
Dennery *St. Lucia*	13°55N 60°54W	89 f
Dennison *U.S.A.*	40°24N 81°19W	82 F3
Denny *U.K.*	56°1N 3°55W	11 E5
Denov *Uzbekistan*	38°16N 67°54E	26 F7
Denpasar *Indonesia*	8°39S 115°13E	37 K18
Denpasar ✈ (DPS) *Indonesia*	8°44S 115°10E	37 K18
Denton *Mont., U.S.A.*	47°19N 109°57W	76 C9
Denton *Tex., U.S.A.*	33°13N 97°8W	84 E6
D'Entrecasteaux, Pt. *Australia*	34°50S 115°57E	61 F2
D'Entrecasteaux △ *Australia*	34°20S 115°33E	61 F2
D'Entrecasteaux Is. *Papua N. G.*	9°0S 151°0E	58 B8
Denver *Colo., U.S.A.*	39°42N 104°59W	76 G11
Denver *Pa., U.S.A.*	40°14N 76°8W	83 F8
Denver City *U.S.A.*	32°58N 102°50W	84 E3
Deoband *India*	29°42N 77°43E	42 E7
Deobhog *India*	19°53N 82°44E	44 E6
Deodrug *India*	16°26N 76°55E	45 F3
Deogarh *Odisha, India*	21°32N 84°45E	44 D7
Deogarh *Raj., India*	25°32N 73°54E	42 G5
Deoghar *India*	24°30N 86°42E	43 G12
Deolali *India*	19°58N 73°50E	44 E1
Deoli = Devli *India*	25°50N 75°20E	42 G6
Deora *India*	26°22N 70°55E	42 F4
Deori *India*	23°24N 79°1E	43 H8
Deoria *India*	26°31N 83°48E	43 F10
Deosai Mts. *Pakistan*	35°40N 75°0E	43 B6
Deosri *India*	26°46N 90°29E	43 F14
Depalpur *India*	22°51N 75°33E	42 H6
Deposit *U.S.A.*	42°4N 75°25W	83 D9
Depuch I. *Australia*	20°37S 117°44E	60 D2
Deputatskiy *Russia*	69°18N 139°54E	27 C14
Dêqên *China*	28°34N 98°51E	34 C2
Deqing *China*	23°8N 111°42E	35 F8
Dera Ghazi Khan *Pakistan*	30°5N 70°43E	42 D4
Dera Ismail Khan *Pakistan*	31°50N 70°50E	42 D4
Derabugti *Pakistan*	29°2N 69°9E	42 E3
Derawar Fort *Pakistan*	28°46N 71°20E	42 E4
Derbent *Russia*	42°5N 48°15E	19 F8
Derby *Australia*	17°18S 123°38E	60 C3
Derby *U.K.*	52°56N 1°28E	12 E6
Derby *Conn., U.S.A.*	41°19N 73°5W	83 E11
Derby *Kans., U.S.A.*	37°33N 97°16W	80 G5
Derby *N.Y., U.S.A.*	42°41N 78°58W	82 D6
Derby City □ *U.K.*	52°56N 1°28E	12 E6
Derby Line *U.S.A.*	45°0N 72°6W	83 B12
Derbyshire □ *U.K.*	53°11N 1°38W	12 D6
Derdepoort *S. Africa*	24°38S 26°24E	56 B4
Dereham *U.K.*	52°41N 0°57E	13 E8
Derg → *U.K.*	54°44N 7°26W	10 B4
Derg, L. *Ireland*	53°0N 8°20W	10 D3
Deridder *U.S.A.*	30°51N 93°17W	84 F8
Dermott *U.S.A.*	33°32N 91°26W	84 E9
Dêrong *China*	28°44N 99°9E	34 C2
Derry = Londonderry *U.K.*	55°0N 7°20W	10 B4
Derry = Londonderry □ *U.K.*	55°0N 7°20W	10 B4
Derry *N.H., U.S.A.*	42°53N 71°19W	83 D13
Derry *Pa., U.S.A.*	40°20N 79°18W	82 F5
Derryveagh Mts. *Ireland*	54°56N 8°11W	10 B3
Derwent → *Cumb., U.K.*	54°39N 3°33W	12 C4
Derwent → *Derby, U.K.*	52°57N 1°28W	12 E6
Derwent → *N. Yorks., U.K.*	53°45N 0°58W	12 D7
Derwent Water *U.K.*	54°35N 3°9W	12 C4
Des Moines *Iowa, U.S.A.*	41°35N 93°37W	80 E7
Des Moines *N. Mex., U.S.A.*	36°46N 103°50W	77 H12
Des Moines *Wash., U.S.A.*	47°24N 122°19W	78 C4
Des Moines → *U.S.A.*	40°23N 91°25W	80 E8
Desaguadero → *Argentina*	34°30S 66°46W	94 C2
Desaguadero → *Bolivia*	16°35S 69°5W	92 G5
Desaru *Malaysia*	1°31N 104°17E	39 d
Descanso, Pta. *Mexico*	32°21N 117°3W	79 N9
Deschaillons-sur-St-Laurent *Canada*	46°32N 72°7W	73 C5
Deschambault L. *Canada*	54°50N 103°30W	71 C8
Deschutes → *U.S.A.*	45°38N 120°55W	76 D3
Dese *Ethiopia*	11°5N 39°40E	49 E2
Deseado → *Argentina*	47°45S 65°54W	96 F3
Deseronto *Canada*	44°12N 77°3W	82 B7
Desert Center *U.S.A.*	33°43N 115°24W	79 M11
Desert Hot Springs *U.S.A.*	33°58N 116°30W	79 M10
Deshnok *India*	27°48N 73°21E	42 F5
Desierto Central de Baja California △ *Mexico*	29°40N 114°50W	86 B2
Desna → *Ukraine*	50°33N 30°32E	17 C16
Desolación, I. *Chile*	53°0S 74°0W	96 G2
Despeñaperros, Paso *Spain*	38°24N 3°30W	21 C4
Dessau *Germany*	51°51N 12°14E	16 C7
Dessye = Dese *Ethiopia*	11°5N 39°40E	49 E2
D'Estrees B. *Australia*	35°55S 137°45E	63 F2
Desuri *India*	25°18N 73°35E	42 G5
Det Udom *Thailand*	14°54N 105°5E	38 E5
Dete *Zimbabwe*	18°38S 26°50E	56 A4
Detmold *Germany*	51°56N 8°52E	16 C5
Detour, Pt. *U.S.A.*	45°40N 86°40W	80 C10
Detroit *U.S.A.*	42°19N 83°12W	82 D1
Detroit Lakes *U.S.A.*	46°49N 95°51W	80 B6
Deua △ *Australia*	35°32S 149°46E	63 F4
Deurne *Neths.*	51°27N 5°49E	15 C5
Deutsche Bucht *Germany*	54°15N 8°0E	16 A5
Deutschland = Germany ■ *Europe*	51°0N 10°0E	16 C6
Deva *Romania*	45°53N 22°55E	17 F12
Devakottai *India*	9°55N 78°45E	45 K4
Devaprayag *India*	30°13N 78°35E	43 D8
Devarkonda *India*	16°42N 78°56E	44 F4
Deventer *Neths.*	52°15N 6°10E	15 B6
Deveron → *U.K.*	57°41N 2°32W	11 D6
Devgad I. *India*	14°48N 74°5E	45 G2
Devgadh Bariya *India*	22°40N 73°55E	42 H5
Devgarh *India*	16°23N 73°23E	45 F1
Devi → *India*	19°59N 86°24E	44 E8
Devikot *India*	26°42N 71°12E	42 F4
Devils Den *U.S.A.*	35°46N 119°58W	78 K7
Devils Hole = Death Valley △ *U.S.A.*	36°29N 117°6W	79 J9
Devils Lake *U.S.A.*	48°7N 98°52W	80 A4
Devils Paw *Canada*	58°47N 134°0W	70 B2
Devils Postpile △ *U.S.A.*	37°37N 119°5W	78 H7
Devil's Pt. *Sri Lanka*	9°26N 80°6E	45 K5
Devils Tower *U.S.A.*	44°35N 104°42W	76 D11
Devils Tower △ *U.S.A.*	44°48N 104°55W	76 D11
Devine *U.S.A.*	29°8N 98°54W	84 G5
Devipattinam *India*	9°29N 78°54E	45 K4
Devizes *U.K.*	51°22N 1°58W	13 F6
Devli *India*	25°50N 75°20E	42 G6
Devon *Canada*	53°24N 113°44W	70 C6
Devon □ *U.K.*	50°50N 3°40W	13 G4
Devon I. *Canada*	75°10N 85°0W	69 B15
Devonport *Australia*	41°10S 146°22E	63 G4
Devonport *N.Z.*	36°49S 174°49E	59 B5
Devrukh *India*	17°3N 73°37E	44 F1
Dewas *India*	22°59N 76°3E	42 H7
Dewetsdorp *S. Africa*	29°33S 26°39E	56 C4
Dewey *Puerto Rico*	18°18N 65°18W	89 d
Dexing *China*	28°46N 117°30E	35 C11
Dexter *Maine, U.S.A.*	45°1N 69°18W	81 C19
Dexter *Mo., U.S.A.*	36°48N 89°57W	80 G9
Dexter *N. Mex., U.S.A.*	33°12N 104°22W	77 K11
Dey-Dey, L. *Australia*	29°12S 131°4E	61 E5
Deyang *China*	31°3N 104°27E	34 B5
Deyhūk *Iran*	33°15N 57°30E	47 C8
Deyyer *Iran*	27°55N 51°55E	47 E6
Dez → *Iran*	31°39N 48°52E	47 D6
Dezadeash L. *Canada*	60°28N 136°58W	70 A1
Dezfūl *Iran*	32°20N 48°30E	47 C6
Dezhneva, Mys *Russia*	66°5N 169°40W	27 C19
Dezhou *China*	37°26N 116°18E	32 F9
Dhadhar → *India*	24°56N 85°24E	43 G11
Dhahiriya = Aẓ Ẓāhirīyah *West Bank*	31°25N 34°58E	48 D3
Dhahran = Aẓ Ẓahrān *Si. Arabia*	26°10N 50°7E	47 E6
Dhak *Pakistan*	32°25N 72°33E	42 C5
Dhaka *Bangla.*	23°43N 90°26E	43 H14
Dhaka □ *Bangla.*	24°25N 90°25E	43 G14
Dhamangaon *India*	20°48N 78°9E	44 D4
Dhamār *Yemen*	14°30N 44°20E	49 E3
Dhamnod *India*	29°19N 78°33E	43 E8
Dhampur *India*	20°47N 86°58E	44 D8
Dhamra → *India*	20°42N 81°35E	44 D5
Dhamtari *India*	23°50N 86°30E	43 H12
Dhanbad *India*	28°55N 80°40E	43 E9
Dhangarhi *Nepal*	26°55N 87°40E	43 F12
Dhankuta *Nepal*	20°20N 80°22E	44 D5
Dhanora *India*	9°11N 79°24E	45 K4
Dhanushkodi *India*	22°35N 75°26E	42 H6
Dhar *India*	31°57N 75°18E	42 H6
Dharampur *India*	30°16N 76°23E	42 C7
Dharamsala = Dharmsala *India*	26°49N 87°17E	43 F12
Dharan *Nepal*	21°1N 75°6E	44 D2
Dharangaon *India*	10°45N 77°34E	45 J3
Dharapuram *India*	31°57N 75°19E	42 D6
Dharla → *Bangla.*	25°46N 89°42E	43 G13
Dharmapuri *India*	12°10N 78°10E	45 H4
Dharmavaram *India*	14°29N 77°44E	45 G3
Dharmjaygarh *India*	22°28N 83°13E	43 H10
Dharni *India*	21°33N 76°53E	42 J7
Dharur *India*	18°3N 76°58E	44 E3
Dharwad *India*	15°30N 75°4E	45 G2
Dhasan → *India*	25°48N 79°24E	43 G8
Dhaulagiri *Nepal*	28°39N 83°28E	43 E10
Dhebar, L. *India*	24°10N 74°0E	42 G6

Dhenkanal India 20°45N 85°35E 44 D7
Dhī Qār □ Iraq 31°0N 46°15E 46 D5
Dhībān Jordan 31°30N 35°46E 48 D4
Dhilwan India 31°31N 75°21E 42 D6
Dhimarkhera India 23°28N 80°22E 43 H9
Dhodhekánisos = Dodecanese
 Greece 36°35N 27°0E 23 F12
Dholka India 22°44N 72°29E 42 H5
Dhond = Daund India 18°26N 74°40E 44 E2
Dhone India 15°25N 77°53E 45 E3
Dhoraji India 21°45N 70°37E 42 J4
Dhorpatan Nepal 28°29N 83°4E 43 E10
Dhrangadhra India 22°59N 71°31E 42 H4
Dhrol India 22°33N 70°25E 42 H4
Dhuburi India 26°2N 89°59E 41 F16
Dhule India 20°58N 74°50E 44 D2
Di Linh Vietnam 11°35N 108°4E 39 G7
Di Linh, Cao Nguyen
 Vietnam 11°30N 108°0E 39 G7
Diablo Range U.S.A. 37°20N 121°25W 78 J5
Diafarabé Mali 14°9N 4°57W 52 F5
Diamante Argentina 32°5S 60°40W 94 C3
Diamante → Argentina 34°30S 66°46W 94 C2
Diamantina Brazil 18°17S 43°40W 93 G10
Diamantina →
 Australia 26°45S 139°10E 63 D2
Diamantina △ Australia 23°33S 141°23E 62 C3
Diamantino Brazil 14°30S 56°30W 93 F7
Diamond Bar U.S.A. 34°1N 117°48W 79 L9
Diamond Harbour India 22°11N 88°14E 43 H13
Diamond Is. Australia 17°25S 151°5E 62 B5
Diamond Mts. U.S.A. 39°40N 115°50W 76 G6
Diamond Springs
 U.S.A. 38°42N 120°49W 78 G6
Dian Chi China 24°50N 102°43E 34 E4
Dianbai China 21°33N 111°0E 35 G8
Diancheng China 21°30N 111°4E 35 G8
Dianjiang China 30°24N 107°20E 34 B6
Diaoyu Dao = Senkaku-Shotō
 E. China Sea 25°45N 123°30E 29 M1
Diaoyu Tai = Senkaku-Shotō
 E. China Sea 25°45N 123°30E 29 M1
Diavolo, Mt. India 12°40N 92°56E 45 H11
Diba = Dibbā al Ḥiṣn
 U.A.E. 25°45N 56°16E 47 E8
Dibai India 28°13N 78°15E 42 E8
Dibaya
 Dem. Rep. of the Congo 6°30S 22°57E 54 F4
Dibaya-Lubue
 Dem. Rep. of the Congo 4°12S 19°54E 54 E3
Dibbā al Ḥiṣn U.A.E. 25°45N 56°16E 47 E8
Dibbeen △ Jordan 32°20N 35°45E 48 C4
D'Iberville, Lac Canada 55°55N 73°15W 72 A5
Dibete Botswana 23°45S 26°32E 56 B4
Dibrugarh India 27°29N 94°55E 41 F19
Dickens U.S.A. 33°37N 100°50W 84 E4
Dickinson U.S.A. 46°53N 102°47W 80 B2
Dickson U.S.A. 36°5N 87°23W 85 C11
Dickson City U.S.A. 41°28N 75°36W 83 E9
Didiéni Mali 13°53N 8°6W 52 F4
Didsbury Canada 51°35N 114°10W 70 C6
Didwana India 27°23N 74°36E 42 F6
Diefenbaker, L. Canada 51°0N 106°55W 71 C7
Diego de Almagro Chile 26°22S 70°3W 94 B1
Diego Suarez = Antsiranana
 Madag. 12°25S 49°20E 55 G9
Diekirch Lux. 49°52N 6°10E 15 E6
Dien Ban Vietnam 15°53N 108°16E 38 E7
Dien Bien Phu Vietnam 21°20N 103°0E 34 G4
Dien Chau, Vinh Vietnam 19°0N 105°55E 38 C5
Dien Khanh Vietnam 12°15N 109°6E 39 F7
Dieppe France 49°54N 1°4E 20 B4
Dierks U.S.A. 34°7N 94°1W 84 D7
Diest Belgium 50°58N 5°4E 15 D5
Dif Somalia 0°59N 40°58E 49 G3
Differdange Lux. 49°31N 5°54E 15 E5
Dig India 27°28N 77°20E 42 F7
Digby Canada 44°38N 65°50W 73 D6
Digges Is. Canada 62°40N 77°50W 69 E16
Diggi India 26°22N 75°26E 42 F6
Dighinala Bangla. 23°15N 92°5E 41 H18
Dighton U.S.A. 38°29N 100°28W 80 F3
Diglur India 18°34N 77°32E 44 E3
Digne-les-Bains France 44°5N 6°12E 20 D7
Digos Phil. 6°45N 125°20E 37 C7
Digranes Iceland 66°4N 14°44W 8 C6
Digras India 20°6N 77°45E 44 D3
Digul → Indonesia 7°7S 138°42E 37 F9
Dihang = Brahmaputra →
 Asia 23°40N 90°35E 43 H13
Dijlah, Nahr → Asia 31°0N 47°25E 46 D5
Dijon France 47°20N 5°3E 20 C6
Dikhil Djibouti 11°8N 42°20E 49 E3
Dikkil = Dikhil Djibouti 11°8N 42°20E 49 E3
Diksmuide Belgium 51°2N 2°52E 15 C2
Dikson Russia 73°40N 80°5E 26 B9
Dikti Oros Greece 35°8N 25°30E 23 G11
Dila Ethiopia 6°21N 38°22E 49 F2
Dili E. Timor 8°39S 125°34E 37 F7
Diligent Strait India 12°40N 92°56E 45 H11
Dilley U.S.A. 28°40N 99°10W 84 G5
Dillingham U.S.A. 59°3N 158°28W 74 D8
Dillon Canada 55°56N 108°35W 71 B7
Dillon Mont., U.S.A. 45°13N 112°38W 76 D7
Dillon S.C., U.S.A. 34°25N 79°22W 85 D15
Dillon → Canada 55°56N 108°56W 71 B7
Dillsburg U.S.A. 40°7N 77°2W 82 F7
Dilolo
 Dem. Rep. of the Congo 10°28S 22°18E 54 G4
Dimapur India 25°54N 93°45E 41 F18
Dimas Mexico 23°43N 106°47W 86 C3
Dimashq Syria 33°30N 36°18E 48 B5
Dimashq □ Syria 33°30N 36°30E 48 B5
Dimbaza S. Africa 32°50S 27°14E 57 D4
Dimboola Australia 36°28S 142°7E 63 F3
Dîmbovița = Dâmbovița →
 Romania 44°12N 26°26E 17 F14
Dimbulah Australia 17°8S 145°4E 62 B4
Dimitrovgrad Bulgaria 42°5N 25°35E 23 C11

Dimitrovgrad Russia 54°14N 49°39E 18 D8
Dimitrovo = Pernik
 Bulgaria 42°35N 23°2E 23 C10
Dimmitt U.S.A. 34°33N 102°19W 84 D3
Dimona Israel 31°2N 35°1E 48 D4
Dinagat I. Phil. 10°10N 125°40E 37 B7
Dinajpur Bangla. 25°33N 88°43E 41 G16
Dinan France 48°28N 2°2W 20 B2
Dīnān Āb Iran 32°4N 56°49E 47 C8
Dinant Belgium 50°16N 4°55E 15 D4
Dinapur India 25°38N 85°5E 43 G11
Dīnār, Kūh-e Iran 30°42N 51°46E 47 D6
Dinara Planina Croatia 44°0N 16°30E 22 C7
Dinard France 48°38N 2°6W 20 B2
Dinaric Alps = Dinara Planina
 Croatia 44°0N 16°30E 22 C7
Dinbych-y-Pysgod = Tenby
 U.K. 51°40N 4°42W 13 F3
Dindi → India 16°24N 78°15E 45 F4
Dindigul India 10°25N 78°0E 45 J4
Dindori India 22°57N 81°5E 43 H9
Ding Xian = Dingzhou
 China 38°30N 114°59E 32 E8
Dinga Pakistan 25°26N 67°10E 42 G2
Ding'an China 19°42N 110°19E 38 C8
Dingbian China 37°35N 107°32E 32 F4
Dingle Ireland 52°9N 10°17W 10 D1
Dingle B. Ireland 52°3N 10°20W 10 D1
Dingle Pen. Ireland 52°12N 10°5W 10 D1
Dingmans Ferry U.S.A. 41°13N 74°55W 83 E10
Dingnan China 24°45N 115°0E 35 E10
Dingo Australia 23°38S 149°19E 62 C4
Dingtao China 35°5N 115°35E 32 G8
Dingwall U.K. 57°36N 4°26W 11 D4
Dingxi China 35°30N 104°33E 32 G3
Dingxiang China 38°30N 112°58E 32 E7
Dingyuan China 32°32N 117°41E 35 A11
Dingzhou China 38°30N 114°59E 32 E8
Dinh, Mui Vietnam 11°22N 109°1E 39 G7
Dinh Lap Vietnam 21°33N 107°6E 34 G6
Dinin → Ireland 52°43N 7°18W 10 D4
Dinira △ Venezuela 9°57N 70°6W 89 E6
Dinokwe Botswana 23°29S 26°37E 56 B4
Dinorwic Canada 49°41N 92°30W 71 D10
Dinosaur △ Canada 50°47N 111°30W 70 C6
Dinosaur △ U.S.A. 40°30N 108°45W 76 F9
Dinuba U.S.A. 36°32N 119°23W 78 J7
Diourbel Senegal 14°39N 16°12W 52 F2
Dipalpur Pakistan 30°40N 73°39E 42 D5
Diplo Pakistan 24°35N 69°35E 42 G3
Dipolog Phil. 8°36N 123°20E 37 C6
Dipperu △ Australia 21°56S 148°42E 62 C4
Dir Pakistan 35°8N 71°59E 40 B7
Dire Dawa Ethiopia 9°35N 41°45E 49 F3
Dirfis Oros Greece 38°40N 23°54E 23 E10
Diriamba Nic. 11°51N 86°19W 88 D2
Dirk Hartog I. Australia 25°50S 113°5E 61 E1
Dirranbandi Australia 28°33S 148°17E 63 D4
Disa India 24°18N 72°10E 42 G5
Disappointment, C.
 U.S.A. 46°18N 124°5W 78 D2
Disappointment, L.
 Australia 23°20S 122°40E 60 D3
Disaster B. Australia 37°15S 149°58E 63 F4
Discovery B. Australia 38°10S 140°40E 63 F3
Discovery B. China 22°18N 114°1E 31 a
Disko = Qeqertarsuaq
 Greenland 69°45N 53°30W 4 C5
Disney Reef Tonga 19°17S 174°7W 59 c
Disneyland Hong Kong
 China 22°18N 114°2E 31 a
Diss U.K. 52°23N 1°7E 13 E9
Disteghil Sar Pakistan 36°20N 75°12E 43 A6
District of Columbia □
 U.S.A. 38°55N 77°0W 81 F15
Distrito Federal □ Brazil 15°45S 47°45W 93 G9
Distrito Federal □
 Mexico 19°15N 99°10W 87 D5
Diu India 20°45N 70°58E 42 J4
Dīvāndarreh Iran 35°55N 47°2E 46 C5
Divi Pt. India 15°59N 81°9E 45 G5
Divide U.S.A. 45°45N 112°45W 76 D7
Dividing Ra. Australia 27°45S 116°0E 61 E2
Divinópolis Brazil 20°10S 44°54W 93 H10
Divnoye Russia 45°55N 43°21E 19 E7
Divo Ivory C. 5°48N 5°15W 52 G4
Dīwāl Kol Afghan. 34°23N 67°52E 42 B2
Dixie Mt. U.S.A. 39°55N 120°16W 78 F6
Dixon Calif., U.S.A. 38°27N 121°49W 78 G5
Dixon Ill., U.S.A. 41°50N 89°29W 80 E9
Dixon Entrance U.S.A. 54°30N 132°0W 68 G5
Dixville Canada 45°4N 71°46W 83 A13
Diyālá □ Iraq 33°45N 44°50E 46 C5
Diyālá → Iraq 33°13N 44°30E 46 C5
Diyarbakır Turkey 37°55N 40°18E 46 B4
Diyodar India 24°8N 71°50E 42 G4
Djamba Angola 16°45S 13°58E 56 A1
Djambala Congo 2°32S 14°30E 54 E2
Djanet Algeria 24°35N 9°32E 52 D7
Djawa = Jawa Indonesia 7°0S 110°0E 36 F3
Djelfa Algeria 34°40N 3°15E 52 B6
Djerba, Î. de Tunisia 33°50N 10°48E 53 B8
Djerid, Chott Tunisia 33°42N 8°30E 52 B7
Djibouti Djibouti 11°30N 43°5E 49 E3
Djibouti ■ Africa 12°0N 43°0E 49 E3
Djolu Dem. Rep. of the Congo 0°35N 22°5E 54 D4
Djougou Benin 9°40N 1°45E 52 G6
Djoum Cameroon 2°41N 12°35E 54 D2
Djourab, Erg du Chad 16°40N 18°50E 53 E9
Djukbinj △ Australia 12°11S 131°2E 60 B5
Djúpivogur Iceland 64°39N 14°17W 8 D6
Dmitriya Lapteva, Proliv
 Russia 73°0N 140°0E 27 B15
Dnepr = Dnipro →
 Ukraine 46°30N 32°18E 19 E5
Dneprodzerzhinsk =
 Dniprodzerzhynsk
 Ukraine 48°32N 34°37E 19 E5
Dnepropetrovsk = Dnipropetrovsk
 Ukraine 48°30N 35°0E 19 E6

Dnestr = Dnister →
 Europe 46°18N 30°17E 17 E16
Dnieper = Dnipro →
 Ukraine 46°30N 32°18E 19 E5
Dniester = Dnister →
 Europe 46°18N 30°17E 17 E16
Dnipro → Ukraine 46°30N 32°18E 19 E5
Dniprodzerzhynsk
 Ukraine 48°32N 34°37E 19 E5
Dnipropetrovsk Ukraine 48°30N 35°0E 19 E6
Dnister → Europe 46°18N 30°17E 17 E16
Dno Russia 57°50N 29°58E 9 H23
Dnyapro = Dnipro →
 Ukraine 46°30N 32°18E 19 E5
Do Gonbadān = Gachsārān
 Iran 30°15N 50°45E 47 D6
Doaktown Canada 46°33N 66°8W 73 C6
Doan Hung Vietnam 21°30N 105°10E 34 G5
Doba Chad 8°40N 16°50E 53 G9
Dobandi Pakistan 31°13N 66°50E 42 D2
Dobbyn Australia 19°44S 140°2E 62 B3
Dobele Latvia 56°37N 23°16E 9 H20
Doberai, Jazirah Indonesia 1°25S 133°0E 37 E8
Doblas Argentina 37°5S 64°0W 94 D3
Dobo Indonesia 5°45S 134°15E 37 F8
Doboj Bos.-H. 44°46N 18°4E 23 B8
Dobrich Bulgaria 43°37N 27°49E 23 C12
Dobruja Europe 44°30N 28°15E 17 F15
Dobrush Belarus 52°25N 31°22E 17 B16
Doc, Mui Vietnam 17°58N 106°30E 38 D6
Docker River = Kaltukatjara
 Australia 24°52S 129°5E 61 D4
Doctor Arroyo Mexico 23°40N 100°11W 86 C4
Doctor Pedro P. Peña
 Paraguay 22°27S 62°21W 94 A3
Doda India 33°10N 75°34E 43 C6
Doda, L. Canada 49°25N 75°13W 72 C4
Doda Betta India 11°24N 76°44E 45 J3
Dodballapur India 13°18N 77°32E 45 H3
Dodecanese = Dodekanisa
 Greece 36°35N 27°0E 23 F12
Dodge City U.S.A. 37°45N 100°1W 80 G3
Dodge L. Canada 59°50N 105°36W 71 B7
Dodgeville U.S.A. 42°58N 90°8W 80 D8
Dodoma Tanzania 6°8S 35°45E 54 F7
Dodsland Canada 51°50N 108°45W 71 C7
Dodson U.S.A. 48°24N 108°15W 76 B9
Doesburg Neths. 52°1N 6°9E 15 B6
Doetinchem Neths. 51°59N 6°18E 15 C6
Dog Creek Canada 51°35N 122°14W 70 C4
Dog L. Man., Canada 51°2N 98°31W 71 C9
Dog L. Ont., Canada 48°48N 89°30W 72 C2
Dogran Pakistan 31°48N 73°35E 42 D5
Doğubayazıt Turkey 39°31N 44°5E 46 B5
Doha = Ad Dawḥah
 Qatar 25°15N 51°35E 47 E6
Dohazari Bangla. 22°10N 92°5E 41 H18
Dohrighat India 26°16N 83°31E 43 F10
Doi Indonesia 2°14N 127°49E 37 D7
Doi Inthanon Thailand 18°35N 98°28E 38 C2
Doi Inthanon △ Thailand 18°33N 98°34E 38 C2
Doi Khuntan △ Thailand 18°33N 99°14E 38 C2
Doi Luang Thailand 18°30N 101°0E 38 C3
Doi Luang △ Thailand 19°22N 99°38E 38 C2
Doi Phukha △ Thailand 19°8N 101°9E 38 C3
Doi Saket Thailand 18°52N 99°9E 38 C2
Doi Suthep Pui △
 Thailand 18°49N 98°53E 38 C2
Doi Toa Thailand 17°55N 98°30E 38 C2
Dois Irmãos, Sa. Brazil 9°0S 42°30W 93 E10
Dokdo = Liancourt Rocks
 Asia 37°15N 131°52E 29 F5
Dokkum Neths. 53°20N 5°59E 15 A5
Dokri Pakistan 27°25N 68°7E 42 F3
Dolak, Pulau Indonesia 8°0S 138°30E 37 F9
Dolbeau-Mistassini
 Canada 48°53N 72°14W 73 C5
Dole France 47°7N 5°31E 20 C6
Dolgellau U.K. 52°45N 3°53W 12 E4
Dolgelley = Dolgellau
 U.K. 52°45N 3°53W 12 E4
Dolinsk Russia 47°21N 142°48E 27 E15
Dollard Neths. 53°20N 7°10E 15 A7
Dolo Ethiopia 4°11N 42°3E 49 G3
Dolomites = Dolomiti
 Italy 46°23N 11°51E 22 A4
Dolomiti Italy 46°23N 11°51E 22 A4
Dolores Argentina 36°20S 57°40W 94 D4
Dolores Uruguay 33°34S 58°15W 94 C4
Dolores U.S.A. 37°28N 108°30W 77 H9
Dolores → U.S.A. 38°49N 108°17W 76 G9
Dolphin, C. Falk. Is. 51°10S 59°0W 96 G5
Dolphin and Union Str.
 Canada 69°5N 114°45W 68 D9
Dom Pedrito Brazil 31°0S 54°40W 95 C5
Domariaganj → India 26°17N 83°44E 43 F10
Dombarovskiy Russia 50°46N 59°32E 26 D6
Dombås Norway 62°4N 9°8E 8 E13
Dome Argus Antarctica 80°50S 76°30E 5 E6
Dome C. Antarctica 75°20S 123°37E 5 D9
Dome Fuji Antarctica 77°20S 39°45E 5 D5
Domel I. = Letsôk-aw Kyun
 Burma 11°30N 98°25E 39 G2
Domeyko Chile 29°0S 71°0W 94 B1
Domeyko, Cordillera
 Chile 24°30S 69°0W 94 A2
Dominador Chile 24°21S 69°20W 94 A2
Dominica ■ W. Indies 15°20N 61°20W 89 C7
Dominica Passage
 W. Indies 15°10N 61°20W 89 C7
Dominican Rep. ■
 W. Indies 19°0N 70°30W 89 C5
Domodóssola Italy 46°7N 8°17E 20 C8
Domville, Mt. Australia 28°1S 151°15E 63 D5
Don → India 16°20N 76°15E 45 F3
Don → Russia 47°4N 39°18E 19 E6
Don → Aberds., U.K. 57°11N 2°5W 11 D6
Don → S. Yorks., U.K. 53°41N 0°52W 12 D7

Don, C. Australia 11°18S 131°46E 60 B5
Don Benito Spain 38°53N 5°51W 21 C3
Don Figuereroa Mts.
 Jamaica 18°5N 77°36W 88 a
Don Sak Thailand 9°18N 99°41E 39 b
Donaghadee U.K. 54°39N 5°33W 10 B6
Donaghmore Ireland 52°52N 7°36W 10 D4
Donald Australia 36°23S 143°0E 63 F3
Donaldsonville U.S.A. 36°59N 90°59W 84 F9
Donalsonville U.S.A. 31°3N 84°53W 85 F12
Donau = Dunărea →
 Europe 45°20N 29°40E 17 F15
Donauwörth Germany 48°43N 10°47E 16 D6
Doncaster U.K. 53°32N 1°6W 12 D6
Dondo Angola 9°45S 14°25E 54 F2
Dondo, Teluk Indonesia 0°50N 120°30E 37 D6
Dondra Head Sri Lanka 5°55N 80°40E 45 M5
Donegal Ireland 54°39N 8°5W 10 B3
Donegal □ Ireland 54°53N 8°0W 10 B4
Donegal B. Ireland 54°31N 8°49W 10 B3
Donets → Russia 47°33N 40°55E 19 E7
Donets Basin Ukraine 49°0N 38°0E 6 F13
Donetsk Ukraine 48°0N 37°45E 19 E6
Dong Ba Thin Vietnam 12°8N 109°13E 39 F7
Dong Dang Vietnam 21°54N 106°42E 34 G6
Dong Giam Vietnam 19°25N 105°31E 38 C5
Dong Ha Vietnam 16°55N 107°8E 38 D6
Dong Hene Laos 16°40N 105°18E 38 D5
Dong Hoi Vietnam 17°29N 106°36E 38 D6
Dong Jiang → China 23°6N 114°0E 35 F10
Dong Khe Vietnam 22°26N 106°27E 38 A6
Dong Phayayen
 Thailand 14°20N 101°22E 38 E3
Dong Ujimqin Qi China 45°32N 116°55E 32 B9
Dong Van Vietnam 23°16N 105°22E 38 A5
Dong Xoai Vietnam 11°32N 106°55E 39 G6
Dong'an China 26°23N 111°12E 35 D8
Dongara Australia 29°14S 114°57E 61 E1
Dongargarh India 21°10N 80°40E 44 D5
Dongbei China 45°0N 125°0E 33 D13
Dongchuan China 26°8N 103°1E 34 D4
Dongfang China 18°50N 108°33E 38 C7
Dongfeng China 42°40N 125°34E 33 C13
Donggala Indonesia 0°30S 119°40E 37 E5
Donggan China 23°22N 105°9E 34 F5
Donggang China 39°52N 124°10E 33 E13
Dongguan China 22°58N 113°44E 35 F9
Dongguang China 37°50N 116°30E 32 F9
Donghae S. Korea 37°29N 129°7E 33 F15
Donghai Dao China 21°0N 110°15E 35 G8
Dongjingcheng China 44°5N 129°10E 33 B15
Dongkou China 27°6N 110°35E 35 D8
Donglan China 24°30N 107°21E 34 E6
Dongliao He → China 42°58N 123°32E 33 C12
Dongliu China 30°13N 116°55E 35 B11
Dongmen China 22°20N 107°48E 34 F6
Dongning China 44°2N 131°5E 33 B16
Dongnyi China 28°3N 100°15E 34 C3
Dongola Sudan 19°9N 30°22E 53 E12
Dongping China 35°55N 116°20E 32 G9
Dongsha Dao
 S. China Sea 20°45N 116°43E 35 G11
Dongshan China 23°43N 117°30E 35 F11
Dongsheng China 39°50N 110°0E 32 E6
Dongtai China 32°51N 120°21E 33 H11
Dongting Hu China 29°18N 112°45E 35 C9
Dongtou China 27°51N 121°10E 35 D13
Dongxiang China 28°11N 116°34E 35 C11
Dongxing China 21°34N 108°0E 34 G7
Dongyang China 29°13N 120°15E 35 C13
Dongying China 37°37N 118°37E 33 F10
Dongyinggang China 37°55N 118°58E 33 F10
Dongzhi China 30°9N 117°0E 35 B11
Donington, C. Australia 34°45S 136°0E 63 E2
Doniphan U.S.A. 36°37N 90°50W 80 G8
Donna Norway 66°6N 12°30E 8 C15
Donna U.S.A. 26°9N 98°4W 84 M5
Donnacona Canada 46°41N 71°41W 73 C5
Donnelly's Crossing
 N.Z. 35°42S 173°38E 59 A4
Donner Pass U.S.A. 39°19N 120°20W 78 F6
Donnybrook Australia 33°34S 115°48E 61 F2
Donnybrook S. Africa 29°59S 29°48E 57 C4
Donora U.S.A. 40°11N 79°52W 82 F5
Donostia = Donostia-San
 Sebastián Spain 43°17N 1°58W 21 A5
Donostia-San Sebastián
 Spain 43°17N 1°58W 21 A5
Donwood Canada 44°19N 78°16W 82 B6
Doomadgee Australia 17°56S 138°49E 62 B2
Doomadgee ☉ Australia 17°56S 138°49E 62 B2
Doon → U.K. 55°27N 4°39W 11 F4
Doon Doon ☉ Australia 16°18S 128°14E 60 C4
Dora, L. Australia 22°0S 123°0E 60 D3
Dora Báltea → Italy 45°11N 8°3E 20 B8
Doran L. Canada 61°13N 108°6W 71 A7
Dorchester, C. Canada 65°27N 77°27W 69 D16
Dordabis Namibia 22°52S 17°38E 56 B2
Dordogne → France 45°2N 0°36W 20 D3
Dordrecht Neths. 51°48N 4°39E 15 C4
Dordrecht S. Africa 31°20S 27°3E 56 D4
Doré L. Canada 54°46N 107°17W 71 C7
Dori Burkina Faso 14°3N 0°2W 52 F5
Doring → S. Africa 31°54S 18°39E 56 D2
Doringbos S. Africa 31°59S 19°16E 56 D2
Dorking U.K. 51°14N 0°19W 13 F7
Dornakal India 17°27N 80°10E 44 F5
Dornbirn Austria 47°25N 9°45E 16 E5
Dornie U.K. 57°17N 5°31W 11 D3
Dornoch Canada 44°18N 80°51W 82 B4
Dornoch U.K. 57°53N 4°2W 11 D4
Dornoch Firth U.K. 57°51N 4°4W 11 D4
Dornogovi □ Mongolia 44°0N 110°0E 32 C6
Doro, Kavo Greece 38°9N 24°38E 23 E11
Dorohoi Romania 47°56N 26°23E 17 E14
Döröö Nuur Mongolia 48°0N 93°0E 30 B7
Dorr Iran 33°17N 50°38E 47 C6
Dorre I. Australia 25°13S 113°12E 61 E1

Dorrigo Australia 30°20S 152°44E 63 E5
Dorris U.S.A. 41°58N 121°55W 76 F3
Dorset Canada 45°14N 78°54W 82 A6
Dorset Ohio, U.S.A. 41°40N 80°40W 82 E4
Dorset Vt., U.S.A. 43°15N 73°5W 83 C11
Dorset □ U.K. 50°45N 2°26W 13 G5
Dortmund Germany 51°30N 7°28E 16 C4
Dörtyol Turkey 36°50N 36°13E 46 B3
Dorūneh Iran 35°10N 57°18E 47 C8
Dos Bahías, C. Argentina 44°58S 65°32W 96 E3
Dos Hermanas Spain 37°16N 5°55W 21 D3
Dos Palos U.S.A. 36°59N 120°37W 78 J6
Dosso Niger 13°0N 3°13E 52 F6
Dothan U.S.A. 31°13N 85°24W 85 F12
Doty U.S.A. 46°38N 123°17W 78 D3
Douai France 50°21N 3°4E 20 A5
Douala Cameroon 4°0N 9°45E 54 D1
Douarnenez France 48°6N 4°21W 20 B1
Double Island Pt.
 Australia 25°56S 153°11E 63 D5
Double Mountain Fork →
 U.S.A. 33°16N 100°0W 84 E4
Doubs → France 46°53N 5°1E 20 C6
Doubtful Sd. N.Z. 45°20S 166°49E 59 F1
Doubtless B. N.Z. 34°55S 173°26E 59 A4
Douglas Canada 45°31N 76°56W 82 A8
Douglas I. of Man 54°10N 4°28W 12 C3
Douglas S. Africa 29°4S 23°46E 56 D3
Douglas Ariz., U.S.A. 31°21N 109°33W 77 L9
Douglas Ga., U.S.A. 31°31N 82°51W 85 F13
Douglas Wyo., U.S.A. 42°45N 105°24W 76 E11
Douglas Apsley △
 Australia 41°45S 148°11E 63 G4
Douglas Chan. Canada 53°40N 129°20W 70 C3
Douglas Pt. Canada 44°19N 81°37W 82 B3
Douglasville U.S.A. 33°45N 84°45W 85 E12
Doumen China 22°10N 113°18E 35 F9
Dounreay U.K. 58°35N 3°44W 11 C5
Dourada, Serra Brazil 13°10S 48°45W 93 F9
Dourados Brazil 22°9S 54°50W 95 A5
Dourados → Brazil 21°58S 54°18W 95 A5
Dourados, Serra dos
 Brazil 23°30S 53°30W 95 A5
Douro → Europe 41°8N 8°40W 21 B1
Dove → U.K. 52°51N 1°36W 12 E6
Dove Creek U.S.A. 37°46N 108°54W 77 H9
Dover Australia 43°18S 147°2E 63 G4
Dover U.K. 51°7N 1°19E 13 F9
Dover Del., U.S.A. 39°10N 75°32W 81 F16
Dover N.H., U.S.A. 43°12N 70°56W 83 C14
Dover N.J., U.S.A. 40°53N 74°34W 83 F10
Dover Ohio, U.S.A. 40°32N 81°29W 82 F3
Dover, Pt. Australia 32°32S 125°32E 61 F4
Dover, Str. of Europe 51°0N 1°30E 13 G9
Dover-Foxcroft U.S.A. 45°11N 69°13W 81 C19
Dover Plains U.S.A. 41°43N 73°35W 83 E11
Dovey = Dyfi → U.K. 52°32N 4°3W 13 E3
Dovrefjell Norway 62°15N 9°33E 8 E13
Dow Rūd Iran 33°28N 49°4E 47 C6
Dowagiac U.S.A. 41°59N 86°6W 80 E10
Dowerin Australia 31°12S 117°2E 61 F2
Dowghā'i Iran 36°54N 58°32E 47 B8
Dowlatābād Kermān, Iran 28°20N 56°40E 47 D8
Dowlatābād Khorāsān,
 Iran 35°16N 59°29E 47 C8
Down □ U.K. 54°23N 6°2W 10 B6
Downey U.S.A. 42°26N 112°7W 76 E7
Downham Market U.K. 52°37N 0°23E 13 E8
Downieville U.S.A. 39°34N 120°50W 78 F6
Downpatrick U.K. 54°20N 5°43W 10 B6
Downpatrick Hd. Ireland 54°20N 9°21W 10 B2
Downsville U.S.A. 42°5N 75°0W 83 D10
Downton, Mt. Canada 52°42N 124°52W 70 C4
Dowsārī Iran 28°25N 57°59E 47 D8
Doyle U.S.A. 40°2N 120°6W 78 E6
Doylestown U.S.A. 40°21N 75°10W 83 F9
Dozois, Rés. Canada 47°30N 77°5W 72 C4
Dra Khel Pakistan 27°58N 66°45E 42 F2
Drâa, C. Morocco 28°47N 11°0W 52 C3
Drâa, Hamada du Algeria 28°30N 11°0W 52 C4
Drâa, Oued → Morocco 28°40N 11°10W 52 C3
Drachten Neths. 53°7N 6°5E 15 A6
Drăgăşani Romania 44°39N 24°17E 17 F13
Dragichyn Belarus 52°15N 25°8E 17 B13
Dragoman, Prokhod
 Bulgaria 42°58N 22°53E 23 C10
Dragon's Mouths
 Trin. & Tob. 11°0N 61°50W 93 K15
Draguignan France 43°32N 6°27E 20 E7
Drain U.S.A. 43°40N 123°19W 76 E2
Drake U.S.A. 47°55N 100°23W 80 B3
Drake Passage S. Ocean 58°0S 68°0W 5 B17
Drakensberg S. Africa 31°0S 28°0E 57 D4
Drama Greece 41°9N 24°10E 23 D11
Drammen Norway 59°42N 10°12E 9 G14
Drangajökull Iceland 66°9N 22°15W 8 C2
Dras India 34°25N 75°48E 43 B6
Drau = Drava → Croatia 45°33N 18°55E 23 B8
Drava → Croatia 45°33N 18°55E 23 B8
Drayton Canada 43°46N 80°40W 82 C4
Drayton Valley Canada 53°12N 114°58W 70 C6
Drenthe □ Neths. 52°52N 6°40E 15 B6
Dresden Canada 42°35N 82°11W 82 D2
Dresden Germany 51°3N 13°44E 16 C7
Dresden U.S.A. 42°41N 76°57W 82 D8
Dreux France 48°44N 1°23E 20 B4
Driffield U.K. 54°0N 0°26W 12 C7
Driftwood U.S.A. 41°20N 78°8W 82 E6
Driggs U.S.A. 43°44N 111°6W 76 E8
Drin → Albania 41°39N 19°32E 23 D8
Drina → Bos.-H. 44°53N 19°21E 23 B8
Drøbak Norway 59°39N 10°39E 9 G14
Drobeta-Turnu Severin
 Romania 44°39N 22°41E 17 F12
Drochia Moldova 48°2N 27°48E 17 D14
Drogheda Ireland 53°43N 6°22W 10 C5
Drogichin = Dragichyn
 Belarus 52°15N 25°8E 17 B13
Drogobych = Drohobych
 Ukraine 49°20N 23°30E 17 D12

Drohobych Ukraine 49°20N 23°30E 17 D12
Droichead Átha = Drogheda
Ireland 53°43N 6°22W 10 C5
Droichead na Bandan = Bandon
Ireland 51°44N 8°44W 10 E3
Droichead Nua = Newbridge
Ireland 53°11N 6°48W 10 C5
Droitwich U.K. 52°16N 2°8W 13 E5
Drôme → France 44°46N 4°46E 20 D6
Dromedary, C. Australia 36°17S 150°10E 63 F5
Dromore Down, U.K. 54°25N 6°9W 10 B5
Dromore Tyrone, U.K. 54°31N 7°28W 10 B4
Dromore West Ireland 54°15N 8°52W 10 B3
Dronfield U.K. 53°19N 1°27W 12 D6
Dronning Maud Land
Antarctica 72°30S 12°0E 5 D3
Dronten Neths. 52°32N 5°43E 15 B5
Druk Yul = Bhutan ■
Asia 27°25N 90°30E 41 F17
Drumbo Canada 43°16N 80°35W 82 C4
Drumcliff Ireland 54°20N 8°29W 10 B3
Drumheller Canada 51°25N 112°40W 70 C6
Drummond U.S.A. 46°40N 113°9W 76 C7
Drummond I. U.S.A. 46°1N 83°39W 81 B12
Drummond Pt. Australia 34°9S 135°16E 63 E2
Drummond Ra.
Australia 23°45S 147°10E 62 C4
Drummondville Canada 45°55N 72°25W 72 C5
Drumright U.S.A. 35°59N 96°36W 84 D6
Druskininkai Lithuania 54°3N 23°58E 9 J20
Drut → Belarus 53°8N 30°5E 17 B16
Druzhina Russia 68°14N 145°18E 27 C15
Dry Harbour Mts. Jamaica 18°19N 77°24W 88 a
Dry Tortugas U.S.A. 24°38N 82°55W 85 J13
Dryander △ Australia 20°13S 148°34E 62 b
Dryden Canada 49°47N 92°50W 71 D10
Dryden U.S.A. 42°30N 76°18W 83 D8
Drygalski I. Antarctica 66°0S 92°0E 5 C7
Drygalski Ice Tongue
Antarctica 75°24S 163°30E 5 D11
Drysdale → Australia 13°59S 126°51E 60 B4
Drysdale I. Australia 11°41S 136°0E 62 A2
Drysdale River △
Australia 14°56S 127°2E 60 B4
Du Gué → Canada 57°21N 70°45W 72 A5
Du He → China 32°48N 110°40E 35 A8
Du Quoin U.S.A. 38°1N 89°14W 80 F9
Du'an China 23°59N 108°3E 34 F7
Duanesburg U.S.A. 42°45N 74°11W 83 D10
Duaringa Australia 23°42S 149°42E 62 C4
Duarte, Pico Dom. Rep. 19°2N 70°59W 89 D5
Dubăsari Moldova 47°15N 29°10E 17 E15
Dubăsari Vdkhr. Moldova 47°30N 29°0E 17 E15
Dubawnt → Canada 64°33N 100°6W 71 A8
Dubawnt L. Canada 63°8N 101°28W 71 A8
Dubbo Australia 32°11S 148°35E 63 E4
Dublin Ga., U.S.A. 32°32N 82°54W 85 E13
Dublin Tex., U.S.A. 32°5N 98°21W 84 E5
Dublin □ Ireland 53°24N 6°20W 10 C5
Dubno Ukraine 50°25N 25°45E 17 C13
Dubois U.S.A. 44°10N 112°14W 76 D7
DuBois Pa., U.S.A. 41°7N 78°46W 82 E6
Dubossary = Dubăsari
Moldova 47°15N 29°10E 17 E15
Dubossary Vdkhr. = Dubăsari
Vdkhr. Moldova 47°30N 29°0E 17 E15
Dubovka Russia 49°5N 44°50E 19 E7
Dubrajpur India 23°48N 87°25E 43 H12
Dubréka Guinea 9°46N 13°31W 52 G3
Dubrovitsa = Dubrovytsya
Ukraine 51°31N 26°35E 17 C14
Dubrovnik Croatia 42°39N 18°6E 23 C8
Dubrovytsya Ukraine 51°31N 26°35E 17 C14
Dubuque U.S.A. 42°30N 90°41W 80 D8
Duc Tho Vietnam 18°32N 105°35E 38 C5
Duchang China 29°18N 116°12E 35 C11
Duchesne U.S.A. 40°10N 110°24W 76 F8
Duchess Australia 21°20S 139°50E 62 C2
Ducie I. Pac. Oc. 24°40S 124°48W 65 K15
Duck → U.S.A. 36°2N 87°52W 85 C11
Duck Cr. → Australia 22°37S 116°53E 60 D2
Duck Lake Canada 52°50N 106°16W 71 C7
Duck Mountain △
Canada 51°45N 101°0W 71 C8
Duckwall, Mt. U.S.A. 37°58N 120°7W 78 H6
Dudhi India 24°15N 83°10E 43 G10
Dudinka Russia 69°30N 86°13E 27 C9
Dudley U.K. 52°31N 2°5W 13 E5
Dudna → India 19°17N 76°54E 44 E3
Dudwa India 28°30N 80°41E 43 E9
Dudwa △ India 28°30N 80°40E 43 E9
Duero = Douro → Europe 41°8N 8°40W 21 B1
Dufftown U.K. 57°27N 3°8W 11 D5
Dugi Otok Croatia 44°0N 15°3E 16 G8
Duisburg Germany 51°26N 6°45E 16 C4
Duiwelskloof = Modjadjiskloof
S. Africa 23°42S 30°10E 57 B5
Dujiangyan China 31°2N 103°38E 34 B4
Dūkdamīn Iran 35°59N 57°43E 47 C8
Dukelský Průsmyk
Slovak Rep. 49°25N 21°42E 17 D11
Dukhān Qatar 25°25N 50°50E 47 E6
Duki Pakistan 30°14N 68°25E 40 D6
Duku Nigeria 10°43N 10°43E 53 F8
Dulan China 36°0N 97°11E 30 D8
Dulce U.S.A. 36°56N 107°0W 77 H10
Dulce → Argentina 30°32S 62°33W 94 C3
Dulce, G. Costa Rica 8°40N 83°20W 88 E3
Dulf Iraq 35°7N 45°51E 46 C5
Duliu China 39°2N 116°55E 32 E9
Dullewala Pakistan 31°50N 71°25E 42 D4
Dullstroom S. Africa 25°27S 30°7E 57 C5
Dulq Maghār Syria 36°22N 38°39E 46 B3
Duluth U.S.A. 46°47N 92°6W 80 B7
Dum Duma India 27°40N 95°40E 41 F19
Dūmā Syria 33°34N 36°24E 48 B5
Dumaguete Phil. 9°17N 123°15E 37 C6
Dumai Indonesia 1°35N 101°28E 36 D2
Dumaran Phil. 10°33N 119°50E 37 B5

Dumas Ark., U.S.A. 33°53N 91°29W 84 E9
Dumas Tex., U.S.A. 35°52N 101°58W 84 D4
Dumayr Syria 33°39N 36°42E 48 B5
Dumbarton U.K. 55°57N 4°33W 11 F4
Dumbleyung Australia 33°17S 117°42E 61 F2
Dumfries U.K. 55°4N 3°37W 11 F5
Dumfries & Galloway □
U.K. 55°9N 3°58W 11 F5
Dumka India 24°12N 87°15E 43 G12
Dumoine → Canada 46°13N 77°51W 72 C4
Dumoine, L. Canada 46°55N 77°55W 72 C4
Dumont d'Urville
Antarctica 66°40S 140°0E 5 C10
Dumont d'Urville Sea
S. Ocean 63°30S 138°0E 5 C9
Dumyât Egypt 31°24N 31°48E 53 B12
Dún Dealgan = Dundalk
Ireland 54°1N 6°24W 10 B5
Dún Garbhán = Dungarvan
Ireland 52°5N 7°37W 10 D4
Duna = Dunărea →
Europe 45°20N 29°40E 17 F15
Dunagiri India 30°31N 79°52E 43 D8
Dunaj = Dunărea →
Europe 45°20N 29°40E 17 F15
Dunakeszi Hungary 47°37N 19°8E 17 E10
Dunărea → Europe 45°20N 29°40E 17 F15
Dunaújváros Hungary 46°58N 18°57E 17 E10
Dunav = Dunărea →
Europe 45°20N 29°40E 17 F15
Dunay Russia 42°52N 132°22E 28 C6
Dunback N.Z. 45°23S 170°36E 59 F3
Dunbar U.K. 56°0N 2°31W 11 E6
Dunblane U.K. 56°11N 3°58W 11 E5
Duncan Canada 48°45N 123°40W 78 B3
Duncan Ariz., U.S.A. 32°43N 109°6W 77 K9
Duncan Okla., U.S.A. 34°30N 97°57W 84 D6
Duncan, L. Canada 53°29N 77°58W 72 B4
Duncan L. Canada 62°51N 113°58W 70 A6
Duncan Passage India 11°0N 92°0E 45 J11
Duncan Town Bahamas 22°15N 75°45W 88 B4
Duncannon U.S.A. 40°23N 77°2W 82 F7
Duncansby Head U.K. 58°38N 3°1W 11 C5
Duncansville U.S.A. 40°25N 78°26W 82 F6
Dund-Us Mongolia 48°1N 91°38E 30 B7
Dundalk Canada 44°10N 80°24W 82 B4
Dundalk Ireland 54°1N 6°24W 10 B5
Dundalk U.S.A. 39°15N 76°31W 81 F15
Dundalk Bay Ireland 53°55N 6°15W 10 C5
Dundas = Uummannaq
Greenland 77°33N 68°52W 69 B18
Dundas Canada 43°17N 79°59W 82 C5
Dundas, L. Australia 32°35S 121°50E 61 F3
Dundas I. Canada 54°30N 130°50W 70 C2
Dundas Str. Australia 11°15S 131°35E 60 B5
Dundee S. Africa 28°11S 30°15E 57 C5
Dundee U.K. 56°28N 2°59W 11 E6
Dundee U.S.A. 42°32N 76°59W 82 D8
Dundee City □ U.K. 56°30N 2°58W 11 E6
Dundgovĭ □ Mongolia 45°10N 106°0E 32 B4
Dundrum U.K. 54°16N 5°52W 10 B6
Dundrum B. U.K. 54°13N 5°47W 10 B6
Dunedin N.Z. 45°50S 170°33E 59 F3
Dunedin U.S.A. 28°1N 82°46W 85 G13
Dunfanaghy Ireland 55°11N 7°58W 10 A4
Dunfermline U.K. 56°5N 3°27W 11 E5
Dungannon Ireland 54°31N 6°46W 10 B5
Dungannon U.K. 54°31N 6°46W 10 B5
Dungarpur India 23°52N 73°45E 42 H5
Dungarvan Ireland 52°5N 7°37W 10 D4
Dungarvan Harbour
Ireland 52°4N 7°35W 10 D4
Dungeness U.K. 50°54N 0°59E 13 G8
Dungiven U.K. 54°56N 6°56W 10 B5
Dunglow Ireland 54°57N 8°21W 10 B3
Dungo, L. do Angola 17°15S 19°0E 56 A2
Dungog Australia 32°22S 151°46E 63 E5
Dungu
Dem. Rep. of the Congo 3°40N 28°32E 54 D5
Dungun Malaysia 4°45N 103°25E 39 K4
Dunhua China 43°20N 128°14E 33 C15
Dunhuang China 40°8N 94°36E 30 C7
Dunk I. Australia 17°59S 146°29E 62 B4
Dunkeld Australia 33°25S 149°29E 63 E4
Dunkeld U.K. 56°34N 3°35W 11 E5
Dunkerque France 51°2N 2°20E 20 A5
Dunkery Beacon U.K. 51°9N 3°36W 13 F4
Dunkirk = Dunkerque
France 51°2N 2°20E 20 A5
Dunkirk U.S.A. 42°29N 79°20W 82 D5
Dunleer Ireland 53°50N 6°24W 10 C5
Dunmanus B. Ireland 51°31N 9°50W 10 E2
Dunmanway Ireland 51°43N 9°6W 10 E2
Dunmarra Australia 16°42S 133°25E 62 B1
Dunmore U.S.A. 41°25N 75°38W 83 E9
Dunmore East Ireland 52°9N 7°0W 10 D5
Dunmore Town
Bahamas 25°30N 76°39W 88 A4
Dunn U.S.A. 35°19N 78°37W 85 D15
Dunnellon U.S.A. 29°3N 82°28W 85 G13
Dunnet Hd. U.K. 58°40N 3°21W 11 C5
Dunning U.S.A. 41°50N 100°6W 80 E3
Dunnville Canada 42°54N 79°36W 82 D5
Dunolly Australia 36°51S 143°44E 63 F3
Dunoon U.K. 55°57N 4°56W 11 F4
Duns U.K. 55°47N 2°20W 11 F6
Dunseith U.S.A. 48°50N 100°3W 80 A3
Dunshaughlin Ireland 53°31N 6°33W 10 C5
Dunsmuir U.S.A. 41°13N 122°16W 76 F2
Dunstable U.K. 51°53N 0°32W 13 F7
Dunstan Mts. N.Z. 44°53S 169°35E 59 F2
Dunster Canada 53°8N 119°50W 70 C5
Dunvegan U.K. 57°27N 6°35W 11 D2
Dunvegan L. Canada 60°8N 107°10W 71 A7
Duolun China 42°12N 116°28E 32 C9
Duong Dong Vietnam 10°13N 103°58E 39 G4
Dupree U.S.A. 45°4N 101°35W 80 C3
Dupuyer U.S.A. 48°13N 112°30W 76 B7
Durack → Australia 15°33S 127°52E 60 C4

Durack Ra. Australia 16°50S 127°40E 60 C4
Durack River Australia 15°32S 127°39E 60 C4
Durance → France 43°55N 4°45E 20 E6
Durand U.S.A. 44°38N 91°58W 80 C8
Durango Mexico 24°3N 104°39W 86 C4
Durango U.S.A. 37°16N 107°53W 77 H10
Durango □ Mexico 24°50N 105°20W 86 C4
Durant Miss., U.S.A. 33°4N 89°51W 85 E10
Durant Okla., U.S.A. 33°59N 96°25W 84 E6
Durazno Uruguay 33°25S 56°31W 94 C4
Durazzo = Durrës
Albania 41°19N 19°28E 23 D8
Durban S. Africa 29°49S 31°1E 57 C5
Durban ✈ (DIA) S. Africa 29°37S 31°7E 57 C5
Durbuy Belgium 50°21N 5°28E 15 D5
Durg = Bhilainagar-Durg
India 21°13N 81°26E 44 D5
Durgapur India 23°30N 87°20E 43 H12
Durham Canada 44°10N 80°49W 82 B4
Durham U.K. 54°47N 1°34W 12 C6
Durham Calif., U.S.A. 39°39N 121°48W 78 F5
Durham N.C., U.S.A. 35°59N 78°54W 85 D15
Durham N.H., U.S.A. 43°8N 70°56W 83 C14
Durham □ U.K. 54°42N 1°45W 12 C6
Durlas = Thurles Ireland 52°41N 7°49W 10 D4
Durmā Si. Arabia 24°37N 46°8E 46 E5
Durmitor Montenegro 43°10N 19°0E 23 C8
Durness U.K. 58°34N 4°45W 11 C4
Durrës Albania 41°19N 19°28E 23 D8
Durrow Ireland 52°51N 7°24W 10 D4
Dursey I. Ireland 51°36N 10°12W 10 E1
Dursley U.K. 51°40N 2°21W 13 F5
Dursunbey Turkey 39°35N 28°37E 23 E13
Durūz, Jabal ad Jordan 32°35N 36°40E 48 C5
D'Urville, Tanjung
Indonesia 1°28S 137°54E 37 E9
D'Urville I. N.Z. 40°50S 173°55E 59 D4
Duryea U.S.A. 41°20N 75°45W 83 E9
Dushak Turkmenistan 37°13N 60°1E 47 B9
Dushan China 25°48N 107°30E 34 E6
Dushanbe Tajikistan 38°33N 68°48E 26 F7
Dushore U.S.A. 41°31N 76°24W 83 E8
Dusky Sd. N.Z. 45°47S 166°30E 59 F1
Dussejour, C. Australia 14°45S 128°13E 60 B4
Düsseldorf Germany 51°14N 6°47E 16 C4
Dutch Harbor U.S.A. 53°53N 166°32W 74 E6
Dutlwe Botswana 23°58S 23°46E 56 B3
Dutton Canada 42°39N 81°30W 82 D3
Dutton → Australia 20°44S 143°10E 62 C3
Dutywa S. Africa 32°8S 28°18E 57 D4
Duwayhin, Khawr
U.A.E. 24°20N 51°25E 47 E6
Duyfken Pt. Australia 12°33S 141°38E 62 A3
Duyun China 26°18N 107°29E 34 D6
Dvina, Severnaya →
Russia 64°32N 40°30E 18 B7
Dvinsk = Daugavpils
Latvia 55°53N 26°32E 9 J22
Dvinskaya Guba Russia 65°0N 39°0E 18 B6
Dwarka India 22°18N 69°8E 42 H3
Dwellingup Australia 32°43S 116°4E 61 F2
Dwight Canada 45°20N 79°1W 82 A5
Dwight U.S.A. 41°5N 88°26W 80 E9
Dyatlovo = Dzyatlava
Belarus 53°28N 25°28E 17 B13
Dyce U.K. 57°13N 2°12W 11 D6
Dyer, C. Canada 66°37N 61°16W 69 D19
Dyer Bay Canada 45°10N 81°20W 82 A3
Dyer Plateau Antarctica 70°45S 65°30W 5 D17
Dyersburg U.S.A. 36°3N 89°23W 85 C10
Dyersville U.S.A. 42°29N 91°8W 80 D8
Dyfi → U.K. 52°32N 4°3W 13 E3
Dymer Ukraine 50°47N 30°18E 17 C16
Dysart U.S.A. 22°32S 148°23E 62 C4
Dzaoudzi Mayotte 12°47S 45°16E 55 a
Dzavhan Gol →
Mongolia 48°54N 93°23E 30 B7
Dzerzhinsk Russia 56°14N 43°30E 18 C7
Dzhalinda Russia 53°26N 124°0E 27 D13
Dzhambul = Taraz
Kazakhstan 42°54N 71°22E 30 C3
Dzhankoy Ukraine 45°40N 34°20E 19 E5
Dzhezkazgan = Zhezqazghan
Kazakhstan 47°44N 67°40E 26 E7
Dzhizak = Jizzax
Uzbekistan 40°6N 67°50E 26 E7
Dzhugdzur, Khrebet
Russia 57°30N 138°0E 27 D14
Dzhungarskiye Vorota =
Dzungarian Gate Asia 45°10N 82°0E 30 B5
Działdowo Poland 53°15N 20°15E 17 B11
Dzibilchaltún Mexico 21°10N 89°35W 87 C7
Dzierżoniów Poland 50°45N 16°39E 17 C9
Dzilam de Bravo Mexico 21°24N 88°53W 87 C7
Dzūkija △ Lithuania 54°10N 24°30E 9 J21
Dzungarian Basin = Junggar Pendi
China 44°30N 86°0E 30 C6
Dzungarian Gate Asia 45°10N 82°0E 30 B5
Dzüünbayan Mongolia 44°29N 110°2E 32 B6
Dzüünharaa Mongolia 48°52N 106°28E 30 B10
Dzüünmod Mongolia 47°45N 106°58E 30 B10
Dzyarzhynsk Belarus 53°40N 27°1E 17 B14
Dzyatlava Belarus 53°28N 25°28E 17 B13

E
E.C. Manning △ Canada 49°5N 120°45W 70 D4
Eabamet L. Canada 51°30N 87°46W 72 B2
Eabametoong Canada 51°30N 88°0W 72 B2
Éadan Doire = Edenderry
Ireland 53°21N 7°4W 10 C4
Eads U.S.A. 38°29N 102°47W 76 G12
Eagar U.S.A. 34°6N 109°17W 77 J9
Eagle Alaska, U.S.A. 64°47N 141°12W 68 E3
Eagle Colo., U.S.A. 39°39N 106°50W 76 G10
Eagle → Canada 53°36N 57°26W 73 B8
Eagle Butte U.S.A. 45°0N 101°10W 80 C3
Eagle Grove U.S.A. 42°40N 93°54W 80 D7
Eagle L. Canada 49°42N 93°13W 71 D10

Eagle L. Calif., U.S.A. 40°39N 120°45W 76 F3
Eagle L. Maine, U.S.A. 46°20N 69°22W 81 B19
Eagle Lake Canada 45°8N 78°29W 82 A6
Eagle Lake Maine, U.S.A. 47°3N 68°36W 81 B19
Eagle Lake Tex., U.S.A. 29°35N 96°20W 84 G6
Eagle Mountain
U.S.A. 33°49N 115°27W 79 M11
Eagle Nest U.S.A. 36°33N 105°16W 77 H11
Eagle Pass U.S.A. 28°43N 100°30W 84 G4
Eagle Pk. U.S.A. 38°10N 119°25W 78 G7
Eagle Pt. Australia 16°11S 124°23E 60 C3
Eagle River Mich., U.S.A. 47°25N 88°18W 80 B9
Eagle River Wis., U.S.A. 45°55N 89°15W 80 C9
Eaglehawk Australia 36°44S 144°15E 63 F3
Eagles Mere U.S.A. 41°25N 76°33W 83 E8
Ear Falls Canada 50°38N 93°13W 71 C10
Earlimart U.S.A. 35°53N 119°16W 79 K7
Earlville U.S.A. 42°44N 75°32W 83 D9
Earn → U.K. 56°21N 3°18W 11 E5
Earn, L. U.K. 56°23N 4°13W 11 E4
Earnslaw, Mt. N.Z. 44°32S 168°27E 59 F2
Earth U.S.A. 34°14N 102°24W 84 D3
Easley U.S.A. 34°50N 82°36W 85 D13
East Anglia U.K. 52°30N 1°0E 12 E9
East Angus Canada 45°30N 71°40W 73 C5
East Antarctica Antarctica 80°0S 90°0E 5 D7
East Aurora U.S.A. 42°46N 78°37W 82 D6
East Ayrshire □ U.K. 55°26N 4°11W 11 F4
East Bengal Bangla. 24°0N 90°0E 41 G17
East Beskids = Vychodné Beskydy
Europe 49°20N 22°0E 17 D11
East Brady U.S.A. 40°59N 79°37W 82 F5
East Branch Clarion River L.
U.S.A. 41°35N 78°35W 82 E6
East C. = Dezhneva, Mys
Russia 66°5N 169°40W 27 C19
East C. N.Z. 37°42S 178°35E 59 B7
East Caroline Basin
Pac. Oc. 4°0N 146°45E 64 G6
East Chicago U.S.A. 41°38N 87°27W 80 E10
East China Sea Asia 30°0N 126°0E 31 F14
East Coulee Canada 51°23N 112°27W 70 C6
East Dereham = Dereham
U.K. 52°41N 0°57E 13 E8
East Dunbartonshire □
U.K. 55°57N 4°13W 11 F4
East Falkland Falk. Is. 51°30S 58°30W 96 G5
East Grand Forks U.S.A. 47°56N 97°1W 80 B5
East Greenwich U.S.A. 41°40N 71°27W 83 E13
East Grinstead U.K. 51°7N 0°0 13 F8
East Hartford U.S.A. 41°46N 72°39W 83 E12
East Haydon Australia 18°0S 141°30E 62 B3
East Helena U.S.A. 46°35N 111°56W 76 C8
East Indies Asia 0°0 120°0E 24 J14
East Kilbride U.K. 55°47N 4°11W 11 F4
East Lansing U.S.A. 42°44N 84°29W 81 D11
East Liverpool U.S.A. 40°37N 80°35W 82 F4
East London S. Africa 33°0S 27°55E 57 E4
East Lothian □ U.K. 55°58N 2°44W 11 F6
East Main = Eastmain
Canada 52°10N 78°30W 72 B4
East Mariana Basin
Pac. Oc. 12°0N 153°0E 64 F7
East Northport U.S.A. 40°53N 73°20W 83 F11
East Orange U.S.A. 40°46N 74°12W 83 F10
East Pacific Rise Pac. Oc. 15°0S 110°0W 65 J17
East Palestine U.S.A. 40°50N 80°33W 82 F4
East Pine Canada 55°48N 120°12W 70 B4
East Providence U.S.A. 41°49N 71°23W 83 E13
East Pt. Br. Virgin Is. 18°40N 64°18W 89 e
East Pt. Canada 46°27N 61°58W 73 C7
East Renfrewshire □ U.K. 55°46N 4°21W 11 F4
East Retford = Retford
U.K. 53°19N 0°56W 12 D7
East Riding of Yorkshire □
U.K. 53°55N 0°30W 12 D7
East Rochester U.S.A. 43°7N 77°29W 82 C7
East St. Louis U.S.A. 38°37N 90°9W 80 F8
East Schelde = Oosterschelde →
Neths. 51°33N 4°0E 15 C4
East Sea = Japan, Sea of
Asia 40°0N 135°0E 28 E7
East Siberian Sea Russia 73°0N 160°0E 27 B17
East Stroudsburg U.S.A. 41°1N 75°11W 83 E9
East Sussex □ U.K. 50°56N 0°19E 13 G8
East Tasman Plateau
Pac. Oc. 43°30S 152°0E 64 M7
East Tawas U.S.A. 44°17N 83°29W 81 C12
East Timor ■ Asia 8°50S 126°0E 37 F7
East Toorale Australia 30°27S 145°28E 63 E4
East Walker → U.S.A. 38°52N 119°10W 78 G7
East Windsor U.S.A. 40°17N 74°34W 83 F10
Eastbourne N.Z. 41°19S 174°55E 59 D5
Eastbourne U.K. 50°46N 0°18E 13 G8
Eastend Canada 49°32N 108°50W 71 D7
Easter Fracture Zone
Pac. Oc. 25°0S 115°0W 65 K16
Easter I. = Pascua, I. de
Chile 27°7S 109°23W 65 K17
Eastern Cape □ S. Africa 32°0S 26°0E 56 E4
Eastern Cr. → Australia 20°40S 141°35E 62 C3
Eastern Desert = Es Sahrâ' Esh
Sharqîya Egypt 27°30N 32°30E 53 C12
Eastern Ghats India 14°0N 78°50E 45 H4
Eastern Group = Lau Group
Fiji 17°0S 178°30W 59 a
Eastern Group Australia 33°30S 124°30E 61 F3
Eastern Guruma ◎
Australia 22°0S 117°30E 60 D2
Eastern Transvaal =
Mpumalanga □ S. Africa 26°0S 30°0E 57 C5
Easterville Canada 53°8N 99°49W 71 C9
Easthampton U.S.A. 42°16N 72°40W 83 D12
Eastlake U.S.A. 41°40N 81°26W 82 E3
Eastleigh U.K. 50°58N 1°21W 13 G6
Eastmain Canada 52°10N 78°30W 72 B4
Eastmain → Canada 52°27N 78°26W 72 B4
Eastman Canada 45°18N 72°19W 83 A12

Eastman U.S.A. 32°12N 83°11W 85 E13
Easton Md., U.S.A. 38°47N 76°5W 81 F15
Easton Pa., U.S.A. 40°41N 75°13W 83 F9
Easton Wash., U.S.A. 47°14N 121°11W 78 C5
Eastport U.S.A. 44°56N 67°0W 81 C20
Eastsound U.S.A. 48°42N 122°55W 78 B4
Eaton U.S.A. 40°32N 104°42W 76 F11
Eatonia Canada 51°13N 109°25W 71 C7
Eatonton U.S.A. 33°20N 83°23W 85 E13
Eatonville U.S.A. 46°52N 122°16W 78 D4
Eau Claire U.S.A. 44°49N 91°30W 80 C8
Eau Claire, L. à l' Canada 56°10N 74°25W 72 A5
Eauripik Rise Pac. Oc. 2°0N 142°0E 64 G6
Ebano Mexico 22°13N 98°24W 87 C5
Ebbw Vale U.K. 51°46N 3°12W 13 F4
Ebeltoft Denmark 56°12N 10°41E 9 H14
Ebensburg U.S.A. 40°29N 78°44W 82 F6
Eberswalde-Finow
Germany 52°50N 13°49E 16 B7
Ebetsu Japan 43°7N 141°34E 28 C10
Ebey's Landing ◌
U.S.A. 48°12N 122°41W 78 B4
Ebian China 29°11N 103°13E 34 C4
Ebinur Hu China 44°55N 82°55E 30 B3
Ebolowa Cameroon 2°55N 11°10E 54 D2
Ebonda
Dem. Rep. of the Congo 2°12N 22°21E 54 D4
Ebre = Ebro → Spain 40°43N 0°54E 21 B6
Ebro → Spain 40°43N 0°54E 21 B6
Ecatepec de Morelos
Mexico 19°36N 99°3W 87 D5
Ecbatana = Hamadān
Iran 34°52N 48°32E 47 C6
Eceabat Turkey 40°11N 26°21E 23 D12
Ech Chéliff Algeria 36°10N 1°20E 52 A6
Echigo-Sammyaku
Japan 36°50N 139°50E 29 F9
Echizen Japan 35°50N 136°10E 29 G8
Echizen-Misaki Japan 35°59N 135°57E 29 G7
Echo Bay N.W.T., Canada 66°5N 117°55W 68 D8
Echo Bay Ont., Canada 46°29N 84°4W 72 C3
Echoing → Canada 55°51N 92°5W 72 B1
Echternach Lux. 49°49N 6°25E 15 E6
Echuca Australia 36°10S 144°45E 63 F3
Écija Spain 37°30N 5°10W 21 D3
Eclipse I. Australia 35°5S 117°58E 61 G2
Eclipse Is. Australia 13°54S 126°19E 60 B4
Eclipse Sd. Canada 72°38N 79°0W 69 C16
Ecuador ■ S. Amer. 2°0S 78°0W 92 D3
Ed Da'ein Sudan 11°26N 26°9E 54 F5
Ed Damazin Sudan 11°46N 34°21E 53 F12
Ed Dâmer Sudan 17°27N 34°0E 53 E12
Ed Dar el Beida = Casablanca
Morocco 33°36N 7°36W 52 B4
Ed Debba Sudan 18°0N 30°51E 53 E12
Ed Déffa Egypt 30°40N 26°30E 53 B11
Ed Dueim Sudan 14°0N 32°10E 53 F12
Edam Canada 53°11N 108°46W 71 C7
Edam Neths. 52°31N 5°3E 15 B5
Edapally India 11°19N 78°3E 45 J4
Eday U.K. 59°11N 2°47W 11 B6
Eddrachillis B. U.K. 58°17N 5°14W 11 C3
Eddystone U.K. 50°11N 4°16W 13 G3
Eddystone Pt. Australia 40°59S 148°20E 63 G4
Ede Neths. 52°4N 5°40E 15 B5
Edehon L. Canada 60°25N 97°15W 71 A9
Eden Australia 37°3S 149°55E 63 F4
Eden N.C., U.S.A. 36°29N 79°53W 85 C15
Eden N.Y., U.S.A. 42°39N 78°55W 82 D6
Eden Tex., U.S.A. 31°13N 99°51W 84 F5
Eden → U.K. 54°57N 3°1W 12 C4
Edenburg S. Africa 29°43S 25°58E 56 C4
Edendale S. Africa 29°39S 30°18E 57 C5
Edenderry Ireland 53°21N 7°4W 10 C4
Edenton U.S.A. 36°4N 76°39W 85 C16
Edenville S. Africa 27°37S 27°34E 57 C4
Eder → Germany 51°12N 9°28E 16 C5
Edessa Greece 40°48N 22°5E 23 D10
Edfu = Idfû Egypt 24°55N 32°49E 53 D12
Edgar U.S.A. 40°22N 97°58W 80 E5
Edgartown U.S.A. 41°23N 70°31W 83 E14
Edge Hill U.K. 52°8N 1°26W 13 E6
Edgefield U.S.A. 33°47N 81°56W 85 E14
Edgeley U.S.A. 46°22N 98°43W 80 B4
Edgemont U.S.A. 43°18N 103°50W 80 D2
Edgeøya Svalbard 77°45N 22°30E 4 B9
Édhessa = Edessa Greece 40°48N 22°5E 23 D10
Edievale N.Z. 45°49S 169°22E 59 F2
Edina U.S.A. 40°10N 92°11W 80 E7
Edinboro U.S.A. 41°52N 80°8W 82 E4
Edinburg U.S.A. 26°18N 98°10W 84 H5
Edinburgh, City of □ U.K. 55°57N 3°17W 11 F5
Edineț Moldova 48°9N 27°18E 17 D14
Edirne Turkey 41°40N 26°34E 23 D12
Edison U.S.A. 48°33N 122°27W 78 B4
Edithburgh Australia 35°5S 137°43E 63 F2
Edmond U.S.A. 35°39N 97°29W 84 H6
Edmonds U.S.A. 47°48N 122°22W 78 C4
Edmonton Australia 17°2S 145°46E 62 B4
Edmonton Canada 53°30N 113°30W 70 C6
Edmund L. Canada 54°45N 93°17W 72 B1
Edmundston Canada 47°23N 68°20W 73 C6
Edna U.S.A. 28°59N 96°39W 84 G6
Edremit Turkey 39°34N 27°0E 23 E12
Edremit Körfezi Turkey 39°30N 26°45E 23 E12
Edson Canada 53°35N 116°28W 70 C5
Eduardo Castex
Argentina 35°50S 64°18W 94 D3
Eduardo Frei Antarctica 62°30S 58°0W 5 C18
Edward → Australia 35°5S 143°30E 63 F3
Edward, L. Africa 0°25S 29°40E 54 E5
Edward VII Land
Antarctica 80°0S 150°0W 5 E13
Edwards Calif., U.S.A. 34°50N 117°40W 79 L9
Edwards N.Y., U.S.A. 44°20N 75°15W 83 B9
Edwards Plateau U.S.A. 30°45N 101°20W 84 F4
Edwardsville U.S.A. 41°15N 75°56W 83 E9

Edzná *Mexico* 19°39N 90°19W **87 D6**
Edzo *Canada* 62°49N 116°4W **70 A5**
Eeklo *Belgium* 51°11N 3°33E **15 C3**
Eenhana *Namibia* 17°30S 16°23E **56 A2**
Eesti = Estonia ■ *Europe* 58°30N 25°30E **9 G21**
Effigy Mounds △ *U.S.A.* 43°5N 91°11W **80 D8**
Effingham *U.S.A.* 39°7N 88°33W **80 F9**
Égadi, Ísole *Italy* 37°55N 12°16E **22 F5**
Egan Range *U.S.A.* 39°35N 114°55W **76 G6**
Eganville *Canada* 45°32N 77°5W **82 A7**
Eger = Cheb *Czech Rep.* 50°9N 12°28E **16 C7**
Eger *Hungary* 47°53N 20°27E **17 E11**
Egersund *Norway* 58°26N 6°1E **9 G12**
Egg L. *Canada* 55°5N 105°30W **71 B7**
Éghezée *Belgium* 50°35N 4°55E **15 D4**
Egilsstaðir *Iceland* 65°16N 14°25W **8 D6**
Egio *Greece* 38°15N 22°5E **23 E10**
Eglinton I. *Canada* 75°48N 118°30W **69 B8**
Egmont *Canada* 49°45N 123°56W **70 D4**
Egmont, C. *N.Z.* 39°16S 173°45E **59 C4**
Egmont, Mt. = Taranaki, Mt.
  N.Z. 39°17S 174°5E **59 C5**
Egmont △ *N.Z.* 39°17S 174°4E **59 C5**
Egra *India* 21°54N 87°32E **43 J12**
Eğridir *Turkey* 37°52N 30°51E **19 G5**
Eğridir Gölü *Turkey* 37°53N 30°50E **46 B1**
Egvekinot *Russia* 66°19N 179°50W **27 C19**
Egypt ■ *Africa* 28°0N 31°0E **53 C12**
Ehime □ *Japan* 33°30N 132°40E **29 H6**
Ehrenberg *U.S.A.* 33°36N 114°31W **79 M12**
Eibar *Spain* 43°11N 2°28W **21 A4**
Eidsvold *Australia* 25°25S 151°12E **63 D5**
Eidsvoll *Norway* 60°19N 11°14E **9 F14**
Eielson *U.S.A.* 64°40N 147°4W **74 C10**
Eifel *Germany* 50°15N 6°50E **16 C4**
Eigg *U.K.* 56°54N 6°10W **11 E2**
Eighty Mile Beach
  Australia 19°30S 120°40E **60 C3**
Eil, L. *U.K.* 56°51N 5°16W **11 E3**
Eildon, L. *Australia* 37°10S 146°0E **63 F4**
Eilean Siar □ *U.K.* 57°30N 7°10W **11 D1**
Einasleigh *Australia* 18°32S 144°5E **62 B3**
Einasleigh → *Australia* 17°30S 142°17E **62 B3**
Eindhoven *Neths.* 51°26N 5°28E **15 C5**
Eire = Ireland ■ *Europe* 53°50N 7°52W **10 C4**
Eiríksjökull *Iceland* 64°46N 20°24W **8 D3**
Eiriosgaigh = Eriskay *U.K.* 57°4N 7°18W **11 D1**
Eirunepé *Brazil* 6°35S 69°53W **92 E5**
Eiseb → *Namibia* 20°33S 20°59E **56 B2**
Eisenach *Germany* 50°58N 10°19E **16 C6**
Eisenerz *Austria* 47°32N 14°54E **16 E8**
Eivissa *Spain* 38°54N 1°26E **21 C6**
Ejutla *Mexico* 16°34N 96°44W **87 D5**
Ekalaka *U.S.A.* 45°53N 104°33W **76 D11**
Ekaterinburg = Yekaterinburg
  Russia 56°50N 60°30E **26 D7**
Ekenäs = Raasepori
  Finland 60°0N 23°26E **9 G20**
Eketahuna *N.Z.* 40°38S 175°43E **59 D5**
Ekibastuz *Kazakhstan* 51°50N 75°10E **26 D8**
Eksjö *Sweden* 57°40N 14°58E **9 H16**
Ekuma → *Namibia* 18°40S 16°2E **56 A2**
Ekwan → *Canada* 53°12N 82°15W **72 B3**
Ekwan Pt. *Canada* 53°16N 82°7W **72 B3**
El Aaiún *W. Sahara* 27°9N 13°12W **52 C3**
El Abanico *Chile* 37°20S 71°31W **94 D1**
El 'Agrūd *Egypt* 30°14N 34°24E **48 E3**
El Alamein *Egypt* 30°48N 28°58E **53 B11**
El 'Aqaba, W. → *Egypt* 30°7N 33°54E **48 E2**
El Arīḥā *West Bank* 31°52N 35°27E **48 D4**
El 'Arīsh *Egypt* 31°8N 33°50E **48 D2**
El 'Arīsh, W. → *Egypt* 31°8N 33°47E **48 D2**
El Asnam = Ech Chéliff
  Algeria 36°10N 1°20E **52 A6**
El Bayadh *Algeria* 33°40N 1°1E **52 B6**
El Bluff *Nic.* 11°59N 83°40W **88 D3**
El Cajon *U.S.A.* 32°48N 116°58W **79 N10**
El Calafate *Argentina* 50°19S 72°15W **96 G2**
El Campo *U.S.A.* 29°12N 96°16W **84 G6**
El Capitan *U.S.A.* 37°44N 119°38E **78 H7**
El Carbón *Honduras* 15°25N 85°32W **88 C2**
El Carmen *Colombia* 9°43N 75°8W **92 B3**
El Centro *U.S.A.* 32°48N 115°34W **79 N11**
El Cerro *Bolivia* 17°30S 61°40W **92 G6**
El Compadre *Mexico* 32°20N 116°14W **79 N10**
El Cuy *Argentina* 39°55S 68°25W **96 D3**
El Cuyo *Mexico* 21°31N 87°41W **87 C7**
El Daheir *Egypt* 31°13N 34°10E **48 D3**
El Descanso *Mexico* 32°12N 116°58W **79 N10**
El Desemboque *Mexico* 30°33N 113°1W **86 A2**
El Diviso *Colombia* 1°22N 78°14W **92 C3**
El Djouf *Mauritania* 21°25N 6°40W **52 D4**
El Dorado *Mexico* 24°17N 107°21W **86 C3**
El Dorado *Ark., U.S.A.* 33°12N 92°40W **84 E8**
El Dorado *Kans., U.S.A.* 37°49N 96°52W **80 G6**
El Dorado *Venezuela* 6°55N 61°37W **92 B6**
El Dorado Springs *U.S.A.* 37°52N 94°1W **80 G6**
El Escorial *Spain* 40°35N 4°7W **21 B3**
El Faiyûm *Egypt* 29°19N 30°50E **53 C12**
El Fâsher *Sudan* 13°33N 25°26E **53 F11**
El Ferrol = Ferrol *Spain* 43°29N 8°15W **21 A1**
El Fuerte *Mexico* 26°30N 108°39W **86 B3**
El Geneina = Al Junaynah
  Sudan 13°27N 22°45E **53 F10**
El Gezira □ *Sudan* 15°0N 33°0E **53 F12**
El Gogorrón △ *Mexico* 21°49N 100°57W **86 C4**
El Goléa *Algeria* 30°30N 2°50E **52 B6**
El Guácharo △ *Venezuela* 10°8N 63°21W **89 D7**
El Guache △ *Venezuela* 9°45N 69°30W **89 E6**
El Iskandarîya *Egypt* 31°13N 29°58E **53 B11**
El Istiwa'iya *Sudan* 5°0N 28°0E **53 G11**
El Jadida *Morocco* 33°11N 8°17W **52 B4**
El Jardal *Honduras* 14°54N 88°50W **88 D2**
El Kef □ *Tunisia* 36°0N 9°0E **53 A7**
El Khârga *Egypt* 25°30N 30°33E **53 C12**
El Khartûm *Sudan* 15°31N 32°35E **53 E12**
El Khartûm Bahri *Sudan* 15°40N 32°31E **53 E12**
El Kuntilla *Egypt* 30°1N 34°45E **48 E3**
El Leoncito △ *Argentina* 31°58S 69°10W **94 C2**

El Lucero *Mexico* 30°37N 106°31W **86 A3**
El Maestrazgo *Spain* 40°30N 0°25W **21 B5**
El Mahalla el Kubra *Egypt* 31°0N 31°0E **53 B12**
El Malpais △ *U.S.A.* 34°53N 108°0W **77 J10**
El Mansûra *Egypt* 31°0N 31°19E **53 B12**
El Ménia = El Goléa
  Algeria 30°30N 2°50E **52 B6**
El Milagro *Argentina* 30°59S 65°59W **94 C2**
El Minyâ *Egypt* 28°7N 30°33E **53 C12**
El Obeid *Sudan* 13°8N 30°10E **53 F12**
El Odaiya *Sudan* 12°8N 28°12E **53 F11**
El Oro *Mexico* 19°51N 100°7W **87 D4**
El Oued *Algeria* 33°20N 6°58E **52 B7**
El Palmar △ *Argentina* 32°10S 58°31W **94 C4**
El Paso *U.S.A.* 31°45N 106°29W **84 F1**
El Paso de Robles = Paso Robles
  U.S.A. 35°38N 120°41W **78 K6**
El Pinacate y Gran Desierto de
  Altar = Gran Desierto del
  Pinacate △ *Mexico* 31°51N 113°32W **86 A2**
El Portal *U.S.A.* 37°41N 119°47W **78 H7**
El Porvenir *Mexico* 31°15N 105°51W **86 A3**
El Progreso *Honduras* 15°26N 87°51W **88 C2**
El Puerto de Santa María
  Spain 36°36N 6°13W **21 D2**
El Qantara *Egypt* 30°51N 32°20E **48 E1**
El Quseima *Egypt* 30°40N 34°15E **48 E3**
El Real de Santa María
  Panama 8°0N 77°40W **92 B3**
El Reno *U.S.A.* 35°32N 97°57W **75 H20**
El Rey △ *Argentina* 24°40S 64°34W **94 A3**
El Río *U.S.A.* 34°14N 119°10W **79 L7**
El Rosario *Mexico* 30°1N 115°45W **86 A1**
El Salto *Mexico* 23°47N 105°22W **86 C3**
El Salvador ■ *Cent. Amer.* 13°50N 89°0W **88 D2**
El Sauce *Nic.* 13°0N 86°40W **88 D2**
El Suweis *Egypt* 29°58N 32°31E **53 C12**
El Tamarâni, W. → *Egypt* 30°7N 34°43E **48 E3**
El Thamad *Egypt* 29°40N 34°28E **48 F3**
El Tigre *Venezuela* 8°44N 64°15W **92 B6**
El Tîh, Gebel *Egypt* 29°40N 33°50E **48 F2**
El Tofo *Chile* 29°22S 71°18W **94 B1**
El Tránsito *Chile* 28°52S 70°17W **94 B1**
El Tûr *Egypt* 28°14N 33°36E **46 D2**
El Turbio *Argentina* 51°45S 72°5W **96 G2**
El Uqsur *Egypt* 25°41N 32°38E **53 C12**
El Vergel *Mexico* 26°28N 106°22W **86 B3**
El Vígía *Venezuela* 8°38N 71°39W **92 B4**
El Wabeira *Egypt* 29°34N 33°6E **48 F2**
El Wuz *Sudan* 15°5N 30°7E **53 E12**
Elamanchili *India* 17°33N 82°50E **44 F6**
Elat *Israel* 29°30N 34°56E **48 F3**
Elâzığ *Turkey* 38°37N 39°14E **46 B3**
Elba *Italy* 42°46N 10°17E **22 C4**
Elba *U.S.A.* 31°25N 86°4W **85 F11**
Elbasan *Albania* 41°9N 20°9E **23 D9**
Elbe *U.S.A.* 46°45N 122°10W **78 D4**
Elbe → *Europe* 53°50N 9°0E **16 B5**
Elbert, Mt. *U.S.A.* 39°7N 106°27W **76 G10**
Elberton *U.S.A.* 34°7N 82°52W **85 D13**
Elbeuf *France* 49°17N 1°2E **20 B4**
Elbing = Elbląg *Poland* 54°10N 19°25E **17 A10**
Elbistan *Turkey* 38°13N 37°15E **46 B3**
Elbląg *Poland* 54°10N 19°25E **17 A10**
Elbow *Canada* 51°7N 106°35W **71 C7**
Elbrus *Russia* 43°21N 42°30E **19 F7**
Elburz Mts. = Alborz, Reshteh-ye
  Kūhhā-ye *Iran* 36°0N 52°0E **47 C7**
Elche *Spain* 38°15N 0°42W **21 C5**
Elcho I. *Australia* 11°55S 135°45E **62 A2**
Elda *Spain* 38°29N 0°47W **21 C5**
Elde → *Germany* 53°7N 11°15E **16 B6**
Eldon *Mo., U.S.A.* 38°21N 92°35W **80 F8**
Eldon *Wash., U.S.A.* 47°33N 123°3W **78 C3**
Eldora *U.S.A.* 42°22N 93°5W **80 D7**
Eldorado *Argentina* 26°28S 54°43W **95 B5**
Eldorado *Canada* 44°35N 77°31W **82 B7**
Eldorado *Ill., U.S.A.* 37°49N 88°26W **80 G9**
Eldorado *Tex., U.S.A.* 30°52N 100°36W **84 F4**
Eldoret *Kenya* 0°30N 35°17E **54 D7**
Eldred *U.S.A.* 41°58N 78°23W **82 E6**
Eleanora, Pk. *Australia* 32°57S 121°9E **61 F3**
Elefantes → *Africa* 24°10S 32°40E **57 B5**
Elektrostal *Russia* 55°41N 38°32E **18 C6**
Elemi Triangle *Africa* 5°0N 35°20E **54 D7**
Elephant Butte Res.
  U.S.A. 33°9N 107°11W **77 K10**
Elephant I. *Antarctica* 61°0S 55°0W **5 C18**
Elephant Pass *Sri Lanka* 9°35N 80°25E **45 K5**
Eleuthera I. *Bahamas* 25°0N 76°20W **88 B4**
Elgin *Canada* 44°36N 76°13W **83 B8**
Elgin *U.K.* 57°39N 3°19W **11 D5**
Elgin *Ill., U.S.A.* 42°2N 88°17W **80 D9**
Elgin *N. Dak., U.S.A.* 46°24N 101°51W **80 B3**
Elgin *Oreg., U.S.A.* 45°34N 117°55W **76 D5**
Elgin *Tex., U.S.A.* 30°21N 97°22W **84 F6**
Elgon, Mt. *Africa* 1°10N 34°30E **54 D6**
Eliase *Indonesia* 8°21S 130°48E **37 F8**
Elim *Namibia* 17°48S 15°31E **56 A2**
Elim *S. Africa* 34°35S 19°45E **56 D2**
Elista *Russia* 46°16N 44°14E **19 E7**
Elizabeth *Australia* 34°42S 138°41E **63 E2**
Elizabeth *U.S.A.* 40°39N 74°12W **83 F10**
Elizabeth City *U.S.A.* 36°18N 76°14W **85 C16**
Elizabethton *U.S.A.* 36°21N 82°13W **85 C13**
Elizabethtown *Ky.,*
  U.S.A. 37°42N 85°52W **81 G11**
Elizabethtown *N.Y.,*
  U.S.A. 44°13N 73°36W **83 B11**
Elizabethtown *Pa., U.S.A.* 40°9N 76°36W **83 F8**
Elk *Poland* 53°50N 22°21E **17 B12**
Elk → *Canada* 49°11N 115°14W **70 C5**
Elk → *U.S.A.* 34°46N 87°16W **85 D11**
Elk City *U.S.A.* 35°25N 99°25W **84 D5**
Elk Creek *U.S.A.* 39°36N 122°32W **78 F4**
Elk Grove *U.S.A.* 38°25N 121°22W **78 G5**
Elk Island △ *Canada* 53°35N 112°59W **70 C6**
Elk Lake *Canada* 47°40N 80°25W **72 C3**
Elk Point *Canada* 53°54N 110°55W **71 C6**

Elk River *Idaho, U.S.A.* 46°47N 116°11W **76 C5**
Elk River *Minn., U.S.A.* 45°18N 93°35W **80 C7**
Elkedra → *Australia* 21°8S 136°22E **62 C2**
Elkhart *Ind., U.S.A.* 41°41N 85°58W **81 E11**
Elkhart *Kans., U.S.A.* 37°0N 101°54W **80 G3**
Elkhorn *Canada* 49°59N 101°14W **71 D8**
Elkhorn → *U.S.A.* 41°8N 96°19W **80 E6**
Elkhovo *Bulgaria* 42°10N 26°35E **23 C12**
Elkin *U.S.A.* 36°15N 80°51W **85 C14**
Elkins *U.S.A.* 38°55N 79°51W **81 F14**
Elkland *U.S.A.* 41°59N 77°19W **82 E7**
Elko *Canada* 49°20N 115°10W **70 D5**
Elko *U.S.A.* 40°50N 115°46W **76 F6**
Elkton *U.S.A.* 43°49N 83°11W **82 C1**
Ellas = Greece ■ *Europe* 40°0N 23°0E **23 E9**
Ellef Ringnes I. *Canada* 78°30N 102°2W **69 B11**
Ellen, Mt. *U.S.A.* 44°9N 72°56W **83 B12**
Ellenburg *U.S.A.* 44°54N 73°48W **83 B11**
Ellendale *U.S.A.* 46°0N 98°32W **80 B4**
Ellensburg *U.S.A.* 46°59N 120°34W **76 C3**
Ellenville *U.S.A.* 41°43N 74°24W **83 E10**
Ellerton *Barbados* 13°7N 59°33W **89 g**
Ellery, Mt. *Australia* 37°28S 148°47E **63 F4**
Ellesmere, L. *N.Z.* 43°47S 172°28E **59 G4**
Ellesmere Island = Quttinirpaaq △
  Canada 82°13N 72°13W **69 A17**
Ellesmere Port *U.K.* 53°17N 2°54W **12 D5**
Ellice Is. = Tuvalu ■
  Pac. Oc. 8°0S 178°0E **58 B10**
Ellicottville *U.S.A.* 42°17N 78°40W **82 D6**
Ellington *U.S.A.* 42°13N 79°6W **82 D5**
Elliot *Australia* 17°33S 133°32E **62 B1**
Elliot *S. Africa* 31°22S 27°48E **57 D4**
Elliot Lake *Canada* 46°25N 82°35W **72 C3**
Elliotdale = Xhora
  S. Africa 31°55S 28°38E **57 D4**
Ellis *U.S.A.* 38°56N 99°34W **80 F4**
Elliston *Australia* 33°39S 134°53E **63 E1**
Ellisville *U.S.A.* 31°36N 89°12W **85 F10**
Ellon *U.K.* 57°22N 2°4W **11 D6**
Ellora *India* 20°1N 75°10E **44 D2**
Ellore = Eluru *India* 16°48N 81°8E **44 F5**
Ellsworth *Kans., U.S.A.* 38°44N 98°14W **80 F4**
Ellsworth *Maine, U.S.A.* 44°33N 68°25W **81 C19**
Ellsworth Land *Antarctica* 76°0S 89°0W **5 D16**
Ellsworth Mts. *Antarctica* 78°30S 85°0W **5 D16**
Ellwood City *U.S.A.* 40°52N 80°17W **82 F4**
Elma *Canada* 49°52N 95°55W **71 D9**
Elma *U.S.A.* 47°0N 123°25E **60 D5**
Elmali *Turkey* 36°44N 29°56E **19 G4**
Elmhurst *U.S.A.* 41°53N 87°56W **80 E10**
Elmira *Canada* 43°36N 80°33W **82 C4**
Elmira *U.S.A.* 42°6N 76°48W **82 D8**
Elmira Heights *U.S.A.* 42°8N 76°50W **82 D8**
Elmore *Australia* 36°30S 144°37E **63 F3**
Elmshorn *Germany* 53°43N 9°40E **16 B5**
Elmvale *Canada* 44°35N 79°52W **82 B5**
Elora *India* 43°41N 80°26W **82 C4**
Eloy *U.S.A.* 32°45N 111°33W **77 K8**
Elphin *Canada* 44°55N 76°37W **83 B8**
Elpitiya *Sri Lanka* 6°17N 80°10E **45 L5**
Elrose *Canada* 51°12N 108°0W **71 C7**
Elsby △ *Australia* 14°55S 133°10E **60 B5**
Elsie *U.S.A.* 45°52N 123°36W **78 E3**
Elsinore = Helsingør
  Denmark 56°2N 12°35E **9 H15**
Eltanin Fracture Zone System
  S. Ocean 54°0S 130°0W **5 B14**
Eltham *N.Z.* 39°26S 174°19E **59 C5**
Eluru *India* 16°48N 81°8E **44 F5**
Elvas *Portugal* 38°50N 7°10W **21 C2**
Elverum *Norway* 60°53N 11°34E **8 F14**
Elvire → *Australia* 17°51S 128°11E **60 C4**
Elvire, Mt. *Australia* 29°22S 119°36E **61 E2**
Elwell, L. = Tiber Res.
  U.S.A. 48°19N 111°6W **76 B8**
Elwood *Ind., U.S.A.* 40°17N 85°50W **81 E11**
Elwood *Nebr., U.S.A.* 40°36N 99°52W **80 E4**
Elx = Elche *Spain* 38°15N 0°42W **21 C5**
Ely *U.K.* 52°24N 0°16E **13 E8**
Ely *Minn., U.S.A.* 47°55N 91°51W **80 B8**
Ely *Nev., U.S.A.* 39°15N 114°54W **76 G6**
Elyria *U.S.A.* 41°22N 82°7W **82 E2**
eMakhazeni *S. Africa* 25°42S 30°2E **57 C5**
eMalahleni *S. Africa* 25°51S 29°14E **57 C4**
Emämrūd *Iran* 36°30N 55°0E **47 B7**
eMbalenhle *S. Africa* 26°31S 29°0E **57 C4**
Embarcación *Argentina* 23°10S 64°0W **94 A3**
Embetsu *Japan* 44°44N 141°47E **28 B10**
Embi *Kazakhstan* 48°50N 58°8E **26 E6**
Embi → *Kazakhstan* 46°55N 53°28E **19 E9**
Embro *Canada* 43°9N 80°54W **82 C4**
Embrun *France* 44°34N 6°30E **20 D7**
Emden *Germany* 53°21N 7°12E **16 B4**
Emei Shan *China* 29°32N 103°46E **34 C4**
Emeishan *China* 29°31N 103°23E **34 C4**
Emerald *Australia* 23°32S 148°10E **62 C4**
Emerald I. *Canada* 76°48N 114°10W **69 B9**
Emerson *Canada* 49°0N 97°10W **71 D9**
Emet *Turkey* 39°20N 29°15E **23 E13**
Emgwenya *S. Africa* 25°42S 30°38E **57 C5**
Emi Koussi *Chad* 19°45N 18°55E **53 E9**
Eminabad *Pakistan* 32°2N 74°8E **42 C6**
Emine, Nos *Bulgaria* 42°40N 27°56E **23 C12**
Emissi, Tarso *Chad* 21°27N 18°36E **53 D9**
Emlenton *U.S.A.* 41°11N 79°43W **82 E5**
Emmaus *S. Africa* 29°2S 25°12E **56 D4**
Emmaus *U.S.A.* 40°32N 75°30W **83 F9**
Emmeloord *Neths.* 52°44N 5°46E **15 B5**
Emmen *Neths.* 52°48N 6°57E **15 B6**
Emmet *Australia* 24°45S 144°30E **62 C3**
Emmetsburg *U.S.A.* 43°7N 94°41W **80 D6**
Emmett *Idaho, U.S.A.* 43°52N 116°30W **76 E5**
Emmett *Mich., U.S.A.* 42°59N 82°46W **82 D2**
Emmonak *U.S.A.* 62°47N 164°31W **74 C7**
Emo *Canada* 48°38N 93°50W **71 D10**

Empalme *Mexico* 27°58N 110°51W **86 B2**
Empangeni *S. Africa* 28°50S 31°52E **57 C5**
Empedrado *Argentina* 28°0S 58°46W **94 B4**
Emperor Seamount Chain
  Pac. Oc. 40°0N 170°0E **64 D9**
Emperor Trough *Pac. Oc.* 43°0N 175°30E **64 D9**
Emporia *Kans., U.S.A.* 38°25N 96°11W **80 F5**
Emporia *Va., U.S.A.* 36°42N 77°32W **81 G15**
Emporium *U.S.A.* 41°31N 78°14W **82 E6**
Empress *Canada* 50°57N 110°0W **71 C7**
Empty Quarter = Rub' al Khālī
  Si. Arabia 19°0N 48°0E **49 D4**
Ems → *Germany* 53°20N 7°12E **16 B4**
Emsdale *Canada* 45°32N 79°19W **82 A5**
Emu *China* 43°40N 128°6E **33 C15**
Emu Park *Australia* 23°13S 150°50E **62 C5**
eMuziwezinto *S. Africa* 30°15S 30°45E **57 D5**
'En 'Avrona *Israel* 29°43N 35°0E **48 F4**
'En Boqeq *Israel* 31°12N 35°21E **47 D4**
'En Gedi *Israel* 31°28N 35°25E **47 D4**
En Nahud *Sudan* 12°45N 28°25E **53 F11**
Ena *Japan* 35°25N 137°25E **29 G8**
Enard B. *U.K.* 58°5N 5°20W **11 C3**
Enara träsk = Inarijärvi
  Finland 69°0N 28°0E **8 B23**
Enarotali *Indonesia* 3°55S 136°21E **37 E9**
Encampment *U.S.A.* 41°12N 106°47W **76 F10**
Encantadas, Serra *Brazil* 30°40S 53°0W **95 C5**
Encarnación *Paraguay* 27°15S 55°50W **95 B4**
Encarnación de Díaz
  Mexico 21°31N 102°14W **86 C4**
Encinitas *U.S.A.* 33°3N 117°17W **79 M9**
Encino *U.S.A.* 34°39N 105°28W **77 J11**
Encounter B. *Australia* 35°45S 138°45E **63 F2**
Endako *Canada* 54°6N 125°2W **70 C3**
Endau Rompin △
  Malaysia 2°27N 103°45E **39 L4**
Ende *Indonesia* 8°45S 121°40E **37 F6**
Endeavour Str. *Australia* 10°45S 142°0E **62 A3**
Enderbury *Kiribati* 3°8S 171°5W **64 H10**
Enderby *Canada* 50°35N 119°10W **70 C5**
Enderby Abyssal Plain
  S. Ocean 60°0S 40°0E **5 C5**
Enderby I. *Australia* 20°35S 116°30E **60 D2**
Enderby Land *Antarctica* 66°0S 53°0E **5 C5**
Enderlin *U.S.A.* 46°38N 97°36W **80 B5**
Endicott *U.S.A.* 42°6N 76°4W **83 D8**
Endicott Mts. *U.S.A.* 68°0N 152°0W **74 B9**
Endwell *U.S.A.* 42°6N 76°2W **83 D8**
Endyalgout I. *Australia* 11°40S 132°35E **60 B5**
Eneabba *Australia* 29°49S 115°16E **61 E2**
Enewetak Atoll
  Marshall Is. 11°30N 162°15E **64 F8**
Enez *Turkey* 40°45N 26°5E **23 D12**
Enfer, Pte. d' *Martinique* 14°22N 60°54W **88 c**
Enfield *Canada* 44°56N 63°32W **73 D7**
Enfield *Conn., U.S.A.* 41°58N 72°36W **83 E12**
Enfield *N.C., U.S.A.* 36°11N 77°41W **85 C16**
Enfield *N.H., U.S.A.* 43°39N 72°9W **83 C12**
Engadin *Switz.* 46°45N 10°10E **20 C9**
Engaño, C. *Dom. Rep.* 18°30N 68°20W **89 C6**
Engaño, C. *Phil.* 18°35N 122°23E **37 A6**
Engaru *Japan* 44°3N 143°31E **28 B11**
Engcobo = Ngcobo
  S. Africa 31°37S 28°0E **57 D4**
Engels *Russia* 51°28N 46°6E **19 D8**
Engemann L. *Canada* 58°0N 106°55W **71 B7**
Enggano *Indonesia* 5°20S 102°40E **36 F2**
England *U.S.A.* 34°33N 91°58W **84 D9**
England □ *U.K.* 53°0N 2°0W **13 E5**
Englee *Canada* 50°45N 56°5W **73 B8**
Englehart *Canada* 47°49N 79°52W **72 C4**
English → *Canada* 49°12N 91°5W **71 C10**
English Bazar = Ingraj Bazar
  India 24°58N 88°10E **43 G13**
English Channel *Europe* 50°0N 2°0W **13 G6**
English Company's Is., The
  Australia 11°50S 136°32E **62 A2**
English River *Canada* 49°14N 91°0W **72 C1**
Enid *U.S.A.* 36°24N 97°53W **84 C6**
Eniwa *Japan* 43°0N 141°30E **28 C10**
Enkhuizen *Neths.* 52°42N 5°17E **15 B5**
Enle *China* 24°0N 101°0E **34 F3**
Enna *Italy* 37°34N 14°16E **22 F6**
Ennadai L. *Canada* 60°58N 101°20W **71 A8**
Ennedi *Chad* 17°15N 22°0E **53 E10**
Enngonia *Australia* 29°21S 145°50E **63 D4**
Ennis *Ireland* 52°51N 8°59W **10 D3**
Ennis *Mont., U.S.A.* 45°21N 111°44W **76 D8**
Ennis *Tex., U.S.A.* 32°20N 96°38W **84 E6**
Enniscorthy *Ireland* 52°30N 6°34W **10 D5**
Enniskillen *U.K.* 54°21N 7°39W **10 B4**
Ennistimon *Ireland* 52°57N 9°17W **10 D2**
Enns → *Austria* 48°14N 14°32E **16 D8**
Eno *Finland* 62°47N 30°10E **8 E24**
Enosburg Falls *U.S.A.* 44°55N 72°48W **83 B12**
Enping *China* 22°16N 112°21E **35 F9**
Enriquillo, L. *Dom. Rep.* 18°20N 71°40W **89 C5**
Enschede *Neths.* 52°13N 6°53E **15 B6**
Ensenada *Argentina* 34°55S 57°55W **94 C4**
Ensenada *Mexico* 31°52N 116°37W **86 A1**
Ensenada de los Muertos
  Mexico 23°59N 109°50W **86 C3**
Enshi *China* 30°18N 109°29E **34 B7**
Entebbe *Uganda* 0°4N 32°28E **54 D6**
Enterprise *Canada* 60°47N 115°45W **70 A5**
Enterprise *Ala., U.S.A.* 31°19N 85°51W **85 F12**
Enterprise *Oreg., U.S.A.* 45°25N 117°17W **76 D5**
Entre Ríos *Bolivia* 21°30S 64°25W **94 A3**
Entre Ríos □ *Argentina* 30°30S 58°30W **94 C4**
Entroncamento *Portugal* 39°28N 8°28W **21 C1**
Enugu *Nigeria* 6°30N 7°30E **52 G7**
Enumclaw *U.S.A.* 47°12N 121°59W **78 C5**
Eochaill = Youghal
  Ireland 51°56N 7°52W **10 E4**
Eólie, Ís. *Italy* 38°30N 14°57E **22 E6**
Epe *Neths.* 52°21N 5°59E **15 B5**
Épernay *France* 49°3N 3°56E **20 B5**
Ephesus *Turkey* 37°55N 27°22E **23 F12**

Ephraim *U.S.A.* 39°22N 111°35W **76 G8**
Ephrata *Pa., U.S.A.* 40°11N 76°11W **83 F8**
Ephrata *Wash., U.S.A.* 47°19N 119°33W **76 C4**
Épinal *France* 48°10N 6°27E **20 B7**
Epsom *U.K.* 51°19N 0°16W **13 F7**
Epukiro *Namibia* 21°40S 19°9E **56 B2**
Equatoria = El Istiwa'iya
  Sudan 5°0N 28°0E **53 G11**
Equatorial Guinea ■ *Africa* 2°0N 8°0E **54 D1**
Er Hai *China* 25°48N 100°11E **34 E3**
Er Rachidia *Morocco* 31°58N 4°20W **52 B5**
Er Rahad *Sudan* 12°45N 30°32E **53 F12**
Er Rif *Morocco* 35°1N 4°1W **52 A5**
Erandol *India* 20°56N 75°20E **44 D2**
Erāwaḍī Myit = Irrawaddy →
  Burma 15°50N 95°6E **41 M19**
Erāwaḍī Myitwanya = Irrawaddy,
  Mouths of the *Burma* 15°30N 95°0E **41 M19**
Erawan △ *Thailand* 14°25N 98°58E **38 E2**
Erbil = Arbīl *Iraq* 36°15N 44°5E **46 B5**
Erçek *Turkey* 38°39N 43°36E **46 B4**
Erciyaş Dağı *Turkey* 38°30N 35°30E **46 B2**
Érd *Hungary* 47°22N 18°56E **17 E10**
Erdao Jiang → *China* 42°37N 128°0E **33 C14**
Erdek *Turkey* 40°23N 27°47E **23 D12**
Erdene = Ulaan-Uul
  Mongolia 46°4N 100°49E **32 B6**
Erdenet *Mongolia* 49°2N 104°5E **32 B6**
Erdenetsogt *Mongolia* 42°55N 106°5E **32 C4**
Erebus, Mt. *Antarctica* 77°35S 167°0E **5 D11**
Erechim *Brazil* 27°35S 52°15W **95 B5**
Ereğli *Konya, Turkey* 37°31N 34°4E **46 B2**
Ereğli *Zonguldak, Turkey* 41°15N 31°24E **19 F5**
Erenhot *China* 43°48N 112°2E **32 C7**
Eresma → *Spain* 41°26N 4°45W **21 B3**
Erfenisdam *S. Africa* 28°30S 26°50E **56 C4**
Erfurt *Germany* 50°58N 11°2E **16 C6**
Ergani *Turkey* 38°17N 39°49E **46 B3**
Ergel *Mongolia* 43°8N 109°5E **32 C5**
Ergeni Vozvyshennost
  Russia 47°0N 44°0E **19 E7**
Ērgļi *Latvia* 56°54N 25°38E **9 H21**
Ergun He = Argun →
  Russia 53°20N 121°28E **31 A13**
Ergun Youqi *China* 50°15N 120°11E **31 A13**
Erhlin *Taiwan* 23°54N 120°22E **35 F13**
Eriboll, L. *U.K.* 58°30N 4°42W **11 C4**
Érice *Italy* 38°2N 12°35E **22 E5**
Erie *U.S.A.* 42°8N 80°5W **82 D4**
Erie, L. *N. Amer.* 42°15N 81°0W **82 D4**
Erie Canal *U.S.A.* 43°5N 78°43W **82 C7**
Erieau *Canada* 42°16N 81°57W **82 D3**
Erigavo = Ceerigaabo
  Somalia 10°35N 47°20E **49 E4**
Eriksdale *Canada* 50°52N 98°7W **71 C9**
Erimanthos *Greece* 37°57N 21°50E **23 F9**
Erimo-Misaki *Japan* 41°50N 143°15E **28 D11**
Erin *Canada* 43°45N 80°7W **82 C4**
Erin Pt. *Trin. & Tob.* 10°3N 61°39W **93 K15**
Erinpura *India* 25°9N 73°3E **42 G5**
Eriskay *U.K.* 57°4N 7°18W **11 D1**
Eritrea ■ *Africa* 14°0N 38°30E **49 D2**
Erlangen *Germany* 49°36N 11°0E **16 D6**
Erldunda *Australia* 25°14S 133°12E **62 D1**
Ermelo *Neths.* 52°18N 5°35E **15 B5**
Ermelo *S. Africa* 26°31S 29°59E **57 C4**
Ermenek *Turkey* 36°38N 33°0E **46 B2**
Ermoupoli *Greece* 37°28N 24°57E **23 F11**
Ernakulam *India* 9°59N 76°22E **45 K3**
Erne → *Ireland* 54°30N 8°16W **10 B3**
Erne, Lower L. *U.K.* 54°28N 7°47W **10 B4**
Erne, Upper L. *U.K.* 54°14N 7°32W **10 B4**
Ernest Giles Ra. *Australia* 27°0S 123°45E **61 E3**
Erode *India* 11°24N 77°45E **45 J3**
Eromanga *Australia* 26°40S 143°11E **63 D3**
Erongo *Namibia* 21°39S 15°58E **56 B2**
Erongo □ *Namibia* 22°20S 15°0E **56 B2**
Erramala Hills *India* 15°30N 78°15E **45 M4**
Errenteria *Spain* 43°19N 1°54W **21 A5**
Errigal *Ireland* 55°2N 8°6W **10 A3**
Errinundra △ *Australia* 37°20S 148°47E **63 F4**
Erris Hd. *Ireland* 54°17N 10°0W **10 B1**
Erskine *U.S.A.* 47°40N 96°0W **80 B6**
Ertan Shuiku *China* 27°5N 101°52E **34 D3**
Ertis = Irtysh → *Russia* 61°4N 68°52E **26 C7**
Erwin *U.S.A.* 36°9N 82°25W **85 C13**
Eryuan *China* 26°7N 99°57E **34 D2**
Erzgebirge *Germany* 50°27N 12°55E **16 C7**
Erzin *Russia* 50°15N 95°10E **27 D10**
Erzincan *Turkey* 39°46N 39°30E **46 B3**
Erzurum *Turkey* 39°57N 41°15E **46 B3**
Es Sahrâ' Esh Sharqîya
  Egypt 27°30N 32°30E **53 C12**
Es Sînâ' *Egypt* 29°0N 34°0E **48 F2**
Esan-Misaki *Japan* 41°40N 141°10E **28 D10**
Esashi *Hokkaidō, Japan* 44°56N 142°35E **28 B11**
Esashi *Hokkaidō, Japan* 41°52N 140°7E **28 D10**
Esbjerg *Denmark* 55°29N 8°29E **9 J13**
Esbo = Espoo *Finland* 60°12N 24°40E **9 F21**
Escalante *U.S.A.* 37°24N 111°10W **77 H8**
Escalante → *U.S.A.* 37°24N 110°57W **77 H8**
Escalón *Mexico* 26°40N 104°20W **86 B4**
Escambia → *U.S.A.* 30°32N 87°11W **85 F11**
Escanaba *U.S.A.* 45°45N 87°4W **80 C10**
Escárcega *Mexico* 18°37N 90°43W **87 D6**
Esch-sur-Alzette *Lux.* 49°32N 6°0E **15 E6**
Escondido *U.S.A.* 33°7N 117°5W **79 M9**
Escuinapa de Hidalgo
  Mexico 22°50N 105°50W **86 C3**
Escuintla *Guatemala* 14°20N 90°48W **88 D1**
Esenguly *Turkmenistan* 37°37N 53°59E **26 F6**
Eşfahān *Iran* 32°39N 51°43E **47 C6**
Eşfahān □ *Iran* 32°50N 51°50E **47 C6**
Esfarāyen *Iran* 37°4N 57°30E **47 B8**
Esfideh *Iran* 33°39N 59°46E **47 C8**
Esh Sham = Dimashq
  Syria 33°30N 36°18E **48 B5**
Esha Ness *U.K.* 60°29N 1°38W **11 A7**
Eshan *China* 24°11N 102°24E **34 E4**

Eshkol △ *Israel* 31°20N 34°30E **48** D3
Eshowe *S. Africa* 28°50S 31°30E **57** C5
Esigodini *Zimbabwe* 20°18S 28°56E **57** B4
Esil = Ishim ⇌ *Russia* 57°45N 71°10E **26** D8
Esk ⇌ *Dumf. & Gall., U.K.* 54°58N 3°2W **11** G5
Esk ⇌ *N. Yorks., U.K.* 54°30N 0°37W **12** C7
Eskān *Iran* 26°48N 63°9E **47** E9
Esker Siding *Canada* 53°53N 66°25W **73** B6
Eskifjörður *Iceland* 65°3N 13°55W **8** D7
Eskilstuna *Sweden* 59°22N 16°32E **9** G17
Eskimo Point = Arviat
  Canada 61°6N 93°59W **71** A10
Eskişehir *Turkey* 39°50N 30°30E **19** G5
Esla ⇌ *Spain* 41°29N 6°3W **21** B2
Eslāmābād-e Gharb *Iran* 34°10N 46°30E **46** C5
Eslāmshahr *Iran* 35°40N 51°10E **47** C6
Eşme *Turkey* 38°23N 28°58E **23** E13
Esmeraldas *Ecuador* 1°0N 79°40W **92** C3
Esna = Isna *Egypt* 25°17N 32°30E **53** C12
Esnagi L. *Canada* 48°36N 84°33W **72** C3
España = Spain ■ *Europe* 39°0N 4°0W **21** B4
Espanola *Canada* 46°15N 81°46W **72** C3
Espanola *U.S.A.* 35°59N 106°5W **77** J10
Esparza *Costa Rica* 9°59N 84°40W **88** E3
Esperance *Australia* 33°45S 121°55E **61** F3
Esperance B. *Australia* 33°48S 121°55E **61** F3
Esperance Harbour
  St. Lucia 14°4N 60°55W **89** f
Esperanza *Antarctica* 65°0S 55°0W **5** C18
Esperanza *Argentina* 31°29S 61°3W **94** C3
Esperanza *Puerto Rico* 18°6N 65°28W **89** d
Espichel, C. *Portugal* 38°22N 9°16W **21** C1
Espigão, Serra do *Brazil* 26°35S 50°30W **95** B5
Espinazo, Sierra del = Espinhaço,
  Serra do *Brazil* 17°30S 43°30W **93** G10
Espinhaço, Serra do
  Brazil 17°30S 43°30W **93** G10
Espinilho, Serra do *Brazil* 28°30S 55°0W **95** B5
Espírito Santo □ *Brazil* 20°0S 40°45W **93** H10
Espírito Santo do Pinhal
  Brazil 22°10S 46°46W **95** A6
Espíritu Santo *Vanuatu* 15°15S 166°50E **58** C9
Espíritu Santo, B. del
  Mexico 19°20N 87°35W **87** D7
Espíritu Santo, I.
  Mexico 24°30N 110°22W **86** C2
Espita *Mexico* 21°1N 88°19W **87** C7
Espoo *Finland* 60°12N 24°40E **9** F21
Espungabera *Mozam.* 20°29S 32°45E **57** B5
Esquel *Argentina* 42°55S 71°20W **96** E2
Esquimalt *Canada* 48°26N 123°25W **78** B3
Esquina *Argentina* 30°0S 59°30W **94** C4
Essaouira *Morocco* 31°32N 9°42W **52** B4
Essen *Belgium* 51°28N 4°28E **15** C4
Essen *Germany* 51°28N 7°2E **16** C4
Essendon, Mt. *Australia* 25°0S 120°29E **61** E3
Essequibo ⇌ *Guyana* 6°50N 58°30W **92** B7
Essex *Canada* 42°10N 82°49W **82** D2
Essex *Calif., U.S.A.* 34°44N 115°15W **79** L11
Essex *N.Y., U.S.A.* 44°19N 73°21W **83** B11
Essex □ *U.K.* 51°54N 0°27E **13** F8
Essex Junction *U.S.A.* 44°29N 73°7W **83** B11
Esslingen *Germany* 48°44N 9°18E **16** D5
Estación Camacho
  Mexico 24°25N 102°18W **86** C4
Estación Simón *Mexico* 24°42N 102°35W **86** C4
Estados, I. de Los
  Argentina 54°40S 64°30W **96** G4
Eştahbānāt *Iran* 29°8N 54°4E **47** D7
Estância *Brazil* 11°16S 37°26W **93** F11
Estancia *U.S.A.* 34°46N 106°4W **77** J10
Estārm *Iran* 28°21N 58°21E **47** D8
Estcourt *S. Africa* 29°0S 29°53E **57** C4
Este △ *Dom. Rep.* 18°14N 68°42W **89** C6
Esteli *Nic.* 13°9N 86°22W **88** D2
Esterhazy *Canada* 50°37N 102°5W **71** C8
Estevan *Canada* 49°10N 102°59W **71** D8
Estevan Group *Canada* 53°3N 129°38W **70** C3
Estherville *U.S.A.* 43°24N 94°50W **80** D6
Eston *Canada* 51°8N 108°40W **71** C7
Estonia ■ *Europe* 58°30N 25°30E **9** G21
Estreito *Brazil* 6°32S 47°25W **93** E9
Estrela, Serra da *Portugal* 40°10N 7°45W **21** B2
Estremoz *Portugal* 38°51N 7°39W **21** C2
Estrondo, Serra do *Brazil* 7°20S 48°0W **93** E9
Esztergom *Hungary* 47°47N 18°44E **17** E10
Et Tidra *Mauritania* 19°45N 16°20W **52** E2
Etah *India* 27°35N 78°40E **43** F8
Étampes *France* 48°26N 2°10E **20** B5
Etanga *Namibia* 17°55S 13°0E **56** A1
Etawah *India* 26°48N 79°6E **43** F8
Etawney L. *Canada* 57°50N 96°50W **71** B9
Etchojoa *Mexico* 26°55N 109°38W **86** B4
eThekwini = Durban
  S. Africa 29°49S 31°1E **57** C5
Ethel *U.S.A.* 46°32N 122°46W **78** D4
Ethelbert *Canada* 51°32N 100°25W **71** C8
Ethiopia ■ *Africa* 8°0N 40°0E **49** F3
Ethiopian Highlands
  Ethiopia 10°0N 37°0E **49** F2
Etive, L. *U.K.* 56°29N 5°10W **11** E3
Etna *Italy* 37°50N 14°55E **22** F6
Etolin Strait *U.S.A.* 60°20N 165°15W **74** C6
Etosha △ *Namibia* 19°0S 16°0E **56** A2
Etosha Pan *Namibia* 18°40S 16°30E **56** A2
Etowah *U.S.A.* 35°20N 84°32W **85** D12
Etrek *Turkmenistan* 37°36N 54°46E **47** B7
Ettelbruck *Lux.* 49°51N 6°5E **15** E6
Ettrick Water ⇌ *U.K.* 55°31N 2°55W **11** F6
Etzná-Tixmucuy = Edzná
  Mexico 19°39N 90°19W **87** D6
Eua *Tonga* 21°22S 174°56W **59** c
Euboea = Evia *Greece* 38°30N 24°0E **23** E11
Eucla *Australia* 31°41S 128°52E **61** F4
Euclid *U.S.A.* 41°34N 81°32W **82** E3
Eucumbene, L. *Australia* 36°2S 148°40E **63** F4
Eudora *U.S.A.* 33°7N 91°16W **84** E9
Eufaula *Ala., U.S.A.* 31°54N 85°9W **85** F12
Eufaula *Okla., U.S.A.* 35°17N 95°35W **84** D7

Eufaula L. *U.S.A.* 35°18N 95°21W **84** D7
Eugene *U.S.A.* 44°5N 123°4W **76** D2
Eugowra *Australia* 33°22S 148°24E **63** E4
Eulo *Australia* 28°10S 145°3E **63** D4
Eungella △ *Australia* 20°57S 148°40E **62** b
Eunice *La., U.S.A.* 30°30N 92°25W **84** F8
Eunice *N. Mex., U.S.A.* 32°26N 103°10W **77** K12
Eupen *Belgium* 50°37N 6°3E **15** D6
Euphrates = Furāt, Nahr al ⇌
  Asia 31°0N 47°25E **46** D5
Eureka *Canada* 80°0N 85°56W **69** B14
Eureka *Calif., U.S.A.* 40°47N 124°9W **76** F1
Eureka *Kans., U.S.A.* 37°49N 96°17W **80** G5
Eureka *Mont., U.S.A.* 48°53N 115°3W **76** B6
Eureka *Nev., U.S.A.* 39°31N 115°58W **76** G6
Eureka *S. Dak., U.S.A.* 45°46N 99°38W **80** C4
Eureka Sd. *Canada* 79°0N 85°0W **69** B15
Euroa *Australia* 36°44S 145°35E **63** F4
Europa, Île *Ind. Oc.* 22°20S 40°22E **57** B7
Europa, Picos de *Spain* 43°10N 4°49W **21** A3
Europa, Pt. *Gib.* 36°3N 5°21W **21** D3
Europe 50°0N 20°0E **6** E10
Europoort *Neths.* 51°57N 4°10E **15** C4
Eustis *U.S.A.* 28°51N 81°41W **85** G14
Eutsuk L. *Canada* 53°20N 126°45W **70** C3
Evale *Angola* 16°33S 15°44E **56** A2
Evans *U.S.A.* 40°23N 104°41W **76** F11
Evans, L. *Canada* 50°50N 77°0W **72** B4
Evans City *U.S.A.* 40°46N 80°4W **82** F4
Evans Head *Australia* 29°7S 153°27E **63** D5
Evansburg *Canada* 53°36N 114°59W **70** C5
Evanston *U.S.A.* 41°16N 110°58W **76** F8
Evansville *U.S.A.* 37°58N 87°35W **80** G10
Evaz *Iran* 27°46N 53°59E **47** E7
Eveleth *U.S.A.* 47°28N 92°32W **80** B7
Evensk *Russia* 62°12N 159°30E **27** C16
Everard, L. *Australia* 31°30S 135°0E **63** E2
Everard Ranges *Australia* 27°5S 132°28E **61** E5
Everest, Mt. *Nepal* 28°5N 86°58E **43** E12
Everett *Pa., U.S.A.* 40°1N 78°23W **82** F6
Everett *Wash., U.S.A.* 47°59N 122°12W **78** C4
Everglades, The *U.S.A.* 25°50N 81°0W **85** J14
Everglades △ *U.S.A.* 25°30N 81°0W **85** J14
Everglades City *U.S.A.* 25°52N 81°23W **85** J14
Evergreen *Ala., U.S.A.* 31°26N 86°57W **85** F11
Evergreen *Mont., U.S.A.* 48°14N 114°17W **76** B6
Evesham *U.K.* 52°6N 1°56W **13** E6
Evia *Greece* 38°30N 24°0E **23** E11
Evje *Norway* 58°36N 7°51E **9** G12
Évora *Portugal* 38°33N 7°57W **21** C2
Evowghlī *Iran* 38°43N 45°13E **46** B5
Évreux *France* 49°3N 1°8E **20** B4
Evros ⇌ *Greece* 41°40N 26°34E **23** D12
Évry *France* 48°38N 2°27E **20** B5
Évvoia = Evia *Greece* 38°30N 24°0E **23** E11
Ewe, L. *U.K.* 57°49N 5°38W **11** D3
Ewing *U.S.A.* 42°16N 98°21W **80** D4
Ewo *Congo* 0°48S 14°45E **54** E2
Exaltación *Bolivia* 13°10S 65°20W **92** F5
Excelsior Springs *U.S.A.* 39°20N 94°13W **80** F6
Exe ⇌ *U.K.* 50°41N 3°29W **13** G4
Exeter *Canada* 43°21N 81°29W **82** C3
Exeter *U.K.* 50°43N 3°31W **13** G4
Exeter *Calif., U.S.A.* 36°18N 119°9W **78** J7
Exeter *N.H., U.S.A.* 42°59N 70°57W **83** D14
Exmoor *U.K.* 51°12N 3°45W **13** F4
Exmoor △ *U.K.* 51°8N 3°42W **13** F4
Exmouth *Australia* 21°54S 114°10E **60** D1
Exmouth *U.K.* 50°37N 3°25W **13** G4
Exmouth G. *Australia* 22°15S 114°15E **60** D1
Exmouth Plateau *Ind. Oc.* 19°0S 114°0E **64** J3
Expedition △ *Australia* 25°41S 149°7E **63** D4
Expedition Ra. *Australia* 24°30S 149°12E **62** C4
Extremadura □ *Spain* 39°30N 6°5W **21** C2
Exuma Sound *Bahamas* 24°30N 76°20W **88** B4
Eyasi, L. *Tanzania* 3°30S 35°0E **54** E7
Eye Pen. *U.K.* 58°13N 6°10W **11** C2
Eyemouth *U.K.* 55°52N 2°5W **11** F6
Eyjafjallajökull *Iceland* 63°38N 19°36W **8** E4
Eyjafjörður *Iceland* 66°15N 18°30W **8** C4
Eyl *Somalia* 8°0N 49°50E **49** F4
Eyre (North), L.
  Australia 28°30S 137°20E **63** D2
Eyre (South), L.
  Australia 29°18S 137°25E **63** D2
Eyre, L. *Australia* 29°30S 137°26E **58** D6
Eyre Mts. *N.Z.* 45°25S 168°25E **59** F2
Eyre Pen. *Australia* 33°30S 136°17E **63** E2
Eysturoy *Færoe Is.* 62°13N 6°54W **8** E9
Eyvān = Jūy Zar *Iran* 33°50N 46°18E **46** C5
Eyvānkī *Iran* 35°24N 51°56E **47** C6
Ezhou *China* 30°23N 114°50E **35** B10
Ezine *Turkey* 39°48N 26°20E **23** E12

F

F.Y.R.O.M. = Macedonia ■
  Europe 41°53N 21°40E **23** D9
Faaa *Tahiti* 17°34S 149°35W **59** d
Faaone *Tahiti* 17°40S 149°21W **59** d
Fabala *Guinea* 9°44N 9°5W **52** G4
Fabens *U.S.A.* 31°30N 106°10W **84** F1
Fabius *U.S.A.* 42°50N 75°59W **83** D9
Fabriano *Italy* 43°20N 12°54E **22** C5
Fachi *Niger* 18°6N 11°34E **53** E8
Fada *Chad* 17°13N 21°34E **53** E10
Fada-n-Gourma
  Burkina Faso 12°10N 0°30E **52** F6
Faddeyevskiy, Ostrov
  Russia 76°0N 144°0E **27** B15
Fadghāmī *Syria* 35°53N 40°52E **46** C4
Faenza *Italy* 44°17N 11°53E **22** B4
Færoe Is. = Føroyar ☑
  Atl. Oc. 62°0N 7°0W **8** F9
Făgăraş *Romania* 45°48N 24°58E **17** F13
Fagersta *Sweden* 60°1N 15°46E **9** F16
Fagnano, L. *Argentina* 54°30S 68°0W **96** G3
Fahlīān *Iran* 30°11N 51°28E **47** D6

Fahraj *Kermān, Iran* 29°0N 59°0E **47** D8
Fahraj *Yazd, Iran* 31°46N 54°36E **47** D7
Fai Tsi Long *Vietnam* 21°0N 107°30E **34** G6
Faial *Azores* 38°34N 28°42W **52** a
Faichan Kangri *India* 35°48N 76°34E **43** B7
Fair Haven *N.Y., U.S.A.* 43°18N 76°42W **83** C8
Fair Haven *Vt., U.S.A.* 43°36N 73°16W **83** C11
Fair Hd. *U.K.* 55°14N 6°9W **10** A5
Fair Isle *U.K.* 59°32N 1°38W **14** B6
Fair Oaks *U.S.A.* 38°39N 121°16W **78** G5
Fairbanks *U.S.A.* 64°51N 147°43W **68** C2
Fairbury *U.S.A.* 40°8N 97°11W **80** E5
Fairfax *U.S.A.* 44°40N 73°1W **83** B11
Fairfield *Ala., U.S.A.* 33°29N 86°55W **85** E11
Fairfield *Calif., U.S.A.* 38°15N 122°3W **78** G4
Fairfield *Conn., U.S.A.* 41°9N 73°16W **83** E11
Fairfield *Idaho, U.S.A.* 43°21N 114°44W **76** E6
Fairfield *Ill., U.S.A.* 38°23N 88°22W **80** F9
Fairfield *Iowa, U.S.A.* 40°56N 91°57W **80** E8
Fairfield *Tex., U.S.A.* 31°44N 96°10W **84** F6
Fairford *Canada* 51°37N 98°38W **71** C9
Fairhope *U.S.A.* 30°31N 87°54W **85** F11
Fairlie *N.Z.* 44°5S 170°49E **59** F3
Fairmead *U.S.A.* 37°5N 120°10W **78** H6
Fairmont *Minn., U.S.A.* 43°39N 94°28W **80** D6
Fairmont *W. Va., U.S.A.* 39°29N 80°9W **81** F13
Fairmount *Calif., U.S.A.* 34°45N 118°26W **79** L8
Fairmount *N.Y., U.S.A.* 43°5N 76°12W **83** C8
Fairplay *U.S.A.* 39°15N 106°2W **76** G10
Fairport *U.S.A.* 43°6N 77°27W **82** C7
Fairport Harbor *U.S.A.* 41°45N 81°17W **82** E3
Fairview *Canada* 56°5N 118°25W **70** B5
Fairview *Mont., U.S.A.* 47°51N 104°3W **76** C11
Fairview *Okla., U.S.A.* 36°16N 98°29W **84** C5
Fairweather, Mt. *U.S.A.* 58°55N 137°32W **70** B1
Faisalabad *Pakistan* 31°30N 73°5E **42** D5
Faith *U.S.A.* 45°2N 102°2W **80** C2
Faizabad *India* 26°45N 82°10E **43** F10
Faizpur *India* 21°14N 75°49E **44** D2
Fajardo *Puerto Rico* 18°20N 65°39W **89** d
Fajr, W. ⇌ *Si. Arabia* 29°10N 38°10E **46** D3
Fakenham *U.K.* 52°51N 0°51E **12** E8
Fakfak *Indonesia* 2°55S 132°18E **37** E8
Faku *China* 42°32N 123°21E **33** C12
Falaise *France* 48°54N 0°12W **20** B3
Falam *Burma* 23°0N 93°45E **41** H18
Falcón, Presa *Mexico* 26°35N 99°10W **87** B5
Falcon Lake *Canada* 49°42N 95°15W **71** D9
Falcon Res. *U.S.A.* 26°34N 99°10W **84** H5
Falconara Marittima
  Italy 43°37N 13°24E **22** C5
Falcone, C. del *Italy* 40°58N 8°12E **22** D3
Falconer *U.S.A.* 42°7N 79°12W **82** D5
Falefa *Samoa* 13°54S 171°31W **59** b
Falelatai *Samoa* 13°55S 171°59W **59** b
Falelima *Samoa* 13°32S 172°41W **59** b
Faleshty = Fălești
  Moldova 47°32N 27°44E **17** E14
Fălești *Moldova* 47°32N 27°44E **17** E14
Falfurrias *U.S.A.* 27°14N 98°9W **84** H5
Falher *Canada* 55°44N 117°15W **70** B5
Falkenberg *Sweden* 56°54N 12°30E **9** H15
Falkirk *U.K.* 56°0N 3°47W **11** F5
Falkirk □ *U.K.* 55°58N 3°49W **11** F5
Falkland Is. ☑ *Atl. Oc.* 51°30S 59°0W **96** G5
Falkland Sd. *Falk. Is.* 52°0S 60°0W **96** G5
Fall River *U.S.A.* 41°43N 71°10W **83** E13
Fallbrook *U.S.A.* 33°23N 117°15W **79** M9
Fallon *U.S.A.* 39°28N 118°47W **76** G4
Falls City *U.S.A.* 40°3N 95°36W **80** E6
Falls Creek *U.S.A.* 41°9N 78°48W **82** E6
Falmouth *Jamaica* 18°30N 77°40W **88** a
Falmouth *U.K.* 50°9N 5°5W **13** G2
Falmouth *U.S.A.* 41°33N 70°37W **83** E14
Falsa, Pta. *Mexico* 27°51N 115°3W **86** B1
False B. *S. Africa* 34°15S 18°40E **56** E2
False Divi Pt. *India* 15°43N 80°50E **45** G5
False Pt. *India* 20°18N 86°48E **44** D8
Falso, C. *Honduras* 15°12N 83°21W **88** C3
Falster *Denmark* 54°45N 11°55E **9** J14
Fălticeni *Romania* 47°21N 26°20E **17** E14
Falun *Sweden* 60°37N 15°37E **8** F16
Famagusta *Cyprus* 35°8N 33°55E **46** C2
Famatina, Sierra de
  Argentina 27°30S 68°0W **94** B2
Family L. *Canada* 51°54N 95°27W **71** C9
Famoso *U.S.A.* 35°37N 119°12W **79** K7
Fan Xian *China* 35°55N 115°38E **32** G8
Fanad Hd. *Ireland* 55°17N 7°38W **10** A4
Fang *Thailand* 19°55N 99°13E **38** C2
Fang Xian *China* 32°3N 110°40E **35** A8
Fangcheng *China* 33°18N 112°59E **32** H7
Fangchang *China* 31°5N 118°4E **35** B12
Fangcheng *China* 33°18N 112°59E **32** H7
Fangchenggang *China* 21°42N 108°21E **34** G7
Fangliao *Taiwan* 22°22N 120°38E **35** F13
Fangshan *Beijing, China* 39°41N 116°0E **32** E9
Fangshan *Shanxi, China* 38°3N 111°25E **32** E6
Fangzi *China* 36°33N 119°10E **33** F10
Fanjiatun *China* 43°40N 125°15E **33** C13
Fanling *China* 22°30N 114°8E **31** a
Fannich, L. *U.K.* 57°38N 4°59W **11** D4
Fannūj *Iran* 26°35N 59°38E **47** E8
Fanø *Denmark* 55°25N 8°25E **9** J13
Fano *Italy* 43°50N 13°1E **22** C5
Fanshi *China* 39°12N 113°20E **32** E7
Fao = Al Fāw *Iraq* 30°0N 48°30E **47** D6
Faqirwali *Pakistan* 29°27N 73°0E **42** E5
Far East = Dalnevostochnyy □
  Russia 67°0N 140°0E **27** C14
Far East *Asia* 40°0N 130°0E **24** E14
Faradje
  Dem. Rep. of the Congo 3°50N 29°45E **54** D5
Farafangana *Madag.* 22°49S 47°50E **55** J9
Farāh *Afghan.* 32°20N 62°7E **40** C3
Farāh □ *Afghan.* 32°25N 62°10E **40** C3
Faranah *Guinea* 10°3N 10°45W **52** F3
Farasān, Jazā'ir *Si. Arabia* 16°45N 41°55E **49** D3
Farasan Is. = Farasān, Jazā'ir
  Si. Arabia 16°45N 41°55E **49** D3

Fareham *U.K.* 50°51N 1°11W **13** G6
Farewell, C. *N.Z.* 40°29S 172°43E **59** D4
Farewell C. = Nunap Isua
  Greenland 59°48N 43°55W **66** D15
Farghona *Uzbekistan* 40°23N 71°19E **26** E8
Fargo *U.S.A.* 46°53N 96°48W **80** B5
Fār'iah, W. al ⇌
  West Bank 32°12N 35°27E **48** C4
Faribault *U.S.A.* 44°18N 93°16W **80** C7
Faridabad *India* 28°26N 77°19E **42** E6
Faridkot *India* 30°44N 74°45E **42** D6
Faridpur *Bangla.* 23°15N 89°55E **43** H13
Faridpur *India* 28°13N 79°33E **43** E8
Farīmān *Iran* 35°40N 59°49E **47** C8
Farleigh *Australia* 21°4S 149°8E **62** b
Farmerville *U.S.A.* 32°47N 92°24W **84** E8
Farmingdale *U.S.A.* 40°12N 74°10W **83** F10
Farmington *Canada* 55°54N 120°30W **70** B4
Farmington *Calif., U.S.A.* 37°55N 120°59W **78** H6
Farmington *Maine, U.S.A.* 44°40N 70°9W **81** C18
Farmington *Mo., U.S.A.* 37°47N 90°25W **80** G8
Farmington *N.H., U.S.A.* 43°24N 71°4W **83** C13
Farmington *N. Mex., U.S.A.* 36°44N 108°12W **77** H9
Farmington *Utah, U.S.A.* 40°59N 111°53W **76** F8
Farmington ⇌ *U.S.A.* 41°51N 72°38W **83** E12
Farmville *U.S.A.* 37°18N 78°24W **81** G14
Farne Is. *U.K.* 55°38N 1°37W **12** B6
Farnham *Canada* 45°17N 72°59W **83** A12
Farnham, Mt. *Canada* 50°29N 116°30W **70** C5
Faro *Brazil* 2°10S 56°39W **93** D7
Faro *Canada* 62°11N 133°22W **68** E5
Faro *Portugal* 37°2N 7°55W **21** D2
Fårö *Sweden* 57°55N 19°5E **9** H18
Farquhar, C. *Australia* 23°50S 113°36E **61** D1
Farrars Cr. ⇌ *Australia* 25°35S 140°43E **62** D3
Farrāshband *Iran* 28°57N 52°5E **47** D7
Farrell *U.S.A.* 41°13N 80°30W **82** E4
Farrokhī *Iran* 33°50N 59°31E **47** C8
Farrukhabad *India* 27°24N 79°34E **44** A4
Fārs □ *Iran* 29°30N 55°0E **47** D7
Farsala *Greece* 39°17N 22°23E **23** E10
Fārsī *Iran* 27°58N 50°11E **47** E6
Farson *U.S.A.* 42°7N 109°26W **76** E9
Farsund *Norway* 58°5N 6°55E **9** G12
Fartak, Râs *Si. Arabia* 28°5N 34°34E **46** D2
Fartak, Ra's *Yemen* 15°38N 52°15E **49** D5
Fartura, Serra da *Brazil* 26°21S 52°52W **95** B5
Fārūj *Iran* 37°14N 58°14E **47** B8
Farvel, Kap = Nunap Isua
  Greenland 59°48N 43°55W **66** D15
Farwell *U.S.A.* 34°23N 103°2W **84** D3
Faryāb □ *Afghan.* 36°0N 65°0E **40** B4
Fasā *Iran* 29°0N 53°39E **47** D7
Fasano *Italy* 40°50N 17°22E **22** D7
Fastiv *Ukraine* 50°7N 29°57E **17** C15
Fastnet Rock *Ireland* 51°22N 9°37W **10** E2
Fastov = Fastiv *Ukraine* 50°7N 29°57E **17** C15
Fatagartuting, Tanjung
  Indonesia 2°46S 131°57E **37** E8
Fatehabad *Haryana, India* 29°31N 75°27E **42** E6
Fatehabad *Ut. P., India* 27°1N 78°19E **42** F8
Fatehgarh *India* 27°25N 79°35E **43** F8
Fatehpur *Bihar, India* 24°38N 85°14E **43** G11
Fatehpur *Raj., India* 28°0N 74°40E **42** F6
Fatehpur *Ut. P., India* 25°56N 81°13E **43** G9
Fatehpur *Ut. P., India* 27°10N 81°13E **43** F9
Fatehpur Sikri *India* 27°6N 77°40E **42** F6
Fathom Five △ *Canada* 45°17N 81°40W **82** A3
Fatima *Canada* 47°24N 61°53W **73** C7
Fátima *Portugal* 39°37N 8°39W **21** C1
Faulkton *U.S.A.* 45°2N 99°8W **80** C4
Faure I. *Australia* 25°52S 113°50E **61** E1
Fauresmith *S. Africa* 29°44S 25°17E **56** D4
Fauske *Norway* 67°17N 15°25E **8** C16
Favara *Italy* 37°19N 13°39E **22** F5
Favignana *Italy* 37°56N 12°20E **22** F5
Fawcett, Pt. *Australia* 11°46S 130°2E **60** B5
Fawn ⇌ *Canada* 55°20N 87°50W **72** A2
Fawnskin *U.S.A.* 34°16N 116°56W **79** L10
Faxaflói *Iceland* 64°29N 23°0W **8** D2
Faya-Largeau *Chad* 17°58N 19°6E **53** E9
Fayd *Si. Arabia* 27°1N 42°52E **46** E4
Fayette *Ala., U.S.A.* 33°41N 87°50W **85** E11
Fayette *Mo., U.S.A.* 39°9N 92°41W **80** F7
Fayetteville *Ark., U.S.A.* 36°4N 94°10W **84** C7
Fayetteville *N.C., U.S.A.* 35°3N 78°53W **85** D15
Fayetteville *N.Y., U.S.A.* 43°1N 76°0W **83** C9
Fayetteville *Tenn., U.S.A.* 35°9N 86°34W **85** D11
Faylakah *Kuwait* 29°27N 48°20E **47** D6
Fazilka *India* 30°27N 74°2E **42** D6
Fazilpur *Pakistan* 29°18N 70°29E **42** E4
Fdérik *Mauritania* 22°40N 12°45W **52** D3
Feale ⇌ *Ireland* 52°56N 9°28W **10** D2
Fear, C. *U.S.A.* 33°50N 77°58W **85** E16
Feather ⇌ *U.S.A.* 38°47N 121°36W **76** G3
Feather Falls *U.S.A.* 39°36N 121°16W **78** F5
Featherston *N.Z.* 41°6S 175°20E **59** D5
Fécamp *France* 49°45N 0°22E **20** B4
Fedala = Mohammedia
  Morocco 33°44N 7°21W **52** B4
Federación *Argentina* 31°0S 57°55W **94** C4
Federal Way *U.S.A.* 47°18N 122°19W **78** C4
Fedeshkūh *Iran* 28°49N 53°50E **47** D7
Fehmarn *Germany* 54°27N 11°7E **16** A6
Fehmarn Bælt *Europe* 54°35N 11°20E **9** J14
Fehmarn Belt = Fehmarn Bælt
  Europe 54°35N 11°20E **9** J14

Feixi *China* 31°43N 117°59E **35** B11
Feixiang *China* 36°30N 114°45E **32** F8
Feldkirch *Austria* 47°15N 9°37E **16** E5
Félicité *Seychelles* 4°19S 55°52E **55** b
Felipe Carrillo Puerto
  Mexico 19°38N 88°3W **87** D7
Felixburg *Zimbabwe* 19°29S 30°51E **57** A5
Felixstowe *U.K.* 51°58N 1°23E **13** F9
Felton *U.S.A.* 37°3N 122°4W **78** H4
Femer Bælt = Fehmarn Bælt
  Europe 54°35N 11°20E **9** J14
Femunden *Norway* 62°10N 11°53E **8** E14
Fen He ⇌ *China* 35°36N 110°42E **32** G6
Fenelon Falls *Canada* 44°32N 78°45W **82** B6
Feng Xian *Jiangsu, China* 34°43N 116°35E **32** G9
Feng Xian *Shaanxi, China* 33°54N 106°40E **32** H4
Fengcheng *Jiangxi,*
  China 28°12N 115°48E **35** C10
Fengcheng *Liaoning,*
  China 40°28N 124°5E **33** D13
Fengdu *China* 29°55N 107°48E **34** C6
Fengfeng *China* 36°28N 114°8E **32** F8
Fenggang *China* 27°58N 107°47E **34** D6
Fenghua *China* 29°40N 121°25E **35** C13
Fenghuang *China* 27°57N 109°29E **34** D7
Fengjie *China* 31°3N 109°31E **34** B7
Fengkai *China* 23°24N 111°30E **35** F8
Fengkang *Taiwan* 22°12N 120°41E **35** F13
Fengle *China* 31°29N 112°29E **35** B9
Fenglin *Taiwan* 23°45N 121°26E **35** F13
Fengning *China* 41°10N 116°33E **32** D9
Fengqing *China* 24°38N 99°55E **34** E2
Fengqiu *China* 35°2N 114°25E **32** G8
Fengrun *China* 39°48N 118°8E **33** E10
Fengshan *Guangxi Zhuangzu,*
  China 24°39N 109°15E **34** E7
Fengshan *Guangxi Zhuangzu,*
  China 24°31N 107°3E **34** E6
Fengshan *Taiwan* 22°38N 120°21E **35** F13
Fengshun *China* 23°46N 116°10E **35** F11
Fengtai *China* 32°50N 116°40E **35** A11
Fengtongzhai △ *China* 30°32N 102°54E **34** B4
Fengxiang *China* 34°29N 107°25E **32** G4
Fengxin *China* 28°41N 115°18E **35** C10
Fengyang *China* 32°51N 117°29E **33** H9
Fengyi *China* 25°37N 100°20E **34** E3
Fengyüan *Taiwan* 24°15N 120°35E **35** F13
Fengzhen *China* 40°25N 113°2E **32** D7
Fenoarivo Atsinanana
  Madag. 17°22S 49°25E **55** H9
Fens, The *U.K.* 52°38N 0°2W **12** E7
Fenton *U.S.A.* 42°48N 83°42W **81** D12
Fenxi *China* 36°40N 111°31E **32** F6
Fenyang *China* 37°18N 111°48E **32** F6
Fenyi *China* 27°45N 114°47E **35** D10
Feodosiya *Ukraine* 45°2N 35°16E **19** E6
Ferbane *Ireland* 53°16N 7°50W **10** C4
Ferdows *Iran* 33°58N 58°2E **47** C8
Ferfer *Somalia* 5°4N 45°9E **49** F4
Fergana = Farghona
  Uzbekistan 40°23N 71°19E **26** E8
Fergus *Canada* 43°43N 80°24W **82** C4
Fergus Falls *U.S.A.* 46°17N 96°4W **80** B5
Ferizaj *Kosovo* 42°23N 21°10E **23** C9
Ferkéssédougou *Ivory C.* 9°35N 5°6W **52** G4
Ferland *Canada* 50°19N 88°27W **72** B2
Ferlo, Vallée du *Senegal* 15°15N 14°15W **52** E3
Fermanagh □ *U.K.* 54°21N 7°40W **10** B4
Fermo *Italy* 43°9N 13°43E **22** C5
Fermont *Canada* 52°47N 67°5W **73** B6
Fermoy *Ireland* 52°9N 8°16W **10** D3
Fernández *Argentina* 27°55S 63°50W **94** B3
Fernandina Beach
  U.S.A. 30°40N 81°27W **85** F14
Fernando de Noronha
  Brazil 4°0S 33°10W **93** D12
Fernando Póo = Bioko
  Eq. Guin. 3°30N 8°40E **54** D1
Ferndale *Canada* 44°58N 81°17W **82** B3
Ferndale *U.S.A.* 48°51N 122°36W **78** B4
Fernie *Canada* 49°30N 115°5W **70** D5
Fernlees *Australia* 23°51S 148°7E **62** C4
Fernley *U.S.A.* 39°36N 119°15W **76** G4
Fernwood *U.S.A.* 43°16N 73°38W **83** C11
Feroke *India* 11°9N 75°46E **45** J2
Ferozepore = Firozpur
  India 30°55N 74°40E **42** D6
Ferrara *Italy* 44°50N 11°35E **22** B4
Ferreñafe *Peru* 6°42S 79°50W **92** E3
Ferret, C. *France* 44°38N 1°15W **20** D3
Ferriday *U.S.A.* 31°38N 91°33W **84** F9
Ferrol *Spain* 43°29N 8°15W **21** A1
Ferron *U.S.A.* 39°5N 111°8W **76** G8
Ferryland *Canada* 47°2N 52°53W **73** C9
Fertile *U.S.A.* 47°32N 96°17W **80** B6
Fès *Morocco* 34°0N 5°0W **52** B5
Fessenden *U.S.A.* 47°39N 99°38W **80** B4
Festus *U.S.A.* 38°13N 90°24W **80** F8
Fetești *Romania* 44°22N 27°51E **17** F14
Fethiye *Turkey* 36°36N 29°6E **19** G4
Fetlar *U.K.* 60°36N 0°52W **11** A8
Feuilles ⇌ *Canada* 58°47N 70°4W **69** F17
Fez = Fès *Morocco* 34°0N 5°0W **52** B5
Fezzan *Libya* 27°0N 13°0E **53** C8
Fiambalá *Argentina* 27°45S 67°37W **94** B2
Fianarantsoa *Madag.* 21°26S 47°5E **55** J9
Ficksburg *S. Africa* 28°51S 27°53E **57** C4
Field ⇌ *Australia* 23°48S 138°0E **62** C2
Field I. *Australia* 12°5S 132°23E **60** B5
Fier *Albania* 40°43N 19°33E **23** D8
Fife □ *U.K.* 56°16N 3°1W **11** E5
Fife Ness *U.K.* 56°17N 2°35W **11** E6
Fifth Cataract *Sudan* 18°22N 33°50E **53** E12
Figeac *France* 44°37N 2°2E **20** D5
Figueira da Foz *Portugal* 40°7N 8°54W **21** B1
Figueres *Spain* 42°18N 2°58E **21** A7
Fiji ■ *Pac. Oc.* 17°20S 179°0E **59** a
Filabus *Zimbabwe* 20°34S 29°20E **57** B4

Filadelfia *Paraguay* 22°21S 60°2W **94** A3
Filchner Ice Shelf *Antarctica* 79°0S 40°0W **5** D1
Filey *U.K.* 54°12N 0°18W **12** C7
Filey B. *U.K.* 54°12N 0°15W **12** C7
Filiatra *Greece* 37°9N 21°35E **23** F9
Filingué *Niger* 14°21N 3°22E **52** F6
Filipstad *Sweden* 59°43N 14°9E **9** G16
Fillmore *Calif., U.S.A.* 34°24N 118°55W **79** L8
Fillmore *Utah, U.S.A.* 38°58N 112°20W **76** G7
Fimbul Ice Shelf *S. Ocean* 69°30S 1°0W **5** C2
Finch *Canada* 45°11N 75°7W **83** A9
Finch Hatton *Australia* 20°25S 148°39E **62** b
Findhorn → *U.K.* 57°38N 3°38W **11** D5
Findlay *U.S.A.* 41°2N 83°39W **81** E12
Fine *U.S.A.* 44°14N 75°8W **83** B9
Finger L. *Canada* 53°33N 93°30W **72** B1
Finger Lakes *U.S.A.* 42°40N 76°30W **83** D8
Fingoè *Mozam.* 15°55S 31°50E **55** G6
Finisterre, C. = Fisterra, C.
   Spain 42°50N 9°19W **21** A1
Finke *Australia* 25°34S 134°35E **62** D1
Finke Gorge △ *Australia* 24°8S 132°49E **60** D5
Finland ■ *Europe* 63°0N 27°0E **8** E22
Finland, G. of *Europe* 60°0N 26°0E **9** G22
Finlay → *Canada* 57°0N 125°10W **70** B3
Finley *Australia* 35°38S 145°35E **63** F4
Finley *U.S.A.* 47°31N 97°50W **80** B5
Finn → *Ireland* 54°51N 7°28W **10** B4
Finnigan, Mt. *Australia* 15°49S 145°17E **62** B4
Finniss, C. *Australia* 33°8S 134°51E **63** E1
Finnmark *Norway* 69°37N 23°57E **8** B20
Finnsnes *Norway* 69°14N 18°0E **8** B18
Finspång *Sweden* 58°43N 15°47E **9** G16
Fiora → *Italy* 42°20N 11°34E **22** C4
Fiordland △ *N.Z.* 45°46S 167°0E **59** F1
Fiq *Syria* 32°46N 35°41E **48** C4
Firat = Furāt, Nahr al →
   Asia 31°0N 47°25E **46** D5
Fire Island △ *U.S.A.* 40°38N 73°8W **83** F11
Firebag → *Canada* 57°45N 111°21W **71** B6
Firebaugh *U.S.A.* 36°52N 120°27W **78** J6
Firedrake L. *Canada* 61°25N 104°30W **71** A8
Firenze *Italy* 43°46N 11°15E **22** C4
Firk, Sha'ib → *Iraq* 30°59N 44°34E **46** D5
Firozabad *India* 27°10N 78°25E **43** F8
Firozpur *India* 30°55N 74°40E **42** D6
Firozpur-Jhirka *India* 27°48N 76°57E **42** F7
Fīrūzābād *Iran* 28°52N 52°35E **47** D7
Fīrūzkūh *Iran* 35°50N 52°50E **47** C7
Firvale *Canada* 52°27N 126°13W **70** C3
Fish → *Namibia* 28°7S 17°10E **56** C2
Fish → *S. Africa* 31°30S 20°16E **56** D3
Fish River Canyon
   Namibia 27°40S 17°35E **56** C2
Fisher B. *Canada* 51°35N 97°13W **71** C9
Fishers I. *U.S.A.* 41°15N 72°0W **83** E13
Fishguard *U.K.* 52°0N 4°58W **13** E3
Fishing L. *Canada* 52°10N 95°24W **71** C9
Fishkill *U.S.A.* 41°32N 73°54W **83** E11
Fisterra, C. *Spain* 42°50N 9°19W **21** A1
Fitchburg *Mass., U.S.A.* 42°35N 71°48W **83** D13
Fitchburg *Wis., U.S.A.* 42°58N 89°28W **80** D9
Fitz Roy *Argentina* 47°0S 67°0W **96** F3
Fitz Roy, Cerro *Argentina* 49°17S 73°5W **96** F2
Fitzgerald *Canada* 59°51N 111°36W **70** B6
Fitzgerald *U.S.A.* 31°43N 83°15W **85** F13
Fitzgerald River △
   Australia 33°53S 119°55E **61** F3
Fitzmaurice → *Australia* 14°45S 130°5E **60** B5
Fitzroy → *Queens.,*
   Australia 23°32S 150°52E **62** C5
Fitzroy → *W. Austral.,*
   Australia 17°31S 123°35E **60** C3
Fitzroy Crossing *Australia* 18°9S 125°38E **60** C4
Fitzwilliam I. *Canada* 45°30N 81°45W **82** A3
Fiume = Rijeka *Croatia* 45°20N 14°21E **16** F8
Five Points *U.S.A.* 36°26N 120°6W **78** J6
Fizi *Dem. Rep. of the Congo* 4°17S 28°55E **54** C5
Flagstaff *Australia* 35°12N 111°39W **77** J8
Flagstaff L. *U.S.A.* 45°12N 70°18W **83** A14
Flaherty I. *Canada* 56°15N 79°15W **72** A4
Flåm *Norway* 60°50N 7°7E **8** F12
Flambeau → *U.S.A.* 45°18N 91°14W **80** C8
Flamborough Hd. *U.K.* 54°7N 0°5W **12** C7
Flaming Gorge △
   U.S.A. 41°10N 109°25W **76** F9
Flaming Gorge Res.
   U.S.A. 41°10N 109°25W **76** F9
Flamingo, Teluk *Indonesia* 5°30S 138°0E **37** F9
Flanders = Flandre *Europe* 50°50N 2°30E **15** B9
Flandre *Europe* 50°50N 2°30E **15** B9
Flandre-Occidentale = West-
   Vlaanderen □ *Belgium* 51°0N 3°0E **15** D2
Flandre-Orientale = Oost-
   Vlaanderen □ *Belgium* 51°5N 3°50E **15** C3
Flandreau *U.S.A.* 44°3N 96°36W **80** C5
Flanigan *U.S.A.* 40°10N 119°53W **78** E7
Flannan Is. *U.K.* 58°9N 7°52W **11** C1
Flåsjön *Sweden* 64°5N 15°40E **8** D16
Flat → *Canada* 61°33N 125°18W **70** A3
Flat I. *Mauritius* 19°53S 57°35E **55** d
Flathead L. *U.S.A.* 47°51N 114°8W **76** C6
Flattery, C. *Australia* 14°58S 145°21E **62** A4
Flattery, C. *U.S.A.* 48°23N 124°29W **78** B2
Flatwoods *U.S.A.* 38°31N 82°43W **81** F12
Fleetwood *U.K.* 53°55N 3°1W **12** D4
Fleetwood *U.S.A.* 40°27N 75°49W **83** F9
Flekkefjord *Norway* 58°18N 6°39E **9** G12
Flemington *U.S.A.* 41°7N 77°28W **82** F7
Flensburg *Germany* 54°47N 9°27E **16** A5
Flers *France* 48°47N 0°33W **20** B3
Flesherton *Canada* 44°16N 80°33W **82** B4
Flesko, Tanjung *Indonesia* 0°29N 124°30E **37** D6
Fleurieu Pen. *Australia* 35°40S 138°5E **63** F2
Flevoland □ *Neths.* 52°30N 5°30E **15** B5
Flin Flon *Canada* 54°46N 101°53W **71** C8
Flinders → *Australia* 17°36S 140°36E **62** B3
Flinders B. *Australia* 34°19S 115°19E **61** F2
Flinders Group *Australia* 14°11S 144°15E **62** A3

Flinders I. *S. Austral.,*
   Australia 33°44S 134°41E **63** E1
Flinders I. *Tas., Australia* 40°0S 148°0E **63** G4
Flinders Ranges
   Australia 31°30S 138°30E **63** E2
Flinders Reefs *Australia* 17°37S 148°31E **62** B4
Flint → *U.K.* 53°15N 3°8W **12** D4
Flint *U.S.A.* 43°1N 83°41W **81** D12
Flint → *U.S.A.* 30°57N 84°34W **85** F12
Flint I. *Kiribati* 11°26S 151°48W **65** J12
Flintshire □ *U.K.* 53°17N 3°17W **12** D4
Flodden *U.K.* 55°37N 2°8W **12** B5
Floodplains △ *Sri Lanka* 8°10N 81°10E **45** K5
Floodwood *U.S.A.* 46°56N 92°55W **80** B7
Flora → *Australia* 14°43S 131°49E **60** B5
Flora *U.S.A.* 38°40N 88°29W **80** F9
Florala *U.S.A.* 31°0N 86°20W **85** F11
Florence = Firenze *Italy* 43°46N 11°15E **22** C4
Florence *Ala., U.S.A.* 34°48N 87°41W **85** D11
Florence *Ariz., U.S.A.* 33°2N 111°23W **77** K8
Florence *Colo., U.S.A.* 38°23N 105°8W **76** G11
Florence *Oreg., U.S.A.* 43°58N 124°7W **76** D1
Florence *S.C., U.S.A.* 34°12N 79°46W **85** D15
Florence, L. *Australia* 28°53S 138°9E **63** D2
Florencia *Colombia* 1°36N 75°36W **92** C3
Florennes *Belgium* 50°15N 4°35E **15** D4
Florenville *Belgium* 49°40N 5°19E **15** E5
Flores *Azores* 39°26N 31°13W **52** a
Flores *Guatemala* 16°59N 89°50W **88** C2
Flores *Indonesia* 8°35S 121°0E **37** F6
Flores I. *Canada* 49°20N 126°10W **70** D3
Flores Sea *Indonesia* 6°30S 120°0E **37** F6
Floreşti *Moldova* 47°53N 28°17E **17** E15
Floresville *U.S.A.* 29°8N 98°10W **84** G5
Floriano *Brazil* 6°50S 43°0W **93** E10
Florianópolis *Brazil* 27°30S 48°30W **95** B6
Florida *Cuba* 21°32N 78°14W **88** B4
Florida *Uruguay* 34°7S 56°10W **95** C4
Florida □ *U.S.A.* 28°0N 82°0W **85** G14
Florida, Straits of *U.S.A.* 25°0N 80°0W **88** B4
Florida B. *U.S.A.* 25°0N 80°45W **88** B3
Florida Keys *U.S.A.* 24°40N 81°0W **85** J14
Florin *U.S.A.* 38°30N 121°24W **78** G5
Florina *Greece* 40°48N 21°26E **23** D9
Florissant *U.S.A.* 38°47N 90°19W **80** F8
Florø *Norway* 61°35N 5°1E **8** F11
Flower Station *Canada* 45°10N 76°41W **83** A8
Flowerpot I. *Canada* 45°18N 81°38W **82** A3
Floydada *U.S.A.* 33°59N 101°20W **84** B4
Fluk *Indonesia* 1°42S 127°44E **37** E7
Flushing = Vlissingen
   Neths. 51°26N 3°34E **15** C3
Fly → *Papua N. G.* 8°25S 143°0E **58** B7
Flying Fish, C. *Antarctica* 72°6S 102°29W **5** D15
Foa *Tonga* 19°45S 174°18W **59** c
Foam Lake *Canada* 51°40N 103°32W **71** C8
Foça *Turkey* 38°39N 26°46E **23** E12
Fochabers *U.K.* 57°37N 3°6W **11** D5
Focşani *Romania* 45°41N 27°15E **17** F14
Fogang *China* 23°52N 113°30E **35** F9
Foggia *Italy* 41°27N 15°34E **22** D6
Fogo *Canada* 49°43N 54°17W **73** C9
Fogo C. Verde Is. 15°5N 24°20W **52** b
Fogo I. *Canada* 49°40N 54°5W **73** C9
Foix *France* 42°58N 1°38E **20** E4
Folda *Nord-Trøndelag,*
   Norway 64°32N 10°30E **8** D14
Folda *Nordland, Norway* 67°38N 14°50E **8** C16
Foley *Botswana* 21°34S 27°21E **56** B4
Foley *U.S.A.* 30°24N 87°41W **85** F11
Foleyet *Canada* 48°15N 82°25W **72** C3
Folgefonna *Norway* 60°3N 6°23E **9** F12
Foligno *Italy* 42°57N 12°42E **22** C5
Folkestone *U.K.* 51°5N 1°12E **13** F9
Folkston *U.S.A.* 30°50N 82°0W **85** F13
Follansbee *U.S.A.* 40°19N 80°35W **82** F4
Folsom *U.S.A.* 38°40N 121°9W **78** G5
Folsom L. *U.S.A.* 38°42N 121°9W **78** G5
Fomboni *Comoros Is.* 12°18S 43°46E **55** a
Fond-du-Lac *Canada* 59°19N 107°12W **71** B7
Fond du Lac *U.S.A.* 43°47N 88°27W **80** D9
Fond-du-Lac → *Canada* 59°17N 106°0W **71** B7
Fonda *U.S.A.* 42°57N 74°22W **83** D10
Fondi *Italy* 41°21N 13°25E **22** D5
Fongafale *Tuvalu* 8°31S 179°13E **58** B10
Fonsagrada = A Fonsagrada
   Spain 43°8N 7°4W **21** A2
Fonseca, G. de
   Cent. Amer. 13°10N 87°40W **88** D2
Fontainebleau *France* 48°24N 2°40E **20** B5
Fontana *U.S.A.* 34°6N 117°26W **79** L9
Fontas → *Canada* 58°14N 121°48W **70** B4
Fonte Boa *Brazil* 2°33S 66°0W **92** D5
Fontenay-le-Comte
   France 46°28N 0°48W **20** C3
Fontur *Iceland* 66°23N 14°32W **8** C6
Fonuafo'ou *Tonga* 20°19S 175°25W **59** c
Fonualei *Tonga* 18°1S 174°19W **59** c
Foochow = Fuzhou
   China 26°5N 119°16E **35** D12
Foping *China* 33°41N 108°0E **32** H5
Foraker, Mt. *U.S.A.* 62°58N 151°24W **74** C9
Forbes *Australia* 33°22S 148°5E **63** E4
Forbesganj *India* 26°17N 87°18E **43** F12
Ford City *Calif., U.S.A.* 35°9N 119°27W **79** K7
Ford City *Pa., U.S.A.* 40°46N 79°32W **82** F5
Førde *Norway* 61°27N 5°53E **8** F11
Fords Bridge *Australia* 29°41S 145°29E **63** D4
Fordyce *U.S.A.* 33°49N 92°25W **84** E8
Forel, Mt. *Greenland* 66°52N 36°55W **4** C6
Foremost *Canada* 49°26N 111°34W **70** D6
Forest *Canada* 43°6N 82°0W **82** D2
Forest City *Iowa, U.S.A.* 43°16N 93°39W **80** D7
Forest City *N.C., U.S.A.* 35°20N 81°52W **85** D14
Forest City *Pa., U.S.A.* 41°39N 75°28W **83** E9
Forest Grove *U.S.A.* 45°31N 123°7W **78** E3
Forestburg *Canada* 52°35N 112°1W **70** C6

Foresthill *U.S.A.* 39°1N 120°49W **78** F6
Forestier Pen. *Australia* 43°0S 148°0E **63** G4
Forestville *Canada* 48°48N 69°2W **73** C6
Forestville *Calif., U.S.A.* 38°28N 122°54W **78** G4
Forestville *N.Y., U.S.A.* 42°28N 79°10W **82** D5
Forfar *U.K.* 56°39N 2°53W **11** E6
Forks *U.S.A.* 47°57N 124°23W **78** C2
Forksville *U.S.A.* 41°29N 76°35W **83** E8
Forlì *Italy* 44°13N 12°3E **22** B5
Forman *U.S.A.* 46°7N 97°38W **80** B5
Formby Pt. *U.K.* 53°33N 3°6W **12** D4
Formentera *Spain* 38°43N 1°27E **21** C6
Formentor, C. de *Spain* 39°58N 3°13E **21** C7
Former Yugoslav Republic of
   Macedonia = Macedonia ■
   Europe 41°53N 21°40E **23** D9
Fórmia *Italy* 41°15N 13°37E **22** D5
Formosa = Taiwan ■
   Asia 23°30N 121°0E **35** F13
Formosa *Argentina* 26°15S 58°10W **94** B4
Formosa *Brazil* 15°32S 47°20W **93** G9
Formosa □ *Argentina* 25°0S 60°0W **94** B4
Formosa, Serra *Brazil* 12°0S 55°0W **93** F8
Føroyar □ *Atl. Oc.* 62°0N 7°0W **8** F9
Forres *U.K.* 57°37N 3°37W **11** D5
Forrest *Australia* 30°51S 128°6E **61** F4
Forrest, Mt. *Australia* 24°48S 127°45E **61** D4
Forrest City *U.S.A.* 35°1N 90°47W **85** D9
Forsayth *Australia* 18°33S 143°34E **62** B3
Forssa *Finland* 60°49N 23°38E **9** F20
Forst *Germany* 51°45N 14°37E **16** C8
Forster *Australia* 32°12S 152°31E **63** E5
Forsyth *U.S.A.* 46°16N 106°41W **76** C10
Fort Abbas *Pakistan* 29°12N 72°52E **42** E5
Fort Albany *Canada* 52°15N 81°35W **72** B3
Fort Assiniboine *Canada* 54°20N 114°45W **70** C6
Fort Augustus *U.K.* 57°9N 4°42W **11** D4
Fort Beaufort *S. Africa* 32°46S 26°40E **56** D4
Fort Benton *U.S.A.* 47°49N 110°40W **76** C8
Fort Bragg *U.S.A.* 39°26N 123°48W **76** G2
Fort Bridger *U.S.A.* 41°19N 110°23W **76** F8
Fort Chipewyan *Canada* 58°42N 111°8W **71** B6
Fort Clatsop = Lewis and Clark △
   U.S.A. 46°8N 123°53W **78** D3
Fort Collins *U.S.A.* 40°35N 105°5W **76** F11
Fort-Coulonge *Canada* 45°50N 76°45W **72** C4
Fort Covington *U.S.A.* 44°59N 74°29W **83** B10
Fort Dauphin = Taolanaro
   Madag. 25°2S 47°0E **55** K9
Fort Davis *U.S.A.* 30°35N 103°54W **84** F3
Fort Defiance *U.S.A.* 35°45N 109°5W **77** J9
Fort Dodge *U.S.A.* 42°30N 94°11W **80** D6
Fort Edward *U.S.A.* 43°16N 73°35W **83** C11
Fort Erie *Canada* 42°54N 78°56W **82** D6
Fort Fairfield *U.S.A.* 46°46N 67°50W **81** B20
Fort Frances *Canada* 48°36N 93°24W **71** D10
Fort Franklin = Déline
   Canada 65°11N 123°25W **68** D7
Fort Garland *U.S.A.* 37°26N 105°26W **77** H11
Fort George = Chisasibi
   Canada 53°50N 79°0W **72** B4
Fort Good Hope *Canada* 66°14N 128°40W **68** C7
Fort Hancock *U.S.A.* 31°18N 105°51W **84** F2
Fort Hope = Eabametoong
   Canada 51°30N 88°0W **72** B2
Fort Irwin *U.S.A.* 35°16N 116°41W **79** K10
Fort Kent *U.S.A.* 47°15N 68°36W **81** B19
Fort Klamath *U.S.A.* 42°42N 122°0W **76** E3
Fort Laramie *U.S.A.* 42°13N 104°31W **76** E11
Fort Liard *Canada* 60°14N 123°30W **70** A4
Fort Liberté *Haiti* 19°42N 71°51W **89** C5
Fort Lupton *U.S.A.* 40°5N 104°49W **76** F11
Fort MacKay *Canada* 57°12N 111°41W **70** B6
Fort Macleod *Canada* 49°45N 113°30W **70** D6
Fort McMurray *Canada* 56°44N 111°7W **70** B6
Fort McPherson *Canada* 67°30N 134°55W **68** D5
Fort Madison *U.S.A.* 40°38N 91°27W **80** E8
Fort Meade *U.S.A.* 27°45N 81°48W **85** H14
Fort Morgan *U.S.A.* 40°15N 103°48W **76** E12
Fort Myers *U.S.A.* 26°39N 81°52W **85** H14
Fort Nelson *Canada* 58°50N 122°44W **70** B4
Fort Nelson → *Canada* 59°32N 124°0W **70** B4
Fort Norman = Tulita
   Canada 64°57N 125°30W **68** E6
Fort Payne *U.S.A.* 34°26N 85°43W **85** D12
Fort Peck *U.S.A.* 48°1N 106°27W **76** B10
Fort Peck Dam *U.S.A.* 48°0N 106°26W **76** C10
Fort Peck L. *U.S.A.* 48°0N 106°26W **76** C10
Fort Pierce *U.S.A.* 27°27N 80°20W **85** H14
Fort Pierre *U.S.A.* 44°21N 100°22W **80** C3
Fort Plain *U.S.A.* 42°56N 74°37W **83** D10
Fort Portal *Uganda* 0°40N 30°20E **54** D6
Fort Providence *Canada* 61°3N 117°40W **70** A5
Fort Qu'Appelle *Canada* 50°45N 103°50W **71** C8
Fort Resolution *Canada* 61°10N 113°40W **70** A6
Fort Ross *U.S.A.* 38°32N 123°13W **78** G3
Fort Rupert = Waskaganish
   Canada 51°30N 78°40W **72** B4
Fort St. James *Canada* 54°30N 124°10W **70** C4
Fort St. John *Canada* 56°15N 120°50W **70** B4
Fort Saskatchewan
   Canada 53°40N 113°15W **70** C6
Fort Scott *U.S.A.* 37°50N 94°42W **80** G6
Fort Severn *Canada* 56°0N 87°40W **72** A2
Fort Shevchenko
   Kazakhstan 44°35N 50°23E **19** F9
Fort Simpson *Canada* 61°45N 121°15W **70** A4
Fort Smith *Canada* 60°0N 111°51W **70** B6
Fort Smith *U.S.A.* 35°23N 94°25W **84** D7
Fort Stockton *U.S.A.* 30°53N 102°53W **84** F3
Fort Sumner *U.S.A.* 34°28N 104°15W **77** J11
Fort Thompson *U.S.A.* 44°3N 99°26W **80** C4
Fort Union △ *U.S.A.* 35°54N 105°1W **77** J11
Fort Valley *U.S.A.* 32°33N 83°53W **85** E13
Fort Vermilion *Canada* 58°24N 116°0W **70** B5
Fort Walton Beach
   U.S.A. 30°25N 86°36W **85** F11

Fort Ware *Canada* 57°26N 125°41W **70** B3
Fort Wayne *U.S.A.* 41°4N 85°9W **81** E11
Fort William *U.K.* 56°49N 5°7W **11** E3
Fort Worth *U.S.A.* 32°43N 97°19W **84** E6
Fort Yates *U.S.A.* 46°5N 100°38W **80** B3
Fort Yukon *U.S.A.* 66°34N 145°16W **68** D2
Fortaleza *Brazil* 3°45S 38°35W **93** D11
Forteau *Canada* 51°28N 56°58W **73** B8
Fortescue → *Australia* 21°0S 116°4E **60** D2
Fortescue River Roadhouse
   Australia 21°17S 116°8E **60** D2
Forth → *U.K.* 56°9N 3°50W **11** E5
Forth, Firth of *U.K.* 56°5N 2°55W **11** E6
Fortrose *U.K.* 57°35N 4°9W **11** D4
Fortuna *Calif., U.S.A.* 40°36N 124°9W **76** F1
Fortuna *N. Dak., U.S.A.* 48°55N 103°47W **80** A2
Fortune *Canada* 47°4N 55°50W **73** C8
Fortune B. *Canada* 47°30N 55°22W **73** C8
Forūr *Iran* 26°17N 54°32E **47** E7
Fosen *Norway* 63°50N 10°20E **8** E14
Fosnavåg *Norway* 62°22N 5°38E **8** E11
Fossano *Italy* 44°33N 7°43E **20** D7
Fossil *U.S.A.* 45°0N 120°9W **76** D3
Fossil Butte △ *U.S.A.* 41°50N 110°27W **76** F8
Foster *Canada* 45°17N 72°30W **83** A12
Foster → *Canada* 55°47N 105°49W **71** B7
Fostoria *U.S.A.* 41°10N 83°25W **81** E12
Fougères *France* 48°21N 1°14W **20** B3
Foul Pt. *Sri Lanka* 8°35N 81°18E **45** K5
Foula *U.K.* 60°10N 2°5W **11** A6
Foulness I. *U.K.* 51°36N 0°55E **13** F8
Fouman *Cameroon* 5°45N 10°50E **54** C2
Foumbouni *Comoros Is.* 11°51S 43°29E **55** a
Fountain *U.S.A.* 38°41N 104°42W **76** G11
Fountain Hills *U.S.A.* 33°37N 111°43W **77** K8
Fountain Springs
   U.S.A. 35°54N 118°51W **79** K8
Four Mountains, Is. of
   U.S.A. 53°0N 170°0W **74** E5
Fouriesburg *S. Africa* 28°38S 28°14E **56** C4
Fourni *Greece* 37°36N 26°32E **23** F12
Fouta Djallon *Guinea* 11°20N 12°10W **52** F3
Foux, Cap-à- *Haiti* 19°43N 73°27W **89** C5
Foveaux Str. *N.Z.* 46°42S 168°10E **59** G2
Fowey *U.K.* 50°20N 4°39W **13** G3
Fowler *Calif., U.S.A.* 36°38N 119°41W **78** J7
Fowler *Colo., U.S.A.* 38°8N 104°2W **76** G11
Fowler, Pt. *Australia* 32°2S 132°3E **61** F5
Fowlers B. *Australia* 31°59S 132°34E **61** F5
Fowman *Iran* 37°13N 49°19E **47** B6
Fox → *Canada* 56°3N 93°18W **71** B10
Fox Creek *Canada* 54°24N 116°48W **70** C5
Fox Is. *U.S.A.* 53°0N 168°0W **74** E6
Fox Lake *Canada* 58°28N 114°31W **70** B6
Fox Valley *Canada* 50°30N 109°25W **71** C7
Foxboro *Canada* 44°14N 77°26W **82** B7
Foxboro *U.S.A.* 42°4N 71°16W **83** D13
Foxdale *Australia* 20°22S 148°35E **62** b
Foxe Basin *Canada* 66°0N 77°0W **69** D16
Foxe Chan. *Canada* 65°0N 80°0W **69** E16
Foxe Pen. *Canada* 65°0N 76°0W **69** E16
Foxford *Ireland* 53°59N 9°7W **10** C2
Foxton *N.Z.* 40°29S 175°18E **59** D5
Foyle, Lough *U.K.* 55°7N 7°4W **10** A4
Foynes *Ireland* 52°37N 9°7W **10** D2
Foz do Cunene *Angola* 17°15S 11°48E **56** A1
Foz do Iguaçu *Brazil* 25°30S 54°30W **95** B5
Frackville *U.S.A.* 40°47N 76°14W **83** F8
Fraile Muerto *Uruguay* 32°31S 54°32W **95** C5
Framingham *U.S.A.* 42°18N 71°24W **83** D13
Franca *Brazil* 20°33S 47°30W **93** H9
Francavilla Fontana
   Italy 40°32N 17°35E **23** D7
France ■ *Europe* 47°0N 3°0E **20** C5
Frances *Australia* 36°41S 140°55E **63** F3
Frances → *Canada* 60°16N 129°10W **70** A3
Frances L. *Canada* 61°23N 129°30W **70** A3
Franceville *Gabon* 1°40S 13°32E **54** E2
Franche-Comté □ *France* 46°50N 5°55E **20** C6
Francis Case, L. *U.S.A.* 43°4N 98°34W **80** D4
Francisco Beltrão *Brazil* 26°5S 53°4W **95** B5
Francisco Ignacio Madero *Coahuila,*
   Mexico 25°48N 103°18W **86** B4
Francisco Ignacio Madero *Durango,*
   Mexico 24°26N 104°18W **86** C4
Francisco Ignacio Madero, Presa
   Mexico 28°10N 105°37W **86** B3
Francistown *Botswana* 21°7S 27°33E **57** B4
François *Canada* 47°35N 56°45W **73** C8
François L. *Canada* 54°0N 125°30W **70** C3
Francois Peron △
   Australia 25°42S 113°33E **61** E1
Francs Pk. *U.S.A.* 43°58N 109°20W **76** E9
Franeker *Neths.* 53°12N 5°33E **15** A5
Frank Hann △ *Australia* 32°52S 120°19E **61** F3
Frankford *Canada* 44°12N 77°36W **82** B7
Frankfort *S. Africa* 27°17S 28°30E **57** C4
Frankfort *Ind., U.S.A.* 40°17N 86°31W **80** E10
Frankfort *Kans., U.S.A.* 39°42N 96°25W **80** F5
Frankfort *Ky., U.S.A.* 38°12N 84°52W **81** F11
Frankfort *N.Y., U.S.A.* 43°2N 75°4W **83** D9
Frankfurt *Brandenburg,*
   Germany 52°20N 14°32E **16** B8
Frankfurt *Hessen, Germany* 50°7N 8°41E **16** C5
Fränkische Alb *Germany* 49°10N 11°23E **16** D6
Frankland → *Australia* 35°0S 116°48E **61** G2
Franklin *Ky., U.S.A.* 36°43N 86°35W **80** G10
Franklin *La., U.S.A.* 29°48N 91°30W **84** G9
Franklin *Mass., U.S.A.* 42°5N 71°24W **83** D13
Franklin *N.H., U.S.A.* 43°27N 71°39W **83** C13
Franklin *N.Y., U.S.A.* 42°20N 75°9W **83** D9
Franklin *Nebr., U.S.A.* 40°6N 98°57W **80** E4
Franklin *Pa., U.S.A.* 41°24N 79°50W **82** E5
Franklin *Va., U.S.A.* 36°41N 76°56W **81** G15
Franklin *W. Va., U.S.A.* 38°39N 79°20W **81** F14
Franklin D. Roosevelt L.
   U.S.A. 48°18N 118°9W **76** B4
Franklin-Gordon Wild Rivers △
   Australia 42°19S 145°51E **63** G4

Franklin I. *Antarctica* 76°10S 168°30E **5** D11
Franklin I. *Canada* 45°24N 80°20W **82** A4
Franklin L. *U.S.A.* 40°25N 115°22W **76** F6
Franklin Mts. *Canada* 65°0N 125°0W **68** D6
Franklin Str. *Canada* 72°0N 96°0W **68** C12
Franklinton *U.S.A.* 30°51N 90°9W **85** F9
Franklinville *U.S.A.* 42°20N 78°27W **82** D6
Frankston *Australia* 38°8S 145°8E **63** F4
Fransfontein *Namibia* 20°12S 15°1E **56** B2
Frantsa Iosifa, Zemlya
   Arctic 82°0N 55°0E **26** A6
Franz *Canada* 48°25N 84°30W **72** C3
Franz Josef Land = Frantsa Iosifa,
   Zemlya *Arctic* 82°0N 55°0E **26** A6
Fraser *U.S.A.* 42°32N 82°57W **82** D2
Fraser → *B.C., Canada* 49°7N 123°11W **78** A4
Fraser → *Nfld. & L.,*
   Canada 56°39N 62°10W **73** A7
Fraser, Mt. *Australia* 25°35S 118°20E **61** E2
Fraser I. *Australia* 25°15S 153°10E **63** D5
Fraser Lake *Canada* 54°0N 124°50W **70** C4
Fraserburg *S. Africa* 31°55S 21°30E **56** E3
Fraserburgh *U.K.* 57°42N 2°1W **11** D6
Fraserdale *Canada* 49°55N 81°37W **72** C3
Fray Bentos *Uruguay* 33°10S 58°15W **94** C4
Fray Jorge △ *Chile* 30°42S 71°40W **94** C1
Frazier Downs ◇
   Australia 18°48S 121°42E **60** C3
Fredericia *Denmark* 55°34N 9°45E **9** J13
Frederick *Md., U.S.A.* 39°25N 77°25W **81** F15
Frederick *Okla., U.S.A.* 34°23N 99°1W **84** D5
Frederick *S. Dak., U.S.A.* 45°50N 98°31W **80** C4
Fredericksburg *Pa.,*
   U.S.A. 40°27N 76°26W **83** F8
Fredericksburg *Tex.,*
   U.S.A. 30°16N 98°52W **84** F5
Fredericksburg *Va.,*
   U.S.A. 38°18N 77°28W **81** F15
Fredericktown *Mo.,*
   U.S.A. 37°34N 90°18W **80** G8
Fredericktown *Ohio,*
   U.S.A. 40°29N 82°33W **82** F2
Frederico Westphalen
   Brazil 27°22S 53°24W **95** B5
Fredericton *Canada* 45°57N 66°40W **73** C6
Fredericton Junction
   Canada 45°41N 66°40W **73** C6
Frederikshåb = Paamiut
   Greenland 62°0N 49°43W **4** C5
Frederikshamn = Hamina
   Finland 60°34N 27°12E **8** F22
Frederikshavn *Denmark* 57°28N 10°31E **9** H14
Frederiksted
   U.S. Virgin Is. 17°43N 64°53W **89** C7
Fredonia *Ariz., U.S.A.* 36°57N 112°32W **77** H7
Fredonia *Kans., U.S.A.* 37°32N 95°49W **80** G6
Fredonia *N.Y., U.S.A.* 42°26N 79°20W **82** D5
Fredrikstad *Norway* 59°13N 10°57E **9** G14
Free State □ *S. Africa* 28°30S 27°0E **56** D4
Freehold *U.S.A.* 40°16N 74°17W **83** F10
Freeland *U.S.A.* 41°1N 75°54W **83** E9
Freels, C. *Nfld. & L.,*
   Canada 49°15N 53°30W **73** C9
Freels, C. *Nfld. & L.,*
   Canada 46°37N 53°32W **73** C9
Freeman *Calif., U.S.A.* 35°35N 117°53W **79** K9
Freeman *S. Dak., U.S.A.* 43°21N 97°26W **80** D5
Freeport *Bahamas* 26°30N 78°47W **88** A4
Freeport *Ill., U.S.A.* 42°17N 89°36W **80** D9
Freeport *N.Y., U.S.A.* 40°39N 73°35W **83** F11
Freeport *Ohio, U.S.A.* 40°12N 81°15W **82** F3
Freeport *Pa., U.S.A.* 40°41N 79°41W **82** F5
Freeport *Tex., U.S.A.* 28°57N 95°21W **84** G7
Freetown *S. Leone* 8°30N 13°17W **52** G3
Frégate, L. de la *Canada* 53°15N 74°45W **72** B5
Fregenal de la Sierra
   Spain 38°10N 6°39W **21** C2
Fregon *Australia* 26°45S 132°1E **61** E5
Freibourg = Fribourg
   Switz. 46°49N 7°9E **20** C7
Freiburg *Germany* 47°59N 7°51E **16** E4
Freire *Chile* 38°54S 72°38W **96** D2
Freirina *Chile* 28°30S 71°10W **94** B1
Freising *Germany* 48°24N 11°45E **16** D6
Freistadt *Austria* 48°30N 14°30E **16** D8
Fréjus *France* 43°25N 6°44E **20** E7
Fremantle *Australia* 32°7S 115°47E **61** F2
Fremont *Calif., U.S.A.* 37°32N 121°57W **78** H4
Fremont *Mich., U.S.A.* 43°28N 85°57W **81** D11
Fremont *Nebr., U.S.A.* 41°26N 96°30W **80** E5
Fremont *Ohio, U.S.A.* 41°21N 83°7W **81** E12
Fremont → *U.S.A.* 38°24N 110°42W **76** G8
French Camp *U.S.A.* 37°53N 121°16W **78** H5
French Cays = Plana Cays
   Bahamas 22°38N 73°30W **89** B5
French Creek → *U.S.A.* 41°24N 79°50W **82** E5
French Frigate Shoals
   U.S.A. 23°45N 166°10W **75** L4
French Guiana □ *S. Amer.* 4°0N 53°0W **93** C8
French Polynesia ☑
   Pac. Oc. 20°0S 145°0W **65** J13
French Riviera = Côte d'Azur
   France 43°25N 7°10E **20** E7
Frenchman Cr. →
   N. Amer. 48°31N 107°10W **76** B10
Frenchman Cr. →
   U.S.A. 40°14N 100°50W **80** E3
Fresco → *Brazil* 7°15S 51°30W **93** E8
Freshfield, C. *Antarctica* 68°25S 151°10E **5** C10
Fresnillo *Mexico* 23°10N 102°53W **86** C4
Fresno *U.S.A.* 36°44N 119°47W **78** J7
Fresno Res. *U.S.A.* 48°36N 109°57W **76** B9
Frew → *Australia* 20°0S 135°38E **62** C2
Frewsburg *U.S.A.* 42°3N 79°10W **82** D5
Freycinet △ *Australia* 42°11S 148°19E **63** G4
Freycinet Pen. *Australia* 42°10S 148°25E **63** G4
Fria *Guinea* 10°27N 13°38W **52** F3
Fria, C. *Namibia* 18°0S 12°0E **56** B1

Friant *U.S.A.* 36°59N 119°43W **78** J7
Frías *Argentina* 28°40S 65°5W **94** B2
Fribourg *Switz.* 46°49N 7°9E **20** C7
Friday Harbor *U.S.A.* 48°32N 123°1W **78** B3
Friedens *U.S.A.* 40°3N 78°59W **82** F6
Friedrichshafen *Germany* 47°39N 9°30E **16** E5
Friendship *U.S.A.* 42°12N 78°8W **82** D6
Friesland □ *Neths.* 53°5N 5°50E **15** A5
Frigate *Seychelles* 4°35S 55°56E **55** b
Frio *U.S.A.* 28°26N 98°11W **84** G5
Frio, C. *Brazil* 22°50S 41°50W **90** F6
Friona *U.S.A.* 34°38N 102°43W **84** D3
Frisco *U.S.A.* 33°9N 96°49W **84** E6
Fritch *U.S.A.* 35°38N 101°36W **84** D4
Frobisher B. *Canada* 62°30N 66°0W **69** E18
Frobisher Bay = Iqaluit
  Canada 63°44N 68°31W **69** E18
Frobisher L. *Canada* 56°20N 108°15W **71** B7
Frohavet *Norway* 64°0N 9°30E **8** E13
Frome *U.K.* 51°14N 2°19W **13** F5
Frome → *U.K.* 50°41N 2°6W **13** G5
Frome, L. *Australia* 30°45S 139°45E **63** E2
Front Range *U.S.A.* 40°25N 105°45W **76** F11
Front Royal *U.S.A.* 38°55N 78°12W **81** F14
Frontenac △ *Canada* 44°32N 76°30W **83** B8
Frontera *Mexico* 18°32N 92°38W **87** D6
Fronteras *Mexico* 30°56N 109°31W **86** A3
Frosinone *Italy* 41°38N 13°19E **22** D5
Frostburg *U.S.A.* 39°39N 78°56W **81** F14
Frostisen *Norway* 68°14N 17°10E **8** B17
Frøya *Norway* 63°43N 8°40E **8** E13
Fruita *U.S.A.* 39°9N 108°44W **76** G9
Frunze = Bishkek
  Kyrgyzstan 42°54N 74°46E **30** C3
Frutal *Brazil* 20°0S 49°0W **93** H9
Frýdek-Místek
  Czech Rep. 49°40N 18°20E **17** D10
Fryeburg *U.S.A.* 44°1N 70°59W **83** B14
Fu Jiang → *China* 30°0N 106°16E **34** C6
Fu Xian = Wafangdian
  China 39°38N 121°58E **33** E11
Fu Xian *China* 36°0N 109°20E **32** G5
Fu'an *China* 27°1N 119°36E **35** D12
Fubian *China* 31°17N 102°22E **34** B4
Fucheng *China* 37°50N 116°10E **32** F9
Fuchou = Fuzhou *China* 26°5N 119°16E **35** D12
Fuchū *Japan* 34°34N 133°14E **29** G6
Fuchuan *China* 24°50N 111°5E **35** E8
Fuchun Jiang → *China* 30°5N 120°5E **35** B13
Fuding *China* 27°20N 120°12E **35** D13
Fuengirola *Spain* 36°32N 4°41W **21** D3
Fuentes de Oñoro *Spain* 40°33N 6°52W **21** B2
Fuerte → *Mexico* 25°54N 109°22W **86** B3
Fuerte Olimpo *Paraguay* 21°0S 57°51W **94** A4
Fuerteventura *Canary Is.* 28°30N 14°0W **52** C3
Fufeng *China* 34°22N 108°0E **32** G5
Fugong *China* 27°5N 98°47E **34** D2
Fugou *China* 34°3N 114°25E **32** G8
Fugu *China* 39°2N 111°3E **32** E6
Fuhai *China* 47°2N 87°25E **30** B6
Fuḥaymī *Iraq* 43°20N 42°10E **46** C4
Fuidhaigh = Wiay *U.K.* 57°24N 7°13W **11** D1
Fuji *Japan* 35°9N 138°39E **29** G9
Fuji-Hakone-Izu △
  Japan 35°15N 138°45E **29** G9
Fuji-San *Japan* 35°22N 138°44E **29** G9
Fuji-Yoshida *Japan* 35°30N 138°46E **29** G9
Fujian □ *China* 26°0N 118°0E **35** E12
Fujinomiya *Japan* 35°10N 138°40E **29** G9
Fujisawa *Japan* 35°22N 139°29E **29** G9
Fujiyama, Mt. = Fuji-San
  Japan 35°22N 138°44E **29** G9
Fukagawa *Japan* 43°43N 142°2E **28** C11
Fukien = Fujian □ *China* 26°0N 118°0E **35** E12
Fukuchiyama *Japan* 35°19N 135°9E **29** G7
Fukue *Japan* 32°41N 128°51E **29** H4
Fukue-Shima *Japan* 32°40N 128°45E **29** H4
Fukui *Japan* 36°5N 136°10E **29** F8
Fukui □ *Japan* 36°0N 136°12E **29** G8
Fukuoka *Japan* 33°39N 130°21E **29** H5
Fukuoka □ *Japan* 33°30N 131°0E **29** H5
Fukushima *Japan* 37°44N 140°28E **28** F10
Fukushima □ *Japan* 37°30N 140°15E **28** F10
Fukuyama *Japan* 34°35N 133°20E **29** G6
Fulaga *Fiji* 19°8S 178°33W **59** a
Fulda *Germany* 50°32N 9°40E **16** C5
Fulda → *Germany* 51°25N 9°39E **16** C5
Fulford Harbour *Canada* 48°47N 123°27W **78** B3
Fuliang *China* 29°23N 117°14E **35** C11
Fuling *China* 29°39N 107°17E **34** C6
Fullerton *Calif., U.S.A.* 33°53N 117°56W **79** M9
Fullerton *Nebr., U.S.A.* 41°22N 97°58W **80** E5
Fulongquan *China* 44°20N 124°42E **33** B13
Fulton *Mo., U.S.A.* 38°52N 91°57W **80** F8
Fulton *N.Y., U.S.A.* 43°19N 76°25W **83** C8
Fumin *China* 25°10N 102°20E **34** E4
Funabashi *Japan* 35°45N 140°0E **29** G10
Funafuti = Fongafale
  Tuvalu 8°31S 179°13E **58** B10
Funan *China* 32°39N 115°42E **35** A10
Funchal *Madeira* 32°38N 16°54W **52** B2
Fundación *Colombia* 10°31N 74°11W **92** A4
Fundão *Portugal* 40°8N 7°30W **21** B2
Fundy, B. of *Canada* 45°0N 66°0W **73** D6
Fundy △ *Canada* 45°35N 65°10W **73** C6
Funhalouro *Mozam.* 23°3S 34°25E **57** B5
Funing *Hebei, China* 39°53N 119°12E **33** E10
Funing *Jiangsu, China* 33°45N 119°50E **33** H10
Funing *Yunnan, China* 23°35N 105°45E **34** F5
Funiu Shan *China* 33°30N 112°20E **34** H7
Funtua *Nigeria* 11°30N 7°18E **52** F7
Fuping *Hebei, China* 38°48N 114°12E **32** E8
Fuping *Shaanxi, China* 34°42N 109°10E **32** G5
Fuqing *China* 25°41N 119°21E **35** E12
Fuquan *China* 26°40N 107°27E **34** D6
Furano *Japan* 43°21N 142°23E **28** C11
Furāt, Nahr al → *Asia* 31°0N 47°25E **46** D5
Fürg *Iran* 28°18N 55°13E **47** D7

Furnas, Represa de
  Brazil 20°50S 45°30W **95** A6
Furneaux Group
  Australia 40°10S 147°50E **63** G4
Furqlus *Syria* 34°36N 37°8E **48** A6
Fürstenwalde *Germany* 52°22N 14°3E **16** B8
Fürth *Germany* 49°28N 10°59E **16** D6
Furukawa = Ōsaki
  Japan 38°34N 140°58E **28** E10
Fury and Hecla Str.
  Canada 69°56N 84°0W **69** D15
Fusagasugá *Colombia* 4°21N 74°22W **92** C4
Fushan *Shandong, China* 37°30N 121°15E **33** F11
Fushan *Shanxi, China* 35°58N 111°51E **32** G6
Fushun *Liaoning, China* 41°50N 123°56E **33** D12
Fushun *Sichuan, China* 29°13N 104°52E **34** C5
Fusong *China* 42°20N 127°15E **33** C14
Fustic *Barbados* 13°16N 59°38W **89** g
Fusui *China* 22°40N 107°56E **34** F6
Futian *China* 22°32N 114°4E **31** a
Fuxian Hu *China* 24°30N 102°53E **34** E4
Fuxin *China* 42°5N 121°48E **33** C11
Fuyang *Anhui, China* 33°0N 115°48E **32** H8
Fuyang *Zhejiang, China* 30°5N 119°57E **35** B12
Fuyang He → *China* 38°12N 117°0E **32** E9
Fuying Dao *China* 26°34N 120°9E **35** D13
Fuyong *China* 22°40N 113°49E **31** a
Fuyu *Heilongjiang, China* 47°49N 124°27E **31** B13
Fuyu *Jilin, China* 45°12N 124°43E **33** B13
Fuyuan *China* 25°40N 104°16E **34** E5
Fuyuan *China* 47°0N 89°28E **30** B6
Fuzhou = Linchuan
  China 27°57N 116°15E **35** D11
Fuzhou *China* 26°5N 119°16E **35** D12
Fyn *Denmark* 55°20N 10°30E **9** J14
Fyne, L. *U.K.* 55°59N 5°23W **11** F3

G

Gaalkacyo *Somalia* 6°30N 47°30E **49** F4
Gabba *Australia* 9°45S 142°38E **62** a
Gabela *Angola* 11°0S 14°24E **54** G2
Gabès *Tunisia* 33°53N 10°2E **53** B8
Gabès, G. de *Tunisia* 34°0N 10°30E **53** B8
Gabon ■ *Africa* 0°10S 10°0E **54** E2
Gaborone *Botswana* 24°45S 25°57E **56** B4
Gabriels *U.S.A.* 44°26N 74°12W **83** B10
Gäbrīk *Iran* 25°44N 58°28E **47** E9
Gabrovo *Bulgaria* 42°52N 25°19E **23** C11
Gāch Sār *Iran* 36°7N 51°19E **47** B6
Gachsārān *Iran* 30°15N 50°45E **47** D6
Gad Hinglaj *India* 16°14N 74°21E **45** F2
Gadag *India* 15°30N 75°45E **45** G2
Gadap *Pakistan* 25°5N 67°28E **42** G2
Gadarwara *India* 22°50N 78°50E **43** H8
Gadhada *India* 22°0N 71°35E **42** J4
Gadra *Pakistan* 25°40N 70°38E **42** G4
Gadsden *U.S.A.* 34°1N 86°1W **85** D11
Gadwal *India* 16°10N 77°50E **45** F3
Gaffney *U.S.A.* 35°5N 81°39W **85** D14
Gafsa *Tunisia* 34°24N 8°43E **53** B7
Gagaria *India* 25°43N 70°46E **42** G4
Gâgâuzia □ *Moldova* 46°10N 28°40E **17** E15
Gagnoa *Ivory C.* 6°56N 5°16W **52** G4
Gagnon *Canada* 51°50N 68°5W **73** B6
Gagnon, L. *Canada* 62°3N 110°27W **71** A6
Gahmar *India* 25°27N 83°49E **43** G10
Gai Xian = Gaizhou
  China 40°22N 122°20E **33** D12
Gail *U.S.A.* 32°46N 101°27W **84** E4
Gaillimh = Galway *Ireland* 53°17N 9°3W **10** C2
Gaines *U.S.A.* 41°46N 77°35W **82** E7
Gainesville *Fla., U.S.A.* 29°40N 82°20W **85** G13
Gainesville *Ga., U.S.A.* 34°18N 83°50W **85** D13
Gainesville *Mo., U.S.A.* 36°36N 92°26W **80** G7
Gainesville *Tex., U.S.A.* 33°38N 97°8W **84** E6
Gainsborough *U.K.* 53°24N 0°46W **12** D7
Gairdner, L. *Australia* 31°30S 136°0E **63** E2
Gairloch *U.K.* 57°43N 5°41W **11** D3
Gairloch, L. *U.K.* 57°43N 5°45W **11** D3
Gaizhou *China* 40°22N 122°20E **33** D12
Gaj → *Pakistan* 26°26N 67°21E **42** F2
Gajendragarh *India* 15°44N 75°59E **45** G2
Gakuch *Pakistan* 36°7N 73°45E **43** A5
Gal Oya △ *Sri Lanka* 7°0N 81°20E **45** L5
Gal Oya Res. *Sri Lanka* 7°5N 81°30E **45** L5
Galán, Cerro *Argentina* 25°55S 66°52W **94** B2
Galápagos = Colón, Arch. de
  Ecuador 0°0 91°0W **90** D1
Galapagos Fracture Zone
  Pac. Oc. 3°0N 110°0W **65** G17
Galapagos Rise *Pac. Oc.* 15°0S 95°0W **65** J18
Galashiels *U.K.* 55°37N 2°49W **11** F6
Galați *Romania* 45°27N 28°2E **17** F15
Galatina *Italy* 40°10N 18°10E **23** D8
Galax *U.S.A.* 36°40N 80°56W **81** G13
Galbīn Govĭ *Mongolia* 43°0N 107°0E **32** C4
Galcaio = Gaalkacyo
  Somalia 6°30N 47°30E **49** F4
Galdhøpiggen *Norway* 61°38N 8°18E **8** F13
Galeana *Chihuahua, Mexico* 30°7N 107°38W **86** A3
Galeana *Nuevo León, Mexico* 24°50N 100°4W **86** B4
Galela *Indonesia* 1°50N 127°49E **37** D7
Galeota Pt. *Trin. & Tob.* 10°8N 60°59W **93** K16
Galera Pt. *Trin. & Tob.* 10°49N 60°54W **93** K16
Galesburg *U.S.A.* 40°57N 90°22W **80** E8
Galestan △ *Iran* 37°30N 56°0E **47** B8
Galeton *U.S.A.* 41°44N 77°39W **82** E7
Galich *Russia* 58°22N 42°24E **18** C7
Galicia □ *Spain* 42°43N 7°45W **21** A2
Galilee = Hagalil *Israel* 32°53N 35°18E **48** C4
Galilee, L. *Australia* 22°20S 145°50E **62** C4
Galilee, Sea of = Yam Kinneret
  Israel 32°45N 35°35E **48** C4
Galina Pt. *Jamaica* 18°24N 76°58W **88** a
Galion *U.S.A.* 40°44N 82°47W **82** F2
Galiuro Mts. *U.S.A.* 32°30N 110°20W **77** K8

Galiwinku *Australia* 12°2S 135°34E **62** A2
Gallan Hd. *U.K.* 58°15N 7°2W **11** C1
Gallatin *U.S.A.* 36°24N 86°27W **85** C11
Galle *Sri Lanka* 6°5N 80°10E **45** L5
Gállego → *Spain* 41°39N 0°51W **21** B5
Gallegos → *Argentina* 51°35S 69°0W **96** G3
Galley Hd. *Ireland* 51°32N 8°55W **10** E3
Gallinas, Pta. *Colombia* 12°28N 71°40W **92** A4
Gallipoli = Gelibolu
  Turkey 40°28N 26°43E **23** D12
Gallipoli *Italy* 40°3N 17°58E **23** D8
Gallipolis *U.S.A.* 38°49N 82°12W **81** F12
Galloo I. *U.S.A.* 43°55N 76°25W **83** C8
Galloway *U.K.* 55°1N 4°29W **11** F4
Galloway, Mull of *U.K.* 54°39N 4°52W **11** G4
Gallup *U.S.A.* 35°32N 108°45W **77** J9
Galmudug *Somalia* 6°30N 48°0E **49** F4
Galoya *Sri Lanka* 8°10N 80°55E **45** K5
Galt *U.S.A.* 38°15N 121°18W **78** G5
Galty Mts. *Ireland* 52°22N 8°10W **10** D3
Galtymore *Ireland* 52°21N 8°11W **10** D3
Galugāh *Iran* 36°43N 53°48E **47** B7
Galva *U.S.A.* 41°10N 90°3W **80** E8
Galveston *U.S.A.* 29°18N 94°48W **84** G7
Galveston B. *U.S.A.* 29°36N 94°50W **84** G7
Gálvez *Argentina* 32°0S 61°14W **94** C3
Galway *Ireland* 53°17N 9°3W **10** C2
Galway □ *Ireland* 53°22N 9°1W **10** C2
Galway B. *Ireland* 53°13N 9°10W **10** C2
Gam → *Vietnam* 21°55N 105°12E **38** B5
Gamagōri *Japan* 34°50N 137°14E **29** G8
Gambat *Pakistan* 27°17N 68°26E **42** F3
Gambhir → *India* 26°58N 77°27E **42** F6
Gambia ■ *W. Afr.* 13°25N 16°0W **52** F2
Gambia → *W. Afr.* 13°28N 16°34W **52** F2
Gambier, C. *Australia* 11°56S 130°57E **60** B5
Gambier, Îs.
  French Polynesia 23°8S 134°58W **65** K14
Gambier Is. *Australia* 35°3S 136°30E **63** F2
Gambo *Canada* 48°47N 54°13W **73** C9
Gamboli *Pakistan* 29°53N 68°24E **42** E3
Gamboma *Congo* 1°55S 15°52E **54** E3
Gamka → *S. Africa* 33°18S 21°39E **56** D3
Gamkab → *Namibia* 28°4S 17°54E **56** D2
Gamlakarleby = Kokkola
  Finland 63°50N 23°8E **8** E20
Gammon → *Canada* 51°24N 95°44W **71** C9
Gammon Ranges △
  Australia 30°38S 139°8E **63** E2
Gampaha *Sri Lanka* 7°5N 79°59E **45** L4
Gampola *Sri Lanka* 7°10N 80°34E **45** L5
Gamtoos → *S. Africa* 33°58S 25°1E **56** D4
Gamzigrad-Romuliana
  Serbia 43°53N 22°11E **23** C10
Gan Jiang → *China* 29°15N 116°0E **35** C11
Ganado *U.S.A.* 35°43N 109°33W **77** J9
Gananoque *Canada* 44°20N 76°10W **83** B8
Ganāveh *Iran* 29°35N 50°35E **47** D6
Gäncä *Azerbaijan* 40°45N 46°20E **19** F8
Gancheng *China* 18°51N 108°37E **38** C7
Gand = Gent *Belgium* 51°2N 3°42E **15** C3
Ganda *Angola* 13°3S 14°35E **55** G2
Gandajika
  Dem. Rep. of the Congo 6°46S 23°58E **54** F4
Gandak → *India* 25°39N 85°13E **43** G11
Gandava *Pakistan* 28°32N 67°32E **42** E2
Gander *Canada* 48°58N 54°35W **73** C9
Gander L. *Canada* 48°58N 54°35W **73** C9
Gandhi Sagar *India* 24°40N 75°40E **42** G6
Gandhinagar *India* 23°15N 72°45E **42** H5
Gandia *Spain* 38°58N 0°9W **21** C5
Ganedidalem = Gani
  Indonesia 0°48S 128°14E **37** E7
Ganga → *India* 23°20N 90°30E **43** H14
Ganga Sagar *India* 21°38N 88°5E **43** J13
Gangakher *India* 18°57N 76°45E **44** E3
Gangan → *India* 28°38N 78°58E **43** E8
Ganganagar *India* 29°56N 73°56E **42** E5
Gangapur *Maharashtra, India* 19°41N 75°1E **44** E2
Gangapur *Raj., India* 26°32N 76°49E **42** F7
Gangaw *Burma* 22°5N 94°5E **41** H19
Gangawati *India* 15°30N 76°36E **45** G3
Gangdisê Shan *China* 31°20N 81°0E **43** D9
Ganges = Ganga →
  India 23°20N 90°30E **43** H14
Ganges *Canada* 48°51N 123°31W **70** D4
Ganges, Mouths of the
  India 21°30N 90°0E **43** J14
Ganggyeong *S. Korea* 36°10N 127°0E **33** F14
Gangneung *S. Korea* 37°45N 128°54E **33** F15
Gangoh *India* 29°46N 77°18E **42** E7
Gangotri *India* 30°50N 79°10E **43** D8
Gangotri △ *India* 30°50N 79°10E **43** D8
Gangseong *S. Korea* 38°24N 128°30E **33** E15
Gangtok *India* 27°20N 88°37E **41** F16
Gangu *China* 34°40N 105°15E **32** G3
Gangyao *China* 44°12N 126°37E **33** B14
Gani *Indonesia* 0°48S 128°14E **37** E7
Ganj *India* 27°45N 78°57E **43** F8
Ganjam *India* 19°23N 85°4E **44** E7
Ganluo *China* 28°58N 102°59E **34** C4
Ganquan *China* 36°20N 109°20E **32** F5
Ganshui *China* 28°40N 106°40E **34** C6
Gansu □ *China* 36°0N 104°0E **32** G3
Ganta *Liberia* 7°15N 8°59W **52** G4
Gantheaume, C. *Australia* 36°4S 137°32E **63** F2
Gantheaume B. *Australia* 27°40S 114°10E **61** E1
Gantsevichi = Hantsavichy
  Belarus 52°49N 26°30E **17** B14
Ganyem = Genyem
  Indonesia 2°46S 140°12E **37** E10
Ganyu *China* 34°50N 119°8E **33** G10
Ganzhou *China* 25°51N 114°56E **35** E10
Gao *Mali* 16°15N 0°5W **52** E5
Gao Xian *China* 28°21N 104°32E **34** C5

Gao'an *China* 28°26N 115°17E **35** C10
Gaobeidian *China* 39°19N 115°51E **32** E8
Gaocheng *China* 38°2N 114°49E **32** E8
Gaochun *China* 31°20N 118°49E **35** B12
Gaohebu *China* 30°43N 116°49E **35** B11
Gaokeng *China* 27°40N 113°58E **35** D9
Gaolan Dao *China* 21°55N 113°10E **35** G9
Gaoligong Shan *China* 24°45N 98°45E **34** E2
Gaomi *China* 36°20N 119°42E **33** F10
Gaoping *China* 35°45N 112°55E **32** G7
Gaotang *China* 36°50N 116°15E **32** F9
Gaoua *Burkina Faso* 10°20N 3°8W **52** F5
Gaoual *Guinea* 11°45N 13°25W **52** F3
Gaoxiong = Kaohsiung
  Taiwan 22°35N 120°16E **35** F13
Gaoyang *China* 38°40N 115°45E **32** E8
Gaoyao *China* 23°3N 112°27E **35** F9
Gaoyou *China* 32°47N 119°26E **35** A12
Gaoyou Hu *China* 32°45N 119°20E **33** H10
Gaoyuan *China* 37°8N 117°58E **33** F9
Gaozhou *China* 21°58N 110°50E **35** G8
Gap *France* 44°33N 6°5E **20** D7
Gapat → *India* 24°30N 82°28E **43** G10
Gapuwiyak *Australia* 12°25S 135°43E **62** A2
Gar *China* 32°10N 79°58E **30** E4
Gara, L. *Ireland* 53°57N 8°26W **10** C3
Garabogazköl Aylagy
  Turkmenistan 41°0N 53°30E **19** F9
Garachiné *Panama* 8°0N 78°12W **88** E4
Garagum *Turkmenistan* 39°30N 60°0E **47** B8
Garah *Australia* 29°5S 149°38E **63** D4
Garanhuns *Brazil* 8°50S 36°30W **93** E11
Garautha *India* 25°34N 79°18E **43** G8
Garawa ✪ *Australia* 16°43S 136°51E **62** B2
Garbiyang *India* 30°8N 80°54E **43** D9
Gard → *France* 43°51N 4°37E **20** E6
Garda, L. di *Italy* 45°40N 10°41E **22** B4
Garde L. *Canada* 62°50N 106°13W **71** A7
Garden City *Ga., U.S.A.* 32°6N 81°9W **85** E14
Garden City *Kans., U.S.A.* 37°58N 100°53W **80** G3
Garden City *Tex., U.S.A.* 31°52N 101°29W **84** F4
Garden Grove *U.S.A.* 33°47N 117°55W **79** M9
Gardēz *Afghan.* 33°37N 69°9E **42** C3
Gardiner *Maine, U.S.A.* 44°14N 69°47W **81** C19
Gardiner *Mont., U.S.A.* 45°2N 110°22W **76** D8
Gardiners I. *U.S.A.* 41°6N 72°6W **83** E12
Gardner *U.S.A.* 42°34N 71°59W **83** D13
Gardner Canal *Canada* 53°27N 128°8W **70** C3
Gardner Pinnacles
  U.S.A. 25°0N 167°55W **75** L6
Gardnerville *U.S.A.* 38°56N 119°45W **78** G7
Gardo = Qardho *Somalia* 9°30N 49°6E **49** F4
Garey *U.S.A.* 34°53N 120°19W **79** L6
Garfield *U.S.A.* 47°1N 117°9W **76** C5
Garforth *U.K.* 53°47N 1°24W **12** D6
Gargantua, C. *Canada* 47°36N 85°2W **81** B11
Gargett *Australia* 21°9S 148°46E **62** b
Garhchiroli *India* 20°10N 80°0E **44** E6
Garibaldi △ *Canada* 49°50N 122°40W **70** D4
Gariep, L. *S. Africa* 30°40S 25°40E **56** D4
Garies *S. Africa* 30°32S 17°59E **56** D2
Garig Gunak Barlu △
  Australia 11°26S 131°58E **60** B5
Garigliano → *Italy* 41°13N 13°45E **22** D5
Garissa *Kenya* 0°25S 39°40E **54** E7
Garland *Tex., U.S.A.* 32°54N 96°38W **84** E6
Garland *Utah, U.S.A.* 41°45N 112°10W **76** F7
Garmāb *Iran* 35°25N 56°45E **47** C8
Garmisch-Partenkirchen
  Germany 47°30N 11°6E **16** E6
Garmsār *Iran* 35°20N 52°25E **47** C7
Garnett *U.S.A.* 38°17N 95°14W **80** F6
Garo Hills *India* 25°30N 90°30E **43** G14
Garoe = Garoowe *Somalia* 8°25N 48°33E **49** F4
Garonne → *France* 45°2N 0°36W **20** D3
Garoowe *Somalia* 8°25N 48°33E **49** F4
Garot *India* 24°19N 75°41E **42** G6
Garoua *Cameroon* 9°19N 13°21E **53** G8
Garrauli *India* 25°5N 79°22E **43** G8
Garrison *Mont., U.S.A.* 46°31N 112°49W **76** C7
Garrison *N. Dak., U.S.A.* 47°40N 101°25W **80** B3
Garrison Res. = Sakakawea, L.
  U.S.A. 47°30N 101°25W **80** B3
Garron Pt. *U.K.* 55°3N 5°59W **11** A6
Garry → *U.K.* 56°44N 3°47W **11** E5
Garry, L. *Canada* 65°58N 100°18W **68** D11
Garrygala *Turkmenistan* 38°31N 56°29E **47** B8
Garson L. *Canada* 56°19N 110°2W **71** B6
Garstang *U.K.* 53°55N 2°46W **12** D5
Garu *India* 23°40N 84°14E **43** H11
Garub *Namibia* 26°37S 16°0E **56** C2
Garut *Indonesia* 7°14S 107°53E **37** G12
Garvie Mts. *N.Z.* 45°30S 168°50E **59** F2
Garwa = Garwa *India* 24°11N 83°47E **43** G10
Garwa *India* 24°11N 83°47E **43** G10
Gary *U.S.A.* 41°36N 87°20W **80** E10
Garzê *China* 31°38N 100°1E **32** H3
Garzón *Colombia* 2°10N 75°40W **92** C3
Gas-San *Japan* 38°32N 140°1E **28** E10
Gasan Kuli = Esenguly
  Turkmenistan 37°37N 53°59E **26** F6
Gascogne *France* 43°45N 0°20E **20** E4
Gascogne, G. de *Europe* 44°0N 2°0W **20** D2
Gascony = Gascogne
  France 43°45N 0°20E **20** E4
Gascoyne → *Australia* 24°52S 113°37E **61** D1
Gascoyne Junction
  Australia 25°2S 115°17E **61** E2
Gashaka *Nigeria* 7°20N 11°29E **53** G8
Gasherbrum *Pakistan* 35°40N 76°40E **43** B7
Gashua *Nigeria* 12°54N 11°0E **53** F8
Gasparillo *Trin. & Tob.* 10°18N 61°26W **93** K15
Gaspé *Canada* 48°52N 64°30W **73** C7
Gaspé, C. de *Canada* 48°48N 64°7W **73** C7
Gaspé Pen. = Gaspésie, Pén. de la
  Canada 48°45N 65°40W **73** C6

Gaspésie, Pén. de la
  Canada 48°45N 65°40W **73** C6
Gaspésie △ *Canada* 48°55N 66°10W **73** C6
Gasteiz = Vitoria-Gasteiz
  Spain 42°50N 2°41W **21** A4
Gastonia *U.S.A.* 35°16N 81°11W **85** D14
Gastre *Argentina* 42°20S 69°15W **96** E3
Gata, C. de *Spain* 36°41N 2°13W **21** D4
Gata, Sierra de *Spain* 40°20N 6°45W **21** B2
Gataga → *Canada* 58°35N 126°59W **70** B3
Gatchina *Russia* 59°35N 30°9E **9** G24
Gatehouse of Fleet *U.K.* 54°53N 4°12W **11** G4
Gates *U.S.A.* 43°9N 77°42W **82** C7
Gatesville *U.S.A.* 31°26N 97°45W **84** F6
Gateshead I. *Canada* 70°36N 100°26W **68** C11
Gateshead *U.K.* 54°57N 1°35W **12** C6
Gatineau *U.S.A.* 45°29N 75°39W **83** A9
Gatineau → *Canada* 45°27N 75°42W **72** C4
Gatineau △ *Canada* 45°40N 76°0W **72** C4
Gatton *Australia* 27°32S 152°17E **63** D5
Gatún, L. *Panama* 9°7N 79°56W **88** E4
Gatwick, London ✈ (LGW)
  U.K. 51°10N 0°11W **13** F7
Gatyana *S. Africa* 32°16S 28°31E **57** D4
Gau *Fiji* 18°2S 179°18E **59** a
Gauer L. *Canada* 57°0N 97°50W **71** B9
Gauhati = Guwahati
  India 26°10N 91°45E **41** F17
Gauja → *Latvia* 57°10N 24°16E **9** H21
Gaujas △ *Latvia* 57°10N 24°50E **9** H21
Gaula → *Norway* 63°21N 10°14E **8** E14
Gauri Phanta *India* 28°41N 80°36E **43** E9
Gauribidanur *India* 13°37N 77°23E **45** H3
Gaustatoppen *Norway* 59°48N 8°40E **9** G13
Gauteng □ *S. Africa* 26°0S 28°0E **57** C4
Gāv Koshī *Iran* 28°38N 57°12E **47** D8
Gāvakān *Iran* 29°37N 53°10E **47** D7
Gavāter *Iran* 25°10N 61°31E **47** E9
Gāvbandī *Iran* 27°12N 53°4E **47** E7
Gavdos *Greece* 34°50N 24°5E **23** G11
Gaviota *U.S.A.* 34°29N 120°13W **79** L6
Gävkhūnī, Bāţlāq-e *Iran* 32°6N 52°52E **47** C7
Gävle *Sweden* 60°40N 17°9E **8** F17
Gawachab *Namibia* 27°4S 17°55E **56** C2
Gawilgarh Hills *India* 21°15N 76°45E **44** D3
Gawler *Australia* 34°30S 138°42E **63** E2
Gawler Ranges *Australia* 32°30S 135°45E **63** E2
Gaxun Nur *China* 42°22N 100°30E **30** C9
Gay *Russia* 51°27N 58°27E **18** D10
Gaya *India* 24°47N 85°4E **43** G11
Gaya *Niger* 11°52N 3°28E **52** F6
Gaylord *U.S.A.* 45°2N 84°41W **81** C11
Gayndah *Australia* 25°35S 151°32E **63** D5
Gaysin = Haysyn
  Ukraine 48°57N 29°25E **17** D15
Gayvoron = Hayvoron
  Ukraine 48°22N 29°52E **17** D15
Gaza *Gaza Strip* 31°30N 34°28E **48** D3
Gaza □ *Mozam.* 23°10S 32°45E **57** B5
Gaza Strip ■ *Asia* 31°29N 34°25E **48** D3
Gazanjyk = Bereket
  Turkmenistan 39°16N 55°32E **47** B7
Gāzbor *Iran* 28°5N 58°51E **47** D8
Gaziantep *Turkey* 37°6N 37°23E **46** B3
Gazimağusa = Famagusta
  Cyprus 35°8N 33°55E **46** C2
Gbadolite
  Dem. Rep. of the Congo 4°1N 21°1E **54** D4
Gbarnga *Liberia* 7°19N 9°13W **52** G4
Gcoverega *Botswana* 19°8S 24°18E **56** B3
Gcuwa *S. Africa* 32°20S 28°11E **57** D4
Gdańsk *Poland* 54°22N 18°40E **17** A10
Gdańska, Zatoka *Poland* 54°30N 19°20E **17** A10
Gdov *Russia* 58°48N 27°55E **9** G22
Gdynia *Poland* 54°35N 18°33E **17** A10
Gebe *Indonesia* 0°5N 129°25E **37** D7
Gebze *Turkey* 40°47N 29°25E **23** D13
Gedaref *Sudan* 14°2N 35°28E **53** F13
Gede, Tanjung *Indonesia* 6°46S 105°12E **37** G11
Gedser *Denmark* 54°35N 11°55E **9** J14
Gedung, Pulau *Malaysia* 5°17N 100°23E **39** c
Geegully Cr. →
  Australia 18°32S 123°41E **60** C3
Geel *Belgium* 51°10N 4°59E **15** C4
Geelong *Australia* 38°10S 144°22E **63** F3
Geelvink B. = Cenderawasih,
  Teluk *Indonesia* 3°0S 135°20E **37** E9
Geelvink Chan. *Australia* 28°30S 114°0E **61** E1
Geesthacht *Germany* 53°26N 10°22E **16** B6
Geidam *Nigeria* 12°57N 11°57E **53** F8
Geikie → *Canada* 57°45N 103°52W **71** B8
Geikie Gorge △ *Australia* 18°3S 125°41E **60** C4
Geistown *U.S.A.* 40°18N 78°52W **82** F6
Gejiu *China* 23°20N 103°10E **34** F4
Gel, Meydān-e *Iran* 29°4N 54°50E **47** D7
Gela *Italy* 37°4N 14°15E **22** F6
Gelang Patah *Malaysia* 1°27N 103°35E **39** d
Gelderland □ *Neths.* 52°5N 6°10E **15** B6
Geldrop *Neths.* 51°25N 5°32E **15** C5
Geleen *Neths.* 50°57N 5°49E **15** D5
Gelib = Jilib *Somalia* 0°29N 42°46E **49** G3
Gelibolu *Turkey* 40°28N 26°43E **23** D12
Gelsenkirchen *Germany* 51°32N 7°6E **16** C4
Gelugur *Malaysia* 5°22N 100°18E **39** c
Gemas *Malaysia* 2°37N 102°36E **39** L4
Gembloux *Belgium* 50°34N 4°43E **15** D4
Gemena
  Dem. Rep. of the Congo 3°13N 19°48E **54** D3
Gemerek *Turkey* 39°15N 36°10E **46** B3
Gemlik *Turkey* 40°26N 29°9E **23** D13
Gemsbok △ *Botswana* 25°10S 25°40E **56** C3
Genale → *Ethiopia* 6°2N 39°1E **49** F2
General Acha *Argentina* 37°20S 64°38W **94** D3
General Alvear *B. Aires,
  Argentina* 36°0S 60°0W **94** D4
General Alvear *Mendoza,
  Argentina* 35°0S 67°40W **94** D2
General Artigas
  Paraguay 26°52S 56°16W **94** B4

122 General Belgrano
INDEX TO WORLD MAPS

General Belgrano Argentina 36°35S 58°47W 94 D4
General Bernardo O'Higgins Antarctica 63°0S 58°3W 5 C18
General Cabrera Argentina 32°53S 63°52W 94 C3
General Carrera, L. S. Amer. 46°35S 72°0W 96 F2
General Cepeda Mexico 25°21N 101°22W 86 B4
General Guido Argentina 36°40S 57°50W 94 D4
General Juan Madariaga Argentina 37°0S 57°0W 94 D4
General La Madrid Argentina 37°17S 61°20W 94 D3
General MacArthur Phil. 11°18N 125°28E 37 B7
General Martin Miguel de Güemes Argentina 24°50S 65°0W 94 A3
General Pico Argentina 35°45S 63°50W 94 D3
General Pinedo Argentina 27°15S 61°20W 94 B3
General Pinto Argentina 34°45S 61°50W 94 C3
General Roca Argentina 39°2S 67°35W 96 D3
General Santos Phil. 6°5N 125°14E 37 C7
General Treviño Mexico 26°14N 99°29W 87 B5
General Trías Mexico 28°21N 106°22W 86 B3
General Viamonte Argentina 35°1S 61°3W 94 D3
General Villegas Argentina 35°5S 63°0W 94 D3
Genesee Idaho, U.S.A. 46°33N 116°56W 76 C5
Genesee Pa., U.S.A. 41°59N 77°54W 82 E7
Genesee → U.S.A. 43°16N 77°36W 82 C7
Geneseo Ill., U.S.A. 41°27N 90°9W 80 E8
Geneseo N.Y., U.S.A. 42°48N 77°49W 82 D7
Geneva = Genève Switz. 46°12N 6°9E 20 C7
Geneva Ala., U.S.A. 31°2N 85°52W 85 F12
Geneva N.Y., U.S.A. 42°52N 76°59W 82 D8
Geneva Nebr., U.S.A. 40°32N 97°36W 80 E5
Geneva Ohio, U.S.A. 41°48N 80°57W 82 E4
Geneva, L. = Léman, L. Europe 46°26N 6°30E 20 C7
Genève Switz. 46°12N 6°9E 20 C7
Gengma China 23°32N 99°20E 34 F2
Genhe China 50°47N 121°31E 31 A13
Genil → Spain 37°42N 5°19W 21 D3
Genk Belgium 50°58N 5°32E 15 D5
Gennargentu, Mti. del Italy 40°1N 9°19E 22 D3
Genoa = Génova Italy 44°25N 8°57E 20 D8
Genoa Australia 37°29S 149°35E 63 F4
Genoa N.Y., U.S.A. 42°40N 76°32W 83 D8
Genoa Nebr., U.S.A. 41°27N 97°44W 80 E5
Genoa Nev., U.S.A. 39°2N 119°50W 78 F7
Génova Italy 44°25N 8°57E 20 D8
Génova, G. di Italy 44°0N 9°0E 22 C3
Genriyetty, Ostrov Russia 77°6N 156°30E 27 B16
Gent Belgium 51°2N 3°42E 15 C3
Genteng Jawa Barat, Indonesia 7°22S 106°24E 37 G12
Genteng Jawa Timur, Indonesia 8°22S 114°9E 37 J17
Genyem Indonesia 2°46S 140°12E 37 E10
Geochang S. Korea 35°41N 127°55E 33 G14
Geographe B. Australia 33°30S 115°15E 61 F2
Geographe Chan. Australia 24°30S 113°0E 61 D1
George, Zemlya Russia 80°30N 49°0E 26 A5
George S. Africa 33°58S 22°29E 56 D3
George → Canada 58°49N 66°10W 73 A6
George, L. N.S.W., Australia 35°10S 149°25E 63 F4
George, L. S. Austral., Australia 37°25S 140°0E 63 F3
George, L. W. Austral., Australia 22°45S 123°40E 60 D3
George, L. Fla., U.S.A. 29°17N 81°36W 85 G14
George, L. N.Y., U.S.A. 43°37N 73°33W 83 C11
George Gill Ra. Australia 24°22S 131°45E 60 D5
George Pt. Australia 20°6S 148°36E 62 b
George River = Kangiqsualujjuaq Canada 58°30N 65°59W 69 F18
George Sound N.Z. 44°52S 167°25E 59 F1
George Town Australia 41°6S 146°49E 63 G4
George Town Bahamas 23°33N 75°47W 88 B4
George Town Cayman Is. 19°20N 81°24W 88 C3
George Town Malaysia 5°25N 100°20E 39 c
George V Land Antarctica 69°0S 148°0E 5 C10
George VI Sound Antarctica 71°0S 68°0W 5 D17
George West U.S.A. 28°20N 98°7W 84 G5
Georgetown = Janjanbureh Gambia 13°30N 14°47W 52 F3
Georgetown Australia 18°17S 143°33E 62 B3
Georgetown Ont., Canada 43°40N 79°56W 82 C5
Georgetown P.E.I., Canada 46°13N 62°24W 73 C7
Georgetown Guyana 6°50N 58°12W 92 B7
Georgetown Calif., U.S.A. 38°54N 120°50W 78 G6
Georgetown Colo., U.S.A. 39°42N 105°42W 76 G11
Georgetown Ky., U.S.A. 38°13N 84°33W 81 F11
Georgetown N.Y., U.S.A. 42°46N 75°44W 83 D9
Georgetown Ohio, U.S.A. 38°52N 83°54W 81 F12
Georgetown S.C., U.S.A. 33°23N 79°17W 85 E15
Georgetown Tex., U.S.A. 30°38N 97°41W 84 F6
Georgia □ U.S.A. 32°50N 83°15W 85 E13
Georgia ■ Asia 42°0N 43°0E 19 F7
Georgia, Str. of N. Amer. 49°25N 124°0W 78 A3
Georgia Basin S. Ocean 50°45S 35°30W 5 B1
Georgian B. Canada 45°15N 81°0W 82 A4
Georgian Bay Islands △ Canada 44°53N 79°52W 82 B5
Georgievka Kazakhstan 49°19N 84°34E 26 E9
Georgina → Australia 23°30S 139°47E 62 C2
Georgina I. Canada 44°22N 79°17W 82 B5
Georgiyevsk Russia 44°12N 43°28E 19 F7
Gera Germany 50°53N 12°4E 16 C7
Geraardsbergen Belgium 50°45N 3°53E 15 D3
Geral, Serra Brazil 26°25S 50°0W 95 B6
Geral de Goiás, Serra Brazil 12°0S 46°0W 93 F9
Geraldine U.S.A. 47°36N 110°16W 76 C8
Geraldton Australia 28°48S 114°32E 61 E1
Geraldton Canada 49°44N 87°10W 72 C2
Gerdine, Mt. U.S.A. 61°35N 152°27W 74 C9
Gereshk Afghan. 31°47N 64°35E 40 D4
Gerik Malaysia 5°50N 101°15E 39 K3
Gering U.S.A. 41°50N 103°40W 80 E2
Gerlach U.S.A. 40°39N 119°21W 76 F4
German Bight = Deutsche Bucht Germany 54°15N 8°0E 16 A5
Germansen Landing Canada 55°43N 124°40W 70 B4
Germantown U.S.A. 35°5N 89°49W 85 D10
Germany ■ Europe 51°0N 10°0E 16 C6
Germī Iran 39°1N 48°3E 47 B6
Gernika-Lumo Spain 43°19N 2°40W 21 A4
Gero Japan 35°48N 137°14E 29 G8
Gerokgak Indonesia 8°11S 114°27E 37 J17
Gerona = Girona Spain 41°58N 2°46E 21 B7
Gerrard Canada 50°30N 117°17W 70 C5
Gersoppa Falls India 14°12N 74°46E 45 G2
Gertak Sanggul Malaysia 5°17N 100°12E 39 c
Gertak Sanggul, Tanjung Malaysia 5°16N 100°11E 39 c
Gerung Indonesia 8°43S 116°7E 37 K19
Geser Indonesia 3°50S 130°54E 37 E8
Gettysburg Pa., U.S.A. 39°50N 77°14W 81 F15
Gettysburg S. Dak., U.S.A. 45°1N 99°57W 80 C4
Getxo Spain 43°21N 2°59W 21 A4
Getz Ice Shelf Antarctica 75°0S 130°0W 5 D14
Gevrai India 19°16N 75°45E 44 E2
Geyser U.S.A. 47°16N 110°30W 76 C8
Geyserville U.S.A. 38°42N 122°54W 78 G4
Gezhouba Dam China 30°40N 111°20E 35 B8
Ghadāf, W. al → Iraq 32°56N 43°30E 46 C4
Ghadāmis Libya 30°11N 9°29E 53 B8
Ghaggar → India 29°30N 74°53E 42 E6
Ghaghara → India 25°45N 84°40E 43 G11
Ghaghat → Bangla. 25°19N 89°38E 43 G13
Ghagra India 23°17N 84°33E 43 H11
Ghagra → India 27°29N 81°9E 43 F9
Ghallamane Mauritania 23°15N 10°0W 52 D4
Ghana ■ W. Afr. 8°0N 1°0W 52 G5
Ghanpokhara Nepal 28°17N 84°14E 43 E11
Ghansor India 22°39N 80°1E 43 H9
Ghanzi Botswana 21°50S 21°34E 56 B3
Ghanzi □ Botswana 22°30S 22°30E 56 B3
Gharb Bahr el Ghazâl = Western Bahr el Ghazâl □ South Sudan 7°30N 25°30E 50 F6
Ghardaïa Algeria 32°20N 3°37E 52 B6
Gharm Tajikistan 39°0N 70°20E 26 F8
Gharyān Libya 32°10N 13°0E 53 B8
Ghāt Libya 24°59N 10°11E 53 D8
Ghatal India 22°40N 87°46E 43 H12
Ghatampur India 26°8N 80°13E 43 F9
Ghatgaon India 21°24N 85°53E 44 D7
Ghatprabha → India 16°15N 75°20E 45 F2
Ghats, Eastern India 14°0N 78°50E 45 H4
Ghats, Western India 14°0N 75°0E 45 H2
Ghatsila India 22°36N 86°29E 43 H12
Ghaṭṭī Si. Arabia 31°16N 37°31E 46 D3
Ghawdex = Gozo Malta 36°3N 14°15E 22 F6
Ghazal, Bahr el → Chad 13°0N 15°47E 53 F9
Ghazal, Bahr el → South Sudan 9°31N 30°25E 53 G12
Ghaziabad India 28°42N 77°26E 42 E7
Ghazipur India 25°38N 83°35E 43 G10
Ghaznī Afghan. 33°30N 68°28E 42 C3
Ghaznī □ Afghan. 32°10N 68°20E 40 C6
Ghent = Gent Belgium 51°2N 3°42E 15 C3
Gheorghe Gheorghiu-Dej = Oneşti Romania 46°17N 26°47E 17 E14
Ghīnah, Wādī al → Si. Arabia 30°27N 38°14E 46 D3
Ghizar → Pakistan 36°15N 73°43E 43 A5
Ghod → India 18°30N 74°35E 44 E2
Ghogha India 21°40N 72°20E 44 D1
Ghotaru India 27°20N 70°1E 42 F4
Ghotki Pakistan 28°5N 69°21E 42 E3
Ghowr □ Afghan. 34°0N 64°20E 40 C4
Ghughri India 22°39N 80°41E 43 H9
Ghugus India 19°58N 79°12E 44 E4
Ghulam Mohammad Barrage Pakistan 25°30N 68°20E 42 G3
Ghūrīān Afghan. 34°17N 61°25E 40 B2
Gia Dinh Vietnam 10°49N 106°42E 39 G6
Gia Lai = Plei Ku Vietnam 13°57N 108°0E 38 F7
Gia Nghia Vietnam 11°58N 107°42E 39 G6
Gia Ngoc Vietnam 14°50N 108°58E 38 E7
Gia Vuc Vietnam 14°42N 108°34E 38 E7
Giamama = Jamaame Somalia 0°4N 42°44E 49 G3
Gianitsa Greece 40°46N 22°24E 23 D10
Giant Forest U.S.A. 36°36N 118°43W 78 J8
Giant Sequoia ⌂ U.S.A. 36°10N 118°35W 78 K8
Giants Causeway U.K. 55°16N 6°29W 10 A5
Giant's Tank Sri Lanka 8°51N 80°2E 45 K5
Gianyar Indonesia 8°32S 115°20E 37 K18
Giarabub = Al Jaghbūb Libya 29°42N 24°38E 53 C10
Giarre Italy 37°43N 15°11E 22 F6
Gibara Cuba 21°9N 76°11W 88 B4
Gibbon U.S.A. 40°45N 98°51W 80 E4
Gibe II Ethiopia 8°0N 37°30E 49 F2
Gibe III Ethiopia 7°0N 37°30E 49 F2
Gibeon Namibia 25°9S 17°43E 56 C2
Gibraltar ◪ Europe 36°7N 5°22W 21 D3
Gibraltar, Str. of Medit. S. 35°55N 5°40W 21 E3
Gibraltar Range △ Australia 29°31S 152°19E 63 D5
Gibson Desert Australia 24°0S 126°0E 60 D4
Gibsons Canada 49°24N 123°32W 70 D4
Gibsonville U.S.A. 39°46N 120°54W 78 F6
Giddalur India 15°20N 78°57E 45 G4
Giddings U.S.A. 30°11N 96°56W 84 F6
Giebnegáisi = Kebnekaise Sweden 67°53N 18°33E 8 C18
Giessen Germany 50°34N 8°41E 16 C5
Gīfān Iran 37°54N 57°28E 47 B8
Gift Lake Canada 55°53N 115°49W 70 B5
Gifu Japan 35°30N 136°45E 29 G8
Gifu □ Japan 35°40N 137°0E 29 G8
Giganta, Sa. de la Mexico 26°0N 111°39W 86 B2
Gigha U.K. 55°42N 5°44W 11 F3
Giglio Italy 42°20N 10°52E 22 C4
Gijón Spain 43°32N 5°42W 21 A3
Gil I. Canada 53°12N 129°15W 70 C3
Gila → U.S.A. 32°43N 114°33W 77 K6
Gila Bend U.S.A. 32°57N 112°43W 77 K7
Gila Bend Mts. U.S.A. 33°10N 113°0W 77 K7
Gila Cliff Dwellings ⌂ U.S.A. 33°12N 108°16W 77 K9
Gīlān □ Iran 37°0N 50°0E 47 B6
Gilbert → Australia 16°35S 141°15E 62 B3
Gilbert Is. Kiribati 1°0N 172°0E 58 A10
Gilbert River Australia 18°9S 142°52E 62 B3
Gilbert Seamounts Pac. Oc. 52°50N 150°10W 4 D18
Gilead U.S.A. 44°24N 70°59W 83 B14
Gilf el Kebîr, Hadabat el Egypt 23°50N 25°50E 53 D11
Gilford I. Canada 50°40N 126°30W 70 C3
Gilgandra Australia 31°43S 148°39E 63 E4
Gilgit India 35°50N 74°15E 43 B6
Gilgit → Pakistan 35°44N 74°37E 43 B6
Gilgit-Baltistan □ Pakistan 36°30N 73°0E 43 A5
Gilimanuk Indonesia 8°10S 114°26E 37 J17
Gillam Canada 56°20N 94°40W 71 B10
Gillen, L. Australia 26°11S 124°38E 61 E3
Gilles, L. Australia 32°50S 136°45E 63 E2
Gillette U.S.A. 44°18N 105°30W 76 D11
Gilliat Australia 20°40S 141°28E 62 C3
Gillingham U.K. 51°23N 0°33E 13 F8
Gilmer U.S.A. 32°44N 94°57W 84 E7
Gilmore, L. Australia 32°29S 121°37E 61 F3
Gilmour Canada 44°48N 77°37W 82 B7
Gilroy U.S.A. 37°1N 121°34W 78 H5
Gimcheon S. Korea 36°11N 128°4E 33 F15
Gimhae S. Korea 35°14N 128°53E 33 G15
Gimhwa S. Korea 38°17N 127°28E 33 E14
Gimie, Mt. St. Lucia 13°54N 61°0W 89 f
Gimje S. Korea 35°48N 126°45E 33 G14
Gimli Canada 50°40N 97°0W 71 C9
Gin → Sri Lanka 6°5N 80°7E 45 L5
Gin Gin Australia 25°0S 151°58E 63 D5
Gingee India 12°15N 79°25E 45 H4
Gingin Australia 31°22S 115°54E 61 F2
Gingindlovu S. Africa 29°2S 31°30E 57 C5
Ginir Ethiopia 7°6N 40°40E 49 F3
Giohar = Jawhar Somalia 2°48N 45°30E 49 G4
Giona, Oros Greece 38°38N 22°14E 23 E10
Gir △ India 21°0N 71°0E 42 J4
Gir Hills India 21°0N 71°0E 42 J4
Girab India 26°2N 70°38E 42 F4
Girâfi, W. → Egypt 29°58N 34°39E 48 F3
Girard St. Lucia 13°59N 60°57W 89 D7
Girard Kans., U.S.A. 37°31N 94°51W 80 G6
Girard Ohio, U.S.A. 41°9N 80°42W 82 E4
Girard Pa., U.S.A. 42°0N 80°19W 82 E4
Girdle Ness U.K. 57°9N 2°3W 11 D6
Giresun Turkey 40°55N 38°30E 19 F6
Girga Egypt 26°17N 31°55E 53 C12
Giri → India 30°28N 77°41E 42 D7
Giridih India 24°10N 86°21E 43 G12
Girne = Kyrenia Cyprus 35°20N 33°20E 46 C2
Giron = Kiruna Sweden 67°52N 20°15E 8 C19
Girona Spain 41°58N 2°46E 21 B7
Gironde → France 45°32N 1°7W 20 D3
Girraween △ Australia 28°46S 151°54E 63 D5
Girringun △ Australia 18°15S 145°32E 62 B4
Giru Australia 19°30S 147°5E 62 B4
Girvan U.K. 55°14N 4°51W 11 F4
Gisborne N.Z. 38°39S 178°5E 59 C7
Gisenyi Rwanda 1°41S 29°15E 54 E5
Gislaved Sweden 57°19N 13°32E 9 H15
Gitega Burundi 3°26S 29°56E 54 E5
Githio Greece 36°46N 22°34E 23 F10
Giuba = Juba → Somalia 1°30N 42°35E 49 G3
Giurgiu Romania 43°52N 25°57E 17 G13
Giyani S. Africa 23°19S 30°43E 57 B5
Gizab Afghan. 33°22N 66°17E 42 C1
Gizhiga Russia 62°3N 160°30E 27 C17
Gizhiginskaya Guba Russia 61°0N 158°0E 27 C16
Giżycko Poland 54°2N 21°48E 17 A11
Gjakovë Kosovo 42°22N 20°26E 23 C9
Gjirokastër Albania 40°7N 20°10E 23 D9
Gjoa Haven Canada 68°38N 95°53W 68 D12
Gjøvik Norway 60°47N 10°43E 8 F14
Glace Bay Canada 46°11N 59°58W 73 C8
Glacier △ Canada 51°15N 117°30W 70 C5
Glacier △ U.S.A. 48°42N 113°48W 76 B7
Glacier Bay U.S.A. 58°40N 136°0W 68 F4
Glacier Bay ⌂ U.S.A. 58°45N 136°30W 70 B1
Glacier Peak U.S.A. 48°7N 121°7W 76 B3
Gladewater U.S.A. 32°33N 94°56W 84 E7
Gladstone Queens., Australia 23°52S 151°16E 62 C5
Gladstone S. Austral., Australia 33°15S 138°22E 63 E2
Gladstone Canada 50°13N 98°57W 71 C9
Gladstone U.S.A. 45°51N 87°1W 80 C10
Gladwin U.S.A. 43°59N 84°29W 81 D11
Glagah Indonesia 8°13S 114°18E 37 J17
Glåma = Glomma → Norway 59°12N 10°57E 9 G14
Gláma Iceland 65°48N 23°0W 8 D2
Glamis U.S.A. 32°55N 115°5W 79 N11
Glamorgan, Vale of □ U.K. 51°28N 3°25W 13 F4
Glasco Kans., U.S.A. 39°22N 97°50W 80 F5
Glasco N.Y., U.S.A. 42°3N 73°57W 83 D11
Glasgow U.K. 55°51N 4°15W 11 F4
Glasgow Ky., U.S.A. 37°0N 85°55W 81 G11
Glasgow Mont., U.S.A. 48°12N 106°38W 76 B10
Glasgow, City of □ U.K. 55°51N 4°12W 11 F4
Glasgow Int. ✕ (GLA) U.K. 55°51N 4°21W 11 F4
Glaslyn Canada 53°22N 108°21W 71 C7
Glastonbury U.K. 51°9N 2°43W 13 F5
Glastonbury U.S.A. 41°43N 72°37W 83 E12
Glazov Russia 58°9N 52°40E 18 C9
Gleichen Canada 50°52N 113°3W 70 C6
Gleiwitz = Gliwice Poland 50°22N 18°41E 17 C10
Glen U.S.A. 44°7N 71°11W 83 B13
Glen Affric U.K. 57°17N 5°1W 11 D3
Glen Canyon U.S.A. 37°30N 110°40W 77 H8
Glen Canyon ⌂ U.S.A. 37°15N 111°0W 77 H8
Glen Canyon Dam U.S.A. 36°57N 111°29W 77 H8
Glen Coe U.K. 56°40N 5°0W 11 E3
Glen Cove U.S.A. 40°51N 73°38W 83 F11
Glen Garry U.K. 57°3N 5°7W 11 D3
Glen Innes Australia 29°44S 151°44E 63 D5
Glen Lyon U.S.A. 41°10N 76°5W 83 E8
Glen Mor U.K. 57°9N 4°37W 11 D4
Glen Moriston U.K. 57°11N 4°52W 11 D4
Glen Robertson Canada 45°22N 74°30W 83 A10
Glen Spean U.K. 56°53N 4°40W 11 E4
Glen Ullin U.S.A. 46°49N 101°50W 80 B3
Glenbeigh Ireland 52°3N 9°58W 10 D2
Glencoe Canada 42°45N 81°43W 82 D3
Glencoe S. Africa 28°11S 30°11E 57 C5
Glencoe U.S.A. 44°46N 94°9W 80 C6
Glencolumbkille Ireland 54°43N 8°42W 10 B3
Glendale U.S.A. 33°32N 112°11W 77 K7
Glendive U.S.A. 47°7N 104°43W 76 C11
Glendo U.S.A. 42°30N 105°2W 76 E11
Glenelg → Australia 38°4S 140°59E 63 F3
Glenfield U.S.A. 43°43N 75°24W 83 C9
Glengad Hd. Ireland 55°20N 7°10W 10 A4
Glengarriff Ireland 51°45N 9°34W 10 E2
Glenmont U.S.A. 40°31N 82°6W 82 F2
Glenmorgan Australia 27°14S 149°42E 63 D4
Glenn U.S.A. 39°31N 122°1W 78 F4
Glennallen U.S.A. 62°7N 145°33W 68 E2
Glennamaddy Ireland 53°37N 8°33W 10 C3
Glenns Ferry U.S.A. 42°57N 115°18W 76 E6
Glenora Canada 44°2N 77°3W 82 B7
Glenorchy Australia 42°49S 147°18E 63 G4
Glenore Australia 17°50S 141°12E 62 B3
Glenreagh Australia 30°2S 153°1E 63 E5
Glenrock U.S.A. 42°52N 105°52W 76 E11
Glenrothes U.K. 56°12N 3°10W 11 E5
Glens Falls U.S.A. 43°19N 73°39W 83 C11
Glenside U.S.A. 40°6N 75°9W 83 F9
Glenties Ireland 54°48N 8°17W 10 B3
Glenveagh △ Ireland 55°3N 8°1W 10 A3
Glenville U.S.A. 38°56N 80°50W 81 F13
Glenwood Canada 49°0N 54°58W 73 C9
Glenwood Ark., U.S.A. 34°20N 93°33W 84 D8
Glenwood Iowa, U.S.A. 41°3N 95°45W 80 E6
Glenwood Minn., U.S.A. 45°39N 95°23W 80 C6
Glenwood Wash., U.S.A. 46°1N 121°17W 78 D5
Glenwood Springs U.S.A. 39°33N 107°19W 76 G10
Glettinganes Iceland 65°30N 13°37W 8 D7
Glin Ireland 52°34N 9°17W 10 D2
Gliwice Poland 50°22N 18°41E 17 C10
Globe U.S.A. 33°24N 110°47W 77 K8
Głogów Poland 51°37N 16°5E 16 C9
Glomma → Norway 59°12N 10°57E 9 G14
Glorieuses, Îs. Ind. Oc. 11°30S 47°20E 55 G9
Glossop U.K. 53°27N 1°56W 12 D6
Gloucester Australia 32°0S 151°59E 63 E5
Gloucester U.K. 51°53N 2°15W 13 F5
Gloucester U.S.A. 42°37N 70°40W 83 D14
Gloucester I. Australia 20°0S 148°30E 62 b
Gloucester Island △ Australia 20°2S 148°30E 62 b
Gloucester Point U.S.A. 37°15N 76°30W 81 G15
Gloucestershire □ U.K. 51°46N 2°15W 13 F5
Gloversville U.S.A. 43°3N 74°21W 83 C10
Glovertown Canada 48°40N 54°3W 73 C9
Glusk Belarus 52°53N 28°41E 17 B15
Glyn Ebwy = Ebbw Vale U.K. 51°46N 3°12W 13 F4
Gmünd Austria 48°45N 15°0E 16 D8
Gmunden Austria 47°55N 13°48E 16 E7
Gniezno Poland 52°30N 17°35E 17 B9
Gnowangerup Australia 33°58S 117°59E 61 F2
Go Cong Vietnam 10°22N 106°40E 39 G6
Gō-no-ura Japan 33°44N 129°40E 29 H4
Goa India 15°33N 73°59E 45 G1
Goa □ India 15°33N 73°59E 45 G1
Goalen Hd. Australia 36°33S 150°4E 63 F5
Goalpara India 26°10N 90°40E 41 F17
Goaltor India 22°43N 87°10E 43 H12
Goalundo Ghat Bangla. 23°50N 89°47E 43 H13
Goat Fell U.K. 55°38N 5°11W 11 F3
Goba Ethiopia 7°1N 39°59E 49 F2
Goba Mozam. 26°15S 32°13E 57 C5
Gobabis Namibia 22°30S 19°0E 56 B2
Gobi Asia 44°0N 110°0E 32 C6
Gobichettipalayam India 11°31N 77°21E 45 J3
Gobō Japan 33°53N 135°10E 29 H7
Gochas Namibia 24°59S 18°55E 56 B2
Godalming U.K. 51°11N 0°36W 13 F7
Godavari → India 16°25N 82°18E 44 F6
Godavari Pt. India 17°0N 82°20E 44 F6
Godbout Canada 49°20N 67°38W 73 C6
Godda India 24°50N 87°13E 43 G12
Goderich Canada 43°45N 81°41W 82 C3
Godfrey Ra. Australia 24°0S 117°0E 61 D2
Godhavn = Qeqertarsuaq Greenland 69°15N 53°38W 4 C5
Godhra India 22°49N 73°40E 42 H5
Godoy Cruz Argentina 32°56S 68°52W 94 C2
Gods → Canada 56°22N 92°51W 72 A1
Gods L. Canada 54°40N 94°15W 72 B1
Gods River Canada 54°50N 94°5W 71 C10
Godthåb = Nuuk Greenland 64°10N 51°35W 67 C14
Goeie Hoop, Kaap die = Good Hope, C. of S. Africa 34°24S 18°30E 56 D2
Goéland, L. au Canada 49°50N 76°48W 72 C4
Goélands, L. aux Canada 55°27N 64°17W 73 A7
Goeree Neths. 51°50N 4°0E 15 C3
Goes Neths. 51°30N 3°55E 15 C3
Goffstown U.S.A. 43°1N 71°36W 83 C13
Gogama Canada 47°35N 81°43W 72 C3
Gogebic, L. U.S.A. 46°30N 89°35W 80 B9
Gogra = Ghaghara → India 25°45N 84°40E 43 G11
Gogriâl South Sudan 8°30N 28°8E 53 G11
Gohana India 29°8N 76°42E 42 E7
Goharganj India 23°1N 77°41E 42 H7
Goi → India 22°4N 74°46E 42 H6
Goiânia Brazil 16°43S 49°20W 93 G9
Goiás Brazil 15°55S 50°10W 93 G8
Goiás □ Brazil 12°10S 48°0W 93 F9
Goio-Erê Brazil 24°12S 53°1W 95 A5
Gojō Japan 34°21N 135°42E 29 G7
Gojra Pakistan 31°10N 72°40E 42 D5
Gokak India 16°11N 74°52E 45 F2
Gokarn India 14°33N 74°17E 45 G2
Gökçeada Turkey 40°10N 25°50E 23 D11
Gökova Körfezi Turkey 36°55N 27°50E 23 F12
Göksu → Turkey 36°19N 34°5E 46 B2
Gokteik Burma 22°26N 97°0E 41 H20
Gokurt Pakistan 29°40N 67°26E 42 E2
Gokwe Zimbabwe 18°7S 28°58E 57 A4
Gola India 28°3N 80°32E 43 E9
Golakganj India 26°8N 89°52E 43 F13
Golan Heights = Hagolan Syria 33°0N 35°45E 48 C4
Golāshkerd Iran 27°59N 57°16E 47 E8
Golconda India 17°24N 78°23E 44 F4
Golconda U.S.A. 40°58N 117°30W 76 F5
Gold U.S.A. 41°52N 77°50W 82 E7
Gold Beach U.S.A. 42°25N 124°25W 76 E1
Gold Coast W. Afr. 4°0N 1°40W 52 H5
Gold Hill U.S.A. 42°26N 123°3W 76 E2
Gold River Canada 49°46N 126°3W 70 D3
Golden Canada 51°20N 116°59W 70 C5
Golden B. N.Z. 40°40S 172°50E 59 D4
Golden Gate Highlands △ S. Africa 28°40S 28°40E 57 C4
Golden Hinde Canada 49°40N 125°44W 70 D3
Golden Lake Canada 45°34N 77°21W 82 A7
Golden Rock India 10°45N 78°48E 45 J4
Golden Spike ⌂ U.S.A. 41°37N 112°33W 76 F7
Golden Vale Ireland 52°33N 8°17W 10 D3
Goldendale U.S.A. 45°49N 120°50W 76 D3
Goldfield U.S.A. 37°42N 117°14W 77 H5
Goldsand L. Canada 57°2N 101°8W 71 B8
Goldsboro U.S.A. 35°23N 77°59W 85 D16
Goldsmith U.S.A. 31°59N 102°37W 84 F3
Goldthwaite U.S.A. 31°27N 98°34W 84 F5
Goleniów Poland 53°35N 14°50E 16 B8
Golestān □ Iran 37°20N 55°25E 47 B7
Golestānak Iran 30°36N 54°14E 47 D7
Goleta U.S.A. 34°27N 119°50W 79 L7
Golfito Costa Rica 8°41N 83°5W 88 E3
Golfo Aranci Italy 40°59N 9°38E 22 D3
Golfo de Santa Clara Mexico 31°42N 114°30W 86 A2
Goliad U.S.A. 28°40N 97°23W 84 G6
Golmud China 36°25N 94°53E 30 D7
Golpāyegān Iran 33°27N 50°18E 47 C6
Golra Pakistan 33°37N 72°56E 42 C5
Golspie U.K. 57°58N 3°59W 11 D5
Goma Dem. Rep. of the Congo 1°37S 29°10E 54 E5
Gomal Pass Pakistan 31°56N 69°20E 42 D3
Gomati → India 25°32N 83°11E 43 G10
Gombe Nigeria 10°19N 11°2E 53 F8
Gomel = Homyel Belarus 52°28N 31°0E 17 B16
Gomera Canary Is. 28°7N 17°14W 52 C2
Gómez Palacio Mexico 25°34N 103°30W 86 B4
Gomīshān Iran 37°4N 54°6E 47 B7
Gomogomo Indonesia 6°39S 134°43E 37 F8
Gomoh India 23°52N 86°10E 43 H12
Gompa = Ganta Liberia 7°15N 8°59W 52 G4
Gonābād Iran 34°15N 58°45E 47 C8
Gonaïves Haiti 19°20N 72°42W 89 C5
Gonâve, G. de la Haiti 19°29N 72°42W 89 C5
Gonâve, Île de la Haiti 18°51N 73°3W 89 C5
Gonbad-e Kāvūs Iran 37°20N 55°25E 47 B7
Gonda India 27°9N 81°58E 43 F9
Gondal India 21°58N 70°52E 42 J4
Gonder Ethiopia 12°39N 37°30E 49 E2
Gondia India 21°23N 80°10E 44 D5
Gönen Turkey 40°6N 27°39E 23 D12
Gong Xian China 28°23N 104°47E 34 C5
Gong'an China 30°7N 112°12E 35 B9
Gongbei China 22°12N 113°32E 31 a
Gongchangling China 41°7N 123°27E 33 D12
Gongcheng China 24°50N 110°49E 35 E8
Gongga Shan China 29°40N 101°55E 34 C3
Gonggar China 29°23N 91°7E 30 F7
Gongguan China 21°48N 109°36E 34 G7
Gonghe China 36°18N 100°32E 30 D9
Gongju S. Korea 36°27N 127°7E 33 F14
Gongming China 22°47N 113°53E 31 a
Gongolgon Australia 30°21S 146°54E 63 E4
Gongshan China 27°43N 98°29E 34 D2
Gongtan China 28°55N 108°20E 34 C7
Gongyi China 34°45N 112°58E 32 G7
Gongzhuling China 43°30N 124°40E 33 C13
Goniri Nigeria 11°30N 12°15E 53 F8
Gonjo China 30°52N 98°17E 34 B2
Gonzales Calif., U.S.A. 36°30N 121°26W 78 J5
Gonzales Tex., U.S.A. 29°30N 97°27W 84 G6
González Mexico 22°48N 98°25W 87 C5
Good Hope, C. of S. Africa 34°24S 18°30E 56 D2
Good Hope Lake Canada 59°16N 129°18W 70 B3
Gooderham Canada 44°54N 78°21W 82 B6
Goodhouse S. Africa 28°57S 18°13E 56 C2
Gooding U.S.A. 42°56N 114°43W 76 E6
Goodland U.S.A. 39°21N 101°43W 80 F3
Goodlands Mauritius 20°25S 57°39E 55 d
Goodlow Canada 56°20N 120°8W 70 B4
Goodooga Australia 29°3S 147°28E 63 D4
Goodsprings U.S.A. 35°49N 115°27W 79 K11

Goole U.K. 53°42N 0°53W 12 D7
Goolgowi Australia 33°58S 145°41E 63 E4
Goomalling Australia 31°15S 116°49E 61 F2
Goomeri Australia 26°12S 152°6E 63 D5
Goondiwindi Australia 28°30S 150°21E 63 D5
Goongarrie, L. Australia 30°3S 121°9E 61 F3
Goongarrie △ Australia 30°7S 121°30E 61 F3
Goonyella Australia 21°47S 147°58E 62 C4
Goose → Canada 53°20N 60°35W 73 B7
Goose Creek U.S.A. 32°59N 80°2W 85 E14
Goose L. U.S.A. 41°56N 120°26W 76 F3
Gooty India 15°7N 77°41E 45 G3
Gop India 22°5N 69°50E 42 H3
Gopalganj India 26°28N 84°30E 43 F11
Göppingen Germany 48°42N 9°39E 16 D5
Gorakhpur India 26°47N 83°23E 43 F10
Goražde Bos.-H. 43°38N 18°58E 23 C8
Gorda, Pta. Nic. 14°20N 83°10W 88 D3
Gordan B. Australia 11°35S 130°10E 60 B5
Gordon U.S.A. 42°48N 102°12W 80 D3
Gordon → Australia 42°27S 145°30E 63 G4
Gordon Bay Canada 45°12N 79°47W 82 A5
Gordon L., Alta., Canada 56°30N 110°25W 71 B6
Gordon L. N.W.T., Canada 63°5N 113°11W 70 A6
Gordonvale Australia 17°5S 145°50E 62 B4
Goré Chad 7°59N 16°31E 53 G9
Gore Ethiopia 8°12N 35°32E 49 F2
Gore N.Z. 46°5S 168°58E 59 G2
Gore Bay Canada 45°57N 82°28W 72 C3
Gorey Ireland 52°41N 6°18W 10 D5
Gorg Iran 29°29N 59°43E 47 D8
Gorgān Iran 36°55N 54°30E 47 B7
Gorgona, I. Colombia 3°0N 78°10W 92 C3
Gorham U.S.A. 44°23N 71°10W 83 B13
Goribidnur = Gauribidanur
  India 13°37N 77°32E 45 H3
Goriganga → India 29°45N 80°23E 43 E9
Gorinchem Neths. 51°50N 4°59E 15 C4
Goris Armenia 39°31N 46°22E 19 G8
Gorizia Italy 45°56N 13°37E 22 B5
Gorkiy = Nizhniy Novgorod
  Russia 56°20N 44°0E 18 C7
Gorkovskoye Vdkhr.
  Russia 57°2N 43°4E 18 C7
Gorleston U.K. 52°35N 1°44E 13 E9
Görlitz Germany 51°9N 14°58E 16 C8
Gorlovka = Horlivka
  Ukraine 48°19N 38°5E 19 E6
Gorman U.S.A. 34°47N 118°51W 79 L8
Gorna Dzhumayo = Blagoevgrad
  Bulgaria 42°2N 23°5E 23 C10
Gorna Oryakhovitsa
  Bulgaria 43°7N 25°40E 23 C11
Gorno-Altay □ Russia 51°0N 86°0E 26 D9
Gorno-Altaysk Russia 51°50N 86°5E 26 D9
Gornozavodsk Russia 46°33N 141°50E 27 E15
Gornyatski Russia 67°32N 64°3E 18 A11
Gornyy Russia 44°57N 133°59E 28 B6
Gorodenka = Horodenka
  Ukraine 48°41N 25°29E 17 D13
Gorodok = Horodok
  Ukraine 49°46N 23°32E 17 D12
Gorokhov = Horokhiv
  Ukraine 50°30N 24°45E 17 C13
Gorong, Kepulauan
  Indonesia 3°59S 131°25E 37 E8
Gorongose → Mozam. 20°30S 34°40E 57 B5
Gorongoza △ Mozam. 18°50S 34°29E 57 A5
Gorontalo Indonesia 0°35N 123°5E 37 D6
Gorontalo □ Indonesia 0°50N 122°20E 37 D6
Gort Ireland 53°3N 8°49W 10 C3
Gorumahisani India 22°20N 86°24E 44 G7
Goryeong S. Korea 35°44N 128°15E 33 G15
Gorzów Wielkopolski
  Poland 52°43N 15°15E 16 B8
Gosford Australia 33°23S 151°18E 63 E5
Goshen Calif., U.S.A. 36°21N 119°25W 78 J7
Goshen Ind., U.S.A. 41°35N 85°50W 81 E11
Goshen N.Y., U.S.A. 41°24N 74°20W 83 E10
Goshogawara Japan 40°48N 140°27E 28 D10
Goslar Germany 51°54N 10°25E 16 C6
Gospič Croatia 44°35N 15°23E 16 F8
Gosport U.K. 50°48N 1°9W 13 G6
Gosse → Australia 19°32S 134°37E 62 B1
Göta älv → Sweden 57°42N 11°54E 9 H14
Göta kanal Sweden 58°30N 15°58E 9 G16
Götaland Sweden 57°30N 14°30E 9 H16
Göteborg Sweden 57°43N 11°59E 9 H14
Gotha Germany 50°56N 10°42E 16 C6
Gothenburg = Göteborg
  Sweden 57°43N 11°59E 9 H14
Gothenburg U.S.A. 40°56N 100°10W 80 E3
Gotland Sweden 57°30N 18°33E 9 H18
Gotō = Fukue Japan 32°41N 128°51E 29 H4
Gotō-Rettō Japan 32°55N 129°5E 29 H4
Gotska Sandön Sweden 58°24N 19°15E 9 G18
Gōtsu Japan 35°0N 132°14E 29 G6
Göttingen Germany 51°31N 9°55E 16 C5
Gottwaldov = Zlín
  Czech Rep. 49°14N 17°40E 17 D9
Goubangzi China 41°20N 121°52E 33 D11
Gouda Neths. 52°1N 4°42E 15 B4
Gouin, Rés. Canada 48°35N 74°40W 72 C5
Goulburn Australia 34°44S 149°44E 63 E4
Goulburn Is. Australia 11°40S 133°20E 62 A1
Goulimine Morocco 28°56N 10°0W 52 C3
Goundam Mali 16°27N 3°40W 52 E5
Gourits → S. Africa 34°21S 21°52E 56 D3
Gourock U.K. 55°57N 4°49W 11 F4
Gouverneur U.S.A. 44°20N 75°28W 83 B9
Gove Peninsula
  Australia 12°17S 136°49E 62 A2
Governador Valadares
  Brazil 18°15S 41°57W 93 G10
Governor's Harbour
  Bahamas 25°10N 76°14W 88 A4
Gowan Ra. Australia 25°0S 145°0E 62 D4
Gowanda U.S.A. 42°28N 78°56W 82 D6

Gower U.K. 51°35N 4°10W 13 F3
Gowna, L. Ireland 53°51N 7°34W 10 C4
Goya Argentina 29°10S 59°10W 94 B4
Goyang S. Korea 37°39N 126°50E 33 F14
Goyder Lagoon Australia 27°3S 138°58E 63 D2
Goyllarisquizga Peru 10°31S 76°24W 92 F3
Goz Beïda Chad 12°10N 21°20E 53 F10
Gozo Malta 36°3N 14°15E 22 F6
Graaff-Reinet S. Africa 32°13S 24°32E 56 D3
Gračac Croatia 44°18N 15°57E 16 F8
Gracias a Dios, C.
  Honduras 15°0N 83°10W 88 D3
Graciosa Azores 39°4N 28°0W 52 a
Grado Spain 43°23N 6°4W 21 A2
Grady U.S.A. 34°49N 103°19W 77 J12
Grafham Water U.K. 52°19N 0°18W 13 E7
Grafton Australia 29°38S 152°58E 63 D5
Grafton N. Dak., U.S.A. 48°25N 97°25W 80 A5
Grafton W. Va., U.S.A. 39°21N 80°2W 81 F13
Graham Canada 49°20N 90°30W 72 C1
Graham U.S.A. 33°6N 98°35W 84 E5
Graham, Mt. U.S.A. 32°42N 109°52W 77 K9
Graham Bell, Ostrov = Greem-Bell,
  Ostrov Russia 81°0N 62°0E 26 A7
Graham I. B.C., Canada 53°40N 132°30W 70 C2
Graham I. Nunavut,
  Canada 77°25N 90°30W 69 B13
Graham Land Antarctica 65°0S 64°0W 5 C17
Grahamstown S. Africa 33°19S 26°31E 56 D4
Grahamsville U.S.A. 41°51N 74°33W 83 E10
Grain Coast W. Afr. 4°20N 10°0W 52 H3
Grajagan Indonesia 8°35S 114°13E 37 K17
Grajaú Brazil 5°50S 46°4W 93 E9
Grajaú → Brazil 3°41S 44°48W 93 D10
Grampian U.S.A. 40°58N 78°37W 82 F6
Grampian Highlands = Grampian
  Mts. U.K. 56°50N 4°0W 11 E5
Grampian Mts. U.K. 56°50N 4°0W 11 E5
Grampians, The
  Australia 37°15S 142°20E 63 F3
Gran Canaria Canary Is. 27°55N 15°35W 52 C2
Gran Chaco S. Amer. 25°0S 61°0W 94 B3
Gran Desierto del Pinacate △
  Mexico 31°51N 113°32W 86 A2
Gran Paradiso Italy 45°33N 7°17E 20 D7
Gran Sasso d'Itália Italy 42°27N 13°42E 22 C5
Granada Nic. 11°58N 86°0W 88 D2
Granada Spain 37°10N 3°35W 21 D4
Granada U.S.A. 38°4N 102°19W 76 G12
Granard Ireland 53°47N 7°30W 10 C4
Granbury U.S.A. 32°27N 97°47W 84 E6
Granby Canada 45°25N 72°45W 83 A12
Granby U.S.A. 40°5N 105°56W 76 F11
Grand → Canada 42°51N 79°34W 82 D5
Grand → Mo., U.S.A. 39°23N 93°7W 80 F7
Grand → S. Dak., U.S.A. 45°40N 100°45W 80 C3
Grand-Anse = Portsmouth
  Dominica 15°34N 61°27W 89 C7
Grand Bahama I.
  Bahamas 26°40N 78°30W 88 A4
Grand Baie Mauritius 20°0S 57°35E 55 d
Grand Bank Canada 47°6N 55°48W 73 C8
Grand Bassam Ivory C. 5°10N 3°49W 52 G5
Grand Bend Canada 43°18N 81°45W 82 C3
Grand-Bourg Guadeloupe 15°53N 61°19W 88 b
Grand Canal = Da Yunhe →
  China 39°10N 117°10E 33 E9
Grand Canyon U.S.A. 36°3N 112°9W 77 H7
Grand Canyon △
  U.S.A. 36°15N 112°30W 77 H7
Grand Canyon-Parashant △
  U.S.A. 36°30N 113°45W 77 H7
Grand Cayman
  Cayman Is. 19°20N 81°20W 88 C3
Grand Coulee U.S.A. 47°57N 119°0W 76 C4
Grand Coulee Dam
  U.S.A. 47°57N 118°59W 76 C4
Grand Falls Canada 48°56N 55°40W 73 C8
Grand Falls-Windsor
  Canada 48°56N 55°40W 73 C8
Grand Forks Canada 49°0N 118°30W 70 D5
Grand Forks U.S.A. 47°55N 97°3W 80 B5
Grand Gorge U.S.A. 42°21N 74°29W 83 D10
Grand Haven U.S.A. 43°4N 86°13W 80 D10
Grand I. Mich., U.S.A. 46°31N 86°40W 80 B10
Grand I. N.Y., U.S.A. 43°0N 78°58W 82 D6
Grand Island U.S.A. 40°55N 98°21W 80 E4
Grand Isle La., U.S.A. 29°14N 90°0W 85 G9
Grand Isle Vt., U.S.A. 44°43N 73°18W 83 B11
Grand Junction U.S.A. 39°4N 108°33W 76 G9
Grand L. N.B., Canada 45°57N 66°7W 73 C6
Grand L., Nfld. & L., Canada 49°0N 57°30W 73 C8
Grand L., Nfld. & L.,
  Canada 53°40N 60°30W 73 B7
Grand L. U.S.A. 29°55N 92°47W 84 G8
Grand Lake U.S.A. 40°15N 105°49W 76 F11
Grand Manan I. Canada 44°45N 66°52W 73 D6
Grand Marais Mich.,
  U.S.A. 46°40N 85°59W 81 B11
Grand Marais Minn.,
  U.S.A. 47°45N 90°25W 72 C1
Grand-Mère Canada 46°36N 72°40W 72 C5
Grand Portage U.S.A. 47°58N 89°41W 80 B9
Grand Prairie U.S.A. 32°44N 96°59W 84 E6
Grand Rapids Canada 53°12N 99°19W 71 C9
Grand Rapids Mich.,
  U.S.A. 42°58N 85°40W 81 D11
Grand Rapids Minn.,
  U.S.A. 47°14N 93°31W 80 B7
Grand St-Bernard, Col du
  Europe 45°50N 7°10E 20 D7
Grand Staircase-Escalante △
  U.S.A. 37°25N 111°33W 77 H8
Grand Teton U.S.A. 43°54N 110°50W 76 E8
Grand Teton △ U.S.A. 43°50N 110°50W 76 E8
Grand Union Canal U.S.A. 52°7N 0°53W 13 E7
Grande → Jujuy, Argentina 24°20S 65°2W 94 A2
Grande → Mendoza,
  Argentina 36°52S 69°45W 94 D2

Grande → Bolivia 15°51S 64°39W 92 G6
Grande → Bahia, Brazil 11°30S 44°30W 93 F10
Grande → Minas Gerais,
  Brazil 20°6S 51°4W 93 H8
Grande, B. Argentina 50°30S 68°20W 96 G3
Grande, Rio → N. Amer. 25°58N 97°9W 84 J6
Grande Anse Seychelles 4°18S 55°45E 55 b
Grande Baleine →
  Canada 55°16N 77°47W 72 A4
Grande Cache Canada 53°53N 119°8W 70 C5
Grande Comore
  Comoros Is. 11°35S 43°20E 55 a
Grande-Entrée Canada 47°30N 61°40W 73 C7
Grande Prairie Canada 55°10N 118°50W 70 B5
Grande-Rivière Canada 48°26N 64°30W 73 C7
Grande-Terre Guadeloupe 16°20N 61°25W 88 b
Grande-Vallée Canada 49°14N 65°8W 73 C6
Grande Vigie, Pte. de la
  Guadeloupe 16°32N 61°27W 88 b
Grandfalls U.S.A. 31°20N 102°51W 84 F3
Grands-Jardins △
  Canada 47°41N 70°51W 73 C5
Grandview Canada 51°10N 100°42W 71 C8
Grandview U.S.A. 46°15N 119°54W 76 C4
Graneros Chile 34°5S 70°45W 94 C1
Grangemouth U.K. 56°1N 3°42W 11 E5
Granger U.S.A. 41°35N 109°58W 76 F9
Grangeville U.S.A. 45°56N 116°7W 76 D5
Granisle Canada 54°53N 126°13W 70 C3
Granite City U.S.A. 38°42N 90°8W 80 F8
Granite Falls U.S.A. 44°49N 95°33W 80 C6
Granite L. Canada 48°8N 57°5W 73 C8
Granite Mt. U.S.A. 33°5N 116°28W 79 M10
Granite Pk. U.S.A. 45°10N 109°48W 76 D9
Graniteville U.S.A. 44°8N 72°29W 83 B12
Granity N.Z. 41°39S 171°51E 59 D3
Granja Brazil 3°7S 40°50W 93 D10
Granollers Spain 41°39N 2°18E 21 B7
Grant U.S.A. 40°50N 101°43W 80 E3
Grant, Mt. U.S.A. 38°34N 118°48W 76 G4
Grant City U.S.A. 40°29N 94°25W 80 E6
Grant I. Australia 11°10S 132°52E 60 B5
Grant Range U.S.A. 38°30N 115°25W 76 G6
Grantham U.K. 52°55N 0°38W 12 E7
Grantown-on-Spey U.K. 57°20N 3°36W 11 D5
Grants U.S.A. 35°9N 107°52W 77 J10
Grants Pass U.S.A. 42°26N 123°19W 76 E2
Grantsville U.S.A. 40°36N 112°28W 76 F7
Granville France 48°50N 1°35W 20 B3
Granville N. Dak., U.S.A. 48°16N 100°47W 80 A3
Granville N.Y., U.S.A. 43°24N 73°16W 83 C11
Granville Ohio, U.S.A. 40°4N 82°31W 82 F2
Granville L. Canada 56°18N 100°30W 71 B8
Graskop S. Africa 24°56S 30°49E 57 B5
Grass → Canada 56°3N 96°33W 71 B9
Grass Range U.S.A. 47°2N 108°48W 76 C9
Grass River △ Canada 54°40N 100°50W 71 C8
Grass Valley Calif., U.S.A. 39°13N 121°4W 78 F6
Grass Valley Oreg.,
  U.S.A. 45°22N 120°47W 76 D3
Grasse France 43°38N 6°56E 20 E7
Grassflat U.S.A. 41°0N 78°6W 82 E6
Grasslands △ Canada 49°11N 107°38W 71 D7
Grassy U.S.A. 40°3S 144°5E 63 G3
Graulhet France 43°45N 1°59E 20 E4
Gravelbourg Canada 49°50N 106°35W 71 D7
's-Gravenhage Neths. 52°7N 4°17E 15 B4
Gravenhurst Canada 44°52N 79°20W 82 B5
Gravesend Australia 29°35S 150°20E 63 D5
Gravesend U.K. 51°26N 0°22E 13 F8
Gravois, Pointe-à- Haiti 18°2N 73°56W 89 C5
Grayling U.S.A. 44°40N 84°43W 81 C11
Grays U.K. 51°28N 0°21E 13 F8
Grays Harbor U.S.A. 46°59N 124°1W 78 D2
Grays L. U.S.A. 43°4N 111°26W 76 E8
Grays River U.S.A. 46°21N 123°37W 78 D3
Graz Austria 47°4N 15°27E 16 E8
Greasy L. Canada 62°55N 122°12W 70 A4
Great Abaco I. = Abaco I.
  Bahamas 26°25N 77°10W 88 A4
Great Artesian Basin
  Australia 23°0S 144°0E 62 C3
Great Australian Bight
  Australia 33°30S 130°0E 61 F5
Great Bahama Bank
  Bahamas 23°15N 78°0W 88 B4
Great Barrier I. N.Z. 36°11S 175°25E 59 B5
Great Barrier Reef
  Australia 18°0S 146°50E 62 B4
Great Barrier Reef △
  Australia 20°0S 150°0E 62 B4
Great Barrington
  U.S.A. 42°12N 73°22W 83 D11
Great Basalt Wall △
  Australia 19°52S 145°43E 62 B4
Great Basin U.S.A. 40°0N 117°0W 76 G5
Great Basin △ U.S.A. 38°56N 114°15W 76 G6
Great Basses Sri Lanka 6°11N 81°29E 45 L5
Great Bear → Canada 65°0N 126°0W 68 E7
Great Bear L. Canada 65°30N 120°0W 68 C7
Great Belt = Store Bælt
  Denmark 55°20N 11°0E 9 J14
Great Bend Kans., U.S.A. 38°22N 98°46W 80 F4
Great Bend Pa., U.S.A. 41°58N 75°45W 83 E9
Great Blasket I. Ireland 52°6N 10°32W 10 D1
Great Britain Europe 54°0N 2°15W 6 E5
Great Camanoe
  Br. Virgin Is. 18°30N 64°35W 89 e
Great Channel Asia 6°0N 94°0E 45 L11
Great Coco I. = Koko Kyunzu
  Burma 14°7N 93°22E 45 G11
Great Codroy Canada 47°51N 59°16W 73 C8
Great Divide, The = Great Dividing
  Ra. Australia 23°0S 146°0E 62 C4
Great Divide Basin U.S.A. 42°0N 108°0W 76 E9
Great Dividing Ra.
  Australia 23°0S 146°0E 62 C4
Great Driffield = Driffield
  U.K. 54°0N 0°26W 12 C7

Great Exuma I. Bahamas 23°30N 75°50W 88 B4
Great Falls U.S.A. 47°30N 111°17W 76 C8
Great Fish = Groot-Vis →
  S. Africa 33°28S 27°5E 56 D4
Great Guana Cay
  Bahamas 24°0N 76°20W 88 B4
Great Himalayan △ India 31°30N 77°30E 42 D7
Great Inagua I. Bahamas 21°0N 73°20W 89 B5
Great Indian Desert = Thar Desert
  India 28°0N 72°0E 42 F5
Great Karoo S. Africa 31°55S 21°0E 56 D3
Great Khingan Mts. = Da Hinggan
  Ling China 48°0N 121°0E 31 B13
Great Lake Australia 41°50S 146°40E 63 G4
Great Lakes N. Amer. 46°0N 84°0W 66 E11
Great Limpopo Transfrontier △
  Africa 23°0S 31°45E 57 B5
Great Malvern U.K. 52°7N 2°18W 13 E5
Great Miami → U.S.A. 39°7N 84°49W 81 F11
Great Nicobar India 7°0N 93°50E 45 L11
Great Ormes Head U.K. 53°20N 3°52W 12 D4
Great Ouse → U.K. 52°48N 0°21E 12 E8
Great Palm I. Australia 18°45S 146°40E 62 B4
Great Pedro Bluff Jamaica 17°51N 77°44W 88 a
Great Pee Dee →
  U.S.A. 33°21N 79°10W 85 E15
Great Plains N. Amer. 47°0N 105°0W 66 E9
Great Ruaha → Tanzania 7°56S 37°52E 54 F7
Great Sacandaga L.
  U.S.A. 43°6N 74°16W 83 C10
Great Saint Bernard Pass = Grand
  St-Bernard, Col du
  Europe 45°50N 7°10E 20 D7
Great Salt Desert = Kavīr, Dasht-e
  Iran 34°30N 55°0E 47 C7
Great Salt L. U.S.A. 41°15N 112°40W 76 F7
Great Salt Lake Desert
  U.S.A. 40°50N 113°30W 76 F7
Great Salt Plains L. U.S.A. 36°45N 98°8W 84 C5
Great Sand Dunes △
  U.S.A. 37°48N 105°45W 77 H11
Great Sandy △ Australia 26°13S 153°2E 63 D5
Great Sandy Desert
  Australia 21°0S 124°0E 60 D3
Great Sangi = Sangihe, Pulau
  Indonesia 3°35N 125°30E 37 D7
Great Sea Reef Fiji 16°15S 179°0E 59 a
Great Sitkin I. U.S.A. 52°3N 176°6W 74 E4
Great Skellig Ireland 51°47N 10°33W 10 E1
Great Slave L. Canada 61°23N 115°38W 70 A5
Great Smoky Mts. △
  U.S.A. 35°40N 83°40W 85 D13
Great Stour = Stour →
  U.K. 51°18N 1°22E 13 F9
Great Victoria Desert
  Australia 29°30S 126°30E 61 E4
Great Wall Antarctica 62°30S 58°0W 5 C18
Great Wall China 38°30N 109°30E 32 E5
Great Whernside U.K. 54°10N 1°58W 12 C6
Great Yarmouth U.K. 52°37N 1°44E 13 E9
Great Zab = Zāb al Kabīr →
  Iraq 36°1N 43°24E 46 B4
Greater Antilles W. Indies 17°40N 74°0W 89 C5
Greater London □ U.K. 51°31N 0°6W 13 F7
Greater Manchester □
  U.K. 53°30N 2°15W 12 D5
Greater Sunda Is. Indonesia 7°0S 112°0E 36 F4
Gredos, Sierra de Spain 40°20N 5°0W 21 B3
Greece U.S.A. 43°13N 77°41W 82 C7
Greece ■ Europe 40°0N 23°0E 23 E9
Greeley Colo., U.S.A. 40°25N 104°42W 76 F11
Greeley Nebr., U.S.A. 41°33N 98°32W 80 E4
Greely Fd. Canada 80°30N 85°0W 69 A15
Greem-Bell, Ostrov Russia 81°0N 62°0E 26 A7
Green → Ky., U.S.A. 37°54N 87°30W 80 G10
Green → Utah, U.S.A. 38°11N 109°53W 76 G9
Green B. U.S.A. 45°0N 87°30W 80 C10
Green Bay U.S.A. 44°31N 88°0W 80 C9
Green C. Australia 37°13S 150°1E 63 F5
Green Cove Springs
  U.S.A. 29°59N 81°42W 85 G14
Green I. = Lütao
  Taiwan 22°40N 121°30E 35 F13
Green Lake Canada 54°17N 107°47W 71 C7
Green Mts. U.S.A. 43°45N 72°45W 83 C12
Green River Utah,
  U.S.A. 38°59N 110°10W 76 G8
Green River Wyo.,
  U.S.A. 41°32N 109°28W 76 F9
Green Valley U.S.A. 31°52N 110°56W 77 L8
Greenbank U.S.A. 48°6N 122°34W 78 B4
Greenbush Mich., U.S.A. 44°35N 83°19W 82 B1
Greenbush Minn., U.S.A. 48°42N 96°11W 80 A5
Greencastle U.S.A. 39°38N 86°52W 80 F10
Greene U.S.A. 42°20N 75°46W 83 D9
Greeneville U.S.A. 36°10N 82°50W 85 C13
Greenfield Calif., U.S.A. 36°19N 121°15E 78 J8
Greenfield Calif., U.S.A. 35°15N 119°0W 79 K8
Greenfield Ind., U.S.A. 39°47N 85°46W 81 F11
Greenfield Iowa, U.S.A. 41°18N 94°28W 80 E6
Greenfield Mass., U.S.A. 42°35N 72°36W 83 D12
Greenfield Mo., U.S.A. 37°25N 93°51W 80 G7
Greenland ☑ N. Amer. 66°0N 45°0W 67 C15
Greenland Sea Arctic 73°0N 10°0W 4 B7
Greenock U.S.A. 55°57N 4°46W 11 F4
Greenore Ireland 54°1N 6°9W 10 B5
Greenore Pt. Ireland 52°14N 6°19W 10 D5
Greenough Australia 28°58S 114°43E 61 E1
Greenough → Australia 28°51S 114°38E 61 E1
Greenough Pt. Canada 44°58N 81°26W 82 B3
Greenport U.S.A. 41°6N 72°22W 83 E12
Greensboro Ga., U.S.A. 33°35N 83°11W 85 E13
Greensboro N.C., U.S.A. 36°4N 79°48W 85 C15
Greensboro Vt., U.S.A. 44°36N 72°18W 83 B12
Greensburg Ind., U.S.A. 39°20N 85°29W 81 F11
Greensburg Kans., U.S.A. 37°36N 99°18W 80 G4
Greensburg Pa., U.S.A. 40°18N 79°33W 82 F5
Greenstone = Geraldton
  Canada 49°44N 87°10W 72 C2

Greenstone Pt. U.K. 57°55N 5°37W 11 D3
Greenvale Australia 18°59S 145°7E 62 B4
Greenville Liberia 5°1N 9°6W 52 G4
Greenville Ala., U.S.A. 31°50N 86°38W 85 F11
Greenville Calif., U.S.A. 40°8N 120°57W 78 E6
Greenville Maine, U.S.A. 45°28N 69°35W 81 C19
Greenville Mich., U.S.A. 43°11N 85°15W 81 D11
Greenville Miss., U.S.A. 33°24N 91°4W 85 E9
Greenville Mo., U.S.A. 37°8N 90°27W 80 G8
Greenville N.C., U.S.A. 35°37N 77°23W 85 D16
Greenville N.H., U.S.A. 42°46N 71°49W 83 D13
Greenville N.Y., U.S.A. 42°25N 74°1W 83 D10
Greenville Ohio, U.S.A. 40°6N 84°38W 81 E11
Greenville Pa., U.S.A. 41°24N 80°23W 82 E4
Greenville S.C., U.S.A. 34°51N 82°24W 85 D13
Greenville Tex., U.S.A. 33°8N 96°7W 84 E6
Greenwater Lake △
  Canada 52°32N 103°30W 71 C8
Greenwich Conn., U.S.A. 41°2N 73°38W 83 E11
Greenwich N.Y., U.S.A. 43°5N 73°30W 83 C11
Greenwich Ohio, U.S.A. 41°2N 82°31W 82 E2
Greenwood Canada 49°10N 118°40W 70 D5
Greenwood Ark., U.S.A. 35°13N 94°16W 84 D7
Greenwood Ind., U.S.A. 39°37N 86°7W 80 F10
Greenwood Miss., U.S.A. 33°31N 90°11W 85 E9
Greenwood S.C., U.S.A. 34°12N 82°10W 85 D13
Greenwood, Mt. Australia 13°48S 130°4E 60 B5
Gregory U.S.A. 43°14N 99°26W 80 D4
Gregory → Australia 17°53S 139°17E 62 B2
Gregory, L. S. Austral.,
  Australia 28°55S 139°0E 63 D2
Gregory, L. W. Austral.,
  Australia 20°0S 127°40E 60 D4
Gregory, L. W. Austral.,
  Australia 25°38S 119°58E 61 E2
Gregory △ Australia 15°38S 131°15E 60 C5
Gregory Downs
  Australia 18°35S 138°45E 62 B2
Gregory Ra. Queens.,
  Australia 19°30S 143°40E 62 B3
Gregory Ra. W. Austral.,
  Australia 21°20S 121°12E 60 D3
Greifswald Germany 54°5N 13°23E 16 A7
Greiz Germany 50°39N 12°10E 16 C7
Gremikha Russia 67°59N 39°47E 18 A6
Grenaa Denmark 56°25N 10°53E 9 H14
Grenada U.S.A. 33°47N 89°49W 85 E10
Grenada ■ W. Indies 12°10N 61°40W 89 D7
Grenadier I. U.S.A. 44°3N 76°22W 83 B8
Grenadines, The
  St. Vincent 12°40N 61°20W 89 D7
Grenen Denmark 57°44N 10°40E 9 H14
Grenfell Australia 33°52S 148°8E 63 E4
Grenfell Canada 50°30N 102°56W 71 C8
Grenoble France 45°12N 5°42E 20 D6
Grenville, C. Australia 12°0S 143°13E 62 A3
Grenville Chan. Canada 53°40N 129°46W 70 C3
Gresham U.S.A. 45°30N 122°25W 78 E4
Gresik Indonesia 7°13S 112°38E 37 G15
Gretna U.K. 55°0N 3°3W 11 F5
Grevenmacher Lux. 49°41N 6°26E 15 E6
Grey → Canada 47°34N 57°6W 73 C8
Grey → N.Z. 42°27S 171°12E 59 E3
Grey, C. Australia 13°0S 136°35E 62 A2
Grey Is. Canada 50°50N 55°35W 69 G20
Grey Ra. Australia 27°0S 143°30E 63 D3
Greybull U.S.A. 44°30N 108°3W 76 D9
Greymouth N.Z. 42°29S 171°13E 59 E3
Greystones Ireland 53°9N 6°5W 10 C5
Greytown N.Z. 41°5S 175°29E 59 D5
Greytown S. Africa 29°1S 30°36E 57 C5
Gribbell I. Canada 53°23N 129°0W 70 C3
Gridley U.S.A. 39°22N 121°42W 78 F5
Griekwastad S. Africa 28°49S 23°15E 56 D3
Griffin U.S.A. 33°15N 84°16W 85 E12
Griffith Australia 34°18S 146°2E 63 E4
Griffith U.S.A. 45°15N 77°10W 82 A7
Griffith I. Canada 44°50N 80°55W 82 B4
Grimaylov = Hrymayliv
  Ukraine 49°20N 26°5E 17 D14
Grimes U.S.A. 39°4N 121°54W 78 F5
Grimsay U.K. 57°29N 7°14W 11 D1
Grimsby Canada 43°12N 79°34W 82 C5
Grimsby U.K. 53°34N 0°5W 12 D7
Grímsey Iceland 66°33N 17°58W 8 C5
Grimshaw Canada 56°10N 117°40W 70 B5
Grimstad Norway 58°20N 8°35E 9 G13
Grindstone I. U.S.A. 44°17N 76°27W 83 B8
Grinnell U.S.A. 41°45N 92°43W 80 E7
Grinnell Pen. Canada 76°40N 95°0W 69 B13
Griomasaigh = Grimsay
  U.K. 57°29N 7°14W 11 D1
Gris-Nez, C. France 50°52N 1°35E 20 A4
Grise Fiord Canada 76°25N 82°57W 69 B15
Groais I. Canada 50°55N 55°35W 73 B8
Groblersdal S. Africa 25°15S 29°25E 57 C4
Grodno = Hrodna
  Belarus 53°42N 23°52E 17 B12
Grodzyanka = Hrodzyanka
  Belarus 53°31N 28°42E 17 B15
Groesbeck U.S.A. 31°31N 96°32W 84 F6
Grójec Poland 51°50N 20°58E 17 C11
Grong Norway 64°25N 12°8E 8 D15
Groningen Neths. 53°15N 6°35E 15 A6
Groningen □ Neths. 53°16N 6°40E 15 A6
Groom U.S.A. 35°12N 101°6W 84 D4
Groot → S. Africa 33°45S 24°36E 56 D3
Groot-Berg → S. Africa 32°47S 18°8E 56 D2
Groot-Brakrivier S. Africa 34°2S 22°18E 56 D3
Groot Karasberge
  Namibia 27°20S 18°40E 56 D2
Groot Kei → S. Africa 32°41S 28°22E 57 D4
Groot-Vis → S. Africa 33°28S 27°5E 56 D4
Grootdrink S. Africa 28°33S 21°42E 56 D3
Groote Eylandt Australia 14°0S 136°40E 62 A2
Groote Peel △ Neths. 51°21N 5°50E 15 C5
Grootfontein Namibia 19°31S 18°6E 56 B2
Grootlaagte → Africa 20°55S 21°27E 56 B3
Grootvloer → S. Africa 30°0S 20°40E 56 D3

Gros C. Canada 61°59N 113°32W 70 A6
Gros Islet St. Lucia 14°5N 60°58W 89 f
Gros Morne △ Canada 49°40N 57°50W 73 C8
Gros Piton St. Lucia 13°49N 61°5W 89 f
Gros Piton Pt. St. Lucia 13°49N 61°5W 89 f
Grosse Point U.S.A. 42°23N 82°54W 82 D2
Grosser Arber Germany 49°6N 13°8E 16 D7
Grosseto Italy 42°46N 11°8E 22 C4
Grossglockner Austria 47°5N 12°40E 16 E7
Groswater B. Canada 54°20N 57°40W 73 B8
Groton Conn., U.S.A. 41°21N 72°5W 83 E12
Groton N.Y., U.S.A. 42°36N 76°22W 83 D8
Groton S. Dak., U.S.A. 45°27N 98°6W 80 C4
Grouard Mission Canada 55°33N 116°9W 70 B5
Groundhog → Canada 48°45N 82°58W 72 C3
Grouw Neths. 53°5N 5°51E 15 A5
Grove City U.S.A. 41°10N 80°5W 82 E4
Grove Hill U.S.A. 31°42N 87°47W 85 F11
Groveland U.S.A. 37°50N 120°14W 78 H6
Grover Beach U.S.A. 35°7N 120°37W 79 K6
Groves U.S.A. 29°57N 93°54W 84 G8
Groveton U.S.A. 44°36N 71°31W 83 B13
Grovetown U.S.A. 33°27N 82°12W 85 E13
Groznyy Russia 43°20N 45°45E 19 F8
Grudziądz Poland 53°30N 18°47E 17 B10
Gruinard B. U.K. 57°56N 5°35W 11 D3
Grundy Center U.S.A. 42°22N 92°47W 80 D7
Gruver U.S.A. 36°16N 101°24W 84 C4
Gryazi Russia 52°30N 39°58E 18 D6
Gryazovets Russia 58°50N 40°10E 18 C7
Grytviken S. Georgia 54°19S 36°33W 96 G9
Gua India 22°18N 85°20E 43 H11
Gua Musang Malaysia 4°53N 101°58E 39 K3
Guacanayabo, G. de Cuba 20°40N 77°20W 88 B4
Guachípas → Argentina 25°40S 65°30W 94 B2
Guadalajara Mexico 20°40N 103°20W 86 C4
Guadalajara Spain 40°37N 3°12W 21 B4
Guadalcanal Solomon Is. 9°32S 160°12E 58 B9
Guadales Argentina 34°30S 67°55W 94 C2
Guadalete → Spain 36°35N 6°13W 21 D2
Guadalquivir → Spain 36°47N 6°22W 21 D2
Guadalupe = Guadeloupe ⊠ W. Indies 16°15N 61°40W 88 b
Guadalupe Mexico 22°45N 102°31W 86 C4
Guadalupe U.S.A. 34°58N 120°34W 79 L6
Guadalupe → U.S.A. 28°27N 96°47W 84 G6
Guadalupe, Sierra de Spain 39°28N 5°30W 21 C3
Guadalupe de Bravo Mexico 31°23N 106°7W 86 A3
Guadalupe I. Pac. Oc. 29°0N 118°50W 66 G8
Guadalupe Mts. △ U.S.A. 31°40N 104°30W 84 F2
Guadalupe Peak U.S.A. 31°50N 104°52W 84 F2
Guadalupe y Calvo Mexico 26°6N 106°58W 86 B3
Guadarrama, Sierra de Spain 41°0N 4°0W 21 B4
Guadeloupe ⊠ W. Indies 16°15N 61°40W 88 b
Guadeloupe △ Guadeloupe 16°10N 61°40W 88 b
Guadeloupe Passage W. Indies 16°50N 62°15W 89 C7
Guadiana → Portugal 37°14N 7°22W 21 D2
Guadix Spain 37°18N 3°11W 21 D4
Guafo, Boca del Chile 43°35S 74°0W 96 E2
Guaico Trin. & Tob. 10°35N 61°9W 93 K15
Guainía → Colombia 2°1N 67°7W 92 C5
Guaíra Brazil 24°5S 54°10W 95 A5
Guaíra □ Paraguay 25°45S 56°30W 94 B4
Guaire = Gorey Ireland 52°41N 6°18W 10 D5
Guaitecas, Is. Chile 44°0S 74°30W 96 E2
Guajará-Mirim Brazil 10°50S 65°20W 92 F5
Guajira, Pen. de la Colombia 12°0N 72°0W 92 A4
Gualán Guatemala 15°8N 89°22W 88 C2
Gualeguay Argentina 33°10S 59°14W 94 C4
Gualeguaychú Argentina 33°3S 59°31W 94 C4
Gualequay → Argentina 33°19S 59°39W 94 C4
Guam ⊠ Pac. Oc. 13°27N 144°45E 64 F6
Guaminí Argentina 37°1S 62°28W 94 D3
Guamúchil Mexico 25°28N 108°6W 86 B3
Guana I. Br. Virgin Is. 18°30N 64°30W 89 e
Guanabacoa Cuba 23°8N 82°18W 88 B3
Guanacaste, Cordillera de Costa Rica 10°40N 85°4W 88 D2
Guanacaste △ Costa Rica 10°57N 85°30W 88 D2
Guanaceví Mexico 25°56N 105°57W 86 B3
Guanahani = San Salvador I. Bahamas 24°0N 74°30W 89 B5
Guanaja Honduras 16°30N 85°55W 88 C2
Guanajay Cuba 22°56N 82°42W 88 B3
Guanajuato Mexico 21°1N 101°15W 86 C4
Guanajuato □ Mexico 21°0N 101°0W 86 C4
Guandacol Argentina 29°30S 68°40W 94 B2
Guandi Shan China 37°53N 111°29E 32 F6
Guane Cuba 22°10N 84°7W 88 B3
Guang'an China 30°28N 106°35E 34 B6
Guangchang China 26°50N 116°21E 35 D11
Guangde China 30°54N 119°25E 35 B12
Guangdong □ China 23°0N 113°0E 35 F9
Guangfeng China 28°20N 118°15E 35 C12
Guanghan China 30°58N 104°17E 34 B5
Guangling China 39°47N 114°22E 32 E8
Guangnan China 24°5N 105°4E 34 E5
Guangning China 23°40N 112°22E 35 F9
Guangrao China 37°5N 118°25E 33 F10
Guangshui China 31°37N 114°0E 35 B9
Guangshun China 26°8N 106°21E 34 D6
Guangwu China 37°48N 105°57E 32 F3
Guangxi Zhuangzu Zizhiqu □ China 24°0N 109°0E 34 F7
Guangyuan China 32°26N 105°51E 32 H3
Guangze China 27°30N 117°12E 35 D11
Guanica Puerto Rico 17°58N 66°55W 89 d
Guanipa → Venezuela 9°56N 62°26W 92 B6
Guanling China 25°56N 105°35E 34 E5
Guannan China 34°8N 119°21E 33 G10
Guantánamo Cuba 20°10N 75°14W 89 B4
Guantánamo B. Cuba 19°59N 75°10W 89 C4
Guantao China 36°42N 115°25E 32 F8
Guanting Shuiku China 40°14N 115°35E 32 D8
Guanyang China 25°30N 111°8E 35 E8
Guanyun China 34°20N 119°18E 33 G10
Guapay = Grande → Bolivia 15°51S 64°39W 92 G6
Guápiles Costa Rica 10°10N 83°46W 88 D3
Guapo B. Trin. & Tob. 10°12N 61°41W 93 K15
Guaporé Brazil 28°51S 51°54W 95 B5
Guaporé → Brazil 11°55S 65°4W 92 F5
Guaqui Bolivia 16°41S 68°54W 92 G5
Guaramacal △ Venezuela 9°13N 70°12W 89 E5
Guarapari Brazil 20°40S 40°30W 95 A7
Guarapuava Brazil 25°20S 51°30W 95 B5
Guaratinguetá Brazil 22°49S 45°9W 95 A6
Guaratuba Brazil 25°53S 48°38W 95 B6
Guarda Portugal 40°32N 7°20W 21 B2
Guardafui, C. = Asir, Ras Somalia 11°55N 51°10E 49 E5
Guárico □ Venezuela 8°40N 66°35W 92 B5
Guarujá Brazil 24°2S 46°25W 95 A6
Guarulhos Brazil 23°29S 46°33W 95 A6
Guasave Mexico 25°34N 108°27W 86 B3
Guasdualito Venezuela 7°15N 70°44W 92 B4
Guatemala Guatemala 14°40N 90°22W 88 D1
Guatemala ■ Cent. Amer. 15°40N 90°30W 88 C1
Guatemala Basin Pac. Oc. 11°0N 95°0W 65 F18
Guatemala Trench Pac. Oc. 14°0N 95°0W 66 H10
Guatopo △ Venezuela 10°5N 66°30W 89 D6
Guatuaro Pt. Trin. & Tob. 10°19N 60°59W 93 K16
Guaviare → Colombia 4°3N 67°44W 92 C5
Guaxupé Brazil 21°10S 47°5W 95 A6
Guayaguayare Trin. & Tob. 10°8N 61°2W 93 K15
Guayama Puerto Rico 17°59N 66°7W 89 d
Guayaquil Ecuador 2°15S 79°52W 92 D3
Guayaquil Mexico 29°59N 115°4W 86 B1
Guayaquil, G. de Ecuador 3°10S 81°0W 92 D2
Guaymas Mexico 27°56N 110°54W 86 B2
Gubbi India 13°19N 76°56E 45 H3
Gubkin Russia 51°17N 37°32E 19 D6
Gubkinskiy Russia 64°27N 76°36E 26 C8
Gucheng China 32°20N 111°30E 35 A8
Gudalur India 11°30N 76°29E 45 J3
Gudbrandsdalen Norway 61°33N 10°10E 8 F14
Guddu Barrage Pakistan 28°30N 69°50E 42 E3
Gudivada India 16°30N 81°3E 45 F5
Gudiyattam India 12°57N 78°55E 45 H4
Gudur India 14°12N 79°55E 45 G4
Guecho = Getxo Spain 43°21N 2°59W 21 A4
Guékédou Guinea 8°40N 10°5W 52 G3
Guelmine = Goulimine Morocco 28°56N 10°0W 52 C3
Guelph Canada 43°35N 80°20W 82 C4
Guerara Algeria 32°51N 4°22E 52 B6
Guéret France 46°11N 1°51E 20 C4
Guerneville U.S.A. 38°30N 123°0W 78 G4
Guernica = Gernika-Lumo Spain 43°19N 2°40W 21 A4
Guernsey U.K. 49°26N 2°35W 13 H5
Guernsey U.S.A. 42°16N 104°45W 76 E11
Guerrero □ Mexico 17°40N 100°0W 87 D5
Gügher Iran 29°28N 56°27E 47 D8
Gui Jiang → China 23°30N 111°15E 35 F8
Guia Lopes da Laguna Brazil 21°26S 56°7W 95 A4
Guiana Highlands S. Amer. 5°10N 60°40W 90 C4
Guichi China 30°39N 117°27E 35 B11
Guiding China 26°34N 107°11E 34 D6
Guidong China 26°7N 113°57E 35 D9
Guidónia-Montecélio Italy 42°1N 12°45E 22 C5
Guigang China 23°8N 109°35E 34 F7
Guijá Mozam. 24°27S 33°0E 57 B5
Guildford U.K. 51°14N 0°34W 13 F7
Guilford U.S.A. 41°17N 72°41W 83 E12
Guilin China 25°18N 110°15E 35 E8
Guillaume-Delisle, L. Canada 56°15N 76°17W 72 A4
Guimarães Portugal 41°28N 8°24W 21 B1
Guimaras □ Phil. 10°35N 122°37E 37 B6
Guinda U.S.A. 38°50N 122°12W 78 G4
Guinea Africa 8°0N 8°0E 50 F4
Guinea ■ W. Afr. 10°20N 11°30W 52 F3
Guinea, Gulf of Atl. Oc. 3°0N 2°30E 51 F4
Guinea-Bissau ■ Africa 12°0N 15°0W 52 F3
Güines Cuba 22°50N 82°0W 88 B3
Guingamp France 48°34N 3°10W 20 B2
Guiping China 23°21N 110°2E 35 F8
Güiria Venezuela 10°32N 62°18W 93 K14
Guiuan Phil. 11°5N 125°55E 37 B7
Guixi China 28°16N 117°15E 35 C11
Guiyang Guizhou, China 26°32N 106°40E 34 D6
Guiyang Hunan, China 25°46N 112°42E 35 E9
Guizhou □ China 27°0N 107°0E 34 D6
Gujar Khan Pakistan 33°16N 73°19E 42 C5
Gujarat □ India 23°20N 71°0E 42 H4
Gujiang China 27°11N 114°47E 35 D10
Gujiao China 37°54N 112°8E 32 F7
Gujō Japan 35°45N 136°57E 29 G8
Gujranwala Pakistan 32°10N 74°12E 42 C6
Gujrat Pakistan 32°40N 74°2E 42 C6
Gulbarga India 17°20N 76°50E 44 F3
Gulbene Latvia 57°8N 26°52E 9 H22
Guledagudda India 16°3N 75°48E 45 F2
Gulf, The = Persian Gulf Asia 27°0N 50°0E 47 E6
Gulf Islands ⌂ U.S.A. 30°10N 87°10W 85 F11
Gulfport U.S.A. 30°22N 89°6W 85 F10
Gulgong Australia 32°20S 149°49E 63 E4
Gulian China 52°56N 122°21E 31 A13
Gulin China 28°1N 105°50E 34 C5
Gulistan Pakistan 30°30N 66°35E 42 D2
Gulja = Yining China 43°58N 81°10E 30 C5
Gull Lake Canada 50°10N 108°29W 71 C7
Güllük Turkey 37°14N 27°35E 23 F12
Gulmarg India 34°3N 74°25E 43 B6
Gülshat Kazakhstan 46°38N 74°21E 26 C8
Gulu Uganda 2°48N 32°17E 54 D6
Gumal → Pakistan 31°40N 71°50E 42 D4
Gumbaz Pakistan 30°2N 69°0E 42 D3
Gumel Nigeria 12°39N 9°22E 52 F7
Gumi S. Korea 36°10N 128°12E 33 F15
Gumla India 23°3N 84°33E 43 H11
Gumlu Australia 19°53S 147°41E 62 B4
Gumma □ Japan 36°30N 138°20E 29 F9
Gumzai Indonesia 5°28S 134°42E 37 F8
Guna India 24°40N 77°19E 42 G7
Gunbalanya Australia 12°20S 133°4E 60 B5
Gundabooka △ Australia 30°30S 145°20E 63 E4
Gundarehi India 20°57N 81°17E 44 D5
Gundlakamma → India 15°30N 80°15E 45 G5
Gundlupet India 11°48N 76°41E 45 J3
Gunisao → Canada 53°56N 97°53W 71 C9
Gunisao L. Canada 53°33N 96°15W 71 C9
Gunjyal Pakistan 32°20N 71°55E 42 C4
Gunnbjørn Fjeld Greenland 68°55N 29°47W 4 C6
Gunnedah Australia 30°59S 150°15E 63 E5
Gunnewin Australia 25°59S 148°33E 63 D4
Gunningbar Cr. → Australia 31°14S 147°6E 63 E4
Gunnison Colo., U.S.A. 38°33N 106°56W 76 G10
Gunnison Utah, U.S.A. 39°9N 111°49W 76 G8
Gunnison → U.S.A. 39°4N 108°35W 76 G9
Gunsan S. Korea 35°59N 126°45E 33 G14
Guntakal India 15°11N 77°27E 45 G3
Gunter Canada 44°52N 77°32W 82 B7
Guntersville U.S.A. 34°21N 86°18W 85 D11
Guntong Malaysia 4°36N 101°3E 39 K3
Guntur India 16°23N 80°30E 45 F5
Gunung Ciremay △ Indonesia 6°53S 108°24E 37 G13
Gunungapi Indonesia 6°45S 126°30E 37 F7
Gunungsitoli Indonesia 1°15N 97°30E 36 D1
Gunupur India 19°5N 83°50E 44 E6
Gunza Angola 10°50S 13°50E 54 G2
Guo He → China 32°59N 117°10E 33 H9
Guoyang China 33°32N 116°12E 32 H9
Gupis Pakistan 36°15N 73°20E 43 A5
Gurbantünggüt Shamo China 45°8N 87°20E 30 B6
Gurdaspur India 32°5N 75°31E 42 C6
Gurdon U.S.A. 33°55N 93°9W 84 E8
Gurgaon India 28°27N 77°1E 42 E7
Gurgueia → Brazil 6°50S 43°24W 93 E10
Gurha India 25°12N 71°39E 42 G4
Guri, Embalse de Venezuela 7°50N 62°52W 92 B6
Gurkha Nepal 28°5N 84°40E 43 E11
Gurla Mandhata = Naimona'nyi Feng China 30°26N 81°18E 43 D9
Gurley Australia 29°45S 149°48E 63 D4
Gurnet Point U.S.A. 42°1N 70°34W 83 D14
Gurun Malaysia 5°49N 100°27E 39 K3
Gürün Turkey 38°43N 37°15E 19 G6
Gurupá Brazil 1°25S 51°35W 93 D8
Gurupá, I. Grande de Brazil 1°25S 51°45W 93 D8
Gurupi Brazil 11°43S 49°4W 93 F9
Gurupi → Brazil 1°13S 46°6W 93 D9
Guruwe Zimbabwe 16°40S 30°42E 57 A5
Gurvan Sayhan Uul Mongolia 43°50N 104°0E 32 C3
Guryev = Atyraū Kazakhstan 47°5N 52°0E 19 E9
Gusau Nigeria 12°12N 6°40E 52 F7
Gushan China 39°50N 123°35E 33 E12
Gushgy = Serhetabat Turkmenistan 35°20N 62°18E 47 C9
Gushi China 32°11N 115°41E 35 A10
Gusinoozersk Russia 51°16N 106°27E 27 D11
Gustavus U.S.A. 58°25N 135°44W 70 B1
Gustine U.S.A. 37°16N 121°0W 78 H6
Güstrow Germany 53°47N 12°10E 16 B7
Gütersloh Germany 51°54N 8°24E 16 C5
Gutha Australia 28°58S 115°55E 61 E2
Guthalungra Australia 19°52S 147°50E 62 B4
Guthrie Canada 44°28N 79°32W 82 B5
Guthrie Okla., U.S.A. 35°53N 97°25W 84 D6
Guthrie Tex., U.S.A. 33°37N 100°19W 84 E4
Gutian China 26°32N 118°43E 35 D12
Guttenberg U.S.A. 42°47N 91°6W 80 D8
Gutu Zimbabwe 19°41S 31°9E 57 A5
Guwahati India 26°10N 91°45E 41 F17
Guy Fawkes River △ Australia 30°0S 152°20E 63 D5
Guyana ■ S. Amer. 5°0N 59°0W 92 C7
Guyane française = French Guiana ⊠ S. Amer. 4°0N 53°0W 93 C8
Guyang China 41°0N 110°5E 32 D6
Guyenne France 44°30N 0°40E 20 D4
Guymon U.S.A. 36°41N 101°29W 84 C4
Guyra Australia 30°15S 151°40E 63 E5
Guyuan Hebei, China 41°37N 115°40E 32 D8
Guyuan Ningxia Huizu, China 36°0N 106°20E 32 F4
Güzelyurt = Morphou Cyprus 35°12N 32°59E 46 C2
Guzhang China 28°42N 109°58E 34 C7
Guzhen China 33°22N 117°18E 33 H9
Guzmán, L. de Mexico 31°20N 107°30W 86 A3
Gwa Burma 17°36N 94°34E 41 L19
Gwabegar Australia 30°37S 148°59E 63 E4
Gwādar Pakistan 25°10N 62°18E 40 G3
Gwaii Haanas △ Canada 52°21N 131°26W 70 C2
Gwalior India 26°12N 78°10E 42 F8
Gwanda Zimbabwe 20°55S 29°0E 55 J5
Gwangju S. Korea 35°9N 126°54E 33 G14
Gwanju = Gwangju S. Korea 35°9N 126°54E 33 G14
Gweebarra B. Ireland 54°51N 8°23W 10 B3
Gweedore Ireland 55°3N 8°14W 10 A3
Gweru Zimbabwe 19°28S 29°45E 55 H5
Gwinn U.S.A. 46°19N 87°27W 80 B10
Gwydir → Australia 29°27S 149°48E 63 D4
Gwynedd □ U.K. 52°52N 4°10W 12 E3
Gyandzha = Gäncä Azerbaijan 40°45N 46°20E 19 F8
Gyangzê China 29°5N 89°47E 30 F6
Gyaring Hu China 34°50N 97°40E 30 E8
Gydanskiy Poluostrov Russia 70°0N 78°0E 26 C8
Gyeongju S. Korea 35°51N 129°14E 33 G15
Gympie Australia 26°11S 152°38E 63 D5
Gyöngyös Hungary 47°48N 19°56E 17 E10
Győr Hungary 47°41N 17°40E 17 E9
Gypsum Pt. Canada 61°53N 114°35W 70 A6
Gypsumville Canada 51°45N 98°40W 71 C9
Gyula Hungary 46°38N 21°17E 17 E11
Gyumri Armenia 40°47N 43°50E 19 F7
Gyzylarbat = Serdar Turkmenistan 39°4N 56°23E 47 B8
Gyzyletrek = Etrek Turkmenistan 37°36N 54°46E 47 B7

H

Ha 'Arava → Israel 30°50N 35°20E 48 E4
Ha Coi Vietnam 21°26N 107°46E 34 G6
Ha Dong Vietnam 20°58N 105°46E 34 G5
Ha Giang Vietnam 22°50N 104°59E 34 F5
Hā Karmel, Har Israel 32°44N 35°3E 48 C4
Ha Karmel △ Israel 32°45N 35°5E 48 C4
Ha Long = Hong Gai Vietnam 20°57N 107°5E 34 G6
Ha Long, Vinh Vietnam 20°56N 107°3E 38 B6
Ha Tien Vietnam 10°23N 104°29E 39 G5
Ha Tinh Vietnam 18°20N 105°54E 38 C5
Ha Trung Vietnam 19°58N 105°50E 38 C5
Haaksbergen Neths. 52°9N 6°45E 15 B6
Ha'ano Tonga 19°41S 174°18W 59 c
Ha'apai Group Tonga 19°47S 174°27W 59 c
Haapiti Moorea 17°34S 149°52W 59 d
Haapsalu Estonia 58°56N 23°30E 9 G20
Haarlem Neths. 52°23N 4°39E 15 B4
Haast → N.Z. 43°50S 169°2E 59 E2
Haasts Bluff Australia 23°22S 132°0E 60 D5
Haasts Bluff ✪ Australia 23°39S 130°34E 60 D5
Hab → Pakistan 24°53N 66°41E 42 G3
Hab Nadi Chauki Pakistan 25°0N 66°50E 42 G2
Habahe China 48°3N 86°23E 30 B6
Habay Canada 58°50N 118°44W 70 B5
Ḩabbānīyah Iraq 33°17N 43°29E 46 C4
Habirag China 42°17N 115°42E 32 C8
Haboro Japan 44°22N 141°42E 28 B10
Ḩabshān U.A.E. 23°50N 53°37E 47 F7
Hachijō-Jima Japan 33°5N 139°45E 29 H9
Hachiman = Gujō Japan 35°45N 136°57E 29 G8
Hachinohe Japan 40°30N 141°29E 28 D10
Hachiōji Japan 35°40N 139°20E 29 G9
Hackettstown U.S.A. 40°51N 74°50W 83 F10
Hadali Pakistan 32°16N 72°11E 42 C5
Hadarba, Ras Sudan 22°4N 36°51E 53 D13
Hadarom □ Israel 31°0N 35°0E 48 E4
Ḩadd, Ra's al Oman 22°35N 59°50E 49 C6
Haddington U.K. 55°57N 2°47W 11 F6
Hadejia Nigeria 12°30N 10°5E 52 F7
Hadera Israel 32°27N 34°55E 48 C3
Hadera, N. → Israel 32°28N 34°52E 48 C3
Haderslev Denmark 55°15N 9°30E 9 J13
Hadgaon India 19°30N 77°40E 44 E3
Hadhramaut = Ḩaḑramawt □ Yemen 15°30N 49°30E 49 D4
Hadībоh Yemen 12°39N 54°2E 49 E5
Hadley B. Canada 72°31N 108°12W 68 C10
Hadong S. Korea 35°5N 127°44E 33 G14
Ḩaḑramawt □ Yemen 15°30N 49°30E 49 D4
Ḩadrānīyah Iraq 35°38N 43°14E 46 C4
Hadrian's Wall U.K. 55°0N 2°30W 12 B5
Hae, Ko Thailand 7°44N 98°22E 39 a
Haeju N. Korea 38°3N 125°45E 33 E13
Hā'ena U.S.A. 22°14N 159°34W 75 L8
Haenam S. Korea 34°34N 126°35E 33 G14
Haenertsburg S. Africa 24°0S 29°50E 57 B4
Haerhpin = Harbin China 45°48N 126°40E 33 B14
Hafar al Bāţin Si. Arabia 28°32N 45°52E 46 D5
Ḩafīrat al 'Aydā Si. Arabia 26°26N 39°12E 46 E3
Hafit Oman 23°59N 55°49E 47 F7
Hafizabad Pakistan 32°5N 73°40E 42 C5
Haflong India 25°10N 93°5E 41 G18
Haft Gel Iran 31°30N 49°32E 47 D6
Hagalil Israel 32°53N 35°18E 48 C4
Hagari → India 15°40N 77°0E 45 G3
Hagemeister I. U.S.A. 58°39N 160°54W 74 D7
Hagen Germany 51°21N 7°27E 16 C4
Hagerman U.S.A. 33°7N 104°20W 77 K11
Hagerman Fossil Beds ⌂ U.S.A. 42°48N 114°57W 76 E6
Hagerstown U.S.A. 39°39N 77°43W 81 F15
Hagersville Canada 42°58N 80°3W 82 D4
Hagfors Sweden 60°3N 13°45E 9 F15
Hagi Japan 34°30N 131°22E 29 G5
Hagolan Syria 33°0N 35°45E 48 C4
Hagondange France 49°16N 6°11E 20 B7
Hags Hd. Ireland 52°57N 9°28W 10 D2
Hague, C. de la France 49°44N 1°56W 20 B3
Hague, The = 's-Gravenhage Neths. 52°7N 4°17E 15 B4
Haguenau France 48°49N 7°47E 20 B7
Hai Duong Vietnam 20°56N 106°19E 34 G6
Hai'an Guangdong, China 20°18N 110°11E 35 G8
Hai'an Jiangsu, China 32°37N 120°27E 35 A13
Haicheng China 40°50N 122°45E 33 D12
Haida Gwaii Canada 53°20N 132°10W 70 C2
Haidar Khel Afghan. 33°58N 68°38E 42 C3
Haidarâbâd = Hyderabad India 17°22N 78°29E 44 F4
Haidargarh India 26°37N 81°22E 43 F9
Haifa = Hefa Israel 32°46N 35°0E 48 C4
Haifeng China 22°58N 115°10E 35 F10
Haikou China 20°1N 110°16E 38 B8
Ḩā'il Si. Arabia 27°28N 41°45E 46 E4
Ḩā'il □ Si. Arabia 26°40N 41°40E 46 E4
Hailar China 49°10N 119°38E 31 B12
Hailey U.S.A. 43°31N 114°19W 76 E6
Haileybury Canada 47°30N 79°38W 72 C4
Hailin China 44°37N 129°30E 33 B15
Hailing Dao China 21°35N 111°47E 35 G8
Hailun China 47°28N 126°50E 31 B14
Hailuoto Finland 65°3N 24°45E 8 D21
Haimen Guangdong, China 23°15N 116°38E 35 F11
Haimen Jiangsu, China 31°52N 121°10E 35 B13
Hainan □ China 19°0N 109°30E 38 C7
Hainan Dao China 19°0N 109°30E 38 C7
Hainan Str. = Qiongzhou Haixia China 20°10N 110°15E 38 B8
Hainaut □ Belgium 50°30N 4°0E 15 D4
Haines Alaska, U.S.A. 59°14N 135°26W 70 B1
Haines Oreg., U.S.A. 44°55N 117°56W 76 D5
Haines City U.S.A. 28°7N 81°38W 85 G14
Haines Junction Canada 60°45N 137°30W 70 A1
Haining China 30°28N 120°40E 35 B13
Haiphong Vietnam 20°47N 106°41E 34 G6
Haitan Dao China 25°30N 119°45E 35 E12
Haiti ■ W. Indies 19°0N 72°30W 89 C5
Haiya Sudan 18°20N 36°21E 53 E13
Haiyan Qinghai, China 36°53N 100°59E 30 D9
Haiyan Zhejiang, China 30°28N 120°58E 35 B13
Haiyang China 36°47N 121°9E 33 F11
Haiyuan Guangxi Zhuangzu, China 22°8N 107°35E 34 F6
Haiyuan Ningxia Huizu, China 36°35N 105°52E 32 F3
Haizhou China 34°37N 119°7E 33 G10
Haizhou Wan China 34°50N 119°20E 33 G10
Haj Ali Qoli, Kavīr Iran 35°55N 54°50E 47 C7
Hajdúböszörmény Hungary 47°40N 21°30E 17 E11
Haji Ibrahim Iraq 36°40N 44°30E 46 B5
Hājjābād Iran 33°37N 60°0E 47 C9
Hajipur India 25°45N 85°13E 43 G11
Ḩajjah Yemen 15°42N 43°36E 49 D3
Ḩājjīābād Iran 28°19N 55°55E 47 D7
Ḩājjīābād-e Zarrīn Iran 33°9N 54°51E 47 C7
Hajnówka Poland 52°47N 23°35E 17 B12
Hakkâri Turkey 37°34N 43°44E 46 B4
Hakken-Zan Japan 34°10N 135°54E 29 G7
Hakkōda San Japan 40°50N 141°0E 28 D10
Hakodate Japan 41°45N 140°44E 28 D10
Hakos Namibia 23°13S 16°21E 56 B2
Hakskeenpan S. Africa 26°48S 20°13E 56 C3
Haku-San Japan 36°9N 136°46E 29 F8
Haku-San △ Japan 36°15N 136°45E 29 F8
Hakui Japan 36°53N 136°47E 29 F8
Hakusan Japan 36°31N 136°34E 29 F8
Hala Pakistan 25°43N 68°20E 42 G3
Ḩalab Syria 36°10N 37°15E 46 B3
Ḩalabjah Iraq 35°10N 45°58E 46 C5
Halaib Sudan 22°12N 36°30E 53 D13
Halaib Triangle Africa 22°30N 35°20E 53 D13
Hālat 'Ammār Si. Arabia 29°10N 36°4E 46 D3
Halbā Lebanon 34°34N 36°6E 48 A5
Halberstadt Germany 51°54N 11°3E 16 C6
Halcombe N.Z. 40°8S 175°30E 59 D5
Halcon, Mt. Phil. 13°16N 121°0E 37 B6
Halde Fjäll = Haltiatunturi Finland 69°17N 21°18E 8 B19
Halden Norway 59°9N 11°23E 9 G14
Haldia Bangla. 22°1N 88°3E 43 H13
Haldwani India 29°31N 79°30E 43 E8
Hale → Australia 24°56S 135°53E 62 C2
Halesowen U.K. 52°27N 2°3W 13 E5
Halesworth U.K. 52°20N 1°31E 13 E9
Haleyville U.S.A. 34°14N 87°37W 85 D11
Half Dome U.S.A. 37°44N 119°32W 78 H7
Halfmoon Bay N.Z. 46°50S 168°5E 59 G2
Halfway → Canada 56°12N 121°32W 70 B4
Halia India 24°50N 82°19E 43 G10
Haliburton Canada 45°3N 78°30W 82 A6
Halifax Australia 18°32S 146°22E 62 B4
Halifax Canada 44°38N 63°35W 73 D7
Halifax U.K. 53°43N 1°52W 12 D6
Halifax U.S.A. 40°25N 76°55W 82 F8
Halifax B. Australia 18°50S 147°0E 62 B4
Halifax I. Namibia 26°38S 15°4E 56 C2
Halik Shan China 42°20N 81°22E 30 C5
Halīl → Iran 27°40N 58°30E 47 E8
Halimun △ Indonesia 6°42S 106°26E 37 G11
Halkida = Chalkida Greece 38°27N 23°42E 23 E10
Halkirk U.K. 58°30N 3°29W 11 C5
Hall Beach Canada 68°46N 81°12W 69 D15
Hall Pen. Canada 63°30N 66°0W 69 E18
Hall Pt. Australia 15°40S 124°23E 60 C3
Halland Sweden 57°8N 12°47E 9 H15
Ḩallāniyat, Jazā'ir al Oman 17°30N 55°58E 49 D6
Hallasan S. Korea 33°22N 126°32E 33 H14
Halle Germany 51°30N 11°56E 16 C6
Hällefors Sweden 59°47N 14°31E 9 G16
Hallett Australia 33°25S 138°55E 63 E2
Hallettsville U.S.A. 29°27N 96°57W 84 G6
Halley Antarctica 75°35S 26°39W 5 D1
Hallia → India 16°55N 79°20E 44 F4
Hallim S. Korea 33°24N 126°15E 33 H14
Hallingdalselva → Norway 60°23N 9°35E 8 F13
Hallock U.S.A. 48°47N 96°57W 80 A5
Halls Creek Australia 18°16S 127°38E 60 C4
Halls Gap Australia 37°8S 142°34E 63 F3
Halls Lake Canada 45°7N 78°45W 82 A6
Hallsberg Sweden 59°5N 15°7E 9 G16
Hallstead U.S.A. 41°58N 75°45W 83 E9
Halmahera Indonesia 0°40N 128°0E 37 D7
Halmstad Sweden 56°41N 12°52E 9 H15
Halong Bay = Ha Long, Vinh Vietnam 20°56N 107°3E 38 B6
Hälsingborg = Helsingborg Sweden 56°3N 12°42E 9 H15

Hälsingland *Sweden* 61°40N 16°5E **8 F17**
Halstead *U.K.* 51°57N 0°40E **13 F8**
Haltiatunturi *Finland* 69°17N 21°18E **8 B19**
Halton □ *U.K.* 53°22N 2°45W **12 D5**
Haltwhistle *U.K.* 54°58N 2°26W **12 C5**
Ḥalūl *Qatar* 25°40N 52°40E **47 E7**
Halvad *India* 23°1N 71°11E **42 H4**
Halvān *Iran* 33°57N 56°15E **47 C8**
Hamab *Namibia* 28°7S 19°16E **56 C2**
Hamada *Japan* 34°56N 132°4E **29 G6**
Hamadān *Iran* 34°52N 48°32E **47 C6**
Hamadān □ *Iran* 35°0N 49°0E **47 C6**
Ḥamāh *Syria* 35°5N 36°40E **46 C3**
Hamamatsu *Japan* 34°45N 137°45E **29 G8**
Hamar *Norway* 60°48N 11°7E **8 F14**
Hamâta, Gebel *Egypt* 24°17N 35°0E **46 E2**
Hamatonbetsu *Japan* 45°10N 142°20E **28 B11**
Hambantota *Sri Lanka* 6°10N 81°10E **45 L5**
Hamber △ *Canada* 52°20N 118°0W **70 C5**
Hamburg *Germany* 53°33N 9°59E **16 B5**
Hamburg *Ark., U.S.A.* 33°14N 91°48W **84 E9**
Hamburg *N.Y., U.S.A.* 42°43N 78°50W **82 D6**
Hamburg *Pa., U.S.A.* 40°33N 75°59W **83 F9**
Ḥamḍ, W. al → *Si. Arabia* 24°55N 36°20E **46 E3**
Hamden *U.S.A.* 41°23N 72°54W **83 E12**
Häme *Finland* 61°38N 25°10E **8 F21**
Hämeenlinna *Finland* 61°0N 24°28E **8 F21**
Hamelin Pool *Australia* 26°22S 114°20E **61 E1**
Hameln *Germany* 52°6N 9°21E **16 B5**
Hamersley Ra. *Australia* 22°0S 117°45E **60 D2**
Hamhŭng *N. Korea* 39°54N 127°30E **33 E14**
Hami *China* 42°55N 93°25E **30 C7**
Hamilton *Australia* 37°45S 142°2E **63 F3**
Hamilton *Canada* 43°15N 79°50W **82 C5**
Hamilton *N.Z.* 37°47S 175°19E **59 B5**
Hamilton *U.K.* 55°46N 4°2W **11 F4**
Hamilton *Ala., U.S.A.* 34°9N 87°59W **85 D11**
Hamilton *Mont., U.S.A.* 46°15N 114°10W **76 C6**
Hamilton *N.Y., U.S.A.* 42°50N 75°33W **83 D9**
Hamilton *Ohio, U.S.A.* 39°24N 84°34W **81 F11**
Hamilton *Tex., U.S.A.* 31°42N 98°7W **84 F5**
Hamilton → *Queens.,*
Australia 23°30S 139°47E **62 C2**
Hamilton → *S. Austral.,*
Australia 26°40S 135°19E **63 D2**
Hamilton City *U.S.A.* 39°45N 122°1W **78 F4**
Hamilton I. *Australia* 20°21S 148°56E **62 b**
Hamilton Inlet *Canada* 54°0N 57°30W **73 B8**
Hamilton Mt. *U.S.A.* 43°25N 74°22W **83 C10**
Hamina *Finland* 60°34N 27°12E **8 F22**
Hamirpur *H.P., India* 31°41N 76°31E **42 D7**
Hamirpur *Ut. P., India* 25°57N 80°9E **43 G9**
Hamlet *U.S.A.* 34°53N 79°42W **85 D15**
Hamley Bridge *Australia* 34°17S 138°35E **63 E2**
Hamlin = Hameln *Germany* 52°6N 9°21E **16 B5**
Hamlin *N.Y., U.S.A.* 43°17N 77°55W **82 C7**
Hamlin *Tex., U.S.A.* 32°53N 100°8W **84 E4**
Hamm *Germany* 51°40N 7°50E **16 C4**
Ḥammār, Hawr al *Iraq* 30°50N 47°10E **46 D5**
Hammerfest *Norway* 70°39N 23°41E **8 A20**
Hammond *Ind., U.S.A.* 41°38N 87°30W **80 E10**
Hammond *La., U.S.A.* 30°30N 90°28W **85 F9**
Hammond *N.Y., U.S.A.* 44°27N 75°42W **83 B9**
Hammondsport *U.S.A.* 42°25N 77°13W **82 D7**
Hammonton *U.S.A.* 39°39N 74°48W **81 F16**
Hampden *N.Z.* 45°18S 170°50E **59 F3**
Hampi *India* 15°18N 76°28E **45 G3**
Hampshire □ *U.K.* 51°7N 1°23W **13 F6**
Hampshire Downs *U.K.* 51°15N 1°10W **13 F6**
Hampton *N.B., Canada* 45°32N 65°51W **73 C6**
Hampton *Ont., Canada* 43°58N 78°45W **82 C6**
Hampton *Ark., U.S.A.* 33°32N 92°28W **84 E8**
Hampton *Iowa, U.S.A.* 42°45N 93°13W **80 D7**
Hampton *N.H., U.S.A.* 42°57N 70°50W **83 D14**
Hampton *S.C., U.S.A.* 32°52N 81°7W **85 E14**
Hampton *Va., U.S.A.* 37°2N 76°21W **81 G15**
Hampton Bays *U.S.A.* 40°53N 72°30W **83 F12**
Hampton Tableland
Australia 32°0S 127°0E **61 F4**
Hamyang *S. Korea* 35°32N 127°42E **33 G14**
Han Jiang → *China* 23°25N 116°40E **35 F11**
Han Pijesak *Bos.-H.* 44°5N 18°57E **23 B8**
Han Shui → *China* 30°34N 114°17E **35 B10**
Hanak *Si. Arabia* 25°32N 37°0E **46 E3**
Hanamaki *Japan* 39°23N 141°7E **28 E10**
Hanau *Germany* 50°7N 8°56E **16 C5**
Hanbogd = Ihbulag
Mongolia 43°11N 107°10E **32 C4**
Hancheng *China* 35°31N 110°25E **32 G6**
Hanchuan *China* 30°40N 113°50E **35 B9**
Hancock *Mich., U.S.A.* 47°8N 88°35W **80 B9**
Hancock *N.Y., U.S.A.* 41°57N 75°17W **83 E9**
Hancock *Vt., U.S.A.* 43°55N 72°50W **83 C12**
Handa *Japan* 34°53N 136°55E **29 G8**
Handa I. *U.K.* 58°23N 5°11W **11 C3**
Handan *China* 36°35N 114°28E **32 F8**
Handwara *India* 34°21N 74°20E **43 B6**
Hanegev *Israel* 30°50N 35°0E **48 E4**
Hanford *U.S.A.* 36°20N 119°39W **78 J7**
Hanford Reach △
U.S.A. 46°40N 119°30W **76 C4**
Hang Chat *Thailand* 18°20N 99°21E **38 C2**
Hangang → *S. Korea* 37°50N 126°30E **33 F14**
Hangayn Nuruu *Mongolia* 47°30N 99°0E **30 B8**
Hangchou = Hangzhou
China 30°18N 120°11E **35 B13**
Hanggin Houqi *China* 40°58N 107°4E **32 D4**
Hanggin Qi *China* 39°52N 108°50E **32 E5**
Hangu *China* 39°18N 117°53E **33 E9**
Hangzhou *China* 30°18N 120°11E **35 B13**
Hangzhou Wan *China* 30°15N 121°0E **35 B13**
Hanh *Mongolia* 51°32N 100°35E **30 A9**
Hanhongor *Mongolia* 43°55N 104°28E **32 C3**
Hania = Chania *Greece* 35°30N 24°4E **23 G11**
Ḥanīdh *Si. Arabia* 26°35N 48°38E **47 E6**
Ḥanīsh *Yemen* 13°45N 42°46E **49 E3**
Hanjiang *China* 25°26N 119°7E **35 E12**
Hankinson *U.S.A.* 46°4N 96°54W **80 B5**

Hankö *Finland* 59°50N 22°57E **9 G20**
Hankou *China* 30°35N 114°30E **35 B10**
Hanksville *U.S.A.* 38°22N 110°43W **76 G8**
Hanle *India* 32°42N 79°4E **43 C8**
Hanmer Springs *N.Z.* 42°32S 172°50E **59 E4**
Hann → *Australia* 17°26S 126°17E **60 C4**
Hann, Mt. *Australia* 15°45S 126°0E **60 C4**
Hanna *Canada* 51°40N 111°54W **70 C6**
Hanna *U.S.A.* 41°52N 106°34W **76 F10**
Hannah B. *Canada* 51°40N 80°0W **72 B4**
Hannibal *Mo., U.S.A.* 39°42N 91°22W **80 F8**
Hannibal *N.Y., U.S.A.* 43°19N 76°35W **83 C8**
Hannover *Germany* 52°22N 9°46E **16 B5**
Hanoi *Vietnam* 21°5N 105°55E **34 G5**
Hanover = Hannover
Germany 52°22N 9°46E **16 B5**
Hanover *Canada* 44°9N 81°2W **82 B3**
Hanover *S. Africa* 31°4S 24°29E **56 E3**
Hanover *N.H., U.S.A.* 43°42N 72°17W **83 C12**
Hanover *Ohio, U.S.A.* 40°4N 82°16W **82 F2**
Hanover *Pa., U.S.A.* 39°48N 76°59W **81 F15**
Hanover, I. *Chile* 51°0S 74°50W **96 G2**
Hans Lollik I.
U.S. Virgin Is. 18°24N 64°53W **89 e**
Hansdiha *India* 24°36N 87°5E **43 G12**
Hanshou *China* 28°56N 111°50E **35 C8**
Hansi *H.P., India* 32°27N 77°50E **42 C7**
Hansi *Haryana, India* 29°10N 75°57E **42 E6**
Hanson, L. *Australia* 31°0S 136°15E **63 E2**
Hanting *China* 36°46N 119°12E **33 F10**
Hanyin *China* 32°54N 108°28E **32 H5**
Hanyuan *China* 29°21N 102°40E **34 C4**
Hanzhong *China* 33°10N 107°1E **34 A6**
Hanzhuang *China* 34°33N 117°23E **33 G9**
Haoxue *China* 30°3N 112°24E **35 B9**
Haparanda *Sweden* 65°52N 24°8E **8 D21**
Happy *U.S.A.* 34°45N 101°52W **84 D4**
Happy Camp *U.S.A.* 41°48N 123°23W **76 F2**
Happy Valley-Goose Bay
Canada 53°15N 60°20W **73 B7**
Hapsu *N. Korea* 41°13N 128°51E **33 D15**
Hapur *India* 28°45N 77°45E **42 E7**
Ḥaql *Si. Arabia* 29°10N 34°58E **48 F3**
Har *Indonesia* 5°16S 133°14E **37 F8**
Har-Ayrag *Mongolia* 45°47N 109°16E **32 B5**
Har Hu *China* 38°20N 97°38E **30 D8**
Har Us Nuur *Mongolia* 48°0N 92°0E **30 B7**
Har Yehuda *Israel* 31°35N 34°57E **48 D3**
Ḥaraḍ *Si. Arabia* 24°22N 49°0E **49 C4**
Haramosh *Pakistan* 35°50N 74°54E **43 B6**
Haranomachi = Minamisōma
Japan 37°38N 140°58E **28 F10**
Harar = Harer *Ethiopia* 9°20N 42°8E **49 F3**
Harare *Zimbabwe* 17°43S 31°2E **55 H6**
Harazé *Chad* 9°57N 20°48E **53 G10**
Harbhanga *India* 20°38N 84°36E **44 D7**
Harbin *China* 45°48N 126°40E **33 B14**
Harbor Beach *U.S.A.* 43°51N 82°39W **82 C2**
Harborcreek *U.S.A.* 42°9N 79°57W **82 D5**
Harbour Breton *Canada* 47°29N 55°50W **73 C8**
Harbour Deep *Canada* 50°25N 56°32W **73 B8**
Harda *India* 22°27N 77°5E **42 H7**
Hardangerfjorden *Norway* 60°5N 6°0E **9 F12**
Hardangervidda *Norway* 60°7N 7°20E **8 F12**
Hardap □ *Namibia* 24°0S 17°0E **56 B2**
Hardap △ *Namibia* 24°29S 17°45E **56 B2**
Hardap Dam *Namibia* 24°32S 17°50E **56 B2**
Hardenberg *Neths.* 52°34N 6°37E **15 B6**
Harderwijk *Neths.* 52°21N 5°38E **15 B5**
Hardey → *Australia* 22°45S 116°8E **60 D2**
Hardin *U.S.A.* 45°44N 107°37W **76 D10**
Harding *S. Africa* 30°35S 29°55E **57 D4**
Harding Ra. *Australia* 16°17S 124°55E **60 C3**
Hardisty *Canada* 52°40N 111°18W **70 C6**
Hardoi *India* 27°26N 80°6E **43 F9**
Hardwar = Haridwar
India 29°58N 78°9E **42 E8**
Hardwick *U.S.A.* 44°30N 72°22W **83 B12**
Hardwood Lake *Canada* 45°12N 77°26W **82 A7**
Hardy, Pen. *Chile* 55°30S 68°20W **96 H3**
Hardy, Pte. *St. Lucia* 14°6N 60°56W **89 f**
Hare B. *Canada* 51°15N 55°45W **73 B8**
Hareid *Norway* 62°22N 6°1E **8 E12**
Harer *Ethiopia* 9°20N 42°8E **49 F3**
Hargeisa *Somalia* 9°30N 44°2E **49 F3**
Hari → *Indonesia* 1°16S 104°5E **36 E2**
Haridwar *India* 29°58N 78°9E **42 E8**
Harihar *India* 14°32N 75°44E **45 G2**
Hariharpur Garhi *Nepal* 27°19N 85°29E **43 F11**
Harim, Jabal al *Oman* 25°58N 56°14E **47 E8**
Haringhata → *Bangla.* 22°0N 89°58E **41 J16**
Haripad *India* 9°14N 76°28E **45 K3**
Harīr, W. al → *Syria* 32°44N 35°59E **48 C4**
Harīrūd → *Asia* 37°24N 60°38E **47 B9**
Härjedalen *Sweden* 62°22N 13°5E **8 E15**
Harlan *Iowa, U.S.A.* 41°39N 95°19W **80 E6**
Harlan *Ky., U.S.A.* 36°51N 83°19W **81 G12**
Harlech *U.K.* 52°52N 4°6W **12 E3**
Harlem *U.S.A.* 48°32N 108°47W **76 B9**
Harlingen *Neths.* 53°11N 5°25E **15 A5**
Harlingen *U.S.A.* 26°12N 97°42W **84 H6**
Harlow *U.K.* 51°46N 0°8E **13 F8**
Harlowton *U.S.A.* 46°26N 109°50W **76 C9**
Harnai *India* 17°48N 73°6E **44 F1**
Harnai *Pakistan* 30°6N 67°56E **42 D2**
Harney Basin *U.S.A.* 43°0N 119°30W **76 E4**
Harney L. *U.S.A.* 43°14N 119°8W **76 E4**
Harney Peak *U.S.A.* 43°52N 103°32W **80 D2**
Härnösand *Sweden* 62°38N 17°55E **8 E17**
Haroldswick *U.K.* 60°48N 0°50W **11 A8**
Harp L. *Canada* 55°5N 61°50W **73 A7**
Harpanahalli *India* 14°47N 76°2E **45 G3**
Harper *Liberia* 4°25N 7°43W **52 H4**
Harper, Mt. *U.S.A.* 64°14N 143°51W **74 C11**
Harrai *India* 22°37N 79°13E **43 H8**
Harrand *Pakistan* 29°28N 70°3E **42 E4**
Harricana → *Canada* 50°56N 79°32W **72 B4**

Harriman *U.S.A.* 35°56N 84°33W **85 D12**
Harrington Harbour
Canada 50°31N 59°30W **73 B8**
Harris *U.K.* 57°50N 6°55W **11 D2**
Harris, L. *Australia* 31°10S 135°10E **63 E2**
Harris, Sd. of *U.K.* 57°44N 7°6W **11 D1**
Harris Pt. *Canada* 43°6N 82°9W **82 C2**
Harrisburg *Ill., U.S.A.* 37°44N 88°32W **80 G9**
Harrisburg *Nebr., U.S.A.* 41°33N 103°44W **80 E2**
Harrisburg *Pa., U.S.A.* 40°16N 76°53W **82 F8**
Harrismith *S. Africa* 28°15S 29°8E **57 C4**
Harrison *Ark., U.S.A.* 36°14N 93°7W **84 C8**
Harrison *Maine, U.S.A.* 44°7N 70°39W **83 B14**
Harrison *Nebr., U.S.A.* 42°41N 103°53W **80 D2**
Harrison, C. *Canada* 54°55N 57°55W **73 B8**
Harrison Bay *U.S.A.* 70°40N 151°0W **74 A9**
Harrison L. *Canada* 49°33N 121°50W **70 D4**
Harrisonburg *U.S.A.* 38°27N 78°52W **81 F14**
Harrisonville *U.S.A.* 38°39N 94°21W **80 F6**
Harriston *Canada* 43°57N 80°53W **82 C4**
Harrisville *Mich., U.S.A.* 44°39N 83°17W **82 B1**
Harrisville *N.Y., U.S.A.* 44°9N 75°19W **83 B9**
Harrisville *Pa., U.S.A.* 41°8N 80°0W **82 E5**
Harrodsburg *U.S.A.* 37°46N 84°51W **81 G11**
Harrogate *U.K.* 54°0N 1°33W **12 C6**
Harrow *Canada* 42°2N 82°55W **82 D2**
Harrowsmith *Canada* 44°24N 76°40W **83 B8**
Harry S. Truman Res.
U.S.A. 38°16N 93°24W **80 F7**
Harsin *Iran* 34°18N 47°33E **46 C5**
Harstad *Norway* 68°48N 16°30E **8 B17**
Harsud *India* 22°6N 76°44E **42 H7**
Hart *U.S.A.* 43°42N 86°22W **80 D10**
Hart, L. *Australia* 31°10S 136°25E **63 E2**
Hartbees → *S. Africa* 28°45S 20°32E **56 C3**
Hartford *Conn., U.S.A.* 41°46N 72°41W **83 E12**
Hartford *Ky., U.S.A.* 37°27N 86°55W **80 G10**
Hartford *S. Dak., U.S.A.* 43°38N 96°57W **80 D5**
Hartford *Vt., U.S.A.* 43°40N 72°20W **83 C12**
Hartford *Wis., U.S.A.* 43°19N 88°22W **80 D9**
Hartford City *U.S.A.* 40°27N 85°22W **81 E11**
Hartland *Canada* 46°20N 67°32W **73 C6**
Hartland Pt. *U.K.* 51°1N 4°32W **13 F3**
Hartlepool *U.K.* 54°42N 1°13W **12 C6**
Hartlepool □ *U.K.* 54°42N 1°17W **12 C6**
Hartley Bay *Canada* 53°25N 129°15W **70 C3**
Hartmannberge *Namibia* 17°0S 13°0E **56 A1**
Hartney *Canada* 49°30N 100°35W **71 D8**
Harts → *S. Africa* 28°24S 24°17E **56 D3**
Harts Range *Australia* 23°6S 134°55E **62 C1**
Hartselle *U.S.A.* 34°27N 86°56W **85 D11**
Hartshorne *U.S.A.* 34°51N 95°34W **84 D7**
Hartstown *U.S.A.* 41°33N 80°23W **82 E4**
Hartsville *U.S.A.* 34°23N 80°4W **85 D14**
Hartswater *S. Africa* 27°34S 24°43E **56 C3**
Hartwell *U.S.A.* 34°21N 82°56W **85 D13**
Harunabad *Pakistan* 29°35N 73°8E **42 E5**
Harur *India* 12°3N 78°29E **45 H4**
Harvand *Iran* 28°25N 55°43E **47 D7**
Harvey *Australia* 33°5S 115°54E **61 F2**
Harvey *U.S.A.* 47°47N 99°56W **80 B4**
Harwich *U.K.* 51°56N 1°17E **13 F9**
Haryana □ *India* 29°0N 76°10E **42 E7**
Haryn → *Belarus* 52°7N 27°17E **17 B14**
Harz *Germany* 51°38N 10°44E **16 C6**
Hasa *Si. Arabia* 25°50N 49°0E **47 E6**
Ḩasā, W. al → *Jordan* 31°4N 35°29E **48 D4**
Ḩasanābād *Iran* 32°8N 52°44E **47 C7**
Hasanparti *India* 18°4N 79°32E **44 E4**
Ḩasb, W. → *Iraq* 31°45N 44°17E **46 D5**
Hasdo → *India* 21°44N 82°44E **43 J10**
Hashimoto *Japan* 34°19N 135°37E **29 G7**
Hashtjerd *Iran* 35°52N 50°40E **47 C6**
Hashtpur = Tālesh *Iran* 37°58N 48°58E **47 B6**
Haskell *U.S.A.* 33°10N 99°44W **84 E5**
Haskovo = Khaskovo
Bulgaria 41°56N 25°30E **23 D11**
Haslemere *U.K.* 51°5N 0°43W **13 F7**
Hassan *India* 13°0N 76°5E **45 H3**
Hasselt *Belgium* 50°56N 5°21E **15 D5**
Hassi Messaoud *Algeria* 31°51N 6°1E **52 B7**
Hässleholm *Sweden* 56°10N 13°46E **9 H15**
Hastings *N.Z.* 39°39S 176°52E **59 C6**
Hastings *U.K.* 50°51N 0°35E **13 G8**
Hastings *Mich., U.S.A.* 42°39N 85°17W **81 D11**
Hastings *Minn., U.S.A.* 44°44N 92°51W **80 C7**
Hastings *Nebr., U.S.A.* 40°35N 98°23W **80 E4**
Hastings Ra. *Australia* 31°15S 152°14E **63 E5**
Hat Lot *Vietnam* 21°15N 104°7E **38 B5**
Hat Yai *Thailand* 7°1N 100°27E **39 J3**
Hatanbulag = Ergel
Mongolia 43°8N 109°5E **32 C5**
Hatay *Turkey* 36°14N 36°10E **46 B3**
Hatch *U.S.A.* 32°40N 107°9W **77 K10**
Hatchet L. *Canada* 58°36N 103°40W **71 B8**
Hateruma-Shima *Japan* 24°3N 123°47E **29 M1**
Hatfield *Australia* 33°54S 143°49E **63 E3**
Hatgal *Mongolia* 50°26N 100°9E **30 A9**
Hathras *India* 27°36N 78°6E **42 F8**
Hatia *Bangla.* 22°30N 91°5E **41 H17**
Hatia *Nepal* 27°43N 87°21E **43 F12**
Hatid *India* 31°32N 76°3E **44 F2**
Hato Mayor *Dom. Rep.* 18°46N 69°15W **89 C6**
Hatta *India* 24°7N 79°36E **43 G8**
Hatta *U.A.E.* 24°45N 56°4E **47 E8**
Hattah *Australia* 34°48S 142°17E **63 E3**
Hattah Kulkyne △
Australia 34°16S 142°33E **63 E3**
Hatteras, C. *U.S.A.* 35°14N 75°32W **85 D17**
Hattiesburg *U.S.A.* 31°20N 89°17W **85 F10**
Hatvan *Hungary* 47°40N 19°45E **17 E10**
Hau → *Vietnam* 9°30N 106°13E **39 H6**
Haugesund *Norway* 59°23N 5°13E **9 G11**
Haukipudas *Finland* 65°12N 25°20E **8 D21**
Haultain → *Canada* 55°51N 106°46W **71 B7**
Hauraki G. *N.Z.* 36°35S 175°5E **59 B5**
Haut Atlas *Morocco* 32°30N 5°0W **52 B4**
Hautes Fagnes = Hohes Venn
Belgium 50°30N 6°5E **15 D6**

Hauts Plateaux *Algeria* 35°0N 1°0E **52 B6**
Havana = La Habana
Cuba 23°8N 82°22W **88 B3**
Havana *U.S.A.* 40°18N 90°4W **80 E8**
Havant *U.K.* 50°51N 0°58W **13 G7**
Havasor = Kığzı *Turkey* 38°18N 43°25E **46 B4**
Havasu, L. *U.S.A.* 34°18N 114°28W **79 L12**
Havel → *Germany* 52°50N 12°3E **16 B7**
Havelian *Pakistan* 34°2N 73°10E **42 B5**
Havelock *Canada* 44°26N 77°53W **82 B7**
Havelock *N.Z.* 41°17S 173°48E **59 D4**
Havelock I. *India* 11°58N 93°0E **45 J11**
Haverfordwest *U.K.* 51°48N 4°58W **13 F3**
Haverhill *U.K.* 52°5N 0°28E **13 E8**
Haverhill *U.S.A.* 42°47N 71°5W **83 D13**
Haveri *India* 14°53N 75°24E **45 G2**
Haverstraw *U.S.A.* 41°12N 73°58W **83 E11**
Havirga *Mongolia* 45°41N 113°5E **32 B7**
Havířov *Czech Rep.* 49°46N 18°20E **17 D10**
Havlíčkův Brod
Czech Rep. 49°36N 15°33E **16 D8**
Havre *U.S.A.* 48°33N 109°41W **76 B9**
Havre-Aubert *Canada* 47°12N 61°56W **73 C7**
Havre-St.-Pierre *Canada* 50°18N 63°33W **73 B7**
Haw → *U.S.A.* 35°36N 79°3W **85 D15**
Hawai'i *U.S.A.* 19°30N 155°30W **75 M8**
Hawai'i □ *U.S.A.* 19°30N 156°30W **75 M8**
Hawaiian Is. *Pac. Oc.* 20°30N 156°0W **65 E12**
Hawaiian Ridge *Pac. Oc.* 24°0N 165°0W **65 E11**
Hawarden *U.S.A.* 43°0N 96°29W **80 D5**
Hawea, L. *N.Z.* 44°28S 169°19E **59 F2**
Hawera *N.Z.* 39°35S 174°19E **59 C5**
Hawi *U.S.A.* 20°14N 155°50W **75 L8**
Hawick *U.K.* 55°26N 2°47W **11 F6**
Hawk Junction *Canada* 48°5N 84°38W **72 C3**
Hawke B. *N.Z.* 39°25S 177°20E **59 C6**
Hawker *Australia* 31°59S 138°22E **63 E2**
Hawke's Bay *Canada* 50°36N 57°10W **73 B8**
Hawkesbury *Canada* 45°37N 74°37W **72 C5**
Hawkesbury I. *Canada* 53°37N 129°3W **70 C3**
Hawkesbury Pt. *Australia* 11°55S 134°5E **62 A1**
Hawkinsville *U.S.A.* 32°17N 83°28W **85 E13**
Hawley *Minn., U.S.A.* 46°53N 96°19W **80 B5**
Hawley *Pa., U.S.A.* 41°28N 75°11W **83 E9**
Ḩawrān, W. → *Iraq* 33°58N 42°34E **46 C4**
Hawsh Mūssá *Lebanon* 33°45N 35°55E **48 B4**
Hawthorne *U.S.A.* 38°32N 118°38W **76 G4**
Hay *Australia* 34°30S 144°51E **63 E3**
Hay → *Australia* 24°50S 138°0E **62 C2**
Hay → *Canada* 60°50N 116°26W **70 A5**
Hay, C. *Australia* 14°5S 129°29E **60 B4**
Hay I. *Canada* 44°53N 80°58W **82 B4**
Hay L. *Canada* 58°50N 118°50W **70 B5**
Hay-on-Wye *U.K.* 52°5N 3°8W **13 E4**
Hay Point *Australia* 21°18S 149°17E **62 C4**
Hay River *Canada* 60°51N 115°44W **70 A5**
Hay Springs *U.S.A.* 42°41N 102°41W **80 D2**
Hayachine-San *Japan* 39°34N 141°29E **28 E10**
Hayastan = Armenia ■
Asia 40°20N 45°0E **19 F7**
Haydān, W. al → *Jordan* 31°29N 35°34E **48 D4**
Hayden *U.S.A.* 40°30N 107°16W **76 F10**
Hayes *U.S.A.* 44°23N 101°1W **80 C3**
Hayes → *Canada* 57°3N 92°12W **72 A1**
Hayes, Mt. *U.S.A.* 63°37N 146°43W **74 C10**
Hayle *U.K.* 50°11N 5°26E **13 G2**
Hayling I. *U.K.* 50°48N 0°59W **13 G7**
Hayrabolu *Turkey* 41°12N 27°5E **23 D12**
Hays *Canada* 50°6N 111°48W **70 C6**
Hays *U.S.A.* 38°53N 99°20W **80 F4**
Haysyn *Ukraine* 48°57N 29°25E **17 D15**
Hayvoron *Ukraine* 48°22N 29°52E **17 D15**
Hayward *Calif., U.S.A.* 37°40N 122°4W **78 H4**
Hayward *Wis., U.S.A.* 46°1N 91°29W **80 B8**
Haywards Heath *U.K.* 51°0N 0°5W **13 G7**
Hazafon □ *Israel* 32°40N 35°20E **48 C4**
Hazar *Turkmenistan* 39°34N 53°16E **19 G9**
Hazārān, Kūh-e *Iran* 29°35N 57°20E **47 D8**
Hazard *U.S.A.* 37°15N 83°12W **81 G12**
Hazaribag *India* 23°58N 85°26E **43 H11**
Hazaribag Road *India* 24°12N 85°57E **43 G11**
Hazelton *Canada* 55°20N 127°42W **70 B3**
Hazelton *U.S.A.* 46°29N 100°17W **80 B3**
Hazen *U.S.A.* 47°18N 101°38W **80 B3**
Hazen, L. *Canada* 81°47N 71°1W **69 A17**
Hazlehurst *Ga., U.S.A.* 31°52N 82°36W **85 F13**
Hazlehurst *Miss., U.S.A.* 31°52N 90°24W **85 F9**
Hazlet *U.S.A.* 40°25N 74°12W **83 F10**
Hazleton *U.S.A.* 40°57N 75°59W **83 F9**
Hazlett, L. *Australia* 21°30S 128°48E **60 D4**
Hazro *Turkey* 38°15N 40°47E **46 B4**
He Xian = Hezhou *China* 24°27N 111°30E **35 E8**
He Xian *China* 31°45N 118°20E **35 B12**
Head of Bight *Australia* 31°30S 131°25E **61 F5**
Head-Smashed-In Buffalo Jump
Canada 49°44N 113°37W **70 D6**
Healdsburg *U.S.A.* 38°37N 122°52W **78 G4**
Healdton *U.S.A.* 34°14N 97°29W **84 D6**
Healesville *Australia* 37°35S 145°30E **63 F4**
Healy *U.S.A.* 63°52N 148°58W **74 C10**
Heany Junction *Zimbabwe* 20°6S 28°54E **57 B4**
Heard I. *Ind. Oc.* 53°6S 72°36E **3 G13**
Hearne *U.S.A.* 30°53N 96°36W **84 F6**
Hearst *Canada* 49°40N 83°41W **72 C3**
Heart → *U.S.A.* 46°46N 100°50W **80 B3**
Heart's Content *Canada* 47°54N 53°27W **73 C9**
Heath, Pte. *Canada* 49°8N 61°40W **73 C7**
Heavener *U.S.A.* 34°53N 94°36W **84 D7**
Hebbronville *U.S.A.* 27°18N 98°41W **84 H5**
Hebei *China* 39°0N 116°0E **32 E9**
Hebei □ *China* 39°0N 116°0E **32 E9**
Hebel *Australia* 28°58S 147°47E **63 D4**
Heber *U.S.A.* 34°30N 110°35W **77 J8**
Heber Springs *U.S.A.* 35°30N 92°2W **84 D8**
Hebgen L. *U.S.A.* 44°52N 111°20W **76 D8**
Hebi *China* 35°57N 114°7E **32 G8**
Hebrides *U.K.* 57°30N 7°0W **6 D4**
Hebrides, Sea of the *U.K.* 57°5N 7°0W **11 D2**

Hebron = Al Khalīl
West Bank 31°32N 35°6E **48 D4**
Hebron *Canada* 58°5N 62°30W **69 F19**
Hebron *N. Dak., U.S.A.* 46°54N 102°3W **80 B2**
Hebron *Nebr., U.S.A.* 40°10N 97°35W **80 E5**
Hecate Str. *Canada* 53°10N 130°30W **70 C2**
Heceta I. *U.S.A.* 55°46N 133°40W **70 B2**
Hechi *China* 24°40N 108°2E **34 E7**
Hechuan *China* 30°2N 106°12E **34 B6**
Hecla *U.S.A.* 45°53N 98°9W **80 C4**
Hecla I. *Canada* 51°10N 96°43W **71 C9**
Hede *Sweden* 62°23N 13°30E **8 E15**
Hedemora *Sweden* 60°18N 15°58E **9 F16**
Heerenveen *Neths.* 52°57N 5°55E **15 B5**
Heerhugowaard *Neths.* 52°40N 4°51E **15 B4**
Heerlen *Neths.* 50°55N 5°58E **15 D5**
Ḥefa *Israel* 32°46N 35°0E **48 C4**
Ḥefa □ *Israel* 32°40N 35°0E **48 C4**
Hefei *China* 31°52N 117°18E **35 B11**
Hefeng *China* 29°55N 109°52E **34 C7**
Hegang *China* 47°20N 130°19E **31 B16**
Heidelberg *Germany* 49°24N 8°42E **16 D5**
Heidelberg *S. Africa* 34°6S 20°59E **56 E3**
Heilbron *S. Africa* 26°30S 28°21E **57 C4**
Heihe *China* 50°10N 127°30E **31 A14**
Heijing *China* 25°22N 101°44E **34 E3**
Heilbron *S. Africa* 27°16S 27°59E **57 C4**
Heilbronn *Germany* 49°9N 9°13E **16 D5**
Heilongjiang □ *China* 48°0N 126°0E **31 B14**
Heilunkiang = Heilongjiang □
China 48°0N 126°0E **31 B14**
Heimaey *Iceland* 63°26N 20°17W **8 E3**
Heinola *Finland* 61°13N 26°2E **8 F22**
Heinze Chaung *Burma* 14°42N 97°52E **38 E1**
Heinze Kyun *Burma* 14°25N 97°45E **38 E1**
Heishan *China* 41°40N 122°5E **33 D12**
Heishui *Liaoning, China* 42°8N 119°30E **33 C10**
Heishui *Sichuan, China* 32°4N 103°2E **34 A4**
Hejaz = Ḥijāz *Si. Arabia* 24°0N 40°0E **46 E3**
Hejian *China* 38°25N 116°5E **32 E9**
Hejiang *China* 28°43N 105°46E **34 C5**
Hejin *China* 35°35N 110°42E **32 G6**
Hekimhan *Turkey* 38°50N 37°55E **46 B3**
Hekla *Iceland* 63°56N 19°35W **8 E4**
Hekou *Gansu, China* 36°10N 103°26E **32 F2**
Hekou *Guangdong, China* 22°13N 112°45E **35 F9**
Hekou *Yunnan, China* 22°30N 103°59E **34 F4**
Helan Shan *China* 38°30N 105°55E **32 E3**
Helen Atoll *Palau* 2°40N 132°0E **37 D8**
Helena *U.S.A.* 46°36N 112°2W **76 C7**
Helena -West Helena
U.S.A. 34°32N 90°36W **85 D9**
Helendale *U.S.A.* 34°44N 117°19W **79 L9**
Helensburgh *U.K.* 56°1N 4°43W **11 E4**
Helensville *N.Z.* 36°41S 174°29E **59 B5**
Helgeland *Norway* 66°7N 13°37E **8 C15**
Helgoland *Germany* 54°10N 7°53E **16 A4**
Heligoland = Helgoland
Germany 54°10N 7°53E **16 A4**
Heligoland B. = Deutsche Bucht
Germany 54°15N 8°0E **16 A5**
Hell Hole Gorge △
Australia 25°31S 144°12E **62 D3**
Hella *Iceland* 63°50N 20°24W **8 E3**
Hellas = Greece ■ *Europe* 40°0N 23°0E **23 E9**
Hellertown *U.S.A.* 40°35N 75°21W **83 F9**
Hellespont = Çanakkale Boğazı
Turkey 40°17N 26°32E **23 D12**
Hellevoetsluis *Neths.* 51°50N 4°8E **15 C4**
Hellin *Spain* 38°31N 1°40W **21 C5**
Hells Canyon △ *U.S.A.* 45°30N 117°45W **76 D5**
Helmand □ *Afghan.* 31°20N 64°0E **40 D4**
Helmand → *Afghan.* 31°12N 61°34E **40 D2**
Helmeringhausen
Namibia 25°54S 16°57E **56 C2**
Helmond *Neths.* 51°29N 5°41E **15 C5**
Helmsdale *U.K.* 58°7N 3°39W **11 C5**
Helmsdale → *U.K.* 58°8N 3°43W **11 C5**
Helong *China* 42°40N 129°0E **33 C15**
Helper *U.S.A.* 39°41N 110°51W **76 G8**
Helsingborg *Sweden* 56°3N 12°42E **9 H15**
Helsingør *Denmark* 56°2N 12°35E **9 H15**
Helston *U.K.* 50°6N 5°17W **13 G2**
Helvellyn *U.K.* 54°32N 3°1W **12 C4**
Helwân *Egypt* 29°50N 31°20E **53 C12**
Hemavati → *India* 12°30N 76°20E **45 H3**
Hemel Hempstead *U.K.* 51°44N 0°28W **13 F7**
Hemet *U.S.A.* 33°45N 116°58W **79 M10**
Hemingford *U.S.A.* 42°19N 103°4W **80 D2**
Hemis △ *India* 34°10N 77°15E **42 B7**
Hemmingford *Canada* 45°3N 73°35W **83 A11**
Hempstead *N.Y., U.S.A.* 40°42N 73°37W **83 F11**
Hempstead *Tex., U.S.A.* 30°6N 96°5W **84 F6**
Hemse *Sweden* 57°15N 18°22E **9 H18**
Henan □ *China* 34°0N 114°0E **32 H8**
Henares → *Spain* 40°24N 3°30W **21 B4**
Henashi-Misaki *Japan* 40°37N 139°51E **28 D9**
Henderson *Argentina* 36°18S 61°43W **94 D3**
Henderson *Ky., U.S.A.* 37°50N 87°35W **80 G10**
Henderson *N.C., U.S.A.* 36°20N 78°25W **85 C15**
Henderson *N.Y., U.S.A.* 43°50N 76°10W **83 C8**
Henderson *Nev., U.S.A.* 36°2N 114°59W **79 K12**
Henderson *Tenn., U.S.A.* 35°26N 88°38W **85 D10**
Henderson *Tex., U.S.A.* 32°9N 94°48W **84 E7**
Henderson I. *Pac. Oc.* 24°22S 128°19W **65 K15**
Hendersonville N.C.,
U.S.A. 35°19N 82°28W **85 D13**
Hendersonville Tenn.,
U.S.A. 36°18N 86°37W **85 D11**
Hendijān *Iran* 30°14N 49°43E **47 D6**
Hendorābī *Iran* 26°40N 53°37E **47 E7**
Heng Jiang → *China* 24°40N 104°25E **34 E5**
Heng Xian *China* 22°40N 109°17E **34 F7**
Hengch'un *Taiwan* 22°0N 120°44E **35 F13**
Hengdaohezi *China* 44°52N 129°0E **33 B15**

126 Hengduan Shan
INDEX TO WORLD MAPS

Hengduan Shan China 28°30N 98°50E 34 C2
Hengelo Neths. 52°16N 6°48E 15 B6
Henggang China 22°39N 114°12E 31 a
Hengmen China 22°33N 113°35E 31 a
Hengshan Hunan, China 27°16N 112°45E 35 D9
Hengshan Shaanxi, China 37°58N 109°5E 32 F5
Hengshui China 37°41N 115°40E 32 F8
Hengyang China 26°59N 112°22E 35 D9
Henley-on-Thames U.K. 51°32N 0°54W 13 F7
Henlopen, C. U.S.A. 38°48N 75°6W 81 F16
Hennenman S. Africa 27°59S 27°1E 56 C4
Hennessey U.S.A. 36°6N 97°54W 84 C6
Henri Pittier △ Venezuela 10°26N 67°37W 89 D6
Henrietta N.Y., U.S.A. 43°4N 77°37W 82 C7
Henrietta Tex., U.S.A. 33°49N 98°12W 84 E5
Henrietta, Ostrov = Genriyetty, Ostrov Russia 77°6N 156°30E 27 B16
Henrietta Maria, C. Canada 55°9N 82°20W 72 A3
Henry U.S.A. 41°7N 89°22W 80 E9
Henry Ice Rise Antarctica 80°35S 62°0W 5 E17
Henry Lawrence I. India 12°9N 93°5E 45 H11
Henryetta U.S.A. 35°27N 95°59W 84 D7
Henryville Canada 45°8N 73°11W 83 A11
Hensall Canada 43°26N 81°30W 82 C3
Hentiesbaai Namibia 22°8S 14°18E 56 B1
Hentiyn Nuruu Mongolia 48°30N 108°30E 31 B10
Henty Australia 35°30S 147°3E 63 F4
Henzada Burma 17°38N 95°26E 41 L19
Heping China 24°29N 115°0E 35 E10
Heppner U.S.A. 45°21N 119°33W 76 D4
Hepu China 21°40N 109°12E 34 G7
Hepworth Canada 44°37N 81°9W 82 B3
Heqing China 26°37N 100°11E 34 D3
Hequ China 39°20N 111°15E 32 E6
Héraðsflói Iceland 65°42N 14°12W 8 D6
Héraðsvötn → Iceland 65°45N 19°25W 8 D4
Heraklion = Iraklio Greece 35°20N 25°12E 23 G11
Herald Cays Australia 16°58S 149°9E 62 B4
Herāt Afghan. 34°20N 62°7E 40 B3
Herāt □ Afghan. 35°0N 62°0E 40 B3
Herbert Canada 50°30N 107°10W 71 C7
Herbert → Australia 18°31S 146°17E 62 B4
Herbertabad India 11°43N 92°37E 45 J11
Herberton Australia 17°20S 145°25E 62 B4
Herbertsdale S. Africa 34°1S 21°46E 56 D3
Herceg-Novi Montenegro 42°30N 18°33E 23 C8
Herchmer Canada 57°22N 94°10W 71 B10
Herðubreið Iceland 65°11N 16°21W 8 D5
Hereford U.K. 52°4N 2°43W 13 E5
Hereford U.S.A. 34°49N 102°24W 84 D3
Herefordshire □ U.K. 52°8N 2°40W 13 E5
Herentals Belgium 51°12N 4°51E 15 C4
Herford Germany 52°7N 8°39E 16 B5
Herington U.S.A. 38°40N 96°57W 80 F5
Herkimer U.S.A. 43°2N 74°59W 83 D10
Herlen → Asia 48°48N 117°0E 31 B12
Herlong U.S.A. 40°8N 120°8W 78 E6
Herm U.K. 49°30N 2°28W 13 H5
Hermann U.S.A. 38°42N 91°27W 80 F8
Hermannsburg Australia 23°57S 132°45E 60 D5
Hermanus S. Africa 34°27S 19°12E 56 D2
Hermidale Australia 31°30S 146°42E 63 E4
Hermiston U.S.A. 45°51N 119°17W 76 D4
Hermon Canada 45°6N 77°37W 82 A7
Hermon U.S.A. 44°28N 75°14W 83 B9
Hermon, Mt. = Shaykh, J. ash Lebanon 33°25N 35°50E 48 B4
Hermosillo Mexico 29°10N 111°0W 86 B2
Hernád → Hungary 47°56N 21°8E 17 D11
Hernandarias Paraguay 25°20S 54°40W 95 B5
Hernandez U.S.A. 36°24N 120°46W 78 J6
Hernando Argentina 32°28S 63°40W 94 C3
Hernando U.S.A. 34°50N 90°0W 85 D10
Herndon U.S.A. 40°43N 76°51W 82 F8
Herne Bay U.K. 51°21N 1°8E 13 F9
Herning Denmark 56°8N 8°58E 9 H13
Heroica Caborca = Caborca Mexico 30°37N 112°6W 86 A2
Heroica Nogales = Nogales Mexico 31°19N 110°56W 86 A2
Heron Bay Canada 48°40N 86°25W 72 C2
Heron I. Australia 23°27S 151°55E 62 C5
Herreid U.S.A. 45°50N 100°4W 80 C3
Herrin U.S.A. 37°48N 89°2W 80 G9
Herriot Canada 56°22N 101°16W 71 B8
Herschel I. Canada 69°35N 139°5W 4 C1
Hershey U.S.A. 40°17N 76°39W 83 F8
Herstal Belgium 50°40N 5°38E 15 D5
Hertford U.K. 51°48N 0°4W 13 F7
Hertfordshire □ U.K. 51°51N 0°5W 13 F7
's-Hertogenbosch Neths. 51°42N 5°17E 15 C5
Hertzogville S. Africa 28°9S 25°30E 56 C4
Hervey B. Australia 25°0S 152°52E 62 C5
Herzliyya Israel 32°10N 34°50E 48 C3
Ḩeşār Fārs, Iran 29°52N 50°16E 47 D6
Ḩeşār Markazī, Iran 35°50N 49°12E 47 C6
Heshan Guangdong, China 22°34N 113°4E 35 F9
Heshan Guangxi Zhuangzu, China 23°50N 108°53E 34 F7
Heshui China 35°48N 108°0E 32 G5
Heshun China 37°22N 113°32E 32 F7
Hesperia U.S.A. 34°25N 117°18W 79 L9
Hesse = Hessen □ Germany 50°30N 9°0E 16 C5
Hessen □ Germany 50°30N 9°0E 16 C5
Hetauda Nepal 27°25N 85°2E 43 F11
Hetch Hetchy Aqueduct U.S.A. 37°29N 122°19W 78 H5
Hetta Enontekiö Finland 68°23N 23°37E 8 B20
Hettinger U.S.A. 46°0N 102°42W 80 B2
Heuksando S. Korea 34°40N 125°30E 33 G13
Heunghae S. Korea 36°12N 129°21E 33 F15
Heuvelton U.S.A. 44°37N 75°25W 83 B9
Hewitt U.S.A. 31°28N 97°12W 84 F6
Hexham U.K. 54°58N 2°4W 12 C5
Hexi Yunnan, China 24°9N 102°38E 34 E4
Hexi Zhejiang, China 27°58N 119°38E 35 D12
Hexigten Qi China 43°18N 117°30E 33 C9
Ḩeydarābād Iran 30°33N 55°38E 47 D7
Heysham U.K. 54°3N 2°53W 12 C5
Heyuan China 23°39N 114°40E 35 F10
Heywood Australia 38°8S 141°37E 63 F3
Heze China 35°14N 115°20E 32 G8
Hezhang China 27°8N 104°41E 34 D5
Hezhou China 24°27N 111°30E 35 E8
Hi Vista U.S.A. 34°45N 117°46W 79 L9
Hiawatha U.S.A. 39°51N 95°32W 80 F6
Hibbing U.S.A. 47°25N 92°56W 80 B7
Hibernia Reef Australia 12°0S 123°23E 60 B3
Hickman U.S.A. 36°34N 89°11W 80 G9
Hickory U.S.A. 35°44N 81°21W 85 D14
Hicks, Pt. Australia 37°49S 149°17E 63 F4
Hicks L. Canada 61°25N 100°0W 71 A9
Hicksville U.S.A. 40°46N 73°32W 83 F11
Hida-Gawa → Japan 35°26N 137°3E 29 G8
Hida-Sammyaku Japan 36°30N 137°40E 29 F8
Hidaka Japan 42°30N 142°10E 28 C11
Hidaka-Sammyaku Japan 42°35N 142°45E 28 C11
Hidalgo □ Mexico 20°30N 99°0W 87 C5
Hidalgo del Parral Mexico 26°56N 105°40W 86 B3
Hierro Canary Is. 27°44N 18°0W 52 C2
Higashiajima-San Japan 37°40N 140°10E 28 F10
Higashiōsaka Japan 34°39N 135°37E 29 G7
Higgins U.S.A. 36°7N 100°2W 84 C4
Higgins Corner U.S.A. 39°2N 121°5W 78 F5
High Bridge U.S.A. 40°40N 74°54W 83 F10
High Desert U.S.A. 43°40N 120°20W 76 E3
High Island Res. China 22°22N 114°21E 31 a
High Level Canada 58°31N 117°8W 70 B5
High Point U.S.A. 35°57N 80°0W 85 D15
High Prairie Canada 55°30N 116°30W 70 B5
High River Canada 50°30N 113°50W 70 C6
High Tatra = Tatry Slovak Rep. 49°20N 20°0E 17 D11
High Veld Africa 27°0S 27°0E 50 J6
High Wycombe U.K. 51°37N 0°45W 13 F7
Highland □ U.K. 57°17N 4°21W 11 D4
Highland Park U.S.A. 42°11N 87°48W 80 D10
Highmore U.S.A. 44°31N 99°27W 80 C4
Highrock L. Canada 55°45N 100°30W 71 B8
Higüey Dom. Rep. 18°37N 68°42W 89 C6
Hiiumaa Estonia 58°50N 22°45E 9 G20
Ḩijārah, Şaḩrā' al Iraq 30°25N 44°30E 46 D5
Ḩijāz Si. Arabia 24°0N 40°0E 46 E3
Hijo = Tagum Phil. 7°33N 125°53E 37 C7
Hikari Japan 33°58N 131°58E 29 H5
Hikkaduwa Sri Lanka 6°8N 80°6E 45 L5
Hiko U.S.A. 37°32N 115°14W 78 H11
Hikone Japan 35°15N 136°10E 29 G8
Hikurangi Gisborne, N.Z. 37°55S 178°4E 59 C6
Hikurangi Northland, N.Z. 35°36S 174°17E 59 A5
Hildesheim Germany 52°9N 9°56E 16 B5
Hill → Australia 30°23S 115°3E 61 F2
Hill City Idaho, U.S.A. 43°18N 115°3W 76 E6
Hill City Kans., U.S.A. 39°22N 99°51W 80 F4
Hill City Minn., U.S.A. 46°59N 93°36W 80 B7
Hill City S. Dak., U.S.A. 43°56N 103°35W 80 D2
Hill Island L. Canada 60°30N 109°50W 71 A7
Hillaby, Mt. Barbados 13°12N 59°35W 89 g
Hillcrest Barbados 13°13N 59°31W 89 g
Hillegom Neths. 52°18N 4°35E 15 B4
Hillsboro Kans., U.S.A. 38°21N 97°12W 80 F5
Hillsboro N. Dak., U.S.A. 47°26N 97°3W 80 B5
Hillsboro Ohio, U.S.A. 39°12N 83°37W 81 F12
Hillsboro Oreg., U.S.A. 45°31N 122°59W 78 E4
Hillsboro Tex., U.S.A. 32°1N 97°8W 84 E6
Hillsborough Grenada 12°28N 61°28W 89 D7
Hillsborough U.S.A. 43°7N 71°54W 83 C13
Hillsborough Channel Australia 20°56S 149°15E 62 b
Hillsdale Mich., U.S.A. 41°56N 84°38W 81 E11
Hillsdale N.Y., U.S.A. 42°11N 73°32W 83 D11
Hillsport Canada 49°27N 85°34W 72 C2
Hillston Australia 33°30S 145°31E 63 E4
Hilo U.S.A. 19°44N 155°5W 75 M8
Hilton U.S.A. 43°17N 77°48W 82 C7
Hilton Head Island U.S.A. 32°13N 80°45W 85 E14
Hilversum Neths. 52°14N 5°10E 15 B5
Himachal Pradesh □ India 31°30N 77°0E 42 D7
Himalaya Asia 29°0N 84°0E 43 E11
Himalchuli Nepal 28°27N 84°38E 43 E11
Himatnagar India 23°37N 72°57E 42 H5
Himeji Japan 34°50N 134°40E 29 G7
Himi Japan 36°50N 136°55E 29 F8
Ḩimş Syria 34°40N 36°45E 48 A5
Ḩimş □ Syria 34°30N 37°0E 48 A6
Hin Khom, Laem Thailand 9°25N 99°56E 39 b
Hinche Haiti 19°9N 72°1W 89 C5
Hinchinbrook I. Australia 18°20S 146°15E 62 B4
Hinchinbrook Island △ Australia 18°14S 146°6E 62 B4
Hinckley U.K. 52°33N 1°22W 13 E6
Hinckley U.S.A. 46°1N 92°56W 80 B7
Hindaun India 26°44N 77°5E 42 F7
Hindmarsh, L. Australia 36°5S 141°55E 63 F3
Hindol India 20°40N 85°10E 44 D7
Hindu Bagh Pakistan 30°56N 67°50E 42 D2
Hindu Kush Asia 36°0N 71°0E 40 B7
Hindupur India 13°49N 77°32E 45 H3
Hines Creek Canada 56°20N 118°40W 70 B5
Hinesville U.S.A. 31°51N 81°36W 85 F14
Hinganghat India 20°30N 78°52E 44 D4
Hingham U.S.A. 48°33N 110°25W 76 B8
Hingir India 21°57N 83°41E 43 J10
Hingoli India 19°41N 77°15E 44 E3
Hinna = Imi Ethiopia 6°28N 42°10E 49 F3
Hinnøya Norway 68°35N 15°50E 8 B16
Hinojosa del Duque Spain 38°30N 5°9W 21 C3
Hinsdale U.S.A. 42°47N 72°29W 83 D12
Hinthada = Henzada Burma 17°38N 95°26E 41 L19
Hinton Canada 53°26N 117°34W 70 C5
Hinton U.S.A. 37°40N 80°54W 81 G13
Hios = Chios Greece 38°27N 26°9E 23 E12
Hirado Japan 33°22N 129°33E 29 H4
Hirakud Dam India 21°32N 83°45E 44 D6
Hiran → India 23°6N 79°21E 43 H8
Hirapur India 24°22N 79°13E 43 G8
Hirara = Miyakojima Japan 24°48N 125°17E 29 M2
Hiratsuka Japan 35°19N 139°21E 29 G9
Hirekerur India 14°28N 75°23E 45 G2
Hiroo Japan 42°17N 143°19E 28 C11
Hirosaki Japan 40°34N 140°28E 28 D10
Hiroshima Japan 34°24N 132°30E 29 G6
Hiroshima □ Japan 34°50N 133°0E 29 G6
Hisar India 29°12N 75°45E 42 E6
Hisb, Sha'ib = Ḩasb, W. → Iraq 31°45N 44°17E 46 D5
Ḩismá Si. Arabia 28°30N 36°0E 46 D3
Hispaniola W. Indies 19°0N 71°0W 89 C5
Hīt Iraq 33°38N 42°49E 46 C4
Hita Japan 33°20N 130°58E 29 H5
Hitachi Japan 36°36N 140°39E 29 F10
Hitchin U.K. 51°58N 0°16W 13 F7
Hitiaa Tahiti 17°36S 149°18W 59 d
Hitoyoshi Japan 32°13N 130°45E 29 H5
Hitra Norway 63°30N 8°45E 8 E13
Hiva Oa French Polynesia 9°45S 139°0W 65 H14
Hixon Canada 53°25N 122°35W 70 C4
Ḩiyyon, N. → Israel 30°25N 35°10E 48 E4
Hjalmar L. Canada 61°33N 109°25W 71 A7
Hjälmaren Sweden 59°18N 15°40E 9 G16
Hjørring Denmark 57°29N 9°59E 9 H13
Hjort Trench S. Ocean 58°0S 157°30E 5 B10
Hkakabo Razi Burma 28°25N 97°23E 34 C1
Hkamti Burma 26°0N 95°39E 41 G19
Hlobane S. Africa 27°42S 31°0E 57 C5
Hluhluwe S. Africa 28°1S 32°15E 57 C5
Hluhluwe ⌓ S. Africa 22°10S 32°5E 57 B5
Hlyboka Ukraine 48°5N 25°56E 17 D13
Ho Ghana 6°37N 0°27E 52 G6
Ho Chi Minh City = Thanh Pho Ho Chi Minh Vietnam 10°58N 106°40E 39 G6
Ho Hoa Binh Vietnam 20°50N 105°0E 34 G5
Ho Thac Ba Vietnam 21°42N 105°1E 38 A5
Ho Thuong Vietnam 19°32N 105°48E 38 C5
Hoa Binh Vietnam 20°50N 105°20E 34 G5
Hoa Hiep Vietnam 11°34N 105°51E 39 G5
Hoai Nhon Vietnam 14°28N 109°1E 38 E7
Hoang Lien △ Vietnam 21°30N 105°32E 38 B5
Hoang Lien Son Vietnam 22°0N 104°0E 34 F4
Hoanib → Namibia 19°27S 12°46E 56 A2
Hoare B. Canada 65°17N 62°30W 69 D19
Hoarusib → Namibia 19°3S 12°36E 56 A2
Hobart Australia 42°50S 147°21E 63 G4
Hobart U.S.A. 35°1N 99°6W 84 D5
Hobbs U.S.A. 32°42N 103°8W 77 K12
Hobbs Coast Antarctica 74°50S 131°0W 5 D14
Hobe Sound U.S.A. 27°4N 80°8W 85 H14
Hobro Denmark 56°39N 9°46E 9 H13
Hoburgen Sweden 56°55N 18°7E 9 H18
Hobyo Somalia 5°25N 48°30E 49 F4
Hochfeld Namibia 21°28S 17°58E 56 B2
Hodaka-Dake Japan 36°17N 137°39E 29 F8
Hodeida = Al Ḩudaydah Yemen 14°50N 43°0E 49 E3
Hodgeville Canada 50°7N 106°58W 71 C7
Hodgson Canada 51°13N 97°36W 71 C9
Hódmezővásárhely Hungary 46°28N 20°22E 17 E11
Hodna, Chott el Algeria 35°26N 4°43E 52 A6
Hodonín Czech Rep. 48°50N 17°10E 17 D9
Hoek van Holland Neths. 52°0N 4°7E 15 C4
Hoengseong S. Korea 37°29N 127°59E 33 F14
Hoeryong N. Korea 42°30N 129°45E 33 C15
Hoeyang N. Korea 38°43N 127°36E 33 E14
Hof Germany 50°19N 11°55E 16 C6
Hofmeyr S. Africa 31°39S 25°50E 56 D4
Höfn Iceland 64°15N 15°13W 8 D6
Hofors Sweden 60°31N 16°15E 9 F17
Hofsjökull Iceland 64°49N 18°48W 8 D4
Hōfu Japan 34°3N 131°34E 29 G5
Hogan Group Australia 39°13S 147°1E 63 F4
Hogarth, Mt. Australia 21°48S 136°58E 62 C2
Hoge Kempen △ Belgium 51°6N 5°35E 15 C5
Hoge Veluwe △ Neths. 52°5N 5°46E 15 B5
Hogenakai Falls India 12°6N 77°50E 45 H3
Hoggar = Ahaggar Algeria 23°0N 6°30E 52 D7
Hogsty Reef Bahamas 21°41N 73°48W 89 B5
Hoh → U.S.A. 47°45N 124°29W 78 C2
Hoh Xil Shan China 36°30N 89°0E 30 D6
Hohenwald U.S.A. 35°33N 87°33W 85 D11
Hoher Rhön = Rhön Germany 50°24N 9°58E 16 C5
Hohes Venn Belgium 50°30N 6°5E 15 D6
Hohhot China 40°52N 111°40E 32 D6
Hoi An Vietnam 15°53N 108°19E 38 E7
Hoi Xuan Vietnam 20°25N 105°9E 34 G5
Hoisington U.S.A. 38°31N 98°47W 80 F4
Hōjō Japan 33°58N 132°46E 29 H6
Hokianga Harbour N.Z. 35°31S 173°22E 59 A4
Hokitika N.Z. 42°42S 171°0E 59 E3
Hokkaidō □ Japan 43°30N 143°0E 28 C11
Hokuto Japan 41°49N 140°39E 28 D10
Holalkere India 14°2N 76°11E 45 G3
Holbrook Australia 35°42S 147°18E 63 F4
Holbrook U.S.A. 34°54N 110°10W 77 J8
Holcomb U.S.A. 42°54N 77°25W 82 D7
Holden U.S.A. 39°6N 112°16W 76 G7
Holdenville U.S.A. 35°5N 96°24W 84 D6
Holdrege U.S.A. 40°26N 99°23W 80 E4
Hole-Narsipur India 12°48N 76°16E 45 H3
Holetown Barbados 13°11N 59°38W 89 g
Holguín Cuba 20°50N 76°20W 88 B4
Hollams Bird I. Namibia 24°40S 14°30E 56 B1
Holland = Netherlands ■ Europe 52°0N 5°30E 15 C5
Holland Mich., U.S.A. 42°47N 86°7W 80 D10
Holland N.Y., U.S.A. 42°38N 78°32W 82 D6
Holland Centre Canada 44°23N 80°47W 82 B4
Holland Patent U.S.A. 43°14N 75°15W 83 C9
Hollandale U.S.A. 33°10N 90°51W 85 E9
Holley U.S.A. 43°14N 78°2W 82 C6
Hollidaysburg U.S.A. 40°26N 78°24W 82 F6
Hollis U.S.A. 34°41N 99°55W 84 D5
Hollister Calif., U.S.A. 36°51N 121°24W 78 J5
Hollister Idaho, U.S.A. 42°21N 114°35W 76 E6
Holly Hill U.S.A. 29°16N 81°3W 85 G14
Holly Springs U.S.A. 34°46N 89°27W 85 D10
Hollywood Ireland 53°6N 6°35W 10 B6
Holman Canada 70°44N 117°44W 68 C8
Hólmavík Iceland 65°42N 21°40W 8 D3
Holmen U.S.A. 43°58N 91°15W 80 D8
Holmes Reefs Australia 16°27S 148°0E 62 B4
Holmsund Sweden 63°41N 20°20E 8 E19
Holon Israel 32°0N 34°46E 48 C3
Holroyd → Australia 14°10S 141°36E 62 A3
Holstebro Denmark 56°22N 8°37E 9 H13
Holsworthy U.K. 50°48N 4°22W 13 G3
Holton Canada 54°31N 57°12W 73 B8
Holton U.S.A. 39°28N 95°44W 80 F6
Holtville U.S.A. 32°49N 115°23W 79 N11
Holwerd Neths. 53°22N 5°54E 15 A5
Holy Cross U.S.A. 62°12N 159°46W 74 C8
Holy I. Anglesey, U.K. 53°17N 4°37W 12 D3
Holy I. Northumberland, U.K. 55°40N 1°47W 12 B6
Holyhead U.K. 53°18N 4°38W 12 D3
Holyoke Colo., U.S.A. 40°35N 102°18W 76 F12
Holyoke Mass., U.S.A. 42°12N 72°37W 83 D12
Holyrood Canada 47°27N 53°8W 73 C9
Homalin Burma 24°55N 95°0E 41 G19
Homand Iran 32°28N 59°37E 47 C8
Homathko → Canada 51°0N 124°56W 70 C4
Hombori Mali 15°20N 1°38W 52 E5
Home B. Canada 68°40N 67°10W 69 D18
Home Hill Australia 19°43S 147°25E 62 B4
Home Reef Tonga 18°59S 174°47W 59 c
Homedale U.S.A. 43°37N 116°56W 76 E5
Homer Alaska, U.S.A. 59°39N 151°33W 68 F1
Homer La., U.S.A. 32°48N 93°4W 84 E8
Homer N.Y., U.S.A. 42°38N 76°10W 83 D8
Homer City U.S.A. 40°32N 79°10W 82 F5
Homestead Australia 20°20S 145°40E 62 C4
Homestead U.S.A. 25°28N 80°29W 85 J14
Homestead ⌓ U.S.A. 40°17N 96°50W 80 E5
Homnabad India 17°45N 77°11E 44 F3
Homoine Mozam. 23°55S 35°8E 57 B6
Homs = Ḩimş Syria 34°40N 36°45E 48 A5
Homyel Belarus 52°28N 31°0E 17 B16
Hon Chong Vietnam 10°25N 104°30E 39 G5
Hon Hai Vietnam 10°0N 109°0E 39 H7
Hon Me Vietnam 19°23N 105°56E 38 C5
Honan = Henan □ China 34°0N 114°0E 32 H8
Honavar India 14°17N 74°27E 45 G2
Honbetsu Japan 43°7N 143°37E 28 C11
Honcut U.S.A. 39°20N 121°32W 78 F5
Honda, Bahía Cuba 22°54N 83°10W 88 B3
Hondeklipbaai S. Africa 30°19S 17°17E 56 D2
Hondo Japan 32°27N 130°12E 29 H5
Hondo U.S.A. 29°21N 99°9W 84 G5
Hondo, Rio → Belize 18°25N 88°21W 87 D7
Honduras ■ Cent. Amer. 14°40N 86°30W 88 D2
Honduras, G. de Caribbean 16°50N 87°0W 88 C2
Hønefoss Norway 60°10N 10°18E 9 F14
Honesdale U.S.A. 41°34N 75°16W 83 E9
Honey Harbour Canada 44°52N 79°49W 82 B5
Honey L. U.S.A. 40°15N 120°19W 78 E6
Honfleur France 49°25N 0°13E 20 B4
Hong → Vietnam 20°16N 106°34E 38 B5
Hong Gai Vietnam 20°57N 107°5E 34 G6
Hong He → China 32°25N 115°35E 32 H8
Hong Hu China 29°54N 113°24E 35 C9
Hong Kong □ China 22°11N 114°14E 31 a
Hong Kong Int. ✈ (HKG) China 22°19N 113°57E 31 a
Hong'an China 31°20N 114°40E 35 B10
Hongcheon S. Korea 37°44N 127°53E 33 F14
Honghai Wan China 22°40N 115°0E 35 F10
Honghe China 23°25N 102°25E 34 F4
Honghu China 29°50N 113°30E 35 C9
Hongjiang China 27°7N 109°59E 34 D7
Hongliu He → China 38°0N 109°50E 32 F5
Hongor Mongolia 45°45N 112°50E 32 B7
Hongseong S. Korea 36°37N 126°38E 33 F14
Hongshan China 36°38N 117°58E 33 F9
Hongshui He → China 23°48N 109°30E 34 F7
Hongtong China 36°16N 111°40E 32 F6
Honguedo, Détroit d' Canada 49°15N 64°0W 73 C7
Hongwon N. Korea 40°0N 127°56E 33 E14
Hongya China 29°57N 103°22E 34 C4
Hongyuan China 32°51N 102°40E 34 A4
Hongze Hu China 33°15N 118°35E 33 H10
Honiara Solomon Is. 9°27S 159°57E 58 B8
Honiton U.K. 50°47N 3°11W 13 G4
Honjō = Yurihonjō Japan 39°23N 140°3E 28 E10
Honnali India 14°15N 75°40E 45 G2
Honningsvåg Norway 70°59N 25°59E 8 A21
Honolulu U.S.A. 21°19N 157°52W 75 L8
Honshū Japan 36°0N 138°0E 28 F9
Hood, Mt. U.S.A. 45°23N 121°42W 76 D3
Hood, Pt. Australia 34°23S 119°34E 61 F2
Hood River U.S.A. 45°43N 121°31W 76 D3
Hoodsport U.S.A. 47°24N 123°9W 78 C3
Hoogeveen Neths. 52°44N 6°28E 15 B6
Hoogezand-Sappemeer Neths. 53°9N 6°45E 15 A6
Hooghly = Hugli → India 21°56N 88°4E 43 J13
Hooghly-Chinsura = Chunchura India 22°53N 88°27E 43 H13
Hook Hd. Ireland 52°7N 6°56W 10 D5
Hook I. Australia 20°4S 149°0E 62 b
Hook of Holland = Hoek van Holland Neths. 52°0N 4°7E 15 C4
Hooker U.S.A. 36°52N 101°13W 84 C4
Hooker Creek = Lajamanu Australia 18°23S 130°38E 60 C5
Hooker Creek ✿ Australia 18°6S 130°23E 60 C5
Hoonah U.S.A. 58°7N 135°27W 70 B1
Hooper Bay U.S.A. 61°32N 166°6W 74 C6
Hoopeston U.S.A. 40°28N 87°40W 80 E10
Hoopstad S. Africa 27°50S 25°55E 56 C4
Hoorn Neths. 52°38N 5°4E 15 B5
Hoover U.S.A. 33°24N 86°49W 85 E11
Hoover Dam U.S.A. 36°1N 114°44W 79 K12
Hooversville U.S.A. 40°9N 78°55W 82 F6
Hop Bottom U.S.A. 41°42N 75°46W 83 E9
Hope Canada 49°25N 121°25W 70 D4
Hope Ariz., U.S.A. 33°43N 113°42W 79 M13
Hope Ark., U.S.A. 33°40N 93°36W 84 E8
Hope, L. S. Austral., Australia 28°24S 139°18E 63 D2
Hope, L. W. Austral., Australia 32°35S 120°15E 61 F3
Hope, Pt. U.S.A. 68°21N 166°47W 66 C3
Hope I. Canada 44°55N 80°11W 82 B4
Hope Town Bahamas 26°35N 76°57W 88 A4
Hope Vale Australia 15°16S 145°20E 62 B4
Hope Vale ✿ Australia 15°8S 145°15E 62 B4
Hopedale Canada 55°28N 60°13W 73 A7
Hopedale U.S.A. 42°8N 71°33W 83 D13
Hopefield S. Africa 33°3S 18°22E 56 D2
Hopei = Hebei □ China 39°0N 116°0E 32 E9
Hopelchén Mexico 19°46N 89°51W 87 D7
Hopetoun Vic., Australia 35°42S 142°22E 63 F3
Hopetoun W. Austral., Australia 33°57S 120°7E 61 F3
Hopetown S. Africa 29°34S 24°3E 56 C3
Hopewell U.S.A. 37°18N 77°17W 81 G15
Hopkins, L. Australia 24°15S 128°35E 60 D4
Hopkinsville U.S.A. 36°52N 87°29W 80 G10
Hopland U.S.A. 38°58N 123°7W 78 G3
Hoquiam U.S.A. 46°59N 123°53W 78 D3
Horana Sri Lanka 6°43N 80°4E 45 L5
Hordern Hills Australia 20°15S 130°0E 60 D5
Horinger China 40°28N 111°48E 32 D6
Horizontina Brazil 27°37S 54°19W 95 B5
Horlick Mts. Antarctica 84°0S 102°0W 5 E15
Horlivka Ukraine 48°19N 38°5E 19 E6
Hormak Iran 29°58N 60°51E 47 D9
Hormoz Iran 27°35N 55°0E 47 E7
Hormoz, Jaz.-ye Iran 27°8N 56°28E 47 E8
Hormozgān □ Iran 27°30N 56°0E 47 E8
Hormuz, Kūh-e Iran 27°27N 55°10E 47 E7
Hormuz, Str. of The Gulf 26°30N 56°30E 47 E8
Horn Austria 48°39N 15°40E 16 D8
Horn → Canada 61°30N 118°1W 70 A5
Horn, Cape = Hornos, C. de Chile 55°50S 67°30W 96 H3
Horn Head Ireland 55°14N 8°0W 10 A3
Horn I. Australia 10°37S 142°17E 62 A3
Horn Plateau Canada 62°15N 119°15W 70 A5
Hornavan Sweden 66°15N 17°30E 8 C17
Hornbeck U.S.A. 31°20N 93°24W 84 F8
Hornbrook U.S.A. 41°55N 122°33W 76 F2
Horncastle U.K. 53°13N 0°7W 12 D7
Hornell U.S.A. 42°20N 77°40W 82 D7
Hornell L. Canada 62°20N 119°25W 70 A5
Hornepayne Canada 49°14N 84°48W 72 C3
Hornings Mills Canada 44°9N 80°12W 82 B4
Hornitos U.S.A. 37°30N 120°14W 78 H6
Hornos, C. de Chile 55°50S 67°30W 96 H3
Hornsby Australia 33°42S 151°2E 63 B5
Hornsea U.K. 53°55N 0°11W 12 D7
Horobetsu = Noboribetsu Japan 42°24N 141°6E 28 C10
Horodenka Ukraine 48°41N 25°29E 17 D13
Horodok Khmelnytskyy, Ukraine 49°10N 26°34E 17 D14
Horodok Lviv, Ukraine 49°46N 23°32E 17 D12
Horokhiv Ukraine 50°30N 24°45E 17 C13
Horqin Youyi Qianqi China 46°5N 122°3E 33 A12
Horqin Zuoyi Zhongqi China 44°8N 123°18E 33 B12
Horqueta Paraguay 23°15S 56°55W 94 A4
Horse Cr. → U.S.A. 41°57N 103°58W 76 F12
Horse I. Canada 53°20N 99°6W 71 C9
Horse Is. Canada 50°15N 55°50W 73 B8
Horsefly L. Canada 52°25N 121°0W 70 C4
Horseheads U.S.A. 42°10N 76°49W 82 D8
Horsens Denmark 55°52N 9°51E 9 J13
Horseshoe Lake Canada 45°17N 79°51W 82 A5
Horsham Australia 36°44S 142°13E 63 F3
Horsham U.K. 51°4N 0°20W 13 F7
Horta Azores 38°32N 28°38W 52 a
Horten Norway 59°25N 10°32E 9 G14
Horti India 17°7N 75°47E 44 F2
Horton U.S.A. 39°40N 95°32W 80 F6
Horton → Canada 69°56N 126°52W 68 D6
Horwood L. Canada 48°5N 82°20W 72 C3
Hosapete = Hospet India 15°15N 76°20E 45 G3
Hosdrug = Kanhangad India 12°21N 74°58E 45 H2
Hosdurga India 13°49N 76°17E 45 H3
Ḩoseynābād Khuzestān, Iran 32°45N 48°20E 47 C6
Ḩoseynābād Kordestān, Iran 35°33N 47°8E 46 C5
Hoshangabad India 22°45N 77°45E 42 H7
Hoshiarpur India 31°30N 75°58E 42 D6
Hoskote India 13°4N 77°48E 45 H3
Hospet India 15°15N 76°20E 45 G3
Hoste, I. Chile 55°0S 69°0W 96 H3
Hosur India 12°43N 77°49E 45 H3
Hot Thailand 18°8N 98°29E 38 C2
Hot Creek Range U.S.A. 38°40N 116°20W 76 G5
Hot Springs Ark., U.S.A. 34°31N 93°3W 84 D8
Hot Springs S. Dak., U.S.A. 43°26N 103°29W 80 D2
Hot Springs △ U.S.A. 34°31N 93°3W 84 D8
Hotagen Sweden 63°59N 14°12E 8 E16
Hotan China 37°25N 79°55E 30 D4
Hotan He → China 40°22N 80°56E 30 C5
Hotazel S. Africa 27°17S 22°58E 56 C3

Hotchkiss *U.S.A.* 38°48N 107°43W 76 G10
Hotham, C. *Australia* 12°2S 131°18E 60 B5
Hoting *Sweden* 64°8N 16°15E 8 D17
Hotte, Massif de la *Haiti* 18°30N 73°45W 89 C5
Hottentotsbaai *Namibia* 26°8S 14°59E 56 C1
Hou Hai *China* 22°32N 113°56E 31 a
Houei Sai *Laos* 20°18N 100°26E 34 G3
Houffalize *Belgium* 50°8N 5°48E 15 D5
Houghton *Mich., U.S.A.* 47°7N 88°34W 80 B9
Houghton *N.Y., U.S.A.* 42°25N 78°10W 82 D6
Houghton L. *U.S.A.* 44°21N 84°44W 81 C11
Houghton-le-Spring *U.K.* 54°51N 1°28W 12 C6
Houhora Heads *N.Z.* 34°49S 173°9E 59 A4
Houlton *U.S.A.* 46°8N 67°51W 81 B20
Houma *China* 35°36N 111°20E 32 G6
Houma *U.S.A.* 29°36N 90°43W 85 G9
Housatonic → *U.S.A.* 41°10N 73°7W 83 E11
Houston *Canada* 54°25N 126°39W 70 C3
Houston *Mo., U.S.A.* 37°22N 91°58W 80 G8
Houston *Tex., U.S.A.* 29°45N 95°21W 84 G7
Hout = Mogwadi → *S. Africa* 23°4S 29°36E 57 B4
Houtkraal *S. Africa* 30°23S 24°5E 56 D3
Houtman Abrolhos *Australia* 28°43S 113°48E 61 E1
Hovd = Dund-Us *Mongolia* 48°1N 91°38E 30 B7
Hove *U.K.* 50°50N 0°10W 13 G7
Hovenweep ⌂ *U.S.A.* 37°20N 109°0W 77 H9
Hoveyzeh *Iran* 31°27N 48°4E 47 D6
Hövsgöl *Mongolia* 43°37N 109°39E 32 C5
Hövsgöl Nuur *Mongolia* 51°0N 100°30E 30 A9
Howar, Wadi → *Sudan* 17°30N 27°8E 53 E11
Howard *Australia* 25°16S 152°32E 63 D5
Howard *Pa., U.S.A.* 41°1N 77°40W 82 F7
Howard *S. Dak., U.S.A.* 44°1N 97°32W 80 C5
Howe *U.S.A.* 43°48N 113°0W 76 E7
Howe, C. *Australia* 37°30S 150°0E 63 F5
Howe, West Cape *Australia* 35°8S 117°36E 61 G2
Howe I. *Canada* 44°16N 76°17W 83 B8
Howell *U.S.A.* 42°36N 83°56W 81 D12
Howick *Canada* 45°11N 73°51W 83 A11
Howick *S. Africa* 29°28S 30°14E 57 C5
Howick Group *Australia* 14°20S 145°30E 62 A4
Howitt, L. *Australia* 27°40S 138°40E 63 D2
Howland I. *Pac. Oc.* 0°48N 176°38W 64 G10
Höxter *Germany* 51°46N 9°22E 16 C5
Hoy *U.K.* 58°50N 3°15W 11 C5
Høyanger *Norway* 61°13N 6°4E 8 F12
Hoyerswerda *Germany* 51°26N 14°14E 16 C8
Hoylake *U.K.* 53°24N 3°10W 12 D4
Hpa-an = Pa-an *Burma* 16°51N 97°40E 41 L20
Hpunan Pass *Asia* 27°30N 96°55E 41 F20
Hpyu = Pyu *Burma* 18°30N 96°28E 41 K20
Hradec Králové *Czech Rep.* 50°15N 15°50E 16 C8
Hrodna *Belarus* 53°42N 23°52E 17 B12
Hrodzyanka *Belarus* 53°31N 28°42E 17 B15
Hron → *Slovak Rep.* 47°49N 18°45E 17 E10
Hrvatska = Croatia ■ *Europe* 45°20N 16°0E 16 F9
Hrymayliv *Ukraine* 49°20N 26°5E 17 D14
Hsenwi *Burma* 23°22N 97°55E 41 H20
Hsiamen = Xiamen *China* 24°25N 118°4E 35 E12
Hsian = Xi'an *China* 34°15N 109°0E 32 G5
Hsinchu *Taiwan* 24°48N 120°58E 35 E13
Hsinhailien = Lianyungang *China* 34°40N 119°11E 33 G10
Hsinkai = Bhamo *Burma* 24°15N 97°15E 41 G20
Hsinying *Taiwan* 23°21N 120°17E 35 F13
Hsopket *Burma* 23°11N 98°26E 34 F2
Hsüchou = Xuzhou *China* 34°18N 117°10E 33 G9
Htawei = Tavoy *Burma* 14°2N 98°12E 38 E2
Hu Xian *China* 34°8N 108°42E 32 G5
Hua Hin *Thailand* 12°34N 99°58E 38 F2
Hua Muang *Laos* 20°13N 103°52E 38 B4
Hua Shan *China* 34°28N 110°4E 32 G6
Hua Xian *Henan, China* 35°30N 114°30E 32 G8
Hua Xian *Shaanxi, China* 34°30N 109°48E 32 G5
Hua'an *China* 25°1N 117°32E 35 E11
Huab → *Namibia* 20°52S 13°25E 56 A2
Huacheng *China* 24°4N 115°37E 35 E10
Huachinera *Mexico* 30°9N 108°55W 86 A3
Huacho *Peru* 11°10S 77°35W 92 F3
Huade *China* 41°55N 113°59E 32 D7
Huadian *China* 43°0N 126°40E 33 C14
Huadu *China* 23°22N 113°12E 35 F9
Huahine, Î. *French Polynesia* 16°46S 150°58W 65 J12
Huai Hat △ *Thailand* 16°52N 104°17E 38 D5
Huai He → *China* 33°0N 118°30E 35 A12
Huai Kha Khaeng ⌂ *Thailand* 15°20N 98°55E 38 E2
Huai Nam Dang △ *Thailand* 19°30N 98°30E 38 C2
Huai Yot *Thailand* 7°45N 99°37E 39 J2
Huai'an *Hebei, China* 40°30N 114°20E 32 D8
Huai'an *Jiangsu, China* 33°30N 119°10E 33 H10
Huaibei *China* 34°0N 116°48E 32 G9
Huaibin *China* 32°32N 115°27E 35 A10
Huaide = Gongzhuling *China* 43°30N 124°40E 33 C13
Huaidezhen *China* 43°48N 124°50E 33 C13
Huaihua *China* 27°32N 109°57E 34 D7
Huaiji *China* 23°55N 112°12E 35 F9
Huainan *China* 32°38N 116°58E 35 A11
Huaining *China* 30°24N 116°40E 35 B11
Huairen *China* 39°48N 113°20E 32 E7
Huairou *China* 40°20N 116°35E 32 D9
Huaiyang *China* 33°40N 114°52E 32 H8
Huaiyin *China* 33°30N 119°2E 33 H10
Huaiyuan *Anhui, China* 32°55N 117°10E 33 H9
Huaiyuan *Guangxi Zhuangzu, China* 24°31N 108°22E 34 E7
Huajuapán de León *Mexico* 17°48N 97°46W 87 D5
Hualapai Peak *U.S.A.* 35°5N 113°54W 79 K13
Hualien *Taiwan* 23°59N 121°36E 35 E13
Huallaga → *Peru* 5°15S 75°30W 92 E3
Huambo *Angola* 12°42S 15°54E 55 G3
Huan Jiang → *China* 34°28N 109°0E 32 G5
Huan Xian *China* 36°33N 107°7E 32 F4
Huancabamba *Peru* 5°10S 79°15W 92 E3
Huancane *Peru* 15°10S 69°44W 92 G5
Huancavelica *Peru* 12°50S 75°5W 92 F3
Huancayo *Peru* 12°5S 75°12W 92 F3
Huanchaca *Bolivia* 20°15S 66°40W 92 H5
Huang Hai = Yellow Sea *China* 35°0N 123°0E 33 G12
Huang He → *China* 37°55N 118°50E 33 F10
Huang Xian *China* 37°38N 120°30E 33 F11
Huangchuan *China* 32°15N 115°10E 35 A10
Huangdao *China* 36°0N 120°7E 33 G11
Huanggang *China* 30°29N 114°52E 35 B10
Huangguoshu *China* 26°0N 105°40E 34 E5
Huanghua *China* 38°22N 117°20E 33 E9
Huanghuagang *China* 38°20N 117°54E 33 E9
Huangling *China* 35°34N 109°15E 32 G5
Huanglong *China* 35°30N 109°59E 32 G5
Huanglong ⌂ *China* 32°44N 103°50E 34 A4
Huanglongtan *China* 32°40N 110°33E 35 A8
Huangmei *China* 30°5N 115°56E 35 B10
Huangpi *China* 30°50N 114°22E 35 B10
Huangping *China* 26°52N 107°54E 34 D6
Huangshan *Anhui, China* 30°8N 118°9E 35 B12
Huangshan *Anhui, China* 29°42N 118°25E 35 C12
Huangshi *China* 30°10N 115°3E 35 B10
Huangsongdian *China* 43°45N 127°25E 33 C14
Huangyan *China* 28°38N 121°19E 35 C13
Huangyangsi *China* 26°33N 111°39E 35 D8
Huaning *China* 24°17N 102°56E 34 E4
Huanjiang *China* 24°50N 108°18E 34 E7
Huanren *China* 41°23N 125°20E 33 D13
Huantai *China* 36°58N 117°56E 33 F9
Huánuco *Peru* 9°55S 76°15W 92 E3
Huaping *China* 26°46N 101°25E 34 D3
Huaraz *Peru* 9°30S 77°32W 92 E3
Huarmey *Peru* 10°5S 78°5W 92 F3
Huarong *China* 29°29N 112°30E 35 C9
Huascarán, Nevado *Peru* 9°7S 77°37W 92 E3
Huasco *Chile* 28°30S 71°15W 94 B1
Huasco → *Chile* 28°27S 71°13W 94 B1
Huasna *U.S.A.* 35°6N 120°24W 79 K6
Huatabampo *Mexico* 26°50N 109°38W 86 B3
Huauchinango *Mexico* 20°12N 98°3W 87 C5
Huautla de Jiménez *Mexico* 18°8N 96°51W 87 D5
Huaxi *China* 26°25N 106°40E 34 D6
Huayin *China* 34°35N 110°5E 32 G6
Huaying *China* 30°8N 106°44E 34 B6
Huayuan *China* 28°37N 109°29E 34 C7
Huazhou *China* 21°33N 110°33E 35 G8
Hubballi = Hubli *India* 15°22N 75°15E 45 G2
Hubbard *Ohio, U.S.A.* 41°9N 80°34W 82 E4
Hubbard *Tex., U.S.A.* 31°51N 96°48W 84 F6
Hubbard Glacier *Canada* 60°18N 139°22W 68 E4
Hubbart Pt. *Canada* 59°21N 94°41W 71 B10
Hubei □ *China* 31°0N 112°0E 35 B9
Hubli *India* 15°22N 75°15E 45 G2
Huch'ang *N. Korea* 41°25N 127°2E 33 D14
Hucknall *U.K.* 53°3N 1°13W 12 D6
Huddersfield *U.K.* 53°39N 1°47W 12 D6
Hudiksvall *Sweden* 61°43N 17°10E 8 F17
Hudson *Canada* 50°6N 92°9W 72 B1
Hudson *Mass., U.S.A.* 42°23N 71°34W 83 D13
Hudson *N.Y., U.S.A.* 42°15N 73°46W 83 D11
Hudson *Wis., U.S.A.* 44°58N 92°45W 80 C7
Hudson *Wyo., U.S.A.* 42°54N 108°35W 76 E9
Hudson → *U.S.A.* 40°42N 74°2W 83 F10
Hudson, C. *Antarctica* 68°21S 153°45E 5 C10
Hudson Bay *Nunavut, Canada* 60°0N 86°0W 69 F14
Hudson Bay *Sask., Canada* 52°51N 102°23W 71 C8
Hudson Falls *U.S.A.* 43°18N 73°35W 83 C11
Hudson Mts. *Antarctica* 74°32S 99°20W 5 D16
Hudson Str. *Canada* 62°0N 70°0W 69 E18
Hudson's Hope *Canada* 56°0N 121°54W 70 B4
Hue *Vietnam* 16°30N 107°35E 38 D6
Huehuetenango *Guatemala* 15°20N 91°28W 88 C1
Huejúcar *Mexico* 22°21N 103°13W 86 C4
Huelva *Spain* 37°18N 6°57W 21 D2
Huentelauquén *Chile* 31°38S 71°33W 94 C1
Huerta, Sa. de la *Argentina* 31°10S 67°30W 94 C2
Huesca *Spain* 42°8N 0°25W 21 A5
Huetamo *Mexico* 18°35N 100°53W 86 D4
Hugh → *Australia* 25°1S 134°1E 62 D1
Hughenden *Australia* 20°52S 144°10E 62 C3
Hughesville *U.S.A.* 41°14N 76°44W 83 E8
Hugli → *India* 21°56N 88°4E 43 J13
Hugo *Colo., U.S.A.* 39°8N 103°28W 76 G12
Hugo *Okla., U.S.A.* 34°1N 95°31W 84 D7
Hugoton *U.S.A.* 37°11N 101°21W 80 G3
Hui Xian = Huixian *China* 35°27N 113°12E 32 G7
Hui Xian *China* 33°50N 106°4E 32 H4
Hui'an *China* 25°1N 118°43E 35 E12
Hui'anbu *China* 37°28N 106°38E 32 F4
Huichang *China* 25°32N 115°45E 35 E10
Huichapan *Mexico* 20°23N 99°39W 87 C5
Huichon *N. Korea* 40°10N 126°16E 33 D14
Huidong *Guangdong, China* 22°58N 114°43E 35 F10
Huidong *Sichuan, China* 26°34N 102°35E 34 D4
Huifa He → *China* 43°0N 127°50E 33 C14
Huila, Nevado del *Colombia* 3°0N 76°0W 92 C3
Huilai *China* 23°0N 116°18E 35 F11
Huili *China* 26°35N 102°17E 34 D4
Huimin *China* 37°27N 117°28E 33 F9
Huinan *China* 42°40N 126°2E 33 C14
Huinca Renancó *Argentina* 34°51S 64°22W 94 C3
Huining *China* 35°38N 105°0E 32 G3
Huinong *China* 39°5N 106°35E 32 E4
Huishui *China* 26°7N 106°38E 34 D6
Huiting *China* 34°5N 116°5E 32 G9
Huitong *China* 26°51N 109°45E 34 D7
Huixian *China* 35°27N 113°12E 32 G7
Huixtla *Mexico* 15°9N 92°28W 87 D6
Huize *China* 26°24N 103°15E 34 D4
Huizhou *China* 23°0N 114°23E 35 F10
Hukawng Valley *Burma* 26°30N 96°30E 41 F20
Hukeri *India* 16°14N 74°36E 45 F2
Hukou *China* 29°45N 116°21E 35 C11
Hukuntsi *Botswana* 23°58S 21°45E 56 B3
Ḥulayfā' *Si. Arabia* 25°58N 40°45E 46 E4
Hulin *China* 45°48N 132°59E 31 B15
Hulin He → *China* 45°0N 122°10E 33 B12
Hull = Kingston upon Hull *U.K.* 53°45N 0°21W 12 D7
Hull *Canada* 45°26N 75°43W 83 A9
Hull → *U.K.* 53°44N 0°20W 12 D7
Hulst *Neths.* 51°17N 4°2E 15 C4
Huludao *China* 40°45N 120°50E 33 D11
Hulun Nur *China* 49°0N 117°30E 31 B12
Hulunbuir = Hailar *China* 49°10N 119°38E 31 B12
Huma, Tanjung *Malaysia* 5°29N 100°16E 39 c
Humacao *Puerto Rico* 18°9N 65°50W 89 d
Humahuaca *Argentina* 23°10S 65°25W 94 A2
Humaitá *Brazil* 7°35S 63°1W 92 E6
Humaitá *Paraguay* 27°2S 58°31W 94 B4
Humansdorp *S. Africa* 34°2S 24°46E 56 D3
Humbe *Angola* 16°40S 14°55E 56 A1
Humber → *U.K.* 53°42N 0°27W 12 D7
Humboldt *Canada* 52°15N 105°9W 71 C7
Humboldt *Iowa, U.S.A.* 42°44N 94°13W 80 D6
Humboldt *Tenn., U.S.A.* 35°50N 88°55W 85 D10
Humboldt → *U.S.A.* 39°59N 118°36W 76 G4
Humboldt Gletscher = Sermersuaq *Greenland* 79°30N 62°0W 69 B19
Hume *U.S.A.* 36°48N 118°54W 78 J8
Hume, L. *Australia* 36°0S 147°5E 63 F4
Humen *China* 22°50N 113°40E 31 a
Humenné *Slovak Rep.* 48°55N 21°50E 17 D11
Humphreys, Mt. *U.S.A.* 37°17N 118°40W 78 H8
Humphreys Peak *U.S.A.* 35°21N 111°41W 77 J8
Humptulips *U.S.A.* 47°14N 123°57W 78 C3
Hūn *Libya* 29°2N 16°0E 53 C9
Hun Jiang → *China* 40°50N 125°38E 33 D13
Húnaflói *Iceland* 65°50N 20°50W 8 D3
Hunan □ *China* 27°30N 112°0E 35 D9
Hunchun *China* 42°52N 130°28E 33 C16
Hundewali *Pakistan* 31°55N 72°38E 42 D5
Hundred Mile House *Canada* 51°38N 121°18W 70 C4
Hunedoara *Romania* 45°40N 22°50E 17 F12
Hung Yen *Vietnam* 20°39N 106°4E 34 G6
Hunga Ha'apai *Tonga* 20°41S 175°7W 59 c
Hungary ■ *Europe* 47°20N 19°20E 17 E10
Hungary, Plain of *Europe* 47°0N 20°0E 6 F10
Hungerford *Australia* 28°58S 144°24E 63 D3
Hŭngnam *N. Korea* 39°49N 127°45E 33 E14
Hungt'ou Hsü = Lan Yü *Taiwan* 22°4N 121°25E 35 F13
Hunjiang *China* 41°54N 126°26E 33 D14
Hunsberge *Namibia* 27°45S 17°12E 56 C2
Hunsrück *Germany* 49°56N 7°27E 16 D4
Hunstanton *U.K.* 52°56N 0°29E 12 E8
Hunsur *India* 12°16N 76°16E 45 H3
Hunter *U.S.A.* 42°13N 74°13W 83 D10
Hunter I. *Australia* 40°30S 144°45E 63 G3
Hunter I. *Canada* 51°55N 128°0W 70 C3
Hunter Ra. *Australia* 32°45S 150°15E 63 E5
Hunterville *N.Z.* 39°56S 175°35E 59 C5
Huntingburg *U.S.A.* 38°18N 86°57W 80 F10
Huntingdon *U.K.* 52°20N 0°11W 13 E7
Huntingdon *U.S.A.* 40°30N 78°1W 82 F6
Huntington *Ind., U.S.A.* 40°53N 85°30W 81 E11
Huntington *N.Y., U.S.A.* 40°52N 73°26W 83 F11
Huntington *Oreg., U.S.A.* 44°21N 117°16W 76 D5
Huntington *Utah, U.S.A.* 39°20N 110°58W 76 G8
Huntington *W. Va., U.S.A.* 38°25N 82°27W 81 F12
Huntington Beach *U.S.A.* 33°40N 118°5W 79 M9
Huntly *N.Z.* 37°34S 175°11E 59 B5
Huntly *U.K.* 57°27N 2°47W 11 D6
Huntsville *Canada* 45°20N 79°14W 82 A5
Huntsville *Ala., U.S.A.* 34°44N 86°35W 85 D11
Huntsville *Tex., U.S.A.* 30°43N 95°33W 84 F7
Hunyuan *China* 39°42N 113°42E 32 E7
Hunza → *India* 35°54N 74°20E 43 B6
Huo Shan *China* 36°26N 111°52E 32 F6
Huo Xian = Huozhou *China* 36°36N 111°42E 32 F6
Huolin Gol *China* 45°32N 119°38E 33 B10
Huong Khe *Vietnam* 18°13N 105°41E 38 C5
Huonville *Australia* 43°0S 147°5E 63 G4
Huoqiu *China* 32°20N 116°12E 35 A11
Huoshan *China* 31°25N 116°20E 35 B11
Huoshao Dao = Lütao *Taiwan* 22°40N 121°30E 35 F13
Huozhou *China* 36°36N 111°42E 32 F6
Hupeh = Hubei □ *China* 31°0N 112°0E 35 B9
Ḥūr *Iran* 30°50N 57°7E 47 D8
Hurānd *Iran* 38°51N 47°22E 46 B5
Ḥuraymīla *Si. Arabia* 25°8N 46°8E 46 E5
Hurd, C. *Canada* 45°13N 81°44W 82 A3
Hure Qi *China* 42°45N 121°45E 33 C11
Hurghada *Egypt* 27°15N 33°50E 53 C12
Hurley *N. Mex., U.S.A.* 32°42N 108°8W 77 K9
Hurley *Wis., U.S.A.* 46°27N 90°11W 80 B8
Huron *Calif., U.S.A.* 36°12N 120°6W 78 J6
Huron *Ohio, U.S.A.* 41°24N 82°33W 82 E2
Huron *S. Dak., U.S.A.* 44°22N 98°13W 80 C4
Huron, L. *U.S.A.* 44°30N 82°40W 82 B2
Huron East *Canada* 43°37N 81°18W 82 C3
Hurricane *U.S.A.* 37°11N 113°17W 77 H7
Hurunui → *N.Z.* 42°54S 173°18E 59 E4
Húsavík *Iceland* 66°3N 17°21W 8 C5
Huşi *Romania* 46°41N 28°7E 17 E15
Hustadvika *Norway* 63°0N 7°0E 8 E12
Hustontown *U.S.A.* 40°3N 78°2W 82 F6
Hutchinson *Kans., U.S.A.* 38°5N 97°56W 80 F5
Hutchinson *Minn., U.S.A.* 44°54N 94°22W 80 C6
Hutiao Xia *China* 27°13N 100°9E 34 D3
Hutte Sauvage, L. de la *Canada* 56°15N 64°45W 73 A7
Hutton, Mt. *Australia* 25°51S 148°20E 63 D4
Huwaki *Indonesia* 7°55S 126°30E 37 F7
Huy *Belgium* 50°31N 5°15E 15 D5
Huzhou *China* 30°51N 120°8E 35 B13
Huzurabad *India* 18°12N 79°25E 44 E4
Huzurnagar *India* 16°54N 79°53E 44 F4
Hvammstangi *Iceland* 65°24N 20°57W 8 D3
Hvar *Croatia* 43°11N 16°28E 22 C7
Hvítá → *Iceland* 64°30N 21°58W 8 D3
Hwacheon-Cheosuji *S. Korea* 38°5N 127°50E 33 E14
Hwang Ho = Huang He → *China* 37°55N 118°50E 33 F10
Hwange *Zimbabwe* 18°18S 26°30E 55 H5
Hwange △ *Zimbabwe* 19°0S 26°30E 56 A4
Hwlffordd = Haverfordwest *U.K.* 51°48N 4°58W 13 F3
Hyannis *Mass., U.S.A.* 41°39N 70°17W 81 E18
Hyannis *Nebr., U.S.A.* 42°0N 101°46W 80 E3
Hyargas Nuur *Mongolia* 49°0N 93°0E 30 B7
Hydaburg *U.S.A.* 55°15N 132°50W 70 B2
Hyde Park *U.S.A.* 41°47N 73°56W 83 E11
Hyden *Australia* 32°24S 118°53E 61 F2
Hyder *U.S.A.* 55°55N 130°5W 70 B2
Hyderabad *India* 17°22N 78°29E 44 F4
Hyderabad *Pakistan* 25°23N 68°24E 42 G3
Hydra *Greece* 37°20N 23°28E 23 F10
Hyères *France* 43°8N 6°9E 20 E7
Hyères, Îs. d' *France* 43°0N 6°20E 20 E7
Hyesan *N. Korea* 41°20N 128°10E 33 D15
Hyland → *Canada* 59°52N 128°12W 70 B3
Hyndman Peak *U.S.A.* 43°45N 114°8W 76 E6
Hyōgo □ *Japan* 35°15N 134°50E 29 G7
Hyrum *U.S.A.* 41°38N 111°51W 76 F8
Hysham *U.S.A.* 46°18N 107°14W 76 C10
Hythe *U.K.* 51°4N 1°5E 13 F9
Hyūga *Japan* 32°25N 131°35E 29 H5
Hyvinge = Hyvinkää *Finland* 60°38N 24°50E 8 F21
Hyvinkää *Finland* 60°38N 24°50E 8 F21

I

I-n-Gall *Niger* 16°51N 7°1E 52 E7
Iaco → *Brazil* 9°3S 68°34W 92 E5
Ialomiţa → *Romania* 44°42N 27°51E 17 F14
Iaşi *Romania* 47°10N 27°40E 17 E14
Ib → *India* 21°34N 83°48E 43 J10
Iba *Phil.* 15°22N 120°0E 37 A6
Ibadan *Nigeria* 7°22N 3°58E 52 G6
Ibagué *Colombia* 4°20N 75°20W 92 C3
Ibar → *Serbia* 43°43N 20°45E 23 C9
Ibaraki □ *Japan* 36°10N 140°10E 29 F10
Ibarra *Ecuador* 0°21N 78°7W 92 C3
Ibb *Yemen* 14°2N 44°10E 49 E3
Ibenga → *Congo* 2°19N 18°9E 54 D3
Ibera, L. *Argentina* 28°30S 57°9W 94 B4
Iberian Peninsula *Europe* 40°0N 5°0W 6 H5
Iberville *Canada* 45°19N 73°17W 83 A11
Iberville, Mt. d' *Canada* 58°50N 63°50W 69 F19
Ibiá *Brazil* 19°30S 46°30W 93 G9
Ibiapaba, Sa. da *Brazil* 4°0S 41°30W 93 D10
Ibicuí → *Brazil* 29°25S 56°47W 95 B4
Ibicuy *Argentina* 33°55S 59°10W 94 C4
Ibiza = Eivissa *Spain* 38°54N 1°26E 21 C6
Ibonma *Indonesia* 3°29S 133°31E 37 E8
Ibotirama *Brazil* 12°13S 43°12W 93 F10
Ibrāhīm → *Lebanon* 34°4N 35°38E 48 A4
'Ibrī *Oman* 23°14N 56°30E 49 C6
Ibu *Indonesia* 1°35N 127°33E 37 D7
Ibusuki *Japan* 31°12N 130°40E 29 J5
Ica *Peru* 14°0S 75°48W 92 F3
Iça → *Brazil* 2°55S 67°58W 92 D5
Icacos Pt. *Trin. & Tob.* 10°3N 61°57W 93 K15
Içana *Brazil* 0°21N 67°19W 92 C5
Içana → *Brazil* 0°26N 67°19W 92 C5
İçel *Turkey* 36°51N 34°36E 46 B2
Iceland ■ *Europe* 64°45N 19°0W 8 D4
Iceland Basin *Atl. Oc.* 61°0N 19°0W 4 C7
Icelandic Plateau *Arctic* 64°0N 10°0W 4 C7
Ichalkaranji *India* 16°40N 74°33E 44 F2
Ich'ang = Yichang *China* 30°40N 111°20E 35 B8
Ichchapuram *India* 19°10N 84°40E 44 E7
Ichhawar *India* 23°1N 77°1E 42 H7
Ichihara *Japan* 35°28N 140°5E 29 G10
Ichilo → *Bolivia* 15°57S 64°50W 92 G6
Ichinohe *Japan* 40°13N 141°17E 28 D10
Ichinomiya *Japan* 35°18N 136°48E 29 G8
Ichinoseki *Japan* 38°55N 141°8E 28 E10
Içoguz *Turkmenistan* 40°11N 58°24E 26 E6
Icy C. *U.S.A.* 70°20N 161°52W 66 B3
Ida Grove *U.S.A.* 42°21N 95°28W 80 D6
Idabel *U.S.A.* 33°54N 94°50W 84 E7
Idaho □ *U.S.A.* 45°0N 115°0W 76 D6
Idaho City *U.S.A.* 43°50N 115°50W 76 E6
Idaho Falls *U.S.A.* 43°30N 112°2W 76 E7
Idalia △ *Australia* 24°49S 144°36E 62 C3
Idar-Oberstein *Germany* 49°43N 7°16E 16 D4
Idensalmi = Iisalmi *Finland* 63°32N 27°10E 8 E22
Idfû *Egypt* 24°55N 32°49E 53 D12
Ídhra = Hydra *Greece* 37°20N 23°28E 23 F10
Idi *Indonesia* 5°2N 97°37E 36 C1
Idi, Oros = Psiloritis, Oros *Greece* 35°15N 24°45E 23 G11
Idiofa *Dem. Rep. of the Congo* 4°55S 19°42E 54 E3
Idlib *Syria* 35°55N 36°36E 46 C3
Idria *U.S.A.* 36°25N 120°41W 78 J6
Idutywa = Dutywa *S. Africa* 32°8S 28°18E 57 D4
Ieper *Belgium* 50°51N 2°53E 15 D2
Ierapetra *Greece* 35°1N 25°44E 23 G11
Iesi *Italy* 43°31N 13°14E 22 C5
Ifakara *Tanzania* 8°8S 36°41E 54 F7
'Ifāl, W. al → *Si. Arabia* 28°7N 35°3E 46 D2
Ife *Nigeria* 7°30N 4°31E 52 G6
Iffley *Australia* 18°53S 141°12E 62 B3
Iforas, Adrar des *Africa* 19°40N 1°40E 52 E6
Ifould, L. *Australia* 30°52S 132°6E 61 F5
Igarapava *Brazil* 20°3S 47°47W 93 H9
Igarka *Russia* 67°30N 86°33E 26 C9
Igatpuri *India* 19°40N 73°35E 44 E1
Iggesund *Sweden* 61°39N 17°10E 8 F17
Iglésias *Italy* 39°19N 8°32E 22 E3
Igloolik = Iglulik *Canada* 69°20N 81°49W 69 D15
Igluligaarjuk = Chesterfield Inlet *Canada* 63°30N 90°45W 68 E13
Iglulik *Canada* 69°20N 81°49W 69 D15
Ignace *Canada* 49°30N 91°40W 72 C1
İğneada Burnu *Turkey* 41°53N 28°2E 23 D13
Igoumenitsa *Greece* 39°32N 20°18E 23 E9
Igrim *Russia* 63°12N 64°30E 26 C7
Iguaçu → *Brazil* 25°36S 54°36W 95 B5
Iguaçu, Cat. del *Brazil* 25°41S 54°26W 95 B5
Iguaçu △ *Brazil* 25°30S 54°0W 95 B5
Iguaçu Falls = Iguaçu, Cat. del *Brazil* 25°41S 54°26W 95 B5
Iguala *Mexico* 18°21N 99°32W 87 D5
Igualada *Spain* 41°37N 1°37E 21 B6
Iguassu = Iguaçu → *Brazil* 25°36S 54°36W 95 B5
Iguatu *Brazil* 6°20S 39°18W 93 E11
Iguazú △ *Argentina* 25°42S 54°22W 95 B5
Iguidi, Erg *Africa* 27°0N 7°0W 52 C4
Iharana *Madag.* 13°25S 50°0E 55 G10
Ihbulag *Mongolia* 43°11N 107°10E 32 C4
Iheya-Shima *Japan* 27°4N 127°58E 29 L3
Ihosy *Madag.* 22°24S 46°8E 55 J9
Ii *Finland* 65°19N 25°22E 8 D21
Ii-Shima *Japan* 26°43N 127°47E 29 L3
Iida *Japan* 35°35N 137°50E 29 G8
Iijoki → *Finland* 65°20N 25°20E 8 D21
Iisalmi *Finland* 63°32N 27°10E 8 E22
Iiyama *Japan* 36°51N 138°22E 29 F9
Iizuka *Japan* 33°38N 130°42E 29 H5
Ijâfene *Mauritania* 20°40N 8°0W 52 D4
Ijebu-Ode *Nigeria* 6°47N 3°58E 52 G6
IJmuiden *Neths.* 52°28N 4°35E 15 B4
Ijo älv = Iijoki → *Finland* 65°20N 25°20E 8 D21
IJssel → *Neths.* 52°35N 5°50E 15 B5
IJsselmeer *Neths.* 52°45N 5°20E 15 B5
Ijuí *Brazil* 28°23S 53°55W 95 B5
Ijuí → *Brazil* 27°58S 55°20W 95 B4
Ikare *Nigeria* 7°32N 5°40E 52 G7
Ikaria *Greece* 37°35N 26°10E 23 F12
Ikeda *Japan* 34°1N 133°48E 29 G6
Ikela *Dem. Rep. of the Congo* 1°6S 23°6E 54 E4
Iki *Japan* 33°45N 129°42E 29 H4
Ikopa → *Madag.* 16°45S 46°40E 55 H9
Ikparjuk = Arctic Bay *Canada* 73°1N 85°7W 69 C14
Iksan *S. Korea* 35°59N 127°0E 33 G14
Ikuntji = Haasts Bluff *Australia* 23°22S 132°0E 60 D5
Ilagan *Phil.* 17°7N 121°53E 37 A6
Īlām *Iran* 33°36N 46°36E 46 C5
Ilam *Nepal* 26°58N 87°58E 43 F12
Īlām □ *Iran* 33°0N 47°0E 46 C5
Ilan *Taiwan* 24°45N 121°44E 35 E13
Ilanskiy *Russia* 56°14N 96°3E 27 D10
Iława *Poland* 53°36N 19°34E 17 B10
Ilayangudi *India* 9°34N 78°37E 45 K4
Ile → *Kazakhstan* 45°53N 77°10E 26 E8
Île-à-la-Crosse *Canada* 55°27N 107°53W 71 B7
Île-à-la-Crosse, Lac *Canada* 55°40N 107°45W 71 B7
Île-de-France □ *France* 49°0N 2°20E 20 B5
Ilebo *Dem. Rep. of the Congo* 4°17S 20°55E 54 E4
Ilek *Russia* 51°32N 53°21E 26 D6
Ilek → *Russia* 51°30N 53°22E 18 D9
Ilesha *Nigeria* 7°37N 4°40E 52 G6
Ilford *Canada* 56°4N 95°35W 71 B9
Ilfracombe *Australia* 23°30S 144°30E 62 C3
Ilfracombe *U.K.* 51°12N 4°8W 13 F3
Ilha Grande, Represa *Brazil* 23°10S 53°5W 95 A5
Ilha Grande △ *Brazil* 23°10S 53°20W 95 A5
Ilhéus *Brazil* 14°49S 39°2W 93 F11
Ili = Ile → *Kazakhstan* 45°53N 77°10E 26 E8
Iliamna L. *U.S.A.* 59°30N 155°0W 74 D8
Iligan *Phil.* 8°12N 124°13E 37 C6
Ilion *U.S.A.* 43°1N 75°2W 83 D9
Ilkal *India* 15°57N 76°8E 45 G3
Ilkeston *U.K.* 52°58N 1°19W 12 E6
Ilkley *U.K.* 53°56N 1°48W 12 D6
Illampu = Ancohuma, Nevado *Bolivia* 16°0S 68°50W 92 G5
Illana B. *Phil.* 7°35N 123°45E 37 C6
Illapel *Chile* 32°0S 71°10W 94 C1
Iller → *Germany* 48°23N 9°58E 16 D6
Illimani, Nevado *Bolivia* 16°30S 67°50W 92 G5
Illinois □ *U.S.A.* 40°15N 89°30W 80 E9
Illinois → *U.S.A.* 38°58N 90°28W 80 F8
Illizi *Algeria* 26°31N 8°32E 52 C7
Ilma, L. *Australia* 29°13S 127°46E 61 E4
Ilmajoki *Finland* 62°44N 22°34E 8 E20
Ilmen, Ozero *Russia* 58°15N 31°10E 18 C5
Ilo *Peru* 17°40S 71°20W 92 G4
Iloilo *Phil.* 10°45N 122°33E 37 B6
Ilomantsi *Finland* 62°38N 30°57E 8 E24
Ilorin *Nigeria* 8°30N 4°35E 52 G6
Ilwaco *U.S.A.* 46°19N 124°3W 78 D2
Imabari *Japan* 34°4N 133°0E 29 G6
Imandra, Ozero *Russia* 67°30N 33°0E 8 C25

128 Imari
INDEX TO WORLD MAPS

Imari Japan 33°15N 129°52E 29 H4
Imatra Finland 61°12N 28°48E 8 F23
imeni 26 Bakinskikh Komissarov = Neftçala Azerbaijan 39°19N 49°12E 47 B6
imeni 26 Bakinskikh Komissarov Turkmenistan 39°22N 54°10E 47 B7
imeni Ismail Samani, Pik Tajikistan 39°0N 72°2E 26 F8
Imeri, Serra Brazil 0°50N 65°25W 92 C5
Imfolozi ⌓ S. Africa 28°18S 31°50E 57 C5
Imi Ethiopia 6°28N 42°10E 49 F3
Imlay U.S.A. 40°40N 118°9W 76 F4
Imlay City U.S.A. 43°2N 83°5W 82 D1
Immingham U.K. 53°37N 0°13W 12 D7
Immokalee U.S.A. 26°25N 81°25W 85 H14
Ímola Italy 44°20N 11°42E 22 B4
Imperatriz Brazil 5°30S 47°29W 93 E9
Impéria Italy 43°53N 8°3E 20 E8
Imperial Canada 51°21N 105°28W 71 C7
Imperial Calif., U.S.A. 32°51N 115°34W 79 N11
Imperial Nebr., U.S.A. 40°31N 101°39W 80 E3
Imperial Beach U.S.A. 32°35N 117°6W 79 N9
Imperial Dam U.S.A. 32°55N 114°25W 79 N12
Imperial Res. U.S.A. 32°53N 114°28W 79 N12
Imperial Valley U.S.A. 33°0N 115°30W 79 N11
Imperieuse Reef Australia 17°36S 118°50E 60 C2
Impfondo Congo 1°40N 18°0E 54 D3
Imphal India 24°48N 93°56E 41 G18
İmroz = Gökçeada Turkey 40°10N 25°50E 23 D11
Imuris Mexico 30°47N 110°52W 86 A2
Imuruan B. Phil. 10°40N 119°10E 37 B5
In Guezzam Algeria 19°37N 5°52E 52 E7
In Salah Algeria 27°10N 2°32E 52 C6
Ina Japan 35°50N 137°55E 29 G8
Inagua △ Bahamas 21°5N 73°24W 89 B5
Inangahua N.Z. 41°52S 171°59E 59 D3
Inanwatan Indonesia 2°8S 132°10E 37 E8
Iñapari Peru 11°0S 69°40W 92 F5
Inari Finland 68°54N 27°1E 8 B22
Inarijärvi Finland 69°0N 28°0E 8 B23
Inawashiro-Ko Japan 37°29N 140°6E 28 F10
tInbhear Mór, An = Arklow Ireland 52°48N 6°10W 10 D5
Inca Spain 39°43N 2°54E 21 C7
Inca de Oro Chile 26°45S 69°54W 94 B2
Incahuasi Argentina 27°2S 68°18W 94 B2
Incahuasi Chile 29°12S 71°5W 94 B1
İnce Burun Turkey 42°7N 34°56E 19 F5
İncesu Turkey 38°38N 35°11E 46 B2
Incheon S. Korea 37°27N 126°40E 33 F14
İncirliova Turkey 37°50N 27°41E 23 F12
Incline Village U.S.A. 39°10N 119°58W 78 F7
Incomáti → Mozam. 25°46S 32°43E 57 C5
Indalsälven → Sweden 62°36N 17°30E 8 E17
Indaw Burma 24°15N 96°5E 41 G20
Independence Calif., U.S.A. 36°48N 118°12W 78 J8
Independence Iowa, U.S.A. 42°28N 91°54W 80 D8
Independence Kans., U.S.A. 37°14N 95°42W 80 G6
Independence Ky., U.S.A. 38°57N 84°33W 81 F11
Independence Mo., U.S.A. 39°6N 94°25W 80 F6
Independence Fjord Greenland 82°10N 29°0W 4 A6
Independence Mts. U.S.A. 41°20N 116°0W 76 F5
Index U.S.A. 47°50N 121°33W 78 C5
Indi India 17°10N 75°58E 44 F2
India ■ Asia 20°0N 78°0E 40 K11
Indian → U.S.A. 27°59N 80°34W 85 H14
Indian Cabins Canada 59°52N 117°40W 70 B5
Indian Harbour Canada 54°27N 57°13W 73 B8
Indian Head Canada 50°30N 103°41W 71 C8
Indian L. U.S.A. 43°46N 74°16W 83 C10
Indian Lake U.S.A. 43°47N 74°16W 83 C10
Indian Springs U.S.A. 36°35N 115°40W 79 J11
Indiana U.S.A. 40°37N 79°9W 82 F5
Indiana ☐ U.S.A. 40°0N 86°0W 81 F11
Indianapolis U.S.A. 39°46N 86°9W 80 F10
Indianola Iowa, U.S.A. 41°22N 93°34W 80 E7
Indianola Miss., U.S.A. 33°27N 90°39W 85 E9
Indiga Russia 67°38N 49°9E 18 A8
Indigirka → Russia 70°48N 148°54E 27 B15
Indio U.S.A. 33°43N 116°13W 79 M10
Indira Gandhi Canal India 28°0N 72°0E 42 F5
Indira Pt. India 6°44N 93°49E 45 L11
Indira Sagar India 22°15N 76°40E 42 H7
Indo-China Asia 15°0N 102°0E 24 G12
Indonesia ■ Asia 5°0S 115°0E 36 F5
Indore India 22°42N 75°53E 42 H6
Indramayu Indonesia 6°20S 108°19E 37 G13
Indravati → India 19°20N 80°20E 44 E5
Indre → France 47°16N 0°11E 20 C4
Indulkana Australia 26°58S 133°5E 63 D1
Indus → Pakistan 24°20N 67°47E 42 G2
Indus, Mouths of the Pakistan 24°0N 68°0E 42 H3
İnebolu Turkey 41°55N 33°40E 19 F5
Infiernillo, Presa del Mexico 18°35N 101°50W 86 D4
Inga, Barrage d' Dem. Rep. of the Congo 5°39S 13°39E 54 F2
Ingenio Santa Ana Argentina 27°25S 65°40W 94 B2
Ingersoll Canada 43°4N 80°55W 82 C4
Ingham Australia 18°43S 146°10E 62 B4
Ingleborough U.K. 54°10N 2°22W 12 C5
Inglewood Queens., Australia 28°25S 151°2E 63 D5
Inglewood Vic., Australia 36°29S 143°53E 63 F3
Inglewood N.Z. 39°9S 174°14E 59 C5
Ingólfshöfði Iceland 63°48N 16°39W 8 E5
Ingolstadt Germany 48°46N 11°26E 16 D6
Ingomar U.S.A. 46°35N 107°23W 76 C10
Ingonish Canada 46°42N 60°18W 73 C7
Ingraj Bazar India 24°58N 88°10E 43 G13
Ingrid Christensen Coast Antarctica 69°30S 76°0E 5 C6
Ingulec = Inhulec Ukraine 47°42N 33°14E 19 E5
Ingushetia ☐ Russia 43°20N 44°50E 19 F8
Ingwavuma S. Africa 27°9S 31°59E 57 C5
Inhaca Mozam. 26°1S 32°57E 57 C5
Inhaca Pen. Mozam. 26°13S 32°55E 57 C5
Inhafenga Mozam. 20°36S 33°53E 57 B5
Inhambane Mozam. 23°54S 35°30E 57 B6
Inhambane ☐ Mozam. 22°30S 34°20E 57 B5
Inharrime Mozam. 24°30S 35°0E 57 B6
Inharrime → Mozam. 24°30S 35°0E 57 B6
Inhulec Ukraine 47°42N 33°14E 19 E5
Ining = Yining China 43°58N 81°10E 30 C5
Inírida → Colombia 3°55N 67°52W 92 C5
Inis = Ennis Ireland 52°51N 8°59W 10 D3
Inishbofin Ireland 53°37N 10°13W 10 C1
Inisheer Ireland 53°3N 9°32W 10 C2
Inishfree B. Ireland 55°4N 8°23W 10 A3
Inishkea North Ireland 54°9N 10°11W 10 B1
Inishkea South Ireland 54°7N 10°12W 10 B1
Inishmaan Ireland 53°5N 9°35W 10 C2
Inishmore Ireland 53°8N 9°45W 10 C2
Inishmurray Ireland 54°26N 8°39W 10 B3
Inishowen Pen. Ireland 55°14N 7°15W 10 A4
Inishshark Ireland 53°37N 10°16W 10 C1
Inishturk Ireland 53°42N 10°7W 10 C1
Inishvickillane Ireland 52°3N 10°37W 10 D1
Injinoo ⚙ Australia 10°56S 142°15E 62 A3
Injune Australia 25°53S 148°32E 63 D4
Inklin → N. Amer. 58°50N 133°10W 70 B2
Inland Kaikoura Ra. N.Z. 41°59S 173°41E 59 D4
Inland Sea = Setonaikai Japan 34°20N 133°30E 29 G6
Inle L. Burma 20°30N 96°58E 41 J20
Inlet U.S.A. 43°45N 74°48W 83 C10
Inn → Austria 48°35N 13°28E 16 D7
Innamincka Australia 27°44S 140°46E 63 D3
Inner Hebrides U.K. 57°0N 6°30W 11 E2
Inner Mongolia = Nei Mongol Zizhiqu ☐ China 42°0N 112°0E 32 D7
Inner Sound U.K. 57°30N 5°55W 11 D3
Innerkip Canada 43°13N 80°42W 82 C4
Innetalling I. Canada 56°0N 79°0W 72 A4
Innisfail Australia 17°33S 146°5E 62 B4
Innisfail Canada 52°2N 113°57W 70 C6
In'noshima Japan 34°19N 133°10E 29 G6
Innsbruck Austria 47°16N 11°23E 16 E6
Inny → Ireland 53°32N 7°51W 10 C4
Inongo Dem. Rep. of the Congo 1°55S 18°30E 54 E3
Inoucdjouac = Inukjuak Canada 58°25N 78°15W 69 F16
Inowrocław Poland 52°50N 18°12E 17 B10
Inscription, C. Australia 25°29S 112°59E 61 E1
Insein Burma 16°50N 96°5E 41 L20
Inta Russia 66°5N 60°8E 18 A11
Intendente Alvear Argentina 35°12S 63°32W 94 D3
Interlaken Switz. 46°41N 7°50E 20 C7
Interlaken U.S.A. 42°37N 76°44W 83 D8
International Falls U.S.A. 48°36N 93°25W 80 A7
Interview I. India 12°55N 92°43E 45 H11
Intiyaco Argentina 28°43S 60°5W 94 B3
Inukjuak Canada 58°25N 78°15W 69 F16
Inútil, B. Chile 53°30S 70°15W 96 G2
Inuvik Canada 68°16N 133°40W 68 D5
Inveraray U.K. 56°14N 5°5W 11 E3
Inverbervie U.K. 56°51N 2°17W 11 E6
Invercargill N.Z. 46°24S 168°24E 59 G2
Inverclyde ☐ U.K. 55°55N 4°49W 11 F4
Inverell Australia 29°45S 151°8E 63 D5
Invergordon U.K. 57°41N 4°10W 11 D4
Inverloch Australia 38°38S 145°45E 63 F4
Invermere Canada 50°30N 116°2W 70 C5
Inverness Canada 46°15N 61°19W 73 C7
Inverness U.K. 57°29N 4°13W 11 D4
Inverness U.S.A. 28°50N 82°20W 85 G13
Inverurie U.K. 57°17N 2°23W 11 D6
Investigator Group Australia 34°45S 134°20E 63 E1
Investigator Str. Australia 35°30S 137°0E 63 F2
Inya Russia 50°28N 86°37E 26 D9
Inyangani Zimbabwe 18°5S 32°50E 55 H6
Inyantue Zimbabwe 18°33S 26°39E 56 A4
Inyo Mts. U.S.A. 36°40N 118°0W 78 J9
Inyokern U.S.A. 35°39N 117°49W 79 K9
Inza Russia 53°55N 46°25E 18 D8
Iō-Jima Japan 30°48N 130°18E 29 J5
Ioannina Greece 39°42N 20°47E 23 E9
Iola U.S.A. 37°55N 95°24W 80 G6
Iona U.K. 56°20N 6°25W 11 E2
Ione U.S.A. 38°21N 120°56W 78 G6
Ionia U.S.A. 42°59N 85°4W 81 D11
Ionian Is. = Ionioi Nisoi Greece 38°40N 20°0E 23 E9
Ionian Sea Medit. S. 37°30N 17°30E 23 E7
Ionioi Nisoi Greece 38°40N 20°0E 23 E9
Ios Greece 36°41N 25°20E 23 F11
Iowa ☐ U.S.A. 42°18N 93°30W 80 D7
Iowa → U.S.A. 41°10N 91°1W 80 E8
Iowa City U.S.A. 41°40N 91°32W 80 E8
Iowa Falls U.S.A. 42°31N 93°16W 80 D7
Iowa Park U.S.A. 33°57N 98°40W 84 E5
Ipameri Brazil 17°44S 48°9W 93 G9
Ipatinga Brazil 19°32S 42°30W 93 G10
Ipiales Colombia 0°50N 77°37W 92 C3
Ipin = Yibin China 28°45N 104°32E 34 C5
Ipixuna Brazil 7°0S 71°40W 92 E4
Ipoh Malaysia 4°35N 101°5E 39 K3
Ippy C.A.R. 6°5N 21°7E 54 C4
İpsala Turkey 40°55N 26°23E 23 D12
Ipswich Australia 27°35S 152°40E 63 D5
Ipswich U.K. 52°4N 1°10E 13 E9
Ipswich Mass., U.S.A. 42°41N 70°50W 83 D14
Ipswich S. Dak., U.S.A. 45°27N 99°2W 80 C4
Ipu Brazil 4°23S 40°44W 93 D10
Iqaluit Canada 63°44N 68°31W 69 E18
Iqaluktuutiaq = Cambridge Bay Canada 69°10N 105°0W 68 D11
Iquique Chile 20°19S 70°5W 92 H4
Iquitos Peru 3°45S 73°10W 92 D4
Irabu-Jima Japan 24°50N 125°10E 29 M2
Iracoubo Fr. Guiana 5°30N 53°10W 93 B8
Īrafshān Iran 26°42N 61°56E 47 E9
Iraklio Greece 35°20N 25°12E 23 G11
Iráklion = Iraklio Greece 35°20N 25°12E 23 G11
Irala Paraguay 25°55S 54°35W 95 B5
Iran ■ Asia 33°0N 53°0E 47 C7
Iran, Pegunungan Malaysia 2°20N 114°50E 36 D4
Iran Ra. = Iran, Pegunungan Malaysia 2°20N 114°50E 36 D4
Iranamadu Tank Sri Lanka 9°23N 80°29E 45 K5
Īrānshahr Iran 27°15N 60°40E 47 E9
Irapuato Mexico 20°41N 101°28W 86 C4
Iraq ■ Asia 33°0N 44°0E 46 C5
Irati Brazil 25°25S 50°38W 95 B5
Irazú, Volcan Costa Rica 10°28N 84°42W 88 D3
Irbid Jordan 32°35N 35°48E 48 C4
Irbid ☐ Jordan 32°30N 35°50E 48 C5
Irebu Dem. Rep. of the Congo 0°40S 17°46E 54 E3
Ireland ■ Europe 53°50N 7°52W 10 C4
Iri = Iksan S. Korea 35°59N 127°0E 33 G14
Irian Jaya = Papua ☐ Indonesia 4°0S 137°0E 37 E9
Irian Jaya Barat ☐ Indonesia 2°5S 132°50E 37 E8
Iringa Tanzania 7°48S 35°43E 54 F7
Irinjalakuda India 10°21N 76°14E 45 J3
Iriomote △ Japan 24°29N 123°53E 29 M1
Iriomote-Jima Japan 24°19N 123°48E 29 M1
Iriona Honduras 15°57N 85°11W 88 C2
Iriri → Brazil 3°52S 52°37W 93 D8
Irish Sea Europe 53°38N 4°48W 12 D3
Irkutsk Russia 52°18N 104°20E 30 A9
Irma Canada 52°55N 111°14W 71 C6
Irō-Zaki Japan 34°36N 138°51E 29 G9
Iron Baron Australia 32°58S 137°11E 63 E2
Iron Gate = Portile de Fier Europe 44°44N 22°30E 17 F12
Iron Knob Australia 32°46S 137°8E 63 E2
Iron Mountain U.S.A. 45°49N 88°4W 80 C9
Iron Range △ Australia 12°34S 143°18E 62 A3
Iron River U.S.A. 46°6N 88°39W 80 B9
Irondequoit U.S.A. 43°13N 77°35W 82 C7
Ironton Mo., U.S.A. 37°36N 90°38W 80 G8
Ironton Ohio, U.S.A. 38°32N 82°41W 81 F12
Ironwood U.S.A. 46°27N 90°9W 80 B8
Ironwood Forest ⌓ U.S.A. 32°32N 111°28W 77 K8
Iroquois Canada 44°51N 75°19W 83 B9
Iroquois Falls Canada 48°46N 80°41W 72 C3
Irpin Ukraine 50°30N 30°15E 17 C16
Irrara Cr. → Australia 29°35S 145°31E 63 D4
Irrawaddy ☐ Burma 17°0N 95°0E 41 L19
Irrawaddy → Burma 15°50N 95°6E 41 M19
Irrawaddy, Mouths of the Burma 15°30N 95°0E 41 M19
Irricana Canada 51°19N 113°37W 70 C6
Irrunytju Australia 26°3S 128°56E 61 E4
Irtysh → Russia 61°4N 68°52E 26 C7
Irún Spain 43°20N 1°52W 21 A5
Iruñea = Pamplona-Iruña Spain 42°48N 1°38W 21 A5
Irvine Canada 49°57N 110°16W 71 D6
Irvine U.K. 55°37N 4°41W 11 F4
Irvine Calif., U.S.A. 33°41N 117°46W 79 M9
Irvine Ky., U.S.A. 37°42N 83°58W 81 G12
Irvinestown U.K. 54°28N 7°39W 10 B4
Irving U.S.A. 32°48N 96°56W 84 E6
Irvona U.S.A. 40°46N 78°33W 82 F6
Irwin → Australia 29°15S 114°54E 61 E1
Irymple Australia 34°14S 142°8E 63 E3
Isa Khel Pakistan 32°41N 71°17E 42 C4
Isaac → Australia 22°55S 149°20E 62 C4
Isabel U.S.A. 45°24N 101°26W 80 C3
Isabel, I. Mexico 21°51N 105°55W 86 C3
Isabela Phil. 6°40N 121°59E 37 C6
Isabela Puerto Rico 18°30N 67°2W 89 d
Isabella, Cord. Nic. 13°30N 85°25W 88 D2
Isabella Ra. Australia 21°0S 121°4E 60 D3
Isachsen, C. Canada 79°20N 105°28W 69 B10
Isachsen Mt. Antarctica 72°8S 26°5E 5 D4
Ísafjarðardjúp Iceland 66°10N 23°0W 8 C2
Ísafjörður Iceland 66°5N 23°9W 8 C2
Isagarh India 24°48N 77°51E 42 G7
Isahaya Japan 32°52N 130°2E 29 H5
Isan → India 26°51N 80°7E 43 F9
Isana = Içana → Brazil 0°26N 67°19W 92 C5
Isar → Germany 48°48N 12°57E 16 D7
Íschia Italy 40°44N 13°57E 22 D5
Ischigualasto △ Argentina 30°0S 68°0W 94 B2
Isdell → Australia 16°27S 124°51E 60 C3
Ise Japan 34°25N 136°45E 29 G8
Ise-Shima △ Japan 34°25N 136°48E 29 G8
Ise-Wan Japan 34°43N 136°43E 29 G8
Isère → France 44°59N 4°51E 20 D6
Isérnia Italy 41°36N 14°14E 22 D6
Isfahan = Eşfahān Iran 32°39N 51°43E 47 C6
Ishigaki Japan 24°26N 124°10E 29 M2
Ishigaki-Shima Japan 24°20N 124°10E 29 M2
Ishikari Japan 43°20N 141°15E 28 C10
Ishikari-Gawa → Japan 43°15N 141°23E 28 C10
Ishikari-Sammyaku Japan 43°30N 143°0E 28 C11
Ishikari-Wan Japan 43°25N 141°1E 28 C10
Ishikawa Japan 26°25N 127°49E 29 L3
Ishikawa ☐ Japan 36°30N 136°30E 29 F8
Ishim Russia 56°10N 69°30E 26 D7
Ishim → Russia 57°45N 71°10E 26 D8
Ishinomaki Japan 38°32N 141°20E 28 E10
Ishioka Japan 36°11N 140°16E 29 F10
Ishkoman Pakistan 36°30N 73°50E 43 A5
Ishpeming U.S.A. 46°29N 87°40W 80 B10
Isil Kul Russia 54°55N 71°16E 26 D8
iSimangaliso ⌓ S. Africa 27°50S 32°32E 57 C5
Isiro Dem. Rep. of the Congo 2°53N 27°40E 54 D5
Isisford Australia 24°15S 144°21E 62 C3
İskenderun Turkey 36°32N 36°10E 46 B3
İskenderun Körfezi Turkey 36°40N 35°50E 19 G6
Iskŭr → Bulgaria 43°45N 24°25E 23 C11
Iskut → Canada 56°45N 131°49W 70 B2
Isla → U.K. 56°32N 3°20W 11 E5
Isla Coiba △ Panama 7°33N 81°36W 88 E3
Isla de Salamanca △ Colombia 10°59N 74°40W 89 D5
Isla Gorge △ Australia 25°10S 149°57E 62 D4
Isla Isabel △ Mexico 21°54N 105°58W 86 C3
Isla Tiburón y San Esteban ⌓ Mexico 29°0N 112°27W 86 B2
Isla Vista U.S.A. 34°25N 119°53W 79 L7
Islam Headworks Pakistan 29°49N 72°33E 42 E5
Islamabad Pakistan 33°40N 73°10E 42 C5
Islamgarh Pakistan 27°51N 70°48E 42 F4
Islamkot Pakistan 24°42N 70°13E 42 G4
Islampur Bihar, India 25°9N 85°12E 43 G11
Islampur Maharashtra, India 17°2N 74°20E 44 F2
Islampur Paschimbanga, India 26°16N 88°12E 43 F13
Island = Iceland ■ Europe 64°45N 19°0W 8 D4
Island L. Canada 53°47N 94°25W 71 C10
Island Lagoon Australia 31°30S 136°40E 63 E2
Island Pond U.S.A. 44°49N 71°53W 83 B13
Islands, B. of Canada 49°11N 58°15W 73 C8
Islands, B. of N.Z. 35°15S 174°6E 59 A5
Islay U.K. 55°46N 6°10W 11 F2
Isle → France 44°55N 0°15W 20 D3
Isle aux Morts Canada 47°35N 59°0W 73 C8
Isle of Wight ☐ U.K. 50°41N 1°17W 13 G6
Isle Royale △ U.S.A. 48°0N 88°55W 80 B9
Isleton U.S.A. 38°10N 121°37W 78 G5
Ismail = Izmayil Ukraine 45°22N 28°46E 17 F15
Ismâ'ilîya Egypt 30°37N 32°18E 53 B12
Isna Egypt 25°17N 32°30E 53 C12
Isparta Turkey 37°47N 30°30E 19 G5
Íspica Italy 36°47N 14°55E 22 F6
Israel ■ Asia 32°0N 34°50E 48 D3
Issoire France 45°32N 3°15E 20 D5
Issyk-Kul = Balykchy Kyrgyzstan 42°26N 76°12E 30 C4
Issyk-Kul, Ozero = Ysyk-Köl Kyrgyzstan 42°25N 77°15E 26 E8
Istiea Greece 38°57N 23°9E 23 E10
Isto, Mt. U.S.A. 69°12N 143°48W 74 B11
Istokpoga, L. U.S.A. 27°23N 81°17W 85 H14
Istra Croatia 45°10N 14°0E 16 F7
Istres France 43°31N 4°59E 20 E6
Istria = Istra Croatia 45°10N 14°0E 16 F7
Itá Paraguay 25°29S 57°21W 94 B4
Itaberaba Brazil 12°32S 40°18W 93 F10
Itabira Brazil 19°37S 43°13W 93 G10
Itabirito Brazil 20°15S 43°48W 95 A7
Itabuna Brazil 14°48S 39°16W 93 F11
Itacaunas → Brazil 5°21S 49°8W 93 E9
Itacoatiara Brazil 3°8S 58°25W 92 D7
Itaipú, Represa de Brazil 25°30S 54°30W 95 B5
Itaituba Brazil 4°10S 55°50W 93 D7
Itajaí Brazil 27°50S 48°39W 95 B6
Itajubá Brazil 22°24S 45°30W 95 A6
Itala ⌓ S. Africa 27°30S 31°7E 57 C5
Italy ■ Europe 42°0N 13°0E 22 C5
Itamaraju Brazil 17°4S 39°32W 93 G11
Itapecuru Mirim Brazil 3°24S 44°20W 93 D10
Itaperuna Brazil 21°10S 41°54W 95 A7
Itapetininga Brazil 23°36S 48°7W 95 A6
Itapeva Brazil 23°59S 48°59W 95 A6
Itapicuru → Bahia, Brazil 11°47S 37°32W 93 F11
Itapicuru → Maranhão, Brazil 2°52S 44°12W 93 D10
Itapipoca Brazil 3°30S 39°35W 93 D11
Itapuá ☐ Paraguay 26°40S 55°40W 95 B4
Itaquí Brazil 29°8S 56°30W 94 B4
Itararé Brazil 24°6S 49°23W 95 A6
Itarsi India 22°36N 77°51E 42 H7
Itatí Argentina 27°16S 58°15W 94 B4
Itatiaia △ Brazil 22°22S 44°38W 95 A7
Itchen → U.K. 50°55N 1°22W 13 G6
Itezhi Tezhi, L. Zambia 15°30S 25°30E 55 H5
Ithaca = Ithaki Greece 38°25N 20°40E 23 E9
Ithaca U.S.A. 42°27N 76°30W 83 D8
Ithaki Greece 38°25N 20°40E 23 E9
Itiquira → Brazil 17°18S 56°44W 93 G7
Itiyuro → Argentina 22°40S 63°50W 94 A3
Itō Japan 34°58N 139°5E 29 G9
Itoigawa Japan 37°2N 137°51E 29 F8
Itonamas → Bolivia 12°28S 64°24W 92 F6
Ittoqqortoormiit Greenland 70°20N 23°0W 4 B6
Itu Brazil 23°17S 47°15W 95 A6
Itu Aba I. S. China Sea 10°23N 114°21E 36 B4
Ituiutaba Brazil 19°0S 49°25W 93 G9
Itumbiara Brazil 18°20S 49°10W 93 G9
Ituna Canada 51°10N 103°24W 71 C8
Iturbe Argentina 23°0S 65°25W 94 A2
Iturup, Ostrov Russia 45°0N 148°0E 27 E15
Ituxi → Brazil 7°18S 64°51W 92 E6
Itzehoe Germany 53°55N 9°31E 16 B5
Ivaí → Brazil 23°18S 53°42W 95 A5
Ivalo Finland 68°38N 27°35E 8 B22
Ivalojoki → Finland 68°40N 27°40E 8 B22
Ivanava Belarus 52°7N 25°29E 17 B13
Ivanhoe Australia 32°56S 144°20E 63 E3
Ivanhoe Canada 44°23N 77°28W 82 B7
Ivanhoe Calif., U.S.A. 36°23N 119°13W 78 J7
Ivanhoe Minn., U.S.A. 44°28N 96°15W 80 C5
Ivano-Frankivsk Ukraine 48°40N 24°40E 17 D13
Ivanovo = Ivanava Belarus 52°7N 25°29E 17 B13
Ivanovo Russia 57°5N 41°0E 18 C7
Ivatsevichy Belarus 52°43N 25°21E 17 B13
Ivdel Russia 60°42N 60°24E 18 B11
Iveragh Pen. Ireland 51°52N 10°15W 10 E1
Ivinheima → Brazil 23°14S 53°42W 95 A5
Ivinhema Brazil 22°10S 53°37W 95 A5
Ivory Coast W. Afr. 4°20N 5°0W 52 H4
Ivory Coast ■ Africa 7°30N 5°0W 52 G4
Ivrea Italy 45°28N 7°52E 20 D7
Ivujivik Canada 62°24N 77°55W 69 E16
Ivvavik △ Canada 69°6N 139°30W 68 D4
Ivybridge U.K. 50°23N 3°56W 13 G4
Iwaizumi Japan 39°50N 141°45E 28 E10
Iwaki Japan 37°3N 140°55E 29 F10
Iwakuni Japan 34°15N 132°8E 29 G6
Iwamizawa Japan 43°12N 141°46E 28 C10
Iwanai Japan 42°58N 140°30E 28 C10
Iwata Japan 34°42N 137°51E 29 G8
Iwate ☐ Japan 39°30N 141°30E 28 E10
Iwate-San Japan 39°51N 141°0E 28 E10
Iwo Nigeria 7°39N 4°9E 52 G6
Iwŏn N. Korea 40°19N 128°39E 33 D15
Ixiamas Bolivia 13°50S 68°5W 92 F5
Ixopo S. Africa 30°11S 30°5E 57 D5
Ixtepec Mexico 16°34N 95°6W 87 D5
Ixtlán del Río Mexico 21°2N 104°22W 86 C4
Iyo Japan 33°45N 132°45E 29 H6
Izabal, L. de Guatemala 15°30N 89°10W 88 C2
Izamal Mexico 20°56N 89°1W 87 C7
Izena-Shima Japan 26°56N 127°56E 29 L3
Izhevsk Russia 56°51N 53°14E 18 C9
Izhma → Russia 65°19N 52°54E 18 A9
Izmayil Ukraine 45°22N 28°46E 17 F15
İzmir Turkey 38°25N 27°8E 23 E12
İzmit = Kocaeli Turkey 40°45N 29°50E 19 F4
İznik Gölü Turkey 40°27N 29°30E 23 D13
Izra Syria 32°51N 36°15E 48 C5
Izu-Hantō Japan 34°45N 139°0E 29 G9
Izu-Shotō Japan 34°30N 140°0E 29 G10
Izúcar de Matamoros Mexico 18°36N 98°28W 87 D5
Izumi Japan 32°5N 130°22E 29 H5
Izumi-Sano Japan 34°23N 135°18E 29 G7
Izumo Japan 35°20N 132°46E 29 G6
Izyaslav Ukraine 50°5N 26°50E 17 C14

J

J.F.K. Int. ✈ (JFK) U.S.A. 40°38N 73°47W 83 F11
J. Strom Thurmond L. U.S.A. 33°40N 82°12W 85 E13
Ja-ela Sri Lanka 7°5N 79°53E 45 L4
Jabalpur India 23°9N 79°58E 43 H8
Jabālya Gaza Strip 31°32N 34°29E 48 D3
Jabbūl Syria 36°4N 37°30E 46 B3
Jabiru Australia 12°40S 132°53E 60 B5
Jablah Syria 35°20N 36°0E 46 C3
Jablonec nad Nisou Czech Rep. 50°43N 15°10E 16 C8
Jaboatão Brazil 8°7S 35°1W 93 E11
Jaboticabal Brazil 21°15S 48°17W 95 A6
Jaca Spain 42°35N 0°33W 21 A5
Jacareí Brazil 23°20S 46°0W 95 A6
Jacarèzinho Brazil 23°5S 49°58W 95 A6
Jack River △ Australia 14°58S 144°19E 62 A3
Jackman U.S.A. 45°37N 70°15W 81 C18
Jacksboro U.S.A. 33°13N 98°10W 84 E5
Jackson Barbados 13°7N 59°36W 89 g
Jackson Ala., U.S.A. 31°31N 87°53W 85 F11
Jackson Calif., U.S.A. 38°21N 120°46W 78 G6
Jackson Ky., U.S.A. 37°33N 83°23W 81 G12
Jackson Mich., U.S.A. 42°15N 84°24W 81 D11
Jackson Minn., U.S.A. 43°37N 95°1W 80 D6
Jackson Miss., U.S.A. 32°18N 90°12W 85 E9
Jackson Mo., U.S.A. 37°23N 89°40W 80 G9
Jackson N.H., U.S.A. 44°10N 71°11W 83 B13
Jackson Ohio, U.S.A. 39°3N 82°39W 81 F12
Jackson Tenn., U.S.A. 35°37N 88°49W 85 D10
Jackson Wyo., U.S.A. 43°29N 110°46W 76 E8
Jackson B. N.Z. 43°58S 168°42E 59 E2
Jackson L. U.S.A. 43°52N 110°36W 76 E8
Jacksons N.Z. 42°46S 171°32E 59 E3
Jackson's Arm Canada 49°52N 56°47W 73 C8
Jacksonville Ala., U.S.A. 33°49N 85°46W 85 E12
Jacksonville Ark., U.S.A. 34°52N 92°7W 84 D8
Jacksonville Calif., U.S.A. 37°52N 120°24W 78 H6
Jacksonville Fla., U.S.A. 30°20N 81°39W 85 F14
Jacksonville Ill., U.S.A. 39°44N 90°14W 80 F8
Jacksonville N.C., U.S.A. 34°45N 77°26W 85 D16
Jacksonville Tex., U.S.A. 31°58N 95°17W 84 F7
Jacksonville Beach U.S.A. 30°17N 81°24W 85 F14
Jacmel Haiti 18°14N 72°32W 89 C5
Jacob Lake U.S.A. 36°43N 112°13W 77 H7
Jacobabad Pakistan 28°20N 68°29E 42 E3
Jacobina Brazil 11°11S 40°30W 93 F10
Jacques-Cartier, Dét. de Canada 50°0N 63°30W 73 C7
Jacques-Cartier, Mt. Canada 48°57N 66°0W 73 C6
Jacques-Cartier ⌓ Canada 47°15N 71°33W 73 C5
Jacuí → Brazil 30°2S 51°15W 95 C5
Jacumba U.S.A. 32°37N 116°11W 79 N10
Jacundá → Brazil 1°57S 50°26W 93 D8
Jadcherla India 16°46N 78°9E 44 F4
Jade City Canada 59°15N 129°37W 70 B3
Jade Dragon Snow Mt. = Yulong Xueshan China 27°6N 100°10E 34 D3
Jade Mt. = Yü Shan Taiwan 23°25N 120°52E 35 F13
Jaén Peru 5°25S 78°40W 92 E3
Jaén Spain 37°44N 3°43W 21 D4
Jafarabad India 20°52N 71°22E 42 J4
Jaffa = Tel Aviv-Yafo Israel 32°4N 34°48E 48 C3

Jaffa, C. Australia 36°58S 139°40E 63 F2
Jaffna Sri Lanka 9°45N 80°2E 45 K5
Jaffrey U.S.A. 42°49N 72°2W 83 D12
Jagadhri India 30°10N 77°20E 42 D7
Jagadishpur India 25°30N 84°21E 43 G11
Jagat Nepal 28°19N 84°53E 43 E11
Jagdalpur India 19°3N 82°0E 44 E6
Jagdaqi China 50°25N 124°7E 31 A13
Jagersfontein S. Africa 29°44S 25°27E 56 C4
Jaghīn → Iran 27°17N 57°13E 47 E8
Jagodina Serbia 44°5N 21°15E 23 C9
Jagraon India 30°50N 75°25E 42 D6
Jagtial India 18°50N 79°0E 44 E4
Jaguariaíva Brazil 24°10S 49°50W 95 A6
Jaguaribe → Brazil 4°25S 37°45W 93 D11
Jagüey Grande Cuba 22°35N 81°7W 88 B3
Jahanabad India 25°13N 84°59E 43 G11
Jahazpur India 25°37N 75°17E 42 G6
Jahrom Iran 28°30N 53°31E 47 D7
Jaigarh India 17°17N 73°13E 44 F1
Jaijon India 31°21N 76°9E 42 D7
Jailolo Indonesia 1°5N 127°30E 37 D7
Jailolo, Selat Indonesia 0°5N 129°5E 37 D7
Jaipur India 27°0N 75°50E 42 F6
Jais India 26°15N 81°32E 43 F9
Jaisalmer India 26°55N 70°54E 42 F4
Jaisinghnagar India 23°38N 78°34E 43 H8
Jaitaran India 26°12N 73°56E 42 F5
Jaithari India 23°14N 78°37E 43 H8
Jajarkot Nepal 28°42N 82°14E 43 E10
Jājarm Iran 36°58N 56°27E 47 B8
Jajpur India 20°53N 86°22E 44 D8
Jakam → India 23°54N 74°13E 42 H6
Jakhal India 29°48N 75°50E 42 E6
Jakhau India 23°13N 68°43E 42 H3
Jakobstad = Pietarsaari
  Finland 63°40N 22°43E 8 E20
Jal U.S.A. 32°7N 103°12W 77 K12
Jalājil Si. Arabia 25°40N 45°27E 46 E5
Jalālābād Afghan. 34°30N 70°29E 42 B4
Jalalabad India 27°41N 79°42E 43 F8
Jalalpur Jattan Pakistan 32°38N 74°11E 42 C6
Jalama U.S.A. 34°29N 120°29W 79 L6
Jalandhar = Jullundur
  India 31°20N 75°40E 42 D6
Jalapa Guatemala 14°39N 89°59W 88 D2
Jalapa Enríquez = Xalapa
  Mexico 19°32N 96°55W 87 D5
Jalasjärvi Finland 62°29N 22°47E 8 E20
Jalaun India 26°8N 79°25E 43 F8
Jaldhaka → Bangla. 26°16N 89°16E 43 F13
Jalesar India 27°29N 78°19E 42 F8
Jaleswar Nepal 26°38N 85°48E 43 F11
Jalgaon India 21°0N 75°42E 44 D2
Jalībah Iraq 30°35N 46°32E 46 D5
Jalingo Nigeria 8°55N 11°25E 53 G8
Jalisco □ Mexico 20°20N 103°40W 86 D4
Jalkot Pakistan 35°14N 73°24E 43 B5
Jalna India 19°48N 75°38E 44 E2
Jalón → Spain 41°47N 1°4W 21 B5
Jalor India 25°21N 72°37E 42 G5
Jalpa Mexico 21°38N 102°58W 86 C4
Jalpaiguri India 26°32N 88°46E 41 F16
Jalpan Mexico 21°14N 99°29W 87 C5
Jaluit I. Marshall Is. 6°0N 169°30E 64 G8
Jalūlā Iraq 34°16N 45°10E 46 C5
Jamaame Somalia 0°4N 42°44E 49 G3
Jamaica ■ W. Indies 18°10N 77°30W 88 a
Jamalpur Bangla. 24°52N 89°56E 41 G16
Jamalpur India 25°18N 86°28E 43 G12
Jamalpurganj India 23°2N 87°59E 43 H13
Jamanxim → Brazil 4°43S 56°18W 93 D7
Jambewangi Indonesia 8°17S 114°7E 37 J17
Jambi Indonesia 1°38S 103°30E 36 E2
Jambi □ Indonesia 1°30S 102°30E 36 E2
Jambongan, Pulau
  Malaysia 6°45N 117°20E 36 C5
Jambusar India 22°3N 72°51E 42 H5
James → S. Dak., U.S.A. 42°52N 97°18W 80 D5
James → Va., U.S.A. 36°56N 76°27W 81 G15
James B. Canada 54°0N 80°0W 72 B3
James Ranges Australia 24°10S 132°30E 60 D5
James Ross I. Antarctica 63°58S 57°50W 5 C18
Jamesabad Pakistan 25°17N 69°15E 42 G3
Jamestown Australia 33°10S 138°32E 63 E2
Jamestown S. Africa 31°6S 26°45E 56 D4
Jamestown N. Dak.,
  U.S.A. 46°54N 98°42W 80 B4
Jamestown N.Y., U.S.A. 42°6N 79°14W 82 D5
Jamestown Pa., U.S.A. 41°29N 80°27W 82 E4
Jamīlābād Iran 34°24N 48°28E 47 C6
Jamira → India 21°35N 88°28E 43 J13
Jamkhandi India 16°30N 75°15E 44 F2
Jamkhed India 18°43N 75°12E 44 E2
Jammalamadugu India 14°51N 78°25E 45 G4
Jammu India 32°43N 74°54E 42 C6
Jammu & Kashmir □
  India 34°25N 77°0E 43 B7
Jamnagar India 22°30N 70°6E 42 H4
Jamner India 20°45N 75°52E 44 D2
Jamni → India 25°13N 78°35E 43 G8
Jampur Pakistan 29°39N 70°40E 42 E4
Jamrud Pakistan 33°59N 71°24E 42 C4
Jämsä Finland 61°53N 25°10E 8 F21
Jamshedpur India 22°44N 86°12E 43 H12
Jamtara India 23°59N 86°49E 43 H12
Jämtland Sweden 63°31N 14°0E 8 E16
Jan L. Canada 54°56N 102°55W 71 C8
Jan Mayen Arctic 71°0N 9°0W 4 B7
Janakpur Nepal 26°42N 85°55E 44 F12
Janaúba Brazil 15°48S 43°19W 93 G10
Jand Pakistan 33°30N 72°6E 42 C5
Jandanku □ Australia 16°20S 135°45E 62 B2
Jandaq Iran 34°3N 54°22E 47 C7
Jandola Pakistan 32°20N 70°9E 42 C4
Jandowae Australia 26°45S 151°7E 63 D5
Janesville U.S.A. 42°41N 89°1W 80 D9
Jangamo Mozam. 24°6S 35°21E 57 B6
Janghai India 25°33N 82°19E 43 G10

Jangheung S. Korea 34°41N 126°52E 33 G14
Jangipur India 24°28N 88°4E 43 G12
Jangoon India 17°44N 79°5E 44 F4
Janjanbureh Gambia 13°30N 14°47W 52 F3
Janjgir India 22°1N 82°34E 43 J10
Janos Mexico 30°54N 108°10W 86 A3
Januária Brazil 15°25S 44°25W 93 G10
Janûb Sînî □ Egypt 29°30N 33°50E 48 F2
Janwada India 18°0N 77°29E 44 E3
Jaora India 23°40N 75°10E 42 H6
Japan ■ Asia 36°0N 136°0E 29 G8
Japan, Sea of Asia 40°0N 135°0E 28 E7
Japen = Yapen Indonesia 1°50S 136°0E 37 E9
Japla India 24°33N 84°1E 43 G11
Japurá → Brazil 3°8S 65°46W 92 D5
Jaquarão Brazil 32°34S 53°23W 95 C5
Jaqué Panama 7°27N 78°8W 88 E4
Jarābulus Syria 36°49N 38°1E 46 B3
Jarama → Spain 40°24N 3°32W 21 B4
Jaranwala Pakistan 31°15N 73°26E 42 D5
Jarash Jordan 32°17N 35°54E 48 C4
Jarash □ Jordan 32°17N 35°54E 48 C4
Jardim Brazil 21°28S 56°2W 94 A4
Jardín América Argentina 27°3S 55°14W 95 B4
Jardine River △ Australia 11°9S 142°21E 62 A3
Jardines de la Reina, Arch. de los
  Cuba 20°50N 78°50W 88 B4
Jargalang China 43°5N 122°55E 33 C12
Jari → Brazil 1°9S 51°54W 93 D8
Jarīr, W. al → Si. Arabia 25°38N 42°30E 46 E4
Jarosław Poland 50°2N 22°42E 17 C12
Jarrahdale Australia 32°24S 116°5E 61 F2
Jarrahi → Iran 30°49N 48°48E 47 D6
Jartai China 39°45N 105°48E 32 E3
Jarud Qi China 44°28N 120°50E 33 B11
Järvenpää Finland 60°29N 25°5E 8 F21
Jarvis Canada 42°53N 80°6W 82 D4
Jarvis I. Pac. Oc. 0°15S 160°5W 65 H11
Jarwa India 27°38N 82°30E 43 F10
Jasdan India 22°2N 71°12E 42 H4
Jashpurnagar India 22°54N 84°9E 43 H11
Jasidih India 24°31N 86°39E 43 G12
Jāsimīyah Iraq 33°45N 44°41E 46 C5
Jasin Malaysia 2°20N 102°26E 39 L4
Jāsk Iran 25°38N 57°45E 47 E8
Jasło Poland 49°45N 21°30E 17 D11
Jaso India 24°30N 80°29E 43 G9
Jasper Alta., Canada 52°55N 118°5W 70 C5
Jasper Ont., Canada 44°52N 75°57W 83 B9
Jasper Ala., U.S.A. 33°50N 87°17W 85 E11
Jasper Fla., U.S.A. 30°31N 82°57W 85 F13
Jasper Ind., U.S.A. 38°24N 86°56W 80 F10
Jasper Tex., U.S.A. 30°56N 94°1W 84 F7
Jasper △ Canada 52°50N 118°8W 70 C5
Jasrasar India 27°43N 73°49E 42 F5
Jászberény Hungary 47°30N 19°55E 17 E10
Jataí Brazil 17°58S 51°48W 93 G8
Jath India 17°3N 75°13E 44 F2
Jati Pakistan 24°20N 68°19E 42 G3
Jatibarang Indonesia 6°28S 108°18E 37 G13
Jatiluwih Indonesia 8°23S 115°8E 37 J18
Játiva = Xàtiva Spain 38°59N 0°32W 21 C5
Jaú Brazil 22°10S 48°30W 95 A6
Jauja Peru 11°45S 75°15W 92 F3
Jaunpur India 25°46N 82°44E 43 G10
Java = Jawa Indonesia 7°0S 110°0E 36 F3
Java Sea Indonesia 4°35S 107°15E 36 E3
Java Trench Ind. Oc. 9°0S 105°0E 36 F3
Javadi Hills India 12°40N 78°40E 45 H4
Javla India 17°18N 75°9E 44 F2
Jawa Indonesia 7°0S 110°0E 36 F3
Jawa Barat □ Indonesia 7°0S 107°0E 37 G12
Jawa Tengah □ Indonesia 7°0S 110°0E 37 G14
Jawa Timur □ Indonesia 8°0S 113°0E 37 G15
Jawad India 24°36N 74°51E 42 G6
Jawhar India 19°55N 73°14E 44 E1
Jawhar Somalia 2°48N 45°30E 49 G4
Jawoyn ◇ Australia 14°16S 132°28E 60 B5
Jay Peak U.S.A. 44°55N 72°32W 83 B12
Jaya, Puncak Indonesia 3°57S 137°17E 37 E9
Jayanti India 26°45N 89°40E 41 F16
Jayapura Indonesia 2°28S 140°38E 37 E10
Jayawijaya, Pegunungan
  Indonesia 5°0S 139°0E 37 F9
Jaynagar India 26°43N 86°9E 43 F12
Jaypur = Jeypore India 18°50N 82°38E 44 E6
Jayrūd Syria 33°49N 36°44E 46 C3
Jayton U.S.A. 33°15N 100°34W 84 F4
Jāz Mūrīān, Hāmūn-e
  Iran 27°20N 58°55E 47 E8
Jazīreh-ye Shīf Iran 29°4N 50°54E 47 D6
Jazminal Mexico 24°52N 101°24W 86 C4
Jazzīn Lebanon 33°31N 35°35E 48 B4
Jean U.S.A. 35°47N 115°20W 79 K11
Jean Marie River
  Canada 61°32N 120°38W 70 A4
Jean-Rabel Haiti 19°50N 73°5W 89 C5
Jeanerette U.S.A. 29°55N 91°40W 84 G9
Jeanette, Ostrov = Zhannetty,
  Ostrov Russia 76°43N 158°0E 27 B16
Jeannette U.S.A. 40°20N 79°36W 82 F5
Jebāl Bārez, Kūh-e Iran 28°30N 58°20E 47 D8
Jebel, Bahr el →
  South Sudan 9°30N 30°25E 53 G12
Jebel Ali = Minā' Jabal 'Alī
  U.A.E. 25°2N 55°8E 47 E7
Jecheon S. Korea 37°8N 128°12E 33 F15
Jedburgh U.K. 55°29N 2°33W 11 F6
Jedda = Jiddah Si. Arabia 21°29N 39°10E 49 C2
Jeddore L. Canada 48°3N 55°55W 73 C8
Jędrzejów Poland 50°35N 20°15E 17 C11
Jefferson Iowa, U.S.A. 42°1N 94°23W 80 D6
Jefferson Ohio, U.S.A. 41°44N 80°46W 82 E4
Jefferson Tex., U.S.A. 32°46N 94°21W 84 E7
Jefferson, Mt. Nev.,
  U.S.A. 38°47N 116°56W 76 G5
Jefferson, Mt. Oreg.,
  U.S.A. 44°41N 121°48W 76 D3

Jefferson City Mo., U.S.A. 38°34N 92°10W 80 F7
Jefferson City Tenn.,
  U.S.A. 36°7N 83°30W 85 C13
Jeffersontown U.S.A. 38°12N 85°35W 81 F11
Jeffersonville U.S.A. 38°17N 85°44W 81 F11
Jeffrey City U.S.A. 42°30N 107°49W 76 E10
Jega Nigeria 12°15N 4°23E 52 F6
Jeju S. Korea 33°31N 126°32E 33 H14
Jeju-do S. Korea 33°29N 126°34E 33 H14
Jēkabpils Latvia 56°29N 25°57E 9 H21
Jekyll I. U.S.A. 31°4N 81°25W 85 F14
Jelenia Góra Poland 50°50N 15°45E 16 C8
Jelgava Latvia 56°41N 23°49E 9 H20
Jemaluang Malaysia 2°16N 103°52E 39 L4
Jember Indonesia 8°11S 113°41E 37 H15
Jena Germany 50°54N 11°35E 16 C6
Jena U.S.A. 31°41N 92°8W 84 F8
Jengish Chokoso = Pobedy, Pik
  Kyrgyzstan 42°0N 79°58E 30 C4
Jenin West Bank 32°28N 35°18E 48 C4
Jenkins U.S.A. 37°10N 82°38W 81 G12
Jenner U.S.A. 38°27N 123°7W 78 G3
Jennings U.S.A. 30°13N 92°40W 84 F8
Jeong-eup S. Korea 35°35N 126°50E 33 G14
Jeongseon S. Korea 37°20N 128°45E 33 F15
Jeonju S. Korea 35°50N 127°4E 33 G14
Jepara Indonesia 7°40S 109°14E 37 G14
Jeparit Australia 36°8S 142°1E 63 F3
Jequié Brazil 13°51S 40°5W 93 F10
Jequitinhonha Brazil 16°30S 41°0W 93 G10
Jequitinhonha →
  Brazil 15°51S 38°53W 93 G11
Jerada Morocco 34°17N 2°10W 52 B5
Jerantut Malaysia 3°56N 102°22E 39 L4
Jerejak, Pulau Malaysia 5°19N 100°19E 39 c
Jérémie Haiti 18°40N 74°10W 89 C5
Jerez, Pta. Mexico 22°58N 97°40W 87 C5
Jerez de García Salinas
  Mexico 22°39N 103°0W 86 C4
Jerez de la Frontera Spain 36°41N 6°7W 21 D2
Jerez de los Caballeros
  Spain 38°20N 6°45W 21 C2
Jericho = El Arīḥā
  West Bank 31°52N 35°27E 48 D4
Jericho Australia 23°38S 146°6E 62 C4
Jerid, Chott el = Djerid, Chott
  Tunisia 33°42N 8°30E 52 B7
Jerilderie Australia 35°20S 145°41E 63 F4
Jermyn U.S.A. 41°32N 75°33W 83 E9
Jerome U.S.A. 42°44N 114°31W 76 E6
Jerramungup Australia 33°55S 118°55E 61 F2
Jersey U.K. 49°11N 2°7W 13 H5
Jersey Shore U.S.A. 41°12N 77°15W 82 E7
Jerseyville U.S.A. 39°7N 90°20W 80 F8
Jervis B. Australia 35°8S 150°46E 63 F5
Jervis Inlet Canada 50°0N 123°57W 70 C4
Jesi = Iesi Italy 43°31N 13°14E 22 C5
Jesup U.S.A. 31°36N 81°53W 85 F14
Jesús Carranza Mexico 17°26N 95°2E 87 D5
Jesús María Argentina 30°59S 64°5W 94 C3
Jetmore U.S.A. 38°4N 99°54W 80 F4
Jetpur India 21°45N 70°10E 42 J4
Jevnaker Norway 60°15N 10°26E 9 F14
Jewett U.S.A. 40°22N 81°2W 82 F3
Jewett U.S.A. 41°36N 71°59W 83 E13
Jeyḥūnābād Iran 34°58N 48°59E 47 C6
Jeypore India 18°50N 82°38E 44 E6
Jha Jha India 24°46N 86°22E 43 G12
Jhaarkand = Jharkhand □
  India 24°0N 85°50E 43 H11
Jhabua India 22°46N 74°36E 42 H6
Jhajjar India 28°37N 76°42E 42 E7
Jhal India 28°17N 67°27E 42 E2
Jhal Jhao Pakistan 26°20N 65°35E 40 F4
Jhalawar India 24°40N 76°10E 42 G7
Jhalida India 23°22N 85°58E 43 H11
Jhalrapatan India 24°33N 76°10E 42 G7
Jhang Maghiana
  Pakistan 31°15N 72°22E 42 D5
Jhansi India 25°30N 78°36E 43 G8
Jhargram India 22°27N 86°59E 43 H12
Jharia India 23°45N 86°26E 43 H12
Jharkhand □ India 24°0N 85°50E 43 H11
Jharsuguda India 21°56N 84°5E 44 D7
Jhelum Pakistan 33°0N 73°45E 42 C5
Jhelum → Pakistan 31°20N 72°10E 42 D5
Jhilmilli India 23°24N 82°51E 43 H10
Jhudo Pakistan 24°58N 69°18E 42 G3
Jhunjhunun India 28°10N 75°30E 42 E6
Ji-Paraná Brazil 10°52S 62°57W 92 F6
Ji Xian China 36°7N 110°40E 32 F6
Jia Xian Henan, China 33°59N 113°12E 32 H7
Jia Xian Shaanxi, China 38°12N 110°28E 32 E6
Jiahe China 25°38N 112°19E 35 E9
Jiaji = Qionghai China 19°15N 110°28E 38 C8
Jialing Jiang → China 29°30N 106°20E 34 C6
Jiamusi China 46°40N 130°26E 31 B15
Ji'an Jilin, China 41°5N 126°10E 33 D14
Ji'an Jiangxi, China 27°6N 114°59E 35 D10
Jianchang China 40°55N 120°35E 33 D11
Jianchuan China 26°38N 99°55E 34 D2
Jiande China 29°23N 119°15E 35 C12
Jiang'an China 28°40N 105°3E 34 C5
Jiangbei China 29°40N 106°34E 34 C6
Jiangcheng China 22°36N 101°52E 34 F3
Jiangchuan China 24°8N 102°39E 34 E4
Jiangdi China 26°57N 103°37E 34 D4
Jiangdu China 32°27N 119°36E 35 A12
Jiange China 32°4N 105°32E 34 A5
Jianghua China 25°0N 111°47E 35 E8
Jiangjin China 29°14N 106°14E 34 C6
Jiangkou China 27°41N 108°49E 34 D7
Jiangle China 26°42N 117°23E 35 D11
Jiangmen China 22°32N 113°0E 35 F9
Jiangning China 31°53N 118°37E 35 B12
Jiangshan China 28°40N 118°37E 35 C12
Jiangsu □ China 33°0N 120°0E 33 H11
Jiangxi □ China 27°30N 116°0E 35 D11

Jiangyan China 32°30N 120°7E 35 A13
Jiangyin China 31°54N 120°17E 35 B13
Jiangyong China 25°20N 111°22E 35 E8
Jiangyou China 31°44N 104°43E 34 B5
Jianhe China 42°2N 126°34E 33 C14
Jianhe China 26°37N 108°31E 34 D7
Jianli China 29°46N 112°56E 35 C9
Jianning China 26°50N 116°50E 35 D11
Jian'ou China 27°3N 118°17E 35 D12
Jianping China 41°53N 119°42E 33 D10
Jianshi China 30°37N 109°38E 34 B7
Jianshui China 23°36N 102°43E 34 F4
Jianyang Fujian, China 27°20N 118°5E 35 D12
Jianyang Sichuan, China 30°24N 104°33E 34 B5
Jiao Xian = Jiaozhou
  China 36°18N 120°1E 33 F11
Jiaohe Hebei, China 38°2N 116°20E 32 E9
Jiaohe Jilin, China 43°40N 127°22E 33 C14
Jiaonan China 35°52N 119°58E 33 G10
Jiaozhou China 36°18N 120°1E 33 F11
Jiaozhou Wan China 36°5N 120°10E 33 F11
Jiaozuo China 35°16N 113°12E 32 G7
Jiawang China 34°28N 117°26E 33 G9
Jiaxian China 35°25N 116°20E 32 G9
Jiaxing China 30°49N 120°45E 35 B13
Jiayi = Chiai Taiwan 23°29N 120°25E 35 F13
Jiayu China 29°55N 113°55E 35 C9
Jiayuguan China 39°49N 98°18E 30 D8
Jibuti = Djibouti ■ Africa 12°0N 43°0E 49 E3
Jicarón, I. Panama 7°10N 81°50W 88 E3
Jiddah Si. Arabia 21°29N 39°10E 49 C2
Jido India 29°2N 94°58E 41 E19
Jieshou China 33°18N 115°22E 32 H8
Jieyang China 23°35N 116°21E 35 F11
Jigalong Australia 23°21S 120°47E 60 D3
Jigalong ◇ Australia 23°21S 120°46E 60 D3
Jigni India 25°45N 79°25E 43 G8
Jihlava Czech Rep. 49°28N 15°35E 16 D8
Jihlava → Czech Rep. 48°55N 16°36E 17 D9
Jijiga Ethiopia 9°20N 42°50E 49 F3
Jilib Somalia 0°29N 42°46E 49 G3
Jilin China 43°44N 126°30E 33 C14
Jilin □ China 44°0N 127°0E 33 C14
Jilong = Chilung Taiwan 25°3N 121°45E 35 E13
Jima Ethiopia 7°40N 36°47E 49 F2
Jimbaran, Teluk Indonesia 8°46S 115°9E 37 K18
Jiménez Mexico 27°8N 104°54W 86 B4
Jimeta Nigeria 9°17N 12°28E 54 C2
Jimo China 36°23N 120°30E 33 F11
Jin Jiang → China 28°24N 115°48E 35 C10
Jin Xian = Jinzhou
  China 38°55N 121°42E 33 E11
Jinan China 36°38N 117°1E 32 F9
Jinchang China 38°30N 102°10E 30 D9
Jincheng China 35°29N 112°50E 32 G7
Jinchuan China 31°30N 102°3E 34 B4
Jind India 29°19N 76°22E 42 E7
Jindabyne Australia 36°25S 148°35E 63 F4
Jinding China 22°22N 113°33E 31 a
Jindo S. Korea 34°28N 126°15E 33 G14
Jindřichův Hradec
  Czech Rep. 49°10N 15°2E 16 D8
Jing He → China 34°27N 109°4E 32 G5
Jing Shan China 31°20N 111°35E 35 B8
Jing Xian China 30°38N 118°25E 35 B12
Jing'an China 28°50N 115°17E 35 C10
Jingbian China 37°20N 108°30E 32 F5
Jingchuan China 35°20N 107°20E 32 G4
Jingde China 30°15N 118°27E 35 B12
Jingdezhen China 29°20N 117°11E 35 C11
Jingdong China 24°23N 100°47E 34 E3
Jinggangshan China 26°58N 114°15E 35 D10
Jinggu China 23°35N 100°41E 34 F3
Jinghai Guangdong,
  China 22°59N 116°31E 35 F11
Jinghai Tianjin, China 38°55N 116°55E 32 E9
Jinghong China 22°0N 100°45E 34 F3
Jinghong Dam China 22°10N 100°46E 34 F3
Jingjiang China 32°2N 120°16E 35 A13
Jingle China 38°20N 111°55E 32 E6
Jingmen China 31°0N 112°10E 35 B9
Jingning China 35°30N 105°43E 32 G3
Jingpo Hu China 43°55N 128°55E 33 C15
Jingshan China 31°1N 113°7E 35 B9
Jingtai China 37°10N 104°6E 32 F3
Jingtanggang China 39°10N 119°5E 33 E10
Jingxi China 23°8N 106°27E 34 F6
Jingyang China 34°30N 108°50E 32 G5
Jingyu China 42°25N 126°45E 33 C14
Jingyuan China 36°30N 104°40E 32 F3
Jingziguan China 33°15N 111°0E 32 H6
Jinhua China 29°8N 119°38E 35 C12
Jining Nei Monggol Zizhiqu,
  China 41°5N 113°0E 32 D7
Jining Shandong, China 35°22N 116°34E 32 G9
Jinja Uganda 0°25N 33°12E 54 D6
Jinji China 37°58N 106°8E 32 F4
Jinjiang Fujian, China 24°43N 118°33E 35 E12
Jinjiang Yunnan, China 26°14N 100°34E 34 D3
Jinju S. Korea 35°12N 128°2E 33 G15
Jinkou China 30°30N 114°8E 35 B10
Jinkouhe China 29°18N 103°4E 34 C4
Jinmu Jiao China 18°9N 109°34E 38 C7
Jinnah Barrage Pakistan 32°58N 71°33E 42 C4
Jinotega Nic. 13°6N 85°59W 88 D2
Jinotepe Nic. 11°50N 86°10W 88 D2
Jinping Guizhou, China 26°41N 109°10E 34 D7
Jinping Yunnan, China 22°45N 103°18E 34 F4
Jinsha China 27°30N 106°14E 34 D6
Jinsha Jiang → China 28°50N 104°36E 34 C5
Jinshi China 29°40N 111°50E 35 C8
Jintan China 31°42N 119°36E 35 B12

Jintur India 19°37N 76°42E 44 E3
Jinxi Jiangxi, China 27°56N 116°45E 35 D11
Jinxi Liaoning, China 40°52N 120°50E 33 D11
Jinxian China 28°26N 116°17E 35 C11
Jinxiang China 35°5N 116°22E 32 G9
Jinyang China 27°28N 103°5E 34 D4
Jinyun China 28°35N 120°5E 35 C13
Jinzhai China 31°40N 115°3E 35 B10
Jinzhong China 37°42N 112°46E 32 F7
Jinzhou Liaoning, China 38°55N 121°42E 33 E11
Jinzhou Liaoning, China 41°5N 121°3E 33 D11
Jiparaná → Brazil 8°3S 62°52W 92 E6
Jipijapa Ecuador 1°0S 80°40W 92 D2
Jiquilpan Mexico 19°59N 102°43W 86 D4
Jirisan S. Korea 35°20N 127°44E 33 G14
Jiroft Iran 28°45N 57°50E 47 D8
Jishan China 35°34N 110°58E 32 G6
Jishou China 28°21N 109°43E 34 C7
Jishui China 27°12N 115°8E 35 D10
Jisr ash Shughūr Syria 35°49N 36°18E 46 C4
Jitarning Australia 32°48S 117°57E 61 F2
Jitra Malaysia 6°16N 100°25E 39 J3
Jiu → Romania 43°47N 23°48E 17 F12
Jiudengkou China 39°56N 106°40E 32 E4
Jiujiang Guangdong, China 22°50N 113°0E 35 F9
Jiujiang Jiangxi, China 29°42N 115°58E 35 C10
Jiuling Shan China 28°40N 114°40E 35 C10
Jiulong China 28°57N 101°31E 34 C3
Jiuquan China 39°50N 98°20E 30 D8
Jiutai China 44°10N 125°50E 33 B13
Jiuxincheng China 39°17N 115°59E 32 E8
Jiuzhaigou △ China 33°8N 103°52E 34 A4
Jiwani Pakistan 25°1N 61°44E 40 G2
Jixi Anhui, China 30°5N 118°34E 35 B12
Jixi Heilongjiang, China 45°20N 130°50E 33 B16
Jiyang China 37°0N 117°12E 33 F9
Jiyuan China 35°7N 112°57E 32 G7
Jīzān Si. Arabia 17°0N 42°20E 49 D3
Jize China 36°54N 114°56E 32 F8
Jizhou China 37°35N 115°30E 32 F8
Jizl, Wādī al → Si. Arabia 25°39N 38°25E 46 E3
Jizō-Zaki Japan 35°34N 133°20E 29 G6
Jizzax Uzbekistan 40°6N 67°50E 26 E7
Joaçaba Brazil 27°5S 51°31W 95 B5
João Pessoa Brazil 7°10S 34°52W 93 E12
Joaquín V. González
  Argentina 25°10S 64°0W 94 B3
Jobat India 22°25N 74°34E 42 H6
Jodhpur India 26°23N 73°8E 42 F5
Jodiya India 22°42N 70°18E 42 H4
Joensuu Finland 62°37N 29°49E 8 E23
Jõetsu Japan 37°12N 138°10E 29 F9
Jofane Mozam. 21°15S 34°18E 57 B5
Jog Falls = Gersoppa Falls
  India 14°12N 74°46E 45 G2
Jogbani India 26°25N 87°15E 43 F12
Jõgeva Estonia 58°45N 26°24E 9 G22
Jogjakarta = Yogyakarta
  Indonesia 7°49S 110°22E 37 G14
Johannesburg S. Africa 35°22N 117°38W 79 K9
Johilla → India 23°37N 81°14E 43 H9
John Crow Mts. Jamaica 18°5N 76°25W 88 a
John Day U.S.A. 44°25N 118°57W 76 D4
John Day → U.S.A. 45°44N 120°39W 76 D3
John Day Fossil Beds △
  U.S.A. 44°33N 119°38W 76 D4
John D'or Prairie Canada 58°30N 115°8W 70 B5
John o' Groats U.K. 58°38N 3°4W 11 C5
Johnnie U.S.A. 36°25N 116°5W 79 J10
John's Ra. Australia 21°55S 133°23E 62 C1
Johnson U.S.A. 44°38N 72°41W 83 B12
Johnson City Kans.,
  U.S.A. 37°34N 101°45W 80 G3
Johnson City N.Y., U.S.A. 42°7N 75°58W 83 D9
Johnson City Tenn.,
  U.S.A. 36°19N 82°21W 85 C13
Johnson City Tex., U.S.A. 30°17N 98°25W 84 F5
Johnsonburg U.S.A. 41°29N 78°41W 82 E6
Johnsondale U.S.A. 35°58N 118°32W 79 K8
Johnsons Crossing
  Canada 60°29N 133°18W 70 A2
Johnston, L. Australia 32°25S 120°30E 61 F3
Johnston Falls = Mambilima Falls
  Zambia 10°31S 28°45E 54 G5
Johnston I. Pac. Oc. 17°10N 169°8W 65 F11
Johnstone Str. Canada 50°28N 126°0W 70 C3
Johnstown Ireland 52°45N 7°33W 10 D4
Johnstown N.Y., U.S.A. 43°0N 74°22W 83 C10
Johnstown Ohio, U.S.A. 40°9N 82°41W 82 F2
Johnstown Pa., U.S.A. 40°20N 78°55W 82 F6
Johor □ Malaysia 2°5N 103°20E 39 M4
Johor, Selat Asia 1°28N 103°47E 39 d
Johor Bahru Malaysia 1°28N 103°46E 39 d
Jõhvi Estonia 59°22N 27°27E 9 G22
Joinville Brazil 26°15S 48°55W 95 B6
Joinville I. Antarctica 65°0S 55°30W 5 C18
Jojutla Mexico 18°37N 99°11W 87 D5
Jokkmokk Sweden 66°35N 19°50E 8 C18
Jökulsá á Bru → Iceland 65°40N 14°16W 8 D6
Jökulsá á Fjöllum →
  Iceland 66°10N 16°30W 8 C5
Jökulsárglúfur △ Iceland 65°56N 16°31W 8 D5
Jolfa Āzarbājān-e Sharqī,
  Iran 38°57N 45°38E 46 B5
Jolfa Eşfahan, Iran 32°58N 51°37E 47 C6
Joliet U.S.A. 41°32N 88°5W 80 E9
Joliette Canada 46°3N 73°24W 72 C5
Jolo Phil. 6°0N 121°0E 37 C6
Jolon U.S.A. 35°58N 121°9W 78 K5
Jombang Indonesia 7°33S 112°14E 37 G15
Jomda China 31°28N 98°12E 34 B2
Jonava Lithuania 55°8N 24°12E 9 J21
Jones Sound Canada 76°0N 85°0W 69 B15
Jonesboro Ark., U.S.A. 35°50N 90°42W 85 D9
Jonesboro La., U.S.A. 32°15N 92°43W 84 E8
Joniškis Lithuania 56°13N 23°35E 9 H20
Jönköping Sweden 57°45N 14°8E 9 H16

Jonquière *Canada* 48°27N 71°14W 73 C5
Joplin *U.S.A.* 37°6N 94°31W 80 G6
Jora *India* 26°20N 77°49E 42 F6
Jordan *Mont., U.S.A.* 47°19N 106°55W 76 C10
Jordan *N.Y., U.S.A.* 43°4N 76°29W 83 C8
Jordan ■ *Asia* 31°0N 36°0E 48 E5
Jordan → *Asia* 31°48N 35°32E 48 D4
Jordan Valley *U.S.A.* 42°59N 117°3W 76 E5
Jorhat *India* 26°45N 94°12E 41 F19
Jörn *Sweden* 65°4N 20°1E 8 D19
Jorong *Indonesia* 3°58S 114°56E 36 E4
Jørpeland *Norway* 59°3N 6°1E 9 G12
Jorquera → *Chile* 28°3S 69°58W 94 B2
Jos *Nigeria* 9°53N 8°51E 52 G7
José Batlle y Ordóñez *Uruguay* 33°20S 55°10W 95 C4
Joseph, L. *Canada* 45°10N 79°44W 82 A5
Joseph Bonaparte G. *Australia* 14°35S 128°50E 60 B4
Joseph L. *Canada* 52°45N 65°18W 73 B6
Joshinath *India* 30°34N 79°34E 43 D8
Joshinetsu-Kōgen △ *Japan* 36°42N 138°32E 29 F9
Joshua Tree *U.S.A.* 34°8N 116°19W 79 L10
Joshua Tree △ *U.S.A.* 33°55N 116°0W 79 M10
Jost Van Dyke I. *Br. Virgin Is.* 18°29N 64°47W 89 e
Jostedalsbreen *Norway* 61°40N 6°59E 8 F12
Jotunheimen *Norway* 61°35N 8°25E 8 F13
Joubertberge *Namibia* 18°30S 14°0E 56 A1
Jourdanton *U.S.A.* 28°55N 98°33W 84 G5
Jovellanos *Cuba* 22°40N 81°10W 88 B3
Ju Xian *China* 36°35N 118°20E 33 F10
Juan Aldama *Mexico* 24°19N 103°21W 86 C4
Juan Bautista Alberdi *Argentina* 34°26S 61°48W 94 C3
Juan de Fuca, Str of. *N. Amer.* 48°15N 124°0W 78 B3
Juán de Nova *Ind. Oc.* 17°3S 43°45E 57 A7
Juan Fernández, Arch. de *Pac. Oc.* 33°50S 80°0W 90 G2
Juan José Castelli *Argentina* 25°27S 60°57W 94 B3
Juan L. Lacaze *Uruguay* 34°26S 57°25W 94 C4
Juankoski *Finland* 63°3N 28°19E 8 E23
Juárez *Mexico* 27°37N 100°44W 86 B4
Juárez, Sa. de *Mexico* 32°0N 115°50W 86 A1
Juàzeiro *Brazil* 9°30S 40°30W 93 E10
Juàzeiro do Norte *Brazil* 7°10S 39°18W 93 E11
Juba *South Sudan* 4°50N 31°35E 53 H12
Juba → *Somalia* 1°30N 42°35E 49 G3
Jubail = Al Jubayl *Si. Arabia* 27°0N 49°50E 47 E6
Jubany *Antarctica* 62°30S 58°0W 5 C18
Jubayl *Lebanon* 34°5N 35°39E 48 A4
Jubbah *Si. Arabia* 28°2N 40°56E 46 D4
Jubbal *India* 31°5N 77°40E 42 D7
Jubbulpore = Jabalpur *India* 23°9N 79°58E 43 H8
Jubilee L. *Australia* 29°0S 126°50E 61 E4
Juby, C. *Morocco* 28°0N 12°59W 52 C3
Júcar = Xúquer → *Spain* 39°5N 0°10W 21 C5
Júcaro *Cuba* 21°37N 78°51W 88 B4
Juchitán de Zaragoza *Mexico* 16°26N 95°1W 87 D5
Judea = Har Yehuda *Israel* 31°35N 34°57E 48 D3
Judith → *U.S.A.* 47°44N 109°39W 76 C9
Judith, Pt. *U.S.A.* 41°22N 71°29W 83 E13
Judith Gap *U.S.A.* 46°41N 109°45W 76 C9
Juigalpa *Nic.* 12°6N 85°26W 88 D2
Juiz de Fora *Brazil* 21°43S 43°19W 95 A7
Jujuy ☐ *Argentina* 23°20S 65°40W 94 A2
Julesburg *U.S.A.* 40°59N 102°16W 76 F12
Juli *Peru* 16°10S 69°25W 92 G5
Julia Cr. → *Australia* 20°0S 141°11E 62 C3
Julia Creek *Australia* 20°39S 141°44E 62 C3
Juliaca *Peru* 15°25S 70°10W 92 G4
Julian *U.S.A.* 33°4N 116°38W 79 M10
Julian, L. *Canada* 54°25N 77°57W 72 B4
Julianatop *Suriname* 3°40N 56°30W 93 C7
Julianehåb = Qaqortoq *Greenland* 60°43N 46°0W 4 C5
Julimes *Mexico* 28°25N 105°27W 86 B3
Jullundur *India* 31°20N 75°40E 42 D6
Julu *China* 37°15N 115°2E 32 F8
Jumbo Pk. *U.S.A.* 36°12N 114°11W 79 J12
Jumentos Cays *Bahamas* 23°0N 75°40W 88 B4
Jumilla *Spain* 38°28N 1°19W 21 C5
Jumla *Nepal* 29°15N 82°13E 43 E10
Jumna = Yamuna → *India* 25°30N 81°53E 43 G9
Jumunjin *S. Korea* 37°55N 128°54E 33 F15
Junagadh *India* 21°30N 70°30E 42 J4
Junan *China* 35°12N 118°53E 33 G10
Junction *Tex., U.S.A.* 30°29N 99°46W 84 F5
Junction *Utah, U.S.A.* 38°14N 112°13W 77 G7
Junction B. *Australia* 11°52S 133°55E 62 A1
Junction City *Kans., U.S.A.* 39°2N 96°50W 80 F5
Junction City *Oreg., U.S.A.* 44°13N 123°12W 76 D2
Junction Pt. *Australia* 11°45S 133°50E 62 A1
Jundah *Australia* 24°46S 143°2E 62 C3
Jundiaí *Brazil* 24°30S 47°0W 95 A6
Juneau *U.S.A.* 58°18N 134°25W 70 B2
Junee *Australia* 34°53S 147°35E 63 E4
Jungar Qi *China* 39°49N 110°57E 32 E6
Jungfrau *Switz.* 46°32N 7°58E 20 C7
Junggar Pendi *China* 44°30N 86°0E 30 C6
Jungshahi *Pakistan* 24°52N 67°44E 42 G2
Juniata → *U.S.A.* 40°24N 77°1W 82 F7
Junín *Argentina* 34°33S 60°57W 94 C3
Junín de los Andes *Argentina* 39°45S 71°0W 96 D2
Jūniyah *Lebanon* 33°59N 35°38E 48 B4
Junlian *China* 28°8N 104°29E 34 C5
Junnar *India* 19°12N 73°58E 44 E1
Juntas *Chile* 28°24S 69°58W 94 B2
Juntura *U.S.A.* 43°45N 118°5W 76 E4
Jur, Nahr el → *South Sudan* 8°45N 29°15E 53 G11
Jura = Jura, Mts. du *Europe* 46°40N 6°5E 20 C7
Jura = Schwäbische Alb *Germany* 48°20N 9°30E 16 D5
Jura *U.K.* 56°0N 5°50W 11 F3
Jura, Mts. du *Europe* 46°40N 6°5E 20 C7
Jura, Sd. of *U.K.* 55°57N 5°45W 11 F3
Jurbarkas *Lithuania* 55°4N 22°46E 9 J20
Jurien Bay *Australia* 30°18S 115°2E 61 F2
Jūrmala *Latvia* 56°58N 23°34E 9 H20
Jurong *China* 31°57N 119°9E 35 B12
Juruá → *Brazil* 2°37S 65°44W 92 D5
Juruena *Brazil* 13°0S 58°10W 92 F7
Juruena → *Brazil* 7°20S 58°3W 92 E7
Juruti *Brazil* 2°9S 56°4W 93 D7
Justo Daract *Argentina* 33°52S 65°12W 94 C2
Jutaí → *Brazil* 2°43S 66°57W 92 D5
Juticalpa *Honduras* 14°40N 86°12W 88 D2
Jutland = Jylland *Denmark* 56°25N 9°30E 9 H13
Juuka *Finland* 63°13N 29°17E 8 E23
Juventud, I. de la *Cuba* 21°40N 82°40W 88 B3
Jūy Zar *Iran* 33°50N 46°18E 46 C5
Juye *China* 35°22N 116°5E 32 G9
Jwaneng *Botswana* 24°45S 24°50E 55 J4
Jylland *Denmark* 56°25N 9°30E 9 H13
Jyväskylä *Finland* 62°14N 25°50E 8 E21

K

K2 *Pakistan* 35°58N 76°32E 43 B7
Kaakha = Kaka *Turkmenistan* 37°21N 59°36E 47 B8
Kaap Plateau *S. Africa* 28°30S 24°0E 56 C3
Kaapkruis *Namibia* 21°55S 13°57E 56 B1
Kabaena *Indonesia* 5°15S 122°0E 37 F6
Kabala *S. Leone* 9°38N 11°37W 52 G3
Kabale *Uganda* 1°15S 30°0E 54 E6
Kabalo *Dem. Rep. of the Congo* 6°0S 27°0E 54 F5
Kabambare *Dem. Rep. of the Congo* 4°41S 27°39E 54 E5
Kabanjahe *Indonesia* 3°6N 98°30E 36 D1
Kabankalan *Phil.* 9°59N 122°49E 37 C6
Kabara *Fiji* 18°59S 178°56W 59 a
Kabardino-Balkaria ☐ *Russia* 43°30N 43°30E 19 F7
Kabarega Falls = Murchison Falls *Uganda* 2°15N 31°30E 54 D6
Kabasalan *Phil.* 7°47N 122°44E 37 C6
Kabat *Indonesia* 8°16S 114°19E 37 J17
Kabbani → *India* 12°13N 76°54E 45 H3
Kabin Buri *Thailand* 13°57N 101°43E 38 F3
Kabinakagami L. *Canada* 48°54N 84°25W 72 C3
Kabinda *Dem. Rep. of the Congo* 6°19S 24°20E 54 F4
Kabompo → *Zambia* 14°11S 23°11E 55 G4
Kabongo *Dem. Rep. of the Congo* 7°22S 25°33E 54 F5
Kabrīt, G. el *Egypt* 29°42N 33°16E 48 F2
Kabūd Gonbad *Iran* 37°5N 59°45E 47 B8
Kābul *Afghan.* 34°28N 69°11E 42 B3
Kābul ☐ *Afghan.* 34°30N 69°0E 40 B6
Kābul → *Pakistan* 33°55N 72°14E 42 C5
Kaburuang *Indonesia* 3°50N 126°30E 37 D7
Kabwe *Zambia* 14°30S 28°29E 55 G5
Kachchh, Gulf of *India* 22°50N 69°15E 42 H3
Kachchh, Rann of *India* 24°0N 70°0E 42 H4
Kachchhidhana *India* 21°44N 78°46E 43 J8
Kachikau *Botswana* 18°8S 24°26E 56 A3
Kachin ☐ *Burma* 26°0N 97°30E 34 D1
Kachīry *Kazakhstan* 53°10N 75°50E 26 D8
Kachnara *India* 23°50N 75°6E 42 H6
Kachot *Cambodia* 11°30N 103°3E 39 G4
Kaçkar *Turkey* 40°45N 41°10E 19 F7
Kadaiyanallur *India* 9°3N 77°22E 45 K3
Kadan Kyun *Burma* 12°30N 98°20E 38 F2
Kadanai → *Afghan.* 31°22N 65°45E 42 D1
Kadavu *Fiji* 19°0S 178°15E 59 a
Kadavu Passage *Fiji* 18°45S 178°0E 59 a
Kade *Ghana* 6°7N 0°56W 52 G5
Kadhimain = Al Kāẓimīyah *Iraq* 33°22N 44°18E 46 C5
Kadi *India* 23°18N 72°23E 42 H5
Kadina *Australia* 33°55S 137°43E 63 E2
Kadipur *India* 26°10N 82°23E 43 F10
Kadirabad *India* 19°51N 75°54E 44 E2
Kadiri *India* 14°12N 78°13E 45 G4
Kadirli *Turkey* 37°23N 36°5E 46 B3
Kadiyevka = Stakhanov *Ukraine* 48°35N 38°40E 19 E6
Kadmat I. *India* 11°14N 72°47E 45 J1
Kadoka *U.S.A.* 43°50N 101°31W 80 D3
Kadoma *Zimbabwe* 18°20S 29°52E 55 H5
Kādugli *Sudan* 11°0N 29°45E 53 F11
Kaduna *Nigeria* 10°30N 7°21E 52 F7
Kadur *India* 13°34N 76°1E 45 H3
Kaédi *Mauritania* 16°9N 13°28W 52 E3
Kaeng Khoi *Thailand* 14°35N 101°0E 38 E3
Kaeng Krachan △ *Thailand* 12°57N 99°23E 38 F2
Kaeng Krung △ *Thailand* 9°30N 98°50E 39 H2
Kaeng Tana △ *Thailand* 15°25N 105°32E 38 E5
Kaesŏng *N. Korea* 37°58N 126°35E 33 F14
Kāf *Si. Arabia* 31°25N 37°29E 46 D3
Kafan = Kapan *Armenia* 39°18N 46°27E 46 B5
Kafanchan *Nigeria* 9°40N 8°20E 52 G7
Kafue *Zambia* 15°46S 28°9E 55 H5
Kafue → *Zambia* 15°30S 29°0E 55 H5
Kaga *Afghan.* 34°14N 70°10E 42 B4
Kaga Bandoro *C.A.R.* 7°0N 19°10E 54 C3
Kagawa ☐ *Japan* 34°15N 134°0E 29 G7
Kagera → *Uganda* 0°57S 31°47E 54 E6
Kağızman *Turkey* 40°5N 43°10E 46 B4
Kagoshima *Japan* 31°35N 130°33E 29 J5
Kagoshima ☐ *Japan* 31°30N 130°30E 29 J5
Kagul = Cahul *Moldova* 45°50N 28°15E 17 F15
Kahak *Iran* 36°6N 49°46E 47 B6
Kahan *Pakistan* 29°18N 68°54E 42 E3
Kahang *Malaysia* 2°12N 103°32E 39 L4
Kahayan → *Indonesia* 3°40S 114°0E 36 E4
Kahemba *Dem. Rep. of the Congo* 7°18S 18°55E 54 F3
Kahnūj *Iran* 27°55N 57°40E 47 E8
Kahoka *U.S.A.* 40°25N 91°44W 80 E8
Kaho'olawe *U.S.A.* 20°33N 156°37W 75 L8
Kahramanmaraş *Turkey* 37°37N 36°53E 46 B3
Kâhta *Turkey* 37°46N 38°36E 46 B3
Kahului *U.S.A.* 20°54N 156°28W 75 L8
Kahurangi △ *N.Z.* 41°10S 172°32E 59 D4
Kahuta *Pakistan* 33°35N 73°24E 42 C5
Kai, Kepulauan *Indonesia* 5°55S 132°45E 37 F8
Kai Besar *Indonesia* 5°35S 133°0E 37 F8
Kai Is. = Kai, Kepulauan *Indonesia* 5°55S 132°45E 37 F8
Kai Kecil *Indonesia* 5°45S 132°40E 37 F8
Kai Xian *China* 31°11N 108°21E 34 B7
Kaiapoi *N.Z.* 43°24S 172°40E 59 E4
Kaidu He → *China* 41°46N 86°31E 30 C6
Kaieteur Falls *Guyana* 5°1N 59°10W 92 B7
Kaifeng *China* 34°48N 114°21E 32 G8
Kaihua *China* 29°12N 118°20E 35 C12
Kaijiang *China* 31°7N 107°55E 34 B6
Kaikohe *N.Z.* 35°25S 173°49E 59 A4
Kaikoura *N.Z.* 42°25S 173°43E 59 E4
Kailash = Kangrinboqe Feng *China* 31°0N 81°25E 43 D9
Kaili *China* 26°33N 107°59E 34 D6
Kailu *China* 43°38N 121°18E 33 C11
Kailua Kona *U.S.A.* 19°39N 155°59W 75 M8
Kaimana *Indonesia* 3°39S 133°45E 37 E8
Kaimanawa Mts. *N.Z.* 39°15S 175°56E 59 C5
Kaimganj *India* 27°33N 79°24E 43 F8
Kaimur Hills *India* 24°30N 82°0E 43 G10
Kainab → *Namibia* 28°32S 19°34E 56 C2
Kainji Res. *Nigeria* 10°1N 4°40E 52 F6
Kainuu ☐ *Finland* 64°30N 29°7E 8 D23
Kaipara Harbour *N.Z.* 36°25S 174°14E 59 B5
Kaiping *China* 22°23N 112°42E 35 F9
Kaipokok B. *Canada* 54°54N 59°47W 73 B8
Kaira *India* 22°45N 72°50E 42 H5
Kairana *India* 29°24N 77°15E 42 E7
Kaironi *Indonesia* 0°47S 133°40E 37 E8
Kairouan *Tunisia* 35°45N 10°5E 53 A8
Kaiserslautern *Germany* 49°26N 7°45E 16 D4
Kaitaia *N.Z.* 35°8S 173°17E 59 A4
Kaitangata *N.Z.* 46°17S 169°51E 59 G2
Kaithal *India* 29°48N 76°26E 42 E7
Kaitu → *Pakistan* 33°10N 70°30E 42 C4
Kaiwi Channel *U.S.A.* 21°15N 157°30W 75 L8
Kaiyang *China* 27°4N 106°59E 34 D6
Kaiyuan *Liaoning, China* 42°28N 124°1E 33 C13
Kaiyuan *Yunnan, China* 23°40N 103°12E 34 F4
Kaiyuh Mts. *U.S.A.* 64°30N 158°0W 74 C8
Kajaani *Finland* 64°17N 27°46E 8 D22
Kajabbi *Australia* 20°0S 140°1E 62 C3
Kajana = Kajaani *Finland* 64°17N 27°46E 8 D22
Kajang *Malaysia* 2°59N 101°48E 39 L3
Kajo Kaji *South Sudan* 3°58N 31°40E 53 H12
Kaka *Turkmenistan* 37°21N 59°36E 47 B8
Kakabeka Falls *Canada* 48°24N 89°37W 72 C2
Kakadu △ *Australia* 12°0S 132°3E 60 B5
Kakamas *S. Africa* 28°45S 20°33E 56 C3
Kakamega *Kenya* 0°20N 34°46E 54 D6
Kakana *India* 9°7N 92°48E 45 K11
Kakanui Mts. *N.Z.* 45°10S 170°30E 59 F3
Kakdwip *India* 21°53N 88°11E 43 J13
Kake = Akiōta *Japan* 34°36N 132°19E 29 G6
Kake *U.S.A.* 56°59N 133°57W 70 B2
Kakegawa *Japan* 34°45N 138°1E 29 G9
Kakeroma-Jima *Japan* 28°8N 129°14E 29 K4
Kākhak *Iran* 34°9N 58°38E 47 C8
Kakhovka *Ukraine* 46°45N 33°30E 19 E5
Kakhovske Vdskh. *Ukraine* 47°5N 34°0E 19 E5
Kakinada *India* 16°57N 82°11E 44 F6
Kakisa *Canada* 60°56N 117°25W 70 A5
Kakisa → *Canada* 61°3N 118°10W 70 A5
Kakisa L. *Canada* 60°56N 117°43W 70 A5
Kakogawa *Japan* 34°46N 134°51E 29 G7
Kakwa → *Canada* 54°37N 118°28W 70 C5
Kāl Gūsheh *Iran* 30°59N 58°12E 47 D8
Kal Sefīd *Iran* 34°52N 47°23E 46 C5
Kala Oya → *Sri Lanka* 8°20N 79°45E 45 K4
Kalaallit Nunaat = Greenland ⊠ *N. Amer.* 66°0N 45°0W 67 C15
Kalabagh *Pakistan* 33°0N 71°28E 42 C4
Kalabahi *Indonesia* 8°13S 124°31E 37 F6
Kalach *Russia* 50°22N 41°0E 19 D7
Kaladan → *Burma* 20°20N 93°5E 41 J18
Kaladar *Canada* 44°37N 77°5W 82 B7
Kalahari *Africa* 24°0S 21°30E 56 B3
Kalahari Gemsbok △ *S. Africa* 25°30S 20°30E 56 C3
Kalajoki *Finland* 64°12N 24°10E 8 D21
Kalakamati *Botswana* 20°40S 27°25E 57 B4
Kalakan *Russia* 55°15N 116°45E 27 D12
K'alak'unlun Shank'ou = Karakoram Pass *Asia* 35°33N 77°50E 43 B7
Kalam *Pakistan* 35°34N 72°30E 43 B5
Kalama *U.S.A.* 46°1N 122°51W 78 E4
Kalamata *Greece* 37°3N 22°10E 23 F10
Kalamazoo *U.S.A.* 42°17N 85°35W 81 D11
Kalamazoo → *U.S.A.* 42°40N 86°10W 80 D10
Kalamb *India* 18°3N 74°48E 44 E2
Kalamnuri *India* 19°40N 77°20E 44 E3
Kalan *Turkey* 39°7N 39°32E 46 B3
Kalannie *Australia* 30°22S 117°5E 61 F2
Kalāntarī *Iran* 32°10N 54°8E 47 C7
Kalao *Indonesia* 7°21S 121°0E 37 F6
Kalaotoa *Indonesia* 7°20S 121°50E 37 F6
Kalasin *Thailand* 16°26N 103°30E 38 D4
Kālat *Iran* 25°29N 59°22E 47 E8
Kalat *Pakistan* 29°8N 66°31E 40 E5
Kalāteh *Iran* 36°33N 55°41E 47 B7
Kalāteh-ye Ganj *Iran* 27°31N 57°55E 47 E8
Kalbā *U.A.E.* 25°5N 56°22E 47 E8
Kalbarri *Australia* 27°40S 114°10E 61 E1
Kalbarri △ *Australia* 27°51S 114°30E 61 E1
Kalburgi = Gulbarga *India* 17°20N 76°50E 44 F3
Kalce *Slovenia* 45°54N 14°13E 16 F8
Kale *Turkey* 37°27N 28°49E 23 F13
Kalegauk Kyun *Burma* 15°33N 97°35E 38 E1
Kalemie *Dem. Rep. of the Congo* 5°55S 29°9E 54 F5
Kalewa *Burma* 23°10N 94°15E 41 H19
Kaleybar *Iran* 38°47N 47°2E 46 B5
Kalghatgi *India* 15°11N 74°58E 45 G2
Kalgoorlie-Boulder *Australia* 30°40S 121°22E 61 F3
Kali → *India* 27°6N 79°55E 43 F8
Kali Sindh → *India* 25°32N 76°17E 42 G6
Kaliakra, Nos *Bulgaria* 43°21N 28°30E 23 C13
Kalianda *Indonesia* 5°50S 105°45E 36 F3
Kalibo *Phil.* 11°43N 122°22E 37 B6
Kalimantan *Indonesia* 0°0 114°0E 36 E4
Kalimantan Barat ☐ *Indonesia* 0°0 110°30E 36 E4
Kalimantan Selatan ☐ *Indonesia* 2°30S 115°30E 36 E5
Kalimantan Tengah ☐ *Indonesia* 2°0S 113°30E 36 E4
Kalimantan Timur ☐ *Indonesia* 1°30N 116°30E 36 D5
Kálimnos *Greece* 37°0N 27°0E 23 F12
Kalimpong *India* 27°4N 88°35E 43 F13
Kalinadi → *India* 14°50N 74°7E 45 G2
Kaliningrad *Russia* 54°42N 20°32E 9 J19
Kalinkavichy *Belarus* 52°12N 29°20E 17 B15
Kalinkovichi = Kalinkavichy *Belarus* 52°12N 29°20E 17 B15
Kalispell *U.S.A.* 48°12N 114°19W 76 B6
Kalisz *Poland* 51°45N 18°8E 17 C10
Kaliveli Tank *India* 12°5N 79°50E 45 H4
Kalix *Sweden* 65°53N 23°12E 8 D20
Kalixälven → *Sweden* 65°50N 23°11E 8 D20
Kalka *India* 30°46N 76°57E 42 D7
Kalkarindji *Australia* 17°30S 130°47E 60 C5
Kalkaska *U.S.A.* 44°44N 85°11W 81 C11
Kalkfeld *Namibia* 20°57S 16°14E 56 B2
Kalkfontein *Botswana* 22°4S 20°57E 56 B3
Kalkrand *Namibia* 24°1S 17°35E 56 B2
Kallakkurichchi *India* 11°44N 79°1E 45 J4
Kallam *India* 18°36N 76°2E 44 E3
Kallavesi *Finland* 62°58N 27°30E 8 E22
Kallidaikurichi *India* 8°38N 77°31E 45 K3
Kallsjön *Sweden* 63°38N 13°0E 8 E15
Kalmar *Sweden* 56°40N 16°20E 9 H17
Kalmunai *Sri Lanka* 7°25N 81°49E 45 L5
Kalmykia ☐ *Russia* 46°5N 46°1E 19 E8
Kalna *India* 23°13N 88°25E 43 H13
Kalnai *India* 22°46N 83°30E 43 H10
Kalocsa *Hungary* 46°32N 19°0E 17 E10
Kalol *Gujarat, India* 22°37N 73°31E 42 H5
Kalol *Gujarat, India* 23°15N 72°33E 42 H5
Kalpeni I. *India* 10°5N 73°38E 45 J1
Kalpi *India* 26°8N 79°47E 43 F8
Kalpitiya *Sri Lanka* 8°14N 79°46E 45 K4
Kalputhi I. *India* 10°49N 72°10E 45 J1
Kalrayan Hills *India* 11°45N 78°40E 45 J4
Kalsubai *India* 19°35N 73°45E 44 E1
Kaltag *U.S.A.* 64°20N 158°43W 74 C8
Kaltukatjara *Australia* 24°52S 129°5E 61 D4
Kalu *Pakistan* 25°5N 67°39E 42 G2
Kaluga *Russia* 54°35N 36°10E 18 D6
Kalumburu *Australia* 13°55S 126°35E 60 B4
Kalumburu ☼ *Australia* 14°17S 126°38E 60 B4
Kalush *Ukraine* 49°3N 24°23E 17 D13
Kalutara *Sri Lanka* 6°35N 80°0E 45 L5
Kalwakurti *India* 16°41N 78°30E 44 F4
Kalya *Russia* 60°15N 59°59E 18 B10
Kalyan *Maharashtra, India* 20°30N 74°3E 44 D2
Kalyan *Maharashtra, India* 19°15N 73°9E 44 E1
Kalyandurg *India* 14°33N 77°6E 45 G3
Kalyani *India* 17°52N 76°57E 44 F3
Kalyansingapuram *India* 19°30N 83°19E 44 E6
Kama *Japan* 33°33N 130°49E 29 H5
Kama → *Russia* 55°45N 52°0E 18 C9
Kamaishi *Japan* 39°16N 141°53E 28 E10
Kamalapurum *India* 14°35N 78°39E 45 G4
Kamalia *Pakistan* 30°44N 72°42E 42 D5
Kaman *India* 27°39N 77°16E 42 F6
Kamanjab *Namibia* 19°35S 14°51E 56 A2
Kamarān *Yemen* 15°21N 42°35E 49 D3
Kamareddi *India* 18°19N 78°21E 44 E4
Kamativi *Zimbabwe* 18°20S 27°6E 56 A4
Kambalda West *Australia* 31°10S 121°37E 61 F3
Kambam *India* 9°45N 77°16E 45 K3
Kambangan, Nusa *Indonesia* 7°40S 108°10E 37 G13
Kambar *Pakistan* 27°37N 68°1E 42 F3
Kambarka *Russia* 56°15N 54°11E 18 C9
Kambove *Dem. Rep. of the Congo* 10°51S 26°33E 54 G5
Kamchatka, Poluostrov *Russia* 57°0N 160°0E 27 D17
Kamchatka Pen. = Kamchatka, Poluostrov *Russia* 57°0N 160°0E 27 D17
Kamchiya → *Bulgaria* 43°4N 27°44E 23 C12
Kameda-Hantō *Japan* 41°50N 141°0E 28 D10
Kamen *Russia* 53°50N 81°30E 26 D9
Kamen-Rybolov *Russia* 44°46N 132°2E 28 B5
Kamenjak, Rt *Croatia* 44°47N 13°55E 16 F7
Kamenka *Russia* 65°58N 44°0E 18 A7
Kamenka Bugskaya = Kamyanka-Buzka *Ukraine* 50°8N 24°16E 17 C13
Kamensk Uralskiy *Russia* 56°25N 62°2E 26 D7
Kamenskoye *Russia* 62°45N 165°30E 27 C17
Kameoka *Japan* 35°0N 135°35E 29 G7
Kamet *India* 30°55N 79°35E 43 D8
Kamiah *U.S.A.* 46°14N 116°2W 76 C5
Kamieskroon *S. Africa* 30°9S 17°56E 56 D2
Kamilukuak L. *Canada* 62°22N 101°40W 71 A8
Kamin-Kashyrskyy *Ukraine* 51°39N 24°56E 17 C13
Kamina *Dem. Rep. of the Congo* 8°45S 25°0E 54 F5
Kaminak L. *Canada* 62°10N 95°0W 71 A10
Kaminoyama *Japan* 38°9N 140°17E 28 E10
Kamla → *India* 25°35N 86°36E 43 G12
Kamloops *Canada* 50°40N 120°20W 70 C4
Kamo *Japan* 37°39N 139°3E 28 F9
Kamoke *Pakistan* 32°4N 74°4E 42 C6
Kampala *Uganda* 0°20N 32°30E 54 D6
Kampar *Malaysia* 4°18N 101°9E 39 K3
Kampar → *Indonesia* 0°30N 103°8E 36 D2
Kampen *Neths.* 52°33N 5°53E 15 B5
Kampene *Dem. Rep. of the Congo* 3°36S 26°40E 54 E5
Kamphaeng Phet *Thailand* 16°28N 99°30E 38 D2
Kampong Cham *Cambodia* 12°0N 105°30E 39 G5
Kampong Chhnang *Cambodia* 12°20N 104°35E 39 F5
Kampong Pengerang *Malaysia* 1°22N 104°7E 39 d
Kampong Punggai *Malaysia* 1°27N 104°18E 39 d
Kampong Saom *Cambodia* 10°38N 103°30E 39 G4
Kampong Saom, Chaak *Cambodia* 10°50N 103°32E 39 G4
Kampong Tanjong Langsat *Malaysia* 1°28N 104°1E 39 d
Kampong Telok Ramunia *Malaysia* 1°22N 104°15E 39 d
Kampot *Cambodia* 10°36N 104°10E 39 G5
Kampuchea = Cambodia ■ *Asia* 12°15N 105°0E 38 F5
Kampung Air Putih *Malaysia* 4°15N 103°10E 39 K4
Kampung Jerangau *Malaysia* 4°50N 103°10E 39 K4
Kampung Raja *Malaysia* 5°45N 102°35E 39 K4
Kampungbaru = Tolitoli *Indonesia* 1°5N 120°50E 37 D6
Kamrau, Teluk *Indonesia* 3°30S 133°36E 37 E8
Kamsack *Canada* 51°34N 101°54W 71 C8
Kamsar *Guinea* 10°40N 14°36W 52 F3
Kamskoye Vdkhr. *Russia* 58°41N 56°7E 18 C10
Kamthi *India* 21°9N 79°19E 44 D4
Kamuchawie L. *Canada* 56°18N 101°59W 71 B8
Kamui-Misaki *Japan* 43°20N 140°21E 28 C10
Kamyanets-Podilskyy *Ukraine* 48°45N 26°40E 17 D14
Kamyanka-Buzka *Ukraine* 50°8N 24°16E 17 C13
Kāmyārān *Iran* 34°47N 46°56E 46 C5
Kamyshin *Russia* 50°10N 45°24E 19 D8
Kanaaupscow → *Canada* 54°2N 76°30W 72 B4
Kanab *U.S.A.* 37°3N 112°32W 77 H7
Kanab Cr. → *U.S.A.* 36°24N 112°38W 77 H7
Kanacea *Lau Group, Fiji* 17°15S 179°6W 59 a
Kanacea *Taveuni, Fiji* 16°59S 179°56E 59 a
Kanaga I. *U.S.A.* 51°45N 177°22W 74 E4
Kanagi *Japan* 40°54N 140°27E 28 D10
Kanairiktok → *Canada* 55°2N 60°18W 73 A7
Kanakapura *India* 12°33N 77°28E 45 H3
Kananga *Dem. Rep. of the Congo* 5°55S 22°18E 54 F4
Kanash *Russia* 55°30N 47°32E 18 C8
Kanaskat *U.S.A.* 47°19N 121°54W 78 C5
Kanastraíon, Ákra = Palioúri, Ákra *Greece* 39°57N 23°45E 23 E10
Kanawha → *U.S.A.* 38°50N 82°9W 81 F12
Kanazawa *Japan* 36°30N 136°38E 29 F8
Kanchanaburi *Thailand* 14°2N 99°31E 38 E2
Kanchenjunga *Nepal* 27°50N 88°10E 43 F13
Kanchenjunga △ *India* 27°42N 88°8E 43 F13
Kanchipuram *India* 12°52N 79°45E 45 H4
Kandaghat *India* 30°59N 77°7E 42 D7
Kandahār *Afghan.* 31°32N 65°43E 40 D4
Kandahar *India* 18°52N 77°12E 44 E3
Kandahār ☐ *Afghan.* 31°0N 65°0E 40 D4
Kandalaksha *Russia* 67°9N 32°30E 8 C25
Kandalakshskiy Zaliv *Russia* 66°0N 35°0E 18 A6
Kandangan *Indonesia* 2°50S 115°20E 36 E5
Kandavu = Kadavu *Fiji* 19°0S 178°15E 59 a
Kandavu Passage = Kadavu Passage *Fiji* 18°45S 178°0E 59 a
Kandhkot *Pakistan* 28°16N 69°8E 42 E3
Kandhla *India* 29°18N 77°19E 42 E7
Kandi *Benin* 11°7N 2°55E 52 F6
Kandi *India* 23°58N 88°5E 43 H13
Kandiaro *Pakistan* 27°4N 68°13E 42 F3
Kandla *India* 23°0N 70°10E 42 H4
Kandos *Australia* 32°45S 149°58E 63 E4
Kandy *Sri Lanka* 7°18N 80°43E 45 L5
Kane *U.S.A.* 41°40N 78°49W 82 E6
Kane Basin *Greenland* 79°1N 70°0W 69 B18
Kang *Botswana* 23°41S 22°50E 56 B3
Kangān *Fārs, Iran* 27°50N 52°3E 47 E7
Kangān *Hormozgān, Iran* 25°48N 57°28E 47 E8
Kangar *Malaysia* 6°27N 100°12E 39 J3
Kangaroo I. *Australia* 35°45S 137°0E 63 F2
Kangaroo Mts. *Australia* 23°29S 141°51E 62 C3
Kangasala *Finland* 61°28N 24°4E 8 F21
Kangāvar *Iran* 34°40N 48°0E 47 C6
Kangding *China* 30°2N 101°57E 34 B3
Kangdong *N. Korea* 39°9N 126°5E 33 E14
Kangean, Kepulauan *Indonesia* 6°55S 115°23E 36 F5
Kangean Is. = Kangean, Kepulauan *Indonesia* 6°55S 115°23E 36 F5
Kanggye *N. Korea* 41°0N 126°35E 33 D14
Kangikajik *Greenland* 70°7N 22°0W 4 B6
Kangiqliniq = Rankin Inlet *Canada* 62°30N 93°0W 68 E13
Kangiqsualujjuaq *Canada* 58°30N 65°59W 69 F18
Kangiqsujuaq *Canada* 61°30N 72°0W 69 E17
Kangiqtugaapik = Clyde River *Canada* 70°30N 68°30W 69 C18

Kangirsuk Canada 60°N 70°0W 69 F18
Kangkar Chemaran
  Malaysia 1°34N 104°12E 39 d
Kangkar Sungai Tiram
  Malaysia 1°35N 103°55E 39 d
Kangkar Teberau
  Malaysia 1°32N 103°51E 39 d
Kangping China 42°43N 123°18E 33 C12
Kangra India 32°6N 76°16E 42 C7
Kangrinboqe Feng China 31°0N 81°25E 43 D9
Kangto China 27°50N 92°35E 41 F18
Kanha △ India 22°15N 80°40E 43 H9
Kanhan → India 21°4N 79°34E 44 D4
Kanhangad India 12°21N 74°58E 45 G2
Kanhar → India 24°28N 83°8E 43 G10
Kaniapiskau = Caniapiscau →
  Canada 56°40N 69°30W 73 A6
Kaniapiskau, L. = Caniapiscau, L.
  Canada 54°10N 69°55W 73 B6
Kanigiri India 15°24N 79°31E 45 G4
Kanin, Poluostrov Russia 68°0N 45°0E 18 A8
Kanin Nos, Mys Russia 68°39N 43°32E 18 A7
Kanin Pen. = Kanin, Poluostrov
  Russia 68°0N 45°0E 18 A8
Kaniva Australia 36°22S 141°18E 63 F3
Kanjut Sar Pakistan 36°7N 75°25E 43 A6
Kankaanpää Finland 61°44N 22°50E 8 E20
Kankakee U.S.A. 41°7N 87°52W 80 E10
Kankakee → U.S.A. 41°23N 88°15W 80 E9
Kankan Guinea 10°23N 9°15W 52 F4
Kankendy = Xankändi
  Azerbaijan 39°52N 46°49E 46 B5
Kanker India 20°10N 81°40E 44 D5
Kankesanturai Sri Lanka 9°49N 80°2E 45 K5
Kankroli India 25°4N 73°53E 42 G5
Kanmaw Kyun Burma 11°40N 98°28E 39 G2
Kannapolis U.S.A. 35°30N 80°37W 85 D14
Kannauj India 27°3N 79°56E 43 F8
Kanniyakumari India 8°5N 77°34E 45 K3
Kannod India 22°45N 76°40E 40 H10
Kannur India 11°53N 75°27E 45 J2
Kannyakumari India 8°3N 77°40E 45 K3
Kano Nigeria 12°2N 8°30E 52 F7
Kan'onji Japan 34°7N 133°39E 29 G6
Kanowit Malaysia 2°14N 112°20E 36 D4
Kanoya Japan 31°25N 130°50E 29 J5
Kanpetlet Burma 21°10N 93°59E 41 J18
Kanpur India 26°28N 80°20E 43 F9
Kansas □ U.S.A. 38°30N 99°0W 80 F4
Kansas → U.S.A. 39°7N 94°37W 80 F6
Kansas City Kans., U.S.A. 39°7N 94°38W 80 F6
Kansas City Mo., U.S.A. 39°6N 94°35W 80 F6
Kansk Russia 56°20N 95°37E 27 D10
Kansu = Gansu □ China 36°0N 104°0E 32 G3
Kantaphor India 22°35N 76°34E 42 H7
Kantharalak Thailand 14°39N 104°39E 38 E5
Kanthi = Contai India 21°54N 87°46E 43 J12
Kantli → India 28°20N 75°30E 42 E6
Kantō □ Japan 36°15N 139°30E 29 F9
Kantō-Sanchi Japan 35°59N 138°50E 29 G9
Kanturk Ireland 52°11N 8°54W 10 D3
Kanuma Japan 36°34N 139°42E 29 F9
Kanus Namibia 27°50S 18°39E 56 C2
Kanye Botswana 24°55S 25°28E 56 C4
Kao Tonga 19°40S 175°1W 59 c
Kao Phara Thailand 8°3N 98°22E 39 a
Kaohsiung Taiwan 22°35N 120°16E 35 F13
Kaokoveld Namibia 19°15S 14°30E 56 A1
Kaolack Senegal 14°5N 16°8W 52 F2
Kaoshan China 44°38N 124°50E 33 B13
Kapa'a U.S.A. 22°5N 159°19W 75 L8
Kapadvanj India 23°5N 73°0E 42 H5
Kapan Armenia 39°18N 46°27E 46 B5
Kapanga
  Dem. Rep. of the Congo 8°30S 22°40E 54 F4
Kapchagai = Qapshaghay
  Kazakhstan 43°51N 77°14E 26 E8
Kapela = Velika Kapela
  Croatia 45°10N 15°5E 16 F8
Kapfenberg Austria 47°26N 15°18E 16 E8
Kapiri Mposhi Zambia 13°59S 28°43E 55 G5
Kāpīsā □ Afghan. 35°0N 69°20E 40 B6
Kapiskau → Canada 52°47N 81°55W 72 B3
Kapit Malaysia 2°0N 112°55E 36 D4
Kapiti I. N.Z. 40°50S 174°56E 59 D5
Kaplan U.S.A. 30°0N 92°17W 84 F8
Kapoe Thailand 9°34N 98°32E 39 H2
Kaposvár Hungary 46°25N 17°47E 17 E9
Kapowsin U.S.A. 46°59N 122°13W 78 D4
Kapps Namibia 22°32S 17°18E 56 B2
Kapsan N. Korea 41°4N 128°19E 33 D15
Kapsukas = Marijampolė
  Lithuania 54°33N 23°19E 9 J20
Kaptai L. Bangla. 22°40N 92°20E 41 H18
Kapuas → Indonesia 0°25S 109°20E 36 E3
Kapuas Hulu, Pegunungan
  Malaysia 1°30N 113°30E 36 D4
Kapuas Hulu Ra. = Kapuas Hulu,
  Pegunungan Malaysia 1°30N 113°30E 36 D4
Kapunda Australia 34°20S 138°56E 63 E2
Kapuni N.Z. 39°29S 174°8E 59 C5
Kapurthala India 31°23N 75°25E 42 D6
Kapuskasing Canada 49°25N 82°30W 72 C3
Kapuskasing → Canada 49°49N 82°0W 72 C3
Kaputar, Mt. Australia 30°15S 150°10E 63 E5
Kara Russia 69°10N 65°0E 26 C7
Kara Bogaz Gol, Zaliv =
  Garabogazköl Aylagy
  Turkmenistan 41°0N 53°30E 19 F9
Kara-Kala = Garrygala
  Turkmenistan 38°31N 56°29E 47 B8
Kara Kalpak Republic =
  Qoraqalpoghistan □
  Uzbekistan 43°0N 58°0E 26 E6
Kara Kum = Garagum
  Turkmenistan 39°30N 60°0E 47 B8
Kara Sea Russia 75°0N 70°0E 26 B8
Karabiğa Turkey 40°23N 27°17E 23 D12

Karabük Turkey 41°12N 32°37E 19 F5
Karaburun Turkey 38°41N 26°28E 23 E12
Karabutak = Qarabutaq
  Kazakhstan 50°0N 60°14E 26 E7
Karacabey Turkey 40°12N 28°21E 23 D13
Karacasu Turkey 37°43N 28°35E 23 F13
Karachey-Cherkessia □
  Russia 43°40N 41°30E 19 F7
Karad India 17°15N 74°10E 44 F2
Karaganda = Qaraghandy
  Kazakhstan 49°50N 73°10E 30 B3
Karagayly = Qaraghayly
  Kazakhstan 49°26N 76°0E 26 E8
Karaginskiy, Ostrov
  Russia 58°45N 164°0E 27 D17
Karagiye, Vpadina
  Kazakhstan 43°27N 51°45E 19 F9
Karagiye Depression = Karagiye,
  Vpadina Kazakhstan 43°27N 51°45E 19 F9
Karagola Road India 25°29N 87°23E 43 G12
Karaikal India 10°59N 79°50E 45 J4
Karaikkudi India 10°5N 78°45E 45 J4
Karaitivu I. Sri Lanka 9°45N 79°52E 45 K4
Karaj Iran 35°48N 51°0E 47 C6
Karajarri ⊙ Australia 19°0S 122°30E 60 C3
Karak Malaysia 3°25N 102°2E 39 L4
Karakalpakstan =
  Qoraqalpoghistan □
  Uzbekistan 43°0N 58°0E 26 E6
Karakelong Indonesia 4°35N 126°50E 37 D7
Karakitang Indonesia 3°14N 125°28E 37 D7
Karakol Kyrgyzstan 42°30N 78°20E 30 C4
Karakoram Pass Asia 35°33N 77°50E 43 B7
Karakoram Ra. Pakistan 35°30N 77°0E 43 B7
Karakuwisa Namibia 18°56S 19°40E 56 A2
Karalon Russia 57°5N 115°50E 27 D12
Karama Jordan 31°57N 35°35E 48 D4
Karaman Turkey 37°14N 33°13E 46 B2
Karamay China 45°30N 84°58E 30 B5
Karambu Indonesia 3°53S 116°6E 36 E5
Karamea Bight N.Z. 41°22S 171°40E 59 D3
Karamnasa → India 25°31N 83°52E 43 G10
Karān Si. Arabia 27°43N 49°49E 47 E6
Karand Iran 34°16N 46°15E 46 C5
Karanganyar Indonesia 7°38S 109°37E 37 G13
Karangasem = Amlapura
  Indonesia 8°27S 115°37E 37 J18
Karanja Maharashtra,
  India 21°11N 78°24E 44 D4
Karanja Maharashtra,
  India 20°29N 77°31E 44 D3
Karanjia India 21°47N 85°58E 43 J11
Karas □ Namibia 27°0S 17°30E 56 C2
Karasburg Namibia 28°0S 18°44E 56 C2
Karasino Russia 66°50N 86°50E 26 C9
Karasjok Norway 69°27N 25°30E 8 B21
Karasuk Russia 53°44N 78°2E 26 D8
Karasuyama Japan 36°39N 140°9E 29 F10
Karatau, Khrebet = Qarataū
  Kazakhstan 43°30N 69°30E 26 E7
Karatax Shan China 35°57N 81°0E 30 D5
Karativu Sri Lanka 8°22N 79°47E 45 K4
Karatsu Japan 33°26N 129°58E 29 H5
Karaul Russia 70°6N 82°15E 26 B9
Karauli India 26°30N 77°4E 42 F7
Karawang Indonesia 6°30S 107°15E 37 G12
Karawanken Europe 46°30N 14°40E 16 E8
Karayaz Turkey 39°41N 42°9E 19 G7
Karazhal = Qarazhal
  Kazakhstan 48°2N 70°49E 26 E8
Karbalā' Iraq 32°36N 44°3E 46 C5
Karcag Hungary 47°19N 20°57E 17 E11
Karcha → Pakistan 34°45N 76°10E 43 B7
Karchana India 25°17N 81°56E 43 G9
Karditsa Greece 39°23N 21°54E 23 E9
Kärdla Estonia 59°0N 22°45E 9 G20
Kardzhali = Kürdzhali
  Bulgaria 41°38N 25°21E 23 D11
Kareeberge S. Africa 30°59S 21°50E 56 D3
Kareha → India 25°44N 86°21E 43 G12
Kareima Sudan 18°30N 31°49E 53 E12
Karelia □ Russia 65°30N 32°30E 18 A5
Karelian Republic = Karelia □
  Russia 65°30N 32°30E 18 A5
Karera India 25°32N 78°9E 42 G8
Kārevāndar Iran 27°53N 60°44E 47 E9
Kargasok Russia 59°3N 80°53E 26 D9
Kargat Russia 55°10N 80°15E 26 D9
Kargil India 34°32N 76°12E 43 B7
Kargopol Russia 61°30N 38°58E 18 B6
Kariān Iran 26°57N 57°14E 47 E8
Kariba Zimbabwe 16°40S 28°25E 55 H5
Kariba, L. Zimbabwe 16°40S 28°25E 55 H5
Kariba Dam Zimbabwe 16°30S 28°35E 55 H5
Kariba Gorge Zambia 16°30S 28°50E 55 H5
Karibib Namibia 22°0S 15°56E 56 B2
Karijini △ Australia 23°8S 118°15E 60 D2
Karimata, Kepulauan
  Indonesia 1°25S 109°0E 36 E3
Karimata, Selat Indonesia 2°0S 108°40E 36 E3
Karimata Is. = Karimata,
  Kepulauan Indonesia 1°25S 109°0E 36 E3
Karimnagar India 18°26N 79°10E 44 E4
Karimun, Pulau Indonesia 1°3N 103°22E 39 d
Karimunjawa, Kepulauan
  Indonesia 5°50S 110°30E 36 F4
Karin Somalia 10°50N 45°52E 49 E4
Karīt Iran 33°29N 56°55E 47 C8
Kariya Japan 34°58N 137°1E 29 G8
Kariyangwe Zimbabwe 18°0S 27°38E 57 A4
Karjala Finland 62°0N 30°25E 8 F24
Karjat India 18°33N 75°0E 44 E2
Karkal India 13°15N 74°56E 45 H2
Karkaralinsk = Qarqaraly
  Kazakhstan 49°26N 75°30E 30 B4
Karkheh → Iran 31°2N 47°29E 46 D5
Karkinitska Zatoka
  Ukraine 45°56N 33°0E 19 E5

Karkinitskiy Zaliv = Karkinitska
  Zatoka Ukraine 45°56N 33°0E 19 E5
Karkük = Kirkük Iraq 35°30N 44°21E 46 C5
Karlantijpa North ⊙
  Australia 19°27S 133°33E 60 C5
Karlantijpa South ⊙
  Australia 20°31S 133°9E 60 D5
Karleby = Kokkola
  Finland 63°50N 23°8E 8 E20
Karlovac Croatia 45°31N 15°36E 16 F8
Karlovo Bulgaria 42°38N 24°47E 23 C11
Karlovy Vary Czech Rep. 50°13N 12°51E 16 C7
Karlsbad = Karlovy Vary
  Czech Rep. 50°13N 12°51E 16 C7
Karlsena, Mys Russia 77°0N 67°42E 26 B7
Karlshamn Sweden 56°10N 14°51E 9 H16
Karlskoga Sweden 59°28N 14°33E 9 G16
Karlskrona Sweden 56°10N 15°35E 9 H16
Karlsruhe Germany 49°0N 8°23E 16 D5
Karlstad Sweden 59°23N 13°30E 9 G15
Karlstad U.S.A. 48°35N 96°31W 80 A5
Karmala India 18°25N 75°12E 44 E2
Karmi'el Israel 32°55N 35°18E 48 C4
Karnak Egypt 25°43N 32°39E 53 C12
Karnal India 29°42N 77°2E 42 E7
Karnali → Nepal 28°45N 81°16E 43 E9
Karnaphuli Res. = Kaptai L.
  Bangla. 22°40N 92°20E 41 H18
Karnaprayag India 30°16N 79°15E 43 D8
Karnataka □ India 13°15N 77°0E 45 H3
Karnes City U.S.A. 28°53N 97°54W 84 G6
Karnische Alpen Europe 46°36N 13°0E 16 E7
Kärnten □ Austria 46°52N 13°30E 16 E8
Karon, Ao Thailand 7°51N 98°17E 39 a
Karonga Malawi 9°57S 33°55E 54 F6
Karoo ⌖ S. Africa 32°18S 22°27E 56 E3
Karoonda Australia 35°1S 139°59E 63 F2
Karor Pakistan 31°15N 70°59E 42 D4
Karora Sudan 17°44N 38°15E 53 E13
Karpathos Greece 35°37N 27°10E 23 G12
Karpinsk Russia 59°45N 60°1E 18 C11
Karpogory Russia 64°0N 44°27E 18 B7
Karpuz Burnu = Apostolos
  Andreas, C. Cyprus 35°42N 34°35E 46 D3
Karratha Australia 20°44S 116°52E 60 D2
Kars Turkey 40°40N 43°5E 19 F7
Karsakpay Kazakhstan 47°55N 66°40E 26 E7
Karshi = Qarshi
  Uzbekistan 38°53N 65°48E 26 F7
Karsiyang India 26°56N 88°18E 43 F13
Karsog India 31°23N 77°12E 42 D7
Kartala Comoros Is. 11°45S 43°21E 55 a
Kartaly Russia 53°3N 60°40E 26 D7
Kartapur India 31°27N 75°32E 42 D6
Karthaus U.S.A. 41°8N 78°9W 82 E6
Karufa Indonesia 3°50S 133°20E 37 E8
Karumba Australia 17°31S 140°50E 62 B3
Kārūn → Iran 30°26N 48°10E 47 D6
Karungu Kenya 0°50S 34°10E 54 E6
Karur India 10°59N 78°2E 45 J4
Karviná Czech Rep. 49°53N 18°31E 17 D10
Karwan → India 27°26N 78°4E 42 F8
Karwar India 14°55N 74°13E 45 G2
Karwi India 25°12N 80°57E 43 G9
Karymskoye Russia 51°36N 114°21E 27 D12
Kasai →
  Dem. Rep. of the Congo 3°30S 16°10E 54 E3
Kasama Zambia 10°16S 31°9E 54 G6
Kasan-dong N. Korea 41°18N 126°55E 33 D14
Kasandra Kolpos Greece 40°5N 23°30E 23 D10
Kasane Namibia 17°34S 24°50E 56 A3
Kasaragod India 12°30N 74°58E 45 G2
Kasba L. Canada 60°20N 102°10W 71 A8
Kāseh Garān Iran 34°5N 46°2E 46 C5
Kasempa Zambia 13°30S 25°44E 55 G5
Kasenga
  Dem. Rep. of the Congo 10°20S 28°45E 54 G5
Kasese Uganda 0°13N 30°3E 54 D6
Kasganj India 27°48N 78°42E 43 F8
Kashabowie Canada 48°40N 90°26W 72 C1
Kashaf Iran 35°58N 61°7E 47 C9
Kāshān Iran 34°5N 51°30E 47 C6
Kashechewan Canada 52°18N 81°37W 72 B3
Kashgar = Kashi China 39°30N 76°2E 30 D4
Kashi China 39°30N 76°2E 30 D4
Kashipur Odisha, India 19°16N 83°3E 44 E6
Kashipur Uttarakhand,
  India 29°15N 79°0E 43 E8
Kashiwazaki Japan 37°22N 138°33E 29 F9
Kashk-e Kohneh Afghan. 34°55N 62°30E 40 B3
Kashkū'īyeh Iran 30°31N 55°40E 47 D7
Kāshmar Iran 35°16N 58°26E 47 C8
Kashmir Asia 34°0N 76°0E 43 C7
Kashmor Pakistan 28°28N 69°32E 42 E3
Kashun Noerh = Gaxun Nur
  China 42°22N 100°30E 30 C9
Kasiari India 22°8N 87°14E 43 H12
Kasimov Russia 54°55N 41°20E 18 D7
Kasiruta Indonesia 0°25S 127°12E 37 E7
Kaskaskia → U.S.A. 37°58N 89°57W 80 G9
Kaskattama → Canada 57°3N 90°4W 71 B10
Kaskinen Finland 62°22N 21°15E 8 E19
Kaskö = Kaskinen
  Finland 62°22N 21°15E 8 E19
Kaslo Canada 49°55N 116°55W 70 D5
Kasmere L. Canada 59°34N 101°10W 71 B8
Kasongo
  Dem. Rep. of the Congo 4°30S 26°33E 54 E5
Kasongo Lunda
  Dem. Rep. of the Congo 6°35S 16°49E 54 F3
Kasos Greece 35°20N 26°55E 23 G12
Kassalâ Sudan 15°30N 36°0E 53 E13
Kassel Germany 51°18N 9°26E 16 C5
Kasson U.S.A. 44°2N 92°45W 80 C7
Kastamonu Turkey 41°25N 33°43E 19 F5
Kasterlee Belgium 51°15N 5°6E 15 C4
Kastoria Greece 40°30N 21°19E 23 D9
Kastrom Mefa'a = Umm al Rasas
  Jordan 31°30N 35°55E 48 D4

Kasumi Japan 35°38N 134°38E 29 G7
Kasur Pakistan 31°5N 74°25E 42 D6
Kata, Ao Thailand 7°48N 98°18E 39 J2
Kata Tjuta Australia 25°20S 130°50E 61 E5
Katahdin, Mt. U.S.A. 45°54N 68°56W 81 C19
Kataka = Cuttack India 20°25N 85°57E 44 D7
Katanga □
  Dem. Rep. of the Congo 8°0S 25°0E 54 F5
Katangi India 21°56N 79°50E 44 D4
Katanning Australia 33°40S 117°33E 61 F2
Katchall India 7°57N 93°22E 45 L11
Katerini Greece 40°18N 22°37E 23 D10
Katghora India 22°30N 82°33E 43 H10
Katha Burma 24°10N 96°30E 41 G20
Katherîna, Gebel Egypt 28°30N 33°57E 46 D2
Katherine Australia 14°27S 132°20E 60 B5
Katherine Gorge = Nitmiluk △
  Australia 14°6S 132°15E 60 B5
Kathi India 21°47N 74°3E 42 J6
Kathiawar India 22°20N 71°0E 42 H4
Kathmandu Nepal 27°45N 85°20E 43 F11
Kathua India 32°23N 75°34E 42 C6
Katihar India 25°34N 87°36E 43 G12
Katima Mulilo Namibia 17°28S 24°13E 56 A3
Katingan = Mendawai →
  Indonesia 3°30S 113°0E 36 E4
Katiola Ivory C. 8°10N 5°10W 52 G4
Katiti ⊙ Australia 25°1S 131°11E 61 E5
Katmandu = Kathmandu
  Nepal 27°45N 85°20E 43 F11
Katni India 23°51N 80°24E 43 H9
Katol India 21°17N 78°38E 44 D4
Katoomba Australia 33°41S 150°19E 63 E5
Katowice Poland 50°17N 19°5E 17 C10
Katrine, L. U.K. 56°15N 4°30W 11 E4
Katrineholm Sweden 59°0N 16°12E 9 G17
Katsina Nigeria 13°0N 7°32E 52 F7
Katsumoto Japan 33°51N 129°42E 29 H4
Katsuura Japan 35°10N 140°20E 29 G10
Katsuyama Japan 36°3N 136°30E 29 F8
Kattegat Denmark 56°40N 11°20E 9 H14
Katwa India 23°30N 88°5E 43 H13
Katwijk Neths. 52°12N 4°24E 15 B4
Kau-Ye Kyun Burma 11°1N 98°32E 39 G2
Kaua'i U.S.A. 22°3N 159°30W 75 L8
Kaudom △ Namibia 18°45S 20°51E 56 A3
Kaufman U.S.A. 32°35N 96°19W 84 E6
Kauhajoki Finland 62°25N 22°10E 8 E20
Kaukauna U.S.A. 44°17N 88°17W 80 C9
Kaukauveld Namibia 20°0S 20°15E 56 A3
Ka'ula I. U.S.A. 21°40N 160°33W 75 L7
Kaunas Lithuania 54°54N 23°54E 9 J20
Kaunia Bangla. 25°46N 89°26E 43 G13
Kautokeino Norway 69°0N 23°4E 8 B20
Kauwapur India 27°31N 82°18E 43 F10
Kavacha Russia 60°16N 169°51E 27 C17
Kavalerovo Russia 44°15N 135°4E 28 B7
Kavali India 14°55N 80°1E 45 G5
Kavār Iran 29°11N 52°44E 47 D7
Kavaratti India 10°34N 72°37E 45 J1
Kavaratti I. India 10°33N 72°38E 45 J1
Kavi India 22°12N 72°38E 42 H5
Kavimba Botswana 18°2S 24°38E 56 A3
Kavīr, Dasht-e Iran 34°30N 55°0E 47 C7
Kavīr △ Iran 34°40N 52°0E 47 C7
Kaw Fr. Guiana 4°30N 52°15W 93 C8
Kawagama L. Canada 45°18N 78°45W 82 A6
Kawagoe Japan 35°55N 139°29E 29 G9
Kawaguchi Japan 35°52N 139°45E 29 G9
Kawah Ijen △ Indonesia 8°3S 114°14E 37 H15
Kawanoe = Shikokuchūō
  Japan 34°1N 133°34E 29 G6
Kawardha India 22°0N 81°17E 43 J9
Kawasi Indonesia 1°38S 127°28E 37 E7
Kawawachikamach
  Canada 54°48N 66°50W 73 B6
Kawerau N.Z. 38°7S 176°42E 59 C6
Kawhia N.Z. 38°4S 174°49E 59 C5
Kawhia Harbour N.Z. 38°5S 174°51E 59 C5
Kawio, Kepulauan
  Indonesia 4°30N 125°30E 37 D7
Kawthaung Burma 10°5N 98°36E 39 H2
Kawthoolei = Kayin □
  Burma 18°0N 97°30E 41 L20
Kawthule = Kayin □
  Burma 18°0N 97°30E 41 L20
Kaya Burkina Faso 13°4N 1°10W 52 F5
Kayah □ Burma 19°15N 97°15E 41 K20
Kayak I. U.S.A. 59°56N 144°23W 74 D11
Kayamkulam India 9°10N 76°33E 45 K3
Kayan → Indonesia 2°55N 117°35E 36 D5
Kaycee U.S.A. 43°43N 106°38W 76 E10
Kayeli Indonesia 3°20S 127°10E 37 E7
Kayenta U.S.A. 36°44N 110°15W 77 H8
Kayes Mali 14°25N 11°30W 52 F3
Kayin □ Burma 18°0N 97°30E 41 L20
Kayoa Indonesia 0°1N 127°28E 37 D7
Kayseri Turkey 38°45N 35°30E 46 B2
Kaysville U.S.A. 41°2N 111°56W 76 F8
Kayts Sri Lanka 9°42N 79°51E 45 K4
Kazachye Russia 70°52N 135°58E 27 B14
Kazakhstan ■ Asia 50°0N 70°0E 26 E8
Kazan Russia 55°50N 49°10E 18 C8
Kazan → Canada 64°3N 95°35W 71 A9
Kazan-Rettō Pac. Oc. 25°0N 141°0E 64 E6
Kazanlâk Bulgaria 42°38N 25°20E 23 C11
Kazatin = Kozyatyn
  Ukraine 49°45N 28°50E 17 D15
Kāzerūn Iran 29°38N 51°40E 47 D6
Kazi Magomed = Qazmämmäd
  Azerbaijan 40°3N 49°0E 47 A6
Kazipet India 17°58N 79°30E 44 E4
Kazuno Japan 40°10N 140°45E 28 D10
Kazym → Russia 63°54N 65°50E 26 C7
Kea Greece 37°35N 24°22E 23 F11
Keady U.K. 54°15N 6°42W 10 B5
Kearney U.S.A. 40°42N 99°5W 80 E4
Kearney ⊙ Australia 20°10S 128°4E 60 D4

Kearny U.S.A. 33°3N 110°55W 77 K8
Kearsarge, Mt. U.S.A. 43°22N 71°50W 83 C13
Keban Turkey 38°50N 38°50E 19 G6
Keban Baraji Turkey 38°41N 38°33E 46 B3
Kebnekaise Sweden 67°53N 18°33E 8 C18
Kebri Dehar Ethiopia 6°45N 44°17E 49 F3
Kebumen Indonesia 7°42S 109°40E 37 G13
Kechika → Canada 59°41N 127°12W 70 B3
Kecskemét Hungary 46°57N 19°42E 17 E10
Kedah □ Malaysia 5°50N 100°40E 39 K3
Kėdainiai Lithuania 55°15N 24°2E 9 J21
Kedarnath India 30°44N 79°4E 43 D8
Kedgwick Canada 47°40N 67°20W 73 C6
Kediri Indonesia 7°51S 112°1E 37 G15
Keeler U.S.A. 36°29N 117°52W 78 J9
Keeley L. Canada 54°54N 108°8W 71 C7
Keeling Is. = Cocos Is.
  Ind. Oc. 12°10S 96°55E 64 J1
Keelung = Chilung
  Taiwan 25°3N 121°45E 35 E13
Keene Canada 44°15N 78°10W 82 B6
Keene Calif., U.S.A. 35°13N 118°33W 79 K8
Keene N.H., U.S.A. 42°56N 72°17W 83 D12
Keene N.Y., U.S.A. 44°16N 73°46W 83 B11
Keep River △ Australia 15°49S 129°8E 60 C4
Keeper Hill Ireland 52°45N 8°16W 10 D3
Keerweer, C. Australia 14°0S 141°32E 62 A3
Keeseville U.S.A. 44°29N 73°30E 83 B11
Keetmanshoop Namibia 26°35S 18°8E 56 C2
Keewatin Canada 49°46N 94°34W 71 D10
Keewatin → Canada 56°29N 100°46W 71 B8
Kefalonia Greece 38°15N 20°30E 23 E9
Kefamenanu Indonesia 9°28S 124°29E 37 F6
Kefar Sava Israel 32°11N 34°54E 48 C3
Keffi Nigeria 8°55N 7°43E 52 G7
Keflavík Iceland 64°2N 22°35W 8 D2
Keg River Canada 57°54N 117°55W 70 B5
Kegalla Sri Lanka 7°15N 80°21E 45 L5
Kegaska Canada 50°9N 61°18W 73 B7
Keighley U.K. 53°52N 1°54W 12 D6
Keila Estonia 59°18N 24°25E 9 G21
Keimoes S. Africa 28°41S 20°59E 56 C3
Keitele Finland 63°10N 26°20E 8 E22
Keith Australia 36°6S 140°20E 63 F3
Keith U.K. 57°32N 2°57W 11 D6
Keiyasi Fiji 17°53S 177°46E 59 a
Kejimkujik △ Canada 44°25N 65°25W 73 D6
Kejserr Franz Joseph Fd.
  Greenland 73°30N 24°30W 4 B6
Kekri India 26°0N 75°10E 42 G6
Kelan China 38°43N 111°31E 32 E6
Kelang = Klang Malaysia 3°1N 101°33E 39 L3
Kelani Ganga → Sri Lanka 6°58N 79°50E 45 L4
Kelantan □ Malaysia 5°10N 102°0E 39 K3
Kelantan → Malaysia 6°13N 102°14E 39 J4
Kelkit Turkey 40°45N 36°32E 19 F6
Kellerberrin Australia 31°36S 117°38E 61 F2
Kellett, C. Canada 72°0N 126°0W 4 B1
Kelleys I. U.S.A. 41°36N 82°42W 82 E2
Kellogg U.S.A. 47°32N 116°7W 76 C5
Kells Ireland 53°44N 6°53W 10 C5
Kélo Chad 9°10N 15°45E 53 G9
Kelowna Canada 49°50N 119°25W 70 D5
Kelsey Creek Australia 20°26S 148°31E 62 b
Kelseyville U.S.A. 38°59N 122°50W 78 G4
Kelso N.Z. 45°54S 169°15E 59 F2
Kelso U.K. 55°36N 2°26W 11 F6
Kelso U.S.A. 46°9N 122°54W 78 D4
Keluang = Kluang
  Malaysia 2°3N 103°18E 39 L4
Kelvington Canada 52°10N 103°30E 71 C8
Kem Russia 65°0N 34°38E 18 B5
Kem → Russia 64°57N 34°41E 18 B5
Kemah Turkey 39°32N 39°5E 46 B3
Kemaman Malaysia 4°12N 103°18E 39 K4
Kemano Canada 53°35N 128°0W 70 C3
Kemasik Malaysia 4°25N 103°27E 39 K4
Kemerovo Russia 55°20N 86°5E 26 D9
Kemi Finland 65°44N 24°34E 8 D21
Kemi älv = Kemijoki →
  Finland 65°47N 24°32E 8 D21
Kemi träsk = Kemijärvi
  Finland 66°43N 27°22E 8 C22
Kemijärvi Finland 66°43N 27°22E 8 C22
Kemijoki → Finland 65°47N 24°32E 8 D21
Kemmerer U.S.A. 41°48N 110°32W 76 F8
Kemp, L. U.S.A. 33°46N 99°9W 84 E5
Kemp Land Antarctica 69°0S 55°0E 5 C5
Kempas Malaysia 1°33N 103°42E 39 d
Kempsey Australia 31°1S 152°50E 63 E5
Kempt, L. Canada 47°25N 74°22W 72 C5
Kempten Germany 47°45N 10°17E 16 E6
Kempton Australia 42°31S 147°12E 63 G4
Kemptville Canada 45°0N 75°38W 83 B9
Ken → India 25°13N 80°27E 43 G9
Kenai U.S.A. 60°33N 151°16W 68 E1
Kenai Mts. U.S.A. 60°0N 150°0W 74 D9
Kendai India 22°45N 82°37E 43 H10
Kendal Indonesia 6°56S 110°14E 37 G14
Kendal U.K. 54°20N 2°44W 12 C5
Kendall Australia 31°35S 152°44E 63 E5
Kendall → Australia 14°4S 141°35E 62 A3
Kendallville U.S.A. 41°27N 85°16W 81 E11
Kendari Indonesia 3°50S 122°30E 37 E6
Kendawangan Indonesia 2°32S 110°17E 36 E4
Kendi, Pulau Malaysia 5°13N 100°12E 39 d
Kendrapara India 20°35N 86°30E 44 D8
Kendrew S. Africa 32°32S 24°30E 56 E3
Kene Thao Laos 17°44N 101°10E 38 D3
Kenedy U.S.A. 28°49N 97°51W 84 G6
Kenema S. Leone 7°50N 11°14W 52 G3
Keng Kok Laos 16°26N 105°12E 38 D5
Keng Tawng Burma 20°45N 98°18E 41 J21
Keng Tung Burma 21°0N 99°30E 41 J21
Kenhardt S. Africa 29°19S 21°12E 56 D3
Kenitra Morocco 34°15N 6°40W 52 B4
Kenli China 37°30N 118°20E 33 F10

Kenmare *Ireland* 51°53N 9°36W 10 E2
Kenmare *U.S.A.* 48°41N 102°5W 80 A2
Kenmare River → *Ireland* 51°48N 9°51W 10 E2
Kennebago Lake *U.S.A.* 45°4N 70°40W 83 A14
Kennebec *U.S.A.* 43°54N 99°52W 80 D4
Kennebec → *U.S.A.* 43°45N 69°46W 81 D19
Kennebunk *U.S.A.* 43°23N 70°33W 83 C14
Kennedy *Zimbabwe* 18°52S 27°10E 56 A4
Kennedy Channel *Arctic* 80°50N 66°0W 69 A18
Kennedy Ra. *Australia* 24°45S 115°10E 61 D2
Kennedy Range △
  Australia 24°34S 115°2E 61 D2
Kennemerduinen △
  Neths. 52°27N 4°33E 15 B4
Kennet → *U.K.* 51°27N 0°57W 13 F7
Kenneth Ra. *Australia* 23°50S 117°8E 61 D2
Kennett *U.S.A.* 36°14N 90°3W 80 G8
Kennewick *U.S.A.* 46°12N 119°7W 76 C4
Kenogami → *Canada* 51°6N 84°28W 72 B3
Kenogamissi Lake *Canada* 48°14N 81°40W 72 C3
Kenora *Canada* 49°47N 94°29W 71 D10
Kenosha *U.S.A.* 42°35N 87°49W 80 D10
Kensington *Canada* 46°28N 63°34W 73 C7
Kent *Ohio, U.S.A.* 41°9N 81°22W 82 E3
Kent *Tex., U.S.A.* 31°4N 104°13W 84 F2
Kent *Wash., U.S.A.* 47°22N 122°14W 78 C4
Kent □ *U.K.* 51°12N 0°40E 13 F8
Kent Group *Australia* 39°30S 147°20E 63 F4
Kent Pen. *Canada* 68°30N 107°0W 68 D10
Kentaū *Kazakhstan* 43°32N 68°36E 26 E7
Kentland *U.S.A.* 40°46N 87°27W 80 E10
Kenton *U.S.A.* 40°39N 83°37W 81 E12
Kentucky □ *U.S.A.* 37°0N 84°0W 81 G11
Kentucky → *U.S.A.* 38°41N 85°11W 81 F11
Kentucky L. *U.S.A.* 37°1N 88°16W 80 G9
Kentville *Canada* 45°6N 64°29W 73 C7
Kentwood *U.S.A.* 30°56N 90°31W 85 F9
Kenya ■ *Africa* 1°0N 38°0E 54 D7
Kenya, Mt. *Kenya* 0°10S 37°18E 54 E7
Kenyir, Tasik *Malaysia* 5°1N 102°54E 39 K4
Keokuk *U.S.A.* 40°24N 91°24W 80 E8
Keoladeo △ *India* 27°0N 77°20E 42 F7
Keonjhargarh *India* 21°28N 85°35E 43 J11
Kep *Cambodia* 10°29N 104°19E 39 G5
Kep *Vietnam* 21°24N 106°16E 38 B6
Kep △ *Cambodia* 10°30N 104°18E 39 G5
Kepala Batas *Malaysia* 5°31N 100°26E 39 c
Kepi *Indonesia* 6°32S 139°19E 37 F9
Kerala □ *India* 11°0N 76°15E 45 J3
Kerama-Rettō *Japan* 26°5N 127°15E 29 L3
Keran *Pakistan* 34°35N 73°59E 43 B5
Kerang *Australia* 35°40S 143°55E 63 F3
Keraudren, C. *Australia* 19°58S 119°45E 60 C2
Kerch *Ukraine* 45°20N 36°20E 19 E6
Kerepakupai-Meru = Angel Falls
  Venezuela 5°57N 62°30W 92 B6
Kerguelen *Ind. Oc.* 49°15S 69°10E 3 G13
Kerian, Kuala *Malaysia* 5°10N 100°25E 39 c
Kericho *Kenya* 0°22S 35°15E 54 E7
Kerinci *Indonesia* 1°40S 101°15E 36 E2
Kerki = Atamyrat
  Turkmenistan 37°50N 65°12E 26 F7
Kerkrade *Neths.* 50°53N 6°4E 15 D6
Kerkyra *Greece* 39°38N 19°50E 23 E8
Kermadec Is. *Pac. Oc.* 30°0S 178°15W 58 E11
Kermadec Trench
  Pac. Oc. 30°30S 176°0W 64 L10
Kermān *Iran* 30°15N 57°1E 47 D8
Kerman *U.S.A.* 36°43N 120°4W 78 J6
Kermān □ *Iran* 30°0N 57°0E 47 D8
Kermān, Biābān-e *Iran* 28°45N 59°45E 47 D8
Kermānshāh *Iran* 34°23N 47°0E 46 C5
Kermānshāh □ *Iran* 34°0N 46°30E 46 C5
Kermit *U.S.A.* 31°52N 103°6W 84 F3
Kern → *U.S.A.* 35°16N 119°18W 79 K7
Kernow = Cornwall □
  U.K. 50°26N 4°40W 13 G3
Kernville *U.S.A.* 35°45N 118°26W 79 K8
Keroh *Malaysia* 5°43N 101°1E 39 K3
Kerrera *U.K.* 56°24N 5°33W 11 E3
Kerrobert *Canada* 51°56N 109°8W 71 C7
Kerrville *U.S.A.* 30°3N 99°8W 84 F5
Kerry □ *Ireland* 52°7N 9°35W 10 D2
Kerry Hd. *Ireland* 52°25N 9°56W 10 D2
Kerulen = Herlen →
  Asia 48°48N 117°0E 31 B12
Kerzaz *Algeria* 29°29N 1°37W 52 C5
Kesagami → *Canada* 51°40N 79°45W 72 B4
Kesagami L. *Canada* 50°23N 80°15W 72 B3
Keşan *Turkey* 40°49N 26°38E 23 D12
Kesennuma *Japan* 38°54N 141°35E 28 E10
Keshit *Iran* 29°43N 58°17E 47 D8
Kesigi = Kosgi *India* 15°51N 77°16E 45 G3
Keskal *India* 20°5N 81°35E 44 D5
Kestenga *Russia* 65°50N 31°45E 8 D24
Keswick *U.K.* 54°36N 3°8W 12 C4
Ket → *Russia* 58°55N 81°32E 26 D9
Ketapang *Jawa Timur,*
  Indonesia 8°9S 114°23E 37 J17
Ketapang *Kalimantan Barat,*
  Indonesia 1°55S 110°0E 36 E4
Ketchikan *U.S.A.* 55°21N 131°39W 70 B2
Ketchum *U.S.A.* 43°41N 114°22W 76 E6
Ketef, Khalig Umm el
  Egypt 23°40N 35°35E 46 F2
Keti Bandar *Pakistan* 24°8N 67°27E 42 G2
Ketri *India* 28°1N 75°50E 42 E6
Kętrzyn *Poland* 54°7N 21°22E 17 A11
Kettering *U.K.* 52°24N 0°43W 13 E7
Kettering *U.S.A.* 39°41N 84°10W 81 F11
Kettle → *Canada* 56°40N 89°34W 71 B11
Kettle Falls *U.S.A.* 48°37N 118°3W 76 B4
Kettle Point *Canada* 43°10N 82°1W 82 C2
Kettle Pt. *Canada* 43°13N 82°1W 82 C2
Kettleman City *U.S.A.* 36°1N 119°58W 78 J7
Keuka L. *U.S.A.* 42°30N 77°9W 82 D7
Keuruu *Finland* 62°16N 24°41E 8 E21

Keware *Nepal* 27°57N 83°47E 43 F10
Kewaunee *U.S.A.* 44°27N 87°31W 80 C10
Keweenaw B. *U.S.A.* 47°0N 88°15W 80 B9
Keweenaw Pen. *U.S.A.* 47°15N 88°15W 80 B9
Keweenaw Pt. *U.S.A.* 47°25N 87°43W 80 B10
Key, L. *Ireland* 54°0N 8°15W 10 C3
Key Lake Mine *Canada* 57°5N 105°32W 71 B7
Key Largo *U.S.A.* 25°5N 80°27W 85 J14
Key West *U.S.A.* 24°33N 81°48W 88 B3
Keynsham *U.K.* 51°24N 2°29W 13 F5
Keyser *U.S.A.* 39°26N 78°59W 81 F14
Kezhma *Russia* 58°59N 101°9E 27 D11
Kezi *Zimbabwe* 20°58S 28°32E 57 B4
Kgalagadi △ *Botswana* 24°30S 22°0E 56 B3
Kgalagadi Transfrontier △
  Africa 25°10S 21°0E 56 C3
Khabarovsk *Russia* 48°30N 135°5E 31 B16
Khabr △ *Iran* 28°51N 56°22E 47 D8
Khābūr → *Syria* 35°17N 40°35E 46 C4
Khachmas = Xaçmaz
  Azerbaijan 41°31N 48°42E 19 F8
Khachrod *India* 23°25N 75°20E 42 H6
Khadro *Pakistan* 26°11N 68°50E 42 F3
Khadzhilyangar = Dahongliutan
  China 35°45N 79°20E 43 B8
Khaga *India* 25°47N 81°7E 43 G9
Khagaria *India* 25°30N 86°32E 43 G12
Khaipur *Pakistan* 29°34N 72°17E 42 E5
Khair *India* 27°57N 77°46E 42 F7
Khairabad *India* 27°33N 80°47E 43 F9
Khairagarh *India* 21°27N 81°2E 43 J9
Khairpur *Pakistan* 27°32N 68°49E 42 F3
Khairpur Nathan Shah
  Pakistan 27°6N 67°44E 42 F2
Khairwara *India* 23°58N 73°38E 42 H5
Khaisor → *Pakistan* 31°17N 68°59E 42 D3
Khajuraho *India* 24°51N 79°55E 43 G8
Khajuri Kach *Pakistan* 32°4N 69°51E 42 C3
Khakassia □ *Russia* 53°0N 90°0E 26 D9
Khakhea *Botswana* 24°48S 23°22E 56 B3
Khalafābād *Iran* 30°54N 49°24E 47 D6
Khalilabad *India* 26°48N 83°5E 43 F10
Khalīlī *Iran* 27°38N 53°17E 47 E7
Khalkhāl *Iran* 37°37N 48°32E 47 B6
Khalkis = Chalkida
  Greece 38°27N 23°42E 23 E10
Khalmer Yu *Russia* 67°58N 65°1E 26 C7
Khalturin *Russia* 58°40N 48°50E 18 C8
Khalūf *Oman* 20°30N 58°13E 49 C6
Kham Keut *Laos* 18°15N 104°43E 38 C5
Khamaria *India* 23°5N 80°48E 43 H9
Khambhaliya *India* 22°14N 69°41E 42 H3
Khambhat *India* 22°23N 72°33E 42 H5
Khambhat, G. of *India* 20°45N 72°30E 40 J8
Khamgaon *India* 20°42N 76°37E 44 D3
Khamir *Iran* 26°57N 55°36E 47 E7
Khamir *Yemen* 16°2N 44°0E 49 D3
Khamīs Mushayţ
  Si. Arabia 18°18N 42°44E 49 D3
Khammam *India* 17°11N 80°6E 44 F5
Khamsa *Egypt* 30°27N 32°23E 48 E1
Khan → *Namibia* 22°37S 14°56E 56 B2
Khān Abū Shāmat *Syria* 33°39N 36°53E 48 B5
Khān Azād *Iraq* 33°7N 44°22E 46 C5
Khān Mujiddah *Iraq* 32°21N 43°48E 46 C4
Khān Shaykhūn *Syria* 35°26N 36°38E 46 C3
Khān Tengri, Pik *Asia* 42°12N 80°10E 30 C5
Khān Yūnis *Gaza Strip* 31°21N 34°18E 48 D3
Khanai *Pakistan* 30°30N 67°8E 42 D2
Khānaqīn *Iraq* 34°23N 45°25E 46 C5
Khānbāghī *Iran* 36°10N 55°25E 47 B7
Khandwa *India* 21°49N 76°22E 44 D3
Khandyga *Russia* 62°42N 135°35E 27 C14
Khanewal *Pakistan* 30°20N 71°55E 42 D4
Khangah Dogran
  Pakistan 31°50N 73°37E 42 D5
Khangchendzonga =
  Kanchenjunga △ *India* 27°42N 88°8E 43 F13
Khanh Duong *Vietnam* 12°44N 108°44E 38 F7
Khaniá = Chania *Greece* 35°30N 24°4E 23 G11
Khaniadhana *India* 25°1N 78°8E 42 G8
Khanka, L. *Asia* 45°0N 132°24E 28 B6
Khankendy = Xankändi
  Azerbaijan 39°52N 46°49E 46 B5
Khanna *India* 30°42N 76°16E 42 D7
Khanozai *Pakistan* 30°37N 67°19E 42 D2
Khanpur *Pakistan* 28°42N 70°35E 42 E4
Khanty-Mansiysk *Russia* 61°0N 69°0E 26 C7
Khao Khitchakut △
  Thailand 12°50N 102°10E 38 F4
Khao Laem △ *Thailand* 14°56N 98°31E 38 E2
Khao Laem Res. *Thailand* 14°50N 98°30E 38 E2
Khao Lak △ *Malaysia* 8°38N 98°16E 39 H2
Khao Luang △ *Thailand* 8°34N 99°42E 39 H2
Khao Nam Khang △
  Thailand 6°32N 100°35E 39 J3
Khao Phlu *Thailand* 9°29N 99°59E 39 b
Khao Pu -Khao Ya △
  Thailand 7°26N 99°57E 39 J2
Khao Sam Roi Yot △
  Thailand 12°13N 99°57E 39 F2
Khao Sok △ *Thailand* 8°55N 98°38E 39 H2
Khao Yai △ *Thailand* 14°21N 101°29E 38 E3
Khaoen Si Nakarin △
  Thailand 14°47N 99°0E 38 E2
Khapalu *Pakistan* 35°10N 76°20E 43 B7
Khapcheranga *Russia* 49°42N 112°24E 27 E12
Khaptao △ *Nepal* 29°20N 81°10E 43 E9
Kharaghoda *India* 23°11N 71°46E 42 H4
Kharagpur *India* 22°20N 87°25E 43 H12
Kharan Kalat *Pakistan* 28°34N 65°21E 40 E4
Kharānaq *Iran* 32°20N 54°45E 47 C7
Kharda *India* 18°40N 75°34E 44 E2
Khardung La *India* 34°20N 77°43E 43 B7
Kharg = Khārk, Jazīreh-ye
  Iran 29°15N 50°28E 47 D6
Khârga, El Wâhât el
  Egypt 25°10N 30°35E 53 C12
Khargon *India* 21°45N 75°40E 44 D2

Khari → *India* 25°54N 74°31E 42 G6
Kharian *Pakistan* 32°49N 73°52E 42 C5
Khārk, Jazīreh-ye *Iran* 29°15N 50°28E 47 D6
Kharkiv *Ukraine* 49°58N 36°20E 19 E6
Kharkov = Kharkiv
  Ukraine 49°58N 36°20E 19 E6
Kharovsk *Russia* 59°56N 40°13E 18 C7
Kharsawangarh *India* 22°48N 85°50E 43 H11
Kharta *Turkey* 40°55N 29°7E 23 D13
Khartoum = El Khartûm
  Sudan 15°31N 32°35E 53 E12
Khartum *Canada* 45°15N 77°5W 82 A7
Khasan *Russia* 42°25N 130°40E 28 C5
Khāsh *Iran* 28°15N 61°15E 47 D9
Khashm el Girba *Sudan* 14°59N 35°58E 53 F13
Khaskovo *Bulgaria* 41°56N 25°30E 23 D11
Khat, Laem *Thailand* 8°6N 98°26E 39 a
Khatanga *Russia* 72°0N 102°20E 27 B11
Khatanga → *Russia* 72°55N 106°0E 27 B11
Khatauli *India* 29°17N 77°43E 42 E7
Khātūnābād *Iran* 30°1N 55°25E 47 D7
Khatyrka *Russia* 62°3N 175°15E 27 C18
Khavda *India* 23°51N 69°43E 42 H3
Khawr Fakkān *U.A.E.* 25°21N 56°22E 47 E8
Khaybar, Ḩarrat
  Si. Arabia 25°30N 39°45E 46 E4
Khāzimiyah *Iraq* 34°46N 43°37E 46 C4
Khe Bo *Vietnam* 19°8N 104°41E 38 C5
Khe Long *Vietnam* 21°29N 104°46E 38 B5
Khe Sanh *Vietnam* 16°37N 106°45E 38 D6
Khed *Maharashtra, India* 17°43N 73°23E 44 F1
Khed *Maharashtra, India* 18°51N 73°56E 44 E1
Khed Brahma *India* 24°7N 73°5E 42 G5
Khekra *India* 28°52N 77°20E 42 E7
Khemarak Phouminville = Krong
  Kaoh Kong *Cambodia* 11°37N 102°59E 39 G4
Khemisset *Morocco* 33°50N 6°1W 52 B4
Khemmarat *Thailand* 16°10N 105°15E 38 D5
Khenāmān *Iran* 30°27N 56°29E 47 D8
Khenchela *Algeria* 35°28N 7°11E 52 A7
Khersān → *Iran* 31°33N 50°22E 47 D6
Kherson *Ukraine* 46°35N 32°35E 19 E5
Kheta → *Russia* 71°54N 102°6E 27 B11
Khewari *Pakistan* 26°36N 68°52E 42 F3
Khilchipur *India* 24°2N 76°34E 42 G7
Khilok *Russia* 51°30N 110°45E 27 D12
Khios = Chios *Greece* 38°27N 26°9E 23 E12
Khirsadoh *India* 22°11N 78°47E 43 H8
Khiuma = Hiiumaa
  Estonia 58°50N 22°45E 9 G20
Khiva = Xiva *Uzbekistan* 41°30N 60°18E 26 E7
Khlong Khlung *Thailand* 16°12N 99°43E 38 D2
Khlong Lan △ *Thailand* 16°12N 99°13E 38 D2
Khlong Phanom △
  Thailand 8°45N 98°38E 39 H2
Khmelnik *Ukraine* 49°33N 27°58E 17 D14
Khmelnytskyy *Ukraine* 49°23N 27°0E 17 D14
Khmelnytskyy □
  Ukraine 49°26N 26°40E 17 D14
Khmer Rep. = Cambodia ■
  Asia 12°15N 105°0E 38 F5
Khoai, Hon *Vietnam* 8°26N 104°50E 39 H5
Khobar = Al Khubar
  Si. Arabia 26°17N 50°12E 47 E6
Khodoriv *Ukraine* 49°24N 24°19E 17 D13
Khodzent = Khüjand
  Tajikistan 40°17N 69°37E 26 E7
Khojak Pass *Afghan.* 30°51N 66°34E 42 D2
Khok Kloi *Thailand* 8°17N 98°19E 39 a
Khok Pho *Thailand* 6°43N 101°6E 39 J3
Khok Samrong *Thailand* 15°3N 100°43E 38 E3
Kholm *Russia* 57°10N 31°15E 18 C5
Kholmsk *Russia* 47°40N 142°5E 27 E15
Khomas □ *Namibia* 23°30S 17°0E 56 B2
Khomas Hochland
  Namibia 22°40S 16°0E 56 B2
Khomeyn *Iran* 33°40N 50°7E 47 C6
Khomeynī Shahr *Iran* 32°41N 51°31E 47 C6
Khomodino *Botswana* 22°46S 23°52E 56 B3
Khon Kaen *Thailand* 16°30N 102°47E 38 D4
Khong → *Cambodia* 13°32N 105°58E 38 F5
Khong Sedone *Laos* 15°34N 105°49E 38 E5
Khonuu *Russia* 66°30N 143°12E 27 C15
Khoper → *Russia* 49°30N 42°20E 19 D6
Khorāsān-e Janūb □ *Iran* 32°0N 59°0E 47 C8
Khorāsān-e Razavī □ *Iran* 35°0N 59°0E 47 C8
Khorāsān-e Shemālī □
  Iran 37°0N 57°0E 47 B8
Khorat = Nakhon Ratchasima
  Thailand 14°59N 102°12E 38 E4
Khorat, Cao Nguyen
  Thailand 15°30N 102°50E 38 E4
Khorixas *Namibia* 20°16S 14°59E 56 B1
Khorramābād *Khorāsān,*
  Iran 33°30N 48°25E 47 C6
Khorramābād *Lorestān,*
  Iran 33°30N 48°25E 47 C6
Khorramshahr *Iran* 30°29N 48°15E 47 D6
Khorugh *Tajikistan* 37°30N 71°36E 26 F8
Khosravī *Iran* 30°48N 51°28E 47 D6
Khosrowābād *Khuzestān,*
  Iran 30°10N 48°25E 47 D6
Khosrowābād *Kordestān,*
  Iran 35°31N 47°38E 46 C5
Khosūyeh *Iran* 28°32N 54°26E 47 D7
Khotang *Nepal* 27°1N 86°51E 43 F12
Khotyn *Ukraine* 48°31N 26°27E 17 D14
Khouribga *Morocco* 32°58N 6°57W 52 B4
Khowst *Afghan.* 33°22N 69°58E 42 C3
Khowst □ *Afghan.* 33°20N 70°0E 40 C6
Khoyniki *Belarus* 51°54N 29°55E 17 C15
Khram, Ko *Thailand* 12°42N 100°47E 38 F3
Khuan Wa *Thailand* 7°53N 98°17E 39 a
Khudzhand = Khüjand
  Tajikistan 40°17N 69°37E 26 E7
Khuff *Si. Arabia* 24°55N 44°53E 46 E5

Khūgīānī *Afghan.* 31°34N 66°32E 42 D2
Khuis *Botswana* 26°40S 21°49E 56 C3
Khuiyala *India* 27°9N 70°25E 42 F4
Khārk, Jazīreh-ye *Iran* 29°15N 50°28E 47 D6
Khūjand *Tajikistan* 40°17N 69°37E 26 E7
Khujner *India* 23°47N 76°36E 42 H7
Khukhan *Thailand* 14°42N 104°12E 38 E5
Khulna *Bangla.* 22°45N 89°34E 41 H16
Khulna □ *Bangla.* 22°25N 89°35E 41 H16
Khumago *Botswana* 20°26S 24°32E 56 B3
Khunjerab △ *Pakistan* 36°40N 75°30E 43 A6
Khunjerab Pass = Kinjirap Daban
  Asia 36°40N 75°25E 40 A9
Khūnsorkh *Iran* 27°9N 56°7E 47 E8
Khunti *India* 23°5N 85°17E 43 H11
Khūr *Iran* 32°55N 58°18E 47 C8
Khurai *India* 24°3N 78°23E 42 G8
Khurayş *Si. Arabia* 25°6N 48°2E 47 E6
Khurda *India* 20°11N 85°37E 44 D7
Khurja *India* 28°15N 77°58E 42 E7
Khūrmāl *Iraq* 35°18N 46°2E 46 C5
Khurr, Wādī al *Iraq* 32°3N 43°52E 46 C4
Khūsf *Iran* 32°46N 58°53E 47 C8
Khushab *Pakistan* 32°20N 72°20E 42 C5
Khust *Ukraine* 48°10N 23°18E 17 D12
Khutse △ *Botswana* 23°31S 24°12E 56 B3
Khuzdar *Pakistan* 27°52N 66°30E 42 F2
Khūzestān □ *Iran* 31°0N 49°0E 47 D6
Khvāf *Iran* 34°33N 60°8E 47 C9
Khvājeh *Iran* 38°9N 46°35E 46 B5
Khvānsār *Iran* 29°56N 54°8E 47 D7
Khvor *Iran* 33°45N 55°0E 47 C7
Khvorgū *Iran* 27°34N 56°27E 47 E8
Khvormūj *Iran* 28°40N 51°30E 47 D6
Khvoy *Iran* 38°35N 45°0E 46 B5
Khwae Noi → *Thailand* 14°1N 99°32E 38 E2
Khyber Pakhtunkhwa □
  Pakistan 34°0N 72°0E 42 C4
Khyber Pass *Afghan.* 34°10N 71°8E 42 B4
Kia *Fiji* 16°15S 179°8E 59 a
Kiadho → *India* 19°37N 77°40E 44 E3
Kiama *Australia* 34°40S 150°50E 63 E5
Kiamba *Phil.* 6°2N 124°46E 37 C6
Kiangsi = Jiangxi □
  China 27°30N 116°0E 35 D11
Kiangsu = Jiangsu □
  China 33°0N 120°0E 33 H11
Kibombo
  Dem. Rep. of the Congo 3°57S 25°53E 54 E5
Kibre Mengist *Ethiopia* 5°54N 38°59E 49 F2
Kıbrıs = Cyprus ■ *Asia* 35°0N 33°0E 46 C2
Kibwezi *Kenya* 2°27S 37°57E 54 E7
Kichha → *India* 28°41N 79°18E 43 E8
Kichmengskiy Gorodok
  Russia 59°59N 45°48E 18 B8
Kicking Horse Pass
  Canada 51°28N 116°16W 70 C5
Kidal *Mali* 18°26N 1°22E 52 E6
Kidderminster *U.K.* 52°24N 2°15W 13 E5
Kidnappers, C. *N.Z.* 39°38S 177°5E 59 C6
Kidsgrove *U.K.* 53°5N 2°14W 12 D5
Kidston *Australia* 18°52S 144°8E 62 B3
Kiel *Germany* 54°19N 10°8E 16 A6
Kiel Canal = Nord-Ostsee-Kanal
  Germany 54°12N 9°32E 16 A5
Kielce *Poland* 50°52N 20°42E 17 C11
Kielder Water *U.K.* 55°11N 2°31W 12 B5
Kieler Bucht *Germany* 54°35N 10°25E 16 A6
Kiev = Kyyiv *Ukraine* 50°30N 30°28E 17 C16
Kiffa *Mauritania* 16°37N 11°24W 52 E3
Kifrī *Iraq* 34°45N 45°0E 46 C5
Kigali *Rwanda* 1°59S 30°4E 54 E6
Kigoma-Ujiji *Tanzania* 4°55S 29°36E 54 E5
Kığzı *Turkey* 38°18N 43°25E 46 B4
Kihnu *Estonia* 58°9N 24°1E 9 G21
Kii-Sanchi *Japan* 34°20N 136°0E 29 G8
Kii-Suidō *Japan* 33°40N 134°45E 29 H7
Kikaiga-Shima *Japan* 28°19N 129°59E 29 K4
Kikiak = Rigolet *Canada* 54°10N 58°23W 73 B8
Kikládhes = Cyclades
  Greece 37°0N 24°30E 23 F11
Kikuchi *Japan* 32°59N 130°47E 29 H5
Kikwit *Dem. Rep. of the Congo* 5°0S 18°45E 54 F3
Kilakkarai *India* 9°12N 78°47E 45 K4
Kilar *India* 33°6N 76°25E 42 C7
Kilbeggan *Ireland* 53°22N 7°30W 10 C4
Kilbrannan Sd. *U.K.* 55°37N 5°26W 11 F3
Kilbuck Mts. *U.S.A.* 60°36N 159°53W 74 C8
Kilchu *N. Korea* 40°57N 129°25E 33 D15
Kilcoy *Australia* 26°59S 152°30E 63 D5
Kildare *Ireland* 53°9N 6°55W 10 C5
Kildare □ *Ireland* 53°10N 6°50W 10 C5
Kildinstroy *Russia* 68°48N 33°6E 8 B25
Kilfinnane *Ireland* 52°21N 8°28W 10 D3
Kilgarvan *Ireland* 51°54N 9°27W 10 E2
Kilgore *U.S.A.* 32°23N 94°53W 84 E7
Kilifi *Kenya* 3°40S 39°48E 54 E7
Kilimanjaro *Tanzania* 3°7S 37°20E 54 E7
Kilindini *Kenya* 4°4S 39°40E 54 E7
Kilinochchi *Sri Lanka* 9°24N 80°25E 45 K5
Kilis *Turkey* 36°42N 37°6E 46 B3
Kiliya *Ukraine* 45°28N 29°16E 17 F15
Kilkee *Ireland* 52°41N 9°39W 10 D2
Kilkeel *U.K.* 54°7N 5°55W 10 B5
Kilkenny *Ireland* 52°39N 7°15W 10 D4
Kilkenny □ *Ireland* 52°35N 7°15W 10 D4
Kilkieran B. *Ireland* 53°20N 9°41W 10 C2
Kilkis *Greece* 40°58N 22°57E 23 D10
Killala *Ireland* 54°13N 9°13W 10 B2
Killala B. *Ireland* 54°16N 9°8W 10 B2
Killaloe *Canada* 45°33N 77°25W 82 A7
Killaloe *Ireland* 52°48N 8°28W 10 D3
Killarney *Australia* 28°20S 152°18E 63 D5
Killarney *Canada* 45°55N 81°30W 72 C3
Killarney *Ireland* 52°4N 9°30W 10 D2
Killary Harbour *Ireland* 53°38N 9°52W 10 C2
Killdeer *U.S.A.* 47°22N 102°45W 80 B2
Killeen *U.S.A.* 31°7N 97°44W 84 F6

Killin *U.K.* 56°28N 4°19W 11 E4
Killington Pk. *U.S.A.* 43°36N 72°49W 83 C12
Killini *Greece* 37°54N 22°25E 23 F10
Killiniq I. *Canada* 60°24N 64°37W 69 E19
Killorglin *Ireland* 52°6N 9°47W 10 D2
Killybegs *Ireland* 54°38N 8°26W 10 B3
Kilmarnock *U.K.* 55°37N 4°29W 11 F4
Kilmore *Australia* 37°25S 144°53E 63 F3
Kilmore Quay *Ireland* 52°10N 6°36W 10 D5
Kilosa *Tanzania* 6°48S 37°0E 54 F7
Kilrush *Ireland* 52°38N 9°29W 10 D2
Kiltan I. *India* 11°29N 73°0E 45 J1
Kilwa Kivinje *Tanzania* 8°45S 39°25E 54 F7
Kilwinning *U.K.* 55°39N 4°43W 11 F4
Kim *U.S.A.* 37°15N 103°21W 77 H12
Kimaam *Indonesia* 7°58S 138°53E 37 F9
Kimba *Australia* 33°8S 136°23E 63 E2
Kimball *Nebr., U.S.A.* 41°14N 103°40W 80 E2
Kimball *S. Dak., U.S.A.* 43°45N 98°57W 80 D4
Kimberley *Australia* 16°20S 127°0E 60 C4
Kimberley *B.C., Canada* 49°40N 115°59W 70 D5
Kimberley *Ont., Canada* 44°23N 80°32W 82 B4
Kimberley *S. Africa* 28°43S 24°46E 56 C3
Kimberly *U.S.A.* 42°32N 114°22W 76 E6
Kimch'aek *N. Korea* 40°40N 129°10E 33 D15
Kimhae = Gimhae
  S. Korea 35°14N 128°53E 33 G15
Kimmirut *Canada* 62°50N 69°50W 69 E18
Kimpese
  Dem. Rep. of the Congo 5°35S 14°26E 54 F2
Kimry *Russia* 56°55N 37°15E 18 C6
Kinabalu, Gunung
  Malaysia 6°3N 116°14E 36 C5
Kinaskan L. *Canada* 57°38N 130°8W 70 B2
Kinbasket L. *Canada* 52°0N 118°10W 70 C5
Kincardine *Canada* 44°10N 81°40W 82 B3
Kincolith *Canada* 55°0N 129°57W 70 C3
Kinde *U.S.A.* 43°56N 83°0W 82 C2
Kinder Scout *U.K.* 53°24N 1°52W 12 D6
Kindersley *Canada* 51°30N 109°10W 71 C7
Kindia *Guinea* 10°0N 12°52W 52 F3
Kindu
  Dem. Rep. of the Congo 2°55S 25°50E 54 E5
Kineshma *Russia* 57°30N 42°5E 18 C7
King, L. *Australia* 33°10S 119°35E 61 F2
King, Mt. *Australia* 25°10S 147°30E 62 D4
King Christian I.
  Canada 77°48N 101°40W 69 B11
King City *U.S.A.* 36°13N 121°8W 78 J5
King Cr. → *Australia* 24°35S 139°30E 62 C2
King Edward →
  Australia 14°14S 126°35E 60 B4
King Edward Point
  S. Georgia 54°17S 36°30W 96 G9
King Frederick VI Land = Kong
  Frederik VI.s Kyst
  Greenland 63°0N 43°0W 4 C5
King George B. *Falk. Is.* 51°30S 60°30W 96 G4
King George I. *Antarctica* 60°0S 60°0W 5 C18
King George Is. *Canada* 57°20N 80°30W 69 F15
King George Sd. *Australia* 35°5S 118°0E 61 G2
King I. = Kadan Kyun
  Burma 12°30N 98°20E 38 F2
King I. *Australia* 39°50S 144°0E 63 F3
King I. *Canada* 52°10N 127°40W 70 C3
King Khalid Military City =
  Madinat al Malik Khālid al
  Askarīyah *Si. Arabia* 27°54N 45°31E 46 E5
King Leopold Ranges
  Australia 17°30S 125°45E 60 C4
King of Prussia *U.S.A.* 40°5N 75°23W 83 F9
King Sd. *Australia* 16°50S 123°20E 60 C3
King Sejong *Antarctica* 62°30S 58°0W 5 C18
King Shaka = Durban ✕ (DIA)
  S. Africa 29°37S 31°7E 57 C5
King William I. *Canada* 69°10N 97°25W 68 D12
King William's Town
  S. Africa 32°51S 27°22E 56 D4
Kingaok = Bathurst Inlet
  Canada 66°50N 108°1W 68 D10
Kingaroy *Australia* 26°32S 151°51E 63 D5
Kingfisher *U.S.A.* 35°52N 97°56W 84 D6
Kingirbān *Iraq* 34°40N 44°54E 46 C5
Kingisepp = Kuressaare
  Estonia 58°15N 22°30E 9 G20
Kingisepp *Russia* 59°25N 28°40E 9 G23
Kingman *Ariz., U.S.A.* 35°12N 114°4W 79 K12
Kingman *Kans., U.S.A.* 37°39N 98°7W 80 G4
Kingoonya *Australia* 30°55S 135°19E 63 E2
Kingri *Pakistan* 30°27N 69°49E 42 D3
Kings → *U.S.A.* 36°3N 119°50W 78 J7
Kings Canyon *Australia* 24°15S 131°34E 60 D5
Kings Canyon △ *U.S.A.* 36°50N 118°40W 78 J8
King's Lynn *U.K.* 52°45N 0°24E 12 E8
Kings Park *U.S.A.* 40°53N 73°16W 83 F11
Kings Peak *U.S.A.* 40°46N 110°23W 76 F8
Kingsbridge *U.K.* 50°17N 3°47W 13 G4
Kingsburg *U.S.A.* 36°31N 119°33W 78 J7
Kingscote *Australia* 35°40S 137°38E 63 F2
Kingscourt *Ireland* 53°54N 6°48W 10 C5
Kingsland *U.S.A.* 30°48N 81°41W 85 F14
Kingsport *U.S.A.* 36°33N 82°33W 85 G13
Kingston *Canada* 44°14N 76°30W 83 B8
Kingston *Jamaica* 17°55N 76°50W 88 a
Kingston *N.Z.* 45°20S 168°43E 59 F2
Kingston *N.H., U.S.A.* 42°56N 71°3W 83 D13
Kingston *N.Y., U.S.A.* 41°56N 73°59W 83 E11
Kingston *Pa., U.S.A.* 41°16N 75°54W 83 E9
Kingston *R.I., U.S.A.* 41°29N 71°30W 83 E13
Kingston Pk. *U.S.A.* 35°44N 115°55W 79 K11
Kingston South East
  Australia 36°51S 139°55E 63 F2
Kingston upon Hull *U.K.* 53°45N 0°21W 12 D7
Kingston upon Hull □
  U.K. 53°45N 0°21W 12 D7
Kingstown *St. Vincent* 13°10N 61°10W 89 D7
Kingstree *U.S.A.* 33°40N 79°50W 85 E15
Kingsville *Canada* 42°2N 82°45W 82 D2

Kingsville U.S.A.	27°31N 97°52W	84 H6
Kingussie U.K.	57°6N 4°2W	11 D4
Kingwood U.S.A.	30°2N 95°16W	84 F7
Kınık Turkey	39°6N 27°24E	23 E12
Kinistino Canada	52°57N 105°2W	71 C7
Kinjirap Daban Asia	36°40N 75°25E	40 A9
Kinkala Congo	4°18S 14°49E	54 E2
Kinki □ Japan	33°45N 136°0E	29 H8
Kinleith N.Z.	38°20S 175°56E	59 C5
Kinlochleven U.K.	56°43N 5°0W	11 E4
Kinmount Canada	44°48N 78°45W	82 B6
Kinna Sweden	57°32N 12°42E	9 H15
Kinnairds Hd. U.K.	57°43N 2°1W	11 D6
Kinngait Canada	64°14N 76°32W	69 E16
Kinniyai Sri Lanka	8°29N 81°11E	45 K5
Kino Nuevo Mexico	28°52N 112°3W	86 B2
Kinoje → Canada	52°8N 81°25W	72 B3
Kinomoto Japan	35°30N 136°13E	29 G8
Kinoosao Canada	57°5N 102°1W	71 B8
Kinross U.K.	56°13N 3°25W	11 E5
Kinsale Ireland	51°42N 8°31W	10 E3
Kinsale, Old Hd. of Ireland	51°37N 8°33W	10 E3
Kinsha = Chang Jiang →		
China	31°48N 121°10E	35 B13
Kinshasa		
Dem. Rep. of the Congo	4°20S 15°15E	54 E3
Kinsley U.S.A.	37°55N 99°25W	80 G4
Kinsman U.S.A.	41°26N 80°35W	82 E4
Kinston U.S.A.	35°16N 77°35W	85 D16
Kintamani Indonesia	8°14S 115°19E	37 J18
Kintore U.K.	57°14N 2°20W	11 D6
Kintore Ra. Australia	23°15S 128°47E	60 D4
Kintyre U.K.	55°30N 5°35W	11 F3
Kintyre, Mull of U.K.	55°17N 5°47W	11 F3
Kinushseo → Canada	55°15N 83°45W	72 A3
Kinuso Canada	55°20N 115°25W	70 B5
Kinvarra Ireland	53°8N 8°56W	10 C3
Kinwat India	19°38N 78°12E	44 E4
Kinzua U.S.A.	41°52N 78°58W	82 E6
Kiosk Canada	46°6N 78°53W	72 C4
Kiowa Kans., U.S.A.	37°1N 98°29W	80 G4
Kiowa Okla., U.S.A.	34°43N 95°54W	84 D7
Kipahigan L. Canada	55°20N 101°55W	71 B8
Kiparissia Greece	37°15N 21°40E	23 F9
Kiparissiakos Kolpos		
Greece	37°25N 21°25E	23 F9
Kipawa, L. Canada	46°50N 79°0W	72 C4
Kipling Canada	50°6N 102°38W	71 C8
Kippure Ireland	53°11N 6°21W	10 C5
Kipushi		
Dem. Rep. of the Congo	11°48S 27°12E	55 G5
Kirandul India	18°33N 81°10E	44 E5
Kirensk Russia	57°50N 107°55E	27 D11
Kirghiz Range Asia	42°40N 73°40E	30 C3
Kirghizia = Kyrgyzstan ■		
Asia	42°0N 75°0E	26 E8
Kirgiziya Steppe Eurasia	50°0N 55°0E	19 E10
Kiri Buru India	22°0N 85°0E	44 D7
Kiribati ■ Pac. Oc.	3°0S 180°0E	58 B10
Kırıkkale Turkey	39°51N 33°32E	19 F5
Kirillov Russia	59°49N 38°24E	18 C6
Kirin = Jilin China	43°44N 126°30E	33 C14
Kirindi Oya → Sri Lanka	6°15N 81°20E	45 L5
Kirinyaga = Kenya, Mt.		
Kenya	0°10S 37°18E	54 E7
Kirirom △ Cambodia	11°18N 104°5E	39 G5
Kirishima Japan	31°44N 130°46E	29 J5
Kirishima Yaku □ Japan	31°24N 130°50E	29 J5
Kiritimati Kiribati	1°58N 157°27W	65 G12
Kirkby U.K.	53°30N 2°54W	12 D5
Kirkby-in-Ashfield U.K.	53°6N 1°14W	12 D6
Kirkby Lonsdale U.K.	54°12N 2°36W	12 C5
Kirkby Stephen U.K.	54°29N 2°21W	12 C5
Kirkcaldy U.K.	56°7N 3°9W	11 E5
Kirkcudbright U.K.	54°50N 4°2W	11 G4
Kirkenes Norway	69°40N 30°5E	8 B24
Kirkfield Canada	44°34N 78°45W	82 B6
Kirkintilloch U.K.	55°56N 4°8W	11 F4
Kirkjubæjarklaustur		
Iceland	63°47N 18°4W	8 E4
Kirkkonummi Finland	60°8N 24°26E	9 F21
Kirkland U.S.A.	47°40N 122°12W	78 C4
Kirkland Lake Canada	48°9N 80°2W	72 C3
Kırklareli Turkey	41°44N 27°15E	23 D12
Kirksville U.S.A.	40°12N 92°35W	80 E7
Kirkūk Iraq	35°30N 44°21E	46 C5
Kirkwall U.K.	58°59N 2°58W	11 C6
Kirkwood S. Africa	33°22S 25°15E	56 D4
Kirlampudi India	17°12N 82°12E	44 F6
Kirov Russia	58°35N 49°40E	18 C8
Kirovabad = Gäncä		
Azerbaijan	40°45N 46°20E	19 F8
Kirovograd = Kirovohrad		
Ukraine	48°35N 32°20E	19 E5
Kirovohrad Ukraine	48°35N 32°20E	19 E5
Kirovsk Russia	67°32N 33°41E	18 A5
Kirovskiy Kamchatka,		
Russia	54°27N 155°42E	27 D16
Kirovskiy Primorsk,		
Russia	45°7N 133°30E	28 B6
Kirovskiy Ukraine	56°41N 3°1W	11 E5
Kirriemuir U.K.	56°41N 3°1W	11 E5
Kirsanov Russia	52°35N 42°40E	18 D7
Kırşehir Turkey	39°14N 34°5E	46 B2
Kirthar △ Pakistan	25°45N 67°30E	42 F2
Kirthar Range Pakistan	27°0N 67°0E	42 F2
Kirtland U.S.A.	36°44N 108°21W	77 H9
Kiruna Sweden	67°52N 20°15E	8 C19
Kiryū Japan	36°24N 139°20E	29 F9
Kisangani		
Dem. Rep. of the Congo	0°35N 25°15E	54 D5
Kisar Indonesia	8°5S 127°10E	37 F7
Kisarazu Japan	35°23N 139°55E	29 G9
Kiselevsk Russia	54°5N 86°39E	26 D9
Kish = Qeys Iran	26°32N 53°58E	47 E7
Kishanganga → Pakistan	34°18N 73°28E	43 B5
Kishanganj India	26°3N 88°14E	43 F13
Kishangarh Raj., India	26°34N 74°52E	42 F6
Kishangarh Raj., India	27°50N 70°30E	42 F4
Kishinev = Chişinău		
Moldova	47°2N 28°50E	17 E15
Kishiwada Japan	34°28N 135°22E	29 G7
Kishtwar India	33°20N 75°48E	42 C6
Kisii Kenya	0°40S 34°45E	54 E6
Kiska I. U.S.A.	51°59N 177°30E	74 E3
Kiskőrös Hungary	46°37N 19°20E	17 E10
Kiskunfélegyháza		
Hungary	46°42N 19°53E	17 E10
Kiskunhalas Hungary	46°28N 19°37E	17 E10
Kislovodsk Russia	43°50N 42°45E	19 F7
Kismaayo Somalia	0°22S 42°32E	49 H3
Kiso-Gawa → Japan	35°20N 136°45E	29 G8
Kiso-Sammyaku Japan	35°45N 137°45E	29 G8
Kisofukushima Japan	35°52N 137°43E	29 G8
Kissidougou Guinea	9°5N 10°5W	52 G3
Kissimmee U.S.A.	28°18N 81°24W	85 G14
Kissimmee → U.S.A.	27°9N 80°52W	85 H14
Kississing L. Canada	55°10N 101°20W	71 B8
Kisumu Kenya	0°3S 34°45E	54 E6
Kit Carson U.S.A.	38°46N 102°48W	76 G12
Kita Mali	13°5N 9°25W	52 F4
Kitaibaraki Japan	36°50N 140°45E	29 F10
Kitakami Japan	39°20N 141°10E	28 E10
Kitakami-Gawa →		
Japan	38°25N 141°19E	28 E10
Kitakami-Sammyaku		
Japan	39°30N 141°30E	28 E10
Kitakata Japan	37°39N 139°52E	28 F9
Kitakyūshū Japan	33°50N 130°50E	29 H5
Kitale Kenya	1°0N 35°0E	54 D7
Kitami Japan	43°48N 143°54E	28 C11
Kitami-Sammyaku		
Japan	44°22N 142°43E	28 B11
Kitchener Canada	43°27N 80°29W	82 C4
Kitee Finland	62°5N 30°8E	8 E24
Kitega = Gitega Burundi	3°26S 29°56E	54 E5
Kithira = Kythira Greece	36°8N 23°0E	23 F10
Kithnos Greece	37°26N 24°27E	23 F11
Kitimat Canada	54°3N 128°38W	70 C3
Kitinen → Finland	67°14N 27°27E	8 C22
Kitsuki Japan	33°25N 131°37E	29 H5
Kittakittaooloo, L.		
Australia	28°3S 138°14E	63 D2
Kittanning U.S.A.	40°49N 79°31W	82 F5
Kittatinny Mt. U.S.A.	41°19N 74°39W	83 E10
Kittery U.S.A.	43°5N 70°45W	83 C14
Kittilä Finland	67°40N 24°51E	8 C21
Kitui Kenya	1°17S 38°0E	54 E7
Kitwanga Canada	55°6N 128°4W	70 B3
Kitwe Zambia	12°54S 28°13E	55 G5
Kivarli India	24°33N 72°46E	42 G5
Kivertsi Ukraine	50°50N 25°28E	17 C13
Kivu, L.		
Dem. Rep. of the Congo	1°48S 29°0E	54 E5
Kiwirrkurra Australia	22°49S 127°45E	60 D4
Kiwirrkurra Ⓐ Australia	22°49S 127°45E	60 D4
Kiyev = Kyyiv Ukraine	50°30N 30°28E	17 C16
Kiyevskoye Vdkhr. = Kyyivske		
Vdskh. Ukraine	51°0N 30°25E	17 C16
Kizel Russia	59°3N 57°40E	18 C10
Kızıl Irmak → Turkey	41°44N 35°58E	19 F6
Kizil Jilga China	35°26N 78°50E	43 B8
Kızıldağ △ Turkey	38°5N 31°20E	46 B1
Kızılkaya Turkey	37°12N 40°35E	46 B4
Kizlyar Russia	43°51N 46°40E	19 F8
Kizyl-Arvat = Serdar		
Turkmenistan	39°4N 56°23E	47 B8
Kjölur Iceland	64°50N 19°25W	8 D4
Kladno Czech Rep.	50°10N 14°7E	16 C8
Klaeng Thailand	12°47N 101°39E	38 F3
Klagenfurt Austria	46°38N 14°20E	16 E8
Klaipėda Lithuania	55°43N 21°10E	9 J19
Klaksvík Færoe Is.	62°14N 6°35W	8 E9
Klamath → U.S.A.	41°33N 124°5W	76 F1
Klamath Falls U.S.A.	42°13N 121°46W	76 E3
Klamath Mts. U.S.A.	41°50N 123°20W	76 F2
Klamono Indonesia	1°8S 131°30E	37 E8
Klang Malaysia	3°2N 101°26E	39 L3
Klappan → Canada	58°0N 129°43W	70 B3
Klarälven → Sweden	59°23N 13°32E	9 G15
Klatovy Czech Rep.	49°23N 13°18E	16 D7
Klawer S. Africa	31°44S 18°36E	56 D2
Klazienaveen Neths.	52°44N 7°0E	15 B6
Kleena Kleene Canada	52°0N 124°59W	70 C4
Klein-Karas Namibia	27°33S 18°7E	56 C2
Kleinbegin S. Africa	28°54S 21°40E	56 C3
Klerksdorp S. Africa	26°53S 26°38E	56 D4
Kletsk = Klyetsk Belarus	53°5N 26°45E	17 B14
Kletskiy Russia	49°16N 43°11E	19 E7
Klickitat U.S.A.	45°49N 121°9W	76 D3
Klickitat → U.S.A.	45°42N 121°17W	78 E5
Klinaklini → Canada	51°21N 125°40W	70 C3
Klip → S. Africa	27°3S 29°3E	57 C4
Klipdale S. Africa	34°19S 19°57E	56 D2
Klipplaat S. Africa	33°1S 24°22E	56 D3
Kłodzko Poland	50°28N 16°38E	17 C9
Klondike Canada	64°0N 139°26W	68 E4
Klong Wang Chao △		
Thailand	16°20N 99°9E	38 D2
Kluane △ Canada	60°45N 139°30W	70 A1
Kluane L. Canada	61°15N 138°40W	68 E5
Kluang Malaysia	2°3N 103°18E	39 L4
Kluczbork Poland	50°58N 18°12E	17 C10
Klukwan U.S.A.	59°24N 135°54W	70 B1
Klungkung Indonesia	8°32S 115°24E	37 K18
Klyetsk Belarus	53°5N 26°45E	17 B14
Klyuchevskaya, Gora		
Russia	55°50N 160°30E	27 D17
Klyuchi Russia	56°18N 160°51E	27 D17
Knaresborough U.K.	54°1N 1°28W	12 C6
Knee L. Man., Canada	55°3N 94°45W	72 A1
Knee L. Sask., Canada	55°51N 107°0W	71 B7
Knight Inlet Canada	50°45N 125°40W	70 C3
Knighton U.K.	52°21N 3°3W	13 E4
Knights Ferry U.S.A.	37°50N 120°40W	78 H6
Knights Landing U.S.A.	38°48N 121°43W	78 G5
Knob, C. Australia	34°32S 119°16E	61 F2
Knock Ireland	53°48N 8°55W	10 C3
Knockmealdown Mts.		
Ireland	52°14N 7°56W	10 D4
Knokke-Heist Belgium	51°21N 3°17E	15 C3
Knossos Greece	35°16N 25°10E	23 G11
Knowlton Canada	45°13N 72°31W	83 A12
Knox U.S.A.	41°18N 86°37W	80 E10
Knox Coast Antarctica	66°30S 108°0E	5 C8
Knoxville Iowa, U.S.A.	41°19N 93°6W	80 E7
Knoxville Pa., U.S.A.	41°57N 77°27W	82 E7
Knoxville Tenn., U.S.A.	35°58N 83°55W	85 D13
Knud Rasmussen Land		
Greenland	78°0N 60°0W	69 B20
Knysna S. Africa	34°2S 23°2E	56 D3
Ko Kha Thailand	18°11N 99°24E	38 C2
Ko Tarutao △ Thailand	6°31N 99°26E	39 J2
Ko Yao Thailand	8°7N 98°35E	39 a
Koartac = Quaqtaq		
Canada	60°55N 69°40W	69 E18
Koba Indonesia	6°37S 134°37E	37 F8
Kobarid Slovenia	46°15N 13°30E	16 E7
Kobayashi Japan	31°56N 130°59E	29 J5
Kōbe Japan	34°41N 135°13E	29 G7
Kōbi-Sho E. China Sea	25°56N 123°41E	29 M1
Koblenz Germany	50°21N 7°36E	16 C4
Kobryn Belarus	52°15N 24°22E	17 B13
Kobuk → U.S.A.	66°54N 160°38W	74 B7
Kocaeli Turkey	40°45N 29°50E	19 F4
Kočani Macedonia	41°55N 22°25E	23 D10
Koch Bihar India	26°22N 89°29E	41 F16
Kochas India	25°15N 83°56E	43 G10
Kochi India	9°58N 76°20E	45 K3
Kōchi Japan	33°30N 133°35E	29 H6
Kōchi □ Japan	33°40N 133°30E	29 H6
Kochiu = Gejiu China	23°20N 103°10E	34 F4
Kodala India	19°38N 84°57E	44 E7
Kodarma India	24°28N 85°36E	43 G11
Koddiyar B. Sri Lanka	8°33N 81°15E	45 K5
Kodiak U.S.A.	57°47N 152°24W	74 D9
Kodiak I. U.S.A.	57°30N 152°45W	74 D9
Kodikkarai = Point Calimere		
India	10°17N 79°49E	45 J4
Kodinar India	20°46N 70°46E	42 J4
Kodinsk Russia	58°40N 99°10E	27 D10
Kodlipet India	12°48N 75°53E	45 H2
Kodungallur = Cranganore		
India	10°13N 76°13E	45 J3
Koedoesberge S. Africa	32°40S 20°11E	56 D3
Koes Namibia	26°0S 19°15E	56 C2
Koffiefontein S. Africa	29°30S 25°0E	56 C4
Kofiau Indonesia	1°11S 129°50E	37 E7
Koforidua Ghana	6°3N 0°17W	52 G5
Kōfu Japan	35°40N 138°30E	29 G9
Koga Japan	36°11N 139°43E	29 F9
Kogaluc → Canada	56°12N 61°44W	73 A7
Køge Denmark	55°27N 12°11E	9 J15
Kogon Uzbekistan	39°43N 64°33E	26 F7
Koh-i-Khurd Afghan.	33°30N 65°59E	42 C1
Koh-i-Maran Pakistan	29°18N 66°50E	42 E2
Koh Ker Cambodia	13°47N 104°32E	38 F5
Koh Wai Thailand	11°54N 102°52E	39 H4
Kohat Pakistan	33°40N 71°29E	42 C4
Kohima India	25°35N 94°10E	41 G19
Kohkīlūyeh va Būyer Aḥmadī		
Iran	31°30N 50°30E	47 D6
Kohler Ra. Antarctica	77°0S 110°0W	5 D15
Kohtla-Järve Estonia	59°20N 27°20E	9 G22
Koi Sanjaq Iraq	36°5N 44°38E	46 B5
Koihoa India	8°12N 93°29E	45 K11
Koilkuntla India	15°14N 78°19E	45 G4
Koillismaa Finland	65°44N 28°36E	8 D23
Koin N. Korea	40°28N 126°18E	33 D14
Kojō N. Korea	38°58N 127°58E	33 E14
Kojonup Australia	33°48S 117°10E	61 F2
Kojūr Iran	36°23N 51°43E	47 B6
Kokand = Qŭqon		
Uzbekistan	40°31N 70°56E	26 E8
Kokang Burma	23°45N 98°30E	34 F2
Kokas Indonesia	2°42S 132°26E	37 E8
Kokchetav = Kökshetaü		
Kazakhstan	53°20N 69°25E	26 D7
Kokemäenjoki →		
Finland	61°32N 21°44E	8 F19
Kokkilai Sri Lanka	9°0N 80°57E	45 K5
Kokkola Finland	63°50N 23°8E	8 E20
Koko Kyunzu Burma	14°7N 93°22E	45 G11
Kokomo U.S.A.	40°29N 86°8W	80 E10
Kokopo Papua N. G.	4°22S 152°19E	64 H7
Koksan N. Korea	38°46N 126°40E	33 E14
Kökshetaü Kazakhstan	53°20N 69°25E	26 D7
Koksoak → Canada	58°30N 68°10W	69 F18
Kokstad S. Africa	30°32S 29°29E	57 D4
Kokubu = Kirishima		
Japan	31°44N 130°46E	29 J5
Kola Indonesia	5°35S 134°30E	37 F8
Kola Russia	68°45N 33°8E	8 B25
Kola Pen. = Kolskiy Poluostrov		
Russia	67°30N 38°0E	18 A6
Kolachel India	8°10N 77°15E	45 K3
Kolachi → Pakistan	27°8N 67°2E	42 F2
Kolahoi India	34°12N 75°22E	43 B6
Kolaka Indonesia	4°3S 121°46E	37 E6
Kolar India	13°12N 78°15E	45 H4
Kolar Gold Fields India	12°58N 78°16E	45 H4
Kolaras India	25°14N 77°36E	42 G6
Kolari Finland	67°20N 23°48E	8 C20
Kolasib India	24°15N 92°45E	41 G18
Kolayat India	27°50N 72°50E	42 F5
Kolda Senegal	12°55N 14°57W	52 F3
Kolding Denmark	55°30N 9°29E	9 J13
Kolepom = Dolak, Pulau		
Indonesia	8°0S 138°30E	37 F9
Kolguyev, Ostrov Russia	69°20N 48°30E	18 A8
Kolhapur India	16°43N 74°15E	44 F2
Kolín Czech Rep.	50°2N 15°9E	16 C8
Kolkas rags Latvia	57°46N 22°37E	9 H20
Kollam India	8°50N 76°38E	45 K3
Kolleru L. India	16°40N 81°10E	44 F5
Kollum Neths.	53°17N 6°10E	15 A6
Kolmanskop Namibia	26°45S 15°14E	56 C2
Köln Germany	50°56N 6°57E	16 C4
Koło Poland	52°14N 18°40E	17 B10
Kołobrzeg Poland	54°10N 15°35E	16 A8
Kolokani Mali	13°35N 7°45W	52 F4
Kolomna Russia	55°8N 38°45E	18 C6
Kolomyya Ukraine	48°31N 25°2E	17 D13
Kolonodale Indonesia	2°0S 121°19E	37 E6
Kolpashevo Russia	58°20N 83°5E	26 D9
Kolpino Russia	59°44N 30°39E	18 C5
Kolskiy Poluostrov Russia	67°30N 38°0E	18 A6
Kolskiy Zaliv Russia	69°23N 34°0E	8 B26
Kolwezi		
Dem. Rep. of the Congo	10°40S 25°25E	54 G5
Kolyma → Russia	69°30N 161°0E	27 C17
Kolymskoye Nagorye		
Russia	63°0N 157°0E	27 C16
Kôm Ombo Egypt	24°25N 32°52E	53 D12
Komandorskiye Is. =		
Komandorskiye Ostrova		
Russia	55°0N 167°0E	27 D17
Komandorskiye Ostrova		
Russia	55°0N 167°0E	27 D17
Komárno Slovak Rep.	47°49N 18°5E	17 E10
Komatipoort S. Africa	25°25S 31°55E	57 C5
Komatsu Japan	36°25N 136°30E	29 F8
Komatsushima Japan	34°0N 134°35E	29 H7
Komi □ Russia	64°0N 55°0E	18 B10
Kommamur Canal India	16°0N 80°25E	45 G5
Kommunarsk = Alchevsk		
Ukraine	48°30N 38°45E	19 E6
Kommunizma, Pik = imeni Ismail		
Samani, Pik Tajikistan	39°0N 72°2E	26 F8
Komodo Indonesia	8°37S 119°20E	37 F5
Komoran, Pulau		
Indonesia	8°18S 138°45E	37 F9
Komoro Japan	36°19N 138°26E	29 F9
Komotini Greece	41°9N 25°26E	23 D11
Kompasberg S. Africa	31°45S 24°32E	56 D3
Kompong Chhnang = Kampong		
Chhnang Cambodia	12°20N 104°35E	39 F5
Kompong Chikreng		
Cambodia	13°5N 104°18E	38 F5
Kompong Kleang		
Cambodia	13°6N 104°8E	38 F5
Kompong Luong		
Cambodia	11°49N 104°48E	39 G5
Kompong Pranak		
Cambodia	13°35N 104°55E	38 F5
Kompong Som = Kampong Saom		
Cambodia	10°38N 103°30E	39 G4
Kompong Som, Chhung =		
Kampong Saom, Chaak		
Cambodia	10°50N 103°32E	39 G4
Kompong Speu		
Cambodia	11°26N 104°32E	39 G5
Kompong Sralau		
Cambodia	14°5N 105°46E	38 E5
Kompong Thom		
Cambodia	12°35N 104°51E	38 F5
Kompong Trabeck		
Cambodia	13°6N 105°14E	38 F5
Kompong Trach		
Cambodia	11°25N 105°48E	39 G5
Kompong Tralach		
Cambodia	11°54N 104°47E	39 G5
Komrat = Comrat		
Moldova	46°18N 28°40E	17 E15
Komsberg S. Africa	32°40S 20°45E	56 D3
Komsomolets, Ostrov		
Russia	80°30N 95°0E	27 A10
Komsomolsk-na-Amur		
Russia	50°30N 137°0E	31 A16
Komsomolskiy Ukraine	50°54N 28°36E	17 C15
Kon Ka Kinh △ Vietnam	14°19N 107°23E	38 E6
Kon Tum Vietnam	14°24N 108°0E	38 E7
Kon Tum, Plateau du		
Vietnam	14°30N 108°30E	38 E7
Konar □ Afghan.	34°30N 71°3E	40 B7
Konarak India	19°54N 86°7E	44 E8
Konārī Iran	28°13N 51°36E	47 D6
Konch India	26°0N 79°10E	43 G8
Kondagaon India	19°35N 81°35E	44 E5
Kondinin Australia	32°34S 118°8E	61 F2
Kondoa Tanzania	4°55S 35°50E	54 E7
Kondopoga Russia	62°12N 34°17E	18 B5
Kondratyevo Russia	57°22N 98°15E	27 D10
Kondukur India	15°12N 79°57E	45 G4
Köneürgench		
Turkmenistan	42°19N 59°10E	26 E6
Konevo Russia	62°8N 39°20E	18 B6
Kong = Khong →		
Cambodia	13°32N 105°58E	38 F5
Kong Ivory C.	8°54N 4°36W	52 G5
Kong, Koh Cambodia	11°20N 103°0E	39 G4
Kong Christian IX.s Land		
Greenland	68°0N 36°0W	4 C6
Kong Christian X.s Land		
Greenland	74°0N 29°0W	4 B6
Kong Frederik IX.s Land		
Greenland	67°0N 52°0W	4 C5
Kong Frederik VI.s Kyst		
Greenland	63°0N 43°0W	4 C5
Kong Frederik VIII.s Land		
Greenland	78°30N 26°0W	4 B6
Kong Oscar Fjord		
Greenland	72°20N 24°0W	4 B6
Konglu Burma	27°13N 97°57E	41 F20
Kongola Namibia	17°45S 23°20E	56 A3
Kongolo		
Dem. Rep. of the Congo	5°22S 27°0E	54 F5
Kongsberg Norway	59°39N 9°39E	9 G13
Kongsvinger Norway	60°12N 12°2E	9 F15
Kongur Shan China	38°34N 75°18E	30 D4
Konin Poland	52°12N 18°15E	17 B10
Konjic Bos.-H.	43°42N 17°58E	23 C7
Konkiep Namibia	26°49S 17°15E	56 C2
Konnur India	16°14N 74°49E	45 F2
Konosha Russia	61°0N 40°5E	18 B7
Kōnosu Japan	36°3N 139°31E	29 F9
Konotop Ukraine	51°12N 33°7E	19 D5
Konqi He → China	41°0N 86°0E	30 C6
Końskie Poland	51°15N 20°23E	17 C11
Konstanz Germany	47°40N 9°10E	16 E5
Kont Iran	26°55N 61°50E	47 E9
Konta India	17°48N 81°23E	44 F5
Kontagora Nigeria	10°23N 5°27E	52 F7
Kontiolahti Finland	62°46N 29°50E	8 E23
Konya Turkey	37°52N 32°35E	46 B2
Koocanusa, L. Canada	49°20N 115°15W	76 B6
Kookynie Australia	29°17S 121°22E	61 E3
Koolyanobbing Australia	30°48S 119°36E	61 F2
Koonibba Australia	31°54S 133°25E	63 E1
Koorawatha Australia	34°2S 148°33E	63 E4
Koorda Australia	30°48S 117°35E	61 F2
Kooskia U.S.A.	46°9N 115°59W	76 C6
Kootenay → U.S.A.	49°19N 117°39W	70 D5
Kootenay L. Canada	49°45N 116°50W	70 D5
Kootjieskolk S. Africa	31°15S 20°21E	56 E3
Kopaonik Serbia	43°10N 20°50E	23 C9
Kopargaon India	19°51N 74°28E	44 E2
Kópavogur Iceland	64°6N 21°55W	8 D3
Koper Slovenia	45°31N 13°44E	16 F7
Kopervik Norway	59°17N 5°17E	9 G11
Kopet Dagh Asia	38°0N 58°0E	47 B8
Kopeysk Russia	55°7N 61°37E	26 D7
Kopi Australia	33°24S 135°40E	63 E2
Köping Sweden	59°31N 16°3E	9 G17
Koppal India	13°33N 75°21E	45 H2
Koppal India	15°23N 76°5E	45 G3
Koppeh Dāgh = Kopet Dagh		
Asia	38°0N 58°0E	47 B8
Koppies S. Africa	27°20S 27°30E	57 D4
Koprivnica Croatia	46°12N 16°45E	22 A7
Köprülü △ Turkey	37°20N 31°5E	46 B1
Kopychyntsi Ukraine	49°7N 25°58E	17 D13
Korab Macedonia	41°44N 20°40E	23 D9
Koral India	21°50N 73°12E	42 J5
Korangal India	17°6N 77°38E	44 F4
Koraput India	18°50N 82°40E	44 E6
Korba India	22°20N 82°45E	43 H10
Korbu, Gunung Malaysia	4°41N 101°18E	39 K3
Korçë Albania	40°37N 20°50E	23 D9
Korčula Croatia	42°56N 16°57E	22 C7
Kord Kūy Iran	36°48N 54°7E	47 B7
Kord Sheykh Iran	28°31N 52°53E	47 D7
Kordestān □ Iran	36°0N 47°0E	46 C5
Kordofân Sudan	13°0N 29°0E	53 F11
Korea, North ■ Asia	40°0N 127°0E	33 E14
Korea, South ■ Asia	36°0N 128°0E	33 G15
Korea Bay Korea	39°0N 124°0E	33 E13
Korea Strait Asia	34°0N 129°30E	33 H15
Koregaon India	17°40N 74°10E	44 F2
Korets Ukraine	50°40N 27°5E	17 C14
Korff Ice Rise Antarctica	79°0S 69°30W	5 D17
Korhogo Ivory C.	9°29N 5°28W	52 G4
Korinthiakos Kolpos		
Greece	38°16N 22°30E	23 E10
Korinthos Greece	37°56N 22°55E	23 F10
Kōriyama Japan	37°24N 140°23E	28 F10
Korneshty = Corneşti		
Moldova	47°21N 28°1E	17 E15
Koro Fiji	17°19S 179°23E	59 a
Koro Ivory C.	8°32N 7°30W	52 G4
Koro Sea Fiji	17°30S 179°45W	59 a
Korogwe Tanzania	5°5S 38°25E	54 F7
Korolevu Fiji	18°12S 177°46E	59 a
Koronadal Phil.	6°12N 124°51E	37 C6
Körös → Hungary	46°43N 20°12E	17 E11
Korosten Ukraine	50°54N 28°36E	17 C15
Korostyshev Ukraine	50°19N 29°4E	17 C15
Korovou Fiji	17°47S 178°32E	59 a
Koroyanitu △ Fiji	17°40S 177°35E	59 a
Korsakov Russia	46°36N 142°42E	27 E15
Korshunovo Russia	58°37N 110°10E	27 D12
Korsør Denmark	55°20N 11°9E	9 J14
Kortrijk Belgium	50°50N 3°17E	15 D3
Korwai India	24°7N 78°5E	42 G8
Koryakskoye Nagorye		
Russia	61°0N 171°0E	27 C18
Kos Greece	36°50N 27°15E	23 F12
Kosan N. Korea	38°52N 127°25E	33 E14
Kościan Poland	52°5N 16°40E	17 B9
Kosciusko U.S.A.	33°4N 89°35W	85 E10
Kosciuszko, Mt.		
Australia	36°27S 148°16E	63 F4
Kosgi Andhra Pradesh,		
India	16°58N 77°43E	44 F3
Kosgi Andhra Pradesh,		
India	15°51N 77°16E	45 G3
Kosha Sudan	20°50N 30°30E	53 D12
Kosi India	27°48N 77°29E	42 F7
Kosi → India	28°41N 78°57E	43 E8
Košice Slovak Rep.	48°42N 21°15E	17 D11
Koslan Russia	63°34N 49°14E	18 B8
Košong N. Korea	38°40N 128°22E	33 E15
Kosovo ■ Europe	42°30N 21°0E	23 C9
Kosovska Mitrovica = Mitrovicë		
Kosovo	42°54N 20°52E	23 C9
Kossou, L. de Ivory C.	6°59N 5°31W	52 G4
Koster S. Africa	25°52S 26°54E	56 C4
Kôstî Sudan	13°8N 32°43E	53 F12
Kostopil Ukraine	50°51N 26°22E	17 C14
Kostroma Russia	57°50N 40°58E	18 C7
Kostrzyn Poland	52°35N 14°39E	16 B8
Koszalin Poland	54°11N 16°8E	16 A9
Kot Addu Pakistan	30°30N 71°0E	42 D4
Kot Kapura India	30°35N 74°50E	42 D6
Kot Moman Pakistan	32°13N 73°0E	42 C5
Kot Sultan Pakistan	30°46N 70°56E	42 D4
Kota India	25°14N 75°49E	42 G6
Kota Barrage India	25°6N 75°51E	42 G6
Kota Belud Malaysia	6°21N 116°26E	36 C5
Kota Bharu Malaysia	6°7N 102°14E	39 J4
Kota Kinabalu Malaysia	6°0N 116°4E	36 C5
Kota Tinggi Malaysia	1°44N 103°53E	39 M4

Kotaagung *Indonesia* 5°38S 104°29E **36** F2
Kotabaru *Indonesia* 3°20S 116°20E **36** E5
Kotabumi *Indonesia* 4°49S 104°54E **36** E2
Kotamobagu *Indonesia* 0°57N 124°31E **37** D6
Kotapad *India* 19°9N 82°21E **44** E6
Kotapinang *Indonesia* 1°53N 100°5E **39** M3
Kotcho L. *Canada* 59°7N 121°12W **70** B4
Kotdwara *India* 29°45N 78°32E **43** E8
Kotelnich *Russia* 58°22N 48°24E **18** C8
Kotelnikovo *Russia* 47°38N 43°8E **19** E7
Kotelnyy, Ostrov *Russia* 75°10N 139°0E **27** B14
Kothapet *India* 19°21N 79°28E **44** E4
Kothari → *India* 25°20N 75°4E **42** G6
Kothi *Chhattisgarh, India* 23°21N 82°3E **43** H10
Kothi *Mad. P., India* 24°45N 80°40E **43** G9
Kotiro *Pakistan* 26°17N 67°13E **42** F2
Kotka *Finland* 60°28N 26°58E **8** F22
Kotlas *Russia* 61°17N 46°43E **18** B8
Kotli *Pakistan* 33°30N 73°55E **42** C5
Kotlik *U.S.A.* 63°2N 163°33W **74** C7
Kotma *India* 23°12N 81°58E **43** H9
Kotor *Montenegro* 42°25N 18°47E **23** C8
Kotovsk *Ukraine* 47°45N 29°35E **17** E15
Kotputli *India* 27°43N 76°12E **42** F7
Kotri *Pakistan* 25°22N 68°22E **42** G3
Kotri → *India* 19°15N 80°35E **44** E5
Kottagudem *India* 17°30N 80°40E **44** F5
Kottayam *India* 9°35N 76°33E **45** K3
Kotto → *C.A.R.* 4°14N 22°2E **54** D4
Kottur *India* 10°34N 76°56E **45** J3
Kotturu *India* 14°45N 76°10E **45** G3
Kotu Group *Tonga* 20°0S 174°45W **59** c
Kotuy → *Russia* 71°54N 102°6E **27** B11
Kotzebue *U.S.A.* 66°53N 162°39W **74** B7
Kotzebue Sound *U.S.A.* 66°20N 163°0W **74** B7
Kouchibouguac △
  Canada 46°50N 65°0W **73** C6
Koudougou *Burkina Faso* 12°10N 2°20W **52** F5
Kougaberge *S. Africa* 33°48S 23°50E **56** D3
Kouilou → *Congo* 4°10S 12°5E **54** E2
Koukdjuak → *Canada* 66°43N 73°0W **69** D17
Koula Moutou *Gabon* 1°15S 12°25E **54** E2
Koulen = Kulen
  Cambodia 13°50N 104°40E **38** F5
Koumala *Australia* 21°38S 149°15E **62** C4
Koumra *Chad* 8°50N 17°35E **53** G9
Kountze *U.S.A.* 30°22N 94°19W **84** F7
Kourou *Fr. Guiana* 5°9N 52°39W **93** B8
Kouroussa *Guinea* 10°45N 9°45W **52** F4
Kousseri *Cameroon* 12°0N 14°55E **53** F8
Koutiala *Mali* 12°25N 5°23W **52** F4
Kouvola *Finland* 60°52N 26°43E **8** F22
Kovdor *Russia* 67°34N 30°24E **8** C24
Kovel *Ukraine* 51°11N 24°38E **17** C13
Kovilpatti *India* 9°10N 77°50E **45** K3
Kovrov *Russia* 56°25N 41°25E **18** C7
Kovur *Andhra Pradesh, India* 17°39N 81°39E **44** F5
Kovur *Andhra Pradesh,
  India* 14°30N 80°1E **45** G5
Kowanyama *Australia* 15°29S 141°44E **62** B3
Kowanyama ☉ *Australia* 15°20S 141°47E **62** B3
Kowŏn *N. Korea* 39°26N 127°14E **33** E14
Koyampattur = Coimbatore
  India 11°2N 76°59E **45** J3
Köyceğiz *Turkey* 36°57N 28°40E **23** F13
Koyukuk → *U.S.A.* 64°55N 157°32W **74** C8
Koza = Okinawa *Japan* 26°19N 127°46E **29** L3
Kozan *Turkey* 37°26N 35°50E **46** B2
Kozani *Greece* 40°19N 21°47E **23** D9
Kozhikode *India* 11°15N 75°43E **45** J2
Kozhva *Russia* 65°10N 57°0E **18** A10
Kōzu-Shima *Japan* 34°13N 139°10E **29** G9
Kozyatyn *Ukraine* 49°45N 28°50E **17** D15
Kozyrevsk *Russia* 56°3N 159°51E **27** D16
Kpalimé *Togo* 6°57N 0°44E **52** G6
Kra, Isthmus of = Kra, Kho Khot
  Thailand 10°15N 99°30E **39** G2
Kra, Kho Khot *Thailand* 10°15N 99°30E **39** G2
Kra Buri *Thailand* 10°22N 98°46E **39** G2
Kraai → *S. Africa* 30°40S 26°45E **56** E4
Krabi *Thailand* 8°4N 98°55E **39** H2
Kracheh = Kratie
  Cambodia 12°32N 106°10E **38** F6
Kragan *Indonesia* 6°43S 111°38E **37** G14
Kragerø *Norway* 58°52N 9°25E **9** G13
Kragujevac *Serbia* 44°2N 20°56E **23** B9
Krakatau = Rakata, Pulau
  Indonesia 6°10S 105°20E **37** G11
Krakatoa = Rakata, Pulau
  Indonesia 6°10S 105°20E **37** G11
Krakor *Cambodia* 12°32N 104°12E **38** F5
Kraków *Poland* 50°4N 19°57E **17** C10
Kraksaan *Indonesia* 7°43S 113°23E **37** G16
Kralanh *Cambodia* 13°35N 103°25E **38** F4
Kraljevo *Serbia* 43°44N 20°41E **23** C9
Kramatorsk *Ukraine* 48°50N 37°30E **19** E6
Kramfors *Sweden* 62°55N 17°48E **8** E17
Kranj *Slovenia* 46°16N 14°22E **16** E8
Krankskop *S. Africa* 28°0S 30°47E **57** C5
Krasavino *Russia* 60°58N 46°29E **18** B8
Krasieo Res. *Thailand* 14°49N 99°30E **38** E2
Kraskino *Russia* 42°44N 130°48E **28** C5
Kraśnik *Poland* 50°55N 22°15E **17** C12
Krasnoarmeysk *Russia* 51°0N 45°42E **26** D5
Krasnodar *Russia* 45°5N 39°0E **19** E6
Krasnokamensk *Russia* 50°3N 118°0E **27** D12
Krasnokamsk *Russia* 58°4N 55°48E **18** C10
Krasnoperekopsk *Ukraine* 46°0N 33°54E **19** E5
Krasnorechenskiy
  Russia 44°41N 135°14E **28** B7
Krasnoselkup *Russia* 65°20N 82°10E **26** C9
Krasnoturinsk *Russia* 59°46N 60°12E **18** C11
Krasnoufimsk *Russia* 56°36N 57°38E **18** C10
Krasnouralsk *Russia* 58°21N 60°3E **18** C11
Krasnovishersk *Russia* 60°23N 57°3E **18** B10
Krasnoyarsk *Russia* 56°8N 93°0E **27** D10
Krasnoyarskoye Vdkhr.
  Russia 56°0N 92°30E **27** D10
Krasnyy Kut *Russia* 50°50N 47°0E **19** D8

Krasnyy Luch *Ukraine* 48°13N 39°0E **19** E6
Krasnyy Yar *Russia* 46°43N 48°23E **19** E8
Kratie *Cambodia* 12°32N 106°10E **38** F6
Krau *Indonesia* 3°19S 140°5E **37** E10
Kravanh, Chuor Phnum
  Cambodia 12°0N 103°32E **39** G4
Krefeld *Germany* 51°20N 6°33E **16** C4
Kremen *Croatia* 44°28N 15°53E **16** F8
Kremenchuk *Ukraine* 49°5N 33°25E **19** E5
Kremenchuksk Vdskh.
  Ukraine 49°20N 32°30E **19** E5
Kremenets *Ukraine* 50°8N 25°43E **17** C13
Kremmling *U.S.A.* 40°4N 106°24W **76** F10
Krems *Austria* 48°25N 15°36E **16** D8
Kretinga *Lithuania* 55°53N 21°15E **9** J19
Kribi *Cameroon* 2°57N 9°56E **54** D1
Krichev = Krychaw
  Belarus 53°40N 31°41E **17** B16
Kril'on, Mys *Russia* 45°53N 142°5E **28** B11
Krishna → *India* 15°57N 80°59E **45** G5
Krishnagiri *India* 12°32N 78°16E **45** H4
Krishnanagar *India* 23°24N 88°33E **43** H13
Krishnaraja Sagar *India* 12°20N 76°30E **45** H3
Kristiansand *Norway* 58°8N 8°1E **9** G13
Kristianstad *Sweden* 56°2N 14°9E **9** H16
Kristiansund *Norway* 63°7N 7°45E **8** E12
Kristiinankaupunki
  Finland 62°16N 21°21E **8** E19
Kristinehamn *Sweden* 59°18N 14°7E **9** G16
Kristinestad = Kristiinankaupunki
  Finland 62°16N 21°21E **8** E19
Kriti *Greece* 35°15N 25°0E **23** G11
Krivoy Rog = Kryvyy Rih
  Ukraine 47°51N 33°20E **19** E5
Krk *Croatia* 45°8N 14°40E **16** F8
Krokodil = Umgwenya →
  Mozam. 25°14S 32°18E **57** C5
Krong Kaoh Kong
  Cambodia 11°37N 102°59E **39** G4
Kronprins Frederik Land
  Greenland 81°0N 45°0W **4** B5
Kronprins Olav Kyst
  Antarctica 69°0S 42°0E **5** C5
Kronprinsesse Märtha Kyst
  Antarctica 73°30S 10°0W **5** D2
Kronshtadt *Russia* 59°57N 29°51E **18** B4
Kroonstad *S. Africa* 27°43S 27°19E **56** C4
Kropotkin *Russia* 45°28N 40°28E **19** E7
Krosno *Poland* 49°42N 21°46E **17** D11
Krotoszyn *Poland* 51°42N 17°23E **17** C9
Kruger △ *S. Africa* 24°0S 31°40E **57** B5
Krugersdorp *S. Africa* 26°5S 27°46E **57** C4
Kruisfontein *S. Africa* 33°59S 24°43E **56** D3
Krupki *Belarus* 54°19N 29°8E **17** A15
Kruševac *Serbia* 43°35N 21°28E **23** C9
Krychaw *Belarus* 53°40N 31°41E **17** B16
Krymskiy Poluostrov = Krymskyy
  Pivostriv *Ukraine* 45°0N 34°0E **19** F5
Krymskyy Pivostriv
  Ukraine 45°0N 34°0E **19** F5
Kryvyy Rih *Ukraine* 47°51N 33°20E **19** E5
Ksar el Kebir *Morocco* 35°0N 6°0W **52** B4
Ksar es Souk = Er Rachidia
  Morocco 31°58N 4°20W **52** B5
Kuah *Malaysia* 6°19N 99°51E **39** J2
Kuala Belait *Malaysia* 4°35N 114°11E **36** D4
Kuala Berang *Malaysia* 5°5N 103°1E **39** K4
Kuala Dungun = Dungun
  Malaysia 4°45N 103°25E **39** K4
Kuala Kangsar *Malaysia* 4°46N 100°56E **39** K3
Kuala Kelawang *Malaysia* 2°56N 102°5E **39** L4
Kuala Kerai *Malaysia* 5°30N 102°12E **39** K4
Kuala Kubu Bharu
  Malaysia 3°34N 101°39E **39** L3
Kuala Lipis *Malaysia* 4°10N 102°3E **39** K4
Kuala Lumpur *Malaysia* 3°9N 101°41E **39** L3
Kuala Nerang *Malaysia* 6°16N 100°37E **39** J3
Kuala Pilah *Malaysia* 2°45N 102°15E **39** L4
Kuala Rompin *Malaysia* 2°49N 103°29E **39** L4
Kuala Selangor *Malaysia* 3°20N 101°15E **39** L3
Kuala Sepetang *Malaysia* 4°49N 100°28E **39** K3
Kuala Terengganu
  Malaysia 5°20N 103°8E **39** K4
Kualajelai *Indonesia* 2°58S 110°46E **36** E4
Kualakapuas *Indonesia* 2°55S 114°20E **36** E4
Kualakurun *Indonesia* 1°10S 113°50E **36** E4
Kualapembuang
  Indonesia 3°14S 112°38E **36** E4
Kualasimpang *Indonesia* 4°17N 98°3E **36** D1
Kuancheng *China* 40°37N 118°30E **33** D10
Kuandang *Indonesia* 0°56N 123°1E **37** D6
Kuandian *China* 40°45N 124°45E **33** D13
Kuanshan *Taiwan* 23°3N 121°9E **35** F13
Kuantan *Malaysia* 3°49N 103°20E **39** L4
Kuba = Quba *Azerbaijan* 41°21N 48°32E **19** F8
Kuban → *Russia* 45°20N 37°30E **19** E6
Kubokawa = Shimanto
  Japan 33°12N 133°8E **29** H6
Kubu *Indonesia* 8°16S 115°35E **37** J18
Kubutambahan *Indonesia* 8°5S 115°10E **37** J18
Kucar, Tanjung
  Indonesia 8°39S 114°34E **37** K18
Kuchaman *India* 27°13N 74°47E **42** F6
Kuchchaveli *Sri Lanka* 8°49N 81°6E **45** K5
Kuchinda *India* 21°44N 84°21E **43** J11
Kuching *Malaysia* 1°33N 110°25E **36** D4
Kuchino-eruba-Jima
  Japan 30°28N 130°12E **29** J5
Kuchino-Shima *Japan* 29°57N 129°55E **29** K4
Kuchinotsu *Japan* 32°36N 130°11E **29** H5
Kucing = Kuching
  Malaysia 1°33N 110°25E **36** D4
Kud → *Pakistan* 26°5N 66°20E **42** F2
Kuda *India* 23°10N 71°15E **42** H4
Kudal *India* 16°2N 73°41E **45** F1
Kudalier → *India* 18°35N 79°48E **44** E4
Kudat *Malaysia* 6°55N 116°55E **36** C5
Kudremukh *India* 13°15N 75°20E **45** H2
Kudus *Indonesia* 6°48S 110°51E **37** G14

Kudymkar *Russia* 59°1N 54°39E **18** C9
Kueiyang = Guiyang
  China 26°32N 106°40E **34** D6
Kufra Oasis = Al Kufrah
  Libya 24°17N 23°15E **53** D10
Kufstein *Austria* 47°35N 12°11E **16** E7
Kugaaruk = Pelly Bay
  Canada 68°38N 89°50W **69** D14
Kugluktuk *Canada* 67°50N 115°5W **68** D8
Kugong I. *Canada* 56°18N 79°50W **72** A4
Kūh Dasht *Iran* 33°32N 47°36E **46** C5
Kūhak *Iran* 27°12N 63°10E **47** E9
Kuhan *Pakistan* 28°19N 67°14E **42** E2
Kūhbonān *Iran* 31°23N 56°19E **47** D8
Kūhestak *Iran* 26°47N 57°2E **47** E8
Kuhin *Iran* 36°22N 49°40E **47** B6
Kūhīrī *Iran* 26°55N 61°2E **47** E9
Kuhmo *Finland* 64°7N 29°31E **8** D23
Kuhn Chae △ *Thailand* 19°8N 99°24E **38** C2
Kūhpāyeh *Eṣfahan, Iran* 32°44N 52°20E **47** C7
Kūhpāyeh *Kermān, Iran* 30°35N 57°15E **47** D8
Kūhrān, Kūh-e *Iran* 26°46N 58°12E **47** E8
Kui Buri *Thailand* 12°3N 99°52E **39** F2
Kuiburi △ *Thailand* 12°10N 99°37E **39** F2
Kuichong *China* 22°38N 114°25E **31** a
Kuiseb → *Namibia* 22°59S 14°31E **56** B1
Kuito *Angola* 12°22S 16°55E **55** G3
Kuiu I. *U.S.A.* 57°45N 134°10W **70** B2
Kujang *N. Korea* 39°57N 126°1E **33** E14
Kuji *Japan* 40°11N 141°46E **28** D10
Kujū-San *Japan* 33°5N 131°15E **29** H5
Kukës *Albania* 42°5N 20°27E **23** C9
Kukup *Malaysia* 1°20N 103°27E **39** d
Kukup, Pulau *Malaysia* 1°18N 103°25E **39** d
Kula *Turkey* 38°32N 28°40E **23** E13
K'ula Shan *Bhutan* 28°14N 90°36E **30** F7
Kulachi *Pakistan* 31°56N 70°27E **42** D4
Kulai *Malaysia* 1°44N 103°35E **39** M4
Kulasekarappattinam *India* 8°20N 78°5E **45** K4
Kuldīga *Latvia* 56°58N 21°59E **9** H19
Kulen *Cambodia* 13°50N 104°40E **38** F5
Kulgam *India* 33°36N 75°2E **43** C6
Kulgera *Australia* 25°50S 133°18E **62** D1
Kulim *Malaysia* 5°22N 100°34E **39** K3
Kulin *Australia* 32°40S 118°2E **61** F2
Kulittalai *India* 10°55N 78°25E **45** J4
Kulkayu = Hartley Bay
  Canada 53°25N 129°15W **70** C3
Kullu *India* 31°58N 77°6E **42** D7
Kŭlob *Tajikistan* 37°55N 69°50E **26** F7
Kulsary = Qulsary
  Kazakhstan 46°59N 54°1E **19** E9
Kulti *India* 23°43N 86°50E **43** H12
Kulunda *Russia* 52°35N 78°57E **26** D8
Kulungar *Afghan.* 34°0N 69°2E **42** C3
Kŭlvand *Iran* 31°21N 54°35E **47** D7
Kulwin *Australia* 35°2S 142°42E **63** F3
Kulyab = Kŭlob *Tajikistan* 37°55N 69°50E **26** F7
Kuma → *Russia* 44°55N 47°0E **19** F8
Kumaganum *Nigeria* 13°8N 10°38E **53** F8
Kumagaya *Japan* 36°9N 139°22E **29** F9
Kumai *Indonesia* 2°44S 111°43E **36** E4
Kumamba, Kepulauan
  Indonesia 1°36S 138°45E **37** E9
Kumamoto *Japan* 32°45N 130°45E **29** H5
Kumamoto □ *Japan* 32°55N 130°55E **29** H5
Kumanovo *Macedonia* 42°9N 21°42E **23** C9
Kumara *N.Z.* 42°37S 171°12E **59** E3
Kumarina Roadhouse
  Australia 24°41S 119°32E **61** D2
Kumasi *Ghana* 6°41N 1°38W **52** G5
Kumba *Cameroon* 4°36N 9°24E **54** D1
Kumbakonam *India* 10°58N 79°25E **45** J4
Kumbarilla *Australia* 27°15S 150°55E **63** D5
Kumbhraj *India* 24°22N 77°3E **42** G7
Kumbia *Australia* 26°41S 151°39E **63** D5
Kumbukkan Oya →
  Sri Lanka 6°35N 81°40E **45** L5
Kŭmch'on *N. Korea* 38°10N 126°29E **33** E14
Kume-Shima *Japan* 26°20N 126°47E **29** L3
Kumertau *Russia* 52°45N 55°57E **18** D10
Kumharsain *India* 31°19N 77°27E **42** D7
Kumo *Nigeria* 10°1N 11°12E **53** F8
Kumo älv = Kokemäenjoki →
  Finland 61°32N 21°44E **8** F19
Kumon Bum *Burma* 26°30N 97°15E **41** F20
Kumta *India* 14°29N 74°25E **45** G2
Kumtag Shamo *China* 39°40N 92°0E **30** D7
Kuna *U.S.A.* 43°30N 116°25W **76** E5
Kunashir, Ostrov *Russia* 44°0N 146°0E **27** E15
Kunchha *Nepal* 28°8N 84°20E **43** E11
Kunda *Estonia* 59°30N 26°34E **9** G22
Kunda *India* 25°43N 81°31E **43** G9
Kundar → *Pakistan* 31°56N 69°19E **42** D3
Kundian *Pakistan* 32°27N 71°28E **42** C4
Kundla *India* 21°21N 71°25E **42** J4
Kunene □ *Namibia* 20°0S 14°0E **56** A1
Kung, Ao *Thailand* 8°5N 98°24E **39** a
Kunga → *Bangla.* 21°46N 89°30E **43** J13
Kunghit I. *Canada* 52°6N 131°3W **70** C2
Kungrad = Qŭnghirot
  Uzbekistan 43°2N 58°50E **26** E6
Kungsbacka *Sweden* 57°30N 12°5E **9** H15
Kungur *Russia* 57°25N 56°57E **18** C10
Kungurri *Australia* 21°4S 148°45E **62** b
Kunhar → *Pakistan* 34°20N 73°30E **43** B5
Kuningan *Indonesia* 6°59S 108°29E **37** G13
Kunlong *Burma* 23°20N 98°50E **34** F2
Kunlun Shan *Asia* 36°0N 86°30E **30** D6
Kunlun Shankou *China* 35°38N 94°0E **30** D7
Kunming *China* 25°1N 102°41E **34** E4
Kunmunya ☉ *Australia* 15°26S 124°42E **60** C3
Kunnamkulam *India* 10°38N 76°7E **45** J3
Kunshan *China* 31°22N 120°58E **35** B13
Kununurra *Australia* 15°40S 128°50E **60** C4
Kunwari → *India* 26°26N 79°11E **43** F8
Kunya-Urgench = Köneürgench
  Turkmenistan 42°19N 59°10E **26** E6
Kuopio *Finland* 62°53N 27°35E **8** E22

Kupa → *Croatia* 45°28N 16°24E **16** F9
Kupang *Indonesia* 10°19S 123°39E **37** F6
Kupreanof I. *U.S.A.* 56°50N 133°30W **70** B2
Kupyansk-Uzlovoi
  Ukraine 49°40N 37°43E **19** E6
Kuqa *China* 41°35N 82°30E **30** C5
Kür → *Azerbaijan* 39°29N 49°15E **19** G8
Kür Dili *Azerbaijan* 39°3N 49°13E **47** B6
Kura = Kür → *Azerbaijan* 39°29N 49°15E **19** G8
Kuranda *Australia* 16°48S 145°35E **62** B4
Kuranga *India* 22°4N 69°10E **42** H3
Kurashiki *Japan* 34°40N 133°50E **29** G6
Kurayoshi *Japan* 35°26N 133°50E **29** G6
Kurayn *Si. Arabia* 27°39N 49°50E **47** E6
Kürchatov *Kazakhstan* 50°45N 78°32E **26** D8
Kurduvadi *India* 18°8N 75°29E **44** E2
Kürdzhali *Bulgaria* 41°38N 25°21E **23** D11
Kure *Japan* 34°14N 132°32E **29** G6
Kure I. *U.S.A.* 28°25N 178°25W **75** K4
Kuressaare *Estonia* 58°15N 22°30E **9** G20
Kurgan *Russia* 55°26N 65°18E **26** D7
Kuri *India* 26°37N 70°43E **42** F4
Kuria Maria Is. = Ḥallāniyat,
  Jazā'ir al *Oman* 17°30N 55°58E **49** D6
Kurichchi *India* 11°36N 77°35E **45** K4
Kuridala *Australia* 21°16S 140°29E **62** C3
Kurigram *Bangla.* 25°49N 89°39E **41** G16
Kurikka *Finland* 62°36N 22°24E **8** E20
Kuril Basin *Pac. Oc.* 47°0N 150°0E **4** E15
Kuril Is. = Kurilskiye Ostrova
  Russia 45°0N 150°0E **27** E16
Kuril-Kamchatka Trench
  Pac. Oc. 44°0N 153°0E **64** C7
Kurilsk *Russia* 45°14N 147°53E **27** E15
Kurilskiye Ostrova
  Russia 45°0N 150°0E **27** E16
Kurino *Japan* 31°57N 130°43E **29** J5
Kurinskaya Kosa = Kür Dili
  Azerbaijan 39°3N 49°13E **47** B6
Kurkheda *India* 20°37N 80°12E **44** D5
Kurlkuta ☉ *Australia* 24°0S 127°5E **60** D4
Kurnool *India* 15°45N 78°0E **45** G4
Kuro-Shima *Kagoshima,
  Japan* 30°50N 129°57E **29** J4
Kuro-Shima *Okinawa,
  Japan* 24°14N 124°1E **29** M2
Kurow *N.Z.* 44°44S 170°29E **59** F3
Kurram → *Pakistan* 32°36N 71°20E **42** C4
Kurri Kurri *Australia* 32°50S 151°28E **63** E5
Kurrimine *Australia* 17°47S 146°6E **62** B4
Kurse Korhi *India* 20°14N 80°46E **44** D5
Kurseong = Karsiyang
  India 26°56N 88°18E **43** F13
Kurshskiy Zaliv *Russia* 55°9N 21°6E **9** J19
Kursk *Russia* 51°42N 36°11E **18** D6
Kuruçay *Turkey* 39°39N 38°29E **46** B3
Kurukshetra = Thanesar
  India 30°1N 76°52E **42** D7
Kuruktag *China* 41°0N 89°0E **30** C6
Kuruman *S. Africa* 27°28S 23°28E **56** C3
Kuruman → *S. Africa* 26°56S 20°39E **56** C3
Kurume *Japan* 33°15N 130°30E **29** H5
Kurunegala *Sri Lanka* 7°30N 80°23E **45** L5
Kurya *Russia* 61°42N 57°9E **18** B10
Kus Gölü *Turkey* 40°10N 27°55E **23** D12
Kuşadası *Turkey* 37°52N 27°15E **23** F12
Kusamba *Indonesia* 8°34S 115°27E **37** K18
Kusatsu *Japan* 36°37N 138°36E **29** F9
Kusawa L. *Canada* 60°20N 136°13W **70** A1
Kushalgarh *India* 23°10N 74°27E **42** H6
Kushalnagar *India* 12°14N 75°57E **45** H2
Kushikino *Japan* 31°44N 130°16E **29** J5
Kushima *Japan* 31°29N 131°14E **29** J5
Kushimoto *Japan* 33°28N 135°47E **29** H7
Kushiro *Japan* 43°0N 144°25E **28** C12
Kushiro-Gawa →
  Japan 42°59N 144°23E **28** C12
Kushiro Shitsugen △
  Japan 43°9N 144°26E **28** C12
Kūshk *Iran* 28°46N 56°51E **47** D8
Kushka = Serhetabat
  Turkmenistan 35°20N 62°18E **47** C9
Kushol *India* 33°40N 76°36E **43** C7
Kushtia *Bangla.* 23°55N 89°5E **41** H16
Kushva *Russia* 58°18N 59°45E **18** C10
Kuskokwim → *U.S.A.* 60°5N 162°25W **74** C7
Kuskokwim B. *U.S.A.* 59°45N 162°25W **74** C7
Kuskokwim Mts. *U.S.A.* 62°30N 156°0W **74** C8
Kusmi *India* 23°17N 83°55E **43** H10
Kusŏng *N. Korea* 39°59N 125°15E **33** E13
Kussharo-Ko *Japan* 43°38N 144°21E **28** C12
Kustanay = Qostanay
  Kazakhstan 53°10N 63°35E **26** D7
Kut, Ko *Thailand* 11°40N 102°35E **39** G4
Kuta *Indonesia* 8°43S 115°11E **37** K18
Kütahya *Turkey* 39°30N 30°2E **19** G5
Kutaisi *Georgia* 42°19N 42°40E **19** F7
Kutaraja = Banda Aceh
  Indonesia 5°35N 95°20E **36** C1
Kutch, Gulf of = Kachchh, Gulf of
  India 22°50N 69°15E **42** H3
Kutch, Rann of = Kachchh, Rann
  of *India* 24°0N 70°0E **42** H4
Kutiyana *India* 21°36N 70°2E **42** J4
Kutno *Poland* 52°15N 19°23E **17** B10
Kutru *India* 19°5N 80°46E **44** E5
Kutse *Botswana* 21°7S 22°16E **56** B3
Kuttabul *Australia* 21°1S 148°54E **62** b
Kutu *Dem. Rep. of the Congo* 2°40S 18°11E **54** E3
Kutum *Sudan* 14°10N 24°40E **53** F10
Kuujjuaq *Canada* 58°6N 68°15W **69** F18
Kuujjuarapik *Canada* 55°20N 77°35W **72** A4
Kuusamo *Finland* 65°57N 29°8E **8** D23
Kuusankoski *Finland* 60°55N 26°38E **8** F22
Kuwait = Al Kuwayt
  Kuwait 29°30N 48°0E **46** D5
Kuwait ■ *Asia* 29°30N 47°30E **46** D5
Kuwana *Japan* 35°5N 136°43E **29** G8
Kuwana → *India* 26°25N 83°15E **43** F10

Kuybyshev = Samara
  Russia 53°8N 50°6E **18** D9
Kuybyshev *Russia* 55°27N 78°19E **26** D8
Kuybyshevskoye Vdkhr.
  Russia 55°2N 49°30E **18** C8
Kuye He → *China* 38°23N 110°46E **32** E6
Kūyeh *Iran* 38°45N 47°57E **46** B5
Kuyto, Ozero *Russia* 65°6N 31°20E **8** D24
Kuytun *China* 44°25N 85°0E **30** C6
Kuyumba *Russia* 60°58N 96°59E **27** C10
Kuzey Anadolu Dağları
  Turkey 41°0N 36°45E **19** F6
Kuzhitturai *India* 8°18N 77°11E **45** K3
Kuznetsk *Russia* 53°12N 46°40E **18** D8
Kuzomen *Russia* 66°22N 36°50E **18** A6
Kvænangen *Norway* 70°5N 21°15E **8** A19
Kvaløya *Norway* 69°40N 18°30E **8** B18
Kvarner *Croatia* 44°50N 14°10E **16** F8
Kvarnerič *Croatia* 44°43N 14°37E **16** F8
Kwabhaca *S. Africa* 30°51S 29°0E **57** C4
Kwai = Khwae Noi →
  Thailand 14°1N 99°32E **38** E2
Kwajalein *Marshall Is.* 9°5N 167°20E **64** G8
Kwakhanai *Botswana* 21°39S 21°16E **56** B3
Kwakoegron *Suriname* 5°12N 55°25W **93** B7
KwaMashu *S. Africa* 29°45S 30°58E **57** C5
Kwando → *Africa* 18°27S 23°32E **56** A3
Kwangdaeri *N. Korea* 40°34N 127°33E **33** D14
Kwango →
  Dem. Rep. of the Congo 3°14S 17°22E **54** E3
Kwangsi-Chuang = Guangxi
  Zhuangzu Zizhiqu □
  China 24°0N 109°0E **34** F7
Kwangtung = Guangdong □
  China 23°0N 113°0E **35** F9
Kwataboahegan →
  Canada 51°9N 80°50W **72** B3
Kwatisore *Indonesia* 3°18S 134°50E **37** E8
KwaZulu Natal □ *S. Africa* 29°0S 30°0E **57** C5
Kweichow = Guizhou □
  China 27°0N 107°0E **34** D6
Kwekwe *Zimbabwe* 18°58S 29°48E **55** H5
Kweneng □ *Botswana* 24°0S 25°0E **56** B3
Kwidzyn *Poland* 53°44N 18°55E **17** B10
Kwilu →
  Dem. Rep. of the Congo 3°22S 17°22E **54** E3
Kwinana *Australia* 32°15S 115°47E **61** F2
Kwoka *Indonesia* 0°31S 132°27E **37** E8
Kyabra Cr. → *Australia* 25°36S 142°55E **63** D3
Kyabram *Australia* 36°19S 145°4E **63** F4
Kyaikto *Burma* 17°20N 97°3E **38** D1
Kyaing Tong = Keng Tung
  Burma 21°18N 99°39E **38** B2
Kyakhta *Russia* 50°30N 106°25E **27** D11
Kyancutta *Australia* 33°8S 135°33E **63** E2
Kyaukpadaung *Burma* 20°52N 95°8E **41** J19
Kyaukpyu *Burma* 19°28N 93°30E **41** K18
Kyaukse *Burma* 21°36N 96°10E **41** J20
Kyburz *U.S.A.* 38°47N 120°18W **78** G6
Kyelang *India* 32°35N 77°2E **42** C7
Kyle *Canada* 50°50N 108°2W **71** C7
Kyle *U.S.A.* 29°59N 97°53W **84** F6
Kyle of Lochalsh *U.K.* 57°17N 5°44W **11** D3
Kymijoki → *Finland* 60°30N 26°55E **8** F22
Kymmene älv = Kymijoki →
  Finland 60°30N 26°55E **8** F22
Kyneton *Australia* 37°10S 144°29E **63** F3
Kynuna *Australia* 21°37S 141°55E **62** C3
Kyō-ga-Saki *Japan* 35°45N 135°15E **29** G7
Kyoga, L. *Uganda* 1°35N 33°0E **54** D6
Kyogle *Australia* 28°40S 153°0E **63** D5
Kyŏngju = Gyeongju
  S. Korea 35°51N 129°14E **33** G15
Kyŏngsŏng *N. Korea* 41°35N 129°36E **33** D15
Kyonpyaw *Burma* 17°12N 95°10E **41** L19
Kyōto *Japan* 35°0N 135°45E **29** G7
Kyōto □ *Japan* 35°15N 135°45E **29** G7
Kypros = Cyprus ■ *Asia* 35°0N 33°0E **46** C2
Kyrenia *Cyprus* 35°20N 33°20E **46** C2
Kyrgyzstan ■ *Asia* 42°0N 75°0E **26** E8
Kyro älv = Kyrönjoki →
  Finland 63°14N 21°45E **8** E19
Kyrönjoki → *Finland* 63°14N 21°45E **8** E19
Kystatyam *Russia* 67°20N 123°10E **27** C13
Kythira *Greece* 36°8N 23°0E **23** F10
Kyunhla *Burma* 23°25N 95°15E **41** H19
Kyuquot Sound *Canada* 50°2N 127°22W **70** D3
Kyūshū *Japan* 33°0N 131°0E **29** H5
Kyūshū □ *Japan* 33°0N 131°0E **29** H5
Kyushu-Palau Ridge
  Pac. Oc. 20°0N 136°0E **64** E5
Kyūshū-Sanchi *Japan* 32°35N 131°17E **29** H5
Kyustendil *Bulgaria* 42°16N 22°41E **23** C10
Kyusyur *Russia* 70°19N 127°30E **27** B13
Kyyiv *Ukraine* 50°30N 30°28E **17** C16
Kyyivske Vdskh. *Ukraine* 51°0N 30°25E **17** C16
Kyzyl *Russia* 51°50N 94°30E **30** A7
Kyzyl Kum *Uzbekistan* 42°30N 65°0E **26** E7
Kyzyl Kyya *Kyrgyzstan* 40°16N 72°8E **26** E8
Kyzyl Orda = Qyzylorda
  Kazakhstan 44°48N 65°28E **26** E7

L

La Alcarria *Spain* 40°31N 2°45W **21** B4
La Amistad △ *Cent. Amer.* 9°28N 83°18W **88** E3
La Asunción *Venezuela* 11°2N 63°51W **92** A6
La Baie *Canada* 48°19N 70°53W **73** C5
La Banda *Argentina* 27°45S 64°10W **94** B3
La Barca *Mexico* 20°17N 102°34W **86** C4
La Barge *U.S.A.* 42°16N 110°12W **76** E8
La Barra *Nic.* 12°54N 83°33W **88** D3
La Belle *U.S.A.* 26°46N 81°26W **85** H14
La Biche → *Canada* 59°57N 123°50W **70** B4
La Biche, L. *Canada* 54°50N 112°3W **70** C6
La Calera *Chile* 32°50S 71°10W **94** C1
La Campana △ *Chile* 32°58S 71°14W **94** C1
La Carlota *Argentina* 33°30S 63°20W **94** C3

La Ceiba *Honduras* 15°40N 86°50W **88** C2
La Chaux-de-Fonds *Switz.* 47°7N 6°50E **20** C7
La Chorrera *Panama* 8°53N 79°47W **88** E4
La Cocha *Argentina* 27°50S 65°40W **94** B2
La Concepción *Panama* 8°31N 82°37W **88** E3
La Concordia *Mexico* 16°5N 92°38W **87** D6
La Coruña = A Coruña
　Spain 43°20N 8°25W **21** A1
La Crescent *U.S.A.* 43°50N 91°18W **80** D8
La Crete *Canada* 58°11N 116°24W **70** B5
La Crosse *Kans., U.S.A.* 38°32N 99°18W **80** F4
La Crosse *Wis., U.S.A.* 43°48N 91°15W **80** D8
La Cruz *Costa Rica* 11°4N 85°39W **88** D2
La Cruz *Mexico* 23°55N 106°54W **86** C3
La Désirade *Guadeloupe* 16°18N 61°3W **88** b
La Digue *Seychelles* 4°20S 55°51E **55** b
La Esperanza *Cuba* 22°46N 83°44W **88** B3
La Esperanza *Honduras* 14°15N 88°10W **88** D2
La Estrada = A Estrada
　Spain 42°43N 8°27W **21** A1
La Fayette *U.S.A.* 34°42N 85°17W **85** D12
La Fé *Cuba* 22°2N 84°15W **88** B3
La Follette *U.S.A.* 36°23N 84°7W **85** C12
La Gi *Vietnam* 10°40N 107°45E **39** G6
La Grande *U.S.A.* 45°20N 118°5W **76** D4
La Grande ↦ *Canada* 53°50N 79°0W **72** B5
La Grande 3, Rés. *Canada* 53°40N 75°10W **72** B4
La Grande 4, Rés. *Canada* 54°0N 73°15W **72** B5
La Grange *Calif., U.S.A.* 37°42N 120°27W **78** H6
La Grange *Ga., U.S.A.* 33°2N 85°2W **85** E12
La Grange *Ky., U.S.A.* 38°24N 85°22W **81** F11
La Grange *Tex., U.S.A.* 29°54N 96°52W **84** G6
La Guaira *Venezuela* 10°36N 66°56W **92** A5
La Habana *Cuba* 23°8N 82°22W **88** B3
La Independencia *Mexico* 16°15N 92°1W **87** D6
La Isabela *Dom. Rep.* 19°58N 71°2W **89** C5
La Junta *U.S.A.* 37°59N 103°33W **76** H12
La Libertad = Puerto Libertad
　Mexico 29°55N 112°43W **86** B2
La Libertad *Guatemala* 16°47N 90°7W **88** C1
La Ligua *Chile* 32°30S 71°16W **94** C1
La Línea de la Concepción
　Spain 36°15N 5°23W **21** D3
La Loche *Canada* 56°29N 109°26W **71** B7
La Louvière *Belgium* 50°27N 4°10E **15** D4
La Lune *Trin. & Tob.* 10°3N 61°22W **93** K15
La Malbaie *Canada* 47°40N 70°10W **73** C5
La Malinche △ *Mexico* 19°15N 98°3W **87** D5
La Mancha *Spain* 39°10N 2°54W **21** C4
La Martre, L. *Canada* 63°15N 117°55W **70** A5
La Mercy = Durban ✈ (DIA)
　S. Africa 29°37S 31°7E **57** C5
La Mesa *Mexico* 32°30N 116°57W **79** N10
La Mesa *U.S.A.* 32°46N 117°1W **79** N9
La Mesilla *U.S.A.* 32°16N 106°48W **77** K10
La Moure *U.S.A.* 46°21N 98°18W **80** B4
La Negra *Chile* 23°46S 70°18W **94** A1
La Oroya *Peru* 11°32S 75°54W **92** F3
La Palma *Canary Is.* 28°40N 17°50W **52** C2
La Palma *Panama* 8°15N 78°0W **88** E4
La Palma del Condado
　Spain 37°21N 6°38W **21** D2
La Paloma *Chile* 30°35S 71°0W **94** C1
La Pampa □ *Argentina* 36°50S 66°0W **94** D2
La Paragua *Venezuela* 6°50N 63°20W **92** B6
La Paz *Entre Ríos,*
　Argentina 30°50S 59°45W **94** C4
La Paz *San Luis, Argentina* 33°30S 67°20W **94** C2
La Paz *Bolivia* 16°20S 68°10W **92** G5
La Paz *Honduras* 14°20N 87°47W **88** D2
La Paz *Mexico* 24°10N 110°18W **86** C2
La Paz Centro *Nic.* 12°20N 86°41W **88** D2
La Pedrera *Colombia* 1°18S 69°43W **92** D5
La Pérade *Canada* 46°35N 72°12W **73** C5
La Perla *Mexico* 28°18N 104°32W **86** B4
La Perouse Str. *Asia* 45°40N 142°0E **28** B11
La Pesca *Mexico* 23°46N 97°47W **87** C5
La Piedad *Mexico* 20°21N 102°0W **86** C4
La Pine *U.S.A.* 43°40N 121°30W **76** E3
La Plata *Argentina* 35°0S 57°55W **94** C4
La Pocatière *Canada* 47°22N 70°2W **73** C5
La Porte *U.S.A.* 29°40N 95°1W **84** G7
La Purísima *Mexico* 26°10N 112°4W **86** B2
La Push *U.S.A.* 47°55N 124°38W **78** C2
La Quiaca *Argentina* 22°5S 65°35W **94** A2
La Rioja *Argentina* 29°20S 67°0W **94** B2
La Rioja □ *Argentina* 29°30S 67°0W **94** B2
La Rioja □ *Spain* 42°20N 2°20W **21** A4
La Robla *Spain* 42°50N 5°41W **21** A3
La Roche-en-Ardenne
　Belgium 50°11N 5°35E **15** D5
La Roche-sur-Yon *France* 46°40N 1°25W **20** C3
La Rochelle *France* 46°10N 1°9W **20** C3
La Roda *Spain* 39°13N 2°15W **21** C4
La Romaine *Canada* 50°13N 60°40W **73** B7
La Romana *Dom. Rep.* 18°27N 68°57W **89** C6
La Ronge *Canada* 55°5N 105°20W **71** B7
La Rumorosa *Mexico* 32°34N 116°6W **79** N10
La Salle *U.S.A.* 41°20N 89°6W **80** E9
La Sarre *Canada* 48°45N 79°15W **72** C4
La Scie *Canada* 49°57N 55°36W **73** C8
La Selva Beach *U.S.A.* 36°56N 121°51W **78** J5
La Serena *Chile* 29°55S 71°10W **94** B1
La Seu d'Urgell *Spain* 42°22N 1°23E **21** A6
La Seyne-sur-Mer *France* 43°7N 5°52E **20** E6
La Soufrière *St. Vincent* 13°20N 61°11W **89** D7
La Spézia *Italy* 44°7N 9°50E **20** D8
La Tagua *Colombia* 0°3N 74°40W **92** C4
La Tortuga, I. *Venezuela* 11°0N 65°22W **89** D6
La Trinité *Martinique* 14°45N 60°58W **88** c
La Tuque *Canada* 47°30N 72°50W **72** C5
La Unión *Chile* 40°10S 73°0W **96** E2
La Unión *El Salv.* 13°20N 87°50W **88** D2
La Unión *Mexico* 17°58N 101°49W **86** D4
La Urbana *Venezuela* 7°8N 66°56W **92** B5
La Vache Pt.
　Trin. & Tob. 10°47N 61°28W **93** K15
La Vall d'Uixó *Spain* 39°49N 0°15W **21** C5
La Vega *Dom. Rep.* 19°20N 70°30W **89** C5

La Vela de Coro
　Venezuela 11°27N 69°34W **92** A5
La Venta *Mexico* 18°5N 94°3W **87** D6
La Vergne *U.S.A.* 36°1N 86°35W **85** C11
La Villa Joiosa = Villajoyosa
　Spain 38°30N 0°12W **21** C5
Laascaanood = Las Anod
　Somalia 8°26N 47°19E **49** F4
Labasa *Fiji* 16°30S 179°27E **59** a
Labdah = Leptis Magna
　Libya 32°40N 14°12E **53** B8
Labe = Elbe ↦ *Europe* 53°50N 9°0E **16** B5
Labé *Guinea* 11°24N 12°16W **52** F3
Laberge, L. *Canada* 61°11N 135°12W **70** A1
Labinsk *Russia* 44°40N 40°48E **19** F7
Labis *Malaysia* 2°22N 103°2E **39** L4
Laborie *St. Lucia* 13°45N 61°2W **89** f
Laboulaye *Argentina* 34°10S 63°30W **94** C3
Labrador *Canada* 53°20N 61°0W **73** B7
Labrador City *Canada* 52°57N 66°55W **73** B6
Labrador Sea *Atl. Oc.* 57°0N 54°0W **69** F21
Lábrea *Brazil* 7°15S 64°51W **92** E6
Labuan □ *Malaysia* 5°20N 115°12E **36** C4
Labuha *Indonesia* 0°30S 127°30E **37** E7
Labuhan *Indonesia* 6°22S 105°50E **37** G11
Labuhanbajo *Indonesia* 8°28S 119°54E **37** F6
Labuhanbilik *Indonesia* 2°31N 100°10E **39** L3
Labuk, Telok *Malaysia* 6°10N 117°50E **36** C5
Labyrinth, L. *Australia* 30°40S 135°11E **63** E2
Labytnangi *Russia* 66°39N 66°21E **18** A12
Lac-Bouchette *Canada* 48°16N 72°11W **73** C5
Lac-Édouard *Canada* 47°40N 72°16W **73** C5
Lac la Biche *Canada* 54°45N 111°58W **70** C6
Lac la Martre = Wha Ti
　Canada 63°8N 117°16W **68** E8
Lac La Ronge △ *Canada* 55°9N 104°41W **71** B7
Lac-Mégantic *Canada* 45°35N 70°53W **73** C5
Lac Thien *Vietnam* 12°25N 108°11E **38** F7
Lacanau *France* 44°58N 1°5W **20** D3
Lacantún ↦ *Mexico* 16°36N 90°39W **87** D6
Laccadive Is. = Lakshadweep Is.
　India 10°0N 72°30E **45** J1
Lacepede B. *Australia* 36°40S 139°40E **63** F2
Lacepede Is. *Australia* 16°55S 122°0E **60** C3
Lacey *U.S.A.* 47°7N 122°49W **78** C4
Lachhmangarh *India* 27°50N 75°4E **42** F6
Lachi *Pakistan* 33°25N 71°20E **42** C4
Lachlan ↦ *Australia* 34°22S 143°55E **63** E3
Lachute *Canada* 45°39N 74°21W **72** C5
Lackagh Hills *Ireland* 54°16N 8°10W **10** B3
Lackawanna *U.S.A.* 42°50N 78°50W **82** D6
Lackawaxen *U.S.A.* 41°29N 74°59W **83** E10
Lacolle *Canada* 45°5N 73°22W **83** A11
Lacombe *Canada* 52°30N 113°44W **70** C6
Lacona *U.S.A.* 43°39N 76°10W **83** C8
Laconia *U.S.A.* 43°32N 71°28W **83** C13
Ladakh Ra. *India* 34°0N 78°0E **43** C8
Ladismith *S. Africa* 33°28S 21°15E **56** D3
Ladnun *India* 28°55N 61°15E **47** D9
Ladoga, L. = Ladozhskoye Ozero
　Russia 61°15N 30°30E **8** F24
Ladozhskoye Ozero
　Russia 61°15N 30°30E **8** F24
Lady Elliott I. *Australia* 24°7S 152°42E **62** C5
Lady Frere *S. Africa* 31°42S 27°14E **56** D4
Lady Grey *S. Africa* 30°43S 27°13E **56** D4
Ladysmith *Canada* 49°0N 123°49W **78** B3
Ladysmith *S. Africa* 28°32S 29°46E **57** C4
Ladysmith *U.S.A.* 45°28N 91°12W **80** C8
Lae *Papua N. G.* 6°40S 147°2E **58** B7
Laem Ngop *Thailand* 12°10N 102°26E **39** F4
Laem Son △ *Thailand* 9°29N 98°24E **39** H2
Læsø *Denmark* 57°15N 11°5E **9** H14
Lafayette *Ind., U.S.A.* 40°25N 86°54W **80** E10
Lafayette *La., U.S.A.* 30°14N 92°1W **84** F8
Lafayette *Tenn., U.S.A.* 36°31N 86°2W **85** C11
Laferte ↦ *Canada* 61°53N 117°44W **70** A5
Lafia *Nigeria* 8°30N 8°34E **52** G7
Lafleche *Canada* 49°45N 106°40W **71** D7
Laful *India* 7°10N 93°52E **45** L11
Lagan ↦ *U.K.* 54°36N 5°55W **10** B6
Lagarfljót ↦ *Iceland* 65°40N 14°18W **8** D6
Lagdo, L. de *Cameroon* 8°40N 14°0E **53** G8
Lågen ↦ *Oppland, Norway* 61°8N 10°25E **8** F14
Lågen ↦ *Vestfold, Norway* 59°3N 10°3E **9** G14
Lages *Brazil* 27°48S 50°20W **95** B5
Laghouat *Algeria* 33°50N 2°59E **52** B6
Lagoa do Peixe △ *Brazil* 31°12S 50°50W **95** C5
Lagoa Vermelha *Brazil* 28°13S 51°32W **95** B5
Lagonoy G. *Phil.* 13°35N 123°50E **37** B6
Lagos *Nigeria* 6°25N 3°27E **52** G6
Lagos *Portugal* 37°5N 8°41W **21** D1
Lagos de Moreno
　Mexico 21°21N 101°55W **86** C4
Lagrange = Bidyadanga
　Australia 18°45S 121°43E **60** C3
Lagrange B. *Australia* 18°38S 121°42E **60** C3
Laguna *Brazil* 28°30S 48°50W **95** B6
Laguna *U.S.A.* 35°2N 107°25W **77** J10
Laguna, Sa. de la
　Mexico 23°35N 109°55W **86** C3
Laguna Beach *U.S.A.* 33°33N 117°47W **79** M9
Laguna de la Restinga △
　Venezuela 10°58N 64°0W **89** D6
Laguna de la Tigre △
　Guatemala 15°55N 90°40W **88** C1
Laguna de Lachuá △
　Guatemala 15°55N 90°40W **88** C1
Laguna del Laja △ *Chile* 37°27S 71°20W **94** D1
Laguna del Tigre △
　Guatemala 17°32N 90°56W **88** C1
Laguna Limpia *Argentina* 26°32S 59°45W **94** B4
Lagunas *Chile* 21°0S 69°45W **94** A2
Lagunas *Peru* 5°10S 75°35W **92** E3
Lagunas de Chacahua △
　Mexico 16°0N 97°43W **87** D5
Lagunas de Montebello △
　Mexico 16°4N 91°42W **87** D6
Lahad Datu *Malaysia* 5°0N 118°20E **37** D5
Lahad Datu, Telok
　Malaysia 4°50N 118°20E **37** D5

Lahan Sai *Thailand* 14°25N 102°52E **38** E4
Lahanam *Laos* 16°16N 105°16E **38** D5
Lahar *India* 26°12N 78°57E **43** F8
Laharpur *India* 27°43N 80°56E **43** F9
Lahat *Indonesia* 3°45S 103°30E **36** E2
Lahewa *Indonesia* 1°22N 97°12E **36** D1
Lahijan *Iran* 37°10N 50°6E **47** B6
Lahn ↦ *Germany* 50°19N 7°37E **16** C4
Laholm *Sweden* 56°30N 13°2E **9** H15
Lahore *Pakistan* 31°32N 74°22E **42** D6
Lahri *Pakistan* 29°11N 68°13E **42** E3
Lahrūd *Iran* 38°30N 47°52E **46** B5
Lahti *Finland* 60°58N 25°40E **8** F21
Lahtis = Lahti *Finland* 60°58N 25°40E **8** F21
Lahugala Kitulana △
　Sri Lanka 6°50N 81°40E **45** L5
Lahad *Chad* 9°25N 16°18E **53** G9
Lai'an *China* 32°28N 118°30E **35** A12
Laibin *China* 23°42N 109°14E **34** F7
Laifeng *China* 29°27N 109°20E **34** C7
Laila = Layla *Si. Arabia* 22°10N 46°40E **49** C4
Laingsburg *S. Africa* 33°9S 20°52E **56** D3
Lainioälven ↦ *Sweden* 67°35N 22°40E **8** C20
Lairg *U.K.* 58°2N 4°24W **11** C4
Laiwu *China* 36°15N 117°40E **33** F9
Laiyang *China* 36°59N 120°45E **33** F11
Laiyuan *China* 39°20N 114°40E **32** E8
Laizhou *China* 37°8N 119°57E **33** F10
Laizhou Wan *China* 37°30N 119°30E **33** F10
Lajamanu *Australia* 18°23S 130°38E **60** C5
Lak Sao *Laos* 18°11N 104°59E **38** C5
Lakaband *Pakistan* 31°2N 69°15E **42** D3
Lake *U.S.A.* 44°33N 110°24W **76** D8
Lake Alpine *U.S.A.* 38°29N 120°0W **78** G7
Lake Andes *U.S.A.* 43°9N 98°32W **80** D4
Lake Arthur *U.S.A.* 30°5N 92°41W **84** F8
Lake Bindegolly △
　Australia 28°0S 144°12E **63** D3
Lake Cargelligo *Australia* 33°15S 146°22E **63** E4
Lake Charles *U.S.A.* 30°14N 93°13W **84** F8
Lake City *Colo., U.S.A.* 38°2N 107°19W **76** G10
Lake City *Fla., U.S.A.* 30°11N 82°38W **85** L4
Lake City *Mich., U.S.A.* 44°20N 85°13W **81** C11
Lake City *Minn., U.S.A.* 44°27N 92°16W **80** C7
Lake City *Pa., U.S.A.* 42°1N 80°21W **82** D4
Lake City *S.C., U.S.A.* 33°52N 79°45W **85** E15
Lake Cowichan *Canada* 48°49N 124°3W **78** D4
Lake District *U.K.* 54°30N 3°21W **12** C4
Lake Elsinore *U.S.A.* 33°38N 117°20W **79** M9
Lake Eyre △ *Australia* 28°40S 137°31E **63** D2
Lake Gairdner △
　Australia 31°41S 135°51E **63** E2
Lake George *U.S.A.* 43°26N 73°43W **83** C11
Lake Grace *Australia* 33°7S 118°28E **61** F2
Lake Gregory ◎
　Australia 20°12S 127°27E **60** D4
Lake Harbour = Kimmirut
　Canada 62°50N 69°50W **69** E18
Lake Havasu City
　U.S.A. 34°27N 114°22W **79** L12
Lake Hughes *U.S.A.* 34°41N 118°26W **79** L8
Lake Isabella *U.S.A.* 35°38N 118°28W **79** K8
Lake Jackson *U.S.A.* 29°3N 95°27W **84** G7
Lake King *Australia* 33°5S 119°45E **61** F2
Lake Lenore *Canada* 52°24N 104°59W **71** C8
Lake Louise *Canada* 51°30N 116°10W **70** C5
Lake Mackay ◎
　Australia 22°30S 129°0E **60** D4
Lake Mead △ *U.S.A.* 36°30N 114°22W **79** K12
Lake Meredith △
　U.S.A. 35°50N 101°50W **84** D4
Lake Mills *U.S.A.* 43°25N 93°32W **80** D7
Lake Placid *U.S.A.* 44°17N 73°59W **83** B11
Lake Pleasant *U.S.A.* 43°28N 74°25W **83** C10
Lake Providence *U.S.A.* 32°48N 91°10W **84** E9
Lake Roosevelt △ *U.S.A.* 48°5N 118°14W **76** B4
Lake St. Peter *Canada* 45°18N 78°2W **82** A6
Lake Stevens *U.S.A.* 48°1N 122°4W **78** B4
Lake Superior △ *Canada* 47°45N 84°45W **72** C3
Lake Torrens △
　Australia 30°55S 137°40E **63** E2
Lake Village *U.S.A.* 33°20N 91°17W **84** E9
Lake Wales *U.S.A.* 27°54N 81°35W **85** H14
Lake Worth *U.S.A.* 26°37N 80°3W **85** H14
Lakeba *Fiji* 18°13S 178°47W **59** a
Lakeba Passage *Fiji* 18°0S 178°45W **59** a
Lakefield *Canada* 44°25N 78°16W **82** B6
Lakefield △ *Australia* 15°24S 144°26E **62** B3
Lakehurst *U.S.A.* 40°1N 74°19W **83** F10
Lakeland *Australia* 15°49S 144°57E **62** B3
Lakeland *U.S.A.* 28°3N 81°57W **85** G14
Lakemba = Lakeba *Fiji* 18°13S 178°47W **59** a
Lakeport *Calif., U.S.A.* 39°3N 122°55W **78** F4
Lakeport *Mich., U.S.A.* 43°7N 82°30W **82** C2
Lakes Entrance *Australia* 37°50S 148°0E **63** F4
Lakeside *Calif., U.S.A.* 32°52N 116°55W **79** N10
Lakeside *Nebr., U.S.A.* 42°3N 102°26W **80** D2
Lakeview *U.S.A.* 42°11N 120°21W **76** E3
Lakeville *U.S.A.* 44°39N 93°14W **80** C7
Lakewood *Colo., U.S.A.* 39°42N 105°4W **76** G11
Lakewood *N.J., U.S.A.* 40°6N 74°13W **83** F10
Lakewood *N.Y., U.S.A.* 42°6N 79°19W **82** D5
Lakewood *Ohio, U.S.A.* 41°28N 81°47W **82** E3
Lakewood *Wash.,*
　U.S.A. 47°11N 122°32W **78** C4
Lakha *India* 26°9N 70°54E **42** F4
Lakhimpur *India* 27°57N 80°46E **43** F9
Lakhisarai *India* 25°11N 86°5E **43** G12
Lakhnadon *India* 22°36N 79°36E **43** H8
Lakhnau = Lucknow
　India 26°50N 81°0E **43** F9
Lakhonpheng *Laos* 15°54N 105°34E **38** E5
Lakhpat *India* 23°48N 68°47E **42** H3
Lakin *U.S.A.* 37°57N 101°15W **80** G3
Lakitusaki ↦ *Canada* 54°21N 82°25W **72** B3
Lakki *Pakistan* 32°36N 70°55E **42** C4
Lakonikós Kólpos
　Greece 36°40N 22°40E **23** F10

Lakor *Indonesia* 8°15S 128°17E **37** F7
Lakota *Ivory C.* 5°50N 5°30W **52** G4
Lakota *U.S.A.* 48°2N 98°21W **80** A4
Laksar *India* 29°46N 78°3E **42** E8
Laksefjorden *Norway* 70°45N 26°50E **8** A22
Lakselv *Norway* 70°2N 25°0E **8** A21
Lakshadweep □ *India* 10°0N 72°30E **45** J1
Lakshadweep Is. *India* 10°0N 72°30E **45** J1
Lakshmanpur *India* 22°58N 83°3E **43** H10
Lakshmeshwar *India* 15°9N 75°28E **45** G2
Lakshmikantapur *India* 22°5N 88°20E **43** H13
Lala Musa *Pakistan* 32°40N 73°57E **42** C5
Lalaganj *India* 25°52N 85°13E **43** G11
Lalago *India* 24°25N 88°15E **43** G13
Lāli *Iran* 32°21N 49°6E **47** C6
Lalibela *Ethiopia* 12°3N 39°0E **49** E2
Lalin *China* 45°12N 127°0E **33** B14
Lalín *Spain* 42°40N 8°5W **21** A1
Lalin He ↦ *China* 45°32N 125°40E **33** B13
Lalitpur *India* 24°42N 78°28E **43** G8
Lalitpur *Nepal* 27°40N 85°20E **43** F11
Lalkua *India* 29°5N 79°31E **43** E8
Lalsot *India* 26°34N 76°20E **42** F7
Lam Nam Nan △
　Thailand 17°55N 100°28E **38** D3
Lam Pao Res. *Thailand* 16°50N 103°15E **38** D4
Lama Kara *Togo* 9°30N 1°15E **52** G6
Lamae *Thailand* 9°51N 99°5E **39** H2
Lamaing *Burma* 15°25N 97°53E **38** E1
Lamar *Colo., U.S.A.* 38°5N 102°37W **76** G12
Lamar *Mo., U.S.A.* 37°30N 94°16W **80** G6
Lamas *Peru* 6°28S 76°31W **92** E3
Lamayuru *India* 34°25N 76°56E **43** B7
Lambaréné *Gabon* 0°41S 10°12E **54** E2
Lambasa = Labasa *Fiji* 16°30S 179°27E **59** a
Lambay I. *Ireland* 53°29N 6°1W **10** C5
Lambert's Bay *S. Africa* 32°5S 18°17E **56** D2
Lambeth *Canada* 42°54N 81°18W **82** D3
Lame Deer *U.S.A.* 45°37N 106°40W **76** D10
Lamego *Portugal* 41°5N 7°52W **21** B2
Lamèque *Canada* 47°45N 64°38W **73** C7
Lameroo *Australia* 35°19S 140°33E **63** F3
Lamesa *U.S.A.* 32°44N 101°58W **84** E4
Lamia *Greece* 38°55N 22°26E **23** E10
Lamington △ *Australia* 28°13S 153°12E **63** D5
Lammermuir Hills *U.K.* 55°50N 2°40W **11** F6
Lamoille ↦ *U.S.A.* 44°38N 73°13W **83** B11
Lamon B. *Phil.* 14°30N 122°20E **37** B6
Lamont *Canada* 53°46N 112°50W **70** C6
Lamont *Calif., U.S.A.* 35°15N 118°55W **79** K8
Lamont *Wyo., U.S.A.* 42°13N 107°29W **76** E10
Lampa *Peru* 15°22S 70°22W **92** G4
Lampang *Thailand* 18°16N 99°32E **38** C2
Lampasas *U.S.A.* 31°4N 98°11W **84** F5
Lampazos de Naranjo
　Mexico 27°1N 100°31W **86** B4
Lampedusa *Medit. S.* 35°36N 12°40E **22** G5
Lampeter *U.K.* 52°7N 4°4W **13** E3
Lamphun *Thailand* 18°40N 99°2E **38** C2
Lampione *Medit. S.* 35°33N 12°20E **22** G5
Lampman *Canada* 49°25N 102°50W **71** D8
Lampung □ *Indonesia* 5°30S 104°30E **36** F2
Lamta *India* 22°8N 80°7E **43** H9
Lamu *Kenya* 2°16S 40°55E **54** E8
Lamy *U.S.A.* 35°29N 105°53W **77** J11
Lan Xian *China* 38°15N 111°35E **32** E6
Lan Yü *Taiwan* 22°4N 121°25E **35** F13
Lāna'i *U.S.A.* 20°50N 156°55W **75** L8
Lanak La *China* 34°27N 79°32E **43** B8
Lanak'o Shank'ou = Lanak La
　China 34°27N 79°32E **43** B8
Lanark *Canada* 45°1N 76°22W **83** A8
Lanark *U.K.* 55°40N 3°47W **11** F5
Lanbi Kyun *Burma* 10°50N 98°20E **39** G2
Lancang *China* 22°36N 99°58E **34** F2
Lancang Jiang ↦ *China* 21°40N 101°10E **34** G3
Lancashire □ *U.K.* 53°50N 2°48W **12** D5
Lancaster *Canada* 45°10N 74°30W **83** A10
Lancaster *U.K.* 54°3N 2°48W **12** C5
Lancaster *Calif., U.S.A.* 34°42N 118°8W **79** L8
Lancaster *Ky., U.S.A.* 37°37N 84°35W **81** G11
Lancaster *N.H., U.S.A.* 44°29N 71°34W **83** B13
Lancaster *Ohio, U.S.A.* 39°43N 82°36W **81** F12
Lancaster *Pa., U.S.A.* 40°2N 76°19W **83** F8
Lancaster *S.C., U.S.A.* 34°43N 80°46W **85** D14
Lancaster *Wis., U.S.A.* 42°51N 90°43W **80** D8
Lancaster Sd. *Canada* 74°13N 84°0W **69** C15
Lancelin *Australia* 31°0S 115°18E **61** F2
Lanchow = Lanzhou
　China 36°1N 103°52E **32** F2
Lanciano *Italy* 42°14N 14°23E **22** C6
Lancun *China* 36°25N 120°10E **33** F11
Land Between the Lakes △
　U.S.A. 36°25N 88°0W **85** G11
Landeck *Austria* 47°9N 10°34E **16** E6
Lander *U.S.A.* 42°50N 108°44W **76** E9
Lander ↦ *Australia* 22°0S 132°0E **60** D5
Landes *France* 44°0N 1°0W **20** D3
Landfall I. *India* 13°40N 93°2E **45** H11
Landi Kotal *Pakistan* 34°7N 71°6E **42** B4
Landisburg *U.S.A.* 40°21N 77°19W **82** F7
Landmannalaugar *Iceland* 63°59N 19°8E **8** E4
Land's End *U.K.* 50°4N 5°44W **13** G2
Landsborough Cr. ↦
　Australia 22°28S 144°35E **62** C3
Landshut *Germany* 48°34N 12°8E **16** D7
Lanesboro *U.S.A.* 41°57N 75°34W **83** E9
Lanett *U.S.A.* 32°52N 85°12W **85** E12
Lang Shan *China* 41°0N 106°30E **32** D4
Lang Son *Vietnam* 21°52N 106°42E **34** G6
Lang Suan *Thailand* 9°57N 99°4E **39** H2
La'nga Co *China* 30°45N 81°15E **43** D9
Langar *Iran* 35°23N 60°25E **47** C9
Langara I. *Canada* 54°14N 133°1W **70** C2
Langarūd *Iran* 37°11N 50°8E **47** B6
Langdai *China* 26°6N 105°21E **34** D5

Langdon *U.S.A.* 48°45N 98°22W **80** A4
Langeberg *S. Africa* 33°55S 21°0E **56** D3
Langeberge *S. Africa* 28°15S 22°33E **56** C3
Langeland *Denmark* 54°56N 10°48E **9** J14
Langenburg *Canada* 50°51N 101°43W **71** C8
Langfang *China* 39°30N 116°41E **32** E9
Langholm *U.K.* 55°9N 3°0W **11** F5
Langjökull *Iceland* 64°39N 20°12W **8** D3
Langkawi, Pulau *Malaysia* 6°25N 99°45E **39** J2
Langklip *S. Africa* 28°12S 20°20E **56** C3
Langkon *Malaysia* 6°30N 116°40E **36** C5
Langley *Canada* 49°7N 122°39W **78** A4
Langoya *Norway* 68°45N 14°50E **8** B16
Langreo *Spain* 43°18N 5°40W **21** A3
Langres *France* 47°52N 5°20E **20** C6
Langres, Plateau de *France* 47°45N 5°3E **20** C6
Langsa *Indonesia* 4°30N 97°57E **36** D1
Langtang △ *Nepal* 28°10N 85°30E **43** E11
Langtou *China* 40°1N 124°19E **33** D13
Langtry *U.S.A.* 29°49N 101°34W **84** G4
Langu *Thailand* 6°53N 99°47E **39** J2
Languedoc *France* 43°58N 3°55E **20** E5
Langwang *China* 22°38N 113°27E **31** a
Langxi *China* 31°10N 119°12E **35** B12
Langzhong *China* 31°38N 105°58E **34** B5
Lanigan *Canada* 51°51N 105°2W **71** C7
Lanjigarh *India* 19°43N 83°23E **44** E6
Lankao *China* 34°48N 114°50E **32** G8
Länkäran *Azerbaijan* 38°48N 48°52E **47** B6
Lannion *France* 48°46N 3°29W **20** B2
L'Annonciation *Canada* 46°25N 74°55W **72** C5
Lanping *China* 26°28N 99°15E **34** D2
Lansang △ *Thailand* 16°45N 99°0E **38** D2
Lansdale *U.S.A.* 40°14N 75°17W **83** F9
Lansdowne *Australia* 31°48S 152°30E **63** E5
Lansdowne *Canada* 44°24N 76°1W **83** B8
Lansdowne *India* 29°50N 78°41E **43** E8
Lansdowne House = Neskantaga
　Canada 52°14N 87°53W **72** B2
L'Anse *U.S.A.* 46°45N 88°27W **80** B9
L'Anse au Loup *Canada* 51°32N 56°50W **73** B8
L'Anse aux Meadows
　Canada 51°36N 55°32W **73** B8
Lansford *U.S.A.* 40°50N 75°53W **83** F9
Lanshan *China* 25°24N 112°10E **35** E9
Lanshantou *China* 35°5N 119°20E **33** G10
Länsi-Turunmaa *Finland* 60°18N 22°18E **9** F20
Lansing *U.S.A.* 42°44N 84°33W **81** D11
Lanta, Ko *Thailand* 7°35N 99°3E **39** J2
Lantau I. *China* 22°15N 113°56E **31** a
Lantian *China* 34°11N 109°20E **32** G5
Lanusei *Italy* 39°52N 9°34E **22** E3
Lanxi *China* 29°13N 119°28E **35** C12
Lanzarote *Canary Is.* 29°0N 13°40W **52** C3
Lanzhou *China* 36°1N 103°52E **32** F2
Lao Cai *Vietnam* 22°30N 103°57E **34** F4
Laoag *Phil.* 18°7N 120°34E **37** A6
Laoang *Phil.* 12°32N 125°8E **37** B7
Laoha He ↦ *China* 43°25N 120°35E **33** C11
Laohekou *China* 32°22N 111°38E **35** A8
Laois □ *Ireland* 52°57N 7°27W **10** D4
Laon *France* 49°33N 3°35E **20** B5
Laona *U.S.A.* 45°34N 88°40W **80** C9
Laos ■ *Asia* 17°45N 105°0E **38** D5
Lapa *Brazil* 25°46S 49°44W **95** B6
Lapeer *U.S.A.* 43°3N 83°19W **81** D12
Lapland = Lappland *Europe* 68°7N 24°0E **8** B21
LaPorte *Ind., U.S.A.* 41°36N 86°43W **80** E10
Laporte *Pa., U.S.A.* 41°25N 76°30W **83** E8
Lappeenranta *Finland* 61°3N 28°12E **8** F23
Lappland *Europe* 68°7N 24°0E **8** B21
Lappo = Lapua *Finland* 62°58N 23°0E **8** E20
Laprida *Argentina* 37°34S 60°45W **94** D3
Lâpseki *Turkey* 40°20N 26°41E **23** D12
Laptev Sea *Russia* 76°0N 125°0E **27** B13
Lapua *Finland* 62°58N 23°0E **8** E20
L'Áquila *Italy* 42°22N 13°22E **22** C5
Lār *Iran* 27°40N 54°14E **47** E7
Laramie *U.S.A.* 41°19N 105°35W **76** F11
Laramie Mts. *U.S.A.* 42°0N 105°30W **76** F11
Laranda = Karaman
　Turkey 37°14N 33°13E **46** B2
Laranjeiras do Sul *Brazil* 25°23S 52°23W **95** B5
Larantuka *Indonesia* 8°21S 122°55E **37** F6
Larat *Indonesia* 7°0S 132°0E **37** F8
Larder Lake *Canada* 48°5N 79°40W **72** C4
Laredo *U.S.A.* 27°30N 99°30W **84** H5
Laredo Sd. *Canada* 52°30N 128°53W **70** C3
Largo *U.S.A.* 27°54N 82°47W **85** H13
Largs *U.K.* 55°47N 4°52W **11** F4
Lariang *Indonesia* 1°26S 119°17E **37** E5
Larimore *U.S.A.* 47°54N 97°38W **80** B5
Larisa *Greece* 39°36N 22°27E **23** E10
Larkana *Pakistan* 27°32N 68°18E **42** F3
Larnaca *Cyprus* 34°55N 33°38E **46** C2
Larne *U.K.* 54°51N 5°51W **10** B6
Larned *U.S.A.* 38°11N 99°6W **84** C5
Larose *U.S.A.* 29°34N 90°23W **85** G9
Larrimah *Australia* 15°35S 133°12E **60** C5
Larsen Ice Shelf *Antarctica* 67°0S 62°0W **5** C17
Larvik *Norway* 59°4N 10°2E **9** G14
Las Animas *U.S.A.* 38°4N 103°13W **76** G12
Las Anod *Somalia* 8°26N 47°19E **49** F4
Las Brenãs *Argentina* 27°5S 61°7W **94** B3
Las Cejas *Argentina* 26°53S 64°44W **96** B4
Las Chimeneas *Mexico* 32°8N 116°5W **79** N10
Las Flores *Argentina* 36°10S 59°7W **94** D4
Las Heras *Argentina* 32°51S 68°49W **94** C2
Las Lajas *Argentina* 38°30S 70°25W **96** D2
Las Lomitas *Argentina* 24°43S 60°35W **94** A3
Las Palmas *Argentina* 27°8S 58°45W **94** B4
Las Palmas *Canary Is.* 28°7N 15°26W **52** C2
Las Palmas ↦ *Mexico* 32°31N 116°58W **79** N10
Las Piedras *Uruguay* 34°44S 56°14W **95** C4
Las Plumas *Argentina* 43°40S 67°15W **96** E3
Las Rosas *Argentina* 32°30S 61°35W **94** C3
Las Tablas *Panama* 7°49N 80°14W **88** E3

Las Toscas *Argentina* 28°21S 59°18W **94 B4**
Las Tunas *Cuba* 20°58N 76°59W **88 B4**
Las Varillas *Argentina* 31°50S 62°50W **94 C3**
Las Vegas *U.S.A.* 35°36N 105°13W **77 J11**
Lascano *Uruguay* 33°35S 54°12W **95 C5**
Lash-e Joveyn *Afghan.* 31°45N 61°30E **40 D2**
Lashburn *Canada* 53°10N 109°40W **71 C7**
Lashio *Burma* 22°56N 97°45E **41 H20**
Lashkar *India* 26°10N 78°10E **42 F8**
Lāsjerd *Iran* 35°24N 53°4E **47 C7**
Lassen Pk. *U.S.A.* 40°29N 121°30W **76 F3**
Lassen Volcanic △
  U.S.A. 40°30N 121°20W **76 F3**
Last Mountain L. *Canada* 51°5N 105°14W **71 C7**
Lastchance Cr. ➘
  U.S.A. 40°2N 121°15W **78 E5**
Lastoursville *Gabon* 0°55S 12°38E **54 E2**
Lastovo *Croatia* 42°46N 16°55E **22 C7**
Lat Yao *Thailand* 15°45N 99°48E **38 E2**
Latacunga *Ecuador* 0°50S 78°35W **92 D3**
Latady I. *Antarctica* 70°45S 74°35W **5 D17**
Latakia = Al Lādhiqīyah
  Syria 35°30N 35°45E **46 C2**
Latchford *Canada* 47°20N 79°50W **72 C4**
Late 18°48S 174°39W **59 c**
Latehar *India* 23°45N 84°30E **43 H11**
Latham *Australia* 29°44S 116°20E **61 E2**
Lathi *India* 27°43N 71°23E **42 F4**
Lathrop Wells *U.S.A.* 36°39N 116°24W **79 J10**
Latina *Italy* 41°28N 12°52E **22 D5**
Latium = Lazio □ *Italy* 42°10N 12°30E **22 C5**
Laton *U.S.A.* 36°26N 119°41W **78 J7**
Latouche Treville, C.
  Australia 18°27S 121°49E **60 C3**
Latrobe *Australia* 41°14S 146°30E **63 G4**
Latrobe *U.S.A.* 40°19N 79°23W **82 F5**
Latur *India* 18°25N 76°40E **44 E3**
Latvia ■ *Europe* 56°50N 24°0E **9 H21**
Lau Group *Fiji* 17°0S 178°30W **59 a**
Lauchhammer *Germany* 51°29N 13°47E **16 C7**
Lauge Koch Kyst
  Greenland 75°45N 57°45W **69 B20**
Laughlin *U.S.A.* 35°10N 114°34W **79 K12**
Laukaa *Finland* 62°24N 25°56E **8 E21**
Launceston *Australia* 41°24S 147°8E **63 G4**
Launceston *U.K.* 50°38N 4°22W **13 G3**
Laune ➘ *Ireland* 52°7N 9°47W **10 D2**
Launglon Bok *Burma* 13°50N 97°54E **38 F1**
Laura *Australia* 15°32S 144°32E **62 B3**
Laurel *Miss., U.S.A.* 31°41N 89°8W **85 F10**
Laurel *Mont., U.S.A.* 45°40N 108°46W **76 D9**
Laurel Hill *U.S.A.* 40°14N 79°6W **82 F5**
Laurencekirk *U.K.* 56°50N 2°28W **11 E6**
Laurens *U.S.A.* 34°30N 82°1W **85 D13**
Laurentian Plateau *Canada* 52°0N 70°0W **73 B6**
Lauria *Italy* 40°2N 15°50E **22 E6**
Laurie L. *Canada* 56°35N 101°57W **71 B8**
Laurinburg *U.S.A.* 34°47N 79°28W **85 D15**
Laurium *U.S.A.* 47°14N 88°27W **80 B9**
Lausanne *Switz.* 46°32N 6°38E **20 C7**
Laut *Indonesia* 4°45N 108°0E **36 D3**
Laut, Pulau *Indonesia* 3°40S 116°10E **36 E5**
Laut Kecil, Kepulauan
  Indonesia 4°45S 115°40E **36 E5**
Lautoka *Fiji* 17°37S 177°27E **59 a**
Lauwersmeer △ *Neths.* 53°22N 6°11E **15 A6**
Lava Beds △ *U.S.A.* 41°40N 121°30W **76 F3**
Lavagh More *Ireland* 54°46N 8°6W **10 B3**
Laval *France* 48°4N 0°48W **20 B3**
Lavalle *Argentina* 28°15S 65°15W **94 B2**
Lāvān *Iran* 26°48N 53°22E **47 E7**
Lavant *Canada* 45°3N 76°42W **83 A8**
Lāvar Meydān *Iran* 30°20N 54°30E **47 D7**
Laverton *Australia* 28°44S 122°29E **61 E3**
Lavras *Brazil* 21°20S 45°0W **95 A7**
Lavrio *Greece* 37°40N 24°4E **23 F11**
Lavumisa *Swaziland* 27°20S 31°55E **57 C5**
Lawaki *Fiji* 17°40S 178°35E **59 a**
Lawas *Malaysia* 4°55N 115°25E **36 D5**
Lawele *Indonesia* 5°13S 122°57E **37 F6**
Lawn Hill = Boodjamulla △
  Australia 18°15S 138°6E **62 B2**
Lawqah *Si. Arabia* 29°49N 42°45E **46 D4**
Lawrence *N.Z.* 45°55S 169°41E **59 F2**
Lawrence *Ind., U.S.A.* 39°50N 86°2W **80 F10**
Lawrence *Kans., U.S.A.* 38°58N 95°14W **80 F6**
Lawrence *Mass., U.S.A.* 42°43N 71°10W **83 D13**
Lawrenceburg *Ind.,*
  U.S.A. 39°6N 84°52W **81 F11**
Lawrenceburg *Tenn.,*
  U.S.A. 35°14N 87°20W **85 D11**
Lawrenceville *Ga.,*
  U.S.A. 33°57N 83°59W **85 E13**
Lawrenceville *Pa., U.S.A.* 41°59N 77°8W **82 E7**
Laws *U.S.A.* 37°24N 118°20W **78 H8**
Lawton *U.S.A.* 34°37N 98°25W **84 D5**
Lawu *Indonesia* 7°40S 111°13E **37 G14**
Laxford, L. *U.K.* 58°24N 5°6W **11 C3**
Laxiwa Dam *China* 36°4N 101°11E **30 D9**
Layla *Si. Arabia* 22°10N 46°40E **49 C4**
Laylān *Iraq* 35°18N 44°31E **46 C5**
Laysan I. *U.S.A.* 25°50N 171°50W **75 K5**
Layton *U.S.A.* 41°4N 111°58W **76 F8**
Laytonville *U.S.A.* 39°41N 123°29W **76 G2**
Lazarev *Russia* 52°13N 141°30E **27 D15**
Lazarev Sea *S. Ocean* 67°30S 3°0W **5 C2**
Lázaro Cárdenas
  Mexico 17°55N 102°11W **86 D4**
Lazio □ *Italy* 42°10N 12°30E **22 C5**
Lazo *Russia* 43°25N 133°55E **28 C6**
Le Bic *Canada* 48°20N 68°41W **73 C6**
Le Creusot *France* 46°48N 4°24E **20 C6**
Le François *Martinique* 14°38N 60°57W **88 c**
Le Gosier *Guadeloupe* 16°14N 61°29W **88 b**
Le Gris Gris *Mauritius* 20°31S 57°32E **55 d**
Le Havre *France* 49°30N 0°5E **20 B4**
Le Lamentin *Martinique* 14°35N 61°2W **88 c**
Le Mans *France* 48°0N 0°10E **20 C4**
Le Marin *Martinique* 14°27N 60°55W **88 c**

Le Mars *U.S.A.* 42°47N 96°10W **80 D5**
Le Mont-St-Michel *France* 48°40N 1°30W **20 B3**
Le Moule *Guadeloupe* 16°20N 61°22W **88 b**
Le Moyne, L. *Canada* 56°45N 68°47W **73 A6**
Le Port *Réunion* 20°56S 55°18E **55 c**
Le Prêcheur *Martinique* 14°50N 61°12W **88 c**
Le Puy-en-Velay *France* 45°3N 3°52E **20 D5**
Le Raysville *U.S.A.* 41°50N 76°10W **83 E8**
Le Robert *Martinique* 14°40N 60°56W **88 c**
Le Roy *U.S.A.* 42°58N 77°59W **82 D7**
Le St-Esprit *Martinique* 14°34N 60°56W **88 c**
Le Sueur *U.S.A.* 44°28N 93°55W **80 C7**
Le Thuy *Vietnam* 17°14N 106°49E **38 D6**
Le Touquet-Paris-Plage
  France 50°30N 1°36E **20 A4**
Le Tréport *France* 50°3N 1°20E **20 A4**
Le Verdon-sur-Mer *France* 45°33N 1°4W **20 D3**
Lea ➘ *U.K.* 51°31N 0°1E **13 F8**
Leach *Cambodia* 12°21N 103°46E **39 F4**
Lead *U.S.A.* 44°21N 103°46W **80 C2**
Leader *Canada* 50°50N 109°30W **71 C7**
Leadville *U.S.A.* 39°15N 106°18W **76 G10**
Leaf ➘ *U.S.A.* 30°59N 88°44W **85 F10**
Leaf Rapids *Canada* 56°30N 99°59W **71 B9**
League City *U.S.A.* 29°31N 95°6W **84 C7**
Leamington *Canada* 42°3N 82°36W **82 D2**
Leamington *U.S.A.* 39°32N 112°17W **76 G7**
Leamington Spa = Royal
  Leamington Spa *U.K.* 52°18N 1°31W **13 E6**
Le'an *China* 27°22N 115°48E **35 D10**
Leander *U.S.A.* 30°34N 97°52W **84 F5**
Leandro Norte Alem
  Argentina 27°34S 55°15W **95 B4**
Leane, L. *Ireland* 52°2N 9°32W **10 D2**
Learmonth *Australia* 22°13S 114°10E **60 D1**
Leask *Canada* 53°5N 106°45W **71 C7**
Leatherhead *U.K.* 51°18N 0°20W **13 F7**
Leavdnja = Lakselv *Norway* 70°2N 25°0E **8 A21**
Leavenworth *Kans.,*
  U.S.A. 39°19N 94°55W **80 F6**
Leavenworth *Wash.,*
  U.S.A. 47°36N 120°40W **76 C3**
Leawood *U.S.A.* 38°58N 94°37W **80 F6**
Lebak *Phil.* 6°32N 124°5E **37 C6**
Lebam *U.S.A.* 46°34N 123°33W **78 D3**
Lebanon *Ind., U.S.A.* 40°3N 86°28W **80 E10**
Lebanon *Kans., U.S.A.* 39°49N 98°33W **80 F4**
Lebanon *Ky., U.S.A.* 37°34N 85°15W **81 G11**
Lebanon *Mo., U.S.A.* 37°41N 92°40W **80 G7**
Lebanon *N.H., U.S.A.* 43°39N 72°15W **83 C12**
Lebanon *Oreg., U.S.A.* 44°32N 122°55W **76 D2**
Lebanon *Pa., U.S.A.* 40°20N 76°26W **83 F8**
Lebanon *Tenn., U.S.A.* 36°12N 86°18W **85 C11**
Lebanon ■ *Asia* 34°0N 36°0E **48 B5**
Lebec *U.S.A.* 34°51N 118°52W **79 L8**
Lebel-sur-Quévillon
  Canada 49°3N 76°59W **72 C4**
Lebomboberge *S. Africa* 24°30S 32°0E **57 B5**
Lębork *Poland* 54°33N 17°46E **17 A9**
Lebowakgomo *S. Africa* 24°12S 29°30E **57 B4**
Lebrija *Spain* 36°53N 6°5W **21 D2**
Lebu *Chile* 37°40S 73°47W **94 D1**
Lecce *Italy* 40°23N 18°11E **23 D8**
Lecco *Italy* 45°51N 9°23E **20 D8**
Lech ➘ *Germany* 48°43N 10°56E **16 D6**
Lechang *China* 25°10N 113°20E **35 E9**
Lecontes Mills *U.S.A.* 41°5N 78°17W **82 E6**
Łęczyca *Poland* 52°5N 19°15E **17 B10**
Ledang, Gunung
  Malaysia 2°22N 102°37E **39 L4**
Ledong *China* 18°41N 109°5E **38 C7**
Leduc *Canada* 53°15N 113°30W **70 C6**
Lee *U.S.A.* 42°19N 73°15W **83 D11**
Lee ➘ *Ireland* 51°53N 8°56W **10 E3**
Lee Vining *U.S.A.* 37°58N 119°7W **78 H7**
Leech L. *U.S.A.* 47°10N 94°24W **80 B6**
Leechburg *U.S.A.* 40°37N 79°36W **82 F5**
Leeds *U.K.* 53°48N 1°33W **12 D6**
Leeds *U.S.A.* 33°33N 86°33W **85 E11**
Leek *Neths.* 53°10N 6°24E **15 A6**
Leek *U.K.* 53°7N 2°1W **12 D5**
Leeman *Australia* 29°57S 114°58E **61 E1**
Leeper *U.S.A.* 41°22N 79°18W **82 E5**
Leer *Germany* 53°13N 7°26E **16 B4**
Leesburg *U.S.A.* 28°49N 81°53W **85 G14**
Leesville *U.S.A.* 31°8N 93°16W **84 F8**
Leeton *Australia* 34°33S 146°23E **63 E4**
Leetonia *U.S.A.* 40°53N 80°45W **82 F4**
Leeu Gamka *S. Africa* 32°47S 21°59E **56 D3**
Leeuwarden *Neths.* 53°15N 5°48E **15 A5**
Leeuwin, C. *Australia* 34°20S 115°9E **61 F2**
Leeuwin Naturaliste △
  Australia 34°6S 115°3E **61 F2**
Leeward Is. *Atl. Oc.* 16°30N 63°30W **89 C7**
Lefka *Cyprus* 35°6N 32°51E **46 C2**
Lefkada *Greece* 38°40N 20°43E **23 E9**
Lefkosia = Nicosia
  Cyprus 35°10N 33°25E **46 C2**
Lefroy *Canada* 44°16N 79°34W **82 B5**
Lefroy, L. *Australia* 31°21S 121°40E **61 F3**
Legazpi *Phil.* 13°10N 123°45E **37 B6**
Legian *Indonesia* 8°42S 115°10E **37 K18**
Legionowo *Poland* 52°25N 20°50E **17 B11**
Legnago *Italy* 45°11N 11°18E **22 B4**
Legnica *Poland* 51°12N 16°10E **16 C9**
Leh *India* 34°9N 77°35E **43 B7**
Lehigh Acres *U.S.A.* 26°36N 81°39W **85 H14**
Lehighton *U.S.A.* 40°50N 75°43W **83 F9**
Lehututu *Botswana* 23°54S 21°55E **56 B3**
Lei Shui ➘ *China* 26°55N 112°35E **35 D9**
Leiah *Pakistan* 30°58N 70°58E **42 D4**
Leibo *China* 28°11N 103°34E **34 C4**
Leicester *U.K.* 52°38N 1°8W **13 E6**
Leicester City *U.K.* 52°38N 1°9W **13 E6**
Leicestershire □ *U.K.* 52°41N 1°17W **13 E6**
Leichhardt ➘ *Australia* 17°35S 139°48E **62 B2**
Leichhardt Ra. *Australia* 20°46S 147°40E **62 C4**

Leiden *Neths.* 52°9N 4°30E **15 B4**
Leie ➘ *Belgium* 51°2N 3°45E **15 C3**
Leimus *Nic.* 14°40N 84°3W **88 D3**
Leine ➘ *Germany* 52°43N 9°36E **16 B5**
Leinster *Australia* 27°51S 120°36E **61 E3**
Leinster □ *Ireland* 53°3N 7°8W **10 C4**
Leinster, Mt. *Ireland* 52°37N 6°46W **10 D5**
Leipzig *Germany* 51°18N 12°22E **16 C7**
Leiria *Portugal* 39°46N 8°53W **21 C1**
Leirvik *Norway* 59°47N 5°28E **9 G11**
Leishan *China* 26°15N 108°20E **34 D7**
Leisler, Mt. *Australia* 23°23S 129°20E **60 D4**
Leith *U.K.* 55°59N 3°11W **11 F5**
Leith Hill *U.K.* 51°11N 0°22W **13 F7**
Leitir Ceanainn = Letterkenny
  Ireland 54°57N 7°45W **10 B4**
Leitrim *Ireland* 54°0N 8°5W **10 B3**
Leitrim □ *Ireland* 54°8N 8°0W **10 B4**
Leixlip *Ireland* 53°22N 6°30W **10 C5**
Leiyang *China* 26°27N 112°45E **35 D9**
Leizhou *China* 20°52N 110°8E **35 G8**
Leizhou Bandao *China* 21°0N 110°0E **34 G7**
Leizhou Wan *China* 20°50N 110°20E **35 G8**
Lek ➘ *Neths.* 51°54N 4°35E **15 C4**
Leka *Norway* 65°5N 11°35E **8 D14**
Leland *Mich., U.S.A.* 45°1N 85°45W **81 C11**
Leland *Miss., U.S.A.* 33°24N 90°54W **85 E9**
Leleque *Argentina* 42°28S 71°0W **96 E2**
Leling *China* 37°44N 117°13E **33 F9**
Lelystad *Neths.* 52°30N 5°25E **15 B5**
Léman, L. *Europe* 46°26N 6°30E **20 C7**
Lembar *Indonesia* 8°45S 116°4E **37 K19**
Lembongan, Nusa
  Indonesia 8°40S 115°27E **37 K18**
Lembuak *Indonesia* 8°36S 116°11E **37 K19**
Lemesós = Limassol
  Cyprus 34°42N 33°1E **46 C2**
Lemhi Ra. *U.S.A.* 44°0N 113°0W **76 D7**
Lemmer *Neths.* 52°51N 5°43E **15 B5**
Lemmon *U.S.A.* 45°57N 102°10W **80 C2**
Lemon Grove *U.S.A.* 32°44N 117°1W **79 N9**
Lemoore *U.S.A.* 36°18N 119°46W **78 J7**
Lemvig *Denmark* 56°33N 8°20E **9 H13**
Lena ➘ *Russia* 72°52N 126°40E **27 B13**
Lenadoon Pt. *Ireland* 54°18N 9°3W **10 B2**
Lenggong *Malaysia* 5°6N 100°58E **39 K3**
Lengshuijiang *China* 27°40N 111°26E **35 D8**
Lengshuitan *China* 26°27N 111°35E **35 D8**
Lengua de Vaca, Pta.
  Chile 30°14S 71°38W **94 C1**
Leninogorsk = Ridder
  Kazakhstan 50°20N 83°30E **26 D9**
Leninsk *Russia* 48°40N 45°15E **19 E8**
Leninsk-Kuznetskiy
  Russia 54°44N 86°10E **26 D9**
Lenkoran = Länkäran
  Azerbaijan 38°48N 48°52E **47 B6**
Lennox *U.S.A.* 43°21N 96°53W **80 D5**
Lennoxville *Canada* 45°22N 71°51W **83 A13**
Lenoir *U.S.A.* 35°55N 81°32W **85 D14**
Lenoir City *U.S.A.* 35°48N 84°16W **85 D12**
Lenore L. *Canada* 52°30N 104°59W **71 C8**
Lenox *U.S.A.* 42°22N 73°17W **83 D11**
Lens *France* 50°26N 2°50E **20 A5**
Lensk *Russia* 60°48N 114°55E **27 C12**
Lentini *Italy* 37°17N 15°0E **22 F6**
Lenwood *U.S.A.* 34°53N 117°7W **79 L9**
Lenya *Burma* 11°33N 98°57E **39 G2**
Leoben *Austria* 47°22N 15°5E **16 E8**
Leodhais = Lewis *U.K.* 58°9N 6°40W **11 C2**
Leola *U.S.A.* 45°43N 98°56W **80 C4**
Leominster *U.K.* 52°14N 2°43W **13 E5**
Leominster *U.S.A.* 42°32N 71°46W **83 D13**
León *Mexico* 21°6N 101°41W **86 C4**
León *Nic.* 12°27N 86°51W **88 D2**
León *Spain* 42°38N 5°34W **21 A3**
Leon *U.S.A.* 40°44N 93°45W **80 E7**
León, Montes de *Spain* 42°30N 6°18W **21 A2**
Leonardtown *U.S.A.* 38°17N 76°38W **81 F15**
Leonardville *Namibia* 23°29S 18°49E **56 B2**
Leone, Amer. Samoa* 14°23S 170°48W **59 b**
Leongatha *Australia* 38°30S 145°58E **63 F4**
Leonora *Australia* 28°49S 121°19E **61 E3**
Leopoldina *Brazil* 21°28S 42°40W **95 A7**
Leopoldsburg *Belgium* 51°7N 5°13E **15 C5**
Leoti *U.S.A.* 38°29N 101°21W **80 F3**
Leova *Moldova* 46°28N 28°15E **17 E15**
Leoville *Canada* 53°39N 107°33W **71 C7**
Lepel = Lyepyel *Belarus* 54°50N 28°40E **9 J23**
Leping *China* 28°47N 117°7E **35 C11**
Lépo, L. do *Angola* 17°0S 19°0E **56 B2**
Leppävirta *Finland* 62°29N 27°46E **8 E22**
Leptis Magna *Libya* 32°40N 14°12E **53 B8**
Léribe *Lesotho* 28°51S 28°3E **57 C4**
Lerwick *U.K.* 60°9N 1°9W **11 A7**
Les Cayes *Haiti* 18°15N 73°46W **89 C5**
Les Coteaux *Canada* 45°15N 74°13W **83 A10**
Les Escoumins *Canada* 48°21N 69°24W **73 C6**
Les Sables-d'Olonne
  France 46°30N 1°45W **20 C3**
Lesbos *Greece* 39°10N 26°20E **23 E12**
Leshan *China* 29°33N 103°41E **34 C4**
Leshukonskoye *Russia* 64°54N 45°46E **18 B8**
Leskov I. *Antarctica* 56°0S 28°0W **5 B1**
Leskovac *Serbia* 43°0N 21°58E **23 C9**
Lesopilnoye *Russia* 46°44N 134°20E **28 A7**
Lesotho ■ *Africa* 29°40S 28°0E **57 C4**
Lesozavodsk *Russia* 45°30N 133°29E **28 B6**
Lesse ➘ *Belgium* 50°15N 4°54E **15 D4**
Lesse et Lomme △ *Belgium* 50°8N 5°9E **15 D5**
Lesser Antilles *W. Indies* 15°0N 61°0W **89 D7**
Lesser Slave L. *Canada* 55°30N 115°25W **70 B5**
Lesser Sunda Is. *Indonesia* 8°0S 120°0E **37 F6**
Lessines *Belgium* 50°42N 3°50E **15 D3**
Lestock *Canada* 51°19N 103°59W **71 C8**
Lesueur I. *Australia* 13°50S 142°23E **62 A3**
Lesueur △ *Australia* 30°11S 115°10E **61 F2**

Lésvos = Lesbos *Greece* 39°10N 26°20E **23 E12**
Leszno *Poland* 51°50N 16°30E **17 C9**
Letaba *S. Africa* 23°59S 31°50E **57 B5**
Letchworth *U.K.* 51°59N 0°13W **13 F7**
Lethbridge *Canada* 49°45N 112°45W **70 D6**
Lethem *Guyana* 3°20N 59°50W **92 C7**
Leti, Kepulauan *Indonesia* 8°10S 128°0E **37 F7**
Leti Is. = Leti, Kepulauan
  Indonesia 8°10S 128°0E **37 F7**
Letiahau ➘ *Botswana* 21°16S 24°0E **56 B3**
Leticia *Colombia* 4°9S 70°0W **92 D5**
Leting *China* 39°23N 118°55E **33 E10**
Letjiesbos *S. Africa* 32°34S 22°16E **56 D3**
Letlhakane *Botswana* 21°27S 25°30E **56 B4**
Letlhakeng *Botswana* 24°0S 24°59E **56 B4**
Letpadan *Burma* 17°45N 95°45E **41 L19**
Letpan *Burma* 19°28N 94°10E **41 K19**
Letsôk-aw Kyun *Burma* 11°30N 98°25E **39 G2**
Letterkenny *Ireland* 54°57N 7°45W **10 B4**
Leucadia *U.S.A.* 33°4N 117°18W **79 M9**
Leuchars *U.K.* 56°24N 2°53W **11 E6**
Leuser, Gunung *Indonesia* 3°46N 97°12E **36 D1**
Leuven *Belgium* 50°52N 4°42E **15 D4**
Leuze-en-Hainaut *Belgium* 50°36N 3°37E **15 D3**
Levanger *Norway* 63°45N 11°19E **8 E14**
Levelland *U.S.A.* 33°35N 102°23W **84 E3**
Leven *U.K.* 56°12N 3°0W **11 E6**
Leven, L. *U.K.* 56°12N 3°22W **11 E5**
Leveque C. *Australia* 16°20S 123°0E **60 C3**
Levice *Slovak Rep.* 48°13N 18°35E **17 D10**
Levin *N.Z.* 40°37S 175°18E **59 D5**
Lévis *Canada* 46°48N 71°9W **73 C5**
Levis, L. *Canada* 62°37N 117°58W **70 A5**
Levittown *N.Y., U.S.A.* 40°44N 73°31W **83 F11**
Levittown *Pa., U.S.A.* 40°9N 74°51W **83 F10**
Levka Oros *Greece* 35°18N 24°3E **23 G11**
Levkás = Lefkada *Greece* 38°40N 20°43E **23 E9**
Levkosía = Karlovo
  Bulgaria 42°38N 24°47E **23 C11**
Levuka *Fiji* 17°34S 179°0E **59 a**
Lewes *U.K.* 50°52N 0°1E **13 G8**
Lewes *U.S.A.* 38°46N 75°9W **81 F16**
Lewis *U.K.* 58°9N 6°40W **11 C2**
Lewis ➘ *U.S.A.* 45°51N 122°48W **78 E4**
Lewis, Butt of *U.K.* 58°31N 6°16W **11 C2**
Lewis and Clark △
  U.S.A. 46°8N 123°53W **78 D3**
Lewis Ra. *Australia* 20°3S 128°50E **60 D4**
Lewis Range *U.S.A.* 48°5N 113°5W **76 B7**
Lewis Run *U.S.A.* 41°52N 78°40W **82 E6**
Lewisburg *Pa., U.S.A.* 40°58N 76°54W **82 F8**
Lewisburg *Tenn., U.S.A.* 35°27N 86°48W **85 D11**
Lewisburg *W. Va.,*
  U.S.A. 37°48N 80°27W **81 G13**
Lewisporte *Canada* 49°15N 55°3W **73 C8**
Lewiston *Idaho, U.S.A.* 46°25N 117°1W **76 C5**
Lewiston *Maine, U.S.A.* 44°6N 70°13W **81 C18**
Lewiston *N.Y., U.S.A.* 43°11N 79°3W **82 C5**
Lewistown *Mont., U.S.A.* 47°4N 109°26W **76 C9**
Lewistown *Pa., U.S.A.* 40°36N 77°34W **82 F7**
Lexington *Ill., U.S.A.* 40°39N 88°47W **80 E9**
Lexington *Ky., U.S.A.* 38°3N 84°30W **81 F11**
Lexington *Mich., U.S.A.* 43°16N 82°32W **82 C2**
Lexington *Mo., U.S.A.* 39°11N 93°52W **80 F8**
Lexington *N.C., U.S.A.* 35°49N 80°15W **85 D14**
Lexington *Nebr., U.S.A.* 40°47N 99°45W **80 E4**
Lexington *Ohio, U.S.A.* 40°41N 82°35W **82 F2**
Lexington *S.C., U.S.A.* 33°59N 81°11W **85 E14**
Lexington *Tenn., U.S.A.* 35°39N 88°24W **85 D10**
Lexington *Va., U.S.A.* 37°47N 79°27W **81 G14**
Lexington Park *U.S.A.* 38°16N 76°27W **81 F15**
Leyburn *U.K.* 54°19N 1°48W **12 C6**
Leyland *U.K.* 53°42N 2°43W **12 D5**
Leyte □ *Phil.* 11°0N 125°0E **37 B7**
Lezhë *Albania* 41°47N 19°39E **23 D8**
Lezhi *China* 30°19N 104°58E **34 B5**
Lhasa *China* 29°25N 90°58E **30 F7**
Lhazê *China* 29°5N 87°38E **30 F6**
L'Hermite, I. *Chile* 55°50S 68°0W **96 H3**
Lhokkruet *Indonesia* 4°55N 95°24E **36 D1**
Lhokseumawe *Indonesia* 5°10N 97°10E **36 C1**
Li *Thailand* 17°48N 98°57E **38 D2**
Li Jiang ➘ *China* 24°40N 110°40E **35 E8**
Li Jiang △ *China* 24°38N 110°38E **35 E8**
Li Shan *China* 35°30N 111°56E **32 G6**
Li Shui ➘ *China* 29°24N 112°1E **35 C9**
Li Xian *Gansu, China* 34°10N 105°5E **32 G3**
Li Xian *Hebei, China* 38°30N 115°35E **32 E8**
Li Xian *Hunan, China* 29°36N 111°42E **35 C8**
Liancheng *China* 25°42N 116°40E **35 E11**
Liancourt Rocks *Asia* 37°15N 131°52E **29 F5**
Lianga *Phil.* 8°38N 126°6E **37 C7**
Liangcheng *Nei Monggol Zizhiqu,*
  China 40°28N 112°25E **32 D7**
Liangcheng *Shandong,*
  China 35°32N 119°37E **33 G10**
Liangdang *China* 33°56N 106°18E **32 H4**
Lianghe *China* 24°50N 98°2E **34 E8**
Lianghekou *China* 29°11N 108°44E **34 C7**
Liangping *China* 30°38N 107°46E **34 B6**
Liangpran *Indonesia* 1°4N 114°23E **36 D4**
Lianhua *China* 27°3N 113°54E **35 D9**
Lianhua Shan *China* 23°40N 115°48E **35 F10**
Lianjiang *Fujian, China* 26°12N 119°27E **35 D12**
Lianjiang *Guangdong,*
  China 21°40N 110°20E **35 G8**
Lianping *China* 24°26N 114°30E **35 E10**
Lianshan *China* 24°38N 112°8E **35 E9**
Lianshanguan *China* 40°53N 123°43E **33 D12**
Lianshui *China* 33°42N 119°20E **33 H10**
Lianyuan *China* 27°40N 111°38E **35 D8**
Lianyungang *China* 34°40N 119°11E **33 G10**
Lianzhou *China* 24°51N 112°22E **35 E9**
Liao He ➘ *China* 41°0N 121°50E **33 D11**
Liaocheng *China* 36°28N 115°58E **32 F8**
Liaodong Bandao *China* 40°0N 122°30E **33 E12**
Liaodong Wan *China* 40°20N 121°10E **33 D11**

Liaoning □ *China* 41°40N 122°30E **33 D12**
Liaotung, G. of = Liaodong Wan
  China 40°20N 121°10E **33 D11**
Liaoyang *China* 41°15N 122°58E **33 D12**
Liaoyuan *China* 42°58N 125°2E **33 C13**
Liaozhong *China* 41°23N 122°50E **33 D12**
Liard ➘ *Canada* 61°51N 121°18W **70 A4**
Liard River *Canada* 59°25N 126°5W **70 B3**
Liari *Pakistan* 25°37N 66°30E **42 G2**
Libanggaon *Nepal* 28°18N 82°38E **43 E10**
Libau = Liepāja *Latvia* 56°30N 21°0E **9 H19**
Libby *U.S.A.* 48°23N 115°33W **76 B6**
Libenge
  Dem. Rep. of the Congo 3°40N 18°55E **54 D3**
Liberal *U.S.A.* 37°3N 100°55W **80 G3**
Liberec *Czech Rep.* 50°47N 15°7E **16 C8**
Liberia *Costa Rica* 10°40N 85°30W **88 D2**
Liberia ■ *W. Afr.* 6°30N 9°30W **52 G4**
Libertador □ *Chile* 34°15S 70°45W **94 C1**
Liberty *Mo., U.S.A.* 39°15N 94°25W **80 F7**
Liberty *N.Y., U.S.A.* 41°48N 74°45W **83 E10**
Liberty *Pa., U.S.A.* 41°34N 77°6W **82 E7**
Liberty *Tex., U.S.A.* 30°3N 94°48W **84 F7**
Liberty-Newark Int. ✖ (EWR)
  U.S.A. 40°42N 74°10W **83 F10**
Lîbîya, Sahrâ' *Africa* 25°0N 25°0E **53 C10**
Libo *China* 25°22N 107°53E **34 E6**
Libobo, Tanjung *Indonesia* 0°54S 128°28E **37 E7**
Libode *S. Africa* 31°33S 29°2E **57 D4**
Libong, Ko *Thailand* 7°15N 99°23E **39 J2**
Libourne *France* 44°55N 0°14W **20 D3**
Libramont *Belgium* 49°55N 5°23E **15 E5**
Libreville *Gabon* 0°25N 9°26E **54 D1**
Libya ■ *N. Afr.* 27°0N 17°0E **53 C9**
Libyan Desert = Lîbîya, Sahrâ'
  Africa 25°0N 25°0E **53 C10**
Libyan Plateau = Ed Déffa
  Egypt 30°40N 26°30E **53 B11**
Licantén *Chile* 35°55S 72°0W **94 D1**
Licata *Italy* 37°6N 13°56E **22 F5**
Licheng *China* 36°28N 113°20E **32 F7**
Lichfield *U.K.* 52°41N 1°49W **13 E6**
Lichinga *Mozam.* 13°13S 35°11E **55 G7**
Lichtenburg *S. Africa* 26°8S 26°8E **56 C4**
Lichuan *Hubei, China* 30°18N 108°57E **34 B7**
Lichuan *Jiangxi, China* 27°18N 116°55E **35 D11**
Licking ➘ *U.S.A.* 39°6N 84°30W **81 F11**
Lida *Belarus* 53°53N 25°15E **17 B13**
Lidköping *Sweden* 58°31N 13°7E **9 G15**
Liebig, Mt. *Australia* 23°18S 131°22E **60 D5**
Liechtenstein ■ *Europe* 47°8N 9°35E **20 C8**
Liège *Belgium* 50°38N 5°35E **15 D5**
Liège □ *Belgium* 50°32N 5°35E **15 D5**
Liegnitz = Legnica *Poland* 51°12N 16°10E **16 C9**
Lieksa *Finland* 63°18N 30°2E **8 E24**
Lienyünchiangshih =
  Lianyungang *China* 34°40N 119°11E **33 G10**
Lienz *Austria* 46°50N 12°46E **16 E7**
Liepāja *Latvia* 56°30N 21°0E **9 H19**
Lier *Belgium* 51°7N 4°34E **15 C4**
Lietuva = Lithuania ■
  Europe 55°30N 24°0E **9 J21**
Lièvre ➘ *Canada* 45°31N 75°26W **72 C4**
Liffey ➘ *Ireland* 53°21N 6°13W **10 C5**
Lifford *Ireland* 54°51N 7°29W **10 B4**
Lifudzin *Russia* 44°21N 134°58E **28 B7**
Lightning Ridge *Australia* 29°22S 148°0E **63 D4**
Ligonier *U.S.A.* 40°15N 79°14W **82 F5**
Liguria □ *Italy* 44°30N 8°50E **20 D8**
Ligurian Sea *Medit. S.* 43°20N 9°0E **22 C3**
Lihou Reefs and Cays
  Australia 17°25S 151°40E **62 B5**
Lihué Calel △ *Argentina* 38°0S 65°10W **94 D2**
Lijiang *China* 26°55N 100°20E **34 D3**
Lik ➘ *Laos* 18°31N 102°30E **38 C4**
Likasi
  Dem. Rep. of the Congo 10°55S 26°48E **54 G5**
L'Île-Rousse *France* 42°38N 8°57E **20 E8**
Liling *China* 27°42N 113°29E **35 D9**
Lille *France* 50°38N 3°3E **20 A5**
Lille Bælt *Denmark* 55°20N 9°45E **9 J13**
Lillehammer *Norway* 61°8N 10°30E **8 F14**
Lillesand *Norway* 58°15N 8°23E **9 G13**
Lillian Pt. *Australia* 27°40S 126°6E **61 E4**
Lillooet *Canada* 50°44N 121°57W **70 C4**
Lillooet ➘ *Canada* 49°15N 121°57W **70 D4**
Lilongwe *Malawi* 14°0S 33°48E **55 G6**
Liloy *Phil.* 8°4N 122°39E **37 C6**
Lim ➘ *Europe* 43°45N 19°15E **23 C8**
Lima *Indonesia* 3°39S 127°58E **37 E7**
Lima *Mont., U.S.A.* 44°38N 112°36W **76 D7**
Lima *N.Y., U.S.A.* 42°54N 77°36W **82 D7**
Lima *Ohio, U.S.A.* 40°44N 84°6W **81 E11**
Lima ➘ *Portugal* 41°41N 8°50W **21 B1**
Limassol *Cyprus* 34°42N 33°1E **46 C2**
Limavady *U.K.* 55°3N 6°56W **10 A5**
Limay ➘ *Argentina* 39°0S 68°0W **96 D3**
Limay Mahuida
  Argentina 37°10S 66°45W **94 D2**
Limbang *Malaysia* 4°42N 115°6E **36 D5**
Limbaži *Latvia* 57°31N 24°42E **9 H21**
Limbdi *India* 22°34N 71°51E **42 H4**
Limbe *Cameroon* 4°1N 9°10E **54 D1**
Limburg *Germany* 50°22N 8°4E **16 C5**
Limburg □ *Belgium* 51°2N 5°25E **15 C5**
Limburg □ *Neths.* 51°20N 5°55E **15 C5**
Limeira *Brazil* 22°35S 47°28W **95 A6**
Limerick *Ireland* 52°40N 8°37E **10 D3**
Limerick *U.S.A.* 43°41N 70°48W **83 C14**
Limerick □ *Ireland* 52°30N 8°50W **10 D3**
Limestone *U.S.A.* 42°2N 78°38W **82 D6**
Limestone ➘ *Canada* 56°31N 94°7W **71 B10**
Limfjorden *Denmark* 56°55N 9°0E **9 H13**
Limia = Lima ➘ *Portugal* 41°41N 8°50W **21 B1**
Limingen *Norway* 64°48N 13°35E **8 D15**
Limmen ◎ *Australia* 15°15S 135°30E **62 B2**
Limmen Bight *Australia* 14°40S 135°35E **62 A2**
Limmen Bight ➘
  Australia 15°7S 135°44E **62 B2**

Limnos *Greece* 39°50N 25°5E **23** E11
Limoges *Canada* 45°20N 75°16W **83** A9
Limoges *France* 45°50N 1°15E **20** D4
Limón *Costa Rica* 10°0N 83°2W **88** E3
Limon *U.S.A.* 39°16N 103°41W **76** G12
Limousin □ *France* 45°30N 1°30E **20** D4
Limoux *France* 43°4N 2°12E **20** E5
Limpopo □ *S. Africa* 24°5S 29°0E **57** B4
Limpopo → *Africa* 25°5S 33°30E **57** C5
Limuru *Kenya* 1°2S 36°35E **54** E7
Lin Xian *China* 37°57N 110°58E **32** F6
Lin'an *China* 30°15N 119°42E **35** B12
Linares *Chile* 35°50S 71°40W **94** D1
Linares *Mexico* 24°52N 99°34W **87** C5
Linares *Spain* 38°10N 3°40W **21** C4
Lincang *China* 23°58N 100°1E **34** F3
Lincheng *China* 37°25N 114°30E **32** F8
Linchuan *China* 27°57N 116°15E **35** D11
Lincoln = Beamsville
   Canada 43°12N 79°28W **82** C5
Lincoln *Argentina* 34°55S 61°30W **94** C3
Lincoln *N.Z.* 43°38S 172°30E **59** E4
Lincoln *U.K.* 53°14N 0°32W **12** D7
Lincoln *Calif., U.S.A.* 38°54N 121°17W **78** G5
Lincoln *Ill., U.S.A.* 40°9N 89°22W **80** E9
Lincoln *Kans., U.S.A.* 39°3N 98°9W **80** F4
Lincoln *Maine, U.S.A.* 45°22N 68°30W **81** C19
Lincoln *N.H., U.S.A.* 44°3N 71°40W **83** B13
Lincoln *N. Mex., U.S.A.* 33°30N 105°23W **77** K11
Lincoln *Nebr., U.S.A.* 40°49N 96°41W **80** E5
Lincoln City *U.S.A.* 44°57N 124°1W **76** D1
Lincoln Hav = Lincoln Sea
   Arctic 84°0N 55°0W **69** A21
Lincoln Sea *Arctic* 84°0N 55°0W **69** A21
Lincolnshire □ *U.K.* 53°14N 0°32W **12** D7
Lincolnshire Wolds *U.K.* 53°26N 0°13W **12** D7
Lincolnton *U.S.A.* 35°29N 81°16W **85** D14
Lind *U.S.A.* 46°58N 118°37W **76** C4
Linda *U.S.A.* 39°8N 121°34W **78** F5
Lindeman I. *Australia* 20°27S 149°3E **62** b
Lindeman Islands △
   Australia 20°28S 149°5E **62** b
Linden *Guyana* 6°0N 58°10W **92** B7
Linden *Ala., U.S.A.* 32°18N 87°48W **85** E11
Linden *Calif., U.S.A.* 38°1N 121°5W **78** G5
Linden *Tex., U.S.A.* 33°1N 94°22W **84** E7
Lindenhurst *U.S.A.* 40°41N 73°23W **83** F11
Lindesnes *Norway* 57°58N 7°3E **9** H12
Lindi *Tanzania* 9°58S 39°38E **54** F7
Lindi →
   Dem. Rep. of the Congo 0°33N 25°5E **54** D5
Lindley *U.S.A.* 42°1N 77°8W **82** D7
Lindos *Greece* 36°6N 28°4E **23** F13
Lindsay *Canada* 44°22N 78°43W **82** B6
Lindsay *Calif., U.S.A.* 36°12N 119°5W **78** J7
Lindsay *Okla., U.S.A.* 34°50N 97°38W **84** H6
Lindsborg *U.S.A.* 38°35N 97°40W **80** F5
Line Islands *Pac. Oc.* 7°0N 160°0W **65** H12
Linesville *U.S.A.* 41°39N 80°26W **82** E4
Linfen *China* 36°3N 111°30E **32** F6
Ling Xian *Hunan, China* 26°29N 113°48E **35** D9
Ling Xian *Shandong,*
   China 37°22N 116°30E **32** F9
Lingal *India* 16°17N 78°31E **45** F4
Linganamakki Res. *India* 14°6N 74°52E **45** G2
Lingao *China* 19°56N 109°42E **38** C7
Lingayen *Phil.* 16°1N 120°14E **37** A6
Lingayen G. *Phil.* 16°10N 120°15E **37** A6
Lingbao *China* 34°31N 110°51E **32** G6
Lingbi *China* 33°33N 117°33E **33** H9
Lingchuan *Guangxi Zhuangzu,*
   China 25°26N 110°21E **35** E8
Lingchuan *Shanxi, China* 35°45N 113°12E **32** G7
Lingding Yang *China* 22°25N 113°44E **31** a
Lingen *Germany* 52°31N 7°19E **16** B4
Lingga *Indonesia* 0°12S 104°37E **36** E2
Lingga, Kepulauan
   Indonesia 0°10S 104°30E **36** E2
Lingga Arch. = Lingga, Kepulauan
   Indonesia 0°10S 104°30E **36** E2
Linghai *China* 41°11N 121°22E **33** D11
Lingle *U.S.A.* 42°8N 104°21W **76** E11
Lingshan *China* 39°28N 114°22E **32** E8
Lingshi *China* 36°48N 111°48E **32** F6
Lingshou *China* 38°20N 114°20E **32** E8
Lingshui *China* 18°27N 110°0E **38** C8
Lingsugur *India* 16°10N 76°31E **45** F3
Lingtai *China* 35°0N 107°40E **32** G4
Linguère *Senegal* 15°25N 15°5W **52** E2
Lingui *China* 25°12N 110°2E **35** E8
Lingwu *China* 38°6N 106°20E **32** E4
Lingyuan *China* 41°10N 119°15E **33** D10
Lingyun *China* 25°2N 106°35E **34** E6
Linhai *China* 28°50N 121°8E **35** C13
Linhares *Brazil* 19°25S 40°4W **93** G10
Linhe *China* 40°48N 107°20E **32** D4
Linjiang *China* 41°50N 127°0E **33** D14
Linköping *Sweden* 58°28N 15°36E **9** G16
Linkou *China* 45°15N 130°18E **33** B16
Linli *China* 29°27N 111°30E **35** C8
Linnhe, L. *U.K.* 56°36N 5°25W **11** E3
Linosa *Medit. S.* 35°51N 12°50E **22** G5
Linqi *China* 35°45N 113°52E **32** G7
Linqing *China* 36°50N 115°42E **32** F8
Linqu *China* 36°25N 118°30E **33** F10
Linquan *China* 33°5N 115°17E **35** A10
Lins *Brazil* 21°40S 49°44W **95** A6
Linshu *China* 34°53N 118°38E **35** G10
Linshui *China* 30°21N 106°57E **34** B6
Linstead *Jamaica* 18°8N 77°2W **88** a
Lintao *China* 35°26N 103°58E **32** G2
Lintong *China* 34°20N 109°10E **32** G5
Linwood *Canada* 43°35N 80°43W **82** C4
Linwu *China* 25°19N 112°31E **35** E9
Linxi *Hebei, China* 39°42N 118°26E **33** E10
Linxi *Liaoning, China* 43°36N 118°2E **33** C10

Linxia *China* 35°36N 103°10E **30** D9
Linxiang *China* 29°28N 113°23E **35** C9
Linyanti → *Africa* 17°50S 25°5E **56** A4
Linyi *Shandong, China* 37°13N 116°54E **32** F9
Linyi *Shandong, China* 35°5N 118°21E **33** G10
Linying *China* 33°48N 113°56E **32** H7
Linz *Austria* 48°18N 14°18E **16** D8
Linzhenzhen *China* 36°30N 109°59E **32** F5
Linzhou *China* 36°4N 113°49E **32** F7
Linzi *China* 36°50N 118°20E **33** F10
Lion, G. du *France* 43°10N 4°0E **20** E6
Lions, G. of = Lion, G. du
   France 43°10N 4°0E **20** E6
Lion's Head *Canada* 44°58N 81°15W **82** B3
Lipa *Phil.* 13°57N 121°10E **37** B6
Lípari *Italy* 38°26N 14°58E **22** E6
Lípari, Is. = Eólie, Ís. *Italy* 38°30N 14°57E **22** E6
Lipcani *Moldova* 48°14N 26°48E **17** D14
Liperi *Finland* 62°31N 29°24E **8** E23
Lipetsk *Russia* 52°37N 39°35E **18** D6
Liping *China* 26°15N 109°7E **34** D7
Lipkany = Lipcani
   Moldova 48°14N 26°48E **17** D14
Lipovets *Ukraine* 49°12N 29°1E **17** D15
Lippe → *Germany* 51°39N 6°36E **16** C4
Lipscomb *U.S.A.* 36°14N 100°16W **84** C4
Liptrap, C. *Australia* 38°50S 145°55E **63** F4
Lipu *China* 24°30N 110°22E **35** E8
Lira *Uganda* 2°17N 32°57E **54** D6
Liria = Lliria *Spain* 39°37N 0°35W **21** C5
Lisala *Dem. Rep. of the Congo* 2°12N 21°38E **54** D4
Lisbon *N. Dak., U.S.A.* 46°27N 97°41W **80** B5
Lisbon *N.H., U.S.A.* 44°13N 71°55W **83** B13
Lisbon *N.Y., U.S.A.* 44°43N 75°19W **83** B9
Lisbon *Ohio, U.S.A.* 40°46N 80°46W **82** F4
Lisbon Falls *U.S.A.* 44°0N 70°4W **81** D18
Lisburn *U.K.* 54°31N 6°3W **10** B5
Lisburne, C. *U.S.A.* 68°53N 166°13W **74** B6
Liscannor B. *Ireland* 52°55N 9°24W **10** D2
Lisdoonvarna *Ireland* 53°2N 9°18W **10** C2
Lishe Jiang → *China* 24°15N 101°35E **34** E3
Lishi *China* 37°31N 111°8E **32** F6
Lishu *China* 43°20N 124°18E **33** C13
Lishui *Jiangsu, China* 31°38N 119°2E **35** B12
Lishui *Zhejiang, China* 28°28N 119°54E **35** C12
Lisianski I. *U.S.A.* 26°2N 174°0W **75** K5
Lisichansk = Lysychansk
   Ukraine 48°55N 38°30E **19** E6
Lisieux *France* 49°10N 0°12E **20** B4
Liski *Russia* 51°3N 39°30E **19** D6
Lismore *Australia* 28°44S 153°21E **63** D5
Lismore *Ireland* 52°8N 7°55W **10** D4
Lista *Norway* 58°7N 6°39E **9** G12
Lister, Mt. *Antarctica* 78°0S 162°0E **5** D11
Liston *Australia* 28°39S 152°6E **63** D5
Listowel *Canada* 43°44N 80°58W **82** C4
Listowel *Ireland* 52°27N 9°29W **10** D2
Litang *Guangxi Zhuangzu,*
   China 23°12N 109°8E **34** F7
Litang *Sichuan, China* 30°1N 100°17E **34** B3
Litang Qu → *China* 28°4N 101°32E **34** C3
Litani → *Lebanon* 33°20N 35°15E **48** B4
Litchfield *Calif., U.S.A.* 40°24N 120°23W **78** E6
Litchfield *Conn., U.S.A.* 41°45N 73°11W **83** E11
Litchfield *Ill., U.S.A.* 39°11N 89°39W **80** F9
Litchfield *Minn., U.S.A.* 45°8N 94°32W **80** C6
Litchfield △ *Australia* 13°14S 131°1E **60** B5
Lithgow *Australia* 33°25S 150°8E **63** E5
Lithino, Ákra *Greece* 34°55N 24°44E **23** G11
Lithuania ■ *Europe* 55°30N 24°0E **9** J21
Lititz *U.S.A.* 40°9N 76°18W **83** F8
Litoměřice *Czech Rep.* 50°33N 14°10E **16** C8
Little Abaco *Bahamas* 26°50N 77°30W **88** A4
Little Andaman I. *India* 10°45N 92°30E **45** J11
Little Barrier I. *N.Z.* 36°12S 175°8E **59** B5
Little Basses *Sri Lanka* 6°24N 81°43E **45** L5
Little Belt Mts. *U.S.A.* 46°40N 110°45W **76** C8
Little Bighorn Battlefield △
   U.S.A. 45°34N 107°25W **76** D10
Little Blue → *U.S.A.* 39°42N 96°41W **80** F5
Little Buffalo → *Canada* 61°0N 113°46W **70** A6
Little Cayman *Cayman Is.* 19°41N 80°3W **88** C3
Little Churchill →
   Canada 57°30N 95°22W **71** B9
Little Coco I. *Burma* 14°0N 93°13E **45** H11
Little Colorado →
   U.S.A. 36°12N 111°48W **77** H8
Little Current *Canada* 45°55N 82°0W **72** C3
Little Current → *Canada* 50°57N 84°36W **72** B3
Little Diomede I. *U.S.A.* 65°45N 168°56W **74** B6
Little Falls *Minn., U.S.A.* 45°59N 94°22W **80** C6
Little Falls *N.Y., U.S.A.* 43°3N 74°51W **83** C10
Little Fork → *U.S.A.* 48°31N 93°35W **80** A7
Little Grand Rapids
   Canada 52°0N 95°29W **71** C9
Little Humboldt →
   U.S.A. 41°1N 117°43W **76** F5
Little Inagua I. *Bahamas* 21°40N 73°50W **89** B5
Little Karoo *S. Africa* 33°45S 21°0E **56** D3
Little Khingan Mts. = Xiao
   Hinggan Ling *China* 49°0N 127°0E **31** B14
Little Lake *U.S.A.* 35°56N 117°55W **79** K9
Little Laut Is. = Laut Kecil,
   Kepulauan *Indonesia* 4°45S 115°40E **36** E5
Little Mecatina = Petit-
   Mécatina → *Canada* 50°40N 59°30W **73** B8
Little Minch *U.K.* 57°35N 6°45W **11** D2
Little Missouri →
   U.S.A. 47°36N 102°25W **80** B2
Little Nicobar *India* 7°20N 93°40E **45** L11
Little Ouse → *U.K.* 52°22N 1°12E **13** E9
Little Rann *India* 23°25N 71°25E **42** H4
Little Red → *U.S.A.* 35°11N 91°27W **84** D9
Little River *N.Z.* 43°45S 172°49E **59** E4
Little Rock *U.S.A.* 34°45N 92°17W **84** D8
Little Sable Pt. *U.S.A.* 43°38N 86°33W **80** D10
Little Sioux → *U.S.A.* 41°48N 96°4W **80** E5
Little Smoky → *Canada* 54°44N 117°11W **70** C5
Little Snake → *U.S.A.* 40°27N 108°26W **76** F9

Little Tobago
   Trin. & Tob. 11°18N 60°30W **93** J16
Little Valley *U.S.A.* 42°15N 78°48W **82** D6
Little Wabash → *U.S.A.* 37°55N 88°5W **80** G9
Little White → *U.S.A.* 43°40N 100°40W **80** D3
Little Zab = Zāb aṣ Şaghīr →
   Iraq 35°17N 43°29E **46** C4
Littlefield *U.S.A.* 33°55N 102°20W **84** E3
Littlehampton *U.K.* 50°49N 0°32W **13** G7
Littleton *U.S.A.* 44°18N 71°46W **83** B13
Liu He → *China* 40°55N 121°35E **33** D11
Liu Jiang → *China* 23°55N 109°30E **34** F7
Liuba *China* 33°38N 106°55E **34** A6
Liucheng *China* 24°38N 109°14E **34** E7
Liugou *China* 40°57N 118°15E **33** D10
Liuhe *China* 42°17N 125°43E **33** C13
Liuheng Dao *China* 29°40N 122°5E **35** C14
Liujiang *China* 24°26N 109°11E **34** E7
Liukang Tenggaja = Sabalana,
   Kepulauan *Indonesia* 6°45S 118°50E **37** F5
Liupan Shan *China* 35°39N 106°12E **32** G4
Liupanshui *China* 26°38N 104°48E **34** D5
Liuwa Plain *Zambia* 14°20S 22°30E **55** G4
Liuyang *China* 28°10N 113°37E **35** C9
Liuzhou *China* 24°22N 109°22E **34** E7
Liuzhuang *China* 33°12N 120°18E **33** H11
Livadia *Greece* 38°27N 22°54E **23** E10
Live Oak *Calif., U.S.A.* 39°17N 121°40W **78** F5
Live Oak *Fla., U.S.A.* 30°18N 82°59W **85** F13
Lively *Canada* 46°26N 81°9W **81** B13
Livermore *U.S.A.* 37°41N 121°47W **78** H5
Livermore, Mt. *U.S.A.* 30°38N 104°11W **84** F2
Livermore Falls *U.S.A.* 44°29N 70°11W **81** C18
Liverpool *Australia* 33°54S 150°58E **63** B5
Liverpool *Canada* 44°5N 64°41W **73** D7
Liverpool *U.K.* 53°25N 3°0W **12** D4
Liverpool *U.S.A.* 43°6N 76°13W **83** C8
Liverpool Bay *U.K.* 53°30N 3°20W **12** D4
Liverpool Ra. *Australia* 31°50S 150°30E **63** E5
Livingston *Guatemala* 15°50N 88°50W **88** C2
Livingston *U.K.* 55°54N 3°30W **11** F5
Livingston *Ala., U.S.A.* 32°35N 88°11W **85** E10
Livingston *Calif., U.S.A.* 37°23N 120°43W **78** H6
Livingston *Mont.,*
   U.S.A. 45°40N 110°34W **76** D8
Livingston *S.C., U.S.A.* 33°38N 81°7W **85** E14
Livingston *Tenn., U.S.A.* 36°23N 85°19W **85** C12
Livingston *Tex., U.S.A.* 30°43N 94°56W **84** F7
Livingston, L. *U.S.A.* 30°50N 95°10W **84** F7
Livingston Manor
   U.S.A. 41°54N 74°50W **83** E10
Livingstone *Zambia* 17°46S 25°52E **55** H5
Livny *Russia* 52°30N 37°30E **18** D6
Livonia *Mich., U.S.A.* 42°23N 83°23W **81** D12
Livonia *N.Y., U.S.A.* 42°49N 77°40W **82** D7
Livorno *Italy* 43°33N 10°19E **22** C4
Livramento *Brazil* 30°55S 55°30W **95** C4
Lixi *China* 26°23N 101°59E **34** D3
Lixian *China* 31°23N 103°13E **34** B4
Lixin *China* 33°8N 116°13E **35** A11
Liyang *China* 31°26N 119°28E **35** B12
Lizard I. *Australia* 14°42S 145°30E **62** A4
Lizard Pt. *U.K.* 49°57N 5°13W **13** H2
Ljubljana *Slovenia* 46°4N 14°33E **16** E8
Ljungan → *Sweden* 62°18N 17°23E **8** E17
Ljungby *Sweden* 56°49N 13°55E **9** H15
Ljusdal *Sweden* 61°46N 16°3E **8** F17
Ljusnan → *Sweden* 61°12N 17°8E **8** F17
Ljusne *Sweden* 61°13N 17°7E **8** F17
Llancanelo, Salina
   Argentina 35°40S 69°8W **94** D2
Llandeilo *U.K.* 51°53N 3°59W **13** F4
Llandovery *U.K.* 51°59N 3°48W **13** F4
Llandrindod Wells *U.K.* 52°14N 3°22W **13** E4
Llandudno *U.K.* 53°19N 3°50W **12** D4
Llanelli *U.K.* 51°41N 4°10W **13** F3
Llanes *Spain* 43°25N 4°50W **21** A3
Llanfair-ym-Muallt = Builth Wells
   U.K. 52°9N 3°25W **13** E4
Llangollen *U.K.* 52°58N 3°11W **12** E4
Llanidloes *U.K.* 52°27N 3°31W **13** E4
Llano *U.S.A.* 30°45N 98°41W **84** F5
Llano → *U.S.A.* 30°39N 98°26W **84** F5
Llano Estacado *U.S.A.* 33°30N 103°0W **84** E3
Llanos *S. Amer.* 5°0N 71°35W **92** C4
Llanos de Challe △ *Chile* 28°8S 71°1W **94** B1
Llanquihue, L. *Chile* 41°10S 72°50W **96** E1
Llanwrtyd Wells *U.K.* 52°7N 3°38W **13** E4
Lleida *Spain* 41°37N 0°39E **21** B6
Llera de Canales *Mexico* 23°19N 99°1W **87** C5
Lleyn Peninsula *U.K.* 52°51N 4°36W **12** E3
Llico *Chile* 34°46S 72°5W **94** C1
Lliria *Spain* 39°37N 0°35W **21** C5
Llobregat → *Spain* 41°19N 2°5E **21** B7
Lloret de Mar *Spain* 41°41N 2°53E **21** B7
Lloyd B. *Australia* 12°45S 143°27E **62** A3
Lloyd L. *Canada* 57°22N 108°57W **71** B7
Lloydminster *Canada* 53°17N 110°0W **71** C7
Llucmajor *Spain* 39°29N 2°53E **21** C7
Llullaillaco, Volcán
   S. Amer. 24°43S 68°30W **94** A2
Llullaillaco △ *Chile* 24°50S 68°51W **94** A2
Lo → *Vietnam* 21°18N 105°25E **38** B5
Loa *U.S.A.* 38°24N 111°39W **76** G8
Loa → *Chile* 21°26S 70°41W **94** A1
Loaita I. *S. China Sea* 10°41N 114°25E **36** B4
Loange →
   Dem. Rep. of the Congo 4°17S 20°2E **54** E4
Lobamba *Swaziland* 26°28S 31°12E **57** C5
Lobatse *Botswana* 25°12S 25°40E **56** C4
Loberia *Argentina* 38°10S 58°40W **94** D4
Lobito *Angola* 12°18S 13°35E **55** G2
Lobos *Argentina* 35°10S 59°0W **94** D4
Lobos, I. *Mexico* 27°20N 110°36W **86** B2
Loc Binh *Vietnam* 21°46N 106°54E **38** B6
Loc Ninh *Vietnam* 11°50N 106°34E **39** G6
Locarno *Switz.* 46°10N 8°47E **20** C8
Loch Garman = Wexford
   Ireland 52°20N 6°28W **10** D5

Loch Lomond and the Trossachs △
   U.K. 56°10N 4°40W **11** E4
Lochaber *U.K.* 56°59N 5°1W **11** E3
Locharbriggs *U.K.* 55°7N 3°35W **11** F5
Lochboisdale *U.K.* 57°9N 7°20W **11** D1
Loche, L. La *Canada* 56°30N 109°30W **71** B7
Lochem *Neths.* 52°9N 6°26E **15** B6
Loches *France* 47°7N 1°0E **20** C4
Lochgilphead *U.K.* 56°2N 5°26W **11** E3
Lochinver *U.K.* 58°9N 5°14W **11** C3
Lochmaddy *U.K.* 57°36N 7°10W **11** D1
Lochnagar *Australia* 23°33S 145°38E **62** C4
Lochnagar *U.K.* 56°57N 3°15W **11** E5
Lochy, L. *U.K.* 57°0N 4°53W **11** E4
Lock *Australia* 33°34S 135°46E **63** E2
Lock Haven *U.S.A.* 41°8N 77°28W **82** E7
Lockeford *U.S.A.* 38°10N 121°9W **78** G5
Lockeport *Canada* 43°47N 65°4W **73** D6
Lockerbie *U.K.* 55°7N 3°21W **11** F5
Lockhart *U.S.A.* 29°53N 97°40W **84** G6
Lockhart, L. *Australia* 33°15S 119°3E **61** F2
Lockhart River *Australia* 12°58S 143°30E **62** A3
Lockhart River ◎
   Australia 12°47S 143°20E **62** A3
Lockney *U.S.A.* 34°7N 101°27W **84** D4
Lockport *U.S.A.* 43°10N 78°42W **82** C6
Lod *Israel* 31°57N 34°54E **48** D3
Lodeinoye Pole *Russia* 60°44N 33°33E **18** B5
Lodge Bay *Canada* 52°14N 55°51W **73** B8
Lodge Grass *U.S.A.* 45°19N 107°22W **76** D10
Lodhran *Pakistan* 29°32N 71°30E **42** E4
Lodi *Italy* 45°19N 9°30E **20** D8
Lodi *Calif., U.S.A.* 38°8N 121°16W **78** G5
Lodi *Ohio, U.S.A.* 41°2N 82°1W **82** E3
Lodja *Dem. Rep. of the Congo* 3°30S 23°23E **54** E4
Lodwar *Kenya* 3°7N 35°36E **54** D7
Łódź *Poland* 51°45N 19°27E **17** C10
Loei *Thailand* 17°29N 101°35E **38** D3
Loeriesfontein *S. Africa* 31°0S 19°26E **56** D2
Lofoten *Norway* 68°30N 13°59E **8** B16
Logan *Iowa, U.S.A.* 41°39N 95°47W **80** E6
Logan *Ohio, U.S.A.* 39°32N 82°25W **81** F12
Logan *Utah, U.S.A.* 41°44N 111°50W **76** F8
Logan *W. Va., U.S.A.* 37°51N 81°59W **81** G13
Logan, Mt. *Canada* 60°34N 140°23W **68** E3
Logandale *U.S.A.* 36°36N 114°29W **79** J12
Logansport *Ind., U.S.A.* 40°45N 86°22W **80** E10
Logansport *La., U.S.A.* 31°58N 94°0W **84** F8
Logone → *Chad* 12°6N 15°2E **53** F9
Logroño *Spain* 42°28N 2°27E **21** A4
Lohardaga *India* 23°27N 84°45E **43** H11
Loharia *India* 23°45N 74°14E **42** H6
Loharu *India* 28°27N 75°49E **42** E6
Lohri Wah → *Pakistan* 27°27N 67°37E **42** F2
Loikaw *Burma* 19°40N 97°17E **41** K20
Loimaa *Finland* 60°50N 23°5E **8** F20
Loir → *France* 47°33N 0°32W **20** C3
Loire → *France* 47°16N 2°10W **20** C2
Loja *Ecuador* 3°59S 79°16W **92** D3
Loja *Spain* 37°10N 4°10W **21** D3
Loji = Kawasi *Indonesia* 1°38S 127°28E **37** E7
Lojung *China* 24°27N 109°36E **34** E7
Lokeren *Belgium* 51°6N 3°59E **15** C3
Lokgwabe *Botswana* 24°10S 21°50E **56** B3
Lokitaung *Kenya* 4°12N 35°48E **54** D7
Lokkan tekojärvi *Finland* 67°55N 27°35E **8** C22
Lokoja *Nigeria* 7°47N 6°45E **52** G7
Lokolo →
   Dem. Rep. of the Congo 1°43S 18°23E **54** E3
Lola, Mt. *U.S.A.* 39°26N 120°22W **78** F6
Lolland *Denmark* 54°45N 11°30E **9** J14
Lolo *U.S.A.* 46°45N 114°5W **76** C6
Lom *Bulgaria* 43°48N 23°12E **23** C10
Lom Kao *Thailand* 16°53N 101°14E **38** D3
Lom Sak *Thailand* 16°47N 101°15E **38** D3
Loma *U.S.A.* 47°56N 110°30W **76** C8
Loma Linda *U.S.A.* 34°3N 117°16W **79** L9
Lomami →
   Dem. Rep. of the Congo 0°46N 24°16E **54** D4
Lomas de Zamora
   Argentina 34°45S 58°24W **94** C4
Lombadina *Australia* 16°31S 122°54E **60** C3
Lombárdia □ *Italy* 45°40N 9°30E **20** D8
Lombardy = Lombárdia □
   Italy 45°40N 9°30E **20** D8
Lomblen *Indonesia* 8°30S 123°32E **37** F6
Lombok *Indonesia* 8°45S 116°30E **36** F5
Lombok, Selat *Indonesia* 8°30S 115°50E **37** K18
Lomé *Togo* 6°9N 1°20E **52** G6
Lomela
   Dem. Rep. of the Congo 2°19S 23°15E **54** E4
Lomela →
   Dem. Rep. of the Congo 0°15S 20°40E **54** E4
Lommel *Belgium* 51°14N 5°19E **15** C5
Lomond *Canada* 50°24N 112°36W **70** C6
Lomond, L. *U.K.* 56°8N 4°38W **11** E4
Lomonosov Ridge *Arctic* 88°0N 140°0E **4** A
Lomphat *Cambodia* 13°30N 106°59E **38** F6
Lompobatang *Indonesia* 5°24S 119°56E **37** F5
Lompoc *U.S.A.* 34°38N 120°28W **79** L6
Łomża *Poland* 53°10N 22°2E **17** B12
Lon, Ko *Thailand* 7°47N 98°23E **39** a
Lonavale *India* 18°46N 73°29E **44** E1
Loncoche *Chile* 39°20S 72°50W **96** D2
Londa *India* 15°30N 74°30E **45** G2
London *Canada* 42°59N 81°15W **82** D3
London *Ky., U.S.A.* 37°8N 84°5W **81** G11
London *Ohio, U.S.A.* 39°53N 83°27W **81** F12
London, Greater □ *U.K.* 51°36N 0°5W **13** F7
London Gatwick ✈ (LGW)
   U.K. 51°10N 0°11W **13** F7
London Stansted ✈ (STN)
   U.K. 51°54N 0°14E **13** F8
Londonderry *U.K.* 55°0N 7°20W **10** B4
Londonderry □ *U.K.* 55°0N 7°20W **10** B4
Londonderry, C.
   Australia 13°45S 126°55E **60** B4
Londonderry, I. *Chile* 55°0S 71°0W **96** H2

Londres *Argentina* 27°43S 67°7W **96** B3
Londrina *Brazil* 23°18S 51°10W **95** A5
Lone Pine *U.S.A.* 36°36N 118°4W **78** J8
Lonely Mine *Zimbabwe* 19°30S 28°49E **57** A4
Long B. *U.S.A.* 33°35N 78°45W **85** E15
Long Beach *Calif.,*
   U.S.A. 33°46N 118°11W **79** M8
Long Beach *N.Y., U.S.A.* 40°35N 73°39W **83** F11
Long Beach *Wash.,*
   U.S.A. 46°21N 124°3W **78** D2
Long Branch *U.S.A.* 40°18N 74°0W **83** F11
Long Creek *U.S.A.* 44°43N 119°6W **76** D4
Long Eaton *U.K.* 52°53N 1°15W **12** E6
Long I. *Australia* 20°22S 148°51E **62** b
Long I. *Bahamas* 23°20N 75°10W **89** B4
Long I. *Canada* 54°50N 79°20W **72** B4
Long I. *Ireland* 51°30N 9°34W **10** E2
Long I. *U.S.A.* 40°45N 73°30W **83** F11
Long Island Sd. *U.S.A.* 41°10N 73°0W **83** E12
Long L. *Canada* 49°30N 86°50W **72** C2
Long L. *U.S.A.* 44°0N 74°25W **83** C10
Long Lake *U.S.A.* 43°58N 74°25W **83** C10
Long Point *Canada* 42°34N 80°25W **82** D4
Long Point B. *Canada* 42°40N 80°10W **82** D4
Long Prairie *U.S.A.* 45°59N 94°52W **80** C6
Long Prairie → *U.S.A.* 46°20N 94°36W **80** B6
Long Pt. *Ont., Canada* 42°35N 80°2W **82** D4
Long Pt. *Ont., Canada* 43°56N 76°53W **83** C8
Long Range Mts. *Canada* 49°30N 57°30W **73** C8
Long Reef *Australia* 14°1S 125°48E **60** B4
Long Sault *Canada* 45°2N 74°53W **83** A10
Long Str. = Longa, Proliv
   Russia 70°0N 175°0E **27** C18
Long Thanh *Vietnam* 10°47N 106°57E **39** G6
Long Xian *China* 34°55N 106°55E **32** G4
Long Xuyen *Vietnam* 10°19N 105°28E **39** G5
Long'an *China* 23°10N 107°40E **34** F6
Longbenton *U.K.* 55°1N 1°31W **12** B6
Longboat Key *U.S.A.* 27°23N 82°39W **85** H13
Longchang *China* 29°18N 105°15E **34** C5
Longchuan *Guangdong,*
   China 24°5N 115°17E **35** E10
Longchuan *Yunnan, China* 24°23N 97°58E **34** E1
Longde *China* 35°30N 106°20E **32** G4
Longford *Australia* 41°32S 147°3E **63** G4
Longford *Ireland* 53°43N 7°49W **10** C4
Longford □ *Ireland* 53°42N 7°45W **10** C4
Longfort, An = Longford
   Ireland 53°43N 7°49W **10** C4
Longhai *China* 24°25N 117°46E **35** E11
Longhua *Guangdong, China* 22°39N 114°0E **31** a
Longhua *Hebei, China* 41°18N 117°45E **33** D9
Longhui *China* 27°7N 111°2E **35** D8
Longiram *Indonesia* 0°5S 115°45E **36** E5
Longjing *China* 42°46N 129°25E **33** C15
Longkou *Jiangxi, China* 26°8N 115°10E **35** D10
Longkou *Shandong,*
   China 37°40N 120°18E **33** F11
Longlac *Canada* 49°45N 86°25W **72** C2
Longli *China* 26°25N 106°58E **34** D6
Longlin *China* 24°47N 105°20E **34** E5
Longling *China* 24°37N 98°39E **34** E2
Longmeadow *U.S.A.* 42°3N 72°34W **83** D12
Longmen *China* 23°40N 114°18E **35** F10
Longmen Shiku *China* 34°28N 112°28E **32** G7
Longming *China* 22°59N 107°7E **34** F6
Longmont *U.S.A.* 40°10N 105°6W **76** F11
Longnan *China* 24°55N 114°47E **35** E10
Longnawan *Indonesia* 1°51N 114°55E **36** D4
Longquan *China* 28°7N 119°10E **35** C12
Longreach *Australia* 23°28S 144°14E **62** C3
Longshan *China* 29°29N 109°25E **34** C7
Longsheng *China* 25°48N 110°0E **35** E8
Longtan Dam *China* 25°5N 107°0E **34** E6
Longview *Tex., U.S.A.* 32°30N 94°44W **84** E7
Longview *Wash., U.S.A.* 46°8N 122°57W **78** D4
Longxi *China* 34°53N 104°40E **32** G3
Longxue Dao *China* 22°41N 113°38E **31** a
Longyan *China* 25°10N 117°0E **35** E11
Longyearbyen *Svalbard* 78°13N 15°40E **4** B8
Longyou *China* 29°1N 119°8E **35** C12
Longzhou *China* 22°22N 106°50E **34** F6
Lonoke *U.S.A.* 34°47N 91°54W **84** D9
Lonquimay *Chile* 38°26S 71°14W **96** D2
Lons-le-Saunier *France* 46°40N 5°31E **20** C6
Looe *U.K.* 50°22N 4°28W **13** G3
Lookout, C. *Canada* 55°18N 83°56W **72** A3
Lookout, C. *U.S.A.* 34°35N 76°32W **85** D16
Loon → *Alta., Canada* 57°8N 115°3W **70** B5
Loon → *Man., Canada* 55°53N 101°59W **71** B8
Loon Lake *Canada* 54°2N 109°10W **71** C7
Loongana *Australia* 30°52S 127°5E **61** F4
Loop Hd. *Ireland* 52°34N 9°56W **10** D2
Lop *China* 37°3N 80°11E **30** D5
Lop Nor = Lop Nur *China* 40°20N 90°10E **30** C7
Lop Nur *China* 40°20N 90°10E **30** C7
Lopatina, Gora *Russia* 50°47N 143°10E **27** D15
Lopatka, Mys *Russia* 50°52N 156°40E **27** D16
Lopburi *Thailand* 14°48N 100°37E **38** E3
Lopez *U.S.A.* 41°27N 76°20W **83** E8
Lopez, C. *Gabon* 0°47S 8°40E **54** E1
Lopphavet *Norway* 70°27N 21°15E **8** A19
Lora → *Afghan.* 31°35N 66°32E **40** D4
Lora, Hāmūn-i- *Pakistan* 29°38N 64°58E **40** E4
Lora Cr. → *Australia* 28°10S 135°22E **63** D2
Lora del Río *Spain* 37°39N 5°33W **21** D3
Lorain *U.S.A.* 41°28N 82°11W **82** E2
Loralai *Pakistan* 30°20N 68°41E **42** D3
Lorca *Spain* 37°41N 1°42W **21** D5
Lord Howe I. *Pac. Oc.* 31°33S 159°6E **58** E8
Lord Howe Rise *Pac. Oc.* 30°0S 162°30E **64** L8
Lord Loughborough I.
   Burma 10°25N 97°54E **39** G1
Lordsburg *U.S.A.* 32°21N 108°43W **77** K9
Lorestān □ *Iran* 33°30N 48°40E **47** C6
Loreto *Brazil* 7°5S 45°10W **93** E9
Loreto *Mexico* 26°0N 111°21W **86** B2
Lorient *France* 47°45N 3°23W **20** C2

Lormi *India* 22°17N 81°41E **43** H9
Lorn *U.K.* 56°26N 5°10W **11** E3
Lorn, Firth of *U.K.* 56°20N 5°40W **11** E3
Lorne *Australia* 38°33S 143°59E **63** F3
Lorraine □ *France* 48°53N 6°0E **20** B7
Los Alamos *Calif., U.S.A.* 34°44N 120°17W **79** L6
Los Alamos *N. Mex.,*
U.S.A. 35°53N 106°19W **77** J10
Los Altos *U.S.A.* 37°23N 122°7W **78** H4
Los Andes *Chile* 32°50S 70°40W **94** C1
Los Angeles *Chile* 37°28S 72°23W **94** D1
Los Angeles Aqueduct
U.S.A. 35°22N 118°5W **79** K9
Los Banos *U.S.A.* 37°4N 120°51W **78** H6
Los Blancos *Argentina* 23°40S 62°30W **94** A3
Los Cabos Int. ✈ (SJD)
Mexico 23°9N 109°43W **86** C3
Los Cardones △ *Argentina* 25°8S 65°55W **94** B2
Los Chiles *Costa Rica* 11°2N 84°43W **88** D3
Los Gatos *U.S.A.* 37°14N 121°59W **78** H5
Los Haïtises △ *Dom. Rep.* 19°4N 69°36W **89** C6
Los Hermanos, Is.
Venezuela 11°45N 64°25W **89** D7
Los Loros *Chile* 27°50S 70°6W **94** B1
Los Lunas *U.S.A.* 34°48N 106°44W **77** J10
Los Mochis *Mexico* 25°45N 108°57W **86** B3
Los Olivos *U.S.A.* 34°40N 120°7W **79** L6
Los Palacios *Cuba* 22°35N 83°15W **88** B3
Los Queñes *Chile* 35°1S 70°48W **94** D1
Los Reyes de Salgado
Mexico 19°35N 102°29W **86** D4
Los Roques, Is. *Venezuela* 11°50N 66°45W **89** D6
Los Teques *Venezuela* 10°21N 67°2W **92** A5
Los Testigos, Is. *Venezuela* 11°23N 63°6W **92** A6
Los Vilos *Chile* 32°10S 71°30W **94** C1
Lošinj *Croatia* 44°30N 14°30E **16** F8
Loskop Dam *S. Africa* 25°23S 29°20E **57** C4
Lossiemouth *U.K.* 57°42N 3°17W **11** D5
Lostwithiel *U.K.* 50°24N 4°41W **13** G3
Lot → *France* 44°18N 0°20E **20** D4
Lota *Chile* 37°5S 73°10W **94** D1
Loffåbåd *Iran* 37°32N 59°20E **47** B8
Lothair *S. Africa* 26°22S 30°27E **57** C5
Lotta → *Europe* 68°42N 31°6E **8** B24
Lotung *Taiwan* 24°41N 121°46E **35** E13
Loubomo *Congo* 4°9S 12°47E **54** E2
Loudi *China* 27°42N 111°59E **35** D8
Loudonville *U.S.A.* 40°38N 82°14W **82** F2
Louga *Senegal* 15°45N 16°5W **52** E2
Loughborough *U.K.* 52°47N 1°11W **12** E6
Lougheed I. *Canada* 77°26N 105°6W **69** B10
Loughrea *Ireland* 53°12N 8°33W **10** C3
Loughros More B. *Ireland* 54°48N 8°32W **10** B3
Louis Trichardt *S. Africa* 23°1S 29°43E **57** B4
Louis XIV, Pte. *Canada* 54°37N 79°45W **72** B4
Louisa *U.S.A.* 38°7N 82°36W **81** F12
Louisbourg *Canada* 45°55N 60°0W **73** C8
Louisburgh *Ireland* 53°46N 9°49W **10** C2
Louise I. *Canada* 52°55N 131°50W **70** C2
Louiseville *Canada* 46°20N 72°56W **72** C5
Louisiade Arch.
Papua N. Guinea 11°10S 153°0E **58** C8
Louisiana *U.S.A.* 39°27N 91°3W **80** F8
Louisiana □ *U.S.A.* 30°50N 92°0W **84** F9
Louisville *Ky., U.S.A.* 38°15N 85°46W **81** F11
Louisville *Miss., U.S.A.* 33°7N 89°3W **85** E10
Louisville *Ohio, U.S.A.* 40°50N 81°16W **82** F3
Louisville Ridge *Pac. Oc.* 31°0S 172°30W **64** L10
Loulé *Portugal* 37°9N 8°0W **21** D1
Loup City *U.S.A.* 41°17N 98°58W **80** E4
Loups Marins, Lacs des
Canada 56°30N 73°45W **72** A5
Lourdes *France* 43°6N 0°3W **20** E3
Lourdes-de-Blanc-Sablon
Canada 51°24N 57°12W **73** B8
Louth *Australia* 30°30S 145°8E **63** E4
Louth *Ireland* 53°58N 6°32W **10** C5
Louth *U.K.* 53°22N 0°1W **12** D7
Louth □ *Ireland* 53°56N 6°34W **10** C5
Louvain = Leuven
Belgium 50°52N 4°42E **15** D4
Louwsburg *S. Africa* 27°37S 31°7E **57** C5
Lovech *Bulgaria* 43°8N 24°42E **23** C11
Loveland *U.S.A.* 40°24N 105°5W **76** F11
Lovelock *U.S.A.* 40°11N 118°28W **76** F4
Lovell *U.S.A.* 44°50N 108°24W **76** D9
Lovisa = Loviisa *Finland* 60°28N 26°12E **8** F22
Lovington *U.S.A.* 32°57N 103°21W **77** K12
Lovisa = Loviisa *Finland* 60°28N 26°12E **8** F22
Low, L. *Canada* 52°29N 76°17W **72** B4
Low Pt. *Australia* 32°25S 127°25E **61** F4
Low Tatra = Nizké Tatry
Slovak Rep. 48°55N 19°30E **17** D10
Lowell *U.S.A.* 42°38N 71°19W **83** D13
Lowellville *U.S.A.* 41°2N 80°32W **82** E4
Löwen → *Namibia* 26°51S 18°17E **56** C2
Lower Alkali L. *U.S.A.* 41°16N 120°2W **76** F3
Lower Arrow L. *Canada* 49°40N 118°5W **70** D5
Lower California = Baja California
Mexico 31°10N 115°12W **86** A1
Lower Hutt *N.Z.* 41°10S 174°55E **59** D5
Lower Lake *U.S.A.* 38°55N 122°37W **78** G4
Lower Manitou L.
Canada 49°15N 93°0W **71** D10
Lower Post *Canada* 59°58N 128°30W **70** B3
Lower Red L. *U.S.A.* 47°58N 95°0W **80** B6
Lower Saxony = Niedersachsen □
Germany 52°50N 9°0E **16** B5
Lower Tunguska = Tunguska,
Nizhnyaya → *Russia* 65°48N 88°4E **27** C9
Lowestoft *U.K.* 52°29N 1°45E **13** E9
Lowgar □ *Afghan.* 34°0N 69°0E **40** B6
Lowicz *Poland* 52°6N 19°55E **17** B10
Lowther I. *Canada* 74°37N 97°0W **69** C12
Lowville *U.S.A.* 43°47N 75°29W **83** C9
Loxton *Australia* 34°28S 140°31E **63** E3
Loxton *S. Africa* 31°30S 22°22E **56** D3

Loyalton *U.S.A.* 39°41N 120°14W **78** F6
Loyalty Is. = Loyauté, Îs.
N. Cal. 20°50S 166°30E **58** D9
Loyang = Luoyang
China 34°40N 112°26E **32** G7
Loyauté, Îs. *N. Cal.* 20°50S 166°30E **58** D9
Loyev = Loyew *Belarus* 51°56N 30°46E **17** C16
Loyew *Belarus* 51°56N 30°46E **17** C16
Ltalaltuma ☉ *Australia* 23°57S 132°25E **60** D5
Lü Shan *China* 29°25N 115°55E **35** C10
Lü Shan △ *China* 29°26N 115°52E **35** C10
Lu Wo *China* 22°33N 114°6E **31** a
Lu'an *China* 31°45N 116°29E **35** B11
Luachimo *Angola* 7°23S 20°48E **54** F4
Luajan → *India* 24°44N 85°1E **43** G11
Lualaba →
Dem. Rep. of the Congo 0°26N 25°20E **54** D5
Luampa →
Dem. Rep. of the Congo 0°50S 23°36E **54** E4
Luan Chau *Vietnam* 21°38N 103°24E **34** G4
Luan He → *China* 39°20N 119°5E **33** E10
Luan Xian *China* 39°40N 118°40E **33** E10
Luancheng *Guangxi Zhuangzu,*
China 22°48N 108°55E **34** F7
Luancheng *Hebei, China* 37°53N 114°40E **32** F8
Luanda *Angola* 8°50S 13°15E **54** F2
Luang, Doi *Thailand* 18°30N 101°15E **38** C3
Luang, Thale *Thailand* 7°30N 100°15E **39** J3
Luang Nam Tha *Laos* 20°58N 101°30E **34** G3
Luang Prabang *Laos* 19°52N 102°10E **34** G4
Luangwa → *Zambia* 14°25S 30°25E **55** G6
Luangwa Valley *Zambia* 13°30S 31°30E **55** G6
Luangwe = Loange →
Dem. Rep. of the Congo 4°17S 20°2E **54** E4
Luanne *China* 40°55N 117°40E **33** D9
Luanping *China* 40°53N 117°23E **33** D9
Luanshya *Zambia* 13°3S 28°28E **55** G5
Luapula → *Africa* 9°26S 28°33E **54** F5
Luarca *Spain* 43°32N 6°32W **21** A2
Luashi
Dem. Rep. of the Congo 10°50S 23°36E **54** G4
Luau *Angola* 10°40S 22°10E **54** G4
Lubana, Ozero = Lubānas Ezers
Latvia 56°45N 27°0E **9** H22
Lubānas Ezers *Latvia* 56°45N 27°0E **9** H22
Lubang Is. *Phil.* 13°50N 120°12E **37** B6
Lubango *Angola* 14°55S 13°30E **55** G2
Lubao
Dem. Rep. of the Congo 5°17S 25°42E **54** F5
Lubbeck *Germany* 53°52N 10°40E **16** B6
Lubero = Luofu
Dem. Rep. of the Congo 0°10S 29°15E **54** E5
Lubicon L. *Canada* 56°23N 115°56W **70** B5
Lubilash →
Dem. Rep. of the Congo 6°2S 23°45E **54** F4
Lublin *Poland* 51°12N 22°38E **17** C12
Lubnān = Lebanon ■ *Asia* 34°0N 36°0E **48** B5
Lubnān, Jabal *Lebanon* 33°45N 35°45E **48** B4
Lubny *Ukraine* 50°3N 32°58E **26** D4
Lubudi
Dem. Rep. of the Congo 9°57S 25°58E **54** F5
Lubuklinggau *Indonesia* 3°15S 102°55E **36** E2
Lubuksikaping *Indonesia* 0°10N 100°15E **36** D2
Lubumbashi
Dem. Rep. of the Congo 11°40S 27°28E **55** G5
Lubutu
Dem. Rep. of the Congo 0°45S 26°30E **54** E5
Lucan *Canada* 43°11N 81°24W **82** C3
Lucan *Ireland* 53°22N 6°28W **10** C5
Lucania, Mt. *Canada* 61°1N 140°27W **68** E3
Lucas Channel = Main Channel
Canada 45°21N 81°45W **82** A3
Lucca *Italy* 43°50N 10°29E **22** C4
Luce Bay *U.K.* 54°45N 4°48W **11** G4
Lucea *Jamaica* 18°27N 78°10W **88** a
Lucedale *U.S.A.* 30°56N 88°35W **85** F10
Lucena *Phil.* 13°56N 121°37E **37** B6
Lucena *Spain* 37°27N 4°31W **21** D3
Lučenec *Slovak Rep.* 48°18N 19°42E **17** D10
Lucerne = Luzern *Switz.* 47°3N 8°18E **20** C8
Lucerne *U.S.A.* 39°6N 122°48W **78** F4
Lucerne Valley *U.S.A.* 34°27N 116°57W **79** L10
Lucheng *China* 36°20N 113°11E **32** F7
Luchuan *China* 22°21N 110°12E **35** F8
Lucia *U.S.A.* 36°2N 121°33W **78** J5
Lucinda *Australia* 18°32S 146°20E **62** B4
Luckenwalde *Germany* 52°5N 13°10E **16** B7
Luckhoff *S. Africa* 29°44S 24°43E **56** D3
Lucknow *Canada* 43°57N 81°31W **82** C3
Lucknow *India* 26°50N 81°0E **43** F9
Lüda = Dalian *China* 38°50N 121°40E **33** E11
Lüderitz *Namibia* 26°41S 15°8E **56** D2
Lüderitzbaai *Namibia* 26°36S 15°8E **56** D2
Ludhiana *India* 30°57N 75°56E **42** D6
Ludian *China* 27°10N 103°33E **34** D4
Luding Qiao *China* 29°53N 102°12E **34** C4
Ludington *U.S.A.* 43°57N 86°27W **80** D10
Ludlow *U.K.* 52°22N 2°42W **13** E5
Ludlow *Calif., U.S.A.* 34°43N 116°10W **79** L10
Ludlow *Pa., U.S.A.* 41°43N 78°56W **82** E6
Ludlow *Vt., U.S.A.* 43°24N 72°42W **83** C12
Ludvika *Sweden* 60°8N 15°14E **8** F16
Ludwigsburg *Germany* 48°53N 9°11E **16** D5
Ludwigshafen *Germany* 49°29N 8°26E **16** D5
Luena *Zambia* 14°47S 23°17E **55** G4
Luena Flats *Zambia* 14°30S 23°30E **55** G4
Lüeyang *China* 33°22N 106°10E **34** A6
Lufeng *Guangdong,*
China 22°57N 115°38E **35** F10
Lufeng *Yunnan, China* 25°0N 102°5E **34** E4
Lufira →
Dem. Rep. of the Congo 9°30S 27°0E **54** F5
Lufkin *U.S.A.* 31°21N 94°44W **84** F7
Luga *Russia* 58°40N 29°55E **9** G23
Lugano *Switz.* 46°1N 8°57E **20** C8
Lugansk = Luhansk
Ukraine 48°38N 39°15E **19** E6
Lugenda → *Mozam.* 11°25S 38°33E **55** G7
Lugh = Luuq *Somalia* 3°48N 42°34E **49** G3
Lugnaquilla *Ireland* 52°58N 6°28W **10** D5
Lugo *Italy* 44°25N 11°54E **22** B4
Lugo *Spain* 43°2N 7°35W **21** A2

Lugoj *Romania* 45°42N 21°57E **17** F11
Lugovoy = Qulan
Kazakhstan 42°55N 72°43E **26** E8
Luhansk *Ukraine* 48°38N 39°15E **19** E6
Luhe *China* 32°19N 118°50E **35** A12
Luhuo *China* 31°21N 100°48E **34** B3
Lui → *Angola* 8°21S 17°33E **54** F3
Luiana *Angola* 17°25S 22°59E **56** A3
Luiana → *Angola* 17°24S 23°3E **55** H4
Luichow Pen. = Leizhou Bandao
China 21°0N 110°0E **34** G7
Luimneach = Limerick
Ireland 52°40N 8°37W **10** D3
Luing *U.K.* 56°14N 5°39W **11** E3
Luís Correia *Brazil* 3°0S 41°35W **93** D10
Luján *Argentina* 34°45S 59°5W **94** C4
Lujiang *China* 31°20N 117°15E **35** B11
Lukang *Taiwan* 24°1N 120°22E **35** E13
Lukanga Swamp *Zambia* 14°30S 27°40E **55** G5
Lukenie →
Dem. Rep. of the Congo 3°0S 18°50E **54** E3
Lukla *Nepal* 27°42N 86°43E **43** F12
Łuków *Poland* 51°55N 22°23E **17** C12
Lülang Shan *China* 38°0N 111°15E **32** F6
Luleå *Sweden* 65°35N 22°10E **8** D20
Luleälven → *Sweden* 65°35N 22°10E **8** D20
Lüleburgaz *Turkey* 41°23N 27°22E **23** D12
Luliang *China* 25°0N 103°40E **34** E4
Luling *U.S.A.* 29°41N 97°39W **84** G6
Lulong *China* 39°53N 118°51E **33** E10
Lulonga →
Dem. Rep. of the Congo 1°0N 18°10E **54** D3
Lulua →
Dem. Rep. of the Congo 4°30S 20°30E **54** E4
Luma *Amer. Samoa* 14°16S 169°33W **59** b
Lumajang *Indonesia* 8°8S 113°13E **37** H15
Lumbala N'guimbo
Angola 14°18S 21°18E **55** G4
Lumberton *N.C., U.S.A.* 34°37N 79°0W **85** D15
Lumberton *Tex., U.S.A.* 30°16N 94°12W **84** F7
Lumsden *Canada* 50°39N 104°52W **71** C8
Lumsden *N.Z.* 45°44S 168°27E **59** F2
Lumut *Malaysia* 4°13N 100°37E **39** K3
Lumut, Tanjung *Indonesia* 3°50S 105°58E **36** E3
Luna *India* 23°43N 69°16E **42** H3
Lunan *China* 24°40N 103°18E **34** E4
Lunavada *India* 23°8N 73°37E **42** H5
Lund *Sweden* 55°44N 13°12E **9** J15
Lundazi *Zambia* 12°20S 33°7E **55** G6
Lundu *Malaysia* 1°40N 109°50E **36** D3
Lune → *U.K.* 54°0N 2°51W **12** C5
Lüneburg *Germany* 53°15N 10°24E **16** B6
Lüneburg Heath = Lüneburger
Heide *Germany* 53°10N 10°12E **16** B6
Lüneburger Heide
Germany 53°10N 10°12E **16** B6
Lunenburg *Canada* 44°22N 64°18W **73** D7
Lunéville *France* 48°36N 6°30E **20** D7
Lunglei *India* 22°55N 92°45E **41** H18
Luni *India* 26°0N 73°6E **42** G5
Luni → *India* 24°41N 71°14E **42** G4
Luninets = Luninyets
Belarus 52°15N 26°50E **17** B14
Luning *U.S.A.* 38°30N 118°11W **76** G4
Luninyets *Belarus* 52°15N 26°50E **17** B14
Lunkaransar *India* 28°29N 73°44E **42** E5
Luo He → *China* 34°35N 110°20E **32** G6
Luocheng *China* 24°48N 108°53E **34** E7
Luochuan *China* 35°45N 109°26E **32** G5
Luoci *China* 25°1N 102°18E **34** E4
Luodian *China* 25°24N 106°43E **34** E6
Luoding *China* 22°45N 111°40E **35** F8
Luofu *Dem. Rep. of the Congo* 0°10S 29°15E **54** E5
Luohe *China* 33°32N 114°2E **32** H8
Luojiang *China* 31°18N 104°33E **34** B5
Luonan *China* 34°5N 110°10E **32** G6
Luoning *China* 34°35N 111°40E **32** G6
Luoshan *China* 32°13N 114°30E **35** A10
Luotian *China* 30°46N 115°22E **35** B10
Luoxiao Shan *China* 26°30N 114°1E **35** D10
Luoyang *China* 34°40N 112°26E **32** G7
Luoyuan *China* 26°28N 119°30E **35** D12
Luozigou *China* 43°42N 130°18E **33** C16
Lupeng *China* 24°53N 104°21E **34** E5
Luquan *Hebei, China* 38°4N 114°17E **32** E8
Luquan *Yunnan, China* 25°35N 102°25E **34** E4
Luque *Paraguay* 25°19S 57°25W **94** B4
Luquillo, Sierra de
Puerto Rico 18°20N 65°47W **89** d
Luray *U.S.A.* 38°40N 78°28W **81** F14
Lurgan *U.K.* 54°28N 6°20W **10** B5
Lusaka *Zambia* 15°28S 28°16E **55** H5
Lusambo
Dem. Rep. of the Congo 4°58S 23°28E **54** E4
Luseland *Canada* 52°5N 109°24W **71** C7
Lushan *Henan, China* 33°45N 112°55E **32** H7
Lushan *Sichuan, China* 30°12N 102°52E **34** B4
Lushi *China* 34°3N 111°3E **32** G6
Lushnjë *Albania* 40°55N 19°41E **23** D8
Lushui *China* 25°58N 98°44E **34** E2
Lusk *U.S.A.* 42°46N 104°27W **76** E11
Lūt, Dasht-e *Iran* 31°30N 58°0E **47** D8
Luta = Dalian *China* 38°50N 121°40E **33** E11
Lütao *Taiwan* 22°40N 121°8E **35** F13
Lutherstadt Wittenberg
Germany 51°53N 12°39E **16** C7
Luton *U.K.* 51°53N 0°24W **13** F7
Luton □ *U.K.* 51°53N 0°24W **13** F7
Lutsel K'e *Canada* 62°24N 110°44W **71** A6
Lutsk *Ukraine* 50°50N 25°15E **17** C13
Lutto = Lotta → *Europe* 68°42N 31°6E **8** B24
Lützow Holmbukta
Antarctica 69°10S 37°30E **5** C4
Lutzputs *S. Africa* 28°3S 20°40E **56** C3
Luuq *Somalia* 3°48N 42°34E **49** G3

Luverne *Ala., U.S.A.* 31°43N 86°16W **85** F11
Luverne *Minn., U.S.A.* 43°39N 96°13W **80** D5
Luvua →
Dem. Rep. of the Congo 6°50S 27°30E **54** F5
Luvuvhu → *S. Africa* 22°25S 31°18E **57** B5
Luwuk *Indonesia* 0°56S 122°47E **37** E6
Luxembourg *Lux.* 49°37N 6°9E **15** E6
Luxembourg □ *Belgium* 49°58N 5°30E **15** E5
Luxembourg ■ *Europe* 49°45N 6°0E **15** E5
Luxembourg ✈ (LUX)
Lux. 49°37N 6°10E **15** E6
Luxi *Hunan, China* 28°20N 110°7E **35** C8
Luxi *Yunnan, China* 24°40N 103°55E **34** E4
Luxi *Yunnan, China* 24°27N 98°36E **34** E2
Luxian *China* 29°9N 105°24E **34** C5
Luxor = El Uqsur *Egypt* 25°41N 32°38E **53** C12
Luyi *China* 33°50N 115°35E **32** H8
Luykau = Loikaw
Burma 19°40N 97°17E **41** K20
Luza *Russia* 60°39N 47°10E **18** B8
Luzern *Switz.* 47°3N 8°18E **20** C8
Luzhai *China* 24°29N 109°42E **34** E7
Luzhi *China* 26°21N 105°16E **34** D5
Luzhou *China* 28°52N 105°20E **34** C5
Luziânia *Brazil* 16°20S 48°0W **93** G9
Luzon *Phil.* 16°0N 121°0E **37** A6
Luzon Strait *Asia* 21°0N 120°40E **35** G13
Lviv *Ukraine* 49°50N 24°0E **17** D13
Lviv □ *Ukraine* 49°30N 24°0E **17** D13
Lvov = Lviv *Ukraine* 49°50N 24°0E **17** D13
Lyakhavichy *Belarus* 53°2N 26°32E **17** B14
Lyakhovskiye, Ostrova
Russia 73°40N 141°0E **27** B15
Lyal I. *Canada* 44°57N 81°24W **82** B3
Lybster *U.K.* 58°18N 3°15W **11** C5
Lycksele *Sweden* 64°38N 18°40E **8** D18
Lydda = Lod *Israel* 31°57N 34°54E **48** D3
Lyddan I. *Antarctica* 74°0S 21°0W **5** D2
Lydenburg *S. Africa* 25°10S 30°29E **57** C5
Lydia *Turkey* 38°48N 28°19E **23** E13
Lyell *U.S.A.* 41°48S 172°4E **59** D4
Lyell I. *Canada* 52°40N 131°35W **70** C2
Lyepyel *Belarus* 54°50N 28°40E **9** J23
Lykens *U.S.A.* 40°34N 76°42W **83** F8
Lyman *U.S.A.* 41°20N 110°18W **76** F8
Lyme B. *U.K.* 50°42N 2°53W **13** G4
Lyme Regis *U.K.* 50°43N 2°57W **13** G5
Lymington *U.K.* 50°45N 1°33W **13** G6
Łyna → *Poland* 54°37N 21°14E **17** A11
Lynchburg *U.S.A.* 37°25N 79°9W **81** G14
Lynd → *Australia* 16°28S 143°18E **62** B3
Lynd Ra. *Australia* 25°30S 149°20E **63** D4
Lynden *Canada* 43°14N 80°9W **82** C4
Lynden *U.S.A.* 48°57N 122°27W **78** B4
Lyndhurst *Australia* 30°15S 138°18E **63** E2
Lyndon → *Australia* 23°29S 114°6E **61** D1
Lyndonville *N.Y., U.S.A.* 43°20N 78°23W **82** C6
Lyndonville *Vt., U.S.A.* 44°31N 72°1W **83** B12
Lyngen *Norway* 69°45N 20°30E **8** B19
Lynher Reef *Australia* 15°27S 121°55E **60** C3
Lynn *U.S.A.* 42°28N 70°57W **83** D14
Lynn Canal *U.S.A.* 58°50N 135°15W **74** D12
Lynn Haven *U.S.A.* 30°15N 85°39W **85** F12
Lynn Lake *Canada* 56°51N 101°3W **71** B8
Lynnwood *U.S.A.* 47°49N 122°18W **78** C4
Lynton *U.K.* 51°13N 3°50W **13** F4
Lyntupy *Belarus* 55°4N 26°23E **9** J22
Lynx L. *Canada* 62°25N 106°15W **71** A7
Lyon *France* 45°46N 4°50E **20** D6
Lyonnais *France* 45°45N 4°15E **20** D6
Lyons = Lyon *France* 45°46N 4°50E **20** D6
Lyons *Ga., U.S.A.* 32°12N 82°19W **85** E13
Lyons *Kans., U.S.A.* 38°21N 98°12W **80** F4
Lyons *N.Y., U.S.A.* 43°5N 77°0W **82** C7
Lyons → *Australia* 25°2S 115°9E **61** E2
Lyons Falls *U.S.A.* 43°37N 75°22W **83** C9
Lys = Leie → *Belgium* 51°2N 3°45E **15** C3
Lysva *Russia* 58°7N 57°49E **18** C10
Lysychansk *Ukraine* 48°55N 38°30E **19** E6
Lytham St. Anne's *U.K.* 53°45N 3°0W **12** D4
Lyttelton *N.Z.* 43°35S 172°44E **59** E4
Lytton *Canada* 50°13N 121°31W **70** C4
Lyubertsy *Russia* 55°40N 37°51E **18** C6
Lyuboml *Ukraine* 51°11N 24°4E **17** C13

M

Ma → *Vietnam* 19°47N 105°56E **34** H5
Ma On Shan *China* 22°24N 114°10E **31** a
Ma'adaba *Jordan* 31°43N 35°47E **48** D4
Ma'alot-Tarshiha *Israel* 33°1N 35°17E **48** B4
Maamba *Zambia* 17°17S 26°28E **56** A4
Ma'ān *Jordan* 30°12N 35°44E **48** E4
Ma'ān □ *Jordan* 30°0N 36°0E **48** F5
Maanselkä *Finland* 63°52N 28°32E **8** C23
Ma'anshan *China* 31°44N 118°29E **35** B12
Maarianhamina = Mariehamn
Finland 60°5N 19°55E **9** F18
Ma'arrat an Nu'mān
Syria 35°43N 36°43E **46** C3
Maas → *Neths.* 51°45N 4°32E **15** C4
Maaseik *Belgium* 51°6N 5°45E **15** C5
Maasin *Phil.* 10°8N 124°50E **37** B6
Maastricht *Neths.* 50°50N 5°40E **15** D5
Maave *Mozam.* 21°4S 34°47E **57** B5
Mababe Depression
Botswana 18°50S 24°15E **56** A3
Mabalane *Mozam.* 23°37S 32°31E **57** C5
Mabel L. *Canada* 50°35N 118°43W **70** C5
Mabian *China* 28°47N 103°37E **34** C4
Mablethorpe *U.K.* 53°20N 0°15E **12** D8
Mabuasehube △ *Botswana* 25°45S 22°0E **56** C3
Mabuiag *Australia* 9°57S 142°11E **62** a
Mac Bac *Vietnam* 9°46N 106°7E **39** H6
Macachin *Argentina* 37°10S 63°43W **94** D3
Macaé *Brazil* 22°20S 41°43W **95** A7
McAlester *U.S.A.* 34°56N 95°46W **84** D7
McAllen *U.S.A.* 26°12N 98°14W **84** H5

MacAlpine L. *Canada* 66°32N 102°45W **68** D11
Macamic *Canada* 48°45N 79°0W **72** C4
Macao = Macau *China* 22°12N 113°33E **35** F9
Macapá *Brazil* 0°5N 51°4W **93** C8
Macarao △ *Venezuela* 10°22N 67°7W **89** D6
McArthur → *Australia* 15°54S 136°40E **62** B2
McArthur, Port *Australia* 16°4S 136°23E **62** B2
Macau *Brazil* 5°15S 36°40W **93** E11
Macau *China* 22°12N 113°33E **35** F9
McBride *Canada* 53°20N 120°19W **70** C4
McCall *U.S.A.* 44°55N 116°6W **76** D5
McCamey *U.S.A.* 31°8N 102°14W **84** F3
McCammon *U.S.A.* 42°39N 112°12W **76** E7
McCauley I. *Canada* 53°40N 130°15W **70** C2
McCleary *U.S.A.* 47°3N 123°16W **78** C3
Macclenny *U.S.A.* 30°17N 82°7W **85** F13
Macclesfield *U.K.* 53°15N 2°8W **12** D5
M'Clintock Chan.
Canada 72°0N 102°0W **68** C11
McClintock Ra.
Australia 18°44S 127°38E **60** C4
McCloud *U.S.A.* 41°15N 122°8W **76** F2
McCluer I. *Australia* 11°5S 133°0E **60** B5
McClure *U.S.A.* 40°42N 77°19W **82** F7
McClure, L. *U.S.A.* 37°35N 120°16W **78** H6
M'Clure Str. *Canada* 75°0N 119°0W **69** C8
McClusky *U.S.A.* 47°29N 100°27W **80** B3
McComb *U.S.A.* 31°15N 90°27W **85** F9
McCook *U.S.A.* 40°12N 100°38W **80** E3
McCreary *Canada* 50°47N 99°29W **71** C9
McCullough Mt.
U.S.A. 35°35N 115°13W **79** K11
McCusker → *Canada* 55°32N 108°39W **71** B7
McDermitt *U.S.A.* 41°59N 117°43W **76** F5
McDonald *U.S.A.* 40°22N 80°14W **82** F4
Macdonald, L. *Australia* 23°30S 129°0E **60** D4
McDonald Is. *Ind. Oc.* 53°0S 73°0E **3** G13
MacDonnell Ranges
Australia 23°40S 133°0E **60** D5
MacDowell L. *Canada* 52°15N 92°45W **72** B1
Macduff *U.K.* 57°40N 2°31W **11** D6
Macedonia *U.S.A.* 41°19N 81°31W **82** E3
Macedonia □ *Greece* 40°39N 22°0E **23** D10
Macedonia ■ *Europe* 41°53N 21°40E **23** D9
Maceió *Brazil* 9°40S 35°41W **93** E11
Macerata *Italy* 43°18N 13°27E **22** C5
McFarland *U.S.A.* 35°41N 119°14W **79** K7
McFarlane → *Canada* 59°12N 107°58W **71** B7
Macfarlane, L. *Australia* 32°0S 136°40E **63** E2
McGehee *U.S.A.* 33°38N 91°24W **84** E9
McGill *U.S.A.* 39°23N 114°47W **76** G6
Macgillycuddy's Reeks
Ireland 51°58N 9°45W **10** E2
McGraw *U.S.A.* 42°36N 76°8W **83** D8
McGregor *U.S.A.* 43°1N 91°11W **80** D8
McGregor Ra. *Australia* 27°0S 142°45E **63** D3
McGuire, Mt. *Australia* 20°18S 148°23E **62** b
Mach *Pakistan* 29°50N 67°20E **42** E2
Mäch Kowr *Iran* 25°48N 61°28E **47** E9
Machado = Jiparaná →
Brazil 8°3S 62°52W **92** E6
Machagai *Argentina* 26°56S 60°2W **94** B3
Machakos *Kenya* 1°30S 37°15E **54** E7
Machala *Ecuador* 3°20S 79°57W **92** D3
Machanga *Mozam.* 20°59S 35°0E **57** B6
Machattie, L. *Australia* 24°50S 139°48E **62** C2
Machava *Mozam.* 25°54S 32°28E **57** C5
Macheke *Zimbabwe* 18°5S 31°51E **57** A5
Macheng *China* 31°12N 115°2E **35** B10
Macherla *India* 16°29N 79°26E **44** F4
Machgaon *India* 20°5N 86°17E **44** D8
Machhu → *India* 23°6N 70°46E **42** H4
Machiara △ *Pakistan* 34°40N 73°30E **42** B5
Machias *Maine, U.S.A.* 44°43N 67°28W **81** C20
Machias *N.Y., U.S.A.* 42°25N 78°29W **82** D6
Machichi → *Canada* 57°3N 92°6W **71** B10
Machilipatnam *India* 16°12N 81°8E **45** F5
Machiques *Venezuela* 10°4N 72°34W **92** A4
Machu Picchu *Peru* 13°8S 72°30W **92** F4
Machynlleth *U.K.* 52°35N 3°50W **13** E4
Macia *Mozam.* 25°2S 33°8E **57** C5
McIlwraith Ra. *Australia* 13°50S 143°20E **62** A3
McInnes L. *Canada* 52°13N 93°45W **71** C10
McIntosh *U.S.A.* 45°55N 101°21W **80** C3
McIntosh L. *Canada* 55°45N 105°0W **71** B8
Macintosh Ra. *Australia* 27°39S 125°32E **61** E4
Macintyre → *Australia* 28°37S 150°47E **63** D5
Mackay *Australia* 21°8S 149°11E **62** K7
Mackay *U.S.A.* 43°55N 113°37W **76** E7
MacKay → *Canada* 57°10N 111°38W **70** B6
Mackay, L. *Australia* 22°30S 129°0E **60** D4
McKay Ra. *Australia* 23°0S 122°30E **60** D3
McKeesport *U.S.A.* 40°20N 79°51W **82** F5
McKellar *Canada* 45°30N 79°55W **82** A5
McKenna *U.S.A.* 46°56N 122°33W **78** D4
Mackenzie = Linden
Guyana 6°0N 58°10W **92** B7
Mackenzie *Canada* 55°20N 123°5W **70** B4
McKenzie *U.S.A.* 36°8N 88°31W **85** C10
Mackenzie → *Australia* 23°38S 149°46E **62** C4
Mackenzie → *Canada* 69°10N 134°20W **68** B6
Mackenzie Bay *Canada* 69°0N 137°30W **66** C6
Mackenzie King I.
Canada 77°45N 111°0W **69** B9
Mackenzie Mts. *Canada* 64°0N 130°0W **66** C6
Mackinac, Straits of
U.S.A. 45°50N 84°40W **81** C11
Mackinaw City *U.S.A.* 45°47N 84°44W **81** C11
McKinlay *Australia* 21°16S 141°18E **62** C3
McKinlay → *Australia* 20°50S 141°28E **62** C3
McKinley, Mt. *U.S.A.* 63°4N 151°0W **68** E1
McKinley Sea *Arctic* 82°0N 0°0 **4** A7
McKinney *U.S.A.* 33°12N 96°37W **84** E6
McKittrick *U.S.A.* 35°18N 119°37W **79** K7
Macklin *Canada* 52°20N 109°56W **71** C7
Macksville *Australia* 30°40S 152°56E **63** E5
McLaughlin *U.S.A.* 45°49N 100°49W **80** C3
Maclean *Australia* 29°26S 153°16E **63** D5

McLean U.S.A. 35°14N 100°36W 84 D4
McLeansboro U.S.A. 38°6N 88°32W 80 F9
Maclear S. Africa 31°2S 28°23E 57 D4
Macleay → Australia 30°56S 153°0E 63 E5
McLennan Canada 55°42N 116°50W 70 B5
McLeod → Canada 54°9N 115°44W 70 C5
MacLeod, L. Australia 24°9S 113°47E 61 D1
MacLeod B. Canada 62°53N 110°0W 71 A7
MacLeod Lake Canada 54°58N 123°0W 70 C4
McLoughlin, Mt. U.S.A. 42°27N 122°19W 76 E2
McMechen U.S.A. 39°57N 80°44W 82 G4
McMinnville Oreg., U.S.A. 45°13N 123°12W 76 D2
McMinnville Tenn., U.S.A. 35°41N 85°46W 85 D12
McMurdo Antarctica 77°51S 166°37E 5 D11
McMurdo Sd. Antarctica 77°0S 170°0E 5 D11
McMurray = Fort McMurray Canada 56°44N 111°7W 70 B6
McMurray U.S.A. 48°19N 122°14W 78 B4
Maçobere Mozam. 21°13S 32°47E 57 B5
Macodoene Mozam. 23°32S 35°5E 57 B6
Macomb U.S.A. 40°27N 90°40W 80 E8
Mâcon France 46°19N 4°50E 20 C6
Macon Ga., U.S.A. 32°51N 83°38W 85 E13
Macon Miss., U.S.A. 33°7N 88°34W 85 E10
Macon Mo., U.S.A. 39°44N 92°28W 80 F7
Macoun L. Canada 56°32N 103°40W 71 B8
Macovane Mozam. 21°30S 35°2E 57 B6
McPherson U.S.A. 38°22N 97°40W 80 F5
McPherson Pk. U.S.A. 34°53N 119°53W 79 L7
McPherson Ra. Australia 28°15S 153°15E 63 D5
Macquarie → Australia 30°7S 147°24E 63 E4
Macquarie Harbour Australia 42°15S 145°23E 63 G4
Macquarie I. Pac. Oc. 54°36S 158°55E 64 N7
Macquarie Ridge S. Ocean 57°0S 159°0E 5 B10
MacRobertson Land Antarctica 71°0S 64°0E 5 D6
Macroom Ireland 51°54N 8°57W 10 E3
MacTier Canada 45°8N 79°47W 82 A5
Macuira △ Colombia 12°9N 71°21W 89 D5
Macumba → Australia 27°52S 137°12E 63 D2
Macuro Venezuela 10°42N 61°55W 93 K15
Macusani Peru 14°4S 70°29W 92 F4
Macuspana Mexico 17°46N 92°36W 87 D6
Macusse Angola 17°48S 20°23E 56 A3
Ma'dabā □ Jordan 31°43N 35°47E 48 D4
Madadeni S. Africa 27°43S 30°3E 57 C5
Madagascar ■ Africa 20°0S 47°0E 55 J9
Madā'in Sālih Si. Arabia 26°46N 37°57E 46 E3
Madakasira India 13°56N 77°16E 45 H3
Madama Niger 22°0N 13°40E 53 D8
Madame, I. Canada 45°30N 60°58W 73 C7
Madanapalle India 13°33N 78°28E 45 H4
Madang Papua N. G. 5°12S 145°49E 58 B7
Madaripur Bangla. 23°19N 90°15E 41 H17
Madauk Burma 17°56N 96°52E 41 L20
Madawaska Canada 45°30N 78°0W 82 A7
Madawaska → Canada 45°27N 76°21W 82 A7
Madaya Burma 22°12N 96°10E 41 H20
Maddalena Italy 41°16N 9°23E 22 D3
Maddur India 12°36N 77°4E 45 H3
Madeira Atl. Oc. 32°50N 17°0W 52 B2
Madeira → Brazil 3°22S 58°45W 92 D7
Madeleine, Îs. de la Canada 47°30N 61°40W 73 C7
Madera Mexico 29°12N 108°7W 86 B3
Madera Calif., U.S.A. 36°57N 120°3W 78 J6
Madera Pa., U.S.A. 40°49N 78°26W 82 F6
Madgaon India 15°12N 73°58E 45 G1
Madha India 18°0N 75°30E 44 F2
Madhavpur India 21°15N 69°58E 42 J3
Madhepura India 26°11N 86°23E 43 F12
Madhira India 16°55N 80°22E 44 F5
Madhubani India 26°21N 86°7E 43 F12
Madhugiri India 13°40N 77°12E 45 H3
Madhupur India 24°16N 86°39E 43 G12
Madhya Pradesh □ India 22°50N 78°0E 42 J8
Madidi → Bolivia 12°32S 66°52W 92 F5
Madikeri India 12°30N 75°45E 45 H2
Madikwe ⌂ S. Africa 27°38S 32°15E 57 C5
Madill U.S.A. 34°6N 96°46W 84 D6
Madimba Dem. Rep. of the Congo 4°58S 15°5E 54 E3
Ma'din Syria 35°45N 39°36E 46 C3
Madinat al Malik Khālid al Askarīyah Si. Arabia 27°54N 45°31E 46 E5
Madingou Congo 4°10S 13°33E 54 E2
Madison Calif., U.S.A. 38°41N 121°59W 78 G5
Madison Fla., U.S.A. 30°28N 83°25W 85 F13
Madison Ind., U.S.A. 38°44N 85°23W 81 F11
Madison Nebr., U.S.A. 41°50N 97°27W 80 E5
Madison Ohio, U.S.A. 41°46N 81°3W 82 E3
Madison S. Dak., U.S.A. 44°0N 97°7W 80 C5
Madison Wis., U.S.A. 43°4N 89°24W 80 D9
Madison → U.S.A. 45°56N 111°31W 76 D8
Madison Heights U.S.A. 37°25N 79°8W 81 G14
Madisonville Ky., U.S.A. 37°20N 87°30W 80 G10
Madisonville Tex., U.S.A. 30°57N 95°55W 84 F7
Madista Botswana 21°15S 25°6E 56 B4
Madiun Indonesia 7°38S 111°32E 37 G14
Madoc Canada 44°30N 77°28W 82 B7
Madoi China 34°46N 98°18E 32 E8
Madona Latvia 56°53N 26°5E 9 H22
Madrakah, Ra's al Oman 19°0N 57°50E 49 D6
Madras = Chennai India 13°8N 80°19E 45 H5
Madras = Tamil Nadu □ India 11°0N 77°0E 45 J3
Madras U.S.A. 44°38N 121°8W 76 D3
Madre, L. U.S.A. 25°15N 97°30W 84 J6
Madre, Sierra Phil. 17°0N 122°0E 37 A6
Madre de Dios → Bolivia 10°59S 66°8W 92 F5
Madre de Dios, I. Chile 50°20S 75°10W 96 G1
Madre del Sur, Sierra Mexico 17°30N 100°0W 87 D5
Madre Occidental, Sierra Mexico 27°0N 107°0W 86 B3
Madre Oriental, Sierra Mexico 25°0N 100°0W 86 C5
Madri India 24°16N 73°32E 42 G5
Madrid U.S.A. 44°45N 75°8W 83 B9
Madura Australia 31°55S 127°0E 61 F4
Madura Indonesia 7°30S 114°0E 37 G15
Madura, Selat Indonesia 7°30S 113°20E 37 G15
Madura Oya △ Sri Lanka 7°20N 81°10E 45 L5
Madurai India 9°55N 78°10E 45 K4
Madurantakam India 12°30N 79°50E 45 H4
Mae Chan Thailand 20°9N 99°52E 38 B2
Mae Charim △ Thailand 18°17N 100°59E 38 C3
Mae Hong Son Thailand 19°16N 97°56E 38 C2
Mae Khlong → Thailand 13°24N 100°0E 38 F3
Mae Moei △ Thailand 17°26N 98°7E 38 D2
Mae Phang △ Thailand 19°7N 99°13E 38 C2
Mae Phrik Thailand 17°27N 99°7E 38 D2
Mae Ping △ Thailand 17°37N 98°51E 38 D2
Mae Ramat Thailand 16°58N 98°31E 38 D2
Mae Rim Thailand 18°54N 98°57E 38 C2
Mae Sai Thailand 20°20N 99°55E 34 G2
Mae Sot Thailand 16°43N 98°34E 38 D2
Mae Suai Thailand 19°39N 99°33E 34 H2
Mae Tha Thailand 18°28N 99°8E 38 C2
Mae Tup Res. Thailand 17°52N 98°45E 38 D2
Mae Wa △ Thailand 17°23N 99°16E 38 D2
Mae Wong △ Thailand 15°54N 99°12E 38 E2
Mae Yom △ Thailand 18°43N 100°15E 38 C3
Maebaru Japan 33°33N 130°12E 29 H5
Maebashi Japan 36°24N 139°4E 29 F9
Maelpaeg L. Canada 48°20N 56°30W 73 C8
Maesteg U.K. 51°36N 3°40W 13 F4
Maestra, Sierra Cuba 20°15N 77°0W 88 B4
Maevatanana Madag. 16°56S 46°49E 55 H9
Mafadi S. Africa 29°12S 29°21E 57 C4
Mafeking = Mafikeng S. Africa 25°50S 25°38E 56 C4
Mafeking Canada 52°40N 101°10W 71 C8
Mafeteng Lesotho 29°51S 27°15E 56 C4
Maffra Australia 37°53S 146°58E 63 F4
Mafia I. Tanzania 7°45S 39°50E 54 F7
Mafikeng S. Africa 25°50S 25°38E 56 C4
Mafra Brazil 26°10S 49°55W 95 B6
Mafra Portugal 38°55N 9°20W 21 C1
Magadan Russia 59°38N 150°50E 27 D16
Magadi India 12°58N 77°14E 45 H3
Magaliesburg S. Africa 26°0S 27°32E 57 C4
Magallanes, Estrecho de Chile 52°30S 75°0W 96 G2
Magangué Colombia 9°14N 74°45W 92 B4
Magdagachi Russia 53°27N 125°48E 27 D13
Magdalen Is. = Madeleine, Îs. de la Canada 47°30N 61°40W 73 C7
Magdalena Argentina 35°5S 57°30W 94 D4
Magdalena Bolivia 13°13S 63°57W 92 F6
Magdalena U.S.A. 34°7N 107°15W 77 J10
Magdalena → Colombia 11°6N 74°51W 92 A4
Magdalena, B. Mexico 24°35N 112°0W 86 C2
Magdalena, I. Mexico 24°40N 112°15W 86 C2
Magdalena, Llano de Mexico 25°0N 111°25W 86 C2
Magdalena de Kino Mexico 30°38N 110°57W 86 A2
Magdeburg Germany 52°7N 11°38E 16 B6
Magdelaine Cays Australia 16°33S 150°18E 62 B5
Magee U.S.A. 31°52N 89°44W 85 F10
Magelang Indonesia 7°29S 110°13E 37 G14
Magellan's Str. = Magallanes, Estrecho de Chile 52°30S 75°0W 96 G2
Magenta, L. Australia 33°30S 119°2E 61 F2
Magerøya Norway 71°3N 25°40E 8 A21
Maggiore, Lago Italy 45°57N 8°39E 20 D8
Maggotty Jamaica 18°9N 77°46W 88 a
Maghâgha Egypt 28°38N 30°50E 53 C12
Maghera U.K. 54°51N 6°41W 10 B5
Magherafelt U.K. 54°45N 6°37W 10 B5
Maghreb N. Afr. 32°0N 4°0W 50 C3
Magistralnyy Russia 56°16N 107°36E 27 D11
Magnetic Pole (North) Arctic 82°18N 113°24W 4 A2
Magnetic Pole (South) Antarctica 64°8S 138°8E 5 C9
Magnitogorsk Russia 53°27N 59°4E 18 D10
Magnolia Ark., U.S.A. 33°16N 93°14W 84 E8
Magnolia Miss., U.S.A. 31°9N 90°28W 85 F9
Mago Fiji 17°26S 179°8W 59 a
Magog Canada 45°18N 72°9W 83 A12
Magpie, L. Canada 51°0N 64°41W 73 B7
Magrath Canada 49°25N 112°50W 70 D6
Maguan China 23°0N 104°21E 34 F5
Maguarinho, C. Brazil 0°15S 48°30W 93 D9
Magude Mozam. 25°2S 32°40E 57 C5
Mağusa = Famagusta Cyprus 35°8N 33°55E 46 C2
Maguse L. Canada 61°37N 95°10W 71 A9
Maguse Pt. Canada 61°20N 93°50W 71 A10
Magvana India 23°13N 69°22E 42 H3
Magwe Burma 20°10N 95°0E 41 J19
Magyarorszag = Hungary ■ Europe 47°20N 19°20E 17 E10
Maha Oya Sri Lanka 7°31N 81°22E 45 L5
Maha Sarakham Thailand 16°12N 103°16E 38 D4
Mahābād Iran 36°50N 45°45E 46 B5
Mahabaleshwar India 17°58N 73°43E 44 F1
Mahabalipuram India 12°37N 80°11E 45 H5
Mahabharat Lekh Nepal 28°30N 82°0E 43 E10
Mahabo Madag. 20°23S 44°40E 55 J8
Mahad India 18°6N 73°29E 44 E1
Mahadeo Hills India 22°20N 78°30E 43 H8
Mahadeopur India 18°48N 80°0E 44 E5
Mahaffey U.S.A. 40°53N 78°44W 82 F6
Mahajan India 28°48N 73°56E 42 E5
Mahajanga Madag. 15°40S 46°25E 55 H9
Mahakam → Indonesia 0°35S 117°17E 36 E5
Mahalapye Botswana 23°1S 26°51E 56 B4
Mahale Mts. Tanzania 6°20S 30°0E 54 F6
Maḩallāt Iran 33°55N 50°30E 47 C6
Māhān Iran 30°5N 57°18E 47 D8
Mahan → India 23°30N 82°50E 43 H10
Mahanadi → India 20°20N 86°25E 44 D8
Mahananda → India 25°12N 87°52E 43 G12
Mahanoro Madag. 19°54S 48°48E 55 H9
Mahanoy City U.S.A. 40°49N 76°9W 83 F8
Maharashtra □ India 20°30N 75°30E 44 D2
Mahasamund India 21°6N 82°6E 44 D6
Mahasham, W. → Egypt 30°15N 34°10E 48 E3
Mahattat ash Shīdīyah Jordan 29°55N 35°55E 48 F4
Mahattat 'Unayzah Jordan 30°30N 35°47E 48 E4
Mahaweli Ganga → Sri Lanka 8°27N 81°13E 45 K5
Mahaxay Laos 17°22N 105°12E 38 D5
Mahbubabad India 17°42N 80°2E 44 F5
Mahbubnagar India 16°45N 77°59E 44 F3
Mahda U.A.E. 25°20N 56°15E 47 E8
Maḩḑah Oman 24°24N 55°59E 47 E7
Mahdia Tunisia 35°28N 11°0E 53 A8
Mahe Jammu & Kashmir, India 33°10N 78°32E 43 C8
Mahé Pondicherry, India 11°42N 75°34E 45 J2
Mahé Seychelles 5°0S 55°30E 55 b
Mahé ✕ (SEZ) Seychelles 4°40S 55°31E 55 b
Mahébourg Mauritius 20°24S 57°42E 55 d
Mahendra Giri India 8°20N 77°30E 45 K3
Mahendragarh India 28°17N 76°14E 42 E7
Mahendranagar Nepal 28°55N 80°20E 43 E9
Mahenge Tanzania 8°45S 36°41E 54 F7
Maheno N.Z. 45°10S 170°50E 59 F3
Mahesana India 23°39N 72°26E 42 H5
Maheshwar India 22°11N 75°35E 42 H6
Mahgawan India 26°29N 78°37E 43 F8
Mahi → India 22°15N 72°55E 42 H5
Mahia Pen. N.Z. 39°9S 177°55E 59 C6
Mahikeng = Mafikeng S. Africa 25°50S 25°38E 56 C4
Mahilyow Belarus 53°55N 30°18E 17 B16
Mahim India 19°39N 72°44E 44 E1
Mahina Tahiti 17°30S 149°27W 59 d
Mahinerangi, L. N.Z. 45°50S 169°56E 59 F2
Mahmud Kot Pakistan 30°16N 71°0E 42 D4
Mahnomen U.S.A. 47°19N 95°58W 80 B6
Maho Sri Lanka 7°49N 80°16E 45 L5
Mahoba India 25°15N 79°55E 43 G8
Mahón = Maó Spain 39°53N 4°16E 21 C8
Mahone Bay Canada 44°27N 64°23W 73 D7
Mahongo ⌂ Namibia 18°0S 23°15E 56 B3
Mahopac U.S.A. 41°22N 73°45W 83 E11
Mahuva India 21°5N 71°48E 42 J4
Mai-Ndombe, L. Dem. Rep. of the Congo 2°0S 18°20E 54 E3
Mai Thon, Ko Thailand 7°40N 98°28E 39 a
Maicuru → Brazil 2°14S 54°17W 93 D8
Maidan Khula Afghan. 33°36N 69°50E 42 C3
Maidenhead U.K. 51°31N 0°42W 13 F7
Maidstone Canada 53°5N 109°20W 71 C7
Maidstone U.K. 51°16N 0°32E 13 F8
Maiduguri Nigeria 12°0N 13°20E 53 F8
Maigh Nuad = Maynooth Ireland 53°23N 6°34W 10 C5
Maihar India 24°16N 80°45E 43 G9
Maikala Ra. India 22°0N 81°0E 44 D5
Mailani India 28°17N 80°21E 43 E9
Mailsi Pakistan 29°48N 72°15E 42 E5
Main → Germany 50°0N 8°18E 16 C5
Main → U.K. 54°48N 6°18W 10 B5
Main Channel Canada 45°21N 81°45W 82 A3
Main Range △ Australia 28°11S 152°27E 63 D5
Main Ridge Trin. & Tob. 11°16N 60°40W 93 J16
Maindargi India 17°28N 76°18E 44 F3
Maine France 48°20N 0°15W 20 C3
Maine □ U.S.A. 45°20N 69°0W 81 C19
Maine → Ireland 52°9N 9°45W 10 D2
Maine, G. of U.S.A. 43°0N 68°30W 75 G26
Maingkwan Burma 26°15N 96°37E 41 F20
Mainistir na Corann = Midleton Ireland 51°55N 8°10W 10 E3
Mainit, L. Phil. 9°31N 125°30E 37 C7
Mainland Orkney, U.K. 58°59N 3°8W 11 C5
Mainland Shet., U.K. 60°15N 1°22W 11 A7
Mainpuri India 27°18N 79°4E 43 F8
Maintirano Madag. 18°3S 44°1E 55 H8
Mainz Germany 50°1N 8°14E 16 C5
Maio C. Verde Is. 15°10N 23°10W 52 b
Maipú Argentina 36°52S 57°50W 94 D4
Maiquetía Venezuela 10°36N 66°57W 92 A5
Mairabari India 26°30N 92°22E 41 F18
Maisí Cuba 20°17N 74°9W 89 B5
Maisí, Pta. de Cuba 20°10N 74°10W 89 B5
Maitland N.S.W., Australia 32°33S 151°36E 63 E5
Maitland S. Austral., Australia 34°23S 137°40E 63 E2
Maitland → Canada 43°45N 81°43W 82 C3
Maitri Antarctica 70°0S 3°0W 5 D3
Maiyuan China 25°34N 117°28E 35 E11
Maíz, Is. del Nic. 12°15N 83°4W 88 D3
Maizuru Japan 35°25N 135°22E 29 G7
Majalengka Indonesia 6°50S 108°13E 37 G13
Majene Indonesia 3°38S 118°57E 37 E5
Majiang China 26°28N 107°32E 34 D6
Majorca = Mallorca Spain 39°30N 3°0E 21 C7
Majuro Marshall Is. 7°9N 171°12E 64 G9
Mak, Ko Thailand 11°49N 102°29E 39 G4
Maka Senegal 13°40N 14°10W 52 F3
Makaha Zimbabwe 17°20S 32°39E 57 A5
Makalamabedi Botswana 20°19S 23°51E 56 B3
Makale Indonesia 3°6S 119°51E 37 E5
Makalu Asia 27°55N 87°8E 43 F12
Makalu-Barun △ Nepal 27°45N 87°10E 43 F12
Makarikari = Makgadikgadi Salt Pans Botswana 20°40S 25°45E 56 B4
Makarov Basin Arctic 87°0N 150°0W 4 A
Makarovo Russia 57°40N 107°45E 27 D11
Makassar Indonesia 5°10S 119°20E 37 F5
Makassar, Selat Indonesia 1°0S 118°20E 37 E5
Makassar, Str. of = Makassar, Selat Indonesia 1°0S 118°20E 37 E5
Makat = Maqat Kazakhstan 47°39N 53°19E 19 E9
Makedonija = Macedonia ■ Europe 41°53N 21°40E 23 D9
Makeni S. Leone 8°55N 12°5W 52 G3
Makeyevka = Makiyivka Ukraine 48°0N 38°0E 19 E6
Makgadikgadi △ Botswana 20°27S 24°47E 56 B3
Makgadikgadi Salt Pans Botswana 20°40S 25°45E 56 B4
Makhachkala Russia 43°0N 47°30E 19 F8
Makhado = Louis Trichardt S. Africa 23°1S 29°43E 57 B4
Makham, Ao Thailand 7°51N 98°25E 39 a
Makhfar al Buşayyah Iraq 30°0N 46°10E 46 D5
Makhmūr Iraq 35°46N 43°35E 46 C4
Makhtal India 16°30N 77°31E 45 E3
Makian Indonesia 0°20N 127°20E 37 D7
Makīnsk Kazakhstan 52°37N 70°26E 26 D8
Makira = San Cristóbal Solomon Is. 10°30S 161°0E 58 C9
Makiyivka Ukraine 48°0N 38°0E 19 E6
Makkah Si. Arabia 21°30N 39°54E 49 C2
Makkovik Canada 55°10N 59°10W 73 A8
Makó Hungary 46°14N 20°33E 17 E11
Makogai Fiji 17°28S 179°0E 59 a
Makokou Gabon 0°40N 12°50E 54 D2
Makrai India 22°2N 77°0E 42 H7
Makran Coast Range Pakistan 25°40N 64°0E 40 G4
Makrana India 27°2N 74°46E 42 F6
Makri India 19°46N 81°55E 44 E5
Mākū Iran 39°15N 44°31E 46 B5
Makunda Botswana 22°30S 20°7E 56 B3
Makung Taiwan 23°34N 119°34E 35 F12
Makurazaki Japan 31°15N 130°20E 29 J5
Makurdi Nigeria 7°43N 8°35E 52 G7
Makushin Volcano U.S.A. 53°53N 166°55W 74 E6
Makūyeh Iran 28°7N 53°9E 47 D7
Makwassie S. Africa 27°17S 26°0E 56 C4
Makwiro Zimbabwe 17°58S 30°25E 57 A5
Mal B. Ireland 52°50N 9°30W 10 D2
Mala = Mallow Ireland 52°8N 8°39W 10 D3
Mala ☼ Australia 21°39S 130°45E 60 D5
Mala, Pta. Panama 7°28N 80°2W 88 E3
Malabar Coast India 11°0N 75°0E 45 J2
Malacca, Straits of Indonesia 3°0N 101°0E 39 L3
Malad City U.S.A. 42°12N 112°15W 76 E7
Maladzyechna Belarus 54°20N 26°50E 17 A14
Málaga Spain 36°43N 4°23W 21 D3
Malagasy Rep. = Madagascar ■ Africa 20°0S 47°0E 55 J9
Malaimbandy Madag. 20°20S 45°36E 55 J9
Malaita Solomon Is. 9°0S 161°0E 58 B9
Malakal South Sudan 9°33N 31°40E 53 G12
Malakanagiri India 18°21N 81°54E 44 E5
Malakand Pakistan 34°40N 71°55E 42 B4
Malakula Vanuatu 16°15S 167°30E 58 C9
Malakwal Pakistan 32°34N 73°13E 42 C5
Malamala Indonesia 3°21S 120°55E 37 E6
Malanda Australia 17°22S 145°35E 62 B4
Malang Indonesia 7°59S 112°45E 37 G15
Malangen Norway 69°24N 18°37E 8 B18
Malangwa Nepal 26°52N 85°34E 43 F11
Malanje Angola 9°36S 16°17E 54 F3
Malappuram India 11°7N 76°11E 45 J3
Mälaren Sweden 59°30N 17°10E 9 G17
Malargüe Argentina 35°32S 69°30W 94 D2
Malartic Canada 48°9N 78°9W 72 C4
Malaryta Belarus 51°50N 24°3E 17 C13
Malaspina Glacier U.S.A. 59°50N 140°30W 74 D11
Malatya Turkey 38°25N 38°20E 46 B3
Malawi ■ Africa 11°55S 34°0E 55 G6
Malawi, L. Africa 12°30S 34°30E 55 G6
Malay Pen. Asia 7°25N 100°0E 39 J3
Malaya Vishera Russia 58°55N 32°25E 18 C5
Malaybalay Phil. 8°5N 125°7E 37 C7
Malāyer Iran 34°19N 48°51E 47 C6
Malaysia ■ Asia 5°0N 110°0E 39 K4
Malazgirt Turkey 39°10N 42°33E 46 B4
Malbon Australia 21°5S 140°17E 62 C3
Malbooma Australia 30°41S 134°11E 63 E1
Malbork Poland 54°3N 19°1E 17 B10
Malcolm Australia 28°51S 121°25E 61 E3
Malcolm, Pt. Australia 33°48S 123°45E 61 F3
Maldah India 25°2N 88°9E 43 G13
Maldegem Belgium 51°14N 3°26E 15 C3
Malden U.S.A. 36°34N 89°57W 80 G9
Malden I. Kiribati 4°3S 155°1W 65 H12
Maldives ■ Ind. Oc. 5°0N 73°0E 25 H9
Maldon U.K. 51°44N 0°42E 13 F8
Maldonado Uruguay 34°59S 55°0W 95 C5
Maldonado, Pta. Mexico 16°20N 98°33W 87 D5
Malé Karpaty Slovak Rep. 48°30N 17°20E 17 D9
Maleas, Akra Greece 36°28N 23°7E 23 F10
Malebo, Pool Africa 4°17S 15°20E 54 E3
Malegaon India 20°30N 74°38E 44 D2
Malek Kandī Iran 37°9N 46°6E 46 B5
Malema Mozam. 14°57S 37°20E 55 G7
Maler Kotla India 30°32N 75°58E 42 D6
Malgomaj Sweden 64°40N 16°30E 8 D17
Malha Sudan 15°8N 25°10E 53 E11
Malhargarh India 24°17N 74°59E 42 G6
Malheur → U.S.A. 44°4N 116°59W 76 D5
Malheur L. U.S.A. 43°20N 118°48W 76 E4
Mali ■ Africa 17°0N 3°0W 52 E5
Mali → Burma 25°42N 97°30E 41 G20
Mali Kyun Burma 13°0N 98°20E 38 F2
Malibu U.S.A. 34°2N 118°41W 79 L8
Maliku = Minicoy I. India 8°17N 73°2E 45 K1
Maliku Indonesia 0°39S 123°16E 37 E6
Malili Indonesia 2°42S 121°6E 37 E6
Malimba, Mts. Dem. Rep. of the Congo 7°30S 29°30E 54 F5
Malin Hd. Ireland 55°23N 7°23W 10 A4
Malin Pen. Ireland 55°20N 7°17W 10 A4
Malindi Kenya 3°12S 40°5E 54 E8
Malines = Mechelen Belgium 51°2N 4°29E 15 C4
Malino Indonesia 1°0N 121°0E 37 D6
Malipo China 23°7N 104°42E 34 F5
Malita Phil. 6°19N 125°39E 37 C7
Maliwun Burma 10°17N 98°40E 39 G2
Maliya India 23°5N 70°46E 42 H4
Malkapur India 20°53N 76°12E 44 D3
Malkara Turkey 40°53N 26°53E 23 D12
Malkhangiri = Malakanagiri India 18°21N 81°54E 44 E5
Mallacoota Inlet Australia 37°34S 149°40E 63 F4
Mallaig U.K. 57°0N 5°50W 11 D3
Mallawan India 27°4N 80°12E 43 F9
Mallawi Egypt 27°44N 30°44E 53 C12
Mallicolo = Malakula Vanuatu 16°15S 167°30E 58 C9
Mallorca Spain 39°30N 3°0E 21 C7
Mallorytown Canada 44°29N 75°53W 83 B9
Mallow Ireland 52°8N 8°39W 10 D3
Malmberget Sweden 67°11N 20°40E 8 C19
Malmédy Belgium 50°25N 6°2E 15 D6
Malmesbury S. Africa 33°28S 18°41E 56 D2
Malmivaara = Malmberget Sweden 67°11N 20°40E 8 C19
Malmö Sweden 55°36N 12°59E 9 J15
Malolo Fiji 17°45S 177°11E 59 a
Malolos Phil. 14°50N 120°49E 37 B6
Malolotja ⌂ Swaziland 26°4S 31°6E 57 C5
Malone U.S.A. 44°51N 74°18W 83 B10
Malong China 25°24N 103°34E 34 E4
Måløy Norway 61°57N 5°6E 8 F11
Malpaso, Presa = Netzahualcóyotl, Presa Mexico 17°8N 93°35W 87 D6
Malpelo, I. de Colombia 4°3N 81°35W 92 C2
Malprabha → India 16°20N 76°5E 45 F3
Malpur India 23°21N 73°27E 42 H5
Malpura India 26°17N 75°23E 42 F6
Malsiras India 17°52N 74°55E 44 F2
Malta Idaho, U.S.A. 42°18N 113°22W 76 E7
Malta Mont., U.S.A. 48°21N 107°52W 76 B10
Malta ■ Europe 35°55N 14°26E 22 G6
Maltahöhe Namibia 24°55S 17°0E 56 B2
Malton U.K. 54°8N 0°49W 12 C7
Maluku Indonesia 1°0S 127°0E 37 E7
Maluku □ Indonesia 3°0S 128°0E 37 E7
Maluku Sea = Molucca Sea Indonesia 0°0 125°0E 37 E6
Malur India 13°0N 77°55E 45 H3
Malvalli India 12°28N 77°8E 45 H3
Malvan India 16°2N 73°30E 45 F1
Malvern U.S.A. 34°22N 92°49W 84 D8
Malvern Hills U.K. 52°0N 2°19W 13 E5
Malvinas, Is. = Falkland Is. ☒ Atl. Oc. 51°30S 59°0W 96 G5
Malyn Ukraine 50°46N 29°3E 17 C15
Malyy Lyakhovskiy, Ostrov Russia 74°7N 140°36E 27 B15
Malyy Taymyr, Ostrov Russia 78°6N 107°15E 27 B11
Mama Russia 58°18N 112°54E 27 D12
Mamanguape Brazil 6°50S 35°4W 93 E11
Mamanuca Group Fiji 17°35S 177°5E 59 a
Mamarr Mitlā Egypt 30°2N 32°54E 48 E1
Mamasa Indonesia 2°55S 119°20E 37 E5
Mamberamo → Indonesia 2°0S 137°50E 37 E9
Mambilima Falls Zambia 10°31S 28°45E 54 G5
Mamburao Phil. 13°13N 120°39E 37 B6
Mameigwess L. Canada 52°35N 87°50W 72 B2
Mamili △ Namibia 18°2S 24°1E 56 A3
Mammoth U.S.A. 32°43N 110°39W 77 K8
Mammoth Cave △ U.S.A. 37°8N 86°13W 80 G10
Mamoré → Bolivia 10°23S 65°53W 92 F5
Mamou Guinea 10°15N 12°0W 52 F3
Mamoudzou Mayotte 12°48S 45°14E 55 a
Mamuju Indonesia 2°41S 118°50E 37 E5
Mamuno Botswana 22°16S 20°1E 56 B3
Man Ivory C. 7°30N 7°40W 52 G4
Man → India 17°31N 75°32E 44 F2
Man, I. of India 8°28N 93°36E 45 K11
Man, I. of U.K. 54°15N 4°30W 12 C3
Man-Bazar India 23°4N 86°39E 43 H12
Man Na Burma 23°27N 97°19E 41 H20
Mänä U.S.A. 22°2N 159°47W 75 L8
Mana → Fr. Guiana 5°45N 53°55W 93 B8
Manaar, G. of = Mannar, G. of Asia 8°30N 79°0E 45 K4
Manacapuru Brazil 3°16S 60°37W 92 D6
Manacor Spain 39°34N 3°13E 21 C7
Manado Indonesia 1°29N 124°51E 37 D6
Managua Nic. 12°6N 86°20W 88 D2
Managua, L. de Nic. 12°20N 86°30W 88 D2
Manakara Madag. 22°8S 48°1E 55 J9
Manali India 32°16N 77°10E 42 C7
Manama = Al Manāmah Bahrain 26°10N 50°30E 47 E6
Mananjary Madag. 21°13S 48°20E 55 J9
Manantavadi India 11°49N 76°1E 45 J3
Manantenina Madag. 24°17S 47°19E 55 J9
Manaos = Manaus Brazil 3°0S 60°0W 92 D7
Manapire → Venezuela 7°42N 66°7W 92 B5
Manapouri N.Z. 45°34S 167°39E 59 F1
Manapouri, L. N.Z. 45°32S 167°32E 59 F1
Manapparai India 10°36N 78°25E 45 J4
Manar → India 18°50N 77°20E 44 E3
Manār, Jabal Yemen 14°2N 44°17E 49 E3
Manas China 44°17N 86°10E 30 C6
Manas → India 26°12N 90°40E 41 F17
Manas He → China 45°38N 85°12E 30 B6
Manaslu Nepal 28°33N 84°33E 43 E11
Manasquan U.S.A. 40°8N 74°3W 83 F10
Manassa U.S.A. 37°11N 105°56W 77 H11
Manatí Puerto Rico 18°26N 66°29W 89 d
Manaus Brazil 3°0S 60°0W 92 D7

Manawan L. *Canada* 55°24N 103°14W **71** B8
Manbij *Syria* 36°31N 37°57E **46** B3
Manchegorsk *Russia* 67°54N 32°58E **26** C4
Manchester *U.K.* 53°29N 2°12W **12** D5
Manchester *Calif.,*
 U.S.A. 38°58N 123°41W **78** G3
Manchester *Conn.,*
 U.S.A. 41°47N 72°31W **83** E12
Manchester *Ga., U.S.A.* 32°51N 84°37W **85** E12
Manchester *Iowa, U.S.A.* 42°29N 91°27W **80** D8
Manchester *Ky., U.S.A.* 37°9N 83°46W **81** G12
Manchester *N.H.,*
 U.S.A. 42°59N 71°28W **83** D13
Manchester *N.Y., U.S.A.* 42°56N 77°16W **82** D7
Manchester *Pa., U.S.A.* 40°4N 76°43W **83** F8
Manchester *Tenn., U.S.A.* 35°29N 86°5W **85** D11
Manchester *Vt., U.S.A.* 43°10N 73°5W **83** C11
Manchester Int. ✈ (MAN)
 U.K. 53°21N 2°17W **12** D5
Manchester L. *Canada* 61°28N 107°29W **71** A7
Manchhar L. *Pakistan* 26°25N 67°39E **42** F2
Manchuria = Dongbei
 China 45°0N 125°0E **33** D13
Manchurian Plain *China* 47°0N 124°0E **24** D14
Mand → *India* 21°42N 83°15E **43** J10
Mand → *Iran* 28°20N 52°30E **47** D7
Mandaguari *Brazil* 23°32S 51°42W **95** A5
Mandah = Töhöm
 Mongolia 44°27N 108°2E **32** B5
Mandal *Norway* 58°2N 7°25E **9** G12
Mandala, Puncak
 Indonesia 4°44S 140°20E **37** E10
Mandalay *Burma* 22°0N 96°4E **41** J20
Mandale = Mandalay
 Burma 22°0N 96°4E **41** J20
Mandalgarh *India* 25°12N 75°6E **42** G6
Mandalgovĭ *Mongolia* 45°45N 106°10E **32** B4
Mandalī *Iraq* 33°43N 45°28E **46** C5
Mandan *U.S.A.* 46°50N 100°54W **80** B3
Mandar, Teluk *Indonesia* 3°32S 119°21E **37** E5
Mandaue *Phil.* 10°20N 123°56E **37** B6
Mandeville *Jamaica* 18°2N 77°31W **88** a
Mandi *India* 31°39N 76°58E **42** D7
Mandi Burewala *Pakistan* 30°9N 72°41E **42** D5
Mandi Dabwali *India* 29°58N 74°42E **42** E6
Mandimba *Mozam.* 14°20S 35°40E **55** G7
Mandioli *Indonesia* 0°40S 127°20E **37** E7
Mandla *India* 22°39N 80°30E **43** H9
Mandorah *Australia* 12°32S 130°42E **60** B5
Mandra *Pakistan* 33°23N 73°12E **42** C5
Mandritsara *Madag.* 15°50S 48°49E **55** H9
Mandsaur *India* 24°3N 75°8E **42** G6
Mandurah *Australia* 32°36S 115°48E **61** F2
Mandvi *India* 22°51N 69°22E **42** H3
Mandya *India* 12°30N 77°0E **45** H3
Mandzai *Pakistan* 30°55N 67°6E **42** D2
Maneh *Iran* 37°39N 57°7E **47** B8
Maner → *India* 18°30N 79°40E **44** E4
Maneroo Cr. →
 Australia 23°21S 143°53E **62** C3
Manfalût *Egypt* 27°20N 30°52E **53** C12
Manfredónia *Italy* 41°38N 15°55E **22** D6
Mangabeiras, Chapada das
 Brazil 10°0S 46°30W **93** F9
Mangaia *Cook Is.* 21°55S 157°55W **65** K12
Mangalagiri *India* 16°26N 80°36E **45** F5
Mangalia *Romania* 43°50N 28°35E **17** G15
Mangalore *India* 12°55N 74°47E **45** H2
Mangaluru = Mangalore
 India 12°55N 74°47E **45** H2
Mangalvedha *India* 17°31N 75°28E **44** F2
Mangan *India* 27°31N 88°32E **43** F13
Mangaon *India* 18°15N 73°20E **44** E1
Mangarrayi ⊙ *Australia* 15°5S 133°10E **62** B1
Mangawan *India* 24°41N 81°33E **43** G9
Mangaweka *N.Z.* 39°48S 175°47E **59** C5
Manggar *Indonesia* 2°50S 108°10E **36** E3
Manggawitu *Indonesia* 4°8S 133°32E **37** E8
Mangghystaŭ Tübegi
 Kazakhstan 44°30N 52°30E **26** E6
Manggis *Indonesia* 8°29S 115°31E **37** J18
Mangkalihat, Tanjung
 Indonesia 1°2N 118°59E **37** D5
Mangkururrpa ⊙
 Australia 20°35S 129°43E **60** D4
Mangla *Pakistan* 33°7N 73°39E **42** C5
Mangla Dam *Pakistan* 33°9N 73°44E **43** C5
Manglaur *India* 29°44N 77°49E **42** E7
Mangnai *China* 37°52N 91°43E **30** D7
Mangnai Zhen *China* 38°24N 90°14E **30** D7
Mango *Togo* 10°20N 0°30E **52** F6
Mango *Tonga* 20°17S 174°29W **59** c
Mangoche *Malawi* 14°25S 35°16E **55** G7
Mangoky → *Madag.* 21°29S 43°41E **55** J8
Mangole *Indonesia* 1°50S 125°55E **37** E7
Mangonui *N.Z.* 35°1S 173°32E **59** A4
Mangrol *Mad. P., India* 21°7N 70°7E **42** J4
Mangrol *Raj., India* 25°20N 76°31E **42** G6
Mangrul Pir *India* 20°19N 77°21E **44** J10
Mangueira, L. da *Brazil* 33°0S 52°50W **95** C5
Mangum *U.S.A.* 34°53N 99°30W **84** D5
Manguri *Australia* 28°58S 134°22E **63** A1
Mangyshlak, Poluostrov =
 Mangghystaŭ Tübegi
 Kazakhstan 44°30N 52°30E **26** E6
Manhattan *U.S.A.* 39°11N 96°35W **80** F5
Manhiça *Mozam.* 25°23S 32°49E **57** C5
Manica *Mozam.* 18°58S 32°59E **57** A5
Manica □ *Mozam.* 19°10S 33°45E **57** A5
Manicoré *Brazil* 5°48S 61°16W **92** E6
Manicouagan → *Canada* 49°30N 68°30W **73** C6
Manicouagan, Rés.
 Canada 51°5N 68°40W **73** B6
Manīfah *Si. Arabia* 27°44N 49°0E **47** E6
Manifold, C. *Australia* 22°41S 150°50E **62** C5
Maniganggo *China* 31°56N 99°10E **34** B2
Manigotagan *Canada* 51°6N 96°18W **71** C9
Manigotagan → *Canada* 51°7N 96°20W **71** C9
Manihari *India* 25°21N 87°38E **43** G12

Manihiki *Cook Is.* 10°24S 161°1W **65** J11
Manihiki Plateau
 Pac. Oc. 11°0S 164°0W **65** J11
Manikpur *India* 25°4N 81°7E **43** G9
Manila *U.S.A.* 40°59N 109°43W **76** F9
Manila B. *Phil.* 14°40N 120°35E **37** B6
Manilla *Australia* 30°45S 150°43E **63** E5
Maningrida *Australia* 12°3S 134°13E **62** A1
Manipur □ *India* 25°0N 94°0E **41** G19
Manipur → *Burma* 23°45N 94°20E **41** H19
Manisa *Turkey* 38°38N 27°30E **23** E12
Manistee *U.S.A.* 44°15N 86°19W **80** C10
Manistee → *U.S.A.* 44°15N 86°21W **80** C10
Manistique *U.S.A.* 45°57N 86°15W **80** C10
Manitoba □ *Canada* 53°30N 97°0W **71** B9
Manitoba, L. *Canada* 51°0N 98°45W **71** C9
Manitou *Canada* 49°15N 98°32W **71** D9
Manitou, L. *Canada* 50°55N 65°17W **73** B6
Manitou Is. *U.S.A.* 45°8N 86°0W **80** C10
Manitou L. *Canada* 52°43N 109°43W **71** C7
Manitou Springs
 U.S.A. 38°52N 104°55W **76** G11
Manitoulin I. *Canada* 45°40N 82°30W **72** C3
Manitouwadge *Canada* 49°8N 85°48W **72** C2
Manitowoc *U.S.A.* 44°5N 87°40W **80** C10
Maniyachi *India* 8°51N 77°55E **45** K3
Manizales *Colombia* 5°5N 75°32W **92** B3
Manjacaze *Mozam.* 24°45S 34°0E **57** B5
Manjakandriana *Madag.* 18°55S 47°47E **55** H9
Manjhand *Pakistan* 25°50N 68°10E **42** G3
Manjimup *Australia* 34°15S 116°6E **61** F2
Manjlegaon *India* 19°9N 76°14E **44** E3
Manjra → *India* 18°49N 77°52E **44** E3
Mankato *Kans., U.S.A.* 39°47N 98°13W **80** F4
Mankato *Minn., U.S.A.* 44°10N 94°0W **80** C6
Mankayane *Swaziland* 26°40S 31°4E **57** D5
Mankera *Pakistan* 31°23N 71°26E **42** D4
Mankota *Canada* 49°25N 107°5W **71** D7
Mankulam *Sri Lanka* 9°8N 80°26E **45** K5
Manlay = Üydzin *Mongolia* 44°9N 107°0E **32** B4
Manmad *India* 20°18N 74°28E **44** D2
Mann Ranges *Australia* 26°6S 130°5E **61** E5
Manna *Indonesia* 4°25S 102°55E **36** E2
Mannahill *Australia* 32°25S 140°0E **63** E3
Mannar *Sri Lanka* 9°1N 79°54E **45** K4
Mannar, G. of *Asia* 8°30N 79°0E **45** K4
Mannar I. *Sri Lanka* 9°5N 79°45E **45** K4
Mannargudi *India* 10°45N 79°51E **45** J4
Mannheim *Germany* 49°29N 8°29E **16** D5
Manning *Canada* 56°53N 117°39W **70** B5
Manning *Oreg., U.S.A.* 45°45N 123°13W **78** E3
Manning *S.C., U.S.A.* 33°42N 80°13W **85** E14
Mannum *Australia* 34°50S 139°20E **63** E2
Manoharpur *India* 22°23N 85°12E **43** H11
Manokwari *Indonesia* 0°54S 134°0E **37** E8
Manombo *Madag.* 22°57S 43°28E **55** J8
Manono
 Dem. Rep. of the Congo 7°15S 27°25E **54** F5
Manono *Samoa* 13°50S 172°5W **59** b
Manorhamilton *Ireland* 54°18N 8°11W **10** B3
Manosque *France* 43°49N 5°47E **20** E6
Manotick *Canada* 45°13N 75°41W **83** A9
Manouane → *Canada* 49°30N 71°10W **73** C5
Manouane, L. *Canada* 50°45N 70°45W **73** B5
Manp'o *N. Korea* 41°6N 126°24E **33** D14
Manpojin = Manp'o
 N. Korea 41°6N 126°24E **33** D14
Manpur *Chhattisgarh,*
 India 23°17N 83°35E **43** H10
Manpur *Chhattisgarh,*
 India 20°22N 80°43E **44** D5
Manresa *Spain* 41°48N 1°50E **21** B6
Mansa *Gujarat, India* 23°27N 72°45E **42** H5
Mansa *Punjab, India* 30°0N 75°27E **42** E6
Mansa *Zambia* 11°13S 28°55E **54** G5
Mansehra *Pakistan* 34°20N 73°15E **42** B5
Mansel I. *Canada* 62°0N 80°0W **69** E15
Mansfield *Australia* 37°4S 146°6E **63** F4
Mansfield *U.K.* 53°9N 1°11W **12** D6
Mansfield *La., U.S.A.* 32°2N 93°43W **84** E8
Mansfield *Mass., U.S.A.* 42°2N 71°13W **83** D13
Mansfield *Ohio, U.S.A.* 40°45N 82°31W **82** F2
Mansfield *Pa., U.S.A.* 41°48N 77°5W **82** E7
Mansfield *Tex., U.S.A.* 32°33N 97°8W **84** E6
Mansfield, Mt. *U.S.A.* 44°33N 72°49W **83** B12
Manson Creek *Canada* 55°37N 124°32W **70** B4
Manta *Ecuador* 1°0S 80°40W **92** D2
Mantalingajan, Mt. *Phil.* 8°55N 117°45E **36** C5
Manteca *U.S.A.* 37°48N 121°13W **78** H5
Mantes-la-Jolie *France* 48°58N 1°41E **20** B4
Mantha *India* 19°40N 76°23E **44** E3
Manthani *India* 18°40N 79°35E **44** E4
Manti *U.S.A.* 39°16N 111°38W **76** G8
Mantiqueira, Serra da
 Brazil 22°0S 44°0W **95** A7
Manton *U.S.A.* 44°25N 85°24W **81** C11
Mántova *Italy* 45°9N 10°48E **22** B4
Mänttä Vilppula *Finland* 62°3N 24°40E **8** E21
Mantua = Mántova *Italy* 45°9N 10°48E **22** B4
Manu → *Peru* 12°10S 70°51W **92** F4
Manú *Peru* 12°16S 70°55W **92** F4
Manu'a Is. *Amer. Samoa* 14°13S 169°35W **59** b
Manuel Alves → *Brazil* 11°19S 48°28W **93** F9
Manui *Indonesia* 3°35S 123°5E **37** E6
Manukau *N.Z.* 37°0S 174°52E **59** B5
Manuripi → *Bolivia* 11°6S 67°36W **92** F5
Manvi *India* 15°57N 76°59E **45** G3
Manwan Dam *China* 24°44N 100°20E **34** E3
Manwath *India* 19°19N 76°32E **44** E3
Many *U.S.A.* 31°34N 93°29W **84** F8
Manyallaluk ⊙
 Australia 14°16S 132°49E **60** B5
Manych-Gudilo, Ozero
 Russia 46°24N 42°38E **19** E7
Manyoni *Tanzania* 5°45S 34°55E **54** F6
Manzai *Pakistan* 32°12N 70°15E **42** C4
Manzanar △ *U.S.A.* 36°44N 118°9W **78** J7

Manzanares *Spain* 39°2N 3°22W **21** C4
Manzanillo *Cuba* 20°20N 77°31W **88** B4
Manzanillo *Mexico* 19°3N 104°20W **86** D4
Manzanillo, Pta. *Panama* 9°30N 79°40W **88** E4
Manzano Mts. *U.S.A.* 34°40N 106°20W **77** J10
Manzariyeh *Iran* 34°53N 50°50E **47** C6
Manzhouli *China* 49°35N 117°25E **31** B12
Manzini *Swaziland* 26°30S 31°25E **57** C5
Manzouli = Manzhouli
 China 49°35N 117°25E **31** B12
Manzur Vadisi △ *Turkey* 39°10N 39°30E **46** B3
Mao *Chad* 14°4N 15°19E **53** F9
Maó *Spain* 39°53N 4°16E **21** C8
Maoke, Pegunungan
 Indonesia 3°40S 137°30E **37** E9
Maolin *China* 43°58N 123°30E **33** C12
Maoming *China* 21°50N 110°54E **35** G8
Maopi T'ou *China* 21°56N 120°43E **35** G13
Mapastepec *Mexico* 15°26N 92°54W **87** D6
Maphrao, Ko *Thailand* 7°56N 98°26E **39** a
Mapia, Kepulauan
 Indonesia 0°50N 134°20E **37** D8
Mapimí *Mexico* 25°49N 103°51W **86** B4
Mapimí, Bolsón de
 Mexico 27°0N 104°15W **86** B4
Maping *China* 31°34N 113°32E **35** B9
Mapinhane *Mozam.* 22°20S 35°0E **57** B6
Maple Creek *Canada* 49°55N 109°29W **71** D7
Maple Valley *U.S.A.* 47°25N 122°3W **78** C4
Mapleton *U.S.A.* 44°2N 123°52W **76** D2
Mapoon ⊙ *Australia* 11°44S 142°8E **62** A3
Mapuera → *Brazil* 1°5S 57°2W **92** D7
Mapulanguene *Mozam.* 24°29S 32°6E **57** B5
Mapungubwe △ *S. Africa* 22°12S 29°22E **57** B4
Maputo *Mozam.* 25°58S 32°32E **57** C5
Maputo → *Mozam.* 26°0S 32°25E **57** C5
Maputo, B. de *Mozam.* 25°50S 32°45E **57** C5
Maputo △ *Mozam.* 26°23S 32°48E **57** C5
Maqat *Kazakhstan* 47°39N 53°19E **19** E9
Maqên *China* 34°24N 100°6E **30** E9
Maqên Gangri *China* 34°55N 99°18E **30** E8
Maqiaohe *China* 44°40N 130°33E **33** B16
Maqna *Si. Arabia* 28°25N 34°50E **46** D2
Maqteïr *Mauritania* 21°50N 11°40W **52** D3
Maqu *China* 33°52N 101°42E **30** E9
Maquan He = Brahmaputra →
 Asia 23°40N 90°35E **43** H13
Maquela do Zombo *Angola* 6°0S 15°15E **54** F3
Maquinchao *Argentina* 41°15S 68°50W **96** E3
Maquoketa *U.S.A.* 42°4N 90°40W **80** D8
Mar *Canada* 44°49N 81°12W **82** B3
Mar, Serra do *Brazil* 25°30S 49°0W **95** B6
Mar Chiquita, L.
 Argentina 30°40S 62°50W **94** C3
Mar del Plata *Argentina* 38°0S 57°30W **94** D4
Mar Menor *Spain* 37°40N 0°45W **21** D5
Maraā *Brazil* 1°52S 65°25W **92** D5
Maraa *Tahiti* 17°46S 149°34W **59** d
Marabá *Brazil* 5°20S 49°5W **93** E9
Maraboon, L. *Australia* 23°41S 148°0E **62** C4
Maracá, I. de *Brazil* 2°10N 50°30W **93** C8
Maracaibo *Venezuela* 10°40N 71°37W **92** A4
Maracaibo, L. de
 Venezuela 9°40N 71°30W **92** B4
Maracaju *Brazil* 21°38S 55°9W **95** A4
Maracas Bay Village
 Trin. & Tob. 10°46N 61°28W **93** K15
Maracay *Venezuela* 10°15N 67°28W **92** A5
Marādah *Libya* 29°15N 19°15E **53** C9
Maradi *Niger* 13°29N 7°20E **52** F7
Marāgheh *Iran* 37°30N 46°12E **46** B5
Marāh *Si. Arabia* 25°0N 45°35E **46** E5
Marajó, I. de *Brazil* 1°0S 49°30W **93** D9
Marākand *Iran* 38°51N 45°16E **46** B5
Marakele △ *S. Africa* 24°30S 25°30E **57** D4
Maralinga *Australia* 30°13S 131°32E **61** F5
Maralinga Tjarutja ⊙
 Australia 29°30S 131°0E **61** E5
Marambio *Antarctica* 64°0S 56°0W **5** C18
Maran *Malaysia* 3°5N 102°45E **39** L4
Marana *U.S.A.* 32°27N 111°13W **77** K8
Maranboy *Australia* 14°40S 132°39E **60** B5
Marand *Iran* 38°30N 45°45E **46** B5
Maranga *Malaysia* 5°12N 103°13E **39** K4
Maranguape *Brazil* 3°55S 38°50W **93** D11
Mariscal Estigarribia
 Paraguay 22°3S 60°40W **94** A3
Maranhão = São Luís
 Brazil 2°39S 44°15W **93** D10
Maranhão □ *Brazil* 5°0S 46°0W **93** E9
Maranoa → *Australia* 27°50S 148°37E **63** D4
Marañón → *Peru* 4°30S 73°35W **92** D4
Marão *Mozam.* 24°18S 34°2E **57** B5
Maraş = Kahramanmaraş
 Turkey 37°37N 36°53E **46** B3
Marathasa *Cyprus* 34°59N 32°51E **25** E11
Marathon *Australia* 20°51S 143°32E **62** C3
Marathon *Canada* 48°44N 86°23W **72** C2
Marathon *N.Y., U.S.A.* 42°27N 76°2W **83** D8
Marathon *Tex., U.S.A.* 30°12N 103°15W **84** F3
Maratua *Indonesia* 2°10N 118°35E **37** D5
Maraval *Trin. & Tob.* 10°42N 61°31W **93** K15
Marāwih *U.A.E.* 24°18N 53°18E **47** E7
Marbella *Spain* 36°30N 4°57W **21** D3
Marble Bar *Australia* 21°9S 119°44E **60** D2
Marblehead *Mass.,*
 U.S.A. 42°29N 70°51W **83** D14
Marblehead *Ohio, U.S.A.* 41°32N 82°44W **82** E2
Marburg *Germany* 50°47N 8°46E **16** C5
Marca, Pta. do *Angola* 16°31S 11°43E **55** H2
March *U.K.* 52°33N 0°5E **13** E8
Marche *France* 46°5N 1°20E **20** C4
Marche-en-Famenne
 Belgium 50°14N 5°19E **15** D5
Marchena *Spain* 37°18N 5°23W **21** D3
Marco Island *U.S.A.* 25°58N 81°44W **85** J14
Marcos Juárez *Argentina* 32°42S 62°5W **94** C3

Marcus Baker, Mt.
 U.S.A. 61°26N 147°45W **74** C10
Marcus I. = Minami-Tori-Shima
 Pac. Oc. 24°20N 153°58E **64** E7
Marcy, Mt. *U.S.A.* 44°7N 73°56W **83** B11
Mardan *Pakistan* 34°20N 72°0E **42** B5
Mardie *Australia* 21°12S 115°59E **60** D2
Mardin *Turkey* 37°20N 40°43E **46** B4
Maree, L. *U.K.* 57°40N 5°26W **11** D3
Mareeba *Australia* 16°59S 145°28E **62** B4
Mareetsane *S. Africa* 26°9S 25°25E **56** C4
Marek = Stanke Dimitrov
 Bulgaria 42°17N 23°9E **23** C10
Marengo *U.S.A.* 41°48N 92°4W **80** E7
Marfa *U.S.A.* 30°19N 104°1W **84** F2
Margao = Madgaon
 India 15°12N 73°58E **45** G1
Margaret → *Australia* 18°9S 125°41E **60** C4
Margaret Bay *Canada* 51°20N 127°35W **70** C3
Margaret L. *Canada* 58°56N 115°25W **70** B5
Margaret River *Australia* 33°57S 115°4E **61** F2
Margarita, I. de *Venezuela* 11°0N 64°0W **92** A6
Margaritovo *Russia* 43°25N 134°45E **28** C7
Margate *S. Africa* 30°50S 30°20E **57** D5
Margate *U.K.* 51°23N 1°23E **13** F9
Marghilon *Uzbekistan* 40°27N 71°42E **26** E8
Märgow, Dasht-e *Afghan.* 30°40N 62°30E **40** D3
Marguerite *Canada* 52°30N 122°25W **70** C4
Mari El □ *Russia* 56°30N 48°0E **18** C8
Mari Indus *Pakistan* 32°57N 71°34E **42** C4
Mari Republic = Mari El □
 Russia 56°30N 48°0E **18** C8
María Elena *Chile* 22°18S 69°40W **94** A2
María Grande *Argentina* 31°45S 59°55W **94** C4
Maria I. *N. Terr.,*
 Australia 14°52S 135°45E **62** A2
Maria I. *Tas., Australia* 42°35S 148°0E **63** G4
Maria Island △ *Australia* 42°38S 148°5E **63** G4
Maria van Diemen, C.
 N.Z. 34°29S 172°40E **59** A4
Mariala △ *Australia* 25°57S 145°2E **63** D4
Marian *Australia* 21°9S 148°57E **62** b
Marian L. *Canada* 63°0N 116°15W **70** A5
Mariana Trench *Pac. Oc.* 13°0N 145°0E **64** F6
Marianna *Ark., U.S.A.* 34°46N 90°46W **85** D9
Marianna *Fla., U.S.A.* 30°46N 85°14W **85** F12
Marias → *U.S.A.* 47°56N 110°30W **76** C8
Marías, Is. *Mexico* 21°25N 106°28W **86** C3
Mariato, Punta *Panama* 7°12N 80°52W **88** E3
Maribor *Slovenia* 46°36N 15°40E **16** E8
Marico → *Africa* 23°35S 26°57E **56** C4
Maricopa *Ariz., U.S.A.* 33°4N 112°3W **77** K7
Maricopa *Calif., U.S.A.* 35°4N 119°24W **79** K7
Marié → *Brazil* 0°27S 66°26W **92** D5
Marie Byrd Land
 Antarctica 79°30S 125°0W **5** D14
Marie-Galante *Guadeloupe* 15°56N 61°16W **88** b
Mariecourt = Kangiqsujuaq
 Canada 61°30N 72°0W **69** E17
Mariehamn *Finland* 60°5N 19°55E **9** F18
Mariembourg *Belgium* 50°6N 4°31E **15** D4
Mariental *Namibia* 24°36S 18°0E **56** B2
Marienville *U.S.A.* 41°28N 79°8W **82** E5
Mariestad *Sweden* 58°43N 13°50E **9** G15
Marietta *Ga., U.S.A.* 33°57N 84°33W **85** E12
Marietta *Ohio, U.S.A.* 39°25N 81°27W **81** F13
Marieville *Canada* 45°26N 73°10W **83** A11
Mariinsk *Russia* 56°10N 87°20E **26** D9
Marijampolė *Lithuania* 54°33N 23°19E **9** J20
Marília *Brazil* 22°13S 50°0W **95** A6
Marín *Spain* 42°23N 8°42W **21** A1
Marina *U.S.A.* 36°41N 121°48W **78** J5
Marine City *U.S.A.* 42°43N 82°30W **82** D2
Marinette *U.S.A.* 45°6N 87°38W **80** C10
Maringá *Brazil* 23°26S 52°2W **95** A5
Marion *Ala., U.S.A.* 32°38N 87°19W **85** E11
Marion *Ark., U.S.A.* 35°13N 90°12W **80** H8
Marion *Ill., U.S.A.* 37°44N 88°56W **80** G9
Marion *Ind., U.S.A.* 40°32N 85°40W **81** E11
Marion *Iowa, U.S.A.* 42°2N 91°36W **80** D8
Marion *Kans., U.S.A.* 38°21N 97°1W **80** F5
Marion *N.C., U.S.A.* 35°41N 82°1W **85** D13
Marion *Ohio, U.S.A.* 40°35N 83°8W **81** E12
Marion *S.C., U.S.A.* 34°11N 79°24W **85** D15
Marion *Va., U.S.A.* 36°50N 81°31W **81** G13
Marion, L. *U.S.A.* 33°28N 80°10W **85** E14
Mariposa *U.S.A.* 37°29N 119°58W **78** H7
Mariscal Estigarribia
 Paraguay 22°3S 60°40W **94** A3
Maritime Alps = Maritimes, Alpes
 Europe 44°10N 7°10E **20** D7
Maritimes, Alpes *Europe* 44°10N 7°10E **20** D7
Maritsa = Evros →
 Greece 41°40N 26°34E **23** D12
Mariupol *Ukraine* 47°5N 37°31E **19** E6
Mariusa △ *Venezuela* 9°24N 61°27W **89** D7
Marīvān *Iran* 35°30N 46°25E **46** C5
Marj 'Uyūn *Lebanon* 33°21N 35°34E **48** B4
Marka *Somalia* 1°48N 44°50E **49** G3
Markam *China* 29°42N 98°38E **34** C2
Markapur *India* 15°44N 79°19E **45** G4
Markazī □ *Iran* 34°0N 49°0E **47** C6
Markdale *Canada* 44°19N 80°39W **82** B4
Marked Tree *U.S.A.* 35°32N 90°25W **85** D9
Market Drayton *U.K.* 52°54N 2°29W **12** E5
Market Harborough *U.K.* 52°29N 0°55W **13** E7
Market Rasen *U.K.* 53°24N 0°20W **12** D7
Markham, Mt. *Antarctica* 83°0S 164°0E **5** E11
Markleeville *U.S.A.* 38°42N 119°47W **78** G7
Markovo *Russia* 64°40N 170°24E **27** C17
Marks *Russia* 51°45N 46°50E **18** D8
Marksville *U.S.A.* 31°8N 92°4W **84** F8
Marla *Australia* 27°19S 133°33E **63** D1
Marlbank *Canada* 44°26N 77°6W **82** B7
Marlboro *U.S.A.* 41°36N 73°59W **83** E11
Marlborough *Australia* 22°46S 149°52E **62** C4
Marlborough *U.K.* 51°25N 1°43W **13** F6
Marlborough *U.S.A.* 42°21N 71°33W **83** D13

Marlborough Downs
 U.K. 51°27N 1°53W **13** F6
Marlin *U.S.A.* 31°18N 96°54W **84** F6
Marlow *U.K.* 51°34N 0°46W **13** F7
Marlow *U.S.A.* 34°39N 97°58W **84** D6
Marmagao *India* 15°25N 73°56E **45** G1
Marmara *Turkey* 40°35N 27°34E **23** D12
Marmara, Sea of = Marmara
 Denizi *Turkey* 40°45N 28°15E **23** D13
Marmara Denizi *Turkey* 40°45N 28°15E **23** D13
Marmaris *Turkey* 36°50N 28°14E **23** F13
Marmion, Mt. *Australia* 29°16S 119°50E **61** E2
Marmion L. *Canada* 48°55N 91°20W **72** C1
Marmolada, Mte. *Italy* 46°26N 11°51E **22** A4
Marmora *Canada* 44°28N 77°41W **82** B7
Marne → *France* 48°47N 2°29E **20** B5
Maro Reef *U.S.A.* 25°25N 170°35W **75** K5
Maroantsetra *Madag.* 15°26S 49°44E **55** H9
Maroelaboom *Namibia* 19°15S 18°53E **56** A2
Marondera *Zimbabwe* 18°5S 31°42E **55** H6
Maroni → *Fr. Guiana* 5°30N 54°0W **93** B8
Maroochydore *Australia* 26°29S 153°5E **63** D5
Maroona *Australia* 37°27S 142°54E **63** F3
Maroua *Cameroon* 10°40N 14°20E **53** F8
Marovoay *Madag.* 16°6S 46°39E **55** H9
Marquard *S. Africa* 28°40S 27°28E **56** C4
Marquesas Fracture Zone
 Pac. Oc. 9°0S 125°0W **65** H15
Marquesas Is. = Marquises, Îs.
 French Polynesia 9°30S 140°0W **65** H14
Marquette *U.S.A.* 46°33N 87°24W **80** B10
Marquis *St. Lucia* 14°2N 60°54W **89** f
Marquises, Îs.
 French Polynesia 9°30S 140°0W **65** H14
Marra, Djebel *Sudan* 13°10N 24°22E **53** F10
Marracuene *Mozam.* 25°45S 32°35E **57** C5
Marrakech *Morocco* 31°9N 8°0W **52** B4
Marrawah *Australia* 40°55S 144°42E **63** G3
Marree *Australia* 29°39S 138°1E **63** D2
Marrimane *Mozam.* 22°58S 33°34E **57** B5
Marromeu *Mozam.* 18°15S 36°25E **57** A6
Marromeu → *Mozam.* 19°0S 36°0E **57** A6
Marrowie Cr. →
 Australia 33°23S 145°40E **63** E4
Marrupa *Mozam.* 13°8S 37°30E **55** G7
Mars Hill *U.S.A.* 46°31N 67°52W **81** B20
Marsá 'Alam *Egypt* 25°5N 34°54E **49** B1
Marsá Matrûh *Egypt* 31°19N 27°9E **53** B11
Marsabit *Kenya* 2°18N 38°0E **54** D7
Marsala *Italy* 37°48N 12°26E **22** F5
Marsden *Australia* 33°47S 147°32E **63** E4
Marseille *France* 43°18N 5°23E **20** E6
Marseilles = Marseille
 France 43°18N 5°23E **20** E6
Marsh I. *U.S.A.* 29°34N 91°53W **84** G9
Marshall *Ark., U.S.A.* 35°55N 92°38W **84** D8
Marshall *Mich., U.S.A.* 42°16N 84°58W **81** D11
Marshall *Minn., U.S.A.* 44°27N 95°47W **80** C6
Marshall *Mo., U.S.A.* 39°7N 93°12W **80** F7
Marshall *Tex., U.S.A.* 32°33N 94°23W **84** E7
Marshall → *Australia* 22°59S 136°59E **62** C2
Marshall Is. ■ *Pac. Oc.* 9°0N 171°0E **58** A10
Marshalltown *U.S.A.* 42°3N 92°55W **80** D7
Marshbrook *Zimbabwe* 18°33S 31°9E **57** A5
Marshfield *Mo., U.S.A.* 37°15N 92°54W **80** G7
Marshfield *Vt., U.S.A.* 44°20N 72°20W **83** B12
Marshfield *Wis., U.S.A.* 44°40N 90°10W **80** C8
Marshūn *Iran* 36°19N 49°23E **47** B6
Märsta *Sweden* 59°37N 17°52E **9** G17
Mart *U.S.A.* 31°33N 96°50W **84** F6
Martaban *Burma* 16°30N 97°35E **41** L20
Martaban, G. of *Burma* 16°5N 96°30E **41** L20
Martapura *Kalimantan Selatan,*
 Indonesia 3°22S 114°47E **36** E4
Martapura *Sumatera Selatan,*
 Indonesia 4°19S 104°22E **36** E2
Marte R. Gómez, Presa
 Mexico 26°10N 99°0W **87** B5
Martelange *Belgium* 49°49N 5°43E **15** E5
Marthapal *India* 19°24N 81°37E **44** E5
Martha's Vineyard
 U.S.A. 41°25N 70°38W **83** E14
Martigny *Switz.* 46°6N 7°3E **20** C7
Martigues *France* 43°24N 5°4E **20** E6
Martin *Slovak Rep.* 49°6N 18°58E **17** D10
Martin *S. Dak., U.S.A.* 43°11N 101°44W **80** D3
Martin *Tenn., U.S.A.* 36°21N 88°51W **85** C10
Martin L. *U.S.A.* 32°41N 85°55W **85** E12
Martina Franca *Italy* 40°42N 17°20E **22** D7
Martinborough *N.Z.* 41°14S 175°29E **59** D5
Martinez *Calif., U.S.A.* 38°1N 122°8W **78** G4
Martinez *Ga., U.S.A.* 33°31N 82°5W **85** E13
Martinique ☑ *W. Indies* 14°40N 61°0W **88** c
Martinique Passage
 W. Indies 15°15N 61°0W **89** C7
Martinópolis *Brazil* 22°11S 51°12W **95** A5
Martins Bay *Barbados* 13°12N 59°29W **89** g
Martins Ferry *U.S.A.* 40°6N 80°44W **82** F4
Martinsburg *Pa., U.S.A.* 40°19N 78°20W **82** F6
Martinsburg *W. Va.,*
 U.S.A. 39°27N 77°58W **81** F15
Martinsville *Ind., U.S.A.* 39°26N 86°25W **80** F10
Martinsville *Va., U.S.A.* 36°41N 79°52W **81** G14
Marton *N.Z.* 40°4S 175°23E **59** D5
Martos *Spain* 37°44N 3°58W **21** D4
Martu ⊙ *Australia* 22°30S 122°30E **60** D3
Marudi *Malaysia* 4°11N 114°19E **36** D4
Maruf *Afghan.* 31°30N 67°6E **40** D5
Marugame *Japan* 34°15N 133°40E **29** G6
Marunga *Angola* 17°28S 20°2E **56** A3
Maruwa ⊙ *Australia* 22°30S 127°42E **60** D4
Marv Dasht *Iran* 29°50N 52°40E **47** D7
Marvast *Iran* 30°30N 54°15E **47** D7
Marvel Loch *Australia* 31°28S 119°29E **61** F2
Marwar *India* 25°43N 73°45E **42** G5
Marwayne *Canada* 53°32N 110°20W **71** C6
Mary *Turkmenistan* 37°40N 61°50E **47** B9
Maryborough = Portlaoise
 Ireland 53°2N 7°18W **10** C4
Maryborough *Queens.,*
 Australia 25°31S 152°37E **63** D5

Maryborough *Vic., Australia* 37°3S 143°44E **63 F3**
Maryfield *Canada* 49°50N 101°35W **71 D8**
Maryland □ *U.S.A.* 39°0N 76°30W **81 F15**
Maryland Junction *Zimbabwe* 17°45S 30°31E **55 H6**
Maryport *U.K.* 54°44N 3°28W **12 C4**
Mary's Harbour *Canada* 52°18N 55°51W **73 B8**
Marystown *Canada* 47°10N 55°10W **73 C8**
Marysville *Calif., U.S.A.* 39°9N 121°35W **78 F5**
Marysville *Kans., U.S.A.* 39°51N 96°39W **80 F5**
Marysville *Mich., U.S.A.* 42°54N 82°29W **82 D2**
Marysville *Ohio, U.S.A.* 40°14N 83°22W **81 E12**
Marysville *Wash., U.S.A.* 48°3N 122°11W **78 B4**
Maryville *Mo., U.S.A.* 40°21N 94°52W **80 E6**
Maryville *Tenn., U.S.A.* 35°46N 83°58W **85 D13**
Masada *Israel* 31°18N 35°21E **48 D4**
Masai *Malaysia* 1°29N 103°55E **39 d**
Masai Steppe *Tanzania* 4°30S 36°30E **54 E7**
Masaka *Uganda* 0°21S 31°45E **54 E6**
Masalembo, Kepulauan *Indonesia* 5°35S 114°30E **36 F4**
Masalima, Kepulauan *Indonesia* 5°4S 117°5E **36 F5**
Masamba *Indonesia* 2°30S 120°15E **37 E6**
Masan *S. Korea* 35°11N 128°32E **33 G15**
Masandam, Ra's *Oman* 26°30N 56°30E **47 E8**
Masasi *Tanzania* 10°45S 38°52E **54 G7**
Masaya *Nic.* 12°0N 86°7W **88 D2**
Masbate *Phil.* 12°21N 123°36E **37 B6**
Mascara *Algeria* 35°26N 0°6E **52 A6**
Mascarene Is. *Ind. Oc.* 22°0S 55°0E **50 J9**
Mascota *Mexico* 20°32N 104°49W **86 C4**
Masela *Indonesia* 8°9S 129°51E **37 F7**
Maseru *Lesotho* 29°18S 27°30E **56 C4**
Mashābih *Si. Arabia* 25°35N 36°30E **46 E3**
Mashan *China* 23°40N 108°11E **34 F7**
Mashang *China* 36°48N 117°57E **33 F9**
Mashatu △ *Botswana* 22°45S 29°5E **57 B4**
Masherbrum *Pakistan* 35°38N 76°18E **43 B7**
Mashhad *Iran* 36°20N 59°35E **47 B8**
Mashīz *Iran* 29°56N 56°37E **47 D8**
Māshkel, Hāmūn-i- *Pakistan* 28°20N 62°56E **47 D9**
Mashki Chāh *Pakistan* 29°5N 62°30E **40 E3**
Mashonaland *Zimbabwe* 16°30S 31°0E **55 H6**
Mashonaland Central □ *Zimbabwe* 17°30S 31°0E **57 A5**
Mashonaland East □ *Zimbabwe* 18°0S 32°0E **57 A5**
Mashonaland West □ *Zimbabwe* 17°30S 29°30E **57 A4**
Mashrakh *India* 26°7N 84°48E **43 F11**
Masi Manimba *Dem. Rep. of the Congo* 4°40S 17°54E **54 E3**
Masig *Australia* 9°45S 143°24E **62 a**
Masindi *Uganda* 1°40N 31°43E **54 D6**
Maşīrah, Jazīrat *Oman* 21°0N 58°50E **49 C6**
Maşīrah, Khalīj *Oman* 20°10N 58°10E **49 C6**
Masisi *Dem. Rep. of the Congo* 1°23S 28°49E **54 E5**
Masjed Soleyman *Iran* 31°55N 49°18E **47 D6**
Mask, L. *Ireland* 53°36N 9°22W **10 C2**
Maski *India* 15°56N 76°46E **45 G3**
Maskin *Oman* 23°44N 56°52E **47 F8**
Masoala, Tanjon' i *Madag.* 15°59S 50°13E **55 H10**
Masohi = Amahai *Indonesia* 3°20S 128°55E **37 E7**
Mason *Nev., U.S.A.* 38°56N 119°8W **78 G7**
Mason *Tex., U.S.A.* 30°45N 99°14W **84 F5**
Mason City *U.S.A.* 43°9N 93°12W **80 D7**
Masqat *Oman* 23°37N 58°36E **49 C6**
Massa *Italy* 44°1N 10°9E **20 D9**
Massachusetts □ *U.S.A.* 42°30N 72°0W **83 D13**
Massachusetts B. *U.S.A.* 42°25N 70°50W **83 D14**
Massakory *Chad* 13°0N 15°49E **53 F9**
Massangena *Mozam.* 21°34S 33°0E **57 B5**
Massango *Angola* 8°2S 16°21E **54 F3**
Massawa = Mitsiwa *Eritrea* 15°35N 39°25E **49 D2**
Massena *U.S.A.* 44°56N 74°54W **83 B10**
Massenya *Chad* 11°21N 16°9E **53 F9**
Masset *Canada* 54°2N 132°10W **70 C2**
Massiah Street *Barbados* 13°9N 59°29W **89 g**
Massif Central *France* 44°55N 3°0E **20 D5**
Massillon *U.S.A.* 40°48N 81°32W **82 F3**
Massinga *Mozam.* 23°15S 35°22E **57 B6**
Massingir *Mozam.* 23°51S 32°4E **57 B5**
Masson-Angers *Canada* 45°32N 75°25W **83 A9**
Masson I. *Antarctica* 66°10S 93°20E **5 C7**
Mastanli = Momchilgrad *Bulgaria* 41°33N 25°23E **23 D11**
Masterton *N.Z.* 40°56S 175°39E **59 D5**
Mastic *U.S.A.* 40°47N 72°54W **83 F12**
Mastuj *Pakistan* 36°20N 72°36E **43 A5**
Mastung *Pakistan* 29°50N 66°56E **40 E5**
Masty *Belarus* 53°27N 24°38E **17 B13**
Masuda *Japan* 34°40N 131°51E **29 G5**
Masuku = Franceville *Gabon* 1°40S 13°32E **54 E2**
Masurian Lakes = Mazurski, Pojezierze *Poland* 53°50N 21°0E **17 B11**
Masvingo *Zimbabwe* 20°8S 30°49E **55 J6**
Maşyāf *Syria* 35°4N 36°20E **46 C3**
Mata-au = Clutha ➛ *N.Z.* 46°20S 169°49E **59 G2**
Matabeleland *Zimbabwe* 18°0S 27°0E **55 H5**
Matachewan *Canada* 47°56N 80°39W **72 C3**
Matadi *Dem. Rep. of the Congo* 5°52S 13°31E **54 F2**
Matagalpa *Nic.* 13°0N 85°58W **88 D2**
Matagami *Canada* 49°45N 77°34W **72 C4**
Matagami, L. *Canada* 49°50N 77°40W **72 C4**
Matagorda B. *U.S.A.* 28°40N 96°12W **84 G6**
Matagorda I. *U.S.A.* 28°15N 96°30W **84 G6**
Mataiea *Tahiti* 17°46S 149°25W **59 d**
Matak *Indonesia* 3°18N 106°16E **36 D3**
Matale *Sri Lanka* 7°30N 80°37E **45 L5**
Matam *Senegal* 15°34N 13°17W **52 E3**
Matamoros *Coahuila, Mexico* 25°32N 103°15W **86 B4**
Matamoros *Tamaulipas, Mexico* 25°53N 97°30W **87 B5**
Ma'ţan as Sarra *Libya* 21°45N 22°0E **53 D10**
Matane *Canada* 48°50N 67°33W **73 C6**
Matang *China* 23°30N 104°7E **34 F5**
Matanomadh *India* 23°33N 68°57E **42 H3**
Matanzas *Cuba* 23°0N 81°40W **88 B3**
Matapa *Botswana* 23°11S 24°39E **56 B3**
Matapan, C. = Tenaro, Akra *Greece* 36°22N 22°27E **23 F10**
Matapédia *Canada* 48°0N 66°59W **73 C6**
Matara *Sri Lanka* 5°58N 80°30E **45 M5**
Mataram *Indonesia* 8°35S 116°7E **37 K19**
Matarani *Peru* 17°0S 72°10W **92 G4**
Mataranka *Australia* 14°55S 133°4E **60 B5**
Matarma, Râs *Egypt* 30°27N 32°44E **48 E1**
Mataró *Spain* 41°32N 2°29E **21 B7**
Matatiele *S. Africa* 30°20S 28°49E **57 D4**
Matatila Dam *India* 25°0N 78°22E **44 B4**
Mataura *N.Z.* 46°11S 168°51E **59 G2**
Matavai, B. de *Tahiti* 17°30S 149°23W **59 d**
Matehuala *Mexico* 23°39N 100°39W **86 C4**
Mateke Hills *Zimbabwe* 21°48S 31°0E **55 J6**
Matelot *Trin. & Tob.* 10°50N 61°7W **93 K15**
Matera *Italy* 40°40N 16°36E **22 D7**
Mathis *U.S.A.* 28°6N 97°50W **84 G6**
Mathraki *Greece* 39°48N 19°31E **23 E8**
Mathura *India* 27°30N 77°40E **42 F7**
Mati *Phil.* 6°55N 126°15E **37 C7**
Matiali *India* 26°56N 88°49E **43 F13**
Matías Romero *Mexico* 16°53N 95°2W **87 D5**
Matiri Ra. *N.Z.* 41°38S 172°20E **59 D4**
Matjiesfontein *S. Africa* 33°14S 20°35E **56 D3**
Matla ➛ *India* 21°40N 88°40E **43 J13**
Matlamanyane *Botswana* 19°33S 25°57E **56 A4**
Matli *Pakistan* 25°2N 68°39E **42 G3**
Matlock *U.K.* 53°9N 1°33W **12 D6**
Mato Grosso □ *Brazil* 14°0S 55°0W **93 F8**
Mato Grosso, Planalto do *Brazil* 15°0S 55°0W **93 G8**
Mato Grosso do Sul □ *Brazil* 18°0S 55°0W **93 G8**
Matochkin Shar, Proliv *Russia* 73°23N 55°12E **26 B6**
Matola *Mozam.* 25°57S 32°27E **57 C5**
Matopo Hills *Zimbabwe* 20°36S 28°20E **55 J5**
Matosinhos *Portugal* 41°11N 8°42W **21 B1**
Matroosberg *S. Africa* 33°23S 19°40E **56 D2**
Maţruḩ *Oman* 23°37N 58°30E **49 C6**
Matsu Tao *Taiwan* 26°8N 119°56E **35 E13**
Matsue *Japan* 35°25N 133°10E **29 G6**
Matsum, Ko *Thailand* 9°22N 99°59E **39 b**
Matsumae *Japan* 41°26N 140°7E **28 D10**
Matsumae-Hantō *Japan* 41°30N 140°15E **28 D10**
Matsumoto *Japan* 36°15N 138°0E **29 F9**
Matsusaka *Japan* 34°34N 136°32E **29 G8**
Matsushima *Japan* 38°20N 141°10E **28 E10**
Matsuura *Japan* 33°20N 129°49E **29 H4**
Matsuyama *Japan* 33°45N 132°45E **29 H6**
Mattagami ➛ *Canada* 50°43N 81°29W **72 B3**
Mattancheri *India* 9°50N 76°15E **45 K3**
Mattawa *Canada* 46°20N 78°45W **72 C4**
Matterhorn *Switz.* 45°58N 7°39E **20 D7**
Matthew Town *Bahamas* 20°57N 73°40W **89 B5**
Matthews Ridge *Guyana* 7°37N 60°10W **92 B6**
Mattice *Canada* 49°40N 83°20W **72 C3**
Mattili *India* 18°33N 82°12E **44 E6**
Mattituck *U.S.A.* 40°59N 72°32W **83 F12**
Mattō = Hakusan *Japan* 36°31N 136°34E **29 F8**
Mattoon *U.S.A.* 39°29N 88°23W **80 F9**
Matuba *Mozam.* 24°28S 32°49E **57 B5**
Matucana *Peru* 11°55S 76°25W **92 F3**
Matugama *Sri Lanka* 6°31N 80°7E **45 L5**
Matuku *Fiji* 19°10S 179°44E **59 a**
Matūn = Khowst *Afghan.* 33°22N 69°58E **42 C3**
Matura B. *Trin. & Tob.* 10°39N 61°1W **93 K15**
Maturín *Venezuela* 9°45N 63°11W **92 B6**
Mau *Mad. P., India* 26°17N 78°41E **43 F8**
Mau *Ut. P., India* 25°56N 83°33E **43 G10**
Mau *Ut. P., India* 25°17N 81°23E **43 G9**
Mau Ranipur *India* 25°16N 79°8E **43 G8**
Maubeuge *France* 50°17N 3°57E **20 A6**
Maubin *Burma* 16°44N 95°39E **41 L19**
Maud, Pt. *Australia* 23°6S 113°45E **60 D1**
Maud Rise *S. Ocean* 66°0S 3°0E **5 C3**
Maude *Australia* 34°29S 144°18E **63 E3**
Maudin Sun *Burma* 16°0N 94°30E **41 M19**
Maués *Brazil* 3°20S 57°45W **92 D7**
Mauganj *India* 24°50N 81°55E **43 G9**
Maughold Hd. *I. of Man* 54°18N 4°18W **12 C3**
Maui *U.S.A.* 20°48N 156°20W **75 L8**
Maulamyaing = Moulmein *Burma* 16°30N 97°40E **41 L20**
Maule □ *Chile* 36°5S 72°30W **94 D1**
Maumee *U.S.A.* 41°34N 83°39W **81 E12**
Maumee ➛ *U.S.A.* 41°42N 83°28W **81 E12**
Maumere *Indonesia* 8°38S 122°13E **37 F6**
Maun *Botswana* 20°0S 23°26E **56 B3**
Mauna Kea *U.S.A.* 19°50N 155°28W **75 M8**
Mauna Loa *U.S.A.* 19°30N 155°35W **75 M8**
Maunath Bhanjan = Mau *India* 25°56N 83°33E **43 G10**
Maungmagan Kyunzu *Burma* 14°0N 97°48E **38 E1**
Maupin *U.S.A.* 45°11N 121°5W **76 D3**
Maurepas, L. *U.S.A.* 30°15N 90°30W **85 F9**
Maurice, L. *Australia* 29°30S 131°0E **61 E5**
Mauricie △ *Canada* 46°45N 73°0W **72 C5**
Mauritania ■ *Africa* 20°50N 10°0W **52 D3**
Mauritius ■ *Ind. Oc.* 20°0S 57°0E **55 d**
Mauston *U.S.A.* 43°48N 90°5W **80 D8**
Mavli *India* 24°45N 73°55E **42 G5**
Mawai *India* 22°30N 81°4E **43 H9**
Mawana *India* 29°6N 77°58E **42 E7**
Mawand *Pakistan* 29°33N 68°38E **42 E3**
Mawjib, W. al ➛ *Jordan* 31°28N 35°36E **48 D4**
Mawkmai *Burma* 20°14N 97°37E **41 J20**
Mawlaik *Burma* 23°40N 94°26E **41 H19**
Mawlamyine = Moulmein *Burma* 16°30N 97°40E **41 L20**
Mawqaq *Si. Arabia* 27°25N 41°8E **46 E4**
Mawson *Antarctica* 67°30S 62°53E **5 C6**
Mawson Coast *Antarctica* 68°30S 63°0E **5 C6**
Max *U.S.A.* 47°49N 101°18W **80 B3**
Maxcanú *Mexico* 20°35N 90°0W **87 C6**
Maxesibeni *S. Africa* 30°49S 29°23E **57 D4**
Maxhamish L. *Canada* 59°50N 123°17W **70 B4**
Maxixe *Mozam.* 23°54S 35°17E **57 B6**
Maxville *Canada* 45°17N 74°51W **83 A10**
Maxwell *U.S.A.* 39°17N 122°11W **78 F4**
Maxwelton *Australia* 20°43S 142°41E **62 C3**
May, C. *U.S.A.* 38°56N 74°58W **81 F16**
May Pen *Jamaica* 17°58N 77°15W **88 a**
Maya ➛ *Russia* 60°28N 134°28E **27 D14**
Maya Mts. *Belize* 16°30N 89°0W **87 D7**
Mayabandar *India* 12°56N 92°56E **45 H11**
Mayaguana I. *Bahamas* 22°30N 72°44W **89 B5**
Mayagüez *Puerto Rico* 18°12N 67°9W **89 d**
Mayāmey *Iran* 36°24N 55°42E **47 B7**
Mayang *China* 27°53N 109°49E **34 D7**
Mayanup *Australia* 33°57S 116°27E **61 F2**
Mayapán *Mexico* 20°29N 89°11W **87 C7**
Mayarí *Cuba* 20°40N 75°41W **89 B4**
Mayaro B. *Trin. & Tob.* 10°14N 60°59W **93 K16**
Mayavaram = Mayiladuthurai *India* 11°3N 79°42E **45 J4**
Maybell *U.S.A.* 40°31N 108°5W **76 F9**
Maybole *U.K.* 55°21N 4°42W **11 F4**
Maydān *Iraq* 34°55N 45°37E **46 C5**
Mayenne ➛ *France* 47°30N 0°32W **20 C3**
Mayer *U.S.A.* 34°24N 112°14W **77 J7**
Mayerthorpe *Canada* 53°57N 115°8W **70 C5**
Mayfield *Ky., U.S.A.* 36°44N 88°38W **80 G9**
Mayfield *N.Y., U.S.A.* 43°6N 74°16W **83 C10**
Mayhill *U.S.A.* 32°53N 105°29W **77 K11**
Mayiladuthurai *India* 11°3N 79°42E **45 J4**
Maykop *Russia* 44°35N 40°10E **19 F7**
Maymyo *Burma* 22°2N 96°28E **38 A1**
Maynard *Mass., U.S.A.* 42°26N 71°27W **83 D13**
Maynard *Wash., U.S.A.* 47°59N 122°55W **78 C4**
Maynard Hills *Australia* 28°28S 119°49E **61 E2**
Mayne ➛ *Australia* 23°40S 141°55E **62 C3**
Maynooth *Canada* 45°13N 77°56W **82 A7**
Maynooth *Ireland* 53°23N 6°34W **10 C5**
Mayo *Canada* 63°38N 135°57W **68 E4**
Mayo □ *Ireland* 53°53N 9°3W **10 C2**
Mayon Volcano *Phil.* 13°15N 123°41E **37 B6**
Mayor I. *N.Z.* 37°16S 176°17E **59 B6**
Mayotte ⊠ *Ind. Oc.* 12°50S 45°10E **55 a**
Maysān □ *Iraq* 31°55N 47°15E **46 D5**
Maysville *U.S.A.* 38°39N 83°46W **81 F12**
Mayu *Indonesia* 1°30N 126°30E **37 D7**
Mayuram = Mayiladuthurai *India* 11°3N 79°42E **45 J4**
Mayville *N. Dak., U.S.A.* 47°30N 97°20W **80 B5**
Mayville *N.Y., U.S.A.* 42°15N 79°30W **82 D5**
Mazabuka *Zambia* 15°52S 27°44E **55 H5**
Mazagán = El Jadida *Morocco* 33°11N 8°17W **52 B4**
Mazagão *Brazil* 0°7S 51°16W **93 D8**
Mazán *Peru* 3°30S 73°0W **92 D4**
Māzandarān □ *Iran* 36°30N 52°0E **47 B7**
Mazapil *Mexico* 24°39N 101°34W **86 C4**
Mazar *China* 36°32N 77°1E **30 D4**
Mazara del Vallo *Italy* 37°39N 12°35E **22 F5**
Mazarrón *Spain* 37°38N 1°19W **21 D5**
Mazaruni ➛ *Guyana* 6°25N 58°35W **92 B7**
Mazatán *Mexico* 29°0N 110°8W **86 B2**
Mazatenango *Guatemala* 14°35N 91°30W **88 D1**
Mazatlán *Mexico* 23°13N 106°25W **86 C3**
Mažeikiai *Lithuania* 56°20N 22°20E **9 H20**
Māzhān *Iran* 32°30N 59°0E **47 C8**
Mazīnān *Iran* 36°19N 56°56E **47 B8**
Mazoe ➛ *Mozam.* 16°20S 33°30E **55 H6**
Mazurski, Pojezierze *Poland* 53°50N 21°0E **17 B11**
Mazyr *Belarus* 51°59N 29°15E **17 B15**
Mba *Fiji* 17°33S 177°41E **59 a**
Mbabane *Swaziland* 26°18S 31°6E **57 C5**
Mbaïki *C.A.R.* 3°53N 18°1E **54 D3**
Mbala *Zambia* 8°46S 31°24E **55 F6**
Mbalabala *Zimbabwe* 20°27S 29°3E **57 B4**
Mbale *Uganda* 1°8N 34°12E **54 D6**
Mbalmayo *Cameroon* 3°33N 11°33E **54 D2**
Mbandaka *Dem. Rep. of the Congo* 0°1N 18°18E **54 D3**
Mbanza Congo *Angola* 6°18S 14°16E **54 F2**
Mbanza Ngungu *Dem. Rep. of the Congo* 5°12S 14°53E **54 F2**
Mbarara *Uganda* 0°35S 30°40E **54 E6**
Mbengga = Beqa *Fiji* 18°23S 178°8E **59 a**
Mbeya *Tanzania* 8°54S 33°29E **54 F6**
Mbhashe ➛ *S. Africa* 32°15S 28°54E **57 D4**
Mbini = Río Muni □ *Eq. Guin.* 1°30N 10°0E **54 D2**
Mbizi *Zimbabwe* 21°23S 31°1E **57 B5**
Mbombela *S. Africa* 25°29S 30°59E **57 C5**
Mbouda *Cameroon* 5°38N 10°15E **52 G8**
M'boukou, L. de *Cameroon* 6°23N 12°50E **54 C2**
Mbour *Senegal* 14°22N 16°54W **52 F2**
Mbuji-Mayi *Dem. Rep. of the Congo* 6°9S 23°40E **54 F4**
Mburucuyá *Argentina* 28°1S 58°14W **94 B4**
Mburucuyá △ *Argentina* 28°1S 58°12W **94 B4**
Mchinji *Malawi* 13°47S 32°58E **55 G6**
Mdantsane *S. Africa* 32°56S 27°46E **57 D4**
Mead, L. *U.S.A.* 36°0N 114°44W **79 J12**
Meade *U.S.A.* 37°17N 100°20W **80 G3**
Meade River = Atqasuk *U.S.A.* 70°28N 157°24W **74 A8**
Meadow Lake *Canada* 54°10N 108°26W **71 C7**
Meadow Lake ⌂ *Canada* 54°27N 109°0W **71 C7**
Meadow Valley Wash ➛ *U.S.A.* 36°40N 114°34W **79 J12**
Meadville *U.S.A.* 41°39N 80°9W **82 E4**
Meaford *Canada* 44°36N 80°35W **82 B4**
Meakan Dake *Japan* 43°15N 144°0E **28 C11**
Mealy Mts. *Canada* 53°10N 58°0W **73 B8**
Meander River *Canada* 59°2N 117°42W **70 B5**
Meares, C. *U.S.A.* 45°37N 124°0W **76 D1**
Mearim ➛ *Brazil* 3°4S 44°35W **93 D10**
Meath □ *Ireland* 53°40N 6°57W **10 C5**
Meath Park *Canada* 53°27N 105°22W **71 C7**
Meaux *France* 48°58N 2°50E **20 B5**
Mebechi-Gawa ➛ *Japan* 40°31N 141°31E **28 D10**
Mebulu, Tanjung *Indonesia* 8°50S 115°5E **37 K18**
Mecca = Makkah *Si. Arabia* 21°30N 39°54E **49 C2**
Mecca *U.S.A.* 33°34N 116°5W **79 M10**
Mechanicsburg *U.S.A.* 40°13N 77°1W **82 F8**
Mechanicville *U.S.A.* 42°54N 73°41W **83 D11**
Mechelen *Belgium* 51°2N 4°29E **15 C4**
Mecheria *Algeria* 33°35N 0°18W **52 B5**
Mecklenburg *Germany* 53°33N 11°40E **16 B7**
Mecklenburger Bucht *Germany* 54°20N 11°40E **16 A6**
Meconta *Mozam.* 14°59S 39°50E **55 G7**
Medak *India* 18°1N 78°15E **44 E4**
Medan *Indonesia* 3°40N 98°38E **36 D1**
Médanos de Coro △ *Venezuela* 11°35N 69°44W **89 D6**
Medanosa, Pta. *Argentina* 48°8S 66°0W **96 F3**
Medawachchiya *Sri Lanka* 8°30N 80°30E **45 K5**
Medchal *India* 17°37N 78°29E **44 F4**
Médéa *Algeria* 36°12N 2°50E **52 A6**
Medellín *Colombia* 6°15N 75°35W **92 B3**
Medelpad *Sweden* 62°33N 16°30E **8 E17**
Medemblik *Neths.* 52°46N 5°8E **15 B5**
Medford *Oreg., U.S.A.* 42°19N 122°52W **76 E2**
Medford *Wis., U.S.A.* 45°9N 90°20W **80 C8**
Medgidia *Romania* 44°15N 28°19E **17 F15**
Media Agua *Argentina* 31°58S 68°25W **94 C2**
Media Luna *Argentina* 34°45S 66°44W **94 C2**
Medianeira *Brazil* 25°17S 54°5W **95 B5**
Mediaş *Romania* 46°9N 24°22E **17 E13**
Medicine Bow *U.S.A.* 41°54N 106°12W **76 F10**
Medicine Bow Mts. *U.S.A.* 40°40N 106°0W **76 F10**
Medicine Hat *Canada* 50°0N 110°45W **71 D6**
Medicine Lake *U.S.A.* 48°30N 104°30W **76 B11**
Medicine Lodge *U.S.A.* 37°17N 98°35W **80 G4**
Medina = Al Madīnah *Si. Arabia* 24°35N 39°52E **46 E3**
Medina *N. Dak., U.S.A.* 46°54N 99°18W **80 B4**
Medina *N.Y., U.S.A.* 43°13N 78°23W **82 C6**
Medina *Ohio, U.S.A.* 41°8N 81°52W **82 E3**
Medina ➛ *U.S.A.* 29°16N 98°29W **84 G5**
Medina del Campo *Spain* 41°18N 4°55W **21 B3**
Medina L. *U.S.A.* 29°32N 98°56W **84 G5**
Medina Sidonia *Spain* 36°28N 5°57W **21 D3**
Medinipur *India* 22°25N 87°21E **43 H12**
Mediterranean Sea *Europe* 35°0N 15°0E **6 H7**
Médoc *France* 45°10N 0°50W **20 D3**
Medveditsa ➛ *Russia* 49°35N 42°41E **19 E7**
Medvezhi, Ostrava *Russia* 71°0N 161°0E **27 B17**
Medvezhyegorsk *Russia* 63°0N 34°25E **18 B5**
Medway □ *U.K.* 51°25N 0°32E **13 F8**
Medway ➛ *U.K.* 51°27N 0°46E **13 F8**
Meekatharra *Australia* 26°32S 118°29E **61 E2**
Meeker *U.S.A.* 40°2N 107°55W **76 F10**
Meerut *India* 29°1N 77°42E **42 E7**
Meeteetse *U.S.A.* 44°9N 108°52W **76 D9**
Mega *Ethiopia* 3°57N 38°19E **49 G2**
Megara *Greece* 37°58N 23°22E **23 F10**
Megasini *India* 21°38N 86°21E **43 J12**
Meghalaya □ *India* 25°50N 91°0E **41 G17**
Meghna ➛ *Bangla.* 22°50N 90°50E **41 H17**
Megion *Russia* 61°3N 76°6E **26 C8**
Mégiscane, L. *Canada* 48°35N 75°55W **72 C4**
Meharry, Mt. *Australia* 22°59S 118°35E **60 D2**
Mehekar *India* 20°9N 76°34E **44 D3**
Mehlville *U.S.A.* 38°31N 90°19W **80 F8**
Mehndawal *India* 26°58N 83°5E **43 F10**
Mehr Jān *Iran* 33°50N 55°6E **47 C7**
Mehrābād *Iran* 36°53N 47°55E **46 B5**
Mehrān *Iran* 33°7N 46°10E **46 C5**
Mehrān ➛ *Iran* 26°45N 55°26E **47 E7**
Mehrgarh *Pakistan* 29°30N 67°30E **42 E2**
Mehrīz *Iran* 31°35N 54°28E **47 D7**
Mei Jiang ➛ *China* 24°25N 116°35E **35 E11**
Mei Xian *China* 34°18N 107°55E **32 G4**
Meicheng *China* 29°29N 119°16E **35 C12**
Meichengzhen *China* 28°9N 111°40E **35 C8**
Meichuan *China* 30°8N 115°31E **35 B10**
Meighen I. *Canada* 80°0N 99°30W **69 B12**
Meigu *China* 28°16N 103°20E **34 C4**
Meihekou *China* 42°32N 125°40E **33 C13**
Meiktila *Burma* 20°53N 95°54E **41 J19**
Meili Xue Shan *China* 28°30N 98°39E **34 C2**
Meimyu = Maymyo *Burma* 22°2N 96°28E **38 A1**
Meishan *China* 30°3N 103°23E **34 B4**
Meissen *Germany* 51°9N 13°29E **16 C7**
Meitan *China* 27°45N 107°29E **34 D6**
Meizhou *China* 24°16N 116°6E **35 E11**
Meja *India* 25°9N 82°7E **43 G10**
Mejillones *Chile* 23°10S 70°30W **94 A1**
Mekele *Ethiopia* 13°33N 39°30E **49 E2**
Mekerghene, Sebkra *Algeria* 26°21N 1°30E **52 C6**
Mekhtar *Pakistan* 30°30N 69°15E **40 D6**
Meknès *Morocco* 33°57N 5°33W **52 B4**
Mekong ➛ *Asia* 9°30N 106°15E **39 H6**
Mekongga *Indonesia* 3°39S 121°15E **37 E6**
Mekvari = Kür ➛ *Azerbaijan* 39°29N 49°15E **19 G8**
Melagiri Hills *India* 12°20N 77°30E **45 H3**
Melaka *Malaysia* 2°15N 102°15E **39 L4**
Melaka □ *Malaysia* 2°15N 102°15E **39 L4**
Melanesia *Pac. Oc.* 4°0S 155°0E **64 H7**
Melanesian Basin *Pac. Oc.* 0°5N 160°35E **64 G8**
Melapalaiyam *India* 8°39N 77°44E **45 K3**
Melaya *Indonesia* 8°17S 114°30E **37 J17**
Melbourne *U.S.A.* 28°5N 80°37W **85 G14**
Melchor Múzquiz *Mexico* 27°53N 101°31W **86 B4**
Melchor Ocampo *Mexico* 24°51N 101°39W **86 C4**
Melekeok *Palau* 7°27N 134°38E **64 G5**
Mélèzes ➛ *Canada* 57°40N 69°29W **72 A5**
Melfort *Canada* 52°50N 104°37W **71 C8**
Melhus *Norway* 63°17N 10°18E **8 E14**
Melilla *N. Afr.* 35°21N 2°57W **21 E4**
Melipilla *Chile* 33°42S 71°15W **94 C1**
Melissa *Canada* 45°24N 79°14W **82 A5**
Melita *Canada* 49°15N 101°0W **71 D8**
Melitopol *Ukraine* 46°50N 35°22E **19 E6**
Melk *Austria* 48°13N 15°20E **16 D8**
Mellansel *Sweden* 63°26N 18°19E **8 E18**
Mellen *U.S.A.* 46°20N 90°40W **80 B8**
Mellerud *Sweden* 58°41N 12°28E **9 G15**
Mellette *U.S.A.* 45°9N 98°30W **80 C4**
Melo *Uruguay* 32°20S 54°10W **95 C5**
Melolo *Indonesia* 9°53S 120°40E **37 F6**
Melouprey *Cambodia* 13°48N 105°16E **38 F5**
Melrhir, Chott *Algeria* 34°13N 6°30E **52 B7**
Melrose *Australia* 32°42S 146°57E **63 E4**
Melrose *U.K.* 55°36N 2°43W **11 F6**
Melrose *Minn., U.S.A.* 45°40N 94°49W **80 C6**
Melrose *N. Mex., U.S.A.* 34°26N 103°38W **77 J12**
Melstone *U.S.A.* 46°36N 107°52W **76 C10**
Melton Mowbray *U.K.* 52°47N 0°54W **12 E7**
Melun *France* 48°32N 2°39E **20 B5**
Melung *Nepal* 27°31N 86°3E **43 F12**
Melur *India* 10°2N 78°23E **45 J4**
Melville *Canada* 50°55N 102°50W **71 C8**
Melville, C. *Australia* 14°11S 144°30E **62 A3**
Melville, L. *Canada* 53°30N 60°0W **73 B8**
Melville B. *Australia* 12°0S 136°45E **62 A2**
Melville B. *Greenland* 75°30N 63°0W **69 B19**
Melville I. *Australia* 11°30S 131°0E **60 B5**
Melville I. *Canada* 75°30N 112°0W **69 B9**
Melville Pen. *Canada* 68°0N 84°0W **69 D15**
Melvin, Lough *Ireland* 54°26N 8°10W **10 B3**
Memba *Mozam.* 14°11S 40°30E **55 G8**
Memboro *Indonesia* 9°30S 119°30E **60 A2**
Memel = Klaipėda *Lithuania* 55°43N 21°10E **9 J19**
Memel *S. Africa* 27°38S 29°36E **57 C4**
Memmingen *Germany* 47°58N 10°10E **16 E6**
Mempawah *Indonesia* 0°30N 109°5E **36 D3**
Memphis *Mich., U.S.A.* 42°54N 82°46W **82 D2**
Memphis *Tenn., U.S.A.* 35°8N 90°2W **85 D9**
Memphis *Tex., U.S.A.* 34°44N 100°33W **84 D4**
Memphrémagog, L. *N. Amer.* 45°8N 72°17W **83 B12**
Mena *U.S.A.* 34°35N 94°15W **84 D7**
Menado = Manado *Indonesia* 1°29N 124°51E **37 D6**
Menai Strait *U.K.* 53°11N 4°13W **12 D3**
Ménaka *Mali* 15°59N 2°18E **52 E6**
Menan = Chao Phraya ➛ *Thailand* 13°40N 100°31E **38 F3**
Menard *U.S.A.* 30°55N 99°47W **84 F5**
Menard Fracture Zone *Pac. Oc.* 43°0S 97°0W **65 M18**
Mendaña Fracture Zone *Pac. Oc.* 16°0S 91°0W **65 J18**
Mendawai ➛ *Indonesia* 3°30S 113°0E **36 E4**
Mende *France* 44°31N 3°30E **20 D5**
Mendeleyev Ridge *Arctic* 80°0N 178°0W **4 B17**
Mendhar *India* 33°35N 74°10E **43 C6**
Mendip Hills *U.K.* 51°17N 2°40W **13 F5**
Mendocino *U.S.A.* 39°19N 123°48W **76 G2**
Mendocino, C. *U.S.A.* 40°26N 124°25W **76 F1**
Mendocino Fracture Zone *Pac. Oc.* 40°0N 142°0W **65 D13**
Mendota *Calif., U.S.A.* 36°45N 120°23W **78 J6**
Mendota *Ill., U.S.A.* 41°33N 89°7W **80 E9**
Mendoyo *Indonesia* 8°23S 114°42E **37 J17**
Mendoza *Argentina* 32°50S 68°52W **94 C2**
Mendoza □ *Argentina* 33°0S 69°0W **94 C2**
Mene Grande *Venezuela* 9°49N 70°56W **92 B4**
Menemen *Turkey* 38°34N 27°3E **23 E12**
Menen *Belgium* 50°47N 3°7E **15 D3**
Mengcheng *China* 33°12N 116°36E **32 H9**
Mengdingjie *China* 23°31N 98°58E **34 F2**
Menggala *Indonesia* 4°30S 105°15E **36 E3**
Menghai *China* 21°49N 100°55E **34 G3**
Mengjin *China* 34°55N 112°45E **32 G7**
Mengla *China* 21°20N 101°25E **34 G3**
Menglian *China* 22°21N 99°27E **34 F2**
Mengshan *China* 24°14N 110°55E **35 E8**
Mengyin *China* 35°40N 117°58E **33 G9**
Mengzhe *China* 22°2N 100°15E **34 F3**
Mengzi *China* 23°20N 103°22E **34 F4**
Menifee *U.S.A.* 33°41N 117°10W **79 M9**
Menihek *Canada* 54°28N 56°36W **73 B6**
Menihek L. *Canada* 54°0N 67°0W **73 B6**
Menin = Menen *Belgium* 50°47N 3°7E **15 D3**
Menindee *Australia* 32°20S 142°25E **63 E3**
Menindee L. *Australia* 32°20S 142°25E **63 E3**
Meningie *Australia* 35°50S 139°18E **63 F2**
Menjangan, Pulau *Indonesia* 8°7S 114°31E **37 J17**
Menlo Park *U.S.A.* 37°27N 122°11W **78 H4**
Menngen ✪ *Australia* 15°21S 131°16E **60 C5**
Menominee *U.S.A.* 45°6N 87°37W **80 C10**
Menominee ➛ *U.S.A.* 45°6N 87°35W **80 C10**
Menomonie *U.S.A.* 44°53N 91°55W **80 C8**
Menongue *Angola* 14°48S 17°52E **55 G3**
Menorca *Spain* 40°0N 4°0E **21 C8**
Mentakab *Malaysia* 3°29N 102°21E **39 L4**
Mentawai, Kepulauan *Indonesia* 2°0S 99°0E **36 E1**
Menton *France* 43°50N 7°29E **20 E7**
Mentor *U.S.A.* 41°40N 81°21W **82 E3**
Menzelinsk *Russia* 55°47N 53°11E **18 C9**
Menzies *Australia* 29°40S 121°2E **61 E3**

Meob B. *Namibia* 24°25S 14°34E **56** B1
Meoqui *Mexico* 28°17N 105°29W **86** B3
Meppel *Neths.* 52°42N 6°12E **15** B6
Merak *Indonesia* 6°10N 106°26E **37** F12
Meramangye, L. *Australia* 28°25S 132°13E **61** E5
Meran = Merano *Italy* 46°40N 11°9E **22** A4
Merano *Italy* 46°40N 11°9E **22** A4
Merauke *Indonesia* 8°29S 140°24E **37** F10
Merbein *Australia* 34°10S 142°2E **63** E3
Merca = Marka *Somalia* 1°48N 44°50E **49** G3
Merced *U.S.A.* 37°18N 120°29W **78** H6
Merced → *U.S.A.* 37°21N 120°59W **78** H6
Merced Pk. *U.S.A.* 37°36N 119°24W **78** H7
Mercedes *B. Aires, Argentina* 34°40S 59°30W **94** C4
Mercedes *Corrientes, Argentina* 29°10S 58°5W **94** B4
Mercedes *San Luis, Argentina* 33°40S 65°21W **94** C2
Mercedes *Uruguay* 33°12S 58°0W **94** C4
Merceditas *Chile* 28°20S 70°35W **94** B1
Mercer *N.Z.* 37°16S 175°5E **59** B5
Mercer *U.S.A.* 41°14N 80°15W **82** E4
Mercer Island *U.S.A.* 47°34N 122°13W **78** C4
Mercury *U.S.A.* 36°40N 115°59W **79** J11
Mercy, C. *Canada* 65°0N 63°30W **69** E19
Mere *U.K.* 51°6N 2°16W **13** F5
Merebuk, Gunung *Indonesia* 8°13S 114°39E **37** J17
Meredith, C. *Falk. Is.* 52°15S 60°40W **96** G4
Meredith, L. *U.S.A.* 35°43N 101°33W **84** D4
Mergui *Burma* 12°26N 98°34E **38** F2
Mergui Arch. = Myeik Kyunzu *Burma* 11°30N 97°30E **39** G1
Mérida *Mexico* 20°58N 89°37W **87** C7
Mérida *Spain* 38°55N 6°25W **21** C2
Mérida *Venezuela* 8°24N 71°8W **92** B4
Mérida, Cord. de *Venezuela* 9°0N 71°0W **92** B4
Meriden *U.K.* 52°26N 1°38W **13** E6
Meriden *U.S.A.* 41°32N 72°48W **83** E12
Meridian *Calif., U.S.A.* 39°9N 121°55W **78** F5
Meridian *Idaho, U.S.A.* 43°37N 116°24W **76** E5
Meridian *Miss., U.S.A.* 32°22N 88°42W **85** E10
Merinda *Australia* 20°2S 148°11E **62** C4
Merir *Palau* 4°10N 132°30E **37** D8
Merirumã *Brazil* 1°15N 54°50W **93** C8
Merkel *U.S.A.* 32°28N 100°1W **84** E4
Mermaid Reef *Australia* 17°6S 119°36E **60** C2
Meroe *India* 7°33N 93°33E **45** L11
Merowe Dam *Sudan* 18°35N 31°56E **53** E12
Merredin *Australia* 31°28S 118°18E **61** F2
Merrick *U.K.* 55°8N 4°28W **11** F4
Merrickville *Canada* 44°55N 75°50W **83** B9
Merrill *Oreg., U.S.A.* 42°1N 121°36W **76** E3
Merrill *Wis., U.S.A.* 45°11N 89°41W **80** C9
Merrimack → *U.S.A.* 42°49N 70°49W **83** D14
Merriman *U.S.A.* 42°55N 101°42W **80** D3
Merritt *Canada* 50°10N 120°45W **70** C4
Merritt Island *U.S.A.* 28°21N 80°42W **85** G14
Merriwa *Australia* 32°6S 150°22E **63** E5
Merry I. *Canada* 55°29N 77°31W **72** A4
Merryville *U.S.A.* 30°45N 93°33W **84** F8
Mersch *Lux.* 49°44N 6°7E **15** E6
Mersea I. *U.K.* 51°47N 0°58E **13** F8
Merseburg *Germany* 51°22N 11°59E **16** C6
Mersey → *U.K.* 53°25N 3°1W **12** D4
Merseyside □ *U.K.* 53°31N 3°2W **12** D4
Mersin = İçel *Turkey* 36°51N 34°36E **46** B2
Mersing *Malaysia* 2°25N 103°50E **39** L4
Merta *India* 26°39N 74°4E **42** F6
Merta Road *India* 26°43N 73°55E **42** F5
Merthyr Tydfil *U.K.* 51°45N 3°22W **13** F4
Merthyr Tydfil □ *U.K.* 51°46N 3°21W **13** F4
Mértola *Portugal* 37°40N 7°40W **21** D2
Mertz Glacier *Antarctica* 67°30S 144°45E **5** C10
Mertzon *U.S.A.* 31°16N 100°49W **84** F4
Meru *Kenya* 0°3N 37°40E **54** D7
Meru *Tanzania* 3°15S 36°46E **54** E7
Meru Betiri △ *Indonesia* 8°27S 113°51E **37** H15
Mesa *U.S.A.* 33°25N 111°50W **77** K8
Mesa Verde △ *U.S.A.* 37°11N 108°29W **77** H9
Mesada = Masada *Israel* 31°18N 35°21E **48** D4
Mesgouez, L. *Canada* 51°20N 75°0W **72** B5
Meshed = Mashhad *Iran* 36°20N 59°35E **47** B8
Meshgīn Shahr *Iran* 38°30N 47°45E **46** B5
Meshoppen *U.S.A.* 41°36N 76°3W **83** E8
Mesilinka → *Canada* 56°6N 124°30W **70** B4
Mesologi *Greece* 38°21N 21°28E **23** E9
Mesopotamia = Al Jazirah *Iraq* 33°30N 44°0E **46** C5
Mesopotamia *U.S.A.* 41°27N 80°57W **82** E4
Mesquite *U.S.A.* 36°48N 114°4W **77** H6
Messaad *Algeria* 34°8N 3°30E **52** B6
Messalo → *Mozam.* 12°25S 39°15E **55** G7
Messina = Musina *S. Africa* 22°20S 30°5E **57** B5
Messina *Italy* 38°11N 15°34E **22** E6
Messina, Str. di *Italy* 38°15N 15°35E **22** E6
Messini *Greece* 37°4N 22°1E **23** F10
Messiniakos Kolpos *Greece* 36°45N 22°5E **23** F10
Mesta = Nestos → *Europe* 40°54N 24°49E **23** D11
Meta → *S. Amer.* 6°12N 67°28W **92** B5
Meta Incognita Pen. *Canada* 62°45N 68°30W **69** E18
Metabetchouan *Canada* 48°26N 71°52W **73** C5
Metaline Falls *U.S.A.* 48°52N 117°22W **76** B5
Metán *Argentina* 25°30S 65°0W **94** B3
Metcalfe *Canada* 45°14N 75°28W **83** A9
Metema *Ethiopia* 12°58N 36°12E **49** E2
Methven *N.Z.* 43°38S 171°40E **59** E3
Metlakatla *U.S.A.* 55°8N 131°35W **68** F5
Metropolis *U.S.A.* 37°9N 88°44W **80** G9
Metropolitana □ *Chile* 33°30S 70°50W **94** C1
Mettuppalaiyam *India* 11°18N 76°59E **45** J3
Mettur *India* 11°48N 77°47E **45** J3
Metu *Ethiopia* 8°18N 35°35E **49** F2

Metz *France* 49°8N 6°10E **20** B7
Meulaboh *Indonesia* 4°11N 96°3E **36** D1
Meureudu *Indonesia* 5°19N 96°10E **36** C1
Meuse → *Europe* 50°45N 5°41E **15** D5
Mexia *U.S.A.* 31°41N 96°29W **84** F6
Mexiana, I. *Brazil* 0°0 49°30W **93** D9
Mexicali *Mexico* 32°40N 115°30W **79** N11
Mexican Plateau *Mexico* 25°0N 104°0W **66** G9
Mexican Water *U.S.A.* 36°57N 109°32W **77** H9
Mexico *Maine, U.S.A.* 44°34N 70°33W **83** B14
Mexico *Mo., U.S.A.* 39°10N 91°53W **80** F8
Mexico *N.Y., U.S.A.* 43°28N 76°14W **83** C8
México □ *Mexico* 19°20N 99°30W **87** D5
Mexico ■ *Cent. Amer.* 25°0N 105°0W **86** C4
Mexico, G. of *Cent. Amer.* 25°0N 90°0W **87** C7
Meydān-e Naftūn *Iran* 31°56N 49°18E **47** D6
Meydani, Ra's-e *Iran* 25°24N 59°6E **47** E8
Meyers Chuck *U.S.A.* 55°45N 132°15W **70** B2
Meymaneh *Afghan.* 35°53N 64°38E **40** B4
Mezen *Russia* 65°50N 44°20E **18** A7
Mezen → *Russia* 65°44N 44°22E **18** A7
Mézenc, Mt. *France* 44°54N 4°11E **20** D6
Mezhdurechensk *Russia* 53°41N 88°3E **26** D9
Mezhdurechenskiy *Russia* 59°36N 65°56E **26** D7
Mezőkövesd *Hungary* 47°49N 20°35E **17** E11
Mezőtúr *Hungary* 47°1N 20°41E **17** E11
Mezquital *Mexico* 23°29N 104°23W **86** C4
Mfolozi → *S. Africa* 28°25S 32°26E **57** C5
Mhow *India* 22°33N 75°50E **42** H6
Miahuatlán *Mexico* 16°20N 96°36W **87** D5
Miami *Okla., U.S.A.* 36°53N 94°53W **84** C7
Miami *Tex., U.S.A.* 35°42N 100°38W **84** D4
Mian Xian *China* 33°10N 106°32E **34** A6
Mianchi *China* 34°48N 111°48E **32** G6
Miāndarreh *Iran* 35°37N 53°39E **47** C7
Miāndowāb *Iran* 37°0N 46°5E **46** B5
Miandrivazo *Madag.* 19°31S 45°29E **55** H9
Miāneh *Iran* 37°30N 47°40E **46** B5
Mianning *China* 28°32N 102°9E **34** C4
Mianwali *Pakistan* 32°38N 71°28E **42** C4
Mianyang *China* 31°22N 104°47E **34** B5
Mianzhu *China* 31°22N 104°7E **34** B5
Miao Ling *China* 26°5N 107°30E **34** D6
Miaodao Qundao *China* 38°10N 120°45E **33** E11
Miaoli *Taiwan* 24°37N 120°49E **35** E13
Miass *Russia* 54°59N 60°6E **18** D11
Mica *S. Africa* 24°10S 30°48E **57** B5
Michalovce *Slovak Rep.* 48°47N 21°58E **17** D11
Michigan □ *U.S.A.* 44°0N 85°0W **81** C11
Michigan, L. *U.S.A.* 44°0N 87°0W **80** D10
Michigan City *U.S.A.* 41°43N 86°54W **80** E10
Michoacán □ *Mexico* 19°10N 101°50W **86** D4
Michurin *Bulgaria* 42°9N 27°51E **23** C12
Michurinsk *Russia* 52°58N 40°27E **18** D7
Micoud *St. Lucia* 13°49N 60°54W **89** f
Micronesia *Pac. Oc.* 11°0N 160°0E **64** G7
Micronesia, Federated States of ■ *Pac. Oc.* 9°0N 150°0E **58** A8
Mid-Indian Ridge *Ind. Oc.* 30°0S 75°0E **64** M1
Mid-Oceanic Ridge *Ind. Oc.* 42°0S 90°0E **64** M1
Mid-Pacific Seamounts *Pac. Oc.* 18°0N 177°0W **64** F10
Midai *Indonesia* 3°0N 107°47E **36** D3
Midale *Canada* 49°25N 103°20W **71** D8
Middelburg *Neths.* 51°30N 3°36E **15** C3
Middelburg *Eastern Cape, S. Africa* 31°30S 25°0E **56** D4
Middelburg *Mpumalanga, S. Africa* 25°49S 29°28E **57** C4
Middelpos *S. Africa* 31°55S 20°13E **56** D3
Middelwit *S. Africa* 24°51S 27°3E **56** B4
Middle Alkali L. *U.S.A.* 41°27N 120°5W **76** F3
Middle America Trench = Guatemala Trench *India* 14°0N 95°0W **66** H10
Middle Andaman I. *India* 12°30N 92°50E **45** H11
Middle Bass I. *U.S.A.* 41°41N 82°48W **82** E2
Middle East *Asia* 35°0N 40°0E **24** E5
Middle Fork Feather → *U.S.A.* 38°33N 121°30W **78** F5
Middle I. *Australia* 34°6S 123°11E **61** F3
Middle Loup → *U.S.A.* 41°17N 98°24W **80** E4
Middleboro *U.S.A.* 41°54N 70°55W **83** E14
Middleburg *Fla., U.S.A.* 30°4N 81°52W **85** F14
Middleburg *Pa., U.S.A.* 40°47N 77°3W **82** F7
Middleburgh *U.S.A.* 42°36N 74°20W **83** D10
Middlebury *U.S.A.* 44°1N 73°10W **83** B11
Middlefield *U.S.A.* 41°27N 81°4W **82** E3
Middlemount *Australia* 22°50S 148°40E **62** C4
Middleport *N.Y., U.S.A.* 43°13N 78°29W **82** C6
Middleport *Ohio, U.S.A.* 39°0N 82°3W **81** F12
Middlesboro *U.S.A.* 36°36N 83°43W **81** G12
Middlesbrough *U.K.* 54°35N 1°13W **12** C6
Middlesbrough □ *U.K.* 54°28N 1°13W **12** C6
Middlesex *Belize* 17°2N 88°31W **88** C2
Middlesex *N.J., U.S.A.* 40°36N 74°30W **83** F10
Middlesex *N.Y., U.S.A.* 42°42N 77°16W **82** D7
Middleton *Australia* 22°22S 141°32E **62** C3
Middleton *Canada* 44°57N 65°4W **73** D6
Middleton Cr. → *Australia* 22°35S 141°51E **62** C3
Middleton I. *U.S.A.* 59°26N 146°20W **74** D10
Middleton *U.K.* 54°17N 6°51W **10** B5
Middletown *Calif., U.S.A.* 38°45N 122°37W **78** G4
Middletown *Conn., U.S.A.* 41°34N 72°39W **83** E12
Middletown *N.Y., U.S.A.* 41°27N 74°25W **83** E10
Middletown *Ohio, U.S.A.* 39°31N 84°24W **81** F11
Middletown *Pa., U.S.A.* 40°12N 76°44W **83** F8
Midge Point *Australia* 20°39S 148°43E **62** b
Midhurst *Canada* 44°26N 79°43W **82** B5

Midhurst *U.K.* 50°59N 0°44W **13** G7
Midi, Canal du → *France* 43°45N 1°21E **20** E4
Midland *Australia* 31°54S 116°1E **61** F2
Midland *Canada* 44°45N 79°50W **82** B5
Midland *Calif., U.S.A.* 33°52N 114°48W **79** M12
Midland *Mich., U.S.A.* 43°37N 84°14W **81** D11
Midland *Pa., U.S.A.* 40°39N 80°27W **82** F4
Midland *Tex., U.S.A.* 32°0N 102°3W **84** F3
Midleton *Ireland* 51°55N 8°10W **10** E3
Midlothian *U.S.A.* 32°30N 97°0W **84** E6
Midlothian □ *U.K.* 55°51N 3°5W **11** F5
Midnapore = Medinipur *India* 22°25N 87°21E **43** H12
Midu *China* 25°18N 100°30E **34** E3
Midway Is. *Pac. Oc.* 28°13N 177°22W **75** K4
Midway Wells *U.S.A.* 32°41N 115°7W **79** N11
Midwest *U.S.A.* 42°0N 90°0W **75** G22
Midwest *Wyo., U.S.A.* 43°25N 106°16W **76** E10
Midwest City *U.S.A.* 35°27N 97°24W **84** D6
Midyat *Turkey* 37°25N 41°23E **46** B4
Midzŏr *Bulgaria* 43°24N 22°40E **23** C10
Mie □ *Japan* 34°30N 136°10E **29** G8
Mieres *Spain* 43°18N 5°48W **21** A3
Międzychód *Poland* 52°35N 15°53E **16** B8
Międzyrzec Podlaski *Poland* 51°58N 22°45E **17** C12
Mielec *Poland* 50°15N 21°25E **17** C11
Mienga *Angola* 17°12S 19°48E **56** A2
Miercurea-Ciuc *Romania* 46°21N 25°48E **17** E13
Mieres *Spain* 43°18N 5°48W **21** A3
Mifflintown *U.S.A.* 40°34N 77°24W **82** F7
Mifraz Ḥefa *Israel* 32°52N 35°0E **48** C4
Migang Shan *China* 35°32N 106°13E **32** G4
Miguasha △ *Canada* 48°5N 66°26W **73** C6
Miguel Alemán, Presa *Mexico* 18°15N 96°32W **87** D5
Miguel Hidalgo, Presa *Mexico* 26°30N 108°34W **86** B3
Mihara *Japan* 34°24N 133°5E **29** G6
Mikhaylovgrad = Montana *Bulgaria* 43°27N 23°16E **23** C10
Mikhaylovka *Russia* 50°3N 43°5E **19** D7
Mikines *Greece* 37°43N 22°46E **23** F10
Mikkeli *Finland* 61°43N 27°15E **8** F22
Mikkwa → *Canada* 58°25N 114°46W **70** B6
Míkonos = Mykonos *Greece* 37°30N 25°25E **23** F11
Mikun *Russia* 62°20N 50°0E **18** B9
Milaca *U.S.A.* 45°45N 93°39W **80** C7
Milagro *Ecuador* 2°11S 79°36W **92** D3
Milan *Mo., U.S.A.* 40°12N 93°7W **80** E7
Milan *Tenn., U.S.A.* 35°55N 88°46W **85** D10
Milâs *Turkey* 37°30N 27°50E **23** F12
Milazzo *Italy* 38°13N 15°15E **22** E6
Milbank *U.S.A.* 45°13N 96°38W **80** C5
Milbanke Sd. *Canada* 52°19N 128°33W **70** C3
Milden *Canada* 51°29N 107°32W **71** C7
Mildenhall *U.K.* 52°21N 0°32E **13** E8
Mildmay *Canada* 44°3N 81°7W **82** B3
Mildura *Australia* 34°13S 142°9E **63** E3
Mile *China* 24°28N 103°20E **34** E4
Miles *Australia* 26°40S 150°9E **63** D5
Miles City *U.S.A.* 46°25N 105°51W **76** C11
Milestone *Canada* 49°59N 104°31W **71** D8
Miletus *Turkey* 37°30N 27°18E **23** F12
Milford *Calif., U.S.A.* 40°10N 120°22W **78** E6
Milford *Conn., U.S.A.* 41°14N 73°3W **83** E11
Milford *Del., U.S.A.* 38°55N 75°26W **81** F16
Milford *Mass., U.S.A.* 42°8N 71°31W **83** D13
Milford *N.H., U.S.A.* 42°50N 71°39W **83** D13
Milford *N.Y., U.S.A.* 42°35N 74°56W **83** D10
Milford *Pa., U.S.A.* 41°19N 74°48W **83** E10
Milford *Utah, U.S.A.* 38°24N 113°1W **76** G7
Milford Haven *U.K.* 51°42N 5°7W **13** F2
Milford Sd. *N.Z.* 44°41S 167°47E **59** F1
Milford Sound *N.Z.* 44°41S 167°55E **59** F1
Milḥ, Baḥr al = Razāzah, Buḥayrat ar *Iraq* 32°40N 43°35E **46** C4
Milikapiti *Australia* 11°26S 130°40E **60** B5
Miling *Australia* 30°30S 116°17E **61** F2
Milk River *Canada* 49°10N 112°5W **70** D6
Mill I. *Antarctica* 66°0S 101°30E **5** C8
Mill I. *Canada* 63°58N 77°49W **69** E16
Mill Valley *U.S.A.* 37°54N 122°32W **78** H4
Millau *France* 44°8N 3°4E **20** D5
Millbridge *Canada* 44°41N 77°36W **82** B7
Millbrook *Canada* 44°10N 78°29W **82** B6
Millbrook *Ala., U.S.A.* 32°29N 86°22W **85** E11
Millbrook *N.Y., U.S.A.* 41°47N 73°42W **83** E11
Mille Lacs, L. des *Canada* 48°45N 90°35W **72** C1
Mille Lacs L. *U.S.A.* 46°15N 93°39W **80** B7
Milledgeville *U.S.A.* 33°5N 83°14W **85** E13
Millen *U.S.A.* 32°48N 81°57W **85** E14
Millennium I. = Caroline I. *Kiribati* 9°58S 150°13W **65** H12
Miller *U.S.A.* 44°31N 98°59W **80** C4
Miller Lake *Canada* 45°6N 81°26W **82** A3
Millersburg *Ohio, U.S.A.* 40°33N 81°55W **82** F3
Millersburg *Pa., U.S.A.* 40°32N 76°58W **82** F8
Millerton *U.S.A.* 41°57N 73°31W **83** E11
Millerton L. *U.S.A.* 37°1N 119°41W **78** J7
Millet *St. Lucia* 13°55N 60°59W **89** f
Millheim *U.S.A.* 40°54N 77°29W **82** F7
Millicent *Australia* 37°34S 140°21E **63** F3
Millington *U.S.A.* 35°20N 89°53W **85** D10
Millinocket *U.S.A.* 45°39N 68°43W **81** C19
Millmerran *Australia* 27°53S 151°16E **63** D5
Millom *U.K.* 54°13N 3°16W **12** C4
Mills L. *Canada* 61°30N 118°20W **70** A5
Millsboro *U.S.A.* 40°0N 80°0W **82** G5
Millstream Chichester △ *Australia* 21°35S 117°6E **60** D2
Millstreet *Ireland* 52°4N 9°4W **10** D2
Milltown Malbay *Ireland* 52°52N 9°24W **10** D2
Millville *Pa., U.S.A.* 41°7N 76°32W **83** E8
Millwood L. *U.S.A.* 33°42N 93°58W **84** E8
Milne → *Australia* 21°10S 137°33E **62** C2
Milo *Canada* 45°15N 68°59W **81** C19
Milos *Greece* 36°44N 24°25E **23** F11

Milparinka *Australia* 29°46S 141°57E **63** D3
Milpitas *U.S.A.* 37°26N 121°55W **78** H5
Milton *N.S., Canada* 44°4N 64°45W **73** D7
Milton *Ont., Canada* 43°31N 79°53W **82** C5
Milton *N.Z.* 46°7S 169°59E **59** G2
Milton *Calif., U.S.A.* 38°3N 120°51W **78** G6
Milton *Fla., U.S.A.* 30°38N 87°3W **85** F11
Milton *Pa., U.S.A.* 41°1N 76°51W **82** F8
Milton *Vt., U.S.A.* 44°38N 73°7W **83** B11
Milton-Freewater *U.S.A.* 45°56N 118°23W **76** D4
Milton Keynes *U.K.* 52°1N 0°44W **13** E7
Milton Keynes □ *U.K.* 52°1N 0°44W **13** E7
Miluo *China* 29°0N 112°59E **35** C9
Milverton *Canada* 43°34N 80°55W **82** C4
Milwaukee *U.S.A.* 43°2N 87°54W **80** D10
Milwaukee Deep *Atl. Oc.* 19°50N 68°0W **89** C6
Milwaukie *U.S.A.* 45°27N 122°38W **78** E4
Mimili *Australia* 27°0S 132°42E **61** E5
Min Jiang → *Fujian, China* 26°0N 119°35E **35** E12
Min Jiang → *Sichuan, China* 28°45N 104°40E **34** C5
Min Xian *China* 34°25N 104°5E **32** G3
Minā' Jabal 'Alī *U.A.E.* 25°2N 55°8E **47** E7
Mina Pirquitas *Argentina* 22°40S 66°30W **94** A2
Mīnā Su'ud *Si. Arabia* 28°45N 48°28E **47** D6
Mīnā'al Aḥmadī *Kuwait* 29°1N 48°9E **47** D6
Minago → *Canada* 54°33N 98°59W **71** C9
Minaki *Canada* 49°59N 94°40W **71** D10
Minamata *Japan* 32°10N 130°30E **29** H5
Minami-Arapusa △ *Japan* 35°30N 138°9E **29** G9
Minami-Tori-Shima *Pac. Oc.* 24°20N 153°58E **64** E7
Minamiaizu *Japan* 37°12N 139°46E **29** F9
Minamiawaji *Japan* 34°10N 134°42E **29** G7
Minamisōma *Japan* 37°38N 140°58E **28** F10
Minas *Uruguay* 34°20S 55°10W **95** C4
Minas, Sierra de las *Guatemala* 15°9N 89°31W **88** C2
Minas Basin *Canada* 45°20N 64°12W **73** C7
Minas Gerais □ *Brazil* 18°50S 46°0W **93** G9
Minatitlán *Mexico* 17°59N 94°31W **87** D6
Minbu *Burma* 20°10N 94°52E **41** J19
Minchinabad *Pakistan* 30°10N 73°34E **42** D5
Mindanao *Phil.* 8°0N 125°0E **37** C7
Mindanao Sea = Bohol Sea *Phil.* 9°0N 124°0E **37** C6
Mindanao Trench *Pac. Oc.* 12°0N 126°6E **37** B7
Mindelo *C. Verde Is.* 16°24N 25°0W **52** b
Minden *Canada* 44°55N 78°43W **82** B6
Minden *Germany* 52°17N 8°55E **16** B5
Minden *La., U.S.A.* 32°37N 93°17W **84** E8
Minden *Nev., U.S.A.* 38°57N 119°46W **78** G7
Mindibungu = Billiluna *Australia* 19°37S 127°41E **60** C4
Mindiptana *Indonesia* 5°55S 140°22E **37** F10
Mindoro *Phil.* 13°0N 121°0E **37** B6
Mindoro Str. *Phil.* 12°30N 120°30E **37** B6
Mine *Japan* 34°12N 131°7E **29** G5
Minehead *U.K.* 51°12N 3°29W **13** F4
Mineola *N.Y., U.S.A.* 40°44N 73°38W **83** F11
Mineola *Tex., U.S.A.* 32°40N 95°29W **84** E7
Mineral King *U.S.A.* 36°27N 118°36W **78** J8
Mineral Wells *U.S.A.* 32°48N 98°7W **84** E5
Miners Bay *Canada* 44°49N 78°46W **82** B6
Minersville *U.S.A.* 40°41N 76°16W **83** F8
Minerva *N.Y., U.S.A.* 43°47N 73°59W **83** C11
Minerva *Ohio, U.S.A.* 40°44N 81°6W **82** F3
Minetto *U.S.A.* 43°24N 76°28W **83** C8
Minfeng *China* 37°4N 82°46E **30** D5
Mingäçevir Su Anbarı *Azerbaijan* 40°57N 46°50E **19** F8
Mingan *Canada* 50°20N 64°0W **73** B7
Mingechaurskoye Vdkhr. = Mingäçevir Su Anbarı *Azerbaijan* 40°57N 46°50E **19** F8
Mingela *Australia* 19°52S 146°38E **62** B4
Mingenew *Australia* 29°12S 115°21E **61** E2
Mingera Cr. → *Australia* 20°38S 137°45E **62** C2
Minggang *China* 32°24N 114°3E **35** A10
Mingguang *China* 32°46N 117°59E **35** A11
Mingin *Burma* 22°50N 94°30E **41** H19
Minglun *China* 25°0N 108°21E **34** E7
Mingo Junction *U.S.A.* 40°19N 80°37W **82** F4
Mingora *Pakistan* 34°48N 72°22E **43** B5
Mingshan *China* 30°6N 103°10E **34** B4
Mingteke Daban = Mintaka Pass *Pakistan* 37°0N 74°58E **43** A6
Mingxi *China* 26°18N 117°12E **35** D11
Mingyuegue *China* 43°2N 128°50E **33** C15
Minhe *China* 36°9N 102°45E **30** D9
Minho = Miño → *Spain* 41°52N 8°40W **21** A2
Minho *Portugal* 41°25N 8°20W **21** B1
Minhou *China* 26°0N 119°15E **35** E12
Minicoy I. *India* 8°17N 73°2E **45** K1
Minidoka *U.S.A.* 42°45N 113°29W **76** E7
Minigwal, L. *Australia* 29°31S 123°14E **61** E3
Minilya → *Australia* 23°45S 114°0E **61** D1
Minilya Roadhouse *Australia* 23°55S 114°0E **61** D1
Minipi L. *Canada* 52°25N 60°45W **73** B7
Minjilang *Australia* 11°8S 132°33E **60** B5
Mink L. *Canada* 61°54N 117°40W **70** A5
Minna *Nigeria* 9°37N 6°30E **52** G7
Minneapolis *Kans., U.S.A.* 39°8N 97°42W **80** F5
Minneapolis *Minn., U.S.A.* 44°57N 93°16W **80** C7
Minnedosa *Canada* 50°14N 99°50W **71** C9
Minnesota □ *U.S.A.* 46°0N 94°15W **80** B7
Minnesota → *U.S.A.* 44°54N 93°9W **80** C7
Minnewaukan *U.S.A.* 48°4N 99°15W **80** A4
Minnipa *Australia* 32°51S 135°9E **63** E2
Minnitaki L. *Canada* 49°57N 92°10W **72** C1
Mino *Japan* 35°32N 136°55E **29** G8
Miño → *Spain* 41°52N 8°40W **21** B1
Minorca = Menorca *Spain* 40°0N 4°0E **21** C8
Minot *U.S.A.* 48°14N 101°18W **80** A3

Minqin *China* 38°38N 103°20E **32** E2
Minqing *China* 26°15N 118°50E **35** D12
Minsk *Belarus* 53°52N 27°30E **17** B14
Mińsk Mazowiecki *Poland* 52°10N 21°33E **17** B11
Mintabie *Australia* 27°15S 133°7E **63** D1
Mintaka Pass *Pakistan* 37°0N 74°58E **43** A6
Minto *Canada* 46°5N 66°5W **73** C6
Minto, L. *Canada* 57°13N 75°0W **72** A5
Minton *Canada* 49°10N 104°35W **71** D8
Minturn *U.S.A.* 39°35N 106°26W **76** G10
Minudasht *Iran* 37°17N 56°7E **47** B8
Minusinsk *Russia* 53°43N 91°20E **27** D10
Minutang *India* 28°15N 96°30E **41** E20
Minvoul *Gabon* 2°9N 12°8E **54** D2
Minya Konka = Gongga Shan *China* 29°40N 101°55E **34** C3
Minzhong *China* 22°37N 113°30E **31** a
Miquelon *Canada* 49°25N 76°27W **72** C4
Miquelon *St-P. & M.* 47°8N 56°22W **73** C8
Mir *Belarus* 53°27N 26°28E **17** B13
Mīr Kūh *Iran* 26°22N 58°55E **47** E8
Mīr Shahdād *Iran* 26°15N 58°29E **47** E8
Mira *Italy* 45°26N 12°8E **22** B5
Mira por vos Cay *Bahamas* 22°9N 74°30W **89** B5
Mirabello, Kolpos *Greece* 35°10N 25°50E **23** G11
Mirador-Río Azul △ *Guatemala* 17°45N 89°50W **88** C2
Miraj *India* 16°50N 74°45E **44** F2
Miram Shah *Pakistan* 33°0N 70°2E **42** C4
Miramar *Argentina* 38°15S 57°50W **94** D4
Miramar *Mozam.* 23°50S 35°35E **57** B6
Miramichi *Canada* 47°2N 65°28W **73** C6
Miramichi B. *Canada* 47°15N 65°0W **73** C7
Miranda *Brazil* 20°10S 56°15W **93** H7
Miranda → *Brazil* 19°25S 57°20W **92** G7
Miranda de Ebro *Spain* 42°41N 2°57W **21** A4
Miranda do Douro *Portugal* 41°30N 6°16W **21** B2
Mirandópolis *Brazil* 21°9S 51°6W **95** A5
Mirani *Australia* 21°8S 148°53E **62** b
Mirassol *Brazil* 20°46S 49°28W **95** A6
Mirbāṭ *Oman* 17°0N 54°45E **49** D5
Miri *Malaysia* 4°23N 113°59E **36** D4
Mirialguda *India* 16°52N 79°35E **44** F4
Miriam Vale *Australia* 24°20S 151°33E **62** C5
Mirigama *Sri Lanka* 7°15N 80°8E **45** L5
Mirim, L. *S. Amer.* 32°45S 52°50W **95** C5
Miriuwung Gajerrong ◇ *Australia* 15°0S 128°45E **60** C4
Mīrjāveh *Iran* 29°1N 61°30E **47** D9
Mirnyy *Antarctica* 66°50S 92°30E **5** C14
Mirnyy *Russia* 62°33N 113°53E **27** C12
Mirokhan *Pakistan* 27°46N 68°6E **42** F3
Mirond L. *Canada* 55°6N 102°47W **71** B8
Mirpur *Pakistan* 33°32N 73°56E **43** C5
Mirpur Batoro *Pakistan* 24°44N 68°12E **42** G3
Mirpur Bibiwari *Pakistan* 28°33N 67°44E **42** E2
Mirpur Khas *Pakistan* 25°30N 69°0E **42** G3
Mirpur Sakro *Pakistan* 24°33N 67°41E **42** G2
Mirs Bay = Tai Pang Wan *China* 22°33N 114°24E **31** a
Mirtağ *Turkey* 38°23N 41°56E **46** B4
Mirtoo Sea *Greece* 37°0N 23°20E **23** F10
Miryang *S. Korea* 35°31N 128°44E **33** G15
Mirzapur *India* 25°10N 82°34E **43** G10
Mirzapur-cum-Vindhyachal = Mirzapur *India* 25°10N 82°34E **43** G10
Misantla *Mexico* 19°56N 96°50W **87** D5
Misawa *Japan* 40°41N 141°24E **28** D10
Miscou I. *Canada* 47°57N 64°31W **73** C7
Misha *India* 7°59N 93°20E **45** L10
Mish'āb, Ra's al *Si. Arabia* 28°15N 48°43E **47** D6
Mishan *China* 45°37N 131°48E **28** B5
Mishawaka *U.S.A.* 41°40N 86°11W **80** E10
Mishima *Japan* 35°10N 138°52E **29** G9
Misión *Mexico* 32°6N 116°53W **79** N10
Misiones □ *Argentina* 27°0S 55°0W **95** B5
Misiones □ *Paraguay* 27°0S 56°0W **94** B4
Miskah *Si. Arabia* 24°49N 42°56E **46** E4
Miskitos, Cayos *Nic.* 14°26N 82°50W **88** D3
Miskolc *Hungary* 48°7N 20°50E **17** D11
Misool *Indonesia* 1°52S 130°10E **37** E8
Mişr = Egypt ■ *Africa* 28°0N 31°0E **53** C12
Mişrātah *Libya* 32°24N 15°3E **53** B9
Missanabie *Canada* 48°20N 84°6W **72** C3
Missinaibi → *Canada* 50°43N 81°29W **72** B3
Missinaibi L. *Canada* 48°23N 83°40W **72** C3
Mission *Canada* 49°10N 122°15W **70** D4
Mission *S. Dak., U.S.A.* 43°18N 100°39W **80** D3
Mission *Tex., U.S.A.* 26°13N 98°20W **84** H5
Mission Beach *Australia* 17°53S 146°6E **62** B4
Mission Viejo *U.S.A.* 33°36N 117°40W **79** M9
Missisa L. *Canada* 52°20N 85°7W **72** B2
Missisicabi → *Canada* 51°14N 79°31W **72** B4
Mississagi → *Canada* 46°15N 83°9W **72** C3
Mississippi □ *U.S.A.* 33°0N 90°0W **85** E9
Mississippi → *U.S.A.* 29°9N 89°15W **85** G10
Mississippi River Delta *U.S.A.* 29°10N 89°15W **85** G10
Mississippi Sd. *U.S.A.* 30°20N 89°0W **85** G10
Missoula *U.S.A.* 46°52N 114°1W **76** C6
Missouri □ *U.S.A.* 38°25N 92°30W **80** F7
Missouri → *U.S.A.* 38°49N 90°7W **80** F8
Missouri City *U.S.A.* 29°37N 95°32W **84** G7
Missouri Valley *U.S.A.* 41°34N 95°53W **80** E6
Mist *U.S.A.* 46°0N 123°15W **78** E3
Mistassibi → *Canada* 48°53N 72°13W **73** B5
Mistassini *Canada* 48°53N 72°12W **73** C5
Mistassini → *Canada* 48°42N 72°20W **73** C5
Mistassini, L. *Canada* 51°0N 73°30W **72** C5
Mistastin L. *Canada* 55°57N 63°20W **73** A7
Mistinibi, L. *Canada* 55°56N 64°17W **73** A7
Mistissini *Canada* 50°30N 73°52W **72** C5
Misty L. *Canada* 58°53N 101°40W **71** B8
Misurata = Mişrātah *Libya* 32°24N 15°3E **53** B9

Mitchell *Australia* 26°29S 147°58E **63** D4
Mitchell *Canada* 43°28N 81°12W **82** C3
Mitchell *Nebr., U.S.A.* 41°57N 103°49W **80** E2
Mitchell *Oreg., U.S.A.* 44°34N 120°9W **76** D3
Mitchell ➤ *Australia* 15°12S 141°35E **62** B3
Mitchell, Mt. *U.S.A.* 35°46N 82°16W **85** D13
Mitchell-Alice Rivers △
  Australia 15°28S 142°5E **62** B3
Mitchell Ra. *Australia* 12°49S 135°36E **62** A2
Mitchelstown *Ireland* 52°15N 8°16W **10** D3
Mitha Tiwana *Pakistan* 32°13N 72°6E **42** C5
Mithi *Pakistan* 24°44N 69°48E **42** G3
Mithrao *Pakistan* 27°28N 69°40E **42** F3
Mitilíni *Greece* 39°6N 26°35E **23** E12
Mitla Pass = Mamarr Mitlā
  Egypt 30°2N 32°54E **48** E1
Mito *Japan* 36°20N 140°30E **29** F10
Mitrovicë *Kosovo* 42°54N 20°52E **23** C9
Mitsamiouli *Comoros Is.* 11°20S 43°16E **55** a
Mitsiwa *Eritrea* 15°35N 39°25E **49** D2
Mitsukaidō *Japan* 36°1N 139°59E **29** F9
Mittagong *Australia* 34°28S 150°29E **63** E5
Mittimatalik = Pond Inlet
  Canada 72°40N 77°0W **69** C16
Mitú *Colombia* 1°15N 70°13W **92** C4
Mitumba, Mts.
  Dem. Rep. of the Congo 7°0S 27°30E **54** F5
Mitwaba
  Dem. Rep. of the Congo 8°2S 27°17E **54** F5
Mixteco ➤ *Mexico* 18°11N 98°30W **87** D5
Miyagi □ *Japan* 38°15N 140°45E **28** E10
Miyah, W. el ➤ *Syria* 34°44N 39°57E **46** C3
Miyake-Jima *Japan* 34°5N 139°30E **29** G9
Miyako *Japan* 39°40N 141°59E **28** E10
Miyako-Jima *Japan* 24°45N 125°20E **29** M2
Miyako-Rettō *Japan* 24°24N 125°0E **29** M2
Miyakojima *Japan* 24°48N 125°17E **29** M2
Miyakonojō *Japan* 31°40N 131°5E **29** J5
Miyani *India* 21°50N 69°26E **42** J3
Miyanoura-Dake *Japan* 30°20N 130°31E **29** J5
Miyazaki *Japan* 31°56N 131°30E **29** J5
Miyazaki □ *Japan* 32°30N 131°30E **29** H5
Miyazu *Japan* 35°35N 135°10E **29** G7
Miyet, Bahr el = Dead Sea
  Asia 31°30N 35°30E **48** D4
Miyi *China* 26°47N 102°9E **34** D4
Miyoshi *Japan* 34°48N 132°51E **29** G6
Miyun *China* 40°28N 116°50E **32** D9
Miyun Shuiku *China* 40°30N 117°0E **33** D9
Mizdah *Libya* 31°30N 13°0E **53** B8
Mizen Hd. *Cork, Ireland* 51°27N 9°50W **10** E2
Mizen Hd. *Wicklow, Ireland* 52°51N 6°4W **10** D5
Mizhi *China* 37°47N 110°12E **32** F6
Mizoram □ *India* 23°30N 92°40E **41** H18
Mizpe Ramon *Israel* 30°34N 34°49E **48** E3
Mizusawa *Antarctica* 70°30S 41°0E **5** D5
Mizusawa = Ōshū *Japan* 39°8N 141°8E **28** E10
Mjölby *Sweden* 58°20N 15°10E **9** G16
Mjøsa *Norway* 60°40N 11°0E **8** F14
Mkhaya △ *Swaziland* 26°34S 31°45E **57** C5
Mkhuze △ *S. Africa* 29°27S 29°30E **57** C4
Mkomazi ➤ *S. Africa* 30°12S 30°50E **57** D5
Mkuze *S. Africa* 27°10S 32°0E **57** D5
Mladá Boleslav *Czech Rep.* 50°27N 14°53E **16** C8
Mlange = Mulanje, Mt.
  Malawi 16°2S 35°33E **55** H7
Mława *Poland* 53°9N 20°25E **17** B11
Mlawula △ *Swaziland* 26°12S 32°2E **57** C5
Mljet *Croatia* 42°43N 17°30E **22** C7
Mmabatho *S. Africa* 25°49S 25°30E **56** C4
Mo i Rana *Norway* 66°20N 14°7E **8** C16
Moa *Australia* 10°11S 142°16E **62** a
Moa *Cuba* 20°40N 74°56W **89** B4
Moa *Indonesia* 8°0S 128°0E **37** F7
Moa ➤ *S. Leone* 6°59N 11°36W **52** G3
Moab *U.S.A.* 38°35N 109°33W **76** G9
Moala *Fiji* 18°36S 179°53E **59** a
Moama *Australia* 36°7S 144°46E **63** F3
Moamba *Mozam.* 25°36S 32°15E **57** D5
Moapa *U.S.A.* 36°40N 114°37W **79** J12
Moate *Ireland* 53°24N 7°44W **10** C4
Mobārakābād *Iran* 28°24N 53°20E **47** D7
Mobaye *C.A.R.* 4°25N 21°5E **54** D4
Moberly *U.S.A.* 39°25N 92°26W **80** F7
Moberly Lake *Canada* 55°50N 121°44W **70** B4
Mobile *U.S.A.* 30°41N 88°3W **85** F10
Mobile B. *U.S.A.* 30°30N 88°0W **85** F11
Mobridge *U.S.A.* 45°32N 100°26W **80** C3
Moc Chau *Vietnam* 20°50N 104°38E **38** B5
Moc Hoa *Vietnam* 10°46N 105°56E **39** G5
Moçambique = Mozambique ■
  Africa 19°0S 35°0E **55** H7
Moçâmedes *Mozam.* 15°3S 40°42E **55** H8
Mocanaqua *U.S.A.* 41°9N 76°8W **83** E8
Moce *Fiji* 18°40S 178°29W **59** a
Mochima △ *Venezuela* 10°30N 64°9W **89** D7
Mochudi *Botswana* 24°27S 26°7E **56** B4
Mocimboa da Praia
  Mozam. 11°25S 40°20E **54** G8
Moclips *U.S.A.* 47°14N 124°13W **78** C2
Mocoa *Colombia* 1°7N 76°35W **92** C3
Mococa *Brazil* 21°28S 47°0W **95** A6
Mocorito *Mexico* 25°29N 107°55W **86** B3
Moctezuma *Mexico* 29°48N 109°42W **86** B3
Moctezuma ➤ *Mexico* 21°59N 98°34W **87** C5
Mocuba *Mozam.* 16°54S 36°57E **55** H7
Modane *France* 45°12N 6°40E **20** D7
Modasa *India* 23°30N 73°21E **42** H5
Modder ➤ *S. Africa* 29°2S 24°37E **56** C3
Modderrivier *S. Africa* 29°2S 24°38E **56** D3
Módena *Italy* 44°40N 10°55E **22** B4
Modena *U.S.A.* 37°48N 113°56W **77** H7
Modesto *U.S.A.* 37°39N 121°0W **78** H6
Módica *Italy* 36°52N 14°46E **22** F6
Modimolle *S. Africa* 24°42S 28°22E **57** B4
Modjadjiskloof *S. Africa* 23°42S 30°10E **57** B5
Moe *Australia* 38°12S 146°19E **63** F4
Moengo *Suriname* 5°45N 54°20W **93** B8

Moenjodaro = Mohenjodaro
  Pakistan 27°19N 68°7E **42** F3
Moffat *U.K.* 55°21N 3°27W **11** F5
Moga *India* 30°48N 75°8E **42** D6
Mogadishu = Muqdisho
  Somalia 2°2N 45°25E **49** G4
Mogador = Essaouira
  Morocco 31°32N 9°42W **52** B4
Mogalakwena ➤
  S. Africa 22°38S 28°40E **57** B4
Mogami-Gawa ➤ *Japan* 38°45N 140°0E **28** E10
Mogaung *Burma* 25°20N 97°0E **41** G20
Mogi-Mirim *Brazil* 22°29S 47°0W **93** H9
Mogilev = Mahilyow
  Belarus 53°55N 30°18E **17** B16
Mogilev-Podolskiy = Mohyliv-
  Podilskyy *Ukraine* 48°26N 27°48E **17** D14
Mogocha *Russia* 53°40N 119°50E **27** D12
Mogoditshane *Botswana* 24°37S 25°51E **56** B4
Mogok *Burma* 23°0N 96°40E **41** H20
Mogollon Rim *U.S.A.* 34°10N 110°50W **77** J8
Mogumber *Australia* 31°2S 116°3E **61** F2
Mogwadi ➤ *S. Africa* 23°4S 29°36E **57** B4
Mohács *Hungary* 45°58N 18°41E **17** F10
Mohala *India* 20°35N 80°44E **44** D5
Mohales Hoek *Lesotho* 30°7S 27°26E **56** D4
Mohali *India* 30°47N 76°41E **42** D7
Mohall *U.S.A.* 48°46N 101°31W **80** A3
Mohammadābād *Iran* 37°52N 59°5E **47** B8
Mohammedia *Morocco* 33°44N 7°21W **52** B4
Mohana *India* 19°27N 84°16E **44** E7
Mohana ➤ *India* 24°43N 85°0E **43** G11
Mohanlalganj *India* 26°41N 80°58E **43** F9
Mohave, L. *U.S.A.* 35°12N 114°34W **79** K12
Mohawk ➤ *U.S.A.* 42°47N 73°41W **83** D11
Mohéli *Comoros Is.* 12°20S 43°40E **55** a
Mohenjodaro *Pakistan* 27°19N 68°7E **42** F3
Moher, Cliffs of *Ireland* 52°58N 9°27W **10** D2
Mohicanville Res. *U.S.A.* 40°45N 82°9W **82** F2
Mohns Ridge *Arctic* 72°30N 5°0W **4** B7
Mohsenābād *Iran* 36°40N 59°35E **47** B8
Mohyliv-Podilskyy
  Ukraine 48°26N 27°48E **17** D14
Moidart, L. *U.K.* 56°47N 5°52W **11** E3
Moinabad *India* 17°44N 77°16E **44** F3
Moira ➤ *Canada* 44°21N 77°24W **82** B7
Moisaküla *Estonia* 58°3N 25°12E **9** G21
Moisie *Canada* 50°12N 66°1W **73** B6
Moisie ➤ *Canada* 50°14N 66°5W **73** B6
Mojave *U.S.A.* 35°3N 118°10W **79** K8
Mojave △ *U.S.A.* 35°7N 115°32W **79** K11
Mojave Desert *U.S.A.* 35°0N 116°30W **79** L10
Moji das Cruzes *Brazil* 23°31S 46°11W **95** A6
Moji-Guaçu ➤ *Brazil* 20°53S 48°10W **95** A6
Mojiang *China* 23°37N 101°35E **34** F3
Mojo *Bolivia* 21°48S 65°33W **94** A2
Mojokerto *Indonesia* 7°28S 112°26E **37** G15
Mokai *N.Z.* 38°32S 175°56E **59** C5
Mokala △ *S. Africa* 29°10S 24°10E **56** C3
Mokau *N.Z.* 38°42S 174°39E **59** C5
Mokelumne ➤ *U.S.A.* 38°13N 121°28W **78** G5
Mokelumne Hill *U.S.A.* 38°18N 120°43W **78** G6
Mokhotlong *Lesotho* 29°22S 29°2E **57** C4
Mokoan, L. *Australia* 36°27S 146°5E **63** C4
Mokokchung *India* 26°15N 94°30E **41** F19
Mokolo ➤ *S. Africa* 23°14S 27°43E **57** B4
Mokopane *S. Africa* 24°10S 28°55E **57** B4
Mokpo *S. Korea* 34°50N 126°25E **33** G14
Mokra Gora *Europe* 42°50N 20°30E **23** C9
Mol *Belgium* 51°11N 5°5E **15** C5
Molakalmuru *India* 14°55N 76°50E **45** G3
Mold *U.K.* 53°9N 3°8W **12** D4
Moldavia = Moldova ■
  Europe 47°0N 28°0E **17** E15
Moldavia *Romania* 46°30N 27°0E **17** E14
Molde *Norway* 62°45N 7°9E **8** E12
Moldova ■ *Europe* 47°0N 28°0E **17** E15
Moldoveanu, Vf.
  Romania 45°36N 24°45E **17** F13
Mole ➤ *U.K.* 51°24N 0°21W **13** F7
Molepolole *Botswana* 24°28S 25°28E **56** B4
Molfetta *Italy* 41°12N 16°36E **22** D7
Moline *U.S.A.* 41°30N 90°31W **80** E8
Molinos *Argentina* 25°28S 66°15W **94** B2
Mollendo *Peru* 17°0S 72°0W **92** G4
Mollerin, L. *Australia* 30°30S 117°35E **61** F2
Molodechno = Maladzyechna
  Belarus 54°20N 26°50E **17** A14
Molodezhnaya *Antarctica* 67°40S 45°51E **5** C9
Moloka'i *U.S.A.* 21°8N 157°0W **75** L8
Molokai Fracture Zone
  Pac. Oc. 28°0N 125°0W **65** E15
Molong *Australia* 33°5S 148°54E **63** E4
Molopo ➤ *Africa* 28°30S 20°12E **56** C3
Molson L. *Canada* 54°22N 96°40W **71** C9
Molteno *S. Africa* 31°22S 26°22E **56** D4
Molu *Indonesia* 6°45S 131°40E **37** F8
Molucca Sea *Indonesia* 0°0 125°0E **37** E6
Moluccas = Maluku
  Indonesia 1°0S 127°0E **37** E7
Moma *Mozam.* 16°47S 39°4E **55** H7
Mombasa *Kenya* 4°3S 39°40E **54** E7
Mombetsu *Japan* 44°21N 143°22E **28** B11
Momchilgrad *Bulgaria* 41°33N 25°23E **23** D11
Mompós *Colombia* 9°14N 74°26W **92** B4
Møn *Denmark* 54°57N 12°20E **9** J15
Mon □ *Burma* 16°0N 97°30E **41** L20
Mona, Canal de la = Mona
  Passage *W. Indies* 18°30N 67°45W **89** C6
Mona, Isla *Puerto Rico* 18°5N 67°54W **89** C6
Mona, Pta. *Costa Rica* 9°37N 82°36E **88** E3
Mona Passage *W. Indies* 18°30N 67°45W **89** C6
Monaca *U.S.A.* 40°41N 80°17W **82** F4
Monaco ■ *Europe* 43°46N 7°23E **20** E7
Monadhliath Mts. *U.K.* 57°10N 4°4W **11** D4
Monadnock, Mt. *U.S.A.* 42°52N 72°7W **83** D12
Monaghan *Ireland* 54°15N 6°57W **10** B5

Monaghan □ *Ireland* 54°11N 6°56W **10** B5
Monahans *U.S.A.* 31°36N 102°54W **84** F3
Monar, L. *U.K.* 57°26N 5°8W **11** D3
Monaragala *Sri Lanka* 6°52N 81°22E **45** L5
Monarch Mt. *Canada* 51°55N 125°57W **70** C3
Monashee Mts. *Canada* 51°0N 118°43W **70** C5
Monasterevin *Ireland* 53°8N 7°4W **10** C4
Monastir = Bitola
  Macedonia 41°1N 21°20E **23** D9
Monastir *Tunisia* 35°50N 10°49E **53** A8
Monbetsu = Hidaka
  Japan 42°30N 142°10E **28** C11
Moncayo, Sierra del *Spain* 41°48N 1°50W **21** B5
Monchegorsk *Russia* 67°54N 32°58E **8** C25
Mönchengladbach
  Germany 51°11N 6°27E **16** C4
Monchique *Portugal* 37°19N 8°38W **21** D1
Moncks Corner *U.S.A.* 33°12N 80°1W **85** E14
Monclova *Mexico* 26°54N 101°25W **86** B4
Moncton *Canada* 46°7N 64°51W **73** C7
Mondego ➤ *Portugal* 40°9N 8°52W **21** B1
Mondeodo *Indonesia* 3°34S 122°9E **37** E6
Mondlo *S. Africa* 27°59S 30°43E **57** C5
Mondovì *Italy* 44°23N 7°49E **20** D7
Mondrain I. *Australia* 34°9S 122°14E **61** F3
Moneague *Jamaica* 18°16N 77°7W **88** a
Moneron, Ostrov
  Russia 46°15N 141°16E **28** A10
Monessen *U.S.A.* 40°9N 79°54W **82** F5
Monett *U.S.A.* 36°55N 93°55W **80** G7
Moneymore *U.K.* 54°41N 6°40W **10** B5
Monforte de Lemos *Spain* 42°31N 7°33W **21** A2
Mong Hpayak *Burma* 20°52N 99°55E **38** B2
Mong Hsat *Shan, Burma* 21°54N 98°30E **34** G2
Mong Hsat *Shan, Burma* 20°31N 99°15E **38** B2
Mong Kung *Burma* 21°35N 97°35E **41** J20
Mong Nai *Burma* 20°32N 97°46E **41** J20
Mong Ping *Burma* 21°22N 99°2E **34** G2
Mong Tai = Shan □
  Burma 21°30N 98°30E **41** J21
Mong Ton *Burma* 20°17N 98°45E **41** J21
Mong Yai *Burma* 22°21N 98°3E **41** H21
Mong Yang *Burma* 21°50N 99°41E **38** B2
Mongalla *South Sudan* 5°8N 31°42E **53** G12
Mongers, L. *Australia* 29°25S 117°5E **61** E2
Monghyr = Munger
  India 25°23N 86°30E **43** G12
Mongibello = Etna *Italy* 37°50N 14°55E **22** F6
Mongo *Chad* 12°14N 18°43E **53** F9
Mongolia ■ *Asia* 47°0N 103°0E **30** B9
Mongolia, Plateau of
  Asia 45°0N 105°0E **24** D12
Mongu *Zambia* 15°16S 23°12E **55** H4
Mõngua *Angola* 16°43S 15°20E **56** A2
Monifieth *U.K.* 56°30N 2°48W **11** E6
Monkey Mia *Australia* 25°48S 113°43E **61** E1
Monkey River *Belize* 16°22N 88°29W **87** D7
Monkland *Canada* 45°11N 74°52W **83** A10
Monkoto
  Dem. Rep. of the Congo 1°38S 20°35E **54** E4
Monkton *Canada* 43°35N 81°5W **82** C3
Monmouth *U.K.* 51°48N 2°42W **13** F5
Monmouth *Ill., U.S.A.* 40°55N 90°39W **80** E8
Monmouth *Oreg.,
  U.S.A.* 44°51N 123°14W **76** D2
Monmouthshire □ *U.K.* 51°48N 2°54W **13** F5
Mono, Pta. *Nic.* 12°0N 83°30W **88** D3
Mono L. *U.S.A.* 38°1N 119°1W **78** H7
Monolith *U.S.A.* 35°7N 118°22W **79** K8
Monongahela *U.S.A.* 40°12N 79°56W **82** F5
Monópoli *Italy* 40°57N 17°18E **22** D7
Monos I. *Trin. & Tob.* 10°42N 61°44W **93** K15
Monroe *La., U.S.A.* 32°30N 92°7W **84** E8
Monroe *Mich., U.S.A.* 41°55N 83°24W **81** E12
Monroe *N.C., U.S.A.* 34°59N 80°33W **85** D14
Monroe *N.Y., U.S.A.* 41°20N 74°11W **83** E10
Monroe *Utah, U.S.A.* 38°38N 112°7W **76** G7
Monroe *Wash., U.S.A.* 47°51N 121°58W **78** C5
Monroe *Wis., U.S.A.* 42°36N 89°38W **80** D9
Monroe City *U.S.A.* 39°39N 91°44W **80** F8
Monroeton *U.S.A.* 41°43N 76°29W **83** E8
Monroeville *Ala., U.S.A.* 31°31N 87°20W **85** F11
Monroeville *Pa., U.S.A.* 40°26N 79°45W **82** F5
Monrovia *Liberia* 6°18N 10°47W **52** G3
Mons *Belgium* 50°27N 3°58E **15** D3
Monse *Indonesia* 4°7S 123°15E **37** E6
Mont-de-Marsan *France* 43°54N 0°31W **20** E3
Mont-Joli *Canada* 48°37N 68°10W **73** C6
Mont-Laurier *Canada* 46°35N 75°30W **72** C4
Mont-Louis *Canada* 49°15N 65°44W **73** C6
Mont-St-Michel, Le
  France 48°40N 1°30W **20** B3
Mont-Tremblant △
  Canada 46°30N 74°30W **72** C5
Montagu *S. Africa* 33°45S 20°8E **56** D3
Montagu I. *Antarctica* 58°25S 26°20W **5** B1
Montague *Canada* 46°10N 62°39W **73** C7
Montague *I. *Mexico* 31°45N 114°48W **86** A2
Montague, I. *U.S.A.* 60°0N 147°30W **74** D10
Montague Ra. *Australia* 27°15S 119°30E **61** E2
Montague Sd. *Australia* 14°28S 125°20E **60** B4
Montalbán *Spain* 40°50N 0°45W **21** B5
Montalvo *U.S.A.* 34°13N 119°12W **79** L7
Montana *Bulgaria* 43°27N 23°16E **23** C10
Montaña *Peru* 6°0S 73°0W **92** E4
Montana □ *U.S.A.* 47°0N 110°0W **76** C9
Montargis *France* 47°59N 2°43E **20** C5
Montauban *France* 44°2N 1°21E **20** D4
Montauk *U.S.A.* 41°3N 71°57W **83** E13
Montauk Pt. *U.S.A.* 41°4N 71°51W **83** E13
Montbéliard *France* 47°31N 6°48E **20** C7
Montceau-les-Mines
  France 46°40N 4°23E **20** C6
Montclair *U.S.A.* 40°49N 74°12W **83** F10
Monte Albán *Mexico* 17°2N 96°46W **87** D5
Monte Alegre *Brazil* 2°0S 54°0W **93** D8
Monte Azul *Brazil* 15°9S 42°53W **93** G10
Monte-Carlo *Monaco* 43°44N 7°25E **20** E7

Monte Caseros *Argentina* 30°10S 57°50W **94** C4
Monte Comán *Argentina* 34°40S 67°53W **94** C2
Monte Cristi *Dom. Rep.* 19°52N 71°39W **89** C5
Monte Lindo ➤
  Paraguay 23°56S 57°12W **94** A4
Monte Patria *Chile* 30°42S 70°58W **94** C1
Monte Quemado
  Argentina 25°53S 62°41W **94** B3
Monte Rio *U.S.A.* 38°28N 123°0W **78** G4
Monte Santu, C. di *Italy* 40°5N 9°44E **22** D3
Monte Vista *U.S.A.* 37°35N 106°9W **77** H10
Monteagudo *Argentina* 27°14S 54°8W **95** B5
Montebello *Canada* 45°40N 74°55W **72** C5
Montebello Is. *Australia* 20°30S 115°45E **60** D2
Montecarlo *Argentina* 26°34S 54°47W **95** B5
Montecito *U.S.A.* 34°26N 119°40W **79** L7
Montecristo *Italy* 42°20N 10°19E **22** C4
Montego Bay *Jamaica* 18°28N 77°55W **88** a
Montélimar *France* 44°33N 4°45E **20** D6
Montello *U.S.A.* 43°48N 89°20W **80** D9
Montemorelos *Mexico* 25°12N 99°49W **87** B5
Montenegro *Brazil* 29°39S 51°29W **95** B5
Montenegro ■ *Europe* 42°40N 19°20E **23** C8
Montepuez *Mozam.* 13°8S 38°59E **55** G7
Monterey *U.S.A.* 36°37N 121°55W **78** J5
Monterey B. *U.S.A.* 36°45N 122°0W **78** J5
Montería *Colombia* 8°46N 75°53W **92** B3
Monteros *Argentina* 27°11S 65°30W **94** B2
Monterrey *Mexico* 25°40N 100°19W **86** B4
Montes Azules △ *Mexico* 16°21S 91°3W **87** D6
Montes Claros *Brazil* 16°30S 43°50W **93** G10
Montesano *U.S.A.* 46°59N 123°36W **78** D3
Montesilvano *Italy* 42°29N 14°8E **22** C6
Montevideo *Uruguay* 34°50S 56°11W **95** C4
Montevideo *U.S.A.* 44°57N 95°43W **80** C6
Montezuma *U.S.A.* 41°35N 92°32W **80** E7
Montezuma Castle △
  U.S.A. 34°39N 111°45W **77** J8
Montgomery *U.K.* 52°34N 3°8W **13** E4
Montgomery *Ala.,
  U.S.A.* 32°23N 86°19W **85** J11
Montgomery *Pa., U.S.A.* 41°10N 76°53W **82** E8
Montgomery *W. Va.,
  U.S.A.* 38°11N 81°19W **81** F13
Montgomery City *U.S.A.* 38°59N 91°30W **80** F8
Monticello *Ark., U.S.A.* 33°38N 91°47W **84** E9
Monticello *Fla., U.S.A.* 30°33N 83°52W **85** F13
Monticello *Ind., U.S.A.* 40°45N 86°46W **80** E10
Monticello *Iowa, U.S.A.* 42°15N 91°12W **80** D8
Monticello *Ky., U.S.A.* 36°50N 84°51W **81** G11
Monticello *Minn., U.S.A.* 45°18N 93°48W **80** C7
Monticello *Miss., U.S.A.* 31°33N 90°7W **85** F9
Monticello *N.Y., U.S.A.* 41°39N 74°42W **83** E10
Monticello *Utah, U.S.A.* 37°52N 109°21W **77** H9
Montijo *Portugal* 38°41N 8°54W **21** C1
Montilla *Spain* 37°36N 4°40W **21** D3
Montluçon *France* 46°22N 2°36E **20** C5
Montmagny *Canada* 46°58N 70°34W **73** C5
Montmartre *Canada* 50°14N 103°27W **71** C8
Montmorillon *France* 46°26N 0°50E **20** C4
Monto *Australia* 24°52S 151°6E **62** C5
Montongbuwoh *Indonesia* 8°33S 116°4E **37** K19
Montoro *Spain* 38°1N 4°27E **21** C3
Montour Falls *U.S.A.* 42°21N 76°51W **82** D8
Montoursville *U.S.A.* 41°15N 76°55W **82** E8
Montpelier *Idaho, U.S.A.* 42°19N 111°18W **76** E8
Montpelier *Ohio, U.S.A.* 41°35N 84°37W **81** E11
Montpelier *Vt., U.S.A.* 44°16N 72°35W **83** B12
Montpellier *France* 43°37N 3°52E **20** E5
Montréal ➤ *Canada* 47°14N 84°39W **72** C3
Montréal L. *Canada* 54°20N 105°45W **71** C7
Montreal Lake *Canada* 54°3N 105°46W **71** C7
Montreux *Switz.* 46°26N 6°55E **20** C7
Montrose *U.K.* 56°44N 2°27W **11** E6
Montrose *Colo., U.S.A.* 38°29N 107°53W **76** G10
Montrose *Pa., U.S.A.* 41°50N 75°53W **83** E9
Monts, Pte. des *Canada* 49°20N 67°12W **73** C6
Montserrat ☒ *W. Indies* 16°40N 62°10W **89** C7
Monywa *Burma* 22°7N 95°11E **41** H19
Monze *Zambia* 16°17S 27°29E **55** H5
Monze, C. *Pakistan* 24°47N 66°37E **42** G2
Monzón *Spain* 41°52N 0°10E **21** B6
Mooers *U.S.A.* 44°58N 73°35W **83** B11
Mooi ➤ *S. Africa* 28°45S 30°34E **57** D5
Mooi River *S. Africa* 29°13S 29°50E **57** C4
Mookgopong *S. Africa* 24°31S 28°44E **57** B4
Moomba *Australia* 28°6S 140°12E **63** A3
Moonah ➤ *Australia* 22°3S 138°33E **62** C2
Moonda, L. *Australia* 25°52S 140°25E **62** D3
Moonie *Australia* 27°46S 150°20E **63** D5
Moonie ➤ *Australia* 29°19S 148°43E **63** D4
Moonta *Australia* 34°6S 137°32E **63** E2
Moora *Australia* 30°37S 115°58E **61** F2
Moorcroft *U.S.A.* 44°16N 104°57W **76** D11
Moore ➤ *Australia* 31°22S 115°30E **61** F2
Moore, L. *Australia* 29°50S 117°35E **61** E2
Moore Falls *Canada* 44°48N 78°48E **82** B6
Moore Park *Australia* 24°43S 152°17E **62** C5
Moore Res. *U.S.A.* 44°20N 71°53W **83** B13
Moore River △ *Australia* 31°7S 115°59E **61** F2
Moorea *French Polynesia* 17°30S 149°50W **59** d
Moorefield *U.S.A.* 39°4N 78°58W **81** F14
Moorfoot Hills *U.K.* 55°44N 3°8W **11** F5
Moorhead *U.S.A.* 46°53N 96°45W **80** B5
Moorpark *U.S.A.* 34°17N 118°53W **79** L8
Mooreesburg *S. Africa* 33°6S 18°38E **56** D2
Moorrinya △ *Australia* 21°42S 144°58E **62** C3
Moose ➤ *Canada* 51°20N 80°25W **72** B3
Moose ➤ *U.S.A.* 43°38N 74°32W **83** C10
Moose Creek *Canada* 45°15N 74°58W **83** A10
Moose Factory *Canada* 51°16N 80°32W **72** B3
Moose Jaw *Canada* 50°24N 105°30W **71** C7
Moose Jaw ➤ *Canada* 50°34N 105°18W **71** C7
Moose Lake *Canada* 53°43N 100°20W **71** C8
Moose Lake *U.S.A.* 46°27N 92°46W **80** B7
Moose Mountain △
  Canada 49°48N 102°25W **71** D8
Moosehead L. *U.S.A.* 45°38N 69°40W **81** C19
Mooselookmeguntic L.
  U.S.A. 44°55N 70°49W **83** B14

Moosilauke, Mt. *U.S.A.* 44°3N 71°40W **83** B13
Moosomin *Canada* 50°9N 101°40W **71** C8
Moosonee *Canada* 51°17N 80°39W **72** B3
Moosup *U.S.A.* 41°43N 71°53W **83** E13
Mopane *S. Africa* 22°37S 29°52E **57** B4
Mopipi *Botswana* 21°6S 24°55E **56** B3
Mopti *Mali* 14°30N 4°0W **52** F5
Moqor *Afghan.* 32°50N 67°42E **42** C2
Moquegua *Peru* 17°15S 70°46W **92** G4
Mora *Sweden* 61°2N 14°38E **8** F16
Mora *Minn., U.S.A.* 45°53N 93°18W **80** C7
Mora *N. Mex., U.S.A.* 35°58N 105°20W **77** J11
Moradabad *India* 28°50N 78°50E **43** E8
Morafenobe *Madag.* 17°50S 44°53E **55** H8
Moramanga *Madag.* 18°56S 48°12E **55** H9
Moran *Kans., U.S.A.* 37°55N 95°10W **80** G6
Moran *Wyo., U.S.A.* 43°50N 110°31W **76** E8
Moranbah *Australia* 22°1S 148°6E **62** C4
Morang = Biratnagar
  Nepal 26°27N 87°17E **43** F12
Morant Bay *Jamaica* 17°53S 76°25W **88** a
Morant Cays *Jamaica* 17°22N 76°0W **88** C4
Morant Pt. *Jamaica* 17°55N 76°12W **88** a
Morar *India* 26°14N 78°14E **42** F8
Morar, L. *U.K.* 56°57N 5°40W **11** E3
Moratuwa *Sri Lanka* 6°45N 79°55E **45** L4
Morava ➤ *Serbia* 44°36N 21°4E **23** B9
Morava ➤ *Slovak Rep.* 48°10N 16°59E **17** D9
Moravia *U.S.A.* 42°43N 76°25W **83** D8
Moravian Hts. = Českomoravská
  Vrchovina *Czech Rep.* 49°30N 15°40E **16** D8
Morawa *Australia* 29°13S 116°0E **61** E2
Morawhanna *Guyana* 8°30N 59°40W **92** B7
Moray □ *U.K.* 57°31N 3°18W **11** D5
Moray Firth *U.K.* 57°40N 3°52W **11** D5
Morbi *India* 22°50N 70°42E **42** H4
Morden *Canada* 49°15N 98°10W **71** D9
Mordovian Republic =
  Mordvinia □ *Russia* 54°20N 44°30E **18** D7
Mordvinia □ *Russia* 54°20N 44°30E **18** D7
Moreau ➤ *U.S.A.* 45°18N 100°43W **80** C3
Morebeng *S. Africa* 23°30S 29°55E **57** B4
Morecambe *U.K.* 54°5N 2°52W **12** C5
Morecambe B. *U.K.* 54°7N 3°0W **12** C5
Moree *Australia* 29°28S 149°54E **63** D4
Morehead *U.S.A.* 38°11N 83°26W **81** F12
Morehead City *U.S.A.* 34°43N 76°43W **85** D16
Morel ➤ *India* 26°13N 76°36E **42** F7
Morelia *Mexico* 19°42N 101°7W **86** D4
Morella *Australia* 23°0S 143°52E **62** C3
Morella *Spain* 40°35N 0°5W **21** B5
Morelos *Mexico* 26°42N 107°40W **86** B3
Morelos □ *Mexico* 18°45N 99°0W **87** D5
Moremi △ *Botswana* 19°18S 23°10E **56** A3
Morena *India* 26°30N 78°4E **42** F8
Morena, Sierra *Spain* 38°20N 4°0W **21** C3
Moreno Valley *U.S.A.* 33°56N 117°14W **79** M10
Moresby I. *Canada* 52°30N 131°40W **70** C2
Moreton I. *Australia* 27°10S 153°25E **63** D5
Moreton Island △
  Australia 27°2S 153°24E **63** D5
Morgan *U.S.A.* 41°2N 111°41W **76** F8
Morgan City *U.S.A.* 29°42N 91°12W **84** G9
Morgan Hill *U.S.A.* 37°8N 121°39W **78** H5
Morganfield *U.S.A.* 37°41N 87°55W **80** G10
Morganton *U.S.A.* 35°45N 81°41W **85** D14
Morgantown *U.S.A.* 39°38N 79°57W **81** F14
Morgenzon *S. Africa* 26°45S 29°36E **57** C4
Morghak *Iran* 29°7N 57°54E **47** D8
Morhar ➤ *India* 25°29N 85°11E **43** G11
Mori *Japan* 42°6N 140°35E **28** C10
Moriarty *U.S.A.* 34°59N 106°3W **77** J10
Morice L. *Canada* 53°50N 127°40W **70** C3
Morinville *Canada* 53°49N 113°41W **70** C6
Morioka *Japan* 39°45N 141°8E **28** E10
Moris *Mexico* 28°10N 108°32W **86** B3
Morlaix *France* 48°36N 3°52W **20** B2
Mormugao = Marmagao
  India 15°25N 73°56E **45** G1
Mornington *Australia* 38°15S 145°5E **63** F4
Mornington, I. *Chile* 49°50S 75°30W **96** F1
Mornington I. *Australia* 16°30S 139°30E **62** B2
Moro *Pakistan* 26°40N 68°0E **42** F2
Moro ➤ *Pakistan* 29°42N 67°22E **42** E2
Moro G. *Phil.* 6°30N 123°0E **37** C6
Morocco ■ *N. Afr.* 32°0N 5°50W **52** B4
Morogoro *Tanzania* 6°50S 37°40E **54** F7
Moroleón *Mexico* 20°8N 101°12W **86** C4
Morombe *Madag.* 21°45S 43°22E **55** J8
Moron *Argentina* 34°39S 58°37W **94** C4
Morón *Cuba* 22°8N 78°39W **88** B4
Mörön *Mongolia* 49°38N 100°9E **30** B9
Morón de la Frontera
  Spain 37°6N 5°28W **21** D3
Morona ➤ *Peru* 4°40S 77°10W **92** D3
Morondava *Madag.* 20°17S 44°17E **55** J8
Morongo Valley *U.S.A.* 34°3N 116°37W **79** L10
Moroni *Comoros Is.* 11°40S 43°16E **55** a
Moroni *U.S.A.* 39°32N 111°35W **76** G8
Morotai *Indonesia* 2°10N 128°30E **37** D7
Moroto *Uganda* 2°28N 34°42E **54** D6
Morpeth *Canada* 42°23N 81°50W **82** D3
Morpeth *U.K.* 55°10N 1°41W **12** B6
Morphou *Cyprus* 35°12N 32°59E **46** C2
Morrilton *U.S.A.* 35°9N 92°44W **84** D8
Morrinhos *Brazil* 17°45S 49°10W **93** G9
Morrinsville *N.Z.* 37°40S 175°32E **59** B5
Morris *Canada* 49°25N 97°22W **71** D9
Morris *Ill., U.S.A.* 41°22N 88°26W **80** E9
Morris *Minn., U.S.A.* 45°35N 95°55W **80** C6
Morris *N.Y., U.S.A.* 42°33N 75°15W **83** D9
Morris *Pa., U.S.A.* 41°35N 77°17W **82** E7
Morris, Mt. *Australia* 26°9S 131°4E **61** E5
Morris Jesup, Kap
  Greenland 83°40N 34°0W **66** A16
Morrisburg *Canada* 44°55N 75°7W **83** B9
Morristown *Ariz.,
  U.S.A.* 33°51N 112°37W **77** K7
Morristown *N.J., U.S.A.* 40°48N 74°29W **83** F10

144 Morristown INDEX TO WORLD MAPS

Morristown N.Y., U.S.A. 44°35N 75°39W 83 B9
Morristown Tenn., U.S.A. 36°13N 83°18W 85 C13
Morrisville N.Y., U.S.A. 42°53N 75°35W 83 D9
Morrisville Pa., U.S.A. 40°13N 74°47W 83 F10
Morrisville Vt., U.S.A. 44°34N 72°36W 83 B12
Morro, Pta. Chile 27°6S 71°0W 94 B1
Morro Bay U.S.A. 35°22N 120°51W 78 K6
Morrocoy △ Venezuela 10°48N 68°13W 89 D6
Morrosquillo, G. de Colombia 9°35N 75°40W 88 E4
Morrumbene Mozam. 23°31S 35°16E 57 B6
Morshansk Russia 53°28N 41°50E 18 D7
Morsi India 21°21N 78°0E 44 D4
Morteros Argentina 30°50S 62°0W 94 C3
Mortlach Canada 50°27N 106°4W 71 C7
Mortlake Australia 38°5S 142°50E 63 F3
Morton Tex., U.S.A. 33°44N 102°46W 84 E3
Morton Wash., U.S.A. 46°34N 122°17W 78 D4
Moruga Trin. & Tob. 10°4N 61°16W 93 K15
Morundah Australia 34°57S 146°19E 63 E4
Moruya Australia 35°58S 150°3E 63 F5
Morvan France 47°5N 4°3E 20 C6
Morven Australia 26°22S 147°5E 63 D4
Morvern U.K. 56°38N 5°44W 11 E3
Morwell Australia 38°10S 146°22E 63 F4
Morzhovets, Ostrov Russia 66°44N 42°35E 18 A7
Mosakahiken = Moose Lake Canada 53°46N 100°8W 71 C8
Moscos Is. Burma 14°0N 97°30E 38 F1
Moscow Idaho, U.S.A. 46°44N 117°0W 76 C5
Moscow Pa., U.S.A. 41°20N 75°31W 83 E9
Mosel → Europe 50°22N 7°36E 20 A7
Moselle = Mosel → Europe 50°22N 7°36E 20 A7
Moses Lake U.S.A. 47°8N 119°17W 76 C4
Mosgiel N.Z. 45°53S 170°21E 59 F3
Moshaweng → S. Africa 26°35S 22°50E 56 C3
Moshchnyy, Ostrov Russia 60°1N 27°50E 9 F22
Moshi Tanzania 3°22S 37°18E 54 E7
Moshupa Botswana 24°46S 25°29E 56 B4
Mosi-oa-Tunya = Victoria Falls Zimbabwe 17°58S 25°52E 55 H5
Mosjøen Norway 65°51N 13°12E 8 D15
Moskenesøya Norway 67°58N 13°0E 8 C15
Moskenstraumen Norway 67°47N 12°45E 8 C15
Mosomane Botswana 24°2S 26°19E 56 B4
Mosonmagyaróvár Hungary 47°52N 17°18E 17 E9
Mosquera Colombia 2°35N 78°24W 92 C3
Mosquero U.S.A. 35°47N 103°58W 77 J12
Mosquitia Honduras 15°20N 84°10W 88 C3
Mosquito Creek L. U.S.A. 41°18N 80°46W 82 E4
Mosquito L. Canada 62°35N 103°20W 71 A8
Mosquitos, G. de los Panama 9°15N 81°10W 88 E3
Moss Norway 59°27N 10°40E 9 G14
Moss Vale Australia 34°32S 150°25E 63 E5
Mossaka Congo 1°15S 16°45E 54 E3
Mossbank Canada 49°56N 105°56W 71 D7
Mossburn N.Z. 45°41S 168°15E 59 F2
Mosselbaai S. Africa 34°11S 22°8E 56 D3
Mossendjo Congo 2°55S 12°42E 54 E2
Mossgiel Australia 33°15S 144°5E 63 E3
Mossman Australia 16°21S 145°15E 62 B4
Mossoró Brazil 5°10S 37°15W 93 E11
Most Czech Rep. 50°31N 13°38E 16 C7
Mostaganem Algeria 35°54N 0°5E 52 A6
Mostar Bos.-H. 43°22N 17°50E 23 C7
Mostardas Brazil 31°2S 50°51W 95 C5
Mostiska = Mostyska Ukraine 49°48N 23°4E 17 D12
Mosty = Masty Belarus 53°27N 24°38E 17 B13
Mostyska Ukraine 49°48N 23°4E 17 D12
Mosul = Al Mawşil Iraq 36°15N 43°5E 46 B4
Motagua → Guatemala 15°44N 88°14W 88 C2
Motala Sweden 58°32N 15°1E 9 G16
Motaze Mozam. 24°48S 32°52E 57 B5
Moth India 25°43N 78°57E 43 G8
Motherwell U.K. 55°47N 3°58W 11 F5
Motihari India 26°30N 84°55E 43 F11
Motozintla de Mendoza Mexico 15°22N 92°14W 87 D6
Motril Spain 36°31N 3°37W 21 D4
Mott U.S.A. 46°23N 102°20W 80 B2
Motueka N.Z. 41°7S 173°1E 59 D4
Motueka → N.Z. 41°5S 173°1E 59 D4
Motul Mexico 21°6N 89°17W 87 C7
Mouchalagane → Canada 50°56N 68°41W 73 B6
Mouding China 25°20N 101°28E 34 E3
Moudros Greece 39°50N 25°18E 23 E11
Mouhoun = Black Volta → Africa 8°41N 1°33W 52 G5
Mouila Gabon 1°50S 11°0E 54 E2
Moulamein Australia 35°3S 144°1E 63 F3
Moule à Chique, C. St. Lucia 13°43N 60°57W 89 f
Moulins France 46°35N 3°19E 20 C5
Moulmein Burma 16°30N 97°40E 41 L20
Moulouya, O. → Morocco 35°5N 2°25W 52 B5
Moultrie U.S.A. 31°11N 83°47W 85 F13
Moultrie, L. U.S.A. 33°20N 80°5W 85 E14
Mound City Mo., U.S.A. 40°7N 95°14W 80 E6
Mound City S. Dak., U.S.A. 45°44N 100°4W 80 C3
Moundou Chad 8°40N 16°10E 53 G9
Moundsville U.S.A. 39°55N 80°44W 82 G4
Moung Cambodia 12°46N 103°27E 38 F4
Mount Airy U.S.A. 36°31N 80°37W 85 C14
Mount Albert Canada 44°8N 79°19W 82 B5
Mount Aspiring △ N.Z. 44°19S 168°47E 59 F2
Mount Barker S. Austral., Australia 35°5S 138°52E 63 F2
Mount Barker W. Austral., Australia 34°38S 117°40E 61 F2
Mount Barnett Roadhouse Australia 16°39S 125°57E 60 C4
Mount Brydges Canada 42°54N 81°29W 82 D3
Mount Burr Australia 37°34S 140°26E 63 F3
Mount Carmel = Ha Karmel △ Israel 32°45N 35°5E 48 C4
Mount Carmel Ill., U.S.A. 38°25N 87°46W 80 F10
Mount Carmel Pa., U.S.A. 40°47N 76°26W 83 F8
Mount Clemens U.S.A. 42°35N 82°53W 82 D2
Mount Coolon Australia 21°25S 147°25E 62 C4
Mount Desert I. U.S.A. 44°21N 68°20W 81 C19
Mount Dora U.S.A. 28°48N 81°38W 85 G14
Mount Ebenezer Australia 25°6S 132°34E 61 E5
Mount Edziza ⌓ Canada 57°30N 130°45W 70 B2
Mount Field △ Australia 42°39S 146°35E 63 G4
Mount Fletcher S. Africa 30°40S 28°30E 57 D4
Mount Forest Canada 43°59N 80°43W 82 C4
Mount Frankland △ Australia 31°47S 116°37E 61 F2
Mount Frederick ❂ Australia 19°39S 129°18E 60 C4
Mount Gambier Australia 37°50S 140°46E 63 F3
Mount Garnet Australia 17°37S 145°6E 62 B4
Mount Holly U.S.A. 39°59N 74°47W 83 G10
Mount Holly Springs U.S.A. 40°7N 77°12W 82 F7
Mount Hope N.S.W., Australia 32°51S 145°51E 63 E4
Mount Hope S. Austral., Australia 34°7S 135°23E 63 E2
Mount Isa Australia 20°42S 139°26E 62 C2
Mount James ❂ Australia 24°51S 116°54E 61 D2
Mount Jewett U.S.A. 41°44N 78°39W 82 E6
Mount Kaputar △ Australia 30°16S 150°10E 63 E5
Mount Kisco U.S.A. 41°12N 73°44W 83 E11
Mount Laguna U.S.A. 32°52N 116°25W 79 N10
Mount Larcom Australia 23°48S 150°59E 62 C5
Mount Lofty Ranges Australia 34°35S 139°5E 63 E2
Mount Magnet Australia 28°2S 117°47E 61 E2
Mount Maunganui N.Z. 37°40S 176°14E 59 B6
Mount Molloy Australia 16°42S 145°20E 62 B4
Mount Morgan Australia 23°40S 150°25E 62 C5
Mount Morris U.S.A. 42°44N 77°52W 82 D7
Mount Pearl Canada 47°31N 52°47W 73 C9
Mount Penn U.S.A. 40°20N 75°54W 83 F9
Mount Perry Australia 25°13S 151°42E 63 D5
Mount Pleasant Iowa, U.S.A. 40°58N 91°33W 80 E8
Mount Pleasant Mich., U.S.A. 43°36N 84°46W 81 D11
Mount Pleasant Pa., U.S.A. 40°9N 79°33W 82 F5
Mount Pleasant S.C., U.S.A. 32°47N 79°52W 85 E15
Mount Pleasant Tenn., U.S.A. 35°32N 87°12W 85 D11
Mount Pleasant Tex., U.S.A. 33°9N 94°58W 84 E7
Mount Pleasant Utah, U.S.A. 39°33N 111°27W 76 G8
Mount Pocono U.S.A. 41°7N 75°22W 83 E9
Mount Rainier △ U.S.A. 46°55N 121°50W 78 D5
Mount Revelstoke △ Canada 51°5N 118°30W 70 C5
Mount Robson ⌓ Canada 53°0N 119°0W 70 C5
Mount St. Helens ⌓ U.S.A. 46°14N 122°11W 78 D4
Mount Selinda Zimbabwe 20°24S 32°43E 57 B5
Mount Shasta U.S.A. 41°19N 122°19W 76 F2
Mount Signal U.S.A. 32°39N 115°37W 79 N11
Mount Sterling Ill., U.S.A. 39°59N 90°45W 80 F8
Mount Sterling Ky., U.S.A. 38°4N 83°56W 81 F12
Mount Surprise Australia 18°10S 144°17E 62 B3
Mount Union U.S.A. 40°23N 77°53W 82 F7
Mount Upton U.S.A. 42°26N 75°23W 83 D9
Mount Vernon Ill., U.S.A. 38°19N 88°55W 80 F9
Mount Vernon Ind., U.S.A. 37°56N 87°54W 75 H22
Mount Vernon Ohio, U.S.A. 40°23N 82°29W 82 F2
Mount Vernon Wash., U.S.A. 48°25N 122°20W 78 B4
Mount William △ Australia 40°56S 148°14E 63 G4
Mountain Ash U.K. 51°40N 3°23W 13 F4
Mountain Center U.S.A. 33°42N 116°44W 79 M10
Mountain City Nev., U.S.A. 41°50N 115°58W 76 F6
Mountain City Tenn., U.S.A. 36°29N 81°48W 85 C14
Mountain Dale U.S.A. 41°41N 74°32W 83 E10
Mountain Grove U.S.A. 37°8N 92°16W 80 G7
Mountain Home Ark., U.S.A. 36°20N 92°23W 84 C8
Mountain Home Idaho, U.S.A. 43°8N 115°41W 76 E6
Mountain Iron U.S.A. 47°32N 92°37W 80 B7
Mountain Pass U.S.A. 35°29N 115°35W 79 K11
Mountain View Ark., U.S.A. 35°52N 92°7W 84 D8
Mountain View Calif., U.S.A. 37°23N 122°5W 78 H4
Mountain Zebra △ S. Africa 32°14S 25°27E 56 D4
Mountainair U.S.A. 34°31N 106°15W 77 J10
Mountbellew Ireland 53°28N 8°31W 10 C3
Mountlake Terrace U.S.A. 47°47N 122°18W 78 C4
Mountmellick Ireland 53°7N 7°20W 10 C4
Mountrath Ireland 53°0N 7°28W 10 D4
Moura Australia 24°35S 149°58E 62 C4
Moura Brazil 1°32S 61°38W 92 D6
Moura Portugal 38°7N 7°30W 21 C2
Mourdi, Dépression du Chad 18°10N 23°0E 53 E10
Mourilyan Australia 17°35S 146°3E 62 B4
Mourne → U.K. 54°52N 7°26W 10 B4
Mourne Mts. U.K. 54°10N 6°0W 10 B5
Mouscron Belgium 50°45N 3°12E 15 D3
Moussoro Chad 13°41N 16°35E 53 F9
Moutong Indonesia 0°28N 121°13E 37 D6
Movas Mexico 28°10N 109°25W 86 B3
Moville Ireland 55°11N 7°3W 10 A4
Mowandjum Australia 17°22S 123°40E 60 C3
Moy → Ireland 54°8N 9°8W 10 B2
Moya Comoros Is. 12°18S 44°18E 55 a
Moyale Kenya 3°30N 39°4E 54 D7
Moyen Atlas Morocco 33°0N 5°0W 52 B4
Moyo Indonesia 8°10S 117°40E 36 F5
Moyobamba Peru 6°0S 77°0W 92 E3
Moyyero → Russia 68°44N 103°42E 27 C11
Moyynqum Kazakhstan 44°12N 71°0E 30 C3
Moyynty Kazakhstan 47°10N 73°18E 26 E8
Mozambique = Moçambique Mozam. 15°3S 40°42E 55 H8
Mozambique ■ Africa 19°0S 35°0E 55 H7
Mozambique Chan. Africa 17°30S 42°30E 57 A7
Mozdok Russia 43°45N 44°48E 19 F7
Mozdūrān Iran 36°9N 60°35E 47 B9
Mozhnābād Iran 34°7N 60°6E 47 C9
Mozyr = Mazyr Belarus 51°59N 29°15E 17 B15
Mpanda Tanzania 6°23S 31°1E 54 F6
Mphoeng Zimbabwe 21°10S 27°51E 57 B4
Mpika Zambia 11°51S 31°25E 55 G6
Mpumalanga S. Africa 29°50S 30°33E 57 C5
Mpumalanga □ S. Africa 26°0S 30°0E 57 C5
Mpwapwa Tanzania 6°23S 36°30E 54 F7
Mqanduli S. Africa 31°49S 28°45E 57 D4
Msaken Tunisia 35°49N 10°33E 53 A8
M'sila Algeria 35°46N 4°30E 52 A6
Mstislavl = Mstsislaw Belarus 54°0N 31°50E 17 A16
Mstsislaw Belarus 54°0N 31°50E 17 A16
Mtamvuna = Mthamvuna → S. Africa 31°6S 30°12E 57 D5
Mthamvuna → S. Africa 31°6S 30°12E 57 D5
Mthatha S. Africa 31°36S 28°49E 57 D4
Mtubatuba S. Africa 28°30S 32°8E 57 C5
Mtwalume S. Africa 30°30S 30°38E 57 D5
Mtwara-Mikindani Tanzania 10°20S 40°20E 54 G8
Mu Gia, Deo Vietnam 17°40N 105°47E 38 D5
Mu Ko Chang △ Thailand 11°59N 102°22E 39 G4
Mu Ko Surin Thailand 9°30N 97°55E 39 H1
Mu Us Shamo China 39°0N 109°0E 32 E5
Muang Beng Laos 20°23N 101°46E 34 G3
Muang Chiang Rai = Chiang Rai Thailand 19°52N 99°50E 34 H2
Muang Et Laos 20°49N 104°1E 38 B5
Muang Hiam Laos 20°5N 103°22E 38 B4
Muang Hongsa Laos 19°43N 101°20E 38 C3
Muang Houn Laos 20°8N 101°23E 34 G3
Muang Kau Laos 15°6N 105°47E 38 E5
Muang Khao Laos 19°38N 103°32E 38 C4
Muang Khong Laos 14°7N 105°51E 38 E5
Muang Khoua Laos 21°5N 102°31E 34 G4
Muang Liap Laos 18°29N 101°40E 38 C3
Muang Mai Thailand 8°5N 98°21E 39 a
Muang May Laos 14°49N 106°56E 38 E6
Muang Na Mo Laos 21°3N 101°49E 34 G3
Muang Ngeun Laos 20°36N 101°3E 34 G3
Muang Ngoi Laos 20°43N 102°41E 34 G4
Muang Nong Laos 16°22N 106°30E 38 D6
Muang Ou Neua Laos 22°18N 101°48E 34 F3
Muang Ou Tay Laos 22°7N 101°48E 34 F3
Muang Pak Beng Laos 19°54N 101°8E 34 H3
Muang Phalane Laos 16°39N 105°34E 38 D5
Muang Phiang Laos 19°6N 101°32E 38 C3
Muang Phine Laos 16°32N 106°2E 38 D6
Muang Saiapoun Laos 18°24N 101°31E 38 C3
Muang Sing Laos 21°11N 101°9E 34 G3
Muang Son Laos 20°27N 103°19E 38 B4
Muang Soui Laos 19°33N 102°52E 38 C4
Muang Va Laos 21°53N 102°19E 34 G4
Muang Va Laos 18°18N 101°20E 38 C3
Muang Xai Laos 20°42N 101°59E 34 G3
Muang Xamteu Laos 19°59N 104°38E 38 C5
Muar Malaysia 2°3N 102°34E 39 L4
Muarabungo Indonesia 1°28S 102°52E 36 E2
Muaraenim Indonesia 3°40S 103°50E 36 E2
Muarajuloi Indonesia 0°12S 114°3E 36 E4
Muarakaman Indonesia 0°2S 116°45E 36 E5
Muaratebo Indonesia 1°30S 102°26E 36 E2
Muaratembesi Indonesia 1°42S 103°8E 36 E2
Muaratewheh Indonesia 0°58S 114°52E 36 E4
Mubarakpur India 26°6N 83°18E 43 F10
Mubarraz = Al Mubarraz Si. Arabia 25°30N 49°40E 47 E6
Mubi Nigeria 10°18N 13°16E 53 F8
Mucajaí → Brazil 2°25N 60°52W 92 C6
Muchinga Mts. Zambia 11°30S 31°30E 55 G6
Muchuan China 28°57N 103°55E 34 C5
Muck U.K. 56°50N 6°15W 11 E2
Muckadilla Australia 26°35S 148°23E 63 D4
Muckaty ❂ Australia 18°37S 133°52E 62 B1
Muckle Flugga U.K. 60°51N 0°54W 11 A8
Mucuri Brazil 18°0S 39°36W 93 G11
Mucusso Angola 18°1S 21°25E 56 A3
Mudanjiang China 44°38N 129°30E 33 B15
Mudanya Turkey 40°25N 28°50E 23 D13
Muddebihal India 16°20N 76°8E 45 F3
Muddy Cr. → U.S.A. 38°24N 110°42W 76 G8
Mudgee Australia 32°32S 149°31E 63 E4
Mudhol Andhra Pradesh, India 18°58N 77°55E 44 E3
Mudhol Karnataka, India 16°21N 75°17E 45 F2
Mudigere India 13°8N 75°38E 45 H2
Mudjatik → Canada 56°1N 107°36W 71 B7
Mudukulattur India 9°21N 78°31E 45 K4
Mudumu △ Namibia 18°5S 23°29E 56 A3
Mueller Ranges Australia 18°18S 126°46E 60 C4
Muerto, Mar Mexico 16°10N 94°10W 87 D6
Mufu Shan China 29°20N 114°30E 35 C10
Mufulira Zambia 12°32S 28°15E 55 G5
Mughal Sarai India 25°18N 83°7E 43 G10
Mughayrā' Si. Arabia 29°17N 37°41E 46 D3
Mugi Japan 33°40N 134°25E 29 H7
Muğla Turkey 37°15N 28°22E 23 F13
Mugu Nepal 29°45N 82°30E 43 E10
Mugu Karnali → Nepal 29°38N 81°51E 43 E9
Muhammad, Râs Egypt 27°44N 34°16E 46 E2
Muhammad Qol Sudan 20°53N 37°9E 53 D13
Muhammadabad India 26°4N 83°25E 43 F10
Mühlhausen Germany 51°12N 10°27E 16 C6
Mühlig Hofmann fjell Antarctica 72°30S 5°0E 5 D3
Muhos Finland 64°47N 25°59E 8 D21
Muhu Estonia 58°36N 23°11E 9 G20
Mui Wo China 22°16N 113°59E 31 a
Muileann gCearr, An = Mullingar Ireland 53°31N 7°21W 10 C4
Muine Bheag = Bagenalstown Ireland 52°42N 6°58W 10 D5
Muineachán = Monaghan Ireland 54°15N 6°57W 10 B5
Muir, L. Australia 34°30S 116°40E 61 F2
Muir of Ord U.K. 57°32N 4°28W 11 D4
Mujeres, I. Mexico 21°13N 86°43W 88 B2
Muka, Tanjung Malaysia 5°28N 100°11E 39 c
Mukacheve Ukraine 48°27N 22°45E 17 D12
Mukachevo = Mukacheve Ukraine 48°27N 22°45E 17 D12
Mukah Malaysia 2°55N 112°5E 36 D4
Mukandwara India 24°49N 75°59E 42 G6
Mukawwa, Geziret Egypt 23°55N 35°53E 46 F2
Mukdahan Thailand 16°32N 104°43E 38 D5
Mukdahan △ Thailand 16°26N 104°45E 38 D5
Mukden = Shenyang China 41°48N 123°27E 33 D12
Mukerian India 31°57N 75°37E 42 D6
Mukher India 18°42N 77°22E 44 E3
Mukinbudin Australia 30°55S 118°5E 61 F2
Muko Phetra △ Thailand 6°57N 99°33E 39 J2
Mukomuko Indonesia 2°30S 101°10E 36 E2
Muktinath Nepal 28°49N 83°53E 43 E10
Muktsar India 30°30N 74°30E 42 D6
Mukur = Moqor Afghan. 32°50N 67°42E 42 C2
Mukutuwa → Canada 53°10N 97°24W 71 C9
Mul India 20°4N 79°40E 44 D4
Mula Spain 38°3N 1°33W 21 C5
Mula → India 18°34N 74°21E 44 E2
Mula → Pakistan 27°57N 67°36E 42 F2
Mulanje, Mt. Malawi 16°2S 35°33E 55 H7
Mulbagal India 13°10N 78°24E 45 H4
Mulchatna → U.S.A. 59°40N 157°7W 74 D8
Mulchén Chile 37°45S 72°20W 94 D1
Mulde → Germany 51°53N 12°15E 16 C7
Mule Creek Junction U.S.A. 43°23N 104°13W 76 E11
Mulegé Mexico 26°53N 111°59W 86 B2
Muleshoe U.S.A. 34°13N 102°43W 84 D3
Mulgrave Canada 45°38N 61°31W 73 C7
Mulgrave I. = Badu Australia 10°7S 142°11E 62 a
Mulhacén Spain 37°4N 3°20W 21 D4
Mulhouse France 47°40N 7°20E 20 C7
Muli China 27°52N 101°8E 34 D3
Mulifanua Samoa 13°50S 171°59W 59 b
Muling China 44°35N 130°10E 33 B16
Mulki India 13°6N 74°48E 45 H2
Mull U.K. 56°25N 5°56W 11 E3
Mull, Sound of U.K. 56°30N 5°50W 11 E3
Mullaittivu Sri Lanka 9°15N 80°49E 45 K5
Mullen U.S.A. 42°3N 101°1W 80 D3
Mullengudgery Australia 31°43S 147°23E 63 B4
Mullens U.S.A. 37°35N 81°23W 81 G13
Muller, Pegunungan Indonesia 0°30N 113°30E 36 D4
Mullet Pen. Ireland 54°13N 10°2W 10 B1
Mullewa Australia 28°29S 115°30E 61 E2
Mulligan → Australia 25°0S 139°0E 62 D2
Mullingar Ireland 53°31N 7°21W 10 C4
Mullins U.S.A. 34°12N 79°15W 85 D15
Mullumbimby Australia 28°30S 153°30E 63 D5
Mulonga Plain Zambia 16°20S 22°40E 55 H4
Mulroy B. Ireland 55°15N 7°46W 10 A4
Mulshi L. India 18°30N 73°48E 44 E1
Multai India 21°50N 78°21E 44 D4
Multan Pakistan 30°15N 71°36E 42 D4
Mulug India 18°11N 79°57E 44 E4
Mulvane U.S.A. 37°29N 97°15W 80 G5
Mulwala, L. Australia 35°59S 146°1E 63 C4
Mun → Thailand 15°19N 105°30E 38 E5
Muna Indonesia 5°0S 122°30E 37 F6
Munabao India 25°45N 70°17E 42 G4
Munamagi Estonia 57°43N 27°4E 9 H22
Munaung Burma 18°45N 93°40E 41 K18
Munaung I. = Cheduba I. Burma 18°45N 93°40E 41 K18
Muncan Indonesia 8°34S 115°11E 37 K18
Muncar Indonesia 8°26S 114°20E 37 J17
Munchen-Gladbach = Mönchengladbach Germany 51°11N 6°27E 16 C4
Muncho Lake Canada 59°0N 125°50W 70 B3
Munch'ŏn N. Korea 39°14N 127°19E 33 E14
Muncie U.S.A. 40°12N 85°23W 81 E11
Muncoonie L. West Australia 25°12S 138°40E 62 D2
Mundabbera Australia 25°36S 151°18E 63 D5
Mundakayam India 9°30N 76°50E 45 K3
Mundal Sri Lanka 7°48N 79°48E 45 L4
Munday U.S.A. 33°27N 99°38W 84 E5
Münden Germany 51°25N 9°38E 16 C5
Mundiwindi Australia 23°47S 120°9E 60 D3
Mundo Novo Brazil 11°50S 40°29W 93 F10
Mundra India 22°54N 69°48E 42 H3
Mundrabilla Australia 31°52S 127°51E 61 F4
Muneru → India 16°45N 80°3E 44 F5
Mungallala Australia 26°28S 147°34E 63 D4
Mungallala Cr. → Australia 28°53S 147°5E 63 D4
Mungana Australia 17°8S 144°27E 62 B3
Mungaoli India 24°24N 78°7E 42 G8
Mungbere Dem. Rep. of the Congo 2°36N 28°28E 54 D5
Mungeli India 22°4N 81°41E 43 H9
Munger India 25°23N 86°30E 43 G12
Mungerannie Australia 28°1S 138°39E 63 A2
Mungilli ❂ Australia 25°14S 124°17E 61 E3
Mungkan Kandju △ Australia 13°35S 142°52E 62 A3
Mungkarta ❂ Australia 20°22S 134°2E 62 C1
Munising U.S.A. 46°25N 86°40W 80 B10
Munku-Sardyk Russia 51°45N 100°20E 27 D11
Munnsville U.S.A. 42°58N 75°35W 83 D9
Muñoz Gamero, Pen. Chile 52°30S 73°5W 96 G2
Munroe L. Canada 59°13N 98°35W 71 B9
Munsan S. Korea 37°51N 126°48E 33 F14
Münster Germany 51°58N 7°37E 16 C4
Munster □ Ireland 52°18N 8°44W 10 D3
Muntadgin Australia 31°45S 118°33E 61 F2
Muntok Indonesia 2°5S 105°10E 36 E3
Muong Nhie Vietnam 22°12N 102°28E 34 F4
Muong Sen Vietnam 19°24N 104°8E 38 C5
Muong Te Vietnam 22°24N 102°49E 34 F4
Muong Xia Vietnam 20°19N 104°50E 38 B5
Muonio Finland 67°57N 23°40E 8 C20
Muonio älv = Muonionjoki → Finland 67°11N 23°34E 8 C20
Muonioälven = Muonionjoki → Finland 67°11N 23°34E 8 C20
Muonionjoki → Finland 67°11N 23°34E 8 C20
Mupa → Mozam. 18°58S 35°54E 57 A6
Muping China 37°22N 121°36E 33 F11
Muqdisho Somalia 2°2N 45°25E 49 G4
Mur → Austria 46°18N 16°52E 17 E9
Murakami Japan 38°14N 139°29E 28 E9
Muralag = Prince of Wales I. Australia 10°40S 142°10E 62 A3
Murallón, Cerro Chile 49°48S 73°30W 96 F2
Murang'a Kenya 0°45S 37°9E 54 E7
Murashi Russia 59°30N 49°0E 18 C8
Murat → Turkey 38°46N 40°0E 19 G7
Muratlı Turkey 41°10N 27°29E 23 D12
Murayama Japan 38°30N 140°25E 28 E10
Murchison → Australia 27°45S 114°0E 61 E1
Murchison, Mt. Antarctica 73°25S 166°20E 5 D11
Murchison Falls Uganda 2°15N 31°30E 54 D6
Murchison Ra. Australia 20°0S 134°10E 62 C1
Murchison Roadhouse Australia 27°39S 116°14E 61 E2
Murcia Spain 38°5N 1°10W 21 D5
Murcia □ Spain 37°50N 1°30W 21 D5
Murdo U.S.A. 43°53N 100°43W 80 D3
Murdoch Pt. Australia 14°37S 144°55E 62 A3
Mureș → Romania 46°15N 20°13E 17 E11
Mureşul = Mureş → Romania 46°15N 20°13E 17 E11
Murewa Zimbabwe 17°39S 31°47E 57 A5
Murfreesboro N.C., U.S.A. 36°27N 77°6W 85 C16
Murfreesboro Tenn., U.S.A. 35°51N 86°24W 85 D11
Murgap Tajikistan 38°10N 74°2E 26 F8
Murgap → Turkmenistan 38°18N 61°12E 47 B9
Murgenella Australia 11°34S 132°56E 60 B5
Murgha Kibzai Pakistan 30°44N 69°25E 42 D3
Murghob = Murgap Tajikistan 38°10N 74°2E 26 F8
Murgon Australia 26°15S 151°54E 63 D5
Muri India 23°22N 85°52E 43 H11
Muria Indonesia 6°36S 110°53E 37 G14
Muriaé Brazil 21°8S 42°23W 95 A7
Müritz Germany 53°25N 12°42E 16 B7
Murliganj India 25°54N 86°59E 43 G12
Murmansk Russia 68°57N 33°10E 8 B25
Murmashi Russia 68°47N 32°42E 8 B25
Murom Russia 55°35N 42°3E 18 C7
Muroran Japan 42°25N 141°0E 28 C10
Muroto Japan 33°18N 134°9E 29 H7
Muroto-Misaki Japan 33°15N 134°10E 29 H7
Murphy U.S.A. 43°13N 116°33W 76 E5
Murphys U.S.A. 38°8N 120°28W 78 G6
Murray Australia 9°56S 144°2E 62 a
Murray Ky., U.S.A. 36°37N 88°19W 80 G9
Murray Utah, U.S.A. 40°40N 111°53W 76 F8
Murray → Australia 35°20S 139°22E 63 F2
Murray, L. U.S.A. 34°3N 81°13W 85 D14
Murray Bridge Australia 35°6S 139°14E 63 F2
Murray Fracture Zone Pac. Oc. 35°0N 130°0W 65 D14
Murray Harbour Canada 46°0N 62°28W 73 C7
Murray River △ Australia 34°23S 140°32E 63 E3
Murraysburg S. Africa 31°58S 23°47E 56 D3
Murree Pakistan 33°56N 73°28E 42 C5
Murrieta U.S.A. 33°33N 117°13W 79 M9
Murrumbidgee → Australia 34°43S 143°12E 63 E3
Murrumburrah Australia 34°32S 148°22E 63 E4
Murrurundi Australia 31°42S 150°51E 63 E5
Murshidabad India 24°11N 88°19E 43 G13
Murtazapur India 20°40N 77°25E 44 D3
Murtle L. Canada 52°8N 119°38W 70 C5
Murtoa Australia 36°35S 142°28E 63 F3
Murud India 18°19N 72°58E 44 E1

Mururoa
  French Polynesia 21°52S 138°55W **65** K14
Murwara *India* 23°46N 80°28E **43** H9
Murwillumbah *Australia* 28°18S 153°27E **63** D5
Murzūq *Libya* 25°53N 13°57E **53** C8
Murzūq, Idehān *Libya* 24°50N 13°51E **53** D8
Mürzzuschlag *Austria* 47°36N 15°41E **16** E8
Muş *India* 9°14N 92°47E **45** K11
Muş *Turkey* 38°45N 41°30E **46** B4
Mūsa, Gebel *Egypt* 28°33N 33°59E **46** D2
Musa Khel *Pakistan* 30°59N 69°52E **42** D3
Mūsa Qal'eh *Afghan.* 32°20N 64°50E **40** C4
Musafirkhana *India* 26°22N 81°48E **43** F9
Musala *Bulgaria* 42°13N 23°37E **23** C10
Musala *Indonesia* 1°41N 98°28E **36** D1
Musan *N. Korea* 42°12N 129°12E **33** C15
Musay'īd *Qatar* 25°0N 51°33E **47** E6
Muscat = Masqaţ *Oman* 23°37N 58°36E **49** C6
Muscatine *U.S.A.* 41°25N 91°3W **80** E8
Muscle Shoals *U.S.A.* 34°45N 87°40W **85** D11
Musgrave Harbour
  Canada 49°27N 53°58W **73** C9
Musgrave Ranges
  Australia 26°0S 132°0E **61** E5
Mushie
  Dem. Rep. of the Congo 2°56S 16°55E **54** E3
Musi → *India* 16°41N 79°40E **44** F4
Musi → *Indonesia* 2°20S 104°56E **36** E2
Musina *S. Africa* 22°20S 30°5E **57** B5
Musiri *India* 10°56N 78°27E **45** J4
Muskeg → *Canada* 60°20N 123°20W **70** A4
Muskegon *U.S.A.* 43°14N 86°16W **80** D10
Muskegon → *U.S.A.* 43°14N 86°21W **80** D10
Muskegon Heights
  U.S.A. 43°12N 86°16W **80** D10
Muskogee *U.S.A.* 35°45N 95°22W **84** D7
Muskoka, L. *Canada* 45°0N 79°25W **82** B5
Muskoka Falls *Canada* 44°59N 79°17W **82** B5
Muskwa → *Canada* 58°47N 122°48W **70** B4
Muslīmiyah *Syria* 36°19N 37°12E **46** B3
Musoma *Tanzania* 1°30S 33°48E **54** E6
Musquaro, L. *Canada* 50°38N 61°5W **73** B7
Musquodoboit Harbour
  Canada 44°50N 63°9W **73** D7
Musselburgh *U.K.* 55°57N 3°2W **11** F5
Musselshell → *U.S.A.* 47°21N 107°57W **76** C10
Mussende *Angola* 10°32S 16°5E **54** G3
Mussoorie *India* 30°27N 78°6E **42** D8
Mussuco *Angola* 17°2S 19°3E **56** A2
Mustafakemalpaşa
  Turkey 40°2N 28°24E **23** D13
Mustang *Nepal* 29°10N 83°55E **43** E10
Musters, L. *Argentina* 45°20S 69°25W **96** F3
Musudan *N. Korea* 40°50N 129°43E **33** D15
Muswellbrook *Australia* 32°16S 150°56E **63** E5
Mût *Egypt* 25°28N 28°58E **53** C11
Mut *Turkey* 36°40N 33°28E **46** B2
Mutanda *Mozam.* 21°0S 33°34E **57** B5
Mutare *Zimbabwe* 18°58S 32°38E **55** H6
Mutawintji △ *Australia* 31°10S 142°30E **63** E3
Muting *Indonesia* 7°23S 140°20E **37** F10
Mutki = Mirtağ *Turkey* 38°23N 41°56E **46** B4
Mutoko *Zimbabwe* 17°24S 32°13E **57** A5
Mutoray *Russia* 60°56N 101°0E **27** C11
Mutsamudu *Comoros Is.* 12°10S 44°25E **55** a
Mutsu *Japan* 41°5N 140°55E **28** D10
Mutsu-Wan *Japan* 41°5N 140°55E **28** D10
Muttaburra *Australia* 22°38S 144°29E **62** C3
Mutton I. *Ireland* 52°49N 9°32W **10** D2
Muttukuru *India* 14°16N 80°6E **45** G5
Mutur *Sri Lanka* 8°27N 81°16E **45** K5
Muweilih *Egypt* 30°42N 34°19E **48** E3
Muy Muy *Nic.* 12°39N 85°36W **88** D2
Muynak *Uzbekistan* 43°44N 59°10E **26** E6
Muyunkum, Peski = Moyynqum
  Kazakhstan 44°12N 71°0E **30** C3
Muz Tag *China* 36°25N 87°25E **30** D6
Muzaffarabad *Pakistan* 34°25N 73°30E **43** B5
Muzaffargarh *Pakistan* 30°5N 71°14E **42** D4
Muzaffarnagar *India* 29°26N 77°40E **42** E7
Muzaffarpur *India* 26°7N 85°23E **43** F11
Muzafīrpur *Pakistan* 30°58N 69°9E **42** D3
Muzhi *Russia* 65°25N 64°40E **18** A11
Muztagh-Ata *China* 38°17N 75°7E **30** D4
Mvuma *Zimbabwe* 19°16S 30°30E **55** H6
Mwali = Mohéli
  Comoros Is. 12°20S 43°40E **55** a
Mwanza
  Dem. Rep. of the Congo 7°55S 26°43E **54** F5
Mwanza *Tanzania* 2°30S 32°58E **54** E6
Mweelrea *Ireland* 53°39N 9°49W **10** C2
Mweka
  Dem. Rep. of the Congo 4°50S 21°34E **54** E4
Mwene-Ditu
  Dem. Rep. of the Congo 6°35S 22°27E **54** F4
Mwenga
  Dem. Rep. of the Congo 3°1S 28°28E **54** E5
Mweru, L. *Zambia* 9°0S 28°40E **54** F5
Mwinilunga *Zambia* 11°43S 24°25E **55** G4
My Son *Vietnam* 15°48N 108°7E **38** E7
My Tho *Vietnam* 10°29N 106°23E **39** G6
Myajlar *India* 26°15N 70°20E **42** F4
Myanaung *Burma* 18°18N 95°22E **41** K19
Myanmar = Burma ■
  Asia 21°0N 96°30E **41** J20
Myaungmya *Burma* 16°30N 94°40E **41** L19
Mycenæ = Mikines
  Greece 37°43N 22°46E **23** F10
Myeik = Mergui *Burma* 12°26N 98°34E **38** F2
Myeik Kyunzu *Burma* 11°30N 97°30E **39** G1
Myerstown *U.S.A.* 40°22N 76°19W **83** F8
Myingyan *Burma* 21°30N 95°20E **41** J19
Myitkyina *Burma* 25°24N 97°26E **41** G20
Mykines *Færoe Is.* 62°7N 7°35W **8** E9
Mykolayiv *Ukraine* 46°58N 32°0E **19** E5
Mykonos *Greece* 37°30N 25°25E **23** F11
Mymensingh *Bangla.* 24°45N 90°24E **41** G17
Mynydd Du *U.K.* 51°52N 3°50W **13** F4
Mýrdalsjökull *Iceland* 63°40N 19°6W **8** E4

Myrtle Beach *U.S.A.* 33°42N 78°53W **85** E15
Myrtle Creek *U.S.A.* 43°1N 123°17W **76** E2
Myrtle Point *U.S.A.* 43°4N 124°8W **76** E1
Mysia *Turkey* 39°50N 27°0E **23** E12
Mysore = Karnataka □
  India 13°15N 77°0E **45** H3
Mysore *India* 12°17N 76°41E **45** H3
Mystic *U.S.A.* 41°21N 71°58W **83** E13
Mysuru = Mysore *India* 12°17N 76°41E **45** H3
Myszków *Poland* 50°45N 19°22E **17** C10
Mytishchi *Russia* 55°50N 37°50E **18** C6
Mývatn *Iceland* 65°36N 17°0W **8** D5
Mzimkulu → *S. Africa* 30°44S 30°28E **57** D5
Mzimvubu → *S. Africa* 31°38S 29°33E **57** D4
Mzuzu *Malawi* 11°30S 33°55E **54** G6

N

Na Clocha Liatha = Greystones
  Ireland 53°9N 6°5W **10** C5
Na Haeo △ *Thailand* 17°31N 100°58E **38** D3
Na Hearadh = Harris
  U.K. 57°50N 6°55W **11** D2
Na Hearadh, Caolas = Harris, Sd.
  of *U.K.* 57°44N 7°6W **11** D1
Na Noi *Thailand* 18°19N 100°43E **38** C3
Na Phao *Laos* 17°35N 105°44E **38** D5
Na Sam *Vietnam* 22°3N 106°37E **34** F6
Na Sceirí = Skerries *Ireland* 53°35N 6°8W **10** C5
Na Thon *Thailand* 9°32N 99°56E **39** b
Naab → *Germany* 49°1N 12°2E **16** D6
Naantali *Finland* 60°29N 22°2E **9** F20
Naas *Ireland* 53°12N 6°40W **10** C5
Nababeep *S. Africa* 29°36S 17°46E **56** C2
Nabadwip = Navadwip
  India 23°34N 88°20E **43** H13
Nabawa *Australia* 28°30S 114°48E **61** E1
Nabberu, L. *Australia* 25°50S 120°30E **61** E3
Naberezhnyye Chelny
  Russia 55°42N 52°19E **18** C9
Nabeul *Tunisia* 36°30N 10°44E **53** A8
Nabha *India* 30°26N 76°14E **42** D7
Nabid *Iran* 29°40N 57°38E **47** D8
Nabire *Indonesia* 3°15S 135°26E **37** E9
Nabisar *Pakistan* 25°8N 69°40E **42** G3
Nabisipi → *Canada* 50°14N 62°13W **73** B7
Nābulus = Nābulus
  West Bank 32°14N 35°15E **48** C4
Naboomspruit *S. Africa* 24°32S 28°40E **57** B4
Nabouwalu *Fiji* 17°0S 178°45E **59** a
Nābulus *West Bank* 32°14N 35°15E **48** C4
Nacala *Mozam.* 14°32S 40°34E **55** G8
Nacaome *Honduras* 13°31N 87°30W **88** D2
Naches *U.S.A.* 46°44N 120°42W **76** C3
Naches → *U.S.A.* 46°38N 120°31W **78** D6
Nachicapau, L. *Canada* 56°40N 68°5W **73** A6
Nachingwea *Tanzania* 10°23S 38°49E **54** G7
Nachna *India* 27°34N 71°41E **42** F4
Nacimiento, L. *U.S.A.* 35°46N 120°53W **78** K6
Naco *Mexico* 31°19N 109°56W **86** A3
Nacogdoches *U.S.A.* 31°36N 94°39W **84** F7
Nácori Chico *Mexico* 29°39N 108°57W **86** B3
Nacozari de García
  Mexico 30°25N 109°38W **86** A3
Nacula *Fiji* 16°54S 177°27E **59** a
Nada = Danzhou *China* 19°31N 109°33E **38** C7
Nådendal = Naantali
  Finland 60°29N 22°2E **9** F20
Nadi *Fiji* 17°42S 177°20E **59** a
Nadiad *India* 22°41N 72°56E **42** H5
Nadūshan *Iran* 32°2N 53°35E **47** C7
Nadvirna *Ukraine* 48°37N 24°30E **17** D13
Nadvoitsy *Russia* 63°52N 34°14E **18** B5
Nadvornaya = Nadvirna
  Ukraine 48°37N 24°30E **17** D13
Nadym *Russia* 65°35N 72°42E **26** C8
Nadym → *Russia* 66°12N 72°0E **26** C8
Nærbø *Norway* 58°40N 5°39E **9** G11
Næstved *Denmark* 55°13N 11°44E **9** J14
Nafpaktos *Greece* 38°24N 21°50E **23** E9
Nafplio *Greece* 37°33N 22°50E **23** F10
Naft-e Safīd *Iran* 31°40N 49°17E **47** D6
Naftshahr *Iran* 34°0N 45°30E **46** C5
Nafud Desert = An Nafūd
  Si. Arabia 28°15N 41°0E **46** D4
Naga *Phil.* 13°38N 123°15E **37** B6
Nagagami *Canada* 50°23N 84°20W **72** B3
Nagahama *Japan* 35°23N 136°16E **29** G8
Nagai *Japan* 38°6N 140°2E **28** E10
Nagaland □ *India* 26°0N 94°30E **41** G19
Nagano *Japan* 36°40N 138°10E **29** F9
Nagano □ *Japan* 36°15N 138°0E **29** F9
Nagaoka *Japan* 37°27N 138°51E **28** F9
Nagaon *India* 26°20N 92°50E **41** F18
Nagappattinam *India* 10°46N 79°51E **45** J4
Nagar → *Bangla.* 24°27N 89°12E **43** G13
Nagar Karnul *India* 16°29N 78°20E **45** F4
Nagar Parkar *Pakistan* 24°28N 70°46E **42** G4
Nagaram *India* 18°21N 80°26E **44** E5
Nagarhole △ *India* 12°0N 76°10E **45** J3
Nagari Hills *India* 13°3N 79°45E **45** H4
Nagarjuna Sagar *India* 16°30N 79°13E **45** F4
Nagasaki *Japan* 32°47N 129°50E **29** H4
Nagasaki □ *Japan* 32°50N 129°40E **29** H4
Nagato *Japan* 34°19N 131°5E **29** G5
Nagaur *India* 27°15N 73°45E **42** F5
Nagbhir *India* 20°34N 79°55E **44** D4
Nagda *India* 23°27N 75°25E **42** H6
Nagercoil *India* 8°12N 77°26E **45** K3
Nagina *India* 29°30N 78°30E **43** E8
Nagineh *Iran* 34°20N 57°15E **47** C8
Nagir *Pakistan* 36°12N 74°42E **43** A6
Nagles Mts. *Ireland* 52°8N 8°30W **10** D3
Nagod *India* 24°34N 80°36E **43** G9
Nagoorin *Australia* 24°17S 151°15E **62** C5
Nagorno-Karabakh □
  Azerbaijan 39°55N 46°45E **46** B5

Nagornyy *Russia* 55°58N 124°57E **27** D13
Nagoya *Japan* 35°10N 136°50E **29** G8
Nagoya ✈ (NGO) *Japan* 34°53N 136°45E **29** G8
Nagpur *India* 21°8N 79°10E **44** D4
Nagqu *China* 31°29N 92°3E **30** E7
Nagua *Dom. Rep.* 19°23N 69°50W **89** C6
Naguabo *Puerto Rico* 18°13N 65°44W **89** d
Nagurunguru ◊
  Australia 16°45S 129°45E **60** C4
Nagykanizsa *Hungary* 46°28N 17°0E **17** E9
Nagykőrös *Hungary* 47°5N 19°48E **17** E10
Naha *Japan* 26°13N 127°42E **29** L3
Nahan *India* 30°33N 77°18E **42** D7
Nahanni △ *Canada* 61°15N 125°48W **70** A4
Nahanni Butte *Canada* 61°2N 123°31W **70** A4
Nahariyya *Israel* 33°1N 35°5E **46** C2
Nahāvand *Iran* 34°10N 48°22E **47** C6
Nahuel Huapi, L.
  Argentina 41°0S 71°32W **96** E2
Nahuelbuta △ *Chile* 37°44S 72°57W **94** D1
Nai Yong *Thailand* 8°14N 98°22E **39** a
Naicá *Mexico* 27°53N 105°31W **86** B3
Naicam *Canada* 52°30N 104°30W **71** C8
Naikoon △ *Canada* 53°55N 131°55W **70** C2
Naikul *India* 21°20N 84°58E **44** D7
Naimisharanya *India* 27°21N 80°30E **43** F9
Naimona'nyi Feng *China* 30°26N 81°18E **43** D9
Nain *Canada* 56°34N 61°40W **73** A7
Nā'īn *Iran* 32°54N 53°0E **47** C7
Naini Tal *India* 29°30N 79°30E **43** E8
Nainpur *India* 22°30N 80°10E **43** H9
Nainwa *India* 25°46N 75°51E **42** G6
Nairai *Fiji* 17°49S 179°15E **59** a
Nairn *U.K.* 57°35N 3°53W **11** D5
Nairobi *Kenya* 1°17S 36°48E **54** E7
Naissaar *Estonia* 59°34N 24°29E **9** G21
Naitaba *Fiji* 17°0S 179°16W **59** a
Naivasha *Kenya* 0°40S 36°30E **54** E7
Najaf = An Najaf *Iraq* 32°3N 44°15E **46** C5
Najafābād *Iran* 32°40N 51°15E **47** C6
Najd *Si. Arabia* 26°30N 42°0E **49** B3
Najibabad *India* 29°40N 78°20E **42** E8
Najin *N. Korea* 42°12N 130°15E **33** C16
Najmah *Si. Arabia* 26°42N 50°6E **47** E6
Najrān *Si. Arabia* 17°34N 44°18E **49** D3
Naju *S. Korea* 35°3N 126°43E **33** G14
Nakadōri-Shima *Japan* 32°57N 129°4E **29** H4
Nakaminato *Japan* 36°21N 140°36E **29** F10
Nakamura = Shimanto
  Japan 32°59N 132°56E **29** H6
Nakano *Japan* 36°45N 138°22E **29** F9
Nakano-Shima *Japan* 29°51N 129°52E **29** K4
Nakashibetsu *Japan* 43°33N 144°59E **28** C12
Nakfa *Eritrea* 16°40N 38°32E **49** D2
Nakhichevan = Naxçıvan
  Azerbaijan 39°12N 45°15E **46** B5
Nakhichevan Rep. = Naxçıvan □
  Azerbaijan 39°25N 45°26E **46** B5
Nakhl *Egypt* 29°55N 33°43E **48** F2
Nakhl-e Taqī *Iran* 27°28N 52°36E **47** E7
Nakhodka *Russia* 42°53N 132°54E **28** C6
Nakhon Nayok *Thailand* 14°12N 101°13E **38** E3
Nakhon Pathom *Thailand* 13°49N 100°3E **38** F3
Nakhon Phanom
  Thailand 17°23N 104°43E **38** D5
Nakhon Ratchasima
  Thailand 14°59N 102°12E **38** E4
Nakhon Sawan *Thailand* 15°35N 100°10E **38** E3
Nakhon Si Thammarat
  Thailand 8°29N 100°0E **39** H3
Nakhon Thai *Thailand* 17°5N 100°44E **38** D3
Nakhtarana *India* 23°20N 69°15E **42** H3
Nakina *Canada* 50°10N 86°40W **72** B2
Nakodar *India* 31°8N 75°31E **42** D6
Naktong → *S. Korea* 35°7N 128°57E **33** G15
Nakuru *Kenya* 0°15S 36°4E **54** E7
Nakusp *Canada* 50°20N 117°45W **70** C5
Nal *Pakistan* 27°40N 66°12E **42** F2
Nal → *Pakistan* 25°20N 65°30E **42** G1
Nalázi *Mozam.* 24°3S 33°20E **57** B5
Nalchik *Russia* 43°30N 43°33E **19** F7
Nalgonda *India* 17°6N 79°15E **44** F4
Nalhati *India* 24°17N 87°52E **43** G12
Naliya *India* 23°16N 68°50E **42** H3
Nallamalai Hills *India* 15°30N 78°50E **45** G4
Nam Can *Vietnam* 8°46N 104°59E **39** H5
Nam-ch'on *N. Korea* 38°15N 126°26E **33** E14
Nam Co *China* 30°30N 90°45E **30** E7
Nam Dinh *Vietnam* 20°25N 106°5E **34** G6
Nam Du, Quan Dao
  Vietnam 9°41N 104°21E **39** H5
Nam Hke → *Burma* 25°34N 95°41E **34** G2
Nam Loi → *Burma* 21°3N 98°27E **34** G3
Nam Nao △ *Thailand* 16°44N 101°32E **38** D3
Nam Ngum Res. *Laos* 18°35N 102°34E **38** C4
Nam-Phan *Vietnam* 10°30N 106°0E **39** G6
Nam Phong *Thailand* 16°42N 102°52E **38** D4
Nam Theun Res. *Laos* 17°51N 105°32E **38** D5
Nam Tok *Thailand* 14°21N 99°4E **38** E2
Nam Un Res. *Thailand* 17°13N 103°44E **38** D4
Namacunde *Angola* 17°18S 15°50E **56** B2
Namacurra *Mozam.* 17°30S 36°50E **57** A6
Namak, Daryācheh-ye
  Iran 34°30N 52°0E **47** C7
Namak, Kavir-e *Iran* 34°30N 57°30E **47** C8
Namakkal *India* 11°13N 78°13E **45** J4
Namakzār, Daryācheh-ye
  Iran 34°0N 60°30E **47** C9
Namaland *Namibia* 26°0S 17°0E **56** C2
Namangan *Uzbekistan* 41°0N 71°40E **30** C3
Namapa *Mozam.* 13°43S 39°50E **55** G7
Namaqua → *S. Africa* 30°0S 17°0E **56** C1
Namaqualand *S. Africa* 30°0S 17°25E **56** D2
Namber *Indonesia* 1°2S 134°49E **37** E8
Nambour *Australia* 26°32S 152°58E **63** D5
Nambouwalu = Nabouwalu
  Fiji 17°0S 178°45E **59** a

Nambucca Heads
  Australia 30°37S 153°0E **63** E5
Nambung △ *Australia* 30°30S 115°5E **61** F2
Namcha Barwa *China* 29°40N 95°10E **30** F8
Namche Bazar *Nepal* 27°51N 86°47E **43** F12
Namchonjōm = Nam-ch'on
  N. Korea 38°15N 126°26E **33** E14
Namenalala *Fiji* 17°8S 179°9E **59** a
Namew L. *Canada* 54°14N 101°56W **71** C8
Namgia *India* 31°48N 78°40E **43** D8
Namhkam *Burma* 23°50N 97°41E **34** E1
Namib Desert *Namibia* 22°30S 15°0E **56** B2
Namib-Naukluft △
  Namibia 24°40S 15°16E **56** B2
Namibe *Angola* 15°7S 12°11E **55** H2
Namibe □ *Angola* 16°35S 12°30E **56** A1
Namibia ■ *Africa* 22°0S 18°9E **56** B2
Namibwoestyn = Namib Desert
  Namibia 22°30S 15°0E **56** B2
Namjeju *S. Korea* 33°14N 126°33E **33** H14
Namlea *Indonesia* 3°18S 127°5E **37** E7
Namoi → *Australia* 30°12S 149°30E **63** E4
Nampa *U.S.A.* 43°34N 116°34W **76** E5
Namp'o *N. Korea* 38°52N 125°10E **33** E13
Nampō-Shotō *Japan* 32°0N 140°0E **29** J10
Nampula *Mozam.* 15°6S 39°15E **55** H7
Namrole *Indonesia* 3°46S 126°46E **37** E7
Namse Shankou *China* 30°0N 82°25E **43** E10
Namsen → *Norway* 64°28N 11°37E **8** D14
Namsos *Norway* 64°29N 11°30E **8** D14
Namtok Chat Trakan △
  Thailand 17°17N 100°40E **38** D3
Namtok Huay Yang △
  Thailand 11°35N 99°30E **39** G2
Namtok Mae Surin △
  Thailand 18°55N 98°2E **38** C2
Namtok Ngao △ *Thailand* 9°58N 98°46E **39** H2
Namtok Phlew △
  Thailand 12°32N 102°13E **38** F4
Namtok Yong △ *Thailand* 8°15N 98°45E **39** H2
Namtsy *Russia* 62°43N 129°37E **27** C13
Namtu *Burma* 23°5N 97°28E **41** H20
Namu *Canada* 51°52N 127°50W **70** C3
Namuka-i-Lau *Fiji* 18°53S 178°37W **59** a
Namur *Belgium* 50°27N 4°52E **15** D4
Namur □ *Belgium* 50°17N 5°0E **15** D4
Namutoni *Namibia* 18°49S 16°55E **56** A2
Namwon *S. Korea* 35°23N 127°23E **33** G14
Namyang *N. Korea* 42°57N 129°52E **33** C15
Nan *Thailand* 18°48N 100°46E **38** C3
Nan → *Thailand* 15°42N 100°9E **38** E3
Nan-ch'ang = Nanchang
  China 28°42N 115°55E **35** C10
Nan Ling *China* 25°0N 112°30E **35** E8
Nan Xian *China* 29°20N 112°22E **35** C9
Nanaimo *Canada* 49°10N 124°0W **70** D4
Nānākuli *U.S.A.* 21°24N 158°9W **75** L8
Nanam *N. Korea* 41°44N 129°40E **33** D15
Nan'an *China* 24°59N 118°21E **35** E12
Nanango *Australia* 26°40S 152°0E **63** D5
Nan'ao *China* 23°28N 117°5E **35** F11
Nanao *Japan* 37°0N 137°0E **29** F8
Nanbu *China* 31°18N 106°3E **34** B6
Nanchang *China* 28°42N 115°55E **35** C10
Nancheng *China* 27°33N 116°35E **35** D11
Nanching = Nanjing
  China 32°2N 118°47E **35** A12
Nanchong *China* 30°43N 106°2E **34** B6
Nanchuan *China* 29°9N 107°6E **34** C6
Nancowry *India* 7°59N 93°32E **45** L11
Nancy *France* 48°42N 6°12E **20** B7
Nanda Devi *India* 30°23N 79°59E **43** D8
Nanda Devi △ *India* 30°30N 79°50E **43** D8
Nanda Kot *India* 30°17N 80°5E **43** D9
Nandan = Minamiawaji
  Japan 34°10N 134°42E **29** G7
Nandan *China* 24°58N 107°29E **34** E6
Nanded *India* 19°10N 77°20E **44** E3
Nandewar Ra. *Australia* 30°15S 150°35E **63** E5
Nandgaon *India* 20°19N 74°39E **44** D2
Nandi = Nadi *Fiji* 17°42S 177°20E **59** a
Nandi *Zimbabwe* 20°58S 31°44E **57** B5
Nandigama *India* 16°47N 80°18E **44** F5
Nandigram *India* 22°1N 87°58E **43** H12
Nandikotkur *India* 15°52N 78°18E **45** G4
Nandura *India* 20°52N 76°25E **44** D3
Nandurbar *India* 21°20N 74°15E **44** D2
Nandyal *India* 15°30N 78°30E **45** G4
Nanfeng *Guangdong,*
  China 23°45N 111°47E **35** F8
Nanfeng *Jiangxi, China* 27°12N 116°28E **35** D11
Nang Rong *Thailand* 14°38N 102°48E **38** E4
Nanga-Eboko *Cameroon* 4°41N 12°22E **54** D2
Nanga Parbat *Pakistan* 35°10N 74°35E **43** B6
Nangapinoh *Indonesia* 0°20S 111°44E **36** E4
Nangarhār □ *Afghan.* 34°20N 70°0E **40** B7
Nangatayap *Indonesia* 1°32S 110°34E **36** E4
Nangong *China* 37°23N 115°22E **32** F8
Nanguneri *India* 8°29N 77°40E **45** K3
Nanhua *China* 25°13N 101°21E **34** E3
Nanhuang *China* 36°58N 121°48E **33** F11
Nanhui *China* 31°5N 121°44E **35** B13
Nanisivik *Canada* 73°2N 84°33W **69** C15
Nanjangud *India* 12°6N 76°43E **45** H3
Nanji Shan *China* 27°27N 121°4E **35** D13
Nanjian *China* 25°2N 100°25E **34** E3
Nanjiang *China* 32°28N 106°51E **34** A6
Nanjing *Fujian, China* 24°25N 117°20E **35** E11
Nanjing *Jiangsu, China* 32°2N 118°47E **35** A12
Nankana Sahib *Pakistan* 31°27N 73°38E **42** D5
Nankang *China* 25°40N 114°45E **35** E10
Nanking = Nanjing
  China 32°2N 118°47E **35** A12
Nankoku *Japan* 33°39N 133°44E **29** H6
Nanlang *China* 22°30N 113°32E **31** a
Nanling *China* 30°55N 118°20E **35** B12
Nannial *India* 19°4N 79°38E **44** E4
Nanning *China* 22°48N 108°20E **34** F7
NanNisa △ *Canada* 54°0N 104°37W **71** C8

Nanpan Jiang → *China* 25°10N 106°5E **34** E6
Nanpara *India* 27°52N 81°33E **43** F9
Nanping *Fujian, China* 26°38N 118°10E **35** D12
Nanping *Henan, China* 29°55N 112°3E **35** C9
Nanri Dao *China* 25°15N 119°25E **35** E12
Nansei-Shotō = Ryūkyū-Rettō
  Japan 26°0N 126°0E **29** M3
Nansen Basin *Arctic* 84°0N 50°0E **4** A10
Nansen Sd. *Canada* 81°0N 91°0W **69** A13
Nansha *China* 22°45N 113°34E **31** a
Nansha Port *China* 22°40N 113°40E **31** a
Nanshan *China* 18°19N 109°10E **38** C7
Nanshan I. *S. China Sea* 10°45N 115°49E **36** B5
Nantawarrinna ◊
  Australia 30°49S 138°58E **63** B2
Nantes *France* 47°12N 1°33W **20** C3
Nanticoke *U.S.A.* 41°12N 76°0W **83** E8
Nanton *Canada* 50°21N 113°46W **70** C6
Nantong *China* 32°1N 120°52E **35** A13
Nantou *China* 22°32N 113°55E **31** a
Nant'ou *Taiwan* 23°55N 120°41E **35** F13
Nantucket *U.S.A.* 41°17N 70°6W **81** E18
Nantucket I. *U.S.A.* 41°16N 70°5W **81** E18
Nantwich *U.K.* 53°4N 2°31W **12** D5
Nanty Glo *U.S.A.* 40°28N 78°50W **82** F6
Nanuku Passage *Fiji* 16°45S 179°15W **59** a
Nanuque *Brazil* 17°50S 40°21W **93** G10
Nanusa, Kepulauan
  Indonesia 4°45N 127°1E **37** D7
Nanutarra Roadhouse
  Australia 22°32S 115°30E **60** D2
Nanxi *China* 28°54N 104°59E **34** C5
Nanxiong *China* 25°6N 114°15E **35** E10
Nanyang *China* 33°11N 112°30E **32** H7
Nanyi Hu *China* 31°5N 119°0E **35** B12
Nanyuan *China* 39°47N 116°24E **32** E9
Nanyuki *Kenya* 0°2N 37°4E **54** D7
Nanzhang *China* 31°45N 111°50E **35** B8
Nanzhang *China* 33°30N 112°20E **32** H7
Nao, C. de la *Spain* 38°44N 0°14E **21** C6
Naococane, L. *Canada* 52°50N 70°45W **73** B5
Naozhou Dao *China* 20°55N 110°20E **35** G8
Napa *U.S.A.* 38°18N 122°17W **78** G4
Napa → *U.S.A.* 38°10N 122°19W **78** G4
Napanee *Canada* 44°15N 77°0W **82** B8
Napanoch *U.S.A.* 41°44N 74°22W **83** E10
Nape *Laos* 18°18N 105°6E **38** C5
Nape Pass = Keo Neua, Deo
  Vietnam 18°23N 105°10E **38** C5
Napier *N.Z.* 39°30S 176°56E **59** C6
Napier Broome B.
  Australia 14°2S 126°37E **60** B4
Napier Pen. *Australia* 12°4S 135°43E **62** A2
Napierville *Canada* 45°11N 73°25W **83** A11
Naples = Nápoli *Italy* 40°50N 14°15E **22** D6
Naples *U.S.A.* 26°8N 81°48W **85** H14
Napo *China* 23°22N 105°50E **34** F5
Napo → *Peru* 3°20S 72°40W **92** D4
Napoleon *N. Dak., U.S.A.* 46°30N 99°46W **80** B4
Napoleon *Ohio, U.S.A.* 41°23N 84°8W **81** E11
Nápoli *Italy* 40°50N 14°15E **22** D6
Naqadeh *Iran* 36°57N 45°23E **46** B5
Naqb, Ra's an *Jordan* 29°48N 35°44E **48** F4
Naqqāsh *Iran* 35°40N 49°6E **47** C6
Nara *Japan* 34°40N 135°49E **29** G7
Nara *Mali* 15°10N 7°20W **52** E4
Nara □ *Japan* 34°30N 136°0E **29** G8
Nara Canal *Pakistan* 24°30N 69°20E **42** G3
Nara Visa *U.S.A.* 35°37N 103°6W **77** J12
Naracoorte *Australia* 36°58S 140°45E **63** F3
Naradhan *Australia* 33°34S 146°17E **63** E4
Naraini *India* 25°11N 80°29E **43** G9
Naranjos *Mexico* 21°21N 97°41W **87** C5
Narasannapeta *India* 18°25N 84°3E **44** E7
Narasapur *India* 16°26N 81°40E **45** F5
Narasaraopet *India* 16°14N 80°4E **45** F5
Narathiwat *Thailand* 6°30N 101°48E **39** J3
Narayanapatnam *India* 18°53N 83°10E **44** E6
Narayangadh = Bharatpur
  Nepal 27°34N 84°10E **43** F11
Narayanganj *Bangla.* 23°40N 90°33E **41** H17
Narayanpet *India* 16°45N 77°30E **44** F3
Narberth *U.K.* 51°47N 4°44W **13** F3
Narbonne *France* 43°11N 3°0E **20** E5
Narcondam I. *India* 13°20N 94°16E **45** H12
Nardín *Iran* 37°3N 55°59E **47** B7
Nardò *Italy* 40°11N 18°2E **23** D8
Narembeen *Australia* 32°7S 118°24E **61** F2
Nares Str. *Arctic* 80°0N 70°0W **69** B18
Naretha *Australia* 31°0S 124°45E **61** F3
Narew → *Poland* 52°26N 20°41E **17** B11
Nari → *Pakistan* 28°0N 67°40E **42** E2
Narin *Afghan.* 36°5N 69°0E **40** A6
Narita *Japan* 35°47N 140°19E **29** G10
Nariva Swamp
  Trin. & Tob. 10°26N 61°4W **93** K15
Narmada → *India* 21°38N 72°36E **42** J5
Narmada Canal *India* 22°20N 73°45E **44** C1
Narnaul *India* 28°5N 76°11E **42** E7
Narodnaya *Russia* 65°5N 59°58E **18** A10
Narooma *Australia* 36°14S 150°4E **63** F5
Narowal *Pakistan* 32°6N 74°52E **42** C6
Narrabri *Australia* 30°19S 149°46E **63** E4
Narran → *Australia* 28°37S 148°12E **63** D4
Narrandera *Australia* 34°42S 146°31E **63** E4
Narrogin *Australia* 32°58S 117°14E **61** F2
Narromine *Australia* 32°12S 148°12E **63** E4
Narrow Hills △ *Canada* 54°0N 104°37W **71** C8
Narsampet *India* 17°57N 79°58E **44** F4
Narsimhapur *India* 22°54N 79°14E **43** H8
Narsinghgarh *India* 23°45N 77°20E **42** H7
Narsinghpur *India* 20°28N 85°5E **44** D7
Narsipatnam *India* 17°40N 82°37E **44** F6
Naruto = Sanmu *Japan* 34°11N 138°12E **29** G8
Narva *Estonia* 59°23N 28°12E **18** C4
Narva → *Russia* 59°27N 28°2E **9** G23
Narva Bay = Narva Laht
  Estonia 59°35N 27°35E **9** G22
Narva Laht *Estonia* 59°35N 27°35E **9** G22

Narvik *Norway* 68°28N 17°26E **8** B17
Narwana *India* 29°39N 76°6E **42** E7
Narwinbi ⊙ *Australia* 16°7S 136°17E **62** B2
Naryan-Mar *Russia* 67°42N 53°12E **18** A9
Narym *Russia* 59°0N 81°30E **26** D9
Naryn *Kyrgyzstan* 41°26N 75°58E **30** C4
Naryn Qum *Kazakhstan* 47°30N 49°0E **26** E7
Nás, An = Naas *Ireland* 53°12N 6°40W **10** C5
Nasa *Norway* 66°29N 15°23E **8** C16
Nasau *Fiji* 17°19S 179°27E **59** a
Nasca *Peru* 14°50S 74°57W **92** F4
Nasca Ridge *Pac. Oc.* 20°0S 80°0W **65** K19
Naseby *N.Z.* 45°1S 170°10E **59** F3
Naselle *U.S.A.* 46°22N 123°49W **78** D3
Naser, Buheirat en *Egypt* 23°0N 32°30E **53** D12
Nashik = Nasik *India* 19°58N 73°50E **44** E1
Nashua *Mont., U.S.A.* 48°8N 106°22W **76** B10
Nashua *N.H., U.S.A.* 42°45N 71°28W **83** D13
Nashville *Ark., U.S.A.* 33°57N 93°51W **84** E8
Nashville *Ga., U.S.A.* 31°12N 83°15W **85** F13
Nashville *Tenn., U.S.A.* 36°10N 86°47W **85** C11
Nasik *India* 19°58N 73°50E **44** E1
Nasirabad *India* 26°15N 74°45E **42** F6
Nasirabad *Pakistan* 28°23N 68°24E **42** E3
Nasiri = Ahvāz *Iran* 31°20N 48°40E **47** D6
Nasiriyah = An Nāşirīyah
  Iraq 31°0N 46°15E **46** D5
Naskaupi → *Canada* 53°47N 60°51W **73** B7
Naşrābād *Iran* 34°8N 51°26E **47** C6
Naşrīān-e Pā'īn *Iran* 32°52N 46°52E **46** C5
Nass → *Canada* 55°0N 129°40W **70** C3
Nassau *Bahamas* 25°5N 77°20W **88** A4
Nassau *U.S.A.* 42°31N 73°37W **83** D11
Nassau, B. *Chile* 55°20S 68°0W **96** H3
Nasser, L. = Naser, Buheirat en
  Egypt 23°0N 32°30E **53** D12
Nässjö *Sweden* 57°39N 14°42E **9** H16
Nastapoka → *Canada* 56°55N 76°33W **72** A4
Nastapoka, Is. *Canada* 56°55N 76°50W **72** A4
Nasushiobara *Japan* 36°58N 140°3E **29** F10
Nata *Botswana* 20°12S 26°12E **56** B4
Nata → *Botswana* 20°14S 26°10E **56** B4
Natal *Brazil* 5°47S 35°13W **93** E11
Natal *Indonesia* 0°35N 99°7E **36** D1
Natal Drakensberg = uKhahlamba
  Drakensberg △
  S. Africa 29°27S 29°30E **57** C4
Naţanz *Iran* 33°30N 51°55E **47** C6
Natashquan *Canada* 50°14N 61°46W **73** B7
Natashquan → *Canada* 50°7N 61°50W **73** B7
Natchez *U.S.A.* 31°34N 91°24W **84** F9
Natchitoches *U.S.A.* 31°46N 93°5W **84** F8
Natewa B. *Fiji* 16°35S 179°40E **59** a
Nathalia *Australia* 36°1S 145°13E **63** F4
Nathdwara *India* 24°55N 73°50E **42** G5
Natimuk *Australia* 36°42S 142°0E **63** F3
Nation → *Canada* 55°30N 123°32W **70** B4
National City *U.S.A.* 32°40N 117°5W **79** N9
Natitingou *Benin* 10°20N 1°26E **52** F6
Natividad, I. *Mexico* 27°52N 115°11W **86** B1
Natkyizin *Burma* 14°57N 97°59E **38** E1
Natron, L. *Tanzania* 2°20S 36°0E **54** C4
Natrona Heights *U.S.A.* 40°37N 79°44W **82** F5
Natukanaoka Pan
  Namibia 18°40S 15°45E **56** A2
Natuna Besar, Kepulauan
  Indonesia 4°0N 108°15E **36** D3
Natuna Is. = Natuna Besar,
  Kepulauan *Indonesia* 4°0N 108°15E **36** D3
Natuna Selatan, Kepulauan
  Indonesia 2°45S 109°0E **36** D3
Natural Bridge *U.S.A.* 44°5N 75°30W **83** B9
Natural Bridges △
  U.S.A. 37°36N 110°0W **77** H9
Naturaliste, C. *Tas.,*
  Australia 40°50S 148°15E **63** G4
Naturaliste, C. *W. Austral.,*
  Australia 33°32S 115°0E **61** F2
Naturaliste Plateau
  Ind. Oc. 34°0S 112°0E **64** L3
Nau Qala *Afghan.* 34°5N 68°5E **42** B3
Naugatuck *U.S.A.* 41°30N 73°3W **83** E11
Naujaat = Repulse Bay
  Canada 66°30N 86°30W **69** D14
Naumburg *Germany* 51°9N 11°47E **16** C6
Naupada *India* 18°34N 84°18E **44** E7
Nauru ■ *Pac. Oc.* 1°0S 166°0E **58** B9
Naushahra = Nowshera
  Pakistan 34°0N 72°0E **40** C8
Naushahro *Pakistan* 26°50N 68°7E **42** F3
Naushon I. *U.S.A.* 41°29N 70°45W **83** E14
Nausori *Fiji* 18°2S 178°32E **59** a
Nauta *Peru* 4°31S 73°35W **92** D4
Nautanwa *India* 27°20N 83°25E **43** F10
Naute △ *Namibia* 26°55S 17°57E **56** C2
Nautla *Mexico* 20°13N 96°47W **87** C5
Nava *Mexico* 28°25N 100°45W **86** B4
Navadwip *India* 23°34N 88°20E **43** H13
Navahrudak *Belarus* 53°40N 25°50E **17** B13
Navajo Res. *U.S.A.* 36°48N 107°36W **77** H10
Navalgund *India* 15°34N 75°22E **45** G2
Navalmoral de la Mata
  Spain 39°52N 5°33W **21** C3
Navan *Ireland* 53°39N 6°41W **10** C5
Navarin, Mys *Russia* 62°15N 179°5E **27** C18
Navarino, I. *Chile* 55°0S 67°40W **96** H3
Navarra □ *Spain* 42°40N 1°40W **21** A5
Navarre *U.S.A.* 40°43N 81°31W **82** F3
Navarro → *U.S.A.* 39°11N 123°45W **78** F3
Navasota *U.S.A.* 30°23N 96°5W **84** F6
Navassa I. *W. Indies* 18°30N 75°0W **89** C5
Naver → *U.K.* 58°32N 4°14W **11** C4
Navibandar *India* 21°26N 69°48E **42** J3
Navidad *Chile* 33°57S 71°50W **94** C1
Naviraí *Brazil* 23°8S 54°13W **95** A5
Naviti *Fiji* 17°7S 177°15E **59** a
Navlakhi *India* 22°58N 70°28E **42** H4
Năvodari *Romania* 44°19N 28°36E **17** F15
Navoi *Uzbekistan* 40°9N 65°22E **26** E7

Navojoa *Mexico* 27°6N 109°26W **86** B3
Navolato *Mexico* 24°47N 107°42W **86** C3
Navsari *India* 20°57N 72°59E **44** D1
Navua *Fiji* 18°12S 178°11E **59** a
Nawa Kot *Pakistan* 28°21N 71°24E **42** E4
Nawab Khan *Pakistan* 30°17N 69°12E **42** D3
Nawabganj *Ut. P., India* 26°56N 81°14E **43** F9
Nawabganj *Ut. P., India* 28°32N 79°40E **43** E8
Nawabshah *Pakistan* 26°15N 68°25E **42** F3
Nawada *India* 24°50N 85°33E **43** G11
Nawakot *Nepal* 27°55N 85°10E **43** F11
Nawalgarh *India* 27°50N 75°15E **42** F6
Nawanshahr *India* 32°33N 74°48E **43** C6
Nawapara *India* 20°46N 82°33E **44** D6
Nawar, Dasht-i- *Afghan.* 33°52N 68°0E **42** C3
Nawoiy = Navoi
  Uzbekistan 40°9N 65°22E **26** E7
Naxçıvan *Azerbaijan* 39°12N 45°15E **46** B5
Naxçıvan □ *Azerbaijan* 39°25N 45°26E **46** B5
Naxos *Greece* 37°8N 25°25E **23** F11
Nay, Mui *Vietnam* 12°54N 109°26E **38** F7
Nāy Band *Büshehr, Iran* 27°20N 52°40E **47** E7
Nāy Band *Khorāsān, Iran* 32°20N 57°34E **47** C8
Nay Pyi Taw = Naypyidaw
  Burma 19°44N 96°12E **30** H8
Nayagarh *India* 20°8N 85°6E **44** D7
Nayakhan *Russia* 61°56N 159°0E **27** C16
Nayarit □ *Mexico* 22°0N 105°0W **86** C4
Nayau *Fiji* 18°6S 178°10E **59** a
Nayong *China* 26°50N 105°20E **34** D5
Nayoro *Japan* 44°21N 142°28E **28** B11
Naypyidaw *Burma* 19°44N 96°12E **30** H8
Nayudupeta *India* 13°54N 79°54E **45** H4
Nayyāl, W. → *Si. Arabia* 28°35N 39°4E **46** D3
Nazaré *Brazil* 13°2S 39°0W **93** F11
Nazareth = Nazerat
  Israel 32°42N 35°17E **48** C4
Nazareth *U.S.A.* 40°44N 75°19W **83** F9
Nazarovo *Russia* 57°2N 90°40E **27** D10
Nazas *Mexico* 25°14N 104°8W **86** B4
Nazas → *Mexico* 25°12N 104°12W **86** B4
Naza = Nasca *Peru* 14°50S 74°57W **92** F4
Naze, The *U.K.* 51°53N 1°18E **13** F9
Nazerat *Israel* 32°42N 35°17E **48** C4
Nāzik *Iran* 39°1N 45°4E **46** B5
Nazilli *Turkey* 37°55N 28°15E **23** F13
Nazko *Canada* 53°1N 123°37W **70** C4
Nazko → *Canada* 53°7N 123°34W **70** C4
Nazret *Ethiopia* 8°32N 39°22E **49** F2
Ndalatando *Angola* 9°12S 14°48E **54** F2
Ndélé *C.A.R.* 8°25N 20°36E **54** C4
Ndjamena *Chad* 12°10N 15°0E **53** F8
Ndola *Zambia* 13°0S 28°34E **55** G5
Ndomo → *S. Africa* 26°52S 32°15E **57** C5
Ndoto Mts. *Kenya* 2°0N 37°0E **54** D7
Neagh, Lough *U.K.* 54°37N 6°25W **10** B5
Neah Bay *U.S.A.* 48°22N 124°37W **78** B2
Neale, L. *Australia* 24°15S 130°0E **60** D5
Neales → *Australia* 28°8S 136°47E **63** D2
Near Is. *U.S.A.* 52°30N 174°0E **74** E2
Neath *U.K.* 51°39N 3°48W **13** F4
Neath Port Talbot □ *U.K.* 51°42N 3°45W **13** F4
Nebine Cr. → *Australia* 29°27S 146°56E **63** D4
Nebitdag = Balkanabat
  Turkmenistan 39°30N 54°22E **47** B7
Nebo *Australia* 21°42S 148°42E **62** C4
Nebraska □ *U.S.A.* 41°30N 99°30W **80** E4
Nebraska City *U.S.A.* 40°41N 95°52W **80** E6
Nébrodi, Monti *Italy* 37°54N 14°35E **22** F6
Necedah *U.S.A.* 44°2N 90°4W **80** C8
Nechako → *Canada* 53°55N 122°42W **70** C4
Neches → *U.S.A.* 29°58N 93°51W **84** G8
Neckar → *Germany* 49°27N 8°29E **16** D5
Necker I. *U.S.A.* 23°35N 164°42W **75** L7
Necochea *Argentina* 38°30S 58°50W **94** D4
Nederland = Netherlands ■
  Europe 52°0N 5°30E **15** C5
Needles *Canada* 49°53N 118°7W **70** D5
Needles *U.S.A.* 34°51N 114°37W **79** L12
Needles, The *U.K.* 50°39N 1°35W **13** G6
Neembucú □ *Paraguay* 27°0S 58°0W **94** B4
Neemuch = Nimach
  India 24°30N 74°56E **42** G6
Neenah *U.S.A.* 44°11N 88°28W **80** C9
Neepawa *Canada* 50°15N 99°30W **71** C9
Neftçala *Azerbaijan* 39°19N 49°12E **47** B6
Neftegorsk *Russia* 53°1N 142°58E **27** D15
Neftekumsk *Russia* 44°46N 44°50E **19** F7
Nefteyugansk *Russia* 61°5N 72°42E **26** C8
Nefyn *U.K.* 52°56N 4°31W **12** E3
Negapatam = Nagappattinam
  India 10°46N 79°51E **45** J4
Negara *Indonesia* 8°22S 114°37E **37** J17
Negaunee *U.S.A.* 46°30N 87°36W **80** B10
Negele *Ethiopia* 5°20N 39°36E **49** F2
Negeri Sembilan □
  Malaysia 2°45N 102°10E **39** L4
Negev Desert = Hanegev
  Israel 30°50N 35°0E **48** E4
Negombo *Sri Lanka* 7°12N 79°50E **45** L4
Negotin *Serbia* 44°16N 22°37E **23** B10
Negra, Pta. *Mauritania* 22°54N 16°18W **52** D2
Negra, Pta. *Peru* 6°6S 81°10W **92** E2
Negrais, C. = Maudin Sun
  Burma 16°0N 94°30E **41** M19
Neva → *Russia* 59°56N 30°20E **18** C5
Negril *Jamaica* 18°22N 78°20W **88** a
Negro → *Argentina* 41°2S 62°47W **96** E4
Negro → *Brazil* 3°0S 60°0W **92** D7
Negro → *Uruguay* 33°24S 58°22W **94** C4
Negros *Phil.* 9°30N 122°40E **37** C6
Neguac *Canada* 47°15N 65°5W **73** C6
Nehalem → *U.S.A.* 45°40N 123°56W **78** D3
Nehāvand *Iran* 35°56N 49°31E **47** C6
Nehbandān *Iran* 31°35N 60°5E **47** D9
Nehe *China* 48°29N 124°50E **31** B13
Nei Mongol Zizhiqu □
  China 42°0N 112°0E **32** D7
Neiafu *Tonga* 18°39S 173°59W **59** c
Neiges, Piton des *Réunion* 21°5S 55°29E **55** c

Neijiang *China* 29°35N 104°55E **34** C5
Neilingding Dao *China* 22°25N 113°48E **31** a
Neill I. *India* 11°50N 93°3E **45** J11
Neillsville *U.S.A.* 44°34N 90°36W **80** C8
Neilton *U.S.A.* 47°25N 123°53W **78** C3
Neiqiu *China* 37°15N 114°30E **32** F8
Neiva *Colombia* 2°56N 75°18W **92** C3
Neixiang *China* 33°10N 111°52E **32** H6
Nejanilini L. *Canada* 59°33N 97°48W **71** B9
Nejd = Najd *Si. Arabia* 26°30N 42°0E **49** B3
Nekā *Iran* 36°39N 53°19E **47** B7
Nekemte *Ethiopia* 9°4N 36°30E **49** F2
Nekso *Denmark* 55°4N 15°8E **9** J16
Nelamangala *India* 13°6N 77°24E **45** H3
Nelia *Australia* 20°39S 142°12E **62** C3
Neligh *U.S.A.* 42°8N 98°2W **80** D4
Nelkan *Russia* 57°40N 136°4E **27** D14
Nellikuppam *India* 11°46N 79°43E **45** J4
Nellore *India* 14°27N 79°59E **45** G4
Nelson *Canada* 49°30N 117°20W **70** D5
Nelson *N.Z.* 41°18S 173°16E **59** D4
Nelson *U.K.* 53°50N 2°13W **12** D5
Nelson *Ariz., U.S.A.* 35°31N 113°19W **77** J7
Nelson *Nev., U.S.A.* 35°42N 114°49W **79** K12
Nelson → *Canada* 54°33N 98°2W **71** C9
Nelson, C. *Australia* 38°26S 141°32E **63** F3
Nelson, Estrecho *Chile* 51°30S 75°0W **96** G2
Nelson Forks *Canada* 59°30N 124°0W **70** B4
Nelson House *Canada* 55°47N 98°51W **71** B9
Nelson L. *Canada* 55°48N 100°7W **71** B8
Nelson Lakes △ *N.Z.* 41°55S 172°44E **59** D4
Nelspoort *S. Africa* 32°7S 23°0E **56** D3
Nelspruit = Mbombela
  S. Africa 25°29S 30°59E **57** C5
Néma *Mauritania* 16°40N 7°15W **52** E4
Neman → *Lithuania* 55°25N 21°10E **9** J19
Neman = Nemunas →
  Lithuania 55°25N 21°10E **9** J19
Nembrala *Indonesia* 10°53S 122°50E **60** B3
Nemeiben L. *Canada* 55°20N 105°20W **71** B7
Nemiscau *Canada* 51°18N 76°54W **72** B4
Nemiscau, L. *Canada* 51°25N 76°40W **72** B4
Nemunas → *Lithuania* 55°25N 21°10E **9** J19
Nemuro *Japan* 43°20N 145°35E **28** C12
Nemuro-Kaikyō *Japan* 43°30N 145°30E **28** C12
Nen Jiang → *China* 45°28N 124°30E **33** B13
Nenagh *Ireland* 52°52N 8°11W **10** D3
Nenana *U.S.A.* 64°34N 149°5W **74** C10
Nenasi *Malaysia* 3°9N 103°23E **39** L4
Nene → *U.K.* 52°49N 0°11E **13** E8
Nenjiang *China* 49°10N 125°10E **31** B14
Neodesha *U.S.A.* 37°25N 95°41W **80** G6
Neora Valley △ *India* 27°0N 88°45E **43** F13
Neosho *U.S.A.* 36°52N 94°22W **80** G6
Neosho → *U.S.A.* 36°48N 95°18W **84** C7
Nepal ■ *Asia* 28°0N 84°30E **43** F11
Nepalganj *Nepal* 28°5N 81°40E **43** E9
Nepalganj Road *India* 28°1N 81°41E **43** E9
Nephi *U.S.A.* 39°43N 111°50W **76** G8
Nephin *Ireland* 54°1N 9°22W **10** B2
Nephin Beg Range *Ireland* 54°0N 9°40W **10** C2
Nerang *Australia* 27°58S 153°20E **63** D5
Nerchinsk *Russia* 52°0N 116°39E **27** D12
Néret, L. *Canada* 54°45N 70°44W **73** B5
Neretva → *Croatia* 43°1N 17°27E **23** C7
Neringa *Lithuania* 55°20N 21°5E **9** J19
Neris → *Lithuania* 55°8N 24°16E **9** J21
Neryungri *Russia* 57°38N 124°28E **27** D13
Nescopeck *U.S.A.* 41°3N 76°12W **83** E8
Neskantaga *Canada* 52°14N 87°53W **72** B2
Neskaupstaður *Iceland* 65°9N 13°42W **8** D7
Ness, L. *U.K.* 57°15N 4°32W **11** D4
Ness City *U.S.A.* 38°27N 99°54W **80** F4
Nesterov = Zhovkva
  Ukraine 50°4N 23°58E **17** C12
Nestos → *Europe* 40°54N 24°49E **23** D11
Nesvizh = Nyasvizh
  Belarus 53°14N 26°38E **17** B14
Netanya *Israel* 32°20N 34°51E **48** C3
Netarhat *India* 23°29N 84°16E **43** H11
Nete → *Belgium* 51°7N 4°14E **15** C4
Netherdale *Australia* 21°10S 148°33E **62** b
Netherlands ■ *Europe* 52°0N 5°30E **15** C5
Netherlands Antilles = ABC
  Islands *W. Indies* 12°15N 69°0W **89** D6
Netrang *India* 21°39N 73°21E **42** J5
Nettilling L. *Canada* 66°30N 71°0W **69** D17
Netzahualcóyotl, Presa
  Mexico 17°8N 93°35W **87** D6
Neubrandenburg
  Germany 53°33N 13°15E **16** B7
Neuchâtel *Switz.* 47°0N 6°55E **20** C7
Neuchâtel, Lac de *Switz.* 46°53N 6°50E **20** C7
Neufchâteau *Belgium* 49°50N 5°25E **15** E5
Neumayer *Antarctica* 71°0S 68°30W **5** D17
Neumünster *Germany* 54°4N 9°58E **16** A5
Neunkirchen *Germany* 49°20N 7°9E **16** D4
Neuquén *Argentina* 38°55S 68°0W **96** D3
Neuquén □ *Argentina* 38°0S 69°50W **94** D2
Neuruppin *Germany* 52°55N 12°48E **16** B7
Neuse → *U.S.A.* 35°6N 76°29W **85** D16
Neusiedler See *Austria* 47°50N 16°47E **17** E9
Neustrelitz *Germany* 53°21N 13°4E **16** B7
Neva → *Russia* 59°56N 30°20E **18** C5
Nevada *Iowa, U.S.A.* 42°1N 93°27W **80** D7
Nevada *Mo., U.S.A.* 37°51N 94°22W **80** G6
Nevada □ *U.S.A.* 39°0N 117°0W **76** G5
Nevada City *U.S.A.* 39°16N 121°1W **78** F6
Nevado, Cerro *Argentina* 35°30S 68°32W **94** D2
Nevado de Colima = Volcán de
  Colima △ *Mexico* 19°30N 103°40W **86** D4
Nevado de Tres Cruces △
  Chile 27°13S 69°5W **94** B2
Nevasa *India* 19°34N 75°0E **44** E2
Nevel *Russia* 56°0N 29°55E **18** C4
Nevelsk *Russia* 46°40N 141°51E **27** E15
Nevers *France* 47°0N 3°9E **20** C5
Nevertire *Australia* 31°50S 147°44E **63** E4

Neville *Canada* 49°58N 107°39W **71** D7
Nevinnomyssk *Russia* 44°40N 42°0E **19** F7
Nevis *St. Kitts & Nevis* 17°0N 62°30W **89** C7
Nevşehir *Turkey* 38°33N 34°40E **46** B2
Nevyansk *Russia* 57°30N 60°13E **18** C11
New → *U.S.A.* 38°10N 81°12W **81** F13
New Aiyansh *Canada* 55°12N 129°4W **70** B3
New Albany *Ind., U.S.A.* 38°18N 85°49W **81** F11
New Albany *Miss.,*
  U.S.A. 34°29N 89°0W **85** D10
New Albany *Pa., U.S.A.* 41°36N 76°27W **83** E8
New Amsterdam *Guyana* 6°15N 57°36W **92** B7
New Baltimore *U.S.A.* 42°41N 82°44W **82** D2
New Bedford *U.S.A.* 41°38N 70°56W **83** E14
New Berlin *N.Y., U.S.A.* 42°37N 75°20W **83** D9
New Berlin *Pa., U.S.A.* 40°50N 76°57W **82** F8
New Bern *U.S.A.* 35°7N 77°3W **85** D16
New Bethlehem *U.S.A.* 41°0N 79°20W **82** F5
New Bight *Bahamas* 24°19N 75°24W **89** B4
New Bloomfield *U.S.A.* 40°25N 77°11W **82** F7
New Boston *U.S.A.* 33°28N 94°25W **84** E7
New Braunfels *U.S.A.* 29°42N 98°8W **84** G5
New Brighton *N.Z.* 43°29S 172°43E **59** E4
New Brighton *U.K.* 40°42N 80°19W **82** F4
New Britain *Papua N. G.* 5°50S 150°20E **58** B8
New Britain *U.S.A.* 41°40N 72°47W **83** E12
New Brunswick *U.S.A.* 40°30N 74°27W **83** F10
New Brunswick □
  Canada 46°50N 66°30W **73** C6
New Caledonia ☑ *Pac. Oc.* 21°0S 165°0E **58** D9
New Caledonia Trough
  Pac. Oc. 30°0S 165°0E **64** L8
New Castile = Castilla-La
  Mancha □ *Spain* 39°30N 3°30W **21** C4
New Castle *Ind., U.S.A.* 39°55N 85°22W **81** F11
New Castle *Pa., U.S.A.* 41°0N 80°21W **82** F4
New City *U.S.A.* 41°9N 73°59W **83** E11
New Concord *U.S.A.* 39°59N 81°54W **82** G3
New Cumberland *U.S.A.* 40°30N 80°36W **82** F4
New Cuyama *U.S.A.* 34°57N 119°38W **79** L7
New Denver *Canada* 50°0N 117°25W **70** D5
New Don Pedro Res.
  U.S.A. 37°43N 120°24W **78** H6
New England *U.S.A.* 43°0N 71°0W **75** G25
New England *N. Dak.,*
  U.S.A. 46°32N 102°52W **80** B2
New England Ra.
  Australia 30°20S 151°45E **63** E5
New Forest △ *U.K.* 50°53N 1°34W **13** G6
New Galloway *U.K.* 55°5N 4°9W **11** F4
New Glasgow *Canada* 45°35N 62°36W **73** C7
New Guinea *Oceania* 4°0S 136°0E **58** B6
New Hamburg *Canada* 43°23N 80°42W **82** C4
New Hampshire □
  U.S.A. 44°0N 71°30W **83** C13
New Hampton *U.S.A.* 43°3N 92°19W **80** D7
New Hanover *S. Africa* 29°22S 30°31E **57** C5
New Hartford *U.S.A.* 43°4N 75°18W **83** C9
New Haven *Conn.,*
  U.S.A. 41°18N 72°55W **83** E12
New Haven *Mich., U.S.A.* 42°44N 82°48W **82** D2
New Haven *N.Y., U.S.A.* 43°28N 76°18W **83** C8
New Hazelton *Canada* 55°20N 127°30W **70** B3
New Hebrides = Vanuatu ■
  Pac. Oc. 15°0S 168°0E **58** C9
New Holland *U.S.A.* 40°6N 76°5W **83** F8
New Iberia *U.S.A.* 30°1N 91°49W **84** F9
New Ireland *Papua N. G.* 3°20S 151°50E **58** B8
New Jersey □ *U.S.A.* 40°0N 74°30W **81** F16
New Kensington *U.S.A.* 40°34N 79°46W **82** F5
New Lexington *U.S.A.* 39°43N 82°13W **81** F12
New Liskeard *Canada* 47°31N 79°41W **72** C4
New London *Conn.,*
  U.S.A. 41°22N 72°6W **83** E12
New London *Ohio, U.S.A.* 41°5N 82°24W **82** E2
New London *Wis., U.S.A.* 44°23N 88°45W **80** C9
New Madrid *U.S.A.* 36°36N 89°32W **80** G9
New Martinsville
  U.S.A. 39°39N 80°52W **81** F13
New Meadows *U.S.A.* 44°58N 116°18W **76** D5
New Melones L. *U.S.A.* 37°57N 120°31W **78** H6
New Mexico □ *U.S.A.* 34°30N 106°0W **77** J11
New Milford *Conn.,*
  U.S.A. 41°35N 73°25W **83** E11
New Milford *Pa., U.S.A.* 41°52N 75°44W **83** E9
New Norcia *Australia* 30°57S 116°13E **61** F2
New Norfolk *Australia* 42°46S 147°2E **63** G4
New Philadelphia *U.S.A.* 40°30N 81°27W **82** F3
New Plymouth *N.Z.* 39°4S 174°5E **59** C5
New Plymouth *U.S.A.* 43°58N 116°49W **76** E5
New Port Richey *U.S.A.* 28°16N 82°43W **85** G13
New Providence
  Bahamas 25°25N 77°35W **88** A4
New Quay *U.K.* 52°13N 4°21W **13** E3
New Radnor *U.K.* 52°15N 3°9W **13** E4
New Richmond *Canada* 48°15N 65°45W **73** C6
New Richmond *U.S.A.* 45°7N 92°32W **80** C7
New River Gorge △
  U.S.A. 37°53N 81°5W **81** G13
New Roads *U.S.A.* 30°42N 91°26W **84** F9
New Rochelle *U.S.A.* 40°55N 73°46W **83** F11
New Rockford *U.S.A.* 47°41N 99°8W **80** B4
New Romney *U.K.* 50°59N 0°57E **13** G8
New Ross *Ireland* 52°23N 6°57W **10** D5
New Salem *U.S.A.* 46°51N 101°25W **80** B3
New Scone = Scone *U.K.* 56°25N 3°24W **11** E5
New Siberian I. = Novaya Sibir,
  Ostrov *Russia* 75°10N 150°0E **27** B16
New Siberian Is. = Novosibirskiye
  Ostrova *Russia* 75°0N 142°0E **27** B15
New Smyrna Beach
  U.S.A. 29°1N 80°56W **85** G14
New South Wales □
  Australia 33°0S 146°0E **63** E4
New Tecumseth = Alliston
  Canada 44°9N 79°52W **82** B5
New Town *U.S.A.* 47°59N 102°30W **80** B3
New Tredegar *U.K.* 51°44N 3°16W **13** F4
New Ulm *U.S.A.* 44°19N 94°28W **80** C6

New Waterford *Canada* 46°13N 60°4W **73** C7
New Westminster
  Canada 49°13N 122°55W **78** A4
New York □ *U.S.A.* 43°0N 75°0W **83** D9
New York J.F. Kennedy Int. ✈
  (JFK) *U.S.A.* 40°38N 73°47W **83** F11
New Zealand ■ *Oceania* 40°0S 176°0E **59** D6
Newaj → *India* 24°24N 76°49E **42** G7
Newark *Del., U.S.A.* 39°41N 75°46W **81** F16
Newark *N.J., U.S.A.* 40°44N 74°10W **83** F10
Newark *N.Y., U.S.A.* 43°3N 77°6W **82** C7
Newark *Ohio, U.S.A.* 40°3N 82°24W **82** F2
Newark Liberty Int. ✈ (EWR)
  U.S.A. 40°42N 74°10W **83** F10
Newark-on-Trent *U.K.* 53°5N 0°48W **12** D7
Newark Valley *U.S.A.* 42°14N 76°11W **83** D8
Newberg *U.S.A.* 45°18N 122°58W **76** D2
Newberry *Mich., U.S.A.* 46°21N 85°30W **81** B11
Newberry *S.C., U.S.A.* 34°17N 81°37W **85** D14
Newberry Springs
  U.S.A. 34°50N 116°41W **79** L10
Newboro L. *Canada* 44°38N 76°20W **83** B8
Newbridge *Ireland* 53°11N 6°48W **10** C5
Newburgh *Canada* 44°19N 76°52W **82** B8
Newburgh *U.S.A.* 41°30N 74°1W **83** E10
Newbury *U.K.* 51°24N 1°20W **13** F6
Newbury *N.H., U.S.A.* 43°19N 72°3W **83** C12
Newbury *Vt., U.S.A.* 44°5N 72°4W **83** B12
Newburyport *U.S.A.* 42°49N 70°53W **83** D14
Newcastle *Australia* 33°0S 151°46E **63** E5
Newcastle *N.B., Canada* 47°1N 65°38W **73** C6
Newcastle *Ont., Canada* 43°55N 78°35W **72** D4
Newcastle *Ireland* 52°27N 9°3W **10** D2
Newcastle *S. Africa* 27°45S 29°58E **57** C4
Newcastle *U.K.* 54°13N 5°54W **10** B6
Newcastle *Calif., U.S.A.* 38°53N 121°8W **78** G5
Newcastle *Wyo.,*
  U.S.A. 43°50N 104°11W **76** E11
Newcastle Emlyn *U.K.* 52°2N 4°28W **13** E3
Newcastle Ra. *Australia* 15°45S 130°15E **60** C5
Newcastle-under-Lyme
  U.K. 53°1N 2°14W **12** D5
Newcastle-upon-Tyne
  U.K. 54°58N 1°36W **12** C6
Newcastle Waters
  Australia 17°30S 133°28E **62** B1
Newcomb *U.S.A.* 43°58N 74°10W **83** C10
Newcomerstown *U.S.A.* 40°16N 81°36W **82** F3
Newdegate *Australia* 33°6S 119°0E **61** F2
Newell *Australia* 16°20S 145°16E **62** B4
Newell *U.S.A.* 44°43N 103°25W **80** C2
Newenham, C. *U.S.A.* 58°39N 162°11W **74** D7
Newfane *U.S.A.* 43°17N 78°43W **82** C6
Newfield *U.S.A.* 42°18N 76°33W **83** D8
Newfound L. *U.S.A.* 43°40N 71°47W **83** C13
Newfoundland *Canada* 49°0N 55°0W **73** C8
Newfoundland *U.S.A.* 41°18N 75°19W **83** E9
Newfoundland & Labrador □
  Canada 52°0N 58°0W **73** B8
Newhaven *U.K.* 50°47N 0°3E **13** G8
Newkirk *U.S.A.* 36°53N 97°3W **84** C6
Newlyn *U.K.* 50°6N 5°34W **13** G2
Newman *Australia* 23°18S 119°45E **60** D2
Newman *U.S.A.* 37°19N 121°1W **78** H5
Newmarket *Canada* 44°3N 79°28W **82** B5
Newmarket *Ireland* 52°13N 9°0W **10** D2
Newmarket *U.K.* 52°15N 0°25E **13** E8
Newmarket *U.S.A.* 43°5N 70°56W **83** C14
Newnan *U.S.A.* 33°23N 84°48W **85** E12
Newport *Ireland* 53°53N 9°33W **10** C2
Newport *I. of W., U.K.* 50°42N 1°17W **13** G6
Newport *Newport, U.K.* 51°35N 3°0W **13** F5
Newport *Ark., U.S.A.* 35°37N 91°16W **84** D9
Newport *Ky., U.S.A.* 39°5N 84°29W **81** F11
Newport *N.H., U.S.A.* 43°22N 72°10W **83** C12
Newport *N.Y., U.S.A.* 43°11N 75°1W **83** C9
Newport *Oreg., U.S.A.* 44°39N 124°3W **76** D1
Newport *Pa., U.S.A.* 40°29N 77°8W **82** F7
Newport *R.I., U.S.A.* 41°29N 71°19W **83** E13
Newport *Tenn., U.S.A.* 35°58N 83°11W **85** D13
Newport *Vt., U.S.A.* 44°56N 72°13W **83** B12
Newport *Wash., U.S.A.* 48°11N 117°3W **76** B5
Newport □ *U.K.* 51°33N 3°1W **13** F4
Newport Beach *U.S.A.* 33°37N 117°56W **79** M9
Newport News *U.S.A.* 36°58N 76°25W **81** G15
Newport Pagnell *U.K.* 52°5N 0°43W **13** E7
Newquay *U.K.* 50°25N 5°6W **13** G2
Newry *U.K.* 54°11N 6°21W **10** B5
Newry Islands △
  Australia 20°51S 148°56E **62** b
Newton *Ill., U.S.A.* 38°59N 88°10W **80** F9
Newton *Iowa, U.S.A.* 41°42N 93°3W **80** E7
Newton *Kans., U.S.A.* 38°3N 97°21W **80** F5
Newton *Miss., U.S.A.* 32°19N 89°10W **85** E10
Newton *N.C., U.S.A.* 35°40N 81°13W **85** D14
Newton *N.J., U.S.A.* 41°3N 74°45W **83** E10
Newton *Tex., U.S.A.* 30°51N 93°46W **84** F8
Newton Abbot *U.K.* 50°32N 3°37W **13** G4
Newton Aycliffe *U.K.* 54°37N 1°34W **12** C6
Newton Falls *N.Y.,*
  U.S.A. 44°12N 74°59W **83** B10
Newton Falls *Ohio,*
  U.S.A. 41°11N 80°59W **82** E4
Newton Stewart *U.K.* 54°57N 4°30W **11** G4
Newtonmore *U.K.* 57°4N 4°8W **11** D4
Newtown *U.K.* 52°31N 3°19W **13** E4
Newtownabbey *U.K.* 54°40N 5°56W **10** B6
Newtownards *U.K.* 54°36N 5°42W **10** B6
Newtownbarry = Bunclody
  Ireland 52°39N 6°40W **10** D5
Newtownstewart *U.K.* 54°43N 7°23W **10** B4
Newville *U.S.A.* 40°10N 77°24W **82** F7
Neya *Russia* 58°21N 43°49E **18** C7
Neyrīz *Iran* 29°15N 54°19E **47** D7
Neyshābūr *Iran* 36°10N 58°50E **47** B8
Neyveli *India* 11°32N 79°29E **45** J4
Neyyattinkara *India* 8°26N 77°5E **45** K3
Nezhin = Nizhyn *Ukraine* 51°5N 31°55E **19** D5
Nezperce *U.S.A.* 46°14N 116°14W **76** C5

Nga, Laem *Thailand* 7°55N 98°27E **39 a**
Ngaanyatjarra ⬡
Australia 22°40S 127°0E **60 D4**
Ngabang *Indonesia* 0°23N 109°55E **36 D3**
Ngabordamlu, Tanjung
Indonesia 6°56S 134°11E **37 F8**
N'Gage *Angola* 7°46S 15°15E **54 F3**
Ngaliwurru Nungali ⬡
Australia 15°42S 130°4E **60 C5**
Ngalurrtju ⬡ *Australia* 22°44S 132°5E **60 D5**
Ngami Depression
Botswana 20°30S 22°46E **56 B3**
Ngamring *China* 29°14N 87°10E **30 F6**
Nganglong Kangri *China* 33°0N 81°0E **43 C9**
Ngao *Thailand* 18°46N 99°59E **38 C2**
Ngaoundéré *Cameroon* 7°15N 13°35E **54 C2**
Ngapara *N.Z.* 44°57S 170°46E **59 F3**
Ngarluma ⬡ *Australia* 21°30S 118°30E **60 D2**
Ngawi *Indonesia* 7°24S 111°26E **37 G14**
Ngcobo *S. Africa* 31°37S 28°0E **57 D4**
Nghia Lo *Vietnam* 21°33N 104°28E **34 G5**
Ngoring Hu *China* 34°55N 97°5E **30 E8**
Ngorongoro *Tanzania* 3°11S 35°32E **54 E7**
Nguigmi *Niger* 14°20N 13°20E **53 F8**
Nguiu *Australia* 11°46S 130°38E **60 B5**
Ngukurr *Australia* 14°44S 134°44E **62 A1**
Ngum → *Laos* 18°31N 102°32E **38 C4**
Ngundu *Zimbabwe* 18°11S 31°15E **57 A5**
Nguru *Nigeria* 12°56N 10°29E **53 F8**
Nguyen Binh *Vietnam* 22°39N 105°56E **34 F5**
Ngwaketse ⬡ *Botswana* 25°0S 25°0E **56 C3**
Nha Bang *Vietnam* 10°37N 105°0E **39 G5**
Nha Trang *Vietnam* 12°16N 109°10E **39 F7**
Nhacoongo *Mozam.* 24°18S 35°14E **57 B6**
Nhamundá → *Brazil* 2°12S 56°41W **93 D7**
Nhangulaze, L. *Mozam.* 24°0S 34°30E **57 B5**
Nharnuwangga, Wajarri and
Ngarlawangga ⬡
Australia 24°50S 118°0E **60 D2**
Nhill *Australia* 36°18S 141°40E **63 F3**
Nho Quan *Vietnam* 20°18N 105°45E **34 G5**
Nhulunbuy *Australia* 12°10S 137°20E **62 A2**
Niafounké *Mali* 16°0N 4°5W **52 E5**
Niagara Falls *Canada* 43°7N 79°5W **82 C5**
Niagara Falls *U.S.A.* 43°5N 79°4W **82 C6**
Niagara-on-the-Lake
Canada 43°15N 79°4W **82 C5**
Niah *Malaysia* 3°58N 113°46E **36 D4**
Niamey *Niger* 13°27N 2°6E **52 F6**
Niangara
Dem. Rep. of the Congo 3°42N 27°50E **54 D5**
Niantic *U.S.A.* 41°20N 72°11W **83 E12**
Nias *Indonesia* 1°0N 97°30E **36 D1**
Nibāk *Si. Arabia* 24°25N 50°50E **47 E7**
Nicaragua ■ *Cent. Amer.* 11°40N 85°30W **88 D2**
Nicaragua, L. de *Nic.* 12°0N 85°30W **88 D2**
Nicastro *Italy* 38°59N 16°19E **22 E7**
Nice *France* 43°42N 7°14E **20 E7**
Niceville *U.S.A.* 30°31N 86°30W **85 F11**
Nichicun, L. *Canada* 53°5N 71°0W **73 B5**
Nichinan *Japan* 31°38N 131°23E **29 J5**
Nicholás, Canal *Caribbean* 23°30N 80°5W **88 B3**
Nicholasville *U.S.A.* 37°53N 84°34W **81 G11**
Nichols *U.S.A.* 42°1N 76°22W **83 D8**
Nicholson *Australia* 18°2S 128°54E **60 C4**
Nicholson *U.S.A.* 41°37N 75°47W **83 E9**
Nicholson → *Australia* 17°31S 139°36E **62 B2**
Nicholson L. *Canada* 62°40N 102°40W **71 A8**
Nicholson Ra. *Australia* 27°15S 116°45E **61 E2**
Nicholville *U.S.A.* 44°41N 74°39W **83 B10**
Nicobar Is. *Ind. Oc.* 8°0N 93°30E **45 L11**
Nicola *Canada* 50°12N 120°40W **70 C4**
Nicolls Town *Bahamas* 25°8N 78°0W **88 A4**
Nicosia *Cyprus* 35°10N 33°25E **46 C2**
Nicoya *Costa Rica* 10°9N 85°27W **88 D2**
Nicoya, G. de *Costa Rica* 10°0N 85°0W **88 E3**
Nicoya, Pen. de *Costa Rica* 9°45N 85°40W **88 E2**
Nidd → *U.K.* 53°59N 1°23W **12 C6**
Niedersachsen □ *Germany* 52°50N 9°0E **16 B5**
Niekerkshoop *S. Africa* 29°19S 22°51E **56 C3**
Niemen = Nemunas →
Lithuania 55°25N 21°10E **9 J19**
Nienburg *Germany* 52°39N 9°13E **16 B5**
Nieu Bethesda *S. Africa* 31°51S 24°34E **56 D3**
Nieuw Amsterdam
Suriname 5°53N 55°5W **93 B7**
Nieuw Nickerie *Suriname* 6°0N 56°59W **93 B7**
Nieuwoudtville *S. Africa* 31°23S 19°7E **56 D2**
Nieuwpoort *Belgium* 51°8N 2°45E **15 C2**
Niğde *Turkey* 37°58N 34°40E **46 B2**
Nigel *S. Africa* 26°27S 28°25E **57 C4**
Niger ■ *W. Afr.* 17°30N 10°0E **52 E7**
Niger → *W. Afr.* 5°33N 6°33E **52 G7**
Nigeria ■ *W. Afr.* 8°30N 8°0E **52 G7**
Nighasin *India* 28°14N 80°52E **43 E9**
Nightcaps *N.Z.* 45°57S 168°2E **59 F2**
Nihoa *U.S.A.* 23°6N 161°58W **75 L7**
Nihon = Japan ■ *Asia* 36°0N 136°0E **29 G8**
Nii-Jima *Japan* 34°20N 139°15E **29 G9**
Niigata *Japan* 37°58N 139°0E **28 F9**
Niigata □ *Japan* 37°15N 138°45E **29 F9**
Niihama *Japan* 33°55N 133°16E **29 H6**
Ni'ihau *U.S.A.* 21°54N 160°9W **75 L7**
Niimi *Japan* 34°59N 133°28E **29 G6**
Niitsu *Japan* 37°48N 139°7E **28 F9**
Nijil *Jordan* 30°32N 35°33E **48 E4**
Nijkerk *Neths.* 52°13N 5°30E **15 B5**
Nijmegen *Neths.* 51°50N 5°52E **15 C5**
Nijverdal *Neths.* 52°22N 6°28E **15 B6**
Nīk Pey *Iran* 36°50N 48°10E **47 B6**
Nikaweratiya *Sri Lanka* 7°45N 80°7E **45 L5**
Nikel *Russia* 69°24N 30°13E **8 B24**
Nikiniki *Indonesia* 9°49S 124°30E **60 A3**
Nikkō *Japan* 36°45N 139°35E **29 F9**
Nikkō △ *Japan* 36°56N 139°37E **29 F9**
Nikolayev = Mykolayiv
Ukraine 46°58N 32°0E **19 E5**

Nikolayevsk *Russia* 50°0N 45°35E **19 E8**
Nikolayevsk-na-Amur
Russia 53°8N 140°44E **27 D15**
Nikolskoye *Russia* 55°12N 166°0E **27 D17**
Nikopol *Ukraine* 47°35N 34°25E **19 E5**
Nīkshahr *Iran* 26°15N 60°10E **47 E9**
Nikšić *Montenegro* 42°50N 18°57E **23 C8**
Nîl, Nahr en → *Africa* 30°10N 31°6E **53 B12**
Nîl el Abyad → *Sudan* 15°38N 32°31E **53 E12**
Nîl el Azraq → *Sudan* 15°38N 32°31E **53 E12**
Nila *Indonesia* 6°44S 129°31E **37 F7**
Nilakkottai *India* 10°10N 77°52E **45 J3**
Nilanga *India* 18°6N 76°46E **44 E3**
Nile = Nîl, Nahr en →
Africa 30°10N 31°6E **53 B12**
Niles *Mich., U.S.A.* 41°50N 86°15W **80 E10**
Niles *Ohio, U.S.A.* 41°11N 80°46W **82 E4**
Nileshwar *India* 12°15N 75°6E **45 H2**
Nilgiri Hills *India* 11°30N 76°30E **45 J3**
Nim Ka Thana *India* 27°44N 75°48E **42 F6**
Nimach *India* 24°30N 74°56E **42 G6**
Nimbahera *India* 24°37N 74°45E **42 G6**
Nîmes *France* 43°50N 4°23E **20 E6**
Nimfaíon, Ákra = Pines, Akra
Greece 40°5N 24°20E **23 D11**
Nimmitabel *Australia* 36°29S 149°15E **63 F4**
Nīnawā *Iraq* 36°25N 43°10E **46 B4**
Nīnawā □ *Iraq* 36°15N 43°0E **46 B4**
Nindigully *Australia* 28°21S 148°50E **63 D4**
Nine Degree Channel *India* 9°0N 73°0E **45 K1**
Ninepin Group *China* 22°16N 114°21E **31 a**
Nineveh = Nīnawā *Iraq* 36°25N 43°10E **46 B4**
Ning Xian *China* 35°30N 107°58E **32 G4**
Ningaloo Marine ⬡
Australia 22°23S 113°32E **60 D1**
Ning'an *China* 44°22N 129°20E **33 B15**
Ningbo *China* 29°51N 121°28E **35 C13**
Ningcheng *China* 41°32N 119°53E **33 D10**
Ningde *China* 26°38N 119°23E **35 D12**
Ningdu *China* 26°25N 115°59E **35 D10**
Ninggang *China* 26°42N 113°55E **35 D9**
Ningguo *China* 30°35N 119°0E **35 B12**
Ninghai *China* 29°15N 121°27E **35 C13**
Ninghua *China* 26°14N 116°45E **35 D11**
Ningjin *China* 37°35N 114°57E **32 F8**
Ningjing Shan *China* 31°0N 98°20E **34 C2**
Ninglang *China* 27°20N 100°55E **34 D3**
Ningling *China* 34°25N 115°22E **32 G8**
Ningming *China* 22°8N 107°4E **34 F6**
Ningnan *China* 27°5N 102°36E **34 D4**
Ningpo = Ningbo
China 29°51N 121°28E **35 C13**
Ningqiang *China* 32°47N 106°15E **32 H4**
Ningshan *China* 33°21N 108°21E **34 A7**
Ningsia Hui A.R. = Ningxia Huizu
Zizhiqu □ *China* 38°0N 106°0E **32 F4**
Ningwu *China* 39°0N 112°18E **32 E7**
Ningxia Huizu Zizhiqu □
China 38°0N 106°0E **32 F4**
Ningxiang *China* 28°15N 112°30E **35 C9**
Ningyang *China* 35°47N 116°45E **32 G9**
Ningyuan *China* 25°37N 111°57E **35 E8**
Ninh Binh *Vietnam* 20°15N 105°55E **34 G5**
Ninh Giang *Vietnam* 20°44N 106°24E **38 B6**
Ninh Hoa *Vietnam* 12°30N 109°7E **38 F7**
Ninh Ma *Vietnam* 12°48N 109°21E **38 F7**
Ninove *Belgium* 50°51N 4°2E **15 D4**
Nioaque *Brazil* 21°5S 55°50W **95 A4**
Niobrara *U.S.A.* 42°45N 98°2W **80 D4**
Niobrara → *U.S.A.* 42°46N 98°3W **80 D5**
Nioro du Sahel *Mali* 15°15N 9°30W **52 E4**
Niort *France* 46°19N 0°29W **20 C3**
Nipani *India* 16°20N 74°25E **45 F2**
Nipawin *Canada* 53°20N 104°0W **71 C8**
Nipigon *Canada* 49°0N 88°17W **72 C2**
Nipigon, L. *Canada* 49°50N 88°30W **72 C2**
Nipishish L. *Canada* 54°12N 60°45W **73 B7**
Nipissing, L. *Canada* 46°20N 80°0W **72 C4**
Nipomo *U.S.A.* 35°3N 120°29W **79 K6**
Nippon = Japan ■ *Asia* 36°0N 136°0E **29 G8**
Nipton *U.S.A.* 35°28N 115°16W **79 K11**
Niquelândia *Brazil* 14°33S 48°23W **93 F9**
Nīr *Iran* 38°2N 47°59E **46 B5**
Nira → *India* 17°58N 75°8E **44 F2**
Nirasaki *Japan* 35°42N 138°27E **29 G9**
Nirmal *India* 19°3N 78°20E **44 E4**
Nirmali *India* 26°20N 86°35E **43 F12**
Niš *Serbia* 43°19N 21°58E **23 C9**
Nisa *Turkmenistan* 37°59N 58°11E **47 B8**
Nişāb *Si. Arabia* 29°11N 44°43E **46 D5**
Nişāb *Yemen* 14°25N 46°29E **49 E4**
Nishino'omote *Japan* 30°43N 130°59E **29 J5**
Nishiwaki *Japan* 34°59N 134°58E **29 G7**
Niskibi → *Canada* 56°29N 88°9W **72 A2**
Nisqually → *U.S.A.* 47°7N 122°42W **78 C4**
Nissum Bredning *Denmark* 56°40N 8°20E **9 H13**
Nistru = Dnister →
Europe 46°18N 30°17E **17 E16**
Nisutlin → *Canada* 60°14N 132°34W **70 A2**
Nitchequon *Canada* 53°10N 70°58W **73 B5**
Nith → *Canada* 43°12N 80°23W **82 C4**
Nith → *U.K.* 55°14N 3°33W **11 F5**
Nitmiluk △ *Australia* 14°6S 132°15E **60 B5**
Nitra *Slovak Rep.* 48°19N 18°4E **17 D10**
Nitra → *Slovak Rep.* 47°46N 18°10E **17 E10**
Niue ☑ *Pac. Oc.* 19°2S 169°54W **65 J11**
Niulan Jiang → *China* 27°30N 103°5E **34 D5**
Niut *Indonesia* 0°55N 109°54E **36 D4**
Niutou Shan *China* 29°5N 121°59E **35 C13**
Niuzhuang *China* 40°58N 122°28E **33 D12**
Nivala *Finland* 63°56N 24°57E **8 E21**
Nivelles *Belgium* 50°35N 4°20E **15 D4**
Nivernais *France* 47°15N 3°30E **20 C5**
Niverville *Canada* 49°36N 97°3W **71 D9**
Niwas *India* 23°3N 80°26E **43 H9**
Nixa *U.S.A.* 37°3N 93°18W **80 G7**
Nixon *U.S.A.* 29°16N 97°46W **84 G6**
Nizam Sagar *India* 18°10N 77°58E **44 E3**

Nizamabad *India* 18°45N 78°7E **44 E4**
Nizamghat *India* 28°20N 95°45E **41 E19**
Nizhne Kolymsk
Russia 68°34N 160°55E **27 C17**
Nizhnekamsk *Russia* 55°38N 51°49E **18 C9**
Nizhneudinsk *Russia* 54°54N 99°3E **27 D10**
Nizhnevartovsk *Russia* 60°56N 76°38E **26 C8**
Nizhniy Bestyakh
Russia 61°57N 129°54E **27 C13**
Nizhniy Novgorod *Russia* 56°20N 44°0E **18 C7**
Nizhniy Tagil *Russia* 57°55N 59°57E **18 C10**
Nizhyn *Ukraine* 51°5N 31°55E **19 D5**
Nizip *Turkey* 37°5N 37°50E **46 B3**
Nízké Tatry *Slovak Rep.* 48°55N 19°30E **17 D10**
Nizwá *Oman* 22°56N 57°32E **49 C6**
Njazidja = Grande Comore
Comoros Is. 11°35S 43°20E **55 a**
Njombe *Tanzania* 9°20S 34°50E **54 F6**
Nkandla *S. Africa* 28°37S 31°5E **57 C5**
Nkawkaw *Ghana* 6°36N 0°49E **52 G5**
Nkhotakota *Malawi* 12°56S 34°15E **55 G6**
Nkongsamba *Cameroon* 4°55N 9°55E **54 D1**
Nkurenkuru *Namibia* 17°42S 18°32E **56 A2**
Nmai → *Burma* 25°30N 97°25E **34 F2**
Noakhali *Bangla.* 22°48N 91°10E **41 H17**
Nobel *Canada* 45°25N 80°6W **82 A4**
Nobeoka *Japan* 32°36N 131°41E **29 H5**
Noblesville *U.S.A.* 40°3N 86°1W **80 E10**
Noboribetsu *Japan* 42°24N 141°6E **28 C10**
Nocera Inferiore *Italy* 40°44N 14°38E **22 D6**
Nocona *U.S.A.* 33°47N 97°44W **84 E6**
Noda *Japan* 35°56N 139°52E **29 G9**
Nogales *Mexico* 31°19N 110°56W **86 A2**
Nogales *U.S.A.* 31°21N 110°56W **77 L8**
Nōgata *Japan* 33°48N 130°44E **29 H5**
Noggerup *Australia* 33°32S 116°5E **61 F2**
Noginsk *Russia* 64°30N 90°50E **27 C10**
Nogliki *Russia* 51°50N 143°10E **27 D15**
Nogoa → *Australia* 23°40S 147°55E **62 C4**
Nogoyá *Argentina* 32°24S 59°48W **94 C4**
Nohar *India* 29°11N 74°49E **42 E6**
Nohta *India* 23°40N 79°34E **43 H8**
Noires, Mts. *France* 48°11N 3°40W **20 B2**
Noirmoutier, Î. de *France* 46°58N 2°10W **20 C2**
Nojane *Botswana* 23°15S 20°14E **56 B3**
Nojima-Zaki *Japan* 34°54N 139°53E **29 G9**
Nok Kundi *Pakistan* 28°50N 62°45E **40 E3**
Nok Ta Phao, Ko *Thailand* 9°23N 99°40E **39 b**
Nokaneng *Botswana* 19°40S 22°17E **56 A3**
Nokia *Finland* 61°30N 23°30E **8 F20**
Nokomis *Canada* 51°35N 105°0W **71 C8**
Nokomis L. *Canada* 57°0N 103°0W **71 B8**
Nola *C.A.R.* 3°35N 16°4E **54 D3**
Noma Omuramba →
Namibia 18°52S 20°53E **56 A3**
Nombre de Dios *Panama* 9°34N 79°28W **88 E4**
Nome *U.S.A.* 64°30N 165°25W **74 C6**
Nomgon *Mongolia* 42°50N 105°8E **32 C3**
Nomo-Zaki *Japan* 32°35N 129°44E **29 H4**
Nomuka *Tonga* 20°17S 174°48W **59 c**
Nomuka Group *Tonga* 20°20S 174°48W **59 c**
Nonacho L. *Canada* 61°42N 109°40W **71 A7**
Nonda *Australia* 20°40S 142°28E **62 C3**
Nong Chang *Thailand* 15°23N 99°51E **38 E2**
Nong Han Res. *Thailand* 17°11N 104°9E **38 D5**
Nong Het *Laos* 19°29N 103°59E **38 C4**
Nong Khai *Thailand* 17°50N 102°46E **38 D4**
Nong'an *China* 44°25N 125°5E **33 B13**
Nongoma *S. Africa* 27°58S 31°35E **57 C5**
Nongsa *Indonesia* 1°11N 104°8E **39 d**
Nonoava *Mexico* 27°28N 106°44W **86 B3**
Nonsan *S. Korea* 36°12N 127°5E **33 F14**
Noonamah *Australia* 12°40S 131°4E **60 B5**
Noondie, L. *Australia* 28°30S 119°30E **61 E2**
Noonkanbah ⬡
Australia 18°30S 124°50E **60 C3**
Noord Brabant □ *Neths.* 51°40N 5°0E **15 C5**
Noord Holland □ *Neths.* 52°30N 4°45E **15 B4**
Noordbeveland *Neths.* 51°35N 3°50E **15 C3**
Noordoostpolder *Neths.* 52°45N 5°45E **15 B5**
Noordwijk *Neths.* 52°14N 4°26E **15 B4**
Noosa Heads *Australia* 26°25S 153°6E **63 D5**
Nootka I. *Canada* 49°32N 126°42W **70 D3**
Nopiming △ *Canada* 50°30N 95°37W **71 C9**
Noralee *Canada* 53°59N 126°26W **70 C3**
Noranda = Rouyn-Noranda
Canada 48°20N 79°0W **72 C4**
Norco *U.S.A.* 33°56N 117°33W **79 M9**
Nord-Ostsee-Kanal
Germany 54°12N 9°32E **16 A5**
Nordaustlandet *Svalbard* 79°14N 23°0E **4 B9**
Nordegg *Canada* 52°29N 116°5W **70 C5**
Norderney *Germany* 53°42N 7°9E **16 B4**
Norderstedt *Germany* 53°42N 10°1E **16 B5**
Nordfjord *Norway* 61°55N 5°30E **8 F11**
Nordfriesische Inseln
Germany 54°40N 8°20E **16 A5**
Nordhausen *Germany* 51°30N 10°47E **16 C6**
Norðoyar *Færoe Is.* 62°17N 6°35W **8 E9**
Nordkapp *Norway* 71°10N 25°50E **8 A21**
Nordkinnhalvøya
Norway 70°55N 27°40E **8 A22**
Nordrhein-Westfalen □
Germany 51°45N 7°30E **16 C4**
Nordvik *Russia* 74°2N 111°32E **27 B12**
Nore → *Ireland* 52°25N 6°58W **10 D4**
Noreland *Canada* 44°43N 78°48W **82 B6**
Norfolk = Simcoe
Canada 42°50N 80°23W **82 D4**
Norfolk *N.Y., U.S.A.* 44°48N 74°59W **83 B10**
Norfolk *Nebr., U.S.A.* 42°2N 97°25W **80 D5**
Norfolk *Va., U.S.A.* 36°50N 76°17W **81 G15**
Norfolk □ *U.K.* 52°39N 0°54E **13 E8**
Norfolk Broads △ *U.K.* 52°45N 1°30E **13 E9**
Norfolk I. *Pac. Oc.* 28°58S 168°3E **58 D9**
Norfolk Ridge *Pac. Oc.* 29°0S 168°0E **64 K8**
Norfork L. *U.S.A.* 36°15N 92°14W **84 C8**

North Olmsted *U.S.A.* 41°25N 81°56W **82 E3**
North Ossetia □ *Russia* 43°30N 44°30E **19 F7**
North Pagai, I. = Pagai Utara,
Pulau *Indonesia* 2°35S 100°0E **36 E2**
North Palisade *U.S.A.* 37°6N 118°31W **78 H8**
North Platte *U.S.A.* 41°8N 100°46W **80 E3**
North Platte → *U.S.A.* 41°7N 100°42W **80 E3**
North Pole *Arctic* 90°0N 0°0 **4 A**
North Portal *Canada* 49°0N 102°33W **71 D8**
North Powder *U.S.A.* 45°2N 117°55W **76 D5**
North Pt. *Barbados* 13°20N 59°37W **89 g**
North Pt. *Trin. & Tob.* 11°21N 60°31W **93 J16**
North Pt. *U.S.A.* 45°2N 83°16W **82 A1**
North Reef I. *India* 13°15N 92°43E **45 H11**
North Rhine Westphalia =
Nordrhein-Westfalen □
Germany 51°45N 7°30E **16 C4**
North River *Canada* 53°49N 57°6W **73 B8**
North Ronaldsay *U.K.* 59°22N 2°26W **11 B6**
North Saskatchewan →
Canada 53°15N 105°5W **71 C7**
North Sea *Europe* 56°0N 4°0E **6 D6**
North Seal → *Canada* 58°50N 98°7W **71 B9**
North Sentinel I. *India* 11°33N 92°15E **45 J11**
North Slope ☆ *U.S.A.* 69°15N 152°0W **74 B9**
North Somerset □ *U.K.* 51°24N 2°45W **13 F5**
North Sydney *Canada* 46°12N 60°15W **73 C7**
North Syracuse *U.S.A.* 43°8N 76°7W **83 C8**
North Taranaki Bight
N.Z. 38°50S 174°15E **59 C5**
North Thompson →
Canada 50°40N 120°20W **70 C4**
North Tonawanda *U.S.A.* 43°2N 78°53W **82 C6**
North Troy *U.S.A.* 45°0N 72°24W **83 B12**
North Twin I. *Canada* 53°20N 80°0W **72 B4**
North Tyne → *U.K.* 55°0N 2°8W **12 B5**
North Uist *U.K.* 57°40N 7°15W **11 D1**
North Vancouver *Canada* 49°19N 123°4W **78 A3**
North Vernon *U.S.A.* 39°0N 85°38W **81 F11**
North Wabasca L.
Canada 56°0N 113°55W **70 B6**
North Walsham *U.K.* 52°50N 1°22E **12 E9**
North West = Severo-Zapadnyy □
Russia 65°0N 40°0E **26 C4**
North West □ *Botswana* 19°0S 22°30E **56 A3**
North-West □ *S. Africa* 27°0S 25°0E **56 D4**
North West C. *Australia* 21°45S 114°9E **60 D1**
North West Christmas I. Ridge
Pac. Oc. 6°30N 165°0W **65 F11**
North West Frontier = Khyber
Pakhtunkhwa □
Pakistan 34°0N 72°0E **42 C4**
North West Highlands
U.K. 57°33N 4°58W **11 D4**
North West River *Canada* 53°30N 60°10W **73 B7**
North Wildwood *U.S.A.* 39°0N 74°48W **81 F16**
North York Moors *U.K.* 54°23N 0°53W **12 C7**
North York Moors △
U.K. 54°27N 0°51W **12 C7**
North Yorkshire □ *U.K.* 54°15N 1°25W **12 C6**
Northam *Australia* 31°35S 116°42E **61 F2**
Northam *S. Africa* 24°56S 27°18E **56 B4**
Northampton *Australia* 28°27S 114°33E **61 E1**
Northampton *U.K.* 52°15N 0°53W **13 E7**
Northampton *Mass.,
U.S.A.* 42°19N 72°38W **83 D12**
Northampton *Pa., U.S.A.* 40°41N 75°30W **83 F9**
Northamptonshire □
U.K. 52°16N 0°55W **13 E7**
Northbridge *U.S.A.* 42°9N 71°39W **83 D13**
Northbrook *Canada* 44°44N 77°9W **82 B7**
Northcliffe *Australia* 34°39S 116°7E **61 F2**
Northeast Pacific Basin
Pac. Oc. 32°0N 145°0W **65 D13**
Northeast Providence Channel
W. Indies 26°0N 76°0W **88 A4**
Northern = Limpopo □
S. Africa 24°5S 29°0E **57 B4**
Northern Areas = Gilgit-
Baltistan □ *Pakistan* 36°30N 73°0E **43 A5**
Northern Circars *India* 17°30N 82°30E **44 F5**
Northern Indian L.
Canada 57°20N 97°20W **71 B9**
Northern Ireland □ *U.K.* 54°45N 7°0W **10 B5**
Northern Lau Group *Fiji* 17°30S 178°59W **59 a**
Northern Light L. *Canada* 48°15N 90°39W **72 C1**
Northern Marianas ☑
Pac. Oc. 17°0N 145°0E **64 F6**
Northern Province □
S. Africa 24°0S 29°0E **57 B4**
Northern Range
Trin. & Tob. 10°46N 61°15W **93 K15**
Northern Sporades
Greece 39°15N 23°30E **23 E10**
Northern Territory □
Australia 20°0S 133°0E **60 D5**
Northfield *Minn., U.S.A.* 44°27N 93°9W **80 C7**
Northfield *Vt., U.S.A.* 44°9N 72°40W **83 B12**
Northgate *Canada* 49°0N 102°16W **71 D8**
Northland □ *N.Z.* 35°30S 173°30E **59 A4**
Northome *U.S.A.* 47°52N 94°17W **80 B6**
Northport *Ala., U.S.A.* 33°14N 87°35W **85 E11**
Northport *Wash., U.S.A.* 48°55N 117°48W **76 B5**
Northumberland □ *U.K.* 55°12N 2°0W **12 B6**
Northumberland, C.
Australia 38°5S 140°40E **63 F3**
Northumberland Is.
Australia 21°30S 149°50E **62 C4**
Northumberland Str.
Canada 46°20N 64°0W **73 C7**
Northville *Canada* 43°10N 80°25W **82 C3**
Northville *U.S.A.* 43°13N 74°11W **83 C10**
Northwest Pacific Basin
Pac. Oc. 32°0N 165°0E **64 D8**
Northwest Providence Channel
W. Indies 26°0N 78°0W **88 A4**
Northwest Territories □
Canada 63°0N 118°0W **68 E8**

Northwich *U.K.* 53°15N 2°31W **12 D5**
Northwood *Iowa, U.S.A.* 43°27N 93°13W **80 D7**
Northwood *N. Dak.,*
  U.S.A. 47°44N 97°34W **80 B5**
Norton *U.S.A.* 39°50N 99°53W **80 F4**
Norton Sd. *U.S.A.* 63°50N 164°0W **74 C7**
Norwalk *Calif., U.S.A.* 33°54N 118°4W **79 M8**
Norwalk *Conn., U.S.A.* 41°7N 73°22W **83 E11**
Norwalk *Iowa, U.S.A.* 41°29N 93°41W **80 E7**
Norwalk *Ohio, U.S.A.* 41°15N 82°37W **82 E2**
Norway *Maine, U.S.A.* 44°13N 70°32W **81 C18**
Norway *Mich., U.S.A.* 45°47N 87°55W **80 C2**
Norway ■ *Europe* 63°0N 11°0E **8 E14**
Norway House *Canada* 53°59N 97°50W **71 C9**
Norwegian B. *Canada* 77°30N 90°0W **69 B14**
Norwegian Basin *Atl. Oc.* 68°0N 2°0W **4 C7**
Norwegian Sea *Atl. Oc.* 66°0N 1°0E **6 B6**
Norwich *Canada* 42°59N 80°36W **82 D4**
Norwich *U.K.* 52°38N 1°18E **13 E9**
Norwich *Conn., U.S.A.* 41°31N 72°5W **83 E12**
Norwich *N.Y., U.S.A.* 42°32N 75°32W **83 D9**
Norwood *Canada* 44°23N 77°59W **82 B7**
Norwood *U.S.A.* 44°45N 75°0W **83 D10**
Nosappu-Misaki *Japan* 45°26N 141°39E **28 C12**
Noshiro *Japan* 40°12N 140°0E **28 D10**
Noşratābād *Iran* 29°55N 60°0E **47 D8**
Noss Hd. *U.K.* 58°28N 3°3W **11 C5**
Nossob → *S. Africa* 26°55S 20°45E **56 C3**
Nosy Varika *Madag.* 20°35S 48°32E **55 J9**
Noteć → *Poland* 52°44N 15°26E **16 B8**
Notikewin → *Canada* 57°2N 117°38W **70 B5**
Noto-Hantō *Japan* 37°15N 136°40E **29 F8**
Notodden *Norway* 59°35N 9°17E **9 G13**
Notre Dame B. *Canada* 49°45N 55°30W **73 C8**
Notre-Dame-de-Koartac =
  Quaqtaq *Canada* 60°55N 69°40W **69 E18**
Notre-Dame-des-Bois
  Canada 45°24N 71°4W **83 A13**
Notre-Dame-d'Ivugivic = Ivujivik
  Canada 62°24N 77°55W **69 E16**
Notre-Dame-du-Nord
  Canada 47°36N 79°30W **72 C4**
Nottawasaga B. *Canada* 44°35N 80°15W **82 B4**
Nottaway → *Canada* 51°22N 78°55W **72 B4**
Nottingham *U.K.* 52°58N 1°10W **12 E6**
Nottingham, City of □
  U.K. 52°58N 1°10W **12 E6**
Nottingham I. *Canada* 63°20N 77°55W **69 E16**
Nottinghamshire □ *U.K.* 53°10N 1°3W **12 D6**
Nottoway → *U.S.A.* 36°33N 76°55W **81 G15**
Notwane → *Botswana* 23°35S 26°58E **56 B4**
Nouâdhibou *Mauritania* 20°54N 17°0W **52 D2**
Nouâdhibou, Râs
  Mauritania 20°50N 17°0W **52 D2**
Nouakchott *Mauritania* 18°9N 15°58W **52 E2**
Nouméa *N. Cal.* 22°17S 166°30E **58 D9**
Noupoort *S. Africa* 31°10S 24°57E **56 D3**
Nouveau Comptoir = Wemindji
  Canada 53°0N 78°49W **72 B4**
Nouvelle Amsterdam, Î.
  Ind. Oc. 38°30S 77°30E **3 F13**
Nouvelle-Calédonie = New
  Caledonia □ *Pac. Oc.* 21°0S 165°0E **58 D9**
Nova Esperança *Brazil* 23°8S 52°24W **95 A5**
Nova Friburgo *Brazil* 22°16S 42°30W **95 A7**
Nova Iguaçu *Brazil* 22°45S 43°28W **95 A7**
Nova Iorque *Brazil* 7°0S 44°5W **93 E10**
Nova Lamego
  Guinea-Biss. 12°19N 14°11W **52 F3**
Nova Mambone *Mozam.* 21°0S 35°3E **57 B6**
Nova Scotia □ *Canada* 45°10N 63°0W **73 C7**
Nova Sofala *Mozam.* 20°7S 34°42E **57 B5**
Nova Venécia *Brazil* 18°45S 40°24W **93 G10**
Nova Zagora *Bulgaria* 42°32N 26°1E **23 C11**
Novar *Canada* 45°27N 79°15W **82 A5**
Novato *U.S.A.* 38°6N 122°35W **78 G4**
Novaya Ladoga *Russia* 60°7N 32°16E **18 B5**
Novaya Lyalya *Russia* 59°4N 60°45E **18 C11**
Novaya Sibir, Ostrov
  Russia 75°10N 150°0E **27 B16**
Novaya Zemlya *Russia* 75°0N 56°0E **26 B6**
Nové Zámky *Slovak Rep.* 48°2N 18°8E **17 D10**
Novgorod = Velikiy Novgorod
  Russia 58°30N 31°25E **18 C5**
Novgorod-Severskiy = Novhorod-
  Siverskyy *Ukraine* 52°2N 33°10E **18 D5**
Novhorod-Siverskyy
  Ukraine 52°2N 33°10E **18 D5**
Novi Lígure *Italy* 44°46N 8°47E **20 D8**
Novi Pazar *Serbia* 43°12N 20°28E **23 C9**
Novi Sad *Serbia* 45°18N 19°52E **23 B8**
Novo Hamburgo *Brazil* 29°37S 51°7W **95 B5**
Novo Mesto *Slovenia* 45°47N 15°12E **22 B6**
Novoaltaysk *Russia* 53°30N 84°0E **26 D9**
Novocherkassk *Russia* 47°27N 40°15E **19 E7**
Novodvinsk *Russia* 55°0N 83°0W **82 E2**
Novogrudok = Navahrudak
  Belarus 53°40N 25°50E **17 B13**
Novohrad-Volynskyy
  Ukraine 50°34N 27°35E **17 C14**
Novokachalinsk *Russia* 45°5N 132°0E **28 B6**
Novokuybyshevsk *Russia* 53°7N 49°58E **18 D8**
Novokuznetsk *Russia* 53°45N 87°10E **26 D9**
Novolazarevskaya *Antarctica* 71°0S 12°0E **5 D3**
Novomoskovsk *Russia* 54°5N 38°15E **18 D6**
Novorossiysk *Russia* 44°43N 37°46E **19 F6**
Novorybnoye *Russia* 72°50N 105°50E **27 B11**
Novoselytsya *Ukraine* 48°14N 26°15E **17 D14**
Novoshakhtinsk *Russia* 47°46N 39°58E **19 E6**
Novosibirsk *Russia* 55°0N 83°5E **26 D9**
Novosibirskiye Ostrova
  Russia 75°0N 142°0E **27 B15**
Novotroitsk *Russia* 51°10N 58°15E **18 D10**
Novouzensk *Russia* 50°32N 48°17E **19 D8**
Novovolynsk *Russia* 50°45N 24°4E **17 C13**
Novska *Croatia* 45°19N 17°0E **22 B7**
Novyy Bor *Russia* 66°43N 52°19E **18 A9**
Novyy Port *Russia* 67°40N 72°30E **26 C8**

Novyy Urengoy *Russia* 65°48N 76°52E **26 C8**
Nowa Sól *Poland* 51°48N 15°44E **16 C8**
Nowata *U.S.A.* 36°42N 95°38W **84 C7**
Nowbarān *Iran* 35°8N 49°42E **47 C6**
Nowghāb *Iran* 33°53N 59°4E **47 C8**
Nowgong = Nagaon
  India 26°20N 92°50E **41 F18**
Nowgong *India* 25°4N 79°27E **43 G8**
Nowra *Australia* 34°53S 150°35E **63 E5**
Nowrangapur *India* 19°14N 82°33E **44 E6**
Nowshera *Pakistan* 34°0N 72°0E **40 C8**
Nowy Sącz *Poland* 49°40N 20°41E **17 D11**
Nowy Targ *Poland* 49°29N 20°2E **17 D11**
Nowy Tomyśl *Poland* 52°19N 16°10E **16 B9**
Noxen *U.S.A.* 41°25N 76°4W **83 E8**
Noyabr'sk *Russia* 64°34N 76°21E **26 C8**
Noyon *France* 49°34N 2°59E **20 B5**
Noyon *Mongolia* 43°2N 102°4E **32 C2**
Nqutu *S. Africa* 28°13S 30°32E **57 C5**
Nsanje *Malawi* 16°55S 35°12E **55 H7**
Nsawam *Ghana* 5°50N 0°24W **52 G5**
Ntaria ⌖ *Australia* 24°0S 132°41E **60 D5**
Nu Jiang → *China* 29°58N 97°25E **34 E2**
Nu Shan *China* 26°0N 99°20E **34 E2**
Nuba Mts. = Nubah, Jibalan
  Sudan 12°0N 31°0E **53 F12**
Nubah, Jibalan *Sudan* 12°0N 31°0E **53 F12**
Nubia *Africa* 21°0N 32°0E **50 D7**
Nubian Desert = Nûbîya, Es Sahrâ
  en *Sudan* 21°30N 33°30E **53 D12**
Nûbîya, Es Sahrâ en
  Sudan 21°30N 33°30E **53 D12**
Nuboai *Indonesia* 2°10S 136°30E **37 E9**
Nubra → *India* 34°35N 77°35E **43 B7**
Nueces → *U.S.A.* 27°51N 97°30W **84 H6**
Nueltin L. *Canada* 60°30N 99°30W **71 A9**
Nuestra Señora del Rosario de
  Caá-Cati *Argentina* 27°45S 57°36W **94 B4**
Nueva Ciudad Guerrero
  Mexico 26°34N 99°12W **87 B5**
Nueva Gerona *Cuba* 21°53N 82°49W **88 B3**
Nueva Palmira *Uruguay* 33°52S 58°20W **94 C4**
Nueva Rosita *Mexico* 27°57N 101°13W **86 B4**
Nueva San Salvador
  El Salv. 13°40N 89°18W **88 D2**
Nuéve de Julio *Argentina* 35°30S 61°0W **94 D3**
Nuevitas *Cuba* 21°30N 77°20W **88 B4**
Nuevo, G. *Argentina* 43°0S 64°30W **96 E4**
Nuevo Casas Grandes
  Mexico 30°25N 107°55W **86 A3**
Nuevo Laredo *Mexico* 27°30N 99°31W **87 B5**
Nuevo León □ *Mexico* 25°20N 100°0W **86 C5**
Nuevo Rocafuerte
  Ecuador 0°55S 75°27W **92 D3**
Nugget Pt. *N.Z.* 46°27S 169°50E **59 G2**
Nuhaka *N.Z.* 39°3S 177°45E **59 C6**
Nukey Bluff *Australia* 32°26S 135°29E **63 E2**
Nukhayb *Iraq* 32°4N 42°3E **46 C4**
Nuku Hiva
  French Polynesia 8°54S 140°6W **65 H13**
Nuku'alofa *Tonga* 21°10S 175°12W **59 c**
Nukus *Uzbekistan* 42°27N 59°41E **26 E6**
Nulato *U.S.A.* 64°43N 158°6W **74 C8**
Nullagine *Australia* 21°53S 120°7E **60 D3**
Nullagine → *Australia* 21°20S 120°20E **60 D3**
Nullarbor *Australia* 31°28S 130°55E **61 F5**
Nullarbor △ *Australia* 32°39S 130°0E **61 F5**
Nullarbor Plain *Australia* 31°10S 129°0E **61 F4**
Numalla, L. *Australia* 28°43S 144°20E **63 D3**
Numan *Nigeria* 9°29N 12°3E **53 G8**
Numata *Japan* 36°45N 139°4E **29 F9**
Numaykoos Lake △
  Canada 57°52N 95°58W **71 B9**
Numazu *Japan* 35°7N 138°51E **29 G9**
Numbulwar *Australia* 14°15S 135°45E **62 A2**
Numfoor *Indonesia* 1°0S 134°50E **37 E8**
Numurkah *Australia* 36°5S 145°26E **63 F4**
Nunaksaluk I. *Canada* 55°49N 60°20W **73 A7**
Nunap Isua *Greenland* 59°48N 43°55W **66 D15**
Nunavik *Greenland* 71°50N 54°55W **69 C21**
Nunavut □ *Canada* 66°0N 85°0W **69 C15**
Nunda *U.S.A.* 42°35N 77°56W **82 D7**
Nuneaton *U.K.* 52°32N 1°27W **13 E6**
Nungarin *Australia* 31°12S 118°6E **61 F2**
Nunivak I. *U.S.A.* 60°10N 166°30W **74 C6**
Nunkun *India* 33°57N 76°2E **43 C7**
Núoro *Italy* 40°20N 9°20E **22 D3**
Nuozhadu Dam *China* 22°39N 100°25E **34 F3**
Nūr *Iran* 36°33N 52°1E **47 B7**
Nūrābād *Hormozgān, Iran* 27°47N 57°12E **47 E8**
Nūrābād *Lorestān, Iran* 34°4N 47°58E **46 C5**
Nuremberg = Nürnberg
  Germany 49°27N 11°3E **16 D6**
Nuri *Mexico* 28°5N 109°22W **86 B3**
Nuriootpa *Australia* 34°27S 139°0E **63 E2**
Nuristān □ *Afghan.* 35°20N 71°0E **40 B7**
Nurmes *Finland* 63°33N 29°10E **8 E23**
Nürnberg *Germany* 49°27N 11°3E **16 D6**
Nurpur *Pakistan* 31°53N 71°54E **42 D4**
Nurran, L. = Terewah, L.
  Australia 29°52S 147°35E **63 D4**
Nurrari Lakes *Australia* 29°1S 130°5E **61 E5**
Nusa Dua *Indonesia* 8°48S 115°14E **37 K18**
Nusa Tenggara Barat □
  Indonesia 8°50S 117°30E **36 F5**
Nusa Tenggara Timur □
  Indonesia 9°30S 122°0E **37 F6**
Nusaybin *Turkey* 37°3N 41°10E **19 G7**
Nuşeirat *Gaza Strip* 31°27N 34°24E **48 D3**
Nushki *Pakistan* 29°35N 66°0E **42 E2**
Nuuk *Greenland* 64°10N 51°35W **67 C14**
Nuupere, Pte. *Moorea* 17°36S 149°47W **59 d**
Nuwakot *Nepal* 28°10N 83°55E **43 E10**
Nuwara Eliya *Sri Lanka* 6°58N 80°48E **45 L5**
Nuwaybi', W. an →
  Si. Arabia 29°18N 34°57E **48 F3**
Nuweiba' *Egypt* 28°59N 34°39E **46 D2**
Nuwerus *S. Africa* 31°8S 18°24E **56 D2**
Nuweveldberge *S. Africa* 32°10S 21°45E **56 D3**

Nuyts, Pt. *Australia* 35°4S 116°38E **61 G2**
Nuyts Arch. *Australia* 32°35S 133°20E **63 E1**
Nxai Pan △ *Botswana* 19°50S 24°46E **56 A3**
Nxaunxau *Botswana* 18°57S 21°4E **56 A3**
Nyabing *Australia* 33°33S 118°9E **61 F2**
Nyack *U.S.A.* 41°5N 73°55W **83 E11**
Nyagan *Russia* 62°30N 65°38E **26 C7**
Nyahururu *Kenya* 0°2N 36°27E **54 D7**
Nyainqêntanglha Shan
  China 30°0N 90°0E **30 F7**
Nyâlâ *Sudan* 12°2N 24°58E **53 F10**
Nyalam *China* 28°32N 86°4E **30 F6**
Nyandoma *Russia* 61°40N 40°12E **18 B7**
Nyangana *Namibia* 18°0S 20°40E **56 A3**
Nyasa, L. = Malawi, L.
  Africa 12°30S 34°30E **55 G6**
Nyasvizh *Belarus* 53°14N 26°38E **17 B14**
Nyaungdon = Yandoon
  Burma 17°0N 95°40E **41 L19**
Nyazepetrovsk *Russia* 56°3N 59°36E **18 C10**
Nybro *Sweden* 56°44N 15°55E **9 H16**
Nyda *Russia* 66°40N 72°58E **26 C8**
Nyeboe Land *Greenland* 82°0N 57°0W **69 A20**
Nyingchi *China* 29°32N 94°25E **30 F7**
Nyíregyháza *Hungary* 47°58N 21°47E **17 E11**
Nykarleby = Uusikaarlepyy
  Finland 63°32N 22°31E **8 E20**
Nykøbing *Nordjylland,*
  Denmark 56°48N 8°51E **9 H13**
Nykøbing *Sjælland,*
  Denmark 54°56N 11°52E **9 J14**
Nykøbing *Sjælland,*
  Denmark 55°55N 11°40E **9 J14**
Nyköping *Sweden* 58°45N 17°1E **9 G17**
Nylstroom = Modimolle
  S. Africa 24°42S 28°22E **57 B4**
Nymagee *Australia* 32°7S 146°20E **63 E4**
Nymboida △ *Australia* 29°38S 152°20E **63 D5**
Nynäshamn *Sweden* 58°54N 17°57E **9 G17**
Nyngan *Australia* 31°30S 147°8E **63 E4**
Nyoma Rap *India* 33°10N 78°40E **43 C8**
Nyoman = Nemunas →
  Lithuania 55°25N 21°10E **9 J19**
Nysa *Poland* 50°30N 17°22E **17 C9**
Nysa → *Europe* 52°4N 14°46E **16 B8**
Nyslott = Savonlinna
  Finland 61°52N 28°53E **8 F23**
Nyssa *U.S.A.* 43°53N 117°0W **76 E5**
Nystad = Uusikaupunki
  Finland 60°47N 21°25E **8 F19**
Nyunzu
  Dem. Rep. of the Congo 5°57S 27°58E **54 F5**
Nyurba *Russia* 63°17N 118°28E **27 C12**
Nzega *Tanzania* 4°10S 33°12E **54 E6**
Nzérékoré *Guinea* 7°49N 8°48W **52 G4**
Nzeto *Angola* 7°10S 12°52E **54 F2**
Nzwani = Anjouan
  Comoros Is. 12°15S 44°20E **55 a**

O

O Le Pupū Pu'e △ *Samoa* 13°59S 171°43W **59 b**
Ō-Shima *Hokkaidō, Japan* 41°30N 139°22E **28 D9**
Ō-Shima *Shizuoka, Japan* 34°44N 139°24E **29 G9**
Oa, Mull of *U.K.* 55°35N 6°20W **11 F2**
Oacoma *U.S.A.* 43°48N 99°24W **80 D4**
Oahe, L. *U.S.A.* 44°27N 100°24W **80 C3**
Oahe Dam *U.S.A.* 44°27N 100°24W **80 C3**
O'ahu *U.S.A.* 21°28N 157°58W **75 L8**
Oak Harbor *U.S.A.* 48°18N 122°39W **78 B4**
Oak Hill *U.S.A.* 37°59N 81°9W **81 G13**
Oak Island *U.S.A.* 33°55N 78°10W **85 E15**
Oak Ridge *U.S.A.* 36°1N 84°16W **85 C12**
Oak View *U.S.A.* 34°24N 119°18W **79 L7**
Oakan-Dake *Japan* 43°27N 144°10E **28 C12**
Oakdale *Calif., U.S.A.* 37°46N 120°51W **78 H6**
Oakdale *La., U.S.A.* 30°49N 92°40W **84 F8**
Oakes *U.S.A.* 46°8N 98°6W **80 B4**
Oakesdale *U.S.A.* 47°8N 117°15W **76 C5**
Oakey *Australia* 27°25S 151°43E **63 D5**
Oakfield *U.S.A.* 43°4N 78°16W **82 C6**
Oakham *U.K.* 52°40N 0°43W **13 E7**
Oakhurst *U.S.A.* 37°19N 119°40W **78 H7**
Oakland *U.S.A.* 41°57N 75°36W **83 E9**
Oakley *Idaho, U.S.A.* 42°15N 113°53W **76 E7**
Oakley *Kans., U.S.A.* 39°8N 100°51W **80 F4**
Oakover → *Australia* 21°0S 120°40E **60 D3**
Oakridge *U.S.A.* 43°45N 122°28W **76 E2**
Oakville *Canada* 43°27N 79°41W **82 C5**
Oakville *U.S.A.* 46°51N 123°14W **78 D3**
Oamaru *N.Z.* 45°5S 170°59E **59 F3**
Oasis *Calif., U.S.A.* 37°29N 117°55W **78 H9**
Oasis *Calif., U.S.A.* 33°28N 116°6W **79 M10**
Oates Land *Antarctica* 69°0S 160°0E **5 C11**
Oatman *U.S.A.* 35°1N 114°19W **79 K12**
Oaxaca *Mexico* 17°3N 96°43W **87 D5**
Oaxaca □ *Mexico* 17°0N 96°30W **87 D5**
Ob → *Russia* 66°45N 69°30E **26 C7**
Oba *Canada* 49°4N 84°7W **72 C3**
Obama *Japan* 35°30N 135°45E **29 G7**
Oban *U.K.* 56°25N 5°29W **11 E3**
Obbia = Hobyo *Somalia* 5°25N 48°30E **49 F4**
Oberá *Argentina* 27°21S 55°2W **95 B4**
Oberhausen *Germany* 51°28N 6°51E **16 C4**
Oberlin *Kans., U.S.A.* 39°49N 100°32W **80 F3**
Oberlin *La., U.S.A.* 30°37N 92°46W **84 F8**
Oberlin *Ohio, U.S.A.* 41°18N 82°13W **82 E2**
Oberon *Australia* 33°45S 149°52E **63 E4**
Obi, Kepulauan *Indonesia* 1°23S 127°45E **37 E7**
Óbidos *Brazil* 1°50S 55°30W **93 D7**
Obihiro *Japan* 42°56N 143°12E **28 C11**
Obilatu *Indonesia* 1°25S 127°20E **37 E7**
Obluchye *Russia* 49°1N 131°4E **27 E14**
Obo *C.A.R.* 5°20N 26°32E **54 C5**
Oboyan *Russia* 51°15N 36°21E **26 D4**
Obozerskaya = Obozerskiy
  Russia 63°34N 40°21E **18 B7**
Obozerskiy *Russia* 63°34N 40°21E **18 B7**
Observatory Inlet
  Canada 55°10N 129°54W **70 B3**

Obshchi Syrt *Russia* 52°0N 53°0E **6 E16**
Obskaya Guba *Russia* 69°0N 73°0E **26 C8**
Obuasi *Ghana* 6°17N 1°40W **52 G5**
Ocala *U.S.A.* 29°11N 82°8W **85 G13**
Ocampo *Chihuahua,*
  Mexico 28°11N 108°23W **86 B3**
Ocampo *Tamaulipas,*
  Mexico 22°50N 99°20W **87 C5**
Ocaña *Spain* 39°55N 3°30W **21 C4**
Occidental, Cordillera
  Colombia 5°0N 76°0W **92 C3**
Occidental, Grand Erg
  Algeria 30°20N 1°0E **52 B6**
Ocean City *Md., U.S.A.* 38°20N 75°5W **81 F16**
Ocean City *N.J., U.S.A.* 39°17N 74°35W **81 F16**
Ocean City *Wash., U.S.A.* 47°4N 124°10W **78 C2**
Ocean Falls *Canada* 52°18N 127°48W **70 C3**
Ocean I. = Banaba
  Kiribati 0°45S 169°50E **64 H8**
Ocean Park *U.S.A.* 46°30N 124°3W **78 D2**
Oceano *U.S.A.* 35°6N 120°37W **79 K6**
Oceanport *U.S.A.* 40°19N 74°3W **83 F10**
Oceanside *U.S.A.* 33°12N 117°23W **79 M9**
Ochil Hills *U.K.* 56°14N 3°40W **11 E5**
Ocho Rios *Jamaica* 18°24N 77°6W **88 a**
Ocilla *U.S.A.* 31°36N 83°15W **85 F13**
Ocmulgee → *U.S.A.* 31°58N 82°33W **85 F13**
Ocnița *Moldova* 48°25N 27°30E **17 D14**
Oconee → *U.S.A.* 31°58N 82°33W **85 F13**
Oconomowoc *U.S.A.* 43°7N 88°30W **80 D9**
Oconto *U.S.A.* 44°53N 87°52W **80 C10**
Oconto Falls *U.S.A.* 44°52N 88°9W **80 C9**
Ocosingo *Mexico* 16°53N 92°6W **87 D6**
Ocotal *Nic.* 13°41N 86°31W **88 D2**
Ocotlán *Jalisco, Mexico* 20°21N 102°46W **86 C4**
Ocotlán *Oaxaca, Mexico* 16°48N 96°40W **87 D5**
Ōda *Japan* 35°11N 132°30E **29 G6**
Ódáðahraun *Iceland* 65°5N 17°0W **8 D5**
Ōdaejin *N. Korea* 41°34N 129°40E **28 D4**
Odate *Japan* 40°16N 140°34E **28 D10**
Odawara *Japan* 35°20N 139°6E **29 G9**
Odda *Norway* 60°3N 6°35E **9 F12**
Odei → *Canada* 56°6N 96°54W **71 B9**
Ödemiş *Turkey* 38°15N 28°0E **23 E13**
Odendaalsrus *S. Africa* 27°48S 26°45E **56 C4**
Odense *Denmark* 55°22N 10°23E **9 J14**
Oder → *Europe* 53°33N 14°38E **16 B8**
Odesa *Ukraine* 46°30N 30°45E **19 E5**
Odessa = Odesa *Ukraine* 46°30N 30°45E **19 E5**
Odessa *Canada* 44°17N 76°43W **83 B8**
Odessa *Tex., U.S.A.* 31°52N 102°23W **84 F3**
Odessa *Wash., U.S.A.* 47°20N 118°41W **76 C4**
Odiakwe *Botswana* 20°12S 25°17E **56 B4**
Odienné *Ivory C.* 9°30N 7°34W **52 G4**
Odintsovo *Russia* 55°40N 37°16E **18 C6**
Odisha □ *India* 20°0N 84°0E **44 E7**
O'Donnell *U.S.A.* 32°58N 101°50W **84 E4**
O'Donnell Pt. *Canada* 45°5N 80°5W **82 A4**
Odorheiu Secuiesc
  Romania 46°21N 25°21E **17 E13**
Odra = Oder → *Europe* 53°33N 14°38E **16 B8**
Odzi *Zimbabwe* 19°0S 32°20E **57 B5**
Odzi → *Zimbabwe* 19°45S 32°23E **57 A5**
Oecussi = Pante Macassar
  E. Timor 9°30S 123°58E **37 F6**
Oeiras *Brazil* 7°0S 42°8W **93 E10**
Oelrichs *U.S.A.* 43°11N 103°14W **80 D2**
Oelwein *U.S.A.* 42°41N 91°55W **80 D8**
Oeno I. *Pac. Oc.* 24°0S 131°0W **65 K14**
Oenpelli = Gunbalanya
  Australia 12°20S 133°4E **60 B5**
Ofanto → *Italy* 41°22N 16°13E **22 D7**
Offa *Nigeria* 8°13N 4°42E **52 G6**
Offaly □ *Ireland* 53°15N 7°30W **10 C4**
Offenbach *Germany* 50°6N 8°44E **16 C5**
Offenburg *Germany* 48°28N 7°56E **16 D4**
Officer Cr. → *Australia* 27°46S 132°30E **61 E5**
Ofolanga *Tonga* 19°38S 174°27W **59 c**
Ofotfjorden *Norway* 68°27N 17°0E **8 B17**
Ofu *Amer. Samoa* 14°11S 169°41W **59 b**
Ōfunato *Japan* 39°4N 141°43E **28 E10**
Oga *Japan* 39°55N 139°50E **28 E9**
Oga-Hantō *Japan* 39°58N 139°47E **28 E9**
Ogaden *Ethiopia* 7°30N 45°30E **49 F3**
Ōgaki *Japan* 35°21N 136°37E **29 G8**
Ogallala *U.S.A.* 41°8N 101°43W **80 E3**
Ogasawara Gunto *Pac. Oc.* 27°0N 142°0E **64 E6**
Ogbomosho *Nigeria* 8°1N 4°11E **52 G6**
Ogden *U.S.A.* 41°13N 111°58W **76 F8**
Ogdensburg *U.S.A.* 44°42N 75°30W **83 B9**
Ogea Driki *Fiji* 19°12S 178°27W **59 a**
Ogea Levu *Fiji* 19°8S 178°24W **59 a**
Ogeechee → *U.S.A.* 31°50N 81°3W **85 F14**
Ogilby *U.S.A.* 32°49N 114°50W **79 N12**
Óglio → *Italy* 45°2N 10°39E **22 B4**
Ogmore *Australia* 22°37S 149°35E **62 C4**
Ogoki *Canada* 51°38N 85°58W **72 B2**
Ogoki → *Canada* 51°38N 85°57W **72 B2**
Ogoki L. *Canada* 50°50N 87°10W **72 B2**
Ogoki Res. *Canada* 50°45N 88°15W **72 B2**
Ogooué → *Gabon* 1°0S 9°0E **54 E1**
Ogowe = Ogooué → *Gabon* 1°0S 9°0E **54 E1**
Ogre *Latvia* 56°49N 24°36E **9 H21**
Ogurja Ada *Turkmenistan* 38°55N 53°2E **47 B7**
Ohai *N.Z.* 45°55S 168°0E **59 F2**
Ohakune *N.Z.* 39°24S 175°24E **59 C5**
Ohangwena □ *Namibia* 17°30S 17°0E **56 A2**
Ohata *Japan* 41°24N 141°10E **28 D10**
Ohau, L. *N.Z.* 44°15S 169°53E **59 F2**
Ohio □ *U.S.A.* 40°15N 82°45W **82 F2**
Ohio → *U.S.A.* 36°59N 89°8W **80 G9**
Ohře → *Czech Rep.* 50°30N 14°10E **16 C8**
Ohrid *Macedonia* 41°8N 20°52E **23 D9**
Ohridsko Jezero *Macedonia* 41°8N 20°52E **23 D9**
Ohrigstad *S. Africa* 24°39S 30°36E **57 B5**
Oi Qu → *China* 39°8N 98°50E **34 C8**
Oiapoque *Brazil* 3°50N 51°50W **93 C8**
Oikou *China* 38°35N 117°42E **35 E9**

Oil Springs *Canada* 42°47N 82°7W **82 D2**
Oildale *U.S.A.* 35°25N 119°1W **79 K7**
Oise → *France* 49°0N 2°4E **20 B5**
Oistins *Barbados* 13°4N 59°33W **89 g**
Oistins B. *Barbados* 13°4N 59°33W **89 g**
Ōita *Japan* 33°14N 131°36E **29 H5**
Ōita □ *Japan* 33°15N 131°30E **29 H5**
Oiticica *Brazil* 5°3S 41°5W **93 E10**
Ojai *U.S.A.* 34°27N 119°15W **79 L7**
Ojhar *India* 20°6N 73°56E **44 D1**
Ojinaga *Mexico* 29°34N 104°25W **86 B4**
Ojiya *Japan* 37°18N 138°48E **29 F9**
Ojo Caliente *Mexico* 22°34N 102°15W **86 C4**
Ojo de Liebre, L. *Mexico* 27°45N 114°15W **86 B2**
Ojos del Salado, Cerro
  Argentina 27°0S 68°40W **94 B2**
Oka → *Russia* 56°20N 43°59E **18 C7**
Okaba *Indonesia* 8°6S 139°42E **37 F9**
Okahandja *Namibia* 22°0S 16°59E **56 B2**
Okakarara *Namibia* 20°35S 17°27E **56 B2**
Okanagan L. *Canada* 50°0N 119°30W **70 D5**
Okandja *Gabon* 0°35S 13°45E **54 E2**
Okanogan *U.S.A.* 48°6N 119°44W **76 B4**
Okanogan → *U.S.A.* 48°6N 119°44W **76 B4**
Okanogan Range
  N. Amer. 49°0N 119°55W **70 D5**
Okaputa *Namibia* 20°5S 17°0E **56 B2**
Okara *Pakistan* 30°50N 73°31E **42 D5**
Okaukuejo *Namibia* 19°10S 16°0E **56 A2**
Okavango □ *Namibia* 18°0S 19°30E **56 A2**
Okavango Delta
  Botswana 18°45S 22°45E **56 A3**
Okavango Swamp = Okavango
  Delta *Botswana* 18°45S 22°45E **56 A3**
Okaya *Japan* 36°5N 138°10E **29 F9**
Okayama *Japan* 34°40N 133°54E **29 G6**
Okayama □ *Japan* 35°0N 133°50E **29 G6**
Okazaki *Japan* 34°57N 137°10E **29 G8**
Okeechobee *U.S.A.* 27°15N 80°50W **85 H14**
Okeechobee, L. *U.S.A.* 27°0N 80°50W **85 H14**
Okefenokee △ *U.S.A.* 30°45N 82°18W **85 F13**
Okefenokee Swamp
  U.S.A. 30°40N 82°20W **85 F13**
Okehampton *U.K.* 50°44N 4°0W **13 G4**
Okha *India* 22°27N 69°42E **42 H3**
Okha *Russia* 53°40N 143°0E **27 D15**
Okhotsk *Russia* 59°20N 143°10E **27 D15**
Okhotsk, Sea of *Asia* 55°0N 145°0E **27 D15**
Okhotskiy Perevoz
  Russia 61°52N 135°35E **27 C14**
Okhtyrka *Ukraine* 50°25N 35°0E **19 D5**
Oki-Shotō *Japan* 36°5N 133°15E **29 F6**
Okiep *S. Africa* 29°39S 17°53E **56 C2**
Okinawa *Japan* 26°19N 127°46E **29 L3**
Okinawa □ *Japan* 26°40N 128°0E **29 L4**
Okinawa-Guntō *Japan* 26°40N 128°0E **29 L4**
Okinawa-Jima *Japan* 26°32N 128°0E **29 L4**
Okino-erabu-Shima
  Japan 27°21N 128°33E **29 L4**
Oklahoma □ *U.S.A.* 35°20N 97°30W **84 D6**
Oklahoma City *U.S.A.* 35°30N 97°30W **84 D6**
Okmulgee *U.S.A.* 35°37N 95°58W **84 D7**
Oknitsa = Ocnița
  Moldova 48°25N 27°30E **17 D14**
Okolona *U.S.A.* 34°0N 88°45W **85 E10**
Okombahe *Namibia* 21°23S 15°22E **56 B2**
Okotoks *Canada* 50°43N 113°58W **70 C6**
Oksovskiy *Russia* 62°33N 39°57E **18 B6**
Oktyabrsk = Qandyaghash
  Kazakhstan 49°28N 57°25E **19 E10**
Oktyabrskiy = Aktsyabrski
  Belarus 52°38N 28°53E **17 B15**
Oktyabrskiy *Bashkortostan,*
  Russia 54°28N 53°28E **18 D9**
Oktyabrskiy *Kamchatka,*
  Russia 52°39N 156°14E **27 D16**
Oktyabrskoy Revolyutsii, Ostrov
  Russia 79°30N 97°0E **27 B10**
Okuru *N.Z.* 43°55S 168°55E **59 E2**
Okushiri-Tō *Japan* 42°15N 139°30E **28 C9**
Okwa → *Botswana* 22°30S 23°0E **56 C3**
Ola *Russia* 59°35N 151°17E **27 D16**
Ola *U.S.A.* 35°2N 93°13W **84 D8**
Ólafsfjörður *Iceland* 66°4N 18°39W **8 C4**
Ólafsvík *Iceland* 64°53N 23°43W **8 D2**
Olancha *U.S.A.* 36°17N 118°1W **79 J8**
Olancha Pk. *U.S.A.* 36°16N 118°7W **79 J8**
Öland *Sweden* 56°45N 16°38E **9 H17**
Olary *Australia* 32°18S 140°19E **63 E3**
Olascoaga *Argentina* 35°15S 60°39W **94 D3**
Olathe *U.S.A.* 38°53N 94°49W **80 F6**
Olavarría *Argentina* 36°55S 60°20W **94 D3**
Oława *Poland* 50°57N 17°20E **17 C9**
Ólbia *Italy* 40°55N 9°31E **22 D3**
Olcott *U.S.A.* 43°20N 78°42W **82 C6**
Old Bahama Chan. = Bahama,
  Canal Viejo de
  W. Indies 22°10N 77°30W **88 B4**
Old Baldy Pk. = San Antonio, Mt.
  U.S.A. 34°17N 117°38W **79 L9**
Old Bridge *U.S.A.* 40°25N 74°22W **83 F10**
Old Castile = Castilla y Leon □
  Spain 42°0N 5°0W **21 B3**
Old Crow *Canada* 67°30N 139°55W **68 B2**
Old Dale *U.S.A.* 34°8N 115°47W **79 L11**
Old Forge *N.Y., U.S.A.* 43°43N 74°58W **83 C10**
Old Forge *Pa., U.S.A.* 41°22N 75°45W **83 E9**
Old Mapoon ⌖ *Australia* 11°5S 142°22E **62 A3**
Old Perlican *Canada* 48°5N 53°1W **73 C9**
Old Speck Mt. *U.S.A.* 44°34N 70°57W **83 B14**
Old Town *U.S.A.* 44°56N 68°39W **81 C19**
Old Washington *U.S.A.* 40°2N 81°27W **82 F3**
Old Wives L. *Canada* 50°5N 106°0W **71 C7**
Oldbury *U.K.* 51°38N 2°33W **13 F5**
Oldcastle *Ireland* 53°46N 7°10W **10 C4**
Oldenburg *Germany* 53°9N 8°13E **16 B5**
Oldenzaal *Neths.* 52°19N 6°53E **15 B6**
Oldham *U.K.* 53°33N 2°7W **12 D5**

Oldman → Canada 49°57N 111°42W 70 D6
Oldmeldrum U.K. 57°20N 2°19W 11 D6
Olds Canada 51°50N 114°10W 70 C6
Öldziyt Mongolia 44°40N 109°1E 32 B5
Olean U.S.A. 42°5N 78°26W 82 D6
Olekma → Russia 60°22N 120°42E 27 C13
Olekminsk Russia 60°25N 120°30E 27 C13
Oleksandriya Ukraine 50°37N 26°19E 17 C14
Olema U.S.A. 38°3N 122°47W 78 G4
Olenegorsk Russia 68°9N 33°18E 8 B25
Olenek Russia 68°28N 112°18E 27 C12
Olenek → Russia 73°0N 120°10E 27 B13
Oléron, Î. d' France 45°55N 1°15W 20 D3
Oleśnica Poland 51°13N 17°22E 17 C9
Olevsk Ukraine 51°12N 27°39E 17 C14
Olga, L. Canada 49°47N 77°15W 72 C4
Olgas, The = Kata Tjuta
   Australia 25°20S 130°50E 61 E5
Ölgiy Mongolia 48°56N 89°57E 30 B6
Olhão Portugal 37°3N 7°48W 21 D2
Olifants = Elefantes →
   Africa 24°10S 32°40E 57 B5
Olifants → Namibia 25°30S 19°30E 56 C2
Olifantshoek S. Africa 27°57S 22°42E 56 C3
Ólimbos, Óros = Olymbos Oros
   Greece 40°6N 22°23E 23 D10
Olimpia Brazil 20°44S 48°54W 95 A6
Olinda Brazil 8°1S 34°51W 93 E12
Oliva Argentina 32°0S 63°38W 94 C3
Olivares, Cerro los
   Argentina 30°18S 69°55W 94 C2
Olive Branch U.S.A. 34°57N 89°49W 85 D10
Olivehurst U.S.A. 39°6N 121°34W 78 F5
Olivenza Spain 38°41N 7°9W 21 C2
Oliver Canada 49°13N 119°37W 70 D5
Oliver L. Canada 56°56N 103°22W 71 B8
Ollagüe Chile 21°15S 68°10W 94 A2
Olmaliq Uzbekistan 40°50N 69°35E 26 E7
Olney Ill., U.S.A. 38°44N 88°5W 80 F9
Olney Tex., U.S.A. 33°22N 98°45W 84 E5
Olomane → Canada 50°14N 60°37W 73 B7
Olomouc Czech Rep. 49°38N 17°12E 17 D9
Olonets Russia 61°0N 32°54E 18 B5
Olongapo Phil. 14°50N 120°18E 37 B6
Olosega Amer. Samoa 14°10S 169°37W 59 b
Olosenga = Swains I.
   Amer. Samoa 11°11S 171°4W 65 J11
Olot Spain 42°11N 2°30E 21 A7
Olovyannaya Russia 50°58N 115°35E 27 D12
Oloy → Russia 66°29N 159°29E 27 C16
Olsztyn Poland 53°48N 20°29E 17 B11
Olt → Romania 43°43N 24°51E 17 G13
Olteniţa Romania 44°7N 26°42E 17 F14
Olton U.S.A. 34°11N 102°8W 84 D3
Oluan Pi Taiwan 21°53N 120°51E 35 G13
Olymbos Oros Greece 40°6N 22°23E 23 D10
Olympia Greece 37°39N 21°39E 23 F9
Olympia U.S.A. 47°3N 122°53W 78 D4
Olympic △ U.S.A. 47°45N 123°43W 78 C3
Olympic Dam Australia 30°30S 136°55E 63 E2
Olympic Mts. U.S.A. 47°55N 123°45W 78 C3
Olympus Cyprus 34°56N 32°52E 46 C2
Olympus, Mt. = Olymbos Oros
   Greece 40°6N 22°23E 23 D10
Olympus, Mt. = Uludağ
   Turkey 40°4N 29°13E 23 D13
Olympus, Mt. U.S.A. 47°48N 123°43W 78 C3
Olyphant U.S.A. 41°27N 75°36W 83 E9
Olyutorskiy, Mys
   Russia 59°55N 170°27E 27 D18
Om → Russia 54°59N 73°22E 26 D8
Om Koi Thailand 17°48N 98°22E 38 D2
Ōma Japan 41°45N 141°5E 28 D10
Ōmachi Japan 36°30N 137°50E 29 F8
Omae-Zaki Japan 34°36N 138°14E 29 G9
Ōmagari = Daisen
   Japan 39°27N 140°29E 28 E10
Omagh U.K. 54°36N 7°19W 10 B4
Omagh □ U.K. 54°35N 7°15W 10 B4
Omaha U.S.A. 41°17N 95°58W 80 E6
Omaheke □ Namibia 21°30S 19°0E 56 B2
Omak U.S.A. 48°25N 119°31W 76 B4
Omalur India 11°44N 78°4E 45 J4
Oman ■ Asia 23°0N 58°0E 49 C6
Oman, G. of Asia 24°30N 58°30E 47 E8
Omaruru Namibia 21°26S 16°0E 56 B2
Omaruru → Namibia 22°7S 14°15E 56 B1
Omate Peru 16°45S 71°0W 92 G4
Ombai, Selat Indonesia 8°30S 124°50E 37 F6
Omboué Gabon 1°35S 9°15E 54 E1
Ombrone → Italy 42°42N 11°5E 22 C4
Omdurmân Sudan 15°40N 32°28E 53 E12
Omemee Canada 44°18N 78°33W 82 B6
Ometepe, I. de Nic. 11°32N 85°35W 88 D2
Ometepec Mexico 16°41N 98°25W 87 D5
Ominato Japan 41°17N 141°10E 28 D10
Omineca → Canada 56°3N 124°16W 70 B4
Omineca Mts. Canada 56°30N 125°30W 70 B3
Omitara Namibia 22°16S 18°2E 56 B2
Ōmiya = Saitama Japan 35°54N 139°38E 29 G9
Ommen Neths. 52°31N 6°26E 15 B6
Omnögovi □ Mongolia 43°15N 104°0E 32 C3
Omo → Ethiopia 6°25N 36°10E 47 F2
Omolon → Russia 68°42N 158°36E 27 C16
Omono-Gawa → Japan 39°46N 140°3E 28 E10
Ompha Canada 45°0N 76°50W 83 B8
Omsk Russia 55°0N 73°12E 26 D8
Omsukchan Russia 62°32N 155°48E 27 C16
Ōmu Japan 44°34N 142°58E 28 B11
Omul, Vf. Romania 45°27N 25°29E 17 F13
Ōmura Japan 32°56N 129°57E 29 H4
Omuramba Omatako →
   Namibia 17°45S 20°25E 56 A2
Omuramba Ovambo →
   Namibia 18°45S 16°59E 56 A2
Omusati □ Namibia 18°30S 15°0E 56 A1
Omuta Japan 33°5N 130°26E 29 H5
Omuthiya Namibia 17°43S 16°13E 56 A2
Onaga U.S.A. 39°29N 96°10W 80 F5

Onalaska U.S.A. 43°53N 91°14W 80 D8
Onancock U.S.A. 37°43N 75°45W 81 G16
Onang, L. Gabon 0°57S 10°4E 54 E2
Onaping L. Canada 47°3N 81°30W 72 C3
Onavas Mexico 28°31N 109°35W 86 B3
Onawa U.S.A. 42°2N 96°6W 80 D5
Oncócua Angola 16°30S 13°25E 56 A1
Onda Spain 39°55N 0°17W 21 C5
Ondangwa Namibia 17°57S 16°4E 56 A2
Ondjiva Angola 16°48S 15°50E 56 A2
Öndörhaan Mongolia 47°19N 110°39E 31 B11
Öndverðarnes Iceland 64°52N 24°0W 8 D2
One Arm Point Australia 16°26S 123°3E 60 C3
One Arm Point ○
   Australia 16°31S 122°53E 60 C3
One Tree Australia 34°11S 144°43E 63 E3
Oneata Fiji 18°26S 178°25W 59 a
Onega Russia 64°0N 38°10E 18 B6
Onega → Russia 63°58N 38°2E 18 B6
Onega, G. of = Onezhskaya Guba
   Russia 64°24N 36°38E 18 B6
Onega, L. = Onezhskoye Ozero
   Russia 61°44N 35°22E 18 B6
Oneida U.S.A. 43°6N 75°39W 83 C9
Oneida L. U.S.A. 43°12N 75°54W 83 C9
O'Neill U.S.A. 42°27N 98°39W 80 D4
Onekotan, Ostrov
   Russia 49°25N 154°45E 27 E16
Oneonta U.S.A. 42°27N 75°4W 83 D9
Oneşti Romania 46°17N 26°47E 17 E14
Onezhskaya Guba Russia 64°24N 36°38E 18 B6
Onezhskoye Ozero Russia 61°44N 35°22E 18 B6
Ongarue N.Z. 38°42S 175°19E 59 C5
Ongea Levu = Ogea Levu
   Fiji 19°8S 178°24W 59 a
Ongers → S. Africa 31°4S 23°13E 56 D3
Ongerup Australia 33°58S 118°28E 61 F2
Ongi Mongolia 45°27N 103°54E 32 B2
Ongjin N. Korea 37°56N 125°21E 33 F13
Ongkharak Thailand 14°8N 101°1E 38 E3
Ongniud Qi China 43°0N 118°38E 33 C10
Ongole India 15°33N 80°2E 45 G5
Ongon = Havirga
   Mongolia 45°41N 113°5E 32 B7
Ongwediva Namibia 17°47S 15°46E 56 A2
Onida U.S.A. 44°42N 100°4W 80 C3
Onilahy → Madag. 23°34S 43°45E 55 J8
Onitsha Nigeria 6°6N 6°42E 52 G7
Ono Fiji 18°55S 178°29E 59 a
Onoda Japan 33°59N 131°11E 29 G5
Onslow Australia 21°40S 115°12E 60 D2
Onslow B. U.S.A. 34°20N 77°15W 85 D16
Ontake-San Japan 35°53N 137°29E 29 G8
Ontario Calif., U.S.A. 34°4N 117°39W 79 L9
Ontario Oreg., U.S.A. 44°2N 116°58W 76 D5
Ontario □ Canada 48°0N 83°0W 72 B2
Ontario, L. N. Amer. 43°20N 78°0W 82 C7
Ontonagon U.S.A. 46°52N 89°19W 80 B9
Onyx U.S.A. 35°41N 118°14W 79 K8
Oodnadatta Australia 27°33S 135°30E 63 D2
Ooldea Australia 30°27S 131°50E 61 F5
Oombulgurri Australia 15°15S 127°45E 60 C4
Oombulgurri ○
   Australia 15°10S 127°50E 60 C4
Oorindi Australia 20°40S 141°1E 62 C3
Oost-Vlaanderen □
   Belgium 51°5N 3°50E 15 C3
Oostende Belgium 51°15N 2°54E 15 C2
Oosterhout Neths. 51°39N 4°47E 15 C4
Oosterschelde → Neths. 51°33N 4°0E 15 C4
Oosterwolde Neths. 53°0N 6°17E 15 B6
Oosteschelde △ Neths. 51°40N 3°40E 15 C3
Ootacamund = Udagamandalam
   India 11°30N 76°44E 45 J3
Ootsa L. Canada 53°50N 126°2W 70 C3
Ooty = Udagamandalam
   India 11°30N 76°44E 45 J3
Op Luang △ Thailand 18°12N 98°32E 38 C2
Opala Dem. Rep. of the Congo 0°40S 24°20E 54 E4
Opanake Sri Lanka 6°35N 80°40E 45 L5
Opasatika Canada 49°30N 82°50W 72 C3
Opasquia △ Canada 53°33N 93°5W 72 B1
Opava Czech Rep. 49°57N 17°58E 17 D9
Opelika U.S.A. 32°39N 85°23W 85 E12
Opelousas U.S.A. 30°32N 92°5W 84 F8
Opémisca, L. Canada 49°56N 74°52W 72 C5
Opheim U.S.A. 48°51N 106°24W 76 B10
Ophthalmia Ra.
   Australia 23°15S 119°30E 60 D2
Opinaca → Canada 52°15N 78°2W 72 B4
Opinaca, Rés. Canada 52°39N 76°20W 72 B4
Opinnagau → Canada 54°12N 82°25W 72 B3
Opiscotéo, L. Canada 53°10N 68°10W 73 B6
Opobo Nigeria 4°35N 7°34E 52 H7
Opole Poland 50°42N 17°58E 17 C9
Oponono L. Namibia 18°8S 15°45E 56 A2
Oporto = Porto Portugal 41°8N 8°40W 21 B1
Opotiki N.Z. 38°1S 177°19E 59 C6
Opp U.S.A. 31°17N 86°16W 85 F11
Oppdal Norway 62°35N 9°41E 8 E13
Opportunity U.S.A. 47°39N 117°15W 76 C5
Opua N.Z. 35°19S 174°9E 59 A5
Opunake N.Z. 39°26S 173°52E 59 C4
Opuwo Namibia 18°3S 13°45E 56 A1
Oracle U.S.A. 32°37N 110°46W 77 K8
Oradea Romania 47°2N 21°58E 17 E11
Öræfajökull Iceland 64°2N 16°39W 8 D5
Orai India 25°58N 79°30E 43 G8
Oral = Zhayyq →
   Kazakhstan 47°0N 51°48E 19 E9
Oral Kazakhstan 51°20N 51°20E 19 D9
Oran Algeria 35°45N 0°39W 52 A5
Orange Australia 33°15S 149°7E 63 E4
Orange France 44°8N 4°47E 20 D6
Orange Calif., U.S.A. 33°47N 117°51W 79 M9
Orange Mass., U.S.A. 42°35N 72°19W 83 D12
Orange Tex., U.S.A. 30°6N 93°44W 84 F8
Orange Va., U.S.A. 38°15N 78°7W 81 F14
Orange → S. Africa 28°41S 16°28E 56 C2

Orange, C. Brazil 4°20N 51°30W 93 C8
Orange Cove U.S.A. 36°38N 119°19W 78 J7
Orange Free State = Free State □
   S. Africa 28°30S 27°0E 56 C4
Orange Grove U.S.A. 27°58N 97°56W 84 H6
Orange Walk Belize 18°6N 88°33W 87 D7
Orangeburg U.S.A. 33°30N 80°52W 85 E14
Orangeville Canada 43°55N 80°5W 82 C4
Orango Guinea-Biss. 11°5N 16°0W 52 F2
Oranje = Orange →
   S. Africa 28°41S 16°28E 56 C2
Oranjemund Namibia 28°38S 16°29E 56 C2
Oranjerivier S. Africa 29°40S 24°12E 56 D3
Oranjestad Aruba 12°32N 70°2W 89 D5
Orapa Botswana 21°15S 25°30E 55 J5
Oras Phil. 12°9N 125°28E 37 B7
Orbetello Italy 42°27N 11°13E 22 C4
Orbisonia U.S.A. 40°15N 77°54W 82 F7
Orbost Australia 37°40S 148°29E 63 F4
Orcadas Antarctica 60°44S 44°37W 5 C18
Orcas I. U.S.A. 48°42N 122°56W 78 B4
Orchard City U.S.A. 38°50N 107°58W 76 G10
Orchard Homes U.S.A. 46°55N 114°4W 76 C6
Orchid I. = Lan Yü
   Taiwan 22°4N 121°25E 35 F13
Orchila, I. Venezuela 11°48N 66°10W 89 D6
Orcutt U.S.A. 34°52N 120°27W 79 L6
Ord U.S.A. 41°36N 98°56W 80 E4
Ord → Australia 15°33S 128°15E 60 C4
Ord, Mt. Australia 17°20S 125°34E 60 C4
Ord Mts. U.S.A. 34°39N 116°45W 79 L10
Orderville U.S.A. 37°17N 112°38W 77 H7
Ordos = Mu Us Shamo
   China 39°0N 109°0E 32 E5
Ordu Turkey 40°55N 37°53E 19 F6
Ordway U.S.A. 38°13N 103°46W 76 G12
Ore Mts. = Erzgebirge
   Germany 50°27N 12°55E 16 C7
Örebro Sweden 59°20N 15°18E 9 G16
Oregon U.S.A. 42°1N 89°20W 80 D9
Oregon □ U.S.A. 44°0N 121°0W 76 E3
Oregon City U.S.A. 45°21N 122°36W 78 E4
Orekhovo-Zuyevo Russia 55°50N 38°55E 18 D6
Orel Russia 52°57N 36°3E 18 D6
Orem U.S.A. 40°19N 111°42W 76 F8
Ören Turkey 37°3N 27°57E 23 F12
Orenburg Russia 51°45N 55°6E 18 D10
Orense = Ourense Spain 42°19N 7°55W 21 A2
Orepuki N.Z. 46°19S 167°46E 59 G1
Orestes Pereyra Mexico 26°30N 105°39W 86 B3
Orestiada Greece 41°30N 26°33E 23 D12
Orfanos Kolpos Greece 40°33N 24°0E 23 D11
Orford Ness U.K. 52°5N 1°35E 13 E9
Organ Pipe Cactus △
   U.S.A. 32°0N 112°52W 77 K7
Orgaz Spain 39°39N 3°53W 21 C4
Orgeyev = Orhei
   Moldova 47°24N 28°50E 17 E15
Orhaneli Turkey 39°54N 28°59E 23 E13
Orhangazi Turkey 40°29N 29°18E 23 D13
Orhei Moldova 47°24N 28°50E 17 E15
Orhon Gol → Mongolia 50°21N 106°0E 30 A10
Oriental, Cordillera
   Colombia 6°0N 73°0W 92 B4
Oriental, Grand Erg Algeria 30°0N 6°30E 52 B7
Oriente Argentina 38°44S 60°37W 94 D3
Orihuela Spain 38°7N 0°55W 21 C5
Orillia Canada 44°40N 79°24W 82 B5
Orinoco → Venezuela 9°15N 61°30W 92 B6
Orion Canada 49°27N 110°49W 71 D6
Oriskany U.S.A. 43°10N 75°20W 83 C9
Orissa = Odisha □ India 20°0N 84°0E 44 E7
Orissaare Estonia 58°34N 23°5E 9 G20
Oristano Italy 39°54N 8°36E 22 E3
Oristano, G. di Italy 39°50N 8°29E 22 E3
Orizaba Mexico 18°51N 97°6W 87 D5
Orizaba, Pico de Mexico 18°58N 97°15W 87 D5
Orkanger Norway 63°18N 9°52E 8 E13
Orkhon = Orhon Gol →
   Mongolia 50°21N 106°0E 30 A10
Orkla → Norway 63°18N 9°51E 8 E13
Orkney S. Africa 26°58S 26°40E 56 D4
Orkney □ U.K. 59°2N 3°13W 11 B5
Orkney Is. U.K. 59°0N 3°0W 11 B6
Orland U.S.A. 39°45N 122°12W 78 F4
Orléanais France 48°0N 2°0E 20 C5
Orléans France 47°54N 1°52E 20 C4
Orleans U.S.A. 44°49N 72°12W 83 B12
Orléans, Î. d' Canada 46°54N 70°58W 73 C5
Ormara Pakistan 25°16N 64°33E 40 G4
Ormoc Phil. 11°0N 124°37E 37 B6
Ormond N.Z. 38°33S 177°56E 59 C6
Ormond Beach U.S.A. 29°17N 81°3W 85 G14
Ormskirk U.K. 53°35N 2°54W 12 D5
Ormstown Canada 45°8N 74°0W 83 A10
Oro N. Korea 40°1N 127°27E 33 D14
Oro → Mexico 25°35N 105°2W 86 B3
Oro Grande U.S.A. 34°36N 117°20W 79 L9
Oro Valley U.S.A. 32°26N 110°58W 77 K8
Orocué Colombia 4°48N 71°20W 92 C4
Orofino U.S.A. 46°29N 116°15W 76 C5
Orohena, Mt. Tahiti 17°37S 149°28W 59 d
Orol Dengizi = Aral Sea
   Asia 45°0N 58°20E 26 E7
Oromocto Canada 45°54N 66°29W 73 C8
Orono Canada 43°59N 78°37W 82 C6
Oronsay U.K. 56°1N 6°15W 11 E2
Oroquieta Phil. 8°32N 123°44E 37 C6
Orosei Italy 40°23N 9°42E 22 D3
Orosháza Hungary 46°32N 20°42E 17 E11
Orosi Italy 40°23N 9°42E 22 D3
Orotukan Russia 62°16N 151°42E 27 C16
Oroville Calif., U.S.A. 39°31N 121°33W 78 F5
Oroville Wash., U.S.A. 48°56N 119°26W 76 B4
Oroville, L. U.S.A. 39°33N 121°29W 78 F5
Orroroo Australia 32°43S 138°38E 63 E2

Orrville U.S.A. 40°50N 81°46W 82 F3
Orsha Belarus 54°30N 30°25E 18 D5
Orsk Russia 51°12N 58°34E 26 D6
Orşova Romania 44°41N 22°25E 17 F12
Ortaca Turkey 36°49N 28°45E 23 F13
Ortegal, C. Spain 43°43N 7°52W 21 A2
Orthez France 43°29N 0°48W 20 E3
Ortigueira Spain 43°40N 7°50W 21 A2
Orting U.S.A. 47°6N 122°12W 78 C4
Ortles Italy 46°31N 10°33E 20 C9
Ortón → Bolivia 10°50S 67°0W 92 F5
Ortonville U.S.A. 45°19N 96°27W 80 C5
Orūmīyeh Iran 37°40N 45°0E 46 B5
Orūmīyeh, Daryācheh-ye
   Iran 37°50N 45°30E 46 B5
Oruro Bolivia 18°0S 67°9W 92 G5
Orust Sweden 58°10N 11°40E 9 G14
Oruzgān □ Afghan. 33°0N 66°0E 40 C5
Orvieto Italy 42°43N 12°7E 22 C5
Orwell N.Y., U.S.A. 43°35N 75°50W 83 C9
Orwell Ohio, U.S.A. 41°32N 80°52W 82 E4
Orwell → U.K. 51°59N 1°18E 13 F9
Orwigsburg U.S.A. 40°38N 76°6W 83 F8
Oryakhovo Bulgaria 43°40N 23°57E 23 C10
Oryol = Orel Russia 52°57N 36°3E 18 D6
Osa Russia 57°17N 55°26E 18 C10
Osa, Pen. de Costa Rica 8°0N 84°0W 88 E3
Osage U.S.A. 43°17N 92°49W 80 D7
Osage → U.S.A. 38°36N 91°57W 80 F8
Osage City U.S.A. 38°38N 95°50W 80 F6
Ōsaki Japan 38°34N 140°58E 28 E10
Osawatomie U.S.A. 38°31N 94°57W 80 F6
Osborne U.S.A. 39°26N 98°42W 80 F5
Osceola Ark., U.S.A. 35°42N 89°58W 85 D10
Osceola Iowa, U.S.A. 41°2N 93°46W 80 E7
Oscoda U.S.A. 44°26N 83°20W 82 B1
Ösel = Saaremaa Estonia 58°30N 22°30E 9 G20
Osgoode Canada 45°8N 75°36W 83 A9
Osh Kyrgyzstan 40°37N 72°49E 30 C3
Oshakati Namibia 17°45S 15°40E 56 H3
Oshana □ Namibia 17°50S 15°40E 56 A2
Oshawa Canada 43°50N 78°50W 82 C6
Oshigambo Namibia 17°45S 16°5E 56 A2
Oshika-Hantō Japan 38°20N 141°30E 28 E10
Oshikoto □ Namibia 18°30S 17°0E 56 A2
Oshivelo Namibia 18°37S 17°10E 56 A2
Oshkosh Nebr., U.S.A. 41°24N 102°21W 80 E2
Oshkosh Wis., U.S.A. 44°1N 88°33W 80 C9
Oshmyany = Ashmyany
   Belarus 54°26N 25°52E 17 A13
Oshnovīyeh Iran 37°2N 45°6E 46 B5
Oshogbo Nigeria 7°48N 4°37E 52 G6
Oshtorīnān Iran 34°1N 48°38E 47 C6
Ōshū Japan 39°8N 141°8E 28 E10
Oshwe
   Dem. Rep. of the Congo 3°25S 19°28E 54 E3
Osijek Croatia 45°34N 18°41E 23 B8
Osipovichi = Asipovichy
   Belarus 53°19N 28°33E 17 B15
Osiyan India 26°43N 72°55E 42 F5
Osizweni S. Africa 27°49S 30°7E 57 C5
Oskaloosa U.S.A. 41°18N 92°39W 80 E7
Oskarshamn Sweden 57°15N 16°27E 9 H17
Öskemen Kazakhstan 50°0N 82°36E 26 D9
Oskélaneo Canada 48°5N 75°15W 72 C4
Oslofjorden Norway 59°20N 10°35E 9 G14
Osmanabad India 18°5N 76°10E 44 E3
Osmaniye Turkey 37°5N 36°10E 46 B3
Osmannagar India 18°32N 79°20E 44 E4
Osnabrück Germany 52°17N 8°3E 16 B5
Osogbo = Oshogbo Nigeria 7°48N 4°37E 52 G6
Osório Brazil 29°53S 50°17W 95 B5
Osorno Chile 40°25S 73°0W 96 E2
Osorno, Vol. Chile 41°0S 72°30W 96 D2
Osoyoos Canada 49°0N 119°30W 70 D5
Osøyro Norway 60°9N 5°30E 8 F11
Ospika → Canada 56°20N 124°0W 70 B4
Osprey Reef Australia 13°52S 146°36E 62 A4
Oss Neths. 51°46N 5°32E 15 C5
Ossa, Mt. Australia 41°52S 146°3E 63 G4
Ossa, Oros Greece 39°47N 22°42E 23 E10
Ossabaw I. U.S.A. 31°50N 81°5W 85 F14
Ossining U.S.A. 41°10N 73°55W 83 E11
Ossipee U.S.A. 43°41N 71°7W 83 C13
Ossokmanuan L. Canada 53°25N 65°0W 73 B7
Ossora Russia 59°20N 163°13E 27 D17
Ostend = Oostende
   Belgium 51°15N 2°54E 15 C2
Oster Ukraine 50°57N 30°53E 17 C16
Österbotten = Pohjanmaa □
   Finland 62°58N 22°50E 8 E20
Osterburg U.S.A. 40°16N 78°31W 82 F6
Österdalälven → Sweden 60°30N 15°7E 8 F15
Østerdalen Norway 61°40N 10°50E 8 F14
Östermyra = Seinäjoki
   Finland 62°40N 22°51E 8 E20
Österreich = Austria ■
   Europe 47°0N 14°0E 16 E8
Östersund Sweden 63°10N 14°38E 8 E16
Ostfriesische Inseln
   Germany 53°42N 7°0E 16 B4
Ostrava Czech Rep. 49°51N 18°18E 17 D10
Ostróda Poland 53°42N 19°58E 17 B10
Ostroh Ukraine 50°20N 26°30E 17 C14
Ostrołęka Poland 53°4N 21°32E 17 B11
Ostrów Mazowiecka
   Poland 52°50N 21°51E 17 B11
Ostrów Wielkopolski
   Poland 51°36N 17°44E 17 C9
Ostrowiec-Świętokrzyski
   Poland 50°55N 21°22E 17 C11
Ostuni Italy 40°44N 17°35E 23 D7
Ōsumi-Kaikyō Japan 30°55N 131°0E 29 J5
Ōsumi-Shotō Japan 30°30N 130°0E 29 J5
Osuna Spain 37°14N 5°8W 21 D3
Oswegatchie → U.S.A. 44°42N 75°30W 83 B9
Oswego U.S.A. 43°27N 76°31W 83 C8
Oswego → U.S.A. 43°27N 76°30W 83 C8
Oswestry U.K. 52°52N 3°3W 12 E4

Oświęcim Poland 50°2N 19°11E 17 C10
Otago □ N.Z. 45°15S 170°0E 59 F2
Otago Harbour N.Z. 45°47S 170°42E 59 F3
Otaheite B. Trin. & Tob. 10°15N 61°30W 93 K15
Ōtake Japan 34°12N 132°13E 29 G6
Ōtaki N.Z. 40°45S 175°10E 59 D5
Otaru Japan 43°10N 141°0E 28 C10
Otaru-Wan = Ishikari-Wan
   Japan 43°25N 141°1E 28 C10
Otavalo Ecuador 0°13N 78°20W 92 C3
Otavi Namibia 19°40S 17°24E 56 A2
Otawara Japan 36°50N 140°0E 29 F10
Otchinjau Angola 16°30S 13°56E 56 A1
Otego U.S.A. 42°23N 75°10W 83 D9
Otelnuk, L. Canada 56°9N 68°12W 73 A6
Othello U.S.A. 46°50N 119°10W 76 C4
Otish, Mts. Canada 52°22N 70°30W 73 B5
Otjinene Namibia 21°8S 18°46E 56 B2
Otjiwarongo Namibia 20°30S 16°33E 56 B2
Otjozondjupa □ Namibia 21°0S 19°0E 56 B2
Oto Tolu Group Tonga 20°21S 174°32W 59 c
Otoineppu Japan 44°44N 142°16E 28 B11
Otorohanga N.Z. 38°12S 175°14E 59 C5
Otoskwin → Canada 52°13N 88°6W 72 B2
Otra → Norway 58°9N 8°1E 9 G13
Otranto Italy 40°9N 18°28E 23 D8
Otranto, C. d' Italy 40°7N 18°30E 23 D8
Otranto, Str. of Italy 40°15N 18°40E 23 D8
Otse S. Africa 25°2S 25°45E 56 C4
Ōtsu Japan 35°0N 135°50E 29 G7
Ōtsuki Japan 35°36N 138°57E 29 G9
Ottapalam India 10°46N 76°23E 45 J3
Ottawa = Outaouais →
   Canada 45°27N 74°8W 72 C5
Ottawa Canada 45°26N 75°42W 83 A9
Ottawa Ill., U.S.A. 41°21N 88°51W 80 E9
Ottawa Kans., U.S.A. 38°37N 95°16W 80 F6
Ottawa Is. Canada 59°35N 80°10W 69 F15
Otter Cr. → U.S.A. 44°13N 73°17W 83 B11
Otter Lake Canada 45°17N 79°56W 82 A5
Otterville Canada 42°55N 80°36W 82 D4
Ottery St. Mary U.K. 50°44N 3°17W 13 G4
Ottosdal S. Africa 26°46S 25°59E 56 C4
Ottumwa U.S.A. 41°1N 92°25W 80 E7
Oturkpo Nigeria 7°16N 8°8E 52 G7
Otway, B. Chile 53°30S 74°0W 96 G2
Otway, C. Australia 38°52S 143°30E 63 F3
Otwock Poland 52°5N 21°20E 17 B11
Ou → Laos 20°4N 102°13E 38 B4
Ou-Sammyaku Japan 39°20N 140°35E 28 E10
Ouachita → U.S.A. 31°38N 91°49W 84 F9
Ouachita, L. U.S.A. 34°34N 93°12W 84 D8
Ouachita Mts. U.S.A. 34°30N 94°30W 84 D7
Ouagadougou
   Burkina Faso 12°25N 1°30W 52 F5
Ouahigouya Burkina Faso 13°31N 2°25W 52 F5
Ouahran = Oran Algeria 35°45N 0°39W 52 A5
Ouallene Algeria 24°41N 1°11E 52 D6
Ouarâne Mauritania 21°0N 10°30W 52 D3
Ouargla Algeria 31°59N 5°16E 52 B7
Ouarra → C.A.R. 5°5N 24°26E 54 C4
Ouarzazate Morocco 30°55N 6°50W 52 B4
Oubangi →
   Dem. Rep. of the Congo 0°30S 17°50E 54 E3
Ouddorp Neths. 51°50N 3°57E 15 C3
Oude Rijn → Neths. 52°12N 4°24E 15 B4
Oudenaarde Belgium 50°50N 3°37E 15 D3
Oudtshoorn S. Africa 33°35S 22°14E 56 E3
Ouessant, Î. d' France 48°28N 5°6W 20 B1
Ouesso Congo 1°37N 16°5E 54 D3
Ouest, Pte. de l' Canada 49°52N 64°40W 73 C7
Ouezzane Morocco 34°51N 5°35W 52 B4
Oughter, L. Ireland 54°1N 7°28W 10 B4
Oughterard Ireland 53°26N 9°18W 10 C2
Ouidah Benin 6°25N 2°0E 52 G6
Oujda Morocco 34°41N 1°55W 52 B5
Oulainen Finland 64°17N 24°47E 8 D21
Oulu Finland 65°1N 25°29E 8 D21
Oulujärvi Finland 64°25N 27°15E 8 D22
Oulujoki → Finland 65°1N 25°30E 8 D21
Oum Chalouba Chad 15°48N 20°46E 53 E10
Oum Hadjer Chad 13°18N 19°41E 53 F9
Ounasjoki → Finland 66°31N 25°40E 8 C21
Ounguati Namibia 22°0S 15°46E 56 B2
Ounianga Kébir Chad 19°4N 20°29E 53 E10
Our → Lux. 49°55N 6°5E 15 E6
Ouray U.S.A. 38°1N 107°40W 77 G10
Ourense Spain 42°19N 7°55W 21 A2
Ouricuri Brazil 7°53S 40°5W 93 E10
Ourinhos Brazil 23°0S 49°54W 95 A6
Ouro Fino Brazil 22°16S 46°25W 95 A6
Ouro Prêto Brazil 20°20S 43°30W 95 A7
Ourthe → Belgium 50°29N 5°35E 15 D5
Ouse → E. Sussex, U.K. 50°47N 0°4E 13 G8
Ouse → N. Yorks., U.K. 53°44N 0°55W 12 D7
Outaouais → Canada 45°27N 74°8W 72 C5
Outapi Namibia 17°30S 15°0E 56 A2
Outardes → Canada 49°24N 69°30W 73 C6
Outer Hebrides U.K. 57°30N 7°15W 11 D1
Outjo Namibia 20°5S 16°7E 56 B2
Outlook Canada 51°30N 107°0W 71 C7
Outokumpu Finland 62°43N 29°1E 8 E23
Ouyen Australia 35°1S 142°22E 63 F3
Ovalau Fiji 17°40S 178°48E 59 a
Ovalle Chile 30°33S 71°18W 94 C1
Ovamboland Namibia 18°30S 16°0E 56 A2
Overflakkee Neths. 51°44N 4°10E 15 C4
Overijssel □ Neths. 52°25N 6°35E 15 B6
Overland Park U.S.A. 38°58N 94°40W 80 F6
Overlander Roadhouse
   Australia 26°19S 114°28E 61 E1
Overton U.S.A. 36°33N 114°27W 79 J12
Övertorneå Sweden 66°23N 23°38E 8 C20
Ovid U.S.A. 42°41N 76°49W 83 D8
Oviedo Spain 43°25N 5°50W 21 A3
Oviši Latvia 57°33N 21°44E 9 H19
Ovoot Mongolia 45°21N 113°45E 32 B7
Övör Hangay □ Mongolia 45°0N 102°30E 32 B2

Øvre Årdal *Norway* 61°19N 7°48E **8** F12
Ovruch *Ukraine* 51°25N 28°45E **17** C15
Owaka *N.Z.* 46°27S 169°40E **59** G2
Owambo = Ovamboland
  Namibia 18°30S 16°0E **56** A2
Owasco L. *U.S.A.* 42°50N 76°31W **83** D8
Owase *Japan* 34°7N 136°12E **29** G8
Owatonna *U.S.A.* 44°5N 93°14W **80** C7
Owbeh *Afghan.* 34°28N 63°10E **40** B3
Owego *U.S.A.* 42°6N 76°16W **83** D8
Owen Sound *Canada* 44°35N 80°55W **82** B4
Owen Stanley Ra.
  Papua N. G. 8°30S 147°0E **58** B7
Oweniny → *Ireland* 54°8N 9°34W **10** B2
Owens → *U.S.A.* 36°32N 117°59W **78** J9
Owens L. *U.S.A.* 36°26N 117°57W **79** J9
Owensboro *U.S.A.* 37°46N 87°7W **80** G10
Owl → *Canada* 57°51N 92°44W **71** B10
Owo *Nigeria* 7°10N 5°39E **52** G7
Owosso *U.S.A.* 43°0N 84°10W **81** D3
Owyhee *U.S.A.* 41°57N 116°6W **76** F5
Owyhee → *U.S.A.* 43°49N 117°2W **76** E5
Owyhee, L. *U.S.A.* 43°38N 117°14W **76** E5
Ox Mts. = Slieve Gamph
  Ireland 54°6N 9°0W **10** B3
Öxarfjörður *Iceland* 66°15N 16°45W **8** C5
Oxbow *Canada* 49°14N 102°10W **71** D8
Oxelösund *Sweden* 58°43N 17°5E **9** G17
Oxford *N.Z.* 43°18S 172°11E **59** E4
Oxford *U.K.* 51°46N 1°15W **13** F6
Oxford *Mass., U.S.A.* 42°7N 71°52W **83** D13
Oxford *Miss., U.S.A.* 34°22N 89°31W **85** D10
Oxford *N.C., U.S.A.* 36°19N 78°35W **85** C15
Oxford *N.Y., U.S.A.* 42°27N 75°36W **83** D9
Oxford L. *Canada* 54°51N 95°37W **71** C9
Oxfordshire □ *U.K.* 51°48N 1°16W **13** F6
Oxnard *U.S.A.* 34°12N 119°11W **79** L7
Oxus = Amudarya →
  Uzbekistan 43°58N 59°34E **26** E6
Oya *Malaysia* 2°55N 111°55E **36** D4
Oyama *Japan* 36°18N 139°48E **29** F9
Oyem *Gabon* 1°34N 11°31E **54** D2
Oyen *Canada* 51°22N 110°28W **71** C6
Oykel → *U.K.* 57°56N 4°26W **11** D4
Oymyakon *Russia* 63°25N 142°44E **27** C15
Oyo *Nigeria* 7°46N 3°56E **52** G6
Oyster Bay *U.S.A.* 40°52N 73°32W **83** F11
Ōyūbari *Japan* 43°1N 142°5E **28** C11
Ozamiz *Phil.* 8°15N 123°50E **37** C6
Ozar = Ojhar *India* 20°6N 73°56E **44** D1
Ozark *Ala., U.S.A.* 31°28N 85°39W **85** F12
Ozark *Ark., U.S.A.* 35°29N 93°50W **84** D8
Ozark *Mo., U.S.A.* 37°1N 93°12W **80** G7
Ozark Plateau *U.S.A.* 37°20N 91°40W **80** G8
Ozarks, L. of the *U.S.A.* 38°12N 92°38W **80** F7
Ózd *Hungary* 48°14N 20°15E **17** D11
Ozernovskiy *Russia* 51°30N 156°31E **27** D16
Ozette, L. *U.S.A.* 48°6N 124°38W **78** B2
Ozieri *Italy* 40°35N 9°0E **22** D3
Ozona *U.S.A.* 30°43N 101°12W **84** F4
Ozuluama *Mexico* 21°40N 97°51W **87** C5

P

Pa-an *Burma* 16°51N 97°40E **41** L20
Pa Mong Dam *Thailand* 18°0N 102°22E **38** D4
Pa Sak → *Thailand* 15°30N 101°0E **38** E3
Paamiut *Greenland* 62°0N 49°43W **4** C5
Paarl *S. Africa* 33°45S 18°56E **56** D2
Pab Hills *Pakistan* 26°30N 66°45E **42** F2
Pabaidh = Pabbay *U.K.* 57°46N 7°14W **11** D1
Pabbay *U.K.* 57°46N 7°14W **11** D1
Pabianice *Poland* 51°40N 19°20E **17** C10
Pabna *Bangla.* 24°1N 89°18E **41** G16
Pacaja → *Brazil* 1°56S 50°50W **93** D8
Pacaraima, Sa. *S. Amer.* 4°0N 62°30W **92** C6
Pacasmayo *Peru* 7°20S 79°35W **92** E3
Pachitea → *Peru* 8°46S 74°33W **92** E4
Pachmarhi *India* 22°28N 78°26E **43** H8
Pachora *India* 20°38N 75°29E **44** D2
Pachpadra *India* 25°58N 72°10E **42** G5
Pachuca *Mexico* 20°7N 98°44W **87** C5
Pacific Antarctic Ridge
  Pac. Oc. 43°0S 115°0W **5** B13
Pacific Grove *U.S.A.* 36°38N 121°56W **78** J5
Pacific Ocean 10°0N 140°0W **65** G14
Pacific Rim △ *Canada* 48°40N 124°45W **78** B2
Pacitan *Indonesia* 8°12S 111°7E **37** H14
Packwood *U.S.A.* 46°36N 121°40W **78** D5
Padaido, Kepulauan
  Indonesia 1°15S 136°30E **37** E9
Padampur *India* 20°59N 83°4E **44** D6
Padang *Riau, Indonesia* 1°30N 102°30E **39** M4
Padang *Sumatera Barat,*
  Indonesia 1°0S 100°20E **36** E2
Padang Endau *Malaysia* 2°40N 103°38E **39** L4
Padangpanjang *Indonesia* 0°40S 100°20E **36** E2
Padangsidempuan
  Indonesia 1°30N 99°15E **36** D1
Paddle Prairie *Canada* 57°57N 117°29W **70** B5
Paderoo *India* 18°5N 82°40E **44** E6
Padma *India* 24°12N 85°22E **43** G11
Pádova *Italy* 45°25N 11°53E **22** B4
Padra *India* 22°15N 73°7E **42** H5
Padrauna *India* 26°54N 83°59E **43** F10
Padre I. *U.S.A.* 27°10N 97°25W **84** H6
Padre Island △ *U.S.A.* 27°0N 97°25W **84** H6
Padstow *U.K.* 50°33N 4°58W **13** G3
Padua = Pádova *Italy* 45°25N 11°53E **22** B4
Paducah *Ky., U.S.A.* 37°5N 88°37W **80** G10
Paducah *Tex., U.S.A.* 34°1N 100°18W **84** D4
Padukka *Sri Lanka* 6°50N 80°6E **45** L5
Padwa *India* 18°27N 82°47E **44** E6
Paea *Tahiti* 17°41S 149°35W **59** d
Paektu-san *N. Korea* 41°59N 128°4E **33** D15
Paeroa *N.Z.* 37°23S 175°41E **59** B5
Pafúri *Mozam.* 22°28S 31°17E **57** B5

Pag *Croatia* 44°25N 15°3E **16** F8
Pagadian *Phil.* 7°55N 123°30E **37** C6
Pagai Selatan, Pulau
  Indonesia 3°0S 100°15E **36** E2
Pagai Utara, Pulau
  Indonesia 2°35S 100°0E **36** E2
Pagalu = Annobón *Atl. Oc.* 1°25S 5°36E **51** G4
Pagara *India* 24°22N 80°1E **43** G9
Pagastikos Kolpos *Greece* 39°15N 23°0E **23** E10
Pagatan *Indonesia* 3°33S 115°59E **36** E5
Page *U.S.A.* 36°57N 111°27W **77** H8
Paget, Mt. *S. Georgia* 54°26S 36°31W **96** G9
Paget I. *India* 13°26N 92°50E **45** H11
Pago Pago *Amer. Samoa* 14°16S 170°43W **59** b
Pagosa Springs *U.S.A.* 37°16N 107°1W **77** H10
Pagri *China* 27°45N 89°10E **30** F6
Pagwa River *Canada* 50°2N 85°14W **72** B2
Pähala *U.S.A.* 19°12N 155°29W **75** M8
Pahang □ *Malaysia* 3°30N 102°45E **39** L4
Pahang → *Malaysia* 3°30N 103°9E **39** L4
Pahiatua *N.Z.* 40°27S 175°50E **59** D5
Pahokee *U.S.A.* 26°50N 80°40W **85** H14
Pahrump *U.S.A.* 36°12N 115°59W **79** J11
Pahute Mesa *U.S.A.* 37°20N 116°45W **78** H10
Pai *Thailand* 19°19N 98°27E **38** C2
Paicines *U.S.A.* 36°44N 121°17W **78** J5
Paide *Estonia* 58°53N 25°33E **9** G21
Paignton *U.K.* 50°26N 3°35W **13** G4
Paiho *Taiwan* 23°21N 120°25E **35** F13
Päijänne *Finland* 61°30N 25°30E **8** F21
Pailani *India* 25°45N 80°26E **43** G9
Pailin *Cambodia* 12°46N 102°36E **38** F4
Painan *Indonesia* 1°21S 100°34E **36** E2
Painesville *U.S.A.* 41°43N 81°15W **82** E3
Paint Hills = Wemindji
  Canada 53°0N 78°49W **72** B4
Paint L. *Canada* 55°28N 97°57W **71** B9
Painted Desert *U.S.A.* 36°0N 111°0W **77** H8
Paintsville *U.S.A.* 37°49N 82°48W **81** G12
País Vasco □ *Spain* 42°50N 2°45W **21** A4
Paisley *Canada* 44°18N 81°16W **82** B3
Paisley *U.K.* 55°50N 4°25W **11** F4
Paisley *U.S.A.* 42°42N 120°32W **76** E3
Paita *Peru* 5°11S 81°9W **92** E2
Paizhou *China* 30°12N 113°55E **35** B9
Pajares, Puerto de *Spain* 42°58N 5°46W **21** A3
Pak Lay *Laos* 18°15N 101°27E **38** C3
Pak Ou *Laos* 20°3N 102°12E **38** B4
Pak Phanang *Thailand* 8°21N 100°12E **39** H3
Pak Sane *Laos* 18°22N 103°39E **38** C4
Pak Song *Laos* 15°11N 106°14E **38** E6
Pak Suang *Laos* 19°58N 102°15E **34** H4
Pak Tam Chung *China* 22°24N 114°19E **31** a
Pak Thong Chai *Thailand* 14°43N 102°1E **38** E4
Pakala *India* 13°29N 79°8E **45** H4
Pakaur *India* 24°38N 87°51E **43** G12
Pakch'ŏn *N. Korea* 39°44N 125°35E **33** E13
Pakenham *Canada* 45°18N 76°18W **83** A8
Pakhuis *S. Africa* 32°9S 19°5E **56** D2
Pakistan ■ *Asia* 30°0N 70°0E **42** E4
Pakkading *Laos* 18°19N 103°59E **38** C4
Pakokku *Burma* 21°20N 95°0E **41** J19
Pakowki L. *Canada* 49°20N 111°0W **71** D6
Pakpattan *Pakistan* 30°25N 73°27E **42** D5
Paktiā □ *Afghan.* 33°30N 69°15E **40** C6
Paktīkā □ *Afghan.* 32°30N 69°0E **40** C6
Pakwach *Uganda* 2°28N 31°27E **54** D6
Pakxe *Laos* 15°5N 105°52E **38** E5
Pal Lahara *India* 21°27N 85°11E **43** J11
Palacios *U.S.A.* 28°42N 96°13W **84** G6
Palagruža *Croatia* 42°24N 16°15E **22** C7
Palakkad *India* 10°46N 76°42E **45** J3
Palakol *India* 16°31N 81°46E **45** F5
Palalankwe *India* 10°52N 92°29E **45** J11
Palam *India* 19°0N 77°0E **44** E3
Palampur *India* 32°10N 76°30E **42** C7
Palana *Australia* 39°45S 147°55E **63** F4
Palana *Russia* 59°10N 159°59E **27** D16
Palanan *Phil.* 17°8N 122°29E **37** A6
Palanan Pt. *Phil.* 17°17N 122°30E **37** A6
Palandri *Pakistan* 33°42N 73°40E **43** C5
Palanga *Lithuania* 55°58N 21°3E **9** J19
Palangkaraya *Indonesia* 2°16S 113°56E **36** E4
Palani *India* 10°30N 77°30E **45** J3
Palani Hills *India* 10°14N 77°33E **45** J3
Palanpur *India* 24°10N 72°25E **42** G5
Palapye *Botswana* 22°30S 27°7E **56** B4
Palar → *India* 12°27N 80°13E **45** H5
Palas *Pakistan* 35°4N 73°14E **43** B5
Palasponga *India* 21°47N 85°34E **43** J11
Palatka *Russia* 60°6N 150°54E **27** C16
Palatka *U.S.A.* 29°39N 81°38W **85** G14
Palau ■ *Palau* 7°30N 134°30E **58** A6
Palauk *Burma* 13°10N 98°40E **38** F2
Palaw *Burma* 12°58N 98°39E **38** F2
Palawan *Phil.* 9°30N 118°30E **36** C5
Palayankottai *India* 8°45N 77°45E **45** K3
Paldiski *Estonia* 59°23N 24°9E **9** G21
Paleleh *Indonesia* 1°10N 121°50E **37** D6
Palembang *Indonesia* 3°0S 104°50E **36** E2
Palencia *Spain* 42°1N 4°34W **21** A3
Palenque *Mexico* 17°29N 92°1W **87** D6
Palermo *Italy* 38°7N 13°22E **22** E5
Palermo *U.S.A.* 39°26N 121°33W **78** F5
Palestine *Chile* 23°50S 69°47W **96** A3
Palestine *Asia* 32°0N 35°0E **48** D4
Palestine *U.S.A.* 31°46N 95°38W **84** F7
Paletwa *Burma* 21°10N 92°50E **41** J18
Palghat = Palakkad *India* 10°46N 76°42E **45** J3
Palgrave, Mt. *Australia* 23°22S 115°58E **60** D2
Pali *India* 25°50N 73°20E **42** G5
Palikir *Micronesia* 6°55N 158°9E **64** G7
Paliouri, Akra *Greece* 39°57N 23°45E **23** E10
Palisades Res. *U.S.A.* 43°20N 111°12W **76** E8
Paliseul *Belgium* 49°54N 5°8E **15** E5
Palitana *India* 21°32N 71°49E **42** J4

Palizada *Mexico* 18°15N 92°5W **87** D6
Palk Bay *Asia* 9°30N 79°15E **45** K4
Palk Strait *Asia* 10°0N 79°45E **45** K4
Palkānah *Iraq* 35°49N 44°26E **46** C5
Palkonda *India* 18°36N 83°48E **44** E6
Palkonda Ra. *India* 13°50N 79°20E **45** H4
Palkot *India* 22°53N 84°39E **43** H11
Pallanza = Verbánia *Italy* 45°56N 8°33E **20** D8
Pallarenda *Australia* 19°12S 146°46E **62** B4
Palleru → *India* 16°45N 80°2E **44** F5
Pallinup → *Australia* 34°27S 118°50E **61** F2
Pallu *India* 28°59N 74°14E **42** E6
Palm Bay *U.S.A.* 28°2N 80°35W **85** G14
Palm Beach *U.S.A.* 26°43N 80°2W **85** H14
Palm Coast *U.S.A.* 29°35N 81°12W **85** G14
Palm Desert *U.S.A.* 33°43N 116°22W **79** M10
Palm-Grove △ *Australia* 24°57S 149°21E **62** C4
Palm Is. *Australia* 18°40S 146°35E **62** B4
Palm Springs *U.S.A.* 33°50N 116°33W **79** M10
Palma, B. de *Spain* 39°30N 2°39E **21** C7
Palma de Mallorca *Spain* 39°35N 2°39E **21** C7
Palma Soriano *Cuba* 20°15N 76°0W **88** B4
Palmares *Brazil* 8°41S 35°28W **93** E11
Palmas *Brazil* 26°29S 52°0W **95** B5
Palmas, C. *Liberia* 4°27N 7°46W **52** H4
Pálmas, G. di *Italy* 39°0N 8°30E **22** E3
Palmdale *U.S.A.* 34°35N 118°7W **79** L8
Palmeira das Missões
  Brazil 27°55S 53°17W **95** B5
Palmeira dos Índios
  Brazil 9°25S 36°37W **93** E11
Palmer *Antarctica* 64°35S 65°0W **5** C17
Palmer *U.S.A.* 61°36N 149°7W **68** E2
Palmer → *Australia* 16°0S 142°26E **62** B3
Palmer Arch. *Antarctica* 64°15S 65°0W **5** C17
Palmer Lake *U.S.A.* 39°7N 104°55W **76** G11
Palmerston *Australia* 12°31S 130°59E **60** B5
Palmerston *Canada* 43°50N 80°51W **82** C4
Palmerston *N.Z.* 45°29S 170°43E **59** F3
Palmerston North *N.Z.* 40°21S 175°39E **59** D5
Palmerton *U.S.A.* 40°48N 75°37W **83** F9
Palmetto *U.S.A.* 27°31N 82°34W **85** H13
Palmi *Italy* 38°21N 15°51E **22** E6
Palmira *Argentina* 32°59S 68°34W **94** C2
Palmira *Colombia* 3°32N 76°16W **92** C3
Palmyra = Tudmur *Syria* 34°36N 38°15E **46** C3
Palmyra *Mo., U.S.A.* 39°48N 91°32W **80** F8
Palmyra *N.J., U.S.A.* 40°0N 75°1W **83** G9
Palmyra *N.Y., U.S.A.* 43°5N 77°18W **82** C7
Palmyra *Pa., U.S.A.* 40°18N 76°36W **83** F8
Palmyra Is. *Pac. Oc.* 5°52N 162°5W **65** G11
Palmyras Pt. *India* 20°46N 87°1E **44** D8
Palo Alto *U.S.A.* 37°27N 122°10W **78** H4
Palo Seco *Trin. & Tob.* 10°4N 61°36W **93** K15
Palo Verde *U.S.A.* 33°26N 114°44W **79** M12
Palo Verde △ *Costa Rica* 10°21N 85°21W **88** D2
Palomar Mt. *U.S.A.* 33°22N 116°50W **79** M10
Palopo *Indonesia* 3°0S 120°16E **37** E6
Palos, C. de *Spain* 37°38N 0°40W **21** D5
Palos Verdes, Pt. *U.S.A.* 33°46N 118°25W **79** M8
Palos Verdes Estates
  U.S.A. 33°48N 118°23W **79** M8
Palu *Indonesia* 1°0S 119°52E **37** E5
Palu *Turkey* 38°45N 40°0E **46** B3
Paluma Ra. *Australia* 19°9S 146°22E **62** B4
Palwal *India* 28°8N 77°19E **42** E7
Pamanukan *Indonesia* 6°16S 107°49E **37** G12
Pamban I. *India* 9°15N 79°20E **45** K4
Pamekasan *Indonesia* 7°10S 113°28E **37** G15
Pamenang *Indonesia* 8°24S 116°6E **37** J19
Pamiers *France* 43°7N 1°39E **20** E4
Pamir *Tajikistan* 37°40N 73°0E **26** F8
Pamlico → *U.S.A.* 35°20N 76°28W **85** D16
Pamlico Sd. *U.S.A.* 35°20N 76°0W **85** D17
Pampa *U.S.A.* 35°32N 100°58W **84** D4
Pampa de las Salinas
  Argentina 32°1S 66°58W **94** C2
Pampanua *Indonesia* 4°16S 120°8E **37** E6
Pampas *Argentina* 35°0S 63°0W **94** D3
Pampas *Peru* 12°20S 74°50W **92** F4
Pamplona *Colombia* 7°23N 72°39W **92** B4
Pamplona-Iruña *Spain* 42°48N 1°38W **21** A5
Pampoenpoort *S. Africa* 31°3S 22°40E **56** E3
Pan de Azúcar *Chile* 24°5S 68°10W **94** A2
Pan de Azúcar △ *Chile* 26°0S 70°40W **94** B1
Pan Xian *China* 25°46N 104°38E **34** E5
Pana *U.S.A.* 39°23N 89°5W **80** F9
Panaca *U.S.A.* 37°47N 114°23W **77** H6
Panagyurishte *Bulgaria* 42°30N 24°15E **23** C11
Panaitan *Indonesia* 6°36S 105°12E **37** G11
Panaji *India* 15°25N 73°50E **45** G1
Panamá *Panama* 9°0N 79°25W **88** E4
Panama ■ *Cent. Amer.* 8°48N 79°55W **88** E4
Panamá, G. de *Panama* 8°4N 79°20W **88** E4
Panama, Isthmus of
  Cent. Amer. 9°0N 79°0W **88** E4
Panama Basin *Pac. Oc.* 5°0N 83°30W **65** G19
Panama Canal *Panama* 9°10N 79°37W **88** E4
Panama City *U.S.A.* 30°10N 85°40W **85** F12
Panamint Range *U.S.A.* 36°20N 117°20W **79** J9
Panamint Springs
  U.S.A. 36°20N 117°28W **79** J9
Panão *Peru* 9°55S 75°55W **92** E3
Panare *Thailand* 6°51N 101°30E **39** J3
Panay *Phil.* 11°10N 122°30E **37** B6
Panay G. *Phil.* 11°0N 122°30E **37** B6
Pančevo *Serbia* 44°52N 20°41E **23** B9
Panch'iao *Taiwan* 25°1N 121°27E **35** E13
Panda *Mozam.* 24°2S 34°45E **57** B5
Pandan *Malaysia* 1°32N 103°46E **39** d
Pandan *Phil.* 11°45N 122°10E **37** B6
Pandan Tampoi = Tampoi
  Malaysia 1°30N 103°39E **39** d
Pandegelang *Indonesia* 6°25S 106°5E **37** G12
Pandhana *India* 21°42N 76°13E **42** J7
Pandharkawada *India* 20°1N 78°32E **44** D4

Pandharpur *India* 17°41N 75°20E **44** F2
Pandhurna *India* 21°36N 78°35E **44** D4
Pando *Uruguay* 34°44S 56°0W **95** C4
Pando, L. = Hope, L.
  Australia 28°24S 139°18E **63** D2
Pandora *Costa Rica* 9°43N 83°3E **88** E3
Panevėžys *Lithuania* 55°42N 24°25E **9** J21
Pang Sida △ *Thailand* 14°5N 102°17E **38** E4
Pangandaran *Indonesia* 7°40S 108°39E **37** G13
Pangandaran △
  Indonesia 7°43S 108°42E **37** G13
Pangani *Tanzania* 5°25S 38°58E **54** F7
Pangfou = Bengbu
  China 32°58N 117°20E **33** H9
Pangga, Tanjung
  Indonesia 8°54S 116°2E **37** K19
Panghsang = Bangkang
  Burma 22°4N 99°1E **34** F2
Pangjiabu *China* 40°38N 115°26E **32** D8
Pangkah, Tanjung
  Indonesia 6°51S 112°33E **37** G15
Pangkai *Burma* 22°49N 98°39E **34** F2
Pangkajene *Indonesia* 4°46S 119°34E **37** E5
Pangkalanbrandan
  Indonesia 4°1N 98°20E **36** D1
Pangkalanbuun *Indonesia* 2°41S 111°37E **36** E4
Pangkalpinang *Indonesia* 2°0S 106°10E **36** E3
Pangkor, Pulau *Malaysia* 4°13N 100°34E **39** K3
Pangniqtuuq = Pangnirtung
  Canada 66°8N 65°43W **69** D18
Pangnirtung *Canada* 66°8N 65°43W **69** D18
Pangody *Russia* 65°52N 74°27E **26** C8
Pangong Tso = Bangong Co
  China 33°45N 78°43E **43** C8
Panguitch *U.S.A.* 37°50N 112°26W **77** H7
Pangutaran Group *Phil.* 6°18N 120°34E **37** C6
Panhala *India* 16°49N 74°7E **44** F2
Panhandle *U.S.A.* 35°21N 101°23W **84** D4
Pani Mines *India* 22°29N 73°50E **42** H5
Panikota I. *India* 20°46N 71°21E **42** J4
Panipat *India* 29°25N 77°2E **42** E7
Panjal Range = Pir Panjal Range
  India 32°30N 76°50E **42** C7
Panjgur *Pakistan* 27°0N 64°5E **40** F4
Panjhra → *India* 21°3N 74°57E **44** D2
Panjim = Panaji *India* 15°25N 73°50E **45** G1
Panjin *China* 41°3N 122°2E **33** D12
Panjnad → *Pakistan* 28°57N 70°30E **42** E4
Panjnad Barrage *Pakistan* 29°22N 71°15E **42** E4
Panjwai *Afghan.* 31°26N 65°27E **42** D1
Panmunjŏm *N. Korea* 37°59N 126°38E **33** F14
Panna *India* 24°40N 80°15E **43** G9
Panna △ *India* 24°40N 80°2E **44** B5
Panna Hills *India* 24°40N 81°15E **43** G9
Pannawonica *Australia* 21°39S 116°19E **60** D2
Pano Akil *Pakistan* 27°51N 69°7E **42** F3
Panorama *Brazil* 21°21S 51°51W **95** A5
Panruti *India* 11°46N 79°35E **45** J4
Pansemal *India* 21°39N 74°42E **42** J6
Panshan = Panjin *China* 41°3N 122°2E **33** D12
Panshi *China* 42°58N 126°5E **33** C14
Pantanal *Brazil* 17°30S 57°40W **92** H7
Pantanos de Centla △
  Mexico 18°25N 92°25W **87** D6
Pantar *Indonesia* 8°28S 124°10E **37** F6
Pante Macassar *E. Timor* 9°30S 123°58E **37** F6
Pantelleria *Italy* 36°50N 11°57E **22** F4
Pánuco *Mexico* 22°3N 98°10W **87** C5
Panvel *India* 18°59N 73°4E **44** E1
Panzhihua *China* 26°33N 101°44E **34** D4
Paola *U.S.A.* 38°35N 94°53W **80** F6
Paonia *U.S.A.* 38°52N 107°36W **76** G10
Paopao *Moorea* 17°30S 149°49W **59** d
Paoting = Baoding
  China 38°50N 115°28E **32** E8
Paot'ou = Baotou *China* 40°32N 110°2E **32** D6
Paoua *C.A.R.* 7°9N 16°20E **54** C3
Pápa *Hungary* 47°22N 17°30E **17** E9
Papa Stour *U.K.* 60°20N 1°42W **11** A7
Papa Westray *U.K.* 59°20N 2°55W **11** B6
Papagayo → *Mexico* 16°46N 99°43W **87** D5
Papagayo, G. de
  Costa Rica 10°30N 85°50W **88** D2
Papagni → *India* 15°35N 77°45E **45** G3
Papakura *N.Z.* 37°4S 174°59E **59** B5
Papantla *Mexico* 20°27N 97°19W **87** C5
Papar *Malaysia* 5°45N 116°0E **36** C5
Papara *Tahiti* 17°43S 149°31W **59** d
Paparoa △ *N.Z.* 42°17S 171°26E **59** E3
Papeete *Tahiti* 17°32S 149°34W **59** d
Papenoo *Tahiti* 17°30S 149°25W **59** d
Papenoo → *Tahiti* 17°30S 149°25W **59** d
Papetoai *Moorea* 17°29S 149°52W **59** d
Paposo *Chile* 25°0S 70°30W **94** B1
Papua □ *Indonesia* 4°0S 137°0E **37** E9
Papua, G. of *Papua N. G.* 9°0S 144°50E **58** B7
Papua New Guinea ■
  Oceania 8°0S 145°0E **58** B7
Papudo *Chile* 32°29S 71°27W **94** C1
Papun *Burma* 18°2N 97°30E **41** K20
Papunya *Australia* 23°15S 131°54E **60** D5
Pará = Belém *Brazil* 1°20S 48°30W **93** D9
Pará □ *Brazil* 3°20S 52°0W **93** D8
Paraburdoo *Australia* 23°14S 117°32E **60** D2
Paracatu *Brazil* 17°10S 46°50W **93** G9
Paracel Is. *S. China Sea* 15°50N 112°0E **36** A4
Parachilna *Australia* 31°10S 138°21E **63** E2
Parachinar *Pakistan* 33°55N 70°5E **42** C4
Paradip *India* 20°15N 86°35E **44** D8
Paradise *U.S.A.* 39°46N 121°37W **78** F5
Paradise → *Canada* 53°27N 57°19W **73** B8
Paradise Hill *Canada* 53°32N 109°28W **71** C7
Paradise River *Canada* 53°27N 57°17W **73** B8
Paradise Valley *U.S.A.* 41°30N 117°32W **76** F5
Paragould *U.S.A.* 36°3N 90°29W **85** C9
Paragua → *Venezuela* 6°55N 62°55W **92** B6
Paraguaçu → *Brazil* 12°45S 38°54W **93** F11
Paraguaçu Paulista
  Brazil 22°22S 50°35W **95** A5

Paraguaná, Pen. de
  Venezuela 12°0N 70°0W **92** A5
Paraguari *Paraguay* 25°36S 57°0W **94** B4
Paraguari □ *Paraguay* 26°0S 57°10W **94** B4
Paraguay ■ *S. Amer.* 23°0S 57°0W **94** A4
Paraguay → *Paraguay* 27°18S 58°38W **94** B4
Paraíba = João Pessoa
  Brazil 7°10S 34°52W **93** E12
Paraíba □ *Brazil* 7°0S 36°0W **93** E11
Paraíba do Sul → *Brazil* 21°37S 41°3W **95** A7
Paraíso *Mexico* 18°24N 93°14W **87** D6
Parak *Iran* 27°38N 52°25E **47** E7
Parakou *Benin* 9°25N 2°40E **52** G6
Paralkote *India* 19°47N 80°41E **44** E5
Paramaribo *Suriname* 5°50N 55°10W **93** B7
Páramos del Batallón y La Negra △
  Venezuela 8°2N 71°55W **89** E5
Paramushir, Ostrov
  Russia 50°24N 156°0E **27** D16
Paran → *Israel* 30°20N 35°10E **48** E4
Paraná *Argentina* 31°45S 60°30W **94** C3
Paraná *Brazil* 12°30S 47°48W **93** F9
Paraná □ *Brazil* 24°30S 51°0W **95** A5
Paraná → *Argentina* 33°43S 59°15W **94** C4
Paranaguá *Brazil* 25°30S 48°30W **95** B6
Paranaíba *Brazil* 19°40S 51°11W **93** H8
Paranaíba → *Brazil* 20°6S 51°4W **93** H8
Paranapanema → *Brazil* 22°40S 53°9W **95** A5
Paranapiacaba, Serra do
  Brazil 24°31S 48°35W **95** A6
Paranavaí *Brazil* 23°4S 52°56W **95** A5
Parang *Maguindanao, Phil.* 7°23N 124°16E **37** C6
Parang *Sulu, Phil.* 5°55N 120°54E **37** C6
Parangippettai *India* 11°30N 79°38E **45** J4
Parângul Mare, Vf.
  Romania 45°20N 23°37E **17** F12
Paranthan *Sri Lanka* 9°26N 80°24E **45** K5
Paraparaumu *N.Z.* 40°57S 175°3E **59** D5
Parbati → *Mad. P., India* 25°50N 76°30E **42** G7
Parbati → *Raj., India* 26°54N 77°53E **42** F7
Parbhani *India* 19°8N 76°52E **44** E3
Parchim *Germany* 53°26N 11°52E **16** B6
Pardes Hanna-Karkur
  Israel 32°28N 34°57E **48** C3
Pardo → *Bahia, Brazil* 15°40S 39°0W **93** G11
Pardo → *Mato Grosso,*
  Brazil 21°46S 52°9W **95** A5
Pardoo Roadhouse
  Australia 20°6S 119°3E **60** D2
Pardubice *Czech Rep.* 50°3N 15°45E **16** C8
Pare *Indonesia* 7°43S 112°12E **37** G15
Parecis, Serra dos *Brazil* 13°0S 60°0W **92** F7
Paren *Russia* 62°30N 163°15E **27** C17
Parenda *India* 18°16N 75°28E **44** E2
Parent *Canada* 47°55N 74°35W **72** C5
Parent, L. *Canada* 48°31N 77°1W **72** C4
Parepare *Indonesia* 4°0S 119°40E **37** E5
Parga *Greece* 39°15N 20°29E **23** E9
Pargas = Länsi-Turunmaa
  Finland 60°18N 22°18E **9** F20
Pargi *India* 17°11N 77°53E **44** E3
Parham *Canada* 44°39N 76°43W **83** B8
Paria → *U.S.A.* 36°52N 111°36W **77** H8
Paria, G. de *Venezuela* 10°30N 61°40W **93** K14
Pariaguán *Venezuela* 8°51N 64°34W **92** B6
Paricutín, Cerro *Mexico* 19°28N 102°15W **86** D4
Parigi *Indonesia* 0°50S 120°5E **37** E6
Parika *Guyana* 6°50N 58°20W **92** B7
Parikkala *Finland* 61°33N 29°31E **8** F23
Parima, Serra *Brazil* 2°30N 64°0W **92** C6
Parinari *Peru* 4°35S 74°25W **92** D4
Pariñas, Pta. *Peru* 4°30S 82°0W **90** D2
Parintins *Brazil* 2°40S 56°50W **93** D7
Pariparit Kyun *Burma* 14°52N 93°41E **45** G11
Paris *Canada* 43°12N 80°25W **82** C4
Paris *France* 48°53N 2°20E **20** B5
Paris *Idaho, U.S.A.* 42°14N 111°24W **76** E8
Paris *Ky., U.S.A.* 38°13N 84°15W **81** F11
Paris *Tenn., U.S.A.* 36°18N 88°19W **85** C10
Paris *Tex., U.S.A.* 33°40N 95°33W **84** E7
Parish *U.S.A.* 43°25N 76°8W **83** C8
Parishville *U.S.A.* 44°38N 74°49W **83** B10
Pariti *Indonesia* 10°1S 123°45E **60** B3
Park *U.S.A.* 48°45N 122°18W **78** B4
Park City *U.S.A.* 37°48N 97°20W **80** G5
Park Falls *U.S.A.* 45°56N 90°27W **80** C8
Park Head *Canada* 44°36N 81°9W **82** B3
Park Hills *U.S.A.* 37°51N 90°51W **80** G8
Park Range *U.S.A.* 40°41N 106°41W **76** F10
Park Rapids *U.S.A.* 46°55N 95°4W **80** B6
Park River *U.S.A.* 48°24N 97°45W **80** A5
Park Rynie *S. Africa* 30°25S 30°45E **57** D5
Parkā Bandar *Iran* 25°55N 59°35E **47** E8
Parkal *India* 18°12N 79°43E **44** E4
Parkano *Finland* 62°1N 23°0E **8** E20
Parker *Ariz., U.S.A.* 34°9N 114°17W **79** L12
Parker *Pa., U.S.A.* 41°5N 79°41W **82** E5
Parker Dam *U.S.A.* 34°18N 114°8W **79** L12
Parkersburg *U.S.A.* 39°16N 81°34W **81** F13
Parkes *Australia* 33°9S 148°11E **63** E4
Parkfield *U.S.A.* 35°54N 120°26W **78** K6
Parkhill *Canada* 43°15N 81°38W **82** C3
Parkland *U.S.A.* 47°9N 122°26W **78** C4
Parkston *U.S.A.* 43°24N 97°59W **80** D5
Parksville *Canada* 49°20N 124°21W **70** D4
Parkway *U.S.A.* 38°32N 121°26W **78** G5
Parla *Spain* 40°14N 3°46W **21** B4
Parlakimidi *India* 18°45N 84°5E **44** E7
Parli *India* 18°50N 76°35E **44** E3
Parma *Italy* 44°48N 10°20E **20** D9
Parma *Idaho, U.S.A.* 43°47N 116°57W **76** E5
Parma *Ohio, U.S.A.* 41°24N 81°43W **82** E3
Parnaguá *Brazil* 10°10S 44°38W **93** F10
Parnaíba *Brazil* 2°54S 41°47W **93** D10
Parnaíba → *Brazil* 3°0S 41°50W **93** D10
Parnassós *Greece* 38°35N 22°30E **23** E10
Parner *India* 19°0N 74°26E **44** E2
Pärnu *Estonia* 58°28N 24°33E **9** G21
Paro Dzong *Bhutan* 27°32N 89°53E **43** F13
Parola *India* 20°47N 75°7E **44** D2

Paroo → Australia 31°28S 143°32E 63 E3
Paros Greece 37°5N 25°12E 23 F11
Parowan U.S.A. 37°51N 112°50W 77 H7
Parral Chile 36°10S 71°52W 94 D1
Parramatta Australia 33°48S 151°1E 63 B5
Parras Mexico 25°25N 102°11W 86 B4
Parrett → U.K. 51°12N 3°1W 13 F4
Parris I. U.S.A. 32°20N 80°41W 85 E14
Parrsboro Canada 45°30N 64°25W 73 C7
Parry Channel Canada 74°15N 94°0W 69 C13
Parry I. Canada 45°18N 80°10W 82 A4
Parry Is. Canada 77°0N 110°0W 69 B10
Parry Sound Canada 45°20N 80°0W 82 A5
Parsnip → Canada 55°10N 123°2W 70 B4
Parsons U.S.A. 37°20N 95°16W 80 G6
Parsons Ra. Australia 13°30S 135°15E 62 A2
Partabpur India 20°0N 80°42E 44 E5
Partinico Italy 38°3N 13°7E 22 E5
Partizansk Russia 43°8N 133°9E 27 E14
Partridge I. Canada 55°59N 87°37W 72 A2
Partry Mts. Ireland 53°40N 9°29W 10 C2
Partur India 19°40N 76°14E 44 E3
Paru → Brazil 1°33S 52°38W 93 D8
Parur India 10°13N 76°14E 45 J3
Parvān □ Afghan. 35°0N 69°0E 40 B6
Parvatipuram India 18°50N 83°25E 44 E6
Parvatsar India 26°52N 74°49E 42 F6
Parys S. Africa 26°52S 27°29E 56 C4
Pas, The Canada 53°45N 101°15W 71 C8
Pasadena Canada 49°1N 57°36W 73 C8
Pasadena U.S.A. 29°43N 95°13W 84 G7
Pasaje → Argentina 25°39S 63°56W 94 B3
Pasar Indonesia 8°27S 114°54E 37 J17
Pasargadae Iran 30°11N 53°10E 47 D7
Pascagoula U.S.A. 30°21N 88°33W 85 F10
Pascagoula → U.S.A. 30°23N 88°37W 85 F10
Paşcani Romania 47°14N 26°45E 17 E14
Paschimbanga □ India 23°0N 88°0E 43 H13
Pasco U.S.A. 46°14N 119°6W 76 C4
Pasco I. Australia 20°57S 115°20E 60 D2
Pascoag U.S.A. 41°57N 71°42W 83 E13
Pascua, I. de Chile 27°7S 109°23W 65 K17
Pasfield L. Canada 58°24N 105°20W 71 B7
Pasir Mas Malaysia 6°2N 102°8E 39 J4
Pasir Putih Malaysia 5°50N 102°24E 39 K4
Pasirian Indonesia 8°13S 113°8E 37 H15
Paskūh Iran 27°34N 61°39E 47 E9
Pasley, C. Australia 33°52S 123°35E 61 F3
Pašman Croatia 43°58N 15°20E 16 G8
Pasni Pakistan 25°15N 63°27E 40 G3
Paso Bravo △ Paraguay 22°32S 57°5W 94 A4
Paso Cantinela Mexico 32°33N 115°47W 79 N11
Paso de Indios Argentina 43°55S 69°0W 96 E3
Paso de los Libres
   Argentina 29°44S 57°10W 94 B4
Paso de los Toros
   Uruguay 32°45S 56°30W 94 C4
Paso Robles U.S.A. 35°38N 120°41W 78 K6
Paspébiac Canada 48°3N 65°17W 73 C6
Pasrur Pakistan 32°16N 74°43E 42 C6
Passage East Ireland 52°14N 7°0W 10 D5
Passage West Ireland 51°52N 8°21W 10 E3
Passau Germany 48°34N 13°28E 16 D7
Passero, C. Italy 36°41N 15°10E 22 F6
Passo Fundo Brazil 28°10S 52°20W 95 B5
Passos Brazil 20°45S 46°37W 93 H9
Pastavy Belarus 55°4N 26°50E 9 J22
Pastaza → Peru 4°50S 76°52W 92 D3
Pasto Colombia 1°13N 77°17W 92 C3
Pasuruan Indonesia 7°40S 112°44E 37 G15
Patagonia Argentina 45°0S 69°0W 96 F3
Patagonia U.S.A. 31°33N 110°45W 77 L8
Patambar Iran 29°45N 60°17E 47 D9
Patan = Lalitpur Nepal 27°40N 85°20E 43 F11
Patan = Somnath India 20°53N 70°22E 42 J4
Patan Gujarat, India 23°54N 72°14E 42 H5
Patan Maharashtra, India 17°22N 73°57E 44 F1
Patani Indonesia 0°20N 128°50E 37 D7
Pataudi India 28°18N 76°48E 42 E7
Patchewollock Australia 35°22S 142°12E 63 F3
Patchogue U.S.A. 40°46N 73°1W 83 F11
Patea N.Z. 39°45S 174°30E 59 C5
Patensie S. Africa 33°46S 24°49E 56 D3
Paternò Italy 37°34N 14°54E 22 F6
Pateros U.S.A. 48°3N 119°54W 76 B4
Paterson U.S.A. 40°54N 74°9W 83 F10
Paterson Ra. Australia 21°45S 122°10E 60 D3
Pathankot India 32°18N 75°45E 42 C6
Pathardi India 19°10N 75°11E 44 E2
Pathein = Bassein
   Burma 16°45N 94°30E 41 L19
Pathfinder Res. U.S.A. 42°0N 106°51W 76 E10
Pathiu Thailand 10°42N 99°19E 39 G2
Pathri India 19°15N 76°27E 44 E3
Pathum Thani Thailand 14°1N 100°32E 38 E3
Pati Indonesia 6°45S 111°1E 37 G14
Patía → Colombia 2°13N 78°40W 92 C3
Patiala Punjab, India 30°23N 76°26E 42 D7
Patiala Ut. P., India 27°43N 79°1E 43 F8
Patkai Bum India 27°0N 95°30E 41 F19
Patmos Greece 37°21N 26°36E 23 F12
Patna India 25°35N 85°12E 43 G11
Patnagarh India 20°43N 83°9E 44 D6
Pato Branco Brazil 26°13S 52°40W 95 B5
Patong, Ao Thailand 7°54N 98°17E 39 a
Patos Brazil 6°55S 37°16W 93 E11
Patos, L. dos Brazil 31°20S 51°0W 95 C5
Patos, Rio de los →
   Argentina 31°18S 69°25W 94 C2
Patos de Minas Brazil 18°35S 46°32W 93 G9
Patquía Argentina 30°2S 66°55W 94 C2
Patra Greece 38°14N 21°47E 23 E9
Patraikos Kolpos Greece 38°17N 21°30E 23 E9
Patras = Patra Greece 38°14N 21°47E 23 E9
Patriot Hills Antarctica 82°20S 81°25W 5 E16
Patrocinio Brazil 18°57S 47°0W 93 G9
Pattadakal India 16°1N 75°42E 45 F2
Pattani Thailand 6°48N 101°15E 39 J3
Pattaya Thailand 12°52N 100°55E 38 F3

Patten U.S.A. 46°0N 68°38W 81 B19
Patterson Calif., U.S.A. 37°28N 121°8W 78 H5
Patterson La., U.S.A. 29°42N 91°18W 84 G9
Patterson, Mt. U.S.A. 38°29N 119°20W 78 G7
Patti Punjab, India 31°17N 74°54E 42 D6
Patti Ut. P., India 25°55N 82°12E 43 G10
Pattoki Pakistan 31°5N 73°52E 42 D5
Patton U.S.A. 40°38N 78°39W 82 F6
Pattukkattai India 10°25N 79°20E 45 J4
Patuakhali Bangla. 22°20N 90°25E 41 H17
Patuanak Canada 55°55N 107°43W 71 B7
Patuca → Honduras 15°50N 84°18W 88 C3
Patuca, Punta Honduras 15°49N 84°14W 88 C3
Patuca △ Honduras 14°30N 85°30W 88 D2
Patur India 20°27N 76°56E 44 D3
Patvinsuo △ Finland 63°7N 30°45E 8 E24
Pátzcuaro Mexico 19°31N 101°38W 86 D4
Pau France 43°19N 0°25W 20 E3
Paudash Canada 44°59N 77°58W 82 B7
Pauk Burma 21°27N 94°30E 41 J19
Paul I. Canada 56°30N 61°20W 73 A7
Paul Smiths U.S.A. 44°26N 74°15W 83 B10
Paulatuk Canada 69°25N 124°0W 68 D7
Paulistana Brazil 8°9S 41°9W 93 E11
Paulo Afonso Brazil 9°21S 38°15W 93 E11
Paulpietersburg S. Africa 27°23S 30°50E 57 C5
Pauls Valley U.S.A. 34°44N 97°13W 84 D6
Pauma Valley U.S.A. 33°16N 116°58W 79 M10
Pauni India 20°48N 79°40E 44 D4
Pauri India 30°9N 78°47E 43 D8
Pavagada India 14°6N 77°16E 45 G3
Pāveh Iran 35°3N 46°22E 46 C5
Pavia Italy 45°7N 9°8E 20 D8
Pavilion U.S.A. 42°52N 78°1W 82 D6
Pāvilosta Latvia 56°53N 21°14E 9 H19
Pavlodar Kazakhstan 52°33N 77°0E 26 D8
Pavlograd = Pavlohrad
   Ukraine 48°30N 35°52E 19 E6
Pavlohrad Ukraine 48°30N 35°52E 19 E6
Pavlovo Russia 55°58N 43°5E 18 C7
Pavlovsk Russia 50°26N 40°5E 19 E7
Pavlovskaya Russia 46°17N 39°47E 19 E6
Pawai, Pulau Singapore 1°11N 103°44E 39 d
Pawayan India 28°4N 80°6E 43 E9
Pawhuska U.S.A. 36°40N 96°20W 84 C6
Pawling U.S.A. 41°34N 73°36W 83 E11
Pawnee U.S.A. 36°20N 96°48W 84 C6
Pawnee City U.S.A. 40°7N 96°9W 80 E5
Pawtucket U.S.A. 41°53N 71°23W 83 E13
Paxi Greece 39°14N 20°12E 23 E9
Paxton U.S.A. 40°27N 88°6W 80 E9
Payakumbuh Indonesia 0°20S 100°35E 36 E2
Payette U.S.A. 44°5N 116°56W 76 D5
Payne Bay = Kangirsuk
   Canada 60°0N 70°0W 69 F18
Payne L. Canada 59°30N 74°30W 69 F17
Paynes Find Australia 29°15S 117°42E 61 E2
Paynesville U.S.A. 45°23N 94°43W 80 C6
Paysandú Uruguay 32°19S 58°8W 94 C4
Payson Ariz., U.S.A. 34°14N 111°20W 77 J8
Payson Utah, U.S.A. 40°3N 111°44W 76 F8
Paz → Guatemala 13°44N 90°10W 88 D1
Paz, B. de la Mexico 24°9N 110°25W 86 C2
Pāzanān Iran 30°35N 49°59E 47 D6
Pazardzhik Bulgaria 42°12N 24°20E 23 C11
Pe Ell U.S.A. 46°34N 123°18W 78 D3
Peabody U.S.A. 42°31N 70°56W 83 D14
Peace → Canada 59°0N 111°25W 70 B6
Peace Point Canada 59°7N 112°27W 70 B6
Peace River Canada 56°15N 117°18W 70 B5
Peach Springs U.S.A. 35°32N 113°25W 77 J7
Peachland Canada 49°47N 119°45W 70 D5
Peachtree City U.S.A. 33°25N 84°35W 85 E12
Peak, The = Kinder Scout
   U.K. 53°24N 1°52W 12 D6
Peak Charles △ Australia 32°42S 121°10E 61 F3
Peak District △ U.K. 53°24N 1°46W 12 D6
Peak Hill Australia 32°47S 148°11E 63 E4
Peak Ra. Australia 22°50S 148°20E 62 C4
Peake Cr. → Australia 28°2S 136°7E 63 D2
Peale, Mt. U.S.A. 38°26N 109°14W 76 G9
Pearblossom U.S.A. 34°30N 117°55W 79 L9
Pearl → U.S.A. 30°11N 89°32W 85 F10
Pearl and Hermes Reef
   U.S.A. 27°55N 175°45W 75 K4
Pearl Banks Sri Lanka 8°45N 79°45E 45 K4
Pearl River = Zhu Jiang
   China 22°45N 113°37E 35 F9
Pearl River U.S.A. 41°4N 74°2W 83 E10
Pearl River Bridge China 22°15N 113°48E 31 a
Pearsall U.S.A. 28°54N 99°6W 84 G5
Peary Land Greenland 82°40N 33°0W 4 A6
Pease → U.S.A. 34°12N 99°2W 84 D5
Peawanuck Canada 55°15N 85°12W 72 A2
Pebane Mozam. 17°10S 38°8E 55 H7
Pebas Peru 3°10S 71°46W 92 D4
Pebble Beach U.S.A. 36°34N 121°57W 78 J5
Peć = Pejë Kosovo 42°40N 20°17E 23 C9
Pechenga Russia 69°29N 31°4E 8 B24
Pechenizhyn Ukraine 48°30N 24°48E 17 D13
Pechora Russia 65°10N 57°11E 18 A10
Pechora → Russia 68°13N 54°15E 18 A9
Pechorskaya Guba Russia 68°40N 54°0E 18 A9
Pechory Russia 57°48N 27°40E 9 H22
Pecos N. Mex., U.S.A. 35°35N 105°41W 77 J11
Pecos Tex., U.S.A. 31°26N 103°30W 84 F3
Pecos → U.S.A. 29°42N 101°22W 84 G4
Pécs Hungary 46°5N 18°15E 17 E10
Pedasí Panama 7°32N 80°2W 88 E3
Pedda Bellala India 19°4N 78°4E 44 E4
Peddapalli India 18°40N 79°24E 44 E4
Peddapuram India 17°6N 82°8E 44 F6
Peddie S. Africa 33°14S 27°7E 57 D4
Pedernales Dom. Rep. 18°2N 71°44W 89 C5
Pedirka Desert Australia 26°47S 134°11E 63 A1
Pedra Azul Brazil 16°2S 41°17W 93 G10
Pedra Lume C. Verde Is. 16°40N 22°52W 52 b

Pedreiras Brazil 4°32S 44°40W 93 D10
Pedro Afonso Brazil 9°0S 48°10W 93 E9
Pedro Cays Jamaica 17°5N 77°48W 88 C4
Pedro de Valdivia Chile 22°55S 69°38W 94 A2
Pedro Juan Caballero
   Paraguay 22°30S 55°40W 95 A4
Pee Dee = Great Pee Dee
   U.S.A. 33°21N 79°10W 85 E15
Peebinga Australia 34°52S 140°57E 63 E3
Peebles U.K. 55°40N 3°11W 11 F5
Peekskill U.S.A. 41°17N 73°55W 83 E11
Peel I. of Man 54°13N 4°40W 12 C3
Peel → Australia 30°50S 150°29E 63 E5
Peel → Canada 67°0N 135°0W 68 D5
Peel Sd. Canada 73°0N 96°0W 68 C12
Peera Peera Poolanna L.
   Australia 26°30S 138°0E 63 D2
Peerless Lake Canada 56°37N 114°40W 70 B6
Peers Canada 53°40N 116°0W 70 C5
Pegasus Bay N.Z. 43°20S 173°10E 59 E4
Pegu Burma 17°20N 96°29E 41 L20
Pegu Yoma Burma 19°0N 96°0E 41 K20
Pehuajó Argentina 35°45S 62°0W 94 D3
Pei Xian China 34°44N 116°55E 32 G9
Peikang Taiwan 23°34N 120°18E 35 F13
Peine Chile 23°45S 68°8W 94 A2
Peine Germany 52°19N 10°14E 16 B6
Peipus, L. = Chudskoye, Ozero
   Russia 58°13N 27°30E 9 G22
Peixe Brazil 12°0S 48°40W 93 F9
Peixe → Brazil 21°31S 51°58W 93 H8
Pejë Kosovo 42°40N 20°17E 23 C9
Pekalongan Indonesia 6°53S 109°40E 37 G13
Pekan Malaysia 3°30N 103°25E 39 L4
Pekan Nenas Malaysia 1°31N 103°31E 39 d
Pekanbaru Indonesia 0°30N 101°15E 36 D2
Pekin U.S.A. 40°35N 89°40W 80 E9
Pekutatan Indonesia 8°25S 114°49E 37 J17
Pelabuhan Ratu, Teluk
   Indonesia 7°5S 106°30E 37 G12
Pelagie, Is. Italy 35°39N 12°33E 22 G5
Pelaihari Indonesia 3°55S 114°45E 36 E4
Peleaga, Vf. Romania 45°22N 22°55E 17 F12
Pelée, Mt. Martinique 14°48N 61°10W 88 c
Pelee, Pt. Canada 41°54N 82°31W 72 D3
Pelee I. Canada 41°47N 82°40W 82 E2
Peleng Indonesia 1°20S 123°30E 37 E6
Pelentong Malaysia 1°32N 103°49E 39 d
Pelican U.S.A. 57°58N 136°14W 70 B1
Pelican L. Canada 52°28N 100°20W 71 C8
Pelican Narrows
   Canada 55°10N 102°56W 71 B8
Peljesac Croatia 42°55N 17°25E 22 C7
Pelkosenniemi Finland 67°6N 27°28E 8 C22
Pella S. Africa 29°1S 19°6E 56 C2
Pello Finland 66°47N 23°59E 8 C20
Pelly → Canada 62°47N 137°19W 70 A1
Pelly Bay Canada 68°38N 89°50W 69 D14
Pelorus Sd. N.Z. 40°59S 173°59E 59 D4
Pelotas Brazil 31°42S 52°23W 95 C5
Pelotas → Brazil 27°28S 51°55W 95 B5
Pelvoux, Massif du France 44°52N 6°20E 20 D7
Pemalang Indonesia 6°53S 109°23E 37 G13
Pemanggil, Pulau
   Malaysia 2°37N 104°21E 39 L5
Pematangsiantar Indonesia 2°57N 99°5E 36 D1
Pemba Mozam. 12°58S 40°30E 55 G8
Pemba I. Tanzania 5°0S 39°45E 54 F7
Pemberton Australia 34°30S 116°0E 61 F2
Pemberton Canada 50°25N 122°50W 70 C4
Pembina → Canada 54°45N 114°17W 70 C6
Pembroke Canada 45°50N 77°7W 72 C4
Pembroke U.K. 51°41N 4°55W 13 F3
Pembrokeshire □ U.K. 51°52N 4°56W 13 F3
Pembrokeshire Coast △
   U.K. 51°50N 5°2W 13 F2
Pen India 18°45N 73°5E 44 E1
Pen-y-bont ar Ogwr = Bridgend
   U.K. 51°30N 3°34W 13 F4
Pen-y-Ghent U.K. 54°10N 2°14W 12 C5
Penal Trin. & Tob. 10°9N 61°29W 93 K15
Penang = Pinang Malaysia 5°25N 100°15E 39 c
Penápolis Brazil 21°30S 50°0W 95 A6
Peñarroya-Pueblonuevo
   Spain 38°19N 5°16W 21 C3
Penarth U.K. 51°26N 3°11W 13 F4
Peñas, C. de Spain 43°42N 5°52W 21 A3
Peñas, G. de Chile 47°0S 75°0W 96 F2
Pench → India 21°17N 79°10E 44 D4
Pench △ India 21°45N 79°20E 43 J8
Pench'i = Benxi China 41°20N 123°48E 33 D12
Pend Oreille → U.S.A. 49°4N 117°37W 76 B5
Pend Oreille, L. U.S.A. 48°10N 116°21W 76 B5
Pendembu S. Leone 9°7N 11°14W 52 G3
Pender B. Australia 16°45S 122°42E 60 C3
Pendleton U.S.A. 45°40N 118°47W 76 D4
Pendra India 22°46N 81°57E 43 H9
Penedo Brazil 10°15S 36°36W 93 F11
Penetanguishene Canada 44°50N 79°55W 82 B5
Penfield U.S.A. 41°13N 78°35W 82 E6
Penfro = Pembroke U.K. 51°41N 4°55W 13 F3
Peng Chau China 22°17N 114°2E 31 a
Peng'an China 31°2N 106°22E 34 B6
Penganga → India 19°53N 79°9E 44 E4
P'enghu Ch'üntou
   Taiwan 23°34N 119°30E 35 F12
Pengjiang China 37°48N 120°42E 33 F11
Pengshan China 30°14N 103°58E 34 B4
Pengshui China 29°17N 108°12E 34 C7
Penguin Australia 41°8S 146°6E 63 G4
Pengxi China 30°44N 105°45E 34 B5
Pengzhou China 31°4N 103°32E 34 B4
Penhalonga Zimbabwe 18°52S 32°40E 55 F3
Peniche Portugal 39°19N 9°22W 21 C1
Penida, Nusa Indonesia 8°45S 115°30E 37 K18
Peninsular Malaysia □
   Malaysia 4°0N 102°0E 39 L4

Penitente, Serra do Brazil 8°45S 46°20W 93 E9
Penkridge U.K. 52°44N 2°6W 12 E5
Penmarch, Pte. de France 47°48N 4°22W 20 C1
Penn Hills U.S.A. 40°28N 79°52W 82 F5
Penn Yan U.S.A. 42°40N 77°3W 82 D7
Pennant Canada 50°32N 108°14W 71 C7
Penner → India 14°35N 80°10E 45 G5
Pennines U.K. 54°45N 2°27W 12 C5
Pennington U.S.A. 39°15N 121°47W 78 F5
Pennsburg U.S.A. 40°23N 75°29W 83 F9
Pennsylvania □ U.S.A. 40°45N 77°30W 81 E15
Penny U.S.A. 53°51N 121°20W 70 C4
Penobscot → U.S.A. 44°30N 68°48W 81 C19
Penobscot B. U.S.A. 44°35N 68°50W 81 C19
Penola Australia 37°25S 140°48E 63 F3
Penong Australia 31°56S 133°1E 61 F5
Penonomé Panama 8°31N 80°21W 88 E3
Penrhyn Cook Is. 9°0S 158°0W 65 H12
Penrith Australia 33°43S 150°38E 63 B5
Penrith U.K. 54°40N 2°45W 12 C5
Penryn U.K. 50°9N 5°7W 13 G2
Pensacola U.S.A. 30°25N 87°13W 85 F11
Pensacola Mts. Antarctica 84°0S 40°0W 5 E1
Pense Canada 50°25N 104°59W 71 C8
Penshurst Australia 37°49S 142°20E 63 F3
Penticton Canada 49°30N 119°38W 70 D5
Pentland Australia 20°32S 145°25E 62 C4
Pentland Firth U.K. 58°43N 3°10W 11 C5
Pentland Hills U.K. 55°48N 3°25W 11 F5
Penukonda India 14°5N 77°38E 45 G3
Penza Russia 53°15N 45°5E 18 D8
Penzance U.K. 50°7N 5°33W 13 G2
Penzhino Russia 63°30N 167°55E 27 C17
Penzhinskaya Guba
   Russia 61°30N 163°0E 27 C17
Peoria Ariz., U.S.A. 33°43N 112°14W 77 K7
Peoria Ill., U.S.A. 40°42N 89°36W 80 E9
Pepani → S. Africa 25°49S 22°47E 56 C3
Pera Hd. Australia 12°55S 141°37E 62 A3
Perabumulih Indonesia 3°27S 104°15E 36 E2
Perak □ Malaysia 5°0N 101°0E 39 K3
Perak → Malaysia 4°0N 100°50E 39 K3
Perancak Indonesia 8°24S 114°37E 37 J17
Percé Canada 48°31N 64°13W 73 C7
Perche, Collines du France 48°30N 0°40E 20 B4
Percival Lakes Australia 21°25S 125°0E 60 D4
Percy Is. Australia 21°39S 150°16E 62 C5
Perdido, Mte. Spain 42°40N 0°5E 21 A6
Perdu, Mt. = Perdido, Mte.
   Spain 42°40N 0°5E 21 A6
Pereira Colombia 4°49N 75°43W 92 C3
Peremul Par India 11°10N 72°4E 45 J1
Perenjori Australia 29°26S 116°16E 61 E2
Pereyaslav-Khmelnytskyy
   Ukraine 50°3N 31°28E 19 D5
Pérez, I. Mexico 22°24N 89°42W 87 C7
Pergamino Argentina 33°52S 60°30W 94 C3
Pergau → Malaysia 5°23N 102°2E 39 K3
Perham U.S.A. 46°36N 95°34W 80 B6
Perhentian, Kepulauan
   Malaysia 5°54N 102°42E 39 K4
Péribonka → Canada 48°45N 72°5W 73 C5
Péribonka, L. Canada 50°1N 71°10W 73 B5
Péribonka, La Centrale de
   Canada 49°30N 71°10W 73 C5
Perico Argentina 24°20S 65°5W 94 A2
Pericos Mexico 25°3N 107°42W 86 B3
Périgueux France 45°10N 0°42E 20 D4
Perijá, Sierra de Colombia 9°30N 73°3W 92 B4
Perijá △ Venezuela 9°20N 72°55E 89 E5
Peringat Malaysia 6°2N 102°17E 39 J4
Perito Moreno Argentina 46°36S 70°56W 96 F2
Periyakulam India 10°5N 77°30E 45 J3
Periyar → India 10°15N 76°10E 45 J3
Periyar, L. India 9°25N 77°10E 45 K3
Periyar △ India 9°25N 77°10E 45 K3
Perkasie U.S.A. 40°22N 75°18W 83 F9
Perlas, Arch. de las
   Panama 8°41N 79°7W 88 E4
Perlas, Punta de Nic. 12°30N 83°30W 88 D3
Perlis □ Malaysia 6°30N 100°15E 39 J3
Perm Russia 58°0N 56°10E 18 C10
Pernambuco = Recife
   Brazil 8°0S 35°0W 93 E12
Pernambuco □ Brazil 8°0S 37°0W 93 E11
Pernatty Lagoon
   Australia 31°30S 137°12E 63 E2
Pernik Bulgaria 42°35N 23°2E 23 C10
Peron Is. Australia 13°9S 130°4E 60 B5
Peron Pen. Australia 26°0S 113°10E 61 E1
Perow Canada 54°35N 126°10W 70 C3
Perpignan France 42°42N 2°53E 20 E5
Perris U.S.A. 33°47N 117°14W 79 M9
Perry Fla., U.S.A. 30°7N 83°35W 85 F13
Perry Ga., U.S.A. 32°28N 83°44W 85 E13
Perry Iowa, U.S.A. 41°51N 94°6W 80 E6
Perry N.Y., U.S.A. 42°44N 78°0W 82 D6
Perry Okla., U.S.A. 36°17N 97°14W 84 C6
Perryton U.S.A. 36°24N 100°48W 84 C4
Perryville U.S.A. 37°43N 89°52W 80 G9
Persepolis Iran 29°55N 52°50E 47 D7
Pershotravensk Ukraine 50°13N 27°40E 17 C14
Persia = Iran ■ Asia 33°0N 53°0E 47 C7
Persian Gulf Asia 27°0N 50°0E 47 E6
Perth Australia 31°57S 115°52E 61 F2
Perth U.K. 56°24N 3°26W 11 E5
Perth & Kinross □ U.K. 56°45N 3°55W 11 E5
Perth Amboy U.S.A. 40°30N 74°15W 83 F10
Perth-Andover Canada 46°44N 67°42W 73 C6
Perth Basin Ind. Oc. 30°0S 95°0E 64 L3
Peru Ind., U.S.A. 40°45N 86°4W 80 E10
Peru N.Y., U.S.A. 44°35N 73°32W 83 B11
Peru ■ S. Amer. 4°0S 75°0W 92 D4
Peru Basin Pac. Oc. 20°0S 95°0W 65 J18
Peru-Chile Trench Pac. Oc. 20°0S 72°0W 92 G3
Perúgia Italy 43°7N 12°23E 22 C5

Pervomaysk Ukraine 48°10N 30°46E 19 E5
Pervouralsk Russia 56°59N 59°59E 18 C10
Pésaro Italy 43°54N 12°55E 22 C5
Pescadores = P'enghu Ch'üntou
   Taiwan 23°34N 119°30E 35 F12
Pescara Italy 42°28N 14°13E 22 C6
Peshawar Pakistan 34°2N 71°37E 42 B4
Peshkopi Albania 41°41N 20°25E 23 D9
Peshtigo U.S.A. 45°3N 87°45W 80 C10
Pesqueira Brazil 8°20S 36°42W 93 E11
Petah Tiqwa Israel 32°6N 34°53E 48 C3
Petaling Jaya Malaysia 3°4N 101°42E 39 L3
Petaluma U.S.A. 38°14N 122°39W 78 G4
Pétange Lux. 49°33N 5°55E 15 E5
Petaro Pakistan 25°31N 68°18E 42 G3
Petatlán Mexico 17°31N 101°16W 86 D4
Petauke Zambia 14°14S 31°20E 55 G6
Petawawa Canada 45°54N 77°17W 72 C4
Petén Itzá, L. Guatemala 16°58N 89°50W 88 C2
Peter I. Br. Virgin Is. 18°22N 64°35W 89 e
Peter I. Øy Antarctica 69°0S 91°0W 5 C16
Peter Pond L. Canada 55°55N 108°44W 71 B7
Peterbell Canada 48°36N 83°21W 72 C3
Peterborough Australia 32°58S 138°51E 63 E2
Peterborough Canada 44°20N 78°20W 82 B6
Peterborough U.K. 52°35N 0°15W 13 E7
Peterborough U.S.A. 42°53N 71°57W 83 D13
Peterborough □ U.K. 52°35N 0°15W 13 E7
Peterculter U.K. 57°6N 2°16W 11 D6
Peterhead U.K. 57°31N 1°48W 11 D7
Peterlee U.K. 54°47N 1°20W 12 C6
Petermann ○ Australia 24°58S 130°0E 61 E4
Petermann Gletscher
   Greenland 80°30N 60°0W 69 A20
Petermann Ranges
   Australia 26°0S 130°30E 61 E5
Petersburg Alaska,
   U.S.A. 56°48N 132°58W 68 F5
Petersburg Pa., U.S.A. 40°34N 78°3W 82 F6
Petersburg Va., U.S.A. 37°14N 77°24W 81 G15
Petersburg W. Va., U.S.A. 39°1N 79°5W 81 F14
Petersfield U.K. 51°1N 0°56W 13 F7
Petit-Canal Guadeloupe 16°25N 61°31W 88 b
Petit-Goâve Haiti 18°27N 72°51W 89 C5
Petit Lac Manicouagan
   Canada 51°25N 67°40W 73 B6
Petit-Mécatina →
   Canada 50°40N 59°30W 73 B8
Petit-Mécatina, Î. du
   Canada 50°30N 59°25W 73 B8
Petit Piton St. Lucia 13°51N 61°5W 89 f
Petit-Saguenay Canada 48°15N 70°4W 73 C5
Petitcodiac Canada 45°57N 65°11W 73 C6
Petite Terre, Îles de la
   Guadeloupe 16°13N 61°9W 88 b
Petitot → Canada 60°14N 123°29W 70 A4
Petitsikapau L. Canada 54°37N 66°25W 73 B6
Petlad India 22°30N 72°45E 42 H5
Peto Mexico 20°8N 88°55W 87 C7
Petone N.Z. 41°13S 174°53E 59 D5
Petorca Chile 32°15S 70°56W 94 C1
Petoskey U.S.A. 45°22N 84°57W 81 C11
Petra Jordan 30°20N 35°22E 48 E4
Petra, Ostrov Russia 76°15N 118°30E 27 B12
Petra Velikogo, Zaliv
   Russia 42°40N 132°0E 28 C6
Petre, Pt. Canada 43°50N 77°9W 82 C7
Petrich Bulgaria 41°24N 23°13E 23 D10
Petrified Forest △ U.S.A. 35°0N 109°30W 77 J9
Petrikov = Pyetrikaw
   Belarus 52°11N 28°29E 17 B15
Petrolândia Brazil 9°5S 38°20W 93 E11
Petrolia Canada 42°54N 82°9W 82 D2
Petrolina Brazil 9°24S 40°30W 93 E10
Petropavl Kazakhstan 54°53N 69°13E 26 D7
Petropavlovsk = Petropavl
   Kazakhstan 54°53N 69°13E 26 D7
Petropavlovsk-Kamchatskiy
   Russia 53°3N 158°43E 27 D16
Petrópolis Brazil 22°33S 43°9W 95 A7
Petroșani Romania 45°28N 23°20E 17 F12
Petrovaradin Serbia 45°16N 19°55E 23 B8
Petrovsk Russia 52°22N 45°19E 18 D8
Petrovsk-Zabaykalskiy
   Russia 51°20N 108°55E 27 D11
Petrozavodsk Russia 61°41N 34°20E 18 B5
Petrus Steyn S. Africa 27°38S 28°8E 57 C4
Petrusburg S. Africa 29°4S 25°26E 56 C4
Peumo Chile 34°21S 71°12W 94 C1
Peureulak Indonesia 4°48N 97°45E 36 D1
Pevek Russia 69°41N 171°19E 27 C18
Pforzheim Germany 48°52N 8°41E 16 D5
Pha Taem △ Thailand 15°32N 105°30E 38 E5
Phagwara India 31°10N 75°40E 42 D6
Phala Botswana 23°45S 26°50E 56 B4
Phalaborwa S. Africa 23°57S 31°7E 57 B5
Phalera = Phulera India 26°52N 75°16E 42 F6
Phalodi India 27°12N 72°24E 42 F5
Phaltan India 17°59N 74°26E 44 F2
Phaluai, Ko Thailand 9°32N 99°41E 39 b
Phan Thailand 19°28N 99°43E 38 C2
Phan Rang-Thap Cham
   Vietnam 11°34N 109°0E 39 G7
Phan Ri Cua Vietnam 11°16N 108°40E 39 G7
Phan Si Pan Vietnam 22°18N 103°46E 38 A4
Phan Thiet Vietnam 11°1N 108°9E 39 G7
Phan Thiet, Vinh
   Vietnam 10°53N 108°5E 39 G7
Phan Wa, Laem Thailand 7°47N 98°25E 39 a
Phanat Nikhom
   Thailand 13°27N 101°11E 38 F3
Phangan, Ko Thailand 9°45N 100°0E 39 H3
Phangnga Thailand 8°28N 98°30E 39 H2
Phangnga, Ao Thailand 8°16N 98°33E 39 a
Phanom Sarakham
   Thailand 13°45N 101°21E 38 F3
Phaphund India 26°36N 79°28E 43 F8
Pharenda India 27°5N 83°17E 43 F10
Pharr U.S.A. 26°12N 98°11W 84 H5

Phatthalung *Thailand* 7°39N 100°6E **39** J3
Phayam, Ko *Thailand* 9°44N 98°25E **39** H2
Phayao *Thailand* 19°11N 99°55E **38** C2
Phelps *U.S.A.* 42°58N 77°3W **82** D7
Phelps L. *Canada* 59°15N 103°15W **71** B8
Phenix City *U.S.A.* 32°28N 85°1W **85** E12
Phet Buri = Phetchaburi
Thailand 13°1N 99°55E **38** F2
Phetchabun *Thailand* 16°25N 101°8E **38** D3
Phetchabun, Thiu Khao
Thailand 16°0N 101°20E **38** E3
Phetchaburi *Thailand* 13°1N 99°55E **38** F2
Phi Phi, Ko *Thailand* 7°45N 98°46E **39** J2
Phiafay *Laos* 14°48N 106°0E **38** E6
Phibun Mangsahan
Thailand 15°14N 105°14E **38** E5
Phichai *Thailand* 17°22N 100°10E **38** D3
Phichit *Thailand* 16°26N 100°22E **38** D3
Philadelphia *Miss.,*
U.S.A. 32°46N 89°7W **85** E10
Philadelphia *N.Y., U.S.A.* 44°9N 75°43W **83** B9
Philadelphia *Pa., U.S.A.* 39°57N 75°9W **83** G9
Philip *U.S.A.* 44°2N 101°40W **80** C3
Philip Smith Mts. *U.S.A.* 68°0N 148°0W **74** B10
Philippeville *Belgium* 50°12N 4°33E **15** D4
Philippi *U.S.A.* 39°9N 80°3W **81** F13
Philippi L. *Australia* 24°20S 138°55E **62** C2
Philippine Basin *Pac. Oc.* 17°0N 132°0E **64** F5
Philippine Sea *Pac. Oc.* 18°0N 125°0E **64** F4
Philippine Trench = Mindanao
Trench *Pac. Oc.* 12°0N 126°6E **37** B7
Philippines ■ *Asia* 12°0N 123°0E **37** B6
Philippolis *S. Africa* 30°15S 25°16E **56** D4
Philippopolis = Plovdiv
Bulgaria 42°8N 24°44E **23** C11
Philipsburg *Canada* 45°2N 73°5W **83** A11
Philipsburg *Mont.,*
U.S.A. 46°20N 113°18W **76** C7
Philipsburg *Pa., U.S.A.* 40°54N 78°13W **82** F6
Philipstown = Daingean
Ireland 53°18N 7°17W **10** C4
Philipstown *S. Africa* 30°28S 24°30E **56** D3
Phillips *U.S.A.* 45°42N 90°24W **80** C8
Phillips *Kans., U.S.A.* 39°45N 99°19W **80** F4
Phillipsburg *N.J., U.S.A.* 40°42N 75°12W **83** F9
Philmont *U.S.A.* 42°15N 73°39W **83** D11
Philomath *U.S.A.* 44°32N 123°22W **76** D2
Phimai *Thailand* 15°13N 102°30E **38** E4
Phitsanulok *Thailand* 16°50N 100°12E **38** D3
Phnom Kulen △
Cambodia 13°38N 104°15E **38** F5
Phnom Penh *Cambodia* 11°33N 104°55E **39** G5
Phnom Penh = Phnom Penh
Cambodia 11°33N 104°55E **39** G5
Pho, Laem *Thailand* 6°55N 101°19E **39** J3
Phoenicia *U.S.A.* 42°5N 74°14W **83** D10
Phoenix *Mauritius* 20°17S 57°30E **55** d
Phoenix *Ariz., U.S.A.* 33°26N 112°4W **77** K7
Phoenix *N.Y., U.S.A.* 43°14N 76°18W **83** C8
Phoenix Is. *Kiribati* 3°30S 172°0W **64** H10
Phoenixville *U.S.A.* 40°8N 75°31W **83** F9
Phon *Thailand* 15°49N 102°36E **38** E4
Phong → *Thailand* 16°23N 102°56E **38** D4
Phong Nha -Ke Bang △
Vietnam 17°30N 106°10E **38** D6
Phong Saly *Laos* 21°42N 102°9E **38** A4
Phong Tho *Vietnam* 22°32N 103°21E **38** A4
Phonhong *Laos* 18°30N 102°25E **38** C4
Phonsavan *Laos* 19°27N 103°10E **38** C4
Phonum *Thailand* 8°49N 98°48E **39** H2
Phosphate Hill *Australia* 21°53S 139°58E **62** C2
Photharam *Thailand* 13°41N 99°51E **38** F2
Phra Nakhon Si Ayutthaya
Thailand 14°25N 100°30E **38** E3
Phra Thong, Ko *Thailand* 9°5N 98°17E **39** H2
Phrae *Thailand* 18°7N 100°9E **38** C3
Phrom Phiram *Thailand* 17°2N 100°12E **38** D3
Phrom Thep, Laem *Thailand* 7°45N 98°19E **39** a
Phu Bia *Laos* 19°10N 103°0E **38** C4
Phu Chong -Na Yoi △
Thailand 14°25N 105°30E **38** E5
Phu Hin Rong Kla △
Thailand 17°0N 100°59E **38** D3
Phu Kao -Phu Phan Kham △
Thailand 16°53N 102°31E **38** D4
Phu Kradung △ *Thailand* 17°12N 101°44E **38** D3
Phu Loi *Laos* 20°14N 103°14E **38** B4
Phu Luang △ *Thailand* 17°15N 101°29E **38** D3
Phu Ly *Vietnam* 20°35N 105°50E **34** G5
Phu My *Vietnam* 14°15N 109°5E **38** E7
Phu Pha Man △
Thailand 16°44N 101°50E **38** D3
Phu Phan △ *Thailand* 17°0N 103°56E **38** D4
Phu Quoc, Dao *Vietnam* 10°20N 104°0E **39** G4
Phu Sa Dok Bua △
Thailand 16°11N 104°45E **38** D5
Phu Sang △ *Thailand* 19°35N 100°19E **38** C3
Phu Tho *Vietnam* 21°24N 105°13E **34** G5
Phu Wiang △ *Thailand* 16°39N 102°23E **38** D4
Phuc Yen *Vietnam* 21°16N 105°45E **34** G5
Phuket *Thailand* 7°53N 98°24E **39** a
Phuket, Ko *Thailand* 8°0N 98°22E **39** a
Phul *India* 30°19N 75°14E **42** D6
Phulad *India* 25°38N 73°49E **42** G5
Phulbani *India* 20°28N 84°14E **44** D7
Phulera *India* 26°52N 75°16E **42** F6
Phulpur *India* 25°31N 82°49E **43** G10
Phunphin *Thailand* 9°7N 99°12E **39** H2
Phuntsholing *Bhutan* 26°51N 89°23E **43** F13
Phuphrabat *Thailand* 17°40N 102°45E **38** D4
Phuthaditjhaba *S. Africa* 28°30S 28°48E **57** D4
Phyu = Pyu *Burma* 18°30N 96°28E **41** K20
Pia △ *Australia* 27°7S 116°23E **61** E2
Piacenza *Italy* 45°1N 9°40E **20** D8
Piai, Tanjung *Malaysia* 1°17N 103°30E **39** d
Pian Cr. → *Australia* 30°2S 148°12E **63** E4
Pianosa *Italy* 42°35N 10°5E **22** C4

Piao'ertun *China* 41°50N 123°47E **33** D12
Piapot *Canada* 49°59N 109°8W **71** D7
Piatra Neamţ *Romania* 46°56N 26°21E **17** E14
Piauí □ *Brazil* 7°0S 43°0W **93** E10
Piauí → *Brazil* 6°38S 42°42W **93** E10
Piave → *Italy* 45°32N 12°44E **22** B5
Pibor Post *South Sudan* 6°47N 33°3E **53** G12
Picardie □ *France* 49°50N 3°0E **20** B5
Picardy = Picardie □
France 49°50N 3°0E **20** B5
Picayune *U.S.A.* 30°32N 89°41W **85** F10
Pichhor *India* 25°58N 78°20E **43** G8
Pichilemu *Chile* 34°22S 72°0W **94** C1
Pichor *India* 25°11N 78°11E **42** G8
Pickerel L. *Canada* 48°40N 91°25W **72** C1
Pickering *U.K.* 54°15N 0°46W **12** C7
Pickering, Vale of *U.K.* 54°14N 0°45W **12** C7
Pickle Lake *Canada* 51°30N 90°12W **72** B1
Pickwick L. *U.S.A.* 35°4N 88°15W **85** D10
Pico *Azores* 38°28N 28°20W **52** a
Pico Bonito △ *Honduras* 15°34N 86°48W **88** C2
Pico Truncado *Argentina* 46°40S 68°0W **96** F3
Picos *Brazil* 7°5S 41°28W **93** E10
Picton *Canada* 44°1N 77°9W **82** B7
Picton *N.Z.* 41°18S 174°3E **59** D5
Pictou *Canada* 45°41N 62°42W **73** C7
Picture Butte *Canada* 49°55N 112°45W **70** D6
Pictured Rocks △
U.S.A. 46°30N 86°30W **80** B10
Picún Leufú *Argentina* 39°30S 69°5W **96** D3
Pidurutalagala *Sri Lanka* 7°10N 80°50E **45** L5
Piedmont = Piemonte □
Italy 45°0N 8°0E **20** D7
Piedmont *Ala., U.S.A.* 33°55N 85°37W **85** E12
Piedmont *S.C., U.S.A.* 34°42N 82°28W **85** D13
Piedras Negras *Mexico* 28°42N 100°31W **86** B4
Pieksämäki *Finland* 62°18N 27°10E **8** E22
Pielinen *Finland* 63°15N 29°40E **8** E23
Piemonte □ *Italy* 45°0N 8°0E **20** D7
Pienaarsrivier *S. Africa* 25°15S 28°18E **57** C4
Piercefield *U.S.A.* 44°13N 74°35W **83** B10
Pierceland *Canada* 54°20N 109°46W **71** C7
Pierpont *U.S.A.* 41°45N 80°34W **82** E4
Pierre *U.S.A.* 44°22N 100°21W **80** C3
Pierrefonds *Canada* 45°29N 73°51W **83** A11
Pierreville *Trin. & Tob.* 10°16N 61°0W **93** K16
Piet Retief *S. Africa* 27°1S 30°50E **57** D5
Pietarsaari *Finland* 63°40N 22°43E **8** E20
Pietermaritzburg *S. Africa* 29°35S 30°25E **57** C5
Pietersburg = Polokwane
S. Africa 23°54S 29°25E **57** B4
Pietrosul, Vf. *Maramureş,*
Romania 47°35N 24°43E **17** E13
Pietrosul, Vf. *Suceava,*
Romania 47°12N 25°18E **17** E13
Pigeon I. *India* 14°2N 74°20E **45** G2
Pigeon L. *Canada* 44°27N 78°30W **82** B6
Piggott *U.S.A.* 36°23N 90°11W **85** C9
Pigüe *Argentina* 37°36S 62°25W **94** D3
Pihani *India* 27°36N 80°15E **43** F9
Pihlajavesi *Finland* 61°45N 28°45E **8** E23
Pijijiapan *Mexico* 15°42N 93°14W **87** D6
Pikangikum *Canada* 51°49N 94°0W **71** C10
Pikes Peak *U.S.A.* 38°50N 105°3W **76** G11
Piketberg *S. Africa* 32°55S 18°40E **56** D2
Pikeville *U.S.A.* 37°29N 82°31W **81** G12
Pikou *China* 39°18N 122°22E **33** E12
Pikwitonei *Canada* 55°35N 97°9W **71** B9
Pila *Poland* 53°10N 16°48E **17** B9
Pilanesberg △ *S. Africa* 25°15S 27°4E **56** C4
Pilani *India* 28°22N 75°33E **42** E6
Pilar *Paraguay* 26°50S 58°20W **94** B4
Pilaya → *Bolivia* 20°55S 64°4W **92** H6
Pilcomaya → *Paraguay* 25°21S 57°42W **94** B4
Pilgrim's Rest *S. Africa* 24°55S 30°44E **57** B5
Pilibhit *India* 28°40N 79°50E **43** E8
Pilica → *Poland* 51°52N 21°17E **17** C11
Pilipinas = Philippines ■
Asia 12°0N 123°0E **37** B6
Pilkhawa *India* 28°43N 77°42E **42** E7
Pilliga *Australia* 30°21S 148°54E **63** E4
Pilos *Greece* 36°55N 21°42E **23** F9
Pilot Mound *Canada* 49°15N 98°54W **71** D9
Pilot Point *U.S.A.* 33°24N 96°58W **84** E6
Pilot Rock *U.S.A.* 45°29N 118°50W **76** D4
Pima *U.S.A.* 32°54N 109°50W **77** K9
Pimba *Australia* 31°18S 136°46E **63** E2
Pimenta Bueno *Brazil* 11°35S 61°10W **92** F6
Pimentel *Peru* 6°45S 79°55W **92** E3
Pimpri Chinchwad *India* 18°37N 73°47E **44** E1
Pin Valley △ *India* 31°50N 77°50E **42** D7
Pinang *Malaysia* 5°25N 100°15E **39** c
Pinang □ *Malaysia* 5°20N 100°20E **39** c
Pinar del Río *Cuba* 22°26N 83°40W **88** B3
Pınarhisar *Turkey* 41°37N 27°30E **23** D12
Pinatubo, Mt. *Phil.* 15°8N 120°21E **37** A6
Pinawa *Canada* 50°9N 95°50W **71** C9
Pinchang *China* 31°36N 107°3E **34** B6
Pincher Creek *Canada* 49°30N 113°57W **70** D6
Pinchi L. *Canada* 54°38N 124°30W **70** C4
Pinckneyville *U.S.A.* 38°5N 89°23W **80** F9
Pińczów *Poland* 50°32N 20°32E **17** C11
Pindar *Australia* 28°30S 115°47E **61** E2
Pindera Downs ○
Australia 29°24S 142°37E **63** A3
Pindi Gheb *Pakistan* 33°14N 72°21E **42** C5
Pindos Oros *Greece* 40°0N 21°0E **23** E9
Pindus Mts. = Pindos Oros
Greece 40°0N 21°0E **23** E9
Pine → *B.C., Canada* 56°8N 120°43W **70** B4
Pine → *Sask., Canada* 58°50N 105°38W **71** B7
Pine Bluff *U.S.A.* 34°13N 92°1W **84** D9
Pine Bluffs *U.S.A.* 41°11N 104°4W **76** F11
Pine City *U.S.A.* 45°50N 92°59W **80** C7
Pine Cr. → *U.S.A.* 41°10N 77°16W **82** E7
Pine Creek *Australia* 13°50S 131°50E **60** B5
Pine Falls *Canada* 50°34N 96°11W **71** C9
Pine Flat L. *U.S.A.* 36°50N 119°20W **78** J7

Pine Grove *U.S.A.* 40°33N 76°23W **83** F8
Pine Hill *Australia* 23°38S 146°57E **62** C4
Pine Island Glacier
Antarctica 76°0S 100°0W **5** D15
Pine Pass *Canada* 55°25N 122°42W **70** B4
Pine Point *Canada* 60°50N 114°28W **70** A6
Pine Ridge *Canada* 51°45N 100°30W **71** C8
Pine River *Canada* 46°43N 94°24W **80** B6
Pine Valley *U.S.A.* 32°50N 116°32W **79** N10
Pinecrest *U.S.A.* 38°12N 120°1W **78** G6
Pinedale *Calif., U.S.A.* 36°50N 119°48W **78** J7
Pinedale *Wyo., U.S.A.* 42°52N 109°52W **76** E9
Pinega → *Russia* 64°30N 44°19E **18** B8
Pinehouse L. *Canada* 55°32N 106°35W **71** B7
Pineimuta → *Canada* 52°8N 88°33W **72** B1
Pinerolo *Italy* 44°53N 7°21E **20** D7
Pines, Akra *Greece* 40°5N 24°20E **23** D11
Pinetop-Lakeside *U.S.A.* 34°9N 109°58W **77** J9
Pinetown *S. Africa* 29°48S 30°54E **57** C5
Pineville *U.S.A.* 31°19N 92°26W **84** F8
Ping → *Thailand* 15°42N 100°9E **38** E3
Pingaring *Australia* 32°40S 118°32E **61** F2
Pingba *China* 26°23N 106°12E **34** D6
Pingbian *China* 23°0N 103°45E **34** F4
Pingchuan *China* 27°35N 101°55E **34** D3
Pingding *China* 37°47N 113°38E **32** F7
Pingdingshan *China* 33°43N 113°27E **32** H7
Pingdu *China* 36°42N 119°59E **33** F10
Pingelly *Australia* 32°32S 117°5E **61** F2
Pingguo *China* 23°19N 107°36E **34** F6
Pinghe *China* 24°17N 117°21E **35** E11
Pinghu *China* 30°40N 121°2E **35** B13
Pingjiang *China* 28°45N 113°36E **35** C9
Pingle *China* 24°40N 110°40E **35** E8
Pingli *China* 32°27N 109°22E **34** A7
Pingliang *China* 35°35N 106°31E **32** G4
Pinglu *China* 39°31N 112°30E **32** E7
Pingluo *China* 38°52N 106°30E **32** E4
Pingnan *Fujian, China* 26°53N 119°0E **35** D12
Pingnan *Guangxi Zhuangzu,*
China 23°33N 110°22E **35** F8
Pingquan *China* 41°1N 118°37E **33** D10
Pingrup *Australia* 33°32S 118°29E **61** F2
Pingshan *China* 28°39N 104°3E **34** C5
Pingtan *China* 25°31N 119°47E **35** E12
Pingtang *China* 25°49N 107°17E **34** E6
P'ingtung *Taiwan* 22°38N 120°30E **35** F13
Pingwu *China* 32°25N 104°30E **32** H3
Pingxiang *Guangxi Zhuangzu,*
China 22°6N 106°46E **34** F6
Pingxiang *Jiangxi, China* 27°43N 113°48E **35** D9
Pingyao *China* 37°12N 112°10E **32** F7
Pingyi *China* 35°30N 117°35E **33** G9
Pingyin *China* 36°20N 116°25E **32** F9
Pingyuan *Guangdong,*
China 24°37N 115°57E **35** E10
Pingyuan *Shandong,*
China 37°10N 116°22E **32** F9
Pingyuanjie *China* 23°45N 103°48E **34** F4
Pinheiro *Brazil* 2°31S 45°5W **93** D9
Pinheiro Machado *Brazil* 31°34S 53°23W **95** C5
Pinhel *Portugal* 40°50N 7°1W **21** B2
Pini *Indonesia* 0°10N 98°40E **36** D1
Pinios → *Greece* 39°55N 22°41E **23** E10
Pinjarra *Australia* 32°37S 115°52E **61** F2
Pink Mountain *Canada* 57°3N 122°52W **70** B4
Pinnacle Is. = Senkaku-Shotō
E. China Sea 25°45N 123°30E **29** M1
Pinnacles △ *U.S.A.* 36°25N 121°12W **78** J5
Pinnaroo *Australia* 35°17S 140°53E **63** F3
Pinon Hills *U.S.A.* 34°26N 117°39W **79** L9
Pinos *Mexico* 22°18N 101°34W **86** C4
Pinos, Mt. *U.S.A.* 34°49N 119°8W **79** L7
Pinos Pt. *U.S.A.* 36°38N 121°57W **73** A5
Pinrang *Indonesia* 3°46S 119°41E **37** E5
Pins, Pte. aux *Canada* 42°15N 81°51W **82** D3
Pinsk *Belarus* 52°10N 26°1E **17** B14
Pintados *Chile* 20°35S 69°40W **92** H5
Pinyang *China* 27°42N 120°31E **35** D13
Pinyug *Russia* 60°5N 48°0E **18** B8
Pioche *U.S.A.* 37°56N 114°27W **77** H6
Piombino *Italy* 42°55N 10°32E **22** C4
Pioner, Ostrov *Russia* 79°50N 92°0E **27** B10
Piopiotaki = Milford Sd.
N.Z. 44°41S 167°47E **59** F1
Piorini, L. *Brazil* 3°15S 62°35W **92** D6
Piotrków Trybunalski
Poland 51°23N 19°43E **17** C10
Pip *Iran* 26°45N 60°10E **47** E9
Pipar *India* 26°25N 73°31E **42** F5
Pipar Road *India* 26°27N 73°27E **42** F5
Piparia *Mad. P., India* 22°45N 78°23E **42** H8
Piparia *Mad. P., India* 21°49N 77°37E **42** J7
Pipestone *U.S.A.* 44°0N 96°19W **80** D5
Pipestone → *Canada* 52°53N 89°23W **72** B2
Pipestone Cr. →
Canada 49°38N 100°15W **71** D8
Piplan *Pakistan* 32°17N 71°21E **42** C4
Piploda *India* 23°37N 74°56E **42** H6
Pipmuacan, Rés. *Canada* 49°45N 70°30W **73** C5
Pippingarra *Australia* 20°27S 118°42E **60** D2
Piqua *U.S.A.* 40°9N 84°15W **81** E11
Piquiri → *Brazil* 24°3S 54°14W **95** A5
Pir Panjal Range *India* 32°30N 76°50E **42** C7
Pir Sohráb *Iran* 25°44N 60°54E **47** E9
Piracicaba *Brazil* 22°45S 47°40W **95** A6
Piracuruca *Brazil* 3°50S 41°50W **93** D10
Pirae *Tahiti* 17°31S 149°33W **59** d
Pirajuí *Brazil* 21°59S 49°29W **95** A6
Piram I. *India* 21°36N 72°21E **42** J5
Pirané *Argentina* 25°42S 59°6W **94** B4
Pīrānshahr *Iran* 36°41N 45°8E **46** B5
Pirapora *Brazil* 17°20S 44°56W **93** G10
Pirawa *India* 24°10N 76°2E **42** G7
Pirgos *Greece* 37°40N 21°27E **23** F9
Piribebuy *Paraguay* 25°26S 57°2W **94** B4
Pirimapun *Indonesia* 6°20S 138°24E **37** F9
Pirin Planina *Bulgaria* 41°40N 23°30E **23** D10

Pírineos = Pyrénées
Europe 42°45N 0°18E **20** E4
Piripiri *Brazil* 4°15S 41°46W **93** D10
Pirlangimpi *Australia* 11°24S 130°26E **60** B5
Pirot *Serbia* 43°9N 22°33E **23** C10
Piru *Indonesia* 3°4S 128°12E **37** E7
Piru *U.S.A.* 34°25N 118°48W **79** L8
Pisa *Italy* 43°43N 10°23E **22** C4
Pisagua *Chile* 19°40S 70°15W **92** G4
Pisco *Peru* 13°50S 76°12W **92** F3
Písek *Czech Rep.* 49°19N 14°10E **16** D8
Pishan *China* 37°30N 78°33E **30** D4
Pīshīn *Iran* 26°6N 61°47E **47** E9
Pishin *Pakistan* 30°35N 67°0E **42** D2
Pishin Lora → *Pakistan* 29°9N 64°5E **42** E1
Pising *Indonesia* 5°8S 121°53E **37** F6
Pismo Beach *U.S.A.* 35°9N 120°38W **79** K6
Pissis, Cerro *Argentina* 27°45S 68°48W **94** B2
Pissouri *Cyprus* 34°40N 32°42E **25** E11
Pisticci *Italy* 40°24N 16°33E **22** D7
Pistóia *Italy* 43°55N 10°54E **22** C4
Pistol B. *Canada* 62°25N 92°37W **71** A10
Pisuerga → *Spain* 41°33N 4°52W **21** B3
Pit → *U.S.A.* 40°47N 122°6W **76** F2
Pitarpunga L. *Australia* 34°24S 143°30E **63** E3
Pitcairn I. *Pac. Oc.* 25°5S 130°5W **65** K14
Pitch L. *Trin. & Tob.* 10°14N 61°39W **93** K15
Piteå *Sweden* 65°20N 21°25E **8** D19
Piteälven → *Sweden* 65°20N 21°25E **8** D19
Piteşti *Romania* 44°52N 24°54E **17** F13
Pithapuram *India* 17°10N 82°15E **44** F6
Pithara *Australia* 30°20S 116°35E **61** F2
Pithora *India* 21°16N 82°31E **44** D6
Pithoragarh *India* 29°35N 80°13E **43** E9
Pithoro *Pakistan* 25°31N 69°23E **42** G3
Pitlochry *U.K.* 56°42N 3°44W **11** E5
Pitt I. *Canada* 53°30N 129°50W **70** C3
Pitti I. *India* 10°50N 72°38E **45** J1
Pittsburg *Calif., U.S.A.* 38°2N 121°53W **78** G5
Pittsburg *Kans., U.S.A.* 37°25N 94°42W **80** G6
Pittsburg *Tex., U.S.A.* 33°0N 94°59W **84** E7
Pittsburgh *U.S.A.* 40°26N 79°58W **82** F5
Pittsfield *Ill., U.S.A.* 39°36N 90°49W **80** F8
Pittsfield *Maine, U.S.A.* 44°47N 69°23W **81** C19
Pittsfield *Mass., U.S.A.* 42°27N 73°15W **83** D11
Pittsfield *N.H., U.S.A.* 43°18N 71°20W **83** C13
Pittston *U.S.A.* 41°19N 75°47W **83** E9
Pittsworth *Australia* 27°41S 151°37E **63** D5
Pituri → *Australia* 22°35S 138°30E **62** C2
Piura *Peru* 5°15S 80°38W **92** E2
Piuthan *Nepal* 28°7N 82°56E **43** E10
Pixian *China* 30°48N 103°52E **34** B4
Pixley *U.S.A.* 35°58N 119°18W **78** K7
Pizhou = Pei Xian *China* 34°44N 116°55E **32** G9
Pizhou *China* 34°18N 117°57E **33** G9
Placentia *Canada* 47°20N 54°0W **73** C9
Placentia B. *Canada* 47°0N 54°40W **73** C9
Placerville *U.S.A.* 38°44N 120°48W **78** G6
Placetas *Cuba* 22°15N 79°44W **88** B4
Plaine des Jarres *Laos* 19°27N 103°10E **38** C4
Plainfield *N.J., U.S.A.* 40°37N 74°25W **83** F10
Plainfield *Ohio, U.S.A.* 40°13N 81°43W **82** F3
Plainfield *Vt., U.S.A.* 44°17N 72°26W **83** B12
Plains *Mont., U.S.A.* 47°28N 114°53W **76** C6
Plains *Tex., U.S.A.* 33°11N 102°50W **84** E3
Plainview *Nebr., U.S.A.* 42°21N 97°47W **80** D5
Plainview *Tex., U.S.A.* 34°11N 101°43W **84** D4
Plainwell *U.S.A.* 42°27N 85°38W **81** D11
Plaistow *U.S.A.* 42°50N 71°6W **83** D13
Plaka, Akra *Greece* 35°11N 26°19E **23** G12
Plana Cays *Bahamas* 22°38N 73°30W **89** B5
Planada *U.S.A.* 37°16N 120°19W **78** H6
Plano *U.S.A.* 33°1N 96°42W **84** E6
Plant City *U.S.A.* 28°1N 82°7W **85** G13
Plaquemine *U.S.A.* 30°17N 91°14W **84** F9
Plasencia *Spain* 40°3N 6°8W **21** B2
Plaster City *U.S.A.* 32°47N 115°51W **79** N11
Plaster Rock *Canada* 46°53N 67°22W **73** C6
Plastun *Russia* 44°45N 136°19E **28** B8
Plata, Río de la →
S. Amer. 34°45S 57°30W **94** C4
Plátani → *Italy* 37°23N 13°16E **22** F5
Platte *U.S.A.* 43°23N 98°51W **80** D4
Platte → *Mo., U.S.A.* 39°16N 94°50W **80** F6
Platte → *Nebr., U.S.A.* 41°4N 95°53W **80** E6
Platteville *U.S.A.* 42°44N 90°29W **80** D8
Plattsburgh *U.S.A.* 44°42N 73°28W **83** B11
Plattsmouth *U.S.A.* 41°1N 95°53W **80** E6
Plauen *Germany* 50°30N 12°8E **16** C7
Plavinas *Latvia* 56°35N 25°46E **9** H21
Playa del Carmen *Mexico* 20°37N 87°4W **87** C7
Playgreen L. *Canada* 54°0N 98°15W **71** C9
Pleasant Bay *Canada* 46°51N 60°48W **73** C7
Pleasant Hill *U.S.A.* 37°57N 122°4W **78** H4
Pleasant Mount *U.S.A.* 41°44N 75°26W **83** E9
Pleasanton *Calif., U.S.A.* 37°39N 121°52W **78** H5
Pleasanton *Tex., U.S.A.* 28°58N 98°29W **84** G5
Pleasantville *N.J.,*
U.S.A. 39°24N 74°32W **81** F16
Pleasantville *Pa., U.S.A.* 41°35N 79°34W **82** E5
Plei Ku *Vietnam* 13°57N 108°0E **38** F7
Plenty → *Australia* 23°25S 136°31E **62** C2
Plenty, B. of *N.Z.* 37°45S 177°0E **59** B6
Plentywood *U.S.A.* 48°47N 104°34W **76** B11
Plesetsk *Russia* 62°43N 40°20E **18** B7
Plessisville *Canada* 46°14N 71°47W **73** C5
Plétipi, L. *Canada* 51°44N 70°6W **73** B5
Pleven *Bulgaria* 43°26N 24°37E **23** C11
Plevna *Canada* 44°58N 76°59W **82** B8
Pljevlja *Montenegro* 43°21N 19°21E **23** C8
Plock *Poland* 52°32N 19°40E **17** B10
Plöckenstein *Germany* 48°46N 13°51E **16** D8
Ploiești *Romania* 44°57N 26°5E **17** F14
Plonge, Lac la *Canada* 55°8N 107°20W **71** B7
Plovdiv *Bulgaria* 42°8N 24°44E **23** C11
Plover Cove Res. *China* 22°28N 114°15E **31** a
Plum *U.S.A.* 40°29N 79°47W **82** F5
Plum I. *U.S.A.* 41°11N 72°12W **83** E12
Plumas *U.S.A.* 39°45N 120°4W **78** F6
Plummer *U.S.A.* 47°20N 116°53W **76** C5

Plumridge Lakes
Australia 29°26S 125°16E **61** E4
Plumtree *Zimbabwe* 20°27S 27°55E **55** J5
Plunge *Lithuania* 55°53N 21°59E **9** J19
Plymouth *Trin. & Tob.* 11°14N 60°48W **93** J16
Plymouth *U.K.* 50°22N 4°10W **13** G3
Plymouth *Calif., U.S.A.* 38°29N 120°51W **78** G6
Plymouth *Ind., U.S.A.* 41°21N 86°19W **80** E10
Plymouth *Mass., U.S.A.* 41°57N 70°40W **83** E14
Plymouth *N.C., U.S.A.* 35°52N 76°43W **85** D16
Plymouth *N.H., U.S.A.* 43°46N 71°41W **83** C13
Plymouth *Pa., U.S.A.* 41°14N 75°57W **83** E9
Plymouth *Wis., U.S.A.* 43°45N 87°59W **80** D10
Plympton-Wyoming = Wyoming
Canada 42°57N 82°7W **82** D2
Plynlimon = Pumlumon Fawr
U.K. 52°28N 3°46W **13** E4
Plyusa *Russia* 58°40N 29°27E **9** G23
Plzeň *Czech Rep.* 49°45N 13°22E **16** D7
Pmere Nyente ○
Australia 24°15S 136°10E **62** C2
Po → *Italy* 44°57N 12°4E **22** B5
Po Hai = Bo Hai *China* 39°0N 119°0E **33** E10
Pobeda *Russia* 65°12N 146°12E **27** C15
Pobedy, Pik *Kyrgyzstan* 42°0N 79°58E **30** C4
Pocahontas *Ark., U.S.A.* 36°16N 90°58W **85** C9
Pocahontas *Iowa, U.S.A.* 42°44N 94°40W **80** D6
Pocatello *U.S.A.* 42°52N 112°27W **76** E7
Pocomoke City *U.S.A.* 38°5N 75°34W **81** F16
Poços de Caldas *Brazil* 21°50S 46°33W **95** A6
Podgorica *Montenegro* 42°30N 19°19E **23** C8
Podile *India* 15°37N 79°37E **45** G4
Podilska Vysochyna
Ukraine 49°0N 28°0E **17** D14
Podolsk *Russia* 55°25N 37°30E **18** C6
Podporozhye *Russia* 60°55N 34°2E **18** B5
Pofadder *S. Africa* 29°10S 19°22E **56** C2
Pogranichnyy *Russia* 44°25N 131°24E **28** B5
Poh *Indonesia* 0°46S 122°51E **37** E6
Pohang *S. Korea* 36°1N 129°23E **33** F15
Pohjanmaa □ *Finland* 62°58N 22°50E **8** E20
Pohnpei *Micronesia* 6°55N 158°10E **64** G7
Pohri *India* 25°32N 77°22E **42** G6
Poinsett, C. *Antarctica* 65°42S 113°18E **5** C8
Point Arena *U.S.A.* 38°55N 123°41W **78** G3
Point Baker *U.S.A.* 56°21N 133°37W **70** B2
Point Calimere *India* 10°17N 79°49E **45** J4
Point Fortin *Trin. & Tob.* 10°10N 61°42W **93** K15
Point Hope *U.S.A.* 68°21N 166°47W **74** B6
Point L. *Canada* 65°15N 113°4W **68** D9
Point Lisas *Trin. & Tob.* 10°24N 61°29W **93** K15
Point Pedro *Sri Lanka* 9°50N 80°15E **45** K5
Point Pelee △ *Canada* 41°57N 82°31W **82** E2
Point Pleasant *N.J., U.S.A.* 40°5N 74°4W **83** F10
Point Pleasant *W. Va.,*
U.S.A. 38°51N 82°8W **81** F12
Point Reyes △ *U.S.A.* 38°10N 122°55W **78** G2
Pointe-à-Pitre *Guadeloupe* 16°15N 61°32W **88** b
Pointe-au-Pic = La Malbaie
Canada 47°40N 70°10W **73** C5
Pointe-Claire *Canada* 45°26N 73°50W **83** A11
Pointe-Gatineau *Canada* 45°27N 75°41W **83** A9
Pointe-Noire *Congo* 4°48S 11°53E **54** E2
Pointe-Noire *Guadeloupe* 16°14N 61°47W **88** b
Poipet *Cambodia* 13°39N 102°33E **38** F4
Poisonbush Ra.
Australia 22°30S 121°30E **60** D3
Poissonnier Pt. *Australia* 19°57S 119°10E **60** C2
Poitiers *France* 46°35N 0°20E **20** C4
Poitou *France* 46°40N 0°10W **20** C3
Pojoaque *U.S.A.* 35°54N 106°1W **77** J10
Pokaran *India* 27°0N 71°50E **42** F4
Pokataroo *Australia* 29°30S 148°36E **63** D4
Pokhara *Nepal* 28°14N 83°58E **43** E10
Poko *Dem. Rep. of the Congo* 3°7N 26°52E **54** D5
Pokrovsk *Russia* 61°29N 129°0E **27** C13
Pola = Pula *Croatia* 44°54N 13°57E **16** F7
Polacca *U.S.A.* 35°50N 110°23W **77** J8
Polan *Iran* 25°30N 61°10E **47** E9
Poland ■ *Europe* 52°0N 20°0E **17** C10
Polar Bear △ *Canada* 55°0N 83°45W **72** A2
Polatsk *Belarus* 55°30N 28°50E **9** J23
Polavaram *India* 17°15N 81°38E **44** F5
Polcura *Chile* 37°17S 71°43W **94** D1
Polesye = Pripet Marshes
Europe 52°10N 27°10E **17** B15
Polevskoy *Russia* 56°26N 60°11E **18** C11
Police *Poland* 53°33N 14°33E **16** B8
Police, Pte. *Seychelles* 4°51S 55°32E **55** b
Poligiros *Greece* 40°23N 23°25E **23** D10
Polillo Is. *Phil.* 14°56N 122°0E **37** B6
Polk *U.S.A.* 41°22N 79°56W **82** E5
Pollachi *India* 10°35N 77°0E **45** J3
Polnovat *Russia* 63°50N 65°54E **26** C7
Polokwane *S. Africa* 23°54S 29°25E **57** B4
Polokwane → *S. Africa* 22°25S 30°5E **57** C5
Polonnaruwa *Sri Lanka* 7°56N 81°0E **45** L5
Polonne *Ukraine* 50°6N 27°30E **17** C14
Polonnoye = Polonne
Ukraine 50°6N 27°30E **17** C14
Polson *U.S.A.* 47°41N 114°9W **76** C6
Poltava *Ukraine* 49°35N 34°35E **19** E5
Põltsamaa *Estonia* 58°39N 25°58E **9** G21
Polunochnoye *Russia* 60°52N 60°25E **26** C7
Polur *India* 12°32N 79°11E **45** H4
Põlva *Estonia* 58°3N 27°3E **9** G22
Polyarny *Russia* 69°8N 33°20E **8** B25
Polyarnyye Zori *Russia* 67°22N 32°30E **8** C25
Polynesia *Pac. Oc.* 10°0S 162°0W **65** F11
Polynésie française = French
Polynesia ☑ *Pac. Oc.* 20°0S 145°0W **65** J13
Pombal *Portugal* 39°55N 8°40W **21** C1
Pomene *Mozam.* 22°53S 35°33E **57** B6
Pomeroy *Ohio, U.S.A.* 39°2N 82°2W **81** F12
Pomeroy *Wash., U.S.A.* 46°28N 117°36W **76** C5
Pomézia *Italy* 41°40N 12°30E **22** D5
Pomona *Australia* 26°22S 152°52E **63** D5
Pomona *U.S.A.* 34°4N 117°45W **79** L9

Pomorskie, Pojezierze
Poland 53°40N 16°37E **17** B9
Pompeys Pillar U.S.A. 45°59N 107°57W **76** D10
Pompeys Pillar △ U.S.A. 46°0N 108°0W **76** D10
Pompton Lakes U.S.A. 41°0N 74°17W **83** F10
Ponape = Pohnpei
Micronesia 6°55N 158°10E **64** G7
Ponask L. Canada 54°0N 92°41W **72** B1
Ponca U.S.A. 42°34N 96°43W **80** D5
Ponca City U.S.A. 36°42N 97°5W **84** C6
Ponce Puerto Rico 18°1N 66°37W **89** d
Ponchatoula U.S.A. 30°26N 90°26W **85** F9
Poncheville, L. Canada 50°10N 76°55W **72** B4
Pond U.S.A. 35°43N 119°20W **79** K7
Pond Inlet Canada 72°40N 77°0W **69** C16
Pondicherry = Puducherry
India 11°59N 79°50E **45** J4
Ponds, I. of Canada 53°27N 55°52W **73** B8
Ponferrada Spain 42°32N 6°35W **21** A2
Ponnaiyar → India 11°50N 79°45E **45** J4
Ponnani India 10°45N 75°59E **45** J2
Ponneri India 13°20N 80°15E **45** H5
Ponnuru India 16°5N 80°34E **45** F5
Ponoka Canada 52°42N 113°40W **70** C6
Ponorogo Indonesia 7°52S 111°27E **37** G14
Ponoy Russia 67°0N 41°13E **18** A7
Ponoy → Russia 66°59N 41°17E **18** A7
Ponta Delgada Azores 37°44N 25°40W **52** a
Ponta Grossa Brazil 25°7S 50°10W **95** B5
Ponta Porã Brazil 22°20S 55°35W **95** A4
Pontarlier France 46°54N 6°20E **20** C7
Pontchartrain, L. U.S.A. 30°5N 90°5W **85** F9
Ponte Nova Brazil 20°25S 42°54W **95** A7
Ponteix Canada 49°46N 107°29W **71** D7
Pontevedra Spain 42°26N 8°40W **21** A1
Pontiac Ill., U.S.A. 40°53N 88°38W **80** E9
Pontiac Mich., U.S.A. 42°38N 83°18W **81** D12
Pontian Kechil Malaysia 1°29N 103°23E **39** d
Pontianak Indonesia 0°3S 109°15E **36** E3
Pontine Is. = Ponziane, Ísole
Italy 40°55N 12°57E **22** D5
Pontine Mts. = Kuzey Anadolu
Dağları Turkey 41°0N 36°45E **19** F6
Pontivy France 48°5N 2°58W **20** B2
Pontoise France 49°3N 2°5E **20** B5
Ponton → Canada 58°27N 116°11W **70** B5
Pontypool Canada 44°6N 78°38W **82** B6
Pontypool U.K. 51°42N 3°2W **13** F4
Ponziane, Ísole Italy 40°55N 12°57E **22** D5
Poochera Australia 32°43S 134°51E **63** E1
Poole U.K. 50°43N 1°59W **13** G6
Poole □ U.K. 50°43N 1°59W **13** G6
Poona = Pune India 18°29N 73°57E **44** E1
Poonamallee India 13°3N 80°10E **45** H5
Pooncarie Australia 33°22S 142°31E **63** E3
Poopelloe L. Australia 31°40S 144°0E **63** E3
Poopó, L. de Bolivia 18°30S 67°35W **92** G5
Popayán Colombia 2°27N 76°36W **92** C3
Poperinge Belgium 50°51N 2°42E **15** D2
Popilta L. Australia 33°10S 141°42E **63** E3
Popio L. Australia 33°10S 141°52E **63** E3
Poplar U.S.A. 48°7N 105°12W **76** B11
Poplar → Canada 53°0N 97°19W **71** C9
Poplar Bluff U.S.A. 36°46N 90°24W **80** G8
Poplarville U.S.A. 30°51N 89°32W **85** F10
Popocatépetl, Volcán
Mexico 19°2N 98°38W **87** D5
Popokabaka
Dem. Rep. of the Congo 5°41S 16°40E **54** F3
Poprad Slovak Rep. 49°3N 20°18E **17** D11
Porali → Pakistan 25°58N 66°26E **42** G2
Porbandar India 21°44N 69°43E **42** J3
Porcher I. Canada 53°50N 130°30W **70** C2
Porcupine → Canada 59°11N 104°46W **71** B8
Porcupine → U.S.A. 66°34N 145°19W **68** D2
Porcupine Gorge △
Australia 20°22S 144°26E **62** C3
Pordenone Italy 45°57N 12°39E **22** B5
Pori Finland 61°29N 21°48E **8** F19
Porkhov Russia 57°45N 29°38E **9** H23
Porlamar Venezuela 10°57N 63°51W **92** A6
Pormpuraaw Australia 14°59S 141°26E **62** A3
Pormpuraaw ◎
Australia 14°55S 141°47E **62** A3
Poronaysk Russia 49°13N 143°0E **31** B17
Poroshiri-Dake Japan 42°41N 142°52E **28** C11
Porpoise B. Antarctica 66°0S 127°0E **5** C9
Porsangerfjorden Norway 70°40N 25°40E **8** A21
Porsgrunn Norway 59°10N 9°40E **9** G13
Port Alberni Canada 49°14N 124°50W **70** D4
Port Alfred S. Africa 33°36S 26°55E **56** D4
Port Alice Canada 50°20N 127°25W **70** C3
Port Allegany U.S.A. 41°48N 78°17W **82** E6
Port Allen U.S.A. 30°27N 91°12W **84** F9
Port Alma Australia 23°38S 150°53E **62** C5
Port Alma Canada 42°10N 82°14W **82** D2
Port Angeles U.S.A. 48°7N 123°27W **78** B3
Port Antonio Jamaica 18°10N 76°26W **88** a
Port Aransas U.S.A. 27°50N 97°4W **84** H6
Port Arthur Australia 43°7S 147°50E **63** G4
Port Arthur U.S.A. 29°54N 93°56W **84** G8
Port au Choix Canada 50°43N 57°22W **73** B8
Port au Port B. Canada 48°40N 58°50W **73** C8
Port-au-Prince Haiti 18°40N 72°20W **89** C5
Port Augusta Australia 32°30S 137°50E **63** E2
Port Austin U.S.A. 44°3N 83°1W **82** B2
Port Blair India 11°40N 92°45E **45** J11
Port Blandford Canada 48°20N 54°10W **73** C9
Port Bradshaw Australia 12°30S 137°20E **62** A2
Port Broughton
Australia 33°37S 137°56E **63** E2
Port Bruce Canada 42°39N 81°0W **82** D4
Port Burwell Canada 42°40N 80°48W **82** D4
Port Campbell India 11°56N 92°57E **45** J11
Port Canning India 22°23N 88°40E **43** H13
Port Carling Canada 45°7N 79°35W **82** A5
Port-Cartier Canada 50°2N 66°50W **73** B6
Port Chalmers N.Z. 45°49S 170°30E **59** F3
Port Charlotte U.S.A. 26°59N 82°6W **85** H13

Port Chester U.S.A. 41°0N 73°40W **83** F11
Port Clements Canada 53°40N 132°10W **70** C2
Port Clinton U.S.A. 41°31N 82°56W **81** E12
Port Colborne Canada 42°50N 79°10W **82** D5
Port Coquitlam Canada 49°15N 122°45W **78** A4
Port Cornwallis India 13°17N 93°5E **45** H11
Port Credit Canada 43°33N 79°35W **82** C5
Port Curtis Australia 23°57S 151°20E **62** C5
Port Dalhousie Canada 43°13N 79°16W **82** C5
Port Darwin Australia 12°24S 130°45E **60** B5
Port Darwin Falk. Is. 51°50S 59°0W **96** G5
Port Davey Australia 43°16S 145°55E **63** G4
Port Dickson Malaysia 2°30N 101°49E **39** L3
Port Douglas Australia 16°30S 145°30E **62** B4
Port Dover Canada 42°47N 80°12W **82** D4
Port Edward Canada 54°12N 130°10W **70** C2
Port Elgin Canada 44°25N 81°25W **82** B3
Port Elizabeth S. Africa 33°58S 25°40E **56** D4
Port Ellen U.K. 55°38N 6°11W **11** F2
Port Erin I. of Man 54°5N 4°45W **12** C3
Port Essington Australia 11°15S 132°10E **60** B5
Port Ewen U.S.A. 41°54N 73°59W **83** E11
Port Fairy Australia 38°22S 142°12E **63** F3
Port Gamble U.S.A. 47°51N 122°34W **78** C4
Port-Gentil Gabon 0°40S 8°50E **54** E1
Port Germein Australia 33°1S 138°1E **63** E2
Port Ghalib Egypt 25°20N 34°50E **46** E2
Port Gibson U.S.A. 31°58N 90°59W **84** F9
Port Glasgow U.K. 55°56N 4°41W **11** F4
Port Harcourt Nigeria 4°40N 7°10E **52** H7
Port Hardy Canada 50°41N 127°30W **70** C3
Port Harrison = Inukjuak
Canada 58°25N 78°15W **69** F16
Port Hawkesbury
Canada 45°36N 61°22W **73** C7
Port Hedland Australia 20°25S 118°35E **60** D2
Port Henry U.S.A. 44°3N 73°28W **83** B11
Port Hood Canada 46°0N 61°32W **73** C7
Port Hope Canada 43°56N 78°20W **82** C6
Port Hope U.S.A. 43°57N 82°43W **82** C2
Port Hope Simpson
Canada 52°33N 56°18W **73** B8
Port Hueneme U.S.A. 34°7N 119°12W **79** L7
Port Huron U.S.A. 42°58N 82°26W **82** D2
Port Jefferson U.S.A. 40°57N 73°3W **83** F11
Port Jervis U.S.A. 41°22N 74°41W **83** E10
Port Kenny Australia 33°10S 134°41E **63** E1
Port Láirge = Waterford
Ireland 52°15N 7°8W **10** D4
Port Lavaca U.S.A. 28°37N 96°38W **84** G6
Port Leyden U.S.A. 43°35N 75°21W **83** C9
Port Lincoln Australia 34°42S 135°52E **63** E2
Port Loko S. Leone 8°48N 12°46W **52** G3
Port-Louis Guadeloupe 16°28N 61°32W **88** b
Port Louis Mauritius 20°10S 57°30E **55** d
Port MacDonnell
Australia 38°5S 140°48E **63** F3
Port McNeill Canada 50°35N 127°6W **70** C3
Port Macquarie
Australia 31°25S 152°25E **63** E5
Port Maria Jamaica 18°22N 76°54W **88** a
Port Matilda U.S.A. 40°48N 78°3W **82** F6
Port McNicoll Canada 44°44N 79°48W **82** B5
Port Mellon Canada 49°32N 123°31W **70** D4
Port-Menier Canada 49°51N 64°15W **73** D7
Port Moody Canada 49°17N 122°51W **78** A4
Port Morant Jamaica 17°54N 76°19W **88** a
Port Moresby Papua N. G. 9°24S 147°8E **58** B7
Port Musgrave Australia 11°55S 141°50E **62** A3
Port Neches U.S.A. 30°0N 93°59W **84** G8
Port Nolloth S. Africa 29°17S 16°52E **56** C2
Port Nouveau-Québec =
Kangiqsualujjuaq
Canada 58°30N 65°59W **69** F18
Port of Climax Canada 49°10N 108°20W **71** D7
Port of Coronach Canada 49°7N 105°31W **71** D7
Port of Spain
Trin. & Tob. 10°40N 61°31W **93** K15
Port Orange U.S.A. 29°9N 80°59W **85** G14
Port Orchard U.S.A. 47°32N 122°38W **78** C4
Port Orford U.S.A. 42°45N 124°30W **76** E1
Port Pegasus N.Z. 47°12S 167°41E **59** G1
Port Perry Canada 44°6N 78°56W **82** B6
Port Phillip B. Australia 38°10S 144°50E **63** F3
Port Pirie Australia 33°10S 138°1E **63** E2
Port Renfrew Canada 48°30N 124°20W **78** B2
Port Roper Australia 14°45S 135°25E **62** A2
Port Rowan Canada 42°40N 80°30W **82** D4
Port Safaga = Bûr Safâga
Egypt 26°43N 33°57E **46** E2
Port Said = Bûr Sa'îd
Egypt 31°16N 32°18E **53** B12
Port St. Joe U.S.A. 29°49N 85°18W **85** G12
Port St. Johns = Umzimvubu
S. Africa 31°38S 29°33E **57** D4
Port St. Lucie U.S.A. 27°18N 80°21W **85** H14
Port Sanilac U.S.A. 43°26N 82°33W **82** C2
Port Severn Canada 44°48N 79°43W **82** B5
Port Shepstone S. Africa 30°44S 30°28E **57** D5
Port Simpson Canada 54°30N 130°20W **70** C2
Port Stanley = Stanley
Falk. Is. 51°40S 59°51W **96** G5
Port Stanley Canada 42°40N 81°10W **82** D3
Port Sudan = Bûr Sûdân
Sudan 19°32N 37°9E **53** E13
Port Sulphur U.S.A. 29°29N 89°42W **85** G10
Port Talbot U.K. 51°35N 3°47W **13** F4
Port Townsend U.S.A. 48°7N 122°45W **78** B4
Port-Vendres France 42°32N 3°8E **20** E5
Port Vila Vanuatu 17°45S 168°18E **58** C9
Port Vladimir Russia 69°25N 33°6E **8** B25
Port Wakefield Australia 34°12S 138°10E **63** E2
Port Washington
U.S.A. 43°23N 87°53W **80** D10
Porta Orientalis Romania 45°6N 22°18E **17** F12
Portacloy Ireland 54°20N 9°46W **10** B2
Portadown U.K. 54°25N 6°27W **10** B5
Portaferry U.K. 54°23N 5°33W **10** B6

Portage Pa., U.S.A. 40°23N 78°41W **82** F6
Portage Wis., U.S.A. 43°33N 89°28W **80** D9
Portage la Prairie
Canada 49°58N 98°18W **71** D9
Portageville U.S.A. 36°26N 89°42W **80** G9
Portalegre Portugal 39°19N 7°25E **21** C2
Portales U.S.A. 34°11N 103°20W **77** J12
Portarlington Ireland 53°9N 7°14W **10** C4
Portbou Spain 42°25N 3°9E **21** A7
Porter L. N.W.T., Canada 61°41N 108°5W **71** A7
Porter L. Sask., Canada 56°20N 107°20W **71** B7
Porterville S. Africa 33°0S 19°0E **56** D2
Porterville U.S.A. 36°4N 119°1W **78** J8
Porth Tywyn = Burry Port
U.K. 51°41N 4°15W **13** F3
Porthcawl U.K. 51°29N 3°42W **13** F4
Porthill U.S.A. 48°59N 116°30W **76** B5
Porthmadog U.K. 52°55N 4°8W **12** E3
Portile de Fier Europe 44°44N 22°30E **17** F12
Portimão Portugal 37°8N 8°32W **21** D1
Portishead U.K. 51°29N 2°46W **13** F5
Portknockie U.K. 57°42N 2°51W **11** D6
Portland N.S.W., Australia 33°20S 150°0E **63** E5
Portland Vic., Australia 38°20S 141°35E **63** F3
Portland Canada 44°42N 76°12W **83** B8
Portland Conn., U.S.A. 41°34N 72°38W **83** E12
Portland Maine, U.S.A. 43°39N 70°16W **81** D18
Portland Mich., U.S.A. 42°52N 84°54W **81** D11
Portland Oreg., U.S.A. 45°32N 122°37W **78** E4
Portland Pa., U.S.A. 40°55N 75°6W **83** F9
Portland Tex., U.S.A. 27°53N 97°20W **84** H6
Portland, I. of U.K. 50°33N 2°26W **13** G5
Portland B. Australia 38°15S 141°45E **63** F3
Portland Bight Jamaica 17°52N 77°5W **88** a
Portland Bill U.K. 50°31N 2°28W **13** G5
Portland Canal U.S.A. 55°56N 130°0W **70** B2
Portland Int. ✈ (PDX)
U.S.A. 45°35N 122°36W **78** E4
Portland Pt. Jamaica 17°42N 77°11W **88** a
Portlaoise Ireland 53°2N 7°18W **10** C4
Portmadoc = Porthmadog
U.K. 52°55N 4°8W **12** E3
Portmore Jamaica 17°53N 76°53W **88** a
Porto France 42°16N 8°42E **20** E8
Porto Portugal 41°8N 8°40W **21** B1
Pôrto Alegre Brazil 30°5S 51°10W **95** C5
Porto de Moz Brazil 1°41S 52°13W **93** D8
Porto Empédocle Italy 37°17N 13°32E **22** F5
Porto Esperança Brazil 19°37S 57°29W **92** G7
Porto Franco Brazil 6°20S 47°24W **93** E9
Porto Inglês C. Verde Is. 15°21N 23°10W **52** b
Porto Mendes Brazil 24°30S 54°15W **95** A5
Porto Murtinho Brazil 21°45S 57°55W **92** H7
Porto Nacional Brazil 10°40S 48°30W **93** F9
Porto-Novo Benin 6°23N 2°42E **52** G6
Porto Primavera, Represa
Brazil 22°10S 52°45W **95** A5
Porto Santo, I. de
Madeira 33°45N 16°25W **52** B2
Porto São José Brazil 22°43S 53°10W **95** A5
Porto Seguro Brazil 16°26S 39°5W **93** G11
Porto Tórres Italy 40°50N 8°24E **22** D3
Porto União Brazil 26°10S 51°10W **95** B5
Porto-Vecchio France 41°35N 9°16E **20** F8
Porto Velho Brazil 8°46S 63°54W **92** E6
Porto Walter Brazil 8°15S 72°40W **92** E4
Portobelo Panama 9°35N 79°42W **88** E4
Portoferráio Italy 42°48N 10°20E **22** C4
Portola U.S.A. 39°49N 120°28W **78** F6
Portoscuso Italy 39°12N 8°24E **22** E3
Portoviejo Ecuador 1°7S 80°28W **92** D2
Portpatrick U.K. 54°51N 5°7W **11** G3
Portree U.K. 57°25N 6°12W **11** D2
Portrush U.K. 55°12N 6°40W **10** A5
Portsmouth Dominica 15°34N 61°27W **89** C7
Portsmouth U.K. 50°48N 1°6W **13** G6
Portsmouth N.H., U.S.A. 43°5N 70°45W **83** C14
Portsmouth Ohio, U.S.A. 38°44N 82°57W **81** F12
Portsmouth R.I., U.S.A. 41°36N 71°15W **83** E13
Portsmouth Va., U.S.A. 36°58N 76°23W **81** G15
Portsmouth □ U.K. 50°48N 1°6W **13** G6
Portsoy U.K. 57°41N 2°41W **11** D6
Portstewart U.K. 55°11N 6°43W **10** A5
Porttipahdan tekojärvi
Finland 68°5N 26°40E **8** B22
Portugal ■ Europe 40°0N 8°0W **21** C1
Portumna Ireland 53°6N 8°14W **10** C3
Portville U.S.A. 42°3N 78°20W **82** D6
Poruma Australia 10°2S 143°4E **62** a
Porvenir Chile 53°10S 70°16W **96** G2
Posadas Argentina 27°30S 55°50W **95** B4
Posht-e Badam Iran 33°2N 55°23E **47** C7
Poso Indonesia 1°20S 120°55E **37** E6
Poso, Danau Indonesia 1°52S 120°35E **37** E6
Posse Brazil 14°4S 46°18W **93** F9
Possession I. Antarctica 72°4S 172°0E **5** D11
Possum Kingdom L.
U.S.A. 32°52N 98°26W **84** E5
Post U.S.A. 33°12N 101°23W **84** E4
Post Falls U.S.A. 47°43N 116°57W **76** C5
Postavy = Pastavy Belarus 55°4N 26°50E **9** J22
Poste-de-la-Baleine =
Kuujjuarapik Canada 55°20N 77°35W **72** A4
Postmasburg S. Africa 28°18S 23°5E **56** C3
Postojna Slovenia 45°46N 14°12E **16** F8
Poston U.S.A. 34°0N 114°24W **79** M12
Postville Canada 54°54N 59°47W **73** B8
Posyet Russia 42°39N 130°48E **28** C5
Potchefstroom S. Africa 26°41S 27°7E **56** C4
Poteau U.S.A. 35°3N 94°37W **84** D7
Poteet U.S.A. 29°2N 98°35W **84** G5
Potenza Italy 40°38N 15°48E **22** D6
Poteriteri, L. N.Z. 46°5S 167°10E **59** G1
Potgietersrus = Mokopane
S. Africa 24°10S 28°55E **57** B4
Poti Georgia 42°10N 41°38E **19** F7
Potiskum Nigeria 11°39N 11°2E **53** F8
Potomac → U.S.A. 38°0N 76°23W **81** F14
Potosí Bolivia 19°38S 65°50W **92** G5

Potosi Mt. U.S.A. 35°57N 115°29W **79** K11
Pototan Phil. 10°54N 122°38E **37** B6
Potrerillos Chile 26°30S 69°30W **94** B2
Potsdam U.S.A. 44°40N 74°59W **83** B10
Potsdam U.S.A. 44°40N 74°59W **83** B10
Pottangi India 18°34N 82°58E **44** E6
Potterville U.S.A. 42°37N 84°44W **81** D11
Pottstown U.S.A. 40°15N 75°39W **83** F9
Pottsville U.S.A. 40°41N 76°12W **83** F8
Pottuvil Sri Lanka 6°55N 81°50E **45** L5
P'otzu Taiwan 23°28N 120°15E **35** F13
Pouce Coupé Canada 55°40N 120°10W **70** B4
Poughkeepsie U.S.A. 41°42N 73°56W **83** E11
Poulaphouca Res. Ireland 53°8N 6°30W **10** C5
Poulsbo U.S.A. 47°44N 122°38W **78** C4
Poultney U.S.A. 43°31N 73°14W **83** C11
Poulton-le-Fylde U.K. 53°51N 2°58W **12** D5
Pouso Alegre Brazil 22°14S 45°57W **95** A6
Pouthisat Cambodia 12°34N 103°50E **38** F4
Považská Bystrica
Slovak Rep. 49°8N 18°27E **17** D10
Povenets Russia 62°50N 34°50E **18** B5
Poverty B. N.Z. 38°43S 178°2E **59** C7
Póvoa de Varzim Portugal 41°25N 8°46W **21** B1
Povorotnyy, Mys Russia 42°40N 133°2E **28** C6
Povungnituk = Puvirnituq
Canada 60°2N 77°10W **69** E16
Powassan Canada 46°5N 79°25W **72** C4
Poway U.S.A. 32°58N 117°2W **79** N9
Powder → U.S.A. 46°45N 105°26W **76** C11
Powder River U.S.A. 43°2N 106°59W **76** E10
Powell U.S.A. 44°45N 108°46W **76** D9
Powell, L. U.S.A. 36°57N 111°29W **77** H8
Powell River Canada 49°50N 124°35W **70** D4
Powers U.S.A. 45°41N 87°32W **80** C10
Pownal U.S.A. 42°45N 73°14W **83** D11
Powys □ U.K. 52°20N 3°20W **13** E4
Poyang Hu China 29°5N 116°20E **35** C11
Poyarkovo Russia 49°36N 128°41E **27** E13
Poza Rica Mexico 20°33N 97°27W **87** C5
Požarevac Serbia 44°35N 21°18E **23** B9
Poznań Poland 52°25N 16°55E **17** B9
Pozo U.S.A. 35°20N 120°24W **79** K6
Pozo Almonte Chile 20°10S 69°50W **92** H5
Pozo Colorado Paraguay 23°30S 58°45W **94** A4
Pozoblanco Spain 38°23N 4°51W **21** C3
Pozzuoli Italy 40°49N 14°7E **22** D6
Prachin Buri Thailand 14°0N 101°25E **38** F3
Prachuap Khirikhan
Thailand 11°49N 99°48E **39** G2
Prado Brazil 17°20S 39°13W **93** G11
Praetprana S. Africa 15°21N 23°34W **52** b
Praia C. Verde Is. 15°2N 23°34W **52** b
Prainha Brazil 1°45S 53°30W **93** D8
Prainha Nova Brazil 7°10S 60°30W **92** E6
Prairie Australia 20°50S 144°35E **62** C3
Prairie City U.S.A. 44°28N 118°43W **76** D4
Prairie Dog Town Fork Red →
U.S.A. 34°34N 99°58W **84** D5
Prairie du Chien U.S.A. 43°3N 91°9W **80** D8
Prairies, L. of the
Canada 51°16N 101°32W **71** C8
Prambanan △ Indonesia 7°45S 110°28E **37** G14
Pran Buri Thailand 12°23N 99°55E **38** F2
Prapat Indonesia 2°41N 98°58E **36** D1
Praslin Seychelles 4°18S 55°45E **55** b
Prata Brazil 19°25S 48°54W **93** G9
Pratabpur India 23°28N 83°15E **43** H10
Pratapgarh Raj., India 24°2N 74°40E **42** G6
Pratapgarh Ut. P., India 25°56N 81°59E **43** G9
Pratas I. = Dongsha Dao
S. China Sea 20°45N 116°43E **35** G11
Prato Italy 43°53N 11°6E **22** C4
Pratt U.S.A. 37°39N 98°44W **80** G4
Prattville U.S.A. 32°28N 86°29W **85** E11
Pravara → India 19°35N 74°45E **44** E2
Pravia Spain 43°30N 6°12W **21** A2
Praya Indonesia 8°39S 116°17E **36** F5
Prayag = Allahabad
India 25°25N 81°58E **43** G9
Preah Vihear Cambodia 14°23N 104°41E **38** E5
Preble U.S.A. 42°44N 76°8W **83** D8
Precipice △ Australia 25°18S 150°5E **63** D5
Precordillera Argentina 30°0S 69°1W **94** C2
Preeceville Canada 51°57N 102°40W **71** C8
Preiļi Latvia 56°18N 26°43E **9** H22
Premont U.S.A. 27°22N 98°7W **84** H5
Prentice U.S.A. 45°33N 90°17W **80** C8
Preobrazheniye Russia 42°54N 133°54E **28** C6
Preparis I. = Pariparit Kyun
Burma 14°52N 93°41E **45** L11
Preparis North Channel
Ind. Oc. 15°27N 94°5E **45** G11
Preparis South Channel
Ind. Oc. 14°33N 93°30E **45** G11
Přerov Czech Rep. 49°28N 17°27E **17** D9
Prescott Canada 44°45N 75°30W **83** B9
Prescott Ariz., U.S.A. 34°33N 112°28W **77** J7
Prescott Ark., U.S.A. 33°48N 93°23W **84** E8
Prescott Valley U.S.A. 34°40N 112°18W **77** J7
Preservation Inlet N.Z. 46°8S 166°35E **59** G1
Presho U.S.A. 43°54N 100°3W **80** D3
Presidencia de la Plaza
Argentina 27°0S 59°50W **94** B4
Presidencia Roque Saenz Peña
Argentina 26°45S 60°30W **94** B3
Presidente Epitácio Brazil 21°56S 52°6W **93** H8
Presidente Hayes □
Paraguay 24°0S 59°0W **94** A4
Presidente Prudente
Brazil 22°5S 51°25W **95** A5
Presidio U.S.A. 29°34N 104°22W **84** G2
Preševo Slovak Rep. 49°0N 21°15E **17** D11
Presidio Texas 46°8S 166°35E **59** G1
Presho U.S.A. 43°54N 100°3W **80** D3
Presteigne U.K. 52°17N 3°0W **13** E5
Preston Canada 43°23N 80°21W **82** C4
Preston U.K. 53°46N 2°42W **12** D5
Preston Idaho, U.S.A. 42°6N 111°53W **76** E8
Preston Minn., U.S.A. 43°40N 92°5W **80** D7
Preston, C. Australia 20°51S 116°12E **60** D2
Prestonburg U.S.A. 37°40N 82°47W **81** G12
Prestwick U.K. 55°29N 4°37W **11** F4
Pretoria S. Africa 25°44S 28°12E **57** C4
Preveza Greece 38°57N 20°45E **23** E9
Prey Veng Cambodia 11°35N 105°29E **39** G5
Pribilof Is. U.S.A. 57°0N 170°0W **74** D6
Příbram Czech Rep. 49°41N 14°2E **16** D8
Price, C. India 13°34N 93°3E **45** H11
Price I. Canada 52°23N 128°41W **70** C3
Prichard U.S.A. 30°44N 88°5W **85** F10
Priekule Latvia 56°26N 21°35E **9** H19
Prienai Lithuania 54°38N 23°57E **9** J20
Prieska S. Africa 29°40S 22°42E **56** C3
Priest L. U.S.A. 48°35N 116°52W **76** B5
Priest River U.S.A. 48°11N 116°55W **76** B5
Priest Valley U.S.A. 36°10N 120°39W **78** J6
Prievidza Slovak Rep. 48°46N 18°36E **17** D10
Prikaspiyskaya Nizmennost =
Caspian Depression
Eurasia 47°0N 48°0E **19** E8
Prilep Macedonia 41°21N 21°32E **23** D9
Priluki = Pryluky
Ukraine 50°30N 32°24E **19** D5
Prime Seal I. Australia 40°3S 147°43E **63** G4
Primo Tapia Mexico 32°16N 116°54W **79** N10
Primorskiy Kray □ Russia 45°0N 135°0E **28** B7
Primrose L. Canada 54°55N 109°45W **71** C7
Prince Albert Canada 53°15N 105°50W **71** C7
Prince Albert S. Africa 33°12S 22°2E **56** D3
Prince Albert △ Canada 54°0N 106°25W **71** C7
Prince Albert Mts.
Antarctica 76°0S 161°30E **5** D11
Prince Albert Pen.
Canada 72°30N 116°0W **68** C8
Prince Albert Sd. Canada 70°25N 115°0W **68** D8
Prince Alfred, C. Canada 74°20N 124°40W **4** B1
Prince Charles I.
Canada 67°47N 76°12W **69** D16
Prince Charles Mts.
Antarctica 72°0S 67°0E **5** D6
Prince Edward Fracture Zone
Ind. Oc. 46°0S 35°0E **5** A4
Prince Edward I. □
Canada 46°20N 63°20W **73** C7
Prince Edward Is. Ind. Oc. 46°35S 38°0E **3** G11
Prince George Canada 53°55N 122°50W **70** C4
Prince of Wales, C.
U.S.A. 65°36N 168°5W **74** B6
Prince of Wales I.
Australia 10°40S 142°10E **62** A3
Prince of Wales I. Canada 73°0N 99°0W **68** C12
Prince of Wales I.
U.S.A. 55°47N 132°50W **68** F5
Prince of Wales Icefield
Canada 78°15N 79°0W **69** B16
Prince of Wales Str.
Canada 73°0N 117°0W **68** C8
Prince Patrick I. Canada 77°0N 120°0W **69** B8
Prince Regent Inlet
Canada 73°0N 90°0W **69** C14
Prince Rupert Canada 54°20N 130°20W **70** C2
Prince William Sd.
U.S.A. 60°40N 147°0W **68** E2
Princes Town
Trin. & Tob. 10°16N 61°23W **93** K15
Princess Charlotte B.
Australia 14°25S 144°0E **62** A3
Princess Elizabeth Trough
S. Ocean 64°10S 83°0E **5** C7
Princess May Ranges
Australia 15°30S 125°30E **60** C4
Princess Royal I. Canada 53°0N 128°40W **70** C3
Princeton Canada 49°27N 120°30W **70** D4
Princeton Calif., U.S.A. 39°24N 122°1W **78** F4
Princeton Ill., U.S.A. 41°23N 89°28W **80** E10
Princeton Ind., U.S.A. 38°21N 87°34W **80** F10
Princeton Ky., U.S.A. 37°7N 87°53W **80** G10
Princeton Mo., U.S.A. 40°24N 93°35W **80** E7
Princeton N.J., U.S.A. 40°21N 74°39W **83** F10
Princeton W. Va., U.S.A. 37°22N 81°6W **81** G13
Principe São Tomé & Príncipe 1°37N 7°25E **50** F4
Príncipe da Beira Brazil 12°20S 64°30W **92** F6
Prineville U.S.A. 44°18N 120°51W **76** D3
Prins Harald Kyst Antarctica 70°0S 35°1E **5** D4
Prinsesse Astrid Kyst
Antarctica 70°45S 12°30E **5** D3
Prinsesse Ragnhild Kyst
Antarctica 70°15S 27°30E **5** D4
Prinzapolca Nic. 13°20N 83°35W **88** D3
Priozersk Russia 61°2N 30°7E **8** F24
Pripet = Prypyat →
Europe 51°20N 30°15E **17** C16
Pripet Marshes Europe 52°10N 27°10E **17** B15
Pripyat Marshes = Pripet Marshes
Europe 52°10N 27°10E **17** B15
Pripyats = Prypyat →
Europe 51°20N 30°15E **17** C16
Prishtinë Kosovo 42°40N 21°13E **23** C9
Priština = Prishtinë
Kosovo 42°40N 21°13E **23** C9
Privas France 44°44N 4°37E **20** D6
Privolzhskaya Vozvyshennost
Russia 51°0N 46°0E **19** D8
Privolzhskiy □ Russia 51°0N 50°0E **28** D6
Prizren Kosovo 42°13N 20°45E **23** C9
Probolinggo Indonesia 7°46S 113°13E **37** G15
Proctor U.S.A. 43°40N 73°2W **83** C11
Proddatur India 14°45N 78°30E **45** G4
Profondeville Belgium 50°23N 4°52E **15** D4
Progreso Coahuila,
Mexico 27°28N 100°59W **86** B4
Progreso Yucatán, Mexico 21°20N 89°40W **87** C7

Progress Antarctica 66°22S 76°22E 5 C12
Progress Russia 49°45N 129°37E 27 E13
Prokopyevsk Russia 54°0N 86°45E 26 D9
Prokuplje Serbia 43°16N 21°36E 23 C9
Prome Burma 18°49N 95°13E 41 K19
Prophet → Canada 58°48N 122°40W 70 B4
Prophet River Canada 58°6N 122°43W 70 B4
Propriá Brazil 10°13S 36°51W 93 F11
Propriano France 41°41N 8°52E 20 F8
Proserpine Australia 20°21S 148°36E 62 b
Prosna → Poland 52°6N 17°44E 17 B9
Prospect U.S.A. 43°18N 75°9W 83 C9
Prosser U.S.A. 46°12N 119°46W 76 C4
Prostějov Czech Rep. 49°30N 17°9E 17 D9
Proston Australia 26°8S 151°32E 63 D5
Provence France 43°40N 5°46E 20 E6
Providence Ky., U.S.A. 37°24N 87°46W 80 G10
Providence R.I., U.S.A. 41°49N 71°24W 83 E13
Providence Bay Canada 45°41N 82°15W 72 C3
Providence Mts.
  U.S.A. 35°10N 115°15W 79 K11
Providencia, I. de
  Colombia 13°25N 81°26W 88 D3
Provideniya Russia 64°23N 173°18W 27 C19
Provincetown U.S.A. 42°3N 70°11W 83 D14
Provins France 48°33N 3°15E 20 B5
Provo U.S.A. 40°14N 111°39W 76 F8
Provost Canada 52°25N 110°20W 71 C6
Prudhoe Bay U.S.A. 70°18N 148°22W 74 A10
Prudhoe I. Australia 21°19S 149°41E 62 C4
Prud'homme Canada 52°20N 105°54W 71 C7
Pruszków Poland 52°9N 20°49E 17 B11
Prut → Romania 45°28N 28°10E 17 F15
Pruzhany Belarus 52°33N 24°28E 17 B13
Prydz B. Antarctica 69°0S 74°0E 5 C6
Pryluky Ukraine 50°30N 32°24E 19 D5
Pryor U.S.A. 36°19N 95°19W 84 C7
Prypyat → Europe 51°20N 30°15E 17 C16
Przemyśl Poland 49°50N 22°45E 17 D12
Przhevalsk = Karakol
  Kyrgyzstan 42°30N 78°20E 30 C4
Psara Greece 38°37N 25°38E 23 E11
Psiloritis, Oros Greece 35°15N 24°45E 23 G11
Pskov Russia 57°50N 28°25E 9 H23
Ptich = Ptsich → Belarus 52°9N 28°52E 17 B15
Ptolemaida Greece 40°30N 21°43E 23 D9
Ptsich → Belarus 52°9N 28°52E 17 B15
Pu Xian China 36°24N 111°6E 32 F6
Pua Thailand 19°11N 100°55E 38 C3
Puán Argentina 37°30S 62°45W 94 D3
Pu'an China 25°46N 104°57E 34 E5
Pu'apu'a Samoa 13°34S 172°9W 59 b
Pubei China 22°16N 109°31E 34 F7
Pucallpa Peru 8°25S 74°30W 92 E4
Pucheng China 27°59N 118°31E 35 D12
Puch'on = Bucheon
  S. Korea 37°28N 126°45E 33 F14
Pudasjärvi Finland 65°23N 26°53E 8 D22
Puding China 26°18N 105°44E 34 D5
Pudozh Russia 61°48N 36°32E 18 B6
Pudu = Suizhou China 31°42N 113°24E 35 B9
Puducherry India 11°59N 79°50E 45 J4
Pudukkottai India 10°28N 78°47E 45 J4
Puebla Mexico 19°3N 98°12W 87 D5
Puebla □ Mexico 18°50N 98°0W 87 D5
Pueblo U.S.A. 38°16N 104°37W 76 G11
Puelches Argentina 38°5S 65°51W 94 D2
Puelén Argentina 37°32S 67°38W 94 D2
Puente Alto Chile 33°32S 70°35W 94 C1
Puente-Genil Spain 37°22N 4°47W 21 D3
Pu'er China 23°0N 101°15E 34 F3
Puerca, Pta. Puerto Rico 18°13N 65°36W 89 d
Puerco → U.S.A. 34°22N 107°50W 77 J10
Puerto Aisén Chile 45°27S 73°0W 96 F2
Puerto Ángel Mexico 15°40N 96°29W 87 D5
Puerto Arista Mexico 15°56N 93°48W 87 D6
Puerto Armuelles Panama 8°20N 82°51W 88 E3
Puerto Ayacucho
  Venezuela 5°40N 67°35W 92 B5
Puerto Barrios Guatemala 15°40N 88°32W 88 C2
Puerto Bermejo
  Argentina 26°55S 58°34W 94 B4
Puerto Bermúdez Peru 10°20S 74°58W 92 F4
Puerto Bolívar Ecuador 3°19S 79°55W 92 D3
Puerto Cabello Venezuela 10°28N 68°1W 92 A5
Puerto Cabezas Nic. 14°0N 83°30W 88 D3
Puerto Cabo Gracias á Dios
  Nic. 15°0N 83°10W 88 D3
Puerto Carreño Colombia 6°12N 67°22W 92 B5
Puerto Castilla Honduras 16°0N 86°0W 88 C2
Puerto Chicama Peru 7°45S 79°20W 92 E3
Puerto Coig Argentina 50°54S 69°15W 96 G3
Puerto Cortés Honduras 15°51N 88°0W 88 C2
Puerto Cumarebo
  Venezuela 11°29N 69°30W 92 A5
Puerto de los Angeles △
  Mexico 23°39N 105°45W 86 C3
Puerto del Rosario
  Canary Is. 28°30N 13°52W 52 C3
Puerto Deseado Argentina 47°55S 66°0W 96 F3
Puerto Escondido Mexico 15°50N 97°3W 87 D5
Puerto Heath Bolivia 12°34S 68°39W 92 F5
Puerto Inírida Colombia 3°53N 67°52W 92 C5
Puerto Juárez Mexico 21°11N 86°49W 87 C7
Puerto La Cruz Venezuela 10°13N 64°38W 92 A6
Puerto Leguízamo
  Colombia 0°12S 74°46W 92 D4
Puerto Lempira
  Honduras 15°16N 83°46W 88 C3
Puerto Libertad Mexico 29°55N 112°43W 86 B2
Puerto Limón Colombia 3°23N 73°30W 92 C4
Puerto Lobos Argentina 42°0S 65°3W 96 E3
Puerto Madryn Argentina 42°46S 65°0W 96 E3
Puerto Maldonado Peru 12°30S 69°10W 92 F5
Puerto Manatí Cuba 21°22N 76°50W 88 B4
Puerto Montt Chile 41°28S 73°0W 96 E2
Puerto Morazán Nic. 12°51N 87°11W 88 D2
Puerto Morelos Mexico 20°50N 86°52W 87 C7
Puerto Natales Chile 51°45S 72°15W 96 G2

Puerto Oscuro Chile 31°24S 71°35W 94 C1
Puerto Padre Cuba 21°13N 76°35W 88 B4
Puerto Páez Venezuela 6°13N 67°28W 92 B5
Puerto Peñasco Mexico 31°20N 113°33W 86 A2
Puerto Pinasco Paraguay 22°36S 57°50W 94 A4
Puerto Plata Dom. Rep. 19°48N 70°45W 89 C5
Puerto Princesa Phil. 9°46N 118°45E 37 C5
Puerto Quepos Costa Rica 9°29N 84°6W 88 E3
Puerto Rico ☑ W. Indies 18°15N 66°45W 89 d
Puerto Rico Trench
  Atl. Oc. 19°50N 66°0W 89 C6
Puerto San Julián
  Argentina 49°18S 67°43W 96 F3
Puerto Santa Cruz
  Argentina 50°0S 68°32W 96 G3
Puerto Sastre Paraguay 22°2S 57°55W 94 A4
Puerto Suárez Bolivia 18°58S 57°52W 92 G7
Puerto Vallarta Mexico 20°37N 105°15W 86 C3
Puerto Varas Chile 41°19S 72°59W 96 E2
Puerto Wilches Colombia 7°21N 73°54W 92 B4
Puertollano Spain 38°43N 4°7W 21 C3
Pueu Tahiti 17°44S 149°13W 59 d
Pueyrredón, L. Argentina 47°20S 72°0W 96 F2
Puffin I. Ireland 51°50N 10°24W 10 E1
Pugachev Russia 52°0N 48°49E 18 D8
Pugal India 28°30N 72°48E 42 E5
Puge China 27°20N 102°31E 34 D4
Pūgönd Iran 25°49N 59°10E 47 E8
Puget Sound U.S.A. 47°50N 122°30W 78 C4
Pugödong N. Korea 42°5N 130°0E 33 C16
Puigcerdà Spain 42°24N 1°50E 21 A6
Puijiang China 30°14N 103°30E 34 B4
Pujiang China 29°29N 119°54E 35 C12
Pujon-ho N. Korea 40°35N 127°35E 33 D14
Pukaki, L. N.Z. 44°4S 170°1E 59 F3
Pukapuka Cook Is. 10°53S 165°49W 65 J11
Pukaskwa △ Canada 48°20N 86°0W 72 C2
Pukatawagan Canada 55°45N 101°20W 71 B8
Pukchin N. Korea 40°12N 125°45E 33 D13
Pukch'ŏng N. Korea 40°14N 128°10E 33 D15
Pukekohe N.Z. 37°12S 174°55E 59 B5
Pukhrayan India 26°14N 79°51E 43 F8
Puksubaek-san
  N. Korea 40°42N 127°45E 33 D14
Pula Croatia 44°54N 13°57E 16 F7
Pulacayo Bolivia 20°25S 66°41W 92 H5
Pulandian China 39°25N 121°58E 33 E11
Pulaski N.Y., U.S.A. 43°34N 76°8W 83 C8
Pulaski Tenn., U.S.A. 35°12N 87°2W 85 D11
Pulaski Va., U.S.A. 37°3N 80°47W 81 G13
Pulau → Indonesia 5°50S 138°15E 37 F9
Pulau Gili Indonesia 8°21S 116°1E 37 K19
Pulawy Poland 51°23N 21°59E 17 C11
Pulga U.S.A. 39°48N 121°29W 78 F5
Pulgaon India 20°44N 78°21E 44 D4
Pulicat India 13°25N 80°19E 45 H5
Pulicat L. India 13°40N 80°15E 45 H5
Pulivendla India 14°25N 78°14E 45 G4
Puliyangudi India 9°11N 77°24E 45 K3
Pullman U.S.A. 46°44N 117°10W 76 C5
Pulog, Mt. Phil. 16°40N 120°50E 37 A6
Pułtusk Poland 52°43N 21°6E 17 B11
Pumlumon Fawr U.K. 52°28N 3°46W 13 E4
Puná, I. Ecuador 2°55S 80°5W 92 D2
Punaauia Tahiti 17°37S 149°34W 59 d
Punakaiki N.Z. 42°7S 171°20E 59 E3
Punakha Dzong Bhutan 27°42N 89°52E 41 F16
Punalur India 9°0N 76°56E 45 K3
Punasar India 27°6N 73°6E 42 F5
Punata Bolivia 17°32S 65°50W 92 G5
Punch India 33°48N 74°4E 43 C6
Punch → Pakistan 33°12N 73°40E 42 C5
Punda Maria S. Africa 22°40S 31°5E 57 B5
Pune India 18°29N 73°57E 44 E1
P'ungsan N. Korea 40°50N 128°9E 33 D15
Puning China 23°20N 116°12E 35 F11
Punjab □ India 31°0N 76°0E 42 D7
Punjab □ Pakistan 32°0N 72°30E 42 E6
Puno Peru 15°55S 70°3W 92 G4
Punpun → India 25°31N 85°18E 43 G11
Punta, Cerro de
  Puerto Rico 18°10N 66°37W 89 d
Punta Alta Argentina 38°53S 62°4W 96 D4
Punta Arenas Chile 53°10S 71°0W 96 G2
Punta del Díaz Chile 28°0S 70°45W 94 B1
Punta Gorda Belize 16°10N 88°45W 87 D7
Punta Gorda U.S.A. 26°56N 82°3W 85 H13
Punta Prieta Mexico 28°58N 114°17W 86 B2
Puntarenas Costa Rica 10°0N 84°50W 88 E3
Puntland Somalia 8°0N 50°0E 49 F4
Punto Fijo Venezuela 11°50N 70°13W 92 A4
Punxsutawney U.S.A. 40°57N 78°59W 82 F6
Pupuan Indonesia 8°19S 115°0E 37 J18
Puqi China 29°40N 113°50E 35 C9
Puquio Peru 14°45S 74°10W 92 F4
Pur → Russia 67°31N 77°55E 26 C8
Puracé, Vol. Colombia 2°21N 76°23W 92 C3
Puralia = Puruliya India 23°17N 86°24E 43 H12
Puranpur India 28°31N 80°9E 43 E9
Purbalingga Indonesia 7°23S 109°21E 37 G13
Purbeck, Isle of U.K. 50°39N 1°59W 13 G5
Purcell U.S.A. 35°1N 97°22W 84 H6
Purcell Mts. Canada 49°55N 116°15W 70 D5
Purdy Canada 45°19N 77°44W 82 A7
Puri India 19°50N 85°58E 44 E7
Purmerend Neths. 52°32N 4°58E 15 B4
Purna → India 19°6N 77°2E 44 E3
Purnia India 25°45N 87°31E 43 G12
Purnululu △ Australia 17°20S 128°20E 60 C4
Pursat = Pouthisat
  Cambodia 12°34N 103°50E 38 F4
Purukcahu Indonesia 0°35S 114°35E 36 E4
Puruliya India 23°17N 86°24E 43 H12
Purus → Brazil 3°42S 61°28W 92 D6
Puruvesi Finland 61°50N 29°30E 8 F23
Purvis U.S.A. 31°9N 89°25W 85 F10
Purwa India 26°28N 80°47E 43 F9
Purwakarta Indonesia 6°35S 107°29E 37 G12
Purwo, Tanjung
  Indonesia 8°44S 114°21E 37 K18

Purwodadi Indonesia 7°7S 110°55E 37 G14
Purwokerto Indonesia 7°25S 109°14E 37 G13
Puryŏng N. Korea 42°5N 129°43E 33 C15
Pus → India 19°55N 77°55E 44 E3
Pusa India 25°59N 85°41E 43 G11
Pusad India 19°56N 77°36E 44 E3
Pusan = Busan S. Korea 35°5N 129°0E 33 G15
Pushkin Russia 59°45N 30°25E 9 G24
Pushkino Russia 51°16N 47°0E 19 D8
Put-in-Bay U.S.A. 41°39N 82°49W 82 E2
Putahow L. Canada 59°54N 100°40W 71 B8
Putao Burma 27°28N 97°30E 41 F20
Putaruru N.Z. 38°2S 175°50E 59 C5
Puteran Indonesia 7°5S 114°0E 37 G15
Putian China 25°23N 119°0E 35 E12
Putignano Italy 40°51N 17°7E 22 D7
Puting, Tanjung Indonesia 3°31S 111°46E 36 E4
Putnam U.S.A. 41°55N 71°55W 83 E13
Putorana, Gory Russia 69°0N 95°0E 27 C10
Putrajaya Malaysia 2°55N 101°40E 39 L3
Puttalam Sri Lanka 8°1N 79°55E 45 K5
Puttalam Lagoon
  Sri Lanka 8°15N 79°45E 45 K4
Puttgarden Germany 54°30N 11°10E 16 A6
Puttur Andhra Pradesh,
  India 13°27N 79°33E 45 H4
Puttur Karnataka, India 12°46N 75°12E 45 H2
Putumayo → S. Amer. 3°7S 67°58W 92 D5
Putuo China 29°56N 122°20E 35 C14
Putussibau Indonesia 0°50N 112°56E 36 D4
Puvirnituq Canada 60°2N 77°10W 69 E16
Puy-de-Dôme France 45°46N 2°57E 20 D5
Puyallup U.S.A. 47°12N 122°18W 78 C4
Puyang China 35°40N 115°1E 32 G8
Pūzeh Rīg Iran 27°20N 58°40E 47 E8
Pweto
  Dem. Rep. of the Congo 8°25S 28°51E 54 F5
Pwllheli U.K. 52°53N 4°25W 12 E3
Pyaozero, Ozero Russia 66°5N 30°58E 8 C5
Pyapon Burma 16°20N 95°40E 41 L19
Pyasina → Russia 73°30N 87°0E 27 B9
Pyatigorsk Russia 44°2N 43°6E 19 F7
Pyay = Prome Burma 18°49N 95°13E 41 K19
Pye = Prome Burma 18°49N 95°13E 41 K19
Pyeongtaek S. Korea 37°1N 127°4E 33 F14
Pyetrikaw Belarus 52°11N 28°29E 17 B15
Pyhäjoki → Finland 64°28N 24°14E 8 D21
Pyin-Oo-Lwin = Maymyo
  Burma 22°2N 96°28E 38 A1
Pyinmana Burma 19°45N 96°12E 41 K20
Pymatuning Res. U.S.A. 41°30N 80°28W 82 E4
Pyŏktong N. Korea 40°50N 125°50E 33 D13
Pyŏnggang S. Korea 38°24N 127°17E 33 E14
P'yŏngsong N. Korea 39°14N 125°52E 33 E13
P'yŏngyang N. Korea 39°0N 125°30E 33 E13
Pyote U.S.A. 31°32N 103°8W 84 F3
Pyramid L. U.S.A. 40°1N 119°35W 76 F4
Pyramid Pk. U.S.A. 36°25N 116°37W 79 J10
Pyrénées Europe 42°45N 0°18E 20 E4
Pyu Burma 18°30N 96°28E 41 K20

Q

Qaanaaq Greenland 77°30N 69°10W 69 B18
Qachasnek S. Africa 30°6S 28°42E 57 D4
Qa'el Jafr Jordan 30°20N 36°25E 48 E5
Qa'emābād Iran 31°44N 60°2E 47 D9
Qā'emshahr Iran 36°30N 52°53E 47 B7
Qagan Nur Jilin, China 45°15N 124°18E 33 B13
Qagan Nur Nei Monggol Zizhiqu,
  China 43°30N 114°55E 32 C8
Qahar Youyi Zhongqi
  China 41°12N 112°40E 32 D7
Qahremānshahr = Kermānshāh
  Iran 34°23N 47°0E 46 C5
Qaidam Pendi China 37°0N 95°0E 30 D8
Qajarīyeh Iran 31°1N 48°22E 47 D6
Qala-i-Jadid = Spīn Būldak
  Afghan. 31°1N 66°25E 42 D2
Qala Viala Pakistan 30°49N 67°17E 42 D2
Qala Yangi Afghan. 34°20N 66°30E 42 B2
Qal'at al Akhḍar Si. Arabia 28°4N 37°9E 46 E3
Qal'at Dīzah Iraq 36°11N 45°7E 46 B5
Qal'at Şāliḥ Iraq 31°31N 47°16E 46 D5
Qal'at Sukkar Iraq 31°51N 46°5E 46 D5
Qamani'tuaq = Baker Lake
  Canada 64°20N 96°3W 68 E12
Qamdo China 31°15N 97°6E 34 B1
Qamea Fiji 16°45S 179°45W 59 a
Qamruddin Karez
  Pakistan 31°45N 68°20E 42 D3
Qandahār = Kandahār
  Afghan. 31°32N 65°43E 40 D4
Qandahār = Kandahār □
  Afghan. 31°0N 65°0E 40 D4
Qandyaghash
  Kazakhstan 49°28N 57°25E 19 E10
Qapān Iran 37°40N 55°47E 47 B7
Qapshaghay Kazakhstan 43°51N 77°14E 26 E8
Qaqortoq Greenland 60°43N 46°0W 4 C5
Qara Qash → China 35°0N 78°30E 43 B8
Qarabutaq Kazakhstan 49°59N 60°14E 26 E7
Qaraghayly Kazakhstan 49°26N 76°0E 26 E8
Qārah Si. Arabia 29°55N 40°3E 46 D4
Qaratau Ongtüstik Qazaqstan,
  Kazakhstan 43°30N 69°30E 26 E7
Qaratau Zhambyl,
  Kazakhstan 43°10N 70°28E 26 E8
Qarazhal Kazakhstan 48°2N 70°49E 26 E8
Qarchak Iran 35°25N 51°34E 47 C6
Qardho Somalia 9°30N 49°6E 49 F4
Qareh → Iran 39°25N 47°22E 46 B5
Qareh Tekān Iran 36°38N 49°29E 47 B6
Qarnein U.A.E. 24°56N 52°52E 47 E7
Qarqan He → China 39°30N 88°30E 30 D6
Qarqaraly Kazakhstan 49°26N 75°30E 30 B4
Qarshi Uzbekistan 38°53N 65°48E 26 F7
Qartabā Lebanon 34°4N 35°50E 48 A4

Qārūh Kuwait 28°49N 48°46E 47 D6
Qaryat al Gharab Iraq 31°27N 44°48E 46 D5
Qaryat al 'Ulyā Si. Arabia 27°33N 47°42E 46 E5
Qasr 'Amra Jordan 31°48N 36°35E 46 D3
Qasr-e Qand Iran 26°15N 60°45E 47 E9
Qasr-e Shīrīn Iran 34°31N 45°35E 46 C5
Qasr Farāfra Egypt 27°0N 28°1E 53 C11
Qasuittuq = Resolute
  Canada 74°42N 94°54W 69 C13
Qatanā Syria 33°26N 36°4E 48 B5
Qatar ■ Asia 25°30N 51°15E 47 E6
Qaṭlīsh Iran 37°50N 57°19E 47 B8
Qattâra, Munkhafed el
  Egypt 29°30N 27°30E 53 C11
Qattâra Depression = Qattâra,
  Munkhafed el Egypt 29°30N 27°30E 53 C11
Qawām al Ḥamzah = Al Ḥamzah
  Iraq 31°43N 44°58E 46 D5
Qāyen Iran 33°40N 59°10E 47 C8
Qazaqstan = Kazakhstan ■
  Asia 50°0N 70°0E 26 E8
Qazimämmäd Azerbaijan 40°3N 49°0E 47 A6
Qazvin Iran 36°15N 50°0E 47 B6
Qazvin □ Iran 36°20N 50°0E 47 B6
Qena Egypt 26°10N 32°43E 53 C12
Qeqertarsuaq Greenland 69°45N 53°30W 4 C5
Qeqertarsuaq Greenland 69°15N 53°38W 4 C5
Qeshlāq Iran 34°55N 46°28E 46 C5
Qeshm Iran 26°55N 56°10E 47 E8
Qeys Iran 26°32N 53°58E 47 E7
Qezel Owzen → Iran 36°45N 49°22E 46 B6
Qezi'ot Israel 30°52N 34°26E 48 E3
Qi Xian China 34°40N 114°48E 32 G8
Qian Gorlos China 45°5N 124°42E 33 B13
Qian Hai China 22°32N 113°54E 31 a
Qian Xian China 34°31N 108°15E 32 G5
Qian'an China 40°0N 118°41E 33 E10
Qiancheng China 27°12N 109°50E 34 D7
Qianjiang Guangxi Zhuangzu,
  China 23°38N 108°58E 34 F7
Qianjiang Hubei, China 30°24N 112°55E 35 B9
Qianjiang Sichuan, China 29°33N 108°47E 34 C7
Qianjin China 47°34N 133°4E 31 B15
Qianshan Anhui, China 30°37N 116°35E 35 B11
Qianshan Guangdong,
  China 22°15N 113°31E 31 a
Qianwei China 29°13N 103°56E 34 C4
Qianxi China 27°3N 106°3E 34 D6
Qianyang Hunan, China 27°18N 110°10E 35 D8
Qianyang Shaanxi, China 34°40N 107°38E 32 G4
Qianyang Zhejiang,
  China 30°11N 119°25E 35 B12
Qi'ao China 22°25N 113°38E 31 a
Qi'ao Dao China 22°25N 113°38E 31 a
Qiaocun China 39°56N 112°55E 32 E7
Qiaojia China 26°56N 102°58E 34 D4
Qichun China 30°18N 115°25E 35 B10
Qidong Hunan, China 26°49N 112°7E 35 D9
Qidong Jiangsu, China 31°48N 121°38E 35 B13
Qiemo China 38°8N 85°32E 30 D6
Qijiang China 28°57N 106°35E 34 C6
Qijiaojing China 43°28N 91°36E 30 C7
Qikiqtarjuaq Canada 67°33N 63°0W 69 D19
Qila Saifullāh Pakistan 30°45N 68°17E 42 D3
Qilian Shan China 38°30N 96°0E 30 D8
Qimen China 29°50N 117°42E 35 C11
Qin He → China 35°1N 113°22E 32 G7
Qin Jiang → Guangxi Zhuangzu,
  China 21°53N 108°35E 34 F7
Qin Jiang → Jiangxi,
  China 26°15N 115°55E 35 D10
Qin Ling = Qinling Shandi
  China 33°50N 108°10E 32 H5
Qin'an China 34°48N 105°40E 32 G3
Qing Xian China 38°35N 116°45E 32 E9
Qingcheng China 37°15N 117°40E 33 F9
Qingcheng Shan China 30°58N 103°31E 34 B4
Qingchuan China 32°36N 105°9E 34 A5
Qingdao China 36°5N 120°20E 33 F11
Qingfeng China 35°52N 115°8E 32 G8
Qinghai □ China 36°0N 98°0E 30 D8
Qinghai Hu China 36°40N 100°10E 30 D9
Qinghecheng China 41°28N 124°15E 33 D13
Qinghemen China 41°48N 121°25E 33 D11
Qingjian China 37°8N 110°8E 32 F6
Qingjiang = Huaiyin
  China 33°30N 119°2E 33 H10
Qingliu China 26°11N 116°48E 35 D11
Qinglong China 25°49N 105°12E 34 E5
Qingping China 26°39N 107°47E 34 D6
Qingshui China 34°48N 106°8E 32 G4
Qingshuihe China 39°55N 111°35E 32 E6
Qingtian China 28°12N 120°15E 35 C13
Qingtongxia China 38°2N 106°3E 32 E4
Qingtongxia Shuiku
  China 37°50N 105°58E 32 F3
Qingxi China 27°8N 108°43E 34 D7
Qingxu China 37°34N 112°22E 32 F7
Qingyang Anhui, China 30°38N 117°50E 35 B11
Qingyang Gansu, China 36°2N 107°55E 32 F4
Qingyi Jiang → China 29°32N 103°44E 34 C4
Qingyuan Guangdong,
  China 23°40N 112°59E 35 F9
Qingyuan Liaoning,
  China 42°10N 124°55E 33 C13
Qingyuan Zhejiang,
  China 27°36N 119°3E 35 D12
Qingyun China 37°45N 117°20E 33 F9
Qingzhen China 26°31N 106°25E 34 D6
Qinhuangdao China 39°56N 119°30E 33 E10
Qinling Shandi China 33°50N 108°10E 32 H5
Qinshui China 35°40N 112°8E 32 G7
Qinyang = Jiyuan China 35°7N 112°57E 32 G7
Qinyang China 35°5N 112°50E 32 G7
Qinyuan China 36°29N 112°20E 32 F7
Qinzhou China 21°58N 108°38E 34 G7
Qionghai China 19°15N 110°26E 38 C8
Qionglai China 30°25N 103°31E 34 B4
Qionglai Shan China 31°0N 102°30E 34 B4

Qiongshan China 19°51N 110°26E 38 C8
Qiongzhou Haixia China 20°10N 110°15E 38 B8
Qiqihar China 47°26N 124°0E 31 B13
Qira China 37°0N 80°48E 30 D5
Qiraîya, W. → Egypt 30°27N 34°0E 48 E3
Qiryat Ata Israel 32°47N 35°6E 48 C4
Qiryat Gat Israel 31°32N 34°46E 48 D3
Qiryat Mal'akhi Israel 31°44N 34°44E 48 D3
Qiryat Shemona Israel 33°13N 35°35E 48 B4
Qiryat Yam Israel 32°51N 35°4E 48 C4
Qishan China 34°25N 107°38E 32 G4
Qitai China 44°2N 89°35E 30 C6
Qitaihe China 45°48N 130°51E 28 B5
Qiubei China 24°2N 104°12E 34 E5
Qixia China 37°17N 120°52E 33 F11
Qiyang China 26°35N 111°50E 35 D8
Qizlağac Körfäzi Azerbaijan 39°9N 49°0E 47 B6
Qods Iran 35°45N 51°15E 47 C6
Qojūr Iran 36°12N 47°55E 46 B5
Qom Iran 34°40N 51°0E 47 C6
Qom □ Iran 34°40N 51°0E 47 C6
Qomolangma Feng = Everest, Mt.
  Nepal 28°5N 86°58E 43 E12
Qomsheh Iran 32°0N 51°55E 47 D6
Qoqek = Tacheng China 46°40N 82°58E 30 B5
Qoqon = Qŭqon
  Uzbekistan 40°31N 70°56E 26 E8
Qoraqalpoghistan □
  Uzbekistan 43°0N 58°0E 26 E6
Qorveh Iran 35°10N 47°48E 46 C5
Qosshaghyl Kazakhstan 46°40N 54°0E 19 E9
Qostanay Kazakhstan 53°10N 63°35E 26 D7
Qu Jiang → China 30°1N 106°24E 34 B6
Qu Xian China 30°48N 106°58E 34 B6
Quabbin Res. U.S.A. 42°20N 72°20W 83 D12
Quairading Australia 32°0S 117°21E 61 F2
Quakenbrück Germany 52°40N 7°39E 16 B4
Quakertown U.S.A. 40°26N 75°21W 83 F9
Qualicum Beach
  Canada 49°22N 124°26W 70 D4
Quambatook Australia 35°49S 143°34E 63 F3
Quambone Australia 30°57S 147°53E 63 E4
Quamby Australia 20°22S 140°17E 62 C3
Quan Long = Ca Mau
  Vietnam 9°7N 105°8E 39 H5
Quanah U.S.A. 34°18N 99°44W 84 D5
Quang Ngai Vietnam 15°13N 108°58E 38 E7
Quang Tri Vietnam 16°45N 107°13E 38 D6
Quang Yen Vietnam 20°56N 106°52E 34 G6
Quannan China 24°45N 114°33E 35 E10
Quantock Hills U.K. 51°8N 3°10W 13 F4
Quanyang China 42°21N 127°32E 33 C14
Quanzhou Fujian, China 24°55N 118°34E 35 E12
Quanzhou Guangxi Zhuangzu,
  China 25°57N 111°5E 35 E8
Qu'Appelle → Canada 50°33N 103°53W 71 C8
Quaqtaq Canada 60°55N 69°40W 69 E18
Quaraí Brazil 30°15S 56°20W 94 C4
Quartu Sant'Élena Italy 39°15N 9°10E 22 E3
Quartzsite U.S.A. 33°40N 114°13W 79 M12
Quatre Bornes Mauritius 20°15S 57°28E 55 d
Quatsino Sd. Canada 50°25N 127°58W 70 C3
Quba Azerbaijan 41°21N 48°32E 19 F8
Qūchān Iran 37°10N 58°27E 47 B8
Queanbeyan Australia 35°17S 149°14E 63 F4
Québec Canada 46°52N 71°13W 73 C5
Québec □ Canada 48°0N 74°0W 73 B6
Quebrada del Condorito △
  Argentina 31°49S 64°40W 94 C3
Queen Alexandra Ra.
  Antarctica 85°0S 170°0E 5 E11
Queen Charlotte City
  Canada 53°15N 132°2W 70 C2
Queen Charlotte Is. = Haida Gwaii
  Canada 53°20N 132°10W 70 C2
Queen Charlotte Sd.
  Canada 51°0N 128°0W 70 C3
Queen Charlotte Strait
  Canada 50°45N 127°10W 70 C3
Queen Elizabeth Is.
  Canada 76°0N 95°0W 69 B13
Queen Mary Land Antarctica 70°0S 95°0E 5 D7
Queen Maud G.
  Canada 68°15N 102°30W 68 D11
Queen Maud Land = Dronning
  Maud Land Antarctica 72°30S 12°0E 5 D3
Queen Maud Mts.
  Antarctica 86°0S 160°0W 5 E12
Queens Channel Australia 15°0S 129°30E 60 C4
Queenscliff Australia 38°16S 144°39E 63 F3
Queensland □ Australia 22°0S 142°0E 62 C3
Queenstown Australia 42°4S 145°35E 63 G4
Queenstown N.Z. 45°1S 168°40E 59 F2
Queenstown S. Africa 31°52S 26°52E 56 D4
Queets U.S.A. 47°32N 124°19W 78 C2
Queguay Grande →
  Uruguay 32°9S 58°9W 94 C4
Queimadas Brazil 11°0S 39°38W 93 F11
Quelimane Mozam. 17°53S 36°58E 55 H7
Quellón Chile 43°7S 73°37W 96 E2
Quelpart = Jeju-do
  S. Korea 33°29N 126°34E 33 H14
Quemado N. Mex.,
  U.S.A. 34°20N 108°30W 77 J9
Quemado Tex., U.S.A. 28°56N 100°37W 84 G4
Quemoy = Chinmen
  Taiwan 24°26N 118°19E 35 E13
Quemú-Quemú Argentina 36°3S 63°36W 94 D3
Quepem India 15°13N 74°3E 45 G2
Quequén Argentina 38°30S 58°30W 94 D4
Querétaro Mexico 20°36N 100°23W 86 C4
Querétaro □ Mexico 21°0N 99°55W 86 C5
Queshan China 32°55N 114°2E 35 A10
Quesnel Canada 53°0N 122°30W 70 C4
Quesnel → Canada 52°58N 122°29W 70 C4
Quesnel L. Canada 52°30N 121°20W 70 C4
Questa U.S.A. 36°42N 105°36W 77 H11
Quetico △ Canada 48°30N 91°45W 72 C1
Quetta Pakistan 30°15N 66°55E 42 D2
Quetzaltenango
  Guatemala 14°50N 91°30W 88 D1

Qufār *Si. Arabia* 27°26N 41°37E **46** E4
Qufu *China* 35°36N 116°58E **32** G9
Qui Nhon *Vietnam* 13°40N 109°13E **38** F7
Quibala *Angola* 10°46S 14°59E **54** G2
Quibaxe *Angola* 8°24S 14°27E **54** F2
Quibdó *Colombia* 5°42N 76°40W **92** B3
Quiberon *France* 47°29N 3°9W **20** C2
Quiet L. *Canada* 61°5N 133°5W **70** A2
Quiindy *Paraguay* 25°58S 57°14W **94** B4
Quilá *Mexico* 24°23N 107°13W **86** C3
Quilcene *U.S.A.* 47°49N 122°53W **78** C4
Quilimari *Chile* 32°5S 71°30W **94** C1
Quilino *Argentina* 30°14S 64°29W **94** C3
Quillabamba *Peru* 12°50S 72°50W **92** F4
Quillagua *Chile* 21°40S 69°40W **94** A2
Quillota *Chile* 32°54S 71°16W **94** C1
Quilmes *Argentina* 34°43S 58°15W **94** C4
Quilon = Kollam *India* 8°50N 76°38E **45** K3
Quilpie *Australia* 26°35S 144°11E **63** D3
Quilpué *Chile* 33°5S 71°33W **94** C1
Quimili *Argentina* 27°40S 62°30W **94** B3
Quimper *France* 48°0N 4°9W **20** B1
Quimperlé *France* 47°53N 3°33W **20** C2
Quinault →, *U.S.A.* 47°21N 124°18W **78** C2
Quincy *Calif., U.S.A.* 39°56N 120°57W **78** F6
Quincy *Fla., U.S.A.* 30°35N 84°34W **85** F12
Quincy *Ill., U.S.A.* 39°56N 91°23W **80** F8
Quincy *Wash., U.S.A.* 47°14N 119°51W **76** C4
Quines *Argentina* 32°13S 65°48W **94** C2
Quintana Roo □ *Mexico* 19°40N 88°30W **87** D7
Quintanar de la Orden
  Spain 39°36N 3°5W **21** C4
Quintero *Chile* 32°45S 71°30W **94** C1
Quirihue *Chile* 36°15S 72°35W **94** D1
Quirindi *Australia* 31°28S 150°40E **63** E5
Quirinópolis *Brazil* 18°32S 50°30W **93** G8
Quissanga *Mozam.* 12°24S 40°28E **55** G8
Quissico *Mozam.* 24°42S 34°44E **57** B5
Quitilipi *Argentina* 26°50S 60°13W **94** B3
Quitman *U.S.A.* 30°47N 83°34W **85** F13
Quito *Ecuador* 0°15S 78°35W **92** D3
Quixadá *Brazil* 4°55S 39°0W **93** D11
Qujing *China* 25°32N 103°41E **34** E4
Qulan *Kazakhstan* 42°55N 72°43E **26** E8
Qul'ân, Jazâ'ir *Egypt* 24°22N 35°31E **46** E2
Qulsary *Kazakhstan* 46°59N 54°1E **19** E9
Qumbu *S. Africa* 31°10S 28°48E **57** D4
Quneitra = Al Qunayţirah
  Syria 33°5N 35°45E **48** B4
Qŭnghirot *Uzbekistan* 43°2N 58°50E **26** E6
Qu'nyido *China* 31°15N 98°6E **34** B2
Quoin I. *Australia* 14°54S 129°32E **60** B4
Quoin Pt. *S. Africa* 34°46S 19°37E **56** D2
Quorn *Australia* 32°25S 138°5E **63** E2
Qŭqon *Uzbekistan* 40°31N 70°56E **26** E8
Qurnat as Sawdâ' *Lebanon* 34°18N 36°6E **48** A5
Quşayba' *Si. Arabia* 26°53N 43°35E **46** E4
Qusaybah *Iraq* 34°24N 40°59E **46** C4
Quseir *Egypt* 26°7N 34°16E **46** E2
Quseir Amra = Qasr 'Amra
  Jordan 31°48N 36°35E **46** D3
Qüshchī *Iran* 37°59N 45°3E **46** B5
Qutang Gorge = Qutang Xia
  China 31°0N 109°40E **34** B7
Qutang Xia *China* 31°0N 109°40E **34** B7
Quthing *Lesotho* 30°25S 27°36E **57** D4
Qūţīābād *Iran* 35°47N 48°30E **47** C6
Quttinirpaaq △ *Canada* 82°13N 72°13W **69** A17
Quwo *China* 35°38N 111°25E **32** G6
Quyang *China* 38°35N 114°40E **32** E8
Quynh Nhai *Vietnam* 21°49N 103°33E **38** B4
Quyon *Canada* 45°31N 76°14W **83** A8
Quzhou *China* 28°57N 118°54E **35** C12
Quzi *China* 36°20N 107°20E **32** F4
Qyzylorda *Kazakhstan* 44°48N 65°28E **26** E7

R

Ra, Ko *Thailand* 9°13N 98°16E **39** H2
Raahe *Finland* 64°40N 24°28E **8** D21
Raalte *Neths.* 52°23N 6°16E **15** B6
Raas *Indonesia* 7°8S 114°33E **37** G16
Raasay *U.K.* 57°25N 6°4W **11** D2
Raasay, Sd. of *U.K.* 57°30N 6°8W **11** D2
Raasepori *Finland* 60°0N 23°26E **9** G20
Rába → *Hungary* 47°38N 17°38E **17** E9
Rabat *Malta* 35°53N 14°24E **22** G6
Rabat *Morocco* 34°2N 6°48W **52** B4
Rabaul *Papua N. G.* 4°24S 152°18E **58** B8
Rabbit Flat *Australia* 20°11S 130°1E **60** D5
Rabbit Lake Mine *Canada* 58°4N 104°54W **71** B8
Rabi *Fiji* 16°30S 179°59W **59** a
Rābigh *Si. Arabia* 22°50N 39°5E **49** C2
Râbniţa *Moldova* 47°45N 29°0E **17** E15
Râbor *Iran* 29°17N 56°55E **47** D8
Rabwah = Chenab Nagar
  Pakistan 31°45N 72°55E **42** D5
Race, C. *Canada* 46°40N 53°5W **73** C9
Racha Noi, Ko *Thailand* 7°30N 98°19E **39** J2
Racha Yai, Ko *Thailand* 7°36N 98°21E **39** J2
Rachid *Mauritania* 18°45N 11°35W **52** E3
Racibórz *Poland* 50°7N 18°18E **17** C10
Racine *U.S.A.* 42°44N 87°47W **80** D10
Rackerby *U.S.A.* 39°26N 121°22W **78** F5
Rădăuţi *Romania* 47°50N 25°59E **17** E13
Radcliff *U.S.A.* 37°51N 85°57W **81** G11
Radekhiv *Ukraine* 50°25N 24°32E **17** C13
Radekhov = Radekhiv
  Ukraine 50°25N 24°32E **17** C13
Radford *U.S.A.* 37°8N 80°34W **81** G13
Radhanpur *India* 23°50N 71°38E **42** H4
Radhwa, Jabal *Si. Arabia* 24°34N 38°18E **46** E3
Radisson *Qué., Canada* 53°47N 77°37W **72** B4
Radisson *Sask., Canada* 52°30N 107°20W **71** C7
Radium Hot Springs
  Canada 50°35N 116°2W **70** C5

Radnor Forest *U.K.* 52°17N 3°10W **13** E4
Radom *Poland* 51°23N 21°12E **17** C11
Radomsko *Poland* 51°5N 19°28E **17** C10
Radomyshl *Ukraine* 50°30N 29°12E **17** C15
Radstock, C. *Australia* 33°12S 134°20E **63** E1
Raduzhnyy *Russia* 62°5N 77°28E **26** C8
Radviliškis *Lithuania* 55°49N 23°33E **9** J20
Rae *Canada* 62°50N 116°3W **70** A5
Rae Bareli *India* 26°18N 81°20E **43** F9
Rae Isthmus *Canada* 66°40N 87°30W **69** D14
Raeren *Belgium* 50°41N 6°7E **15** D6
Raeside, L. *Australia* 29°20S 122°0E **61** E3
Raetihi *N.Z.* 39°25S 175°17E **59** C5
Rafaela *Argentina* 31°10S 61°30W **94** C3
Rafah *Gaza Strip* 31°18N 34°14E **48** D3
Rafḩā *Si. Arabia* 29°35N 43°35E **46** D4
Rafsanjān *Iran* 30°30N 56°5E **47** D8
Raft Pt. *Australia* 16°4S 124°26E **60** C3
Râga *South Sudan* 8°28N 25°41E **53** G11
Ragachow *Belarus* 53°8N 30°5E **17** B16
Ragama *Sri Lanka* 7°0N 79°50E **40** R11
Ragged, Mt. *Australia* 33°27S 123°25E **61** F3
Ragged Pt. *Barbados* 13°10N 59°26W **89** g
Raghunathpalli *India* 22°14N 84°48E **43** H11
Raghunathpur *India* 23°33N 86°40E **43** H12
Raglan *N.Z.* 37°55S 174°55E **59** B5
Ragusa *Italy* 36°55N 14°44E **22** F6
Raha *Indonesia* 4°55S 123°0E **37** E6
Rahaeng = Tak *Thailand* 16°52N 99°8E **38** D2
Rahat *Israel* 31°24N 34°45E **48** D3
Rahatgarh *India* 23°47N 78°22E **43** H8
Rahimyar Khan *Pakistan* 28°30N 70°25E **42** E4
Rāhjerd *Iran* 34°22N 50°22E **47** C6
Rahon *India* 31°3N 76°7E **42** D7
Rai, Hon *Vietnam* 9°48N 104°38E **39** H5
Raiatéa, Î.
  French Polynesia 16°50S 151°25W **65** J12
Raichur *India* 16°10N 77°20E **45** F3
Raiganj *India* 25°37N 88°10E **43** G13
Raigarh *India* 21°56N 83°25E **44** J5
Raighar *India* 19°51N 82°6E **44** E6
Raijua *Indonesia* 10°37S 121°36E **37** F6
Raikot *India* 30°41N 75°42E **42** D6
Railton *Australia* 41°25S 146°28E **63** G4
Rainbow Bridge △
  U.S.A. 37°5N 110°58W **77** H8
Rainbow Lake *Canada* 58°30N 119°23W **70** B5
Rainier *U.S.A.* 46°53N 122°41W **78** D4
Rainier, Mt. *U.S.A.* 46°52N 121°46W **78** D5
Rainy L. *Canada* 48°42N 93°10W **71** D10
Rainy River *Canada* 48°43N 94°29W **71** D10
Raippaluoto *Finland* 63°13N 21°14E **8** E19
Raipur *India* 21°17N 81°45E **44** D5
Rairakhol *India* 21°4N 84°21E **44** D7
Raisen *India* 23°20N 77°48E **42** H8
Raisio *Finland* 60°28N 22°11E **9** F20
Raj Nandgaon *India* 21°5N 81°5E **44** D5
Raj Nilgiri *India* 21°28N 86°46E **43** J12
Raja, Ujung *Indonesia* 3°40N 96°25E **36** D1
Raja Ampat, Kepulauan
  Indonesia 0°30S 130°0E **37** E8
Rajahmundry *India* 17°1N 81°48E **44** F5
Rajaji △ *India* 30°10N 78°20E **42** D8
Rajampet *India* 14°11N 79°10E **45** G4
Rajang → *Malaysia* 2°30N 112°0E **36** D4
Rajanpur *Pakistan* 29°6N 70°19E **42** E4
Rajapalaiyam *India* 9°25N 77°35E **45** K3
Rajapur *India* 16°40N 73°31E **44** F1
Rajasthan □ *India* 26°45N 73°30E **42** F5
Rajasthan Canal = Indira Gandhi
  Canal *India* 28°0N 72°0E **42** F5
Rajauri *India* 33°25N 74°21E **43** C6
Rajendranagar *India* 17°18N 78°27E **44** F4
Rajgarh *Mad. P., India* 24°2N 76°45E **42** G7
Rajgarh *Raj., India* 27°14N 76°38E **42** F7
Rajgarh *Raj., India* 28°40N 75°25E **42** E6
Rajghat Dam *India* 24°45N 78°20E **44** B4
Rajgir *India* 25°2N 85°25E **43** G11
Rajim *India* 20°58N 81°53E **44** D5
Rajkot *India* 22°15N 70°56E **42** H4
Rajmahal Hills *India* 24°30N 87°30E **43** G12
Rajpipla *India* 21°50N 73°30E **44** D1
Rajpur *India* 22°18N 74°21E **42** H6
Rajpura *India* 30°25N 76°32E **42** D7
Rajsamand = Kankroli
  India 25°4N 73°53E **42** G5
Rajshahi *Bangla.* 24°22N 88°39E **41** G16
Rajshahi □ *Bangla.* 25°0N 89°0E **43** G13
Rajula *India* 21°3N 71°26E **42** J4
Rajur *India* 20°7N 78°55E **44** D4
Rajura *India* 19°47N 79°22E **44** E4
Rakaia *N.Z.* 43°45S 172°1E **59** E4
Rakaia → *N.Z.* 43°36S 172°15E **59** E4
Rakan, Ra's *Qatar* 26°10N 51°20E **47** E6
Rakaposhi *Pakistan* 36°10N 74°25E **43** A6
Rakata, Pulau *Indonesia* 6°10S 105°20E **37** G11
Rakhine □ *Burma* 19°0N 94°15E **41** K18
Rakhiv *Ukraine* 48°3N 24°12E **17** D13
Rakhni *Pakistan* 30°4N 69°56E **42** D3
Rakhni → *Pakistan* 29°31N 69°36E **42** E3
Rakiraki *Fiji* 17°22S 178°11E **59** a
Rakitnoye *Russia* 45°36N 134°17E **28** B7
Rakiura = Stewart I.
  N.Z. 46°58S 167°54E **59** G1
Rakiura △ *N.Z.* 47°0S 167°50E **59** G1
Rakops *Botswana* 21°1S 24°28E **56** B3
Rakvere *Estonia* 59°20N 26°25E **9** G22
Raleigh *U.S.A.* 35°47N 78°39W **85** D15
Ralik Chain *Pac. Oc.* 8°0N 168°0E **64** G8
Ralls *U.S.A.* 33°41N 101°24W **84** E4
Ralston *U.S.A.* 41°30N 76°57W **82** E8
Ram → *Canada* 62°1N 123°41W **70** A4
Rama *Nic.* 12°9N 84°15W **88** D3
Ramachandrapuram *India* 16°50N 82°4E **44** F6
Ramagiri Udayagiri *India* 19°5N 84°18E **44** E7
Ramagundam *India* 18°55N 79°15E **44** E4
Ramakona *India* 21°43N 78°50E **43** J8

Raman *Thailand* 6°29N 101°18E **39** J3
Ramanathapuram *India* 9°25N 78°55E **45** K4
Ramanujganj *India* 23°48N 83°42E **43** H10
Ramas C. *India* 15°5N 73°55E **45** G1
Ramat Gan *Israel* 32°4N 34°48E **48** C3
Ramatlhabama *S. Africa* 25°37S 25°33E **56** C4
Ramban *India* 33°14N 75°12E **43** C6
Rambipuji *Indonesia* 8°12S 113°37E **37** H15
Ramdurg *India* 15°58N 75°22E **45** G2
Rame Hd. *Australia* 37°47S 149°30E **63** F4
Ramechhap *Nepal* 27°25N 86°10E **43** F12
Rameswaram *India* 9°17N 79°18E **45** K4
Ramganga → *India* 27°5N 79°58E **43** F8
Ramgarh *Jharkhand,*
  India 23°40N 85°35E **43** H11
Ramgarh *Raj., India* 27°16N 75°14E **42** F6
Ramgarh *Raj., India* 27°30N 70°36E **42** F4
Ra's al 'Ayn *Syria* 36°45N 40°12E **46** B4
Ra's al Khaymah *U.A.E.* 25°50N 55°59E **47** E7
Ra's aţ Ţib *Tunisia* 37°1N 11°2E **22** F4
Rasa, Pta. *Argentina* 36°20S 56°41W **94** D4
Raseiniai *Lithuania* 55°25N 23°5E **9** J20
Rashmi *India* 25°4N 74°22E **42** G6
Rasht *Iran* 37°20N 49°40E **47** B6
Rasi Salai *Thailand* 15°20N 104°9E **38** E5
Rasipuram *India* 11°30N 78°15E **45** J4
Raskot *Nepal* 29°14N 81°39E **43** E9
Rason L. *Australia* 28°45S 124°25E **61** E3
Rasra *India* 25°50N 83°50E **43** G10
Rasua Garhi *Nepal* 28°17N 85°23E **43** E11
Rasul *Pakistan* 32°42N 73°34E **42** C5
Râmnicu Sărat *Romania* 45°26N 27°3E **17** F14
Râmnicu Vâlcea *Romania* 45°9N 24°21E **17** F13
Ramona *U.S.A.* 33°2N 116°52W **79** M10
Ramore *Canada* 48°30N 80°25W **72** C3
Ramotswa *Botswana* 24°50S 25°52E **56** B4
Rampur *H.P., India* 31°26N 77°43E **42** D7
Rampur *Mad. P., India* 23°25N 73°53E **42** H5
Rampur *Odisha, India* 21°48N 83°58E **44** D6
Rampur *Ut. P., India* 28°50N 79°5E **43** E8
Rampur Hat *India* 24°10N 87°50E **43** G12
Rampura *India* 24°30N 75°27E **42** G6
Ramree I. *Burma* 19°0N 93°40E **41** K19
Ramsar *Iran* 36°53N 50°41E **47** B6
Ramsey *I. of Man* 54°20N 4°22E **12** C3
Ramsey *Canada* 41°4N 74°9W **83** E10
Ramsey L. *Canada* 47°13N 82°15W **72** C3
Ramsgate *U.K.* 51°20N 1°25E **13** F9
Ramtek *India* 21°20N 79°15E **44** D4
Rana Pratap Sagar Dam
  India 24°58N 75°38E **42** G6
Ranaghat *India* 23°15N 88°35E **43** H13
Ranahu *Pakistan* 25°55N 69°45E **42** G3
Ranau *Malaysia* 6°2N 116°40E **36** C5
Rancagua *Chile* 34°10S 70°50W **94** C1
Rancheria → *Canada* 60°13N 129°7W **70** A3
Ranchester *U.S.A.* 44°54N 107°10W **76** D10
Ranchi *India* 23°19N 85°27E **43** H11
Rancho Cordova *U.S.A.* 38°36N 121°18W **78** G5
Rancho Cucamonga
  U.S.A. 34°10N 117°30W **79** L9
Rander *India* 21°14N 72°47E **44** D1
Randers *Denmark* 56°29N 10°1E **9** H14
Randfontein *S. Africa* 26°8S 27°45E **57** C4
Randle *U.S.A.* 46°32N 121°57W **78** D5
Randolph *Mass., U.S.A.* 42°10N 71°2W **83** D13
Randolph *N.Y., U.S.A.* 42°10N 78°59W **82** D6
Randolph *Utah, U.S.A.* 41°40N 111°11W **76** F8
Randolph *Vt., U.S.A.* 43°55N 72°40W **83** C12
Randsburg *U.S.A.* 35°22N 117°39W **79** K9
Råneälven → *Sweden* 65°50N 22°20E **8** D20
Rangae *Thailand* 6°19N 101°44E **39** J3
Rangaunu B. *N.Z.* 34°51S 173°15E **59** A4
Rangeley *U.S.A.* 44°58N 70°39W **83** B14
Rangeley L. *U.S.A.* 44°55N 70°43W **83** B14
Rangely *U.S.A.* 40°5N 108°48W **76** F9
Ranger *U.S.A.* 32°28N 98°41W **84** E5
Rangia *India* 26°28N 91°38E **41** F17
Rangiora *N.Z.* 43°19S 172°36E **59** E4
Rangitaiki → *N.Z.* 37°54S 176°49E **59** B6
Rangitata → *N.Z.* 43°45S 171°15E **59** E3
Rangitoto ke te tonga = D'Urville I.
  N.Z. 40°50S 173°55E **59** D4
Rangkasbitung
  Indonesia 6°21S 106°15E **37** G12
Rangoon *Burma* 16°45N 96°20E **41** L20
Rangpur *Bangla.* 25°42N 89°22E **41** G16
Rangsang *Indonesia* 1°20N 103°5E **39** M4
Ranibennur *India* 14°35N 75°30E **45** G2
Raniganj *Paschimbang,*
  India 23°40N 87°5E **41** H15
Raniganj *Ut. P., India* 27°3N 82°13E **43** F9
Ranikhet *India* 29°39N 79°25E **43** E8
Ranippettai *India* 12°56N 79°23E **45** H4
Raniwara *India* 24°50N 72°10E **42** G5
Rāniyah *Iraq* 36°15N 44°53E **46** B5
Ranka *India* 23°59N 83°47E **43** H10
Ranken → *Australia* 20°31S 137°36E **62** C2
Rankin *U.S.A.* 31°13N 101°56W **84** F4
Rankin Inlet *Canada* 62°30N 93°0W **68** E13
Rankins Springs
  Australia 33°49S 146°14E **63** E4
Rannoch, L. *U.K.* 56°41N 4°20W **11** E4
Rannoch Moor *U.K.* 56°38N 4°48W **11** E4
Ranohira *Madag.* 22°29S 45°24E **55** J9
Ranong *Thailand* 9°56N 98°40E **39** H2
Ranpur *India* 21°15S 105°10E **42** J5
Rānsa *Iran* 33°39N 48°18E **47** C6
Ransiki *Indonesia* 1°30S 134°10E **37** E8
Rantau Abang *Malaysia* 4°52N 103°24E **39** K4
Rantauprapat *Indonesia* 2°15N 99°50E **36** D1
Rantemario *Indonesia* 3°15S 119°57E **37** E5
Ranthambore △ *India* 26°0N 76°45E **42** F7
Rantoul *U.S.A.* 40°19N 88°9W **80** E9
Raohe *China* 46°47N 134°0E **28** A7
Raoping *China* 23°42N 117°5E **35** F11
Raoyang *China* 38°15N 115°45E **32** E8
Rap, Ko *Thailand* 9°19N 99°58E **39** b

Rapa *French Polynesia* 27°35S 144°20W **65** K13
Rapa Nui = Pascua, I. de
  Chile 27°7S 109°23W **65** K17
Rapallo *Italy* 44°21N 9°14E **20** D8
Rapar *India* 23°34N 70°38E **42** H4
Rāpch *Iran* 25°40N 59°15E **47** E8
Rapel, Lago *Chile* 34°20S 71°14W **94** C1
Raper, C. *Canada* 69°44N 67°6W **69** D18
Rapid City *U.S.A.* 44°5N 103°14W **80** C2
Rapid River *U.S.A.* 45°55N 86°58W **80** C10
Rapla *Estonia* 59°1N 24°52E **9** G21
Rapti → *India* 26°18N 83°41E **43** F10
Raquette → *U.S.A.* 45°0N 74°42W **83** B10
Raquette Lake *U.S.A.* 43°49N 74°40W **83** C10
Rara △ *Nepal* 29°30N 82°10E **43** E10
Rarotonga *Cook Is.* 21°30S 160°0W **65** K12
Ra's al 'Ayn *Syria* 36°45N 40°12E **46** B4
Rasa, Pta. *Argentina* 36°20S 56°41W **94** D4
Rasht *Iran* 37°20N 49°40E **47** B6
Razāzah, Buḩayrat ar
  Iraq 32°40N 43°35E **46** C4
Razāzah, L. = Razāzah, Buḩayrat
  ar *Iraq* 32°40N 43°35E **46** C4
Razdel'naya = Rozdilna
  Ukraine 46°50N 30°2E **17** E16
Razdolnoye *Russia* 43°30N 131°52E **28** C5
Razeh *Iran* 32°47N 48°9E **47** C6
Razgrad *Bulgaria* 43°33N 26°34E **23** C12
Razim, Lacul *Romania* 44°50N 29°0E **17** F15
Razmak *Pakistan* 32°45N 69°50E **42** C3
Re, Cu Lao *Vietnam* 15°22N 109°8E **38** E7
Ré, Î. de *France* 46°12N 1°30W **20** C3
Reading *U.K.* 51°27N 0°58W **13** F7
Reading *U.S.A.* 40°20N 75°56W **83** F9
Reading □ *U.K.* 51°27N 0°58W **13** F7
Realicó *Argentina* 35°0S 64°15W **94** D3
Ream *Cambodia* 10°34N 103°39E **39** G4
Ream △ *Cambodia* 10°30N 103°45E **39** G4
Reay Forest *U.K.* 58°22N 4°55W **11** C4
Rebecca, L. *Australia* 30°0S 122°15E **61** F3
Rebi *Indonesia* 6°23S 134°7E **37** F8
Rebiana, Sahrâ' *Libya* 24°30N 21°0E **53** D10
Reboly *Russia* 63°49N 30°47E **8** E24
Rebun-Tō *Japan* 45°23N 141°2E **28** B10
Recherche, Arch. of the
  Australia 34°15S 122°50E **61** F3
Rechna Doab *Pakistan* 31°35N 73°30E **42** D5
Rechytsa *Belarus* 52°21N 30°24E **17** B16
Recife *Brazil* 8°0S 35°0W **93** E12
Recife *Seychelles* 4°36S 55°42E **55** b
Reckong Peo *India* 31°32N 78°16E **42** D8
Reconquista *Argentina* 29°10S 59°45W **94** B4
Recreo *Argentina* 29°25S 65°10W **94** B2
Red = Hong → *Vietnam* 20°16N 106°34E **38** B5
Red →, *U.S.A.* 31°1N 91°45W **84** F9
Red Bank *U.S.A.* 40°21N 74°5W **83** F10
Red Bay *Canada* 51°44N 56°25W **73** B8
Red Bluff *U.S.A.* 40°11N 122°15W **76** F2
Red Bluff Res. *U.S.A.* 31°54N 103°55W **77** L12
Red Cliffs *Australia* 34°19S 142°11E **63** E3
Red Cloud *U.S.A.* 40°5N 98°32W **80** E4
Red Creek *U.S.A.* 43°14N 76°45W **83** C8
Red Deer *Canada* 52°20N 113°50W **70** C6
Red Deer → *Alta.,*
  Canada 50°58N 110°0W **71** C7
Red Deer → *Man.,*
  Canada 52°53N 101°1W **71** C8
Red Deer L. *Canada* 52°55N 101°20W **71** C8
Red Hook *U.S.A.* 41°55N 73°53W **83** E11
Red Indian L. *Canada* 48°35N 57°0W **73** C8
Red L. *Canada* 51°3N 93°49W **71** C10
Red Lake *Canada* 51°3N 93°49W **71** C10
Red Lake Falls *U.S.A.* 47°53N 96°16W **80** B5
Red Lake Road *Canada* 49°59N 93°25W **71** C10
Red Lodge *U.S.A.* 45°11N 109°15W **76** D9
Red Mountain *U.S.A.* 35°37N 117°38W **79** K9
Red Oak *U.S.A.* 41°1N 95°14W **80** E6
Red River of the North →
  N. Amer. 49°0N 97°15W **80** A5
Red Rock *Canada* 48°55N 88°15W **72** C2
Red Rock, L. *U.S.A.* 41°22N 92°59W **80** E7
Red Rocks Pt. *Australia* 32°13S 127°32E **61** F4
Red Sea *Asia* 25°0N 36°0E **49** C2
Red Slate Mt. *U.S.A.* 37°31N 118°52W **78** H8
Red Sucker L. *Canada* 54°9N 93°40W **72** B1
Red Tower Pass = Turnu Roşu, P.
  Romania 45°33N 24°17E **17** F13
Red Wing *U.S.A.* 44°34N 92°31W **80** C7
Redang, Pulau *Malaysia* 5°49N 103°2E **39** K4
Redange *Lux.* 49°46N 5°52E **15** E5
Redcar *U.K.* 54°37N 1°4W **12** C6
Redcar & Cleveland □
  U.K. 54°29N 1°0W **12** C7
Redcliff *Canada* 50°10N 110°50W **76** A8
Redcliffe *Australia* 27°12S 153°6E **63** D5
Redcliffe, Mt. *Australia* 28°30S 121°30E **61** E3
Reddersburg *S. Africa* 29°41S 26°10E **56** C4
Redding *U.S.A.* 40°35N 122°24W **76** F2
Redditch *U.K.* 52°18N 1°55W **13** E6
Redfield *U.S.A.* 44°53N 98°31W **80** C4
Redford *U.S.A.* 44°38N 73°48W **83** B11
Redhead *Trin. & Tob.* 10°44N 60°58E **93** K16
Redlands *U.S.A.* 34°4N 117°11W **79** M9
Redmond *Oreg., U.S.A.* 44°17N 121°11W **76** D3
Redmond *Wash., U.S.A.* 47°40N 122°7W **78** C4
Redon *France* 47°40N 2°6W **20** C2
Redonda *Antigua & B.* 16°58N 62°19W **89** C7
Redondela *Spain* 42°15N 8°38W **21** A1
Redondo Beach *U.S.A.* 33°50N 118°23W **79** M8
Redoubt Volcano
  U.S.A. 60°29N 152°45W **74** C9
Redruth *U.K.* 50°14N 5°14W **13** G2
Redvers *Canada* 49°35N 101°40W **71** D8
Redwater *Canada* 53°55N 113°6W **70** C6
Redwood *U.S.A.* 44°18N 75°48W **83** B9
Redwood △ *U.S.A.* 41°40N 124°5W **76** F1
Redwood City *U.S.A.* 37°30N 122°15W **78** H4
Redwood Falls *U.S.A.* 44°32N 95°7W **80** C6
Ree, L. *Ireland* 53°35N 8°0W **10** C3
Reed City *U.S.A.* 43°53N 85°31W **81** D11
Reed L. *Canada* 54°38N 100°30W **71** C8
Reedley *U.S.A.* 36°36N 119°27W **78** J7
Reedsburg *U.S.A.* 43°32N 90°0W **80** D8
Reedsport *U.S.A.* 43°42N 124°6W **76** E1
Reedsville *U.S.A.* 40°39N 77°35W **82** F7
Reefton *N.Z.* 42°6S 171°51E **59** E3
Reese → *U.S.A.* 40°48N 117°4W **76** F5
Refugio *U.S.A.* 28°18N 97°17W **84** G6
Regensburg *Germany* 49°1N 12°6E **16** D7
Reggâne = Zaouiet Reggâne
  Algeria 26°32N 0°3E **52** C6
Réggio di Calábria *Italy* 38°6N 15°39E **22** E6
Réggio nell'Emília *Italy* 44°43N 10°36E **22** B4
Reghin *Romania* 46°46N 24°42E **17** E13
Regina *Canada* 50°27N 104°35W **71** C8
Regina Beach *Canada* 50°47N 105°0W **71** C8
Registro *Brazil* 24°29S 47°49W **95** A6
Rehar → *India* 23°55N 82°40E **43** H10

Rehli *India* 23°38N 79°5E **43** H8
Rehoboth *Namibia* 23°15S 17°4E **56** B2
Rehovot *Israel* 31°54N 34°48E **48** D3
Reichenbach *Germany* 50°37N 12°17E **16** C7
Reid *Australia* 30°49S 128°26E **61** F4
Reidsville *U.S.A.* 36°21N 79°40W **85** C15
Reigate *U.K.* 51°14N 0°12W **13** F7
Reims *France* 49°15N 4°1E **20** B6
Reina Adelaida, Arch. *Chile* 52°20S 74°0W **96** G2
Reindeer → *Canada* 55°36N 103°11W **71** B8
Reindeer I. *Canada* 52°30N 98°0W **71** C9
Reindeer L. *Canada* 57°15N 102°15W **71** B8
Reinga, C. *N.Z.* 34°25S 172°43E **59** A4
Reinosa *Spain* 43°2N 4°15W **21** A3
Reitz *S. Africa* 27°48S 28°29E **57** C4
Reivilo *S. Africa* 27°36S 24°8E **56** C3
Reliance *Canada* 63°0N 109°20W **71** A7
Remanso *Brazil* 9°41S 42°4W **93** E10
Remarkable, Mt. *Australia* 32°48S 138°10E **63** E2
Rembang *Indonesia* 6°42S 111°21E **37** G14
Remedios *Panama* 8°15N 81°50W **88** E3
Remeshk *Iran* 26°55N 58°50E **47** E8
Remich *Lux.* 49°32N 6°22E **15** E6
Ren Xian *China* 37°8N 114°40E **32** F8
Rendang *Indonesia* 8°26S 115°25E **37** J18
Rendsburg *Germany* 54°17N 9°39E **16** A5
Renfrew *Canada* 45°30N 76°40W **83** A8
Renfrewshire □ *U.K.* 55°49N 4°38W **11** F4
Rengat *Indonesia* 0°30S 102°45E **36** E2
Rengo *Chile* 34°24S 70°50W **94** C1
Renhua *China* 25°5N 113°40E **35** E9
Renhuai *China* 27°48N 106°24E **34** D6
Reni = Taranagar *India* 28°43N 74°50E **42** E6
Reni *Ukraine* 45°28N 28°15E **17** F15
Renigunta *India* 13°38N 79°30E **45** H4
Renmark *Australia* 34°11S 140°43E **63** E3
Rennell Sd. *Canada* 53°23N 132°35W **70** C2
Renner Springs *Australia* 18°20S 133°47E **62** B1
Rennes *France* 48°7N 1°41W **20** B3
Rennick Glacier *Antarctica* 70°30S 161°45E **5** D11
Rennie L. *Canada* 61°32N 105°35W **71** A7
Reno *U.S.A.* 39°31N 119°48W **78** F7
Reno → *Italy* 44°38N 12°16E **22** B5
Renovo *U.S.A.* 41°20N 77°45W **82** E7
Renqiu *China* 38°43N 116°5E **32** E9
Renshou *China* 29°59N 104°9E **34** C5
Rensselaer *Ind., U.S.A.* 40°57N 87°9W **80** E10
Rensselaer *N.Y., U.S.A.* 42°38N 73°45W **83** D11
Renton *U.S.A.* 47°28N 122°12W **78** C4
Renukoot *India* 24°12N 83°2E **43** G10
Reotipur *India* 25°33N 83°45E **43** G10
Repalle *India* 16°2N 80°45E **45** F5
Republic *Mo., U.S.A.* 37°7N 93°29W **80** G7
Republic *Wash., U.S.A.* 48°39N 118°44W **76** B4
Republican → *U.S.A.* 39°4N 96°48W **80** F5
Repulse B. *Australia* 20°35S 148°46E **62** b
Repulse Bay *Canada* 66°30N 86°30W **69** D14
Requena *Peru* 5°5S 73°52W **92** E4
Requena *Spain* 39°30N 1°4W **21** C5
Reserve *U.S.A.* 33°43N 108°45W **77** K9
Resht = Rasht *Iran* 37°20N 49°40E **47** B6
Resistencia *Argentina* 27°30S 59°0W **94** B4
Reşiţa *Romania* 45°18N 21°53E **17** F11
Reso = Raisio *Finland* 60°28N 22°11E **9** F20
Resolute *Canada* 74°42N 94°54W **69** C13
Resolution I. *Canada* 61°30N 65°0W **69** E19
Resolution I. *N.Z.* 45°40S 166°40E **59** F1
Ressano Garcia *Mozam.* 25°25S 32°0E **57** C5
Reston *Canada* 49°33N 101°6W **71** D8
Retalhuleu *Guatemala* 14°33N 91°46W **88** D1
Retford *U.K.* 53°19N 0°56W **12** D7
Rethimno *Greece* 35°18N 24°30E **23** G11
Reti *Pakistan* 28°5N 69°48E **42** E3
Réunion ☒ *Ind. Oc.* 21°0S 56°0E **55** c
Reus *Spain* 41°10N 1°5E **21** B6
Reutlingen *Germany* 48°29N 9°12E **16** D5
Reval = Tallinn *Estonia* 59°22N 24°48E **9** G21
Revda *Russia* 56°48N 59°57E **18** C10
Revelganj *India* 25°50N 84°40E **43** G11
Revelstoke *Canada* 51°0N 118°10W **70** C5
Reventazón *Peru* 6°10S 80°58W **92** E2
Revillagigedo, Is. de *Pac. Oc.* 18°40N 112°0W **86** D2
Rewa *India* 24°33N 81°25E **43** G9
Rewari *India* 28°15N 76°40E **42** E7
Rexburg *U.S.A.* 43°49N 111°47W **76** E8
Rey, I. del *Panama* 8°20N 78°30W **88** E4
Rey, L. del *Mexico* 27°1N 103°26W **86** B4
Rey Malabo *Eq. Guin.* 3°45N 8°50E **54** D1
Reyðarfjörður *Iceland* 65°2N 14°13W **8** D6
Reyes, Pt. *U.S.A.* 38°0N 123°0W **78** H3
Reykjahlið *Iceland* 65°40N 16°55W **8** D5
Reykjanes *Iceland* 63°48N 22°40W **8** E2
Reykjavík *Iceland* 64°10N 21°57W **8** D3
Reynolds Ra. *Australia* 22°30S 133°0E **60** D5
Reynoldsville *U.S.A.* 41°6N 78°53W **82** E6
Reynosa *Mexico* 26°7N 98°18W **87** B5
Rēzekne *Latvia* 56°30N 27°17E **9** H22
Rezvān *Iran* 27°34N 56°6E **47** E8
Rhayader *U.K.* 52°18N 3°29W **13** E4
Rhein → *Europe* 51°52N 6°2E **15** C6
Rhein-Main-Donau-Kanal *Germany* 49°1N 11°27E **16** D6
Rheine *Germany* 52°17N 7°26E **16** B4
Rheinland-Pfalz □ *Germany* 50°0N 7°0E **16** C4
Rhin = Rhein → *Europe* 51°52N 6°2E **15** C6
Rhine = Rhein → *Europe* 51°52N 6°2E **15** C6
Rhinebeck *U.S.A.* 41°56N 73°55W **83** E11
Rhineland-Palatinate = Rheinland-Pfalz □ *Germany* 50°0N 7°0E **16** C4
Rhinelander *U.S.A.* 45°38N 89°25W **80** C9
Rhinns Pt. *U.K.* 55°40N 6°29W **11** F2
Rhir, Cap *Morocco* 30°38N 9°54W **52** B4
Rhode Island □ *U.S.A.* 41°40N 71°30W **83** E13
Rhodes *Greece* 36°15N 28°10E **23** F13
Rhodope Mts. = Rhodopi Planina *Bulgaria* 41°40N 24°20E **23** D11
Rhodopi Planina *Bulgaria* 41°40N 24°20E **23** D11
Rhön *Germany* 50°24N 9°58E **16** C5
Rhondda *U.K.* 51°39N 3°31W **13** F4
Rhondda Cynon Taff □ *U.K.* 51°42N 3°27W **13** F4
Rhône → *France* 43°28N 4°42E **20** E6
Rhum = Rùm *U.K.* 57°0N 6°20W **11** E2
Rhydaman = Ammanford *U.K.* 51°48N 3°59W **13** F4
Rhyl *U.K.* 53°20N 3°29W **12** D4
Riachão *Brazil* 7°20S 46°37W **93** E9
Riang, Laem *Thailand* 8°7N 98°27E **39** a
Riasi *India* 33°10N 74°50E **43** C6
Riau □ *Indonesia* 0°0 102°35E **36** E2
Riau, Kepulauan □ *Indonesia* 0°30N 104°20E **36** D2
Riau Arch. = Riau, Kepulauan □ *Indonesia* 0°30N 104°20E **36** D2
Ribadeo *Spain* 43°35N 7°5W **21** A2
Ribas do Rio Pardo *Brazil* 20°27S 53°46W **93** H8
Ribble → *U.K.* 53°52N 2°25W **12** D5
Ribe *Denmark* 55°19N 8°44E **9** J13
Ribeira Grande *C. Verde Is.* 17°0N 25°4W **52** b
Ribeirão Prêto *Brazil* 21°10S 47°50W **95** A6
Riberalta *Bolivia* 11°0S 66°0W **92** F5
Riccarton *N.Z.* 43°32S 172°37E **59** E4
Rice *U.S.A.* 34°5N 114°51W **79** L12
Rice L. *Canada* 44°12N 78°10W **82** B6
Rice Lake *U.S.A.* 45°30N 91°44W **80** C8
Rich, C. *Canada* 44°43N 80°38W **82** B4
Richards Bay *S. Africa* 28°48S 32°6E **57** C5
Richardson → *Canada* 58°25N 111°14W **71** B6
Richardson Lakes *U.S.A.* 44°46N 70°58W **81** C18
Richardson Springs *U.S.A.* 39°51N 121°46W **78** F5
Riche, C. *Australia* 34°36S 118°47E **61** F2
Richey *U.S.A.* 47°39N 105°4W **76** C11
Richfield *U.S.A.* 38°46N 112°5W **76** G7
Richfield Springs *U.S.A.* 42°51N 74°59W **83** D10
Richford *U.S.A.* 45°0N 72°40W **83** B12
Richibucto *Canada* 46°42N 64°54W **73** C7
Richland *Ga., U.S.A.* 32°5N 84°40W **85** E12
Richland *Wash., U.S.A.* 46°17N 119°18W **76** C4
Richland Center *U.S.A.* 43°21N 90°23W **80** D8
Richlands *U.S.A.* 37°6N 81°48W **81** G13
Richmond *Australia* 20°43S 143°8E **62** C3
Richmond *N.Z.* 41°20S 173°12E **59** D4
Richmond *U.K.* 54°25N 1°43W **12** C6
Richmond *Calif., U.S.A.* 37°56N 122°21W **78** H4
Richmond *Ind., U.S.A.* 39°50N 84°53W **81** F11
Richmond *Ky., U.S.A.* 37°45N 84°18W **81** G11
Richmond *Mich., U.S.A.* 42°49N 82°45W **82** D2
Richmond *Mo., U.S.A.* 39°17N 93°58W **80** F7
Richmond *Tex., U.S.A.* 29°35N 95°46W **84** G7
Richmond *Utah, U.S.A.* 41°56N 111°48W **76** F8
Richmond *Va., U.S.A.* 37°33N 77°27W **81** G15
Richmond *Vt., U.S.A.* 44°24N 72°59W **83** B12
Richmond Hill *Canada* 43°52N 79°27W **82** C5
Richmond Ra. *Australia* 29°0S 152°45E **63** D5
Richmondville *U.S.A.* 42°38N 74°33W **83** D10
Richtersveld △ *S. Africa* 28°15S 17°10E **56** C2
Richville *U.S.A.* 44°25N 75°23W **83** B9
Richwood *U.S.A.* 38°14N 80°32W **81** F13
Ridder *Kazakhstan* 50°20N 83°30E **26** D9
Riddlesburg *U.S.A.* 40°9N 78°15W **82** F6
Rideau → *Canada* 45°27N 75°42W **83** A9
Ridgecrest *U.S.A.* 35°38N 117°40W **79** K9
Ridgefield *Conn., U.S.A.* 41°17N 73°30W **83** E11
Ridgefield *Wash., U.S.A.* 45°49N 122°45W **78** E4
Ridgeland *Miss., U.S.A.* 32°26N 90°8W **85** E9
Ridgeland *S.C., U.S.A.* 32°29N 80°59W **85** E14
Ridgetown *Canada* 42°26N 81°52W **82** D3
Ridgewood *U.S.A.* 40°59N 74°7W **83** F10
Ridgway *U.S.A.* 41°25N 78°44W **82** E6
Riding Mountain △ *Canada* 50°50N 100°0W **71** C9
Ridley, Mt. *Australia* 33°12S 122°7E **61** F3
Riebeek-Oos *S. Africa* 33°10S 26°10E **56** D4
Ried *Austria* 48°14N 13°30E **16** D7
Riesa *Germany* 51°17N 13°17E **16** C7
Riet → *S. Africa* 29°0S 23°54E **56** C3
Rietbron *S. Africa* 32°54S 23°10E **56** D3
Rietfontein *Namibia* 21°58S 20°58E **56** B3
Rieti *Italy* 42°24N 12°51E **22** C5
Rif = Er Rif *Morocco* 35°1N 4°1W **52** A5
Riffe L. *U.S.A.* 46°32N 122°26W **78** D4
Rifle *U.S.A.* 39°32N 107°47W **76** G10
Rift Valley *Africa* 7°0N 30°0E **50** G7
Rīga *Latvia* 56°53N 24°8E **9** H21
Riga, G. of *Latvia* 57°40N 23°45E **9** H20
Rīgān *Iran* 28°37N 58°58E **47** D8
Rīgas Jūras Līcis = Riga, G. of *Latvia* 57°40N 23°45E **9** H20
Rigaud *Canada* 45°29N 74°18W **83** A10
Rigby *U.S.A.* 43°40N 111°55W **76** E8
Rīgestān *Afghan.* 30°15N 65°0E **40** D4
Riggins *U.S.A.* 45°25N 116°19W **76** D5
Rigolet *Canada* 54°10N 58°23W **73** B8
Rihand Dam *India* 24°9N 83°2E **43** G10
Riihimäki *Finland* 60°45N 24°48E **8** F21
Riiser-Larsen-halvøya *Antarctica* 68°0S 35°0E **5** C4
Riiser-Larsen Ice Shelf *S. Ocean* 74°0S 19°0W **5** D2
Riiser-Larsen Sea *S. Ocean* 67°30S 22°0E **5** C4
Rijeka *Croatia* 45°20N 14°21E **16** F8
Rijssen *Neths.* 52°19N 6°31E **15** B6
Rikuchū-Kaigan △ *Japan* 39°20N 142°0E **28** E11
Rikuzentakada *Japan* 39°0N 141°40E **28** E10
Riley *U.S.A.* 43°32N 119°28W **76** E4
Rima → *Nigeria* 13°4N 5°10E **52** F7
Rimah, Wadi ar → *Si. Arabia* 26°5N 41°30E **46** E4
Rimau, Pulau *Malaysia* 5°15N 100°16E **39** c
Rimbey *Canada* 52°35N 114°15W **70** C6
Rimersburg *U.S.A.* 41°3N 79°30W **82** E5
Rímini *Italy* 44°3N 12°33E **22** B5
Rimouski *Canada* 48°27N 68°30W **73** C6
Rimrock *U.S.A.* 46°40N 121°7W **78** D5
Rinca *Indonesia* 8°45S 119°35E **37** F5
Rincón de Romos *Mexico* 22°14N 102°18W **86** C4
Rinconada *Argentina* 22°26S 66°10W **94** A2
Rind → *India* 25°53N 80°33E **43** G9
Ringas *India* 27°21N 75°34E **42** F6
Ringgold Is. *Fiji* 16°15S 179°25W **59** a
Ringkøbing *Denmark* 56°5N 8°15E **9** H13
Ringvassøya *Norway* 69°56N 19°15E **8** B18
Ringwood *U.S.A.* 41°7N 74°15W **83** E10
Rinjani, Gunung *Indonesia* 8°24S 116°28E **36** F5
Rio Branco *Brazil* 9°58S 67°49W **92** E5
Río Branco *Uruguay* 32°40S 53°40W **95** C5
Río Bravo *Mexico* 25°59N 98°6W **87** B5
Río Bravo ⌓ *N. Amer.* 29°2N 102°45W **86** B4
Río Bravo del Norte → *Mexico* 25°57N 97°9W **87** B5
Rio Brilhante *Brazil* 21°48S 54°33W **95** A5
Rio Claro *Brazil* 22°19S 47°35W **95** A6
Rio Claro *Trin. & Tob.* 10°20N 61°10W **93** K15
Río Colorado *Argentina* 39°0S 64°0W **96** D4
Río Cuarto *Argentina* 33°10S 64°25W **94** C3
Rio das Pedras *Mozam.* 23°8S 35°28E **57** B6
Rio de Janeiro *Brazil* 22°54S 43°12W **95** A7
Rio de Janeiro □ *Brazil* 22°50S 43°0W **95** A7
Rio do Sul *Brazil* 27°13S 49°37W **95** B6
Río Dulce △ *Guatemala* 15°43N 88°50W **88** C2
Río Gallegos *Argentina* 51°35S 69°15W **96** G3
Río Grande *Argentina* 53°50S 67°45W **96** G3
Rio Grande *Brazil* 32°0S 52°20W **95** C5
Río Grande *Mexico* 23°50N 103°2W **86** C4
Río Grande *Puerto Rico* 18°23N 65°50W **89** d
Rio Grande → *N. Amer.* 25°58N 97°9W **84** J6
Rio Grande City *U.S.A.* 26°23N 98°49W **84** H5
Río Grande de Santiago → *Mexico* 21°36N 105°26W **86** C3
Rio Grande do Norte □ *Brazil* 5°40S 36°0W **93** E11
Rio Grande do Sul □ *Brazil* 30°0S 53°0W **95** C5
Río Hato *Panama* 8°22N 80°10W **88** E3
Río Lagartos *Mexico* 21°36N 88°10W **87** C7
Rio Largo *Brazil* 9°28S 35°50W **93** E11
Río Mulatos *Bolivia* 19°40S 66°50W **92** G5
Río Muni □ *Eq. Guin.* 1°30N 10°0E **54** D2
Rio Negro *Brazil* 26°0S 49°55W **95** B6
Rio Pardo *Brazil* 30°0S 52°30W **95** C5
Río Pilcomayo △ *Argentina* 25°5S 58°5W **94** B4
Río Plátano ⌓ *Honduras* 15°45N 85°0W **88** C3
Rio Rancho *U.S.A.* 35°14N 106°41W **77** J10
Río Segundo *Argentina* 31°40S 63°59W **94** C3
Río Tercero *Argentina* 32°15S 64°8W **94** C3
Rio Verde *Brazil* 17°50S 51°0W **93** G8
Río Verde *Mexico* 21°56N 99°59W **87** C5
Rio Vista *U.S.A.* 38°10N 121°42W **78** G5
Ríobamba *Ecuador* 1°50S 78°45W **92** D3
Ríohacha *Colombia* 11°33N 72°55W **92** A4
Ríosucio *Colombia* 7°27N 77°7W **92** B3
Riou L. *Canada* 59°7N 106°25W **71** B7
Ripley *Canada* 44°4N 81°35W **82** B3
Ripley *Calif., U.S.A.* 33°32N 114°39W **79** M12
Ripley *N.Y., U.S.A.* 42°16N 79°43W **82** D5
Ripley *Tenn., U.S.A.* 35°45N 89°32W **85** D10
Ripley *W. Va., U.S.A.* 38°49N 81°43W **81** F13
Ripon *U.K.* 54°9N 1°31W **12** C6
Ripon *Calif., U.S.A.* 37°44N 121°7W **78** H5
Ripon *Wis., U.S.A.* 43°51N 88°50W **80** D9
Rishā', W. ar → *Si. Arabia* 25°33N 44°5E **46** E5
Rishikesh *India* 30°7N 78°19E **42** D8
Rishiri-Rebun-Sarobetsu △ *Japan* 45°26N 141°30E **28** B10
Rishiri-Tō *Japan* 45°11N 141°15E **28** B10
Rishon le Ẕiyyon *Israel* 31°58N 34°48E **48** D3
Rison *U.S.A.* 33°58N 92°11W **84** E8
Risør *Norway* 58°43N 9°13E **9** G13
Rita Blanca Cr. → *U.S.A.* 35°40N 102°29W **84** D3
Ritchie's Arch. *India* 12°14N 93°10E **45** H11
Ritter, Mt. *U.S.A.* 37°41N 119°12W **78** H7
Rittman *U.S.A.* 40°58N 81°47W **82** F3
Ritzville *U.S.A.* 47°8N 118°23W **76** C4
Riva del Garda *Italy* 45°53N 10°50E **22** B4
Rivadavia *B. Aires, Argentina* 35°29S 62°59W **94** D3
Rivadavia *Mendoza, Argentina* 33°13S 68°30W **94** C2
Rivadavia *Salta, Argentina* 24°5S 62°54W **94** A3
Rivadavia *Chile* 29°57S 70°35W **94** B1
Rivas *Nic.* 11°30N 85°50W **88** D2
Rivash *Iran* 35°28N 58°26E **47** C8
River Cess *Liberia* 5°30N 9°32W **52** G4
River Jordan *Canada* 48°26N 124°3W **78** B2
Rivera *Argentina* 37°12S 63°14W **94** D3
Rivera *Uruguay* 31°0S 55°50W **95** C4
Riverbank *U.S.A.* 37°44N 120°56W **78** H6
Riverdale *U.S.A.* 36°26N 119°52W **78** J7
Riverhead *U.S.A.* 40°55N 72°40W **83** F12
Riverhurst *Canada* 50°55N 106°50W **71** C7
Rivers *Canada* 50°2N 100°14W **71** C8
Rivers Inlet *Canada* 51°42N 127°15W **70** C3
Riversdale *Canada* 44°5N 81°20W **82** B3
Riversdale *S. Africa* 34°7S 21°15E **56** D3
Riverside *U.S.A.* 33°59N 117°22W **79** M9
Riversleigh *Australia* 19°5S 138°40E **62** B2
Riverton *Australia* 34°10S 138°46E **63** E2
Riverton *Canada* 51°1N 97°0W **71** C9
Riverton *N.Z.* 46°21S 168°0E **59** G2
Riverton *U.S.A.* 43°2N 108°23W **76** E9
Riviera = Côte d'Azur *France* 43°25N 7°10E **20** E7
Riviera *U.S.A.* 35°4N 114°35W **79** K12
Riviera di Levante *Italy* 44°15N 9°30E **20** D8
Riviera di Ponente *Italy* 44°10N 8°20E **20** D8
Rivière-au-Renard *Canada* 48°59N 64°23W **73** C7
Rivière-du-Loup *Canada* 47°50N 69°30W **73** C6
Rivière-Pentecôte *Canada* 49°57N 67°1W **73** C6
Rivière-Pilote *Martinique* 14°26N 60°53W **88** c
Rivière St-Paul *Canada* 51°28N 57°45W **73** B8
Rivière-Salée *Martinique* 14°31N 61°0W **88** c
Rivne *Ukraine* 50°40N 26°10E **17** C14
Rivne □ *Ukraine* 51°15N 26°30E **17** C14
Rívoli *Italy* 45°3N 7°31E **20** D7
Rivoli B. *Australia* 37°32S 140°3E **63** F3
Riyadh = Ar Riyāḍ *Si. Arabia* 24°41N 46°42E **46** E5
Rize *Turkey* 41°0N 40°30E **19** F7
Rizhao *China* 35°25N 119°30E **33** G10
Rizzuto, C. *Italy* 38°53N 17°5E **22** E7
Rjukan *Norway* 59°54N 8°33E **9** G13
Road Town *Br. Virgin Is.* 18°27N 64°37W **89** e
Roan Plateau *U.S.A.* 39°20N 109°20W **76** G9
Roanne *France* 46°3N 4°4E **20** C6
Roanoke *Ala., U.S.A.* 33°9N 85°22W **85** E12
Roanoke *Va., U.S.A.* 37°16N 79°56W **81** G14
Roanoke → *U.S.A.* 35°57N 76°42W **85** D16
Roanoke I. *U.S.A.* 35°53N 75°39W **85** D17
Roanoke Rapids *U.S.A.* 36°28N 77°40W **85** C16
Roatán *Honduras* 16°18N 86°35W **88** C2
Robāt Sang *Iran* 35°35N 59°10E **47** C8
Robāţkarīm *Iran* 35°25N 50°59E **47** C6
Robben I. *S. Africa* 33°46S 18°22E **56** D2
Robbins I. *Australia* 40°42S 145°0E **63** G4
Robe → *Australia* 21°42S 116°15E **60** D2
Robert Bourassa, Rés. *Canada* 53°40N 76°55W **72** B4
Robert Lee *U.S.A.* 31°54N 100°29W **84** F4
Robertsdale *U.S.A.* 40°11N 78°6W **82** F6
Robertsganj *India* 24°44N 83°4E **43** G10
Robertson *S. Africa* 33°46S 19°50E **56** D2
Robertson I. *Antarctica* 65°15S 59°30W **5** C18
Robertson Ra. *Australia* 23°15S 121°0E **60** D3
Robertstown *Australia* 33°58S 139°5E **63** E2
Roberval *Canada* 48°32N 72°15W **73** C5
Robeson Chan. *N. Amer.* 82°0N 61°30W **69** A19
Robesonia *U.S.A.* 40°21N 76°8W **83** F8
Robinson *U.S.A.* 39°0N 87°44W **80** F10
Robinson → *Australia* 16°3S 137°16E **62** B2
Robinson Crusoe I. *Pac. Oc.* 33°38S 78°52W **90** F2
Robinson Ra. *Australia* 25°40S 119°0E **61** E2
Robinvale *Australia* 34°40S 142°45E **63** E3
Roblin *Canada* 51°14N 101°21W **71** C8
Roboré *Bolivia* 18°10S 59°45W **92** G7
Robson, Mt. *Canada* 53°10N 119°10W **70** C5
Robstown *U.S.A.* 27°47N 97°40W **84** H6
Roca, C. da *Portugal* 38°40N 9°31W **21** C1
Roca Partida, I. *Mexico* 19°1N 112°2W **86** D2
Rocas, Atol das *Brazil* 4°0S 34°1W **93** D12
Rocha *Uruguay* 34°30S 54°25W **95** C5
Rochdale *U.K.* 53°38N 2°9W **12** D5
Rochefort *Belgium* 50°9N 5°12E **15** D5
Rochefort *France* 45°56N 0°57W **20** D3
Rochelle *U.S.A.* 41°56N 89°4W **80** E9
Rocher River *Canada* 61°23N 112°44W **70** A6
Rochester *U.K.* 51°23N 0°31E **13** F8
Rochester *Ind., U.S.A.* 41°4N 86°13W **80** E10
Rochester *Minn., U.S.A.* 44°1N 92°28W **80** C7
Rochester *N.H., U.S.A.* 43°18N 70°59W **83** C14
Rochester *N.Y., U.S.A.* 43°10N 77°37W **82** C7
Rock → *Canada* 60°7N 127°7W **70** A3
Rock, The *Australia* 35°15S 147°2E **63** F4
Rock Creek *U.S.A.* 41°40N 80°52W **82** E4
Rock Falls *U.S.A.* 41°47N 89°41W **80** E9
Rock Hill *U.S.A.* 34°56N 81°1W **85** D14
Rock Island *U.S.A.* 41°30N 90°34W **80** E8
Rock Port *U.S.A.* 40°25N 95°31W **80** E6
Rock Rapids *U.S.A.* 43°26N 96°10W **80** D5
Rock Sound *Bahamas* 24°54N 76°12W **88** B4
Rock Springs *Mont., U.S.A.* 46°49N 106°15W **76** C10
Rock Springs *Wyo., U.S.A.* 41°35N 109°14W **76** F9
Rock Valley *U.S.A.* 43°12N 96°18W **80** D5
Rockall *Atl. Oc.* 57°37N 13°42W **6** D3
Rockdale *Tex., U.S.A.* 30°39N 97°0W **84** F6
Rockdale *Wash., U.S.A.* 47°22N 121°28W **78** C5
Rockeby = Mungkan Kandju △ *Australia* 13°35S 142°52E **62** A3
Rockefeller Plateau *Antarctica* 76°0S 130°0W **5** E14
Rockford *U.S.A.* 42°16N 89°6W **80** D9
Rockglen *Canada* 49°11N 105°57W **71** D7
Rockhampton *Australia* 23°22S 150°32E **62** C5
Rockingham *Australia* 32°15S 115°38E **61** F2
Rockingham *N.C., U.S.A.* 34°57N 79°46W **85** D15
Rockingham *Vt., U.S.A.* 43°11N 72°29W **83** C12
Rockingham B. *Australia* 18°5S 146°10E **62** B4
Rocklake *U.S.A.* 48°47N 99°15W **80** A4
Rockland *Canada* 45°33N 75°17W **83** A9
Rockland *Idaho, U.S.A.* 42°34N 112°53W **76** E7
Rockland *Maine, U.S.A.* 44°6N 69°7W **81** C19
Rockland *Mich., U.S.A.* 46°44N 89°11W **80** B9
Rocklin *U.S.A.* 38°48N 121°14W **78** G5
Rockly B. *Trin. & Tob.* 11°9N 60°46W **93** J16
Rockmart *U.S.A.* 34°1N 85°3W **85** D12
Rockport *Mass., U.S.A.* 42°39N 70°37W **83** D14
Rockport *Tex., U.S.A.* 28°2N 97°3W **84** G6
Rocksprings *U.S.A.* 30°1N 100°13W **84** F4
Rockville *Conn., U.S.A.* 41°52N 72°28W **83** E12
Rockville *Md., U.S.A.* 39°5N 77°9W **81** F15
Rockwall *U.S.A.* 32°56N 96°28W **84** E6
Rockwell City *U.S.A.* 42°24N 94°38W **80** D6
Rockwood *Canada* 43°37N 80°8W **82** C4
Rockwood *Maine, U.S.A.* 45°41N 69°45W **81** C19
Rockwood *Tenn., U.S.A.* 35°52N 84°41W **85** D12
Rocky Ford *U.S.A.* 38°3N 103°43W **76** G12
Rocky Gully *Australia* 34°30S 116°57E **61** F2
Rocky Harbour *Canada* 49°36N 57°55W **73** C8
Rocky Island L. *Canada* 46°55N 83°0W **72** C3
Rocky Lane *Canada* 58°31N 116°22W **70** B5
Rocky Mount *U.S.A.* 35°57N 77°48W **85** D16
Rocky Mountain △ *U.S.A.* 40°25N 105°45W **76** F11
Rocky Mountain House *Canada* 52°22N 114°55W **70** C6
Rocky Mts. *N. Amer.* 49°0N 115°0W **76** B6
Rocky Point *Namibia* 19°3S 12°30E **56** A2
Rod *Pakistan* 28°10N 63°5E **40** E3
Rødbyhavn *Denmark* 54°39N 11°22E **9** J14
Roddickton *Canada* 50°51N 56°8W **73** B8
Rodez *France* 44°21N 2°33E **20** D5
Ródhos = Rhodes *Greece* 36°15N 28°10E **23** F13
Rodna ✪ *Australia* 23°45S 132°4E **60** D5
Rodney *Canada* 42°34N 81°41W **82** D3
Rodney, C. *N.Z.* 36°17S 174°50E **59** B5
Rodrigues *Ind. Oc.* 19°45S 63°20E **3** E13
Roe → *U.K.* 55°6N 6°59W **10** A5
Roebling *U.S.A.* 40°7N 74°47W **83** F10
Roebourne *Australia* 20°44S 117°9E **60** D2
Roebuck B. *Australia* 18°5S 122°20E **60** C3
Roebuck Roadhouse *Australia* 17°59S 122°36E **60** C3
Roermond *Neths.* 51°12N 6°0E **15** C6
Roes Welcome Sd. *Canada* 65°0N 87°0W **69** E14
Roeselare *Belgium* 50°57N 3°7E **15** D3
Rogachev = Ragachow *Belarus* 53°8N 30°5E **17** B16
Rogagua, L. *Bolivia* 13°43S 66°50W **92** F5
Rogatyn *Ukraine* 49°24N 24°36E **17** D13
Rogers *U.S.A.* 36°20N 94°7W **84** C7
Rogers City *U.S.A.* 45°25N 83°49W **81** C12
Rogersville *Canada* 46°44N 65°26W **73** C6
Roggan → *Canada* 54°24N 79°25W **72** B4
Roggan L. *Canada* 54°8N 77°50W **72** B4
Roggeveen Basin *Pac. Oc.* 31°30S 95°30W **65** L18
Roggeveldberge *S. Africa* 32°10S 20°10E **56** D3
Rogoaguado, L. *Bolivia* 13°0S 65°30W **92** F5
Rogojampi *Indonesia* 8°19S 114°17E **37** J17
Rogue → *U.S.A.* 42°26N 124°26W **76** E1
Roha *India* 18°26N 73°7E **44** E1
Rohnert Park *U.S.A.* 38°16N 122°40W **78** G4
Rohri *Pakistan* 27°45N 68°51E **42** F3
Rohri Canal *Pakistan* 26°15N 68°27E **42** F3
Rohtak *India* 28°55N 76°43E **42** E7
Roi Et *Thailand* 16°4N 103°40E **38** D4
Roja *Latvia* 57°29N 22°43E **9** H20
Rojas *Argentina* 34°10S 60°45W **94** C3
Rojo, C. *Mexico* 21°33N 97°20W **87** C5
Rokan → *Indonesia* 2°0N 100°50E **36** D2
Rokiškis *Lithuania* 55°55N 25°35E **9** J21
Rolândia *Brazil* 23°18S 51°23W **95** A5
Rolla *Mo., U.S.A.* 37°57N 91°46W **80** G8
Rolla *N. Dak., U.S.A.* 48°52N 99°37W **80** A4
Rolleston *Australia* 24°28S 148°35E **62** C4
Rollingstone *Australia* 19°2S 146°24E **62** B4
Roma *Australia* 26°32S 148°49E **63** D4
Roma *Sweden* 57°32N 18°26E **9** H18
Roma-Los Saenz *U.S.A.* 26°24N 99°1W **84** H5
Romain, C. *U.S.A.* 33°0N 79°22W **85** E15
Romaine → *Canada* 50°18N 63°47W **73** B7
Roman *Romania* 46°57N 26°55E **17** E14
Romang *Indonesia* 7°30S 127°20E **37** F7
Romāni *Egypt* 30°59N 32°38E **48** E1
Romania ■ *Europe* 46°0N 25°0E **17** F12
Romano, Cayo *Cuba* 22°0N 77°30W **88** B4
Romans-sur-Isère *France* 45°3N 5°3E **20** D6
Romanzof C. *U.S.A.* 61°49N 166°6W **74** C6
Romblon *Phil.* 12°33N 122°17E **37** B6
Rome *Ga., U.S.A.* 34°15N 85°10W **85** D12
Rome *N.Y., U.S.A.* 43°13N 75°27W **83** C9
Rome *Pa., U.S.A.* 41°51N 76°21W **83** E8
Romney *U.S.A.* 39°21N 78°45W **81** F14
Romney Marsh *U.K.* 51°2N 0°54E **13** F8
Rømø *Denmark* 55°10N 8°30E **9** J13
Romorantin-Lanthenay *France* 47°21N 1°45E **20** C4
Rompin → *Malaysia* 2°49N 103°29E **39** L4
Romsdalen *Norway* 62°25N 7°52E **8** E12
Romsey *U.K.* 51°0N 1°29W **13** G6
Ron *India* 15°40N 75°44E **45** G2
Ron *Vietnam* 17°53N 106°27E **38** D6
Rona *U.K.* 57°34N 5°59W **11** D3
Ronan *U.S.A.* 47°32N 114°6W **76** C6
Roncador, Cayos *Colombia* 13°32N 80°4W **88** D3
Roncador, Serra do *Brazil* 12°30S 52°30W **93** F8
Ronda *Spain* 36°46N 5°12W **21** D3
Rondane *Norway* 61°57N 9°50E **8** F13
Rondônia □ *Brazil* 11°0S 63°0W **92** F6
Rondonópolis *Brazil* 16°28S 54°38W **93** G8
Rondu *Pakistan* 35°32N 75°10E **43** B6
Rong, Koh *Cambodia* 10°45N 103°15E **39** G4
Rong Jiang → *China* 24°35N 109°20E **34** E7
Rong Xian *China* 22°50N 110°31E **35** F8
Rong'an *China* 25°14N 109°22E **34** E7
Rongchang *China* 29°20N 105°32E **34** C5
Rongcheng *China* 37°9N 122°23E **33** F12
Ronge, L. la *Canada* 55°6N 105°17W **71** B7
Rongjiang *China* 25°57N 108°28E **34** E7
Rongshui *China* 25°5N 109°12E **34** E7
Rongxian *China* 29°23N 104°22E **34** C5
Rønne *Denmark* 55°6N 14°43E **9** J16
Ronne Ice Shelf *Antarctica* 77°30S 60°0W **5** D18
Ronsard, C. *Australia* 24°46S 113°10E **61** D1
Ronse *Belgium* 50°45N 3°35E **15** D3
Roodepoort *S. Africa* 26°11S 27°54E **57** C4
Roof Butte *U.S.A.* 36°28N 109°5W **77** H9
Rooiboklaagte → *Namibia* 20°50S 21°0E **56** B3
Rooniu, Mt. *Tahiti* 17°49S 149°12W **59** d
Roorkee *India* 29°52N 77°59E **42** E7
Roosendaal *Neths.* 51°32N 4°29E **15** C4
Roosevelt *U.S.A.* 40°18N 109°59W **76** F9
Roosevelt → *Brazil* 7°35S 60°20W **92** E6
Roosevelt, Mt. *Canada* 58°26N 125°20W **70** B3
Roosevelt I. *Antarctica* 79°30S 162°0W **5** D12
Roper → *Australia* 14°43S 135°27E **62** A2
Roper Bar *Australia* 14°43S 134°44E **62** A1
Roper River = St. Vidgeon's ✪ *Australia* 14°47S 134°53E **62** A1

Roque Pérez *Argentina* 35°25S 59°24W **94** D4
Roquetas de Mar *Spain* 36°46N 2°36W **21** D4
Roraima □ *Brazil* 2°0N 61°30W **92** C6
Roraima, Mt. *Venezuela* 5°10N 60°40W **92** B6
Røros *Norway* 62°35N 11°23E **8** E14
Ros Comáin = Roscommon
    Ireland 53°38N 8°11W **10** C3
Ros Mhic Thriúin = New Ross
    Ireland 52°23N 6°57W **10** D5
Rosa, Monte *Europe* 45°57N 7°53E **20** D7
Rosalia *U.S.A.* 47°14N 117°22W **76** C5
Rosamond *U.S.A.* 34°52N 118°10W **79** L8
Rosario *Argentina* 33°0S 60°40W **94** C3
Rosário *Brazil* 3°0S 44°15W **93** D10
Rosario *Mexico* 22°58N 105°53W **86** C3
Rosario *Paraguay* 24°30S 57°35W **94** A4
Rosario de la Frontera
    Argentina 25°50S 65°0W **94** B3
Rosario de Lerma
    Argentina 24°59S 65°35W **94** A2
Rosario del Tala
    Argentina 32°20S 59°10W **94** C4
Rosário do Sul *Brazil* 30°15S 54°55W **95** C5
Rosarito *Baja Calif.,*
    Mexico 32°20N 117°2W **79** N9
Rosarito *Baja Calif.,*
    Mexico 28°38N 114°1W **86** B2
Roscoe *U.S.A.* 41°56N 74°55W **83** E10
Roscommon *Ireland* 53°38N 8°11W **10** C3
Roscommon □ *Ireland* 53°49N 8°23W **10** C3
Roscrea *Ireland* 52°57N 7°49W **10** D4
Rose → *Australia* 14°16S 135°45E **62** A2
Rose, L. *Bahamas* 21°0N 73°30W **89** B5
Rose Belle *Mauritius* 20°24S 57°36E **55** d
Rose Blanche *Canada* 47°38N 58°45W **73** C8
Rose Hill *Mauritius* 20°14S 57°27E **55** d
Rose Pt. *Canada* 54°11N 131°39W **70** C2
Rose Valley *Canada* 52°19N 103°49W **71** C8
Roseau *Dominica* 15°17N 61°24W **89** C7
Roseau *U.S.A.* 48°51N 95°46W **80** A6
Rosebery *Australia* 41°46S 145°33E **63** G4
Rosebud *S. Dak., U.S.A.* 43°14N 100°51W **80** D3
Rosebud *Tex., U.S.A.* 31°4N 96°59W **84** F6
Roseburg *U.S.A.* 43°13N 123°20W **76** E2
Rosedale *U.S.A.* 33°51N 91°2W **85** E9
Rosehearty *U.K.* 57°42N 2°7W **11** D6
Roseires Res. *Sudan* 11°51N 34°23E **53** F12
Roseland *U.S.A.* 38°25N 122°43W **78** G4
Rosemary *Canada* 50°46N 112°5W **70** C6
Rosenberg *U.S.A.* 29°34N 95°49W **84** G7
Rosenheim *Germany* 47°51N 12°7E **16** E7
Roses, G. de *Spain* 42°10N 3°15E **21** A7
Rosetown *Canada* 51°35N 107°59W **71** C7
Roseville *Calif., U.S.A.* 38°45N 121°17W **78** G5
Roseville *Mich., U.S.A.* 42°30N 82°56W **82** D2
Roseville *Pa., U.S.A.* 41°51N 76°57W **83** E8
Rosewood *Australia* 27°38S 152°36E **63** D5
Roshkvār *Iran* 34°58N 59°37E **47** C8
Rosignano Maríttimo
    Italy 43°24N 10°28E **22** C4
Rosignol *Guyana* 6°15N 57°30W **92** B7
Roșiori de Vede *Romania* 44°9N 25°0E **17** F13
Roskilde *Denmark* 55°38N 12°3E **9** J15
Roslavl *Russia* 53°57N 32°55E **18** D5
Rosmead *S. Africa* 31°29S 25°8E **56** D4
Ross *Australia* 42°2S 147°30E **63** G4
Ross *N.Z.* 42°53S 170°49E **59** E3
Ross Dependency
    Antarctica 76°0S 170°0W **5** D12
Ross I. *Antarctica* 77°30S 168°0E **5** D11
Ross Ice Shelf *Antarctica* 80°0S 180°0E **5** E12
Ross L. *U.S.A.* 48°44N 121°4W **76** B3
Ross-on-Wye *U.K.* 51°54N 2°34W **13** F5
Ross River *Australia* 23°44S 134°30E **62** C1
Ross River *Canada* 62°30N 131°30W **70** A2
Ross Sea *Antarctica* 74°0S 178°0E **5** D11
Rossall Pt. *U.K.* 53°55N 3°3W **12** D4
Rossan Pt. *Ireland* 54°42N 8°47W **10** B3
Rossano *Italy* 39°36N 16°39E **22** E7
Rossburn *Canada* 50°40N 100°49W **71** C8
Rosseau *Canada* 45°16N 79°39W **82** A5
Rosseau, L. *Canada* 45°10N 79°35W **82** A5
Rosses, The *Ireland* 55°2N 8°20W **10** A3
Rossignol, L. *Canada* 52°43N 73°40W **72** B5
Rossignol L. *Canada* 44°12N 65°10W **73** D6
Rossiya = Russia ■
    Eurasia 62°0N 105°0E **27** C11
Rossland *Canada* 49°6N 117°50W **70** D5
Rosslare *Ireland* 52°17N 6°24W **10** D5
Rosslare Europort = Rosslare
    Harbour *Ireland* 52°15N 6°20W **10** D5
Rosslare Harbour *Ireland* 52°15N 6°20W **10** D5
Rossmore *Canada* 44°8N 77°23W **82** B7
Rosso *Mauritania* 16°40N 15°45W **52** E2
Rossosh *Russia* 50°15N 39°28E **19** D6
Røssvatnet *Norway* 65°45N 14°5E **8** D16
Røst *Norway* 67°32N 12°10E **8** C15
Rosthern *Canada* 52°40N 106°20W **71** C7
Rostock *Germany* 54°5N 12°8E **16** A7
Rostov *Don, Russia* 57°14N 39°25E **18** C6
Rostov *Yaroslavl, Russia* 57°14N 39°25E **18** C6
Roswell *Ga., U.S.A.* 34°2N 84°22W **85** D12
Roswell *N. Mex., U.S.A.* 33°24N 104°32W **77** K11
Rotan *U.S.A.* 32°51N 100°28W **84** E4
Rote *Indonesia* 10°50S 123°0E **37** F6
Rother → *U.K.* 50°59N 0°45E **13** G8
Rothera *Antarctica* 67°34S 68°8W **5** C17
Rotherham *U.K.* 53°26N 1°20W **12** D6
Rothes *U.K.* 57°32N 3°13W **11** D5
Rothesay *Canada* 45°23N 66°0W **73** C6
Rothesay *U.K.* 55°50N 5°3W **11** F3
Roti = Rote *Indonesia* 10°50S 123°0E **37** F6
Roto *Australia* 33°0S 145°30E **63** E4
Rotondo, Mte. *France* 42°14N 9°8E **20** E8
Rotoroa, L. *N.Z.* 41°55S 172°39E **59** D4
Rotorua *N.Z.* 38°9S 176°16E **59** C6
Rotorua, L. *N.Z.* 38°5S 176°18E **59** C6
Rotterdam *Neths.* 51°55N 4°30E **15** C4
Rotterdam *U.S.A.* 42°48N 74°1W **83** D10

Rottnest I. *Australia* 32°0S 115°27E **61** F2
Rottumeroog *Neths.* 53°33N 6°34E **15** A6
Rottweil *Germany* 48°9N 8°37E **16** D5
Rotuma *Fiji* 12°25S 177°5E **58** C10
Roubaix *France* 50°40N 3°10E **20** A5
Rouen *France* 49°27N 1°4E **20** B4
Rouleau *Canada* 50°10N 104°56W **71** C8
Roulpmaulpma ☉
    Australia 23°52S 133°0E **60** D5
Round I. *Mauritius* 19°51S 57°45E **55** d
Round Mountain *U.S.A.* 38°43N 117°4W **76** G5
Round Mt. *Australia* 30°26S 152°16E **63** E5
Round Rock *U.S.A.* 30°31N 97°41W **84** F6
Roundup *U.S.A.* 46°27N 108°33W **76** C9
Rousay *U.K.* 59°10N 3°2W **11** B5
Rouses Point *U.S.A.* 44°59N 73°22W **83** B11
Rouseville *U.S.A.* 41°28N 79°42W **82** E5
Rousse = Ruse *Bulgaria* 43°48N 25°59E **23** C12
Roussillon *France* 42°30N 2°35E **20** E5
Rouxville *S. Africa* 30°25S 26°50E **56** D4
Rouyn-Noranda *Canada* 48°20N 79°0W **72** C4
Rovaniemi *Finland* 66°29N 25°41E **8** C21
Rovereto *Italy* 45°53N 11°3E **22** B4
Rovigo *Italy* 45°4N 11°47E **22** B4
Rovinj *Croatia* 45°5N 13°40E **16** F7
Rovno = Rivne *Ukraine* 50°40N 26°10E **17** C14
Rovuma = Ruvuma →
    Tanzania 10°29S 40°28E **54** G8
Row'ān *Iran* 35°8N 48°51E **47** C6
Rowena *Australia* 29°48S 148°55E **63** D4
Rowley I. *Canada* 69°6N 77°52W **69** D16
Rowley Shoals *Australia* 17°30S 119°0E **60** C2
Roxas *Phil.* 11°36N 122°49E **37** B6
Roxboro *U.S.A.* 36°24N 78°59W **85** C15
Roxborough *Trin. & Tob.* 11°15N 60°35W **93** J16
Roxburgh *N.Z.* 45°33S 169°19E **59** F2
Roxbury *N.Y., U.S.A.* 42°17N 74°33W **83** D10
Roxbury *Pa., U.S.A.* 40°6N 77°39W **82** F7
Roxby Downs *Australia* 30°43S 136°46E **63** E2
Roy *Mont., U.S.A.* 47°20N 108°58W **76** C9
Roy *Utah, U.S.A.* 41°10N 112°2W **76** F7
Royal Bardia △ *Nepal* 28°20N 81°20E **43** E9
Royal Canal *Ireland* 53°30N 7°13W **10** C4
Royal Chitawan △
    Nepal 26°30N 84°30E **43** F11
Royal Geographical Society Is.
    Canada 68°56N 100°15W **68** D11
Royal Leamington Spa
    U.K. 52°18N 1°31W **13** E6
Royal Natal △ *S. Africa* 28°43S 28°51E **57** C4
Royal Tunbridge Wells
    U.K. 51°7N 0°16E **13** F8
Royale, Isle *U.S.A.* 48°0N 88°54W **80** B9
Royan *France* 45°37N 1°2W **20** D3
Royston *U.K.* 52°3N 0°0 **13** E7
Rozdilna *Ukraine* 46°50N 30°2E **17** E16
Rozhyshche *Ukraine* 50°54N 25°15E **17** C13
Rtishchevo *Russia* 52°18N 43°46E **18** D7
Ruacaná *Namibia* 17°27S 14°21E **56** A1
Ruahine Ra. *N.Z.* 39°55S 176°2E **59** C6
Ruapehu *N.Z.* 39°17S 175°35E **59** C5
Ruapuke I. *N.Z.* 46°46S 168°31E **59** G2
Ruâq, W. → *Egypt* 30°0N 33°49E **48** F2
Rub' al Khālī *Si. Arabia* 19°0N 48°0E **49** D4
Rubh a' Mhail *U.K.* 55°56N 6°8W **11** F2
Rubha Hunish *U.K.* 57°42N 6°20W **11** D2
Rubha Robhanais = Lewis, Butt of
    U.K. 58°31N 6°16W **11** C2
Rubicon → *U.S.A.* 38°53N 121°4W **78** G5
Rubio *Venezuela* 7°43N 72°22W **92** B4
Rubtsovsk *Russia* 51°30N 81°10E **30** A5
Ruby L. *U.S.A.* 40°10N 115°28W **76** F6
Ruby Mts. *U.S.A.* 40°30N 115°20W **76** F6
Rubyvale *Australia* 23°25S 147°42E **62** C4
Rucheng *China* 25°33N 113°38E **35** E9
Rūd Sar *Iran* 37°8N 50°18E **47** B6
Rudall *Australia* 33°43S 136°17E **63** E2
Rudall → *Australia* 22°34S 122°13E **60** D3
Rudall River △ *Australia* 22°38S 122°30E **60** D3
Rudbar *Iran* 36°48N 49°23E **47** B6
Rudnyy *Kazakhstan* 52°57N 63°7E **26** D7
Rudolfa, Ostrov *Russia* 81°45N 58°30E **26** A6
Rudong *China* 32°0N 121°12E **35** A13
Rudrapur *India* 28°59N 79°24E **43** E8
Rudyard *U.S.A.* 46°14N 84°36W **81** B11
Ruffling Pt. *Br. Virgin Is.* 18°44N 64°27W **89** e
Rufiji → *Tanzania* 7°50S 39°15E **54** F7
Rufino *Argentina* 34°20S 62°50W **94** C3
Rugao *China* 32°23N 120°31E **35** A13
Rugby *U.K.* 52°23N 1°16W **13** E6
Rugby *U.S.A.* 48°22N 100°0W **80** A4
Rügen *Germany* 54°22N 13°24E **16** A7
Ruhnu *Estonia* 57°48N 23°15E **9** H20
Ruhr → *Germany* 51°27N 6°43E **16** C4
Rui'an *China* 27°47N 120°40E **35** D13
Ruichang *China* 29°40N 115°39E **35** C10
Ruidoso *U.S.A.* 33°20N 105°41W **77** K11
Ruijin *China* 25°48N 116°0E **35** E10
Ruili *China* 24°6N 97°46E **34** E1
Rujm Tal'at al Jamā'ah
    Jordan 30°24N 35°30E **48** E4
Ruk *Pakistan* 27°50N 68°42E **42** F3
Rukhla *Pakistan* 32°27N 71°57E **42** C4
Ruki →
    Dem. Rep. of the Congo 0°5N 18°17E **54** E3
Rukumkot *Nepal* 28°37N 82°37E **43** E10
Rukwa □ *Tanzania* 8°0S 32°20E **54** F6
Rukwa, L. *Tanzania* 8°0S 32°20E **54** F6
Rulhieres, C. *Australia* 13°56S 127°22E **60** B4
Rum *Jordan* 29°39N 35°26E **48** F4
Rùm *U.K.* 57°0N 6°20W **11** E2
Rum Cay *Bahamas* 23°40N 74°58W **89** B5
Rum Jungle *Australia* 13°0S 130°59E **60** B5
Rumāh *Si. Arabia* 25°29N 47°10E **46** E5
Rumania = Romania ■
    Europe 46°0N 25°0E **17** F12
Rumaylah *Iraq* 30°47N 47°37E **46** D5
Rumbêk *South Sudan* 6°54N 29°37E **53** G11
Rumford *U.S.A.* 44°33N 70°33W **83** B14

Rumia *Poland* 54°37N 18°25E **17** A10
Rumoi *Japan* 43°56N 141°39E **28** C10
Rumson *U.S.A.* 40°23N 74°0W **83** F11
Runan *China* 33°0N 114°30E **32** H8
Runanga *N.Z.* 42°25S 171°15E **59** E3
Runaway, C. *N.Z.* 37°32S 177°59E **59** B6
Runaway Bay *Jamaica* 18°27N 77°20W **88** a
Runcorn *U.K.* 53°21N 2°44W **12** D5
Rundu *Namibia* 17°52S 19°43E **56** A2
Rungwe *Tanzania* 9°11S 33°32E **50** G7
Rungwe, Mt. *Tanzania* 9°8S 33°40E **54** F6
Runton Ra. *Australia* 23°31S 123°6E **60** D3
Ruo Shui → *China* 41°0N 100°16E **30** C9
Ruokolahti *Finland* 61°17N 28°50E **8** F23
Ruoqiang *China* 38°55N 88°10E **30** D6
Rupa *India* 27°15N 92°21E **41** F18
Rupar *India* 31°2N 76°38E **42** D7
Rupat *Indonesia* 1°45N 101°40E **36** D2
Rupen → *India* 23°28N 71°31E **42** H4
Rupert → *Canada* 51°29N 78°45W **72** B4
Rupert B. *Canada* 51°35N 79°0W **72** B4
Rupert House = Waskaganish
    Canada 51°30N 78°40W **72** B4
Rupsa *India* 21°37N 87°1E **43** J12
Rurrenabaque *Bolivia* 14°30S 67°32W **92** F5
Ruschuk = Ruse
    Bulgaria 43°48N 25°59E **23** C12
Ruse *Bulgaria* 43°48N 25°59E **23** C12
Rush *Ireland* 53°31N 6°6W **10** C5
Rushan *China* 36°56N 121°30E **33** F11
Rushden *U.K.* 52°18N 0°35W **13** E7
Rushikulya → *India* 19°23N 85°5E **44** E7
Rushmore, Mt. *U.S.A.* 43°53N 103°28W **80** D2
Rushville *Ill., U.S.A.* 40°7N 90°34W **80** E8
Rushville *Ind., U.S.A.* 39°37N 85°27W **81** F11
Rushville *Nebr., U.S.A.* 42°43N 102°28W **80** D2
Russas *Brazil* 4°55S 37°50W **93** D11
Russell *Canada* 50°50N 101°20W **71** C8
Russell *Kans., U.S.A.* 38°54N 98°52W **80** F4
Russell *N.Y., U.S.A.* 44°27N 75°9W **83** B9
Russell *Pa., U.S.A.* 41°56N 79°8W **82** E5
Russell Cave △ *U.S.A.* 34°59N 85°49W **85** D12
Russell L. *Man., Canada* 56°15N 101°30W **71** B8
Russell L. *N.W.T., Canada* 63°5N 115°44W **70** A5
Russellkonda *India* 19°57N 84°42E **44** E7
Russellville *Ala., U.S.A.* 34°30N 87°44W **85** D11
Russellville *Ark., U.S.A.* 35°17N 93°8W **84** D8
Russellville *Ky., U.S.A.* 36°51N 86°53W **80** G10
Russia ■ *Eurasia* 62°0N 105°0E **27** C11
Russian → *U.S.A.* 38°27N 123°8W **78** G3
Rustam Shahr *Pakistan* 26°58N 66°6E **42** F2
Rustavi *Georgia* 41°30N 45°0E **19** F8
Rustenburg *S. Africa* 25°41S 27°14E **56** C4
Ruston *U.S.A.* 32°32N 92°38W **84** E8
Ruteng *Indonesia* 8°35S 120°30E **37** F6
Rutenga *Zimbabwe* 21°15S 30°44E **57** B5
Ruth *U.S.A.* 43°42N 82°45W **82** C2
Rutherford *U.S.A.* 38°26N 122°24W **78** G4
Rutland *U.S.A.* 43°37N 72°58W **83** C12
Rutland □ *U.K.* 52°38N 0°40W **13** E7
Rutland I. *India* 11°25N 92°10E **45** J11
Rutland Water □ *U.K.* 52°39N 0°38W **13** E7
Rutledge → *Canada* 61°4N 112°0W **71** A6
Rutledge L. *Canada* 61°33N 110°47W **71** A6
Rutog *China* 33°27N 79°42E **30** E4
Rutshuru
    Dem. Rep. of the Congo 1°13S 29°25E **54** E5
Ruvuma → *Tanzania* 10°29S 40°28E **54** G8
Ruwais *U.A.E.* 24°5N 52°50E **47** E7
Ruwenzori *Africa* 0°30N 29°55E **54** D5
Ruya → *Zimbabwe* 16°27S 32°5E **57** A5
Ruyang *China* 34°9N 112°27E **32** G7
Ruyuan *China* 24°46N 113°16E **35** E9
Ruzhou *China* 34°11N 112°52E **32** G7
Ružomberok *Slovak Rep.* 49°3N 19°17E **17** D10
Rwanda ■ *Africa* 2°0S 30°0E **54** E5
Ryan, L. *U.K.* 55°0N 5°2W **11** G3
Ryazan *Russia* 54°40N 39°40E **18** D6
Ryazhsk *Russia* 53°45N 40°3E **18** D7
Rybachiy Poluostrov
    Russia 69°43N 32°0E **8** B25
Rybachye = Balykchy
    Kyrgyzstan 42°26N 76°12E **30** C4
Rybinsk *Russia* 58°5N 38°50E **18** C6
Rybinskoye Vdkhr.
    Russia 58°30N 38°25E **18** C6
Rybnitsa = Râbnița
    Moldova 47°45N 29°0E **17** E15
Rycroft *Canada* 55°45N 118°40W **70** B5
Ryde *U.K.* 50°43N 1°9W **13** G6
Ryderwood *U.S.A.* 46°23N 123°3W **78** D3
Rye *U.K.* 50°57N 0°45E **13** G8
Rye → *U.K.* 54°11N 0°44W **12** C7
Rye Bay *U.K.* 50°52N 0°49E **13** G8
Rye Patch Res. *U.S.A.* 40°28N 118°19W **76** F4
Ryegate *U.S.A.* 46°18N 109°15W **76** C9
Ryley *Canada* 53°17N 112°26W **70** C6
Rylstone *Australia* 32°46S 149°58E **63** E4
Ryn Peski = Naryn Qum
    Kazakhstan 47°30N 49°0E **26** E5
Ryōtsu *Japan* 38°5N 138°26E **28** E9
Rypin *Poland* 53°3N 19°25E **17** B10
Ryūgasaki *Japan* 35°54N 140°11E **29** G10
Ryukyu Is. = Ryūkyū-Rettō
    Japan 26°0N 126°0E **29** M3
Ryūkyū-Rettō *Japan* 26°0N 126°0E **29** M3
Rzeszów *Poland* 50°5N 21°58E **17** C11
Rzhev *Russia* 56°20N 34°20E **18** C5

S

Sa Dec *Vietnam* 10°20N 105°46E **39** G5
Sa Kaeo *Thailand* 13°49N 102°4E **38** F4
Sa Pa *Vietnam* 22°20N 103°47E **38** A4
Sa'ādat Shahr *Iran* 30°10N 53°5E **47** D7
Sa'ādatābād *Hormozgān,*
    Iran 28°3N 55°53E **47** D7
Sa'ādatābād *Kermān, Iran* 29°40N 55°51E **47** D7

Saale → *Germany* 51°56N 11°54E **16** C6
Saalfeld *Germany* 50°38N 11°21E **16** C6
Saanich *Canada* 48°29N 123°26W **78** B3
Saar → *Europe* 49°41N 6°32E **15** E6
Saarbrücken *Germany* 49°14N 6°59E **16** D4
Saaremaa *Estonia* 58°30N 22°30E **9** G20
Saarijärvi *Finland* 62°43N 25°16E **8** E21
Sab 'Ābar *Syria* 33°46N 37°41E **46** C3
Saba *W. Indies* 17°38N 63°14W **89** C7
Šabac *Serbia* 44°48N 19°42E **23** B8
Sabadell *Spain* 41°28N 2°7E **21** B7
Sabah □ *Malaysia* 6°0N 117°0E **36** C5
Sabak Bernam *Malaysia* 3°46N 100°58E **39** L3
Sabalān, Kūhhā-ye *Iran* 38°15N 47°45E **46** B5
Sabalana, Kepulauan
    Indonesia 6°45S 118°50E **37** F5
Sabana de la Mar
    Dom. Rep. 19°7N 69°24W **89** C6
Sábanalarga *Colombia* 10°38N 74°55W **92** A4
Sabang *Indonesia* 5°50N 95°15E **36** C1
Sabarmati → *India* 22°18N 72°22E **42** H5
Sabattis *U.S.A.* 44°6N 74°40W **83** B10
Saberania *Indonesia* 2°5S 138°18E **37** E9
Sabhā *Libya* 27°9N 14°29E **53** C8
Sabi → *India* 28°29N 76°44E **42** E7
Sabie *S. Africa* 25°10S 30°48E **57** C5
Sabinal *Mexico* 29°19N 99°28W **84** G5
Sabinas *Mexico* 27°51N 101°7W **86** B4
Sabinas → *Mexico* 27°37N 100°42W **86** B4
Sabinas Hidalgo *Mexico* 26°30N 100°10W **86** B4
Sabine → *U.S.A.* 29°59N 93°47W **84** G8
Sabine L. *U.S.A.* 29°53N 93°51W **84** G8
Sabine Pass *U.S.A.* 29°44N 93°54W **84** G8
Sablayan *Phil.* 12°50N 120°50E **37** B6
Sable *Canada* 55°30N 68°21W **73** A6
Sable, C. *Canada* 43°29N 65°38W **73** D6
Sable, C. *U.S.A.* 25°9N 81°8W **88** A3
Sable I. *Canada* 44°0N 60°0W **73** D8
Sabrina Coast *Antarctica* 68°0S 120°0E **5** C9
Sabulubek *Indonesia* 1°36S 98°40E **36** E1
Sabzevār *Iran* 36°15N 57°40E **47** B8
Sabzvārān = Jiroft *Iran* 28°45N 57°50E **47** D8
Sac City *U.S.A.* 42°25N 95°0W **80** D6
Săcele *Romania* 45°37N 25°41E **17** F13
Sacheon *S. Korea* 35°0N 128°6E **33** G15
Sachigo → *Canada* 55°6N 88°58W **72** A2
Sachigo, L. *Canada* 53°50N 92°12W **72** B1
Sachimbo *Angola* 9°14S 20°16E **54** F4
Sachin *India* 21°5N 72°53E **46** E1
Sachsen □ *Germany* 50°55N 13°10E **16** C7
Sachsen-Anhalt □
    Germany 52°0N 12°0E **16** C7
Sackets Harbor *U.S.A.* 43°57N 76°7W **83** C8
Sackville *Canada* 45°54N 64°22W **73** C7
Saco *Maine, U.S.A.* 43°30N 70°27W **83** C14
Saco *Mont., U.S.A.* 48°28N 107°21W **76** B10
Sacramento *U.S.A.* 38°35N 121°29W **78** G5
Sacramento → *U.S.A.* 38°3N 121°56W **78** G5
Sacramento Mts.
    U.S.A. 32°30N 105°30W **77** K11
Sacramento Valley
    U.S.A. 39°30N 122°0W **78** G5
Sada-Misaki *Japan* 33°20N 132°5E **29** H6
Sadabad *India* 27°27N 78°3E **42** F8
Sadao *Thailand* 6°38N 100°26E **39** J3
Sadaseopet *India* 17°38N 77°59E **44** F3
Sadd el Aali *Egypt* 23°54N 32°54E **53** D12
Saddle Mt. *U.S.A.* 45°58N 123°41W **78** E3
Saddle Pk. *India* 13°9N 93°1E **45** H11
Sado *Japan* 38°0N 138°25E **28** F9
Sadra *India* 23°21N 72°43E **42** H5
Sadri *India* 25°11N 73°26E **42** G5
Saegertown *U.S.A.* 41°43N 80°9W **82** E4
Şafājah *Si. Arabia* 26°25N 39°0E **46** E3
Safata B. *Samoa* 14°0S 171°50W **59** b
Säffle *Sweden* 59°8N 12°55E **9** G15
Safford *U.S.A.* 32°50N 109°43W **77** K9
Saffron Walden *U.K.* 52°1N 0°16E **13** E8
Safi *Morocco* 32°18N 9°20W **52** B4
Şafiābād *Iran* 36°45N 57°58E **47** B8
Safid Dasht *Iran* 33°27N 48°11E **47** C6
Safid Kūh *Afghan.* 34°45N 63°0E **40** B3
Safid Rūd → *Iran* 37°23N 50°11E **47** B6
Safipur *India* 26°44N 80°21E **43** F9
Şafītā *Syria* 34°48N 36°7E **46** C3
Safune *Samoa* 13°25S 172°21W **59** b
Şafwān *Iraq* 30°7N 47°43E **46** D5
Sag Harbor *U.S.A.* 41°0N 72°18W **83** F12
Saga *Japan* 33°15N 130°16E **29** H5
Saga □ *Japan* 33°15N 130°20E **29** H5
Sagae *Japan* 38°22N 140°17E **28** E10
Sagaing *Burma* 21°52N 95°59E **41** J19
Sagamore *U.S.A.* 40°46N 79°14W **82** F5
Saganaga L. *Canada* 48°14N 90°52W **80** A8
Saganthit Kyun *Burma* 11°56N 98°29E **38** G2
Sagar *Karnataka, India* 16°38N 76°48E **44** F3
Sagar *Karnataka, India* 14°14N 75°6E **45** G2
Sagar *Mad., India* 23°50N 78°44E **43** H8
Sagarmatha = Everest, Mt.
    Nepal 28°5N 86°58E **43** E12
Sagarmatha △ *Nepal* 27°55N 86°45E **43** F12
Saginaw *U.S.A.* 43°26N 83°56W **81** D12
Saginaw B. *U.S.A.* 43°50N 83°40W **81** D12
Saglouc = Salluit
    Canada 62°14N 75°38W **69** E16
Sagone *France* 42°7N 8°42E **20** E8
Sagua la Grande *Cuba* 22°50N 80°10W **88** B3
Saguache *U.S.A.* 38°5N 106°8W **76** G10
Saguaro △ *U.S.A.* 32°12N 110°38W **77** K8
Saguenay → *Canada* 48°22N 71°0W **73** C5
Sagunt *Spain* 39°42N 0°18W **21** C5
Sagunto = Sagunt *Spain* 39°42N 0°18W **21** C5
Sagwara *India* 23°41N 74°1E **42** H6
Sahagún *Spain* 42°18N 5°2W **21** A3
Saham al Jawlān *Syria* 32°45N 35°55E **48** C4
Sahand, Kūh-e *Iran* 37°44N 46°27E **46** B5
Sahara *Africa* 23°0N 5°0E **52** D6

Saharan Atlas = Saharien, Atlas
    Algeria 33°30N 1°0E **52** B6
Saharanpur *India* 29°58N 77°33E **42** E7
Sahariën, Atlas *Algeria* 33°30N 1°0E **52** B6
Saharsa *India* 25°53N 86°36E **43** G12
Sahaswan *India* 28°5N 78°45E **43** E8
Saheira, W. el → *Egypt* 30°5N 33°25E **48** E2
Sahel *Africa* 16°0N 5°0E **52** E5
Sahibganj *India* 25°12N 87°40E **43** G12
Sāhilīyah *Iraq* 33°43N 42°42E **46** C4
Sahiwal *Pakistan* 30°45N 73°8E **42** D5
Şahneh *Iran* 34°29N 47°41E **46** C5
Sahrawi = Western Sahara ■
    Africa 25°0N 13°0W **52** D3
Sahuaripa *Mexico* 29°3N 109°14W **86** B3
Sahuarita *U.S.A.* 31°57N 110°58W **77** L8
Sahuayo de Díaz *Mexico* 20°4N 102°43W **86** C4
Sai → *India* 25°39N 82°47E **43** G10
Sai Buri *Thailand* 6°43N 101°45E **39** J3
Sai Thong △ *Thailand* 15°56N 101°10E **38** E3
Sai Yok △ *Thailand* 14°25N 98°40E **38** E2
Saibai I. *Australia* 9°25S 142°40E **62** a
Sa'id Bundâs *South Sudan* 8°24N 24°48E **53** G10
Sa'īdābād = Sīrjān *Iran* 29°30N 55°45E **47** D7
Sa'īdābād *Iran* 36°8N 54°11E **47** B7
Saidpur *Bangla.* 25°48N 89°0E **41** G16
Saidpur *India* 25°33N 83°11E **43** G10
Saidu Sharif *Pakistan* 34°43N 72°24E **43** B5
Saigō *Japan* 36°12N 133°20E **29** F6
Saigon = Thanh Pho Ho Chi Minh
    Vietnam 10°58N 106°40E **39** G6
Saijō *Japan* 33°55N 133°11E **29** H6
Saikai □ *Japan* 33°12N 129°36E **29** H4
Saikhoa Ghat *India* 27°50N 95°40E **41** F19
Saiki *Japan* 32°58N 131°51E **29** H5
Sailana *India* 23°28N 74°55E **42** H6
Sailolof *Indonesia* 1°15S 130°46E **37** E8
Sailu *India* 19°28N 76°28E **44** E3
Saimaa *Finland* 61°15N 28°15E **8** F23
Saimen = Saimaa *Finland* 61°15N 28°15E **8** F23
Şa'in Dezh *Iran* 36°40N 46°25E **46** B5
St. Abb's Head *U.K.* 55°55N 2°8W **11** F6
St. Alban's *Canada* 47°51N 55°50W **73** C8
St. Albans *U.K.* 51°45N 0°19W **13** F7
St. Albans *Vt., U.S.A.* 44°49N 73°5W **83** B11
St. Albans *W. Va.,*
    U.S.A. 38°23N 81°50W **81** F13
St. Alban's Head *U.K.* 50°34N 2°4W **13** G5
St. Albert *Canada* 53°37N 113°32W **70** C6
St-André *Réunion* 20°57S 55°39E **55** c
St. Andrew's *Canada* 47°45N 59°15W **73** C8
St. Andrews *U.K.* 56°20N 2°47W **11** E6
St-Anicet *Canada* 45°8N 74°22W **83** A10
St. Annes *Canada* 49°40N 96°39W **71** D9
St. Anns B. *Canada* 46°22N 60°25W **73** C7
St. Ann's Bay *Jamaica* 18°26N 77°12W **88** a
St. Anthony *Canada* 51°22N 55°35W **73** B8
St. Anthony *U.S.A.* 43°58N 111°41W **76** E8
St-Antoine *Canada* 46°22N 64°45W **73** C7
St. Arnaud *Australia* 36°40S 143°16E **63** F3
St-Augustin *Canada* 51°13N 58°38W **73** B8
St-Augustin → *Canada* 51°16N 58°40W **73** B8
St. Augustine *U.S.A.* 29°54N 81°19W **85** G14
St. Austell *U.K.* 50°20N 4°47W **13** G3
St. Barbe *Canada* 51°12N 56°46W **73** B8
St-Barthélemy ☑
    W. Indies 17°50N 62°50W **89** C7
St. Barts = St-Barthélemy ☑
    W. Indies 17°50N 62°50W **89** C7
St. Bees Hd. *U.K.* 54°31N 3°38W **12** C4
St. Bees I. *Australia* 20°56S 149°26E **62** b
St-Benoît *Réunion* 21°2S 55°43E **55** c
St. Bride's *Canada* 46°56N 54°10W **73** C9
St. Brides B. *U.K.* 51°49N 5°9W **13** F2
St-Brieuc *France* 48°30N 2°46W **20** B2
St. Catharines *Canada* 43°10N 79°15W **82** C5
St. Catherines I. *U.S.A.* 31°40N 81°10W **85** F14
St. Catherine's Pt. *U.K.* 50°34N 1°18W **13** G6
St-Chamond *France* 45°28N 4°31E **20** D6
St. Charles *Ill., U.S.A.* 41°54N 88°19W **80** E9
St. Charles *Md., U.S.A.* 38°36N 76°56W **81** F15
St. Charles *Mo., U.S.A.* 38°47N 90°29W **80** F8
St. Charles *Va., U.S.A.* 36°48N 83°4W **81** G12
St. Christopher-Nevis = St. Kitts &
    Nevis ■ *W. Indies* 17°20N 62°40W **89** C7
St. Clair *Mich., U.S.A.* 42°50N 82°30W **82** D2
St. Clair *Pa., U.S.A.* 40°43N 76°12W **83** F8
St. Clair → *U.S.A.* 42°38N 82°31W **82** D2
St. Clair, L. *N. Amer.* 42°27N 82°39W **82** D2
St. Clairsville *U.S.A.* 40°5N 80°54W **82** F4
St. Claude *Canada* 49°40N 98°20W **71** D9
St. Clears *U.K.* 51°49N 4°31W **13** F3
St-Clet *Canada* 45°21N 74°13W **83** A10
St. Cloud *Fla., U.S.A.* 28°15N 81°17W **85** G14
St. Cloud *Minn., U.S.A.* 45°34N 94°10W **80** C6
St. Cricq, C. *Australia* 25°17S 113°6E **61** E1
St. Croix *U.S. Virgin Is.* 17°45N 64°45W **89** C7
St. Croix → *U.S.A.* 44°45N 92°48W **80** C8
St. Croix Falls *U.S.A.* 45°24N 92°38W **80** C7
St. David's *Canada* 48°12N 58°52W **73** C8
St. David's *U.K.* 51°53N 5°16W **13** F2
St. David's Head *U.K.* 51°54N 5°19W **13** F2
St-Denis *Réunion* 20°52S 55°27E **55** c
St-Denis ✈ (RUN) *Réunion* 20°53S 55°32E **55** c
St-Dizier *France* 48°38N 4°56E **20** B6
St. Elias, Mt. *U.S.A.* 60°18N 140°56W **68** E3
St. Elias Mts. *N. Amer.* 60°33N 139°28W **70** A1
St-Étienne *France* 45°27N 4°22E **20** D6
St. Eugène *Canada* 45°30N 74°28W **83** A10
St. Eustatius *W. Indies* 17°20N 63°0W **89** C7
St-Félicien *Canada* 48°40N 72°25W **72** C5
St-Flour *France* 45°2N 3°6E **20** D5
St. Francis *U.S.A.* 39°47N 101°48W **80** F3
St. Francis → *U.S.A.* 34°38N 90°36W **85** D9
St. Francis, C. *S. Africa* 34°14S 24°49E **56** D3
St. Francisville *U.S.A.* 30°47N 91°23W **84** F9
St-François, L. *Canada* 45°10N 74°22W **83** A10
St-Gabriel *Canada* 46°17N 73°24W **72** C5
St. Gallen = Sankt Gallen
    Switz. 47°26N 9°22E **20** C8

St-Gaudens *France* 43°6N 0°44E **20 E4**
St. George *Australia* 28°1S 148°30E **63 D4**
St. George *N.B., Canada* 45°11N 66°50W **73 C6**
St. George *Ont., Canada* 43°15N 80°15W **82 C4**
St. George *S.C., U.S.A.* 33°11N 80°35W **85 E14**
St. George *Utah, U.S.A.* 37°6N 113°35W **77 H7**
St. George, C. *Canada* 48°30N 59°16W **73 C8**
St. George, C. *Canada* 29°40N 85°5W **85 G12**
St. George I. *U.S.A.* 56°35N 169°35W **74 D6**
St. George Ra. *Australia* 18°40S 125°0E **60 C4**
St. George's *Canada* 48°26N 58°31W **73 C8**
St-Georges *Canada* 46°8N 70°40W **73 C5**
St. George's *Grenada* 12°5N 61°43W **89 D7**
St. George's B. *Canada* 48°24N 58°53W **73 C8**
St. Georges Basin *N.S.W., Australia* 35°7S 150°36E **63 F5**
St. Georges Basin *W. Austral., Australia* 15°23S 125°2E **60 C4**
St. George's Channel *Europe* 52°0N 6°0W **10 E6**
St. George's Channel *India* 7°15N 93°43E **45 L11**
St. Georges Hd. *Australia* 35°12S 150°42E **63 F5**
St. Gotthard P. = San Gottardo, P. del *Switz.* 46°33N 8°33E **20 C8**
St. Helena *Atl. Oc.* 15°58S 5°42W **50 H3**
St. Helena *U.S.A.* 38°30N 122°28W **78 G4**
St. Helena, Mt. *U.S.A.* 38°40N 122°36W **78 G4**
St. Helena B. *S. Africa* 32°40S 18°10E **56 D2**
St. Helens *Australia* 41°20S 148°15E **63 G4**
St. Helens *U.K.* 53°27N 2°44W **12 D5**
St. Helens *U.S.A.* 45°52N 122°48W **78 E4**
St. Helens, Mt. *U.S.A.* 46°12N 122°12W **78 D4**
St. Helier *U.K.* 49°10N 2°7W **13 H5**
St-Hyacinthe *Canada* 45°40N 72°58W **72 C5**
St. Ignace *U.S.A.* 45°52N 84°44W **81 C11**
St. Ignace I. *Canada* 48°45N 88°0W **72 C2**
St. Ignatius *U.S.A.* 47°19N 114°6W **76 C6**
St. Ives *Cambs., U.K.* 52°20N 0°4W **13 E7**
St. Ives *Corn., U.K.* 50°12N 5°30W **13 G2**
St. James *U.S.A.* 43°59N 94°38W **80 D6**
St-Jean → *Canada* 50°17N 64°20W **73 B7**
St-Jean, L. *Canada* 48°40N 72°0W **73 C5**
St-Jean-Port-Joli *Canada* 47°15N 70°13W **73 C5**
St-Jean-sur-Richelieu *Canada* 45°20N 73°20W **83 A11**
St-Jérôme *Canada* 45°47N 74°0W **72 C5**
St. John *Canada* 45°20N 66°8W **73 C6**
St. John → *N. Amer.* 45°12N 66°5W **81 C20**
St. John, C. *Canada* 50°0N 55°32W **73 C8**
St. John I. *U.S. Virgin Is.* 18°20N 64°42W **89 e**
St. John's *Antigua & B.* 17°6N 61°51W **89 C7**
St. John's *Canada* 47°35N 52°40W **73 C9**
St. Johns *Ariz., U.S.A.* 34°30N 109°22W **77 J9**
St. Johns *Mich., U.S.A.* 43°0N 84°33W **81 D11**
St. Johns → *U.S.A.* 30°24N 81°24W **85 F14**
St. John's Pt. *Ireland* 54°34N 8°27W **10 B3**
St. Johnsbury *U.S.A.* 44°25N 72°1W **83 B12**
St. Johnsville *U.S.A.* 43°0N 74°43W **83 C10**
St. Joseph *Canada* 43°24N 81°42W **82 C3**
St-Joseph *Martinique* 14°39N 61°4W **88 c**
St. Joseph *Réunion* 21°22S 55°37E **55 c**
St. Joseph *La., U.S.A.* 31°55N 91°14W **84 F9**
St. Joseph *Mo., U.S.A.* 39°46N 94°50W **80 F6**
St. Joseph → *U.S.A.* 42°7N 86°29W **80 D10**
St. Joseph, I. *Canada* 46°12N 83°58W **72 C3**
St. Joseph, L. *Canada* 51°10N 90°35W **72 B1**
St. Kilda *U.K.* 57°49N 8°34W **14 C2**
St. Kitts & Nevis ■ *W. Indies* 17°20N 62°40W **89 C7**
St. Laurent *Canada* 50°25N 97°58W **71 C9**
St. Lawrence *Australia* 22°16S 149°31E **62 C4**
St. Lawrence *Canada* 46°54N 55°23W **73 C8**
St. Lawrence → *Canada* 49°30N 66°0W **73 C6**
St. Lawrence, Gulf of *Canada* 48°25N 62°0W **73 C7**
St. Lawrence I. *U.S.A.* 63°30N 170°30W **74 C5**
St. Lawrence Islands △ *Canada* 44°27N 75°52W **83 B9**
St. Léonard *Canada* 47°12N 67°58W **73 C6**
St-Leu *Réunion* 21°9S 55°18E **55 c**
St. Lewis → *Canada* 52°26N 56°11W **73 B8**
St-Lô *France* 49°7N 1°5W **20 B3**
St-Louis *Guadeloupe* 15°56N 61°19W **88 b**
St-Louis *Réunion* 21°16S 55°25E **55 c**
St-Louis *Senegal* 16°8N 16°27W **52 E2**
St. Louis *U.S.A.* 38°37N 90°11W **80 F8**
St. Louis → *U.S.A.* 46°44N 92°9W **80 B7**
St-Luc *Canada* 45°22N 73°18W **83 A11**
St. Lucia ■ *W. Indies* 14°0N 60°57W **89 f**
St. Lucia, L. *S. Africa* 28°5S 32°30E **57 D5**
St. Lucia △ *S. Africa* 28°6S 32°27E **57 C5**
St. Lucia Channel *W. Indies* 14°15N 61°0W **89 D7**
St. Maarten ☑ *W. Indies* 18°2N 63°5W **89 C7**
St. Magnus B. *U.K.* 60°25N 1°35W **11 A7**
St-Malo *France* 48°39N 2°1W **20 B2**
St-Marc *Haiti* 19°10N 72°41W **89 C5**
St. Maries *U.S.A.* 47°19N 116°35W **76 C5**
St-Martin ☑ *W. Indies* 18°0N 63°0W **89 C7**
St-Martin, C. *Martinique* 14°52N 61°14W **88 c**
St. Martin, L. *Canada* 51°40N 98°30W **71 C9**
St. Martins *Barbados* 13°5N 59°28W **89 g**
St. Mary Is. *India* 13°20N 74°35E **45 H2**
St. Mary Pk. *Australia* 31°32S 138°34E **63 E2**
St. Marys *Australia* 41°35S 148°11E **63 G4**
St. Marys *Canada* 43°20N 81°10W **82 C3**
St. Mary's *Corn., U.K.* 49°55N 6°18W **13 H1**
St. Mary's *Orkney, U.K.* 58°54N 2°54W **11 C6**
St. Marys *Ga., U.S.A.* 30°44N 81°33W **85 F14**
St. Marys *Pa., U.S.A.* 41°26N 78°34W **82 E6**
St. Mary's, C. *Canada* 46°50N 54°12W **73 C9**
St. Mary's B. *Canada* 46°50N 53°50W **73 C9**
St. Mary's Bay *Canada* 44°25N 66°10W **73 D6**
St-Mathieu, Pte. *France* 48°20N 4°45W **20 B1**
St. Matthew I. *U.S.A.* 60°24N 172°42W **74 C5**
St-Maurice → *Canada* 46°21N 72°31W **72 C5**
St. Mawes *U.K.* 50°10N 5°2W **13 G2**
St-Nazaire *France* 47°17N 2°12W **20 C2**

St. Neots *U.K.* 52°14N 0°15W **13 E7**
St-Omer *France* 50°45N 2°15E **20 A5**
St-Pamphile *Canada* 46°58N 69°48W **73 C6**
St-Pascal *Canada* 47°32N 69°48W **73 C6**
St. Paul *Canada* 54°0N 111°17W **70 C6**
St-Paul *Réunion* 20°59S 55°17E **55 c**
St-Paul *Minn., U.S.A.* 44°56N 93°5W **80 C7**
St. Paul *Nebr., U.S.A.* 41°13N 98°27W **80 E4**
St-Paul → *Canada* 51°27N 57°42W **73 B8**
St. Paul, Î. *Ind. Oc.* 38°55S 77°34E **3 F13**
St. Paul I. *Canada* 47°12N 60°9W **73 C7**
St. Paul I. *U.S.A.* 57°10N 170°15W **74 D5**
St. Peter *U.S.A.* 44°20N 93°57W **80 C7**
St. Peter Port *U.K.* 49°26N 2°33W **13 H5**
St. Peters *N.S., Canada* 45°40N 60°53W **73 C7**
St. Peters *P.E.I., Canada* 46°25N 62°35W **73 C7**
St. Petersburg *Russia* 27°46N 82°40W **85 H13**
St-Phillippe *Réunion* 21°21S 55°44E **55 c**
St-Pie *Canada* 45°30N 72°54W **83 A12**
St-Pierre *Martinique* 14°45N 61°10W **88 c**
St-Pierre *Réunion* 21°19S 55°28E **55 c**
St-Pierre *St-P. & M.* 46°46N 56°12W **73 C8**
St-Pierre, L. *Canada* 46°12N 72°52W **72 C5**
St-Pierre-et-Miquelon ☑ *N. Amer.* 46°55N 56°10W **73 C8**
St-Quentin *Canada* 47°30N 67°23W **73 C6**
St-Quentin *France* 49°50N 3°16E **20 B5**
St. Regis *U.S.A.* 47°18N 115°6W **76 C6**
St. Regis Falls *U.S.A.* 44°40N 74°32W **83 B10**
St-Siméon *Canada* 47°51N 69°54W **73 C6**
St. Simons I. *U.S.A.* 31°12N 81°15W **85 F14**
St. Simons Island *U.S.A.* 31°9N 81°22W **85 F14**
St. Stephen *Canada* 45°16N 67°17W **73 C6**
St. Thomas *Canada* 42°45N 81°10W **82 D3**
St. Thomas I. *U.S. Virgin Is.* 18°20N 64°55W **89 e**
St-Tite *Canada* 46°45N 72°34W **72 C5**
St-Trond = Sint-Truiden *Belgium* 50°48N 5°10E **15 D5**
St-Tropez *France* 43°17N 6°38E **20 E7**
St. Vidgeon's △ *Australia* 14°47S 134°53E **62 A1**
St. Vincent = São Vicente *C. Verde Is.* 17°0N 25°0W **52 b**
St. Vincent, G. *Australia* 35°0S 138°0E **63 F2**
St. Vincent & the Grenadines ■ *W. Indies* 13°0N 61°10W **89 D7**
St. Vincent Passage *W. Indies* 13°30N 61°0W **89 D7**
St-Vith *Belgium* 50°17N 6°9E **15 D6**
St. Walburg *Canada* 53°39N 109°12W **71 C7**
Saintala *India* 20°26N 83°20E **44 D6**
Ste-Agathe-des-Monts *Canada* 46°3N 74°17W **72 C5**
Ste-Anne *Guadeloupe* 16°13N 61°24W **88 b**
Ste-Anne *Seychelles* 4°36S 55°31E **55 b**
Ste-Anne, L. *Canada* 50°0N 67°42W **73 B6**
Ste-Anne-des-Monts *Canada* 49°8N 66°30W **73 C6**
Ste. Genevieve *U.S.A.* 37°59N 90°2W **80 G8**
Ste-Marguerite → *Canada* 50°9N 66°36W **73 B6**
Ste-Marie *Canada* 46°26N 71°0W **73 C5**
Ste-Marie *Martinique* 14°48N 61°1W **88 c**
Ste-Marie *Réunion* 20°53S 55°33E **55 c**
Ste-Marie, Ile = Boraha, Nosy *Madag.* 16°50S 49°55E **55 H9**
Ste-Rose *Guadeloupe* 16°20N 61°45W **88 b**
Ste-Rose *Réunion* 21°8S 55°45E **55 c**
Ste. Rose du Lac *Canada* 51°4N 99°30W **71 C9**
Saintes *France* 45°45N 0°37W **20 D3**
Saintes, Îs. des *Guadeloupe* 15°50N 61°35W **88 b**
Saintfield *U.K.* 54°28N 5°49W **10 B6**
Saintonge *France* 45°40N 0°50W **20 D3**
Saipal *Nepal* 29°50N 81°40E **43 E9**
Saipan *N. Marianas* 15°12N 145°45E **64 F6**
Sairang *India* 23°50N 92°45E **41 H18**
Sairecábur, Cerro *Bolivia* 22°43S 67°54W **94 A2**
Saitama *Japan* 35°54N 139°38E **29 G9**
Saitama □ *Japan* 36°25N 139°30E **29 F9**
Saiyid *Pakistan* 33°7N 73°2E **42 C5**
Sajama *Bolivia* 18°7S 69°0W **92 G5**
Sajószentpéter *Hungary* 48°12N 20°44E **17 D11**
Sajum *India* 33°20N 79°0E **43 C8**
Sak → *S. Africa* 30°52S 20°25E **56 D3**
Sakai *Japan* 34°19N 133°50E **29 G6**
Sakaiminato *Japan* 35°38N 133°11E **29 G6**
Sakākah *Si. Arabia* 30°0N 40°8E **46 D4**
Sakakawea, L. *U.S.A.* 47°30N 101°25W **80 B3**
Sakami → *Canada* 53°40N 76°40W **72 B4**
Sakami, L. *Canada* 53°15N 77°0W **72 B4**
Sakartvelo = Georgia ■ *Asia* 42°0N 43°0E **19 F7**
Sakarya *Turkey* 40°48N 30°25E **19 F5**
Sakashima-Guntō *Japan* 24°46N 124°0E **29 M2**
Sakata *Japan* 38°55N 139°50E **28 E9**
Sakchu *N. Korea* 40°23N 125°2E **33 D13**
Sakha □ *Russia* 66°0N 130°0E **27 C14**
Sakhalin *Russia* 51°0N 143°0E **27 D15**
Sakhalinskiy Zaliv *Russia* 54°0N 141°0E **27 D15**
Sakhi Gopal *India* 19°58N 85°50E **44 E7**
Šakiai *Lithuania* 54°59N 23°2E **9 J20**
Sakon Nakhon *Thailand* 17°10N 104°9E **38 D5**
Sakrand *Pakistan* 26°10N 68°15E **42 F3**
Sakri *Maharashtra, India* 26°13N 86°5E **43 F12**
Sakri *Maharashtra, India* 21°2N 74°20E **44 D2**
Sakrivier *S. Africa* 30°54S 20°28E **56 D3**
Sakti *India* 22°2N 82°58E **43 H10**
Sakuma *Japan* 35°3N 137°49E **29 G8**
Sakurai *Japan* 34°30N 135°51E **29 G7**
Sal → *Russia* 46°5N 43°30E **19 E7**
Sal Rei *C. Verde Is.* 16°11N 22°53W **52 b**
Sala *Sweden* 59°58N 16°35E **9 G17**
Sala Consilina *Italy* 40°23N 15°36E **22 D6**
Sala-y-Gómez *Pac. Oc.* 26°28S 105°28W **65 K17**
Sala y Gómez Ridge *Pac. Oc.* 25°0S 98°0W **65 K18**
Salaberry-de-Valleyfield *Canada* 45°15N 74°8W **83 A10**

Salada, L. *Mexico* 32°20N 115°40W **77 K6**
Saladas *Argentina* 28°15S 58°40W **94 B4**
Saladillo *Argentina* 35°40S 59°55W **94 D4**
Salado → *B. Aires, Argentina* 35°44S 57°22W **94 D4**
Salado → *La Pampa, Argentina* 37°30S 67°0W **96 D3**
Salado → *Santa Fe, Argentina* 31°40S 60°41W **94 C3**
Salado → *Mexico* 26°52N 99°19W **84 H5**
Salaga *Ghana* 8°31N 0°31W **52 G5**
Sālah *Syria* 32°40N 36°45E **48 C5**
Salālah *Oman* 16°56N 53°59E **49 D5**
Salamanca *Chile* 31°46S 70°59W **94 C1**
Salamanca *Spain* 40°58N 5°39W **21 B3**
Salamanca *U.S.A.* 42°10N 78°43W **82 D6**
Salamina *Greece* 37°56N 23°30E **23 F10**
Salar de Atacama *Chile* 23°30S 68°25W **94 A2**
Salar de Uyuni *Bolivia* 20°30S 67°45W **92 H5**
Salatiga *Indonesia* 7°19S 110°30E **37 G14**
Salavat *Russia* 53°21N 55°55E **18 D10**
Salaverry *Peru* 8°15S 79°0W **92 E3**
Salawati *Indonesia* 1°7S 130°52E **37 E8**
Salawin △ *Thailand* 18°18N 97°40E **38 C1**
Salaya *India* 22°19N 69°35E **42 H3**
Salayar *Indonesia* 6°7S 120°30E **37 F6**
Salcombe *U.K.* 50°14N 3°47W **13 G4**
Saldanha *S. Africa* 33°0S 17°58E **56 D2**
Saldanha B. *S. Africa* 33°6S 18°0E **56 D2**
Saldus *Latvia* 56°38N 22°30E **9 H20**
Sale *Australia* 38°6S 147°6E **63 F4**
Salé *Morocco* 34°3N 6°48W **52 B4**
Sale *U.K.* 53°26N 2°19W **12 D5**
Salekhard *Russia* 66°30N 66°35E **26 C7**
Salelologa *Samoa* 13°41S 172°11W **59 b**
Salem *India* 11°40N 78°11E **45 J4**
Salem *Ill., U.S.A.* 38°38N 88°57W **80 F9**
Salem *Ind., U.S.A.* 38°36N 86°6W **80 F10**
Salem *Mass., U.S.A.* 42°31N 70°53W **83 D14**
Salem *Mo., U.S.A.* 37°39N 91°32W **80 G8**
Salem *N.H., U.S.A.* 42°45N 71°12W **83 D13**
Salem *N.J., U.S.A.* 39°34N 75°28W **81 F16**
Salem *N.Y., U.S.A.* 43°10N 73°20E **83 C11**
Salem *Ohio, U.S.A.* 40°54N 80°52W **82 F4**
Salem *Oreg., U.S.A.* 44°56N 123°2W **76 D2**
Salem *S. Dak., U.S.A.* 43°44N 97°23W **80 D5**
Salem *Va., U.S.A.* 37°18N 80°3W **81 G13**
Salerno *Italy* 40°41N 14°47E **22 D6**
Salford *U.K.* 53°30N 2°18W **12 D5**
Salgótarján *Hungary* 48°5N 19°47E **17 D10**
Salgueiro *Brazil* 8°4S 39°6W **93 E11**
Salher *India* 20°40N 73°55E **44 D1**
Salibabu *Indonesia* 3°51N 126°40E **37 D7**
Salibea = Salybia *Trin. & Tob.* 10°43N 61°2W **93 K15**
Salida *U.S.A.* 38°32N 106°0W **76 G10**
Salihli *Turkey* 38°28N 28°8E **23 E13**
Salihorsk *Belarus* 52°51N 27°27E **17 B14**
Salima *Malawi* 13°47S 34°28E **55 G6**
Salina *Italy* 38°34N 14°50E **22 E6**
Salina *Kans., U.S.A.* 38°50N 97°37W **80 F5**
Salina *Utah, U.S.A.* 38°58N 111°51W **76 G8**
Salina Cruz *Mexico* 16°10N 95°12W **87 D5**
Salinas *Brazil* 16°10S 42°10W **93 G10**
Salinas *Ecuador* 2°10S 80°58W **92 D2**
Salinas *U.S.A.* 36°40N 121°39W **78 J5**
Salinas → *Guatemala* 16°28N 90°31W **87 D6**
Salinas → *U.S.A.* 36°45N 121°48W **78 J5**
Salinas, B. de *Nic.* 11°4N 85°45W **88 D2**
Salinas, Pampa de las *Argentina* 31°58S 66°42W **94 C2**
Salinas Ambargasta *Argentina* 29°0S 65°0W **94 B3**
Salinas de Hidalgo *Mexico* 22°38N 101°43W **86 C4**
Salinas Grandes *Argentina* 30°0S 65°0W **94 C3**
Salinas Pueblo Missions △ *U.S.A.* 34°6N 106°4W **77 J10**
Salinas Valley *U.S.A.* 36°15N 121°15W **78 J5**
Saline → *Ark., U.S.A.* 33°10N 92°8W **84 E8**
Saline → *Kans., U.S.A.* 38°52N 97°30W **80 F5**
Salinópolis *Brazil* 0°40S 47°20W **93 D9**
Salisbury *Australia* 34°46S 138°38E **63 E2**
Salisbury *U.K.* 51°4N 1°47W **13 F6**
Salisbury *Md., U.S.A.* 38°22N 75°36W **81 F16**
Salisbury *N.C., U.S.A.* 35°40N 80°29W **85 D14**
Salisbury I. *Canada* 63°30N 77°0W **69 E16**
Salisbury Plain *U.K.* 51°14N 1°55W **13 F6**
Şalkhad *Syria* 32°29N 36°43E **48 C5**
Salla *Finland* 66°50N 28°49E **8 C23**
Sallent = Coral Harbour *Canada* 64°8N 83°10W **69 E15**
Sallisaw *U.S.A.* 35°28N 94°47W **84 D7**
Salluit *Canada* 62°14N 75°38W **69 E16**
Sallyana *Nepal* 28°22N 82°10E **43 E9**
Salmās *Iran* 38°11N 44°47E **46 B5**
Salmo *Canada* 49°10N 117°20W **70 D5**
Salmon *U.S.A.* 45°11N 113°54W **76 D7**
Salmon → *Canada* 54°3N 122°40W **70 C4**
Salmon → *U.S.A.* 45°51N 116°47W **76 D5**
Salmon Arm *Canada* 50°40N 119°15W **70 C5**
Salmon Gums *Australia* 32°59S 121°38E **61 F3**
Salmon Pt. *Canada* 43°52N 77°15W **82 C7**
Salmon River Mts. *U.S.A.* 45°0N 115°30W **76 D6**
Salmon River Res. *U.S.A.* 43°32N 75°55W **83 C9**
Salo *Finland* 60°22N 23°10E **9 F20**
Salome *U.S.A.* 33°47N 113°37W **79 M13**
Salon *India* 26°2N 81°27E **43 F9**
Salon-de-Provence *France* 43°39N 5°6E **20 E6**
Salonica = Thessaloniki *Greece* 40°38N 22°58E **23 D10**
Salonta *Romania* 46°49N 21°42E **17 E11**
Salpausselkä *Finland* 61°0N 26°30E **8 F22**
Salsacate *Argentina* 31°20S 65°5W **94 C2**
Salsk *Russia* 46°28N 41°30E **19 E7**

Salso → *Italy* 37°6N 13°57E **22 F5**
Salt → *Canada* 60°0N 112°25W **70 B6**
Salt → *U.S.A.* 33°23N 112°19W **77 K7**
Salt Fork Red → *U.S.A.* 34°27N 99°21W **84 D5**
Salt L. *Australia* 30°6S 142°8E **63 E3**
Salt Lake City *U.S.A.* 40°45N 111°53W **76 F8**
Salt Range *Pakistan* 32°30N 72°25E **42 C5**
Salta *Argentina* 24°57S 65°25W **94 A2**
Salta □ *Argentina* 24°48S 65°30W **94 A2**
Saltash *U.K.* 50°24N 4°14W **13 G3**
Saltburn by the Sea *U.K.* 54°35N 0°58W **12 C7**
Saltcoats *U.K.* 55°38N 4°47W **11 F4**
Saltee Is. *Ireland* 52°7N 6°37W **10 D5**
Saltfjellet *Norway* 66°40N 15°15E **8 C16**
Saltfjorden *Norway* 67°15N 14°10E **8 C16**
Saltillo *Mexico* 25°25N 101°0W **86 B4**
Salto *Argentina* 34°20S 60°15W **94 C3**
Salto *Uruguay* 31°27S 57°50W **94 C4**
Salto → *Italy* 42°26N 12°25E **22 C5**
Salto del Guairá *Paraguay* 24°3S 54°17W **95 A5**
Salton City *U.S.A.* 33°18N 115°57W **M11**
Salton Sea *U.S.A.* 33°15N 115°45W **79 M11**
Saltsburg *U.S.A.* 40°29N 79°27W **82 F5**
Saluda → *U.S.A.* 34°1N 81°4W **85 D14**
Saluin *Egypt* 31°31N 25°7E **53 B11**
Salur *India* 18°27N 83°18E **44 E6**
Salvador *Brazil* 13°0S 38°30W **93 F11**
Salvador, El ■ *Cent. Amer.* 13°50N 89°0W **88 D2**
Salvador, L. *U.S.A.* 29°43N 90°15W **85 G9**
Salween → *Burma* 16°31N 97°37E **41 L20**
Salyan *Azerbaijan* 39°33N 48°59E **47 B6**
Salybia *Trin. & Tob.* 10°43N 61°2W **93 K15**
Salzach → *Austria* 48°12N 12°56E **16 D7**
Salzburg *Austria* 47°48N 13°2E **16 E7**
Salzgitter *Germany* 52°9N 10°19E **16 B6**
Salzwedel *Germany* 52°52N 11°10E **16 B6**
Sam *India* 26°50N 70°31E **42 F4**
Sam Neua *Laos* 20°29N 104°5E **34 G5**
Sam Ngao *Thailand* 17°18N 99°0E **38 D2**
Sam Rayburn Res. *U.S.A.* 31°4N 94°5W **84 F7**
Sam Son *Vietnam* 19°44N 105°54E **38 C5**
Sama de Langreo = Langreo *Spain* 43°18N 5°40W **21 A3**
Samagaltay *Russia* 50°36N 95°3E **27 D10**
Samales Group *Phil.* 6°0N 122°0E **37 C6**
Samalkot *India* 17°3N 82°13E **44 F6**
Samana *India* 30°10N 76°13E **42 D7**
Samana Cays *Bahamas* 23°3N 73°45W **89 B5**
Samangán □ *Afghan.* 36°15N 68°3E **40 B5**
Samani *Japan* 42°7N 142°56E **28 C11**
Samar *Phil.* 12°0N 125°0E **37 B7**
Samara *Russia* 53°8N 50°6E **18 D9**
Samaria = Shōmrōn *West Bank* 32°15N 35°13E **48 C4**
Samarinda *Indonesia* 0°30S 117°9E **36 E5**
Samarkand = Samarqand *Uzbekistan* 39°40N 66°55E **26 F7**
Samarqand *Uzbekistan* 39°40N 66°55E **26 F7**
Sāmarrā' *Iraq* 34°12N 43°52E **46 C4**
Samastipur *India* 25°50N 85°50E **43 G11**
Samba *India* 32°32N 75°10E **43 C6**
Samba *Indonesia* 38°58N 111°51W **76 G8**
Sambalpur *India* 21°28N 84°4E **44 D7**
Sambar, Tanjung *Indonesia* 2°59S 110°19E **36 E4**
Sambas *Indonesia* 1°20N 109°20E **36 D3**
Sambhajinagar = Aurangabad *India* 19°50N 75°23E **44 E2**
Sambhal *India* 28°35N 78°37E **43 E8**
Sambhar *India* 26°52N 75°6E **42 F6**
Sambhar L. *India* 26°55N 75°12E **42 F6**
Sambiase *Italy* 38°58N 16°17E **22 E7**
Sambir *Ukraine* 49°30N 23°10E **17 D12**
Sambor *Cambodia* 12°46N 106°0E **38 F6**
Sambor Prei Kuk *Cambodia* 12°46N 105°58E **38 F5**
Samborombón, B. *Argentina* 36°5S 57°20W **94 D4**
Samcheok *S. Korea* 37°30N 129°10E **33 F15**
Samet, Ko *Thailand* 12°34N 101°27E **38 F3**
Samfya *Zambia* 11°22S 29°31E **55 E2**
Samnah *Si. Arabia* 25°10N 37°15E **46 E3**
Samo Alto *Chile* 30°22S 71°0W **94 C1**
Samoa ■ *Pac. Oc.* 14°0S 172°0W **59 b**
Samoan Is. *Pac. Oc.* 14°0S 171°0W **59 b**
Samokov *Bulgaria* 42°18N 23°35E **23 C10**
Samos *Greece* 37°45N 26°50E **23 F12**
Samothráki = Mathraki *Greece* 39°48N 19°31E **23 E8**
Samothráki *Greece* 40°28N 25°28E **23 D11**
Sampacho *Argentina* 33°20S 64°50W **94 C3**
Sampalan *Indonesia* 8°41S 115°34E **37 K18**
Sampang *Indonesia* 7°11S 113°13E **37 G15**
Sampit *Indonesia* 2°34S 113°0E **36 E4**
Sampit, Teluk *Indonesia* 3°5S 113°3E **36 E4**
Samrong *Cambodia* 14°15N 103°30E **38 E4**
Samsø *Denmark* 55°50N 10°35E **9 J14**
Samsun *Turkey* 41°15N 36°22E **19 F6**
Samui, Ko *Thailand* 9°30N 100°0E **39 b**
Samut Prakan *Thailand* 13°32N 100°40E **38 F3**
Samut Sakhon *Thailand* 13°31N 100°13E **38 F3**
Samut Songkhram *Thailand* 13°24N 100°1E **38 F3**
Samwari *Pakistan* 28°30N 66°46E **42 E2**
San *Mali* 13°15N 4°57W **52 F5**
San → *Cambodia* 13°32N 105°57E **38 F5**
San → *Poland* 50°45N 21°51E **17 C11**
San Agustin, C. *Phil.* 6°20N 126°13E **37 C7**
San Agustín de Valle Fértil *Argentina* 30°35S 67°30W **94 C2**
San Ambrosio *Pac. Oc.* 26°28S 79°53W **90 F3**
San Andreas *U.S.A.* 38°12N 120°41W **78 G6**
San Andrés, I. de *Caribbean* 12°42N 81°46W **88 D3**
San Andres Mts. *U.S.A.* 33°0N 106°30W **77 K10**
San Andrés Tuxtla *Mexico* 18°27N 95°13W **87 D5**
San Anselmo *U.S.A.* 37°59N 122°34W **78 H4**

San Antonio *Belize* 16°15N 89°2W **87 D7**
San Antonio *Chile* 33°40S 71°40W **94 C1**
San Antonio *N. Mex., U.S.A.* 33°55N 106°52W **77 K10**
San Antonio *Tex., U.S.A.* 29°25N 98°29W **84 G5**
San Antonio → *U.S.A.* 28°30N 96°54W **84 G6**
San Antonio, C. *Argentina* 36°15S 56°40W **94 D4**
San Antonio, C. de *Cuba* 21°50N 84°57W **88 B3**
San Antonio, Mt. *U.S.A.* 34°17N 117°38W **79 L9**
San Antonio de los Baños *Cuba* 22°54N 82°31W **88 B3**
San Antonio de los Cobres *Argentina* 24°10S 66°17W **94 A2**
San Antonio Oeste *Argentina* 40°40S 65°0W **96 E4**
San Ardo *U.S.A.* 36°1N 120°54W **78 J6**
San Augustine *U.S.A.* 31°32N 94°7W **84 F7**
San Benedetto del Tronto *Italy* 42°57N 13°53E **22 C5**
San Benedicto, I. *Mexico* 19°18N 110°49W **86 D2**
San Benito *U.S.A.* 26°8N 97°38W **84 H6**
San Benito → *U.S.A.* 36°53N 121°34W **78 J5**
San Benito Mt. *U.S.A.* 36°22N 120°37W **78 J6**
San Bernardino *U.S.A.* 34°7N 117°19W **79 L9**
San Bernardino Mts. *U.S.A.* 34°10N 116°45W **79 L10**
San Bernardino Str. *Phil.* 12°30N 124°10E **37 B7**
San Bernardo *Chile* 33°40S 70°50W **94 C1**
San Bernardo, I. de *Colombia* 9°45N 75°50W **92 B3**
San Blas *Mexico* 26°5N 108°46W **86 B3**
San Blas, Arch. de *Panama* 9°50N 78°31W **88 E4**
San Blas, C. *U.S.A.* 29°40N 85°21W **85 G12**
San Borja *Bolivia* 14°50S 66°52W **92 F5**
San Buenaventura = Ventura *U.S.A.* 34°17N 119°18W **79 L7**
San Buenaventura *Mexico* 27°5N 101°32W **86 B4**
San Carlos *Argentina* 33°50S 69°0W **94 C2**
San Carlos *Chile* 36°10S 72°0W **94 D1**
San Carlos *Baja Calif. S., Mexico* 24°47N 112°7W **86 C2**
San Carlos *Coahuila, Mexico* 29°1N 100°51W **86 B4**
San Carlos *Nic.* 11°12N 84°50W **88 D3**
San Carlos *Phil.* 10°29N 123°25E **37 B6**
San Carlos *Uruguay* 34°46S 54°58W **95 C5**
San Carlos *U.S.A.* 33°21N 110°27W **77 K8**
San Carlos *Venezuela* 9°40N 68°36W **92 B5**
San Carlos de Bariloche *Argentina* 41°10S 71°25W **96 E2**
San Carlos de Bolívar *Argentina* 36°15S 61°6W **94 D3**
San Carlos del Zulia *Venezuela* 9°1N 71°55W **92 B4**
San Clemente *Chile* 35°30S 71°29W **94 D1**
San Clemente *U.S.A.* 33°26N 117°37W **79 M9**
San Clemente I. *U.S.A.* 32°53N 118°29W **79 N8**
San Cristóbal *Argentina* 30°20S 61°10W **94 C3**
San Cristóbal *Dom. Rep.* 18°25N 70°6W **89 C5**
San Cristóbal *Solomon Is.* 10°30S 161°0E **58 C9**
San Cristóbal *Venezuela* 7°46N 72°14W **92 B4**
San Cristóbal de las Casas *Mexico* 16°45N 92°38W **87 D6**
San Diego *Calif., U.S.A.* 32°42N 117°9W **79 N9**
San Diego *Tex., U.S.A.* 27°46N 98°14W **84 H5**
San Diego, C. *Argentina* 54°40S 65°10W **96 G3**
San Diego de la Unión *Mexico* 21°28N 100°52W **86 C4**
San Diego Int. ✈ (SAN) *U.S.A.* 32°44N 117°11W **79 N9**
San Estanislao *Paraguay* 24°39S 56°26W **94 A4**
San Felipe *Chile* 32°43S 70°42W **94 C1**
San Felipe *Mexico* 31°1N 114°52W **86 A2**
San Felipe *Venezuela* 10°20N 68°44W **92 A5**
San Felipe → *U.S.A.* 33°10N 115°49W **79 M11**
San Félix *Chile* 28°56S 70°28W **94 B1**
San Félix *Pac. Oc.* 26°23S 80°0W **90 F2**
San Fernando *Chile* 34°30S 71°0W **94 C1**
San Fernando *Mexico* 24°51N 98°10W **87 C5**
San Fernando *La Union, Phil.* 16°40N 120°23E **37 A6**
San Fernando *Pampanga, Phil.* 15°5N 120°37E **37 A6**
San Fernando *Spain* 36°28N 6°17W **21 D2**
San Fernando *Trin. & Tob.* 10°16N 61°28W **93 K15**
San Fernando *U.S.A.* 34°17N 118°26W **79 L8**
San Fernando de Apure *Venezuela* 7°54N 67°15W **92 B5**
San Fernando de Atabapo *Venezuela* 4°3N 67°42W **92 C5**
San Francisco *Argentina* 31°30S 62°5W **94 C3**
San Francisco → *U.S.A.* 32°59N 109°22W **77 K9**
San Francisco, C. de *Colombia* 6°18N 77°29W **90 C3**
San Francisco, Paso de *S. Amer.* 27°0S 68°0W **94 B2**
San Francisco de Macorís *Dom. Rep.* 19°19N 70°15W **89 C5**
San Francisco del Monte de Oro *Argentina* 32°36S 66°8W **94 C2**
San Francisco del Oro *Mexico* 26°52N 105°51W **86 B3**
San Francisco Int. ✈ (SFO) *U.S.A.* 37°37N 122°22W **78 H4**
San Gabriel *Chile* 33°47S 70°15W **94 C1**
San Gabriel Chilac *Mexico* 18°19N 97°21W **87 D5**
San Gabriel Mts. *U.S.A.* 34°17N 117°38W **79 L9**
San Gavino Monreale *Italy* 39°33N 8°47E **22 E3**

San German *Puerto Rico* 18°4N 67°4W 89 d
San Gorgonio Mt.
 U.S.A. 34°6N 116°50W 79 L10
San Gottardo, P. del *Switz.* 46°33N 8°33E 20 C8
San Gregorio *Uruguay* 32°37S 55°40W 95 C4
San Gregorio *U.S.A.* 37°20N 122°23W 78 H4
San Guillermo △
 Argentina 27°50S 69°45W 94 B2
San Ignacio *Belize* 17°10N 89°5W 87 D7
San Ignacio *Bolivia* 16°20S 60°55W 92 G6
San Ignacio *Mexico* 27°27N 112°51W 86 B2
San Ignacio *Paraguay* 26°52S 57°3W 94 B4
San Ignacio, L. *Mexico* 26°54N 113°13W 86 B2
San Ildefonso, C. *Phil.* 16°0N 122°1E 37 A6
San Isidro *Argentina* 34°29S 58°31W 94 C4
San Jacinto *U.S.A.* 33°47N 116°57W 79 M10
San Javier *Misiones,*
 Argentina 27°55S 55°5W 95 B4
San Javier *Santa Fe,*
 Argentina 30°40S 59°55W 94 C4
San Javier *Bolivia* 16°18S 62°30W 92 G6
San Javier *Chile* 35°40S 71°45W 94 D1
San Jerónimo Taviche
 Mexico 16°44N 96°35W 87 D5
San Joaquin *U.S.A.* 36°36N 120°11W 78 J6
San Joaquin → *U.S.A.* 38°4N 121°51W 78 G5
San Joaquin Valley
 U.S.A. 37°20N 121°0W 78 J6
San Jon *U.S.A.* 35°6N 103°20W 77 J12
San Jorge *Argentina* 31°54S 61°50W 94 C3
San Jorge, B. *Mexico* 31°20N 113°20W 86 A2
San Jorge, G. *Argentina* 46°0S 66°0W 96 F3
San José *Argentina* 32°12S 58°15W 94 C4
San José *Costa Rica* 9°55N 84°2W 88 E3
San José *Guatemala* 14°0N 90°50W 88 D1
San Jose *Mind. Occ., Phil.* 12°27N 121°4E 37 B6
San Jose *Nueva Ecija,*
 Phil. 15°45N 120°55E 37 A6
San Jose *U.S.A.* 37°20N 121°53W 78 H5
San Jose → *U.S.A.* 34°25N 106°45W 77 J10
San José, I. *Mexico* 25°0N 110°38W 86 C2
San Jose de Buenavista
 Phil. 10°45N 121°56E 37 B6
San José de Chiquitos
 Bolivia 17°53S 60°50W 92 G6
San José de Feliciano
 Argentina 30°26S 58°46W 94 C4
San José de Jáchal
 Argentina 30°15S 68°46W 94 C2
San José de Mayo
 Uruguay 34°27S 56°40W 94 C4
San José del Cabo *Mexico* 23°3N 109°41W 86 C3
San José del Guaviare
 Colombia 2°35N 72°38W 92 C4
San Juan *Argentina* 31°30S 68°30W 94 C2
San Juan *Puerto Rico* 18°28N 66°7W 89 d
San Juan *Trin. & Tob.* 10°39N 61°29W 93 K15
San Juan □ *Argentina* 31°9S 69°0W 94 C2
San Juan → *Argentina* 32°20S 67°25W 94 C2
San Juan → *Nic.* 10°56N 83°42W 88 D3
San Juan → *U.S.A.* 37°16N 110°26W 77 H8
San Juan Bautista
 Paraguay 26°37S 57°6W 94 B4
San Juan Bautista
 U.S.A. 36°51N 121°32W 78 J5
San Juan Capistrano
 U.S.A. 33°30N 117°40W 79 M9
San Juan Cr. → *U.S.A.* 35°40N 120°22W 78 J5
San Juan de Guadalupe
 Mexico 24°38N 102°44W 86 C4
San Juan de la Costa
 Mexico 24°20N 110°41W 86 C2
San Juan de los Lagos
 Mexico 21°15N 102°18W 86 C4
San Juan de los Morros
 Venezuela 9°55N 67°21W 92 B5
San Juan del Norte *Nic.* 10°58N 83°40W 88 D3
San Juan del Norte, B. de
 Nic. 11°0N 83°40W 88 D3
San Juan del Río *Mexico* 20°23N 100°0W 87 C5
San Juan del Sur *Nic.* 11°20N 85°51W 88 D2
San Juan I. *U.S.A.* 48°32N 123°5W 78 B3
San Juan Island △
 U.S.A. 48°35N 123°8W 78 B4
San Juan Mts. *U.S.A.* 37°30N 107°0W 77 H10
San Justo *Argentina* 30°47S 60°30W 94 C3
San Kamphaeng *Thailand* 18°45N 99°8E 38 C2
San Lázaro, C. *Mexico* 24°50N 112°18W 86 C2
San Leandro *U.S.A.* 37°44N 122°9W 78 H4
San Lorenzo *Argentina* 32°45S 60°45W 94 C3
San Lorenzo *Ecuador* 1°15N 78°50W 92 C3
San Lorenzo *Paraguay* 25°20S 57°32W 94 B4
San Lorenzo → *Mexico* 24°15N 107°24W 86 C3
San Lorenzo, I. *Mexico* 28°38N 112°51W 86 B2
San Lorenzo, Mte.
 Argentina 47°40S 72°20W 96 F2
San Lucas = Cabo San Lucas
 Mexico
San Lucas *Bolivia* 20°5S 65°7W 92 H5
San Lucas *Mexico* 27°10N 112°14W 86 B2
San Lucas *U.S.A.* 36°8N 121°1W 78 J5
San Lucas, C. *Mexico* 22°52N 109°53W 86 C3
San Luis *Argentina* 33°20S 66°20W 94 C2
San Luis *Cuba* 22°17N 83°46W 88 B3
San Luis *Guatemala* 16°14N 89°27W 88 C2
San Luis *Ariz., U.S.A.* 32°29N 114°47W 77 K6
San Luis *Colo., U.S.A.* 37°12N 105°25W 77 H11
San Luis □ *Argentina* 34°0S 66°0W 94 C2
San Luis, I. *Mexico* 29°58N 114°26W 86 B2
San Luis, Sierra de
 Argentina 32°30S 66°10W 94 C2
San Luis de la Paz
 Mexico 21°18N 100°31W 86 C4
San Luis Obispo *U.S.A.* 35°17N 120°40W 79 K6
San Luis Potosí *Mexico* 22°9N 100°59W 86 C4
San Luis Potosí □ *Mexico* 23°0N 101°0W 86 C4
San Luis Res. *U.S.A.* 37°4N 121°5W 78 H5
San Luis Río Colorado
 Mexico 32°29N 114°58W 86 A2

San Manuel *U.S.A.* 32°36N 110°38W 77 K8
San Marcos *Guatemala* 14°59N 91°52W 88 D1
San Marcos *Calif., U.S.A.* 33°9N 117°10W 79 M9
San Marcos *Tex., U.S.A.* 29°53N 97°56W 84 G6
San Marcos, I. *Mexico* 27°13N 112°6W 86 B2
San Marino *San Marino* 43°55N 12°30E 16 G7
San Marino ■ *Europe* 43°56N 12°25E 22 C5
San Martín *Antarctica* 68°11S 67°0W 5 C17
San Martín *Argentina* 33°5S 68°28W 94 C2
San Martín → *Bolivia* 13°8S 63°43W 92 F6
San Martín, L. *Argentina* 48°50S 72°50W 96 F2
San Martin de los Andes
 Argentina 40°10S 71°20W 96 E2
San Mateo *U.S.A.* 37°34N 122°19W 78 H4
San Matías *Bolivia* 16°25S 58°20W 92 G7
San Matías, G. *Argentina* 41°30S 64°0W 96 E4
San Miguel *El Salv.* 13°30N 88°12W 88 D2
San Miguel *Panama* 8°27N 78°55W 88 E4
San Miguel *U.S.A.* 35°45N 120°42W 78 K6
San Miguel → *Bolivia* 13°52S 63°56W 92 F6
San Miguel de Tucumán
 Argentina 26°50S 65°20W 94 B2
San Miguel del Monte
 Argentina 35°23S 58°50W 94 D4
San Miguel I. *U.S.A.* 34°2N 120°23W 79 L6
San Nicolás de los Arroyos
 Argentina 33°25S 60°10W 94 C3
San Nicolas I. *U.S.A.* 33°15N 119°30W 79 M7
San Onofre *U.S.A.* 33°22N 117°34W 79 M9
San Pablo *Bolivia* 21°43S 66°38W 94 A2
San Pablo *U.S.A.* 37°58N 122°21W 78 H4
San Pedro *B. Aires,*
 Argentina 33°40S 59°40W 94 C4
San Pedro *Misiones,*
 Argentina 26°30S 54°10W 95 B5
San Pedro *Chile* 33°54S 71°28W 94 C1
San Pedro *Ivory C.* 4°50N 6°33W 52 H4
San Pedro □ *Paraguay* 24°0S 57°0W 94 A4
San Pedro → *Chihuahua,*
 Mexico 28°21N 105°25W 86 B3
San Pedro → *Nayarit,*
 Mexico 21°45N 105°30W 86 C3
San Pedro → *U.S.A.* 32°59N 110°47W 77 K8
San Pedro, Pta. *Chile* 25°30S 70°38W 94 B1
San Pedro Channel
 U.S.A. 33°30N 118°25W 79 M8
San Pedro de Atacama
 Chile 22°55S 68°15W 94 A2
San Pedro de Jujuy
 Argentina 24°12S 64°55W 94 A3
San Pedro de las Colonias
 Mexico 25°45N 102°59W 86 B4
San Pedro de Macorís
 Dom. Rep. 18°30N 69°18W 89 C6
San Pedro del Norte *Nic.* 13°4N 84°33W 88 D3
San Pedro del Paraná
 Paraguay 26°43S 56°13W 94 B4
San Pedro Mártir, Sa. de
 Mexico 30°45N 115°13W 86 A1
San Pedro Ocampo = Melchor
 Ocampo *Mexico* 24°51N 101°39W 86 C4
San Pedro Pochutla
 Mexico 15°44N 96°28W 87 D5
San Pedro Sula *Honduras* 15°30N 88°0W 88 C2
San Pedro Tututepec
 Mexico 16°9N 97°38W 87 D5
San Pietro *Italy* 39°8N 8°17E 22 E3
San Rafael *Argentina* 34°40S 68°21W 94 C2
San Rafael *Calif., U.S.A.* 37°58N 122°32W 78 H4
San Rafael *N. Mex.,*
 U.S.A. 35°7N 107°53W 77 J10
San Rafael Mt. *U.S.A.* 34°41N 119°52W 79 L7
San Rafael Mts. *U.S.A.* 34°40N 119°50W 79 L7
San Ramón de la Nueva Orán
 Argentina 23°10S 64°20W 94 A3
San Remo *Italy* 43°49N 7°46E 20 E7
San Roque *Argentina* 28°25S 58°45W 94 B4
San Roque *Spain* 36°17N 5°21W 21 D3
San Rosendo *Chile* 37°16S 72°43W 94 D1
San Saba *U.S.A.* 31°12N 98°43W 84 F5
San Salvador *El Salv.* 13°40N 89°10W 88 D2
San Salvador de Jujuy
 Argentina 24°10S 64°48W 94 A3
San Salvador I. *Bahamas* 24°0N 74°30W 89 B5
San Sebastián = Donostia-San
 Sebastián *Spain* 43°17N 1°58W 21 A5
San Sebastián *Argentina* 53°10S 68°30W 96 G3
San Sebastián *Puerto Rico* 18°20N 66°59W 89 d
San Severo *Italy* 41°41N 15°23E 22 D6
San Simeon *U.S.A.* 35°39N 121°11W 78 K5
San Simon *U.S.A.* 32°16N 109°14W 77 K9
San Telmo *Mexico* 30°58N 116°6W 86 A1
San Tiburcio *Mexico* 24°8N 101°32W 86 C4
San Valentin, Mte. *Chile* 46°30S 73°30W 96 F2
San Vicente de Cañete
 Peru 13°8S 76°30W 92 F3
San Vicente de la Barquera
 Spain 43°23N 4°29W 21 A3
San Vito *Costa Rica* 8°50N 82°58W 88 E3
Sana'a = San'ā' *Yemen* 15°27N 44°12E 49 D3
San'ā' *Yemen* 15°27N 44°12E 49 D3
Sana → *Bos.-H.* 45°3N 16°23E 16 F9
Sanaa = San'ā' *Yemen* 15°27N 44°12E 49 D3
Sanae IV *Antarctica* 70°20S 9°0W 5 D2
Sanaga → *Cameroon* 3°35N 9°38E 54 D1
Sanak I. *U.S.A.* 54°25N 162°40W 74 E7
Sanalona, Presa *Mexico* 24°49N 107°8W 86 B3
Sanana *Indonesia* 2°4S 125°58E 37 E7
Sanand *India* 22°59N 72°25E 42 H5
Sanandaj *Iran* 35°18N 47°1E 46 C5
Sanandita *Bolivia* 21°40S 63°45W 94 A3
Sanawad *India* 22°11N 76°5E 42 H7
Sancha He → *China* 26°48N 106°7E 34 D6
Sanchahe *China* 44°50N 126°2E 33 B14
Sánchez *Dom. Rep.* 19°15N 69°36W 89 C6
Sanchi *India* 23°28N 77°44E 42 H7
Sanchor *India* 24°45N 71°55E 42 G4
Sancti Spíritus *Cuba* 21°52N 79°33W 88 B4

Sancy, Puy de *France* 45°32N 2°50E 20 D5
Sand = Polokwane →
 S. Africa 22°25S 30°5E 57 B5
Sand Hills *U.S.A.* 42°10N 101°30W 80 D3
Sand Lakes △ *Canada* 57°51N 98°32W 71 B9
Sand Springs *U.S.A.* 36°9N 96°7W 84 C6
Sanda *Japan* 34°53N 135°14E 29 G7
Sandakan *Malaysia* 5°53N 118°4E 36 C5
Sandan = Sambor
 Cambodia 12°46N 106°0E 38 F6
Sandanski *Bulgaria* 41°35N 23°16E 23 D10
Sanday *U.K.* 59°16N 2°31W 11 B6
Sandefjord *Norway* 59°10N 10°15E 9 G14
Sanders *U.S.A.* 35°13N 109°20W 77 J9
Sanderson *U.S.A.* 30°9N 102°24W 84 F3
Sandersville *U.S.A.* 32°59N 82°48W 85 E13
Sandfire Roadhouse
 Australia 19°45S 121°15E 60 C3
Sandfly L. *Canada* 55°43N 106°6W 71 B7
Sandfontein *Namibia* 23°48S 19°1E 56 B2
Sandheads, The *India* 21°10N 88°20E 43 J13
Sandía *Peru* 14°10S 69°30W 92 F5
Sandila *India* 27°5N 80°31E 43 F9
Sandnes *Norway* 58°50N 5°45E 9 G11
Sandnessjøen *Norway* 66°2N 12°38E 8 C15
Sandoa
 Dem. Rep. of the Congo 9°41S 23°0E 54 F4
Sandomierz *Poland* 50°40N 21°43E 17 C11
Sandover → *Australia* 21°43S 136°32E 62 C2
Sandoway = Thandwe
 Burma 18°20N 94°30E 41 K19
Sandoy *Færoe Is.* 61°52N 6°46W 8 F9
Sandpoint *U.S.A.* 48°17N 116°33W 76 B5
Sandray *U.K.* 56°53N 7°31W 11 E1
Sandringham *U.K.* 52°51N 0°31E 12 E8
Sandstone *Australia* 27°59S 119°16E 61 E2
Sandu *China* 26°0N 107°52E 34 E6
Sandur *India* 15°6N 76°33E 45 F3
Sandusky *Mich., U.S.A.* 43°25N 82°50W 82 C2
Sandusky *Ohio, U.S.A.* 41°27N 82°42W 82 E2
Sandveld *Namibia* 21°25S 20°0E 56 B3
Sandviken *Sweden* 60°38N 16°46E 8 F17
Sandwich, C. *Australia* 18°14S 146°18E 62 B4
Sandwich B. *Canada* 53°40N 57°15W 73 B8
Sandwich B. *Namibia* 23°25S 14°20E 56 B1
Sandy *Oreg., U.S.A.* 45°24N 122°16W 78 E4
Sandy *Pa., U.S.A.* 41°6N 78°46W 82 E6
Sandy *Utah, U.S.A.* 40°32N 111°50W 76 F8
Sandy Bay *Canada* 55°31N 102°19W 71 B8
Sandy Bight *Australia* 33°50S 123°20E 61 F3
Sandy C. *Queens.,*
 Australia 24°42S 153°15E 62 C5
Sandy C. *Tas., Australia* 41°25S 144°45E 63 G3
Sandy Cay *Bahamas* 23°13N 75°18W 89 B4
Sandy Cr. → *Australia* 31°54S 145°18E 63 B4
Sandy Cr. → *U.S.A.* 41°51N 109°47W 76 F9
Sandy Creek *U.S.A.* 43°38N 76°5W 83 C8
Sandy L. *Canada* 53°2N 93°0W 72 B1
Sandy Lake *Canada* 53°0N 93°15W 72 B1
Sandy Point *India* 10°32N 92°22E 45 J11
Sandy Valley *U.S.A.* 35°49N 115°38W 79 K11
Sanford *Fla., U.S.A.* 28°48N 81°16W 85 G14
Sanford *Maine, U.S.A.* 43°27N 70°47W 83 C14
Sanford *N.C., U.S.A.* 35°29N 79°10W 85 D15
Sanford → *Australia* 27°22S 115°53E 61 E2
Sanford, Mt. *U.S.A.* 62°13N 144°8W 68 C5
Sang-i-Masha *Afghan.* 33°8N 67°27E 42 C2
Sanga → *Congo* 1°5S 17°0E 54 E3
Sangamner *India* 19°37N 74°15E 44 E2
Sangān *Iran* 34°23N 60°15E 47 C9
Sangar *Afghan.* 32°56N 65°30E 42 C1
Sangar *Russia* 64°2N 127°31E 27 C13
Sangar Sarai *Afghan.* 34°27N 70°35E 42 B4
Sangareddi *India* 17°38N 78°7E 44 F4
Sangarh → *Pakistan* 30°43N 70°44E 42 D4
Sangay *Ecuador* 2°0S 78°20W 92 D3
Sangeang *Indonesia* 8°12S 119°6E 37 F5
Sanger *U.S.A.* 36°42N 119°33W 78 J7
Sangerhausen *Germany* 51°28N 11°18E 16 C6
Sanggan He → *China* 38°12N 117°15E 32 E9
Sanggau *Indonesia* 0°5N 110°30E 36 D4
Sanghar *Pakistan* 26°2N 68°57E 42 F3
Sangihe, Kepulauan
 Indonesia 3°0N 125°30E 37 D7
Sangihe, Pulau *Indonesia* 3°35N 125°30E 37 D7
Sangiran *Indonesia* 7°27S 110°50E 37 g
Sangju *S. Korea* 36°25N 128°10E 33 F15
Sangkapura *Indonesia* 5°52S 112°40E 36 F4
Sangkha *Thailand* 14°37N 103°52E 38 E4
Sangkhla Buri *Thailand* 14°57N 98°28E 38 E2
Sangkulirang *Indonesia* 0°59N 117°58E 36 D5
Sangla *Pakistan* 31°43N 73°23E 42 D5
Sangli *India* 16°55N 74°33E 44 F2
Sangmélima *Cameroon* 2°57N 12°1E 54 D2
Sango *Zimbabwe* 18°44S 31°44E 57 A5
Sangod *India* 24°55N 76°17E 42 G7
Sangole *India* 17°26N 75°12E 44 F2
Sangre de Cristo Mts.
 U.S.A. 37°30N 105°20W 77 H11
Sangre Grande
 Trin. & Tob. 10°35N 61°8W 93 K15
Sangrur *India* 30°59N 75°25E 42 D6
Sangudo *Canada* 53°50N 114°54W 70 C6
Sangue → *Brazil* 11°1S 58°39W 92 F7
Sangzhi *China* 29°25N 110°12E 35 C8
Sanibel *U.S.A.* 26°27N 82°1W 85 H13
Sanikiluaq *Canada* 56°32N 79°14W 72 A4
Sanin-Kaigan △ *Japan* 35°39N 134°37E 29 G7
Sanirajak = Hall Beach
 Canada 68°46N 81°12W 69 D15
Sanjawi *Pakistan* 30°17N 68°21E 42 D3
Sanjiang *China* 25°48N 109°37E 34 E7
Sanjo *Japan* 37°37N 138°57E 28 F9
Sankarankovil *India* 9°10N 77°35E 45 K3
Sankeshwar *India* 16°23N 74°32E 45 F2
Sankh → *India* 22°15N 84°48E 43 H11
Sankt Gallen *Switz.* 47°26N 9°22E 20 C8
Sankt Michel = Mikkeli
 Finland 61°43N 27°15E 8 F22

Sankt Moritz *Switz.* 46°30N 9°51E 20 C8
Sankt Pölten *Austria* 48°12N 15°38E 16 D8
Sankuru →
 Dem. Rep. of the Congo 4°17S 20°25E 54 E4
Sanliurfa *Turkey* 37°12N 38°50E 46 B3
Sanlúcar de Barrameda
 Spain 36°46N 6°21W 21 D2
Sanmen *China* 29°5N 121°35E 35 C13
Sanmenxia *China* 34°47N 111°12E 32 G6
Sanming *China* 26°15N 117°40E 35 D11
Sanmu *Japan* 34°11N 134°37E 29 G7
Sanndraigh = Sandray
 U.K. 56°53N 7°31W 11 E1
Sannicandro Gargánico
 Italy 41°50N 15°34E 22 D6
Sânnicolau Mare
 Romania 46°5N 20°39E 17 E11
Sannieshof *S. Africa* 26°30S 25°47E 56 C4
Sannīn, J. *Lebanon* 33°57N 35°52E 48 B4
Sanniquellie *Liberia* 7°19N 8°38W 52 G4
Sano *Japan* 36°19N 139°35E 29 F9
Sanok *Poland* 49°35N 22°10E 17 D12
Sanqingshan △ *China* 28°54N 118°3E 35 C12
Sanquhar *U.K.* 55°22N 3°54W 11 F5
Sans Souci *Trin. & Tob.* 10°50N 61°0W 93 K16
Sansha *China* 26°58N 120°12E 35 D13
Sanshui *China* 23°10N 112°56E 35 F9
Sansui *China* 26°58N 108°39E 34 D7
Sant Antoni de Portmany
 Spain 38°59N 1°19E 21 C6
Sant Feliu de Guíxols *Spain* 41°45N 3°1E 21 B7
Sant Jordi, G. de *Spain* 40°53N 1°2E 21 B6
Santa Ana *Bolivia* 13°50S 65°40W 92 F5
Santa Ana *El Salv.* 14°0N 89°31W 88 D2
Santa Ana *Mexico* 30°33N 111°7W 86 A2
Santa Ana *U.S.A.* 33°46N 117°52W 79 M9
Santa Ana de los Rios de Cuenca =
 Cuenca *Ecuador* 2°50S 79°9W 92 D3
Sant' Antíoco *Italy* 39°4N 8°27E 22 E3
Santa Bárbara *Chile* 37°40S 72°1W 94 D1
Santa Bárbara *Honduras* 14°53N 88°14W 88 D2
Santa Bárbara *Mexico* 26°48N 105°49W 86 B3
Santa Barbara *U.S.A.* 34°25N 119°42W 79 L7
Santa Barbara Channel
 U.S.A. 34°15N 120°0W 79 L7
Santa Barbara I. *U.S.A.* 33°29N 119°2W 79 M7
Santa Catalina, Gulf of
 U.S.A. 33°10N 117°50W 79 N9
Santa Catalina, I.
 Mexico 25°40N 110°47W 86 B2
Santa Catalina I.
 U.S.A. 33°23N 118°25W 79 M8
Santa Catarina □ *Brazil* 27°25S 48°30W 95 B6
Santa Catarina, I. de
 Brazil 27°30S 48°40W 95 B6
Santa Cecília *Brazil* 26°56S 50°18W 95 B5
Santa Clara *Cuba* 22°20N 80°0W 88 B4
Santa Clara *Calif.,*
 U.S.A. 37°21N 121°57W 78 H5
Santa Clara *Utah, U.S.A.* 37°8N 113°39W 77 H7
Santa Clara *N.Y., U.S.A.* 44°38N 74°27W 83 B10
Santa Clara → *Mexico* 29°51N 107°6W 86 A3
Santa Clara de Olimar
 Uruguay 32°50S 54°54W 95 C5
Santa Clara Valley
 U.S.A. 36°50N 121°30W 78 J5
Santa Clarita *U.S.A.* 34°24N 118°33W 79 L8
Santa Clotilde *Peru* 2°33S 73°45W 92 D4
Santa Cruz *Bolivia* 17°43S 63°10W 92 G6
Santa Cruz *Chile* 34°38S 71°27W 94 C1
Santa Cruz *Costa Rica* 10°15N 85°35W 88 D2
Santa Cruz *Phil.* 14°20N 121°24E 37 B6
Santa Cruz → *Argentina* 50°10S 68°20W 96 G3
Santa Cruz de Mompox = Mompós
 Colombia 9°14N 74°26W 92 B4
Santa Cruz de Tenerife
 Canary Is. 28°28N 16°15W 52 C2
Santa Cruz del Norte
 Cuba 23°9N 81°55W 88 B3
Santa Cruz del Sur *Cuba* 20°44N 78°0W 88 B4
Santa Cruz do Rio Pardo
 Brazil 22°54S 49°37W 95 A6
Santa Cruz do Sul *Brazil* 29°42S 52°25W 95 B5
Santa Cruz I. *U.S.A.* 34°1N 119°43W 79 M7
Santa Cruz Is. *Solomon Is.* 10°30S 166°0E 58 C9
Santa Cruz Mts. *Jamaica* 17°58N 77°43W 88 a
Santa Elena *Argentina* 30°58S 59°47W 94 C4
Santa Elena, C.
 Costa Rica 10°54N 85°56W 88 D2
Santa Fé *Argentina* 31°35S 60°41W 94 C3
Santa Fe *U.S.A.* 35°41N 105°57W 77 J11
Santa Fé □ *Argentina* 31°50S 60°55W 94 C3
Santa Fé do Sul *Brazil* 20°13S 50°56W 93 H8
Santa Filomena *Brazil* 9°6S 45°50W 93 E9
Santa Inês *Brazil* 13°17S 39°48W 93 F11
Santa Inés, I. *Chile* 54°0S 73°0W 96 G2
Santa Isabel *Argentina* 36°10S 66°54W 94 D2
Santa Isabel do Morro
 Brazil 11°34S 50°40W 93 F8
Santa Lucía *Corrientes,*
 Argentina 28°58S 59°5W 94 B4
Santa Lucía *San Juan,*
 Argentina 31°30S 68°30W 94 C2
Santa Lucia *Uruguay* 34°27S 56°24W 94 C4
Santa Lucia Range
 U.S.A. 36°0N 121°20W 78 K5
Santa Luzia *C. Verde Is.* 16°50N 24°35W 52 b
Santa Margarita
 Argentina 38°28S 61°35W 94 D3
Santa Margarita *U.S.A.* 35°23N 120°37W 78 K6
Santa Margarita →
 U.S.A. 33°13N 117°23W 79 M9
Santa Margarita, I.
 Mexico 24°27N 111°50W 86 C2
Santa María *Argentina* 26°40S 66°0W 94 B2
Santa Maria *Brazil* 29°40S 53°48W 95 B5
Santa Maria *C. Verde Is.* 16°31N 22°53W 52 b

Santa Maria *U.S.A.* 34°57N 120°26W 79 L6
Santa María → *Mexico* 31°0N 107°14W 86 A3
Santa María, B. de *Mexico* 25°4N 108°6W 86 B3
Santa Maria da Vitória
 Brazil 13°24S 44°12W 93 F10
Santa Maria di Léuca, C.
 Italy 39°47N 18°22E 23 E8
Santa Marta *Colombia* 11°15N 74°13W 92 A4
Santa Marta, Sierra Nevada de
 Colombia 10°55N 73°50W 92 A4
Santa Marta Grande, C.
 Brazil 28°43S 48°50W 95 B6
Santa Maura = Lefkada
 Greece 38°40N 20°43E 23 E9
Santa Monica Mts. △
 U.S.A. 34°4N 118°44W 79 L8
Santa Paula *U.S.A.* 34°21N 119°4W 79 L7
Santa Rosa *La Pampa,*
 Argentina 36°40S 64°17W 94 D3
Santa Rosa *San Luis,*
 Argentina 32°21S 65°10W 94 C2
Santa Rosa *Brazil* 27°52S 54°29W 95 B5
Santa Rosa *Calif., U.S.A.* 38°26N 122°43W 78 G4
Santa Rosa *N. Mex.,*
 U.S.A. 34°57N 104°41W 77 J11
Santa Rosa and San Jacinto Mts. △
 U.S.A. 33°28N 116°20W 79 M10
Santa Rosa de Copán
 Honduras 14°47N 88°46W 88 D2
Santa Rosa de Río Primero
 Argentina 31°8S 63°20W 94 C3
Santa Rosa del Sara
 Bolivia 17°7S 63°35W 92 G6
Santa Rosa I. *Calif.,*
 U.S.A. 33°58N 120°6W 79 M6
Santa Rosa I. *Fla.,*
 U.S.A. 30°20N 86°50W 85 F11
Santa Rosa Range
 U.S.A. 41°45N 117°40W 76 F5
Santa Rosalía *Mexico* 27°19N 112°17W 86 B2
Santa Sylvina *Argentina* 27°50S 61°10W 94 B3
Santa Tecla = Nueva San Salvador
 El Salv. 13°40N 89°18W 88 D2
Santa Teresa *Argentina* 33°25S 60°47W 94 C3
Santa Teresa *Australia* 24°8S 134°22E 62 C1
Santa Teresa *Mexico* 25°17N 97°51W 87 B5
Santa Teresa → *Uruguay* 33°33S 53°31W 95 C5
Santa Teresa △ *Uruguay* 33°57S 53°30W 95 C5
Santa Teresita *Argentina* 36°32S 56°41W 94 D4
Santa Vitória do Palmar
 Brazil 33°32S 53°25W 95 C5
Santa Ynez → *U.S.A.* 34°41N 120°36W 79 L6
Santa Ynez Mts. *U.S.A.* 34°30N 120°0W 79 L6
Santa Ysabel *U.S.A.* 33°7N 116°40W 79 M10
Santai *China* 31°5N 104°58E 34 B5
Santana, Coxilha de
 Brazil 30°50S 55°35W 95 C4
Santana do Livramento
 Brazil 30°55S 55°30W 95 C4
Santander *Spain* 43°27N 3°51W 21 A4
Santander Jiménez
 Mexico 24°13N 98°28W 87 C5
Santanilla, Is. *Honduras* 17°22N 83°57W 88 C3
Santaquin *U.S.A.* 39°59N 111°47W 76 G8
Santarém *Brazil* 2°25S 54°42W 93 D8
Santarém *Portugal* 39°12N 8°42W 21 C1
Santaren Channel
 W. Indies 24°0N 79°30W 88 B4
Santee *U.S.A.* 32°50N 116°58W 79 N10
Santee → *U.S.A.* 33°7N 79°17W 85 E15
Santiago = Río Grande de
 Santiago → *Mexico* 21°36N 105°26W 86 C3
Santiago = São Tiago
 C. Verde Is. 15°0N 23°40W 52 b
Santiago *Brazil* 29°11S 54°52W 95 B5
Santiago *Panama* 8°0N 81°0W 88 E3
Santiago *Phil.* 16°41N 121°33E 37 A6
Santiago → *Peru* 4°27S 77°38W 92 D3
Santiago de Compostela
 Spain 42°52N 8°37W 21 A1
Santiago de Cuba *Cuba* 20°0N 75°49W 88 C4
Santiago de los Caballeros
 Dom. Rep. 19°30N 70°40W 89 C5
Santiago del Estero
 Argentina 27°50S 64°15W 94 B3
Santiago del Estero □
 Argentina 27°40S 63°15W 94 B3
Santiago Ixcuintla
 Mexico 21°49N 105°13W 86 C3
Santiago Jamiltepec
 Mexico 16°17N 97°49W 87 D5
Santiago Papasquiaro
 Mexico 25°3N 105°25W 86 C3
Santiago Pinotepa Nacional
 Mexico 16°19N 98°1W 87 D5
Santiaguillo, L. de
 Mexico 24°48N 104°48W 86 C4
Santo Amaro *Brazil* 12°30S 38°43W 93 F11
Santo Anastácio *Brazil* 21°58S 51°39W 95 A5
Santo André *Brazil* 23°39S 46°29W 95 A6
Santo Ângelo *Brazil* 28°15S 54°15W 95 B5
Santo Antão *C. Verde Is.* 16°52N 25°10W 52 b
Santo Antônio do Içá
 Brazil 3°5S 67°57W 92 D5
Santo Antônio do Leverger
 Brazil 15°52S 56°5W 93 G7
Santo Domingo
 Dom. Rep. 18°30N 69°59W 89 C6
Santo Domingo *Mexico* 25°29N 111°55W 86 B2
Santo Domingo *Nic.* 12°14N 84°59W 88 D3
Santo Domingo, Cay
 Bahamas 21°25N 75°45W 88 B4
Santo Domingo de los Colorados
 Ecuador 0°15S 79°9W 92 D3
Santo Domingo Pueblo
 U.S.A. 35°31N 106°22W 77 J10
Santo Domingo Tehuantepec =
 Tehuantepec *Mexico* 16°21N 95°13W 87 D5
Santo Tomás *Mexico* 31°33N 116°24W 86 A1
Santo Tomás *Peru* 14°26S 72°8W 92 F4

Santo Tomé *Argentina* 28°40S 56°5W **95 B4**
Santo Tomé de Guayana = Ciudad
  Guayana *Venezuela* 8°0N 62°30W **92 B6**
Santoña *Spain* 43°29N 3°27W **21 A4**
Santorini *Greece* 36°23N 25°27E **23 F11**
Santos *Brazil* 24°0S 46°20W **95 A6**
Santos Dumont *Brazil* 22°55S 43°10W **95 A7**
Santuario de Aves Laguna
  Colorada △ *Bolivia* 22°10S 67°45W **94 A2**
Sanuki *Japan* 34°19N 134°10E **29 G7**
Sanur *Indonesia* 8°41S 115°15E **37 K18**
Sanwer *India* 22°59N 75°50E **42 H6**
Sanxia Shuiku *China* 30°3N 107°58E **34 B6**
Sanxiang *China* 22°21N 113°25E **31 a**
Sanya *China* 18°14N 109°29E **38 C7**
Sanyuan *China* 34°35N 108°58E **32 G5**
São Bernardo do Campo
  Brazil 23°45S 46°34W **95 A6**
São Borja *Brazil* 28°39S 56°0W **95 B4**
São Carlos *Brazil* 22°0S 47°50W **95 A6**
São Cristóvão *Brazil* 11°1S 37°15W **93 F11**
São Domingos *Brazil* 13°25S 46°19W **93 F9**
São Filipe *C. Verde Is.* 15°2N 24°30W **52 b**
São Francisco *Brazil* 16°0S 44°50W **93 G10**
São Francisco → *Brazil* 10°30S 36°24W **93 F11**
São Francisco do Sul
  Brazil 26°15S 48°36W **95 B6**
São Gabriel *Brazil* 30°20S 54°20W **95 C5**
São Gonçalo *Brazil* 22°48S 43°5W **95 A7**
São João da Boa Vista
  Brazil 22°0S 46°52W **95 A6**
São João da Madeira
  Portugal 40°54N 8°30W **21 B1**
São João del Rei *Brazil* 21°8S 44°15W **95 A7**
São João do Araguaia
  Brazil 5°23S 48°46W **93 E9**
São João do Piauí *Brazil* 8°21S 42°15W **93 E10**
São Joaquim *Brazil* 28°18S 49°56W **95 B6**
São Joaquim △ *Brazil* 28°12S 49°37W **95 B6**
São Jorge *Azores* 38°38N 28°3W **52 a**
São José *Brazil* 27°38S 48°39W **95 B5**
São José do Norte *Brazil* 32°1S 52°3W **95 C5**
São José do Rio Preto
  Brazil 20°50S 49°20W **95 A6**
São José dos Campos
  Brazil 23°7S 45°52W **95 A6**
São Leopoldo *Brazil* 29°50S 51°10W **95 B5**
São Lourenço *Brazil* 22°7S 45°3W **95 A6**
São Lourenço → *Brazil* 17°53S 57°27W **93 G7**
São Lourenço do Sul
  Brazil 31°22S 51°58W **95 C5**
São Luís *Brazil* 2°39S 44°15W **93 D10**
São Luís Gonzaga *Brazil* 28°25S 55°0W **95 B5**
São Marcos → *Brazil* 18°15S 47°37W **93 G9**
São Marcos, B. de *Brazil* 2°0S 44°0W **93 D10**
São Mateus *Brazil* 18°44S 39°50W **93 G11**
São Mateus do Sul *Brazil* 25°52S 50°23W **95 B5**
São Miguel *Azores* 37°47N 25°30W **52 a**
São Miguel do Oeste
  Brazil 26°45S 53°34W **95 B5**
São Nicolau *C. Verde Is.* 16°20N 24°20W **52 b**
São Paulo □ *Brazil* 22°0S 49°0W **95 A6**
São Paulo de Olivença
  Brazil 3°27S 68°48W **92 D5**
São Roque, C. de *Brazil* 5°30S 35°16W **93 E11**
São Sebastião, I. de
  Brazil 23°50S 45°18W **95 A6**
São Sebastião do Paraíso
  Brazil 20°54S 46°59W **95 A6**
São Tiago *C. Verde Is.* 15°0N 23°40W **52 b**
São Tomé
  São Tomé & Príncipe 0°10N 6°39E **50 F4**
São Tomé, C. de *Brazil* 22°0S 40°59W **95 A7**
São Tomé & Príncipe ■
  Africa 0°12N 6°39E **51 F4**
São Vicente *Brazil* 23°57S 46°23W **95 A6**
São Vicente *C. Verde Is.* 17°0N 25°0W **52 b**
São Vicente, C. de *Portugal* 37°0N 9°0W **21 D1**
Saona, I. *Dom. Rep.* 18°10N 68°40W **89 C6**
Saône → *France* 45°44N 4°50E **20 D6**
Saonek *Indonesia* 0°22S 130°55E **37 E8**
Sapam, Ao *Thailand* 8°0N 98°26E **39 a**
Saparua *Indonesia* 3°33S 128°40E **37 E7**
Sape *Indonesia* 8°34S 118°59E **37 F5**
Sapele *Nigeria* 5°50N 5°40E **52 G7**
Sapelo I. *U.S.A.* 31°25N 81°12W **85 F14**
Saposoa *Peru* 6°55S 76°45W **92 E3**
Sapphire *Australia* 23°28S 147°43E **62 C4**
Sappho *U.S.A.* 48°4N 124°16W **78 B2**
Sapporo *Japan* 43°0N 141°21E **28 C10**
Sapt Kosi → *Nepal* 26°32N 86°56E **43 F12**
Sapudi *Indonesia* 7°6S 114°20E **37 G16**
Sapulpa *U.S.A.* 35°59N 96°5W **84 D6**
Saqqez *Iran* 36°15N 46°20E **46 B5**
Sar Dasht *Āzarbāyjān-e Gharbī,*
  Iran 36°9N 45°28E **46 B5**
Sar Dasht *Khuzestan, Iran* 32°32N 48°52E **47 C6**
Sar-e Pol □ *Afghan.* 36°20N 65°50E **40 B4**
Sar Gachīneh = Yāsūj
  Iran 30°31N 51°31E **47 D6**
Sar Planina *Macedonia* 42°0N 21°0E **23 C9**
Sara Buri = Saraburi
  Thailand 14°30N 100°55E **38 E3**
Saráb *Iran* 37°55N 47°40E **46 B5**
Sarābādī *Iraq* 33°1N 44°48E **46 C5**
Saraburi *Thailand* 14°30N 100°55E **38 E3**
Saradiya *India* 21°34N 70°2E **42 J4**
Saragossa = Zaragoza
  Spain 41°39N 0°53W **21 B5**
Saraguro *Ecuador* 3°35S 79°16W **92 D3**
Sarai Naurang *Pakistan* 32°50N 70°47E **42 C4**
Saraikela *India* 22°42N 85°56E **43 H11**
Saraipali *India* 21°20N 82°59E **44 D6**
Sarajevo *Bos.-H.* 43°52N 18°26E **23 C8**
Sarakhs = Sarahs
  Turkmenistan 36°32N 61°13E **47 B9**
Saran, Gunung *Indonesia* 0°30S 111°25E **36 E4**
Saranac Lake *U.S.A.* 44°20N 74°10W **83 B10**

Saranac Lakes *U.S.A.* 44°20N 74°28W **83 B10**
Sarandí del Yi *Uruguay* 33°18S 55°38W **95 C4**
Sarandí Grande *Uruguay* 33°44S 56°20W **94 C4**
Sarangani B. *Phil.* 6°0N 125°13E **37 C7**
Sarangani Is. *Phil.* 5°25N 125°25E **37 C7**
Sarangarh *India* 21°30N 83°5E **44 D6**
Saransk *Russia* 54°10N 45°10E **18 D8**
Sarapul *Russia* 56°28N 53°48E **18 C9**
Sarasota *U.S.A.* 27°20N 82°32W **85 H13**
Saratoga *Calif., U.S.A.* 37°16N 122°2W **78 H4**
Saratoga *Wyo., U.S.A.* 41°27N 106°49W **76 F10**
Saratoga △ *U.S.A.* 43°0N 73°38W **83 D11**
Saratoga L. *U.S.A.* 43°1N 73°44W **83 C11**
Saratoga Springs *U.S.A.* 43°5N 73°47W **83 C11**
Saratok *Malaysia* 1°55N 111°17E **36 D4**
Saratov *Russia* 51°30N 46°2E **19 D8**
Sarävän *Iran* 27°25N 62°15E **47 E9**
Saravane *Laos* 15°43N 106°25E **38 E6**
Sarawak □ *Malaysia* 2°0N 113°0E **36 D4**
Saray *Turkey* 41°26N 27°55E **23 D12**
Sarayköy *Turkey* 37°55N 28°54E **23 F13**
Sarbāz *Iran* 26°38N 61°19E **47 E9**
Sarbīsheh *Iran* 32°30N 59°40E **47 C8**
Sarda → *India* 27°21N 81°23E **43 F9**
Sardar Sarovar Dam
  India 21°50N 73°50E **44 D1**
Sardarshahr *India* 28°30N 74°29E **42 E6**
Sardegna □ *Italy* 40°0N 9°0E **22 D3**
Sardhana *India* 29°9N 77°39E **42 E7**
Sardinia = Sardegna □ *Italy* 40°0N 9°0E **22 D3**
Sardis *Turkey* 38°28N 27°58E **23 E12**
Sārdūīyeh = Dar Mazār
  Iran 29°14N 57°20E **47 D8**
Saren *Indonesia* 8°26S 115°34E **37 J18**
Sarera, G. of *Indonesia* 2°0S 135°0E **58 B6**
Sargasso Sea *Atl. Oc.* 27°0N 72°0W **66 G13**
Sargodha *Pakistan* 32°10N 72°40E **42 C5**
Sarh *Chad* 9°5N 18°23E **53 G9**
Sārī *Iran* 36°30N 53°4E **47 B7**
Saria *India* 21°38N 83°22E **43 J10**
Sariab *Pakistan* 30°6N 66°59E **42 D2**
Sarıgöl *Turkey* 38°14N 28°41E **23 E13**
Sarikei *Malaysia* 2°8N 111°30E **36 D4**
Sarila *India* 25°46N 79°41E **43 G8**
Sarina *Australia* 21°22S 149°13E **62 C4**
Sarita *U.S.A.* 27°13N 97°47W **84 H6**
Sariwŏn *N. Korea* 38°31N 125°46E **33 E13**
Sarju → *India* 27°21N 81°23E **43 F9**
Sark *U.K.* 49°25N 2°22W **13 H5**
Sarkari Tala *India* 27°39N 70°52E **42 F4**
Şarköy *Turkey* 40°36N 27°6E **23 D12**
Sarlat-la-Canéda *France* 44°54N 1°13E **20 D4**
Sarmi *Indonesia* 1°49S 138°44E **37 E9**
Sarmiento *Argentina* 45°35S 69°5W **96 F3**
Särna *Sweden* 61°41N 13°8E **8 F15**
Sarnia *Canada* 42°58N 82°23W **82 D2**
Sarolangun *Indonesia* 2°19S 102°42E **36 E2**
Saronikos Kolpos *Greece* 37°45N 23°45E **23 F10**
Saros Körfezi *Turkey* 40°30N 26°15E **23 D12**
Sarpsborg *Norway* 59°16N 11°7E **9 G14**
Sarqan *Kazakhstan* 45°24N 79°55E **30 B4**
Sarre = Saar → *Europe* 49°41N 6°32E **15 E6**
Sarreguemines *France* 49°5N 7°4E **20 B7**
Sartell *U.S.A.* 45°37N 94°12W **80 C6**
Sarthe → *France* 47°33N 0°31W **20 C3**
Saruna → *Pakistan* 26°31N 67°7E **42 F2**
Sarvar *India* 26°4N 75°0E **42 F6**
Sarvestān *Iran* 29°20N 53°10E **47 D7**
Sary-Tash *Kyrgyzstan* 39°44N 73°15E **26 F8**
Saryshaghan *Kazakhstan* 46°12N 73°38E **26 E8**
Sarykolab *Russia* 71°55N 114°1E **27 B12**
Saslaya △ *Nic.* 13°45N 85°4W **88 D2**
Sasolburg *S. Africa* 26°46S 27°49E **57 D4**
Sasovo *Russia* 54°25N 41°55E **18 D7**
Sassandra *Ivory C.* 4°55N 6°8W **52 H4**
Sassandra → *Ivory C.* 4°58N 6°5W **52 H4**
Sássari *Italy* 40°43N 8°34E **22 D3**
Sassie *Australia* 10°2S 142°51E **62 a**
Sassnitz *Germany* 54°29N 13°39E **16 A7**
Sassuolo *Italy* 44°33N 10°47E **22 B4**
Sastamala *Finland* 61°20N 22°54E **8 F20**
Sasvad *India* 18°20N 74°2E **44 E2**
Sasyk, Ozero *Ukraine* 45°45N 29°40E **17 F15**
Sata-Misaki *Japan* 31°0N 130°40E **29 J5**
Satadougou *Mali* 12°25N 11°25W **52 F3**
Satakunta □ *Finland* 61°45N 23°0E **8 F20**
Satara *India* 17°44N 73°58E **44 F1**
Satara *S. Africa* 24°29S 31°47E **57 B5**
Satbarwa *India* 23°55N 84°16E **43 H11**
Satevó *Mexico* 27°57N 106°7W **86 B3**
Satilla → *U.S.A.* 30°59N 81°29W **85 F14**
Satka *Russia* 55°3N 59°1E **18 C10**
Satmala Hills *Andhra Pradesh,*
  India 19°45N 78°45E **44 E4**
Satmala Hills *Maharashtra,*
  India 20°15N 74°40E **44 D2**
Satna *India* 24°35N 80°50E **43 G9**
Sátoraljaújhely *Hungary* 48°25N 21°41E **17 D11**
Satpura △ *India* 22°40N 78°15E **42 H8**
Satpura Ra. *India* 21°25N 76°10E **44 D3**
Satsuma-Sendai *Japan* 31°50N 130°20E **29 J5**
Satsuna-Shotō *Japan* 30°0N 130°0E **29 K5**
Sattahip *Thailand* 12°41N 100°54E **38 F3**
Sattenapalle *India* 16°25N 80°6E **45 F5**
Satu Mare *Romania* 47°46N 22°55E **17 E12**
Satui *Indonesia* 3°50S 115°27E **36 E5**
Satun *Thailand* 6°43N 100°2E **39 J3**
Satupa'itea *Samoa* 13°45S 172°18W **59 b**
Saturnina → *Brazil* 12°15S 58°10W **92 F7**
Sauce *Argentina* 30°5S 58°46W **94 C4**
Sauceda *Mexico* 25°46N 101°19W **86 B4**

Saucillo *Mexico* 28°1N 105°17W **86 B3**
Sauda *Norway* 59°40N 6°20E **9 G12**
Sauðarkrókur *Iceland* 65°45N 19°40W **8 D4**
Saudi Arabia ■ *Asia* 26°0N 44°0E **46 B3**
Sauerland *Germany* 51°12N 7°59E **16 C4**
Saugeen → *Canada* 44°30N 81°22W **82 B3**
Saugerties *U.S.A.* 42°5N 73°57W **83 D11**
Saugus *U.S.A.* 34°25N 118°32W **79 L8**
Sauk Centre *U.S.A.* 45°44N 94°57W **80 C6**
Sauk Rapids *U.S.A.* 45°35N 94°10W **80 C6**
Sault Ste. Marie *Canada* 46°30N 84°20W **72 C3**
Sault Ste. Marie *U.S.A.* 46°30N 84°21W **81 B11**
Saumlaki *Indonesia* 7°55S 131°20E **37 F8**
Saumur *France* 47°15N 0°5W **20 C3**
Saundatti *India* 15°47N 75°7E **45 G2**
Saunders, C. *N.Z.* 45°53S 170°45E **59 F3**
Saunders I. *Antarctica* 57°48S 26°28W **5 B1**
Saunders Pt. *Australia* 27°52S 125°38E **61 E4**
Savá *Honduras* 15°32N 86°15W **88 C2**
Sava → *Serbia* 44°50N 20°26E **23 B9**
Savage *U.S.A.* 47°27N 104°21W **76 C11**
Savage I. = Niue ☑
  Pac. Oc. 19°2S 169°54W **65 J11**
Savage River *Australia* 41°31S 145°14E **63 G4**
Savai'i *Samoa* 13°28S 172°24W **59 b**
Savalou *Benin* 7°57N 1°58E **52 G6**
Savane *U.S.A.* 42°5N 90°8W **80 D8**
Savanna-la-Mar *Jamaica* 18°10N 78°10W **88 a**
Savannah *Ga., U.S.A.* 32°5N 81°6W **85 E14**
Savannah *Mo., U.S.A.* 39°56N 94°50W **80 F6**
Savannah *Tenn., U.S.A.* 35°14N 88°15W **85 D10**
Savannah → *U.S.A.* 32°2N 80°53W **85 E14**
Savannakhet *Laos* 16°30N 104°49E **38 D5**
Savant L. *Canada* 50°16N 90°44W **72 B1**
Savant Lake *Canada* 50°14N 90°40W **72 B1**
Savantvadi *India* 15°55N 73°54E **45 G1**
Savanur *India* 14°59N 75°21E **45 G2**
Savarkundla = Kundla
  India 21°21N 71°25E **42 J4**
Savda *India* 21°9N 75°56E **44 D2**
Save → *Mozam.* 21°16S 34°0E **57 B5**
Sāveh *Iran* 35°2N 50°20E **47 C6**
Savelugu *Ghana* 9°38N 0°54W **52 G5**
Savo *Finland* 62°45N 27°30E **8 E22**
Savoie □ *France* 45°26N 6°25E **20 D7**
Savolax = Savo *Finland* 62°45N 27°30E **8 E22**
Savona *Italy* 44°17N 8°30E **20 D8**
Savona *U.S.A.* 42°17N 77°13W **82 D7**
Savonlinna *Finland* 61°52N 28°53E **8 F23**
Savoy = Savoie □ *France* 45°26N 6°25E **20 D7**
Savur *Turkey* 37°34N 40°53E **46 B4**
Savusavu *Fiji* 16°34S 179°15E **59 a**
Savusavu B. *Fiji* 16°45S 179°15E **59 a**
Sawahlunto *Indonesia* 0°40S 100°52E **36 E2**
Sawai *Indonesia* 3°0S 129°5E **37 E7**
Sawai Madhopur *India* 26°0N 76°25E **42 G7**
Sawaleke *Fiji* 17°59S 179°18E **59 a**
Sawang Daen Din
  Thailand 17°28N 103°28E **38 D4**
Sawankhalok *Thailand* 17°19N 99°50E **38 D2**
Sawara *Japan* 35°55N 140°30E **29 G10**
Sawatch Range *U.S.A.* 39°0N 106°30W **76 G10**
Sawel Mt. *U.K.* 54°50N 7°2W **10 B4**
Sawi *Thailand* 10°14N 99°5E **39 G2**
Sawu *Indonesia* 10°35S 121°50E **37 F6**
Sawu Sea *Indonesia* 9°30S 121°50E **37 F6**
Saxby → *Australia* 18°25S 140°53E **62 B3**
Saxmundham *U.K.* 52°13N 1°30E **13 E9**
Saxony = Sachsen □
  Germany 50°55N 13°10E **16 C7**
Saxony, Lower = Niedersachsen □
  Germany 52°50N 9°0E **16 B5**
Saxton *U.S.A.* 40°13N 78°15W **82 F6**
Sayabec *Canada* 48°35N 67°41W **73 C6**
Sayaboury *Laos* 19°15N 101°45E **38 C3**
Sayán *Peru* 11°8S 77°12W **92 F3**
Sayan, Vostochnyy *Russia* 54°0N 96°0E **27 D10**
Sayan, Zapadnyy *Russia* 52°30N 94°0E **30 A7**
Sayanogorsk *Russia* 53°5N 91°23E **27 D10**
Saydā *Lebanon* 33°35N 35°25E **48 B4**
Sayhandulaan = Öldziyt
  Mongolia 44°40N 109°1E **32 B5**
Sayḩūt *Yemen* 15°12N 51°10E **49 D5**
Saylac *Somalia* 11°21N 43°30E **49 E3**
Saynshand = Buyant-Uhaa
  Mongolia 44°55N 110°11E **32 B6**
Sayre *Okla., U.S.A.* 35°18N 99°38W **84 D5**
Sayre *Pa., U.S.A.* 41°59N 76°32W **83 E8**
Sayreville *U.S.A.* 40°28N 74°22W **83 F10**
Sayula *Mexico* 19°52N 103°36W **86 D4**
Sayward *Canada* 50°21N 125°55W **70 C3**
Sazanit *Albania* 40°30N 19°20E **23 D8**
Sázava → *Czech Rep.* 49°53N 14°24E **16 D8**
Sazin *Pakistan* 35°35N 73°30E **43 B5**
Scafell Pike *U.K.* 54°27N 3°14W **12 C4**
Scalloway *U.K.* 60°9N 1°17W **11 A7**
Scalpay *U.K.* 57°18N 6°0W **11 D3**
Scandia *Canada* 50°20N 112°2W **70 C6**
Scandicci *Italy* 43°45N 11°11E **22 C4**
Scapa Flow *U.K.* 58°53N 3°3W **11 C5**
Scappoose *U.S.A.* 45°45N 122°53W **78 E4**
Scarba *U.K.* 56°11N 5°43W **11 E3**
Scarborough
  Trin. & Tob. 11°11N 60°42W **93 J16**
Scarborough *U.K.* 54°17N 0°24W **12 C7**
Scariff I. *Ireland* 51°44N 10°15W **10 E1**
Scarp *U.K.* 58°1N 7°8W **11 C1**
Scebeli = Shabeelle →
  Somalia 2°0N 44°0E **49 G3**
Schaffhausen *Switz.* 47°42N 8°39E **20 C8**
Schagen *Neths.* 52°49N 4°48E **15 B4**
Schaghticoke *U.S.A.* 42°54N 73°35W **83 D11**
Schefferville *Canada* 54°48N 66°50W **73 B6**
Schelde → *Belgium* 51°15N 4°16E **15 C4**
Schell Creek Ra. *U.S.A.* 39°25N 114°40W **76 G6**

Schellsburg *U.S.A.* 40°3N 78°39W **82 F6**
Schenectady *U.S.A.* 42°49N 73°57W **83 D11**
Schenevus *U.S.A.* 42°33N 74°50W **83 D10**
Schiedam *Neths.* 51°55N 4°25E **15 C4**
Schiermonnikoog *Neths.* 53°30N 6°15E **15 A6**
Schiermonnikoog △
  Neths. 53°30N 6°15E **15 A6**
Schio *Italy* 45°43N 11°21E **22 B4**
Schleswig *Germany* 54°31N 9°34E **16 A5**
Schleswig-Holstein □
  Germany 54°30N 9°30E **16 A5**
Schœlcher *Martinique* 14°36N 61°7W **88 c**
Schoharie *U.S.A.* 42°40N 74°19W **83 D10**
Schoharie Cr. → *U.S.A.* 42°57N 74°18W **83 D10**
Schokland *Neths.* 52°38N 5°46E **15 B5**
Scholls *U.S.A.* 45°24N 122°56W **78 E4**
Schouten I. *Australia* 42°20S 148°20E **63 G4**
Schouten Is. = Supiori
  Indonesia 1°0S 136°0E **37 E9**
Schouwen *Neths.* 51°43N 3°45E **15 C3**
Schreiber *Canada* 48°45N 87°20W **72 C2**
Schroffenstein *Namibia* 27°11S 18°42E **56 C2**
Schroon Lake *U.S.A.* 43°50N 73°46W **83 C11**
Schuler *Canada* 50°20N 110°6W **71 C6**
Schumacher *Canada* 48°30N 81°16W **72 C3**
Schurz *U.S.A.* 38°57N 118°49W **76 G4**
Schuyler *U.S.A.* 41°27N 97°4W **80 E5**
Schuylerville *U.S.A.* 43°6N 73°35W **83 C11**
Schuylkill → *U.S.A.* 39°53N 75°12W **83 G9**
Schuylkill Haven *U.S.A.* 40°37N 76°11W **83 F8**
Schwäbische Alb *Germany* 48°20N 9°30E **16 D5**
Schwaner, Pegunungan
  Indonesia 1°0S 112°30E **36 E4**
Schwarzrand *Namibia* 25°37S 16°50E **56 C2**
Schwarzwald *Germany* 48°30N 8°20E **16 D5**
Schwatka Mts. *U.S.A.* 67°20N 156°30W **74 B8**
Schwedt *Germany* 53°3N 14°16E **16 B8**
Schweinfurt *Germany* 50°3N 10°14E **16 C6**
Schweizer-Reneke
  S. Africa 27°11S 25°18E **56 C4**
Schwenningen = Villingen-
  Schwenningen *Germany* 48°3N 8°26E **16 D5**
Schwerin *Germany* 53°36N 11°22E **16 B6**
Schwyz *Switz.* 47°2N 8°39E **20 C8**
Sciacca *Italy* 37°31N 13°3E **22 F5**
Scilla *Italy* 38°15N 15°43E **22 E6**
Scilly, Isles of *U.K.* 49°56N 6°22W **13 H1**
Scioto → *U.S.A.* 38°44N 83°1W **81 F12**
Scituate *U.S.A.* 42°12N 70°44W **83 D14**
Scobey *U.S.A.* 48°47N 105°25W **76 B11**
Scone *Australia* 32°5S 150°52E **63 E5**
Scone *U.K.* 56°25N 3°24W **11 E5**
Scoresbysund = Ittoqqortoormiit
  Greenland 70°20N 23°0W **4 B6**
Scotia *Calif., U.S.A.* 40°29N 124°6W **76 F1**
Scotia *N.Y., U.S.A.* 42°50N 73°58W **83 D11**
Scotia Sea *Antarctica* 56°5S 56°0W **5 B18**
Scotland *Canada* 43°1N 80°22W **82 C4**
Scotland □ *U.K.* 57°0N 4°0W **11 E5**
Scott *Antarctica* 77°0S 166°45E **5 D11**
Scott, C. *Australia* 13°30S 129°49E **60 B4**
Scott City *U.S.A.* 38°29N 100°54W **80 F4**
Scott Glacier *Antarctica* 66°15S 100°5E **5 C8**
Scott I. *Antarctica* 67°0S 179°0E **5 C11**
Scott Is. *Canada* 50°48N 128°40W **70 C3**
Scott L. *Canada* 59°55N 106°18W **71 B7**
Scott Reef *Australia* 14°0S 121°50E **60 B3**
Scottburgh *S. Africa* 30°15S 30°47E **57 D5**
Scottdale *U.S.A.* 40°6N 79°35W **82 F5**
Scottish Borders □ *U.K.* 55°35N 2°50W **11 F6**
Scotts Valley *U.S.A.* 37°3N 122°1W **78 H4**
Scottsbluff *U.S.A.* 41°52N 103°40W **80 E2**
Scottsboro *U.S.A.* 34°40N 86°2W **85 D11**
Scottsburg *U.S.A.* 38°41N 85°47W **81 F11**
Scottsdale *Australia* 41°9S 147°31E **63 G4**
Scottsdale *U.S.A.* 33°40N 111°53W **77 K8**
Scottsville *Ky., U.S.A.* 36°45N 86°11W **80 G10**
Scottsville *N.Y., U.S.A.* 43°2N 77°47W **82 C7**
Scottville *U.S.A.* 43°58N 86°17W **80 D10**
Scranton *U.S.A.* 41°25N 75°40W **83 E9**
Scugog, L. *Canada* 44°10N 78°55W **82 B6**
Scunthorpe *U.K.* 53°36N 0°39W **12 D7**
Scutari = Shkodër *Albania* 42°4N 19°32E **23 C8**
Sea Is. *U.S.A.* 31°30N 81°7W **85 F14**
Seabrook, L. *Australia* 30°55S 119°40E **61 F2**
Seaford *U.K.* 50°47N 0°7E **13 G8**
Seaford *U.S.A.* 38°39N 75°37W **81 F16**
Seaforth *Australia* 20°55S 148°57E **62 b**
Seaforth *Canada* 43°35N 81°25W **82 C3**
Seaforth, L. *U.K.* 57°52N 6°36W **11 D2**
Seaham *U.K.* 54°50N 1°20W **12 C6**
Seagraves *U.S.A.* 32°57N 102°34W **84 E3**
Seal → *Canada* 59°4N 94°48W **71 B10**
Seal L. *Canada* 54°20N 61°30W **73 B7**
Sealy *U.S.A.* 29°47N 96°9W **84 G6**
Searchlight *U.S.A.* 35°28N 114°55W **79 K12**
Searcy *U.S.A.* 35°15N 91°44W **84 D9**
Searles L. *U.S.A.* 35°44N 117°21W **79 K9**
Seascale *U.K.* 54°24N 3°29W **12 C4**
Seaside *Calif., U.S.A.* 36°37N 121°50W **78 J5**
Seaside *Oreg., U.S.A.* 46°0N 123°56W **78 E3**
Seaspray *Australia* 38°25S 147°15E **63 F4**
Seattle *U.S.A.* 47°36N 122°19W **78 C4**
Seattle-Tacoma Int. ✈ (SEA)
  U.S.A. 47°27N 122°18W **78 C4**
Seba *Indonesia* 10°29S 121°50E **60 B3**
Sebago L. *U.S.A.* 43°52N 70°34W **83 C14**
Sebago Lake *U.S.A.* 43°51N 70°34W **83 C14**
Sebastián Vizcaíno, B.
  Mexico 28°0N 114°30W **86 B2**
Sebastopol = Sevastopol
  Ukraine 44°35N 33°30E **19 F5**
Sebastopol *U.S.A.* 38°24N 122°49W **78 G4**
Sebewaing *U.S.A.* 43°44N 83°27W **82 C1**
Sebha = Sabhā *Libya* 27°9N 14°29E **53 C8**
Şebinkarahisar *Turkey* 40°22N 38°28E **19 F6**

Sebring *Fla., U.S.A.* 27°30N 81°27W **85 H14**
Sebring *Ohio, U.S.A.* 40°55N 81°2W **82 F3**
Sebringville *Canada* 43°24N 81°4W **82 C3**
Sebta = Ceuta *N. Afr.* 35°52N 5°18W **21 E3**
Sebuku *Indonesia* 3°30S 116°25E **36 E5**
Sechelt *Canada* 49°25N 123°42W **70 D4**
Sechura, Desierto de *Peru* 6°0S 80°30W **92 E2**
Secretary I. *N.Z.* 45°15S 166°56E **59 F1**
Secunderabad *India* 17°28N 78°30E **44 F4**
Security *U.S.A.* 38°45N 104°45W **76 G2**
Sedalia *U.S.A.* 38°42N 93°14W **80 F7**
Sedan *India* 17°11N 77°17E **44 F3**
Sedan *France* 49°43N 4°57E **20 B6**
Sedan *U.S.A.* 37°8N 96°11W **80 G5**
Sedbergh *U.K.* 54°20N 2°31W **12 C5**
Seddon *N.Z.* 41°40S 174°7E **59 D5**
Seddonville *N.Z.* 41°33S 172°1E **59 D4**
Sedé Boqér *Israel* 30°52N 34°47E **48 E3**
Sedeh *Fārs, Iran* 30°45N 52°11E **47 D7**
Sedeh *Khorāsān, Iran* 33°20N 59°14E **47 C8**
Sederot *Israel* 31°32N 34°37E **48 D3**
Sédhiou *Senegal* 12°44N 15°30W **52 F2**
Sedley *Canada* 50°10N 104°0W **71 C8**
Sedona *U.S.A.* 34°52N 111°46W **77 J8**
Sedova, Pik *Russia* 73°29N 54°58E **26 B6**
Sedro-Woolley *U.S.A.* 48°30N 122°14W **78 B4**
Seeheim *Namibia* 26°50S 17°45E **56 C2**
Seeis *Namibia* 22°29S 17°39E **56 B2**
Seekoei → *S. Africa* 30°18S 25°1E **56 E4**
Seeley's Bay *Canada* 44°29N 76°14W **83 B8**
Seferihisar *Turkey* 38°10N 26°50E **23 E12**
Sefophe *Botswana* 22°11S 27°58E **57 B4**
Seg-ozero *Russia* 63°20N 33°46E **18 B5**
Segamat *Malaysia* 2°30N 102°50E **39 L4**
Segesta *Italy* 37°56N 12°50E **22 F5**
Seget *Indonesia* 1°24S 130°58E **37 E8**
Segezha *Russia* 63°44N 34°19E **18 B5**
Ségou *Mali* 13°30N 6°16W **52 F4**
Segovia = Coco →
  Cent. Amer. 15°0N 83°8W **88 D3**
Segovia *Spain* 40°57N 4°10W **21 B3**
Segre → *Spain* 41°40N 0°43E **21 B6**
Seguam I. *U.S.A.* 52°19N 172°30W **74 E5**
Séguéla *Ivory C.* 7°55N 6°40W **52 G4**
Seguin *U.S.A.* 29°34N 97°58W **84 G6**
Segundo → *Argentina* 30°53S 62°44W **94 C3**
Segura → *Spain* 38°3N 0°44W **21 C5**
Seh Konj, Kūh-e *Iran* 30°6N 57°30E **47 D8**
Seh Qal'eh *Iran* 33°40N 58°24E **47 C8**
Sehitwa *Botswana* 20°30S 22°30E **56 B3**
Sehlabathebe △ *Lesotho* 29°53S 29°7E **57 C4**
Sehore *India* 23°10N 77°5E **42 H7**
Sehwan *Pakistan* 26°28N 67°53E **42 F2**
Seikan Tunnel *Japan* 41°28N 140°10E **28 D10**
Seil *U.K.* 56°18N 5°38W **11 E3**
Seiland *Norway* 70°25N 23°15E **8 A20**
Seiling *U.S.A.* 36°9N 98°56W **84 C5**
Seinäjoki *Finland* 62°40N 22°51E **8 E20**
Seine → *France* 49°26N 0°26E **20 B4**
Seistan = Sīstān *Asia* 30°50N 61°0E **47 D9**
Seistan, Daryācheh-ye = Sīstān,
  Daryācheh-ye *Iran* 31°0N 61°0E **47 D9**
Sekayu *Indonesia* 2°51S 103°51E **36 E2**
Sekondi-Takoradi *Ghana* 4°58N 1°45W **52 H5**
Sekuma *Botswana* 24°36S 23°50E **56 C3**
Selah *U.S.A.* 46°39N 120°32W **76 C3**
Selama *Malaysia* 5°12N 100°42E **39 K3**
Selangor □ *Malaysia* 3°10N 101°30E **39 L3**
Selaru *Indonesia* 8°9S 131°0E **37 F8**
Selatan, Selat *Malaysia* 5°15N 100°20E **39 c**
Selawik L. *U.S.A.* 66°30N 160°45W **74 B7**
Selby *U.K.* 53°47N 1°5W **12 D6**
Selby *U.S.A.* 45°31N 100°2W **80 C3**
Selçuk *Turkey* 37°56N 27°22E **23 F12**
Sele → *Italy* 40°29N 14°56E **22 D6**
Selebi-Phikwe *Botswana* 21°58S 27°48E **57 B4**
Selemdzha → *Russia* 51°42N 128°53E **27 D13**
Selenga = Selenge Mörön →
  Asia 52°16N 106°16E **30 A10**
Selenge Mörön → *Asia* 52°16N 106°16E **30 A10**
Seletan, Tanjung
  Indonesia 4°10S 114°40E **36 E4**
Sélibabi *Mauritania* 15°10N 12°15W **52 E3**
Seligman *U.S.A.* 35°20N 112°53W **77 J7**
Selima *Sudan* 21°22N 29°19E **53 D11**
Selinda Spillway
  Botswana 18°35S 23°10E **56 A3**
Selinsgrove *U.S.A.* 40°48N 76°52W **82 F8**
Selkirk *Man., Canada* 50°10N 96°55W **71 C9**
Selkirk *Ont., Canada* 42°49N 79°56W **82 D5**
Selkirk *U.K.* 55°33N 2°50W **11 F6**
Selkirk I. = Horse I.
  Canada 53°20N 99°6W **71 C9**
Selkirk Mts. *Canada* 51°15N 117°40W **68 C8**
Sellafield *U.K.* 54°25N 3°29W **12 C4**
Sells *U.S.A.* 31°55N 111°53W **77 L8**
Selma *Ala., U.S.A.* 32°25N 87°1W **85 E11**
Selma *Calif., U.S.A.* 36°34N 119°37W **78 J7**
Selma *N.C., U.S.A.* 35°32N 78°17W **85 D15**
Selmer *U.S.A.* 35°10N 88°36W **85 D10**
Selpele *Indonesia* 0°1S 130°5E **37 E8**
Seltso *Russia* 53°22N 34°4E **18 D5**
Selu *Indonesia* 7°32S 130°55E **37 F8**
Selva *Argentina* 29°50S 62°0W **94 B3**
Selva Lancandona = Montes
  Azules △ *Mexico* 16°21N 91°3W **87 D6**
Selvagens, Ilhas *Madeira* 30°5N 15°55W **52 B2**
Selvas *Brazil* 6°30S 67°0W **92 E5**
Selwyn L. *Canada* 60°0N 104°30W **71 A8**
Selwyn Mts. *Canada* 63°0N 130°0W **68 B6**
Selwyn Ra. *Australia* 21°10S 140°0E **62 C3**
Seman → *Albania* 40°47N 19°30E **23 D8**
Semarang *Indonesia* 7°0S 110°26E **37 G14**
Semarapura = Klungkung
  Indonesia 8°32S 115°24E **37 K18**
Sembung *Indonesia* 8°28S 115°11E **37 J18**

Semey *Kazakhstan* 50°30N 80°10E **30** A5
Seminoe Res. *U.S.A.* 42°9N 106°55W **76** E10
Seminole *Okla., U.S.A.* 35°14N 96°41W **84** D6
Seminole *Tex., U.S.A.* 32°43N 102°39W **84** E3
Seminole Draw → *U.S.A.* 32°27N 102°20W **84** E3
Semipalatinsk = Semey *Kazakhstan* 50°30N 80°10E **30** A5
Semirara Is. *Phil.* 12°0N 121°20E **37** B6
Semisopochnoi I. *U.S.A.* 51°55N 179°36E **74** E3
Semitau *Indonesia* 0°29N 111°57E **36** D4
Semmering *P. Austria* 47°41N 15°45E **16** E8
Semnān *Iran* 35°40N 53°23E **47** C7
Semnān □ *Iran* 36°0N 54°0E **47** C7
Semporna *Malaysia* 4°30N 118°33E **37** D5
Semuda *Indonesia* 2°51S 112°58E **36** E4
Sen → *Cambodia* 12°32N 104°28E **38** F5
Senā *Iran* 28°27N 51°36E **47** D6
Sena Madureira *Brazil* 9°5S 68°45W **92** E5
Senador Pompeu *Brazil* 5°40S 39°20W **93** E11
Senang, Pulau *Singapore* 1°11N 103°52E **39** d
Senanga *Zambia* 16°7S 23°16E **55** H4
Senatobia *U.S.A.* 34°37N 89°58W **85** D10
Sendai = Satsuma-Sendai *Japan* 31°50N 130°20E **29** J5
Sendai *Japan* 38°15N 140°53E **28** E10
Sendai-Wan *Japan* 38°15N 141°0E **28** E10
Sendhwa *India* 21°41N 75°6E **42** J6
Sendurjana *India* 21°32N 78°17E **44** D4
Seneca *U.S.A.* 34°41N 82°57W **85** D13
Seneca Falls *U.S.A.* 42°55N 76°48W **83** D8
Seneca L. *U.S.A.* 42°40N 76°54W **82** D8
Senecaville L. *U.S.A.* 39°55N 81°25W **82** G3
Senegal ■ *W. Afr.* 14°30N 14°30W **52** F3
Sénégal → *W. Afr.* 15°48N 16°32W **52** E2
Senegambia *Africa* 12°45N 12°0W **50** E2
Senekal *S. Africa* 28°20S 27°36E **57** C4
Senge Khambab = Indus → *Pakistan* 24°20N 67°47E **42** G2
Senggigi *Indonesia* 8°29S 116°2E **37** J19
Senhor-do-Bonfim *Brazil* 10°30S 40°10W **93** F10
Senigállia *Italy* 43°43N 13°13E **22** C5
Senj *Croatia* 45°0N 14°58E **16** F8
Senja *Norway* 69°25N 17°30E **8** B17
Senkaku-Shotō *E. China Sea* 25°45N 123°30E **29** M1
Senlis *France* 49°13N 2°35E **20** B5
Senmonorom *Cambodia* 12°27N 107°12E **38** F6
Senneterre *Canada* 48°25N 77°15W **72** C4
Seno *Laos* 16°35N 104°50E **38** D5
Senqu = Orange → *S. Africa* 28°41S 16°28E **56** C2
Sens *France* 48°11N 3°15E **20** B5
Senta *Serbia* 45°55N 20°3E **23** B9
Sentinel *U.S.A.* 32°52N 113°13W **77** K7
Senwabarana *S. Africa* 23°17S 29°7E **57** B4
Seo de Urgel = La Seu d'Urgell *Spain* 42°22N 1°23E **21** A6
Seogwipo *S. Korea* 33°13N 126°34E **33** H14
Seohara *India* 29°15N 78°33E **43** E8
Seonath → *India* 21°44N 82°28E **43** J10
Seondha *India* 26°9N 78°48E **43** F8
Seongnam *S. Korea* 37°26N 127°8E **33** F14
Seoni *India* 22°5N 79°30E **43** H8
Seoni Malwa *India* 22°27N 77°28E **42** H8
Seonsan *S. Korea* 36°14N 128°17E **33** F15
Seoriuarayan *India* 21°45N 82°34E **44** D6
Seosan *S. Korea* 36°47N 126°27E **33** F14
Sepīdān *Iran* 30°20N 52°5E **47** D7
Sepo-ri *N. Korea* 38°57N 127°25E **33** E14
Sepone *Laos* 16°45N 106°13E **38** D6
Sept-Îles *Canada* 50°13N 66°22W **73** B6
Sequim *U.S.A.* 48°5N 123°6W **78** B3
Sequoia △ *U.S.A.* 36°30N 118°30W **78** J8
Seraing *Belgium* 50°35N 5°32E **15** D5
Seram *Indonesia* 3°10S 129°0E **37** E7
Seram Sea *Indonesia* 2°30S 128°30E **37** E7
Serampore = Shrirampur *India* 22°44N 88°21E **43** H13
Serang *Indonesia* 6°8S 106°10E **37** G12
Serasan *Indonesia* 2°29N 109°4E **36** D3
Serbia ■ *Europe* 43°20N 20°0E **23** B9
Serdar *Turkmenistan* 39°4N 56°23E **47** B8
Serdobsk *Russia* 52°28N 44°10E **18** D7
Seremban *Malaysia* 2°43N 101°53E **39** L3
Serengeti Plain *Tanzania* 2°40S 35°0E **54** E7
Sereth = Siret → *Romania* 45°24N 28°1E **17** F14
Sergeya Kirova, Ostrova *Russia* 77°30N 89°0E **27** B10
Sergino *Russia* 62°25N 65°12E **26** C7
Sergipe □ *Brazil* 10°30S 37°30W **93** F11
Sergiyev Posad *Russia* 56°20N 38°10E **18** C6
Serhetabat *Turkmenistan* 35°20N 62°18E **47** C9
Seria *Brunei* 4°37N 114°23E **36** D4
Serian *Malaysia* 1°10N 110°31E **36** D4
Serifos *Greece* 37°9N 24°30E **23** F11
Sérigny → *Canada* 56°47N 66°0W **73** A6
Seringapatam Reef *Australia* 13°38S 122°5E **60** B3
Seririt *Indonesia* 8°12S 114°56E **37** J17
Serkout *Algeria* 23°56N 6°47E **52** D7
Sermata *Indonesia* 8°15S 128°50E **37** F7
Sermersuaq *Greenland* 79°30N 62°0W **69** B19
Serov *Russia* 59°29N 60°35E **18** C11
Serowe *Botswana* 22°25S 26°43E **56** B4
Serpentine Lakes *Australia* 28°30S 129°10E **61** E4
Serpent's Mouth = Sierpe, Bocas de la *Venezuela* 10°0N 61°30W **93** L15
Serpukhov *Russia* 54°55N 37°28E **18** D6
Serra do Navio *Brazil* 0°59N 52°3W **93** C8
Serranía San Luís △ *Paraguay* 22°35S 57°22W **94** A4
Serranía San Rafael △ *Paraguay* 26°30S 56°0W **95** B4
Serres *Greece* 41°5N 23°31E **23** D10
Serrezuela *Argentina* 30°40S 65°20W **94** C2

Serrinha *Brazil* 11°39S 39°0W **93** F11
Sertanópolis *Brazil* 23°4S 51°2W **95** A5
Sêrtar *China* 32°20N 100°41E **34** A3
Serua *Indonesia* 6°18S 130°1E **37** F8
Serui *Indonesia* 1°53S 136°10E **37** E9
Serule *Botswana* 21°57S 27°20E **56** B4
Sesepe *Indonesia* 1°30S 127°59E **37** E7
Sesfontein *Namibia* 19°7S 13°39E **56** A1
Sesheke *Zambia* 17°29S 24°13E **56** A3
Setana *Japan* 42°26N 139°51E **28** C9
Sète *France* 43°25N 3°42E **20** E5
Sete Lagoas *Brazil* 19°27S 44°16W **93** G10
Seti → *Nepal* 28°59N 81°8E **43** E9
Sétif *Algeria* 36°9N 5°26E **52** A7
Seto *Japan* 35°14N 137°6E **29** G8
Setonaikai *Japan* 34°20N 133°30E **29** G6
Setonaikai △ *Japan* 34°15N 133°15E **29** G6
Settat *Morocco* 33°0N 7°40W **52** B4
Setting L. *Canada* 55°0N 98°38W **71** C9
Settle *U.K.* 54°5N 2°16W **12** C5
Settlement, The *Br. Virgin Is.* 18°43N 64°22W **89** e
Settlers *S. Africa* 25°2S 28°30E **57** C4
Setúbal *Portugal* 38°30N 8°58W **21** C1
Setúbal, B. de *Portugal* 38°40N 8°56W **21** C1
Seul, Lac *Canada* 50°20N 92°30W **72** B1
Sevan, Ozero = Sevana Lich *Armenia* 40°30N 45°20E **46** A5
Sevana Lich *Armenia* 40°30N 45°20E **46** A5
Sevastopol *Ukraine* 44°35N 33°30E **19** F5
Seven Sisters *Canada* 54°56N 128°10W **70** C3
Severn → *Canada* 56°2N 87°36W **72** A2
Severn → *U.K.* 51°35N 2°40W **13** F5
Severnaya Zemlya *Russia* 79°0N 100°0E **27** B11
Severnyye Uvaly *Russia* 60°0N 50°0E **18** C8
Severo-Kurilsk *Russia* 50°40N 156°8E **27** D16
Severo-Yeniseyskiy *Russia* 60°22N 93°1E **27** C10
Severo-Zapadnyy □ *Russia* 65°0N 40°0E **26** C4
Severobaykalsk *Russia* 55°39N 109°19E **27** D11
Severodvinsk *Russia* 64°27N 39°58E **18** B6
Severomorsk *Russia* 69°5N 33°27E **8** B25
Severouralsk *Russia* 60°9N 59°57E **18** B10
Seversk *Russia* 56°36N 84°49E **26** D9
Sevier → *U.S.A.* 39°4N 113°6W **76** G7
Sevier Desert *U.S.A.* 39°40N 112°45W **76** G7
Sevier L. *U.S.A.* 38°54N 113°9W **76** G7
Sevilla *Spain* 37°23N 5°58W **21** D2
Seville = Sevilla *Spain* 37°23N 5°58W **21** D2
Sevlievo *Bulgaria* 43°2N 25°6E **23** C11
Sewani *India* 28°58N 75°39E **42** E6
Seward *Alaska, U.S.A.* 60°7N 149°27W **68** E2
Seward *Nebr., U.S.A.* 40°55N 97°6W **80** E5
Seward *Pa., U.S.A.* 40°25N 79°1W **82** F5
Seward Peninsula *U.S.A.* 65°30N 166°0W **74** B6
Sewell *Chile* 34°10S 70°23W **94** C1
Sewer *Indonesia* 5°53S 134°40E **37** F8
Sewickley *U.S.A.* 40°32N 80°12W **82** F4
Sexsmith *Canada* 55°21N 118°47W **70** B5
Seychelles ■ *Ind. Oc.* 5°0S 56°0E **55** b
Seyðisfjörður *Iceland* 65°16N 13°57W **8** D7
Seydişehir *Turkey* 37°25N 31°51E **19** G5
Seydvān *Iran* 38°34N 45°2E **46** B5
Seyhan → *Turkey* 36°43N 34°53E **46** B2
Seym → *Ukraine* 51°27N 32°34E **19** D5
Seymour *Australia* 37°2S 145°10E **63** F4
Seymour *S. Africa* 32°33S 26°46E **57** D4
Seymour *Conn., U.S.A.* 41°24N 73°4W **83** E11
Seymour *Ind., U.S.A.* 38°58N 85°53W **81** F11
Seymour *Tex., U.S.A.* 33°35N 99°16W **84** E5
Sfântu Gheorghe *Romania* 45°52N 25°48E **17** F13
Sfax *Tunisia* 34°49N 10°48E **53** B8
Sha Tau Kok *China* 22°33N 114°13E **31** a
Sha Xi → *China* 26°35N 118°0E **35** D12
Sha Xian *China* 26°23N 117°45E **35** D11
Shaanxi □ *China* 35°0N 109°0E **32** G5
Shaba = Katanga □ *Dem. Rep. of the Congo* 8°0S 25°0E **54** F5
Shabeelle → *Somalia* 2°0N 44°0E **49** G3
Shabogamo L. *Canada* 53°15N 66°30W **73** B6
Shabunda *Dem. Rep. of the Congo* 2°40S 27°16E **54** E5
Shackleton Fracture Zone *S. Ocean* 60°0S 60°0W **5** B18
Shackleton Ice Shelf *Antarctica* 66°0S 100°0E **5** C8
Shackleton Inlet *Antarctica* 83°0S 160°0E **5** E11
Shādegān *Iran* 30°40N 48°38E **47** D6
Shadi *China* 26°7N 114°47E **35** D10
Shadi *India* 33°24N 77°14E **43** C7
Shadrinsk *Russia* 56°5N 63°32E **26** D7
Shadyside *U.S.A.* 39°58N 80°45W **82** G4
Shafter *U.S.A.* 35°30N 119°16W **79** K7
Shaftesbury *U.K.* 51°0N 2°11W **13** F5
Shaftsbury *U.S.A.* 43°0N 73°11W **83** D11
Shagram *India* 36°24N 72°20E **43** A5
Shah Alam *Malaysia* 3°5N 101°32E **39** L3
Shah Alizai *Pakistan* 29°25N 66°33E **42** E2
Shah Bunder *Pakistan* 24°13N 67°56E **42** G2
Shahabad *Karnataka, India* 17°10N 76°54E **44** F3
Shahabad *Punjab, India* 30°10N 76°55E **42** D7
Shahabad *Raj., India* 25°15N 77°11E **42** G7
Shahabad *Ut. P., India* 27°36N 79°56E **43** F8
Shahada *India* 21°33N 74°30E **44** D2
Shahadpur *Pakistan* 25°55N 68°35E **42** G3
Shahapur *India* 15°50N 74°34E **45** G2
Shahbā' *Syria* 32°52N 36°38E **48** C5
Shahdād *Iran* 30°30N 57°40E **47** D8
Shahdād, Namakzār-e *Iran* 30°20N 58°20E **47** D8
Shahdadkot *Pakistan* 27°50N 67°55E **42** F2
Shahdol *India* 23°19N 81°26E **43** H9
Shahe *China* 37°0N 114°32E **32** F8
Shahganj *India* 26°3N 82°44E **43** F10
Shahgarh *India* 27°15N 69°50E **42** F3
Shāhīn Shahr *Iran* 32°49N 51°32E **47** C6
Shahjahanpur *India* 27°54N 79°57E **43** F8

Shahpur = Salmās *Iran* 38°11N 44°47E **46** B5
Shahpur *Karnataka, India* 16°40N 76°48E **44** F3
Shahpur *Mad. P., India* 22°12N 77°58E **42** H7
Shahpur *Baluchistan, Pakistan* 28°46N 68°27E **42** E3
Shahpur *Punjab, Pakistan* 32°17N 72°26E **42** C5
Shahpur Chakar *Pakistan* 26°9N 68°39E **42** F3
Shahpura *Mad. P., India* 23°10N 80°45E **43** H9
Shahpura *Raj., India* 25°38N 74°56E **42** G6
Shahr-e Bābak *Iran* 30°7N 55°9E **47** D7
Shahr-e Kord *Iran* 32°15N 50°55E **47** C6
Shāhrakht *Iran* 33°38N 60°16E **47** C9
Shāhrezā = Qomsheh *Iran* 32°0N 51°55E **47** D6
Shahrig *Pakistan* 30°15N 67°40E **42** D2
Shāhrūd = Emāmrūd *Iran* 36°30N 55°0E **47** B7
Shahukou *China* 40°20N 112°18E **32** D7
Shaikhabad *Afghan.* 34°2N 68°45E **42** B3
Shajapur *India* 23°27N 76°21E **42** H7
Shajing *China* 22°44N 113°48E **31** a
Shakargarh *Pakistan* 32°17N 75°10E **42** C6
Shakawe *Botswana* 18°28S 21°49E **56** A3
Shaker Heights *U.S.A.* 41°28N 81°32W **82** E3
Shakhtersk *Russia* 49°10N 142°8E **27** E15
Shakhty *Russia* 47°40N 40°16E **19** E7
Shakhunya *Russia* 57°40N 46°46E **18** C8
Shaki *Nigeria* 8°41N 3°21E **52** G6
Shakotan-Hantō *Japan* 43°10N 140°30E **28** C10
Shaksam Valley *Asia* 36°0N 76°20E **43** A7
Shallow Lake *Canada* 44°36N 81°5W **82** B3
Shalqar *Kazakhstan* 47°48N 59°39E **26** E6
Shaluli Shan *China* 30°40N 99°55E **34** B3
Shām *Iran* 26°39N 57°21E **47** E8
Shām, Bādiyat ash *Asia* 32°0N 40°0E **46** C3
Shamāl □ *Sinī □ Egypt* 30°30N 33°30E **48** E2
Shamattawa *Canada* 55°51N 92°5W **72** A1
Shamattawa → *Canada* 55°1N 85°23W **72** A2
Shamil *Iran* 27°30N 56°55E **47** E8
Shāmkūh *Iran* 35°47N 57°50E **47** C8
Shamli *India* 29°32N 77°18E **42** E7
Shammar, Jabal *Si. Arabia* 27°40N 41°0E **46** E4
Shamo = Gobi *Asia* 44°0N 110°0E **32** C6
Shamo, L. *Ethiopia* 5°45N 37°30E **49** F2
Shamokin *U.S.A.* 40°47N 76°34W **83** F8
Shamrock *Canada* 45°23N 76°50W **83** A8
Shamrock *U.S.A.* 35°13N 100°15W **84** D4
Shan □ *Burma* 21°30N 98°30E **41** J21
Shan Xian *China* 34°50N 116°5E **32** G9
Shanchengzhen *China* 42°20N 125°20E **33** C13
Shāndak *Iran* 28°28N 60°27E **47** D9
Shandan *China* 38°45N 101°15E **30** D9
Shandon *U.S.A.* 35°39N 120°23W **78** K6
Shandong □ *China* 36°0N 118°0E **33** G10
Shandong Bandao *China* 37°0N 121°0E **33** F11
Shandur Pass *Pakistan* 36°4N 72°31E **43** A5
Shang Xian = Shangzhou *China* 33°50N 109°58E **32** H5
Shangani *Zimbabwe* 19°41S 29°20E **57** A4
Shangani → *Zimbabwe* 18°41S 27°10E **55** H5
Shangbancheng *China* 40°50N 118°1E **33** D10
Shangchuan Dao *China* 21°40N 112°50E **35** G9
Shangdu *China* 41°30N 113°30E **32** D7
Shanggao *China* 28°17N 114°55E **35** C10
Shanghai Shi □ *China* 31°0N 121°30E **35** B13
Shanghang *China* 25°2N 116°23E **35** E11
Shanghe *China* 37°20N 117°10E **33** F9
Shanglin *China* 23°27N 108°33E **34** F7
Shangnan *China* 33°32N 110°50E **32** H6
Shangqiu *China* 34°26N 115°36E **32** G8
Shangrao *China* 28°25N 117°59E **35** C11
Shangri-La = Zhongdian *China* 27°48N 99°42E **34** D2
Shangshui *China* 33°32N 114°35E **32** H8
Shangsi *China* 22°8N 107°58E **34** F6
Shangyi *China* 41°4N 113°57E **32** D7
Shangyou *China* 25°48N 114°32E **35** E10
Shangyu *China* 30°3N 120°52E **35** B13
Shangzhou *China* 33°50N 109°58E **32** H5
Shanhetun *China* 44°33N 127°15E **33** B14
Shankou *China* 22°30N 113°55E **31** a
Shanklin *U.K.* 50°38N 1°11W **13** G6
Shannon *N.Z.* 40°33S 175°25E **59** D5
Shannon → *Ireland* 52°35N 9°30W **10** D2
Shannon × (SNN) *Ireland* 52°42N 8°57W **10** D3
Shannon, Mouth of the *Ireland* 52°30N 9°55W **10** D2
Shannon △ *Australia* 34°35S 116°25E **61** F2
Shannonbridge *Ireland* 53°17N 8°3W **10** C3
Shansi = Shanxi □ *China* 37°0N 112°0E **32** F7
Shantar, Ostrov Bolshoy *Russia* 55°9N 137°40E **27** D14
Shantipur *India* 23°17N 88°25E **43** H13
Shantou *China* 23°18N 116°40E **35** F11
Shantung = Shandong □ *China* 36°0N 118°0E **33** G10
Shanwei *China* 22°48N 115°22E **35** F10
Shanxi □ *China* 37°0N 112°0E **32** F7
Shanyang *China* 33°31N 109°55E **32** H5
Shanyin *China* 39°25N 112°56E **32** E7
Shaodong *China* 27°15N 111°43E **35** D8
Shaoguan *China* 24°48N 113°35E **35** E9
Shaoshan *China* 27°55N 112°33E **35** D9
Shaowu *China* 27°22N 117°28E **35** D11
Shaoxing *China* 30°0N 120°35E **35** C13
Shaoyang *Hunan, China* 26°59N 111°20E **35** D8
Shaoyang *Hunan, China* 27°14N 111°25E **35** D8
Shap *U.K.* 54°32N 2°40W **12** C5
Shapinsay *U.K.* 59°3N 2°51W **11** B6
Shaqra' *Si. Arabia* 25°15N 45°16E **46** E5
Sharafkhāneh *Iran* 38°11N 45°29E **46** B5
Sharavati → *India* 14°20N 74°40E **45** G2
Sharbot Lake *Canada* 44°46N 76°41W **83** B8
Shari *Japan* 43°55N 144°40E **28** C12
Sharjah = Ash Shāriqah *U.A.E.* 25°23N 55°26E **47** E7
Shark B. *Australia* 25°30S 113°32E **61** E1
Shark Bay △ *Australia* 25°15S 113°30E **61** E1
Sharm el Sheikh *Egypt* 27°53N 34°18E **53** C12
Sharon *Canada* 44°6N 79°26W **82** B5

Sharon *Mass., U.S.A.* 42°7N 71°11W **83** D13
Sharon *Pa., U.S.A.* 41°14N 80°31W **82** E4
Sharon Springs *Kans., U.S.A.* 38°54N 101°45W **80** F3
Sharon Springs *N.Y., U.S.A.* 42°48N 74°37W **83** D10
Sharp Pt. *Australia* 10°58S 142°43E **62** A3
Sharpe L. *Canada* 54°24N 93°40W **72** B1
Sharpsville *U.S.A.* 41°15N 80°29W **82** E4
Sharqi, Al Jabal ash *Lebanon* 33°40N 36°10E **48** B5
Sharya *Russia* 58°22N 45°20E **18** C8
Shashemene *Ethiopia* 7°13N 38°33E **49** F2
Shashi *Botswana* 21°15S 27°27E **57** A4
Shashi → *Africa* 21°14S 29°20E **57** A4
Shasta, Mt. *U.S.A.* 41°25N 122°12W **76** F2
Shasta L. *U.S.A.* 40°43N 122°25W **76** F2
Shatsky Rise *Pac. Oc.* 34°0N 157°0E **64** D7
Shatt al Arab *Asia* 29°57N 48°34E **47** D6
Shaunavon *Canada* 49°35N 108°25W **71** D7
Shaver L. *U.S.A.* 37°9N 119°18W **78** H7
Shawan *Iran* 37°9N 120°53E **33** F11
Shawanaga *Canada* 45°31N 80°17W **82** A4
Shawano *U.S.A.* 44°47N 88°36W **80** C9
Shawinigan *Canada* 46°35N 72°50W **72** C5
Shawmari, J. ash *Jordan* 30°35N 36°35E **48** E5
Shawnee *Canada* 35°20N 96°55W **84** D6
Shay Gap *Australia* 20°30S 120°10E **60** D3
Shayang *China* 30°42N 112°29E **35** B9
Shaybārā *Si. Arabia* 25°26N 36°47E **46** E3
Shaykh, J. ash *Lebanon* 33°25N 35°50E **48** B4
Shaykh Miskīn *Syria* 32°49N 36°9E **48** C5
Shaykh Sa'd *Iraq* 32°34N 46°17E **46** C5
Shāzand *Iran* 33°56N 49°24E **47** C6
Shchūchīnsk *Kazakhstan* 52°56N 70°12E **26** D8
She Xian *Anhui, China* 29°50N 118°25E **35** C12
She Xian *Hebei, China* 36°30N 113°40E **32** F7
Shebele = Shabeelle → *Somalia* 2°0N 44°0E **49** G3
Sheboygan *U.S.A.* 43°46N 87°45W **80** D10
Shediac *Canada* 46°14N 64°32W **73** C7
Sheelin, L. *Ireland* 53°48N 7°20W **10** C4
Sheenjek → *U.S.A.* 66°45N 144°33W **74** B11
Sheep Haven *Ireland* 55°11N 7°52W **10** A4
Sheep Range *U.S.A.* 36°35N 115°15W **79** J11
Sheerness *U.K.* 51°26N 0°47E **13** F8
Sheet Harbour *Canada* 44°56N 62°31W **73** D7
Sheffield *U.K.* 53°23N 1°28W **12** D6
Sheffield *Ala., U.S.A.* 34°46N 87°41W **85** D11
Sheffield *Mass., U.S.A.* 42°5N 73°21W **83** D11
Sheffield *Pa., U.S.A.* 41°42N 79°3W **82** E5
Shegaon *India* 20°48N 76°47E **44** D3
Shehong *China* 30°54N 105°18E **34** B5
Sheikhpura *India* 25°9N 85°53E **43** G11
Sheikhupura *Pakistan* 31°42N 73°58E **42** D5
Shekou *China* 22°30N 113°55E **31** a
Shelburne *N.S., Canada* 43°47N 65°20W **73** D6
Shelburne *Ont., Canada* 44°4N 80°15W **82** B4
Shelburne *U.S.A.* 44°23N 73°14W **83** B11
Shelburne B. *Australia* 11°50S 142°50E **62** A3
Shelburne Falls *U.S.A.* 42°36N 72°45W **83** D12
Shelby *Mich., U.S.A.* 43°37N 86°22W **80** D10
Shelby *Miss., U.S.A.* 33°57N 90°46W **85** E9
Shelby *Mont., U.S.A.* 48°30N 111°51W **76** B8
Shelby *N.C., U.S.A.* 35°17N 81°32W **85** D14
Shelby *Ohio, U.S.A.* 40°53N 82°40W **82** F2
Shelbyville *Ill., U.S.A.* 39°24N 88°48W **80** F9
Shelbyville *Ind., U.S.A.* 39°31N 85°47W **81** F11
Shelbyville *Ky., U.S.A.* 38°13N 85°14W **81** F11
Shelbyville *Tenn., U.S.A.* 35°29N 86°28W **85** D11
Sheldon *U.S.A.* 43°11N 95°51W **80** D6
Sheldrake *Canada* 50°20N 64°51W **73** B7
Shelikhova, Zaliv *Russia* 59°30N 157°0E **27** D16
Shelikof Strait *U.S.A.* 57°30N 155°0W **74** D9
Shell Lakes *Australia* 29°20S 127°30E **61** E4
Shellbrook *Canada* 53°13N 106°24W **71** C7
Shellharbour *Australia* 34°31S 150°51E **63** E5
Shelter I. *U.S.A.* 41°4N 72°20W **83** E12
Shelton *Conn., U.S.A.* 41°19N 73°5W **83** E11
Shelton *Wash., U.S.A.* 47°13N 123°6W **78** C3
Shen Xian *China* 36°15N 115°40E **32** F8
Shenandoah *Iowa, U.S.A.* 40°46N 95°22W **80** E6
Shenandoah *Pa., U.S.A.* 40°49N 76°12W **83** F8
Shenandoah → *U.S.A.* 39°19N 77°44W **81** F15
Shenandoah △ *U.S.A.* 38°35N 78°22W **81** F14
Shenchi *China* 39°8N 112°10E **32** E7
Shencottah *India* 8°59N 77°18E **45** K3
Shendam *Nigeria* 8°49N 9°30E **52** G7
Shendi *Sudan* 16°46N 33°22E **53** E12
Shendurni *India* 20°39N 75°36E **44** D2
Shengfang *China* 39°3N 116°42E **32** E9
Shengzhou *China* 29°35N 120°50E **35** C13
Shenjingzi *China* 44°40N 124°30E **33** B13
Shenmu *China* 38°50N 110°29E **32** E6
Shennongjia *China* 31°43N 110°44E **35** B8
Shenqiu *China* 33°25N 115°5E **32** H8
Shensi = Shaanxi □ *China* 35°0N 109°0E **32** G5
Shenyang *China* 41°48N 123°27E **33** D12
Shenzhen *China* 22°32N 114°5E **35** F10
Shenzhen Bao'an Int. × (SZX) *China* 22°41N 113°49E **31** a
Shenzhen Shuiku *China* 22°34N 114°8E **31** a
Shenzhen Wan *China* 22°27N 114°2E **31** a
Sheo *India* 26°11N 71°15E **42** F4
Sheopur Kalan *India* 25°40N 76°40E **42** G7
Shepetivka *Ukraine* 50°10N 27°10E **17** C14
Shepparton *Australia* 36°23S 145°26E **63** F4
Sheppey, I. of *U.K.* 51°25N 0°48E **13** F8
Shepton Mallet *U.K.* 51°11N 2°33W **13** F5
Sheqi *China* 33°12N 112°57E **32** H7
Sher Qila *Pakistan* 36°7N 74°2E **43** A6
Sherborne *U.K.* 50°57N 2°31W **13** G5
Sherbro I. *S. Leone* 7°30N 12°40W **52** G3
Sherbrooke *N.S., Canada* 45°8N 61°59W **73** C7
Sherbrooke *Qué., Canada* 45°28N 71°57W **83** A13

Sherburne *U.S.A.* 42°41N 75°30W **83** D9
Shergarh *India* 26°20N 72°18E **42** F5
Sherghati *India* 24°34N 84°47E **43** G11
Sheridan *Ark., U.S.A.* 34°19N 92°24W **84** D8
Sheridan *Wyo., U.S.A.* 44°48N 106°58W **76** D10
Sheringham *U.K.* 52°56N 1°13E **12** E9
Sherkin I. *Ireland* 51°28N 9°26W **10** E2
Sherkot *India* 29°22N 78°35E **43** E8
Sherlovaya Gora *Russia* 50°34N 116°15E **27** D12
Sherman *N.Y., U.S.A.* 42°9N 79°35W **82** D5
Sherman *Tex., U.S.A.* 33°38N 96°36W **84** E6
Sherpur *India* 25°34N 83°47E **43** G10
Sherridon *Canada* 55°8N 101°5W **71** B8
Shertallai = Cherthala *India* 9°42N 76°20E **45** K3
Sherwood Forest *U.K.* 53°6N 1°7W **12** D6
Sherwood Park *Canada* 53°31N 113°19W **70** C6
Sheslay → *Canada* 58°48N 132°5W **70** B2
Shethanei L. *Canada* 58°48N 97°50W **71** B9
Shetland □ *U.K.* 60°30N 1°30W **11** A7
Shetland Is. *U.K.* 60°30N 1°30W **11** A7
Shetrunji → *India* 21°19N 72°7E **42** J5
Sheung Shui *China* 22°31N 114°7E **31** a
Shevaroy Hills *India* 11°58N 78°12E **45** J4
Shevgaon *India* 19°21N 75°14E **44** E2
Shey-Phoksundo △ *Nepal* 29°30N 82°45E **43** E10
Sheyang *China* 33°48N 120°29E **33** H11
Sheyenne → *U.S.A.* 47°2N 96°50W **80** B5
Shiashkotan, Ostrov *Russia* 48°49N 154°6E **27** E16
Shibām *Yemen* 15°59N 48°36E **49** D4
Shibata *Japan* 37°57N 139°20E **28** F9
Shibecha *Japan* 43°17N 144°36E **28** C12
Shibetsu *Hokkaidō, Japan* 43°30N 145°10E **28** C12
Shibetsu *Hokkaidō, Japan* 44°10N 142°23E **28** B11
Shibing *China* 27°2N 108°7E **34** D7
Shibogama L. *Canada* 53°35N 88°15W **72** B2
Shibushi *Japan* 31°25N 131°8E **29** J5
Shicheng *China* 26°22N 116°20E **35** D11
Shickshinny *U.S.A.* 41°9N 76°9W **83** E8
Shickshock Mts. = Chic-Chocs, Mts. *Canada* 48°55N 66°0W **73** C6
Shidao *China* 36°50N 122°25E **33** F12
Shidian *China* 24°40N 99°5E **34** E2
Shido = Sanuki *Japan* 34°19N 134°10E **29** G7
Shiel, L. *U.K.* 56°48N 5°34W **11** E3
Shield, C. *Australia* 13°20S 136°20E **62** A2
Shieli *Kazakhstan* 44°20N 66°15E **26** E7
Shifang *China* 31°8N 104°18E **34** B5
Shiga □ *Japan* 35°20N 136°0E **29** G8
Shigu *China* 26°51N 99°56E **34** D2
Shiguaigou *China* 40°52N 110°15E **32** D6
Shihchiachuangi = Shijiazhuang *China* 38°2N 114°28E **32** E8
Shihezi *China* 44°15N 86°2E **30** C6
Shijiazhuang *China* 38°2N 114°28E **32** E8
Shijiu Hu *China* 31°25N 118°50E **35** B12
Shikarpur *India* 28°17N 78°7E **42** E8
Shikarpur *Pakistan* 27°57N 68°39E **42** F3
Shikohabad *India* 27°6N 78°36E **43** F8
Shikokuchō *Japan* 34°1N 133°34E **29** G6
Shikoku □ *Japan* 33°30N 133°30E **29** H6
Shikoku-Sanchi *Japan* 33°30N 133°30E **29** H6
Shikotan, Ostrov *Asia* 43°47N 146°44E **27** E15
Shikotsu-Ko *Japan* 42°45N 141°25E **28** C10
Shikotsu-Tōya △ *Japan* 44°4N 145°8E **28** C12
Shiliguri *India* 26°45N 88°25E **41** F16
Shiliu = Changjiang *China* 19°12N 108°55E **38** C7
Shilka *Russia* 52°0N 115°55E **27** D12
Shilka → *Russia* 53°20N 121°26E **27** D13
Shillelagh *Ireland* 52°45N 6°32W **10** D5
Shillington *U.S.A.* 40°18N 75°58W **83** F9
Shillong *India* 25°35N 91°53E **41** G17
Shilo *West Bank* 32°4N 35°18E **48** C4
Shilong *China* 23°5N 113°52E **35** F9
Shilou *China* 37°0N 110°48E **32** F6
Shimabara *Japan* 32°48N 130°20E **29** H5
Shimada *Japan* 34°49N 138°10E **29** G9
Shimane □ *Japan* 35°0N 132°30E **29** G6
Shimanovsk *Russia* 52°15N 127°30E **27** D13
Shimanto *Kōchi, Japan* 33°12N 133°9E **29** H6
Shimanto *Kōchi, Japan* 32°59N 132°56E **29** H6
Shimbiris *Somalia* 10°44N 47°14E **49** E4
Shimen *China* 29°35N 111°20E **35** C8
Shimenjie *China* 29°29N 116°48E **35** C11
Shimian *China* 29°17N 102°23E **34** C4
Shimizu *Japan* 35°0N 138°30E **29** G9
Shimla *India* 31°2N 77°9E **42** D7
Shimodate *Japan* 36°20N 139°55E **29** F9
Shimoga *India* 13°57N 75°32E **45** H2
Shimokita-Hantō *Japan* 41°20N 141°0E **28** D10
Shimonoseki *Japan* 33°58N 130°55E **29** H5
Shimpuru Rapids *Namibia* 17°45S 19°55E **56** A2
Shimsha → *India* 13°15N 77°10E **45** H3
Shin, L. *U.K.* 58°5N 4°30W **11** C4
Shinan *China* 22°44N 109°53E **34** F7
Shinano-Gawa → *Japan* 36°50N 138°30E **29** F9
Shināṣ *Oman* 24°46N 56°28E **47** E8
Shīndand *Afghan.* 33°12N 62°8E **40** C3
Shinglehouse *U.S.A.* 41°58N 78°12W **82** E6
Shingū *Japan* 33°40N 135°55E **29** H7
Shingwidzi *S. Africa* 23°5S 31°25E **57** B5
Shinjō *Japan* 38°46N 140°18E **28** E10
Shinkolobwe *Dem. Rep. of the Congo* 11°10S 26°40E **54** G5
Shinshār *Syria* 34°36N 36°43E **48** A5
Shinyanga *Tanzania* 3°45S 33°27E **54** E6
Shio-no-Misaki *Japan* 33°25N 135°45E **29** H7
Shiogama *Japan* 38°19N 141°1E **28** E10
Shiojiri *Japan* 36°6N 137°58E **29** F8
Shipchenski Prokhod *Bulgaria* 42°45N 25°15E **23** C11
Shiphoirt, L. = Seaforth, L. *U.K.* 57°52N 6°36W **11** D2

Shiping *China* 23°45N 102°23E **34** F4
Shippagan *Canada* 47°45N 64°45W **73** C7
Shippensburg *U.S.A.* 40°3N 77°31W **82** F7
Shippenville *U.S.A.* 41°15N 79°28W **82** E5
Shiprock *U.S.A.* 36°47N 108°41W **77** H9
Shiqian *China* 27°32N 108°13E **34** D7
Shiqma, N. → *Israel* 31°37N 34°30E **48** D3
Shiquan *China* 33°5N 108°15E **34** A7
Shiquan He = Indus →
   Pakistan 24°20N 67°47E **42** G2
Shīr Kūh *Iran* 31°39N 54°3E **47** D7
Shiragami-Misaki
   Japan 41°24N 140°12E **28** D10
Shirakawa *Fukushima,*
   Japan 37°7N 140°13E **29** F10
Shirakawa *Gifu, Japan* 36°17N 136°56E **29** F8
Shirane-San *Gumma,*
   Japan 36°48N 139°22E **29** F9
Shirane-San *Yamanashi,*
   Japan 35°42N 138°9E **29** G9
Shiraoi *Japan* 42°33N 141°21E **28** C10
Shīrāz *Iran* 29°42N 52°30E **47** D7
Shire → *Africa* 17°42S 35°19E **55** H7
Shiren *China* 41°57N 126°34E **33** D14
Shiretoko △ *Japan* 44°15N 145°15E **28** B12
Shiretoko-Misaki *Japan* 44°21N 145°20E **28** B12
Shirinab → *Pakistan* 30°15N 66°28E **42** D2
Shiriya-Zaki *Japan* 41°25N 141°30E **28** D10
Shiroishi *Japan* 38°0N 140°37E **28** F10
Shirol *India* 16°47N 74°41E **44** F2
Shirpur *India* 21°21N 74°57E **44** D2
Shirshov Ridge *Pac. Oc.* 58°0N 170°0E **64** B8
Shīrvān *Iran* 37°30N 57°50E **47** B8
Shirwa, L. = Chilwa, L.
   Malawi 15°15S 35°40E **55** H7
Shishaldin Volcano
   U.S.A. 54°45N 163°58W **74** E7
Shishi *China* 24°44N 118°37E **35** E12
Shishou *China* 29°38N 112°22E **35** C9
Shitai *China* 30°12N 117°25E **35** B11
Shivamogga = Shimoga
   India 13°57N 75°32E **45** H2
Shivpuri *India* 25°26N 77°42E **42** G7
Shixian *China* 43°5N 129°50E **33** C15
Shixing *China* 24°46N 114°5E **35** E10
Shiyan *Guangdong, China* 22°42N 113°56E **31** a
Shiyan *Hubei, China* 32°35N 110°45E **35** A8
Shiyan Shuiku *China* 22°42N 113°54E **31** a
Shizhu *China* 29°58N 108°7E **34** C7
Shizong *China* 24°50N 104°0E **34** E5
Shizuishan *China* 39°15N 106°50E **32** E4
Shizuoka *Japan* 34°57N 138°24E **29** G9
Shizuoka □ *Japan* 35°15N 138°40E **29** G9
Shklov = Shklow
   Belarus 54°16N 30°15E **17** A16
Shklow *Belarus* 54°16N 30°15E **17** A16
Shkodër *Albania* 42°4N 19°32E **23** C8
Shkumbini → *Albania* 41°2N 19°31E **23** D8
Shmidta, Ostrov *Russia* 81°0N 91°0E **27** A10
Shō-Gawa → *Japan* 36°47N 137°4E **29** F8
Shoal L. *Canada* 49°33N 95°1W **71** D9
Shoal Lake *Canada* 50°30N 100°35W **71** C8
Shōdo-Shima *Japan* 34°30N 134°15E **29** G7
Sholapur = Solapur *India* 17°43N 75°56E **44** F2
Shōmrōn *West Bank* 32°15N 35°13E **48** C4
Shoranur *India* 10°46N 76°19E **45** J3
Shorapur *India* 16°31N 76°48E **45** F3
Shoreham *U.S.A.* 43°53N 73°18W **83** C11
Shoreham by Sea *U.K.* 50°50N 0°16W **13** G7
Shori → *Pakistan* 28°29N 69°44E **42** E3
Shorkot *Pakistan* 30°50N 72°0E **42** D4
Shorkot Road *Pakistan* 30°47N 72°15E **42** D5
Shortt's I. *India* 20°47N 87°4E **44** D8
Shoshone *Calif., U.S.A.* 35°58N 116°16W **79** K10
Shoshone *Idaho, U.S.A.* 42°56N 114°25W **76** E6
Shoshone L. *U.S.A.* 44°22N 110°43W **76** D8
Shoshone Mts. *U.S.A.* 39°20N 117°25W **76** G5
Shoshong *Botswana* 22°56S 26°31E **56** B4
Shoshoni *U.S.A.* 43°14N 108°7W **76** E9
Shou Xian *China* 32°37N 116°42E **35** A11
Shouchang *China* 29°18N 119°12E **35** C12
Shouguang *China* 37°52N 118°45E **33** F10
Shouning *China* 27°27N 119°31E **35** D12
Shouyang *China* 37°54N 113°8E **32** F7
Show Low *U.S.A.* 34°15N 110°2W **77** J8
Shqipëria = Albania ■
   Europe 41°0N 20°0E **23** D9
Shreveport *U.S.A.* 32°31N 93°45W **84** E8
Shrewsbury *U.K.* 52°43N 2°45W **13** E5
Shri Mohangarh *India* 27°17N 71°18E **42** F4
Shrigonda *India* 18°37N 74°41E **44** E2
Shrirampur *India* 22°44N 88°21E **43** H13
Shropshire □ *U.K.* 52°36N 2°45W **13** E5
Shū *Kazakhstan* 43°36N 73°42E **26** E8
Shuangbai *China* 24°42N 101°38E **34** E3
Shuangcheng *China* 45°20N 126°15E **33** B14
Shuangfeng *China* 27°29N 112°11E **35** D9
Shuanggou *China* 34°2N 117°30E **33** G9
Shuangjiang *China* 23°26N 99°58E **34** F2
Shuangliao *China* 43°29N 123°30E **33** C12
Shuangshanzi *China* 40°20N 119°8E **33** D10
Shuangyang *China* 43°28N 125°40E **33** C13
Shuangyashan *China* 46°28N 131°5E **31** B15
Shucheng *China* 31°28N 116°57E **35** B11
Shuiji *China* 27°13N 118°20E **35** D12
Shujalpur *India* 23°18N 76°46E **42** H7
Shukpa Kunzang *India* 34°22N 78°22E **43** B8
Shulan *China* 44°28N 127°0E **33** B14
Shule *China* 39°25N 76°3E **30** D4
Shule He → *China* 40°20N 92°50E **30** C7
Shumagin Is. *U.S.A.* 55°7N 160°30W **74** D7
Shumen *Bulgaria* 43°18N 26°55E **23** C12
Shumikha *Russia* 55°10N 63°15E **26** D7
Shūnān *Japan* 34°3N 131°50E **29** G5
Shunchang *China* 26°54N 117°48E **35** D11
Shunde *China* 22°42N 113°14E **35** F9
Shungnak *U.S.A.* 66°52N 157°9W **74** B8

Shuozhou *China* 39°20N 112°33E **32** E7
Shuqrā' *Yemen* 13°22N 45°44E **49** E4
Shūr → *Fārs, Iran* 28°30N 55°0E **47** D7
Shūr → *Kermān, Iran* 30°52N 57°37E **47** D8
Shūr → *Yazd, Iran* 31°45N 55°15E **47** D7
Shūr Āb *Iran* 34°23N 51°11E **47** C6
Shūr Gaz *Iran* 29°10N 59°20E **47** D8
Shūrāb *Iran* 33°43N 56°29E **47** C8
Shūrjestān *Iran* 31°24N 52°25E **47** D7
Shurugwi *Zimbabwe* 19°40S 30°0E **55** H6
Shūsf *Iran* 31°50N 60°5E **47** D9
Shūshtar *Iran* 32°0N 48°50E **47** D6
Shuswap L. *Canada* 50°55N 119°3W **70** C5
Shute Harbour △
   Australia 20°17S 148°47E **62** b
Shuyang *China* 34°10N 118°42E **33** G10
Shūzū *Iran* 29°52N 54°30E **47** D7
Shwebo *Burma* 22°30N 95°45E **41** H19
Shwegu *Burma* 24°15N 96°26E **41** G20
Shweli → *Burma* 23°45N 96°45E **41** H20
Shyamnagar *India* 13°21N 92°57E **45** H11
Shymkent *Kazakhstan* 42°18N 69°36E **26** E7
Shyok *India* 34°13N 78°12E **43** B8
Shyok → *Pakistan* 35°13N 75°53E **43** B6
Si Kiang = Xi Jiang →
   China 22°5N 113°20E **35** F9
Si Lanna △ *Thailand* 19°17N 99°12E **38** C2
Si Nakarin Res. *Thailand* 14°35N 99°0E **38** E2
Si-ngan = Xi'an *China* 34°15N 109°0E **32** G5
Si Phangnga *Thailand* 9°8N 98°29E **39** H2
Si Prachan *Thailand* 14°37N 100°9E **38** E3
Si Racha *Thailand* 13°10N 100°48E **38** F3
Si Sa Ket *Thailand* 15°8N 104°23E **38** E5
Siachen Glacier *Asia* 35°20N 77°30E **43** B7
Siahan Range *Pakistan* 27°30N 64°40E **40** F4
Siak Sri Indrapura
   Indonesia 0°51N 102°0E **36** D2
Sialkot *Pakistan* 32°32N 74°30E **42** C6
Siam = Thailand ■ *Asia* 16°0N 102°0E **38** E4
Sian = Xi'an *China* 34°15N 109°0E **32** G5
Sian Ka'an △ *Mexico* 19°35N 87°40W **87** D7
Siantan *Indonesia* 3°10N 106°15E **36** D3
Siāreh *Iran* 28°5N 60°14E **47** D9
Siargao I. *Phil.* 9°52N 126°3E **37** C7
Siasi *Phil.* 5°34N 120°50E **37** C6
Siau *Indonesia* 2°50N 125°25E **37** D7
Šiauliai *Lithuania* 55°56N 23°15E **9** J20
Siavonga *Zambia* 16°33S 28°42E **57** A4
Sibâi, Gebel el *Egypt* 25°45N 34°10E **46** E3
Sibang *Indonesia* 8°34S 115°13E **37** K18
Sibay *Russia* 52°42N 58°39E **18** D10
Sibayi, L. *S. Africa* 27°20S 32°45E **57** D5
Šibenik *Croatia* 43°48N 15°54E **22** C6
Siberia = Sibirskiy □
   Russia 58°0N 90°0E **27** D10
Siberia *Russia* 60°0N 100°0E **24** B12
Siberut *Indonesia* 1°30S 99°0E **36** E1
Sibi *Pakistan* 29°30N 67°54E **42** E2
Sibirskiy □ *Russia* 58°0N 90°0E **27** D10
Sibirtsevo *Russia* 44°12N 132°26E **28** B5
Sibiti *Congo* 3°38S 13°19E **54** E2
Sibiu *Romania* 45°45N 24°9E **17** F13
Sibley *U.S.A.* 43°24N 95°45W **80** D6
Sibolga *Indonesia* 1°42N 98°45E **36** D1
Siborongborong *Indonesia* 2°13N 98°58E **39** L2
Sibsagar *India* 27°0N 94°36E **41** F19
Sibu *Malaysia* 2°18N 111°49E **36** D4
Sibuco *Phil.* 7°20N 122°10E **37** C6
Sibuguey B. *Phil.* 7°50N 122°45E **37** C6
Sibut *C.A.R.* 5°46N 19°10E **54** C3
Sibutu *Phil.* 4°45N 119°30E **37** D5
Sibutu Passage *E. Indies* 4°50N 120°0E **37** D6
Sibuyan I. *Phil.* 12°25N 122°40E **37** B6
Sibuyan Sea *Phil.* 12°30N 122°20E **37** B6
Sicamous *Canada* 50°49N 119°0W **70** C5
Sichon *Thailand* 9°0N 99°54E **39** H2
Sichuan □ *China* 30°30N 103°0E **34** B5
Sichuan Pendi *China* 31°0N 105°0E **34** B5
Sicilia *Italy* 37°30N 14°30E **22** F6
Sicily = Sicilia *Italy* 37°30N 14°30E **22** F6
Sicily, Str. of *Medit. S.* 37°35N 11°56E **22** F4
Sico → *Honduras* 15°58N 84°58W **88** C3
Sicuani *Peru* 14°21S 71°10W **92** F4
Siddapur *India* 14°20N 74°53E **45** G2
Siddhapur *India* 23°56N 72°25E **42** H5
Siddipet *India* 18°5N 78°51E **44** E4
Sidhauli *India* 27°17N 80°50E **43** F9
Sidhi *India* 24°25N 81°53E **43** G9
Sidi-bel-Abbès *Algeria* 35°13N 0°39W **52** A5
Sidi Ifni *Morocco* 29°29N 10°12W **52** C3
Sidikalang *Indonesia* 2°45N 98°19E **39** L2
Sidlaw Hills *U.K.* 56°32N 3°2W **11** E5
Sidley, Mt. *Antarctica* 77°2S 126°2W **5** D14
Sidmouth *U.K.* 50°40N 3°15W **13** G4
Sidmouth, C. *Australia* 13°25S 143°36E **62** A3
Sidney *Canada* 48°39N 123°24W **78** B3
Sidney *Mont., U.S.A.* 47°43N 104°9W **76** C11
Sidney *N.Y., U.S.A.* 42°19N 75°24W **83** D9
Sidney *Nebr., U.S.A.* 41°8N 102°59W **80** E2
Sidney *Ohio, U.S.A.* 40°17N 84°9W **81** E11
Sidney Lanier, L. *U.S.A.* 34°10N 84°4W **85** D12
Sidoarjo *Indonesia* 7°27S 112°43E **37** G15
Sidon = Saydā *Lebanon* 33°35N 35°25E **48** B4
Sidra = Surt *Libya* 31°11N 16°39E **53** B9
Sidra, G. of = Surt, Khalīj
   Libya 31°40N 18°30E **53** B9
Siedlce *Poland* 52°10N 22°20E **17** B12
Sieg → *Germany* 50°46N 7°6E **16** C4
Siegen *Germany* 50°51N 8°0E **16** C5
Siem Pang *Cambodia* 14°7N 106°23E **38** E6
Siem Reap = Siemreab
   Cambodia 13°20N 103°52E **38** F4
Siemreab *Cambodia* 13°20N 103°52E **38** F4
Siena *Italy* 43°19N 11°21E **22** C4
Sieradz *Poland* 51°37N 18°41E **17** C10
Sierpe, Bocas de la
   Venezuela 10°0N 61°30W **93** L15

Sierra Blanca *U.S.A.* 31°11N 105°22W **84** F2
Sierra Blanca Peak
   U.S.A. 33°23N 105°49W **77** K11
Sierra City *U.S.A.* 39°34N 120°38W **78** F6
Sierra Colorada *Argentina* 40°35S 67°50W **96** E3
Sierra de Agalta △
   Honduras 15°1N 85°48W **88** C2
Sierra de Bahoruco △
   Dom. Rep. 18°10N 71°25W **89** C5
Sierra de La Culata △
   Venezuela 8°45N 71°10W **89** E5
Sierra de Lancandón △
   Guatemala 16°59N 90°23W **88** C1
Sierra de las Quijadas △
   Argentina 32°29S 67°5W **94** C2
Sierra de San Luis △
   Venezuela 11°20N 69°43W **89** D6
Sierra de San Pedro Mártir △
   Mexico 31°10N 115°30W **86** A1
Sierra Gorda *Chile* 22°50S 69°15W **94** A2
Sierra Leone ■ *W. Afr.* 9°0N 12°0W **52** G3
Sierra Madre *Mexico* 16°0N 93°0W **87** D6
Sierra Madre Occidental
   Mexico 27°0N 107°0W **86** B3
Sierra Madre Oriental
   Mexico 25°0N 100°0W **86** C5
Sierra Mojada *Mexico* 27°18N 103°41W **86** B4
Sierra Nevada *Spain* 37°3N 3°15W **21** D4
Sierra Nevada *U.S.A.* 39°0N 120°30W **78** H8
Sierra Nevada △
   Venezuela 8°35N 70°45W **89** E5
Sierra Nevada de Santa Marta △
   Colombia 10°56N 73°36W **89** D5
Sierra Vista *U.S.A.* 31°33N 110°18W **77** L8
Sierraville *U.S.A.* 39°36N 120°22W **78** F6
Sifnos *Greece* 37°0N 24°45E **23** F11
Sifton *Canada* 51°21N 100°8W **71** C8
Sifton Pass *Canada* 57°52N 126°15W **70** B3
Sig *Algeria* 35°32N 0°12W **52** A5
Sigatoka *Fiji* 18°8S 177°32E **59** a
Sighetu-Marmaţiei
   Romania 47°57N 23°52E **17** E12
Sighişoara *Romania* 46°12N 24°50E **17** E13
Sigiriya *Sri Lanka* 7°57N 80°45E **45** L5
Sigli *Indonesia* 5°25N 96°0E **36** C1
Siglufjörður *Iceland* 66°12N 18°55W **8** C4
Signal de Botrang *Belgium* 50°29N 6°4E **15** D6
Signal Pk. *U.S.A.* 33°20N 114°2W **79** M12
Signy I. *Antarctica* 60°43S 45°36W **5** C18
Sigsig *Ecuador* 3°0S 78°50W **92** D3
Sigüenza *Spain* 41°3N 2°40W **21** B4
Siguiri *Guinea* 11°31N 9°10W **52** F4
Sigulda *Latvia* 57°10N 24°55E **9** H21
Siguniangshan *China* 31°15N 103°10E **34** B4
Sihawa *India* 20°19N 81°55E **44** D5
Sihong *China* 33°27N 118°16E **33** H10
Sihora *India* 23°29N 80°6E **43** H9
Sihui *China* 23°20N 112°40E **35** F9
Siikajoki → *Finland* 64°50N 24°43E **8** D21
Siilinjärvi *Finland* 63°4N 27°39E **8** E22
Sika *India* 22°26N 69°47E **42** H3
Sikanni Chief →
   Canada 57°47N 122°15W **70** B4
Sikao *Thailand* 7°34N 99°21E **39** J2
Sikar *India* 27°33N 75°10E **42** F6
Sikasso *Mali* 11°18N 5°35W **52** F4
Sikeston *U.S.A.* 36°53N 89°35W **80** G9
Sikhote Alin, Khrebet
   Russia 45°0N 136°0E **28** B8
Sikhote Alin Ra. = Sikhote Alin,
   Khrebet *Russia* 45°0N 136°0E **28** B8
Sikinos *Greece* 36°40N 25°8E **23** F11
Sikkim □ *India* 27°50N 88°30E **41** F16
Sil → *Spain* 42°27N 7°43W **21** A2
Silacayoapan *Mexico* 17°30N 98°9W **87** D5
Silawad *India* 21°54N 74°54E **42** J6
Silchar *India* 24°49N 92°48E **41** G18
Silent Valley △ *India* 11°10N 76°20E **45** J3
Siler City *U.S.A.* 35°44N 79°28W **85** D15
Sileru → *India* 17°49N 81°24E **44** F5
Silesia = Śląsk *Poland* 51°0N 16°30E **16** C9
Silgarhi Doti *Nepal* 29°15N 81°0E **43** E9
Silghat *India* 26°35N 93°0E **41** F18
Silhouette *Seychelles* 4°29S 55°12E **55** b
Siliana *India* 22°0S 130°46E **60** D5
Silifke *Turkey* 36°22N 33°58E **46** B2
Siliguri = Shiliguri *India* 26°45N 88°25E **41** F16
Siling Co *China* 31°50N 89°20E **30** E6
Silistra *Bulgaria* 44°6N 27°19E **23** B12
Silivri *Turkey* 41°4N 28°14E **23** D13
Siljan *Sweden* 60°55N 14°45E **8** F16
Silkeborg *Denmark* 56°10N 9°32E **9** H13
Silkwood *Australia* 17°45S 146°2E **62** B4
Sillajhuay, Cordillera
   Chile 19°46S 68°40W **92** G5
Sillamäe *Estonia* 59°24N 27°45E **9** G22
Sillod *India* 20°18N 75°39E **44** D2
Silloth *U.K.* 54°52N 3°23W **12** C4
Siloam Springs *U.S.A.* 36°11N 94°32W **84** C7
Silopi *Turkey* 37°15N 42°27E **46** B4
Šilutė *Lithuania* 55°21N 21°33E **9** J19
Silvan *Turkey* 38°7N 41°2E **46** B4
Silvani *India* 23°18N 78°25E **43** H8
Silvassa *India* 20°16N 73°1E **44** D1
Silver City *U.S.A.* 32°46N 108°17W **77** K9
Silver Cr. → *U.S.A.* 43°16N 119°13W **76** E4
Silver Creek *U.S.A.* 42°33N 79°10W **82** D5
Silver L. *U.S.A.* 38°39N 120°6W **78** G6
Silver Lake *Calif., U.S.A.* 35°21N 116°7W **79** K10
Silver Lake *Oreg., U.S.A.* 43°8N 121°3W **76** E3
Silvermine Mts. *Ireland* 52°47N 8°15W **10** D3
Silverton *Colo., U.S.A.* 37°49N 107°40W **77** H10
Silverton *Tex., U.S.A.* 34°28N 101°19W **84** D4
Silvies → *U.S.A.* 43°34N 119°2W **76** E4
Simaltala *India* 24°43N 86°33E **43** G12
Simanggang = Bandar Sri Aman
   Malaysia 1°15N 111°32E **36** D4
Simao *China* 22°47N 101°5E **34** F3
Simard, L. *Canada* 47°40N 78°40W **72** C4
Simav *Turkey* 39°4N 28°58E **23** E13

Simbirsk = Ulyanovsk
   Russia 54°20N 48°25E **18** D8
Simcoe *Canada* 42°50N 80°20W **82** D4
Simcoe, L. *Canada* 44°25N 79°20W **82** B5
Simdega *India* 22°37N 84°31E **43** H11
Simeria *Romania* 45°51N 23°1E **17** F12
Simeulue *Indonesia* 2°45N 95°45E **36** D1
Simferopol *Ukraine* 44°55N 34°3E **19** F5
Simi *Greece* 36°35N 27°50E **23** F12
Simi Valley *U.S.A.* 34°16N 118°47W **79** L8
Simikot *Nepal* 30°0N 81°50E **43** E9
Simla = Shimla *India* 31°2N 77°9E **42** D7
Simlipal △ *India* 21°45N 86°30E **43** J12
Simmie *Canada* 49°56N 108°6W **71** D7
Simmler *U.S.A.* 35°21N 119°59W **79** K7
Simo älv = Simojoki →
   Finland 65°35N 25°1E **8** D21
Simojoki → *Finland* 65°35N 25°1E **8** D21
Simojovel *Mexico* 17°12N 92°38W **87** D6
Simonette → *Canada* 55°9N 118°15W **70** B5
Simonstown *S. Africa* 34°14S 18°26E **56** D2
Simpang Empat *Malaysia* 5°27N 100°29E **39** c
Simplonpass *Switz.* 46°15N 8°3E **20** C8
Simpson Desert *Australia* 25°0S 137°0E **62** D2
Simpson Desert △
   Australia 24°59S 138°21E **62** C2
Simpson Pen. *Canada* 68°34N 88°45W **69** D14
Simrishamn *Sweden* 55°33N 14°22E **9** J16
Simsbury *U.S.A.* 41°53N 72°48W **83** E12
Simushir, Ostrov
   Russia 46°50N 152°30E **27** E16
Sin Cowe I. *S. China Sea* 9°53N 114°19E **36** C4
Sina → *India* 17°30N 75°55E **44** F2
Sina Dhago *Somalia* 5°50N 47°0E **49** F4
Sinabang *Indonesia* 2°30N 96°24E **36** D1
Sinai = Es Sînâ' *Egypt* 29°0N 34°0E **48** F2
Sinai, Mt. = Mûsa, Gebel
   Egypt 28°33N 33°59E **46** D2
Sinaloa □ *Mexico* 25°0N 107°30W **86** C3
Sinaloa de Leyva
   Mexico 25°50N 108°14W **86** B3
Sinan *China* 27°56N 108°13E **34** D7
Sincelejo *Colombia* 9°18N 75°24W **92** B3
Sinch'ang *N. Korea* 40°7N 128°28E **33** D15
Sinch'ŏn *N. Korea* 38°17N 125°21E **33** E13
Sinclair *U.S.A.* 41°47N 107°7W **76** F10
Sinclair Mills *Canada* 54°5N 121°40W **70** C4
Sinclair's B. *U.K.* 58°31N 3°5W **11** C5
Sinclairville *U.S.A.* 42°16N 79°16W **82** D5
Sincorá, Serra do *Brazil* 13°30S 41°0W **93** F10
Sind = Sindh □ *Pakistan* 26°0N 69°0E **42** G3
Sind → *Jammu & Kashmir,*
   India 34°18N 74°45E **43** B6
Sind → *Mad. P., India* 26°26N 79°13E **43** F8
Sind Sagar Doab *Pakistan* 32°0N 71°30E **42** D4
Sindangan *Phil.* 8°10N 123°5E **37** C6
Sindangbarang *Indonesia* 7°27S 107°1E **37** G12
Sindewahi *India* 20°17N 79°39E **44** D4
Sindgi *India* 16°55N 76°14E **44** F3
Sindh = Indus →
   Pakistan 24°20N 67°47E **42** G2
Sindh □ *Pakistan* 26°0N 69°0E **42** G3
Sindhnur *India* 15°47N 76°46E **45** F3
Sindhuli Garhi *Nepal* 27°16N 85°58E **43** F11
Sindi *India* 20°48N 78°52E **44** D4
Sindri *India* 23°45N 86°42E **43** H12
Sines *Portugal* 37°56N 8°51W **21** D1
Sines, C. de *Portugal* 37°58N 8°53W **21** D1
Sing Buri *Thailand* 14°53N 100°25E **38** E3
Singa *Sudan* 13°10N 33°57E **53** F12
Singalila △ *India* 27°10N 88°5E **43** F13
Singanallur *India* 11°2N 77°1E **45** J3
Singapore ■ *Asia* 1°17N 103°51E **39** d
Singapore, Straits of *Asia* 1°15N 104°0E **39** d
Singaraja *Indonesia* 8°7S 115°6E **37** J18
Singatoka = Sigatoka *Fiji* 18°8S 177°32E **59** a
Singida *Tanzania* 4°49S 34°48E **54** E6
Singkang *Indonesia* 4°8S 120°1E **37** E6
Singkawang *Indonesia* 1°0N 108°57E **36** D3
Singkep *Indonesia* 0°30S 104°25E **36** E2
Singkil *Indonesia* 2°17N 97°49E **39** L1
Singkuang *Indonesia* 1°3N 98°55E **39** L2
Singleton *Australia* 32°33S 151°0E **63** E5
Singleton, Mt. *N. Terr.,*
   Australia 22°0S 130°46E **60** D5
Singleton, Mt. *W. Austral.,*
   Australia 29°27S 117°15E **61** E2
Singoli *India* 25°0N 75°22E **42** G6
Singora = Songkhla
   Thailand 7°13N 100°37E **39** J3
Singrauli *India* 24°7N 82°23E **43** G10
Sinharaja *Sri Lanka* 6°25N 80°30E **45** L5
Sinhgarh *India* 18°22N 73°45E **44** F1
Sinhŭng *N. Korea* 40°11N 127°34E **33** D14
Siniscóla *Italy* 40°34N 9°41E **22** D3
Sinjai *Indonesia* 5°7S 120°20E **37** F6
Sinjär *Iraq* 36°19N 41°52E **46** B4
Sinkat *Sudan* 18°55N 36°49E **53** E13
Sinkiang = Xinjiang Uygur
   Zizhiqu □ *China* 42°0N 86°0E **30** C6
Sinmak *N. Korea* 38°25N 126°14E **33** E14
Sinmi-do *N. Korea* 39°33N 124°53E **33** E13
Sinnamary *Fr. Guiana* 5°25N 53°0W **93** B8
Sinnar *India* 19°48N 74°0E **44** E2
Sinni → *Italy* 40°8N 16°41E **22** D7
Sinop *Turkey* 42°1N 35°11E **19** F6
Sinor *India* 21°55N 73°20E **42** J5
Sinp'o *N. Korea* 40°0N 128°13E **33** E15
Sinsk *Russia* 61°8N 126°48E **27** C13
Sint-Hubert *Belgium* 50°2N 5°23E **15** D5
Sint-Niklaas *Belgium* 51°10N 4°8E **15** C4
Sint-Truiden *Belgium* 50°48N 5°10E **15** D5
Sintang *Indonesia* 0°5N 111°35E **36** D4
Sinton *U.S.A.* 28°2N 97°31W **84** G6
Sintra *Portugal* 38°47N 9°25W **21** C1
Siniŭju *N. Korea* 40°5N 124°24E **33** D13
Siocon *Phil.* 7°40N 122°10E **37** C6
Siófok *Hungary* 46°54N 18°3E **17** E10
Sion *Switz.* 46°14N 7°20E **20** C7
Sion Mills *U.K.* 54°48N 7°29W **10** B4

tSionainn, An = Shannon →
   Ireland 52°35N 9°30W **10** D2
Sioux Center *U.S.A.* 43°5N 96°11W **80** D5
Sioux City *U.S.A.* 42°30N 96°24W **80** D5
Sioux Falls *U.S.A.* 43°33N 96°44W **80** D5
Sioux Lookout *Canada* 50°10N 91°50W **72** B1
Sioux Narrows *Canada* 49°25N 94°10W **71** D10
Sipadan *Malaysia* 4°6N 118°38E **37** D5
Siparia *Trin. & Tob.* 10°8N 61°31W **93** K15
Siping *China* 43°8N 124°21E **33** C13
Sipiwesk L. *Canada* 55°5N 97°35W **71** B9
Sipra → *India* 23°55N 75°28E **42** H6
Sipsongpanna = Xishuangbanna
   China 22°5N 101°1E **34** F3
Sipur *India* 21°11N 85°9E **44** D7
Sipura *Indonesia* 2°18S 99°40E **36** E1
Siquia → *Nic.* 12°10N 84°20W **88** D3
Siquijor *Phil.* 9°12N 123°35E **37** C6
Siquirres *Costa Rica* 10°6N 83°30W **88** D3
Şīr Abu Nu'ayr *U.A.E.* 25°20N 54°20E **47** E7
Şīr Banī Yās *U.A.E.* 24°19N 52°37E **47** E7
Sir Edward Pellew Group
   Australia 15°40S 137°10E **62** B2
Sir Graham Moore Is.
   Australia 13°53S 126°34E **60** B4
Sir James MacBrien, Mt.
   Canada 62°7N 127°41W **68** C6
Sira *India* 13°41N 76°49E **45** H3
Sira → *Norway* 58°23N 6°34E **9** G12
Siracusa *Italy* 37°4N 15°17E **22** F6
Sirajganj *Bangla.* 24°25N 89°47E **43** G13
Sirathu *India* 25°39N 81°19E **43** G9
Sīrdān *Iran* 36°39N 49°12E **47** B6
Siren *U.S.A.* 45°47N 92°24W **80** C7
Siret → *Romania* 45°24N 28°1E **17** F14
Sirghāyā *Syria* 33°51N 36°8E **48** B5
Sirikit Res. *Thailand* 17°45N 100°34E **38** C3
Sirinat △ *Thailand* 8°6N 98°17E **39** a
Sīrjān *Iran* 29°30N 55°45E **47** D7
Sirkali = Sirkazhi *India* 11°15N 79°41E **45** J4
Sirkazhi *India* 11°15N 79°41E **45** J4
Sirmaur *India* 24°51N 81°23E **43** G9
Sirmilik △ *Canada* 72°50N 80°35W **69** C15
Sirohi *India* 24°52N 72°53E **42** G5
Sironj *India* 24°5N 77°39E **42** G7
Síros = Ermoupoli
   Greece 37°28N 24°57E **23** F11
Sirpur *India* 19°29N 79°36E **44** E4
Sirr, Nafud as *Si. Arabia* 25°33N 44°35E **46** E5
Sirretta Pk. *U.S.A.* 35°56N 118°19W **79** K8
Sīrrī *Iran* 25°55N 54°32E **47** E7
Sirsa *India* 29°33N 75°4E **42** E6
Sirsa → *India* 26°51N 79°4E **43** F8
Sirsi *India* 14°40N 74°49E **45** G2
Sirsilla *India* 18°23N 78°50E **44** E4
Sirte = Surt *Libya* 31°11N 16°39E **53** B9
Siruguppa *India* 15°38N 76°54E **45** F3
Sirur *India* 18°50N 74°23E **44** F2
Şirvan *Azerbaijan* 39°59N 48°52E **47** B6
Sisak *Croatia* 45°30N 16°21E **16** F9
Sishen *S. Africa* 27°47S 22°59E **56** C3
Sishui *China* 35°42N 117°18E **33** G9
Sisipuk L. *Canada* 55°45N 101°50W **71** B8
Sisophon *Cambodia* 13°38N 102°59E **38** F4
Sisseton *U.S.A.* 45°40N 97°3W **80** C5
Sīstān *Asia* 30°50N 61°0E **47** D9
Sīstān, Daryācheh-ye *Iran* 31°0N 61°0E **47** D9
Sīstān va Balūchestān □
   Iran 27°0N 62°0E **47** E9
Sisters *U.S.A.* 44°18N 121°33W **76** D3
Sisters, The *Seychelles* 4°16S 55°52E **55** b
Siswa Bazar *India* 27°9N 83°46E **43** F10
Sitamarhi *India* 26°37N 85°30E **43** F11
Sitapur *India* 27°38N 80°45E **43** F9
Siteki *Swaziland* 26°32S 31°58E **57** C5
Sitges *Spain* 41°17N 1°47E **21** B6
Sitia *Greece* 35°13N 26°6E **23** G12
Sitito-Ozima Ridge *Pac. Oc.* 23°0N 143°0E **64** E6
Sitka *U.S.A.* 57°3N 135°20W **70** B1
Sitkaing = Sagaing
   Burma 21°52N 95°59E **41** J19
Sitoti *Botswana* 23°15S 23°40E **56** B3
Sittang Myit → *Burma* 17°20N 96°45E **41** L20
Sittard *Neths.* 51°0N 5°52E **15** C5
Sittingbourne *U.K.* 51°21N 0°45E **13** F8
Sittoung = Sittang Myit →
   Burma 17°20N 96°45E **41** L20
Sittwe *Burma* 20°18N 92°45E **41** J18
Situbondo *Indonesia* 7°42S 113°56E **37** G16
Si'umu *Samoa* 14°1S 171°48W **59** b
Siuna *Nic.* 13°37N 84°45W **88** D3
Siuri *India* 23°50N 87°34E **43** H12
Sivaganga *India* 9°50N 78°28E **45** K4
Sivagiri *India* 9°16N 77°26E **45** K3
Sivakasi *India* 9°24N 77°47E **45** K3
Sīvand *Iran* 30°5N 52°55E **47** D7
Sivas *Turkey* 39°43N 36°58E **46** B3
Sivasamudram *India* 12°37N 77°10E **45** H3
Siverek *Turkey* 37°50N 39°19E **46** B3
Sivomaskinskiy *Russia* 66°40N 62°35E **18** A11
Sivrihisar *Turkey* 39°30N 31°35E **19** G5
Sīwa *Egypt* 29°11N 25°31E **53** C11
Sīwa, El Wâhât es *Egypt* 29°10N 25°30E **50** D6
Siwa Oasis = Sīwa, El Wâhât es
   Egypt 29°10N 25°30E **50** D6
Siwalik Range *Nepal* 28°0N 83°0E **43** F10
Siwan *India* 26°13N 84°21E **43** F11
Siwana *India* 25°38N 72°25E **42** G5
Six Cross Roads *Barbados* 13°7N 59°28W **89** g
Sixian *China* 33°30N 117°50E **33** H9
Sixmilebridge *Ireland* 52°44N 8°46W **10** D3
Sixth Cataract *Sudan* 16°20N 32°42E **53** E12
Siyabuswa *S. Africa* 25°7S 29°3E **57** C4
Siyah Kuh, Kavīr-e *Iran* 32°55N 53°55E **47** C7
Siyang *China* 33°42N 118°40E **33** H10
Siziwang Qi *China* 41°25N 111°40E **32** D6
Sjælland *Denmark* 55°30N 11°30E **9** J14
Sjumen = Shumen
   Bulgaria 43°18N 26°55E **23** C12

Skadarsko Jezero *Europe* 42°10N 19°20E **23** C8
Skaftafell *Iceland* 64°1N 17°0W **8** D5
Skaftafell △ *Iceland* 64°9N 16°50W **8** D5
Skagafjörður *Iceland* 65°54N 19°35W **8** D4
Skagaströnd *Iceland* 65°50N 20°19W **8** D3
Skagen *Denmark* 57°43N 10°35E **9** H14
Skagerrak *Denmark* 57°30N 9°0E **9** H13
Skagit → *U.S.A.* 48°23N 122°22W **78** B4
Skagway *U.S.A.* 59°28N 135°19W **68** F4
Skala-Podilska *Ukraine* 48°50N 26°15E **17** D14
Skalat *Ukraine* 49°23N 25°55E **17** D13
Skåne *Sweden* 55°59N 13°30E **9** J15
Skaneateles *U.S.A.* 42°57N 76°26W **83** D8
Skaneateles L. *U.S.A.* 42°51N 76°22W **83** D8
Skardu *Pakistan* 35°20N 75°44E **43** B6
Skarżysko-Kamienna
  Poland 51°7N 20°52E **17** C11
Skeena → *Canada* 54°9N 130°5W **70** C2
Skeena Mts. *Canada* 56°40N 128°30W **70** B3
Skegness *U.K.* 53°9N 0°20E **12** D8
Skeleton Coast *Namibia* 20°0S 13°0E **55** J2
Skeleton Coast △ *Namibia* 20°0S 13°0E **56** B1
Skellefteå *Sweden* 64°45N 20°50E **8** D19
Skellefteälven → *Sweden* 64°45N 21°10E **8** D19
Skelleftehamn *Sweden* 64°40N 21°9E **8** D19
Skellig Michael = Great Skellig
  Ireland 51°47N 10°33W **10** E1
Skerries *Ireland* 53°35N 6°8W **10** C5
Skerries, The *U.K.* 53°25N 4°36W **12** D3
Ski *Norway* 59°43N 10°52E **9** G14
Skiathos *Greece* 39°12N 23°30E **23** E10
Skibbereen *Ireland* 51°33N 9°16W **10** E2
Skiddaw *U.K.* 54°39N 3°9W **12** C4
Skidegate *Canada* 53°15N 132°1W **70** C2
Skien *Norway* 59°12N 9°35E **9** G13
Skierniewice *Poland* 51°58N 20°10E **17** C11
Skihist, Mt. *Canada* 50°12N 121°54W **70** C4
Skikda *Algeria* 36°50N 6°58E **52** A7
Skipton *U.K.* 53°58N 2°3W **12** D5
Skirmish Pt. *Australia* 11°59S 134°17E **62** A1
Skiros *Greece* 38°55N 24°34E **23** E11
Skive *Denmark* 56°33N 9°2E **9** H13
Skjálfandafljót → *Iceland* 65°59N 17°25W **8** D5
Skjálfandi *Iceland* 66°5N 17°30W **8** C5
Skole *Ukraine* 49°3N 23°30E **17** D12
Skopelos *Greece* 39°9N 23°47E **23** E10
Skopje *Macedonia* 42°1N 21°26E **23** C9
Skövde *Sweden* 58°24N 13°50E **9** G15
Skovorodino *Russia* 54°0N 124°0E **27** D13
Skowhegan *U.S.A.* 44°46N 69°43W **81** C19
Skull *Ireland* 51°32N 9°34W **10** E2
Skunk → *U.S.A.* 40°42N 91°7W **80** E8
Skuodas *Lithuania* 56°16N 21°33E **9** H19
Skvyra *Ukraine* 49°44N 29°40E **17** D15
Skye *U.K.* 57°15N 6°10W **11** D2
Skykomish *U.S.A.* 47°42N 121°22W **76** C3
Skyros = Skiros *Greece* 38°55N 24°34E **23** E11
Slade Point *Australia* 21°4S 149°13E **62** b
Slade Pt. *Australia* 21°5S 149°13E **62** b
Slættaratindur *Færoe Is.* 62°18N 7°1W **8** E9
Slagelse *Denmark* 55°23N 11°19E **9** J14
Slamet *Indonesia* 7°16S 109°8E **37** G13
Slane *Ireland* 53°42N 6°33W **10** C5
Slaney → *Ireland* 52°26N 6°33W **10** D5
Slangberge *S. Africa* 31°32S 20°48E **56** D3
Śląsk *Poland* 51°0N 16°30E **16** C9
Slate Is. *Canada* 48°40N 87°0W **72** C2
Slatina *Romania* 44°28N 24°22E **17** F13
Slatington *U.S.A.* 40°45N 75°37W **83** F9
Slaton *U.S.A.* 33°26N 101°39W **84** E4
Slave → *Canada* 61°18N 113°39W **70** A6
Slave Coast *W. Afr.* 6°0N 2°30E **52** G6
Slave Lake *Canada* 55°17N 114°43W **70** B6
Slave Pt. *Canada* 61°11N 115°56W **70** A5
Slavgorod *Russia* 53°1N 78°37E **26** D8
Slavonski Brod *Croatia* 45°11N 18°1E **23** B8
Slavuta *Ukraine* 50°15N 27°2E **17** C14
Slavyanka *Russia* 42°53N 131°21E **28** C5
Slavyansk = Slovyansk
  Ukraine 48°55N 37°36E **19** E6
Slawharad *Belarus* 53°27N 31°0E **17** B16
Slea Hd. *Ireland* 52°6N 10°27W **10** D1
Sleaford *U.K.* 53°0N 0°24W **12** D7
Sleaford B. *Australia* 34°55S 135°45E **63** E2
Sleat, Sd. of *U.K.* 57°5N 5°47W **11** D3
Sleeper Is. *Canada* 58°30N 81°0W **69** F15
Sleeping Bear Dunes △
  U.S.A. 44°50N 86°5W **80** C10
Sleepy Eye *U.S.A.* 44°18N 94°43W **80** C6
Slemon L. *Canada* 63°13N 116°4W **70** A5
Slide Mt. *U.S.A.* 42°0N 74°25W **83** E10
Slidell *U.S.A.* 30°17N 89°47W **85** F10
Slieve Aughty *Ireland* 53°4N 8°30W **10** C3
Slieve Bloom *Ireland* 53°4N 7°40W **10** C4
Slieve Donard *U.K.* 54°11N 5°55W **10** B6
Slieve Gamph *Ireland* 54°6N 9°0W **10** B3
Slieve Gullion *U.K.* 54°7N 6°26W **10** B5
Slieve League *Ireland* 54°40N 8°42W **10** B3
Slieve Mish *Ireland* 52°12N 9°50W **10** D2
Slievenamon *Ireland* 52°25N 7°34W **10** D4
Sligeach = Sligo *Ireland* 54°16N 8°28W **10** B3
Sligo *Ireland* 54°16N 8°28W **10** B3
Sligo □ *Ireland* 54°8N 8°42W **10** B3
Sligo B. *Ireland* 54°18N 8°40W **10** B3
Slippery Rock *U.S.A.* 41°4N 80°3W **82** E4
Slite *Sweden* 57°42N 18°48E **9** H18
Sliven *Bulgaria* 42°42N 26°19E **23** C12
Sloan *U.S.A.* 35°57N 115°13W **79** K11
Sloansville *U.S.A.* 42°45N 74°22W **83** D10
Slobodskoy *Russia* 58°40N 50°6E **18** C9
Slobozia *Romania* 44°34N 27°23E **17** F14
Slocan *Canada* 49°48N 117°28W **70** D5
Slonim *Belarus* 53°4N 25°19E **17** B13
Slough *U.K.* 51°30N 0°36W **13** F7
Slough □ *U.K.* 51°30N 0°36W **13** F7
Sloughhouse *U.S.A.* 38°26N 121°12W **78** G5
Slovak Rep. ■ *Europe* 48°30N 20°0E **17** D10

Slovakia = Slovak Rep. ■
  Europe 48°30N 20°0E **17** D10
Slovakian Ore Mts. = Slovenské
  Rudohorie *Slovak Rep.* 48°45N 20°0E **17** D10
Slovenia ■ *Europe* 45°58N 14°30E **16** F8
Slovenija = Slovenia ■
  Europe 45°58N 14°30E **16** F8
Slovenska = Slovak Rep. ■
  Europe 48°30N 20°0E **17** D10
Slovenské Rudohorie
  Slovak Rep. 48°45N 20°0E **17** D10
Slovyansk *Ukraine* 48°55N 37°36E **19** E6
Sluch → *Ukraine* 51°37N 26°38E **17** C14
Sluis *Neths.* 51°18N 3°23E **15** C3
Słupsk *Poland* 54°30N 17°3E **17** A9
Slurry *S. Africa* 25°49S 25°42E **56** C4
Slutsk *Belarus* 53°2N 27°31E **17** B14
Slyne Hd. *Ireland* 53°25N 10°10W **10** C1
Slyudyanka *Russia* 51°40N 103°40E **27** D11
Småland *Sweden* 57°15N 15°25E **9** H16
Smalltree L. *Canada* 61°0N 105°0W **71** A8
Smallwood Res. *Canada* 54°5N 64°30W **73** B7
Smarhon *Belarus* 54°20N 26°24E **17** A14
Smartt Syndicate Dam
  S. Africa 30°45S 23°10E **56** D3
Smartville *U.S.A.* 39°13N 121°18W **78** F5
Smeaton *Canada* 53°30N 104°49W **71** C8
Smederevo *Serbia* 44°40N 20°57E **23** B9
Smerwick Harbour
  Ireland 52°12N 10°23W **10** D1
Smethport *U.S.A.* 41°49N 78°27W **82** E6
Smidovich *Russia* 48°36N 133°49E **27** E14
Smith *Canada* 55°10N 114°0W **70** B6
Smith Center *U.S.A.* 39°47N 98°47W **80** F4
Smith I. *India* 13°20N 93°4E **45** H11
Smith Islands △ *Australia* 20°40S 149°9E **62** b
Smith River → *U.S.A.* 41°55N 124°0W **76** F2
Smithburne → *Australia* 17°3S 140°57E **62** B3
Smithers *Canada* 54°45N 127°10W **70** C3
Smithfield *S. Africa* 30°9S 26°30E **57** D4
Smithfield *N.C., U.S.A.* 35°31N 78°21W **85** D15
Smithfield *Utah, U.S.A.* 41°50N 111°50W **76** F8
Smithton *Australia* 40°53S 145°6E **63** G4
Smithville *Canada* 43°6N 79°33W **82** C5
Smithville *U.S.A.* 30°1N 97°10W **84** F6
Smoke Creek Desert
  U.S.A. 40°30N 119°40W **76** F4
Smoky → *Canada* 56°10N 117°21W **70** B5
Smoky Bay *Australia* 32°22S 134°13E **63** E1
Smoky Hill → *U.S.A.* 39°4N 96°48W **80** F5
Smoky Hills *U.S.A.* 39°15N 99°30W **80** F4
Smoky Lake *Canada* 54°10N 112°30W **70** C6
Smøla *Norway* 63°23N 8°3E **8** E13
Smolensk *Russia* 54°45N 32°5E **18** D5
Smolikas, Oros *Greece* 40°9N 20°58E **23** D9
Smolyan *Bulgaria* 41°36N 24°38E **23** D11
Smooth Rock Falls
  Canada 49°17N 81°37W **72** C3
Smoothstone L. *Canada* 54°40N 106°50W **71** C7
Smorgon = Smarhon
  Belarus 54°20N 26°24E **17** A14
Smyley I. *Antarctica* 72°55S 78°0W **5** D17
Smyrna = İzmir *Turkey* 38°25N 27°8E **23** E12
Smyrna *U.S.A.* 39°18N 75°36W **81** F16
Snæfell *Iceland* 64°48N 15°34W **8** D6
Snaefell *I. of Man* 54°16N 4°27W **12** C3
Snæfellsjökull *Iceland* 64°49N 23°46W **8** D2
Snake → *U.S.A.* 46°12N 119°2W **76** C4
Snake I. *Australia* 38°47S 146°33E **63** F4
Snake Range *U.S.A.* 39°0N 114°20W **76** G6
Snake River Plain *U.S.A.* 42°50N 114°0W **76** E7
Snåsavatnet *Norway* 64°12N 12°0E **8** D15
Sneek *Neths.* 53°2N 5°40E **15** A5
Sneem *Ireland* 51°50N 9°54W **10** E2
Sneeuberge *S. Africa* 31°46S 24°20E **56** E3
Snelling *U.S.A.* 37°31N 120°26W **78** H6
Snežka *Europe* 50°41N 15°50E **16** C8
Snizort, L. *U.K.* 57°33N 6°28W **11** D2
Snøhetta *Norway* 62°19N 9°16E **8** E13
Snohomish *U.S.A.* 47°55N 122°6W **78** C4
Snoqualmie *U.S.A.* 47°31N 121°49W **78** C5
Snoqualmie Pass *U.S.A.* 47°25N 121°25W **78** C5
Snoul *Cambodia* 12°4N 106°26E **39** F6
Snover *U.S.A.* 43°27N 82°58W **82** C2
Snow Hill *U.S.A.* 38°11N 75°24W **81** F16
Snow Lake *Canada* 54°52N 100°3W **71** C8
Snow Mt. *Calif., U.S.A.* 39°23N 122°45W **78** F4
Snow Mt. *Maine, U.S.A.* 45°18N 70°48W **83** A14
Snow Shoe *U.S.A.* 41°2N 77°57W **82** E7
Snowbird L. *Canada* 60°45N 103°0W **71** A8
Snowdon *U.K.* 53°4N 4°5W **12** D3
Snowdonia △ *U.K.* 53°7N 3°59W **12** D4
Snowdrift = Łutsel K'e
  Canada 62°24N 110°44W **71** A6
Snowdrift → *Canada* 62°24N 110°44W **71** A6
Snowflake *U.S.A.* 34°30N 110°5W **77** J8
Snowshoe Pk. *U.S.A.* 48°13N 115°41W **76** B6
Snowtown *Australia* 33°46S 138°14E **63** E2
Snowville *U.S.A.* 41°58N 112°43W **76** F7
Snowy → *Australia* 37°46S 148°30E **63** F4
Snowy Mt. *U.S.A.* 43°42N 74°23W **83** C10
Snowy Mts. *Australia* 36°30S 148°20E **63** F4
Snug Corner *Bahamas* 22°33N 73°52W **89** B5
Snug Harbour *Canada* 45°22N 80°17W **82** A4
Snyatyn *Ukraine* 48°27N 25°38E **17** D13
Snyder *Okla., U.S.A.* 34°40N 98°57W **84** D5
Snyder *Tex., U.S.A.* 32°44N 100°55W **84** E4
Soalala *Madag.* 16°6S 45°20E **55** H9
Soan → *Pakistan* 33°1N 71°44E **42** C4
Sobat, Nahr →
  South Sudan 9°22N 31°33E **53** G12
Sobhapur *India* 22°47N 78°17E **42** H8
Sobradinho, Represa de
  Brazil 9°30S 42°0W **93** E10
Sobral *Brazil* 3°50S 40°20W **93** D10
Soc Giang *Vietnam* 22°54N 106°1E **34** F6
Soc Trang *Vietnam* 9°37N 105°50E **39** H5

Socastee *U.S.A.* 33°41N 78°59W **85** E15
Soch'e = Shache *China* 38°20N 77°10E **30** D4
Sochi *Russia* 43°35N 39°40E **19** F6
Société, Îs. de la
  French Polynesia 17°0S 151°0W **65** J12
Society Is. = Société, Îs. de la
  French Polynesia 17°0S 151°0W **65** J12
Socompa, Portezuelo de
  Chile 24°27S 68°18W **94** A2
Socorro *N. Mex., U.S.A.* 34°4N 106°54W **77** J10
Socorro *Tex., U.S.A.* 31°39N 106°18W **84** F1
Socorro, I. *Mexico* 18°45N 110°58W **86** D2
Socotra *Yemen* 12°30N 54°0E **49** E5
Soda L. *U.S.A.* 35°10N 116°4W **79** K10
Soda Plains *India* 35°30N 79°0E **43** B8
Soda Springs *U.S.A.* 42°39N 111°36W **76** E8
Sodankylä *Finland* 67°29N 26°40E **8** C22
Soddy-Daisy *U.S.A.* 35°17N 85°10W **85** D12
Söderhamn *Sweden* 61°18N 17°10E **8** F17
Söderköping *Sweden* 58°31N 16°20E **9** G17
Södermanland *Sweden* 58°56N 16°55E **9** G17
Södertälje *Sweden* 59°12N 17°39E **9** G17
Sodiri *Sudan* 14°27N 29°0E **53** F11
Sodus *U.S.A.* 43°14N 77°4W **82** C7
Sodwana Bay △ *S. Africa* 27°35S 32°43E **57** C5
Soe *Indonesia* 9°52S 124°17E **60** A3
Soekmekaar = Morebeng
  S. Africa 23°30S 29°55E **57** B4
Soest *Neths.* 52°9N 5°19E **15** B5
Sofala □ *Mozam.* 19°30S 34°30E **57** A5
Sofia = Sofiya *Bulgaria* 42°45N 23°20E **23** C10
Sofia → *Madag.* 15°27S 47°23E **55** H9
Sofiya *Bulgaria* 42°45N 23°20E **23** C10
Sōfu-Gan *Japan* 29°49N 140°21E **29** K10
Sogamoso *Colombia* 5°43N 72°56W **92** B4
Sogār *Iran* 25°53N 58°6E **47** E8
Sogndalsfjøra *Norway* 61°14N 7°5E **8** F12
Søgne *Norway* 58°5N 7°48E **9** G12
Sognefjorden *Norway* 61°10N 5°50E **8** F11
Soh *Iran* 33°26N 51°27E **47** C6
Sohâg *Egypt* 26°33N 31°43E **53** C12
Sohagpur *India* 22°42N 78°12E **42** H8
Sohar = Şuḩār *Oman* 24°20N 56°40E **47** E8
Sohela *India* 21°18N 83°24E **44** D6
Soheuksando *S. Korea* 34°4N 125°7E **33** G13
Soignies *Belgium* 50°35N 4°5E **15** D4
Soissons *France* 49°25N 3°19E **20** B5
Sōja *Japan* 34°40N 133°45E **29** G6
Sojat *India* 25°55N 73°45E **42** G5
Sokal *Ukraine* 50°31N 24°15E **17** C13
Sokcho *S. Korea* 38°12N 128°36E **33** E15
Söke *Turkey* 37°48N 27°28E **23** F12
Sokhumi *Georgia* 43°0N 41°0E **19** F7
Soko Is. *China* 22°10N 113°54E **31** a
Sokodé *Togo* 9°0N 1°11E **52** G6
Sokol *Russia* 59°30N 40°5E **18** C7
Sokółka *Poland* 53°25N 23°30E **17** B12
Sokołów Podlaski
  Poland 52°25N 22°15E **17** B12
Sokoto *Nigeria* 13°2N 5°16E **52** F7
Sol Iletsk *Russia* 51°10N 55°0E **18** D10
Solan *India* 30°55N 77°7E **42** D7
Solana Beach *U.S.A.* 32°58N 117°16W **79** N9
Solander I. *N.Z.* 46°34S 166°54E **59** G1
Solapur *India* 17°43N 75°56E **44** F2
Soldotna *U.S.A.* 60°29N 151°3W **68** E1
Soledad *Colombia* 10°55N 74°46W **92** A4
Soledad *U.S.A.* 36°26N 121°20W **78** J5
Soledad *Venezuela* 8°10N 63°34W **92** B6
Solent, The *U.K.* 50°45N 1°25W **13** G6
Solfonntaggen *Norway* 60°2N 6°57E **9** F12
Solhan *Turkey* 38°57N 41°3E **46** B4
Soligalich *Russia* 59°5N 42°10E **18** C7
Soligorsk = Salihorsk
  Belarus 52°51N 27°27E **17** B14
Solihull *U.K.* 52°26N 1°47W **13** E6
Solikamsk *Russia* 59°38N 56°50E **18** C10
Solimões = Amazonas →
  S. Amer. 0°5S 50°0W **93** D8
Solingen *Germany* 51°10N 7°5E **16** C4
Sollefteå *Sweden* 63°12N 17°20E **8** E17
Sóller *Spain* 39°46N 2°43E **21** C7
Solo → *Indonesia* 6°47S 112°22E **37** G15
Sologne *France* 47°40N 1°45E **20** C4
Solok *Indonesia* 0°45S 100°40E **36** E2
Sololá *Guatemala* 14°49N 91°10W **88** D1
Solomon, N. Fork →
  U.S.A. 39°29N 98°26W **80** F4
Solomon, S. Fork →
  U.S.A. 39°25N 99°12W **80** F4
Solomon Is. ■ *Pac. Oc.* 6°0S 155°0E **58** B8
Solomon Rise *Pac. Oc.* 1°0N 157°0E **64** D7
Solon *China* 46°32N 121°10E **31** B13
Solon Springs *U.S.A.* 46°22N 91°49W **80** B8
Solor *Indonesia* 8°27S 123°0E **37** F6
Solothurn *Switz.* 47°13N 7°32E **20** C7
Solovetskiye Ostrova
  Russia 65°5N 35°40E **18** B6
Šolta *Croatia* 43°24N 16°15E **22** C7
Solṭānābād *Khorāsān, Iran* 34°13N 59°58E **47** C8
Solṭānābād *Khorāsān, Iran* 36°29N 58°5E **47** B8
Solṭāniyeh *Iran* 36°26N 48°47E **47** B6
Solunska Glava
  Macedonia 41°44N 21°31E **23** D9
Solvang *U.S.A.* 34°36N 120°8W **79** L6
Solvay *U.S.A.* 43°3N 76°13W **83** C8
Solvesborg *Sweden* 56°5N 14°35E **9** H16
Solvychegodsk *Russia* 61°21N 46°56E **18** B8
Solway Firth *U.K.* 54°49N 3°35W **12** C4
Solwezi *Zambia* 12°11S 26°21E **55** G5
Sōma *Japan* 37°40N 140°50E **28** F10
Soma *Turkey* 39°10N 27°35E **23** E12
Somabhula *Zimbabwe* 19°42S 29°40E **57** A4
Somali Pen. *Africa* 7°0N 46°0E **50** F8
Somalia ■ *Africa* 7°0N 47°0E **49** F4
Somaliland □ *Somalia* 10°0N 46°0E **49** F4
Sombor *Serbia* 45°46N 19°9E **23** B8
Sombra *Canada* 42°43N 82°29W **82** D2
Sombrerete *Mexico* 23°38N 103°39W **86** C4

Sombrero *Anguilla* 18°37N 63°30W **89** C7
Sombrero Channel *India* 7°41N 93°35E **45** L11
Somdari *India* 25°47N 72°38E **42** G5
Somers *U.S.A.* 48°5N 114°13W **76** B6
Somerset *Ky., U.S.A.* 37°5N 84°36W **81** G11
Somerset *Mass., U.S.A.* 41°47N 71°8W **83** E13
Somerset *Pa., U.S.A.* 40°1N 79°5W **82** F5
Somerset □ *U.K.* 51°9N 3°0W **13** F5
Somerset East *S. Africa* 32°42S 25°35E **56** D4
Somerset I. *Canada* 73°30N 93°0W **68** C13
Somerset West *S. Africa* 34°8S 18°50E **56** D2
Somersworth *U.S.A.* 43°16N 70°52W **83** C14
Somerton *U.S.A.* 32°36N 114°43W **77** K6
Somerville *U.S.A.* 40°35N 74°38W **83** F10
Someş → *Romania* 47°49N 22°43E **17** D12
Somme → *France* 50°11N 1°38E **20** A4
Somnath *India* 20°53N 70°22E **42** J4
Somosierra, Puerto de
  Spain 41°4N 3°35W **21** B4
Somosomo *Fiji* 16°47S 179°58E **59** a
Somosomo Str. *Fiji* 16°0S 180°0E **59** a
Somoto *Nic.* 13°28N 86°37W **88** D2
Somport, Túnel de *Spain* 42°48N 0°31W **20** E3
Somvarpet *India* 12°36N 75°52E **45** H2
Son → *India* 25°42N 84°52E **43** G11
Son, Laem *Thailand* 7°59N 98°16E **39** a
Son Ha *Vietnam* 15°3N 108°34E **38** E7
Son La *Vietnam* 21°20N 103°50E **34** G4
Son Tay *Vietnam* 21°8N 105°30E **34** G5
Son Tinh *Vietnam* 15°10N 108°40E **38** E7
Soná *Panama* 8°0N 81°20W **88** E3
Sonamarg *India* 34°18N 75°21E **43** B6
Sonamukhi *India* 23°18N 87°27E **43** H12
Sonar → *India* 24°24N 79°56E **43** G8
Sŏnch'ŏn *N. Korea* 39°48N 124°55E **33** E13
Sondags → *S. Africa* 33°44S 25°51E **56** D4
Sønderborg *Denmark* 54°55N 9°49E **9** J13
Sóndrio *Italy* 46°10N 9°52E **20** C8
Sondur → *India* 20°40N 82°1E **44** D6
Sonepur *India* 20°55N 83°50E **44** D6
Song *Thailand* 18°28N 100°11E **38** C3
Song Cau *Vietnam* 13°27N 109°18E **38** F7
Song Ma *Vietnam* 20°56N 103°53E **34** G4
Song Xian *China* 34°12N 112°8E **32** G7
Songadh *India* 21°9N 73°33E **44** D1
Songan *Indonesia* 8°13S 115°24E **37** J18
Songea *Tanzania* 10°40S 35°40E **54** G7
Songgang *China* 22°46N 113°50E **31** a
Songhua Hu *China* 43°35N 126°50E **33** C14
Songhua Jiang →
  China 47°45N 132°30E **31** B15
Songimvelo △ *S. Africa* 25°50S 31°2E **57** C5
Songjiang *China* 31°1N 121°12E **33** B13
Songjianghe *China* 42°10N 127°29E **33** C14
Songnim *N. Korea* 38°45N 125°39E **33** E13
Songo *Mozam.* 15°34S 32°38E **57** A5
Songpan *China* 32°40N 103°30E **34** A4
Songtao *China* 28°11N 109°10E **34** C7
Songxi *China* 27°31N 118°44E **35** D12
Songzi *China* 30°12N 111°45E **35** B8
Sonhat *India* 23°29N 82°31E **43** H10
Sonid Youqi *China* 42°45N 112°48E **32** C7
Sonid Zuoqi *China* 43°50N 113°42E **32** C7
Sonipat *India* 29°0N 77°5E **42** E7
Sonkach *India* 22°59N 76°21E **42** H7
Sonmiani *Pakistan* 25°25N 66°40E **42** G2
Sonmiani B. *Pakistan* 25°15N 66°30E **42** G2
Sono → *Brazil* 9°58S 48°11W **93** E9
Sonoma *U.S.A.* 38°18N 122°28W **78** G4
Sonoma *Calif., U.S.A.* 37°59N 120°23W **78** H6
Sonora *Tex., U.S.A.* 30°34N 100°39W **84** F4
Sonora □ *Mexico* 29°20N 110°40W **86** B2
Sonora → *Mexico* 29°5N 110°55W **86** B2
Sonoran Desert *U.S.A.* 33°40N 113°30W **79** L12
Sonoyta *Mexico* 31°51N 112°50W **86** A2
Soochow = Suzhou
  China 31°19N 120°38E **35** B13
Sooke *Canada* 48°13N 123°43W **78** B3
Soomaaliya = Somalia ■
  Africa 7°0N 47°0E **49** F4
Sop Hao *Laos* 20°33N 104°27E **34** G5
Sop Prap *Thailand* 17°53N 99°20E **38** D2
Sopi *Indonesia* 2°34N 128°28E **37** D7
Sopot *Poland* 54°27N 18°31E **17** A10
Sopron *Hungary* 47°45N 16°32E **17** E9
Sopur *India* 34°18N 74°27E **43** B6
Sør-Rondane *Antarctica* 72°0S 25°0E **5** D4
Sorab *India* 14°23N 75°6E **45** G2
Sorada *India* 19°45N 84°26E **44** E7
Sorah *Pakistan* 27°13N 68°56E **42** F3
Soraon *India* 25°37N 81°51E **43** G9
Sorel-Tracy *Canada* 46°0N 73°10W **72** C5
Sórgono *Italy* 40°1N 9°6E **22** D3
Soria *Spain* 41°43N 2°32W **21** B4
Soriano *Uruguay* 33°24S 58°19W **94** C4
Sorkh, Kuh-e *Iran* 35°40N 58°30E **47** C8
Soroca *Moldova* 48°8N 28°12E **17** D15
Sorocaba *Brazil* 23°31S 47°27W **95** A6
Sorochinsk *Russia* 52°26N 53°10E **18** D9
Soroki = Soroca *Moldova* 48°8N 28°12E **17** D15
Sorong *Indonesia* 0°55S 131°15E **37** E8
Soroti *Uganda* 1°43N 33°35E **54** D6
Sørøya *Norway* 70°40N 22°30E **8** A20
Sørøysundet *Norway* 70°25N 23°0E **8** A20
Sorrell *Australia* 42°47S 147°34E **63** G4
Sorrento *Italy* 40°37N 14°22E **22** D6
Sorsele *Sweden* 65°31N 17°30E **8** D17
Sorsogon *Phil.* 13°0N 124°0E **37** B6
Sortavala *Russia* 61°42N 30°41E **8** F24
Sortland *Norway* 68°42N 15°25E **8** B16
Soscumica, L. *Canada* 50°15N 77°27W **72** B4
Sosnogorsk *Russia* 63°37N 53°51E **18** B9
Sosnowiec *Poland* 50°20N 19°10E **17** C10

Sossus Vlei *Namibia* 24°40S 15°23E **56** B2
Sŏsura *N. Korea* 42°16N 130°36E **33** C16
Sot → *India* 27°27N 79°37E **43** F8
Sotavento *C. Verde Is.* 15°0N 24°0W **52** b
Sotkamo *Finland* 64°8N 28°23E **8** D23
Soto la Marina *Mexico* 23°46N 98°13W **87** C5
Soto la Marina →
  Mexico 23°45N 97°45W **87** C5
Sotuta *Mexico* 20°36N 89°1W **87** C7
Souanké *Congo* 2°10N 14°3E **54** D2
Soudas, Ormos *Greece* 35°25N 24°10E **23** G11
Souderton *U.S.A.* 40°19N 75°19W **83** F9
Soufrière *Guadeloupe* 16°5N 61°40W **88** b
Soufrière *St. Lucia* 13°51N 61°3W **89** f
Soufrière Bay *Dominica* 15°13N 61°22W **89** f
Soukhouma *Laos* 14°38N 105°48E **38** E5
Sound, The *U.K.* 50°20N 4°10W **13** G3
Sound I. *India* 12°58N 92°59E **45** H11
Sources, Mt. aux *Lesotho* 28°45S 28°50E **57** C4
Soure *Brazil* 0°35S 48°30W **93** D9
Souris *Man., Canada* 49°40N 100°20W **71** D8
Souris *P.E.I., Canada* 46°21N 62°15W **73** C7
Souris → *N. Amer.* 49°40N 99°34W **80** A4
Sousa *Brazil* 6°45S 38°10W **93** E11
Sousse *Tunisia* 35°50N 10°38E **53** A8
Sout → *S. Africa* 31°35S 18°24E **56** E2
South Africa ■ *Africa* 32°0S 23°0E **56** D3
South America 10°0S 60°0W **90** E5
South Andaman *India* 11°45N 92°20E **45** J11
South Aulatsivik I.
  Canada 56°45N 61°30W **73** A7
South Australia □
  Australia 32°0S 139°0E **63** E2
South Australian Basin
  Ind. Oc. 38°0S 126°0E **64** L4
South Ayrshire □ *U.K.* 55°18N 4°41W **11** F4
South Baldy Pk. *U.S.A.* 34°6N 107°11W **77** J10
South Bass I. *U.S.A.* 41°39N 82°49W **82** E2
South Bend *Ind., U.S.A.* 41°41N 86°15W **80** E10
South Bend *Wash.,*
  U.S.A. 46°40N 123°48W **78** D3
South Boston *U.S.A.* 36°42N 78°54W **81** G14
South Branch *Canada* 47°55N 59°2W **73** C8
South Brook *Canada* 49°26N 56°5W **73** C8
South Brother, I. *India* 10°56N 92°37E **45** J11
South Bruny I. *Australia* 43°20S 147°15E **63** G4
South Carolina □ *U.S.A.* 34°0N 81°0W **85** E14
South Charleston
  U.S.A. 38°22N 81°44W **81** F13
South China Sea *Asia* 10°0N 113°0E **36** C4
South Cumberland Is. △
  Australia 20°42S 149°11E **62** b
South Dakota □ *U.S.A.* 44°15N 100°0W **80** C4
South Dayton *U.S.A.* 42°21N 79°3W **82** D5
South Deerfield *U.S.A.* 42°29N 72°37W **83** D12
South Downs *U.K.* 50°52N 0°25W **13** G7
South Downs △ *U.K.* 50°50N 0°50W **13** G7
South East C. *Australia* 43°40S 146°50E **63** G4
South East Is. *Australia* 34°17S 123°30E **61** F3
South Esk → *U.K.* 56°43N 2°31W **11** E6
South Fiji Basin *Pac. Oc.* 26°0S 175°0E **64** K9
South Foreland *U.K.* 51°8N 1°24E **13** F9
South Fork American →
  U.S.A. 38°57N 120°59W **78** G5
South Fork Feather →
  U.S.A. 39°17N 121°36W **78** F5
South Fork Grand →
  U.S.A. 45°43N 102°17W **80** C2
South Fork Milk →
  U.S.A. 48°4N 106°19W **76** B10
South Fork Republican →
  U.S.A. 40°3N 101°31W **80** E3
South Georgia *Antarctica* 54°30S 37°0W **96** G4
South Gloucestershire □
  U.K. 51°32N 2°28W **13** F5
South Hadley *U.S.A.* 42°16N 72°35W **83** D12
South Haven *U.S.A.* 42°24N 86°16W **80** D10
South Henik L. *Canada* 61°30N 97°20W **71** A9
South Horr *Kenya* 2°12N 36°56E **54** D7
South I. *India* 10°3N 72°17E **45** J1
South I. *N.Z.* 44°0S 170°0E **59** F3
South Indian Lake
  Canada 56°47N 98°56W **71** B9
South Invercargill *N.Z.* 46°26S 168°23E **59** G2
South Knife → *Canada* 58°55N 94°37W **71** B10
South Koel → *India* 22°32N 85°14E **43** H11
South Korea ■ *Asia* 36°0N 128°0E **33** G15
South Lake Tahoe
  U.S.A. 38°57N 119°59W **78** G6
South Lanarkshire □
  U.K. 55°37N 3°53W **11** F5
South Loup → *U.S.A.* 41°4N 98°39W **80** E4
South Magnetic Pole
  Antarctica 64°8S 138°8E **5** C9
South Milwaukee
  U.S.A. 42°55N 87°52W **80** D10
South Molton *U.K.* 51°1N 3°51W **13** F4
South Moose L. *Canada* 53°49N 100°1W **71** C8
South Nahanni →
  Canada 61°3N 123°21W **70** A4
South Nation → *Canada* 45°34N 75°6W **83** A9
South Natuna Is. = Natuna
  Selatan, Kepulauan
  Indonesia 2°45N 109°0E **36** D3
South Negril Pt. *Jamaica* 18°16N 78°22W **88** a
South Orkney Is. *Antarctica* 63°0S 45°0W **5** C18
South Ossetia □ *Georgia* 42°21N 44°2E **19** F7
South Otselic *U.S.A.* 42°38N 75°46W **83** D9
South Pagai, I. = Pagai Selatan,
  Pulau *Indonesia* 3°0S 100°15E **36** E2
South Paris *U.S.A.* 44°14N 70°31W **83** B14
South Pittsburg *U.S.A.* 35°1N 85°42W **85** D12
South Platte → *U.S.A.* 41°7N 100°42W **80** E3
South Pole *Antarctica* 90°0S 0°0E **5** E
South Porcupine *Canada* 48°30N 81°12W **72** C3
South Portland *U.S.A.* 43°38N 70°15W **83** C14
South Pt. *Barbados* 13°2N 59°32W **89** g
South Pt. *U.S.A.* 44°52N 83°19W **82** B1

South River *Canada* 45°52N 79°23W **72** C4
South River *U.S.A.* 40°27N 74°23W **83** F10
South Ronaldsay *U.K.* 58°48N 2°58W **11** C6
South Sandwich Is.
Antarctica 57°0S 27°0W **5** B1
South Sandwich Trench
Atl. Oc. 56°0S 24°0W **5** B1
South Saskatchewan →
Canada 53°15N 105°5W **71** C7
South Seal → *Canada* 58°48N 98°8W **71** B9
South Sentinel I. *India* 10°59N 92°14E **45** J11
South Shetland Is.
Antarctica 62°0S 59°0W **5** C18
South Shields *U.K.* 55°0N 1°25W **12** C6
South Sioux City *U.S.A.* 42°28N 96°24W **80** D5
South Sister *U.S.A.* 44°4N 121°51W **76** D3
South Sudan ■ *Africa* 8°0N 30°0E **53** G11
South Taranaki Bight
N.Z. 39°40S 174°5E **59** C5
South Tasman Rise
S. Ocean 48°0S 146°0E **5** A10
South Thompson →
Canada 50°40N 120°20W **70** C4
South Twin I. *Canada* 53°7N 79°52W **72** B4
South Tyne → *U.K.* 54°59N 2°8W **12** C5
South Uist *U.K.* 57°20N 7°15W **11** D1
South Valley *U.S.A.* 35°1N 106°41W **77** J10
South Wellesley Is.
Australia 16°58S 139°17E **62** B2
South West C. *Australia* 43°34S 146°3E **63** G4
South West C. *N.Z.* 47°17S 167°28E **59** G1
South Williamsport
U.S.A. 41°13N 77°0W **82** E8
South Yorkshire □ *U.K.* 53°27N 1°36W **12** D6
Southampton *Canada* 44°30N 81°25W **82** B3
Southampton *U.K.* 50°54N 1°23W **13** G6
Southampton *U.S.A.* 40°53N 72°23W **83** F12
Southampton □ *U.K.* 50°54N 1°23W **13** G6
Southampton I. *Canada* 64°30N 84°0W **69** E15
Southaven *U.S.A.* 34°59N 90°0W **85** D9
Southbank *Canada* 54°2N 125°46W **70** C3
Southbridge *N.Z.* 43°48S 172°16E **59** E4
Southbridge *U.S.A.* 42°5N 72°2W **83** D12
Southend *Canada* 56°19N 103°22W **71** B8
Southend-on-Sea *U.K.* 51°32N 0°44E **13** F8
Southend-on-Sea □ *U.K.* 51°32N 0°44E **13** F8
Southern = Yuzhnyy □
Russia 44°0N 40°0E **26** E5
Southern Alps *N.Z.* 43°41S 170°11E **59** E3
Southern Cross *Australia* 31°12S 119°15E **61** F2
Southern Indian L.
Canada 57°10N 98°30W **71** B9
Southern Lau Group *Fiji* 18°40S 178°40W **59** a
Southern Ocean 62°0S 60°0E **5** C6
Southern Pines *U.S.A.* 35°11N 79°24W **85** D15
Southern Uplands *U.K.* 55°28N 3°52W **11** F5
Southington *U.S.A.* 41°36N 72°53W **83** E12
Southland □ *N.Z.* 45°30S 168°0E **59** F1
Southold *U.S.A.* 41°4N 72°26W **83** E12
Southport *Australia* 27°58S 153°25E **63** D5
Southport *U.K.* 53°39N 3°0W **12** D4
Southport *U.S.A.* 42°3N 76°49W **82** D8
Southwest △ *Australia* 43°8S 146°5E **63** G4
Southwest Pacific Basin
Pac. Oc. 40°0S 140°0W **5** A12
Southwold *U.K.* 52°20N 1°41E **13** E9
Southwood △ *Australia* 27°48S 150°8E **63** D5
Soutpansberg *S. Africa* 23°0S 29°30E **57** B4
Sovetsk *Kaliningrad, Russia* 55°6N 21°50E **9** J19
Sovetsk *Kirov, Russia* 57°38N 48°53E **18** C8
Sovetskaya Gavan
Russia 48°58N 140°18E **27** E15
Sowma'eh Sarā *Iran* 37°17N 49°18E **47** B6
Sōya-Kaikyō = La Perouse Str.
Asia 45°40N 142°0E **28** B11
Sōya-Misaki *Japan* 45°30N 141°55E **28** B10
Soyo *Angola* 6°13S 12°20E **54** F2
Sozh → *Belarus* 51°57N 30°48E **17** B16
Spa *Belgium* 50°29N 5°53E **15** D5
Spaatz I. *Antarctica* 73°10S 75°0W **5** D17
Spain ■ *Europe* 39°0N 4°0W **21** B4
Spalding *Australia* 33°30S 138°37E **63** E2
Spalding *U.K.* 52°48N 0°9W **12** E7
Spanaway *U.S.A.* 47°6N 122°26W **78** C4
Spangler *U.S.A.* 40°39N 78°48W **82** F6
Spanish *Canada* 46°12N 82°20W **72** C3
Spanish Fork *U.S.A.* 40°7N 111°39W **76** F8
Spanish Town
Br. Virgin Is. 18°26N 64°26W **89** e
Spanish Town *Jamaica* 18°0N 76°57W **88** a
Sparks *U.S.A.* 39°32N 119°45W **78** F7
Sparta = Sparti *Greece* 37°5S 22°25E **23** F10
Sparta *Mich., U.S.A.* 43°10N 85°42W **81** D11
Sparta *N.J., U.S.A.* 41°2N 74°38W **83** E10
Sparta *Wis., U.S.A.* 43°56N 90°49W **80** D8
Sparti *Greece* 37°5N 22°25E **23** F10
Spartanburg *U.S.A.* 34°56N 81°57W **85** D14
Spartivento, C. *Calabria, Italy* 37°55N 16°4E **22** F7
Spartivento, C. *Sard., Italy* 38°53N 8°50E **22** E3
Sparwood *Canada* 49°44N 114°53W **70** D6
Spassk Dalniy *Russia* 44°40N 132°48E **28** B6
Spatha, Akra *Greece* 35°42N 23°43E **23** G10
Spatsizi → *Canada* 57°42N 128°7W **70** B3
Spatsizi Plateau Wilderness △
Canada 57°40N 128°0W **70** B3
Spean → *U.K.* 56°55N 4°59W **11** E4
Spearfish *U.S.A.* 44°30N 103°52W **80** C2
Spearman *U.S.A.* 36°12N 101°12W **84** C4
Speculator *U.S.A.* 43°30N 74°22W **83** C10
Speightstown *Barbados* 13°15N 59°39W **89** g
Spence Bay = Taloyoak
Canada 69°32N 93°32W **68** D13
Spencer *Idaho, U.S.A.* 44°22N 112°11W **76** D7
Spencer *Iowa, U.S.A.* 43°9N 95°9W **80** D6
Spencer *N.Y., U.S.A.* 42°13N 76°30W **83** D8
Spencer, C. *Australia* 35°20S 136°53E **63** F2
Spencer B. *Namibia* 25°30S 14°47E **56** C1

Spencer G. *Australia* 34°0S 137°20E **63** E2
Spencerville *Canada* 44°51N 75°33W **83** B9
Spences Bridge *Canada* 50°25N 121°20W **70** C4
Spennymoor *U.K.* 54°42N 1°36W **12** C6
Spenser Mts. *N.Z.* 42°15S 172°45E **59** E4
Sperrin Mts. *U.K.* 54°50N 7°0W **10** B5
Spey → *U.K.* 57°40N 3°6W **11** D5
Speyer *Germany* 49°29N 8°25E **16** D5
Spezand *Pakistan* 29°59N 67°0E **42** E2
Spiddle *Ireland* 53°15N 9°18W **10** C2
Spirit Lake *U.S.A.* 46°15N 122°9W **78** D4
Spirit River *Canada* 55°45S 118°50W **70** B5
Spiritwood *Canada* 53°24N 107°33W **71** C7
Spithead *U.K.* 50°45N 1°10W **13** G6
Spitzbergen = Svalbard
Arctic 78°0N 17°0E **4** B8
Spjelkavik *Norway* 62°28N 6°22E **8** E12
Split *Croatia* 43°31N 16°26E **22** C7
Split L. *Canada* 56°8N 96°15W **71** B9
Split Lake *Canada* 56°8N 96°15W **71** B9
Spofford *U.S.A.* 29°10N 100°25W **84** G4
Spokane *U.S.A.* 47°40N 117°24W **76** C5
Spoleto *Italy* 42°44N 12°44E **22** C5
Spooner *U.S.A.* 45°50N 91°53W **80** C8
Sporoy Navolok, Mys
Russia 75°50N 68°40E **26** B7
Sprague *U.S.A.* 47°18N 117°59W **76** C5
Spratly I. *S. China Sea* 8°38N 111°55E **36** C4
Spratly Is. *S. China Sea* 8°20N 112°0E **36** C4
Spray *U.S.A.* 44°50N 119°48W **76** D4
Spree → *Germany* 52°32N 13°12E **16** B7
Sprengisandur *Iceland* 64°52N 18°7W **8** D4
Spring City *U.S.A.* 40°11N 75°33W **83** F9
Spring Creek *U.S.A.* 40°44N 115°35W **76** F6
Spring Garden *U.S.A.* 39°52N 120°47W **78** F6
Spring Hall *Barbados* 13°18N 59°36W **89** g
Spring Hill *U.S.A.* 28°27N 82°41W **85** G13
Spring Mts. *U.S.A.* 36°0N 115°45W **79** J11
Spring Valley *U.S.A.* 32°44N 116°59W **79** N10
Springbok *S. Africa* 29°42S 17°54E **56** C2
Springboro *U.S.A.* 41°48N 80°22W **82** E4
Springdale *Canada* 49°30N 56°6W **73** C8
Springdale *U.S.A.* 36°11N 94°8W **84** C7
Springer *U.S.A.* 36°22N 104°36W **77** H11
Springerville *U.S.A.* 34°8N 109°17W **77** J9
Springfield *Canada* 42°50N 80°56W **82** D4
Springfield *N.Z.* 43°19S 171°56E **59** E3
Springfield *Colo.,
U.S.A.* 37°24N 102°37W **77** H12
Springfield *Ill., U.S.A.* 39°48N 89°39W **80** F9
Springfield *Mass., U.S.A.* 42°6N 72°35W **83** D12
Springfield *Mo., U.S.A.* 37°13N 93°17W **80** G7
Springfield *Ohio, U.S.A.* 39°55N 83°49W **81** F12
Springfield *Oreg., U.S.A.* 44°3N 123°1W **76** D2
Springfield *Tenn., U.S.A.* 36°31N 86°53W **85** C11
Springfield *Vt., U.S.A.* 43°18N 72°29W **83** C12
Springfontein *S. Africa* 30°15S 25°40E **56** D4
Springhill *Canada* 45°40N 64°4W **73** C7
Springhill *U.S.A.* 33°0N 93°28W **84** E8
Springhouse *Canada* 51°56N 122°7W **70** C4
Springlands = Corriverton
Guyana 5°55N 57°20W **92** B7
Springs *S. Africa* 26°13S 28°25E **57** C4
Springsure *Australia* 24°8S 148°6E **62** C4
Springvale *Australia* 43°28N 70°48W **83** C14
Springville *Calif., U.S.A.* 36°8N 118°49W **78** J8
Springville *N.Y., U.S.A.* 42°31N 78°40W **82** D6
Springville *Utah, U.S.A.* 40°10N 111°37W **76** F8
Springwater *U.S.A.* 42°38N 77°35W **82** D7
Spruce-Creek *U.S.A.* 40°36N 78°9W **82** F6
Spruce Knob-Seneca Rocks △
U.S.A. 38°50N 79°30W **81** F14
Spruce Mt. *U.S.A.* 44°12N 72°19W **83** B12
Sprucedale *Canada* 45°29N 79°28W **82** A5
Spur *U.S.A.* 33°28N 100°52W **84** E4
Spurn Hd. *U.K.* 53°35N 0°8E **12** D8
Spuzzum *Canada* 49°37N 121°23W **70** D4
Squam L. *U.S.A.* 43°45N 71°32W **83** C13
Squamish *Canada* 49°45N 123°10W **70** D4
Square Islands *Canada* 52°47N 55°47W **73** B8
Squires, Mt. *Australia* 26°14S 127°28E **61** E4
Srbija = Serbia ■ *Europe* 43°20N 20°0E **23** B9
Sre Ambel *Cambodia* 11°8N 103°46E **39** G4
Sre Khtum *Cambodia* 12°10N 106°52E **39** F6
Sre Umbell = Sre Ambel
Cambodia 11°8N 103°46E **39** G4
Srebrenica *Bos.-H.* 44°6N 19°18E **23** B8
Sredinnyy Khrebet
Russia 57°0N 160°0E **27** D17
Sredinnyy Ra. = Sredinnyy
Khrebet *Russia* 57°0N 160°0E **27** D17
Srednekolymsk *Russia* 67°27N 153°40E **27** C16
Śrem *Poland* 52°6N 17°2E **17** B9
Sremska Mitrovica *Serbia* 44°59N 19°38E **23** B8
Srepok → *Cambodia* 13°33N 106°16E **38** F6
Sretensk *Russia* 52°10N 117°40E **27** D12
Sri Aman = Bandar Sri Aman
Malaysia 1°15N 111°32E **36** D4
Sri Kalahasti *India* 13°45N 79°44E **45** H4
Sri Lanka ■ *Asia* 7°30N 80°50E **45** L5
Sri Pada = Adam's Peak
Sri Lanka 6°48N 80°30E **45** L5
Sriharikota I. *India* 13°40N 80°20E **45** H5
Srikakulam *India* 18°14N 83°58E **44** E6
Srinagar *India* 34°5N 74°50E **43** B6
Srivardhan *India* 18°4N 73°3E **44** E1
Srivilliputtur *India* 9°31N 77°40E **45** K3
Srono *Indonesia* 8°24S 114°16E **37** J17
Srungavarapukota *India* 18°7N 83°10E **44** E6
Staaten → *Australia* 16°24S 141°17E **62** B3
Staaten River △
Australia 16°15S 142°40E **62** B3
Stade *Germany* 53°35N 9°29E **16** B5
Stadskanaal *Neths.* 53°4N 6°55E **15** A6
Staffa *U.K.* 56°27N 6°21W **11** E2
Stafford *U.K.* 52°49N 2°7W **12** E5
Stafford *U.S.A.* 37°58N 98°36W **80** G4

Stafford Springs *U.S.A.* 41°57N 72°18W **83** E12
Staffordshire □ *U.K.* 52°53N 2°10W **12** E5
Staines *U.K.* 51°26N 0°29W **13** F7
Stakhanov *Ukraine* 48°35N 38°40E **19** E6
Stalowa Wola *Poland* 50°34N 22°3E **17** C12
Stalybridge *U.K.* 53°28N 2°3W **12** D5
Stamford *Australia* 21°15S 143°46E **62** C3
Stamford *U.K.* 52°39N 0°29W **13** E7
Stamford *Conn., U.S.A.* 41°3N 73°32W **83** E11
Stamford *N.Y., U.S.A.* 42°25N 74°38W **83** D10
Stamford *Tex., U.S.A.* 32°57N 99°48W **84** E5
Stampriet *Namibia* 24°20S 18°28E **56** C2
Stamps *U.S.A.* 33°22N 93°30W **84** E8
Standerton *S. Africa* 26°55S 29°7E **57** C4
Standish *U.S.A.* 43°59N 83°57W **81** D12
Stanford *S. Africa* 34°26S 19°29E **56** D2
Stanford *U.S.A.* 47°9N 110°13W **76** C8
Stanger *S. Africa* 29°27S 31°14E **57** C5
Stängselåsen = Salpausselkä
Finland 61°3N 26°15E **8** F22
Stanislaus → *U.S.A.* 37°40N 121°14W **78** H5
Stanke Dimitrov *Bulgaria* 42°17N 23°9E **23** C10
Stanley *Australia* 40°46S 145°19E **63** G4
Stanley *Falk. Is.* 51°40S 59°51W **96** G5
Stanley *U.K.* 54°53N 1°41W **12** C6
Stanley *Idaho, U.S.A.* 44°13N 114°56W **76** D6
Stanley *N. Dak., U.S.A.* 48°19N 102°23W **80** A2
Stanley *N.Y., U.S.A.* 42°48N 77°6W **82** D7
Stanley Mission *Canada* 55°25N 104°33W **71** B8
Stanley Res. *India* 11°50N 77°40E **45** J3
Stannards *U.S.A.* 42°5N 77°55W **82** D7
Stanovoy Khrebet *Russia* 55°0N 130°0E **27** D14
Stanovoy Ra. = Stanovoy Khrebet
Russia 55°0N 130°0E **27** D14
Stansmore Ra. *Australia* 21°23S 128°33E **60** D4
Stansted, London ✈ (STN)
U.K. 51°54N 0°14E **13** F8
Stanthorpe *Australia* 28°36S 151°59E **63** D5
Stanton *U.S.A.* 32°8N 101°48W **84** E4
Stanwood *U.S.A.* 48°15N 122°23W **78** B4
Staples *Canada* 42°10N 82°35W **82** D2
Staples *U.S.A.* 46°21N 94°48W **80** B6
Stapleton *U.S.A.* 41°29N 100°31W **80** E3
Star City *Canada* 52°50N 104°20W **71** C8
Star Lake *U.S.A.* 44°10N 75°2W **83** B9
Stara Planina *Bulgaria* 43°15N 23°0E **23** C10
Stara Zagora *Bulgaria* 42°26N 25°39E **23** C11
Starachowice *Poland* 51°3N 21°2E **17** C11
Staraya Russa *Russia* 57°58N 31°23E **18** C5
Starbuck I. *Kiribati* 5°37S 155°55W **65** H12
Starcke △ *Australia* 14°56S 145°2E **62** A4
Stargard Szczeciński
Poland 53°20N 15°0E **16** B8
Staritsa *Russia* 56°33N 34°55E **18** C5
Starke *U.S.A.* 29°57N 82°7W **85** G13
Starkville *U.S.A.* 33°28N 88°49W **85** E10
Starogard Gdański
Poland 53°59N 18°30E **17** B10
Starokonstantinov =
Starokonstyantyniv
Ukraine 49°48N 27°10E **17** D14
Starokonstyantyniv
Ukraine 49°48N 27°10E **17** D14
Start Pt. *U.K.* 50°13N 3°39W **13** G4
Staryy Chartoryysk
Ukraine 51°15N 25°54E **17** C13
Staryy Oskol *Russia* 51°19N 37°55E **19** D6
State College *U.S.A.* 40°48N 77°52W **82** F7
Stateline *U.S.A.* 38°57N 119°56W **78** G7
Staten, I. = Estados, I. de Los
Argentina 54°40S 64°30W **96** G4
Staten I. *U.S.A.* 40°35N 74°9W **83** F10
Statesboro *U.S.A.* 32°27N 81°47W **85** E14
Statesville *U.S.A.* 35°47N 80°53W **85** D14
Statia = St. Eustatius
W. Indies 17°20N 63°0W **89** C7
Stauffer *U.S.A.* 34°45N 119°3W **79** L7
Staunton *Ill., U.S.A.* 39°1N 89°47W **80** F9
Staunton *Va., U.S.A.* 38°9N 79°4W **81** F14
Stavanger *Norway* 58°57N 5°40E **9** G11
Staveley *N.Z.* 43°40S 171°32E **59** E3
Stavelot *Belgium* 50°23N 5°55E **15** D5
Stavern *Norway* 59°0N 10°1E **9** G14
Stavoren *Neths.* 52°53N 5°22E **15** B5
Stavropol *Russia* 45°5N 42°0E **19** E7
Stawell *Australia* 37°5S 142°47E **63** F3
Stawell → *Australia* 20°20S 142°55E **62** C3
Stayner *Canada* 44°25N 80°5W **82** B4
Stayton *U.S.A.* 44°48N 122°48W **76** D2
Steamboat Springs
U.S.A. 40°29N 106°50W **76** F10
Steele *U.S.A.* 46°51N 99°55W **80** B4
Steelton *U.S.A.* 40°14N 76°50W **82** F8
Steen River *Canada* 59°40N 117°12W **70** B5
Steens Mt. *U.S.A.* 42°35N 118°40W **76** E4
Steenwijk *Neths.* 52°47N 6°7E **15** B6
Steep Pt. *Australia* 26°8S 113°8E **61** E1
Steep Rock *Canada* 51°30N 98°48W **71** C9
Stefanie L. = Chew Bahir
Ethiopia 4°40N 36°50E **49** G2
Stefansson Bay *Antarctica* 67°20S 59°8E **5** C5
Steiermark □ *Austria* 47°26N 15°0E **16** E8
Steilacoom *U.S.A.* 47°10N 122°36W **78** C4
Steilrandberge *Namibia* 17°45S 13°20E **56** A1
Steinbach *Canada* 49°32N 96°40W **71** D9
Steinhausen *Namibia* 21°49S 18°20E **56** C2
Steinkjer *Norway* 64°1N 11°31E **8** D14
Steinkopf *S. Africa* 29°18S 17°43E **56** D2
Stellarton *Canada* 45°32N 62°30W **73** C7
Stellenbosch *S. Africa* 33°58S 18°50E **56** D2
Stendal *Germany* 52°36N 11°53E **16** B6
Steornabhaigh = Stornoway
U.K. 58°13N 6°23W **11** C2
Stepanakert = Xankändi
Azerbaijan 39°52N 46°49E **46** B5
Stephens Creek *Australia* 31°50S 141°30E **63** E3
Stephens I. *Canada* 54°10N 130°45W **70** C2
Stephens L. *Canada* 56°32N 95°0W **71** B9

Stephenville *Canada* 48°31N 58°35W **73** C8
Stephenville *U.S.A.* 32°13N 98°12W **84** E5
Steppe *Asia* 50°0N 50°0E **24** C7
Sterkstroom *S. Africa* 31°32S 26°32E **56** D4
Sterling *Colo., U.S.A.* 40°37N 103°13W **76** F12
Sterling *Ill., U.S.A.* 41°48N 89°42W **80** E9
Sterling *Kans., U.S.A.* 38°13N 98°12W **80** F4
Sterling City *U.S.A.* 31°51N 101°0W **84** F4
Sterling Heights *U.S.A.* 42°35N 83°0W **81** D12
Sterling Run *U.S.A.* 41°25N 78°12W **82** E6
Sterlitamak *Russia* 53°40N 56°0E **18** D10
Stettin = Szczecin *Poland* 53°27N 14°27E **16** B8
Stettiner Haff *Germany* 53°47N 14°15E **16** B8
Stettler *Canada* 52°19N 112°40W **70** C6
Steubenville *U.S.A.* 40°22N 80°37W **82** F4
Stevenage *U.K.* 51°55N 0°13W **13** F7
Stevens Point *U.S.A.* 44°31N 89°34W **80** C9
Stevenson *U.S.A.* 45°42N 121°53W **78** E5
Stevenson → *Australia* 27°6S 135°33E **63** D2
Stevenson L. *Canada* 53°55N 96°0W **71** C9
Stevensville *U.S.A.* 46°30N 114°5W **76** C6
Stewart *Canada* 55°56N 129°57W **70** B3
Stewart *U.S.A.* 39°5N 119°46W **78** F7
Stewart → *Canada* 63°19N 139°26W **68** E4
Stewart, C. *Australia* 11°57S 134°56E **62** A1
Stewart, I. *Chile* 54°50S 71°15W **96** G2
Stewart I. *N.Z.* 46°58S 167°54E **59** G1
Stewarts Point *U.S.A.* 38°39N 123°24W **78** G3
Stewartville *U.S.A.* 43°51N 92°29W **80** D7
Stewiacke *Canada* 45°9N 63°22W **73** C7
Steynsburg *S. Africa* 31°15S 25°49E **56** D4
Steyr *Austria* 48°3N 14°25E **16** D8
Steytlerville *S. Africa* 33°17S 24°19E **56** D3
Stigler *U.S.A.* 35°15N 95°8W **84** D7
Stikine → *Canada* 56°40N 132°30W **70** B2
Stilfontein *S. Africa* 26°51S 26°50E **56** C4
Stillwater *N.Z.* 42°27S 171°20E **59** E3
Stillwater *N.Y., U.S.A.* 42°55N 73°41W **83** D11
Stillwater *Okla., U.S.A.* 36°7N 97°4W **84** C6
Stillwater Range *U.S.A.* 39°50N 118°5W **76** G4
Stillwater Res. *U.S.A.* 43°54N 75°3W **83** C9
Stilwell *U.S.A.* 35°49N 94°38W **84** D7
Stînga Nistrului □
Moldova 47°20N 29°15E **17** E15
Ştip *Macedonia* 41°42N 22°10E **23** D10
Stirling *Canada* 44°18N 77°33W **82** B7
Stirling *U.K.* 56°8N 3°57W **11** E5
Stirling □ *U.K.* 56°12N 4°18W **11** E4
Stirling Ra. *Australia* 34°23S 118°0E **61** F2
Stirling Range △
Australia 34°26S 118°20E **61** F2
Stittsville *Canada* 45°15N 75°55W **83** A9
Stjernøya *Norway* 70°20N 22°40E **8** A20
Stjørdalshalsen *Norway* 63°29N 10°51E **8** E14
Stockerau *Austria* 48°24N 16°12E **16** D9
Stockport *U.K.* 53°25N 2°9W **12** D5
Stocksbridge *U.K.* 53°29N 1°35W **12** D6
Stockton *Calif., U.S.A.* 37°58N 121°17W **78** H5
Stockton *Kans., U.S.A.* 39°26N 99°16W **80** F4
Stockton *Mo., U.S.A.* 37°42N 93°48W **80** G7
Stockton-on-Tees *U.K.* 54°35N 1°19W **12** C6
Stockton-on-Tees □ *U.K.* 54°35N 1°19W **12** C6
Stockton Plateau
U.S.A. 30°30N 102°30W **84** F3
Stoeng Treng *Cambodia* 13°31N 105°58E **38** F5
Stoer, Pt. of *U.K.* 58°16N 5°23W **11** C3
Stoke-on-Trent *U.K.* 53°1N 2°11W **12** D5
Stoke-on-Trent □ *U.K.* 53°1N 2°11W **12** D5
Stokes △ *Australia* 33°45S 121°11E **61** F3
Stokes Bay *Canada* 45°0N 81°28W **82** B3
Stokes Pt. *Australia* 40°10S 143°56E **63** G3
Stokes Ra. *Australia* 15°50S 130°50E **60** C5
Stokksnes *Iceland* 64°14N 14°58W **8** D6
Stokmarknes *Norway* 68°34N 14°54E **8** B16
Stolac *Bos.-H.* 43°5N 17°59E **23** C7
Stolbovoy, Ostrov
Russia 74°44N 135°14E **27** B14
Stolbtsy = Stowbtsy
Belarus 53°30N 26°43E **17** B14
Stolin *Belarus* 51°53N 26°50E **17** C14
Stone *U.K.* 52°55N 2°9W **12** E5
Stoneboro *U.S.A.* 41°20N 80°7W **82** E4
Stonehaven *U.K.* 56°59N 2°12W **11** E6
Stonehenge *Australia* 24°22S 143°17E **62** C3
Stonehenge *U.K.* 51°9N 1°45W **13** F6
Stonewall *Canada* 50°10N 97°19W **71** C9
Stony I. *U.S.A.* 43°53N 76°19W **83** C8
Stony L. *Man., Canada* 58°51N 98°40W **71** B9
Stony L. *Ont., Canada* 44°30N 78°5W **82** B6
Stony Point *U.S.A.* 41°14N 73°59W **83** E11
Stony Pt. *U.S.A.* 43°50N 76°18W **83** C8
Stony Rapids *Canada* 59°16N 105°50W **71** B7
Stony Tunguska = Tunguska,
Podkamennaya →
Russia 61°50N 90°13E **27** C10
Stonyford *U.S.A.* 39°23N 122°33W **78** F4
Stora Lulevatten *Sweden* 67°10N 19°30E **8** C18
Storavan *Sweden* 65°45N 18°10E **8** D18
Stord *Norway* 59°52N 5°23E **9** G11
Store Bælt *Denmark* 55°20N 11°0E **9** J14
Storkerson Pen.
Canada 72°30N 106°30W **68** C10
Storm B. *Australia* 43°10S 147°30E **63** G4
Storm Lake *U.S.A.* 42°39N 95°13W **80** D6
Stormberge *S. Africa* 31°16S 26°17E **56** D4
Stormsrivier *S. Africa* 33°59S 23°52E **56** D3
Stornoway *U.K.* 58°13N 6°23W **11** C2
Storozhinets = Storozhynets
Ukraine 48°14N 25°45E **17** D13
Storozhynets *Ukraine* 48°14N 25°45E **17** D13
Storrs *U.S.A.* 41°49N 72°15W **83** E12
Storsjön *Sweden* 63°9N 14°30E **8** E16
Storuman *Sweden* 65°5N 17°10E **8** D17
Storuman, L. *Sweden* 65°13N 16°50E **8** D17
Stouffville *Canada* 43°58N 79°15W **82** C5
Stoughton *Canada* 49°40N 103°0W **71** D8
Stour → *Dorset, U.K.* 50°43N 1°47W **13** G6
Stour → *Kent, U.K.* 51°18N 1°22E **13** F9
Stour → *Suffolk, U.K.* 51°57N 1°4E **13** F9

Stourbridge *U.K.* 52°28N 2°8W **13** E5
Stout L. *Canada* 52°0N 94°40W **71** C10
Stove Pipe Wells Village
U.S.A. 36°35N 117°11W **79** J9
Stow *U.S.A.* 41°10N 81°27W **82** E3
Stowbtsy *Belarus* 53°30N 26°43E **17** B14
Stowmarket *U.K.* 52°12N 1°0E **13** E9
Strabane *U.K.* 54°50N 7°27W **10** B4
Strahan *Australia* 42°9S 145°20E **63** G4
Stralsund *Germany* 54°18N 13°4E **16** A7
Strand *S. Africa* 34°9S 18°48E **56** D2
Stranda *Møre og Romsdal,
Norway* 62°19N 6°58E **8** E12
Stranda *Nord-Trøndelag,
Norway* 63°33N 10°14E **8** E14
Strangford L. *U.K.* 54°30N 5°37W **10** B6
Stranorlar *Ireland* 54°48N 7°46W **10** B4
Stranraer *U.K.* 54°54N 5°1W **11** G3
Strasbourg *Canada* 51°4N 104°55W **71** C8
Strasbourg *France* 48°35N 7°42E **20** B7
Stratford *Canada* 43°23N 81°0W **82** C4
Stratford *N.Z.* 39°20S 174°19E **59** C5
Stratford *Calif., U.S.A.* 36°11N 119°49W **78** J7
Stratford *Conn., U.S.A.* 41°12N 73°8W **83** E11
Stratford *Tex., U.S.A.* 36°20N 102°4W **84** C3
Stratford-upon-Avon
U.K. 52°12N 1°42W **13** E6
Strath Spey *U.K.* 57°9N 3°49W **11** D5
Strathalbyn *Australia* 35°13S 138°53E **63** F2
Strathaven *U.K.* 55°40N 4°5W **11** F4
Strathcona △ *Canada* 49°38N 125°40W **70** D3
Strathmore *Canada* 51°5N 113°18W **70** C6
Strathmore *U.K.* 56°37N 3°7W **11** E5
Strathmore *U.S.A.* 36°9N 119°4W **78** J7
Strathnaver *Canada* 53°20N 122°33W **70** C4
Strathpeffer *U.K.* 57°35N 4°32W **11** D4
Strathroy *Canada* 42°58N 81°38W **82** D3
Strathy Pt. *U.K.* 58°36N 4°1W **11** C4
Strattanville *U.S.A.* 41°12N 79°19W **82** E5
Stratton *U.S.A.* 45°8N 70°26W **83** A14
Stratton Mt. *U.S.A.* 43°4N 72°55W **83** C12
Straubing *Germany* 48°52N 12°34E **16** D7
Straumnes *Iceland* 66°26N 23°8W **8** C2
Strawberry → *U.S.A.* 40°10N 110°24W **76** F8
Streaky B. *Australia* 32°48S 134°13E **63** E1
Streaky Bay *Australia* 32°51S 134°18E **63** E1
Streator *U.S.A.* 41°8N 88°50W **80** E9
Streetsboro *U.S.A.* 41°14N 81°21W **82** E3
Streetsville *Canada* 43°35N 79°42W **82** C5
Streng → *Cambodia* 13°12N 103°37E **38** F4
Strezhevoy *Russia* 60°42N 77°34E **26** C8
Strimonas → *Greece* 40°46N 23°51E **23** D10
Strokestown *Ireland* 53°47N 8°5W **10** C3
Stroma *U.K.* 58°41N 3°7W **11** C5
Strómboli *Italy* 38°47N 15°13E **22** E6
Stromeferry *U.K.* 57°21N 5°33W **11** D3
Stromness *U.K.* 58°58N 3°17W **11** C5
Stromsburg *U.S.A.* 41°7N 97°36W **80** E5
Strömstad *Sweden* 58°56N 11°10E **9** G14
Strömsund *Sweden* 63°51N 15°33E **8** E16
Strongsville *U.S.A.* 41°19N 81°50W **82** E3
Stronsay *U.K.* 59°7N 2°35W **11** B6
Stroud *U.K.* 51°45N 2°13W **13** F5
Stroud Road *Australia* 32°18S 151°57E **63** E5
Stroudsburg *U.S.A.* 40°59N 75°12W **83** F9
Struer *Denmark* 56°30N 8°35E **9** H13
Strugi Krasnyye *Russia* 58°21N 29°1E **9** G23
Strumica *Macedonia* 41°28N 22°41E **23** D10
Struthers *U.S.A.* 41°4N 80°39W **82** E4
Stryker *U.S.A.* 48°41N 114°46W **76** B6
Stryy *Ukraine* 49°16N 23°48E **17** D12
Strzelecki Cr. →
Australia 29°37S 139°59E **63** D2
Strzelecki Desert
Australia 29°30S 140°0E **63** D3
Stuart *Fla., U.S.A.* 27°12N 80°15W **85** H14
Stuart *Nebr., U.S.A.* 42°36N 99°8W **80** D4
Stuart → *Canada* 54°0N 123°35W **70** C4
Stuart Bluff Ra. *Australia* 22°50S 131°52E **60** D5
Stuart L. *Canada* 54°30N 124°30W **70** C4
Stuart L. *Canada* 54°30N 124°30W **70** C4
Stuart Ra. *Australia* 29°10S 134°56E **63** D1
Stull L. *Canada* 54°24N 92°34W **72** B1
Stung Treng = Stoeng Treng
Cambodia 13°31N 105°58E **38** F5
Stupart → *Canada* 56°0N 93°25W **72** A1
Sturge I. *Antarctica* 67°26S 164°47E **5** C11
Sturgeon B. *Canada* 52°0N 97°50W **71** C9
Sturgeon Bay *U.S.A.* 44°50N 87°23W **80** C10
Sturgeon Falls *Canada* 46°25N 79°57W **72** C4
Sturgeon L. *Alta., Canada* 55°6N 117°32W **70** B5
Sturgeon L. *Ont., Canada* 50°0N 90°45W **72** C1
Sturgeon L. *Ont., Canada* 44°28N 78°43W **82** B6
Sturgis *Canada* 51°56N 102°36W **71** C8
Sturgis *Mich., U.S.A.* 41°48N 85°25W **81** E11
Sturgis *S. Dak., U.S.A.* 44°25N 103°31W **80** C2
Sturt △ *Australia* 27°17S 141°37E **63** D3
Sturt Cr. → *Australia* 19°8S 127°50E **60** C4
Sturt Stony Desert
Australia 28°30S 141°0E **63** D3
Stutterheim *S. Africa* 32°33S 27°28E **56** D4
Stuttgart *Germany* 48°48N 9°11E **16** D5
Stuttgart *U.S.A.* 34°30N 91°33W **84** D9
Stuyvesant *U.S.A.* 42°23N 73°45W **83** D11
Stykkishólmur *Iceland* 65°2N 22°40W **8** D2
Styria = Steiermark □
Austria 47°26N 15°0E **16** E8
Su Xian = Suzhou *China* 33°41N 116°59E **32** H9
Suakin *Sudan* 19°8N 37°20E **53** E13
Suamico *U.S.A.* 44°38N 88°2W **80** C9
Suan *N. Korea* 38°42N 126°22E **33** E14
Suana *Indonesia* 8°44S 115°36E **37** K18
Suar *India* 29°2N 79°3E **43** E8
Subã *Si. Arabia* 27°10N 35°40E **46** E2
Subang *Indonesia* 6°34S 107°45E **37** G12
Subansiri → *India* 26°48N 93°50E **41** F18
Subarnagiri *India* 19°50N 83°15E **44** K6
Subarnarekha → *India* 22°34N 87°24E **43** H12

Subayhah Si. Arabia 30°2N 38°50E 46 D3
Subi Indonesia 2°58N 108°50E 36 D3
Subotica Serbia 46°6N 19°39E 23 A8
Suceava Romania 47°38N 26°16E 17 E14
Suchan = Partizansk
Russia 43°8N 133°9E 27 E14
Suchil Mexico 23°39N 103°54W 86 C4
Suchou = Suzhou
China 31°19N 120°38E 35 B13
Süchow = Xuzhou
China 34°18N 117°10E 33 G9
Suck → Ireland 53°17N 8°3W 10 C3
Sucre Bolivia 19°0S 65°15W 92 G5
Sucuriú → Brazil 20°47S 51°38W 93 H8
Sud, Pte. du Canada 49°3N 62°14W 73 C7
Sud-Ouest, Pte. Canada 49°23N 63°36W 73 C7
Sud Ouest, Pte. Mauritius 20°28S 57°18E 55 d
Sudan ■ Africa 15°0N 30°0E 53 E11
Sudbury Canada 46°30N 81°0W 72 C3
Sudbury U.K. 52°2N 0°45E 13 E8
Sudd South Sudan 8°20N 30°0E 53 G12
Suden Mts. = Sudety
Europe 50°20N 16°45E 17 C9
Sudety Europe 50°20N 16°45E 17 C9
Suðuroy Færoe Is. 61°32N 6°50W 8 F9
Sudirman, Pegunungan
Indonesia 4°30S 137°0E 37 E9
Sudong, Pulau Singapore 1°13N 103°44E 39 d
Sueca Spain 39°12N 0°21W 21 C5
Suemez I. U.S.A. 55°15N 133°20W 70 B2
Suez = El Suweis Egypt 29°58N 32°31E 53 C12
Suez, G. of = Suweis, Khalig el
Egypt 28°40N 33°0E 53 C12
Suez Canal = Suweis, Qanâ es
Egypt 31°0N 32°20E 53 B12
Suffield Canada 50°12N 111°10W 70 C6
Suffolk U.S.A. 36°44N 76°35W 81 G15
Suffolk □ U.K. 52°16N 1°0E 13 E9
Sugaing = Sagaing
Burma 21°52N 95°59E 41 J19
Sugar Grove U.S.A. 41°59N 79°20W 82 E5
Sugarcreek U.S.A. 41°25N 79°52W 82 E5
Sugarive → India 26°16N 86°24E 43 F12
Sugluk = Salluit Canada 62°14N 75°38W 69 E16
Suḥār Oman 24°20N 56°40E 47 E8
Sühbaatar Mongolia 50°17N 106°10E 30 A10
Sühbaatar □ Mongolia 45°30N 114°0E 32 B8
Suheli Par India 10°5N 72°17E 45 J1
Suhl Germany 50°36N 10°42E 16 C6
Sui Pakistan 28°37N 69°19E 42 E3
Sui Xian China 34°25N 115°2E 32 G8
Suichang China 28°29N 119°15E 35 C12
Suichuan China 26°20N 114°32E 35 D10
Suide China 37°30N 110°12E 32 F6
Suifenhe China 44°25N 131°10E 33 B16
Suihua China 46°32N 126°55E 31 B14
Suijiang China 28°40N 103°59E 34 C4
Suining Hunan, China 26°35N 110°10E 35 D8
Suining Jiangsu, China 33°56N 117°58E 33 H9
Suining Sichuan, China 30°26N 105°35E 34 B5
Suiping China 33°10N 113°59E 32 H7
Suir → Ireland 52°16N 7°9W 10 D4
Suisse = Switzerland ■
Europe 46°30N 8°0E 20 C8
Suisun City U.S.A. 38°15N 122°2W 78 G4
Suixi China 21°19N 110°18E 35 G8
Suiyang Guizhou, China 27°58N 107°18E 34 D6
Suiyang Heilongjiang,
China 44°30N 130°56E 33 B16
Suizhong China 40°21N 120°20E 33 D11
Suizhou China 31°42N 113°24E 35 B9
Sujangarh India 27°42N 74°31E 42 F6
Sujiatun China 41°39N 123°20E 33 D12
Sukabumi Indonesia 6°56S 106°50E 37 G12
Sukadana Indonesia 1°10S 110°0E 36 E4
Sukagawa Japan 37°17N 140°23E 29 F10
Sukamade Indonesia 8°30S 113°52E 37 H15
Sukaraja Indonesia 2°28S 110°25E 36 E4
Sukawati Indonesia 8°35S 115°17E 37 K18
Sukch'ŏn N. Korea 39°22N 125°35E 33 E13
Sukhna → Russia 61°15N 46°39E 18 C6
Sukhothai Thailand 17°1N 99°49E 38 D2
Sukhumi = Sokhumi
Georgia 43°0N 41°0E 19 F7
Sukkur Pakistan 27°42N 68°54E 42 F3
Sukkur Barrage Pakistan 27°40N 68°50E 42 F3
Sukma India 18°24N 81°45E 44 E5
Sukri → India 25°4N 71°43E 42 G4
Sukumo Japan 32°56N 132°44E 29 H6
Sukunka → Canada 55°45N 121°15W 70 B4
Sula, Kepulauan Indonesia 1°45S 125°0E 37 E7
Sulaco → Honduras 15°2N 87°44W 88 C2
Sulaiman Range Pakistan 30°30N 69°50E 42 D3
Sülär Iran 31°53N 51°54E 47 D6
Sulawesi Indonesia 2°0S 120°0E 37 E6
Sulawesi Barat □ Indonesia 3°0S 119°0E 37 E5
Sulawesi Sea = Celebes Sea
Indonesia 3°0N 123°0E 37 D6
Sulawesi Selatan □
Indonesia 2°30S 120°0E 37 E6
Sulawesi Tengah □
Indonesia 1°30S 121°0E 37 E6
Sulawesi Tenggara □
Indonesia 3°50S 122°0E 37 E6
Sulawesi Utara □ Indonesia 1°0N 120°0E 37 D6
Sulima S. Leone 6°58N 11°32W 52 G3
Sulina Romania 45°10N 29°40E 17 F15
Sulitjelma Norway 67°9N 16°3E 8 C17
Sullana Peru 4°52S 80°39W 92 D2
Sullivan Ill., U.S.A. 39°36N 88°37W 80 F9
Sullivan Ind., U.S.A. 39°6N 87°24W 80 F2
Sullivan Mo., U.S.A. 38°13N 91°10W 80 F8
Sullivan Bay Canada 50°55N 126°50W 70 C3
Sullivan I. = Lanbi Kyun
Burma 10°50N 98°20E 39 G2
Sullom Voe U.K. 60°27N 1°20W 11 A7
Sulphur La., U.S.A. 30°14N 93°23W 84 F8
Sulphur Okla., U.S.A. 34°31N 96°58W 84 D6

Sulphur Pt. Canada 60°56N 114°48W 70 A6
Sulphur Springs U.S.A. 33°8N 95°36W 84 E7
Sultan Canada 47°36N 82°47W 72 C3
Sultan U.S.A. 47°52N 121°49W 78 C5
Sultanābād = Arāk Iran 34°0N 49°40E 47 C6
Sultanpur Mad. P., India 23°9N 77°56E 42 H8
Sultanpur Punjab, India 31°13N 75°11E 42 D6
Sultanpur Ut. P., India 26°18N 82°4E 43 F10
Sulu Arch. Phil. 6°0N 121°0E 37 C6
Sulu Sea E. Indies 8°0N 120°0E 37 C6
Sulūq Libya 31°44N 20°14E 53 B10
Suluru India 13°42N 80°1E 45 H5
Sulzberger Ice Shelf
Antarctica 78°0S 150°0W 5 E13
Sumalata Indonesia 1°0N 122°31E 37 D6
Sumampa Argentina 29°25S 63°29W 94 B3
Sumatera Indonesia 0°40N 100°20E 36 D2
Sumatera Barat □ Indonesia 1°0S 101°0E 36 E2
Sumatera Selatan □
Indonesia 3°0S 104°0E 36 E2
Sumatera Utara □
Indonesia 2°30N 98°0E 36 D1
Sumatra = Sumatera
Indonesia 0°40N 100°20E 36 D2
Sumba Indonesia 9°45S 119°35E 37 F5
Sumba, Selat Indonesia 9°0S 118°40E 37 F5
Sumbawa Indonesia 8°26S 117°30E 36 F5
Sumbawa Besar Indonesia 8°30S 117°26E 36 F5
Sumbawanga □ Tanzania 8°0S 31°30E 54 F6
Sumbe Angola 11°10S 13°48E 54 G2
Sumburgh Hd. U.K. 59°52N 1°17W 11 B7
Sumdeo India 31°26N 78°44E 43 D8
Sumdo China 35°6N 78°41E 43 B8
Sumedang Indonesia 6°52S 107°55E 37 G12
Šumen = Shumen
Bulgaria 43°18N 26°55E 23 C12
Sumenep Indonesia 7°1S 113°52E 37 G15
Sumgait = Sumqayıt
Azerbaijan 40°34N 49°38E 19 F8
Summer L. U.S.A. 42°50N 120°45W 76 E3
Summerland Canada 49°32N 119°41W 70 D5
Summerside Canada 46°24N 63°47W 73 C7
Summersville U.S.A. 38°17N 80°51W 81 F13
Summerville Ga., U.S.A. 34°29N 85°21W 85 D12
Summerville S.C., U.S.A. 33°1N 80°11W 85 E14
Summit Lake Canada 54°20N 122°40W 70 C4
Summit Peak U.S.A. 37°21N 106°42W 77 H10
Sumner Iowa, U.S.A. 42°51N 92°6W 80 D7
Sumner Wash., U.S.A. 47°12N 122°14W 78 C4
Sumoto Japan 34°21N 134°54E 29 G7
Šumperk Czech Rep. 49°59N 16°59E 17 D9
Sumqayıt Azerbaijan 40°34N 49°38E 19 F8
Sumter U.S.A. 33°55N 80°21W 85 E14
Sumy Ukraine 50°57N 34°50E 19 D5
Sun City S. Africa 25°17S 27°3E 56 C4
Sun City Center U.S.A. 27°43N 82°21W 85 H13
Sun Kosi → Nepal 26°59N 87°8E 43 F12
Sun Lakes U.S.A. 33°10N 111°52W 77 K8
Sun Valley U.S.A. 43°42N 114°21W 76 E6
Sunagawa Japan 43°29N 141°55E 28 C10
Sunan N. Korea 39°15N 125°40E 33 E13
Sunart, L. U.K. 56°42N 5°43W 11 E3
Sunburst U.S.A. 48°53N 111°55W 76 B8
Sunbury Australia 37°35S 144°44E 63 F3
Sunbury U.S.A. 40°52N 76°48W 83 F8
Sunchales Argentina 30°58S 61°35W 94 C3
Suncheon S. Korea 34°52N 127°31E 33 G14
Suncho Corral Argentina 27°55S 63°27W 94 B3
Sunch'on N. Korea 39°25N 125°56E 33 E13
Suncook U.S.A. 43°8N 71°27W 83 C13
Sunda, Selat Indonesia 6°20S 105°30E 36 F3
Sunda Is. Indonesia 5°0S 105°0E 64 H2
Sunda Str. = Sunda, Selat
Indonesia 6°20S 105°30E 36 F3
Sunda Trench = Java Trench
Ind. Oc. 9°0S 105°0E 36 F3
Sundance Canada 56°32N 94°4W 71 B10
Sundance U.S.A. 44°24N 104°23W 76 D11
Sundar Nagar India 31°32N 76°53E 42 D7
Sundarbans Asia 22°0N 89°0E 41 J16
Sundarbans △ India 22°0N 88°45E 43 J13
Sundargarh India 22°4N 84°5E 44 C7
Sundays = Sondags →
S. Africa 33°44S 25°51E 56 D4
Sunderland Canada 44°16N 79°4W 82 B5
Sunderland U.K. 54°55N 1°23W 12 C6
Sundown △ Australia 28°49S 151°38E 63 D5
Sundre Canada 51°49N 114°38W 70 C6
Sundsvall Sweden 62°23N 17°17E 8 E17
Sungai Acheh Malaysia 5°8N 100°30E 39 c
Sungai Kolok Thailand 6°2N 101°58E 39 J3
Sungai Lembing Malaysia 3°55N 103°3E 39 L4
Sungai Petani Malaysia 5°37N 100°30E 39 K3
Sungaigerong Indonesia 2°59S 104°52E 36 E2
Sungailiat Indonesia 1°51S 106°8E 36 E3
Sungaipenuh Indonesia 2°1S 101°20E 36 E2
Sungari = Songhua Jiang →
China 47°45N 132°30E 31 B15
Sunghua Chiang = Songhua
Jiang → China 47°45N 132°30E 31 B15
Sunland Park U.S.A. 31°50N 106°40W 77 L10
Sunndalsøra Norway 62°40N 8°33E 8 E13
Sunnyside U.S.A. 46°20N 120°0W 76 C3
Sunnyvale U.S.A. 37°23N 122°2W 78 H4
Suntar Russia 62°15N 117°30E 27 C12
Suomenselkä Finland 62°52N 24°0E 8 E21
Suomi = Finland ■ Europe 63°0N 27°0E 8 E22
Suomussalmi Finland 64°54N 29°10E 8 D23
Suoyarvi Russia 62°3N 32°20E 18 B5
Supai U.S.A. 36°15N 112°41W 77 H7
Supaul India 26°10N 86°40E 43 F12
Superior Ariz., U.S.A. 33°18N 111°6W 77 K8
Superior Mont., U.S.A. 47°12N 114°53W 76 C6
Superior Nebr., U.S.A. 40°1N 98°4W 80 E4
Superior Wis., U.S.A. 46°44N 92°6W 80 B7
Superior, L. N. Amer. 47°0N 87°0W 72 C2
Suphan Buri Thailand 14°14N 100°10E 38 E3
Suphan Dağı Turkey 38°54N 42°48E 46 B4
Supiori Indonesia 1°0S 136°0E 37 E9

Supung Shuiku China 40°35N 124°50E 33 D13
Sūq ash Shuyūkh Iraq 30°53N 46°28E 46 D5
Sūq Suwayq Si. Arabia 24°23N 38°27E 46 E3
Suqian China 33°54N 118°8E 33 H10
Suqutra = Socotra Yemen 12°30N 54°0E 49 E5
Sūr Lebanon 33°19N 35°16E 48 B4
Şūr Oman 22°34N 59°32E 49 C6
Sur, Pt. U.S.A. 36°18N 121°54W 78 J5
Sura → Russia 56°6N 46°0E 18 C8
Surab Pakistan 28°25N 66°15E 42 E2
Surabaja = Surabaya
Indonesia 7°17S 112°45E 37 G15
Surabaya Indonesia 7°17S 112°45E 37 G15
Surakarta Indonesia 7°35S 110°48E 37 G14
Surat Australia 27°10S 149°6E 63 D4
Surat India 21°12N 72°55E 44 D1
Surat Thani Thailand 9°6N 99°20E 39 H2
Suratgarh India 29°18N 73°55E 42 E5
Surathkal India 12°58N 74°46E 45 H2
Şuraymilā Si. Arabia 25°7N 46°7E 46 E5
Surendranagar India 22°45N 71°40E 42 H4
Surf U.S.A. 34°41N 120°36W 79 L6
Surfers Paradise Australia 28°0S 153°25E 63 D5
Surgana India 20°34N 73°37E 44 D1
Surgut Russia 61°14N 73°20E 26 C8
Suri India 23°54N 87°43E 43 H12
Suriapet India 17°10N 79°40E 44 E4
Surigao Phil. 9°47N 125°29E 37 C7
Surin Thailand 14°50N 103°34E 38 E4
Surinam = Suriname ■
S. Amer. 4°0N 56°0W 93 C7
Suriname ■ S. Amer. 4°0N 56°0W 93 C7
Suriname → Suriname 5°50N 55°15W 93 B7
Surjagarh India 19°36N 80°25E 44 E5
Sürmaq Iran 31°3N 52°48E 47 D7
Surprise U.S.A. 33°38N 112°19W 77 K7
Surrey Canada 49°7N 122°45W 78 A4
Surrey □ U.K. 51°15N 0°31W 13 F7
Sursand India 26°39N 85°43E 43 F11
Sursar → India 26°14N 87°3E 43 F12
Surt Libya 31°11N 16°39E 53 B9
Surt, Khalīj Libya 31°40N 18°30E 53 B9
Surtanaha Pakistan 26°22N 70°0E 42 F4
Surtsey Iceland 63°20N 20°30W 8 E3
Suruga-Wan Japan 34°45N 138°30E 29 G9
Süsah Libya 32°52N 21°59E 53 B10
Susaki Japan 33°22N 133°17E 29 H6
Susanerd Iran 31°35N 48°6E 47 D6
Susanville U.S.A. 40°25N 120°39W 76 F3
Susner India 23°57N 76°5E 42 H7
Susong China 30°10N 116°5E 35 B11
Susquehanna U.S.A. 41°57N 75°36W 83 E9
Susquehanna → U.S.A. 39°33N 76°5W 83 G8
Susques Argentina 23°35S 66°25W 94 A2
Sussex Canada 45°45N 65°37W 73 C6
Sussex U.S.A. 41°13N 74°37W 83 E10
Sussex, E. □ U.K. 51°0N 0°20E 13 G8
Sussex, W. □ U.K. 51°0N 0°30W 13 G7
Sustut → Canada 56°20N 127°30W 70 B3
Susuman Russia 62°47N 148°10E 27 C15
Susunu Indonesia 3°7S 133°39E 37 E8
Susurluk Turkey 39°54N 28°8E 23 E13
Sutay Uul Asia 46°35N 93°38E 30 B7
Sutherland S. Africa 32°24S 20°40E 56 D3
Sutherland U.K. 58°12N 4°50W 11 C4
Sutherland U.S.A. 41°10N 101°8W 80 E3
Sutherland Falls N.Z. 44°48S 167°46E 59 F1
Sutherlin U.S.A. 43°23N 123°19W 76 E2
Suthri India 23°3N 68°55E 42 H3
Sutlej → Pakistan 29°23N 71°3E 42 E4
Sutter U.S.A. 39°10N 121°45W 78 F5
Sutter Buttes U.S.A. 39°12N 121°49W 78 F5
Sutter Creek U.S.A. 38°24N 120°48W 78 G6
Sutton Canada 45°6N 72°37W 83 A12
Sutton Nebr., U.S.A. 40°36N 97°52W 80 E5
Sutton W. Va., U.S.A. 38°40N 80°43W 81 F13
Sutton → Canada 55°15N 83°45W 72 A3
Sutton Coldfield U.K. 52°35N 1°49W 13 E6
Sutton in Ashfield U.K. 53°8N 1°16W 12 D6
Sutton L. Canada 54°15N 84°42W 72 B3
Suttor → Australia 21°36S 147°2E 62 C4
Suttsu Japan 42°48N 140°14E 28 C10
Sutwik I. U.S.A. 56°34N 157°12W 74 D8
Suva Fiji 18°6S 178°30E 59 a
Suva Planina Serbia 43°10N 22°5E 23 C10
Suvorov Is. = Suwarrow Is.
Cook Is. 13°15S 163°5W 65 J11
Suwałki Poland 54°8N 22°59E 17 A12
Suwannaphum Thailand 15°33N 103°47E 38 E4
Suwannee → U.S.A. 29°17N 83°10W 85 G13
Suwanose-Jima Japan 29°38N 129°43E 29 K4
Suwarrow Is. Cook Is. 13°15S 163°5W 65 J11
Suweis, Khalīg el Egypt 28°40N 33°0E 53 C12
Suweis, Qanâ es Egypt 31°0N 32°20E 53 B12
Suwon S. Korea 37°17N 127°1E 33 F14
Suzdal Russia 56°29N 40°26E 18 C7
Suzhou Anhui, China 33°41N 116°59E 32 H9
Suzhou Jiangsu, China 31°19N 120°38E 35 B13
Suzu Japan 37°25N 137°17E 29 F8
Suzu-Misaki Japan 37°31N 137°21E 29 F8
Suzuka Japan 34°55N 136°36E 29 G8
Svalbard Arctic 78°0N 17°0E 4 B8
Svalbard Radio = Longyearbyen
Svalbard 78°10N 15°40E 4 B8
Svappavaara Sweden 67°40N 21°3E 8 C19
Svartisen Norway 66°40N 13°59E 8 C15
Svay Chek Cambodia 13°48N 102°58E 38 F4
Svay Rieng Cambodia 11°9N 105°45E 39 G5
Svealand Sweden 60°20N 15°0E 9 F16
Sveg Sweden 62°2N 14°21E 8 E16
Svendborg Denmark 55°4N 10°35E 9 J14
Sverdrup Chan. Canada 79°56N 96°25W 69 B12
Sverdrup Is. Canada 79°0N 97°0W 66 B10
Sverige = Sweden ■ Europe 57°0N 15°0E 9 H16
Svetlaya Russia 46°33N 138°18E 28 A9
Svetlogorsk = Svyetlahorsk
Belarus 52°38N 29°46E 17 B15
Svir → Russia 60°30N 32°48E 18 B6
Svishtov Bulgaria 43°36N 25°23E 23 C11
Svislach Belarus 53°3N 24°2E 17 B13

Svizzera = Switzerland ■
Europe 46°30N 8°0E 20 C8
Svobodnyy Russia 51°20N 128°0E 27 D13
Svolvær Norway 68°15N 14°34E 8 B16
Svyetlahorsk Belarus 52°38N 29°46E 17 B15
Swabian Alps = Schwäbische Alb
Germany 48°20N 9°30E 16 D5
Swaffham U.K. 52°39N 0°42E 13 E8
Swains Is. Amer. Samoa 11°11S 171°4W 65 J11
Swainsboro U.S.A. 32°36N 82°20W 85 E13
Swakop → Namibia 22°38S 14°36E 56 B2
Swakopmund Namibia 22°37S 14°30E 56 B1
Swale → U.K. 54°5N 1°20W 12 C6
Swaamihalli India 14°52N 76°38E 45 G3
Swan → Australia 32°3S 115°45E 61 F2
Swan → Canada 52°30N 100°45W 71 C8
Swan Hill Australia 35°20S 143°33E 63 F3
Swan Hills Canada 54°43N 115°24W 70 C5
Swan Is. = Santanilla, Is.
Honduras 17°22N 83°57W 88 C3
Swan L. Man., Canada 52°30N 100°40W 71 C8
Swan L. Ont., Canada 54°16N 91°11W 72 B1
Swan R. U.S.A. 48°0N 113°45W 76 C7
Swan River Canada 52°10N 101°16W 71 C8
Swanage U.K. 50°36N 1°58W 13 G6
Swansea Australia 42°8S 148°4E 63 G4
Swansea U.K. 51°37N 3°57W 13 F4
Swansea □ U.K. 51°38N 4°3W 13 F3
Swartberge S. Africa 33°20S 22°0E 56 D3
Swartmodder S. Africa 28°1S 20°32E 56 C3
Swartnossob → Namibia 23°8S 18°42E 56 B2
Swartruggens S. Africa 25°39S 26°42E 56 C4
Swastika Canada 48°7N 80°6W 72 C3
Swat → Pakistan 34°40N 72°5E 43 B5
Swatow = Shantou
China 23°18N 116°40E 35 F11
Swaziland ■ Africa 26°30S 31°30E 57 C5
Sweden ■ Europe 57°0N 15°0E 9 H16
Sweet Grass U.S.A. 48°59N 111°58W 76 B8
Sweet Home U.S.A. 44°24N 122°44W 76 D2
Sweetwater Nev., U.S.A. 38°27N 119°9W 78 G7
Sweetwater Tenn.,
U.S.A. 35°36N 84°28W 85 D12
Sweetwater Tex., U.S.A. 32°28N 100°25W 84 E4
Sweetwater → U.S.A. 42°31N 107°2W 76 E10
Swellendam S. Africa 34°1S 20°26E 56 D3
Świdnica Poland 50°50N 16°30E 17 C9
Świdnik Poland 51°13N 22°39E 17 C12
Świebodzin Poland 52°15N 15°31E 16 B8
Świecie Poland 53°25N 18°30E 17 B10
Swift Current Canada 50°20N 107°45W 71 C7
Swift Current →
Canada 50°38N 107°44W 71 C7
Swilly, L. Ireland 55°12N 7°33W 10 A4
Swindon U.K. 51°34N 1°46W 13 F6
Swindon □ U.K. 51°34N 1°46W 13 F6
Swinemünde = Świnoujście
Poland 53°54N 14°16E 16 B8
Swinford Ireland 53°57N 8°58W 10 C3
Świnoujście Poland 53°54N 14°16E 16 B8
Switzerland ■ Europe 46°30N 8°0E 20 C8
Swoyerville U.S.A. 41°18N 75°53W 83 E9
Sydenham → Canada 42°33N 82°25W 82 D2
Sydney Canada 46°7N 60°7W 73 C7
Sydney L. Canada 50°41N 94°25W 71 C10
Sydney Mines Canada 46°18N 60°15W 73 C7
Sydprøven = Alluitsup Paa
Greenland 60°30N 45°35W 4 C5
Sydra, G. of = Surt, Khalīj
Libya 31°40N 18°30E 53 B9
Sykesville U.S.A. 41°3N 78°50W 82 E6
Syktyvkar Russia 61°45N 50°40E 18 B9
Sylacauga U.S.A. 33°10N 86°15W 85 E11
Sylarna Sweden 63°2N 12°13E 8 E15
Sylhet Bangla. 24°54N 91°52E 41 G17
Sylhet □ Bangla. 24°50N 91°50E 41 G17
Sylt Germany 54°54N 8°22E 16 A5
Sylvan Beach U.S.A. 43°12N 75°44W 83 C9
Sylvan Lake Canada 52°20N 114°3W 70 C6
Sylvania Ga., U.S.A. 32°45N 81°38W 85 E14
Sylvania Ohio, U.S.A. 41°43N 83°42W 81 E12
Sylvester U.S.A. 31°32N 83°50W 85 F13
Sym Russia 60°20N 88°18E 26 C9
Synnot Ra. Australia 16°30S 125°20E 60 C4
Syowa Antarctica 68°50S 12°0E 5 C5
Syracuse Kans., U.S.A. 37°59N 101°45W 80 G3
Syracuse N.Y., U.S.A. 43°3N 76°9W 83 C8
Syracuse Nebr., U.S.A. 40°39N 96°11W 80 E5
Syrdarya → Kazakhstan 46°3N 61°0E 26 E7
Syria ■ Asia 35°0N 38°0E 46 C3
Syrian Desert = Shām, Bādiyat ash
Asia 32°0N 40°0E 46 C3
Syros = Ermoupoli
Greece 37°28N 24°57E 23 F11
Syzran Russia 53°12N 48°30E 18 D8
Szczecin Poland 53°27N 14°27E 16 B8
Szczecinek Poland 53°43N 16°41E 17 B9
Szczeciński, Zalew = Stettiner Haff
Germany 53°47N 14°15E 16 B8
Szczytno Poland 53°33N 21°0E 17 B11
Szechuan = Sichuan □
China 30°30N 103°0E 34 B5
Szechuan Basin = Sichuan Pendi
China 31°0N 105°0E 34 B5
Szeged Hungary 46°16N 20°10E 17 E11
Székesfehérvár Hungary 47°15N 18°25E 17 E10
Szekszárd Hungary 46°22N 18°42E 17 E10
Szentes Hungary 46°39N 20°21E 17 E11
Szolnok Hungary 47°10N 20°15E 17 E11
Szombathely Hungary 47°14N 16°38E 17 E9

T

Ta Khli Thailand 15°15N 100°21E 38 E3
Ta Lai Vietnam 11°24N 107°23E 39 G6
Ta Phraya △ Thailand 14°11N 102°49E 38 E4
Taamissaari = Raasepori
Finland 60°0N 23°26E 9 G20
Tabacal Argentina 23°15S 64°15W 94 A3

Tabaco Phil. 13°22N 123°44E 37 B6
Ṭabah Si. Arabia 26°55N 42°38E 46 E4
Tabanan Indonesia 8°32S 115°8E 37 K18
Ṭabas Khorāsān, Iran 32°48N 60°12E 47 C9
Ṭabas Yazd, Iran 33°35N 56°55E 47 C8
Tabasará, Serranía de
Panama 8°35N 81°40W 88 E3
Tabasco □ Mexico 18°0N 92°40W 87 D6
Tābāsīn Iran 31°12N 57°54E 47 D8
Tabatinga, Serra da
Brazil 10°30S 44°0W 93 F10
Taber Canada 49°47N 112°8W 70 D6
Tablas I. Phil. 12°25N 122°2E 37 B6
Table, Pte. de la Réunion 21°14S 55°48E 55 c
Table B. Canada 53°40N 56°25W 73 B8
Table I. Burma 14°12N 93°22E 45 G11
Table Rock L. U.S.A. 36°36N 93°19W 84 D7
Tabletop, Mt. Australia 23°24S 147°11E 62 C4
Tábor Czech Rep. 49°25N 14°39E 16 D8
Tabora Tanzania 5°2S 32°50E 54 F6
Tabou Ivory C. 4°30N 7°20W 52 H4
Tabrīz Iran 38°7N 46°20E 46 B5
Tabuaeran Kiribati 3°51N 159°22W 65 G12
Tabūk Si. Arabia 28°23N 36°36E 46 D3
Tabūk □ Si. Arabia 27°40N 36°50E 46 E3
Tacámbaro de Codallos
Mexico 19°14N 101°28W 86 D4
Tacheng China 46°40N 82°58E 30 B5
Tach'i Taiwan 24°53N 121°17E 35 E13
Tachia Taiwan 24°25N 120°28E 35 E13
Tachilek Burma 20°49N 99°52E 38 B2
Tach'ing Shan = Daqing Shan
China 40°40N 111°0E 32 D6
Tacloban Phil. 11°15N 124°58E 37 B6
Tacna Peru 18°0S 70°20W 92 G4
Tacoma U.S.A. 47°14N 122°26W 78 C4
Tacuarembó Uruguay 31°45S 56°0W 95 C4
Tademaït, Plateau du
Algeria 28°30N 2°30E 52 C6
Tadjoura Djibouti 11°50N 42°55E 49 E3
Tadmor N.Z. 41°27S 172°45E 59 D4
Tadoba △ India 20°30N 78°20E 44 D4
Tadoule L. Canada 58°36N 98°20W 71 B9
Tadoussac Canada 48°11N 69°42W 73 C6
Tadpatri India 14°55N 78°1E 45 G4
Tadzhikistan = Tajikistan ■
Asia 38°30N 70°0E 26 F8
Taegu = Daegu
S. Korea 35°50N 128°37E 33 G15
Taegwan N. Korea 40°13N 125°12E 33 D13
Taejŏn = Daejeon
S. Korea 36°20N 127°28E 33 F14
Taen, Ko Thailand 9°22N 99°57E 39 b
Tafalla Spain 42°30N 1°41W 21 A5
Tafermaar Indonesia 6°47S 134°10E 37 F8
Tafi Viejo Argentina 26°43S 65°17W 94 B2
Tafīhān Iran 29°25N 52°39E 47 D7
Tafresh Iran 34°45N 49°57E 47 C6
Taft Iran 31°45N 54°14E 47 D7
Taft Phil. 11°57N 125°30E 37 B7
Taft U.S.A. 35°8N 119°28W 79 K7
Taftan Pakistan 29°0N 61°30E 40 E2
Taftān, Kūh-e Iran 28°40N 61°0E 47 D9
Tafwap India 7°23N 93°43E 45 L11
Taga Samoa 13°46S 172°28W 59 b
Taga Dzong Bhutan 27°5N 89°55E 41 F16
Taganrog Russia 47°12N 38°50E 19 E6
Tagbilaran Phil. 9°39N 123°51E 37 C6
Tagish Canada 60°19N 134°16W 70 A2
Tagish L. Canada 60°10N 134°20W 70 A2
Tagliamento → Italy 45°38N 13°6E 22 B5
Taguatinga Brazil 12°27S 46°22W 93 F10
Tagum Phil. 7°33N 125°53E 37 C7
Tagus = Tejo → Europe 38°40N 9°24W 21 C1
Tahakopa N.Z. 46°30S 169°23E 59 G2
Tahan, Gunung Malaysia 4°34N 102°17E 39 K4
Tahat Algeria 23°18N 5°33E 52 D7
Tāherī Iran 27°43N 52°20E 47 E7
Tahiti French Polynesia 17°37S 149°27W 59 d
Tahiti, I. Tahiti 17°37S 149°27W 59 d
Tahlequah U.S.A. 35°55N 94°58W 84 D7
Tahoe, L. U.S.A. 39°6N 120°2W 78 G6
Tahoe City U.S.A. 39°10N 120°9W 78 F6
Tahoka U.S.A. 33°10N 101°48W 84 E4
Taholah U.S.A. 47°21N 124°17W 78 C2
Tahoua Niger 14°57N 5°16E 52 F7
Tahrūd Iran 29°26N 57°49E 47 D8
Tahsis Canada 49°55N 126°40W 70 D3
Tahta Egypt 26°44N 31°32E 53 C12
Tahulandang Indonesia 2°27N 125°23E 37 D7
Tahuna Indonesia 3°38N 125°30E 37 D7
Tai Hu China 31°5N 120°10E 35 B12
Tai Mo Shan China 22°25N 114°7E 31 a
Tai O China 22°15N 113°52E 31 a
Tai Pang Wan China 22°33N 114°24E 31 a
Tai Po China 22°27N 114°10E 31 a
Tai Rom Yen △ Thailand 8°45N 99°30E 39 H2
Tai Yue Shan = Lantau I.
China 22°15N 113°56E 31 a
Tai'an China 36°12N 117°8E 33 F9
Taiarapu, Presqu'île de
Tahiti 17°47S 149°14W 59 d
Taibai Shan China 33°57N 107°45E 32 H4
Taibei = T'aipei Taiwan 25°4N 121°29E 35 E13
Taibus Qi China 41°54N 115°22E 34 D8
Taicang China 31°30N 121°16E 35 B13
T'aichung Taiwan 24°9N 120°37E 35 E13
Taieri → N.Z. 46°3S 170°12E 59 G3
Taigu China 37°28N 112°30E 32 F7
Taihang Shan China 36°0N 113°30E 32 G7
Taihape N.Z. 39°41S 175°48E 59 C5
Taihe Anhui, China 33°20N 115°42E 32 H8
Taihe Jiangxi, China 26°47N 114°52E 35 D10
Taihu China 30°22N 116°20E 35 B11
Taijiang China 26°39N 108°21E 34 D7
Taikang China 34°5N 114°50E 32 G8
Tailem Bend Australia 35°12S 139°29E 63 F2
T'ailuko Taiwan 24°9N 121°37E 35 E13

Taimyr Peninsula = Taymyr,
  Poluostrov *Russia* 75°0N 100°0E **27 B11**
Tain *U.K.* 57°49N 4°4W **11 D4**
T'ainan *Taiwan* 23°0N 120°10E **35 F13**
Taining *China* 26°54N 117°9E **35 D11**
Taipa *China* 22°10N 113°35E **31 a**
T'aipei *Taiwan* 25°4N 121°29E **35 E13**
Taiping *China* 30°15N 118°6E **35 B12**
Taiping *Malaysia* 4°55N 100°44E **39 K3**
Taipingchuan *China* 44°23N 123°11E **33 B12**
Taipingzhen *China* 33°35N 111°42E **32 H6**
Taishan *Guangdong,
  China* 22°14N 112°41E **35 F9**
Taishan *Shandong, China* 36°25N 117°20E **33 F9**
Taishun *China* 27°30N 119°42E **35 D12**
Taitao, Pen. de *Chile* 46°30S 75°0W **96 F2**
T'aitung *Taiwan* 22°43N 121°4E **35 F13**
Taivalkoski *Finland* 65°33N 28°12E **8 D23**
Taiwan ■ *Asia* 23°30N 121°0E **35 F13**
Taiwan Strait *Asia* 24°40N 120°0E **35 E12**
Taixing *China* 32°11N 120°0E **35 A13**
Taiyiba *Israel* 32°36N 35°27E **48 C4**
Taiyuan *China* 37°52N 112°33E **32 F7**
Taizhong = T'aichung
  Taiwan 24°9N 120°37E **35 E13**
Taizhou *Jiangsu, China* 32°28N 119°55E **35 A12**
Taizhou *Zhejiang, China* 28°40N 121°24E **35 C13**
Taizhou Liedao *China* 28°30N 121°55E **35 C13**
Ta'izz *Yemen* 13°35N 44°2E **49 E3**
Taj Mahal *India* 27°10N 78°2E **42 F8**
Tājābād *Iran* 30°2N 54°24E **47 D7**
Tajikistan ■ *Asia* 38°30N 70°0E **26 F8**
Tajima = Minamiaizu
  Japan 37°12N 139°46E **29 F9**
Tajo = Tejo → *Europe* 38°40N 9°24W **21 C1**
Tak *Thailand* 16°52N 99°8E **38 D2**
Takāb *Iran* 36°24N 47°7E **46 B5**
Takachiho *Japan* 32°42N 131°18E **29 H5**
Takachu *Botswana* 22°37S 21°58E **56 B3**
Takada *Japan* 37°7N 138°15E **29 F9**
Takahagi *Japan* 36°43N 140°45E **29 F10**
Takaka *N.Z.* 40°51S 172°50E **59 D4**
Takamaka *Seychelles* 4°50S 55°30E **55 b**
Takamatsu *Japan* 34°20N 134°5E **29 G7**
Takaoka *Japan* 36°47N 137°0E **29 F8**
Takapuna *N.Z.* 36°47S 174°47E **59 B5**
Takasaki *Japan* 36°20N 139°0E **29 F9**
Takatsuki *Japan* 34°51N 135°37E **29 G7**
Takayama *Japan* 36°18N 137°11E **29 F8**
Take-Shima *Japan* 30°49N 130°26E **29 J5**
Takefu = Echizen *Japan* 35°50N 136°10E **29 G8**
Takengon *Indonesia* 4°45N 96°50E **36 D1**
Takeo *Cambodia* 10°59N 104°47E **39 G5**
Takeo *Japan* 33°12N 130°1E **29 H5**
Takeshima = Liancourt Rocks
  Asia 37°15N 131°52E **29 F5**
Tākestān *Iran* 36°0N 49°40E **47 C6**
Taketa *Japan* 32°58N 131°24E **29 H5**
Takh *India* 33°6N 77°32E **43 C7**
Takhmau *Cambodia* 11°29N 104°57E **39 G5**
Takht-e Soleymān *Iran* 36°36N 47°14E **46 B5**
Takht-Sulaiman *Pakistan* 31°40N 69°58E **42 D3**
Takikawa *Japan* 43°33N 141°54E **28 C10**
Takla L. *Canada* 55°15N 125°45W **70 B3**
Takla Landing *Canada* 55°30N 125°50W **70 B3**
Taklamakan *China* 38°0N 83°0E **30 D5**
Taklamakan Shamo =
  Taklamakan *China* 38°0N 83°0E **30 D5**
Taksimo *Russia* 56°20N 114°52E **27 D12**
Taku → *Canada* 58°30N 133°50W **70 B2**
Takua Thung *Thailand* 8°24N 98°27E **39 a**
Tal Halāl *Iran* 28°54N 55°1E **47 D7**
Tala *Uruguay* 34°21S 55°46W **95 C4**
Talagang *Pakistan* 32°55N 72°25E **42 C5**
Talagante *Chile* 33°40S 70°50W **94 C1**
Talaimannar *Sri Lanka* 9°6N 79°43E **45 K4**
Talamanca, Cordillera de
  Cent. Amer. 9°20N 83°20W **88 E3**
Talampaya △ *Argentina* 29°43S 67°42W **94 B2**
Talara *Peru* 4°38S 81°18W **92 D2**
Talas *Kyrgyzstan* 42°30N 72°13E **26 E8**
Talâta *Egypt* 30°36N 32°20E **48 E1**
Talaud, Kepulauan
  Indonesia 4°30N 126°50E **37 D7**
Talaud Is. = Talaud, Kepulauan
  Indonesia 4°30N 126°50E **37 D7**
Talavera de la Reina
  Spain 39°55N 4°46W **21 C3**
Talayan *Phil.* 6°52N 124°24E **37 C6**
Talbandh *India* 22°3N 86°20E **43 H12**
Talbot, C. *Australia* 13°48S 126°43E **60 B4**
Talbragar → *Australia* 32°12S 148°37E **63 E4**
Talca *Chile* 35°28S 71°40W **94 D1**
Talcahuano *Chile* 36°40S 73°10W **94 D1**
Talcher *India* 21°0N 85°18E **44 D7**
Taldy Kurgan = Taldyqorghan
  Kazakhstan 45°10N 78°45E **30 B4**
Taldyqorghan *Kazakhstan* 45°10N 78°45E **30 B4**
Tälesh *Iran* 37°58N 48°58E **47 B6**
Tälesh, Kühhä-ye *Iran* 37°42N 48°55E **47 B6**
Talguppa *India* 14°13N 74°56E **45 G2**
Tali Post *South Sudan* 5°55N 30°44E **53 G12**
Taliabu *Indonesia* 1°50S 125°0E **37 E6**
Talibon *Phil.* 10°9N 124°20E **37 B6**
Talihina *U.S.A.* 34°45N 95°3W **84 D7**
Talikota *India* 16°29N 76°17E **45 F3**
Talipparamba *India* 12°3N 75°12E **45 H2**
Taliwang *Indonesia* 8°50S 116°55E **36 F5**
Talkot *Nepal* 29°37N 81°2E **43 E9**
Tall 'Afar *Iraq* 36°22N 42°27E **46 B4**
Tall Kalakh *Syria* 34°41N 36°15E **48 A5**
Talladega *U.S.A.* 33°26N 86°6W **85 E11**
Tallahassee *U.S.A.* 30°27N 84°17W **85 F12**
Tallangatta *Australia* 36°15S 147°19E **63 F4**
Tallering Pk. *Australia* 28°6S 115°37E **61 E2**
Talli *Pakistan* 29°32N 68°8E **42 E3**
Tallinn *Estonia* 59°22N 24°48E **9 G21**
Tallmadge *U.S.A.* 41°6N 81°27W **82 E3**
Tallulah *U.S.A.* 32°25N 91°11W **84 E9**

Talnakh *Russia* 69°29N 88°22E **27 C9**
Taloda *India* 21°34N 74°11E **44 D2**
Taloyoak *Canada* 69°32N 93°32W **68 D13**
Talpa de Allende
  Mexico 20°23N 104°51W **86 C4**
Talparo *Trin. & Tob.* 10°30N 61°17W **93 K15**
Talsi *Latvia* 57°10N 22°30E **9 H20**
Taltal *Chile* 25°23S 70°33W **94 B1**
Taltson → *Canada* 61°24N 112°46W **70 A6**
Talwood *Australia* 28°29S 149°29E **63 D4**
Talyawalka Cr. →
  Australia 32°28S 142°22E **63 E3**
Tam Dao △ *Vietnam* 21°45N 105°45E **38 B5**
Tam Ky *Vietnam* 15°34N 108°29E **38 E7**
Tam Quan *Vietnam* 14°35N 109°3E **38 E7**
Tama *U.S.A.* 41°58N 92°35W **80 E7**
Tama Abu, Banjaran
  Malaysia 3°50N 115°5E **36 D5**
Tamale *Ghana* 9°22N 0°50W **52 G5**
Taman Negara △
  Malaysia 4°38N 102°26E **39 K4**
Tamano *Japan* 34°29N 133°59E **29 G6**
Tamanrasset *Algeria* 22°50N 5°30E **52 D7**
Tamaqua *U.S.A.* 40°48N 75°58W **83 F9**
Tamar → *U.K.* 50°27N 4°15W **13 G3**
Tamarin *Mauritius* 20°19S 57°20E **55 d**
Tamashima *Japan* 34°32N 133°40E **29 G6**
Tamatave = Toamasina
  Madag. 18°10S 49°25E **55 H9**
Tamaulipas □ *Mexico* 24°0N 98°45W **87 C5**
Tamaulipas, Sierra de
  Mexico 23°30N 98°20W **87 C5**
Tamazula *Mexico* 24°57N 106°57W **86 C3**
Tamazunchale *Mexico* 21°16N 98°47W **87 C5**
Tambacounda *Senegal* 13°45N 13°40W **52 F3**
Tambaram *India* 12°55N 80°7E **45 H5**
Tambelan, Kepulauan
  Indonesia 1°0N 107°30E **36 D3**
Tambellup *Australia* 34°4S 117°37E **61 F2**
Tambo *Australia* 24°54S 146°14E **62 C4**
Tambo de Mora *Peru* 13°30S 76°8W **92 F3**
Tambohorano *Indonesia* 8°12S 118°5E **36 F5**
Tambov *Russia* 52°45N 41°28E **18 D5**
Tambuku *Indonesia* 7°8S 113°40E **37 G15**
Tâmega → *Portugal* 41°5N 8°21W **21 B1**
Tamenglong *India* 25°0N 93°35E **41 G18**
Tamiahua, L. de *Mexico* 21°35N 97°35W **87 C5**
Tamil Nadu □ *India* 11°0N 77°0E **45 J3**
Tamluk *India* 22°18N 87°58E **43 H12**
Tammerfors = Tampere
  Finland 61°30N 23°50E **8 F20**
Tampa *U.S.A.* 27°56N 82°27W **85 H13**
Tampa, Tanjung
  Indonesia 8°55S 116°12E **37 K19**
Tampa B. *U.S.A.* 27°50N 82°30W **85 H13**
Tampere *Finland* 61°30N 23°50E **8 F20**
Tampico *Mexico* 22°13N 97°51W **87 C5**
Tampin *Malaysia* 2°28N 102°13E **39 L4**
Tampoi *Malaysia* 1°30N 103°39E **39 d**
Tamsagbulag *Mongolia* 47°14N 117°21E **31 B12**
Tamu *Burma* 24°13N 94°12E **41 G19**
Tamworth *Australia* 31°7S 150°58E **63 E5**
Tamworth *Canada* 44°29N 77°0W **82 B8**
Tamworth *U.K.* 52°39N 1°41W **13 E6**
Tan An *Vietnam* 10°32N 106°25E **39 G6**
Tan Chau *Vietnam* 10°48N 105°12E **39 G5**
Tan Hiep *Vietnam* 10°27N 106°21E **39 G6**
Tan-Tan *Morocco* 28°29N 11°1W **52 C3**
Tan Yen *Vietnam* 22°4N 105°3E **38 A5**
Tana → *Kenya* 2°32S 40°31E **54 E8**
Tana → *Norway* 70°30N 28°14E **8 A23**
Tana, L. *Ethiopia* 13°5N 37°30E **49 E2**
Tanabe *Japan* 33°44N 135°22E **29 H7**
Tanafjorden *Norway* 70°45N 28°25E **8 A23**
Tanaga I. *U.S.A.* 51°48N 177°53W **74 E4**
Tanah Merah *Malaysia* 5°48N 102°9E **39 K4**
Tanahbala *Indonesia* 0°30S 98°30E **36 E1**
Tanahgrogot *Indonesia* 1°55S 116°15E **36 E5**
Tanahjampea *Indonesia* 7°10S 120°35E **37 F6**
Tanahmasa *Indonesia* 0°12S 98°39E **36 E1**
Tanahmerah *Indonesia* 6°5S 140°16E **37 F10**
Tanakpur *India* 29°5N 80°7E **43 E9**
Tanami *Australia* 19°59S 129°43E **60 C4**
Tanami Desert *Australia* 18°50S 132°0E **60 C5**
Tanamalwila *Sri Lanka* 6°26N 81°8E **45 L5**
Tanana *U.S.A.* 65°10N 152°4W **74 B9**
Tanana → *U.S.A.* 65°10N 151°58W **68 D1**
Tananarive = Antananarivo
  Madag. 18°55S 47°31E **55 H9**
Tánaro → *Italy* 44°55N 8°40E **20 D8**
Tancheng *China* 34°25N 118°20E **33 G10**
Tanch'ŏn *N. Korea* 40°27N 128°54E **33 D15**
Tanda *Ut. P., India* 28°57N 78°56E **43 E8**
Tanda *Ut. P., India* 26°33N 82°35E **43 F10**
Tandag *Phil.* 9°4N 126°9E **37 C7**
Tandaué *Angola* 16°58S 18°5E **56 A2**
Tandil *Argentina* 37°15S 59°6W **94 D4**
Tandil, Sa. del *Argentina* 37°30S 59°0W **94 D4**
Tandlianwala *Pakistan* 31°3N 73°9E **42 D5**
Tando Adam *Pakistan* 25°45N 68°40E **42 G3**
Tando Allahyar *Pakistan* 25°28N 68°43E **42 G3**
Tando Bago *Pakistan* 24°47N 68°58E **42 G3**
Tando Mohommed Khan
  Pakistan 25°8N 68°32E **42 G3**
Tandou L. *Australia* 32°40S 142°5E **63 E3**
Tandoureh △ *Iran* 37°50N 59°0E **47 B8**
Tandragee *U.K.* 54°21N 6°24W **10 B5**
Tandula → *India* 21°6N 81°14E **44 D5**
Tandula Tank *India* 20°40N 81°12E **44 D5**
Tandur *Andhra Pradesh,
  India* 19°11N 79°30E **44 E4**
Tandur *Andhra Pradesh,
  India* 17°14N 77°35E **44 F3**
Tane-ga-Shima *Japan* 30°30N 131°0E **29 J5**
Taneatua *N.Z.* 38°4S 177°1E **59 C6**
Tanen Tong Dan = Dawna Ra.
  Burma 16°30N 98°30E **38 D2**
Tanezrouft *Algeria* 23°9N 0°11E **52 D6**
Tang, Koh *Cambodia* 10°16N 103°7E **39 G4**
Tang, Ra's-e *Iran* 25°21N 59°52E **47 E8**

Tang Krasang *Cambodia* 12°34N 105°3E **38 F5**
Tanga *Tanzania* 5°5S 39°2E **54 F7**
Tangalla *Sri Lanka* 6°1N 80°48E **45 L5**
Tanganyika, L. *Africa* 6°40S 30°0E **54 F6**
Tangasseri *India* 8°53N 76°35E **45 K3**
Tanger *Morocco* 35°50N 5°49W **52 A4**
Tangerang *Indonesia* 6°11S 106°37E **37 G12**
Tanggu *China* 39°2N 117°40E **33 E9**
Tanggula Shan *China* 32°40N 92°10E **30 E7**
Tanggula Shankou *China* 32°42N 92°27E **30 E7**
Tanghe *China* 32°47N 112°50E **32 H7**
Tanghla Range = Tanggula Shan
  China 32°40N 92°10E **30 E7**
Tangi *India* 19°56N 85°24E **44 E7**
Tangier = Tanger
  Morocco 35°50N 5°49W **52 A4**
Tangjia *China* 22°22N 113°35E **31 a**
Tangjia Wan *China* 22°21N 113°36E **31 a**
Tangorin *Australia* 21°47S 144°12E **62 C3**
Tangra Yumco *China* 31°0N 86°38E **30 E6**
Tangshan *China* 39°38N 118°10E **33 E10**
Tangtou *China* 35°28N 118°30E **33 G10**
Tangxi *China* 29°17N 119°42E **35 C12**
Tangyan He → *China* 28°54N 108°19E **34 C7**
Tangyin *China* 35°54N 114°21E **32 G8**
Taniantaweng Shan
  China 31°20N 98°0E **34 B2**
Tanimbar, Kepulauan
  Indonesia 7°30S 131°30E **37 F8**
Tanimbar Is. = Tanimbar,
  Kepulauan *Indonesia* 7°30S 131°30E **37 F8**
Taninthayri = Tenasserim
  Burma 12°6N 99°3E **39 F2**
Tanjay *Phil.* 9°30N 123°5E **37 C6**
Tanjong Pelepas *Malaysia* 1°21N 103°33E **39 d**
Tanjore = Thanjavur
  India 10°48N 79°12E **45 J4**
Tanjung *Kalimantan Selatan,
  Indonesia* 2°10S 115°25E **36 E5**
Tanjung *Nusa Tenggara Barat,
  Indonesia* 8°21S 116°9E **37 J19**
Tanjung Malim *Malaysia* 3°42N 101°31E **39 L3**
Tanjung Tokong *Malaysia* 5°28N 100°18E **39 c**
Tanjungbalai *Indonesia* 2°55N 99°44E **36 D1**
Tanjungbatu *Indonesia* 2°23N 118°3E **36 D5**
Tanjungkarang Telukbetung =
  Bandar Lampung
  Indonesia 5°20S 105°10E **36 F3**
Tanjungpandan *Indonesia* 2°43S 107°38E **36 E3**
Tanjungpinang *Indonesia* 1°5N 104°30E **36 D2**
Tanjungredeb *Indonesia* 2°9N 117°29E **36 D5**
Tanjungselor *Indonesia* 2°55N 117°25E **36 D5**
Tank *Pakistan* 32°14N 70°25E **42 C4**
Tankhala *India* 21°58N 73°47E **42 J5**
Tankwa-Karoo △
  S. Africa 32°14S 19°50E **56 E2**
Tannersville *U.S.A.* 41°3N 75°18W **83 E9**
Tannu Ola *Asia* 51°0N 94°0E **27 D10**
Tannum Sands *Australia* 23°57S 151°22E **62 C5**
Tanout *Niger* 14°50N 8°55E **52 F7**
Tanshui *Taiwan* 25°10N 121°28E **35 E13**
Tansing *Nepal* 27°52N 83°33E **43 F10**
Tanta *Egypt* 30°45N 30°57E **53 B12**
Tantoyuca *Mexico* 21°21N 98°14W **87 C5**
Tantung = Dandong
  China 40°10N 124°20E **33 D13**
Tanuku *India* 16°45N 81°44E **44 F5**
Tanunda *Australia* 34°30S 139°0E **63 E2**
Tanur *India* 11°1N 75°52E **45 J2**
Tanzania ■ *Africa* 6°0S 34°0E **54 F6**
Tanzhou *China* 22°16N 113°28E **31 a**
Tanzilla → *Canada* 58°8N 130°43W **70 B2**
Tao, Ko *Thailand* 10°5N 99°52E **39 G2**
Tao'an = Taonan
  China 45°22N 122°40E **33 B12**
Tao'er He → *China* 45°45N 124°5E **33 B13**
Taohua Dao *China* 29°50N 122°20E **35 C14**
Taolanaro *Madag.* 25°2S 47°0E **55 K9**
Taole *China* 38°48N 106°40E **32 E4**
Taonan *China* 45°22N 122°40E **33 B12**
Taos *U.S.A.* 36°24N 105°35W **77 H11**
Taoudenni *Mali* 22°40N 3°55W **52 D5**
Taoyuan *China* 28°55N 111°16E **35 C8**
Taoyüan *Taiwan* 25°0N 121°4E **35 E13**
Tapa *Estonia* 59°15N 25°50E **9 G21**
Tapa Shan = Daba Shan
  China 32°0N 109°0E **34 B7**
Tapachula *Mexico* 14°54N 92°17W **87 E6**
Tapah *Malaysia* 4°12N 101°15E **39 K3**
Tapajós → *Brazil* 2°24S 54°41W **93 D8**
Tapaktuan *Indonesia* 3°15N 97°10E **36 D1**
Tapanahoni → *Suriname* 4°20N 54°25W **93 C8**
Tapanui *N.Z.* 45°56S 169°18E **59 F2**
Tapauá → *Brazil* 5°40S 64°21W **92 E6**
Tapes *Brazil* 30°40S 51°23W **95 C5**
Tapeta *Liberia* 6°29N 8°52W **52 G4**
Taphan Hin *Thailand* 16°13N 100°26E **38 D3**
Tapirapecó, Serra
  Venezuela 1°10N 65°0W **92 C6**
Taplejung *Nepal* 27°1N 86°16E **43 F12**
Tapo-Capara △ *Venezuela* 7°11N 71°55W **89 E5**
Tapti → *India* 21°8N 72°41E **44 D1**
Tapuae-o-Uenuku *N.Z.* 42°0S 173°39E **59 E4**
Tapul Group *Phil.* 5°35N 120°50E **37 C6**
Tapurucuará *Brazil* 0°24S 65°2W **92 D5**
Taqtaq *Iraq* 35°53N 44°35E **46 C5**
Taquara *Brazil* 29°36S 50°46W **95 B5**
Taquari → *Brazil* 19°15S 57°17W **92 G7**
Tara *Australia* 27°17S 150°31E **63 D5**
Tara *Canada* 44°28N 81°9W **82 B3**
Tara *Russia* 56°55N 74°24E **26 D8**
Tara → *Montenegro* 43°21N 18°51E **23 C8**
Tara *Zambia* 16°58S 26°45E **55 F2**
Tarābulus *Lebanon* 34°31N 35°50E **48 A4**
Tarābulus *Libya* 32°49N 13°7E **53 B8**
Tarābulus *Libya* 31°0N 13°0E **53 B8**
Taradehi *India* 23°18N 79°21E **43 H8**
Tarakan *Indonesia* 3°20N 117°35E **36 D5**
Tarama-Jima *Japan* 24°39N 124°42E **29 M2**
Taran, Mys *Russia* 54°56N 19°59E **9 J18**

Taranagar *India* 28°43N 74°50E **42 E6**
Taranaki □ *N.Z.* 39°25S 174°30E **59 C5**
Taranaki, Mt. *N.Z.* 39°17S 174°5E **59 C5**
Tarancón *Spain* 40°1N 3°1W **21 B4**
Táranto *Italy* 40°28N 17°14E **22 D7**
Táranto, G. di *Italy* 40°8N 17°20E **22 D7**
Tarapacá *Colombia* 2°56S 69°46W **92 D5**
Tarapacá □ *Chile* 20°45S 69°30W **94 A2**
Tarapoto *Peru* 6°30S 76°20W **92 E3**
Tararua Ra. *N.Z.* 40°45S 175°25E **59 D5**
Tarashcha *Ukraine* 49°30N 30°31E **17 D16**
Tarauacá *Brazil* 8°6S 70°48W **92 E4**
Tarauacá → *Brazil* 6°42S 69°48W **92 E5**
Taravao *Tahiti* 17°43S 149°19W **59 d**
Taravao, Isthme de
  Tahiti 17°43S 149°19W **59 d**
Tarawa *Kiribati* 1°30N 173°0E **64 G9**
Tarawera *N.Z.* 39°2S 176°36E **59 C6**
Tarawera, L. *N.Z.* 38°13S 176°27E **59 C6**
Taraz *Kazakhstan* 42°54N 71°22E **30 C3**
Tarazona *Spain* 41°55N 1°43W **21 B5**
Tarbagatay, Khrebet
  Kazakhstan 48°0N 83°0E **30 B5**
Tarbat Ness *U.K.* 57°52N 3°47W **11 D5**
Tarbela Dam *Pakistan* 34°8N 72°52E **42 B5**
Tarbert *Ireland* 52°34N 9°22E **10 D2**
Tarbert *Argyll & Bute, U.K.* 55°52N 5°25W **11 F3**
Tarbert *W. Isles, U.K.* 57°54N 6°49W **11 D2**
Tarbes *France* 43°15N 0°3E **20 E4**
Tarboro *U.S.A.* 35°54N 77°32W **85 D16**
Tarcoola *Australia* 30°44S 134°36E **63 E1**
Tarcoon *Australia* 30°15S 146°43E **63 E4**
Taree *Australia* 31°50S 152°30E **63 E5**
Tarfaya *Morocco* 27°55N 12°55W **52 C3**
Târgovişte *Romania* 44°55N 25°27E **17 F13**
Târgu Jiu *Romania* 45°5N 23°19E **17 F12**
Târgu Mureş *Romania* 46°31N 24°38E **17 E13**
Tarif *U.A.E.* 24°3N 53°46E **47 E7**
Tarifa *Spain* 36°1N 5°36W **21 D3**
Tarija *Bolivia* 21°30S 64°40W **94 A3**
Tarija □ *Bolivia* 21°30S 63°30W **94 A3**
Tariku → *Indonesia* 2°55S 138°26E **37 E9**
Tarim Basin = Tarim Pendi
  China 40°0N 84°0E **30 C5**
Tarim He → *China* 39°30N 88°30E **30 D6**
Tarim Pendi *China* 40°0N 84°0E **30 C5**
Taritatu → *Indonesia* 2°54S 138°27E **37 E9**
Tarka → *S. Africa* 32°10S 26°0E **56 E4**
Tarka La *Bhutan* 27°12N 89°44E **43 F13**
Tarkastad *S. Africa* 32°0S 26°16E **56 D4**
Tarkhankut, Mys
  Ukraine 45°25N 32°30E **19 E5**
Tarko Sale *Russia* 64°55N 77°50E **26 C8**
Tarkwa *Ghana* 5°20N 2°0W **52 G5**
Tarlac *Phil.* 15°29N 120°35E **37 A6**
Tarma *Peru* 11°25S 75°45W **92 F3**
Tarn → *France* 44°5N 1°6E **20 E4**
Târnăveni *Romania* 46°19N 24°13E **17 E13**
Tarnobrzeg *Poland* 50°35N 21°41E **17 C11**
Tarnów *Poland* 50°3N 21°0E **17 C11**
Tarnowskie Góry *Poland* 50°27N 18°54E **17 C10**
Tärom *Iran* 28°11N 55°46E **47 D7**
Taroom *Australia* 25°36S 149°48E **63 D4**
Taroudannt *Morocco* 30°30N 8°52W **52 B4**
Tarpon Springs *U.S.A.* 28°9N 82°45W **85 G13**
Tarrafal *C. Verde Is.* 15°18N 23°39W **52 b**
Tarragona *Spain* 41°5N 1°17E **21 B6**
Tarraleah *Australia* 42°17S 146°26E **63 G4**
Tarrasa = Terrassa *Spain* 41°34N 2°1E **21 B7**
Tarrytown *U.S.A.* 41°4N 73°52W **83 E11**
Tarsus *Turkey* 36°58N 34°55E **46 B2**
Tartagal *Argentina* 22°30S 63°50W **94 A3**
Tartu *Estonia* 58°20N 26°44E **9 G22**
Ţarţūs *Syria* 34°55N 35°55E **46 C2**
Tarumizu *Japan* 31°29N 130°42E **29 J5**
Tarutao = Ko Tarutao △
  Thailand 6°31N 99°26E **39 J2**
Tarutao, Ko *Thailand* 6°33N 99°40E **39 J2**
Tarutung *Indonesia* 2°0N 98°54E **36 D1**
Taseko → *Canada* 52°8N 123°45W **70 C4**
Tasgaon *India* 17°3S 74°39E **44 F2**
Tash-Kömür *Kyrgyzstan* 41°40N 72°10E **28 E8**
Tashauz = Daşoguz
  Turkmenistan 41°49N 59°58E **26 E6**
Tashi Chho Dzong = Thimphu
  Bhutan 27°31N 89°45E **41 F16**
Tashk, Daryācheh-ye
  Iran 29°45N 53°35E **47 D7**
Tashkent = Toshkent
  Uzbekistan 41°20N 69°10E **28 E7**
Tashtagol *Russia* 52°47N 87°53E **26 D9**
Tasiilaq *Greenland* 65°40N 37°20W **4 C6**
Tasikmalaya *Indonesia* 7°18S 108°12E **37 G13**
Tåsjön *Sweden* 64°15N 15°40E **8 D16**
Taskan *Russia* 62°59N 150°20E **27 C16**
Tasman B. *N.Z.* 40°59S 173°25E **59 D4**
Tasman Basin *Pac. Oc.* 46°0S 158°0E **64 M7**
Tasman Mts. *N.Z.* 41°3S 172°25E **59 D4**
Tasman Pen. *Australia* 43°10S 148°0E **63 G4**
Tasman Sea *Pac. Oc.* 36°0S 160°0E **64 L8**
Tasmania □ *Australia* 42°0S 146°30E **63 G4**
Tasmanian Wilderness World
  Heritage Area △
  Australia 43°0S 146°0E **63 G4**
Tassili n' Ajjer *Algeria* 25°47N 8°1E **52 C7**
Tassili-Oua-n-Ahaggar
  Algeria 20°41N 5°30E **52 D7**
Tat Ton △ *Thailand* 15°57N 102°2E **38 E4**
Tata *Morocco* 29°46N 7°56W **52 C4**
Tatabánya *Hungary* 47°32N 18°25E **17 E10**
Tataouine *Tunisia* 32°57N 10°29E **53 B8**
Tatar Republic = Tatarstan □
  Russia 55°30N 51°30E **18 C9**
Tatarbunary *Ukraine* 45°50N 29°39E **17 F15**
Tatarsk *Russia* 55°14N 76°0E **26 D8**
Tatarskiy Proliv *Russia* 50°0N 141°0E **27 E15**

Tatarstan □ *Russia* 55°30N 51°30E **18 C9**
Tatatua, Pte. *Tahiti* 17°44S 149°8W **59 d**
Tateyama *Japan* 35°0N 139°50E **29 G9**
Tathlina L. *Canada* 60°33N 117°39W **70 A5**
Tathra *Australia* 36°44S 149°59E **63 F4**
Tatinnai L. *Canada* 60°55N 97°40W **71 A9**
Tatla Lake *Canada* 52°0N 124°20W **70 C4**
Tatnam, C. *Canada* 57°16N 91°0W **71 B10**
Tatra = Tatry *Slovak Rep.* 49°20N 20°0E **17 D11**
Tatry *Slovak Rep.* 49°20N 20°0E **17 D11**
Tatshenshini →
  Canada 59°28N 137°45W **70 B1**
Tatshenshini-Alsek △
  Canada 59°55N 137°45W **70 B1**
Tatsuno *Japan* 34°52N 134°33E **29 G7**
Tatta = Thatta *Pakistan* 24°42N 67°55E **42 G2**
Tatuī *Brazil* 23°25S 47°53W **95 A6**
Tatum *U.S.A.* 33°16N 103°19W **77 K12**
Tat'ung = Datong *China* 40°6N 113°18E **32 D7**
Tatvan *Turkey* 38°31N 42°15E **46 B4**
Ta'ū *Amer. Samoa* 14°15S 169°30W **59 b**
Taubaté *Brazil* 23°0S 45°36W **95 A6**
Tauern *Austria* 47°15N 12°40E **16 E7**
Taumarunui *N.Z.* 38°53S 175°15E **59 C5**
Taumaturgo *Brazil* 8°54S 72°51W **92 E4**
Taung *S. Africa* 27°33S 24°47E **56 D4**
Taungdwingyi *Burma* 20°1N 95°40E **41 J19**
Taunggyi *Burma* 20°50N 97°0E **41 J20**
Taungoo = Tounggoo
  Burma 19°0N 96°30E **41 K20**
Taungup *Burma* 18°51N 94°14E **41 K19**
Taunsa *Pakistan* 30°42N 70°39E **42 D4**
Taunsa Barrage *Pakistan* 30°42N 70°50E **42 D4**
Taunton *U.K.* 51°1N 3°5W **13 F4**
Taunton *U.S.A.* 41°54N 71°6W **83 E13**
Taunus *Germany* 50°13N 8°34E **16 C5**
Taupo *N.Z.* 38°41S 176°7E **59 C6**
Taupo, L. *N.Z.* 38°46S 175°55E **59 C5**
Tauragė *Lithuania* 55°14N 22°16E **9 J20**
Tauranga *N.Z.* 37°42S 176°11E **59 B6**
Tauranga Harb. *N.Z.* 37°30S 176°5E **59 B6**
Taureau, Rés. *Canada* 46°46N 73°50W **72 C5**
Taurianova *Italy* 38°21N 16°1E **22 E7**
Taurus Mts. = Toros Dağları
  Turkey 37°0N 32°30E **46 B2**
Tautira *Tahiti* 17°44S 149°9W **59 d**
Tauyskaya Guba
  Russia 59°20N 150°20E **27 D16**
Tavan Bogd Uul *Mongolia* 49°10N 87°49E **30 B6**
Tavastehus = Hämeenlinna
  Finland 61°0N 24°28E **8 F21**
Tavda *Russia* 58°7N 65°8E **26 D7**
Tavda → *Russia* 57°47N 67°18E **26 D7**
Taverner B. *Canada* 67°12N 72°25W **69 D17**
Taveuni *Fiji* 16°51S 179°58W **59 a**
Tavira *Portugal* 37°8N 7°40W **21 D2**
Tavistock *Canada* 43°19N 80°50W **82 C4**
Tavistock *U.K.* 50°33N 4°9W **13 G3**
Tavoy *Burma* 14°2N 98°12E **38 E2**
Tavoy Pt. *Burma* 13°32N 98°10E **38 F2**
Tavrichanka *Russia* 43°18N 131°59E **28 C5**
Tavua *Fiji* 17°37S 177°5E **59 a**
Tavuki *Fiji* 19°7S 178°8E **59 a**
Taw → *U.K.* 51°4N 4°4W **13 F3**
Tawa → *India* 22°48N 77°48E **42 H8**
Tawa Res. *India* 22°35N 78°5E **44 C4**
Tawas City *U.S.A.* 44°16N 83°31W **81 C12**
Tawau *Malaysia* 4°20N 117°55E **36 D5**
Tawi-tawi I. *Phil.* 5°10N 120°15E **37 C6**
Tawu *Taiwan* 22°22N 120°54E **35 F13**
Taxco *Mexico* 18°33N 99°36E **87 D5**
Taxila *Pakistan* 33°42N 72°52E **42 C5**
Taxkorgan Tajik Zizhixian
  China 37°49N 75°14E **30 D4**
Tay → *U.K.* 56°37N 3°38W **11 E5**
Tay, Firth of *U.K.* 56°25N 3°8W **11 E5**
Tay, L. *Australia* 32°55S 120°48E **61 F3**
Tay, L. *U.K.* 56°32N 4°8W **11 E4**
Tay Ninh *Vietnam* 11°20N 106°5E **39 G6**
Tayabamba *Peru* 8°15S 77°16W **92 E3**
Taygetos Oros *Greece* 37°0N 22°23E **23 F10**
Taylakova *Russia* 59°13N 74°0E **26 D8**
Taylor *Canada* 56°13N 120°40W **70 B4**
Taylor *Nebr., U.S.A.* 41°46N 99°23W **80 E4**
Taylor *Pa., U.S.A.* 41°23N 75°43W **83 E9**
Taylor *Tex., U.S.A.* 30°34N 97°25W **84 F6**
Taylor, Mt. *U.S.A.* 35°14N 107°37W **77 J10**
Taylorville *U.S.A.* 39°33N 89°18W **80 F9**
Taymā *Si. Arabia* 27°35N 38°45E **46 E3**
Taymyr, Oz. *Russia* 74°20N 102°0E **27 B11**
Taymyr, Poluostrov
  Russia 75°0N 100°0E **27 B11**
Taypaq *Kazakhstan* 49°0N 51°47E **19 E9**
Tayport *U.K.* 56°27N 2°52W **11 E6**
Tayrona △ *Colombia* 11°20N 74°2W **89 D5**
Tayshet *Russia* 55°58N 98°1E **27 D10**
Taytay *Phil.* 10°45N 119°30E **37 B5**
Tāyyebād *Iran* 34°45N 60°45E **47 C9**
Tāyyebād □ *Iran* 34°44N 60°44E **47 C9**
Taz → *Russia* 67°32N 78°40E **26 C8**
Taza *Morocco* 34°16N 4°6W **52 B5**
Tāza Khurmātū *Iraq* 35°18N 44°20E **46 C5**
Tazerbo *Libya* 25°45N 21°0E **53 C10**
Tazin → *Canada* 59°48N 109°55W **71 B7**
Tazin L. *Canada* 59°44N 108°42W **71 B7**
Tazovskiy *Russia* 67°30N 78°44E **26 C8**
Tbilisi *Georgia* 41°43N 44°50E **19 F7**
Tchad = Chad ■ *Africa* 15°0N 17°15E **53 F8**
Tchad, L. *Chad* 13°30N 14°30E **53 F8**
Tch'eng-tou = Chengdu
  China 30°38N 104°2E **34 B5**
Tchentlo L. *Canada* 55°15N 125°0W **70 B4**
Tchibanga *Gabon* 2°45S 11°0E **54 E2**
Tch'ong-k'ing = Chongqing
  China 29°35N 106°25E **34 C6**

Tczew _Poland_ 54°8N 18°50E **17** A10
Te Anau, L. _N.Z._ 45°15S 167°45E **59** F1
Te Aroha _N.Z._ 37°32S 175°44E **59** B5
Te Awamutu _N.Z._ 38°1S 175°20E **59** C5
Te Ika a Maui = North I.
  _N.Z._ 38°0S 175°0E **59** C5
Te Kuiti _N.Z._ 38°20S 175°11E **59** C5
Te Puke _N.Z._ 37°46S 176°22E **59** B6
Te Waewae B. _N.Z._ 46°13S 167°33E **59** G1
Te Wai Pounamu = South I.
  _N.Z._ 44°0S 170°0E **59** F3
Teague _U.S.A._ 31°38N 96°17W **84** F6
Teahupoo _Tahiti_ 17°50S 149°16W **59** d
Teapa _Mexico_ 17°33N 92°57W **87** D6
Tebakang _Malaysia_ 1°6N 110°30E **36** D4
Teberau → _Malaysia_ 1°30N 103°42E **39** d
Tébessa _Algeria_ 35°22N 8°8E **52** A7
Tebicuary → _Paraguay_ 26°36S 58°16W **94** B4
Tebingtinggi _Riau,_
  Indonesia 1°0N 102°45E **36** E2
Tebingtinggi _Sumatera Utara,_
  Indonesia 3°20N 99°9E **36** D1
Tecate _Mexico_ 32°34N 116°38W **79** N10
Tecka _Argentina_ 43°29S 70°48W **96** E2
Tecomán _Mexico_ 18°55N 103°53W **86** D4
Tecopa _U.S.A._ 35°51N 116°13W **79** K10
Tecoripa _Mexico_ 28°37N 109°57W **86** B3
Tecuala _Mexico_ 22°23N 105°27W **86** C3
Tecuci _Romania_ 45°51N 27°27E **17** F14
Tecumseh _Canada_ 42°19N 82°54W **82** D2
Tecumseh _Mich., U.S.A._ 42°0N 83°57W **81** D12
Tecumseh _Okla., U.S.A._ 35°15N 96°56W **84** D6
Tedzhen = Tejen
  Turkmenistan 37°23N 60°31E **26** F7
Tees → _U.K._ 54°37N 1°10W **12** C6
Tees B. _U.K._ 54°40N 1°9W **12** C6
Teeswater _Canada_ 43°59N 81°17W **82** C3
Tefé _Brazil_ 3°25S 64°50W **92** D6
Tegal _Indonesia_ 6°52S 109°8E **37** G13
Tegallalang _Indonesia_ 8°27S 115°17E **37** J18
Tegalsari _Indonesia_ 8°25S 114°8E **37** J17
Tegid, L. = Bala, L. _U.K._ 52°53N 3°37W **12** E4
Tegucigalpa _Honduras_ 14°5N 87°14W **88** D2
Tehachapi _U.S.A._ 35°8N 118°27W **79** K8
Tehachapi Mts. _U.S.A._ 35°0N 118°30W **79** L8
Tehoru _Indonesia_ 3°23S 129°30E **37** E7
Tehrān □ _Iran_ 35°30N 51°30E **47** C6
Tehri _India_ 30°23N 78°29E **43** D8
Tehuacán _Mexico_ 18°27N 97°23W **87** D5
Tehuantepec _Mexico_ 16°21N 95°13W **87** D5
Tehuantepec, G. de
  Mexico 15°50N 95°12W **87** D5
Tehuantepec, Istmo de
  Mexico 17°15N 94°30W **87** D6
Teifi → _U.K._ 52°5N 4°41W **13** E3
Teign → _U.K._ 50°32N 3°32W **13** G4
Teignmouth _U.K._ 50°33N 3°31W **13** G4
Tejakula _Indonesia_ 8°8S 115°20E **37** J18
Tejen _Turkmenistan_ 37°23N 60°31E **26** F7
Tejen → _Turkmenistan_ 37°24N 60°38E **47** B9
Tejo → _Europe_ 38°40N 9°24W **21** C1
Tejon Pass _U.S.A._ 34°49N 118°53W **79** L8
Tekamah _U.S.A._ 41°47N 96°13W **80** E5
Tekapo, L. _N.Z._ 43°53S 170°33E **59** E3
Tekax _Mexico_ 20°12N 89°17W **87** C7
Tekeli _Kazakhstan_ 44°50N 79°0E **26** E8
Tekeze → _Ethiopia_ 13°10N 38°45E **49** E2
Tekirdağ _Turkey_ 40°58N 27°30E **23** D12
Tekkali _India_ 18°37N 84°15E **44** E7
Tekoa _U.S.A._ 47°14N 117°4W **76** C5
Tekong Besar, Pulau
  Singapore 1°25N 104°3E **39** d
Tel → _India_ 20°50N 83°54E **44** D6
Tel Aviv ✈ (TLV) _Israel_ 32°5N 34°49E **48** C3
Tel Aviv-Yafo _Israel_ 32°4N 34°48E **48** C3
Tel Lakhish _Israel_ 31°34N 34°51E **48** D3
Tel Megiddo _Israel_ 32°35N 35°11E **48** C4
Tela _Honduras_ 15°40N 87°28W **88** C2
Telanaipura = Jambi
  Indonesia 1°38S 103°30E **36** E2
Telangana _India_ 17°30N 78°30E **44** F4
Telavi _Georgia_ 42°0N 45°30E **19** F8
Telegraph Creek _Canada_ 58°0N 131°10W **70** B2
Telekhany = Tsyelyakhany
  Belarus 52°30N 25°46E **17** B13
Telemark _Norway_ 59°15N 7°40E **9** G12
Telén _Argentina_ 36°15S 65°31W **94** D2
Teleng _Iran_ 25°47N 61°3E **47** E9
Teles Pires → _Brazil_ 7°21S 58°3W **92** E7
Telescope Pk. _U.S.A._ 36°10N 117°5W **79** J9
Telford _U.K._ 52°40N 2°27W **13** E5
Telford and Wrekin □
  _U.K._ 52°45N 2°27W **12** E5
Telkwa _Canada_ 54°41N 127°5W **70** C3
Tell City _U.S.A._ 37°57N 86°46W **80** G10
Teller _U.S.A._ 65°16N 166°22W **74** B6
Tellicherry = Thalassery
  India 11°45N 75°30E **45** J2
Telluride _U.S.A._ 37°56N 107°49W **77** H10
Teloloapán _Mexico_ 18°21N 99°51E **87** D5
Telpos Iz _Russia_ 63°16N 59°13E **18** B10
Telsen _Argentina_ 42°30S 66°50W **96** E3
Telšiai _Lithuania_ 55°59N 22°14E **9** J20
Teluk Anson = Teluk Intan
  Malaysia 4°3N 101°0E **39** K3
Teluk Bahang _Malaysia_ 5°28N 100°13E **39** c
Teluk Betung = Bandar Lampung
  Indonesia 5°20S 105°10E **36** F3
Teluk Intan _Malaysia_ 4°3N 101°0E **39** K3
Teluk Kumbar _Malaysia_ 5°18N 100°14E **39** c
Telukbutun _Indonesia_ 4°13N 108°12E **36** D3
Telukdalam _Indonesia_ 0°33N 97°50E **36** D1
Tema _Ghana_ 5°41N 0°0 **52** G5
Temagami, L. _Canada_ 47°0N 80°10W **72** C3
Temax _Mexico_ 21°9N 88°56W **87** C7
Temba _S. Africa_ 25°20S 28°17E **57** C4
Tembagapura _Indonesia_ 4°20S 137°0E **37** E9
Tembe □ _S. Africa_ 26°51S 32°24E **57** C5
Temblor Range _U.S.A._ 35°20N 119°50W **79** K7

Teme → _U.K._ 52°11N 2°13W **13** E5
Temecula _U.S.A._ 33°30N 117°9W **79** M9
Temengor, Tasik
  Malaysia 5°4N 101°18E **39** K3
Temerloh _Malaysia_ 3°27N 102°25E **39** L4
Teminabuan _Indonesia_ 1°26S 132°1E **37** E8
Temir _Kazakhstan_ 49°1N 57°14E **19** E10
Temirtau _Kazakhstan_ 50°5N 72°56E **30** A3
Témiscamie → _Canada_ 50°59N 73°5W **73** B5
Témiscaming _Canada_ 46°44N 79°5W **72** C4
Témiscamingue, L.
  Canada 47°10N 79°25W **72** C4
Temosachic _Mexico_ 28°57N 107°51W **86** B3
Tempe _U.S.A._ 33°24N 111°54W **77** K8
Tempiute _U.S.A._ 37°39N 115°38W **78** H11
Temple _U.S.A._ 31°6N 97°21W **84** F6
Temple B. _Australia_ 12°15S 143°3E **62** A3
Templemore _Ireland_ 52°47N 7°51W **10** D4
Templeton _U.S.A._ 35°33N 120°42W **78** K6
Templeton → _Australia_ 21°0S 138°40E **62** C2
Tempoal de Sánchez
  Mexico 21°31N 98°23W **87** C5
Temuco _Chile_ 38°45S 72°40W **96** D2
Temuka _N.Z._ 44°14S 171°17E **59** F3
Ten Degree Channel
  India 10°0N 92°30E **45** K11
Tenabo _Mexico_ 20°3N 90°14W **87** C6
Tenaha _U.S.A._ 31°57N 94°15W **84** F7
Tenakee Springs _U.S.A._ 57°47N 135°13W **70** B1
Tenali _India_ 16°15N 80°35E **45** F5
Tenancingo _Mexico_ 18°58N 99°38W **87** D5
Tenango del Valle _Mexico_ 19°7N 99°33W **87** D5
Tenaro, Akra _Greece_ 36°22N 22°27E **23** F10
Tenasserim _Burma_ 12°6N 99°3E **39** F2
Tenasserim □ _Burma_ 14°0N 98°30E **38** F2
Tenasserim → _Burma_ 12°24N 98°37E **38** F2
Tenby _U.K._ 51°40N 4°42W **13** F3
Tenda, Colle di _France_ 44°7N 7°36E **20** D7
Tendaho _Ethiopia_ 11°48N 40°54E **49** E3
Tendō _Japan_ 38°20N 140°30E **28** E10
Tendukhera _India_ 23°24N 79°33E **43** H8
Ténéré, Erg du _Niger_ 17°35N 10°55E **53** E8
Tenerife _Canary Is._ 28°15N 16°35W **52** C2
Teng Xian _Guangxi Zhuangzu,_
  China 23°21N 110°56E **35** F8
Teng Xian _Shandong,_
  China 35°5N 117°10E **33** G9
Tengah, Kepulauan
  Indonesia 7°5S 118°15E **36** F5
Tengchong _China_ 25°0N 98°28E **34** E2
Tengchowfu = Penglai
  China 37°48N 120°42E **33** F11
Tenggarong _Indonesia_ 0°24S 116°58E **36** E5
Tengger Shamo _China_ 38°0N 104°10E **32** F3
Tenggol, Pulau _Malaysia_ 4°48N 103°41E **39** K4
Tengiz Köli _Kazakhstan_ 50°30N 69°0E **30** A2
Tengzhou _China_ 35°4N 117°9E **33** G9
Teniente Enciso △
  Paraguay 21°5S 61°8W **94** A3
Tenino _U.S.A._ 46°51N 122°51W **78** D4
Tenkasi _India_ 8°55N 77°20E **45** K3
Tennant Creek _Australia_ 19°30S 134°15E **62** B1
Tennessee □ _U.S.A._ 36°0N 86°30W **85** D11
Tennessee → _U.S.A._ 37°4N 88°34W **85** C10
Tenojoki = Tana →
  Norway 70°30N 28°14E **8** A23
Tenom _Malaysia_ 5°4N 115°57E **36** C5
Tenosique _Mexico_ 17°29N 91°26W **87** D6
Tenryū-Gawa → _Japan_ 35°39N 137°48E **29** G8
Tenterden _U.K._ 51°4N 0°42E **13** F8
Tenterfield _Australia_ 29°0S 152°0E **63** D5
Teófilo Otoni _Brazil_ 17°50S 41°30W **93** G10
Tepa _Indonesia_ 7°52S 129°31E **37** F7
Tepalcatepec → _Mexico_ 18°35N 101°59W **86** D4
Tepehuanes _Mexico_ 25°21N 105°44W **86** B3
Tepetongo _Mexico_ 22°28N 103°9W **86** C4
Tepic _Mexico_ 21°30N 104°54W **86** C4
Teplice _Czech Rep._ 50°40N 13°48E **16** C7
Tequila _Mexico_ 20°54N 103°47W **86** C4
Ter → _Spain_ 42°2N 3°12E **21** A7
Ter Apel _Neths._ 52°53N 7°5E **15** B7
Téra _Niger_ 14°0N 0°45E **52** F6
Teraina _Kiribati_ 4°43N 160°25W **65** G12
Terang _Australia_ 38°15S 142°55E **63** F3
Terang, Teluk _Indonesia_ 8°44S 116°0E **37** K19
Tercero → _Argentina_ 32°58S 61°47W **94** C3
Terdal _India_ 16°33N 75°3E **44** F2
Terebovlya _Ukraine_ 49°18N 25°44E **17** D13
Terek → _Russia_ 44°0N 47°30E **19** F8
Terengganu □ _Malaysia_ 4°55N 103°0E **39** K4
Terepaima △ _Venezuela_ 9°58N 69°17W **89** E6
Teresina _Brazil_ 5°9S 42°45W **93** E10
Teressa _India_ 8°15N 93°10E **45** K11
Teridgerie Cr. →
  Australia 30°25S 148°50E **63** E4
Termas de Río Hondo
  Argentina 27°29S 64°52W **94** B3
Términi Imerese _Italy_ 37°59N 13°42E **22** F5
Términos, L. de _Mexico_ 18°37N 91°33W **87** D6
Termiz _Uzbekistan_ 37°15N 67°15E **26** F7
Térmoli _Italy_ 42°0N 15°0E **22** C6
Ternate _Indonesia_ 0°45N 127°25E **37** D7
Terneuzen _Neths._ 51°20N 3°50E **15** C3
Terney _Russia_ 45°3N 136°37E **28** B8
Terni _Italy_ 42°34N 12°37E **22** C5
Ternopil _Ukraine_ 49°30N 25°40E **17** D13
Ternopil □ _Ukraine_ 48°10N 25°10E **17** D13
Ternopol = Ternopil
  Ukraine 49°30N 25°40E **17** D13
Terowie _Australia_ 33°8S 138°55E **63** E2
Terra Bella _U.S.A._ 35°58N 119°3W **79** K7
Terra Nova △ _Canada_ 48°33N 53°55W **73** C9
Terrace _Canada_ 54°30N 128°35W **70** C3
Terrace Bay _Canada_ 48°47N 87°5W **72** C2
Terracina _Italy_ 41°17N 13°15E **22** D5
Terralba _Italy_ 39°43N 8°39E **22** E3

Terrassa _Spain_ 41°34N 2°1E **21** B7
Terre Haute _U.S.A._ 39°28N 87°25W **80** F10
Terrebonne B. _U.S.A._ 29°5N 90°35W **85** G9
Terrell _U.S.A._ 32°44N 96°17W **84** E6
Terrenceville _Canada_ 47°40N 54°44W **73** C9
Terry _U.S.A._ 46°47N 105°19W **76** C11
Terryville _U.S.A._ 41°41N 73°3W **83** E11
Terschelling _Neths._ 53°25N 5°20E **15** A5
Teruel _Spain_ 40°22N 1°8W **21** B5
Tervola _Finland_ 66°6N 24°49E **8** C21
Teryaweynya L.
  Australia 32°18S 143°22E **63** E3
Teshio _Japan_ 44°53N 141°44E **28** B10
Teshio-Gawa → _Japan_ 44°53N 141°45E **28** B10
Tesiyn Gol → _Mongolia_ 50°40N 93°20E **30** A7
Teslin _Canada_ 60°10N 132°43W **70** A2
Teslin → _Canada_ 61°34N 134°35W **70** A2
Teslin L. _Canada_ 60°15N 132°57W **70** A2
Tessalit _Mali_ 20°12N 1°0E **52** D6
Tessaoua _Niger_ 13°47N 7°56E **52** F7
Test → _U.K._ 50°56N 1°29W **13** G6
Testigos, Is. Los _Venezuela_ 11°23N 63°7W **89** D7
Tetachuck L. _Canada_ 53°18N 125°55W **70** C3
Tetas, Pta. _Chile_ 23°31S 70°38W **94** A1
Tete _Mozam._ 16°13S 33°33E **55** H6
Teterev → _Ukraine_ 51°1N 30°5E **17** C16
Teteven _Bulgaria_ 42°58N 24°17E **23** C11
Tethul → _Canada_ 60°35N 112°12W **70** A6
Tetiyev _Ukraine_ 49°22N 29°38E **17** D15
Tetlit Zheh = Fort McPherson
  Canada 67°30N 134°55W **68** D5
Teton → _U.S.A._ 47°56N 110°31W **76** C8
Tétouan _Morocco_ 35°35N 5°21W **52** A4
Tetovo _Macedonia_ 42°1N 20°59E **23** C9
Teuco → _Argentina_ 25°35S 60°11W **94** B3
Teulon _Canada_ 50°23N 97°16W **71** C9
Teun _Indonesia_ 6°59S 129°8E **37** F7
Teuri-Tō _Japan_ 44°26N 141°19E **28** B10
Teutoburger Wald _Germany_ 52°5N 8°22E **16** B5
Tevere → _Italy_ 41°44N 12°14E **22** D5
Teverya _Israel_ 32°47N 35°32E **48** C4
Teviot → _U.K._ 55°29N 2°38W **11** F6
Tewantin _Australia_ 26°27S 153°3E **63** D5
Tewkesbury _U.K._ 51°59N 2°9W **13** F5
Texada I. _Canada_ 49°40N 124°25W **70** D4
Texarkana _Ark., U.S.A._ 33°26N 94°2W **84** E7
Texarkana _Tex., U.S.A._ 33°26N 94°3W **84** E7
Texas _Australia_ 28°49S 151°9E **63** D5
Texas □ _U.S.A._ 31°40N 98°30W **84** F5
Texas City _U.S.A._ 29°24N 94°54W **84** G7
Texel _Neths._ 53°5N 4°50E **15** A4
Texline _U.S.A._ 36°23N 103°2W **84** A3
Texoma, L. _U.S.A._ 33°50N 96°34W **84** E6
Teyateyaneng _Lesotho_ 29°7S 27°34E **55** K5
Tezin _Afghan._ 34°24N 69°30E **42** B3
Teziutlán _Mexico_ 19°49N 97°21W **87** D5
Tezpur _India_ 26°40N 92°45E **41** F18
Tezzeron L. _Canada_ 54°43N 124°30W **70** C4
Tha-anne → _Canada_ 60°31N 94°37W **71** A10
Tha Deua _Laos_ 17°57N 102°53E **38** D4
Tha Deua _Laos_ 19°26N 101°50E **38** C3
Tha Li _Thailand_ 17°37N 101°25E **38** D3
Tha Pla _Thailand_ 17°48N 100°32E **38** D3
Tha Rua _Thailand_ 14°34N 100°44E **38** E3
Tha Sala _Thailand_ 8°40N 99°56E **39** H2
Tha Song Yang _Thailand_ 17°34N 97°55E **38** D1
Thaba Putsoa _Lesotho_ 29°45S 28°0E **57** C4
Thaba-Tseka _Lesotho_ 29°32S 28°36E **57** C4
Thabana Ntlenyana
  Lesotho 29°30S 29°16E **57** C4
Thabazimbi _S. Africa_ 24°40S 27°21E **57** B4
Thādiq _Si. Arabia_ 25°18N 45°52E **46** E5
Thai Binh _Vietnam_ 20°35N 106°1E **34** G6
Thai Muang _Thailand_ 8°24N 98°16E **39** H2
Thai Nguyen _Vietnam_ 21°35N 105°55E **34** G5
Thailand ■ _Asia_ 16°0N 102°0E **38** E4
Thailand, G. of _Asia_ 11°30N 101°0E **39** G3
Thakhek _Laos_ 17°25N 104°45E **38** D5
Thal _Pakistan_ 33°28N 70°33E **42** C4
Thal Desert _Pakistan_ 31°10N 71°30E **42** D4
Thala La = Hkakabo Razi
  Burma 28°25N 97°23E **34** C1
Thalabarivat _Cambodia_ 13°33N 105°57E **38** F5
Thalang = Amphoe Thalang
  Thailand 8°1N 98°20E **39** a
Thalang _Thailand_ 8°2N 98°20E **39** h2
Thalara _Nepal_ 29°29N 80°59E **43** E9
Thalassery _India_ 11°45N 75°30E **45** J2
Thale Sap Songkhla
  Thailand 7°12N 100°28E **39** J3
Thallon _Australia_ 28°39S 148°49E **63** D4
Thalu, Ko _Thailand_ 9°26N 99°54E **39** b
Tham Lot _Thailand_ 19°34N 98°16E **38** C2
Thames _N.Z._ 37°7S 175°34E **59** B5
Thames → _Canada_ 42°20N 82°25W **82** D2
Thames → _U.K._ 51°29N 0°34E **13** F8
Thames → _U.S.A._ 41°18N 72°5W **83** E12
Thames Estuary _U.K._ 51°29N 0°52E **13** F8
Thamesford _Canada_ 43°4N 81°0W **82** C4
Thamesville _Canada_ 42°33N 81°59W **82** D3
Than _India_ 22°34N 71°11E **42** H4
Than Kyun _Burma_ 9°49N 98°41E **39** H1
Than Uyen _Vietnam_ 22°0N 103°54E **38** B4
Thana Gazi _India_ 27°25N 76°19E **42** F7
Thandla _India_ 23°0N 74°34E **42** H6
Thandwe _Burma_ 18°20N 94°30E **41** K19
Thane _India_ 19°12N 72°59E **44** K1
Thanesar _India_ 30°1N 76°52E **42** D7
Thanet, I. of _U.K._ 51°21N 1°20E **13** F9
Thangool _Australia_ 24°38S 150°42E **62** C5
Thanh Hoa _Vietnam_ 19°48N 105°46E **38** C5
Thanh Hung _Vietnam_ 9°41N 105°43E **39** H5
Thanh Pho Ho Chi Minh
  Vietnam 10°58N 106°40E **39** G6
Thanh Thuy _Vietnam_ 22°55N 104°51E **38** A5
Thanjavur _India_ 10°48N 79°12E **45** J4
Thanlwin = Salween →
  Burma 16°31N 97°37E **41** L20

Thano Bula Khan
  Pakistan 25°22N 67°50E **42** G2
Thanya Buri _Thailand_ 14°1N 100°45E **38** E3
Thaoge → _Botswana_ 20°27S 22°36E **56** B3
Thap Lan △ _Thailand_ 14°15N 102°16E **38** E4
Thap Sakae _Thailand_ 11°30N 99°37E **39** G2
Thap Than _Thailand_ 15°27N 99°54E **38** E2
Thar Desert _India_ 28°0N 72°0E **42** F5
Tharad _India_ 24°30N 71°44E **42** G4
Thargomindah _Australia_ 27°58S 143°46E **63** D3
Tharp Fracture Zone
  S. Ocean 54°0S 135°0W **5** B14
Tharrawaddy _Burma_ 17°38N 95°48E **41** L19
Tharthār, Buḥayrat ath
  Iraq 34°0N 43°15E **46** C4
Tharthār, L. = Tharthār, Buḥayrat
  ath _Iraq_ 34°0N 43°15E **46** C4
Tharthār, W. ath → _Iraq_ 34°32N 43°4E **46** C4
Thasos _Greece_ 40°40N 24°40E **23** D11
That Khe _Vietnam_ 22°16N 106°28E **34** F6
Thatcher _Ariz., U.S.A._ 32°51N 109°46W **77** K9
Thatcher _Colo., U.S.A._ 37°33N 104°7W **77** H11
Thaton _Burma_ 16°55N 97°22E **41** L20
Thatta _Pakistan_ 24°42N 67°55E **42** G2
Thaungdut _Burma_ 24°30N 94°40E **41** G19
Thayawthadangy Kyun
  Burma 12°19N 98°0E **38** F1
Thayer _U.S.A._ 36°31N 91°33W **80** G8
Thayetmyo _Burma_ 19°20N 95°10E **41** K19
Thazi _Burma_ 21°0N 96°5E **41** J20
Thbeng Meanchey
  Cambodia 13°49N 104°58E **38** F5
The Bahamas ■ _N. Amer._ 24°0N 75°0W **89** B5
The Broads _U.K._ 52°45N 1°30E **12** E9
The Everglades _U.S.A._ 25°50N 81°0W **85** J14
The Gambia ■ _W. Afr._ 13°25N 16°0W **52** F2
The Gulf = Persian Gulf
  Asia 27°0N 50°0E **47** E6
The Hague = 's-Gravenhage
  Neths. 52°7N 4°17E **15** B4
The Pas _Canada_ 53°45N 101°15W **71** C8
The Wash _U.K._ 52°58N 0°20E **12** E8
The Weald _U.K._ 51°4N 0°20E **13** F8
Thebes = Thiva _Greece_ 38°19N 23°19E **23** E10
Thebes _Egypt_ 25°40N 32°35E **53** C12
Thedford _U.S.A._ 41°59N 100°35W **80** E3
Theebine _Australia_ 25°57S 152°34E **63** D5
Thekulthili L. _Canada_ 61°3N 110°0W **71** A7
Thelon → _Canada_ 64°16N 96°4W **71** A8
Theodore _Australia_ 24°55S 150°3E **62** C5
Theodore _Canada_ 51°26N 102°55W **71** C8
Theodore _U.S.A._ 30°33N 88°10W **85** F10
Theodore Roosevelt △
  _U.S.A._ 47°0N 103°25W **80** B2
Theodore Roosevelt L.
  _U.S.A._ 33°40N 111°10W **77** K8
Thepha _Thailand_ 6°52N 100°58E **39** J3
Theresa _U.S.A._ 44°13N 75°48W **83** B9
Thermopolis _U.S.A._ 43°39N 108°13W **76** E9
Thermopylæ _Greece_ 38°48N 22°35E **23** E10
Thessalon _Canada_ 46°20N 83°30W **72** C3
Thessalonica, Gulf of =
  Thessaloniki Kolpos
  Greece 40°15N 22°45E **23** D10
Thessaloniki _Greece_ 40°38N 22°58E **23** D10
Thessaloniki Kolpos
  Greece 40°15N 22°45E **23** D10
Thetford _U.K._ 52°25N 0°45E **13** E8
Thetford Mines _Canada_ 46°8N 71°18W **73** C5
Theun → _Laos_ 18°19N 104°0E **38** C5
Theunissen _S. Africa_ 28°26S 26°43E **56** C4
Thevenard _Australia_ 32°9S 133°38E **63** E1
Thibodaux _U.S.A._ 29°48N 90°49W **85** G9
Thicket Portage _Canada_ 55°19N 97°42W **71** B9
Thief River Falls _U.S.A._ 48°7N 96°10W **80** A5
Thiel Mts. _Antarctica_ 85°15S 91°0W **5** E16
Thiers _France_ 45°52N 3°33E **20** D5
Thiès _Senegal_ 14°50N 16°51W **52** F2
Thika _Kenya_ 1°1S 37°5E **54** E7
Thimphu _Bhutan_ 27°31N 89°45E **41** F16
Thina → _S. Africa_ 31°18S 29°13E **57** D4
Þingvallavatn _Iceland_ 64°11N 21°9W **8** D3
Thionville _France_ 49°20N 6°10E **20** B7
Thira = Santorini _Greece_ 36°23N 25°27E **23** F11
Third Cataract _Sudan_ 19°42N 30°20E **53** E12
Thirsk _U.K._ 54°14N 1°19W **12** C6
Thiruvananthapuram
  India 8°41N 77°0E **45** K3
Thiruvarur _India_ 10°46N 79°38E **45** J4
Thisted _Denmark_ 56°58N 8°40E **9** H13
Thistle I. _Australia_ 35°0S 136°8E **63** F2
Thithia = Cicia _Fiji_ 17°45S 179°18W **59** a
Thiva _Greece_ 38°19N 23°19E **23** E10
Þjórsá → _Iceland_ 63°47N 20°48W **8** E3
Thlewiaza → _Canada_ 60°29N 94°40W **71** A10
Thmar Puok _Cambodia_ 13°57N 103°4E **38** F4
Tho Chu, Dao _Vietnam_ 9°20N 103°28E **39** H4
Tho Vinh _Vietnam_ 19°16N 105°42E **38** C5
Thoa → _Canada_ 60°31N 109°47W **71** A7
Thoen _Thailand_ 17°43N 99°12E **38** D2
Thoeng _Thailand_ 19°41N 100°12E **38** C3
Thohoyandou _S. Africa_ 22°58S 30°29E **55** J6
Thomas _U.S.A._ 35°45N 98°45W **84** D5
Thomas, L. _Australia_ 26°4S 137°58E **63** D2
Thomas Hubbard, C.
  Canada 82°0N 94°25W **69** A13
Thomaston _U.S.A._ 32°53N 84°20W **85** E12
Thomasville _Ala., U.S.A._ 31°55N 87°44W **85** F11
Thomasville _Ga., U.S.A._ 30°50N 83°59W **85** F13
Thomasville _N.C., U.S.A._ 35°53N 80°5W **85** D15
Thompson _Canada_ 55°45N 97°52W **71** B9
Thompson _U.S.A._ 41°52N 75°31W **83** E9
Thompson → _Canada_ 50°15N 121°24W **70** C4
Thompson → _U.S.A._ 39°46N 93°37W **80** F7
Thompson Falls _U.S.A._ 47°36N 115°21W **76** C6
Thompson Pk. _U.S.A._ 41°0N 123°2W **76** F2
Thompson Springs
  _U.S.A._ 38°58N 109°43W **76** G9

Thompsontown _U.S.A._ 40°33N 77°14W **82** F7
Thomson _U.S.A._ 33°28N 82°30W **85** E13
Thomson → _Australia_ 25°11S 142°53E **62** C3
Thong Yang _Thailand_ 9°28N 99°56E **39** b
Thoothukudi = Tuticorin
  India 8°50N 78°12E **45** K4
Þórisvatn _Iceland_ 64°20N 18°55W **8** D4
Thornaby on Tees _U.K._ 54°33N 1°18W **12** C6
Thornbury _Canada_ 44°34N 80°26W **82** B4
Thorne _U.K._ 53°37N 0°57W **12** D7
Thornton _Canada_ 44°16N 79°43W **82** B5
Thornton _U.S.A._ 39°52N 104°58W **76** G11
Thorold _Canada_ 43°7N 79°12W **82** C5
Þórshöfn _Iceland_ 66°12N 15°20W **8** C6
Thouin, C. _Australia_ 20°20S 118°10E **60** D2
Thousand Islands _U.S.A._ 44°20N 76°0W **83** B9
Thousand Oaks _U.S.A._ 34°10N 118°50W **79** L8
Thrace _Turkey_ 41°0N 27°0E **23** D12
Three Forks _U.S.A._ 45°54N 111°33W **76** D8
Three Gorges Dam
  China 30°45N 111°15E **35** B8
Three Gorges Res. = Sanxia
  Shuiku _China_ 30°N 107°58E **34** B6
Three Hills _Canada_ 51°43N 113°15W **70** C6
Three Hummock I.
  Australia 40°25S 144°55E **63** G3
Three Pagodas Pass _Asia_ 15°20N 98°30E **38** E2
Three Points, C. _Ghana_ 4°42N 2°6W **52** H5
Three Rivers _Calif.,_
  _U.S.A._ 36°26N 118°54W **78** J8
Three Rivers _Tex., U.S.A._ 28°28N 98°11W **84** G5
Three Springs _Australia_ 29°32S 115°45E **61** E2
Thrissur _India_ 10°30N 76°18E **45** J3
Throssell, L. _Australia_ 27°33S 124°10E **61** E3
Throssell Ra. _Australia_ 22°3S 121°43E **60** D3
Thrushton △ _Australia_ 27°47S 147°40E **63** D4
Thu Dau Mot _Vietnam_ 10°58N 106°39E **39** G6
Thua → _Kenya_ 1°31S 39°30E **54** E7
Thuamal Rampur _India_ 19°23N 82°56E **44** E6
Thuan Hoa _Vietnam_ 8°58N 105°30E **39** H5
Thubun Lakes _Canada_ 61°30N 112°0W **71** A6
Thuin _Belgium_ 50°20N 4°17E **15** D4
Thule = Qaanaaq
  Greenland 77°30N 69°10W **69** B18
Thule Air Base = Uummannaq
  Greenland 77°33N 68°52W **69** B18
Thun _Switz._ 46°45N 7°38E **20** C7
Thunder B. _U.S.A._ 45°0N 83°20W **82** B1
Thunder Bay _Canada_ 48°20N 89°15W **72** C2
Thung Salaeng Luang △
  Thailand 16°43N 100°50E **38** D3
Thung Song _Thailand_ 8°10N 99°40E **39** H2
Thungyai = Amphoe
  Thailand 15°20N 98°55E **38** E2
Thunkar _Bhutan_ 27°55N 91°0E **41** F17
Thuong Tra _Vietnam_ 16°2N 107°42E **38** D6
Thüringer Wald _Germany_ 50°35N 11°0E **16** C6
Thuringowa △ _Australia_ 19°18S 146°43E **62** B4
Thurles _Ireland_ 52°41N 7°49W **10** D4
Thurrock □ _U.K._ 51°31N 0°23E **13** F8
Thursday I. _Australia_ 10°30S 142°3E **62** A3
Thurso _Canada_ 45°36N 75°15W **72** C4
Thurso _U.K._ 58°36N 3°32W **11** C5
Thurso → _U.K._ 58°36N 3°32W **11** C5
Thurston I. _Antarctica_ 72°0S 100°0W **5** D16
Thutade L. _Canada_ 57°0N 126°55W **70** B3
Ti-Tree _Australia_ 22°5S 133°22E **62** C1
Tian Shan _Asia_ 40°30N 76°0E **30** E6
Tianchang _China_ 32°40N 119°0E **35** A12
Tiandeng _China_ 23°6N 107°7E **34** F6
Tiandong _China_ 23°36N 107°8E **34** F6
Tian'e _China_ 25°1N 107°9E **34** E6
Tianhe _China_ 24°48N 108°40E **34** E7
Tianjin _China_ 39°7N 117°12E **33** E9
Tianjin Shi □ _China_ 39°8N 117°12E **33** E9
Tianjun _China_ 38°0N 98°30E **30** D8
Tianlin _China_ 24°21N 106°12E **34** E6
Tianmen _China_ 30°39N 113°9E **35** B9
Tianquan _China_ 30°7N 102°43E **34** B4
Tianshifu _China_ 41°17N 124°22E **33** D13
Tianshui _China_ 34°32N 105°40E **34** G3
Tiantai _China_ 29°10N 121°2E **35** C13
Tianya _China_ 18°18N 109°20E **38** C7
Tianyang _China_ 23°42N 106°53E **34** F6
Tianzhen _China_ 40°24N 114°5E **32** D8
Tianzhu _China_ 26°54N 109°11E **34** D7
Tianzhuangtai _China_ 40°43N 122°5E **33** D12
Tiarei _Tahiti_ 17°32S 149°20W **59** d
Tiaret _Algeria_ 35°20N 1°21E **52** A6
Tibagi _Brazil_ 24°30S 50°24W **95** A5
Tibagi → _Brazil_ 22°47S 51°1W **95** A5
Tibastī, Sarīr _Libya_ 22°50N 18°30E **53** D9
Tibati _Cameroon_ 6°22N 12°30E **54** C2
Tiber = Tevere → _Italy_ 41°44N 12°14E **22** D5
Tiber Res. _U.S.A._ 48°19N 111°6W **76** B8
Tiberias = Teverya _Israel_ 32°47N 35°32E **48** C4
Tiberias, L. = Yam Kinneret
  Israel 32°45N 35°35E **48** C4
Tibesti _Chad_ 21°0N 17°30E **53** D9
Tibet = Xizang Zizhiqu
  China 32°0N 88°0E **30** E6
Tibet, Plateau of _Asia_ 32°0N 86°0E **24** E10
Tibnī _Syria_ 35°36N 39°50E **46** C3
Tibooburra _Australia_ 29°26S 142°1E **63** D3
Tibrikot _Nepal_ 29°3N 82°48E **43** E10
Tiburón, I. _Mexico_ 29°0N 112°25W **86** B2
Ticino → _Italy_ 45°9N 9°14E **20** D8
Ticonderoga _U.S.A._ 43°51N 73°26W **83** C11
Ticul _Mexico_ 20°24N 89°32W **87** C7
Tidaholm _Sweden_ 58°12N 13°58E **9** G15
Tiddim _Burma_ 23°28N 93°45E **41** H18
Tiden _India_ 7°15N 93°33E **45** L11
Tidioute _U.S.A._ 41°41N 79°24W **82** E5
Tidjikja _Mauritania_ 18°29N 11°35W **52** E3
Tidore _Indonesia_ 0°40N 127°25E **37** D7
Tiefa _China_ 42°28N 123°26E **33** C12
Tiegang Shuiku _China_ 22°37N 113°53E **31** a
Tiel _Neths._ 51°53N 5°26E **15** C5
Tieli _China_ 46°57N 128°3E **31** B14

Tieling *China* 42°20N 123°55E **33** C12
Tielt *Belgium* 51°0N 3°20E **15** C3
Tien Shan = Tian Shan
  Asia 40°30N 76°0E **30** C4
Tien-tsin = Tianjin *China* 39°7N 117°12E **33** E9
Tien Yen *Vietnam* 21°20N 107°24E **38** B6
T'ienching = Tianjin
  China 39°7N 117°12E **33** E9
Tienen *Belgium* 50°48N 4°57E **15** D4
Tientsin = Tianjin *China* 39°7N 117°12E **33** E9
Tieri *Australia* 23°2S 148°21E **62** C4
Tierra Amarilla *Chile* 27°28S 70°18W **94** B1
Tierra Amarilla *U.S.A.* 36°42N 106°33W **77** H10
Tierra Colorada *Mexico* 17°11N 99°32W **87** D5
Tierra de Campos *Spain* 42°10N 4°50W **21** A3
Tierra del Fuego, I. Grande de
  Argentina 54°0S 69°0W **96** G3
Tiétar → *Spain* 39°50N 6°1W **21** C3
Tieté → *Brazil* 20°40S 51°35W **95** A5
Tiffin *U.S.A.* 41°7N 83°11W **81** E12
Tifton *U.S.A.* 31°27N 83°31W **85** F13
Tifu *Indonesia* 3°39S 126°24E **37** E7
Tiger Leaping Gorge = Hutiao Xia
  China 27°13N 100°9E **34** D3
Tighina *Moldova* 46°50N 29°30E **17** E15
Tigil *Russia* 57°49N 158°40E **27** D16
Tigiria *India* 20°29N 85°31E **44** D7
Tignish *Canada* 46°58N 64°2W **73** C7
Tigre → *Peru* 4°30S 74°10W **92** D4
Tigre → *Venezuela* 9°20N 62°30W **92** B6
Tigris = Dijlah, Nahr →
  Asia 31°0N 47°25E **46** D5
Tigyaing *Burma* 23°45N 96°10E **41** H20
Tihāmah *Asia* 15°3N 41°55E **49** D3
Tijara *India* 27°56N 76°31E **42** F7
Tijuana *Mexico* 32°32N 117°1W **79** N9
Tikal *Guatemala* 17°13N 89°24W **88** C2
Tikal △ *Guatemala* 17°23N 89°34W **88** C2
Tikamgarh *India* 24°44N 78°50E **43** G8
Tikchik Lakes *U.S.A.* 60°0N 159°0W **74** D8
Tikhoretsk *Russia* 45°56N 40°5E **19** E7
Tikhvin *Russia* 59°35N 33°30E **18** C5
Tikirarjuaq = Whale Cove
  Canada 62°10N 92°34W **71** A10
Tikrīt *Iraq* 34°35N 43°37E **46** C4
Tiksi *Russia* 71°40N 128°45E **27** B13
Tilā' al 'Alī *Jordan* 32°0N 35°52E **48** D4
Tilamuta *Indonesia* 0°32N 122°23E **37** D6
Tilburg *Neths.* 51°31N 5°6E **15** C5
Tilbury *Canada* 42°17N 82°23W **82** D2
Tilbury *U.K.* 51°27N 0°22E **13** F8
Tilcara *Argentina* 23°36S 65°23W **94** A2
Tilden *U.S.A.* 42°3N 97°50W **80** D5
Tilhar *India* 28°0N 79°45E **43** F8
Tilichiki *Russia* 60°27N 166°5E **27** C17
Till → *U.K.* 55°41N 2°13W **12** B5
Tillamook *U.S.A.* 45°27N 123°51W **76** D2
Tillanchong I. *India* 8°30N 93°37E **45** K11
Tillsonburg *Canada* 42°53N 80°44W **82** D4
Tilos *Greece* 36°27N 27°27E **23** F12
Tilpa *Australia* 30°57S 144°24E **63** E3
Tilt → *U.K.* 56°46N 3°51N **11** E5
Tilton *U.S.A.* 43°27N 71°36W **83** C13
Tiltonsville *U.S.A.* 40°10N 80°41W **82** F4
Timanskiy Kryazh *Russia* 65°58N 50°5E **18** A9
Timaru *N.Z.* 44°23S 171°14E **59** F3
Timber Creek *Australia* 15°40S 130°29E **60** C5
Timber Lake *U.S.A.* 45°26N 101°5W **80** C3
Timber Mt. *U.S.A.* 37°6N 116°28W **78** H10
Timbué, Ponta *Mozam.* 18°47S 36°22E **57** A6
Timbuktu = Tombouctou
  Mali 16°50N 3°0W **52** E5
Timika *Indonesia* 4°47S 136°32E **37** E9
Timimoun *Algeria* 29°14N 0°16E **52** C6
Timiris, Râs *Mauritania* 19°21N 16°30W **52** E2
Timiskaming, L. =
  Témiscamingue, L.
  Canada 47°10N 79°25W **72** C4
Timișoara *Romania* 45°43N 21°15E **17** F11
Timmins *Canada* 48°28N 81°25W **72** C3
Timok → *Serbia* 44°10N 22°40E **23** B10
Timoleague *Ireland* 51°39N 8°46W **10** E3
Timor *Asia* 9°0S 125°0E **37** F7
Timor Leste = East Timor ■
  Asia 8°50S 126°0E **37** F7
Timor Sea *Ind. Oc.* 12°0S 127°0E **60** B4
Tin Can Bay *Australia* 25°56S 153°0E **63** D5
Tin Mt. *U.S.A.* 36°50N 117°10W **78** J9
Tin Shui Wai *China* 22°28N 114°0E **31** a
Tina = Thina → *S. Africa* 31°18S 29°13E **57** E4
Tina, Khalig el *Egypt* 31°10N 32°40E **48** D1
Tinaca Pt. *Phil.* 5°30N 125°25E **37** C7
Tindal *Australia* 14°31S 132°22E **60** B5
Tindivanam *India* 12°15N 79°41E **45** H4
Tindouf *Algeria* 27°42N 8°10W **52** C4
Tinfunque △ *Paraguay* 23°55S 60°17W **94** A3
Ting Jiang → *China* 24°45N 116°35E **35** E11
Tinggi, Pulau *Malaysia* 2°18N 104°7E **39** L5
Tingo María *Peru* 9°10S 75°54W **92** E3
Tingrela *Ivory C.* 10°27N 6°25E **52** F4
Tingri *China* 28°34N 86°38E **30** F6
Tinh Bien *Vietnam* 10°36N 104°57E **39** G5
Tinian *N. Marianas* 15°0N 145°38E **64** F6
Tinnevelly = Tirunelveli
  India 8°45N 77°45E **45** K3
Tinogasta *Argentina* 28°5S 67°32W **94** B2
Tinos *Greece* 37°33N 25°8E **23** F11
Tinpahar *India* 24°59N 87°44E **43** G12
Tintina *Argentina* 27°2S 62°45W **94** B3
Tintinara *Australia* 35°48S 140°2E **63** F3
Tiobraid Árann = Tipperary
  Ireland 52°28N 8°10W **10** D3
Tioga *N. Dak., U.S.A.* 48°24N 102°56W **80** A2
Tioga *Pa., U.S.A.* 41°55N 77°8W **82** E7
Tioman, Pulau *Malaysia* 2°50N 104°10E **39** L5
Tionesta *U.S.A.* 41°30N 79°28W **82** E5
Tipperary *Ireland* 52°28N 8°10W **10** D3
Tipperary □ *Ireland* 52°37N 7°55W **10** D4
Tipton *Calif., U.S.A.* 36°4N 119°19W **78** J7

Tipton *Iowa, U.S.A.* 41°46N 91°8W **80** E8
Tipton Mt. *U.S.A.* 35°32N 114°12W **79** K12
Tiptonville *U.S.A.* 36°23N 89°29W **85** C10
Tiptur *India* 13°15N 76°26E **45** H3
Tīrān *Iran* 32°45N 51°8E **47** C6
Tiranë *Albania* 41°18N 19°49E **23** D8
Tirari Desert *Australia* 28°22S 138°7E **63** D2
Tiraspol *Moldova* 46°55N 29°35E **17** E15
Tire *Turkey* 38°5N 27°45E **23** E12
Tirebolu *Turkey* 40°58N 38°45E **19** F6
Tiree *U.K.* 56°31N 6°55W **11** E2
Tiree, Passage of *U.K.* 56°30N 6°30W **11** E2
Tîrgoviște = Târgoviște
  Romania 44°55N 25°27E **17** F13
Tîrgu Jiu = Târgu Jiu
  Romania 45°5N 23°19E **17** F12
Tîrgu Mureș = Târgu Mureș
  Romania 46°31N 24°38E **17** E13
Tirich Mir *Pakistan* 36°15N 71°55E **40** A7
Tiritiri o te Moana = Southern
  Alps *N.Z.* 43°41S 170°11E **59** E3
Tirna → *India* 18°4N 76°57E **44** E3
Tírnavos *Greece* 39°45N 22°18E **23** E10
Tirodi *India* 21°40N 79°44E **44** D4
Tirol □ *Austria* 47°3N 10°43E **16** E6
Tirrukkovil *Sri Lanka* 7°7N 81°51E **45** L5
Tirso → *Italy* 39°53N 8°32E **22** E3
Tirtagangga *Indonesia* 8°24S 115°35E **37** J18
Tirthahalli *India* 13°42N 75°14E **45** H2
Tiruchchendur *India* 8°30N 78°11E **45** K4
Tiruchchirappalli *India* 10°45N 78°45E **45** J4
Tirukkoyilur *India* 11°57N 79°12E **45** J4
Tirumangalam *India* 9°49N 77°58E **45** K3
Tirumayam *India* 10°14N 78°45E **45** J4
Tirunelveli *India* 8°45N 77°45E **45** K3
Tirupati *India* 13°39N 79°25E **45** H4
Tiruppattur *Tamil Nadu,*
  India 10°8N 78°37E **45** J4
Tiruppattur *Tamil Nadu,*
  India 12°30N 78°30E **45** H4
Tiruppur *India* 11°5N 77°22E **45** J3
Tirur *India* 10°54N 75°55E **45** J2
Tiruttani *India* 13°11N 79°58E **45** H4
Tirutturaippundi *India* 10°32N 79°41E **45** J4
Tiruvadaimarudur *India* 11°2N 79°27E **45** J4
Tiruvalla *India* 9°23N 76°34E **45** K3
Tiruvallar *India* 13°9N 79°57E **45** H4
Tiruvannamalai *India* 12°15N 79°5E **45** H4
Tiruvettipuram *India* 12°39N 79°33E **45** H4
Tiruvottiyur *India* 13°10N 80°22E **45** H5
Tisa *India* 32°50N 76°9E **42** C7
Tisa → *Serbia* 45°15N 20°17E **23** B9
Tisdale *Canada* 52°50N 104°0W **71** C8
Tishomingo *U.S.A.* 34°14N 96°41W **84** D6
Tissamaharama *Sri Lanka* 6°17N 81°17E **45** L5
Tisza = Tisa → *Serbia* 45°15N 20°17E **23** B9
Tit-Ary *Russia* 71°55N 127°2E **27** B13
Tithwal *Pakistan* 34°21N 73°50E **43** B5
Titicaca, L. *S. Amer.* 15°30S 69°30W **92** G5
Titiwa *Nigeria* 12°14N 12°53E **53** F8
Titlagarh *India* 20°15N 83°11E **44** D6
Titule
  Dem. Rep. of the Congo 3°15N 25°31E **54** D5
Titusville *Fla., U.S.A.* 28°37N 80°49W **85** G5
Titusville *Pa., U.S.A.* 41°38N 79°41W **82** E5
Tivaouane *Senegal* 14°56N 16°45W **52** F2
Tiverton *Canada* 44°16N 81°32W **82** B3
Tiverton *U.K.* 50°54N 3°29W **13** G4
Tívoli *Italy* 41°58N 12°45E **22** D5
Tiwi *Australia* 11°33S 130°42E **60** B5
Tizi-Ouzou *Algeria* 36°42N 4°3E **52** A6
Tizimín *Mexico* 21°9N 88°9W **87** C7
Tiznit *Morocco* 29°48N 9°45W **52** C4
Tjeggelvas *Sweden* 66°37N 17°45E **8** C17
Tjieggelvas = Tjeggelvas
  Sweden 66°37N 17°45E **8** C17
Tjirebon = Cirebon
  Indonesia 6°45S 108°32E **37** G13
Tjirrkarli ☉ *Australia* 26°0S 125°28E **61** E4
Tjluring *Indonesia* 8°25S 114°13E **37** J17
Tjörn *Sweden* 58°0N 11°35E **9** H14
Tjukayirla Roadhouse
  Australia 27°9S 124°34E **61** E3
Tjurabalan ☉ *Australia* 20°0S 128°0E **60** C4
Tlacotalpan *Mexico* 18°37N 95°40W **87** D5
Tlahualilo de Zaragoza
  Mexico 26°7N 103°27W **86** B4
Tlaquepaque *Mexico* 20°39N 103°19W **86** C4
Tlaxcala *Mexico* 19°19N 98°14W **87** D5
Tlaxcala □ *Mexico* 19°25N 98°10W **87** D5
Tlaxiaco *Mexico* 17°25N 97°35W **87** D5
Tlemcen *Algeria* 34°52N 1°21W **52** B5
Tlokweng *Botswana* 24°40S 25°58E **56** B4
To Bong *Vietnam* 12°45N 109°16E **38** F7
Toad → *Canada* 59°25N 124°57W **70** B4
Toad River *Canada* 58°51N 125°14W **70** B3
Toamasina *Madag.* 18°10S 49°25E **55** H9
Toay *Argentina* 36°43S 64°38W **94** D3
Toba *China* 31°19N 97°42E **34** B1
Toba, Danau *Indonesia* 2°30N 98°30E **36** D1
Toba Kakar *Pakistan* 31°30N 69°0E **42** D3
Toba Tek Singh *Pakistan* 30°55N 72°25E **42** D5
Tobago *Trin. & Tob.* 11°10N 60°30W **93** J16
Tobelo *Indonesia* 1°45N 127°56E **37** D7
Tobercurry *Ireland* 54°3N 8°44W **10** B3
Tobermory *Canada* 45°12N 81°40W **82** A3
Tobermory *U.K.* 56°38N 6°5W **11** E2
Tobi *Palau* 2°40N 131°10E **37** D8
Tobi-Shima *Japan* 41°12N 139°34E **28** D9
Tobin, L. *Australia* 21°45S 125°49E **60** D4
Tobin L. *Canada* 53°35N 103°30W **71** C8
Tobol → *Russia* 58°10N 68°12E **26** D7
Toboali *Indonesia* 3°0S 106°25E **36** E3
Tobol → *Russia* 58°10N 68°10E **26** D7
Toboli *Indonesia* 0°38S 120°5E **37** E6
Tobolsk *Russia* 58°15N 68°10E **26** D7
Tobruk = Tubruq *Libya* 32°7N 23°55E **53** B10
Tobyhanna *U.S.A.* 41°11N 75°25W **83** E9
Tobyl = Tobol → *Russia* 58°10N 68°12E **26** D7

Tocantinópolis *Brazil* 6°20S 47°25W **93** E9
Tocantins □ *Brazil* 10°0S 48°0W **93** F9
Tocantins → *Brazil* 1°45S 49°10W **93** D9
Toccoa *U.S.A.* 34°35N 83°19W **85** D13
Tochi → *Pakistan* 32°49N 70°41E **42** C4
Tochigi *Japan* 36°25N 139°45E **29** F9
Tochigi □ *Japan* 36°45N 139°45E **29** F9
Toco *Trin. & Tob.* 10°49N 60°57W **93** K16
Toconao *Chile* 23°11S 68°1W **94** A2
Tocopilla *Chile* 22°5S 70°10W **94** A1
Tocumwal *Australia* 35°51S 145°31E **63** F4
Tocuyo → *Venezuela* 11°3N 68°23W **92** A5
Todd → *Australia* 24°52S 135°48E **62** C2
Todeli *Indonesia* 1°40S 124°29E **37** E6
Todgarh *India* 25°42N 73°58E **42** G5
Todos os Santos, B. de
  Brazil 12°48S 38°38W **93** F11
Todos Santos *Mexico* 23°26N 110°13W **86** C2
Toe Hd. *U.K.* 57°50N 7°8W **11** D1
Tofield *Canada* 53°25N 112°40W **70** C6
Tofino *Canada* 49°11N 125°55W **70** D3
Tofua *Tonga* 19°45S 175°5W **59** c
Tōgane *Japan* 35°33N 140°22E **29** G10
Togian, Kepulauan
  Indonesia 0°20S 121°50E **37** E6
Togliatti *Russia* 53°32N 49°24E **18** D8
Togo ■ *W. Afr.* 8°30N 1°35E **52** G6
Togtoh *China* 40°15N 111°10E **32** D6
Tohiea, Mt. *Moorea* 17°33S 149°49W **59** d
Tōhoku □ *Japan* 39°50N 141°45E **28** E10
Tōhōm *Mongolia* 44°27N 108°2E **32** B5
Toibalewe *India* 10°32N 92°30E **45** J11
Toinya *South Sudan* 6°17N 29°46E **53** G11
Toiyabe Range *U.S.A.* 39°30N 117°0W **76** G5
Tojikiston = Tajikistan ■
  Asia 38°30N 70°0E **26** F8
Tōjō *Japan* 34°53N 133°16E **29** G6
Tok *U.S.A.* 63°20N 142°59W **68** E3
Tokachi-Dake *Japan* 43°17N 142°5E **28** C11
Tokachi-Gawa →
  Japan 42°44N 143°42E **28** C11
Tokala *Indonesia* 1°30S 121°40E **37** E6
Tokamachi *Japan* 37°8N 138°43E **29** F9
Tokanui *N.Z.* 46°34S 168°56E **59** G2
Tokara-Rettō *Japan* 29°37N 129°43E **29** K4
Tokarahi *N.Z.* 44°56S 170°39E **59** F3
Tokashiki-Shima *Japan* 26°11N 127°21E **29** L3
Tokat *Turkey* 40°22N 36°35E **19** F6
Tŏkchŏn *N. Korea* 39°45N 126°18E **33** E14
Tokdo = Liancourt Rocks
  Asia 37°15N 131°52E **29** F5
Tokeland *U.S.A.* 46°42N 123°59W **78** D3
Tokelau Is. ☑ *Pac. Oc.* 9°0S 171°45W **64** H10
Tokmak *Kyrgyzstan* 42°49N 75°15E **26** E8
Toko Ra. *Australia* 23°5S 138°20E **62** C2
Tokoro-Gawa → *Japan* 44°7N 144°5E **28** B12
Toku *Tonga* 18°10S 174°11W **59** c
Tokuno-Shima *Japan* 27°56N 128°55E **29** L4
Tokushima *Japan* 34°4N 134°34E **29** G7
Tokushima □ *Japan* 33°55N 134°0E **29** H7
Tokuyama = Shunan
  Japan 34°3N 131°50E **29** G5
Tolaga Bay *N.Z.* 38°21S 178°20E **59** C7
Tolbukhin = Dobrich
  Bulgaria 43°37N 27°49E **23** C12
Toledo *Brazil* 24°44S 53°45W **95** A5
Toledo *Spain* 39°50N 4°2E **21** C3
Toledo *Ohio, U.S.A.* 41°39N 83°33W **81** E12
Toledo *Oreg., U.S.A.* 44°37N 123°56W **76** D2
Toledo *Wash., U.S.A.* 46°26N 122°51W **78** D4
Toledo, Montes de *Spain* 39°33N 4°20W **21** C3
Toledo Bend Res. *U.S.A.* 31°11N 93°34W **84** F8
Tolga *Australia* 17°15S 145°29E **62** B4
Toliara *Madag.* 23°21S 43°40E **55** J8
Tolima *Colombia* 4°40N 75°19W **92** C3
Tolitoli *Indonesia* 1°5N 120°50E **37** D6
Tollhouse *U.S.A.* 37°1N 119°24W **78** H7
Tolmachevo *Russia* 58°56N 29°51E **9** G23
Tolo, Teluk *Indonesia* 2°20S 122°10E **37** E6
Tolo Harbour *China* 22°27N 114°12E **31** a
Toluca *Mexico* 19°17N 99°40W **87** D5
Tolyatti = Togliatti
  Russia 53°32N 49°24E **18** D8
Tom Burke *S. Africa* 23°5S 28°0E **57** C4
Tom Price *Australia* 22°40S 117°48E **60** D2
Tomah *U.S.A.* 43°59N 90°30W **80** D8
Tomahawk *U.S.A.* 45°28N 89°44W **80** C9
Tomakomai *Japan* 42°38N 141°36E **28** C10
Tomales *U.S.A.* 38°15N 122°53W **78** G4
Tomales B. *U.S.A.* 38°15N 123°58W **78** G3
Tomanivi *Fiji* 17°37S 178°1E **59** a
Tomar *Portugal* 39°36N 8°25W **21** C1
Tomaszów Mazowiecki
  Poland 51°30N 20°2E **17** C10
Tomatlán *Mexico* 19°56N 105°15W **86** D3
Tombador, Serra do *Brazil* 12°0S 58°0W **92** F7
Tombigbee → *U.S.A.* 31°8N 87°57W **85** F11
Tombouctou *Mali* 16°50N 3°0W **52** E5
Tombstone *U.S.A.* 31°43N 110°4W **77** L8
Tombua *Angola* 15°55S 11°55E **55** H2
Tomé *Chile* 36°36S 72°57W **94** D1
Tome *Japan* 38°40N 141°20E **28** E10
Tomelloso *Spain* 39°10N 3°2W **21** C4
Tomini *Indonesia* 0°30N 120°30E **37** D6
Tomini, Teluk *Indonesia* 0°10S 121°0E **37** E6
Tomintoul *U.K.* 57°15N 3°23W **11** D5
Tomkinson Ranges
  Australia 26°11S 129°5E **61** E4
Tommot *Russia* 59°4N 126°20E **27** D13
Tomnop Ta Suos
  Cambodia 11°20N 104°15E **39** G5
Tomo → *Colombia* 5°20N 67°48W **92** B5
Toms Place *U.S.A.* 37°34N 118°41W **78** H8
Toms River *U.S.A.* 39°58N 74°12W **83** G10
Tomsk *Russia* 56°30N 85°5E **26** D9
Tonalá *Chiapas, Mexico* 16°4N 93°45W **87** D6
Tonalá *Jalisco, Mexico* 20°37N 103°14W **86** C4
Tonantins *Brazil* 2°45S 67°45W **92** D5
Tonasket *U.S.A.* 48°42N 119°26W **76** B4

Tonawanda *U.S.A.* 43°1N 78°53W **82** D6
Tonb *Iran* 26°15N 55°15E **47** E7
Tonbridge *U.K.* 51°11N 0°17E **13** F8
Tondano *Indonesia* 1°35N 124°54E **37** D6
Tondi *India* 9°45N 79°4E **45** K4
Tone → *Australia* 34°25S 116°25E **61** F2
Tone → *Japan* 35°44N 140°51E **29** F9
Tonekābon *Iran* 36°45N 51°12E **47** B6
Tong Xian *China* 39°55N 116°35E **32** E9
Tong-yeong *S. Korea* 34°50N 128°20E **33** G15
Tonga ■ *Pac. Oc.* 19°50S 174°30W **59** c
Tonga Trench *Pac. Oc.* 18°0S 173°0W **64** J10
Tongaat *S. Africa* 29°33S 31°9E **57** C5
Tong'an *China* 24°37N 118°8E **35** E12
Tongareva = Penrhyn
  Cook Is. 9°0S 158°0W **65** H12
Tongariro △ *N.Z.* 39°8S 175°33E **59** C5
Tongatapu *Tonga* 21°10S 175°10W **59** c
Tongatapu Group *Tonga* 21°0S 175°0W **59** c
Tongbai *China* 32°20N 113°0E **35** A9
Tongcheng *Anhui, China* 31°4N 116°56E **35** B11
Tongcheng *Hubei, China* 29°15N 113°50E **35** C9
Tongchuan *China* 35°6N 109°3E **32** G5
Tongdao *China* 26°10N 109°42E **34** D7
Tongeren *Belgium* 50°47N 5°28E **15** D5
Tonggu *China* 28°31N 114°20E **35** C10
Tonggu Jiao *China* 22°22N 113°37E **31** a
Tongguan *China* 34°40N 110°25E **32** G6
Tonghai *China* 24°10N 102°53E **34** E4
Tonghua *China* 41°42N 125°58E **33** D13
Tongjiang *Heilongjiang,*
  China 47°40N 132°27E **31** B15
Tongjiang *Sichuan, China* 31°58N 107°11E **34** B6
Tongjosŏn Man *N. Korea* 39°30N 128°0E **33** E15
Tongking, G. of = Tonkin, G. of
  Asia 20°0N 108°0E **38** C7
Tongliang *China* 29°50N 106°3E **34** C6
Tongliao *China* 43°38N 122°18E **33** C12
Tongling *China* 30°55N 117°48E **35** B11
Tonglu *China* 29°45N 119°37E **35** C12
Tongnan = Anyue *China* 30°9N 105°50E **34** B5
Tongoy *Chile* 30°16S 71°31W **94** C1
Tongren *Guizhou, China* 27°43N 109°11E **34** D7
Tongren *Qinghai, China* 35°25N 102°5E **30** D9
Tongres = Tongeren
  Belgium 50°47N 5°28E **15** D5
Tongsa Dzong *Bhutan* 27°31N 90°31E **41** F17
Tongshi *China* 18°30N 109°20E **38** C7
Tongue *U.K.* 58°29N 4°25W **11** C4
Tongue → *U.S.A.* 46°25N 105°52W **76** C11
Tongwei *China* 35°0N 105°5E **34** G3
Tongxiang *China* 30°39N 120°34E **35** B13
Tongxin *China* 36°59N 105°58E **32** F3
Tongyang *N. Korea* 39°9N 126°53E **33** E14
Tongyu *China* 44°45N 123°4E **33** B12
Tongzhou *China* 32°12N 121°2E **35** A13
Tongzi *China* 28°9N 106°49E **34** C6
Tonj *South Sudan* 7°20N 28°44E **53** G11
Tonk *India* 26°6N 75°54E **42** F6
Tonkawa *U.S.A.* 36°41N 97°18W **84** C6
Tonkin = Bac Phan
  Vietnam 22°0N 105°0E **34** G5
Tonkin, G. of *Asia* 20°0N 108°0E **38** C7
Tonlé Sap *Cambodia* 13°0N 104°0E **38** F5
Tono *Japan* 39°19N 141°32E **28** E10
Tonopah *U.S.A.* 38°4N 117°14W **77** G5
Tonosi *Panama* 7°20N 80°20W **88** E3
Tons → *Haryana, India* 30°30N 77°39E **42** D7
Tons → *Ut. P., India* 26°1N 83°33E **43** F10
Tønsberg *Norway* 59°19N 10°25E **9** G14
Tonto △ *U.S.A.* 33°39N 111°7W **77** K8
Tonumea *Tonga* 20°30S 174°30W **59** c
Toobanna *Australia* 18°42S 146°9E **62** B4
Toodyay *Australia* 31°34S 116°28E **61** F2
Tooele *U.S.A.* 40°32N 112°18W **76** F7
Toompine *Australia* 27°15S 144°19E **63** D3
Toora *Australia* 38°39S 146°23E **63** F4
Toora-Khem *Russia* 52°28N 96°17E **27** D10
Toowoomba *Australia* 27°32S 151°56E **63** D5
Top Springs *Australia* 16°37S 131°51E **60** C5
Topaz *U.S.A.* 38°41N 119°30W **78** G7
Topeka *U.S.A.* 39°3N 95°40W **80** F6
Topley *Canada* 54°49N 126°18W **70** C3
Topocalma, Pta. *Chile* 34°10S 72°2W **94** C1
Topock *U.S.A.* 34°46N 114°29W **79** L12
Topol'čany *Slovak Rep.* 48°35N 18°12E **17** D10
Topolobampo *Mexico* 25°36N 109°3W **86** B3
Topozero, Ozero *Russia* 65°35N 32°0E **8** D25
Toppenish *U.S.A.* 46°23N 120°19W **76** C3
Torata *Peru* 17°23S 70°1W **92** G4
Torbalı *Turkey* 38°10N 27°21E **23** E12
Torbat-e Heydārīyeh *Iran* 35°15N 59°12E **47** C8
Torbat-e Jām *Iran* 35°16N 60°35E **47** C9
Torbay *Canada* 47°40N 52°42W **73** C9
Torbay □ *U.K.* 50°26N 3°31W **13** G4
Tordesillas *Spain* 41°30N 5°0W **21** B3
Torfaen □ *U.K.* 51°43N 3°3W **13** F4
Torgau *Germany* 51°34N 13°0E **16** C7
Torhout *Belgium* 51°5N 3°7E **15** C3
Tori-Shima *Japan* 30°29N 140°19E **29** J10
Torilla Pen. *Australia* 22°29S 150°5E **62** C5
Torino *Italy* 45°3N 7°40E **20** D7
Torit *South Sudan* 4°27N 32°31E **53** H12
Torkamān *Iran* 37°35N 47°23E **46** B5
Tormes → *Spain* 41°18N 6°29W **21** B2
Tornado Mt. *Canada* 49°55N 114°40W **70** D6
Torneå = Tornio *Finland* 65°50N 24°12E **8** D21
Torneälven → *Europe* 65°50N 24°12E **8** D21
Torneträsk *Sweden* 68°24N 19°15E **8** B18
Torngat Mountains Nat. Park △
  Canada 59°0N 63°40W **69** F19
Torngat Mts. *Canada* 59°0N 63°40W **69** F19
Tornio *Finland* 65°50N 24°12E **8** D21
Tornionjoki = Torneälven →
  Europe 65°50N 24°12E **8** D21
Tornquist *Argentina* 38°8S 62°15W **94** D3
Toro, Cerro del *Chile* 29°10S 69°50W **94** B2
Toro Pk. *U.S.A.* 33°34N 116°24W **79** M10

Toronto *U.S.A.* 40°28N 80°36W **82** F4
Toropets *Russia* 56°30N 31°40E **18** C5
Tororo *Uganda* 0°45N 34°12E **54** D6
Toros Dağları *Turkey* 37°0N 32°30E **44** B2
Torpa *India* 22°57N 85°6E **43** H11
Torquay *U.K.* 50°27N 3°32W **13** G4
Torrance *U.S.A.* 33°50N 118°20W **79** M8
Torre de Moncorvo
  Portugal 41°12N 7°8W **21** B2
Torre del Greco *Italy* 40°47N 14°22E **22** D6
Torrejón de Ardoz *Spain* 40°27N 3°29W **21** B4
Torrelavega *Spain* 43°20N 4°5W **21** A3
Torremolinos *Spain* 36°38N 4°30W **21** D3
Torrens, L. *Australia* 31°0S 137°50E **63** E2
Torrens Cr. → *Australia* 22°23S 145°9E **62** C4
Torrens Creek *Australia* 20°48S 145°3E **62** C4
Torrent *Spain* 39°27N 0°28W **21** C5
Torreón *Mexico* 25°33N 103°26W **86** B4
Torres *Brazil* 29°21S 49°44W **95** B5
Torres *Mexico* 28°46N 110°47W **86** B2
Torres Strait *Australia* 9°50S 142°20E **62** a
Torres Vedras *Portugal* 39°5N 9°15W **21** C1
Torrevieja *Spain* 37°59N 0°42W **21** D5
Torrey *U.S.A.* 38°18N 111°25W **76** G8
Torridge → *U.K.* 51°0N 4°13W **13** G3
Torridon, L. *U.K.* 57°35N 5°50W **11** D3
Torrington *Conn., U.S.A.* 41°48N 73°7W **83** E11
Torrington *Wyo., U.S.A.* 42°4N 104°11W **76** E11
Tórshavn *Faroe Is.* 62°5N 6°56W **8** F9
Tortola *Br. Virgin Is.* 18°19N 64°45W **89** e
Tortosa *Spain* 40°49N 0°31E **21** B6
Tortosa, C. *Spain* 40°41N 0°52E **21** B6
Tortue, Î. de la *Haiti* 20°5N 72°57W **89** B5
Tortuguero △ *Costa Rica* 10°31N 83°29W **88** D3
Torūd *Iran* 35°25N 55°5E **47** C7
Toruń *Poland* 53°2N 18°39E **17** B10
Tory Hill *Canada* 44°58N 78°16W **82** B6
Tory I. *Ireland* 55°16N 8°14W **10** A3
Tosa *Japan* 33°24N 133°23E **29** H6
Tosa-Shimizu *Japan* 32°52N 132°58E **29** H6
Tosa-Wan *Japan* 33°15N 133°30E **29** H6
Toscana □ *Italy* 43°25N 11°0E **22** C4
Toshka Lakes *Egypt* 22°50N 31°0E **53** D12
Toshkent *Uzbekistan* 41°20N 69°10E **26** E7
Tostado *Argentina* 29°15S 61°50W **94** B3
Tosu *Japan* 33°22N 130°31E **29** H5
Toteng *Botswana* 20°22S 22°58E **56** B3
Totma *Russia* 60°0N 42°40E **18** C7
Totnes *U.K.* 50°26N 3°42W **13** G4
Totness *Suriname* 5°53N 56°19W **93** B7
Totonicapán *Guatemala* 14°58N 91°12W **88** D1
Totoya, I. *Fiji* 18°57S 179°50W **59** a
Totten Glacier *Antarctica* 66°45S 116°10E **5** C8
Tottenham *Australia* 32°14S 147°21E **63** E4
Tottenham *Canada* 44°1N 79°49W **82** B5
Tottori *Japan* 35°30N 134°15E **29** G7
Tottori □ *Japan* 35°30N 134°12E **29** G7
Toubkal, Djebel *Morocco* 31°0N 8°0W **52** B4
Tougan *Burkina Faso* 13°11N 2°58W **52** F5
Touggourt *Algeria* 33°6N 6°4E **52** B7
Toul *France* 48°40N 5°53E **20** B6
Touliu *Taiwan* 23°42N 120°31E **35** F13
Toulon *France* 43°10N 5°55E **20** E6
Toulouse *France* 43°37N 1°27E **20** E4
Toummo *Niger* 22°45N 14°8E **53** D8
Tounan *Taiwan* 23°41N 120°28E **35** F13
Tounggoo *Burma* 19°0N 96°30E **41** K20
Touraine *France* 47°20N 0°30E **20** C4
Touran = Tūrān △ *Iran* 35°45N 56°30E **47** C8
Tourcoing *France* 50°42N 3°10E **20** A5
Touriñán, C. *Spain* 43°3N 9°18W **21** A1
Tournai *Belgium* 50°35N 3°25E **15** D3
Tournon-sur-Rhône *France* 45°4N 4°50E **20** D6
Tours *France* 47°22N 0°40E **20** C4
Toussoro, Mt. *C.A.R.* 9°7N 23°14E **54** C4
Touws → *S. Africa* 33°45S 21°11E **56** E3
Touwsrivier *S. Africa* 33°20S 20°2E **56** E3
Towada *Japan* 40°37N 141°13E **28** D10
Towada-Hachimantai △
  Japan 40°20N 140°55E **28** D10
Towada-Ko *Japan* 40°28N 140°55E **28** D10
Towanda *U.S.A.* 41°46N 76°27W **83** E8
Tower *U.S.A.* 47°48N 92°17W **80** B7
Towerhill Cr. →
  Australia 22°28S 144°35E **62** C3
Towner *U.S.A.* 48°21N 100°25W **80** A3
Townsend *U.S.A.* 46°19N 111°31W **76** C8
Townsville *Australia* 19°15S 146°45E **62** B4
Towraghondī *Afghan.* 35°13N 62°16E **40** B3
Towson *U.S.A.* 39°24N 76°36W **81** F15
Towuti, Danau *Indonesia* 2°45S 121°32E **37** E6
Tōya-Ko *Japan* 42°35N 140°51E **28** C10
Toyama *Japan* 36°40N 137°15E **29** F8
Toyama □ *Japan* 36°45N 137°30E **29** F8
Toyama-Wan *Japan* 37°0N 137°30E **29** F8
Toyapakeh *Indonesia* 8°41S 115°29E **37** K18
Toyohashi *Japan* 34°45N 137°25E **29** G8
Toyokawa *Japan* 34°48N 137°27E **29** G8
Toyonaka *Japan* 34°35N 134°49E **29** G7
Toyooka *Japan* 35°35N 134°48E **29** G7
Toyota *Japan* 35°3N 137°7E **29** G8
Tozeur *Tunisia* 33°56N 8°8E **52** B7
Trá Li = Tralee *Ireland* 52°16N 9°42W **10** D2
Trá Mhór = Tramore
  Ireland 52°10N 7°10W **10** D4
Tra On *Vietnam* 9°58N 105°55E **39** H5
Tra Vinh *Vietnam* 9°50N 106°15E **39** H6
Trabzon *Turkey* 41°0N 39°45E **19** F6
Tracadie *Canada* 47°30N 64°55W **73** C7
Tracy *Canada* 46°1N 73°9W **72** C5
Tracy *Calif., U.S.A.* 37°44N 121°26W **78** H5
Tracy *Minn., U.S.A.* 44°14N 95°37W **80** C6
Trafalgar, C. *Spain* 36°10N 6°2W **21** D2
Trail *Canada* 49°5N 117°40W **70** D5
Trainor L. *Canada* 60°24N 120°17W **70** A4
Trakai △ *Lithuania* 54°30S 25°10E **9** J21
Tralee *Ireland* 52°16N 9°42W **10** D2
Tralee B. *Ireland* 52°17N 9°55W **10** D2
Tram Chim △ *Vietnam* 10°43N 105°31E **39** G5

Tramore *Ireland* 52°10N 7°10W **10** D4
Tramore B. *Ireland* 52°9N 7°10W **10** D4
Tran Ninh, Cao Nguyen
　Laos 19°30N 103°10E **38** C4
Tranås *Sweden* 58°3N 14°59E **9** G16
Trancas *Argentina* 26°11S 65°20W **94** B2
Trang *Thailand* 7°33N 99°38E **39** J2
Trangan *Indonesia* 6°40S 134°20E **37** F8
Trangie *Australia* 32°4S 148°0E **63** E4
Trani *Italy* 41°17N 16°25E **22** D7
Tranoroa *Madag.* 24°42S 45°4E **55** J9
Tranqueras *Uruguay* 31°13S 55°45W **95** C4
Transantarctic Mts.
　Antarctica 85°0S 170°0W **5** E12
Transilvania *Romania* 46°30N 24°0E **17** E12
Transilvanian Alps = Carpaţii
　Meridionali *Romania* 45°30N 25°0E **17** F13
Transnistria = Stînga Nistrului □
　Moldova 47°20N 29°15E **17** E15
Transylvania = Transilvania
　Romania 46°30N 24°0E **17** E12
Trápani *Italy* 38°1N 12°29E **22** E5
Trapper Pk. *U.S.A.* 45°54N 114°18W **76** D6
Traralgon *Australia* 38°12S 146°34E **63** F4
Trasimeno, L. *Italy* 43°8N 12°6E **22** C5
Trat *Thailand* 12°14N 102°33E **39** F4
Tratani → *Pakistan* 29°19N 68°20E **42** E3
Traun *Austria* 48°14N 14°15E **16** D8
Travellers L. *Australia* 33°20S 142°0E **63** E3
Travemünde *Germany* 53°57N 10°52E **16** B6
Travers, Mt. *N.Z.* 42°1S 172°45E **59** E4
Traverse City *U.S.A.* 44°46N 85°38W **81** C11
Travis, L. *U.S.A.* 30°24N 97°55W **84** F6
Travnik *Bos.-H.* 44°17N 17°39E **23** B7
Trawbreaga B. *Ireland* 55°20N 7°25W **10** A4
Trébbia → *Italy* 45°4N 9°41E **20** D8
Třebíč *Czech Rep.* 49°14N 15°55E **16** D8
Trebinje *Bos.-H.* 42°44N 18°22E **23** C8
Trebonne *Australia* 18°37S 146°5E **62** B4
Trefaldwyn = Montgomery
　U.K. 52°34N 3°8W **13** E4
Trefynwy = Monmouth
　U.K. 51°48N 2°42W **13** F5
Tregaron *U.K.* 52°14N 3°56W **13** E4
Tregrosse Is. *Australia* 17°41S 150°43E **62** B5
Treherne *Canada* 49°38N 98°42W **71** D9
Treinta y Tres *Uruguay* 33°16S 54°17W **95** C5
Trelawney *Zimbabwe* 17°30S 30°30E **57** A5
Trelew *Argentina* 43°10S 65°20W **96** E3
Trelleborg *Sweden* 55°20N 13°10E **9** J15
Tremadog Bay *U.K.* 52°51N 4°18W **12** E3
Tremonton *U.S.A.* 41°43N 112°10W **76** F7
Tremp *Spain* 42°10N 0°52E **21** A6
Trenche → *Canada* 47°46N 72°53W **72** C5
Trenčín *Slovak Rep.* 48°52N 18°4E **17** D10
Trenggalek *Indonesia* 8°3S 111°43E **37** H14
Trenque Lauquen
　Argentina 36°5S 62°45W **94** D3
Trent → *Canada* 44°6N 77°34W **82** B7
Trent → *U.K.* 53°41N 0°42W **12** D7
Trento *Italy* 46°4N 11°8E **22** A4
Trenton *Canada* 44°10N 77°34W **82** B7
Trenton *Mo., U.S.A.* 40°5N 93°37W **80** E7
Trenton *N.J., U.S.A.* 40°14N 74°46W **83** F10
Trenton *Nebr., U.S.A.* 40°11N 101°1W **80** E3
Trepassey *Canada* 46°43N 53°25W **73** C9
Tres Arroyos *Argentina* 38°26S 60°20W **94** D3
Três Corações *Brazil* 21°44S 45°15W **95** A6
Três Lagoas *Brazil* 20°50S 51°43W **93** H8
Tres Lomas *Argentina* 36°27S 62°51W **94** D3
Tres Montes, C. *Chile* 46°50S 75°30W **96** F1
Tres Pinos *U.S.A.* 36°48N 121°19W **78** J5
Três Pontas *Brazil* 21°23S 45°29W **95** A6
Tres Puentes *Chile* 27°50S 70°15W **94** B1
Tres Puntas, C. *Argentina* 47°0S 66°0W **96** F3
Três Rios *Brazil* 22°6S 43°15W **95** A7
Tres Valles *Mexico* 18°15N 96°8W **87** D5
Tresco *U.K.* 49°57N 6°20W **13** H1
Treviso *Italy* 45°40N 12°15E **22** B5
Triabunna *Australia* 42°30S 147°55E **63** G4
Triangle *Zimbabwe* 21°2S 31°28E **57** B5
Tribal Areas □ *Pakistan* 33°0N 70°0E **42** C4
Tribulation, C. *Australia* 16°5S 145°29E **62** B4
Tribune *U.S.A.* 38°28N 101°45W **80** F3
Trichinopoly = Tiruchchirappalli
　India 10°45N 78°45E **45** J4
Trichur = Thrissur *India* 10°30N 76°18E **45** J3
Trichy = Tiruchchirappalli
　India 10°45N 78°45E **45** J4
Trida *Australia* 33°1S 145°1E **63** E4
Trier *Germany* 49°45N 6°38E **16** D4
Trieste *Italy* 45°40N 13°46E **22** B5
Triglav *Slovenia* 46°21N 13°50E **16** E7
Trikala *Greece* 39°34N 21°47E **23** E9
Trikora, Puncak
　Indonesia 4°15S 138°45E **37** E9
Trim *Ireland* 53°33N 6°48W **10** C5
Trimbak *India* 19°56N 73°33E **44** E1
Trimmu Dam *Pakistan* 31°10N 72°8E **42** D5
Trincomalee *Sri Lanka* 8°38N 81°15E **45** K5
Trindade *Atl. Oc.* 20°20S 29°50W **2** F8
Trindade *Brazil* 16°40S 49°30W **93** G9
Trinidad *Bolivia* 14°46S 64°50W **92** F6
Trinidad *Cuba* 21°48N 80°0W **88** B4
Trinidad *Trin. & Tob.* 10°30N 61°15W **93** K15
Trinidad *Uruguay* 33°30S 56°50W **94** C4
Trinidad *U.S.A.* 37°10N 104°31W **77** H11
Trinidad & Tobago ■
　W. Indies 10°30N 61°20W **93** K15
Trinity *Canada* 48°59N 53°55W **73** C9
Trinity *U.S.A.* 30°57N 95°22W **84** F7
Trinity → *Calif., U.S.A.* 41°11N 123°42W **76** F2
Trinity → *Tex., U.S.A.* 29°45N 94°43W **84** G7
Trinity B. *Canada* 48°20N 53°10W **73** C9
Trinity Hills *Trin. & Tob.* 10°7N 61°7W **93** K15
Trinity Is. *U.S.A.* 56°33N 154°25W **74** D9
Trinity Range *U.S.A.* 40°10N 118°40W **76** F4
Trinkat *India* 8°5N 93°30E **45** K11
Trinkitat *Sudan* 18°45N 37°51E **53** E13

Trinway *U.S.A.* 40°9N 82°1W **82** F2
Triolet *Mauritius* 20°4S 57°32E **55** d
Tripoli = Tarābulus
　Lebanon 34°31N 35°50E **48** A4
Tripoli = Tarābulus *Libya* 32°49N 13°7E **53** B8
Tripoli *Greece* 37°31N 22°25E **23** F10
Tripolitania = Tarābulus
　Libya 31°0N 13°0E **53** B8
Tripura □ *India* 24°0N 92°0E **41** H18
Tristan da Cunha *Atl. Oc.* 37°6S 12°20W **51** K2
Trisul *India* 30°19N 79°47E **43** D8
Trivandrum =
　Thiruvananthapuram
　India 8°41N 77°0E **45** K3
Trnava *Slovak Rep.* 48°23N 17°35E **17** D9
Trochu *Canada* 51°50N 113°13W **70** C6
Trodely I. *Canada* 52°15N 79°26W **72** B4
Troglav *Croatia* 43°56N 16°36E **22** C7
Troilus, L. *Canada* 50°50N 74°35W **72** B5
Trois-Pistoles *Canada* 48°5N 69°10W **73** C6
Trois-Rivières *Canada* 46°25N 72°34W **72** C5
Trois-Rivières *Guadeloupe* 15°57N 61°40W **88** b
Troitsk *Russia* 54°10N 61°35E **26** D7
Troitsko Pechorsk
　Russia 62°40N 56°10E **18** B10
Troll *Antarctica* 72°0S 2°30E **5** D3
Trölladyngja *Iceland* 64°54N 17°16W **8** D5
Trollhättan *Sweden* 58°17N 12°20E **9** G15
Trollheimen *Norway* 62°46N 9°1E **8** E13
Trombetas → *Brazil* 1°55S 55°35W **93** D7
Tromsø *Norway* 69°40N 18°56E **8** B18
Tron *Thailand* 17°28N 100°7E **38** D3
Trona *U.S.A.* 35°46N 117°23W **79** K9
Tronador, Mte. *Argentina* 41°10S 71°50W **96** E2
Trøndelag *Norway* 64°17N 11°50E **8** D14
Trondheim *Norway* 63°36N 10°25E **8** E14
Trondheimsfjorden
　Norway 63°35N 10°30E **8** E14
Troon *U.K.* 55°33N 4°39W **11** F4
Tropic *U.S.A.* 37°37N 112°5W **77** H7
Trostan *U.K.* 55°3N 6°10W **10** A5
Trou Gras Pt. *St. Lucia* 13°51N 60°53W **89** f
Trout → *Canada* 61°19N 119°51W **70** A5
Trout L. *N.W.T., Canada* 60°40N 121°14W **70** A4
Trout L. *Ont., Canada* 51°20N 93°15W **71** C10
Trout Lake *Canada* 56°30N 114°32W **70** B6
Trout Lake *U.S.A.* 46°0N 121°32W **78** E5
Trout River *Canada* 49°29N 58°8W **73** C8
Trout Run *U.S.A.* 41°23N 77°3W **82** E7
Trouville-sur-Mer *France* 49°21N 0°5E **20** B4
Trowbridge *U.K.* 51°18N 2°12W **13** F5
Troy *Turkey* 39°57N 26°12E **23** E12
Troy *Ala., U.S.A.* 31°48N 85°58W **85** F12
Troy *Kans., U.S.A.* 39°47N 95°5W **80** F7
Troy *Mo., U.S.A.* 38°59N 90°59W **80** F8
Troy *Mont., U.S.A.* 48°28N 115°53W **76** B6
Troy *N.Y., U.S.A.* 42°44N 73°41W **83** D11
Troy *Ohio, U.S.A.* 40°2N 84°12W **81** E11
Troy *Pa., U.S.A.* 41°47N 76°47W **83** E8
Troyes *France* 48°19N 4°3E **20** B6
Truchas Pk. *U.S.A.* 35°58N 105°39W **77** J11
Trucial States = United Arab
　Emirates ■ *Asia* 23°50N 54°0E **47** F7
Truckee *U.S.A.* 39°20N 120°11W **78** F6
Trudovoye *Russia* 43°17N 132°5E **28** C6
Trujillo *Honduras* 16°0N 86°0W **88** C2
Trujillo *Peru* 8°6S 79°0W **92** E3
Trujillo *Spain* 39°28N 5°55W **21** C3
Trujillo *U.S.A.* 35°32N 104°42W **77** J11
Trujillo *Venezuela* 9°22N 70°38W **92** B4
Truk *Micronesia* 7°25N 151°46E **64** G7
Trumann *U.S.A.* 35°41N 90°31W **85** D9
Trumansburg *U.S.A.* 42°33N 76°40W **83** D8
Trumbull, Mt. *U.S.A.* 36°25N 113°19W **77** H7
Trundle *Australia* 32°53S 147°35E **63** E4
Trung Lon, Hon *Vietnam* 8°36N 106°8E **39** H6
Trung-Phan *Vietnam* 17°0N 109°0E **38** D6
Truro *Canada* 45°21N 63°14W **73** C7
Truro *U.K.* 50°16N 5°4W **13** G2
Truskavets *Ukraine* 49°17N 23°30E **17** D12
Trutch *Canada* 57°44N 122°57W **70** B4
Truth or Consequences
　U.S.A. 33°8N 107°15W **77** K10
Trutnov *Czech Rep.* 50°37N 15°54E **16** C8
Tryonville *U.S.A.* 41°42N 79°48W **82** E5
Tsandi *Namibia* 17°42S 14°50E **56** A1
Tsaratanana *Madag.* 16°47S 47°39E **55** G9
Tsau *Botswana* 20°8S 22°22E **56** B3
Tsavo *Kenya* 2°59S 38°28E **54** E7
Tsentralnyy □ *Russia* 52°0N 40°0E **26** D4
Tses *Namibia* 25°58S 18°8E **56** C2
Tsetserleg *Mongolia* 47°36N 101°32E **30** B9
Tsévié *Togo* 6°25N 1°20E **52** G6
Tshabong *Botswana* 26°2S 22°29E **56** C3
Tshane *Botswana* 24°5S 21°54E **56** B3
Tshela *Dem. Rep. of the Congo* 4°57S 13°4E **54** E2
Tshesebe *Botswana* 21°51S 27°32E **57** B4
Tshikapa
　Dem. Rep. of the Congo 6°28S 20°48E **54** F4
Tshwane = Pretoria
　S. Africa 25°44S 28°12E **57** C4
Tshwane *Botswana* 22°24S 22°1E **56** B3
Tsigara *Botswana* 20°22S 25°54E **56** B4
Tsihombe *Madag.* 25°10S 45°41E **55** K9
Tsiigehtchic *Canada* 67°15N 134°0W **68** D5
Ts'il-os △ *Canada* 51°9N 123°59W **70** C4
Tsimlyansk Res. = Tsimlyanskoye
　Vdkhr. *Russia* 48°0N 43°0E **19** E7
Tsimlyanskoye Vdkhr.
　Russia 48°0N 43°0E **19** E7
Tsinan = Jinan *China* 36°38N 117°1E **32** F9
Tsinan *S. Africa* 27°5S 23°5E **56** C3
Tsinghai = Qinghai □
　China 36°0N 98°0E **30** D8
Tsingtao = Qingdao
　China 36°5N 120°20E **33** F11
Tsirigo = Kythira *Greece* 36°8N 23°0E **23** F10
Tsitsikamma △ *S. Africa* 34°3S 23°40E **56** D3
Tskhinvali *Georgia* 42°14N 44°1E **19** F7

Tsna → *Russia* 54°55N 41°58E **18** D7
Tso Moriri, L. *India* 32°50N 78°20E **43** C8
Tsobis *Namibia* 19°27S 17°30E **56** A2
Tsodilo Hills *Botswana* 18°49S 21°43E **56** A3
Tsogttsetsiy = Baruunsuu
　Mongolia 43°43N 105°35E **32** C3
Tsolo *S. Africa* 31°18S 28°37E **57** D4
Tsomo *S. Africa* 32°0S 27°42E **57** D4
Tsu *Japan* 34°45N 136°25E **29** G8
Tsu L. *Canada* 60°40N 111°52W **70** A6
Tsuchiura *Japan* 36°5N 140°15E **29** F10
Tsugaru-Hantō *Japan* 41°0N 140°30E **28** D10
Tsugaru-Kaikyō *Japan* 41°35N 141°0E **28** D10
Tsumeb *Namibia* 19°9S 17°44E **56** A2
Tsumis *Namibia* 23°39S 17°29E **56** B2
Tsuruga *Japan* 35°45N 136°2E **29** G8
Tsurugi-San *Japan* 33°51N 134°6E **29** H7
Tsuruoka *Japan* 38°44N 139°50E **28** E9
Tsushima *Gifu, Japan* 35°10N 136°43E **29** G8
Tsushima *Nagasaki,
　Japan* 34°20N 129°20E **29** G4
Tsuyama *Japan* 35°3N 134°0E **29** G7
Tsyelyakhany *Belarus* 52°30N 25°46E **17** B13
Tuam = Tuam *Ireland* 53°31N 8°51W **10** C3
Tual *Indonesia* 5°38S 132°44E **37** F8
Tualatin *U.S.A.* 45°23N 122°45W **78** E4
Tuam *Ireland* 53°31N 8°51W **10** C3
Tuamotu, Is.
　French Polynesia 17°0S 144°0W **65** J13
Tuamotu Arch. = Tuamotu, Is.
　French Polynesia 17°0S 144°0W **65** J13
Tuamotu Ridge *Pac. Oc.* 20°0S 138°0W **65** K14
Tuan Giao *Vietnam* 21°35N 103°25E **38** B4
Tuanfeng *China* 30°38N 114°52E **35** B10
Tuanxi *China* 27°28N 107°8E **34** D6
Tuao *Phil.* 17°45N 121°22E **37** A6
Tuapse *Russia* 44°5N 39°10E **19** F6
Tuatapere *N.Z.* 46°8S 167°41E **59** G1
Tuba City *U.S.A.* 36°8N 111°14W **77** H8
Tuban *Indonesia* 6°54S 112°3E **37** G15
Tubani *Botswana* 24°46S 24°18E **56** B3
Tubarão *Brazil* 28°30S 49°0W **95** B6
Tūbās *West Bank* 32°20N 35°22E **48** C4
Tubas → *Namibia* 22°54S 14°35E **56** B2
Tübingen *Germany* 48°31N 9°4E **16** D5
Tubou *Fiji* 18°13S 178°48W **59** a
Tubruq *Libya* 32°7N 23°55E **53** B10
Tubuaï, Is.
　French Polynesia 25°0S 150°0W **65** K13
Tuc Trung *Vietnam* 11°1N 107°12E **39** G6
Tucacas *Venezuela* 10°48N 68°19W **92** A5
T'uch'ang *Taiwan* 24°35N 121°29E **35** E13
Tuchitua *Canada* 60°55N 129°13W **70** A3
Tuchodi → *Canada* 58°17N 123°42W **70** B4
Tuckanarra *Australia* 27°7S 118°5E **61** E2
Tucson *U.S.A.* 32°13N 110°58W **77** K8
Tucumán □ *Argentina* 26°48S 66°2W **94** B2
Tucumcari *U.S.A.* 35°10N 103°44W **77** J12
Tucupita *Venezuela* 9°2N 62°3W **92** B6
Tucuruí *Brazil* 3°42S 49°44W **93** D9
Tucuruí, Represa de *Brazil* 4°0S 49°30W **93** D9
Tudela *Spain* 42°4N 1°39W **21** A5
Tudmur *Syria* 34°36N 38°15E **46** C3
Tudor, L. *Canada* 55°50N 65°25W **73** A6
Tuen Mun *China* 22°24N 113°59E **31** a
Tug Hill Plateau *U.S.A.* 43°45N 75°50W **83** C9
Tugela → *S. Africa* 29°14S 31°30E **57** C5
Tugela Falls *S. Africa* 28°42S 29°51E **57** C4
Tuguegarao *Phil.* 17°35N 121°42E **37** A6
Tugur *Russia* 53°44N 136°45E **27** D14
Tui *Spain* 42°3N 8°39W **21** A1
Tukangbesi, Kepulauan
　Indonesia 6°0S 124°0E **37** F6
Tukarak I. *Canada* 56°15N 78°45W **72** A4
Tukayyid *Iraq* 29°47N 45°36E **46** D5
Tuktoyaktuk *Canada* 69°27N 133°2W **68** D5
Tuktut Nogait △ *Canada* 69°15N 122°0W **68** D7
Tukums *Latvia* 56°58N 23°10E **9** H20
Tukuyu *Tanzania* 9°17S 33°35E **54** F6
Tula *Hidalgo, Mexico* 20°3N 99°21W **87** C5
Tula *Tamaulipas, Mexico* 23°0N 99°43W **87** C5
Tula *Russia* 54°13N 37°38E **18** D6
Tulach Mhór = Tullamore
　Ireland 53°16N 7°31W **10** C4
Tulancingo *Mexico* 20°5N 98°22W **87** C5
Tulare *U.S.A.* 36°13N 119°21W **78** J7
Tulare Lake Bed *U.S.A.* 36°0N 119°48W **78** K7
Tularosa *U.S.A.* 33°5N 106°1W **77** K10
Tulbagh *S. Africa* 33°16S 19°6E **56** D2
Tulcán *Ecuador* 0°48N 77°43W **92** C3
Tulcea *Romania* 45°13N 28°46E **17** F15
Tulchyn *Ukraine* 48°41N 28°49E **17** D15
Tūleh *Iran* 34°35N 52°33E **47** C7
Tulemalu L. *Canada* 62°58N 99°25W **71** A9
Tulia *U.S.A.* 34°32N 101°46W **84** D4
Tulita *Canada* 64°57N 125°30W **68** E6
Tullahoma *U.S.A.* 35°22N 86°13W **85** D11
Tullamore *Australia* 32°39S 147°36E **63** E4
Tullamore *Ireland* 53°16N 7°31W **10** C4
Tulle *France* 45°16N 1°46E **20** D4
Tullow *Ireland* 52°49N 6°45E **10** D5
Tully *Australia* 17°56S 145°55E **62** B4
Tully *U.S.A.* 42°48N 76°7W **83** D8
Tulsa *U.S.A.* 36°10N 95°55W **84** C7
Tulsequah *Canada* 58°39N 133°35W **70** B2
Tuluá *Colombia* 4°6N 76°11W **92** C3
Tulum *Mexico* 20°13N 87°28W **87** C7
Tulun *Russia* 54°32N 100°35E **27** D11
Tulungagung *Indonesia* 8°5S 111°54E **37** H14
Tuma → *Nic.* 13°6N 84°35W **88** D3
Tumacacori △ *U.S.A.* 31°35N 111°6W **77** L8
Tumaco *Colombia* 1°50N 78°45W **92** C3
Tumakuru = Tumkur
　India 13°18N 77°6E **45** H3
Tumatumari *Guyana* 5°20N 58°55W **92** B7
Tumba *Sweden* 59°12N 17°48E **9** G17
Tumba, L.
　Dem. Rep. of the Congo 0°50S 18°0E **54** E3

Tumbarumba *Australia* 35°44S 148°0E **63** F4
Tumbaya *Argentina* 23°50S 65°26W **94** A2
Tumbes *Peru* 3°37S 80°27W **92** D2
Tumbler Ridge *Canada* 55°8N 121°0W **70** B4
Tumby Bay *Australia* 34°21S 136°8E **63** E2
Tumd Youqi *China* 40°30N 110°30E **32** D6
Tumen *China* 43°0N 129°50E **28** C4
Tumen Jiang → *China* 42°20N 130°35E **33** C16
Tumeremo *Venezuela* 7°18N 61°30W **92** B6
Tumkur *India* 13°18N 77°6E **45** H3
Tump *Pakistan* 26°7N 62°16E **40** F3
Tumpat *Malaysia* 6°11N 102°10E **39** J4
Tumsar *India* 21°26N 79°45E **44** D4
Tumu *Ghana* 10°56N 1°56W **52** F5
Tumucumaque, Serra
　Brazil 2°0N 55°0W **93** C8
Tumut *Australia* 35°16S 148°13E **63** F4
Tumwater *U.S.A.* 47°1N 122°54W **78** C4
Tuna *India* 22°59N 70°5E **42** H4
Tunapuna *Trin. & Tob.* 10°38N 61°24W **93** K15
Tunas de Zaza *Cuba* 21°39N 79°34W **88** B4
Tunbridge Wells = Royal
　Tunbridge Wells *U.K.* 51°7N 0°16E **13** F8
Tunchang *China* 19°21N 110°5E **38** C8
Tuncurry *Australia* 32°17S 152°29E **63** E5
Tundla *India* 27°12N 78°17E **42** F8
Tundzha → *Bulgaria* 41°40N 26°35E **23** C11
Tung Chung *China* 22°17N 113°57E **31** a
Tunga → *India* 15°0N 75°50E **45** G2
Tungabhadra → *India* 15°57N 78°15E **45** G4
Tungabhadra Dam *India* 15°0N 75°50E **45** G2
Tungla *Nic.* 13°24N 84°21W **88** D3
Tungsha Tao = Dongsha Dao
　S. China Sea 20°45N 116°43E **35** G11
Tungshih *Taiwan* 24°12N 120°43E **35** E13
Tungsten *Canada* 61°57N 128°16W **70** A3
Tunguska, Nizhnyaya →
　Russia 65°48N 88°4E **27** C9
Tunguska, Podkamennaya →
　Russia 61°50N 90°13E **27** C10
Tuni *India* 17°22N 82°36E **44** F6
Tunica *U.S.A.* 34°41N 90°23W **85** D9
Tunis *Tunisia* 36°50N 10°11E **53** A8
Tunisia ■ *Africa* 33°30N 9°10E **53** A7
Tunja *Colombia* 5°33N 73°25W **92** B4
Tunkhannock *U.S.A.* 41°32N 75°57W **83** E9
Tunliu *China* 36°13N 112°52E **32** F7
Tunnel Creek △
　Australia 17°41S 125°18E **60** C4
Tunnsjøen *Norway* 64°45N 13°25E **8** D15
Tunungayualok I. *Canada* 56°0N 61°0W **73** A7
Tunuyán *Argentina* 33°35S 69°0W **94** C2
Tunuyán → *Argentina* 33°33S 67°30W **94** C2
Tunxi = Huangshan
　China 30°8N 118°9E **35** B12
Tuo Jiang → *China* 28°50N 105°35E **34** C5
Tuolumne *U.S.A.* 37°58N 120°15W **78** H6
Tuolumne → *U.S.A.* 37°36N 121°13W **78** H5
Tūp Āghāj *Iran* 36°3N 47°50E **46** B5
Tupã *Brazil* 21°57S 50°28W **95** A5
Tupelo *U.S.A.* 34°16N 88°43W **85** D10
Tupinambarana, I. *Brazil* 3°0S 58°0W **92** D7
Tupiza *Bolivia* 21°30S 65°40W **94** A2
Tupman *U.S.A.* 35°18N 119°21W **79** K7
Tupper *Canada* 55°32N 120°1W **70** B4
Tupper L. *U.S.A.* 44°10N 74°32W **83** B10
Tupper Lake *U.S.A.* 44°14N 74°28W **83** B10
Tupungato, Cerro
　S. Amer. 33°15S 69°50W **94** C2
Tuquan *China* 45°18N 121°38E **33** B11
Túquerres *Colombia* 1°5N 77°37W **92** C3
Tura *Russia* 64°20N 100°17E **27** C11
Turabah *Si. Arabia* 28°20N 43°15E **46** D4
Tūrān *Iran* 35°39N 56°42E **47** C8
Turan *Russia* 51°55N 94°0E **27** D10
Tūrān □ *Iran* 35°45N 56°30E **47** C8
Turayf *Si. Arabia* 31°41N 38°39E **46** D3
Turda *Romania* 46°34N 23°47E **17** E12
Turek *Poland* 52°3N 18°30E **17** B10
Turén *Venezuela* 9°17N 69°6W **92** B5
Turfan = Turpan *China* 43°58N 89°10E **30** C6
Turfan Basin = Turpan Pendi
　China 42°40N 89°25E **30** C6
Turfan Depression = Turpan Pendi
　China 42°40N 89°25E **30** C6
Turgeon → *Canada* 50°0N 78°56W **72** C4
Türgovishte *Bulgaria* 43°17N 26°38E **23** C12
Turgutlu *Turkey* 38°30N 27°43E **23** E12
Turgwe → *Zimbabwe* 21°31S 32°15E **57** B5
Turia → *Spain* 39°27N 0°19W **21** C5
Turiaçu *Brazil* 1°40S 45°19W **93** D9
Turiaçu → *Brazil* 1°36S 45°19W **93** D9
Turin = Torino *Italy* 45°3N 7°40E **20** D7
Turkana, L. *Africa* 3°30N 36°5E **54** D7
Turkestan = Türkistan
　Kazakhstan 43°17N 68°16E **26** E7
Turkey ■ *Eurasia* 39°0N 36°0E **19** G6
Turkey Creek = Warmun
　Australia 17°2S 128°12E **60** C4
Türkistan *Kazakhstan* 43°17N 68°16E **26** E7
Turkmenabat
　Turkmenistan 39°6N 63°34E **47** B9
Turkmenbashi
　Turkmenistan 40°5N 53°5E **47** A7
Turkmenistan ■ *Asia* 39°0N 59°0E **26** F6
Turks & Caicos Is. ☑
　W. Indies 21°20N 71°20W **89** B5
Turks Island Passage
　Turks & Caicos 21°25N 71°19W **89** B5
Turku *Finland* 60°30N 22°19E **9** F20
Turkwel → *Kenya* 3°6N 36°6E **54** D7
Turlock *U.S.A.* 37°30N 120°51W **78** H6
Turnagain → *Canada* 59°12N 127°35W **70** B3
Turnagain, C. *N.Z.* 40°28S 176°38E **59** D6
Turneffe Is. *Belize* 17°20N 87°50W **87** D7
Turner *U.S.A.* 48°51N 108°24W **76** B9
Turner Pt. *Australia* 11°47S 133°32E **62** A1
Turner Valley *Canada* 50°40N 114°17W **70** C6

Turners Falls *U.S.A.* 42°36N 72°33W **83** D12
Turnhout *Belgium* 51°19N 4°57E **15** C4
Turnor L. *Canada* 56°35N 108°35W **71** B7
Türnovo = Veliko Tŭrnovo
　Bulgaria 43°5N 25°41E **23** C11
Turnu Măgurele
　Romania 43°46N 24°56E **17** G13
Turnu Roşu, P. *Romania* 45°33N 24°17E **17** F13
Turpan *China* 43°58N 89°10E **30** C6
Turpan Pendi *China* 42°40N 89°25E **30** C6
Turriff *U.K.* 57°32N 2°27W **11** D6
Tursāq *Iraq* 33°27N 45°47E **46** C5
Turtle Head I. *Australia* 10°56S 142°37E **62** A3
Turtle L. *Canada* 53°36N 108°38W **71** C7
Turtle Lake *U.S.A.* 47°31N 100°53W **80** B3
Turtleford *Canada* 53°23N 108°57W **71** C7
Turuépano △ *Venezuela* 10°34N 62°43W **89** D7
Turukhansk *Russia* 65°21N 88°5E **27** C9
Tuscaloosa *U.S.A.* 33°12N 87°34W **85** E11
Tuscany = Toscana □
　Italy 43°25N 11°0E **22** C4
Tuscarawas → *U.S.A.* 40°24N 81°25W **82** F3
Tuscarora Mt. *U.S.A.* 40°55N 77°55W **82** F7
Tuscola *Ill., U.S.A.* 39°48N 88°17W **80** F9
Tuscola *Tex., U.S.A.* 32°12N 99°48W **84** E5
Tuscumbia *U.S.A.* 34°44N 87°42W **85** D11
Tuskegee *U.S.A.* 32°25N 85°42W **85** E12
Tuticorin *India* 8°50N 78°12E **45** K4
Tutóia *Brazil* 2°45S 42°20W **93** D10
Tutong *Brunei* 4°47N 114°40E **36** D4
Tutrakan *Bulgaria* 44°2N 26°40E **23** B12
Tuttle Creek L. *U.S.A.* 39°15N 96°36W **80** F5
Tuttlingen *Germany* 47°58N 8°48E **16** E5
Tutuala *E. Timor* 8°25S 127°15E **37** F7
Tutuila *Amer. Samoa* 14°19S 170°50W **59** b
Tutume *Botswana* 20°30S 27°5E **55** J5
Tuul Gol → *Mongolia* 48°30N 104°25E **30** B9
Tuva □ *Russia* 51°30N 95°0E **27** D10
Tuvalu ■ *Pac. Oc.* 8°0S 178°0E **58** B10
Tuvuca *Fiji* 17°40S 178°48W **59** a
Tuxpan *Mexico* 20°57N 97°24W **87** C5
Tuxtla Gutiérrez *Mexico* 16°45N 93°7W **87** D6
Tuy = Tui *Spain* 42°3N 8°39W **21** A1
Tuy Duc *Vietnam* 12°15N 107°27E **39** F6
Tuy Phong *Vietnam* 11°14N 108°43E **39** G7
Tuya L. *Canada* 59°7N 130°35W **70** B2
Tuyen Hoa *Vietnam* 17°50N 106°10E **38** D6
Tuyen Quang *Vietnam* 21°50N 105°10E **34** G5
Tüysarkän *Iran* 34°33N 48°27E **47** C6
Tuz Gölü *Turkey* 38°42N 33°18E **19** G5
Ţūz Khurmātū *Iraq* 34°56N 44°38E **46** C5
Tuzigoot △ *U.S.A.* 34°46N 112°2W **77** J7
Tuzla *Bos.-H.* 44°34N 18°41E **23** B8
Tver *Russia* 56°55N 35°59E **18** C6
Twain *U.S.A.* 40°1N 121°3W **78** E5
Twain Harte *U.S.A.* 38°2N 120°14W **78** G6
Twee River *Namibia* 25°27S 19°27E **56** C2
Tweed *Canada* 44°29N 77°19W **82** B7
Tweed → *U.K.* 55°45N 2°0W **11** F6
Tweed Heads *Australia* 28°10S 153°31E **63** D5
Tweedsmuir △ *Canada* 53°0N 126°20W **70** C3
Twentynine Palms
　U.S.A. 34°8N 116°3W **79** L10
Twillingate *Canada* 49°42N 54°45W **73** C9
Twin Bridges *U.S.A.* 45°33N 112°20W **76** D7
Twin Falls *Canada* 53°30N 64°32W **73** B7
Twin Falls *U.S.A.* 42°34N 114°28W **76** E6
Twin Valley *U.S.A.* 47°16N 96°16W **80** B5
Twinsburg *U.S.A.* 41°19N 81°26W **82** E3
Twitchell Res. *U.S.A.* 34°59N 120°19W **79** L6
Two Harbors *U.S.A.* 47°2N 91°40W **80** B8
Two Hills *Canada* 53°43N 111°52W **70** C6
Two Rivers *U.S.A.* 44°9N 87°34W **80** C10
Two Rocks *Australia* 31°30S 115°35E **61** F2
Twofold B. *Australia* 37°8S 149°59E **63** F4
Twyfelfontein *Namibia* 20°34S 14°22E **56** B1
Tyachiv *Ukraine* 48°1N 23°35E **17** D12
Tychy *Poland* 50°9N 18°59E **17** C10
Tyler *Minn., U.S.A.* 44°17N 96°8W **80** C5
Tyler *Tex., U.S.A.* 32°21N 95°18W **84** E7
Tynda *Russia* 55°10N 124°43E **27** D13
Tyndall *U.S.A.* 43°0N 97°50W **80** D5
Tyne → *U.K.* 54°59N 1°32W **12** C6
Tyne & Wear □ *U.K.* 55°6N 1°17W **12** B6
Tynemouth *U.K.* 55°1N 1°26W **12** B6
Tyre = Sür *Lebanon* 33°19N 35°16E **48** B4
Tyrifjorden *Norway* 60°2N 10°8E **9** F14
Tyrol = Tirol □ *Austria* 47°3N 10°43E **16** E6
Tyrone *U.S.A.* 40°40N 78°14W **82** F6
Tyrone □ *U.K.* 54°38N 7°11W **10** B4
Tyrrell → *Australia* 35°26S 142°51E **63** F3
Tyrrell, L. *Australia* 35°20S 142°50E **63** F3
Tyrrell L. *Canada* 63°7N 105°27W **71** A7
Tyrrhenian Sea *Medit. S.* 40°0N 12°30E **22** E5
Tysfjorden *Norway* 68°7N 16°25E **8** B17
Tyulgan *Russia* 52°22N 56°12E **18** D10
Tyumen *Russia* 57°11N 65°29E **26** D7
Tywi → *U.K.* 51°48N 4°21W **13** F3
Tywyn *U.K.* 52°35N 4°5W **13** E3
Tzaneen *S. Africa* 23°47S 30°9E **57** B5
Tzukong = Zigong
　China 29°15N 104°48E **34** C5

U

U.S.A. = United States of
　America ■ *N. Amer.* 37°0N 96°0W **75** H20
U.S. Virgin Is. ☑ *W. Indies* 18°20N 65°0W **89** e
Uaimh, An = Navan
　Ireland 53°39N 6°41W **10** C5
Uanle Uen = Wanleweyne
　Somalia 2°37N 44°54E **49** G3
Uatumã → *Brazil* 2°26S 57°37W **92** D7
Uaupés *Brazil* 0°8S 67°5W **92** D5
Uaupés → *Brazil* 0°2N 67°16W **92** C5
Uaxactún *Guatemala* 17°25N 89°29W **88** C2
Ubá *Brazil* 21°8S 43°0W **95** A7
Ubaitaba *Brazil* 14°18S 39°20W **93** F11
Ubangi = Oubangi →
　Dem. Rep. of the Congo 0°30S 17°50E **54** E3

Ubauro *Pakistan* 28°15N 69°45E **42** E3
Ubayyiḍ, W. al ➤ *Iraq* 32°34N 43°48E **46** C4
Ube *Japan* 33°56N 131°15E **29** H5
Úbeda *Spain* 38°3N 3°23W **21** C4
Uberaba *Brazil* 19°50S 47°55W **93** G9
Uberlândia *Brazil* 19°0S 48°20W **93** G9
Ubly *U.S.A.* 43°42N 82°55W **82** C2
Ubolratna Res. *Thailand* 16°45N 102°30E **38** D4
Ubombo *S. Africa* 27°31S 32°4E **57** C5
Ubon Ratchathani
  Thailand 15°15N 104°50E **38** E5
Ubort ➤ *Belarus* 52°6N 28°30E **17** B15
Ubud *Indonesia* 8°30S 115°16E **37** J18
Ubundu
  Dem. Rep. of the Congo 0°22S 25°30E **54** E5
Ucayali ➤ *Peru* 4°30S 73°30W **92** D4
Uchab *Namibia* 19°47S 17°42E **56** A2
Uchiura-Wan *Japan* 42°25N 140°40E **28** C10
Uchquduq *Uzbekistan* 41°50N 62°50E **26** E7
Uchur ➤ *Russia* 58°48N 130°35E **27** D14
Ucluelet *Canada* 48°57N 125°32W **70** D3
Uda ➤ *Russia* 54°42N 135°14E **27** D14
Uda Walawe △ *Sri Lanka* 6°20N 81°0E **45** L5
Udachnyy *Russia* 66°25N 112°24E **27** C12
Udagamandalam *India* 11°30N 76°44E **45** J3
Udainagar *India* 22°33N 76°13E **42** H7
Udaipur *India* 24°36N 73°44E **42** G5
Udaipur Garhi *Nepal* 27°0N 86°35E **43** F12
Udala *India* 21°35N 86°34E **43** J12
Udayagiri *Andhra Pradesh,*
  India 14°52N 79°19E **45** G4
Udayagiri *Odisha, India* 20°8N 84°23E **44** D7
Uddevalla *Sweden* 58°21N 11°55E **9** G14
Uddjaure *Sweden* 65°56N 17°49E **8** D17
Uden *Neths.* 51°40N 5°37E **15** C5
Udgir *India* 18°25N 77°5E **44** E3
Udhampur *India* 33°0N 75°5E **43** C6
Údine *Italy* 46°3N 13°14E **22** A5
Udintsev Fracture Zone
  S. Ocean 57°0S 145°0W **5** B13
Udmurtia □ *Russia* 57°30N 52°30E **18** C9
Udon Thani *Thailand* 17°29N 102°46E **38** D4
Udskaya Guba *Russia* 54°50N 135°45E **27** D14
Udu Pt. *Fiji* 16°9S 179°57W **59** a
Udumalaippettai *India* 10°35N 77°15E **45** J3
Udupi *India* 13°25N 74°42E **45** H2
Udva *India* 20°5N 73°0E **44** D1
Udzungwa Range *Tanzania* 9°30S 35°10E **54** F7
Ueda *Japan* 36°24N 138°16E **29** F9
Uedineniya, Os. *Russia* 78°0N 85°0E **4** B12
Uele ➤
  Dem. Rep. of the Congo 3°45N 24°45E **54** D4
Uelen *Russia* 66°10N 170°0W **27** C19
Uelzen *Germany* 52°57N 10°32E **16** B6
Ufa *Russia* 54°45N 55°55E **18** D10
Ufa ➤ *Russia* 54°40N 56°0E **18** D10
Ugab ➤ *Namibia* 20°55S 13°30E **56** B1
Ugalla ➤ *Tanzania* 5°8S 30°42E **54** F6
Uganda ■ *Africa* 2°0N 32°0E **54** D6
Ugie *S. Africa* 31°10S 28°13E **57** D4
Uglegorsk *Russia* 49°5N 142°2E **27** E15
Uglich *Russia* 57°33N 38°20E **18** C6
Ugljan *Croatia* 44°12N 15°10E **16** F8
Ugolnye Kopi *Russia* 64°44N 177°42E **27** C18
Uhlenhorst *Namibia* 23°45S 17°55E **56** B2
Uhrichsville *U.S.A.* 40°24N 81°21W **82** F3
Uibhist a Deas = South Uist
  U.K. 57°20N 7°15W **11** D1
Uibhist a Tuath = North Uist
  U.K. 57°40N 7°15W **11** D1
Uig *U.K.* 57°35N 6°21W **11** D2
Uíge *Angola* 7°30S 14°40E **54** F2
Uiha *Tonga* 19°54S 174°25W **59** c
Uijeongbu *S. Korea* 37°44N 127°2E **33** F14
Ŭiju *N. Korea* 40°15N 124°35E **33** D13
Uinta Mts. *U.S.A.* 40°45N 110°30W **76** F8
Uis *Namibia* 21°8S 14°49E **56** B1
Uiseong *S. Korea* 36°21N 128°45E **33** F15
Uitenhage *S. Africa* 33°40S 25°28E **56** D4
Uithuizen *Neths.* 53°24N 6°41E **15** A6
Ujh ➤ *India* 32°10N 75°18E **42** C6
Ujhani *India* 28°0N 79°6E **43** F8
Uji-guntō *Japan* 31°15N 129°25E **29** J4
Ujjain *India* 23°9N 75°43E **42** H6
Ujung Kulon △
  Indonesia 6°46S 105°19E **37** G11
Ujung Pandang = Makassar
  Indonesia 5°10S 119°20E **37** F5
Uka *Russia* 57°50N 162°0E **27** D17
Ukai Sagar *India* 21°20N 73°43E **44** D1
Uke-Shima *Japan* 28°2N 129°14E **29** K4
uKhahlamba Drakensberg △
  S. Africa 29°27S 29°30E **57** C4
Ukhrul *India* 25°10N 94°25E **41** G19
Ukhta *Russia* 63°34N 53°41E **18** B9
Ukiah *U.S.A.* 39°9N 123°13W **78** F3
Ukmergė *Lithuania* 55°15N 24°45E **9** J21
Ukraine ■ *Europe* 49°0N 32°0E **19** E5
Ukwi *Botswana* 23°29S 20°30E **56** B3
Ulaan Nuur *Mongolia* 44°13N 103°30E **32** B2
Ulaan-Uul *Mongolia* 44°6N 100°49E **32** B6
Ulaanbaatar *Mongolia* 47°55N 106°53E **30** B10
Ulaangom *Mongolia* 50°5N 92°10E **30** A7
Ulaanjirem *Mongolia* 45°5N 105°30E **32** B3
Ulak I. *U.S.A.* 51°22N 178°57W **74** E4
Ulan Bator = Ulaanbaatar
  Mongolia 47°55N 106°53E **30** B10
Ulan Ude *Russia* 51°45N 107°40E **31** A10
Ulanhad = Chifeng
  China 42°18N 118°58E **33** C10
Ulanhot = Horqin Youyi Qianqi
  China 46°5N 122°3E **33** A12
Ulansuhai Nur *China* 40°53N 108°51E **32** D5
Ulco *S. Africa* 28°21S 24°15E **56** C3
Ule älv = Oulujoki ➤
  Finland 65°1N 25°30E **8** D21
Ule träsk = Oulujärvi
  Finland 64°25N 27°15E **8** D22

Uleåborg = Oulu *Finland* 65°1N 25°29E **8** D21
Ulefoss *Norway* 59°17N 9°16E **9** G13
Ulhasnagar *India* 19°15N 73°10E **44** E1
Uliastay *Mongolia* 47°56N 97°28E **30** B8
Uljin *S. Korea* 36°59N 129°24E **33** F15
Ulladulla *Australia* 35°21S 150°29E **63** F5
Ullal *India* 12°48N 74°51E **45** H2
Ullapool *U.K.* 57°54N 5°9W **11** D3
Ulleungdo *S. Korea* 37°30N 130°30E **29** F5
Ullswater *Canada* 45°12N 79°29W **82** A5
Ullswater *U.K.* 54°34N 2°52W **12** C5
Ulm *Germany* 48°23N 9°58E **16** D5
Ulmarra *Australia* 29°37S 153°4E **63** D5
Ulricehamn *Sweden* 57°46N 13°26E **9** H15
Ulsan *S. Korea* 35°20N 129°15E **33** G15
Ulsta *U.K.* 60°30N 1°9W **11** A7
Ulster □ *U.K.* 54°35N 6°30W **10** B5
Ulubat Gölü *Turkey* 40°9N 28°35E **23** D13
Uludağ *Turkey* 40°4N 29°13E **23** D13
Ulundi *S. Africa* 28°20S 31°25E **57** C5
Ulungur He ➤ *China* 47°1N 87°24E **30** B6
Ulungur Hu *China* 47°20N 87°10E **30** B6
Uluru *Australia* 25°23S 131°5E **61** E5
Uluru-Kata Tjuta △
  Australia 25°19S 131°1E **61** E5
Ulutau *Kazakhstan* 48°39N 67°1E **26** E7
Uluwatu *Indonesia* 8°50S 115°5E **37** K18
Ulva *U.K.* 56°29N 6°13W **11** E2
Ulverston *U.K.* 54°13N 3°5W **12** C4
Ulverstone *Australia* 41°11S 146°11E **63** G4
Ulya *Russia* 59°10N 142°0E **27** D15
Ulyanovsk *Russia* 54°20N 48°25E **18** D8
Ulyasutay = Uliastay
  Mongolia 47°56N 97°28E **30** B8
Ulysses *Kans., U.S.A.* 37°35N 101°22W **80** G3
Ulysses *Pa., U.S.A.* 41°54N 77°46W **82** E7
Ulysses, Mt. *Canada* 57°20N 124°5W **70** B4
Umala *Bolivia* 17°25S 68°5W **92** G5
'Umān = Oman ■ *Asia* 23°0N 58°0E **49** C6
Uman *Ukraine* 48°40N 30°12E **17** D16
Umaria *India* 23°35N 80°50E **43** H9
Umarkhed *India* 19°37N 77°46E **44** E3
Umarkot *Pakistan* 25°15N 69°40E **42** G3
Umarpada *India* 21°27N 73°30E **42** J5
Umatilla *U.S.A.* 45°55N 119°21W **76** D4
Umba *Russia* 66°42N 34°11E **18** A5
Umbagog L. *U.S.A.* 44°46N 71°3W **83** B13
Umbakumba *Australia* 13°47S 136°50E **62** A2
Umbrella Mts. *N.Z.* 45°35S 169°5E **59** F2
Umeå *Sweden* 63°45N 20°20E **8** E19
Umeälven ➤ *Sweden* 63°45N 20°20E **8** E19
Umera *Indonesia* 0°12S 129°37E **37** E7
Umgwenya ➤ *Mozam.* 25°14S 32°18E **57** C5
Umkomaas *S. Africa* 30°13S 30°48E **57** D5
Umlazi *S. Africa* 29°59S 30°54E **55** L6
Umm ad Daraj, J. *Jordan* 32°18N 35°48E **48** C4
Umm al Qaywayn *U.A.E.* 25°30N 55°35E **47** E7
Umm al Qittayn *Jordan* 32°18N 36°40E **48** C5
Umm al Rasas *Jordan* 31°30N 35°55E **48** D4
Umm Bāb *Qatar* 25°12N 50°48E **47** E6
Umm Durman = Omdurmân
  Sudan 15°40N 32°28E **53** E12
Umm el Fahm *Israel* 32°31N 35°9E **48** C4
Umm Keddada *Sudan* 13°33N 26°35E **53** F11
Umm Lajj *Si. Arabia* 25°0N 37°23E **46** E3
Umm Qasr *Iraq* 30°1N 47°58E **46** D5
Umm Ruwaba *Sudan* 12°50N 31°20E **53** F12
Umm Tais △ *Qatar* 26°7N 51°15E **47** E6
Umnak I. *U.S.A.* 53°15N 168°20W **74** E6
Umniati ➤ *Zimbabwe* 16°49S 28°45E **55** H5
Umpqua ➤ *U.S.A.* 43°40N 124°12W **76** E1
Umred *India* 20°51N 79°18E **44** D4
Umreth *India* 22°41N 73°4E **42** H5
Umri *India* 19°2N 77°39E **44** E3
Umtata = Mthatha
  S. Africa 31°36S 28°49E **57** D4
Umuarama *Brazil* 23°45S 53°20W **95** A5
Umvukwe Ra. *Zimbabwe* 16°45S 30°45E **55** H6
Umzimvubu *S. Africa* 31°38S 29°33E **57** D4
Umzinto = eMuziwezinto
  S. Africa 30°15S 30°45E **57** D5
Una *India* 20°46N 71°8E **42** J4
Una ➤ *Bos.-H.* 45°0N 16°20E **16** F9
Unadilla *U.S.A.* 42°20N 75°19W **83** D9
Unalakleet *U.S.A.* 63°52N 160°47W **74** C7
Unalaska *U.S.A.* 53°53N 166°32W **74** E6
Unalaska I. *U.S.A.* 53°35N 166°50W **74** E6
'Unayzah *Si. Arabia* 26°6N 43°58E **46** E4
'Unayzah, J. *Asia* 32°12N 39°18E **46** C3
Uncía *Bolivia* 18°25S 66°40W **92** G5
Uncompahgre Peak
  U.S.A. 38°4N 107°28W **76** G10
Uncompahgre Plateau
  U.S.A. 38°20N 108°15W **76** G9
Undara Volcanic △
  Australia 18°14S 144°41E **62** B3
Underbool *Australia* 35°10S 141°51E **63** F3
Underwood *Canada* 44°18N 81°29W **82** B3
Ungarie *Australia* 33°38S 146°56E **63** E4
Ungarra *Australia* 34°12S 136°2E **63** E2
Ungava, Pén. d' *Canada* 60°0N 74°0W **69** F17
Ungava B. *Canada* 59°30N 67°30W **69** F18
Ungeny = Ungheni
  Moldova 47°11N 27°51E **17** E14
Unggi *N. Korea* 42°16N 130°28E **33** C16
Ungheni *Moldova* 47°11N 27°51E **17** E14
União da Vitória *Brazil* 26°13S 51°5W **95** B5
Unimak I. *U.S.A.* 54°45N 164°0W **74** E7
Unimak Pass. *U.S.A.* 54°15N 164°30W **74** E7
Union *Miss., U.S.A.* 32°34N 89°7W **85** E10
Union *Mo., U.S.A.* 38°27N 91°0W **80** F8
Union *S.C., U.S.A.* 34°43N 81°37W **85** D14
Union City *Calif., U.S.A.* 37°36N 122°1W **78** H4
Union City *Pa., U.S.A.* 41°54N 79°51W **82** E5
Union City *Tenn., U.S.A.* 36°26N 89°3W **85** C10
Union Dale *U.S.A.* 41°43N 75°29W **83** E9
Union Gap *U.S.A.* 46°33N 120°28W **76** C3
Union Springs *Ala.,*
  U.S.A. 32°9N 85°43W **85** E12

Union Springs *N.Y.,*
  U.S.A. 42°50N 76°41W **83** D8
Uniondale *S. Africa* 33°39S 23°7E **56** D3
Uniontown *U.S.A.* 39°54N 79°44W **81** F14
Unionville *U.S.A.* 40°29N 93°1W **80** E7
United Arab Emirates ■
  Asia 23°50N 54°0E **47** F7
United Kingdom ■ *Europe* 53°0N 2°0W **14** E6
United States of America ■
  N. Amer. 37°0N 96°0W **75** H20
Unity *Canada* 52°30N 109°5W **71** C7
University Park *U.S.A.* 32°17N 106°45W **77** K10
University Place *U.S.A.* 47°14N 122°33W **78** C4
Unjha *India* 23°46N 72°24E **42** H5
Unnao *India* 26°35N 80°30E **43** F9
Unst *U.K.* 60°44N 0°53W **11** A8
Unuk ➤ *Canada* 56°5N 131°3W **70** B2
Unzen-Amakusa △
  Japan 32°15N 130°10E **29** H5
Uong Bi *Vietnam* 21°2N 106°47E **38** B6
Uotsuri-Shima
  E. China Sea 25°45N 123°29E **29** M1
Uozu *Japan* 36°48N 137°24E **29** F8
Upata *Venezuela* 8°1N 62°24W **92** B6
Upemba, L.
  Dem. Rep. of the Congo 8°30S 26°20E **54** F5
Upernavik *Greenland* 72°49N 56°20W **4** B5
Upington *S. Africa* 28°25S 21°15E **56** C3
Upleta *India* 21°46N 70°16E **42** J4
'Upolu *Samoa* 13°58S 172°0W **59** b
Upper Alkali L. *U.S.A.* 41°47N 120°8W **76** F3
Upper Arrow L. *Canada* 50°30N 117°50W **70** C5
Upper Daly ◎ *Australia* 14°26S 131°3E **60** B5
Upper Darby *U.S.A.* 39°55N 75°16W **81** F16
Upper Foster L. *Canada* 56°47N 105°20W **71** B7
Upper Hutt *N.Z.* 41°8S 175°5E **59** D5
Upper Klamath L.
  U.S.A. 42°25N 121°55W **76** E3
Upper Lake *U.S.A.* 39°10N 122°54W **78** F4
Upper Liard *Canada* 60°3N 128°54W **70** A3
Upper Manzanilla
  Trin. & Tob. 10°31N 61°4W **93** K15
Upper Missouri Breaks △
  U.S.A. 47°50N 109°55W **76** C9
Upper Musquodoboit
  Canada 45°10N 62°58W **73** C7
Upper Red L. *U.S.A.* 48°8N 94°45W **80** A6
Upper Sandusky *U.S.A.* 40°50N 83°17W **81** E12
Upper Volta = Burkina Faso ■
  Africa 12°0N 1°0W **52** F5
Uppland *Sweden* 59°59N 17°48E **9** G17
Uppsala *Sweden* 59°53N 17°38E **9** G17
Upshi *India* 33°48N 77°52E **43** C7
Upton *U.S.A.* 44°6N 104°38W **76** D11
Uqsuqtuuq = Gjoa Haven
  Canada 68°38N 95°53W **68** D12
Ur *Iraq* 30°55N 46°25E **46** D5
Urad Qianqi *China* 40°40N 108°30E **32** D5
Urahoro *Japan* 42°50N 143°40E **28** C11
Urakawa *Japan* 42°9N 142°47E **28** C11
Ural = Uralskiy □ *Russia* 64°0N 70°0E **26** C7
Ural = Zhayyq ➤
  Kazakhstan 47°0N 51°48E **19** E9
Ural Mts. = Uralskie Gory
  Eurasia 60°0N 59°0E **18** C10
Uralla *Australia* 30°37S 151°29E **63** E5
Uralsk = Oral *Kazakhstan* 51°20N 51°20E **19** D9
Uralskie Gory *Eurasia* 60°0N 59°0E **18** C10
Uralskiy □ *Russia* 64°0N 70°0E **26** C7
Urambo *Tanzania* 5°4S 32°0E **54** F6
Urandangi *Australia* 21°32S 138°14E **62** C2
Uranium City *Canada* 59°34N 108°37W **71** B7
Urania *Brazil* 13°0S 58°10W **92** F7
Urapuntja = Utopia
  Australia 22°14S 134°33E **62** C1
Uraricoera ➤ *Brazil* 3°2N 60°30W **92** C6
Urasoe *Japan* 26°15N 127°43E **29** L3
Uravakonda *India* 14°57N 77°12E **45** G3
Urawa = Saitama *Japan* 35°54N 139°38E **29** G9
Uray *Russia* 60°5N 65°15E **26** C7
'Uray'irah *Si. Arabia* 25°57N 48°53E **47** E6
Urbana *Ill., U.S.A.* 40°7N 88°12W **80** E9
Urbana *Ohio, U.S.A.* 40°7N 83°45W **81** E12
Urbandale *U.S.A.* 41°38N 93°43W **80** E7
Urbino *Italy* 43°43N 12°38E **22** C5
Urbión, Picos de *Spain* 42°1N 2°52E **21** A4
Urcos *Peru* 13°40S 71°38W **92** F4
Urdinarrain *Argentina* 32°37S 58°52W **94** C4
Ure ➤ *U.K.* 54°5N 1°20W **12** C6
Urengoy *Russia* 65°58N 78°22E **26** C8
Ures *Mexico* 29°26N 110°24W **86** B2
Urewera △ *N.Z.* 38°29S 177°7E **59** C6
Urfa = Sanlıurfa *Turkey* 37°12N 38°50E **46** B3
Urganch *Uzbekistan* 41°40N 60°41E **26** E7
Urgench = Urganch
  Uzbekistan 41°40N 60°41E **26** E7
Ürgüp *Turkey* 38°38N 34°56E **46** B6
Uri *India* 34°8N 74°2E **43** B6
Uribia *Colombia* 11°43N 72°16W **92** A4
Uriondo *Bolivia* 21°41S 64°41W **94** A3
Urique *Mexico* 27°13N 107°55W **86** B3
Urk *Neths.* 52°39N 5°36E **15** B5
Urla *Turkey* 38°20N 26°47E **23** E12
Urmia = Orūmīyeh *Iran* 37°40N 45°0E **46** B5
Uroševac = Ferizaj
  Kosovo 42°23N 21°10E **23** C9
Uroyan, Montanas de
  Puerto Rico 18°12N 66°50W **89** d
Urrampinyi Iltjiltarri ◎
  Australia 24°20S 132°10E **60** D5
Uruaçu *Brazil* 14°30S 49°10W **93** F9
Uruapan *Mexico* 19°24N 102°3W **86** D4
Urubamba ➤ *Peru* 10°43S 73°48W **92** F4
Urucará *Brazil* 2°32S 57°45W **92** D7
Uruçuí *Brazil* 7°20S 44°28W **93** E10
Uruguai ➤ *Brazil* 26°0S 53°30W **95** B5
Uruguaiana *Brazil* 29°50S 57°0W **94** B4
Uruguay ■ *S. Amer.* 32°30S 56°30W **94** C4

Uruguay ➤ *S. Amer.* 34°12S 58°18W **94** C4
Urumchi = Ürümqi *China* 43°45N 87°45E **30** C6
Ürümqi *China* 43°45N 87°45E **30** C6
Uruna ◎ *Australia* 24°3S 133°1E **60** D5
Urup, Ostrov *Russia* 46°0N 151°0E **27** E16
Ürzhar *Kazakhstan* 47°5N 81°38E **26** E9
Usa ➤ *Russia* 66°16N 59°49E **18** A10
Uşak *Turkey* 38°43N 29°28E **19** G4
Usakos *Namibia* 21°54S 15°31E **56** B2
Usedom *Germany* 53°55N 14°2E **16** B8
Useless Loop *Australia* 26°8S 113°23E **61** E1
Ushakova, Ostrov *Russia* 82°0N 80°0E **27** A8
Ushant = Ouessant, Î. d'
  France 48°28N 5°6W **20** B1
'Ushayrah *Si. Arabia* 25°35N 45°47E **46** E5
Ushibuka *Japan* 32°11N 130°1E **29** H5
Ushtöbe *Kazakhstan* 45°16N 78°0E **26** E8
Ushuaia *Argentina* 54°50S 68°23W **96** G3
Ushumun *Russia* 52°47N 126°32E **27** D13
Usinsk *Russia* 65°57N 57°27E **18** A10
Usk *Canada* 54°38N 128°26W **70** C3
Usk ➤ *U.K.* 51°33N 2°58W **13** F5
Uska *India* 27°12N 83°7E **43** F10
Usman *Russia* 52°5N 39°48E **18** D6
Usolye-Sibirskoye
  Russia 52°48N 103°40E **27** D11
Uspallata, P. de *Argentina* 32°37S 69°22W **94** C2
Ussuriysk *Russia* 43°48N 131°59E **28** C5
Ussurka *Russia* 45°12N 133°31E **28** B6
Ust-Chaun *Russia* 68°47N 170°30E **27** C18
Ust-Ilimsk *Russia* 58°3N 102°39E **27** D11
Ust-Ishim *Russia* 57°45N 71°10E **26** D8
Ust-Kamchatsk *Russia* 56°10N 162°28E **27** D17
Ust-Kamenogorsk = Öskemen
  Kazakhstan 50°0N 82°36E **26** D9
Ust-Khayryuzovo
  Russia 57°15N 156°45E **27** D16
Ust-Kut *Russia* 56°50N 105°42E **27** D11
Ust-Kuyga *Russia* 70°1N 135°43E **27** B14
Ust-Maya *Russia* 60°30N 134°28E **27** C14
Ust-Mil *Russia* 59°40N 133°11E **27** D14
Ust-Nera *Russia* 64°35N 143°15E **27** C15
Ust-Nyukzha *Russia* 56°34N 121°37E **27** D13
Ust-Olenek *Russia* 73°0N 120°5E **27** B12
Ust-Omchug *Russia* 61°9N 149°38E **27** C15
Ust-Port *Russia* 69°40N 84°26E **26** C9
Ust-Tsilma *Russia* 65°28N 52°11E **18** A9
Ust-Urt = Ustyurt Plateau
  Asia 44°0N 55°0E **26** E6
Ust-Usa *Russia* 66°2N 56°57E **18** A10
Ust-Vorkuta *Russia* 67°24N 64°0E **18** A11
Ústí nad Labem *Czech Rep.* 50°41N 14°3E **16** C8
Ústica *Italy* 38°42N 13°11E **22** E5
Ustinov = Izhevsk *Russia* 56°51N 53°14E **18** C9
Ustyurt Plateau *Asia* 44°0N 55°0E **26** E6
Usu *China* 44°27N 84°40E **30** C5
Usuki *Japan* 33°8N 131°49E **29** H5
Usulután *El Salv.* 13°25N 88°28W **88** D2
Usumacinta ➤ *Mexico* 18°24N 92°38W **87** D6
Usumbura = Bujumbura
  Burundi 3°16S 29°18E **54** E5
Usutuo ➤ *Mozam.* 26°48S 32°7E **57** C5
Uta *Indonesia* 4°33S 136°0E **37** E9
Utah □ *U.S.A.* 39°20N 111°30W **76** G8
Utah L. *U.S.A.* 40°12N 111°48W **76** F8
Utara, Selat *Malaysia* 5°28N 100°20E **39** c
Utarni *India* 26°5N 71°58E **42** F4
Utatlan *Guatemala* 15°2N 91°11W **88** C1
Ute Creek ➤ *U.S.A.* 35°21N 103°50W **77** J12
Utena *Lithuania* 55°27N 25°40E **9** J21
Uthai Thani *Thailand* 15°22N 100°3E **38** E3
Uthal *Pakistan* 25°44N 66°40E **42** G2
Utiariti *Brazil* 13°0S 58°10W **92** F7
Utica *N.Y., U.S.A.* 43°6N 75°14W **83** C9
Utica *Ohio, U.S.A.* 40°14N 82°27W **82** F2
Utikuma L. *Canada* 55°50N 115°30W **70** B5
Utila *Honduras* 16°6N 86°56W **88** C2
Utkela *India* 20°6N 83°10E **44** D6
Utnur *India* 19°22N 78°46E **44** E4
Utopia *Australia* 22°14S 134°33E **62** C1
Utraula *India* 27°19N 82°25E **43** F10
Utrecht *Neths.* 52°5N 5°8E **15** B5
Utrecht *S. Africa* 27°38S 30°20E **57** C5
Utrecht □ *Neths.* 52°6N 5°7E **15** B5
Utrera *Spain* 37°12N 5°48W **21** D3
Utsjoki ➤ *Finland* 69°51N 26°59E **8** B22
Utsunomiya *Japan* 36°30N 139°50E **29** F9
Uttar Pradesh □ *India* 27°0N 80°0E **43** F9
Uttaradit *Thailand* 17°36N 100°5E **38** D3
Uttarakhand □ *India* 30°0N 79°30E **43** D8
Utterson *Canada* 45°12N 79°19W **82** A5
Uttoxeter *U.K.* 52°54N 1°52W **12** E6
Utuado *Puerto Rico* 18°16N 66°42W **89** d
Uummannaq *Avannaarsua,*
  Greenland 77°33N 68°52W **69** B18
Uummannaq *Kitaa,*
  Greenland 70°58N 52°17W **4** B5
Uummannarsuaq = Nunap Isua
  Greenland 59°48N 43°55W **66** D15
Uusikaarlepyy *Finland* 63°32N 22°31E **8** E20
Uusikaupunki *Finland* 60°47N 21°25E **8** F19
Uva *Russia* 56°59N 52°13E **18** C9
Uvalde *U.S.A.* 29°13N 99°47W **84** G5
Uvat *Russia* 59°5N 68°50E **26** D7
Uvinza *Tanzania* 5°5S 30°24E **54** F6
Uvira *Dem. Rep. of the Congo* 3°22S 29°3E **54** E5
Uvs Nuur *Mongolia* 50°20N 92°30E **30** A7
'Uwainīdh, Ḥarrat al
  Si. Arabia 26°50N 38°0E **46** E3
Uwajima *Japan* 33°10N 132°35E **29** H6
Uweinat, Jebel *Sudan* 21°54N 24°58E **53** D10
Uxbridge *Canada* 44°6N 79°7W **82** B5
Uxin Qi *China* 38°50N 109°5E **32** E5
Uxmal *Mexico* 20°22N 89°46W **87** C7
Üydzin *Mongolia* 44°9N 107°0E **32** B4
Uyo *Nigeria* 5°1N 7°53E **52** G7
Uyuni *Bolivia* 20°28S 66°47W **92** H5
Uzbekistan ■ *Asia* 41°30N 65°0E **26** E7

Uzboy ➤ *Turkmenistan* 39°30N 55°0E **47** B7
Uzen, Mal ➤ *Kazakhstan* 49°4N 49°44E **19** E8
Uzerche *France* 45°25N 1°34E **20** D4
Uzh ➤ *Ukraine* 51°15N 30°12E **17** C16
Uzhgorod = Uzhhorod
  Ukraine 48°36N 22°18E **17** D12
Uzhhorod *Ukraine* 48°36N 22°18E **17** D12
Užice *Serbia* 43°55N 19°50E **23** C8
Uzunköprü *Turkey* 41°16N 26°43E **23** D12

V

Vaal ➤ *S. Africa* 29°4S 23°38E **56** C3
Vaal Dam *S. Africa* 27°0S 28°14E **57** D4
Vaalwater *S. Africa* 24°15S 28°8E **57** B4
Vaasa *Finland* 63°6N 21°38E **8** E19
Vác *Hungary* 47°49N 19°10E **17** E10
Vacaria *Brazil* 28°31S 50°52W **95** B5
Vacata *Fiji* 17°15S 179°31W **59** a
Vacaville *U.S.A.* 38°21N 121°59W **78** G5
Vach = Vakh ➤ *Russia* 60°45N 76°45E **26** C8
Vache, Î. à *Haiti* 18°2N 73°35W **89** C5
Vacoas *Mauritius* 20°18S 57°29E **55** d
Vada *India* 19°39N 73°8E **44** E1
Vadakara *India* 11°35N 75°40E **45** J2
Vadnagar *India* 23°47N 72°40E **42** H5
Vadodara *India* 22°20N 73°10E **42** H5
Vadsø *Norway* 70°3N 29°50E **8** A23
Vaduj *India* 17°36N 74°27E **44** F2
Vaduz *Liech.* 47°8N 9°31E **20** C8
Værøy *Norway* 67°40N 12°40E **8** C15
Vágar *Færoe Is.* 62°5N 7°15W **8** E9
Vågsfjorden *Norway* 68°50N 16°50E **8** B17
Váh ➤ *Slovak Rep.* 47°43N 18°7E **17** D9
Vahsel B. *Antarctica* 75°0S 35°0W **5** D1
Váhtjer = Gällivare
  Sweden 67°9N 20°40E **8** C19
Vaigai ➤ *India* 9°15N 79°10E **45** K4
Vaihiria, L. *Tahiti* 17°40S 149°25W **59** d2
Vaijapur *India* 19°58N 74°45E **44** E2
Vaikam *India* 9°45N 76°25E **45** K3
Vail *U.S.A.* 39°40N 106°20W **76** G10
Vaippar ➤ *India* 9°0N 78°25E **45** K4
Vairao *Tahiti* 17°47S 149°17W **59** d
Vaisali ➤ *India* 26°28N 78°53E **43** F8
Vaitogi *Amer. Samoa* 14°24S 170°44W **59** b
Vajpur *India* 21°24N 73°17E **44** D1
Vakarai *Sri Lanka* 8°8N 81°26E **45** K5
Vakh ➤ *Russia* 60°45N 76°45E **26** C8
Val-d'Or *Canada* 48°7N 77°47W **72** C4
Val Marie *Canada* 49°15N 107°45W **71** D7
Valaam *Russia* 61°22N 30°57E **8** F24
Valahia *Romania* 44°35N 25°0E **17** F13
Valaichenai *Sri Lanka* 7°54N 81°32E **45** L5
Valandovo *Macedonia* 41°19N 22°34E **23** D10
Valatie *U.S.A.* 42°24N 73°40W **83** D11
Valcheta *Argentina* 40°40S 66°8W **96** E3
Valdai Hills = Valdayskaya
  Vozvyshennost *Russia* 57°0N 33°30E **18** C5
Valdayskaya Vozvyshennost
  Russia 57°0N 33°30E **18** C5
Valdepeñas *Spain* 38°43N 3°25W **21** C4
Valdés, Pen. *Argentina* 42°30S 63°45W **96** E4
Valdez *U.S.A.* 61°7N 146°16W **68** E2
Valdivia *Chile* 39°50S 73°14W **96** D2
Valdivia Abyssal Plain
  S. Ocean 62°30S 70°0E **5** C6
Valdosta *U.S.A.* 30°50N 83°17W **85** F13
Valdres *Norway* 61°5N 9°5E **8** F13
Vale *U.S.A.* 43°59N 117°15W **76** E5
Vale of Glamorgan □
  U.K. 51°28N 3°25W **13** F4
Valemount *Canada* 52°50N 119°15W **70** C5
Valença *Brazil* 13°20S 39°5W **93** F11
Valença do Piauí *Brazil* 6°20S 41°45W **93** E10
Valence *France* 44°57N 4°54E **20** D6
Valencia *Spain* 39°27N 0°23W **21** C5
Valencia *Trin. & Tob.* 10°39N 61°11W **93** K15
Valencia *U.S.A.* 34°48N 106°43W **77** J10
Valencia *Venezuela* 10°11N 68°0W **92** A5
Valencia, G. de *Spain* 39°30N 0°20E **21** C6
Valencia de Alcántara
  Spain 39°25N 7°14W **21** C2
Valencia I. *Ireland* 51°54N 10°22W **10** E1
Valenciennes *France* 50°20N 3°34E **20** A5
Valentim, Sa. do *Brazil* 6°0S 43°30W **93** E10
Valentine *Nebr., U.S.A.* 42°52N 100°33W **80** D3
Valentine *Tex., U.S.A.* 30°35N 104°30W **84** F2
Valera *Venezuela* 9°19N 70°37W **92** B4
Valga *Estonia* 57°47N 26°2E **9** H22
Valier *U.S.A.* 48°18N 112°16W **76** B7
Valjevo *Serbia* 44°18N 19°53E **23** B8
Valka *Latvia* 57°46N 26°3E **9** H22
Valkeakoski *Finland* 61°16N 24°2E **8** F21
Valkenswaard *Neths.* 51°21N 5°29E **15** C5
Vall de Uxó = La Vall d'Uixó
  Spain 39°49N 0°15W **21** C5
Valladolid *Mexico* 20°41N 88°12W **87** C7
Valladolid *Spain* 41°38N 4°43W **21** B3
Valle de la Pascua
  Venezuela 9°13N 66°0W **92** B5
Valle de las Palmas
  Mexico 32°20N 116°43W **79** N10
Valle de Santiago
  Mexico 20°23N 101°12W **86** C4
Valle de Zaragoza
  Mexico 27°25N 105°50W **86** B3
Valle Fértil, Sierra del
  Argentina 30°20S 68°0W **94** C2
Valle Hermoso *Mexico* 25°35N 97°40W **87** B5
Valle Nacional *Mexico* 17°47N 96°18W **87** D5
Valledupar *Colombia* 10°29N 73°15W **92** A4
Vallejo *U.S.A.* 38°7N 122°14W **78** G4
Vallenar *Chile* 28°30S 70°50W **94** B1
Valletta *Malta* 35°54N 14°31E **22** G6
Valley Center *U.S.A.* 33°13N 117°2W **79** M9
Valley City *U.S.A.* 46°55N 98°0W **80** B5

Valley Falls Oreg., U.S.A. 42°29N 120°17W 76 E3
Valley Falls R.I., U.S.A. 41°54N 71°24W 83 E13
Valley of Flowers △ India 30°50N 79°40E 43 D8
Valley Springs U.S.A. 38°12N 120°50W 78 G6
Valley View U.S.A. 40°39N 76°33W 83 F8
Valley Wells U.S.A. 35°27N 115°46W 79 K11
Valleyview Canada 55°5N 117°17W 70 B5
Vallimanca, Arroyo Argentina 35°40S 59°10W 94 D4
Valls Spain 41°18N 1°15E 21 B6
Valmiera Latvia 57°37N 25°29E 9 H21
Valognes France 49°30N 1°28W 20 B3
Valona = Vlorë Albania 40°32N 19°28E 23 D8
Valozhyn Belarus 54°3N 26°30E 17 A14
Valparai India 10°22N 76°58E 45 J3
Valparaíso Chile 33°2S 71°40W 94 C1
Valparaíso Mexico 22°46N 103°34W 86 C4
Valparaiso U.S.A. 41°28N 87°4W 80 E10
Valparaíso □ Chile 33°2S 71°40W 94 C1
Valpoy India 15°32N 74°8E 45 G2
Vals → S. Africa 27°23S 26°30E 56 C4
Vals, Tanjung Indonesia 8°26S 137°25E 37 F9
Valsad India 20°40N 72°58E 44 D1
Valverde del Camino Spain 37°35N 6°47W 21 D2
Vambori India 19°17N 74°44E 44 E2
Vammala = Sastamala Finland 61°20N 22°54E 8 F20
Vamsadhara → India 18°21N 84°8E 44 E7
Van Turkey 38°30N 43°20E 46 B4
Van, L. = Van Gölü Turkey 38°30N 43°0E 46 B4
Van Alstyne U.S.A. 33°25N 96°35W 84 E6
Van Blommestein Meer Suriname 4°45N 55°5W 93 C7
Van Buren Canada 47°10N 67°55W 73 C6
Van Buren Ark., U.S.A. 35°26N 94°21W 84 D7
Van Buren Maine, U.S.A. 47°10N 67°58W 81 B20
Van Buren Mo., U.S.A. 37°0N 91°1W 80 G8
Van Canh Vietnam 13°37N 109°0E 38 F7
Van Diemen, C. N. Terr., Australia 11°9S 130°24E 60 B5
Van Diemen, C. Queens., Australia 16°30S 139°46E 62 B2
Van Diemen G. Australia 11°45S 132°0E 60 B5
Van Gölü Turkey 38°30N 43°0E 46 B4
Van Horn U.S.A. 31°3N 104°50W 84 F2
Van Ninh Vietnam 12°42N 109°14E 38 F7
Van Rees, Pegunungan Indonesia 2°35S 138°15E 37 E9
Van Tivu India 8°51N 78°15E 45 K4
Van Wert U.S.A. 40°52N 84°35W 81 E11
Van Yen Vietnam 21°4N 104°42E 34 G5
Van Zylsrus S. Africa 26°52S 22°4E 56 C3
Vanadzor Armenia 40°48N 44°30E 19 F7
Vanavara Russia 60°22N 102°16E 27 C11
Vancouver Canada 49°15N 123°7W 78 A3
Vancouver U.S.A. 45°38N 122°40W 78 E4
Vancouver, C. Australia 35°2S 118°11E 61 G2
Vancouver I. Canada 49°50N 126°0W 78 B2
Vancouver Int. ✈ (YVR) Canada 49°10N 123°10W 78 A3
Vandalia Ill., U.S.A. 38°58N 89°6W 80 F9
Vandalia Mo., U.S.A. 39°19N 91°29W 80 F8
Vandavasi India 12°30N 79°30E 45 H4
Vandeloos B. Sri Lanka 8°0N 81°45E 45 L5
Vandenberg Village U.S.A. 34°43N 120°28W 79 L6
Vandergrift U.S.A. 40°36N 79°34W 82 F5
Vanderhoof Canada 54°0N 124°0W 70 C4
Vanderkloof Dam S. Africa 30°4S 24°40E 56 D3
Vanderlin I. Australia 15°44S 137°2E 62 B2
Vänern Sweden 58°47N 13°30E 9 G15
Vänersborg Sweden 58°26N 12°19E 9 G15
Vang Vieng Laos 18°58N 102°32E 38 C4
Vangaindrano Madag. 23°21S 47°36E 55 J9
Vanguard Canada 49°55N 107°20W 71 D7
Vanino Russia 48°50N 140°5E 27 E15
Vanivilasa Sagara India 13°45N 76°30E 45 H3
Vaniyambadi India 12°46N 78°44E 45 H4
Vankleek Hill Canada 45°32N 74°40W 83 A10
Vännäs Sweden 63°58N 19°48E 8 E18
Vannes France 47°40N 2°47W 20 C2
Vannøya Norway 70°6N 19°50E 8 A18
Vanrhynsdorp S. Africa 31°36S 18°44E 56 D2
Vansada India 20°47N 73°25E 44 D1
Vansbro Sweden 60°32N 14°15E 9 F16
Vansittart B. Australia 14°3S 126°17E 60 B4
Vansittart I. Canada 65°50N 84°0W 69 D15
Vanua Balavu Fiji 17°12S 178°55W 59 a
Vanua Levu Fiji 16°33S 179°15E 59 a
Vanua Vatu Fiji 18°22S 179°15W 59 a
Vanuatu ■ Pac. Oc. 15°0S 168°0E 58 C9
Vanwyksvlei S. Africa 30°18S 21°49E 56 D3
Vapi India 20°22N 72°54E 44 D1
Vapnyarka Ukraine 48°32N 28°45E 17 D15
Var → France 43°39N 7°12E 20 E7
Varada → India 15°0N 75°40E 45 G2
Varāmīn Iran 35°20N 51°39E 47 C6
Varāmīn □ Iran 35°18N 51°35E 47 B6
Varanasi India 25°22N 83°0E 43 G10
Varangerfjorden Norway 70°3N 29°25E 8 A23
Varangerhalvøya Norway 70°25N 29°30E 8 A23
Varaždin Croatia 46°20N 16°20E 16 E9
Varberg Sweden 57°6N 12°20E 9 H15
Vardak □ Afghan. 34°0N 68°0E 40 B6
Vardar = Axios → Greece 40°57N 22°35E 23 D10
Varde Denmark 55°38N 8°29E 9 J13
Vardø Norway 70°23N 31°5E 8 A24
Varella, Mui = Nay, Mui Vietnam 12°54N 109°26E 38 F7
Varėna Lithuania 54°12N 24°30E 9 J21
Varese Italy 45°48N 8°50E 20 D8
Varginha Brazil 21°33S 45°25W 95 A6
Varillas Chile 24°0S 70°10W 94 A1
Varkaus Finland 62°19N 27°50E 8 E22
Varna Bulgaria 43°13N 27°56E 23 C12
Varna → India 16°48N 74°32E 44 F2
Värnamo Sweden 57°10N 14°3E 9 H16
Varnjarga = Varangerhalvøya Norway 70°25N 29°30E 8 A23
Vars Canada 45°21N 75°21W 83 A9
Varysburg U.S.A. 42°46N 78°19W 82 D6
Varzaneh Iran 32°25N 52°40E 47 C7
Vasa = Vaasa Finland 63°6N 21°38E 8 E19
Vasa Barris → Brazil 11°10S 37°10W 93 F11
Vasai-Virar India 19°28N 72°48E 44 E1
Vascongadas = País Vasco □ Spain 42°50N 2°45W 21 A4
Vasht = Khāsh Iran 28°15N 61°15E 47 D9
Vasilevichi Belarus 52°15N 29°50E 17 B16
Vasilkov = Vasylkiv Ukraine 50°7N 30°15E 17 C16
Vaslui Romania 46°38N 27°42E 17 E14
Vassar Canada 49°10N 95°55W 71 D9
Vassar U.S.A. 43°22N 83°35W 81 D12
Västerås Sweden 59°37N 16°38E 9 G17
Västerbotten Sweden 64°36N 20°4E 8 D19
Västerdalälven → Sweden 60°30N 15°7E 8 F16
Västervik Sweden 57°43N 16°33E 9 H17
Västmanland Sweden 59°45N 16°20E 9 G17
Vasto Italy 42°8N 14°40E 22 C6
Vasylkiv Ukraine 50°7N 30°15E 17 C16
Vat Phou Laos 14°51N 105°49E 38 E5
Vatersay U.K. 56°55N 7°32W 11 E1
Vatiu = Atiu Cook Is. 20°0S 158°10W 65 J12
Vatnajökull Iceland 64°30N 16°48W 8 D5
Vatra-Dornei Romania 47°22N 25°22E 17 E13
Vatrak → India 23°9N 73°2E 42 H5
Vättern Sweden 58°25N 14°30E 9 G16
Vatu Vara Fiji 17°26S 179°31W 59 a
Vatulele Fiji 18°33S 177°37E 59 a
Vaudreuil-Dorion Canada 45°23N 74°3W 83 A10
Vaughn Mont., U.S.A. 47°33N 111°33W 76 C8
Vaughn N. Mex., U.S.A. 34°36N 105°13W 77 J11
Vaujours L. Canada 55°27N 74°15W 72 A5
Vaupés = Uaupés → Brazil 0°2N 67°16W 92 C5
Vaupés □ Colombia 1°0N 71°0W 92 C4
Vauxhall Canada 50°5N 112°9W 70 C6
Vav India 24°22N 71°31E 42 G4
Vava'u Tonga 18°36S 174°0W 59 c
Vava'u Group Tonga 18°40S 174°0W 59 c
Vavuniya Sri Lanka 8°45N 80°30E 45 K5
Vawkavysk Belarus 53°9N 24°30E 17 B13
Växjö Sweden 56°52N 14°50E 9 H16
Vayalpad India 13°39N 78°38E 45 H4
Vaygach, Ostrov Russia 70°0N 60°0E 26 C7
Veaikevárri = Svappavaara Sweden 67°40N 21°3E 8 C19
Vechte → Neths. 52°34N 6°6E 15 B6
Vedaranniyam India 10°25N 79°50E 45 J4
Vedea → Romania 43°42N 25°41E 17 G13
Vedia Argentina 34°30S 61°31W 94 C3
Veendam Neths. 53°5N 6°52E 15 A6
Veenendaal Neths. 52°2N 5°34E 15 B5
Vefsna → Norway 65°48N 13°10E 8 D15
Vega Norway 65°40N 11°55E 8 D14
Vega U.S.A. 35°15N 102°26W 84 D3
Vega Baja Puerto Rico 18°27N 66°23W 89 d
Vegreville Canada 53°30N 112°5W 70 C6
Vejer de la Frontera Spain 36°15N 5°59W 21 D3
Vejle Denmark 55°43N 9°30E 9 J13
Velachha India 21°26N 73°1E 44 D1
Velanai I. Sri Lanka 9°45N 79°45E 45 K4
Velas, C. Costa Rica 10°21N 85°52W 88 D2
Velasco, Sierra de Argentina 29°20S 67°10W 94 B2
Velddrif S. Africa 32°42S 18°11E 56 D2
Velebit Planina Croatia 44°50N 15°20E 16 F8
Veles Macedonia 41°46N 21°47E 23 D9
Vélez-Málaga Spain 36°48N 4°5W 21 D3
Vélez Rubio Spain 37°41N 2°5W 21 D4
Velhas → Brazil 17°13S 44°49W 93 G10
Velika Kapela Croatia 45°10N 15°5E 16 F8
Velikaya → Russia 57°48N 28°10E 18 C4
Velikaya Kema Russia 45°30N 137°12E 28 B8
Veliki Ustyug Russia 60°47N 46°20E 18 B8
Velikiy Novgorod Russia 58°30N 31°25E 18 C5
Velikiye Luki Russia 56°25N 30°32E 18 C5
Veliko Tŭrnovo Bulgaria 43°5N 25°41E 23 C11
Velikonda Range India 14°45N 79°10E 45 G4
Vellar → India 11°30N 79°36E 45 J4
Velletri Italy 41°41N 12°47E 22 D5
Vellore India 12°57N 79°10E 45 H4
Velsk Russia 61°10N 42°5E 18 B7
Veluwezoom △ Neths. 52°5N 6°0E 15 B6
Velva U.S.A. 48°4N 100°56W 80 A3
Vembanad L. India 9°36N 76°15E 45 K3
Venado Mexico 22°56N 101°6W 86 C4
Venado Tuerto Argentina 33°50S 62°0W 94 C3
Vendée □ France 46°50N 1°35W 20 C3
Vendôme France 47°47N 1°3E 20 C4
Venézia Italy 45°27N 12°21E 22 B5
Venézia, G. di Italy 45°15N 13°0E 22 B5
Venezuela ■ S. Amer. 8°0N 66°0W 92 B5
Venezuela, G. de Venezuela 11°30N 71°0W 92 A4
Vengurla India 15°53N 73°45E 45 G1
Vengurla Rocks India 15°55N 73°22E 45 G1
Venice = Venézia Italy 45°27N 12°21E 22 B5
Venice U.S.A. 27°6N 82°27W 85 H13
Venkatagiri India 14°0N 79°35E 45 H4
Venkatapuram India 18°20N 80°30E 44 E5
Venlo Neths. 51°22N 6°11E 15 C6
Vennachar Junction Canada 45°5N 77°14W 82 A7
Vennesla Norway 58°15N 7°59E 9 G12
Venray Neths. 51°31N 6°0E 15 C6
Ventana, Sa. de la Argentina 38°0S 62°30W 94 D3
Ventersburg S. Africa 28°7S 27°9E 56 C4
Venterstad S. Africa 30°47S 25°48E 56 D4
Ventnor U.K. 50°36N 1°12W 13 G6
Ventoténe Italy 40°47N 13°25E 22 D5
Ventoux, Mt. France 44°10N 5°17E 20 D6
Ventspils Latvia 57°25N 21°32E 9 H19
Ventuarí → Venezuela 3°58N 67°2W 92 C5
Ventucopa U.S.A. 34°50N 119°29W 79 L7
Ventura U.S.A. 34°17N 119°18W 79 L7
Vénus, Pte. Tahiti 17°29S 149°29W 59 d
Venus B. Australia 38°40S 145°42E 63 F4
Venustiano Carranza Mexico 30°25N 115°53W 86 A1
Venustiano Carranza, Presa Mexico 27°30N 100°37W 86 B4
Vera Argentina 29°30S 60°20W 94 B3
Vera Spain 37°15N 1°51W 21 D5
Veracruz Mexico 19°11N 96°8W 87 D5
Veracruz □ Mexico 19°0N 96°15W 87 D5
Veraval India 20°53N 70°27E 42 J4
Verbánia Italy 45°56N 8°33E 20 D8
Vercelli Italy 45°19N 8°25E 20 D8
Verdalsøra Norway 63°48N 11°30E 8 E14
Verde → Argentina 41°56S 65°5W 96 E3
Verde → Goiás, Brazil 18°1S 50°14W 93 G8
Verde → Mato Grosso do Sul, Brazil 21°25S 52°20W 93 H8
Verde → Chihuahua, Mexico 26°39N 107°11W 86 B3
Verde → Jalisco, Mexico 20°42N 103°14W 86 C4
Verde → Oaxaca, Mexico 15°59N 97°50W 87 D5
Verde → Paraguay 23°9S 57°37W 94 A4
Verde → U.S.A. 33°33N 111°40W 77 K8
Verde, Cay Bahamas 23°0N 75°5W 88 B4
Verden Germany 52°55N 9°14E 16 B5
Verdi U.S.A. 39°31N 119°59W 78 F7
Verdun France 49°9N 5°24E 20 B6
Vereeniging S. Africa 26°38S 27°57E 57 C4
Verga, C. Guinea 10°30N 14°10W 52 F3
Vergara Uruguay 32°56S 53°57W 95 C5
Vergemont Cr. → Australia 24°16S 143°16E 62 C3
Vergennes U.S.A. 44°10N 73°15W 83 B11
Veria Greece 40°34N 22°12E 23 D10
Verín Spain 41°57N 7°27W 21 B2
Verkhnetulomskoye Vdkhr. Russia 68°36N 31°12E 8 B24
Verkhnevilyuysk Russia 63°27N 120°18E 27 C13
Verkhniy Baskunchak Russia 48°14N 46°44E 19 E8
Verkhoyansk Russia 67°35N 133°25E 27 C14
Verkhoyansk Ra. = Verkhoyanskiy Khrebet Russia 66°0N 129°0E 27 C13
Verkhoyanskiy Khrebet Russia 66°0N 129°0E 27 C13
Vermilion Canada 53°20N 110°50W 71 C6
Vermilion U.S.A. 41°25N 82°22W 82 E2
Vermilion → Canada 53°22N 110°51W 71 C6
Vermilion B. U.S.A. 29°42N 92°0W 84 G9
Vermilion Bay Canada 49°51N 93°34W 71 D10
Vermilion L. U.S.A. 47°53N 92°26W 80 B7
Vermillion U.S.A. 42°47N 96°56W 80 D5
Vermillion → Canada 47°38N 72°56W 72 C5
Vermont □ U.S.A. 44°0N 73°0W 83 C12
Vernadsky Antarctica 65°0S 64°0W 5 C17
Vernal U.S.A. 40°27N 109°32W 76 F9
Vernalis U.S.A. 37°36N 121°17W 78 H5
Verner Canada 46°25N 80°8W 72 C3
Verneukpan S. Africa 30°0S 21°0E 56 D3
Vernon Canada 50°20N 119°15W 70 C5
Vernon U.S.A. 34°9N 99°17W 84 D5
Vernonia U.S.A. 45°52N 123°11W 78 E3
Vero Beach U.S.A. 27°38N 80°24W 85 H14
Véroia = Veria Greece 40°34N 22°12E 23 D10
Verona Canada 44°29N 76°42W 83 B8
Verona Italy 45°27N 10°59E 22 B4
Vert, C. Senegal 14°45N 17°30W 52 F2
Verulam S. Africa 29°38S 31°2E 57 C5
Verviers Belgium 50°37N 5°52E 15 D5
Veselovskoye Vdkhr. Russia 46°58N 41°25E 19 E7
Vesoul France 47°40N 6°11E 20 C7
Vesterålen Norway 68°45N 15°0E 8 B16
Vestfjorden Norway 67°55N 14°0E 8 C16
Vestmannaeyjar Iceland 63°27N 20°15W 8 E3
Vestvågøya Norway 68°18N 13°50E 8 B15
Vesuvio Italy 40°49N 14°26E 22 D6
Vesuvius, Mt. = Vesuvio Italy 40°49N 14°26E 22 D6
Veszprém Hungary 47°8N 17°57E 17 E9
Vetapalem India 15°47N 80°18E 45 G5
Vetlanda Sweden 57°24N 15°3E 9 H16
Vetlugu → Russia 56°36N 46°4E 18 C8
Vettore, Mte. Italy 42°49N 13°16E 22 C5
Veurne Belgium 51°5N 2°40E 15 C2
Veys Iran 31°30N 49°0E 47 D6
Vezhen Bulgaria 42°50N 24°20E 23 C11
Vi Thanh Vietnam 9°42N 105°26E 39 H5
Viacha Bolivia 16°39S 68°18W 92 G5
Viamão Brazil 30°5S 51°0W 95 C5
Viana Brazil 3°13S 44°55W 93 D10
Viana do Alentejo Portugal 38°17N 7°59W 21 C2
Viana do Castelo Portugal 41°42N 8°50W 21 B1
Vianden Lux. 49°56N 6°12E 15 E6
Viangchan = Vientiane Laos 17°58N 102°36E 38 D4
Vianópolis Brazil 16°40S 48°35W 93 G9
Viaréggio Italy 43°52N 10°14E 22 C4
Vibo Valéntia Italy 38°40N 16°6E 22 E7
Viborg Denmark 56°27N 9°23E 9 H13
Vic Spain 41°58N 2°19E 21 B7
Vicenza Italy 45°33N 11°33E 22 B4
Vich = Vic Spain 41°58N 2°19E 21 B7
Vichada → Colombia 4°55N 67°50W 92 C5
Vichy France 46°9N 3°26E 20 C5
Vicksburg Ariz., U.S.A. 33°45N 113°45W 79 M13
Vicksburg Miss., U.S.A. 32°21N 90°53W 85 E9
Victor India 21°0N 71°30E 42 J4
Victor Harbor Australia 35°30S 138°37E 63 F2
Victoria Argentina 32°40S 60°10W 94 C3
Victoria Canada 48°30N 123°25W 78 B3
Victoria Chile 38°13S 72°20W 96 D2
Victoria Seychelles 4°38S 55°28E 55 b
Victoria Kans., U.S.A. 38°52N 99°9W 80 F4
Victoria Tex., U.S.A. 28°48N 97°0W 84 G6
Victoria □ Australia 37°0S 144°0E 63 F3
Victoria → Australia 15°10S 129°40E 60 C4
Victoria, Grand L. Canada 47°31N 77°30W 72 C4
Victoria, L. Africa 1°0S 33°0E 54 E6
Victoria, L. Australia 33°57S 141°15E 63 E3
Victoria, Mt. Burma 21°14N 93°55E 41 J18
Victoria Beach Canada 50°40N 96°35W 71 C9
Victoria de Durango = Durango Mexico 24°3N 104°39W 86 C4
Victoria de las Tunas = Las Tunas Cuba 20°58N 76°59W 88 B4
Victoria Falls Zimbabwe 17°58S 25°52E 55 H5
Victoria Harbour Canada 44°45N 79°45W 82 B5
Victoria I. Canada 71°0N 111°0W 68 C9
Victoria L. Canada 48°20N 57°27W 73 C8
Victoria Ld. Antarctica 75°0S 160°0E 5 D11
Victoria Pk. Belize 16°48N 88°37W 87 D7
Victoria River Australia 16°25S 131°0E 60 C5
Victoria Str. Canada 69°31N 100°30W 68 D11
Victoria West S. Africa 31°25S 23°4E 56 D3
Victoriaville Canada 46°4N 71°56W 73 C5
Victorica Argentina 36°20S 65°30W 94 D2
Victorville U.S.A. 34°32N 117°18W 79 L9
Vicuña Chile 30°0S 70°50W 94 C1
Vicuña Mackenna Argentina 33°53S 64°25W 94 C3
Vidal U.S.A. 34°7N 114°31W 79 L12
Vidalia U.S.A. 32°13N 82°25W 85 E13
Viddolatno = Vindelälven → Sweden 63°55N 19°50E 8 E18
Vidin Bulgaria 43°59N 22°50E 23 C10
Vidisha India 23°28N 77°53E 42 H7
Vidzy Belarus 55°23N 26°37E 9 J22
Viedma Argentina 40°50S 63°0W 96 E4
Viedma, L. Argentina 49°30S 72°30W 96 F2
Vielsalm Belgium 50°17N 5°54E 15 D5
Vieng Pou Kha Laos 20°41N 101°4E 34 G3
Vienna Canada 42°41N 80°48W 82 D4
Vienna Ill., U.S.A. 37°25N 88°54W 80 G9
Vienna Mo., U.S.A. 38°11N 91°57W 80 F8
Vienne France 45°31N 4°53E 20 D6
Vienne → France 47°13N 0°5E 20 C4
Vientiane Laos 17°58N 102°36E 38 D4
Vientos, Paso de los Caribbean 20°0N 74°0W 89 C5
Vieques Puerto Rico 18°8N 65°25W 89 d
Vierge Pt. St. Lucia 13°49N 60°53W 89 f
Vierzon France 47°13N 2°5E 20 C5
Viet Quang Vietnam 22°30N 104°48E 34 F5
Viet Tri Vietnam 21°18N 105°25E 38 B5
Vietnam ■ Asia 19°0N 106°0E 38 C6
Vieux Fort St. Lucia 13°46N 60°58W 89 f
Vigan Phil. 17°35N 120°28E 37 A6
Vigévano Italy 45°19N 8°51E 20 D8
Vigia Brazil 0°50S 48°5W 93 D9
Vigo Spain 42°12N 8°41W 21 A1
Vihowa Pakistan 31°8N 70°30E 42 D4
Vihowa → Pakistan 31°8N 70°41E 42 D4
Vijayadurg India 16°30N 73°25E 44 F1
Vijayawada India 16°31N 80°39E 44 F5
Vijosë → Albania 40°37N 19°24E 23 D8
Vík Iceland 63°25N 19°1W 8 E4
Vikarabad India 17°20N 77°54E 44 E3
Vikeke = Viqueque E. Timor 8°52S 126°23E 37 F7
Viking Canada 53°7N 111°50W 70 C6
Vikna Norway 64°55N 10°58E 8 D14
Vila da Ribeira Brava C. Verde Is. 16°32N 24°25W 52 b
Vila do Bispo Portugal 37°5N 8°53W 21 D1
Vila Franca de Xira Portugal 38°57N 8°59W 21 C1
Vila Gomes da Costa Mozam. 24°20S 33°37E 57 B5
Vila Nova de Gaia Portugal 41°8N 8°37W 21 B1
Vila Real Portugal 41°17N 7°48W 21 B2
Vila-Real Spain 39°55N 0°3W 21 C5
Vila Real de Santo António Portugal 37°10N 7°28W 21 D2
Vila Velha Brazil 20°20S 40°17W 95 A7
Vilagarcía de Arousa Spain 42°34N 8°46W 21 A1
Vilaine → France 47°30N 2°27W 20 C2
Vilanandro, Tanjona Madag. 16°11S 44°27E 55 H8
Vilanculos Mozam. 22°1S 35°17E 57 B6
Vilanova i la Geltrú Spain 41°13N 1°40E 21 B6
Vilcheka, Ostrov Russia 80°0N 58°31E 26 B6
Vilcheka, Zemlya Russia 80°30N 60°30E 4 A11
Vileyka Belarus 54°30N 26°53E 17 A14
Vilhelmina Sweden 64°35N 16°39E 8 D17
Vilhena Brazil 12°40S 60°5W 92 F6
Viliya = Neris → Lithuania 55°8N 24°16E 9 J21
Viljandi Estonia 58°28N 25°30E 9 G21
Vilkitskogo, Proliv Russia 78°0N 103°0E 27 B11
Vilkovo = Vylkove Ukraine 45°28N 29°32E 17 F15
Villa Abecia Bolivia 21°0S 68°18W 94 A2
Villa Ana Argentina 28°28S 59°40W 94 B4
Villa Angela Argentina 27°34S 60°45W 94 B3
Villa Bella Bolivia 10°25S 65°22W 92 F5
Villa Cañás Argentina 34°0S 61°35W 94 C3
Villa Constitución Argentina 33°15S 60°20W 94 C3
Villa de Arriaga Mexico 21°56N 101°20W 86 C4
Villa de María Argentina 29°55S 63°43W 94 B3
Villa de Méndez Mexico 25°7N 98°34W 87 B5
Villa Dolores Argentina 31°58S 65°15W 94 C2
Villa Gesell Argentina 37°15S 56°55W 94 D4
Villa Guillermina Argentina 28°15S 59°29W 94 B4
Villa Hayes Paraguay 25°5S 57°20W 94 B4
Villa Hidalgo Mexico 24°15N 99°26W 87 C5
Villa Iris Argentina 38°12S 63°12W 94 D3
Villa María Argentina 32°20S 63°10W 94 C3
Villa Mazán Argentina 28°40S 66°30W 94 B2
Villa Montes Bolivia 21°10S 63°30W 94 A3
Villa Ocampo Argentina 28°30S 59°20W 94 B4
Villa Ocampo Mexico 26°27N 105°31W 86 B3
Villa Ojo de Agua Argentina 29°30S 63°44W 94 B3
Villa San Martín Argentina 28°15S 64°9W 94 B3
Villa Unión Mexico 23°12N 106°14W 86 C3
Villacarrillo Spain 38°7N 3°3W 21 C4
Villach Austria 46°37N 13°51E 16 E7
Villagrán Mexico 24°29N 99°29W 87 C5
Villaguay Argentina 32°0S 59°0W 94 C4
Villahermosa Mexico 17°59N 92°55W 87 D6
Villajoyosa Spain 38°30N 0°12W 21 C5
Villalba Spain 43°26N 7°40W 21 A2
Villanueva U.S.A. 35°16N 105°22W 77 J11
Villanueva de la Serena Spain 38°59N 5°50W 21 C3
Villanueva y Geltrú = Vilanova i la Geltrú Spain 41°13N 1°40E 21 B6
Villarreal = Vila-Real Spain 39°55N 0°3W 21 C5
Villarrica Chile 39°15S 72°15W 96 D2
Villarrica Paraguay 25°40S 56°30W 94 B4
Villarrobledo Spain 39°18N 2°36W 21 C4
Villavicencio Argentina 32°28S 69°0W 94 C2
Villavicencio Colombia 4°9N 73°37W 92 C4
Villaviciosa Spain 43°32N 5°27W 21 A3
Villazón Bolivia 22°0S 65°35W 94 A2
Ville-Marie Canada 47°20N 79°30W 72 C4
Ville Platte U.S.A. 30°41N 92°17W 84 F8
Villena Spain 38°39N 0°52W 21 C5
Villeneuve-d'Ascq France 50°38N 3°9E 20 A5
Villeneuve-sur-Lot France 44°24N 0°42E 20 D4
Villiers S. Africa 27°2S 28°36E 57 C4
Villingen-Schwenningen Germany 48°3N 8°26E 16 D5
Villmanstrand = Lappeenranta Finland 61°3N 28°12E 8 F23
Villupuram India 11°59N 79°31E 45 J4
Vilna Canada 54°7N 111°55W 70 C6
Vilnius Lithuania 54°38N 25°19E 9 J21
Vilyuchinsk Russia 52°55N 158°24E 27 D16
Vilyuy → Russia 64°24N 126°26E 27 C13
Vilyuysk Russia 63°40N 121°35E 27 C13
Vilyuyskoye Vdkhr. Russia 63°0N 112°0E 27 C12
Viña del Mar Chile 33°0S 71°30W 94 C1
Vinarós Spain 40°30N 0°27E 21 B6
Vincennes U.S.A. 38°41N 87°32W 80 F10
Vincennes Bay S. Ocean 66°0S 109°0E 5 C8
Vincent U.S.A. 34°33N 118°11W 79 L8
Vinchina Argentina 28°45S 68°15W 94 B2
Vindelälven → Sweden 63°55N 19°50E 8 E18
Vindeln Sweden 64°12N 19°43E 8 D18
Vindhya Ra. India 22°50N 77°0E 42 H7
Vineland U.S.A. 39°29N 75°2W 81 F16
Vinh Vietnam 18°45N 105°38E 38 C5
Vinh Long Vietnam 10°16N 105°57E 39 G5
Vinh Moc Vietnam 21°18N 105°1E 38 B5
Vinh Yen Vietnam 21°21N 105°35E 34 G5
Vinita U.S.A. 36°39N 95°9W 84 C7
Vinkovci Croatia 45°19N 18°48E 23 B8
Vinnitsa = Vinnytsya Ukraine 49°15N 28°30E 17 D15
Vinnytsya Ukraine 49°15N 28°30E 17 D15
Vinnytsya □ Ukraine 49°20N 28°15E 17 D15
Vinson Massif Antarctica 78°35S 85°25W 5 D16
Vinton Calif., U.S.A. 39°48N 120°10W 78 F6
Vinton Iowa, U.S.A. 42°10N 92°1W 80 D7
Vinton La., U.S.A. 30°11N 93°35W 84 F8
Vinukonda India 16°4N 79°45E 44 F4
Violet Valley ✪ Australia 17°10S 127°55E 60 C4
Vioolsdrif S. Africa 28°46S 17°39E 56 C2
Viqueque E. Timor 8°52S 126°23E 37 F7
Virac Phil. 13°30N 124°20E 37 B6
Virachey Cambodia 13°59N 106°49E 38 F6
Virachey △ Cambodia 14°14N 106°55E 38 E6
Virago Sd. Canada 54°0N 132°30W 70 C2
Virajpet = Virarajendrapet India 12°10N 75°50E 45 H2
Viramgam India 23°5N 72°0E 42 H5
Viranşehir Turkey 37°13N 39°45E 46 B3
Virarajendrapet India 12°10N 75°50E 45 H2
Virawah Pakistan 24°31N 70°46E 42 G4
Virden Canada 49°50N 100°56W 71 D8
Vire France 48°50N 0°53W 20 B3
Vírgenes, C. Argentina 52°19S 68°21W 96 G3
Virgin → U.S.A. 36°28N 114°21W 77 H6
Virgin Gorda Br. Virgin Is. 18°30N 64°26W 89 e
Virgin Is. (British) ⊠ W. Indies 18°30N 64°30W 89 e
Virgin Is. (U.S.) ⊠ W. Indies 18°20N 65°0W 89 e
Virgin Islands △ U.S. Virgin Is. 18°21N 64°43W 89 C7
Virginia S. Africa 28°8S 26°55E 56 C4
Virginia U.S.A. 47°31N 92°32W 80 B7
Virginia □ U.S.A. 37°30N 78°45W 81 G14
Virginia Beach U.S.A. 36°49N 76°9W 81 F16
Virginia City Mont., U.S.A. 45°18N 111°56W 76 D8
Virginia City Nev., U.S.A. 39°19N 119°39W 78 F7
Virginia Falls Canada 61°38N 125°42W 70 A3
Virginiatown Canada 48°9N 79°36W 72 C4
Viroqua U.S.A. 43°34N 90°53W 80 D8
Virovitica Croatia 45°51N 17°21E 22 B7
Virpur India 21°51N 70°42E 42 J4
Virton Belgium 49°35N 5°32E 15 E5
Virudunagar India 9°30N 77°58E 45 K3
Vis Croatia 43°4N 16°10E 22 C7

Visalia *U.S.A.* 36°20N 119°18W **78** J7
Visayan Sea *Phil.* 11°30N 123°30E **37** B6
Visby *Sweden* 57°37N 18°18E **9** H18
Viscount Melville Sd.
  Canada 74°10N 108°0W **69** C10
Visé *Belgium* 50°44N 5°41E **15** D5
Vise, Ostrov *Russia* 79°33N 76°50E **26** B8
Višegrad *Bos.-H.* 43°47N 19°17E **23** C8
Viseu *Brazil* 1°10S 46°5W **93** D9
Viseu *Portugal* 40°40N 7°55W **21** B2
Vishakhapatnam *India* 17°45N 83°20E **44** F6
Visnagar *India* 23°45N 72°32E **42** H5
Viso, Mte. *Italy* 44°38N 7°5E **20** D7
Visokoi I. *Antarctica* 56°43S 27°15W **5** B1
Vista *U.S.A.* 33°12N 117°14W **79** M9
Vistula = Wisła ↦
  Poland 54°22N 18°55E **17** A10
Vita *India* 17°17N 74°33E **44** F2
Vitebsk = Vitsyebsk
  Belarus 55°10N 30°15E **18** C5
Viterbo *Italy* 42°25N 12°6E **22** C5
Viti Levu *Fiji* 17°30S 177°30E **59** a
Vitigudino *Spain* 41°1N 6°26W **21** B2
Vitim *Russia* 59°28N 112°35E **27** D12
Vitim ↦ *Russia* 59°26N 112°34E **27** D12
Vitória *Brazil* 20°20S 40°22W **93** H10
Vitória da Conquista
  Brazil 14°51S 40°51W **93** F10
Vitória de Santo Antão
  Brazil 8°10S 35°20W **93** E11
Vitoria-Gasteiz *Spain* 42°50N 2°41W **21** A4
Vitsyebsk *Belarus* 55°10N 30°15E **18** C5
Vittória *Italy* 36°57N 14°32E **22** F6
Vittório Véneto *Italy* 45°59N 12°18E **22** B5
Viveiro *Spain* 43°39N 7°38W **21** A2
Vivian *U.S.A.* 32°53N 93°59W **84** E8
Viwa *Fiji* 17°10S 177°58E **59** a
Vizcaíno, Desierto de
  Mexico 27°30N 113°45W **86** B2
Vizcaíno, Sierra *Mexico* 27°30N 114°0W **86** B2
Vize *Turkey* 41°34N 27°45E **23** D12
Vizianagaram *India* 18°6N 83°30E **44** E6
Vlaardingen *Neths.* 51°55N 4°21E **15** C4
Vladikavkaz *Russia* 43°0N 44°35E **19** F7
Vladimir *Russia* 56°15N 40°30E **18** C7
Vladimir Volynskiy = Volodymyr-
  Volynskyy *Ukraine* 50°50N 24°18E **17** C13
Vladivostok *Russia* 43°10N 131°53E **28** C5
Vlieland *Neths.* 53°16N 4°55E **15** A4
Vlissingen *Neths.* 51°26N 3°34E **15** C3
Vlorë *Albania* 40°32N 19°28E **23** D8
Vltava ↦ *Czech Rep.* 50°21N 14°30E **16** D8
Vo Dat *Vietnam* 11°9N 107°31E **39** G6
Voe *U.K.* 60°21N 1°16W **11** A7
Vogelkop = Doberai, Jazirah
  Indonesia 1°25S 133°0E **37** E8
Vogelsberg *Germany* 50°31N 9°12E **16** C5
Voghera *Italy* 44°59N 9°1E **20** D8
Vohibinany *Madag.* 18°49S 49°4E **55** H9
Vohimarina = Iharana
  Madag. 13°25S 50°0E **55** G10
Vohimena, Tanjon' i
  Madag. 25°36S 45°8E **55** K9
Vohipeno *Madag.* 22°22S 47°51E **55** J9
Voi *Kenya* 3°25S 38°32E **54** E7
Voiron *France* 45°22N 5°35E **20** D6
Voisey B. *Canada* 56°15N 61°50W **73** A7
Vojmsjön *Sweden* 65°0N 16°24E **8** D17
Vojvodina □ *Serbia* 45°20N 20°0E **23** B9
Volborg *U.S.A.* 45°51N 105°41W **76** D11
Volcán de Colima △
  Mexico 19°30N 103°40W **86** D4
Volcano Is. = Kazan-Rettō
  Pac. Oc. 25°0N 141°0E **64** E6
Volda *Norway* 62°9N 6°5E **8** E12
Volga = Privolzhskiy □
  Russia 56°0N 50°0E **26** D6
Volga ↦ *Russia* 46°0N 48°30E **19** E8
Volga Hts. = Privolzhskaya
  Vozvyshennost *Russia* 51°0N 46°0E **19** D8
Volgodonsk *Russia* 47°33N 42°5E **19** E7
Volgograd *Russia* 48°40N 44°25E **19** E7
Volgogradskoye Vdkhr.
  Russia 50°0N 45°20E **19** D8
Volkhov ↦ *Russia* 60°8N 32°20E **18** B5
Volkovysk = Vawkavysk
  Belarus 53°9N 24°30E **17** B13
Volksrust *S. Africa* 27°24S 29°53E **57** C4
Volochanka *Russia* 71°0N 94°28E **27** B10
Volodymyr-Volynskyy
  Ukraine 50°50N 24°18E **17** C13
Vologda *Russia* 59°10N 39°45E **18** C6
Volos *Greece* 39°24N 22°59E **23** E10
Volosovo *Russia* 59°27N 29°32E **9** G23
Volovets *Ukraine* 48°43N 23°11E **17** D12
Volozhin = Valozhyn
  Belarus 54°3N 26°30E **17** A14
Volsk *Russia* 52°5N 47°22E **18** D8
Volta ↦ *Ghana* 5°46N 0°41E **50** F4
Volta, L. *Ghana* 7°30N 0°0 **52** G6
Volta Redonda *Brazil* 22°31S 44°5W **95** A7
Voltaire, C. *Australia* 14°16S 125°35E **60** B4
Volterra *Italy* 43°24N 10°51E **22** C4
Volturno ↦ *Italy* 41°1N 13°55E **22** D5
Volyn □ *Ukraine* 51°15N 24°30E **17** C13
Volzhskiy *Russia* 48°56N 44°46E **19** E7
Vomo *Fiji* 17°30S 177°15E **59** a
Vopnafjörður *Iceland* 65°45N 14°50W **8** D6
Vorkuta *Russia* 67°48N 64°20E **18** A11
Vormsi *Estonia* 59°1N 23°13E **9** G20
Voronezh *Russia* 51°40N 39°10E **19** D6
Võrts järv *Estonia* 58°16N 26°3E **9** G22
Võru *Estonia* 57°48N 26°54E **9** H22
Vosges *France* 48°20N 7°10E **20** B7
Voss *Norway* 60°38N 6°26E **8** F12
Vostok *Antarctica* 78°30S 106°50E **5** D8
Vostok I. *Kiribati* 10°5S 152°23W **65** J12
Votkinsk *Russia* 57°0N 53°55E **18** C9

Votkinskoye Vdkhr.
  Russia 57°22N 55°12E **18** C10
Vouga ↦ *Portugal* 40°41N 8°40W **21** B1
Voyageurs △ *U.S.A.* 48°32N 93°0W **80** A7
Voynitsa *Russia* 65°10N 30°20E **8** D24
Voyvozh *Russia* 62°56N 54°56E **26** C6
Vozhe, Ozero *Russia* 60°45N 39°0E **18** B6
Voznesensk *Ukraine* 47°35N 31°21E **19** E5
Voznesenye *Russia* 61°0N 35°28E **18** B6
Vrangel *Russia* 42°43N 133°5E **28** C6
Vrangelya, Ostrov *Russia* 71°0N 180°0E **27** B18
Vranje *Serbia* 42°34N 21°54E **23** C9
Vratsa *Bulgaria* 43°15N 23°30E **23** C10
Vrbas ↦ *Bos.-H.* 45°8N 17°29E **22** B7
Vrede *S. Africa* 27°24S 29°6E **57** C4
Vredefort *S. Africa* 27°0S 27°22E **56** C4
Vredenburg *S. Africa* 32°56S 18°0E **56** D2
Vredendal *S. Africa* 31°41S 18°35E **56** D2
Vriddhachalam *India* 11°30N 79°20E **45** J4
Vrindavan *India* 27°37N 77°40E **42** F7
Vršac *Serbia* 45°8N 21°30E **23** B9
Vryburg *S. Africa* 26°55S 24°45E **56** C3
Vryheid *S. Africa* 27°45S 30°47E **57** C5
Vu Liet *Vietnam* 18°43N 105°23E **38** C5
Vukovar *Croatia* 45°21N 18°59E **23** B8
Vuktyl *Russia* 63°52N 57°20E **26** C6
Vulcan *Canada* 50°25N 113°15W **70** C6
Vulcan *Romania* 45°23N 23°17E **17** F12
Vulcaneşti *Moldova* 45°41N 28°18E **17** F15
Vulcano *Italy* 38°24N 14°58E **22** E6
Vulkaneshty = Vulcaneşti
  Moldova 45°41N 28°18E **17** F15
Vung Tau *Vietnam* 10°21N 107°4E **39** G6
Vunidawa *Fiji* 17°50S 178°21E **59** a
Vunisea *Fiji* 19°3S 178°10E **59** a
Vyara *India* 21°8N 73°28E **44** D1
Vyartsilya *Russia* 62°8N 30°45E **8** E24
Vyatka = Kirov *Russia* 58°35N 49°40E **18** C8
Vyatka ↦ *Russia* 55°37N 51°28E **18** C9
Vyatskiye Polyany *Russia* 56°14N 51°5E **18** C9
Vyazemskiy *Russia* 47°32N 134°45E **27** E14
Vyazma *Russia* 55°10N 34°15E **18** C5
Vyborg *Russia* 60°43N 28°47E **8** F23
Vychegda ↦ *Russia* 61°18N 46°36E **18** B8
Vychodné Beskydy
  Europe 49°20N 22°0E **17** D11
Vyg-ozero *Russia* 63°47N 34°29E **18** B5
Vylkove *Ukraine* 45°28N 29°32E **17** F15
Vynohradiv *Ukraine* 48°9N 23°2E **17** D12
Vypin *India* 10°10N 76°15E **45** J3
Vyrnwy, L. *U.K.* 52°48N 3°31W **12** E4
Vyshniy Volochek *Russia* 57°30N 34°30E **18** C5
Vyshza = imeni 26 Bakinskikh
  Komissarov
  Turkmenistan 39°22N 54°10E **47** B7
Vyškov *Czech Rep.* 49°17N 17°0E **17** D9
Vytegra *Russia* 61°0N 36°27E **18** B6

W

W.A.C. Bennett Dam
  Canada 56°2N 122°6W **70** B4
Wa *Ghana* 10°7N 2°25W **52** F5
Waal ↦ *Neths.* 51°37N 5°0E **15** C5
Waalwijk *Neths.* 51°42N 5°4E **15** C5
Waanyi-Garawa ◇
  Australia 18°2S 137°33E **62** B2
Wabakimi △ *Canada* 50°43N 89°29W **72** B2
Wabana *Canada* 47°40N 53°0W **73** C9
Wabasca ↦ *Canada* 58°22N 115°20W **70** B5
Wabasca-Desmarais
  Canada 55°57N 113°56W **70** B6
Wabash *U.S.A.* 40°48N 85°49W **81** E11
Wabash ↦ *U.S.A.* 37°48N 88°2W **80** G9
Wabigoon L. *Canada* 49°44N 92°44W **71** D10
Wabowden *Canada* 54°55N 98°38W **71** C9
Wabu Hu *China* 32°20N 116°50E **35** A11
Wabuk Pt. *Canada* 55°20N 85°5W **72** A2
Wabush *Canada* 52°55N 66°52W **73** B6
Waco *U.S.A.* 31°33N 97°9W **84** F6
Waconichi, L. *Canada* 50°8N 74°0W **72** B5
Wad Hamid *Sudan* 16°30N 32°45E **53** E12
Wad Medanî *Sudan* 14°28N 33°30E **53** F12
Wad Thana *Pakistan* 27°22N 66°23E **42** F2
Wadayama *Japan* 35°19N 134°52E **29** G7
Waddeneilanden *Neths.* 53°25N 5°10E **15** A5
Waddenzee *Neths.* 53°6N 5°10E **15** A5
Waddington *Canada* 44°52N 75°12W **83** B9
Waddington, Mt.
  Canada 51°23N 125°15W **70** C3
Waddy Pt. *Australia* 24°58S 153°21E **63** C5
Wadebridge *U.K.* 50°31N 4°51W **13** G3
Wadena *Canada* 51°57N 103°47W **71** C8
Wadena *U.S.A.* 46°26N 95°8W **80** B6
Wadeye *Australia* 14°28S 129°52E **60** B4
Wadgaon *India* 18°44N 73°39E **44** E1
Wadhams *Canada* 51°30N 127°30W **70** C3
Wadhwan *India* 22°42N 71°41E **42** H4
Wadi *India* 17°4N 76°54E **44** F3
Wādī as Sīr *Jordan* 31°56N 35°49E **48** D4
Wadi Halfa *Sudan* 21°53N 31°19E **53** D12
Wādī Rum △ *Jordan* 29°30N 35°20E **48** F4
Wadian *China* 32°42N 112°29E **35** A9
Wadsworth *Nev., U.S.A.* 39°38N 119°17W **76** G4
Wadsworth *Ohio, U.S.A.* 41°2N 81°44W **82** E3
Waegwan *S. Korea* 35°59N 128°23E **33** G15
Wafangdian *China* 39°38N 121°58E **33** E11
Wafrah *Kuwait* 28°33N 47°56E **46** D5
Wagait ◇ *Australia* 13°1S 130°5E **60** B5
Wageningen *Neths.* 51°58N 5°40E **15** C5
Wager B. *Canada* 65°26N 88°40W **69** D14
Wagga Wagga *Australia* 35°7S 147°24E **63** F4
Waghete *Indonesia* 4°10S 135°50E **37** E9
Wagin *Australia* 33°17S 117°25E **61** F2
Wagner *U.S.A.* 43°5N 98°18W **80** D4
Wagon Mound *U.S.A.* 36°1N 104°42W **77** H11
Wagoner *U.S.A.* 35°58N 95°22W **84** D7

Wah *Pakistan* 33°45N 72°40E **42** C5
Wahai *Indonesia* 2°48S 129°35E **37** E7
Wâhid *Egypt* 30°48N 32°21E **48** E1
Wahnai *Afghan.* 32°40N 65°50E **42** C1
Wahoo *U.S.A.* 41°13N 96°37W **80** E5
Wahpeton *U.S.A.* 46°16N 96°36W **80** B5
Wai *India* 17°56N 73°57E **44** F1
Waialua *U.S.A.* 21°34N 158°8W **75** L8
Waiau ↦ *N.Z.* 42°47S 173°22E **59** E4
Waiawe Ganga ↦
  Sri Lanka 6°15N 81°0E **45** L5
Waibeem *Indonesia* 0°30S 132°59E **37** E8
Waigeo *Indonesia* 0°20S 130°40E **37** E8
Waihi *N.Z.* 37°23S 175°52E **59** B5
Waihou ↦ *N.Z.* 37°15S 175°40E **59** B5
Waikabubak *Indonesia* 9°45S 119°25E **37** F5
Waikaremoana, L. *N.Z.* 38°49S 177°9E **59** C6
Waikari *N.Z.* 42°58S 172°41E **59** E4
Waikato ↦ *N.Z.* 37°23S 174°43E **59** B5
Waikelo *Indonesia* 9°24S 119°19E **60** A2
Waikerie *Australia* 34°9S 140°0E **63** E3
Waikokopu *N.Z.* 39°3S 177°52E **59** C6
Waikouaiti *N.Z.* 45°36S 170°41E **59** F3
Waimakariri ↦ *N.Z.* 43°24S 172°42E **59** E4
Waimate *N.Z.* 44°45S 171°3E **59** F3
Wainganga ↦ *India* 18°50N 79°55E **44** E4
Waingapu *Indonesia* 9°35S 120°11E **37** F6
Waini ↦ *Guyana* 8°20N 59°50W **92** B7
Wainwright *Canada* 52°50N 110°50W **71** C6
Wainwright *U.S.A.* 70°38N 160°2W **74** A7
Waiouru *N.Z.* 39°28S 175°41E **59** C5
Waipara *N.Z.* 43°3S 172°46E **59** E4
Waipawa *N.Z.* 39°56S 176°38E **59** C6
Waipiro *N.Z.* 38°2S 178°22E **59** C7
Waipoua Forest *N.Z.* 35°39S 173°33E **59** A4
Waipu *N.Z.* 35°59S 174°29E **59** A5
Waipukurau *N.Z.* 40°1S 176°33E **59** D6
Wairakei *N.Z.* 38°37S 176°6E **59** C6
Wairarapa, L. *N.Z.* 41°14S 175°15E **59** D5
Wairoa *N.Z.* 39°3S 177°25E **59** C6
Waitaki ↦ *N.Z.* 44°56S 171°7E **59** F3
Waitangi *N.Z.* 35°16S 174°5E **59** A5
Waitara *N.Z.* 38°59S 174°15E **59** C5
Waitomo Caves *N.Z.* 38°16S 175°7E **59** C5
Waitsburg *U.S.A.* 46°16N 118°9W **76** C4
Waiuku *N.Z.* 37°15S 174°45E **59** B5
Wajima *Japan* 37°30N 137°0E **29** F8
Wajir *Kenya* 1°42N 40°5E **54** D8
Wakasa *Japan* 35°20N 134°24E **29** G7
Wakasa-Wan *Japan* 35°40N 135°30E **29** G7
Wakatipu, L. *N.Z.* 45°5S 168°33E **59** F2
Wakaw *Canada* 52°39N 105°44W **71** C7
Wakaya *Fiji* 17°37S 179°0E **59** a
Wakayama *Japan* 34°15N 135°15E **29** G7
Wakayama □ *Japan* 33°50N 135°30E **29** H7
Wake Forest *U.S.A.* 35°59N 78°30W **85** D15
Wake I. *Pac. Oc.* 19°18N 166°36E **64** F8
Wakefield *Jamaica* 18°26N 77°42W **88** a
Wakefield *N.Z.* 41°24S 173°5E **59** D4
Wakefield *U.K.* 53°41N 1°29W **12** D6
Wakefield *U.S.A.* 46°29N 89°56W **80** B9
Wakkanai *Japan* 45°28N 141°35E **28** B10
Wakkerstroom *S. Africa* 27°24S 30°10E **57** C5
Wakool *Australia* 35°28S 144°23E **63** F3
Wakool ↦ *Australia* 35°5S 143°33E **63** F3
Wakre *Indonesia* 0°19S 131°5E **37** E8
Wakuach, L. *Canada* 55°34N 67°32W **73** A6
Walagunya ◇ *Australia* 23°10S 120°50E **60** D3
Wałbrzych *Poland* 50°45N 16°18E **16** C9
Walbury Hill *U.K.* 51°21N 1°28W **13** F6
Walcha *Australia* 30°55S 151°31E **63** E5
Walcheren *Neths.* 51°30N 3°55E **15** C3
Walcott *U.S.A.* 41°46N 106°51W **76** F10
Wałcz *Poland* 53°17N 16°27E **16** B9
Waldburg Ra. *Australia* 24°40S 117°35E **61** D2
Walden *Colo., U.S.A.* 40°44N 106°17W **76** F10
Walden *N.Y., U.S.A.* 41°34N 74°11W **83** E10
Waldport *U.S.A.* 44°26N 124°4W **76** D1
Waldron *U.S.A.* 34°54N 94°5W **84** D7
Walebing *Australia* 30°41S 116°13E **61** F2
Wales □ *U.K.* 52°19N 4°43W **13** E3
Wales I. *Canada* 68°1N 86°40W **69** D14
Walgett *Australia* 30°0S 148°5E **63** E4
Walgreen Coast
  Antarctica 75°15S 105°0W **5** D15
Walker *U.S.A.* 47°6N 94°35W **80** B6
Walker, L. *Canada* 50°20N 67°11W **73** B6
Walker L. *Canada* 54°42N 95°57W **71** C9
Walker L. *U.S.A.* 38°42N 118°43W **76** G4
Walkerston *Australia* 21°11S 149°8E **62** b
Walkerton *Canada* 44°10N 81°10W **82** B3
Wall *U.S.A.* 44°0N 102°8W **80** C2
Walla Walla *U.S.A.* 46°4N 118°20W **76** C4
Wallace *Idaho, U.S.A.* 47°28N 115°56W **76** C6
Wallace *N.C., U.S.A.* 34°44N 77°59W **85** D16
Wallaceburg *Canada* 42°34N 82°23W **82** D2
Wallachia = Valahia
  Romania 44°35N 25°0E **17** F13
Wallal *Australia* 26°32S 146°7E **63** D4
Wallam Cr. ↦ *Australia* 28°40S 147°20E **63** D4
Wallambin, L. *Australia* 30°57S 117°35E **61** F2
Wallangarra *Australia* 28°56S 151°58E **63** D5
Wallaroo *Australia* 33°56S 137°39E **63** E2
Wallenpaupack, L.
  U.S.A. 41°25N 75°15W **83** E9
Wallingford *Conn.,*
  U.S.A. 41°27N 72°50W **83** E12
Wallingford *Vt., U.S.A.* 43°28N 72°58W **83** C12
Wallis & Futuna, Îs. □
  Pac. Oc. 13°18S 176°10W **58** C11
Wallowa *U.S.A.* 45°34N 117°32W **76** D5
Wallowa Mts. *U.S.A.* 45°20N 117°30W **76** D5
Walls *U.K.* 60°14N 1°33W **11** A7
Walls of Jerusalem △
  Australia 41°56S 146°15E **63** G4
Wallula *U.S.A.* 46°5N 118°54W **76** C4
Wallumbilla *Australia* 26°33S 149°9E **63** D4

Walmsley L. *Canada* 63°25N 108°36W **71** A7
Walney, I. of *U.K.* 54°6N 3°15W **12** C4
Walnut Canyon △
  U.S.A. 35°15N 111°20W **77** J8
Walnut Creek *U.S.A.* 37°54N 122°4W **78** H4
Walnut Ridge *U.S.A.* 36°4N 90°57W **85** C9
Walpole *Australia* 34°58S 116°44E **61** F2
Walpole *U.S.A.* 42°9N 71°15W **83** D13
Walpole-Nornalup △
  Australia 35°0S 116°45E **61** G2
Walsall *U.K.* 52°35N 1°58W **13** E6
Walsenburg *U.S.A.* 37°38N 104°47W **77** H11
Walsh ↦ *Australia* 16°31S 143°42E **62** B3
Walsingham *Canada* 42°40N 80°31W **82** D4
Waltair *India* 17°44N 83°23E **44** F6
Walter F. George Res.
  U.S.A. 31°38N 85°4W **85** F12
Walterboro *U.S.A.* 32°55N 80°40W **85** E14
Walters *U.S.A.* 34°22N 98°19W **84** H5
Waltman *U.S.A.* 43°4N 107°12W **76** E10
Walton *U.S.A.* 42°10N 75°8W **83** D9
Walton-on-the-Naze *U.K.* 51°51N 1°17E **13** F9
Walvis Bay *Namibia* 23°0S 14°28E **56** B1
Walvisbaai = Walvis Bay
  Namibia 23°0S 14°28E **56** B1
Wamba
  Dem. Rep. of the Congo 2°10N 27°57E **54** D5
Wambardi ◇ *Australia* 16°2S 130°55E **60** C5
Wamego *U.S.A.* 39°12N 96°18W **80** F5
Wamena *Indonesia* 4°4S 138°57E **37** E9
Wampana Karlantijpa ◇
  Australia 17°45S 132°10E **60** C5
Wampaya ◇ *Australia* 17°20S 135°0E **62** B2
Wampsville *U.S.A.* 43°4N 75°42W **83** C9
Wamsutter *U.S.A.* 41°40N 107°58W **76** F10
Wamulan *Indonesia* 3°27S 126°7E **37** E7
Wan Tup *Burma* 21°13N 98°42E **34** G2
Wan Xian *China* 38°47N 115°7E **32** E8
Wana *Pakistan* 32°20N 69°32E **42** C3
Wanaaring *Australia* 29°38S 144°9E **63** D3
Wanaka *N.Z.* 44°42S 169°9E **59** F2
Wanaka, L. *N.Z.* 44°33S 169°7E **59** F2
Wan'an *China* 26°26N 114°49E **35** D10
Wanapitei L. *Canada* 46°45N 80°40W **72** C3
Wandel Sea = McKinley Sea
  Arctic 82°0N 0°0 **4** A7
Wandhari *Pakistan* 27°42N 66°48E **42** F2
Wanding *China* 24°5N 98°4E **34** E2
Wandoan *Australia* 26°5S 149°55E **63** D4
Wandur Marine △ *India* 11°35N 92°40E **45** J11
Wanfu *China* 40°8N 122°38E **33** D12
Wang ↦ *Thailand* 17°8N 99°2E **38** D2
Wang Noi *Thailand* 14°13N 100°44E **38** E3
Wang Saphung *Thailand* 17°18N 101°46E **38** D3
Wang Thong *Thailand* 16°50N 100°26E **38** D3
Wanganella *Australia* 35°6S 144°49E **63** F3
Wanganui *N.Z.* 39°56S 175°3E **59** C5
Wangaratta *Australia* 36°21S 146°19E **63** F4
Wangary *Australia* 34°35S 135°29E **63** E2
Wangcang *China* 32°18N 106°20E **34** A6
Wangcheng *China* 28°22N 112°49E **35** C9
Wangcun *China* 36°41N 117°41E **33** F9
Wangdu *China* 38°40N 115°7E **32** E8
Wangerooge *Germany* 53°47N 7°54E **16** B4
Wangiwangi *Indonesia* 5°22S 123°37E **37** F6
Wangjiang *China* 30°10N 116°42E **35** B11
Wangmo *China* 25°11N 106°5E **34** E6
Wangqing *China* 43°12N 129°42E **33** C15
Wani *India* 20°5N 78°55E **44** D4
Wanimiyn ◇ *Australia* 15°55S 130°49E **60** C5
Wanjina Wunggurr Wilinggin
  Australia 16°0S 127°0E **60** C4
Wankaner *India* 22°35N 71°0E **42** H4
Wanless *Canada* 54°11N 101°21W **71** C8
Wanleweyne *Somalia* 2°37N 44°54E **49** G3
Wanneroo *Australia* 31°42S 115°46E **61** F2
Wanning *China* 18°48N 110°22E **38** C8
Wanon Niwat *Thailand* 17°38N 103°46E **38** D4
Wanqinsha *China* 22°43N 113°33E **31** a
Wanquan *China* 40°50N 114°40E **32** D8
Wanrong *China* 35°25N 110°50E **32** G6
Wanshan *China* 27°30N 109°12E **34** D7
Wanshan Qundao *China* 21°57N 113°45E **31** a
Wansheng *China* 28°57N 106°53E **34** C6
Wantage *U.K.* 51°35N 1°25W **13** F6
Wanxian *China* 30°42N 108°20E **34** B7
Wanyuan *China* 32°4N 108°3E **34** A7
Wanzai *Guangdong, China* 22°12N 113°31E **31** a
Wanzai *Jiangxi, China* 28°7N 114°30E **35** C10
Wapakoneta *U.S.A.* 40°34N 84°12W **81** E11
Wapato *U.S.A.* 46°27N 120°25W **76** C3
Wapawekka L. *Canada* 54°55N 104°40W **71** C8
Wapikopa L. *Canada* 52°56N 87°53W **72** B2
Wapiti ↦ *Canada* 55°5N 118°18W **70** B5
Wappingers Falls
  U.S.A. 41°36N 73°55W **83** E11
Wapsipinicon ↦ *U.S.A.* 41°44N 90°19W **80** E9
Wapusk △ *Canada* 57°46N 93°22W **71** B10
Warakurna *Australia* 24°59S 128°17E **61** D4
Warangal *India* 17°58N 79°35E **44** E4
Waraseoni *India* 21°45N 80°2E **43** J9
Waratah *Australia* 41°30S 145°30E **63** G4
Waratah B. *Australia* 38°54S 146°5E **63** F4
Warburton *Vic.,*
  Australia 37°47S 145°42E **63** F4
Warburton *W. Austral.,*
  Australia 26°8S 126°35E **61** E4
Warburton ◇ *Australia* 26°7S 126°34E **61** E4
Warburton ↦ *Australia* 28°4S 137°28E **63** D2
Warburton Groove
  Australia 28°18S 137°8E **63** A2
Warburton Ra. *Australia* 25°55S 126°28E **61** E4
Ward *N.Z.* 41°49S 174°11E **59** D5
Ward ↦ *Australia* 26°28S 146°6E **63** D4

Ward Mt. *U.S.A.* 37°12N 118°54W **78** H8
Warden *S. Africa* 27°50S 29°0E **57** C4
Wardha *India* 20°45N 78°39E **44** D4
Wardha ↦ *India* 19°57N 79°11E **44** E4
Wardsville *Canada* 42°39N 81°45W **82** D3
Ware *U.K.* 51°49N 0°0 **13** F8
Ware *U.S.A.* 42°16N 72°14W **83** D12
Waregem *Belgium* 50°53N 3°27E **15** D3
Wareham *U.S.A.* 41°46N 70°43W **83** E14
Waremme *Belgium* 50°43N 5°15E **15** D5
Warialda *Australia* 29°29S 150°33E **63** D5
Warin Chamrap
  Thailand 15°12N 104°53E **38** E5
Warkopi *Indonesia* 1°12S 134°9E **37** E8
Warm Springs *U.S.A.* 38°10N 116°20W **77** G5
Warman *Canada* 52°19N 106°30W **71** C7
Warmbad = Bela Bela
  S. Africa 24°51S 28°19E **57** B4
Warmbad *Namibia* 28°25S 18°42E **56** C2
Warminster *U.K.* 51°12N 2°10W **13** F5
Warminster *U.S.A.* 40°12N 75°6W **83** F9
Warmun *Australia* 17°2S 128°12E **60** C4
Warner Mts. *U.S.A.* 41°40N 120°15W **76** F3
Warner Robins *U.S.A.* 32°37N 83°36W **85** E13
Waroona *Australia* 32°50S 115°58E **61** F2
Warora *India* 20°14N 79°1E **44** D4
Warrabri ◇ *Australia* 21°1S 134°19E **62** C1
Warracknabeal *Australia* 36°9S 142°26E **63** F3
Warragul *Australia* 38°10S 145°58E **63** F4
Warrego ↦ *Australia* 30°24S 145°21E **63** E4
Warrego Ra. *Australia* 24°58S 146°0E **62** C4
Warren *Australia* 31°42S 147°51E **63** E4
Warren *Ark., U.S.A.* 33°37N 92°4W **84** E8
Warren *Mich., U.S.A.* 42°28N 83°1W **81** D12
Warren *Minn., U.S.A.* 48°12N 96°46W **80** A5
Warren *Ohio, U.S.A.* 41°14N 80°49W **82** E4
Warren *Pa., U.S.A.* 41°51N 79°9W **82** E5
Warrenpoint *U.K.* 54°6N 6°15W **10** B5
Warrensburg *Mo., U.S.A.* 38°46N 93°44W **80** F7
Warrensburg *N.Y.,*
  U.S.A. 43°29N 73°46W **83** C11
Warrenton *S. Africa* 28°9S 24°47E **56** C3
Warrenton *U.S.A.* 46°10N 123°56W **78** D3
Warri *Nigeria* 5°30N 5°41E **52** G7
Warrington *U.K.* 53°24N 2°35W **12** D5
Warrington *U.S.A.* 30°23N 87°17W **85** F11
Warrnambool *Australia* 38°25S 142°30E **63** F3
Warroad *U.S.A.* 48°54N 95°19W **80** A6
Warruwi *Australia* 11°36S 133°20E **62** A1
Warsak Dam *Pakistan* 34°11N 71°19E **42** B4
Warsaw *Ind., U.S.A.* 41°14N 85°51W **81** E11
Warsaw *N.Y., U.S.A.* 42°45N 78°8W **82** D6
Warsaw *Ohio, U.S.A.* 40°20N 82°0W **82** F3
Warta ↦ *Poland* 52°35N 14°39E **16** B8
Warthe = Warta ↦
  Poland 52°35N 14°39E **16** B8
Waru *Indonesia* 3°30S 130°36E **37** E8
Warud *India* 21°30N 78°16E **44** D4
Warumungu ◇
  Australia 19°15S 134°44E **62** B1
Warwick *Australia* 28°10S 152°1E **63** D5
Warwick *U.K.* 52°18N 1°35W **13** E6
Warwick *N.Y., U.S.A.* 41°16N 74°22W **83** E10
Warwick *R.I., U.S.A.* 41°42N 71°28W **83** E13
Warwickshire □ *U.K.* 52°14N 1°38W **13** E6
Wasaga Beach *Canada* 44°31N 80°1W **82** B4
Wasagaming *Canada* 50°39N 99°58W **71** C9
Wasatch Ra. *U.S.A.* 40°0N 111°30W **76** F8
Wasbank *S. Africa* 28°15S 30°9E **57** C5
Wasco *Calif., U.S.A.* 35°36N 119°20W **79** K7
Wasco *Oreg., U.S.A.* 45°36N 120°42W **76** D3
Waseca *U.S.A.* 44°5N 93°30W **80** C7
Wasekamio L. *Canada* 56°45N 108°45W **71** B7
Wasgomuwa △ *Sri Lanka* 7°45N 81°0E **45** L5
Wash, The *U.K.* 52°58N 0°20E **12** E8
Washago *Canada* 44°45N 79°20W **82** B5
Washburn *N. Dak.,*
  U.S.A. 47°17N 101°2W **80** B3
Washburn *Wis., U.S.A.* 46°40N 90°54W **80** B8
Washim *India* 20°3N 77°0E **44** D3
Washington *U.K.* 54°55N 1°30W **12** C6
Washington *Ga., U.S.A.* 33°44N 82°44W **85** E13
Washington *Ind., U.S.A.* 38°40N 87°10W **80** F10
Washington *Iowa, U.S.A.* 41°18N 91°42W **80** E8
Washington *Mo., U.S.A.* 38°33N 91°1W **80** F8
Washington *N.C., U.S.A.* 35°33N 77°3W **85** D16
Washington *N.J., U.S.A.* 40°46N 74°59W **83** F10
Washington *Pa., U.S.A.* 40°10N 80°15W **82** F4
Washington *Utah, U.S.A.* 37°8N 113°31W **77** H7
Washington □ *U.S.A.* 47°30N 120°30W **76** C3
Washington, Mt.
  U.S.A. 44°16N 71°18W **83** B13
Washington Court House
  U.S.A. 39°32N 83°26W **81** F12
Washington I. *U.S.A.* 45°23N 86°54W **80** C10
Washougal *U.S.A.* 45°35N 122°21W **78** E4
Washpool △ *Australia* 29°22S 152°20E **63** D5
Wasian *Indonesia* 1°47S 133°19E **37** E8
Wasilla *U.S.A.* 61°35N 149°26W **68** C5
Wasior *Indonesia* 2°43S 134°30E **37** E8
Wasiri *Indonesia* 7°30S 126°30E **37** F7
Wāsiţ □ *Iraq* 32°50N 45°50E **46** C5
Waskaganish *Canada* 51°30N 78°40W **72** B4
Waskaiowaka L. *Canada* 56°33N 96°23W **71** B9
Waskesiu Lake *Canada* 53°55N 106°5W **71** C7
Wasserkuppe *Germany* 50°29N 9°55E **16** C5
Waswanipi *Canada* 49°40N 76°29W **72** C4
Waswanipi, L. *Canada* 49°35N 76°40W **72** C4
Watampone *Indonesia* 4°29S 120°25E **37** E6
Watarrka △ *Australia* 24°20S 131°30E **60** D5
Water Park Pt. *Australia* 22°56S 150°47E **62** C5
Water Valley *U.S.A.* 34°10N 89°38W **85** D10
Waterberg Plateau △
  Namibia 20°25S 17°18E **56** B2
Waterberge *S. Africa* 24°10S 28°0E **57** B4
Waterbury *Conn., U.S.A.* 41°33N 73°3W **83** E11
Waterbury *Vt., U.S.A.* 44°20N 72°46W **83** B12

INDEX TO WORLD MAPS Wieluń 173

Waterbury L. *Canada* 58°10N 104°22W 71 B8
Waterdown *Canada* 43°20N 79°53W 82 C5
Waterford *Canada* 42°56N 80°17W 82 D4
Waterford *Ireland* 52°15N 7°8W 10 D4
Waterford *Calif., U.S.A.* 37°38N 120°46W 78 H6
Waterford *Pa., U.S.A.* 41°57N 79°59W 82 E5
Waterford □ *Ireland* 52°10N 7°40W 10 D4
Waterford Harbour *Ireland* 52°8N 6°58W 10 D5
Waterhen L. *Canada* 52°10N 99°40W 71 C9
Waterloo *Ont., Canada* 43°30N 80°32W 82 C4
Waterloo *Qué., Canada* 45°22N 72°32W 83 A12
Waterloo *Ill., U.S.A.* 38°20N 90°9W 80 F8
Waterloo *Iowa, U.S.A.* 42°30N 92°21W 80 D7
Waterloo *N.Y., U.S.A.* 42°54N 76°52W 82 D8
Watersmeet *U.S.A.* 46°16N 89°11W 80 B9
Waterton Lakes △ *Canada* 48°45N 115°0W 70 D6
Watertown *Conn., U.S.A.* 41°36N 73°7W 83 E11
Watertown *N.Y., U.S.A.* 43°59N 75°55W 83 C9
Watertown *S. Dak., U.S.A.* 44°54N 97°7W 80 C5
Watertown *Wis., U.S.A.* 43°12N 88°43W 80 D9
Waterval-Boven = Emgwenya *S. Africa* 25°40S 30°18E 57 C5
Waterville *Canada* 45°16N 71°54W 83 A13
Waterville *Maine, U.S.A.* 44°33N 69°38W 81 C19
Waterville *N.Y., U.S.A.* 42°56N 75°23W 83 D9
Waterville *Pa., U.S.A.* 41°19N 77°21W 82 E7
Waterville *Wash., U.S.A.* 47°39N 120°4W 76 C3
Watervliet *U.S.A.* 42°44N 73°42W 83 D11
Wates *Indonesia* 7°51S 110°10E 37 G14
Watford *Canada* 42°57N 81°53W 82 D3
Watford *U.K.* 51°40N 0°24W 13 F7
Watford City *U.S.A.* 47°48N 103°17W 80 B2
Wathaman → *Canada* 57°16N 102°59W 71 B8
Wathaman L. *Canada* 56°58N 103°44W 71 B8
Watheroo *Australia* 30°15S 116°5E 61 F2
Watheroo △ *Australia* 30°19S 115°48E 61 F2
Wating *China* 35°40N 106°38E 32 G4
Watkins Glen *U.S.A.* 42°23N 76°52W 82 D8
Watling I. = San Salvador I. *Bahamas* 24°0N 74°30W 89 B5
Watonga *U.S.A.* 35°51N 98°25W 84 D5
Watrous *Canada* 51°40N 105°25W 71 C7
Watrous *U.S.A.* 35°48N 104°59W 77 J11
Watsa *Dem. Rep. of the Congo* 3°4N 29°30E 54 D5
Watseka *U.S.A.* 40°47N 87°44W 80 E10
Watson *Canada* 52°10N 104°30W 71 C8
Watson Lake *Canada* 60°6N 128°49W 70 A3
Watsontown *U.S.A.* 41°5N 76°52W 82 E8
Watsonville *U.S.A.* 36°55N 121°45W 78 J5
Wattiwarriganna Cr. → *Australia* 28°57S 136°10E 63 D2
Watuata = Batuata *Indonesia* 6°12S 122°42E 37 F6
Watubela, Kepulauan *Indonesia* 4°28S 131°35E 37 E8
Watubela Is. = Watubela, Kepulauan *Indonesia* 4°28S 131°35E 37 E8
Wau *South Sudan* 7°45N 28°1E 53 G11
Waubamik *Canada* 45°27N 80°1W 82 A4
Waubay *U.S.A.* 45°20N 97°18W 80 C5
Wauchope *N.S.W., Australia* 31°28S 152°45E 63 E5
Wauchope *N. Terr., Australia* 20°36S 134°15E 62 C1
Wauchula *U.S.A.* 27°33N 81°49W 85 H14
Waukarlycarly, L. *Australia* 21°18S 121°56E 60 D3
Waukegan *U.S.A.* 42°22N 87°50W 80 D10
Waukesha *U.S.A.* 43°1N 88°14W 80 D9
Waukon *U.S.A.* 43°16N 91°29W 80 D8
Waupaca *U.S.A.* 44°21N 89°5W 80 C9
Waupun *U.S.A.* 43°38N 88°44W 80 D9
Waurika *U.S.A.* 34°10N 98°0W 84 D6
Wausau *U.S.A.* 44°58N 89°38W 80 C9
Wautoma *U.S.A.* 44°4N 89°18W 80 C9
Wauwatosa *U.S.A.* 43°2N 88°0W 80 D9
Wave Hill = Kalkarindji *Australia* 17°30S 130°47E 60 C5
Wave Rock ⌓ *Australia* 32°26S 118°53E 61 F2
Waveney → *U.K.* 52°35N 1°39E 13 E9
Waverley *N.Z.* 39°46S 174°37E 59 C5
Waverly *Iowa, U.S.A.* 42°44N 92°29W 80 D7
Waverly *N.Y., U.S.A.* 42°1N 76°32W 83 E8
Wavre *Belgium* 50°43N 4°38E 15 D4
Wâw = Wau *South Sudan* 7°45N 28°1E 53 G11
Wāw al Kabīr *Libya* 25°20N 16°43E 53 C9
Wawa *Canada* 47°59N 84°47W 72 C3
Wawanesa *Canada* 49°36N 99°40W 71 D9
Wawona *U.S.A.* 37°32N 119°39W 78 H7
Waxahachie *U.S.A.* 32°24N 96°51W 84 E6
Way, L. *Australia* 26°45S 120°16E 61 E3
Waya *Fiji* 17°19S 177°10E 59 a
Waycross *U.S.A.* 31°13N 82°21W 85 F13
Wayland *U.S.A.* 42°34N 77°35W 82 D7
Wayne *Nebr., U.S.A.* 42°14N 97°1W 80 D5
Wayne *W. Va., U.S.A.* 38°13N 82°27W 81 F12
Waynesboro *Ga., U.S.A.* 33°6N 82°1W 85 E13
Waynesboro *Miss., U.S.A.* 31°40N 88°39W 85 F10
Waynesboro *Pa., U.S.A.* 39°45N 77°35W 81 F15
Waynesboro *Va., U.S.A.* 38°4N 78°53W 81 F14
Waynesburg *U.S.A.* 39°54N 80°11W 81 F13
Waynesville *U.S.A.* 35°28N 82°58W 85 D13
Waynoka *U.S.A.* 36°35N 98°53W 84 C5
Wazirabad *Pakistan* 32°30N 74°8E 42 C6
Waziristan *Pakistan* 33°0N 70°0E 42 C4
We *Indonesia* 5°51N 95°18E 36 C1
Weald, The *U.K.* 51°4N 0°20E 13 F8
Wear → *U.K.* 54°55N 1°23W 12 C6
Weatherford *Okla., U.S.A.* 35°32N 98°43W 84 D5
Weatherford *Tex., U.S.A.* 32°46N 97°48W 84 E6
Weaverville *U.S.A.* 40°44N 122°56W 76 F2
Webb City *U.S.A.* 37°9N 94°28W 80 G6
Webequie *Canada* 52°59N 87°21W 72 B2
Webster *Mass., U.S.A.* 42°3N 71°53W 83 D13
Webster *N.Y., U.S.A.* 43°13N 77°26W 82 C7
Webster *S. Dak., U.S.A.* 45°20N 97°31W 80 C5
Webster City *U.S.A.* 42°28N 93°49W 80 D7
Webster Springs *U.S.A.* 38°29N 80°25W 81 F13
Weda *Indonesia* 0°21N 127°50E 37 D7
Weda, Teluk *Indonesia* 0°20N 128°0E 37 D7
Weddell Abyssal Plain *S. Ocean* 65°0S 20°0W 5 C2
Weddell I. *Falk. Is.* 51°50S 61°0W 96 G4
Weddell Sea *Antarctica* 72°30S 40°0W 5 D1
Wedderburn *Australia* 36°26S 143°33E 63 F3
Wedgeport *Canada* 43°44N 65°59W 73 D6
Wee Waa *Australia* 30°11S 149°26E 63 E4
Weed *U.S.A.* 41°25N 122°23W 76 F2
Weed Heights *U.S.A.* 38°59N 119°13W 78 G7
Weedsport *U.S.A.* 43°2N 76°33W 83 C8
Weedville *U.S.A.* 41°17N 78°30W 82 E6
Weenen *S. Africa* 28°48S 30°7E 57 C5
Weerribben △ *Neths.* 52°47N 5°58E 15 B5
Weert *Neths.* 51°15N 5°43E 15 C5
Wei He → *Hebei, China* 36°10N 115°45E 32 F8
Wei He → *Shaanxi, China* 34°38N 110°15E 32 G6
Weichang *China* 41°58N 117°49E 33 D9
Weichuan *China* 34°20N 113°59E 32 G7
Weiden *Germany* 49°41N 12°10E 16 D7
Weifang *China* 36°44N 119°7E 33 F10
Weihai *China* 37°30N 122°6E 33 F12
Weihui *China* 35°25N 114°3E 32 G8
Weimar *Germany* 50°58N 11°19E 16 C6
Weinan *China* 34°31N 109°29E 32 G5
Weining *China* 26°50N 104°17E 34 D5
Weipa *Australia* 12°40S 141°50E 62 A3
Weir → *Australia* 28°20S 149°50E 63 D4
Weir → *Canada* 56°54N 93°21W 71 B10
Weir River *Canada* 56°49N 94°6W 71 B10
Weirton *U.S.A.* 40°24N 80°35W 82 F4
Weiser *U.S.A.* 44°15N 116°58W 76 D5
Weishan *Shandong, China* 34°47N 117°5E 33 G9
Weishan *Yunnan, China* 25°12N 100°20E 34 E3
Weishan Hu *China* 34°35N 117°14E 33 G9
Weixi *China* 27°10N 99°10E 34 D2
Weixin *China* 27°48N 105°3E 34 D5
Weiyuan *Gansu, China* 35°7N 104°10E 32 G3
Weiyuan *Sichuan, China* 29°35N 104°36E 34 C5
Weizhou Dao *China* 21°0N 109°5E 34 G7
Wejherowo *Poland* 54°35N 18°12E 17 A10
Wekusko L. *Canada* 54°40N 99°50W 71 C9
Welch *U.S.A.* 37°26N 81°35W 81 G13
Welford △ *Australia* 25°5S 143°16E 62 D3
Weligama *Sri Lanka* 5°58N 80°25E 45 M5
Welkom *S. Africa* 28°0S 26°46E 56 C4
Welland *Canada* 43°0N 79°15W 82 D5
Welland → *U.K.* 52°51N 0°5W 13 E7
Wellawaya *Sri Lanka* 6°44N 81°6E 45 L5
Wellesley Is. *Australia* 16°42S 139°30E 62 B2
Wellesley Islands ✿ *Australia* 16°32S 139°23E 62 B2
Wellingborough *U.K.* 52°19N 0°41W 13 E7
Wellington *Australia* 32°35S 148°59E 63 E4
Wellington *Canada* 43°57N 77°20W 82 C7
Wellington *N.Z.* 41°19S 174°46E 59 D5
Wellington *S. Africa* 33°38S 19°1E 56 D2
Wellington *Somst., U.K.* 50°58N 3°13W 13 G4
Wellington *Telford & Wrekin, U.K.* 52°42N 2°30W 13 E5
Wellington *Colo., U.S.A.* 40°42N 105°0W 76 F11
Wellington *Kans., U.S.A.* 37°16N 97°24W 80 G5
Wellington *Nev., U.S.A.* 38°45N 119°23W 78 G7
Wellington *Ohio, U.S.A.* 41°10N 82°13W 82 E2
Wellington *Tex., U.S.A.* 34°51N 100°13W 84 D4
Wellington, I. *Chile* 49°30S 75°0W 96 F2
Wellington, L. *Australia* 38°6S 147°20E 63 F4
Wellington Chan. *Canada* 75°0N 93°0W 69 C13
Wells *U.K.* 51°13N 2°39W 13 F5
Wells *Maine, U.S.A.* 43°20N 70°35W 83 C14
Wells *N.Y., U.S.A.* 43°24N 74°17W 83 C10
Wells *Nev., U.S.A.* 41°7N 114°58W 76 F6
Wells, L. *Australia* 26°44S 123°15E 61 E3
Wells, Mt. *Australia* 17°25S 127°8E 60 C4
Wells Gray ⌓ *Canada* 52°30N 120°15W 70 C4
Wells-next-the-Sea *U.K.* 52°57N 0°51E 12 E8
Wells River *U.S.A.* 44°9N 72°4W 83 B12
Wellsboro *U.S.A.* 41°45N 77°18W 82 E7
Wellsburg *U.S.A.* 40°16N 80°37W 82 F4
Wellsville *N.Y., U.S.A.* 42°7N 77°57W 82 D7
Wellsville *Ohio, U.S.A.* 40°36N 80°39W 82 F4
Wellsville *Utah, U.S.A.* 41°38N 111°56W 76 F8
Wellton *U.S.A.* 32°40N 114°8W 77 K6
Wels *Austria* 48°9N 14°1E 16 D8
Welshpool *U.K.* 52°39N 3°8W 13 E4
Welwyn Garden City *U.K.* 51°48N 0°12W 13 F7
Wem *U.K.* 52°52N 2°44W 12 E5
Wemindji *Canada* 53°0N 78°49W 72 B4
Wemyss *Canada* 44°52N 76°23W 83 B8
Wen Xian *Gansu, China* 32°43N 104°36E 32 H3
Wen Xian *Henan, China* 34°55N 113°5E 32 G7
Wenatchee *U.S.A.* 47°25N 120°19W 76 C3
Wenchang *China* 19°38N 110°42E 38 C8
Wencheng *China* 27°46N 120°4E 35 D13
Wenchi *Ghana* 7°46N 2°8W 52 G5
Wenchow = Wenzhou *China* 28°0N 120°38E 35 D13
Wenchuan *China* 31°22N 103°35E 34 B4
Wenden *U.S.A.* 33°49N 113°33W 79 M13
Wendeng *China* 37°15N 122°5E 33 F12
Wendesi *Indonesia* 2°30S 134°17E 37 E8
Wendover *U.S.A.* 40°44N 114°2W 76 F6
Weng'an *China* 27°5N 107°25E 34 D6
Wengcheng *China* 24°22N 113°50E 35 E9
Wengyuan *China* 24°20N 114°9E 35 E10
Wenling *China* 28°21N 121°20E 35 C13
Wenlock → *Australia* 12°2S 141°55E 62 A3
Wenshan *China* 23°20N 104°18E 34 F5
Wenshang *China* 35°45N 116°30E 32 G9
Wenshui *China* 37°26N 112°1E 32 F7
Wensleydale *U.K.* 54°17N 2°0W 12 C6
Wensu *China* 41°15N 80°10E 30 C5
Wensum → *U.K.* 52°40N 1°15E 12 E8
Wentworth *Australia* 34°2S 141°54E 63 E3
Wentzel L. *Canada* 59°2N 114°28W 70 B6
Wenut *Indonesia* 3°11S 133°19E 37 E8
Wenxi *China* 35°20N 111°10E 32 G6
Wenzhou *China* 28°0N 120°38E 35 D13
Weott *U.S.A.* 40°20N 123°55W 76 F2
Wepener *S. Africa* 29°42S 27°3E 56 C4
Werda *Botswana* 25°24S 23°15E 56 C3
Weri *Indonesia* 3°10S 132°38E 37 E8
Werra → *Germany* 51°24N 9°39E 16 C5
Werrimull *Australia* 34°25S 141°38E 63 E3
Werris Creek *Australia* 31°18S 150°38E 63 E5
Weser → *Germany* 53°36N 8°28E 16 B5
Weslaco *U.S.A.* 26°10N 97°58W 84 H6
Weslemkoon L. *Canada* 45°2N 77°25W 82 A7
Wesleyville *Canada* 49°9N 53°33W 73 C9
Wesleyville *U.S.A.* 42°9N 80°1W 82 D4
Wessel, C. *Australia* 10°59S 136°46E 62 A2
Wessel Is. *Australia* 11°10S 136°45E 62 A2
Wessex *U.K.* 51°0N 2°0W 13 F5
Wessington Springs *U.S.A.* 44°5N 98°34W 80 C4
West *U.S.A.* 31°48N 97°6W 84 F6
West → *U.S.A.* 42°52N 72°33W 83 D12
West Allis *U.S.A.* 43°1N 88°0W 80 D9
West Antarctica *Antarctica* 80°0S 90°0W 5 D15
West Baines → *Australia* 15°38S 129°59E 60 C4
West Bank ■ *Asia* 32°6N 35°13E 48 C4
West Bend *U.S.A.* 43°25N 88°11W 80 D9
West Bengal = Paschimbanga □ *India* 23°0N 88°0E 43 H13
West Berkshire □ *U.K.* 51°25N 1°17W 13 F6
West Beskids = Západné Beskydy *Europe* 49°30N 19°0E 17 D10
West Branch *U.S.A.* 44°17N 84°14W 81 C11
West Branch Susquehanna → *U.S.A.* 40°53N 76°48W 83 F8
West Bromwich *U.K.* 52°32N 1°59W 13 E6
West Burra *U.K.* 60°5N 1°21W 11 A7
West Canada Cr. → *U.S.A.* 43°1N 74°58W 83 C10
West Caroline Basin *Pac. Oc.* 4°0N 138°0E 64 G5
West Chazy *U.S.A.* 44°49N 73°28W 83 B11
West Chester *U.S.A.* 39°58N 75°36W 83 G9
West Coast ⌓ *Namibia* 21°53S 14°14E 56 B1
West Coast △ *S. Africa* 33°13S 18°0E 56 D2
West Columbia *U.S.A.* 29°9N 95°39W 84 G7
West Covina *U.S.A.* 34°4N 117°54W 79 L9
West Des Moines *U.S.A.* 41°35N 93°43W 80 E7
West Dunbartonshire □ *U.K.* 55°59N 4°30W 11 F4
West End *Bahamas* 26°41N 78°58W 88 A4
West Falkland *Falk. Is.* 51°40S 60°0W 96 G4
West Fargo *U.S.A.* 46°52N 96°54W 80 B5
West Fiji Basin *Pac. Oc.* 17°0S 173°0E 64 J9
West Fjord = Vestfjorden *Norway* 67°55N 14°0E 8 C16
West Fork Trinity → *U.S.A.* 32°48N 96°54W 84 E6
West Frankfort *U.S.A.* 37°54N 88°55W 80 G9
West Grand L. *U.S.A.* 45°14N 67°51W 81 C20
West Hartford *U.S.A.* 41°45N 72°44W 83 E12
West Haven *U.S.A.* 41°17N 72°57W 83 E12
West Hazleton *U.S.A.* 40°58N 76°0W 83 F9
West Hurley *U.S.A.* 41°59N 74°7W 83 E10
West Ice Shelf *Antarctica* 67°0S 85°0E 5 C7
West Indies *Cent. Amer.* 15°0N 65°0W 89 D7
West Jordan *U.S.A.* 40°36N 111°56W 76 F8
West Linn *U.S.A.* 45°21N 122°36W 78 E4
West Lorne *Canada* 42°36N 81°36W 82 D3
West Lothian □ *U.K.* 55°54N 3°36W 11 F5
West MacDonnell △ *Australia* 23°38S 132°59E 60 D5
West Mariana Basin *Pac. Oc.* 15°0N 137°0E 64 F5
West Memphis *U.S.A.* 35°8N 90°10W 85 D9
West Midlands □ *U.K.* 52°26N 2°0W 13 E6
West Mifflin *U.S.A.* 40°21N 79°52W 82 F5
West Milford *U.S.A.* 41°8N 74°22W 83 E10
West Milton *U.S.A.* 41°1N 76°50W 82 E8
West Monroe *U.S.A.* 32°31N 92°9W 84 E8
West Newton *U.S.A.* 40°14N 79°46W 82 F5
West Odessa *U.S.A.* 31°50N 102°30W 84 F3
West Palm Beach *U.S.A.* 26°43N 80°3W 85 H14
West Plains *U.S.A.* 36°44N 91°51W 80 G8
West Point *Miss., U.S.A.* 33°36N 88°39W 85 E10
West Point *N.Y., U.S.A.* 41°24N 73°58W 83 E11
West Point *Nebr., U.S.A.* 41°51N 96°43W 80 E5
West Point *Va., U.S.A.* 37°32N 76°48W 81 G15
West Point L. *U.S.A.* 33°8N 85°0W 85 E12
West Pt. = Ouest, Pte. de l' *Canada* 49°52N 64°40W 73 C7
West Pt. *Australia* 35°1S 135°56E 63 F2
West Road → *Canada* 53°18N 122°53W 70 C4
West Rutland *U.S.A.* 43°36N 73°3W 83 C11
West Schelde = Westerschelde → *Neths.* 51°25N 3°25E 15 C3
West Seneca *U.S.A.* 42°51N 78°48W 82 D6
West Siberian Plain *Russia* 62°0N 75°0E 24 B9
West Sussex □ *U.K.* 50°55N 0°30W 13 G7
West-Terschelling *Neths.* 53°22N 5°13E 15 A5
West Valley City *U.S.A.* 40°42N 111°58W 76 F8
West Virginia □ *U.S.A.* 38°45N 80°30W 81 F13
West-Vlaanderen □ *Belgium* 51°0N 3°0E 15 D2
West Walker → *U.S.A.* 38°54N 119°9W 78 G7
West Wyalong *Australia* 33°56S 147°10E 63 E4
West Yellowstone *U.S.A.* 44°40N 111°6W 76 D8
West Yorkshire □ *U.K.* 53°45N 1°40W 12 D6
Westall, Pt. *Australia* 32°55S 134°4E 63 E1
Westbrook *U.S.A.* 43°41N 70°22W 81 D18
Westbury *Australia* 41°30S 146°51E 63 G4
Westby *U.S.A.* 48°52N 104°3W 76 B11
Westend *U.S.A.* 35°42N 117°24W 79 K9
Westerland *Germany* 54°54N 8°17E 16 A5
Westerly *U.S.A.* 41°22N 71°50W 83 E13
Western Australia □ *Australia* 25°0S 118°0E 61 E2
Western Bahr el Ghazâl □ *South Sudan* 7°30N 25°30E 50 F6
Western Cape □ *S. Africa* 34°0S 20°0E 56 D3
Western Dvina = Daugava → *Latvia* 57°4N 24°3E 9 H21
Western Ghats *India* 14°0N 75°0E 45 H2
Western Isles = Eilean Siar □ *U.K.* 57°30N 7°10W 11 D1
Western Sahara ■ *Africa* 25°0N 13°0W 52 D3
Western Samoa = Samoa ■ *Pac. Oc.* 14°0S 172°0W 59 b
Western Sierra Madre = Madre Occidental, Sierra *Mexico* 27°0N 107°0W 86 B3
Westernport *U.S.A.* 39°29N 79°3W 81 F14
Westerschelde → *Neths.* 51°25N 3°25E 15 C3
Westerwald *Germany* 50°38N 7°56E 16 C4
Westfield *Mass., U.S.A.* 42°7N 72°45W 83 D12
Westfield *N.Y., U.S.A.* 42°20N 79°35W 82 D5
Westfield *Pa., U.S.A.* 41°55N 77°32W 82 E7
Westhill *U.K.* 57°9N 2°19W 11 D6
Westhope *U.S.A.* 48°55N 101°1W 80 A3
Westland △ *N.Z.* 43°16S 170°16E 59 E2
Westland Bight *N.Z.* 42°55S 170°5E 59 E3
Westlock *Canada* 54°9N 113°55W 70 C6
Westmar *Australia* 27°55S 149°44E 63 D4
Westmeath □ *Ireland* 53°33N 7°34W 10 C4
Westminster *Calif., U.S.A.* 33°45N 118°0W 79 M8
Westminster *Colo., U.S.A.* 39°50N 105°2W 76 G11
Westminster *Md., U.S.A.* 39°34N 76°59W 81 F15
Westmont *U.S.A.* 40°19N 78°58W 82 F6
Westmoreland *Barbados* 13°13N 59°37W 89 g
Westmorland *U.S.A.* 33°2N 115°37W 79 M11
Weston *Oreg., U.S.A.* 45°49N 118°26W 76 D4
Weston *W. Va., U.S.A.* 39°2N 80°28W 81 F13
Weston I. *Canada* 52°33N 79°36W 72 B4
Weston-super-Mare *U.K.* 51°21N 2°58W 13 F5
Westover *U.S.A.* 40°45N 78°40W 82 F6
Westport *Canada* 44°40N 76°25W 83 B8
Westport *Ireland* 53°48N 9°31W 10 C2
Westport *N.Z.* 41°46S 171°37E 59 D3
Westport *N.Y., U.S.A.* 44°11N 73°26W 83 B11
Westport *Oreg., U.S.A.* 46°8N 123°23W 78 D3
Westport *Wash., U.S.A.* 46°53N 124°6W 78 D2
Westray *Canada* 53°36N 101°24W 71 C8
Westray *U.K.* 59°18N 3°0W 11 B5
Westree *Canada* 47°26N 81°34W 72 C3
Westville *U.S.A.* 39°8N 120°42W 78 F6
Westwood *U.S.A.* 40°18N 121°0W 76 F3
Wetar *Indonesia* 7°48S 126°30E 37 F7
Wetaskiwin *Canada* 52°55N 113°24W 70 C6
Wete *Tanzania* 5°4S 39°43E 54 F7
Wetherby *U.K.* 53°56N 1°23W 12 D6
Wethersfield *U.S.A.* 41°42N 72°40W 83 E12
Wetteren *Belgium* 51°0N 3°53E 15 D3
Wetzlar *Germany* 50°32N 8°31E 16 C5
Wewoka *U.S.A.* 35°9N 96°30W 84 D6
Wexford *Ireland* 52°20N 6°28W 10 D5
Wexford □ *Ireland* 52°20N 6°25W 10 D5
Wexford Harbour *Ireland* 52°20N 6°25W 10 D5
Weyburn *Canada* 49°40N 103°50W 71 D8
Weymouth *Canada* 44°30N 66°1W 73 D6
Weymouth *U.K.* 50°37N 2°28W 13 G5
Weymouth *U.S.A.* 42°13N 70°58W 83 D14
Weymouth, C. *Australia* 12°37S 143°27E 62 A3
Wha Ti *Canada* 63°8N 117°16W 68 E8
Whakaari *N.Z.* 37°30S 177°13E 59 B6
Whakatane *N.Z.* 37°57S 177°1E 59 B6
Whale = Baleine → *Canada* 58°15N 67°40W 73 A6
Whale B. *Burma* 11°37N 98°38E 39 G2
Whale Cove *Canada* 62°10N 92°34W 71 A10
Whales, B. of *Antarctica* 78°0S 160°0W 5 D12
Whalsay *U.K.* 60°22N 0°59W 11 A8
Whangamata *N.Z.* 37°12S 175°53E 59 B5
Whangamomona *N.Z.* 39°8S 174°44E 59 C5
Whanganui △ *N.Z.* 39°17S 174°53E 59 C5
Whangarei *N.Z.* 35°43S 174°21E 59 A5
Whangarei Harb. *N.Z.* 35°45S 174°28E 59 A5
Wharekauri = Chatham Is. *Pac. Oc.* 44°0S 176°40W 64 M10
Wharfe → *U.K.* 53°51N 1°9W 12 D6
Wharfedale *U.K.* 54°6N 2°1W 12 C5
Wharton *N.J., U.S.A.* 40°54N 74°35W 83 F10
Wharton *Pa., U.S.A.* 41°31N 78°1W 82 E6
Wharton *Tex., U.S.A.* 29°19N 96°6W 84 G6
Wharton Basin *Ind. Oc.* 22°0S 92°0E 64 K1
Wheatland *Calif., U.S.A.* 39°1N 121°25W 78 F5
Wheatland *Wyo., U.S.A.* 42°3N 104°58W 76 E11
Wheatley *Canada* 42°6N 82°27W 82 D2
Wheaton *Md., U.S.A.* 39°3N 77°3W 81 F15
Wheaton *Minn., U.S.A.* 45°48N 96°30W 80 C5
Wheelbarrow Pk. *U.S.A.* 37°26N 116°5W 78 H10
Wheeler *Oreg., U.S.A.* 45°41N 123°53W 76 D2
Wheeler *Tex., U.S.A.* 35°27N 100°16W 84 D4
Wheeler → *Canada* 57°2N 67°13W 73 A6
Wheeler L. *U.S.A.* 34°48N 87°23W 85 D11
Wheeler Pk. *N. Mex., U.S.A.* 36°34N 105°25W 77 H11
Wheeler Pk. *Nev., U.S.A.* 38°57N 114°15W 76 G6
Wheeler Ridge *U.S.A.* 35°0N 118°57W 79 L8
Wheelersburg *U.S.A.* 38°44N 82°51W 81 F12
Wheeling *U.S.A.* 40°4N 80°43W 82 F4
Whernside *U.K.* 54°14N 2°24W 12 C5
Whiddy I. *Ireland* 51°41N 9°31W 10 E2
Whim Creek *Australia* 20°50S 117°49E 60 D2
Whiskey Jack L. *Canada* 58°23N 101°55W 71 B8
Whiskeytown-Shasta-Trinity ⌓ *U.S.A.* 40°45N 122°15W 76 F2
Whistleduck Cr. → *Australia* 20°15S 135°18E 62 C2
Whistler *Canada* 50°7N 122°58W 70 C4
Whitby *Canada* 43°52N 78°56W 82 C6
Whitby *U.K.* 54°29N 0°37W 12 C7
White → *Ark., U.S.A.* 33°57N 91°5W 84 E9
White → *Ind., U.S.A.* 38°25N 87°45W 80 F10
White → *S. Dak., U.S.A.* 43°42N 99°27W 80 D4
White → *Tex., U.S.A.* 33°14N 100°56W 84 E4
White → *Utah, U.S.A.* 40°4N 109°41W 76 F9
White → *Vt., U.S.A.* 43°37N 72°20W 83 C12
White → *Wash., U.S.A.* 47°12N 122°15W 78 C4
White, L. *Australia* 21°9S 128°56E 60 D4
White B. *Canada* 50°0N 56°35W 73 C8
White Bird *U.S.A.* 45°46N 116°18W 76 D5
White Butte *U.S.A.* 46°23N 103°18W 80 B2
White City *U.S.A.* 42°26N 122°51W 76 E2
White Cliffs *Australia* 30°50S 143°10E 63 E3
White Hall *U.S.A.* 39°26N 90°24W 80 F8
White Haven *U.S.A.* 41°4N 75°47W 83 E9
White Horse, Vale of *U.K.* 51°37N 1°30W 13 F6
White I. = Whakaari *N.Z.* 37°30S 177°13E 59 B6
White L. *Canada* 45°18N 76°31W 83 A8
White L. *U.S.A.* 29°44N 92°30W 84 G8
White Lake *Canada* 45°21N 76°29W 83 A8
White Mountain Peak *U.S.A.* 37°38N 118°15W 79 H8
White Mts. *Calif., U.S.A.* 37°30N 118°15W 78 H8
White Mts. *N.H., U.S.A.* 44°15N 71°15W 83 B13
White Mts. △ *Australia* 20°43S 145°12E 62 C4
White Nile = Nîl el Abyad → *Sudan* 15°38N 32°31E 53 E12
White Otter L. *Canada* 49°5N 91°55W 72 C1
White Pass *U.S.A.* 46°38N 121°24W 78 D5
White Plains *U.S.A.* 41°2N 73°46W 83 E11
White River *Canada* 48°35N 85°20W 72 C2
White River *U.S.A.* 43°34N 100°45W 80 D3
White Rock *Canada* 49°2N 122°48W 78 A4
White Rock *U.S.A.* 35°50N 106°12W 77 J10
White Russia = Belarus ■ *Europe* 53°30N 27°0E 17 B14
White Sands ⌓ *U.S.A.* 32°46N 106°20W 77 K10
White Sea = Beloye More *Russia* 66°30N 38°0E 18 A6
White Sulphur Springs *Mont., U.S.A.* 46°33N 110°54W 76 C8
White Sulphur Springs *W. Va., U.S.A.* 37°48N 80°18W 81 G13
White Swan *U.S.A.* 46°23N 120°44W 78 D6
Whitecliffs *N.Z.* 43°26S 171°55E 59 E3
Whitecourt *Canada* 54°10N 115°45W 70 C5
Whiteface Mt. *U.S.A.* 44°22N 73°54W 83 B11
Whitefield *U.S.A.* 44°23N 71°37W 83 B13
Whitefish *U.S.A.* 48°25N 114°20W 76 B6
Whitefish B. *U.S.A.* 46°40N 84°55W 72 C3
Whitefish L. *Canada* 62°41N 106°48W 71 A7
Whitefish Pt. *U.S.A.* 46°45N 84°59W 81 B11
Whitegull, L. = Goélands, L. aux *Canada* 55°27N 64°17W 73 A7
Whitehall *Mich., U.S.A.* 43°24N 86°21W 80 D10
Whitehall *Mont., U.S.A.* 45°52N 112°6W 76 D7
Whitehall *N.Y., U.S.A.* 43°33N 73°24W 83 C11
Whitehall *Wis., U.S.A.* 44°22N 91°19W 80 C8
Whitehaven *U.K.* 54°33N 3°35W 12 C4
Whitehorse *Canada* 60°43N 135°3W 70 A1
Whitemark *Australia* 40°7S 148°3E 63 G4
Whiteriver *U.S.A.* 33°50N 109°58W 77 K9
Whitesand → *Canada* 60°9N 115°45W 70 A5
Whitesands *S. Africa* 34°23S 20°50E 56 D3
Whitesboro *N.Y., U.S.A.* 43°7N 75°18W 83 C9
Whitesboro *Tex., U.S.A.* 33°39N 96°54W 84 E6
Whiteshell ⌓ *Canada* 50°0N 95°40W 71 D9
Whiteville *U.S.A.* 34°20N 78°42W 85 D15
Whitewater *U.S.A.* 42°50N 88°44W 80 D9
Whitewater Baldy *U.S.A.* 33°20N 108°39W 77 K9
Whitewater L. *Canada* 50°50N 89°10W 72 B2
Whitewood *Australia* 21°28S 143°30E 62 C3
Whitewood *Canada* 50°20N 102°20W 71 C8
Whithorn *U.K.* 54°44N 4°26W 11 G4
Whitianga *N.Z.* 36°47S 175°41E 59 B5
Whitman *U.S.A.* 42°5N 70°56W 83 D14
Whitmore Mts. *Antarctica* 82°35S 104°30W 5 E15
Whitney *Canada* 45°31N 78°14W 82 A6
Whitney, Mt. *U.S.A.* 36°35N 118°18W 78 J8
Whitney Point *U.S.A.* 42°20N 75°58W 83 D9
Whitstable *U.K.* 51°21N 1°3E 13 F9
Whitsunday I. *Australia* 20°15S 149°4E 62 b
Whitsunday Islands △ *Australia* 20°15S 149°0E 62 b
Whittier *U.S.A.* 60°47N 148°41W 74 C10
Whittlesea *Australia* 37°27S 145°9E 63 F4
Wholdaia L. *Canada* 60°43N 104°20W 71 A8
Whyalla *Australia* 33°2S 137°30E 63 E2
Wiang Kosai △ *Thailand* 17°54N 99°29E 38 D2
Wiang Sa *Thailand* 18°34N 100°45E 38 C3
Wiarton *Canada* 44°40N 81°10W 82 B3
Wiay *U.K.* 57°24N 7°13W 11 D1
Wibaux *U.S.A.* 46°59N 104°11W 76 C11
Wichian Buri *Thailand* 15°39N 101°7E 38 E3
Wichita *U.S.A.* 37°42N 97°20W 80 G5
Wichita Falls *U.S.A.* 33°54N 98°30W 84 E5
Wick *U.K.* 58°26N 3°5W 11 C5
Wickenburg *U.S.A.* 33°58N 112°44W 77 K7
Wickepin *Australia* 32°50S 117°30E 61 F2
Wickham *Australia* 20°42S 117°11E 60 D2
Wickham, C. *Australia* 39°35S 143°57E 63 F3
Wickliffe *U.S.A.* 41°36N 81°28W 82 E3
Wicklow *Ireland* 52°59N 6°3W 10 D5
Wicklow □ *Ireland* 52°57N 6°25W 10 D5
Wicklow Hd. *Ireland* 52°58N 6°0W 10 D6
Wicklow Mts. *Ireland* 52°58N 6°26W 10 C5
Wicklow Mts. △ *Ireland* 53°6N 6°21W 10 C5
Widgeegoara Cr. → *Australia* 28°51S 146°34E 63 D4
Widgiemooltha *Australia* 31°30S 121°34E 61 F3
Widnes *U.K.* 53°23N 2°45W 12 D5
Wieluń *Poland* 51°15N 18°34E 17 C10

Wiener Neustadt Austria 47°49N 16°16E 16 E9
Wiesbaden Germany 50°4N 8°14E 16 C5
Wigan U.K. 53°33N 2°38W 12 D5
Wiggins Colo., U.S.A. 40°14N 104°4W 76 F11
Wiggins Miss., U.S.A. 30°51N 89°8W 85 F10
Wight, I. of U.K. 50°41N 1°17W 13 G6
Wigston U.K. 52°35N 1°6W 13 E6
Wigton U.K. 54°50N 3°10W 12 C4
Wigtown U.K. 54°53N 4°27W 11 G4
Wigtown B. U.K. 54°46N 4°15W 11 G4
Wik and Wikway People ◊
 Australia 13°55S 142°28E 62 A3
Wilber U.S.A. 40°29N 96°58W 80 E5
Wilberforce Canada 45°2N 78°13W 82 A6
Wilberforce, C. Australia 11°54S 136°35E 62 A2
Wilburton U.S.A. 34°55N 95°19W 84 D7
Wilcannia Australia 31°30S 143°26E 63 E3
Wilcox U.S.A. 41°35N 78°41W 82 E6
Wildomar U.S.A. 33°36N 117°16W 79 M9
Wildrose U.S.A. 36°14N 117°11W 79 J9
Wildspitze Austria 46°53N 10°53E 16 E6
Wilge → S. Africa 27°3S 28°20E 57 C4
Wilhelm II Coast Antarctica 68°0S 90°0E 5 C7
Wilhelmshaven Germany 53°31N 8°7E 16 B5
Wilhelmstal Namibia 21°58S 16°21E 56 B2
Wilis Indonesia 7°51S 111°48E 37 G15
Wilkes-Barre U.S.A. 41°15N 75°53W 83 E9
Wilkes Land Antarctica 69°0S 120°0E 5 D9
Wilkie Canada 52°27N 108°42W 71 C7
Wilkins Ice Shelf
 Antarctica 70°30S 72°0W 5 C17
Wilkinsburg U.S.A. 40°26N 79°52W 82 F5
Wilkinson Lakes
 Australia 29°40S 132°39E 61 E5
Willandra Creek →
 Australia 33°22S 145°52E 63 E4
Willapa B. U.S.A. 46°40N 124°0W 78 D3
Willapa Hills U.S.A. 46°35N 123°25W 78 D3
Willard U.S.A. 41°3N 82°44W 82 E2
Willare Bridge Roadhouse
 Australia 17°43S 123°38E 60 C3
Willcox U.S.A. 32°15N 109°50W 77 K9
Willemstad Curaçao 12°5N 68°55W 89 D6
William → Canada 59°8N 109°19W 71 B7
William 'Bill' Dannelly Res.
 U.S.A. 32°6N 87°24W 85 E11
William Creek Australia 28°58S 136°22E 63 D2
Williams Australia 33°2S 116°52E 61 F2
Williams Ariz., U.S.A. 35°15N 112°11W 77 J7
Williams Calif., U.S.A. 39°9N 122°9W 78 F4
Williams Harbour
 Canada 52°33N 55°47W 73 B8
Williams Lake Canada 52°10N 122°10W 70 C4
Williamsburg Ky.,
 U.S.A. 36°44N 84°10W 81 G11
Williamsburg Pa., U.S.A. 40°28N 78°12W 82 F6
Williamsburg Va.,
 U.S.A. 37°16N 76°43W 81 G15
Williamson N.Y., U.S.A. 43°14N 77°11W 82 C7
Williamson W. Va.,
 U.S.A. 37°41N 82°17W 81 G12
Williamsport U.S.A. 41°15N 77°1W 82 E7
Williamston U.S.A. 35°51N 77°4W 85 D16
Williamstown Ky.,
 U.S.A. 38°38N 84°34W 81 F11
Williamstown Mass.,
 U.S.A. 42°43N 73°12W 83 D11
Williamstown N.Y.,
 U.S.A. 43°26N 75°53W 83 C9
Willimantic U.S.A. 41°43N 72°13W 83 E12
Willingboro U.S.A. 40°3N 74°54W 81 E16
Williston S. Africa 31°20S 20°53E 56 D3
Williston Fla., U.S.A. 29°23N 82°27W 85 G13
Williston N. Dak., U.S.A. 48°9N 103°37W 80 A2
Williston L. Canada 56°0N 124°0W 70 B4
Willits U.S.A. 39°25N 123°21W 76 G2
Willmar U.S.A. 45°7N 95°3W 80 C6
Willmore Wilderness △
 Canada 53°45N 119°30W 70 C5
Willoughby U.S.A. 41°39N 81°24W 82 E3
Willow Bunch Canada 49°20N 105°35W 71 D7
Willow L. Canada 62°10N 119°8W 70 A5
Willow Wall, The China 42°10N 122°0E 33 C12
Willowick U.S.A. 41°38N 81°28W 82 E3
Willowlake → Canada 62°42N 123°8W 70 A4
Willowmore S. Africa 33°15S 23°30E 56 E3
Willowvale = Gatyana
 S. Africa 32°16S 28°31E 57 E4
Wills, L. Australia 21°25S 128°51E 60 D4
Wills Cr. → Australia 22°43S 140°2E 62 C3
Willsboro U.S.A. 44°21N 73°24W 83 B11
Willunga Australia 35°15S 138°30E 63 F2
Wilmington Australia 32°39S 138°7E 63 E2
Wilmington Del., U.S.A. 39°45N 75°33W 81 F16
Wilmington N.C.,
 U.S.A. 34°14N 77°55W 85 D16
Wilmington Ohio,
 U.S.A. 39°27N 83°50W 81 F12
Wilmington Vt., U.S.A. 42°52N 72°52W 83 D12
Wilmslow U.K. 53°19N 2°13W 12 D5
Wilpattu △ Sri Lanka 8°20N 79°50E 45 K4
Wilpena Cr. → Australia 31°25S 139°29E 63 E2
Wilsall U.S.A. 45°59N 110°38W 76 D8
Wilson N.C., U.S.A. 35°44N 77°55W 85 D16
Wilson N.Y., U.S.A. 43°19N 78°50W 82 C6
Wilson Pa., U.S.A. 40°41N 75°15W 83 F9
Wilson → Australia 16°48S 128°16E 60 C4
Wilson Bluff Australia 31°41S 129°0E 61 F4
Wilson Inlet Australia 35°0S 117°22E 61 G2
Wilsons Promontory
 Australia 38°59S 146°23E 63 F4
Wilton U.S.A. 47°10N 100°47W 80 B3
Wilton → Australia 14°45S 134°33E 62 A1
Wiltshire □ U.K. 51°18N 1°53W 13 F6
Wiltz Lux. 49°57N 5°55E 15 E5
Wiluna Australia 26°36S 120°14E 61 E3
Wimborne Minster U.K. 50°48N 1°59W 13 G6

Wimmera → Australia 36°8S 141°56E 63 F3
Winburg S. Africa 28°30S 27°2E 56 C4
Winchendon U.S.A. 42°41N 72°3W 83 D12
Winchester U.K. 51°4N 1°18W 13 F6
Winchester Idaho,
 U.S.A. 46°14N 116°38W 76 C5
Winchester Ind., U.S.A. 40°10N 84°59W 81 E11
Winchester Ky., U.S.A. 37°59N 84°11W 81 G11
Winchester N.H., U.S.A. 42°46N 72°23W 83 D12
Winchester Tenn., U.S.A. 35°11N 86°7W 85 D11
Winchester Va., U.S.A. 39°11N 78°10W 81 F14
Wind → U.S.A. 43°12N 108°12W 76 E9
Wind Cave △ U.S.A. 43°32N 103°17W 80 D2
Wind River Range
 U.S.A. 43°0N 109°30W 76 E9
Windamere, L. Australia 32°48S 149°51E 63 B4
Windau = Ventspils
 Latvia 57°25N 21°32E 9 H19
Windber U.S.A. 40°14N 78°50W 82 F6
Winder U.S.A. 34°0N 83°45W 85 D13
Windermere U.K. 54°23N 2°55W 12 C5
Windhoek Namibia 22°35S 17°4E 56 B2
Windidda ◊ Australia 26°23S 122°12E 61 E3
Windjana Gorge △
 Australia 17°51S 125°0E 60 C3
Windom U.S.A. 43°52N 95°7W 80 D6
Windorah Australia 25°24S 142°36E 62 D3
Window Rock U.S.A. 35°41N 109°3W 77 J9
Windrush → U.K. 51°43N 1°24W 13 F6
Windsor Australia 33°37S 150°50E 63 E5
Windsor N.S., Canada 44°59N 64°5W 73 D7
Windsor Ont., Canada 42°18N 83°0W 82 D2
Windsor U.K. 51°29N 0°36W 13 F7
Windsor Calif., U.S.A. 38°33N 122°49W 78 G4
Windsor Colo., U.S.A. 40°29N 104°54W 76 F11
Windsor Conn., U.S.A. 41°50N 72°39W 83 E12
Windsor Mo., U.S.A. 38°32N 93°31W 80 F7
Windsor N.Y., U.S.A. 42°5N 75°37W 83 D9
Windsor Vt., U.S.A. 43°29N 72°24W 83 C12
Windsor & Maidenhead □
 U.K. 51°29N 0°40W 13 F7
Windsorton S. Africa 28°16S 24°44E 56 C3
Windward Is. W. Indies 13°0N 61°0W 89 D7
Windward Passage = Vientos,
 Paso de los Caribbean 20°0N 74°0W 89 C5
Winefred L. Canada 55°30N 110°30W 71 B6
Winfield U.S.A. 37°15N 96°59W 80 G6
Wingate Mts. Australia 14°25S 130°40E 60 B5
Wingellina = Irruntyju
 Australia 26°3S 128°56E 61 E4
Wingham Australia 31°48S 152°22E 63 E5
Wingham Canada 43°55N 81°20W 82 D3
Winisk → Canada 55°17N 85°5W 72 A2
Winisk L. Canada 52°55N 87°22W 72 B2
Wink U.S.A. 31°45N 103°9W 84 F3
Winkler Canada 49°10N 97°56W 71 D9
Winlock U.S.A. 46°30N 122°56W 78 D4
Winneba Ghana 5°25N 0°36W 52 G5
Winnebago, L. U.S.A. 44°0N 88°26W 80 D9
Winnecke Cr. →
 Australia 18°35S 131°34E 60 C5
Winnemucca U.S.A. 40°58N 117°44W 76 F5
Winnemucca L. U.S.A. 40°7N 119°21W 76 F4
Winner U.S.A. 43°22N 99°52W 80 D4
Winnett U.S.A. 47°0N 108°21W 76 C9
Winnfield U.S.A. 31°56N 92°38W 84 F8
Winnibigoshish, L.
 U.S.A. 47°27N 94°13W 80 B6
Winnipeg Canada 49°54N 97°9W 71 D9
Winnipeg → Canada 50°38N 96°19W 71 C9
Winnipeg, L. Canada 52°0N 97°0W 71 C9
Winnipeg Beach Canada 50°30N 96°58W 71 C9
Winnipegosis Canada 51°39N 99°55W 71 C9
Winnipegosis L. Canada 52°30N 100°0W 71 C9
Winnipesaukee, L.
 U.S.A. 43°38N 71°21W 83 C13
Winnisquam L. U.S.A. 43°33N 71°31W 83 C13
Winnsboro La., U.S.A. 32°10N 91°43W 84 E9
Winnsboro S.C., U.S.A. 34°23N 81°5W 85 D14
Winnsboro Tex., U.S.A. 32°58N 95°17W 84 E7
Winokapau, L. Canada 53°15N 62°50W 73 B7
Winona Minn., U.S.A. 44°3N 91°39W 80 C8
Winona Miss., U.S.A. 33°29N 89°44W 85 E10
Winooski U.S.A. 44°29N 73°11W 83 B11
Winooski → U.S.A. 44°32N 73°17W 83 B11
Winschoten Neths. 53°9N 7°3E 15 A7
Winsford U.K. 53°12N 2°31W 12 D5
Winslow = Bainbridge Island
 U.S.A. 47°38N 122°32W 78 C4
Winslow U.S.A. 35°2N 110°42W 77 J8
Winsted U.S.A. 41°55N 73°4W 83 E11
Winston-Salem U.S.A. 36°6N 80°15W 85 C14
Winter Garden U.S.A. 28°34N 81°35W 85 G14
Winter Haven U.S.A. 28°1N 81°44W 85 G14
Winter Park U.S.A. 28°36N 81°20W 85 G14
Winterhaven U.S.A. 32°44N 114°38W 79 N12
Winters U.S.A. 38°32N 121°58W 78 G5
Winterset U.S.A. 41°20N 94°1W 80 E6
Wintersville U.S.A. 40°23N 80°42W 82 F4
Winterswijk Neths. 51°58N 6°43E 15 C6
Winterthur Switz. 47°30N 8°44E 20 C8
Winthrop U.S.A. 48°28N 120°10W 76 B3
Winton Australia 22°24S 143°3E 62 C3
Winton N.Z. 46°8S 168°20E 59 G2
Wirlyajarrayi ◊
 Australia 21°45S 132°35E 60 D5
Wirrulla Australia 32°24S 134°31E 63 E1
Wisbech U.K. 52°41N 0°9E 13 E8
Wisconsin □ U.S.A. 44°45N 89°30W 80 C9
Wisconsin → U.S.A. 43°0N 91°15W 80 D8
Wisconsin Rapids U.S.A. 44°23N 89°49W 80 C9
Wisdom U.S.A. 45°37N 113°27W 76 D7
Wiseman U.S.A. 67°25N 150°6W 74 B9
Wishaw U.K. 55°46N 3°54W 11 F5
Wishek U.S.A. 46°16N 99°33W 80 B4
Wisła → Poland 54°22N 18°55E 17 A10
Wismar Germany 53°54N 11°29E 16 B6

Wisner U.S.A. 41°59N 96°55W 80 E5
Witbank = eMalahleni
 S. Africa 25°51S 29°14E 57 C4
Witches Gorge = Wu Xia
 China 31°2N 110°10E 35 B8
Witdraai S. Africa 26°58S 20°48E 56 C3
Witham U.K. 51°48N 0°40E 13 F8
Witham → U.K. 52°59N 0°2W 12 E7
Withernsea U.K. 53°44N 0°1E 12 D8
Witjira △ Australia 26°22S 135°37E 63 D2
Witless Bay Canada 47°17N 52°50W 73 C9
Witney U.K. 51°48N 1°28W 13 F6
Witnossob → Namibia 23°55S 18°45E 56 C3
Witriver S. Africa 25°20S 31°0E 57 C5
Wittenberge Germany 53°0N 11°45E 16 B6
Wittenoom Australia 22°15S 118°20E 60 D2
Witvlei Namibia 22°23S 18°32E 56 B2
Wiwon N. Korea 40°54N 126°3E 33 D14
Wkra → Poland 52°27N 20°44E 17 B11
Wlingi Indonesia 8°5S 112°25E 37 H15
Włocławek Poland 52°40N 19°3E 17 B10
Wlodawa Poland 51°33N 23°31E 17 C12
Wodian China 32°50N 112°35E 32 H7
Wodonga Australia 36°5S 146°50E 63 F4
Woinbogoin China 32°51N 98°39E 34 A2
Wokam Indonesia 5°45S 134°28E 37 F8
Woking U.K. 51°19N 0°34W 13 F7
Wokingham U.K. 51°24N 0°49W 13 F7
Wokingham □ U.K. 51°25N 0°51W 13 F7
Wolf → Canada 60°17N 132°33W 70 A2
Wolf Creek U.S.A. 47°0N 112°4W 76 C7
Wolf L. Canada 60°24N 131°40W 70 A2
Wolf Point U.S.A. 48°5N 105°39W 76 B11
Wolfe Creek Crater △
 Australia 19°10S 127°47E 60 C4
Wolfe I. Canada 44°7N 76°20W 83 B8
Wolfeboro U.S.A. 43°35N 71°13W 83 C13
Wolfsberg Austria 46°50N 14°52E 16 E8
Wolfsburg Germany 52°25N 10°48E 16 B6
Wolin Poland 53°50N 14°37E 16 B8
Wollaston, Is. Chile 55°40S 67°30W 96 H3
Wollaston L. Canada 58°7N 103°10W 71 B8
Wollaston Lake Canada 58°3N 103°33W 71 B8
Wollaston Pen. Canada 69°30N 115°0W 68 D9
Wollongong Australia 34°25S 150°54E 63 E5
Wolmaransstad S. Africa 27°12S 25°59E 56 C4
Wolseley S. Africa 33°26S 19°7E 56 D2
Wolsey U.S.A. 44°25N 98°28W 80 C4
Wolstenholme, C.
 Canada 62°35N 77°30W 66 C12
Wolvega Neths. 52°52N 6°0E 15 B6
Wolverhampton U.K. 52°35N 2°7W 13 E5
Wondai Australia 26°20S 151°49E 63 D5
Wongalarroo L. Australia 31°32S 144°0E 63 E3
Wongan Hills Australia 30°51S 116°37E 61 F2
Wonju S. Korea 37°22N 127°58E 33 F14
Wonosari Indonesia 7°58S 110°36E 37 G14
Wonosobo Indonesia 7°22S 109°54E 37 G13
Wonowon Canada 56°44N 121°48W 70 B4
Wŏnsan N. Korea 39°11N 127°27E 33 E14
Wonthaggi Australia 38°37S 145°37E 63 F4
Wood Buffalo △ Canada 59°0N 112°0W 70 B6
Wood Is. Australia 16°24S 123°19E 60 C3
Wood L. Canada 55°17N 103°17W 71 B8
Woodah, I. Australia 13°27S 136°10E 62 A2
Woodbourne U.S.A. 41°46N 74°36W 83 E10
Woodbridge U.S.A. 52°6N 1°20E 13 E9
Woodburn Australia 29°6S 153°23E 63 A5
Woodburn U.S.A. 45°9N 122°51W 76 D2
Woodenbong Australia 28°24S 152°39E 63 D5
Woodend Australia 37°20S 144°33E 63 F3
Woodford Australia 26°58S 152°47E 63 D5
Woodfords U.S.A. 38°47N 119°50W 78 G7
Woodlake U.S.A. 36°25N 119°6W 78 J7
Woodland Calif., U.S.A. 38°41N 121°46W 78 G5
Woodland Maine, U.S.A. 45°9N 67°25W 81 C20
Woodland Wash., U.S.A. 45°54N 122°45W 78 E4
Woodland Caribou △
 Canada 51°0N 94°45W 71 C10
Woodlands, The U.S.A. 30°9N 95°29W 84 F7
Woodonga Australia 36°10S 146°50E 63 F4
Woodroffe, Mt. Australia 26°20S 131°45E 61 E5
Woods, L. Australia 17°50S 133°30E 62 B1
Woods, L. of the
 N. Amer. 49°15N 94°45W 71 D10
Woods Bay Canada 45°8N 79°59W 82 A5
Woodstock Australia 19°35S 146°50E 62 B4
Woodstock N.B., Canada 46°11N 67°37W 73 C6
Woodstock Ont., Canada 43°10N 80°45W 82 C4
Woodstock U.K. 51°51N 1°20W 13 F6
Woodstock Ill., U.S.A. 42°19N 88°27W 80 D9
Woodstock N.Y., U.S.A. 42°2N 74°7W 83 D10
Woodstock Vt., U.S.A. 43°37N 72°31W 83 C12
Woodsville U.S.A. 44°9N 72°2W 83 B13
Woodville N.Z. 40°20S 175°53E 59 D5
Woodville Miss., U.S.A. 31°6N 91°18W 84 F9
Woodville Tex., U.S.A. 30°47N 94°25W 84 F7
Woodward U.S.A. 36°26N 99°24W 84 C5
Woody → Canada 52°31N 100°51W 71 C8
Woody U.S.A. 35°42N 118°50W 79 K8
Woolacombe U.K. 51°10N 4°13W 13 F3
Woolamai, C. Australia 38°30S 145°23E 63 F4
Woolgoolga Australia 30°6S 153°11E 63 E5
Woomera Australia 31°5S 136°50E 63 E2
Woonsocket R.I., U.S.A. 42°0N 71°31W 83 E13
Woonsocket S. Dak.,
 U.S.A. 44°3N 98°17W 80 C4
Wooramel → Australia 25°47S 114°10E 61 E1
Wooramel Roadhouse
 Australia 25°45S 114°17E 61 E1
Wooroonooran △
 Australia 16°25S 146°1E 62 B4
Wooster U.S.A. 40°48N 81°56W 82 F3
Worcester S. Africa 33°39S 19°27E 56 E2

Worcester U.K. 52°11N 2°12W 13 E5
Worcester Mass., U.S.A. 42°16N 71°48W 83 D13
Worcester N.Y., U.S.A. 42°36N 74°45W 83 D10
Worcestershire □ U.K. 52°13N 2°10W 13 E5
Workington U.K. 54°39N 3°33W 12 C4
Worksop U.K. 53°18N 1°7W 12 D6
Workum Neths. 52°59N 5°26E 15 B5
Worland U.S.A. 44°1N 107°57W 76 D10
Worms Germany 49°37N 8°21E 16 D5
Worsley Canada 56°31N 119°8W 70 B5
Wortham U.S.A. 31°47N 96°28W 84 F6
Worthing Barbados 13°5N 59°35W 89 g
Worthing U.K. 50°49N 0°21W 13 G7
Worthington Minn.,
 U.S.A. 43°37N 95°36W 80 D6
Worthington Pa., U.S.A. 40°50N 79°38W 82 F5
Wosi Indonesia 0°15S 128°0E 37 E7
Wotjalum ◊ Australia 16°30S 123°45E 60 C3
Wotjobaluk ◊ Australia 37°0S 142°0E 63 C3
Wou-han = Wuhan
 China 30°31N 114°18E 35 B10
Wousi = Wuxi China 31°33N 120°18E 35 B13
Wowoni Indonesia 4°5S 123°5E 37 E6
Wrangel I. = Vrangelya, Ostrov
 Russia 71°0N 180°0E 27 B18
Wrangell U.S.A. 56°28N 132°23W 70 B2
Wrangell Mts. U.S.A. 61°30N 142°0W 68 E3
Wrath, C. U.K. 58°38N 5°1W 11 C3
Wray U.S.A. 40°5N 102°13W 76 F12
Wrekin, The U.K. 52°41N 2°32W 13 E5
Wrens U.S.A. 33°12N 82°23W 85 E13
Wrexham U.K. 53°3N 3°0W 12 D4
Wrexham □ U.K. 53°1N 2°58W 12 D5
Wright Fla., U.S.A. 30°27N 86°38W 85 F11
Wright Wyo., U.S.A. 43°45N 105°28W 76 E11
Wright Pt. Canada 43°48N 81°44W 82 C3
Wrightmyo India 11°47N 92°43E 45 J11
Wrightson, Mt. U.S.A. 31°42N 110°51W 77 L8
Wrightwood U.S.A. 34°22N 117°38W 79 L9
Wrigley Canada 63°16N 123°37W 68 C7
Wrocław Poland 51°5N 17°5E 17 C9
Września Poland 52°21N 17°36E 17 B9
Wu Jiang → China 29°40N 107°20E 34 C6
Wu Kau Tang China 22°30N 114°14E 31 a
Wu Xia China 31°2N 110°10E 35 B8
Wu'an China 36°40N 114°15E 32 F8
Wubalawun ◊ Australia 15°28S 133°1E 60 C5
Wubin Australia 30°6S 116°37E 61 F2
Wubu China 37°28N 110°42E 32 F6
Wuchang China 44°55N 127°5E 33 B14
Wucheng China 37°12N 116°20E 32 F9
Wuchuan Guangdong,
 China 21°33N 110°43E 35 G8
Wuchuan Guizhou, China 28°25N 108°3E 34 C7
Wuchuan Nei Monggol Zizhiqu,
 China 41°5N 111°28E 32 D6
Wuda China 39°29N 106°42E 32 E4
Wudang Shan China 32°23N 111°2E 35 A8
Wudi China 37°40N 117°35E 33 F9
Wuding China 25°24N 102°21E 34 E4
Wuding He → China 37°2N 110°23E 32 F6
Wudinna Australia 33°0S 135°22E 63 E2
Wudu China 33°22N 104°54E 32 H3
Wufeng China 30°12N 110°42E 35 B8
Wugang China 26°44N 110°35E 35 D8
Wugong Shan China 27°30N 114°0E 35 D9
Wuguishan China 22°25N 113°25E 31 a
Wuhai China 39°39N 106°48E 32 E4
Wuhan China 30°31N 114°18E 35 B10
Wuhe China 33°10N 117°50E 33 H9
Wuhsi = Wuxi China 31°33N 120°18E 35 B13
Wuhu China 31°22N 118°21E 35 B12
Wujiang China 31°9N 120°38E 35 B13
Wukari Nigeria 7°51N 9°42E 52 G7
Wulajie China 44°6N 126°33E 33 B14
Wulanbulang China 41°5N 110°55E 32 D6
Wular L. India 34°20N 74°30E 43 B6
Wulian China 35°40N 119°12E 33 G10
Wulian Feng China 27°48N 103°36E 34 D4
Wuliang Shan China 24°30N 100°40E 34 E3
Wuliaru Indonesia 7°27S 131°0E 37 F8
Wuling Shan China 30°0N 110°0E 34 C7
Wulingyuan △ China 29°20N 110°30E 35 C8
Wulong China 29°22N 107°43E 34 C6
Wulong △ China 31°8N 103°5E 34 B4
Wulumuchi = Ürümqi
 China 43°45N 87°45E 30 C6
Wumeng Shan China 26°48N 104°0E 34 D5
Wuming China 23°12N 108°18E 34 F7
Wuning China 29°17N 115°5E 35 C10
Wunna → India 20°18N 78°48E 44 D4
Wunnummin L. Canada 52°55N 89°10W 72 B2
Wuntho Burma 23°55N 95°45E 41 H19
Wupatki △ U.S.A. 35°35N 111°20W 77 J8
Wuping China 25°5N 116°5E 35 E11
Wuppertal Germany 51°16N 7°12E 16 C4
Wuppertal S. Africa 32°13S 19°12E 56 E2
Wuqing China 39°23N 117°4E 33 E9
Wurralibi ◊ Australia 15°43S 137°1E 62 B2
Wurtsboro U.S.A. 41°35N 74°29W 83 E10
Würzburg Germany 49°46N 9°55E 16 D5
Wushan China 34°43N 104°53E 32 G3
Wushi China 41°9N 79°13E 30 C4
Wutai China 38°40N 113°12E 32 E7
Wutai Shan China 39°3N 113°32E 32 E7
Wuting = Huimin China 37°27N 117°28E 33 F9
Wutong China 25°5N 116°5E 35 E11
Wutonghaolai China 42°50N 120°5E 33 C11
Wutongqiao China 29°22N 103°50E 34 C4
Wuwei Anhui, China 31°18N 117°54E 35 B11
Wuwei Gansu, China 37°57N 102°34E 30 D9
Wuxi Jiangsu, China 31°33N 120°18E 35 B13
Wuxi Sichuan, China 31°23N 109°35E 34 B7
Wuxiang China 36°49N 112°50E 32 F7
Wuxuan China 23°34N 109°38E 34 F7

Wuxue China 29°52N 115°30E 35 C10
Wuyang China 33°25N 113°35E 32 H7
Wuyi Hebei, China 37°46N 115°56E 32 F8
Wuyi Zhejiang, China 28°52N 119°50E 35 C12
Wuyi Shan China 27°0N 117°0E 35 D11
Wuyishan China 27°55N 117°54E 35 D11
Wuyishan △ China 27°55N 117°54E 35 D11
Wuyuan Jiangxi, China 29°15N 117°50E 35 C11
Wuyuan Nei Monggol Zizhiqu,
 China 41°2N 108°20E 32 D5
Wuzhai China 38°54N 111°48E 32 E6
Wuzhi Shan China 18°45N 109°45E 38 C7
Wuzhong China 38°2N 106°12E 32 E4
Wuzhou China 23°30N 111°18E 35 F8
Wuzishan = Tongshi
 China 18°30N 109°20E 38 C7
Wyaaba Cr. → Australia 16°27S 141°35E 62 B3
Wyalkatchem Australia 31°8S 117°22E 61 F2
Wyalusing U.S.A. 41°40N 76°16W 83 E8
Wyandotte U.S.A. 42°12N 83°9W 81 D12
Wyandra Australia 27°12S 145°56E 63 D4
Wyangala, L. Australia 33°54S 149°0E 63 E4
Wyara, L. Australia 28°42S 144°14E 63 D3
Wycheproof Australia 36°5S 143°17E 63 F3
Wycliffe Well Australia 20°48S 134°14E 62 C1
Wye → U.K. 51°38N 2°40W 13 F5
Wyemandoo Australia 28°28S 118°29E 61 E2
Wymondham U.K. 52°35N 1°7E 13 E9
Wymore U.S.A. 40°7N 96°40W 80 E5
Wyndham Australia 15°33S 128°3E 60 C4
Wyndham N.Z. 46°20S 168°51E 59 G2
Wynne U.S.A. 35°14N 90°47W 85 D9
Wynyard Australia 41°5S 145°44E 63 G4
Wynyard Canada 51°45N 104°10W 71 C8
Wyola L. Australia 29°8S 130°17E 61 E5
Wyoming Canada 42°57N 82°7W 82 D2
Wyoming □ U.S.A. 43°0N 107°30W 76 E10
Wyomissing U.S.A. 40°20N 75°59W 83 F9
Wyong Australia 33°14S 151°24E 63 E5
Wytheville U.S.A. 36°57N 81°5W 81 G13

X

Xaafuun Somalia 10°25N 51°16E 49 E5
Xaafuun, Ras Somalia 10°27N 51°24E 49 E5
Xaçmaz Azerbaijan 41°31N 48°42E 19 F8
Xai-Xai Mozam. 25°6S 33°31E 57 C5
Xaignabouri = Sayaboury
 Laos 19°15N 101°45E 38 C3
Xainza China 30°58N 88°35E 30 E6
Xalapa Mexico 19°32N 96°55W 87 D5
Xangongo Angola 16°45S 15°5E 56 B2
Xankändi Azerbaijan 39°52N 46°49E 46 B5
Xanthi Greece 41°10N 24°58E 23 D11
Xanxerê Brazil 26°53S 52°23W 95 B5
Xapuri Brazil 10°35S 68°35W 92 F5
Xar Moron He →
 China 43°25N 120°35E 33 C11
Xátiva Spain 38°59N 0°32W 21 C5
Xau, L. Botswana 21°15S 24°44E 56 C3
Xavantina Brazil 21°15S 52°48W 95 A5
Xebert China 44°2N 122°0E 33 B12
Xenia U.S.A. 39°41N 83°56W 81 F12
Xhora S. Africa 31°55S 28°38E 57 E4
Xhumo Botswana 21°7S 24°35E 56 B3
Xi Jiang → China 22°5N 113°20E 35 F9
Xi Ujimqin Qi China 44°32N 117°40E 33 B9
Xi Xian Henan, China 32°20N 114°43E 35 A10
Xi Xian Shanxi, China 36°41N 110°58E 32 F6
Xia Xian China 35°8N 111°12E 32 G6
Xiachengzi China 44°40N 130°18E 33 B16
Xiachuan Dao China 21°40N 112°40E 35 G9
Xiaguan China 25°32N 100°16E 34 E3
Xiajiang China 27°30N 115°10E 35 D10
Xiajin China 36°56N 116°0E 32 F9
Xiamen China 24°25N 118°4E 35 E12
Xi'an China 34°15N 109°0E 32 G5
Xian Xian China 38°12N 116°6E 32 E9
Xianfeng China 29°40N 109°8E 34 C7
Xiang Jiang → China 28°55N 112°50E 35 C9
Xiang Khouang Laos 19°17N 103°25E 38 C4
Xiangcheng Henan,
 China 33°50N 113°27E 32 H7
Xiangcheng Sichuan,
 China 28°53N 99°47E 34 C2
Xiangdu China 23°13N 106°58E 34 F6
Xiangfan China 32°2N 112°8E 35 A9
Xianggang = Hong Kong □
 China 22°11N 114°14E 31 a
Xianghuang Qi China 42°2N 113°50E 32 C7
Xiangjiaba Dam China 28°37N 104°17E 34 C5
Xiangning China 35°58N 110°50E 32 G6
Xiangquan China 36°30N 113°1E 32 F7
Xiangquan He = Sutlej →
 Pakistan 29°23N 71°3E 42 E4
Xiangshan China 29°29N 121°51E 35 C13
Xiangshui China 34°12N 119°33E 33 G10
Xiangtan China 27°51N 112°54E 35 D9
Xiangxiang China 27°43N 112°28E 35 D9
Xiangyin China 28°38N 112°54E 35 C9
Xiangyun China 25°34N 100°35E 34 E3
Xiangzhou China 23°58N 109°40E 34 F7
Xianju China 28°51N 120°44E 35 C13
Xianshui He → China 30°10N 100°59E 34 B3
Xiantao China 30°25N 113°25E 35 B9
Xianyang China 34°20N 108°40E 32 G5
Xianyou China 25°22N 118°38E 35 E12
Xiao Hinggan Ling China 49°0N 127°0E 31 B14
Xiao Xian China 34°15N 116°55E 32 G9
Xiaofeng China 30°35N 119°32E 35 B12
Xiaogan China 30°52N 113°55E 35 B9
Xiaojin China 30°50N 102°21E 34 B4
Xiaolan China 22°38N 113°13E 35 F9
Xiaowan Dam China 24°42N 100°5E 34 E3
Xiaowutai Shan China 39°51N 114°59E 32 E8
Xiaoyi China 37°8N 111°48E 32 F6

Xiapu China 26°54N 119°59E 35 D12
Xiashan = Zhanjiang China 21°15N 110°20E 35 G8
Xiawa China 42°35N 120°38E 33 C11
Xiayi China 34°15N 116°10E 32 G9
Xichang China 27°51N 102°19E 34 D4
Xichong China 30°57N 105°54E 34 B5
Xichou China 23°25N 104°42E 34 E5
Xichuan China 33°0N 111°30E 32 H6
Xide China 28°8N 102°19E 34 D4
Xiemahe China 31°38N 111°12E 35 B8
Xifei He → China 32°45N 116°42E 35 H9
Xifeng Gansu, China 35°40N 107°40E 32 G4
Xifeng Guizhou, China 27°7N 106°42E 34 D6
Xifeng Liaoning, China 42°42N 124°45E 33 C13
Xifengzhen = Xifeng China 35°40N 107°40E 32 G4
Xigazê China 29°5N 88°45E 30 F6
Xihe China 34°2N 105°20E 32 G3
Xihua China 33°45N 114°30E 32 H8
Xili Shuiku China 22°36N 113°57E 31 a
Xiliao He → China 43°32N 123°35E 33 C12
Xilin China 24°30N 105°6E 34 E5
Xiling Gorge = Xiling Xia China 30°54N 110°48E 35 B8
Xiling Xia China 30°54N 110°48E 35 B8
Xilinhot China 43°52N 116°2E 32 C9
Xiluodu Dam China 28°12N 103°34E 34 C4
Ximeng China 22°50N 99°27E 34 F2
Ximiao China 40°59N 100°12E 30 C9
Xin Jiang → China 28°45N 116°35E 35 C11
Xin Xian = Xinzhou China 38°22N 112°46E 32 E7
Xin'anjiang Shuiku China 29°33N 118°56E 35 C12
Xinavane Mozam. 25°2S 32°47E 57 C5
Xinbin China 41°40N 125°2E 33 D13
Xincai China 32°43N 114°58E 35 A10
Xinchang China 29°28N 120°52E 35 C13
Xincheng Guangxi Zhuangzu, China 24°5N 108°39E 34 E7
Xincheng Jiangxi, China 26°48N 114°6E 35 D10
Xinfeng Guangdong, China 24°5N 114°16E 35 E10
Xinfeng Jiangxi, China 27°7N 116°11E 35 D11
Xinfeng Jiangxi, China 25°27N 114°58E 35 E10
Xinfengjiang Shuiku China 23°52N 114°30E 35 F10
Xing Xian China 38°27N 111°7E 32 E6
Xing'an Guangxi Zhuangzu, China 25°38N 110°40E 35 E8
Xingan Jiangxi, China 27°46N 115°20E 35 D10
Xingcheng China 40°40N 120°45E 33 D11
Xingguo China 26°21N 115°21E 35 D10
Xinghe China 40°55N 113°55E 32 D7
Xinghua China 32°58N 119°48E 33 H10
Xinghua Wan China 25°15N 119°20E 35 E12
Xinglong China 40°25N 117°30E 33 D9
Xingning China 24°3N 115°42E 35 E10
Xingping China 34°20N 108°28E 32 G5
Xingren China 25°24N 105°11E 34 E5
Xingshan China 31°15N 110°45E 35 B8
Xingtai China 37°3N 114°32E 32 F8
Xingu → Brazil 1°30S 51°53W 93 D8
Xingwen China 28°22N 104°50E 34 C5
Xingxingxia China 41°47N 95°0E 30 C7
Xingyang China 34°45N 112°52E 32 G7
Xingyi China 25°3N 104°59E 34 E5
Xinhe China 37°30N 115°15E 32 F8
Xinhua China 27°42N 111°13E 35 D8
Xinhuang China 27°21N 109°12E 34 D7
Xinhui China 22°25N 113°0E 35 F9
Xining China 36°34N 101°40E 30 D9
Xinji China 37°55N 115°13E 32 F8
Xinjian China 28°37N 115°46E 35 C10
Xinjiang China 35°34N 111°11E 32 G6
Xinjiang Uygur Zizhiqu □ China 42°0N 86°0E 30 C6
Xinjin = Pulandian China 39°25N 121°58E 33 E11
Xinjin China 30°24N 103°47E 34 B4
Xinkai He → China 43°32N 123°35E 33 C12
Xinken China 22°39N 113°36E 31 a
Xinlitun China 38°25N 114°40E 32 E8
Xinlong China 30°57N 100°12E 34 B3
Xinmi China 34°30N 113°25E 32 G7
Xinmin China 41°59N 122°50E 33 D12
Xinning China 26°28N 110°50E 35 D8
Xinping China 24°5N 101°59E 34 E3
Xinshao China 27°21N 111°26E 35 D8
Xintai China 35°55N 117°45E 33 G9
Xintian China 25°55N 112°13E 35 E9
Xinwan China 22°47N 113°40E 31 a
Xinxiang China 35°18N 113°50E 32 G7
Xinxing China 22°35N 112°15E 35 F9
Xinyang China 32°6N 114°3E 35 A10
Xinye China 32°20N 112°21E 35 A9
Xinyi Guangdong, China 22°25N 111°0E 35 F8
Xinyi Nei Mongol Zizhiqu, China 24°23N 118°21E 33 G10
Xinyu China 27°49N 114°58E 35 D10
Xinzhan China 43°50N 127°18E 33 C14
Xinzheng China 34°20N 113°45E 32 G7
Xinzhou Hainan, China 19°43N 109°17E 38 C7
Xinzhou Hubei, China 30°50N 114°48E 35 B10
Xinzhou Shanxi, China 38°22N 112°46E 32 E7
Xingyuecheng China 40°12N 122°33E 33 D12
Xiping Henan, China 33°22N 114°5E 32 H8
Xiping Henan, China 33°25N 111°8E 32 H6
Xique Zhejiang, China 28°16N 119°29E 35 C12
Xique-Xique Brazil 10°50S 42°40W 93 F10
Xisha Qundao = Paracel Is. S. China Sea 15°50N 112°0E 36 A4
Xishuangbanna China 22°5N 101°1E 34 F3
Xishui Guizhou, China 28°19N 106°9E 34 C6
Xishui Hubei, China 30°30N 115°15E 35 B10
Xiu Shui → China 29°13N 114°0E 35 C10

Xiuning China 29°45N 118°10E 35 C12
Xiuren China 24°27N 110°12E 35 E8
Xiushan China 28°25N 108°57E 34 C7
Xiushui China 29°2N 114°33E 35 C10
Xiuwen China 26°49N 106°32E 34 D6
Xiuyan China 40°18N 123°11E 33 D12
Xiva Uzbekistan 41°30N 60°18E 26 E7
Xixabangma Feng China 28°20N 85°40E 43 E11
Xixia China 33°25N 111°29E 32 H6
Xixiang Guangdong, China 22°34N 113°52E 31 a
Xixiang Shaanxi, China 33°0N 107°44E 32 H4
Xixón = Gijón Spain 43°32N 5°42W 21 A3
Xiyang China 37°38N 113°38E 32 F7
Xizang Zizhiqu □ China 32°0N 88°0E 30 E6
Xochob Mexico 19°21N 89°48W 87 D7
Xu Jiang → China 28°0N 116°25E 35 D11
Xuan Loc Vietnam 10°56N 107°14E 39 G6
Xuan'en China 30°0N 109°30E 34 C7
Xuanhan China 31°18N 107°38E 34 B6
Xuanhua China 40°40N 115°2E 32 D8
Xuanwei China 26°15N 103°59E 34 C5
Xuanzhou China 30°56N 118°43E 35 B12
Xuchang China 34°2N 113°48E 32 G7
Xuefeng Shan China 27°5N 110°35E 35 D8
Xuejiaping China 31°39N 110°16E 35 B8
Xun Jiang → China 23°35N 111°30E 35 F8
Xun Xian China 35°42N 114°33E 32 G8
Xundian China 25°36N 103°15E 34 E4
Xunwu China 24°54N 115°37E 35 E10
Xunyang China 32°48N 109°22E 32 H5
Xunyi China 35°8N 108°20E 32 G5
Xupu China 27°53N 110°32E 35 D8
Xúquer → Spain 39°5N 0°10W 21 C5
Xushui China 39°2N 115°40E 32 E8
Xuwen China 20°20N 110°10E 35 G8
Xuyi China 32°55N 118°32E 35 A12
Xuyong China 28°10N 105°22E 34 C5
Xuzhou China 34°18N 117°10E 33 G9

Y

Y Drenewydd = Newtown U.K. 52°31N 3°19W 13 E4
Y Fenni = Abergavenny U.K. 51°49N 3°1W 13 F4
Y Gelli Gandryll = Hay-on-Wye U.K. 52°5N 3°8W 13 E4
Y Trallwng = Welshpool U.K. 52°39N 3°8W 13 E4
Ya Xian = Sanya China 18°14N 109°29E 38 C7
Yaamba Australia 23°8S 150°22E 62 C5
Ya'an China 29°58N 103°5E 34 C4
Yaapeet Australia 35°45S 142°3E 63 F3
Yablonovyy Khrebet Russia 53°0N 114°0E 27 D12
Yablonovyy Ra. = Yablonovyy Khrebet Russia 53°0N 114°0E 27 D12
Yabrai Shan China 39°40N 103°0E 32 E2
Yabrūd Syria 33°58N 36°39E 48 B5
Yabucoa Puerto Rico 18°3N 65°53W 89 d
Yacambú △ Venezuela 9°42N 69°27W 89 E6
Yacheng China 18°22N 109°6E 38 C7
Yacuiba Bolivia 22°0S 63°43W 94 A3
Yacuma → Bolivia 13°38S 65°23W 92 F5
Yadgir India 16°45N 77°5E 44 F3
Yadkin → U.S.A. 35°23N 80°4W 85 D15
Yadua Fiji 16°49S 178°18E 59 a
Yaeyama-Rettō Japan 24°30N 123°40E 29 M1
Yagasa Cluster Fiji 18°57S 178°28W 59 a
Yagodnoye Russia 62°33N 149°40E 27 C15
Yahk Canada 49°6N 116°10W 70 D5
Yahuma Dem. Rep. of the Congo 1°0N 23°10E 54 D4
Yaita Japan 36°48N 139°56E 29 F9
Yajiang China 30°2N 100°57E 34 B3
Yakeshi China 49°17N 120°44E 31 B13
Yakima U.S.A. 46°36N 120°31W 76 C3
Yakima → U.S.A. 46°15N 119°14W 76 C4
Yakishiri-Jima Japan 44°26N 141°25E 28 B10
Yakobi I. U.S.A. 58°0N 136°30W 70 B1
Yakovlevka Russia 44°26N 133°28E 28 B6
Yaku-Shima Japan 30°20N 130°30E 29 J5
Yakumo Japan 42°15N 140°16E 28 C10
Yakutat U.S.A. 59°33N 139°44W 68 F4
Yakutat B. U.S.A. 59°45N 140°45W 74 D11
Yakutia = Sakha □ Russia 66°0N 130°0E 27 C14
Yakutsk Russia 62°5N 129°50E 27 C13
Yala Thailand 6°33N 101°18E 39 J3
Yala △ Sri Lanka 6°20N 81°30E 45 L5
Yalata Australia 31°55S 132°6E 61 F5
Yalata ⊙ Australia 31°35S 132°7E 61 F5
Yalboroo Australia 20°50S 148°40E 62 b
Yale U.S.A. 43°8N 82°48W 82 C2
Yalgorup △ Australia 32°39S 115°38E 61 F2
Yalinga C.A.R. 6°33N 23°10E 54 C4
Yalkubul, Pta. Mexico 21°32N 88°37W 87 C7
Yalleroi Australia 24°3S 145°42E 62 C4
Yalobusha → U.S.A. 33°33N 90°10W 85 E9
Yalong China 21°12N 109°42E 38 C7
Yalong Jiang → China 26°40N 101°55E 34 D3
Yalova Turkey 40°41N 29°15E 23 D13
Yalpirakinu ⊙ Australia 22°24S 132°15E 60 D5
Yalta Ukraine 44°30N 34°10E 19 F5
Yalu Jiang → China 39°55N 124°19E 33 E13
Yam Australia 9°54S 142°46E 62 a
Yam Ha Melah = Dead Sea Asia 31°30N 35°30E 48 D4
Yam Kinneret Israel 32°45N 35°35E 48 C4
Yamada = Kama Japan 33°33N 130°49E 29 H5
Yamagata Japan 38°15N 140°15E 28 E10
Yamagata □ Japan 38°30N 140°0E 28 E10
Yamaguchi Japan 34°10N 131°32E 29 G5
Yamaguchi □ Japan 34°20N 131°40E 29 G5
Yamal, Poluostrov Russia 71°0N 70°0E 26 B8
Yamal Pen. = Yamal, Poluostrov Russia 71°0N 70°0E 26 B8
Yamanashi □ Japan 35°40N 138°40E 29 G9

Yamantau, Gora Russia 54°15N 58°6E 18 D10
Yamato Ridge Sea of Japan 39°20N 135°0E 28 E7
Yamba Australia 29°26S 153°23E 63 D5
Yambarran Ra. Australia 15°10S 130°25E 60 C5
Yâmbiô South Sudan 4°35N 28°16E 53 H11
Yambol Bulgaria 42°30N 26°30E 23 C12
Yamburg Russia 68°21N 77°8E 26 C8
Yamdena Indonesia 7°45S 131°20E 37 F8
Yame Japan 33°13N 130°35E 29 H5
Yamethin Burma 20°29N 96°18E 41 J20
Yamma Yamma, L. Australia 26°16S 141°20E 63 D3
Yamoussoukro Ivory C. 6°49N 5°17W 52 G4
Yampa → U.S.A. 40°32N 108°59W 76 F9
Yampi Sd. Australia 16°8S 123°38E 60 C3
Yampil Moldova 48°15N 28°15E 17 D15
Yampil = Yampil Moldova 48°15N 28°15E 17 D15
Yamu, Laem Thailand 7°59N 98°28E 39 a
Yamuna → India 25°30N 81°53E 43 G9
Yamunanagar India 30°7N 77°17E 42 D7
Yamzho Yumco China 28°48N 90°35E 30 F4
Yan Oya → Sri Lanka 9°0N 81°10E 45 K5
Yana → Russia 71°30N 136°0E 27 B14
Yanagawa Japan 33°10N 130°24E 29 H5
Yanai Japan 33°58N 132°7E 29 H6
Yan'an China 36°35N 109°26E 32 F5
Yanaul Russia 56°25N 55°0E 18 C10
Yanbian China 26°47N 101°31E 34 D3
Yanchang China 36°43N 110°1E 32 F6
Yancheng Henan, China 33°35N 114°0E 32 H8
Yancheng Jiangsu, China 33°23N 120°8E 33 H11
Yanchep Australia 31°33S 115°37E 61 F2
Yanchi China 37°48N 107°20E 32 F4
Yanchuan China 36°51N 110°10E 32 F6
Yanco Cr. → Australia 35°14S 145°35E 63 F4
Yandang Shan China 28°0N 120°25E 35 D13
Yandeyarra ⊙ Australia 21°17S 118°24E 60 D2
Yandicoogina Australia 22°49S 119°12E 60 D2
Yandoon Burma 17°0N 95°40E 41 L19
Yanfeng China 25°52N 101°8E 34 E3
Yang Xian China 33°15N 107°30E 34 A6
Yang-yang S. Korea 38°4N 128°38E 33 E15
Yangambi Dem. Rep. of the Congo 0°47N 24°24E 54 D4
Yangbi China 25°41N 99°58E 34 E2
Yangcheng China 35°28N 112°22E 32 G7
Yangch'ü = Taiyuan China 37°52N 112°33E 32 F7
Yangchun China 22°11N 111°48E 35 F8
Yanggao China 40°21N 113°55E 32 D7
Yanggu China 36°8N 115°43E 32 F8
Yangjiang China 21°50N 111°59E 35 G8
Yangliuqing China 39°2N 117°5E 33 E9
Yangon = Rangoon Burma 16°45N 96°20E 41 L20
Yangping China 31°12N 111°25E 35 B8
Yangpingguan China 32°58N 106°5E 34 A6
Yangquan China 37°58N 113°31E 32 F7
Yangshan China 24°30N 112°40E 35 E9
Yangshuo China 24°48N 110°29E 35 E8
Yangtse = Chang Jiang → China 31°48N 121°10E 35 B13
Yangtze Kiang = Chang Jiang → China 31°48N 121°10E 35 B13
Yangxin China 29°50N 115°12E 35 C10
Yangyuan China 40°1N 114°10E 32 D8
Yangzhong China 32°22N 119°22E 35 A12
Yangzhou China 32°21N 119°26E 35 A12
Yanhe China 28°31N 108°29E 34 C7
Yanji China 42°59N 129°30E 33 C15
Yanjin China 28°5N 104°18E 34 C5
Yanjing China 29°7N 98°33E 34 C2
Yankton U.S.A. 42°53N 97°23W 80 D5
Yankunytjatjara-Antakirinja Australia 27°20S 134°30E 63 A1
Yanqi China 42°5N 86°35E 30 C6
Yanqing China 40°30N 115°58E 32 D8
Yanshan Hebei, China 38°4N 117°22E 33 E9
Yanshan Jiangxi, China 28°15N 117°41E 35 C11
Yanshan Yunnan, China 23°35N 104°20E 34 F5
Yanshou China 45°28N 128°22E 33 B15
Yantabulla Australia 29°21S 145°0E 63 D4
Yantai China 37°34N 121°22E 33 F11
Yantian China 22°35N 114°16E 31 a
Yanting China 31°11N 105°24E 34 B5
Yantongshan China 43°17N 126°0E 33 C14
Yanuca Fiji 18°24S 178°0E 59 a
Yanwa China 27°35N 98°55E 34 D2
Yanyuan China 27°25N 101°30E 34 D3
Yanzhou China 35°35N 116°49E 32 G9
Yao Xian China 34°55N 108°59E 32 G5
Yao Yai, Ko Thailand 8°7N 98°37E 39 a
Yao'an China 25°31N 101°18E 34 E3
Yaowan China 34°15N 118°3E 33 G10
Yap Pac. Oc. 9°30N 138°10E 64 G5
Yapen Indonesia 1°50S 136°0E 37 E9
Yapen, Selat Indonesia 1°20S 136°10E 37 E9
Yapero Indonesia 4°59S 137°11E 37 E9
Yappar → Australia 18°22S 141°16E 62 B3
Yaqaga Fiji 16°35S 178°36E 59 a
Yaqui → Mexico 27°37N 110°39W 86 B2
Yar-Sale Russia 66°50N 70°50E 26 C8
Yaraka Australia 24°53S 144°3E 62 C3
Yaransk Russia 57°22N 47°49E 18 C8
Yare → U.K. 52°35N 1°38E 13 E9
Yaremcha Ukraine 48°27N 24°33E 17 D13
Yaren Nauru 0°33S 166°55E 57 B9
Yarensk Russia 62°11N 49°15E 18 B8
Yarí → Colombia 0°20S 72°20W 92 D4
Yarkand = Shache China 38°20N 77°10E 30 D4
Yarkant He → China 40°26N 80°59E 30 C5
Yarker Canada 44°23N 76°46W 83 B8
Yarkhun → Pakistan 36°17N 72°30E 43 A5

Yarlung Ziangbo Jiang = Brahmaputra → Asia 23°40N 90°35E 43 H13
Yarmouth Canada 43°50N 66°7W 73 D6
Yarmūk → Syria 32°42N 35°40E 48 C4
Yarqa, W. → Egypt 30°0N 33°49E 48 F2
Yaroslavl Russia 57°35N 39°55E 18 C6
Yarra Yarra Lakes Australia 29°40S 115°45E 61 E2
Yarram Australia 38°29S 146°39E 63 F4
Yarraman Australia 26°50S 152°0E 63 D5
Yarras Australia 31°25S 152°20E 63 E5
Yarrie Australia 20°45S 120°12E 60 D3
Yartsevo Russia 60°20N 90°0E 27 C10
Yarumal Colombia 6°58N 75°24W 92 B3
Yasawa Fiji 16°47S 177°31E 59 a
Yaselda Belarus 52°7N 26°28E 17 B14
Yasin Pakistan 36°24N 73°23E 43 A5
Yasinski, L. Canada 53°16N 77°35W 72 B4
Yasinya Ukraine 48°16N 24°21E 17 D13
Yasothon Thailand 15°50N 104°10E 38 E5
Yass Australia 34°49S 148°54E 63 E4
Yāsūj Iran 30°31N 51°31E 47 D6
Yatağan Turkey 37°20N 28°10E 23 F13
Yates Center U.S.A. 37°53N 95°44W 80 G6
Yathkyed L. Canada 62°40N 98°0W 71 A9
Yatsushiro Japan 32°30N 130°40E 29 H5
Yauco Puerto Rico 18°2N 66°51W 89 d
Yauri = Sanya China 18°14N 109°29E 38 C7
Yavari → Peru 4°21S 70°2W 92 D4
Yávaros Mexico 26°42N 109°31W 86 B3
Yavatmal India 20°20N 78°15E 44 D4
Yavne Israel 31°52N 34°45E 48 D3
Yavoriv Ukraine 49°55N 23°20E 17 D12
Yavorov = Yavoriv Ukraine 49°55N 23°20E 17 D12
Yawatahama Japan 33°27N 132°24E 29 H6
Yawri B. S. Leone 8°22N 13°0W 52 G3
Yaxi China 27°33N 106°41E 34 D6
Yaxian = Sanya China 18°14N 109°29E 38 C7
Yazd Iran 31°55N 54°27E 47 D7
Yazd □ Iran 32°0N 55°0E 47 D7
Yazd-e Khvāst Iran 31°31N 52°7E 47 D7
Yazman Pakistan 29°8N 71°45E 42 E4
Yazoo → U.S.A. 32°22N 90°54W 85 E9
Yazoo City U.S.A. 32°51N 90°25W 85 E9
Ybycuí △ Paraguay 26°5S 56°46W 94 B4
Ybyturuzú △ Paraguay 25°51S 56°11W 94 B4
Ye Burma 15°15N 97°15E 38 E1
Ye Xian China 33°35N 113°25E 32 H7
Yebyu Burma 14°15N 98°13E 38 E2
Yecheng China 37°54N 77°26E 30 D4
Yecheon S. Korea 36°39N 128°27E 33 F15
Yecla Spain 38°35N 1°5W 21 C5
Yécora Mexico 28°20N 108°58W 86 B3
Yedintsy = Edineț Moldova 48°9N 27°18E 17 D14
Yegros Paraguay 26°20S 56°25W 94 B4
Yehbuah Indonesia 8°23S 114°45E 37 J17
Yehuda, Midbar Israel 31°35N 35°15E 48 D4
Yei South Sudan 4°9N 30°40E 53 H12
Yekaterinburg Russia 56°50N 60°30E 26 D7
Yelandur India 12°6N 77°0E 45 H3
Yelarbon Australia 28°33S 150°38E 63 D5
Yelets Russia 52°40N 38°30E 18 D6
Yelin = Lingshui China 18°27N 110°0E 38 C8
Yelizavetgrad = Kirovohrad Ukraine 48°35N 32°20E 19 E5
Yelizovo Russia 53°11N 158°23E 27 D16
Yell U.K. 60°35N 1°5W 11 A7
Yell Sd. U.K. 60°33N 1°15W 11 A7
Yellamanchili = Elamanchili India 17°33N 82°50E 44 F6
Yellandu India 17°39N 80°23E 44 F5
Yellapur India 14°58N 74°43E 45 G2
Yellareddi India 18°12N 78°2E 44 E4
Yellow = Huang He → China 37°55N 118°50E 33 F10
Yellow Sea China 35°0N 123°0E 33 G12
Yellowhead Pass Canada 52°53N 118°25W 70 C5
Yellowknife Canada 62°27N 114°29W 70 A6
Yellowknife → Canada 62°31N 114°19W 70 A6
Yellowstone → U.S.A. 47°59N 103°59W 76 C12
Yellowstone △ U.S.A. 44°40N 110°30W 76 D8
Yellowstone L. U.S.A. 44°27N 110°22W 76 D8
Yelsk Belarus 51°50N 29°10E 17 C15
Yemen ■ Asia 15°0N 44°0E 49 E3
Yemmiganur India 15°44N 77°29E 45 G3
Yen Bai Vietnam 21°42N 104°52E 34 G5
Yenangyaung Burma 20°30N 95°0E 41 J19
Yenbo = Yanbu 'al Bahr Si. Arabia 24°0N 38°5E 46 F3
Yenda Australia 34°13S 146°14E 63 E4
Yenice Turkey 39°55N 27°17E 23 E12
Yenisey → Russia 71°50N 82°40E 26 B9
Yeniseysk Russia 58°27N 92°13E 27 D10
Yeniseyskiy Zaliv Russia 72°20N 81°0E 26 B9
Yenyuka Russia 57°57N 121°15E 27 D13
Yeo → U.K. 51°2N 2°49W 13 G5
Yeo, L. Australia 28°0S 124°30E 61 E3
Yeo I. Canada 45°24N 81°48W 82 A3
Yeola India 20°2N 74°30E 44 D2
Yeong-wol S. Korea 37°11N 128°28E 33 F15
Yeongcheon S. Korea 35°58N 128°56E 33 G15
Yeongdeok S. Korea 36°24N 129°22E 33 F15
Yeongdong S. Korea 36°10N 127°46E 33 F14
Yeongju S. Korea 36°50N 128°40E 33 F15
Yeosu S. Korea 34°47N 127°15E 33 G14
Yeotmal = Yavatmal India 20°20N 78°15E 44 D4
Yeovil U.K. 50°57N 2°38W 13 G5
Yeppoon Australia 23°5S 150°47E 62 C5
Yerbent Turkmenistan 39°19N 58°36E 47 B8
Yerbogachen Russia 61°16N 108°0E 27 C11
Yerevan Armenia 40°10N 44°31E 46 B6
Yerington U.S.A. 38°59N 119°10W 76 G4
Yerla → India 16°50N 74°30E 44 F2

Yermo U.S.A. 34°54N 116°50W 79 L10
Yeropol Russia 65°15N 168°40E 27 C17
Yershov Russia 51°23N 48°27E 19 D8
Yes Tor U.K. 50°41N 4°0W 13 G4
Yesan S. Korea 36°41N 126°51E 33 F14
Yeso U.S.A. 34°26N 104°37W 77 J11
Yessey Russia 68°29N 102°10E 27 C11
Yetman Australia 28°56S 150°48E 63 D5
Yeu, Î. d' France 46°42N 2°20W 20 C2
Yevpatoriya Ukraine 45°15N 33°20E 19 E5
Yeysk Russia 46°40N 38°12E 19 E6
Yezd = Yazd Iran 31°55N 54°27E 47 D7
Ygatimi Paraguay 24°5S 55°40W 95 A4
Yhati Paraguay 25°45S 56°35W 94 B4
Yhú Paraguay 25°0S 56°0W 95 B4
Yí → Uruguay 33°7S 57°8W 94 C4
Yi 'Allaq, G. Egypt 30°21N 33°31E 48 E2
Yi He → China 34°10N 118°8E 33 G10
Yi Xian Anhui, China 29°55N 117°57E 35 C11
Yi Xian Hebei, China 39°20N 115°30E 32 E8
Yi Xian Liaoning, China 41°30N 121°22E 33 D11
Yibin China 28°45N 104°32E 34 C5
Yicheng Henan, China 31°41N 112°12E 35 B9
Yicheng Shanxi, China 35°42N 111°40E 32 G6
Yichuan China 36°2N 110°10E 32 F6
Yichun Heilongjiang, China 47°44N 128°52E 31 B14
Yichun Jiangxi, China 27°48N 114°22E 35 D10
Yidu China 36°43N 118°28E 33 F10
Yidun China 30°22N 99°21E 34 B2
Yifeng China 28°22N 114°45E 35 C10
Yijun China 35°28N 109°8E 32 G5
Yilan China 46°19N 129°34E 31 B15
Yıldız Dağları Turkey 41°48N 27°36E 23 D12
Yilehuli Shan China 51°20N 124°20E 31 A13
Yiliang Yunnan, China 27°38N 104°2E 34 D5
Yiliang Yunnan, China 24°56N 103°11E 34 E4
Yilong China 31°34N 106°23E 34 B6
Yima China 34°44N 111°53E 32 G6
Yimen China 24°40N 102°10E 34 E4
Yimianpo China 45°7N 128°2E 33 B15
Yin Xu China 36°7N 114°18E 32 F8
Yi'nan China 35°31N 118°24E 33 G10
Yinchuan China 38°30N 106°15E 32 E4
Yindarlgooda, L. Australia 30°40S 121°52E 61 F3
Yindjibarndi ⊙ Australia 22°0S 118°35E 60 D2
Ying He → China 32°30N 116°30E 32 H9
Ying Xian China 39°32N 113°10E 32 E7
Yingcheng China 30°56N 113°35E 35 B9
Yingde China 24°10N 113°25E 35 E9
Yingjiang China 24°41N 97°55E 34 E1
Yingkou China 40°37N 122°18E 33 D12
Yingpanshui China 37°26N 104°18E 32 F3
Yingshan Hubei, China 30°41N 115°32E 35 B10
Yingshan Sichuan, China 31°4N 106°35E 34 B6
Yingshang China 32°38N 116°12E 35 A11
Yingtan China 28°12N 117°0E 35 C11
Yingualyalya ⊙ Australia 18°49S 129°12E 60 C4
Yining China 43°58N 81°10E 30 C5
Yiningarra ⊙ Australia 20°53S 129°27E 60 D4
Yinmabin Burma 22°10N 94°55E 41 H19
Yipinglang China 25°10N 101°52E 34 E3
Yirga Alem Ethiopia 6°48N 38°22E 49 F2
Yirrkala Australia 12°14S 136°56E 62 A2
Yishan China 24°28N 108°38E 34 E7
Yishui China 35°47N 118°30E 33 G10
Yitong China 43°13N 125°20E 33 C13
Yiwu China 29°20N 120°3E 35 C13
Yixing China 31°21N 119°48E 35 B12
Yiyang Henan, China 34°27N 112°10E 32 G7
Yiyang Hunan, China 28°35N 112°18E 35 C9
Yiyang Jiangxi, China 28°22N 117°20E 35 C11
Yizhang China 25°27N 112°57E 35 E9
Yizheng China 32°18N 119°10E 35 A12
Yli-Kitka Finland 66°8N 28°30E 8 C23
Ylitornio Finland 66°19N 23°39E 8 C20
Ylivieska Finland 64°4N 24°28E 8 D21
Yoakum U.S.A. 29°17N 97°9W 84 G6
Yog Pt. Phil. 14°6N 124°12E 37 B6
Yogyakarta Indonesia 7°49S 110°22E 37 G14
Yogyakarta □ Indonesia 7°48S 110°22E 37 G14
Yoho △ Canada 51°25N 116°30W 70 C5
Yojoa, L. de Honduras 14°53N 88°0W 88 D2
Yok Don △ Vietnam 12°50N 107°40E 38 F6
Yokadouma Cameroon 3°26N 14°55E 54 D2
Yokkaichi Japan 34°55N 136°38E 29 G8
Yoko Cameroon 5°32N 12°20E 54 C2
Yokohama Japan 35°27N 139°28E 29 G9
Yokosuka Japan 35°20N 139°40E 29 G9
Yokote Japan 39°20N 140°30E 28 E10
Yola Nigeria 9°10N 12°29E 53 G8
Yolaina, Cordillera de Nic. 11°30N 84°0W 88 D3
Yölöten Turkmenistan 37°18N 62°21E 47 B9
Yom → Thailand 15°35N 100°1E 38 E3
Yonago Japan 35°25N 133°19E 29 G6
Yonaguni-Jima Japan 24°27N 123°0E 29 M1
Yonan N. Korea 37°55N 126°11E 33 F14
Yonezawa Japan 37°57N 140°4E 28 F10
Yong-in S. Korea 37°14N 127°12E 33 F14
Yong Peng Malaysia 2°0N 103°3E 39 M4
Yong Sata Thailand 7°8N 99°41E 39 J2
Yongamp'o N. Korea 39°56N 124°23E 33 E13
Yong'an China 38°17N 102°7E 30 D9
Yongcheng China 33°55N 116°20E 32 H9
Yongchuan China 29°17N 105°55E 34 C5
Yongchun China 25°16N 118°20E 35 E12
Yongde China 24°5N 99°25E 34 E2
Yongdeng China 36°38N 103°25E 32 F2
Yongding China 24°43N 116°45E 35 E11
Yongfeng China 27°20N 115°22E 35 D10
Yongfu China 24°59N 109°59E 34 E7

Yonghe *China* 36°46N 110°38E **32** F6
Yŏnghŭng *N. Korea* 39°31N 127°18E **33** E14
Yongji *Jilin, China* 43°33N 126°13E **33** C14
Yongji *Shanxi, China* 34°52N 110°28E **32** G6
Yongjia *China* 28°10N 120°45E **35** C13
Yongkang *Yunnan, China* 24°9N 99°20E **34** E2
Yongkang *Zhejiang, China* 28°55N 120°2E **35** C13
Yongnian *China* 36°47N 114°29E **32** F8
Yongning *Guangxi Zhuangzu, China* 22°44N 108°28E **34** F7
Yongning *Ningxia Huizu, China* 38°15N 106°14E **32** E4
Yongping *China* 25°27N 99°38E **34** E2
Yongren *China* 26°4N 101°40E **34** D3
Yongshan *China* 28°11N 103°35E **34** C4
Yongsheng *China* 26°38N 100°46E **34** D3
Yongshun *China* 29°2N 109°51E **34** C7
Yongtai *China* 25°49N 118°58E **35** E12
Yongxin = Jinggangshan *China* 26°58N 114°15E **35** D10
Yongxing *China* 26°9N 113°8E **35** D9
Yongxiu *China* 29°2N 115°42E **35** C10
Yongzhou *China* 26°17N 111°37E **35** D8
Yonibana *S. Leone* 8°30N 12°19W **52** G3
Yonne → *France* 48°23N 2°58E **20** B5
York *Australia* 31°52S 116°47E **61** F2
York *U.K.* 53°58N 1°6W **12** D6
York *Ala., U.S.A.* 32°29N 88°18W **85** E10
York *Nebr., U.S.A.* 40°52N 97°36W **80** E5
York *Pa., U.S.A.* 39°58N 76°44W **81** F15
York, C. *Australia* 10°42S 142°31E **62** A3
York, City of □ *U.K.* 53°58N 1°6W **12** D6
York, Kap *Greenland* 75°55N 66°25W **69** B18
York, Vale of *U.K.* 54°15N 1°25W **12** C6
York Sd. *Australia* 15°0S 125°5E **60** C4
Yorke Pen. *Australia* 34°50S 137°40E **63** E2
Yorkshire Dales △ *U.K.* 54°12N 2°10W **12** C5
Yorkshire Wolds *U.K.* 54°8N 0°31W **12** C7
Yorkton *Canada* 51°11N 102°28W **71** C8
Yorkville *U.S.A.* 38°52N 123°13W **78** G3
Yoro *Honduras* 15°9N 87°7W **88** C2
Yoron-Jima *Japan* 27°2N 128°26E **29** L4
Yos Sudarso, Pulau = Dolak, Pulau *Indonesia* 8°0S 138°30E **37** F9
Yosemite △ *U.S.A.* 37°45N 119°40W **78** H7
Yosemite Village *U.S.A.* 37°45N 119°35W **78** H7
Yoshino-Kumano △ *Japan* 34°12N 135°55E **29** H8
Yoshkar Ola *Russia* 56°38N 47°55E **18** C8
Yotvata *Israel* 29°55N 35°2E **48** F4
You Jiang → *China* 22°50N 108°6E **34** F6
You Xian *China* 27°1N 113°17E **35** D9
Youbou *Canada* 48°53N 124°13W **78** B2
Youghal *Ireland* 51°56N 7°52W **10** E4
Youghal B. *Ireland* 51°55N 7°49W **10** E4
Young *Australia* 34°19S 148°18E **63** E4
Young *Canada* 51°47N 105°45W **71** C7
Young *Uruguay* 32°44S 57°36W **94** C4
Young I. *Antarctica* 66°25S 162°24E **5** C11
Younghusband, L. *Australia* 30°50S 136°5E **63** E2
Younghusband Pen. *Australia* 36°0S 139°25E **63** F2
Youngstown *Canada* 51°35N 111°10W **71** C6
Youngstown *N.Y., U.S.A.* 43°15N 79°3W **82** C5
Youngstown *Ohio, U.S.A.* 41°6N 80°39W **82** E4
Youngsville *U.S.A.* 41°51N 79°19W **82** E5
Youngwood *U.S.A.* 40°14N 79°34W **82** F5
Youxi *China* 26°10N 118°13E **35** D12
Youyang *China* 28°47N 108°42E **34** C7
Youyu *China* 40°10N 112°20E **32** D7
Yozgat *Turkey* 39°51N 34°47E **19** G5
Ypacaraí △ *Paraguay* 25°18S 57°19W **94** A4
Ypané → *Paraguay* 23°29S 57°19W **94** A4
Ypres = Ieper *Belgium* 50°51N 2°53E **15** D2
Yr Wyddgrug = Mold *U.K.* 53°9N 3°8W **12** D4
Yreka *U.S.A.* 41°44N 122°38W **76** F2
Ystad *Sweden* 55°26N 13°50E **9** J15
Ysyk-Köl = Balykchy *Kyrgyzstan* 42°26N 76°12E **30** C4
Ysyk-Köl *Kyrgyzstan* 42°25N 77°15E **26** E8
Ythan → *U.K.* 57°19N 1°59W **11** D7
Ytyk-Kuyuel *Russia* 62°30N 133°45E **27** C14
Yu Jiang → *China* 23°22N 110°3E **34** F7
Yü Shan *Taiwan* 23°25N 120°52E **35** F13
Yu Xian = Yuzhou *China* 34°10N 113°28E **32** G7
Yu Xian *Hebei, China* 39°50N 114°35E **32** E8
Yu Xian *Shanxi, China* 38°5N 113°20E **32** E7
Yuan Jiang → *Hunan, China* 28°55N 111°50E **35** C8
Yuan Jiang → *Yunnan, China* 22°20N 103°59E **34** F4
Yuan'an *China* 31°3N 111°34E **35** B8
Yuanjiang *Hunan, China* 28°47N 112°21E **35** C9
Yuanjiang *Yunnan, China* 23°32N 102°0E **34** F4
Yüanli *Taiwan* 24°27N 120°39E **35** E13
Yüanlin *Taiwan* 23°58N 120°30E **35** F13
Yuanling *China* 28°29N 110°22E **35** C8
Yuanmou *China* 25°42N 101°52E **34** D3
Yuanping *China* 38°42N 112°46E **32** E7
Yuanqu *China* 35°18N 111°40E **32** G6
Yuanyang *Henan, China* 35°3N 113°58E **32** G7
Yuanyang *Yunnan, China* 23°10N 102°43E **34** F4
Yuba → *U.S.A.* 39°8N 121°36W **78** F5
Yuba City *U.S.A.* 39°8N 121°37W **78** F5
Yübari *Japan* 43°4N 141°59E **28** C10
Yübetsu *Japan* 44°13N 143°50E **28** B11
Yucatán □ *Mexico* 20°50N 89°0W **87** C7
Yucatán, Canal de *Caribbean* 22°0N 86°30W **88** B2
Yucatán, Península de *Mexico* 19°30N 89°0W **66** H11
Yucatan Basin *Cent. Amer.* 19°0N 86°0W **87** D7
Yucatan Channel = Yucatán, Canal de *Caribbean* 22°0N 86°30W **88** B2
Yucca *U.S.A.* 34°52N 114°9W **79** L12

Yucca Valley *U.S.A.* 34°8N 116°27W **79** L10
Yucheng *China* 36°55N 116°32E **32** F9
Yuci = Jinzhong *China* 37°42N 112°46E **32** F7
Yudu *China* 25°59N 115°30E **35** E10
Yuen Long *China* 22°26N 114°2E **31** a
Yuendumu *Australia* 22°16S 131°49E **60** D5
Yuendumu ☉ *Australia* 22°21S 131°40E **60** D5
Yueqing *China* 28°9N 120°59E **35** C13
Yueqing Wan *China* 28°5N 121°20E **35** D13
Yuexi *Anhui, China* 30°50N 116°20E **35** B11
Yuexi *Sichuan, China* 28°37N 102°26E **34** C4
Yueyang *China* 29°21N 113°5E **35** C9
Yugan *China* 28°43N 116°37E **35** C11
Yugorenok *Russia* 59°47N 137°40E **27** D14
Yuhuan *China* 28°9N 121°12E **35** C13
Yühuan Dao *China* 28°5N 121°15E **35** C13
Yujiang *China* 28°10N 116°43E **35** C11
Yukon *U.S.A.* 35°31N 97°45W **84** D6
Yukon → *U.S.A.* 62°32N 163°54W **74** a
Yukon Flats *U.S.A.* 66°40N 145°45W **74** B10
Yukon Territory □ *Canada* 63°0N 135°0W **68** E5
Yukta *Russia* 63°26N 105°42E **27** C11
Yukuhashi *Japan* 33°44N 130°59E **29** H5
Yulara *Australia* 25°10S 130°55E **61** E5
Yule → *Australia* 20°41S 118°17E **60** D2
Yuleba *Australia* 26°37S 149°24E **63** D4
Yüli *Taiwan* 23°20N 121°18E **35** F13
Yulin *Guangxi Zhuangzu, China* 22°40N 110°8E **35** F8
Yulin *Hainan, China* 18°10N 109°31E **38** C7
Yulin *Shaanxi, China* 38°20N 109°30E **32** E5
Yulong Xueshan *China* 27°6N 100°10E **34** D3
Yuma *Ariz., U.S.A.* 32°43N 114°37W **79** N12
Yuma *Colo., U.S.A.* 40°8N 102°43W **76** F12
Yuma, B. de *Dom. Rep.* 18°20N 68°35W **89** C6
Yumen *China* 39°50N 97°30E **30** D8
Yun Gui Gaoyuan *China* 26°0N 104°0E **34** D5
Yun Ling Shan *China* 27°0N 99°20E **34** D2
Yun Xian *Hubei, China* 32°50N 110°46E **32** H6
Yun Xian *Yunnan, China* 24°27N 100°8E **34** E3
Yuna *Australia* 28°20S 115°0E **61** E2
Yunan *China* 23°12N 111°30E **35** F8
Yuncheng *Henan, China* 35°36N 115°57E **32** G8
Yuncheng *Shanxi, China* 35°2N 111°0E **32** G6
Yunfu *China* 22°50N 112°5E **35** F9
Yungang Shiku *China* 40°6N 113°7E **32** D7
Yungas *Bolivia* 17°0S 66°0W **92** G5
Yungay *Chile* 37°10S 72°5W **94** D1
Yunhe *China* 28°8N 119°33E **35** C12
Yunkai Dashan *China* 22°30N 111°0E **35** F8
Yunkanjini ☉ *Australia* 22°33S 131°6E **60** D5
Yunling Shan *China* 28°30N 99°30E **34** D2
Yunlong *China* 25°57N 99°13E **34** E2
Yunmeng *China* 31°2N 113°43E **35** B9
Yunnan □ *China* 25°0N 102°0E **34** E4
Yunta *Australia* 32°34S 139°36E **63** E2
Yunxi *China* 33°0N 110°22E **32** H6
Yunxiao *China* 23°59N 117°18E **35** F11
Yunyang *Chongqing, China* 31°2N 108°51E **34** B7
Yunyang *Henan, China* 33°26N 112°42E **35** A9
Yupanqui Basin *Pac. Oc.* 19°0S 101°0W **65** J17
Yuping *China* 27°13N 108°57E **34** D6
Yuqing *China* 27°13N 107°53E **34** D6
Yuraygir △ *Australia* 29°45S 153°15E **63** D5
Yurga *Russia* 55°42N 84°51E **26** D9
Yurihonjo *Japan* 39°23N 140°8E **28** E10
Yurimaguas *Peru* 5°55S 76°7W **92** E3
Yurubí △ *Venezuela* 10°26N 68°42W **89** D6
Yuscarán *Honduras* 13°58N 86°45W **88** D2
Yushan *China* 28°42N 118°10E **35** C12
Yushanzhen *China* 28°28N 108°22E **34** C7
Yushe *China* 37°4N 112°58E **32** F7
Yushu *Jilin, China* 44°43N 126°38E **33** B14
Yushu *Qinghai, China* 33°5N 96°55E **30** E8
Yutai *China* 35°0N 116°45E **32** G9
Yutian *Hebei, China* 39°53N 117°45E **32** E9
Yutian *Sinkiang-Uigur, China* 36°52N 81°42E **30** D5
Yuxarı Qarabağ = Nagorno-Karabakh □ *Azerbaijan* 39°55N 46°45E **46** B5
Yuxi *China* 24°30N 102°35E **34** E4
Yuyao *China* 30°3N 121°10E **35** B13
Yuzawa *Japan* 39°10N 140°30E **28** E10
Yuzhno-Kurilsk *Russia* 44°1N 145°51E **27** E15
Yuzhno-Sakhalinsk *Russia* 46°58N 142°45E **31** B17
Yuzhnyy □ *Russia* 44°0N 40°0E **26** E5
Yuzhou *China* 34°10N 113°28E **32** G7
Yvetot *France* 49°37N 0°44E **20** B4

Z

Zāb al Kabīr → *Iraq* 36°1N 43°24E **46** B4
Zāb aş Şaghīr → *Iraq* 35°17N 43°29E **46** C4
Zabaykalsk *Russia* 49°40N 117°25E **27** E12
Zabol *Iran* 31°0N 61°32E **47** D9
Zābol □ *Afghan.* 32°0N 67°0E **40** D5
Zāboli *Iran* 27°10N 61°35E **47** E9
Zabrze *Poland* 50°18N 18°50E **17** C10
Zacapa *Guatemala* 14°59N 89°31W **88** D2
Zacapu *Mexico* 19°50N 101°43W **86** D4
Zacatecas *Mexico* 22°47N 102°35W **86** C4
Zacatecas □ *Mexico* 23°0N 103°0W **86** C4
Zacatecoluca *El Salv.* 13°29N 88°51W **88** D2
Zachary *U.S.A.* 30°39N 91°9W **84** F9
Zacoalco de Torres *Mexico* 20°14N 103°35W **86** C4
Zacualtipán *Mexico* 20°39N 98°36W **87** C5
Zadar *Croatia* 44°8N 15°14E **16** F8
Zadetkyi Kyun *Burma* 10°0N 98°25E **39** G2
Zafarqand *Iran* 33°11N 52°29E **47** C7
Zafra *Spain* 38°26N 6°30W **21** C2
Żagań *Poland* 51°39N 15°22E **16** C8
Zagaoua *Chad* 15°30N 22°24E **53** E10
Zagazig *Egypt* 30°40N 31°30E **53** B12

Zāgheh *Iran* 33°30N 48°42E **47** C6
Zagreb *Croatia* 45°50N 15°58E **16** F9
Zāgros, Kūhhā-ye *Iran* 33°45N 48°5E **47** C6
Zagros Mts. = Zāgros, Kūhhā-ye *Iran* 33°45N 48°5E **47** C6
Zāhedān *Fārs, Iran* 28°46N 53°52E **47** D7
Zāhedān *Sīstān va Balūchestān, Iran* 29°30N 60°50E **47** D9
Zahirabad *India* 17°43N 77°37E **44** F3
Zahlah *Lebanon* 33°52N 35°50E **48** B4
Zaïre = Congo → *Africa* 6°4S 12°24E **54** F2
Zaječar *Serbia* 43°53N 22°18E **23** C10
Zaka *Zimbabwe* 20°20S 31°29E **57** B5
Zakamensk *Russia* 50°23N 103°17E **27** D11
Zakhodnaya Dzvina = Daugava → *Latvia* 57°4N 24°3E **9** H21
Zākhū *Iraq* 37°10N 42°50E **46** B4
Zakinthos = Zakynthos *Greece* 37°47N 20°54E **23** F9
Zakopane *Poland* 49°18N 19°57E **17** D10
Zakynthos *Greece* 37°47N 20°54E **23** F9
Zalaegerszeg *Hungary* 46°53N 16°47E **17** E9
Zalantun *China* 48°0N 122°43E **31** B13
Zalari *Russia* 53°33N 102°30E **27** D11
Zalău *Romania* 47°12N 23°3E **17** E12
Zaleshchiki = Zalishchyky *Ukraine* 48°45N 25°45E **17** D13
Zalew Wiślany *Poland* 54°20N 19°50E **17** A10
Zalingei *Sudan* 12°51N 23°29E **53** F10
Zalishchyky *Ukraine* 48°45N 25°45E **17** D13
Zama L. *Canada* 58°45N 119°5W **70** B5
Zambeze → *Africa* 18°35S 36°20E **55** H7
Zambezi = Zambeze → *Africa* 18°35S 36°20E **55** H7
Zambezi *Zambia* 13°30S 23°15E **55** G4
Zambia ■ *Africa* 15°0S 28°0E **55** H5
Zamboanga *Phil.* 6°59N 122°3E **37** C6
Zamora *Mexico* 19°59N 102°16W **86** D4
Zamora *Spain* 41°30N 5°45W **21** B3
Zamość *Poland* 50°43N 23°15E **17** C12
Zamtang *China* 32°26N 101°6E **34** A3
Zanda *China* 31°32N 79°50E **30** E4
Zandvoort *Neths.* 52°22N 4°32E **15** B4
Zanesville *U.S.A.* 39°56N 82°1W **82** G2
Zangābād *Iran* 38°26N 46°44E **46** B5
Zanjān *Iran* 36°40N 48°35E **47** B6
Zanjān □ *Iran* 37°20N 49°30E **47** B6
Zanjān → *Iran* 37°8N 47°47E **47** B6
Zante = Zakynthos *Greece* 37°47N 20°54E **23** F9
Zanthus *Australia* 31°2S 123°34E **61** F3
Zanzibar *Tanzania* 6°12S 39°12E **54** F7
Zaouiet El-Kala = Bordj Omar Driss *Algeria* 28°10N 6°40E **52** C7
Zaouiet Reggâne *Algeria* 26°32N 0°3E **52** C6
Zaoyang *China* 32°10N 112°45E **35** A9
Zaozhuang *China* 34°50N 117°35E **33** G9
Zap Suyu = Zāb al Kabīr → *Iraq* 36°1N 43°24E **46** B4
Zapadnaya Dvina = Daugava → *Latvia* 57°4N 24°3E **9** H21
Západné Beskydy *Europe* 49°30N 19°0E **17** D10
Zapala *Argentina* 39°0S 70°5W **96** D2
Zapaleri, Cerro *Bolivia* 22°49S 67°11W **94** A2
Zapata *U.S.A.* 26°55N 99°16W **84** H5
Zapolyarnyy *Russia* 69°26N 30°51E **8** B24
Zapopán *Mexico* 20°43N 103°24W **86** C4
Zaporizhzhya *Ukraine* 47°50N 35°10E **19** E6
Zaporozhye = Zaporizhzhya *Ukraine* 47°50N 35°10E **19** E6
Zara *Turkey* 39°58N 37°43E **46** B3
Zaragoza *Coahuila, Mexico* 28°29N 100°55W **86** B4
Zaragoza *Nuevo León, Mexico* 23°58N 99°46W **87** C5
Zaragoza *Spain* 41°39N 0°53W **21** B5
Zarand *Kermān, Iran* 30°46N 56°34E **47** D8
Zarand *Markazī, Iran* 35°18N 50°25E **47** C6
Zaranj *Afghan.* 30°55N 61°55E **40** D2
Zarasai *Lithuania* 55°40N 26°20E **9** J22
Zárate *Argentina* 34°7S 59°0W **94** C4
Zard, Kūh-e *Iran* 32°22N 50°4E **47** C6
Zāreh *Iran* 35°7N 49°9E **47** C6
Zaria *Nigeria* 11°0N 7°40E **52** F7
Zarneh *Iran* 33°55N 46°10E **46** C5
Zarqā', Nahr az → *Jordan* 32°10N 35°37E **48** C4
Zarrīn *Iran* 32°46N 54°37E **47** C7
Zaruma *Ecuador* 3°40S 79°38W **92** D3
Zarzis *Tunisia* 33°31N 11°2E **53** B8
Zaskar → *India* 34°13N 77°20E **43** B7
Zaskar Mts. *India* 33°15N 77°30E **43** C7
Zastron *S. Africa* 30°18S 27°7E **56** D4
Zāvareh *Iran* 33°29N 52°28E **47** C7
Zave *Zimbabwe* 17°6S 30°1E **57** A5
Zavitinsk *Russia* 50°10N 129°20E **27** D13
Zavodovski I. *Antarctica* 56°0S 27°45W **5** B1
Zawiercie *Poland* 50°30N 19°24E **17** C10
Zāwiyat al Bayḑā = Al Bayḑā *Libya* 32°50N 21°44E **53** B10
Zāyā *Iraq* 33°33N 44°13E **46** C5
Zāyandeh → *Iran* 32°35N 52°0E **47** C7
Zaysan *Kazakhstan* 47°28N 84°52E **26** E9
Zaysan Köli *Kazakhstan* 48°0N 83°0E **26** E9
Zayü *China* 28°48N 97°27E **41** E20
Zbarazh *Ukraine* 49°43N 25°44E **17** D13
Zdolbuniv *Ukraine* 50°30N 26°15E **17** C14
Zduńska Wola *Poland* 51°37N 18°59E **17** C10
Zeballos *Canada* 49°59N 126°50W **70** D3
Zebediela *S. Africa* 24°20S 29°17E **57** B4
Zeebrugge *Belgium* 51°19N 3°12E **15** C3
Zeehan *Australia* 41°52S 145°25E **63** G4
Zeeland □ *Neths.* 51°30N 3°50E **15** C3
Zeerust *S. Africa* 25°31S 26°4E **56** C4
Zefat *Israel* 32°58N 35°29E **48** C4
Zehak *Iran* 30°53N 61°42E **47** D9
Zeil, Mt. *Australia* 23°30S 132°23E **60** D5
Zeila = Saylac *Somalia* 11°21N 43°30E **49** E3
Zeist *Neths.* 52°5N 5°15E **15** B5

Zeitz *Germany* 51°2N 12°7E **16** C7
Zelenogorsk *Russia* 60°12N 29°43E **8** F23
Zelenograd *Russia* 56°1N 37°12E **18** C6
Zelienople *U.S.A.* 40°48N 80°8W **82** F4
Zempoala *Mexico* 19°27N 96°23W **87** D5
Zemun *Serbia* 44°51N 20°25E **23** B9
Zengcheng *China* 23°13N 113°52E **35** F9
Zenica *Bos.-H.* 44°10N 17°57E **23** B7
Žepče *Bos.-H.* 44°28N 18°2E **23** B8
Zevenaar *Neths.* 51°56N 6°5E **15** C6
Zeya *Russia* 53°48N 127°14E **27** D13
Zeya → *Russia* 51°42N 128°53E **27** D13
Zeyskoye Vdkhr. *Russia* 54°30N 127°30E **27** D13
Zêzere → *Portugal* 39°28N 8°20W **21** C1
Zghartā *Lebanon* 34°21N 35°53E **48** A4
Zgorzelec *Poland* 51°10N 15°0E **16** C8
Zhabinka *Belarus* 52°13N 24°2E **17** B13
Zhambyl = Taraz *Kazakhstan* 42°54N 71°22E **30** C3
Zhangaözen *Kazakhstan* 43°18N 52°48E **19** F9
Zhangaqazaly *Kazakhstan* 45°48N 62°6E **26** E7
Zhangbei *China* 41°10N 114°45E **32** D8
Zhangguangcai Ling *China* 45°0N 129°0E **33** B15
Zhangjiabian *China* 22°33N 113°28E **31** a
Zhangjiagang *China* 31°55N 120°30E **35** a
Zhangjiakou *China* 40°48N 114°55E **32** D8
Zhangping *China* 25°17N 117°23E **35** E11
Zhangshu *China* 28°4N 115°29E **35** C10
Zhangye *China* 38°50N 100°23E **30** D9
Zhangzhou *China* 24°30N 117°35E **35** E11
Zhanhua *China* 37°40N 118°8E **33** F10
Zhanjiang *China* 21°15N 110°20E **35** G8
Zhannetty, Ostrov *Russia* 76°43N 158°0E **27** B16
Zhanyi *China* 25°38N 103°48E **34** E4
Zhanyu *China* 44°30N 122°30E **33** B12
Zhao Xian *China* 37°43N 114°45E **32** F8
Zhao'an *China* 23°41N 117°10E **35** F11
Zhaocheng *China* 36°22N 111°38E **32** F6
Zhaodong *China* 46°4N 125°59E **31** B13
Zhaojue *China* 28°1N 102°49E **34** C4
Zhaoping *China* 24°11N 110°48E **35** E8
Zhaoqing *China* 23°0N 112°20E **35** F9
Zhaotong *China* 27°20N 103°44E **34** D4
Zhaoyang Hu *China* 35°4N 116°47E **32** G9
Zhaoyuan *Heilongjiang, China* 45°27N 125°0E **33** B13
Zhaoyuan *Shandong, China* 37°20N 120°23E **33** F11
Zhari Namco *China* 31°6N 85°36E **30** E6
Zhashkiv *Ukraine* 49°15N 30°5E **17** D16
Zhashui *China* 33°40N 109°8E **32** H5
Zhayylma *Kazakhstan* 51°37N 61°33E **26** D7
Zhayyq → *Kazakhstan* 47°0N 51°48E **19** E9
Zhdanov = Mariupol *Ukraine* 47°5N 37°31E **19** E6
Zhecheng *China* 34°7N 115°20E **32** G8
Zhegao *China* 31°46N 117°45E **35** B11
Zhejiang □ *China* 29°0N 120°0E **35** C13
Zheleznodorozhnyy *Russia* 62°35N 50°55E **18** B9
Zheleznogorsk-Ilimskiy *Russia* 56°34N 104°8E **27** D11
Zhen'an *China* 33°27N 109°9E **34** A7
Zhenba *China* 32°27N 107°42E **34** A6
Zhenfeng *China* 25°22N 105°40E **34** E5
Zheng'an *China* 28°32N 107°27E **34** C6
Zhengding *China* 38°8N 114°32E **32** E8
Zhenghe *China* 27°20N 118°50E **35** D12
Zhengyang *China* 32°37N 114°22E **35** A10
Zhengyangguan *China* 32°30N 116°29E **35** A11
Zhengzhou *China* 34°45N 113°34E **32** G7
Zhenhai *China* 29°59N 121°42E **35** C13
Zhenjiang *China* 32°11N 119°26E **35** A12
Zhenkang *China* 23°58N 99°0E **34** F2
Zhenlai *China* 45°50N 123°5E **33** B12
Zhenning *China* 26°4N 105°45E **34** D5
Zhenping *Henan, China* 33°10N 112°16E **32** H7
Zhenping *Shaanxi, China* 31°59N 109°31E **34** A7
Zhenxiong *China* 27°27N 104°50E **34** D5
Zhenyuan *Gansu, China* 35°35N 107°30E **34** G4
Zhenyuan *Guizhou, China* 27°4N 108°21E **34** D7
Zherong *China* 27°15N 119°52E **35** D12
Zhetiqara *Kazakhstan* 52°11N 61°12E **26** D7
Zhezqazghan *Kazakhstan* 47°44N 67°40E **26** E7
Zhicheng *China* 30°25N 111°27E **35** B8
Zhidan *China* 36°48N 108°48E **32** F5
Zhigansk *Russia* 66°48N 123°27E **27** C13
Zhijiang *Hubei, China* 30°32N 111°42E **35** B8
Zhijiang *Hunan, China* 27°7N 109°42E **34** D7
Zhijin *China* 26°38N 105°45E **34** D5
Zhilinda *Russia* 70°0N 114°20E **27** C12
Zhitomir = Zhytomyr *Ukraine* 50°20N 28°40E **17** C15
Zhlobin *Belarus* 52°55N 30°0E **17** B16
Zhmerynka *Ukraine* 49°2N 28°2E **17** D15
Zhob *Pakistan* 31°20N 69°31E **42** D3
Zhob → *Pakistan* 32°4N 69°50E **42** C3
Zhodino *Russia* 54°5N 28°17E **17** A15
Zhokhova, Ostrov *Russia* 76°4N 152°40E **27** B16
Zhongba *China* 29°39N 84°10E **30** E6
Zhongdian *China* 27°48N 99°42E **34** D2
Zhongdong *China* 22°48N 107°47E **34** F6
Zhongdu *China* 24°0N 109°40E **34** E7
Zhongjiang *China* 30°53N 104°46E **34** B5
Zhongning *China* 37°29N 105°40E **32** F3
Zhongshan *Antarctica* 69°0S 39°50E **5** C6
Zhongshan *Guangdong, China* 22°26N 113°20E **35** a
Zhongshan *Guangxi Zhuangzu, China* 24°29N 111°18E **35** E8
Zhongshankou *China* 22°35N 113°29E **31** a
Zhongtiao Shan *China* 35°0N 111°10E **32** G6
Zhongwei *China* 37°30N 105°12E **32** F3

Zhongxian *China* 30°18N 107°58E **34** B6
Zhongxiang *China* 31°12N 112°34E **35** B9
Zhongyang *China* 37°20N 111°11E **32** F6
Zhosaly *Kazakhstan* 45°29N 64°4E **26** E7
Zhoucun *China* 36°47N 117°48E **33** F9
Zhoukou *China* 33°38N 114°38E **32** H8
Zhoukoudian *China* 39°41N 115°56E **32** E8
Zhouning *China* 27°12N 119°20E **35** D12
Zhoushan *China* 30°1N 122°6E **35** B14
Zhoushan Dao *China* 30°5N 122°10E **35** C14
Zhouzhi *China* 34°10N 108°12E **32** G5
Zhovkva *Ukraine* 50°4N 23°58E **17** C12
Zhu Jiang → *China* 22°45N 113°37E **35** F9
Zhuanghe *China* 39°40N 123°0E **33** E12
Zhucheng *China* 36°0N 119°27E **33** G10
Zhugqu *China* 33°40N 104°30E **34** A5
Zhuhai *China* 22°17N 113°34E **35** F9
Zhuji *China* 29°40N 120°10E **35** C12
Zhujiang Kou *China* 22°20N 113°45E **35** F9
Zhumadian *China* 32°59N 114°2E **35** H8
Zhuo Xian = Zhuozhou *China* 39°28N 115°58E **32** E8
Zhuolu *China* 40°20N 115°12E **32** D8
Zhuozhou *China* 39°28N 115°58E **32** E8
Zhuozi *China* 41°0N 112°25E **32** D7
Zhushan *China* 32°15N 110°13E **35** A8
Zhuxi *China* 32°25N 109°40E **34** A7
Zhuzhou *China* 27°49N 113°12E **35** D9
Zhytomyr *Ukraine* 50°20N 28°40E **17** C15
Zhytomyr □ *Ukraine* 50°50N 28°10E **17** C14
Zi Shui → *China* 28°40N 112°40E **35** C9
Ziarat *Pakistan* 30°25N 67°49E **42** D2
Zibo *China* 36°47N 118°3E **33** F10
Zichang *China* 37°18N 109°40E **32** F5
Zidi = Wandhari *Pakistan* 27°42N 66°48E **42** F2
Zielona Góra *Poland* 51°57N 15°31E **16** C8
Zierikzee *Neths.* 51°40N 3°55E **15** C3
Zigong *China* 29°15N 104°48E **34** C5
Ziguéy *Chad* 14°43N 15°50E **53** F9
Ziguinchor *Senegal* 12°35N 16°20E **52** F2
Zihuatanejo *Mexico* 17°39N 101°33W **86** D4
Zijin *China* 23°33N 115°8E **35** F10
Zixi *China* 27°45N 117°4E **35** D11
Zixing *China* 25°59N 113°21E **35** E9
Ziyang *Shaanxi, China* 32°32N 108°31E **34** H5
Ziyang *Sichuan, China* 30°6N 104°40E **34** B5
Ziyun *China* 25°45N 106°5E **34** E5
Zizhong *China* 29°48N 104°47E **34** C5
Zlatograd *Bulgaria* 41°22N 25°7E **23** D11
Zlatoust *Russia* 55°10N 59°40E **18** C10
Zlin *Czech Rep.* 49°14N 17°40E **17** D9
Zmeinogorsk *Kazakhstan* 51°10N 82°13E **26** D9
Znojmo *Czech Rep.* 48°50N 16°2E **16** D9
Zobeyrī *Iran* 34°10N 46°40E **46** C5
Zoetermeer *Neths.* 52°3N 4°30E **15** B4
Zogang *China* 29°55N 97°47E **34** C1
Zohreh → *Iran* 30°16N 51°15E **47** D6
Zolochiv *Ukraine* 49°45N 24°51E **17** D13
Zomba *Malawi* 15°22S 35°19E **55** H7
Zongo *Dem. Rep. of the Congo* 4°20N 18°35E **54** D3
Zonguldak *Turkey* 41°28N 31°50E **19** F5
Zongyang *China* 30°42N 117°12E **35** B11
Zorritos *Peru* 3°43S 80°40W **92** D2
Zou Xiang *China* 35°30N 116°58E **32** G9
Zouar *Chad* 20°30N 16°32E **53** D8
Zouérate = Zouîrât *Mauritania* 22°44N 12°21W **52** D3
Zoutkamp *Neths.* 53°20N 6°18E **15** A6
Zrenjanin *Serbia* 45°22N 20°23E **23** B9
Zufar *Oman* 17°40N 54°0E **49** D5
Zug *Switz.* 47°10N 8°31E **20** C8
Zugspitze *Germany* 47°25N 10°59E **16** E6
Zuid-Holland □ *Neths.* 52°0N 4°35E **15** C4
Zuidbeveland *Neths.* 51°30N 3°50E **15** C3
Zuidhorn *Neths.* 53°15N 6°23E **15** A6
Zula *Eritrea* 15°17N 39°40E **49** D2
Zumbo *Mozam.* 15°35S 30°26E **55** H6
Zumpango *Mexico* 19°48N 99°6W **87** B5
Zunhua *China* 40°18N 117°58E **33** D9
Zuni Pueblo *U.S.A.* 35°4N 108°51W **77** J9
Zunyi *China* 27°42N 106°53E **34** D6
Zuoquan *China* 37°5N 113°22E **32** F7
Zuozhou *China* 22°42N 107°27E **34** F6
Zurbātīyah *Iraq* 33°9N 46°3E **46** C5
Zürich *Switz.* 47°22N 8°32E **20** C8
Zutphen *Neths.* 52°9N 6°12E **15** B6
Zuurberg △ *S. Africa* 33°12S 25°32E **56** D4
Zūzan *Iran* 34°22N 59°53E **47** C8
Zvishavane *Zimbabwe* 20°17S 30°2E **55** J6
Zvolen *Slovak Rep.* 48°33N 19°10E **17** D10
Zwettl *Austria* 48°35N 15°9E **16** D8
Zwickau *Germany* 50°44N 12°30E **16** C7
Zwolle *Neths.* 52°31N 6°6E **15** B6
Zwolle *U.S.A.* 31°38N 93°39W **84** F7
Żyrardów *Poland* 52°3N 20°28E **17** B11
Zyryan = Zyryan *Kazakhstan* 49°43N 84°20E **26** E9
Zyryanka *Russia* 65°45N 150°51E **27** C16
Zyryanovsk = Zyryan *Kazakhstan* 49°43N 84°20E **26** E9
Żywiec *Poland* 49°42N 19°10E **17** D10